MISE EN BOUTEILLES
E. GUIGAL AMPUIS
1991
CLOUDY BAY
1987
DOMAINE
LOUIS JADOT
DOISY-DAËNE BARSAC
CHATEAU DOISY-DAËNE BARSAC
LA SOUMADE 84110
CLOUDY BAY ESTATE BOTTLED
STERLING VINEYARDS
MESSO IN BOTTIGLIA
DES MOINES
MOSSWOOD
ST-JULIEN 1970
RASTEAU

The OXFORD COMPANION TO WINE

The OXFORD COMPANION TO WINE

EDITED BY

JANCIS ROBINSON

Oxford New York
OXFORD UNIVERSITY PRESS

Oxford University Press, Walton Street, Oxford OX2 6DP

Oxford New York
Athens Auckland Bangkok Bombay
Calcutta Cape Town Dar es Salaam Delhi
Florence Hong Kong Istanbul Karachi
Kuala Lumpur Madras Madrid Melbourne
Mexico City Nairobi Paris Singapore
Taipei Tokyo Toronto

and associated companies in
Berlin Ibadan

Oxford is a trade mark of Oxford University Press

First published 1994

British Library Cataloguing in Publication Data
Data available

Library of Congress Cataloging in Publication Data
Robinson, Jancis.
The Oxford companion to wine / Jancis Robinson.
p. cm.
Includes bibliographical references and index.
1. Wine and wine making. I. Title.
641.2'2—dc20 TP548.R6455 1994 94–26509
ISBN 0–19–866159–2

3 5 7 9 10 8 6 4

Typeset by Selwood Systems, Midsomer Norton
Printed in Great Britain
on acid-free paper by
Butler & Tanner Ltd.
Frome, Somerset

PREFACE

It is a great compliment to Wine that Oxford University Press has chosen it as a suitable subject for an Oxford Companion, thus joining such art forms as English Literature, Music, and Art itself, and such areas of scientific concern as the Mind and Medicine. But the compliment is entirely justifiable, for wine is not only capable of providing unparalleled sensory stimulation; it is also a rewarding and unusually multidisciplinary subject for study. It is both a living thing and yet able to link us with past generations of wine-makers; it is a subject which demands a broad grasp of history, geography, economics, and a wide range of scientific disciplines, as demonstrated by the contents of this book.

The aim has been to provide a single volume of reference that will be of use over the long term. With over 3,000 alphabetically arranged entries, this book is intended not just for the wine fanatic (who, it is hoped, will find here a substantial amount of unfamiliar material, particularly historical and scientific) and the wine professional, but for everyone who enjoys drinking wine at any level and wants to know more about it. It is not a buyers' guide; there are many excellent books of this sort already, whose contents date all too rapidly; nor is it merely a vineyard gazetteer: a strictly geographical approach to wine necessarily omits an increasing proportion of what makes wine so fascinating. Rather, this book aims to set wine in a much wider context, to explain where it fits into the worlds of, for example, botany, commerce, geology, and literature. There are, I hope, entries under all the terms you would expect, as well as all the places and likely names (although individual wine producers merit a separate entry only when they have played a significant role in the history, possibly quite recent, of wine). But there are also entries on other, less obvious topics, such as animals (their function as vine pests), auctions, the specific influence of the British, and Australians, on the world of wine, fashion, fraud, health, numbers and wine, the influence of rivers on the history of wine, global overproduction, wine in literature and art, and the role of water throughout wine production.

I hope that this book sheds light on some of the increasingly important discoveries in the fields of viticulture and oenology which have tended to remain obscured in the academic literature, as well as stimulating appreciation of just how much wine has touched, and continues to touch, the course of history. Well over a third of the book is concerned with specific wines and wine regions, with about an eighth devoted to each of oenology (including a detailed look at oak and cooperage) and viticulture (including considerable examination of the influence of soil, climate, and weather). Other quantitatively important themes include the history of wine and details of specific vine varieties.

With this book Oxford University Press may have honoured its subject, but it has honoured its editor more, and very much less deservedly. Editing the first edition of such a work has been the greatest challenge of my life. Oxford University Press and my literary agent Caradoc King must take credit for proposing the book in the first place. It has given me an excuse to plunder the expertise of all of those named below as contributors and consultants, as well as prevailing upon the goodwill of others too numerous to mention. Although I have tried to become as knowledgeable as they are in their individual disciplines, I am all too aware of my own limitations and take full responsibility for any shortcomings in this new Companion.

I am extremely grateful to all at OUP who have worked on this book. Pam Coote and Alysoun Owen of OUP have been quite dazzlingly erudite and hard-working (a rare combination); Jackie and Edwin Pritchard raised my expectations of copy editors to an entirely new plane; and Anne-Marie Ehrlich was indefatigably diligent and cheerful in her search for suitable illustrations.

The people to whom I owe the greatest debt, however, are of course my immediate family, four very long-suffering Landers, one of whom has yet to experience a life beyond the shadow of the Companion, and another of whom temporarily shouldered the burdens of a single parent with his usual remarkable stoicism and generosity.

JANCIS ROBINSON

London, June 1994

ACKNOWLEDGMENTS

MORE than half the entries in this book have been contributed by those whose knowledge is considerably greater than that of the editor. Overall Oenology Editor is Professor A. Dinsmoor Webb, now retired from the University of California at Davis. Professor Pascal Ribéreau-Gayon provided some entries with a European perspective, while Professor Terry H. Lee, director of the Australian Wine Research Institute, and Dr Tony Jordan, past president of the Australian Society of Viticulture and Oenology injected considerable Australian expertise. Viticulture Editor is Dr Richard Smart, whose reputation, experience, and perspective are truly international. Dr Bryan Coombe and Dr John Gladstones were important contributors in their respective fields of vine physiology and the influence of soil and climate.

Historical entries are mainly the result of a substantial number of individual specialists, some of them leaders in their field. Hanneke Wirtjes, however, has contributed first-class articles on a dazzlingly wide variety of regions in both ancient and medieval periods, as well as commenting on a number of other topics. Roger Brock and Jeremy Paterson were important contributors on their respective Greek and Roman specialities.

Some regional specialists helped enormously by providing detailed, original information upon which the relevant entries are based. Abi Duhr was an invaluable source of both wines and statistics from Luxembourg. James and John Gillespie worked extremely hard and here convey their love and knowledge of Romanian wine. Professor Alejandro Hernandez provided considerable information about the wines of Chile, and Monsieur et Madame Didier Joris helped to fill the gaps in my knowledge of Swiss wine. The book's coverage of the burgeoning Latin American wine industry would have been very much weaker but for Maria Isabel Mijares et Garcia-Pelayo, a Madrid-based, Bordeaux-trained oenologist, writer and teacher, whose consultancy work regularly takes her to Latin America, in particular to Bolivia, Colombia, and Peru. Her associate José Antonio Saez Illobre also played a major part in furnishing detailed, original, and up-to-date information on Latin America.

Hamish Aird, Nicholas Faith, Richard Smart, Daniel Thomases, Nigel Wilson, and Hanneke Wirtjes were all particularly helpful in their comments on the book as it painfully evolved.

People who kindly read and commented on entries, from one to scores of them, or set me on the right track are: Julian Barnes, Sybille Bedford, David Bird MW, William Bolter, Professor Denis Boubals, Matthew Boucher, Simon Brewin, Peter Bright, Jim Budd, Ulf Buxrud, Mme Casado, Eduardo Chadwick, Pam Coote, Abi Duhr, Jean-Louis Escudier, George Espie, Dereck Foster, John and James Gillespie, Sue Harris, Nancy Lady Henley, Paul Henschke, Professor Alejandro Hernandez, James Herrick, Merlin Holland, Peter Jackson Cousin, Andrew Jefford, Brian Jordan, Didier Joris, Kathryn McWhirter, Catherine Manac'h, Carlos Tizio Mayer, Giles MacDonogh, Charles Metcalfe, Hazel Murphy, Jill Norman, Michael Prónay, Edmund Penning-Rowsell, David Russell, Victor de la Serna, Peter Schleimer, Catherine Scott, Charles Sydney, Robert Tinlot, Miguel Torres, Tim Unwin, Jeremy Watson, Richard Ward, Alan West, Nigel Wilson, Warren Winiarski,

John Worontschak, plus various men from the Ministry of Agriculture, Fisheries and Food in London and scores of others whose help has been too fundamental or too obvious to recall.

Charles Withington and Lynne Sherriff MW both bore grapes from South Africa for photographing.

The Publishers are grateful to Anne-Marie Ehrlich for her picture research, and to Russell Birkett who produced the diagrams.

Contributors

Oenology Editor: Professor A. Dinsmoor Webb *Viticulture Editor*: Dr Richard Smart

Listed in alphabetical order of surname. MW stands for Master of Wine. Unsigned entries are written by the Editor.

H.H.A. Hamish Aird is a classicist and Sub-Warden of Radley College, Oxfordshire in England.

T.A. Tony Aspler, Canada's most widely read wine writer, wine columnist, and educator.

S.A. Susy Atkins is a free-lance wine writer who travels widely from her base in London.

H.G.B. Bill Baker, wine merchant whose distinctive wine list has long been decorated with unusual vinous quotations.

N.J.B. Nicolas Belfrage MW is a wine merchant and wine writer specializing in Italian wines.

E.J.R.B. Elizabeth Berry MW, wine merchant and author whose books include *The Wines of Alsace*.

H.B. Helen Bettinson, television producer, researcher for Hugh Johnson's *Story of Wine*.

J.A.B. Dr Jeremy Black was formerly Director of the British School of Archaeology in Iraq and is now a Fellow of Wolfson College, Oxford, and University Lecturer in Akkadian. He is the author of several studies on Sumerian and Babylonian literature and ancient philology.

W.B. William Bolter, Bordeaux-based wine merchant, author, and wine-maker who worked for Alexis Lichine (q.v.) from 1958 to 1964.

J.M.B. Michael Broadbent MW, head of Christie's Wine Department and author (see entry).

R.B. Dr Roger Brock is a Lecturer in Classics at the University of Leeds and specialist in Greek history and historiography.

S.B. Stephen Brook, journalist and author whose works include *Liquid Gold: Dessert Wines of the World*.

L.B. Larry Brooks studied plant pathology at the University of California at Davis and has been wine-maker at Acacia winery in the Napa Valley since 1981.

R.N.H.B. Robin Butler, antique dealer with a particular interest in wine, he co-wrote *The Book of Wine Antiques* in 1986.

R.F.C. Bob Campbell MW, New Zealand's best-known wine writer and founder of an exceptional wine school in Auckland.

B.G.C. Dr Bryan Coombe, author, recently retired lecturer and researcher specializing in grapevine physiology at Waite Agricultural Research Institute, Adelaide. The American Society of Enology and Viticulture awarded him Best Paper of the Year for viticulture in 1987, and oenology in 1991.

B.C. Professor Barry Cunliffe has been Professor of European Archaeology at the Institute of Archaeology, University of Oxford since 1972.

J.&M.D. Professor James Douglas was Visiting Professor of Political Science in various American universities while Professor Mary Douglas was Professor of Social Anthropology at the University of London.

P.R.D. Peter Dry, Senior Lecturer, Department of Horticulture, Viticulture and Oenology on the Waite Campus of the University of Adelaide.

A.J.D. Dr Anne Duggan is Senior Lecturer in Medieval History at King's College, University of London.

M.J.E. MARGARET EMERY has been a librarian at Roseworthy Agricultural College (q.v.) since 1975 and holds a Graduate Diploma in Wine.

N.F. NICHOLAS FAITH is a financial journalist whose several specialities include wine and brandy. He has written two important books on cognac and other brandies.

C.C.F. CHRISTOPHER FIELDEN is a British wine merchant and collector of wine books whose travels have on three occasions taken him to, and hurriedly from, Albania.

D.G. DENIS GASTIN, once Senior Trade Commissioner in the Australian Embassy in Tokyo and now Australian wine exporter and writer specializing in Japan.

R.G. ROSEMARY GEORGE MW, wine writer, one of the first women to become a Master of Wine (q.v.), whose books include the award-winning *Chablis*.

D.J.G. DAVID GILL MW, wine merchant who played an important part in developing Britain as Bulgaria's biggest export market.

J.G. DR JOHN GLADSTONES, author of *Viticulture and Environment* and former Senior Lecturer in the University of Western Australia Department of Agriculture.

P.A.H. DR PETER HALLGARTEN trained as a chemist before taking over the family wine business in London. His specialist areas include Germany, Rhône, Burgundy, and Israel.

J.H. JAMES HALLIDAY, Australia's most prolific and most respected wine writer, an ex-lawyer who also finds time to run Coldstream Hills winery in the Yarra Valley.

J.M.H. PROFESSOR JAKE HANCOCK is Professor of Geology at Imperial College, University of London and a member of the editorial board of the *Journal of Wine Research*.

J.H.H. DR JUDITH HARVEY became a medical practitioner after a distinguished career as a research scientist.

L.A.H.-S. DR LEOFRANC HOLFORD-STREVENS is a classical scholar and author of *Aulus Gellius* who works for Oxford University Press.

I.J. IAN JAMIESON is a wine merchant-turned-wine writer who passed the Master of Wine examinations in 1970 and is best known for his articles and books on German wines.

H.J. HUGH JOHNSON is the world's most successful wine writer and was introduced to specialist wine writing by the late André Simon (see entries on both).

R.J. RUSSELL JOHNSTONE, viticulturist working for and liaising between the Australian Wine Research Institute and the Division of Horticulture of the Commonwealth Scientific and Industrial Research Organization in Adelaide specializing in agrochemical residues.

T.J. DR TONY JORDAN, oenological consultant and managing director of Domaine Chandon, Australia and previously lecturer in chemistry and research scientist in the USA, UK, France, Spain, and Germany.

E.K. EVA KALUZYNSKA, Brussels-based free-lance journalist with a special interest in wine and a consultant to the European Commission.

J.K. JANE KAY spent three years at the Bordeaux Institute of Oenology (see entry on Bordeaux University) before working as wine-maker in Corsica and, eventually, joining an important British retailer as wine technologist/buyer.

P.K. PHILIP KENNEDY is based at the Oriental Institute of Oxford University where he completed a doctorate in classical Arabic poetry.

J.D.K. JOHN KESBY, social anthropologist with a particular interest in metaphysical systems and myths, who teaches at the University of Kent.

M.K. MEL KNOX is based in California where he has sold wine since 1972, taught wine appreciation classes at the University of California since 1974, and sold French barrels since 1980.

N.L.L. NICHOLAS LANDER, *Financial Times* restaurant writer, author, and ex-restaurateur.

G.J.L. GARETH LAWRENCE is Registrar of the Wine & Spirit Education Trust in London and has a particular interest in the wines of central and south eastern Europe.

T.H.L. PROFESSOR TERRY LEE, Director of the Australian Wine Research Institute in Adelaide (q.v.).

H.L. HARRIET LEMBECK, noted wine educator and writer based in New York.

D.V.L. PROFESSOR DENNIS LINDLEY was until his retirement Professor of Statistics and Head of the Department of Statistics at University College, London, having previously occupied similar positions at Cambridge University and the University College of Wales.

S.P.D.L. SIMON LOFTUS, English wine merchant and award-winning author.

Z.L. ZELMA LONG, second woman to enrol in the Department of Enology at the University of California at Davis, once Head Enologist at the Robert Mondavi Winery and now President of Simi Winery.

M.McN. MAGGIE MCNIE MW, international wine consultant and head of the Greek Wine Bureau in London.

R.J.M. RICHARD MAYSON, wine writer and author of *Portugal's Wines and Wine-makers*.

M.M.-F. MARK MICELI-FARRUGIA has imported wine into Malta, exported wine from Italy, promoted and distributed wine in Canada; his ambition is to produce world-class wine in Malta.

J.T.C.M. JASPER MORRIS MW, joint editor of the *Journal of Wine Research*, wine merchant and author specializing in Burgundy.

A.H.M. ANGELA MUIR MW is a British-based roving wine-making consultant with a particular interest in central and eastern Europe.

R.M.B. ROSE MURRAY BROWN trained as a wine and wine antiques specialist with auctioneers Sotheby's and is now a wine writer with a particular interest in modern China and India.

L.N. LOUISE NICHOLSON is a writer, lecturer, and adviser specializing in India which she has visited more than 50 times.

J.J.P. JEREMY PATERSON, Senior Lecturer in Ancient History at the University of Newcastle-upon-Tyne, is a specialist in Roman economic and social history with particular interest in the Roman wine trade on which he has published.

E.P.-R. EDMUND PENNING-ROWSELL, one of the world's most respected wine writers, author of *The Wines of Bordeaux* (see entry).

T.P. PROFESSOR THOMAS PINNEY, Professor of English at Pomona College in Claremont, California and author of *A History of Wine in America: from the Beginnings to Prohibition*.

J.P. JOHN PLATTER became a South African wine farmer and wine writer after a career as a foreign correspondent for United Press International. *John Platter's Guide to South African Wines* is the country's best-selling wine book.

J.V.P. DR JOHN POSSINGHAM has degrees from the universities of Adelaide and Oxford and was foundation Chief of CSIRO's Division of Horticulture in Australia.

J.R. JAN READ was a research chemist who worked for Fritz Lang among others in the film industry before becoming a wine writer specializing in Spain, Portugal, and Chile.

J.M.R. DR JANE RENFREW (Lady Renfrew of Kaimsthorn) is Vice-President of Lucy Cavendish College, Cambridge. She is a prehistorian and palaeoethnobotanist and is an affiliated lecturer in the Department of Archaeology, University of Cambridge.

P.R.-G. PROFESSOR PASCAL RIBÉREAU-GAYON, author, consultant, and internationally respected Director of the Institut d'Oenologie at the University of Bordeaux.

J.Ro. Signals a significant additional contribution from the editor.

A.H.L.R. ANTHONY ROSE, British lawyer-turned-wine writer who has written regularly on auctions and investment in wine for publications which include the wine trade magazine *Wine & Spirit*.

R.R. ROSEMARY RUDDLE, journalist and author of a book on the recipes and traditions of the French wine harvest.

V.R. VIACHESLAV RYBINSTEV was appointed Deputy Director of Research at the Magaratch (q.v.) wine research institute in Yalta in 1986 and has studied viticulture in Ukraine, Russia, Moldova, Kazakhstan, Uzbekistan, Georgia, Armenia, Azerbaijan, Turkmenistan, Germany, and the south of France.

M.S. MARK SAVAGE MW, wine taster since Oxford University days, wine merchant, and recognized authority on the wines of the Pacific Northwest.

M.W.E.S. MICHAEL SCHUSTER, writer who runs his own wine school in London and has translated the work of Professor Émile Peynaud.

T.S. Dr Tom Scott, part-time wine merchant and Reader in History at the University of Liverpool, specializing in the economic and agrarian history of Germany 1300–1650.

R.E.S. Dr Richard Smart, world-famous Australian viticulturist and author, particularly well known for his work on canopy management.

D.F.S. David Stevens MW was the first Chief Executive of the Institute of Masters of Wine (q.v.) and pioneered British importation of Argentine wines in the 1960s.

K.S. Keith Sutton is Senior Lecturer in Geography at the University of Manchester and has spent 20 years researching Algeria's socio-economic development.

G.T. Geoffrey Taylor is an analytical chemist specializing in wine analysis and has been involved with the British wine trade since 1976.

D.T. Daniel Thomases, American wine writer based in Florence who has worked closely with Luigi Veronelli (q.v.) for many years.

P.T.H.U. Dr Tim Unwin, Reader in Geography at Royal Holloway, University of London, joint editor of *Journal of Wine Research* and author of *Wine and the vine: an historical geography of viticulture and the wine trade.*

P.V.P. Pamela Vandyke Price, prolific English author, and one of the first women wine writers (see entry).

B.M.W. Dr Bernard Watney is a retired physician whose many interests include wine, wine labels, and corkscrews. He co-wrote *Corkscrews for Collectors* which has since been translated into French and German.

A.D.W. Professor A. Dinsmoor Webb retired in 1982 as Professor Emeritus from the University of California at Davis and continues to write and to act as consultant oenologist world-wide.

A.G.W. Andrew Williams established the first British company to specialize in importing organic wines before becoming a wine writer.

N.G.W. Nigel Wilson, Fellow and Tutor in Classics at Lincoln College, Oxford where *inter alia* he looks after the college cellar. His main work as a classical scholar has been as an expert in Greek palaeography.

H.M.W. Hanneke Wirtjes teaches medieval English at Wadham College, Oxford and has written a book on wine in classical antiquity and the Middle Ages.

Maps of Wine Regions

List of Colour Plates

Note to the Reader

Entries are arranged in letter-by-letter alphabetical order up to the first punctuation in the headword, except that names beginning with Mc are ordered as if they were spelt Mac, and St and Ste (French) are arranged as if they were spelt Saint and Sainte. Château and châteaux appear in full as headwords, but are abbreviated to ch and chx elsewhere. Entries appear under the name of the château, and not under C.

Cross-references are denoted by small capitals and indicate the entry headword to which attention is being directed. Cross-references appear only where reference is likely to amplify or increase understanding of the entry being read. They are not given in all instances where a headword appears in the text.

All wine-producing countries have an entry. The more significant ones also have individual entries for regions, or in the case of Australia and the USA for states. German wines, since they carry the name of their region of origin on the bottle label, are discussed within regional entries. Each wine-producing state of former Yugoslavia and the former Soviet Union has its own entry. Individual wine producers and properties which have played an important part in the history of wine have an entry, as do all appellations from France, Spain, and Portugal. Italy is extensively covered by a mixture of individual denominations and regional entries.

Measurements are given in metric accompanied by the United States equivalent. The abbreviation hl stands for hectolitres and ha for hectares.

A

ABBOCCATO, Italian for medium sweet (less sweet than AMABILE) or, literally, 'palatable' from *bocca* or 'mouth'. See also SWEETNESS.

ABOCADO, Spanish for medium sweet.

ABOURIOU is a minor south western dark-berried vine variety that is slowly disappearing from France's vineyards. It is still allowed into Côtes du MARMANDAIS but only just and is also found in many red VINS DE PAYS of the south west. It achieved some degree of international fame in 1976 when French AMPELOGRAPHER Paul Truel identified as Abouriou cuttings sent to Australia from California as Early Burgundy but these were subsequently uprooted to make way for something more marketable.

ABRUZZI, mountainous region in central ITALY with a significant coastline on the Adriatic sea to the south of the MARCHES, and an important producer of wine (see map p. 517). The Abruzzi is seventh among Italy's 20 regions in terms of volume of wine produced, which is almost as much as in PIEDMONT.

Despite the presence of two qualitatively important vine varieties (Montepulciano d'Abruzzo and Trebbiano d'Abruzzo), despite the warm climate, and despite favourable vineyard sites where the hills descend towards the Adriatic and enjoy the benefits of summer heat and solar radiation from the sea, most of the region's production is undistinguished, and less than five per cent of the Abruzzi's 3.3 million hl/87 million gal produced each year are DOC wines. The DOCs themselves are not particularly well conceived, with excessively generous production limits—100 hl/ha (5.7 ton/acre) for Montepulciano d'Abruzzo and over 120 hl/ha for Trebbiano d'Abruzzo—and little attempt to define suitable subzones for the varieties: either Trebbiano or Montepulciano can be planted in any of the region's four provinces. The only limitation is that of ALTITUDE, with 500 m/1,640 ft being the maximum for most vineyards, although southern exposures up to 600 m can be planted; ripening either Trebbiano or Montepulciano at these heights can be a hazardous business indeed.

In spite of this rickety legislative framework, good wine is produced in the Abruzzi, with an important tradition of fine, often keenly priced Montepulciano existing in such townships as Brecciarola, Città Sant'Angelo, Controguerra, Loreto, Tocco da Casauria, Torano Nuovo, and Vasto. The MONTEPULCIANO grape itself, at its best, gives wines of deep colour, substantial EXTRACT, firm TANNINS, and low ACIDITY. It was once much prized as a blending wine in the north of Italy, particularly in TUSCANY and, in this context, the DOC limits of extract, between 18 and 27 g/l, seem to have little logic behind them. The wine frequently has a detectable animal quality to it, which can range from the attractively 'sweaty saddle' to the intolerably gamey, but it is not clear if this element is due to the TERROIR, to the way in which the wine is fermented, or to the kind of WOOD in which it is aged. CASK AGEING was virtually universal before the Second World War but has been less practised recently as some producers, particularly the CO-OPERATIVES, have aimed at a simple quaffing style which hardly demonstrates the innate character of the variety.

Trebbiano d'Abruzzo, mentioned as a wine of high quality by Cervantes in his *Novelas ejemplares*, is not made from Trebbiano at all but rather from the BOMBINO, a variety widely employed in APULIA. Better Trebbiano d'Abruzzo is a pleasant, if not memorable, wine, but in the hands of one producer, Edoardo Valentini, who combines low YIELDS with a severe selection in the cellar, and ferments and ages his wine entirely in wood, it is one of Italy's outstanding, and certainly its longest-lived, dry white wines. Valentini's Trebbiano d'Abruzzo is so startlingly different from that of his peers that it is difficult to decide whether it is a quirk of fate or the hand of genius that has revealed the true potential of an otherwise quite obscure grape variety. D.T.

Anderson, B., *The Wine Atlas of Italy* (London and New York, 1990).
Gleave, D., *The Wines of Italy* (London and New York, 1989).

ABSCISIC ACID, a HORMONE that occurs naturally in vines and regulates growth and physiology. Its synthesis is encouraged by physiological stresses including short days and by WATER STRESS. In the vine, abscisic acid is involved in LEAF FALL, stunted shoots, bud dormancy, opening of STOMATA, and the biosynthesis of PHENOLICS during grape ripening. It has also been suggested that abscisic acid is involved in the initiation of grape RIPENING. R.E.S.

Champagnol, F., *Éléments de physiologie de la vigne et de viticulture générale* (Saint-Gely-du-Fesc, 1984).
Mullins, M. G., Bouquet, A., and Williams, L., *Biology of the Vine* (Cambridge, 1992).

ABU NUWAS (d. AD 814), half Arab/half Persian, was court poet and close friend of the Abbasid Caliph al-Amīn (reigned AD 809–813). He was one of the greatest ARAB POETS of classical Arabic/Islamic culture and, despite his eloquence in all the poetic genres, is remembered principally in the Arabic tradition for his wine poems (the *Khamriyyāt*). His ribaldry, much of it legendary, captured the imagination of succeeding generations, hence his appearance as boon companion of Hārūn al-Rashīd (the most famous Abbasid caliph) in four of the stories in *The Thousand and One Nights*. P.K.

ABYMES, named CRU just south of CHAMBÉRY (famous for its VERMOUTH) whose name may be added to the eastern French appellation Vin de SAVOIE. The wines are typically light, dry whites made from the local JACQUÈRE grape, although there has been some experimentation with Chardonnay.

AC, sometimes **AOC,** common abbreviation for APPELLATION CONTRÔLÉE, the French quality wine category.

ACADEME, originally a Greek word for a site of scholastic endeavour, and today a term embracing all that is achieved there. It impinges considerably on the world of wine.

Wine-making was already a sophisticated practical art by the beginning of the 19th century, but in the second half of the century the seminal work of Louis PASTEUR heralded its transition to an applied science worthy of academic study. Vine-growing and wine-making were soon recognized as academic disciplines and in 1880, coincidentally, both the University of California (now established at DAVIS) and the Institut d'Oenologie at BORDEAUX UNIVERSITY began teaching and researching VITICULTURE and OENOLOGY. The devastation caused in the mid 19th century by FUNGAL DISEASES and the PHYLLOXERA pest may help to explain the coincidence.

During the 20th century academic institutions throughout the world have worked in tandem with their local wine industries both to teach the scientific principles of vine-growing and wine-making (increasingly regarded as the single discipline of wine-growing) and to research refinements and solutions. Other academic institutions of importance to wine include ADELAIDE, CHANGINS, CONEGLIANO, DIJON, GEILWEILERHOF, GEISENHEIM, KLOSTERNEUBURG, MAGARATCH, MONTPELLIER, ROSEWORTHY, SAN MICHELE ALL'ADIGE, STELLENBOSCH, and WÄDENSWIL. Many of these are government funded, although grants for specific research projects are increasingly sought from industry.

In traditional wine regions wine-growing was taught by apprenticeship and apprentices were taught to respect TRADITION above SCIENCE. Formal academic training has long been the norm in the New World, on the other hand. By the late 20th century, however, it was customary for even a seventh generation Old World wine producer to have received some sort of formal academic training, certainly in his or her own region and very possibly abroad. This not only reflects a fundamental change of attitude towards the science of wine production on the part of Old World producers, but also played a crucial role in the widespread improvement in wine quality during the 1970s and 1980s. Increased travel has taught many New World producers, on the other hand, to augment the science taught by academe with practical experience.

ACCAD, GUY, Lebanese viticulturist and oenologist with a controversial approach to red wine-making, based in Nuits-St-Georges, BURGUNDY, and active since the mid 1980s. Accad is convinced that quality is closely linked to the ability to age and that great red burgundies should be made to last. Much of his advice, both viticultural and oenological, is uncontroversial: very ripe grapes, low YIELDS, high fermentation TEMPERATURES rising to a maximum of 30 °C, and a modest use of new WOOD for ageing. The heart of the controversy over Accad's method lies in the long cold MACERATION period before fermentation, five to 15 days at 8–14 °C/46–57 °F (in some cases longer) and in the high doses of SULPHUR applied to the grapes at this stage, at least 0.1 g/l, two or three times the normal amount. The rationale is that water in the juice, aided by the solvent properties of SULPHUR DIOXIDE, extracts considerable ANTHOCYANS (important for a wine's keeping potential) and that it is a much more discriminating solvent for AROMAS and TANNINS than ALCOHOL; for the same reason there is also no need for further alcoholic maceration of the wine once fermentation is complete. When young these wines seem exceptionally dark for Burgundy and unusually sweet to smell (critics accuse them of being 'RHÔNE-like'), and there is also a certain similarity of style from the systematic use of selected YEAST. There is no question that Accad's motives are irreproachable and that the domains which use him are serious; nor is there any doubt that fine, well-structured, and distinctive wines have been made under his guidance. Equally, many experienced Burgundy tasters have real doubts as to their typicity and, indeed, their quality. However, these are meant to be wines for the long term, and, whilst one may remain unconvinced, it is certainly too early to be definitively dismissive about them. M.W.E.S.

Parker, R., *Burgundy* (New York, 1990).

ACETALDEHYDE, the most common member of the group of chemical compounds known as ALDEHYDES, a constituent of nearly all plant material, including grapes. In pure liquid form acetaldehyde has a particularly penetrating and unpleasant aroma. At the dilute concentrations normally present in wines, and mixed with wine's many other odorants, it is not unpleasant but above a certain level can make the wine smell 'flat' and vapid. At slightly higher concentrations, it is the distinctive and characteristic smell of FINO sherry and other FLOR wines.

Because it is the first compound formed when OXYGEN reacts with the ETHANOL in wine, wine-makers are careful to minimize delicate white wines' exposure to air. (This is not so critical with heavier red wines because their TANNINS are even readier to react with oxygen.) Special care must be taken while BOTTLING white wines as this is when the introduction of oxygen can most easily damage the delicate aromas.

As most wine consumers know, the aroma of a white wine is particularly fragile. When a bottle of white wine is only partially emptied, the freshness of its aroma is rapidly lost and replaced by a vapid OXIDIZED smell that is due to the conversion of ethanol to acetaldehyde. The formation of perceptible acetaldehyde, accompanied by a browning of colour, is a typical sign of OXIDATION.

Acetaldehyde is the next to last substance involved in the FERMENTATION pathway (and is therefore a minor constituent in bread as well as wine). Post-fermentation traces of acetaldehyde remain in all wines and all distilled spirits, including BRANDY. A.D.W.

ACETALS, name given by scientists to a large group of natural organic chemical compounds formed by reactions between ALDEHYDES and ALCOHOLS. Since this reaction is encouraged in acid solutions, it occurs in wines. Acid also facilitates the reverse reaction by which acetals are hydrolysed (with water) to the aldehyde and the alcohol. The balance between their formation and the hydrolysis reactions in the wine medium is such that only small amounts of the acetals are present.

Acetal (the name assigned to acetaldehyde diethyl acetal) has an odour that is roughly similar to that of ACETALDEHYDE but a bit less harsh and penetrating. Relatively small amounts of acetals are found in most table wines because of their relatively low concentrations of aldehydes. Oxidized wines, however, such as some SHERRY and the VIN JAUNE of the Jura, have greater concentrations of acetals because of their greater concentrations of aldehydes. Fortified wines (see FORTIFICATION) in general tend to have higher concentrations of acetals derived from the fortifying spirit. A.D.W.

ACETIC ACID, the most common of the VOLATILE ACIDS, one of the more common organic chemicals encountered in foods, and the sour-tasting two-carbon acid which is the main flavour constituent of VINEGAR. **Acetification** of a wine begins when it is exposed to OXYGEN, which allows ACETOBACTER bacteria to transform the wine's ALCOHOL into acetic acid. Such a wine may be described as **acetic**. Acetic acid may also be directly produced during primary FERMENTATION; many white wines have detectable acetic acid levels which are the result of regular YEAST activity. Acetic acid is the simplest member of a large family of organic acids which, when reacted with GLYCEROL, constitute the natural fats of plants and animals. A.D.W. & T.J.

ACETOBACTER, group of BACTERIA capable of affecting wine by converting it into VINEGAR and therefore highly undesirable. Because acetobacter can only survive in OXYGEN they are described as 'obligate aerobes'. They are also one of the very few groups of bacteria which can live in the high acid (low PH) environment of wine (although see also LACTIC BACTERIA).

Ideal conditions for the growth of acetobacter are temperatures between 30° and 40 °C (104 °F), relatively high pH values of between 3.5 and 4.0, low alcohol concentrations, absence of SULPHUR DIOXIDE, and generous supplies of oxygen. For this reason, safe wine-making favours low storage temperatures, good levels of ACIDITY and alcohol, use of sulphur dioxide as a disinfectant, and barrels, vats, and tanks kept full at all times, and the use of CARBON DIOXIDE, NITROGEN, or INERT GAS MIXTURE blanketing.

Certain acetobacter are capable of oxidizing ETHANOL all the way to CARBON DIOXIDE and water without stopping at the usual intermediate ACETIC ACID so necessary in vinegar production. Not surprisingly, these acetobacter are not favoured by producers of wine vinegar. A.D.W.

ACID, when used as an adjectival wine-tasting term rather than a chemical noun (see ACIDS), is usually pejorative and means that the wine has too much ACIDITY.

ACID ADJUSTMENT. See ACIDIFICATION.

ACIDIFICATION, often referred to more diplomatically as **acid adjustment**, is the wine-making process of increasing the ACIDITY in a grape must or wine. This is a common practice in warm wine regions (as common as ENRICHMENT, or CHAPTALIZATION, in cool wine regions), and is often the only course open to a wine-maker wanting to make a balanced wine from grapes which have been allowed a growing season long enough to develop flavour by reaching full physical RIPENESS. A good level of ACIDS (and therefore low PH) not only increases the apparent freshness and fruitiness of many wines, it also protects the wine against attack from BACTERIA and improves COLOUR (as explained under acidity).

Acidification is usually sanctioned by local wine regulations within carefully delineated limits in order to prevent stretching of wine by adding sugar and water along with the permitted acid. In temperate zones such as Bordeaux and Burgundy, acidification is allowed, but with the understandable proviso that no wine may be both acidified and enriched.

Timing of the acid addition varies, but adding acid usually lowers pH so that an addition before FERMENTATION results in better microbiological control of subsequent processes and favours the formation of desirable aroma substances. Fine tuning of acid levels may take place at the final BLENDING stage.

Regulations vary from country to country but the most common permitted additives for acidification are, in descending order, TARTARIC ACID, CITRIC ACID, and MALIC ACID. Tartaric is the acid of choice for adding to grape juice before fermentation because, unlike both citric and malic acid which can be attacked by LACTIC BACTERIA, tartaric acid is rarely degraded. Tartaric acid has the disadvantages, however, that it is the most expensive of the three and that significant amounts of the acid may be precipitated as TARTRATES and lost from the wine. Malic acid is used infrequently because of its microbiological instability and its cost. Citric acid, while also being susceptible to microbiological attack, has the merit of being the least expensive and is used widely for inexpensive wines. It is often chosen for late acid additions because, unlike tartaric acid, it does not affect cold STABILIZATION.

See also DEACIDIFICATION, a less common wine-making measure used in cool climates. A.D.W.

ACIDITY is a general term for the fresh, tart, or sour taste produced by the natural organic ACIDS present in a liquid. Wines, together with most other refreshing or appetizing drinks, owe their attractive qualities to a proper balance between this acidic character and the sweet and bitter sensations of other components. All refreshing drinks contain some acidity, which is typically sensed on the human palate by a prickling sensation on the sides of the tongue (see TASTING).

The acidity of the original grape juice has an important influence on wine quality because of its direct influence on COLOUR (see below), its effect on the growth of YEASTS and BACTERIA (harmful and beneficial), and its inherent effects on flavour qualities.

Grape juice acidity is highest just at the beginning of GRAPE RIPENING, at which stage grapes have half as much acid as lemons. (Because of this high acidity, some vine-growers in tropical regions, such as Thailand, sell the thinned green berries as an acidic ingredient for relishes.)

Acidity is one of the most important components in both grape juice and wine, and is also easily quantifiable. What is measured, although in different ways in different countries, is usually the TOTAL ACIDITY, which is the sum of the FIXED ACIDS and the VOLATILE ACIDS. To a scientist, acidity is the extent to which a solution is acid, caused by protons (hydrogen ions or H^+), which may be present in either free or bound forms. Another way of measuring acidity is to measure the concentration of hydrogen ions (H^+) free in solution, using the logarithmic PH scale. The higher a wine's acidity, the lower its pH.

Acidity helps to preserve the colour of red wines because the pH affects the ionization of ANTHOCYANS and the ionized form has a different colour from the un-ionized form. The lower the pH, the redder (less blue) the colour is and the greater the colour stability. As pH values rise (in less acid wines), pigments become increasingly blue and the colour becomes less stable with pigments eventually assuming muddy grey forms. Red wines from warmer regions have colours that are bluer than those from colder regions which produce wines with higher acidity. Higher pH values also cause the PHENOLICS of white wines to darken and eventually to polymerize as brown deposits.

Excessive acidity—resulting either from excessive concentrations of natural plant acids in the grape due to insufficient heat during ripening or, more rarely, from overenthusiastic ACIDIFICATION in the winery—makes wines sharp, tart, and sometimes physically uncomfortable to drink. Too little acidity, on the other hand—the consequence of picking too late, or such heat during ripening that the natural plant acids are largely decomposed—results in wines that are flat, uninteresting, and described typically by wine tasters as 'flabby'.

See TOTAL ACIDITY for more details. A.D.W. & B.G.C.

ACIDS, members of a group of chemical compounds which are responsible for the sharp or sour taste of all drinks and foods, including wine. The most important acids contained in grapes are TARTARIC ACID and, in slightly lower concentrations, MALIC ACID. Malic acid occurs in many different plants and fruits, but vines are among the very few plants with large concentrations of tartaric acid in their fruit. The principal acid component in most plants is CITRIC ACID but VINIFERA vines are also unusual among plants in accumulating only very small amounts of citric acid.

Grapes contain a large number of acids other than their major constituents tartaric and malic acids. Present in low concentrations are several of the fatty acids, of which the most common is ACETIC ACID, one of the VOLATILE ACIDS. Acetic acid is responsible for the sour taste of VINEGAR but in grapes it is involved in many of the metabolic processes during the ripening of the fruit.

Another group of acids involved in the growth of vines and the production of grapes, and in the metabolic activity of yeasts, is the keto-acid group. These compounds are involved in the final metabolism of sugars to yield energy for the many activities of living systems. They are present in grapes and wines in small concentrations.

Some other acids involved in the growth of vines accumulate in the berry in very small amounts and some of these persist into the wine. Other acids found in wines, while possibly present in traces in grapes, are formed mainly during FERMENTATION. Among those present in the largest concentrations are LACTIC ACID, SUCCINIC ACID, and carbonic acid.

Various acids are also occasionally added during winemaking. (See ASCORBIC ACID, SORBIC ACID, and sulphurous acid, which is SULPHUR DIOXIDE.)

Acids are important in wine not just because, in moderation, they make it taste refreshing, but also because they ward off harmful BACTERIA and can keep it microbiologically stable. Most bacteria, and all of those of greatest danger to man, are incapable of living in distinctly acid solutions such as wines. Two groups of bacteria are major exceptions to this rule, however, the ACETOBACTER and the various LACTIC BACTERIA.

A wine's concentration of acids is called its ACIDITY, which can be measured in various ways. Acidity is closely, if inversely, related to PH. A.D.W.

ACIDULATION, wine-making process more commonly known as ACIDIFICATION.

ADEGA, Portuguese word for cellar or winery.

ADELAIDE, usual abbreviation in the wine world for the **University of Adelaide,** in South Australia, with which ROSEWORTHY Agricultural College was merged in 1991 to form the Department of Horticulture, Viticulture, and Oenology, Australia's principal and influential centre of wine education and research (see ACADEME and AUSTRALIAN INFLUENCE).

A new four-year Bachelor of Agricultural Science degree, with majors in VITICULTURE and OENOLOGY, was introduced in

Adega: From Vizetelly's *Facts about Madeira and Port* (1880).

1992 to replace the more specialized three-year Roseworthy degree. Much of this degree is taught in the South Australian capital city of Adelaide where students have access to the Commonwealth Scientific and Industrial Research Organization (CSIRO) Division of Horticulture and the Australian Wine Research Institute, both organizations having established a considerable international reputation for research in viticulture and oenology respectively. T.H.L.

Adelaide Hills, fashionable, relatively high, cool wine region in AUSTRALIA. For more detail see SOUTH AUSTRALIA.

adulteration and fraud have dogged the wine trade throughout its history. The variability and value of wine have traditionally made it a target for unscrupulous operators, as catalogued in the LITERATURE OF WINE. The long human chain stretching from grower to consumer affords many opportunities for illegal practices. It is important to remember, however, that at various times the law has viewed the same practices differently, sometimes condoning, sometimes condemning them. What we know as adulteration, our ancestors may have classed as a legitimate part of the wine-making process.

The simplest and most obvious form of adulterating wine is to add water. This is not necessarily fraudulent. In Ancient GREECE, for example, no civilized man would dream of drinking undiluted wine. The practice becomes illegal when done surreptitiously to cheat the consumer or defraud the taxman.

Another means of stretching wine is to 'cut', or blend, it with spirits or other (usually poorer-quality) wines. BORDEAUX merchants in the 18th century cut fine clarets with rough, stronger wine imported from Spain, the Rhône, or the Midi to increase profits, but also because it was genuinely believed that the resulting fuller bodied concoction was more to the English taste. JULLIEN describes this common practice as *travail à l'anglaise*. Similarly merchants in 18th-century OPORTO began to adulterate port with brandy. The systematization of this process by the Portuguese government eventually led to an accepted method of 'adulteration', entirely lawful, to produce PORT as we know it today.

Other ways of altering the nature of a wine were perfectly legal. In the past wines turned sour after a year or two and techniques used to cure or disguise 'sick' wines were commonplace. Classical and medieval recipes suggested adding a range of substances ranging from milk (perhaps a precursor of FINING with CASEIN) and mustard to ashes, nettles, and LEAD. Although home doctoring was routine, when these techniques were employed by merchants or taverners deliberately to mislead the customer, the practice was as illegal as it was ubiquitous. In the first century AD PLINY the Elder bemoaned the fact that 'not even our nobility ever enjoys wines that are genuine'.

One particular method of altering the nature of wine remains controversial; the addition of sugar during fermentation to increase the eventual ALCOHOLIC STRENGTH, known as CHAPTALIZATION after the French minister CHAPTAL, who gave it respectability at the beginning of the 19th century. Producers in wine regions warm enough to need no such assistance tend to be scornful of the practice (although they may well indulge in ACIDIFICATION to increase the ACIDITY of their wines).

It is assumed today that, unless explicitly stated otherwise, wine is the product of naturally fermented grape juice. However, the practice of fabricating wine, as opposed to simply doctoring it, has a long and chequered history, often most prolific and ingenious at times when true grape wine has been difficult to obtain. In 1709 Joseph Addison wrote in the *Tatler* of the 'fraternity of chymical operators . . . who squeeze Bourdeaux out of a sloe and draw Champagne from an apple', apparently a profession of long standing. Although other fruits were often the basis of these concoctions, 'wine' was sometimes completely manufactured from a mixture of water, sugar, dyes, and other chemicals, as has reputedly (and mysteriously in an era of wine surplus) been known in more recent times.

Wines were also fabricated from raisins. In the 1880s and 1890s the scourge of PHYLLOXERA led to a serious shortage of wine in France. In response, a thriving industry manufacturing wine from imported raisins sprang up on the Mediterranean coast. During American PROHIBITION in the 1920s various methods were contrived to circumvent the law by producing wines at home from raisins, dried grape 'bricks', and tinned GRAPE CONCENTRATE (using techniques common to HOME WINE-MAKING today).

One of the most common forms of fraud does not involve any doctoring or fabricating of the wine, but merely the label. Once a region made a name for its wines, others tried to steal it. In Roman times ordinary wines were passed off as valuable FALERNIAN. From the 19th century vine-growers have fought for the legal apparatus to protect their names (see APPELLATION CONTRÔLÉE).

The adulteration or fraudulent sale of wine can be dangerous. The consumer may even be put medically at risk, by the use of lead in ancient times and by METHANOL contamination in the 20th century. The use of lead in wine for many centuries is an obvious example. Pliny wrote: 'So many poisons are employed to force wine to suit our taste—and we are surprised that it is not wholesome'. In 1833 the influential English wine writer Cyrus REDDING recommended: 'The best test against adulterated wine is a perfect acquaintance with that which is good.'

Illegal practices frequently hurt the grower and merchant. Once the reputation of a wine has been jeopardized, economic hardship may result. The flagrant adulteration of port wine in the 18th century resulted in a rapid and dramatic fall in demand. The Portuguese government stepped in and formed a state company to control the trade.

Consumers, growers, and merchants are not alone in trying to prevent adulteration and fraud. Local authorities and (in this century) governments have fought it. Regulations and legislation have been passed for many reasons: to protect the consumer; to preserve the good name of the local wine; or to facilitate TAXATION.

In medieval London it was illegal for taverners to keep French or Spanish wines in the same cellar as those from Germany to prevent mixing or substitution. A vintner found selling corrupt wine was forced to drink it, then banned from the trade. German punishments of the time were more severe, ranging from beatings and branding to hanging.

The legal apparatus existing to combat fraud and adulteration today is the culmination of many battles waged by both consumers and trade. In 1820 Frederick Accum published his *Treatise* stating that wine was the commodity most

Adulteration: illustration from the 1836 edition of Cyrus REDDING's influential *A History and Description of Modern Wines.*

at risk. Thirteen years later Cyrus Redding reported no improvement and it was not until 1860 that the first British Food and Drug Act was passed.

As for wine-producing countries, the economic distress caused by PHYLLOXERA was the main stimulus to legislation. The French government produced a legal definition of wine in 1889, the Germans framed their first national wine law in 1892 (superseded by the more thorough 1909 version), and the Italians in 1904. The French appellation contrôlée system, defining wines by geography rather than simply composition, did not become nationally viable until the 1930s.

Although once rife, adulteration and fraud have been considerably rarer in the wine trade since the adoption of CONTROLLED APPELLATION systems and methods by which to enforce them such as France's Service de la Répression des Fraudes. There have been examples of CONTAMINANTS in wine, both deliberate and accidental, but passing off has become increasingly difficult and, just possibly, less rewarding as wine consumers become ever more sophisticated and more concerned with inherent wine quality than the hierarchy of famous names. Consumers may with justification feel that the wine trade has attracted more than its fair share of charlatans because fraud in any field in which expertise is difficult to acquire and viewed with suspicion (such as wine and fine art) makes an exceptionally good story and attracts more media attention than most other types of commercial fraud. Nevertheless, the Commission of the EUROPEAN UNION was sufficiently concerned about potential fraud over its compulsory DISTILLATION scheme in 1993 that it specifically cited the need to police the system effectively as one of its four major proposals for reform.

See also CONTAMINANTS. H.B. & J.R.

Accum, F., *Treatise on Adulteration of Food and Culinary Poisons* (London, 1820).
Barr, A., *Wine Snobbery: An Insider's Guide to the Booze Business* (London, 1988).
Johnson, H., *The Story of Wine* (London and New York, 1989).
Jullien, A., *Topographie de tous les vignobles connus* (Paris, 1816).
Loubère, L. A., *The Red and the White: A History of Wine in France and Italy in the Nineteenth Century* (Albany, NY, 1978).
Redding, C., *The History and Description of Modern Wines* (London, 1833).

AEGEAN ISLANDS, islands in the Aegean Sea between modern GREECE and TURKEY. From 1050 BC onwards most of these islands were populated by Greeks. Some of the best Greek wine came from these islands, with Chian wine, from the island of Chios, ranked highly in both Ancient Greece and Ancient ROME. Wines from Lesbos, Thasos, and Cos also featured strongly. Chian wine was still highly valued in the Middle Ages and traded in quantity by the GENOANS, for example. H.H.A.

AERATION, the deliberate and controlled exposure of a substance to air, and particularly to its reactive component OXYGEN.

The aeration of wine during WINE-MAKING must be carefully controlled, since excessive exposure to oxygen can result in OXIDATION and the possible formation of excess ACETIC ACID. At the beginning of FERMENTATION some aeration is necessary since YEAST needs oxygen for growth. The cellar operation of TOPPING UP can expose the wine to an amount of oxygen that contributes to the BARREL MATURATION process. The amount of aeration involved in the cellar technique of RACKING wine from one container, usually a BARREL, to another can also be positively beneficial to a wine's development. Specifically, aeration can often cure wines suffering from REDUCTION and can usually remove malodorous and volatile HYDROGEN SULPHIDE, MERCAPTANS, and some other SULPHIDES from young wines. Often for the same reasons, some aeration before SERVING can also benefit some wines after BOTTLE AGEING.

See also DECANTING.

AFGHANISTAN, Middle Eastern country in which about 50,000 ha/123,500 acres of vines are officially cultivated for TABLE GRAPES and DRYING GRAPES. At one time wine may have been made and shipped along the old Silk Road to India.

AGE in a wine is not necessarily a virtue. See AGEING. See also VINE AGE.

AGEING of wine, an important aspect of wine connoisseurship, and one which distinguishes wine from almost every other drink.

History

When a fine wine is allowed to age spectacular changes can occur which increase both its complexity and monetary value. Ageing is dependent on several factors: the wine must be intrinsically capable of it; it must be correctly stored (in a cool place and out of contact with air); and some form of capital INVESTMENT is usually necessary.

Although the BIBLE suggests that Luke understood that old wine was finer than new wine, the Romans (see Ancient ROME and, specifically, HORACE) were the first connoisseurs systematically to appreciate fine wines which had been allowed to age, although there is some evidence of wine ageing in Ancient GREECE. Certain wines (DRIED GRAPE WINES, for example) were suitable for ageing because of their high sugar content and were stored in sealed earthenware jars or AMPHORAE. The best, FALERNIAN and SURRENTINE wines, required 15 to 20 years before they were considered at their best and were sometimes kept for decades.

The Greek physician GALEN (b. AD 130) noted that an 'aged' wine need not necessarily be old, but might simply have the characteristics of age. In other words it was possible, indeed very common, to age wines prematurely by means of heating or smoking them (see Ancient ROME). At one time the smoky taste of 'aged' wines became a vogue in itself, though Galen warned that they were not as wholesome as naturally old wines.

After the collapse of the Roman Empire the appreciation of aged wines disappeared for a millennium. The thin, low alcohol wines of northern Europe were good for only a few months, after which they turned sour and were sold cheap. The only wines that could be enjoyed a little longer were the sweeter and more alcoholic wines of the Mediterranean such as MALMSEY and SACK.

By the 16th century exceptions to this rule could be found in the huge casks of top-quality wine made from RIESLING wine kept beneath German palaces (see GERMAN HISTORY). These wines were preserved through a combination of sweetness and ACIDITY in the must, the coldness of the cellar, and the cellarmaster's habit of constantly TOPPING UP the cask to avoid OXIDATION.

The real breakthrough came with the introduction in the 17th century of glass BOTTLES and CORKS. The ageing of wine in bottle was pioneered in England by connoisseurs of fine CLARET and port. English wine drinkers rediscovered pleasures largely unknown since Roman times. As binning (see BIN) and storing wine became commonplace during the course of the 18th century, the wine bottle evolved into the cylindrical shape we know today.

Other methods of preserving wine were developed or rediscovered: the addition of spirits to a partially fermented wine to produce fortified wines (see FORTIFICATION); the systematic topping up of a SOLERA system to produce wines like sherry; and the heating of madeira.

Demand for mature wines transformed the wine trade. Aside from a few wealthy owners, most vine-growers could not afford to keep stocks of past vintages. Only MERCHANTS could do that, and their economic power and hold over the producers increased during the 18th and 19th centuries. This was most demonstrably the case in BORDEAUX, BEAUNE, and OPORTO, where merchants amassed huge stocks, vast fortunes, and powerful reputations. H.B.

Johnson, H., *The Story of Wine* (London, 1989).
Younger, W., *Gods, Men and Wine* (London, 1966).

Which wines to age

The ageing of wine is an important element in getting the most from it but, contrary to popular opinion, only a small subgroup of wines benefit from extended BOTTLE AGEING. The great bulk of wine sold today, red as well as white and pink, is designed to be drunk within a year, or at most two, of BOTTLING. Before bottling most wines are usually aged for several months in tanks or wooden COOPERAGE but they are not expected to undergo the subtle evolution involved in bottle ageing.

Wines which generally do not improve with time spent in bottle, and which are usually best consumed as soon as possible after bottling (although after a few weeks in bottle has eliminated any BOTTLE SICKNESS) include the following—although all of the following is only the most approximate generalization: wines packaged in any containers other than bottles—BOXES, for example; wines designated TABLE WINES in the EUROPEAN UNION, JUG WINES in the USA, and their everyday, commercial equivalents elsewhere; almost all branded wines, with the possible exception of some red bordeaux; most FIGHTING VARIETALS with the possible exception of the best made from Cabernet Sauvignon grapes; most German QBA wines almost all French VINS DE PAYS; almost all wine coloured pink; all wines released within less than six months of the vintage such as those labelled NOUVEAU and the like; FINO and MANZANILLA and similar light, dry sherries; most wines labelled MOSCATO and all ASTI SPUMANTE.

Even among finer wines, different wines mature at different rates, according to individual VINTAGE characteristics, their exact provenance, and how they were made. Such factors as BARREL FERMENTATION for whites and BARREL MATURATION for wines of any colour play a part in the likely life cycle of the wine. In general, the lower a wine's PH, the longer it is capable of evolving. Among reds, generally speaking the higher the level of FLAVOUR COMPOUNDS and PHENOLICS, particularly TANNINS, the longer it is capable of being aged. Wines made from the Cabernet Sauvignon and Nebbiolo grapes, for example, and many of those made from Syrah, should be aged longer than those based on Merlot or Pinot Noir—and certainly much longer than the average wine made from Gamay or Grenache. Among white wines, partly because of their higher acidity and their aroma and BOUQUET precursors, the finest Riesling and Loire Chenin Blanc evolve more slowly than wines based on Chardonnay.

In general terms, better-quality wines made from the following grape varieties should benefit from some bottle age, with a *very* approximate number of years in bottle in brackets:

Red wines

Cabernet Sauvignon (4–20)
Merlot (2–10)
Tannat of Madiran (4–12)
Raboso of Piave (4–8)
Pinot Noir (2–8)
Syrah/Shiraz (4–16)
Nebbiolo (4–20)
Sangiovese (2–8)
Zinfandel (2–6)
Aglianico of Taurasi (4–15)
Baga of Barraida (4–8)
Kadarka of Hungary (3–7)
Plavac Mali of Croatia (4–8)
Melnik of Bulgaria (3–7)
Saperavi of Russia (3–10)
Xynomavro of Greece (4–10)

White wines

Riesling (2–30)
Chardonnay (2–6)
Loire Chenin Blanc (4–30)
Petit Manseng of Jurançon (3–10)
Furmint of Hungary (3–25)
and all botrytized wines (5–25)

Most fortified wines and their like, such as VINS DOUX NATURELS and VINS DE LIQUEUR, are bottled when their producers think they are ready to drink. Exceptions to this are the extremely rare bottle-aged sherries, vintage PORT (which is expressly designed for many years' bottle ageing), single quinta ports, and crusted port.

Producers of SPARKLING WINES usually claim that their wines are ready to drink on release, but experience has shown that release dates have in some instances relied more on commercial considerations than on a wine's maturity. Even if yeast AUTOLYSIS ceases when the wine is disgorged, better-quality young sparkling wines with their high levels of acidity can often improve considerably with an additional year or so in bottle. And top-quality champagne has been known to withstand several decades in bottle, even if it can be appreciated only by those who share the GOÛT anglais.

BRANDY like almost all spirits, does not benefit from bottle ageing.

STORING wine in particular conditions can also affect the rate at which wine ages; the lower the TEMPERATURE, the slower the maturation. Conversely, ageing can be hastened by stripping a young wine of its solids (by very heavy FILTRATION or FINING, for example), and by storing wine in warmer conditions. Also, in general, the smaller the bottle, the faster its contents mature, presumably because of the greater proportion of OXYGEN in the bottle, as a result of the bottling process and during ageing via the pump action which results from the effects of temperature variations on the cork. The greater glass surface to wine volume ratio may also have an effect, but this is not established.

How wine ages

The descriptions below concern only those wines designed specifically to be aged. A high proportion of wines in commercial circulation are ready to drink when sold.

Red wines To the untutored taster, older red wines seem to be softer and gentler than harsh, inky young ones. Those who notice such things will also observe a change in colour, typically from deep purple to light brick red. There should also be more SEDIMENT in an old wine than a young one. All these phenomena are related, and are related in particular to the behaviour of phenolics, the compounds in grape skins which include the blue/red ANTHOCYANS responsible for a red wine's COLOUR, bitter and astringent tannins which act as wine preservatives, and some flavour compounds.

Most phenolics are leeched out of the grape skins and

seeds during RED WINE-MAKING. They react with each other in young wine, initially under the influence of the wine's ACIDS and later, during barrel maturation and bottle ageing, under the influence of the small amounts of oxygen dissolved in the wine during such processes as RACKING, topping up, and, later, bottling. Under these influences, POLYMERIZATION takes place so that the phenolic molecules agglomerate to form much more complex, larger molecules. There is some evidence that this polymerization starts during the primary FERMENTATION process, and by about 18 months later the anthocyans have mostly bound with tannins to form complexes responsible for the colour of older red wines. A fine red wine ready for bottling, therefore, may contain tannins, anthocyans, tannin-anthocyan complexes, and more complex COLLOIDS such as tannin-polysaccharides, tannin-salts, and polymerized anthocyans. Polymerization continues in bottle. When these polymers reach a certain size they are too heavy to be held in solution and precipitate as dark reddish-brown sediment, leaving wine that is progressively less astringent, some of the red/blue anthocyans having been precipitated and the tannins having oxidized. Thus, to a certain extent, holding a bottle of wine up to the light to determine how much sediment it has precipitated can give some indication of its maturity (although the amount of sediment deposited is a function not just of time, but of storage temperature and the charge of phenolics left in the wine when it was bottled).

At the same time as these visible changes occur, the impact of the wine on the nose and palate also evolves. The various acids attached to the glucose detach themselves and contribute their individual flavour characteristics to the older wine.

The flavour compounds responsible for the initial primary AROMAS of the grape and those of fermentation (sometimes called secondary aroma, or secondary bouquet) are also interacting, with each other and with other phenolics so that gradually the smell of the wine is said to be transformed into a bouquet, of tertiary aromas, a very much more subtle array and arrangement of flavours which can be sensed by the nose (see TASTING).

ALDEHYDES are oxidized. ESTERS are formed from combinations of the increasingly complex array of wine ACIDS with ALCOHOLS. Continued esterification in bottle produces another range of possible aromas, all the more unpredictable since the esters are formed at very different rates. Esterification also makes the wine taste less acid (until the point at which other perceptible wine constituents have diminished to such an extent that the wine's acidity, which remains almost constant throughout bottle age, once more dominates its impact on the palate).

The rate at which all these things happen is influenced by a host of factors: storage conditions (particularly temperature), the state of the cork, the ULLAGE when the wine was bottled, its pH level, and SULPHUR DIOXIDE concentration, both of which can inhibit or slow the all-important influence of oxygen.

OENOLOGISTS understand this much about the maturation of age-worthy red wine, but are unable to predict with any degree of certainty when such a wine is likely to reach that complex stage called full MATURITY, when it has dispensed with its uncomfortably harsh tannins and acquired maximum complexity of flavour without starting to decay. This may be of minority interest since relatively few wine consumers are interested in storing wine and maintaining their own cellar (which is why so much research has been conducted into making red wines taste lower in tannins in recent years). Part of the joy of wine has long been said to be the monitoring of the progress of a case of wine, bottle by bottle, but this is strictly a rich person's sport.

White wines If our understanding of red wine maturation is incomplete, even less is known about the ageing process in white wines. They begin life in bottle with a much lower tally of phenolics, although those they have strongly influence colour and apparent astringency. White wines become browner with age, presumably because of the slow oxidation of their phenolic content. They may also throw a sediment, although very, very much less than a red wine of similar quality.

Ageing potential is clearly not directly related to a white wine's obvious concentration of phenolics since fine Rieslings, which are relatively low in phenolics, can in general age much longer than comparable Chardonnays, which contain more phenolics.

Experienced tasters, however, often note that wines affected by NOBLE ROT have a much greater ability to last than their non-botrytized counterparts. Experience also seems to suggest that white wines which undergo barrel fermentation also seem capable of lasting longer than those fermented in inert containers and then transferred to barrel for barrel maturation.

Most white wines which can mature over several decades rather than years are notably high in acidity, and few of them undergo MALOLACTIC FERMENTATION. Many of those venerable wines which demonstrate exceptional ageing ability today may well have been bottled with higher levels of sulphur dioxide than are acceptable to the modern consumer.

Artificial ageing

This wine-making technique has been practised with varying degrees of enthusiasm according to the demands of the market. Current FASHION dictates that wine should be as 'natural' as possible, and so very few table wines are ever subjected to artificial ageing (even if many modern WINE-MAKING techniques are in fact designed to hasten some natural processes). Wine can be artificially aged by exposing it to oxygen or extremes of temperature, by shaking it to encourage effects of dissolved oxygen, or by exposing it to radiation or ultra-sonic waves. The making of MADEIRA and some other RANCIO wines deliberately incorporates exposure to high temperatures, while storing wine in some modern domestic conditions can expose wine to high temperatures rather less deliberately.

See ANTHOCYANS, ESTER, PH, PHENOLICS, TANNINS; also MATURITY and STORING WINE.

AGIORGITIKO, red grape variety, also known as St George, native to Nemea in the Peloponnese in GREECE, whose wines may be made from no other variety. It blends well with other varieties (notably with Cabernet Sauvignon grown many miles north in Metsovo to make the popular table wine Katoi) and can also produce good-quality rosé. The wine produced by Agiorgitiko is fruity but can lack acidity. Grapes grown on the higher vineyards of Nemea can yield long-lived reds, however.

AGLIANICO, a dark-skinned Italian grape variety of Greek origin (the name itself is a corruption of the word Ellenico, the Italian word for Hellenic), is cultivated in the mountainous centre of Italy's south, in particular in the provinces of Avellino and Benevento in CAMPANIA, and in the provinces of Potenza and Matera in the BASILICATA. Scattered traces of this early budding vine variety can also be found in CALABRIA, in APULIA, and on the island of Procida near Naples. The grape seems to prefer soils of volcanic origin and achieves its finest results in the two DOCs of TAURASI in Campania and AGLIANICO DEL VULTURE in Basilicata. These two wines share the deep ruby colour, the full aromas, and the powerful, intense flavours which make the variety, at least potentially, one of Italy's finest, even if the potential has so far been realized only in limited quantities. There were about 13,000 ha/32,000 acres of Aglianico planted at the last count, in 1990. D.T.

AGLIANICO DEL VULTURE is BASILICATA's only DOC wine but is also one of the most important wines of Italy's south, showing the potential, in its finest bottles, to offer worthy competition to a fine Sangiovese of Tuscany or Nebbiolo of Piedmont. The DOC zone consists of close to 1,200 ha/2,960 acres, but it has been greatly expanded from the historic core of Barile, Rionero, Ginestra, and Ripacandida, all on soil of volcanic origin from Mount Vulture in the north western part of the zone and at an altitude of 450 to 600 m (1,970 ft) which gives the necessary nocturnal coolness. The expanded zone, particularly in the townships of Venosa, Forenza, Acerenza, Genzano, and Palazzo San Gervasio, lower in altitude and with considerable clay in the soil, was formerly devoted almost entirely to cereal cultivation, together with a few vineyards planted principally to give wine for home consumption.

The larger size of the DOC zone has not resulted in higher production of wine; of the potential 100,000 hl/2.6 million gal from the more than 1,400 ha/3,460 acre DOC, fewer than 8,000 hl/211,000 gal of Aglianico del Vulture are produced in a normal year, and much of the wine is sold either in bulk or for blending. Marketing of the wine is controlled by NÉGOCIANT houses in the zone, an inevitable consequence of a system of landholding in which almost 1,200 growers divide the 1,400 ha of vineyards, but the major négociants have demonstrated an admirable commitment to Aglianico during the 1980s. They have largely replaced chestnut casks, previously produced in the local township of Barile ('barrel' in Italian) from the chestnut forests of nearby Melfi and Monticchio, with OAK casks, experimented with small BARREL MATURATION, and generally improved the quality of their product. The zone is handicapped by an ageing work-force, by its distance from major markets, and by the general obscurity of its grape and its wine, but there are signs that the potential of Aglianico del Vulture is gradually being recognized by informed and discriminating consumers. D.T.

Anderson, B., *The Wine Atlas of Italy* (London and New York, 1990).
Gleave, D., *The Wines of Italy* (London and New York, 1989).

AGRICULTURAL TREATISES are the source of much of our evidence for wine in Ancient GREECE and Ancient ROME. HESIOD was the first Greek to write on agriculture, in the eighth century BC. CATO, VARRO, COLUMELLA, PLINY, and VIRGIL were all important Roman writers.

AGROCHEMICALS, the materials used in agriculture to control pests and diseases. They include FUNGICIDES, insecticides, HERBICIDES, bird repellents, plant GROWTH REGULATORS, rodenticides, and soil fumigants. A broader definition might also include FERTILIZERS.

Viticulture requires fewer agrochemicals than many other field crops, partly because such a high proportion of vines are grown in warm, dry summer environments in which FUNGAL DISEASES are relatively rare, and also because vines require fewer fertilizers than most other crops (see VINE NUTRITION). Vines grown in humid, warm summers may require as many as 10 SPRAYINGS, however, although vine-growers, like other farmers, are in general becoming less reliant on agrochemicals as a result of increased environmental awareness, and because some diseases, notably BOTRYTIS BUNCH ROT, develop tolerance to the repeated use of chemicals. This may take the form of INTEGRATED PEST MANAGEMENT (IPM) programmes which aim to apply chemicals more rationally, or the adoption of some form of ORGANIC VITICULTURE.

The use of agrochemicals in viticulture is strictly regulated by governments. The process of registering a new agrochemical with a government is lengthy and exacting. Before an agrochemical is registered for use, studies are conducted by the producer to assess possible toxicity to man.

Studies are also conducted to assess the danger the agrochemical may present to the wider environment. This includes the risk to non-target organisms, such as fish or bees, and the agrochemical's fate in the environment. This latter is assessed by monitoring the progress of metabolites (breakdown products) of the agrochemical in various soil types. Ideally the agrochemical will be broken down into harmless RESIDUES.

Having established the risk that an agrochemical may present to humans and to the environment, the manufacturer conducts field trials to establish the ideal application rate, appropriate timing of application, efficacy against the target organism, withholding period, and the tolerance, or maximum residue limit (MRL). For most pests and diseases the timing of application is important. The application of an insecticide in the early part of the growing season, for example, may be entirely inappropriate if the insect pest is only prevalent near harvest. This information must be on the label as a restriction to use. The withholding period, or preharvest interval, is the time that must elapse after an agrochemical is applied before the crop is harvested. This withholding period is important to allow residues of the agrochemical to diminish to very low concentrations.

In the case of wine, the effect the agrochemical may have on FERMENTATION is also assessed. For example, the fungicide folpet, which is used to protect vines against DOWNY MILDEW, may delay, or even prevent, fermentation. When this effect was observed, the withholding period was increased to an appropriate level.

All of the above data are then submitted to government in support of the application for registration of the formulation. A registration may then be granted by government after assessment of all information available. The cost of these trials and registration is now such that only multinational companies may consider developing new materials.

Because an official maximum residue limit (MRL) may not exist for an agrochemical in all countries, world trade may be adversely affected. For example, the fungicide procymidone, which has been used in parts of Europe, is not registered in the USA for use on any crop. When they detected residues of procymidone in some European wines in early 1990, the American authorities banned the importation of any European wine containing residues of procymidone in excess of 20 μg/kg, although the French MRL for procymidone is 5,000 μg/kg. This had a serious effect on many sectors of the European wine trade.

Codex Alimentarius (meaning 'food code' in Latin) was established by the Food and Agricultural Organization (FAO) and the World Health Organization (WHO) to upgrade and simplify international food regulations and to avoid such incidents. *Codex* MRLs have been set for some agrochemicals in a range of crops, and several countries accept *Codex* MRLs in the absence of their own. The USA does not recognize *Codex* MRLs, however.

One or more agrochemicals, plus other materials including wetting agents, emulsifiers, and inert diluents, may be present in a formulation. Although an agrochemical may be present in formulations bearing different proprietary names, it usually has a single common name that is recommended by standards organizations. For example, the fungicide Rovral® (from manufacturers Rhône Poulenc) contains the agrochemical iprodione that is also used in the manufacture of several other fungicides.

See also RESIDUES. R.J.

Cabras, P., Meloni, M., and Pirisi, F. M., 'Pesticide fate from vine to wine' in G. W. Ware (ed.), *Reviews of Environmental Contamination and Toxicology*, 99 (New York, 1987).

Hassall, K. A., *The biochemistry and uses of pesticides: structure metabolism, mode of action and uses in crop protection.* (2nd edn., Weinheim, NY, 1990).

Lemperle, E., 'Fungicide residues in musts and wine' in R. E. Smart, R. J. Thornton, S. B. Rodriguez, and J. E. Young (eds.), *Proceedings of the Second International Symposium for Cool Climate Viticulture and Oenology: 11–15 January 1988 Auckland, New Zealand* (Auckland, 1988).

AGUARDENTE, Portuguese word for high-proof grape spirit made in a CONTINUOUS STILL.

AGUARDIENTE, Spanish word for high-proof grape spirit made in a CONTINUOUS STILL. See BRANDY, Spanish.

AHR, small wine region of 430 ha/1,063 acres in GERMANY specializing in red wine and named after the river, which flows east from the hills of the Eifel to join the Rhine near Remagen (see map on p. 442). The most westerly vineyards are in dramatic, rocky, wooded scenery near Altenahr, where the steep slopes on either side of the river reach up to 300 m/980 ft above sea level, and sometimes narrow to the dimensions of a gorge. Many are covered in slate and grey wacke clay of volcanic origin, well suited to Spätburgunder (PINOT NOIR), but the vines grow in a variety of soils. The region lies between 50 and 51 degrees of LATITUDE, so that a good MESOCLIMATE is needed to ripen the grapes. Most of the best sites face south east to south west (see TOPOGRAPHY). The dark soil (see SOIL COLOUR), the reflected heat from the curious rock formations, and the protection from north winds that blow above the valley help to ensure the necessary summer warmth. Spätburgunder covers 40 per cent of the area under vine and is spreading steadily, while PORTUGIESER, RIESLING, and MÜLLER-THURGAU vine varieties are on the decline. Many producers still offer soft, late-picked, medium sweet Spätburgunder with about 36 g/l of RESIDUAL SUGAR. Fully fermented, dry, BARRIQUE-aged, tannic, Spätburgunder of good colour and from a low yield in the modern German style is rare, but sells with ease and at a high price to enthusiastic wine lovers. Almost 95 per cent of the region's grape harvest is processed by five CO-OPERATIVE cellars, and the state of Rheinland-Pfalz owns the largest estate, 20 ha/49 acres based on the 13th century Kloster Marienthal. These, and the few private estate bottlers, sell most of their wine directly to the consumer and, in particular, to the hordes of visiting tourists from the Ruhr district and the Benelux countries.

I.J.

AIRÉN, Spain's most planted vine variety, and one that is planted at such a low VINE DENSITY that its vineyards cover more area than any other vine variety in the world, 476,300 ha/1.2 milion acres in the late 1980s according to some Spanish statistics. This light-skinned grape variety accounts for almost a third of all Spain's vineyards, being by far the most planted variety in La MANCHA and VALDEPEÑAS, where it is the major ingredient in the important Spanish BRANDY business, and has been blended with dark-skinned Cencibel (TEMPRANILLO) grapes to produce light red wines. It is increasingly vinified as a white wine, however, not just in the traditional way to yield heavy wines often marked by OXIDATION, but also using modern temperature-controlled methods to yield crisp, slightly neutral dry white wines for early consumption. In several ways, therefore, Airén is the Spanish equivalent of France's UGNI BLANC. Airén vines are trained into low BUSHES and have remarkable resistance to the DROUGHTS

Harvesting the low yield **Airén** grapes in La Mancha, central Spain.

which plague central Spanish viticulture. The variety is also grown in ANDALUCÍA, where it is known as Lairén.

AIX-EN-PROVENCE, COTEAUX D'. Mainly red and dry rosé wines are made, often in spectacularly situated vineyards among the lavender and *garrigue* of PROVENCE, many of them quite distant from this famous university town. The extensive area entitled to this relatively recent appellation (1985) stretches from the extraordinary clifftop gastronomic shrine Les Baux in the west as far as the Coteaux VAROIS, but also includes land all round the Étang de Berres, the lagoon dominated by Marseilles's airport. Within the area a total of about 3,000 ha/7,400 acres of vineyards produce serviceable, usually quite fruity reds and pale pink wines for early, often local consumption. CO-OPERATIVES are relatively important here, but a number of individual estates are trying to establish a distinctive style from blends of Grenache, Cinsaut, Mourvèdre, the local Counoise, limited amounts of Carignan, and increasing amounts of Syrah and Cabernet Sauvignon grapes. Ch Vignelaure in the far west of the appellation was one of the first properties to achieve some degree of fame outside the region (by grafting Bordeaux techniques and some grape varieties on to the Provençal terrain).

Arguably the most successful estate is Domaine de Trevallon, producing a blend of Cabernet Sauvignon and Syrah on the soils of the Coteaux de Baux, the particularly exciting western end of the appellation. Wines made on this harshly dramatic clay-limestone terrain were entitled to the somewhat cumbersome appellation **Coteaux d'Aix-en-Provence Coteaux des Baux** in the late 1980s and early 1990s, but it seems likely that, given the high overall quality of wine producers there, the Coteaux des Baux will eventually be awarded their own appellation.

Rosés made within the greater appellation represent about one bottle in every three and a small amount of rarely distinguished dry white wine is made from Grenache Blanc, Ugni Blanc, Sémillon, and Sauvignon Blanc grapes.

ORGANIC VITICULTURE has established a significant hold in this arid, mediterranean climate.

Parker, R. M., *The Wines of the Rhône Valley and Provence* (New York, 1987).

ALAMBIC, alternative word for ALEMBIC.

ALBA, town which provides a focus for the famous wines of the LANGHE hills in Piedmont in north west Italy. Regarded as the region's red wine, and white truffle, capital. See also ROERO and NEBBIOLO D'ALBA.

ALBALONGA is a Riesling x Silvaner vine crossing grown to a very limited extent in Germany, notably the RHEINHESSEN. If it escapes rot it can produce some vigorous AUSLESE in good years.

ALBANA, white grape variety mentioned in the 13th century by PETRUS DE CRESCENTIIS and now widely planted in EMILIA-ROMAGNA, where it is most notably responsible for ALBANA DI ROMAGNA. The thick-skinned Albana Gentile di Bertinoro is the most common clone, which results in relatively deep coloured wines. Although Greco and Greco di Ancona are two of its synonyms, it is unrelated to GRECO di Tufo. A total of about 4,500 ha / 11,100 acres were planted with Albana in 1990.

ALBANA DI ROMAGNA, dry white wine made in ROMAGNA in Central Italy from the ALBANA grape which was, amid much incredulity, awarded DOCG status in 1986. Albana di Romagna is Romagna's third most important VARIETAL wine, some way behind SANGIOVESE DI ROMAGNA and TREBBIANO DI ROMAGNA in terms of quantity produced. Albana, which needs good water supplies for ripening, has shown little aptitude either for heavy clay soils or for zones with little precipitation. Its high susceptibility to GREY ROT has further limited its cultivation to areas with a certain circulation of air to dry the bunches after heavy rainfall. Although the DOCG zone includes the Apennine strip of the provinces of Bologna, Forlì, and Ravenna, the best Albana comes almost entirely from the red clay soils of the hills between Faenza and the river Ronco to the east of Forlì; the sole exception is the subzone of Bertinoro with heavily calcareous soils where the variety (here called Albana Gentile) produces much less vegetation and considerablly smaller bunches, characteristics which have led some AMPELOGRAPHERS to consider this a separate variety, rather than simply a CLONE, of Albana. The Albana of Bertinoro enjoyed a significant renown in the past, and the words of Roman Empress Galla Placidia, that the wine should be drunk in gold goblets (*berti in oro*) are allegedly the origin of the township's name. The extreme vegetative VIGOUR of the normal Albana has led to claims that the variety must be allowed to produce abundantly, a philosophy reflected in the DOCG rules which permit yields of 100 hl/ha (5.7 tons/acre). The decision to award Albana di Romagna DOCG status in 1986 was greeted with polemical, and futile, declarations that these production limits were incompatible with the supposed purpose of the DOCG, namely to distinguish Italy's finest wines.

As a wine Albana di Romagna comes in three different styles: secco (dry), amabile (medium dry), and dolce (sweet). Dry Albana is a rather neutral, characterless wine, and although modern cellar techniques have partially solved the chronic problems of OXIDATION which existed in the past, they have not succeeded in giving the wines significant flavour. Medium dry Albana normally seems neither fish nor fowl. The future of the grape seems to lie in the dessert version, achieved either with raisined grapes or, in more recent experiments, with NOBLE ROT and small BARREL MATURATION. These can be wines of surprisingly good quality, although they represent a minuscule portion of the total annual production of 37,000 hl/976,800 gal from the 1,800 ha/4,450 acres of DOCG vineyards. D.T.

Anderson, B., *The Wine Atlas of Italy* (London and New York, 1990).
Gleave, D., *The Wines of Italy* (London and New York, 1989).

Janneau's pot stills, or **alambics**, in the Armagnac region.

ALBANI, COLLI, white wines from the hills south east of Rome. For more information see CASTELLI ROMANI.

ALBANIA, small European country on the Adriatic Sea, for much of the 20th century under hard-line communist control with YUGOSLAVIA to the north and GREECE to the south. Albania claims one of the longest histories of European viticulture, but more recent history has meant that wine production is now only of minor importance. Albania's annual harvest is less than 250,000 hl/6.6 million gal of wine and domestic consumption is small. Despite the fact that atheism was for many years officially imposed by the government, the majority of the population is Muslim and prohibited by the rules of ISLAM from consuming alcohol.

Production is based on the Red Star Co-operative Cellar outside the main port of Durres, where wines are made from such grape varieties as CABERNET FRANC, WELSCHRIESLING, and the native Balkan grape MAVRUD. Albania's most individual wine is Kagor, a dessert wine made in the style of MARSALA around the town of Sarande in the south of the country.

Albania can claim with some justification to be the cradle of European viticulture. The French historian Henri Enjalbert considers that Albania, together with the Ionian islands of Greece and southern Dalmatia in what is now BOSNIA HERCEGOVINA, might well have been the last European refuge of the vine after the Ice Age. Certainly there are written accounts of the vine being cultivated in Illyria, as it was known in classical times, as early as the eighth century BC. Early Latin writers also cite Illyria as the source of a high-yielding grape variety that was introduced into Italy.

The future for Albanian viticulture appears to be brighter, as the government has employed the Spanish oenologist Isabel Mijares as a consultant, and political liberalization should open up further export markets.

Albania is also an old name for the central Asian republic of AZERBAIJAN. C.C.F.

Enjalbert, H., *Histoire de la vigne et du vin* (Paris, 1975).
Frasheri, K., *The History of Albania* (Tiranë, 1964).

ALBARIÑO, the Spanish name of a distinctive white grape variety grown in GALICIA (and, as ALVARINHO in the north of Portugal's Vinho Verde region). The grapes' thick skins help them withstand the particularly damp climate, and can result in wines notably high in alcohol, acidity, and flavour. Albariño is one of the few Spanish white grape varieties encountered on the labels of VARIETAL wines. The variety is most common in Spain in the RIAS BAIXAS zone, where it has become so popular (and probably the most expensive white wine in Spain) that it accounts for about 90 per cent of all plantings. The wines can have a peachy aroma.

ALBARIZA, a local, Andalucian term for the white, chalky-looking soil typical of parts of the JEREZ region in southern Spain. Grapes grown on this soil type produce some of the finest FINO and MANZANILLA sherries. The soil has a high LIMESTONE content, about 40 per cent, the remainder being CLAY and SAND. It appears dazzling white in summer, and has the characteristic of drying without caking, slowly releasing moisture to the vines during the growing season. This soil type is also present in the PENEDÈS region of north east Spain, where some of the best Spanish sparkling wine is produced (see CAVA). M.J.E.

ALBERELLO, Italian term to describe free-standing BUSH VINES trained according to the GOBELET system.

ALBILLO, white grape variety grown in various parts of Spain, most notably RIBEIRO and around MADRID. It produces wines that are neutral in flavour although they can be quite high in GLYCEROL.

ALCOBACA, an IPR in western Portugal. See OESTE for more details.

ALCOHOL, the common name for ETHANOL. The term alcohol, which can be applied to any of the ALCOHOLS, derives from the Arabic *al-kuhl*, meaning 'the fine powder used to stain eyelids' (today's kohl), and thus by extension any kind of fine impalpable powder that represents the concentration, or quintessence, of the raw material involved. It was then more widely applied to fluids that represented the essence, or spirit, of something, and thus to any product of DISTILLATION.

Alcohol is the most potent component of wine (and the most obvious of those that distinguish it from GRAPE JUICE) but it is probably the least discussed by wine consumers (unless in the context of hangovers). The sense of TASTE sometimes identifies an excess of alcohol with a hot or burning sensation after wine has been swallowed, or spat out. Alcohol is closely related to the tasting concept BODY.

See ALCOHOLIC STRENGTH for the varied concentrations of alcohol to be found in different wines, and see HEALTH AND WINE for the effects of alcohol consumption in the form of wine.

ALCOHOLIC, usually pejorative tasting term for a wine which tastes 'hot' and seems to contain excess ethyl alcohol, or ETHANOL.

ALCOHOLIC STRENGTH, an important measurement of any wine, is its concentration of the intoxicant ethyl alcohol, or ETHANOL. It can be measured in several different ways, the most common being the DEGREE first defined in France by Gay-Lussac in 1884. This was the number of litres of pure ethanol in 100 litres of wine, both measured at 15 °C/59 °F. Later a more precise definition, using 20 °C/68 °F as the reference temperature and some other minor refinements, was adopted in France and by most international organizations. The degree of alcohol is equivalent to its percentage by volume. In most countries it is mandatory to specify the alcoholic strength of all wines on the label, although it may be written either % or occasionally ° (see also DEGREE).

The alcoholic strength of wine that has not had alcohol added by FORTIFICATION is usually between nine and 15 per cent, with the great majority of wines being between 11 and 13 per cent alcohol. In Europe, fermented grape juice must usually reach at least 8.5 per cent alcohol before it legally constitutes wine, although exceptions are made for better-quality wines that have traditionally been low in alcohol such as German QMP wines and Italian MOSCATO. The technical European legal maximum alcoholic strength for wines that have had no alcohol added is 15 per cent, but derogations are frequently made at this upper limit too, notably for Italy's strongest wines such as AMARONE. In the United States, grape-based table wine must legally be between seven and 14 per cent, while DESSERT WINES must be between 14 and 24 per cent.

Since alcohol is the product by FERMENTATION of grape sugar, itself the product of PHOTOSYNTHESIS driven by sunlight, the alcoholic strength of a wine is, very generally, proportional to the proximity of its provenance to the equator, although many other factors play a part. High vineyard ALTITUDE, poor WEATHER in a particular year, high YIELD, and any RESIDUAL SUGAR, are just some of the factors which may decrease alcoholic strength. Severe PRUNING in the vineyard and cellar techniques such as ENRICHMENT, CONCENTRATION, and fortification allow man to manipulate alcoholic strength upwards. Some OLOROSO sherries, for example, can reach alcoholic strengths approaching 24 per cent after EVAPORATION. (See also DRIED GRAPE WINES.)

The alcoholic strength of spirits is also measured as a percentage of alcohol by volume, and most spirits are sold at a strength of around 40 per cent, although some special bottlings of COGNAC or ARMAGNAC, notably those bottled straight from cask without any added water, may be rather higher than this.

The alcoholic strength of beers has traditionally been measured either in terms of specific gravity (see DENSITY) or in percentage by weight, which differs slightly from the equivalent percentage by volume. Beers are typically around 4 per cent alcohol.

See also REDUCED ALCOHOL WINES.

ALCOHOLS, those natural organic chemicals usually consisting of carbon, hydrogen, and oxygen atoms arranged so that there is one linkage of carbon to oxygen to hydrogen, that is, there is an -OH group present.

Many different alcohols are used in commerce and industry but the most common is ethyl alcohol, or ETHANOL, the alcohol that is the important, and intoxicating, ingredient in wines and spirits. The small amounts of ethanol in foods and beverages, commonly referred to simply as 'alcohol', are the product of yeast FERMENTATION of natural sugars. Industrial ethanol is usually a by-product of refining petroleum through a series of processes ending with the hydration of ethylene, although in countries such as New Zealand it is produced from whey, as a by-product of the dairy industry.

Other common alcohols are METHANOL, also known as wood alcohol; isopropyl (rubbing alcohol); and isoamyl alcohol, used as a solvent in many paints and polishes.

Alcohols that are the product of fermentation and contain more than two carbon atoms of ethanol are sometimes called higher alcohols, or FUSEL OILS. The higher alcohols separated from ethanol by DISTILLATION are normally used as solvents in industrial processes. The major constituent of higher alcohols or fusel oils is the five-carbon isoamyl alcohol which is one by-product of the normal alcoholic fermentation during which yeasts have to find nitrogen to build proteins of their cells and the fusel oils are by-products of this metabolic process. Other alcohols such as propyl, isobutyl, hexyl, and 2-phenethyl are used as solvents or as intermediates in syntheses of perfumes, medicines, and numerous household products.

Although alcohol does not have a taste, it has an effect, not just on the human nervous system, but on how a wine tastes. The alcohol content in a perfectly balanced wine should be unfathomable, but wines that are slightly too high in alcohol can have a hot after-taste. As a general rule, wines described as 'full bodied' (see BODY) are high in alcohol, while those described as 'light' are low in alcohol.

For more on concentrations and effects of ethanol in wines and spirits, see ALCOHOLIC STRENGTH. A.D.W.

ALDEHYDES, a class of chemical compounds midway between the ALCOHOLS and the organic acids in their state of OXIDATION. They are formed during any phase of processing in which an alcoholic beverage is exposed to air. ACETALDEHYDE is the aldehyde of most interest to wine producers.

Those aldehydes with lower molecular weights smell pungently unpleasant in their pure, concentrated forms. However, they are present in only trace concentrations in wines and spirits, and in this much more dilute state these same aldehydes contribute harmoniously to overall character. An **aldehydic** aroma is characteristic of many a SHERRY labelled FINO or MANZANILLA, for example, where it is produced by FLOR yeast growing on the wine's surface in a partially filled barrel. The aldehydes containing more carbon atoms in their structure are, in general, much more palatable.

Indeed, some of them play a part in the perfumes of fruits and flowers. Vanillin, for example, is a fairly complicated organic molecule present in the vanilla bean and some other plants, where it is combined with a molecule of sugar. When the sugar divides from the vanillin, the characteristic and widely used flavouring material is liberated. Vanillin also occurs as a component of the lignin structure of OAK wood. Oak casks are used for wine maturation partly in order to dissolve some of this vanillin from the wood to add complexity to the wine (see WOOD FLAVOUR).

In BRANDY production, the lower molecular weight aldehydes tend to concentrate in the early HEADS portion of the distillate. If there are higher concentrations of aldehydes in the distilling material, significant portions may appear in the distillate. While these aldehydes contribute to the overall aroma, their presence in more than trace amounts can induce unpleasant headaches in the drinker. This is because aldehydes are in general considerably more toxic to the human system than are ETHANOL or other constituents of wines and brandies. The higher molecular weight aldehydes, with their pleasant aromas, tend to appear in the product during POT STILL distillation. In the CONTINUOUS STILL, however, they concentrate mostly with the FUSEL OIL fraction which is usually separated and discarded.

See also HERBACEOUS for the part played by **leaf aldehydes**.

A.D.W.

ALEATICO, Italian red grape variety with a strong MUSCAT aroma. PETRUS DE CRESCENTIIS referred, as early as the 14th century, to the 'Livatica' vine which today is sometimes called Leatico or Agliano. It may well be a dark-berried mutation of the classic MUSCAT BLANC À PETITS GRAINS and certainly has the potential to produce fine, if somewhat esoteric, fragrant wine, as an example made by Avignonesi from Tuscan Maremma fruit has demonstrated. Two DOCS enshrine the word Aleatico in the wine lexicon of Latium and Apulia, but the variety is becoming increasingly rare. Sweet red Aleatico is one of the few wines to be exported from the island of ELBA, and the variety is grown on the island of Corsica, although it is not authorized for any APPELLATION CONTRÔLÉE wine. Aleatico is also surprisingly popular in the central Asian republics of the CIS, notably KAZAKHSTAN and UZBEKISTAN.

ALELLA, town near Barcelona in CATALONIA (see map on p. 907) which gives its name to a small Spanish wine zone making mainly white wines in increasingly urbanized countryside. In order to compensate for loss of agricultural land, this tiny DO was extended northwards in 1989 but four years later there were still only 550 ha / 1,360 acres of vineyard, a third of the area planted in 1956 when Alella was first awarded DO status. A single co-operative dominates the zone which used to be known for its old-fashioned, cask-aged, medium sweet white wines. The chief grape variety is the Pansá Blanca, the local name for XAREL-LO, which is now grown along with some CHENIN BLANC and CHARDONNAY to make both CAVA sparkling wines and dry, still white wine. The reputation of Alella has been salvaged by a single producer, Parxet / Marqués de Alella, which pioneered these new styles of wine.

R.J.M.

ALEMBIC, word for a POT STILL derived from the Arabic word *al-anbiq* for a still (just as the word ALCOHOL has Arab origins; see DISTILLATION). Thus an alembic, and sometimes alambic, BRANDY is one distilled in a pot still.

ALENQUER, an IPR in western Portugal. See OESTE for more details.

ALENTEJO, promising Portuguese wine region. The undulating Alentejo plains south and east of Lisbon cover a third of mainland Portugal and most of the country south of the river Tagus (Tejo in Portuguese)—although see also RIBATEJO, and map on p. 750. In complete contrast to the north, this is a sparsely populated region where cereal farms stretch as far as the eye can see. Nicknamed 'land of bread', Alentejo has also been called, somewhat unfairly in the light of recent progress, 'land of bread and bad wine'.

For centuries, Alentejo's main link with wine was CORK. Over half the world's supply of cork is grown in Portugal and almost all of it is stripped from the cork oaks that fleck the vast Alentejo wheat fields. Southern Portugal bore the brunt of the military-led revolution that rocked the Lisbon establishment in 1974 and 1975. In Alentejo, many large privately owned cork estates were occupied by local farm workers who ran them as self-styled co-operatives. These quickly degenerated as many farms faced bankruptcy. Cork trees were prematurely stripped of their bark and the region's scattered vineyards were pruned with quantity rather than quality in mind as many workers' co-operatives became desperate for cash.

At the beginning of the 1980s, Alentejo was in complete disarray, but over the next decade or so five vineyard enclaves emerged from the chaos and confusion. The towns of Portalegre, Borba, Redondo, Reguengos de Monsaraz, Granja, and Vidigueira each had CO-OPERATIVE wineries built with government support in the pre-revolutionary 1960s and early 1970s. Until recently they produced wines for the undemanding local market but, with financial assistance from the EUROPEAN UNION, they have begun to tap Alentejo's winemaking potential and export their wines. Likewise single estates, mostly returned to their former owners, are emerging with new wines.

The climate in Alentejo is hardly conducive to wine production, but modern technology can now compensate for natural deficiencies. IRRIGATION supplements an annual rainfall total which rarely reaches 600 mm / 23 in. Temperatures in the summer months frequently exceed 35 or even 40 °C (104 °F), so, for grapes which ripen as early as the end of August or the beginning of September, sophisticated TEMPERATURE CONTROL systems are necessary to prevent FERMENTATIONS from running out of control. The production of red wine, principally from ARAGONEZ, Trincadeira, MORETO, and CASTELÃO FRANCES grapes, exceeds white, although some growers see potential in white varieties such as ROUPEIRO and Perrum. Seven IPR regions were designated in the Alentejo around the six co-operatives listed above, together with Evora, and a number of them are expected to be promoted to DOC status.

R.J.M.

ALEXANDER VALLEY. California wine region and AVA. See SONOMA.

ALEZIO, DOC for robust red wine made mainly from NEGROAMARO grapes in south east Italy. For more details see APULIA.

ALFROCHEIRO PRETO, Portuguese grape variety which can add useful colour to red wine blends. It is grown in ALENTEJO, BAIRRADA, RIBATEJO, and, particularly, DÃO.

ALGARVE, the southernmost province of PORTUGAL, now better known for tourism than for wine (see map on p. 750). There is, however, evidence of a long wine-making tradition in the Algarve. H. Warner Allen in his book *The Wines of Portugal* contends that Osey, a fortified wine popular in England in the 14th and 15th centuries, originated in Algarve. The Adega Co-operativa de Lagoa continues to make a small amount of dry, fortified wine from locally grown Crato Branco grapes. It ages in a SOLERA under a film of FLOR which lends the wine a nutty character so that it resembles a coarse MONTILLA or FINO sherry. The Algarvean climate is generally better suited to growing CORK oaks and sun-bathing than wine-making, however—indeed the economy of the region was transformed in the late 17th century by the cultivation of QUERCUS *suber*.

Other wines, predominantly red and made by the region's four co-operatives, are high in alcohol and undistinguished. The Algarve was demarcated in 1980 (one suspects political motives) and has since been split into four DOC districts—Lagos, Portimão, Lagoa, and Tavira. A discussion is under way to demote them to IPRS. R.J.M.

Warner Allen, H., *The Wines of Portugal* (London, 1963).

ALGERIA has known world renown in its turbulent recent history as a wine producer but is currently grappling with the economic and cultural problems posed by having almost as great an area under vine as Germany or South Africa, for example, but in an increasingly fervent ISLAMIC environment. A colonial legacy has become a problem of economic dependency.

In the late 1950s France depended heavily on Algerian wine to provide its everyday blended red (and some smarter wines) with strength, colour, and concentration—all of them attributes entirely lacking in the ARAMON then grown so prolifically in the LANGUEDOC. Together with neighbouring MOROCCO and TUNISIA, Algeria accounted for two-thirds of international wine trade in the 1950s. As a legacy of this era, the quayside in the important French wine port of Sète is called the Quai d'Alger.

Although vine-growing was practised in pre-colonial Algeria, and indeed flourished in classical times, it was the French PHYLLOXERA crisis of the 1870s that was to convert the agriculture of this North African colony to vineyards (although there had been a certain influx of wine-growers from Baden in the mid 19th century—see GERMAN HISTORY). In the late 19th century Algeria was so successfully developed as the prime alternative source for France's voracious wine drinkers that parts of the country grew nothing but the vine. Algeria's total viticultural area grew from 16,688 ha/41,240 acres in 1872 to 110,042 ha/271,910 acres in 1890, largely thanks to settlers whose own European vineyards had been devastated by phylloxera, which eventually reached Algeria.

Vineyards reached their maximum extent of 400,000 ha/988,400 acres in 1938, when Algeria produced more than 21 million hl/550 million gal of wine. By then viticulture had shaped Algerian colonial society and by the year of independence, 1962, a dozen crus were accorded the honour of official VDQS recognition by the French. To the European vineyard owners, the so-called *pieds noirs*, or 'black feet', it gave economic and political power; for non-Europeans it provided valuable employment, but also dependance as the wine trade more than anything else integrated the colony with metropolitan France.

By the start of Algeria's war of independence in the mid 1950s, viticulture was still the leading sector of the colonial economy accounting for half of Algeria's exports by value. Its relatively high labour requirements provided a fifth of the country's total agricultural employment and, more significantly, two-thirds of the paid employment in the modern, commercialized sector of agriculture. In regions such as the Mitidja plain inland of Algiers and in parts of Oranais, around Ain-Temouchent for example, viticulture had acquired monocultural status.

At Algerian independence in 1962 nearly a million French settlers left as well as a sizeable army of occupation. Algeria's domestic wine market promptly collapsed and the inappropriateness of an Islamic country's heavy economic reliance on wine production became an immediate problem. The mass exodus of European technical skills adversely affected both quality and productivity. Most vineyards passed into a form of collective agriculture as total vineyard and, especially, total wine production began to decline. This posed

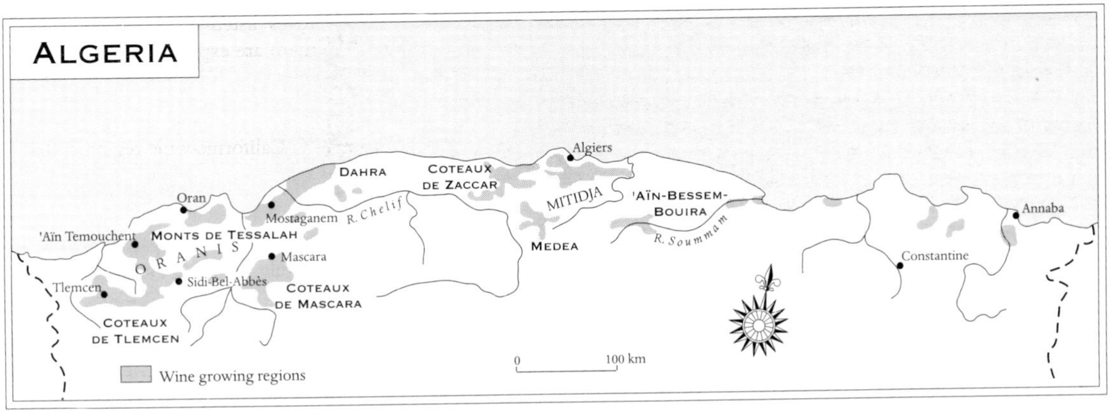

economic problems as by the mid 1960s wine was still Algeria's second export commodity, after the country's burgeoning oil industry, and viticulture still provided half the man-days worked in the modern, commercialized sector of agriculture.

Marketing problems soon emerged after independence. France immediately reduced its imports of Algerian wine from 14.6 million hl/385 million gal in 1962 (about a fifth of France's own total production) to only 6.8 million hl in 1963. This reduction, while entirely understandable in terms of France's own SURPLUS of ordinary wine, breached the terms of the independence agreement. A new five-year accord was agreed but France soon reneged and continued to reduce its imports from Algeria, where stocks of wine reached crisis levels. The USSR's agreement to buy 5 million hl a year between 1969 and 1975 eased these marketing difficulties somewhat but the agreed price represented less than half the prevailing world market rate. Negotiations with the EUROPEAN UNION resulted in reduced quantities of Algerian wine allowed into Europe.

These problems prompted various schemes in the late 1960s for the reconversion and reconstitution of Algeria's uneconomically ageing vineyards. The essential problem was however, that few replacement crops such as cereals could match viticulture's employment opportunities. Only in the 1970s when the area under vine was steadily reduced was a real effort made to face up to the economic realities of the lack of markets. Urban and industrial expansion in the Mitidja plain behind Algiers also helped swallow up vineyards.

By 1979 the area under vine had declined to 208,570 ha/515,380 acres and this grubbing up has since continued. By 1990 only 102,000 ha of vines remained, about one-quarter of the maximum extent in the 1930s. A growing proportion of these vineyards now provide table grapes rather than wine, about 60 per cent in 1990. Wine production levels have therefore fallen even more drastically than vineyard area, from between 1.8 and 2.8 million hl in the 1978–81 period to only 0.5 million hl in 1989 and 0.3 million hl of the admittedly poor 1990 vintage. Although reduced vineyard area, lower yields, and lower prices have combined to make the relict Algerian wine industry a shadow of its former self, wine exports are still the country's third most important, after hydrocarbons and iron and steel products.

In regional terms, by the early 1980s western Algeria accounted for over 80 per cent of the area under vines, notably the districts of 'Aïn Temouchent, Mascara, Mostaganem, Sidi Bel-Abbes, and Tlemcen. Seven regions have been designated quality zones by the country's Office National de Commercialisation des Produits Viticoles (ONCV). From west to east they are (see map) the Coteaux de Tlemcen, the Monts du Tessalah, the Coteaux de Mascara, the Dahra hills region, the Coteaux du Zaccar inland from Algiers, the Medea region, and the 'Aïn Bessem-Bouira region.

These viticultural regions all lie within the littoral Mediterranean climate zone of Algeria with its mild winters and hot, dry, and sunny summers. To the south and east of Algiers annual rainfall exceeds 600 mm/23 in while further west, around Tlemcen and Mascara, it usually exceeds 400 mm/23 in. Climatically this is similar to much of southern and eastern Spain, although it is not as arid as Murcia in south-eastern Spain.

These recognized quality zones produce mostly relatively concentrated red wines from old vines of those varieties planted, typically, in the 1950s. In 1962 at the time of independence Algeria had 140,000 ha/345,900 acres of Carignan, 75,000 ha of Alicante Bouschet, 60,000 ha of Cinsaut, and 10,000 of Grenache planted, all producing fiery stuff that almost certainly contributed substantially to a high proportion of the wine then sold as burgundy as well as to everyday table wine. If Algerian wine has a fault today it may be a lack of acidity or an overdose of alcohol but in no other country could the term VIEILLES VIGNES be so widely and literally applied.

Most wine is still vinified on a semi-industrial scale that demands fast fermentations and early bottling. The country has seen practically zero investment in technology in the second half of the 20th century, although its mechanization and hot country technology at one time provided inspiration for many. The AUTOVINIFICATION tanks of the DOURO, for example, were developed in Algeria, where they were known as the Ducellier system.

The centralized ONCV, which exercises a near monopoly, markets several standard labels, liberally adorned with such expressions as 'grand cru', but their prestige brand, Cuvée du Président, reveals nothing about the origin of the wine other than its region, if that. An increasing emphasis on quality has been recognized by awards at the occasional international wine fair, however.

Algeria's colonial viticultural legacy has therefore become first an economic liability and more recently a cultural anachronism in this increasingly Islamic state. The aspiring Islamic Salvation Front seems unfettered by a sense of irony. One of its stated economic policies is to boost the country's wine exports, while banning domestic alcohol consumption.

Algeria's role in the modern wine world is perhaps greater as a producer of CORKS, albeit mainly processed in Portugal and Spain, than of wine. K.S.

Galet, P., *Cépages et vignobles de France* (2nd edn., Montpellier, 1990).
Isnard, H., 'Vigne et décolonisation en Algérie', in A. Huetz de Lemps (ed.), *Géographie historique des vignobles: actes du colloque de Bordeaux: octobre 1977* (Paris, 1978), vol. i.
Sutton, K., 'Algeria's vineyards: an Islamic dilemma and a problem of decolonisation', *Journal of Wine Research*, 1/2 (1990), 101–20.

ALICANTE, city on Spain's Mediterranean coast long associated with strong, rustic wines which now gives its name to a denominated wine zone. This DO in the LEVANTE extends from the city towards YECLA on the foothills of Spain's central plateau (see map on p. 907) and allows eight different styles of wine including DOBLE-PASTA, fortified wines, and a SOLERA-aged wine called Fondillon made from very sweet, deliberately overripened grapes. The climate becomes progressively hotter and the landscape more arid away from the coast and YIELDS rarely exceed 20 hl/ha (1.1 ton/acre). The principal grape variety, the red MONASTRELL, frequently ripens to produce wines with 16 to 18 per cent natural alcohol. Other red varieties well suited to the MEDITERRANEAN climate include GARNACHA and BOBAL along with the undistinguished white MERSEGUERA. Ninety per cent of the region's wine is produced in poorly equipped CO-OPERATIVES. Most is sold in bulk, although Bodegas Eval is experimenting with TEMPRANILLO and CABERNET SAUVIGNON vines. R.J.M.

ALICANTE BOUSCHET, often known simply as **Alicante**, the most widely planted of France's red-fleshed TEINTURIER grape varieties. Although it declined in importance throughout the 1980s, it was in 1988 still the country's eleventh most planted black grape variety with 15,800 ha/39,000 acres, mainly in the Languedoc-Roussillon (especially in the Hérault and Gard *départements*) but also in Provence and as far north as cognac country.

It was bred between 1865 and 1885 by Henri BOUSCHET from his father's crossing of Petit Bouschet with the popular Grenache and was an immediate success. Thanks to its deep red flesh, the wine it produced was about 15 times as red as that of the productive and rapidly spreading ARAMON (and much redder than that of its stablemate GRAND NOIR DE LA CALMETTE). In France at least it has tended to be planted alongside the pale but prolific Aramon to add colour in blends. It is also relatively high yielding and on fertile soils can easily produce more than 200 hl/ha (12 ton/acre) of wine with 12 per cent alcohol, if little character.

Alicante Bouschet also played a major role in late 19th and early 20th century viticulture as parent of a host of other Teinturiers, the products almost exclusively of crossings with non-VINIFERA varieties. In the second half of the 20th century it has profited from its status as the sole Teinturier to be a *Vitis vinifera*, and therefore officially sanctioned by the French authorities. This useful but somewhat spurious variety is expected to disappear eventually as a result of EUROPEAN UNION policy of grubbing up Aramon. Nevertheless it was still being planted in the late 1980s: as many as 1,400 ha/3,500 acres in France between 1986 and 1988. This is usually the first variety to be harvested in the south of France, in late August, and is blended with other varieties for colour or sometimes used for GRAPE JUICE.

Outside France it is perhaps most widely cultivated in Spain where it is also known as Garnacha Tintorera and covered more than 16,000 ha/39,000 acres in 1990. It is particularly common in Almansa. Why Henri Bouschet should have chosen to name this hugely successful variety after a Spanish city is not known.

Alicante is also grown in Corsica, Tuscany, Calabria in southern Italy, Yugoslavia, Israel, and North Africa; and there were still 2,000 acres/800 ha of it in California in 1992, mainly in the hot Central Valley. Papagni's Alicante Bouschet surely took the concept of VARIETAL wine to its limit.

Galet, P., *Cépages et vignobles de France* (2nd edn., Montpellier, 1990).

ALIGOTÉ, the second white grape variety of Burgundy. It is very much Chardonnay's underdog but in a fine year, when ripeness can compensate for its characteristic ACIDITY, Aligoté is not short of champions. Its roots almost certainly lie in Burgundy, where it was recorded at the end of the 18th century.

The vine is vigorous and its yield varies enormously according to the vineyard site. If grown on Burgundy's best slopes on the poorest soils in warmer years, Aligoté could produce fine dry whites with more nerve than most Chardonnays, but it would not be nearly as profitable. Aligoté is, typically, an angular wine short on obvious flavour and usually too spindly to subject to oak ageing.

In the Côte d'Or it is being replaced by the two obviously nobler grape varieties Chardonnay and Pinot Noir, and there were only 500 ha/1200 acres left in 1988. It is now largely relegated to the highest and lowest vineyards, where it produces light, early maturing wines allowed only the Bourgogne Aligoté appellation and drunk either with simple meals, by penny-pinchers, or, traditionally, mixed with blackcurrant liqueur as a KIR. Only the village of Bouzeron, where some of the finest examples are produced, has its own appellation for Aligoté, Bourgogne Aligoté-Bouzeron, in which the maximum yield is only 45 hl/ha (2.5 ton/acre) as opposed to the 60 hl/ha allowed for Bourgogne Aligoté.

To the north and south of the Côte d'Or, however, total plantings of Aligoté have remained relatively stable with 500 ha to the south and 200 ha in Chablis country, where it makes everyday dry white wine.

Aligoté is extraordinarily popular in eastern Europe. Bulgaria for example had 2,500 ha/6,100 acres of it in the 1980s—far more than France—and presumably prized it for its high natural acidity. In ROMANIA more than 10,000 ha of the vine may be productively cultivated, mainly for varietal wines on its fertile plains, while in the CIS it is grown in substantial quantities, on as many as 50,000 ha according to some estimates, particularly in RUSSIA, UKRAINE, MOLDOVA, GEORGIA, AZERBAIJAN, and KAZAKHSTAN. It is Russia's second most planted white wine grape and is prized as an ingredient in SOVIET SPARKLING WINE. Aligoté is also grown in Chile and to a very limited extent in California.

ALLERGIES to wines of various sorts are by no means unknown. The most common **allergens**, chemicals capable of causing an allergic reaction in humans, are proteinaceous compounds. Among possible allergens in wines are traces of the natural PROTEINS not precipitated and removed with the dead yeast cells after FERMENTATION, and traces of proteins from a FINING agent used to clarify and stabilize the wine. One amine, HISTAMINE, was once thought to be a cause of allergic reactions to red wines.

The most common wine allergies are a sensitivity to either white wine or red wine. Since red wine contains a much wider range of constituents than white wine, having been fermented with the grape SKINS and other grape solids, an allergic reaction to all red wines and no whites seems more easily comprehensible than vice versa—although this has not been the subject of much detailed research, perhaps because those who determine wine research are almost by definition unlikely to be allergic to wine themselves. SULPHUR DIOXIDE, used at higher concentrations in making white wines than red, has been suggested as a cause of so-called white wine allergies, and a minuscule proportion of the population, notably asthmatics, is sensitive to SULPHITES. Controlled experiments have yet to add any scientific weight to either red or white wine allergy as a phenomenon and some scientists suspect psychosomatic causes, at least in part.

Some people, particularly members of some ethnic groups, experience some form of allergic reaction such as face flushing and high pulse rate to even quite moderate amounts of ETHANOL.

See also HEALTH AND WINE.

ALLIER is the name of a *département* in central France best known in the world of wine for its OAK, although it also provides the wines of ST-POURÇAIN.

ALLUVIUM, type of sediment which can be described as **alluvial**, giving rise to soils which are often fine grained and typically fertile consisting of mud, SILT, SAND, and sometimes GRAVEL or stones deposited by flowing water on flood plains, in river beds, in deltas, and in estuaries. Alluvial soils are variable in texture, DRAINAGE, and maturity, and often such changes can be seen over a few metres. Where these soils are stony and sandy they are highly valued for viticulture as in the MÉDOC region of France and Marlborough in NEW ZEALAND. See entries prefixed SOIL. R.E.S.

ALMACENISTA. From the Spanish word *almacén* meaning store, an almacenista is the term for a SHERRY stockholder who sells wine to shippers. It has been used as a marketing term by the sherry firm of Lustau, who buy in and bottle wines from almacenistas.

ALMANSA, small denominated wine zone in the eastern corner of CASTILLA-LA MANCHA in central Spain (see map on p. 907). The Almansa DO borders the LEVANTE regions JUMILLA and YECLA which produce similarly strong, sturdy red wines principally from MONASTRELL and GARNACHA Tintorera grapes. The climate is extreme. Temperatures rise to 40 °C (104 °F) in summer but can dip below 0 °C (32 °F) in winter. Producers in Almansa have always had a ready market for their wines in the merchants of TARRAGONA and VALENCIA on the coast. The bulk of the wine is not therefore made to be drunk in its natural state but is designed to be blended with other, lighter wines from cooler parts of Spain. From the late 1980s, Bodegas Piqueras has been making consistently good wine using Cencibel (TEMPRANILLO) to lighten the load of Almansa's traditionally overripe grapes. R.J.M.

ALOXE-CORTON, a small village of charm at the northern end of the Côte de Beaune in Burgundy. First references to vineyards in Aloxe date back to 696, while in 775 CHARLEMAGNE ceded vines to the Abbey of St-Andoche at Saulieu. Aloxe is dominated by the hill of Corton, planted on three sides with vineyards including the GRANDS CRUS Corton (almost all red) and Corton-Charlemagne (white).

Corton is the sole grand cru appellation for red wine in the CÔTE DE BEAUNE and covers several vineyards which may be described simply as Corton or as Corton hyphenated with their names. While all Corton tends to be a dense, closed wine when young, Bressandes is noted for its comparative suppleness and charm; Renardes for its rustic, gamey character; Perrières for extra finesse; and Clos du Roi for the optimum balance between weight and elegance. It is often regarded as superior to Le Corton itself. Other Corton vineyards are Le Charlemagne, Les Pougets, and Les Languettes, all of which more often produce white Corton-Charlemagne, and Les Chaumes, Les Grèves, Les Fiètres, Les Meix, Clos de la Vigne au Saint, and part of Les Paulands and Les Maréchaudes. Further Corton vineyards extend into LADOIX-Serrigny. Although Corton is planted almost entirely with Pinot Noir vines, a tiny amount of white Corton is made, including the HOSPICES DE BEAUNE cuvée Paul Chanson from Chardonnay.

The great white wines, however, are those made within the **Corton-Charlemagne** appellation which stretches in a narrow band around the top of the hill from Ladoix-Serrigny, through Aloxe-Corton to PERNAND-VERGELESSES, where it descends down the western edge of the hillside. The MESOCLIMATE governing Corton-Charlemagne is fractionally cooler than that of Corton and the soils are different. Whereas red Corton is mainly produced on reddish chalky clay which is rich in marl, the soil at the top of the hill and on the western edge is lighter and whiter, its stoniness believed locally to impart a gunflint edge to the wines of Corton-Charlemagne.

There remains some Pinot Blanc in the otherwise Chardonnay-dominated Corton-Charlemagne vineyards which formerly were widely planted with Pinot Beurot (see PINOT GRIS) and Aligoté. Legend has it that white wine vines were initially planted at the insistence of Charlemagne's wife Hildegard, who disapproved of red wine stains on his beard.

A great Corton may seem ungainly in its sturdiness when young but should have the power to develop into a rich wine with complex, gamey flavours at eight to 10 years old. Cortons should, with POMMARD, be the most intense and longest-lived wines of the Côte de Beaune. A great Corton-Charlemagne also needs time to develop its exceptional character of breed, backbone, and racy power. Needing a minimum of five years, a good example will be better for a full decade in bottle and can last substantially thereafter.

Although more than half the vineyard area is given over to the grand crus, Aloxe-Corton also has its share of PREMIER CRU and village vineyards producing mainly red wines which can be supple and well coloured but mostly do not justify their significant premium over the wines of SAVIGNY-LÈS-BEAUNE. Apart from Les Guérets and Les Vercots, which are adjacent to Les Fichots in the commune of Pernand-Vergelesses, the premier crus of Aloxe-Corton form a band just below the swathe of grand cru vineyards, extending into Ladoix-Serrigny.

See also CÔTE D'OR and its map. J.T.C.M.

Chapuis, C., *Aloxe Corton* (Dijon, 1988), in French.

ALQUITARA, Spanish term for BRANDY distilled (either once or twice) in a POT STILL.

ALSACE, historically much-disputed region now on the eastern border of France, producing a unique style of largely VARIETAL wine, over 90 per cent of which is white. For much of its existence it has been the western German region Elsass, and, because of its geographic location, has been the subject of many a territorial dispute between France and Germany. Now separated from Germany by the river RHINE, and from France by the Vosges mountains, the language and culture of Alsace owe much to both origins, but are at the same time unique. Many families speak Alsacien, a dialect peculiar to the region, quite different from either French or German.

Of all the regions of France this is the one in which it is still easiest to find villages outwardly much as they were in the Middle Ages, with traditional half-timbered houses and extant fortifications. The hilltops of the lower Vosges are dotted with ruined castles and fortresses, witnesses to past invasions.

Up to 2,000 growers bottle and sell their own wines, although over 80 per cent of the total volume is produced by just 175 companies. Even the large companies are usually family owned, however. One of the unique aspects of Alsace is that even the smallest growers regularly produce at least six to eight different wines each year, whilst the larger producers may extend to a range of 20 to 30 different bottlings.

All Alsace wines are, by law, bottled in the region of production in tall BOTTLES called *flûtes*.

History

For details of the earlier history of the region see GERMAN HISTORY. Annexed by France in the 17th century, Alsace was reclaimed, with part of Lorraine, by the new German empire in 1871. The vineyards were used to produce cheap blending wines. After the twin crises of oïdium (POWDERY MILDEW) and PHYLLOXERA, HYBRIDS to give large trouble-free crops were planted on the flat, easily accessible land on the plains. The finer, steeper, HILLSIDE sites, formerly revered, were largely abandoned.

Following the First World War, when Alsace returned to French rule, up to a third of these better sites were replanted with the noble VINIFERA varieties. A setback occurred with the Second World War, when export was impossible, and the area was once again overrun by Germany. Replanting of the better sites gathered momentum in the 1960s and 1970s, when Alsace once again started to build up export markets.

Geography and climate

Alsace lies between LATITUDES 47.5 degrees and 49 degrees north of the equator, giving a long, cool growing season. It is important for the vineyards to make the most of the sun's rays, and so most of the best vineyards are on south, south west, or south east facing slopes, sheltered from the wind by the Vosges. Average annual RAINFALL is one of the lowest in France, due to the influence of the Vosges mountains: 500 mm / 19 in in Colmar. Rainfall varies considerably according to the vineyard sites, and isolated rain, HAIL, and thunderstorms are liable to occur in random areas, without affecting the remainder of the region. Most vineyards are at an ALTITUDE of between 175 m and 420 m (2,017 ft), above which level much of the mountainside is covered with pine forests. Autumn humidity allows for the production of late-picked VENDANGE TARDIVE wines in good vintages.

The narrow vineyard strip runs from north to south, along the lower contours of the Vosges mountains, and spans the two French *départements* of Haut-Rhin and Bas-Rhin. The majority of large producers are based in the more southerly Haut-Rhin *département*, which is generally associated with better quality, especially for Gewürztraminer (often spelt Gewurztraminer in Alsace) and Pinot Gris, producing fatter, more powerful wines towards the south of the region. In the Bas-Rhin, individual vineyard sites become even more important to ensure full RIPENESS.

There are at least 20 major soil formations within the Alsace wine region, covering several eras. Higher, steeper slopes of the Vosges have thin topsoil, with subsoils of weathered gneiss, GRANITE, SANDSTONE, SCHIST, and VOLCANIC sediments. The gentler lower slopes, derived from the Rhine delta bed, have deeper topsoils, over subsoils of CLAY, MARL, LIMESTONE, and SANDSTONE. One of the most important subsoils is the pink grès de Vosges, Vosges sandstone, which was used extensively in the construction of churches and cathedrals, and which is much in evidence in Strasbourg. The plains at the foot of the Vosges are of ALLUVIAL soils, eroded from the Vosges, and are rich and fertile, generally more suited to the production of crops other than vines.

Winters can be very cold, spring is generally mild, and the summer is warm and sometimes very dry, with heavy hail and thunderstorms possible in summer and autumn. In some vintages summer DROUGHT can be a problem, and younger vines planted in the drier, sandy soils can suffer, whereas vineyards on the water-retentive clay soils have an advantage.

As a general rule, the heavier clay and marl soils give a wine with broader flavours, more body and weight, whilst a lighter limestone or sand soil gives more elegance and finesse. Flint, schist, shale, and slate soils tend to give wines with a characteristic oily, minerally aroma reminiscent of petrol and sometimes described as 'gunflint', especially those made from the Riesling grape.

Viticulture

The varied styles of training in use depend partly on the steepness of the vineyard. The APPELLATION regulations allow a maximum of 12 buds per square metre, although in practice this allows too great a YIELD for high quality. Either single GUYOT, with up to 15 buds left on the cane, or double guyot, with up to eight buds on each cane, may be found, with a VINE DENSITY of between 4,400 and 4,800 vines per ha (1,940 per acre). There are also some CORDON-trained vines, with SPUR PRUNING, generally on older vines. A few vineyards are experimenting with LYRE and GENEVA DOUBLE CURTAIN vine-training systems. The permitted yield is set at 100 hl/ha (6 ton/acre), higher than for any other APPELLATION CON-

TRÔLÉE—with the customary Plafond Limité de Classement (see PLC) of an extra 20 per cent, provided that wines are submitted for sampling, and show a certain TYPICITY. Each year the permitted yield can be altered upwards or downwards by decree.

Quality-conscious producers will prune for a yield markedly lower than this, generally of between 40 and 50 hl/ha. SUMMER PRUNING may be carried out to ensure a smaller harvest of riper grapes.

Vines are generally trained at a height of between 60 and 90 cm (35 in) above ground, depending on the site. Vines on the plain are generally trained high to avoid FROSTS, whilst sloping vineyards can be trained closer to the ground, benefiting to the maximum from the available SUNLIGHT. Stoves and sprinklers may be used against spring frosts on the flatter vineyards (see FROST).

The steepest vineyard slopes may be TERRACED, as for example the GRAND CRU sites of Rangen and Kastelberg, or vines may be planted in rows either following the contours of the slope, or vertically from top to bottom, depending on the risk of SOIL EROSION. COVER CROPS may be planted to prevent erosion and to give more of a grip to tractors on moderate slopes.

Although MECHANICAL HARVESTING is used on the plains, many vineyards are too steep for machines, and many grapes are still hand picked. The vintage is always protracted, with varieties ripening at different times. Generally, harvesting starts in mid September, and often continues well into November.

A few growers have experimented with late-picked, BOTRYTIZED wines, not merely for the four permitted varietals (see Vendange Tardive below), but also with such diverse varieties as Auxerrois and Sylvaner, which can make outstanding wines. One or two growers produce a small quantity of VIN DE PAILLE, from healthy, ripe grapes picked in October, and dried on straw over the winter months. There have also been experiments with EISWEIN, from healthy grapes picked in December, and even in early January.

Vine varieties

At the beginning of the 20th century the many varieties planted in Alsace were divided into 'noble' and others. The number has been rationalized over the years, and now the region produces eight major varietal wines: RIESLING, GEWÜRZTRAMINER, PINOT GRIS, PINOT NOIR, PINOT BLANC, MUSCAT, CHASSELAS, and SYLVANER. Chasselas is generally used for blending, and only a handful of producers still bottle it as a varietal. AUXERROIS is also planted, and is usually blended with Pinot Blanc, although it increasingly features on a label. There is also an increasing interest in planting the ubiquitous CHARDONNAY, forbidden by law, but tolerated when labelled as Pinot Blanc, or used in the sparkling wine CRÉMANT d'Alsace.

Most growers, wherever in the region they are based, plant all of the above varieties. As some varieties fetch higher prices, and some are much more fussy about vineyard site, each grower must make an economic as well as a practical decision when deciding what to plant where. Early ripening varieties

The Clos St-Urban in the vertiginous Rangen vineyard of **Alsace**, overlooked by the toppled tower of Drachenfelds castle.

are more adaptable. Pinot Blanc and Auxerrois, both growing in popularity, are amongst the first to ripen, and are viticulturally easy to please. The later ripening Riesling and Sylvaner need to be planted on a sheltered site, and are amongst the most fussy. Muscat and Gewürztraminer are the most unreliable producers; unsettled weather at FLOWERING time can decimate the crop, so the site should be sheltered.

Riesling is one of the most widely planted varieties, accounting for over 20 per cent of the area under vine. Plantations are steadily increasing, mainly in place of Sylvaner, which is losing ground, but which still accounts for nearly 20 per cent of the area planted, with higher proportions in the Bas-Rhin than the Haut-Rhin. Pinot Blanc and Auxerrois are also on the increase, accounting for another 20 per cent between them. Gewürztraminer represents a similar acreage of plantation, but usually a smaller percentage of the production, which can fluctuate alarmingly. Its average yield is the smallest of all the varieties.

The largest plantations of Gewürztraminer are in the Haut-Rhin. Pinot Gris accounts for only around five per cent of the total area under vine, but is registering a slow increase. Pinot Noir is also increasing its share, rather more rapidly, as the only red varietal of Alsace. It represented about eight per cent of the total vineyard area in the early 1990s. The remaining vineyard area is planted with MUSCAT D'ALSACE, MUSCAT OTTONEL, Chasselas, Chardonnay, and small amounts of old plantings, of varieties no longer permitted but not yet replaced.

Wine-making

As in Germany, wine-makers measure the sugar content of the grapes, or MUST WEIGHT, in degrees OECHSLE. Most Alsace wines are CHAPTALIZED, with the notable exception of Vendange Tardive wines, which must rely totally on natural sugars present in the grape. Indigenous YEASTS are generally sufficient, and few wine-makers add yeast cultures, except in an abnormally wet vintage. ACIDIFICATION is not practised.

The number of different varieties, all to be vinified separately, can present a logistical problem. Small operations with one PRESS (increasingly a bladder press, which gives cleaner juice) will organize picking to allow each variety sufficient time in the press before the next variety is picked. Large NÉGOCIANTS and CO-OPERATIVES have a number of presses, and give growers a schedule of what may be brought to the winery on which dates.

Most wine-makers deliberately prevent MALOLACTIC FERMENTATION in white wines by keeping them cool and lightly sulphured, preferring to keep the fresh grape aromas. Only Pinot Noir goes through this secondary, softening fermentation, and for this reason is usually kept in an isolated part of the cellar to prevent cross-contamination from LACTIC BACTERIA.

Because over 95 per cent of the wine is white, and because wine-makers are emphasizing the primary grape flavours, most wine is vinified and stored in inert containers, and new wood is very seldom used. Traditional cellars have large oval wood *cuves*, many over 100 years of age, literally built into the cellar. Traditionally the same cask will be used each year for the same varietal. The build up of TARTRATES forms a glass-like lining to the cask, and there is no likelihood of wood flavours masking the wine's character. If a cask has to be replaced, the new cask will be well washed out to remove as much as possible of the WOOD FLAVOUR, and will be used for Edelzwicker until all wood flavours have disappeared. A few growers are experimenting with BARREL MATURATION, most widely for Pinot Noir, but also occasionally with Pinot Blanc, Pinot Gris, Auxerrois, and even Sylvaner. Whilst this is considered acceptable for red and experimental wines, many growers and wine critics find it inappropriate for classic whites; one grower's BARRIQUE-aged Grand Cru Pinot Gris has been regularly rejected by tasting panels of his peers.

The cellars are generally quite cold by the time FERMENTATION is taking place, so many cellars have no cooling system.

Growers have found that the BOUQUET and AGEING potential can be enhanced by fermenting Riesling, Sylvaner, and Muscat at between 14 and 16 °C (61 °F), whilst Gewürztraminer will take a warmer temperature, of up to 21 °C (70 °F).

Alsace wines are generally fermented dry, and the only wines with significant RESIDUAL SUGAR are Vendange Tardive. A few growers, however, like to leave 3 to 4 g/l of residual sugar in their wines to give a softer flavour.

Most wines are bottled within a year of the vintage, to retain freshness.

Some specific wines

Alsace was awarded AC status in 1962, with the one appellation Alsace, or Vin d'Alsace. The appellation Crémant d'Alsace was added in 1976, and Grand Cru in 1983. In addition, laws for Vendange Tardive wines were drawn up in 1983. For the still wines, the appellation Alsace can stand on its own, but is usually accompanied by one of the following names.

Riesling Considered by growers to be the most noble variety, Alsace Riesling is almost invariably bone dry. Young Riesling can display floral aromas, although it is sometimes fairly neutral. With age it takes on complex, gunflint, mineral aromas, with crisp steely acidity and very pure fruit flavours. It is one of the most difficult varieties for beginners, but one of the most rewarding wines for connoisseurs.

Gewürztraminer Usually dry to off-dry, but its low ACIDITY, combined with high alcohol and GLYCEROL, give an impression of sweetness. Gewürztraminer has a distinctive spicy aroma and flavour, with hints of lychees and grapefruit. The naturally high sugar levels of Gewürztraminer make it ideal for late harvest sweet wines, and this is the most frequent varietal found as Vendange Tardive. The high sugar can, however, put some wines out of BALANCE, and poorly made examples can be blowsy, flat, and over-alcoholic. Gewürztraminer from the southern end of Alsace, around Eguisheim southwards, tends to have quite a different character, and is generally more aromatic as well as richer in weight.

Pinot Gris Traditionally known as Tokay-Pinot Gris or Tokay d'Alsace, Pinot Gris is to be the only accepted name according to a 1993 agreement between Hungary and the EUROPEAN UNION. Pinot Gris is a very underrated variety in Alsace. It combines some of the spicy flavours of Gewürztraminer with the firm backbone of acidity found in Riesling, giving a wine which ages very well. Young Pinot Gris is reminiscent of peaches and apricot, with a hint of smoke, developing biscuity, buttery flavours with age. It is very successful in a Vendange Tardive style.

Muscat Two varieties of Muscat are found in the Alsace region: MUSCAT BLANC À PETITS GRAINS, known as Muscat d'Alsace, and Muscat Ottonel. Most wines are a blend of the two. Alsace Muscat is always dry, and has a fresh grapey aroma and flavour. The taste should be reminiscent of biting into a fresh grape, with young, crisp fruitiness. Muscat is low in alcohol, and quite low in acidity. Because of its sensitivity to poor weather at flowering, Muscat only produces well in favourable vintages, and may only produce top-quality wine in five or six vintages out of 10.

Sylvaner Sylvaner suffers from bad press in Alsace. It is difficult to grow, needs a good site, yet fetches comparatively little money. Good Sylvaner has a slightly bitter, slightly perfumed aroma and flavour, with very firm acidity. It has moderate alcohol, and is at its best when it is young and fresh. Sylvaner is at its best in hot vintages.

Pinot Blanc Also labelled Clevner or Klevner, Pinot Blanc is the workhorse of Alsace. As well as forming the base wine for Crémant d'Alsace, Pinot Blanc can produce very good, clean, dry white that is not particularly aromatic but has good acidity, with moderate alcohol. It is often blended with Auxerrois, giving a fuller flavoured, broader, more spicy wine.

Pinot Noir The only red varietal of Alsace seldom achieves a particularly deep colour in this northerly climate. Many a Rouge d'Alsace has a light strawberry pink colour, whilst some Rosé d'Alsace can be deeper. Alsace Pinot Noir was always light, fresh quaffing wine, with raspberry fruit flavours, but increasingly it has suffered an identity crisis, with many growers experimenting with OAK AGEING. Although some very good oak matured wines have resulted, many growers have produced over-oaked, dried-out thin wines.

Edelzwicker Literally, this is German for 'noble mixture'. A blend of more than one variety can be labelled as Edelzwicker, or more occasionally, as Gentil. It can also be given a general name, such as 'Fruits de Mer'. Usually Edelzwicker is one of the cheapest wines in the range. Most are pleasant and bland, some may have attractive richness and spiciness. Some growers are reverting to the practice of naming an individual vineyard site, and blending the wine from more than one variety, in which case the wine may not be cheap. This was quite common practice in the last century, and some of these wines can be extremely good.

Auxerrois This variety is rarely mentioned on the label, although it may form the total or the majority of some wines labelled as Pinot Blanc, Klevner, or Clevner. A wine from pure Auxerrois is spicy, soft, and quite broad, with low acidity and good alcohol. It is occasionally vinified in oak, quite successfully.

Chasselas This variety's name is also seldom seen on the label. It is usually used for Edelzwicker, although the few growers who bottle Chasselas as a varietal can produce a very pretty, quite lightweight wine, dry with soft grapey fruit, low acidity, and light alcohol.

Klevener de Heiligenstein The village of Heiligenstein in the Bas-Rhin has always been known for its 'Klevener', a local name for a variety long forgotten in the rest of Alsace, similar if not identical to the SAVAGNIN Rose of the Jura, but also probably related to Gewürztraminer. Only about 35 ha/86 acres are grown, although the vineyard area is increasing. Klevener has a lightly spicy, sometimes slightly buttery flavour. It is dry, less scented than Gewürztraminer, with less alcohol and a little more acidity. In good vintages it can age well.

Crémant d'Alsace An increasing amount of sparkling wine is produced in Alsace, under this appellation Crémant. Any variety may in theory be used, with the exception of Gewürztraminer, which would give too overpowering a flavour. In practice, most Crémant is from a base of Pinot Blanc, although some particularly good (white) Crémants are produced from Pinot Noir. See CRÉMANT for more details.

Vendange Tardive Late-picked wines have always been produced in small quantities in outstanding vintages. They were formerly sold as 'Spätlese', 'Auslese', and 'Beerenauslese', and the grower was free to decide which category he would choose. It was only in 1983, however, that legislation was passed to give a legal definition to Alsace's late-picked, sweet wines. To be labelled as Vendange Tardive, a wine must come from a single vintage, from one of the four permitted varieties Riesling, Muscat, Gewürztraminer, or Pinot Gris. The wine must not be ENRICHED in any way, and the minimum sugar concentration at harvest must be 220 g/l (95° Oechsle) for Riesling or Muscat, and 243 g/l (105° Oechsle) for Gewürztraminer or Pinot Gris. Picking must take place after a certain date, determined annually by the authorities, who must be informed beforehand of the grower's intention to pick a Vendange Tardive wine, and will inspect the vineyard at the time of picking to check the sugar concentration and quantity produced. The wine must also undergo an analysis and tasting after bottling, before the label is granted. Vendange Tardive wines do not have to be BOTRYTIS affected. The most commonly found varietal for Vendange Tardive wines is Gewürztraminer, which can easily attain very high sugar levels. Pinot Gris is the next varietal for ease of production, although as less is grown, it is only made in small quantities. Riesling, too, is only made in limited amounts, as producers must usually wait until November to attain the must weights needed. Muscat is the rarest of all, and is only possible in occasional vintages. Vendange Tardive wine is not necessarily sweet, and may vary from bone dry to medium sweet, and labels signify what style of wine to expect only very rarely. Although few producers made Vendange Tardive wines prior to 1983, many more are now attempting this style.

Sélection des Grains Nobles SGN is a further refinement of Vendange Tardive, where the grapes have reached even higher sugar levels. Wines labelled as Sélection des Grains Nobles, however, nearly always contain a proportion of grapes affected by botrytis, or NOBLE ROT. The same four varieties are permitted, with minimum sugar levels of 256 g/l (110° Oechsle) for Riesling and Muscat, and 279 g/l (120° Oechsle) for Gewürztraminer and Pinot Gris. The same legislation as for Vendange Tardive governs production (see above). Sélection des Grains Nobles wine is sweet, although there is a variation in richness, depending on the grape and the grower.

In the mid 1990s there were probably too many late-picked wines produced in Alsace, as producers tried to cash in on a lucrative market. It takes skill to vinify a wine with high sugar and from botrytis-affected grapes, and many producers do not have this skill. Prices and quality vary considerably, some wines scraping in with the minimum sugar levels, whilst others far surpass these minima, and are wines of extraordinary richness and complexity.

Alsace Grand Cru The Alsace Grand Cru appellation, created in 1983, signifies a wine from a single named vineyard site, a single vintage, from one of four permitted varieties, Riesling, Muscat, Gewürztraminer, or Pinot Gris. Yields are lower than for the basic appellation Alsace, with a maximum of 70 hl/ha (4 tons/acre). Moves are afoot to lower this still further. Wines must undergo technical analysis and tasting for typicality. Minimum sugar levels are higher than for basic Alsace.

Certain vineyards have always had a high reputation for the style and quality of their wines, due to the unique combination of SOIL, TOPOGRAPHY, and ASPECT of the vineyard, encompassed by the French word TERROIR. A list of the best sites was drawn up with the help of growers, and historical documents were unearthed to prove the reputation of the nominated sites.

The appellation is the subject of much controversy. Out of 94 sites originally considered, 25 were initially chosen in 1983, and by the mid 1990s there were more than 50 Grand Cru vineyard sites in Alsace, and some of the boundaries were still under discussion. Some of the nominated sites are of only moderate quality. Some named vineyards cover an unreasonably large area, often extending over a number of hillsides, including a number of soils and aspects, some greatly superior to others. Some parts of Kaefferkopf, for example, face north. Growers who have used the vineyard name for many years do not wish to lose that right. Additionally, some growers do not want to reduce their yield for the sake of the Grand Cru appellation.

Whilst single-vineyard wines are an excellent way forward for quality wine production, much depends on the attitude of the grower, as well as on the quality of the vineyard site. The best sites and growers have undoubtedly benefited from the Grand Cru appellation, but many growers and co-operatives are producing wines of average quality, cashing in on the Grand Cru name. Some of the top négociants have Grand Cru vineyard sites, but prefer to use the names by which they have historically sold such wines: Trimbach's famous Clos Ste-Hune Riesling comes from the Grand Cru Rosacker, while Beyer's Riesling Cuvée Particulière is from the Grand Cru Pfersigberg. Some Grand Cru sites are only outstanding when planted with one or two of the four permitted varietals. On Kastelberg, for example, only Riesling is permitted. Many more should be further delimited in this way. Some of the sites more recently admitted into the classification already had a reputation for a variety other than the four permitted for Grand Cru, and it would be a shame to lose wines as fine and characterful as Zotzenberg Sylvaner, for example, a fine, vibrant wine, often from old vines. Sylvaner is now being removed in favour of Riesling and Gewürztraminer, both producing adequate wines on the Zotzenberg, but replacing a very individual wine.

In the following list, compiled in late 1993, an approximate size has been indicated for those Grand Cru sites not yet fully delimited.

Altenberg de Bergbieten, Bergbieten, Bas-Rhin, 27.26 ha / 67.3 acres
Altenberg de Bergheim, Bergheim, Haut-Rhin, 35.06 ha
Altenberg de Wolxheim, Wolxheim, Haut-Rhin, approx. 28 ha
Brand, Turckheim, Haut-Rhin, 55.21 ha
Bruderthal, Molsheim, Bas-Rhin, approx. 19 ha
Eichberg, Eguisheim, Haut-Rhin, 57.6 ha
Engelberg, Dahlenheim, Bas-Rhin, approx. 11 ha
Florimont, Ingersheim, Haut-Rhin, approx. 15 ha
Frankstein, Dambach-la-Ville, Bas-Rhin, approx. 53 ha
Froehn, Zellenberg, Haut-Rhin, approx. 13 ha
Furstentum, Kientzheim, Sigolsheim, Haut-Rhin, 27.65 ha
Geisberg, Ribeauvillé, Haut-Rhin, 8.53 ha
Gloeckelberg (or Kloeckelberg), Rodern, St-Hippolyte, Haut-Rhin, 23.4 ha
Goldert, Gueberschwihr, Haut-Rhin, 45.35 ha
Hatschbourg, Hattstatt, Voegtlinshoffen, Haut-Rhin, 47.36 ha
Hengst, Wintzenheim, Haut-Rhin, 75.74 ha
Kaefferkopf, Ammerschwihr, Haut-Rhin, approx. 60 ha
Kanzlerberg, Bergheim, Haut-Rhin, 3.23 ha
Kastelberg, Andlau, Bas-Rhin, 5.82 ha
Kessler, Guebwiller, Haut-Rhin, 28.53 ha
Kirchberg de Barr, Barr, Bas-Rhin, 37.13 ha
Kirchberg de Ribeauvillé, Haut-Rhin, 11.4 ha
Kitterlé, Guebwiller, Haut-Rhin, 25.79 ha
Mambourg, Sigolsheim, Haut-Rhin, approx. 65 ha
Mandelberg, Mittelwihr, Haut-Rhin, approx. 12 ha
Marckrain, Bennwihr, Sigolsheim, Haut-Rhin, approx. 45 ha
Moenchberg, Andlau, Eichhoffen, Bas-Rhin, 11.83 ha
Muenchberg, Nothalten, Bas-Rhin, 25 ha
Ollwiller, Wuenheim, Haut-Rhin, 35.86 ha
Osterberg, Ribeauvillé, Haut-Rhin, approx. 24 ha
Pfersigberg, Eguisheim, Haut-Rhin, approx. 56 ha
Pfingstberg, Orschwihr, Haut-Rhin, approx. 28 ha
Praelatenberg, Orschwiller, Kintzheim, Bas-Rhin, approx. 12 ha
Rangen, Thann, Vieux Thann, Haut-Rhin, 18.81 ha
Rosacker, Hunawihr, Haut-Rhin, 27.24 ha
Saering, Guebwiller, Haut-Rhin, 26.75 ha
Schlossberg, Kayserberg, Kientzheim, Haut-Rhin, 80 ha
Schoenenbourg, Riquewihr, Haut-Rhin, approx. 40 ha
Sommerberg, Niedermorschwihr, Katzenthal, Haut-Rhin, 27.76 ha
Sonnenglanz, Beblenheim, Haut-Rhin, 32.8 ha
Spiegel, Bergholtz, Guebwiller, Haut-Rhin, 18.28 ha
Sporen, Riquewihr, Haut-Rhin, approx. 22 ha
Steinert, Pfaffenheim, Haut-Rhin, 38 ha
Steingrubler, Wettolsheim, Haut-Rhin, approx. 19 ha
Steinklotz, Marlenheim, Bas-Rhin, 24 ha
Vorbourg, Rouffach, Westhalten, Haut-Rhin, approx. 72 ha
Wiebelsberg, Andlau, Bas-Rhin, 10.32 ha
Wineck-Schlossberg, Katzenthal, Ammerschwihr, Haut-Rhin, approx. 24 ha
Winzenberg, Blienschwiller, Bas-Rhin, approx. 5 ha
Zinnkoepflé, Westhalten, Soultzmatt, Haut-Rhin, approx. 62 ha
Zotzenberg, Mittelbergheim, Bas-Rhin, approx. 34 ha

See also MARC and CRÉMANT. E.J.R.B.

Berry, E. J. R., *The Wines of Alsace: A Buyer's Guide* (London, 1989).
Duijker, H., *Loire, Alsace and Champagne* (London, 1983).
Stevenson, T., *The Wines of Alsace* (London, 1993).
Vandyke Price, P., *Alsace Wines* (London, 1984).

ALTERNARIA. Vine disease. See BUNCH ROTS.

ALTERNATIVE VITICULTURE, a series of vineyard practices which differ from conventional, commercial viticulture for which the principal objectives are the maximization of yield or quality. Alternative viticultural practices usually aim to minimize environmental degradation, and are very similar to those used in ORGANIC VITICULTURE, for which 'alternative viticulture' is in many ways a more accurate description. See also SUSTAINABLE VITICULTURE. R.E.S.

ALTESSE, synonym for the Savoie fine white grape variety ROUSSETTE.

ALTITUDE, the height above sea level of a site, can have important effects on its climate and therefore on its viticultural potential. Other things being equal, temperature falls by about 0.6 °C (1.1 °F) per 100 m (330 ft) greater altitude. See also ELEVATION.

The lower temperatures at higher altitudes retard both vine BUDBREAK and, in particular, RIPENING. Temperatures during ripening can therefore be reduced much more than over the season as a whole. Small differences in elevation can have surprisingly big effects on wine quality and, indeed, on the ability of individual grape varieties to ripen at all. Becker summarizes and refers to a major Rhine valley study illustrating this. Lower temperatures can be further compounded by the generally greater rainfall and cloudiness at higher altitudes.

Such effects are most marked in cool viticultural climates, where the rates of vine and berry development are directly limited by temperature through all or most of the season. Similar altitude differences have much less effect in warmer climates (although they are sufficiently significant to explain, for example, why grapes may not always ripen fully in parts of TUSCANY). Gladstones quantifies these relationships.

With the increased market prominence of table wines relative to fortified wines since the 1960s, many of the new plantings in the world's warmer viticultural regions have been at higher altitudes, as a means of attaining the cooler conditions most appropriate for their production (see CLIMATE AND WINE QUALITY and TEMPERATURE). Large-scale plantings in the ADELAIDE HILLS regions in South Australia are a notable example of this, as are some newer vineyards in ARGENTINA. Similar examples can be seen in HILLSIDE VINEYARDS in California, Chile, South Africa, Sicily, and Greece.

Whether diminishing concentrations of atmospheric CARBON DIOXIDE with altitude are a significant disadvantage for these plantings remains to be seen. On average the atmospheric carbon dioxide concentration falls by about one per cent for each 100 m/330 ft greater altitude, a fact which undoubtedly affects vines as it does other plants. Theoretically this should tend to reduce the yield, and possibly the quality, of wines from high-altitude vineyards. Certainly almost all the world's best wines have come historically from vineyards below 500 m. On the other hand, current and future general rises in atmospheric carbon dioxide concentration may well largely override any such differences. See also CLIMATE CHANGE.

BOLIVIA has vines planted at up to 2,500 m/8,200 ft. Vineyards in MEXICO may be as high as 2,100 m/6,900 ft above sea level, while PERU has vines planted up to 1,500 m and some newer vineyards in ARGENTINA are as high as 1,200 m. The highest European vineyards are probably those of the ALTO ADIGE, which may be up to 1,000 m and SWITZERLAND, which boasts one vineyard at an altitude of 1,100 m. J.G. & R.E.S.

Becker, H., 'Site climate effects on development, fruit maturation and harvest quality', in R. E. Smart *et al.* (eds.), *Proceedings of the Second International Symposium for Cool Climate Viticulture and Oenology: 11–15 January 1988 Auckland, New Zealand* (Auckland, 1988), 11–15.

Gladstones, J., *Viticulture and Environment* (Adelaide, 1992).

ALTO ADIGE is the northern, predominantly German-speaking part of the TRENTINO-ALTO ADIGE region, bordering on the Austrian Tyrol. It was ceded to Italy only after the First World War and most of its inhabitants, who enjoy a certain amount of autonomy, call it the Südtirol, or South Tyrol. (Throughout this article, German names appear after Italian names in brackets.) The region owes its Italian name to the river Adige (Etsch), which flows through it on its way to the Adriatic. Viticulture follows the mountainous local TOPOGRAPHY, vine-growing being a feasible proposition only in the valleys of the Adige and Isarco (Eisach) rivers which meet at Bolzano (Bozen) to form a Y-shaped growing zone. Despite its septentrional position, the Alto Adige enjoys a warm summer climate in the valleys and in the hills just off of the valley floors, and the towns of Bolzano and Merano (Meran) are frequently among Italy's hottest in July and August. Virtually the entire production of wine qualifies as DOC; only 60 of the region's total 5,000 ha/12,350 acres of vineyards grow VINO DA TAVOLA grapes. The annual production of about 350,000 hl/9.2 million gal is dominated by CO-OPERATIVES which control about two-thirds of the total output, but many of these co-ops, in particular those of Colterenzio and Appiano, are run with high professional and managerial standards and produce excellent wine.

SCHIAVA (Vernatsch) is the dominant grape in the Alto Adige, accounting for close to 60 per cent of the total wine produced and giving a light to medium bodied red wine with a hint of violets in the nose and almonds on the finish. It is the base of the Caldaro (Kalterer), Colli di Bolzano (Bozner Leiten), Meranese (Meraner), and SANTA MADDALENA (Sankt Magdalener) DOCs, and is the most important varietal DOC within the overall Alto Adige appellation. The DOC structure of the Alto Adige closely resembles that of the TRENTINO: a variety of geographically specific DOC zones together with a general DOC which embraces the entire zone, whose wines are further identified by VARIETAL, 18 in all. There are two other specific and delimited DOC zones in addition to these Schiava-dominated zones: Valle Isarco (Eisacktaler), where production is dominated by SILVANER and MÜLLER-THURGAU in addition to small amounts of GEWÜRZTRAMINER (itself supposedly a native of this region); and Terlano (Terlaner), a white DOC based on PINOT BIANCO, and with limited but high-quality production of SAUVIGNON Blanc.

Schiava accounts for a third of the overall production in the general Alto Adige DOC; other varieties of some significance are PINOT GRIGIO, CHARDONNAY, and Pinot Bianco amongst the whites plus LAGREIN, PINOT NOIR, and—to a lesser extent—CABERNET and MERLOT amongst the reds. Lagrein is frequently added to both Schiava and Pinot Noir to deepen the colour and supply extra tannins and structure, giving a characteristic bitter finish.

Apart from the almost ubiquitous Schiava, the Alto Adige is best known for clean, crisp, fruity white wines made in a modern style with low temperature fermentation, and solid, if somewhat rustic, reds. The whites compare quite favourably, at a considerably lower price, with the more famous products of FRIULI.

Styles began to change in the 1980s, however, with producers seeking a richer and fuller style in the whites and a more polished character in the reds. BARRIQUES are increasingly used to add dimension.

A substantial part of the improvement in the overall quality level has been the result of better matching of varieties to subzones, a matching which in many cases merely confirms the historic tradition of certain TERROIRS for certain grapes: Magré (Margreid) and Cortaccia (Kurtatsch) in the south west and Settequerce (Siebeneich) to the west of Bolzano for Cabernet and Merlot; Mazzon and Montagna (Montan) in the valley's south east and Cornaiano (Girlan) to the south west of Bolzano for Pinot Noir (unlike in BURGUNDY, Pinot Noir prefers a south western ASPECT in this hotter region); Terlano (Terlan) for Sauvignon; Appiano (Eppan) and Monte (Berg) for Pinot Bianco; Ora (Auer) and the sandy and gravelly soils adjacent to Bolzano for Lagrein; Termeno (Tramin), Caldaro (Kaltern), and Cortaccia in addition to Santa Maddalena for Schiava; Cortaccia, Magré, and Salorno for Pinot Grigio.

See also SANTA MADDALENA, and compare with TRENTINO.

D.T.

ALVARINHO, the Portuguese name of a distinctive white grape variety grown in the north of Portugal's VINHO VERDE country (and, as ALBARIÑO, in GALICIA). The grapes' thick skins help them withstand the particularly damp climate, and can result in wines notably high in alcohol, acidity, and flavour. Alvarinho is one of the few Portuguese white grape varieties encountered on the labels of VARIETAL wines.

AMABILE, Italian for sweet (sweeter than ABBOCCATO) or, literally, 'lovable'. See also SWEETNESS.

AMARONE, the most famous of Italy's dry DRIED GRAPE WINES, is produced from identical grape varieties and in the same production zone as VALPOLICELLA, with the same distinction between the classical zone, where Amarone Classico is produced, and an enlarged zone where simple Amarone is produced. No longer obliged to call itself RECIOTO Amarone, it has become one of Italy's DOC wines in its own right.

Although the wine was once produced from the upper lobes or 'ears' of the bunches, it is now made from selected superior whole bunches which are dried or raisined in special drying lodges or chambers. Here the grapes are spread out on mats or wickerwork shelving, or are strung up from the ceiling or rafters. It is increasingly common to dry the grapes in the slatted packing cases in which they were harvested. The length of the drying period varies from producer to producer. It was often prolonged until late February or March with ample development of BOTRYTIS, which became increasingly common during the 1970s and 1980s as the vineyards and production facilities of Valpolicella descended from the drier hills to the more humid valley floor. There has been a tendency to shorten the raisining period in recent years, however, in order to produce a wine less obviously affected by botrytis. Some producers now eliminate botrytis-affected grapes completely in order to produce a fresher, fruitier wine without the OXIDIZED flavours which once characterized the wine. After the drying process is finished, the grapes are pressed and fermented dry, and the wine aged in wooden casks. Smaller casks of new OAK are being experimented with, *demi-muids* (see BARREL TYPES) enjoying a certain vogue. The finished wine easily reaches 15 per cent of alcohol and is rarely released until five years after the vintage, even though this is not legally required.

Prior to the Second World War Amarone was considered a kind of failure, a sweet wine *manqué* in which the RESIDUAL SUGARS had inadvertently been fermented. The first attempts to market Amarone date from the early 1950s and were carried out by such leading houses as Santa Sofia, Bertani, Bolla, and Allegrini, with other labels following—considerably later—in their wake. The elevated price of the wine, caused by its high production costs and low yield in terms of juice (40 per cent is the legal maximum), its high ALCOHOLIC STRENGTH, and the characteristic oxidized aromas and flavours created by the noble rot, created some difficulties in marketing the wine in the 1980s, although Amarone still has a hard core of admirers. The experiments at creating a fruitier, less oxidized style are thus best seen as a search for new customers and new markets. Current production is approximately 15,000 hl/396,000 gal a year.

D.T.

AMATEUR WINE-MAKING. See HOME WINE-MAKING.

AMELIORATION, which strictly means improvement, is a euphemism for chemical intervention in wine-making with the express purpose of compensating for nature's deficiencies. Thus in cooler wine regions the term is commonly used interchangeably with ENRICHMENT or CHAPTALIZATION, the addition of extra fermentable sugars to grape juice or MUST with the intention of increasing the alcoholic strength of the resultant wine. Amelioration is sometimes used more widely to include both ACIDIFICATION and DEACIDIFICATION, and sometimes for any chemical adjustment to the constituents naturally present in grape juice or wine.

Authorities in almost all wine regions have enacted strict regulations concerning such possible adjustments in order to preclude exaggerations and, even, the possibility of making a wine-like liquid from SUGARS, synthetic ACIDS, commercial

TANNINS, artificial COLOUR, and WATER. Ameliorating operations condoned by each region's authorities tend to be those required, and vice versa, but limits are set.

The French often use their word *amélioration* to mean enrichment, while the direct German equivalent is *Verbesserung*.

AMERICAN HYBRIDS, group of vine HYBRIDS developed in the eastern United States, mainly in the early and mid 19th century and in some cases earlier. The term encompasses both hybrids between different native AMERICAN VINE SPECIES of the vine genus VITIS such as the *labrusca–aestivalis* Norton, or, more commonly, an American species crossed with a variety of the European vine species VINIFERA, such as Black Spanish, Herbemont, Delaware, and Othello. The hybrids' most common parents are the American species *V labrusca* and *V aestivalis*, along with *V vinifera*. More recently the binomial *V labruscana* has been used for natural hybrids of *V labrusca* with other species, including *V vinifera*, of which CONCORD is the most famous variety.

These varieties are used to some extent for wine production and for TABLE GRAPES, but most are used commercially for unfermented GRAPE JUICE and jelly. The fruit is typically highly flavoured, and palates accustomed to the taste of *vinifera* varieties find the FOXY character of American vines strong and objectionable.

As outlined in UNITED STATES, history, the early European settlers in America imported *vinifera* cuttings from Europe repeatedly. Although these early vineyards were eventually killed by extreme winter cold and indigenous diseases, during flowering there was natural hybridization by pollen exchange with the native American species. The hybrid offspring of these accidental (or natural) crosses was first noticed in the mid 18th century, when a grape later called the Alexander was found in Pennsylvania. The hybrid nature of the variety Alexander was not understood, but the grape became the basis of the first commercially successful wine-making in North America (200 years after commercial wine production began in SOUTH AMERICA).

In the early 19th century, many more chance-produced American hybrids were found and used for wine, among them Catawba, Isabella, and Delaware. In the mid 19th century, deliberate, controlled breeding of hybrids began in America, and many thousands of hybrid varieties were created including Elvira, Niagara, and Diamond.

Following the devastation wreaked by the pest PHYLLOXERA in Europe at the end of the 19th century, the French began experimental hybridizing of *vinifera* with American species, producing the so-called FRENCH HYBRIDS or direct producers.

T.P. & R.E.S.

Galet, P., and Morton, L. T., *A Practical Ampelography* (Ithaca, NY, and London, 1979).

Hedrick, U. P., *The Grapes of New York* (Albany, NY, 1908).

Mullins, M. G., Bouquet, A., and Williams, L., *Biology of the Grapevine* (Cambridge, 1992).

Pinney, T., *A History of Wine in America* (Berkeley, Calif., 1989).

AMERICAN VINES, loose term for both AMERICAN VINE SPECIES and also AMERICAN HYBRIDS.

AMERICAN VINE SPECIES, those members of the grapevine genus VITIS which originate in North America, Mexico, and the Caribbean. About half the vine species of the world are native to America, but they are poorly suited to WINE-MAKING. When, however, all efforts to grow the imported European vine species *Vitis* VINIFERA failed through disease or climatic extreme (see UNITED STATES, history), wine was made in North America of necessity from these species, detailed below.

After the discovery of AMERICAN HYBRIDS and the successful cultivation of *V vinifera* vines in CALIFORNIA, native vines were no longer used for wine, with two notable exceptions: the *V labrusca* CONCORD grape and some varieties of *V rotundifolia*, notably the SCUPPERNONG. The Concord has evolved a style of sweet, sometimes KOSHER, wine which is distinctively American (see NEW YORK), and the Scuppernong is also used for a sweet, musky wine popular in the southern United States where it is grown.

The most important role for the American species has been to provide the genetic basis for ROOTSTOCKS on to which European *vinifera* vines may be grafted. This became a necessity in most of the world's wine regions at the end of the 19th

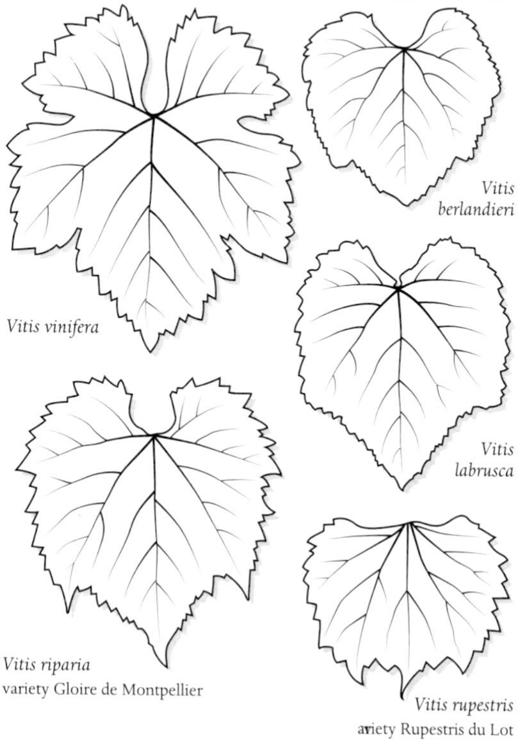

American (and European) **vine species**

century to counter the predations of the PHYLLOXERA louse, native to America and to which most American vine species had therefore developed resistance. The species *V riparia* and *V rupestris* are particularly important in this regard, and most of the world's vineyards now grow on roots derived from them.

These are some of the more important American vine species (although others are listed under VITIS):

Vitis labrusca Vine species found in the north eastern United States producing strongly flavoured, dark berries whose almost rank aroma is sometimes described as FOXY. The berries fall easily when ripe and are called 'slip-skin' in that a berry squeezed between fingers will eject the flesh as a complete ball (non slip-skin varieties, which are the norm, are squashed when squeezed in this way). Most of the fruit of this species is black, and the leaves are large, thick, and covered on the lower surface with dense white or brown hairs. *Vitis labrusca* is a common parent in American hybrids. *Vitis labruscana* is a term for natural hybrids of *Vitis labrusca* with other species, of which Concord is the most important variety by far, thought to have one *vinifera* parent.

Vitis aestivalis Vine species grown in the south eastern United States which, like *Vitis labrusca*, is a common parent in American hybrids. The fruit, however, is juicier and sweeter, and the grape skins are always black. This species shows good resistance to DOWNY MILDEW and POWDERY MILDEW and is therefore a common parent in VINE BREEDING programmes.

Vitis riparia This vigorous, tall growing vine species is usually found along streams (its Latin name means river bank) and is widely distributed from Canada in the north to the Gulf of Mexico in the south. The grape has a black skin and its juice is acid without strong flavours. A common parent of many commercially important rootstocks, which are often early and of low to moderate vigour.

Vitis rupestris Unusual vine species in being a small shrub found typically on gravelly banks of streams or in watercourses in Texas. The leaves are small and kidney shaped and roots tend to grow vertically downwards rather than spread horizontally. A common parent of many commercially important rootstocks because of its phylloxera resistance.

Vitis berlandieri Vine species found on the limestone soils of Texas and Mexico. The grape is black and its juice is high in sugar and acid without strong flavours. This species is known for being difficult to root from cuttings, but because of high phylloxera and lime resistance it is a common parent of many commercially important rootstocks.

Other American species include *V cinerea*, *cordifolia*, *candicans*, *longii*, *champini*, *monicola*, and *V caribaea*. R.E.S.

Antcliff, A. J., 'Taxonomy: the grapevine as a member of the plant kingdom', in B. G. Coombe and P. R. Dry (eds.), *Viticulture*, *Resources in Australia* (Adelaide, 1988).

Galet, P., and Morton, L. T., *A Practical Ampelography* (Ithaca, NY, and London, 1979).

AMERICAN VITICULTURAL AREA. See AVA.

AMERINE, MAYNARD (1911–), American OENOLOGIST, teacher, and writer, was trained as a plant physiologist at Berkeley in CALIFORNIA before joining the revived Department of Viticulture and Enology at DAVIS in 1935. There he participated in some of the most important branches of its work, including the assessment of VINE VARIETIES for the different regions of California and the re-education of the wine industry to restore and advance the technical knowledge lost during PROHIBITION. With A. J. WINKLER, Amerine developed the system of classifying wine regions by measuring heat summation. The list of his publications extends to nearly 400 items. In his writings, Amerine has addressed nearly everyone interested in wine: oenologists, VITICULTURISTS, owners and operators, politicians, connoisseurs, and the public generally. His *Wine: An Introduction for Americans* (1965, with Vernon Singleton) is a popular authority; he has also made substantial contributions to the literature of such subjects as wine JUDGING methods, wine and must ANALYSIS, COLOUR in wines, the AGEING of wine, the control of FERMENTATION, and the LITERATURE OF WINE. His combination of practical and theoretical scientific knowledge, connoisseurship, erudition, and prolific output made him, to the American public, the pre-eminent member of that group of Davis scientists who renewed research on vines and wines after Repeal of Prohibition. His contribution to the improvement of WINE-MAKING standards in California following Repeal is of fundamental importance.

Amerine served as chairman of his department from 1957 until 1962 and retired from the University in 1974. He has remained active as a writer and a recognized general expert on wine, particularly wine in California. T.P.

AMINO ACIDS, the basic building blocks of PROTEINS, chemicals essential to all living systems. There are 20 amino acids involved in constructing thousands of proteins of living materials. When these proteins act as catalysts for specific biochemical reaction, they are called ENZYMES.

In ripe grapes, NITROGEN-containing compounds constitute about 1 g/l of juice, of which amino acids make up about half. The most common are proline, arginine, and glutamic acid. Of the others the most prominent are alanine, a-aminobutyric acid, aspartic acid, serine, and threonine. During grape RIPENING, the concentrations of amino acids increase, arginine and proline especially; proline increases more than arginine if the fruit is exposed to light. High concentrations of arginine, resulting from soils with a high nitrogen content, present the danger of production of the carcinogen urethane (ethyl CARBAMATE) in wine.

YEASTS are able to make all the amino acids they require, but they will also use intact amino acids from the medium in which they find themselves if they are available. Thus FUSEL OILS are formed in wine as by-products of the nitrogen metabolism of the yeast cells living in grape juice. After fermentation has finished, yeast proteins break down, secreting smaller peptide units and amino acids into the wine if it is left in the presence of the LEES or dead yeast cells. Bottle-fermented SPARKLING WINES owe some of their special flavour to the presence of substances associated with yeast breakdown, peptides, and amino acids (see AUTOLYSIS).

A.D.W. & B.G.C.

Rantz, J. A. (ed.), 'Nitrogen in Grapes and Wine', Proc. Int. Symposium, Seattle, June 1991, *Amer. Soc. for Enol. and Vitic.* (Davis, Calif., 1991).

AMONTILLADO, Spanish word which originally described sherry in the style of MONTILLA. Today it has two related meanings in the sherry-making process. The basic FINO wines become amontillado (Spanish for 'like Montilla') when the FLOR yeast dies and the wine is exposed to oxygen. This happens automatically if a fino type of sherry is fortified to 16 per cent since the flor yeast cannot work in such an alcoholic environment. The wine turns amber and tastes richer and nuttier. A true Amontillado-style sherry is therefore an aged Fino. Cheaper Amontillados, the most common Amontillado encountered commercially, are created artificially by blending and are usually sweetened. They tend to be quintessentially medium. For more details see SHERRY.

AMPELOGRAPHY, the science of description and identification of the vine species VITIS and its cultivated VINE VARIETIES. A volume of vine descriptions is also called an ampelography, the word coming from the Greek *ampelos* for vine, and *graphe* for writing. Some system of distinguishing between vine varieties (and thus grape varieties) is clearly necessary since the early French **ampelographers** Viala and Vermorel (see below) were able to list about 24,000 names of varieties and their synonyms in their seven-volume *Ampelographie* published between 1902 and 1910. Some system of vine identification is particularly necessary in the modern era of VARIETAL wines (see below for examples of mistaken identification, especially in the NEW WORLD).

There has long been an awareness of differences between vine varieties, and PLINY the Elder could already produce vine descriptions and state that synonyms were creating confusion in Ancient ROME. While regional ampelographies which emphasized the aptitudes of various cultivated varieties already existed in medieval Europe, it was not until the second half of the 19th century that a need for more systematic study developed. When serious vine diseases and pests were introduced to Europe from America (POWDERY MILDEW in 1852, PHYLLOXERA in 1863, DOWNY MILDEW in 1878, and BLACK ROT in 1885), it became essential to identify those species and varieties which showed most resistance to these hazards.

Early ampelographic works emphasized fruit characters, and did not provide a key for classification, so that it was impossible to determine the name of a variety in a systematic fashion. Further, the distinguishing features of the vine varieties themselves were not emphasized. The vegetative parts of the vine were not used for identification since they were thought too variable and not stable. The Austrian ampelographer Hermann Goethe proposed measuring the angle between leaf veins as an identifying character in 1876, and this concept was developed by the French ampelographer Louis Ravaz when in 1902 he published his, presumably much-needed, book *Les Vignes américaines*. Several large regional ampelographies were published near the turn of the century, including Pulliat (1888) and also Viala and Vermorel (1902–10) in France; Goethe (1878) in Austria; Rovasenda (1881) and Molon (1906) in Italy; and Hedrick (1908) and Munson (1909) in the USA.

The most famous modern ampelographer, Professor Pierre GALET of MONTPELLIER, began his studies in 1944 by inspecting ROOTSTOCK plantings, and this led to the publication of a distinguishing key in 1946. These studies were extended to include wine and table grape varieties and in 1952 his *Précis d'ampélographie pratique* was published, followed by, among other works, *Cépages et vignobles de France*. Galet formalized the study of the morphology of the growing shoot tips, leaves, and shoots, including qualitative descriptions of leaf hair types and quantitative descriptions of leaf shape.

Vine characteristics which ampelographers use to differentiate species and varieties include colour and hairiness of shoot, shoot tip, petiole, and young and mature leaves; the shape, contour, texture, and indentation of leaves; the sex of flowers; shape and compactness of bunches; and shape, colour, taste, and seed presence of grapes. These characteristics are more or less subjective but once an observer becomes familiar with the terminology they are easy to use. Grape flavour is admittedly subjective, but at the other end of the scale of objectivity is Galet's comprehensive quantitative description of leaf shape by measuring the lengths and angles of the veins, the ratio of length to width, and the depth of sinuses. Other characters have been considered for identification, including the timing of phenological or development stages such as BUDBREAK, fruit maturation, or even LEAF FALL. Such features are known to be controlled by the environment, however, and can be used only in a relative sense for vine varieties in a single region.

The disadvantages of the technique are that, while some characteristics are quite stable, others, such as leaf shape, can vary markedly even on one vine. Major differences can be caused by environmental factors, but also and to a lesser degree by variation between different CLONES, plant age, and the influence of pests and vine DISEASES. There are, however, five characters which are quite stable: sex of the flower; grape skin colour; pulp colour; the taste of berries; and the presence of seeds. There is a need for a simple, precise, and reproducible system with well-defined terms in several major languages.

Experience has shown that ampelography is a field of systematic botany requiring very specialized skills and interpretative ability, as well as an extraordinary memory. There are very few people who can walk into any vineyard and unequivocally identify varieties. Some modern acknowledged experts apart from Pierre Galet are his colleague Paul Truel and successor Jean-Michel Boursiquot of Montpellier, and Alan Antcliff of Australia.

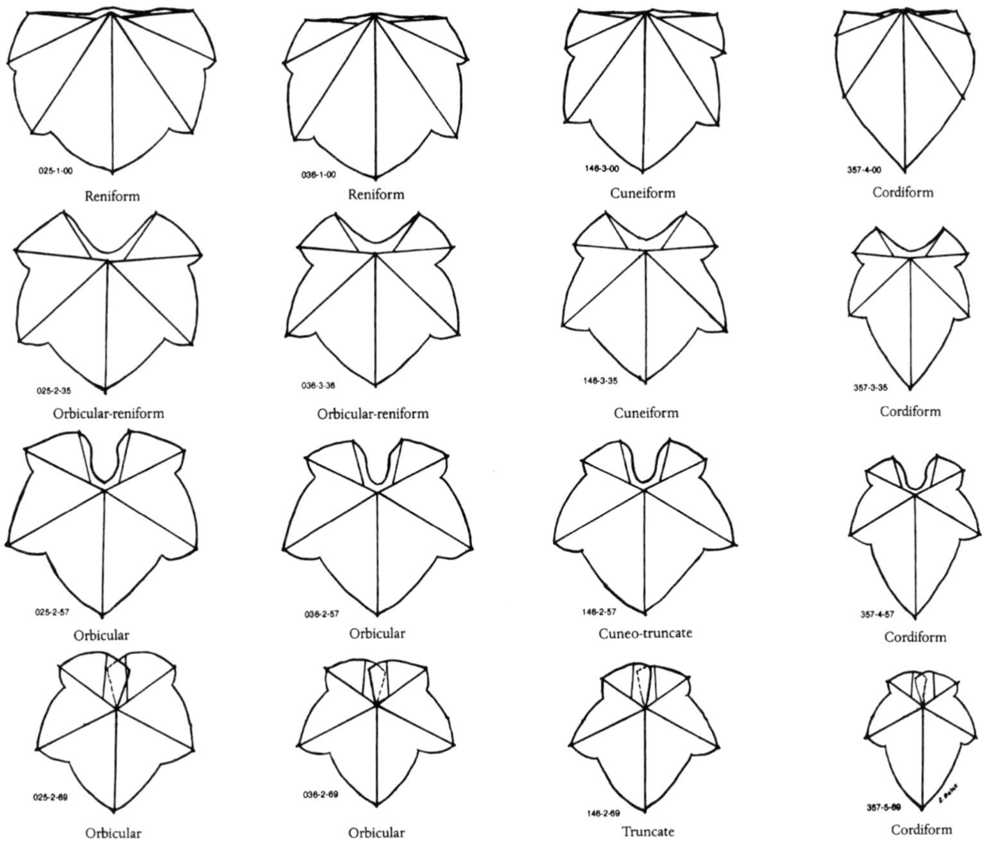

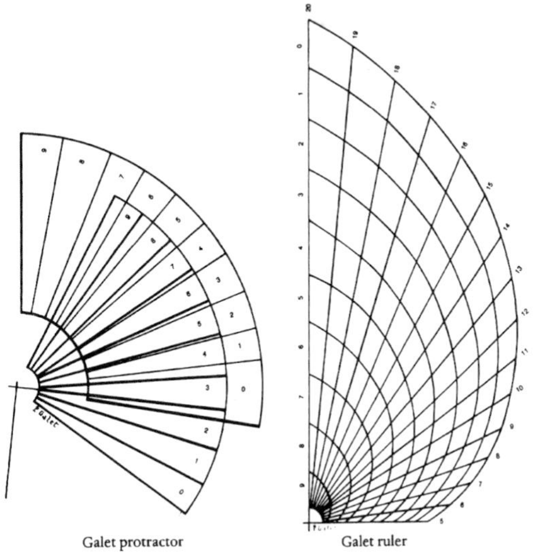

Galet's **ampelographic** codes for some basic vine leaf shapes and the ruler and protractor used to measure them.

Three international ampelographic codes are currently in use. A complex ampelographic procedure was proposed by the Office International de la Vigne et du Vin (OIV) in 1951, based on 65 morphological characters and 267 levels of expression. The International Board of Plant Genetic Resources (IBPGR) and l'Union International pour la Protection des Obtentions Végétales (UPOV) have also produced lists of descriptors and all three international systems have been harmonized by the introduction of numeric codes. The OIV list now includes 130 characters, and the UPOV list has a minimum of 36 characters for description. Ampelographic studies have recently been facilitated by application of computers and electronic data storage and retrieval, but final identification still relies heavily on the judgement of ampelographers.

BLIND TASTING tests on VARIETAL wines have demonstrated that the human palate does not reliably identify different vine varieties. More recently, attempts have been made to develop objective, laboratory-based tests for vine identification, including isozyme analysis and gel electrophoresis of enzyme banding patterns. The most recent are DNA 'FINGERPRINTING' methods.

Unfortunately, mistakes in naming grapevine varieties are common, especially in the New World, in government collections as well as in commercial nurseries. Some of the early introductions of vine cuttings to these regions were made before European vine-growers had correctly identified their own varieties. Sometimes name tags on bundles of vine cuttings, all of which look remarkably similar, were simply misplaced or transposed. In other cases, confusion was caused by different synonyms in different European regions. James BUSBY's celebrated vine collection introduced to colonial Australia in 1832, for example, probably contained CINSAUT cuttings under seven different regional synonyms, and CHENIN BLANC under three. The noted French ampelographer Paul Truel studied a large collection of French varieties at Vassal on the Mediterranean coast in the 1960s and 1970s and found that as many as six distinct varieties grown in different parts of France were the one variety under different names, and there is even more variation in nomenclature between countries. The GRACIANO of Spain, for example, is the same as France's Morrastel while the Ottavianello of Italy is the same as CINSAUT of France, but more complex examples abound.

Because its nursery has been able to provide virus-free, high-health vines, the University of California at DAVIS has been an important source of varieties for many establishing New World countries. Naming mistakes in this collection are legion, and have caused inconvenience for both the California wine industry and importers of plant material from Davis. Some examples of such errors cited in California by French ampelographers Galet and Boursiquot, in Australia by Truel, and in New Zealand by Zuur include Abouriou (incorrectly called Early Burgundy), Petit Verdot (Gros Manseng), one clone of Pinot Noir (Gamay Beaujolais), Négrette (Pinot St George), Valdiguié (Napa Gamay), Melon (Pinot Blanc), Muscadelle (Sauvignon Vert), Tempranillo (Valdepeñas), a clone of Sauvignon Blanc (Savagnin Musqué), Trousseau Gris (Grey Riesling), and Touriga (Alvarelhão).

Roman **amphora** used to transport wine in classical times.

Generally ROOTSTOCKS are more difficult to differentiate, so it is not surprising that problems have also occurred with their naming. In the 1990s, California has been forced to replace the rootstock AXR1, as it succumbed to phylloxera. This effort was thwarted by finding that the rootstock SO4 was in fact 5C Teleki, and Riparia Gloire was mixed with Couderc 1616.

Since the early 1970s many countries have recognized these problems and have attempted to reduce the confusion. Invalid synonyms are discouraged, as is incorrect naming. Problems inevitably arise, however, when incorrect names become established commercially (see Sauvignon in CHILE, for example). R.E.S.

Galet, P., *Cépages et vignobles de France* (2nd edn., Montpellier, 1990).

Galet, P., and Morton, L. T., *A Practical Ampelography* (Ithaca, NY, and London, 1979).

Huglin, P., *Biologie et écologie de la vigne* (Paris, 1986).

AMPHORA, Latin word from the Greek for a vessel with two handles. Although the term may refer sometimes to fine wares, it is normally used to describe the large pottery containers which were used for the bulk transport of many goods and liquids, including wine, in the Mediterranean world throughout classical antiquity (see Ancient EGYPT, for example). Despite the considerable variety of shape in amphorae, they mainly shared the characteristics of the two handles, a mouth narrow enough to be stoppered, and a bottom which tapered to a point (only a few, notably those of southern France, had flat bottoms). When full, many amphorae were a considerable weight; so the spike on the bottom served as a third handle, an essential point of purchase, when lifting and pouring. To carry wine the inner surface of the porous amphora was sealed with a coating of pine resin (see RESINATED WINES). To stop the mouth, either CORK or a lid of fired clay was pushed down the neck and then secured with a sealing of mortar. Many amphorae were stamped with names or symbols before firing; these usually identified the pottery and its owner. The mortar seal in the mouth of the amphora could also be stamped, frequently with the names of the merchants whose goods were being carried. Further details of the contents could be painted on the body of the amphora. Modern study of amphorae began after the Second World War, when the use of the aqualung led to the discovery of many wrecks carrying cargoes of amphorae (see CELTS, for example). Later research has concentrated on the identification of kiln sites, where the vessels were produced. As a result, a much clearer picture of the pattern of trade in goods, such as wine, has emerged. The term amphora also became an expression of capacity, a cubic Roman foot, about 26 l/7 gal, although the actual vessels did not by any means conform to this. Indeed, it is likely that goods, such as wine, were frequently sold wholesale by weight and there were formulae for converting the weight of different goods into capacity. J.J.P.

Peacock, D. P. S., and Williams, D. F., *Amphorae and the Roman Economy* (London, 1986).

AMPURDÁN-COSTA BRAVA, denominated wine zone in the extreme north east corner of Spanish CATALONIA separated from ROUSSILLON only by the French border (see maps on p. 907). The zone, now a DO, has a long history of wine production which was nearly extinguished when PHYLLOXERA swept through the vineyards in the 1900s. Many of the TERRACES that climb the low foothills of the Pyrenees were never replanted. The climate is MEDITERRANEAN, although strong winds blow all year round which protect the vineyards from FROST and VINE DISEASES, but can subject vines unprotected with WINDBREAKS to severe stress.

Ampurdán-Costa Brava (Empordà-Costa Brava in Catalan) used to produce heavy RANCIOS, sometimes called Garnatxa, the Catalan name for the GRENACHE grape. This vine variety and Cariñena (CARIGNAN) still account for 80 per cent of production, although they are mostly turned into bulk rosé for the local market. The white XAREL-LO and MACABEO vines grown here produce a small quantity of CAVA sparkling wines. During the 1980s a number of producers turned to making Vi Novell or NOUVEAU style wines, although these have met with a mixed reception. Exports amount to no more than two per cent of the region's production. R.J.M.

AMTLICHE PRÜFUNGSNUMMER. See AP NUMBER.

AMURENSIS, an Asian vine species of the VITIS genus which takes its name from the Amur valley of northern China. The exceptionally cold climate in which it originates makes it useful to vine breeders seeking to introduce genes for cold hardiness. Professor Helmut BECKER in particular developed HYBRIDS which shared some RIESLING characteristics, using *V amurensis*.

AMYL ALCOHOLS. See FUSEL OILS.

ANALYSIS of grapes, must, and wine is a regular and important part of the WINE-MAKING process.

Grapes and must

Analysis of grapes and must is chiefly concerned with just three components: sugar, acid, and pH. The grapes should ideally contain SUGARS capable of producing wines with a final ALCOHOLIC STRENGTH between about 10 and 13 per cent by volume, which means that the grapes should have between 18 and 22 per cent of fermentable sugar by weight (see MUST WEIGHT for the various ways in which this can be measured).

The ACIDITY of the grapes or must should also ideally be such that the TOTAL ACIDITY is in the general range of 7 to 10 g/l expressed as tartaric acid. (Some acid is always lost during wine-making, primarily as the alcohol content of the wine increases and the solubility of wine acids decreases. Acidity may be further reduced by MALOLACTIC FERMENTATION and cold STABILIZATION. It is therefore necessary to start with more acid in the grapes than is eventually wanted in the wine.)

It has been recently understood that the chemistry of AGEING is strongly influenced by PH, and, although there is a close relationship between pH and total acidity, it is important to measure pH separately. Two samples with the same total acidity can have different pH readings because of the buffering effect of POTASSIUM.

Sugars are most simply measured by determining the DENSITY of a sample of clarified grape juice. Measurement of the juice's index of refraction (see REFRACTOMETER) can also provide a close estimate of its sugar content. In establishments with particularly well-equipped laboratories, modern chromatography can provide an extremely accurate sugar measurement. This is the measurement of most concern in cool wine regions, as an indication of when a viable minimum or likely maximum level has been reached, and as a useful piece of information on which to base any calculations involving ENRICHMENT.

In warm wine regions the accumulation of sugars poses a different problem; indeed frequent and accurate estimates of the sugar concentration are needed to ensure that the resulting wines do not have excessive alcohol and insufficient acid.

Particularly in hot, dry weather, sugar synthesis (see PHOTOSYNTHESIS) and acid loss occur so rapidly that picking decisions have to be taken fast, and frequent field analysis may be necessary, involving a hand refractometer for sugar and approximate field TITRATION for acidity. B.G.C.

Wine

Analysis of wine involves the specific wine-making operation of measuring various of those characteristics of a wine which relate to its quality and to legal requirements, ideally in a well-equipped laboratory. In most specialist wine laboratories, wine analysis also includes a critical tasting to ensure that the wine conforms to type and quality.

Common measurements include those of alcoholic strength, total acidity, VOLATILE ACIDITY, pH, density, RESIDUAL SUGAR, and SULPHUR DIOXIDE. Laboratories in larger wineries may also be equipped to test for mineral elements such as IRON, COPPER, SODIUM, and POTASSIUM. All these parameters either play an important part in assessing quality or are limited by law.

Not all wineries determine all these constituents, and many of the smaller ones have no laboratory at all and have to rely on samples sent to professional analysts.

More unusual determinations, such as detecting pesticide RESIDUES or, from the late 1980s, fraudulent CONTAMINANTS such as METHANOL, SORBITOL, and methylisothiocyanate are only usually undertaken by specialist commercial laboratories.

Stability prediction tests for TARTRATES, PROTEIN, COLOUR sedimentation and microbiology are also crucial analyses to ensure a commercially sound and stable product.

Modern analytical methods have become so sensitive that some trace components can be measured at concentrations of one part per million million, levels unimaginable even as recently as the early 1980s. The wine analyst's increasingly difficult role is to assess which of the many hundreds of chemicals in finished wine at these very low concentrations are of constructive interest.

See also NUCLEAR MAGNETIC RESONANCE; and SOIL TESTING for the analysis of soils. A.D.W. & G.T.

ANBAUGEBIET, wine region in GERMANY, of which there are 13. The A in QBA stands for Anbaugebiet and these regions are fundamental to Germany's wine labelling and GERMAN WINE LAW.

ANCENIS, COTEAUX D', small VDQS zone in the Loire around the historic town of Ancenis between Nantes and Angers. It is used for a limited number of VARIETAL wines, and the name of the variety must be stated on the label: Pineau de la Loire or Chenin Blanc; Malvoisie or Pinot Beurot (Pinot Gris); Gamay; or Cabernet. In fact the great majority of wine produced here is light red or pink made from Gamay, and some Cabernet, but some serious medium sweet white wine is also produced.

See also LOIRE and map on pp. 576–7.

ANCIENT MEDITERRANEAN. By classical times vines were grown for wine in almost all the countries bordering the Mediterranean Sea and on many of the islands; from Spain in the west to BYBLOS in the east, from northern Italy to Egypt, the vine made inexorable progress, with AMPHORAE traversing the sea regularly.

ANCIENT VINE VARIETIES. THEOPHRASTUS (*c.*370–*c.*287 BC) remarked that there were as many kinds of grapes as there were kinds of soil (*Historia plantarum* 2. 5. 7; also *De causis plantarum* 4. 11. 6). He does not elaborate, but his remark shows how difficult it is to discuss VINE VARIETIES in the classical world. Are varieties that classical authors describe as different really different varieties, or are they examples of the same variety behaving differently in different conditions? Soil is only one factor; climate and wine-making methods methods are others. We cannot resort to tasting samples or nursery specimens; all we possess are CLASSICAL TEXTS written by authors who were not modern, scientifically trained AMPELOGRAPHERS.

The Greeks did not write systematic treatises on wine so we must turn to the Latin writers on agriculture and natural history, particularly VIRGIL, PLINY, and COLUMELLA (CATO and Varro do not discuss the subject in detail). Virgil's treatment, in *Georgics* 2. 98–108, is the briefest and least systematic of the three, and he does not distinguish different wines, such as Lesbos, from different grape varieties, such as Aminnean and Bumastus (the latter primarily a TABLE GRAPE). There are so many varieties, he concludes, that no one knows the number.

Only Democritus knew how many grape varieties existed, Pliny says (14. 20), but his account does not survive. Pliny himself announces that he will give us only the most important vine varieties. Pride of place among the Italian grapes goes to the Aminnean, which has five subvarieties, then to the Nomentan, and third comes the Apian, which has two subvarieties and is the preferred grape of Etruria. All other vine varieties, Pliny asserts confidently, are imports from GREECE. Of these, the Graecula, from Chios or Thasos, is as good as the Aminnean. Eugenia is good but only when planted in the Colli ALBANI. Elsewhere it does not produce good wine. The same goes for Rhaetic, which grows well in a cool climate, and the Allobrogian, which apparently ripens well in frost. These three grape varieties produce red wines which go lighter with age. The remaining varieties Pliny mentions are ones that he judges to be without distinction as wine grapes.

Columella agrees with Pliny for the most part but there are differences (3. 2. 7–31). He regards the Aminnean as the best grape and puts the Nomentan second. He also recommends the Eugenian and Allobrogian wines, with the same reservation as Pliny, and the Apian. Then he mentions other varieties which are noted for their productivity rather than their flavour. He does not think highly of the Rhaetic, and he does not rank the Graecula with the Aminnean. Vines were still being imported: Columella mentions three grapes which have only lately come to his notice so that he cannot give an opinion on their wines and also another grape which

Ancient World: part of a Roman column depicting soldiers unloading a supply of barrels for the Roman army.

he says is a recent Greek import named Dracontion. Columella's aim is not to give a long and comprehensive list, for that would be impossible (he quotes Virgil's words, *Georgics* 2. 104–6). One should not quibble about names, he concludes, and, knowing that a variety can change out of all recognition if it is planted somewhere new, one should not approve a new grape until it has been tried and tested.

Columella's remarks indicate that farmers were prepared to experiment with new varieties, some of them imported from Greece. Some varieties were probably brought over with the Greek colonists from the 8th century BC onwards, others were growing in Italy long before they arrived. A Greek name is not a guarantee of Greek origin: some Greek names may be names given to Italian grapes which the Greeks of Sicily and southern Italy used when they started producing wine in their colonies. If so, these names reflect no more than the fact that the Greeks exploited the potential of these grapes commercially before the natives did. One thing is certain: any search for the exact ancient ancestors of modern varieties whether in Italy, Greece, or elsewhere, must be fruitless. Documentary evidence is of no help, and in any case *Vitis* VINIFERA mutates so easily that the varieties themselves cannot have survived for so long in the same form.

Columella also praises the Biturica, for example, which he regards as close to the very best. Pliny thinks less highly of it, but they agree that its wine ages well. It has been claimed that Biturica equals Vidure, a synonym for CABERNET SAUVIGNON. Even if this were philologically possible, there would be other objections. The name need not apply to the same vine variety, and if it did we have to bear in mind that *Vitis vinifera* mutates too easily for the resemblance to be exact. Besides, we have no conclusive evidence that the tribe of the Bituriges grew vines in the Bordeaux region where they lived. Our earliest evidence for viticulture in Bordeaux is the poet Ausonius writing in the 4th century (see BORDEAUX, history). H.M.W.

André, J., 'Contribution au vocabulaire de la viticulture: les noms de cépages', *Revue des études latines* 30 (1952), 126–56.

Tchernia, A., *Le Vin de l'Italie romaine* (Paris, 1986).

ANCIENT WORLD. See Ancient ARMENIA, ASIA MINOR, CANAAN, CHINA, EGYPT, GREECE, INDIA, IRAN, MESOPOTAMIA, PHOENICIA, ROME, SUMER.

ANDALUCÍA, or **Andalusia,** the southernmost of Spain's autonomous regions encompassing eight provinces and the DO regions of JEREZ, MÁLAGA, MONTILLA-MORILES, and CONDADO DE HUELVA (see map on p. 907). Andalucía is the hottest part of Spain and has traditionally been associated with strong, alcoholic wines which have been exported from the Atlantic port of Cádiz since the PHOENICIANS first established their trading links around 1100 BC (see SPAIN, history). Wine continued to be produced during seven centuries of Moorish domination when Andalucía became one of most prosperous parts of southern Europe. Since the 16th century, however, when cities such as Seville, Granada, and Cordoba were stepping stones to the new colonies in SOUTH AMERICA, Andalucía has become one of the most impoverished regions of Spain.

The wines of Andalucía bear a strong resemblance to each other, and particularly to SHERRY, which has fashioned the region's wine industry since the city of Jerez was won back from the Moors in 1264. Most are FORTIFIED, although grapes from the arid plateau around Cordoba and Jaén are often so rich in natural sugar that they do not require the addition of spirit to reach an ALCOHOLIC STRENGTH of between 14 and 18 per cent. Until laws were tightened up following the foundation of the Jerez Consejo Regulador in 1934, wines from other parts of Andalucía would frequently find their way into sherry blends. Nowadays wines made outside the four DO regions around Bailén, Almería, and Cordoba are mostly sold in bulk for blending. R.J.M.

ANDERSON VALLEY. California wine region and AVA. See MENDOCINO.

ANGELS' SHARE. See EVAPORATION.

ANIMALS can cause serious damage in the vineyard, most obviously but not exclusively by eating grapes and foliage. Any reductions in foliage can prejudice fruit RIPENING and wine quality.

Most animals may be kept out by fencing, but fences have to be sunk into the soil for smaller, burrowing animals, and high and cantilevered for animals as large and mobile as kangaroos. The following are some of the most common vineyard animal pests, but wild boar have been known to damage vines in the DOURO valley in Portugal, and to eat an entire EISWEIN crop in Germany, while some vine-growers in New Zealand use electric fencing and sheep to perform judicious LEAF REMOVAL.

Deer

Deer can be a persistent pest in some North American vineyards where state game management laws limit control methods. Deer damage vines by eating the leaves, especially the new growth. They may almost strip vines of foliage. If deer repeatedly feed on vines, they can severely stunt them, and they can also break and scar them by rubbing their antlers on vine trunks, arms, or cordon branches. The best method of control is to fence the vineyard area to keep deer outside. A woven wire fence, 1.5 to 2 m (6 ft) in height, is usually sufficient, or electric fences can be used.

Kangaroos

Kangaroos may be a tourist attraction, but they are also a problem for young vineyards in some areas of Australia. Like rabbits, they feed on leaves, but also on canes at wire height, destroying buds for future growth. They may be controlled by shooting, for which a permit is required. In areas where there are large populations of kangaroos, fences are necessary. They should be erected before vines are planted, and usually involve considerable height, and cantilevered tops with barbed wires.

Rabbits and hares

Rabbits and hares (or jack rabbits) can be a serious pest in some regions, particularly while vineyards are being established. In some parts of southern France and Australia, for example, rabbits require expensive control. Rabbits can kill young vines by chewing the bark and leaves. Even vines only slightly damaged seem to recover slowly. Vineyards can be fenced with wire netting to keep rabbits out but, to make the fence rabbitproof, about 15 cm/6 in of wire netting must be buried in the ground to prevent burrowing. Individual vine guards of mesh or solid material can be used. Poisoning by laying toxic baits is still a practical method of control for large numbers of rabbits in some areas. Shooting can also be an effective means of control in some circumstances, while chemical repellents may provide temporary relief. Choice of control methods depends on the nature and urgency of the situation; but rabbit populations can increase rapidly.

Squirrels

Ground squirrels may nibble on bark or eat grapes in vineyards in some areas of the United States. They seldom cause much damage, although they live in colonies, and nuisance damage can increase if populations are not controlled. In addition to damage by gnawing vines, their burrowing can destroy root systems, and the mounds and burrow openings can disturb machinery and harvesting. No fencing will exclude them, nor are repellants effective. Toxic fumigants, poison baits, or traps are the only effective controls.

Rodents

Voles, field mice, and meadow mice feed readily on young vines, and can cause severe damage and kill vines, especially in young plantings which provide a favourable habitat. Clean cultivation, and weed control on fence lines and roadsides are important preventive measures, while poison baits are the only way to eliminate them once they have infiltrated. Guards can be used around young vines to protect them, and these also protect against rabbits.

Gophers can damage vines in some areas of North America. They can girdle vines just below the surface of the ground, and dig furrows in the soil which can cause water loss and other watering problems. They can be controlled by trapping, or by poison baits. If numbers of gophers are high, a mechanical gopher bait applicator may even be used to lay the poison. Herbicides can reduce gopher populations by decreasing the food supply. It is necessary to control populations in areas adjacent to vineyards, because young animals will disperse into vineyards.

See also BIRDS. M.J.E.

Flaherty, D. L., *et al.* (eds.), *Grape Pest Management* (2nd edn., Oakland, 1992).

ANJOU, important and varied wine region in the western Loire centred on the town of Angers, whose influence once extended all over north west France. Anjou was the birthplace of Henri II, and its wines were some of France's most highly regarded in the Middle Ages (see LOIRE, history). It was the DUTCH WINE TRADE, however, that developed the sweet white wine production of the region in the 16th and 17th centuries, and it would be some centuries before the citizens of Paris rather than Rotterdam had the pick of each Angevin vintage. White grapes predominated until the 19th century, when the Anjou vignoble reached its peak and PHYLLOXERA arrived. Since then a wide variety of less noble grape varieties have been planted, including a number of HYBRIDS, and the ENCÉP-

AGEMENT of this region is beginning to show some stability, with the total vineyard having shrunk by a half from its peak. White wine represents hardly a fifth of Anjou's total wine production, and rosé still dominates the region's output.

The region is relatively mild, being influenced by the Atlantic and protected by the woods of the Vendée to the south west (rather as the MÉDOC is protected by the Landes). RAINFALL is particularly low here, with annual totals of just 500 mm/19 in.

The GROLLEAU vine, and the sickly **Rosé d'Anjou** it all too often produced, are in retreat—although as much Rosé d'Anjou was still being made in 1990 as the much more refined, and incredibly long-lasting, rosé **Cabernet d'Anjou**, which must be made from Cabernet Sauvignon or much more likely, Cabernet Franc grapes. It can be quite sweet but usually has very high acidity which can preserve it for decades and makes it an interesting partner for a wide range of savoury dishes.

Cabernet Franc represents about one vine in three in Anjou and is increasingly favoured by growers there, encouraged by the creation in 1987 of the serious red wine appellation **Anjou-Villages**, which can provide luscious, and often better priced, alternatives to the more famous Cabernet Franc-dominated red Loires of SAUMUR-CHAMPIGNY to the east. Best areas for such reds are immediately south of Angers in the Coteaux de l'Aubance. There is increasing experimentation with CANOPY MANAGEMENT and use of PUMPING OVER and BARREL MATURATION. Lighter reds are produced as **Anjou-Gamay**, from the Gamay grape of Beaujolais, and **Anjou Rouge** is the catch-all appellation for lighter, often quite crisp, red wines.

Of dry white wines, **Anjou Blanc** is the most common, and is most successful when produced on the SCHIST close to the river. The wine must contain at least 80 per cent Chenin Blanc, but increasing proportions of Chardonnay, and Sauvignon, are included in the blend. Tiny amounts of sweet white **Anjou-Coteaux de la Loire**, made exclusively from Chenin Blanc, are also made.

Within the Anjou region are certain areas which have produced white wines of such quality that they have earned their own appellations: Coteaux de l' AUBANCE; BONNEZEAUX; Coteaux du LAYON; QUARTS DE CHAUME for sweet wines and SAVENNIÈRES for dry wines.

See also LOIRE and map on pp. 576–7.

ANNUAL GROWTH CYCLE of the vine. See VINE GROWTH CYCLE.

AÑO, Spanish word for year. Some wines, particularly RIOJA, were sold without a VINTAGE year but with the number of years' AGEING prior to bottling indicated on the label. **Ano** is the Portuguese word.

ANSONICA, alternative name for Sicily's white INZOLIA grape used particularly in the Tuscan Maremma, where it can produce wines of real character.

ANTHER, the pollen-bearing part of the STAMEN of a flower such as that of the vine. Each of the five anthers of the grape has sacs in which a large number of pollen mother cells develop into pollen grains about two to three weeks before FLOWERING. The small, dry grains of POLLEN are released, possibly before the CALYPTRA or flower caps have fallen (see POLLINATION). In deliberate VINE BREEDING stamens and caps are removed early, before caps would normally fall, to prevent self-pollination and permit deliberate cross-pollination.

B.G.C.

ANTHOCYANS, members of a complex group of natural organic chemical compounds responsible for the red to purple colours of grapes and wines, including **anthocyanins**, **anthocyanidins**, and **pro-anthocyanidins**. These water-soluble blue, purple, or red pigments occur in the cell sap and, in grape skin, constitute the colour of black and red grape varieties. Anthocyans and TANNINS are the main PHENOLICS found in grapes and wines and, although anthocyans are not found in white wines, they are related to the flavones, which are yellow pigments. Anthocyans are common in the natural world and are responsible for the red to blue colours of leaves, fruits, and flowers. The word comes from *anthos*, Greek for flower, together with the Greek-derived 'cyan' blue.

Chemical study reveals that a very large number of pigment anthocyan structures are possible. The particular mixture ocurring in grapes varies from species to species and from grape variety to grape variety. Indeed, chemical determination of the particular mixture of pigments present in an unidentified grape berry can aid vine identification in several cases. Members of the PINOT family, for example, do not have any acid molecules attached to the sugars of their anthocyanins. Pure VINIFERA varieties have anthocyan pigments with only one molecule of glucose attached to a certain portion, while many of the AMERICAN VINES used in breeding ROOTSTOCKS and AMERICAN HYBRIDS frequently have two (a fact which greatly aided detection of non-*vinifera* wine in France in the mid 20th century; see BORDEAUX UNIVERSITY).

Anthocyans have another interesting characteristic. They are capable of changing form slightly, depending upon the PH, or degree of ACIDITY, of the medium in which they are dissolved, the forms having slightly different colours. In general, the more acid the grape juice or wine, the greater the degree of ionization of the anthocyans, and the brighter red (and more microbiologically and chemically stable) the liquid. Less acid wines tend to shade through dull purple to almost blueish colours as the acidity diminishes and rises. Gardeners will recognize similar behaviour in the colour of hydrangea flowers after adjustment of soil acidity.

The anthocyan pigments are formed in the grapevine by a complicated series of reactions and are first visible when the berry begins to expand. The onset of this stage in the vine's metabolism is called VERAISON and is characterized by rapid growth and accumulation of sugar in the berry together with the starting of colouring in darker coloured berries. It seems likely that the signal for the start of this colouring process is given by a certain level of glucose, the sugar in the anthocyanin, in the outer cells of the grape skin. The sucrose transferred from the leaves to the berry is split into its constituent parts GLUCOSE and FRUCTOSE at the junction between the PEDICEL and the inside of the berry.

The concentration of the pigments in the grape skin increases as the level of sugar increases in the grapes during ripening. The increase is intensified if sunlight falls on the berries, that is, if the berries are in an open CANOPY MICROCLIMATE.

The pulp of most dark-berried grapes is the same colour as the pulp of light-berried grapes, however. During veraison the anthocyan pigments are formed in the berry skins' outer cell layers in all but a few dark-berried grape varieties (see TEINTURIERS) which have a portion of the pigment dissolved in the pulp of the berry as well as in the skin.

One important operation during the FERMENTATION of most red wines, therefore, is to transfer these pigments from the skin cells to the wine. Fortunately, anthocyan pigments are more soluble in alcohol than in aqueous solutions, so colour transfer occurs as fermentation proceeds. Alcohol also makes the skin cell walls more permeable to the diffusion of pigment molecules. Colour transfer is thus achieved by keeping the skins adequately mixed with the fermenting wine during and after fermentation (see MACERATION).

One might reasonably expect that the pigments in the new wine would be identical to those found in the grape skin. This may be the case for a few hours, but once the anthocyans are mixed with the ACIDS of the pulp and the many products of the reactions involved in fermentation, they begin a series of interactions leading to much larger and more complicated molecules. Within a few years only traces of the relatively simple grape skin anthocyans remain and, with enough age, the bright red colour of young wine is replaced with a paler, yellower colour. These changes in the pigments also affect flavour to some extent. The glucose molecule of the anthocyan is liberated and softens the taste. The various acids attached to the glucose detach themselves and contribute their individual flavour characteristics to the older wine. As the anthocyan molecules polymerize and agglomerate, they become larger and heavier so that some of them exceed their solubility in the wine and are precipitated as SEDIMENT. See AGEING.

A.D.W. & B.G.C.

Somers, T. C., and Verette, E., 'Phenolic composition of natural wine types', in H. F. Linskens and J. F. Jackson (eds.), *Wine Analysis* (Modern methods of plant analysis, NS 6) (Berlin, 1988), 219–72.

ANTHRACNOSE, one of the FUNGAL DISEASES of European origin which affects vines. It is also known as bird's eye rot or black spot. The disease is spread world-wide but is a particular problem in humid regions. Before the introduction of DOWNY MILDEW and POWDERY MILDEW it was the most serious grape fungal disease in Europe, but since BORDEAUX MIXTURE was introduced in 1885 it has been controllable. The disease is caused by the fungus *Elsinoe ampelina*. Small black lesions are produced on the leaves and this area can die and drop out so that the leaves look as though peppered with gunshot. Small dark coloured spots are also produced on young shoots, flower cluster stems, and berries. Anthracnose can reduce both the yield and quality of the fruit. The disease can be controlled by fungicides applied early in the growing season.

R.E.S.

ANTINORI, the most important NÉGOCIANT firm in TUSCANY, and probably in the whole of ITALY. The modern wine firm was founded by brothers Lodovico and Piero Antinori in 1895, although the Antinori family can trace their history in the wine trade back to 1385, when Giovanni di Pietro Antinori enrolled in the Vintners Guild of Florence; like the vast majority of the Florentine nobility, the Antinori were, for centuries, producers of wine on their substantial country properties.

The work of the 19th century brothers was continued by Piero's son Niccolò, who extended the house's commercial network both in Italy and into foreign markets and purchased the Castello della Sala estate near ORVIETO in Umbria. The house made a certain reputation for its white wines, sold under the Villa Antinori label, and for its Chianti, made in a soft and fruity style, by focusing its purchases of wine on various areas of the province of Florence, a style in contrast to the more austere wines of RICASOLI, the dominant Chianti

Marchese Piero **Antinori** at the Antinori headquarters, the Palazzo Antinori in the Piazza Antinori in Florence.

house of the period and headquartered in Gaiole in the province of Siena. A vineyard was also planted with the Bordeaux grape variety CABERNET SAUVIGNON and cultivated during the 1930s. Although the family fortunes flourished, Antinori was only a medium-sized operation, with a yearly production of approximately 1 million bottles, in 1966 when Piero Antinori, the son of Niccolò Antinori, assumed the direction of the firm's activities. By the early 1990s he had increased the annual production 14-fold, giving the house a commanding position in Tuscany, a position based both on the excellent quality of all the firm's wines at various price levels and, above all, on the innovative work of Antinori and house OENOLOGIST Giacomo Tachis in creating a new category of outstanding wines at the top of the range: Tignanello, the prototype SUPERTUSCAN which eliminated white grapes from the basic blend of Tuscan reds and introduced small BARREL MATURATION for wines made from the local SANGIOVESE grape; Solaia, which, together with SASSICAIA (initially marketed by the Antinori and whose development was assisted by Tachis), showed the potential for outstanding Cabernet in Tuscany; Cervaro, a white wine produced at the Castello della Sala based on CHARDONNAY grapes and, then unusual for Italy, BARREL FERMENTATION.

Piero's brother Lodovico Antinori independently produces internationally famous VINI DA TAVOLA such as Ornellaia and the all-Merlot Masseto at his own estate near BOLGHERI. D.T.

ANTIQUES AND ARTEFACTS. While some people collect wine (see COLLECTING), others collect **wine antiques**, objects associated with wine, particularly those with some historical value. An enormous variety and quantity of decorative and utilitarian craftsmanship was undertaken to add pleasure and efficiency to the business of STORING, SERVING, and drinking wine. This has been the case for hundreds of years.

Generally, it was in those countries in which wine was most valued that the greatest artistic effort and ingenuity were employed in making, and preserving, wine-related artefacts. This means that some of the finest wine antiques are to be found in Britain, which has a long tradition of importing wine in quantity and has long had a substantial middle class to provide a market for them. It also helps to explain why Britain has the greatest concentration of specialist dealers in wine antiques.

Perhaps the greatest testament to the designs and craftsmanship involved in making wine antiques is that many are as useful and relevant today as they were when they were crafted 200 or more years ago.

Specific categories of wine antiques in which individual collectors may specialize include BIN LABELS, BOTTLES, CORKSCREWS, DECANTERS, DECANTER LABELS, LABELS, TASTEVINS, wine COASTERS, wine COOLERS, wine FUNNELS, and a variety of DRINKING VESSELS. Others include:

Wine fountains

These grand silver objects, usually dating from within 50 years of 1700, were usually made to accompany cisterns (wine COOLERS) with which they formed an important ensemble. They were large lidded urns with taps and were probably used for water as well as wine although they have long been called wine fountains. Some late ones were made of glass in a barrel shape and mounted on silver frames.

Wine glass coolers

From *c.*1660 silver punch bowls were often fitted with detachable notched rims so that they could be used to cool wine glasses. The stems would rest in the notches with the bowls immersed in iced water. Such vessels were called Monteiths (apparently after a Scot who wore his cloak scalloped at the hem). The custom of cooling glasses communally (as well as the wine) persisted in Europe until the mid 19th century and vessels (*verrières*) were made specifically for the purpose. They were made in silver (gilt and white), pewter, brass, porcelain, and tôle peint (painted tinware).

Typically they were oval in outline. The British from *c.*1780 preferred individual coolers made of glass that closely resembled finger bowls but with a lip or two to locate the wine glass stems.

Bottle carriers, tilters, wagons, and wine furniture

From *c.*1760 deep-sided trays with between two and 10 divisions specifically to hold bottles were made for the transport of wine from the cellar to the eating room. Most held the bottles horizontally but others, perhaps for decanters, held them vertically. Similar trays on legs, being of sophisticated design, can be presumed to be for the display of wine in the eating room. Bottle cradles held a single bottle at the ideal angle for drawing the cork.

Decanting machines of more or less mechanical contrivance made the job of decanting more smooth and precise, brass and steel being popular in Burgundy and Portugal, while some English ones of mahogany resembled cannon. Wine siphons in silver allowed the decanting of wine without tilting the bottle.

From *c.*1790–1840, U-shaped drinking tables were made to fit around a fireplace and, equipped with integral decanter wagons, were made for gentlemen to drink wine at the end of dinner. Sideboards, too, often had cellarets (boxes in which wine bottles could reach room temperature) and wine coolers incorporated in cupboards and drawers. R.N.H.B.

Bickerton, L. M., *18th Century Drinking Glasses* (2nd edn., Woodbridge, 1986).

Butler, R., and Walking, G., *The Book of Wine Antiques* (Woodbridge, 1986).

Charleston, R. J., *English Glass* (London, 1984).

Clayton, M., *Collectors Dictionary of the Silver & Gold of Great Britain & North America* (revised edn., Woodbridge, 1985).

Dumbrell, R., *Understanding Antique Wine Bottles* (Woodbridge, 1983).

Hernmarck, C., *The Art of the European Silversmith 1430–1830* (London, 1977).

AOSTA, or the **Valle d'Aosta** (**Vallée d'Aoste** to the region's many French speakers), is Italy's smallest region (see map on p. 517). The long, narrow valley formed by the river

Dora Baltea as it courses through the mountains of Italy's extreme north west is Italy's connecting link to France and Switzerland and to the north of Europe beyond. This rugged alpine terrain is more suited to the grazing of animals than to the cultivation of the vine, and the vineyards—for the most part on HILLSIDES on either side of the Dora Baltea before the land rises to impossible altitudes—are frequently terraced into dizzingly steep slopes. No more than 40,000 hl / 1 million gal of wine is produced in an average year, of which only about 3,000 hl/79,200 gal qualifies as DOC. A good deal of it is sold privately either to the thriving tourist trade or to the intense flow of motorists which passes through the region.

At the crossroads between northern and southern Europe, the Valle d'Aosta has found itself with an extremely rich diversity of vine varieties. Native regional and other Italian varieties include NEBBIOLO, DOLCETTO, Petit and Gros Rouge, Fumin, Vien de Nus, Prëmetta, Moscato di Chambave, and Blanc de Morgex. French varieties include PINOT NOIR, GAMAY, SYRAH, GRENACHE, PINOT GRIS or Malvoisie, PINOT BLANC, and CHARDONNAY. There is also the Petite Arvine of SWITZERLAND and the MÜLLER-THURGAU of Germany.

The most interesting wines being made in the early 1990s were the Nebbiolo-based Donnas or Donnaz, produced close to CAREMA across the border in Piedmont and more interesting than the neighbouring Nebbiolo-based Arnad-Monjovet; the family of fruity reds with Petit Rouge as their base which encompassed Enfer d'Arvier, Torrette, and Chambave Rosso; the Nus Rosso, made from Vien de Nus and with Petit Rouge (spicier and more herbaceous than the Petit Rouge-based reds); the Moscato of Chambave, particularly in the PASSITO or dessert version; Gamay, fruity and soft but with some bitterness on the after-taste which is not present in BEAUJOLAIS; Müller-Thurgau; the floral Blanc de Morgex et La Salle, produced in some of the highest vineyards in Europe, up to 1,300 m/4,260 ft, in whose aromas its devotees profess to find the aromas of alpine meadows. The dessert version of Pinot Gris (called Malvoisie in the Valle d'Aosta), a passito, was a legendary wine of the past, but has virtually gone out of production. Local producers are showing a new interest in the Fumin, the grape which supplies structure and intensity in many of the Petit Rouge-based blends, and interesting experiments with small BARREL MATURATION of VARIETAL Fumin wines have begun.

The overall viticultural production of the valley is almost entirely consumed within the regional confines and, as for the finest wines of Switzerland just across the border, an export trade seems highly unlikely to develop in view of the small quantities and high prices. D.T.

AOÛTEMENT, French term for CANE RIPENING derived from *août*, French for August, the month in which it generally takes place in the northern hemisphere.

APERITIFS, drinks served before a meal to 'open' (from the Latin *aperire*) the digestive system and stimulate the appetite. Wines commonly served as aperitifs are dry, white, and not too alcoholic: CHAMPAGNE or any brut SPARKLING WINE; FINO and MANZANILLA sherry; MOSEL wines up to SPÄTLESE level of sweetness; less rich ALSACE whites; MUSCADET, CHABLIS, and virtually any light, dry, still white wine. Customs vary nationally, however, and the French have customarily served spirits, FORTIFIED WINES, VINS DOUX NATURELS, VINS DE LIQUEUR, and strong, sweet wines such as SAUTERNES before meals (and dry champagne with the sweet course). A common all-purpose aperitif, apparently acceptable to French and non-French alike, is the KIR, or *vin blanc cassis*, as well as a blend of white wine and sparkling water sometimes known as a spritzer.

APHIDS, small insects of the *Aphidiodae* family that feed by sucking the juices from plants. Several species of aphids attack grapes, but apart from PHYLLOXERA, they seldom cause serious damage in vineyards. Natural enemies usually hold aphids in check. M.J.E.

AP NUMBER, or Amtliche Prüfungsnummer, adorns the label of every bottle of German quality wine, whether QBA or QMP. This 10- to 12-digit number is an outward sign that the wine has passed GERMANY's much-vaunted official testing procedure, which involves submitting samples of the wine to ANALYSIS and a BLIND TASTING test in which the wine is checked for FAULTS by a changing panel of fellow wine-makers and other tasters. The test is hardly the most stringent procedure; the pass rate is well above 90 per cent. The first digit signifies which of the country's testing stations awarded the AP number (1 for Koblenz, 2 for Bernkastel, 3 for Trier (all three in the MOSEL-SAAR-RUWER), 4 for Alzey in RHEINHESSEN, 5 for Neustadt in PFALZ, no 6, and 7 for Bad Kreuznach in NAHE, where wines from SAALE-UNSTRUT and SACHSEN were also tested in the mid 1990s). The next code signifies the location of the vineyard and precedes the bottler's own code. The final two digits signify the year in which the wine was tested and the number immediately before this one is the number of the particular bottling in that year.

APOPLEXY. Vine disease. See ESCA.

APPELLATION. See CONTROLLED APPELLATION.

APPELLATION CONTRÔLÉE, short for **appellation d'origine contrôlée**, is France's prototype CONTROLLED APPELLATION, her much-imitated system of designating and controlling her all-important geographically based names, not just of wines, but also of spirits such as COGNAC, ARMAGNAC, and calvados, as well as of certain foodstuffs. This inherently protectionist and highly successful system is administered by the INAO, a powerful Paris-based body which controls an increasing proportion of French wine production (about 40 per cent in the early 1990s).

History

France's role as a wine producer had been gravely affected by the viticultural devastation caused by POWDERY MILDEW, DOWNY MILDEW, and PHYLLOXERA in the second half of the 19th century (see FRANCE, history). Fine wines were available in much-reduced quantity, but the LANGUEDOC and ALGERIA had become vast factories for the production of very ordinary wine at very low prices. Laws passed in the first two decades of the 20th century were aimed at bringing an end to the ADULTERATION AND FRAUD that was by then widespread. These were based simply on the principle of geographical DELIMITATION, and specified particular areas within which certain wines had to be produced. Bordeaux, Banyuls, and Clairette de Die were among the first; disagreement about exactly which districts should be allowed to produce France's most famous sparkling wine led to riots (see CHAMPAGNE, history).

It rapidly became clear, however, that France's famous wines depended on more than geography. The wrong grape varieties and careless wine-making would not result in a suitable expression of these carefully delimited TERROIRS. By 1923, Baron le Roy, the most influential and well-connected producer of CHÂTEAUNEUF-DU-PAPE, was implementing in his part of the southern Rhône a much more detailed set of rules including not just geographical delimitation but a specification of permitted VINE VARIETIES, PRUNING, and vine-TRAINING methods, and minimum ALCOHOLIC STRENGTH. (The Châteauneuf rules also insisted on a compulsory rejection or TRIAGE of imperfect grapes, and that no rosé be produced within the zone.)

The French appellation contrôlée system evolved into a national reality in the 1930s when economic depression, widespread cultivation of HYBRIDS, and a serious wine SURPLUS increased the incentive for wine merchants to indulge in nefarious blending. The producers of genuine Pommard, for example, had a very real interest in limiting the use of their name to themselves. In 1935 the INAO was created with the express mission of drawing up and enforcing specifications for individual AOCs, or ACs, which broadly followed the Châteauneuf prototype, and in principle banned hybrids from AC wine (if not spirit; see ARMAGNAC) production.

The great majority of the appellation regulations for France's most famous wines and spirits are therefore dated 1936 or 1937, although they have been continuously revised since. The VDQS category for wines deemed just below AC status was created in 1949 and is also administered by the INAO. The scheme was extended to cheeses in 1955 and now includes Puy lentils, Grenoble walnuts, Bresse poultry, certain butters, and Provençal lavender oil.

The French system of categorizing wine, including its main plank appellation contrôlée, has been taken as a model for EUROPEAN UNION wine legislation, and AC is France's equivalent of what the European authorities consider a QUALITY WINE. The legal powers of the INAO, both within France and in its dealings with the EU and beyond, were strengthened substantially in 1990, when it took the conscious decision to build the future of French wine on the concept of geographical appellations (eschewing even the mention of vine varieties on the main label) and adopted the specific aim of preserving agricultural activity in certain zones. It wages unceasing war on all misused GENERIC wine and spirit names and such products as Turkey's 'St-Émilion', Yugoslavia's 'Calvados', and Davidoff's 'Château Margaux' cigars.

The regulations' scope

The INAO's complete list of wine and spirit appellation regulations is an unwieldy, annually revised tome, divided regionally with up to four tightly written pages of specification for each appellation and VDQS, covering the following aspects.

Production area All those communes allowed to produce the wine or spirit in question are listed, but within each of these communes only certain plots of land are deemed worthy, details of which are lodged with each commune's all-important *mairie* or administrative centre. Vines grown elsewhere within the commune are normally entitled only to be sold as a less specific appellation, a VIN DE PAYS or VIN DE TABLE.

Vine varieties The permitted grapes are specified in great detail, along with permitted maximum and minimum proportions. Many appellation regulations include long lists of half-forgotten local varieties. White grape varieties are permitted to a certain extent in a number of red wine appellations.

Ripeness and alcoholic strength Specific MUST WEIGHTS are generally cited for freshly picked grapes before any CHAPTALIZATION, generally given in g/l of sugar. A maximum ALCOHOLIC STRENGTH after any chaptalization, if allowed, is also usually specified.

Yields Control of YIELDS is a fundamental tenet of the appellation contrôlée system, however sceptical some New World viticulturists are of the concept. The maximum yields cited in the regulations were almost routinely increased, however, by about 20 per cent throughout the 1970s and 1980s, so that study of these sections of appellation regulations informs only about relative not absolute productivity (see PLC). In 1993 the INAO announced its intention of curbing yields (as the EU has done).

This section usually includes information on a minimum VINE AGE allowed for appellation contrôlée production (which explains some of the more famous names on labels of VIN DE TABLE in, particularly, the recently expanded appellations of the northern Rhône).

Viticulture This usually specifies a minimum VINE DENSITY, the approved PRUNING regime down to the number of buds, and the permitted vine-TRAINING SYSTEM. In some southern appellations the (limited) extent to which IRRIGATION is allowed may be outlined.

Wine-making and distillation This long section may well specify such aspects as compulsory DESTEMMING, method of ROSÉ WINE-MAKING (usually by SAIGNÉE), although there is generous use of the vague phrase 'usages locaux'. Precise DISTILLATION techniques are usually specified for spirits.

Pros and cons

France's appellation contrôlée designation is in general a very much more reliable guide to the country's best wines than, for example, the QBA category of 'quality wines' in Germany, the liberally applied DOC designation in Italy and Portugal, and its DO counterpart in Spain (all of the last three modelled in the AC system). The French system is by no means perfect, however. Policing remains a problem, and the Service de la Répression des Fraudes is probably understaffed. Contraventions of the regulations, particularly over-chaptalization, or chaptalization and ACIDIFICATION of the same wine, are difficult to detect (although a complex bureaucracy controls over-production). Misdemeanours are only very rarely publicized, and then usually only as a result of local politics.

A more serious disadvantage of the appellation contrôlée system is the extent to which it limits the sorts of wines that can be produced, and stifles experimentation. In dramatic contrast to the New World, vine-growers may plant only certain vine varieties. Those wishing to experiment may be restricted to selling the wine not merely as a vin de pays, but as an anonymous, undated vin de table.

The appellation contrôlée regulations have been drawn up not with a clean slate and a pencil devoted to the best possible options, but to legitimize the best current practices. In the various GRANDS CRUS and PREMIERS CRUS of the CÔTE D'OR, few would argue with the restriction that Pinot Noir and Chardonnay grapes should be cultivated; Burgundians have had at least seven centuries to test this hypothesis. In southern France, however, particularly in the LANGUEDOC-ROUSSILLON (far from INAO headquarters), there is widespread dissatisfaction with regulations which are based on declining but dominant proportions of the controversial CARIGNAN vine, planted in great quantity earlier this century for reasons of expediency rather than quality. Other, perhaps more paranoid, growers resent the stranglehold on the internationally famous Cabernet Sauvignon vine which Bordeaux appears to exercise.

It is also fanciful to suggest that every wine produced within an appellation inevitably produces wines which uniquely betray their geographical provenance. Few blind tasters would unhesitatingly identify a Côtes du MARMANDAIS, for example. And then there are the catch-all appellations such as BORDEAUX AC and CHAMPAGNE whose quality variation is simply frustrating.

See also FRANCE, INAO, LABELLING, and VDQS.

APREMONT, named CRU just south of CHAMBÉRY (famous for its VERMOUTH) whose name be added to the eastern French appellation Vin de SAVOIE. The wines are typically light, dry whites made from the local JACQUÈRE grape, although some Chardonnay is also grown.

APULIA, or Puglia in Italian, long (350 km/1210 miles) and fertile region along the Adriatic coast in Italy's extreme south east (see map on p. 517) which has long been of major importance for the production of wine and TABLE GRAPES. A MEDITERRANEAN CLIMATE and a predominance of soils well suited to grape-growing (a CALCAREOUS base from the Cretaceous era overlain by topsoils rich in iron oxide from the Tertiary and Quartenary eras) have created an ideal viticultural environment. Close to 190,000 ha/470,000 acres of land is dedicated to the vine, and annual wine production in the late 1980s reached almost 13 million hl/343 million gal (more than three times as much as the entire production of Chile, for example). Only Sicily rivals Apulia as Italy's most productive wine region.

Quantity has been in inverse proportion to quality in Apulia, however, and a large part of the region's viticultural production is utilized, now as in the past, for anonymous ingredients in BLENDING that are usefully high in alcohol, as a base for VERMOUTH, or are either compulsorily distilled or transformed into GRAPE CONCENTRATE for ENRICHMENT as part of EUROPEAN UNION efforts to drain the European WINE LAKE. Production of DOC wines in Apulia wines rarely exceeds two per cent of the regional total, and less than a quarter of the regional production is ever sold in bottle. Although Apulia is fortunate in its landscape, with a virtual absence of the hard-to-cultivate rocky, arid hills and mountains which dominate neighbouring CAMPANIA, MOLISE, and BASILICATA, over 70 per cent of vineyards are in the plains, where evenings and nights offer little relief from the torrid daytime TEMPERATURES. High YIELDS are the rule, and a significant number of DOCs have lost credibility with excessively tolerant production limits: 98–105 hl/ha (6–7 tons/acre) in the Castel del Monte DOC, 98–126 hl/ha in many of the various DOCs where NEGROAMARO, Puglia's most interesting native variety, is cultivated. Even the Primitivo di Manduria DOC, with a more reasonable limit of 63 hl/ha, seems to hold little attraction for local producers. Of a potential total declaration of more than 24,000 hl/633,600 gal from the 540 ha/1,330 acres designated for this DOC, fewer than 2,000 hl/52,800 gal are declared in a typical vintage.

Apulia's finest wines are produced in the Salento peninsula, the heel of the boot, where distinctively full but not unappetizingly alcoholic wines are made from the conjunction of CLIMATE, VINE VARIETY, and vine-TRAINING SYSTEM. The proximity of both the Adriatic and the Ionian seas brings a welcome cooling at night (see TOPOGRAPHY). The Negroamaro is principally grown, with some supplementary MALVASIA Nera of Brindisi or Lecce. When the GOBELET trained vines are limited in yield, the resulting wines are not unlike a savoury CHÂTEAUNEUF-DU-PAPE. Eight DOCs share this soil and these varieties: Alezio, Brindisi, Copertino, Leverano, Matino, Nardò, Salice Salento, and Squinzano.

The PRIMITIVO grape, almost certainly California's ZINFANDEL, suffers from a poorly conceived DOC in its home territory of Manduria: a minimum alcohol level of 14 per cent for the regular production and higher alcohol or *liquoroso* versions (both sweet and dry) which reach a leg-wobbling 17.5 to 18 per cent. The UVA DI TROIA grape, used in several DOCs (the large one of Castel del Monte and the small ones of Rosso Barletta, Rosso Canossa, Rossi di Cerignola, Cacc'e Mmitte di Lucera) is considered by many a variety with real potential, so far ignored due to its relatively low productivity.

MONTEPULCIANO d'Abruzzo and BOMBINO BIANCO are both cultivated in the northern part of the region, in the province of Foggia, but bear little resemblance to the better ABRUZZO wines from these grapes. Sporadic attempts at cultivating

Arab poets: Public tavern scene from Arab manuscript *Al Hariri XII Maqama*, dated 1237.

INTERNATIONAL VARIETIES are being made both in the province of Foggia and in Minervino Murge, a high-altitude area of the province of Bari, but in the mid 1990s seemed more curiosities than a serious alternative to local varieties. The low acidity and lack of aromatic character of white international varietals suggest, on the contrary, that Puglia's fierce summer heat may be incompatible with fine white wines.

The region's principal problem in the 1990s is less what to cultivate than the constant drop in per capita consumption of wine, a phenomenon which is having drastic effects on regional production, which dropped below 7 million hl/185 million gal in 1990 before rebounding to over 9 million hl in 1991. These effects, which have been multiplied by the financial difficulties of many of the regional CO-OPERATIVES which produce and market over 60 per cent of Apulia's production, have directed producers' minds more to the question of survival than to questions of quality. D.T.

AQUILEIA, or **Aquileia del Friuli,** one of the more variable and less exported DOCs of the FRIULI region in north east Italy. The principal town is named after the Roman city which predated it.

ARAB POETS. The classical period of Arab civilization spawned a rich corpus of BACCHIC poetry which had its roots in pre-Islamic Arabia (AD 530 until the emergence of ISLAM).

Wine was celebrated as one of a number of standard topics in the composite odes of pre-Islamic poetry. In its treatment, wine was underpinned by the rigid ethical code (*Muruwwa*, approximately *virtus*) that predicated the desert *Weltanschauung*, and thus gave voice to exaggerated notions of generosity. It was in this period, when wine was often compared to the saliva of women (to represent a kiss), that the seeds of the erotic register of later Arabic wine poetry were sown. Interestingly one such simile is even contained in the ode composed by Hassān Ibn Thābit, the Prophet's bard, to celebrate the conquest of Mecca shortly before Muhammad's death in AD 632. Traditional Muslim commentary, basing itself on the Islamic injunction against the consumption of wine, suggests that the simile is interpolated. But this argument is not entirely convincing; for Islam, while criticizing aspects of the culture of poetry, seems to have had little effect in censoring the poetic repertoire.

The essential model provided by this bedouin canon, which constituted the corner-stone of Arabian cultural and tribal identity, was absorbed virtually in its entirety into the nascent Islamic/Arab community; for this reason wine survived as a theme. Soon its treatment came to stand independently from the composite ode and, whilst the descriptive elements of Bacchic verse were based around a core of inherited imagery, a new defiant and anti-religious attitude was introduced that is reflected in a verse by the poet from al-Tā'if, Abū Mihjan al-Thaqafī: 'If I die bury me by the vine, so that its roots may satiate the thirst of my bones.' This solipsistic dirge, that shows the poet to have acquired notions of life after death, ignores the new imposing religious eschatology of the nascent Islamic community.

Islam did, of course, have a profound effect on the poets of Bacchism; for after a time, usually with the onset of old age, they would repent of their erring in pious Islamic terms. To replace them there was always a new generation of libertines, who were commonly men of high standing, such as governors and even, during the Umayyad period, caliphs. Al-Walīd ibn Yazīd, one of the last Umayyad caliphs (d. AD 744), was a notorious hedonist (although perhaps maligned by later Abbasid propaganda) whose attitude in some Bacchic fragments is aggressively atheistic: 'Give wine [to drink] . . . for I know there is no Hell-fire!' In this period Bacchism became an urban phenomenon, notably amongst the libertines of Kufa (modern Iraq), and was eventually to gain a high profile in the Abbasid court circle of Baghdad, particularly during the reign of al-Amīn (reigned AD 809–13). This son of Hārūn al-Rashīd is famous in literary history as patron and boon companion of the great ABU NUWAS (d. AD 814).

In his wine poetry Abu Nuwas synthesized a variety of impulses to produce sometimes complex poems which articulated all the issues relevant to the social dialectic of wine culture in an Islamic society: he expanded both the fantastical and mimetic descriptive repertoire of the *khamriyya*; he fused the Bacchic and erotic registers of poetry to create well-wrought seduction poems that gave voice to a sceptical world-view; he structured his poems in such a way as to support the simple rhetoric in defence of wine; finally, with literary sleights of hand, he reconciled the hedonistic ethic with Islamic dogma. It has rightly been said about the finest of these poems that they parallel the impulses and complexity of some English Metaphysical poetry.

From the descriptions of Abu Nuwas and other poets we gain a detailed picture of Bacchic culture: we are familiarized with the wine itself (its provenance, preparation, colour, bouquet, taste, and age—although here a mythological dimension enters into the poet's expression); its effects (physical, psychic, and spiritual); the personages (the boon companion, the pourer, the singing girl, the taverner (Jewish, Christian, or Persian), and the servant girl); the decorum of drinking (generosity, aristocracy, the quest for freedom, the Satanic pact, and, ultimately, belief in divine mercy); the venues of drinking (the caliphal palace, the tavern, the monastery, gardens, and the vine itself); finally we learn about the variety of vessels (for drinking: glass, silver and gold cups or goblets, ewers; for storage: jars, tanks or casks, and leather bottles).

After Abu Nuwas poets who treated wine (throughout the Islamic lands, including al-Andalus in southern Spain) had little new to say; they simply reworked the imagery he had established, whilst discarding the careful structure of his finest poems. It was only amongst Sufi mystics that a new, important dimension was added to Bacchic poetry. Foremost amongst these was Ibn al-Fārid (d. 1235). For these ascetics DRUNKENNESS represented divine intoxication; they simply borrowed the imagery of Bacchic culture to articulate the otherwise ineffable states of mystical experience. Although Abu Nuwas himself was a ribald, Sufi sensitivity is perhaps foreshadowed in some of his most ethereal descriptions of wine:

> [Last night I could not sleep] so give me to drink of the maiden wine who has donned the grey locks of old age whilst still in the womb;
> A wine which [when poured] is replenished with youth . . .
> One preserved for a day when its [seal] is pierced, though it is the confidant of Time itself;
> It has been aged, such that if it were possessed of an eloquent tongue,
> It would sit proudly amongst people and tell a tale of an ancient time . . .

P.K.

'*Khamriyya*', *The Encyclopaedia of Islam* (new edn.), vol. iv (Leiden, 1978), 998–1009.

ARAGON, known as **Aragón** in Spanish. Once a powerful kingdom whose sphere of influence stretched from the LEVANTE in the west as far as NAPLES and SICILY in the east, Aragon is now one of Spain's 17 autonomous regions. In the north east of the country, it spans the broad valley of the River Ebro which is flanked by mountains on either side (see map on p. 907). The north is dominated by the Pyrenees which feed water on to arid Ebro plain. To the south and east the climate becomes progressively extreme as the land rises towards the central Spanish plateau.

The wines of Aragon have traditionally been strong, strapping potions with natural alcohol reaching levels as high as 17 or 18 per cent. Red wines, made predominantly from the GARNACHA grape, were mostly sold in bulk for blending. However four DO regions designated between 1980 and 1990 are helping to raise the profile of Aragon wines. SOMONTANO in the lush Pyrenean foothills east of the city of Huesca certainly has the most potential but south of the Ebro, wines from the DOs of CAMPO DE BORJA, CARIÑENA, and CALATAYUD are starting to benefit from investment in modern winemaking technology. Throughout much of Aragon, large CO-OPERATIVES continue to dominate production buying in grapes from smallholders. R.J.M.

ARAGONEZ, Portuguese name for the Spanish red grape variety TEMPRANILLO used particularly in the Alentejo region.

ARAK, anise-flavoured spirit produced in the LEBANON where it is considerably more popular than wine, from which it should be produced. Base wine is distilled three times, the third time with aniseed. The best may be aged in terracotta jars; the worst may be distilled from molasses. As Lebanese demand for wine declined during the turmoil of the 1980s, an increasing proportion of the country's vineyard was dedicated to arak, as well as dried fruit and table grapes. The spirit tastes similar to the raki of Turkey, rakia of Bulgaria, and ouzo of Greece.

ARAMON is now, happily, a remnant of French viticultural history, a vine variety that burgeoned throughout the Midi in the second half of the 19th century and was displaced as France's most popular only in the 1960s by CARIGNAN. For decades, particularly after the development of railway links with the populous north of France, Aramon vines were encouraged to spew forth light, everyday wine-for-the-workers that was with good reason called *petit rouge*.

Aramon's great attribute, apart from its prodigious productivity (up to 400 hl/ha (22.8 tons/acre) on the fertile plains of the Languedoc), was its resistance to POWDERY MILDEW, the scourge of what were France's established wine regions in the mid 19th century. The variety was taken up with great enthusiasm and rapidly spread over terrain previously considered too flat and fertile for viticulture.

Galet notes that its effects were particularly noticeable in the Hérault, where, between 1849 and 1869, the land under vine more than doubled, to 214,000 ha/528,800 acres, while its annual output of wine quadrupled, to 15 million hl/396 million gal.

Unless planted on poor soils and pruned extremely severely, Aramon produces some of the lightest red wine that could be considered red, often with a blue-black tinge and notably low in alcohol, extract, and character. To render the *rouge* sufficiently *rouge* for the French consumer, Aramon had invariably to be bolstered by such red-fleshed grapes as one of the TEINTURIERS, most often ALICANTE BOUSCHET. This gave Aramon a grave disadvantage compared with the deep, alcoholic reds of North Africa, and its popularity began to decline in the mid 20th century, a trend exacerbated by its toll from the 1956 and 1963 frosts. Aramon suffers from the twin disadvantages of budding early and ripening late and is therefore limited to hotter wine regions.

Not surprisingly, this variety has not been in great demand elsewhere (although it has been known in Algeria and Argentina and its origins are thought by some to be Spanish). The last French agricultural census noted that Aramon was still France's sixth most planted vine variety in 1988, its 34,700 ha/85,700 acres of vineyard (almost exclusively in the Midi and half of them still in the Hérault) covering more ground than total French plantings of either Gamay, Cabernet Franc, Syrah, or Pinot Noir. It is to be hoped that the next census reveals a more thorough scourge, thanks to financial inducements to pull out these worthless vines.

Aramon Gris and **Aramon Blanc**, lighter-berried mutations, can still be found, particularly in the Hérault.

Galet, P., *Cépages et vignobles de France* (2nd edn., Montpellier, 1990).

ARBIN, named CRU just south east of the vermouth town CHAMBÉRY whose name can be added to the eastern French appellation Vin de SAVOIE. Arbin is particularly well known for the power and concentration of its red wine from the local MONDEUSE grape.

ARBOIS, the most important appellation in the JURA region in eastern France, named after the region's main wine town. Until recently, Arbois was the name most commonly given to Jura wines. The scientist Louis PASTEUR was brought up in the town, and conducted observations here when invited to turn his attention to wine health. More recently Arbois has been famous as the location of the Jura's most famous wine producer, the energetic Henri Maire, whose BRAND Vin Fou has been much advertised all over France. So important is this NÉGOCIANT that it grows or buys, blends, sometimes bubbles by the TRANSFER METHOD, and then sells about half of the entire Jura wine production.

Arbois may be any colour, particularly *corail* or *rubis*, intermediate hues between pink and red which result from applying normal RED WINE-MAKING techniques to the light-coloured POULSARD grape which is a speciality here (although Pinot Noir and the local Trousseau are also grown). From more than 750 ha/1,850 acres of vines, white wine production has been increasing so that it represented about half of the appellation's output by the early 1990s. White wines are often VARIETAL Chardonnay, and those in which some of the local SAVAGNIN, or Naturé, is included can taste distinctly nutty. A significant proportion of wine is made bubbly by the champagne method of SPARKLING WINE-MAKING and sold as **Arbois Mousseux.** Wines made from grapes grown within the commune of Pupillin have the right to the appellation **Arbois Pupillin**.

See also VIN JAUNE and VIN DE PAILLE, both of which rarities are made within this appellation.

Arbois is also the name of a white grape variety of which about 700 ha/1,730 acres were grown in the Loire in the late 1980s to produce such wines as VALENÇAY and CHEVERNY. Arbois is also a permitted ingredient in white wines labelled TOURAINE (and, in theory, Vouvray). The variety is declining in importance but was still the third most important variety of any colour in the Loir-et-Cher *département* in 1988. Often called Menu Pineau or Petit Pineau, it is a vigorous vine whose wines are softer than those of the Chenin Blanc that is more common in the middle Loire valley.

ARBOUR, an overhead trellis structure used for VINE TRAINING, particularly in southern Italy. See TENDONE.

ARCHAEOLOGY has been of great importance in tracing the ORIGINS OF VITICULTURE and plays a part in the ancient history of most wine regions. For a discussion of the techniques available and some of the more significant finds, see PALAEOETHNOBOTANY. For some more specific aspects, see also AMPHORAE and the CELTS.

ARCHIVE WINE, term used particularly in eastern Europe, for wines deliberately aged in bottle to be sold at a premium, usually on the domestic market. See also Portugal's GARRAFEIRA.

ARDÈCHE, region of France on the right bank of the Rhône between the main concentrations of vineyards which constitute the northern and southern Rhône valley in south east France. Its steadily improving wines are sold as VIN DE PAYS des Coteaux de l'Ardèche, from the southern VIVARAIS area, or Vin de Pays des Collines Rhodaniennes from the much larger surrounding region. VARIETAL Chardonnay and Viognier have been particularly successful here.

ARGENTINA, the most important wine-producing country in South America and one of the few remaining major wine-producing countries of the world yet to be fully exploited. To understand this one has to look no further than the country's turbulent political and economic recent history.

In the 1920s Argentina was the eighth richest nation in the world, but the subsequent economic depression led to a steep decline in foreign investments and a disastrous drop in the export price of its primary products. While the landowning classes continued to prosper, or salted away their capital overseas, there was growing unrest among the largely disenfranchised, poorly paid urban masses. It became imperative for the country to develop its own infrastructure and when General Juan Domingo Perón came to power in 1943 he appealed directly to the workers with promises of rapid industrialization, better working conditions, and organized, state-controlled unions. He was strongly influenced by his ambitious and charismatic wife Eva, and for a while the fortunes of Argentina revived. But Perón's origins were military and, when in the mid 1950s it became obvious that his populist power base was becoming a threat to the long-term interests and image of the armed forces, he was quickly deposed. From then on a succession of opportunist military governments led the country into spiralling decline. Throughout the 1960s and 1970s Argentina had become so enmeshed in stifling bureaucracy that this was to lead to widespread corruption and ultimately to social and political unrest. The Argentine people, noted for their natural self-confidence and sense of national pride, became regressive and dispirited while the country itself grew increasingly isolated. By the early 1980s with hyper-inflation running at nearly 1,000 per cent a year, Argentina had dropped to 15th place in the league of developed countries. It is not surprising that Argentina's wine industry has felt the effects of these changes in fortune. In the early 1980s, only France, Italy, Spain, and what was the USSR produced more wine than Argentina, but then most Argentine wine producers were content to supply cheap, rustic VINO DE MESA to a domestic market that boasted the third highest per capita consumption of wine in the world. In the late 1960s and early 1970s, at a time when the UK was drinking approximately 3 l per capita per year and the Americans even less, the Argentines, despite all their troubles, were quaffing 90 l of wine per head. By 1992 that figure had dropped dramatically to 50 l per capita and is still falling.

Faced with this dramatic drop in home consumption, added to the pressing need to earn foreign currency, the more enlightened producers decided to go upmarket and in the late 1980s, for the first time, gave serious consideration to the possibilities of exporting, helped by political and economic stability not experienced for decades. Under President Menem business confidence in Argentina's future was revitalized at home and abroad and encouraged investment in a wine industry where time had stood still (see also CHILE).

However, before Argentina can claim its place alongside the other emerging New World wine-producing countries, there is much to be done, particularly in the vineyard, and in understanding which vine varieties can realistically be grown where to produce wine of export quality (although some pioneering work was done by Pedro Zuluaga *et al.* at the National University of Cuyo in 1968). Contrary to popular belief, long hot summers are not sufficient to guarantee wine quality. The vineyards of the Andes are blessed with a prolonged and relatively trouble-free ripening season under clear skies. The abundance of water from melting snow in the high mountains and from deep boreholes in an area where the average annual rainfall is just 200 mm/8 in has made possible a massive and highly efficient IRRIGATION system in the vineyards. This results in such spectacular vegetative growth that it is easy to forget that surrounding this fertile garden there is unclaimed and inhospitable desert. However, skilful vineyard siting is vital in the drive for quality and other viticultural practices such as scientifically chosen ROOTSTOCK, CLONAL SELECTION, CANOPY MANAGEMENT, and suitable VINE DENSITY are all still to be fully understood and exploited by an industry that for generations equated success solely with the production of maximum YIELDS.

It is a measure of changing attitudes that during the 1970s Argentina regularly produced well over 20 million hl/528 million gal of wine but by the early 1990s production had stabilized at around 15 million hl. This was largely brought about by a reduction of a third during the 1980s in the total

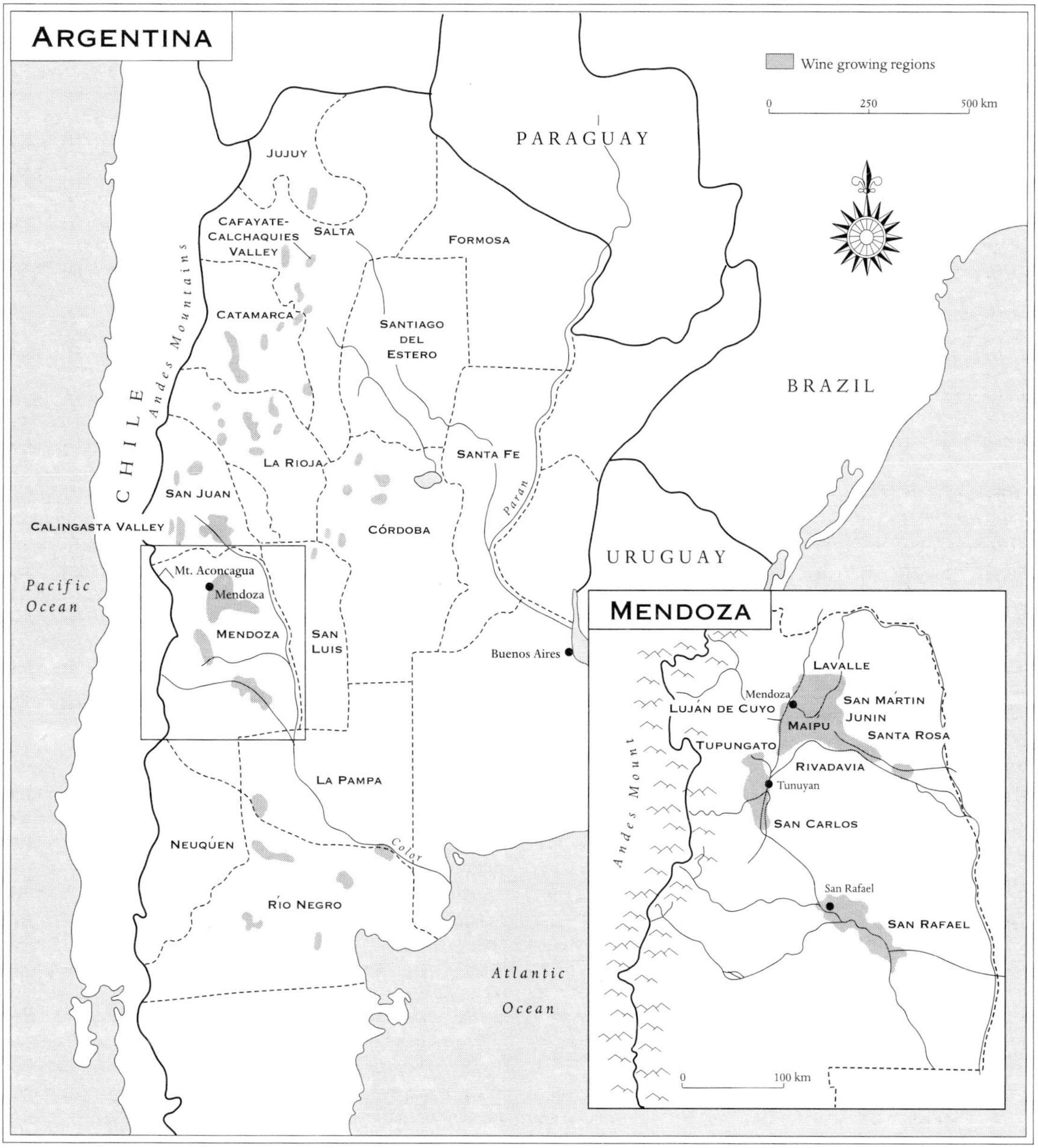

area planted with vines, especially red wine grape varieties. Despite the historic association of alcoholic, red wines with good red Argentine beef, there was a noticeable swing to white wine drinking as the emerging middle class began to develop a life-style and taste of their own. In the 1960s about 50,000 ha/123,500 acres were planted to Argentina's most distinctive red variety MALBEC, but uneconomically low prices for Malbec grapes in the 1970s and 1980s encouraged a reduction of this area to less than 10,000 ha in 1990, just as the potential of the variety became apparent.

By far the most planted varieties in Argentina are still the prolific, pink-skinned CRIOLLA and CEREZA, workhorse varieties brought by the original settlers. The common white table wine made from these grapes is cheap but has become unfashionable, however, and their importance is likely to decline.

Of the 200,000 ha/494,200 acres of vineyard dedicated to wine production in 1990 (by far the most important grape use), approximately 50 per cent was planted with pink-skinned varieties, 30 per cent with white-skinned varieties, and just 20 per cent with red-skinned varieties. But by the mid 1990s the new wave of optimism began to reverse this trend, with the emphasis increasingly on finding premium varieties and styles that will allow Argentina wine producers to compete successfully internationally.

Some red wines were already able to compete favourably in quality and price with those from neighbouring Chile on the west of the Andes and the warmer regions of Australia and California. White wines tend to lack natural acidity (an attribute not highly valued by Argentine consumers); growing white wine varieties at higher altitudes helps, and finding the right rootstock and clones will probably be more effective in the long run. Some of the richer producers have recently started to use French oak barriques to give added complexity to their wine, but this fashionable, and in some cases possibly unsuitable, expedient greatly increases costs.

A few Argentine wineries, including the largest, Peñaflor, have contrived to equip themselves with stainless steel tanks, pneumatic presses, refrigeration, and small oak barrels, despite the difficulties imposed by hyper-inflation and the lack of foreign currency. Only in the early 1990s, however, was there even any thought of investment in the vineyard and in current viticultural trends. In the main, the Argentine wine industry is still suffering from years of chronic under-funding, introspection, and isolation from the rest of the world. It is likely to be the turn of the century before Argentine wine producers are ready to compete on equal terms.

History

Unlike North America where explorers and early settlers found vitis *labrusca* growing in abundance, South America depended on the Spanish colonizers for imported European vinifera vines. The vine probably arrived in Argentina by four different routes. The first was directly from Spain in 1541 when vines are thought to have been cultivated, without great success, on the Atlantic coast around the river Plate. A year later, seeds of dried grapes were germinated as a result of an expedition from Peru to the current wine regions immediately east of the Andes. Another expedition from Peru in 1550 also imported vines to Argentina, while the fourth and most important vine importation came from Chile in 1556, just two years after the vine was introduced to Chile's Central valley. (See south america, history for more details.)

One of the most important grape varieties systematically cultivated for wine in South America was almost certainly the forerunner of Argentina's Criolla Chica, California's mission, and Chile's pais, which were to be the backbone of South American wine production for the next 300 years.

Although Argentina was settled from both the east and the west, it was in the foothills of the Andes that the Jesuit missionaries found the best conditions for vine-growing. The first recorded vineyard was planted at Santiago del Estero in 1557. The city of Mendoza was founded in 1561 and vineyards in the province of San Juan to the north were established on a commercial scale between 1569 and 1589.

By the skilful use of dams and irrigation channels, the early settlers were able to produce sufficient wine to meet the needs of a growing population and they also learned how to produce wine that could stand up to long wagon train journeys to the centres of population to the east.

In the 1820s, following the freeing of Argentina from Spanish colonial rule by General San Martín, there was a massive influx of European immigrants. In 1885 the railway between Buenos Aires and Mendoza was completed, lending still greater importance to the vineyards in the foothills of the Andes, and by 1900 a second wave of immigrants, many from wine-producing areas of Italy, Spain, and France, brought with them many new vine varieties and their own regional vine-growing and wine-making skills. The old colonial methods were quickly dispensed with, except the historic and essential irrigation system, and the foundations for Argentina's mammoth domestic wine industry were laid.

Climate

Argentina's wine regions are widely dispersed, but are almost entirely confined to the western strip of the country bordering the foothills of the Andes. The vineyard area extends from the tropic of Capricorn in the north to the 40th parallel in the south. Apart from the southern, largely fruit-growing areas of the Río Negro and Neuquén, the climate is semi-desert with annual rainfall rarely more than 250 mm/10 in. The seasons are well defined, allowing the vines to rest.

Summer temperatures vary from 10 °C/50 °F at night to as much as 40 °C/104 °F during the day. Summers are hot in the regions of San Juan (except for the Calingasta valley), La Rioja, Catamarca, and the east of Mendoza (Santa Rosa, Rivadavia, San Martín, and Lavalle). In the Calchaquies valley (Cafayate), upper Mendoza (Luján de Cuyo), Uco valley (Tupungato), and Río Negro, summers are temperate to warm, making them Regions II and III in the Winkler system of climate classification. In winter temperatures can drop below 0 °C/32 °F, although frost is rare, except where vines have been grown at altitude.

What little rain there is falls mainly in the summer months, often as hail, but heavy winter snow in the high Andes is important as this ensures plentiful supplies of water for the irrigation system on which the vines depend.

The air is dry and particularly unpolluted, unlike the smog that is sometimes trapped over the Chilean vineyards closest to the capital, Santiago, just a short flight away over the Andes. Vine flowering may occasionally be adversely affected by a hot, dry, hurricane-force storm called the *zonda* which blows down from the north west in early summer. Grapes almost invariably reach full maturity and the lack of humidity reduces the risk of fungal diseases, obviating the need for frequent and costly spraying.

Viticulture

Until the mid 1990s more emphasis was placed on wine-making techniques and the equipment required for processing the huge yields of the Criolla Grande vine than on experimentation and innovation in the vineyards.

Spraying is an important vineyard operation in most climates, especially in damp ones where the risk of **fungal diseases** is high. **Tractors** have been specially designed to straddle low, neat rows of vines such as here in Mesnil-sur-Oger in Champagne.

Warm, dry summers, clear skies, and ample supplies of water for irrigation can lead to very high yields. Figures of 250 to 400 hl/ha (22.8 tons/acre) were not unusual in the 1970s when domestic consumption was at its peak. The drop in home sales in the 1980s and the growing realization among Argentine producers that they must export to survive is leading to a closer study of the art of the possible in their existing vineyards and a search for new areas more suitable for the production of better-quality wine.

Almost all vines in Argentina are ungrafted, planted on their own roots. The root louse PHYLLOXERA has made only limited predations in Argentina, perhaps because the biotype present in the country is a relatively mild one, perhaps because there is a relatively high proportion of SAND in vineyard soils. The average vine life cycle in Argentina has been 50 years so that rootstocks with particular resistances and attributes are likely to be introduced relatively slowly, if at all.

Before the construction of a new vineyard or the replanting of an old one can begin, the ground is cleared by bulldozer to leave slight slopes to facilitate the flow of the all-important water which is stored nearby in strategically placed reservoirs and distributed by an intricate network of canals and ditches. Argentina's water distribution system is still one of the best in the world, despite having its origins in the 16th century. In more recent times, the channels of water that flow from the permanently snow-capped peaks of the high Andes have been augmented by the drilling of deep boreholes. These take water from between 60 and 120 m (390 ft) below the surface and can produce as much as 250,000 l/66,000 gal per hour. The landscape is unique, the cultivated areas resembling green oases in the scorched desert surroundings (as in the irrigated vineyards of AUSTRALIA but with the Andes as a backdrop).

Three methods of irrigation are used. Most common is flood irrigation, whereby measured amounts of water are channelled into flat vineyards. Furrow irrigation involves the channelling of water along the furrows in which the vines are planted. Drip irrigation is a relatively new technique in Argentina, and is relatively expensive.

Soil structure varies from region to region but a loose greyish sandy texture predominates with substrates of GRAVEL, LIMESTONE, and CLAY. The Instituto Nacional de Vitiviniculture (INV), the Government's controlling body, and the National Institute of Agriculture Technology (INTA) were originally guided by DAVIS in California in selecting the right clones for the soil, but many vineyard owners subsequently looked to Australasia for advice on the type of vine to plant.

Although the immigrants who arrived in the early 20th century brought with them the vertical *espaldera* VINE-TRAINING SYSTEM of low training of vines along three wires, the need for greater volume led most vineyard owners to adopt the *parral cuyano* trellis system in the 1950s and 1960s (see TENDONE). *Parral* trained vines rise to about 2 m/6 ft off the ground and are planted at low vine densities of between 1,600 and 2,000 vines per ha (650–800 per acre). The advantages afforded by the *parral* system include high yields, ease of picking, control of WEEDS, and protection from frost and reflected soil heat. As in Chile, however, the classic method is increasingly favoured once again, in order to facilitate both canopy management and drip irrigation, although Cereza and Criolla Grande vines are still likely to be *parral* trained.

Spraying against FUNGAL DISEASES is minimal compared to more humid countries. From BUDBREAK to HARVEST takes an average of five months and the long ripening season normally ensures grapes of full maturity. The INV declares the date of the harvest, which usually begins in mid February and, depending on the variety and the region, can extend until April. Towards the end of the 1980s some producers picked their white grapes early in order to increase the fresh, fruity aromas and the natural acidity in the must but the practice has not always been a success, particularly with *parral*-trained vines. Large bunches hanging down below a dense canopy risk lacking full ripeness and therefore the necessary level of alcohol to ensure stability. Other ideas include using mobile crushing machines for white grapes in the vineyard in order to reduce the risk of OXIDATION that takes place in the road tanker on the way to a distant winery, but this increases the PHENOLICS in the finished wine and off-flavours can result.

Many of the large new vineyards are several hours' drive from the wineries and, unless MECHANICAL HARVESTING (which is still rare) enables picking in the cool of the night, the wine should ideally be processed in the immediate vineyard area. Itinerant, low-paid grape pickers were once plentiful but the cost of living rose dramatically from the late 1980s.

Much more rigorous control of yields, the gradual introduction of mechanical harvesting, and the building of wine-making facilities in the vineyard are likely to be the main viticultural developments of the late 1990s.

Wine-making

The overwhelming demands of the domestic market in the late 1960s and early 1970s meant that wine-making techniques were geared to processing the vast yields of Criolla Grande, Criolla Chica, and Cereza grapes. The big producers concentrated their efforts and resources into perfecting a simple, somewhat brutal, but highly efficient system for receiving, destemming, crushing, macerating, and fermenting up to 2.5 million kg/2,500 tons of grapes a day. Even in the 1990s it is not unusual at the peak of the harvest to see a line of 50 or more grape-laden trucks waiting patiently in the winery approaches to be weighed before tipping their loads into the giant crushers, often leading to dangerously oxidized fruit. Red wines would be picked at 21 to 23° BRIX, crushed, fermented in concrete fermentation vessels, RACKED off the skins, at 10° Brix, fermented to dryness off the skins, and then left for up to four years in large old wooden tanks before BOTTLING according to market demand.

Changes are afoot, however. The export-led drive for improved quality is forcing even the biggest producers of

With topography and architecture typical of **Alsace**, Hunawihr is most famous with wine enthusiasts for the grand cru vineyard Rosacker and **Trimbach's** great enclave of Riesling vines, Clos Ste-Hune, within it.

cheap wine into a reappraisal of their wine-making techniques in order to supply international demand for sound VARIETAL wines such as the Chardonnay and Cabernet Sauvignon.

Vine varieties

Although in the early 1990s the high-yielding Criolla and Cereza (see Pinks below) still accounted for more than half the total crop, and are likely to do so for some time to come, vineyard owners were slowly increasing their production of the classic varieties originating in Europe. They are typically planted in flat vineyards in the deep, fertile, heavily irrigated soils of the warmer wine regions. Argentina's signature variety, MALBEC, on the other hand, is more likely to be planted in the less fertile Andean foothills.

The vines brought by the second and third wave of immigrants in the 1880s and at the turn of the 20th century may or may not have been precisely what they were called then or even today. The AMPELOGRAPHER Alberto Alcalde at INTA, Mendoza, has made considerable progress in vine identification in Argentina, as well as developing suitable plant material by MASS SELECTION of popular high-quality varieties.

Certainly the science of selecting vine varieties to suit the soil, climate, and growing conditions has, until recently, been largely ignored in Argentina. Now purer, more suitable strains are being sought with the help of viticultural schools such as those at DAVIS, MONTPELLIER, BORDEAUX, and DIJON. The variety introduced as Sauvignon Blanc years ago, for example, was, as in Chile, almost certainly the Tocai Friuliano (as were some cuttings called Riesling), whose end product is a far cry from the crisp, dry, grassy wines of the Loire or New Zealand's South Island.

White The swing to white wine consumption in the late 1980s generated a need for relatively inexpensive neutral styles of wine. UGNI BLANC often serves, and CHENIN BLANC, oddly called Pinot de la Loire here, is also grown successfully, albeit demonstrating the somewhat anodyne characteristics of a California rather than Loire example. It provides much of the base wine for the sparkling wine popular with Argentines.

The Pedro Giménez (not identical to Spain's PEDRO XIMÉNEZ) is the most planted white grape variety, grown particularly in Mendoza and the province of San Juan, where it yields alcoholic, full-bodied wine suitable for blending. It is also used for making GRAPE CONCENTRATE, which Argentina exports in vast quantities to JAPAN.

Second most planted light-skinned variety in 1990 was Moscatel de Alejandria, or MUSCAT OF ALEXANDRIA, but perhaps the most interesting, and certainly the most distinctive, white wine grape variety is the third most important, TORRONTÉS, of which, of the three different strains, Torrontés Riojano, from La Rioja province, is by far the most common. Others are Torrontés Mendocino and Torrontés Sanjuanino. There is no evidence that Argentina's Torrontés is the same as that grown in GALICIA, north west Spain, but it is the nearest thing to an indigenous white variety in Argentina and produces a light wine with a strong MUSCAT aroma. Use of the right strains of yeast and careful temperature control during fermentation can result in a Torrontés wine of great universal appeal. Originally it was planted almost exclusively in the northern province of Salta, particularly in the Calchaquies Valley and around Cafayate. It can now be found in the province of Mendoza, where it is often used for blending. Its flowery, strongly aromatic character makes it ideal for this purpose.

The climate does not lend itself to the successful growing of the RIESLING grape, although some producers are making a passable wine in the richer, fuller bodied Australian mode. True SAUVIGNON Blanc, which the more enlightened producers believe they must try to produce if they are to carve out a niche in the world market, is as yet unproven and relatively rare. Careful siting helps but aspiring Sauvignon Blanc growers would probably do better to study what is being done in their own hemisphere in Australia and South Africa, for instance, rather than rely on guidance from California.

CHARDONNAY is the wine that everyone wants to produce and the Argentines are no exception, particularly with their eye on the US and British markets. Although Argentina has its own Chardonnay clone developed at Davis in California, the so-called Mendoza clone (see MILLERANDAGE), which is widely used in Australia, the style and character of the Chardonnay coming from the eponymous province is not yet entirely convincing. Some Chardonnays grown in selected vineyards and at a good altitude, such as the Tupungato area at 1,200 m/3940 ft, are beginning to produce wines of style, sometimes the result of BARREL FERMENTATION, but many wines are still too bland in character and have a tendency to oxidation. Of all the classic grape varieties, Chardonnay has proved to be one of the most adaptable, even though fewer than 1,000 ha/2,470 acres were producing wine in 1990. It is reasonable to suppose that Argentina will be producing significant quantities of good Chardonnay in the next century.

Other varieties include Chenin Blanc, Ugni Blanc, and SÉMILLON.

Red Paradoxically the predominant red wine grape variety in Argentina is one that has never achieved greatness in its original birthplace in the south west of France. The Malbec, often spelt Malbeck, of Bordeaux BOURG, BLAYE, and CAHORS seems to have discovered its true home in upper Mendoza. There it produces a deep coloured, robust, and fruity red wine with enough alcohol, weight, and structure to benefit from OAK ageing. Cabernet Sauvignon is as popular with Argentine wine growers as any others, but there is no doubt that the Malbec produces by far the best and most balanced red wine and, with careful nurturing and strict temperature control during fermentation, it could develop into a wine of quality and style that would be unique to Argentina.

So enthusiastically was Malbec pulled out in the 1970s and 1980s, however, that by 1990 there was slightly more vineyard, 12,000 ha/29,600 acres, planted with a variety called BONARDA, whose exact identity is still the subject of some debate among ampelographers. Most think it is the CHARBONO of California, while others believe it is CROATINA. This variety, along with many other Italian varieties (most notably SANGIOVESE and BARBERA but also FREISA, NEBBIOLO, RABOSO, DOLCETTO, and LAMBRUSCO), was brought to the country by the substantial numbers of Italian immigrants. Also important is the Spanish variety TEMPRANILLO, known here as Tempranilla, often used to make light, fruity wines by CARBONIC MACERATION.

CABERNET SAUVIGNON, rather like Chardonnay, has been much slower to find its niche. The wines have tended to lack fruit, perhaps because of relatively unsophisticated wine-making techniques, including prolonged CASK AGEING, but average quality is rapidly improving. There were nearly 2,500 ha / 6,200 acres of productive Cabernet vines in 1990.

Other red wine varieties include the MERLOT, which some more adventurous producers are beginning to blend Bordeaux-style with Cabernet Sauvignon to soften the hard TANNINS and provide fruit, and the PINOT NOIR, whose often unrecognizable produce suggests that the variety may be unsuited to Argentina's climate and soil types.

Several viticulturists consider SYRAH, or Shiraz, of which there were nearly 700 ha in 1990, might do well in Argentina's climate and soil, and it is expected to be more widely planted.

Pinks The grapes of this, Argentina's most quantitatively important category of vine varieties can hardly be described as either white skinned or dark skinned since at full ripeness their skins are distinctly pink. The CRIOLLA GRANDE, CRIOLLA CHICA, and CEREZA are some of Argentina's oldest varieties. Cereza and Criolla Grande are the country's two most planted vine varieties, with 43,000 ha / 106,200 acres and 37,000 ha / 91,400 acres respectively in 1990. The much less important Criolla Chica is identical to the PAIS of Chile, and probably descended from the seeds of dried grapes brought by the Conquistadores. Both Criolla and Cereza are extremely productive varieties of which one bunch on a well-irrigated vineyard can weigh as much as 4 kg / 9 lbs. Moscatel Rosada is another important pink-skinned variety, of which there were a total of 15,000 ha in 1990. The wine produced from these varieties is usually very deeply coloured white, occasionally pink, often quite sweet, and sold at the bottom end of the market, either in bulk or in litre bottles or cardboard cartons, as everyday wine within Argentina, or blended with basic Malbec to produce a light red.

Regions

See map on p. 47.

Mendoza In the far west of the country, only a (substantial) mountain range from Santiago in Chile, this is by far the biggest and most important wine-growing province in Argentina, covering over 150,000 square km / 58,000 square miles and with a population exceeding 1.2 million, most of whom live in the modern city of Mendoza and its immediate surroundings. The white-capped tops of the Andes range dominate the western skyline, with Mount Aconcagua, at over 7,000 m / 23,000 ft, the highest mountain in the Americas, rising above the rest.

The evolution of the vineyard area can be seen from the table, which reflects the substantial drop in Malbec production. The province of Mendoza still accounts for over 70 per cent of all Argentina's wine production, although the area planted declined from a peak of 255,000 ha in 1980 to about 150,000 ha in 1992. This shrinkage can be attributed quite simply to a drop in demand for the prolific Criolla Grande as a result of economic factors and it can be assumed that the area under cultivation will continue to drop as domestic consumption falls even further.

Year	Total area of vineyards (ha / acres)
1890	6,000 / 14,830
1910	45,000 / 111,200
1936	100,000 / 247,100
1963	190,000 / 469,500
1977	250,000 / 617,700
1989	177,999 / 439,800
1992	150,000 / 370,600

The climate and soil structure in Mendoza province are the best in Argentina for grape production. The climate is CONTINENTAL, with the four seasons clearly defined but without any extremes of temperature. Rainfall occurs mostly in the summer months, which encourages growth, but it seldom exceeds 300 mm / 12 in a year with 200 mm / 8 in being the average. Early summer HAIL is the main risk to the vines and frost is rare. A combination of both late in 1992 resulted in a 50 per cent reduction in the 1993 crop. Average altitudes are about 500 to 800 m (1,600–2,600 ft) above sea level.

The topsoil in Mendoza is of a loose, sandy, ALLUVIAL type with clay substructures. Water is in ample supply from five mountain rivers flowing from glaciers in the high Andes and 17,000 deep boreholes equal the flow of two additional rivers. The long rows of protective trees that line the vineyards and make summer temperatures of 36 °C / 97 °F bearable are testimony to the effective and well-orchestrated system of reservoirs, canals, and IRRIGATION channels.

The most important wine-producing areas in and around Mendoza are:

Maipú department: Cruz de Piedra, Barrancas, Russell, Coquimbito, Lunlunta, and Maipú districts.

Luján department: Carrodilla, Chacras de Coria, Mayor Drummond, Luján, Vistalba, Las Compuertas, Pedriel, Agrelo, Ugarteche, Carrizal, Tres Esquinas, Anchoris.

San Martín to the east and San Raphael to the south of the region are also major centres of production, although less important than formerly following the swing to classic varieties.

Luján de Cuyo (which created Argentina's first controlled appellation in 1993) is in the upper Mendoza valley at altitudes between 800 and 1,100 m. Average rainfall is about 190 mm a year and the mean annual temperature is 15 °C. The Malbec vine does particularly well here.

Red wine grape varieties account for about a third of all

Mendoza plantings with the Malbec predominating but Italian varieties and Tempranillo are also important. Cabernet Sauvignon is beginning to catch up. White wine varieties such as Chardonnay and Sauvignon Blanc are increasingly common, especially in high altitude vineyards, such as those of Tupungato, which can be as high as 1,200 m.

San Juan This is Argentina's second biggest wine-producing region and had more than 46,000 ha / 113,600 acres of vineyards in 1990. The capital of the province, San Juan, is 150 km / 90 miles north of Mendoza. The climate is much hotter than that of Mendoza, with summer temperatures of 42 °C / 107 °F not uncommon and with rainfall averaging only 150 mm / 6 in per annum.

Apart from one or two potential quality wine areas, such as the high-altitude Barreal vineyard in the Calingasta valley 120 km west of San Juan in the Andean foothills, San Juan province is facing an identity crisis. For long the home of high-yielding pink and white varieties whose high sugar content made them ideal for wine blending, concentrating, or for selling as fresh table grapes or raisins, the area now has very little to offer the modern wine market. A rapid reduction in the volume of wine produced has already taken place and is likely to continue. Between 1966 and 1989 San Juan province regularly produced as much as 6 million hl / 158 million gal of wine, but since then the figure had dropped dramatically to under 3.5 million by 1992. GRAPE CONCENTRATE production has been the mainstay of San Juan for some years but, unless investment is made in new plant to produce grape concentrate at competitive prices, even this could be under threat. Peñaflor have shown the way with new FLOTATION processes to clear juice, and THERMOVINIFICATION of reds. It should be noted, however, that San Juan produces perfectly acceptable sherry style wines and also provides the base for most of Argentina's BRANDY and VERMOUTHS.

The best areas are in the Ullun, Zonda, and Tulum valleys.

La Rioja Historically the oldest of the wine-producing provinces, La Rioja had only 5,800 ha / 14,300 acres of vineyard in 1990. By world standards the area is unimportant, although aromatic white wines from the TORRONTÉS grape can be good, and wines made from the Moscatel de Alexandria (MUSCAT OF ALEXANDRIA) have a following in Argentina itself. The lack of water for irrigation purposes makes wine-making a marginal activity.

Salta, Jujuy, and Catamarca These three provinces cover 500,000 square km / 193,000 square miles and, although Catamarca has the biggest area under vine, it is in the province of Salta that the best wine is produced. Here the Torrontés Riojano is very much at home. Around Cafayate in the Calchaquies valley it is producing an outstandingly aromatic, full bodied, dryish white wine. The vineyards are northerly, lying between 24 degrees and 26 degrees latitude, and can be 1,500 m / 4,900 ft above sea level. The climate and soil are not dissimilar to Mendoza but the MESOCLIMATE there ensures a combination of good sugar levels at harvest (from 21° to 25° Brix) and above average TOTAL ACIDITY, thereby ensuring a wine of depth and balance.

Of the other grape varieties grown in Salta, Cabernet Sauvignon is the most successful, producing a young wine with good fruit and concentration without the benefit of oak ageing.

Río Negro and Neuquén This area of Patagonia is much cooler than the higher-yielding areas to the north and, although there were some 5,300 ha / 13,000 acres under vine by the early 1990s, it has yet to reach its full potential. Historically the Río Negro has been the fruit-growing centre of Argentina, producing particularly apples, but the cooler climate and chalky soil combined with a long warm ripening season under clear skies make it ideal for the production of good-quality white wine (notably Torrontés Riojano and Semillon) and for sparkling wine base material. Investment in wine-making equipment and viticultural ideas has been minimal. Sauvignon Blanc and Chardonnay should do particularly well in this region and of all the regions of Argentina the Río Negro and Neuquén have the most potential and are most likely to be developed by multinational companies in the future. The distinguished de la Motta family, associated with Weinert winery in Mendoza, have established an experimental vineyard in the Bolzon valley of Río Negro. D.F.S.

Wine trade organization

The majority of Argentina's vineyards are in the hands of specialist grape-growers, of which many are relatively large commercial concerns. Wine producers exert increasing control on the grapes they buy in, however, and almost all of them own at least some vineyards.

The great majority of Argentina's wineries, like the country's vineyards, are in Mendoza province, often on the outskirts of the city of Mendoza itself. The largest companies have traditionally had sales offices in the distant capital Buenos Aires, but the largest producer by far, Peñaflor, now masterminds its export campaign from Mendoza. At its show-piece winery at Coquimbito just outside Mendoza and under the Trapiche label it produces such spearhead lines as the Medalla range and Fond de Cave.

Bianchi, situated in San Rafael in the south of Mendoza province, is another producer to have exported successfully, particularly to the USA, as have Finca Flichman and Pascual Toso, substantial vineyard owners Bodegas Lopez and Bodegas Esmeralda, and Weinert, whose speciality is not viticulture but maturing particularly concentrated red wines. Regional specialists with some degree of success outside Argentina include Etchart of Salta and Canale in the Río Negro.

Unlike Chile, Argentina failed to attract a substantial wave of foreign investors in the late 1980s and early 1990s, but the POMEROL oenologist Michel Rolland is developing in the small El Recreo winery in Cafayate and the Italian vermouth producers Martini & Rossi have long had Argentine investments,

Argentina: Flood irrigation in some of Peñaflor's Trapiche vineyards, the water supplied by melting snow from the distant Andes.

as have MOËT Hennessy, whose wholly owned subsidiary Chandon has been the biggest producer of sparkling 'Champaña' in Argentina for three decades. Other foreign investors include the champagne houses of Mumm, Deutz, and Piper-Heidsieck. Bodega Norton of Luján de Cuyo was acquired by Austrian interests in 1989.

Alcalde, A. J., *Cultivadores vitícolas argentinas* (Mendoza, 1989).

Foster, D. H. N., 'Fortifying a vintage industry', *Americas*, 40–2 (Apr.–May 1988).

Queyrat, E., *Guia de los Vinos Argentinos* (2nd edn. Buenos Aires, 1993).

ARGOLS, another word for TARTRATES.

ARINTO, Portuguese white grape variety most commonly encountered in BUCELAS in which it must constitute at least 75 per cent of the blend. It is also grown in many other parts of Portugal, including RIBATEJO. Arinto is most notable for its high acidity and can yield wines which gain interest and, sometimes, a citrus quality with age. Arinto Miudo and Arinto Cachudo are subvarieties. As an ingredient in VINHO VERDE it is known as Pedernã.

Arinto do Dão is a different, less distinguished variety.

ARISTOPHANES, Greek writer of comedies at the end of the fifth century BC. In his plays he extols the hard-working peasant farmer in the fields around Athens. One of his characters is a vine-dresser, or early vineyard worker (Trygaios in *The Peace*), and the goddess of peace is called wine-loving and 'giver of grapes'. Aristophanes criticizes the young for idling and drinking too much. Women also come in for criticism as topers in several of his plays. H.H.A.

ARM, viticultural term for that part of the vine's woody framework from which the CANES and SPURS arise. The location of arms depends on the vine-TRAINING system used. They may be borne along CORDONS, positioned at intervals so that the buds, after PRUNING, are placed to space the bearing shoots desirably. Alternatively, the arms may be positioned on a short HEAD at the top of the trunk as happens with some CANE PRUNING systems. B.G.C.

ARMAGNAC, grape spirit, or BRANDY, distilled in the Armagnac region of Gascony, SOUTH WEST FRANCE. As the local Gascons will often inform even the most casual visitor, armagnac is at once the oldest and the youngest spirit in France. The oldest because it was first distilled in the 15th century and a still was set up by the Maniban family at their Ch de Brusca in the mid 17th century, youngest because the armagnac producers are still arguing over how to distil it. For armagnac, sometimes to an exaggerated extent, is a better reflection of French individuality at work than any other spirit. As a result it remains one of the least industrialized of spirits, the one where amateurs can most legitimately hope to find a neglected bottle which they can cherish because it offers unique qualities, probably not shared even by a bottle from the next cask in the cellar where it was lodged. At its best armagnac offers the drinker a depth, a natural sweetness, and a fullness unmatched by even the finest COGNAC. Armagnac is underrated, however, because far too high a proportion is sold young.

It is also underrated because, unlike cognac, it does not come from a region which has lived off trade for a millennium or more but from the depths of GASCONY, 160 km/100 miles south of Bordeaux, and away from navigable waters. Its rise to fame dates only from the middle of the 19th century when the river Baise was canalized and the Armagnacais gained direct access to Bordeaux for the first time. Geologically it is produced on the churned-up mess of SAND and CLAY left behind by the ebb and flow of the sea that once reached the foot of the Pyrenees. But, curiously, the best is produced to the west of the Armagnac region, on the edge of the pine forests of the Landes. This makes armagnac one of the few distinguished alcoholic products from sandy soil, or rather from the ALLUVIAL deposits which cover a subsoil of sand and clay.

This western section is the heart of the Bas Armagnac, whose brandies evoke associations of plums and prunes. To the east is the Tenarèze district, whose soil, a mixture of chalk and clay, produces fine floral armagnacs that are often reminiscent of violets. Furthest east is the Haut Armagnac district, where the grapes are now used almost exclusively for wine, most noticeably VIN DE PAYS des Côtes de Gascogne.

Although cooled by breezes from the Bay of Biscay, Armagnac is warmer than the cognac region and its grapes ripen earlier and more fully, thus making them more suitable raw material for wine than the more acid grapes of the cognac region.

The Armagnac grapes are also rather different. Although the dreary UGNI BLANC, which is ubiquitous in Cognac, is also widely planted in Armagnac, the region also retains a little of the decidedly superior FOLLE BLANCHE, a little also of the relatively aromatic COLOMBARD, and much more of the only hybrid allowed in any APPELLATION CONTRÔLÉE wine or spirit, BACO 22A, whose parents are Folle Blanche and the infamous and over-productive NOAH. Baco 22A will have to be phased out by the year 2010, but in the meantime provides the older spirits with a unique combination: the florality of the Folle Blanche and the rather foxy strength of the Noah.

Until the mid 19th century armagnac was distilled in tiny POT STILLS. But when Edouard Adam of Montpellier invented a type of CONTINUOUS STILL in the early 19th century, the Armagnacais immediately seized on its potential for producing greater, and thus more commercial quantities of spirit than their existing installations. It is this type which has come to be regarded as the traditional still in the region. Nevertheless armagnac is distilled today in a variety of ways: like cognac, twice in a copper pot still, in a number of different fashions in a Coffey still, each of them regarded as traditional: truly continuously; or semi-continuously, with the *secondes*, or heavier elements, returned to the still to be redistilled; or in a still with three or four plates which provides a semi-continuous flow, which is stopped only to enable the still to be emptied and cleaned.

A *bouilleur de cru* producing **armagnac** as a cottage industry.

In all the stills the wine is heated to between 92 and 93° C (199 °F), the point at which wine of 10 per cent alcohol boils (to get a higher-strength spirit you allow a slightly cooler wine). The strength of the final spirit depends on the number of plates in the still. The maximum is, say, 15, which will produce a spirit of 70 per cent alcohol, while the traditional still, with five plates, will produce a spirit of a mere 60 per cent alcohol.

The older stills had even fewer plates. They were also small, and rarely cleaned, and the spirit they produced was heady with congeners, especially if the wine was distilled only to 52 or 53 per cent alcohol. This made an enormous difference. Wine distilled to 52 per cent contains twice as much of the congener-heavy *queues*, or tails, than one distilled to the 60 per cent or so that is normal in modern stills, a difference in potential richness (and potential impurities) far greater than that between spirits distilled to 60 and the 70 per cent that is normal in the pot stills used for cognac.

As with cognac, however, after armagnac is distilled, wood maturation (see OAK AND BRANDY) is the essential next step in production and the spirit is generally left to mature in cask until being bottled. Younger armagnac, like almost all cognac, is 'broken down' with water to the commercial selling strength of 40 per cent, but some older armagnacs are bottled at cask strength.

Armagnacs made in the old form still were hardly drinkable under 10 years old and, in the view of the writer, are at their best after 40 years or so. Unfortunately, the producers often kept them in old wood too long, so many of the older armagnacs on the market are far too woody. But this is an uncommon problem with armagnac. By a quirk of French law, armagnac, which matures so much more slowly than cognac, can be sold even younger, from two years (as opposed to three for cognac), while five-year-old armagnacs can be labelled VO, VSOP, or Réserve, and six-year-old armagnacs qualify as Extra, Napoléon, XO, Vieille Réserve, or indeed any other name which takes the producer's fancy.

Unfortunately the fortunes of this incomparable spirit have suffered a number of set-backs in the century since it shared in the general popularity enjoyed by all French wines and spirits in the middle of the 19th century. First came that universal plague, PHYLLOXERA. In Armagnac the devastation was complete, the recovery minimal. By 1937, after the worst of the world economic slump, the region was producing a mere 22,000 hl/581,000 gal of spirit annually, a quarter of the pre-phylloxera level. There were two false dawns, after each of the two world wars. The recovery after the First World War was minimal, so the let-down was not dramatic. But the surge of sales immediately after 1945 was dramatic—and dramatically short lived because too much young armagnac was sold in the immediate post-war years (inevitably at low prices). The result was to give armagnac a lasting reputation as a poor relation of cognac.

In the 1950s and 1960s a number of cognac houses established themselves in the region, took one look at the situation, and decided that the major problem lay precisely in the time it took for brandy distilled by traditional armagnac methods to mature. So, in the early 1970s, after a struggle with the authorities, they were allowed to introduce their own pot stills. As can be imagined, these do indeed produce a more acceptable, if rather characterless armagnac which needs fewer years in wood. But it is too early to judge if these brandies mature as well.

The extent of this cognac-inspired experimentation was limited, and did not affect the bulk of armagnac production. It had the beneficial effect, however, of encouraging the native armagnac producers to experiment with their own type of continuous stills, trying to retain the characteristic richness of flavour, while losing some of the impurities traditionally associated with it. Such experiments can be conducted effectively on a limited scale because most armagnacs not made by the very few major firms such as Janneau, Sempé, and Clé des Ducs are actually distilled by a core of specialists who distil on behalf of individual growers. These specialist distillers are far more responsible for the style of the region's brandies than are the individual proprietors who mature and sell the resulting spirit. The more reputable houses naturally mature their brandies for longer than the legal minimum, but this does not help greatly. A more rational (if inevitably less immediately profitable) policy would have been to prevent the sale of armagnacs less than five years old.

In the 1970s and 1980s armagnac's reputation was greatly helped by Armagnac's ability to offer the single-VINTAGE spirits that were not then permitted by the cognac regulations. Armagnac producers were able to offer a seemingly limitless supply of single-vintage brandies, most of which include a majority of spirits distilled within a few years of the date on the bottle. The cynicism of this judgement is justified because few producers have enough casks of any particular vintage to top up these casks through the years. The Armagnac authorities have been working on the sort of strict regulatory framework established in Cognac in 1989 for vintage-dated spirits. The fault may, however, lie more with buyers' insistance, say, on brandy from their birth year, rather than with the armagnacs themselves, which, in most cases, are worthy of the charming region from which they spring.

N.F.

Faith, N., *Nicholas Faith's Guide to Cognac & Other Brandies* (London, 1992).

Samalens, J., and Samalens, G., *Armagnac*, ed. and embellished by J. Goolden (London, 1980).

ARMAZÉM, Portuguese word literally meaning warehouse or store. In the towns of Vila Nova da Gaia (see OPORTO) and Funchal (see MADEIRA), armazém are the long, low LODGES where PORT and madeira are left to age.

ARMENIA, relatively small mountainous, inland CIS republic on TURKEY's north east border. One of the oldest viticultural regions, its altitude compensates for its latitude, which is five to seven degrees more southerly than the famous vineyards of France. It specializes in high-strength white wines and brandies, but is not today one of the more important CIS wine producers.

History

The Transcaucasian region, including Armenia, is one of the world's oldest centres of viticulture. Ancient Armenia was much bigger than modern Armenia and in classical times included much of eastern Turkey, AZERBAIJAN, and GEORGIA in the area between the Black Sea and the Caspian Sea. The vine was an indigenous plant in the valleys of Armenia, where the climate was particularly suitable for it. The wild vine *Vitis vinifera silvestris* (ancestor of the cultivated VINIFERA vine species) was established there over a million years ago. Carbonized or petrified grape pips have been found at several Neolithic sites in the Caucasus, especially on the western (Black Sea) side. See PALAEOETHNOBOTANY and ORIGINS OF VITICULTURE.

Archaeological evidence has also revealed irrigation canals, wine cellars with processing facilities, and large clay jugs (*karas*). Raisins and grape seeds reminiscent of the varieties Voskeat, Makhali, and Garandmak cultivated today in the Ararat plain south west of Erevan were unearthed during excavations of the Teishebaini fortress from the 10th century BC. Wine cups and SULPHUR sticks used in the 7th century BC were also found in the fortress.

Argishti I (785–753 BC), the king of Urartu (an ancient state which is regarded by modern Armenians as a predecessor of their homeland), made his capital Tushpa into a pleasant garden city planted with vineyards. An inscription of his descendant Rusa II (680–639 BC), who built Teishebaini (modern Karmir Blur), states, 'By command of the god Haldi I have planted these vineyards.' At Teishebaini wine cellars were excavated, with rows of *pithoi* (large ceramic wine jars) buried up to the neck and stamped with the year of production and the quality of the wine. Herodotus (*Histories* I. 194, see Ancient GREECE) described the river trade on the Tigris carried on by merchants operating from Armenia all the way downstream by the ASSYRIANS. Transported on circular leather-covered rafts (like the modern *gufas* which could until recently still be seen on the river) was wine (*oinos* and therefore made from grapes; see WINE, etymology) in what he described as palm-wood casks.

But the Ancient Armenians fermented more than grapes. XENOPHON (*Anabasis* 4. 5. 26) describes how during his epic journey through the Near East he found in Armenia villages, 'also wheat, barley and beans; and barley-wine in *kraters* [see CRATER]. The actual grains of barley floated level with the brim, and reeds of various lengths but without nodes were in the bowls. When you were thirsty, you had to put one of these in your mouth and suck. It was a very strong wine, unless you mixed it with water. Once you got used to it, it was a very pleasant drink.'

Old manuscripts confirm Armenia's high level of viticultural development, yet this art often suffered periods of decline due to war and Arab, Turkish, and Persian invasions (see ISLAM).

By the end of the 19th century Armenia's viticulture was on a small scale. In 1913 vineyards covered 9,200 ha/22,700 acres and wine and brandy production was 18,800 hl/496,300 gal and 4,800 hl/126,700 gal respectively. After the First World War the vineyard area was reduced to 5,100 ha. In that period the average area of a peasant farm was just 1 ha.

In the 1920s private wineries were nationalized and amalgamated into the large Ararat wine trust, which later established a network of wine-processing plants in RUSSIA and in UKRAINE.

In 1940 the vineyard area reached 16,300 ha, the wine and brandy production being 104,800 and 6,600 hl, respectively. In the post-war period grape culture was developed mainly on land that had not been cultivated before, and specialized state farms were established based on collective farms. By 1990 Armenia had 29,000 ha of vineyards.

Modern viticulture

Bounded by the Small Caucasus in the north and east and by the narrow Ararat plain in the south west, Armenia grows vines commercially at an altitude of 400 to 1,700 m (1,300–5,580 ft). The average annual temperature fluctuates in the range of 9.2 to 14.3 °C (48.5–57.7 °F), the average January temperature is 0.3–0.6 °C (Megri and Debedashen) to 5.5–6.4 °C (Ararat plain); the average July temperature is 21 to 26 °C. The active temperature summation is 2,500 to 4,000 °C. The climate varies vertically; it is dry and continental to dry subtropical, the annual rainfall being less than 500 mm/19 in.

Armenia has five viticultural zones: the Ararat plain (65 per cent of vineyards and most of the wineries), the foothills above the Ararat plain (18 per cent), the Daralagez zone (three per cent), the Zangezur zone (two per cent), and the north east zone (12 per cent, on grafted vines). Climatic differences are found within each zone as a direct result of altitude, exposition of slopes, relief, and the water table. These zones suffer much from late spring and autumn FROSTS, which can reach −17 °C (0 °F) even in the middle of November, when vines are not sufficiently cold hardened to withstand them.

Vineyards equipped for both WINTER PROTECTION and IRRIGATION account for about 85 per cent of the total vine area. Vine-training systems are vertical trellises with the most common being fan-shaped from a point just above ground level. Frost-resistant varieties are being introduced in commercial culture, however, so that the area of high-trunked vineyards is increasing.

Forty-eight recognized grape varieties (30 wine varieties among them) are cultivated on a commercial scale in Armenia. The largest areas are planted to such wine varieties as Voskeat, Garandmak, Mekhali, RKATSITELI, Kakhet, Areni Cherny, and Adisi. Table grape varieties occupy 10 per cent of vineyards.

Armenia's wine industry specializes in the production of strong wines and brandy. Small quantities of table wines are produced, mostly for local consumption. Wineries are mainly in the Ararat valley and in the hills just above it, and produced 150,000 hl/3.9 million gal of wine from 29,000 ha/71,600 acres of vineyard in 1990. J.A.B. & V.R.

Arzumanian, P. R., 'The Soviet Socialist Republic of Armenia' (Russian), in A. I. Timush (ed.), *Encyclopaedia of Viticulture* (Kishinev, 1986).

Piotrovski, B. B., and Janpoladian, L. M., 'Viticulture in Urartu' (Russian), *Vinodelie i vinogradarstvo SSSR*, 1 (1956), 23–6.

ARMILLARIA ROOT ROT, world-wide FUNGAL DISEASE which lives in woody plant materials in the soil and attacks a wide range of plants including vines. It is sometimes called the mushroom, oak, or shoestring root rot. It is frequently a problem on land where vines have replaced trees. Infected vines occur typically in groups and slowly decline or sometimes die suddenly. The causal fungus, *Armillaria mellea*, produces white fungal mats with a distinct mushroom-like smell under the bark of the vine's lower trunk and roots. The land can be fumigated to ward off this fungus, for which there are no tolerant rootstocks. R.E.S.

ARNALDUS DE VILLANOVA, sometimes called **Arnaud de Villeneuve**, was a Catalan who died in 1311. He taught medicine at MONTPELLIER, the most important medical school, with Salerno, in medieval Europe. He had an eventful life, attending the sick beds of popes and kings and engaging in theological controversy. He was an influential physician, and his writings were still reprinted in the 16th century.

Arnaldus is not interested in wine for its own sake: his concern is with the medical proprieties of wine (see MEDICINE). One of his books, the *Liber de vinis* ('Book on Wines'), deals exclusively with wine as medicine, but references to wine appear throughout his works. The *Liber de vinis* is short: in the 16th century editions of the complete works it occupies no more than 10 folio pages. To a modern reader it is bound to appear a strange mixture: Galen and the Arab philosopher Avicenna; alchemy and astrology; some first-hand observation. Arnaldus' medicine draws heavily on the voluminous writings of Galen (129–99 BC), physician to the Emperor Marcus Aurelius, but Galen was a far better scientist. Galen wrote in Greek, but knowledge of Greek was rare in the medieval west: some of his works were, however, translated into Arabic and thence into Latin. Through Moorish SPAIN, Arabic influence on European influence was strong: hence Arnaldus' references to Avicenna and other Arabic authors.

Arnaldus praises wine as a remedy against melancholy and says that it is good for the liver, the urinary tract, and the veins, because it purifies the blood. He recommends it to the old, especially in winter, because it warms the kidneys as well as the entire body, it reduces the swelling of haemorrhoids, it is beneficial to digestion, gives one a healthy complexion, comforts the mind, and, best of all, slows down the greying of one's hair. Most of his remedies, however, do not involve the drinking of neat or watered wine. He uses wines FLAVOURED with rosemary or borage, recipes which go back to classical antiquity and which were supposed to cure a wide variety of ills; he exploits the antiseptic quality of wine for making poultices and, since the water was not usually reliable, to dissolve other medical substances.

One would not have been safe in Arnaldus' hands. An aside about making wine is spot on, however: the wooden casks in which wine was kept should be clean and free of odours, the grapes should mature properly, and any unripe grapes must be discarded.

He is popularly credited with introducing the first still to France, probably from Salerno, and George (1990) notes that he was granted a patent for his discovery of MUTAGE (which spawned wines such as those now known as VINS DOUX NATURELS) in 1299 from the powerful king of Majorca.

H.M.W.

George, R., *French Country Wines* (London, 1990).

Lucia, S. P., *A History of Wine as Therapy* (New York, 1963).

Sigerist, H. E., *The Earliest Printed Book on Wine* (New York, 1943).
Thorndike, L., *A History of Magic and Experiential Science* 7 vols. (New York and London, 1923–57) ii. 841–61.

ARNEIS, white grape variety and dry, scented VARIETAL wine of PIEDMONT in north west Italy. Originally from ROERO, where it may be used to soften the dark NEBBIOLO in red wines, it is also sometimes called BAROLO Bianco, or white Barolo, by some of its more fervent admirers. Although the wine has a certain history in Piedmont, it seemed on the verge of disappearing in the early 1970s when only two houses, Vietti and Bruno Giacosa, were bottling Arneis. In the 1980s, however, thanks to growing demand for white wine in Piedmont, particularly from houses more renowned for their important reds such as Barolo and BARBARESCO, there was an explosion of interest in Arneis, although total plantings are still very limited. The wine received DOC status in 1989 and production is rising towards an annual total of 2 million bottles, as consumers have come to appreciate its herbaceous aromas and the almond flavours on the palate and after-taste. If Arneis, at its best, can undoubtedly be a pleasing wine, it suffers from a lack of acidity when the grapes ripen properly and an inability, in the vast majority of cases, to age well. By the early 1990s demand had slackened, and grape prices dropped by more than 50 per cent between 1990 and 1992, raising the question of whether Arneis is truly here to stay or merely a passing fancy. DOC regulations also permit a sparkling Arneis, virtually never encountered; experiments with a PASSITO version have given interesting initial results.
D.T.

Anderson, B., *The Wine Atlas of Italy* (London and New York, 1990).
Gleave, D., *The Wines of Italy* (London and New York, 1989).

AROMA, imprecise tasting term for a smell that is relatively simple such as that of a grape, fermenting MUST, or young wine. The word comes originally from Greek and its original meaning was 'spice'. Its meaning has evolved so that in generally current English it means 'pleasant smell' (as opposed to odours which may be distinctly nasty). Wine-tasting professionals tend to use the word aroma to distinguish the smells associated with young wines from the word BOUQUET, which is used for the more complex flavour compounds which result from extended BOTTLE AGE. In Australia the word aroma is often used to refer specifically to VARIETAL characteristics rather than those associated with wine-making. Those who distinguish between aroma and bouquet differ in the point in a wine's life cycle which divides use of the two terms. For tasters schooled at BORDEAUX UNIVERSITY, bouquet includes fermentation smells, for example, as well as all those associated with oak ageing and bottle ageing. Others, particularly Burgundians, may refer to grape aromas and primary aromas, fermentation and oak ageing aromas as secondary aromas, and bottle ageing aromas as either tertiary aromas or bouquet. See also AROMA WHEEL, FLAVOUR COMPOUNDS, and ESTER.
A.D.W.

AROMA COMPOUNDS. See FLAVOUR COMPOUNDS.

AROMATIZED WINES. See FLAVOURED WINES.

AROMA WHEEL, graphical representation of TASTING terms used for AROMA, devised at the University of California at DAVIS by Ann C. Noble and others in the early 1980s. Her research into sensory evaluation of wine had indicated that there was no general agreement either on terminology or on its application. The aroma wheel was developed to provide a lexicon which can be used to describe wine aroma in non-judgemental terms, grouping specific terms which can be defined to provide a basis for communication. In its attempt at clarification and categorization it provides, and is widely used in the wine industry, a good basis on which tasting terms for aroma can be taught to novices. With experience, however, most individuals use many precise descriptive terms which are not on the aroma wheel. The aroma wheel does not include judgemental terms (such as 'elegant' and 'supple') which are necessary for overall assessment of wine quality.

Noble, A. C., Arnold, R. A., Buechsenstein, J., Leach, E. J., Schmidy, J. O., and Stern, P. M., 'Modification of a standardized system of wine aroma terminology', *American Journal of Enology and Viticulture*, 38/2 (1987).

ARRÁBIDA. The Serra da Arrábida range of limestone hills are the main feature on the SETÚBAL peninsula between the Tagus and Sado estuaries in southern PORTUGAL whose warm, maritime climate is well suited to wine-making (see map on p. 750).

In the 19th century the north facing slopes around the village of Azeitão were planted with a number of different Moscatel (MUSCAT) grape varieties to make sweet, fortified Setúbal but, since this wine has declined in popularity, other varieties have taken their place.

Although there are many individual growers, production is largely concentrated in the hands of two firms, José Maria da FONSECA Successores in Azeitão and João Pires just outside the district at Pinhal Novo. In the 1980s two skilled OENOLOGISTS, trained respectively at DAVIS in California and ROSEWORTHY in Australia, helped to modernize wine-making in Arrábida and other parts of southern Portugal. As a result of experiments that were partly inspired by the NEW WORLD, Arrábida produces a wide range of different wines. The most important red grapes are the indigenous varieties CASTELÃO FRANCES (here nicknamed Periquita), ESPADEIRO, and Monvedro but imported varieties such as Cabernet Sauvignon and Merlot are making inroads. MUSCAT OF ALEXANDRIA (called Moscatel de Setúbal locally) is the most significant white variety, together with ARINTO and ESGAÑA Cão. Chardonnay, Riesling, and Gewürtraminer have also been grown successfully.

Arrábida was officially designated an IPR in 1990 but as most of the wines are sold with well-established brand names, producers are less than eager to adopt the new legislation.

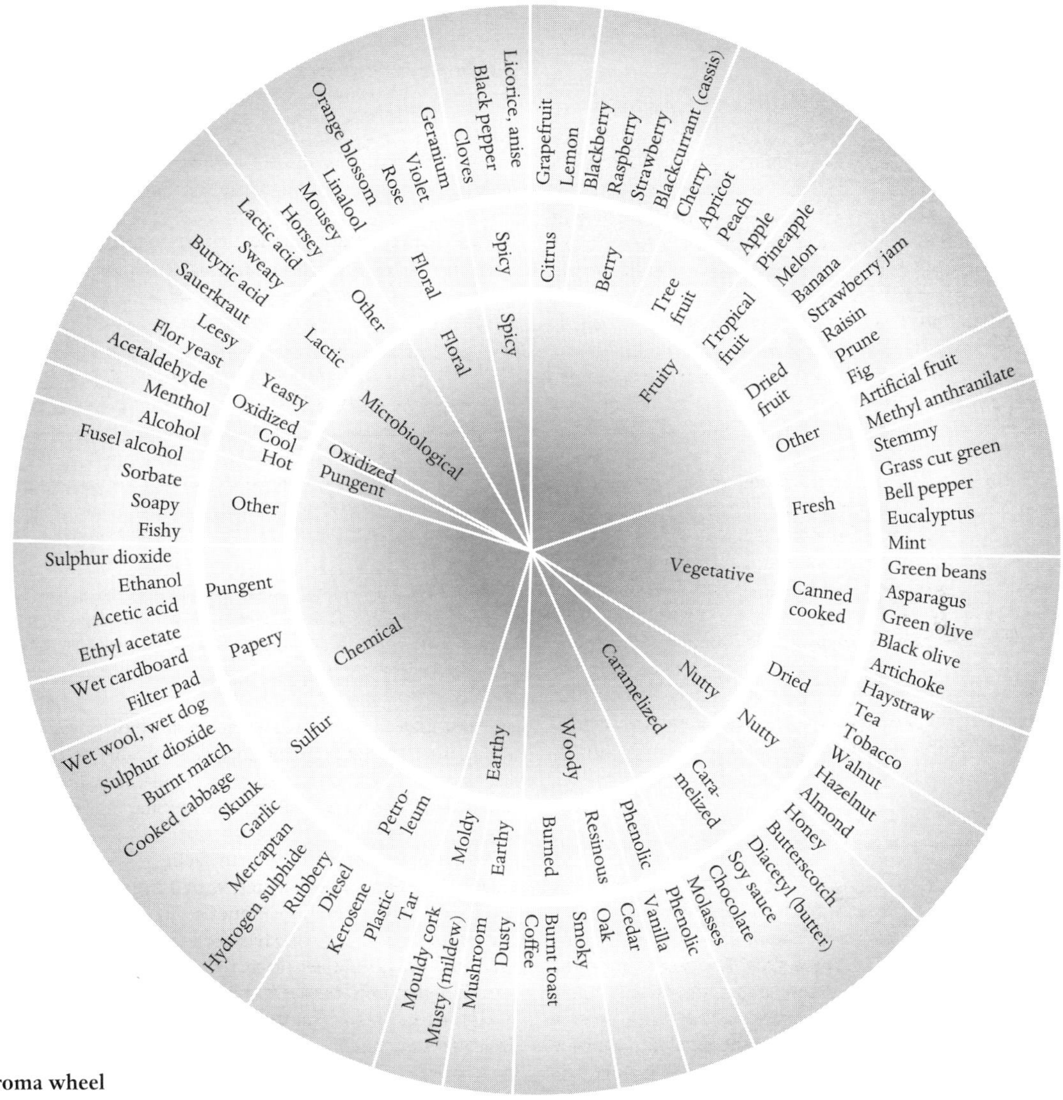

Aroma wheel

See also PALMELA, another recently demarcated region on the Setúbal peninsula.

R.J.M.

ARRACHAGE, French term for RIPPING OUT vines. The *prime d'arrachage*, payment for participating in the European VINE PULL SCHEME became a topic of much discussion in southern France in the late 1980s.

ARROPE, a syrup used for sweetening wine in Spain, especially SHERRY, made by boiling down and concentrating unfermented grape juice. See GRAPE CONCENTRATE.

ARROYO GRANDE. California wine region and AVA. See SAN LUIS OBISPO.

ARROYO SECO. California wine region and AVA. See MONTEREY.

ARRUDA, an IPR in western Portugal. See OESTE for more details.

ARRUFIAC or **Arrufiat.** See RUFFIAC.

ARTISTS' LABELS, wine LABELS illustrated by works of art, often a different one for each vintage. Baron Philippe de ROTHSCHILD instituted this custom at Ch MOUTON-ROTHSCHILD for the 1945 vintage, with the result that COLLECTORS may seek particular missing labels, thereby adding value even to Mouton-Rothschild in earlier maturing vintages (of which most bottles tend to have been opened).

En hommage à Francis Bacon
qui offrit à Mouton l'une de ses dernières oeuvres
Francis Bacon
1990
Philippine de Rothschild
toute la récolte a été mise
en bouteilles au Château
Château
Mouton Rothschild
PAUILLAC
12.5% Vol.
75 cl
APPELLATION PAUILLAC CONTROLEE
Baronne Philippine de Rothschild g.f.a.
PRODUCE OF FRANCE
PROPRIETAIRE

Artists' labels: The 1990 Ch Mouton-Rothschild label incorporates one of Francis Bacon's last paintings.

ASCORBIC ACID, vitamin C, one of the first VITAMINS to be discovered, and a wine-making additive used chiefly as an antioxidant. As well as being essential to man's diet, it is involved in plant metabolic processes. The green grape contains significant levels of vitamin C but much is lost during fruit ripening and later wine-making operations. In a wine context, ascorbic acid is of chief importance not to the wine drinker but to the wine-maker as a permitted additive, within limits, for its ability to prevent OXIDATION. It is added chiefly to light white wines, at the same time as SULPHUR DIOXIDE, and the resulting antioxidant couple has played an important part in enabling fresh white wines to be made in the NEW WORLD. Erythorbic or iso-ascorbic acid is often used, especially in Australia, as a less expensive alternative to ascorbic acid. A.D.W. & T.J.

ASEPTIC BOTTLING. See STERILE BOTTLING.

ASIA MINOR, much of modern TURKEY, the land lying between the Black Sea and the Mediterranean.

In Ancient Asia Minor grapes were harvested in September and October. In business documents of the Old ASSYRIAN trading colonies in Asia Minor (dating to approximately the 19th century BC) this season of the year was called *qitip karānim*, or 'grape picking'. The location of the ancient vine-growing areas is uncertain, although they may well have been, as today, along the four great river valleys north of Adana, in the vicinities of Niğde, Nevşehir, Kayseri, Yozgat, and Sungurlu in central Turkey, towns which lie in a line between the east coast of the Black Sea and the east coast of the Mediterranean.

Among the Hittites, the Anatolian civilization in western Turkey in the second millennium BC, a grape harvesting festival took place every year. Viticulture was certainly important during the Hittite Old Kingdom (*c.*18th–15th centuries BC). The king's merit in the eyes of the storm god (who was regarded as the owner of the land) was reflected in the produce of the vineyards and in grain and livestock production. Wine was under the control of royal officials who distributed 'good wine' to certain pensioners (who complained when the quality was not satisfactory). Certain officials during the Old Kingdom bore a title which can be translated as 'wine chief', originally supervisor of the vineyards but later an exalted military rank comparable with general or field marshal.

In Hittite laws (also of the Old Kingdom) the price of grapes was regulated, together with the prices of barley and emmer (a species of wheat). One law makes provisions for damage caused to vines: the offender has to take the damaged vine himself and let the plaintiff take grapes from one of his own good vines at harvest time.

Another law prescribes penalties for the theft of a vine: six shekels for a free man, three if the offender was a slave. Previously the fine was lower, but the offender had been obliged to undergo corporal punishment in addition. Six shekels was also the fine for a free man who damaged another's vine by fire.

Viticultural images were used in ritual magic. In an archaic ritual performed during the foundation of a new palace, for example: 'They lay out a vine tendril and say, "Just as the vine puts down roots and sends up tendrils, so may the king and queen put down roots and send up tendrils!"'

Similarly in so-called 'vanishing god' texts we read: 'O Telepinu [a god of agriculture], hold goodness in your mind and heart, just as the grape holds wine in its heart!' J.A.B.

Hoffner, H. A., jr., *Alimenta Hethaeorum: Food Production in Hittite Asia Minor*, American Oriental Series 55 (New Haven, Conn., 1974).

ASPECT, the direction in which a slope faces, an important characteristic of any vineyard site that is not completely flat. For more details, see TOPOGRAPHY.

ASPERGILLUS. Vine disease. See BUNCH ROTS.

ASPIRAN, very old dark-skinned grape variety of the LANGUEDOC which once represented about a quarter of all vines planted in the Hérault *département*, but was not replanted on any great scale after PHYLLOXERA because it is not particularly productive. It yields limited quantities of light but perfumed red wine and is a permitted grape variety in MINERVOIS.

Assemblage, French word for the important operation in the production of fine wines of deciding which lots will be assembled to make up the final blend. It plays a crucial role in SPARKLING WINE-MAKING when some CUVÉES may be assembled from several hundred different components. Here the complementary nature of each component is of great importance, as is, for NON-VINTAGE wines, adherence to a house style.

Assemblage is of almost ritual significance in BORDEAUX, where many CHÂTEAUX make their so-called GRAND VIN carrying the château name by selecting and BLENDING only the best lots. The rejected lots may either be blended together to make a SECOND WINE (and occasionally even a third wine) or be sold off in bulk to a NÉGOCIANT carrying only the local APPELLATION (Margaux or St-Julien, for example).

This selection process typically takes place between the third and sixth month after the HARVEST (much later in SAUTERNES) and involves the MAÎTRE-DE-CHAI (wine-maker), any OENOLOGIST regularly working for the property, and the proprietor who must bear the considerable financial sacrifice of exclusions from the *grand vin*, which may sell for three or more times the price of the associated second wine. It is at this stage that a decision is taken over whether to incorporate any PRESS WINE.

The normal procedure is to taste samples from each *cuve* or FERMENTATION VESSEL and then simply decide whether it is of sufficiently high quality for the *grand vin*. It is assumed that any blend of wines from the same property is likely to be harmonious. In most other Old World wine regions, especially BURGUNDY, holdings are too small to allow this selectivity, although Chave of HERMITAGE is notable for keeping lots from different parcels of vineyard separate until a final assembly just before bottling.

In the New World such a process is likely to involve the assembly of blends of various different quality levels and character. In this case there may be extensive experiments with small samples of each lot known as bench blending before final blends are decided upon. In this case the wine-maker is concerned not just with each lot's inherent quality but also with its affinity with other components in the blend.

Assyria was for the writers of Ancient GREECE the whole area between the mountains of Ancient ARMENIA and Ancient PERSIA and the Syro-Arabian desert: the viticulturally important area dominated by the rivers Tigris and Euphrates and also called MESOPOTAMIA. The ancient kingdom at the centre of the Assyrian Empire covered the northern part of Mesopotamia with its capital at Assur (*c*.1000–612 BC). H.H.A.

Assyrtiko, top-quality white grape variety grown increasingly widely in GREECE. Its origins lie on the island of SANTORINI but its ability to retain acidity in a hot climate have encouraged successful experimentation with it elsewhere, notably on the north eastern mainland around Halkidiki. It may also help to compensate for the relatively low acidity of the SAVATIANO grape grown widely in Attica.

Asti, town and province in PIEDMONT in north west Italy whose name appears in those of fruity local VARIETAL wines made from the likes of BARBERA, DOLCETTO, FREISA, GRIGNOLINO, MALVASIA, and MOSCATO D'ASTI, which is the superior version of the famous ASTI SPUMANTE (both of which are produced in a much wider area than the province of Asti).

Asti Spumante, light, sweet SPUMANTE which, like the superior MOSCATO D'ASTI, is produced from the MOSCATO Bianco grape in the provinces of Asti, Cuneo, and Alessandria. The total area cultivated, which was 92,000 ha/227,000 acres worked by 80,000 vine-growers in the early 1960s, had 30 years later declined to 40,000 ha worked by 37,000 growers. This contraction of the cultivated surface and of the manpower working has not been mirrored by a dramatic fall in wine produced, however, since most of the land that has gone out of production has been in marginal sites, while the remaining vineyard surface is more energetically exploited.

As a blended wine produced in extremely large quantities (nearly 650,000 hl/17 million gal per year, by far the largest single Italian DOC, more than half as much again as SOAVE, Italy's second most important DOC), Asti Spumante is dominated by the large commercial houses of PIEDMONT, most if not all clustered around the town of Canelli, where production of Asti Spumante began in the 1850s. The 18 largest houses control approximately 80 per cent of the total production, which has now surpassed 75 million bottles per year according to official figures, the great majority of them exported. The combination of large-volume production and small-scale viticulture has necessarily made Asti Spumante a blended wine from many sources, a fact which has tended to mask the significant quality differences from zone to zone and the different characteristics of the Moscato Bianco grape in a variety of TERROIRS. Thus far the NÉGOCIANT houses, unlike their counterparts in CHAMPAGNE, have shown no interest in any demarcation of subzones or of separate bottlings of wine of distinctive or superior provenances. A certain blandness and uniformity in the final product has been the inevitable result, but the striking commercial success of Asti Spumante has created little incentive to change what appears to be a winning formula.

Asti Spumante differs significantly from its cousin, Moscato d'Asti: its ALCOHOLIC STRENGTH is higher (between 7 and 9.5 per cent against the maximum 5.5 per cent of Moscato d'Asti), as is its FIZZINESS (3.5–4 atmospheres of pressure in the bottle against a maximum of one atmosphere in Moscato d'Asti). As a more alcoholic wine with a smaller quantity of RESIDUAL SUGAR, Asti Spumante should, in theory, taste drier than Moscato d'Asti; in practice, the sweetness is even more marked due to the less pronounced aromas and flavours that are the inevitable result of blending, and to a significant use of base material from zones that have been planted more to supply the needs of the négociant houses than for any verifiable aptitude for producing fine Moscato.

In 1994 Asti Spumante was elevated to DOCG status and renamed **Asti**. D.T.

ATHENAEUS (flourished *c.*AD 200), early gastronomic chronicler, was born in Naucratis, a Greek city in the Nile Delta in Egypt, and wrote in Greek. Nothing is known about his life, and his surviving work, the *Deipnosophistae*, meaning 'The masters of the art of dining', can be dated only from internal evidence. It describes at length how 23 men dine together in Ancient ROME and records their conversations, which are mainly about food. Two of the participants are the physician Galen and the lawyer Ulpian of Tyre; the others are not based on real persons. The work consists of 15 books, but the first two and part of the third survive only in excerpts.

Although it is largely a collection of quotations from earlier literature, it contains a great deal of information about the kinds of wine that were available in Athenaeus' day, where they were grown, which were most highly regarded, what they looked like, whether they were sweet or dry, and other characteristics. When the *Deipnosophistae* was written, Italian wine was generally regarded as superior to Greek wine: hence Athenaeus is interested mainly in the Italian wines of his own time and not so much in the famous Greek wines of the past. In his opinion, the best wines were FALERNIAN and Alban. Falernian needs a minimum of 10 years' ageing, is best after 15 to 20, and, if any older, gives headaches. Alban is best at 15 years old. CAECUBAN, highly acclaimed by PLINY, is no longer held in high regard: all Athenaeus says about it is that it is heavy and overpowering and needs many years. He mentions that Falernian can be sweet or dry, whereas in Pliny's day good wine appears to be sweet. H.M.W.

AUBANCE, COTEAUX DE L', small but excellent sweet white wine appellation in Anjou on the left bank of the river Loire just south of the town of Angers and immediately north of Coteaux du LAYON. It takes its name from the Aubance, a tributary of the Loire. Total production is hardly more than that of SAVENNIÈRES across the river to the west, but the best results come from Chenin planted on outcrops of heat-retaining SLATE. The standard of wine-making is high, and a high proportion of the racy, sweet white Chenin Blanc wines made here are snapped up locally or in Paris. Red and dry white ANJOU make up the bulk of production in this zone, but Coteaux de l'Aubance can be just as noble as the Loire's more famous sweet whites, and must owe their sweetness to a succession of TRIES through the vineyard, picking only the ripest grapes, a discipline, unusually, overseen by the INAO. According to the vintage, the wines may be BOTRYTIZED, as in 1990, or partly raisined on the vine. The wines must have a RESIDUAL SUGAR level of at least 17 g/l; any lower and they must be declassified to Anjou Blanc.

See also LOIRE and map on pp. 576–7.

AUBUN is a not especially distinguished black-berried vine variety of the southern Rhône (not to be confused with the almost extinct Moselle white-berried Aubin). After a strange increase in popularity noted by the French agricultural census of 1979, it is now in decline but was still among France's top twenty red wine vines in the early 1990s.

In the vineyard it looks extremely similar to COUNOISE, which is officially approved as an ingredient in many appellations of the southern Rhône, eastern Languedoc, and Provence (including CHÂTEAUNEUF-DU-PAPE), whereas Aubun is not recognized by the INAO authorities. The wine it produces is a sort of softer, lesser CARIGNAN but it also yields well and buds late, offering good resistance to spring frosts. It is found in the southern Rhône, Gard, and the Aude, but is being systematically pulled up as a vine with no useful future for quality wine production.

Aubun (and Counoise) formed part of the vine collection imported into Australia by James BUSBY and isolated plantings can still be found there.

AUCTIONS of wine are the sale of wine by lots by an auctioneer acting as agent for the seller or, in certain instances, as the seller in his own right.

History

Auctions have long been an integral a part of the wine TRADE. Wine was sold by auction in Ancient ROME and, in the Middle Ages, before it became commonplace for buyers to visit wine regions, wine shipped in barrel to its final destination (see CONTAINERS) was frequently sold by auction as well as by private contract. In Britain, wine auctions were common at trading ports such as Leith in Edinburgh, Scotland, where the auction room in The Vaults testifies to a once lively auction trade in casks of fine bordeaux. In Germany, the practice of selling wine by auction under the names of village and vintage became well established in the 18th century. The Nassauer'sche Domäne in the Rheingau was among the first to initiate the movement towards establishing conditions of sale by auction in the 1830s.

As wine trading became increasingly competitive with improved transportation and more sophisticated communications, the need for producers to sell their wine by auction diminished. Whereas historically wine auctions were used as a means of selling young or relatively young wine in barrel, today's commercial auction trade relies on bottled wines at all stages of maturity. Once wine was packaged in BOTTLES stoppered with CORKS from the end of the 17th century, it became capable of BOTTLE AGEING and full maturation. With, literally, a new lease of life for fine wine, exceeding decades and, in rare instances, even a century or more, fine wine transcended its previous status as a short-term commodity.

Once wine became capable of being traded across generations, it naturally attracted admirers, collectors, and investors (see INVESTMENT). It became something that, at its finest, could be regarded with the same admiration as a work of art or any other classic auction room collectible. Wine captured in bottle led to a market in older wines whose reputation, based on VINTAGE and name, created a comprehensible and measurable scale of values. More recently, the establishment of wine departments from the mid 1960s at Britain's leading auction houses, Christie's and Sotheby's, has provided a forum, not just for the acquisition and disposal of mature

Perhaps the most famous wine **auction** of all, the annual Hospices de Beaune sale of the new Burgundy vintage in late November.

wines, but also for a lively trade in younger wines. The wheel has turned full circle.

Some notable annual auctions

Nevertheless, traditional auctions survive, most notably that of the HOSPICES DE BEAUNE. This former medieval hospice in Burgundy derives a substantial proportion of income for the modern hospital associated with it from the sale of wines produced from vineyards given as bequests over the centuries. Every third Sunday in November, the Hospices holds an annual charity auction accompanied by a long weekend of gargantuan feasting and decadent celebration. At the traditional candle auction, lots named after the Hospices' benefactors, each comprising a number of new 228-l/60-gal barrels, are sold. The auction is unique in that not only is it a public stage for the NÉGOCIANTS of Beaune to demonstrate their magnanimity, but it also acts as a barometer of the market price for the new vintage in BURGUNDY. The success of the Hospices de Beaune auction in combining the sale of wines with the glare of publicity has been the role model for a number of latter-day imitators particularly in California, but also in other French towns such as LIMOUX.

In Germany at KLOSTER EBERBACH on the Rhine, Die Glorreiche Tage is a modern three-day event organized in the image of the Hospices de Beaune by the CHARTA group of Riesling producers around the traditional annual auction of German wines at this Cistercian abbey in the heart of the RHEINGAU. In South Africa, wine producer Nederburg enhanced its reputation for producing high-quality wines by establishing the Nederburg auction in 1965, at which small lots of its top bottlings are sold by auction. The Nederburg sale in turn spawned the annual auction of the Cape Independent Winemakers' Guild, a group of small growers that started selling small lots of its top wines at auction in 1985. In the United States, distillers Heublein established the first New World wine auction in Chicago in 1969. Since then a combination of strict licensing laws and distinct tax advantages to buyers have led to an American charity auction boom, although owing to the inflated prices paid, they cannot be taken as indicators of the market value of the wines.

The professionals

Christie's is the oldest established wine auctioneer. Wine was a prominent feature in James Christie's first sale on 5 December 1766 which, along with household furniture, jewellery, and firearms, included the sale of 'a large quantity of Madeira and high Flavour'd Claret, late the Property of Noble Personage (Deceas'd)'. Three years later, on 7 and 8 September, James Christie held his first sale entirely devoted to wine, a collection of 'Old Hock, Rich Burgundy, Calcavella

[Portugal's CARCAVELOS], Malaga and TENT, the property of Captain Fletcher from the West Indies'.

Today's commercial auction scene is dominated by regular sales conducted by the professional auction houses, Christie's and Sotheby's, whose headquarters are in London, although both houses hold occasional or one-off auctions in other countries. Commercial auctions are conducted in the United States, principally by Butterfield & Butterfield of San Francisco and the Chicago Wine Company, although restrictive licensing laws effectively limit the location of American wine auctions to the states of Illinois and California. Commercial auctions are also held to a certain extent in other countries, notably France, Belgium, Switzerland, and Australia, with occasional sales in Japan.

London is widely acknowledged as the hub of the wine auction trade world-wide. The healthy rivalry of Sotheby's and Christie's has helped to create a ready market and given both sellers and buyers the best chance to obtain a market price for their wines. Christie's established its wine department in 1966, when Michael BROADBENT was recruited from the Bristol wine merchant HARVEYS to build up the department to meet the demands of an increasingly specialized and sophisticated international market. The first auction of the new era was held on 11 October 1966 and the first season achieved sales amounting to £220,634. Not to be outdone, Sotheby's entered the fray in 1970, holding the first auction of their newly formed wine department on 16 September 1970 in Glasgow.

At this time, the combined turnover of the major London auction houses was £900,000. By the 1979/80 auction season, turnover had grown to £5 million and by the end of the 1980s, had registered a further increase to £13 million. An infrastructure of wine auction facilities from broking to warehousing has grown up around the two companies. The fact that customers can buy wines at market prices as well as store and ship them with the minimum of difficulty has drawn a dominant proportion of wine auction business through the London salerooms.

At the height of the investment boom of the 1980s, the Chicago Wine Company established a third major auction operation in London, International Wine Auctions, which was an offshoot of a wine investment company. But, as the economic situation deteriorated and a glut of fine wines came on to the market, International Wine Auctions stopped operating in the late 1980s. A small number of minor British auction houses hold occasional wine sales, notably Bonhams in London and a handful of British country auctioneers, among them Lacy Scott (Bury St Edmunds), Bigwood (Stratford-on-Avon), and J. Straker Chadwick (Abergavenny). Phillips of Oxford held wine auctions until 1991.

Trade structure

Broadly speaking, wine auction customers are split between private individuals and the wine trade. Private buyers may have any number of different reasons for buying wine, from buying for personal consumption, for collection of a certain wine, bottle size, or type of wine, or for INVESTMENT. Trade buyers may also buy for investment, to fill gaps in a restaurant or merchant wine list, or as BROKERS for trade or private clients. Reasons for selling wine vary equally. Private customers may want or need to sell in order to realize the value of their cellar, or part of it, or to finance further purchases, or as executors selling on behalf of an estate. The wine trade may sell to dispose of surplus or bankrupt stock.

For the 1992 auction season, Christie's, with the biggest of the auction houses' wine departments, conducted a survey into the profile of their suppliers and customers from both the United Kingdom and overseas. At their main branch at King Street, London, they found that private buyers made up 76 per cent of their trade by number although they accounted for only only 55 per cent of purchases by value. Trade buyers who numbered 24 per cent thus bought 45 per cent of lots by value.

Private cellars too accounted for the lion's share of their source of supplies with 77 per cent of private sellers accounting for 71 per cent of the value of the business. Exactly the same numbers of buyers as sellers, 75 per cent in both instances, were from the United Kingdom, although how many of those were buying or selling on behalf of overseas clients is more difficult to ascertain. Among overseas buyers, Americans have been consistent buyers in the London salerooms, with increasing interest from buyers from the Far East in the 1980s.

Wines traded

Red bordeaux, or CLARET, is the staple of the wine auction rooms, accounting for more than 60 per cent of saleroom throughput. It is long lived, enjoys widespread appeal, and it is in relatively plentiful supply. And the relative value of a particular red bordeaux is more readily identifiable than that of any other wine style, the 1855 CLASSIFICATION of bordeaux being the key to the most widely traded red bordeaux châteaux in the saleroom.

The five FIRST GROWTHS in wine's most prestigious classification are Chx LAFITE, LATOUR, MARGAUX, MOUTON-ROTHSCHILD, and HAUT-BRION. Although not considered as important at the time, St-Émilion's two top classified châteaux, AUSONE and CHEVAL BLANC, and Pomerol's unclassified Ch PÉTRUS, are undisputed members of this élite today. Owing to the classification's rigid composition, a secondary, informal leading group of properties has emerged, commonly referred to as SUPER SECONDS. Qualification for this group requires not only the strictest commitment to quality, but a record of consistent prices, at least since the 1960s, which reflects that policy.

Red bordeaux apart, vintage PORT is a saleroom regular, albeit on a far smaller scale, with TAYLOR, FONSECA, Graham, Warre, Dow, CROFT, COCKBORN, and Quinta do NOVAL the unofficial 'first growths', as it were, of a group of some 40 or more port houses. The legendary staying power of MADEIRA and Hungary's Imperial TOKAY ensures their regular appearance at auction. The remaining auction stalwarts are divided for the most part between the top wines of BURGUNDY, SAUTERNES, CHAMPAGNE, and GERMANY. In recent years, the fashion for the finest wines of the Rhône, HERMITAGE and CÔTE-RÔTIE, has seen an increase in popularity and prices, largely as a result of American demand. The wines of the New World have yet to make a big impact within the traditional trade, but once individual wines' track record for AGEING is more widely established, their appearance at auction is likely to become increasingly frequent.

Pre-phylloxera clarets, red bordeaux from the last century made before the devastation of the vineyards by the PHYLLOXERA louse, are among the most highly prized items in the sale catalogue. Unique *grands formats* (large bottles) of old vintages, particularly of first growths, are much sought after by collectors (see BOTTLE SIZE). Specific VINTAGES play an important part too, with the price of wines from consecutive years often fluctuating by a factor of three according to the reputation of the vintage. The greatest pre-war vintages of the 20th century are 1900, 1920, 1926, 1928, and 1929. In the immediate post-war period, 1945, 1947, and 1949 were a trio of great vintages. In the second half of the 20th century, 1953, 1959, 1961, and 1982 rank as the outstanding vintages, while 1985, 1986, 1989, and 1990 run them close.

Record prices

Red bordeaux is the consistent pace-setter for wine auction prices, with almost all the red wine records being held by these wines. The record price for a bottle of wine at auction was achieved at Christie's on 5 December 1985, when the late Malcolm Forbes, an American publishing magnate, paid £105,000 for a bottle of 1787 Ch Lafitte (*sic*). This bottle, said by its owner Hardy Rodenstock to have been found in a bricked-up cellar in Paris, and wheel-engraved with the markings '1787 Lafitte Th.J', was believed to have been a bottle of 1787 Ch Lafite belonging to Thomas JEFFERSON, the third president of the United States.

Although the circumstances surrounding the find of the cache have never been disclosed, this has not prevented two more of the so-called Jefferson bottles from achieving world records. A half-bottle of 1784 Ch Margaux was sold for 180,000 French francs (about £18,000 at the prevailing exchange rate) to the American publisher Marvin Shanken at the Vinexpo Wine Fair in Bordeaux in 1987, and in 1986 a world record was set for a bottle of white wine when a 1784 Ch d'Yquem was sold at Christie's to Iyad Shiblaq, a Jordanian collector, for £36,000. Other 20th century records include the equivalent of £9,350 for a 1924 impériale (an eight-bottle bottle) sold by Sotheby's in Geneva in 1984 and £13,000 for a case of 1961 Ch Pétrus sold by Sotheby's in 1991.

How to buy and sell at auction

The public forum of the auction room and the intrinsically competitive aspect of bidding for lots often creates an atmosphere of tension and excitement in the saleroom in which it is easy for inexperienced participants to get carried away. All the information required about a particular auction is contained in the auction catalogue, an increasingly glossy publication thanks to the rivalry between Christie's and Sotheby's. The catalogue contains details of the lots, estimated prices, conditions of sale, and other general information on such matters as FILL LEVELS, bottlings, delivery charges, premiums, and other additions to the hammer price such as value added tax and excise duties payable where applicable.

The wines to be sold are contained in numbered lots. Apart from a number and an estimated price band from lowest to highest, the description of each lot identifies the wine by name, bottle size, and vintage where applicable. The more reputable the auction house, the more it takes steps to guarantee the provenance of the wine to protect both the buyer and its own reputation. Given the importance of the condition of the wine, especially older wines, and since wines are not generally available for inspection, the catalogue specifies exact fill, or ULLAGE levels ('mid shoulder' or 'bottom neck', for example, levels illustrated in the catalogue), the condition of the LABEL, whether the wine comes in its own wooden CASE (sometimes abbreviated to 'owc.'), and will generally mention if a cellar is of exceptional pedigree or in previously undisturbed condition.

Auction house policy may vary on the condition of the wine to be sold. Sotheby's do not open original wooden cases, while Christie's do unless the wines are young. Pre-sale tastings are not the lavish affairs they once were, but limited pre-sale tastings are still the practice. Lots which are of special interest may be supplemented by the auctioneer's tasting notes. Bidding may be by hand or, more often today, by waving a numbered paddle to attract the auctioneer's attention. Bidding is, unless otherwise stated, per dozen bottles.

Advance commission bids form a substantial proportion of bids received. Both Christie's and Sotheby's estimate that they may receive anything from 800 to 2,000 commission bids per sale (which usually includes between 600 and 800 lots), but on average nearly two-thirds of lots are sold in the saleroom. Commission bids are treated in exactly the same way as bids in the room. The successful bidder obtains his lot at one increment above the underbidder. In the event of two commission bids of the same amount, it is the one received first that takes precedence. A.H.L.R.

AUSBRUCH, famous wine style of AUSTRIA, a speciality of the town of RUST on the Neusiedlersee in Burgenland. Ausbruch is a close etymological relative of Aszú, a term commonly used in TOKAY, where Hungary's most famous sweet wine is made. Tokay and Ausbruch were probably developed at very much the same time, probably in the late 17th century. Ausbruch is traditionally made by adding the juice of freshly picked grapes to that of, often FURMINT, grapes concentrated by NOBLE ROT, whose incidence is encouraged by the proximity of the shallow lake and the warm climate of the Pannonian plain. Modern Austrian wine law requires Ausbruch to be made entirely from grapes affected by noble rot which reach a MUST WEIGHT of 138 OECHSLE, but Furmint is only rarely grown.

AUSLESE, one of the riper Prädikats in the QMP quality wine category defined by the GERMAN WINE LAW. Auslese means literally 'selected harvest' and, from the 1994 vintage, the grapes should have been picked at least a week after a preliminary picking of less ripe grapes (until the 1994 vintage the less ripe SPÄTLESE was the only Prädikat for which this was explicitly required). Specific minimum MUST WEIGHTS are laid down for each combination of vine variety and region and the tendency is to increase them. At their best, these are sweet, often BOTRYTIZED wines which can be sold at lower prices than the even riper and considerably rarer BEERENAUSLESE and TROCKENBEERENAUSLESE Prädikats. (Auslese is usually better dedicated to SWEET WINES than TROCKEN as the resulting alcohol can be so high as to be out of BALANCE, and in any case NOBLE ROT character sits uneasily with dry wines.) Auslesen made from most of the new GERMAN CROSSINGS should be treated with suspicion as they rarely have the ACIDITY to balance the sweetness, but Riesling Auslesen can be some of Germany's finest and most characteristic wines, best savoured without food. They can last for decades.

See also AUSTRIA.

AUSONE, CHÂTEAU, minuscule but exceptionally fine estate on the edge of the town of ST-ÉMILION. Named in 1781 after the Roman poet Ausonius who certainly had a vineyard in the Gironde, but probably one facing the river GARONNE rather than in St-Émilion. Recorded in the 1868 Cocks et Feret's *Bordeaux et ses vins* (see LITERATURE OF WINE) as belonging to M. Cantenats, it then passed to a nephew, M. Lafargue, and then to his nephew, Edouard Dubois-Challon, who raised the reputation of the château to the leading position in St-Émilion up to the 1920s, when it was challenged by Ch CHEVAL-BLANC. Today 50 per cent is owned by Mme Dubois-Challon, widow of Edouard, and 50 per cent by M. Vauthier, who married Edouard's daughter Cécile. Of 12 premiers grands crus classés in the official CLASSIFICATION of St-Émilion in 1955, two were ranked 'A'—Ausone and Cheval-Blanc—the other 10 being ranked 'B'. From 1939 to the mid 1970s Ausone was not, with a few exceptional vintages, producing wines of the longevity of their 19th century predecessors. There has been a marked improvement since the arrival of a new RÉGISSEUR, Pascal Delbeck, in 1976.

The vineyard consists of a mere 7 ha / 18 acres—50 per cent MERLOT vines and 50 per cent CABERNET FRANC—on the steep slopes of the Côtes (see ST-ÉMILION) that run along the right bank of the DORDOGNE just below the town. The cellars are in deep limestone caves, originally excavated to provide stone for building the town. In 1916 the adjoining vineyard of Ch Belair was bought. The wines are made separately but matured in oak in the same cellars. Production of Ausone averages 2,000 cases. E.P.-R.

Coates, C., 'Ch Ausone', *The Vine*, 38 (1988).

AUSTRALIA, the 11th largest wine producer in the world (averaging 450,000 hl / 12 million gal a year) making every one of the major wine styles from aromatic, dry white table wine through to wines fashioned in the image of vintage port. Some of its wines—the unwooded Semillons of the Hunter Valley, the fortified Muscats and Tokays of north east Victoria—have no direct equivalent elsewhere, but overall the wines manage to be at once distinctively Australian yet fit easily into the world scene.

Nearly 800 wineries are spread through every state and territory; there is even a vineyard at Alice Springs in the hot, arid Northern Territory. Most of the wineries are small; 80 per cent of the annual crush comes from the four largest companies, headed by the vast PENFOLDS Wine Group (renamed Southcorp Wines in 1994) with a market share of 35 per cent.

As in California, over 500 of those small wineries have come into existence since the late 1960s, offering weekend or retirement occupations for people from all walks of life, notably doctors and lawyers. In typical Australian style, the owners have frequently appointed themselves as winemakers. Nevertheless, perhaps due to the trickle-down effect of the renowned Australian Wine Research Institute at ADELAIDE and the university wine schools (see ROSEWORTHY), standards are extremely high.

The Australian wine show system (see COMPETITIONS) has also played a major role in promoting technical excellence and in shaping style. Each state has a series of regional shows, but the most important are the capital city shows, typically attracting around 2,000 entries. The trophies and medals awarded to the more successful exhibitors are used extensively in marketing and promotion, and are accepted as reliable indicators of quality by retailers and consumers alike. But the greater long-term benefit has been for the winemaker judges, drawn from the leading wineries and schooled by chairmen such as Len EVANS.

The lessons of the show ring have been reinforced by the well-known penchant Australians have for travel. Indeed, Australia spawned the so-called FLYING WINE-MAKERS, a group of oenological guns for hire who follow the vintage around the world. On a less formal basis, many Australian winemakers have made a point of travelling and working overseas, principally in Europe. See AUSTRALIAN INFLUENCE.

Add this experience to the technological base, take in the effect of the sunny Australian climate, and allow for the surge in plantings of such popular grape varieties as Chardonnay and Cabernet Sauvignon, and it is not hard to see why Australian exports increased tenfold between 1984 and 1992, and were expected to increase by a further 400 per cent by the year 2000. It is not too fanciful to suggest that the wines have an openness, a confident, user-friendly style which reflects the national character (and climate). Australian makers have opted to preserve as much as possible of the flavour of the grape, yet to do so with a delicacy of touch, producing intensely fruity white wines and soft, mouth-filling red wines which appeal to the heart as much as to the mind. In so doing they have (willingly) sacrificed structural complexity at the altar of simple fruit flavour.

As in the rest of the world, white wine sales have soared since 1975 while those of red wines have remained static, and those of FORTIFIED wines have declined (over a longer period) from 70 to 9 per cent. In turn, 70 per cent of all Australian wine sold locally is packaged in the ubiquitous wine 'cask', (see BOXES) usually in a 4.5-l (1.2-gal) configuration. It should come as no surprise to find that Australia has the highest annual per capita wine consumption in the English-speaking world, peaking at 21.6 l in 1986 before declining to a low of 17.6 l in 1991.

History

'On 24th January two bunches of grapes were cut in the Governor's garden from cuttings of vines brought three years before from the Cape of Good Hope.' The year was 1791, the chronicler Watkin Tench, and the site of the garden is now occupied by the Hotel Inter-Continental in Sydney's Macquarie Street.

Between 1820 and 1840 commercial viticulture was progressively established in New South Wales, Tasmania, Western Australia, Victoria, and finally South Australia. It was based upon comprehensive collections of *Vitis* VINIFERA vines imported from Europe: there are no native vines in Australia, and neither CROSSINGS nor HYBRIDS have ever taken root.

By 1870 South Australia, Victoria, and New South Wales all had substantial industries: that year they produced 8.7 million l/2.3 million gal of wine. Twenty years later Victoria alone was making twice that amount, more than the other two states combined. But PHYLLOXERA (discovered near Geelong in 1877), changing land use, a swing from dry wine production to fortified wine, the establishment of irrigated vineyards along the Murray river, and the removal of state trade barriers after Federation in 1901 saw South Australia comprehensively usurp Victoria's dominant position. (Phylloxera has never invaded South Australia nor the main producing areas of New South Wales, although it remains active in much of Victoria.)

By 1930 South Australia was producing over 75 per cent of Australia's wine and the Barossa Valley had become the centre of production, processing not only its own grapes but much of those grown in the Riverlands, then and now the engine-room of Australian bulk wine production in the same way as California's SAN JOAQUIN VALLEY. As the geographic

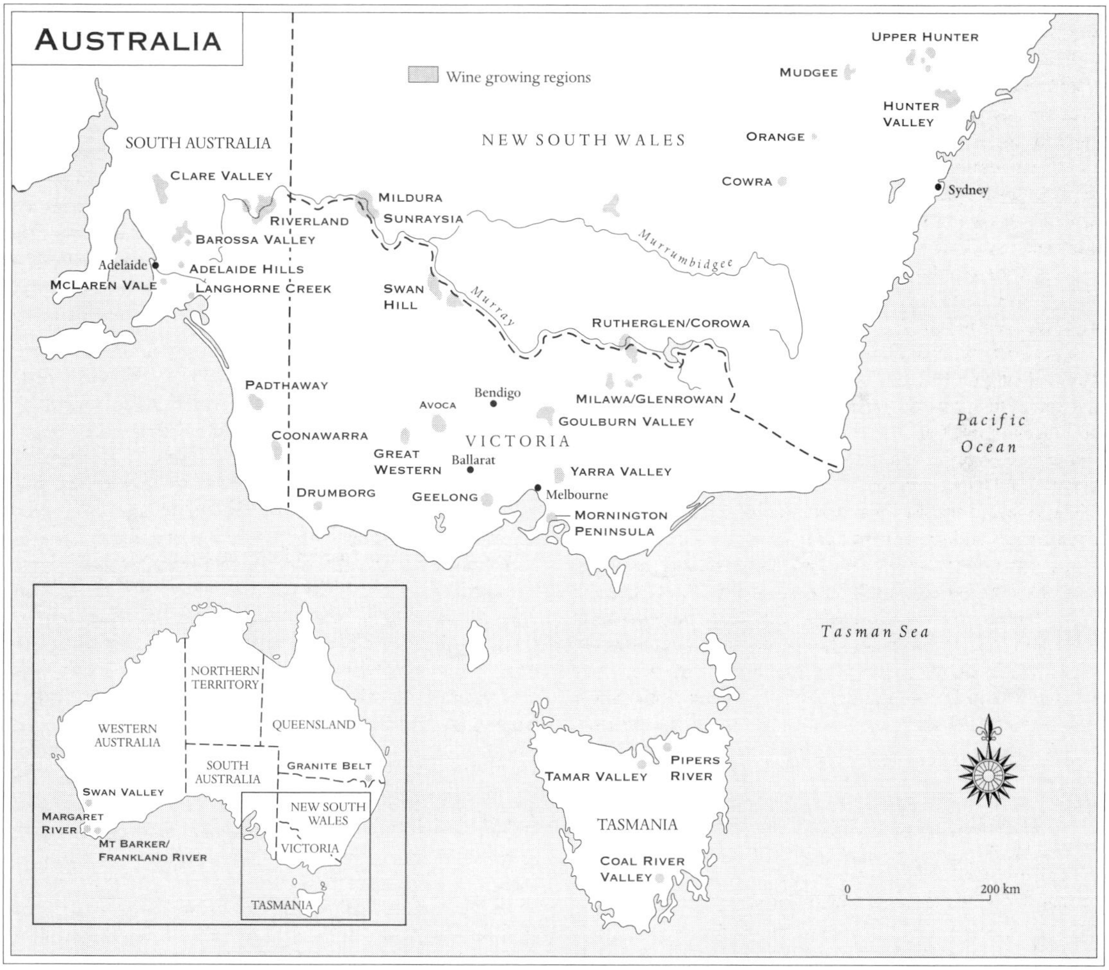

base moved from the cooler parts of Victoria to the warmer regions of South Australia, and specifically as the Murray and then Murrumbidgee Riverlands came into production, so the type of wine being produced changed.

Between 1927 and 1939 inclusive, mainly because of the Imperial Preference system which created trading advantages within the British Commonwealth, Australia exported more wine to the United Kingdom than did France. Most of this wine was fortified, the remainder being massively alcoholic and ferruginous red wine from north east Victoria, the Barossa Valley and the Southern Vales marketed (*inter alia*) under the Emu wine brand.

The industry of today started to take shape in the mid 1950s. Cold fermentation of white wine in STAINLESS STEEL was pioneered (see REFRIGERATION); the big wine companies moved into Coonawarra and (a decade later) nearby Padthaway; and the decline in fortified wine production and consumption contrasted with spectacular growth in the consumption of red table wine (up to 1970) and thereafter white table wine. The 1970s witnessed the arrival of the wine cask, of Cabernet Sauvignon and Chardonnay, the phenomenon of the boutique winery, and the re-establishment of viticulture across the cool corner of south eastern Australia, running east from Coonawarra and Padthaway right through Victoria.

The 1980s saw more of the same: the fine wines of today bear no resemblance to those of 50 years ago. The next 50 years will bring further refinement, a continuation of the trend towards quality, and a decrease in the use of chemicals in all aspects of grape-growing and wine-making. But only the bravest prophet would suggest a further degree of change equivalent to that of the second half of the 20th century.

Climate

With a land mass similar to that of the United States of America, winter snowfields larger than those of Switzerland, and with viticulture in every state, one-line descriptions of the Australian climate are hazardous. For all that, there are two basic weather patterns, one affecting Western Australia, South Australia, Victoria, and Tasmania (the southern states), the other governing Queensland and New South Wales.

The southern states experience a winter–spring rainfall pattern, with a dry summer and early autumn. Ridges of high pressure sweep across the southern half of the continent from Perth to Melbourne during the vines' growing season, uninterrupted by mountain ranges; daytime temperatures typically range between 25 °C/77 °F and 35 °C/95 °F.

There is a less profound maritime influence than in California; the sea temperature is warmer, and the diurnal temperature ranges are less. The resultant even accumulation of heat in the premium wine regions is seen by Australia researchers to be a major factor in promoting wine quality (and, more controversially, style).

Using the California heat degree system developed by WINKLER, the climate varies between Region I and mid Region III, with a preponderance in Region II. Because of the lack of summer rainfall, IRRIGATION is considered as important for quality as for quantity. In the much hotter and drier Riverland of South Australia, Victoria, and New South Wales it becomes as essential as it is in California's San Joaquin Valley, and is unashamedly used to boost production.

The other, more northerly weather system derives from the tropics. It provides a more even rainfall pattern, higher temperatures, and higher humidity. The Hunter Valley is prone to receive rather too much of its annual rainfall during HARVEST, only to suffer the subsequent dual burden of winter and spring drought. Its redeeming feature is the humidity and afternoon cloud cover which reduces stress on the vines and ameliorates the impact of its Region IV heat load (see CLIMATE CLASSIFICATION for details).

Geography

Vine-growing in Australia is concentrated in the south eastern corner of this vast country although there are vineyards in cooler spots elsewhere such as the lone vineyards in the Northern Territory and the geographically curious CANBERRA district. For more detail see under the state or territory names which are, in declining order of importance as grape growers, SOUTH AUSTRALIA, NEW SOUTH WALES, VICTORIA, WESTERN AUSTRALIA, TASMANIA, and QUEENSLAND. Considerable quantities of grapes and wine are trucked over state boundaries, however, for blending and bottling. EUROPEAN UNION laws demand that VARIETAL wines, labelled with a grape variety, be labelled with an officially recognized region. **South Eastern Australia** was created for this purpose and is a vast area encompassing all three of the most important wine states, including the important irrigated regions RIVERLAND and MURRUMBIDGEE Irrigation Area, or Riverina. This somewhat vague description is one of the most common on Australian wine labels in export markets.

Viticulture

Equal pay for women, introduced in the latter part of the 1960s, had some unforeseen consequences. One was a major stimulus to the development of mechanized viticulture, initially with harvesting but in due course extending to pruning and, in the latter part of the 1980s, to all aspects of CANOPY MANAGEMENT during the growing season. Machines which trim the canopy, lift and clip the foliage wires, pluck leaves in the fruiting zone, while simultaneously spraying herbicides were already common by the early 1990s.

International cost comparisons carried out in the early 1990s for the Penfold Wine Group established what common sense suggested: Australia is able to grow and harvest grapes more economically than California, France, or South Africa (although not necessarily more economically than Chile or Argentina). This big-company, broad-acre approach to viticulture was carried to its logical conclusion with the development of so-called MINIMAL PRUNING in the late 1970s. This involves no winter pruning at all; the vine is allowed to grow unchecked save for light trimming and skirting during the summer months, demonstrating a hitherto unsuspected capacity for self-regulation.

At the other end of the spectrum, Australasian viticulturists and researchers have been at the forefront in developing advanced TRELLIS SYSTEMS and canopy man-

Even in South **Australia's** McLaren Vale, viticulture is by no means the only land use.

agement systems. While these glory under such science fiction names as RT2T and TK2T, they can be seen as doing no more than recognizing what the French have practised for centuries: namely, that SUNLIGHT interception on buds and grape bunches is essential, as is a proper balance between CANOPY and crop level, or YIELD.

As in California, Oregon, and elsewhere, new vineyards in premium areas, particularly those in cooler regions, are being established with VINE DENSITIES two or three times greater than traditionally used, and with specifically adapted trellis systems. The aim is better-quality grapes at yields which may in fact be greater than those of traditional plantings.

The other major development is the move towards what is loosely called SUSTAINABLE VITICULTURE with phrases such as Integrated Pest Management coming into general (viticultural) usage. The Australian climate may prove less amenable than that of California (rather more growing season rainfall, higher humidity, and the scourge of DOWNY MILDEW), but there is an ineluctable move away from fungicides, pesticides, and herbicides towards more 'natural' grape growing (see ORGANIC VITICULTURE).

While the Australian climate is less suited to sustainable viticulture than might appear at first sight, the overall health of the vineyards appears to be excellent. PHYLLOXERA has never entered the state of South Australia, nor most of New South Wales (including the Hunter Valley), and is not present in the bulk wine-producing Riverland. Small parts of Victoria remain affected, but very strict quarantine legislation, actively enforced and respected by viticulturists, prevented any spread from infested areas during the second half of the 20th century, with only one small exception. Grafted vines are most commonly used in areas infested with VIRUS DISEASES, the main vineyard scourge being the two fungus diseases, downy mildew and POWDERY MILDEW.

Grafting, not as protection against phylloxera but for the entirely different purpose of changing vine variety, is practised (see TOP WORKING), and is playing a role in the shift towards premium grape varieties. However, the greater impetus comes from replanting and new plantings rather than this form of viticultural top working.

Wine-making

The typical medium-sized modern Australian winery is comprehensively equipped, especially in comparison with its counterpart in Europe. It has a laboratory capable of carrying out most basic ANALYSIS; a powerful REFRIGERATION system for cooling fermentation in insulated stainless steel fermenters, probably computer-controlled; and a must chiller to cool white grapes immediately after they have been crushed (unless they were machine harvested at night). The CRUSHER, PRESS, and FILTRATION equipment are usually of French, German, or Italian design and fabrication; and it is highly probable that there will be several large ROTOFERMENTERS supplementing the normal array of FERMENTATION VESSELS, including the Australian-designed Potter fermenters (see below).

The winery will routinely work 24 hours a day through the six to eight weeks of harvest using two shifts. The chief wine-maker often works an 18-hour day. Scrupulous attention is paid to HYGIENE with caustic soda and citric acid solutions having replaced chlorine-based products.

Up to this point there is nothing particularly unusual in an international context, unless it be the extent of the refrigeration capacity and the rotofermenter capacity. It is the way Australian wine-makers use the equipment, and the underlying technology, which differentiates them (and their wines) from wine-makers (and wines) in most other parts of the world.

The basic aims of the maximum preservation of varietal fruit flavour, and an essentially soft and supple structure for both wood-matured white and wood-matured red wines, are achieved in a number of ways.

Primary FERMENTATION and the secondary MALOLACTIC FERMENTATION are initiated speedily by the use of cultured YEASTS; only a handful of makers rely on wild yeasts. White wine fermentations are carried out at relatively low temperatures (typically 12–14 °C/53–7 °C), usually with clear juice which has been cold-settled (see SETTLING), or filtered and protected against prefermentation oxidation (see PROTECTIVE WINE-MAKING). The more complex, so-called 'dirty French' BARREL FERMENTATION of cloudy juice, LEES CONTACT, and so forth is used for the small percentage of the best Chardonnay varietals and a handful of Sauvignon Blancs. The majority of white wines are made without malolactic fermentation, and are bottled within six to nine months after the harvest.

Because the grapes reach chemical RIPENESS and PHYSIOLOGICAL RIPENESS with relatively low levels of acidity, TARTARIC ACID is routinely added during the primary fermentation. Australian wine-makers believe that if the ACIDIFICATION takes place at this stage, rather than later (and specifically rather than at BOTTLING), it cannot be distinguished from natural ACIDITY. CHAPTALIZATION, by contrast, is prohibited, even in the coolest regions, although certain forms of ENRICHMENT are permitted.

Red wines are fermented at intermediate temperatures (22–5 °C) in a wide variety of fermentation vessels. The once-popular Potter fermenter (with a central vertical sieve cylinder for draining and pumping over) has been superseded by newer designs with single slope floors and sieves which hug either wall or floor, often with provision for wooden header boards which hold the CAP of grape skins submerged. The handling of PINOT NOIR grapes is more complex: in this case open-top fermenters are common, although only a few wineries have the luxury of pneumatic devices for PUNCHING DOWN.

Extended MACERATION after fermentation is less commonly practised than in Europe or the United States, and is bypassed altogether with classic wines such as Penfolds Grange, which, like a significant proportion of fine Australian red wines, is pressed and put into barrel while still actively fermenting. The Australian belief is that post-fermentation maceration initially extracts more TANNINS, which entails extending the maceration to soften (by POLYMERIZATION) those tannins, and that this process dulls the fruit aroma and flavour, polymerization being an OXIDATIVE process.

French OAK is preferred for top-quality white wines, for Pinot Noir, and much of the Cabernet Sauvignon produced. American oak is widely used for SHIRAZ, Cabernet-Shiraz blends, and for some Cabernet Sauvignon. For lesser-quality wines, the use of OAK CHIPS (in conjunction with older barrels) is becoming increasingly widespread.

Chemical additions of all kinds are decreasing. The viticulturists are seeking to provide grapes with the correct chemical composition (reducing the need for acidification while the wine-makers are reducing already low SULPHUR DIOXIDE additions. Fewer and fewer wine-makers add any sulphur to red must or wines prior to the completion of the malolactic fermentation. For dry white and red wines the aim is to limit the total sulphur dioxide level to 50 parts per million (ppm) and free sulphur dioxide to 20 ppm, less than half the internationally set legal limits. Sulphur-free red wines are being made, and may become more common, relying on the preservative action of their tannins. Making sulphur-free white wines with an acceptable shelf life is rather more difficult, but research work is continuing.

Vine varieties

The following are the country's most widely planted varieties, red wine varieties first, in descending order of volume of wine produced.

Shiraz For long Australia's premier red wine grape in terms of area planted (5,760 ha/14,200 acres in 1992), Shiraz's output was forecast to increase by 25 per cent by 1995. It is grown in virtually every wine region, responding generously to the varying imperatives of TERROIR and climate. The variety is identical to the SYRAH of France and has a long Australian history. During the period in which Cabernet Sauvignon came into vogue, the familiarity of Shiraz led to its being treated with a thoroughly undeserved degree of contempt. However, the old DRYLAND (non-irrigated) plantings of the Barossa Valley (producing spicy Rhône-like wines) and the traditional Hunter Valley wines (which become silky with age) led to a surge of popularity in both domestic and export markets in the late 1980s.

Cabernet Sauvignon Although Cabernet is second to Shiraz in terms of plantings (5,465 ha/13,500 acres in 1992), it leads it in terms of both reputation and geographical spread. The thick-skinned small berries stand up to rain, and impart distinctive varietal flavour in almost all growing conditions. The total area under this particular vine has grown from less than 100 ha/250 acres in 1960, and production was forecast to increase by 75 per cent between 1992 and 1995, although its lower average yield will still see it languish behind Shiraz in tonnage. Partly due to the excess demand of the 1960s and 1970s, the blending of Cabernet and Shiraz—or, more probably, Shiraz with a little Cabernet—became widespread, but with a few notable exceptions the trend for premium wines is towards the traditional bordeaux blend with MERLOT (622 ha in Australia in 1992) and CABERNET FRANC (396 ha in 1992). The rate of increase in the planting of these latter two varieties exceeds all others, and varietal Merlots, uncommon at the start of the 1990s, are proliferating.

Grenache As is so often the case, this red-skinned variety is treated as a workhorse and grown in warm to hot conditions, frequently with the aid of irrigation to augment naturally abundant yields. The 2,000 ha/4,900 acres of 1992 are expected to decline slowly as the shift to premium varieties continues. MOURVÈDRE (622 ha and often called Mataro) is used in precisely the same fashion, and has the same destiny.

Pinot Noir Total 1992 plantings of 1,256 ha/3,100 acres put Pinot Noir in a surprise fourth position as an Australian red wine grape, and production was expected to double by 1995. Much is used in making sparkling wine; only in a few cool regions around Melbourne, Victoria, the Adelaide Hills, Albany in Western Australia, and Tasmania does it produce table wine of genuine, at times exhilarating, distinction.

Sultana It depends on the exigencies of the vintage as to how much of the Sultana crop of relatively flavourless white grapes is made into wine, how much is sold fresh, and how much is dried. However, not infrequently more Sultana is vinified than any other white grape variety. It is grown entirely in the Riverlands and is destined for the cheapest table and fortified wine. In 1992, for example, 54,000 tonnes/53,100 tons were used in wine-making, 335,000 tonnes were dried, and 25,000 tonnes sold as fresh table grapes. See both SULTANA and THOMPSON SEEDLESS.

Muscat Gordo Blanco Australia's MUSCAT OF ALEXANDRIA is the white grape equivalent of Grenache with 3,497 ha/8,600 acres planted in 1992 producing 89,000 tonnes (87,500 tons), 78,000 tonnes of which was used in wine-making. It provides a more positively flavoured wine than does Sultana, but production will not increase and hence its ranking as a wine producer will steadily decline.

Chardonnay In Australia as elsewhere in the world, Chardonnay is seen as the grape of today and of tomorrow. Plantings soared from a negligible level in 1970 to 5,194 ha/12,800 acres in 1992. Production was expected to double by 1995, touching 80,000 tonnes. It is grown in every wine region, bending as much to the wills of the viticulturists and winemakers as to the influence of climate and terroir. The style varies from simple to complex and quality from mediocre to excellent, parameters increasingly recognized by a widening range of prices. Market demand engendered blends with Semillon, Colombard, and almost any other white grape variety in the 1980s.

Riesling The great grape of GERMANY, traditionally known as Rhine Riesling in Australia, finally yielded pride of place to Chardonnay among premium white grapes in 1992, with 3,570 ha/8,800 acres under vine. Its chief home is South Australia; its qualitative home-away-from-home the Lower Great Southern region of Western Australia. Most is made dry or near dry (less than 7.5 g/l of RESIDUAL SUGAR), producing a very distinctive Australian style which is better understood (and appreciated) within the country than outside it. Small quantities of delicious BOTRYIZED Riesling are made which are of world quality but (as with those of Germany and California) have a minuscule, if devoted, following.

Semillon Semillon (rarely written Sémillon in the New World) is Australia's traditional counterpart to Shiraz. The nation's 2,860 ha/7,000 acres (1992) is shared between many regions, however much the variety may be identified with the Hunter Valley in New South Wales. As with Shiraz and Cabernet, Semillon is emerging from the shadow of Chardonnay, and production was expected to increase by 30 per cent by 1995. Classic Hunter Semillon was made without the use of new OAK, relying on extended BOTTLE AGEING to weave its magic. Latter-day variations incorporate BARREL FERMENTATION and BARREL MATURATION, or blending with SAUVIGNON Blanc (990 ha in 1992). The latter is another recent arrival on the scene, essentially since 1980, and production is rapidly increasing, spurred on by competition from NEW ZEALAND.

Colombard The ability of this variety to retain ACIDITY has the same attractions in the warmer regions of Australia as in California, although its 1992 plantings of 836 ha/2,000 acres are nowhere on the same scale as those in California. It is used chiefly as a blend component for cheap GENERIC bottled table wines and casks, or wine BOXES.

Other Australian vine variety specialities include the red crossing TARRANGO and a richly historic legacy of Iberian varieties that is rapidly being replaced with more fashionable or productive varieties.

Labelling laws

Australia has had the major components of an APPELLATION system since 1963, initially through the framework of state legislation, but since 1987 effectively embodied in federal law, and since 1990 actively enforced by the official Wine and Brandy Corporation through the Label Integrity Programme (LIP). LIP annually carries out both general and specific audits, variously covering regions, varieties, and individual wineries, utilizing detailed production records which wineries must keep.

This is designed to ensure that where a variety or a region is specified, at least 85 per cent of the wine is of that variety and/or of that region; that 95 per cent is of the stated vintage; and, if more than one variety or region are specified, that they are listed in descending order. Thus Cabernet-Shiraz means the wine has more Cabernet Sauvignon grapes than Shiraz; Shiraz-Cabernet the reverse.

The only missing link as at 1994 was a legislative definition of the boundaries of each region. At a *de facto* level, those boundaries had been agreed, and legislation planned for the mid 1990s, spurred on by the wine agreement signed between the EU and Australia in 1994.

Mudgee in New South Wales, the Margaret River in Western Australia, and Tasmania pioneered regional appellation schemes at various times from the late 1970s onwards, but these are being subsumed into the federal framework as a result of accords with the EU.

The once widespread but now largely discredited use of generic names such as claret, burgundy, champagne, port, and sherry are being progressively phased out under the terms of this EU wine agreement. Such names were never permitted on export labels (so that, for example, the famous Penfolds Grange Hermitage was renamed Grange for European customers), but are progressively disappearing from wine labels within Australia.

Wine trade organization

The Australian wine market is dominated by one group and a few other large companies. The majority of the largest wineries in the country are in South Australia. In the Barossa Valley are Penfolds, Orlando, Seppelt (also part of the Penfolds Wine Group) in the first rank; Wolf Blass, Yalumba, Saltram, Peter Lehmann, and Krondorf in the second rank. Hardy BRL is the amalgamated Thomas Hardy/Berri Renmano group spanning the South Australian Riverland and the Southern Vales. The notable absentee is Lindemans, another Penfolds company, which is based at Karadoc in the Riverlands of VICTORIA not far from the South Australian border.

The sale of wine within Australia is relatively simple, and notably free of the restraints which apply in the United States. Movement between the states is unhindered, and wine producers can sell to whomever they wish (distributors, retailers, or the public), wherever they wish. One of the particular freedoms of Australia is the BYO restaurant, 'BYO' standing for Bring Your Own. In Victoria, indeed, 'Licensed and BYO' restaurants, which are licensed but which generously encourage patrons to bring their own wine, are common. This ethic spreads across all restaurants in Australia. Most will permit patrons to bring their own wine upon payment of a CORKAGE fee, if the request is made in appropriate fashion.

See also Australian BRANDY. J.H.

Evans, L., *Complete Book of Australian Wine* (3rd edn., Adelaide, 1990).

Halliday, J., numerous works including *The Wine Atlas of Australia and New Zealand* (Sydney and London, 1991).

AUSTRALIAN INFLUENCE on wine production in the 1990s is difficult to overestimate. When the chips are finally counted, Australia will be credited with having had an enormous influence on the wine world of the late 20th century. Their VITICULTURISTS have pioneered sophisticated CANOPY MANAGEMENT techniques and all sorts of tricks such as MINIMAL PRUNING and soil slotting (respectively, leaving vines to grow wild and adding nutrients by digging deep). Their winemakers now travel the world— especially the northern hemisphere where the HARVEST conveniently takes place during their quiet time—quietly infiltrating all manner of wineries with Australian technology, obsession with HYGIENE, and record WATER usage (see FLYING WINE-MAKERS). One of their distinguishing marks is their commitment to long hours, ignoring weekends and evenings, at the critical periods during and immediately after harvest. Graduates of oenology and viticulture courses at Australian colleges such as ROSEWORTHY are now dispersed around the world, and the Australian Wine Research Institute at ADELAIDE is increasingly recognized as one of the most important, and practical, forces in ACADEME.

AUSTRIA, increasingly important wine-producing country in central Europe with an annual production of about 3 million hl/79 million gal, often more than a third as much as GERMANY to the north, with which it shares many grape varieties, wine styles, and labelling customs. The wines themselves are more varied and full bodied than the German norm, however, often enlivened by characteristics shared with vineyards just across Austria's borders with, respectively, CZECHOSLOVAKIA, HUNGARY, and SLOVENIA. The majority of wines are white, dry, and VARIETAL, but there is also a keen appreciation of geographical variation, particularly among Austria's own growing connoisseur class. Widespread adulteration on the part of certain merchants, resulting in a major wine scandal in 1985, led to major reforms in wine law and a determination to emphasize quality at the expense of quantity; average Austrian YIELDS from the country's 58,000 ha/143,000 acres of vines (in 1993) are half those in Germany. Austria is also famous for the quality of its wine GLASSES, the result of post-communist migration from BOHEMIA.

History

The CELTS are believed to have grown vines for wine in what is now Austria five centuries before the Christian era, and viticulture continued under Roman domination in what were then the Roman provinces of Noricum and Pannonia in the south east of modern Austria.

The Pannonian plain was repeatedly raided by waves of barbarians (almost defined by their lack of respect for viticulture), but by the era of CHARLEMAGNE vines flourished once more, in many of what are still today regarded as the most important sites, under the influence of MONKS AND MONASTERIES, most concentratedly around Krems on the Danube west of Vienna. Monasteries, often founded by Cistercians from BURGUNDY, and whose viticultural associations date from the Middle Ages, include Göttweig, Zwettl, Güssing, Heiligenkreuz, Klosterneuburg, and Melk. At this time (as in Germany) the total area under vine was about 10 times what it is today, and Austrian wines were widely exported. So great was this surplus production that a series of protectionist measures was undertaken in the 14th, 15th, and 16th centuries (when selling 'foreign' non-indigenous wines was prohibited from lower Austria).

Once Hungary was also part of the Habsburg empire, Hungary's most famous wine TOKAY somewhat overshadowed the reputation of other sweet wines produced within the Austro-Hungarian empire, even AUSBRUCH wines from Rust in the Neusiedlersee-Hügelland district of Burgenland (see below).

The Napoleonic wars did not leave Austrian vineyards unscathed, but the 19th century saw, as elsewhere, enthusiastic botanical experimentation, with perceptible effects on the development of Austria's vine varieties. Austria established its first viticultural and oenological school and research centre at KLOSTERNEUBURG in 1860.

The most important event in 20th century history was the discovery in 1985 that a small but highly publicized proportion of Austrian wine had been adulterated by DIETHYLENE GLYCOL, a harmless but illegal additive designed to add apparent BODY and to make sweet wines taste sweeter. Prior to 1985, well over half of all Austrian wine exports went to Germany. Analyses designed to sniff out diethylene glycol demonstrated just how much of this Austrian wine had been used to bolster sweet wines labelled as 100 per cent German. Germany's reputation as a wine producer was not as seriously harmed by this revelation as Austria's. In the year after the scandal, Austria's wine exports were less than a fifth those of the year before. Hundreds of vine-growers found their produce unwanted outside Austria as a result of misdeeds on the part of some larger wine producers and blenders. Swingeing reforms were enacted and Austrian wine laws are currently some of the most exacting.

Climate

Austria's climate is decidedly continental, with much harsher winters but hotter, drier summers than those of France, for example. Average winter temperatures in the wine regions are only just above freezing point, ranging from 0.1 °C to just 0.6 °C (33 °F). Average summer temperatures, however, range from 18.5 °C/65 °F in Retz almost on the northern, Czechoslovakian border in the Weinviertel to 19.3 °C/67 °F in Klöch in Styria (Steiermark) on the southern, Slovenian border.

Annual rainfall varies considerably more, with an average of 430 mm (16 in) in Retz but 854 (33 in) in Klöch. The Weinviertel (and indeed southern Moravia; see CZECHOSLOVAKIA) is one of the driest wine regions in Europe, while rain in the much wetter Styrian climate tends to fall mainly in summer. The most marked climate is in the Wachau region, source of Austria's most prized dry Rieslings, where the average annual rainfall in nearby Krems is 539 mm/21 in.

Styria in the south enjoys the sunniest climate, with 1,956 hours of sunshine in an average year, almost the same as at Rust in Burgenland, while Gumpoldskirchen just south of Vienna has an average of only 1,805 hours.

Viticulture

Austria's fame viticulturally is as birthplace of the LENZ MOSER 'high culture' system whereby vines are trained far from the ground. This is by far the most common system of vine training in Austria, although new vineyards are more likely to be planned with a higher VINE DENSITY and a lower training system.

Average YIELDS, of about 55 hl/ha (3 tons/acre), are much lower than in Germany, but higher than in neighbouring eastern European vineyards (see CZECHOSLOVAKIA, HUNGARY, and SLOVENIA), where yields have declined because of neglect.

As in Germany, the great majority of vineyard is tended by part-time vine-growers, 30,000 of the Austrian total of 45,000 owning less than 1 ha of vines. (CO-OPERATIVES are therefore important, producing about 15 per cent of all Austrian wine.)

Major climatological hazards are late spring FROSTS throughout Austria; HAIL in Styria; winter frosts in some sites with very little wind, although the Lenz Moser system offers some protection. On the terraces of the Wachau IRRIGATION is occasionally employed, in drought years such as 1992. Harvest dates vary from mid September in very ripe years until late October, except for late harvest wines which may be picked even later. Mechanization is relatively rare in Austrian vineyards.

Viticultural research is centred on KLOSTERNEUBURG, where some of Austria's most successful crossings such as Zweigelt were developed.

Wine-making

Dry wines with both EXTRACT and pronounced ACIDITY are fashionable with connoisseurs even more markedly in Austria than Germany so that the most sought after wines are those labelled TROCKEN (dry). All but the great sweet wines of Burgenland are fermented to almost complete dryness, with a RESIDUAL SUGAR level under 4 g/l (increased to a maximum level of 9 g/l in 1994 to bring it into line with German labelling).

Most wineries are well equipped and use stainless steel or large old wooden vats for fermentation and ageing. Bottling usually takes place in the spring following the vintage.

Many Austrian wine-makers have travelled, however, and practices common in the fine wine regions of the world are increasingly employed by the more innovative producers. The most obvious wine-making development of the 1980s was the introduction of MALOLACTIC FERMENTATION for red wines. Even in the early 1990s by no means all of Austria's red wine producers had mastered the technique. Producers in Burgenland and Styria of a wide range of red wines, and many of those who produce Chardonnay, or Morillon, are also experimenting with BARRIQUES, of BARREL MATURATION and, for some fuller bodied white wines, BARREL FERMENTATION.

Chemical ACIDIFICATION is sometimes allowed in very ripe vintages, usually with TARTARIC ACID within strict limits, while DEACIDIFICATION is occasionally practised in lesser years. ENRICHMENT of alcohol levels is allowed for Qualitätswein (see Wine labelling below) but not for wines of Kabinett quality or above.

Austrian wine research and teaching is centred on Klosterneuburg in Donauland-Carnuntum. Austrian specialities include HEURIGE wine, G'spritzer (Heurige wine mixed with an equal quantity of sparkling soda water), Schilcher (see Weststeiermark below), and Sturm, still-fermenting grape must, often made from BOUVIER grapes, that is a popular, sweet, cloudy drink in Austria at harvest time.

Despite the fashion for dry wines, MUST WEIGHT measurement is the key to wine labelling (see below) and wine quality in Austria, as it is in Germany. The Austrians have their own system of measuring must weight, expressed as degrees on the Klosterneuburg scale. One degree 'KMW' is equivalent to one per cent by weight of sugar in the must, or 5° OECHSLE.

Vine varieties

Austria's varietal mix reflects the country's geographical position between Germany on the one hand and Hungary and Slovenia on the other. Austria's most planted variety is a national speciality, however, GRÜNER VELTLINER which in 1993 was planted in more than 35 per cent of Austria's total vineyard area. It is particularly important in lower Austria, Vienna, and, to a lesser extent, Burgenland. MÜLLER-THURGAU is declining in importance but was still the country's second most planted vine variety in the early 1990s, even if rarely producing wines of real excitement. Third most important variety WELSCHRIESLING can produce sweet wines of great quality in Burgenland, and many perfectly respectable dry wines too. The indigenous red wine grape ZWEIGELT is the country's fourth most planted variety and is found in all districts. Almost as much land is planted with the central European red grape varieties Blauer PORTUGIESER and BLAUFRÄNKISCH, however, with the former predominating in lower Austria and the latter in Burgenland. Weissburgunder (PINOT BLANC) is another widely planted white wine variety. CHARDONNAY was still a fashionable novelty in the early 1990s in most districts, although it has been grown and known as Morillon in Styria for at least a century, this old CHABLIS synonym offering a possible clue to the original provenance of the cuttings imported into Styria. The specifically Austrian NEUBURGER was a speciality of Neusiedlersee, Thermenregion, and the Wachau, where RIESLING reigns, as it does in Kamptal-Donauland and Vienna. Muskat Ottonel (see MUSCAT OTTONEL) is Austria's most commonly planted Muscat variety (although the superior (Gelber) Muskateller, planted in Styria, enjoys more respect). Both TRAMINER and GEWÜRZTRAMINER are widely planted, if often underestimated, while PINOT GRIS (known, as in Germany, both as Grauer Burgunder and Ruländer) is grown mainly in the southern wine districts, as is Sauvignon Blanc (sometimes still called Muskat-Sylvaner). ZIERFANDLER (or Spätrot) and ROTGIPFLER are the curious white wine grape specialities of Gumpoldskirchen in Thermenregion, while Blauer WILDBACHER is a light red grape grown almost exclusively in western Styria. CABERNET SAUVIGNON is a relatively new arrival, concentrated in Burgenland, but Blauer Burgunder (PINOT NOIR) is relatively well established, if on a limited scale, in lower Austria and Burgenland. ST-LAURENT is a useful variant of it particularly well adapted to conditions in lower Austria and Burgenland. Other less common vine varieties include FRÜHROTER VELTLINER and Roter Veltliner (see GRÜNER VELTLINER), BOUVIER, GOLDBURGER, SYLVANER, and SÄMLING 88 (see SCHEUREBE).

Wine regions

Almost all of Austria's vineyards are, like most of the country's agriculture, in the east of the country, far from the mountains that draw skiers from all over the world and constitute the majority of the country—although Styria's vineyards are in the Southern alps, on inclines up to 60 per cent and at altitudes of up to 650 m / 2,130 ft. The boundaries and names of the country's wine regions (see map on p. 75) were reorganized in the *putsch* of 1985.

Nearly six in every ten bottles produced come from Niederösterreich, or lower Austria, on the fertile Danube plain in the north eastern corner of the country. Lower Austria includes, in declining order of the amount of wine produced, the districts of Weinviertel, Kamptal-Donauland, Donauland-Carnuntum, Thermenregion, and the highly respected Wachau.

Burgenland, on the Hungarian border in the far east, makes more than a third of all Austrian wine, and a far higher proportion of Austria's best reds and sweet whites. Neusiedlersee on the eastern shores of the eponymous lake (or 'See') is by far the most important district, followed by Neusiedlersee-Hügelland on the western shores. Some wine is also produced in Mittelburgenland, Austria's red wine corner, and Südburgenland in the middle and south of the region respectively.

Styria is a mountainous viticultural district with more in common with SLOVENIA over the border than with the rest of Austria. It is officially divided into south, south east, and west (Süd-, Süd-Ost-, and West- respectively) districts which combine to produce less than five per cent of an average Austrian vintage.

The city of Vienna, or Wien, is given its own status as a wine region, climatically a particularly favoured enclave within Donauland-Carnuntum.

Weinviertel Austria's largest wine district, the so-called 'wine quarter' with 18,000 ha / 44,500 acres of vineyards, is also the least distinguished. Much of the land is flat, fertile, and very dry. The region typically produces relatively light, dry to off-dry white wines from Austria's signature Grüner Veltliner grape produced at yields considerably higher than the national average. The Müller-Thurgau and Welschriesling vines common here also help to bolster the volume produced. Some fine Weissburgunder (PINOT BLANC) is produced here, however, in villages such as Retz, Röschitz, and Hollabrunn in the west and Falkenstein, Poysdorf, Wolkersdorf, Matzen, and Mannersdorf in the east. Mailberg, almost due north of Vienna, has earned itself a particular reputation for its confident red wines, notably from the Malteser estate managed by LENZ MOSER. Much of Austria's sparkling wine, or SEKT, is produced here, along the Brünner Strasse, the road north from Vienna to Brno in Moravia.

Kamptal-Donauland (renamed Kremstal, Kamptal, and Donauland in 1994) This 6,500-ha / 16,000-acre district, named after the rivers Kamp and Danube which dissect it, is centred on the important wine centres of Krems and Langenlois, where huge quantities of wine were made under monastic auspices in the Middle Ages. Some of Austria's finest, most concentrated Grüner Veltliner comes from this district where LOESS is a common geological feature and seems to imbue the finest Veltliners with a fiery density of their own. Some fine Rieslings are also made here, notably on vineyards based on primary rock formation similar to

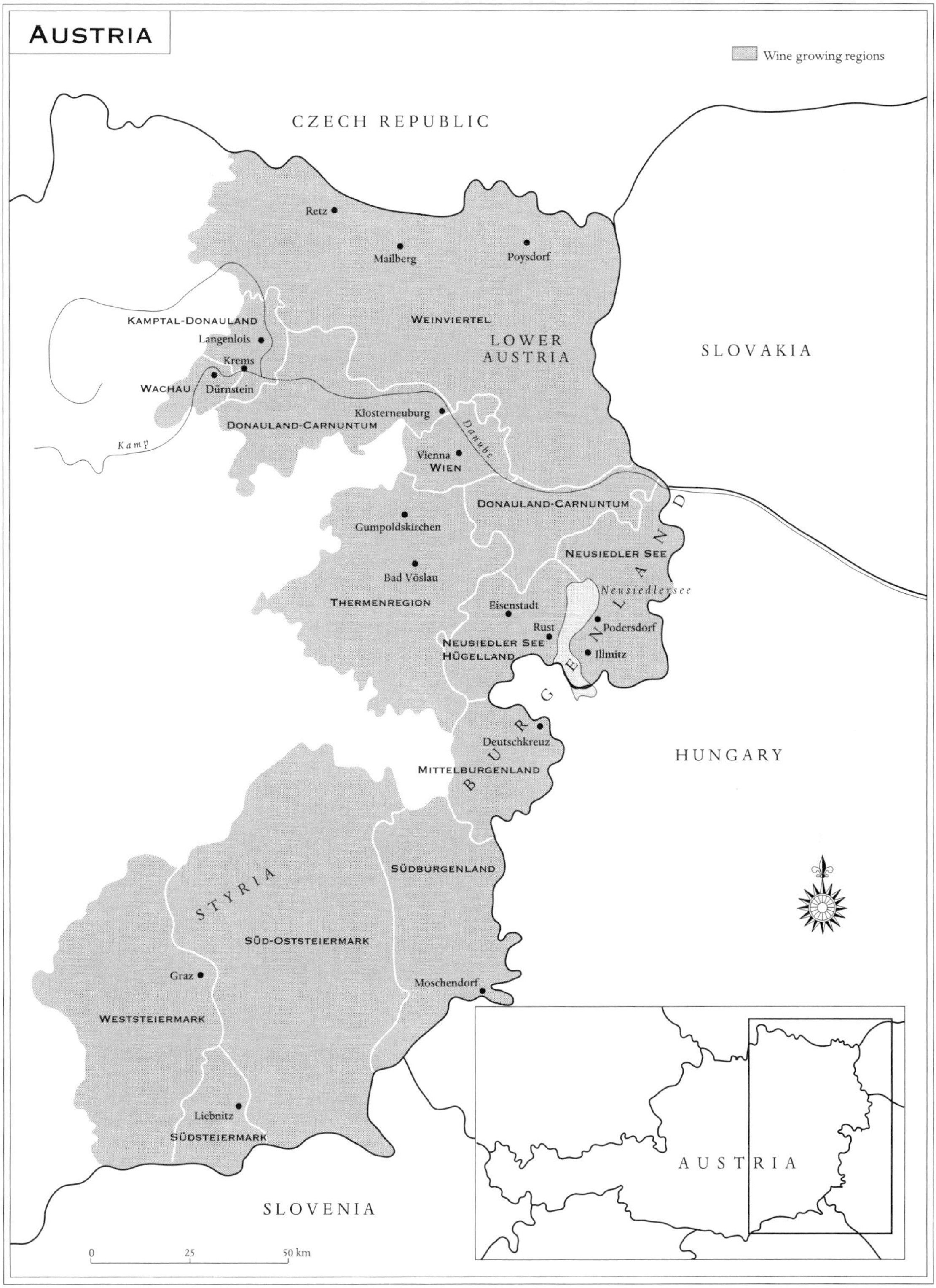
AUSTRIA
Wine growing regions
CZECH REPUBLIC
SLOVAKIA
HUNGARY
SLOVENIA
Retz
Mailberg
Poysdorf
WEINVIERTEL
LOWER AUSTRIA
KAMPTAL-DONAULAND
Langenlois
Krems
WACHAU
Dürnstein
DONAULAND-CARNUNTUM
Kamp
Klosterneuburg
Danube
Vienna
WIEN
DONAULAND-CARNUNTUM
Gumpoldskirchen
Bad Vöslau
THERMENREGION
NEUSIEDLER SEE
Neusiedlersee
Eisenstadt
Rust
Podersdorf
Illmitz
NEUSIEDLER SEE HÜGELLAND
BURGENLAND
Deutschkreuz
MITTELBURGENLAND
SÜDBURGENLAND
STYRIA
SÜD-OSTSTEIERMARK
Graz
WESTSTEIERMARK
Moschendorf
Liebnitz
SÜDSTEIERMARK
0
25
50 km
AUSTRIA

some of the best in the famous and adjoining Wachau district. The most famous Riesling site is probably the Zöbinger Heiligenstein. The headquarters of Lenz Moser, probably the producer best known outside the country, is in Kamptal-Donauland, at Rohrendorf. The district is also associated with a number of Austria's most innovative wine-makers (Malat, Jurtschitsch, Retzl, and Bründlmayer, for example), keen to join the international wine market by playing by the same rules.

Donauland-Carnuntum (renamed Carnuntum in 1994) This large (more than 4,000-ha / 9,900-acre) district stretches along the Danube both east and west of Vienna and is more of a bureaucratic convenience than a homogeneous viticultural entity. The impressively classical suffix comes from the old Roman fortress town of Carnuntum on the Danube east of Vienna, but if the district has a wine centre (apart from Vienna itelf which is officially regarded as autonomous) it is Klosterneuburg which abbey is both centre of ACADEME and a wine producer, with monastic origins, in its own right. Other better-known villages in the Donauland-Carnuntum include Fels, Göttlesbrunn, and Herzogenburg, and the soils of Wagram, almost in Kamptal-Donauland, are particularly rich in loess. Vine varieties planted vary considerably, although white wine varieties predominate west of Vienna.

Thermenregion This is the relatively new name for the 3,000-ha/7,400-acre district centred on the once world-famous village of Gumpoldskirchen on the Südbahn, southbound rail line from Vienna which gave its name to the region in the pre-1985 era. This is the warmest part of lower Austria and can boast the longest uninterrupted tradition of vine-growing since Cistercians planted vineyards here in the 12th century. It is also one of the most distinctive wine regions in the world, dependent for its best wines on two specially adapted grape varieties found nowhere else (and here only in very limited quantity), ZIERFANDLER (or Spätrot) and ROTGIPFLER. Wines made from Spätrot-Rotgipfler grown in Gumpoldskirchen and ripened to AUSLESE level are rich, spicy, and potentially long-lived whites in quite a different style from the lean raciness evinced by the famous Rieslings of the Wachau, or even the BOTRYTIZED sweet wines of Burgenland. Neuburger is also planted here as well as the full range of Austria's red wine varieties. Other wine villages in the regions include Traiskirchen, Baden, Tattendorf, Sooss, and Bad Vöslau.

Wachau Austria's westernmost wine district is, with about 1,400 ha/3,500 acres of vines, lower Austria's smallest. It is also the one of which many Austrian connoisseurs are most proud, on account of the elegance and refinement of its dry RIESLINGS, and GRÜNER VELTLINERS, made from terraces sculpted from the steep banks of the river Danube as it flows through some of this beautiful country's most beautiful scenery. Primary rock formations, with occasional layers of loess, yield fine white wines with high levels of both EXTRACT and ACIDITY—Austria's (more consistent) answer to German RHEINGAU perhaps. As in the Rheingau, most of the vineyards are on the steeper northern bank of the broad river, and presumably benefit from some reflected sunlight. The climate is very particular here where a narrow spur of the southern Pannonian zone meets cooler, moister, oxygen-enriched air from the northern forests. The effect is permanent air circulation, and the Danube stores heat and acts as an effective temperature regulator. More than any other Austrian wine region, the Wachau is marked by wide variations between day and night temperatures, which help to preserve aroma and acidity. Vineyards in the heartland of this region, which styles itself Vinea Wachau Nobilis Districtus, range hardly more than 10 km/6 miles as the crow flies from Schwallenbach in the west, downstream through Spitz, Weissenkirchen, Dürnstein (where the admirable and important co-operative Freie Weingärtner Wachau is based), and Loiben to Mautern. Some of these grapes are vinified by producers in the town of Krems just over the border in Kamptal-Donauland, but respected family estates such as Alzinger, F. X. Pichler, Prager, Knoll, Jamek, and Hirtzberger which did much to create the Vinea Wachau association and affirm the district's commitment to quality in 1985 are all based in the medieval wine villages of the Wachau itself. The association has established three quality levels of their own for their distinctively racy dry white wines. Steinfeder is the lightest, made from grapes which, without ENRICHMENT, have a MUST WEIGHT between 73 and 83° Oechsle and a maximum alcohol content of 10.7 per cent, while Federspiel wines are usually in the 83 to 90° Oechsle range and should be no more than 11.9 per cent alcohol. The most concentrated, and alcoholic, are those which qualify as Smaragd by notching up more than 90° Oechsle, and therefore an alcoholic strength of more than 12 per cent. In very ripe years, sweet wines may also be made, and some producers are beginning to make BOTRYTIZED wines.

Neusiedlersee The shallow lake of Neusiedlersee, surrounded by sandy marshes, is the natural focus for Austria's Burgenland, and the district named after it consists of more than 11,000 ha/27,000 acres of vines on the warm Pannonian plain between the lake and the Hungarian border, the Seewinkel, and the strip of land north of the lake. Mainly sandy, rich soils produce some very fine, full bodied Weissburgunder (Pinot Blanc) together with Traminer and, especially, Welschriesling of all levels of sweetness, from dry and fiery to late harvest TROCKENBEERENAUSLESE, often superior to that produced anywhere else in the world. The lake and its surrounding marshes encourage the formation of NOBLE ROT so that very sweet wines are a speciality of the lakeshore vineyards and, in the best vintages, have a balance and structure that can rival the world's finest sweet wines. Strohwein (straw wines) and EISWEIN are local sweet wine specialities. Some of Austria's more ambitious red wines come, in small quantities, from Neusiedlersee. ZWEIGELT is the most common red wine vine variety but Cabernet Sauvignon is encroaching. Apetlon, Neusiedl, Podersdorf, Frauenkirchen, Halbturn, Illmitz, and Gols are some of the more important wine villages. Some of the more dynamic producers include Stiegelmar, Kracher, Umathum, and hypercreative Willi Opitz, whose inventions include special Italianate bottles and Schilfwein, or reed wine, from grapes dried on reeds from the lake (see DRIED GRAPE WINES). The Pannonischer Reigen is one of the most successful wine producer associations in Austria.

Neusiedlersee-Hügelland This is the name given to the wine region on the western shore of the lake, where soils are higher in loam around Eisenstadt and Mattersburg. The range of wines produced, from full bodied dry and very sweet whites to increasingly 'international' reds, is very similar to that of the Neusiedlersee region on the opposite shore, with the addition of the famous sweet white AUSBRUCH wines from the town of Rust almost directly on the lake, and just over the border from the Sopron vineyards of Hungary. Specialists in this historic wine style include Feiler, Landauer, Schandl, and Wenzel. There are many family wine holdings here dedicated to both quality and innovation and it is not unusual for the likes of the Triebaumer brothers and Anton Kollwentz at the Römerhof to make wines as varied as a Sauvignon Blanc, Chardonnay, Welschriesling Eiswein, Cabernet Sauvignon, and perhaps an oak-aged Blaufränkisch. Welschriesling, Pinot Blanc, and Neuburger are also common in this district where total vineyard area is about 7,000 ha / 17,300 acres.

Mittelburgenland The central Burgenland district, immediately south of the Neusiedlersee-Hügelland, harbours about 2,000 ha / 5,000 acres of vineyard on mainly loamy flat land extending to the Hungarian border, sheltered by hills. With its warm climate, it has long been associated with red grapes, which constitute an unusually high proportion of those grown, about 70 per cent. Mittelburgenland has its own association, the Verband Blaufränkisch, dedicated to extracting maximum quality from this lively eastern European red grape variety. But the district has more recently become a hotbed of experimentation and increasing sophistication. Deep coloured, intensely flavoured and often oak-aged wines are made in quantity from Blaufränkisch grapes as well as from various combinations of Blaufränkisch and Zweigelt with St Laurent, Pinot Noir, and, particularly, Cabernet Sauvignon by producers such as Gesellmann and Igler based in Deutschkreutz. Neckenmarkt and Horitschon are the other important areas.

Südburgenland Southern Burgenland sprawls along the Hungarian border between Styria and Mittelburgenland but the total area planted with vines is less than 500 ha / 1,200 acres and producers have remained largely unaffected by fashions in wine-making and consumer taste. Best-known wines are Blaufränkisch made in the Eisenberg area, where, as German speakers will deduce, the soils are high in iron, and dry Welschrieslings from around Rechnitz. Uhudler is a curious speciality of the far south, well removed from the bureaucrats of Vienna, made from a wide range of AMERICAN HYBRIDS which have been grown around the villages of Moschendorf and Heiligenbrunn (famous for its Kellergassen, clusters of thatched presshouses) since the 19th century, when they were presumably imported to offer resistance to the PHYLLOXERA louse. Krutzler is probably the best producer of the region, specializing in red wines in which Blaufränkisch plays an important part.

Südsteiermark The wines of Styria, representing hardly five per cent of Austria's total production, became particularly fashionable after the 1985 scandal; since Styrian wines are quintessentially dry and fragrant, no one had been tempted to adulterate them with diethylene glycol. The smallest of the Styrian districts, southern Styria around Leibnitz and some of it within sight of Slovenia, is the most important in terms of wine production, but even its 1,500 ha / 3,700 acres of vines are widely scattered, grown vertically up steep, south-facing slopes in particularly sheltered spots, at altitudes of between 250 and 650 m (2,100 ft). The region has long cultivated two of the most popular 'international' vine varieties, Sauvignon Blanc (occasionally still called Muskat-Silvaner) and Chardonnay (here usually called Morillon). Welschriesling, Pinot Blanc (called Klevner here), and Gelber Muskateller (MUSCAT BLANC À PETITS GRAINS) are also grown and all of these varieties can produce distinctively crisp yet full and aromatic white wines, an Austrian answer to Alsace but with more obvious acidity. Sattlerhof, Reinhold Polz, Alois Gross, and Tement are some of the best-known producers.

Süd-Oststeiermark South east Styria is a vast area in which there are about 1,000 ha / 2,500 acres of widely dispersed vineyards, notably on the volcanic soils of Klöch, where Traminer is a speciality. Welschriesling, Pinot Blanc, Ruländer, Gewürztraminer, and Müller-Thurgau are also cultivated in this relatively warm area.

Weststeiermark Western Styria, where there are fewer than 300 ha of vines, has its own extremely local speciality, Schilcher rosé made from lightly pressed Blauer Wildbacher grapes, known only here and, to a much more limited extent, in the VENETO. The district produces little else, and exports little other than its fame beyond its own boundaries.

Vienna Vienna boasts of being the only capital city with a serious wine industry within its boundaries (although PARIS could at one time have made the same claim). Strict laws protect the city's 700 ha of vines, which were even more extensive in the Middle Ages, thanks to the influence of CHARLEMAGNE. Both monastic and aristocratic wine producers served the local populace with wine from specially built cellars, the precursors of Austria's unique HEURIGE tradition. Attractively youthful, relatively simple wines, typically made from Grüner Veltliner, are served to locals and tourists alike in these wine taverns in outlying suburbs such as Grinzing, Nussdorf, Neustift, and Sievering on the right bank of the Danube, and Stammersdorf, Strebersdorf, and Jedlersdorf on the left bank. Vienna also produces wines of real quality and ageing potential, however, notably those made from Riesling and various Pinot grapes grown on vineyards such as the Nussberg at Döbling, and those of Bisamberg and Kahlenbergerdorf. Traditional customs are maintained in many less ambitious vineyards still cultivated with a mixture of grape varieties which are vinified together. Franz Mayer and Wieninger are two of Vienna's best producers.

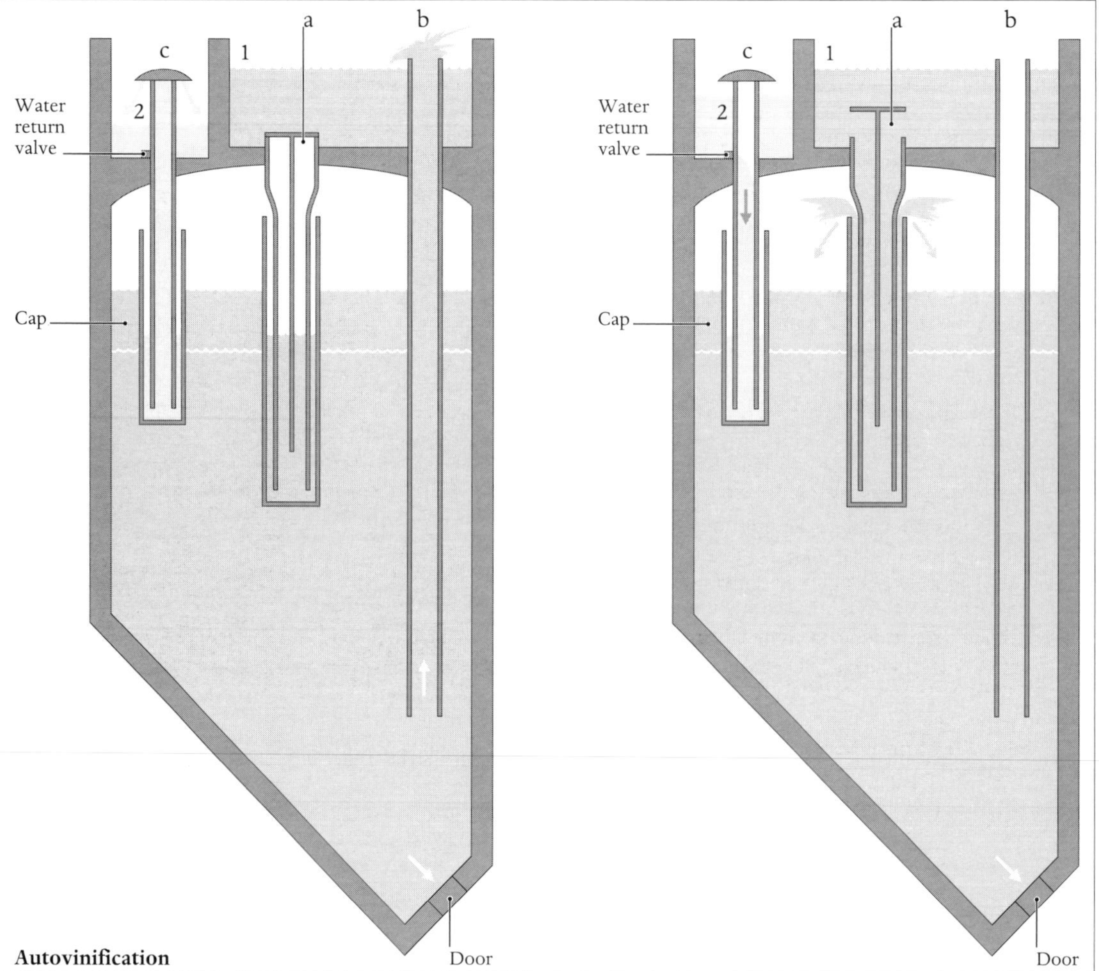

Autovinification

Wine labelling

Wine laws drawn up since 1985 are some of the strictest in the world. They share much of the nomenclature of the GERMAN WINE LAW but standards in general and minimum MUST WEIGHTS in particular are higher (although warmer summers mean that it is easier to achieve higher Oechsle levels in most Austrian wine districts than in Germany). Qualitätswein is a genuinely exclusive category, for example, and Kabinett is regarded as a subcategory of Qualitätswein rather than a fully fledged Prädikatswein, as only Spätlese, Auslese, Strohwein, Eiswein, Beerenauslese, Auslese, and Trockenbeerenauslese are in Austria. All Austrian wines should have a red and white striped 'Banderole' around the neck or on top of the cork, which must be purchased by the producer to ensure that official quotas are not breached and to provide some sort of tracking system.

Wines are also labelled according to sugar content. A trocken wine must have a residual sugar level of no more than 4 g/l, a medium or halbtrocken wine 4 to 9 g/l, a medium sweet, halbsüss or lieblich wine 9 to 18 g/l, and a sweet or süss wine more than 18 g/l. Wines carrying the name of a grape variety or a vintage date must be composed of at least 85 per cent of that grape variety and 85 per cent of wine from that vintage.

Tafelwein The bottom rung, and the great majority of all wine produced, is represented by TAFELWEIN, for which grapes must achieve a must weight of 63° Oechsle. No Tafelwein other than BERGWEIN, wine produced on steeper slopes, may be sold in regular bottles. This is by far the most common wine category, accounting for more than half of all wine produced in a normal vintage.

Landwein One step up from Tafelwein, LANDWEIN must be made from certain specified grape varieties, must reach 68° Oechsle, and be sold either in 25-cl (9-fl oz), 1-l, or 2-l bottles. ALCOHOLIC STRENGTH must be less than 11.5 per cent and residual sugar cannot exceed 6 g/l. Only about five per cent of all Austrian wine qualifies as Landwein.

Qualitätswein This is the name both of a category which includes the subcategory Kabinett (below) and of a subcategory itself which, depending on the vintage characteristics, can represent as much as 1 million hl/26 million gal. To qualify as Qualitätswein, the wine must come from a single district specified on the label and must demonstrate the characteristics of the recognized grape variety from which it is made. The must weight must reach 73° Oechsle and, after enrichment within certain limits, a white wine must have 8.5 per cent alcohol (9 per cent for reds). As in Germany, wines are tasted, analysed, and awarded a code that is the Austrian equivalent of Germany's AP NUMBER.

Kabinett Regarded as merely a Qualitätswein in Austria, Kabinett wines, like Prädikatswein below, may nevertheless not be chaptalized (see ENRICHMENT). Oechsle levels must reach 84° and residual sugar cannot exceed 9 g/l.

Spätlese All Prädikatswein must be from one wine district, must be vintage dated, and must have its must weight officially certified. As in Germany, no Prädikatswein may be chaptalized. No Austrian Spätlese may be sweetened by added SÜSSRESERVE; all alcohol and residual sugar must be the result of natural grape sugars. A Spätlese must be made from fully ripe grapes picked at a minimum must weight of 94° Oechsle.

Auslese Must weight must be at least 105° Oechsle and any unripe or unhealthy grapes must be excluded.

Strohwein 'Straw wine' made from overripe grapes with a must weight of at least 127° Oechsle which are dried on straw or reeds for at least three months (see DRIED GRAPE WINES).

Eiswein 'Ice wine' should be made from grapes with a must weight of 127° Oechsle, picked and pressed while still frozen (see ICE WINE).

Beerenauslese Sweet wine made from grapes that are overripe and affected by noble rot with a must weight of at least 127° Oechsle.

Ausbruch A speciality of Rust in Neusiedlersee-Hügelland, made from grapes with a must weight of at least 138° Oechsle that are naturally shrivelled, overripe, and affected by noble rot. See also AUSBRUCH.

Trockenbeerenauslese Very sweet wine made from grapes with a must weight of at least 168° Oechsle that are naturally shrivelled, overripe and affected by noble rot.

Hollzer, F., Schima, W., and Sedlaczek, R., *Unser Wein 1992/93* (Vienna, 1992).
MacDonogh, G., *The Wine & Food of Austria* (London, 1992).
Pigott, S., *Riesling* (London and New York, 1991).
Steurer, R., *Oesterreichischer Weinführer: 1992/93* (Vienna, 1992).

AUTOLYSIS, the destruction of cells by their own ENZYMES. In a wine-making context the term most commonly applies to the action of dead YEAST cells, or lees, after a second fermentation has taken place during SPARKLING WINE-MAKING. Its effects are greatest if wine is left in contact with the lees of a second fermentation in bottle for at least five years, and minimal if LEES CONTACT lasts for less than 18 months.

Peter Symington checking the depth of colour at the top of an **autovinifier** at the Quinta do Bomfim in the Douro valley.

Charpentier, C., and Feuillat, M., 'Yeast autolysis', in G. H. Fleet, (ed.), *Wine Microbiology and Biotechnology* (Switzerland, 1993).

AUTOVINIFICATION, method of vinification designed to extract maximum COLOUR from red grapes and used primarily in the production of red port. Autovinification, a process involving automatic PUMPING OVER, was developed in ALGERIA in the 1960s, where it was known as the Ducellier system. Faced with a shortage of labour in the 1960s, port producers were forced to abandon the traditional practice of treading grapes by foot in LAGARES. Many isolated QUINTAS had no electricity and so shippers built central wineries. The power supply was erratic and too weak for sophisticated pumps or presses so the shippers installed autovinification tanks in order to extract sufficient colour and TANNINS in the short FERMENTATION period prior to FORTIFICATION. Autovinification is a self-perpetuating process induced by the buildup of pressure; no external power source is needed.

Grapes which have been crushed and partially destemmed are pumped into specially constructed autovinification vats (see diagram on p. 78) which are filled to within about 75 cm (29 in) of the top. The vat is closed and the autovinification unit (*a*) is screwed into place. As the fermentation begins, CARBON DIOXIDE is given off and pressure builds up inside the vat. This drives the fermenting must up an escape valve (*b*) which spills out into an open reservoir (1) on top of the vat. At the same time the pressure forces water out of a second valve (*c*) in to a smaller, separate reservoir (2). When all the water has been expelled, the carbon dioxide that has built up in the vat escapes with explosive force through valve (*c*). The fermenting must in reservoir (1) falls back into the vat down the central autovinification unit (*a*), spraying the floating CAP of grape skins with considerable force, so extracting colour and tannin. At the same moment, the water in reservoir (2) returns to valve (*c*) for the process to repeat itself. The cycle continues until the wine-maker judges that sufficient grape sugar has been fermented to alcohol, and sufficient COLOUR has been extracted, at which time the wine is run off and fortified just as described in PORT, wine-making.

At the start of fermentation, when a small amount of carbon dioxide is given off, the autovinification cycle is slow. But when the fermentation is in full swing the pressure build-up is such that the cycle takes only 10 to 15 minutes to complete.

Originally autovinification vats were built from cement and lined with resin-painted concrete. However, significant modifications have accompanied improvements in both wine-making technology and the power supply to the DOURO valley, where port is produced. Modern autovinification tanks are made from STAINLESS STEEL and are equipped with REFRIGERATION units to prevent the must from overheating. Some shippers have resorted to traditional pumping over, or *remontage*, although this generally provides insufficient EXTRACTION for better-quality port. Other shippers have successfully combined pumping over with autovinification, thereby giving the wine-maker greater control over port fermentation than ever before. R.J.M.

AUVERGNE, CÔTES D', VDQS which is administratively considered part of the greater LOIRE region, and basin, but these Massif Central vineyards, around Clermont-Ferrand, are in fact closer to the vineyards of the northern RHÔNE than they are to the river Loire itself. From about 500 ha/1,200 acres of mainly Gamay and Chardonnay vines light reds, pinks, and whites are made in quantity, with considerable skill from some of the many small enterprises here. Gamay has long been grown here and this was one of the most important wine regions of France in the 19th century, before which Pinot Noir was grown in preference to Gamay. The names of the communes Boudes, Chanturgue, Châteaugay, Corent, and Madargues may be appended to Côtes d'Auvergne on wine labels. Most wines are consumed locally; none is expensive.

George, R., *French Country Wines* (London, 1990).

AUVERNAT, synonym for various Pinots and other grape varieties used in the Loire. Auvernat Noir is PINOT NOIR; Auvernat Gris is usually MEUNIER, sometimes PINOT GRIS; and Auvernat Blanc is CHARDONNAY.

AUXERRE, once an important city in the Yonne *département* of north east France. Today CHABLIS is the Yonne's only famous and substantial wine appellation, but in the time of CHARLEMAGNE the region centred on Auxerre 20 km/12 miles west had many more vineyards, being a larger centre of population and being conveniently situated on a river which leads directly into the Seine and thence to the PARIS basin. It is perhaps not surprising, given its historic importance, that so many vine varieties have the name or synonym AUXERROIS, meaning 'of Auxerre'.

The so-called **Côtes d'Auxerre** produce light red and white wines made in the mould of light BURGUNDY and CHABLIS respectively. The zone includes Chitry, Coulanges-la-Vineuse, Épineuil, and Irancy. They may all append their names to the BOURGOGNE appellation.

AUXERROIS is both the name used for the black-berried MALBEC in CAHORS where it is the dominant vine variety and the name of a relatively important white-berried variety in Alsace. And as if that were not confusing enough, Auxerrois Gris is a synonym for PINOT GRIS in Alsace while Chardonnay, before it became so famous, was once known as Auxerrois Blanc in the Moselle—as distinct from Auxerrois Blanc de Laquenexy which is the variety today called Auxerrois in north east France (including Alsace) and LUXEMBOURG.

Galet refutes 19th century suggestions that the variety has some connection with either Chardonnay, Sylvaner, or Melon and maintains it is a distinct variety originally studied at the Laquenexy viticultural station near Metz on the MOSELLE in the far north east of France. There are still minuscule plantings of Auxerrois in the Loire but today it is most important in Alsace, the French Moselle (including Côtes de TOUL) and Luxembourg where it is most valued, particularly for its low acidity. If yields are suppressed, which they rarely are, the variety can produce excitingly rich wines in both Moselle regions that are worth ageing until they achieve a bouquet with a honeyed note like that of mature Chablis, the wine which today could be described as 'from Auxerre' or, in French, Auxerrois.

Auxerrois is Alsace's *éminence grise*, whose 1,500 ha/3,700 acres (in France's 1988 census) covered considerably more Alsace vineyard than any one of the three true PINOTS planted there. Rarely seen on a label, it produces slightly flabby, broad wines which are blended into many a PINOT BLANC. Auxerrois can add substance if not subtlety to over-produced or underripened Pinot Blanc. Many Alsace wine enthusiasts have never heard of Auxerrois, which in 1988 constituted nearly 10 per cent of all vines planted in the Bas-Rhin and more than 12 per cent of all vineyard in the region's heartland, the Haut-Rhin—half as much again as plantings of the Pinot Blanc so much more familiar on wine labels. An Alsace wine labelled 'Pinot Blanc' could contain nothing but Auxerrois, which is also a major ingredient in EDELZWICKER.

Germany's plantings of Auxerrois declined steadily in the

The famous Cluny tapestries reveal the importance of wine and, here, the grape harvest in early 16th century **Burgundy**. This section illustrates (bottom left) how black-skinned grapes (almost certainly **Pinot Noir** even this long ago) were transported to an open-topped fermentation vat (foreground) where the foot was used in an early form of **pigeage** to encourage **extraction** before the remaining grape skins were pressed (back centre) and the wine kept in **barrels** remarkably like those used today (back right).

1970s and are mainly concentrated in Baden, where there were still nearly 50 ha of relatively antique vines in 1990.

The variety achieved international fame in the 1980s when it was discovered that the first Chardonnay cuttings officially promulgated in SOUTH AFRICA were in fact nothing more glamorous than Auxerrois.

Galet, P., *Cépages et vignobles de France* (2nd edn., Montpellier, 1990).

AUXEY-DURESSES, a village in Burgundy producing medium-priced red and white wines not dissimilar to neighbouring VOLNAY and MEURSAULT respectively, although more austere in style. The vineyards, which include those of the hamlets of Petit Auxey and Melin, are located on either side of a valley subject to cooler winds than the main Côte de BEAUNE. PINOT NOIR vineyards, including such PREMIERS CRUS as Les Duresses and Le Climat de Val, are grown on the south east slope of the Montagne du Bourdon. White wines, made from CHARDONNAY, account for just above a quarter of the production, covering the slopes adjacent to Meursault. Some vines, atypically for Burgundy, are trained high.

In the past wines from Auxey-Duresses were likely to have been sold under the names of grander neighbours. Many are now labelled as Côte de Beaune Villages, although the village appellation is becoming more popular.

See also CÔTE D'OR and its map. J.T.C.M.

AUXINS, one of a number of groups of natural HORMONES present in vines which regulate growth. Auxins' effects were first demonstrated in 1926. They are produced in vine parts which are actively growing, such as shoot and root tips. Auxins favour cell growth over cell division, but are also involved in inhibiting the growth of LATERAL SHOOTS. Many chemicals have been synthesized which are chemically related and have a similar biological function. For example, the compounds 2,4-D and 2,4,5-T are auxin-like and form the basis of some HERBICIDES. Vines, like tomatoes, are very sensitive to 2,4-D vapours and growth abnormalities may be caused by its presence in spray drift from such herbicides applied to other agricultural crops, even in very small concentrations, many miles away. R.E.S.

AVA, the acronym for **American Viticultural Area** and the UNITED STATES' so far rudimentary answer to France's APPELLATION CONTRÔLÉE system of permitted geographical designation. The US federal government began developing this system in 1983 through its Bureau of Alcohol, Tobacco, and Firearms. Under existing regulations AVAs are defined by geographic and climatic boundaries, as opposed to pre-existing political ones. Before AVAs, counties were the prevailing appellations. The newer system requires no limitations on varieties planted, YIELDS, or other specifics familiar to those who know France's AC or Italy's DOC laws. The only requirement for their use is that 85 per cent of the grapes in a wine labelled with an AVA come from that region; if the wine is a VARIETAL, the legal minimum of 75 per cent of the named variety must come from the named AVA. (Unlike the AC, or DOC system, however, neither the expression 'AVA' nor 'American Viticultural Area' appears on wine labels.)

Some observers have criticized these early rules as too lax. This position ignores the immaturity of the United States wine industry. Most AVAs are too young as vineyard districts for anyone to know which varieties will fare best in them, or what crop yields will give the finest wines. Even in CALIFORNIA, which has much the longest and most extensive viticultural history of any American state, many regions now designated as AVAs were first planted in the 1970s, and then only sparsely. Given that, the very existence of AVAs is, usefully, driving growers and wine-makers to refine their observations about suitability of grape variety to site, and relationship of crop yield to wine quality.

Between 1983 and 1991, BATF approved more than 100 AVAs in the country at large, more than 60 of those in California.

AVERY, RONALD (1899–1976), came from an old Cornish family which partly moved to Bristol, then an important port in the west of England, towards the end of the 18th century. The family wine merchants Avery & Co dates its origin from 1793. Born in the celebrated BORDEAUX vintage of 1899, he remained faithful to CLARET as his favourite red wine throughout his life. His time at Cambridge was cut short by the death of an uncle, who with his father ran the firm. To gain experience in the trade at a time when nearly all wine was imported in cask and bottled in Britain, he worked in the cellars of the London agents of the Bordeaux house of BARTON & Guestier, in the latter's premises in Bordeaux, and also in OPORTO. He effectively took over the running of Averys in 1923.

In those days, wine merchants mostly bought from British agents or their principals, and only visited the wine regions for social purposes. But Avery had a keen, enquiring, even suspicious mind, became an excellent taster, and paid frequent visits abroad, particularly to Bordeaux. There he selected the casks he preferred, and when they arrived in Bristol docks was not averse to topping them up with another wine altogether. By the late 1930s Averys produced an exceptionally extensive list with a large range of German wines and 100 clarets extending back 20 years, including unusually good stocks of 1923 BURGUNDY and 1929 bordeaux whose quality he was astute enough to discern. At one time the list included seven vintages, back to the famous 1921, of Ch CHEVAL-BLANC, a wine then little known in Britain but of which he was very fond. After the Second World War he and Harry WAUGH, a friend and rival then working for HARVEYS of Bristol, were the first to import Ch PÉTRUS into a distinctly unimpressed Britain. At this time he also became specially interested in burgundy in order to secure authentic wines, much subject then to blending from sources in southern France and

Bordeaux first growth Ch **Margaux** is one of relatively few wine estates still to indulge in the luxury of having its own cooper.

Ronald **Avery** (right) in the firm's Bristol cellars with long-serving cellarmaster Teddy Tamlin.

ALGERIA. Many of the world's serious personal cellars contain Averys bottlings.

Until the abolition of resale price maintenance in the British drinks trade in 1963, and the development of licensed supermarkets, the wine trade was very much an occupation for gentlemen, and Ronald Avery was an eccentric example. Habitually unpunctual, he seldom arrived at his office before 1 p.m., but then stayed late, writing heavily annotated letters of recommendation that turned many customers into friends. At this period most amateurs of fine wine in Britain had an account with Averys, which also had a large hotel and restaurant trade, especially in the west of England.

An excellent navigator, Ronald Avery frequently crossed the English Channel to France in his large motor yacht, which he had to sell to reduce the borrowings entailed by his enthusiastic investment in the Bordeaux vintages of the late 1940s and 1950s. He died in 1976, after which time the firm was run by his son John, although it lost its independence in 1987. E.P.-R.

Averys Bicentennial Wine List (Bristol, 1993).

AVESSO, Iberian white grape variety used for VINHO VERDE. It produces scented, relatively full bodied wine and is most common in the south of the Vinho Verde region. See also JAÉN.

AYZE, named, isolated CRU just outside Bonneville east of Geneva whose name may be added to the eastern French appellation Vin de SAVOIE. The wine is typically a light white sparkling wine.

AZAL BRANCO, Portuguese white grape variety which brings acidity to VINHO VERDE. **Azal Tinto** is the dark-skinned version which is used for red Vinho Verde.

AZEOTROPE, a mixture of liquid chemicals which has a boiling point either higher or lower than any one of its components. The principal volatile components of wine tend to form azeotropes of two, three, or more components. Water, ETHANOL, volatile organic ACIDS, ALDEHYDES, ESTERS, ACETALS, and ketones, all powerfully aromatic, are among the azeotrope components in wines. The multiplicity of volatile compounds present in wine and our lack of detailed knowledge of all of the azeotropes possible makes it difficult to predict the composition of distillates (which depend on the varied boiling points of components).

Just as the formation of azeotropic mixtures in a liquid governs the boiling point and composition of the vapour during DISTILLATION, so it governs the composition of the vapours above a liquid in a glass at room temperature. When we smell a wine, our noses are recording the impression created by the azeotropic mixture rather than that of any single component. A.D.W.

AZERBAIJAN, eastern wine-producing republic in the CIS situated between ARMENIA and the Caspian Sea. Divided into the mountain system of the large and small Caucasus and the Kura and Araka lowlands, it includes the Republics of Nakhichevan and Nagorno Karabakh.

History

Grape-growing is the oldest branch of Azerbaijan's economy. Archaeology has revealed seeds of cultured grapes, stones for crushing grape berries, and stone fermentation and storage vessels dating back to the second millennium BC in the settlements of Kültan, Galabaglar, and Galajig (Nakhichevan).

HERODOTUS describing a campaign of the SCYTHIAN chief Madyas in ASIA MINOR in the seventh century BC, mentioned that viticulture and wine-making were already developed in that region. The Greek geographer Strabo, in the first century BC, reported on grape culture in 'Albania', the old name of part of Azerbaijan.

The Arabian historians and geographers Abulfedy, Masudi, Khaukal, and El Mugaddasi recorded that vineyards existed near the towns of Gianji and Bardy during Arab domination. Viticulture of that region declined in the periods of war and revived in the time of peace. Viticulture was on a commercial scale after 1814, and developed especially fast at the end of the 19th century when two railways were built which provided access to the enormous wine market of RUSSIA.

By the beginning of the 20th century small viticultural farms were established in the Kirovabad-Kazakh region as well as much larger enterprises in specialized zones of commercial grape and wine production. In 1913 15 districts of Azerbaijan had 26,500 ha/65,500 acres of vineyards and produced 400,000 hl/10 million gal of wine. In 1931 the first state farms growing grapes and producing wine were established. In 1940, the total vineyard area was 33,000 ha, but the Second World War reduced this total to 21,000 ha by 1947. Revival came in 1954, when expansion in grape cultivation began once more and gross yields also increased.

Climate and geography

The climate and the soils of mountainous regions are determined to a considerable extent by latitude, altitude, relief, and exposition of slopes. The climate of Azerbaijan varies between moderately warm with dry winters, to cold with abundant rainfall.

The average annual temperature is 10.5 to 15.5 °C (51–60 °F). The active temperature summation is between 3,000 and 4,600 °C in its varied wine regions. Annual rainfall in the low and premountainous parts of the country, where grapes are grown, is 250 and 600 mm (23 in) respectively.

Modern viticulture is concentrated in the Kirovabad-Kazakh and Shirvan regions, in the Republics of Nagorno-Karabakh and Nakhichevan, and in microregions of several other zones.

Viticulture

Vineyards account for about seven per cent of the country's cultivated land, grapes representing 30 to 40 per cent of total agricultural output. Only about 10 per cent of the vineyards, mainly in Nakhichevan, need the WINTER PROTECTION that is so necessary in Russian vineyards. About half of all vineyards need IRRIGATION and only about 20 per cent of them are grafted on to PHYLLOXERA-resistant ROOTSTOCKS. Irrigated vineyards are mainly in the Khanlar, Agdam, Mardakert, Tauz, Kazakh, Fizuli, and Shamkhor regions as well as in several zones of Nakhichevan.

Vine varieties

The country has 17 vine varieties officially recognized for wine production—and 16 table grape varieties are planted, accounting for 15 per cent of the total vineyard area. The most common varieties are RKATSITELI and PINOT NOIR.

New vineyards are planted to PINOT BLANC, ALIGOTÉ, Podarok Magaratcha, Pervenets Magaratcha (both developed at the Institute MAGARATCH), Doina, Viorica, Ranni Magaracha, and Kishmish Moldavski.

Industry organization

In 1990 Azerbaijan's 181,000 ha/447,000 acres of vineyard yielded 1,196,000 tons of grapes and just 661,000 hl/17.5 million gal of wine, 18.2 million bottles of Soviet sparkling wine and 114,000 hl/3 million gal of brandy. A high proportion of vineyard production is shipped west to slake Russian thirst.

The leading wine enterprises of the country, which produce more than 90 different brands of wine and brandy, are the two Baku wineries, the Baku sparkling wines enterprise, and the Khanlar winery. V.R.

Asadulayev, A. N., and Suleimanov, D. S., 'The intensification of viticulture of Azerbaijan' (Russian), *Vinodelie i vinogradarstvo SSSR*, 2 (1985), 24–7.

Negrul, A. M. (ed.), *Ampelography of Azerbaijan* (Baku, 1973).

Suleimanov, D. S., 'The Soviet Socialist Republic of Azerbaijan' (Russian), in A. I. Timush (ed.), *Encyclopaedia of Viticulture* (Kishinëv, 1986).

AZIENDA, Italian for a business. An **azienda agricola** is a farm and the phrase should appear on a wine label only if the grapes were grown and the wine produced on that estate, as opposed to an **azienda vinicola** which may buy in grapes from elsewhere.

B

BABYLONIA, kingdom in southern MESOPOTAMIA in what is now mainly IRAQ. Babylonia inherited much of its knowledge from Ancient SUMER, and attained its highest prosperity 626–539 BC before being conquered by the PERSIANS.

BACCHUS, common name in Ancient ROME for the classical god of wine whom the Greeks called Bacchos but, more usually, DIONYSUS. The **Bacchanalia** was the Roman festival of Bacchus and the word **bacchanal** has come to mean any form of drunken revelry. **Bacchic** poetry is verse with a vinous theme, a speciality of the ARAB POETS. Because the Romans concentrated on the vinous aspect of this much more complex god, and possibly because the word Bacchus is considerably easier to say and spell than Dionysus, the Roman name is much more commonly used in modern times, and is regarded as a word rich in wine connotations. The United States has its Society of Bacchus for committed wine enthusiasts, and the word is used emotively around the world to conjure up various conjunctions of wine and pleasure.

Bacchus in the Villa Borghese, Rome.

Bacchus is also the name of an important German white grape variety, one of the few modern crossings that was still gaining ground at the beginning of the 1990s. It was bred from a Silvaner × Riesling crossing and the lacklustre MÜLLER-THURGAU and in good years can provide growers with musts notching up the all-important numbers on the OECHSLE scale as well as powerful flavours and character, and is therefore useful for blending with Müller-Thurgau. Unlike the more aristocratic and more popular crossing KERNER, however, the wine produced lacks acidity and is not even useful for blending with high-acid musts in poor years since it too needs to be fully ripe before it can express its own exuberant flavours.

Bacchus's great allure for growers, however, is that it can be planted on sites on which Riesling is an unreliable ripener and will ripen as early and as productively as Müller-Thurgau. There were 3,500 ha/8,650 acres of it in Germany in 1990, about a third more than a decade previously, and more than half of this total were in the Rheinhessen, where its substance is valued as an ingredient in QBA blends. The Mosel-Saar-Ruwer and Nahe valleys also grow more than 200 ha/490 acres, almost exclusively as a sort of alternative to the later ripening MORIO-MUSKAT for blending purposes, while Franken produces some respectable varietal wines from its increasing area of more than 600 ha.

Bacchus is also the fourth most planted grape variety in ENGLAND where it can produce relatively full, currant-flavoured wines.

BACK BLENDING, wine-making term used either synonymously with BLENDING, or more specifically for an operation involving some form of blending relatively late in the WINE-MAKING process. Back blending is most commonly used for the addition of SWEET RESERVE to sweeten or soften a wine high in ACIDITY. It is also used for adding a small portion of an older wine to give complexity to young wines or, even more rarely, for adding a small portion of young wine to refresh an older blend. A.D.W.

BACO, FRANÇOIS, was, like BOUSCHET, a nurseryman who saw his name live on in the names of some of the most successful of the vine varieties he bred. Baco's specialities were hybrids and his most successful was **Baco Blanc**, sometimes called **Baco 22A**, which was hybridized in 1898 and was, for much of the 20th century until the late 1970s, the prime ingredient in ARMAGNAC (a role now occupied by UGNI BLANC but previously occupied by FOLLE BLANCHE). Baco Blanc was Baco's solution to Folle Blanche's reluctance to be grafted after the predations of PHYLLOXERA, a crossing of Folle Blanche with the sturdy NOAH. Baco Blanc, once planted quite widely in western France, is now being fast pulled up, however, as the French authorities seek to purge hybrids from their vineyards. New Zealand grew Baco Blanc in some quantity at one time but here too evidence of a hybrid past is being rapidly eradicated.

Baco Noir, or **Baco 1**, resulted from crossing Folle Blanche with a variety of *Vitis riparia* in 1894 and was at one time cultivated in such disparate French wine regions as Burgundy, Anjou, and the Landes. It has also been widely planted in the eastern United States (see NEW YORK and CANADA), where its relatively fruity wines are not marked by the FOXY flavours associated with *Vitis* LABRUSCA and are sometimes harnessed to make NOUVEAU reds.

BACTERIA, very small micro-organisms which have serious implications in both viticulture and wine-making. It is they that are responsible for spreading a wide range of BACTERIAL DISEASES of the vine. In wine-making, however, just two groups of bacteria are important, ACETOBACTER and LACTIC BACTERIA.

The great majority of bacteria function best in neutral environments which, like water, are neither very acidic nor alkaline, and are close to the temperature of the human body. In nature they survive in or on soil, plant debris, seeds, insects, or infected plants. Bacteria are spread in the vineyard by water, wind, insects, by humans through transport of soil, infected plants, or even by vineyard equipment. Some bacteria are limited to certain tissues in the vine.

Since grape juice and wine are both high in ACIDITY, the great majority of bacteria are incapable of living in them and, if introduced, do not survive. (Drinks such as cider, perry, orange juice, and beer are all much less acid than wine, are thereby subject to many forms of BACTERIAL SPOILAGE to which wine is immune, and therefore lack wine's AGEING potential.) The only exceptions to this are acetobacter and a group of lactic bacteria which can survive in higher acid concentrations. No known human pathogenic bacteria can survive in wine, however, which is one of the reasons why it has been such a safe drink (safer than water at some times and in some places) through the ages.

Acetobacter (which do not harm humans) can turn wine, or any other dilute solution containing ETHANOL, into VINEGAR. Acetobacter require OXYGEN for growth and survival and they die in the absence of oxygen (which is why care is taken to exclude oxygen from certain stages of wine-making and all stages of wine preservation—see LEFTOVER WINE).

Lactic bacteria produce LACTIC ACID and grow best in environments where there is a very small amount of oxygen. They are important as the agents of MALOLACTIC FERMENTATION in wines, by which harsh MALIC ACID is decomposed. A.D.W. & R.E.S.

Kunkee, R., 'Bacteria in wine', in *Technology of Wine Making* (Westport, Conn., 1979).

BACTERIAL BLIGHT, vine BACTERIAL DISEASE caused by the bacterium *Xanthomonas ampelina*, so serious that it has led some Greek and French growers to abandon stricken vineyards. This disease shows its presence by retarding and killing young shoots. It is spread by rain and also by pruning tools. It can be controlled by removing and destroying infected plants and by disinfecting pruning tools between vines, as well as by copper sprays. R.E.S.

BACTERIAL DISEASES, group of grapevine diseases caused by BACTERIA, small organisms which do not commonly attack vines but which can be deadly and are difficult to control. Of the bacterial diseases, PIERCE'S DISEASE is the most important and quarantine authorities around the world are anxious to stop it spreading from America. There are places in North and Central America (southern California, Florida, and eastern Texas, for instance) where viticulture is prejudiced by the natural presence of this disease. Other economically important bacterial diseases are BACTERIAL BLIGHT and CROWN GALL. R.E.S.

Flaherty, D. L., *et al.* (eds.), *Grape Pest Management* (Berkeley, Calif., 1981).
Pearson, R. C., and Goheen, A. C., *Compendium of Grape Diseases* (St Paul, Minn., 1988).

BACTERIAL SPOILAGE, range of wine maladies or FAULTS including gas, haze, cloud, and off-flavours generated by the activity of BACTERIA in wine. These bacteria are either ACETOBACTER or LACTIC BACTERIA. Acetobacter's tendency to transform wine into vinegar can be checked by keeping air away from wine, on the part of both wine-maker and wine drinker (see LEFTOVER WINE). Lactic bacteria are more varied in their effects, which include a wide range of unpleasant-smelling compounds, depending on the type of bacterium. These are relatively rarely seen today since great care is taken by wine-makers (see STABILIZATION and HYGIENE) to guard against spoilage by lactic bacteria in the winery and to minimize the risk of a wine's being bottled with any spoilage bacteria (see FILTRATION, PASTEURIZATION, STERILE BOTTLING). If lactic bacteria do attack a wine in bottle, the results are usually detrimental to the taste and clarity of the wine, and gas is usually given off. A.D.W.

BADEN, GERMANY's longest wine region, stretching over 400 km / 250 miles from the border with FRANKEN in the north to Lake Constance (the Bodensee) and German-speaking SWITZERLAND in the south (see map on p. 442). The general and local climate, the varying soils, and the height above sea level have a marked effect on the wines of Baden's eight districts, or BEREICH.

Baden is the southernmost region of Germany, with some of its vineyards at lower LATITUDES than those in ALSACE across the river RHINE in France. As a result, an ALCOHOLIC STRENGTH a little higher than that of other German regions is characteristic of Baden wine. This natural tendency is recognized by EUROPEAN UNION law, which has placed Baden in its administrative Zone B alongside the northern wine regions of France, while the rest of Germany is in Zone A. The annual RAINFALL rises to 1,200 mm/47 in in the Bereich Ortenau on the slopes of the Black Forest. It tends to rain briefly but powerfully, with water pouring out of the sky and then rushing through the storm channels that lead across the plain to the river Rhine. EROSION would have been a serious problem without the substantial vineyard modernization since the Second World War. Of those vineyards in the state of Baden-Württemberg where modernization (FLURBEREINIGUNG) has been possible, two-thirds have been reconstructed.

The Bereich **Badisches Frankenland** covers 680 ha/1,680 acres that intermittently follow the river Tauber until the confluence with the Main at Westheim. Here, spring FROSTS are a great danger so that the vines (65 per cent MÜLLER-THURGAU) are grown mainly on slopes above the cool valley floor (see HILLSIDE VINEYARDS). The wine is similar to that of FRANKEN and for historical reasons the QUALITÄTSWEIN is sold in its neighbour's flagon-shaped BOCKSBEUTEL.

East across the Odenwald, the 1,980 ha/4,893 acres of the Bereich **Badische Bergstrasse/Kraichgau** vineyards run north and south of Heidelberg. The first part of the composite district is simply a continuation of the HESSISCHE BERGSTRASSE. In this southern stretch of the Bergstrasse, RIESLING is less widely grown and Müller-Thurgau is the leading vine. The northern Baden wines have good acidity with Riesling on the granite soil showing charm and delicacy. Most of the harvest is handled by co-operative cellars and there are fewer private estates of note than in the Bereich Ortenau, south of Baden-Baden.

There are two Bereiche in Baden whose wines are especially well known amongst wine lovers in Germany. In **Kaiserstuhl** and in the **Ortenau** the names of some communities carry the same weight in the German wine world as the better-known villages of the MOSEL-SAAR-RUWER. This may be because almost the entire grape harvest of some villages is vinified by one good co-operative cellar. Such establishments are regarded as the equals of the large, private estates of the northern German regions. Their more expensive wines bear striking labels and are treated with increasing seriousness in Germany.

South of Baden-Baden there are a few villages which, like those in the Badisches Frankenland, sell their wines in the Bocksbeutel. Riesling predominates and certainly cheaper versions can be found further south in the Bereich Ortenau, away from the inflationary effect of Baden-Baden. The steep vineyards of Neuweier and Varnhalt are impressive and lie on the spurs of the Black Forest which run west, towards the Rhine. At nearby Bühl, Sasbachwalden, Kappelrodeck, and Waldulm, good Spätburgunder (PINOT NOIR) is produced at prices which reflect its quality. If wines are aged in new BARRIQUES, or come from vines older than 20 years, a premium is liable to be asked, whether or not it is justified. However, many of these wines are destined for the top German restaurants, where a mark-up as high as 400 per cent blurs nuances in ex-cellars prices.

Durbach near Offenburg is one of the best and most versatile Ortenau wine villages. There is a large area planted in Spätburgunder, and the Riesling (known locally as Klingelberger) has that vital ingredient in Germany of good ACIDITY. Durbach also claims more Traminer (see GEWÜRZTRAMINER), or Clevner as it is called in the Ortenau, than any other village in the country. Besides a good co-operative cellar there are at least 11 successful private estates, with vineyards on extremely steep and high slopes directly above the village.

Low YIELDS contribute to the quality of better Baden wine today. Village co-operatives encourage the production of a crop far smaller than the maximum legal amount, through the way in which they pay their members. Nevertheless, yields from the white wine varieties are often greater in Baden than they are in Alsace, and the wines are usually not so concentrated as a result. Less sugar is added to them to increase the alcohol content (see ENRICHMENT) and many Baden wines are lighter in style. With the red wines the situation is different and the better Baden Spätburgunder is impressive, a dark coloured wine with a wealth of flavour.

Between Offenburg and Freiburg, the capital of the Baden wine trade, the Bereich **Breisgau** rolls across the rural foothills of the Black Forest. Private estate bottlers are rare and much of the wine is made by the vast central co-operative cellars in Kaiserstuhl, the Badischer Winzerkeller. The CO-OPERATIVES are responsible for some 85 per cent of Baden's wine production, and the Badischer Winzerkeller receives grapes from 5,000 ha/12,350 acres of vineyard. The range it offers is understandably enormous, and each year 500 or so wines are individually vinified. Half of the turnover, however, is concentrated on 20 wines only.

The wines of the Bereich **Tuniberg** are lighter than those of Kaiserstuhl and virtually all are produced by the Badischer Winzerkeller. South of Freiburg, the pleasant landscape of the Bereich **Markgräflerland** is known for its easy-to-drink wine from Gutedel (CHASSELAS), and near Lake Constance the wines of the Bereich **Bodensee** have more acidity and elegance. Baden-Württemberg has a fine DOMÄNE overlooking the lake at Meersburg, with 59 ha planted 50 per cent in Spätburgunder and 34 per cent in Müller-Thurgau.

The many visitors to Baden buy wine directly from the producer, so where the scenery is at its prettiest, such as in the Glottertal in the Breisgau, or by Lake Constance, retail and wine bar sales are at their highest. The few private estates also supply restaurants and wine merchants, and village co-operatives achieve national distribution through supermarkets. If the northern German regions will always have the largest offer of stylish Rieslings, the structure of the best Baden Burgunder or PINOT wines, in particular, makes them potentially well suited to the export market. I.J.

Harvesting **Baga** grapes from Luis Pato's 70-year-old vines in the **Bairrada** region.

BAGA, the most common grape variety planted in the BAIRRADA region of Portugal and probably Portugal's most planted single variety for it is also commonly grown in the Dão and Ribatejo regions too, sometimes called Tinta Bairrada. The name means 'berry' in Portuguese, and its berries are notable for their thick skins and the high levels of TANNINS and ACIDITY in the wines they produce (particularly when, as was traditionally the case, there is no DESTEMMING). The finest examples can age well and vinification techniques are in the process of modification.

BAGACEIRA, Portuguese term for POMACE BRANDY, a brandy made from grape pomace rather than wine. See also MARC and GRAPPA.

BAGHDAD, the capital of modern IRAQ, was founded by the first Abbasid caliph, al-Mansur, in AD 762. Early in its history the city became the focus of a Bacchic culture (see ARAB POETS), celebrated most eloquently by the poet ABU NUWAS. Although wine was imbibed in the Caliphal court and some outlying districts of the city (al-Karkh, for example), most wine was consumed where it was produced, in the small monasteries and towns that lay outside the city in various parts of Iraq. Their names are preserved in poetry and other sources ('Āna, Hīt, Qutrubbul in the vicinity of the city, for example, and Tīzanabādh further south near Kufa). P.K.

BAG-IN-BOX. See BOXES.

BAIRRADA, wine region in northern PORTUGAL (see map on p. 750). The coastal belt south of OPORTO has been producing wine since Portugal gained independence from the Moors in the 10th century. By the early 1700s Bairrada's dark, tannic red wines were widely drunk in Britain, masquerading as or blended with PORT from the DOURO valley to the north. Then in 1756, as part of his measures to protect the authenticity of port (see DELIMITATION), the marquis of Pombal, Portugal's powerful prime minister, ordered that Bairrada's vineyards should be uprooted.

It has taken Bairrada more than two centuries to recover. The district was excluded from the list of wine regions demarcated by the Portuguese government in 1908. After constant pressure from growers, Bairrada was awarded Região Demarcada status in 1979 and, like Portugal's other RDs, it is now designated a Denominação de Origem Controlada (DOC).

Like much of northern Portugal, Bairrada is an area of agricultural smallholdings. Cereals, beans, and vines thrive in between clumps of eucalyptus on the heavy but fertile clay soils. Most growers send their grapes to one of six CO-OPERATIVES but more than 20 merchants also have cellars in the region where wines from Bairrada and neighbouring DÃO are bought in for AGEING and BLENDING. Recently a number of larger individual estates have started to produce their own wines.

Bairrada is unusual in Portugal in that it is almost a one-grape region. Over 70 per cent of the wines are red, made principally from the BAGA vine. This small, dark, thick-skinned grape produces solid wines that often suffer from an excess of TANNINS, a characteristic exacerbated on those properties without DESTEMMING equipment. But wine styles are changing and firms such as Aliança and Sogrape (who produce MATEUS Rosé in Bairrada) are adapting their vinification methods to make their wines softer and more approachable. White grapes, mostly Maria Gomes (or FERNÃO PIRES) and BICAL, are grown to produce traditional method sparkling wines, although these are not entitled to the denomination.

On the edge of the region, the Palace Hotel at Buçaco blends its own red and white wines from grapes bought from growers in Dão and Bairrada. These are widely regarded as some of the best table wines in Portugal but are available only to guests dining at the hotel or one of its few associated establishments, apart from those few bottles which occasionally crop up at AUCTION. R.J.M.

BALANCE is essential for quality in both vine and wine.

Vines

Vine balance is a viticultural concept little appreciated by wine consumers, yet one which is essential for producing good-quality grapes for premium wine-making. A vine is in balance when the LEAF TO FRUIT RATIO is favourable, and also when both are in a favourable ratio to the vine's reserves of CARBOHYDRATES, which limit early growth in the spring. Vine balance concerns VIGOUR and its management by the VITICULTURIST. The rate of growth of vine shoots in the spring is a good measure of vine balance relative to reserves. If shoots grow very vigorously, then their numbers are too low, while if spring growth of shoots is sluggish, then shoot numbers may be too high. The viticulturist is responsible for this state of affairs by choosing the number of buds to leave after winter PRUNING, although it can also be affected by the weather. That decision is aided by the viticulturist's experience of the vineyard, but can alternatively be calculated using BALANCED PRUNING criteria. R.E.S.

Wines

Wine tasters say that a wine has balance, or is well **balanced**, if its ALCOHOLIC STRENGTH, ACIDITY, RESIDUAL SUGAR, and TANNINS complement each other so that no single one of them is obtrusive on the PALATE. It is a wine characteristic quite unrelated to FLAVOUR.

BALANCED PRUNING. The number of buds to be left at PRUNING should be judged relative to the vine's capacity to support the growth of shoots early in the growing season from its reserves of CARBOHYDRATES. A common method is to weigh the CANES (the shoots which grew the previous year) and to use this figure to judge the appropriate bud numbers to leave at winter pruning. For example, one formula is to keep around 30 buds for each kg/2 lb of pruning weight. Experienced vine pruners can achieve a similar effect by looking at each vine, judging how it grew last growing season, and adjusting this year's number of buds accordingly.

If too few buds are left on the vine, then shoots in spring

Balance

Vegetative cycle

Canopies tend to become more and more shaded and vegetative, leading to yield and quality reductions. Typical of vineyards on high potential soils with an inadequate trellis.

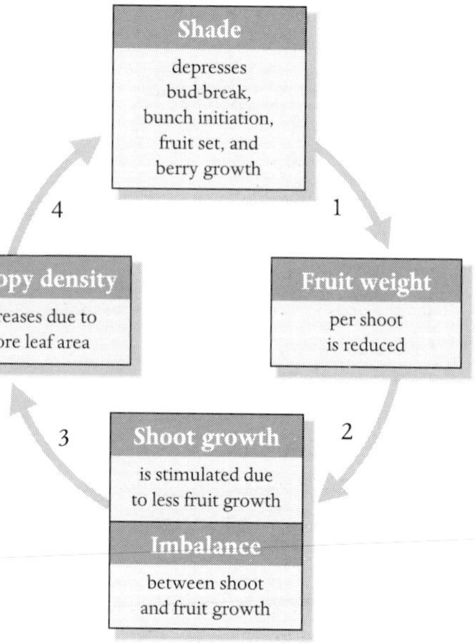

Balanced cycle

Light stimulates shoot fruitfulness leading to balance between shoot and fruit growth. Typical of vineyards trellised according to vigour.

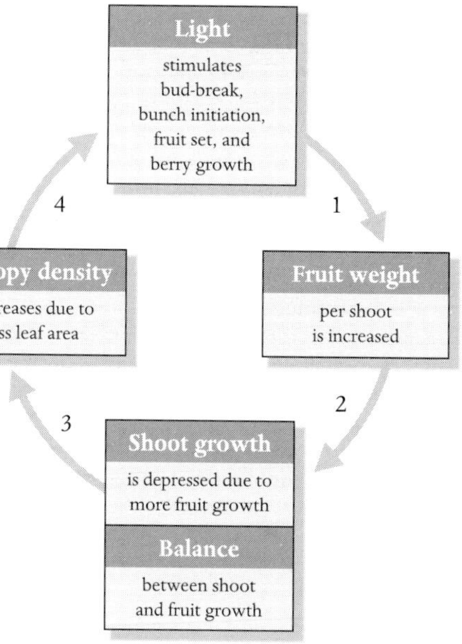

will grow quickly and have leaves which are too large and stems which are too thick. The vine will have a high LEAF TO FRUIT RATIO, which may result from poor fruit set (see COULURE). In any event the leaf to fruit imbalance normally leads to a shaded CANOPY MICROCLIMATE and attendant problems of loss of YIELD and quality. Such a situation is common for vines planted close together on fertile soil.

On the other hand, if vines are pruned to many buds then the resulting large number of shoots will develop only slowly in spring. The leaves will be small and the stems spindly. The danger here is that the leaf area will be too low for the weight of grapes, which will ripen slowly and wine quality will suffer. This condition is often described as OVERCROPPING.

See also PRUNING. R.E.S.

Smart, R. E., and Robinson, M., *Sunlight into Wine: A Handbook for Winegrape Canopy Management* (Adelaide, 1991).

Tassie, E., and Freeman, B. M., 'Pruning', in B. G. Coombe and P. R. Dry (eds.), *Viticulture, i: Resources in Australia* (Adelaide, 1988).

Winkler, A. J., *et al.*, *General Viticulture* (2nd edn., Berkeley, Calif., 1974).

BALLING, scale of measuring total dissolved compounds in grape juice, and therefore its approximate concentration of grape sugars. It is very similar to the BRIX scale used in the United States. For more details, see MUST WEIGHT.

BANAT RIESLING or **Banat Rizling**, white grape variety grown in ROMANIA and just across the border with what was Yugoslavia in VOJVODINA. Its produce tends to be somewhat heavy, a sort of LASKI RIZLING without the lift.

BANDOL, the most serious wine of PROVENCE, typically a deep flavoured, lush red blend dominated by the Mourvèdre grape. Like CHÂTEAUNEUF-DU-PAPE, Bandol produces quintessentially Mediterranean red wines which are easy to appreciate despite their longevity.

The appellation is named after the port from which they were once shipped all over the world. Bandol is now a Mediterreanean resort town with little to offer the wine tourist, and the vineyards are on south-facing terraces well above the coast called locally *restanques*. As in the smaller appellation of CASSIS just along the coast, the vines are protected from the cold north winds, but have to fight property developers for their right to continued existence.

This particularly well-favoured southern corner is one of the few parts of France in which Mourvèdre can be relied upon to ripen. Other dark-berried varieties grown include Grenache and Cinsaut, much used for the local herby rosés which account for about one bottle of Bandol in three, together with strictly limited additions of Syrah and Carignan. A small quantity of white Bandol is made from Bourboulenc, Clairette, and Ugni Blanc with a maximum of 40 per cent Sauvignon Blanc, but little of it escapes the region's fish restaurants.

The Bandol appellation managed to produce a total of 40,000 hl / 1.05 million gal in 1990 and all too little of this often magnificent red wine, and enticing rosé, was exported. Winemaking techniques are traditional but evolving. All reds must have at least 18 months in cask. Mechanical harvesting is banned. Domaine Tempier is one of the few domaines to have a well-established market outside France.

Lynch, K., *Adventures along the Wine Route* (New York, 1988).

BANYULS and **Banyuls Grand Cru** are the appellations for France's finest and certainly most complex VINS DOUX NATURELS, made from vertiginous terraced vineyards above the Mediterranean at the southern limit of ROUSSILLON, and indeed mainland France. The dry but powerful red wine produced in the same vineyards is entitled to the appellation COLLIOURE, Banyuls-sur-Mer and Collioure being two of the four dramatic seaside communes included in these two appellations.

Banyuls differs from RIVESALTES, Roussillon's catch-all vin doux naturel, not only in terms of quality but also in style. Grenache Noir must dominate the blend, constituting at least 50 per cent of a Banyuls and 75 per cent of a Banyuls Grand Cru (which latter appellation is ignored by individual producers of the calibre of Dr Parcé of Domaine du Mas Blanc, who could be said to have re-energized the appellation in the mid 20th century). The grapes yield poorly and are often part shrivelled before being picked in early October. Alcohol is added while the must is still on the skins so that a wide range of flavour compounds are absorbed into the young wine, which, after perhaps five weeks' further maceration, is then subjected to one of a wide range of ÉLEVAGE techniques. A Banyuls Grand Cru must be matured in wood for at least 30 months. Others may be kept for as long as the producer desires and can afford, in glass BONBONNES or in barrels of all sizes, either carefully topped up in cool, damp conditions or deliberately evaporating, sometimes outdoors to achieve RANCIO flavours, or even in a local version of a SOLERA system.

Some Banyuls is made to preserve the heady aromas of macerated red fruits; others to display the characteristics of a particularly successful and long-past year (sometimes labelled RIMAGE); while other Banyuls demonstrate the extraordinary levels of concentration that can be achieved by Grenache, heat, and time. Such wines are some of the few that go well with chocolate, although many a French chef has created savoury dishes, often with a hint of sweetness, to be served expressly with a particular Banyuls. This is the only French wine region able to offer 20- and 30-year-old wines as a serious proportion of its total production. See also MAURY.

George, R., *French Country Wines* (London, 1990).

BARBARESCO, powerful red wine based on the NEBBIOLO grape grown around the village of Barbaresco in the PIEDMONT region in north west Italy. For long considered very much the junior of BAROLO in terms of its size and the power and prestige of its wines, Barbaresco emerged from Barolo's shadow in the 1960s to win recognition of its own striking qualities of elegance and aromatic intensity.

The wine is, in fact, a younger one than Barolo: it was not

Snow is by no means uncommon in the vineyards of **Barbaresco**.

until the mid 1890s that Domizio Cavazza, professor at the Onological School of ALBA and director of the Co-operative Winery of Barbaresco, succeeded in fermenting all of the sugars and producing a completely dry wine, replicating the work of Louis Oudart in Barolo 50 years earlier. Barbaresco did not enjoy Barolo's connection with the House of Savoy and the nobility of the royal court in Turin, and suffered relative commercial obscurity until the efforts of Giovanni GAJA and Bruno Giacosa in the 1960s demonstrated the full potential of the wine.

The production zone of Barbaresco is to the north east and east of the city of Alba and is considerably smaller than that of Barolo. With 484 ha / 1,200 acres currently in production, the Barbaresco DOCG is just over 40 per cent of the area planted in the Barolo DOCG zone. The wine is produced in the townships of Barbaresco, Treiso (formerly part of Barbaresco), Neive, and a fragment of Alba, although 95 per cent of the cultivated vineyards lie in the first three. Neive calls itself 'the township of four wines' (the others being MOSCATO, BARBERA, DOLCETTO), and Nebbiolo only consolidated its position there after the Second World War. Even today Neive has fewer than 100 ha of Nebbiolo, less than that of Barbera or Dolcetto and half the area planted with Moscato.

The soil of the Barbaresco zone is fundamentally a calcareous marl of the Tortonian epoch and the wines, in their relative softness and fruitiness and their perfumed aromas, bear a certain resemblance to Barolo produced on similar soils around the villages of La Morra and Barolo, although it is rare to find a Barbaresco with the body and concentration of a fine Cannubi or Brunate. A few positions in Neive, however—notably Santo Stefano and Bricco di Neive—do give wines which, in local parlance, *baroleggiano*, or resemble a Barolo.

Nebbiolo ripens earlier in Barbaresco than in Barolo, a factor which frequently saves at least a part of the Barbaresco harvest in the rainy Octobers which dilute Barolo; there are therefore likely to be more successful vintages in a given decade in Barbaresco than in Barolo.

Wine-making techniques, which had previously favoured extremely prolonged MACERATION and CASK AGEING, evolved in the 1970s and 1980s, much as in Barolo, towards considerably shorter periods in cask in an effort to respond to modern tastes for rounder, fruitier wines. If Barbaresco is generally a lighter bodied wine than Barolo (although these are wines which must have a minimum ALCOHOLIC STRENGTH of 12.5° and easily reach 13.5°), it is not lacking in the TANNINS and ACIDITY that mark the Nebbiolo grape; young Barbaresco is by no means an inevitably pleasurable glass of wine. It does mature more rapidly than Barolo, however, and rarely ages as well. Barbaresco is normally at its best between five and 10 years of age, with the exception of the above-mentioned vineyards in Neive. The general level of wine-making skills is lower in Barbaresco than in Barolo, a fact that is probably a reflection of the later emergence of the former as a fine wine zone of significance, the lower prices paid for the wines over the years, and the slower development of estate bottling by small producers. In partial compensation, the zone does benefit from the presence of an important co-operative winery in Barbaresco itself. Produttori del Barbaresco is Italy's finest co-operative, which has established admirable quality levels in both its blended Barbaresco and its designated-vineyard selections; its example has been followed by the co-operative of Treiso.

Single-vineyard bottlings are a relatively recent phenomenon, in Barbaresco as in the rest of Italy. The first efforts date from 1967, and there is a less firmly established written record of CRU designation here than in Barolo. Lorenzo Fantini's monograph on Piedmontese viticulture of the late 19th century indicates no 'choice positions' in Barbaresco, and the first attempts to list and rate the finest positions date from the 1960s (Luigi VERONELLI) and the 1970s (Renato Ratti). NÉGOCIANTS' willingness to pay higher prices for grapes from certain vineyards, however, does establish the existence of a certain consensus existing in the zone, a tradition which gave an undeniable prestige to Asili, Montefico, Montestefano, and Rabajà in Barbaresco; Albesani and Gallina in Neive; and Pajorè in Treiso. A certain number of the most famous vineyards—San Lorenzo, Tildin, and Martinenga in Barbaresco, Santo Stefano in Neive—are, in effect, 'man-made' crus which have gained their current prestige from the dedicated work and exacting standards of producers such as GAJA and Marchese di Gresy, and have no historical tradition behind them (see also GUIGAL of Côte-Rôtie in France). Barbaresco suffered less than Barolo from the proliferation of single-vineyard names and resulting consumer confusion in the 1980s; it has suffered more from the imprecision and lack of controls over vineyard demarcation and boundaries which has led to an inflated use of certain names, Rabajà in particular. New legislation, approved in early 1992, is designed to put an end to this phenomenon in Barbaresco and elsewhere.

Ultra-short fermentations and BARRIQUE ageing of the wines were introduced to Barbaresco in the mid 1980s, although the former phenomenon has found fewer converts than in Barolo; the softer quality of Nebbiolo in Barbaresco—conserved by a shorter, one-year minimum ageing period in wood—makes radical innovations in wine-making techniques less of a necessity. The use of new OAK spread rapidly, however, due to the powerful influence of Angelo Gaja, headquartered in Barbaresco itself, and its spicy and aromatic qualities seem to blend well with the character of the wine, although by far the majority of Barbaresco continues to be aged in the zone's traditional large oval casks. D.T.

Anderson, B., *The Wine Atlas of Italy* (London and New York, 1990).
Gleave, D., *The Wines of Italy* (London and New York, 1989).

BARBARIANS, uncivilized ancient European people who were introduced to wine, and therefore considered civilized, by CLASSICAL civilizations. See CELTS.

BARBAROSSA, red grape variety planted, and occasionally made into VARIETAL wine, in Emilia-Romagna and Corsica. In PROVENCE it is known as Barberoux and is a permitted, if little planted, grape variety in Côtes de Provence.

BARBERA, productive and versatile red grape variety which is challenged only by SANGIOVESE in its many forms as Italy's most planted dark-berried vine. There were nearly 50,000 ha/123,500 acres of Barbera planted in Italy in 1990, but it has travelled widely, most notably to the Americas.

The Monferrato in PIEDMONT is frequently cited as the variety's birthplace, although the AMPELOGRAPHER Pierre Viala cites OLTREPÒ PAVESE in Lombardy as its original home. In any case, the archives of the cathedral chapters of Casale Monferrato conserve contracts leasing vineyard land between 1246 and 1277 provided that 'de bonis vitibus barbexinis' were planted.

Barbera ripens relatively late, as much as two weeks after the other 'lesser' black grape variety of Piedmont DOLCETTO—although still in advance of the stately NEBBIOLO. Its chief characteristic is its high level of natural acidity even when fully ripe, which has helped its popularity in hot climates. Such a widely planted variety (see below) has understandably developed various strains in its various spheres of Italian influence, Piedmont, Oltrepò Pavese, EMILIA-ROMAGNA, and the Mezzogiorno.

A white-berried **Barbera Bianca** is also known.

Piedmont

Barbera is sometimes called 'the people's wine' of Piedmont for its versatility and its abundant production; it usually accounts for more than half of all the wine produced in the region in a given year, close to 55 per cent of the total red DOC production, and 70 per cent of all the grapes produced for VINO DA TAVOLA, totalling over 2 million hl/5.2 million gal in a favourable vintage. The wine comes in a bewildering range of styles, from the young and spritzy to powerful and intense wines that need extended cellaring, reflecting the extreme heterogeneousness of the soils and MESOCLIMATES of the zones where it is planted.

Certain characteristics are constant none the less: a deep ruby colour (the wine was frequently used in the past to 'correct' the colour of Nebbiolo grapes grown in BAROLO and BARBARESCO); a full body with notably low levels of TANNINS; pronounced ACIDITY which is aggravated by over-production, Barbera being a variety of exemplary vigour and productivity. The use of southern Italian blending wine to compensate for the thinness and sharpness of overcropped Barbera, a common practice in the past, seems to be coming to an end as yields drop. The DOC regulations regrettably permit generous yields (70 hl/ha), relatively low ALCOHOLIC STRENGTH (12° in Alba and Asti, 11.5° in the Monferrato), and high minimum acidity in relation to the alcohol and body of the wines, and therefore do little to restrain yields or exalt the better characteristics of the wine.

Alba, Asti, and the Monferrato give their names to the three DOC zones of Piedmont, although the zones tend to sprawl across rather vast extensions of territory: there are 171 townships in the Asti DOC and 215 townships in the Monferrato DOC (with the two zones overlapping to a certain extent). A number of leading producers in these two DOC zones have, in fact, refused DOC status for their wines, preferring to label them vino da tavola on the grounds that the net has been far too widely cast. Given the enormous acreage devoted to Barbera, it is no surprise that little mapping of the most suitable subzones has occurred, but, at the level of folk knowledge, the hills immediately to the north and south of Alba and Monforte d'Alba in the Alba DOC and, in the province of Asti, the area from Nizza Monferrato north west towards Vinchio, Belveglio, and Rocchetta Tánaro are considered classic zones for Barbera. Much remains to be done, obviously, in matching variety and TERROIR.

A small number of Barberas have undergone a significant metamorphosis during the 1980s as producers, in a parallel development to the Sangiovese-based SUPERTUSCANS, have begun to age their wines in small oak barrels. The pioneering and, to a certain extent, still paradigmatic effort was Giacomo Bologna's Bricco dell'Uccellone (although Émile PEYNAUD, while consulting for the ASTI SPUMANTE house of Gancia in the early 1970s, had also suggested using BARRIQUES for Barbera, much to local bewilderment). There can be no question that new oak substantially modifies the character of Barbera, adding a real spiciness to its rather neutral aromas and a certain quantity of ligneous tannins which firm up its structure and soften the impact of its acidity. It should be remembered, however, that these new wave Barberas, being invariably the product of low yields and careful vinification, already have more body and flavour than traditional Barbera, even of a better sort, and that small barrels are unlikely to become a panacea for this grape. The new wave Barberas which rather self-consciously strive for greatness have also doubtless created some confusion for consumers used to regarding Barbera merely as a hearty and warming glass to accompany the traditionally robust fare of the Piedmontese kitchen. D.T.

Elsewhere in Italy

Barbera dominates much of Lombardy, in particular the vineyards of Oltrepò Pavese, where it makes VARIETAL wines of varying quality and degrees of fizziness, some fine and lively, as well as being blended with the softer local Croatina or BONARDA grape. It is a minor ingredient in FRANCIACORTA and is found, as elsewhere in Italy, in oceans of basic VINO DA TAVOLA.

Barbera is also much planted immediately south east of Piedmont in the Colli Piacentini, the hills above Piacenza, of EMILIA-ROMAGNA. Here too it is often blended with Bonarda, particularly in the Val Tidone for the DOC red Gutturnio. It is also planted in the Bologna and Parma hills, the Colli Bolognesi and Colli di Parma, where it may also produce a VARIETAL wine which rarely has the concentration of Piedmont's best. Most of central Italy's Barbera plays a minor role in blends with more locally indigenous varieties, not always adding useful acidity, although that is its real purpose in the deep south.

A Barbera Sarda is grown in SARDINIA, where some argue that the local Perricone, or Pignatello, is also Barbera.

Outside Italy

Only just outside Italy, Barbera is also grown over the border with what was Yugoslavia in SLOVENIA, chiefly in the Primorski coastal zone.

Elsewhere in Europe it is barely known, but Italian immigrants took Barbera with them to both North and, particularly, South America. It is planted in Argentina where there are several thousand hectares, mainly in Mendoza and San Juan provinces. The variety is planted to a much more limited extent in the rest of South America. In California, however, particularly in the hot SAN JOAQUIN VALLEY, there are nearly 10,000 acres/4,050 ha. Among grape varieties hopefully brought to California from Piedmont, Barbera has consistently outperformed the nobler Nebbiolo, and yet has still not managed to win many friends or influence many people. In the NORTH COAST counties it has yielded a few memorable wines (notably made by Louis M. Martini), several of the finest of them blended with PETITE SIRAH. However, most of the Napa and Sonoma plantings have disappeared, leaving the vast preponderance in the San Joaquin Valley, where winemakers value the variety in blending for its ability to maintain acid levels in hot climates.

Anderson, B., *The Wine Atlas of Italy* (London and New York, 1990).
Gleave, D., *The Wines of Italy* (London and New York, 1989).

BARDOLINO, cheerful and uncomplicated light red wine from the south eastern shores of Lake Garda in the VENETO region of north east Italy. It is produced from CORVINA, Rondinella, and Molinara grapes. As in the other two important Veneto DOCS SOAVE and VALPOLICELLA, the original production zone is that known as CLASSICO (Bardolino, Garda, Lazise, Affa, Costermano, and Cavaion), extended to a considerably larger zone whose wines may be called simply Bardolino. Exact TERROIR seems to have rather less effect on the quality of this relatively simple wine than it does on Soave and Valpolicella, and good Bardolino is regularly produced outside the Classico zone, notably in Sommacampagna.

At the beginning of the 1990s, about 200,000 hl/5.3 million gal of Bardolino were produced each year, with 45 per cent coming from the Bardolino Classico heartland. Although the DOC blend, in terms of both the indicated grapes and the percentages to be employed, differs little from Valpolicella, Bardolino producers tend to use less Corvina (the variety which gives body and structure) and more of the somewhat neutral Rondinella than their neighbours in Valpolicella.

The rosé version of the wine is called Bardolino Chiaretto. Bardolino Superiore, a slightly headier wine with an extra one per cent of alcohol, must be aged a year before being released. Bardolino NOVELLO, an attempt to ape Beaujolais NOUVEAU, was born in the late 1980s, but the competition of similar novello wines from every grape and corner of Italy considerably lessened the marketing impact of the move. D.T.

BAROLO, the most powerful and dramatic expression of the NEBBIOLO grape, takes its name from the village of the same name 15 km/9 miles to the south of the town of Alba in the region of PIEDMONT in north west Italy.

In the mid 19th century the local viticultural output was transformed from a sweet to a dry wine, assuming the character it has maintained to this day. Up to this point the elevated sugar content of the late maturing Nebbiolo grape, the cold cellars of Piedmont in November and December, and the unavailability of prepared YEASTS had combined to make a certain quantity of RESIDUAL SUGAR in the wines all but inevitable. The metamorphosis of the wines in the cellars of Giulietta Falletti, marquise of Barolo, was effected by the French OENOLOGIST Louis Oudart, called to the zone by Camillo Cavour, the architect of Italian unity and mayor of Grinzano Cavour in the Barolo zone.

The wine, (one of several) widely termed 'the wine of kings, the king of wines' by its more avid admirers, enjoyed a privileged position from the very beginning, not merely among the nobility of Turin but also with the ruling House of Savoy (see PIEDMONT). Carlo Alberto di Savoia, who greatly appreciated the wines of Giulietta Falletti, purchased and developed the properties of the castles of Verduno and Roddi, both in the modern Barolo zone, while Vittorio Emanuele II's son by the royal mistress Rosa Vercellana, Emanuele, count of Mirafiori, developed the vineyards around the hunting lodge of Fontanafredda in Serralunga d'Alba. This association with what was then Italy's reigning dynasty has given Barolo an aura and a mystique which it has retained to this day.

The core of Barolo has always been the townships of Barolo, La Morra, Castiglione Falletto, Serralunga d'Alba, and the northern half of Monforte d'Alba, supplemented by outlying areas in a variety of other townships which have changed over the course of time. The Agricultural Commission of Alba added Grinzano, part of Verduno, and a section of Novello in 1909, confirming the previous DELIMITATION work of the Ministry of Agriculture in 1896. This became the official definition of the zone in 1934, not without protests from Barolo and Castiglione Falletto, which considered themselves the true standard-bearers of authentic Barolo. Parts of Diano d'Alba, Roddi, and Cherasco were added in the DOC decree of 1966, an error at least on paper, although growers in the zone have generally been careful to plant Nebbiolo only where it can ripen properly, and the villages of Roddi and Cherasco have respectively a mere 10.77 and 1.26 ha (26.4 and 3.1 acres) planted to Nebbiolo for Barolo.

The five core townships mentioned above, in fact, contain 87 per cent of the total Barolo area. This sensible demarcation of the zone, disciplined YIELDS (56 hl/ha (3.2 tons/acre) maximum), and reasonable requirements for CASK AGEING (originally three years, subsequently lowered to two years with a pending proposal to lower it to one year) make this DOC (promoted to DOCG in 1980) one of Italy's most intelligent. These sensible restraints have also curbed the multiplicity of superior wines labelled VINO DA TAVOLA characteristic of other areas of Italy (see SUPERTUSCAN, for example).

Although Barolo is always a rich, concentrated, and heady wine, with pronounced TANNINS and ACIDITY, significant stylistic differences among the various wines of the zone do exist and tend to reflect the two major soil types of the zone which are conveniently separated by the Alba–Barolo road which runs along the valley floor, separating La Morra and Barolo to the west from Castiglione Falletto, Monforte d'Alba, and Serralunga d'Alba to the east. The first soil type, calcareous marls of the Tortonian epoch which are relatively compact, fresher, and more fertile, characterize the vineyards of the townships of La Morra and Barolo and result in softer, fruitier, aromatic wines which age relatively rapidly for a Barolo. The second soil type, from the Helvetian epoch, with a higher proportion of compressed sandstone, is less compact, poorer, and less fertile, with the result that the townships of Castiglione Falletto, Monforte d'Alba, and Serralunga d'Alba yield more intense, structured wines that mature more slowly.

All fine Barolo, however, shares certain common traits: a garnet hue, tending toward ruby in Tortonian soils and towards brick in Helvetian soils; complex and expansive aromas of plums, dried roses, tar, liquorice, and—according to a few fortunate connoisseurs—the local white truffles. Full flavours are backed by substantial tannins, a dense texture, and real alcoholic warmth. (Barolo from Helvetian soils easily surpasses 14°, and an ALCOHOLIC STRENGTH of over 15° is by no means rare in superior vintages.) Excessive EXTRACTION and/or cask ageing can easily lead to overly tannic and bitter wines, and obtaining the proper richness while maintaining a certain drinkability is the fundamental, and not easy, task of the individual producer, a balancing act which is not rendered easier by the late ripening character of the Nebbiolo grape.

Two developments have marked contemporary, post-DOC Barolo: the move towards estate bottling and single-vineyard bottling (principally by small producers), and an attempt to find a fruitier, less austere style of Barolo more in tune with modern palates. The marketing of the wine was dominated by NÉGOCIANT houses until 1960, unsurprisingly in a production zone where the average property is little more than 1 ha (1,107 growers divided 1164 ha/2,875 acres in 1990). Estate bottling represented both an attempt by peasant proprietors to reap greater economic benefits from the production cycle and a desire to put their name, as well as that of their holdings, before the public eye. Négociant houses, dealing in large quantities, necessarily blended the wines of different provenances into a house Barolo (just like their counterparts in BURGUNDY. When skilfully done, this did—and still does—accomplish the creation of balanced and harmonious wines which will exemplify the general characteristics of Barolo. It is none the less true that certain privileged positions have long enjoyed a greater prestige and given more distinctive wines in both the written tradition (from Lorenzo Fantini in the late 19th century to modern writers such as Luigi VERONELLI and Renato Ratti) and in the oral tradition of the zone, opinions made concretely significant by the higher prices paid by négociants for the grapes and wines of certain vineyards. While there is no absolute unanimity, most shortlists of the finest CRUS include Rocche and Cerequio in La Morra; Cannubi, Sarmazza, and Brunate in Barolo (this latter vineyard shared, *à la bourguignonne*, with La Morra); Rocche, Villero, and Monprivato in Castiglione Falletto; Bussia, Ginestra, and Santo Stefano di Perno in Monforte d'Alba; Lazzarito and Vigna Rionda in Serralunga d'Alba.

The multiplicity of single-vineyard bottlings in the 1980s,

in the absence of an official CLASSIFICATION, has had the paradoxical result of focusing attention on and reinforcing confidence in the brand names of single producers. It should be remembered that estate bottling and single-vineyard bottling are parallel and not interlocking phenomena: small producers, in many cases, have continued to offer a generic Barolo in addition to those from a selected vineyard, and virtually all of the négociant houses could offer a selection of Barolo crus alongside their blended Barolo by the late 1980s.

Like many of the world's powerful and age-worthy red wines, Barolo has had to come to terms in the 1970s and 1980s with market demands for fruitier, less tannic wines that can more easily be drunk while young—not an easy transition for a zone where FERMENTATION and MACERATION have regularly lasted as long as two months. The leaders of the movement towards a softer style of Barolo were Renato Ratti, Paolo Cordero di Montezemolo, and the house of Ceretto. Their methods consisted of shorter fermentations (generally 10 to 14 days) and an abbreviated ageing period in wood followed by extended BOTTLE AGEING prior to commercial release.

'Modernists' and 'traditionalists' continue to coexist in the zone, at times uneasily and polemically, although results thus far tend to confirm that Barolo, always rich in tannins and acidity, best benefits from abbreviated fermentation and cask ageing when producers accept the discipline of smaller yields to give adequate flavour concentration. That 'modern' Barolo ages less well and oxidizes more easily (see OXIDATION) than 'traditional' Barolo is, however, beyond discussion. A group of young Turks appeared in the 1980s to push the principles of the modernists even further: fermentation times of a week or less; minimal cask ageing; the use of new small oak barrels. This last phenomenon is as yet unproven, although the preliminary results—ham-handed in many cases, imperceptible in others—suggest that Barolo and new oak are more likely to be a marriage of convenience than a marriage made in heaven.

See also BARBARESCO. D.T.

Anderson, B., *The Wine Atlas of Italy* (London and New York, 1990).
Garner, M., and Merritt, P., *Barolo: Tar and Roses* (London, 1990).
Gleave, D., *The Wines of Italy* (London and New York, 1989).

BAROQUE is the intensely local grape variety of which white TURSAN must be made. Although it is now grown almost exclusively in the Landes *département*, it was at one time known throughout south west France and was valued by growers in the early 20th century for its resistance to POWDERY MILDEW. The total area planted with Baroque was quite literally decimated in the 1970s and 1980s by Landais disaffection with viticulture, but recent investment in the Tursan appellation by the proprietor of the famously epicurean establishment at Eugénie-les-Bains may help save this characterful variety from extinction.

The wine produced displays the unusual combination of high alcohol and fine aroma, something akin to ripe pears. Galet claims that the variety was brought back from Spain by pilgrims to Santiago de Compostela.

Galet, P., *Cépages et vignobles de France* (2nd edn., Montpellier, 1990).

BAROSSA VALLEY, the heart of the Australian wine industry, the most famous wine region in AUSTRALIA, and the one in which most wine is produced, even if a high proportion of it is shipped in from vineyards outside the valley itself. There is an increasing trend towards planting off the valley floor and on the **Barossa Ranges**. The Barossa District includes both Eden Valley and Barossa Valley. For more detail see SOUTH AUSTRALIA.

BARREL, cylindrical container traditionally made from WOOD and historically used for the storage and transportation of a wide range of goods. Today, barrels are used almost exclusively in the production of fine wines and spirits, and are almost invariably made of wood (although TORRES and others have unsuccessfully experimented with various combinations of STAINLESS STEEL and wood in an effort to cut costs). The bulge, or bilge, of barrels means that they can be rolled and spun easily, and that, when they are kept horizontal, any sediment naturally collects in one place, from which the wine can easily be separated by RACKING.

Barrels come in many sizes (see BARREL TYPES) and qualities (see BARREL MAKING), although the word barrel is conventionally used for a wooden container small enough to be moved, while VATS are larger, permanent containers, sometimes with an open top. COOPERAGE is the collective noun for all wooden containers, whether barrels or vats, and the word CASK is used for wooden containers of all sizes. Some Britons use the word cask deliberately in place of the more American word barrel.

BARREL MATURATION is the term used in this book for ageing a wine in a barrel, while CASK AGEING has been used as a general term for keeping a wine in a larger wooden container. BARREL FERMENTATION is the technique of fermenting a white wine in barrel.

A barrel is made up of STAVES shaped into a bulging cylinder, with hoops round it, a flat circular head at either end, and at least one hole for a BUNG. See BARREL MAKING for details.

History

Although HERODOTUS refers to palm-wood casks being used to carry Armenian wine to Babylon in Mesopotamia, it is generally accepted that it was the Iron Age communities of northern Europe, notably the CELTS, who developed the wooden barrel for the large-scale transport of goods. Its origins cannot now be recovered but Julius Caesar encountered barrels during his campaigns in France in the 50s BC. In the second half of the 1st century AD PLINY described transport barrels in GAUL in a way that suggests they would have been unfamiliar to his Roman audience. The Latin term *cupa*, which later came to mean barrel, at this time normally referred to wood storage tanks, the remains of one of which have been found at POMPEII, near Naples. Barrels or barrel staves have been preserved in waterlogged conditions on sites in Britain (at Silchester), and along the RHINE and the Danube. The wood used was frequently silver fir.

Famous monuments such as that from Neumagen on the German river MOSEL testify to the use of barrels for the transport of goods. When the Roman army served in northern Europe, it used barrels regularly; they are frequently illustrated in scenes from the columns of Trajan and Marcus Aurelius which commemorated the campaigns of these emperors in the 2nd century AD. From the middle of the 3rd century references in literature and art to the use of barrels in Italy and, to a lesser extent, elsewhere in the Mediterranean are much more frequent. It is possible that the more widespread use of the barrel explains the disappearance of various types of AMPHORAE in this period. It also means that from this period on it is much more difficult to trace trade routes, since wood is much less likely to survive on archaeological sites. Barrels were certainly used for the transport of wine, but also for other liquids and goods such as salt.

See also BARREL MAINTENANCE, CELTS, GRAIN, OAK, TOAST, WOOD FLAVOUR, WOOD INFLUENCE, WOOD TYPES. J.J.P.

BARREL FERMENTATION, wine-making technique of fermenting grape juice or must in small BARRELS rather than in a larger FERMENTATION VESSEL. The technique is used principally for white wines because of the difficulty of extracting through a barrel's small BUNG hole the mass of skins and seeds which necessarily remains after red wine fermentation. In Burgundy, California, and Australia, however, some winemakers deliberately put pressed red wines which still retain some unfermented sugars into barrel, thus allowing completion of red wine FERMENTATION in barrel in an attempt to make more approachable wines.

The technique seems particularly well adapted to wine made from CHARDONNAY grapes and some of the finest SWEET WINES. Its advantages are that it protects the wine from OXYGEN during fermentation, offers the possibility of extracting a controlled amount of WOOD FLAVOUR into the wine, and, since barrels have a large surface to volume ratio, artificial TEMPERATURE CONTROL is rarely needed. It also provides a natural prelude to BARREL MATURATION and LEES STIRRING since the lees and the wine are already in the same container.

White wine which is fermented and stored in oak with its yeast solids, or LEES, has a softened, less obvious, and more integrated oak flavour than wine that has been fermented in a larger container before being matured in barrels. This is because the YEAST acts on the highly aromatic oak flavour molecules to transform them biochemically into much less aromatic substances. (The secondary fermentation aromas, however, such as result from ESTERS, fatty acids, and higher alcohols, are substantially unaffected by barrel fermentation.) FINING also removes some oak compounds. Fermentation in barrel also gives large increases in polysaccharides, or complex SUGARS, which add richness and apparent LENGTH of flavour on the palate. The amount of yeast mass in the barrel and the frequency of stirring have a direct and considerable effect on the quantity of polysaccharides formed.

White wines matured for a few months on their lees in barrel usually have a much lighter colour than those put into barrel after fermentation to mature. Certain COLLOIDS are liberated during fermentation and LEES CONTACT which stabilize some of the PHENOLICS extracted from the oak, causing pigment to be precipitated.

Stirring up the lees in the barrel also affects wood flavour. If the lees are stirred, they act as an even more effective buffer between the wine and the wood, limiting the extent to which wood TANNINS, and colouring matter, are extracted into the wine. Wines subjected to lees stirring therefore tend to be much paler and less tannic than those whose lees are not stirred.

Fermentation in barrel can also have secondary flavour effects due to temperature, lot size, and precise level of TOAST. The generally higher temperature of fermentation in barrel rather than vat causes a loss of floral flavours and a reduction of the most obvious white wine fermentation AROMAS reminiscent of tropical fruit. There are fewer fatty acid ESTERS and fatty acids which are described as perfumed or soapy, and more higher alcohols, which makes the wine taste fuller bodied. And because each fermentation even of identical juice has a slightly different flavour outcome, the larger number of small volume lots that are common in barrel fermentation create more complexity. A 10,000-l/2,642-gal lot would create one fermentation flavour if it were fermented in one tank, for example, but the same lot fermented in 70 barrels would produce a much more complex array of flavours.

The disadvantages of barrel fermentation are the relatively small size of the barrel and the time and effort required to clean, fill, and empty it, although the extra degree of complexity gained by the wine is usually worth any extra production costs. The cost of new barrels themselves is such, however, that the technique is restricted to higher-priced wines. With so many fermentations in a non-sterile material, it is always possible that some barrels may be infected with BACTERIA or undesirable yeasts, so extra vigilance is required to eliminate any defective wines. A.D.W. and L.B.

Dubourdieu, D., 'Vinification des vins blanc secs en barriques', in *Le Bois et la qualité des vins et eaux-de-vie* (Bordeaux, 1992).

BARREL MAINTENANCE. BARRELS are an important investment for a winery, in terms of both their cost and their precious contents. The contents of a barrel may well have a wholesale value of thousands of dollars, while some new barrels were selling for more than $US600 in 1992. The preparation of new barrels and the maintenance of used ones is therefore an important activity for wine-makers, and can play a part in determining WOOD INFLUENCE.

Preparation for use

Barrels are treated prior to use both to check for leaks and to ensure that the barrel offers the right flavours to the wine. In Burgundy, where the barrels are filled with either white grape MUST in the case of white wines or just-pressed wine in the case of reds, treatment is minimal. Usually the barrel is merely rinsed or filled with cold water to check for leaks. In Bordeaux barrels are traditionally filled with 15 to 20 l/4 to 5 gal of hot water. The barrel is spun and shaken so that, in theory, some of the rough TANNINS are washed out as the steam created during the spinning process exposes any leaks. (If a small leak is found, it can usually be plugged with a small piece of wood. A leak near the head may indicate that some adjustment is necessary. Occasionally a stave may have to be replaced.)

New World wine regions are less systematic in their barrel preparation. In the late 1970s it was still common to use soda ash, supposedly to remove unpleasant tannins, although it is now clear that soda ash prematurely ages the barrel and at the same time removes the barrel's TOAST and makes the wine taste more tannic. Most wine-makers are wary of filling a barrel with lukewarm water as BACTERIA grow easily under such conditions. Nearly all wine-makers will at least rinse the barrel prior to use and in parts of Europe ammonia is often used which, though a harsh cleanser, can provide nutrients for fermentation. Ammonia may also be used deliberately to prepare barrels for a light vintage, supposedly to remove some of the wood tannins. At some point prior to first use, the exterior of the barrel is often coated with linseed oil or a commercial product such as Mildecide to combat MOULDS, although this is done principally for aesthetic reasons.

Identification

At many larger wineries a card is attached to the head of the barrel so as to enable the wine-maker to follow the life of each individual barrel. In larger New World wineries it is not uncommon to see the sort of bar code used by supermarkets, along with computerized tracking. In smaller wineries a few letters may suffice. In Burgundy, for example, the chalked letters 'CM/R' might serve to denote 'Chassagne Montrachet, Ruchottes'. And in very small cellars, the single individual in charge may know every barrel so intimately that formal markings are unnecessary.

Temperature and humidity

Storage conditions of full barrels are important (and see below for unused barrels). If the cellar is too cold, the wine will not develop. If it is too warm, off-flavours and harmful bacteria may develop, and the wine may age too rapidly. If the cellars are too dry, too much wine can evaporate and the barrels themselves can dry out. The ideal temperature is usually around 10 to 13 °C/50 to 55 °F, with a humidity over 70 per cent. Below 75 per cent, water evaporates, but above that figure alcohol evaporates. In warm regions wine-makers like to keep the humidity high, but not so high that it becomes impossible to control the growth of moulds.

If the humidity is too high, the barrel will have mould problems. The wine-maker must consider the dew point, that combination of temperature and humidity at which evaporation occurs. Storing empty barrels (and full ones too) at temperatures higher than 65 °F invites problems, and storing barrels over 70 °F for more than three weeks runs the risk of BACTERIAL BLIGHT and the formation of VOLATILE ACIDS.

Bungs

See BUNG.

Storage

The question of storage of all these barrels has both aesthetic and practical ramifications. In most wineries there are visitors to impress, although they tend to find efficient modern reality less impressive than cobwebbed tradition. Some much-visited wineries fill their barrels in full view of the tourists before trucking them down the road to a clinical modern barrel warehouse, carefully regulated for both temperature and humidity, until the wine is ready for bottling.

Touristic considerations aside, most wineries usually employ one of the following techniques: (1) Barrels are placed on metal pallets and fork-lifted into place. This looks industrial but is actually easiest on the cellar staff. Barrels can be stored either rolled to the side or with the bung straight up. (2) Barrels are piled one, two, or even three high in neat rows. (3) Barrels are stacked in huge pyramids. These may look good but the barrels are hard to work as disassembling the stack is a daunting task. Sometimes, as a result of this, the barrels are not properly cleaned. (4) A single row of barrels is rolled on to fixed barrel racks, which also look good but are often inefficient in terms of labour costs and use of space.

Topping up

When the barrels are full, wine-makers like to keep them full to prevent excessive oxygenation. Most wineries 'top up' the barrels frequently to compensate for evaporation. The rate of wine evaporation is directly proportional to the temperature, which should be about 50 to 55 °F: not so cold as to hinder development but not so warm as to encourage bacterial growth. Constancy of temperature is not as important as it is in a cellar for full bottles, and a winter drop in temperature assists precipitation and therefore CLARIFICATION. See also TOPPING UP.

Unused barrels

Storage of empty barrels is always problematic, particularly because of the possible growth of harmful ACETOBACTER, and barrels may well be sheathed in plastic before being shipped long distances to minimize spoilage. Traditionally empty barrels were rinsed, dried, treated with SULPHUR DIOXIDE, then bunged up. Recent experiments suggest that sulphuring an inverted barrel but not bunging up results in a much lower level of VOLATILE ACIDS since bunging up creates a humid environment, ideal for the growth of bacteria. Barrels so treated must be stored under the same conditions of low temperature and high, but not too high, humidity as full barrels.

Most wine-makers prefer to avoid the cost and risks associated with the long-term storage of empty barrels by ordering very precise quantities and filling them as soon as possible.

M.K. & L.B.

Taransaud, J., *Le Livre de la tonnellerie* (Paris, 1976).

BARREL MAKING involves far more than mere mechanics and the ability to fashion a watertight container out of nothing but bent wood. As outlined in detail in WOOD INFLUENCE, every stage of barrel manufacture has an impact on wine matured in that barrel. First, the tree is cut down, usually during the autumn or winter when the sap is down. COOPERS usually buy long sections of trunk, from trees that are ideally between 100 and 150 years old, and then the process that turns logs into stave wood begins.

Cutting: sawing versus splitting

Logs of appropriate lengths are cut and then split into four lengthwise. The bark and sap wood are cut off so that STAVES may be cut from transversal (rather than tangential) sections of wood.

Because American OAK is so much less porous than European, staves of American oak can simply be sawn from each quarter using a curved-band barrel saw, as shown in Fig. 1, so as to maximize the yield of each log. This is traditional quarter sawing. Some American coopers saw from half rather than quarter logs.

European oak could well leak if thus sawn, however, and staves have to be cut, or split, much more carefully, minimizing the risk of leakage by following the oak GRAIN. Traditionally therefore European oak was split by hand, as in Fig. 2, so that the axe blade could follow the grain. Nowadays mechanically operated axes are guided through the wood sections and the resulting staves trimmed, still following the grain.

There is also a second method called quarter sawing, whereby European oak is split in four lengthwise, as usual, then into eighths and then staves of varying widths are cut using a band saw, as shown in Fig. 3, leaving much less waste than in traditional 'hand' splitting with an axe blade. This has the disadvantage that some staves may have grains running perpendicular to the barrel.

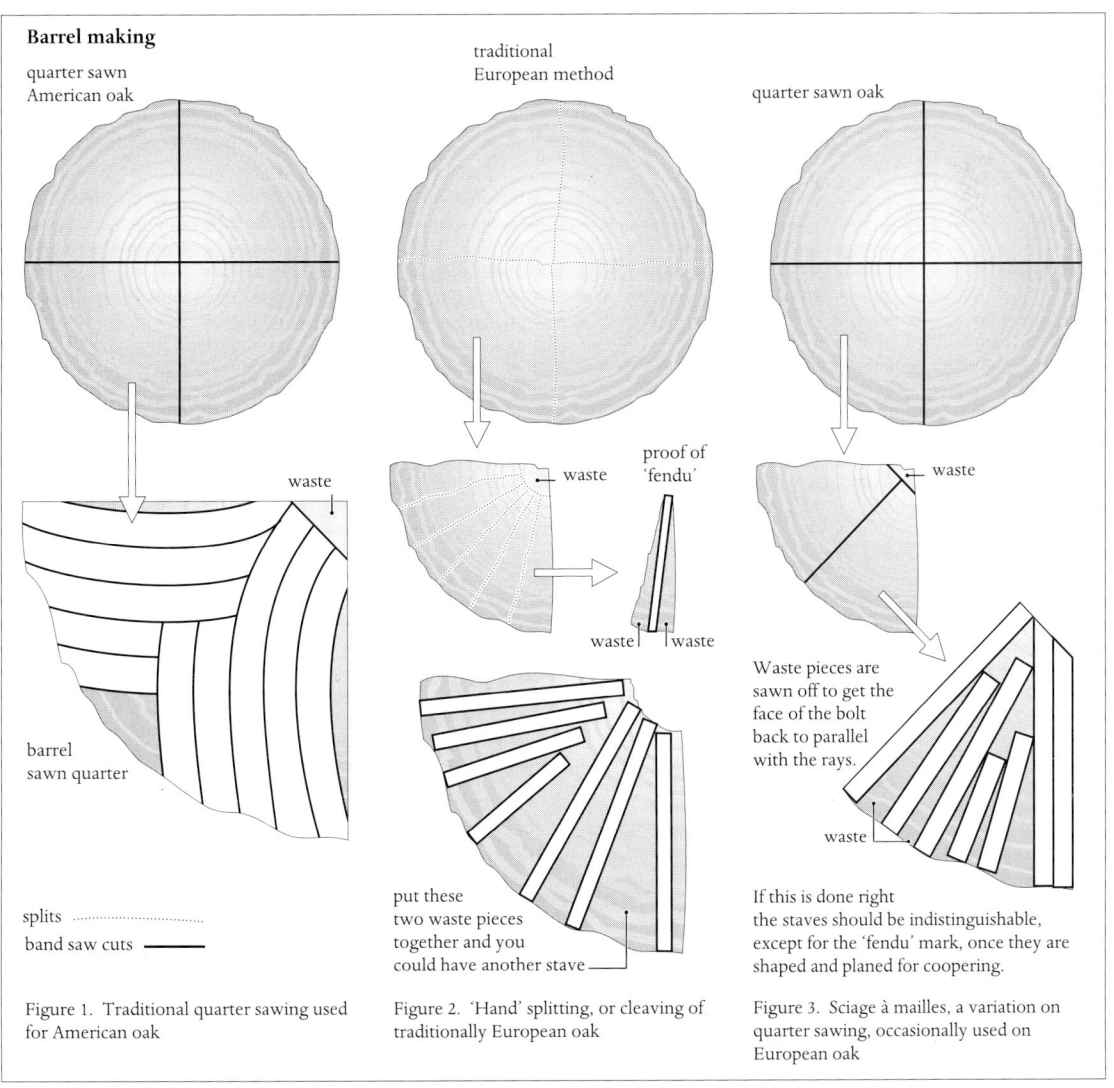

Barrel making

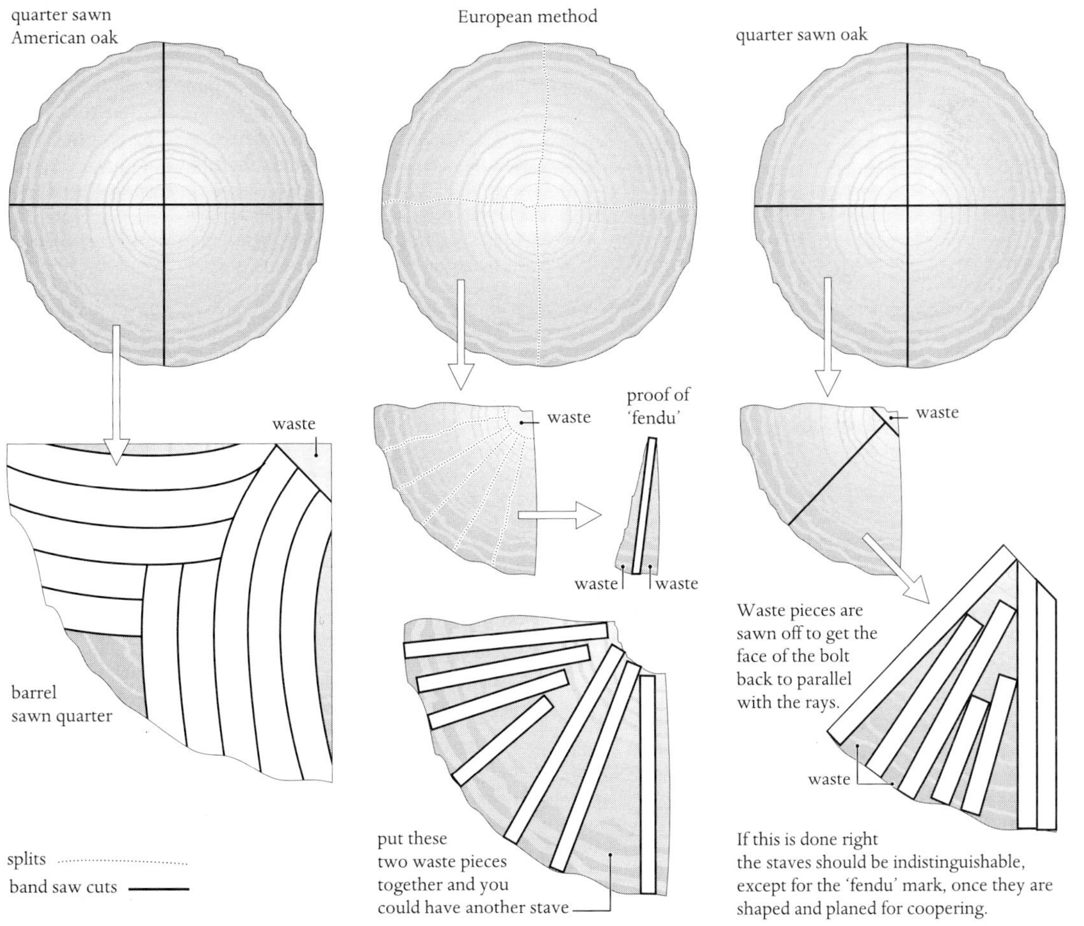
quarter sawn
American oak
traditional
European method
quarter sawn oak
waste
waste
proof of
'fendu'
waste
waste
waste
barrel
sawn quarter
Waste pieces are
sawn off to get the
face of the bolt
back to parallel
with the rays.
waste
splits
band saw cuts
put these
two waste pieces
together and you
could have another stave
If this is done right
the staves should be indistinguishable,
except for the 'fendu' mark, once they are
shaped and planed for coopering.

Figure 1. Traditional quarter sawing used for American oak

Figure 2. 'Hand' splitting, or cleaving of traditionally European oak

Figure 3. Sciage à mailles, a variation on quarter sawing, occasionally used on European oak

A variation on this method is called *sciage à mailles* in France, and is considered better than traditional quarter sawing, but not as good as 'hand' splitting. It is more efficient because a saw is used rather than an axe blade, and the yield per log is higher, but since the saw does not follow the grain, the resulting staves may leak even though the original log appeared to have very straight grains. It has the inconvenience, therefore, that only those rare and expensive logs with very straight grains and no knots or imperfections can be used.

A fourth sawing technique involves simply cutting the log as though cutting up the tree for use in construction. While very efficient in terms of yield, this method is the worst for barrel making since it maximizes the risk of leaks.

Some coopers do saw European wood and may paint the end of the staves, the chime, to block end-grain leaks. Since twice as many staves are produced by sawing as by hand-splitting, the waste involved in traditional European COOPERAGE practices is considerable. French oak is so relatively expensive (the wood cost in a barrel was approaching FF1,400 in the early 1990s) that sawn French barrels seem an economically alluring proposition. Experiments so far, however, suggest that experienced tasters systematically prefer wines from French barrels made from traditionally hand-split staves—perhaps because sawing oak exposes more grains, and therefore more raw TANNINS, to the wine. This may explain why barrels made from quarter-sawn French oak staves seem to perform almost as well as those made from hand-split wood in blind tastings of wines matured in them. Proponents of sawing maintain that the wood is worked so much during manufacture it does not matter how the wood is cut.

In France wood split by hand from logs for use as staves is known as *merrain* and the men who do this work are known as *merrandiers*. Traditionally this work was done near the forest, but nowadays many cooperages have their own stave-splitting facilities.

Drying: air versus kiln

After the wood has been split or sawn, it must be dried. Otherwise the wood continues to dry and wine may leak out of the barrel. The drying process can be achieved either naturally in the open air or artificially using kilns. French oak has traditionally been air dried one year for every 10 mm/0.4 in width so that it takes between 18 and 36 months to 'season' wood by drying it, in stacks of potential staves, in the open, preferably on a site far from any industrial activity or any other source of pollution. This ties up so much capital that many cooperages have been forced to substitute artificial drying techniques which generally take no more than 12 months.

Many quality-conscious wine-makers will pay a premium for wood dried in the open air, however. First, it is felt that kiln-dried wood does not dry properly and that the barrel made from these staves will leak more than those made from naturally seasoned staves. Second, natural drying tends to reduce the stable extractable compounds of the wood while heightening its aromatic potential. It has for long been thought that, as wood is seasoned outdoors and turns grey, darkening the ground beneath it, harsh tannins are being leached out of the wood. Wine matured in air-dried wood certainly tends to taste less aggressively tannic than the same wine matured in kiln-dried wood. Australian research by Sefton and others, however, indicates that tannin levels in wood do not in fact change during seasoning, but that their sensory effect does, with French oak tannins becoming much less noticeable with seasoning and American oak tannins more so.

Unpublished studies by Nicolas Vivas of BORDEAUX UNIVERSITY indicate that moulds and enzymes formed on and in the wood during air drying play crucial roles in oak and consequent wine flavour. Moulds formed on the surface of the wood liberate exocellular ENZYMES, principally heterosidases. They permit the transformation of certain bitter components into molecules which taste more neutral. At the same time, glucose and polysaccharides are liberated from the structural elements of the wood.

Some cooperages maintain that it is not the duration of the air-drying process that is important but the wood's exposure to rain and the temperature at which the wood is dried. Their wood may therefore be watered to simulate rain, but there has been little scientific analysis of results.

Assembling

Once the staves are dry enough, they can be assembled into barrels. Barrel making is made possible by the fact that wood can be bent when it has been heated. If the staves are shaped properly, the result will be a barrel. All edges will meet properly and the barrel will hold liquid without any agent other than the hoops which hold the staves together.

First, the staves are sized and trimmed into oblong lengths that might be called a double taper. Traditionally this work, known as 'dressing' the staves, was done by hand. The stave was 'listed', that is given the double taper shape, with a cooper's axe, known as a *doloire* in French. Then, the inside of the stave was 'scalloped' with a two-handled hollowing knife to allow for easier bending. Finally the staves were joined on a jointer, known as a *colombe* in French. Here the staves were given their final shape—rounded at the bilge (the middle) and narrowed at the heads (the ends)—giving the barrel its proper shape. Nowadays most of this work is done with machines, even in France, at great savings of time and energy.

Finally, the cooper fits the staves in a frame so that each barrel will have the same circumference. An especially strong and wide stave is chosen for the stave into which the BUNG-hole will eventually be drilled (see below). Then he arranges these staves around an iron 'raising up' hoop, the result looking like a skirt or a teepee splayed out from the hoop at the top. This job calls for great manual dexterity, although in many American cooperages machines can do much of this work.

Shaping and toasting

Research has shown that the heating process is one of the most important in barrel manufacture, modifying the wood's physical and chemical composition and profoundly influencing any wine stored in the barrel.

Various sources of heat can be used to shape the barrel: natural gas, steam and boiling water, or the fire of wood chips. Some cooperages combine techniques and shape the barrel with the aid of boiling water or steam, then finish the barrel with a fire toasting.

The spectacle of the fire and the coopers knocking down the hoops and bending the barrels is exciting. A high degree of co-ordination is required. The would-be barrel is rolled over a cylindrical, vented metal firepot, known as a *chaufferette*, in which small oak chips are burned. The coopers walk round the barrel knocking down the temporary iron hoops. Each cooper pounds his hammer on a hoop driver—a short block of wood with a flat metal end—while slapping a wet rag on the wood to keep it from getting too toasted too quickly. After the top of the barrel has been shaped, the coopers wrap cables around the base of the barrel and use a capstan to cinch up the base.

Natural gas, boiling water, and steam will heat the wood effectively and allow the cooper to bend the staves without the creation of blisters on the inside of the staves. Many wine-makers prefer this technique as the barrel is easier to clean. Other wine-makers prefer barrels shaped over a fire of wood chips, as the TOAST on the inside of the barrel provides an interesting 'toasty' flavour to the wine. These wine-makers feel that any extra effort in BARREL MAINTENANCE is justified by the special flavour provided by this technique. The amount of time the barrel sits on the fire and the heat of the fire both have a dramatic impact on the appearance of the barrel's interior and on resultant wine flavour. Nowadays wine-makers can order barrels 'toasted' to order. Some cooperages use an electric ambient heater or a wood fire to toast the heads too, although these are usually left untoasted.

The heads

After the body of the barrel has been formed, then the heads, or barrel-ends, must be made and fitted. Five or six head staves are fitted together with wooden dowels or stainless steel gudgeons (headless nails). Then the head is cut to size, usually slightly oval in shape. Near each end of body of the barrel, a groove, called the croze, is cut into the inside of the barrel. The head is cut at the edges so that it will fit into the croze.

Formerly all of this work was done by hand, but now virtually all of it is done on machines which have replaced an array of traditional cooper's tools with names (adze, chiv, etc.) to delight the dedicated Scrabble player. Finally the head is fitted into the barrel. To do this the hoops are loosened and the head is inserted into the croze.

Finishing

Before the barrel can be sold or shipped, its outside must be planed so that splinters will not dog cellar work. The barrel is tested for leaks, usually with steam or hot water injected through a small hole drilled in the bung stave. If the barrel passes the test, the small hole is drilled to bung-hole size and cauterized. The temporary iron hoops are removed and the final ones, usually made of metal and sometimes of chestnut, are fitted.

Developments

American cooperages have been experimenting with air drying rather than kiln drying, with promising results.

The fact that expensive barrels lose their value so quickly has initiated various schemes for reuse. The process of 'shaving' barrels is quite popular in the New World. A cooper removes the heads and removes all the pigmented wood from inside the barrel with a plane or grouter. In some cases the barrel is allowed to dry out a bit, and then the cooper retoasts the inside in order to maintain the all-important buffer of toast between the wine and the wood. Barrels that are shaved but not toasted yield extremely astringent tannins to their wines because there is no toast buffer between wood and wine. The difficulty is that it is not dry wood that is being toasted, as was done originally, but wood into which alcohol has permeated. Retoasting seems most effective on relatively young (two- to three-year-old) barrels. Wine aged in shaved and retoasted older barrels rarely pleases.

Another technique involves removing the head of the barrel and inserting a food-grade device reminiscent of the tray in an automatic dishwasher. This insert holds small oak boards which may be renewed every other year or so. This idea is not perfect, as sooner or later the barrel falls apart from the repeated torture, and getting the right amount of new oak is difficult. This technique can result in much better wines than shaving old barrels, however.

See also BARREL TYPES, OAK, and WOOD INFLUENCE. M.K.

Chatonnet, P., 'Origin and processing of oak used in cooperage' and 'Aromatic compounds yielded by oak into wine', in *Le Bois et la qualité des vins et eaux-de-vie* (Bordeaux, 1992).

Kilby, K., *The Cooper and his Trade* (London, 1971).

Sefton, M. A., *et al.*, 'Influence of seasoning on the sensory characteristics and composition of oak extracts', in *International Oak Symposium* (San Francisco, 1993).

Taransaud, J., *Le Livre de la tonnellerie* (Paris, 1976).

BARREL MATURATION is the wine-making operation of storing a fermented wine in wooden BARRELS so that the wood exerts some wood influence and, possibly, imparts some WOOD FLAVOUR. This is an increasingly common practice for superior-quality still wines of all colours and styles, providing them, as it does, with the ideal preparation for BOTTLE AGEING.

The most obvious advantage of barrel maturation is that it encourages CLARIFICATION and STABILIZATION of the wine in the most natural, if not necessarily the fastest, way. It also helps to deepen and stabilize the COLOUR, to soften the TANNINS, and to increase the complexity of the flavour compounds.

Although some wood flavour is extracted directly into the wine, one of the more obvious secondary flavour effects of maturing a wine in barrel results from the slow oxygenation of the wine. When barrels are filled, stoppered, and rolled, they receive a small but significant amount of OXYGEN. Leaving barrels upright and topping up the evaporated wine weekly can triple the amount of oxygen the wine receives. This uptake of oxygen, however slow or fast, tends to reduce fresh, grapey primary AROMAS and also causes small tannin molecules to agglomerate, which changes COLOUR towards gold in whites and softens astringency in both reds and whites. Oxygen causes the colouring material of reds, ANTHOCYANS, to change their yellow and colourless forms so that the red intensifies. However, at the same time oxygen aids in the formation of anthocyan-tannin complexes which are more permanent than the anthocyans alone. For more details see AGEING.

WOOD INFLUENCE outlines the factors that govern this process: size, age, and wood type of the barrel, techniques used in BARREL MAKING, storage conditions, characteristics of the vintage, wine-making techniques, and time. See also TOAST for details of how this plays a part in providing a buffer between the alcohol and the wood's PHENOLICS.

The better properties in BORDEAUX provide the paradigm for the barrel maturation of wines based on CABERNET SAUVIGNON and MERLOT grapes. Here top-quality wines are put into barrels with a light to medium toast immediately after MALOLACTIC FERMENTATION and left to mature for up to two years. RACKING every three or four months helps clarification, softens the wood flavour, and inevitably involves some oxygenation. Oxygenation is positively encouraged during the first six months by leaving the barrels with the BUNG up. Thereafter they are rotated so that oxygenation is reduced. FINING takes place at the beginning of the second year, further encouraging stabilization. The timing of BOTTLING is the final crucial human input of barrel maturation.

In the early 1980s it was common for New World wine-makers to practice these same techniques on wines made from the PINOT NOIR grape, but, because they lack the tannic structure of wines made from Cabernet Sauvignon or Merlot, such wines tasted bitter and excessively tannic. Heavier toast on the inside of the barrel can also act as a buffer between wood and wine. By racking Pinot Noir into barrel immediately after alcoholic fermentation and allowing malolactic fermentation to take place in barrel, much better integration of wood and wine has been achieved, together with greater complexity of flavour.

As a result of this success, some California wine-makers began to apply this Pinot Noir technique to varieties such as Cabernet Sauvignon, ZINFANDEL, and the RHÔNE varieties. Whereas in Bordeaux red wine is racked into barrel only after malolactic fermentation, a significant proportion of New World Cabernet, Syrah, Zinfandel, and Merlot is now racked straight into barrel after primary alcoholic fermentation with the result that wine and wood flavours are better integrated.

All over the world, many top quality white wines are subjected to BARREL FERMENTATION prior to barrel maturation, another practice which tends to result in much better integration of wood and wine than putting white wine into barrel only after fermentation.

An alternative to barrel maturation for wines of all hues is CASK AGEING, whereby wine is stored in large, old wooden containers which impart no wood flavour but exert some of the favourable aspects of wood influence, provided they are kept clean. Other alternatives, and possible supplements, to barrel maturation are ageing in inert CONTAINERS; BOTTLE AGEING; and bottling almost immediately after fermentation as in NOUVEAU wines.

See BARREL MAINTENANCE for more details of some of the important practical aspects of barrel maturation.

M.K. & L.B.

Naudin, R., *L'Élevage des vins de Bourgogne en fûts neufs* (Beaune, 1989).

Pontallier, P., 'Pratiques actuelles de l'élevage en barriques des grands vins rouges', in *Le Bois et la qualité des vins et eaux-de-vie* (Bordeaux, 1992).

Sefton, M. A., 'How does oak barrel maturation contribute to wine flavor?', *Australian and NZ Industry Journal* (Feb. 1991).

Singleton, V. L., 'Some aspects of the wooden container as a factor in wine maturation', in *Chemistry of Winemaking*, American Chemical Society (Washington, DC, 1974).

BARREL TYPES vary considerably and this list includes some terms used for COOPERAGE, or wooden containers, that are, strictly speaking, larger than BARRELS.

Before concrete, STAINLESS STEEL, and other inert materials replaced WOOD as the most common material for wine FERMENTATION VESSELS and storage CONTAINERS in the 1960s, each wine region had its own legion of barrel types. Even today such terms as feuillette, TONNEAU, and FUDER may be used to measure volumes of wine long after the actual containers themselves have been abandoned. As recently as 1976 Jean Taransaud was able to list four pages of different barrel types used in various French wine regions (see below).

France

Barrel types, as most things French, are intensely regionalized. In many cases their capacity has changed over the years.

Bordeaux The **barrique bordelaise**, designated 225 l/59 gal for more than a century, is probably the most famous barrel of all and is now used widely outside the region. It is about 95 cm/37 in high and the staves are only about 20 mm/0.8 in thick (although the export version may be a cm or two lower and have rather thicker staves). The traditional BARRIQUE, sometimes called the 'château' model, has a wooden crossbar at each head and both a top and a racking BUNG.

The TONNEAU, at 900 l equivalent to four barriques, or 100 cases of wine, is still much used as a measurement by the Bordeaux trade, but this large cask no longer exists.

Burgundy Here the standard barrel is the 228-l **pièce**, which is relatively low (88 cm) and squat, supposedly for practicality given the narrow doorways and small scale of many Burgundian cellars, and to provide a deeper bilge for the LEES which accumulate in this region where RACKING is generally less frequent than in Bordeaux, for example. The staves are usually notably thicker than those of barriques, about 27 mm. Traditionally these barrels had chestnut hoops or iron hoops painted black, although some domaines have followed the American taste for more workmanlike galvanized hoops which need no repainting.

The traditional barrel in CHABLIS was the **feuillette**, at 132 l about half the size of the pièce. This is still the unit in which prices are commonly given, even though the barrel itself is increasingly rare.

Some domaines on the CÔTE D'OR may still have their own size of feuillette, holding 114 l, or even a **quartaut** holding 57 l, used primarily for TOPPING UP.

Cognac The standard cognac barrel now holds 350 l, although in 1900 it held only about 275 l, and only 200 l before the French Revolution. Cognac coopers make a wide range of different barrels for other wine regions.

Champagne A 205-l barrel is traditional here but those few houses which persist with BARREL FERMENTATION may also buy in Burgundy barrels.

Elsewhere in France A wide range of different barrel types is used in the Loire and the Rhône, from small new oak barrels to large wooden vats such as the 600-l **demi-muid** used in Châteauneuf-du-Pape. In Alsace, large ovals, or **foudres** of varying capacities, are most common.

Germany
Although Germany has formed its own group of daring iconoclasts, the Barrique Forum, most of the cooperage used is large, old, and typically on the Mosel a **Fuder** holding 1,000 l or on the Rhine a **Stück** of 1,200 l. A **Halbfuder** and **Halbstück** are half these sizes respectively.

Spain
Spain's most characteristic barrel is the BUTT used for SHERRY. The American oak barrels used in RIOJA, and elsewhere, are 225-l **barricas bordelesas** modelled on Bordeaux barriques. Spanish cooperage can vary considerably in size and shape, however, and new wood is not generally prized.

Portugal
The PIPE is Portugal's most famous wine measure. Portuguese cooperage, which can vary considerably in size and shape, may be made from French, American, or even Portuguese oak.

Italy
The large **botti**, or old wooden casks, traditionally used in Italy are typically made from Slovenian oak and have varying capacities. The barrique is increasingly common, however, sometimes called a **carato**, while the small barrels traditionally used for VIN SANTO are **caratelli** holding between 50 and 225 l. Large wooden casks standing vertical rather than being laid horizontal may be called **tini**. See BARRIQUE for a discussion of the use of this French barrel type in Italy today.

Hungary
Gönci holding 136 l are traditional in the production of TOKAY and are named after the village in which they were usually made.

United States
Before the USA became the world's best customer for exported French oak barrels (see COOPERAGE), American wine-makers bought 50 gal/190 l American oak barrels produced for the whiskey business. A decline in bourbon sales in the 1980s led to American cooperages tailoring an increasing proportion of their output to wineries' needs, however, although variations on the barrique and pièce imported from France are the most desired, and most common, barrels used by American wine-makers.

Australia and New Zealand
The **hogshead** is used quite widely, with 300 l being a common size, along with traditional barriques and pièces imported whole from France or made up from imported staves. **Puncheons** holding 450 or 500 l may also be found in New World wineries but they are too large to manœuvre with ease and do not impart WOOD FLAVOUR as fast as many wine-makers desire. M.K. & J.R.

Taransaud, J., *Le Livre de la tonnellerie* (Paris, 1976).

BARRICA, Spanish term for a BARRIQUE. A *barrica bordelesa* is the specific term for a Bordeaux barrique, the most common BARREL TYPE used in Spain.

BARRIQUE, the most famous of the BARREL TYPES, Bordeaux's relatively tall 225-l/59-gal wooden cask with thinner STAVES than the Burgundian pièce and most other barrels.

In the Middle Ages the commercially acute Bordelais virtually trade-marked their distinctive barrique bordelaise, carefully designating its dimensions and prohibiting its use outside the region. By the end of the 18th century it had replaced the unwieldy TONNEAU four times the size for transportation as well as storage, and in 1866 it was officially decreed that it must hold 225 l, rather than between 215 and 230 l as previously. Even as recently as this it was common for some of the most highly regarded wines of Bordeaux to be shipped in barrique for bottling, if not by the NÉGOCIANTS of Bordeaux, then by wine merchants outside France, particularly in Britain.

Today the word barrique is often used, particularly outside France, for all manner of wooden BARRELS. In Germany and Italy, for example, the word is closely and emotively associated with iconoclasts who employ BARREL MATURATION in small, new OAK rather than traditional CASK AGEING in large, old, wooden casks. Germany has its Barrique Forum of innovators, and some Italian traditionalists are careful to use the Italian word *carati* for small wooden barrels in place of the French term employed by many internationalists. J.Ro.

A note on Italy
Barrique, the Bordeaux name for the small oak barrels used for ageing the wines of the better châteaux, has been almost unanimously adopted in Italy to indicate these containers, to the exclusion of pièce, fût, or the other names which the French use. It is also improperly used in Italy not just for the 225-l size of Bordelais barrel, but for virtually any small format of oak cask, including **demi-muids, muids**, and other sizes. Small barrel ageing of wines began on a small scale in TUSCANY

The second year *chai* at Ch Margaux is filled with traditional **barriques** bordelaises. The new, upright ones will be filled with wine from the first year *chai* upstairs.

in the late 1960s and early 1970s. The two pioneering wines, TIGNANELLO and SASSICAIA, were of such outstanding quality and effected such a radical improvement on previous Italian versions of SANGIOVESE and CABERNET grapes that the advantages of barrique ageing became immediately evident to more open-minded Italian producers. Their use in Italy was none the less slow to increase in the 1970s and their suitability to Italian varieties was by no means universally accepted; a vocal school of native critics was not slow to denounce their use with indigenous varieties as a betrayal of the authentic character of the wines.

The 1980s saw a widespread and rapid expansion of barrique ageing, a key event being a 1981 tour of California by the influential Italian wine writer Luigi VERONELLI, accompanied by important producers Maurizio Zanella of FRANCIACORTA, Giacomo Bologna of PIEDMONT, and Mario Schiopetto of FRIULI, all amongst the most influential figures in Italian viticulture. Their conversion to the cause can only be compared to that of St Paul on the road to Damascus, and their vocal advocacy of the advantages of new oak and small formats had an immeasurable effect upon their return. Bologna was the pioneer in demonstrating how well the humble BARBERA could marry with new oak, and similar demonstrations, if with less uniform success, were first carried out for NEBBIOLO by Angelo Gaja, Aldo Conterno, and Elio Altare. By the end of the 1980s the use of barriques had been extended to a large number of Italy's most important varieties, red and white: GARGANEGA, CORVINA, CORTESE, VERNACCIA, AGLIANICO, GAGLIOPPO, NERO D'AVOLA, and NEGROAMARO. The resulting wines have not always been a subtle blending of oak and varietal character, but an overall assessment of these wines as heavy handed or overly oaky would be inaccurate and unfair, however, much still needs to be learned about a correct employment of new oak with Italian grapes.

The new popularity of barriques in the 1980s has also led to major changes in the style and personality of Italian versions of INTERNATIONAL VARIETIES. Once almost exclusively made in a fresh and fruity style, many have taken on a fuller and more powerful character as producers came to realize that barriques and light, refreshing wines were incompatible. D.T.

BARSAC, important sweet white wine appellation in BORDEAUX on the left bank of the river GARONNE just over the climatologically important cool river Ciron from the even bigger and more famous Sauternes appellation. All wines produced within Barsac are also entitled to use the appellation Sauternes (although the reverse is not the case). In the 1990 vintage, for example, 580 ha / 1,432 acres of vineyard were declared as producing wine for the Barsac appellation, as opposed to nearly 1,400 ha for the Sauternes appellation. It is traditionally said that the wines of Barsac are slightly lighter than those of Sauternes, perhaps because the soils are richer in sand and limestone, and because the land is flatter, but much depends on individual properties and wine-making policies too. For more detail of viticultural and wine-making practices, see SAUTERNES. See also the Barsac properties included in the Sauternes CLASSIFICATION.

BARTONS, prominent family in BORDEAUX, originally from Lancashire in the north of England, which joined the Tudor Protestant Ascendancy in Ireland. Unlike most others who joined the BORDEAUX wine TRADE from abroad, the Bartons maintained their nationality, religion, and family connections with their country of origin. Thomas Barton arrived in Bordeaux in 1725, played a leading part in shipping fine CLARET back to Britain, and died in 1780 a very rich man. His son William (1723–99), with whom he bitterly quarrelled, formed his own company and was prominent in the trade on his own account. His son Hugh (1766–1854) married Anna, daughter of another prosperous merchant, Nathaniel Johnston. The association with Daniel Guestier of a Breton Huguenot family began in 1795 and Barton & Guestier, still an important NÉGOCIANT, was formed in 1802.

Anthony **Barton**, of Chx Langoa-Barton and Léoville-Barton.

Highly successful, Hugh Barton bought Ch Langoa in ST-JULIEN in 1821, and acquired in 1826 part of the Léoville vineyard that was to become Ch Léoville-Barton, an even more prominent St-Julien. He died in England, having been succeeded by his son Nathaniel (1799–1867). Barton & Guestier continued to play a leading role in the Bordeaux trade, but PHYLLOXERA, the consequent shortage of authentic bordeaux, and the slump in English demand prior to the First World War led to unprecedented problems. Nathaniel's son Bertram Francis (1830–1904) worked first in the London office but came in 1873 to live in Bordeaux, rather than at Langoa. It was his third successor Ronald Barton (1902–86) who made Langoa his home. Business was difficult between the World Wars, and on the fall of France in 1940 Ronald had hurriedly to leave Langoa, which was soon occupied by the Germans. They did not pillage the cellars as Daniel Guestier told them that the estate belonged to a neutral Irishman, who, however, volunteered for the British army. Although the quality and reputation of second growth (see CLASSIFICATION) Ch Léoville-Barton and third growth Ch Langoa-Barton steadily improved, the profitability of Barton & Guestier gradually declined, and in 1954 the American firm of Seagram took half the shares and later acquired complete control.

Ronald Barton's nephew Anthony (1930–) joined Barton & Guestier in 1951, and subsequently left to form his own merchant business. In 1986 he moved into Langoa and took over complete control of the two classed growths, whose wines are both made at Langoa and have become models of fairly priced claret made for the long term. E.P.-R.

Barton, A., and Petit-Castelli, C., *La Saga des Bartons* (Bordeaux, 1991).

Ray, C., *Fide et fortitudine: The Story of a Vineyard: Langoa-Léoville Barton 1821–1971* (Oxford, 1971).

BASE BUDS, or **basal buds**, the group of barely visible buds at the bottom of a shoot or cane. These were formed in the previous growing season in the developing buds, but the internodes between them do not expand, so they sit as a ring of inconspicuous buds at the base of the shoot. Normally they do not burst as buds higher on the cane burst preferentially. R.E.S.

BASILICATA, a mountainous, virtually land-locked area of southern Italy, is the country's third least populated region, with approximately 600,000 inhabitants. Its name has become synonymous with the extreme poverty in, and abandonment of, much of Italy's deep south. Its largest city, Potenza, has a population of less than 70,000 and Matera, its only other city of any size, has a population of just over 50,000. Little

commercial or industrial activity exists, and the countryside has been drained by emigration since the end of the Second World War. Little exists in the way of viticulture, with the region's total wine production amounting to less than 200,000 hl/5.3 million gal, of which less than 10 per cent is of DOC status. The Basilicata, in fact, has only one DOC wine, AGLIANICO del Vulture, although the Aglianico grape also gives interesting, if not superior, results in other areas of Basilicata such as near Matera and in the Colli Lucani in the east of the region. The most significant viticultural zone is undoubtedly that of the Vulture, an extinct volcano 56 km/35 miles to the north of Potenza, where, in addition to Aglianico, limited qualities of MALVASIA (dry, sweet, or sparkling) and MOSCATO (usually both sweet and lightly sparkling) are also produced.
D.T.

Anderson, B., *The Wine Atlas of Italy* (London and New York, 1990).
Gleave, D., *The Wines of Italy* (London and New York, 1989).

BASQUE country produces wines in Spain and France on either side of the western Pyrenees.

Spain

The Basque country (País Vasco in Castilian, Euskadi in Basque) is the most ferociously independent of all Spain's 17 autonomous regions. This densely populated, heavily industrialized strip of country facing the Bay of Biscay is not normally associated with wine, even though the important RIOJA region stretches north of the river Ebro into the Basque province of Alava. Wine is also made in the hills of the Alto Ebro. The only wholly Basque DO is the tiny region of CHACOLÍ DE GUETARIA on the coast 25 km/15 miles west of San Sebastián.

France

See BÉARN and IROULÉGUY.

BASTARDO, Portuguese name for a much travelled, dark-skinned grape variety known as TROUSSEAU in the Jura, south east France. In the Douro it is regarded as usefully productive but one of the less exciting ingredients in PORT; it ripens to high sugar levels but cannot contribute any great complexity of flavour. It is also grown in the Dão and Bairrada regions of Portugal and a variety called Bastardo was certainly cultivated at one time on the island of MADEIRA. It has also been planted, under a variety of aliases, in Australia and California.

BÂTARD-MONTRACHET, great white GRAND CRU in Burgundy's CÔTE D'OR. For more details, see MONTRACHET.

BATF, initials which spell bureaucracy for American wine producers and importers or, more precisely, Bureau of Alcohol, Tobacco, and Firearms, the wine trade's regulatory body in the United States.

BÂTONNAGE, French term for the wine-making operation of LEES STIRRING.

BAUMÉ, scale of measuring total dissolved compounds in grape juice, and therefore its approximate concentration of grape sugars (see MUST WEIGHT). It is used in much of Europe, including France, and Australia and, like other scales used elsewhere (see BRIX and OECHSLE), it can be measured with either a REFRACTOMETER or HYDROMETER. The Baumé scale is particularly useful in wine-making since the number of degrees Baumé indicates the POTENTIAL ALCOHOL in percentage by volume. (Grape juice of 12° Baumé, for example, would produce a wine of about 12 per cent alcohol if fermented out to dryness.) The rate of fall in Baumé is one method used to follow the course of an alcoholic FERMENTATION, but it should be noted that its product, ETHANOL, has a low DENSITY and progressively depresses hydrometer readings.
B.G.C.

BAUX, LES. Spectacular and famous small hilltop settlement in the far west of PROVENCE dominated by Michelin-starred restaurants and their customers' cars. It lends its name to wines produced round about, some of them excellent, as **Coteaux des Baux**. For more details, see Coteaux d'AIX-EN-PROVENCE.

BEARER, viticultural term used when pruning for what is effectively the fruiting unit of the vine, the selected long or shortened canes bearing the buds that will produce the next season's shoots and crop. See also PRUNING.

BÉARN, wine made in SOUTH WEST FRANCE either in the MADIRAN or JURANÇON zones, or in a third zone of 13 communes around Salies-de-Béarn and Bellocq dedicated exclusively to the production of **Béarn-Bellocq**. Characterful reds (often very similar to Madiran) and some firm rosés are made with up to 60 per cent Tannat grapes blended with Cabernet Franc, Cabernet Sauvignon, Fer, Manseng Noir, and Courbu Noir, while the very rare, tangy white wines may be made from such classic south west white grape varieties as Manseng, Courbu, Lauzet, Camaralet (as in Jurançon), which together with Raffiat de Moncade (as well as Sauvignon), are conserved in the letter of the appellation law if not in the reality of the vineyard. Nearly 200 ha/494 acres of vineyards are dedicated to the wines of Béarn (most of which are quite concentrated enough to go with a steak and Béarn's famous sauce), and the great majority of the wine is made by the CO-OPERATIVE at Bellocq.

BEAUJOLAIS, quantitatively extremely important wine region in east central France producing a single, unique style of wine. For administrative purposes, Beaujolais is often included as part of the greater BURGUNDY, but in terms of climate, topography, soil types, and even distribution of grape varieties, it is quite different. In a typical vintage Beaujolais produces more than the whole of the rest of greater Burgundy to the north put together, well over a million hl of wine, almost all of which is produced from a single red grape variety, GAMAY Noir à Jus Blanc. Beaujolais at its best provides the yardstick for all the world's attempts to put red refreshment into a bottle, being a wine that is essentially fruity, with a juicy aroma which, combined with its promise of appetizing acidity, is sufficient to release the gastric juices before even a mouthful of the wine has been drunk. In modern France Beaujolais has become almost a commodity, however, with attendant pressures on prices, so that generic blended Beaujolais can simply be a thin, inky liquid that is in all senses lacklustre. As Harry WAUGH discovered so many years ago, a DOMAINE BOTTLED wine may well be the most direct route to quality (although see also Georges DUBŒUF, whose importance is that of a major NÉGOCIANT, but whose philosophy was based on an attempt to be true to TERROIR).

To the Burgundian, Beaujolais wines are *les vins du Rhône*, not because they are from the RHÔNE valley, but because the vineyards of the Beaujolais hills fall within the Rhône *département* that surrounds the city of Lyon.

History

The region is on the ancient Roman trade route up the Rhône and Saône valleys. It is hardly surprising, therefore, that there are records of Roman vineyards in the region, notably on Mont Brouilly (Brulliacus), just the sort of HILLSIDE VINEYARD site favoured by the Romans, and Morgon. Benedictine MONKS developed vineyards here as early as the 7th century and for much of the medieval period Beaujolais, in wine terms at least, was simply the southern neighbour of the great duchy of Burgundy.

Beaujolais is named after Beaujeu, the town in its western hills founded in the 10th century, and was ruled by the Dukes of Beaujeu before being ceded to the Bourbonnais for a time. The region achieved real viticultural identity when Philip the Bold issued his famous edict against the growing of Gamay in Burgundy proper. He was right in that Gamay performs so much better on the granite hillsides of Beaujolais than on the limestone escarpment of the CÔTE D'OR.

The Gamay wines of Beaujolais continued to flow down the Saône to Lyons so that Beaujolais became known as the city's third river, after the Rhône and Saône. When communications with Paris by canal and then RAILWAY were developed, demand for Beaujolais the wine increased yet further, and the region expanded to include much less suitable land in the south, the Bas Beaujolais. Beaujolais is a relatively recent wine of note. REDDING in the early 19th century does not mention the word and cites, of today's well-known names, only St-Amour and Moulin-à-Vent, noting that they sold for relatively low prices, and that they should be drunk young.

Geography and climate

The total vineyard area is well over 20,000 ha/49,420 acres and includes nearly 100 communes with the MÂCONNAIS on its northern boundary (indeed some vineyards may be classified either as Beaujolais Blanc or ST-VÉRAN). The climate is TEMPERATE and semi-CONTINENTAL; snow may fall in the foothills of the Massif Central to the immediate west by the time Beaujolais Nouveau is launched, but summers are sufficiently hot for the local houses to have the shutters and gentle, tiled roofs of the south of France.

In the northern, narrower part of the region, the TOPOGRAPHY is very varied, the landscape made up of gentle, rolling hills, based on GRANITE and SCHIST with some limestone, while the flatter, southern, more recently developed sector south of Villefranche has much richer soils, often with some clay, making much lighter wines, typically for earlier consumption, on the plains which stretch down towards Lyon. The result of the more favourable MESOCLIMATES on the granite hillsides is that ripening is always more advanced in the north so that, apparently paradoxically, picking begins with the better-quality wines.

The appellations

About half of all Beaujolais is sold under the basic appellation **Beaujolais**, which comes from the Bas Beaujolais and the flatter land to the immediate west of the main north–south *autoroute* around Belleville. A small amount may be sold as **Beaujolais Supérieur**, for which the minimum POTENTIAL ALCOHOL of the grapes when picked must be 10.5 rather than 10 per cent.

The second most important Beaujolais appellation is **Beaujolais-Villages**, which accounts for about a quarter of total production. Beaujolais-Villages must come from the hillier, northern part of the Beaujolais region, its vineyards pushing up into the foothills of the Massif Central. If a Beaujolais-Villages is the produce of just one village or commune, it can append the name of that commune. In the finest sectors of this superior, northern part are the so-called **Beaujolais Crus**, 10 named communes of CRUS whose wines are considered so distinctive, and so good, that they have earned their own appellations. Some of these have the most evocative names in the wine lexicon, but their existence as separate entities can be very confusing for newcomers to wine since there is rarely mention of the word Beaujolais on their labels. For more details of individual Crus, see, approximately from north to south ST-AMOUR, JULIÉNAS, CHÉNAS, MOULIN-À-VENT, FLEURIE, CHIROUBLES, MORGON, REGNIÉ, BROUILLY, and Côte de Brouilly.

A small amount of **Beaujolais Blanc** and **Beaujolais-Villages Blanc** is made each year, mainly from Chardonnay grapes, although Aligoté is also allowed. White grapes do best on patches of limestone and are planted mainly on these outcrops in the north of the region so that they are effectively southern neighbours of MÂCON Blanc and taste exactly like it. Growers are supposed to devote no more than 10 per cent of their vineyard to white grape varieties. Even smaller amounts of refreshing **Beaujolais Rosé** are made.

Basic maximum permitted YIELDS are 55 hl/ha (3.1 tons/acre) for Beaujolais AC, Beaujolais Supérieur, and white wines, 50 hl/ha for Beaujolais-Villages, with a curiously modest reduction to 48 hl/ha for the Beaujolais Crus. The additional 20 per cent (PLC) has in practice been used to the maximum.

Another extremely important sort of Beaujolais is that sold as NOUVEAU, which may carry the appellation Beaujolais, Beaujolais Supérieur, or Beaujolais-Villages. When demand for **Beaujolais Nouveau** reached its peak, in 1992, nearly half of all Beaujolais AC was sold in this youthful state, for

Beaujolais: Picking Gamay grapes near Brouilly.

immediate consumption and, from the point of view of the producer, as an immediate generator of cash flow.

Viticulture

The GOBELET vine-training method is traditional in Beaujolais but in fact single GUYOT is much more likely in the southern Bas Beaujolais, with up to 12 buds. For Beaujolais-Villages as well as the Crus, PRUNING methods must be much more restrained, either *en gobelet* or *éventail* (see TRAINING SYSTEMS). VINE DENSITY here is one of the highest in the world, between 9,000 and 13,000 vines per ha usually. All picking, typically in late September, has to be manual because whole bunches are needed for Beaujolais's wine-making technique.

Vine varieties

Gamay Noir à Jus Blanc (so called to distinguish it from the relatively widely planted red-fleshed Gamay TEINTURIERS) accounts for about 98 per cent of the Beaujolais vineyard, which makes Beaujolais the most *monocépagiste* region of any size in France. Virtually all the rest is Chardonnay. According to the official regulations, up to 15 per cent of white varieties may be included in most Beaujolais appellations.

Considerable research into CLONAL SELECTION has taken place since 1960 so that the modern grower can choose from six approved clones, the best quality coming from small, thick-skinned berries.

ROOTSTOCKS used are SO 4, 3309, or, the Beaujolais speciality for granitic soils, Vialla.

Wine-making

Beaujolais is distinguished not just by the Gamay grape, but by its characteristic wine-making method, CARBONIC MACERATION or, more likely, SEMI-CARBONIC MACERATION. Only in Beaujolais is this technique used so widely, and, thanks to the commercial success of Nouveau, with such speed.

Another controversial issue in Beaujolais is CHAPTALIZATION. In recent years the trend was to pick grapes at the legal minimum ripeness of 10 per cent potential alcohol (10.5 per cent for Beaujolais-Villages and Crus), and then add sugar to bring the actual alcoholic strength dangerously close to the 13 (13.5) per cent maximum permitted final alcohol content.

Whole bunches arrive at the cellars and are emptied into cement or stainless steel FERMENTATION VESSELS generally of between 40 and 300 hl/1,056 and 7,920 gal capacity. The bottom 10 to 30 per cent of grapes are crushed by the weight above them and ferment in the normal way. This proportion increases with time. CARBON DIOXIDE is given off by this fermentation, and leaves the upper grapes bathed in the gas so that they undergo intracellular fermentation and produce the sort of aromas reminiscent of pear drops and bananas so closely associated with Beaujolais.

This combination of two different sorts of fermentation, together with MACERATION of the lower grapes and must, continues for perhaps as little as four days for Beaujolais Nouveau and 10 days for Cru wines destined for the long term. The pomace is then pressed and, unlike other regions, the PRESS WINE is automatically included in the final blend. MALOLACTIC FERMENTATION is then *de rigueur*, especially since the effect of carbonic fermentation is to increase malic acid. After some form of STABILIZATION, the wine is bottled either at under two months, in the case of Nouveaux, or perhaps not until the second Christmas after the vintage for the most concentrated, long-lived Crus. Bottling often takes place in the cellars of the négociants who soak up 90 per cent of the region's entire production (every BEAUNE merchant has to have its Beaujolais), or at one of the village CO-OPERATIVES which produce about a third of all the region's wine, or in a grower's cellar, using a mobile BOTTLING line.

Some Beaujolais, particularly in the Crus, is made at a much more leisurely pace, given some CASK AGEING, and possibly even bottled by hand from individual barrels. North Beaujolais is a region where TRADITION and the best of peasant culture survive, looking down, perhaps with wry amusement, at the frenetic production of Nouveau in the Bas Beaujolais.

Serving Beaujolais

Beaujolais has traditionally been served in a special 46-cl/1.2-gal bottle known as a *pôt*. European standardization may not approve of this but the essential point is that most Beaujolais is designed to be *drunk* rather than discussed or collected. This is the archetypal lubrication wine, and can be particularly *gouleyant*, or gulpable, if served cellar cool. Most Beaujolais is best drunk within a year of harvest, most Beaujolais-Villages within two, most Crus within three, although traditionally vinified wines, particularly Morgon, Moulin-à-Vent, Chénas, and Juliénas, can improve in bottle for up to 10 years from a good vintage. The tendency with time, however, is for a serious old Beaujolais Cru to taste increasingly like a red burgundy.

See also the individual Beaujolais Cru appellations BROUILLY, CHÉNAS, CHIROUBLES, FLEURIE, JULIÉNAS, MOULIN-À-VENT, MORGON, RÉGNIÉ, ST-AMOUR, as well as NOUVEAU.

Arlott, J., and Fielden, C., *Burgundy Vines and Wines* (London, 1978).
Hanson, A., *Burgundy* (2nd edn., London, 1994).

BEAUMES-DE-VENISE is a pretty village in Vaucluse that produces serviceable southern red Cotes-du-Rhône Villages (see RHÔNE) but is most famous for its unusually fragrant, sweet, pale gold VIN DOUX NATUREL. Muscat de Beaumes-de-Venise was particularly popular in northern Europe in the 1970s and early 1980s and could at that time be said to have been more widely appreciated than the great sweet whites of Bordeaux and Germany. It certainly launched to much of the restaurant trade the notion of wine by the glass as a tenable and profitable proposition and may well have been a catalyst for the mid 1980s renaissance in appreciation of sweet wines of all sorts.

Like the Muscats of the Languedoc (see FRONTIGNAN, LUNEL, MIREVAL, and, particularly, ST-JEAN-DE-MINERVOIS), this southern Rhône Muscat is made exclusively from the best Muscat variety, MUSCAT BLANC À PETITS GRAINS, and occasionally its darker-berried mutation. (This appellation represents the Rhône's only dalliance with Muscat except for the vineyards that produce CLAIRETTE DE DIE to the north which have so successfully been invaded by the same variety.) Fermentation is arrested by the addition of alcohol to produce a wine of just over 15 per cent but Beaumes-de-Venise is usually more delicate and refreshing than the Languedoc Muscats, partly because its minimum residual level is 110 g/l, as opposed to 125 g/l. Some of the vineyards, such as that of Domaine de Durban, are particularly high and yield especially concentrated, aromatic wine. Most of the northern Rhône NÉGOCIANTS such as CHAPOUTIER, JABOULET, and Delas sell their own bottling of this popular appellation which, apart from the extremely rare and expensive VIN DE PAILLE, is the Rhône's only sweet, still white (although see RASTEAU). Like all Muscats, this wine should be drunk as young as possible and is best served chilled. The French prefer it as an aperitif, while most anglophones prefer it with or after dessert.

BEAUNE, vinous capital of BURGUNDY giving its name to the Côte de Beaune section of the CÔTE D'OR vineyards. Beaune was founded as a Roman camp by Julius Caesar, became the seat of the dukes of Burgundy until the 13th century, and, although losing political supremacy to Dijon thereafter, has always been the centre of the Burgundian wine industry. In the 18th century the first merchant houses such as Champy (1720) and Bouchard (1731) were established and Beaune remains home to such leading NÉGOCIANTS as Louis JADOT, Joseph DROUHIN, Louis LATOUR, and BOUCHARD Père et Fils.

Beaune wines are almost all red, made from Pinot Noir grapes. They are usually no more than medium bodied, best drunk between five and 10 years old. While neither as powerful as POMMARD nor as elegant as VOLNAY, Beaune wines are more supple than Corton (see ALOXE-CORTON) and can be a charming introduction to good burgundy.

Before the enforcement of APPELLATION CONTRÔLÉE regulations many local wines were sold as Beaune as a readily marketable label of convenience. Now the town has a good rather than great reputation for its wines, perhaps because there are few outstanding domaines in an appellation

Quintessential **Beaune**—the courtyard of the Hôtel Dieu.

dominated by merchants. However, Beaune is blessed with an unusually high proportion, nearly three-quarters, of PREMIER CRU vineyards. Indeed those of village status are the exception, being limited to small parcels of land clinging to unsuitable upper slopes and some low-lying vineyards with richer soils. Otherwise the vineyards of Beaune form a broad swathe of premiers crus from the border with SAVIGNY-LÈS-BEAUNE to Pommard.

The finest vineyards are regarded as those situated almost directly between the town and the hill of Les Mondes Rondes: Les Grèves, Les Bressandes, Les Teurons, Les Avaux, and Les Champs Pimont. Beaune-Grèves includes Bouchard's noted Vigne de l'Enfant Jésus vineyard while Beaune-Boucherottes includes Louis Jadot's Clos des Ursules.

Other noted premier cru vineyards are Les Marconnets and Clos du Roi near the border with Savigny, and Clos des Mouches abutting Pommard. Although the red wines from this vineyard are not always memorable, Joseph Drouhin makes a rich, complex, and age-worthy white Clos des Mouches which is highly sought after.

In 1443 Nicolas Rolin founded the Hôtel Dieu, Beaune's principal tourist attraction. For more details, especially of the famous annual auction, see HOSPICES DE BEAUNE.

See also CÔTE D'OR and its map.

J.T.C.M.

BEAUNE, CÔTE DE. The Côte de Beaune is the southern half of the escarpment of the CÔTE D'OR, named after the important town and wine centre of Beaune. The greatest white wines of Burgundy and some very fine reds are grown on this stretch. The principal appellations, from north to south, are Corton and Corton-Charlemagne (see ALOXE-CORTON), BEAUNE, POMMARD, VOLNAY, MEURSAULT, PULIGNY-MONTRACHET, and CHASSAGNE-MONTRACHET. See also the separate entry under MONTRACHET.

Red wines from the lesser villages of the Côte may be sold under their own names or as **Côte de Beaune Villages**. This appellation is available for the wines of AUXEY-DURESSES, Chassagne-Montrachet, CHOREY-LÈS-BEAUNE, LADOIX-SERRIGNY, Meursault, MONTHÉLIE, PERNAND-VERGELESSES, Puligny-Montrachet, ST-AUBIN, ST-ROMAIN, SANTENAY, and SAVIGNY-LÈS-BEAUNE. See also MARANGES.

Whereas wines labelled Beaune come from the appellation adjoining the town, there is a small group of vineyards on the hill above whose wines are sold under the confusing appellation Côte de Beaune. Of these the best known are Clos des Monsnières and Les Topes Bizot. Both red and white wines are produced.

See also NUITS, CÔTE DE and map on p. 163. J.T.C.M.

BECKER, HELMUT (1927–89), academic and exceptionally cosmopolitan VITICULTURIST who was chief of the GEISENHEIM Grape Breeding Institute in Germany from 1964 until his death. Although he travelled, lectured, and learned extensively, he was essentially of this small town in the Rheingau region, having been born and educated there before studying biology at the nearby University of Mainz. He continued his academic career with a Ph.D. thesis on the biology of the PHYLLOXERA pest and then worked as a research scientist at the Neustadt viticultural station, where he was introduced to the field of VINE BREEDING, which was to dominate his work.

At Geisenheim from 1964, he continued the work of his predecessor Professor Heinrich Birk in CLONAL SELECTION and SCION breeding, but emphasized the need for deliberate cross-breeding for resistance to DOWNY MILDEW and POWDERY MILDEW. To achieve this end he used not only resistance genes from AMERICAN VINES, as many other vine breeders had, but also those from Asian species of VITIS, in particular *V amurensis*. Under his leadership, the wine-making facilities of the institute were extended and became a model for small-scale wine-making in breeding stations around the world. The products of these micro-vinifications were filed like library books in the research institute's deep, cool cellar, in bottles closed with the crown caps (see STOPPERS) of which Becker was a great proponent. Here Professor Becker would regale visitors with tastings of fine, Riesling-like wine made from

NEW VARIETIES which were effectively HYBRIDS because of their non-VINIFERA genes, and therefore officially outlawed.

He also intensified breeding of ROOTSTOCKS, aiming for complete phylloxera resistance rather than tolerance. This work yielded Börner, the first registered NEMATODE- and phylloxera-resistant rootstock (released after his death). Largely as a result of work undertaken under Becker's direction, Geisenheim holds the licences of about half of the scion and rootstock material propagated in Germany. Becker's studies of GRAFTING led to the introduction of special cover for CALLUS boxes, and a patented disinfectant which enables long-term storage of PROPAGATION material.

Apart from his research work, Helmut Becker was also a passionate teacher, lecturing not only at Geisenheim but also at the Universities of Bonn and Giessen. He always saw viticulture from a global point of view and collaborated with numerous scientists around the world, participating in and organizing conferences as a platform for scientific discussion. Thanks to his willingness to travel, his often iconoclastic views, and lively delivery in several languages (including some colourful English learned while a 17-year-old prisoner of war), he was probably the most internationally famous viticultural authority in much of the 1970s and 1980s. Helmut Becker's legacy to the viticultural community around the world is not only a wide range of breeding stock of scion and rootstock varieties, but also the request to continue to intensify scientific discussion and collaboration.

BEER. This alcoholic drink made, like wine, by FERMENTATION, but of cereals rather than grapes has impinged on wine mainly as a commercial competitor, the rivalry having ancient roots. Both beverages were enjoyed in the civilizations of MESOPOTAMIA, Ancient IRAN, and Ancient EGYPT, where brewing was associated with bread-making. Although beer was occasionally used for religious purposes it was generally the drink of the common people, whereas the aristocracy and priesthood drank wine.

The Greeks and Romans (see Ancient GREECE and Ancient ROME) reinforced wine's ancient supremacy, considering beer a barbarian drink fit only for the CELTIC and Germanic tribes they conquered. As wine became known through Europe, its strong association with religious ritual (pagan then Christian, see RELIGION) contributed to its prestige and its commercial success with the aristocracy and tavern drinkers. Beer lacked these religious and aristocratic connections.

The turning-point for beer came in the Middle Ages, when hops were added for bitterness and aroma. This new style of beer tasted different from traditional ale and was received with initial suspicion in England. Henry VIII banned his brewer from adding hops to the royal brew, but as wine became more expensive the popularity of hopped beer grew.

Similarly, hopped beer was hugely successful in those areas of Europe where wine could not be grown easily and had always been imported, notably northern Germany and Holland. During the course of the 18th and 19th centuries, brewing became big business.

See also COFFEE HOUSES for details of other drinks which were historically in commercial competition with wine. See SPARKLING WINES for one area in which the concerns of the beer industry parallel those of some wine-makers. H.B.

Forbes, R. J., 'Food and drink', in C. Singer (ed.), *A History of Technology*, ii (Oxford, 1956).
Lutz, H. F., *Viticulture and Brewing in the Ancient Orient* (Leipzig and New York, 1922).
Monckton, H. A., *A History of English Ale and Beer* (London, 1966).

BEERENAUSLESE, sometimes known as BA, one of the two rare and very ripe Prädikats in the QMP quality wine category defined by the GERMAN WINE LAW. In many VINTAGES hardly any Beerenauslese wine is produced anywhere in Germany. This rich, usually deep golden wine should be made from individually selected overripe grapes (**Beeren** means 'berries' in German), usually affected by NOBLE ROT. Specific minimum MUST WEIGHTS are laid down for each combination of vine variety and region and vary from about 110 to 128° OECHSLE. These rarities command extremely high prices but taste like honey-soaked raisins, essences of the relevant grape variety. Riesling in general produces the most refined and long-lasting examples, although Huxelrebe can also reach the necessary ripeness. Beerenauslesen from such vintages as 1975 and 1976 were mainly fermented very long and very slowly so that they were high in sugar and very low in alcohol (often lower than the technical minimum ALCOHOLIC STRENGTH) but Beerenauslese from, say, the 1989 and 1990 vintages are more likely to be slightly drier and more alcoholic. Some TROCKEN, or dry, Beerenauslesen have also been produced, but there is a certain element of perversion in their production.

See also AUSTRIA.

BEETLES, insects of the *Coleoptera* order, several of which attack grapevines as well as other horticultural crops and pastures. While particular species of beetles are often specific to a country or even region, beetles are a pest to grapevines world-wide. Black beetles (*Heteronychus arator*) attack young vines in spring, and can cause ring barking. They are native to South Africa, and are also known as African black beetles, but cause damage in other countries such as Australia.

Apple curculio beetle (*Otiorhyncus cribricollis*), thought to be a native of Europe, and vegetable weevil (*Listorderes costirostris*) also attack young vines in late spring and early summer, causing damage by eating vine leaves and/or young shoots. Beetles of importance in France are *Altica ampelophaga* and *Adoxus vitis*, which eat leaves, and *Otiorhyncus sulcatus*, which eats young shoots and buds. *Rhynchites betuleti* is called *cigarier* in French because it damages PETIOLES so the leaves roll up like cigars. Control of beetles, if necessary, is by application of the appropriate insecticide. See also BORERS.

M.J.E. & R.E.S.

Flaherty, D. L., *et al.* (eds.), *Grape Pest Management* (2nd edn., Oakland, Calif., 1992).
Galet, P., *Précis de viticulture* (4th edn., Montpellier, 1983).

BELGIUM, north European country which regularly imports more bordeaux than any other country, nurturing a particular passion for Pomerol, and which produces a minuscule amount of wine of its own, about 2,000 hl/52,800 gal a year, despite its LATITUDE.

Most vineyards are hardly more than 1 ha, produce wine merely for local sale, and were, typically, planted in the 1970s. There are two enterprises which have about 4 ha of vines, however: the renowned Hagelander near Aarschot, which produces a firm, dry Müller-Thurgau and Clos de la Zolette, which dates back to 1951. Belgian wine is made with varying degrees of competence but is, typically, light, dry, and similar to that made just over the border in the southern NETHERLANDS. Varieties planted include MÜLLER-THURGAU, AUXERROIS, various Pinots (including PINOT NOIR), various German crossings bred to ripen in cool climates such as OPTIMA, and such local specialities as Leopold III, Maréchal Joffre, and Loonse Vroege. Most but not all Belgian wine is white.

The wine industry of LUXEMBOURG to the south east is much bigger, more successful, and older, having been established in Roman times. Belgian viticulture has a long, if not continuous, history, however. In the era of CHARLEMAGNE vines were grown extensively in southern Belgium to provide wine for MONKS and were not abandoned until the 15th century, when a combination of CLIMATE CHANGE and the increasing influence of BURGUNDY prejudiced the continuation of Belgian viticulture.

BELLET, historic and distinctive appellation in the far south east of PROVENCE based on just 45 ha/111 acres of vines in the hills above Nice which have somehow survived the urban encroachment. (There are similarities with COLARES in Portugal.) It would presumably be possible to sell every one of the 10,000 or so cases of Bellet made in a good year in the hotels of Nice alone. It takes determination to find a bottle outside the Côte d'Azur, and even greater determination to find the vineyards themselves perched about 300 m/980 ft above the Mediterranean up the Var valley in the city's hinterland. Almost equal quantities of all three colours are produced. The scented, full bodied whites made from the local Rolle grapes with some Chardonnay are the appellation's most distinctive wines, and reflect well the MESOCLIMATE of these hillside vineyards, which is slightly cooler than in much of the rest of Provence. Rosés may be made from Braquet (the BRACHETTO of Piedmont across the Italian border) while the intriguing Folle Noire (Fuella) is traditional for red wines, although it is often supplemented by Grenache and Cinsaut. Ch de Crémat and Ch de Bellet are the principal producers.

George, R., *French Country Wines* (London, 1990).

BENCH BLENDING. See ASSEMBLAGE.

BENCH GRAFTING, the viticultural operation of GRAFTING vines indoors rather than in the field. It permits mechanization and factory-style operations leading to mass production. The procedure is widely used in Europe, especially Italy and southern France, where it is an important industry. Dormant cuttings are saved for bench grafting, stored in the cold; after soaking in fungicide solution, ROOTSTOCK cuttings are disbudded and SCION cuttings are cut into one-node pieces. Cuts of matching shape are made at the bottom surface of the scion and at the top of the rootstock, using cuttings of similar diameter. With a GRAFTING MACHINE, variously shaped cuts are used, such as 'omega' or 'saw-tooth'. After fitting, the newly grafted cuttings are packed with a moistened, coarse-grained medium in boxes and stacked in humid, warm rooms (28–9 °C/82–4 °F) until the union has CALLUSED (in about two weeks). Once they have hardened, grafts are waxed to reduce water loss, then planted out, usually in a NURSERY. Many variations of this procedure are used, but attention is always paid to preventing FUNGAL DISEASES. B.G.C.

BENDIGO, small, isolated but historic (see GOLD RUSHES) wine region in the state of VICTORIA in AUSTRALIA.

BENTONITE, a montmorillonite clay found principally in the state of Wyoming in the western United States, and in many other areas of the world. Like most clays, bentonite is a hydrated compound of aluminium and silicon oxides, but it differs in ways that are useful to wine-makers. When mixed with water it swells and assumes a form that has significant powers of adsorption.

Bentonite, so called because it was first discovered in the Fort Benton rock series, is widely used in the NEW WORLD to ensure PROTEIN stability, particularly to remove heat-unstable proteins from white wines such as MUSCATS, which normally contain them.

Bentonite fining is also used in making everyday white wines for the CLARIFICATION of MUST before or, for more commercial wines, during FERMENTATION to remove solids that would otherwise make the wine look darker, taste coarser, and possibly form clouds in bottle. It is not used at this stage for top-quality white grape must whose constituents should have a beneficial effect on flavour. Bentonite is frequently used for fining after fermentation, however, to hasten the settling of LEES and thereby reduce the time between rackings. Bentonite is not generally used for red wines because their higher concentration of TANNINS removes proteins and naturally aids rapid clarification.

Even the most sophisticated wine drinker prefers a clear white to a hazy one, however strange the idea of a Wyoming clay treatment may seem. Care should be taken when fining with bentonite that a wine's complexity is not diminished by fining too heavily. A.D.W.

BEREICH, German for a district, bigger than a GROSSLAGE but smaller than a region or ANBAUGEBIET. The boundaries of these wine-making units in GERMANY are often drawn more for political than geographical reasons. A wine labelled Bereich Something (Bernkastel, for example) is unlikely to be very exciting.

BERGERAC, the biggest wine appellation in SOUTH WEST FRANCE producing red, dry white, and sweet white wines in the image of BORDEAUX to the immediate west of the region. The greater Bergerac region, named after the principal town at its centre on the river DORDOGNE, is the principal appellation of the Dordogne *département*, and can boast more beautiful and varied countryside than that of its vinously more glamorous neighbour. Lacking distinctions other than touristic (and gastronomic; Périgord is the home of the truffle), it has long been difficult for the wines of Bergerac to escape from the shadow of Bordeaux's more serious wine reputation.

The climate here is somewhere between MARITIME and CONTINENTAL, but overripeness is a rare characteristic of Bergerac grapes and wines. Soils vary from alluvial silt to clay and, on the higher terraces, limestone.

Within the region are smaller districts, generally on higher sites with more obvious potential, which have their own appellations for specific wine types. MONBAZILLAC on the left bank of the river is potentially the greatest of these, and could make fine BOTRYTIZED wine if producers could afford to take the necessary risks. MONTRAVEL on the right bank makes lightish dry and sweet white wines in the west of the region. Both these appellations were created in the late 1930s just after the creation of the Bergerac appellation. PÉCHARMANT won its own red wine appellation in 1946, as did the almost extinct sweet wine appellation of ROSETTE, while the SAUSSIGNAC sweet white wine appellation was created in 1982. Partly because these names, with the exception of Monbazillac, are hardly the most famous in the wine world, many producers choose to sell their wines simply as Bergerac.

The vine was grown in the region in Roman times but the wines were most obviously exported and appreciated in the Middle Ages, when viticulture thrived under the influence of the monasteries (see MONKS AND MONASTERIES). The history of BORDEAUX outlines why the English were so fond of them, and why, as wines of the HAUT PAYS, they were discriminated against by the Bordeaux merchants. After the HUNDRED YEARS WAR the DUTCH WINE TRADE dominated exports of Bergerac, developing the production of SWEET WINES here, as elsewhere, from the 16th century and, especially, after Protestant refugees left Périgord for northern Europe after the Edict of Nantes in 1685.

Bergerac was slow to recover from PHYLLOXERA and today's total of 13,500 ha/33,360 acres is just a fraction of the area planted with vines in the early 1870s. Vines grown are the classic Bordeaux varieties: Cabernets and Merlot for red wines and Sauvignon, Sémillon, and Muscadelle for whites. Sémillon is still the most planted variety, accounting for one vine in every three, although Merlot is pressing for second place. Cabernet Sauvignon and Cabernet Franc were more widely planted than Sauvignon Blanc at the end of the 1980s.

The most common form of Bergerac is as a still red wine generally very similar to red BORDEAUX AC. A small amount of red is sold as **Côtes de Bergerac**, which has a higher minimum ALCOHOLIC STRENGTH (11 rather than 10 per cent). Effective wood ageing was still relatively rare in the region in the mid 1990s. A little bit of **Bergerac Rosé** is made, but the second most common form of Bergerac is the dry white **Bergerac Sec**, increasingly well made thanks to the application of some of the techniques employed for better dry white bordeaux. About a quarter of all white wine is sweet, made mainly from Sémillon, and sold as **Côtes de Bergerac Mœlleux**, but this is rarely a sophisticated or deep flavoured wine.

See also MONBAZILLAC, MONTRAVEL, PÉCHARMANT, ROSETTE, and SAUSSIGNAC.

BERGWEIN, term in AUSTRIA for wine made on slopes steeper than 26 per cent, most common in the Wachau and Styria. Unlike wine made from flatter land, it may be sold in a regular 75-cl/27-fl oz bottle even without satisfying Qualitätswein requirements.

BERRY, botanical term for a class of fleshy fruit lacking a stony layer, so that all of the fruit wall is fleshy or pulpy. The grape berry, popularly known as the grape, is a prime example. It consists of two carpels, denoted by its two locules (internal spaces) in each of which are borne two ovules which may develop into SEEDS, giving in most cases a maximum of four seeds per berry. For more details, see GRAPE.

BERRY ROTS. See BUNCH ROTS.

BERRY SIZE is considered by many to be a factor in wine quality, in that smaller berries contribute to better wine quality, especially for red wines, since the ANTHOCYANS, PHENOLICS, and FLAVOUR COMPOUNDS are mostly contained in the skins. Smaller berries' higher surface to volume ratio results in a higher concentration of these skin compounds in the juice and hence in the wine.

Good-quality wine grape varieties typically have small berries, at least compared to both lower-quality varieties and TABLE GRAPES. The average weight of a premium wine grape at full ripeness is 1 to 2 g, whereas others weigh 3 to 10 g/0.35 oz. These values doubtless represent the natural selection of VINE VARIETIES for their end use, which has continued for centuries. This fact in itself would seem to support the idea that small berries are a prerequisite for premium wine production.

It is not the case, however, that any vineyard management practice which leads to smaller berries will necessarily improve wine quality. Certainly, WATER STRESS causes small berries, although some of the effects on wine quality may be the result of water stress on VINE PHYSIOLOGY rather than the direct result of small berries. The other simple means of reducing berry size is PRUNING to many buds in winter, but this is contrary to BALANCED PRUNING, and is likely to reduce wine quality since the vine has to struggle to ripen grapes with insufficient leaf area for efficient PHOTOSYNTHESIS.

R.E.S.

BIANCO means white in Italian and the names of many Italian white wines therefore begin Bianco d'/da/di/del Place-name. For more details see under the place-name.

Note, however, that Bianco is also the name of a small town in CALABRIA and that GRECO di Bianco can be an exceptional sweet white wine.

BIBLE. The vine, including its chief product, wine, is mentioned more often in the Bible than any other plant. The Book of Genesis presents the invention of viticulture as a step in the development of civilization. 'And Noah began to be an husbandman, and he planted a vineyard. And he drank of the wine and was drunken' (Gen. 9. 20–1). The original Hebrew text and its translations state clearly that Noah was the first to make wine, just as Abel was the first shepherd, Cain the first city builder, Jabel the first dweller in tents and keeper of cattle, Jubal the first musician, and Tubal-cain the first smith (Gen. 4. 2–22). By becoming the first wine-maker, Noah fulfils his father's prophecy: 'this same shall comfort us concerning our work and toil of our hands, because of the ground which the Lord hath cursed' (Gen. 5. 29). VITICULTURE is divinely ordained: the art of WINE-MAKING will soften the rigours of human existence in a fallen world.

But wine is intoxicating if taken in excess: the invention of wine is also the occasion of the first DRUNKENNESS. Noah 'was uncovered within his tent'. Yet Genesis does not condemn Noah for his drunkenness and indecent exposure: it is Ham, the son who draws attention to his father's nakedness instead of respectfully covering it as Japheth and Shem do, who gets the blame. The impropriety is Ham's, not Noah's, and Noah curses Ham's offspring.

Even if Genesis was not troubled by drunkenness, the early Christian commentators were. The Church Fathers found all manner of excuses for Noah's behaviour: that Noah did not know the possible effects of wine, for example; that he drank to blot out his sorrow at the death and devastation wrought by the Flood; or that he was not drunk in a literal sense. Allegorically, Noah's drunkenness signifies divine ecstasy, the joy experienced by the Christian at the EUCHARIST, when wine is drunk. This interpretation is first offered by St Cyprian (d. 258), and, once it had been adopted by St Ambrose in the 4th century, it became the standard gloss on this text. Going yet further, because events in the Old Testament are read as foreshadowing parts of the life of Christ, Noah prefigures Christ. The wine that Noah drinks is the cup that God the Father would not allow to pass from Christ in the Garden of Gethsemane (Matt. 26. 39; cf. Mark 14. 35, Luke 22. 41–2), as St Augustine stated in Book 16 of *The City of God* (written in 429). In the eyes of Augustine and those of medieval commentators after him, because Noah's drunkenness points forward to Christ's Passion, it is to be praised. Similarly, the speaker of Isaiah 63. 3, who has 'trodden the wine press alone', is interpreted as Christ, the man of sorrows (Isa. 53. 3).

In the Middle Ages Christ in his Passion is often depicted as a man treading grapes or even—but not in English art—crushed in a wine press. These numerous mentions of grapes, wine, and the vintage in the Old Testament are allegorized as representing Christ's Passion: the bunch of grapes from the Promised Land (Num. 13. 24), for example; the vineyard in Isaiah 5. 1–7; and the wine in the Song of Songs.

Nowadays this method of biblical interpretation, known technically as typology, is used much less often: we may still hear Moses mentioned occasionally as a type of Christ but not Noah: modern biblical scholars restrict themselves to pointing out that in a primitive society lack of respect for one's elders is a far more serious offence than drunkenness.

The Bible is not suitable reading for teetotallers. As the Psalmist says, 'wine maketh glad the heart of man' (Ps. 104. 15). Although we may not realize it, Psalm 23, 'The Lord is my Shepherd', sings the praises of wine. In the line which is familiar to most English speakers as 'My cup runneth over', the cup contains wine, and the original version, followed by the various Latin translations, speaks approvingly of its intoxicating properties. To be deprived of wine is a terrible thing. Whenever the Prophets threaten doom and destruction, they say that the Lord will withhold the benefits of the vintage from the Israelites, as in Micah 6. 15, Amos 4. 9, Isaiah 17. 6, and Joel 1. 10. In the New Testament Timothy is advised to give up drinking water and instead to 'use a little wine for thy stomach's sake and thine often infirmities' (1 Tim. 5. 23, now no longer thought to be by St Paul).

A rare disapproving reference would seem to be Acts 2. 13, when sceptical observers dismiss the Pentecostal miracle of speaking in tongues as drunkenness: the apostles 'are full of new wine', but the disapproval is aimed at the unseemly babble, not at wine; in any case, Pentecost is not the time of the vintage so the insult is perhaps not to be taken literally. 'New wine' evokes images of joyful abandon and drunken revelry, as in Joel 1. 5, where the Israelites, Joel prophesies, will labour in vain: 'Awake, ye drunkards, and weep, and howl, all ye drinkers of wine, because of the new wine, for it is cut off from your mouth.' But as a sign of God's mercy 'the mountains shall drop down new wine' (Joel 3. 18).

Old wine is never mentioned in the Old Testament, but it is in the New. Where the Synoptic Gospels explain that new wine should not be put into old 'bottles', wineskins in fact, as a matter of hygiene (Luke 5. 37–9, Matt. 9. 16–17, Mark 2. 21–2), only Luke adds, 'No man also, having drunk old wine, straightaway desireth new; for he saith, The old is better.' The old wine would not of course have been stored and aged in a wineskin but in a sealed non-permeable container such as an AMPHORA. In the hot climate of the Holy Land old wine would have been better than new, especially if it was a heavy tannic red. Compare Greek and Latin authors, who always prefer old wine to new (see Ancient GREECE and CLASSICAL TEXTS).

On one occasion Christ himself expresses a desire to drink new wine. At the Last Supper, as the Synoptic Gospels tell us (Matt. 26. 29, Mark 14. 25, Luke 22. 18), he will not drink the wine until he drinks it new in the kingdom of his Father (Luke omits 'new'). These passages describe how the Eucharist was instituted. The new wine which Christ will drink when God's everlasting kingdom has come carried with it all the

This illustration to Gen. 9. 20–1, from the Holkam **Bible** *c*.1320–30, shows Noah and his sons harvesting grapes, whose fermented juice takes its toll on Noah.

pres q̃ Noe out uines plaunte. Hi crescerent grapes: a grant plente. E tens
venist de les vendenger. Adunk Noe: les fist cuiller: E en hottes: al oustel porter:
n graunz cuves: les alla fuller. E fesoit vin lon: si enleuoit. Dount meistenant
le estoit. E chest dormir: tut decouvert. Se membre apparuth tut apert.
am son deusime enfaunt. Son pere trova: issi dormant. Il sen moca: ne le
usist couerir. Porceo estoit son fiz le pire. Ves alla: ses freres quere. Por
pere hounte fere. Sem le eisne. le alla couerir. Mal de son pere: ne vousist
Japhet le ieuene se returna. E ne vousist regarder: endreit la. Ben tot apres
e velliat, E de ceo q'il: estoit tut nuth, Por son fiz: q'de luy mocka. E tot il dit
am ween ceo chea. ton fiz Canaan seit maudit. Por le tu mecal en despit.

Like many traditional cellars, that of Ch Margaux is fitted with concrete **bins**.

associations of the joy of the vintage. And Christ was aware of the importance of wine. His first miracle was to turn water into wine at the marriage in Cana, when the wine had run out. The governor of the feast, who does not know where the wine has come from, says to the bridegroom, 'Every man at the beginning doth set forth good wine and, when men have well drunk, then that which is worse; but thou hast kept the good wine until now' (John 2. 10). One would dearly like to know what this wine was like. But how delightful that Christ should be portrayed as a man of taste and discernment and that this should be the first tangible proof of his glory and the miracle that convinced the disciples. 'This beginning of miracles did Jesus in Cana, of Galilee, and manifested forth his glory; and his disciples believed in him' (John 2. 11).

H.M.W.

Daube, D., *Wine in the Bible*, St Paul's Lecture (London, 1974).
Zapletal, V., *Der Wein in dem Bible* (Freiburg im Breisgau, 1920).

BICAL, Portuguese white grape variety grown mainly in BAIRRADA, and DÃO, where it is called Borrado das Moscas, or fly droppings. The wines have good acidity and can be persuaded to display some aroma in a few still VARIETAL versions, although the grapes are typically used in blends for sparkling wines.

BIENVENUES-BÂTARD-MONTRACHET, a great white GRAND CRU in Burgundy's CÔTE D'OR. For more details, see MONTRACHET.

BIERZO, or **El Bierzo**, small DO region in north west Spain which administratively forms part of CASTILE-LEÓN (see map on p. 907). The river Sil which bisects it, however, is a tributary of the Miño (Minho in Portugal) and the wines have more in common with those of GALICIA than those of the DOURO 140 km/88 miles to the south. Sheltered from the climatic excesses of the Atlantic and the central plateau, Bierzo shows promise as a wine region. The MENCÍA grape is capable of producing balanced, fruity red wines in the well-drained soils on the SLATE and GRANITE of this part of Spain. In the mid 1990s some modernization of production methods and winery equipment was still needed for Bierzo to fulfil its potential.

R.J.M.

BIFERNO, effectively the only DOC in the Italian MOLISE region.

BIN, traditional term for a collection of wine bottles, normally stacked horizontally on top of each other, or the process of so storing, or **binning**, them. Thus these bins needed BIN LABELS, and a **bin end** has come to signify a small quantity of wine bottles left over from a larger lot.

BIN LABELS were necessitated by the practice of BINNING unlabelled bottles.

The most common form of bin label was made of pottery and was approximately the shape of a coat hanger some 3–5 in/7–13 cm wide. At the apex there was an additional lug, pierced so that it formed a suspension ring. As many were nailed to the cellar masonry, they were often broken or cracked during removal.

Early English bin labels (dating to the mid 18th century) are delftware (tin-glazed earthenware) with blue or deep magenta calligraphy (upper case) on a white to pale blue ground. Almost all later ones have black lettering on white pottery, although coloured lettering is very occasionally seen.

European labels came in a variety of forms and often with polychrome decoration; the language of the writing usually provides an obvious clue to the country of origin.

By the 19th century, labels developed rounded shoulders, the earlier ones being angled. Many had a portion of the face left unglazed where more precise details of the bin contents might be written. Home-made labels were sometimes fashioned from wood or slate and would likewise have written information.

In very large cellars and in commercial ones where the bin contents changed frequently, it was established practice to use circular bin labels with numbers that would cross-refer to the cellar records. Many of these, and the coat hanger variety, are marked with the manufacturer's name (Wedgwood, Copeland, etc.) or the vendor's name (e.g. Farrow & Jackson), almost invariably impressed during manufacture. Bin labels are not much collected in the world of wine ANTIQUES but the most sought after are delftware examples, those with spelling mistakes, and rarities of name, colour, or form. R.N.H.B.

Butler, R., *The Philoenic Antiquary* (1978).

—— and Walkling, G., *The Book of Wine Antiques* (Woodbridge, 1986).

W. & A. Gilbey Ltd., *The Compleat Imbiber* (London, 1957).

Johnson, H., Janson, D. J., and McFadden, D. R., *Wine Celebration and Ceremony* (New York, 1985).

Weinhold, R., *Vivat Bacchus*, trans. by N. Jones (Watford, 1978).

BINISSALEM, sometimes spelt **Benissalem**. Wines from Spain's first offshore DO on the Mediterranean island of MAJORCA are mostly destined for the Balearic holiday resorts. Binissalem's dominant grape, the Manto Negro, is reputed to be capable of making well-balanced reds, but most suffer from a heavy-handed approach to wine-making. The most common white variety is the Moll, also called Prensal Blanc, which produces bland, neutral wines. R.J.M.

BIODYNAMIC VITICULTURE, sometimes called *biodynamie* in France, is the most extreme and ideological of all alternative approaches to viticulture, and is heavily influenced by the theories of Rudolf Steiner. Biodynamic viticulture emphasizes soil fertility, as do many other ORGANIC VITICULTURE philosophies, but has added dimensions of the 'cosmic background' of astronomy. Thus vineyard (and winery) operations are governed by positions of the planets and phases of the moon. Conventional AGROCHEMICALS and FERTILIZERS are absolutely forbidden, although BORDEAUX MIXTURE and SULPHUR are permitted. Used also are liquid extracts of products of vegetable origin, including yarrow, camomile, nettle, oak, dandelion, and valerian, typically applied as very dilute concentrations in applications as low 40 l/ha (4 gal/acre). Domaines converted to biodynamic viticulture in the early 1990s included Domaine Leflaive of PULIGNY-MONTRACHET, Domaine LEROY of Vosne-Romanée, Coulée de Serrant of SAVENNIÈRES, and Domaine Huet of VOUVRAY. See also ORGANIC VITICULTURE, SUSTAINABLE VITICULTURE. R.E.S.

BIOLOGICAL VITICULTURE, a loose term since all viticulture involves biology, but for more details of the general philosophy implied, see ORGANIC VITICULTURE. In France, many ORGANIC WINES are sold as *vins biologiques*.

BIONDI-SANTI, family popularly credited with establishing the repute of BRUNELLO DI MONTALCINO in Tuscany, central Italy.

BIOTECHNOLOGY. See GENETIC ENGINEERING for some examples of viticultural biotechnology.

BIRDS are a more serious modern vine pest than PHYLLOXERA. Birds can be a serious vineyard pest during grape RIPENING because they love to eat grapes, which is hardly surprising since, before grapevines were domesticated, they may well have formed soft, flavoured, sugary fruit in order to attract birds, so that vines might be spread and propagated by seeds in the birds' excreta. For small vineyards in isolated regions, and particularly for early ripening vine varieties, birds may destroy an entire crop. Unfortunately, the birds begin their destruction as soon as the grapes begin to ripen, so early harvest is not a solution. As well as the potential crop loss, bird pecks provide entry points for all sorts of BUNCH ROTS. Control measures (see below) are expensive and bird damage can make some vineyards uneconomic. Birds are often the greatest problem facing vineyards in new viticultural regions, especially if the vineyards are isolated (as in Long Island in NEW YORK and ENGLAND, for example).

The species of birds which attack grapes vary from region to region. The ubiquitous starling is one of the most widespread problem species but blackbirds, partridges, robins, sparrows, thrushes, and finches are also common. Starlings, for example, can eat 60 to 80 g/2.8 oz of grapes a day. The planting of a vineyard and the consequent provision of an extra food source can actually lead to a population increase of birds. Many growers notice that bird damage depends on the availability of alternative food sources. In the MARGARET RIVER region of Western Australia, for example, silvereye birds do more damage to vineyards when nectar from local eucalyptus trees and saltbush berries are limited. Where vineyards are extensive, and the varieties ripen together, then damage to individual vineyards is minor.

Effective bird control measures depend first on recognition of the species and then on knowledge of its habits. Some birds are extremely mobile; starlings may travel 25–30 km/16–19 miles from the roost to feed. Birds usually approach a vineyard from one direction, usually on one flight path. Trees or shrubs adjacent to the vineyard provide cover to survey the vineyard, and some species such as waxeyes, sparrows, and finches are difficult to scare as they fly from one shrub or tree to another *en route* to the vineyard. Thus trees near a vineyard can contribute to bird feeding.

Many bird protection devices are based on scaring birds. In time, birds become accustomed to new objects or noises in a vineyard so that, for example, the traditional immobile scarecrow can rapidly lose effectiveness. Other scaring

Economically vital **bird** scarer at Yeringberg in Australia's Yarra Valley.

devices include a wide range of auditory devices, guns, gas-powered cannons, tape across the vineyards, cats, etc. Variation of devices is effective, and tape can be effective, especially if given a few turns which cause it to move and roar in the wind. Trapping birds can be useful, but it leaves the owner with the difficult decision as to what to do with the caught birds.

Netting of vineyards is becoming increasingly common. The nets are made of woven string or perforated plastic and typically cover individual rows. While this protection is expensive, the nets can often be reused and tractor-mounted rollers assist installation and removal. Since the nets provide for virtually 100 per cent effective control yet do not harm birds, they are acceptable to growers and environmentalists alike.

Some local bird populations are affected by eating insects or grapes which contain pesticides used in vineyards, which bird lovers view as an argument against the use of AGROCHEMICALS. R.E.S.

Buchanan, G. A., and Amos, T. G., 'Grape pests', in B. G. Coombe and P. R. Dry (eds.), *Viticulture, ii: Practices* (Adelaide, 1992).

BIRD'S EYE ROT. Vine disease. See ANTHRACNOSE.

BITTER ROT, a FUNGAL DISEASE of ripe grapes that is active in warm, humid conditions. It is found on damaged and almost senescent tissues, and the bitter fruit flavour can be detected in the finished wine. The cause is the fungus *Greeneria uvicola* and the disease is widespread in the eastern United States, Asia, Australasia, and South Africa but not in France or Germany. The disease affects only damaged grapes and is easily controlled by most fungicides. R.E.S.

BLACK KNOT. Vine disease. See CROWN GALL.

BLACK MEASLES. Vine disease. See ESCA.

BLACK ROT, FUNGAL DISEASE which is one of the most economically important diseases of vines in the north eastern United States, Canada, and parts of Europe and South America. The disease is native to North America and was probably introduced to other countries by contaminated cuttings. It was introduced to France, for example, on PHYLLOXERA-tolerant rootstocks in 1885. The disease is caused by the fungus *Guignardia bidwelli*, which attacks young shoots, leaves, and berries. The disease spreads only in mild, wet weather. Crop losses can be high, up to 80 per cent. Control of the disease is based on fungicides sprayed from spring up to fruit ripening. As might be expected from the origin of the disease, some native American species are tolerant. R.E.S.

BLACK SPOT. Vine disease. See ANTHRACNOSE.

BLAGNY, small village in Burgundy's CÔTE D'OR. For more details, see both MEURSAULT and PULIGNY-MONTRACHET.

BLANC DE BLANCS, French for 'white of whites', may justifiably be used to describe white wines made from pale-skinned grapes, as the great majority of them are. The term has real significance, however, only when used for white SPARKLING WINES, in the production of which dark-skinned grapes often predominate. A blanc de blancs CHAMPAGNE, for example, is, unusually, made exclusively from CHARDONNAY grapes.

BLANC DE NOIRS, French for 'white of blacks', describes a white wine made from dark-skinned grapes by pressing them very gently and running the pale juice off the skins as early as possible. Many such still wines have a slightly pink tinge (see DÔLE Blanche and WHITE ZINFANDEL, for example). The term has a specific meaning in the Champagne region, where it is used to describe a CHAMPAGNE made exclusively from PINOT NOIR and MEUNIER grapes.

BLANC FUMÉ is a French synonym for SAUVIGNON BLANC, notably in Pouilly-sur-Loire, centre of the POUILLY-FUMÉ, or Blanc Fumé de Pouilly, appellation, many of whose aromatic dry whites do indeed have a smoky, if not exactly smoked, perfume. Thanks to one imaginative American, FUMÉ BLANC is today a much more widely known term.

BLANCO, Spanish term for white as in *vino blanco*, or white wine.

BLANDY, a name that is synonymous with MADEIRA, both the island and the wine. The Blandy family has extensive interests on Madeira, including ownership of the famous Reid's Hotel. John Blandy of Dorset came to live on the island in 1811, having been introduced to the island and its wines while serving in the navy. His son Charles was astute enough to buy up considerable stocks of mature wine during the outbreak of POWDERY MILDEW in 1852, which contributed to the success of the madeira wine firm Blandy Brothers & Co. in the second half of the 19th century. In 1874 Charles's daughter married a Cossart, of the other important madeira wine firm COSSART GORDON. The tourist show-piece of the madeira wine industry, the old São Francisco lodge in Funchal, was once the Blandy family home and offices.

The difficult years of the early 20th century saw the formation of the Madeira Wine Association, which Blandy's joined in the 1920s and eventually acquired a controlling interest. The group is now known as the Madeira Wine Company, includes all the British madeira firms (Cossart Gordon, Leacock, Rutherford & Miles), and produces more than half of all exported island bottled madeira. The SYMINGTON family, a major force in the port wine trade, acquired a controlling interest in the Madeira Wine Company in 1988.

Cossart, N., *Madeira: The Island Vineyard* (London, 1984).

BLANKETING, wine-making term for protecting grapes, juice, or wine, particularly from OXYGEN, by applying a gas, usually INERT GAS or sometimes CARBON DIOXIDE.

BLANQUETTE DE LIMOUX. See LIMOUX.

BLAU or **Blauer** is the adjective meaning 'blue' in German, often used for darker-berried vine varieties. Blauer Burgunder is PINOT NOIR, for example, while Weisser Burgunder is PINOT BLANC.

BLAUBURGUNDER or even **Blauer Burgunder** is one German name for PINOT NOIR, for example, although Spätburgunder (occasionally Blauer Spätburgunder) is more common.

BLAUER SPÄTBURGUNDER, an Austrian synonym for the PINOT NOIR grape.

BLAUFRÄNKISCH is the Austrian name for the middle European black grape variety the Germans call LIMBERGER. From pre-medieval times it was common to divide grape varieties into the (superior) 'fränkisch', whose origins lay with the Franks, and the rest. It is today one of Austria's most widely planted dark-berried varieties producing wines of real character, if notably high acidity, when carefully grown. Its good colour, tannin, and raciness encourage the most ambitious Austrian producers to lavish new oak on it and treat it like SYRAH. Outsiders however can find its build reminiscent of, say, the MONDEUSE of Savoie or one of the denser Crus of BEAUJOLAIS and for many years it was thought to be the Beaujolais grape GAMAY. Bulgarians still call it Gamé, while Hungarians translate its Austrian name more directly as KÉKFRANKOS.

Its Austrian home is Burgenland where most of its nearly 3,000 ha/7,400 acres are situated. It is grown particularly on the warm shores of the Neusiedlersee, on the Hungarian side of which it also grows, as Kékfrankos, in Sopron, whose porty version even has the distinction of having been singled out for mention by Napoleon. Today it is increasingly recognized by Austrian wine-makers as worthy of attention, ageing, and,

Blandy: From Vizetelly's *Facts about Madeira and Port* (1880).

often, BARREL MATURATION. While Austrian plantings of INTERNATIONAL VARIETIES are limited, Blaufränkisch is being used to add fruit to blends of Cabernet Sauvignon and Pinot Noir. The variety called Frankovka in CZECHOSLOVAKIA and VOJVODINA is one and the same and here can produce lively, fruity, vigorous wines for early consumption. In FRIULI in the far north eastern corner of Italy, the variety is called Franconia and can yield wines with zip and fruit.

The vine buds early and ripens late and can therefore thrive only in a relatively warm climate. It can suffer spring frost damage but is very vigorous and is not particularly disease prone. Yields are therefore quite high, around 75 hl/ha/4.3 tons/acre.

BLAYE, fortified town on the north bank of the Gironde estuary just opposite Margaux in the BORDEAUX region which has been exporting wine much longer than the famous MÉDOC across the water. Today it lends its name to several of the so-called BORDEAUX CÔTES appellations, although at the beginning of the 20th century it produced mainly white wine for distillation into COGNAC to the immediate north. Today by far the most important wine produced here is robust red **Premières Côtes de Blaye**, made on 3,400 ha/8,400 acres of vineyard, mainly from MERLOT grapes supplemented by CABERNET SAUVIGNON. Such wines vary in quality but the region is rich in conscientious PETITS CHÂTEAUX which can provide increasingly good value for early drinking. Soils vary considerably (much more than in neighbouring Côtes de BOURG). White wine may be called **Blaye**, **Blayais**, or **Côtes de Blaye**, the latter limited to a higher minimum ALCOHOLIC STRENGTH and lower maximum YIELD. Although plantings of SAUVIGNON Blanc are increasing, the much more neutral UGNI BLANC and COLOMBARD grapes predominate here and some of their produce is distilled into FINE de Bordeaux. A little red Blaye is also made.

BLEEDING. Vines are said to bleed when they lose fluid in spring from pruning cuts. This event can take place over several days, and is generally seen following the first few days of warm spring weather. Individual vines can lose up to 5 l/1.3 gal of water. The liquid which drips from the pruning cuts is mostly water, with low concentrations of MINERALS, SUGARS, organic acids, and HORMONES. This is the first visible sign of the start of the new VINE GROWTH CYCLE. Bleeding is in fact the first sign of renewed activity of the root system, and is related to the rise in soil temperature, although the soil temperature at which this occurs depends on the variety of ROOTSTOCK. Osmotic forces create root pressure, which forces water up through the plant. This was measured for the first time in 1725 by Hales, who found that root pressure could push water 7 m/23 ft up a tube. R.E.S.

Galet, P., *Précis de viticulture* (4th edn., Montpellier, 1983).

BLENDING different batches of wine, or *coupage* as it is known in French, is a practice more distrusted than understood. Almost all of the world's finest wines are made by blending the contents of different vats and different barrels (see ASSEMBLAGE); CHAMPAGNE and SHERRY are examples of wines which are quintessentially blends. It is often the case, as has been proven by the most rigorous of experiments, that a wine blend is superior to any one of its component parts.

Blending earned its dubious reputation before the mid 20th century when wine laws were either non-existent or under-enforced, and 'stretching' a superior wine by blending it with inferior wines was commonplace (see ADULTERATION). Blending of different lots of the same wine as it is commonly practised today to ensure that quality is maximal and consistent was not possible before the days of large blending vats; before then wine was bottled from individual casks or vats, which is one explanation of the much higher degree of BOTTLE VARIATION in older vintages.

Modern blending, important in the production of both fine and everyday wines, may combine wines with different but complementary characteristics: heavily oak-influenced lots aged in new barrels may be muted by blending with less oaky lots of the same wine; wines that have undergone MALOLACTIC FERMENTATION may be blended with crisper ones that have not. In the case of ordinary table wines, blending is an important ingredient in smoothing out the difference between one VINTAGE and its successor. Such practices are by no means unknown in the realm of fine wine production, whether legally sanctioned or not. The wine regulations in many regions permit the addition of a certain proportion of another vintage to a vintage-dated wine, as they sometimes do a certain proportion of wine from a region or even grape variety other than that specified on the label.

In a competitive and quality-conscious wine market, motivation for blending is more often improvement than deception.

Perhaps the most enthusiastic blenders are the AUSTRALIANS, who regularly blend, to produce what they regard as a QUALITY WINE, the produce of three different wine regions, possibly many hundreds of miles apart. There are philosophical differences between them and the European authorities, but some compromise solution to allow the importation of such wines into Europe was reached in the mid 1990s.

For details of **fractional blending**, see SOLERA. See also ASSEMBLAGE and BACK BLENDING.

BLIND TASTING, a particularly masochistic but potentially rewarding form of wine TASTING whereby the taster attempts to identify wines without knowing their identity. Only by blind tasting can a true assessment of a wine's style and quality be made, so powerful is SUBJECTIVISM in the wine-tasting process.

The blind taster generally attempts to identify VINE VARIETY, geographical provenance, and VINTAGE. The first of these should be the easiest but, while wines from different varieties are generally considered to be distinctive, trained tasters have been found unable correctly to identify varieties in University of California blind tasting tests. The percentage of correct identification was high for characteristic varieties such as Muscat at 59 per cent; the success rate with Cabernet Sauvignon was 39 per cent, while some minor varieties could not be identified at all. Some well-known varieties with non-distinctive flavours were recognized only infrequently, such as Chenin Blanc's 15 per cent and Merlot's 14 per cent. Vintage variation was also considerable; Gewürztraminer was identified correctly from one vintage on 50 per cent of occasions, but on only six per cent from the following year.

In some cases, a wine's geographical provenance can be easier to detect than specific grape variety or blend of varieties. Red bordeaux and white Alsace, for example, tend to express place before grape.

In identifying vintage and general maturity, a wine's COLOUR can be particularly helpful, although, given the extent of vintage variation, of course a vintage several years from the actual one may well be a better guess than a consecutive one.

The OPTIONS GAME was devised by Len EVANS as a way of combining the arcane process of blind tasting with general entertainment. Beginners often make the best blind tasters; experience can confuse.

BLOOM on a grape's skin (*pruine* in French) is the whitish covering consisting of waxes and cutin which protects the berry against water loss and helps stop the penetration of spores.

BLUE FINING, largely outmoded wine-making process whereby excess copper and iron are removed from wine by FINING with potassium ferrocyanide. The process works because soluble copper and iron form insoluble compounds with the ferrocyanide ion. A century ago, before STAINLESS STEEL was widely available, winery equipment was often made of iron, copper, or bronze, an alloy of copper and tin. They would be attacked by the ACIDS in wine. Wines containing more than 10 mg/l of iron or 0.25 mg/l of copper could easily form a haze, so blue fining was needed to remove the excess copper and iron dissolved from the equipment after prolonged contact with the metals.

The process was developed by the German chemist Möslinger at the end of the 19th century and was legally used, under strict controls, for many years in Germany. It is now outlawed in most wine regions because of fears that poisonous PRUSSIC ACID (hydrogen cyanide) could be formed and remain in the wine. A.D.W.

BLUE NUN, the most successful German wine BRAND, a LIEBFRAUMILCH owned by H. SICHEL Söhne of Mainz. It was developed, mainly in Britain and America, between the two World Wars, when there was a certain resistance to anything German (although German wines had previously enjoyed greater prestige than they do today), as a more accessible product than the host of German bottles adorned with Gothic script and long, complicated names. A label was developed for the easy, medium dry style of young white wine sold in inns throughout Germany which initially showed two nuns in brown habits against a bright blue sky. The label, and

subsequently the brand, became known as Blue Nun, featuring a single, alluring nun in a blue habit. Long before MATEUS Rosé, Blue Nun became a substantial commercial success as a result of heavy investment in advertising which preyed on the fears of what was then an unsophisticated wine drinking public. Blue Nun was advertised as the wine you could drink 'right through the meal', thereby solving the awkward problem of food and wine matching. It began to grow rapidly in the 1950s, and at its zenith, in 1984/5, annual sales in the USA alone were 1.25 million cases, with a further 750,000 cases sold elsewhere. Quality was reliably high, despite the quantities needed to satisfy world sales, and blending at the Mainz headquarters was conscientiously undertaken (at this stage by Rainer Lingenfelder among others, who went on to established a reputation for himself as one of the best estate producers in Germany's PFALZ region). A static wine market, economic recession, and increasing sophistication on the part of wine consumers saw worldwide sales fall to less than a million cases in the early 1990s, although there were attempts to widen the range of Blue Nun products, even into French red wine.

BLUSH wine is pale pink and made by using black-skinned grapes as if to make white wine. A marketing triumph emanating from California in the late 1980s (the name was originally coined by Mill Creek winery), it differs from ROSÉ mainly in ethos rather than substance, having become fashionable just when and where rosé was losing its market appeal (although in very general terms a blush wine is likely to be paler than a rosé). WHITE ZINFANDEL was initially the dominant type in this class, but it spawned many other pinks-from-reds such as VARIETALS labelled White Grenache, Cabernet Blanc, Merlot Blanc, Blanc de Pinot Noir, as well as GENERICS called Blanc de Noirs. Most are sweet, vaguely aromatic and faintly fizzy. CALIFORNIA produces a few dry, oaked blush wines, most of them called VIN GRIS. See also SAIGNÉE.

BOAL, name of several Portuguese white grape varieties, grown on the mainland but also, most famously, on the island of MADEIRA, where its name was Anglicized to BUAL.

BOBAL, important Spanish dark-skinned grape variety which produces deep coloured red wines and even GRAPE CONCENTRATE in ALICANTE, UTIEL-REQUENA, and other regions for bulk wine production in south east Spain. It is widely planted, perhaps on as much as 100,000 ha/247,000 acres, even though not associated with fine wine. It retains its acidity better than MONASTRELL, with which it is often grown, and is notably lower in alcohol.

BOCA, rare but historically important red wine DOC in the Novara hills in the subalpine north of the PIEDMONT region of north west Italy. GHEMME, SIZZANO, and FARA, also in Novara, are similar, as are LESSONA and BRAMATERRA in the Vercelli hills across the river Sesia. For more details, see SPANNA.

BOCKSBEUTEL. Special bottle in the shape of a flattened flask used in the German wine region of FRANKEN and four communes in the northern Ortenau area of BADEN. The name probably derived from the Low German *Bockesbeutel*, a pouch to carry prayer-books and the like, rather than from any ostensible resemblance to a goat's scrotum (the literal translation). T.S.

BODEGA, Spanish term for a wine CELLAR, a WINERY, or a tavern or grocery store selling wine.

BODY, tasting term for the perceived 'weight'—the sensation of fullness, resulting from DENSITY or VISCOSITY—of a wine on the palate. Wines at either end of the scale are described as **full bodied** and **light bodied**.

Next to water, ALCOHOL is the major constituent of wines. It has a much higher viscosity than water and is the major component responsible for the sensation of fullness, or body, as a wine is rinsed around the mouth. ALCOHOLIC STRENGTH is therefore clearly an important factor: the more potent a wine the more full bodied it is usually said to be.

The dissolved solids in a wine, its EXTRACT, can also contribute significantly to body, although sweet wines are not necessarily full bodied (ASTI SPUMANTE, for example, being sweet but very light bodied, thanks to its low alcohol content).

Contrary to popular conception, GLYCEROL makes only a very minor contribution to density, viscosity and therefore to body (although it does have a slight effect on apparent sweetness).

Body is not related to wine quality, BALANCE being more important in a wine than whether it is full or light bodied. One of the less desirable effects of the increase in comparative TASTING, however, is that full bodied wines make a more obvious impression and therefore tend to be glorified.

Amerine, M. A., and Roessler, E. B., *Wines: Their Sensory Evaluation* (2nd edn., New York, 1982).

BOHEMIA, part of the Czech Republic in the west of what was CZECHOSLOVAKIA and best known for beer and the production of GLASSES.

BOLGHERI, small town on the coastal strip of TUSCANY which gives its name to a DOC for relatively ordinary white

One of the **bodegas** in which Alvear matures its Montilla.

and rosé wines (including one from ANTINORI holdings here), and provides a geographical reference point for at least two of Italy's most famous SUPERTUSCANS, Sassicaia and Ornellaia (see VINO DA TAVOLA), made by cousins and members of the extended ANTINORI family.

BOLIVIA in SOUTH AMERICA has a long history of vine-growing but its modern wine industry is as yet undeveloped. Viticulture was brought to the high valleys of Bolivia from neighbouring PERU in the 16th century by Augustine MISSIONARIES. Between 1550 and 1570 they had reached the districts of Pilaya, Paspalla, and Cinti and had spread as far south as Tarija by 1600.

PHYLLOXERA and NEMATODES severely hampered Bolivian viticulture in much of the 20th century. Resistant ROOTSTOCKS and good-quality VINIFERA cuttings were imported in the 1980s in an effort to restore vineyard health and the proportion of grafted vines is increasing.

The climate here is both CONTINENTAL and TROPICAL, modified by ALTITUDE in that the majority of vines are planted at 2,000 to 2,500 m / 8,200 ft above sea level. Modern Bolivian viticulture extends only to about 1,000 ha / 2,470 acres, mainly but not exclusively in the southern zone of Camargo and, especially, Tarija, where soils are predominantly fertile and ALLUVIAL. Tarija's wine zones would be classified as Region III or IV according to the WINKLER system, and annual RAINFALL can reach 700 mm / 27 in, much of it during the growing season from December to March, which encourages a range of FUNGAL DISEASES. (The traditional system of training vines up the indigenous pepper tree (*schinus molle*) helped retard the development of such diseases, but ESPALIER vine-training systems are more common today.) IRRIGATION is widely practised.

MUSCAT OF ALEXANDRIA represents about 80 per cent of all light coloured VINIFERA grape varieties planted, and is widely used for distillation into the aromatic local brandy *singani*, which can be a fine counterpart to the PISCO of Peru and Chile. Table wines are also produced from Muscat although plantings of a wide range of other varieties associated throughout the world with good-quality red and white wine are increasing. Some creditable Cabernet / Merlot blends are produced, and examples of varietal Torrontés, Riesling, and Chenin Blanc.

The wine produced for domestic consumption by foot treading and vinification in clay jars is called *patero*.

BOLLINGER, independent Champagne house producing a range of top-quality wines based on Pinot Noir grapes. Bollinger was formed from the de Villermont family's holdings in the village of Ay near Rheims, where the company is still based. In 1829, Jacques Joseph Placide Bollinger, youngest son of a noblewoman and a legal officer in Württemberg, formed a partnership with Amiral Comte Athanase Louis Emmanuel de Villermont and Paul-Joseph Renaudin to form the house of Champagne Renaudin, Bollinger & Cie. In 1837, Jacques Bollinger married de Villermont's daughter Louise Charlotte and became a French citizen. In 1865, the house started to ship low DOSAGE champagne to Britain, which was unusual for a period in which most champagne reaching the country was sweet. Champagne Bollinger received the Royal Warrant as Official Purveyor of Champagne to Queen Victoria in 1884.

Control of the house eventually passed to Jacques's grandson (also named Jacques), who died young, leaving his widow Elizabeth Law 'Lily' Bollinger (1899–1977) in charge. Lily oversaw the family vineyards on foot and bicycle for four decades, enduring the 1944 German bombardment of Ay while sleeping in the Bollinger cellars. After the Second World War, she acquired the Beauregard vineyard at Mutigny as well as vineyards in Grauves, Bisseuil, and Champvoisy, bringing Bollinger's land holdings to 144 ha / 356 acres, about 70 per cent of production needs. By the time of her death in 1977, Lily had seen sales double to 1 million bottles a year. She believed that nothing should change the traditional Bollinger style, which is achieved with a backbone of Pinot Noir from the Ay vineyards, a certain proportion of BARREL FERMENTATION (unusual for sparkling wine), and TIRAGE in bottles stoppered with corks rather than crown caps, often for a decade or more. Bollinger Tradition RD ('recently disgorged', with marked AUTOLYSIS as a result of being aged for a minimum of eight years) is only released in great vintages, and only the best of these witness production of Année Rare RD. Rarest of all the Bollinger range of champagnes is the Vieilles Vignes Françaises, a BLANC DE NOIRS produced exclusively from ungrafted Pinot Noir vines that grow in a vineyard never affected by PHYLLOXERA behind Bollinger's headquarters.

In 1985 Bollinger took a 40 per cent share of the Australian Petaluma winery, with particular involvement in the development of the associated sparkling wine operation at Bridgewater Mill in the ADELAIDE HILLS. While other Champagne houses became defensive, Bollinger rose admirably to the challenge posed by critics of champagne in the early 1990s by issuing the Bollinger Charter of Ethics and Quality, in which it volunteered conditions for the production of its wines which protected both wine quality and the Bollinger name. Chief architect of the Bollinger Charter was the outspoken Christian Bizot, president of the house and nephew of Lily Bollinger.

See also CHAMPAGNE. S.A.

Ray, C., *Bollinger: Tradition of a Champagne Family* (3rd edn., London, 1988).

BOLOGNESI, COLLI, small DOC zone in the hills of Bologna in north central Italy. See EMILIA-ROMAGNA for more details.

BOLZANO, or **Bozen** in German, the main town of the ALTO ADIGE in northern Italy. Local light red wines may carry the name **Colli di Bolzano** or **Bozner Leiten**.

BOMBINO BIANCO, important white grape variety, especially in APULIA in southern Italy. Bombino Bianco is probably the most planted white grape variety in the productive and heavily milked vineyards of Apulia but is also

Bollinger's headquarters, not in Épernay or Rheims, but in the small town of Ay.

planted in EMILIA-ROMAGNA, LATIUM, MARCHES, and the ABRUZZI, where it is thought to be the true identity of the variety that is so common that it is, confusingly, called Trebbiano d'Abruzzo, even though it is distinctly less acidic than true TREBBIANO. A sign of how unimportant white grape varieties are in southern Italy, however, is that the Italian vineyard survey of 1990 found only 3,700 ha/9,140 acres of Bombino Bianco, hardly more than a tenth of the area planted with the southern red varieties Montepulciano and Negroamaro, for example.

The vine may have originated in Spain. It ripens late and yields extremely high quantities of relatively neutral wine, much of which has been shipped north, particularly to the energetic blenders of Germany. Many an ordinary SEKT or EUROPEAN UNION TABLE WINE is made up substantially of Bombino Bianco, perhaps scented with a particularly aromatic German variety such as MORIO-MUSKAT. Some of its synonyms, Pagedebit and Straccia Cambiale in particular, allude to its profitability to the vine-grower. There is also a much less common dark-berried **Bombino Nero** in Apulia.

BONARDA, Italian red grape variety, or more accurately the name of three distinct varieties: (1) the Bonarda of the OLTREPÒ PAVESE and COLLI PIACENTINI which is, in fact, not Bonarda at all but rather the CROATINA grape; (2) the Bonarda Novarese, used to soften SPANNA in its range of DOC reds in the Novara and Vercelli hills, which again is not Bonarda, but UVA RARA, a variety more widely employed in the Oltrepò Pavese; and (3) the so-called Bonarda Piemontese, an aromatic variety which has been virtually abandoned because of its small bunches and low productivity, although it covered 30 per cent of the region's vineyard before the advent of PHYLLOXERA. Scattered patches remain on the left bank of the Tanaro, particularly in the township of Govone. In the mid 1990s attempts were made to revive this last variety, in the belief that it will add aromatic interest when blended with the BARBERA grape.

The only DOC wines in production which bear the name Bonarda are from the Oltrepò Pavese and are made from Croatina. D.T.

Bonarda is also the name of the most widely grown red wine grape variety in ARGENTINA, where so much Malbec was pulled out in the 1980s that it fell into second place behind Bonarda's 1990 total of more than 12,000 ha/29,650 acres. This means that Argentina has six times as much Bonarda planted as Italy, although some authorities believe Argentine Bonarda is in fact the variety known as CHARBONO in California.

BONBONNE, a large glass jar or carboy, typically holding 25 l/6.6 gal, used as a neutral container to store wine, VIN DOUX NATUREL, or BRANDY, often after a period of wood ageing.

BONDED WAREHOUSE or **bonded winery**, one in which no DUTY has been paid on the goods inside it. Prices for wines and, especially, spirits held **in bond** (IB) are therefore considerably lower than those quoted duty paid, or duty paid and delivered (DPD). It is sensible for any foreigner buying wine to store for possible shipment outside that country to buy it in bond.

BONNE ŒUVRE, French expression meaning literally 'good work', also means DESUCKERING.

BONNES MARES, great red GRAND CRU in Burgundy's CÔTE D'OR. For more details, see CHAMBOLLE-MUSIGNY and MOREY-ST-DENIS.

BONNEZEAUX, particularly well-favoured enclave for sweet white wine production within the Coteaux du LAYON appellation in the Anjou district of the Loire. In this respect Bonnezeaux resembles QUARTS DE CHAUME to the north west but, despite its greater extent (about 70 ha/173 acres), it has not enjoyed such fame. A Bonnezeaux from a reliable producer such as Ch de Fesles, the most important, can be a deep green-gold nectar at 10 to 20 years old. The wines are made exclusively from Chenin Blanc grapes grown on steep slopes near Thouarcé which should ideally be attacked by NOBLE ROT, or at the very least have been picked only after several TRIS through the vineyard. POTENTIAL ALCOHOL should be at least 13.5 per cent, half a per cent more than Quarts de Chaume, and yields are usually very low.

See also LOIRE and map on pp. 576–7.

BOOKS ON WINE. See the LITERATURE OF WINE and WINE WRITING. For references to wine in some more obviously literary works, see ENGLISH LITERATURE.

BORBA, town in southern Portugal whose CO-OPERATIVE is establishing a certain reputation for its wines. See ALENTEJO for more details.

BORDEAUX, important French port on the GARONNE river leading to the GIRONDE estuary on the west coast. Bordeaux gives its name to a wine region which includes the vineyards of the Gironde *département* and, as such, the wine region which produces more top-quality wine than any other, from a total vineyard area of about 100,000 ha/247,000 acres divided among 13,000 producers. Bordeaux has a higher proportion of large estates than any other French wine region. Red bordeaux is known in Britain as CLARET. The most famous examples, which represent less than five per cent of the region's total production, are characterized by their ability to evolve after years, sometimes decades, of BOTTLE AGEING. About a quarter of all bordeaux is white, however, some sweet as well as dry. Small quantities of rosé, light red CLAIRET, sparkling CRÉMANT, and FINE brandy are also made. The total quantity of wine produced each year is about 660 million bottles, which represents more than a quarter of France's total APPELLATION CONTRÔLÉE wine production, but the total can vary quite considerably owing to the vagaries of the climate. See BORDEAUX AC for bordeaux wine at its most basic, BORDEAUX TRADE for an account of the workings of the wine trade in Bordeaux, and BORDEAUX UNIVERSITY for details of its important Institut d'Oenologie.

History to medieval times

The Latin poet Ausonius (*c.*AD 310–393/4) is not only the first author to mention that wine was grown in his native Bordeaux, he was also the region's first known wine-grower. In his poem 'De herediolo' ('On his small inheritance'), dated 379, he tells us that he grows 100 *iugera* (a *iugerum* is approximately two-thirds of an acre or 0.25 ha) of vines. His estate was probably at Bazas, near the river Garonne (although some have suggested St-Émilion). In two of his other poems, 'Mosella' ('On the Moselle'), and 'Ordo urbium nobilium' ('The list of distinguished cities'), he describes the banks of the Garonne overgrown with vines. Ch AUSONE is named after him.

Although Ausonius' descriptions indicate that viticulture was well established in Bordeaux in his lifetime, no definite earlier evidence exists. Given that the Allobroges tribe were growing wine around Vienne in the RHÔNE valley in the 1st century AD, the Bituriges may have been doing the same in Bordeaux, but Strabo, author of the *Geography* (completed in 7 BC), merely says that Bordeaux ('Burdigala' in Latin and in Strabo's Greek) was a place of commerce, and PLINY, writing *c.*AD 77, does not tell us clearly that the Bituriges grew wine (although he does refer to a Biturica vine, which may have been associated with either the Bituriges tribe of Bordeaux or the other to the west of Bourges), so the likelihood is that viticulture spread to Bordeaux after it had come to the Rhône.

We know little about Bordeaux in the centuries following the fall of the Roman empire. The area was overrun by the Visigoths in the 5th century and when Clovis had defeated the Visigoths in 507 it became part of the Frankish kingdom. CHARLEMAGNE is said to have displayed a temporary interest in FRONSAC. With the economic expansion in Europe which started in the 11th century, demand for wine grew. Initially, the new port of LA ROCHELLE, on the Atlantic coast north of Bordeaux, brought wealth to the region in the 12th century; consequently, Bordeaux increased both its trade and its production. By 1200 wine was grown in BLAYE, BOURG, the lower DORDOGNE and the Garonne valley, and in the GRAVES. The Graves was the largest producer, with Ch Pape-Clément as its oldest named vineyard. In 1305 Archbishop Bertrand de Goth, who was to become Pope Clement V, presented it to the see of Bordeaux. Throughout the Bordeaux region more red wine was grown than white, but SAUTERNES and CÉRONS probably had white wine, although these white wines cannot have been like the botrytis-affected wines of today, for the deliberate commercial use of NOBLE ROT in Sauternes and Cérons dates from after the Middle Ages. Until the late 17th century the MÉDOC was too marshy to produce much wine and was known mainly for its corn: there were just a few vineyards in what is now called the Bas-Médoc, north of ST-ESTÈPHE. ST-ÉMILION was already a wine-growing district,

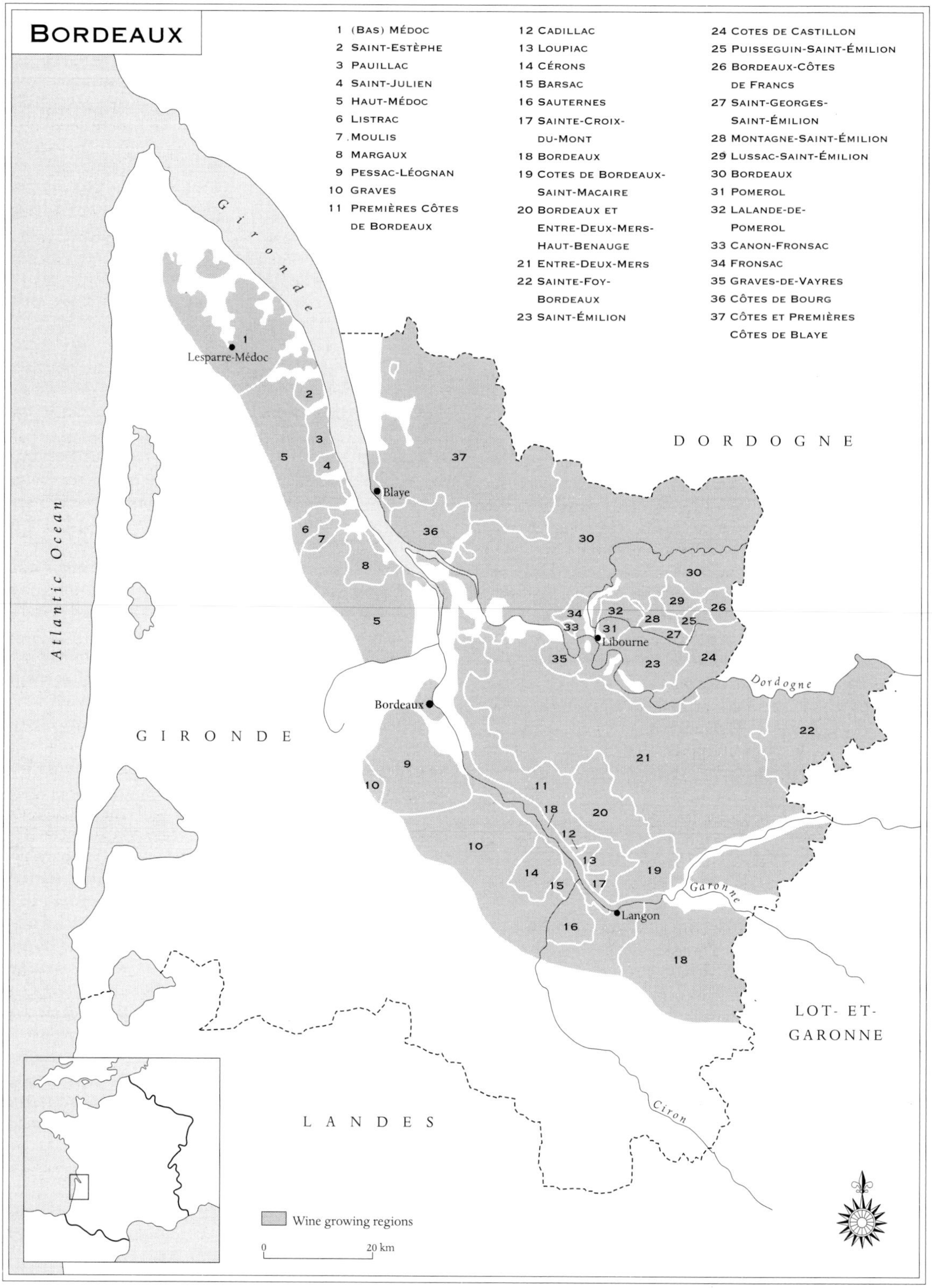
BORDEAUX
1 (Bas) Médoc
2 Saint-Estèphe
3 Pauillac
4 Saint-Julien
5 Haut-Médoc
6 Listrac
7 Moulis
8 Margaux
9 Pessac-Léognan
10 Graves
11 Premières Côtes de Bordeaux
12 Cadillac
13 Loupiac
14 Cérons
15 Barsac
16 Sauternes
17 Sainte-Croix-du-Mont
18 Bordeaux
19 Cotes de Bordeaux-Saint-Macaire
20 Bordeaux et Entre-Deux-Mers-Haut-Benauge
21 Entre-Deux-Mers
22 Sainte-Foy-Bordeaux
23 Saint-Émilion
24 Cotes de Castillon
25 Puisseguin-Saint-Émilion
26 Bordeaux-Côtes de Francs
27 Saint-Georges-Saint-Émilion
28 Montagne-Saint-Émilion
29 Lussac-Saint-Émilion
30 Bordeaux
31 Pomerol
32 Lalande-de-Pomerol
33 Canon-Fronsac
34 Fronsac
35 Graves-de-Vayres
36 Côtes de Bourg
37 Côtes et Premières Côtes de Blaye
Gironde
Lesparre-Médoc
Blaye
Atlantic Ocean
DORDOGNE
Libourne
Dordogne
Bordeaux
GIRONDE
Garonne
Langon
LOT-ET-GARONNE
LANDES
Ciron
Wine growing regions
0
20 km

however. Some of the wine of Bordeaux was neither white nor red but a mixture of white and red grapes fermented together called 'clairet' in Old French, which is the origin of the modern English word CLARET.

Bordeaux's pre-eminence began as a result of the English connection. In 1152 Eleanor of Aquitaine married Henry Plantagenet, who in 1154 became king of England (and duke of Normandy) as well as acquiring Eleanor's territories, GASCONY and most of western France. In order to win the favour of the citizens of Bordeaux, King John (1199–1216) granted them numerous privileges. The most important of these was exemption from the Grand Coutume, the export tax imposed on ships sailing from Bordeaux. Also, Gascon merchants were given favoured treatment in London. All this made Gascon wine cheaper for the English than any other imported wine. In the 14th century, most French wine consumed in England was from Gascony, and a quarter of Bordeaux's wine exports went to England. Against these protective measures La Rochelle could not compete, despite its superior position right on the coast, while Bordeaux was 60 miles / 100 km up river. And when La Rochelle fell to the French in 1224, it ceased to be a commercial threat to Bordeaux.

Not all the wines sold by the Gascon merchants were from the immediate Bordeaux area. In the HAUT PAYS (Gaillac, Quercy, Nérac, and Bergerac) the climate was more reliable and these wines were stronger than those of Bordeaux. The Haut Pays wines were more expensive because they were taxed in Bordeaux; and those from the parts of the Haut Pays which had fallen to the French were not allowed into Bordeaux until St Martin's Day, 11 November, or even until Christmas, so that Bordeaux wines dominated the wines available for the fleet which arrived each autumn to deliver the year's new wine to England, Scotland, Ireland, the Low Countries, and the Hanseatic ports. The wine of GAILLAC was especially prized in England.

In 1453, at the end of the HUNDRED YEARS WAR, Gascony reverted to French rule; yet its trade with England soon picked up again, even though it never regained its 14th century volume. Bordeaux had been a major port before it became a wine-producing area to feed its wine trade. Its winemakers were not patient monks, as they had often been in Burgundy, but opportunistic laymen, whose aim was to cash in on the huge demand for Bordeaux's chief export product, and so they switched from grain to wine. The thin wines of Bordeaux, which before the advent of glass BOTTLES and CORKS did not last from one vintage to the next, cannot have been anything like modern bordeaux. H.M.W.

James, M. K., *Studies in the Medieval Wine Trade* (Oxford, 1971).
Penning-Rowsell, E., *The Wines of Bordeaux* (6th edn., London, 1989).
Simon, A. L., *The History of the Wine Trade in England*, 3 vols. (London, 1906–9).

Modern history

Trade with Britain continued after the English were expelled, but the DUTCH WINE TRADE gradually became dominant, not so much in wines for their own consumption but in inexpensive white wines for the rest of northern Europe and the Hanseatic states. The Bordeaux merchants had to fight hard to maintain their position in northern Europe, for the Dutch also bought from the Mediterranean countries.

It was the Dutch who drained the marshy MÉDOC in the mid 17th century, thereby creating the basis for the fine wines that made Bordeaux's reputation throughout the world. Before this the best wines were to be found in the well-drained GRAVES near the city, notably Ch HAUT-BRION. Today's leading Médocain estates—Chx LAFITE, LATOUR, and MARGAUX—were probably planted in the last third of the 17th century, and reached England, to be offered at auction in the COFFEE HOUSES of London, only after consignments had been captured at sea in the Anglo-French wars at the beginning of the 18th century.

The simultaneous trade war between Britain and France led to ever-increasing duties on French wines and the Anglo-Portuguese Methuen Treaty of 1703. In return for a Portuguese promise to admit British woollen goods in perpetuity, the British government agreed that duty on French wines should never be less than 50 per cent higher than on the wines of Portugal (and, in fact, Spain). Officially, British wine imports from Bordeaux declined sharply but smuggling must have been rife, to judge from the prevalence of bordeaux in the household sales conducted by Christie's (see AUCTIONS) after their foundation in 1766. Conditions in both Bordeaux and Britain were ripe for the development of trade in fine CLARET: in the Gironde there was a new affluent bourgeoisie, members of the legal Bordeaux Parlement, with the means to plant and maintain expensive vineyards, while in Britain bordeaux's almost exclusive market was created by a wealthy, landowning aristocracy and, soon, the new industrial middle class.

The necessary link was a Bordeaux merchant class, sufficiently well established to be able to buy, cellar, and export these 'new French clarets'. These merchants came largely from Britain, and Germany, which had long been prominent in the inexpensive red bordeaux trade. BARTON & Guestier originally started in 1725; William, later Nathaniel, Johnston began in 1734; and BROKERS Tastet & Lawton in 1740. These are some of the longer survivors of many more. The German firms of standing appear to have arrived later: CRUSE from Danish Schleswig-Holstein, later incorporated into Germany, arrived in 1819; Eschenauer in 1821; and Kressmann in 1858. A substantial French merchant, with its roots in the RHÔNE valley, was Calvet, which opened a Bordeaux office in 1870. It is also significant that the trade's 'bible' was the creation, in 1850, of an English teacher, Charles Cocks (see LITERATURE OF WINE).

Until well into the second half of the 20th century, most of these firms had their premises in the suburb of Les Chartrons, named after a medieval Carthusian monastery. The Quai des Chartrons, facing the river Garonne, and its side-streets, was the headquarters of the so-called *aristocratie du bouchon* (aristocracy of the cork).

In 1852 Bordeaux was struck by oidium, or POWDERY MILDEW, the first of a series of vine plagues which were to devastate many other wine regions too. First noted in the

Some of the cellars under **Bordeaux's** Quai des Chartrons, such as those of Peter Sichel, are so extensive that they are traversed by bicycle rather than on foot.

sweet wine areas near the Garonne, it spread through the Graves and then into the Médoc. Between 1854 and 1856, all the properties which were rated CLASSED GROWTHS in the 1855 CLASSIFICATION produced a total of only 3,400 TONNEAUX of wine, not much more than half the crop in a prolific year. By 1858 this fungal disease was conquered by spraying with SULPHUR, a practice which continues to this day.

Trade with Britain increased as a result of the Anglo-French Treaty of 1860, for in the following year Gladstone, then Chancellor of the Exchequer, reduced duty on French wines to 2d. (less than 1p) a bottle. This was a particularly prosperous time for Bordeaux, which had also developed substantial markets in South America and Russia, and a small one in North America.

However, the severe onset of PHYLLOXERA in the late 1870s, followed by DOWNY MILDEW in the following decade, proved a serious set-back to the trade in everyday GENERIC red and white bordeaux. For the first time ever an import BOND was established in Bordeaux, largely supplied with blending wine from the new vineyards of ALGERIA. On the other hand excessive FERTILIZATION by important châteaux proprietors to compensate for losses by disease led to large crops of inferior quality and to a fall in reputation and price. In 1910, nevertheless, two out of every three bottles of French wine imported into Britain came from the Gironde. They totalled 110,000 hl/2.9 million gal, approximately the same as for BELGIUM, although Germany imported almost twice as much. In 1911 the Gironde *département* was delimited, leading eventually to the establishment of Bordeaux's APPELLATION CONTRÔLÉE system in 1936.

A serious slump followed soon after the First World War, with many châteaux changing hands, and this continued in the 1930s. After the First World War the Russian market had disappeared, the South American one was much reduced, and the US market was closed by PROHIBITION between 1919 and 1933, when it hardly had time to recover before the Second World War.

At this time the market for fine wines was largely confined to the Médoc and the châteaux in the Graves near to Bordeaux. It was not until after the Second World War—during which Bordeaux, and many large châteaux, were occupied by the German army—that any ST-ÉMILION property other than Ch CHEVAL BLANC was widely known outside France, and the same was true of POMEROL, even Ch PÉTRUS, although there was a good market for inexpensive St-Émilions in Belgium.

It was not until the end of the 1950s that those châteaux with an international reputation made sufficient profits to begin serious replanting and the installation of modern equipment, notably FERMENTATION VESSELS made of STAINLESS STEEL, although this was an option which many châteaux, including Lafite, Margaux, and MOUTON-ROTHSCHILD, did not take. From the mid 1960s the United States market became increasingly important, particularly for the classed growths. This was particularly marked with the successful 1970 vintage when large American purchases were made of FUTURES, followed some years later in Britain by 'opening offers'. Previously, if a vintage was considered likely to be very fine, the BORDEAUX TRADE would sometimes buy SUR SOUCHE, but otherwise a vintage would not be marketed until shortly before or after BOTTLING, either by the château or by the Bordeaux merchants. In 1972 CHÂTEAU BOTTLING became compulsory for the classed growths, and was generally applied to the more important properties in the Graves, St-Émilion, and Pomerol. The leading red and white Graves had first been classified in 1953, and the St-Émilions in 1955 (see CLASSIFICATIONS). The Pomerols remain unclassified.

These EN PRIMEUR campaigns reflected the changed financial situation in Bordeaux (although the generic wines, accounting for up to half the annual crop, continued, and continue, to be sold chiefly within 12 months of the harvest). No longer could most châteaux afford to hold several vintages in stock; nor could the Bordeaux merchants or their customers in France or abroad. For the most part in the 1970s and 1980s, consumers had to bear the financial responsibility of AGEING young red bordeaux, and some leading sweet wines.

The 'energy crisis' of 1973, in which Middle East oil producers greatly raised their prices, caused havoc in Bordeaux, where recent vintages had been sold en primeur at excessively high prices. This had applied at all quality levels, and one result was that in order to meet contracts for generic red bordeaux the distinguished house of CRUSE had bought wine from outside the region, involving altered appellation contrôlée documents. A sharp fall in prices occurred, as well as subsequent mass disposals of stock by both merchants and leading châteaux. Some of the traditional firms were saved from bankruptcy only by foreign ownership, and the old world of the Chartronnais disappeared for ever. Later, classed growth châteaux passed into the financial control of such outsiders as insurance companies and multinational corporations.

The succession of fine vintages in the 1980s improved the situation of many châteaux, but competition was so keen on the Bordeaux market that the merchants were unable as in the past to build up the financial reserves to tide them over poor years. So when Bordeaux was hit by the heavily FROST-damaged 1991 vintage and the record, diluted 1992, the en primeur trade virtually ceased internationally, and considerable financial problems arose—although the chiefly domestic trade in generic and humble appellation wines continued much as usual.

From the 18th century until 1939 the Bordeaux trade normally called the price tune, and with the exception of the *belle époque* from 1858 to 1878 the châteaux owners had to fall into line. For the 30 years from 1961 the leading proprietors then held the whip hand in allocating their new wines to more than 100 Bordeaux merchants, but an increasingly competitive wine-producing world has transferred power to the consumer of the 1990s. E.P.-R.

Faith, N., *The Winemasters* (London, 1978).

Penning-Rowsell, E., *The Wines of Bordeaux* (6th edn., London, 1989).

Geography

The wine districts of Bordeaux hug the Gironde estuary and the rivers DORDOGNE and GARONNE which flow into it (see map on p. 124). The largest and most important appellation is BORDEAUX AC, but there are 54 appellations in all, although many of them are rarely seen outside the region. The notably flat Bordeaux vineyards are rarely at altitudes of more than a few metres above sea level.

Conventionally, in terms of the all-important fine red wines at least, the whole region is split into 'left bank' and 'right bank', or MÉDOC and GRAVES on the one hand, and ST-ÉMILION and POMEROL on the other, leaving the vast ENTRE-DEUX-MERS ('between two seas') district in the middle. Within the Haut-Médoc, the superior land closer to Bordeaux, are the world-famous communes MARGAUX, ST-JULIEN, PAUILLAC, and ST-ESTÈPHE, together with the slightly less illustrious and, significantly, more inland appellations of LISTRAC and MOULIS. Most of the finest wines of the Graves, on the other hand, have come from an enclave awarded its own appellation in 1987, PESSAC-LÉOGNAN. Pomerol and St-Émilion have their 'satellite' appellations: LALANDE-DE-POMEROL; and Montagne-St-Émilion, Lussac-St-Émilion, St-Georges-St-Émilion, and Puisseguin-St-Émilion (for details of which see ST-ÉMILION). And just west of Pomerol are the increasingly respected appellations of FRONSAC and Canon-Fronsac.

Although a certain amount of white wine is made between the two rivers, most of Bordeaux's best white wines are made south of the river Garonne: dry wines from Graves and Pessac-Léognan, and sweet white wines which include some of the finest in the world from SAUTERNES and BARSAC. (See Climate below for a more detailed explanation.)

Also important quantitatively, however, are the so-called BORDEAUX CÔTES, the PREMIÈRES CÔTES DE BORDEAUX along the right bank of the Garonne; the GRAVES DE VAYRES enclave near Libourne on the left bank of the Dordogne; Côtes de BOURG across the wide Gironde estuary from Margaux; BLAYE, Côtes de Blaye, and Premières Côtes de Blaye in Côtes de Bourg's green, hilly hinterland; and the appellations which lie between Bordeaux and Bergerac to the east: Côtes de CASTILLON, Bordeaux Côtes de FRANCS, and STE-FOY-Bordeaux (not technically part of the Bordeaux Côtes).

The most famous vineyards are on particularly well-drained soils, notably gravels in the Médoc and Graves, and more calcareous terrain in parts of St-Émilion and Ste-Croix-du-Mont. For more details of local soils and conditions, see under these appellation names.

Climate

The mild climate of Bordeaux is tailor-made to produce mild wines, wines that are marked more by subtlety than power. (It is the vine varieties, described below, which endow the wines with longevity.) Unlike the much more continental climate of inland France, or the more arid Mediterranean influence in the south of the country, the vineyards of Bordeaux are moderated and heavily influenced by their proximity to the Atlantic, here warmed by the Gulf Stream, and this gentle oceanic regulation of the climate extends well inland, thanks to the wide Gironde estuary. Most years the maritime climate protects the vines from severe FROST damage in winter (although February 1956 was so cold that many vines were killed by sub-zero temperatures in February) and spring (although April 1991 was so cold that much of that year's growth was frozen to extinction and the crop much reduced).

Spring is generally mild and damp, providing ample supplies of water for the growing season. Bordeaux's climate is hardly marginal, in that most grapes are usually ripened, but the region's weather is sufficiently unpredictable that the period of the FLOWERING in June is critical, with unsettled weather, especially cold rain and strong winds, seriously prejudicing the quantity of the forthcoming crop. COULURE and MILLERANDAGE are perennial threats, especially to the Merlot crop, although average rainfall in June is markedly lower than in any other month.

Summers are usually hot, with occasional storms but rarely prolonged rainfall. The forests of the Landes to the south help to moderate temperatures (and to protect the wine districts from strong winds off the Atlantic), which reach an average maximum of 26 °C/79 °F in August, the hottest month. July is usually the driest and sunniest month. Annual average sunshine is well over 2,000 hours. Occasionally, as in 1989 and 1990, some periods in August can be so hot that the ripening process stops altogether, but generally Bordeaux's grapes ripen steadily, swollen by occasional rainfall, until a harvest between mid September and mid October. Rainfall can vary considerably from vintage to vintage and within the Bordeaux region itself, with the Médoc being wetter overall, with an average annual rainfall of 950 mm/37 in, than more inland districts.

Excessive rain is the chief hazard at harvest, especially in a year during which full ripeness has yet to be achieved. In the sweet wine areas, on the other hand, humidity is sought in autumn, particularly morning mists which evaporate during the day to encourage the spread of NOBLE ROT. It is no coincidence that Bordeaux's sweet white wine districts are clustered together on either side of the Garonne about 20 miles upstream of the city where the river Ciron flows into the Garonne. The waters of the Ciron, shaded for most of its length by the forests of the Landes, are invariably cooler than those of the Garonne and encourage the autumn morning mists which promote the BOTRYTIS fungus. In years when these are followed by warm, dry afternoons, the benevolent form of botrytis, noble rot, forms and great sweet white wine may be made. In damp years the malevolent form, GREY ROT, simply rots the fruit.

Vine varieties

Bordeaux's most famous, and best travelled, grape variety is that on which the Médoc and Graves depend for their red wines, CABERNET SAUVIGNON. Bordeaux's most planted variety by far, however, is MERLOT, which by the end of the 1980s occupied 40 per cent of all vineyard land. It predominates not just in the famous right bank appellations of St-Émilion and Pomerol but more importantly in the Entre-Deux-Mers and throughout the Bordeaux Côtes, in whose damper, cooler soils Cabernet Sauvignon can be difficult to ripen. CABERNET FRANC, also important on the right bank where it is often called Bouchet, is the third most planted grape variety. PETIT VERDOT is the only other red grape variety of any importance, playing a minor, but in ripe vintages useful, role in the Médoc. Cot, Pressac, or MALBEC is an ingredient in some right bank wines on the other hand, although it is declining in importance. CARMENÈRE is a red grape variety of historical importance.

In the early 1970s Bordeaux's single most planted grape variety of either colour was SÉMILLON but it has become progressively less important since then, especially in the Entre-Deux-Mers, so that total Sémillon plantings had halved by 1988. SAUVIGNON Blanc is Sémillon's traditional minor blending partner in sweet white bordeaux but is used increasingly for dry white wines, often unblended. The only other white grape variety fully sanctioned by the appellation laws is the Bordeaux speciality MUSCADELLE, but small quantities of UGNI BLANC, COLOMBARD, and Merlot Blanc are also planted and used in white BORDEAUX AC.

In stark contrast to France's other famous fine wine, BURGUNDY, red bordeaux is quintessentially a wine made from a blend of different vine varieties. This is only partly because Merlot and Cabernet are complementary, the flesh of the former filling in the frame of the latter. It is also an insurance policy on the part of growers in an unpredictable climate. Merlot grapes bud, flower, and ripen earlier than Cabernet Sauvignon, and are much more susceptible to COULURE, which can seriously affect quantity. Cabernet Sauvignon, on the other hand, ripens so late that a cool, cloudy late summer can seriously affect its quality. Having several grape varieties mitigates the climatological disasters which struck Merlot in 1984 and 1991, for example, and Cabernet Sauvignon in 1992. Although the ENCÉPAGEMENT, the exact proportions of different vine varieties, varies from château to château, a typical Médoc recipe is 70 per cent Cabernet Sauvignon, 15 per cent Cabernet Franc, 15 per cent Merlot, while a typical St-Émilion recipe might be 60 per cent Merlot, 30 per cent Cabernet Franc, and 10 per cent Cabernet Sauvignon.

Among dry white wines, the recipe is less predictable, although some all-Sauvignon wines are produced. The classic recipe for sweet white wines is 80 per cent Sémillon to 20 per cent Sauvignon Blanc.

Viticulture

With their neat, low rows of densely planted, GUYOT trained, low-vigour vines, Bordeaux's vineyards are some of the world's most recognizable. Vine TRIMMING is a perennial activity, and VINE DENSITY averages between 5,000 and 6,000 vines per ha, although it is often as high as 10,000 vines per ha/4,000 per acre in the Médoc. The LYRE trellis system may have been developed by INRA at Bordeaux but has hardly been embraced by the region's vine-growers.

FUNGAL DISEASES thrive in Bordeaux's damp climate, and frequent SPRAYING is a fact of life here. (This may explain the relative rarity of ORGANIC VITICULTURE in Bordeaux.) The incidence of EUTYPA DIEBACK became a serious preoccupation in the 1980s. BOTRYTIS BUNCH ROT is one of the most common hazards, although in sweet wine districts it is encouraged in its benevolent form as NOBLE ROT.

Fertilizers (including manure from specially reared herds at some top properties) and pesticides played their part in increasing YIELDS in the 1970s and 1980s. CROP THINNING during the growing season was widely employed in the late 1980s and early 1990s.

The flat, well-drained vineyards would submit easily to MECHANIZATION, although few have rows sufficiently widely spaced to permit MECHANICAL HARVESTING.

Traditionally the Bordeaux harvest would begin 100 days after the flowering, but since the mid 1980s the tendency has been to leave the grapes on the vine to achieve full ripeness, or even overripeness (*surmaturité* in French), not just high SUGARS but fully ripe PHENOLICS. It has not been uncommon therefore to start picking 110 days or more after the flowering. Identifying the date of optimum maturity of each parcel of grapes, and managing to pick them as quickly as possible on and after that date was one of the chief preoccupations in Bordeaux in the early 1990s.

The harvest generally starts in September, although 1989 was so hot that Ch HAUT-BRION began picking on 31 August, and ripening may be so slow in summers as cool as, for example, 1984 and 1977, that the grapes are kept on the vine until October in the hope of boosting sugar levels in the grapes. Grapes for dry white wines and Merlot are in general picked before Cabernet Sauvignon and, especially, grapes for sweet white wines, which may not be picked until late October or even November in SAUTERNES.

Bordeaux must be the only region able to command prices high enough to justify hiring HELICOPTERS in an attempt to agitate cold air during spring FROSTS, or dry grapes during a wet vintage, as Chx MOUTON-ROTHSCHILD and PÉTRUS have been known to do. In the more difficult vintages of the early 1990s, a high proportion of properties invested in SORTING tables in an attempt to maximize wine quality.

Wine-making

Wine-making techniques in Bordeaux's top estates are regarded as the paradigm by producers of Cabernet and Merlot wines, and fine sweet white wines, throughout the world. Under the guidance of BORDEAUX UNIVERSITY, these techniques underwent considerable modernization in the 1970s and are continually being refined. Émile PEYNAUD in particular led the way towards much more approachable, more concentrated red wines. And the way in which dry white bordeaux is made was revolutionized in the 1980s, notably by Denis DUBOURDIEU.

Red wines Classic vinification of red bordeaux involves time and, because of the size of most top estates, considerable space in which to house the wine as it slowly makes itself (see RED WINE-MAKING). The process begins in the vat hall or cuvier, then moves to a first-year CHAI in which a year's production is stored in barrel, continues in the second-year *chai*, and may well necessitate an area for bottle storage.

Grapes are almost invariably destemmed before CRUSHING, and fermented in large FERMENTATION VESSELS, known as CUVES in Bordeaux, which may be made of cement, stainless steel, or even wood, for between five and 10 or more days. Some form of TEMPERATURE CONTROL was installed at most properties in the 1970s or early 1980s, but is needed for only the hotter vintages; indeed it is increasingly common practice to heat the *cuves* at the beginning of FERMENTATION. Fermentation TEMPERATURES are generally slightly higher in Bordeaux than in the NEW WORLD, with 30 °C/86 °F being a common maximum during fermentation. The concentration of PHENOLICS in ripe Bordeaux Cabernet Sauvignon grapes is such that EXTRACTION is an extremely important aspect of vinification. Much modern research is concentrated on the relative merits of various PUMPING OVER regimes, usually several times a day. The post-fermentation MACERATION is therefore seen as crucial by most wine-makers, who allow the newly made wine at least a week 'on the skins'.

Some degree of CHAPTALIZATION is commonplace, and generally well judged, in Bordeaux, although CONCENTRATION techniques, including both osmosis and reverse osmosis, were increasingly practised alternatives in the early 1990s. Natural YEASTS are the norm and vines have been such an important crop in Bordeaux for so long that the indigenous yeast population is reliable and well adapted.

After fermentation and maceration the FREE-RUN WINE is racked off the solids into another large vessel, either by PUMPING or, in the most meticulously or fortuitously designed properties, by gravity. If the free-run wine is drained into a lower tank, the volume of harsher PRESS WINE can be reduced from more than 15 per cent to about 10 per cent, and the wine tastes softer and riper.

After MALOLACTIC FERMENTATION, the wine is racked into BARRELS made of French OAK, often LIMOUSIN with the typical Bordeaux barrel being called a BARRIQUE. The luxury of new barrels was introduced only in the 1980s, and the proportion of new barrels used even at top estates tends to be lower than in the most lavish New World wineries: rarely more than 60 per cent, and even fewer in less ripe vintages. During the first year the wine is racked off its LEES into a fresh barrel every three months or so, as well as being clarified by egg-white FINING. The wine is traditionally moved to a separate second year *chai*, where it remains until the wine is blended immediately prior to BOTTLING, usually in early summer. The wine then undergoes the all-important period of BOTTLE AGEING, although this is likely, depending on the state of the market, to take place in the cellars of the BORDEAUX TRADE, the wine merchant, and, typically, the consumer.

The ASSEMBLAGE is a crucial operation, undertaken in the first few months after fermentation, during which it is decided which lots of wine will be blended together to form the principal *grand vin* for that year, which lots will form the SECOND WINE, and which may be sold off at an even lower level, either in bulk or in bottle.

The procedure above is that followed by the CLASSED GROWTHS and those who aspire to that quality level. Most wine which qualifies merely as BORDEAUX AC is more likely to be fairly ruthlessly filtered than fined, and is not given any BARREL MATURATION, but is bottled after a few months in tank. Some PETITS CHÂTEAUX may treat their wines to a stint in barrique, but such barrels are likely to be hand-me-downs from properties whose wines sell at a higher price.

For Bordeaux's exclusively red wine appellations, see MÉDOC, HAUT-MÉDOC, ST-ESTÈPHE, PAUILLAC, ST-JULIEN, MARGAUX, LISTRAC, MOULIS, ST-ÉMILION, POMEROL, FRONSAC, and CASTILLON.

Dry whites WHITE WINE-MAKING is relatively unremarkable in Bordeaux, except that the region was one of the last in France to cling to high doses of SULPHUR in finished dry wines (perhaps because of its long history of turning its white grapes into sweet wines, which do need more sulphur), and in the upper echelons of white Graves and Pessac-Léognan BARREL MATURATION has one of the longest histories in the world here. Bordeaux is also the home of cryomaceration, whereby additional flavour is imbued by prefermentation SKIN CONTACT at low temperatures, known here as macération pelliculaire.

For Bordeaux's principal dry white wine appellations see PESSAC-LÉOGNAN, GRAVES, ENTRE-DEUX-MERS, BLAYE, and GRAVES DE VAYRES.

Sweet whites Bordeaux's sweet white wine appellations are, in very approximate descending order of quality, SAUTERNES, BARSAC, STE-CROIX-DU-MONT, LOUPIAC, CÉRONS, CADILLAC, PREMIÈRES CÔTES DE BORDEAUX, GRAVES Supérieures, STE-FOY-Bordeaux, and Bordeaux ST-MACAIRE and Bordeaux Supérieur (for which see BORDEAUX AC).

Basic sweet white bordeaux, often described as *moelleux*, is a simple, sugary wine, typically made either by fermenting the grapes out to produce a regular dry wine which is then sweetened by adding concentrated grape must, or by enthusiastic ENRICHMENT followed by stopping the alcoholic FERMENTATION by chilling or with high doses of sulphur. Winemakers in Sauternes and Barsac, however, and their more ambitious counterparts elsewhere, aim to make very rich BOTRYTIZED wines from grapes at the full limit of ripeness, which may be described as LIQUOREUX. This involves a considerably more painstaking wine-making regime, even more dependent than any other on events in the vineyard, which is described in SAUTERNES. The wine's selling PRICE, which has in the 20th century been depressed by the whims of FASHION, may also play a part in determining whether its maker is able or prepared to take the risks involved in trying to maximize ripeness of the grapes. Since the late 1980s some producers have also introduced the supplementary and controversial technique CRYOEXTRACTION in order to concentrate sugars by freezing.

CONCENTRATION of all sorts is becoming more common for all types of bordeaux.

Parker, R., *Bordeaux* (2nd edn., New York, 1991).
Penning-Rowsell, E., *The Wines of Bordeaux* (6th edn., London, 1989).
Peppercorn, D., *Bordeaux* (2nd edn., London, 1991).

BORDEAUX AC. The most important sort of wine produced in Bordeaux, quantitatively if not qualitatively, is that which qualifies for the simple appellation Bordeaux. Approximately 40 per cent of all red APPELLATION CONTRÔLÉE wine produced in the region, and almost 70 per cent of all white, is straightforward Bordeaux AC. This wine is typically produced outside the more specific commune or regional appellations, although a great deal of red Bordeaux AC comes from the ENTRE-DEUX-MERS region, whose eponymous appellation applies only to white wine. (A counterpoint to this is the fact that the appellations of the Médoc apply only to red wines, so that even the Médoc's smartest white wines, such as Pavillon Blanc du Ch MARGAUX, are not allowed any appellation grander than Bordeaux AC.) The other area with the greatest concentration of vineyard dedicated to the production of Bordeaux and Bordeaux Supérieur (see below) is that north of the Libourne between BLAYE and ST-ÉMILION, where Merlot grapes predominate. In total, about 31,000 ha/76,600 acres of Bordeaux vineyard is dedicated to the production of red Bordeaux AC, 11,000 ha to white Bordeaux AC, and 10,000 ha to red Bordeaux Supérieur.

The great majority of Bordeaux AC produced is made, often by CO-OPERATIVES, to be sold for blending anonymously into humble GENERIC wines, of very varying quality, but there are also individual properties, so called PETITS CHÂTEAUX, which lie outside any grander appellation but which express their own TERROIR and practise CHÂTEAU BOTTLING. About two-thirds of all Bordeaux AC produced is red, and the white, which may be called **Bordeaux Sec**, is invariably dry. Bordeaux is relatively low in alcohol, the minimum ALCOHOLIC STRENGTH after FERMENTATION being 10 per cent (although most wines are between 11 and 12.5).

More specific appellations which incorporate the word Bordeaux include **Bordeaux Supérieur**, whose minimum permitted alcoholic strength is half a per cent higher than Bordeaux AC and which is mainly red, but is occasionally sweet and white; **Bordeaux** CLAIRET, which is a light red recalling the precursors of CLARET; the bottle-fermented sparkling wine **Bordeaux Mousseux**, which is being replaced by CRÉMANT de Bordeaux; and a minor oddity, **Bordeaux Haut-Benauge**, which appellation applies to basic dry white wines made in a small district in the south of the Entre-Deux-Mers. (These last wines may also be labelled, by real devotees of the hyphen, Entre-Deux- Mers-Haut-Benauge.)

Most of these wines are designed to be drunk within a year of bottling if white, rosé, or clairet and within two or three years if red. The better examples are unmistakably lighter versions of Bordeaux's grander wines, while the worst can taste like homeless TABLE WINE. Few producers can afford to age wines at this level in OAK, and even fewer of the wines have the concentration to benefit from it, although exceptions are becoming more numerous. Most of the Bordeaux BRANDS are Bordeaux AC, most notably MOUTON CADET, which started off life with the much grander and more specific appellation of PAUILLAC.

The Bordeaux authorities call the above appellations the 'Bordeaux regional appellations' (all of which may much more simply be labelled Bordeaux), and include with them the Entre-Deux-Mers, STE-FOY-Bordeaux, and Côtes de Bordeaux-ST-MACAIRE appellation, which applies to the everyday sweet white wines made in a small district immediately south west of Haut-Benauge.

Other appellations which incorporate or have at one time incorporated the word Bordeaux are Bordeaux Côtes de CASTILLON, Bordeaux Côtes de FRANCS, and PREMIÈRES CÔTES DE BORDEAUX, all of which belong to the subgroup of Bordeaux appellations known as the BORDEAUX CÔTES.

BORDEAUX CÔTES, local name in BORDEAUX for appellations on the, often historic, outer fringes of the region: BLAYE, Côtes de Blaye, Premières Côtes de Blaye; Côtes de BOURG; PREMIÈRES CÔTES DE BORDEAUX; Côtes de CASTILLON; Bordeaux Côtes de FRANCS; and GRAVES DE VAYRES. These wines tend to have considerably more personality than regular BORDEAUX AC, the result perhaps of local pride, and can provide some of Bordeaux's best wine value.

BORDEAUX MIXTURE, once much-used mixture of lime, copper sulphate, and water first recorded in 1885 by Alexis Millardet, Professor of Botany at Bordeaux University, as an effective control of DOWNY MILDEW. Use of the mixture was an historic event since it was to become the most important chemical for the control of both FUNGAL DISEASES and BACTERIAL DISEASES for 50 years. It has subsequently been replaced by other fungicides, many of them containing copper. It is still used today by very traditional growers in some regions and it is one of the few preparations permitted in ORGANIC VITICULTURE.

There is some debate as to how the treatment was discovered. It was common for Bordeaux vignerons to spray the outside vineyard rows with the blue-staining copper sulphate to deter thieves. No doubt it was noticed that this practice halted the devastation caused by downy mildew which had begun in 1883. Continued use of Bordeaux mixture can lead to accumulation of COPPER in the soil which can reach toxic levels especially in acidic soils. Some vineyards affected by copper toxicity in the Bordeaux area are much reduced in vigour, but the problem can be overcome by adding LIME to the soil. Also, copper sprayed within 14 days of harvest can produce browning, turbidity, and SULPHIDE characters in the wine and can result in incomplete FERMENTATIONS. R.E.S.

Figiel, R., 'Bouillie bordelaise: the other gift from Bordeaux vineyards', *Practical Winery and Vineyard*, 11/3 (1990), 27–9.

BORDEAUX TRADE. The sheer quantity of wine produced in Bordeaux, the fact that so much bordeaux requires AGEING, and the historical importance of Bordeaux as a wine port (see BORDEAUX, history), mean that the Bordeaux wine trade is more stratified than most—even if wine is no longer the city's economically most important commodity.

Bordeaux wines have always been produced by one category of people and sold by another. The wine producers of the region range from world-famous estates with 200 ha/500 acres under vine, to owners of 2.5 ha or less whose grapes are delivered to one of the region's wine CO-OPERATIVES, or vinified in conditions of precarious HYGIENE for personal consumption.

The wine merchants, or NÉGOCIANTS, sometimes called *négociants-éleveurs* for their role in wine ÉLEVAGE, traditionally brought most of the wines they bought into their CHAIS in or around Bordeaux (notably its Quai des Chartrons) to be matured and shipped out to export customers, notably in Britain and Scandinavia, either in barrels, or after bottling. They were joined in the early 20th century by merchants in LIBOURNE, who concentrated on markets in northern France and northern Europe (see POMEROL).

So great was the quantity of wine to be traded that numbers of middlemen were needed between producers and the merchants, of whom professional brokers, or *courtiers*, such as Tastet & Lawton have become an essential part of Bordeaux's vinous commercial structure. What the merchant supplied in addition to the mere buying and selling of wine was technical ability (his cellarmaster and team were likely to be considerably better technicians than the producers'), and the financing of the grower.

This way of doing business changed considerably after 1945, when even some of the FIRST GROWTHS were still made available to the merchants in bulk, and most of the CLASSED GROWTHS have since 1959 been sold to the merchants on the condition that they are CHÂTEAU BOTTLED.

Since 1945, improvements in wine-making at all levels and, since the 1980s, PRICE increases and inflation levels which have made it impossible for even the biggest merchants to finance large quantities of wine, have transformed the role of the merchant from principal to broker. This was most marked in the 1980s when EN PRIMEUR buying reached a new peak.

With the economic problems of the 1990s, and increased competition from other wine regions of the world, it seems likely that the merchants' other justification as adviser and selector, the intermediary who transmits changes in consumer tastes to producers, will once again become important.

For examples of specific Bordeaux merchants, see BARTON, CRUSE, SICHEL, and MOUEIX. W.B.

Faith, N., *The Winemasters* (London, 1978).
Loftus, S., *Anatomy of the Wine Trade* (London, 1985).
Penning-Rowsell, E., *The Wines of Bordeaux* (6th edn., London, 1989).

BORDEAUX UNIVERSITY, university complex within sight of Ch HAUT-BRION on the outskirts of the city, whose Institut d'Oenologie is a centre of oenological ACADEME of world renown. (Viticultural research is conducted under the auspices of INRA.)

The institute was founded in 1880 (the same year as the research institute that was to become the University of California at DAVIS) as a mere *station agronomique*, when Ulysse Gayon, the sole Professor of Chemistry at the associated University of Bordeaux, became its director.

Gayon had studied and worked with Louis PASTEUR, the founder of scientific OENOLOGY. He considered the *station*'s function was to promulgate sound methods of making and maturing wine. In addition to this contributions to the

Bordeaux trade: Poster advertising wines of Bordeaux, late 19th century.

ANALYSIS of wines, he worked with Alexis Millardet on the development of the copper-based vine treatment designed to combat FUNGAL DISEASES which was to be known as BORDEAUX MIXTURE.

During the 40 years Gayon directed the *station*, its tradition of identifying the practical applications which could be made from research results was established, as was the importance of transmitting information to wine-makers in unscientific language.

From 1927 the most significant research on wine and related subjects in the world was carried out at the University of Bordeaux through a collaboration between Jean Ribéreau-Gayon, the grandson of Ulysse Gayon, and Émile PEYNAUD, who did not officially join the University until 1949. From 1949, when Jean Ribéreau-Gayon became director of the *station*, the results of basic and extensive research became apparent to wine-maker and consumer alike. Chromatography provided legally convincing evidence of the use of HYBRIDS in any wine sample, and encouraged their replacement by 'noble' VINIFERA vine varieties in the vineyards of Bordeaux, and thereby a great improvement in the quality of the region's basic BORDEAUX AC wines. At the same time, the understanding of the process of MALOLACTIC FERMENTATION gave wine producers the knowledge they needed to control a fundamental step in wine-making and gave them much greater control over the style and quality of the wines they made.

The importance of the education of OENOLOGISTS was officially recognized in 1956 with the creation of an École Supérieure d'Oenologie empowered to award a wine-maker's diploma. This became the Institut d'Oenologie in 1963. During this period oenology achieved full recognition as a new science and in 1971 the institute formally became part of the University, its work and educational titles enjoying full academic status.

The work of the institute has continued since 1976 under the direction of Pascal Ribéreau-Gayon, the son of the previous director. Since 1905 there has been close collaboration between the research carried out by the institute and a laboratory founded in that year by the French Ministry of Agriculture. The primary business of this laboratory is to check that French wine laws are respected by ensuring, for example, that all alcohol is grape based, that no fruits other than grapes have been used, that wines have not been subjected to both ACIDIFICATION and ENRICHMENT, and that a wine has not been stretched by dilution.

The institute is currently engaged in research on subjects which vary from explorations of the nature and effects of different YEASTS to investigations into the characteristics of different TANNINS. The most significant result of the institute's research in the 1980s was arguably the dramatic improvement in aroma and subtlety of dry white bordeaux, in which field DUBOURDIEU deserves much credit.

In addition to training oenologists who make wine throughout the world and belong to what is outside France referred to as the 'Bordeaux school' of wine-making, the institute supervises doctorates on vinous subjects and is the only French organization to enjoy this privilege. A prominent feature of the professional training at the institute is the importance attached to tasting wines and analysing their characteristics. Since 1949 the institute has also given series of tastings and lectures for growers and cellar workers without scientific training.

The institute is housed in its own buildings on the grounds of Bordeaux University. Although some viticultural research is conducted under INRA auspices at Bordeaux, and some viticulture is certainly taught by the institute's lecturers, MONTPELLIER has long been regarded as France's centre of viticultural academe. W.B.

Bordo, occasional north-east Italian name for CABERNET FRANC.

borers, usually beetles or their larvae, which bore into the woody parts of plants. A number of these cause damage to grapevines which can be fatal. The branch and twig borer, *Melalqus confertus*, occurs throughout California and parts of Oregon and damages grape canes. The adults bore into the canes and cause severe pruning. The larvae bore into wood of dead or dying parts of the vine, and feed on living and dead tissue. Control is usually by cultural methods, by keeping vines healthy, pruning off all dying and dead parts and infested wood in winter. Beetle larvae causing problems to vineyards can be quite regionally specific. The fig longicorn (*Dihammus vastator*) beetle larvae causes vine damage only in the Hunter Valley region of Australia, for example. M.J.E.

Flaherty, D. L. *et al.* (eds.), *Grape Pest Management* (2nd edn., Oakland, Calif., 1992).

boron, a mineral element required in minute quantities for healthy vine growth, and thus a so-called trace element. Boron deficiencies in vines are commonly found where SOIL ACIDITY and RAINFALL are high. Boron is required for the movement of SUGARS and the synthesis of AUXINS in the plant. A major effect of boron deficiency is poor FRUIT SET caused by the effect on POLLEN tube growth affecting germination, which can result in substantial reductions in YIELD. A quality gain from having more and smaller berries (see BERRY SIZE) is possible, but this effect has not been proven.

Boron as a vine nutrient is very different from many others in that there is a relatively small range in soil concentration between deficiency levels and toxicity, and it is not uncommon for the vine-grower to poison the soil by overtreating deficient vines with boron fertilizer. Excess boron can also come from IRRIGATION water. Boron deficiency is treated by adding a boron salt either to the soil or leaves in small amounts of about 3 kg/ha (2.6 lb/acre). See also FERTILIZERS. R.E.S.

Bosnia Hercegovina, central coastal regions of what was YUGOSLAVIA, whose vineyards are in Hercegovina in the south. So much of the territory in the centre of the former Yugoslavia is wild, dry pastoral upland that these vineyards cover only a relatively small 5,000 ha/12,350 acres of territory down towards the coast around Mostar, inland and to the north of Dubrovnik.

The region has its own grape types: the white ZILAVKA, famed for its generous alcohol levels combined with unusually refreshing ACIDITY; and the much less impressive red Blatina. Zilavka has begun to be planted in neighbouring territories. A.H.M.

botanical classification, a system of classifying plants—including vines, yeasts, and the organisms responsible for FUNGAL DISEASES of the vine—which shows their relationship one to the other, and which also allows them to be uniquely described and identified. The basic unit of classification is the species; related species are sometimes grouped into sections, and sections into genera (plural of genus); related genera into families; and related families into orders.

Individual members of a single species are called varieties, or occasionally cultivars, and VINE VARIETIES can be further divided into three PROLES, according to their geographical origins. Different CLONES of individual varieties have also been identified. To summarize:

Order	Species
Family	Variety
Genus	Clone
Section	

Classifications are created by botanists. Most commercially important grapevine varieties used for wine production, for example, are members of the genus VITIS, created in 1700 by Tournefort, and the species VINIFERA, first studied by Linnaeus in 1735. The full botanical binomial of the most common wine-producing vine species is therefore *Vitis vinifera L.*, often abbreviated to *V vinifera* or just *vinifera* (the person who describes the species often being listed, usually as initials, after the scientific name). Another convention is the use of Latin, often confected, and italics.

To start at the macro-level, vines belong to the order *Rhamnales*, and the family *Vitaceae*. There are two other families in the order *Rhamnales*: the *Rhamnaceae* family, which includes mostly shrubs or trees with dry fruit, together with such fleshy-fruited plants as the jujube and the plant thought to be the lotus of ancient Greece; and the *Leeaceae* family, which consists mostly of shrubs, also with fruit, and some species, such as are found in the monsoonal north of Australia, which can be seen to be related to the grapevine.

The family *Vitaceae* contains the GRAPEVINE. The genus *Vitis* is one of 14 (some authorities say 12) genera, and *vinifera* is one of about 700 species. This plant family is very widespread, with members in both tropical and temperate regions. Most of the plants are climbers and have tendrils opposite leaves on the shoots, the grapevine being representative. Galet lists 13 genera other than *Vitis* in this family (excluding two extinct species); the largest genus is *Cissus* with about 350 species, from succulent species such as cacti to the lianas of tropical jungles. *Ampelopsis* and *Parthenocissus* are two more genera closely related to each other and which include virginia creepers, observably similar to grapevines.

The order *Rhamnales*

Vitaceae	*Leeacea*
Rhamnaceae	

The family *Vitaceae* (according to Galet)

Vitis	*Rhoicissus*
Cissus	*Ampelopsis*
Cayratia	*Parthenocissus*
Clematicissus	*Acareosperma*
Tetrastigma	*Pterocissus*
Ampelocissus	*Landukia*
Pterisanthes	*Cyphostemma*

There are also the fossil genera *Cissites* and *Paleovitis*.

The *Vitis* genus has traditionally been divided into two distinct sections called *Euvitis* (now *Vitis*) and *Muscadinia*. (It should be noted, however, that some botanists consider *Muscadinia* as a separate genus to *Vitis*.) Galet's convention of the 14 extant genera listed above is used here. The two sections may be differentiated not only on the basis of appearance but also by chromosome number. *Muscadinia* has 40 chromosomes while *Vitis* has only 38. (This is a frustration to VINE BREEDERS, who would welcome ready access to the many pest and disease resistance genes of *Muscadinia*.)

The genus *Vitis*

There are many species of *Vitis*, most of which are native to North America (see AMERICAN VINE SPECIES). The common wine grape species *Vitis vinifera* is native to Europe and west Asia. It shows great diversity as a result of cultivation by man, and two basic groups of varieties, or proles, reflect differences between origin and end use. See VITIS and VINIFERA for more details.

The full botanical pedigree of a bottle of wine made from Cabernet Sauvignon grapes might therefore be: order *Rhamnales*, family *Vitaceae*, genus *Vitis*, section *Vitis*, species *vinifera*, proles *Occidentalis*, variety Cabernet Sauvignon, clone INRA BX 5197. R.E.S.

Antcliff, A. J., 'Taxonomy: the grapevine as a member of the plant kingdom', in B. G. Coombe and P. R. Dry (eds.), *Viticulture, i: Resources in Australia* (Adelaide, 1988).

Galet, P., *Précis de viticulture* (4th edn., Montpellier, 1983).

Mullins, M. G., Bouquet, A., and Williams, L., *Biology of the Grapevine* (Cambridge, 1992).

BOTRYTIS, without the capital B it botanically deserves, is commonly used as an abbreviation for BOTRYTIS BUNCH ROT, for the fungus that causes it *Botrytis cinerea*, for its benevolent form NOBLE ROT, and occasionally for its malevolent form GREY ROT. Grapes affected by noble rot and the wines produced from them are often called BOTRYTIZED, or **botrytis affected.**

BOTRYTIS BUNCH ROT, vine disease which, of all FUNGAL DISEASES, has the greatest potential effect on wine quality. The disease can have a disastrous effect on both yield and quality when the fungus affects unripe or damaged grapes, or in humid weather. This malevolent form is known as grey rot, the most common of the BUNCH ROTS. On the other hand, if it affects ripe, healthy, whole, light-skinned grapes, and the weather conditions are favourable, botrytis develops in a benevolent form called noble rot, which is responsible for some of the world's finest sweet wines. (If it affects red grapes, it always damages PIGMENTS, resulting in wines with a greyish tinge and, often, off-odours associated with rot.)

The causal fungus for both forms of botrytis bunch rot is *Botrytonia fuckelinia* of which only a certain form (the so-called conidial form), termed *Botrytis cinerea*, is found in vineyards. The disease is widespread as it attacks not only vines but many cultivated and wild plants, and also survives on dying and dead plant tissue.

Botrytis rot is a particular problem for vineyards in damp climates. In particular, rainfall near harvest causes severe infections (see BUNCH ROTS), and thus can be a major climatic factor affecting the quality of a particular vintage. Botrytis spores germinate either on wet surfaces or where the ambient humidity is at least 90 per cent. Optimal infection temperatures are 15 to 20 °C/59–68 °F.

Although it most commonly affects bunches, the botrytis fungus can infect parts of the vine other than the berry such as emerging shoots in spring and reddish patches can form on the edge of young leaves. Similarly, under appropriate weather conditions, young bunches may be infected so that they rot and fall off with obvious effects on yield. The more common problem, however, is when flower parts are infected and remain trapped in the developing bunches. Infections of the fungus can spread in the bunch as it approaches maturity. Stage of ripeness is important, and infections before VERAISON are rare. From veraison onwards, however, the grape berries are infected directly through the intact berry skin, or through wounds. The fungi can penetrate even healthy berries, gaining access through minute breathing pores called stomates, but more commonly the entry is through the broken skin. Such injuries may be caused by bird pecks, insect damage, mechanical abrasion, or by tightly compressed berries which burst when the vine takes up water after rainfall.

The mould spreads progressively through the whole bunch, especially when berries are in close contact, as with vine varieties with compact bunches. If the weather turns dry, infected berries tend to dry out, and major changes to the fruit's chemistry can result in grapes suitable for classic botrytized wines influenced by noble rot. In continuing wet weather, however, the fungus rapidly spreads as grey rot, and the grape crop can literally rot before the owner's eyes. This explains the urgency of harvest when weather conditions are inclement. Wines in such years are typically lower in alcohol as the fruit is harvested earlier.

Botrytis is a problem in other areas of viticulture. It is a common rot developing in stored TABLE GRAPES and also causes problems during GRAFTING operations in nurseries.

Vine varieties, and indeed various CLONES of vine varieties, differ in their susceptibility to botrytis depending on how tightly packed the berries are in the bunch, on the thickness of the skin, and to some extent also on the chemical composition of the berries. Varieties with compact bunches of high sugar content are the most susceptible. Sémillon, Sauvignon Blanc, Muscadelle, Carignan, Pinot Noir, and Merlot are particularly susceptible to botrytis bunch rot, with Chardonnay moderately susceptible and Cabernet Sauvignon quite tolerant.

Interestingly, some varieties are made more resistant by producing PHYTOALEXINS which inhibit the fungus. Modern control measures take two forms. The first, the 'natural' approach, is to avoid excessive leafiness around the fruit, which means that bunches are better exposed to sun and wind which dry the fruit after rain or dew. CANOPY MANAGEMENT practices such as leaf removal and improved trellis are most useful. Chemical control is the second route and the number of sprays required depends on the climate. In wet regions, more than half a dozen sprayings may be used, beginning at FLOWERING and ending before harvest. The last sprayings cannot be applied too close to harvest as yeast activity during fermentation may be inhibited, quite apart from any potentially harmful chemical RESIDUES.

While a relatively large range of chemicals is now used for botrytis control, the fungus seems to be waging a war against the chemist. New chemicals only seem to be used for a few years before they become less effective, as the fungus develops tolerance. Growers are now being forced to rely less on chemicals and to use more natural means of control. Newly bred varieties commonly have greater disease tolerance, and researchers are also attempting to control botrytis with an antagonistic fungus, *Trichoderma harzianum*.

See GREY ROT and NOBLE ROT for more details of the two different forms of botrytis. For details of how nobly rotten grapes are transformed into wine, and of the resulting wines, see BOTRYTIZED WINES. R.E.S.

Galet, P., *Précis de viticulture* (Montpellier, 1983).

Pearson, R. C., and Goheen, A. C., *Compendium of Grape Diseases* (St Paul, Minn., 1988).

Winkler, A. J., *et al.*, *General Viticulture* (Berkeley, Calif., 1974).

BOTRYTIZED, or **botrytis-affected, wines** are those made from white grapes affected by the benevolent form of BOTRYTIS BUNCH ROT, known in English as NOBLE ROT. The French call them *liquoreux*, as distinct from simply *moelleux*. Distinctively scented in youth, and with considerably more EXTRACT than most wines, they are the most complex and longest lived of all the sweet, white table wines. The noble rot smell is often described as honeyed, but it can also have an (attractive) overtone of boiled cabbage.

History

There is no firm evidence that botrytized wines were recognized in antiquity, although Olney points out that a particularly fine Ancient Greek wine produced on Chios in the 5th century BC is described as *saprian* by ATHENAEUS, and that the literal translation of this may be 'rotten, putrid'. Noble rot is much more likely to occur in more humid climates than the MEDITERRANEAN CLIMATE of the Aegean islands, however, and the extremely unpleasant appearance of grapes infected by noble rot, and the difficulty with which they ferment, must have deterred many early wine-makers.

Three important centres of botrytized wine production have their own accounts of the discovery that this particular sort of mouldy grape could be transformed into exceptional wine.

That of the TOKAY region of north east Hungary is the oldest, dating from 1650 when the priest-cum-wine-maker on a particular estate there delayed the HARVEST because of the threat of attack by the Turks. This allowed the development of noble rot and the grapes were duly vinified separately, as one would expect, and the resulting wine much admired. For diplomatic purposes it was introduced to the French court in the early 18th century, long before French vine-growers had recognized the existence of the noble fungus.

In Germany, the principle of picking selected bunches of grapes (AUSLESE) was understood in the 18th century, but that of the widespread picking of grapes affected by NOBLE ROT dates, in the Rheingau region which became most famous for botrytized wines, from about 1820. In spite of popular beliefs to the contrary, precisely when and where vine-growers first realized the value of noble rot is not certain, although the discovery in Germany is thought to have been in the particularly suitable climate of the Rheingau. SCHLOSS JOHANNISBERG has certainly promulgated its own claim that in 1775 the traditional harvest messenger, as usual licensed to deliver permission to pick from the owner, the distant prince-abbot of Fulda, was delayed, thereby supposedly allowing a noble rot infection to proceed, and resulting in Germany's first botrytized SPÄTLESE.

The sweet wines of Bordeaux and the Loire were much treasured in the Middle Ages, particularly by the DUTCH, but without any specific mention of a special fungus, or acknowledgement of any special attribute. The principal French legend concerning the 'discovery' of noble rot—and legend it is widely believed to be—dates from as recently as 1847, at Ch d'YQUEM (although the quality, style, and youthfulness of earlier vintages of Yquem suggest that noble rot may have played an important part in wine production there before that date).

The risks and costs involved in making naturally botrytized wine make it necessarily expensive. It has therefore been an economical proposition only when sweet wines are highly valued. Germany's botrytized wines have always been regarded as precious rarities for which a ready market can be found within Germany. France's output of botrytized wines is potentially much greater, but when sweet wines were regarded as out of FASHION in the 1960s and 1970s enthusiasm for producing them inevitably waned, only to be rekindled in the 1980s.

Geography and climate

Many conditions have to be met before botrytized wines can be produced. Not only is a MESOCLIMATE which favours misty mornings and warm afternoons in autumn needed, but producers must have the knowledge and the will to sacrifice quantity for nothing more certain than possible quality. Botrytized wines are very much a product of psyche as well as nature.

The district with the potential to produce the greatest quantity of top-quality botrytized wine is SAUTERNES (although it all depends, as everywhere, on the precise WEATHER of the year). The confluence of the rivers Ciron and GARONNE provide an ideal mesoclimate for the satisfactory development of noble rot. Nearby sweet white wine districts CÉRONS, LOUPIAC, CADILLAC, and STE-CROIX-DU-MONT may also produce small quantities of botrytized wines, although the price fetched by these appellations rarely justifies the additional production costs.

In extremely good vintages such as 1976 and 1990, some botrytized wine may be, and famously was, made in MONBAZILLAC, and occasionally even in BERGERAC on the river DORDOGNE.

On the river Loire, appellations such as Coteaux de l'AUBANCE, Coteaux du LAYON, QUARTS DE CHAUME, BONNEZEAUX, MONTLOUIS, and VOUVRAY can produce botrytized wines in good years, and they are given even greater ageing potential for being made from the acidic Chenin Blanc grape.

Botrytized wines may also be made from such varied grapes as Mâconnais Chardonnays and Alsace Rieslings in exceptional years.

Germany is the other famous source of botrytized wines, usually labelled BEERENAUSLESE or TROCKENBEERENAUSLESE, although the quantities made vary enormously according to vintage. Noble rot infections are much more reliable in the Burgenland district of AUSTRIA, where, thanks to the influence of the Neusiedlersee, considerable quantities of botrytized Beerenauslesen and Trockenbeerenauslesen are made most years, although relatively few of the wines are exported. Over the border in Hungary, TOKAY is still closely associated with botrytized wine-making, as are various parts of ROMANIA, notably COTNARI.

Botrytized wine-making is an embryonic art in Italy, Spain, and most of Portugal, where producers and consumers tend to favour either DRIED GRAPE WINES or FORTIFIED wines.

In the New World, botrytized wines are made with increasing frequency. Griffith in NEW SOUTH WALES was producing botrytized Pedro Ximénez as early as the late 1950s, while Edelkeur was a South African prototype which enjoyed international acclaim in the 1970s. In Australia and in California particularly, a host of botrytized Rieslings have emerged.

California has also seen attempts to simulate noble rot, by growing spores of the botrytis fungus in a laboratory and spraying them on picked, healthy, ripe grapes before subjecting them to alternately humid and warm conditions for a couple of weeks. The first of these wines was made in the late 1950s by Myron Nightingale in the Livermore Valley. The result was called Premiere Semillon and has been followed by a series of similar wines made at Beringer in the Napa Valley.

As awareness of noble rot and botrytized wines grows, the number of wine-makers anxious to experiment also increases, even if they are usually at the mercy of the weather. Even ENGLAND has succeeded in producing botrytized wine.

Vine varieties

Any white grape variety may be infected benevolently by the botrytis fungus; red varieties simply lose their colour. Certain varieties seem particularly sensitive to the fungus and well adapted to the production of botrytized wines, however: Sémillon, Sauvignon Blanc, Chenin Blanc, Riesling, Gewürztraminer, and Furmint are traditional.

Viticulture

The chief viticultural aspect of making botrytized wines is the number of passages or TRIS through the vineyard which may have to be made in order to pick grapes only at the optimum point of botrytis infection, because noble rot is so crucial to quality. See SAUTERNES for a description of the likely routine there. In a year as difficult as 1974 at Ch d'YQUEM (admittedly the most conscientious Sauternes estates) 11 *tris* were made over a 10-week period. In 1990, on the other hand, noble rot spread rapidly and uniformly and the grapes were picked by early October. Hand picking of these varied but usually disgusting-looking grapes is essential, and the cost of LABOUR is one important element in the price of botrytized wines.

In wet vintages, some producers use modern freeze concentration techiques, called *cryoextraction* in French.

Wine-making

If picking botrytized grapes is painstaking, obtaining their juice and persuading it to ferment is at least as difficult

Chianti Rufina gaining valuable **bottle age** at the expense of Selvapiana in Tuscany.

because of its composition (see NOBLE ROT). PRESSING is a physically difficult operation, and, contrary to the usual practice, later pressings yield juice superior to the first pressing because it is richer in sugar and the chemical compounds produced by the botrytis fungus. The most dehydrated grapes in the press may not in any case yield juice until being pressed twice or three times.

A certain variety of wine-making methods are used, including the classic method described in SAUTERNES. Fermentation is necessarily extremely slow. The juice seems almost designed to inhibit YEASTS, being so high in sugar and antibiotics such as botryticine. Fermentation may be allowed to stop itself, or SULPHUR DIOXIDE addition may be used. Care must be taken that these wines, which often have a RESIDUAL SUGAR level equivalent to about six per cent alcoholic strength, do not suffer a SECOND FERMENTATION, and bottling, whether after two winters in new BARRIQUES as in the top Sauternes properties, or the following spring as in the Loire and many German cellars, has to be undertaken with care.

Botrytized wines are capable of extremely long BOTTLE AGEING, for many decades in some cases.

Brook, S., *Liquid Gold: Dessert Wines of the World* (London, 1987).
Olney, R., *Yquem* (Paris, 1985, and London, 1986).

BOTTE, Italian word for a large wooden cask, presumably from the same root as BUTT. The plural is **botti**.

BOTTLE AGEING, the process of deliberately maturing a wine after BOTTLING, whether for a few weeks as a conscious effort on the part of the bottler to allow the wine to recover from BOTTLE SICKNESS or, in the case of very fine wines, for many years in order to allow the wine to mature. Fine wines are usually vinified expressly so that they will benefit from ageing in bottle, with generous amounts of alcohol, ACIDS, PHENOLICS, and FLAVOUR COMPOUNDS extracted from the skins. These can often make them unattractive when consumed young, but provide them with all the necessary ingredients for bottle ageing. In some cases the high sugar, acid, and flavour compound levels, as in great Rieslings which may not contain much alcohol, can benefit greatly from bottle ageing.

The exact identification of the compounds produced during bottle ageing and responsible for the complex BOUQUET of a mature wine is yet to be completely resolved, although pioneering work has been conducted by the Australian Wine Research Institute in ADELAIDE. It has been suggested, however, that in this sealed container they are all substances that are chemically in a state of REDUCTION. The substances that are oxidized in the coupled reaction involved in reduction are almost certainly the phenolics which we know are oxidized during their polymerization, after which they drop out as SEDIMENT. Although scientists call these coupled reactions oxidation-reduction, or redox reactions, no oxygen from the air is involved. Indeed, if oxygen somehow enters bottled wine through a poor cork, no ageing compounds will be formed.

See also AGEING. A.D.W.

BOTTLE FERMENTED, description of some SPARKLING WINES made either by the champagne method, or by the transfer method. See SPARKLING WINE-MAKING for full details.

BOTTLES, by far the most common CONTAINERS for finished wine. Being made of glass, bottles are inconveniently fragile and relatively heavy, but, importantly for long-term AGEING, they are inert. A standard bottle contains 75 cl/27 fl oz although see also BOTTLE SIZES.

History

Today it may be taken for granted that wine bottles of different colours and shapes will hold a precise capacity. Nor is it questioned that a paper LABEL will be firmly fixed to the bottle to give a plethora of information, much of it required by law. These are recent developments.

In classical antiquity wine was stored and transported in large, long jars called AMPHORAE. They varied considerably in

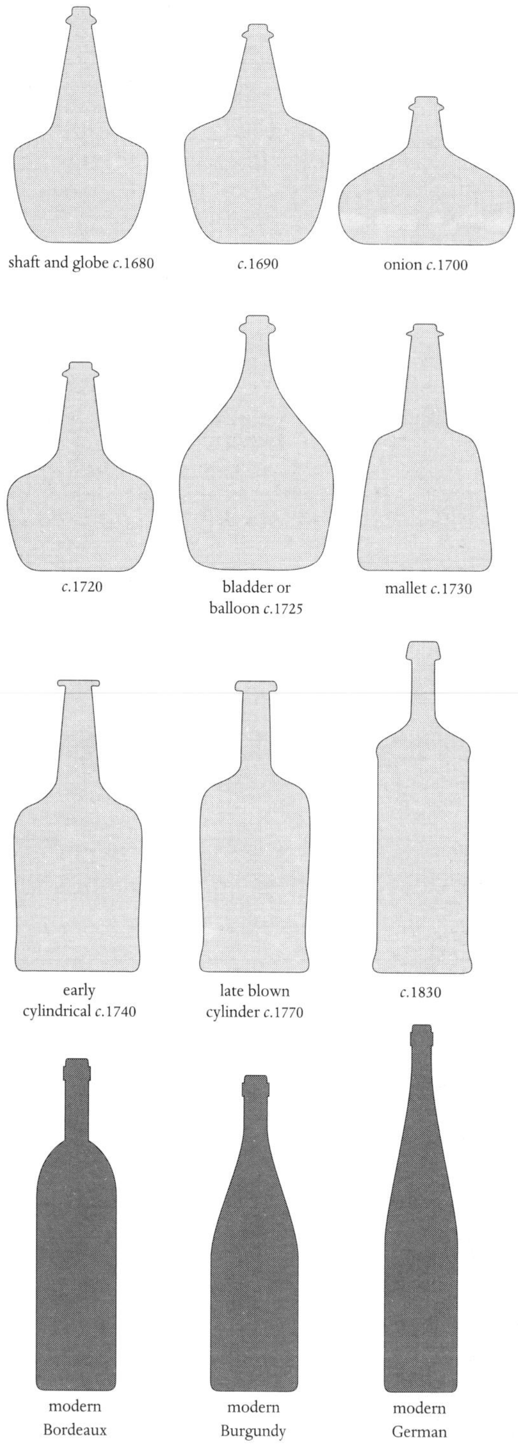

Bottles

size but it would certainly be difficult to pour a drinking quantity from such an awkward and big vessel, without using some sort of intermediate container. The Romans invented the technique of blowing glass bottles and some of these may well have been used to serve wine.

Pottery and stoneware jugs were used for centuries in Europe for serving wine, but glass took over as technology to make glass in commercial quantities spread in the 17th century, and by the end of it glass bottles were plentiful, although reserved for the upper classes.

Shape Early bottles have more or less globular bodies with long conical necks. The form developed (see illustration), becoming lower and wider in Britain, while on mainland Europe the flask-shape with an oval cross-section was popular. From *c.*1690 to 1720, the outline of a bottle resembled that of an onion—a wide compressed globular body with a short neck. Larger bottles were made too, whose shape resembled an inflated balloon or bladder. It is thought that all these forms were stored in beds of sand. By the 1720s the 'onion' became taller and the sides flatter—a form known by collectors (old bottles have become wine ANTIQUES) as a 'mallet'. Naturally occurring impurities in the constituent ingredients gave glass an olive green hue which varied from pale to almost black and was beneficial to the bottled wine as it excluded light. Most bottles had an applied ring of glass just below the neck which gave an anchorage to the string used to hold in a variety of stoppers. These bottles were of substantial weight and thickness too.

Wine drinkers made an important discovery in the 1730s. While it was known that some vintages of wine were better than others even in prehistory, their keeping and consequent maturing qualities were not realized until the introduction of BINNING, the storing of wine in bottles laid on their sides. The effectiveness of CORK as a stopper was thereby enhanced because it was kept wet and expanded by the wine. All this was achieved by the abandoning of onion-, bladder-, and mallet-shaped bottles in favour of cylindrical ones which stack easily. Early cylindrical bottles have short wide bodies with tall necks, but as the century progressed the modern shape evolved. In 1821 Ricketts of Bristol patented a machine for moulding bottles of uniform size and shape, early examples of which are impressed 'patent' on the shoulder of the bottle and the legend 'H Ricketts & Co. Glassworks Bristol' on the base. Thus the modern wine bottle had evolved, all later shapes and colours being decided as a question of aesthetics rather than technical limitation.

Identification From 1636, at about the time of the first appearance of glass bottles in post-Roman Britain, it was illegal to sell wine by the bottle. This consumer protection measure was on account of vintners' willingness to take advantage of the varying capacity of blown bottles! From that time and for the next 230 years, wine was sold by the measure and then bottled. Customers who bought regularly had their own bottles and had them marked in order to distinguish them from any others that might be at the vintner's premises waiting to be filled. The usual marking was the attachment at the end of the production process of a disc seal of the same glass as the bottle, upon which was impressed the owner's initials, name, or heraldic device, often accompanied by the date. Innkeepers and taverners had appropriately marked, or 'sealed', bottles too. It may be noted here that these seals did not indicate the contents.

Sealed bottles are avidly collected today, the most prized being 17th century ones, particularly those with dates incorporated in the seal. Named examples are preferred to one with initials, and earlier ones to later.

Bottles with paper labels indicating the contents, first hand written and later printed, emerged during the opening years of the 19th century, but in Britain the law prohibiting wine from being sold by the bottle was not relaxed until 1860. Bottles with paper labels printed with pre-1860 vintages are probably relabelled or were intended for non-British markets.

Other materials Bottles in media other than glass are known, particularly in the 17th century, when glass was an expensive and scarce commodity. Leather bottles, jugs, and other vessels are sometimes associated with ale and beer but many will have been used in the service of wine. A large group of serving bottles is known, made in London, of white tin-glazed earthenware (termed delftware). They are onion shaped with handles and vary from about half to $1\frac{1}{2}$-bottle capacity. Their most charming feature is the calligraphy, usually opposite the handle, for 'CLARET', 'Whit Wine' (*sic*), 'SACK', or, more rarely, 'PORT' or other wine. They are frequently dated (from *c.*1630 to 1660) and the legend is often embellished with a curlicue.

Size The size and shape of early bottles was, to an extent, a hit and miss affair. Perhaps the 'standard' size was the natural result of a lungful of air, but bottles were made in a variety of sizes from early times. The onion or bladder shape can sometimes be found in extremely large sizes holding up to 30 bottles. The general term for a large early bottle is a carboy but the word magnum was also used somewhat impressively for a bottle of about double normal capacity. For a long while a bottle was more or less $1\frac{1}{4}$ UK pints (70 cl or 25 fl oz) and a magnum was a quart (1.12 l or 40 fl oz). Until the 1970s, when EUROPEAN UNION and other legislation enforced standardization, bottles varied from about 65 to 85 cl, CHAMPAGNE

Onion wine **bottle** *c.*1740 (right), and cylindrical bottle with the seal of R. Jones Esq., *c.*1790, both on display at Harveys Wine Museum in Bristol, England.

and BURGUNDY tending to be larger than those for BORDEAUX, while SHERRY bottles were often smaller. R.N.H.B.

Butler, R., and Walkling, G., *The Book of Wine Antiques* (Woodbridge, 1986).
Davis, D. C., *English Bottles & Decanters 1650–1900* (1st American edn., New York, 1972).
Dumbrell, R., *Understanding Antique Wine Bottles* (Woodbridge, 1983).
Johnson, H., *The Story of Wine* (London and New York, 1989).
Morgan, R., *Sealed Bottles: Their History & Evolution (1630–1930)* (Burton-on-Trent, n.d.).
Ruggles-Brise, S., *Sealed Bottles* (London, 1949).

Modern bottles

Choice of LABEL and FOIL are not the only ways in which a wine producer can make a visual statement to a potential customer. Wine bottles are now made in an almost bewildering array of shapes, weights, colours of glass, and design, quite apart from their capacity (see BOTTLE SIZES).

In some regions one specific bottle has been adopted by all but the most anarchic producers, and indeed adoption of a special local, regional, or appellational bottle became particularly fashionable in the 1980s. Examples of special bottles are the heavy, embossed CHÂTEAUNEUF-DU-PAPE bottle; the BOCKSBEUTEL of FRANKEN; the Ch-Grillet bottle peculiar to a single property; and the long-necked green bottle particular to MUSCADET.

In general Italians, with their firm belief in the importance of design, offer the most dazzling range of wine bottles. Some of the particularly artful shapes used for GRAPPA have been adopted by wine producers in Austria and further afield especially for halves of sweet wine. Weight and darkness of glass seem to be highly valued by the Italians in particular, although it is a general rule throughout the wine world that, the heavier a bottle, the greater the aspirations of the producer of the wine for its longevity. Bottling wine in the lightest, cheapest glass is one way of paring production costs to a minimum.

The problem with some special bottle shapes, however, is that they may well be difficult to store, both on the shelf (many a special bottle is simply too tall for the average supermarket display) and, particularly, in a wine rack designed for standard bottles.

Bottle shapes Special designs apart, there are certain standard bottle shapes associated most commonly with certain regions or, increasingly, styles of wine associated with those regions. Ambitiously made Chardonnays the world over, for example, tend to be put into burgundy bottles. Since the geographical provenance of most wines should be clear from the label, understanding bottle shapes is most useful for the clues they provide as to the intended style of the wine inside them. Some RIOJA producers, for example, put their Garnacha-dominated, richer blends into burgundy bottles, while their Tempranillo wines designed for longer ageing are put into bordeaux bottles. The red bordeaux bottle itself, incidentally, has been the subject of much research and revision to increase the durability of the wine stored inside it (see also Bottle colour below).

Many German wine producers in particular have employed bottle shapes as their most eloquent marketing tool in distancing drier, non-aromatic styles of wine from traditional German wines sold in the elongated bottle shape which has come to be associated with aromatic wines. The precise elongation of that shape evolved considerably in the 1970s and 1980s. Mass market retailers objected to the inconvenient height of the traditional German bottle and so it was reduced by many, only to be increased again as a defiant statement of their reverence for tradition by some of the most quality-conscious German producers.

Most champagne and sparkling wines are sold in much the same shape of bottle, moulded to be thick and strong enough to withstand the pressure of up to six atmospheres inside each bottle. Considerable energy and money is expended, however, on designing special bottles for PRESTIGE CUVÉES, the Dom Pérignon bottle of MOËT & CHANDON having set a formidable standard. The precise shape of the lip of a champagne bottle indicates whether the second fermentation took place under a crown cap or under a cork, as it does in some very rare cases.

Bottles vary in the extent to which they have a punt, or inverse indentation in their base. Most champagne and sparkling wine bottles have a particularly deep indentation because of the need to stack inverted bottles one on top of the other during the traditional method of SPARKLING WINE-MAKING. Punts are less obviously useful for still wines—although they can make 75-cl capacity bottles look bigger and more impressive—and deep punts can provide useful purchase for the thumb when SERVING wine from a bottle.

Bottle colour Wine keeps best in dark glass—as the Champenois, the most energetic researchers into the effects of bottle choice on wine, have found (ROEDERER Cristal, which has traditionally been sold in clear glass, is always swathed in an orange wrap designed to filter out ultraviolet light). On the other hand, dark glass prevents the consumer from being impressed by the colour of a wine. For this reason, most ROSÉS, not designed for BOTTLE AGEING in any case, are sold in clear glass. It is less clear why SAUTERNES and other sweet white bordeaux is sold in clear glass; tradition is the explanation. Most wine bottles are, for reasons of both tradition and the orientation of glass furnaces, some shade of green, from pale blue green to a colour that to all intents and purposes is black. For traditional reasons again, brown glass is used for some Italian wines, for fortified wines, and was the traditional way of telling a HOCK or Rhine wine from a MOSELLE in green glass. German producers are increasingly using powerfully blue-green glass, however, a nod to Victorian times when blue glass was often used. One of the most distinctive glass colours for wine bottles is the yellow-green used for white burgundy, called *feuille morte* in France and therefore 'dead leaf' in much of the New World. As CHARDONNAY became the most fashionable wine in the world in the 1980s, so the dead leaf burgundy bottle became the most sought-after wine bottle, with especial frustration by producers in New World regions far from France until supply lines were established.

Bottle sizes: The range of bottles used for champagne is one of the most extensive. From left to right are Salmanazar, Nebuchadnezzar, Methuselah, standard bottle, magnum, half-bottle, Jéroboam, Balthazar, although only bottles and magnums are generally used for the all-important ageing process. (The Rehoboam is no longer made.)

More clues from the bottle
Most wine bottles are moulded with the mark of their manufacturers, sometimes with their capacity, and all wine sold within Europe from the 1990s should have a LOT MARKING, a small code stamped on the label, foil, or bottle, so that each bottle can be traced back to its precise BOTTLING and dispatch.

BOTTLE SICKNESS, also known less politely as **bottle stink**, unpleasant smell apparent in a wine immediately on opening which dissipates after a few minutes.

Off-odour compounds such as MERCAPTANS and SULPHUR DIOXIDE may occasionally be formed by moulds embedded in poor CORKS, or by a small amount of wine which has escaped through the cork or capsule and is then acetified or otherwise subjected to BACTERIAL SPOILAGE. This is the principal reason why some people advocate allowing a bottle of wine to BREATHE before serving (and one of the reasons why it is wise to wipe the top of an opened bottle clean). DECANTING can achieve the same end.

A similar phenomenon should perhaps more properly be called 'bottling sickness' as it is usually an unpleasant smell that results directly from the BOTTLING process. Other than under perfect conditions, bottling may be a rough business involving so much aeration and agitation that a certain amount of potentially harmful OXYGEN is frequently dissolved in the wine. To counter possible OXIDATION, many bottlers add SULPHUR DIOXIDE at this stage. If the wine is tasted in the first few weeks after bottling, the smell of sulphur dioxide may well be obtrusive and it is wise to wait until the sulphur dioxide has reacted with the oxygen and the wine once more tastes as it did prior to bottling.

BOTTLE SIZES are standardized in most countries. A bottle containing 75 cl (27 fl oz) is now accepted almost universally as the standard wine (but not spirits, which is more usually 70 cl) bottle, with the magnum being 1.5 l, exactly twice the capacity. The standard bottle is about the same size as the first bottles (see BOTTLES, history), whose size may have been determined by the size of container conveniently blown by a (glassblower's) lungful of air. The bottle has in its time been described as a suitable ration of wine for one person at a sitting, one person per day, and two people at a sitting (see CONSUMPTION).

Half-bottles usually contain 37.5 cl and tend to hasten wine AGEING, partly because they contain more OXYGEN per centilitre of wine since the bottle neck and ULLAGE are the same as for a full bottle. Most wine bottlers have viewed halves and other bottles smaller than the standard bottle as an unwelcome inconvenience, and BOTTLING technology has been focused on standard bottles, but there continues to be strong demand for half-bottles, particularly in restaurants. There have been various attempts to launch a 50-cl bottle.

Capacity (l)	Bordeaux	Champagne/Burgundy
1.5 (2 bottles)	magnum	magnum
2.25 (3 bottles)	Marie-Jeanne	not found
3 (4 bottles)	double magnum	Jéroboam
4.5 (6 bottles)	Jéroboam	Rehoboam
6 (8 bottles)	Impériale	Methuselah
9 (12 bottles)	not found	Salmanazar
16 bottles	not found	Balthazar
20 bottles	not found	Nebuchadnezzar

The bottle capacities permitted within Europe for still wines are 10 cl, 25 cl, 37.5 cl, 50 cl, 75 cl, and 1, 1.5, 2, 3, 4, 5, 6, 8, 9, and 10 litres (and 18.7 cl bottles may be served aboard trains, planes, and the like). Sparkling wine bottles come in 12.5-, 20-, 37.5- and 75-cl and 1.5-, 3-, 4.5-, 6- and 9-litre capacities.

The larger-sized bottles, some of them no longer in production, have different names in different regions.

Bordeaux COLLECTORS particularly treasure larger bottles (often known as 'large formats') up to Impériale size, as they favour slow but subtle wine AGEING. Giant champagne bottles, on the other hand, tend to favour publicity rather than wine quality, and sizes larger than a magnum tend to be filled with wine made in smaller bottles.

BOTTLE VARIATION is one of the more tantalizing aspects of wine appreciation. It is only to be expected with a product as sensitive to STORAGE conditions as wine that bottles of the same wine will differ—perhaps because one has been exposed to higher temperatures or greater humidity. There can, however, be a perceptible difference in quality and character between bottles from the very same CASE. SUBJECTIVISM may play a part, as well as a difference in levels, but the individual wines before they went into bottle may have differed, as indeed did bottling conditions. It was not until the 1970s, for example, that it became commonplace for Bordeaux châteaux to ensure that a uniform blend was made before bottling; some of the world's more artisanal producers still bottle by hand from cask to cask. Similarly, wines bottled on two different occasions may find themselves packed in the same case (although modern LOT NUMBER marking provides more clues in this respect).

BOTTLING, vital wine-making operation for all wines other than those packaged in containers other than bottles (see BOXES and CANS) and those few served straight as BULK WINE from a cask or tank.

Bottling techniques vary greatly according to the size, resources, technical ability, and modernity of the winery, although since the 1960s it has been customary almost everywhere to blend all casks or vats of a given lot of wine together before bottling, and to bottle it all at once. (Prior to this there could be considerable BOTTLE VARIATION between different bottlings of even FIRST GROWTHS.)

Until recently, the high-speed, efficient bottling lines used for everyday wine subjected the wine to considerable AERATION and agitation so that wines would not taste as they should for some weeks after bottling, when the dissolved OXYGEN had fully reacted with the wine components, including added SULPHUR DIOXIDE (as explained in BOTTLE SICKNESS). And wines containing RESIDUAL SUGAR may well have been subjected to PASTEURIZATION and 'hot bottled' to ensure microbiological stability. An increasing proportion of even inexpensive wine is bottled more carefully today, however, borrowing technology from the brewing industry.

Producers of high-quality wine with the means to invest in a bottling line (by no means all of them) use much more complicated and expensive equipment which subjects the wine to minimal aeration and agitation. NITROGEN or CARBON DIOXIDE is used to eliminate exposure to oxygen, and bottles are filled slowly so that there is no splashing or foaming. High-quality, low alcohol, slightly sweet young wines may well be treated to STERILE BOTTLING.

Some small-scale wineries still follow the ancient tradition of bottling wine from casks or even individual barrels in the cellar. Many other small wineries, especially in France where *mis en bouteille au domaine* has considerable cachet, depend upon the services of outside mobile bottling lines, bottling equipment mounted in a truck or lorry which can be brought to the winery for a day or more.

The specific steps involved in bottling are the preparation of the wine itself (BLENDING, ANALYSIS, and possibly final FILTRATION) together with the preparation of the bottling line (sterilization and the preparation of the filler, corker or capper, labeller, capsuler, and casing machines, as appropriate). High-quality wines suitable for BOTTLE AGEING may not be labelled as soon as they are bottled, because they are stored for some time before being released.

Bottling may take place either at any time from a few weeks after HARVEST (as with NOUVEAU wines) or when the wine is many years old (as in some of the most traditional Iberian BODEGAS). On smaller wine estates, bottling normally takes place at an otherwise quiet time for cellar staff such as in the spring or early summer.

Place of bottling may be many thousands of miles from where the grapes were originally grown, and even from where the wine was made, since BULK TRANSPORT is so very much cheaper than transporting wine in bottle. In eastern Europe and the Soviet Union in particular, bottling has traditionally taken place much closer to centres of population than to the vineyard. Producers of hand-crafted, top-quality wines, however, usually prefer to conduct the bottling operation themselves. See BOTTLING INFORMATION for the significance of various bottling claims on the label.

As with any mechanical process, many things can go wrong during the bottling operation. The bottled wine itself can develop problems which were not previously apparent. Most result from incomplete STABILIZATION, but other contaminants may also intervene, such as those associated with CORKS.

See also BOTTLES. A.D.W. & J.Ro.

BOTTLING INFORMATION. Most wine labels should divulge where the wine was bottled. Wines bottled in the same place as they were vinified are described under CHÂTEAU BOTTLED, DOMAINE BOTTLED, ESTATE BOTTLED, ERZEUGERABFÜLLUNG, or GUTSABFÜLLUNG.

Common phrases for 'bottled' are *mis en bouteille* in French, *imbottigliato* in Italian, *embotellado* in Spanish, and *engarrafado* in Portuguese.

Many of the wines bottled by an enterprise other than the one which made the wine are labelled relatively obliquely. Within the EUROPEAN UNION a bottler's address may not be specified on the label of a basic TABLE WINE if it incorporates the name of a QUALITY WINE; the bottler's postal code is usually employed instead. This is one of those well- intentioned rules designed to minimize the possibility of passing off, but it does make labels less informative to those not conversant with, for example, French *département* numbers or the two letters used for each Italian province.

A relatively primitive **bottling** line.

BOUCHALÈS is a dark-berried vine variety still grown to a limited extent in Bordeaux and in the Lot-et-Garonne *département*. It is not particularly easy to graft or grow and total French plantings fell from over 4,000 ha/9,900 acres in 1968 to less than 500 ha 20 years later.

BOUCHARD, PÈRE ET FILS, one of Beaune's large merchant houses, and the most important vineyard owner on Burgundy's Côte de BEAUNE. Based since 1731 in the 15th century Ch de Beaune, a landmark in this medieval wine town, the house is now run by the ninth generation of Bouchards (and is quite distinct from Bouchard Aîné). The house was established by Michel Bouchard, a Dauphiné textile merchant, and land has been acquired over the centuries so that by the mid 1990s it totalled more than 90 ha/230 acres. Bouchard have holdings in 25 different Beaune vineyards, including their exclusivities Beaune-Grèves, Vigne de l'Enfant Jésus and Beaune, Clos de la Mousse. They are also particularly proud of their 1.1-ha/2.7-acre holding in Le MONTRACHET, their particularly significant share of Chevalier-Montrachet in their holding of 2.33 ha, and their exclusive distribution rights to the VOSNE-ROMANÉE GRAND CRU La Romanée. In all, 71 of their 92 ha are in grands crus or PREMIERS CRUS.

Wines from their own vineyards are undoubtedly Bouchard's best, although rarely Burgundy's most concentrated. For the much larger NÉGOCIANT business, the firm buys in considerable quantities of grapes (including all of those grown in the Clos-St-Marc premier cru in Nuits-St-Georges), must (notably in Chablis), and young wines for ÉLEVAGE in the medieval cellars on several levels below the Ch de Beaune. The firm is run by Jean-François Bouchard, and his cousin Christophe, in charge of vinification, is introducing advances in both cellar and vineyard, thanks to the firm's annual research programme.

BOUCHET, the name for CABERNET FRANC used in St-Émilion and elsewhere on the right bank of the GIRONDE.

BOUCHON is French for CORK and **bouchonné** describes a faulty, CORKED wine.

BOUCHY, the local name for the CABERNET FRANC grape when grown in MADIRAN.

BOUQUET, oft-ridiculed tasting term for the smell of a wine, particularly that of a mature or maturing wine. Although its original French meaning was 'small wood' (from the same root as the Italian *bosco* and the English bosky), bouquet is a French word for a bunch of flowers which has been used to describe the perfume of a wine since the first half of the 19th century. It is used loosely by many wine tasters to describe any pleasant wine smell or smells but, just as a bouquet (rather than a bunch) of flowers suggests a composition of several varied elements, many wine professionals distinguish between the simple AROMA of the grape and the bouquet of the more complex compounds which evolve as a result of FERMENTATION, ÉLEVAGE, and BOTTLE AGEING. There is little consistency in usage, however, and many authorities differ about which point in a wine's life cycle represents the point at which a wine's smell stops being an aroma and becomes a bouquet. See also AGEING, ESTER, and FLAVOUR COMPOUNDS.

BOURBOULENC is an ancient white grape variety that may well have originated in Greece, as the now rarely seen Asprokondoura, and has been grown throughout southern France for centuries. Ripening late but keeping its acidity well, it is allowed into a wide variety of Provençal and southern Rhône appellations (including Châteauneuf-du-Pape) but is rarely encountered as a dominant variety other than in the distinctive whites of La CLAPE in the Languedoc. France's total area planted with Bourboulenc halved in the 1970s and then doubled again, to about 800 ha/2,000 acres, in the 1980s thanks in part to a re-evalution in the Languedoc where it is also, confusingly, known as Malvoisie. Its tight bunches of large grapes can make it prone to rot in more difficult years but Bourboulenc, together with Maccabéo, should constitute more than 50 per cent of the blend for any white Minervois, and the two, with Grenache Blanc, should dominate Corbières Blanc.

BOURG, small town in the BORDEAUX region on the right bank of the river DORDOGNE, just up river of its confluence with the Garonne, which is surrounded by the **Côtes de Bourg** appellation. In most years about 200,000 hl/5.3 million gal of Côtes de Bourg red is produced, more than any other BORDEAUX CÔTES appellation. Grape varieties and organization are very similar to the larger BLAYE area to the immediate north, but the clay-limestone soils tend to be less varied in Bourg, and those vineyards on the edge of the Gironde estuary are particularly well protected from FROST damage, thanks to the maritime influence. Almost all wine produced is red, based on MERLOT grapes, and designed to last slightly longer than Premières Côtes de Blaye, to be consumed at four to six or even more years old. The average quality of Bourg's PETITS CHÂTEAUX (some of them not that small) has been improving. A little dry white wine is also made, chiefly from the eminently distillable UGNI BLANC and COLOMBARD grapes which still predominate here, even though it is decades since the region's wines were sent north to produce COGNAC. Some of them today are distilled into FINE de Bordeaux.

For more details see BORDEAUX.

BOURGEON is French for BUD, and **bourgeonnage** is the viticultural practice of thinning surplus developing buds before FLOWERING, a form of early CROP THINNING.

BOURGOGNE, the French name for both the region of BURGUNDY (La Bourgogne) and burgundy, the wines thereof (*le bourgogne*), which are red, white, and very occasionally rosé. In particular Bourgogne refers to the most basic, generic category of APPELLATIONS in Burgundy.

For white wines the generic appellations are BOURGOGNE ALIGOTÉ, **Bourgogne Blanc** (made from Chardonnay grapes, although Pinot Blanc and Pinot Gris are tolerated), and **Bourgogne Grand Ordinaire** which may contain Chardonnay, Aligoté, Melon de Bourgogne, and (in the Yonne, the Chablis *département*) Sacy.

For red wines the generic appellations are BOURGOGNE PASSETOUTGRAINS, **Bourgogne Grand Ordinaire**, and **Bourgogne Rouge**. The latter is usually pure Pinot Noir, although it may technically include the César and Tressot once grown in the Yonne, and may be made from Gamay grapes if grown in one of the BEAUJOLAIS crus. Bourgogne Passetoutgrains is a blend of Gamay and Pinot Noir, requiring a minimum of one-third of the latter. Bourgogne Grand Ordinaire may include Pinot, Gamay, César, and Tressot.

Some vineyards also carry a geographical suffix, as in Bourgogne Hautes Côtes de Nuits, Bourgogne Hautes Côtes de Beaune, Bourgogne Côte Chalonnaise, and, around AUXERRE, Bourgogne from Irancy, Côte St-Jacques, Coulanges-la-Vineuse, Chitry, and Épineuil.

Thus it is evident that the scope of 'Bourgogne', be it white or red, encompasses wide variations in provenance, quality, and style of wine, which may not be clear from the label. A Bourgogne Rouge or Bourgogne Blanc made by a grower in one of the major villages of the Côte d'Or (such as MEURSAULT for whites and VOLNAY or CHAMBOLLE-MUSIGNY for reds) is likely to be reliably fashioned in the image of classic CÔTE D'OR burgundy, however, and may well represent excellent value. There is every chance that the wine will be made from vines only just outside the village appellation yet selling at half the price.

A small amount of pink wine is sold as **Bourgogne Rosé** or **Bourgogne Clairet**. In practice this may be the result of a SAIGNÉE of a red wine from a major vineyard in order to concentrate it—although by law this is not possible, since to declassify part of the crop into Bourgogne Rosé would necessitate declassifying the remainder into Bourgogne Rouge.

CRÉMANT de Bourgogne is the generic appellation for sparkling Burgundy, either white or rosé, while the now rare red version is classified as **Bourgogne Mousseux**.

See also BOURGOGNE ALIGOTÉ and BOURGOGNE PASSETOUTGRAINS. J.T.C.M.

BOURGOGNE ALIGOTÉ, a generic appellation in Burgundy for white wines made from the ALIGOTÉ grape. These wines vary between refreshingly crisp and disagreeably tart although the latter characteristic suits their role as the basis for *vin blanc cassis*, known as 'Kir' after the canon of Dijon who perfected this aperitif. Aligoté is primarily for early consumption although wines from the best locations such as Chitry in the Yonne, PERNAND-VERGELESSES in the Côte de Beaune, and Bouzeron in the Côte CHALONNAISE can age well. Since 1979 Bouzeron has enjoyed a specific appellation, Bourgogne Aligoté de Bouzeron. J.T.C.M.

BOURGOGNE PASSETOUTGRAINS, red thirst quencher from Burgundy made from Pinot Noir (minimum one-third) and Gamay grapes. Often deep in colour and rather savagely animal when young, Passetoutgrains with age can attain greater refinement as the Pinot Noir flavours start to dominate. The best examples come from vineyards in the CÔTE D'OR lying in the plain beyond the main RN74 road which divides the finer vineyards from the generic. J.T.C.M.

BOURGOGNE, UNIVERSITÉ DE. See DIJON.

BOURGUEIL, potentially captivating red wines made on the north bank of the Loire in the west of the TOURAINE district. The climate here is particularly gentle and rainfall is low, as in much of ANJOU to the immediate west. Most of the 1,200 ha/2,960 acres of vineyard are on a plateau of sand, gravel, and limestone about 5 km/3 miles north of the Loire, bisected by the Changeon tributary.

The CABERNET FRANC grape is exclusively responsible for these medium bodied wines which are typically marked by a more powerful aroma (reminding some of raspberries) and slightly more noticeable tannins than the wines of CHINON to the south. Bourgueil can be aged for five or many more years in ripe VINTAGES such as 1989, while **St-Nicolas-de-Bourgueil**, produced on about 800 ha of lighter soils in the west of the region, is generally a lighter, earlier maturing wine. These fragrant wines are extremely popular in Paris and northern France but have yet to be discovered by most non-French wine lovers.

A little dry rosé Bourgueil is also made, but the appellation does not, unlike Chinon, encompass white wines.

See LOIRE and map on pp. 576–7.

BOUSCHET is, like Müller, Sheu, and Seibel, a vine-breeder's surname that lives on in the name of his creations, although in this case there were two Bouschets, a 19th century father and son whose work, perhaps unfortunately, made the spread of ARAMON possible. In 1824 Louis Bouschet de Bernard combined the productivity of Aramon with the colour expected of a red wine by crossing Aramon with TEINTURIER du Cher and modestly calling the result Petit Bouschet. This expedient crossing was popular in France throughout the second half of the 19th century and is still to be found in parts of North Africa and, according to GALET, Portugal. Louis's son Henri carried on where his father left off, producing most durably ALICANTE BOUSCHET and GRAND NOIR DE LA CALMETTE as well as a Carignan Bouschet.

BOUVIER, minor white grape variety bred as a TABLE GRAPE and now grown mainly in the Burgenland region of AUSTRIA, where it is particularly used for Sturm, the cloudy, part-fermented sweet grape juice that is a local speciality at harvest time. It is also grown in the Mátra Foothills of HUNGARY.

BOUZERON, village in the Côte Chalonnaise famous for its BOURGOGNE ALIGOTÉ.

BOXES, WINE. In the 1970s an entirely new way of packaging wine was developed, expressly to provide a significant volume of wine in a package that is not as breakable or heavy as a bottle, and is better able to preserve any wine left over in the container. It comprises a collapsable laminated bag inside a strong carton with a handle, and wine is drawn out of a tap specially designed to minimize the ingress of potentially harmful OXYGEN. Filling and packaging costs for **bag-in-box** wines, together with the difficulty of making the wine container completely airtight, have been the main brakes on what was a remarkably rapid sales success. The package, commonly holding four litres of wine, is particularly popular in Australia and New Zealand, where it is known flatteringly as the 'cask' or, more prosaically, 'bladder pack'. Wine boxes have also enjoyed success in northern Europe, notably 3-l boxes, which accounted for just over 10 per cent of all wine sold in Great Britain in 1990. Boxes are generally filled with less expensive wines designed for early drinking and are bought either in bulk for parties or by those who want to enjoy a simple wine one glass at a time over several weeks and who do not object to or notice the deterioration in quality towards the end of that period. The wine inside a bag, even one whose tap has remained sealed, is best immediately after filling, and has usually deteriorated quite markedly 12 months after filling, which is why most wine boxes are dated. (See LEFTOVER WINE for details of devices for preserving wine in partially empty bottles.)

BRACHETTO, light red grape variety found particularly round Asti, Roero, and Alessandria, where it is particularly successful, in the PIEDMONT region of Italy. It produces wines, notably **Brachetto d'Acqui**, that are fizzy, relatively alcoholic, and have both the colour and flavour of strawberries. Brachetto is the Italian name for **Braquet**, which the French consider an old variety of PROVENCE and which is a valued ingredient in the red and pink wines of BELLET near Nice. Yields are low and the vine is relatively delicate but the wine is truly distinctive.

BRAMATERRA, a lighter variation on the NEBBIOLO theme of LESSONA in the PIEDMONT region of north west Italy. See SPANNA, the local name for Nebbiolo, for more details. See also the nearby BOCA, GHEMME, SIZZANO, and FARA in Novara.

BRANCO, Portuguese word meaning white. A *vinho branco* is therefore white wine.

BRANDEWIJN (**brandvin**, **brandywijn**), a Dutch word meaning literally 'burnt', or distilled, wine. The word is derived from the German *Gebrandtwein*. The Dutch, the dominant western European commercial force in the late 16th century (see DUTCH WINE TRADE), sought a cheap source of distilling material to provide their sailors with potable liquids. They imported huge quantities of wine, and later spirit, from various parts of western France, including the MUSCADET, COGNAC, and ARMAGNAC regions. So important did this trade become that *brandewijn* became the international term for the spirit produced by distilling wine, evolving eventually into the word BRANDY—proof that the Dutch were the pioneers of the commercialization of alcohol.

BRANDS, products marketed on the basis of their name and image rather than on their inherent qualities, have a less secure place in the late 20th century wine market than branded goods do in many others. Most sectors of the wine market are extremely fragmented (although the fortified wine business is not and has been built on brands, see FORTIFICATION), so that brand promotion is difficult to make cost effective, and can leave **branded wines** looking extremely poor value. Wine brands offer a familiar lifeline to new wine consumers baffled by a multiplicity of unfamiliar, often foreign, proper names. But as wine drinkers become more sophisticated, they learn to decode what initially seems the arcane language of wine names, usually by identifying the major VARIETALS and some of the more important place-names. Thus, brands are most in demand in embryonic and fast-growing markets, such as northern Europe and the rest of the English-speaking world between the 1950s and the 1980s, and in Africa, South America, and some Asian countries in the 1990s.

It may be difficult to market branded wines in a competitive market, but it can be even more difficult to maintain consistency of a product as variable as wine. Supplies are strictly limited to an annual batch production process. Wine cannot be manufactured to suit demand, and different vintages impose their own characteristics on the product regardless of consumer taste.

A high proportion of all wine drinkers were introduced to wine through brands, and it is to the credit of those brand owners most dedicated to maintaining quality standards whenever the introduction was a happy one.

Most national wine markets of any size have their own particularly successful brands: in the United Kingdom Lutomer Riesling (in fact a Laski Rizling, from SLOVENIA) was an enormous success in the 1970s, while today the French VIN DE TABLE Piat d'Or outsells all of its Beaujolais (on which the house of Piat was founded) many times over.

Notably successful international wine brands are relatively few, and they have perforce to be based on wine of which there is no shortage of supply. MOUTON CADET is by far the world's best-known CLARET, selling an estimated 1.5 million cases a year world-wide in the early 1990s. It was slowly and skilfully developed by Baron Philippe de ROTHSCHILD in the mid 20th century.

The relatively vague wine style LIEBFRAUMILCH, created by German exporters, lends itself well to branding, and BLUE NUN has been the most successful Liebfraumilch of all on an international basis, although, after rapid growth from the 1950s, sales peaked at 2 million cases in the mid 1980s.

The table wine exports of an entire country, Portugal, were founded on two brands created during the Second World War. The success of LANCERS and MATEUS owed much to the fact that the neophyte wine drinkers of the mid 20th century were reassured by the fact that these medium sweet, pale pink, slightly sparkling blends, each marketed in its own easily recognizable bottle, were neither red nor white, still nor sparkling, sweet nor dry and thus in theory offered protection from solecism. The sales of Mateus alone were more than 3 million cases in the late 1980s.

In the more static wine market of the 1990s, more experienced consumers tend to eschew brands for more individual wines, although there are those who argue that the grape variety CHARDONNAY, for example, has become a brand in its own right, so strong is consumer recognition of the name. Others claim that in certain markets buyers' own brands have become so important, and so cleverly marketed, that some supermarkets' names have established themselves as brands.

The definition of a wine brand is a loose one. In some respects, the New French CLARETS, named for the estate which produced them, were the first wine brands. And any definition which incorporates the notion of relatively elastic supply and some studied promotion would allow that the most successful wine brands of all are the so-called *grande marque* (which translates directly as 'big brand') CHAMPAGNES.

BRANDY, a much abused term whose proper meaning is grape-based spirit, of which the most noble and most famous forms are COGNAC and ARMAGNAC from south west France. Despite its etymologically vinous origins (see BRANDEWIJN), however, brandy can be made from a wide variety of fruits, as in peach brandy, apricot brandy, and apple brandy (of which the calvados of Normandy is the most famous).

In the 1970s and 1980s some distillers played the name false, however, by using the term for any distilled spirit, even those whose taste and character could not be traced back to the original raw materials subjected to DISTILLATION, including spirits made from industrial alcohol artificially flavoured to resemble a brandy made from fruit. Until more stringent European legislation was introduced in 1989 (see BRANDY AND THE EUROPEAN UNION), most so-called French brandy was nothing more than flavoured neutral alcohol, of negligible interest to connoisseurs. The commercially successful Greek spirit Metaxa is similar.

Nowadays, within the EU, at least, a spirit labelled brandy must be grape based and must have been aged for at least six months in OAK. Any other products of wine origin, such as cognac or armagnac, may be added to this rather neutral spirit to improve its flavour and quality. See French brandy below.

Of more interest, and considerably more character, are those brandies technically known as POMACE BRANDIES, made out of the residue of wine-making. Such a brandy is called MARC in France, GRAPPA in Italy, and BAGACEIRA in Portugal. Such brandies are distinctive, often noble, and almost always underrated.

American brandy

Brandy has a long and not especially distinguished history in the USA, virtually confined to California. Until PROHIBITION brandy formed a normal part of the range of most major wine-makers in California, along with 'port' and 'sherry'. But it was not generally thought of as a separate, quality product. Instead it occupied a fall-back position, made from wines which were not good enough to be sold as such. It was important, however, and when in the 1870s James Shorb, a typical pioneer, found that many of the million bottles of wine he was making every year proved unsaleable, he reverted to selling only brandy. (The same fate befell the grapes produced by Governor Leland Stanford at his Viña vineyard.)

But there were exceptions, like one Henry Nagele, who in the 1860s was making brandy from Riesling and Pinot Noir in the Santa Clara Valley south of San Francisco. He consistently won prizes, especially for the brandy made from Pinot Noir, which he called 'Burgundy brandy'.

After Repeal of Prohibition, brandy remained a relatively ordinary product although its commercial importance grew over the decades. Moreover the shortage of wine grapes ensured that most California brandies were (and are) made from two varieties, Flame Tokay and, above all, the prolific but neutral THOMPSON SEEDLESS, grown and distilled not in a quality wine-making area but in the SAN JOAQUIN VALLEY. Although a few distillers use the POT STILL, most California brandies are continuously distilled and then immediately diluted to 50 per cent before being matured in casks made of American oak, generally ones which have previously been charred and used to mature bourbon whiskey, and so contribute to these brandies' richness.

The making of California brandy is regulated. Only California grapes can be used, and the spirit must be distilled to below a maximum of 85 per cent alcohol. The spirit can be flavoured by up to 2.5 per cent of what are confusingly called 'rectifying agents', which include caramel, liquid sugar, fortified wines, and the juice of prunes and other fruit, fresh as well as dried. The result naturally tends to be brandy made in the Spanish style (see Spanish brandy below), although most of them are rather lighter, and are designed to be drunk, not neat, but as a mixer. Indeed the greatest success story of American brandies has been the brandy made by GALLO, a light, unremarkable spirit made in continuous stills, and marketed specially to be drunk with orange juice. The longest established brand, Christian Brothers, is a much lighter and more characterful spirit.

But the future of good-quality California brandy lies with a handful of brave pioneers who are trying to make a quality product using fine wine grapes. The first was Russell Woodbury, who started distilling from Ugni Blanc, the cognac variety, in the early 1970s, producing fine, light cognac-type brandies. Another pioneer, RMS, wholly owned by RÉMY MARTIN, uses a number of varieties, including the Colombard once used in Cognac, and others have decided that the Ugni Blanc does not provide enough character in California conditions and have reverted to Henry Nagele's ideas. Typically the brandy made with enthusiasm by Hubert Germain-Robin, a descendant of the Jules Robin family which was once a power in Cognac, is made from Gamay and Pinot Noir. The result is indeed complex and interesting enough to suggest a considerable, and highly individual, future for the new California brandies.

Australian brandy

Australia has been producing brandy for over a century. For half a century before that the Australians were producing grape spirit to reduce a surplus of SULTANA grapes and then to provide spirit for Australia's FORTIFIED wines. The production of true brandy started in SOUTH AUSTRALIA, where a local coppersmith produced his own type of POT STILL. Brandy production is strictly regulated. The spirit cannot be sold until it is two years old; 'old' brandies must be five years old and 'very old' 10 years old. Some of the best Australian brandies, curiously underrated by Australians, are made by wine producers HARDY'S and can be compared with a light COGNAC from the Fins Bois.

Cyprus brandy

Cyprus brandy is rich and unremarkable, typical of the island's vinous products, and of the brandies made industrially in Germany and Italy. It is distilled on a large scale, either in old pot stills as at Keo, or in large continuous stills as by the SODAP CO-OPERATIVE winery.

Eastern European brandy

Traditionally, brandy has been made from grapes, and a wide range of other fruits, throughout Eastern Europe. Today the only wine-based spirit widely sold internationally comes from Bulgaria, where brandy is distilled from UGNI BLANC, RKATSITELI, and DIMIAT grapes. They are then matured for at least three years in oak casks.

French brandy

Only the least interesting and cheapest French brandy is actually labelled as such. (The best are labelled COGNAC and ARMAGNAC.) It comes from a single, controlled source, the Société des Alcools Viticoles based close to POMEROL in Libourne, and provides a useful outlet for some of Europe's WINE LAKE. This neutral spirit must be aged for at least a year in wood and owners of the better brands may try to improve them by adding a small portion of a superior spirit. Packaging, marketing, and, sometimes, the sly insinuation of a connection with a superior sort of brandy are all in this sector of the market. In many traditional French wine regions, however, notably Champagne and Burgundy, some wine considered suitable for DISTILLATION is made into a local FINE. Such spirits should be distinguished from POMACE BRANDY which in France is called MARC.

German brandy

German brandies are almost invariably unauthentic and uninteresting, if perfectly wholesome and correctly made. Their lack of distinction derives from the fact that they are not made from the local wines, apart from the Pfalzer Weinbrand made by Pabst & Richarz in Pfalz. They are usually rich and sweet, rather heavy, and aromatic in a non-grapey way. They are a mass industrial product, made by a handful of major firms such as Asbach and Eckes, distillers of Mariacron, one of the world's best-selling brandies. Spirits for serious sipping they are not. They are made from wines imported from a variety of countries, mostly France and Italy. Some of these base wines, especially the considerable proportion from the

Cognac region, are already FORTIFIED by the addition of spirit. This ensures stability, but removes the final product yet further from any of the tastes or aromas associated with the original raw material.

German brandies are strictly regulated. They can be distilled in either a POT STILL or CONTINUOUS STILL. Standard blends must be aged for at least six months, and older brandies (Alter Weinbrand or Uralt, for example) for at least a year. Typical is the best-selling Uralt made by Asbach, which is aged for a year in small oak casks and for six further months in larger wooden tanks.

Israeli brandy
The early Jewish immigrants to what was then Palestine needed a source of KOSHER brandy. As early as 1882 Baron de ROTHSCHILD imported French vines into the country and the first wine- and brandy-making co-operative was established. Since then an industry has grown up which continues to have a tied market in Jewish communities outside Israel as well as in the country itself. But the distillers retain the rather sweet, rich character originally favoured by poor eastern European immigrants.

Italian brandy
Although the Italians claim that the word 'brandy' is derived from the Piedmontese word *branda*, their heart is not with brandy, the distilled product of wine, typically preferring their distinctive GRAPPA produced from grape pomace. Italian brandies are industrial products born not of native love or ingenuity but, like Spanish brandies, of the market opportunity which opened when PHYLLOXERA hit the Charentes and supplies of cognac dried up. Indeed until 1948 the Italians called brandies 'cognac', not unreasonably since they make their brandies out of the same grape variety that is called UGNI BLANC in France but TREBBIANO in Italy.

So Italian brandy is treated as an industrial product, and, fortunately for its reputation, its production is covered by the same, strict regulations which govern the pharmaceutical industry. The wines must come from strictly defined regions; they are analysed before distillation; and they can be distilled only to a relatively low strength to retain the fruitiness of the grapes. Additives are strictly limited to caramel and one per cent of a sweetening agent. To be sold as 'brandy' the spirit has to be aged for a year. Younger than this, it can be marketed only as *acquavite*, *distillato*, or *arzente*. The Italian government encourages the ageing of brandies by taxing older spirits more lightly than younger ones.

But all these restrictions do not add up to a remarkable product. Italian brandies may be more authentic, less remorselessly sticky than their (equally industrial) German competitors, but they are still not great spirits. Rather, they are light, bland, relatively standardized, albeit agreeable, reliable, and easily quaffable brands, mostly from the two firms Buton (who market Vecchia Romagna) and Stock.

Latin American brandy
Wine-based brandies are produced in a number of Latin American countries. The most important producer is MEXICO, where the Presidente brand produced by a subsidiary of DOMECQ is one of the world's best-selling brandies. Chile, Bolivia, and Peru produce their own type of aromatic brandy; see PISCO.

Portuguese brandy
The Portuguese could make good brandy, and occasionally do, because they have a ready, cheap supply of sharp white wine, which they normally use for VINHO VERDE. In reality most Portuguese grape spirit is simply that: distilled by the Portuguese government and then supplied to the port houses for use in PORT production.

Most commercially available Portuguese brandies are still made from BAGA, the thick-skinned, astringent black grape used for Bairrada and Dão wines. A few firms, such as Aveleda, Imperio, and Sogrape, are now using properly acid grapes to make brandies and also, in one or two cases, decent BAGACEIRA, their version of POMACE BRANDY.

South African brandy
South African brandy has a long, and generally disreputable history in South Africa, where the country's two white races both enjoy it: the Dutch invented BRANDEWIJN, and the British Uitlanders who arrived in the late 19th century to work the gold and diamond deposits on the Rand were thirsty folk. For two centuries the Dutch produced only a peculiarly fierce form of POMACE BRANDY known variously as dop (short for dopbrandewyn, or husk brandy), Cape smoke, or witblits (an Afrikaans word meaning white lightning).

During the 19th century a handful of more conscientious distillers tried to make better-quality Cape brandy, a natural step because Cape wines were then greatly prized in Europe. (King Louis XVI's cellar contained more CONSTANTIA than claret). A former cavalry officer of French origins, René Santhagens, imported the first POT STILL and he and Francis Collison, a noted wine-maker, began to distil fine brandies. Nevertheless the inhabitants, even Barney Barnato, one of the richest of the Randlords, remained faithful to Cape smoke.

Since then the industry has become very much more organized. In the 1920s controls were imposed and distillation centralized in KWV, the co-operative which dominates the wine and spirit business in South Africa. There is a general surplus of wine for distillation, and so the stills have a ready supply of classic varieties such as Ugni Blanc and Colombard. Yet despite its monopoly the KWV encourages quality. Continuous stills are allowed only for exported grape spirit and brandy for home consumption must contain at least 30 per cent of spirit distilled by pot still. Brandies matured for at least three years are known as 'rebate brandies' because they are entitled to a rebate on the duty level.

Spanish brandy
Spain is a major producer of brandies, some of them very distinctive. The Spaniards are second only to the people of the Cognac region in the quantity of brandy they make, and they drink far more of their own brandy than the French do cognac. Around 100 million bottles of Spanish brandy are consumed in Spain each year, and large quantities are

exported, not only to the rest of the Spanish-speaking world, but also to Germany and Italy. Most Spanish brandy is distinctively rich grape-based spirit matured in JEREZ in the far south of Spain and sold as Brandy de Jerez.

In Catalonia in northern Spain, however, two producers, TORRES and the much smaller but innovative Mascaro, produce often excellent spirits according to the normal formula for high-grade brandies (see COGNAC). They use local, acidic grapes (in this case the PARELLADA), double-distil them—for better-quality brandies, anyway—and end up with brandies which have the same style as cognac, and show well in any comparative tasting.

But for most of the world (and virtually all Spaniards) the term Spanish brandy is confined to the rich, popular brandies matured and sold by the sherry firms in Jerez which bear little or no resemblance to cognac. Their history is one of the most curious in the world of grape-based spirits. Their generally rich, flavoursome warmth is underrated, largely because they do not conform to the norms imposed by Anglo-Saxon drinkers.

Thanks to their absorption of so much Arab culture (see SPAIN, history), Spaniards were among the first Europeans to learn the art of DISTILLATION. They still use a number of Arab-based words, such as *alquitara*, meaning brandy. In modern times the Spaniards were content to provide raw spirit for the Dutch (hence the word *holandas* for one type of Spanish brandy—see below) until PHYLLOXERA hit Cognac in the early 1880s. At that point Jerez-produced brandy increased in popularity as a readily available alternative to French brandies. The Spanish brandy industry was given a further boost by the demands of troops in the Spanish Civil War, and by the needs of the industrial proletariat spawned by the post-war economic boom. As elsewhere, sales of basic Spanish grape spirit have dropped recently, but drinkers, and not only in Spain, continue to appreciate the better qualities on offer.

The success of Spanish brandy is due not only to its inherent qualities, but also to the fact that production is firmly in the hands of the major SHERRY producers. They are big enough, and proud enough, to ensure that the quality is regular and that the brandies are properly promoted, not only in Spain but, increasingly, throughout the world. Indeed during the 1960s and 1970s, when the Rumasa empire was rapidly built on selling huge volumes of sherry at uneconomic prices, many of the locally owned firms such as Bobadilla and Osborne survived only through the profits from their brandies.

The name Brandy de Jerez, used by most Jerez producers, is slightly misleading. The brandy is indeed matured in Jerez, in old sherry casks, or BUTTS, using the same SOLERA system used for sherry maturation. But the wine comes not from Jerez (which would be far too dear) but from the AIRÉN grape grown on such a massive scale on the dusty plain of La MANCHA 240 km/150 miles south of Madrid. Like the wines used for other fine brandies, Airén wine is acid and relatively characterless. It is higher in alcohol than most base wines for brandy, however, often reaching the still at over 12 per cent, heavily sulphured not only because of its strength, but also because much of it is stored for many months after fermentation. It was the opening of a RAILWAY line in 1945 which facilitated this business opportunity for the Jerezanos.

Spanish brandy is special in that it can be distilled in any one of four ways, although the word AGUARDIENTE may be applied to the products of all of them. The base wine may be distilled either once or twice in pot stills; or continuously distilled either up to the legal EU maximum of 86 per cent alcohol, when it is called *destilados de vino*; or to about 70 per cent alcohol, the same strength as cognac, in which case it is called *holandas*. The Spaniards are delightfully vague about all this; only a handful of technicians in each firm seem to know which method is being used.

But all the Jerez firms mature their brandies in soleras using American oak casks. What the locals call their 'dynamic' system matures the spirit much faster than the 'static' way in which other brandies are matured in a single cask. The brandy is cascaded down the casks in the solera at least three or four times a year (depending on the final house style required) and is therefore deliberately exposed to air several times annually. As a result a year-old *holandas* is already drinkable, while a two-year-old brandy matured in a solera is as mature as a three- or four-year-old cognac. As with sherry, the solera system also guarantees a consistent house style. In the late 1980s the Jerezanos codified the rules—which most firms were following anyway. To be called Brandy de Jerez Solera the spirit has to be matured for at least six months, Reservas for a year, and a Gran Reserva for at least three.

House styles start in the solera with the choice of casks (those previously used for OLOROSO sherry give a naturally rich final result). The house with the richest style is Osborne (pronounced Osbornay) which adds specially grown and macerated plums, almonds, and other fruits and nuts to its brandies at an early stage in the maturation process, and uses dry warehouses to retain the brandies' strength. At the other extreme is GONZALEZ BYASS, with light, often elegant, rather un-Spanish brandies. In the middle comes DOMECQ, whose basic brand Fundador is synonymous with Spanish brandy outside Spain. It is a worthy ambassador, since Domecq is more sophisticated than its rivals. Even Fundador is mostly *holandas*, and Domecq also distils on the lees, using a hot water spray on them to boost the brandy's natural richness.

The firms' pride and joy are their luxury products. The Conde d'Osborne is chiefly remarkable for coming in the only liquor bottle ever designed by Salvador Dali, while the sweetness and richness of Domecq's Marqués de Domecq clearly comes from the grape and the wood rather than from any additive.

Most of the others have names associated with the great age of Spain. The brandy most favoured by rich Hispanics (in Latin America as well as in Spain itself) is the rich, naturally sweet Cardinal Mendoza from Sanchez Romate which is double-distilled and kept in oloroso casks. It is named after the belligerent prelate who finally chased the Arabs from Granada. The rich but unremarkable Gran Duque d'Alba is named after the viceroy who butchered so many Dutch rebels. Bobadilla's rich and creamy Gran Capitan celebrates the memory of Pizarro, who conquered Peru, while Gonzalez Byass's Lepanto, Spain's most delicate and distinguished brandy, recalls the sea battle which dispatched the Turks from the western Mediterranean in 1571. N.F.

Faith, N., *Nicholas Faith's Guide to Cognac and Other Brandies* (London, 1992).

Gonzalez Gordon, M., chapter in *Sherry: The Noble Wine* (London, 1972).

BRANDY AND THE EUROPEAN UNION. On 12 June, 1989 the EUROPEAN UNION promulgated a set of regulations covering the official definition of BRANDIES within the Union. Brandies were defined in one of three ways:

GRAPE SPIRIT, *eau-de-vie de vin* in French, is produced by the DISTILLATION (or redistillation) of wine, FORTIFIED or unfortified, to no more than 86 per cent ALCOHOL by volume. For every hectolitre of pure alcohol, wine spirit also had to contain at least 125 g of volatile substances (other than ETHANOL and METHANOL), and a maximum of 200 g of methanol.

BRANDY, or *Weinbrand* in German, has the same specification as grape spirit except that it can be distilled up to 94.8 per cent alcohol. It has to contain at least 200 rather than 125 g of volatile substances, and has to be aged for at least one year in large OAK containers, or for at least six months in oak casks holding less than 1,000 l/26,400 gal.

POMACE BRANDY, or marc in French, has to be produced exclusively by the distillation of grape POMACE, with or without added water. A percentage of LEES may be added. The whole has to be distilled to no more than 86 per cent alcohol, so that the distillate retains the aromatic contents of the raw materials. For every hectolitre of pure alcohol, the spirit must contain a minimum of 140 g of volatile substances (other than ethanol and methanol), and a maximum of 1,000 g of methanol. The term GRAPPA can be applied only to grape marc spirit produced in Italy. N.F.

BRAQUET, scented red grape variety used for BELLET. See also BRACHETTO, its Italian incarnation.

BRAZIL, vast country and third most important wine producer in SOUTH AMERICA, after Argentina and Chile, with an average annual production of about 3 million hl/79 million gal in the late 1980s and early 1990s.

The vine was introduced in São Paulo state by the Portuguese as early as 1532. Spanish vines were introduced by the Jesuits in Rio Grande do Sul in 1626, but viticulture was abandoned after the destruction of Jesuit missions in the south of the country. In the 18th century settlers from the Azores tried for a third time to establish VINIFERA vine cuttings brought from Madeira and the Azores, but encountered severe problems in the hot, humid climate. The first vines to be successfully cultivated in Brazil were the HYBRID Isabella that was first planted on the south coast of Rio Grande in 1840, but it was not until the arrival of Italian immigrants in the high Serra Gaucha region in the north east of Rio Grande do Sul that viticulture was definitively established in Brazil, and even then, in the late 1870s, it was mainly Isabella that was cultivated, subsequently supplemented by Italian varieties such as Barbera, Bonarda, Moscato, and Trebbiano.

Only in the early 20th century was any sort of national wine market established, with the development of communications between the centres of population such as Rio de Janeiro and the wine regions in the far south. The first CO-OPERATIVES were established in the late 1920s.

Wines with serious claims to quality were not developed until the 1970s, when several important multinational corporations, including MOËT & CHANDON and MARTINI & ROSSI, established wine companies in Brazil and invested in modern wine-making equipment such as automatic TEMPERATURE CONTROL, STAINLESS STEEL, and imported BARRIQUES. Vine varieties such as Chardonnay, Welschriesling (Riesling Italico), Sémillon, Gewürztraminer, Cabernet Franc, Merlot, and Cabernet Sauvignon were also imported, and a programme of viticultural improvements embarked upon.

Modern Brazilian viticulture is concentrated in the extreme south of the country in the state of Rio Grande do Sul, principally on the high, hilly Serra Gaucha region, north and inland of the state capital Pôrto Alegre, and also in the much smaller, newer Frontera wine region on the border with URUGUAY and Argentina.

Serra Gaucha incorporates about 33,000 ha/81,500 acres of vineyard, at an average ALTITUDE of 700 m/2,300 ft, which is difficult to mechanize, and shared between so many small farmers that the average vineyard holding is just 3 ha. The relatively acid soils are shallow, not particularly fertile, and have a high proportion of water-retaining clay. Average RAINFALL here is very high for a wine region, about 1,800 mm/70 in, of which 700 mm falls during the growing season of September to February. The resulting effect on grape RIPENING means that ENRICHMENT of some sort, usually CHAPTALIZATION, is almost always necessary. FUNGAL DISEASES are a constant threat in this humid climate, and more than three-quarters of all vines are hybrids, still chiefly Isabella, grown to produce GRAPE JUICE, TABLE GRAPES, and wine of the most basic quality.

The most common vine-TRAINING SYSTEMS are TENDONE to minimize the ROT that is a perennial problem and ESPALIER to encourage ripening of red wine varieties. For the *vinifera* varieties such as Trebbiano, Chardonnay, Cabernet Sauvignon, Cabernet Franc, Merlot, Petite Sirah, and a number of Muscats, efforts are being made to reduce YIELDS, however, in attempts to maximize wine quality.

The grapes are often picked before full ripeness is reached and the white wines of Serra Gaucha are usually high in MALIC ACID without being unpleasantly tart. Different wineries have different policies on the desirability of MALOLACTIC FERMENTATION for white wines. Red wines are, inevitably in this climate, relatively light and acid, although there has been some experimentation with new OAK.

Within Serra Gaucha, Garibaldi, where the Moët subsidiary Provifin (an important producer of still and sparkling wine) is based, is the centre for sparkling wine production, many of these wines being made in the image of SPUMANTE, for Italian influence is strong in the region. Farroupilha can produce good-quality grapes for red wine (and substantial quantities for local VERMOUTH), while Flores de Cunha is the source of much everyday wine. Bento Gonçalves is a sort of tourist centre for the wine industry.

Between 1975 and the early 1990s about 800 ha of vines, all *vinifera* varieties, had been planted in the new Frontera wine region on the border with Uruguay, chiefly in the communes of Santana do Livramento and Pinheiro Machado. This is much flatter country, used substantially for pasture and cereal crops, with sandy soils and good DRAINAGE. Most vines are trained using some sort of espalier system, and the average annual rainfall is 1,400 mm, less than Sierra Gaucha but still high enough to prejudice ripening. It is too early to pass judgement on this new wine region.

Small amounts of wine are also made from the 1,500 ha of vines grown in the San Francisco Valley region in the arid north of the country near Recife in Pernambuco state. TROPICAL VITICULTURE is the rule at this LATITUDE of just nine degrees. The cycle of grape vine growth is controlled by PRUNING and IRRIGATION, and up to five crops can be produced in a two-year period. The grapes here, mainly Piróvano, are chiefly sold as table grapes but some particularly alcoholic wine, both red and white, is made.

Local wine is a relatively recent addition to Brazilian culture, and average consumption is still low except in the predominantly European communities of the south, although interest in Brazilian wine both domestically and on export markets is growing.

BREATHING, an activity, believed beneficial, attributed by some consumers to wine standing for a few hours in an opened bottle before it is served. In fact, in such circumstances the wine can take only the most minimal of 'breaths', and any change is bound to be imperceptible (except possibly in the case of BOTTLE SICKNESS). The surface area of wine exposed to the air is so small that the effects of any AERATION and OXIDATION are negligible. See also DECANTING.

BREEDING. See VINE BREEDING.

BREGANZE, DOC zone for a range of red and white often VARIETAL wines in the VENETO region of north east Italy. Although some of the vineyards are in the foothills of the alps to the north of the city of Vicenza, a large percentage of them are in the gravel soils of the plain. Some rather anonymous wines based on TOCAI, PINOT BLANC, VESPAIOLA, CABERNET, MERLOT, and PINOT NOIR are made, none of which is widely known outside the zone itself. Such international fame as the zone has is due to the efforts of a single producer, Fausto Maculan, who has travelled widely in France and California, planted CABERNET SAUVIGNON, CHARDONNAY, and SAUVIGNON Blanc, invested heavily in small oak barrels, and experimented with densely planted vineyards on French models, as well as producing important dessert wines from grapes with NOBLE ROT (the rare Acininobili, and the Torcolato mentioned under DRIED GRAPE WINES). Despite the excellence of his products, he has remained an isolated figure in Breganze. D.T.

BRETON, name used in the middle Loire for the CABERNET FRANC grape. The reference is not to Brittany but to Abbot Breton, who is reputed to have disseminated the vine in the 17th century.

BRETTANOMYCES, sometimes called **Brett**, one of the YEAST genera found occasionally on grapes and in wines. It is usually considered a spoilage yeast since it can produce off-flavours in wines variously described as 'mousey' and 'metallic' (see FAULTS for an explanation of how this fault is not immediately apparent). Nearly all of the *Brettanomyces* species are very sensitive to SULPHUR DIOXIDE so its presence in a winery may indicate less than perfect HYGIENE, or a low-sulphur wine-making regime. Once it is embedded in COOPERAGE, or obvious in a wine, it can be difficult to eliminate. A low level of *Brettanomyces* flavour in a wine may not be unpleasant, indeed it has been known to beguile some tasters in some wines. See also DEKKERA. A.D.W.

Heresztyn, T., 'Formation of substituted tetrahydropyridines by species of *Brettanomyces* and *Lactobacillus* isolated from mousey wines', *American Journal of Enology and Viticulture*, 37 (1986), 127–32.

BRÉZÈME, curious small area just south of Valence in the northern RHÔNE which claims the right to prefix its name to the Côtes-du-Rhône appellation and produces sturdy, rather rustic reds from Syrah grapes.

BRICCO, or *bric* in the dialect of the north west Italian region of PIEDMONT, indicates the highest part of an elevation in the landscape or, in particular, a vineyard with a steep gradient at the top of a hill. The term was first used on a wine label by Luciano de Giacomi in 1969 for his Bricco del Drago, a blend of DOLCETTO and NEBBIOLO grapes from Alba, and has been extensively used for the other wines of Piedmont ever since. D.T.

BRINDISI, Adriatic port and DOC for robust red wine made mainly from NEGROAMARO grapes in south east Italy. For more details see APULIA.

BRITAIN, or **Great Britain**, has long been one of the most important international markets for wine. In the late 1980s and early 1990s it imported more wine than any country other than Germany. Its long wine MERCHANT tradition has made it one of the most fastidious, yet open-minded, wine-consuming nations. Domestic vine-growing in England and Wales is on too small a scale to affect consumers who expect to find the wines of the world on the shelves of their specialist merchants and, increasingly, supermarkets. A certain amount of wine is also made from imported grape concentrate (see BRITISH WINE).

Historically, Britain's commercial influence helped shape the very existence of such wines as claret, madeira, marsala, port, and sherry (see BRITISH INFLUENCE).

See also ENGLAND (especially for history and modern viticulture), SCOTLAND, and WALES.

BRITISH INFLUENCE ON THE WINE TRADE. For centuries wine consumption in Britain has had significant ramifications in many of the world's most important wine regions. A cool, wet climate has limited the production of ENGLISH WINE, so that British wine drinkers have had no choice but to look overseas for their supplies. Since they owe no permanent allegiance to any one wine region or wine-producing country, they have traditionally had a broad range from which to choose, although that choice has been dictated by convenience, FASHION, and politics as often as by taste.

British influence on the wine trade resulted from more complex circumstances than a simple lack of native wines, however. (Otherwise, British influence on the wine trade would be no greater than, for example, Swedish or Danish—although see DUTCH WINE TRADE.) Britain enjoyed a unique combination of factors: relative prosperity and political power, a world-wide commercial empire supported by a strong navy, and a steadily increasing middle class. These circumstances not only helped to foster an interest in imported wines, but also provided the economic clout to acquire them. And at certain times in history, in specific wine regions, the British market was so influential that wine styles evolved, or completely new wines were invented, to satisfy its demands.

The first region fully to devote itself to British needs was SOUTH WEST FRANCE, when it belonged to the English crown. Indeed it could be argued that for 300 years, from 1152, Britain did have her own vines. During this medieval period BORDEAUX was transformed into the most important wine centre in France. Vineyards were planted or extended around the city and far up the rivers Garonne and Dordogne to quench the English thirst. The loss of Bordeaux to the French in 1453 saw a decline in exports to England but this part of France was by now well established as a commercial wine region.

During the Middle Ages wine was relatively cheap and plentiful in Britain. Wines from Germany, Portugal, Spain, Italy, Greece, the Mediterranean islands, and the Holy Land (see CRUSADES) could all be found in London taverns, as well as those from France. It was not until the 16th century, however, that British merchants found, in southern Spain, a wine region to compensate for the loss of Bordeaux. Known collectively as SACK, the wines of Andalucía became immensely fashionable in Tudor times despite wars with Spain. Thousands of BUTTS of wine were sent back to England by British merchants settled in Sanlúcar and MÁLAGA. British taste and investment laid the foundations of what was to become the SHERRY industry.

The 17th century brought many problems for wine. The introduction of exotic new beverages such as coffee, chocolate, and teas (see COFFEE HOUSES), as well as the growing popularity of 'hopped' beer, threatened the wine trade (see BEER). The situation was not eased by the fact that the cost of wine had steadily grown to such a point that only the middle and upper classes could afford it. Crippling customs duties exacerbated the crisis. If the wine trade was to survive in Britain some drastic changes needed to be effected.

Medieval CLAIRET and Tudor SACK had been staple beverages enjoyed by many Englishmen. British influence at the end of the 17th century was felt by a different sort of wine producer and encouraged the development of sophisticated superior-quality wines which only a limited clientele could afford. This select English market had particular influence in two areas of France: Bordeaux and CHAMPAGNE.

After the Restoration of Charles II in 1660, all things French were extremely fashionable in London. At this time individual producers in both Champagne and Bordeaux were making efforts to improve the quality of their wines. Champagne was promoted in London by French exiles (although it was English aristocrats who developed the taste for sparkling wine when French connoisseurs decried it as an aberration). Meanwhile a wealthy landowner from Bordeaux, Arnaud de Pontac, succeeded in creating a stir when he opened a restaurant in London, Pontack's Head in Abchurch Street, to sell the wines of his Graves estate of HAUT-BRION.

The English aristocracy were delighted by these new styles of French wines, CLARET, and paid through the nose for them. Thus London became the chief market for fine wine and in turn influenced the quality of the wines themselves, for in the wine trade it is export that makes reputations, raises standards, and, above all, provides the driving force for investment. New vineyards were planted in Champagne and in the MÉDOC to exploit these refined English palates and purses.

The next great instance of a British-inspired wine was PORT. The exorbitant cost of champagne and good-quality claret, combined with the supply difficulties that resulted from WAR with France, caused British merchants to look elsewhere. Political rapprochement with Portugal signalled the possibility of a new, and cheap, source of wine. The British moved into OPORTO, prospected the DOURO valley for wine and vine-growing potential, and started a boom. Huge quantities of port were sent to Britain from the early 1700s, and as the century progressed the nature of the wine evolved to suit. Originally a rough red table wine, it was soon discovered to be improved by the addition of brandy, which made it even more palatable to the English, and considerably more stable for the sea voyage required. A whole new industry was created and the steep sides of the Douro valley terraced and planted to victual the English shires.

Similarly, Sicily's MARSALA wine industry was developed by the British when, in the early years of the 19th century, Napoleon set up his Continental System hoping that, by depriving his enemies of French wine (among other things), he could cause British morale to collapse.

In 1860 William Gladstone stated that an Englishman's taste in wine 'is not an immutable, but a mutable thing'. He meant that British palates were capable of adapting to whatever was most available or pleasing at any particular period. A host of factors influenced taste and in turn demand influenced supply. Of all wine-drinking societies, Britain showed these developments most strikingly. Top-quality claret, sparkling champagne, and distinguished vintage port are today sought after by a world-wide clientele. But ties of tradition and affection remain strong with the British market, a reminder of the fundamental part it played in the evolution of these and many other wines, and the wine trade in general.

In the late 1980s and early 1990s, Great Britain has been targeted by many of the world's wine producers as one of the few substantial wine markets in which per capita wine consumption is not falling. Only Germany imports more wine than Great Britain, but a substantial proportion of this is basic wine for processing into TAFELWEIN or SEKT, some of which is re-exported.

The presence of the principal wine auctioneers (see AUCTIONS) has made London the focus of the fine wine market, just as it is of wine trade education by virtue of the Institute of MASTERS OF WINE. H.B.

Francis, A. D., *The Wine Trade* (London, 1972).
Johnson, H., *The Story of Wine* (London and New York, 1989).
Simon, A. L., *The History of the Wine Trade in England* (London, 1906–9).

BRITISH WINE, a curious alcoholic drink made in the image of WINE from GRAPE CONCENTRATE imported into Great BRITAIN. It is known as MADE WINE, and a decidedly manufactured product it is. Grape must in concentrated form is imported in bulk throughout the year from wherever happens to be able to supply the best value (CYPRUS was a notable source in the early 1990s). The must, concentrated to the consistency of thin honey, is eventually reconstituted by adding water and is fermented using selected YEAST strains, under the most rigorous technical controls, according to the wine style required. Until the 1980s almost all British wine produced was FORTIFIED, and made to resemble SHERRY or PORT, or flavoured with ginger or other spices or fruits. British wine-makers have done their best to replicate the relevant wine-making techniques, including some old COOPERAGE for wood maturation and even a FLOR solera for a British version of FINO. Since the early 1980s British wines of normal table wine strength have also been made, much to the dismay of the producers of British wine, with whose products made from freshly picked grapes there is considerable confusion.

The British wine producers, few and relatively industrial, claim as initial historical precedent a Francis Chamberleyne who was granted a charter by Charles I in 1635 to make wine from imported raisins. Wine continued to be made from imported raisins, but the real catalyst for the establishment of an economically viable British wine trade came when a technique for the CONCENTRATION of GRAPE JUICE was perfected by Emmanuel Roche of Toulouse, south west France. Two Greek brothers Mitzotakis, members of his wife's family, had come to London in 1900 trying to sell a surplus stock of Greek grapes and grape juice that was no longer required by their previous customer in France. As soon as Roche had perfected a way of transporting grape juice safely and cheaply, so thick and sugary that it was completely stable, and much less bulky than grapes or unconcentrated juice to boot, the Mitzotakis brothers established the Crown Grape Wine Company (on the site of a previous VINEGAR plant) in Fulham, south west London. By 1908 they were producing about a million bottles a year, and the company, now called Vine Products, had soon to move to larger premises outside the capital in Kingston-upon-Thames, described in the 1960s, in a reference to its production of SHERRY style wines, as 'the biggest BODEGA in Europe'. This highly profitable concern was eventually taken over by Allied Breweries and, by the 1970s, was being run, somewhat incongruously, in tandem with HARVEYS of Bristol, the principal producers of real sherry.

Abbott, J. H. C., *British Wines* (London, 1975).

BRIX, scale of measuring total dissolved compounds in grape juice, and therefore its approximate concentration of grape sugars. It is used in the United States and, like other scales used elsewhere (see BAUMÉ and OECHSLE), it can be measured with either a REFRACTOMETER or HYDROMETER. Degrees Brix indicate the percentage of solutes (of which about 90 per cent are sugars in ripe grapes) by weight in the liquid, at a temperature specified for the instrument used. One degree Brix corresponds approximately to 18 g/l sugar.

The **Balling** scale is similar although the specified temperature may differ. B.G.C.

BROADBENT, J. MICHAEL (1927–), wine taster, writer, and auctioneer known particularly for his experience of fine, old wines. Broadbent trained initially as an architect in London but was not as enthused by its more prosaic aspects as by the fine wines to which a family friend had introduced him. He joined the late Tommy Layton as a wine trade trainee in 1952. Three years later he joined HARVEYS of Bristol, then in its heyday, where he worked for Harry WAUGH and eventually became UK sales director. In 1966, partly as a result of his own personal enterprise in corresponding with the chairman, Broadbent was taken on by Christie's to revive their wine AUCTION business. Since then he has been director of Christie's wine department and in that capacity has traded in and tasted a greater number of fine wines than anyone else in the world.

Naturally didactic, he has been lecturing on wine since the late 1950s and it is as a conductor of wine tastings that he is distinguished. He sees it as his duty to ensure that tasting conditions are correct, and has no inhibitions about airing his elegant wine vocabulary in public. His passion is not for wine consumption, or for the relaxed sociability associated with it, but for the rigorous analysis of each measured mouthful of wine (he sees his wristwatch as an important TASTING accessory, monitoring how a wine evolves in the glass). In his architect's handwriting, he has recorded his disciplined impressions of every wine tasted, over 60,000 of them in more than 100 notebooks.

It is these notebooks, retyped by his equally hard-working wife Daphne, which form the basis for Broadbent's *Great Vintage Wine Book*, a unique record of wine-tasting history which stretches back to wines of the early 18th century. Unlike PARKER, his most obvious young rival, Broadbent eschews

Michael **Broadbent**, with madeira.

scoring wines with NUMBERS between 50 and 100, but does award up to five stars to each wine.

As a result of his prominence as a literate and articulate wine taster, he has been invited to attend and often conduct most important wine tastings, many of them arranged specifically around his frenetic international schedule. With Hugh JOHNSON and others he is a consultant to British Airways.

Broadbent's life has been marked by competition, particularly with Sotheby's, and ambition. While at Christie's he not only wrote his own classic on the subject of *Wine Tasting*, first published in 1968 and much republished since, but instituted and directed Christie's Wine Publications, which issued many invaluable books—including the *Christie's Wine Review* anthologies—during the 1970s and 1980s. He has also written a monthly column of tasting notes for the British magazine *Decanter* since its inception.

Incurably active and apparently indefatigable, he became a MASTER OF WINE in 1960, a freeman of the City of London in 1964, chairman of the Institute of Masters of Wine in 1970, international president of the INTERNATIONAL WINE & FOOD SOCIETY in 1986, master of the City of London's Distillers' Company in 1990, council chairman of the Wine & Spirit Trades Benevolent Society in 1991, and even stood as sheriff of the City of London in 1993. He was made a Chevalier de l'Ordre du Mérite National in 1979.

Parnell, C.,'Michael Broadbent: man of great taste', *Decanter* (Mar. 1992).

Suckling, J., 'The world's most experienced taster' *The Wine Spectator* (15 Nov., 1991).

BROKERS, important members of any trade, including the wine trade. Known charmingly as *courtiers* in French, brokers can play a vital role as middlemen between vine-growers and merchants, or NÉGOCIANTS, collecting and exhibiting hundreds of samples, or *échantillons*, taking a small percentage of any eventual sale. Another class of brokers, further along the distribution chain, guide those who sell wine through the maze of those who produce it, some of them nursing 'stables' of producers rather in the manner of a literary agent representing a rollcall of authors. And then, just one or two links away from those who actually pull the cork, there are the fine wine brokers, those who sell from a list of glamorous properties and vintages which may, but often do not, belong to them.

BROUILLIS, spirit of about 30 per cent alcohol produced by the first distillation in a POT STILL.

BROUILLY, largest of the Beaujolais Crus, produces some of the most robust, most textured of these red wines. About 1,200 ha/29,600 acres of vineyards flank the volcanic Mont Brouilly. **Côte de Brouilly** is an entirely separate appellation including just 290 ha of land higher up the hillside. The wine produced tends to be more concentrated and longer lived than that of Brouilly.

BRULHOIS, CÔTES DU, red wine VDQS in SOUTH WEST FRANCE. About 160 ha/395 acres of Bordeaux vine varieties plus the Gascon TANNAT are still grown in the rolling farmland down river of Moissac on both sides of the river Garonne. From medieval times the Brulhois wines of the HAUT PAYS were blended with those of Bordeaux down river but the ravages of PHYLLOXERA in the late 19th century were followed by widespread planting of HYBRIDS. The district's wines made from recently replanted VINIFERA vines were given VIN DE PAYS status initially before an elevation to VDQS in 1985. The wines are usually well coloured and the best can offer a good meeting-point between Gascon and Bordelais influences. Most are consumed locally.

BRUNELLO, conventionally the name for a strain of SANGIOVESE particularly well adapted to the vineyards of Montalcino in TUSCANY in central Italy producing most notably, therefore, BRUNELLO DI MONTALCINO. The 1990 vineyards survey of Italy found just over 1,000 ha/2,470 acres planted with this particular subvariety.

BRUNELLO DI MONTALCINO is the youngest of Italy's prestigious red wines, having been invented as a wine in its own right by Ferruccio BIONDI-SANTI, the first to bottle it and give it a distinctive name, in 1888. Conventional descriptions of the birth of the wine stress Biondi-Santi's successful isolation of a superior CLONE of SANGIOVESE, the Sangiovese Grosso or BRUNELLO, but enthusiastic descriptions of the wines of Montalcino by Cosimo Ridolfi (1831), and the fact that a wine of Clemente Santi, described as a 'select red wine (brunello)', had been a prize-winning entry in the agricultural fair of Montepulciano in 1865, indicate that genetically superior material was available in the zone at an earlier date. (And some records show the wines of Montalcino referred to as Brunello as early as the 14th century; see TUSCANY, history.)

Climate is perhaps a more significant factor than specific clones in creating the characteristics of the wine: the town of Montalcino, 112 km/70 miles south of Florence, enjoys a warmer, drier climate than the various zones of CHIANTI, and the open countryside around it ensures both excellent ventilation and cool evenings and nights. The Sangiovese reaches its maximum ripeness here, giving fuller, richer wines than anywhere else in Tuscany, whose ALCOHOLIC STRENGTH is frequently over 14° and whose levels of dry EXTRACT approach 30 g/l. Brunello di Montalcino is the only important Tuscan red wine whose Sangiovese has never been blended with other varieties.

The oenological practices of first Ferruccio Biondi-Santi and then his son Tancredi Biondi-Santi—prolonged FERMENTATION and five to six years' CASK AGEING for the superior RISERVA—established a model of Brunello as a full, intense, and long-lasting wine. Only four vintages—1888, 1891, 1925, 1945—were declared in the first 57 years of production, contributing an aura of rarity to the wine that translated into high prices and, in Italy at least, incomparable prestige. The Biondi-Santi were the only commercial producers until after the Second World War and a government report of 1932 named Brunello as an exclusive product of the family and estimated its total production at just 200 hl/5,280 per year.

Even in 1960 there were only 11 bottlers, rising to 25 in 1970, 53 in 1980, and 87 in 1990. The total area planted was a mere 63.5 ha/157 acres in 1960, but it had jumped to 626 ha in 1980 and reached almost 1,250 ha by 1993. Substantial amounts of outside capital entered the zone in the 1970s and 1980s, restoring vineyards and wine-making facilities; a considerable number of small peasant proprietors also began to bottle their own Brunello. Although the better products have been widely in demand at high prices, quality levels have undeniably been irregular. The dubious condition of many of the casks and the lengthy obligatory ageing periods regardless of the characteristics of the vintage have unquestionably not helped the wine.

The DOC regulations of 1960 established a minimum period of cask ageing of 42 months, confirmed in 1980 by the DOCG rules. A campaign to lower this period gained support, not without vocal opposition, in the latter half of the 1980s, and the minimum ageing period was lowered to 36 months in 1990. The total ageing period of 48 months has remained, however, and the financial burden of holding wine for four years has reduced actual production (41,178 hl in 1989) below the total potential production of 50,178 hl/1.32 million gal.

There has been a corresponding increase in the production of Rosso di Montalcino, a red DOC wine that can be marketed after one year, with an estimated 1.8 million bottles produced in 1990. The availability of a second DOC into which lesser wines can be declassified is expected to have a positive impact on the quality of Brunello, in addition to its obvious advantages for the cash flow of producers.

See also VINO NOBILE DI MONTEPULCIANO. D.T.

Anderson, B., *The Wine Atlas of Italy* (London and New York, 1990).
Gleave, D., *The Wines of Italy* (London and New York, 1989).

BRUSH, the flesh remaining attached to the top of the berry stalk, or stem, after a grape is pulled off the bunch, as occurs during MECHANICAL HARVESTING or DESTEMMING, for example. The brush's size varies between vine varieties, from a barely discernible bit of flesh to a 'tongue' up to 5 mm/0.2 in long. The brush is caused by strong adhesion between the berry and stem, causing tearing of the skin, combined with particular characteristics of the zone of the flesh at the base of the berry; microscopically, this tissue has a core of vascular fibres embedded in small, rounded cells with large air spaces between. The cells of the brush are rich in TANNINS. Berries lack a brush if they develop a corky abscission layer at the junction of the grape and the stem, as occurs with some varieties, or if a berry is partially injured during RIPENING. The French term is *pinceau*.

The word brush is also used in the USA for the total cane growth evident after leaf fall. B.G.C.

BRUT, French word meaning 'crude' or 'raw', adapted by the CHAMPAGNE industry for wines made without (much) added sweetening or DOSAGE. It has come to be used widely for any SPARKLING WINE to indicate one that tastes bone dry. Technically a brut champagne should contain fewer than 15 g/l RESIDUAL SUGAR, a maximum level which, in less naturally acidic still wines, would seem medium dry (see SWEETNESS). A wine labelled **extra brut** should contain less than 6 g/l residual sugar and may incorporate no dosage at all. Particularly dry wines may also be labelled **brut natur(e)**. The word **bruto** may be used in Portugal.

BUAL, Anglicized form of BOAL, name of several Portuguese white grape varieties much planted in the 19th century. Most famously, Bual came to represent a style of MADEIRA, richer than SERCIAL and VERDELHO, yet not as sweet as that called MALMSEY. In reality, total plantings of any form of Boal were extremely small, and were almost exclusively Boal Cachudo clustered around Câmara de Lobos on the south coast. For more information, see MADEIRA.

BUÇACO, range of forested hills between DÃO and BAIRRADA in central Portugal where the Palace Hotel bottles some of the country's most sought-after wines. For more details, see BAIRRADA.

BUCELAS, historic white wine enjoying a revival of interest in its native PORTUGAL, sometimes spelt **Bucellas**. It is thought to be Shakespeare's Charneco, mentioned in *Henry VI, Part II* and named after one of the local villages. The duke of Wellington popularized the wine in Britain following the Peninsular Wars and for a time Bucelas was widely sold and appreciated in Victorian Britain as Portuguese Hock. (This undoubtedly helped to perpetuate the story that the ARINTO grape, the main variety in Bucelas, was related to Germany's RIESLING, a theory that does not stand up to AMPELOGRAPHIC scrutiny. Both Arinto and its aptly named partner ESGANA CÃO, meaning 'dog strangler', share the ability to make acidic, dry white wine in a sub-mediterranean climate.) After such an illustrious past, this tiny white wine denomination just north of Lisbon, Portugal's capital city (see map on p. 750), had almost disappeared by the early 1980s, the production of Bucelas having been concentrated in the hands of a single firm who let standards slip. In the early 1990s, new enterprises are helping to revive an old tradition. R.J.M.

BUD, a primordial shoot covered by leaf-like structures and borne in the axils of leaves. *Bourgeon* is French for bud. Grapevine buds are classified as compound and fruitful; their development is complex. B.G.C.

BUDBREAK, or **budburst**, a stage of annual vine development during which small shoots emerge from vine buds in the spring. This process begins the new growing season and signals the end of DORMANCY, their period of winter sleep. The first sign that budbreak is imminent is BLEEDING, when the vines begin to drip water from pruning cuts. The buds left at winter pruning begin to swell in the few weeks prior to budbreak, and budbreak itself is marked by the first signs of green in the vineyard, as the young leaves unfold and push through the buds. Although changing only gradually at first, the buds are soon opened fully and small shoots are evident, growing a little longer and producing new leaves every few days.

Budbreak takes place in early spring in cool climates, when the average air temperature is about 10 °C/50 °F. For many northern hemisphere regions budbreak occurs in March, and for the southern hemisphere in September. Budbreak is more uniform when winters are cold but not subject to WINTER FREEZE. In warm to hot regions budbreak is earlier, and in cooler regions it is delayed. In fact in the tropics (see TROPICAL VITICULTURE) the vines do not become properly dormant, and budbreak can take place at any time of the year. IRRIGATION, manipulation of PRUNING times, and GROWTH REGULATORS are used in these regions to control the time of budbreak.

Not all varieties show budbreak at the same temperature. For example, French studies indicate that for the early table grape Pearl of Csaba budbreak occurs at 5.6 °C, MERLOT at 9.4 °C, and UGNI BLANC at 11.0 °C. However, budbreak does not occur in the same variety on the same date or even at the same mean temperature each year. This probably depends on the degree of cold in the preceding winter, with lower winter temperatures causing it to happen more uniformly when budbreak is eventually encouraged by the warmer spring weather. Late pruning in winter delays budbreak, and this can be used to reduce the risk of winter FROST.

In temperate regions with warm winters, a few warm days, even in midwinter, can be enough to induce budbreak. One of the very few places around the world to show this problem is the MARGARET RIVER region in Western Australia. Because of the nearby moderating effects of the Indian Ocean, the midwinter (July) mean temperature is a warm 13 °C. CHARDONNAY vines are particularly prone to this premature budbreak, with only a few buds breaking on the vine in midwinter, and the rest somewhat erratically later in spring.

For vines which are properly pruned (see BALANCED PRUNING) most of the buds left at winter pruning will burst, and budbreak is near 100 per cent. Budbreak is, however, normally lower for buds in the middle of long CANES. When vines are left unpruned, as in MINIMAL PRUNING, it is the buds near the ends of canes which burst preferentially, as do the buds which are at the highest positions. This example of adaptive physiology helps vines to climb trees, important in their quest for light in their evolutionary forest habitat. Much the same effects are seen in modern vineyards. Buds which nearly always burst are the two buds on either side of the cane just below the pruning cut. This is connected with the flow of HORMONES in the plant and is the reason for pruning to two bud spurs. When the vine is lightly pruned, with many buds left, then the proportion of buds bursting is much less than 100 per cent. Thus, the vine in its natural unpruned state will not exhaust finite stored reserves of CARBOHYDRATES.

For the vine-grower, budbreak represents the beginning of about eight months' work before HARVEST, during which the vine must be protected from pests, VINE DISEASES, and climatological disaster. The biggest problem for many vineyards at this time of the year is spring FROST, to which the young shoot growth is particularly sensitive. If young shoots are killed by frost then the vines will push, or burst, more buds. However, since the most FRUITFUL buds burst first, the second growth of buds are sure to produce less than the one lost to the frost. R.E.S.

Huglin, P., *Biologie et écologie de la vigne* (Paris, 1986).
Winkler, A. J., *et al.*, *General Viticulture* (2nd edn., Berkeley, Calif., 1974).

BUDDING, the viticultural operation of GRAFTING where only a single bud is inserted. The term is also used in the context of BUDBREAK.

BUDWOOD, name give to vine CUTTINGS when they are destined for GRAFTING. Alternatively, cuttings may be planted directly into the nursery to grow one-year-old plants, or ROOTLINGS. Depending on the cutting length and bud spacing, four to 12 buds may be taken from each cutting. The budwood is typically put into cold storage to await grafting in the spring.

BUGEY, VINS DU, collective name for the wines of the Ain *département* just west of SAVOIE in eastern France. Many of the same grape varieties are grown here, although some from nearby JURA are also grown on this VDQS wine's total of nearly 400 ha/990 acres. Bugey was once part of Burgundy and under the medieval influence of MONKS AND MONASTERIES the area was an important wine producer. Today, almost all of its varied wines are consumed locally. About half of all wines are white, but there are rosés as well as light reds, fully sparkling **Vin du Bugey Mousseux** and lightly sparkling **Vin du Bugey Pétillant**, varietal wines as in ROUSSETTE du Bugey, and wines to which the name of a CRU may be suffixed, as, for example, **Vin du Bugey Cerdon** (which comes in still, pétillant, and mousseux versions!). The vines are widely dispersed and, among reds, may be the POULSARD (Mescle) of Jura, the MONDEUSE of Savoie, the Gamay of Beaujolais, or the Pinot Noir of Burgundy. White grapes grown are Burgundy's Chardonnay, Pinot Gris, and Aligoté: Savoie's ROUSSETTE (Altesse), MOLETTE, JACQUÈRE, and even a Mondeuse Blanche (Dongine). Wines sold as VARIETALS are made exclusively from that variety. Most of these wines are drunk locally, notably with the local cuisine of Bresse. A particular speciality among this disparate collection of grape varieties, wine styles, and TERROIRS is Rosé de Cerdon, which is usually lightly sparkling. These were the wines with which the notable gastronome Anthelme Brillat-Savarin grew up.

George, R., *French Country Wines* (London, 1990).

BUKETTRAUBE, white grape variety used mainly in South Africa for sweet and occasionally BOTRYTIZED dessert wines, with a slightly grapey aroma. The precise parentage of this German import is unclear, but there is an Alsace variety, originating in Würzburg, known as Bouquettraube. Several hundred hectares are planted mainly in cooler coastal areas. J.P.

BULGARIA, eastern European wine producer whose commercial success in the 1980s was built on inexpensive VARIETAL wines, especially Cabernet Sauvignon. Through its Thracian heritage (Thrace was an important wine region in Ancient GREECE), Bulgaria lays claim to being the birthplace of winemaking. Viniculture has been practised in this part of the world for more than three millennia, even if it was interrupted occasionally by Ottoman domination (see ISLAM). The Turks retained substantial vineyards for TABLE GRAPE production, however, so that vine-growing has been consistently one of Bulgaria's principal agricultural activities.

Geography and climate

Bulgaria is a small country just 400 km/250 miles from the western border to the Black Sea and 300 km/200 miles from Romania to the north and Greece and Turkey to the south. With the exception of the Balkan mountain range which runs east to west, vines are planted all over the country, although the modern wine industry has been based on rolling fertile flatlands. On the Transdanubian and upper Thracian plains, for example, the vineyards lie mainly between 100 and 300 m in altitude, although some south western vineyards are as high as 1000 m/3,280 ft.

Summers tend to be hot with temperatures up to 40 °C/104 °F while the temperature can fall to −25 °C in winter. Although the Black Sea has a moderating effect on the eastern side of the country, the climate tends to be dramatically continental.

The most common climatological hazards are FUNGAL DISEASES caused by humidity. In non-drought years rainfall and high temperatures combine to promote rot and both sorts of mildew which, thanks to Bulgaria's limited resources, are combated with nothing more sophisticated than SULPHUR sprays and BORDEAUX MIXTURE, depending on the health of the other crops farmed by individual agricultural co-operatives. Irrigation is not generally necessary and nor, thanks to hot summers, is CHAPTALIZATION.

History

Despite its long vinous heritage, underlined by archaeological evidence of neolithic wine production, Bulgaria's present wine industry is less than a century old and has undergone many changes in the last 100 years. While some of these changes have been responses to the market, many of them are the result of political interference, most notably the effects of the rise, and fall, of communism and of Comecon economics and politics.

At the beginning of the 20th century, most Bulgarian wineries were CO-OPERATIVES with many smallholders pooling their resources. Private estates existed but tended to be somewhat inward looking. Then in the 1930s the import and export of both wine and table grapes, at this stage a much more important export than wine, was given over to a single state monopoly, Vinprom. The new communist government, established in 1947, also nationalized wine production and quickly set about rationalizing the vineyards. Holdings of barely half a hectare gave way to much larger new co-operative enterprises. These were further developed in the 1960s when agro-industrial complexes were set up to grow crops as well as producing fertilizers, pesticides, and other agrochemicals. Vineyards, therefore, were tended by co-operatives also producing cereals, rice, and a host of other fruit and vegetables.

Even so, in the 1960s new grape varieties were introduced. Native varieties MAVRUD, MELNIK, PAMID, and Gamza gave way to Cabernet Sauvignon and Merlot. Among white varieties, RKATSITELI and WELSCHRIESLING yielded to proper Riesling, Chardonnay, and Sauvignon Blanc. It was this decision, allied to Vinprom's control of production and, to a certain extent, marketing, that set the scene for Bulgarian wine in the 1980s.

The vines were planted in vast vineyards, with high training and wide spacing to allow mechanization as well as hand picking. A standard CORDON, or occasionally double GUYOT system of vine training replaced the straggly bush systems previously used for the likes of Mavrud. The ethos of Bulgarian wine production changed from small peasant farming to vine-growing on a major industrial scale.

At the same time, wineries were also set up by Vinprom, independently of vine-growing, to take advantage of the new, better-quality grape produce. Initially the emphasis was on red wine production, so no great influx of new equipment was needed, although Soviet demand for sparkling and sweet wines was so great that investment in stainless steel tanks, proper FILTRATION systems, and glass-lined cement vats was initially financed by the Soviet Union, for long the principal export market for Bulgarian wine. Subsequently, new technology was subsidized by cheap loans from the Bulgarian government. New REFRIGERATION systems, improved filters, and better BOTTLING lines were all bought without western money.

Western expertise came with the men from Pepsico, the giant American cola manufacturers. Eager to trade their soft drink concentrate for a saleable product, they provided links with California's wine faculty at DAVIS, with Professor Maynard AMERINE, and with other western establishments and wineries. Much of the theory of modern wine production in Bulgaria is therefore California in origin, although many of the better technical winery staff also spent time in Europe, as well as at Bulgaria's own wine schools. Some wineries such as Suhindol, Russe, Sliven, Preslav, and Burgas benefited greatly from this, continuously learning and upgrading, immersing themslves in the culture of quality control to meet western standards. Others, for reasons of management culture, were unwilling or unable to modernize.

Recent developments

Between the mid 1960s and mid 1980s, the Bulgarian wine industry was making significant progress, in terms of both quality and exports of inexpensive but competently made varietals to the west, especially to Britain. Gorbachev's arrival as Soviet premier, however, had dire consequences for Bulgarian wine. His campaign to curb alcohol consumption in the USSR involved uprooting huge tracts of Bulgarian vineyard, some but not all of inferior quality.

Grape prices were then fixed every year, irrespective of quality, which encouraged the co-operatives to turn their attention away from vines to other crops. Dead, dying, or diseased vines were not replaced. Many vineyards were simply abandoned, and few were treated to any systematized training or pruning systems. Although there is some regional variation, by the early 1990s between 20 and 40 per cent of Bulgarian vines were either under-producing or dead, resulting in a shortage of grapes for quality wine production. In 1985 Bulgaria produced 4.5 million hl of wine, but in 1990, probably the best-quality vintage in 45 years, the total crop was just 1.8 million hl/119 million gal, and this at a time when exports to the west were at record levels. Average yield statistics can be relatively meaningless in the more neglected vineyards but in better-run vineyards such as those near Russe they are about 60 hl/ha/3.4 tons/acre for regular Cabernets, 90 hl/ha for varietal white wines, and 45 hl/ha for Controliran wines (see Quality categories below).

In the same year the wine sector was suddenly liberalized and Vinprom disbanded, as part of the free market reforms introduced in the wake of the fall of communism in 1989 when Bulgaria's Stalinist dictator Zhivkov was finally deposed. This has strengthened ties between vine-growing and wine production, most notably at the Suhindol winery in the north (although other wineries such as Assenovgrad continue to be marooned in an urban setting far from any vineyard).

In the early 1990s the Bulgarian wine industry was in disarray. The reformist government's promise to restore land to those who could prove they owned it before 1947 cast a shadow of uncertainty over both vineyards and wineries. Rampant inflation took its toll on the domestic market and the export market was in the throes of substantial and sometimes painful reorganization in response to the realities of the new free market economy. The USSR disappeared, both as a political entity and as a major customer for Bulgarian wine, leaving large volumes of unwanted sweet and sparkling wines together with outmoded equipment in many wineries. Investment in technology, as well as in vineyards, was urgently needed but understandably difficult to generate.

Grape varieties

Unusually for a whole country, Bulgaria's vineyards are dominated by Cabernet Sauvignon, Merlot, and, to a lesser extent, Pinot Noir. In many cases they are regarded as everyday grapes and vinified as such, although some Controliran wines achieve distinction. Some wineries have made a speciality of combinations that in France would be unthinkable, such as Sliven's blend of Merlot and Pinot Noir. Gamza, the KADARKA of Hungary, is widely planted in the north of the country, where it has a tendency to over-produce but can produce interestingly spicy wines if the growing season is long enough. More interesting to many palates are the indigenous red grape varieties MAVRUD and MELNIK, which may also be called Shiroka Melnishka Losa. The most widely planted indigenous red grape variety, however, is the undistinguished PAMID. There is also some SAPERAVI imported from the Soviet Union and a little of the variety known as Senzo, or Senso (CINSAUT).

Bulgaria grows a curious mix of white grape varieties, showing evidence of Serbian influence in its everyday DIMIAT, Georgian influence in its plantings of RKATSITELI, Romanian influence in its FETEASCA (often written Fetiaska), and general central European influence in its WELSCHRIESLING and MUSCAT OTTONEL. MISKET is a peculiarly Bulgarian crossing of Dimiat and Riesling and a red Misket is also a common ingredient in grapey white wines, most notably in the eastern region. Chardonnay, Riesling, Sauvignon, and Gewürztraminer are also planted, as well as Aligoté and Ugni Blanc, which may be blended together as at Varna. Bulgaria's white wines have betrayed the shortfall in winery investment more obviously than its reds.

The regions

Although vines are grown all over Bulgaria, there are five distinct wine regions with about 45 separate winery complexes. The only region which has no real wine production is the area round the capital Sofia, which does, however, have a large winery for processing and finishing. The winery, and its level of equipment, expertise, and commitment, is for the moment the most important quality determinant for Bulgarian wine.

Northern region This important area runs from Vidin in the north west across to Russe and south to the Balkan foothills. The region's wineries, of which some are very important, take their grapes from the rolling Transdanubian Plain, the Danube to the north providing water and moderation of summer temperatures. Key wineries include:

Russe: A promising winery at Bulgaria's fourth city, on the Danube and the Romanian border. One of the few wineries to draw grapes from HILLSIDE sites, this winery produces sound commercial whites as well as reds, most notably Cabernet Sauvignon from the Yantra valley whose first Controliran vintage was 1987.

Suhindol: Bulgaria's showcase winery, the rock upon which western markets were built, specializing in red wines, particularly Gamza but also Cabernet and Merlot in vast quantities. Real control is exercised over vineyards thanks to the formation of a larger co-operative with local growers. Wine is produced alongside local spirits *rakia*, usually a sort of MARC, and apple brandy, soft drinks, and salami for the domestic market.

Svishtov: Right on the Danube, specializes in Cabernet Sauvignon.

Eastern region The heart of white wine country where the climate is moderated by the Black Sea. Key wineries include:

Preslav, Khan Krum, Novi Pazar, Schumen: These nearby inland wineries produce a high proportion of Bulgaria's higher-priced white wine, especially Chardonnay, some of which is oak aged and even, at Preslav, barrel fermented. Some of these wineries are also trying hard with their Sauvignon Blanc, Gewürztraminer, and Riesling.

Varna: Bulgaria's major port also has a winery which specializes in more aromatic whites. The prestige Ch Euxinograd produces small quantities of promising Chardonnay.

Burgas, Pomorie: Neighbours on the Black Sea producing considerable quantities of white and increasing quantities of red wine, from Muscat Ottonel, Aligoté, Ugni Blanc, a little Chardonnay, Cabernet Sauvignon, and Merlot. Burgas rosé a speciality.

Sub-Balkan region The most mountainous region.

Slaviantzi: Most noted for its Sungurlare wines made from Chardonnay and Misket.

Sliven: On the south eastern foothills of the Balkans and therefore bordering on the diverse southern region (see below), Bulgaria's largest wine producer making spirits as well as Cabernet, Merlot, Chardonnay, Misket, and some Pinot Noir in huge quantities.

Southern region Vast area on the flat upper Thracian Plain from the Pirin mountains to the Black Sea producing cereals, rice, and a wide range of crops other than grapes. Main wineries include:

Haskovo, Stambolovo, Sakar: In the deep south of the country specializing in Merlot with those of Sakar being richer than those of Stambolovo.

Bulk transport: Bulk wine destined for bottling in Sweden travels half-way round the world from Penfolds base in Nuriootpa in South Australia.

Peruschitza, Assenovgrad: Neighbouring wineries near Plovdiv, Bulgaria's second city, best known for reds, with robust Mavrud an Assenovgrad speciality.

Stara Zagora: Most famous for its Cabernet and Merlot from the Oriachovitza region.

South western region This hot region by the Greek border is most notable for the picturesque town of Melnik, which gives its name to the indigenous distinctive vine of the same name, grown on nearby rugged hillsides and capable of much more concentration and longevity than is the current Bulgarian norm. Wineries which may eventually capitalize on this are at Harsovo, Petrich, and Damianitza.

Quality categories

A scheme drawn up in 1978 delineated four main categories of Bulgarian quality wine. Country wines are the equivalent of France's VIN DE PAYS (the name indicating Bulgaria's major market for such wines). Varietal wines of denominated geographical origin are the equivalent of France's VDQS while Reserve and Special Reserve wines are superior varietal wines aged for at least two years in the case of whites and three in the case of reds. Controliran is Bulgaria's answer to France's APPELLATION CONTRÔLÉE, wines from named varieties in specific vineyard sites. About 27 Controlirans had been registered by the end of the 1980s, by submitting three consecutive vintages to the state authority and conforming to this standard in subsequent vintages.

See also eastern European BRANDY. D.J.G.

Philpott, D., *The Wine & Food of Bulgaria* (London, 1989).

BULK METHOD, alternative name for the Charmat or tank method of SPARKLING WINE-MAKING.

BULK STORAGE of wine is important in the production and BLENDING of everyday commercial wines. Large storage tanks are usually made of stainless steel and may hold as much as 800,000 l/211,000 gal. OXIDATION is always a risk, and, if the tank is not completely filled with wine, the head space must be filled with an INERT GAS. The lower its storage temperature, the better such a wine will keep. Many commercial blends are bottled throughout the year from such tanks, which are kept at relatively low temperatures. If consumers were to become more demanding of individuality in their wines, these large storage containers would become rarer and the wineries of the future may have only small and medium-sized storage containers. A.D.W.

BULK TRANSPORT of wine is the movement of large quantities of wine within a single winery or from one place to another, typically where it was held in BULK STORAGE to the BOTTLING location.

Traditional, and traditionally minded, wineries are often sited on hillsides so that gravity can be used to move wine between successive processing sites. Most modern wineries rely on PUMPS instead.

The bulk transport of wine from one installation to another is most commonly done today by road tanker and/or ocean-going tank ships, although rail and barge are not unknown as means of transporting wine over long distances (while pipelines are occasionally used over short distances).

Whenever wine is moved, it is important to guard against OXIDATION. Danger points include the seals on pumps. Wine being delivered to a receiving tank should be filled from the bottom to prevent excessive aeration of the wine. If the tank must be filled from the top, then the tank should be filled with an INERT GAS such as nitrogen or carbon dioxide to displace any OXYGEN. A.D.W.

BULK WINE, or wine *en vrac*, as the French call it, is wine that is at or near the end of its ÉLEVAGE, and therefore ready to drink, but has not been put into smaller CONTAINERS such as BOTTLES. This may be because it is about to be packaged, or because it will be sold to another producer. BULK TRANSPORT is by far the cheapest way of moving wine and it is common for wine to move in bulk between producer and blender or bottler, possibly between continents and hemispheres.

Such wine may even be sold in measured quantities drawn off from some form of BULK STORAGE. In southern Europe it is still commonplace to take a container, perhaps a BONBONNE or large plastic container, to be filled with bulk wine, which is charged by the litre.

BULLAS, wine-producing zone in Spain's LEVANTE.

BULL'S BLOOD, branded red wine from HUNGARY which enjoyed notable success in the 1970s. It was then produced exclusively by the state-owned Egervin winery of EGER which shrouded the product in possibly convenient mystery. The principal grape variety was said to be KADARKA, but this was replaced by increasing proportions of KÉKFRANKOS, supplemented by CABERNET SAUVIGNON, MERLOT (here called Médoc Noir), and KÉKOPORTO. The wines were the product of longer MACERATION than was perhaps common at the time, and the blend was certainly given some age before bottling. Bikavér is Hungarian for Bull's Blood and a (sometimes different) blend is sold within Hungary as Egri Bikavér. From the early 1990s, the term Bull's Blood was used to denote a style of wine rather than being associated exclusively with Eger.

BUNCH, or cluster, the viticultural term for that part of the grapevine to which berries are attached. *Grappe* is the French term. Before the berries SET each berry position is occupied by a flower; a bunch is an INFLORESCENCE of the vine after berries have set. In the grapevine the inflorescence grows at the node on the side of the stem opposite to a leaf, an unusual position within the plant kingdom. It is closely related to a TENDRIL, both deriving from the same embryonic organ, the Anlage. Anlagen which develop in late spring often become inflorescences and grow slowly during that same summer, but more rapidly after budburst the following spring to become mature inflorescences about a year after their INITIATION. Anlagen which develop as the shoot tips lengthen after budburst evolve directly into TENDRILS. Anlagen on lateral shoots, however, where tip dominance is muted, may develop inflorescences which become what is known as a SECOND CROP. Unlike the main crop, these bunches are formed during the same summer.

Like a tendril, a grape bunch has two arms, called outer and inner. The inner arm develops the bulk of the bunch, while the outer arm may vary from a large, well-set 'wing' (as in the UGNI BLANC variety) to a small tendril arm without berries, or it may even abort. Berries on wings sometimes ripen differently from those on the main crop.

Bunches vary hugely in size depending on that year's FRUIT SET and VINE VARIETY, from a few grams to many kilograms. They also vary in shape and tightness depending on the lengthening and flexibility of the BUNCHSTEM and branches and, of course, on setting and BERRY SIZE. B.G.C.

BUNCH ROTS, or **berry rots**, occur in vines all over the world and can be caused by many species of fungi including YEASTS and BACTERIA. Yield losses can be as high as 80 per cent and wine made from rotten fruit often smells and tastes tainted, often mouldy, with a perceptible loss of fruit flavour. Vineyards badly infected with bunch rots themselves have a distinctive and unpleasant smell. Wet weather at HARVEST causes the worst cases of bunch rot, especially if grape skins are broken. The best known of the bunch rots is BOTRYTIS BUNCH ROT.

Some fungi, such as botrytis, alternaria, and cladosporium, can infect healthy berries and these are called 'primary invaders'. 'Secondary invaders' such as aspergillus, rhizopus, and penicillium gain access to berries split by rain, bird or insect attack, or diseases such as DOWNY MILDEW and POWDERY MILDEW, ESCA, or HAIL disease. So-called SOUR ROT is due to a mix of fungi, yeasts, acetic acid bacteria, and fruit fly larvae. Control measures can include bunch thinning, increasing fruit exposure to wind and sun (see CANOPY MANAGEMENT), and avoiding other pests and diseases which can break berry skins. (See also FUNGAL DISEASES). R.E.S.

Emmett, R. W., Harris, A. R., Taylor, R. H., and McGechan, J. K., 'Grape diseases and vineyard protection', in B. G. Coombe and P. R. Dry (eds.), *Viticulture, ii: Practices* (Adelaide, 1992).

Pearson, R. C., and Goheen, A. C., *Compendium of Grape Diseases* (St Paul, Minn., 1988).

BUNCHSTEM, the stem of a grapevine inflorescence, or bunch of grapes, known by botanists as the peduncle and in French as a *rafle*. The form of the bunchstem, especially the position and length of lateral branches, determines the shape of the BUNCH and is one of many characters used to identify vine varieties in the science of AMPELOGRAPHY. Collectively, bunchstems are referred to as stems or stalks. B.G.C.

BUNG. A bung, made of glass, plastic, rubber, earthenware, silicone, or wood, is a barrel's stopper, analogous to the cork of a bottle. It is inserted in a **bung-hole**. If a barrel is stored so that the bung is at its highest point, this position is called **bung up** and the bung may be left so that gas can escape from the bung-hole. Some bungs even incorporate a device that encourages this. If a barrel is stored with the bung at either two or 10 o'clock, the position is called **bung over**.

Since OXYGEN tends to enter a barrel around the bung-hole, silicone bungs are sometimes used to keep a particularly tight fit. These silicone bungs also have the advantage of being gentler on the **bung stave**, the stave in which the bung-hole is drilled, which is weakened and sometimes cracked by the constant hammering needed on wooden bungs.

Depending on the amount of evaporation (see BARREL MAINTENANCE and WOOD INFLUENCE), and the spare time available to the winery staff, TOPPING UP is done anywhere from twice a week to once every six weeks. In Bordeaux the bung is left at the top of the barrel so as to maximize AERATION of the young wine for the first six months, after which the barrel is rolled to one side so that the bung is in the so-called bung-over position. Thus the bung and bung-hole region are kept moist and aeration is reduced. Many New World wineries have adopted this practice, even for Burgundian varieties, as it is much less labour intensive than constant topping up.

Traditionally in Bordeaux and Burgundy barrels are filled through the top bung but racked via a RACKING bung on the head of the barrel. M.K.

BURGENLAND, the second most important wine region in AUSTRIA, in the far east of the country on the Hungarian border, most famous for sweet white and red wines.

BURGER, white grape variety that was once very important in CALIFORNIA where it was the state's most planted VINIFERA variety, having been promoted by one pioneer as greatly superior to the MISSION grape. The ampelographer GALET has identified it as the almost extinct southern French variety Monbadon that was cultivated to a limited extent in the Languedoc until the 1980s. It produces sizeable quantities of neutral wine. In the early 1990s there were more than 2,000 acres / 810 ha of Burger, mainly in the hot SAN JOAQUIN VALLEY, many of them planted in the early 1980s.

BURGUNDER, common suffix in German, meaningly literally 'of BURGUNDY', for such grape variety members of the PINOT family as Spätburgunder, Blauer Spätburgunder, Blauburgunder, or Blauer Burgunder (PINOT NOIR); Weissburgunder or Weisser Burgunder (PINOT BLANC); and Grauburgunder (drier styles of PINOT GRIS).

BURGUNDY, known as BOURGOGNE in French, province of eastern France famous for its great red and white wines produced mostly from PINOT NOIR and CHARDONNAY grapes respectively. The province includes the viticultural regions of the Côte de Nuits and Côte de Beaune in the *département* of the CÔTE D'OR (which had a total of 8,450 ha / 20,880 acres of vineyards in 1990), and the Côte CHALONNAISE and MÂCONNAIS in the Saône-et-Loire (11,323 ha).

BEAUJOLAIS in the Rhône *département* (21,550 ha) and CHABLIS and the AUXERROIS in the Yonne *département* (totalling 3,910 ha) are distinct regions viticulturally, if not administratively, and are treated separately.

Ancient history

When the Romans (see Ancient ROME) conquered Gaul in 51 BC, they probably found the CELTS inhabiting what is now Burgundy already growing wine, although definite archaeological evidence for this goes back no further than the 2nd century AD. A tombstone in the village church of Corgoloin depicts what appears to be a Celtic god with a vine in his right hand; other gravestones have carvings of grapes. Also, archaeologists have found no Italian AMPHORAE of the mid 2nd century or later in Burgundy, which may indicate that from then on the region was producing enough wine of its own. From at least the 3rd century onwards, however, wine was transported from Italy in wooden BARRELS instead of amphorae, and wood is far more perishable than pottery.

The earliest literary evidence dates from AD 312. In a panegyric addressed to the Emperor Constantine the Great on the occasion of his visit to Autun (Augustodeunum), the citizens plead poverty. Part of the grim picture their orator paints is abandoned vineyards, the roots of the old vines so thickly intertwined that it would be impossible for a farmer to dig ditches. However old the vines were—and a mere human lifetime's worth of neglect would account for their tangled state—commercial viticulture had clearly been well established by the early 4th century.

As the Roman empire disintegrated, Burgundy came once more under barbarian rule, by the Franks, the Alamans and the Vandals. The Burgundians, Scandinavians by origin, founded a kingdom in the RHÔNE valley, later including Lyons and Dijon, in 456; they were defeated by the Franks under Clovis's sons in 534. The first recorded words in praise of Burgundian wine date from the Merovingian period. Gregory of Tours, who finished his History of the Franks in 591, says that the hills to the west of Dijon produce a noble wine that is like FALERNIAN—the highest praise possible from a Dark Age latinist. That wine, and the clear water flowing from the springs around the city, are sufficient reasons why in his opinion Dijon should become an episcopal see. In 587 King Guntramn, grandson of Clovis and son of Lothar I, gave a vineyard to the Abbey of St Benignus at Dijon, and in 630 the duke of Lower Burgundy donated vineyards at Gevrey, Vosne, and Beaune to the Abbey of Bèze, near Gevrey. The beginnings of monastic viticulture in Burgundy were in these Merovingian times.

Monastic influence

Nobles, peasants, and monks cultivated the vine under CHARLEMAGNE, when political stability brought prosperity. Med-

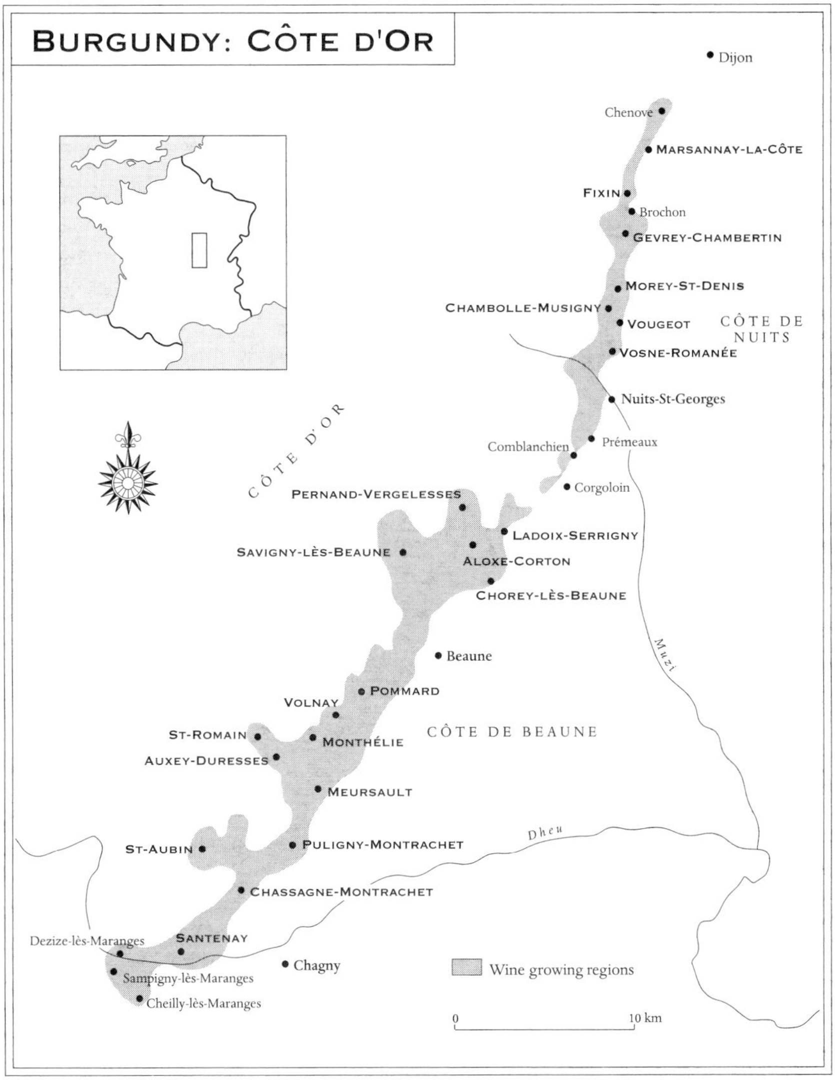

ieval Burgundy owes its reputation as a producer of excellent wines largely to the MONKS AND MONASTERIES. The monks had several advantages over lay growers: they had cellars and store rooms in which to mature their wine; and, most importantly, they kept records and had the time and the degree of organization necessary to engage in systematic improvement. The first group of monks to acquire vineyards in Burgundy on a large scale were the Benedictines of Cluny. The foundation in 910 of the Abbey at Cluny in the Mâconnais was the beginning of the Benedictine reform movement. Between 927 and 1157 Cluny became a vast organization with hundreds of dependent priories, not only in France but also in England, Germany, Spain, and Italy. Through benefactions from pious laymen, Cluny came to own all the vineyards around Gevrey by 1273, and in 1232 the duchess of Burgundy granted the Abbey of St-Vivant the vineyards now known as Romanée-Conti, La Romanée, La Tâche, Richebourg and Romanée-St-Vivant (see also DOMAINE DE LA ROMANÉE-CONTI). It also owned Pommard and vineyards at Auxey and Santenay.

The other group of monks to have a lasting effect on Burgundian viticulture were the Cistercians, an order founded in 1098 which took its name from the site of its first monastery, Cîteaux, east of modern Nuits-St-Georges. Although austerity and asceticism were the aims of the order, in contrast to the luxury and ostentation of the Benedictines, the Cistercians, often through donations, became rich and important landowners.

The Cistercians' first vineyard was given to them by the duke of Burgundy in 1098, not long after their foundation. Soon they were buying vineyards as well: in 1118 the

Cistercians of Pontigny on the river Serein purchased, after much haggling, vineyards from the Benedictine monks of St-Martin at Tours from which they produced a white wine, the first CHABLIS. In 1110 the monks of Cîteaux were given land at Vougeot and went on to acquire more land there: it took them until 1336 to acquire enough to form one large vineyard, which they surrounded with a wall, the CLOS DE VOUGEOT. They bought or were given more vineyards all over the CÔTE D'OR and trained their lay brothers to work them: Beaune, Chambolle, Fixin, Pommard, and many more.

Aided by their skilled work-force, the monks had the time, the experience, and the learning necessary to experiment, record, and compare. By observing how different plots of vines produced different wines, the Cistercians discovered the importance of TERROIR and began to acknowledge different CRUS.

In the 12th and 13th centuries white wine was preferred to red. In an age of murky drinking water, carefully made white wine was valued for its clarity. The wines that were most highly reputed, however, were not those of Burgundy but those of the Île-de-France centred on PARIS, which could easily be transported by RIVERS. Burgundy, on the other hand, was cut off, and its wines, which could only be transported north with much expense and difficulty along bumpy roads, were as yet little known. In medieval French texts, 'vin de Bourgogne' was from Auxerre, whose wines could easily reach Paris along the river Yonne: transport by boat was cheaper, easier, and less harmful to the wine than being carried by horse-drawn cart along bumpy roads. Until the 15th century what we call burgundy was known as 'Beaune'.

Upon his election in 1305 Clement V moved the papal court to Avignon. During this 'Babylonian captivity', which lasted until 1377, the court of the Avignonese popes was famous for its extravagance as well as its corruption, and demand for the wines of Burgundy to the north surged. The wines of 'Beaune' came generally to be regarded as second to none. Urban V (1362–70) went to Rome for three years in 1367 but, exasperated by the political infighting there, he returned to Avignon. In a letter, Petrarch made a vain attempt to persuade him to go back to Rome but had to admit that the best Burgundy was not to be had south of the alps. The Babylonian captivity ended with Urban's successor Gregory XI, but the wines of Burgundy retained their high reputation.

The dukes of Burgundy

From a byword for largesse in Avignon, Burgundian wine became a status symbol with the Valois dukes, four generations of which governed Burgundy from 1363 to 1477. The first duke, Philip the Bold (1363–1404), son of King John of France, took a keen interest in the wine of the region, its most important export. In 1395 he issued a decree declaring the GAMAY grape variety to be harmful to human beings and its planting contrary to Burgundian practice. The first mention of the PINOT NOIR grape, named NOIRIEN, dates only from the 1370s, but in all probability the grape had been in use longer. Modern Gamay has a far higher yield than Pinot Noir, and documentary evidence suggests that the same was true in the 14th century. In the same decree Philip inveighs against the use of organic FERTILIZERS, presumably because it also increased YIELDS. Philip was trying to maintain quality, while many growers thought that manure and Gamay would make for easy profits. Although Philip the Bold wanted every single Gamay plant uprooted by the next Easter, we find his grandson Philip the Good (1429–67) still thundering against the inferior vine, which he says is a threat to both the wines and the dukes of Burgundy. Fearing for his immortal soul, Philip the Good's rapacious Chancellor Nicolas Rolin built the famous HOSPICES DE BEAUNE in 1443.

But what were these famous wines really like? The white wines of Burgundy were probably made from the grape that also produced the highly reputed white wines of north eastern France, the Fromenteau, which had pale red berries and white juice, and could well be the ancestor of our PINOT GRIS. (The CHARDONNAY of modern white burgundy did not appear in the region until after the Middle Ages.) Also, in the Middle Ages wines were drunk in the year following the vintage, so properly matured burgundy would then have been unknown. H.M.W.

Derlow, R. K., 'The "disloyal grape": the agrarian crisis of late fourteenth century Burgundy', *Agricultural History*, 56 (1982), 426–38.

Dion, Roger, *Histoire de la vigne et du vin en France* (Paris, 1959).

Modern burgundy

The duchy of Burgundy was once so proud of having the finest wines and finest court in Christendom that it developed into a state, and very nearly a kingdom in its own right. The defeat and death of the over-ambitious Charles the Rash, however, led to its being reincorporated into the kingdom of France. As the monarchy became stronger the power of the Church declined slowly, so that during the 17th century many of the famous vineyards donated to the Church during the Middle Ages were sold to the increasingly important bourgeoisie in Dijon.

Although transport difficulties (see RIVERS) still hindered burgundy's fame abroad, the famous giant Pierre Brosse managed to interest Louis XIV in his Mâcon and the Sun King's physician, Fagon, prescribed old burgundy instead of champagne as the most suitable wine for his monarch's health. Roads began to improve in the 18th century and the tolls and tribulations inherent in road travel diminished, encouraging the start of commercial traffic in Burgundy. The first NÉGOCIANT (merchant) houses were founded in the 1720s and 1730s, including Champy (1720) and BOUCHARD (1731), names which have survived to this day.

The earliest major work on the wines of Burgundy, Claude Arnoux's *Dissertation on the Situation of Burgundy . . .* was published in 1728. It demonstrates the fame of the red wines of the Côte de Nuits and the special reputation of the *œil de perdrix* (partridge-eye) pink wines of Volnay, while the existence of white wine in the Côte de Beaune earns only a brief mention.

Most vineyards remained in the hands of Church or nobility until the French Revolution. From 1791 the vineyards were sold off, often split between several owners. Since then they have further fragmented as a result of the law of equal inheritance among children laid down in the Napoleonic Code. This process has caused much of the difficulty in understanding burgundy: the consumer must familiarize himself not only with a plethora of village and vineyard names but also with the relative merits of possibly dozens of producers of each one.

Burgundy prospered in the early 19th century, although wine PRICES were low even for the fine vineyards. In addition, there was widespread planting of the inferior GAMAY grape to provide wine that was plentiful and cheap, albeit mediocre. Transport conditions continued to improve with the opening of a canal system in Burgundy, and the Paris–Dijon railway in 1851.

Easy prosperity was first checked, however, by the spread of POWDERY MILDEW in the 1850s and then destroyed by the arrival of the PHYLLOXERA louse in the 1870s. This calamity was finally admitted in the Côte d'Or in 1878 when an infested vineyard in Meursault was surrounded by soldiers. The Burgundians did not find it easy to come to terms with the problem: there were riots in Bouze-lès-Beaune between factions in favour of treating vineyards and those against; a posse of growers in Chenôve actually attacked a team sent in to spray the vines; American ROOTSTOCKS, the eventual saviours of French vineyards, were banned from the region between 1874 and 1887. Eventually, however, common sense prevailed and by the 1890s post-phylloxera wines were again on the market. Only the best vineyards were worth replanting after the predations of phylloxera, a valuable side benefit of the disaster.

The Burgundians were well aware of the considerable variation in quality of the wines produced by different plots of land, or *climats*, as they are known in Burgundy. In 1855 Dr Lavalle published his influential *History and Statistics of the Côte d'Or*, which included an informal CLASSIFICATION of the best vineyards. This was formalized in 1861 by the Beaune Committee of Agriculture, which, with Lavalle's assistance, devised three classes. Most of the first class were in due course enfranchised as GRANDS CRUS when the APPELLATION CONTRÔLÉE system was introduced in the 1930s.

Most burgundy was sold through the flourishing merchant houses until the years of hardship after the First World War. The economic depression of the 1920s and early 1930s threatened to ruin many small growers. One solution was the CO-OPERATIVE, particularly useful in the Mâconnais, where prices were lower. Another was for proprietors to bottle their own produce, a move which met with opposition from the merchants when growers such as the Marquis d'Angerville, Henri Gouges, and Armand Rousseau pioneered the concept of DOMAINE BOTTLING in the 1930s. Whereas in 1962 wines produced and bottled by growers accounted for only 15 per cent of production, by 1990 nearly half of all Côte d'Or wines were domaine bottled.

BURGUNDY GRANDS CRUS
(listed from north to south)

Commune	Grand Cru
Côtes de Nuits (all for red wine unless otherwise stated)	
Gevrey-Chambertin	MAZIS-CHAMBERTIN
	RUCHOTTES-CHAMBERTIN
	CHAMBERTIN CLOS-DE-BÈZE
	CHAPELLE-CHAMBERTIN
	GRIOTTE-CHAMBERTIN
	CHARMES-CHAMBERTIN
	LE CHAMBERTIN
	LATRICIÈRES-CHAMBERTIN
Morey-St-Denis	CLOS DE LA ROCHE
	CLOS ST-DENIS
	CLOS DES LAMBRAYS
	CLOS DE TART
	BONNES MARES (some)
Chambolle-Musigny	BONNES MARES (most)
	LE MUSIGNY (some white wine too)
Vougeot	CLOS DE VOUGEOT
Flagey-Échezeaux	GRANDS ÉCHEZEAUX
	ÉCHEZEAUX
Vosne-Romanée	RICHEBOURG
	ROMANÉE-ST-VIVANT
	ROMANÉE-CONTI
	LA ROMANÉE
	LE GRANDE RUE
	LA TÂCHE
Côte de Beaune (all for white wine unless otherwise stated)	
Aloxe-Corton	LE CORTON (almost all red)
Ladoix-Serrigny	CORTON-CHARLEMAGNE
Puligny-Montrachet	CHEVALIER-MONTRACHET
	BIENVENUES-BÂTARD-MONTRACHET
with Chassagne-Montrachet	LE MONTRACHET
	BÂTARD-MONTRACHET
Chassagne-Montrachet	CRIOTS-BÂTARD-MONTRACHET

Geography and climate

The vineyards of Burgundy are based on LIMESTONE originating in the Jurassic period. This takes the form of undulating CHALK hills in Chablis; a long narrow escarpment running south and a touch west from Dijon to Chagny, the CÔTE D'OR; more isolated limestone outcrops in the Côte Chalonnaise and Mâconnais; with the vineyards of POUILLY-FUISSÉ beneath the imposing crags of Solutré and Vergisson in the extreme south.

The climate in Burgundy is broadly CONTINENTAL. In contrast to BORDEAUX, Burgundy is noticeably colder in the winter months, similar in temperature in the spring, but a little cooler during the summer. Although usually dry in winter, Burgundy tends to suffer from particularly heavy rainfall in May and June and again in October, which may or may not fall after the HARVEST. Spring FROST can be a problem (especially in CHABLIS), while HAIL causes local damage almost every year.

Overall, there is a shorter and more variable summer than in Bordeaux (which is why only early ripening grape varieties can be grown there). And whereas the hardy CHARDONNAY vine can thrive under these conditions, producing what are widely considered the finest full bodied dry white wines in the world, the temperamental PINOT NOIR vine is less regularly successful. For more details of Burgundy's special aptitude for top-quality wine production, see CLIMATE AND WINE QUALITY.

Burgundy is at the limit of successful RIPENING, the red wines of Auxerrois rarely achieving much depth or body. The great red wines of Burgundy are produced on the escarpment of the Côte d'Or, especially in the Côte de Nuits sector. Even here several vintages in a decade may lack sufficient sun to ripen properly.

Among the white wines of Burgundy, the wines of Chablis, reflecting their northern origin, are green tinted in colour and comparatively austere to taste. The most revered white wines are those of the Côte de Beaune, there being practically none in the Côte de Nuits, while the whites of the Côte Chalonnaise are lighter and attractive to drink young. Further south the white wines of the Mâconnais enjoy enough sun to make fat and ripe wines, although many of them lack finesse.

J.T.C.M.

Viticulture

For details, see CÔTE D'OR; CHALONNAISE; and MÂCONNAIS.

Wine-making

For details, see CÔTE D'OR; CHALONNAISE; and MÂCONNAIS.

Vine varieties

Burgundy has one of the world's least varied ranges of vine varieties. Almost all of the region's best red and white wines are made from Pinot Noir and Chardonnay respectively. On the Côte d'Or, more than seven in every 10 vines planted was Pinot Noir in the late 1980s, while Chardonnay plantings were increasing so that even at the most recent vineyard census of 1988 they represented nearly two in every 10 vines. Gamay and ALIGOTÉ, the 'lesser' red and white wine vines respectively, were in hasty retreat, although BOURGOGNE ALIGOTÉ has its followers.

In the Côte Chalonnaise and Mâconnais, Chardonnay plantings increased notably during the 1970s and 1980s when the variety overtook Gamay as most important, and became an important source of wine labelled Bourgogne Blanc. In 1988 the Saône-et-Loire *département* which includes these two southern Burgundy wine districts had 4,500 ha / 11,100 acres of Chardonnay (three times more than the Côte d'Or). Gamay plantings were just over 3,000 ha while those of Pinot Noir were 2,800 ha. There were also about 500 ha of Aligoté, approximately the same area as the Côte d'Or.

Organization of Burgundian vineyards

The vineyards of Burgundy, especially those of the Côte d'Or, are the most minutely parcellated in the world. This is mainly because the land has been continuously managed and owned by individual smallholders—there was no influx of outside capital with which to establish great estates as in BORDEAUX. But the combination of the Napoleonic Code, with its insistence on equal inheritance for every family member, and the fact that the land has proved so valuable, has meant that small family holdings have been divided and subdivided over generations. One vineyard, or *climat*, as it is known in this, the cradle of TERROIRS, may therefore be owned by scores of different individual owners, each of them cultivating sometimes just a row or two of vines (see CLOS DE VOUGEOT, for example).

Organization of trade

Unlike the BORDEAUX wine TRADE with its large volume of single appellations, and many stratifications of those who sell it, the Burgundian wine trade is polarized between growers and NÉGOCIANTS, or merchants. Because the laws of equal inheritance have been strictly applied in a region of such valuable vineyards, individual growers may for example produce just one barrel, enough to fill just 25 cases, of a particular appellation. The market for burgundy was built by the merchants who would buy grapes and wine from many different growers before blending and selling the results. Behind a merchant's Aloxe-Corton label, for example, may well be the produce of many different plots and cellars. Although in some cases these blends may be better than any individual ingredient, and in most cases today the merchants have better equipment and wine-making skills than the average Burgundian vine-grower, such blends have met increasing consumer resistance. Wine merchants such as Frank SCHOONMAKER and Alexis LICHINE introduced particularly the American public to the notion of DOMAINE BOTTLED burgundy in the 1950s and 1960s, creating a demand which resulted in a widespread improvement in the quality and authenticity of the merchants' produce. The merchants increasingly own their own vineyards, and are able to label the wines they produce 'mise en bouteille au domaine'. (Because few growers can afford their own BOTTLING equipment, mobile bottling units are much used in Burgundy.) In the early 1990s both merchants and all but the most famous growers found to their cost that burgundy prices had risen too fast in the 1980s.

See also HOSPICES DE BEAUNE and see BOURGOGNE for details of Burgundy's generic appellations. For the names of individual appellations, see BEAUNE; NUITS; CHALONNAISE; and MÂCONNAIS.

CHABLIS and BEAUJOLAIS are treated separately.

Hanson, A. D., *Burgundy* (2nd edn., London, 1995).
Norman, R. H., *The Great Domaines of Burgundy* (London, 1992).
Pitiot, S., and Servant, J.-C., *Les Vins de Bourgogne* (11th edn. of P. Poupon's original, Paris, 1992).

BUSBY, JAMES (1801–71), the so-called 'father' of Australian viticulture, although more recently the term 'prophet' has been considered more appropriate. James Busby was born in Edinburgh and became interested in agriculture in Ireland, where his father managed estates. Before leaving Scotland for Australia, Busby became convinced of the future of the colony in viticulture, and so spent several months studying viticulture and wine-making in France. This allowed him to write his first book, *Treatise on the Culture of the Vine*, on the five-month voyage on the *Triton*. At 24, therefore, Busby was already an author of a viticultural textbook, although at the time it was considered too scientific and lacking in simple directions. A land grant of 800 ha/1,980 acres was made to Busby on the Hunter river in NEW SOUTH WALES in 1824, and the property was named Kirkton. Busby was initially employed to teach viticulture at the Male Orphan School near Liverpool, and to manage its 5,000-ha estate. Unfortunately the school was soon closed down, and in between several other posts Busby published in 1830 his second and much more successful book *A Manual of Plain Directions for Planting and Cultivating Vineyards and for Making Wine in New South Wales*. Busby, like others of his time, extolled the virtues of wine drinking compared with the then common excesses with spirits in the colony. His book contains the much quoted 'The man who could sit under the shade of his own vine, with his wife and children about him, and the ripe clusters hanging within their reach, in such a climate as this, and not feel the highest enjoyment, is incapable of happiness and does not know what the word means.'

Busby's greatest contribution to Australian viticulture was yet to be made. In 1831 he returned to England, and spent four months touring the Continent, primarily to make a collection of vine cuttings for Australia. His collection included cuttings for about 680 VINE VARIETIES (not necessarily all different) from the botanical gardens of MONTPELLIER, Luxembourg in Paris, and Kew in London, as well as from other parts of France and Spain. This collection was shipped to Sydney along with seeds of various vegetables, and by January 1833 was reported to be growing in the Sydney Botanic Gardens. In 1833 Busby published another book about his tour to Spain and France, and listed the varieties in his collection.

Busby's life entered a new dimension in 1833 with his appointment as the first British Resident at the Bay of Islands in New Zealand. The nearby town of Russell was a trading port for visiting whalers, and described as 'the hell hole of the Pacific'. Busby had neither the magisterial powers nor the constabulary to impose any order but, through his and others' efforts, New Zealand became a British possession in February 1840 with the signing of the Treaty of Waitangi by some fifty Maori chiefs. Busby had little time for viticulture in New Zealand, although he did establish a vineyard at Waitangi which was destroyed in 1845 during clashes with the Maoris.

Unfortunately, the Sydney vine collection was not tended as it might have been. Some of the vines were distributed to Kirkton in the Hunter, and some to the Adelaide Botanic Gardens in South Australia. Many of Busby's imports were to become the basis of the Australian wine industry which subsequently developed; indeed some CLONES of vine varieties such as Chardonnay and Shiraz that are important in the 1990s can be traced to Busby's imports. Busby died in England in 1871, and in his later life he was aggrieved to discover that much of the credit for his vine introductions was erroneously given to William Macarthur, another pioneer of the Australian wine industry. Busby's great contribution to the Australian wine industry was his vine importations, his writings, and his enthusiasm for the notion that Australia should develop as John Bull's (England's) vineyard of the Antipodes. R.E.S.

Evans, L., *Australian Complete Book of Wine* (Sydney, 1977).
Halliday, J., and Jarratt, R., *The Wines & History of the Hunter Valley* (Sydney, 1979).

BUSH VINES, an alternative term to describe GOBELET trained vines or HEAD TRAINING. The comparison with a bush is apt: the vines are trained to a short trunk, normally free standing (without a trellis system), and are pruned to a few spurs commonly arranged in a ring on short arms from the trunk. The term bush vines is used in Australia and South Africa, although most of these old, and typically low-vigour, vineyards are being replaced by vines with a TRELLIS SYSTEM. R.E.S.

BUTT, BARREL TYPE associated particularly with SHERRY production in the Jerez region. It is usually made from American oak and has a capacity of between 600 and 650 l/172 gal. A *bota chica* or shipping butt holds 500 l and is sometimes used as a unit of measurement. New butts are an inconvenience in the sherry-making process and have to be seasoned by being used for the FERMENTATION of lower-quality wines.

BUTTERFLIES, regarded as pests in some vineyards. See MOTHS.

BUZET, known until 1988 as **Côtes de Buzet**, archetypically Gascon red wine appellation in SOUTH WEST FRANCE up the Garonne river from BORDEAUX energetically producing notably bordeaux-like wines. The recent history of the appellation, created in 1973, is inextricably intertwined with the dynamism of the local CO-OPERATIVE, Les Vignerons Réunis de Buzet, which makes all but a tiny proportion of Buzet. Notably ambitious, the co-operative laid the foundation stones of a barrel-ageing cellar in 1958, for which their own COOPER today makes more than 500 BARRIQUES a year from specially chosen and seasoned French OAK. Thus, the average Buzet is given much more sophisticated ÉLEVAGE than the average BORDEAUX AC, without an enormous price differential.

The region, which extends along the left bank of the Garonne between Agen and Marmande, has known viticulture since Roman times but vine-growing was developed under monastic influence in the Middle Ages. The fortunes of the district's wines suffered during the HUNDRED YEARS WAR, when the district supported the English crown. The district was further hampered by the restrictions imposed by

Picking Verdejo grapes from the widely spaced **bush vines** of Rueda in Spain.

the Bordelais on all HAUT PAYS, or 'high country', wines, when the wines of the village of Nérac were particularly well known. PHYLLOXERA seriously affected viticulture in the late 19th century, and a ruling in the early 20th century that Bordeaux wines had to come from within the GIRONDE *département* was a further blow to a district which had habitually supplied BLENDING wines to the Bordeaux merchants.

About 1,500 ha/3,700 acres on the gravels and clays of these inland hills were planted in the mid 1990s with classic red Bordeaux vine varieties CABERNET SAUVIGNON, CABERNET FRANC, and, especially, MERLOT. The co-operative has invested heavily in the most modern wine-making equipment, and its policy is to make strict selections according to TERROIR and quality each VINTAGE so that, although all Buzet should receive at least a year's BARREL MATURATION, the finest wines are blended to produce their top bottling Cuvée Napoléon. The co-operative also vinifies the produce of a number of individual parcels of land and bottles them separately as CHÂTEAU wines, such as Chx Balesté, de Gueyze, and du Bouchet.

BYBLOS, ancient town in the LEBANON 40 km/25 miles north of modern Beirut. It had the reputation of being the oldest town in the world and was a PHOENICIAN centre of trading. Its wines were famous in classical times.

BYO stands for 'Bring Your Own' (Wine) and is a type of restaurant most common in Australia and New Zealand, where the term was coined. The term is associated with maximum wine-drinking pleasure at minimum cost to the restaurant-goer (in tandem with reduced profit to the restaurateur). New Zealanders claim that the BYO evolved in 1976 when the New Zealand authorities, still notably cautious about the distribution of alcoholic drinks, devised the Bring Your Own licence for restaurants at which diners would be allowed to take their own wine. Australians in the state of Victoria, also famously restrictive in its legislative attitude to alcoholic drinks, maintain that Melbourne had BYO establishments in the 1960s. Wherever its origins, this arrangement has become common for a wide range of restaurants in Australia, New Zealand, and further afield, the wine often being bought in a nearby retail establishment.

C

Cabardès. This small wine region to the north of Carcassonne in south west France produces red and some rosé wines that testify to its location on the cusp of Atlantic and Mediterranean influences. The grape varieties planted also represent a Bordeaux/Languedoc cocktail of Cabernet Sauvignon, Cabernet Franc, Merlot, Cot (Malbec), and some Fer Servadou (of MARCILLAC), spiced and fleshed out with the more meridional Syrah, Grenache, Cinsaut (mainly for rosé) and a limited, and declining, proportion of Carignan. The Bordelais varieties tend to prosper on the western, wetter, deeper soils, while wines produced from the hotter, shallower soils of the eastern Cabardès are more likely to have a high proportion of Mediterranean varieties. Winds almost constantly buffet the small hills punctuated by pines and *garrigue*, and minimize the local wine producers' dependence on agrochemicals. In contrast to the somewhat similar Côtes de la MALEPÈRE to the south of Carcassonne, production here is mainly in the hands of a small but committed band of individuals constrained by low financial returns. Wine-making equipment and methods are far from sophisticated, with destalking machines and BARRIQUES still a rarity in the early 1990s, but the wines boast an originality and potential for longevity that is unusual for this part of France (which officials tend to classify as SOUTH WEST FRANCE rather than the LANGUEDOC to which its immediate eastern neighbour the Minervois belongs).

Cabernet is loosely used as an abbreviation for either or both of the black grape varieties CABERNET FRANC and CABERNET SAUVIGNON. In north east Italy in particular there has been a certain lack of precision about the precise identity of the Cabernet grown and allowed into the many Cabernet DOCs, although Cabernet Franc has tended to predominate. Elsewhere, Cabernet is more likely to be an abbreviation for Cabernet Sauvignon.

Cabernet Franc, French black grape variety, much blended with and overshadowed by the more widely planted CABERNET SAUVIGNON. Only in Anjou-Touraine in the Loire valley and on the right bank of the Gironde in Bordeaux is it more important than Cabernet Sauvignon.

In the vineyard it can be distinguished from Cabernet Sauvignon by its less dramatically indented leaves but the two share so many characteristics that it seems likely that Cabernet Franc is a particularly well-established mutation of the other Cabernet, possibly one particularly well adapted to the right bank's cooler, damper conditions.

By the end of the 18th century Cabernet Franc was already documented as producing high-quality wine in the Libournais vineyards of St-Émilion, Pomerol, and Fronsac where it is often called Bouchet today.

Long before this, however, according to Odart, it had already been selected by Cardinal Richelieu, as a well-respected vine of south west France, to be planted at the Abbaye de St-Nicolas-de-Bourgueil in the Loire by an abbot called Breton whose name persists as the Loire synonym for Cabernet Franc to this day.

Cabernet Franc is particularly well suited to cool, inland climates such as the middle Loire and the Libournais. It buds and matures more than a week earlier than Cabernet Sauvignon, which makes it more susceptible to COULURE, but it is easier to ripen fully and is much less susceptible to poor weather during harvest. In the Médoc and Graves districts of Bordeaux, where Cabernet Franc constitutes about 15 per cent of a typical vineyard and is always blended with other varieties, it is regarded as a form of insurance against the weather's predations on Cabernet Sauvignon and Merlot grapes. Most Libournais bet on Cabernet Franc in preference to the later, and therefore riskier, Cabernet Sauvignon to provide a framework for Merlot, Bordeaux's most planted variety.

In Bordeaux plantings of Cabernet Franc and Cabernet Sauvignon were almost equal, at about 10,000 ha/25,000 acres, in the late 1960s but Cabernet Sauvignon was so often chosen in preference to Cabernet Franc by those replacing unprofitable white wine vineyards that 20 years later Cabernet Sauvignon covered almost twice Cabernet Franc's total area of 13,400 ha.

As a wine, Cabernet Franc tends to be rather lighter in colour and tannins, and therefore earlier maturing, than Cabernet Sauvignon although CHEVAL BLANC, the world's grandest Cabernet Franc-dominated wine, proves that majestic durability is also possible. Cabernet Franc is, typically, light to medium bodied with more immediate fruit than Cabernet Sauvignon and some of the herbaceous aromas evident in unripe Cabernet Sauvignon.

Cabernet Franc is still planted all over south west France, although, in appellations such as Bergerac and Madiran (where Cabernet Franc is known as Bouchy), Cabernet Sauvignon is gaining ground.

If Cabernet Franc was France's eighth most planted black grape variety in the 1988 census, this was largely thanks to its ascendancy in the Loire (where it was the single most planted grape variety with 11,000 ha in 1988). Steadily increasing appreciation of relatively light, early maturing reds such as Saumur-Champigny, Bourgueil, Chinon, and Anjou-Villages fuelled demand for Cabernet Franc in the Loire at the expense of the competing Rosé d'Anjou and Chenin Blanc whites, whose popularity now declined.

Cabernet Franc is also well established in Italy, particularly in the north east (see FRIULI in particular), where it has typically been encouraged to yield such a quantity that over-herbaceous aromas scent wines that can be decidedly short on fruit. The 1990 Italian vineyard survey found nearly 6,000 ha of Cabernet Franc in Italy (as opposed to only 2,400 of Cabernet Sauvignon). It is occasionally called Cabernet Frank or even Bordo, but more usually labelled simply Cabernet once in the bottle. Italian vine-growers tend to be as insouciant about the distinction between the two Cabernets as their counterparts over the border in SLOVENIA and further east. In the early 1990s Cabernet Franc was relatively common in KOSOVO and was the only western grape to be grown for red wine production in ALBANIA. Within the CIS it is grown only in KAZAKHSTAN, according to available information.

Elsewhere, Cabernet Franc tends to be grown for the express purpose of blending with Cabernet Sauvignon, following the Bordeaux recipe whether or not the climate suggests that such insurance would be wise. Cabernet Franc plantings have slowly increased in New World wine regions as wine-makers embrace the sophistication of Bordeaux blends as opposed to single VARIETALS. In 1990, for example, a third of Australia's 300 ha/750 acres of Cabernet Franc (and two thirds of its 400 ha of Merlot) was too young to bear a crop.

Although there was some early confusion between Cabernet Franc and Merlot, Californians have been rearing Cabernet Franc since the late 1960s, and with zeal since the 1980s. This is more on the vague assumption that their part of the state somehow mirrors Bordeaux than out of recognized shortcomings in their vineyards. Some varietal Cabernet Franc is made in CALIFORNIA but it is mainly used in MERITAGE-like blends. The state's total acreage was 1,700 in 1992 (700 ha), most of it in Napa and Sonoma counties and one-third of it too young to bear fruit. It is expected to play an increasingly important role in California.

The vine is increasingly planted in South America. ARGENTINA now grows Cabernet Franc with more than 500 ha/1,200 acres planted by the early 1990s, most of it in Mendoza.

New World wine regions that have shown a particular aptitude for well-balanced, fruity wines based predominantly on Cabernet Franc include Long Island in NEW YORK STATE and WASHINGTON State in the far Pacific Northwest. NEW ZEALAND also shows promise.

Enjalbert, H., *Les Grands Vins de Saint-Émilion, Pomerol et Fronsac* (Paris, 1983).
Galet, P., *Cépages et vignobles de France* (2nd edn., Montpellier, 1990).
Odart, A.-P., *Ampélographie universelle* (Paris, 1845).

CABERNET FRANK, occasional northeast Italian name for CABERNET FRANC.

CABERNET SAUVIGNON, the world's most renowned grape variety for the production of fine red wine. From its power base in Bordeaux, where it is almost invariably blended with other grapes, it has been taken up in other French wine regions and in much of the Old and New Worlds, where it has been blended with traditional native varieties and often used to produce pure VARIETAL wine.

Perhaps the most extraordinary aspect of Cabernet Sauvignon is its ability to travel, to set down its roots in distant lands and still produce something that is recognizably Cabernet, whatever the circumstances. And what makes Cabernet Sauvignon remarkable to taste is not primarily its exact fruit flavour—although that is often likened to blackcurrants, its aroma sometimes to green bell peppers—but its structure and its ability to provide the perfect vehicle for individual vintage characteristics, wine-making and ÉLEVAGE techniques, and local physical attributes, or TERROIR. In this respect it resembles the equally popular and almost as ubiquitous CHARDONNAY, to whose 'vanilla' Cabernet Sauvignon is often compared as 'chocolate'.

It is Cabernet Sauvignon's remarkable concentration of PHENOLICS that really sets it aside from most other widely grown vine varieties. It is therefore easily capable of producing deeply coloured wines worthy of long maceration and wood ageing for the long term. Over the centuries it has demonstrated a special but by no means exclusive affinity for densely textured French OAK. The particular appeal of Cabernet Sauvignon lies much less in primary fruit aromas (with which other varieties such as Gamay and Pinot Noir are more obviously associated) than in the much more subtle flavour compounds that evolve over years of BOTTLE AGEING from complex interaction between compounds derived from fruit, fermentation, alcohol, and oak. It is also true, however, that so distinctive is Cabernet Sauvignon's imprint on the palate memory that part of the reason why it is so widely planted is that even when irrigated to greedily high yields and hastily vinified without even a glimpse of wood, it can produce a wine with some recognizable relationship to the great Bordeaux growths of the Médoc and Graves on which its reputation has been built. (In this respect it is quite different from Chardonnay which can taste extremely neutral, and only rarely resembles great white burgundy when planted outside the Côte d'Or.)

Cabernet Sauvignon's origins will almost always remain shrouded in mystery. One of its early synonyms, well-established by the 17th century, is Bidure. This has led to the tempting theory that it is the direct descendant of the vine called Biturica by PLINY after the Bituriges tribes which had settled both in the BORDEAUX region and near Bourges in the first century AD. There has been even more speculation about the likely identity of Biturica than the many other ANCIENT VINE VARIETIES to which Pliny and COLUMELLA tantalizingly refer. What seems more likely, however, is that the vine's 17th century synonyms Bidure and Vidure (a corruption of *vigne dure*?) refer to the hardness of the vine's wood, which today makes it such a suitable candidate for mechanical harvesting.

Certainly there were two Vidures listed in the well-documented vine collection of 18 black- and 20 white-berried varieties at Cadillac near Bordeaux recorded by the Abbé Bellet in 1736. However, Cabernet's relatively low productivity, and prevailing preference for wines (often white) for early consumption, meant that it was not until the end of the 18th century that Cabernet Sauvignon started to make any significant impact on the vineyards of Bordeaux, when the great estates were built up and wine with real longevity emerged (see BORDEAUX, history). Baron Hector de Brane, once owner of Ch Mouton, together with his neighbour Armand d'Armailhacq, is credited with its promulgation, if not introduction, in the MÉDOC.

The distinguishing marks of the Cabernet Sauvignon berry are its small size, its high ratio of pip to pulp (one to 12, according to Peynaud, as opposed to one to 25 for Sémillon), and the thickness of its skins, so distinctively blue, as opposed to red or even purple, on the vine. The pips are a major factor in Cabernet Sauvignon's high TANNIN level while the skins account for the depth of colour that is the tell-tale sign of a Cabernet Sauvignon in so many blind tastings. The thickness of the skins also makes the vine relatively resistant to rot.

The vine is susceptible however to OIDIUM, which can be treated quite easily, and the wood diseases EUTYPA and EXCORIOSE, which cannot. It is extremely vigorous and should ideally be grafted on to a weak ROOTSTOCK to keep its leaf growth in check. It both buds and ripens late, one to two weeks after Merlot and Cabernet Franc, the two varieties with which it is typically blended in Bordeaux. Cabernet Sauvignon ripens slowly, which has the advantage that picking dates are less crucial than with other varieties (such as Syrah, for example); but this has the disadvantage that Cabernet Sauvignon simply cannot be relied upon to ripen in the coolest wine regions, especially when its energy can so easily be diverted into producing dangerously shady leaves such as in Tasmania or New Zealand unless CANOPY MANAGEMENT is employed. Cabernet Sauvignon that fails to reach full ripeness can taste eerily like Cabernet Franc (just as unripe Sémillon, coincidentally, resembles Sauvignon Blanc).

Even in the temperate climate of Bordeaux, the flowering of the vine can be dogged by cold weather and the ripening by rain, so that Bordeaux's vine-growers have traditionally hedged their bets by planting a mix of early and late local varieties, typically in the Médoc and Graves districts 75 per cent of Cabernet Sauvignon plus a mixture of Merlot, Cabernet Franc, and sometimes a little Petit Verdot. (See CABERNET FRANC for reasons why the Cabernet in St-Émilion and Pomerol is much less likely to be Cabernet Sauvignon.)

A practice that had its origins in canny fruit farming has proved itself in the blending vat. The plump, fruity, earlier maturing Merlot is a natural blending partner for the more rigorous Cabernet Sauvignon, while Petit Verdot can add extra spice (if only in the sunniest years) and Cabernet Franc can perfume the blend to a certain extent. Wines made solely from Cabernet Sauvignon can lack charm and stuffing; the framework is sensational but tannin and colour alone make poor nourishment. As demonstrated by the increasing popularity of Merlot and Cabernet Franc and even Petit Verdot cuttings, newer wine regions have begun to follow the Bordeaux example of blending their Cabernet Sauvignon with other varieties, although the Médoc recipe is by no means the only one. In Tuscany it is commonly blended with Sangiovese. In Australia and, increasingly but with very different results, in Provence it is blended with SYRAH (SHIRAZ).

Cabernet Sauvignon is by quite a margin the most planted top-quality vine variety in the world (if one excludes Grenache, which, in its most common form Garnacha, rarely performs at the peak of its potential). In fact as the world's wine regions have been introduced to the demands of the modern international market-place, one of the first signs of 'modernization' of a wine region has been its importation of and experimentation with Cabernet Sauvignon cuttings. Only those regions, such as England, Germany, and Luxembourg, disbarred for reasons of climate, have resisted joining this particular club on any significant scale. Cabernet production has become almost a rite of passage for the modern wine-maker wishing to make his mark.

French plantings of Cabernet Sauvignon increased enormously in the 1980s so that by 1988 there were 36,500 ha/90,000 acres, of which two-thirds were in the Bordeaux *département* the Gironde (although within the Gironde the agriculturally more dependable Merlot has been consistently and considerably more popular). The vine's stronghold is the left bank of the river Gironde, most notably the famously well-drained gravels of the Médoc and Graves CRUS classés, whose selling price can well justify the efficacious luxury of ageing their wine in small, often new, oak casks. Chx Latour and Mouton-Rothschild, two of the most famous wine farms in the world and both of them FIRST GROWTHS in Pauillac, are famous for their high proportion of Cabernet Sauvignon: approximately four vines in every five, although nowadays planted in parcels of individual varieties rather than ready-blended in the vineyard. The wines of both, although differing in character, are known for their solidity and longevity.

Cabernet Sauvignon, although little planted north of the river Dordogne, is now much more common in the ENTRE-DEUX-MERS between the Gironde and Dordogne rivers as less profitable white varieties have been uprooted. Such is the size of the Entre-Deux-Mers district that there is more Cabernet Sauvignon planted there, 11,000 ha recorded in 1988, than in any other Bordeaux district, including the Médoc (although there is considerably more Merlot in Entre-Deux-Mers than Cabernet Sauvignon).

The vine is also planted over much of SOUTH WEST FRANCE, often as an optional ingredient in its red, and occasionally rosé, wines. Only in BERGERAC and BUZET does it play a substantial part. In more internationally styled wines, however, it may add structure to the Malbec of CAHORS, the Négrette of GAILLAC and Côtes du frontonnais, and the Tannat of BÉARN, IROULÉGUY, and MADIRAN. In 1988 there were 1,300 ha of Cabernet Sauvignon in the Bergerac *département* of Dordogne (as opposed to 2,800 ha of Merlot and 1,500 ha of Cabernet Franc) and 300 ha in the Gers where it is being increasingly planted to add substance to the red Côtes de ST-MONT.

Plantings in the Languedoc-Roussillon increased

substantially in the 1980s to a total of nearly 12,000 ha by 1993, but Cabernet Sauvignon has not been nearly so successful here as Syrah which covered a total of 24,000 ha by the same year. Cabernet Sauvignon does not tolerate very dry conditions without more substantial irrigation than is condoned by the French authorities. Varietal Cabernet Sauvignon wines made in the Languedoc-Roussillon have tended towards herbaceousness and suffered lack of substance, but the vines may well have been encouraged to over-produce.

The most obviously successful southern French Cabernet Sauvignons are those used as ingredients in low-yield blends with Syrah and other Rhône varieties, such as Mas de Daumas Gassac in the Hérault or, further east in Provence, Domaine de Trévallon and Ch Vignelaure.

Provence and the southern Rhône are no more impervious to the winds of fashion than they are to the famous local mistral and by 1988 there were already 900 ha of Cabernet Sauvignon in the Var, 500 ha in the Bouches-du-Rhône, and 400 ha in the Ardèche. The variety has also been gaining ground and reputation in Corsica.

Cabernet Sauvignon's only other French territory is the Loire, but, despite the freedom allowed by most appellation regulations to choose either Cabernet Franc or Cabernet Sauvignon or both for local reds, most vine-growers prefer the regularity of the former to the risks involved with growing the latter in relatively cool conditions. Of the Loire *départements*, only the Maine-et-Loire ANJOU-SAUMUR has any substantial area of Cabernet Sauvignon (1,000 ha in 1988)—far less than of Cabernet Franc, or even than of Grolleau or Gamay.

Outside France

If current estimates are correct, the CIS has approximately 30,000 ha/75,000 acres of Cabernet Sauvignon (some of the most impressive bottle-aged examples have come from MOLDOVA). It is widely planted in RUSSIA and UKRAINE, although in Russia's cooler wine regions the cold-hardy hybrid CABERNET SEVERNY is becoming increasingly popular. Cabernet Sauvignon is also grown in GEORGIA, AZERBAIJAN, KAZAKHSTAN, TAJIKISTAN, and KYRGYZSTAN.

Another country with an important area planted with the world's noblest black grape variety is Chile, whose grand total of, ungrafted, Cabernet Sauvignon is well over 12,000 ha, making it by far the country's third most important vine variety after PAIS and Semillon. Here the fruit is exceptionally healthy and the wine, if made carefully in one of the more modern wineries, almost rudely exuberant. See CHILE for more on Chilean Cabernet Sauvignon.

Not surprisingly, Cabernet Sauvignon also flourishes in the rest of South America's vineyards: in ARGENTINA; where in terms of quantity it is dwarfed by Malbeck (the same grape, MALBEC, that has declined in Bordeaux); in BRAZIL, URUGUAY, MEXICO, PERU, and BOLIVIA.

Cabernet Sauvignon, even less surprisingly, has been the bedrock of that construct called California collectable. In 1992 the state could boast more than 33,000 acres/13,300 ha of it, very slightly less in 1991 than of the most widely planted black grape variety Zinfandel, but much less than plantings of any of the white wine varieties Chardonnay, Colombard, or Chenin Blanc. Late in 1991 the pendulum of American consumer preference swung back with a vengeance towards red wine, however, and plantings, or at least graftings-over (see TOP WORKING), of Cabernet Sauvignon subsequently increased apace.

Although Cabernet Sauvignon was no stranger to California, it was during the wine boom of the 1970s and early 1980s that plantings multiplied rapidly, especially in the premium North Coast sites of Sonoma and, especially, Napa. During this period, little expense was spared in replicating what were commonly thought to be the wine-making methods of a top Bordeaux château, although it was only from the mid 1980s that tannin, fruit, and alcohol levels were brought into harmony on a wide scale, and blending with Merlot and Cabernet Franc became at all common. For more detail on the golden state's Cabernet achievements, see CALIFORNIA.

Cabernet Sauvignon is also one of WASHINGTON state's two major black grape varieties, along with the hugely successful Merlot, each of them accounting for about 1,500 acres/600 ha and gaining ground rapidly in 1991, but almost invariably bottled as 100 per cent varietals. Cabernet Sauvignon's vigour and late ripening make it unattractive to growers in damp, cool Oregon but it has been most successful in other American states including Arizona and TEXAS. Even the wine industry in CANADA with its natural climatic disadvantages persists with the variety.

If Californians decided early on that the Napa Valley was their Cabernet Sauvignon hotspot, Australians did the same about Coonawarra. They, however, have for decades employed a much less reverential policy towards blending their Cabernet. Cabernet–Shiraz blends (a recipe recommended in Provence as long ago as 1865 by Dr GUYOT) have been popular items in the Australian market-place since the 1960s. The richness and softness of Australian Shiraz is such that it fills in the gaps left by Cabernet Sauvignon even more effectively than the French Syrah recommended by Dr Guyot can do. The classic Bordeaux blend is still very much rarer, on the other hand, as one might expect from wine producers more determined than the Californians to go their own way independently of Europe. Australian Cabernet Franc and Merlot plantings totalled only 800 ha in 1990, while plantings of Cabernet Sauvignon were 4,600 ha/11,400 acres, one-fifth of it too young to bear fruit. See AUSTRALIA for more detail on Australian Cabernet Sauvignon.

Cabernet Sauvignon has long played a part in the NEW ZEALAND wine industry, and with 475 ha it was the country's fourth most planted vine variety in 1990. It was not until the mid to late 1980s, however, that Cabernet's tendency to transform energy into excess foliage rather than ripe fruit was mastered, thanks to canopy management, and fully ripe colours and flavours in New Zealand Cabernets became an attractive reality.

SOUTH AFRICA's early problems with Cabernet also involved colour; the wines lacked depth and tended to brown early. Now, thanks to better understanding of PH, much of the produce of South Africa's 2,400 ha (in 1990), of Cabernet

Sauvignon is suitably deep crimson for the first four of five years of its life at least (provided it is not irrigated too enthusiastically), and it is increasingly being blended with other Bordeaux varieties such as Merlot and Cabernet Franc. In North Africa there are very limited plantings of the vine in Morocco.

Cabernet Sauvignon has been an increasingly popular choice for internationally minded wine producers in both Portugal and, particularly, Spain, however. In Spain it was planted by the Marqués de Riscal at his Rioja estate in the late 19th century, and could also be found in the vineyards of VEGA SICILIA, but was otherwise virtually unknown on the Iberian peninsula until the 1960s, when it was imported into Penedès by both Miguel TORRES, Jr and Jean León. It is slowly broadening its base in Spain, not just for wines dominated by it but for blending. And in Portugal it could already be found by the mid 1980s, blended with indigenous grape varieties in a handful of lush red wines made in the Lisbon area.

Italy, where Cabernet Sauvignon was introduced, via Piedmont, in the early 19th century, now has a very substantial area of Cabernet vineyard, although Italians have been somewhat cavalier about distinguishing between the two very different sorts of Cabernet either on the label or, sometimes, in the vineyard. The 1990 vineyard survey identified just 2,400 ha of Cabernet Sauvignon (a considerable increase on the 1982 figure) as compared with a total of nearly 6,000 ha of Cabernet Franc. Remarkably few of the denominations which begin with the word Cabernet specify which should be used and in what proportions. Cabernet Sauvignon is increasingly recognized as superior to the grassy Cabernet Franc in Friuli, however, and the vine, which continues to spread southwards through Italy and even as far as the islands, features in many of Italy's more cosmopolitan producers' most cherished wines. Cabernet Sauvignon has played a considerable role in the emergence of SUPERTUSCANS, and can be found as a seasoning in an increasing proportion of CHIANTI. It is officially sanctioned, and individually specified, in such DOCS as CARMIGNANO in Tuscany; Colli BOLOGNESI in Emilia-Romagna; in TRENTINO; in LISON-PRAMAGGIORE in the Veneto, and in Friuli COLLI ORIENTALI, COLLIO, GRAVE DEL FRIULI, ISONZO, and Latisana. Cabernet Sauvignon is a major ingredient in such Tuscan wines as Solaia, Sassicaia, Venegazzù, and Castello di Rampolla's Sammarco, and is increasingly common (occasionally blended with BARBERA grapes) in the NEBBIOLO territory of Piedmont in such bottlings as Darmagi from GAJA and Alberto Bertelli's I Fossaretti.

East of Italy there are many thousands of hectares of Cabernet Sauvignon, which plays an important part in the wine industries of BULGARIA in particular, ROMANIA, and what was YUGOSLAVIA. Even when expected to produce relatively high yields, eastern European Cabernet Sauvignon is unmistakably Cabernet, and the best Romanian and Bulgarian wines have real depth of flavour as well as colour. There are smaller amounts of Cabernet Sauvignon grown in HUNGARY, AUSTRIA, and GREECE, where it was first planted, in modern times at least, at the Carras domaine.

Perhaps the most tenacious Cabernet Sauvignon grower has been Serge Hochar of Ch Musar in the LEBANON, and there are other, rather less war-torn, pockets of Cabernet Sauvignon vines all over the eastern Mediterranean in TURKEY, ISRAEL, and CYPRUS. In the Far East, there have been experiments with the vine in both CHINA and in JAPAN where its strong links with the famous châteaux of Bordeaux are particularly prized.

Wherever there is any vine-grower with any grounding in the wines of the world, and late ripening grapes are economically viable, he is almost certain to try Cabernet Sauvignon—unless he inhabits one of Bordeaux's great rival regions Burgundy and the Rhône. It is perhaps significant that, in contrast to many other black grape varieties, no white, pink, or grey version of this definitive red wine inspiration exists.

Eyres, H., *Cabernet Sauvignon* (London, 1991).
Galet, P., *Cépages et vignobles de France* (2nd edn., Montpellier, 1990).
Johnson, H., *The Story of Wine* (London, 1989).
Lake, M., *Cabernet* (Sydney, 1977).
Peynaud, E., *Connaissance et travail du vin* (Paris, 1981).

CABERNET SEVERNY, red wine grape variety specially bred for cold climates at the All-Russia Potapenko Institute in the Rostov region of RUSSIA. It was created by pollination of a hybrid of Galan × VITIS *amurensis* with a pollen mixture of other hybrid forms involving both the European vine species *Vitis* VINIFERA and the famously cold-hardy Mongolian vine species *Vitis amurensis*.

CABINET, historical term for superior German wines, whose origins are disputed. Wines made in Germany prior to the GERMAN WINE LAW of 1971 were labelled Cabinet if thought to be better than average and, by tradition, worthy of space in the producer's own Cabinet or cellar. The description was then abandoned in favour of KABINETT. The term Cabinet to indicate a wine of reserve quality is first encountered at KLOSTER EBERBACH in the Rheingau in 1712.

CABRIÈRES, village and named TERROIR within the Coteaux du LANGUEDOC in southern France, just east of FAUGÈRES and within the CLAIRETTE DU LANGUEDOC zone. The CO-OPERATIVE dominates production, which has historically favoured rosé.

CADILLAC, small sweet white appellation just north of LOUPIAC in the BORDEAUX region, once particularly popular with the Dutch, named after the walled town built by the English in the 12th century. Until 1973 it was part of the surrounding PREMIÈRES CÔTES DE BORDEAUX appellation but its special combination of chalk and gravel theoretically justifies a distinction which is still too rarely found in the wines. Low selling prices make high-quality production methods such as those practised in SAUTERNES difficult to justify, and few producers are brave enough to try to make BOTRYTIZED WINES.

CAECUBAN wine was ranked by the connoisseurs of Ancient ROME among the finest wines of Italy for the last century BC and the first half of the first century AD. Caecuban wine was produced on a small vineyard in the low-lying marshy region, south of Terracina, on the west coast of central Italy, between the sea and the Lago di Fondi. The vines were trained up poplars. Caecuban was a white wine, which following standard Roman practice was aged for a number of years, during which it deepened to a 'flame' colour. It was described as 'sinewy' and 'packing a punch' by the medical writer Galen. The vineyard was largely destroyed in the middle of the first century AD by the ambitious, though abortive, scheme of the Emperor Nero to dig a canal to link the bay of Naples with the Tiber. Caecuban never recovered and the name became simply a generic term for wine with the characteristic colour of the true wine. Small quantities of undistinguished red wine called Cécubo are produced in the district today. J.J.P.

CAHORS, significant wine region in the Quercy district in SOUTH WEST FRANCE, producing exclusively red wine, uniquely dependent on the MALBEC or Cot grape. The wine producers of Cahors long suffered from the protectionist measures against such HAUT PAYS wines inflicted on Cahors by the merchants of Bordeaux. The RIVER Lot provided an ideal trade route from the town of Cahors to the markets of northern Europe via the GARONNE and Bordeaux, and Cahors was making wines noted for their colour and BODY from at least the early Middle Ages. There are records of Cahors being sold in London in the early 13th century, but the HUNDRED YEARS WAR disrupted patterns of trade.

Cahors is influenced by the Mediterranean as well as by the Atlantic, and, although winters are rather colder than in Bordeaux, the wines tend to be more concentrated. They were appreciated as suitable blending material with the lighter wines of Bordeaux, and in the early 19th century were famed as the 'black wines of Cahors'. (Such was Cahors's international renown in the 19th century that imitation 'Cahors' was made at at least one of the Russian model wineries in the CRIMEA.) A method of making the wines even blacker had been adopted whereby a portion of the grape juice was boiled to concentrate its colour and fermentable sugars. The produce of this technique was designed specifically for blending rather than drinking. At this time there were almost 40,000 ha/80,000 acres of vineyards in the greater Cahors region, but PHYLLOXERA was to more than decimate this total, and resulted in considerable replanting with HYBRIDS. The arrival of the RAILWAYS also gave the populous north ready access to the cheap and plentiful wines of the LANGUEDOC. Cahors fell into decline.

The establishment of the Caves d'Olt CO-OPERATIVE at Parnac in 1947 marked the modest beginning of a new era during which the proportion of noble grape varieties and the incidence of good wine-making equipment and technology has steadily increased so that by the early 1990s more than 3,500 ha of vines were producing Cahors, awarded full APPELLATION CONTRÔLÉE status in 1971. Within South West France only BERGERAC makes more wine. Vines for Cahors may be planted either on the notably thin topsoil of the arid, limestone plateau, the *causses*, or on the sand and gravel terraces between the plateau and the river, the *coteaux*. The suitability of each is much debated (according to the location of the debater's own vines), although most agree that the *causses* tend to produce wine for long ageing, a more traditional style of Cahors, while the wine made on the *coteaux* can be drunk much younger.

The notorious WINTER FREEZE of 1956 had a marked effect on the Cahors *vignoble* and provided a clean slate at an appropriate moment in the appellation's evolution. By far the largest number of growers planted an overwhelming majority of Malbec, called here for obscure reasons Auxerrois, a traditional Cahors variety which is nowhere else associated with particularly long-living wines. The appellation rules stipulate at least 70 per cent Auxerrois, supplemented by the tannic TANNAT and/or the supple MERLOT. A strictly local variety known as Jurançon Noir is being phased out, and most vines are now trained to a single GUYOT system (which is appropriate since this 19th century scientist was particularly critical of the traditional GOBELET method for Auxerrois). Again, debate rages over the most suitable mix of grape varieties (although, like vineyard location, this is hardly a variable in practice, more a matter of long-term fact). Cahors is exceptional among the important South West French appellations in that neither Cabernet vine is allowed.

In the winery, MACERATION times are a genuine variable and can have a considerable effect on wine style, as of course does BARREL MATURATION, still a relatively rare phenomenon in the early 1990s. This has been changing, however, since Cahors has attracted more than its fair share of well-heeled outsiders. Cahors was still in flux in the mid 1990s, attempting to find a style that would suit the impatient modern consumer, while remaining faithful to the region's long viticultural history.

The local VIN DE PAYS, a speciality of the co-operative, is Vin de Pays des Coteaux de Quercy.

Bespaloff, A., 'Cahors', *Fine Wine Folio* 3/8 (1991).

CAIRANNE, probably the best of the Côtes-du-Rhône Villages. See RHÔNE.

CALABRESE, meaning 'of Calabria', is a common synonym for the NERO D'AVOLA Sicilian red grape variety.

CALABRIA, the rugged toe of the boot of Italy, is closer to SICILY than to Rome in every way. (In antiquity, Calabria was the name of the heel of Italy, part of modern APULIA.) It has lagged behind the rest of Italy in its agricultural and industrial development with a per capita income barely half the national average. It is not surprising, therefore, that its wines have made little impact and have little significance in national and international markets.

Only five per cent of the total surface area of the region's agricultural land is planted with vines, most of them close to the northern, Tyrrhenian coast or the southern, Ionian coast.

The 35,000 ha/86,500 acres currently dedicated to vineyards—two-thirds of which are officially classified as hillside sites, with another 15 per cent promisingly mountainous but difficult to work—produce an average 1.8 million hl/48 million gal of wine a year. The average size of the properties, whether in DOC zones or not, is hardly more than half a hectare, most of them yielding a particularly low annual income. The total DOC production of the region is only three per cent of the region's annual wine crop and almost 90 per cent of the wine produced is red.

The most important DOC by far is Cirò (on the sole of Italy's boot), where a certain viticultural tradition exists and where Tancredi BIONDI-SANTI of MONTALCINO operated as a consultant during the decades immediately following the Second World War. Even Cirò produces only a quarter of its potential, however, with barely 670 ha of the 2,500 ha of DOC Cirò vineyards planted actually employed in the production of a strong, dark, DOC wine.

So uncommitted is Calabria to the business of making wine officially regarded as of superior quality that certain DOC wines have virtually disappeared from the market: Melissa Bianco, Donnici, Savuto (10 producers, and close to 200 hl/5,300 gal produced in the official production declarations in the mid 1990s), Sant'Anna Isola Capo Rizzuto—and Pollino reappeared with less than 400 hl. In a certain sense, therefore, the DOC system has ceased to function in Calabria.

GAGLIOPPO, the principal red grape of the region, is the base of Cirò, Savuto, and Pollino and seems to have real potential; interesting experiments with small oak BARREL MATURATION have begun in Cirò in an effort to give the wine a more international character. It may be blended with red and white GRECO, TREBBIANO, and NERELLO grapes to produce Calabria's hefty reds and rosés. The white Greco grape, partially dried, produces a strong, coppery dessert wine of real interest and personality in its DOC zone around the town of Bianco almost at the tip of the boot, making the confusingly named Greco di Bianco Calabria's most distinguished wine. Cabernet Sauvignon and Cabernet Franc, Chardonnay, and Sauvignon Blanc are being experimented with in a desultory fashion, although real conviction and truly convincing results are rare. This is all too predictable in a region where, in the early 1990s, only three firms among the 65,000 registered grape-growers managed to export their wines. D.T.

Anderson, B., *The Wine Atlas of Italy* (London and New York, 1990).
Gleave, D., *The Wines of Italy* (London and New York, 1989).

CALADOC is a black grape variety created by French AMPELOGRAPHER Paul Truel under INRA auspices by crossing Grenache and Côt (Malbec) to produce a Grenache-like crossing less prone to COULURE. It has been planted in the southern Rhône but is not allowed into any APPELLATION CONTRÔLÉE wine, although it may be used to add TANNIN and aroma to red VINS DE PAYS in Provence. It is grown only in limited quantities.

CALANDRE, a system of DISTILLATION in which the raw material is first heated by steam in three interconnected vessels each holding about 400 l/105 gal. The fumes they give off, which are about 20 per cent alcohol, are then distilled to about 70 per cent. The biggest installation is at the Distillerie Goyard at Ay, which buys all the surplus wine and lees from the Champagne region. N.F.

CALATAYUD, denominated wine zone in ARAGON in north east Spain, in arid country on either side of the river Jalon, a tributary of the Ebro (see map on p. 907). As in much of central Spain, YIELDS rarely rise above 20 hl/ha (1 ton/acre). The DO regulations limit growers to indigenous grape varieties, which are mostly sold to one of nine local CO-OPERATIVES. The GARNACHA grape which accounts for around two-thirds of the Calatayud's production makes heady, potent red wine, although TEMPRANILLO is slowly gaining in popularity among the more quality-conscious producers. Investment in new technology, particularly STAINLESS STEEL and REFRIGERATION, is increasing the proportion of crisp white wines made from VIURA and Garnacha-based rosés, but in 1993 few wines had yet reached an exportable standard. R.J.M.

CALCAIRE, French word for LIMESTONE, a rock largely made up of calcium carbonate, which may in English be described as **calcareous**. The term is used to describe, for example, the vineyard soils of the CHAMPAGNE region of France, as well as some of those in the south of BEAUJOLAIS. Soils described in French as *argilo-calcaire* are a mixture of clay and limestone. See entries prefixed SOIL. M.J.E.

CALCIUM, a major element required for vine growth, but one in which vineyards are hardly ever deficient. Calcium is very important to many aspects of the vine's metabolism, not least as a basic constituent of cell walls. The calcium content of soils is important in affecting SOIL STRUCTURE, encouraging as it does good friability and hence water infiltration. All CALCAREOUS soils are high in calcium. A high LIMESTONE content can affect vine health because of lime-induced CHLOROSIS. R.E.S.

CALDARO, or **Kaltern** in German, township in the ALTO ADIGE of northern Italy. It gives its name to **Lago di Caldaro** or **Kalterersee**, a large DOC zone for lightish red wines which extends into neighbouring TRENTINO.

CALIFORNIA, state on the Pacific coast of the UNITED STATES and the largest source of American wine by far, producing 90 per cent of all American wine in the early 1990s. California was also for years the only source of *vinifera* wine in the USA: it is deservedly called 'the Wine State'. California wine, like most things Californian, has arrived at its current position by a series of bold investments, natural disasters, scientific achievements, external pressures, and political calamities. That the USA is not a nation of wine drinkers has tended to exaggerate the cycle of giant strides and general retreats, and even relatively recent events can fast become history (see below).

This personalized numberplate advertising Renaissance Vineyard and Winery of northern **California** is one of many devised by the state's wine-making population.

History

Franciscan MISSIONARIES planted the first *vinifera* vines in California around 1779 (the native *Vitis californica* and *Vitis girdiana* are unfit for wine). For the next hundred years the Franciscans' MISSION grape remained the basis of California wine-growing, which passed from the missions to small growers in and around Los Angeles, which was then, sleepy pueblo though it was, California's centre of population. After the American annexation of California in 1847, wine-growing spread throughout the state and California's fame as a new wine region spread even as far as North Caucasus (see RUSSIA).

Following the GOLD RUSH of 1849, both population and vineyards shifted northwards to San Francisco Bay and its surrounds. SONOMA County was the centre of wine-making activity and in 1891 had 22,683 acres/9,180 ha under vine to the NAPA Valley's 18,000 acres. At the end of the 19th century an extraordinary burst of investment in vineyards and wineries benefited not just these NORTH COAST counties, but also LIVERMORE VALLEY and SANTA CLARA VALLEY.

By the end of the century nearly every region currently producing wine in California had been tried, and production was over 30 million gal/1.1 million hl, largely from the northern part of the state, especially Sonoma, Napa, and Santa Clara counties. The great central SAN JOAQUIN VALLEY began to develop for the large-scale production of inexpensive wines from the 1870s, especially in Fresno and Madera counties. The state had officially encouraged wine-growing from the earliest years, recognizing it as one of California's most distinctive contributions to the US economy. A board of State Viticultural Commissioners did useful work from 1880 to 1895, and the wine research and education of the University of California (first at Berkeley and subsequently in the warmer, more suitable location of DAVIS) began in 1880 and continues to the present.

California had neither viticultural traditions nor an entrenched peasantry in its early era, so aggressive research and education by E. W. Hilgard and Frederic T. Bioletti at the University produced immediate results. No later than 1881, scholars and growers alike saw clearly that the coastal counties were for finer table wines, the San Joaquin for everyday table wines and, perhaps, dessert wines of quality. Already California grew more than 300 *vinifera* varieties with CHASSELAS, ZINFANDEL, BURGER, and of course Mission, predominating, even if most of the nearly 800 wineries producing at California's 19th century peak (about the same number as a century later) sold their wines anonymously in bulk to a handful of blender/bottlers who offered broad ranges of wine types to the trade.

Already in 1880, however, there were the early signs of PHYLLOXERA, the first major set-back to this burgeoning industry, which was to devastate California's wine production. PROHIBITION, legally in force between 1920 and 1933, destroyed its market. It was many decades before some areas recovered their pre-Prohibition status as wine regions, unlike Napa and Sonoma to the north and the Central Valley which endured this second set-back relatively robustly.

Immediately after the Repeal of Prohibition, the market demanded mostly sweet wines. Relatively few, small producers attempted to make superior table wines from superior varieties, with little recognition. By the end of the Second World War, wineries that bottled their own production were the norm. By then overall numbers had dwindled to about 120 producing wineries. A trade far more familiar with whiskey than wine enouraged the survivors to produce 'full lines' echoing, not the old blender/bottlers, but importers who were now bringing in broad arrays of wines from Europe sold under GENERIC names. In the three-tiered system of distributors (national or regional), district wholesalers, and local retailers, it may have been the retailers who were most to blame for wanting to keep their domestic orders as simple as their import invoices, reinforced by the general ignorance of the American drinking public. California thus produced wines sold under such generic names as Burgundy and Chablis.

After a period of struggle that lingered beyond the Great Depression and the Second World War, a second grand burst of investment was evident between 1970 and 1985, most obviously in Napa but also in Sonoma. (It was to be a new strain of phylloxera coupled with a new wave of prohibitionist sentiments that from the late 1980s helped cool this second burst too.) Growing populations around San Francisco pushed the new wave of vineyard planting south into MONTEREY, SAN LUIS OBISPO, and SANTA BARBARA counties.

In the 1970s and early 1980s America became interested in wine. New wineries proliferated, production rose, better varieties were extensively planted, higher standards aimed at, and market demand swiftly answered. While California had fewer than 100 acres of Cabernet Sauvignon and practically no Chardonnay immediately after Prohibition in 1933, and only 600 and under 100 acres of these two major vine varieties by 1960, California's total plantings of Cabernet and Char-

Wall paintings executed in Ancient **Egypt** have provided some remarkably detailed illustrations of wine-making techniques 3,500 years ago. The tomb of Sennufer, mayor of Thebes during the 18th Dynasty (1567–1320 BC), was decorated so that he and his wife could remain forever beneath an arbour of vines.

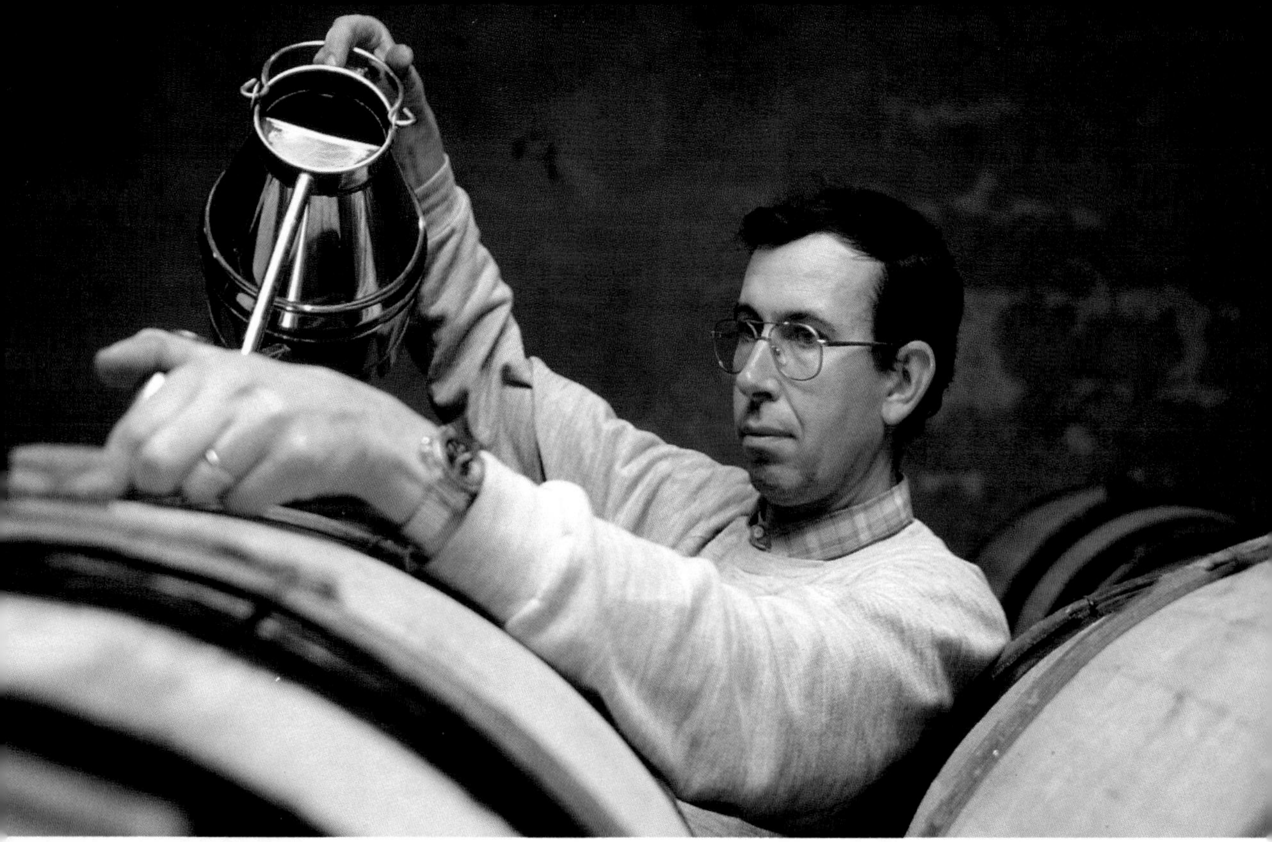

D'ESTOURNEL
MARTYNS ERRAZU
HOSTEIN CHARMOLUE
GINESTET PRATS

donnay had reached 34,000 acres/13,700 ha and 56,000 acres/22,700 ha (about as much as the French national total) respectively by 1991.

By the early 1990s the state was producing more than 400 million gal/15 million hl from nearly 700,000 acres of vines of grape-bearing age. Only 290,000 acres of these produced specifically wine grapes, however, and, even as recently as in 1989, nearly 20 per cent of the grapes crushed for wine were raisin and table varieties such as THOMPSON SEEDLESS.

As both consumers and trade matured in the 1970s, there was a proliferation of California wineries specializing in just two or three wines, most of them labelled as VARIETAL wines closely tied to their region of origin, a distinct step up from the generic wines that had dominated the state's production since Prohibition. By 1990 the number of wine companies in the state was once again nearing 800, almost all of them this time selling their production under their own labels.

It has to be said that California's matching of vine variety to region remains so relatively immature that people continue to be more important than place. In the 19th century immigrant Germans and Frenchmen showed the way for a larger population of Anglo-Americans. A later wave of Italian immigrants kept things going during and after Prohibition. And in the second half of the 20th century the wine industry has been populated by an eclectic gathering of engineers, painters, physicians, pilots, retired industrialists, reformed hippies, and other second careerists who somehow found a calling in wine, and who have driven themselves with the same energy that made them successes in other fields, sometimes in spite of location rather than because of it.

Vine varieties (see below) are not necessarily planted because they are known to be the best adapted to that region—although there is a new awareness of the importance of matching site and variety (see Geography/Regions below and AVA). In many areas the devastation wrought by phylloxera in the early 1990s made this an urgent practicality rather than a theoretical aim. T.P.

Adams, L., *The Wines of America* (4th edn., New York, 1990).
Carosso, V., *The California Wine Industry: A Study of the Formative Years* (Berkeley, Calif., 1951).
Muscatine, D., Amerine, M. A., and Thompson, B. (eds.), *The University of California/Sotheby Book of California Wine* (Berkeley, Calif., 1984).
Pinney, T., *A History of Wine in America* (Berkeley, Calif., 1989).

Climate

Those unfamiliar with California assign it a two-season MEDITERRANEAN CLIMATE. This is but a partial truth. Offshore ocean currents cause a nearly perpetual fog-bank along California's coast, creating large areas too cold and wet to grow any grapes at all. These fogs do not penetrate far inland, leaving the San Joaquin Valley too warm and sunny—too mediterranean if you will—to grow fine table wines. However, in the sharply hilly in-between of the Coast Ranges, jumbled terrain and variable fog produce more and less perfect growing season echoes of Castellina-in-CHIANTI, ST-ESTÈPHE, BEAUNE, and even Hattenheim in the RHEINGAU. There is no linear pattern. Napa, across the bay from San Francisco, is one of the warmer, drier regions on the coast. Parts of Santa Barbara County, 200 miles to the south, are cooler and foggier than any part of Napa, while much of Mendocino, nearly 80 miles north of Napa, has hotter summers. Openings to the Pacific Ocean in the Coast Ranges indicate the cool spots, while mountain barriers locate the warmer ones.

The rainy season follows a more orderly pattern. Total annual RAINFALL north of San Francisco is between 24 and 45 in (615–1,150 mm) while from San Francisco southwards totals range from 20 in to the low teens. Rainfalls aside, winters in California's grape-growing regions are mild to outright balmy. Damaging WINTER FREEZES are unheard of.

Spring FROSTS vex growers more than any other fact of climate. Although late cold snaps occur infrequently, growers in the North Coast are geared to mitigate the effects with SMUDGE POTS, overhead SPRINKLERS, and WIND MACHINES, huge fans that keep cold air moving in the vineyards. Spring rains sometimes interfere with flowering and fruit set, but never in disastrous proportion.

California has been, somewhat crudely, divided into five climatological regions by AMERINE and WINKLER (for more details, see CLIMATE CLASSIFICATION).

Geography

In the early 1990s California's wine regions extended over more than 600 miles/960 km of the state's length from north to south. The clear demarcation of regions and the establishment of regional specialities is an important task begun as recently as 1983. Before then California's geographical appellations, by and large, were its counties. Those much used in practice on wine labels have been, in very approximate descending order of popularity, Napa, Sonoma, MENDOCINO, Monterey, Santa Barbara, San Luis Obispo, and LAKE. Other, usually larger and often vaguer, geographical descriptions in use are NORTH COAST, CENTRAL COAST, SOUTH COAST, San Joaquin Valley, SANTA CRUZ MOUNTAINS, and SIERRA FOOTHILLS.

In 1983 came the first steps towards a system of more specific appellations of origin driven by soil and climate. These American Viticultural Areas (AVAs) are initially rudimentary, imposing no restrictions on varieties planted or vineyard practices. By 1990, California had more than 60 (out of a national total of 115), many such complete unknowns that Napa, Sonoma, Mendocino, Santa Barbara, and a few other county names remain more effective at communicating vineyard location. Still, AVAs have helped tasters notice details that have long been there. Most dramatically, many can now spot the distinctions between North and Central Coast in many wines when tasted BLIND. Throughout the 1990s that process continued to elaborate itself within each of those broad regions, although not without complications and contradictions.

To many producers the cask, or **barrel**, is the most important wine-making tool. Perfectionists such as Jean-François Coche of Coche-Dury know that frequent **topping-up** is essential in his small cellar in the Burgundy village of **Meursault**, while large Bordeaux estates such as Ch Cos d'Estournel (below), second growth **St-Estèphe**, make their major annual investment in new oak **barriques**.

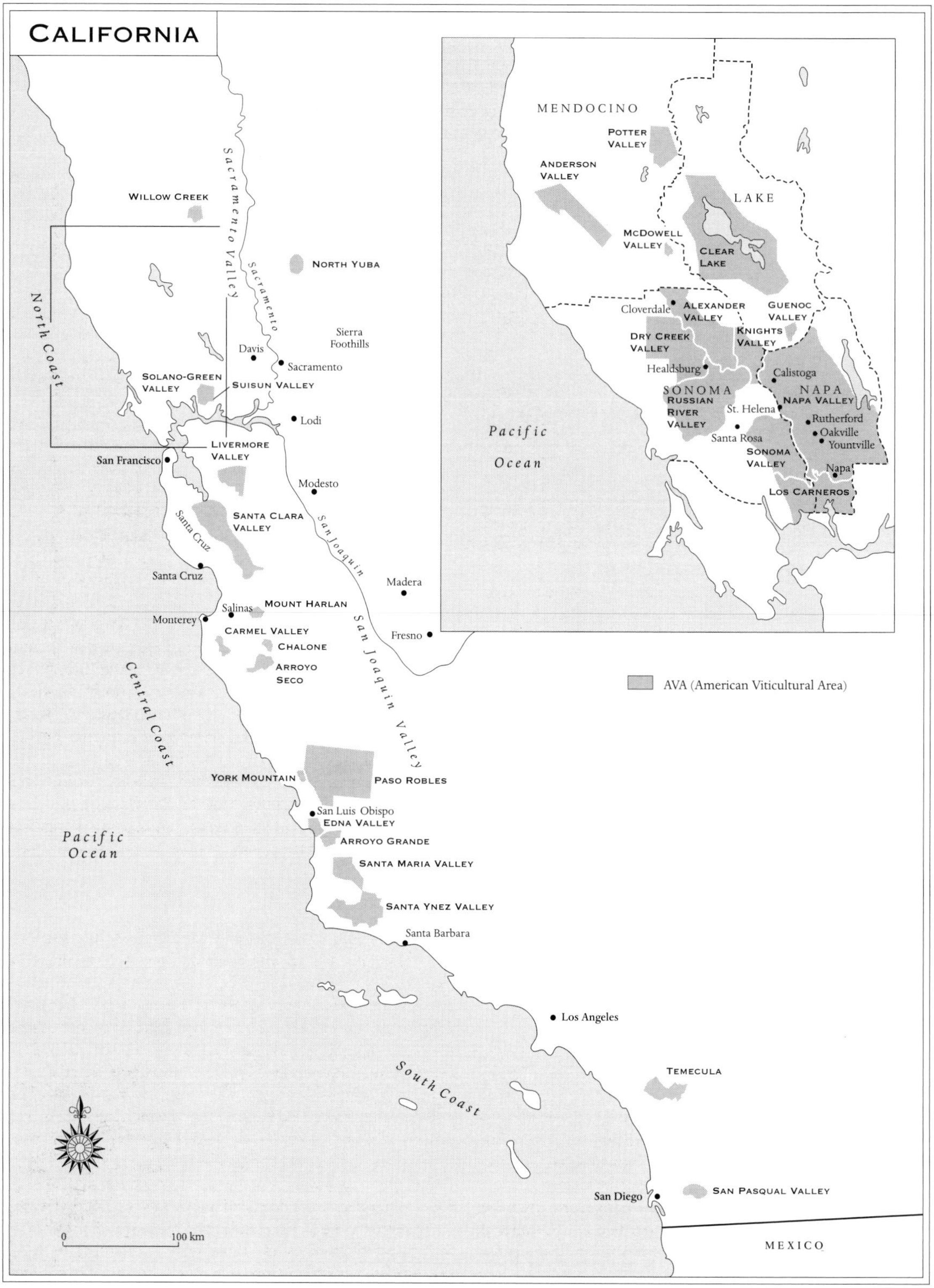
CALIFORNIA
Willow Creek
North Yuba
Sacramento Valley
Sacramento
Sierra Foothills
Davis
Sacramento
North Coast
Solano-Green Valley
Suisun Valley
Lodi
San Francisco
Livermore Valley
Modesto
Santa Clara Valley
Santa Cruz
San Joaquin
Santa Cruz
Madera
Salinas
Mount Harlan
Monterey
Carmel Valley
Chalone
Arroyo Seco
Fresno
San Joaquin Valley
Central Coast
York Mountain
Paso Robles
San Luis Obispo
Edna Valley
Arroyo Grande
Pacific Ocean
Santa Maria Valley
Santa Ynez Valley
Santa Barbara
Los Angeles
South Coast
Temecula
San Diego
San Pasqual Valley
Mexico
0
100 km
AVA (American Viticultural Area)
Mendocino
Potter Valley
Anderson Valley
Lake
McDowell Valley
Clear Lake
Cloverdale
Alexander Valley
Guenoc Valley
Dry Creek Valley
Knights Valley
Healdsburg
Calistoga
Sonoma
Napa
Russian River Valley
St. Helena
Napa Valley
Rutherford
Oakville
Yountville
Pacific Ocean
Santa Rosa
Sonoma Valley
Napa
Los Carneros

Individual AVAs are detailed under the name of the county or larger geographical unit in which they fall, except for the following AVAs, of varying sizes, which have their own individual entries: CARNEROS, Livermore Valley, NORTH YUBA, SAN PASQUAL VALLEY, Santa Clara Valley, SOLANO-GREEN VALLEY, SUISUN VALLEY, TEMECULA, and WILLOW CREEK.

Kramer, M., *Making Sense of California Wine* (New York, 1992).
Thompson, B., *Wine Atlas of California and Traveller's Guide to the Vineyards* (London and New York, 1993).

Viticulture

In the years following Repeal of Prohibition, California viticultural practices were relatively uniform: head trained, SPUR PRUNED vines spaced about 8 ft apart on rows about 10 ft/3 m apart. Dry farming was the rule in the North Coast, while flood IRRIGATION was the universal practice in the San Joaquin Valley.

During the 1960s vine TRAINING began to move on to wires, with cane PRUNING for lighter bearing vine varieties and CORDON for heavier yielders. Overhead sprinkler systems for irrigation became more common, especially in the emerging Central Coast. AXR1 became the ROOTSTOCK of choice because of its vigour and near universal adaptability and heavy, dense canopies were the norm. Vine spacing remained at or near 8 × 10, or between 400 and 600 vines per acre (1,000 to 1,500 vines per ha).

Towards the mid 1980s all of the old rules went by the way, impelled partly by a new mutation of phylloxera, the so-called biotype B, partly by a recurrence of PIERCE'S DISEASE, and, more significantly, by closer observation of the variables caused by California's turbulent geology. It was not uncommon in the early 1990s to see single properties on the North Coast with three or four different vine spacings, ranging between 800 and 2,000 vines per acre, and as many different systems of CANOPY MANAGEMENT. The aim was to take advantage of variations in soil structures and exposures as well as vine varieties. Since AXR1's resistance to phylloxera had proved disastrously low, rootstock selection was becoming a new art. The 1990s saw a major replanting programme, particularly in Napa and Sonoma, as a direct result of phylloxera and vine disease.

The quickened pace of change in vineyard management and in the market-place was, at the time, driving wineries to buy, lease, or otherwise control ever-increasing proportions of the vineyards throughout the coast counties. In most, wineries actively farm between 65 and 80 per cent of the total acreage. The San Joaquin Valley, true to long practice, remained largely committed to the system of independent growers selling their grapes under contract to wineries.

Wine-making

Without tradition as either guide or limitation, most California wine-makers have consistently looked to achieve the kind of reproducible results their university training exalts. Understanding a process and then controlling it are, thus, the first two goals of the state's typical OENOLOGIST. Of all the steps in wine-making, FERMENTATION has received the most vigorous attention.

Temperature-controlled fermentation began in California in the 1940s. With the advent of STAINLESS STEEL tanks and more integral cooling systems in the 1960s, there came 'designed' fermentation curves for each major grape variety. Ultra-hygienic, infinitely controllable stainless steel tanks allowed MALOLACTIC FERMENTATIONS to be brought under control at the same time.

Until the early 1980s ACIDIFICATION was the norm throughout the state, but it is increasingly unusual in coastal regions, where grapes often have higher natural ACIDITY than their counterparts in Bordeaux or Burgundy. DEACIDIFICATION and ENRICHMENT, although permitted, are rarely practised, and never in the vineyards of the Central Valley.

OAK barrels from French forests came into play as ageing vessels at the beginning of the 1960s; within a decade BARREL FERMENTATION of white wines was highly fashionable. Chardonnay was and remains foremost among the varieties so fermented, but no white grape variety is immune.

With rare exceptions, red wines continue to be fermented in TANK, most often in stainless steel but sometimes in the open-topped redwood or cement tanks that were common before the advent of stainless steel. After years of separating MUST from CAP just as the fermentation approached dryness, the vogue of the 1980s and 1990s has been extended MACERATION for as long as 25 days after the end of fermentation.

YEASTS, the very engine of fermentation, are also much studied and carefully monitored. For years pure strains of specially cultured yeast ruled in California. Towards the end of the 1980s, however, wine-makers began to use various combinations of these strains, and were increasingly prepared to experiment with natural yeast, the local population of so-called wild yeasts which, over the wine-making years, are effectively tamed to field yeast suitable for fermenting wine. The stated goal is greater aromatic complexity.

Ageing in oak became a whole art form in itself, with wine-makers diligently matching COOPERS, TOAST levels, and new versus used BARRELS to wine types and regions. Length of time in oak also became a subject of much debate and experimentation.

Wine types

The most important California wine type is the VARIETAL, the principal sorts of which are outlined below (see Vine varieties).

The production of inexpensive wines, largely from the Central or San Joaquin Valley, is in the hands of a relatively few very large wineries. Most of the state's wineries concentrate on more expensive wines, many of limited production and available only in a few markets. Throughout the 1980s, production of red table wines, to which the state is well adapted, declined precipitously in response to the vagaries of the market. Only 14 per cent of the table wines shipped from California in 1989 were red, the rest being white (53 per cent), rosé (16 per cent), and so-called BLUSH wines (17 per cent).

American wine diction tends to be based more on tax rates than wine characteristics. Table wine is anything with an ALCOHOLIC STRENGTH of up to 13.9 per cent. Even the finest late harvest imitations of TBAs (see TROCKENBEERENAUSLESE), the ones with 40 per cent residual sugar, are table wines to the taxman. Quality, or lack of it, is not implied by nomenclature as it is in Europe. Dessert wine, meanwhile, is anything with more than 16 per cent of alcohol, even the driest of SHERRY types. Sparkling wine, sensibly, is the stuff with bubbles.

That mastered, California offers a few other terms not found elsewhere, or else mutated too little to require explanation, although see also FIGHTING VARIETAL, GENERIC, JUG WINE, and MERITAGE. In addition there are the proprietary blends, which were originally only tarted up generics. A Rhine would become Rhine Castle, a Chablis would become Golden Chablis, or somesuch. Some of those continue to exist. However, the advent of fighting varietals in the late 1980s called the supremacy of varietals into question and spawned a new breed of high-priced proprietaries based on blends of classic grape varieties that were traditional in Europe. Meritages, for example, imitate BORDEAUX and there are also equivalent counterparts to RHÔNE blends.

There is also a long and complex history of producing sparkling wine in California, which has had few inhibitions about calling it champagne. HARASZTHY began attempts to make sparkling wines of quality in the 1870s, using the champagne method. F. Korbel & Bros. came right behind, with rather more success.

In the years since 1970, European- and especially French-owned firms have come to dominate production of California champagne method wines made by traditional techniques using traditional grape varieties (see CMCV). Domaine Chandon was the forerunner. Piper-Sonoma, Mumm-Napa Valley, Roederer Estate, Maison Deutz, Domaine Carneros (Taittinger), and Scharffenberger (Pommery) have followed from France, Gloria Ferrer (Freixenet) and Codorníu Napa from Spain. There remains a strong domestic element led by Schramsberg, Iron Horse, and, more recently, Jordan.

These are the sources of complexity in sparkling wines. Producers of inexpensive mass-market bubblies make less complicated wines yet complicate the story. American law permits wines made from a wide range of non-traditional grape varieties, made sparkling either by the Charmat CUVE CLOSE process or the Carstens TRANSFER process, to be called Champagne so long as that word is accompanied by a clear appellation of origin (almost always 'California') and indication of the method used. Such wines are the sparkling equivalents of generic table wines.

Vine varieties

California's mix of vine varieties is one of the world's most fluid, thanks to its high proportion of professional grape farmers selling their produce to wineries in free market conditions, thanks to innate American flexibility, and thanks to the technique of FIELD GRAFTING.

The most planted varieties are Chardonnay, whose total area of 57,000 acres / 23,000 ha finally overtook that of FRENCH COLOMBARD in 1991, Zinfandel, matched by Cabernet Sauvignon in the same year, and Chenin Blanc. Of these Cabernet Sauvignon and Chardonnay dominate labels, while the other three are more often non-trumpeted ingredients in less expensive blends, the great majority of them either white or blush. There are also substantial total acreages of Sauvignon Blanc, Grenache, Carignane (as CARIGNAN is spelt in California), and Barbera. Italian influence is again likely to increase in California's vineyards, most particularly with Sangiovese. Other varieties enjoying modish popularity in the early 1990s were the Bordeaux bit players Merlot and Cabernet Franc, and some which have origins in the Rhône; Syrah and Viognier are foremost.

Varieties that constitute a California speciality, many of them specifically bred in and for the state, are CARNELIAN, CHARBONO, EMERALD RIESLING, FLORA, GREEN HUNGARIAN, PETITE SIRAH, RUBY CABERNET, SYMPHONY, ZINFANDEL.

AMPELOGRAPHY, the science of vine identification by human observation, has never been a popular sport with Californians. Nineteenth century Californians were altogether casual about the identities of the vines they imported and grew. Modern researchers at Davis are using more sophisticated techniques of vine identification such as DNA 'FINGERPRINTING' to try to sort out the ancestry of the varieties known in California as Petite Sirah (probably not DURIF, as was originally thought), Valdepeñas (probably TEMPRANILLO), Pinot Blanc (MELON, the Muscadet grape, whose California existence is outlined below), Sauvignon Vert (MUSCADELLE), and Gray Riesling (TROUSSEAU Gris). Gamay presents a particularly confused picture in California. The variety known as Gamay Beaujolais is probably a poor clone of PINOT NOIR, while that called either Napa Gamay or just plain Gamay may either be true GAMAY Noir à Jus Blanc or, at least as likely, the obscure VALDIGUIÉ from south west France. Muscat Blanc should mean MUSCAT BLANC À PETITS GRAINS, although before a BATF ruling in the early 1990s it was also known as Muscat Frontignan and Muscat Canelli. Orange Muscat is a darker-berried mutation. Malvasia Bianca is a minor variety but has produced some impressive bottles of sweet wine, not all of them fortified.

The following are the most important varieties found on California wine labels, listed alphabetically. For details of other California vine varieties, see under the variety name.

Cabernet Sauvignon Of all the transplants of European varieties to California, it is Cabernet Sauvignon that seems most at home, particularly in the Napa Valley. Cabernet had surfaced as a leading success in Napa by the 1880s according to producers and critics of the time. Its primacy there has been recognized by authorities ever since, although not always by the consuming public. Other parts of the state have been trying to catch Napa since the 1880s, and most convincingly since the 1970s. The result is a state total of 34,000 acres / 13,800 ha in 1991, of which Napa's share, despite vigorous increases in Cabernet acreage, is less than a third.

Early in the 1960s one of the notables in the English wine trade called Napa Cabernet Sauvignon 'California's Burgundy'. Varietal flavour may have gone over his head, but he struck a right note all the same, because Napa Cabernet has much of the alcohol-induced weight of BURGUNDY. He would have been closer to the mark if he had called it California's Rhône, however, the tannins in Cabernet being what they are. Since then, expanded plantings alongside rainy forests and in deserts, on mountain slopes and old river beds, and in scores of sites less extreme have stretched Cabernet's varietal character to wide limits. Some of the fattest, most alcoholic models from California's hottest districts (see SAN JOAQUIN VALLEY) come perilously close to port. Some thin, sharp-featured examples from notably chilly districts taste not merely herbaceous, but dowright vegetative.

The best ones offer rich textures and an entrancing tennis match of opposing flavours, berries on one side, herbs on the other. Whether by natural gift or historic dominance, Napa produces most of the memorably distinctive, age-worthy examples from California. Some show off particular subzones such as the Rutherford-Oakville west side (of which two of the first to establish their credentials were Beaulieu Vineyard's Georges DeLatour bottling and Heitz Cellars' Martha's Vineyard) or Stags Leap District (from which a Stag's Leap Wine Cellars offering famously 'beat' some of the great names of France at a much-reported tasting in Paris in 1976). A long list of others come from less defined regions or are blended from vineyards in differing parts of the valley.

Sonoma does not lag far behind with its finest examples, but they are fewer and more scattered in provenance. Its superior districts appear to be Alexander Valley and Sonoma Valley. The other North Coast counties show a kinship in growing conditions with similar wines. They are MENDOCINO and LAKE. The Central Coast is a different kettle of fish. While flavours of fruit and herb play against each other in North Coast Cabernet Sauvignons, their Central Coast counterparts pit herb against vegetable. Or at least so the first 20 vintages have done, although growers say they are modifying vineyard practices (see CANOPY MANAGEMENT) and with them the flavours.

Laube, J., *California's Great Cabernets* (San Francisco, 1989).

Chardonnay The great white grape variety of Burgundy came late to California but, once arrived, it swiftly came to play vanilla to Cabernet Sauvignon's chocolate. It has become so ubiquitous that many consumers use the name almost synonymously with white wine. However, grown in appropriate vineyards and made with care, it is still the premier white varietal wine of the state.

Wente Bros resolutely grew and made Chardonnay in LIVERMORE VALLEY during the 1940s. They were almost alone until 1952, when Napa's Stony Hill winery brought new attention to the varietal wine. With its celebrated 1957, Hanzell added the effects of new oak barrels to those of the vineyard, inspiring first dozens then scores to clamber on to that bandwagon. After a 1973 from Ch Montelena came first against some respectable white burgundies in a famous blind tasting in Paris in 1976, a whole new gold rush was on. Best estimates are that, by the late 1980s, California wineries were producing more than 700 different Chardonnays in each vintage.

As in Burgundy, indeed because of Burgundy, California Chardonnay is made as much or more in the cellar as in the vineyard. Barrel fermentation and OAK ageing, malolactic fermentation, and all the other tricks in the wine-maker's bag go into a wide range of styles from outright butterscotchy to straightforwardly fruity, with every stage in between. Most are dry, but a considerable number offer a softening dollop of sweetness (such as Kendall-Jackson's, whose supposed 'recipe' was the subject of a famous 1992 court case). California's greatest problem is a lack of semantic distinctions; buyers must divine style from sources other than the label.

The grape variety has proven remarkably adaptable, growing well throughout the coastal counties, and not badly in the SIERRA FOOTHILLS. Chardonnay is most widely planted in Napa, Monterey, and Sonoma counties, in almost equal measure.

Laube, J., *California's Great Chardonnays* (San Francisco, 1990).

Gewürztraminer The California history of this distinctive ALSACE variety, most often spelt without the umlaut here, is relatively short. It did not come into its own as a varietal wine until the 1950s, and it remains limited in acreage. The variety takes on a particular flavour in California: floral, almost sweet pea, in most of Napa and the warmer parts of Sonoma; very close to lychee in the cooler climates of Carneros, the Russian River Valley, and, above all, Mendocino County's Anderson Valley. Vineyards in the Central Coast show about the same range of flavours, although in less predictable geographic patterns. A substantial majority of California producers opt for off-dry styles, but a solid core make the wine dry. By and large, the dry wines are the ones to age in order to bring Gewürztraminer's perfumes to their most concentrated.

Merlot A scant historical record suggests that Merlot succeeded rarely and excelled never in California in the years before Prohibition. The practical result was that it virtually disappeared from the state between 1919 and 1969, when, at last, a few curious growers began experimenting with it as a possible blending grape to soften the tannins in Cabernet Sauvignon. Since the mid 1970s it has been the subject of an increasingly significant explosion of interest. It remains less than clear where in California Merlot will make its fame as a varietal wine. The variety has in part been held back by a widely held assumption that it is supposed to be a less tannic alternative to Cabernet Sauvignon rather than the sort of wine that comes naturally from this place or that. More broadly, it has yielded the bland sort of wines that caused it to disappear in the first place. However, more skilful growers and more determined winery owners have pushed scattered examples to heights heretofore not achieved. Of all the districts in which it has been tried to date, the most promising appear to be Napa's Stags Leap District, the Russian River Valley, and the Santa Ynez Valley. Much of the annual crop still goes into blends with Cabernet Sauvignon, usually in the amount of 10 to 15 per cent, or into MERITAGE-like blends in larger proportions.

Pinot Blanc Grapes and wines that go by this name in California may either be true PINOT BLANC or Melon de

Bourgogne, the Muscadet grape. Almost certainly existing vineyards contain some of each. Many plantings come from vine cuttings brought to California in the 1870s and 1880s; of these many bear closer resemblance to today's Melon than Pinot Blanc. Others are recent imports of authentic Pinot Blanc. Only a few patches of the sparse acreage of California Pinot Blanc have ever produced wines of real interest but these have had sufficient depth and longevity to maintain the variety's status. The most singular examples came long ago from Spring Mountain in the Napa Valley, more recently from the Santa Cruz Mountains, and Redwood Valley in Mendocino County. Sonoma County, Livermore Valley, and Monterey County are other sources.

Pinot Noir The secrets of Pinot Noir in California turned out to be two: fog in the vineyards and less time in wood in the cellars than it was given in the early 1980s. Pinot Noir perplexed California wine-makers for decades by producing truly outstanding wine once in a great while, but dull stuff most of the time. André TCHELISTCHEFF symbolizes the struggle, never having equalled by his own judgement the splendid pair he made for Beaulieu Vineyard in 1946 and 1947. The harder people tried to make something grand, the more often they fell short. In the 1970s the search for more suitable vineyards began to move ever closer to tidal shores. By the end of the 1980s, three districts had emerged, if not triumphant then at least much closer to triumph. Unified only by the persistence of their fogs, they are Carneros, the Russian River Valley of Sonoma, and Santa Barbara County, especially its Santa Maria Valley. On a slightly later curve, more and more wineries were trimming the time they left their Pinot Noirs in French oak barrels from two years or more to one year or less. With rare exceptions, long wood ageing diminishes California-grown Pinot Noirs to extinction. They emerge browning, raisiny, and dried out. The shorter span confers complexity of bouquet, yet leaves the wines richer in texture and readier to age well in bottle.

Riesling In the 1960s Riesling was, with Cabernet Sauvignon, Chardonnay, and Pinot Noir, one of the Big Four in California. Beginning in the 1970s its reputation began to decline, as an explosion in differing sweetness levels lacked a coherent set of semantic explanations. There may be a connection. During the 1980s both sales and acreage tumbled, and scores of wineries abandoned Germany's noblest grape, leaving it in the hands of a few stubborn supporters. It had already survived a longer-lasting identity crisis, having been popularly christened Johannisberg Riesling and academically named White Riesling—to distinguish it from Gray Riesling (TROUSSEAU), Franken Riesling (SILVANER), and California's own crossing EMERALD RIESLING.

California Riesling cannot be mistaken for its German counterparts, being riper in flavour and weightier with higher alcohol. It certainly is no competitor as an aperitif, but dry versions can outstrip most German Rieslings with meals because of a balance closer to traditional dry white wines from Italy or France. Its finest homes in California include Mendocino's Anderson Valley, Sonoma's Russian River Valley, and parts of the Napa Valley. It has sometimes done well in Monterey and Santa Barbara County. Although a fascination by wine-makers with BOTRYTIS-affected sweet wines may have helped cause its downfall as a drier wine, examples of the former have been memorable from the likes of Freemark Abbey, Chateau St Jean, and Joseph Phelps.

Sauvignon Blanc Dr Maynard A. AMERINE, long a voice of conscience for California wine-makers from his post at the University of California at Davis, has called Sauvignon Blanc California's greatest white grape. He has also confessed that the variety's forceful flavours may need tempering to appeal to the public. There, in a nutshell, is its career, whether under its own name or under the California-coined synonym FUMÉ BLANC. It makes outstanding wines that many find too specific to enjoy, especially against the milder charms of Chardonnay. Some age their Sauvignons in new oak, disguising it as a sort of poor man's Chardonnay. Some blend in proportions of Semillon to temper the flavour and fill out a characteristically light body. Some do both.

Certainly no other white wine variety is so widely adapted in the state. Memorable examples have come from Livermore Valley, Sonoma Valley, Napa Valley, and Santa Barbara. Scores of producers compete well; nearly every region in the state produces at least agreeably balanced wines from the variety. Generally speaking, straightforwardly styled Central Coast Sauvignon Blancs (Santa Ynez Valley, Monterey) smack sharply of the herbaceous or grassy flavours for which the Sauvignon is so widely noted. Their North Coast counterparts are more subtly herbaceous from the cooler zones (Russian River Valley, lower Napa Valley), almost melony from warmer areas (upper Napa Valley, upper Alexander Valley). Both the Sierra Foothills and Temecula give a curiously floral twist to the flavours.

In recent years, an ever-increasing number of growers have been allowing grapes to become botrytis affected for sweet wines styled after SAUTERNES. Early results have charmed in youth, but tended to fade quickly.

Zinfandel The 'native' variety for long suffered from an image problem. Lacking a specific European forebear (see ZINFANDEL) it must be taken on its own terms. Few critics have had the independence of mind to do so, and so it has struggled to find a style.

Although sometimes deliberately vinified to minimize this characteristic, Zinfandel can easily be chewier than a Cabernet. Beyond its robust textures, Zinfandel at the height of its powers tastes of a berry not unlike but more wonderful than the wild blackberries found only in burned-over foothills in the Pacific Northwest and, maybe, one strain of raspberry. Although it often has the structure and balance to age well, time does not replace its glorious flavours of berry with anything as pleasing. Flavours from oak barrels can also be difficult to work into harmony with the taste of berries. All the foregoing means that Zinfandel must come from a superior vineyard or be ordinary. Since it must compete for territory with Cabernet Sauvignon, the recent commercial success of red Zinfandel has been modest indeed.

The variety finds its most congenial home in Sonoma's Dry Creek Valley, with close competition from Sonoma Valley, Alexander Valley, and, though the fact is little recognized, the Napa Valley. San Luis Obispo County's Paso Robles AVA has a long, strong history with Zinfandel, as does the Sierra Foothills AVA. Both of these tend to make headier, riper wines than Sonoma and heady, port-style wines made from late harvested old Zinfandel vines in the Sierra Foothills, particularly Amador County, enjoyed a brief vogue in the early 1970s. See also WHITE ZINFANDEL.

Darlington, D., *Angel's Visits: An Inquiry into the Mystery of Zinfandel* (New York, 1991).

See also American BRANDY.

Adams, L., *The Wines of America* (4th edn., New York, 1990).
Muscatine, D., Amerine, M. A., and Thompson, B. (eds.), *The University of California / Sotheby Book of California Wine* (Berkeley, Calif., 1984).
Thompson, B., *Notes on a California Cellarbook* (New York, 1988).
—— *Wine Atlas of California and Traveller's Guide to the Vineyards* (London and New York, 1993).

CALLUS, the white, formless tissue that grows at cut and wounded surfaces on stems and roots. Its development is important during vine GRAFTING since it signifies that the conditions for cell division are favourable and that the underlying graft or bud has united, or that the cutting base has the right conditions for formation of new roots at the CAMBIUM layer within the stem tissues. High humidity, oxygen supply, and warm temperatures are the major requirements for rapid callus development. In the field these conditions may be achieved by waxing or by wrapping the tissues tightly with plastic grafting tape. After BENCH GRAFTING the cuttings are packed with moist material and held in a warm, humid room. Old callus becomes rust coloured. (See also TISSUE CULTURE.) B.G.C.

Hartmann, H. T., and Kester, D. E., *Plant Propagation: Principles and Practices* (3rd edn., Englewood Cliffs, NJ, 1975).

CALUSO, town in northern PIEDMONT most famous for its sweet white ERBALUCE.

CALYPTRA, or flower cap, of the vine flower consists of the five petals fused in the form of an inverted cup. The cap separates as a unit and falls from the grape flower at FLOWERING and exposes the STAMENS, which produce pollen, and the STIGMA, which receives pollen. Full bloom, or full flowering, is said to be when a large proportion (about two-thirds) of the caps have fallen. Caps tend to fall between 6 and 9 a.m. and between 2 and 4 p.m. The rate of capfall is slowed by cold and rain; the duration of capfall can stretch from a normal seven to 10 days to as long as 15 to 20 days. FRUIT SET is impaired if the caps are retained. B.G.C.

CÂMARA DE LOBOS, or **Cama de Lobos**, occasionally found on bottles of ancient MADEIRA, is a wine district west of the capital Funchal on the south coast of the island associated with noble vine varieties and fine wine.

CAMBIUM, a zone of dividing cells in plants involved in the secondary growth of stems and roots. In the vascular cambium of plants such as the grapevine, the inner cells develop into XYLEM and later differentiate into wood, while the outer cells develop PHLOEM and, later, bark. Cutting the bark through to the cambium, as is done in CINCTURING or girdling a vine, severs phloem connections at that point and interrupts the flow of nutrients (provided the ring encircles the trunk). The matching of cambial zones is important to the success of BUDDING and GRAFTING.

Another secondary cambium is the CORK cambium which cuts off non-living suberized cells yielding bark, as during vine CANE RIPENING, and cork oak stems yield the commodity so valued as wine bottle STOPPERS. B.G.C.

CAMPANIA, region of south west Italy of which Naples is the capital. In the ancient world Campania was the home of some of the most renowned wines of Italy, if not of the whole Mediterranean basin: SURRENTINE, Calenian, MASSIC, and, most famous of all, FALERNIAN. Modern reality is considerably more modest: only 1,100 ha / 2,700 acres of the region's total 48,000 ha / 118,600 acres of vineyards are in DOC zones, and the regional production of 34,000 hl / 898,000 gal of DOC wines is less than two per cent of the region's total production, the lowest proportion of any of Italy's 20 regions.

Campania's natural beauty can be deceptive: the bay of Naples, Capri, and the Amalfi coast do not reflect the grinding poverty of the depopulated interior, which has also been severely damaged in recent earthquakes, and the desperate *plebs* of its regional capital of Naples, Italy's third largest city, offer little in terms of an interesting market. The possibility of good-quality viticulture none the less exists: abundant sunshine and hillside sites for vineyards, volcanic soil quite suitable for vine-growing, and, most important of all, local vine varieties of real interest. AGLIANICO produces red wine of unquestionable character in the TAURASI DOC near Avellino, and non-DOC Aglianico wines of some potential can also be found in the province of Avellino (in the townships of Sabato, Bonito, Fontanarosa, Grottaminarda, Montefredane, Santa Lucia di Serino, Solofra, and Tufo) and in the province of Benevento, where the so-called Aglianico del Sannio is produced in the townships of Castelpoto, Paupisi, and Sant'Agata dei Goti.

The Solopaca DOC in the province of Benevento, with almost 500 ha / 12,300 acres, produces an interesting, if rustic, red wine with occasional notes of tobacco, from a blend of 45 to 60 per cent SANGIOVESE grapes, AGLIANICO (10 to 20 per cent), PIEDIROSSO (20 to 25 per cent), and other red varieties. Attempts to revive the glory of Falernian are under way, with the new Falerno del Massico DOC on the slopes of Monte Massico near Mondragone stipulating a blend of Aglianico (60 to 80 per cent), Piedirosso (20 to 40 per cent), plus PRIMITIVO or BARBERA (up to a maximum of 20 per cent). White and all-Primitivo versions are also made. The wines are still too young to be judged, although it seems safe to say that they will not match the 100-year-old Falernian served by Trimalchio in Petronius' *Satyricon*.

White wines are less significant in Campania, although FIANO d'Avellino and Greco di Tufo, both from the province of Avellino, have their devotees. Fiano d'Avellino, which takes its name from the variety the Romans called *Vitis apiana*, vine beloved of bees, is said to be redolent of pears and hazelnuts and bottles frequently carry the classical diction 'apianum'. Greco di Tufo, made from a clone of the GRECO vine grown around the village of Tufo, is said to recall peaches and almonds. Both of these descriptions correspond to the epoch in which the wines underwent some ageing in wood. Now made in a lighter, fresher style, they have become more technically correct, if less pronounced in flavour (although they can still display considerably more character than the average Italian white).

While the once-renowned viticulture of the island of Capri has virtually disappeared before the Gadarene onrush of modern tourism, ISCHIA has managed to maintain 165 ha of DOC vineyards, producing small quantities of white and minuscule quantities of red wine. D.T.

Anderson, B., *The Wine Atlas of Italy* (London and New York, 1990).
Gleave, D., *The Wines of Italy* (London and New York, 1989).

CAMPO DE BORJA, Spanish wine zone in the undulating plains around the town of Borja (named after the Borgia family) in the ARAGON region in the north east (see map on p. 907), producing mainly coarse, alcoholic red wines. This is one of the most arid parts of the country and low-yielding vineyards planted predominantly with GARNACHA vines produce intensely sweet, dark grapes which are made into heady red wines whose minimum permitted natural ALCOHOLIC STRENGTH is 13 per cent and may be as high as 18 per cent. Wine-making is concentrated in the hands of six, poorly equipped CO-OPERATIVES, although in the early 1990s the EUROPEAN UNION was funding some wine-making improvements. Some of the younger, fresher styles are exported. R.J.M.

CANAAN was the coastal region comprising a tiny part of modern TURKEY, the coast of modern SYRIA, LEBANON, and ISRAEL, from Gaza in the south to Hamath in the north, *c*.1000 BC. The pharaohs of Ancient EGYPT were struggling to maintain their control of this area during the 14th century BC, as we can read in the Amarna letters, an extensive correspondence between the pharaohs and the local puppet rulers and officials of Canaan. 'See that much food and wine—everything in great quantities—is made available for the archers of the king,' writes one Egyptian monarch.

Records on cuneiform tablets from the kingdom centres on the city of Ugarit (*c*.1200 BC; modern Ras Rhamra near Latakia about 160 km/100 miles north of the vineyards of modern Lebanon) indicate extensive viticulture. A standard formulation in describing properties for real estate transactions at this date mentions 'a house, together with its [watch-]tower, its olive grove and its vineyard'. However, life was as difficult in this area then as it was in the 1980s, since a complaint addressed by the prefect of Ugarit to a local great king, who was acting as mediator, stated that the people of Siyannu, a neighbouring city, 'have cut down our vines'. The people of Ugarit were obliged to swear not to cut down the vines of Siyannu, and moreover to swear (somewhat ingenuously) that they knew nothing of the identity of the perpetrators of such acts in the past. A similar dispute was adjudicated on the same occasion, this time concerning an allegation that wine from Ugarit had been stolen and sold unofficially to dealers at Beirut, down the coast. J.A.B.

CANADA. Largely unnoticed by the rest of the world, Canada grows wine in four of its 10 provinces: Ontario, British Columbia, Quebec, and Nova Scotia. The combined vineyards total more than 20,000 acres/8,000 ha. Most of the vines are winter-hardy HYBRIDS such as SEYVAL BLANC and VIDAL for white wines and MARÉCHAL FOCH and BACO Noir for reds. Since the late 1980s, however, growers have put greater emphasis on *vinifera* varieties, including CHARDONNAY, RIESLING, GAMAY, PINOT NOIR, CABERNET SAUVIGNON, and CABERNET FRANC. Thanks to the severity of Canadian winters, 'Icewine' is routinely made each year (from Vidal and Riesling) in much the same way as EISWEIN. Such wines regularly win prizes in international competitions and, thanks to predictable winter temperatures of −8 °C, Canada now produces more ICE WINE than any other country.

Geographically, the major concentration of Canadian vineyards is on the same latitude as the LANGUEDOC and CHIANTI, but polar temperatures in winter, and unpredictable weather in spring and at HARVEST, rank Canada as a COOL CLIMATE wine region, with all the wine-making problems that entails.

History

The Canadian wine industry dates from the early 19th century (although see also VÍNLAND). In 1811 a retired German corporal, Johann Schiller, domesticated the LABRUSCA vines he found growing along the Credit river west of Toronto and planted a 20-acre vineyard. In 1866 the country's first major winery Vin Villa was established at Canada's most southerly point, on Pelee Island on Lake Erie, by three gentlemen farmers from Kentucky who planted 20 acres/8 ha of ISABELLA vines. By 1890 there were 41 commercial wineries across the country, 35 in Ontario.

PROHIBITION, which began in Canada in 1916, spurred the wine trade. Thanks to some fancy political lobbying by the grape-growers, wine was exempted from the general interdiction against alcohol. By the time the Great Experiment was brought to an end in 1927 (six years before Repeal in the United States), 57 winery licences had been granted in Ontario alone.

In that year another experiment began, the creation of the provincial liquor board system, government MONOPOLIES which still control the sale and distribution of all beverage alcohol sold in Canada and collect millions of dollars in tax revenues. (By the 1990s Alberta and British Columbia had some privately owned wine merchant stores competing with government monopolies.)

Until the mid 1970s, Canadian wines were sweet, highly alcoholic products made from *labrusca* varieties and labelled Sherry or Port, depending on the colour.

The advent of the 'boutique' (small, usually owner-managed) winery was signalled in 1975 when Inniskillin, near Niagara Falls, was granted the first commercial licence since Prohibition. This coincided with a shift in public taste towards drier, less alcoholic, TABLE WINE. The wineries that followed in Ontario and British Columbia were dedicated to the proposition that *vinifera* grapes could be grown in the right soils in spite of the harsh winters and unpredictable springs.

In 1988 an APPELLATION system was introduced, first in Ontario and then in British Columbia. Called Vintners Quality Alliance (VQA), it stressed minimum MUST WEIGHTS but not minimum YIELDS. VQA wines must contain only locally grown grapes. In Ontario, Canada's most important wine region with 17,000 acres/6,900 ha under vine, wineries may also bottle wines which contain up to 75 per cent of grapes or grape-based material produced outside Canada (Chile became a popular source in the 1980s).

The Canadian wine industry has spawned a considerable number of 'farmgate wineries' in which grape-growers are developing agri-tourism by offering bed and breakfast accommodation and winery restaurants as well as wine.

Ontario

The climate, similar to that of the Finger Lakes region in NEW YORK state, is ameliorated by two bodies of water, Lakes Ontario and Erie. The major concentration of vineyards around the Niagara Peninsula is further protected by an escarpment, the shore of an Ice Age lake. This bluff above the vineyards encourages onshore winds which dissipate fog and minimize frost damage. Climatically similar to BURGUNDY, the region produces Chardonnay in the style of CHABLIS and Riesling grapes which, in GERMANY, would vary from KABINETT to BEERENAUSLESE degrees of ripeness. Pinot Noir, the great red burgundy grape, should in the right sites eventually produce wines that emulate VOLNAY, while early successes with the Cabernet Sauvignon, MERLOT, and Cabernet Franc grapes of Bordeaux augur well. Hybrids still predominate, however.

British Columbia

The BC wine industry is thousands of miles west of Ontario, much nearer the vineyards of WASHINGTON state in the United States than any other Canadian wine region. It is centred on the arid Okanagan valley in the south east of British Columbia where the deep Okanagan Lake warms the vineyards in winter. The pressures of free trade with the USA have forced many grape-growers to uproot their vines and in the early 1990s only 1,000 acres/400 ha of vineyard remained. The emphasis is mainly on white varieties such as the *vinifera* Riesling, GEWÜRZTRAMINER, PINOT BLANC, EHRENFELSER, BACCHUS, and Chardonnay, and the SEIBEL hybrid Verdelet. The style of wine-making here tends more towards the German model than the French.

Quebec

Cottage wineries (about 15 in the early 1990s) struggle to produce hybrid wines and a little Chardonnay along the American border around the town of Durham, with more of an eye to tourism than the production of great wines from its 250 acres of vines. Seyval Blanc is the main white wine variety while Maréchal Foch and CHANCELLOR are commonly used for reds. Some ice wine is also produced. The wines are sold almost exclusively from the cellar door.

Nova Scotia

The first small winery in Nova Scotia on Canada's Atlantic seaboard was Grand Pré in the Annapolis valley, where the bay of Fundy creates a suitable MESOCLIMATE for grape-growing. Russian grape varieties Michurnitz and Severnyi (probably VITIS *amurensis*, the result of a deal in which Nova Scotian raspberries were bartered for vine cuttings from RUSSIA) are cultivated here as well as the ubiquitous Maréchal Foch. Grand Pré has since been joined by two other wineries in the province around Malagesh on the Northumberland Strait. T.A.

Aspler, T., *Vintage Canada* (Toronto, 1993).
—— 'A Vine Mess', *Canadian Business* (May 1989), 37–42, 83–7.
Bramble, L., and Darling, S., *Discovering Ontario's Wine Country* (Toronto, 1992).
Schreiner, J., *The World of Canadian Wine* (Vancouver, 1984).

CANAIOLO, or **Canaiolo Nero**, red grape variety grown all over central Italy and, perhaps most famously, a permitted ingredient in the controversial recipe for CHIANTI, in which it played a more important part than SANGIOVESE in the 18th century. It has declined considerably in popularity since it was relatively difficult to graft in the wake of PHYLLOXERA, and suffered from poor, or CLONAL SELECTION. The decline in popularity of the GOVERNO wine-making trick has also hastened its decline since Canaiolo, without either the structure of Sangiovese or the scent or MAMMOLO, was most prized for its resistance to rot while being dried for *governo* use. Canaiolo is also grown, to an even more limited extent, in LATIUM, SARDINIA, and the MARCHES. Italy's total plantings of Canaiolo Nero declined from 6,600 ha/16,300 acres to 4,300 ha in the the 1980s, although the variety is specified in the regulations for 17 DOC wines.

A light-berried **Canaiolo Bianco** is also grown in Umbria, where, in ORVIETO, it is known as Drupeggio, but has also been declining in popularity.

CANARY ISLANDS, Spanish islands in the Atlantic ocean off the coast of Morocco which were famous in Shakespearian England, as witness Sir Toby Belch's call for 'a cup of canary' in *Twelfth Night*. Today most of the wine produced is mediocre and consumed by the hordes of tourists attracted to Tenerife and surrounding, smaller islands. The Canaries used to be famed for their sweet Malvasia-based wines, especially those made on Lanzarote, but production has declined and they have never been granted a DO. TACORONTE-ACENTEJO is the only denominated wine zone on the islands.

CANBERRA, the capital of AUSTRALIA, is ringed by wineries which together constitute a wine region called the Canberra district even if, because freeholds are not granted in the Australian Capital Territory itself, they are all over the border in NEW SOUTH WALES.

CANE, the stem of a mature grapevine shoot after the bark becomes tan-coloured and starts its overwintering form (see CANE RIPENING and CAMBIUM). After leaves have fallen, the canes of a vine display the total vegetative growth it made during the previous season (called the 'brush' in the USA). The number of canes and their weight and average size are important guides to decisions about BALANCED PRUNING and CANOPY MANAGEMENT tactics. The canes are cut at winter PRUNING to reduce the number of buds and to select their position. The cutting may be to SPURS of less than five buds or to canes of five to 16 buds. B.G.C.

CANE PRUNING, a form of winter vine PRUNING in which the buds are retained on longer bearers called CANES, typically including six to 15 buds. This pruning system usually takes longer to perform than the alternative SPUR PRUNING, and cannot be mechanized. Cane pruning is typically used for those varieties which have fewer FRUITFUL buds at the base of canes. For more details see GUYOT pruning. R.E.S.

CANE RIPENING, or *aoûtement* in French, viticultural term used to describe a stage in the development of the shoot when the stem matures and changes colour from green to yellow and thence to brown. At this time, the stem becomes a cane. The change involves the formation of corky tissue known as periderm and cellular changes including the accumulation of CARBOHYDRATE reserves, which collectively prepare the stem to withstand the cold of winter. The process begins at the base of the shoot and progresses up towards the tip, as does the dormancy status of its buds. VERAISON, the change in colour of the grapes, usually occurs at about the same time. B.G.C.

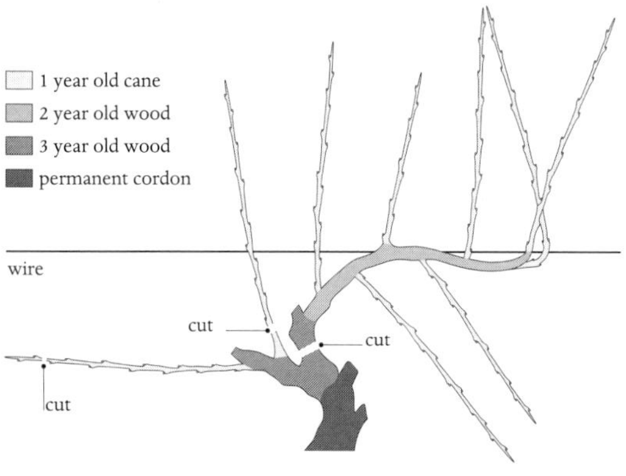

Cane pruning: at pruning the cane retained during the previous winter is removed. The mature shoots from the replacement spur are cut so as to produce a unit comprising a two node (replacement) spur and a 10 to 15 node cane.

CANNONAU, sometimes spelt **Cannonao**, the SARDINIAN name for the widely planted red grape variety known in Spain as Garnacha and in France as GRENACHE. A high proportion of the grapes are grown on the east of the island to produce a varietal **Cannonau di Sardegna** which comes in several forms, but most commonly as a full throttle dryish red. Although the variety is being pulled out by some Sardinian growers, there were still more than 11,000 ha/27,000 acres of Cannonau on the island in 1990.

CANON-FRONSAC, underrated Bordeaux wine appellation. See FRONSAC for more details.

CANOPY, that part of the vine above the ground, which includes leaves and fruit. See CANOPY MANAGEMENT.

CANOPY MANAGEMENT, a portfolio of vineyard management techniques used to improve vineyard YIELD, wine QUALITY, and the control of VINE DISEASES where vines are particularly vigorous. These techniques essentially alter the exposure of leaves and fruit to the sun. The phrase became popular in many parts of the New World in the 1980s and early 1990s as part of a growing awareness of the way in which CANOPY MICROCLIMATE affects vineyards. This awareness was not restricted to the New World. Considerable experimental work was also conducted in Europe, and the effects of canopy microclimate are now recognized as an explanation for the ability of distinguished vineyards to produce great wines (see VITICULTURE).

Although some of the concepts of canopy management can be traced to early Roman writings, the principles were best formulated by the experimental work of Professor Nelson Shaulis of Cornell University in New York state. During the 1960s he experimented with CONCORD vines and showed that increased fruit and leaf exposure to sunlight improved both yield and fruit composition. These early studies were also much involved with introducing MECHANICAL HARVESTERS and winter PRUNING. Shaulis influenced researchers from other countries, who extended this work to VINIFERA vine varieties and also considered effects on wine quality. Studies in Bordeaux by Dr Alain Carbonneau demonstrated wine quality benefits of canopy manipulation in the mid 1970s. Other notable early studies were by Intrieri in Italy, Kliewer in California, and Smart in Australia and New Zealand.

Canopy management techniques are essentially aimed at producing a desirable canopy microclimate, which is characterized by good leaf and fruit exposure to the sun and other climate elements. The benefits of such a microclimate include improvements to wine quality and yield, and a significant reduction in diseases such as POWDERY MILDEW and BOTRYTIS BUNCH ROT. Interest in overcoming the common problems of excessively vigorous vines caused canopy management techniques to become popular. This was particularly marked in the New World, where a lack of experience to guide site selection and management practices resulted in some vineyards whose vines were so leafy and the fruit so shaded that it affected ripeness and wine quality. These problems were exacerbated by the AGROCHEMICALS developed after the Second World War to control pests, diseases, and weeds, which, along with practices such as FERTILIZATION and IRRIGATION, stimulated shoot growth, often excessively. Canopy management techniques can offset the negative effects of vines with excess VIGOUR, but are not applicable to low-vigour vineyards such as those found in most of the classic fine wine regions of Europe.

A common feature of all vineyards with a reputation for producing high-quality wines is that they are of moderate to low vigour, and that the canopy microclimate is characterized by good exposure of leaves and fruit to the sun. Canopy management techniques can emulate this microclimate. For example, by altering TRELLIS SYSTEMS, it is possible to alter the fruit position from the deep shade of the canopy interior to the outside of the canopy in the sun. Canopy management can also increase yield, which is reduced by densely shaded conditions. In particular, BUDBREAK and FRUITFULNESS are reduced by shade, no doubt an example of adaptive physiology which allowed WILD VINES to fruit only when they had climbed to the top of forest canopies. With increasing global concern about the use of agricultural chemicals there is a swing towards using canopy management to help control FUNGAL DISEASES and reduce reliance on sprays. Not only is it difficult and wasteful to force sprays to penetrate to the centre of dense canopies, but shaded conditions also encourage diseases such as botrytis bunch rot and powdery mildew.

There are a range of canopy management techniques, the applicability of which varies from vineyard to vineyard. The simplest of these are TRIMMING, which cuts off excessive shoot growth in the summer, SHOOT THINNING which removes unwanted shoots early in the season, LEAF REMOVAL in the fruit zone, which allows more exposure to sun and wind, and SHOOT POSITIONING, which makes trimming and leaf removal easy and effective. PRUNING also affects canopy density, as well as vine BALANCE. These practices may be termed 'Bandaid viticulture' in the sense that they overcome the problem only in the season during which they are applied, and need to be reapplied each year. More permanent solutions are found by altering the trellis system, which affects the canopy shape, size, and density. The changes to the trellis usually involve increasing the canopy surface area and decreasing canopy density. For example, dense canopies in vineyards where rows are as much as 3.5 m / 11.5 ft apart can be converted to a trellis system such as GENEVA DOUBLE CURTAIN, which effectively results in a canopy twice as long as the row. This is achieved by dividing the canopy into two curtains, thereby doubling the canopy surface area.

Many New World viticulturists are adopting the simpler canopy management techniques, but changes to trellis systems are slower because generally the costs are greater and can involve investments in plant machinery such as machine harvesters.

Canopy management: The canopy of Petaluma's Pinot Noir vines in South Australia is held up by special wires to maximize the leaves' exposure to the sun.

There is less scope in the Old World for canopy management since ROW SPACING is traditionally less, and trimming and leaf removal are used anyway. Centuries of trial and error have demonstrated the benefits of open canopies to improve wine quality and reduce vine diseases. Many German vineyard canopies, for example, could well be emulated in many New World situations. However, in the Old World the benefits of canopy management are often not recognized as such by traditional viticulturists, many of whom ascribe the quality and disease effects solely to the associated lower yield or vigour. By the early 1990s, however, there were already examples in Old World commercial viticulture—in France, Italy, and Spain—where trellises had been altered for canopy management reasons. R.E.S.

Smart, R. E., and Robinson, M., *Sunlight into Wine: A Handbook of Winegrape Canopy Management* (Adelaide, 1991).

CANOPY MICROCLIMATE, the climate within and immediately around the CANOPY. This is the third stage of climate definition (see also MACROCLIMATE, MESOCLIMATE). The canopy microclimate at the outside of the canopy is obviously affected by the macroclimate and mesoclimate, but that within the canopy depends on the way the canopy itself alters the climate. Bright sunlight falling on a dense canopy with few gaps in California's Napa Valley may be considered as an example. Suppose a leaf facing the sun at midday receives 100 relative units of sunlight. The second leaf in the canopy will receive less than 10 units and the third will receive less than one. So the second leaf in the canopy has a light climate like that of a northern European vineyard on an overcast day. In other words, the canopy density can have even more effect than can vineyard location on sunlight levels on the leaves. This drastic reduction in sunlight levels in the canopy is caused by the vine leaves absorbing and reflecting more than 90 per cent of light falling on the upper surface; less than 10 per cent penetrates through to the lower surface.

This illustrates the importance of canopy microclimate, and indeed how its effects can override those of regional CLIMATE, CLONE, ROOTSTOCK, and so on. (See VITICULTURE.) A feature of vineyards with a high reputation, be they in the Old World or the New, is that they are typically of low VIGOUR and as a result the canopies are not dense or shaded. Many vineyards with a high VINE AGE are also like this. Leaves and fruit are well exposed to the sun, so the microclimate in the centre of the canopy is not too different from that of the canopy outside. For vigorous and high-yielding vineyards, on the other hand, the canopy interior is a dark, humid, cool place by day. Not only are the processes of fruit RIPENING affected, but FUNGAL DISEASES such as BOTRYTIS BUNCH ROT and POWDERY MILDEW are encouraged. CANOPY MANAGEMENT techniques can be used to provide high-vigour vineyards with the same canopy microclimate as that of low-vigour vineyards.

Of the various climatological elements such as SUNLIGHT, HUMIDITY, TEMPERATURE, RAINFALL, EVAPORATION, and WIND, the canopy has greatest effect on sunlight, wind, and evaporation. The values of these three elements in the centre of a dense canopy can be less than one-tenth of those above the canopy, while temperature and humidity values are more similar to those outside the canopy. It is the leaves of the vine canopy that are responsible for creating the distinctive canopy microclimate. They strongly absorb sunlight and the energy (strictly, momentum) of wind so that values below just one leaf are very different from those above it. Since evaporation depends on sunlight and wind, it is easy to appreciate that these values will also be reduced below the first leaf layer.

It is obvious therefore that the amount of vine leaf area has a significant effect on canopy microclimate. If there is no shortage of visible gaps in the vine canopy, with most leaves and fruit exposed, then the canopy microclimate values will not be too different from those above the canopy. If, on the other hand, the canopy is dense and the majority of leaves and bunches are not visible, then it is fair to conclude that wine QUALITY and YIELD are both below the vineyard's potential. That a visual impression of the canopy can be so definitive in terms of the vineyard's ability to produce good-quality wines is the basis of a system of vineyard SCORING used to assess vineyard potential to produce quality wine. R.E.S.

Smart, R. E., and Robinson, M., *Sunlight into Wine: A Handbook of Winegrape Canopy Management* (Adelaide, 1991).

CANS. Ordinary wine is occasionally packaged in cans which have no harmful effect on wine destined for early consumption. The advantages are that cans are lighter and less fragile than BOTTLES, but the material from which they are made is not, unlike GLASS, inert.

CANTINA, Italian for a cellar, a wine shop (although the word ENOTECA is more promising), and a winery (and, tellingly, a hovel). A **cantina sociale** is a CO-OPERATIVE winery.

CAP (*chapeau* in French), the layer of grape solids that floats on the liquid surface during red wine FERMENTATION. It usefully limits the amount of OXYGEN available to the YEAST, thereby encouraging the formation of alcohol, but has to be broken up and submerged in order to encourage the extraction of the desirable PHENOLICS which add colour, flavour, and longevity to a wine. See MACERATION, PUMPING OVER, and PUNCHING DOWN.

CAP stands for Common Agricultural Policy, a plank of EUROPEAN UNION policy which has had enormous effects on world wine production.

CAPE RIESLING, South African name for the French white grape variety CROUCHEN Blanc that is virtually extinct in its native France but is grown in Australia as Clare Riesling. Also known as Paarl Riesling and South African Riesling, but much less distinguished than true RIESLING, which is also known as Weisser Riesling in South Africa, Cape Riesling produces an unexceptional dry white, its popularity due to a combination of the name, its undemanding blandness, and reasonable price. Nearly 3,500 ha / 8,600 acres were planted in South Africa in the early 1990s. J.P.

CAPITOLARE, name given in 1993 by a group of producers in TUSCANY to a special group of wines previously described as PREDICATO. It means chapter or classification, and refers to wines made from INTERNATIONAL vine VARIETIES using BARREL MATURATION.

CAPSULE, French and occasional English name for the sheath over the top of a cork and bottle-neck, otherwise known as a FOIL, just as the **capsule cutter** is more widely known as a foil cutter. French wine released for sale within

Capsules (foils) made from (left to right) plastic, tin, and the traditional lead model on a bottle of red bordeaux at the back.

France, as opposed to export, must have its capsules embossed with a customs seal, known as a **capsule congé**.

CARAMANY is a commune constituting a special, named enclave in the area designated for Côtes du ROUSSILLON Villages. At least 60 per cent of the total blend, including any Carignan used, must be vinified by CARBONIC MACERATION, which technique was pioneered in the area by the Caramany CO-OPERATIVE.

CARBAMATES, or **urethanes**, relatively simple organic compounds found in very low concentrations in some foods and wines. Ethyl carbamate, or ethyl urethane, formed by complex routes from compounds containing NITROGEN in grapes from vineyards given excess nitrogen FERTILIZERS, were in the late 1980s added to the growing list of compounds suspected of human carcinogenicity on the basis of animal tests.

Most wine types contain ethyl carbamate concentrations well below the limit suggested by US authorities of 10 mg per litre. High alcohol, sweet wines which have been heated during production (such as MADEIRA) are likely to be the wines with the highest levels of ethyl carbamate. A.D.W.

CARBOHYDRATES, organic compounds made up of carbon, oxygen, and hydrogen and which include sugars, starch, and cellulose. Of particular interest to the wine consumer are the simple sugar molecules glucose and FRUCTOSE, which together make up the SUGARS in grape juice, which are subsequently fermented into the alcohol which distinguishes wine from grape juice. Sucrose is the sugar molecule made up of glucose and fructose and is manufactured in the leaves of plants, including vines, by PHOTOSYNTHESIS. Sucrose can be converted to all other forms of carbohydrates, such as starch, as a storage compound in the roots and trunks, and cellulose, which is present in all cells. Sucrose is also the basic plant biochemical building block, and can be converted to proteins, fats, and organic acids.

A vine's reserves of carbohydrates are an important factor in its healthy annual growth cycle. STARCH is the principal form of carbohydrate reserve which is stored in the woody vine parts in the autumn. The starch is converted into SUGARS which, via RESPIRATION, provide the chemical energy for growing shoots early the following spring. The reason perennial plants, such as vines, can grow to such a large size is this ability to store surplus chemical energy each growing season, which is then available for shoot growth the following season.

At about VERAISON, when the fruit starts to ripen, the vine begins to replace carbohydrate reserves used earlier that growing season. Sugars are moved into the trunk, arms, and roots, where they are converted to the insoluble storage material starch. As shoots accumulate starch they change colour, from green to brown; this is called CANE RIPENING. Ideally there should be a period of warm, sunny weather after HARVEST during which the leaves can manufacture the sugars to provide the final topping up of starch reserves. However, this ideal state of affairs can be disrupted, for example by large crops of grapes or late season shoot growth which slows ripening and limits the amounts of starch formed. Similarly, an autumn FROST which destroys leaves can interrupt the orderly buildup of reserves in the vine. High levels of carbohydrate reserves of sugars and starches make vines better able to withstand WINTER FREEZE, providing them with a sort of biological antifreeze mechanism. Although starch is the main carbohydrate storage compound, there are some other minor compounds such as AMINO ACIDS and carboxylic acids which show the same pattern of autumn accumulation and spring depletion.

Early shoot growth in spring is entirely dependent on these stored reserves, which are mobilized in the woody parts and moved to the developing shoots. If there are too many new shoots growing for the reserves available then new growth will be checked. The concept of BALANCED PRUNING ensures that the number of buds retained is proportional to the reserves available. The new shoots become independent of these reserves when the leaves reach about half their final size, and photosynthesis is sufficient to support further growth.

See also WOOD, in which the carbohydrate cellulose plays an important part. R.E.S.

Winkler, A. J., *et al.*, *General Viticulture* (2nd edn., Berkeley, Calif., 1974).

CARBON, ACTIVE. See CHARCOAL.

CARBON DIOXIDE, or CO_2, a naturally occurring atmospheric gas, commonly encountered as the sparkle in soft drinks, beers, and SPARKLING WINES. Its content in the atmosphere is only about 0.03 of a per cent; yet upon that small amount depends the growth of all living systems, including man, vines, yeasts, bacteria, all plants, and the existence of all fauna depending on them for food. Not least, it is the ultimate raw material of wine, via a biochemical chain which sees its elaboration (with water) into sugars in the vine leaves by PHOTOSYNTHESIS; conversion in the leaves and berries of some of that sugar into a variety of compounds, including those directly or indirectly responsible for ACIDS, COLOUR, and FLAVOUR in the grapes and wine; and, as the final step, transformation of the grapes into wine by FERMENTATION. It returns whence it came with the metabolism of the alcohol and other wine constituents back to carbon dioxide and water, or with the ultimate (in wine drinkers, usually much delayed) decomposition of the happy consumer's last mortal remains.

Carbon dioxide passes into vine leaves through small pores, or STOMATA. The greater the atmospheric concentration, the more can pass in, and the greater the potential growth and yield of the wine (provided that other factors such as water, light, temperature, or nutrients are not more directly limiting). Advanced commercial glasshouse culture of many fruits and vegetables uses artificially enhanced carbon dioxide concentrates two or three times those in the outside atmosphere, thereby attaining both higher yields and better product quality (Mortensen 1987).

Carbon dioxide concentrations in the earth's atmosphere have increased by some 25 per cent since the beginning of the Industrial Revolution, largely through the burning of fossil fuels. By analogy, it seems certain that this has already helped to increase the yields of grapevines, and, very possibly, grape and wine quality. Theoretical arguments have been advanced that it may also have tended to raise the optimum ripening temperatures for grape and wine quality.

See CLIMATE CHANGE. J.G.

Mortensen, L. M., 'Review: CO_2 enrichment in glasshouses: crop responses', *Scientia horticulturae*, 33 (1987), 1–25.

In wine-making

Carbon dioxide is used throughout the wine-making process to displace oxygen from contact with crushed grapes or wine. At some wineries carbon dioxide is deliberately pumped over white grapes as they are received at the winery and pass through the destemmer in order to minimize OXIDATION. Draining tanks, presses, storage and blending vats, filters, and bottling lines are all examples where carbon dioxide may be applied by fastidious wine-makers.

Carbon dioxide also plays an important role in fermentation of all wines. Like man, YEAST metabolizes starches and sugars to produce water and carbon dioxide. In the human case, carbon dioxide from muscle or brain activity dissolves in the blood, is transferred to the lungs and then to the atmosphere as exhaled breath. In the case of yeast's metabolic activity in six-carbon sugar solutions such as grape juice, the three main by-products are water, ETHANOL, and carbon dioxide. If excess oxygen is available, the yeast obtains more cell-building energy from the sugar by converting it to carbon dioxide and water. With only a moderate oxygen supply, the yeast produces carbon dioxide and the ethanol that distinguishes wine from grape juice.

As winery visitors during vintage time may discover, while wine is fermenting, substantial quantities of carbon dioxide are given off which, while not being inherently toxic to man, displace oxygen so that, in a confined space such as a FERMENTATION VESSEL, suffocation is all too possible. Winery workers must exercise particular caution in this respect.

In most still wines this carbon dioxide is encouraged to dissipate leaving only very small amounts in the finished wine—although the more PROTECTIVE the wine-making, the more substantial these traces may be, as in, for example, many German and other light, aromatic, white wines. (Wine-makers may, however, choose to remove carbon dioxide from such wines by SPARGING them with NITROGEN just before bottling.)

In sparkling wines, however, substantial quantities of dissolved carbon dioxide, between two and six atmospheres, are encouraged to remain in the bottle by one of the methods outlined in SPARKLING WINE-MAKING. Lesser quantities of carbon dioxide, between one and two atmospheres, may be encouraged in wines such as those labelled PERLANT, PÉTILLANT, or FRIZZANTE by inducing a second but less violent fermentation and preserving the carbon dioxide produced.

Since the 1960s, however, a number of wine-makers in hotter, particularly New World, regions pursue a deliberate policy of bottling wine, particularly white wine, with up to one atmosphere of carbon dioxide dissolved in it. This is because carbon dioxide, as it vaporizes from the wine, carries with it many ESTERS and thus tends to increase a wine's freshness and fruitiness, attributes which the wine-maker may well wish to enhance. This is done by processing the wine at very low temperatures where carbon dioxide is much more soluble in wine, and bottling it early in order to preserve some of the gas given off during fermentation. The warmer the wine is served, the more obvious is the carbon dioxide to the taster.

While most tasters would be surprised and probably shocked to notice any carbon dioxide in a mature red bordeaux (in which case it could even be taken to be an unwelcome sign of FERMENTATION IN BOTTLE), it is not necessarily a fault in most types of white and rosé wines. Portugal's VINHO VERDE provides many examples of this deliberate wine style, and some Italian red wines contain a perceptible level of carbon dioxide, sometimes as a result of the GOVERNO practice of adding dried grapes to provoke a second fermentation.

Carbon dioxide also plays an essential role in CARBONIC MACERATION. A.D.W.

CARBONIC ACID is the acid form when CARBON DIOXIDE is dissolved in water, H_2CO_3.

CARBONIC MACERATION, red wine-making process which transforms a small amount of SUGAR IN GRAPES to

ETHANOL without the intervention of yeasts, and without even crushing the grapes. It is used typically to produce light-bodied, brightly-coloured, fruity red wines for early consumption, most famously but by no means exclusively in the Beaujolais region of France.

Whole bunches or clusters of grapes are deliberately placed, with care to ensure that the berries are not broken, in an anaerobic atmosphere, generally obtained by using CARBON DIOXIDE to exclude OXYGEN. An intracellular fermentation takes place within the intact berry and a small amount of ethanol is formed, along with traces of many flavourful aromatic compounds. All of these contribute to the distinctive flavour and aroma of the resultant wines. The maceration period in this anaerobic environment and phase, where these aromatic compounds are produced, depends on temperature, and can be from one to three weeks. (The process is not normally applied to white grapes as undesirable flavours are formed.)

Louis PASTEUR observed in 1872 that grape berries held in air differed in flavour from those held in a carbon dioxide atmosphere (although he, wrongly, suspected that grapes held in carbon dioxide would produce wines for long ageing).

It is likely that the same metabolic pathways are involved in carbonic maceration as in normal alcoholic fermentation but the flavour differences suggest that other processes are also concerned. Michel Flanzy, whose work dates from 1936, and other French researchers have observed that ordinary grapes held intact for several days under a carbon dioxide atmosphere and then crushed and allowed to ferment produce a wine which is much brighter-coloured, less tannic and more distinctively perfumed than one made normally.

Detailed studies suggest that whole grapes held under carbon dioxide lose about a fifth of their sugar, gain about two per cent in ALCOHOLIC STRENGTH, show a tenfold gain in GLYCEROL, lose about half of their harsh MALIC ACID, and show an increase in PH of about 0.25, all within the intact berry. These measurements exclude any changes in FLAVOUR COMPOUNDS. It is thought that the distinguishing volatile compounds include the volatile PHENOLS, benzaldehyde, vinylbenzene, ethyl cinnamate, ethyl vanillate, and methyl vanillate.

In practical terms it is almost impossible to produce a wine that depends wholly on carbonic maceration. Whole clusters are poured into a vat which is then filled with carbon dioxide and sealed. The weight of the upper grapes breaks open the bottom layer of grapes which begin to ferment in the normal way with oxygen excluded. In the middle layer are whole grapes surrounded by juice, and only on the top layer are whole grapes surrounded by carbon dioxide which undergo full carbonic maceration. The grapes in the middle layer undergo similar intracellular transformations, but at a much slower rate.

In traditional wine-making it was common for uncrushed grapes at the top of a closed fermentation vessel to undergo carbonic maceration since the fermenting crushed grapes at the bottom would give off carbon dioxide which would exclude oxygen from the top of the vat. Thus, alcoholic fermentation and carbonic maceration would proceed simultaneously. This also applies to some red burgundy made today using WHOLE GRAPE fermentations.

The technique is open to much regional and personal modification (see SEMI-CARBONIC MACERATION as an example). Some wine-makers allow one or two days' maceration in carbon dioxide while others, or those same ones in different vintages, may prefer a week or two under the gas. The less ripe the year, the longer the carbonic maceration needed because of its work in removing malic acid.

Although Beaujolais is the most famous wine region where carbonic maceration is the most common wine-making technique, it is also widely used for the Beaujolais grape Gamay in other parts of France, for more commercial reds in the southern Rhône, and has been a major factor in persuading the tough Carignan grape to yield red wines for early drinking in the Languedoc-Roussillon in southern France (although there is an increasing tendency to blend these with traditionally made wines). Its use in the New World has been limited to some novel products such as the 'CabMac' designed as Australia's answer to Beaujolais. The wines produced tend to have a very particular, aroma which some find reminiscent of bananas, others of kirsch. Researchers, notably Ducruet in the early 1980s, suggest that this is due to the formation of compounds formed during the anaerobic metabolism of acid phenolics which may include benzaldehyde, vinylbenzene, ethyl vanillate, and methyl vanillate, and, especially, ethyl cinnamate. A.D.W.

Sneyd, T. N., 'Carbonic maceration: an overview', *Australian and New Zealand Wine Industry Journal*, 4 (1989), 281–5.

CARBONIZATION, the cheapest and least effective method of SPARKLING WINE-MAKING involving the simple pumping of CARBON DIOXIDE into a tank of wine.

CARCAVELOS, one of just over a dozen regions in PORTUGAL awarded DOC status, although the vineyards have almost been obliterated by the westward expansion of the capital city Lisbon along the Tagus estuary (see map on p. 750). A cynic's view of Carcavelos is that it was created by the marquis of Pombal, Portugal's autocratic 18th century prime minister, because he had to do something with the grapes from his country residence at nearby Oeiras. He even flouted his own regulations and permitted Carcavelos to be blended with PORT. However, Pombal established the reputation of Carcavelos as a FORTIFIED wine which enjoyed a brief period of popularity in Britain in the early part of the 19th century (and see AUCTIONS for evidence of its renown even earlier). The wine may be made from a blend of up to nine different red and white grapes. It is usually fermented dry and fortified with GRAPE SPIRIT up to an ALCOHOLIC STRENGTH of 18 to 20 per cent. A small amount of *vinho abafado* (fermenting grape must preserved by the addition of alcohol) is added after FERMENTATION to sweeten the wine. Between three and five years' CASK AGEING give the wine a nutty character akin to a tawny port. Carcavelos was demarcated in 1908 but, of the land originally included, only Pombal's palace and one vineyard remain. R.J.M.

CAREMA, almost alpine red wine zone of PIEDMONT in north west Italy, bordering on the Valle d'AOSTA, is the northernmost zone of Piedmont in which the great NEBBIOLO grape—present here in the Picutener and Pugnet clones, the approximate equivalents of the Lampia and Michet of the LANGHE—is cultivated (although see also VALTELLINA). Viticulture is not an easy task in this mountainous region, and the vineyards have been wrested from steep gradients by means of TERRACES and supporting stone walls similar to those of CÔTE RÔTIE or CONDRIEU, although the low VINE DENSITY and the TENDONE training system bear no resemblance to the north RHÔNE. The wine itself has a recognizably Nebbiolo character, with a higher ACIDITY and less body than the better wines of the Langhe or of GATTINARA, but interesting, perfumed, and pleasurable wines are regularly made in hot years. The total potential vineyard area is 120 ha/300 acres, although only 60 were planted in the mid 1990s, and of these only 40 produced a DOC wine, approximately 200 hl/5,300 gal annually. The 40 ha are divided among over 120 growers, for most of whom viticulture is of course only a part-time activity at best; the resulting wines have been of variable quality in the past, although mastery of MALOLACTIC FERMENTATION has resulted in better and more consistent wines from the local co-operative winery. Producer Luigi Ferrando works hard at maintaining the wine's reputation. D.T.

Anderson, B., *The Wine Atlas of Italy* (London and New York, 1990).
Gleave, D., *The Wines of Italy* (London and New York, 1989).

CARIGNAN, known as **Carignane** in the USA, **Carignano** in Italy, and **Cariñena** in Spain, late-ripening black grape variety which could fairly be called the bane of the European wine industry. Carignan, distinguished only by its disadvantages, has dug its roots into so much of the southern French *vignoble* that even the most generous of European Union bribes are having their work cut out to eradicate it. It is better than the ARAMON it replaced, however.

Throughout the 1960s it infiltrated the Midi, then rapidly trying to fill the void left in the national blending vat by the independence of Algeria, to such an extent that it has been France's most planted black grape variety ever since the mid 1960s and, although declining rapidly (almost half of all Carignan vines are well over 30 years old) is still almost twice as popular as its nearest rival Grenache Noir. Of all vines ripped out during the 1980s and 1990s under the EU's scheme to rid Europe of its wine surplus, Carignan has quite rightly been the most common casualty.

From the perspective of the 1990s, Carignan seems a very odd choice indeed, although presumably it seemed obvious to many *pieds noirs* returning from Algeria, where the wine industry depended at one time on its 140,000 ha/350,000 acres of Carignan. Its wine is high in everything—acidity, tannins, colour, bitterness—but finesse and charm. This gives it the double inconvenience of being unsuitable for early consumption yet unworthy of maturation. The vine is not even particularly easy to grow. It is extremely sensitive to POWDERY MILDEW, quite sensitive to DOWNY MILDEW, prone to rot, and prey to infestation by grape worms. Its diffusion has been extremely beneficial to the agrochemical industry. Its bunches keep such a tenacious hold on the vine that it does not adapt well to mechanical harvesting, but then the majority of Carignan is not trained on wires anyway but grows in gnarled old bushes that do not share the stability of GRENACHE.

There must have been some attribute to have Carignan disseminated so exclusively throughout the Midi in the 1950s and 1960s, and there was: yield. The vine can quite easily be persuaded to produce almost 200 hl/ha (11 tons/acre), ideal for a thirsty but not discriminating market. It also buds late, which gave it extra allure as a substitute for the much lighter Aramon, previously France's number one vine, which had been badly affected by the frosts of 1956 and 1963. It ripens late too, however, limiting its cultivation to Mediterranean wine regions. The French agricultural census of 1988 found that more than 70 per cent of France's total area of Carignan, 167,000 ha, was in the two major Languedoc *départements* of the Aude and Hérault. It is also the dominant variety in Gard and Pyrénées-Orientales and is planted in quantity all over southeastern France too. The south west has been saved from Carignan by its cooler, wetter autumns.

The regulations for the Languedoc-Roussillon's appellations have been forced to embrace the ubiquitous Carignan, which still accounts for almost half of all vines planted there. But it is hard to argue that, for example, Minervois or Corbières are improved by their (continually reduced) Carignan component. Those wines that depend most heavily on the 'improving' varieties such as Syrah and Mourvèdre and least on Carignan are almost invariably the most successful.

Only the most carefully farmed old vines on well-placed, low-yielding sites such as Fernand Vaquer's in Roussillon can produce Carignan with real character. Elsewhere, the widespread introduction of CARBONIC MACERATION has helped disguise, if not exactly compensate for, Carignan's lack of youthful charm. The astringence of basic vin de table has owed much to this vine, although blending with Cinsaut or Grenache helps considerably.

The white mutation **Carignan Blanc** can still be found in some vineyards of the Languedoc and, in particular, Roussillon.

Although the vine (like Grenache) originated in Spain in the province of Aragon, it is not widely planted there today. Carignan is not even the principal grape variety in the wine that carries its Spanish synonym CARIÑENA. It is grown chiefly in Catalonia today although it was historically, as Mazuelo, a not particularly distinguished ingredient in Rioja. It also plays a major part in the wines of Costers del Segre, Penedès, Tarragona, and Terra Alta, so that Spain had total plantings of around 12,000 ha/30,000 acres in the early 1990s.

The vine, gaining a vowel as Carignane, has been import-

Typically overburdened old **Carignan** vines at Arboras, Hérault, in the Languedoc.

ant in the Americas. Although rarely seen today as a varietal, there were still more than 10,000 acres / 4,000 ha in California's hotter regions in 1992 for the vine's productivity and vigour are valued by growers, if not consumers. Galet reports total plantings of 13,500 ha in Mexico and Carignan is also grown (to a much lesser extent) in Argentina, Chile, and Uruguay.

Because of its late ripening habits, Carignan can thrive only in relatively hot climates. At one time it underpinned Israel's wine industry and it is by no means unknown in Italy. As Carignano it is grown in Latium and most commonly in Sardinia, perhaps as a result of that island's long dominance by Aragon, where it makes strong reds and rosés. Italy's total plantings of Carignano had fallen to about 2,500 ha by 1990.

The Carignan era is surely long past.

Galet, P., *Cépages et vignobles de France* (2nd edn., Montpellier, 1990).

CARIÑENA, town in north east SPAIN which lends its name to both a denominated wine zone and a vine variety, widely grown in southern France as CARIGNAN. Although it is known to originate in the area, the vine (also called Mazuelo) has been widely abandoned in its native region in favour of GARNACHA, which seems better suited to the arid growing conditions in this, the largest of the four DO zones of the ARAGON region (see map on p. 907). Until the 1980s most of Cariñena's hefty red wines were sold in bulk for blending with lighter wines from other parts of Spain. Natural alcohol levels of 18 and sometimes 19 per cent were not uncommon. But Cariñena, like so many other regions of Spain, is trying to break with the past. The minimum ALCOHOLIC STRENGTH permitted by DO regulations for red Cariñena was reduced from 14 to 12 per cent in 1990, while Garnacha vines are gradually being uprooted and replaced by TEMPRANILLO as well as some Mazuelo. Among the white vine varieties that cover a fifth of Cariñena's total vineyard area, VIURA and Garnacha Blanca have been joined by PARELLADA from PENEDÈS. The CO-OPERATIVES which produce over three-quarters of all the Cariñena's wines are playing their part in this modernization process. Besides encouraging their members to plant better VINE VARIETIES, they are investing in equipment designed to raise the quality of Cariñena's wines to an exportable standard. One of the few non-Catalan CAVA sparkling wines is made here.

R.J.M.

CARMEL VALLEY, California wine region and AVA. See MONTEREY.

CARMENÈRE is rarely encountered in the vineyards of Bordeaux today but was, according to Daurel, widely cultivated in the Médoc in the early 18th century and, with Cabernet Franc, established the reputations of its best properties. He reports that the vine is vigorous and used to produced exceptionally good wine but was abandoned because of its susceptibility to COULURE and resultant low yields. Its name may well be related to the word 'carmine' and even today it yields small quantities of exceptionally deep coloured, full bodied wines and may even be, like PETIT VERDOT, the subject of a revival.

Daurel, J., *Les Raisins de cuve de la Gironde et du sud-ouest de la France* (Bordeaux, 1892).

CARMENET, a Médocain synonym for CABERNET FRANC, which has also been adopted as the name of a winery in northern California.

CARMIGNANO, historic central Italian red wine made 16 km/10 miles north west of Florence in a zone noted as one of TUSCANY's finest for red wine production since the Middle Ages. The vineyards are located on a series of low hills between 50 and 200 m (160–650 ft) above sea level, unusually low for the SANGIOVESE grape which forms the base of the blend and gives wines with lower ACIDITY and firmer TANNINS than the wines of CHIANTI CLASSICO. The relatively low altitudes allow Sangiovese to ripen fully here in this relatively northern zone for the variety.

The wines were given legal status by Cosimo III de'Medici— himself a major proprietor in the Carmignano zone at the villa of Artimino—who included them in his selection of four areas of superior wine production in an edict of 1716 which prohibited other wines from using the names of the selected areas. The grandical wines were sent regularly to Queen Anne of England, who apparently appreciated their quality. The wines were also praised by Giovanni Cosimo Villifranchi (1773) and Cosimo Ridolfi (1831), and began to be bottled and distributed on a national and international scale by Marquis Ippolito Niccolini and by the Fattoria di Artimino in the 19th century.

The report of the Dalmasso Commission in 1932 (see ITALY and TUSCANY) assigned Carmignano to the nearby zone of Chianti Montalbano, where cooler temperatures and higher altitudes result in Chianti wines of lighter body and higher acidity more suitable for drinking when young. Independent status was won in 1975, however, with the granting of a DOC for Carmignano, the first Tuscan DOC to permit the inclusion of CABERNET SAUVIGNON in the wines (many years before that of Chianti). The alleged tradition of Cabernet Sauvignon in the zone was of major assistance in detaching it from Chianti Montalbano, although there is good reason to treat the assertions of continuous cultivation of this variety in Carmignano as spurious; the vineyards of Ugo Contini-Bonacossi, the zone's major producer, were grafted with cuttings from Château LAFITE in the 1970s, in fact, and not with locally available Cabernet.

Current production is slightly under 3,000 hl/79,000 gal from the zone's approximately 110 ha/270 acres of vineyards. A few producers have begun to experiment with small oak barrels, though the phenomenon has not become generalized as it has in Chianti Classico. With the 1988 vintage, Carmignano was awarded DOCG status. D.T.

CARNELIAN, black grape variety developed in and specifically for California by Dr H. P. Olmo of DAVIS. It is the result of crossing a 1936 crossing of Carignan and Cabernet Sauvignon with Grenache and was released in 1972. It was supposed to be a hot-climate Cabernet but too many of the Grenache characteristics predominate to make it easy to pick. Its California influence is limited, and limited to the SAN JOAQUIN VALLEY, where the liberal produce of its 1,000 acres/400 ha goes into blends. Curiously, one of its loftiest expressions has come from a Texas vineyard, Fall Creek.

CARNEROS, also known as **Los Carneros**, a particularly cool, foggy CALIFORNIA wine region, an AVA that spans the extreme south of both NAPA and SONOMA counties. Carneros sprang to public notice in and outside California in the mid 1980s, partly on the strength of some impressive Pinot Noirs and as much or more because of traditionally made sparkling wines blended from Chardonnay and Pinot Noir grown in Carneros. Acacia, Buena Vista, Carneros Creek, and Saintsbury were important producers of still wines throughout the 1980s; Gloria Ferrer, Domaine Carneros, and Codorníu Napa were the pioneer sparkling wine producers.

In fact this is one of the state's older wine districts. Agoston HARASZTHY planted grapes in it before 1870. A property originally called Stanly Ranch was famous as a vineyard by 1880. However, persistent fog and wind made vine-growing difficult and, when PHYLLOXERA struck hard in the 1880s, there began a swift slide into a long night. The Stanly Ranch was bought and replanted in 1942 by wine producer Louis M. Martini, but the push that brought Carneros both fame and more than 3,000 acres/1,200 ha of vineyard did not begin until the 1970s.

Carneros sprawls across the last, low hills of the Mayacamas Range before it slips beneath San Francisco Bay. The larger part of the AVA lies within Sonoma County; grapes from that portion can also use the Sonoma Valley AVA. The smaller segment, in Napa County, is equally entitled to use Napa Valley as an AVA. In addition to Chardonnay and Pinot Noir, Carneros is gaining a reputation for Merlot, and could have one for Gewürztraminer.

Growers and wineries within the AVA have banded together in a promotional body called the Carneros Quality Alliance, the seal of which appears on many wines from it.

CAROTENOIDS, important class of plant PIGMENTS whose red, orange, and yellow colours complement the green of chlorophyll and the blue and red of ANTHOCYANS. They come from the chloroplasts in green grapes. Carotenoids are TERPENOIDS with 40 carbons and belong to the LIPID group of organic compounds. They include two main groups—xanthophylls and carotenes—which are prominent in grapes and provide the skin colour of so-called white grapes; carotenes also form a substrate for synthesis of many important regulatory and FLAVOUR COMPOUNDS. Carotenoids serve as accessory pigments in the process of PHOTOSYNTHESIS. B.G.C.

CARSO, zone in FRIULI in north east Italy very close to Trieste and the border with SLOVENIA producing mainly red wines from the Terrano/Teran (REFOSCO) grape, and some whites from MALVASIA, which are not often exported.

CARTAGENA, wine-producing zone in Spain's LEVANTE.

CARTAGÈNE is the largely domestically produced strong sweet aperitif of the Languedoc made, rather like a VIN DE LIQUEUR, by adding grape spirit to barely fermenting grape juice.

CARTHAGE, ancient city on the north coast of Africa just east of modern Tunis, whose part in the history of viticulture was a curious and incidental one. It was most probably the early PHOENICIAN settlers at Carthage who introduced viticulture to that region of North Africa. A famous passage of the historian Diodorus (20. 8) paints a vivid picture of the country estates of the Carthaginian elite of the late fourth century BC, flourishing on the fertile soils around Carthage with a mix of farming, which included viticulture. However, at no period did Carthaginian wine figure prominently in trade. It was eclipsed by North Africa's importance as a producer of corn and olive oil, most particularly in the period when it was part of the Roman empire. Still, there can be little doubt that Carthage's élite shared the same interest in viticulture as the rest of the Mediterranean world.

It was for them that a large work, written in Punic, of 28 books on agriculture was produced by a certain Mago. Nothing is known of the writer or of his date; but his work fits most easily into the great explosion of handbooks on agriculture written in the Hellenistic period, particularly in the third and second centuries BC. Like these other works, Mago's treatise is lost; our knowledge of its contents is entirely derived from references to it and quotations from it in the later writers. Of these the largest number are about vines, although it would be dangerous to infer from this very fragmentary selection that viticulture had particular prominence in his work. While Mago's work probably contained much that was taken from the earlier AGRICULTURAL TREATISES produced in the Greek world, it was not without information based on personal observation. As COLUMELLA (*De re rustica* 3. 12. 5–6) noted, Mago's advice to plant vines on north-facing slopes is particularly appropriate to Africa (see TOPOGRAPHY). Large extracts from Mago were translated into Greek and incorporated in a treatise on agriculture by Cassius Dionysius of Utica, near Carthage (VARRO, *De re rustica* 1. 1. 10). More surprisingly a decree of the senate ordered a translation of Mago into Latin (Columella, *De re rustica* 1. 1. 13). The most likely occasion for this must be in connection with one of the schemes for Roman settlement in North Africa in the period after Rome's destruction of Carthage in 146 BC. Columella was to call Mago 'the father of country matters', probably primarily because his work in its Latin version gave Romans convenient access to the vast literature on agriculture from the Hellenistic world.

The most famous Carthaginian of all is commemorated in the name of the co-operative and principal producer of CHÂTILLON-EN-DIOIS in the foothills of the French alps, the Cellier Hannibal. J.J.P.

Gsell, S., *Histoire ancienne de l'Afrique du nord* (Paris, 1951), iv. 1–169.

CARTONS. Method of packaging wine in what are effectively cardboard 'bricks' that has been particularly popular for everyday wines in Latin American countries such as CHILE.

CASA VINICOLA on the label of an Italian wine indicates a producer who buys in grapes or wine, like a French NÉGOCIANT.

CASE. BEER and milk may be sold in crates but wine is sold in cases. A case holds a dozen bottles, the basic trading unit in the fine wine trade and much of the wholesale wine trade. It is posited that the case contains 12 bottles because that is as many as a man can comfortably carry. Most cases are made of cardboard outers, with cardboard vertical or papier mâché horizontal dividers. Wine merchants truly dedicated to the mail order business ensure that they use only particularly strong cases especially designed to minimize breakage. Most (but not all) fine wines designed for prolonged BOTTLE AGEING are dispatched from their producers in thick wooden cases, usually made of rough pine, branded with the name, and often logo, of the producer on the **case ends** (which can be attractive enough for future use). These cases are usually nailed down and can only be opened with a chisel or screwdriver and hammer, often breaking the wooden lid. Wine sold in unopened cases is presumed, in the fine wine market, to be worth sufficient premium that they are usually designated 'o.w.c.', or 'original wooden cases'.

The German wine trade has long sold wine in six-bottle cartons and many COLLECTORS find 12 bottles about six too many for their own personal consumption. A **split case** may be one that is torn, but may be one that contains six bottles of each of two different wines, or four bottles of each of three different wines. One bottle of each of 12 different wines becomes a **mixed case**.

CASEIN, the principal milk PROTEIN, is used by wine-makers as a FINING agent particularly useful for removing brown colours from white wines. It is also used to a lesser extent in the general CLARIFICATION of young wines. Precipitated from milk by the addition of ACIDS, casein is chiefly used in the form of sodium or potassium caseinate. When this salt is added to cloudy wine, it reacts with some of the wine acid forming a curd which adsorbs and precipitates most of the very small particles, including the PIGMENTS causing discolouration. A.D.W.

CASK, wooden container for wine, often used interchangeably with BARREL (particularly by the British), a cylindrical container small enough to be rolled. The term is also used less precisely, however, for any form of COOPERAGE, i.e. wooden containers of any size, whether larger, immobile,

Traditional oval **casks** in Trimbach's cellars in Ribeauvillé, Alsace.

storage containers such as the ovals common in German and Alsace, or the *botte* of Italy, and also including quite large, immovable containers which may or may not be open topped.

In the 1970s the Australian wine industry neatly, if misleadingly, coined the term **cask wine** for wine packaged in a bag packed inside a cardboard BOX, a wine type highly unlikely to have been either made or aged in wood of any sort (although OAK CHIPS could have played a part in some).

CASK AGEING, wine-making practice of ageing a wine after fermentation (see ÉLEVAGE) in a large wooden container usually too old to impart any WOOD FLAVOUR. It may well, however, exert some WOOD INFLUENCE and help considerably to achieve natural CLARIFICATION and STABILIZATION. White wines subjected to cask ageing for several months include some of the great white wines of the LOIRE, GERMANY, and ALSACE. Red wines subjected to cask ageing, sometimes for several years, include many of the traditional wines of the RHÔNE, ITALY, SPAIN, PORTUGAL, and GREECE.

The alternatives, and possible supplements, to cask ageing are BARREL MATURATION; AGEING in inert CONTAINERS such as stainless steel tanks; BOTTLE AGEING; and BOTTLING almost immediately after FERMENTATION as in NOUVEAU wines.

CASSIS is French for blackcurrant and is used often as a tasting note for red wines, particularly red wines based on Cabernet Sauvignon grapes. Dry white wine mixed with some blackcurrant liqueur is known as both a **vin blanc cassis** and KIR (while red wine mixed with blackcurrant liqueur is sometimes called a cardinal).

CASSIS, an appellation in PROVENCE. Greater Marseilles is rapidly advancing on the old fishing village of Cassis so that the total area under vine gives way each year to a new encroachment of villas (as in BANDOL just along the coast). In the early 1990s there were about 160 ha / 400 acres of vineyard in this sheltered amphitheatre, protected from the mistral by the Cap Canaille to the east, one of the highest cliffs in France.

Three-quarters of the wine produced from Cassis's 160 ha of vineyards is white, made from Clairette, Ugni Blanc, Marsanne, and some Sauvignon Blanc grapes, which at its best is dry, perfumed, and full bodied, given a slight twang of the RHÔNE by the Marsanne. A little red and rosé is also made, mainly from Mourvèdre (which ripens easily here), Grenache, and Cinsaut. Most Cassis, however, finds a ready market within only a few miles of its source; local white wines, even those without the cachet of Cassis, are seized upon by the annual influx of summer visitors.

CASTELÃO FRANCES, dark-skinned grape variety planted all over southern Portugal and known variously as PERIQUITA in Arrábida, Palmela, and Ribatejo; as João de Santarém or Santarém in parts of Ribatejo; Mortágua in the Oeste; and even Trincadeira Preta in parts of the country. This versatile vine can produce fruity, relatively fleshy red wines which can be drunk young or aged.

CASTEL DEL MONTE, DOC in the far south east of Italy. For more details, see APULIA.

CASTELLI ROMANI, general term for the white wines of the VOLCANIC hills south east of Rome in the region of LATIUM (see map on p. 517) which stretch from just outside the city gates (some of the vineyards are in fact within the administrative borders of the city) into the province of Latina, south of the township of Velletri. Over 10,000 ha / 25,000 acres of DOC vineyards fall within the zone and are divided into six different appellations: Colli Albani (almost 1,450 ha of vineyards in the early 1990s), Colli Lanuvini (over 1,700 ha), FRASCATI (some 2,800 ha), Marino (1,600 ha), Montecompatri (245 ha), and Velletri (2,200 ha). The wines are made principally from MALVASIA grapes with usually at least 25 per cent TREBBIANO. BOMBINO (here also called Bonvino) and Bellone are also permitted in the blend, up to a maximum of 10 per cent, and can add a welcome note of complexity, but these vines are less suitable to the TENDONE training systems that have come to dominate the zone and are gradually being abandoned by growers. Malvasia di Candia is more widely utilized than Malvasia di Lazio, principally for its high productivity, although some producers prefer the quality level of the latter. A wide variety of different strains of Trebbiano are employed (Verde, Giallo, Toscano, Romagnolo, di Soave); the first of these, if theoretically more interesting, is not necessarily preferred in the vineyard. High YIELDS—ranging from the 98 hl/ha (6 tons/acre) of the Colli Lanuvini to the more than 115 hl/ha of the Colli Albani and Marino—make many of the discussions of blends and subvarieties purely nugatory; interesting wines from Malvasia and Trebbiano cannot be made in these quantities. The wines of the separate DOCs tend to resemble one another closely, in fact, although Marino, with a more westerly ASPECT than most, can be somewhat fuller than its neighbours. Over three-quarters of the total production is in the hands of CO-OPERATIVES, the rest principally in the hands of large commercial wineries. Both have followed a marketing strategy based on high volume and low prices, counting on the advantages of the proximity of the large Roman market and on the more extended recognition that has come from the millions of visitors who flock to the city each year and encounter the wines in the city's taverns and *trattorie*.

If the Castelli Romani wines are principally intended for the guzzling needs of their public, the character of the wines themselves has changed rather drastically, just as the vineyards have been transformed from GUYOT and CORDON training systems to tendone. Once fermented on their skins, these wines were golden in colour, full in flavour and aroma. The colour deepened as the Malvasia, a variety whose wines oxidize quite rapidly, began to age, and the aromas and flavours followed suit. The results were not always wines of great finesse, but they provided an excellent accompaniment to the flavoursome cuisine of Rome. Modern Castelli Romani wines, cold fermented off the skins, filtered, and stabilized, are a product without the defects of old but without the character of the past, a character which made them an integral part of the life and culture of Rome. D.T.

CASTELLÓN, wine-producing zone in Spain's LEVANTE.

CASTILE, Castilla in Spanish, old central Spanish kingdom divided by mountains into CASTILE-LA MANCHA, or New Castile, in the south and CASTILE-LEÓN, or Old Castile, in the north.

CASTILE-LA MANCHA, known as **Castilla-La Mancha** in Spanish and New Castile in English, the lower, southern half of the plateau that makes up central SPAIN (see map on p. 907). At altitudes between 500 and 700 m (1,650–2,300 ft) above sea level, this is Spain at her most extreme. Winters are long and cold with temperatures often falling below 0 °C/ 32 °F for days on end. In summer the heat is gruelling. The thermometer regularly rises above 35 °C, even 40 °C (104 °F), and little if any rain falls between May and September. The vast expanse of country which is green in the spring quickly turns to a shade of burnt ochre in July and August as all but the deepest river beds dry up completely. The locals say that they suffer 'nine months of winter and three months of hell'. Despite these fierce conditions, Castile-La Mancha produces half of all the wine made in Spain. Around 700,000 ha / 1.7 million acres of vineyard yield an average of 18 million hl / 475 million gal of wine (averaging yields of just over 25 hl / ha (1.4 tons / acre)). Two of Castile-La Mancha's four DO regions, VALDEPEÑAS and LA MANCHA itself, are planted mainly with the robust white wine vine AIRÉN.

There are an estimated 130,000 ha of Airén in La Mancha alone, making it the world's most widely planted vine variety. Cencibel (alias TEMPRANILLO) comes a poor second in this region behind the DROUGHT-resistant Airén, while north west of Toledo MÉNTRIDA produces rough and ready reds from overripe Garnacha (GRENACHE). Although the fourth DO, ALMANSA, belongs administratively to Castile-La Mancha, the style of wine-making there is closer to that of the LEVANTE. MONASTRELL, Cencibel, and the red-fleshed Garnacha Tintorera produce big, alcoholic red wines.

Until the 1970s the wines from Castile-La Mancha were mainly sold in bulk to be drunk by undiscerning palates in bars all over Spain. But in the 1970s and 1980s parts of the region were quietly revolutionized. Attracted by the availability of grapes and low production costs, a number of large companies moved to the region bringing new wine-making technology with them. Although much of the production is still concentrated in the hands of old-fashioned CO-OPERATIVES obliged by the EUROPEAN UNION to send a high proportion of their wine for compulsory distillation (see WINE LAKE), a new generation of cleanly made and often inexpensive red and white wine from Castile-La Mancha is finding favour with buyers both at home and abroad. R.J.M.

CASTILE-LEÓN, known as **Castilla-León** in Spanish and often known as Old Castile in English, is the largest of the 17 autonomous regions of SPAIN. This northern part of Spain's central plateau, rising to between 880 and 1,000 m (2,900–3,300 ft) above sea level, takes up about a fifth of the entire country. Centred on its capital, the university city of Valladolid, most of Castile-León is thinly populated table land almost encircled by mountains. It is separated from the hub of Spain (MADRID and CASTILE-LA MANCHA or New Castile) by the central mountain range which rises to over 2,000 m near Avila and Segovia (see map on p. 907). To the north, the Cordillera Cantabrica, which peaks at over 2,600 m deflects the maritime influence of the Bay of Biscay.

The climate here is harsh. Short, hot summers are followed by long, cold winters when temperatures can drop to −10 °C/14 °F. Under often clear skies, temperatures drop quickly after sunset and, even in summer, nights are cool. FROST continues to be a threat until mid May. Rain falls mainly in winter and amounts to between 400 and 500 mm (15–19 in) a year. Much of the land is poor and unable to support anything other than nomadic flocks of sheep. However the river Duero (known as DOURO in Portugal), which cuts a broad valley in the rather featureless plain, provides a natural water source. Grain, sugar beet, and vines are grown along its length.

A regional variant of the red TEMPRANILLO vine, variously called Tinta del País, Tinto Fino, and Tinto de Toro, is the chief good-quality grape variety in three of the five DO wine regions in Castile-León. The largest of these is RIBERA DEL DUERO, which extends for about 100 km/60 miles either side of the river and is internationally known for its red wines. Downstream of Ribera del Duero, RUEDA made enormous progress in its white wine production in the 1980s, while TORO, straddling the Duero near the Portuguese border, resolutely sticks to making fiery reds. CIGALES, north of Valladolid, specializes in rosé wine. BIERZO, abutting GALICIA in the north west, shows promise but has yet to find a role outside the immediate vicinity. Other wine zones awaiting official recognition in the mid 1990s were Cebreros in the mountains north of Madrid, and León itself, where the unfortunately named producer VILE sells wines under the Palacio de León and other labels. R.J.M.

CASTILLON, CÔTES DE CASTILLON, once **Bordeaux Côtes de Castillon**, is a good value red wine appellation in the BORDEAUX region immediately east of ST-ÉMILION. Much bigger than its northern neighbour Côtes de FRANCS, Castillon produces similarly sturdy red wines with generally better structure than regular red BORDEAUX AC, although using the same vine varieties and techniques. The vine-growers here elected in 1989 to establish their own identity rather than depend on the name of Bordeaux. VINE DENSITY on the 2,700 ha/6,700 acres of vineyard is 5,000 vines per ha and those vineyards closest to the river DORDOGNE tend to produce more supple wine than those at higher altitudes such as Ch de Belcier, one of the more important producers. The region is named after the town of Castillon-la-Bataille, the battle being that which brought an end to the HUNDRED YEARS WAR.

CATALONIA, a proud and industrious region on the Mediterranean coast which encompasses a part of southern France and a part of north east Spain (see maps on pp. 399 and 907), whose inhabitants consider themselves neither French, nor Spanish, but Catalan. The region has suffered a turbulent past, fighting for separation first from ARAGON to the south and then from CASTILE and the national capital Madrid. Self-government was achieved in 1977, when Catalonia became one of Spain's 17 autonomous regions. Barcelona, the second largest city in Spain and the busiest port on the Mediterranean, became the Catalan capital. Centuries of political infighting have left Catalonia with a strong sense of independence. The Catalan language derived from the French *langue d'oc* (see LANGUEDOC), often suppressed in the past in favour of Castilian Spanish, has now been restored as the official language and Catalonia (**Cataluña** in Castilian, **Catalunya** in Catalan) is now officially bilingual (which leads to some confusion and anomalies in proper names). For details of French Catalonia, see ROUSSILLON.

Barcelona and its densely populated hinterland is a hive of enterprise and industry. A fifth of Spain's industrial output comes from the city alone. It is therefore no coincidence that Catalonia has been at the vanguard of Spain's 20th century wine-making revolution. The region began to stir in the early 1870s when José Raventos began making sparkling wine by the CHAMPAGNE METHOD in the small town of San Sadurni de Noya (Sant Sadurni d'Anoia in Catalan). He founded the giant CODORNÍU firm, and his foresight generated the Catalan CAVA industry which earned its own Denominación de Origen (see DO) in 1986.

Alongside Cava, Catalonia produces an eclectic range of wines from traditional, powerful reds to ultra-modern, cool-fermented dry whites. With Barcelona close at hand, wine producers have always found it relatively easy to raise finance and Catalonia was consequently the first region in Spain to introduce STAINLESS STEEL and its accompanying technology.

Much of the credit for the transformation of Catalonia's wine industry in recent years must go to the late Don Miguel Torres Carbo and his son Miguel A. TORRES, who imported INTERNATIONAL VINE VARIETIES to plant alongside indigenous varieties such as GARNACHA, MONASTRELL, and TEMPRANILLO (called Ull de Llebre in Catalan), and the Cava grapes, PARELLADA, MACABEO, and XAREL-LO.

The climate in Catalonia is strongly influenced by the Mediterranean. The coastal belt is warm and equable with moderate rainfall but conditions become progressively more arid and extreme further inland. There are eight DO regions: ALELLA, AMPURDÁN-COSTA BRAVA, CONCA DE BARBERÁ, COSTERS DEL SEGRE, PENEDÈS, PRIORATO, TARRAGONA, and TERRA ALTA. Of these, Penedès is the most important in terms of both quantity and quality.

In the early 1990s Catalonia was expected to become a DO

in its own right, probably including everything but Ampurdán-Costa Brava.

Catalonia has long been an important centre of CORK production and is a particularly important source of corks for sparkling wines. R.J.M.

CATARRATTO, Sicilian white grape variety which was identified as the second most planted single variety in all of Italy in the 1990 agricultural census. According to official returns, there were about 65,000 ha / 1,600 acres of **Catarratto Bianco Comune** and nearly 10,000 ha of **Catarratto Bianco Lucido**, the latter, the superior in terms of wine quality, having given up ground to the former during the 1980s. (Total plantings of SANGIOVESE were 86,000 ha.)

The variety is planted almost exclusively in the far western province of Trapani and has in the past been much used for the production of MARSALA. Today, it can be expected that much of the vine's produce is regarded as SURPLUS and is therefore either compulsorily distilled by the EUROPEAN UNION, or transformed into GRAPE CONCENTRATE. Despite its profusion, this variety is specified in the regulations of just three DOC zones. Some characterful white table wines are produced, however. See SICILY for more details.

CATAWBA, deep pink-skinned grape variety grown to a great extent in NEW YORK state. It is a VITIS *labruscana*, a cross between LABRUSCA and VINIFERA identified in North Carolina in 1802, even before CONCORD. It can produce wines of all shades of pink, and can even yield light reds after THERMOVINIFICATION.

CATION EXCHANGE, see ION EXCHANGE.

CATO, MARCUS (234–149 BC), Roman statesman advanced as a writer on agricultural and viticulture matters, known as 'Cato the Elder' or 'Cato the Censor' to distinguish him from his great-grandson. He grew up on his father's farm near Reate, north east of Rome, then fought against CARTHAGE in the Second Punic War and afterwards had a distinguished political career. He became known as a strict moralist, castigating the 'new' extravagance, ostentation, and luxury and advocating a return to the 'old' virtues of austerity, honesty, and hard work. He wrote books on many subjects and published his speeches. PLINY the Elder praises him for the breadth of his learning (*Natural History* 25. 4), and COLUMELLA (*De re rustica* 1. 1. 12) and Cicero (*Brutus* 16. 61) honour him as the father of Latin prose. His only surviving work, *De agri cultura* ('Concerning the cultivation of the land'), also known as *De re rustica* ('Concerning country matters'), is important not only because it is the first lengthy prose work in Latin. *De agri cultura* is not divided into books or arranged systematically in any other way: Cato's remarks on viticulture and wine-making are scattered throughout the treatise. The advice he gives is of a severely practical kind. His prime concern is making farming, including wine-growing, profitable through hard work and careful management. For instance, he stresses that the grapes should always be thoroughly ripe when harvested, or one's wine will lose its good reputation. And in the making and storing of wine he was aware of the importance of HYGIENE to prevent the wine turning to VINEGAR. After the vintage, the wine jars should be wiped twice a day, each with its own broom. After 30 days, when FERMENTATION is complete, the jars should be sealed or the wine can be drawn off its LEES if desired as an alternative to LEES CONTACT. The type of estate he has in mind produces chiefly wine and olive oil: hence his extensive section on the construction of presses. H.M.W.

Astin, A. S., *Cato the Censor* (Oxford, 1978)
Thielschen, P., *Des Marcus Catos Belehrung über die Landwirtschaft* (Berlin, 1963).

CAVA, Spanish SPARKLING WINES made using the traditional CHAMPAGNE METHOD. The term Cava was adopted by the Spanish in 1970 when they agreed to abandon the use of the potentially misleading term Champaña. The word originates in CATALONIA, which produces most but not all Cava, where it means cellar. It was here in the town of San Sadurni de Noya that José Raventos, head of the family firm of CODORNÍU, made the first bottles of champagne method sparkling wine after a visit to France in 1872. Early growth in the industry coincided with the arrival of the PHYLLOXERA louse, which first appeared in Catalan vineyards in the 1880s. Vineyards that had once made sturdy red wines had to be uprooted and were replanted with MACABEO, PARELLADA, and XAREL-LO, the triad of grape varieties which is the mainstay of the Cava industry to this day. In 1889 the Raventos family were joined by Pedro Ferrer, who founded the firm of FREIXENET. Codorníu and Freixenet, both still family owned, are now two of the largest sparkling wine producers in the world, with their own winery outposts in CALIFORNIA.

Unlike any other Spanish DO, the Cava denominación is not restricted to a single delimited area. However, since Spain joined the EUROPEAN UNION in 1986, the EU authorities have insisted that Cava should be made from grapes grown in prescribed regions. As a result, the use of the term Cava is restricted to sparkling wines from a list of municipalities in CATALONIA, VALENCIA, ARAGON, NAVARRA, RIOJA, and the BASQUE country. Probable additions to this list include municipalities where sparkling wines are made in CASTILE-LEÓN and EXTREMADURA. Ninety-five per cent of all Cava is made in Catalonia, however, mostly in and around the town of San Sadurni de Noya. Total production amounts to over 1 million hl / 26 million gal a year.

The somewhat neutral Macabeo (the Viura of Rioja) comprises about half of the blend for a typical Cava, its late budbreak making it a popular choice for vineyards prone to spring frosts. The productive and indigenous Xarel-lo vine is the second most important, and its earthy aroma has been one of Cava's distinguishing features, although it thrives only at relatively low altitudes. Parellada performs better above 300 m / 900 ft, where it produces finer wines relatively low in BODY. Plantings of the French vine CHARDONNAY, officially authorized for Cava in 1986, are increasing rapidly.

To qualify for the DO, Cava must be made according to the local, and in some respects less rigorous, adaptation of the champagne method. The wine must spend at least nine months on its lees before DISGORGEMENT, achieve at least four atmospheres of pressure, and attain an ALCOHOLIC STRENGTH of between 10.8 and 12.8 per cent by volume. YIELDS, set at a maximum of 1 hl of must per 150 kg of grapes are higher than CHAMPAGNE.

Production methods, which used to be crude and heavy handed, have been refined and automated in recent years. Most REMUAGE is now carried out automatically in a *girasol* or GYROPALETTE, a Spanish invention which enables hundreds of bottles to be handled at a time. The best Cavas tend to be produced by the larger firms who control their own vinification rather than those producers who buy in ready-made base wine from one of the large but often outdated CO-OPERATIVES that continue to flourish all over Catalonia. R.J.M.

CAVE, French for a CELLAR or wine-making establishment, virtually the equivalent of a WINERY. A **caviste** is French for a specialist wine retailer, of which there are surprisingly few in France, presumably since so many consumers buy direct from the producer.

CAVE CO-OPÉRATIVE, French for one of France's more than 1,000 wine CO-OPERATIVES.

CAYETANA, high-yielding Spanish white grape variety which produces neutral flavoured wine. It is particularly popular in the EXTREMADURA region, where much of its produce is distilled into BRANDY de Jerez. In Rioja it may be known as Cazagal.

CEBREROS, wine zone in north west Spain. See CASTILE-LEÓN.

CELL, the structural unit of living organisms, the smallest unit capable of independent existence. YEAST and BACTERIA are examples of single cells while one grapevine has billions of cells. Each plant cell consists of a protoplast surrounded by a cell wall, but it can be differentiated into a host of forms. A cell in the flesh of a ripe grape berry, for example, can be 0.5 mm in length with a thin, wavy cell wall lined by an equally thin cytoplasm surrounding the vacuole, a 'sea' of water with dissolved sugars, acids, and hundreds of other solutes, otherwise known as grape juice. Other cells within the berry can be entirely different. A PHLOEM element aligns end to end with others to form a tube through which elaborated sap moves in a network throughout the plant. Adjacent fibre cells are long and slim with thick walls hardened by the wood polymer, lignin. The complex functioning of the leaf provides other examples of cell forms: STOMATAL cells function to allow carbon dioxide in and oxygen and water vapour out; others function as the 'carbohydrate factory'; and cells in its dense network of veins are designed to move water and minerals up from the roots (in the XYLEM) and to move sugars and other elaborated organic nutrients out to the rest of the plant (in the phloem).

Despite this diversity, all cells of a plant have the same genetic information in their nuclei and, with some exceptions, may be separated and cultured as single protoplasts. By TISSUE CULTURE methods, these can then be used for the regeneration of another plant like the parent. The genetic material in each cell will therefore be 'tuned' for its differentiation and functioning by the dictate of its neighbours in that tissue and by its reaction to signals received from other tissues and organs.

Cell walls are made of cellulose and other polymers but, despite appearances, these walls are by no means inert. They respond in form to pressures exerted by surrounding cells and to osmotic pressure from the vacuolar sap which leads to cell expansion, or growth, depending on the wall's plasticity. B.G.C.

Taiz, L., and Zeiger, E., *Plant Physiology* (Redwood City, Calif., 1991)

CELLAR, widely used word that is roughly the English counterpart to CAVE, CANTINA, and BODEGA in French, Italian, and Spanish respectively. It can therefore be applied to wine shops and wine-making premises, but is here considered only in its domestic sense, as a collection of wine and the place in which it is stored.

Location

Traditional underground cellars have the great advantages of being secure, dark, at a constant low temperature, slightly damp, and rarely disturbed. As outlined in STORING WINE, these constitute ideal conditions. Few modern dwellings have anywhere that enjoys all these advantages, and to re-create them it may be necessary to spend lavishly on specialist advice on constructing or adapting quarters with low lighting levels and specially controlled temperature and humidity (and as few visitors as the expender of all this money and effort can bear). It is also possible to buy special cabinets which look like refrigerators and can be programmed to maintain certain temperature and humidity levels, but they are expensive relative to their capacity. Less expensive options include insulating a small room or large cupboard, insulating a space under some stairs, using a dark corner of a distant spare room or a closet against an outside wall, or a secure outhouse (although care must be taken that the TEMPERATURE never falls so low as to freeze the wine and push the corks out). It is important that any makeshift cellar is far from any heat source, even a hot water pipe and, especially, a boiler, but a constant medium temperature is less harmful than a place in which there are violent temperature swings. Those living on ground level can even excavate, and depend on a trapdoor.

Accessibility is an advantage or disadvantage depending on the cellar owner's personality and attitude towards the cellar. Paying for professional storage may be the only realistic option for some, but in this case cellar records (see below) are essential.

Small bins designed to hold 12 bottles are a good storage solution for private **cellars**, although there is usually a stack of wooden cases ready to be unpacked.

Design

Wine can be stored in the CASES in which it is bought, but this is practical only for wines years away from being ready to drink, and very steady and sturdy shelves are needed if more than one layer of cases is to be stacked. Some form of wine rack is usually most user-friendly, allowing the bottles to be kept horizontal and withdrawn easily. Racks with slots for individual bottles are best for very mixed cellars (metal and wood is the usual combination of materials used for these racks) but larger compartments, or BINS, can be used for larger quantities of bottles of the same wine.

It of course makes sense to keep the wines nearest MATURITY in the most accessible positions and vice versa (which dictates how wines may be kept in double-depth racks). There will be a slight temperature variation between the top and bottom of the cellar. Light levels are also likely to be higher at the top than the bottom, so there are at least two reasons why the fullest, least fragile, slowest maturing wines such as vintage port should be stored at the top and bottles as sensitive as, say, those containing sparkling wines should be stored close to floor level.

Contents

There is little point in devoting space and capital to storing wine unless it is difficult to replace, or will positively improve as a result of BOTTLE AGEING. It may therefore be worthwhile keeping the last bottle of nuptial champagne or holiday souvenir purely for sentimental reasons, but in general it is wise to be ruthless about cellar space, and accord it only to wines which are available only for a brief period (such as EN PRIMEUR rarities) or the wines recommended as worth AGEING. Space in wine books and magazines is often devoted to a concept called the 'ideal cellar' and the recommendations usually make interesting reading, but in truth there is no such thing and an individual's ideal depends entirely on his or her tastes and consumption patterns. Even the advice that NON-VINTAGE champagne is always improved by a year or so in a personal cellar may be questionable in an era of champagne glut.

Records

Cellar records are not necessary but they can add to the pleasure of wine COLLECTORS with a love of order and memorabilia. (The other school enjoys the twin elements of chaos and serendipity in plundering their wine cellars.) The ideal cellar record has a good-sized page for each case of wine acquired, stating price, supplier, and date of purchase. Below this a dated tasting note for each bottle tasting can be inserted, together perhaps with details of the circumstances in which it was opened. The pages can be grouped by wine type (red bordeaux, for example) and individual bottles can be grouped appropriately together on pages. (Those using professional wine storage need, for obvious reasons, to keep full details of where and since when the wine has been stored.)

Personal computers offer other, often more sophisticated, possibilities for cellar record-keeping but it is worth remembering that cellars are usually kept for many years longer than a pc.

See also STORING WINE.

Thorn, J., *The Good Cellar Guide* (London, 1990).

CELLAR WORK, general term for all the processing steps requiring human intervention or monitoring in WINE-MAKING. In its most general sense it encompasses all operations included in wine-making. In the narrower human sense of what cellar workers actually do, apart from overseeing grape reception, DESTEMMING, CRUSHING, FERMENTATION, CLARIFICATION, FILTRATION, BLENDING, STABILIZATION, and BOTTLING, it generally entails operating PUMPS, adding FINING agents and other additions, and almost constant cleaning (see HYGIENE). Cellars in which small barrels are used for both fermentation and maturation involve the most physical work, including filling, RACKING and moving barrels, TOPPING UP, and possibly STIRRING. See also ÉLEVAGE.

CELTS, peoples who inhabited western Europe before the rise of Ancient ROME. Many of them were introduced to wine by the Romans, when some were already skilled COOPERS.

The first clear evidence that wine drinking with its attendant rituals was penetrating to the courts of the prehistoric barbarian élites in western central Europe (eastern France, southern Germany, and Switzerland) appears in the archaeological record in the sixth century BC.

Griffon-headed cauldrons, CRATERS, jugs and strainers, and fine painted Attic cups, all of which would have been used at a Greek SYMPOSIUM, were shipped to Mediterranean ports such as Massilia (Marseilles). From there they were transported along the navigable RIVERS into the hinterland to be used in the complex systems of gift exchange which bound these peoples to the Greek and Etruscan traders of the south. Along with these trappings of civilization came wine. How much of it, if any, was at this stage Greek or Italian is difficult to tell. What is certain is that the large ceramic AMPHORAE in which the wine was transported inland were manufactured along the coast of southern France in the vicinity of Marseilles, suggesting, but not proving, that most of the wine consumed was locally manufactured.

The courts of the élite, places such as Mont Lassois on the main south–north trade route between Burgundy and Paris (where the celebrated Vix crater, a bronze vase 1.64 m/5.4 ft high and clearly made in Ancient GREECE, was found), and Heuneburg in Germany, lasted for a comparatively short time. They were flourishing in the 530s and 520s BC but had ceased to exist by the end of the next century as the old social order collapsed in a turmoil of unrest caused by migrating bands of Celts who were to thrust deep into Italy, Greece, and Turkey.

By the end of the third century a new order was beginning to emerge in the western Mediterranean. Rome was growing rapidly in power and had won a decisive victory over the CARTHAGINIANS in Spain, but their military involvement was to last for almost two centuries before the peninsula could be regarded as fully conquered. This meant a continuous movement of military detachments, supplies, and officials using the ports and the roads in southern France linking Italy and Spain. Inevitably the cities and the native tribes of Provence and Languedoc got used to this traffic and no doubt profited from it. So too did Roman entrepreneurs keen to exploit the new markets being opened up. For them the love of wine which the Celtic tribes of the interior so evidently

Celts: The Vix crater, at 2 m/7 ft high the largest ever found, was made in Greece at the end of the 6th century BC and unearthed in northern France in 1952.

possessed was a heaven-sent opportunity to offload, with profit, the considerable wine surpluses being generated by the large estates of northern and western Italy. As one contemporary writer somewhat incredulously remarked of the Celts of GAUL, 'They will give you a slave for an amphora of wine thus exchanging the cupbearer for the cup.' While this does not necessarily imply the actual exchange rate it shows which surpluses the two societies were prepared to exchange with each other for mutual benefit.

In the Celtic world it was important for those aspiring to power to host elaborate feasts to entertain their followers and others. The more exotic the commodities offered, the greater the status of the host. Wine from the south was in considerable demand and was avidly consumed. The drunken Celt who took his wine undiluted—something no civilized man would have done—was several times remarked upon by contemporary writers.

Wine was usually transported by sea in large ceramic amphorae made in distinctive styles and fabrics which can be quite closely dated and assigned to specific localities of manufacture. This means that it is possible to study the developing wine trade in some detail, and, since several of the estates produced amphorae with their own identifying stamps, individual marketing strategies can be identified. By studying the relative proportions of Italic and local amphorae in the successive levels of settlement sites in southern France it is possible to show that throughout the second century BC, when Provence and Languedoc were finally annexed by Rome, there is little trace in the archaeological record that local wine was drunk at all. In parallel with this the number of shipwrecks containing amphorae found off the southern French coast increases noticeably, presumably reflecting the corresponding increase in the volume of trade.

Once offloaded at ports such as Massilia and Narbo (Narbonne) the amphorae were transported inland by road or river. *En route* a *portorium* (or transport tax) was charged at each settlement through which the wine passed, trebling the price charged by the time it eventually reached the native consumers. From the borders of Provincia of Ancient Rome, modern Provence, the wine penetrated the territory of the neighbouring tribes. At two locations, one just outside Toulouse and the other at Chalon-sur-Saône, substantial quantities of discarded Italian amphorae have been found. No precise count can now be made but estimates in the tens of thousands are unlikely to be far from the truth. These must surely be major transshipment points where wine was decanted into skins or BARRELS (for which the Celts of the CAHORS region were particularly famed) for the more arduous journeys by cart into the wild interior. Not all wine was decanted, however. Considerable numbers of amphorae have been recovered from major native *oppida* (towns) at Montmerlhe, Essalois, Jœuvres, and Mont-Beuvray between 20 and 100 km (12–62 miles) beyond the frontier. From here much of it passed into the hands of the local nobility to be consumed with relish in their lavish feasts.

The volume of wine imported into Gaul at this time is difficult to estimate in detail but a conservative assessment suggests that it may have reached 100,000 hl / 2.6million gal a year. When it is remembered that the largest trading system operating in pre-industrial Europe—the Gascon wine trade to Britain and Flanders in the 14th century (see BORDEAUX)—was 750,000 hl / 20 million gal a year, the intensity of the Roman operation can be appreciated.

By the end of the second century BC Italian wine was reaching all parts of France mainly along the navigable rivers but some, still in its amphorae, was being reloaded on to ships in the GIRONDE estuary to be transported along the Atlantic coast of France to Brittany. There much of it was consumed, but a small quantity was carried by Breton sailors on the last leg of its journey via Guernsey to the British port on Hengistbury Head, overlooking Christchurch harbour, constituting the earliest attested importation of wine to ENGLAND, or Britain. One wonders whether after such a journey it was even barely drinkable. B.C.

Cuncliffe, B., *Greeks, Romans & Barbarians: spheres of Interaction* (London, 1988).

Tchernia, A., *Le Vin de l'Italie romaine* (Paris, 1986).

—— 'Italian Wine in Gaul at the end of the Republic', in P. Garnsey, K. Hopkins, and C. R. Whittaker (eds.), *Trade in the Ancient Economy* (London, 1983).

Cencibel, synonym for the Spanish black grape variety TEMPRANILLO, especially in central and southern Spain, notably in La Mancha and Valdepeñas, where it is the principal dark-skinned variety.

Central Coast, one of CALIFORNIA's umbrella AVAS, this large wine region encompasses all of the major vineyards in eight thoroughly disparate counties from Contra Costa in the north to SANTA BARBARA in the south. The counties (and their AVAs) are Alameda (LIVERMORE VALLEY); Contra Costa; MONTEREY (Arroyo Seco, Carmel Valley, Chalone, San Lucas); SAN BENITO (Cienega Valley, Lime Kiln Valley, Mount Harlan, Paicines); SAN LUIS OBISPO (Arroyo Grande, Edna Valley, Paso Robles, York Mountain); SANTA CLARA (most of Santa Cruz Mountains, San Ysidro); and Santa Barbara (Santa Maria Valley, Santa Ynez Valley).

Central Valley. In CALIFORNIA this great expanse is divided into the SACRAMENTO Valley in the north, which produces small quantities of wine, and the vast SAN JOAQUIN VALLEY in the south, which supplies the majority of the state's bulk wine (and table grapes and raisins). CHILE also has a Central Valley, although in this case it is the source of a high proportion of Chile's best wine.

centrifugation, once-fashionable wine-making operation of CLARIFICATION using a **centrifuge**. Occasionally used to clarify white grape juice before FERMENTATION, the process is relatively expensive and lengthy. It is more effective when used to clarify new wines because of the greater difference in DENSITY between the yeast cells and the liquid than between the grape solids and the liquid.

While the force used in natural clarification is gravity, the

Centrifuge in the Residenz cellar in Würzburg, Franken in south eastern Germany.

centrifugal force used in centrifugation is 5,000 to 10,000 times greater and requires large amounts of electrical power while managing to process only relatively small amounts of wine per hour. Because centrifuges are so expensive to buy and maintain, and because some wine-makers feel they submit wine to a physically shocking process, they are used relatively rarely nowadays. A.D.W.

CENTURIAN, CALIFORNIA vine crossing with same parentage as CARNELIAN but released three years later in 1975. The state's total acreage was static throughout the 1980s at just over 500 acres/200 ha, all in the central SAN JOAQUIN VALLEY. It has viticultural advantages over Carnelian but no organoleptic distinction.

CÉPAGE, French for VINE VARIETY. A VARIETAL wine, one that is sold by the name of the principal grape variety from which it is made, is known as a **vin de cépage** within France, a term which has had some pejorative sense in comparison with a geographically named wine which qualifies as APPEL-

LATION CONTRÔLÉE. AC wines may not, in general, specify the name of a vine variety on the main label.

CERCEAL, name of several white Portuguese grape varieties, whose Anglicized form is SERCIAL, a variety most commonly associated with the island of MADEIRA. Forms of Cerceal are planted in many mainland wine regions, where, because of the grapes' high acidity, they are often called Esgana Cão, or 'dog strangler'. **Cerceal do Dão** is a quite distinct ingredient in white DÃO.

CEREZA, pink-skinned grape variety of historical interest in ARGENTINA which takes its name from the Spanish for cherry. Like the even more widely planted CRIOLLA Grande, it is thought to be descended from the seeds of grapes imported by the early Spanish settlers, although it produces larger berries which result in paler wine than Criolla. It is declining in importance but there were still about 40,000 ha/99,000 acres of it at the end of the 1980s, most notably in San Juan province. It produces red, white, and dark rosé wine of extremely mediocre quality for early consumption.

CÉRONS, the least important sweet white wine appellation in the BORDEAUX region, on the left bank of the river GARONNE. Just north of BARSAC and SAUTERNES, it produces wines which rarely demonstrate either the finesse of the first or the concentration of the second of these two more famous appellations, possibly partly because YIELDS of 40 hl/ha (2 tons/acre) are allowed, as opposed to a maximum of 25 hl/ha in Barsac and Sauternes. In effect Cérons is a buffer zone between Barsac and the GRAVES, and indeed it produces dry wines entitled to the Graves appellation as well as its own sweet wine which enjoys a long history (see BORDEAUX, history). The best bottlings from the likes of Ch de Cérons can demonstrate real vivacity but apathy and depressed prices have discouraged many producers from making the investments of faith and equipment needed to make great sweet wine. Clay is slightly more common here than in Barsac and Sauternes and the generally flatter land may also play a part in reducing the likelihood of BOTRYTIZED WINES.

CERTIFIED PLANTING MATERIAL, budwood, cuttings, or grafted plants which have normally been through a form of quality assurance to ensure trueness to type, freedom from known virus diseases, and typically designated clonal origin. Various bodies, often government controlled, offer such certification programmes around the world. The planting of certified material is an important first step in developing vineyards with high yield and quality potential, and is a preferred practice to planting haphazardly selected budwood. See CLONE, CLONAL SELECTION, and VINE IMPROVEMENT.

R.E.S.

Coombe, B. G., and Dry, P. R., *Viticulture*, i: *Resources in Australia* (Adelaide, 1988).

CESANESE, the red grape variety apparently indigenous to LATIUM (for ancient historical reasons, one might expect great things from it). The superior **Cesanese d'Affile** is more common but is losing ground and was planted on barely 1,300 ha/3,200 acres of vineyard in 1990. **Cesanese Comune** has larger berries and is also known as Bonvino Nero. See LATIUM for more details.

CHABLIS is the steely, dry, white wine of the most northern vineyards of BURGUNDY in north east France, made like all fine white Burgundy, from Chardonnay grapes. Paradoxically, however, in the New World, particularly in North America and Australia, the name Chablis has been borrowed and abused so that it is more often used to describe a dry white wine of uncertain provenance and no specific grape variety bearing no resemblance other than its colour to true Chablis (see GENERIC wine).

The appellation covers some 3,000 ha/7,500 acres around the small town of Chablis and 19 other villages and hamlets in the *département* of the Yonne, near the city of AUXERRE. The appellation, which was created in 1938, comprises four ranks of which the top is grand cru Chablis, with seven named vineyards. Then come the premiers crus, including 40 vineyard names, then Chablis, by far the most common appellation, and finally Petit Chablis, the lowliest. The best vineyard sites are on the south west facing slopes of the valley of the Serein, the small river that flows through the quiet town of Chablis to join the Yonne.

Chablis is quite separate from the rest of Burgundy, divided from the CÔTE D'OR by the hills of the Morvan, so that BEAUNE, for example, is over 100 km to the south. In fact the vineyards of Chablis are much closer to CHAMPAGNE and its southernmost vineyards in the Aube *département*, than to the rest of Burgundy, and until early in this century it was not unusual for wine from Chablis to find its way into the champagne makers' cellars in Rheims and Épernay.

History

Although it was the Romans who introduced vines to Chablis, as to so many other parts of FRANCE, it was the medieval church, notably the Cistercian MONKS of the nearby abbey of Pontigny, who firmly established viticulture as an essential part of the rural economy, possibly even introducing the Chardonnay vine. See BURGUNDY, history.

Towards the end of the 19th century the Yonne as a whole was a flourishing wine region, with some 40,000 ha of vines. Vineyards lined the banks of the river Yonne, as far as Joigny and Sens. The best known of these Yonne wines was Chablis and the name was used to describe the ample quantities of dry white wine that was transported with great convenience along the rivers Yonne and Seine to satisfy the vast and thirsty Parisian market. At the end of the 20th century there are barely 4,000 ha of vines in the Yonne, mainly in Chablis but also other peripheral Auxerrois appellations such as Irancy, Coulanges-la-Vineuse, and Epineuil.

Three factors were responsible for the sharp decline in the vineyard area at the end of the 19th century: first POWDERY MILDEW which appeared in Chablis in 1886, for which a cure had already been found, as had one for PHYLLOXERA which first reached Chablis in 1887. However, many growers were reluctant to replant their vineyards, for the opening of the

The town of **Chablis**, with the grand cru vineyards of Valmur and Les Clos beyond.

Paris–Lyons–Marseilles RAILWAY in 1856 considerably reduced their share of the Paris market. Thanks to the railways, Chablis lost its advantage of proximity to the capital and was simply unable to compete with the cheap wines of the MIDI, which could now be transported easily to the capital. Consequently the vineyard area gradually declined until it reached a mere 500 ha in the mid 1950s, before the fortunes of the appellation revived.

Climate

Climate has always played an important role in determining the success and quality of Chablis. Essentially the climate is semi-CONTINENTAL, with no maritime influence, so that the winters are long and hard and the summers often, but not always, fairly hot. There is all the climatic uncertainty, and therefore vintage variation, both in quality and quantity, of a vineyard far from the equator.

One of the key factors in determining how much wine will be produced is the possibility of spring FROSTS, which can cause enormous damage to the young vine shoots. Depending on how advanced the vegetation is, the vineyards are vulnerable from the end of March until well into May. Since the end of the 1950s, after a decade of vintages particularly badly affected by frost, various methods of protection evolved. Heaters, or SMUDGE POTS, may be lit in the vineyards; they are expensive but efficient. The alternative technique of using SPRINKLERS, or aspersion, to spray the vines with water from the moment the temperature drops to freezing point may also be practised. The water freezes to form a protective coating of ice round the young vine buds, in the same way that snow can protect a seemingly fragile snowdrop. Wind can seriously prejudice the effectiveness of aspersion, however. In the often parcellated vineyards of Chablis it can be all too easy to protect a neighbour's vines rather than one's own. Spraying must continue all the time the temperature is at 0°C/32°F or below. If there is any interruption, for any reason, such as a blocked pipe, then even more damage is caused to the vines than if no precautions had been taken in the first place.

However both heaters and aspersion are sufficiently effective to make the difference in some years between a crop of reasonable quantity and virtually no crop at all. It is now perfectly possible to make a viable living from vines in Chablis, whereas in the 1950s you needed both eternal optimism and another crop, so that polyculture was common.

Vineyard expansion

The development of effective frost protection in the early 1960s was followed by a tremendous increase in the vineyard area of Chablis, which has not been without controversy, with those who believe that the vineyards should be restricted in area arguing their cause as fervently as those who favour the expansion of the appellation. The seven grands crus total just 100 ha and are all on one slope facing south west just outside the town. They are Les Clos, Blanchots, Bougros, Vaudésir, Valmur, Preuses, and Grenouilles. There is also, in true Burgundian fashion, an anomaly. The tiny vineyard of La Moutonne is partly in Vaudésir and partly in Preuses, but for some illogical and doubtless bureaucratic reason does not have the status of a grand cru in its own right, even though its wines certainly demonstrate that it qualifies.

Much of the dispute over the vineyard expansion has centred on the premiers crus. By the mid 1990s there were 40 in all, totalling nearly 700 ha out of a delimited 750. Some are often seen on labels, while others are more obscure, and some such as Vaudevey came into existence only with the expansion of the appellation. Their protagonists argue that they are on slopes that were planted before the phylloxera crisis and that their TERROIR closely resembles that of the long-established premiers crus. Some of the lesser known vineyards may use a better known umbrella name, so that for example L'Homme Mort may be sold as Fourchaume, as follows, with umbrella names followed by their associated premiers crus:

Mont de Milieu
Montée de Tonnerre: *Chapelot, Pied d'Aloue, Côte de Bréchain*
Fourchaume: *Vaupulent, Côte de Fontenay, L'Homme Mort, Vaulorent*
Vaillons: *Châtains, Séchet, Beugnons, Les Lys, Mélinots, Roncières, Les Epinottes*
Montmains: *Forêt, Butteaux*
Côte de Léchet
Beauroy: *Troesme, Côte de Savant*
Vauligneau
Vaudevey: *Vaux Ragons*
Vaucoupin
Vosgros: *Vaugiraut*
Les Fourneaux: *Morein, Côte de Prés Girots*
Côte de Vaubarousse
Berdiot
Chaume de Talvat
Côte de Jouan
Les Beauregards: *Côte de Cuissy*

Nearly 2,300 ha out of a possible 2,600 of AC Chablis are planted and it is in the village appellation that there has been the greatest growth, with the planting of vines on much of the arable land. In the mid 1990s there were only just over 200 ha of Petit Chablis vineyard, but 1,800 ha are permitted within the delimited area. There have been some moves to change the name of this category, for to some it sounds petty rather than petit, but for the moment its status and size are likely to remain unchanged.

Soil is another significant factor in determining not only the unique flavour of Chablis, but also the vineyard area. Chablis lies on the edge of the Paris basin, where the rocks date back to the Upper Jurassic age, some 180 million years ago. On the other side of the basin is the Dorset village of Kimmeridge in southern England which gives its name to the particular geological formation and period known as 'Kimmeridgean'. Basically the soil is what the French call *argilo-calcaire*, a mixture of limestone and clay, containing a multitude of tiny fossilized oyster shells. The next geological layer is Portlandien, which is very similar in structure to Kimmeridge, but is generally deemed not to give as much finesse to the wine. The grand cru vineyards are all on Kimmeridge while Portlandien constitutes most of the outlying vineyards of Petit Chablis.

Viticultural practices in Chablis are very similar to those in the rest of Burgundy, apart from the overriding need to protect the vines from frost.

The use of oak

In the cellar, as elsewhere in France, wine-making techniques improved enormously in the 1970s and 1980s, so that there is a better understanding of such elements as MALOLACTIC FERMENTATION and the need for TEMPERATURE CONTROL during fermentation. The most interesting and controversial aspect of vinification in Chablis is the use of OAK. This is a most significant factor in influencing the taste of a Chablis, for it is where the wine-maker can make the most impact. Chablis is the one fine wine area where Chardonnay is not automatically given some contact with oak.

In the 1960s oak barrels were used simply for storage. Although in Chablis prices are still quoted per *feuillette*, the region's traditional barrel size of 132 l (half the size of the Burgundian pièce; see BARREL TYPES), *feuillettes* are in practice found increasingly rarely in the cellars of Chablis. Concrete vats, then steel and more recently stainless steel have all provided more inert materials for containers. Some producers abandoned their oak barrels in favour of stainless steel, which although expensive, is very much easier to use, allowing for impeccable hygiene and a meticulous control of temperature. Inert vats have no effect on the taste of Chablis and allow the wine to express the terroir of a particular cru, without any external influence. Those who favour stainless steel want the purest flavour of Chablis, with the firm streak of acidity and the mineral quality that the French describe as *goût de pierre à fusil*, or gunflint. Louis Michel's is generally considered to be the epitome of this style, although others who employ it successfully include Jean Durup, Jean-Marc Brocard, A. Régnard and Long-Depaquit.

Other producers, such as René and Vincent Dauvissat, and François and Jean-Marie Raveneau, have never completely abandoned their barrels. They may ferment their wine in vats and then once the alcoholic FERMENTATION is finished, the wine goes into oak for a few months' BARREL MATURATION. Those who favour the use of oak barrels believe that the gentle process of oxygenation adds an extra dimension of complexity to the flavour of their wine. However, oak barrels are much more demanding in terms of labour; hygiene in the cellar must be impeccable; the barrels require careful maintenance and if you replace your barrels on a regular three yearly rotation, they are expensive. The proportion of new barrels in a cellar in Chablis can vary. Some producers buy very few each year, wishing to avoid the marked vanilla flavours that new wood can impart. Others such as William Fèvre regularly replace a third of their barrels.

Experimentation with oak reached almost fever pitch in the early 1990s. Some who had abandoned it have returned to it, or their children have. Some, such as Gilles Collet, Jean-Paul Droin, and Domaine Laroche for some crus, ferment in barrel; others just age their wine in oak, with annual variations according to the quality of the wine. Few wines other than the grands crus and premiers crus are matured in wood, however, for it is generally recognized that a wine needs a certain structure and extract to avoid being overwhelmed by the taste of oak, as is the case with some Chablis *cuvée bois*, the product of barrel maturation. LEES STIRRING, degrees of barrel TOAST, origins of oak and coopers (see COOPERAGE) are all topics of consideration, and there are of course no conclusive answers. Paradoxically it is not unknown for a Chablis that has seen no wood, to take on as it matures, a certain firm nuttiness that suggests some ageing in oak. Ultimately as with all Burgundy, where vineyards and crus are split amongst several families, the choice of a bottle depends on the name of the grower and the estate on the label.

The Chablis market

Surprisingly perhaps until the early 1980s Chablis was hardly appreciated in France itself as most of it was sold on the export market, usually through the large NÉGOCIANTS of Burgundy, based mainly in Beaune. Currently nearly a third of all Chablis is vinified by the local co-operative, La Chablisienne, which works well for its appellation. There are also five négociants based in the town, some with vineyards and some without. However, the trend of the last decade or two has been for an increasing number of producers, who originally sold their wine in bulk to négociants, to bottle and sell their wine themselves. Consequently the négociants have tended to decline in importance and the choice of Chablis producers has grown significantly.

Chablis has always been affected by significant variations in the size of the vintage. At times it seems that the swings between glut and penury can never be mastered, and prices fluctuate accordingly (much more dramatically, for example, than in the more regulated but climatically similar Champagne market). However, some of the commercial instability has disappeared with the growth in the vineyard area, so that there is more Chablis available to satisfy world demand. Generally Chablis is a more prosperous appellation than it was in the 1970s, for with the possibility of frost protection the growers are much more certain of making a viable living from their vines than ever before.

Chablis remains one of the great white wines of the world. It is sometimes overshadowed by the greater opulence of a fine Meursault or Corton Charlemagne, but it has an individuality of its own that sets it apart from the great white burgundies of the Côte d'Or. There is a unique streak of steely acidity, a firm flintiness and a mineral quality that is not found elsewhere in Burgundy. Like all great white burgundy, it benefits from but all too rarely receives BOTTLE AGEING. A premier cru will be at its best at 10 years, while a grand cru could easily benefit from 15 or more years of maturation. A 1947 Côte de Léchet, not one of the best premiers crus, but from a great vintage, was still showing a remarkable depth of flavour with the characteristic *goût de pierre à fusil*, when it was 40 years old. Perhaps the 1990 vintage, with its excellent balance of concentration and acidity, will eventually prove to have the same potential.

Bro, L., *Chablis, Porte d'or de la Bourgogne* (Paris, 1959).
Fèvre, W., *Le Vrai Chablis et les autres* (Chablis, 1978).
George, R., *Chablis* (London, 1984).

CHACOLÍ DE GUETARIA, Spain's smallest DO region and a matter of considerable pride to those few BASQUE farmers who stubbornly refuse to give in to the elements and continue to farm less than 50 ha/120 acres of vines on the rocky Biscay coast west of San Sebastian (see map on p. 907). A century ago over 1,000 ha of vines stretched from Bayonne to Bilbao, but after PHYLLOXERA ravaged the region, few vineyards were replanted. With cool summers, and an annual RAINFALL of 1,500 mm/58 in, this is hardly ideal grape-growing country. The high trained Hondarribi Zuri white grape variety, which accounts for 85 per cent of Chacolí, produces thin, acid wines. A small amount of red is made from the Hondarribi Beltz. Nearly all the wine is drunk in local seafood restaurants and Chacolí is almost unknown outside Basque country. R.J.M.

CHAI, French, and particularly Bordelais, term for a place where wine and occasionally brandy is stored, typically in BARREL. Thus a smart Bordeaux CHÂTEAU will have (perhaps) the château building itself with no direct wine-making function, a CUVERIE in which fermentation takes place, a first-year *chai* in which the most recent vintage's crop undergoes ÉLEVAGE, and a second-year *chai* to which it is moved at some point before the end of the year in order to make way for the next year's crop. The New World counterpart to the *chai* is sometimes called the barrel hall.

CHALK, a soft and crumbly, highly porous (35 to 40 per cent) type of pure white LIMESTONE. Chalk-derived SOILS are valued in viticulture for their excellent DRAINAGE, combined with a capacity of the SUBSOIL to store substantial amounts of water. Because vine ROOTS can usually penetrate to chalk bedrock, continuity of moisture supply is assured regardless of short-term fluctuations in RAINFALL. Pure chalk is of low fertility, resulting in a rather low vine VIGOUR and naturally good CANOPY MICROCLIMATE.

True chalk is much less common under vineyards than most wine books suggest, chiefly because CALCAREOUS has been taken to mean chalky. Apart from some vineyards in southern ENGLAND, the principal wine region with chalk is CHAMPAGNE. Even here, the better vineyards are mostly on

Merlot grapes are delivered to Domaine de la Baume, a winery outside Béziers in the Languedoc revitalized by the South Australian company Thomas Hardy in the early 1990s as part of a European expansion scheme—all part of **Australian influence** on the world of wine.

CLAYS, with only the longer roots reaching the underlying chalk.

There is also a long-standing myth that the quality of COGNAC is directly related to the 'chalkiness' of the soil in the Charentes. Although there is a swathe of real chalk some distance south of the town of Cognac, largely outside Grande Champagne, the circular boundaries drawn between supposed different qualities of the spirit do not follow the pattern of the geology.

Similarly, it is widely believed that the SHERRY region around Jerez in south west Spain is on chalk, although the bedrock is not even pure limestone. The fact that Jerez, Cognac, and Champagne produce more or less exclusively white wines is one of the bases for the widely held misapprehension that there is a correlation between wine colour and SOIL COLOUR.

(See also DEACIDIFICATION for the use of chalk in winemaking.) J.M.H. & J.G.

Hancock, J., and Price, M., 'Real chalk balances the water supply', *Journal of Wine Research*, 1/1 (1990), 45–60.

CHALK HILL, California wine region and AVA. See SONOMA.

CHALONE, California single winery wine region and AVA. See MONTEREY.

CHALONNAISE, CÔTE, red and white wine-producing region in the Saône-et-Loire *département* of BURGUNDY between the CÔTE D'OR and the Mâconnais (see map on p. 163). The Côte Chalonnaise takes its name from the town of Chalon-sur-Saône, which had been an important CELTIC trading centre in Ancient GAUL. As well as generic BOURGOGNE Côte Chalonnaise, mostly red from the Pinot Noir grape, and BOURGOGNE ALIGOTÉ de Bouzeron, there are four village appellations: MERCUREY, which stands apart in both quality and price, produces mostly Pinot Noir with small quantities of white wine; GIVRY the same; MONTAGNY is exclusively a white wine appellation growing the Chardonnay grape; while RULLY offers both red and white wines and is a centre for the sparkling wine industry in a small way.

Although the soils in the Côte Chalonnaise are similar to those of the Côte d'Or, being based on limestone with a complex admixture of other elements, the vineyards are more scattered since there is no regular escarpment to provide continuity of suitable slopes.

Viticultural practices are broadly similar to those in the Côte d'Or. Vinification is sometimes carried out in barrels, although only the best producers use any new OAK. Bottling normally takes place in the summer before the new vintage.

Maximum yields for Mercurey are the same as those for VILLAGE WINES in the Côte d'Or, whereas the other appellations of the Côte Chalonnaise may produce an additional 5 hl/ha (0.3 tons/acre). Although cheerfully fruity while young, few wines from this region have enough body to age well. J.T.C.M.

CHAMBERTIN, Chambertin-Clos de Bèze, Chapelle-Chambertin, Charmes-Chambertin, Griottes-Chambertin, Latricières-Chambertin, Mazis-Chambertin, and **Ruchottes-Chambertin,** great red GRANDS CRUS in Burgundy's CÔTE D'OR. For more details, see GEVREY-CHAMBERTIN.

CHAMBÉRY, not a wine at all but a delicate, aromatic VERMOUTH made in the French alps. Of the huge volume of vermouth produced and assiduously marketed each year, the relatively rare Chambéry is one subtle enough to appeal to the wine drinker.

CHAMBOLLE-MUSIGNY, village and appellation of particular charm in the Côte de Nuits district of Burgundy producing red wines from Pinot Noir grapes. A fine Chambolle-Musigny has a rich, velvety elegance which rivals the finesse of Vosne-Romanée or the power of Gevrey-Chambertin. There are two GRAND CRU vineyards, Le Musigny and Bonnes Mares (in part), and some exceptional PREMIERS CRUS worthy of promotion.

Le **Musigny** ranks with Romanée-Conti, La Tâche, Richebourg, Chambertin, and Chambertin Clos de Bèze as one of the pinnacles of great burgundy (see DOMAINE DE LA ROMANÉE-CONTI, VOSNE-ROMANÉE, and GEVREY-CHAMBERTIN for details of these). The vineyard lies between the scrubland at the top of the slope and the upper part of CLOS DE VOUGEOT, on a slope of eight to 10 per cent which drains particularly well through the oolitic limestone. The soil is more chalk than clay, covered by a fine silt, a combination which leads to the exceptional grace and power of Le Musigny, an iron fist in a velvet glove.

Of the 10.7 ha/26 acres of Le Musigny which is split between Musigny, Petits Musigny, and La Combe d'Orveau, seven are owned by Domaine Comte de Vogüé. Other significant producers are the Château de Chambolle Musigny, Joseph Drouhin, and Domaine Jacques Prieur.

Adjacent to Le Musigny lies the premier cru Les Amoureuses, whose reputation and price suggest that this vineyard is worthy of elevation to grand cru. If a little less powerful than Le Musigny itself, the wines of Les Amoureuses demonstrate a very similar style. The next most sought after premier cru, and the largest, is Les Charmes.

The other grand cru of Chambolle Musigny is **Bonnes Mares**, situated to the north of the village and overflowing into MOREY-ST-DENIS. The wines show more sturdiness than silkiness, less graceful than Le Musigny but with evident power and structure. Bonnes Mares is noted for its ageing capacity. Ownership is spread over more than 30 proprietors, the largest being again Domaine Comte de Vogüé. This producer also makes a very small quantity of white Musigny.

See also CÔTE D'OR and its map. J.T.C.M.

Vines in early spring outside the French-owned Clos du Val winery in the **Napa** Valley. In this famous northern California wine region, **hillside vineyards** are relatively rare and vines cluster on the valley floor.

CHAMBOURCIN is a relatively recent dark-berried FRENCH HYBRID commercially available only since 1963 and popular in the 1970s, particularly in the MUSCADET area, where it was still the third most planted variety, although admittedly a long way behind Melon and Folle Blanche, according to the 1988 agricultural census (which found a total of 1,200 ha/3,000 acres in France). This extremely vigorous, productive vine produces better-quality wine than most hybrids, being deep coloured and full of relatively aromatic flavour, although it is not officially allowed even into the local VINS DE PAYS. It has also been grown on an experimental basis in New South Wales in Australia in a culture unfettered by anti-hybrid prejudice.

CHAMBRÉ, French word also used in English to describe a wine that has been deliberately warmed to room TEMPERATURE before serving (from *chambre*, 'room').

CHAMPAGNE, name derived from the Latin term *campania*, originally used to describe the rolling open countryside just north of Rome (see CAMPANIA). In the early Middle Ages it became applied to a province in north east France (see map on p. 399). It is now divided into the so-called 'Champagne pouilleuse' the once-barren but now cereal-growing chalky plains east of Rheims, and the 'Champagne viticole' (capital letters indicate the geographical descriptions, while lower case is used for the wine). The term Champagne is also used for the chalkier parts of the COGNAC region in South West France.

Champagne, with its two champagne towns Rheims and Épernay, was the first region to make SPARKLING WINE in any quantity and historically the name champagne became synonymous with the finest, although Champagne is now responsible for less than one bottle in 12 of total world production of all sparkling wine. In common with other French regions making fine wines, notably Burgundy and Bordeaux, champagne formed the model for other aspiring wine-makers, especially in Australia and the west coast of the United States, employing the same grapes, and the same SPARKLING WINE-MAKING method, as the French originals. This form of imitation, while flattering, became decidedly awkward for the Champenois in the late 1980s. Their response was to tighten up the regulations regarding their own wines, and thus substantially increase the average quality.

History

Champagne was at the crossroads of two major trade routes, north–south between Flanders and Switzerland and east–west from Paris to the Rhine. Its position made it prosperous, but also ensured that it has been fought over many times in the course of the past 1,500 years. One of the most important battles in history was fought at Châlons-sur-Marne in AD 455, when Attila the Hun was finally repulsed. Subsequent battles included a savage civil war, the Fronde in the middle of the 17th century. As late as 1914 the famous 'Taxis de la Marne' brought French reinforcements from Paris to repulse the German invaders, who had (briefly) occupied Épernay and reached the outskirts of Rheims. But successive conflicts merely interrupted the progress of the vineyard.

Although there are numerous legends concerning earlier vineyards, the first serious mention is at the time of St Rémi at the end of the fifth century AD. For nearly nine centuries after Hugh Capet was crowned as king of France in Rheims cathedral in 987, the city's position as the spiritual centre of France naturally boosted its fame.

Vines had already been planted around the city, mainly by the numerous local abbeys and by the local nobility. But until the 17th century there was no generic 'vin de Champagne'. Since the ninth century, wines from the Montagne de Reims south of the city had been known as 'vins de Reims', those from the Marne valley as 'vins de la rivière', or river wines. A number of villages, notably Bouzy and Verzenay on the Montagne, and Ay and Épernay in the Marne valley, were already being singled out for the quality of their wines. The wine trade was centred on Rheims and Châlons-sur-Marne, and the wines had the great advantage of immediate access to the Marne, which joined the Seine just east of PARIS (see RIVERS).

But the wines did not sparkle: they were light, pinkish still wines made from the Pinot Noir grape. In the last half of the 17th century wine-making greatly improved, under the auspices of leading clerical wine-makers, led by Dom PÉRIGNON, who transformed the Abbey of Hautvillers, above Épernay, into the region's leading centre of viticultural progress. The wines' fame grew greatly in the second half of the 17th century when they were introduced to the Court of Versailles, notably by the Marquis de Sillery, a large landowner in the region, and by the Marquis de St-Évremond, who introduced champagne to London society after he was banished to Britain in 1662.

In the cold winters normal in the region the wines had a tendency to stop FERMENTATION and then to start refermenting in the spring. For a long time this was considered something of a nuisance, as the resulting release of CARBON DIOXIDE was often strong enough to break the flimsy bottles normal at the time. The development of stronger BOTTLES by British glassmakers permitted drinkers to enjoy the resulting sparkle. Indeed it was the café society of London, encouraged by St-Évremond, which probably first enjoyed true 'sparkling champagne' (see contemporary references in ENGLISH LITERATURE).

The habit was taken up by the licentious court round the duke of Orléans, who became regent of France after the death of Louis XIV in 1715, but serious wine-makers (and their clients) continued to believe that sparkling champagne was inferior to the still wines of the region. Moreover even the stronger bottles could not reliably withstand the pressure generated by the SECOND FERMENTATION. So, throughout the 18th century, only a few thousand bottles were produced every year, and up to half of them would break.

The champagne business we know today was born in the first 40 years of the 19th century. The first notable step was taken by Madame (VEUVE) CLICQUOT. One of her employees developed the system of PUPITRES to assist in the REMUAGE

Pickers at work near Verzenay on **Champagne's** Montagne de Reims.

process. CORKS were improved, and a corking machine developed. Understanding, and then mastering, the second fermentation took longer. The scientist and minister CHAPTAL had understood that 'sparkling wines owe their tendency to sparkle only to the fact that they have been enclosed in a bottle before they have completed their fermentation'. But it took a young pharmacist from Châlons-sur-Marne, André François, to enable wine-makers to measure the precise quantity of sugar required to induce a second fermentation in the bottle without inducing an explosive force.

François died in 1838, shortly after he had published his formulae. But within a generation Champagne had become the home of the world's first 'wine industry', one dominated by a number of internationally famous brand names. Most of these were those of young entrepreneurs from the Rhineland, such as Messrs KRUG, BOLLINGER, and ROEDERER, who showed greater commercial nous than the local merchants, only a few of whom, apart from Madame Clicquot and Monsieur MOËT, survived.

But for over half a century, until well into the 1950s, Champagne suffered from a number of problems which clouded its earlier successes. The important RUSSIAN market collapsed in 1917 and two World Wars, separated by the slump, closed the export markets on which the region depended so heavily. The arrival of the PHYLLOXERA louse in Champagne in 1890 intensified competition from other sparkling wines, from Germany as well as from other French wine-makers, and intensified the fraudulent habits of some of the region's more unscrupulous merchants, who were wont to import juice and wine for bottling and sale as champagne.

The fraud compounded the misery caused by phylloxera to the region's growers and caused a near civil war in 1911. This was sparked off by the first attempts to define the region entitled to produce champagne. When the French Assembly included the Aube, a separate wine region 110 km/70 miles south east of Épernay, riots broke out in the Champagne region proper. Eventually the Aube was included as a separate 'second zone', although it was included when the boundaries were finally fixed in 1927.

The events of 1911 shook the whole wine-making community, and 25 years later the resulting desire for common action resulted in the combined group of growers and merchants known as the Commission de Châlons, set up in 1935 under the impetus of the remarkable Robert-Jean de Vogüé, head of Moët. At a time when growers were virtually giving away their grapes, the Commission provided them with some stability. Six years later the desire for joint action led to the formation of the CIVC, the Comité Interprofessionnel du Vin de Champagne, the pioneering attempt, much copied elsewhere, to provide wine-making regions with an organism which represented all the interests involved.

In the 40 years after 1950 the region enjoyed unprecedented prosperity with sales quadrupling to over 200 million bottles. Traditional export markets, like Britain, the United States, Belgium, and Switzerland, took increasing quantities. Nevertheless the French market, which grew more than sixfold between 1950 and 1980, overwhelmed exports and came to account for two-thirds of sales. This emphasis had important structural implications, since the traditional BRANDS were less dominant in the domestic market than outside France, where they still account for over 90 per cent of sales.

In the domestic market nearly half total sales are made by individual GROWERS, CO-OPERATIVES, and co-operative unions. The first co-operatives in Champagne were founded just before the First World War. They grew rapidly in the early 1960s and by 1989 the region's 140 co-operatives represented over half the growers and a third of the area under vines. Some co-operatives merely press grapes, others make wine (much of which is returned to members for sale under their own label, a fact signified by the letters CM before the grower's code on the label). Two or three co-operative unions, producing up to 10 million bottles annually, became major forces, particularly in supplying buyers' own brands.

The competition from the co-operatives added to the pressure on the, usually family-owned, MERCHANTS. In the 1960s and 1970s Moët absorbed Mercier and Ruinart, the oldest firm in the region. The Canadian liquor firm Seagram bought Mumm, Perrier-Jouët, and Heidsieck Monopole, while two of the most famous family firms, Lanson and Pommery & Greno, were bought first by an entrepreneur related to the Lansons, Xavier Gardinier, then by the major French group BSN, before becoming part of the Veuve Clicquot group which in 1987 became part of LVMH, which now accounts for over two-fifths of the total exports of champagne. The boom provided the opportunity for a number of newcomers. These included the Taittinger family, Bernard de Nonancourt, who built Laurent Perrier from virtually nothing into one of the biggest brands in Champagne, and Pierre Burtin, whose firm, Marne & Champagne, supplied supermarkets and other major buyers with their own-label wines.

The growers' increasing power was reflected in a rapid rise of grape prices during the 1980s and the inflexibility with which grapes were allotted to the merchants. In 1990, under the impetus of Moët, the market was freed. Since then price has been indicative, not legally binding. Between 1990 and 1993 the indicative maximum price fell from FF32 to FF20.50 per kg of grapes and merchants were increasingly able to control the quality of the grapes they bought. By then Champagne had been hit by the recession, first in Britain, where sales had quadrupled in a decade to reach nearly 23 million bottles in 1989. As a result a number of firms, especially those without their own vineyards, experienced difficulties and were sold and resold a number of times. So the trade has become increasingly concentrated, with the seven biggest merchants accounting for 70 per cent of the total.

Geography and climate

The region permitted to call its wines 'champagne' was strictly defined by the INAO in 1927. It sprawls from Charly a mere 30 miles east of Paris in the Marne valley to Rheims and south from Épernay along the Côte des Blancs and its southern extension, the Côtes de Sézanne. A separate region is the Aube, 112 km south east of Épernay. It was first DELIMITED in 1927 and over the years the acreage actually planted has varied widely, dropping to 11,000 ha/27,000 acres during the 1930s. In 1993 the appellation covered 27,500 ha of vines in 301 communes in five *départements*: 19,500 ha in the Marne; 2,500 in the Aisne (and Seine-et-Marne); and 5,500 in the Aube (and the Haute Marne). The mid 1990s area is the result of a recent increase of 5,000 ha, spread over a 10-year period, an increase granted after a shortage of grapes at the end of the 1970s. Only a tenth of the vines are owned by merchants, who can now add to their holdings only under very strict conditions. The remainder is owned by nearly 20,000 growers, many of whom own less than a hectare of vines.

Much of the appellation (and Champagne is now the only major French region to have just one appellation), and all the better CRUS, are on the slopes of the hills typical of Champagne region. The vines' roots dig deep into CHALKY depths, providing ideal conditions of DRAINAGE and HUMIDITY. The Champagne vineyard's exposure to the cold northern winter inevitably makes grape-growing a precarious operation, with the quality of the wines varying from year to year. As a result champagne is traditionally a wine blended, not only from a number of different villages, but also from several vintages. The poverty of the soil requires constant addition of FERTILIZER, either the *cendres noirs*, the natural compost found on the region's hilltops, or finely ground (and curiously multicoloured) household rubbish from Rheims, or even Paris.

The different qualities of grapes from the region's 301 widely spread CRUS has led to the establishment of a scale of prices. Originally the scale was from 50 to 100 per cent of the fixed price. Since a revision in 1985 it has been merely from 80 to 100 per cent, that level allowed only to grapes from 17 'grand cru' communes. Grapes from a further 38 communes, called premiers crus, are sold at between 90 and 98 per cent of the maximum price.

Vine varieties

In the past a number of grape varieties were planted in Champagne. But today the whole vineyard is planted with three, Pinot Noir, Meunier, and Chardonnay. The Pinot Noir, which accounts for just over a third of the total acreage, is no longer as dominant as it was, but still provides the basic structure and depth of fruit in the blend. In Champagne the Chardonnay, planted in a quarter of the vineyard, was traditionally grown on the east-facing slopes of the Côte des Blancs but has proved suitable in many other subregions, especially the Côtes de Sézanne. In Champagne it grows vigorously and buds early, thus making it susceptible to spring FROSTS. It imparts a certain austerity and elegance to young champagnes, but is long lived and matures to a fine fruitiness. The remaining third is planted with Pinot MEUNIER, a variety widely grown only in Champagne, particularly in the Valley of the Marne. It provides many champagnes with an early maturing richness and fruitiness.

Thanks to new CLONES and viticultural methods, the yield of grapes has grown greatly: from an average of 3,670 kg/ha in the 1940s to 9,910 in the 1980s (or from 24 to 66 hl/ha (1.3–

3.7 tons/acre). The first limit was set in 1935. Since 1992 yields have been limited to 10,400 kg/ha (with the usual additional 20 per cent PLC in exceptional years). Since 1992 160 (rather than the earlier limit of 150) kg of grapes are required to produce 100 l of juice, which means that the basic permitted yield is 65 hl/ha.

VINE DENSITY is notably high, and vines are replanted after between 25 and 30 years. The grapes are picked in late September, on dates now fixed village by village. They cannot be harvested unless they contain that year's fixed minimum level of POTENTIAL ALCOHOL. But since the level can be as low as eight per cent, sugar can be added to provide another degree and a half (see CHAPTALIZATION), and the second fermentation supplements the final ALCOHOLIC STRENGTH by up to another two per cent. Most champagne is about 12.5 per cent alcohol.

Wine-making

The pressing of the grapes is difficult, since the juice of what is to be a white wine must not be tainted by the skin of the mainly black grapes used. The traditional champagne PRESS was vertical, holding 4,000 kg/8,800 lb of grapes, a quantity known as a *marc* and a standard unit of measurement in the region. These presses are also called 'Coquard' presses after the name of the manufacturer. A number of other types of press have since been introduced and the CIVC allows both hydraulic and pneumatic horizontal presses.

Since 1990 all pressing centres have had to comply with certain minimum standards. Traditionally 2,666 l/704 gal were extracted from every *marc*: the first 2,050 l were the cuvée, the next 410 l the *premières tailles*, while the final 205 l were the *deuxièmes tailles*. The total yield has now been reduced by 115 l to 2,550 l and the *deuxièmes tailles* abolished.

The juice is allowed to settle for between 12 and 48 hours, at a low temperature. A few firms use oak FERMENTATION VESSELS for some or all of their grapes, but the overwhelming majority of the grapes are fermented in STAINLESS STEEL vats holding between 50 and 1,200 hl (1,320–31,700 gal). The fermentation TEMPERATURE also varies, between 12 and 25 °C (54–77 °F). Most wine-makers use a strain of YEAST specially developed by the CIVC.

Immediately after the first fermentation most, but by no means all, champagnes now undergo MALOLACTIC FERMENTATION. The result is called *vin clair*. Traditionally champagne has been made from wines from a number of different vineyards within the appellation although large numbers of growers (and a few firms) make wines from a single commune or vineyard. Major firms use wines from between 50 and 200 communes for their blend. They also use a percentage varying between 10 and 50 per cent of *vins de réserve* from earlier vintages, generally stored in stainless steel or cement vats.

Before the wine is bottled a measured dose of bottling liquor (*liqueur de tirage*), a mixture of wine, sugar, and specially developed yeasts, is added to the wine. The bottles are then capped, usually with a crown cap lined with plastic. Following TIRAGE, LEES CONTACT, RIDDLING, and DISGORGEMENT, a sweetening DOSAGE is usually added before final corking. A few champagnes are sold without any added sugar at all, but most are BRUT.

For more information, see in SPARKLING WINE-MAKING, champage method.

Styles of champagne

In addition to their basic wine, their non-vintage brut, major firms also make single **vintage champagnes** from the produce of three or four of the better years in every decade. BLANC DE BLANCS are made exclusively from the Chardonnay grape while BLANC DE NOIRS are made exclusively from black grapes. Pink or **rosé champagne** is made either by adding a small proportion of red wine to the blend or, less usually, by letting the juice remain in contact with the skin of the grapes for a short time during fermentation. Until 1992 the Champenois could market as Crémant wines made under lower pressure: generally three atmospheres rather than the normal six. But today only wines made in other French wine-growing regions are allowed to use the term (see CRÉMANT). All the major firms have now followed the example of Roederer with their Cristal bottling and Moët & Chandon with Dom Pérignon and produce 'luxury', 'de luxe', or PRESTIGE CUVÉES to show their house styles at their best.

The small proportion of still wines made in the region are sold under the appellations Coteaux CHAMPENOIS and the rare pink ROSÉ DES RICEYS. MARC, EAU-DE-VIE, and RATAFIA are also made. N.F.

Bonal, F., *Le Livre d'or de Champagne* (Lausanne, 1984).
Faith, N., *The Story of Champagne* (London, 1988).
Forbes, P., *Champagne: The Wine, the Land and the People* (London 1967).
Stevenson, T., *Champagne* (London, 1986).

CHAMPAGNE METHOD. See SPARKLING WINE-MAKING for this, the most meticulous way of making a wine sparkle and the one employed throughout CHAMPAGNE. On labels it is generally referred to as Méthode Traditionnelle, Méthode Classique, Traditional Method, Classic Method, or Bottle Fermented (although this last term is ambiguous and could be used of TRANSFER METHOD sparkling wines).

CHAMPENOIS, COTEAUX. Appellation used for the unusual still wines of CHAMPAGNE in northern France. For every one bottle of still white Coteaux Champenois produced, perhaps 20 of still red Coteaux Champenois are produced (in a good vintage), and 16,000 bottles of sparkling champagne. The wines of this cool region with their naturally high acidity and naturally light body are much improved by dissolved CARBON DIOXIDE. It is difficult to justify the production of white Coteaux Champenois, from expensive Chardonnay grapes, but easier to understand why the Champenois like to be able to drink the odd bottle of local still red from time to time. The village of Bouzy on the MONTAGNE DE REIMS has a particular reputation for its red Coteaux Champenois, partly perhaps because of the appeal of the name Bouzy Rouge, as do Ay, Cumières, and Ambonnay.

These red wines are of interest to outsiders only in the ripest vintages, while the whites and rosés serve only to compliment the Champenois on their wise decision to concentrate on sparkling wines.

See also ROSÉ DES RICEYS.

CHANCELLOR, productive red wine grape variety that is a FRENCH HYBRID developed from two Seibel parents. For long it was known as Seibel 7053, but was named Chancellor in NEW YORK in 1970. See SEIBEL for more details.

CHANGINS, viticultural research station in French-speaking SWITZERLAND near Nyon on Lake Geneva. It is principally concerned with improving plant material, including CLONAL SELECTION; matching VINE VARIETY to specific TERROIR in both French-speaking Switzerland and Italian-speaking Switzerland; and developing viticultural techniques which reduce costs, improve wine quality, and minimize chemical inputs (see ORGANIC VITICULTURE). Areas of OENOLOGICAL research in the mid 1990s included techniques for must SETTLING of white wines, red wine MACERATION, YEASTS, MALOLACTIC FERMENTATION, FILTRATION, and ENRICHMENT.

The research station's counterpart in German-speaking Switzerland is WÄDENSWIL.

CHAPITEAU, the small, round container which traps the alcoholic vapours emanating from a POT STILL, literally a circus tent or 'big top'.

CHAPOUTIER, family-owned merchant-grower based at Tain-l'HERMITAGE in France's northern RHÔNE. One of the Rhône valley's great names, established in 1808 and owning some 75 ha / 180 acres of vineyard, notably 26 ha of Hermitage. The house used to be particularly well known for its white Hermitage, Chante Alouette, and for its Grande Cuvée wines, high-quality blends of one appellation but more than one vintage. During the 1980s, however, when Chapoutier's peers (GUIGAL and JABOULET, for example) and numerous small growers were catching the imagination of the wine world with the improving quality of their wines, Chapoutier wines stood out precisely because they seemed unexceptional by comparison. This situation changed dramatically when Max Chapoutier's sons Marc and Michel took over the running of the company full time in 1988. All wines are now vintage dated, and great attention is paid to detail at every stage from vineyard management to bottling. Viticulture is ORGANIC, YIELDS are low, the wines are aged in OAK (new as appropriate) rather than old chestnut barrels, and the top reds are subjected to neither FINING nor FILTRATION. As a result the wines have more concentration, polish, and distinction, and Chapoutier's Hermitage, CÔTE RÔTIE, and CHÂTEAUNEUF-DU-PAPE can once again compete with the very best from the region. M.W.E.S.

Livingstone-Learmonth, J., *The Wines of the Rhône* (3rd edn., London, 1992).

CHAPTAL, JEAN-ANTOINE (1756–1832), French chemist, statesman, and essential polymath who rose from humble beginnings to become Minister of the Interior under Napoleon. In 1799 he wrote the article on wine for the monumental *Dictionnaire d'agriculture* of the Abbé Rozier, but is better known for his *l'Art de faire le vin* (1807) and his support for the concept of increasing the ALCOHOLIC STRENGTH of wine by adding sugar to the must, the procedure now known as CHAPTALIZATION. Some wine-makers throughout history sought to enhance either the quality or quantity of their product by adulterating the basic raw material, grapes, with other products. However, after the French Revolution of 1789 there was a considerable increase in the amount of poor-quality wine made in France. This provided the incentive for Chaptal to compile his famous *Traité théorique et pratique sur la culture de la vigne* (1801). Although he is best known for having introduced the metric system of weights and measures into France, as a practical scientist Chaptal was particularly concerned at the declining reputation of French wines, with increasing ADULTERATION AND FRAUD in the wine trade, and with the ignorance of many French wine producers of the scientific advances that could help them. He was of the firm belief that it was perfectly natural, and desirable, to add sugar to wine in order to improve it. Although he encouraged farmers to use GRAPE CONCENTRATE, he recognized that sugar from cane or beet was also capable of having a similar effect. (Another of Chaptal's many achievements was his development of techniques for extracting sugar from sugar beet.) P.T.H.U.

Chaptal, J. A., *Traité théorique et pratique sur la culture de la vigne* (Paris, 1801).
Johnson, H., *The Story of Wine* (London, 1989).
Loubère, L. A., *The Red and the White: A History of Wine in France and Italy in the Nineteenth Century* (Albany, NY, 1978).

CHAPTALIZATION, common wine-making practice, named after its French promulgator Jean-Antoine CHAPTAL, whereby the final ALCOHOLIC STRENGTH of a wine is increased by the addition of sugar to the grape juice or must, before and/or during FERMENTATION.

Amelioration is a common English euphemism for chaptalization. The French sometimes call it *amélioration*; the Germans, who were introduced to the technique by the chemist Ludwig Gall in the mid 19th century, call it *Verbesserung*; while most southern Europeans consider it an appalling practice, chiefly because, thanks to their warmer climate, they have no need of it.

Although the practice is still commonplace, and is indeed the norm in northern Europe, potential alcoholic strength is increasingly raised by adding products other than beet or cane sugar (particularly grape products of which there is a surplus in many wine regions). The addition of sugar, grape must, concentrated grape must, and rectified concentrated grape must (RCGM) in order to increase a wine's alcoholic strength are collectively known as enrichment, the general term for chaptalization and all related techniques and that officially sanctioned in EUROPEAN UNION parlance.

The **Chapoutiers** are not the only ones to have used the famous hill of Hermitage above Tain in the north Rhône as a hoarding.

In 1993 the European Union, concerned about its wine SURPLUS, officially announced its disapproval of chaptalization and its intention to curb the practice because it tended to encourage higher YIELDS.

See ENRICHMENT for more details.

CHAR. Term sometimes used of barrels. See TOAST.

CHARBONO, CALIFORNIA's obscure black grape variety may well be the DOLCETTO of Italy, according to GALET. Charbonneau is a synonym of the virtually extinct Douce Noire of the SAVOIE region in the French alps, which Galet at least argues is one and the same as Dolcetto Nero. The California version called Charbono clings to existence on a handful of acres on the NORTH COAST, especially in the NAPA Valley. As varietal wine (made chiefly by Inglenook) it can be difficult to distinguish from BARBERA grown under similar circumstances. See also the BONARDA of Argentina.

Galet, P., *Cépages et vignobles de France* (2nd edn., Montpellier, 1990).

CHARCOAL, absorbent material occasionally used in wine processing to remove COLOUR and COLLOIDS.

Charcoal is an impure amorphous carbon obtained by the dry distillation of wood or some other material containing carbon (bones, peat, and plant debris have all been used). The sort of charcoal most freqently used in wine-making is generally known as **active carbon** and is much purer than the charcoal in common use as a fuel in 17th century England.

Because of its very porous nature, charcoal has the particularly high ratio of surface area to weight required of an absorptive material. In wine-making it is used mainly to absorb the colloidal pigment polymers responsible for amber or brown colours in white wines, particularly in the manufacture of Pale Cream SHERRY. Off-flavours in wine are occasionally removed using a grade of active charcoal with a smaller pore size, transforming an unsaleable wine into a neutral one for use in a basic blend. Small amounts of active charcoal mixed with diatomaceous earth are sometimes used during final FILTRATION in the hope of removing unstable colloids which could potentially form a haze. A.D.W.

CHARDONNAY, white grape variety, and the one vine variety that has successfully escaped the confines of botanical nomenclature to become a brand, a wine name as familiar and popular as any to which consumers have been exposed for more than a century longer. In its Burgundian homeland, Chardonnay was for long the sole vine responsible for all of the finest white burgundy. As such, in a region devoted to geographical labelling, its name was known only to vine-growers. In the late 20th century, however, it was transplanted in most of the world's wine regions—where VARIETAL labelling has become the norm—with such a high degree of success that Chardonnay was by the 1990s a name known to far more wine consumers than MEURSAULT or MONTRACHET, two of Burgundy's greatest white wines.

But it is not just wine drinkers who appreciate the broad, easy charms of golden Chardonnay. Vine-growers appreciate the ease with which, in a wide range of climates, they can coax relatively high yields from this vine (whose natural vigour may need to be curbed by either dense planting or CANOPY MANAGEMENT). Wine quality is severely prejudiced however at yields above 80 hl/ha (4.5 tons/acre) and yields of 30 hl/ha (1.7 tons/acre) or less are needed for seriously fine wine. Their only major reservation is that it buds quite early, just after Pinot Noir, which regularly puts the coolest vineyards of Chablis and Champagne at risk from spring frosts. It can suffer from COULURE and occasionally MILLERANDAGE and the grapes' relatively thin skins can encourage rot if there is rain at harvest time, but it can thrive in climates as diverse as those of Chablis in northern France and California's hot Central Valley. Picking time is crucial for, unlike Cabernet Sauvignon, Chardonnay can lose its crucial acidity fast in the latter stages of ripening. In Burgundy, Chardonnay tends to ripen the week after its red counterpart Pinot Noir but with more regularity and, usually, with conveniently higher alcohol levels. A Montrachet with a natural alcohol content of more than 13 per cent is by no means uncommon—although the natural Burgundian inclination is to CHAPTALIZE.

Wine-makers love Chardonnay for its reliably high ripeness levels and its malleability. It will happily respond to a far wider range of wine-making techniques than most white varieties. The Mosel or Vouvray wine-making recipe of a long, cool fermentation followed by early bottling can be applied to Chardonnay. Or it can be fermented and aged in small oak barrels, some of the highest-quality fruit being able to stand up to new oak. It accommodates each individual wine-maker's policy on MALOLACTIC FERMENTATION and LEES STIRRING without demur. Chardonnay is also a crucial ingredient in most of the world's best sparkling wine, not just in Champagne, demonstrating its ability to age in bottle even when picked early. And, picked late, it has even been known to produce some creditable BOTRYTIZED sweet wines, notably in the Mâconnais, Romania, and New Zealand, from grapes attacked by NOBLE ROT (which helps counteract falling acidity levels).

Chardonnay also manages to retain a remarkable amount of its own character even when blended with other less fashionable varieties such as Chenin Blanc, Sémillon, or Colombard to meet demand at the lower end of the market. But perhaps this is because its own character is, unlike that of the other ultra-fashionable white, Sauvignon Blanc, not too pronounced. Chardonnay from young or over-productive vines can taste almost aqueous. Basic Chardonnay may be vaguely fruity (apples or melons) but at its best Chardonnay, like Pinot Noir, is merely a vehicle for the character of the vineyard in which it is grown. In many other ambitious wines fashioned in the image of top white burgundy, its 'flavour' is actually that of the oak in which it was matured, or the relics of the wine-making techniques used. When the vineyard site is right, yields are not too high, acid not too low, and wine-making skilled, Chardonnay can produce wines that will continue to improve in bottle for one, two, or, exceptionally, more decades but—unlike Riesling, the best Chenin Blanc, and botrytized Sémillon—it is not a variety capable of making whites for the very long term.

Chardonnay's origins are obscure. For long it was thought to be a white mutation of Pinot Noir, and it has often been called Pinot Chardonnay, but GALET cites good AMPELOGRAPHICAL evidence for Chardonnay's being a variety in its own right. A village in the Mâconnais called Chardonnay has excited various theories, while others speculate that Chardonnay's origins may be Middle Eastern, evincing its long history in the vineyards of LEBANON, where it is sufficiently well established to have at least two local synonyms, Meroué and Obaideh. There is a rare but distinct pink-berried mutation, Chardonnay Rose, as well as a headily perfumed Chardonnay Blanc MUSQUÉ version which is still grown by some Mâconnais and other growers to scent wines for early consumption.

Some of the 34 official French clones of Chardonnay have a similarly grapey perfume; notably 77 and 809, which are now quite widely disseminated, can add a rather incongruously aromatic note to blends with other clones of the variety. The arguably over-enthusiastic application of CLONAL SELECTION techniques in Burgundy means that growers can now choose from a wide range of Chardonnay clones specially selected for their productivity, particularly 75, 78, 121, 124, 125, and 277. Those seeking quality rather than quantity are more likely to choose 76, 95, and 96.

Chardonnay cuttings are sought after the world over and in many countries—France, America, even fiercely quarantined Australia, New Zealand, and South Africa—this is the white variety for which nurserymen found the greatest demand in the late 1980s, fuelled partly by consumer demand for full bodied white wines with the magic word Chardonnay on the label, but also by the dramatic expansion of the world's sparkling wine industry. Such is Chardonnay's glamour that it has probably been the variety of which most cuttings have been smuggled by ambitious wine producers thwarted by plant quarantine regulations.

Although, in total area planted, this superior-quality white variety is dwarfed by those traditionally used for brandy production such as AIRÉN and TREBBIANO, its popularity in the late 1980s was sufficient to propel it to first or second place in terms of area planted in each of France, California, Washington state, Australia, and New Zealand in the early 1990s. It thereby overtook Sémillon and Riesling in the 1980s to occupy more of the world's vineyard than any white-berried variety other than Airén, Trebbiano, and RKATSITELI—a remarkable feat for a vine credited with such nobility.

In France, for example, Chardonnay plantings had reached 20,000 ha/50,000 acres by the end of the 1980s, an increase of more than 50 per cent in the space of a decade. This was substantially due to the expansion of the CHAMPAGNE vineyard, where Chardonnay now represents as much as a third of all vines planted, an increase fuelled by the price premium paid for Chardonnay grapes that has spread Chardonnay much more widely around the region than its traditional base in the Côte des Blancs. There was a similar expansion of the total CHABLIS *vignoble*, whose Chardonnay plantings increased from 1,600 to 3,000 ha (7,400 acres) in the 1980s. Improvements in FROST protection techniques may have played a part in encouraging both these expansions.

In the Burgundian heartland, the CÔTE D'OR, Chardonnay plantings increased by one-quarter in the 1980s to a grand total of 1,400 ha—just half as much Chardonnay as was actually planted in a single year, 1988, in California! Perhaps it is not so surprising that Meursault is a name unknown to legions of Chardonnay drinkers when the former is produced in such limited quantity. Although Chardonnay, sometimes called Beaunois or Aubaine in Burgundy, has gradually been replacing GAMAY and ALIGOTÉ, Pinot Noir vines still outnumber Chardonnay vines more than four to one on the Côte d'Or. Much more Chardonnay is grown on the Côte de BEAUNE than on the Côte de NUITS. Famous white wine appellations include, from north to south, CORTON-CHARLEMAGNE, Meursault, PULIGNY-MONTRACHET, CHASSAGNE-MONTRACHET, and any name that includes the word Montrachet. For more on individual wines, see BURGUNDY.

In the Saône-et-Loire *département* which encompasses both the Côte CHALONNAISE and the MÂCONNAIS, total Chardonnay plantings overtook those of Gamay in the 1980s so that there were 4,500 ha/11,000 acres by 1988. From the Côte Chalonnaise, the whites of RULLY, MERCUREY, and MONTAGNY can offer real value in comparison with those of the Côte d'Or. The Mâconnais produces not just white MÂCON with a range of geographical suffixes but also various Pouillys, most famously POUILLY-FUISSÉ. From further south still come ST-VÉRAN and BEAUJOLAIS Blanc. Although the regulations allow Aligoté into Beaujolais Blanc and PINOT BLANC into wines labelled BOURGOGNE and Mâcon, most of these less expensive white burgundies are in practice made predominantly from Chardonnay. Much to the horror of the INAO there has been an increasing trend towards slipping the word Chardonnay on to white burgundy labels to increase their appeal to non-French consumers.

Although 90 per cent of French Chardonnay is still in either Champagne or Greater Burgundy, the variety has been sweeping south and west from this base. It is embraced by an ever-wider variety of appellations and plantings can be found in ALSACE, the ARDÈCHE, JURA, SAVOIE, in much of the LOIRE, and in the Languedoc, where it was first planted to add international appeal to Blanquette de LIMOUX. It has since been gaining ground in the Aude and Hérault for use in varietal vins de pays, whose quality is increasing as growers are persuaded to prune more severely and wine-makers' tendency to exhibitionism with new techniques is curbed. Total plantings in the LANGUEDOC-ROUSSILLON increased from 1,100 ha in 1988 to 5,300 ha in 1993.

Nowhere was the wine-making exhibitionism associated with Chardonnay more marked than in California in the 1970s and early 1980s when the accepted wine style veered sharply from outrageously rich and full-blown to meagrely early picked to, in some cases, all too obviously the product of full malolactic fermentation. Few would have believed in 1980, when California had just 18,000 acres/7,200 ha of Chardonnay, that by 1988 the state's total plantings would overtake the (rapidly increasing) French total so that by 1991 California had 56,600 acres/22,640 ha of Chardonnay, more than a fifth of which was less than three years old. The rate of new plantings reached a peak in 1988, however, and the early 1990s brought a new red wine fashion for California grape-growers to grapple with. Nearly half of all California Chardonnay is concentrated in Sonoma, Napa, and Monterey counties but there are also sizeable plantings further south in Santa Barbara and San Luis Obispo. See under CALIFORNIA for more detail of the wines.

Chardonnay has been embraced with equal fervour throughout the rest of North America, from CANADA to Long Island, NEW YORK. In 1990 it overtook Riesling to become the most planted variety of any hue in Washington state with 2,600 acres and it is also popular in Oregon and Texas. See under state names for details of wine styles produced.

The scale of America's romance with Chardonnay in general and oak-aged Chardonnay in particular has had a profound effect on the structure and viability of the international COOPERAGE business.

Various South American countries have been flirting with Chardonnay and are seeking out the cooler spots to imbue it with real concentration. CHILE, where plantings are increasing from a base that is tiny compared with Chile's area of white bordeaux varieties, has had greatest success, but even here Chilean Chardonnay can taste eerily like some Chilean Sauvignon. ARGENTINA had 800 ha/12,000 acres of Chardonnay in 1989, mainly in Mendoza, but plantings are increasing rapidly as Argentine wine producers are turning their attentions to exporting.

In the southern hemisphere it is the Australian wine industry whose all-important export trade has been centred on its peculiarly user-friendly style of Chardonnay. Rich fruit flavours, often disciplined by added acid and enlivened by oak influence of some sort are available at carefully judged prices. Such was the strength of demand for Australian Chardonnay in the late 1980s that the area of Chardonnay vines increased more than fivefold during the decade so that in 1990 Chardonnay, with its 4,300 ha, became Australia's most planted white wine grape variety (although 1,300 ha was too young to bear fruit). See AUSTRALIA for more detail on Chardonnay's location and wine styles.

It would be surprising if New Zealand had escaped Chardonnay-mania and indeed the variety was so enthusiastically embraced by New Zealand grape-growers in the late 1980s that there were 1,000 ha in total, one-sixth of the nation's total vineyard, by 1992 and only the more traditional MÜLLER-THURGAU covered more ground. New Zealand's Chardonnays have perceptibly more natural acid than their trans-Tasman neighbours. For more detail see NEW ZEALAND.

Chardonnay has had a chequered history in South Africa, with the first official cuttings so named being eventually identified as the very much less fashionably exciting AUXERROIS. This single ampelographical misfortune set back South Africa's entry into the international market-place by many years, so important is Chardonnay to the world's wine consumers. True Chardonnay was therefore slow to take hold, but see SOUTH AFRICA for more details.

Although Chardonnay can thrive in relatively hot climates (such as Australia's irrigation zones), it has to be picked before acids plummet (often before the grapes have developed much real character) and it does require relatively sophisticated technique, and access to cooling equipment, in the cellar. This is why it is not nearly so well suited to the less developed Mediterranean wine regions than such black grape varieties as GRENACHE and CINSAUT. Even in Lebanon, where local strains of Chardonnay are well entrenched, the wine tends to betray its torrid origins. With human skill and investment in technology, however, more well-balanced Chardonnays with the real interest of isolated examples from ISRAEL will emerge.

The variety continues to be planted widely—indeed it is almost a badge for those who would like to be recognized as members of the modern wine world. Italy, however, has a long history of Chardonnay cultivation, especially on its subalpine slopes in the north. For decades Italians were as casual about distinguishing between their Pinot Bianco (PINOT BLANC, also known as Weissburgunder in ALTO ADIGE) and their Chardonnay (traditionally called Gelber, or Golden, Weissburgunder in the Italian Tyrol) as they were about distinguishing between the two Cabernets. Indeed the Italian agricultural census of 1982 failed to distinguish a single Chardonnay vine, while that of 1990 located more than 6,000 ha.

International market forces eventually convinced Italians that the distinction could be worthwhile, although the Italian authorities were slow to recognize this dangerously Gallic grape as a name officially allowed into any DOC. Alto Adige Chardonnay was the first accorded DOC status, in 1984, although the vine has been working its magic on producers all over Italy from APULIA TO PIEDMONT and, of course, AOSTA towards the French border.

Nowadays much of Italy's Chardonnay is produced, often without much distinction, in FRIULI, TRENTINO, and, to a more limited extent, the VENETO, where much of it is used as ballast for GARGANEGA. Some fine examples are produced in favoured sites in both Friuli and Trentino but a considerable proportion is siphoned off to become SPUMANTE, as it is in LOMBARDY. Most of Italy's most ambitious still Chardonnays, exhibiting every possible wine-making technique, are white versions of SUPERTUSCANS (typically a BARRIQUE-aged VINO DA TAVOLA from Tuscany) with some counterparts in UMBRIA too. Chardonnay is gaining ground rapidly in Italy, being planted in Tuscan spots where Sangiovese is difficult to ripen and in Piedmont replacing Dolcetto, which can be difficult to sell. See under these geographical names for more details of Italian Chardonnays.

Chardonnay is of course well suited to many vineyards immediately north and east of Italy. See SWITZERLAND for more details of its performance over the alps. To the east wine-makers in AUSTRIA, anxious to prove their international worth, have been keen experimenters with this foreign import that was originally known as Morillon in Styria and Feinburgunder in Vienna and Burgenland and was not identified as the modish Chardonnay until the late 1980s (when Styria had well over 200 ha of it). Austria's Chardonnays include relatively rich, oak-matured versions; lean, aromatic styles modelled on their finest Rieslings; and even sweet AUSBRUCH wines.

BULGARIA has a vast area of Chardonnay vineyard but, perhaps because of over-production or for wine-making reasons, is rarely able to demonstrate real Chardonnay character in the bottle. There are limited plantings in SLOVENIA, HUNGARY, and ROMANIA (whence late harvest Chardonnays have been exported), but it seems that the Soviet Union's political turbulence during the late 1980s may have saved it from the major Chardonnay invasion that took place almost everywhere else at that time. Official statistics in 1993 found that it had infiltrated only MOLDOVA and GEORGIA, and played an extremely minor role relative to, for example, the white grape varieties RKATSITELI, RIESLING, and Chardonnay's Burgundian rival ALIGOTÉ.

Germany was one of the last wine-producing countries to admit Chardonnay to the ranks of accepted vine varieties, which is perhaps not surprising, since giving over one of Germany's favoured sites to this quintessentially French variety is inevitably viewed by some as a defeat for Germany's signal white variety Riesling. It was only in 1991 that Chardonnay was officially permitted, although small quantities grown from imported cuttings, officially totalling just 4 ha, were tolerated on an experimental basis before that.

Such is Chardonnay's fame and popularity that it is grown to a certain extent in climates as dissimilar as those of ENGLAND and eastern Switzerland on the one hand and Spain and Portugal on the other. In PENEDÈS Chardonnay has added class and an internationally recognizable flavour to CAVA as well as producing some relatively fat still wines both here and in COSTERS DEL SEGRE. There is also limited experimentation with the variety in SOMONTANO as well as to an even more limited extent in central Portugal.

It would seem that, of all the world's vine-growers, only France's *vignerons* with their slavish devotion to the appellation contrôlée system, constraints and all, limit themselves in their experimentation with what is still, despite red wines' resurgence, the most popular vine variety of all.

See also FASHION.

Atkin, T., *Chardonnay* (London, 1992).
Galet, P., *Cépages et vignobles de France* (2nd edn., Montpellier, 1990).

CHARLEMAGNE, king of the Franks 768–814, crowned Holy Roman Emperor in 800, the man who ushered in civilization, order, and prosperity after the long Dark Ages, ruling a Christian kingdom based at Aachen (Aix-la-Chapelle) which included virtually all of France, Belgium, Germany, and Switzerland.

Charlemagne's name is associated by modern wine drinkers with one of the greatest white burgundies, Corton-Charlemagne, produced on land he gave to the Abbey of Saulieu in 775 (see ALOXE-CORTON for more detail). Charlemagne's secretary and biographer Einhard tells us, however, that Charlemagne was a moderate man: he never drank more than three cups of wine with dinner, and he hated to see people drunk (*Life of Charlemagne* ch. 24). Only a temperate man is truly interested in wine: when he renamed the 12 months of the year in his native language, he called October 'windume-manoth', the month of the wine harvest (Einhard ch. 28)—which was presumably true of the vineyards then established in parts of northern Europe considered too cool for viable wine production today.

This Old FRANKEN name reflects the growing importance of wine in the Carolingian era, for under Charlemagne and his heirs more and more wine began to be grown. Viticulture had of course been long established in a large part of Charlemagne's empire. The Greek colonists had introduced winegrowing to Massilia (now Marseilles) from 600 BC onwards. When the Romans, under Julius Caesar, conquered Gaul in 51 BC, they gradually expanded the small-scale viticulture of the Gauls, who had drunk mainly BEER. The Roman settlers planted their first vineyards in southern Gaul, and by the 2nd century wine was grown extensively in most of Gaul. The Romans also planted vines in the Moselle valley, on the left bank of the Rhine, and in the areas we now know as Alsace, Pfalz, and Rheinhessen.

The spread of Christianity was one reason for the expansion of viticulture that took place during Charlemagne's reign and continued for another two centuries afterwards. The Church needed a daily supply of wine to celebrate the EUCHARIST. Also, monasteries, many of which were new foundations, needed wine for the monks and their guests (see MONKS AND MONASTERIES) and vineyards were planted all over northern France and even southern Belgium.

The Rule of St Benedict permitted a modest daily ration of wine, and more on holy days and feast days; important guests who stayed at the monastery had to be suitably entertained, for they might one day repay the monks generously for their hospitality. Monasteries usually had their own vineyards, and often these had been donated by local landowners who hoped for a place in heaven. Bishops also wanted wine, not just for the day-to-day running of their households but as a status symbol to put themselves on a par with the nobility of the district. Bishops, like monks, had their own vineyards, and some bishops may even have moved their sees to be nearer vineyards: at least, this may explain why the bishopric of Langres moved south to Dijon (at the north of the CÔTE D'OR), that of Tongres to Liège in modern Belgium, and that of St-Quentin to Noyon north of Paris. Thus Christianity fostered the production of two grades of wine, wine for daily consumption and a superior kind that was designed to impress prestigious guests.

In 816 the Council of Aachen added a third category of ecclesiastical viticulture. The Council prescribed that a college of canons, living under monastic rule, should be attached to every cathedral and that the canons should grow wine. Often they tended vineyards adjacent to those of their bishops; collegiate churches could be founded elsewhere in the diocese as well, and they also acquired their own vineyards.

Unlike education, viticulture was not the preserve of the Church, however: laymen also grew wine. The factor that decided where they established their new vineyards was not TERROIR but ease of transport. If the enterprise was to be commercially viable, the area had to be near a navigable RIVER or within each reach, by road, of a major town or city. This is why so much wine was grown around PARIS, AUXERRE, and in CHAMPAGNE, despite the fact that it was too cold there for the vine to yield ripe and abundant fruit. If the summer had not been hot, there was nothing for it but to drink thin, acidic wine until the following autumn, unless one could afford to buy better wine from elsewhere.

An interesting document from the last decade of the 8th century deals with the management of vineyards in secular ownership. It is known as the 'Capitulare de villis', or 'Concerning estates' (a capitulary being a collection of ordinances). Linguistic evidence and local references show that it was drawn up for Aquitaine, which was administered by Charlemagne's son Louis the Pious before he succeeded his father. The list of plants and herbs which it says must be grown in the estate's market garden owes more to the library than to real horticulture, but the advice it gives on wine-growing is sound and practical. Not only should the king's inspectors claim the portion of the vintage that is the royal household's due, they should also oversee hygienic procedures in the vineyard. Wine

PRESSES should be clean, and grapes should not be trodden with the feet. Wine that is to be sent to the palace should be put into proper wooden BARRELS instead of leather wineskins. An inventory of the entire estate should be drawn up each Christmas, including the wine it has produced that autumn and any older wine left over.

The 'Capitulare de villis' has no connection with Charlemagne himself, and there is no solid evidence that he initiated the planting of any vineyard, although parts of France and the Rheingau were first planted in his day. Viticulture flourished, not because of a *dirigiste* policy but because political unity had brought prosperity. External threats, most importantly from the Moors and the Magyars, could not be prevented and had to be dealt with, but, within the frontiers of the Holy Roman Empire, peace reigned, and viticulture was so successful that there was a surplus of wine. Landowners had to resort to the right of 'banvin', by which none of their tenants was allowed to sell his wine until the lord had sold his own. In the south wine was part of everyday life; in the north it was more of a luxury item but it could still be obtained readily.

How different things were in England! When the English scholar Alcuin, friend of Charlemagne and tutor to his court at Aachen, went back to his native country for a visit, he complained bitterly in a letter, dated 790, to a Frankish ex-pupil. The wine has run out, and his stomach aches with sour beer: please send wine. Beer has its uses, but it is not a civilized drink. In the 8th century the Frankish kingdom was a better place for a wine drinker to be than Anglo-Saxon England.

See also GERMAN HISTORY. H.M.W.

Bassermann-Jordan, F., *Geschichte des Weinbaus*, 3 vols., i (1907).
Dion, R., *Histoire de la vigne et du vin en France* (France, 1959; rpt. 1977).
Duby, G., *Historie de la France rurale*, 4 vols., i (1975).
Einhard and Notker the Stammerer, *Two Lives of Charlemagne*, tr. Lewis Thorpe (London, 1969).
Latouche, R., *The Birth of Western Economy* (London, 1961).

CHARMAT, the name of a bulk SPARKLING WINE-MAKING process which involves provoking a second fermentation in wine stored in a pressure tank. Also called cuve close or tank method.

CHARTA (pronounced 'karta'), important organization of more than 30 RHEINGAU wine producers in Germany dedicated to making a certain style of dry to off-dry RIESLING according to much stricter rules than those imposed by the GERMAN WINE LAW. It was founded in 1984 by Bernhard Breuer and, unlike the VDP association of estates for example, distinguishes individual wines as reaching Charta quality. The wines must be made entirely of Riesling grapes and taste like a dryish, concentrated HALBTROCKEN. RESIDUAL SUGAR cannot be more than 3 g/l TOTAL ACIDITY. Selection is on the basis of blind tastings during which an impressive proportion of samples are rejected. The successful wines are bottled in a tall brown bottle embossed with Charta's symbol of a double romanesque arch and also carry a Charta label on the back of the bottle. This style of wine, particularly in years with high natural ACIDITY, improves considerably in bottle and no Charta wine may be sold until 18 months after the vintage. A Charta wine from a Charta-classified vineyard may be described on the label as 'Klassifizierten Ersten Lagen' (classified top vineyard) if the YIELD is no more than 50 hl/ha (3 tons/acre), and the wine is released at least two years after the harvest.

CHASAN is a crossing of Palomino (known in France as LISTÁN) and Chardonnay made under INRA auspices by French AMPELOGRAPHER Paul Truel. The resulting wine bears a lightweight imprint of Chardonnay while the vine buds early. It is planted on a limited scale in the Midi, particularly in the Aude *département*.

CHASSAGNE-MONTRACHET, village in the Côte de Beaune district of Burgundy's Côte d'Or more famed for its white wines from the Chardonnay grape than for its equally plentiful red wines from Pinot Noir. Until the mid 1980s the village produced more red wine than white, but the significant premium for white Chassagne led to considerable planting of Chardonnay, even on relatively unsuitable soils.

The better soil for Pinot Noir, limestone marl with a red gravel content, lies mainly on the south side of the village towards Santenay and incorporates most of the village appellation, although La Boudriotte and Morgeot, among the PREMIERS CRUS, make excellent red wines, as can Clos St-Jean to the north of village. Red Chassagne-Montrachet tends to be somewhat hard and earthy when young, mellowing with age but rarely achieving the delicacy of truly fine red burgundy.

The fame of Chassagne rests with the white wines at village, premier cru, and especially GRAND CRU level. Chassagne shares the Le Montrachet and Bâtard-Montrachet vineyards with neighbouring Puligny and enjoys sole possession of a third grand cru, Criots-Bâtard-Montrachet (see MONTRACHET for more details). Among the premiers crus, the best known are Les Chenevottes, Clos de la Maltroie, En Cailleret, and Les Ruchottes. Suitable white wine soil tends to have more oolitic limestone and less marl in its make-up.

The white wines of Chassagne are noted for their steely power, less flattering than Meursault when young, sometimes too similar to Puligny-Montrachet to tell apart. Good vintages from good producers should age from five to ten years.

See also CÔTE D'OR and its map. J.T.C.M.

CHASSELAS, even if by no means the most revered white grape variety, is widely planted around the world and has a long, intriguing history. Some authorities cite Middle Eastern, even Egyptian origins. Some point instead to the village of Chasselas in the Mâconnais in eastern France. Others suggest that Chasselas travelled to SWITZERLAND, where it certainly produces its finest wines today, from the famous Chasselas vine that was planted for the French king at Fontainebleau outside Paris in the mid 18th century. Others

Pauillac's Ch Pichon-Longueville (Baron) has one of the most romantic 19th century **château** buildings, supplemented in the early 1990s by a defiantly modernistic winery and tourist centre.

again, particularly the Swiss, argue that Chasselas's origins are Swiss and that the name FENDANT, its common synonym in the Valais, can be found in monastic records well before the 16th century.

In France it is rather despised, not least because, as Chasselas Doré or Golden Chasselas, it is France's most common table grape. It is rapidly disappearing from Alsace, where it is regarded as the lowest of the low and is generally sold as Edelzwicker or under some proprietary name that excludes mention of any grape variety. Planted in the area responsible for Pouilly-Fumé, it makes the distinctly inferior white labelled Pouilly-sur-Loire and, as might be expected, approaches respectability only as it approaches Switzerland, in SAVOIE. Here it is at its most noble in CRÉPY, where it has a long, sometimes noble, history.

Here on the shores of Lake Geneva, as on the other side of the lake in Switzerland, care has to be taken with the choice of ROOTSTOCK so as to avoid the variety's dangerous tendencies towards early budding and too much VIGOUR. But skilfully grown Chasselas can yield good quantities of fairly neutral, soft wine which achieves a peak of concentration in isolated sites such as some round the village of Dézaley. Its Vaud name is Dorin and overall Chasselas is by far Switzerland's most planted variety.

The variety's long history has enabled it to spread far and wide. In Germany, where it is known as Weisser GUTEDEL, it has been known since the 16th century. It was once revered in the PFALZ region and there were still more than 1,300 ha/3,200 acres planted in Germany in 1990. In Austria it is known, but not widely grown, as Moster and Wälscher. It is reputedly grown widely in Romania, in Hungary, to a limited extent in Moldova and Ukraine, in both the north and far south of Italy (where it is sometimes called Marzemina Bianca), around the Mediterranean including North Africa, in Chile, and was at one time curiously important in New Zealand.

CHÂTEAU may be French for 'castle' but in wine parlance it usually means a vine-growing, wine-making estate, to include the vineyards, the cellars, often the wine itself, and any building or buildings on the property, which can range from the non-existent (as in the case of Ch Léoville-BARTON, for example), through the most rudimentary shack, to the sumptuous classical edifice called Ch MARGAUX. The term is most commonly used in BORDEAUX, where the 13th edition of the Féret guide (see LITERATURE OF WINE) lists 7,000 châteaux, although common use of the term developed only in the second half of the 19th century, when the owners of the great estates could afford to build grand lodgings to go with them. Only five of the original 79 properties in the Médoc, Graves, and Sauternes listed in the famous 1855 CLASSIFICATION, for example, are described as châteaux. Bordeaux proprietors soon learnt the value of a Château prefix, and have long adopted the policy of renaming properties almost at will, in particular suffixing their own surname as, for example, Ch Prieuré-LICHINE and Chx Mouton- and Lafite-ROTHSCHILD

The word Château is by no means uncommon outside Bordeaux, however, mainly within but sometimes outside FRANCE. According to current French law, the word Château may be used only of a specified plot of land, which means that it is perfectly possible for CO-OPERATIVES, for example, to produce a wine labelled as Château Quelquechose (see CHÂTEAU BOTTLING). Some producers make a range of wines carrying the name of the property, but reserve the word Château for their top bottlings. NEW WORLD chateaux tend to dispense with their circumflexes.

CHÂTEAU BOTTLING, the relatively recent practice of BOTTLING the produce of a CHÂTEAU on that property. Such a wine is said to be **château bottled**, or *mis(e) en bouteille au château* in French, an expression used throughout France but particularly in BORDEAUX. (Its counterpart in BURGUNDY is DOMAINE BOTTLED, while in the NEW WORLD the term ESTATE BOTTLED is often used.)

Initially all wine was sold in bulk, and subsequently it was up to the MERCHANTS, whether in the region of consumption or production, to put the wine into bottle. Even as recently as the mid 20th century, the great majority of wine left the property on which it was produced in BARRELS (some of which were so useful to the Scotch whisky industry that even today they deliberately have barrels seasoned on their behalf in JEREZ). ADULTERATION AND FRAUD was therefore all too easy among less scrupulous merchants, and particularly tempting in the wake of the world wine shortages which followed OIDIUM and PHYLLOXERA at the end of the 19th century.

The bottom line on this label is a guarantee of **château bottling**.

It was the young Baron Philippe de ROTHSCHILD who did most to promote château bottling when he took over Ch MOUTON-ROTHSCHILD in the early 1920s. He succeeded in persuading all the first growths (and Ch Mouton-Rothschild of course) of the wisdom of bottling all of their principal output, the so-called *grand vin*, on their own territory. This involved a certain amount of investment, but the resulting reliability and cachet more than compensated. Although Ch MARGAUX had to opt out for 20 years in 1930, the first growths set and maintained an example for quality-conscious wine producers everywhere.

Good BOTTLING lines require a level of investment that is unrealistic for many a small wine property, however, so contract bottlers and mobile bottling lines are much in demand, and a producer may not be able to bottle at the precise time he would prefer. Others still bottle by hand, some with scant regard for HYGIENE and consistency. Such considerations mean that bottling at source is not necessarily superior to careful BULK TRANSPORT of the wine to a top-quality bottling plant, but such cases are rare.

Today, a producer of château bottled wine, described on the label as *mis(e) en bouteille au château*, is likely to care about quality. It is worth noting in addition that wines made from specific plots of land but vinified and bottled by CO-OPERATIVES may also be described as château bottled.

See also DOMAINE BOTTLING and ESTATE BOTTLING.

CHÂTEAU-CHALON, extraordinary wine made in the JURA region of eastern France with its own appellation named after the hilltop village where it is produced. Unlike other Jura appellations, Ch-Chalon must be a VIN JAUNE and must be made exclusively from SAVIGNIN grapes grown on the local limestone and, especially, MARL. (Other wines produced by local growers are entitled to the Côtes du JURA appellation.) It must reach a slightly higher POTENTIAL ALCOHOL than other Jura *vins jaunes*, 12 rather than 11.5 per cent (but in practice this is usually much surpassed). It must also be kept for at least six years and three months in partially filled, untouched casks under the famous *voile*, or local benevolent FILM-FORMING YEAST. The resulting wine, exceptionally nutty, deep golden brown, and long lasting, is allowed to use a special *clavelin* bottle containing 62 cl, supposedly the amount of wine produced by a litre of wine kept in a cask in Ch-Chalon for six years. The result is a wine that shares many taste characteristics with SHERRY but is more actively promoted as a gastronomic partner (especially with the local poultry of Bresse, also APPELLATION CONTRÔLÉE products) and as a candidate for BOTTLE AGEING. The total *vignoble* was just 50 ha / 120 acres in 1990, of which 15 ha were relatively recently planted. In some years in this quality-conscious appellation the producers (known as *castel-Chalonnais*), nobly decide that the quality does not merit the production of any wine from the appellation.

CHÂTEAU-GRILLET, one of France's smallest wine appellations and one of the few with a single owner (although see also DOMAINE DE LA ROMANÉE-CONTI). Ch-Grillet's 4 ha of vineyard represent an enclave within the CONDRIEU zone in the north of the northern RHÔNE (see map on p. 796). A virtual amphitheatre carved out of the granite shelters the narrow terraces of VIOGNIER vines from the north winds which can so seriously prejudice both quantity and quality in Condrieu. Already appreciated by Thomas JEFFERSON in the late 18th century, Ch-Grillet has always been in single ownership and, although the family name Neyret-Gachet appears on the label, André Canet has run the property since the early 1960s, extending the vineyard so that production from just 3.8 ha / 9 acres in 1990, for example, was 15,800 l / 4,200 gal, or nearly 2,000 cases of Château-Grillet's distinctive brown bottle, which was one of the last to grow from 70 to 75 cl.

Since the 1970s, the wine has maintained its high price more by its rarity than because it is one of France's finest wines. The grapes have traditionally been picked rather earlier than in Condrieu so that the wine is usually more austere and less headily perfumed than the best Condrieu. The wine is kept in cask and is not usually bottled until well after the next harvest, considerably later than most Condrieu is bottled. The result is a restrained, taut, longer-living wine which, unlike Condrieu, may improve in bottle for a decade or even two. The potential of the vineyard is undoubted, as earlier eulogies testify.

CHÂTEAUMEILLANT, small, isolated red and rosé wine VDQS zone in central France around the town of Châteaumeillant between ST-POURÇAIN-sur-Sioule and TOURAINE (see map on p. 399). Total production is only about 30,000 cases, mainly the produce of Gamay vines (although Pinot Noir and Pinot Gris are allowed) grown on about 100 ha / 250 acres of VOLCANIC soils. VIN GRIS is a local speciality, and one CO-OPERATIVE dominates production.

CHÂTEAUNEUF-DU-PAPE, the most important appellation in the southern RHÔNE in terms of quality, producing mainly rich, spicy, full bodied red wines which can be some of the most alluring expressions of warm climate viticulture. About one in every 16 distinctively heavy and embossed Châteauneuf-du-Pape bottles contains white wine.

The wine takes its name, which means 'Pope's new castle', from the relocation of the papal court to Avignon in the 14th century, and in particular from the construction of summer quarters just north of the city in a village once known as Calcernier for its limestone quarry. It is now called Châteauneuf-du-Pape. The Gascon Pope Clément V (after whom Ch Pape-Clément in PESSAC-LÉOGNAN is named) arrived at Avignon in 1309 and is supposed to have ordered the planting of vines, but it was his successor John XXII who is credited with developing a papal vineyard in Châteauneuf-du-Pape.

The history of Châteauneuf-du-Pape as such is relatively recent, however. As Livingstone-Learmonth points out, the region's wine was known simply as *vin d'Avignon* in the 18th century, when it was shipped northwards up river. In the early 19th century a wine called Châteauneuf-du-Pape-Calcernier emerges, but from JULLIEN's description it sounds a much lighter wine than the Châteauneuf-du-Pape of today. Châteauneuf-du-Pape's reputation steadily grew within France until the arrival of the PHYLLOXERA louse began seriously to affect wine production, in the early 1870s, before most other French wine regions.

Reconstruction of the vineyards was financially devastating, and the Châteauneuf-du-Pape vignerons were just some of those affected by the ADULTERATION AND FRAUD that were rife in the early 20th century. By 1923 the most energetic and well connected of their number, Baron Le Roy of Ch Fortia, had successfully drawn up a set of rules for the production of Châteauneuf-du-Pape, with the co-operation of his peers, which was the prototype for the entire APPELLATION CONTRÔLÉE system. Among what have now become the usual regulations, it involved the first geographical DELIMITATION of a table wine area, land being defined as suitable, by now in a much larger area, if it were so infertile and arid that thyme and lavender would grow on it. Another notable feature was the minimum specified ALCOHOLIC STRENGTH, at 12.5 per cent still the highest in France, and in the southern Rhône this must be achieved without the aid of external sugar addition, or CHAPTALIZATION. TRIAGE of picked grapes was mandatory and ROSÉ was outlawed (with a nod to the vignerons of TAVEL just across the river). When GIGONDAS drew up its own appellation rules, it incorporated many of these exigencies.

Perhaps it is because of the antiquity of Châteauneuf-du-Pape's wine regulations that quite so many VINE VARIETIES are theoretically permitted by the Châteauneuf-du-Pape appellation (because vines are such a long-term crop, appellation laws have to countenance the status quo to a certain extent). Three more varieties were added to the original 10 in 1936. The Châteauneuf-du-Pape grape *par excellence* is GRENACHE and conversely Châteauneuf-du-Pape is its finest expression. Grenache dominates plantings in the Châteauneuf-du-Pape vineyards and on their impoverished soils, with yields officially restricted to a base rate of just 35 hl/ha (2 tons/acre), it can produce wines which combine concentration with the usual sweet fruit of Grenache.

MOURVÈDRE also plays a part at many properties, although it needs the warmest MESOCLIMATES to ripen fully, while SYRAH from the northern Rhône has also been planted by a number of producers who admire its TANNINS and structure, although, unlike Grenache and Mourvèdre, it needs care to avoid over-ripeness. CINSAUT is also grown, but to a declining extent. Of the other permitted red wine varieties Muscardin, Vaccarèse, PICPOUL, TERRET Noir, and COUNOISE, only the last is gown to any significant extent, and has its admirers, particularly at Ch de Beaucastel, one of the most rigorous producers of Châteauneuf-du-Pape, and one of the few to cultivate the entire 13 permitted varieties. For white Châteauneuf-du-Pape, there is considerable variation in the proportions of Grenache Blanc, CLAIRETTE, BOURBOULENC, and ROUSSANNE planted, although Ch de Beaucastel have demonstrated that a VARIETAL Roussanne can be a worthy candidate for BARREL MATURATION. Picardan, which is not widely planted, produces light, relatively neutral wine.

The Châteauneuf-du-Pape appellation extends over more than 3,000 ha/7,500 acres of relatively flat vineyards at varying altitudes and expositions above the river in Châteauneuf-du-Pape and the neighbouring communes of Bédarrides, Courthézon, Orange, and Sorgues. The terrain is traditionally characterized by the large pebbles, or *galets*, some of them several inches across, which cover many of the more photographed vineyards, supposedly retaining heat and speeding the ripening process of the traditionally low trained GOBELET vines. Soils in Châteauneuf-du-Pape are more varied than this, however, and those at the celebrated Ch Rayas, for example, are sandy CALCAREOUS without a *galet* in sight. And on south-facing slopes, any reradiated night-time heat could well be too much, so, on very pebbly ground, the best vineyards may face at least partly north to moderate this.

Indeed the key with red Châteauneuf-du-Pape in general is to balance the accumulation of SUGAR IN GRAPES, and therefore alcohol content, with the PHENOLICS, and tannins in particular. Traditionally DESTEMMING has been avoided, and fairly hot fermentations have been accompanied by frequent PUNCHING DOWN or PUMPING OVER, so that some wines have been tannic, although it is also easy for others to be too alcoholic without the flavour and structure to support it. Since the 1970s a number of producers have used CARBONIC MACERATION or SEMI-CARBONIC MACERATION to produce lighter, fruitier wines which can be drunk with pleasure from about three years rather than from five or six. This is by no means a high-tech wine region, however.

White Châteauneuf-du-Pape is a relative rarity, and may be made according to a wide range of formulas. Only the very best are worth their price premium, although the overall quality is steadily increasing. The wines are always full bodied and the less successful lack acidity and BOUQUET.

See also RHÔNE.

Livingstone-Learmonth, J., *The Wines of the Rhône* (3rd edn., London, 1992).

Parker, R. M., *The Wines of the Rhône Valley and Provence* (New York, 1987).

CHÂTILLON-EN-DIOIS, small appellation of nearly 60 ha/150 acres in the DIOIS area round Die in the far east of the greater RHÔNE region in the cooler reaches of the Drôme valley for still wines: light, Gamay-based reds and light whites made from Aligoté and Chardonnay.

CHAUTAGNE, named CRU in the upper Rhône valley just north of Chambéry whose name be added to the French appellation Vin de SAVOIE. Production is dominated by the co-operative, and some fine red wines are made, from Gamay, Pinot Noir, and, especially, the local Mondeuse.

CHÉNAS, the smallest of the 10 BEAUJOLAIS Crus in the far north of the region. Its 260 ha/640 acres of vines are divided between the villages of Chénas and La Chapelle de Guinchay.

CHENIN or **Chenin Blanc**, in its native region often called Pineau or Pineau de la Loire, is probably the world's most versatile grape variety, capable of producing some of the finest, longest-living sweet whites although more usually harnessed to the yoke of basic New World table wine production. In between these two extremes it is responsible for a considerable volume of sparkling wine and, in SOUTH AFRICA, where it is by far the most planted vine, it is even used as the base for a wide range of fortified wines and spirits. Although, in its high-yield, New World form, its distinctive flavour reminiscent of honey and damp straw is usually lost, it retains the naturally high acidity that dogs it in some of the Loire's less ripe vintages but can be so useful in hot climates.

South Africa now has more than three times as much Chenin planted as France and the Cape's strain of the variety, often called STEEN, constitutes nearly 30 per cent of the country's entire vineyard. It was not until 1965 that the connection was made between Chenin and 'Steen', then the Cape's third most planted variety, prized for its productivity and good resistance to disease and wind, but the vine was almost certainly one of the original collection imported in 1655 by Jan van Riebeeck. In the late 1960s and early 1970s it provided ideal material for new low-temperature, high-tech wine-making techniques so that a flood of off-dry, refreshingly crisp, but otherwise rather bland white washed over the South African wine market, as it continues to do, although Chenin's star is now well eclipsed in terms of esteem by South Africa's more recent imports.

CALIFORNIA also has more Chenin planted than France, and uses it for much the same purposes as South Africa, as the often anonymous base for everyday commercial blends of reasonably crisp white of varying degrees of sweetness, often blended with the even more widely planted French COLOMBARD. Both of these workhorse varieties are planted primarily in the hot Central Valley, a setting that might be described as the antithesis of Chenin's Loire homeland. (It also presumably helps extend quantities of and add acidity to cheaper wines labelled Chardonnay.) Only a handful of producers take Chenin seriously enough to try to make wines worth ageing from it. In the Clarksburg AVA at the north end of the SAN JOAQUIN VALLEY it can take on a distinctive melony, musky flavour.

One or two try to make a wine in the image of the great sweet Loire Chenins, as do one or two producers in NEW ZEALAND, where there were 200 ha/500 acres in the early 1990s, mainly in the North Island. AUSTRALIA had three times as much, much of it misidentified in its time, but treats it largely with disdain as suitably acid blending material, usually extending Chardonnay, or even spiking a blend of Chardonnay and Semillon.

Chenin is widely planted throughout the Americas for no perceptible reason other than that it will obligingly produce a decent yield of relatively crisp wine. There are perhaps as many as 4,000 ha/10,000 acres of Chenin in Argentina, whose heavily irrigated vineyards yield an even more blurred expression of the variety's character, as well as substantial plantings in Chile. In Mexico, Brazil, and Uruguay it is still more usually called Pinot Blanco, as it still is by some Argentine growers. It is also common though not particularly popular in many North American states outside California. In Washington, for example, almost half of all Chenin vines were pulled out in the late 1980s but it still comprised five per cent of the state's vineyard in 1991, covering a total area only slightly smaller than Sauvignon Blanc.

The variety was also exported to Israel to establish vineyards there at the end of the 19th century.

If Chenin appears to lead a double life—biddable workhorse in the New World, superstar in Anjou-Touraine—it seems clear that the explanation lies in a combination of climate, soil, and yield. In California's Central Valley the vine is often expected to yield 10 tons per acre (175 hl/ha), while even the most basic Anjou Blanc should not be produced from vines that yield more than 45 hl/ha. It is hardly surprising that Chenin's character seems diluted outside the Loire.

GALET suggests that it may have been well established in Anjou as long ago as the 9th century and that it was exported to Touraine in the 15th. Rabelais certainly wrote about Chenin both as Chenin and its already familiar synonym of Pineau, often Pineau d'Anjou. See also LA ROCHELLE.

The vine is vigorous and has a tendency to bud early and ripen late, both of which are highly inconvenient attributes in the cool Loire valley (though hardly noticeable characteristics in the hotter vineyards of the New World). Clones that minimize these inconveniences have been selected and six had been officially sanctioned in France by the 1990s.

About a third of all France's, which means the middle Loire's, Chenin was abandoned in the 1970s, often in favour of the red Cabernet Franc in Anjou-Touraine and to make way for the (temporarily?) more fashionable Gamay and Sauvignon de Touraine in the east of the middle Loire. It is today the second most planted variety in the heart of Anjou-Touraine, as well it might be to judge from the superlative quality of the best wines of such appellations as ANJOU, BONNEZEAUX, Coteaux de l'AUBANCE, Coteaux du LAYON, JASNIÈRES, MONTLOUIS, QUARTS DE CHAUME, SAUMUR, SAVENNIÈRES, VOUVRAY, and CRÉMANT de Loire.

In most of the best wines, and certainly all of the great sweet wines, Chenin is unblended, but up to 20 per cent of Chardonnay or Sauvignon is allowed into an Anjou or a Saumur and even more catholic blends are allowed into whites labelled Touraine—although even here Chardonnay's pervasive influence is officially limited to 20 per cent of the total blend. If middle Loire white has any character at all it is that of Chenin, however traduced in the rest of the world.

While basic Loire Chenin exhibits simply vaguely floral aromas and refreshingly high acidity (together with too much sulphur if made in one of the more old-fashioned cellars), the best have a physically thrilling concentration of honeyed flavour, whether the wine is made sweet (MOELLEUX), dry or demi-sec, together with Chenin's characteristically vibrant acidity level.

It is undoubtedly this acid, emphasized by a conscious distaste for MALOLACTIC FERMENTATION and concentrated in some years by BOTRYTIS, that helps preserve the finest Chenins for decades after their relatively early bottling. (In all of these respects, together with lateness of ripening and a wide range of sweetness levels that are customary, Chenin is France's answer to Germany's Riesling.)

Chenin with its high acidity is a useful base for a wide range of sparkling wines, most importantly Saumur Mousseux but also Crémant de Loire and even some rich sparkling Vouvrays which, like their still counterparts, can age beautifully. Treasured for its reliably high acidity, and useful perfume, it is also an ingredient, with Mauzac and, increasingly, Chardonnay, in the sparkling wines of LIMOUX.

The twin great vintages for middle Loire sweet whites of 1989 and 1990 did something to raise the profile, and price, of great Chenin, but a variety whose best wines demand time to be fully appreciated inevitably suffers in the late 20th century.

Chenin Noir is a rarely used synonym for PINEAU D'AUNIS, a dark-berried grape variety.

CHESTE once qualified as a Spanish DO in its own right but is now part of the VALENCIA denomination.

CHEVAL BLANC, CHÂTEAU, very fine BORDEAUX property in ST-ÉMILION. In 1832 Ch Figeac sold 15 ha/37 acres to M. Laussac-Fourcaud, including part of the narrow gravel ridge that runs through Figeac and neighbouring vineyards and reaches Ch PÉTRUS just over the border in POMEROL. This became Ch Cheval Blanc which, in the International London and Paris Exhibitions in 1862 and 1867, won the medals still prominent on its labels. In 1892 Albert reversed the order of his double surname, and it has remained in the Fourcaud-Laussac family ever since. In 1970 M. Jacques Hébrard, who had married one of the Fourcaud-Laussac daughters, took over but in 1989 it was taken over by three other sisters, headed by Mme Claude de Labarre. Pierre, one of the young LURTONS, was made RÉGISSEUR in 1991.

The vineyard is of 41 ha, with 36 ha under vines: 66 per cent CABERNET FRANC vines, 33 per cent MERLOT, and one per cent MALBEC. The average production is about 11,500 cases. The unusual ENCÉPAGEMENT is a result of the special soil and the fact that it adjoins Pomerol's leading vineyards, La Conseillante and L'Évangile, giving it a deep colour and a rich, concentrated blackcurrant bouquet and flavour. Although excellent wines were made towards the end of the 19th century and before the First World War, the property's international reputation was made with the 1921, which had enormous concentration and sweetness. Other very successful wines were made in the 1920s, and even in 1934 and 1937, but its more modern fame was achieved with the rich, porty 1947. Consistently good wines have been made with few exceptions ever since, although, like other St-Émilions and Pomerols, they usually do not last as long as the top red wines from MÉDOC and GRAVES. E.P.-R.

Coates, C., 'Ch Cheval Blanc', *The Vine*, 4 (1985).

CHEVALIER, DOMAINE DE, important CHÂTEAU in Bordeaux producing top-quality red and white wines. For more details, see PESSAC-LÉOGNAN.

CHEVALIER-MONTRACHET, great white GRAND CRU in Burgundy's CÔTE D'OR. For more details, see MONTRACHET.

CHEVERNY. The most important of the VDQS zones of the middle Loire was promoted to full APPELLATION CONTRÔLÉE status in 1993 and produces a wide range of wines in an enclave in the north east corner of TOURAINE near Blois. Light reds may be made from Cabernet Franc, Gamay, or Pinot Noir, while Pineau d'Aunis and Grolleau are allowed for the small quantity of rosé produced. Whites are as common as red Cheverny, and are usually keen, lean Sauvignons which can offer good value northern ripostes to Sancerre and Pouilly-Fumé. Both Chenin Blanc and Chardonnay are also allowed, and wines made from the local ROMORANTIN grape have their own appellation **Cour Cheverny**.

See also LOIRE and map on pp. 576–7.

CHIAN wine, from the island of **Chios**, was highly prized in both ancient and medieval times. See AEGEAN ISLANDS for more details.

CHIANTI, the name of a specific geographical area between Florence and Siena in the central Italian region of Tuscany, associated with tangy, dry red wines of very varied quality. The Chianti zone is first identified in documents of the second half of the 13th century which named the high hills between Baliaccia and Monte Luco 'the Chianti mountains'. The name was later applied to the townships of Castellina, Radda, and Gaiole that formed the nucleus of the medieval League of Chianti under Florentine jurisdiction. The earliest known recorded mention of Chianti the wine, in 1398, refers to a white wine (see TUSCANY, history).

Oenological Chianti covers a much wider area than this historic zone. Seven zones of Tuscany can call their wines Chianti: CHIANTI CLASSICO; Chianti Montalbano; the Florentine hills (Chianti Colli Fiorentini); CHIANTI RUFINA; the hills of Siena (Colli Senesi); the Pisan hills (Colline Pisane); and the hills of Arezzo (Colli Aretini). There are also peripheral zones which can call their wines simply Chianti without an additional appellative.

This vast enlargement of the production zone was prefigured in the report of the Dalmasso Commission in 1932 (see TUSCANY), which preferred to consider Chianti as a generic type of wine, without distinctions or hierarchies. Dalmasso and his colleagues defined a common ground of climactic and geological conditions, of grapes employed (a SANGIOVESE base with additions of CANAIOLO and the white grapes TREBBIANO and MALVASIA—and, very occasionally, some MAMMOLO and COLORINO), and of oenological practices. He declared that a generalization of the name Chianti was desirable in so far as Chianti was to be considered 'a fine table wine and not a superior table wine . . . not a wine for a small aristocratic clientele, but a wine for larger public both in Italy and abroad'. This democratic philosophy, enshrined in a DOC and DOCG status granted simultaneously in 1984 to both Chianti Classico and the extended Chianti zones, may well have been intended to work for the greater common good by transferring some of the prestige and historical reputation of the Classico zone to secondary or generic Chianti, but in practice the results have been precisely the opposite; mere 'Chianti' has sunk, in terms of consumer image and producer remuneration, to the level of a quaffing wine without notable characteristics of quality and with little ability to be cellared and aged. D.T.

CHIANTI CLASSICO, the heartland of the CHIANTI zone, was given its fundamental geographical DELIMITATION by the Medici Grand Duke Cosimo III in an edict of 1716, one of the first examples of such legislation, and was defined as the townships of Radda, Gaiole, and Castellina in addition to the township of Greve (including Panzano) as far as the hill of Spedaluzza 3 km/2 miles to the north of Greve. This area was expanded in the law of July 1932 (later to be confirmed by the DOC regulations of 1966) which established a legal framework for the various types of Chianti in Tuscany; the zone was enlarged to the west to include parts of San Casciano Val di Pesa and Barberino Val d'Elsa and, more damagingly, to the north to include Chiocchio, Strada in Chianti, and San Polo in Robbiano. This latter area allowed in substantial amounts of lighter wines, more similar to the wines of the Florentine hills (Colli Fiorentini), less suitable for ageing, which have not helped Chianti Classico's reputation for longevity.

Little is known of the precise varietal composition of the wines before the 19th century, although the work of Cosimo Villifranchi (1773) would seem to indicate that the wine was a blend of CANAIOLO in the largest part with lesser amounts of SANGIOVESE, MAMMOLO, and MARZEMINO. Modern Chianti can be said to have been invented in a certain sense by Baron Bettino RICASOLI who, in a letter of 1872, synthesized decades of experimentation and recommended that the wine be based on Sangiovese ('for bouquet and vigour') with the addition of Canaiolo to soften the wine. MALVASIA was suggested as appropriate for wines to be drunk young; its use was discouraged for wines intended for ageing. Villifranchi, however, had mentioned the use of both 'Tribbiano and San Colombano' as blending wines for Chianti. The DOC regulations of 1967, which canonized a mythical 'Ricasoli formula' which included between 10 and 30 per cent of the white grapes TREBBIANO and Malvasia, unquestionably reflected the oenological practices of the zone at that time, practices aimed principally at producing large quantities of fast-maturing, rather facile wines. The DOC seemed designed precisely to produce this type of wine: generous permitted YIELDS of 80 hl/ha (4.5 tons/acre), no limits on production per vine, no penalties for overcropping, and low minimum EXTRACT levels (from 20 g/l).

The replanting of the vineyards in the 1960s and 1970s, which transformed them from mixed cultivation to a vine monoculture with the vines trained on wires, was generally done with little attention to CLONAL SELECTION or proper considerations of SITE suitability (notably exposure). The overall result was a general lowering of the quality of the wine between 1965 and 1980, difficult economic conditions for producers, and a general tendency for many houses to decline DOC status for better products and label them vino da tavola.

Total production in the Chianti Classico zone in the early 1930s was 171,800 hl/4.5 million gal from 37,372 ha/92,300 acres of vineyards, although it must be remembered that the common system of mixed cultivation did not imply the modern, monocultural vineyards established subsequently. Production rose to 323,378 hl/8.5 million gal in the late 1980s from nearly 7,000 ha of vineyards, although the end of the 1980s began to see a slight but gradual decrease in production as growers sought to improve quality with smaller yields.

The DOCG regulations of 1984, in addition to lowering the minimum requirement of white grapes to a cosmetic two per cent, lowered yields to 52.5 hl/ha with a maximum of 3 kg of fruit per vine, established 23 g/l as the minimum extract level, and forced producers to declassify the entire crop when yields exceeded legal limits by 20 per cent. Wine from vineyards less than five years old can no longer be used for DOCG wine. A general improvement in the quality level has resulted from this stricter legal framework, as well as from a generally greater openness to experimentation.

The 1984 regulations permitted the addition of up to 10 per cent of non-traditional grapes to the final blend, leading to frequent use of CABERNET SAUVIGNON (see VINO DA TAVOLA). MERLOT and SYRAH are also being used as minor ingredients in Chianti Classico blends, although to a lesser extent. The use of small barrel ageing for Chianti Classico and for Chianti Classico Riserva in particular is increasing, although in many cases this represents a mere recycling of BARRIQUES previously used for vini da tavola. The standard casks for ageing, none

Bottles of **Chianti Classico** are distinguished from those of Chianti by the black rooster seal.

the less, remain the large ovals of Yugoslav oak, BOTTI, with a capacity which varies from 30 to 100 hl (790–2,600 gal). By no means all of these are in pristine condition and lengthy periods of CASK AGEING required for RISERVA wines have not always been to their benefit. D.T.

CHIANTI RUFINA, north eastern zone of CHIANTI, was first identified as an area of superior production in Cosimo III de'Medici's grandducal edict of 1716, which names the zone 'Pomino' after the famous estate of the Albizi family. Pomino, now owned substantially by FRESCOBALDI, has its own DOC, but the delimited zone of the DOC of 1967 followed to a substantial extent the territory first delimited by Cosimo III, with an extension of the zone, however, to the west of the confluence of the Sieve and Arno rivers. This happens to be one case where the always popular measure of enlarging the production zone was based on sound principles.

The soil of Rufina is remarkably similar to the clay and limestone marls of Panzano in Chianti; the vineyards, protected by a series of low mountains to the north, benefit from a warm, dry MESOCLIMATE. The Chianti produced here has always enjoyed an excellent reputation and has been cited for its superior qualities by Lapo Ricci, Cosimo Ridolfi, A. Bizzari, A. Brutini, and other authorities; Fernando Paoletti, in 1744, remarked upon the wine's outstanding longevity, a characteristic which has continued to distinguish it. Production levels have remained low, aided by an important proportion of old vineyards, with average YIELDS of little over 32 hl/ha (1.8 tons/acre) from the 573 ha/1,400 acres of vineyards now classified DOCG.

Despite these advantages, the wines have experienced a certain generalized obscurity attendant on all Chianti with the exception of Chianti Classico. Prices have remained modest, even for producers with international markets and recognition, and the cellars of the zone are badly in need of significant investments to renew and improve both FERMENTATION equipment and casks for ageing. D.T.

Anderson, B., *The Wine Atlas of Italy* (London and New York, 1990).
Gleave, D., *The Wines of Italy* (London and New York, 1989).

CHIAVENNASCA, synonym for the noble NEBBIOLO vine and grape in VALTELLINA.

CHIGNIN, named CRU just south of Chambéry whose name can be added to the eastern French appellation Vin de SAVOIE. Most Chignin is a scented dry white made from the local JACQUÈRE grape variety. A wine labelled **Chignin Bergeron** is made from the superior white ROUSSANNE grape, Bergeron being a local name for it.

CHILE, long, exceptionally narrow country down the south west coast of SOUTH AMERICA. The Spanish conquistadores were responsible for the introduction of the wine-producing vine, *Vitis* VINIFERA, to Chile in the mid 16th century (see SOUTH AMERICA, history), but France was to have a greater influence on shaping Chilean wine industry. The country is most famous viticulturally for being free of DOWNY MILDEW and PHYLLOXERA, which frees vine-growers from the costs of frequent SPRAYING, and of GRAFTING young vines on to resistant ROOTSTOCKS. Chile's dry summers tend to yield exceptionally healthy fruit. The wines exported from Chile have been almost exclusively VARIETAL, with a preponderance of fruitily uncomplicated CABERNET SAUVIGNON, although in the mid 1990s the Chilean wine industry was in its own ferment, the result of the opening of new markets in Europe and North America, and of an economy at last regarded as sufficiently stable to justify long-term investment.

Precise record-keeping is a relatively recent art and statistics should be read with caution. They suggest, however, that Chile's wine production fell considerably between the early 1980s and the early 1990s when annual production was about 4 million h/105 million gal. Argentina produces nearly four times as much, and Brazil almost as much, as Chile.

History

The *vinifera* vine, and deliberate cultivation of it for wine, was brought to the Americas by the Spanish (see SOUTH AMERICA, history). Cortés imported vine cuttings, or more probably seeds, directly from Spain to Mexico where the first successful American vintage was produced, but it is not clear whether the vines first cultivated in the mid 16th century at Cuzco in PERU, the progenitors of the Chilean wine industry, came from Mexico or directly from Spain or Portugal. It is generally agreed, however, that Spanish settlers brought the vine to Chile some time in the 1550s, the vine probably arriving in the Central Valley with Juan Jufre et Diego Garcia de Cárceres in 1554. This was partly so that the early Spanish settlers could celebrate the EUCHARIST with its produce. Specific grape varieties mentioned by the Jesuit priest Alonso Ovalle include Muscatel, Torontel, Albilho, Mollar, and 'the common black grape' (presumably related to the PAIS).

Some early vineyards were ransacked by native Indians, notably in the far south of the country, but the capital Santiago has been associated with continuous wine production for more than four centuries. In the 17th century Spain attempted to protect its export trade of wine to South America by banning new plantings of vineyards there, but

Don Melchor de Concha y Toro was one of the 19th century founders of the modern wine industry in **Chile**.

with little success. Indeed in 1678 the Chilean governor recommended that not only should this ban be lifted but vineyards should be actively encouraged so that more farms, or estancias, would be established. In the 18th century Chile was known for the quantity and cheapness of wine it produced, much to the dismay of some Spanish wine producers.

The vine varieties grown and wine-making techniques of the early 19th century were well documented and fairly primitive by modern standards, the wines commonly being sweetened with boiled, concentrated must, for example. It was Chile's great good fortune that an energetic Frenchman, Claudio Gay, persuaded the Chilean government to set up the Quinta Normal, an experimental nursery for all manner of exotic botanical specimens, including European vines, as early as 1830. This meant that Chile had its own collection of *vinifera* cuttings safely banked in viticultural isolation before the onset of the world's late 19th century vineyard scourges of POWDERY MILDEW and phylloxera, although it was private enterprise which, as so often, provided the spur to the nation's wine industry.

Now independent of Spanish domination, rich Chileans began to travel and experience a wider world, which included the fine wines of Europe, markedly different from the rustic produce of Pais and Moscatel grapes. One of these was Silvestre Ochagavía Echazarreta, who in 1851 personally imported, along with a French wine-maker, a range of those vine varieties regarded today as the most classic and internationally respected. These cuttings were to form the basis of Chile's modern wine industry. A class of gentlemen farmers was emerging in Chile, some of whom had made their fortunes as a result of Chile's rich mineral deposits. Owning a vine-growing country estate on the fertile land outside Santiago, preferably run by one of the many French refugees from phylloxera, was a sign of success in 19th century Chile.

It was not long before Chile could boast the world's only healthy wine industry, both viticulturally and financially, run effectively by 10 rich, often Basque, families and their descendants. As almost every other wine-producing country succumbed successively to the ravages of mildew and phylloxera, the Chilean wine industry enjoyed the rudest of health. The industry, still (as today) substantially in private hands, was so profitable, and per capita wine consumption so high, that it was increasingly energetically taxed and constricted as the 20th century wore on.

Domestic demand for Chile's basic wines declined, and wine prices plummeted in the 1970s and early 1980s. About half of Chile's vineyards were pulled up, some of them in quite suitable locations. The unsettled nature of Chile's politics and economics provided a natural brake on the progress of this unique industry, until the successful establishment of free market policies and the return of democracy in the 1980s stimulated growth in this potentially important aspect of the Chilean economy. Between 1987 and 1993, more than 10,000 ha/25,000 acres of vineyard were planted with premium vine varieties, significant investments were made in new wine-making technology, and the focus of the wine industry switched completely from quantity for the domestic market to quality for export markets.

Geography and climate

With its 5,000 km/3,000 miles of coastline to the west, the Andes at heights of up to 7,000 m/23,000 ft to the east, extensive desert to the north, and Antarctic region in the south, Chile is unusually isolated, and this has undoubtedly played a major part in keeping phylloxera at bay.

The healthy fruit-growing climate of Chile, and ready access to ports (cf. Argentina), make the country an important exporter of TABLE GRAPES, with 49,000 ha/121,000 acres of vineyard dedicated to them, not far short of the 61,500 ha dedicated to wine production in the early 1990s. In general it is the hotter, more northerly vineyards that produce table grapes. The two northernmost regions, Atacama and, especially, Coquimbo, produce far more table grapes than wine, and they also specialize in the production of Chile's own controlled appellation grapey spirit PISCO, to which more than 6,000 ha of vineyards were dedicated in the early 1990s.

The great majority of Chilean wine is produced between the latitudes of 32 degrees 308 minutes and 38 degrees. A northern hemisphere counterpart of these latitudes might be North Africa and southern Spain, but in Chile temperatures are considerably mitigated by the influence of the Pacific, in sharp contrast to the climate in ARGENTINA's wine regions across the Andes. Chilean wine producers describe their climate as somewhere between those of California's NAPA Valley and Bordeaux.

Although the coastal area of Casablanca is being energetically developed, most of Chile's wine has traditionally come from the Central Valley, a 1,000-km-long plateau which reaches as far south as Puerto Montt and is separated from the Pacific Ocean to the west by a relatively low coastal range (whose peaks at 300 to 800 m (1,000–2,600 ft) are high enough to precipitate rainfall in their immediate shadow), and separated from the Argentine Mendoza wine region to the east by the Andes, which can reach altitudes of 6,000 m here. Vines will grow up to an ALTITUDE of 600 m on the western slopes of the Central Valley, and 1,000 m on the sunnier eastern slopes of the Andes. This Central Valley is dissected by rivers which, during the growing season, carry torrents of melted snow from the Andes to the Pacific: IRRIGATION made easy.

Although there are distinct variations between individual regions and even subregions (see Maipo, Rapel, Maule, and BÍO-BÍO), the climate in the Central Valley is generally mediterranean, with warm, dry summers, and rainfall, averaging between 350 and 800 mm (14–31 in) a year, restricted to the winter, thanks to the effect of the Pacific high-pressure area. Rainfall in the Central Valley tends to increase both in the south and west, in the rain shadow of the coastal range. On the western edge of the valley, summer temperatures average 15 to 18 °C (59–64 °F) and may rise to 30 °C/86 °F, with clear skies, strong sunlight, and relatively low humidity of just 55 to 60 per cent. On the eastern edge of the valley, however, under the influence of cold air drainage from the Andes at night, there is higher humidity and much greater temperature variation resulting in particularly good levels of ACIDITY and colour in the ripe grapes.

The southern Central Valley regions of Maule and, especially Bío-Bío are as yet undeveloped, partly because of their distance from the major wineries. In carefully selected sites, vines may well yield good white wines, although frost and excessive rain may prejudice quality south of Temuco.

Regions and soils

The great bulk of Chile's wine is grown in the southern wine regions. Some wine is produced in the northerly Atacama and Coquimbo regions, although they are are very hot and dry and are much more important producers of table grapes and pisco. From north to south the main wine regions, with their subregions, are (see map on facing page):

Aconcagua: Casablanca;
Maipo: Santiago, Talagante, Pirque, Llano del Maipo, Buin;
Rapel: Cachapoal, Colchagua, Santa Cruz, Peralillo;
Maule: Curicó (including Lontué), Talca, Cauquenes, Linares, Parral;
Bío-Bío: Ñuble (including Chillán).

In general, Chile's vineyards are planted on flat, fertile land where water is readily available either naturally or through irrigation, so that vine root systems are relatively shallow. Alluvial soils predominate in Aconcagua and are also present to the south in Maipo, although here there are loams and occasionally clay soils too. In both the Maipo region and the Cachapoal district of northern Rapel, there are mixtures of loam, clay, and even mud, some of which may be subject to EROSION as a result of irrigation. Some TUFFEAU soils are found in southern Rapel and in Maule, while volcanic soils extend from south of Curicó to the Bío-Bío region, interrupted only by sand and sandy loam around Linares. Some parts of the eastern slopes of the Coastal range in Maule and Bío-Bío suffer from relatively poor drainage and can be quite swampy.

Aconcagua The most northerly of Chile's wine regions, named after the river which bisects it, lies between PISCO country and the capital Santiago and is made up of two very distinct zones. The interior of Aconcagua is Chile's hottest, driest wine region. In the summer clouds are rarely seen, and temperatures are often above 30 °C/86 °F. Soils are mainly alluvial and the region produces some good red wines. Errazuriz is one of the few important wine exporters to have its base in this region, at Panquehue in the much gentler intermediate region, cooled by coastal breezes. On the coast, however, is the cool, relatively recently established Casablanca region near Valparaiso.

Casablanca One of the coolest and newest wine regions in Chile, on the coast close to Valparaiso. Officially part of the Aconcagua region, it is quite different from the vineyards of the hot interior. Casablanca's vineyards are cooled to WINKLER Region I by cool morning fogs, the result of the Pacific's icy Humboldt current (which has a similar effect thousands of miles up the coast in CARNEROS in California). Frequent cloud slows ripening and reduces the average number of clear days per year to 180, as opposed to between 240 and 300 in the interior (mirroring the climatic contrast between Carneros and California's SAN JOAQUIN VALLEY). The first vines were planted in the cool Casablanca valley in 1982 but by 1993 there were nearly 1,500 ha/3,700 acres of vines, thanks to extensive plantings, mainly of CHARDONNAY vines, by both wine producers (notably Concha y Toro and Franciscan of California) and specialist grape growers. Spring FROSTS are a real hazard here.

Maipo The most famous wine region in Chile just south of the capital Santiago is also one of the smallest. About 2,500 ha/6,200 acres of vines were recorded in 1991, and are split quite evenly between red and white grapes, of which CABERNET SAUVIGNON and SÉMILLON are the most important, according to official 1992 statistics, although SAUVIGNON is also important. Annual rainfall averages just 300 mm/12 in a year, most of which is the result of sporadic storms. Irrigation is common, although the water can be high in salt around the Maipo river from which the region takes its name. Potassium levels tend to be low throughout the region. Official subregions are Santiago, Talagante, Pirque, Llano del Maipo, and Buin. Although this is quantitatively one of the less important wine regions in Chile, it is one often named on export labels, perhaps because, being closest to Santiago, it houses the headquarters of so many of the major companies.

Rapel Wine region in Chile comprising about 7,000 ha/17,300 acres of vineyard dedicated to wine production, the majority of which grow red grapes. The region is officially divided into the subregions Cachapoal and Colchagua. SÉMILLON and CABERNET SAUVIGNON are the most planted grape varieties according to official 1992 statistics, and the region has a particularly good reputation for full flavoured red wines. Los Vascos winery, in which Ch LAFITE-Rothschild has an important stake, is at Peralillo. The region overall is hotter than Maule to the immediate south. Large wineries such as Santa Emiliana, Santa Rita, Undurraga, and the smaller Discover Wine (Montes) operation made considerable vineyard investments in the Colchagua subregion in the early 1990s.

Maule Important wine region in Chile which includes the subregions of Curicó, Talca, Cauquenes, Linares, Lontue, and Parral. According to official 1991 records, there were 24,000 ha/59,300 acres of wine vines. Well to the south of Santiago, this region is one of Chile's cooler and cloudier, thanks to the Pacific influence, although it is hotter and drier than Bío-Bío to the south. The rustic PAIS vine variety dominates plantings, especially in the rain-fed areas, although Sémillon, Sauvignon, and Cabernet Sauvignon are also important. Vineyards in the rain-fed western areas often suffer from serious deficiencies of nutrients, especially NITROGEN and to a lesser extent POTASSIUM. Spanish wine-maker Miguel TORRES' purchase of vineyards in the Curicó area, in 1979, was interpreted as an unusual act of faith in the region, although San Pedro also have their headquarters here.

Bío-Bío The most southerly and most extensive wine region in Chile, where nearly two-thirds of the 27,000 ha/66,700 acres of vineyards were planted with red grape varieties

according to official statistics in 1991. At the south of the Central Valley, Bío-Bío is more open than Maipo and Rapel to the north, lacking the protection of a high coastal range, so that rainfall is higher and average temperature and sunshine hours are lower. Official subregions are Ñuble in the north, around Chillán and Quillón, and Bío-Bío around Yumbel and Mulchén. By far the most planted vine variety is the humble PAIS, although Moscatel Alejandria (MUSCAT OF ALEXANDRIA) is also widely grown for basic wine to be consumed within Chile. A significant proportion of vineyards planted in the west of the region are in swampland, capable of producing high quantities of undistinguished wine. Research in the early 1990s in the Chillán area, however, suggested that, with drip irrigation and appropriate training systems such as the LYRE, some good-quality wine from the best-known international vine varieties could be made here.

Viticulture

IRRIGATION is essential in nearly half of all Chilean vineyards and, as in Argentina, is made possible by the melting snows of the Andes, diverted along a series of canals and channels. Drip irrigation was introduced only in the early 1990s. As a result of this ready and plentiful water supply, most vineyards have better access to water during the growing season than during the supposed rainy season, the winter. The irrigated vineyards are mainly in the north of the Central Valley, in the interior of the Aconcagua, Maipo, Rapel, and Maule regions. On the slopes of the coastal range in the west of these regions, rainfall is often sufficient, as it is in most of the often swampy Bío-Bío region. The common PAIS vine is cultivated in the swampiest parts of these rain-fed wine regions and yields prolifically there.

FERTILIZERS are widely needed, especially in the Maipo and Aconcagua regions and, even more so, in the rain-fed areas of Maule and Bío-Bío. Drip irrigation allows FERTIGATION in some of the more viticulturally developed areas.

Average YIELDS in Chile are about 70 hl/ha (4 tons/acre). Over-irrigated, high-yielding vines can experience difficulties in ripening. This is particularly true of varieties which ripen relatively late, such as Cabernet Sauvignon, or of high TRAINING SYSTEMS. There is a predictably rich cultural diversity of training and trellis systems in Chile. Some vines, particularly those dedicated to table grapes, are trained in variations on the TENDONE system in the high, arbour-like *parron* trellis which encourages shade (like the *parral* of ARGENTINA).

The standard Spanish practice of growing unstaked vines as free-standing bushes, trained into a GOBELET shape has been common since the Spanish conquest and is the method usually adopted for the Pais vine. The height of such spur-pruned vines varies according to vine variety, vigour, and region. On the wetter southern hills of Bío-Bío, many Pais vineyards are cultivated under what is known as *tresbolillo* in Chile, whereby the vines are not planted in rows, and LAYERING is practised, whereby one-year-old shoots are buried during the winter in order to establish their own root systems.

The Bordeaux post-PHYLLOXERA immigrants introduced head trellising to Chile at the end of the 19th century and this has evolved in two distinct ways. Low, narrow rows of vines that are traditional in Europe tend to be double GUYOT pruned and used mainly to produce better-quality wines. More common for basic wine production are widely spaced vines with crosspieces, sometimes described as Californian, which permit the increasingly common phenomenon of vineyard MECHANIZATION. In the 1990s most new plantings have been of long narrow rows between 2 and 2.5 m (6.5–8 ft) apart, with vines planted 1.2 to 1.5 m apart. CANOPY MANAGEMENT techniques were introduced in some vineyards in the early 1990s.

Harvest of wine grapes begins at the end of February for such early maturing varieties as Chardonnay, continues through to the end of April for Cabernet Sauvignon, and can last well into May for Pais grown in the southern regions of Maule and Bío-Bío.

No Chilean vine-grower feels he needs to study rootstocks since the country is free of phylloxera and the consequent need for grafting. Some FIELD GRAFTING has been undertaken, however, in the rush to increase the proportion of fashionable grape varieties planted. And such is the prevalence of NEMATODES in Chilean vineyards, because of *vinifera*'s low resistance to them relative to American vine species, that some authorities suggest using American rootstocks to combat this problem. Chile's vines are by no means free of VIRUS DISEASES.

Chile may be famously free of two major vineyard hazards, but powdery mildew and BOTRYTIS BUNCH ROT are annual and potentially extremely costly vine diseases, with VERTICILLIUM WILT another serious vine health hazard.

Vine varieties

Vine variety identification is an underdeveloped science in Chile. Conscious of its unique status as a wine-producing country as yet unravaged by two of the most famous and widespread vine hazards, Chile imposes a particularly strict QUARANTINE on imported plant material, which has helped to maintain certain aspects of its viticultural isolation. The quality and identification of the vines grown is the most dramatic example of this.

The great majority of the vines called SAUVIGNON by the Chileans, for example, are almost certainly Sauvignon Vert (or TOCAI Friulano) and occasionally Sauvignon Gris, rather than the more familiar, and more aromatic, Sauvignon Blanc. Only a very small proportion of Sauvignon Blanc, almost exclusively based on clones developed in California, had been planted by the early 1990s.

The most commonly planted grape variety, however, is the dark-skinned PAIS, found only in Chile and thought to be, like the Criolla of Argentina and the MISSION of California, a direct descendant of vine cuttings imported by the Spanish colonists. Official statistics recorded nearly 30,000 ha/74,000 acres of Pais in 1992, constituting almost half the total vineyard. The great majority is planted, often on poorly drained, almost swamp land, in the southern Maule and Bío-Bío regions.

The same survey found 9,000 ha of Moscatel Alejandria (MUSCAT OF ALEXANDRIA), and 8,000 ha of CABERNET SAUVIGNON, as well as 6,000 and 4,500 ha of varieties called locally SÉMILLON and SAUVIGNON respectively. Other varieties, in declining order of total area planted, were TORONTEL, MERLOT, CHARDONNAY, CARIGNAN, CHASSELAS, COT, RIESLING, and Pinot Negro (PINOT NOIR). Torontel is the local form of the Torrontés of Argentina, although the variety known as Moscatel de Austria in Chile is the Torrontés Sanjuanino of Argentina.

Such a survey is likely to be inaccurate and out of date, however. At least 5,000 ha of vineyards were planted in Chile between 1989 and 1992, of which approximately half were Chardonnay, a third were Cabernet Sauvignon, and a sixth Merlot. Some SYRAH has also been planted.

Such new plant material as is allowed in has come mainly from DAVIS, but European investors such as Miguel TORRES, a couple from Chablis, and Ch LAFITE-Rothschild are increasingly importing their own cuttings directly from Europe, under strict quarantine regulations.

Wine-making

Chile is undergoing possibly the most dramatic technological revolution in the wine world. Wineries were for decades underfunded as the domestic market could be satisfied with often oxidized white wines and faded reds made with the most traditional of equipment. All wines were made from grapes trucked, often in very high temperatures with scant regard for OXIDATION, to wineries equipped with little in the way of temperature control, and made exclusively in vats made either of cement or the coarse local *rauli*, or evergreen beech, WOOD, usually coopered many decades previously. In the late 1980s, however, both government and the wine industry made a commitment to the long-term future of Chile as a wine exporter and began to invest in the equipment necessary for that goal. Outside investors assisted the influx of both equipment and expertise, and since then the wineries of Chile have been invaded, at a pace usually determined by the enterprise's size and cash flow, by pneumatic PRESSES, oak BARRELS, STAINLESS STEEL, and modern filters. (One of the larger companies, Santa Rita, for example, views its purchase of 7,000 French and American oak barrels in 1988 as a milestone in its corporate history.) Often one of the most necessary improvements has been one of the technically least complicated: the provision of cool storage facilities.

Industry organization

Most of the big wine-exporting companies, many of them run by descendants of the wine dynasties of the mid 19th century, have their headquarters in Santiago or nearby in the Maipo region. Some of the biggest are Concha y Toro, Santa Rita, and Santa Carolina. Many own several wineries and many different vineyards, although it is also the norm to buy in most grapes from a wide range of growers. The estate wineries such as the historic Cousiño Macul, Los Vascos, Montes, Portal del Alto, Santa Monica, and Santa Inés, for which practically all grapes used are grown by the owner/wine-makers, are relatively rare. Foreign investment has come from California, France, Spain, and the Far East, presumably attracted by the relatively low cost of land, vineyard establishment, and running costs in Chile, although this is offset by the need to import all sophisticated equipment and cooperage.

Wine styles

Wines exported from Chile are, typically, extremely fruity and clean but did not until the early 1990s display the structure which can only be imposed by low yields and/or BARREL MATURATION. Yields are still relatively high, although there are some plots of very old vines which produce concentrated wine. Cabernet Sauvignon and Cabernet blends dominate Chile's red wine exports and can provide extremely good-value wines for drinking within two or three years, although an increasing proportion of wine capable of BOTTLE AGEING is likely to be made.

The new generation of white wines has been clean and well made rather than strongly characteristic of any particular grape variety, although this was evolving dramatically with each vintage in the early 1990s. Pink and sweet wines are certainly made (Concha y Toro make a late harvest 'Sauterne'), and Alberto Valdivieso was the first to make sparkling wines using CHAMPAGNE techniques, as early as 1879.

There has been a sharp distinction in Chile between wine of export quality (much of which is difficult to obtain even in Santiago) and wine for the domestic market, which is, typically, made from Pais, Sultanina (SULTANA), and other TABLE GRAPES. It is mainly light red and rustic, sold in Tetrapak cardboard bricks or giant bottles. Export-quality wine is increasingly sold in Chilean liquor stores, however.

Table grapes may be vinified and sold as wine in Chile and the grape varieties Sultana and Ribier, or Alphonse Lavallé, are most commonly used for this purpose. Most of this wine is sold locally, or is exported in bulk. Wine made from a table grape variety sold locally should be labelled with the name of the variety.

It is fair to say, however, that Chile lacks a wine style to call its own. Argentina may have lush Malbec, serviceable Bonarda, and aromatic Torrontés in quantity; California can field a host of Zinfandels; even Uruguay has some surviving Tannat as a relic of its Basque invasion. Chile is still to a certain extent the Bordeaux of the southern hemisphere.

Hernandez, A., and Contreras, G., *Wine and Vineyards of Chile* (Santiago, 1993).
Read, J., *Chilean Wines* (2nd edn., London, 1994).

CHINA, vast Asian country with its own indigenous vine species (see VITIS) but a relatively short tradition of growing VINIFERA grapes to make wine. The preferred stimulant, or rather relaxant, was for long rice-based wine, followed by brandy, introduced by Europeans in the 19th century.

Ancient China

Chinese literary accounts of the introduction of grapes to China have a strong legendary element, but it seems that grape seeds were brought back from Ferghana in modern UZBEKISTAN by General Chang Chien during the Han dynasty between 121 and 136 BC and planted in Xinjiang and Shaanxi (Xian). In the second century AD grape wine imported from the west was highly prized. It is possible that wine was made from grapes in China before the T'ang Dynasty (AD 618–907), although the industry seems not to have been highly developed. But by the beginning of the T'ang era it is well established that the Chinese were importing quantities of wine from the area of Tashkent in modern Uzbekistan. This central Asian wine was claimed to be drinkable for up to 10 years. After the Chinese conquest of Turfan on the Chinese side of the Sino-Russian frontier in 640, Snake and Dragon Pearl and Mare's Teat (the former red and also known as Cabernet Gernischet, the latter a white table grape variety known as Maru in Chinese) were imported and successfully cultivated in China. Thereafter viticulture prospered in China, especially in Kansu and Shansi provinces in central China. Shansi wine continued to be popular after the decline of the import trade following a break in relations with central Asia. It was not long before wine was being made also from a small native grape (*Vitis thunbergii*) which grows wild in Shantung province, north of Shanghai.

In earlier periods, two alcoholic beverages, *chiu* and *li*, were made from rice or wheat. At feasts they were set out for guests in separate containers: *chiu* was dark, probably stronger, and seems to have been more popular, while *li* was white, sweeter, with a higher proportion of rice, and could be made overnight. Labelled wine jars indicate that 'wine' could be made from millet or other grains as well. Strictly speaking, however, these beverages are beers (brewed from cereals) rather than wines (fermented from fruits). The grade of the 'wine' was not dependent on the kind of cereal but on the thickness: the thicker liquids were more highly prized. During the Han Dynasty (206 BC–AD 220) wine was served at the beginning of a feast, when the music began but before the guests took their seats. The evidence suggests that wine was not drunk on its own but always with some sort of food. If drinking was to continue after the cooked food had been exhausted, dried meat and fish were served. Wine cups were made in a variety of fixed sizes: 1, 1½, 2, and 4 measures respectively.

In the very earliest periods (pre-Han) the term used is *yin* 'drink', which includes alcoholic drink and water. In upper-class circles in the later Chou Dynasty (12th century BC–221 BC), *yin* was drunk with meals, at which the procedures were extremely formalized. Guests ate and drank kneeling on mats; their drinks were placed to their right, while other rules governed the position of foods and condiments. Archaeological excavations have revealed wine drinking cups made from bronze, pottery, lacquered wood, and bottle-gourds, and wine containers of bronze, pottery, and wood. J.A.B.

More recent times

Viticulture continued in China (JULLIEN classified the wines of what he called Chinese Tartary). In 1892 Zhang Bi Shi, an officer in the Ching government, returned to China and established the Chang Yu winery in Yantai. He introduced 150 *vinifera* vine varieties from Europe, including Welschriesling, and apparently employed the then Austrian consul as his wine-maker. Quingdao, the other winery established by Germans at that time, was first known as the Melco winery. Shang Yi winery (today's Beijing winery) was set up by French Catholics, and Tung Hua winery at Jilini was managed by the Japanese. The wines produced by them were made mainly to cater for the foreign communities in China.

In 1949 the wineries were expanded by the government, who, for reasons of economy, blended grape wine with water, fermented cereals, and colouring. Because of this, the term 'wine' is still widely misunderstood in China today.

China's 65,000 ha/161,000 acres of vineyards are spread across provinces north of the Yangtze river, from Xinjiang in the extreme north west to the coastal regions of Shandong, Tianjin, Liaoning, and Jilin in the north east. Due to the general lack of exposure to western wine culture and extreme continental conditions inland, production in all regions is still largely concentrated on table grapes and DRYING GRAPES. China's 200 state 'alcohol manufacturing factories' vinify only about one-fifth of the total grape harvest (240,000 tons of grape wine in 1991).

Temperatures in the coastal provinces of Shandong, Hebei and Tianjin, which lie on the same latitude as California, appear most favourable for wine production. Cool Pacific breezes moderate humidity levels and temperatures range from 3 °C/37 °F in winter to 26 °C/79 °F in summer. Monsoons and typhoons which sweep in from the South China Sea can prove hazardous (a typhoon destroyed vineyards on the Shandong peninsula in 1985), although monsoon winds rapidly aerate vines. Springs are generally dry, but an average 700 mm/27 in rainfall between June and August means summers and autumns can be muggy and wet, promoting FUNGAL DISEASES.

The most suitable climate for advanced viticulture, with cooler inland temperatures, is in the centre of the Shandong peninsula near Pingdu. Here China's easterly range of mountains, the Dazashen, have ideal south east- and south west-facing slopes with decomposed granite overlying limestone, low in nutrients. Vineyards are planted here at altitudes of 150–250 m (490–820 ft) on free-draining soils. On the peninsula's south coast around Qingdao and north coast near Yantai, soils are sandier, with plantings at altitudes of 80–100 m.

Jesuit MISSIONARIES are believed to have been the first to encourage the planting of vineyards here specifically to make wine in the mid 19th century. During the German and Japanese occupation of northern China at the turn of the century, the foundations of the terraced vineyards were laid and the first two wineries at Yantai and Qingdao were established. However, still and sparkling wine production in the five largest state wineries—Qingdao, Yantai Chang Yu, Henan Min Chuan, Beijing Eastern Rural, and Jilin Tung Fa—remained very unsophisticated until 1978 when China opened again to the outside world.

Since 1979, several moves have been made to allow foreign investors to install a modern wine industry in north east China. In May 1980, Cognac giant RÉMY MARTIN set up the first joint venture winery, Sino-French Corporative winery, with the Tianjin Farm Bureau. The Huadong (East China) winery was established at Qingdao in 1986 by a Hong Kong wine merchant and subsequently run by the multinational Allied-Lyons. Another multinational, Pernod Ricard, set up the Beijing Friendship winery in 1987 and an Italian venture set up the Marco Polo winery at Yantai in 1990. Other joint venture wineries include Summer Palace, in which American distiller Seagram is involved. All imported advanced vinification equipment, European *vinifera* vine cuttings, and foreign OENOLOGISTS to produce the first 'western style' grape wines in China, suitable for the domestic and export markets. State wineries are slowly following their lead.

Thousands of native grape varieties exist in northern China, many from wild species (see VITIS), as breeding is a preoccupation of Chinese research institutions. The most widely planted table grapes, used by state wineries for low-quality sweet table wines, are the cold-resistant Beichun (hybrid of *V. amurensis*); high-yielding white Long Yan (Dragon's Eye); and Ju Feng Noir, also known as Jifeng (hybrid of Japanese Koho and Jixiang developed by Dalian Institute in 1973).

There are widespread plantings imported from RUSSIA, of MUSCAT HAMBURG and RKATSITELI, here, where it has reasonable potential for quality, known as Baiyu. Alongside large acreages of Italian Riesling (see WELSCHRIESLING), these varieties have formed the backbone of China's modern wine industry. In the 1980s, classic European varieties were introduced by foreign investors and the Beijing Friendship winery planted 33 ha of 16 imported varieties in 1987. By the early 1990s Huadong winery had established over 50 ha/120 acres of CHARDONNAY, with small experimental plots of other European varieties in Shandong.

The grapes, supplied on contract through collective agencies, are grown on intensively subdivided lands. Individual farmers work less than an acre each and are entitled to choose their own crop, often preferring less viticulturally risky table grapes or more profitable agricultural crops. China's parallel systems of planned and market-driven economy and deep-rooted peasant traditions clearly hinder modernization. The traditional fan trellis system, dense foliage, excessive YIELDS, heavy summer IRRIGATION, peanut COVER CROPS, early picking to avoid ROT, and grape prices determined by weight alone are typical. Many vineyards planted in low-lying valleys alongside rice-fields have high water-tables and a high risk of flooding.

The majority of vines are ungrafted, with no widespread PHYLLOXERA problem encountered to date. The strong summer rains, humidity levels over 85 per cent, and typically dense CANOPY encourage many vine diseases. ANTHRACNOSE, mildew, OIDIUM, DEAD ARM, and WHITE ROT are commonplace, controlled by modern fungicides when available. Bitter rot (*Greeneria uvicola*) is also a major problem, as a low level of infection affects the wine.

Modern viticultural developments have been introduced in Shandong for imported classic varieties to combat disease and increase quality, under Australasian expertise. With cheap and plentiful labour, all work is done manually with very limited MECHANIZATION. The low water-holding capacity and dry spring weather necessitate irrigation, controlled manually with pump and hose.

Lack of modern equipment, absence of western influence, and a desire for strong, sweet drinks had made syrupy MADERIZED wines the norm in state wineries. Vaslin presses, REFRIGERATION, STAINLESS STEEL tanks, and cultural exchanges introduced into joint venture wineries are now starting to revolutionize wine styles. The Sino-French brand Dynasty is a commercial medium dry white blend from Muscat Hamburg, Italian Riesling, and SYLVANER. The Huadong winery is pioneering dry VARIETAL wines with Australian expertise. Quality will clearly improve as more INTERNATIONAL VARIETIES bear fruit, foreign investment increases, and China moves gradually towards westernization.

The largest vineyard area in China (39 per cent of plantings in 1991) is on the same latitude as the south of France, but as far away from western influence as possible (and about 650 km/400 miles east of the vineyards of KAZAKHSTAN). On the northern Silk Route in Xinjiang province in the extreme north west, vineyards are centred around the Turpan Depression

Newly acquired skills being used on fashionable Chardonnay vines at the Huadong winery at Qingdao, **China**.

oases, which can be 154 m/500 ft below sea level. Here viticultural and vinification practices differ greatly due to climatic extremes, as they do in northerly vineyards of Jilin, Heilongjiang, and Liaoning bordering Mongolia.

Xinjiang's winter temperatures fall to −40 °C/−7 °F, making cold-resistant rootstocks of *V amurensis* essential. *Vinifera* vines are buried with desert sands or covered with straw during winter. Summer temperatures reach 48 °C/118 °F, with annual rainfall at only 19.6 mm/0.8 in. Here vineyards are irrigated by the 2,000-year-old Persian Karez irrigation system, which taps subterranean water from melted snow off the Tianshan mountains and conveys it in man-made underground channels to avoid evaporation in the desert sun.

Only cold- and drought-resistant vine varieties can survive in Xinjiang: Beichun, Longyan (probably the same as the Ryugan of JAPAN), and Sultanine. Here production is almost entirely devoted to raisin and table grapes. Only a small proportion of Sultanine is made into unappetizingly sweet OXIDIZED dessert wines by Xinjiang's five state wineries, without any means of temperature control. R.M.B.

Chang, K. C. (ed.), *Food in Chinese Culture: Anthropological and Historical Perspectives* (New Haven, Conn., and London, 1977).

Murray Brown, R., 'China's melting pot', *Wine*, 41–2 (Sept. 1992).

—— 'The sleeping giant', *Wine and Spirit International*, 23–7 (Dec. 1992).

Vignau, L., 'Chine: des vignes près des rizières', *Bulletin de l'OIV*, 735–6 (1992), 442–5.

CHINON, significant red wine appellation in the TOURAINE district of the Loire in which a small amount of rosé, and an even smaller amount of white wine from Chenin Blanc grapes, is produced from an area of about 1,800 ha/4,500 acres. The vineyards extend south of the Loire on the banks of the Vienne, not far east of the fashionable red Saumur-Champigny, another product of CABERNET FRANC grapes, here often called Breton.

The region's most famous son, the early 16th century writer Rabelais, did much to promulgate the wines of Chinon. In modern times, it is the gastronomic writers of Paris who have done much to increase demand for Chinon, and increase the extent of the vineyards that produce it (which had fallen to a few hundred hectares in the 1950s).

Two distinct styles of Chinon are made. A fuller, long-term BOURGUEIL-like wine comes from sites on the TUFFEAU limestone slopes and plateaux, most notably the south-facing slopes of Cravant-les-Coteaux, and the plateau above Beaumont. Lighter wines are made from sand and gravel vineyards near the river (in effect the old flood plains of the Loire and Vienne), with the most elegant examples coming from the gravel beds around Panzoult. These wines are closer to St Nicolas-de-Bourgueil in style.

Chinon is quintessentially a wine of refreshment, being light to medium bodied, often extravagantly scented (lead pencils is one common tasting note), and with an appetizing combination of fruit and acidity. The best wines can benefit from BOTTLE AGEING, but that is not the point of the wine, which keeps the Chinon market free of foreign speculation on the part of COLLECTORS. Chinon is essentially a Frenchman's wine, and it takes some local knowledge to seek out the best, often artisanal, bottlings from the likes of Charles Joguet and Olga Raffault. A high proportion of the wine is sold to merchants, whose blends vary considerably in quality.

See also LOIRE and map on pp. 576–7.

CHIP BUDDING, a popular method for the BUDDING of vines, with a long history. It is known as the yema bud in Europe and California. During the first growing season of the ROOTSTOCK, a piece is cut from its original wood and a matching chip piece with a bud is cut from a scion cutting. The chip is inserted in the stock with CAMBIUM zones matching, then wrapped tightly with budding tape. The timing of chip budding during the year is flexible. Chip budding may also be used for TOP WORKING. See also FIELD GRAFTING.

B.G.C.

CHIROUBLES, highest of the BEAUJOLAIS Crus producing some of the lightest but most genuinely refreshing wines. The soils are very similar to those of neighbouring FLEURIE and these wines are best drunk young. Perhaps the most archetypically Beaujolais of all the Crus. There are about 350 ha/860 acres.

CHITRY, commune just west of Chablis. See Côtes d'AUXERRE for more information.

CHLOROSIS, vine disorder in which parts or all of the foliage turn yellow due to lack of chlorophyll. The most common and extreme chlorosis is that which is visible in spring and early summer and is caused by IRON deficiency, which is common on soils high in LIMESTONE. Lime-induced chlorosis became a problem in parts of France as a consequence of PHYLLOXERA invasion at the end of the 19th century, since AMERICAN VINE SPECIES used as phylloxera-resistant ROOTSTOCKS were more prone to iron deficiency than were the original VINIFERA root systems. This problem, known in French as **chlorose calcaire**, has been largely overcome now by the selection of lime-tolerant rootstocks suitable for calcareous soils, such as 41B or the newer Fercal. In Burgundy and Champagne, where soils tend to be high in limestone, it has been difficult to find rootstocks with sufficient lime tolerance for healthy vine growth. This sensitivity of early post-phylloxera rootstocks to lime-induced chlorosis may provide part of the explanation for an apparent drop in quality in post-phylloxera wines, according to some historical authorities.

Chlorosis is a common symptom of deficiencies of other nutrients such as NITROGEN, SULPHUR, and MAGNESIUM. It can also be caused by some VINE DISEASES. The effect may be general, as for FANLEAF DEGENERATION virus, or more localized, as in, for example, the so-called oil spot on leaves due to DOWNY MILDEW infection.

R.E.S.

CHOREY-LÈS-BEAUNE, village near (*lès* in old French) Beaune in Burgundy producing red wines from Pinot Noir grapes. Chorey lies in the plain below the main RN74 road, as do most of the appellation's vineyards. There are no vineyards of PREMIER CRU status, and much of the wine is sold as Côte de BEAUNE Villages. Notable exceptions are the Ch de Chorey and Domaine Tollot Beaut. A good Chorey is similar to a village SAVIGNY-LÈS-BEAUNE or a lesser ALOXE-CORTON. A tiny quantity of white Chorey-lès-Beaune is made from Chardonnay.

See also CÔTE D'OR and its map.

J.T.C.M.

CHRISTIANITY AND WINE. See EUCHARIST, RELIGION, BIBLE, MONKS AND MONASTERIES, and MISSIONARIES.

CHUSCLAN, the most famous of the Côtes-du-RHÔNE Villages on the right bank of the river. As in nearby Tavel, its rosé is particularly appreciated.

CIENEGA VALLEY, small California wine region and AVA in SAN BENITO County.

CIGALES, wine zone in northern Spain, north of Valladolid in CASTILLA-LEÓN (see map on p. 907). This DO has staked its future on dry rosé wines made from Tinto del Pais (TEMPRANILLO) and GARNACHA grapes. Few wines are seen outside the immediate vicinity.

R.J.M.

CILIEGIOLO, central Italian red grape variety of Tuscan origin named after its supposed cherry-like flavour and colour. It is declining in popularity and total Italian plantings of the vine were just 5,000 ha/12,000 acres in 1990, although it can make some excellent wines, and could be a usefully soft blending partner for SANGIOVESE.

CINCTURING, viticultural practice involving removing, with a knife or special tool, a ring (3 to 8 mm (0.1–0.3 in) wide) of conducting tissue (PHLOEM) around a trunk, cane, or shoot,

Chip budding

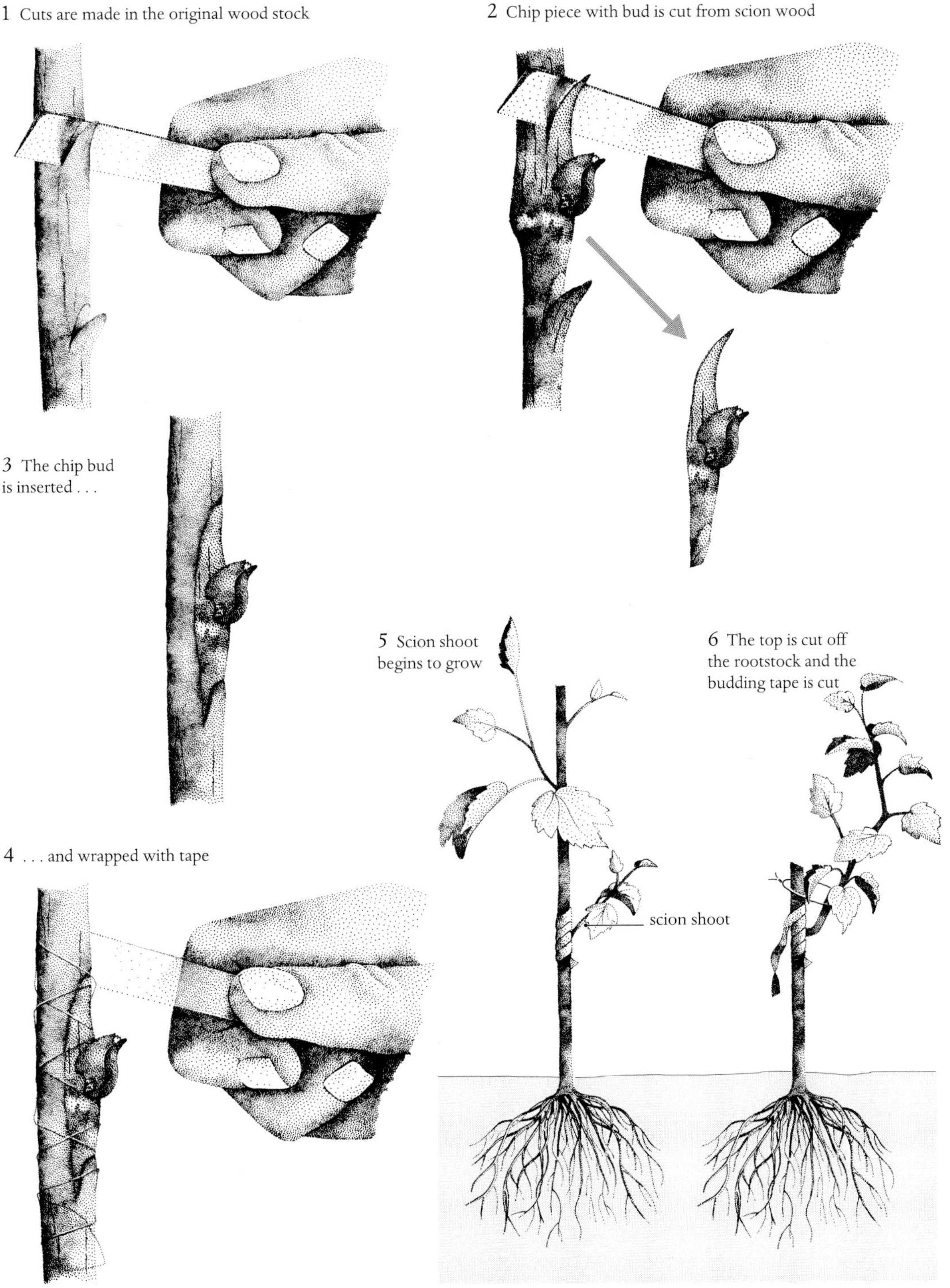
1 Cuts are made in the original wood stock
2 Chip piece with bud is cut from scion wood
3 The chip bud is inserted . . .
4 . . . and wrapped with tape
5 Scion shoot begins to grow
scion shoot
6 The top is cut off the rootstock and the budding tape is cut

normally to improve FRUIT SET. Also called girdling or ringing in English and *incision annulaire* in French, the technique is more widely used for TABLE GRAPES than for wine-growing. It is said that the effect was discovered with the abrasion caused by a mule tied to a vine which set fruit better than its neighbours. Cincturing also gives the benefit of producing bigger berries and advancing RIPENING. The benefit is mainly seen with seedless varieties, such as the table grapes Black Corinth, Sultana, and Perlette. Cincturing stops both the upwards and downwards flow of nutrients and plant hormones, until the wound heals over. The practice demands a large input of labour and so is not usually justified for wine grapes, although it is practised commercially for table grapes. R.E.S.

Winkler, A. J., *et al.*, *General Viticulture* (2nd edn., Berkeley, Calif., 1974).

CINSAUT, sometimes written **Cinsault**, is a red grape variety known for centuries in the Languedoc region of southern France that has much in common with GRENACHE. Although it has good drought resistance and its best wines by far come from vines that yield less than 40 hl/ha (2.3 tons/acre), it can all too easily be persuaded to yield generously and unremarkably. The wines it produces tend to be lighter, softer, and, in extreme youth, more aromatic than most reds. Although prone to rot, it is particularly well adapted for rosé production and is widely planted throughout southern France, and Corsica, where it is the dominant vine variety. It differs from Grenache by virtue of its long history, its shorter growing season, and its easier adaptation to mechanical harvesting.

There was a threefold increase in French plantings in the 1970s, when Cinsaut was officially sanctioned as an 'improving' grape variety with which to replace ARAMON and ALICANTE BOUSCHET, mainly in the Aude and Hérault *départements*. Since then, the economic realities of quality's supremacy over quantity have slowed Cinsaut's fortunes and Languedoc producers have been much more likely to plant a variety with as much character and cachet as Syrah, Merlot, Mourvèdre, or Cabernet Sauvignon. Cinsaut is used almost exclusively to add suppleness, perfume, and immediate fruit to blends (typically of the ubiquitous but curmudgeonly Carignan), although some all-Cinsaut rosés exist.

It is an approved but hardly venerated ingredient in the CHÂTEAUNEUF-DU-PAPE cocktail and is often found further east in Provence, as well as in the north of Corsica, where it has been widely pulled up in favour of more profitable crops.

Total French plantings of Cinsaut fell throughout the 1980s to less than 50,000 ha/123,500 acres (still more vineyard than Cabernet Sauvignon). The variety was most important in the 1950s and early 1960s when ALGERIA, then constitutionally part of France, was an important wine producer and depended particularly heavily on its healthily productive 60,000 ha of Cinsaut. Since Algerian wine was then used primarily for blending in France, notoriously for adding body to less reputable burgundies, some of this North African Cinsaut may still be found in a few older bottles of 'burgundy'. The variety is still cultivated quite extensively in Morocco (and has long played a part in the Lebanese wine industry).

Cinsaut has in its time played a major part in South as well as North Africa. Having been imported from southern France in the mid 19th century, it was South Africa's most planted grape variety until the mid 1960s and is still by far the Cape's most popular red grape variety, with more than 6,000 ha/14,800 acres planted in 1990. Cinsaut was known carelessly as Hermitage in South Africa (although there is no Cinsaut in the northern Rhône). Thus South Africa's own grape variety speciality, a crossing of Pinot Noir with Cinsaut, was named PINOTAGE, now a much more respected South African vine variety than Cinsaut.

In both France and Australia (where its fortunes waned rapidly in the 1970s and 1980s) Cinsaut has occasionally been sold as a table grape under the name Œillade. In southern Italy, it is probably the same as the Ottavianello, planted around Brindisi and producing light, unremarkable red wines. Cinsaut can also be found in various corners of eastern Europe.

CIRÒ, the only DOC of any quantitative significance in the southern Italian region of CALABRIA.

CIS, or **Confederation of Independent States**, approximates to what was once the Russian empire and was known for much of the 20th century as the Soviet Union, or USSR, the world's largest country. With the fall of communism towards the end of the 1980s, the Union fragmented into its separate republics which acquired, or regained, administrative and economic independence. Some republics—Georgia, Lithuania, Latvia, and Estonia (the last three of importance in the world of wine only for the Baltic OAK they once supplied for cooperage)—declared independence from the CIS right from the start. Others retain an affiliation.

Those which produce considerable quantities of wine grapes, in descending order of the area of vines planted for wine production (including the determinedly independent remnants of the Soviet Union), are MOLDOVA, UKRAINE and the CRIMEA, RUSSIA (including Belarus, Belorussia, or White Russia), AZERBAIJAN, and GEORGIA. Small amounts of wine (about the same as ISRAEL, or LUXEMBOURG in a good year) are also produced by ARMENIA, KYRGYZSTAN, TAJIKISTAN, KAZAKHSTAN, UZBEKISTAN, and TURKMENISTAN. There has traditionally been considerable movement of wine, grapes, and grape juice between the republics (as suggested by the table opposite). The Central Asian republics of Uzbekistan, Turkmenistan, Tajikistan, Kazakhstan, and Kyrgyzstan have a climate and grape variety mix that is quite different from that of the most 'European' republic Moldova, for example, and the first three produce predominantly DRYING GRAPES and TABLE GRAPES from their vineyards.

Unlike that other great empire-turned-communist superstate CHINA, the Soviet Union was an important producer of wine, which has long been an integral part of its culture. Indeed, both Georgia and Armenia are part of the general area most closely associated with the ORIGINS OF VITICULTURE.

The vine was cultivated in the Russian empire for many centuries, even if Ottoman rule interrupted wine production in many regions (see ISLAM). The Russian empire's vineyards accounted for about three per cent of the world's vineyards and about two per cent of the world's wine production at the beginning of the 20th century. The tsars and the imperial court at St Petersburg were important consumers of some of Europe's finest wines, most notably relatively sweet CHAMPAGNE (especially Roederer) and SAUTERNES (especially Ch d'YQUEM). Imports of champagne reached a peak of more than 800,000 bottles in 1897, despite relatively high import taxes which eventually stimulated a domestic sparkling wine industry (see SOVIET SPARKLING) initially based on both base wines in barrel and production techniques imported directly from France. Wine-producing centres such as Abrau-Durso, Tsinandali, and MASSANDRA were designed to supply the imperial court with superior wines, most of them sweet and many of them named after European wine types.

The country's vineyards were badly damaged during the First World War and civil war so that the total vineyard area declined from 230,000 ha/568,000 acres in 1913 to 132,000 ha in 1921.

Communism and collectivization were vigorously applied in the early years of the Soviet period with size of enterprise and YIELD the chief aims. Many viticultural practices were mechanized, particularly on the flatter terrain of Russia and Ukraine. Vine TRELLISING was widely adopted and means of pest and disease control were developed. By 1940 there were 425,000 ha of vines and 146 specialized viticultural farms, where, typically, FERMENTATION would take place. The wine would subsequently be shipped in bulk to vast 'secondary vinification enterprises' close to population centres for finishing and BOTTLING. During Soviet involvement in the Second World War, however, vineyards in Moldova, Ukraine, and North Caucasus were badly damaged.

Accelerated development of viticulture came after 1953 when there were the first serious attempts to match vine variety to MESOCLIMATE and the use to which the grapes would eventually be put. Total vineyard area increased by about a third in 20 years to reach 1.32 million ha/3.26 million acres in 1980. Then came yet another set-back: President Gorbachev's 1985–8 national campaign against alcohol abuse. Measures were energetically directed not just against vodka consumption but also against the production of wine (and therefore BRANDY), so that the country's total vineyard area fell back to around the 1960 level of just over 1 million ha in 1990. (This dramatic programme of vine pulling was echoed in countries from which the Soviet Union had been importing huge quantities of wine; see BULGARIA and CYPRUS.) Despite this reduction in output, in 1990 the Soviet Union accounted for 12 per cent of the world's total area of vineyard, nine per cent of the grapes harvested, and five per cent of the wine produced.

In 1990 the republics with the most land planted with vines (many of them, especially in the five Central Asian republics, for table grapes, RAISINS, or other non-wine grape products) were, in descending order, Moldova, Azerbaijan, Ukraine, Russia, Uzbekistan, and Georgia. Vine-growing makes an important financial and social contribution in many regions. The Soviet Union had 206 recognized viticultural zones, of which 196 were regarded as having real potential for wine and 10 for table grapes only.

Republic	1990	
	1,000 hl wine produced	1,000 ha vineyard planted
Russia (incl. Belarus)	8,130	147
Moldova	4,000	182
Ukraine (incl. Crimea)	2,720	175
Georgia	960	113
Azerbaijan	660	181
Kazakhstan	660	25
Uzbekistan	640	133
Tajikistan	150	37
Kyrgyzstan	150	9
Armenia	150	29
Turkmenistan	120	27
Latvia	120	—
Lithuania	74	—
Estonia	17	—
Total	15,700	1,080

Vineyards in Russia, some of the Ukraine, and most of central Asia need WINTER PROTECTION because the winters are so harsh, and IRRIGATION because summers are so dry. Moldova has the most suitable climate, and range of vine varieties planted, for regular production of European VARIETALS, while the central Asian republics are more likely to be planted with indigenous vine varieties producing heavier, sweeter wines.

The wine grape varieties regarded as specialities of the CIS are the white RKATSITELI and the red SAPERAVI, both of which are also widely planted elsewhere in eastern Europe. Of varieties imported from classic European wine regions, RIESLING is surprisingly widely planted, even in some relatively hot regions, as are ALIGOTÉ and, perhaps more usefully on the international market-place, CABERNET SAUVIGNON. Some particularly cold-hardy crossings of classic varieties have been developed especially for Russia's cold winters and are usually described as *Severny*, or Northern.

In the late 1980s, the Soviet Union was producing an average of about 16 million hl/420 million gal of wine each year in total, together with 240 million bottles of the country's passion, Soviet sparkling wine (until the early 1990s labelled *champanskoje*) and a million hl of brandy.

Research into both viticulture and wine-making has long been a concern with the Institute MAGARATCH in Yalta in the Crimea, founded in 1828, being one of the most venerable centres of vinous academe. Others include experimental stations at Odessa and Platniansk, the Sakarsk vine nursery in Georgia, and the Kostiuzhensk experimental vineyard in Moldova.

The breakup of the Soviet Union affected the international wine market to a certain extent and the eastern European wine market enormously. Eastern bloc countries such as Bulgaria, ROMANIA, and HUNGARY suddenly had to find new customers for an important proportion of their annual wine production, customers who would certainly be more demanding than their Soviet predecessors. Wine produced within the CIS, on the other hand, was viewed by some republics as a potential earner of hard currency, by others as useful barter.

Outsiders drafted in to new CIS republics in the early 1990s to lend expertise to vine-growing and wine-making were often surprised by the lack of winery hygiene and equipment (even bottles were scarce in many areas, let alone sterile bottling lines) and disappointed by the poor health of many vineyards. Vineyards with missing, dying, or diseased vines were relatively common. As in other commercial sectors, the transition to a free market economy has been difficult for wine producers, not helped by the problem of transferring land ownership from state to individuals. The first example of outside wine investment was the Australian company PENFOLDS' joint venture in Moldova, announced in 1993.

For more detail see under the names of individual republics. V.R.

Dokuchayeva, E. N. (ed.), *Grape Varieties* (Russian) (Kiev, 1986).
Kishkovski, Z. N., and Merjanian, A. A., *Technology of Wine* (Russian) (Moscow, 1984).
Negrul, A. M., *Viticulture with Basic Principles of Ampelography and Breeding* (Russian) (3rd edn., Moscow, 1959).
Valouiko, G. G. (ed.), *Modern Methods for Grape Wine Production* (Russian) (Moscow, 1984).
Vernovski, E. A., *The Technolgoy of Grape Cultivation and Use* (Russian) (Moscow, 1990).

CITRIC ACID, a common plant acid, abundant in some fleshy fruits such as lemons, but rare in grapes. The grape is unusual among fruits in that its major acid is TARTARIC ACID (and MALIC ACID), rather than citric acid, whose concentration in the juice of most grape varieties is only about one-twentieth that of tartaric acid.

Citric acid is also one of the ACIDS used in wine-making for the purposes of ACIDIFICATION. It is inexpensive but unsubtle and is used almost exclusively for inexpensive wines. It is produced commercially by fermenting SUCROSE solutions; very small amounts are recovered from processing citrus fruits. It is also used for cleaning. B.G.C. & A.D.W.

CIVC. Thanks to the **Comité Interprofessionnel du Vin de Champagne,** CHAMPAGNE is one of the most thoroughly organized wine regions in the world. The CIVC was established in 1941 as a co-operative organization grouping GROWERS and MERCHANTS under the auspices of the government (now represented by a commissioner appointed by the French Ministry of Agriculture). Growers and merchants each have a president to represent them. The CIVC is charged with organizing and controlling the production, distribution, and promotion of the wines of Champagne, as well as undertaking fundamental research for the region. Until 1990 it set a price for the grapes and still intervenes to regulate the size of the harvest and decide whether any of it should be 'blocked', or retained as juice rather than vinified and sold. The CIVC is financed by a levy on production and a tax on champagne sales.

The CIVC has also been responsible for defending the Champenois's exclusive right to use the word 'champagne'. A notable victory was won in the English courts in 1959 and since then the name has achieved legal protection in most major markets, although not in the United States. The EUROPEAN UNION has also awarded the Champenois the monopoly of the term *méthode champenoise* (French for CHAMPAGNE METHOD), previously much used on sparkling wine labels. The CIVC has fought a number of battles to ensure that the name Champagne is not used for other products, including a cigarette and a brand of perfume. N.F.

CLAIRET, dark pink wine style that is a speciality of the BORDEAUX region, recalling the sort of red wines that were shipped in such quantity in the Middle Ages from BORDEAUX to ENGLAND, and which originally inspired the English word CLARET. Dark-skinned grapes are fermented in contact with the skins for about 24 hours before fermentation of this lightly coloured wine continues to dryness. Small quantities of potentially refreshing wine are bottled to be sold under the appellation Bordeaux Clairet, and should be drunk as young as possible. It is said to have originated in Quinsac in the PREMIÈRES CÔTES DE BORDEAUX.

CLAIRETTE is a much-used name for southern French white grape varieties. Clairette Ronde, for example, is the Languedoc name for the ubiquitous UGNI BLANC, and various Clairettes serve as synonyms for the much finer BOURBOULENC.

True Clairette Blanc, however, is a decidedly old-fashioned variety, producing slightly flabby, alcoholic whites that MADERIZE easily, but it is allowed into a wide range of southern Rhône, Provençal, and Languedoc appellations, even lending its name to three (see below). Clairette is a traditional variety well suited to poor, dry soils, for long grown in what Galet calls 'the land of the olive tree'. It needs a non-vigorous rootstock to avoid COULURE and is susceptible to mildew and grape worms. Its small, thick- skinned grapes ripen relatively late, but can ripen dangerously fast at the end of the growing season. Total French plantings fell by more than half during the 1970s and there were just 4,000 ha/9,900 acres at the end of the 1980s, a decade during which consumers acquired a taste for whites that in many ways are the antithesis of Clairette. It is still, usually enlivened by Ugni Blanc and Terret, one of the principal ingredients in the Languedoc's white VINS DE PAYS.

Its presence in many southern white appellations such as LIRAC (in whose white wines Clairette must constitute at least a third), Côtes-du-RHÔNE, COSTIÈRES DE NÎMES, and PALETTE explains why Ugni Blanc is also needed in these blends, to add counterbalancing acid. Its other common partner in the blending vat, and often vineyard, GRENACHE Blanc, certainly does nothing to compensate for Clairette's weight and premature senility, although low-temperature fermentation and minimal exposure to oxidation can do something to offset these tendencies. Clairette is widely distributed throughout the eastern Midi, especially in the Gard, where it produces CLAIRETTE DE BELLEGARDE and in the Hérault for CLAIRETTE DU LANGUEDOC, two of the Languedoc's earliest controlled appellations, presumably because these white wines were so unlike, rather than superior to, the typical produce of the Midi. Clairette's noblest incarnation is undoubtedly the usually sparkling CLAIRETTE DE DIE of the mid-Rhône, although it must be admitted that the most interesting examples are those which rely more on Muscat than Clairette.

In previous eras, when consumers expected their whites to look pale brown and taste halfway to sherry, Clairette was clearly relatively important. With the more acid PICPOUL it formed the basis of PICARDAN, an extraordinarily popular wine exported in enormous quantities northwards from the Languedoc in the 17th and 18th centuries. It is hardly surprising that the variety spread far and wide in the 19th and early 20th centuries. At one time there were sizeable plantings in Algeria. It is known as Clairette Blanche in South Africa, whose relatively important area, at 3,500 ha/8,600 acres almost as much as the French total, makes a useful ingredient in basic sparkling wine or good blending material. It can still be found in Australia's Hunter Valley, where it is known as Blanquette but is declining fast. It is also planted in Romania, Israel, Tuscany, and Sardinia, where it is a permitted ingredient in NURAGUS di Cagliari.

A Clairette is grown in RUSSIA in some quantity.

Clavel, J., *Vins et cuisine de terroir en Languedoc* (Toulouse, 1988).
Galet, P., *Cépages et vignobles de France* (2nd edn., Montpellier, 1990).

Clairette de Bellegarde is a small enclave of exclusively white wine production in the south of the COSTIÈRES DE NÎMES appellation in the eastern Languedoc. Like CLAIRETTE DU LANGUEDOC it is made entirely of the somewhat flabby CLAIRETTE grape and needs all the streamlining that modern vinification can impart to make this old-fashioned wine appeal to wine drinkers outside the region. Inhabitants of the small town of Bellegarde may be used to their own nutty, deep coloured whites, but they are likely to continue to constitute the major market for this anomalous appellation since total production is low, declining, and dominated by the Bellegarde co-operative. This wine demands to be drunk as young as possible.

Clairette de Die is a sparkling white appellation centred on the town of DIE on the Drôme tributary east of the Rhône between Valence and Montélimar. According to PLINY, wine has been made here since Roman times. Die's gently fizzing wines may pre-date those of Champagne. Clairette de Die is a drink much more likely to refresh than either of the Languedoc's Clairettes (see above and below), but often despite rather than because of the CLAIRETTE grape. As well as a small quantity of still Clairette, a bit like CLAIRETTE DE BELLEGARDE but with the benefit of a slightly cooler climate, two very different sorts of sparkling Clairette de Die have been made, from Clairette and MUSCAT BLANC À PETITS GRAINS grapes.

The more distinctive and more important is Clairette de Die (Tradition), a refreshingly grapey fizz that underpins Italianate Moscato flavours with Rhône weight, and is made by the *méthode dioise* which should be signalled on the label. In this wine Muscat should dominate the blend and the aroma, concentrated by a second fermentation in bottle (see SPARKLING WINE-MAKING) activated, unusually, by the inherent grape sugar rather than added sugar and yeast. After at least four months on the grapey lees of this process, the wine is decanted off and rebottled under pressure, leaving varying degrees of residual sweetness. No last-minute adjustments with DOSAGE are allowed.

The more ordinary but usually well-made brut version made by the CHAMPAGNE METHOD, mainly from Clairette grapes, has been called Clairette de Die Brut, but must, from 1999, be called CRÉMANT de Die.

The local co-operative, geographically justified in calling itself the Cellier Hannibal, has been responsible for dynamizing the appellation and makes three in every four bottles carrying it. Perhaps it is significant that their top cuvée, and that of some smaller producers, contains no Clairette at all.

Other local still red and whites may qualify as CHÂTILLON-EN-DIOIS.

Clairette du Languedoc is a slightly more important appellation than CLAIRETTE DE BELLEGARDE, again exclusively from the overweight Clairette grape. It is one of the named subappellations of the southern French Coteaux du LANGUEDOC appellation. Clairette du Languedoc has suffered an extremely confused image as, despite its relatively small production, a wide array of different wine styles have been produced, and are officially sanctioned, within the appellation. The wine can be anything from an ultra-modern, early-picked, yellowish green, dry wine for drinking almost before the end of the year in which it was harvested, to a deep brown RANCIO sweet, alcoholic VIN DE LIQUEUR to suit French taste in aperitifs. The area qualifying for this confused appellation lies to the north east of Pézenas, where Clairette and other even more outdated Languedoc varieties are rapidly being displaced by flashier imports from wine regions to the north such as Syrah, Merlot, Chardonnay, and Sauvignon Blanc. Although co-operatives dominate production quantitatively, by the 1980s it was left to the Jany family at the Condamine-Bertrand domain to uphold the qualitative honour of the appellation, which they express as a flavourful dry white for early drinking. PICPOUL DE PINET made just to the south shares many of these characteristics.

Clape, La, named TERROIR within the Coteaux du LANGUEDOC in southern France. La Clape was once an island off the busy Roman port of Narbo. Today it is a quintessentially Mediterranean coastal mountain just south of Narbonne which has one of France's highest average annual totals of sunshine. On the southern slopes of the mountain the climate is heavily influenced by the sea. Altitudes of vineyards can vary by as much as 200 m/980 ft. La Clape is particularly well suited to growing Bourboulenc, and the production of sea-scented white wines, although these represent a distinct minority of the wine produced from about 1,000 ha/2,500 acres of vineyard within the appellation and most La Clape is full blooded red, virtually indistinguishable from maritime CORBIÈRES.

CLARE RIESLING. See CROUCHEN.

CLARET, English term generally used to describe red wines from the BORDEAUX region, or red bordeaux. Claret has also been used as a GENERIC term for a vaguely identified class of red table wines supposedly drier, and possibly higher in TANNINS, than those wines sold as generic burgundy (although, in the history of Australian wine shows, it has been known for the same wine to win both claret and burgundy classes).

History

In medieval France, most red wine was the result of a short FERMENTATION, usually of no more than one or two days. The short period of contact with the grape skins meant that the resultant wines were pale in colour, and were probably very similar to the rosés of today. Such wines exported from Bordeaux were known as *vinum clarum*, *bin clar*, or CLAIRET, and it is from the last of these that the English term claret is derived. Other much darker wines were also made by pressing the remaining skins, effectively the same as modern PRESS WINE, and these were known as *vinum rubeum purum*, *bin vermelh*, or *pinpin*.

Although the term *clairet* was widely used during the medieval period in France, the word claret does not appear to have been used at all extensively in England until the 16th century. In the second half of the 17th century a new type of wine, of much higher quality and deeper colour, began to be produced in the GRAVES and on the sands and gravels of the MÉDOC to the north west of Bordeaux. These wines, the provenance of specific properties, where close attention was paid to grape selection, improved methods of vinification, and the use of new oak BARRELS, became known by the beginning of the 18th century as New French Clarets, and the earliest and most famous of them were HAUT-BRION, LAFITE, LATOUR, and MARGAUX (see BORDEAUX, history). P.T.H.U.

Marquette, J., 'La Vinification dans les domaines de l'archevêque de Bordeaux à la fin du Moyen Âge', in A. Huetz de Lemps (ed.), *Géographie historique des vignobles*, i (Bordeaux, 1978).

Pijassou, R., *Un grand vignoble de qualité: le Médoc* (Paris, 1980).

CLARETE is a Spanish term for a particularly Spanish hue of wine somewhere between a rosé (which the Spaniards would call rosado) and a light red. It is etymologically, though not oenologically, related to CLARET and derives from *claro*, the Spanish word meaning clear. The term used to appear regularly on labels until it was prohibited following Spain's accession to the EUROPEAN Community UNION in 1986, but clarete is still used in Spanish as a descriptive term.

CLARET JUGS. See DECANTERS.

CLARE VALLEY, fine wine region near the important Barossa Valley in AUSTRALIA. For more detail see SOUTH AUSTRALIA.

CLARIFICATION, wine-making operation which removes suspended and insoluble material from grape juice, or new wine, in which these solids are known as LEES.

Clarification proper may be the removal only of insoluble solids such as the dead yeast cells and fragments of grape skins, stems, seeds, and pulp, but is frequently understood to encompass also the removal of dispersed COLLOIDS and other materials which exist in supersaturated concentration in the must or new wine, and in older wine that has not been stabilized. These latter substances include excess TARTRATES, pectins and gums, some PROTEINS, MALIC ACID, and small numbers of micro-organisms such as YEAST and BACTERIA. Removal of all these substances, which are not visible to the unaided eye, is frequently called STABILIZATION, since no subsequent clarification is needed.

Clarification can usually be accomplished naturally by simply holding the liquid in a storage tank until the larger particles settle (see SETTLING, or *débourbage*) and then siphoning, or RACKING, the clear upper layer from the compact layer of solids at the bottom on the tank. This takes time, however, especially if the wine is stored in small barrels where full clarification may take a year or two and several rackings.

Most wine-makers, therefore, and certainly all concerned with high-volume production, choose to speed the process by intervening with one or more of FILTRATION, CENTRIFUGATION, FLOTATION, and the much cheaper though slower process of FINING, the addition of agents which aid agglomeration and settling of colloids in the must or new wine.

One important white wine-making decision is the extent to which grape solids should be removed from the must before FERMENTATION. With Chardonnays, for example, a relatively high proportion of grape solids may be desirable which produce various characters during fermentation. Wine-makers may wish to eliminate most grape solids from the juice of more aromatic varieties in order to accentuate varietal fruit flavours. Juice for everyday white wines may be clarified before fermentation simply to speed and ease processing afterwards. This clarification can be done by simply holding the cooled and SULPHUR DIOXIDE-treated juice in a tank for 24 hours or so. More often pectin-splitting ENZYMES and fining agents such as BENTONITE will be added along with the sulphur dioxide in order to aid the clarification.

Flotation is a more recent technique of must clarification, borrowed from the ore refining and concentrating industry. If very small bubbles of air are introduced at the bottom of a vat of must, easily oxidized PHENOLICS in the juice will react and some will be removed along with the other suspended solids which are carried to the tank top by the finely divided air bubbles. Oxidized phenolics, which are brown, not removed by flotation will probably be adsorbed and removed with the lees after fermentation. The advantage of this technique is that the resultant wine resists further oxidative browning.

For a long time neither centrifugation nor filtration was practical for removing solids from must. Centrifugation, which depends upon differing densities between the solids and the liquid, is impractically inefficient because of the high density of the sugar-laden juice. Before the development of ROTARY DRUM VACUUM FILTERS, the finely divided grape solids would quickly plug the small holes of a filter, making the process prohibitively expensive. Today, however, rotary filters may be used on lees which contain up to 15 per cent solids.

Red wines are not commonly clarified before fermentation because the skins are fermented with the juice in order to provide colour and flavour. In some cases, however, pectin-splitting enzymes are added to red must before fermentation to aid subsequent clarification and increase the eventual yield of FREE-RUN wine. Many everyday new red wines are processed in order to prevent the subsequent precipitation of tartrates and some will have the malic acid removed or reduced by a MALOLACTIC FERMENTATION to assure reasonable stability in bottle.

See also the similar but distinct processes associated with STABILIZATION. A.D.W.

Clarksburg, California wine region and AVA. See SAN JOAQUIN VALLEY.

classed growth is a vineyard, estate, or château included in a wine CLASSIFICATION. The term is used almost exclusively in BORDEAUX for those châteaux included in the 1855 classification of the Médoc and Sauternes, the 1955 classification of Graves, and sometimes for those properties included in the constantly revised St-Émilion classification. The term is a direct translation of the French term CRU classé.

classical art, wine in. Wine was so deeply embedded in the culture of the classical world that it is inevitable that it would figure prominently in all its aspects in the art of that world. The vessels used for mixing and drinking wine (see CRATER, for example) were frequently decorated with scenes which played on the association with wine. So, most notably, the fine Attic Black and Red Figure pottery of the 6th and 5th centuries BC sometimes contain rural scenes of men harvesting grapes and treading them, as well as scenes from the *komos* (revels) and the SYMPOSIUM, in which the craters and cups are depicted in use. Sometimes it is possible to suspect an ironic commentary taking place. A famous Red Figure cup by the so-called Dokimasia painter has scenes of revelry around the outside with the awkward spaces under the handles filled by men crouched or crawling, the worse for drink, while inside the cup an old man is depicted being sick. Another playful irony is that nearly all these scenes can be found translated to another world, in which men are replaced by satyrs, uninhibited by the conventions of human society and presided over by the god DIONYSUS. Not surprisingly, Dionysus achieves a greater prominence in the art of the world of drinking than his place in the pantheon would suggest as his due. Feasting and banquets with wine also form the subject of some of the most memorable frescos from the tombs of the ETRUSCANS, where, for example, the Tomb of the Leopards at Tarquinia beautifully illustrates the funeral meal held near the tomb in honour of the dead.

Scenes of the vintage and the pressing of the grapes, with the role of humans frequently played by *amorini*, cupids, are found in great numbers at all periods throughout the Roman world, in paintings, sculptured reliefs, sarcophagi, decorated glass, and ivory plaques. Part of the explanation for the popularity of the themes, particularly on sarcophagi, is the obvious mystical symbolism of the vine and wine. Scenes of country life, including vines and the vintage, play a significant part in Roman painting from the 1st century BC onwards. Scenes such as these are most elaborately and impressively illustrated in mosaic. The vintage and tasks connected with viticulture, such as pruning and the cleaning and pitching of DOLIA, are often found in mosaics which illustrate the seasons or the tasks of the rural calendar. As a genre these had a long history, which went back to the Hellenistic period in mosaic and may be connected with illustrated manuscript calendars. Fine examples in mosaic come from GAUL (St-Romain-en-Gal) and North Africa (the Maison des Mois at El Djem). From the 3rd century AD the élite of North Africa adorned their houses with mosaics which reflected the work of their estates. One of the most remarkable examples of realism in classical art must be the mosaic of the Labours of the Fields from Cherchel in Algeria, with men hoeing between TRELLISED vines.

The potential of the vine and wine as mystical symbols also explains why this was one of the themes of classical art which was most easily taken over by Christianity. A key monument is the church of Santa Costanza on the Via Nomentana in the north of Rome, a work of such rare beauty as to justify on its own a visit to that city. Santa Costanza was the mausoleum of Constantina, the daughter of Constantine, the first Christian emperor. Her huge porphyry sarcophagus has cherubs engaged in the vintage, a theme which is taken up by the remarkable mosaics which run round the ceiling of the ambulatory. The themes are traditional. Nothing is specifically Christian in these mosaics, but they are given a Christian connotation by the other, more overtly Christian, mosaics which would have adorned the dome. J.J.P.

Berard, C., *et al.*, *A City of Images* (Princeton, NJ, 1989).
Dunbabin, K. M. D., *The Mosaics of Roman North Africa* (Oxford, 1978).

classical texts. The vine and the olive are the plants that characterize Mediterranean civilization. To grow them is the sign of a settled, not a nomadic, existence. Their

Classical art: Pigeage in Roman times.

products can be used as part of the daily routine, olive oil for cooking and washing, wine for drinking, or to mark a special occasion in the life of a community, when people would anoint their heads with fragrant oil and drink the best wine. In wine-producing countries wine can be an ordinary drink or a luxury item: classical literature reflects both.

This starts with HOMER (the end of the 8th century BC) and HESIOD (*c*.700 BC), the earliest Greek authors. Wine is mentioned frequently in the grander context. In Hesiod's *Works and Days* the cultivation of the vine is part of the order of nature as laid down by the gods: the secular and the religious were not distinct spheres. HERODOTUS' *Histories* (5th century BC) have many observations on wine and its uses among foreign nations. The Greeks had no books on agriculture, but THEOPHRASTUS (*c*.370–*c*.287 BC) could be called the first systematic botanist. A very late Greek author, ATHENAEUS (fl. AD 200) is a good source of information on the wines of his day.

Among the Romans, VIRGIL (70–19 BC), HORACE (65–8 BC), and MARTIAL (*c*.AD 30–103/4) are the poets who display a particular interest in wine: Virgil chiefly in the *Georgics*, Horace throughout his poems, and Martial in many of his epigrams on the mores of his time. PLINY the Elder (AD 23/4–79) devoted an entire book of his *Natural History* to all aspects of wine. Other prose writers wrote treatises on agriculture: CATO (234–149 BC), VARRO (116–27 BC), COLUMELLA (1st century AD), and the derivative PALLADIUS (4th century AD). H.M.W.

CLASSICAL VINE VARIETIES. See ANCIENT VINE VARIETIES.

CLASSICAL WINES. See GREECE and ROME for general comments, as well as CAECUBAN, FALERNIAN, MASSIC, OPIMIAN, and SURRENTINE wines specifically.

CLASSICAL WORLD. See Ancient GREECE and Ancient ROME.

CLASSICO, Italian term appended to the names of various DOC or DOCG wines to indicate that they have been produced in the historic zone which gave the wine its name, the zone which, at least in theory, offers the ideal conditions of soil and climate for the grape or grapes to express themselves.

In reality, the name of the wine *without* the adjective Classico is usually applied to a significant expansion of the original production zone into areas which cultivate the same grape but in different, and usually less satisfactory, conditions of soil and climate. The origins of this practice, which occurred well before the establishment of the DOC system in the 1960s, lie in the regulation of the use of the name CHIANTI established by the Dalmasso Commission in 1932: large areas of Tuscany, some far distant from CHIANTI CLASSICO, were permitted to use the name Chianti, while other historic areas of production of fine wine, Rufina and CARMIGNANO in particular, were obliged to add the word Chianti to their name. (Carmignano has since detached itself from the Chianti zone.)

This precedent was widely followed as the various DOCs came into being between 1967 and 1975, since when a significant number of Italy's historically important wines are now produced in both a Classico and a regular version. These include BARDOLINO, CALDARO, CHIANTI CLASSICO, CIRÒ, ORVIETO, SANTA MADDALENA, SOAVE, TERLANO, VALPOLICELLA, and VERDICCHIO.

The practice reflects a permanent tension in Italy's DOC system itself. Instead of choosing, like France, a geographical system of appellations, or choosing a VARIETAL system of nomenclature as California has done, Italy has, in effect, chosen to do both by giving an appellation name to a wine produced with the same grapes outside the original appellation; the geographical expansion of production zones under DOC regulation has been the chosen instrument for carrying out this policy. D.T.

Anderson, B., *The Wine Atlas of Italy* (London and New York, 1990).

CLASSIFICATION of various wine estates and vineyards is in general a relatively recent phenomenon, dictated by the increasingly sophisticated wine market of the late 19th and 20th centuries. It has to a certain extent been superseded by the even more recent phenomenon of SCORING individual wines.

There were earlier instances of classifying individual vineyards, however. The vineyards of JURANÇON in South West France were officially evaluated as early as the 14th century, and in 1644 the council of Würzburg in FRANKEN rigorously ranked the city's vineyards according to the quality of wine they produced (see GERMAN HISTORY).

Bordeaux

BORDEAUX, with its plethora of fine, long-lasting wine from well-established estates and its well-organized market, is the wine region which has been most subject to classification of individual châteaux. The most famous wine classification in the world is that drawn up in 1855 of what became known as the CLASSED GROWTHS of the MÉDOC, and one GRAVES (see p. 246). In response to a request from Napoleon III's 1855 Exposition Universelle in Paris (possibly so that dignitaries there should effectively know what to be impressed by), the Bordeaux BROKERS formalized their own and the market's ranking with a five-class classification of 61 of the leading Médoc châteaux and the particularly famous and historic Graves, HAUT-BRION; and a two-class classification of SAUTERNES and BARSAC. This classification merely codified the market's view of relative quality as expressed by the prices fetched by individual estates' wines. (It also formalized previous informal lists of those wines widely regarded as the best by the likes of Thomas JEFFERSON, Wilhelm Franck, Alexander HENDERSON, and Cyrus REDDING.) The brokers issued the 1855 classification through the Bordeaux Chamber of Commerce, and were careful to explain that it was based on a century's experience. Within each of their classes, from FIRST GROWTHS, or PREMIERS CRUS down to fifth growths, or cinquièmes CRUS, the brokers listed châteaux in descending order of average price fetched. Thus, it is widely believed, Ch LAFITE, the 'premier des premiers', headed the list because it commanded prices in excess even of LATOUR, MARGAUX, and Haut-Brion (although others have argued that the first growths were simply listed in alphabetical order). In the original classification, the term CHÂTEAU was rarely used.

The 1855 classification has endured remarkably well considering the many and various changes to the management and precise extent of individual properties since it was compiled, with only Chx MOUTON-ROTHSCHILD and Léoville-BARTON in the same hands. The vineyards of third growth Ch Desmirail, for example, have for long been subsumed into Ch Palmer, while another Margaux Ch Ferrière hardly exists as a third growth wine (although the label is used by the owners of Ch Lascombes), and Ch Dubignon-Talbot has not produced wine since the arrival of PHYLLOXERA in the late 19th century. Edmund PENNING-ROWSELL notes that Palmer's low ranking may have been influenced by the fact that the property was in receivership in 1855, and that Cantemerle, a property relatively new to the Bordeaux market, was added to the bottom of the list in a different hand. The only official revision of this much discussed list took place in 1973 when, after much lobbying on the part of Baron Philippe de ROTHSCHILD, Ch Mouton-Rothschild made the all-important leap from top of the second growths to become a first growth (although see also SUPER SECOND). It could be argued that such a classification contains an element of self-preservation in that highly classified properties are thereby able to command prices which sustain the investment needed to maintain their status, although the history of Ch Margaux in the 1960s and 1970s demonstrates that other factors may affect this hypothesis, and in the 1980s and 1990s many Bordeaux proprietors were driven by competition and ambition to invest at a level above that suggested by their official ranking.

The 1855 classification of Sauternes and Barsac is also printed on p. 247. Reflecting price and the *réclame* then attached to sweet wines, it elevated Ch d'YQUEM to grand premier cru, a rank higher even than any of the red wine first growths, and listed 11 châteaux as first growths and 12 as seconds.

Bordeaux

THE OFFICIAL CLASSIFICATION OF MEDOC AND GRAVES OF 1855

First Growths (Premiers Crus)

	Commune	*Appellation*
CH LAFITE-ROTHSCHILD	Pauillac	Pauillac
CH MARGAUX	Margaux	Margaux
CH LATOUR	Pauillac	Pauillac
CH HAUT-BRION*	Pessac	Graves, now Pessac-Léognan
CH MOUTON-ROTHSCHILD**	Pauillac	Pauillac

Second Growths (Deuxièmes Crus)

	Commune	*Appellation*
CH RAUSAN-SEGLA	Margaux	Margaux
CH RAUZAN-GASSIES	Margaux	Margaux
CH LÉOVILLE-LAS CASES	St-Julien	St-Julien
CH LÉOVILLE-POYFERRÉ	St-Julien	St-Julien
CH LÉOVILLE-BARTON	St-Julien	St-Julien
CH DURFORT-VIVENS	Margaux	Margaux
CH GRUAUD-LAROSE	St-Julien	St-Julien
CH LASCOMBES	Margaux	Margaux
CH BRANE-CANTENAC	Cantenac	Margaux
CH PICHON-LONGUEVILLE (BARON)	Pauillac	Margaux
CH PICHON-LONGUEVILLE, COMTESSE DE LALANDE	Pauillac	Pauillac
CH DUCRU-BEAUCAILLOU	St-Julien	St-Julien
CH COS D'ESTOURNEL	St-Estèphe	St-Estèphe
CH MONTROSE	St-Estèphe	St-Estèphe

Third Growths (Troisièmes Crus)

	Commune	*Appellation*
CH KIRWAN	Cantenac	Margaux
CH D'ISSAN	Cantenac	Margaux
CH LAGRANGE	St-Julien	St-Julien
CH LANGOA-BARTON	St-Julien	St-Julien
CH GISCOURS	Labarde	Margaux
CH MALESCOT ST-EXUPÉRY	Margaux	Margaux
CH BOYD-CANTENAC	Cantenac	Margaux
CH CANTENAC-BROWN	Cantenac	Margaux
CH PALMER	Cantenac	Margaux
CH LA LAGUNE	Ludon	Haut-Médoc
CH DESMIRAIL	Margaux	Margaux
CH CALON-SEGUR	St-Estèphe	St-Estèphe
CH FERRIÈRE	Margaux	Margaux
CH MARQUIS D'ALESME BECKER	Margaux	Margaux

Fourth Growths (Quatrième Crus)

	Commune	*Appellation*
CH ST-PIERRE	St-Julien	St-Julien
CH TALBOT	St-Julien	St-Julien
CH BRANAIRE-DUCRU	St-Julien	St-Julien
CH DUHART-MILON-ROTHSCHILD	Pauillac	Pauillac
CH POUGET	Cantenac	Margaux
CH LA TOUR-CARNET	St-Laurent	Haut-Médoc
CH LAFON-ROCHET	St-Estèphe	St-Estèphe
CH BEYCHEVELLE	St-Julien	St-Julien
CH PRIEURÉ-LICHINE	Cantenac	Margaux
CH MARQUIS-DE-TERME	Margaux	Margaux

Fifth Growths (Cinquièmes Crus)

	Commune	*Appellation*
CH PONTET-CANET	Pauillac	Pauillac
CH BATAILLEY	Pauillac	Pauillac
CH HAUT-BATAILLEY	Pauillac	Pauillac
CH GRAND-PUY-LACOSTE	Pauillac	Pauillac
CH GRAND-PUY-DUCASSE	Pauillac	Pauillac
CH LYNCH-BAGES	Pauillac	Pauillac
CH LYNCH-MOUSSAS	Pauillac	Pauillac
CH DAUZAC	Labarde	Margaux
CH D'ARMAILHAQ***	Pauillac	Pauillac
CH DU TERTRE	Arsac	Margaux
CH HAUT-BAGES-LIBERAL	Pauillac	Pauillac
CH PÉDESCLAUX	Pauillac	Pauillac
CH BELGRAVE	St-Laurent	Haut-Médoc
CH DE CAMENSAC	St-Laurent	Haut-Médoc
CH COS-LABORY	St-Estèphe	St-Estèphe
CH CLERC-MILON	Pauillac	Pauillac
CH CROIZET-BAGES	Pauillac	Pauillac
CH CANTEMERLE	Macau	Haut-Médoc

* This wine, although a Graves, was universally recognized and classified as one of the four first-growths.

** This wine was decreed a first-growth in 1973.

*** Previously Ch Mouton-Baron-Philippe, then Ch Mouton-Baronne-Philippe.

THE OFFICIAL CLASSIFICATION OF SAUTERNES-BARSAC OF 1855

First Great Growth (1er Cru Supèrieur)	*Commune*
CH D'YQUEM	Sauternes

First Growths (Premier Crus)	*Commune*
CH LA TOUR-BLANCHE	Bommes
CH LAFAURIE-PEYRAGUEY	Bommes
CH CLOS HAUT-PEYRAGUEY	Bommes
CH DE RAYNE-VIGNEAU	Bommes
CH SUDUIRAUT	Preignac
CH COUTET	Barsac

First Growths (Premier Crus)	*Commune*
CH CLIMENS	Barsac
CH GUIRAUD	Sauternes
CH RIEUSSEC	Fargues
CH RABAUD-PROMIS	Bommes
CH SIGALAS-RABAUD	Bommes

Second Growths (Deuxième Crus)	*Commune*
CH DE MYRAT	Barsac
CH DOISY-DAËNE	Barsac
CH DOISY-DUBROCA	Barsac
CH DOISY-VEDRINES	Barsac
CH D'ARCHE	Sauternes
CH FILHOT	Sauternes
CH BROUSTET	Barsac

Second Growths (Deuxième Crus)	*Commune*
CH NAIRAC	Barsac
CH CAILLOU	Barsac
CH SUAU	Barsac
CH DE MALLE	Preignac
CH ROMER-DU-HAYOT	Fargues
CH LAMOTHE-DESPUJOLS	Sauternes
CH LAMOTHE-GUIGNARD	Sauternes

GRAVES: 1959 OFFICIAL CLASSIFICATION

Classified Red Wines of Graves	*Commune*
CH BOUSCAUT	Cadaujac
CH HAUT-BAILLY	Léognan
CH CARBONNIEUX	Léognan
CH DE CHEVALIER	Léognan
DOMAINE DE CHEVALIER	Léognan
CH DE FIEUZAL	Léognan
CH D'OLIVIER	Léognan

Classified Red Wines of Graves	*Commune*
CH MALARTIC-LAGRAVIÈRE	Léognan
CH LA TOUR-MARTILLAC	Martillac
CH SMITH-HAUT-LAFITTE	Martillac
CH HAUT-BRION	Pessac
CH LA MISSION-HAUT-BRION	Talence
CH PAPE-CLÉMENT	Pessac
CH LATOUR-HAUT-BRION	Talence

Classified White Wines of Graves	*Commune*
CH BOUSCAUT	Cadaujac
CH CARBONNIEUX	Léognan
CH DOMAINE DE CHEVALIER	Léognan
CH D'OLIVIER	Léognan
CH MALARTIC-LAGRAVIÈRE	Léognan

Classified White Wines of Graves	*Commune*
CH LA TOUR-MARTILLAC	Martillac
CH LAVILLE-HAUT-BROWN	Talence
CH COUHINS-LURTON	Villenave d'Ornon
CH COUHINS	Villenave d'Ornon
CH HAUT-BRION	Pessac*

* Added to the list in 1960.

ST-ÉMILION 1955 OFFICIAL CLASSIFICATION (OFFICIALLY RECLASSIFIED 1985)

Premiers Grands Crus Classés

(A) CH AUSONE
CH CHEVAL BLANC

(B) CH BEAUSÉJOUR-DUFFAU LA GARROSSE
CH BELAIR
CH CANON
CLOS FOURTET
CH FIGEAC
CH LA GAFFELIÈRE
CH MAGDELAINE
CH PAVIE
CH TROTTEVIEILLE

Grands Crus Classés

CH L'ANGELUS
CH L'ARROSÉE
CH BALESTARD LA TONNELLE
CH BEAUSEJOUR-BECOT
CH BELLEVUE
CH BERGAT
CH BERLIQUET
CH CADET PIOLA
CH CANON-LA-GAFFELIÈRE
CH CAP DE MOURLIN
CH LE CHATELET
CH CHAUVIN
CH CLOS DES JACOBINS
CH CLOS LA MADELEINE
CH CLOS DE L'ORATOIRE
CH CLOS SAINT-MARTIN
CH LA CLOTTE
CH LA CLUSIÈRE
CH CORBIN
CH CORBIN MICHOTTE
CH COUVENT DES JACOBINS
CH CROQUE-MICHOTTE
CH CURÉ-BON-LA-MADELEINE
CH DASSAULT
CH LA DOMINIQUE
CH FAURIE DE SOUCHARD
CH FONPLÉGADE
CH FONROQUE
CH FRANC-MAYNE
CH GRAND-BARRAIL-LAMARZELLE-FIGEAC
CH GRAND-CORBIN
CH GRAND-CORBIN DESPAGNE
CH GRAND-MAYNE
CH GRAND-PONTET
CH GAUDET-SAINT-JULIEN
CH HAUT-CORBIN
CH HAUT-SARPE
CH LANIOTE
CH LARCIS-DUCASSE
CH LAMARZELLE
CH LARMANDE
CH LAROZE
CH MATRAS
CH MAUVEZIN
CH MOULIN-DU-CADET
CH L'ORATOIRE
CH PAVIE-DECESSE
CH PAVIE-MACQUIN
CH PAVILLON-CADET
CH PETIT-FAURIE-DE-SOUTARD
CH LE PRIEURÉ
CH RIPEAU
CH SAINT-GEORGES-COTE-PAVIE
CH SANSONNET
CH LA SERRE
CH SOUTARD
CH TERTRE-DAUGAY
CH LA TOUR-DU-PIN-FIGEAC (GIRAUD-BELIVIER)
CH LA TOUR-DU-PIN-FIGEAC (MOUEIX)
CH LA TOUR-FIGEAC
CH TRIMOULET
CH TROPLONG-MONDOT
CH VILLEMAURINE
CH YON-FIGEAC

Other than Haut-Brion's inclusion in the 1855 Médoc classification, the red wines of the GRAVES district were not officially classified until 1953. This one-class list, together with an official classification of the white wines made in 1959, appears on p. 247. It avoided some possible controversy by employing a democratically alphabetical order (Ch Haut-Brion Blanc was added in 1960). It should be said, however, that there is a wide differential between the prices commanded by Ch Haut-Brion and its close rival Ch La Mission-Haut-Brion, and those fetched by Chx Bouscaut and de Fieuzal, for example. The Graves district was subsequently divided into Graves and PESSAC-LÉOGNAN.

The classification of ST-ÉMILION, formally drawn up in 1955, is most frequently amended. There were modifications in both 1969 and 1985 and these are likely to continue on the basis of monitoring of wine quality, vineyard boundaries, and the like (vineyards cannot be extended between re-classifications). The St-Émilion classification's laudable topicality is mitigated by over-generosity, however. The top two properties Chx CHEVAL BLANC and AUSONE are ranked, somewhat inelegantly, premiers grands crus classés A, while nine (10 until 1985) properties qualify as premiers grands crus classés B. Below this are more than 60 grands crus classés, whose quality can vary considerably, and then in each vintage, on the basis of tastings, the deceptively grandiose rank of GRAND CRU (minus the classé) is awarded to scores of individual wines from properties below grand cru classé status. The 1985 classification is reproduced on p. 248; a revision based on tastings of wines made between 1984 and 1994 is expected to be published in 1996.

POMEROL is the only important fine wine district of Bordeaux never to have been classified, although its star Ch PÉTRUS is conventionally included with Chx Lafite, Latour, Margaux, Haut-Brion, Mouton-Rothschild, Cheval Blanc, and Ausone as a first growth.

There have been regular attempts to revise and assimilate the various classifications of Bordeaux, most notably that drawn up by Alexis LICHINE in 1959. Most serious writers on bordeaux make their own revisions, more or less confirmed by the market.

See also CRU BOURGEOIS for those MÉDOC properties classified as just below the status of a fifth growth.

Burgundy

Burgundians were also well aware of the considerable variation in quality of the wines produced by different plots of land, or *climats*, as they are known in Burgundy. In 1855 Dr Lavalle published his influential *History and Statistics of the Côte d'Or* which included an informal classification of the best vineyards. This was formalized in 1861 by the Beaune Committee of Agriculture, which, with Lavalle's assistance, devised three classes. Most *climats* included in the first class eventually became grands crus when the APPELLATION CONTRÔLÉE system was introduced in the 1930s. See p. 165 for a full list of Burgundian grands crus, and see under individual village names for details of their premiers crus.

Elsewhere

Few other regions of France have anything approaching an official classification, although see ALSACE for a list of those vineyards accorded grand cru status, and CHAMPAGNE for some details of the classification of individual villages there.

There have been attempts, typically by wine writers and/or wine waiters, to produce classifications of the best vineyards, or best wines, of many countries, notably Germany and Italy (see VERONELLI), but these have so far been too controversial to be generally adopted. With the exception of the DOURO, where individual vineyards have been classified for the quality of port they produce, the wine regions of Portugal and Spain are in too great a state of flux to submit satisfactorily to classification, like those of eastern Europe and the rest of the Mediterranean.

In the New World, Australia prefers to classify not vineyards but individual wines, often much blended between areas, by awarding them medals and trophies in their famous SHOWS, while classification may never appeal to the democratic California wine industry.

See also CLIMATE CLASSIFICATION.

Penning-Rowsell, E., *The Wines of Bordeaux* (6th edn., London, 1989).

Pitiot, S., and Servant, J.-C., *Les Vins de Bourgogne; Collection Pierre Poupon* (11th edn., Paris, 1992).

CLAY, description of sediment or soil which is made up of particularly small particles. See SOIL TEXTURE, and GEOLOGY, for more details of this particular form of soil classification. The terms used in this classification are unrelated to the soil's mineral composition—although in general soils whose texture is described as clay tend to be dominated by clay minerals (a geological term with a technical meaning), while they may also contain considerable quantities of clay grade (particularly small particles of) quartz. To have a stable SOIL STRUCTURE, a soil must contain at least a moderate amount of clay. In viticultural terms, clay is especially celebrated as a vineyard SUBSOIL, often being more important than is obvious from the surface of the soils, as in parts of POMEROL, for example. J.G.

CLEANLINESS, an important quality in wine (a wine should not have any off-odours) and in wineries, for which see HYGIENE.

CLEAR LAKE, CALIFORNIA wine region and AVA. See LAKE COUNTY.

CLEFT GRAFTING, a popular method for changing VINE VARIETY in the vineyard (see FIELD GRAFTING). The severing of the trunk may be at ground level or just below the head; the latter is preferred because DESUCKERING is simpler, less vine training is required, and the extra wood of the trunk aids the rapid establishment of the new vine. The trunk is cut horizontally in early spring and the stump split across the middle to about 5 cm/2 in depth. SCION pieces of one or two nodes are prepared from dormant canes with a long-tapered

Cleft grafting

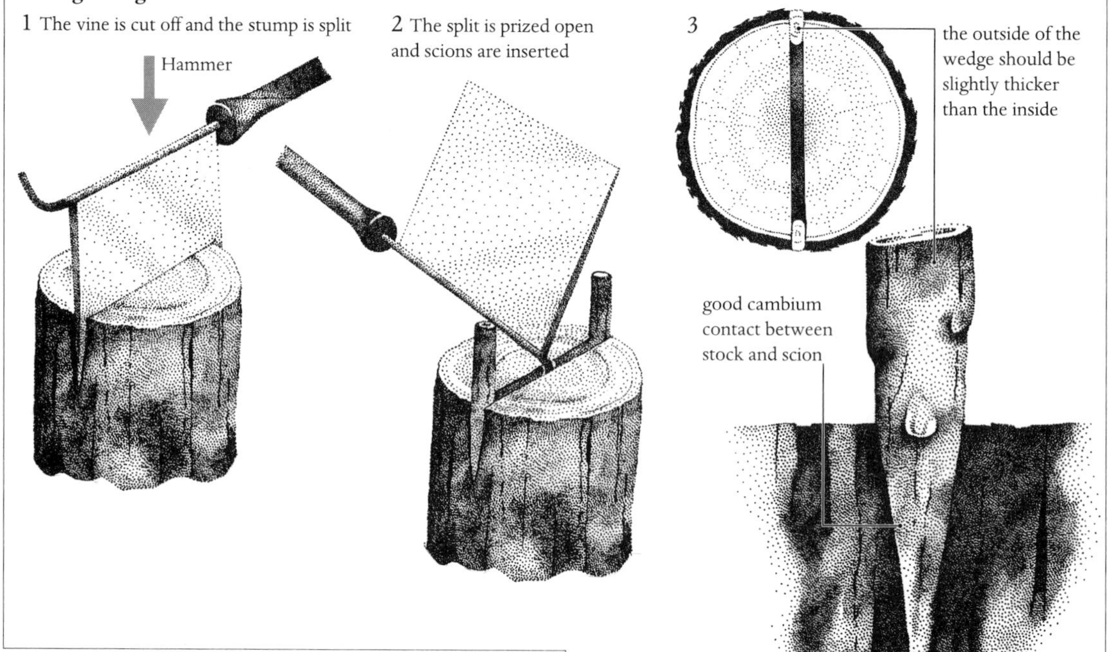
1 The vine is cut off and the stump is split
Hammer
2 The split is prized open and scions are inserted
3
the outside of the wedge should be slightly thicker than the inside
good cambium contact between stock and scion

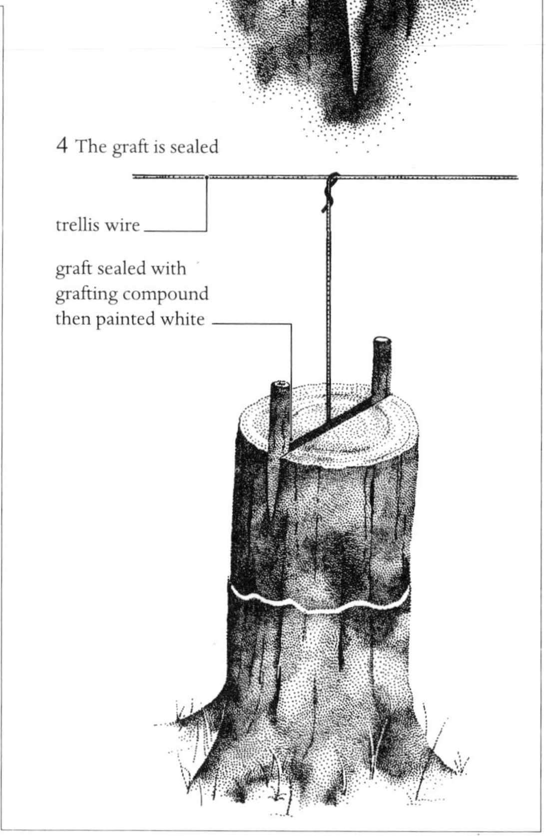
4 The graft is sealed
trellis wire
graft sealed with grafting compound then painted white

wedge. After the trunk is split and spread, the pieces are inserted one on each side so that CAMBIUMS of ROOTSTOCK and scion are matched to facilitate their bonding. The wounds are sealed with grafting mastic, then with paint. NOTCH GRAFTING is an alternative. See illustration. B.G.C.

CLEVNER, grape variety, usually part of the PINOT family. In SWITZERLAND the name is often applied to PINOT NOIR or Blauburgunder grown in the canton of Zurich. See also KLEVNER.

CLIMAT, French, particularly Burgundian, term for a specific vineyard site defined by, as the name suggests, all of its climatological as well as geographical characteristics, otherwise known as TERROIR. Thus the Burgundian grower uses the word *climat* interchangeably with 'vineyard'. A *climat* is generally smaller than a specific appellation, and most appellations have over the centuries been subdivided into small parcels of a few hectares, each with its own name, known by local geographers as a *lieu-dit*.

CLIMATE, long-term WEATHER pattern of an area, and an extremely important variable in the wine-making equation. For more details see MACROCLIMATE in particular, but also CLIMATE CLASSIFICATION, CLIMATE CHANGE, CONTINENTALITY, COOL CLIMATE, LATITUDE, MEDITERRANEAN CLIMATE, RAINFALL, SUNLIGHT, TEMPERATE, TEMPERATURE, TEMPERATURE VARIABILITY, and, importantly, CLIMATE AND WINE QUALITY. For details of climate on a smaller scale, see MESOCLIMATE and MICROCLIMATE.

CLIMATE AND WINE QUALITY. Climate of course influences the styles (as opposed to quality) of wine that an area can produce best. At the extremes a climate can be so unsuitable for grape-growing that to produce good wines regularly is impossible or, at best, uneconomic. But within the normal limits of viticulture a wide range of styles is possible, ranging from the light, delicate table wines that are in general best produced in cool viticultural climates, to the full bodied, sweet FORTIFIED wines that need warm and very sunny climates.

Although the quality of any one of these wines can be judged only against that of others of comparable style, there are criteria for quality that are valid across the full range of styles. Most important is fruit FLAVOUR and AROMA, derived from GRAPE JUICE, WINE-MAKING techniques, and from storage conditions. There should also be a balance of ACIDS, ALCOHOL, and PHENOLICS which is appropriate for the wine's style and commercial purpose.

All these things can be influenced by factors other than climate but climate dominates. And, as viticultural and wine-making methods are progressively refined, so climate might increasingly be expected to govern the remaining differences in both wine quality and wine style. Climatic influences are therefore crucial to future developments in the wine industry. For more detail than appears below, see Gladstones.

Temperature

Average mean TEMPERATURE during ripening strongly influences potential wine style. Defining grape maturity as that appropriate to making dry table wines, mean temperatures averaging above about 21 °C/70 °F in the final month to maturity lead to a rapid loss of MALIC ACID from the grapes, and to lower TOTAL ACIDITY and generally higher PH in the juice. Conversely, an average mean temperature below about 15 °C in the final month minimizes acid loss to the point that acid levels may be too high. There is also often a risk that the grapes will not ripen fully at all. Becker gives examples of this for inferior sites at the cool limit of viticulture in Germany.

Shortcomings in juice and must composition that result from ripening (or failing to ripen fully) outside optimum temperature limits can usually be overcome to some extent by wine-making practice. Nevertheless the necessary measures can seldom substitute fully for having a perfect natural balance in the grapes to start with. And that, for dry table wines, is most readily achieved when moderate YIELDS and good vine CANOPY MANAGEMENT are combined with average mean temperatures during the last month of ripening of between about 15 and 21 °C.

Within that range the natural styles vary from light, fresh, and aromatic at the cooler end, to full bodied and full flavoured at the warmer end. Regions with the coolest ripening temperatures produce almost exclusively delicate white wines; those with warm ripening, full bodied wines that might be either white or red. Thus 15 to 16 °C is a typical average mean for the final ripening month in the warmer vineyards of Germany and Switzerland; in Alsace, Champagne, and the cooler parts of the Loire valley in France; in the Willamette Valley of Oregon, USA; and near the north east coasts of Tasmania and the South Island of New Zealand. Average ripening month means of 18 to 20 °C are typical for Bordeaux and the northern Rhône in France, and for many of the best areas for full bodied table wines in California and Australia. Beyond that, average means from 21 to about 24 °C during the ripening month are best suited to sweet fortified wines, provided that there is also enough sunlight (see below). However, with appropriate ACIDIFICATION and REFRIGERATION, table wine quality can still be quite good at these ripening temperatures, provided also that TEMPERATURE VARIABILITY during ripening is sufficiently moderate (see below).

Average conditions during ripening cannot be estimated directly from raw climatic statistics, because they depend in part on when ripening occurs. That, in turn, depends on the heat requirements of individual VINE VARIETIES to reach maturity. Some are early maturing and have a relatively low total heat requirement to reach maturity. These will ripen successfully in cool climates, and in hot climates ripen very early. Late maturing varieties need a long, warm growing season and a high heat total to ripen at all. Gladstones (ch. 7) classifies the main wine grape varieties into eight maturing groups.

Beyond that, individual grape varieties differ in their optimum ripening temperatures for quality. Many of the early maturing varieties are best when ripened under relatively cool conditions. The berries of some of them are very sensitive to heat, particularly red wine varieties such as Pinot Noir. Such varieties nevertheless need warmth during ripening to give enough colour and body for red wines, a contradiction which explains their limited and specialized climatic adaptations. Other equally early maturing varieties, usually for white wine, can tolerate considerable heat during ripening and can give good quality across a wide range of climates. Chardonnay, Verdelho, and to a lesser extent Sauvignon Blanc are good examples. Late maturing varieties such as Grenache, Mourvèdre, Carignan, and Muscat of Alexandria need not only high heat totals to reach maturity, but also moderately high temperatures during ripening for maximum wine quality.

Temperature variability

Whereas potential wine style depends broadly on average mean temperature during ripening, quality appears to be related at least as much to short-term temperature variability both between night and day, and from day to day. The less variable (or more equable) the ripening temperatures, the better is likely to be the wine quality.

Ecological evidence for this can be seen in the regional and site characteristics of the world's acknowledged great vineyards. All provide equable temperature through the growing season, and especially during ripening. Furthermore, the best individual sites have features of both topography and soil type that accentuate equability still further, chiefly by maintaining the greatest possible warmth at vine and fruit height through the night and under temporary cloud cover. See TOPOGRAPHY, TERROIR, STONES AND ROCKS, MESOCLIMATE.

From the viewpoint of the vine the reasons are clear enough. Highly variable temperatures result in greater damage, both by frosts after budburst and by extremes of heat in summer. For fruit quality alone there is a further theoretical argument. The compounds responsible for COLOUR, flavour, and aroma in the grapes and wine are formed from sugars by chemical reactions depending on ENZYMES, which in temperate plants such as the vine appear to be most active at about 20–4 °C (68–75 °F). Activity is much less marked both above and below this range. Periods of extremely high temperatures can also cause permanent enzyme inactivation, and partial or total failure of flavour ripening. Even in the absence of this, high day temperatures might be expected to accelerate the loss of volatile FLAVOUR COMPOUNDS from the ripening grapes, as well as loss of acidity. Low night temperatures, on the other hand, will slow metabolism and the formation of all flavour, aroma, and pigment compounds, while at the same time encouraging the accumulation of SUGAR IN GRAPES and therefore potential wine alcohol. The combined result is an optimum temperature during ripening of about 20 °C to combine suitably moderate sugar and alcohol contents with the fullest flavour and adequate natural acidity for table wine. Mean temperatures a little lower are appropriate for light, freshly acid, and aromatic wine styles. But the important thing is that during ripening there should be as little variation as possible around the respective optimum temperatures through the 24 hours, and from day to day. The berries then reach flavour ripeness rapidly, while retaining flavour compounds and a high natural acid level; juice POTASSIUM accumulation and pH levels are minimized; and because maturation is rapid, there is least chance of the berries suffering any kind of damage or decay before they reach that total flavour ripeness that is essential for making great wines.

Continentality

CONTINENTALITY is measured as the range between the average mean temperate for the hottest month and that of the coldest month. Despite its role in CLIMATE CLASSIFICATION, the implications of continentality for wine style and quality remain speculative. It has been suggested that the steeply falling temperatures and sunlight hours of the cooler continental climates towards the end of grape ripening could have advantages for SWEET WINES. Such conditions allow final ripening and juice concentration under the influence of NOBLE ROT infection in equably low temperatures, thereby conserving both natural acid and volatile flavour compounds. Against that, the margin between full ripening and not ripening at all is narrow, leading to marked vintage variation with only normal climatic fluctuations.

'Maritime' climates (those with a low index of continentality) have a more prolonged and thus generally more reliable period available for ripening. This may give a higher average quality, although perhaps without the potential for certain styles of sweet table wines as described above for the best continental seasons.

Sunlight

Contrary to common perception, cool viticultural climates are probably more limited by their low temperatures than by lack of SUNLIGHT. Heat as summed over the season determines which grape varieties, if any, reach a satisfactory degree of PHYSIOLOGICAL RIPENESS. Sunlight duration acts mainly by controlling sugar in grapes and therefore potential wine alcohol content at a given stage of physiological ripening. In practice, however, the relative contributions of sunlight and temperature are hard to distinguish, because low temperatures and low sunlight hours tend to go together. Poor seasons in cool climates are usually both sunless and cold.

Paradoxically, sunlight duration appears to limit wine style and (sometimes) quality fully as much in warm as in cool climates, even though their sunlight hours over the season are usually greater. The explanation lies in rates of RESPIRATION. Vines respire more sugar at high temperatures for their normal metabolism, but do not photosynthesize any faster; they therefore need more sunlight hours to generate a sugar surplus for ripening the fruit. It is why, for instance, Australia's often cloudy HUNTER VALLEY produces only table wines despite being very warm; and why mild to warm, but cloudy, regions of northern NEW ZEALAND such as Auckland produce predominantly light table wines. Similar factors appear to apply through much of central and northern Italy.

Regions with unlimited sunlight hours and intensity are nevertheless not necessarily at an advantage because they commonly suffer from excessive temperature variability (see above) and low relative humidities and strong moisture stresses (see below). But in the absence of these adverse factors, ample sunlight does appear to be universally beneficial. A strong and constant sugar flow to the ripening berries assures not only their sweetness and sufficient alcohol in the wine, but also that colour, flavour, and aroma compounds are not limited by a lack of sugar substrate for their formation.

Timing of the sunlight is important. Studies such as that of Gadille in Burgundy show that the most critical period for quality is around the start of ripening (August in most European viticultural regions). Good conditions then assure an ample reserve of sugar in the vine, both for early conversion in the leaves and berries into flavour and aroma compounds, or their precursors, and so that sugar and flavour ripening of the berries can continue unabated under the cooler and less sunny conditions normally encountered later.

Rainfall

The general implications of rain for viticulture are discussed under RAINFALL.

Rain early in the season can be beneficial or otherwise for quality, depending on how it affects vegetative VIGOUR, FRUIT SET, and the balance between the two. Much rain after fruit set can reduce quality if, in conjunction with other factors, it encourages the vines to remain too vegetative into the ripening period.

Associated lack of sunshine around the start of ripening appears especially detrimental to quality (see above).

Opinions differ as to optimum rainfall amounts during ripening. Most agree that any severe WATER STRESS at that stage is deleterious. On the other hand, heavy rain can lead to temporary juice dilution and sometimes to incomplete ripening, especially if accompanied by lack of sunshine. Wet ripening periods commonly signal poor vintages. Heavy rain close to maturity is especially damaging, because it can cause berry splitting and subsequent fungal infection of the bunches (see BOTRYTIS BUNCH ROT). This occurs most typically in certain varieties with tight bunches, such as Chenin Blanc and Zinfandel, and where the vines were under drought stress prior to the rain. Hail at this time can be totally devastating.

Relative humidity and evaporation

Strong evaporative demands place the vines under water stress which, in extreme cases, can cause leaf loss and substantial collapse of vine metabolism. Obvious fruit damage often follows through excessive exposure to the overhead sun. Milder moisture stress can still reduce PHOTOSYNTHESIS and sugar production in the leaves, and hence reduce both quantity and fruit quality. Mechanisms are discussed more fully under EVAPORATION and HUMIDITY.

Virtually all of the world's acknowledged great table wines come from regions with moderately high relative humidities and low evaporation. This is partly because of their lack of stress (see above) and through their usually restricted temperature variability. Gladstones, however, postulates a further mechanism which is based on general principles of crop physiology, but has not yet been directly documented in grapevines: the greater uptake and TRANSPIRATION of water per unit of growth and yield by vines growing in arid atmospheres will be paralleled, to at least some degree, by a greater uptake of POTASSIUM per unit of yield; and thence, other things being equal, by a higher potassium concentration in the fruit.

Excess potassium in the grapes and juice leads directly during fermentation to loss of TARTARIC ACID, and thus to high pH in the wine. Results include dull wine colours and flavours, and an enhanced liability to OXIDATION and BACTERIAL SPOILAGE, precisely the features for which table wines from arid climates have traditionally been criticized.

These defects have commonly been attributed to the IRRIGATION usually needed in such climates. However, Smart and others have now shown that the main disadvantage of irrigation lies in the canopy crowding and internal leaf SHADING caused by the extra vegetative growth that follows, unless matching improvements are made in trellising and CANOPY MANAGEMENT. With proper canopy management, judicious irrigation in a dry climate can in fact improve both yield and fruit quality. But that does not fully overcome the problem of low relative humidity and strong evaporation. The broad evidence suggests that these can still directly limit grape and wine quality in such climates.

Wind

The effects of WIND STRESS are largely on vine health and yield, via reduced disease incidence on the one hand, and closure of the leaf STOMATA and especially direct physical damage on the other. Dry winds can probably also reduce wine quality through increased evaporation, as explained above.

On the other hand, the daily alternating land and sea breezes of the summer months that occur with some regularity in coastal regions of the dry continents markedly benefit both vine physiological functioning and wine quality. They are especially important in Australia and west coastal United States, and are doubly advantageous. Dry land winds at night and in the early morning reduce the risk of FUNGAL DISEASES. Then mild, humid afternoon sea breezes reduce stresses on the vines and greatly improve day conditions for photosynthesis and ripening. The same applies on a reduced scale around inland lakes and rivers. See TOPOGRAPHY and TERROIR.

Summary

Many climatic elements influence grape and wine quality, and no existing climate perfectly fulfils all the requirements. Indeed, some desirable climatic elements tend towards being mutually exclusive. The best viticultural climates are therefore anomalous and rare.

Two climatic types appear to offer the best compromises for both viticulture and wine quality. The first is that with cool to mild growing season temperatures and uniform to predominantly summer rainfall, such as is found in western and central Europe. Within that context, the best vineyard sites have specialized MESOCLIMATES with more than usual sunshine, warmth, and length of frost-free period. Such sites are often found on sheltered east-facing slopes behind major hill or mountain ranges, as in the RHINE valley or BURGUNDY; or else close to west- or south-facing coasts. Examples of the latter are BORDEAUX and the lower LOIRE valley of France, and the northern shores of Lake Geneva in SWITZERLAND, and Lake Balaton in HUNGARY.

The second broad climatic type, extending more or less contiguously from the first, comprises the cooler and more humid of the summer-dry MEDITERRANEAN CLIMATES, whenever summer heat is regularly moderated by afternoon sea breezes, and irrigation can be supplied in late summer if needed and permitted. Advantages over the uniform and summer-rainfall climates include more reliable summer sunshine and less risk of excessive rain and humidity during the ripening period. In its warmer parts, this climate type merges into that most suitable for fortified wines, as in the LANGUEDOC-ROUSSILLON of southern France, the DOURO valley of Portugal, WESTERN AUSTRALIA, and SOUTH AUSTRALIA.

The world's greatest table wines have traditionally come from the cool to mild temperate climates with uniform to summer-dominant rainfall. Partly this was because the limitations of frost and lack of warmth automatically confined viticulture there to the most equable mesoclimates, which happened also to have the best temperature regimes for wine quality. Mediterranean-type climates had fewer such absolute limitations, enabling viticulture to be practised on qualitatively inferior (but often more productive) sites. Indeed, sites with deep and water-retentive soil were largely essential to avoid extreme water stress in summer.

Better knowledge of the climate and terroir requirements

for wine quality, together with improved irrigation technology and canopy management, is now changing this situation. Production of high-quality table wines is rapidly spreading into mediterranean climates, a movement which, it has been argued, may in future be further assisted by increasing concentrations of CARBON DIOXIDE in the atmosphere.

See also COOL CLIMATE VITICULTURE and CLIMATE CHANGE.

J.G. & R.E.S.

Becker, N., 'Site climate effects on development, fruit maturation and harvest quality', in R. E. Smart, *et al.* (eds.), *Proceedings of the Second International Symposium for Cool Climate Viticulture and Oenology: 11–15 January 1988 Auckland, New Zealand* (Auckland, 1988).

Gadille, R., *Le Vignoble de la Côte Bourguignonne* (Paris, 1967), cited by H. Johnson, *The World Atlas of Wine* (London, 1971).

Gladstones, J., *Viticulture and Environment* (Adelaide, 1992).

CLIMATE CHANGE, or **climatological history**. The lifetimes of individual vines, are usually measured in decades, and those of vineyards or vineyard areas often in centuries. The prospects of long-term climatic change are therefore crucial to viticultural planning.

Past changes in the growing season temperatures have almost certainly played a role in shaping central and western European viticulture, from Roman times onwards. Pfister and Gladstones have attempted to trace these changes in more detail than is feasible here, on the basis of recorded vintage dates and other historical evidence as described by writers such as Lamb.

Viticulture was first introduced into north western Europe by the Romans in the 3rd and 4th centuries AD, spreading northwards and reaching the MOSEL-SAAR-RUWER region of Germany, the Meuse valley of southern BELGIUM, and the south of England. This appears to have corresponded with the time of greatest warmth in the era of Ancient ROME. Following the cooling and climate deterioration of the succeeding Dark Ages, re-establishment started about the 8th century, which appears to have been the beginning of a renewed period of warmth. This reached its peak in the High Middle Ages of the 12th and early 13th centuries, when northern viticulture flourished (see ENGLAND, PARIS, NETHERLANDS, and LA ROCHELLE). According to Pfister the average vintage was nearly a month earlier than in the 20th century, and it can be estimated that growing season temperatures must have been at least 1.0 °C/1.8 °F higher.

Viticulture in northern Germany reached its furthest recorded extent a little later, in the 15th and early 16th centuries. Weinhold described Thuringia and the Electorate of Saxony (today's SACHSEN) as then being flourishing wine provinces, with vineyards ringing towns such as Erfurt and Dresden (see GERMAN HISTORY and the map on p. 431). Viticulture even extended into the Baltic states of Holstein, Mecklenburg, Pomerania, and West and East Prussia.

Temperatures in the west had by then already started to fall from their medieval heights, however. Following some temporary climatic upsets in the second half of the 13th century, a sharp temperature drop in the early 14th century brought famine and the Black Death in its wake, and contributed to a southward contraction of viticulture in many parts. Subsequent climatic recovery was followed by a further major cold period covering most of the first half of the 15th century, when the then extensive vineyards of the Paris region were badly hit. Further cold, still worse than before, lasted throughout the second half of the 16th century, and occasioned the first major viticultural retreat from northern Germany. It marked the beginning of the so-called Little Ice Age, which lasted, with intermissions, until about 1830. Perhaps Shakespeare had particular reason when, in 1598, he had the bibulous Sir John Falstaff complain so bitterly on the subject of 'thin potations', and enjoin his listeners to addict themselves instead to Spanish SACK. (Such climate changes may well also have helped to develop the market for the rich, sweet wines of the Mediterranean; see VENICE, MALVASIA, SANTORINI, GREECE.)

Following what must have been a relatively warm half-century up to about 1660, during which CHAMPAGNE flourished as a growing producer of red wines, the coldest spell of the Little Ice Age came in the last decades of the 17th century. This was the time when the English river Thames froze repeatedly, and ice fairs were held on it. BORDEAUX had a run of four vintage disasters (1692–5). Champagne started making sparkling white wine from its Pinot Noir grapes, instead of the still red wines for which it had previously been famous. Average temperatures were probably 1.0 to 1.5 °C (1.8 to 2.7 °F) lower than now. Perhaps more than politics was involved in the fact that this was also when England started to look to PORTUGAL for its wines, instead of France, culminating in the second Methuen Treaty of 1703. It was also at this time that the sweet wines of CONSTANTIA, COTNARI, and TOKAY were so particularly prized.

The most recent southward retreat of European viticulture came following the severe winter freeze of 1708/9, just as the seasons had started to improve again (although Lamb believes that the winters continued, on average, to be cold through much of the rest of the 18th century). A substantial proportion of vines were killed by WINTER FREEZE and many of the more northerly vineyards were not replanted. From then on French viticultural expansion was in southern areas, such as Bordeaux. The northern limits of German viticulture finally became fixed more or less as at present.

There were to be no further major temperature drops in the European viticultural regions, apart from one relatively brief and mild one in the second and early third decades of the 19th century, the 'years of the Dickensian winters'. Temperature records since 1850 have shown a progressive increase of about 0.5 °C/0.9 °F world-wide, although the reality of this for vineyard and other non-urban areas has been disputed (below). Minor, medium-term fluctuations of temperature are well documented, however. The 1860s and early 1870s, which produced the great PRE-PHYLLOXERA vintages, were markedly warm. The late 1870s and 1880s were cooler, and it seems very likely that the poor European vintages of the period, widely blamed on the new phylloxera-

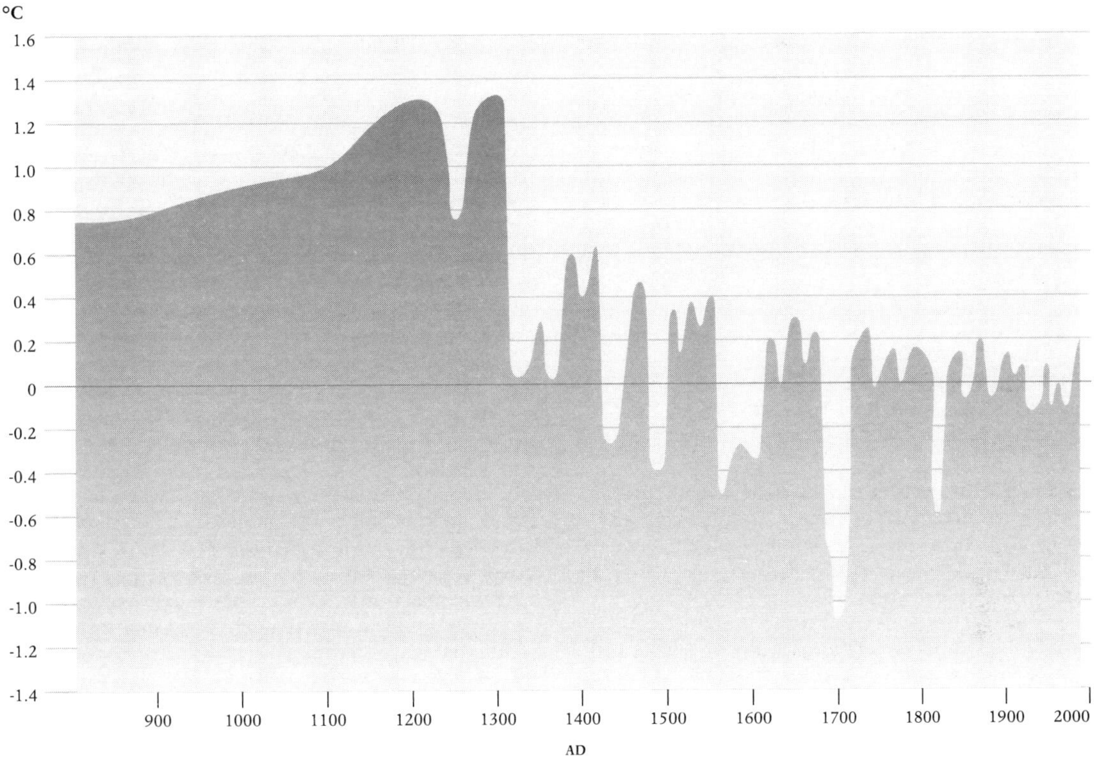

Climate change: estimated vine growing season temperatures in central and western Europe since AD 800, relative to the average for the first half of the 20th century.

resistant ROOTSTOCKS, were partly due to the climate. Warmer and cooler periods of up to a decade or so have since then been associated with predominantly good and poor vintages respectively, culminating in the warm and generally outstanding decade of the 1980s. Penning-Rowsell documents the Bordeaux vintages up to that time.

The future course of TEMPERATURES, locally and worldwide, cannot fail to have a profound influence on viticulture. One lesson to be learned from history is that growing season temperatures can drop suddenly, and remain low for years or decades. The effects on viticulture towards its cool limit can be drastic.

What, then, of the immediate future? A study of recent medium-term temperature fluctuations, and their possible causes, suggests that the warm 1980s probably represented a temperature peak. If so, a moderate cyclic fall could follow. Students of longer-term fluctuations have further predicted the possibility of a full return to Little Ice Age conditions, for at least a period, sometime early in the 21st century.

Against this must be balanced the forecasts of global warming due to a 'greenhouse effect', caused by increasing atmospheric concentrations of CARBON DIOXIDE and various other gases produced by fossil fuel burning and industry. The most recent consensus forecast by viridomologists (proponents of the greenhouse effect) has been for a temperature rise of some 2 °C/3.6 °F by the mid 21st century, which, if fulfilled, will override even the largest natural fluctuations. The expected result would then be a poleward migration of viticulture, to and probably beyond the limits reached in the Middle Ages. Regions such as England, northern France and Germany, Oregon, Washington, and British Colombia, southern Argentina and Chile, and Tasmania and southern New Zealand would become the main table wine producers of the mid to late 21st century under such conditions. Kenny and Harrison present detailed projections for Europe. Existing warm to hot viticultural regions will presumably become less tenable, especially for table wines. Warm, summer rainfall climates, such as the east coast of Australia, could suffer doubly, with an increase in RAINFALL during the ripening period and therefore in the risk of VINE DISEASE.

Gladstones argues a contrary case. He finds no sign in recent viticultural history of the 0.5 °C global warming claimed to have occurred already, and sides with those who believe the apparent warming has been due to a disproportionate placing of thermometers in growing towns and cities, which create their own local warming. He maintains that, if anything, the record of European vintages suggests a slight average cooling since 1850 in the open countryside. He further argues that any future temperature increases due to rising atmospheric carbon dioxide concentrations are likely to be small; that the main effect of more carbon dioxide will be to improve both vine YIELD and wine quality; and that the greatest benefits will be in warm and sunny climates. Typical of the regions expected to benefit most in these circumstances are southern France, Portugal, California, Chile, mainland Australia, and South Africa. Indeed, they may already have done so.

J.G.

Gladstones, J., *Viticulture and Environment* (Adelaide, 1992).
Kenny, G. J., and Harrison, P. A., 'The effects of climate variability and change on grape suitability in Europe', *Journal of Wine Research*, 3 (1992), 163–83.
Lamb, H. H., *Climate, Past, Present and Future*, ii: *Climatic History and the Future* (London, 1977).
Penning-Rowsell, E., *The Wines of Bordeaux* (6th edn., London, 1989).
Pfister, C., 'Variations in the spring–summer climate of Central Europe from the High Middle Ages to 1980', in W. Wanner and U. Siegenthaler (eds.), *Long and Short Term Variability of Climate* (Berlin, 1988).
Weinhold, R., *Vivat Bacchus: A History of the Vine and its Wine*, trans. from the German by N. Jones (Watford, 1978).

CLIMATE CLASSIFICATION, the description and grouping of climates for viticultural purposes.

History

The first influential scientific study of viticultural climates was that of the French researcher A. P. de Candolle in the mid 19th century, a time when reliable climatic data were just starting to become available. De Candolle observed that the spring start of vine growth in European vineyards corresponded closely with the dates on which average mean temperature reached 10 °C/50 °F. On that basis he proposed that useful heat for vine growth and RIPENING could be measured by the amount that actual mean temperatures exceed 10 °C. A summation of the excesses (if any) for all individual days would give a measure of the total usable heat for the year.

Subsequent French research has paid surprisingly little attention to developing systematic methods, or models, for classifying viticultural climates (Seguin). Perhaps this is understandable, in that French viticulture is long established in its given environments. Because it has not traditionally sought to expand to new environments, there is little need to establish general principles on which to base such expansion. Some ideas on the role of day length at high latitudes, associated with researchers such as J. Branas and P. Huglin, are mentioned under LATITUDE. Leaving them aside, however, it is hardly surprising to find that the greatest interest in this field has been in the NEW WORLD, where the need for principles to evaluate potential new viticultural environments has been both pressing and obvious.

California heat summation

The first extensive practical use of de Candolle's method was in California, where AMERINE and Winkler, in 1944, delineated five viticultural regions on the basis of their Fahrenheit temperature summations over 50 °F/10 °C. One advance over de Candolle was to confine the summations to an assumed vine growth and ripening season extending from 1 April to 31 October. The resulting comparisons are more relevant and reliable than those taking in all months of the year.

The California summations (like most others) are in practice calculated from monthly averages, each month's total being its average excess of the mean over 50 °F, multiplied by the number of days in the month. Amerine and Winkler's five regions, in terms of the total Fahrenheit 'degree days' for the seven months, are as follows.

Region I (the coolest) having less than 2,500 ° days F;
Region II, 2,500–3,000 ° days F;
Region III, 3,000–3,500 ° days F;
Region IV, 3,500–4,000 ° days F;
Region V, over 4,000 ° days F.

Regions I and II are found in general to produce California's best dry table wines, with light to medium body and good natural balance. Region III produces full bodied dry and sweet wines. Region IV is reckoned to be best for FORTIFIED wines, with table wines mainly inferior. Region V, typified by the irrigated inland valleys, such as the hottest parts of SAN JOAQUIN VALLEY, is best for TABLE GRAPES and DRYING GRAPES, producing mainly low-quality table wines.

Although successful in California, Amerine and Winkler's system, sometimes called heat summation (or simply by Winkler's name), is not fully accepted elsewhere. We now know that it works well in California partly because temperatures there are quite closely correlated with other climatic factors of possibly equal importance to viticulture and wine quality: directly with TEMPERATURE VARIABILITY and total SUNLIGHT, and inversely with HUMIDITY (see also CLIMATE AND WINE QUALITY). Temperature alone thus gives an adequate index of all the relevant climatic variables. The correlations are much less close in most other environments. In some they are largely absent: in east coastal Australia and New Zealand, and in central and northern Italy, for instance. In these regions temperature alone is a poor indicator of their viticultural climates.

Some other systems based on temperature have been simpler. Prescott found that the average mean temperature of the warmest month gave essentially as good a climatic indication as the seasonal temperature summation. Average mean temperature for the whole seven months (see COOL CLIMATES) likewise gives a reasonable measure of growing season temperature regimes. All such indices, however, suffer from the same shortcomings as temperature summations.

An Australian alternative

Recent major proposals for viticultural climate classification have sought to place them on broader bases. The most widely used is that of Smart and Dry, developed for use in Australia.

This involves five separate dimensions, but is still tolerably simple and workable. Following Prescott's earlier Australian work, Smart and Dry preferred to use the simple statistic of average mean temperature for January (July in the northern hemisphere) as a measure of usable heat. It is complemented by an index of CONTINENTALITY (the difference between mean summer and winter temperatures) to show the amplitude of swings in temperatures through the 12 months, together with indices of sunlight and water relations. The five elements of the classification are:

- Average mean January (July) temperature (five categories);
- continentality (five categories);
- total seasonal sunlight hours (four categories);
- aridity, based on the difference between rainfall and 0.5 of measured EVAPORATION (four categories);
- relative humidity, as measured at 0900 hours (four categories).

The resulting five-way classification gives a reasonable overview of viticultural climates, if still hardly detailed enough for some of the more important practical uses. It does not, for example, incorporate the possibly important factor of temperature variability.

This writer's own proposal goes beyond simple categories, and is too complex to cover in full here. Briefly, a method to predict an average ripening date for any defined grape maturity type in any environment is developed. Like Amerine and Winkler's method (above) it employs growing season temperature summations over a 10 °C/50 °F base, but with refinements to improve the fit to known vine behaviour across existing viticultural environments. These entail:

- imposing an upper limit (19 °C) on the monthly average mean temperatures, beyond which no further increases are credited;
- a correction factor proportional to the average day length of each month (long days giving greater biological effectiveness for a given greater mean temperature; see LATITUDE);
- a correction for each month's average daily temperature range (a narrow range resulting in greater effectiveness, for a given mean).

Having arrived at a predicted ripening date, average conditions of temperature, sunshine, rainfall, and relative humidity for the final ripening month can be estimated. Conditions then are held to be those most influential in determining the quality characteristics of grapes and therefore of the potential wine (or at least to be sufficiently indicative of them for practical purposes). Calculated separately for each grape maturity group, the ripening month conditions become the direct basis for evaluating or comparing environments as to their likely grape variety adaptations, potential for wine quality, and most natural wine styles. J.G.

Amerine, M. A., and Winkler, A. J., 'Composition and quality of musts and wines of California grapes', *Hilgardia*, 15 (1944), 493–575.

Gladstones, J., *Viticulture and Environment* (Adelaide, 1992).

Prescott, J. A., 'The climatology of the vine (Vitis vinifera). 3. A comparison of France and Australia on the basis of the warmest month', *Transactions of the Royal Society of South Australia*, 93 (1969), 7–15.

Seguin, B., 'Synthèse des travaux de recherche sur l'influence du climat, du microclimat et du sol sur la physiologie de la vigne, avec quelques éléments sur les arbres fruitiers', *Vignes & Vins*, special number *Agrométéorologie et Vigne* (Sept. 1982), 13–21.

Smart, R. E., and Dry, P. R., 'A climatic classification for Australian viticultural regions', *Australian Grapegrower and Winemaker*, 196 (1980), 8, 10, 16.

CLIMATE EFFECTS ON VINE DISEASES. The climate has a major effect on VINE DISEASES, and indeed is a major factor determining where grapes are grown worldwide. The most commercially important vine diseases are due to fungi, and these are normally encouraged by warm, humid, and rainy conditions. Most of the world's viticulture is therefore carried out in regions with dry summers, the Mediterranean area being a classic example. However, as the risk of fungal disease decreases, the likelihood of DROUGHT and, in those parts of Europe where irrigation is prohibited (such as Spain), the effects of drought can be substantial. Some regions such as California, Chile, and Western Australia can be so dry that DOWNY MILDEW, one of the worst vine fungal diseases, is not present at all.

RAINFALL (and sometimes dew) has a major effect on diseases. Water is important for spore germination and dispersal by splashing, as for downy mildew and DEAD ARM, and so a rainy spring can cause epidemics of both these diseases. Rain near the time of harvest causes grape berries to split, and so many BUNCH ROT fungi and bacteria can gain entry and ruin the fruit. Many fungi spores such as those of BOTRYTIS BUNCH ROT and downy mildew germinate in high humidity. The fungal disease POWDERY MILDEW develops in the shade of dense vine canopies, and is also encouraged by overcast weather.

TEMPERATURE is a major factor in disease development and spread, with temperatures of 20 to 27 °C favour the germination of powdery mildew spores. Freezing winter temperatures can cause vine trunks to split, allowing the entry of the CROWN GALL bacterium.

WIND is important in spreading diseases: for example BACTERIAL BLIGHT is spread in wet, windy weather.

Climate has such a large effect on wine quality because of disease, and there is no more important example than that of botrytis bunch rot. Intermittent rainy, humid, and warm weather near the time of harvest causes anguish to the grapegrower and wine-maker alike, because of the risk of losing both yield and quality. Furthermore, costs of grape production are higher when the weather induces disease. R.E.S.

Pearson, R. C., and Goheen, A. C., *Compendium of Grape Diseases* (St Paul, Minn., 1988).

CLONAL SELECTION, one of the two principal means of improving a vine variety (the other being the elimination of VIRUS DISEASES). Clonal selection is the practice of selecting a superior plant in the vineyard (typically from the point of view of YIELD or fruit RIPENESS) and then taking cuttings from this vine for PROPAGATION.

New grapevines, in common with many other perennial

crops, are produced by vegetative propagation, that is by using cuttings or buds, whereas agricultural field crops are multiplied by seed. Cuttings from the one vine are genetically identical, whereas seedlings are different one from another. Indeed, sexual reproduction leading to the production of seedlings is the means by which NEW VARIETIES are created. In vegetative propagation, each bud from a so-called 'mother vine' gives rise to a plant of the same CLONE.

Clonal selection was first demonstrated in Germany in 1926, and has been most widely practised in that country. Other European countries have also developed clonal selection initiatives, but the practice is less well developed in some countries of the New World.

Clonal selection depends on the fact that adjacent vines in a vineyard may be different, sometimes discernibly different. Differences on this scale would not normally be expected from soil variation. There are two possible explanations: the first being a difference in genetic make-up between vines; the second being a difference in the incidence of virus diseases in the vines. Spontaneous MUTATIONS can sometimes occur and cause small but perceptible changes to a vine's genetic make-up. The disease agents are transmitted by careless selection of the BUDWOOD or ROOTSTOCK material used at GRAFTING (and thus a human influence), but it may also reflect the effect of viruses and/or VIROIDS transmitted by NEMATODES or INSECTS. In any event, virus infection can have a major impact on yield, fruit ripening, and wine quality.

There has been disagreement between viticultural scientists working in this area as to the relative importance of genetic difference *vis-à-vis* virus diseases. Professor Helmut BECKER, an acknowledged authority on clonal selection based at the GEISENHEIM Institute in Germany, argued for the genetic difference principle, while the virologists led by Austin Goheen of the University of California at DAVIS believed that virus infection was the more important. (More recently the possibility has been raised that differing viroid incidence may be responsible for clonal variation.) Most workers in the field would now agree that both influences are important, but these views have had significant consequences. For example, some European centres have been slow to test for and eliminate virus diseases, whereas in California the emphasis has been on virus elimination, typically by HEAT TREATMENT, rather than on clonal selection and evaluation in the field (which has its disadvantages for California's replanting programme necessitated in the 1990s by PHYLLOXERA). In countries such as Australia, New Zealand, and South Africa, efforts to improve vines acknowledge both viewpoints.

The process of clonal selection is necessarily long and requires considerable investment of resources. To make reliable field selections requires several years of records (up to nine are used in Germany) followed by comparative trials of many different clones of the one variety for evaluation. After waiting three years for the first harvest, five to 10 more years are necessary to monitor yields and fruit ripeness. These trials are often conducted in several locations and with several rootstocks. Clonal selection should also involve making trial wine to assure trueness to varietal type. Selected clones may not therefore be released until 15 or more years after the initial selection in the field. And, given the possibilities of both mutation and the spread of viruses by natural means, clonal selection should be an ongoing process. There has already been a release of second generation clones in Germany; fields originally planted to one clone have been selected again for 'clones of clones'.

There is no doubt that clonal selection has played an important part in improving both yield and wine quality from modern vineyards. When grafting became popular in the 1880s to overcome phylloxera, virus diseases were inadvertently spread. Many vineyards of both the Old World and the New World planted as late as the 1960s contained off-types, rogue vines, and virus diseases. As more healthy and true to type planting material becomes available as a result of clonal selection, then these problems disappear. Many reputable nurserymen world-wide will provide only plants propagated from clonally selected rootstocks and scions.

Mechanisms for clonal selection and propagation vary from country to country. Generally the studies are conducted by government-funded scientists (although it is not unusual for a leading Bordeaux château, for example, to be doing its own clonal selection from vines naturally adapted to that property). In France the extent to which planting material was infected by viruses up to the mid 1940s led to the formation of the Institut des Vins de Consommation Courante (IVCC). This organization and its affiliates test selected clones and supply CERTIFIED PLANTING MATERIAL. Certification in Germany was introduced voluntarily after the First World War, and the scheme later became law. The EUROPEAN UNION adopted guidelines for propagation material through the EU in the early 1990s. In Australia, South Africa, and New Zealand there are well-established VINE IMPROVEMENT programmes utilizing clonal selection as well as virus elimination.

For many vine varieties, the differences in appearance and performance between clones with the same virus status is small. This suggests that genetic differences are generally minor and that the mutation rate is low. Some varieties, such as Pinot Noir, show extreme variation between clones, which suggest that multiple selections were initially made from the wild and/or a high mutation rate.

It is difficult to understand the effect of clonal selection on commercial wine quality since so many vineyards are still of mixed clones. While most Old World countries have a wide range of clones available, sometimes, because of limited importations, a New World country might have only a few for any one variety. An extreme example is Sauvignon Blanc in New Zealand, where all commercial plantings up until the early 1990s can be traced to one clone imported from the United States of America. Some producers are critical of the limited availability of only improved clones from nurserymen. They argue that a range of clones is desirable from a wine quality point of view, and that virus-free, high-yielding clones impair wine quality. As with much debate about wine quality, it is difficult to separate the perception from truth. Certainly there is concern among most clonal selectors to guarantee that wine quality is enhanced rather than diminished by clonal selection, by rigorous field testing and winemaking studies. Unfortunately, some improved planting material was not thoroughly evaluated before release which has fuelled suspicion about wine quality implications. R.E.S.

Clone in a viticultural context is a population of vines all derived by vegetative PROPAGATION from cuttings or buds from a single vine called a MOTHER VINE. Different clones of the same VINE VARIETY come from different mother vines, and may differ one from another because of genetic differences due to MUTATION, and/or different VIRUS DISEASE or VIROID status (because such diseases are transmitted in cuttings and by GRAFTING).

Vine nurseries may sell a range of different clones of each vine variety, individually identified by numbers and/or names. In Germany, for example, there is a formal process of clonal evaluation and a systematic numbering system. Normally government agencies are involved in selection, evaluation, and distribution to nurserymen, and often the availability of clones and their acceptance varies regionally. Some clones are so outstanding that they become internationally distributed. Clones of Riesling from GEISENHEIM in Germany are examples of this. In the 1990s there was considerable interest in Burgundian clones of Chardonnay and, particularly, Pinot Noir, which can vary considerably between different clones.

By the late 1980s many quality-conscious wine producers were wary of being dependent on a single clone of a particular variety.

See also CLONAL SELECTION. R.E.S. & B.G.C.

Galet, P., *Cépages et vignobles de France* (2nd edn., Montpellier, 1990).
Mullins, M. G., Bouquet, A., and Williams, L., *Biology of the Grapevine* (Cambridge, 1992).

Clos is French for enclosed, and any vineyard described as a Clos should be enclosed, generally by a wall. This is a particularly common term in Burgundy, but is also used elsewhere. Similarly, the term CUVE CLOSE refers to the need to used a sealed tank for this bulk method of sparkling winemaking. The term is also associated with the most ambitious small producers of PRIORATO.

Clos de la Roche, great red GRAND CRU in Burgundy's CÔTE D'OR. For more details, see GEVREY-CHAMBERTIN.

Clos de Tart, Clos des Lambrays, and **Clos St-Denis,** red GRANDS CRUS in Burgundy's CÔTE D'OR. For more details, see MOREY-ST-DENIS.

Clos de Vougeot, also frequently known as **Clos Vougeot**, famous walled vineyard in BURGUNDY created originally by the monks (see MONKS AND MONASTERIES) of Cîteaux. Between the 12th and early 14th centuries the Cistercians purchased or received as donations the land, much of which needed clearing and planting, which subsequently became known as the Clos de Vougeot. By 1336 the 50-ha/120-acre plot was complete and enclosed by stone walls on all sides.

The Cistercians maintained ownership until the French Revolution, when all clerical estates were dispossessed, although Dom Goblet, the monk responsible for the vineyards and the wine, had a sufficiently fine reputation to retain his job in the short term. In due course Clos de Vougeot was sold on to Julien-Jules Ouvrard in 1818, the year before he bought ROMANÉE-Conti, and remained in single ownership until 1889. Since then ownership has fragmented so that today there are over 80 proprietors.

A small chapel and rudimentary buildings, damaged during the religious wars, were rebuilt and enlarged in 1551, becoming the current Ch du Clos de Vougeot, a major tourist attraction. It is also home to the CONFRÉRIE des Chevaliers du Tastevin, a brotherhood which organizes copious feasts and the tastings for the Tastevinage. For this producers submit wines to a jury; those selected are entitled to use the 'tastevіné' label, which should enable the wine to be sold more easily or at a higher price.

For more historical detail, see BURGUNDY, history. The vineyard and wines of Clos de Vougeot are described under VOUGEOT. J.T.C.M.

Closures, wine bottle. See STOPPERS.

Cloudy wine. See FAULTS and STABILIZATION.

Cloudy Bay, seminal winery in the Marlborough region of NEW ZEALAND, the brainchild of David Hohnen of Cape Mentelle in WESTERN AUSTRALIA. Its debut release of a moodily labelled varietal Sauvignon Blanc in 1986 on export markets created a reputation for Marlborough Sauvignon and a cult

A pair of silver wine **coasters** made by Robert Hennell in London in 1772.

following for Cloudy Bay almost overnight, even though initially the grapes were bought in and the wine made under contract at another winery. The enterprise, based in its own premises, became a distant offshoot of the VEUVE CLICQUOT, and hence LVMH, empire in 1990.

CLUSTER, alternative, viticultural term for a BUNCH of grapes.

CM/CV, abbreviates Classic Methods/Classic Varieties, the name of a CALIFORNIA voluntary producer association of many of that state's most CHAMPAGNE-like sparkling wines. The CM/CV trademark appears on the packaging of many member wines. The organization, founded in 1990, is patterned on the Comité Interprofessionel du Vin de Champagne (CIVC of France's Champagne region). Eight of nine charter member-producers were wholly or partially owned by Champagne houses. The double goal is to promote California sparkling wines and to establish standards for their production. Initial standards limit vineyard location to the three coolest regions in the five-region system described under California, climate; limit grape varieties to Chardonnay, Pinot Blanc, Pinot Meunier, and Pinot Noir; limit juice yield to 160 gal (605 l) per ton of grapes (slightly stricter than that permitted in the Champagne region); and specify permitted types of PRESS and ranges of sweetness for brut, extra dry, and other label designations.

COASTERS. To those interested in wine ANTIQUES, **wine coasters** are small, circular, high-sided trays for DECANTERS which prevent damage by spillage. They also help to protect the decanter from damage. The earliest of them date from the late 1750s and within 20 years they had become very popular. Many are made of silver with wooden bases, the best-quality ones having silver bases too. Treen (turned wood) examples were a cheaper alternative, as were those in papier mâché. Of the latter many were decorated in gilt against a black or red background while others were embellished with horizontal ribs and Sheffield plated mounts. Glass coasters seldom survive and the few rolled-paperwork ones that do have lost much of their original bright colour.

Coasters for magnums and half-bottles are hugely outnumbered by those for bottle-sized decanters. The 19th century saw a general elaboration of design and, as decanters changed shape, so coasters followed, with progressively everted sides often accompanied by cast borders. Sheffield and electroplated coasters became very popular from *c.*1820. Like wine FUNNELS, coasters were little made after the mid 19th century until the modern era, when they became very popular, probably because of the diminishing use of the tablecloth.

Double coasters, in the form of boats or wagons in silver and papier mâché, enjoyed a brief popularity around the turn of the 18th and 19th centuries. Some Irish examples were for three decanters. In that country, too, there was a vogue for incorporating coasters in dumb waiters. In 1847 Richard Redgrave patented a papier mâché tray of shaped outline that incorporated a pair of coasters. At the end of the century appeared very high-sided coasters in electroplated copper which were designed to hide a bottle. This popular model had a long production run. R.N.H.B.

Butler, R., and Walkling, G., *The Book of Wine Antiques* (Woodbridge, 1986).

Clayton, M., *Collectors Dictionary of the Silver and Gold of Great Britain and North America* (rev. edn., Woodbridge, 1985).

Hernmarck, K., *The Art of the European Silversmith 1430–1830* (London, 1977).

Weinhold, R., *Vivat Bacchus*, trans. by N. Jones (Watford, 1978).

COCHYLIS, a flying insect which can damage vines. See MOTHS.

COCKBURN, port house which, in the second half of the 20th century, made the transition from bulk shipper to brand leader in the important British market. The house was founded in 1815 by Robert Cockburn and George Wauchope, who were joined in 1828 by Captain William Greig. A year later, Robert Cockburn's sons Archibald and Alexander joined the company and opened an office in London. In 1845, the brothers Henry and John Smithies joined the company which became Cockburn Smithies and Co. John Smithies initiated an organized system of records for blending. He married Eleanor Cobb and both Smithies and Cobb families remained in the firm for many generations; Peter Cobb joined Cockburn's in 1960 and has been a director of the company in Oporto since 1980. In 1962, Cockburn's became an associate company of HARVEYS of Bristol and, subsequently, part of the Allied-Lyons conglomerate. A year previously Harveys had bought Martinez Gassiot, transforming the two houses from fierce competitors to something more like a joint venture. Gordon Guimaraens (brother of Bruce Guimaraens of Fonseca Guimaraens) became chief wine-maker of both. Cockburn's most important brand, in volume sales, is Fine Ruby, although the vintage character port Special Reserve has benefited from widespread advertising and promotion to become the more easily recognized flagship wine of the house. The house has taken some unconventional views on declaring vintage port: it released the lighter 1967 rather than

Cockburn's winery at Tua where young port is stored temporarily in 'balloons' before being shipped down the Douro river to be matured in Vila Nova de Gaia.

1966 against the popular vote (Martinez joined it) but decided against declaring 1977 and 1980 before releasing an exceptionally good wine in 1983. In 1975, amid political turbulence in Portugal, Cockburn's made a major investment in land and buildings at Quinta de Santa Maria, near Regua. The house continued its tradition of using land in the higher reaches of DOURO with the purchase, in 1978, of 300 ha/750 acres of vineyards at Vilariça, where important viticultural experiments are being carried out. In 1989 the company acquired Quinta dos Canais, a 300-ha property on the north bank of the Douro, which has long provided the backbone of Cockburn's vintage port. S.A.

COCKS ET FÉRET, important directory of Bordeaux châteaux which was first published in 1846 as *Bordeaux, its Wines and the Claret Country* by the Englishman Charles Cocks who died in 1854 (see LITERATURE OF WINE). It was translated into *Bordeaux et ses vins*, with the emphasis on classifying wines in order of merit, by Féret in 1850. A second edition appeared in 1868 and provides a useful historical record of the evolution of different properties' and districts' reputations. (The 1868 edition, for example, ranks Ch PÉTRUS as a mere CRU BOURGEOIS.) It continues, as Féret, to this day.

Féret, C., *Bordeaux and its Wines* (13th edn., Bordeaux, 1986).

CODORNÍU, the world's largest producer of bottle-fermented SPARKLING WINES made by the traditional champagne method. The Codorníu group, which incorporates the Spanish CAVA brands Codorníu and Rondel, and the still wines Raimat (see COSTERS DEL SEGRE) and Masia Bach, sells over 45 million bottles of wine in its domestic market and over 60 million world-wide, with an annual turnover of more than 30 billion pesetas. The history of Codorníu dates back to 1551, when the Codorníu family established their first winery in San Sadurni de Noya, PENEDÈS, in Spanish Catalonia. In 1659 the heiress to the Codorníu winery, María Ana Codorníu, married a member of the Raventos family. A direct descendant, José Raventos, decided to produce sparkling wine, uncorking the first bottle of Spanish wine made in the image of CHAMPAGNE in 1872. Within 10 years, the style was popular across Spain, and, as a result, Codorníu can claim to be the wine on which the Cava industry was founded. The group's Cava is made from Parelleda, Macabeo, and Xarel-lo grapes (no still wine is bought in) and 10 per cent of the blend is usually older reserve wine. A vintage premium Cava made substantially from Chardonnay was launched in 1992, named Anna de Codorníu after María Ana. In 1992 the group opened Codorníu Napa, a new winery in the CARNEROS district of California, which makes CM/CV sparkling wine. More than $50 million have been invested in a winery at Raimat, plus land, vineyards, and properties in other parts of Spain. Viticultural research, ROOTSTOCKS, and vine material are supplied by the group's own nursery, known as Agro 2000. S.A.

COFFEE HOUSES. The traditional drink of Arabs, coffee was introduced to western Europe in the mid 17th century. Like tea and chocolate, it was soon to pose a serious threat to the popularity of wine.

The first English coffee house was reputedly opened in a room in the Angel Inn in Oxford's High Street in 1650 and within a couple of years the trend had taken hold in London. Coffee was lauded in the *Publick Adviser* (1657) as 'a very wholesome and physical drink' with numerous medicinal properties.

By the 1660s coffee houses were challenging the traditional English tavern, and not only because they served this novel beverage which was very cheap and had the added advantage of not making you drunk. Samuel Pepys, among others, frequented these 'penny universities' in order to catch up on the city's gossip or join a political debate.

The king's government reacted uneasily to the coffee houses' popularity, fearing them a hotbed of political dissent and 'the great resort of idle and disaffected persons'. However, a proclamation (1675) to ban them eventually came to nothing.

Each coffee house had its own regular clientele—be it literary, clerical, aristocratic, or commercial. Some of the more popular survive as gentlemen's clubs, whilst coffee houses in Europe evolved into that ubiquitous institution, the café. H.B.

Aubertin-Potter, N., and Bennett, A., *Oxford Coffee Houses 1651–1800* (Oxford, 1987).
Ellis, A., *The Penny Universities: A History of the Coffee Houses* (London, 1956).
Lillywhite, B., *London Coffee Houses* (London, 1963).

COFFEY STILL, the model of CONTINUOUS STILL used most commonly to produce spirits ever since it was invented by Aeneas Coffey, an Irish customs agent who patented his continuous still in 1831. Its introduction inaugurated a new era in the history of spirits involving a clear distinction between continuously distilled spirits which were mass produced, and those hand crafted spirits, described by the French as *artisanale*, which are mostly made in batches using the POT STILL. N.F.

COGNAC, France's and therefore the world's most prized grape-based spirit, or BRANDY, produced in a delimited part of south west France within the *départements* of Charente and Charente-Maritime. Cognac has held the high ground as the world's finest distilled spirit for over 300 years. This superiority is firmly based on the systematic exploitation by man of the Cognac region's natural advantages. As a result the little town of Cognac, which housed barely 5,000 souls at the time of its rise to fame towards the end of the 17th century, is probably better known than any other French place-name, Paris alone excepted. The town remains compact, its heart a picturesque huddle of lanes bounded by often rather dilapidated warehouses. These warehouses, like those of Cognac's sister town Jarnac, are recognizable from their roofs, blackened by the presence of *Torula compniacensis richon*, the mould, specific to the region, which thrives on the

Recently replaced tiles on warehouses in **Cognac** are unblackened by the region's characteristic brandy-nurtured fungus.

aromatic fumes from hundreds of casks of maturing cognac (see illustration above).

All the brandy in these warehouses is capable of retaining more of the character of the original fruit, a crucial test of any product of the vine, than that distilled anywhere else in the world. But, naturally, Cognac's fame reposes most securely on its finest products, which represent a very small proportion of the total. After 30 years or more in oak casks (see OAK AND BRANDY), brandies from the semicircle south of Cognac known as the Champagnes offer an incomparable richness of fruit, balanced by an equally unique elegance and delicacy. But the Cognac region also produces two other brandies superior to any others made outside it (ARMAGNAC alone excepted): from the Borderies district to the immediate north and west of the town of Cognac, and from the Fins Bois district round Jarnac, a few miles further up the river Charente.

History

Cognac's exploitation of its natural advantages started centuries before its first wines were distilled. Its position on the Charente provided it with a major trade in salt, and then in the wine from the slopes above the town, wine which helped to satisfy the English thirst for wine during the medieval centuries when the king of England also ruled over Aquitaine. Politically Cognac was also lucky. The French king Francis II was born in the town in 1492 and naturally favoured his birthplace. Moreover Cognac was on the Catholic side during the wars of religion which raged through the 16th century (unlike Jarnac, which was a major centre of Protestantism).

But Cognac's breakthrough came thanks to the Dutch (see DUTCH WINE TRADE), who wanted *brandewijn*, or distilled wine, rather than wine for their sailors, and it was they who first bought the wine for distillation at home and then installed their own stills in the Cognac region to distil the wine nearer the source. By the middle of the 17th century even the fine wines from the Champagnes were being used for distillation, because it had been realized that these wines resulted in pure brandies after only two distillations, while rival French wines for distillation needed many more passes through the stills to eliminate nauseous impurities, but which also removed their grapey characteristics.

Brandy from Cognac soon found a market which was to dominate the fine end of the trade for nearly three centuries, for it took only a few years for the London connoisseurs of the late 17th century to grasp the fact that brandy from Cognac, 'Coniac', or 'Coniack' (spelling has never been the strong suit of the British upper classes) was superior to that from bigger centres of the wine trade, such as 'Nants', LA ROCHELLE, or BORDEAUX, the source of another newly fashionable drink, mature claret.

In the following century the trade attracted a number of notable entrepreneurs, most crucially the former smuggler Jean MARTELL and Richard HENNESSY, a former officer in the French army. They helped to ensure that the basic quality of cognac has always been higher than that of any other distilled spirit—at the expense, perhaps of a certain amount of the picturesque individuality associated with armagnac.

Geography

Cognac's natural advantages start with its TERROIR. The basic league table based on terroir has an even firmer base in the

Cognac region than almost anywhere else in the world of wine and spirits. Cognac is produced only in a strictly delimited region extending inland from the Gironde estuary north of Bordeaux and the Bay of Biscay towards Angoulême, 80 km / 50 miles inland. But the town originally made its name from the brandies produced on a semicircle of slopes to the south of Cognac and Jarnac.

After a few years in cask, brandies made from the same type of wine but from different districts within the Cognac region, distilled in the same stills, being matured in the same casks, take on very different characteristics. The finest come from the slopes of Campanian CHALK from the inner semicircle, the Grande Champagne. Then come those from the outer semicircle, the Petite Champagne, largely composed of Santonian chalk (a name derived from the old name for the region, the Saintonge). The Borderies, a small clay-chalk rectangle north and west of Cognac, produce an unmistakable brandy of their own, offering the same intensely fruity nuttiness found in fine tawny port. The best brandies from the Fins Bois which surround the Champagnes produce a light, flowery, elegant type of brandy, traditionally associated with the town of Jarnac.

The region is blessed with an equable climate. Long, but not excessively hot, summer days ensure that the grapes do not ripen and lose their acidity too quickly (which means that in cooler years the local wine, VIN DE PAYS des Charentes, can be remarkably thin and acid). Ideally the grapes should be relatively fruity and contain between eight and nine per cent potential alcohol when harvested. If they are stronger then the final brandy tends to be flabby and does not contain nearly as strong a concentration of the qualities found in the original fruit (for the obvious reason that a wine of 12 per cent alcohol distilled to 70 per cent is only concentrated six times, whereas a wine of 9 per cent is concentrated nearly eight times). At the other end of the scale, grapes containing less than 8 per cent alcohol will simply be too green to have developed the right potential aromas.

Production techniques

The makers of cognac are working with a limited palette. In the 18th century much brandy was distilled from the COLOMBARD grape still extensively grown in Armagnac, and in the 19th century it was made predominantly from the particularly aromatic FOLLE BLANCHE. But this proved to be even more prone to rot when grafted after the PHYLLOXERA epidemic and today virtually all the wine used for cognac comes from the same, rather characterless, grape, known variously as the UGNI BLANC, St-Émilion, or TREBBIANO.

The wine is fermented without using SULPHUR, which would emerge as an undesirable element in the final brandy, and is distilled as soon as possible after fermentation—preferably during the winter months (unlike the technique outlined in BRANDY, Spanish). The copper cognac POT STILL and the DISTILLATION process have changed remarkably little over the years, except for the method of heating. The heat source remains outside the still, but first coal, and more recently natural gas, have replaced wood, providing an ideal source of heat that is controllable and, above all, uniform, ensuring that the brandy is not burnt.

Crucially the distillation is in two stages. The wine is heated in a still that is now, as always, made of copper, and the lighter alcohol fumes are the first to emerge from the top of the still. To produce a raw cognac, which is about 70 per cent alcohol (nearly double the strength of the final, drinkable, spirit) the wine has to be heated twice. The first distillation produces what is known as the *brouillis*, which contains all the essential elements for the final product. The second distillation, in stills holding not more than 25 hl (660 gal or about 3,000 bottles' worth) merely concentrates and separates the essential elements.

The stills may not vary much, but the distiller can control the quality of the brandy. The lower the strength of the raw brandy, the richer it will be in the delicious, fruity, hangover-inducing CONGENERS which provide all spirits with their fundamental character. So a house like Bisquit, looking for a fruity style even in its superior VS brandy, will leave the tap running—and thus extract lower-strength brandy—longer than, say, Martell, which is looking for relatively neutral raw spirit. The difference is not great, a matter of half a degree or so, but it counts.

Newly distilled cognac is pretty rough stuff, and not only because of its strength. It lacks a crucial dimension, which can be provided only by maturation in small oak casks which allow a subtle chemical process with the brandy slowly absorbing the tannins and vanillins from the oak (see OAK AND BRANDY).

The major cognac firms know this perfectly well and have taken care to control the manufacture of their casks very closely. Hennessy and RÉMY MARTIN own Taransaud and Seguin-Moreau respectively, two of France's biggest firms of coopers. All Cognac is matured in French OAK, but the style from the TRONÇAIS forest in the very centre of France differs from LIMOUSIN near Limoges. Rémy uses Limousin oak, rich in tannin, to accelerate the maturation of its 'Champagne' brandies, mostly destined to be sold younger than purists would advise. Martell, by contrast, uses Tronçais oak, which is tougher and less generous with its tannins, in its continuing search for a certain austerity of style.

The choice between new and old oak is even more fundamental. Those houses looking for a light style, most obviously Delamain, use no new casks, but most other firms keep their newly distilled brandies in new oak for up to a year. At the other extreme Frapin, which sells mostly brandies from well-placed estates in the Grande Champagne, characterful enough to be able to absorb a lot of tannin, keeps its brandies in new wood for up to two years.

The maturing brandies are housed in hundreds of warehouses. For obvious reasons of transport convenience, the older cellars were all by the Charente RIVER. These damp cellars favoured maturation by reducing the strength rather than the volume of the spirit. Evaporation is faster (and accompanied by a slower loss of strength) in a dry cellar, resulting in an undesirably harsh style of brandy. Even today all the Cognac houses avoid dry cellars. Indeed, when Bisquit moved from the banks of the Charente to a new site on the slopes some miles away, it ensured that the new *chais* were properly humidified.

The 'early landed, late bottled' brandies sold to the aristocratic end of the British market in the early 20th century by traditional British wine merchants were matured in even more humid warehouses near the docks in London and Bristol (see EVAPORATION). After 20 to 40 years in cask they were bottled and sold under the names of both the supplier and the merchant. This British cask maturation of cognac continues on a much more limited scale today.

The Cognacais take particular care in reducing their brandies to the 40 per cent strength at which they are sold. Distilled water (or a type of low-strength spirits known as *petits eaux*) are used and the brandy is then left for several months to settle before being bottled.

Styles of cognac

Over the years a hierarchy has emerged within Cognac, based on a combination of the geographical origin of the grapes and the length of time the cognac has spent in cask. Brandies from the Fins Bois or the Borderies districts are at their best after less than two decades and even those from the Champagnes do not develop any further after 40 years or so in wood (age snobbery is just that, snobbery). Nevertheless the finest cognacs need at least 20 years to develop the lovely ripe, rich qualities called in the region RANCIO.

Even the most basic cognac, the VS (better known under its historic name of ***, or three star), cannot contain any brandy less than three years old, while the VSOP (originally named after the Very Special Old Pale brandies sold in London in Victorian times) cannot be less than five years old. But the authorities lose track of brandies after they are six years old, and buyers have to rely on the reputation of the firm when choosing between the proliferation of superior grades—the Napoleons, the Extras, the XOs, and the like—for such names provide no stylistic guarantee and there is great variation in the age of the cognacs involved.

The duopoly created by Messrs Martell and Hennessy has been successfully challenged only by two other firms: COURVOISIER and RÉMY MARTIN. Between them the Big Four now account for four-fifths of the cognac sold outside France. The French themselves are less concerned with quality than with price, buying mostly cheap, young supermarket cognacs. In the late 1980s even these rose rapidly in price because the growers, particularly in the outer subregions such as the Bois Communs, had taken such enthusiastic advantage of the premiums paid by the European Union for pulling up surplus vines. The resulting shortage, especially of mature cognacs, was exacerbated by the damage caused by the vine disease EUTYPA DIEBACK.

For some houses, the most important stylistic weapons they wield are the additives they employ. They all use a small quantity of caramel to smooth out colour variations from cask to cask. Because caramel has no effect on taste, a dry, dark-brown brandy is certainly a theoretical possibility. But because buyers are conditioned to associate brown with sweetness, the houses use colour as a signal of taste—especially to the Chinese, great cognac drinkers, who love the cognac with which they accompany their meals to be dark and, by association, rich and sweet.

Sugar syrup is used to sweeten and enrich young cognacs, particularly by firms such as Courvoisier, which has a notably rounded style. Both caramel and sugar syrup are legal and freely discussed additives. But there is one unregulated, largely unmentioned, but extremely important shaper of cognac style, *boisé*, oak chips soaked in old cognac and left in cask for months or years. To cognac connoisseurs, the richness *boisé* imparts to the brandy is rather hard and tannic and cannot be mistaken for real rancio.

Cognac today

Recently brandies have reverted to their older, heavier, stickier, 'browner' style in response to demand from the Far East, most notably from the Japanese and from the prosperous Chinese communities throughout south east Asia who drink cognac with water throughout their meals. Indeed more cognac is drunk per head in Hong Kong than anywhere else in the world, and the total consumption from the prosperous and thirsty Chinese in Taiwan, Thailand, Singapore, and Malaysia makes them, collectively, the biggest single market for cognac.

Unfortunately the cognac producers have relied on glamour, mystique, their name, and the guarantee it provides of superiority over brandies from any other source. The dominance of a handful of firms, however reliable their products, has prevented cognac from developing the specialist appeal which it had, and which some armagnacs still have—largely because the armagnac producers have never had the same commercial sense as the cognac houses, so there are no mass-produced house styles of armagnac. As a result, outside the Far East, cognac was on the decline in the early 1990s, not only because of the marked swing away from spirits in general and towards 'lighter' spirits such as vodka, but because so few firms have managed to inject any excitement into the business of buying or drinking cognac.

For some years a few growers, notably the two branches of the Ragnaud family, had shown that there was a market for fine old brandies from individual estates in the heart of the Grande Champagne. Fortunately the cognac regulators have also recognized the need for single VINTAGE cognacs, an important marketing point since British drinkers in particular attach great importance to the idea of a drink's vintage. New regulations, first introduced at the time of the 1989 vintage, allow vintage-dated cognacs. A few houses such as Croizet and, above all, Hine, are now producing such brandies.

N.F.

Faith, N., *Cognac* (London, 1986).
—— *Nicholas Faith's Guide to Cognac & Other Brandies* (London, 1992).

COL, literally the neck of a POT STILL. It used to be straight, but is now elegantly curved into a *col de cygne*, or swan's neck.

COLARES, exceptional but minuscule DOC wine region on the west coast of PORTUGAL just north of the capital Lisbon buffeted by relentless winds from the Atlantic (see map on p. 750). These vineyards were spared from the PHYLLOXERA pest in the 19th century (thanks to their sandy composition) but look unlikely to survive the commercial pressures of the 20th. RAMISCO, the Colares vine, is probably the only VINIFERA grape variety never to have been grafted. It is to be found planted only in a narrow strip of sand dunes on the clifftops above the Atlantic, its roots anchored in the clay below. It is ironic that the soils that saved Colares are making them today less and less viable. When a Colares vineyard is replanted, a trench 2 to 3 m deep has to be excavated to reach the clay, risking suffocation on the part of the digger, should the sandy sides of the trench give way. It is not surprising that few people are prepared to go to such lengths today.

From the 1930s, Portuguese government legislation obliged all growers to send grapes to the Adega Regional (a co-operative winery) for their wine to be entitled to the Colares denomination. This was established in order to stamp out fraud, but standards slipped and the ruling had the effect of merely stifling initiative. In 1990 the EUROPEAN UNION forced the government to abolish the Adega Regional's monopoly (soon after a similar move in Dão), but this was probably too late to save the wine from virtual extinction. Three different styles of wine are permitted to use the name Colares: two red and one white. The most highly prized comes from the sandiest soils and the Ramisco grape must make up 80 per cent of the blend. A second red comes from the firmer ground away from the coast, although this is usually sold in bulk for blending. A small amount of white Colares is also made, principally from MALVASIA grapes. R.J.M.

COLHEITA, Portuguese word meaning crop or HARVEST and, by extension, VINTAGE. It is also the name of a style of PORT from a single year aged for at least seven years in wood before bottling. R.J.M.

COLLAGE, French term for FINING.

COLLAR ROT, one of the FUNGAL DISEASES of the vine which particularly attacks young vines growing in cool, moist soil via the *Pythium* fungus. The vines are weakened and may die. Vines grafted on to Rupestris St George ROOTSTOCKS are most susceptible. Control is achieved by removing soil from the base of the trunk and reducing soil moisture. R.E.S.

COLLECTING WINE became a popular hobby in the 1980s. Americans tend to call anyone who buys fine wine a **collector** rather than a wine enthusiast, connoisseur, or *amateur* (the French term), suggesting that the thrill lies in acquisition rather than in consumption. Ever since the development of cylindrical BOTTLES in the 1730s, when it first became possible to maintain a personal CELLAR, there have been individuals whose purchasing patterns amounted to building up a specific **collection** of certain wines. The rapid economic growth of the late 1970s and 1980s, however, together with a succession of good vintages to be bought EN PRIMEUR and the emergence of a truly international consumer wine press (see Robert PARKER, for example), resulted in the emergence of a significant group of serious wine collectors around the globe (notably in the United States, Germany, and the Far East). They communicate and trade with each other through the AUCTION houses and the specialist fine wine traders, and for many of them the purpose of collecting is to enable occasional but usually sumptuous marathon TASTING events.

COLLI, also written **colline** and **collio**, the Italian word for hills, and its use in a wine name indicates that the wine is produced on slopes of a certain altitude (it is an almost direct analogy of France's CÔTE, Côtes, and Coteaux). Accordingly, articles about Colli Somewhere are listed not under Colli, but under S for Somewhere.

Elevation is obviously in the eye of the beholder, however, and the word Colli is used to describe both mere knolls and near-mountainous viticulture at altitudes of over 500 m / 1,600 ft. Colli and its variations can be found not only as the title of various DOCS but also as a part of their descriptive apparatus: CHIANTI, for example, is produced in the Colli Senesi and the Colline Pisane (Chianti dei Colli Senesi, Chianti delle Colline Pisane). The absence of the word does not imply that a given wine is produced in the flatlands; much of Italy's finest wine—BARBARESCO, BAROLO, BRUNELLO DI MONTALCINO, VINO NOBILE DI MONTEPULCIANO—is produced from HILLSIDE VINEYARDS without that fact being indicated in the wine's name. D.T.

COLLIO, more properly **Collio Goriziano**, is a qualitatively important, predominantly white wine DOC zone on the north eastern border of Italy with Slovenia. Collio has done much to increase Italians' confidence in their ability to make fine white wine.

Collio, a corruption of the Italian word for hills (see COLLI), is in the province of Gorizia (hence Colli Goriziano) and was only reunified with Italy after the First World War. Within the region of FRIULI it is the third biggest DOC in terms of area planted and volume of production after GRAVE DEL FRIULI and COLLI ORIENTALI del Friuli, but its fragrant and lively white wines, which account for 85 per cent of total production, have created an image of quality for Friuli thoughout the world. Collio's red wines, overwhelmingly from MERLOT and CABERNET, tend to resemble LOIRE reds, at times with an identical vegetal quality underlined by a certain lightness of body and texture.

The territory itself extends across the hills from the Judrio river in the west—the former boundary between Austria and Italy and now Collio's boundary with the climatologically similar Colli Orientali—to the Slovenian border in the east. Vines are planted on a calcareous marl alternating with layers of sandstone called 'flysch of Cormons' after an important township in the heart of the zone.

The zone's current white wine style is relatively recent and was introduced not only to Collio but to all of Friuli by Mario Schiopetto, who had studied cold fermentation techniques in

Germany. The strongly innovative character of his wines, coupled with their high quality and purity of varietal expression, gave direction to the entire zone and to the neighbouring Colli Orientali. The cellars of Collio and of the Colli Orientali tend to be extremely well equipped, with an abundance of REFRIGERATION units, pneumatic PRESSES, and all that is required for CENTRIFUGATION and STERILE BOTTLING. When pushed to extremes this technological approach, together with relatively high yields (maximum permitted is 77 hl/ha (4.4 tons/acre) for all varieties except for the quantitatively insignificant TRAMINER), has created a certain blandness and monotony in the wines, with primary fermentation AROMAS and flavours getting the upper hand over the varietal character. A certain readjustment has taken place since the mid 1980s, as producers have begun to search for a fuller, more characterized style, and a small minority has begun to strive for a more international style using BARRIQUES. The exceptional commercial success of Collio over the past 20 years, with the wines fetching extremely remunerative prices, seems to have convinced most producers, however, to proceed with due caution.

The grape variety mix is very similar to that in the Colli Orientali to the immediate west. TOCAI is the dominant variety of the DOC with 370 of the total 1,550 ha/3,800 acres planted in 1993; PINOT GRIGIO (294 ha), SAUVIGNON Blanc (241 ha), PINOT BIANCO (164 ha), and CHARDONNAY (83 ha) are also significantly represented. Merlot accounts for 119 of the 210 ha of red grapes planted, with Cabernet accounting for 65 of the remaining 90 ha. CABERNET FRANC, whose herbaceousness is much appreciated in the zone, is 10 times as common as CABERNET SAUVIGNON. Desultory attempts at a more important style of red wine, complete with new oak barrels, have been made, with mixed results, although good quality has been attained by some producers in Brazzano and Oslavia.

See also SLOVENIA, which is capable of producing some extremely similar wines. D.T.

Anderson, B., *The Wine Atlas of Italy* (London and New York, 1990).
Gleave, D., *The Wines of Italy* (London and New York, 1989).

COLLI ORIENTALI del Friuli, literally the eastern hills of the FRIULI region in north east Italy, is the region's second largest DOC. Its 2,100 ha/5,200 acres of vineyard give it 40 per cent more land dedicated to the vine than the COLLIO DOC between it and the Slovenian border, but the Colli Orientali have only a third as much vineyard as GRAVE DEL FRIULI on the plain. It is the most versatile of the three, however, producing interesting white wines, high-quality dessert wines, and what are indisputably the finest, longest-lived red wines of Friuli. In a region known principally for its white wines, the Colli Orientali has 35 per cent of its vineyards planted to such red varieties as the international CABERNET and MERLOT as well as the renascent natives REFOSCO, SCHIOPPETTINO, and PIGNOLO. The area between Buttrio, Cividale, and Manzano has long been considered prime territory for superior reds, providing excellent growing conditions for all these varieties.

The territory of the DOC begins, as its name implies, to the east of the city of Udine and continues to the border of the province of Udine. The dividing line between the Colli Orientali and Collio is neither geological nor climatic, but simply historical: Udine and its province became part of Italy in 1866 while the neighbouring area of Collio, in the province of Gorizia, was not reunified with the rest of Italy until the end of the First World War. The contiguous zones in fact have the same sort of soil: the so-called 'flysch of Cormons', with alternating strata of calcareous marls and sandstone.

Wine has a documented history here, as in most parts of Italy, since the days of the Roman empire, but the zone first began to attract significant attention in the 1970s, when cold fermentation techniques began to produce here, and in the Collio DOC, significant quantities of fresh, fruity, and aromatic white wines, pioneering efforts for Italy. Significant development of red wines came in the 1980s as producers began to move away from lighter, fruitier styles towards a fuller, more structured style more worthy of ageing, a move that was frequently accompanied by the use of small oak barrels. A certain number of these more ambitious reds were released as an ambitiously priced VINO DA TAVOLA, because individual producers wanted either to distance the wines from their more facile antecedents, to make an unorthodox blend of varieties, or to emphasize their own name or that of Friuli. White wine, particularly from CHARDONNAY or PINOT BIANCO, was either fermented or aged in BARRIQUES; these wines were also marketed as vini da tavola to distinguish them from the fresher style of whites, which remained the backbone of production.

Current production is dominated by TOCAI among the whites, with 465 of the 1,375 ha/3,400 acres planted to white varieties in 1993, followed by SAUVIGNON BLANC, VERDUZZO, PINOT GRIGIO, and Pinot Bianco. Small quantities of the sweet white PICOLIT are also made. Merlot is by far the most significant red variety representing more than half of all red grape plantings, with Cabernet, Refosco, and minor quantities of PINOT NOIR and Schioppettino making up the rest. D.T.

COLLIOURE to tourists is one of the prettiest seaside villages on the Mediterranean coast just north of the Franco-Spanish border. To wine lovers it is a rare, particularly heady, deep red table wine whose aromas of overripe fruits and spice reflect the fact that the Collioure comes from exactly the same area as BANYULS, France's most concentrated VIN DOUX NATUREL. They span the communes of, Spainwards down the coast, Collioure, Port-Vendres, Banyuls-sur-Mer, and Cerbère. The characteristics of the vintage determine how each vineyard's produce is apportioned between Collioure and Banyuls, but the grapes for Collioure are certainly picked before those destined to become vin doux naturel.

The region's MOURVÈDRE is grown expressly for Collioure, however, as it and Grenache Noir are the principal grape varieties in the table wine, with between 25 and 40 per cent made up of the 'complementary' grape varieties Syrah, Cinsaut, and Carignan. As in Banyuls, yields from these terraced bush-like vines are some of the lowest in France, although 40 hl/ha (2.3 tons/acre) is decreed the official maximum. There is also, unusually, an official maximum alcohol level, 15 per cent, as well as a maximum RESIDUAL SUGAR level of 5gm/l—although many of these wines taste so ripe that they do give the impression of sweetness.

COLLOIDS, substance consisting of ultramicroscopic particles, usually solids but occasionally liquids or gases. Wine colloids are very finely divided solids in particles with diameters ranging from about five nanometres to one micrometre. These are principally large organic molecules, most of which are polymers made up of smaller molecules of the PECTINS, PHENOLICS, ANTHOCYANS, and TANNINS (see POLYMERIZATION).

Colloids are major contributors to a wine's VISCOSITY, the extent to which the wine resists movement.

Colloids can be removed by FINING and by FILTRATION. The fewer colloids are removed, the more BODY a wine will seem to have, the more astringent it may taste in youth, the slower it will mature, but the more complex it should taste when at its peak. A.D.W.

COLOMBARD was originally a Charentais white grape variety used with Ugni Blanc (TREBBIANO) and FOLLE BLANCHE, but considered inferior to both, as an ingredient in COGNAC. As Colombard's star waned in France, almost half of total plantings being pulled up in the 1970s, it waxed quite spectacularly in California, where, as FRENCH COLOMBARD, it became the state's most planted variety of all, providing generous quantities of reasonably neutral but reliably crisp base wine for commercial, often quite sweet, white blends.

Its disadvantages of being quite prone to rot and oidium are much lesser inconveniences in hot Central Valley, where almost all of California's Colombard is planted (official statistics record just 43 acres/17 ha of the variety ever planted in the smart Napa Valley). And Colombard's disadvantages for the distillers of Charentes, that its wine is more alcoholic and less acid than that of the other cognac varieties, are positive advantages for consumers of the wine in its undistilled state (although Colombard is also used for California brandy).

Annual rate of planting of Colombard in California slowed considerably during the 1980s so that, during the year 1990, for example, just 29 acres of Colombard were planted to Chardonnay's 4,944 and it would seem that Colombard's burst of popularity in this wine region is now over, although the variety is found in other American states, notably Texas.

It would take some sorcery to transform Colombard into an exciting wine, but pleasantly lively innocuousness is well within reach for those equipped with stainless steel and temperature control. In a nice example of transatlantic switchback, the producers of the ARMAGNAC region set about duplicating California's modern wine-making transformation of the dull Colombard grape on their own varieties surplus to brandy production, thus creating the hugely successful VIN DE PAYS des Côtes de Gascogne. Colombard, still third most important variety in the region after Ugni Blanc and BACO Blanc, which are particularly well-suited to distillation, has been a prime ingredient in this hugely successful wine. The Charentais, who grow only a third as much Colombard as their rival brandy producers to the south, later tried to work the same magic to produce their own version Vin de Pays Charentais, often from Colombard.

More than half of the 5,000 ha/12,300 acres of Colombard still cultivated in France by the end of the 1980s was in either cognac or, particularly, armagnac country, but there were still 1,700 ha in the Bordeaux region, particularly in the north west around BOURG and BLAYE, where much of it acts as a subordinate ingredient in dull blended BORDEAUX Blanc. It is still planted to a limited extent in much of SOUTH WEST FRANCE.

The variety, once important to the local brandy industry, also reached a peak of popularity for cheap, commercial off-dry white in SOUTH AFRICA. There were still 5,700 ha of Colombar(d) left in 1990, making it the country's fifth most important variety, and some wine-makers here use more ingenuity than most in attempting to fashion various silk purses from this sow's ear of a vine.

In Australia too there were still 600 ha in the early 1990s, although it is usually blended with more fashionable grape varieties, often adding useful natural acidity.

COLOMBIA, South American country with a TROPICAL climate and a relatively short history of viticulture. For long Colombia depended on imported wines and spirits from Spain and developed a taste for sweet fortified wines such as MÁLAGA. The initial output of the first vines planted here in the 1920s and 1930s was therefore directed towards aping these sort of products, as well as to the production of TABLE GRAPES. Since wine imports from non-South American countries were banned in 1984, however, consumers have become accustomed to the dry table wines of Chile and Argentina and in the early 1990s Colombia was beginning to produce small quantities of dry wines from VINIFERA vines—although by far the majority of vines grown, especially in the northern zone of Santa Marta, are HYBRIDS and destined for the table. The main wine grape zone is in the south east of the country in the upper Cauca valley, where there are about 1,500 ha/3,700 acres of vineyards. Vines have to be defoliated by hand in order to provide a short 'winter' DORMANCY. A vine is in full production at just 15 months of age. Annual rainfall is 1,000 mm/39 in, although there are dry periods between December and March and between June and September. DOWNY MILDEW is the principle hazard. ISABELLA and Italia table grapes are grown in the main but there are experimental plantings of Cabernet Sauvignon, Chardonnay, and other INTERNATIONAL VARIETIES. The bulk of production is wine-based aperitifs and fortified wines and brandies, but a subsidiary of Pedro DOMECQ is at the forefront of experimentation with dry vinifera table wines.

COLORINO, rare, deep coloured dark grape variety used traditionally in Tuscany for the wine-making GOVERNO technique.

COLOUR OF WINES. Wines are classified as red, white, or rosé but can vary widely in colour within these broad categories, sometimes with little obvious distinction between a light red and a dark rosé.

Red wines

Red wines owe their colour to the natural organic red/blue ANTHOCYAN pigments, of which there are varying concentrations in the skins of darker-skinned grapes (only TEINTURIER grape varieties have red pulp). These concentrations depend on the VINE VARIETY, the RIPENESS of the grape, and the weather conditions of the VINTAGE year. The amount of anthocyans leached into the resulting wine depends on many factors including BERRY SIZE, homogeneity of berry ripeness, length and temperature of the MACERATION of skins and new wine, together with the extent to which techniques to encourage EXTRACTION such as PUMPING OVER and PUNCHING DOWN are used. All these factors influence the intensity of colour in a young red wine.

The actual hue of a young red wine is influenced partly by the grape variety (Cabernet Sauvignon grape skins, for example, are blue-black, while those of Grenache are much more crimson), although much less than one might expect (see ANTHOCYANS). A more important influence is the acidity of the grape juice. In low PH solutions anthocyans exist in bright red coloured forms, while as pH rises they change to a more colourless form and, in very high pH solutions, exist in greyish forms. In general, therefore, the more acid the grape juice, the brighter the colour—although very high acid grapes may be unripe and deficient in available anthocyans.

Red wines which undergo BARREL MATURATION also tend to have more stable colour than those which do not, because of the effect of small amounts of OXYGEN on the wine's PHENOLICS (including anthocyans).

During AGEING, this slow phenolic OXIDATION process continues, forming ever larger molecules made up of anthocyans, TANNINS, and other phenolics. The result of this POLYMERIZATION is that the larger ones precipitate as SEDIMENT, leaving the wine increasingly pale, less blue, and more yellow.

The antioxidant effect of SULPHUR DIOXIDE also means that red wines with a high level of free sulphur dioxide tend to be paler than they would be with a lower level. Also, if red wines are bottled with high sulphur dioxide levels, the normal chemical interactions among the phenolics and other wine constituents to generate BOUQUET are disrupted.

The colour of a young red wine can vary from blackish purple (as in a vintage PORT, for example) through many hues of crimson to ruby. With age, red wines take on brick and then amber hues, lightening with time. The colour at the rim of a glassful of wine can give the most telling indication of the hue and therefore age of a wine, while looking straight down through a glassful of wine from above can clearly indicate the intensity of colour (see TASTING).

See also RED WINE-MAKING and RED WINES for more information, including names for red wines in languages other than English.

White wines

Although red wines are red, white wines are not white. Very occasionally they are colourless, but they usually range from pale green, through straw, pale copper, and deep gold to amber.

The stems, skins, and pulp of the light-skinned grapes used for making white wines contain a large and complex mixture of phenolics similar to the red/blue coloured anthocyans except that they are not capable of the multiplicity of forms which result in red colour. The absorption of these white grape phenolics into white wine occurs mainly in the ultraviolet range, but extends into the visible range sufficiently to cause a light yellow colour in the wines we call 'white'. After CRUSHING of the grapes, these phenolics are exposed to oxygen and to the acids and other constituents of the grape juice, which causes a number of chemical reactions (including oxidation and polymerization) which result in changes of colour from light yellow to amber and eventually to brown.

Different 'white' grape varieties contain a slightly different array of phenolics, which results in differently coloured wines. Palomino and Pinot Blanc, for example, are particularly prone to oxidation and browning, while Riesling has traces of non-phenolic compounds which can cause a greenish tinge to the basic yellow. Some white grape varieties contain leucoanthocyans which under some circumstances can produce a pink tinge to the basic yellow. Some varieties used for white wines such as Gewürztraminer and Pinot Gris have greyish pink to purple skins and tend to result in deeply coloured wines with a strong pinkish yellow hue.

During fermentation yeast cells can absorb some of the brown polymerized materials which are then removed with the LEES. (Much the same phenomenon allows the use of quite distinctly pale pink base wines from Pinot Noir and Meunier in the blend for bottle fermented sparkling wines which, after disgorging, are white.) White wines may be made from dark-skinned grape varieties using minimum skin contact and this phenomenon and/or CHARCOAL treatments.

The names of the fundamental phenolics on which each group of complex compounds is built are the benzoic acid group, the cinnamic acid group, the flavan-3-ols, and the flavan-3, 4-diols (these last two frequently being called tannins).

With age, small amounts of oxygen act on these phenolic compounds to brown them and apparently deepen a white wine's colour. With extreme BOTTLE AGEING of many decades, a very old white wine can be the same medium intensity amber colour as a red wine of the same age.

White wine colour is also affected by the wine's levels of pH and sulphur dioxide, low pH and high sulphur dioxide levels tending to have a bleaching effect.

Wines made from grapes affected by NOBLE ROT tend to have a particularly deep golden colour. Those which have been given extended SKIN CONTACT tend to brown relatively early, while young white wines subjected to BARREL FERMENTATION and LEES CONTACT tend to be markedly paler than those fermented in STAINLESS STEEL and then transferred to cask for barrel maturation because darker pigments are absorbed by the lees.

See also WHITE WINE-MAKING and WHITE WINES.

Rosé wines

These wines owe their combination of pink colour and white wine characteristics either to a very short skin contact with dark-skinned grapes, or, for some everyday wines and pink sparkling wines, to the BLENDING of red and white wines.

Wines that are pale bluish pink are likely to be the results of protective techniques, while those with an orange tinge may well have been exposed to some, possibly deliberate, OXIDATION. While a blindfold taster can in some circumstances find it difficult to distinguish between low tannin red wines and fuller bodied white wines, it can be almost impossible to distinguish a rosé wine from a white one.

See also ROSÉ WINE-MAKING, ROSÉ WINES, and AGEING.

COLUMBARD is how the white variety COLOMBARD is occasionally spelt on labels.

COLUMELLA, LUCIUS JUNIUS MODERATUS, important but, for long, uncredited source of information on wine production in Ancient ROME. Little is known about his life except that he was born in Gades (Cádiz near JEREZ) and that he was an officer in the Roman army in Syria. He composed his treatise on farming, *De re rustica*, in AD 60–5. It is divided into 12 books, all in prose except the tenth, on gardens. This book was written in hexameter verse as an addition to VIRGIL's *Georgics*, which Columella admired. Columella's work shows by far the best grasp of technical detail of all the surviving Roman treatises on farming, and this is particularly clear in his treatment of VITICULTURE. Books 3 and 4, the most important of the treatise, deal with vine-growing, but much practical advice on wine-making is also contained in Book 12, which outlines the duties of the bailiff's wife. He discusses what grape variety to use in which type of soil; yield in relation to labour and capital outlay (he assumes that a well-managed vineyard will yield at least 20 AMPHORAE *per iugerum*, approximately 20 hl/ha (1.1 tons/acre), and possibly 30); planting; propagating; pruning; training and dressing; grafting (Books 3–4); the vintage, and wine-making (Book 12). Half of an earlier, shorter, work called *De arboribus* ('On trees') also survives: it has a section on vines which is much briefer than the corresponding sections of *De re rustica*.

H.M.W.

Martin, R., *Recherches sur les agronomes latins* (Paris, 1971).
White, K. D., *Roman Farming* (London, 1970).

COMITÉ INTERPROFESSIONNEL, body representing all interests concerned with the production of a certain wine and the French counterpart to the CONSORZIO of Italy and the CONSEJO REGULADOR. The model for all such organizations was the CIVC of champagne.

COMMANDARIA, a dark dessert wine speciality of the island of CYPRUS with a honeyed, raisiny flavour and alcohol content usually around 15 per cent, produced from partially raisined grapes.

The name Commandaria dates from the Lusignan period of the island's history (1192–1489) and was derived from the Knights of St John of Jerusalem's chief feudal holding, called the Grand Commandery, within which lay the vineyards producing the wine. This type of wine, however, was already well known centuries before the time of the Crusades. As long ago as 800 BC the Greek poet HESIOD described a sweet Cypriot wine, produced from sun-dried grapes. Cyprus Nama, the forerunner of Commandaria, was famed throughout the classical world (see DRIED GRAPE WINES).

In 1993 Commandaria became the first Cypriot wine to be granted full, legal protection covering both its geographical origin and production techniques. Commandaria must be produced within a strictly defined region comprising fourteen wine-producing villages on the Troodos foothills about 30 km/20 miles north of Limassol, from the Mavro (red) and Xynisteri (white) grape varieties, trained in the traditional low bush form. White grapes bring increased subtlety to Commandaria.

The vintage usually takes place in mid September. When picked, the grapes must be capable of giving juice with a minimum sugar level of 212 g/l for Xynisteri, and 258 g/l for Mavro. After picking the grapes are dried in the sun for at least one week. At the end of this period the sugar content of the juice must lie within the range of 390 g/l to 450 g/l.

FERMENTATION, which must take place within the Commandaria region, stops naturally long before all the sugar is converted into alcohol, leaving a wine with considerable residual sweetness and a minimum ALCOHOLIC STRENGTH of 10 per cent. At this stage the wine is normally moved to one of the large wineries in Limassol to mature (rather as PORT is shipped down the Douro to Vila Nova de Gaia).

Once fermentation has been completed, the alcohol content of the wine may be increased by the addition of pure grape spirit (95 per cent alcohol) or wine distillate (at least 70 per cent alcohol), but the wine's actual alcohol must not exceed 20 per cent, while its total POTENTIAL ALCOHOL must be at least 22.5 per cent. Commandaria must be matured in oak casks for at least two years. In practice it is usually matured, in underground cellars, for considerably longer than this. Some producers use a three-tier SOLERA system.

Though of limited commercial importance, even within Cyprus, Commandaria is one of the world's classic wines, and may well have the longest continuous history of any wine still in production. A premium version should be of real interest.

G.J.L.

COMMON MARKET, EUROPEAN. See EUROPEAN UNION for details of this international organization of member countries.

COMMUNE, French for village or parish.

CONFEDERATION OF INDEPENDENT STATES. See CIS.

COMPETITIONS, WINE. Well-run reputable wine competitions can play an important part in the sales success of a wine producer, which is why some wine labels are adorned with MEDALS and the like, and some wine merchants' lists are dotted with lists of awards. Care should be taken when studying these claims that the competition was a recent and respected one, and that successful wine was exactly the same as the one being offered. One of the most ambitious and successful international wine competitions is that held every May in London under the auspices of *WINE* magazine. It attracts many thousands of entries from around the world and most of its gold medal winning wines are of genuinely superior quality. It should be remembered, however, that few of the world's most revered producers enter such competitions, and certainly none of those who produce very limited quantities. It is difficult to imagine there will ever be a wine competition which will identify the best, rather than the best of those who have something to gain by entering.

For more details of how competitions work, see JUDGING WINE.

COMPLETER, ancient white grape variety grown in Graubünden in eastern SWITZERLAND. The wine produced, pungent, acidic, and full bodied, is a speciality of Herrschaft.

COMPOST, the name given to the product of microbial action on organic wastes under controlled conditions. Compost can be created from winery wastes, typically MARC, and it may be mixed for example with animal manures which encourages microbial action and resultant high temperatures. Compost is applied to vineyard soils and, being rich in ORGANIC MATTER and NUTRIENTS, improves vine growth. However, compost making and distribution requires handling large quantities of material, and for this reason most vine-growers around the world use manufactured FERTILIZERS. The use of compost and other organic soil amendments is, however, an integral part of ORGANIC VITICULTURE.

R.E.S.

CONCA DE BARBERÁ, small but promising wine zone in Spanish CATALONIA, sandwiched in between PENEDÈS, COSTERS DEL SEGRE, and TARRAGONA (see map on p. 907). At around 500 m/1,600 ft above sea level, this DO experiences cold winters, and hot summer days are tempered by cool winds from the sea. Miguel TORRES of Penedès recognized the grape-growing potential of the LIMESTONE country around the Castillo de Milmanda and some of his best CABERNET, PINOT NOIR, and CHARDONNAY grapes are sourced in the zone. Torres has been attempting to form a federation between Conca de Barberá and Penedès 40 km/25 miles away. Some interesting rosé wines are also made from the local Trepat vine.

Most of Conca de Barberá's grapes are used to produce CAVA, however, and consequently few wines carry the name of the DO on the label. In the early 1990s negotiations were well under way to draw up a federation between Conca de Barberá and nearby Penedès, leading to a possible future merger between the two regions.

R.J.M.

CONCENTRATED GRAPE MUST. See GRAPE CONCENTRATE.

CONCENTRATION, umbrella term for any wine-making operation which serves to remove volatile substances, mainly water, from grape juice or wine. Its most common application has been in the production of GRAPE CONCENTRATE but a range of more sophisticated concentration techniques is increasingly used on grapes and musts, often only on a certain portion of the total must, in order to produce more concentrated wines.

One component in a mixture can be concentrated either using differences in boiling points, in freezing points, or in molecular size. The usual technique for making grape concentrate is to use differences in boiling points in a low-pressure, low-temperature evaporator. While very effective in concentrating sugar, this technique has the disadvantage of also removing volatile FLAVOUR COMPOUNDS.

A more recent and more sophisticated technique, used since 1989 in some parts of France as an alternative to ENRICHMENT, involves evaporating grape must under vacuum. Under vacuum, the water in the must evaporates at temperatures of about 20 °C/68 °F, no hotter than fermentation temperatures and therefore involving no dangerous loss of flavour. The equipment needed is relatively expensive, but less labour intensive than the alternatives outlined below.

Freeze concentration, using differences in freezing points, is used to make a range of sweet wines of varying qualities. The EISWEIN of Germany and Austria and the ICE WINE of Canada and elsewhere is made by picking frozen grapes from the vine, crushing them, and filtering the juice without allowing the mixture to thaw so that water is removed in the form of ice. Ice crystals are collected on the filter along with the more usual grape solids (skins etc.) and the result is grape juice with a lower concentration of water, but a higher concentration of sugars, acids, and other soluble solids.

Natural freezing on the vine is replicated by producers in such different regions as SAUTERNES (where it is called CRYOEXTRACTION) and NEW ZEALAND. Freshly picked grapes may be frozen in special chillers prior to crushing and filtering. This technique is often practised selectively, not just for sweet white wines, but also on grapes destined to make dry white wines, not all of which are fully ripe. Since just-ripe grapes freeze at 0 °C/32 °F but fully ripe grapes freeze only at −6 °C or below, the mixture of grapes is chilled before crushing to an intermediate temperature so that it yields only the ripest juice (although it will yield nothing if there are no ripe grapes in the first place). The technique can only be practised on individual batches of grapes, however, so is relatively labour intensive.

Differences in molecular size have long been used to purify substances other than wine. The development of physically strong plastic membrane filters with very small pores of nearly uniform size means that the technique can be applied to purifying drinking water, and concentrating wine. Osmotic pressure is that minimum pressure necessary to prevent pure solvent from passing through the membrane into a solution prepared with the same solvent. The alcohol in wine can be concentrated using a membrane separating wine from water through which alcohol cannot pass. If there were the same pressure on both sides of the membrane, water would go through to the wine since its concentration is less in the wine. But if the pressure on the wine side of the membrane is increased considerably, water passes from the wine side to the pure water side, a process called reverse osmosis, since the behaviour is the reverse of that observed when pressure is the same on each side of the membrane.

One final method of concentrating grape must is also the oldest: desiccation. See DRIED GRAPE WINES.

Because in general these methods remove only water from the grapes or must, all other components are concentrated. An increased concentration of fermentable SUGARS results in a wine with a higher ALCOHOLIC STRENGTH. Increased concentrations of PHENOLICS in many cases result in wines with more BODY, potential for AGEING, and possibly more flavour. Increased ACIDITY, however, can result in wines that are aggressively tart, especially in less ripe years or in cooler wine regions. In some cases, particularly in cooler areas, musts which have been concentrated may have to be further subjected to DEACIDIFICATION, although in temperate climates TOTAL ACIDITY is usually only very slightly raised once TARTRATES have been precipitated.

McWhirter, K., 'The End of Chaptalisation?', *Wine & Spirit* (Mar. 1993), 75.

CONCORD, the most important vine variety grown in the eastern United States, notably in NEW YORK state. It belongs to the American vine species *Vitis labrusca* and the pronounced FOXY flavour of its juice make its wine an acquired taste for those raised on the produce of VINIFERA vines. It was named after Concord, Massachusetts, by Ephraim W. Bull, who introduced it, having planted the seeds of a WILD VINE there in 1843. It is particularly important for the production of GRAPE JUICE and grape jelly, but it produces a wide range of wines, often with some considerable RESIDUAL SUGAR. Viticulturally, the vine is extremely well adapted to the low temperatures of New York and is both productive and vigorous. Some Concord has also been grown in Brazil. See also VITIS and LABRUSCA.

CONDADO DE HUELVA, Spanish denominated wine zone in ANDALUCÍA, close to the city of Huelva between the JEREZ region and the Portuguese border (see map on p. 750). Nowadays few of its wines, which have typically been FORTIFIED and made in the image of its neighbour SHERRY, are exported but the region has a long history (see SPAIN, history). In 'The Pardoner's Tale' Chaucer refers to the wines of Lepe, a small town just outside the modern Condado de Huelva DO and a notorious source of blending wine, and by the early 16th century the wines of Huelva were being exported to northern Europe and the emerging colonies in South America. But from the 17th century much of Huelva's production was sold to Jerez, where it was blended anonymously into sherry SOLERAS. Huelva became a DO in its own right in 1964. The principal grape is the rather neutral ZALEMA along with smaller quantities of PALOMINO.

Three styles of wine are made. Condado Palido is a pale, dry fortified wine matured in a solera under a blanket of FLOR so that it resembles a coarse FINO sherry. Condado Viejo is a RANCIO style of wine aged in a solera resembling a somewhat rustic Jerez OLOROSO. Vino Joven, on the other hand, is a slightly bland, unfortified, table wine on which the local cooperative has been working. It is often fermented cool and bottled young and by the mid 1990s accounted for around a third of the region's total production. R.J.M.

CONDRIEU, distinctive white wine made in minuscule quantities in the northern RHÔNE. It is made exclusively from the VIOGNIER grape, whose successful wines manage the unusual combination of a pronounced yet elusive perfume with substantial BODY. The variety was planted all over southern France in the 1980s and early 1990s, often on the strength of the vigneron's enthusiasm for Condrieu.

This small appellation encompasses seven right bank communes (which happen to span three *départements*, the Rhône, Loire, and Ardèche) just south of the red wine appellation CÔTE-RÔTIE where the river turns a bend and the best vineyards are exposed to the south (see map on p. 796). The vine has probably been cultivated here for two millennia, since nearby Vienne was an important Roman city, although the total Condrieu *vignoble* fell to fewer than 10 ha/25 acres in the 1960s, when the wine was virtually unknown outside local restaurants, and when other fruit crops were much more profitable.

Since the 1970s, however, Condrieu's fame and price have risen steadily, and an increasing number of growers have been prepared to reconstruct small patches of vineyard on the steep, often granitic slopes, the best of which are traditionally said to have a topsoil of *arzelle*, or decomposed mica. The best sites should also be sheltered from the north wind, which can decimate the potential crop at FLOWERING, but little can be done to combat the inevitable SOIL EROSION. Average yields here are notoriously low (and very much lower than for Viognier planted further south), which is one reason why Condrieu is relatively expensive for a wine that is best drunk young, at between two and four years in general.

At one time Condrieu was a sweet or medium sweet wine but almost all is made dry today. Vinification standards are extremely variable, particularly since some vignerons are relative newcomers (even if their grandfathers were experienced in making Condrieu). Two of the most experienced wine-makers are Multier at Ch du Rozay and Georges Vernay. Policies on such fundamentals as the desirability of MALOLACTIC FERMENTATION and use of OAK vary considerably in Condrieu.

In 1990 there were 40 ha/100 acres of vineyard old enough to produce AC wine, but the total area under vine grew so rapidly in the early 1990s that bottlings from Viognier vines too young for full appellation status were almost as common as Condrieu itself.

CH-GRILLET, France's other all-Viognier appellation, is an enclave within the Condrieu zone.

CONEGLIANO, base of the main experimental viticultural station in the VENETO region of north east Italy. The Istituto Sperimentale per la Viticoltura was established in 1923. Six years later it expanded its operations to include OENOLOGY and its first director was Professor Dalmasso, whose Dalmasso Commission made a significant report on the state of the Italian wine industry (see ITALY). In 1933 Conegliano became involved in combating ADULTERATION AND FRAUD in an area which was expanded in 1965 to include not just Veneto but also FRIULI. At the same time an experimental winery was established at Conegliano.

A 9-ha nursery for an ampelographical collection of vine varieties had been established in 1951, and another estate of 20 ha/50 acres was acquired nearby in 1963. From 1967 the institute's work was focused on viticulture, with four central units concerned with AMPELOGRAPHY and VINE IMPROVEMENT, biology and protection, PROPAGATION, and cultivation techniques. There are further units located around Italy and the institute is responsible for CLONAL SELECTION, research into ROOTSTOCKS, and an ampelographic collection of more than 2,000 VINE VARIETIES.

Conegliano's influence extends all over Italy, and not just because many of the country's better producers and consultant OENOLOGISTS have trained here. Important concerns include vine improvement (of TABLE GRAPES as well as scions and rootstocks), research into FUNGAL DISEASES and insect PESTS, propagating techniques, and environmental influences on grape quality and yield.

CONFRÉRIES, French 'brotherhoods' or associations, dedicated in particular to advancing the cause of various foods and drinks throughout France. More than 150 of them, most of them founded in the second half of the 20th century, are devoted to such various products as macaroons, jams, olives, and local shellfish. A high proportion of them, almost half, are based on specific wines and other alcoholic drinks. One of the most famous is the Confrérie des Chevaliers de Tastevin in Burgundy (see CLOS DE VOUGEOT). The Commanderie du Bontemps du MÉDOC et des Graves in Bordeaux is also well known. It was founded in 1949 by the energetic Henri Martin, and even markets its own Cuvée de la Commanderie du Bontemps Médoc. The oldest of these confréries, the Jurade de ST-ÉMILION, owes its origins to the late 12th century, when the town councillors of this ancient town were given particular powers and responsibilities by the English crown, which then governed it (see BORDEAUX, history). It was reconstituted in 1947. These confréries are devoted to an annual programme of pageantry, feasting, and the *intronisation* (enthronement) of honorary converts to the cause. The *intronisation* process of the Commanderie du Bontemps du Médoc et des Graves involves public, but assisted, BLIND TASTING.

The Chevaliers de Tastevin, one of the most famous **confréries**, whose 'intronisation' of new members takes place amid much pomp at the Clos de Vougeot.

CONGENERS, a general term, from the same Latin root as the word 'generic', for the many and various impurities found in a spirit, whatever its origin, when it is distilled below 100 per cent alcohol. The lower the ALCOHOLIC STRENGTH to which the raw material is distilled, the higher the proportion of these impurities, reaching a maximum of just over two per cent of the total in ARMAGNAC distilled in the older type of still to just over 50 per cent alcohol.

These impurities, however, are precisely the ingredients which provide spirits with their character, and thus their interest to the drinker. Hence the need to arrive at a delicate balance to include as many of the aromatic congeners as possible, while excluding the noxious ones. The distiller's task is further complicated because these congeners vary widely, and include ALDEHYDES, PHENOLICS, and more or less aromatic ESTERS. Up to 150 different congeners may be present in a newly distilled spirit, whether it be whisky or BRANDY, and the combination of the spirit with WOOD produces up to a further 200 congeners, the result of OXIDATION and reactions between the spirit and wood components, most notably lignins and TANNINS.

Although they are present only in minute doses in FORTIFIED wines and spirits, they contribute, in mysterious and still barely understood ways, to the quality and likely effects of the final product. They are thought to make a significant contribution to hangovers. N.F.

CONNOISSEURSHIP of wine is an art in search of a less emotive name. The word **connoisseur** in English, and its counterpart *connaisseur* in French, conjures up a frightening vision of an elderly male so steeped in wine, wine knowledge, and wine prejudices as to be completely unapproachable. Much more attractive and widely acceptable terms are those which convey not just knowledge but an element of relish such as wine lover, wine enthusiast, or, the common and attractive French term *amateur du vin*. None of these terms, incidentally, has any connotation of gender.

Whatever the drawbacks of the term, connoisseurship or wine expertise is an art that can give pleasure, and involves less an arid grasp of the precise ENCÉPAGEMENT of each vineyard and fermentation regimes for each vintage than an intelligent appreciation of how wines are likely to taste in a given environment, at a certain stage in their evolution, before or after other wines, and, importantly, with different foods. This is what consumers rather than producers are for. Experience can contribute to connoisseurship, but only if the consumer tastes with attention and an open mind. Some newcomers to wine have an instinctive grasp of connoisseurship.

See wine TASTING, AGEING, SERVING, and FOOD AND WINE.

CONSEJO REGULADOR, Spanish term meaning 'regulating council'. Spanish wine law is administered through a network of Consejos Reguladores representing each and every DO. They comprise vine-growers, wine producers, and merchants who between them decide on the ground rules for their region.

CONSORZIO, Italian word for a consortium or association, notably of wine-growers dedicated to regulation. The most famous in Italian wine is the **Consorzio Chianti Classico**, which has been instrumental in promoting and defending the wines of CHIANTI CLASSICO. Its counterpart in France is the COMITÉ INTERPROFESSIONNEL; in Spain the CONSEJO REGULADOR.

CONSTANTIA, legendary, aromatic, concentrated 18th century dessert wines from the Cape, SOUTH AFRICA, then a Dutch colony. Their fame was never matched by any other New World wines and at their height they commanded more prestige, more fabulous prices, and enjoyed more crowned patronage than the most celebrated wines of Europe. Save one, Hungarian TOKAY. Constantia was even ordered by Napoleon from his exile on the island of St Helena!

The Cape wines were grown at the 750-ha/1,850-acre Constantia Estate just outside Cape Town, in the lee of Table Mountain, founded in 1685 by an early Dutch governor, Simon van der Stel. But it was Constantia's subsequent owners who achieved acclaim and prosperity, principally Hendrik Cloete, who purchased and restored it in 1778. Quality and fame gradually began to fade after the British occupied the Cape following the Napoleonic Wars and Cape wine in general faced decline and neglect after 1861, when the Gladstone government removed empire preferential tariffs.

The sweet wines of Constantia, both red and white, the latter the more expensive, were made principally from MUSCAT BLANC À PETITS GRAINS and its dark-berried mutation, probably including the lesser MUSCAT OF ALEXANDRIA together with the dark red PONTAC. Analyses of recently opened bottles (still perfumed with a 'tang of citrus and smoky richness' according to South African writer Michael Fridjhon) show they were unfortified although high in alcohol, apparently confirming records that the grapes were left on the vines long after ripeness to achieve shrivelled, but not BOTRYTIZED, concentration (see DRIED GRAPE WINES for more details of the

The original Cape Dutch homestead at Groot **Constantia**.

technique). Other stories suggest the wines may have been fortified by shippers for protection on the long, rough, and hot journey across the equator to Europe.

An 18th century Cape society diarist, Lady Anne Barnard, provides one of the most detailed reports of this era. 'What struck me most', she said after watching the pressing of the Constantia desserts of Hendrik Cloete, 'was the beautiful antique forms, perpetually changing and perpetually graceful, of the three bronze figures, half naked, who were dancing in the wine press beating the drum (as it were) with their feet in perfect time. Of these presses, there were four with three slaves in each.'

Groot Constantia has been a government wine estate since 1885 but in 1993 the government announced plans to privatize it within a few years. In recent times, Constantia has made sound, unexciting conventional wines. A neighbouring privately owned estate, Klein (Little) Constantia, a subdivision of the original farm, has been first to take up the challenge to re-enact the legend. It replanted vineyards of Muscat of Frontignan in 1980 and now produces naturally high-alcohol white dessert wines (also without botrytis—in the manner of the old Constantia's) to some local acclaim.

See also SOUTH AFRICA, history. J. P.

Burman, J., *Wine of Constantia* (Cape Town, 1979).
Johnson, H., 'Groot Constantia', in *The Story of Wine* (London, 1989).
Leipold, C. L., *Three Hundred Years of Cape Wines* (Cape Town, 1952).

CONSULTANTS are used with increasing frequency in wine production, selling, and occasionally consumption. Consultant VITICULTURISTS are particularly useful since they can work for much of the year and those who operate on an international scale can import knowledge gleaned from a wide variety of different vine-growing environments. They are commonly used to introduce new CANOPY MANAGEMENT techniques to established vineyards, or to advise, for example, on suitable ROOTSTOCKS for new vineyards. Like viticulturists, the more energetic consultant OENOLOGISTS can use their expertise in both hemispheres, although their work is necessarily limited by the timing of HARVEST. One of the most famous international wine-making consultants is Professor Émile PEYNAUD, although there are now many who travel more extensively and perhaps take a more active role in wine-making processes (see FLYING WINE-MAKERS).

Many restaurateurs and hoteliers, most airlines, and even some wine retailers employ consultants in their wine selection.

CONSUMPTION of wine throughout the world is about 230 million hl / 6,000 million gal a year and has in general been falling rapidly since the mid 1980s. Since PRODUCTION has remained stable or has declined much more slowly, this has resulted in a serious global wine SURPLUS that is most acute in Europe, the most important producer and consumer of wine.

The countries with the highest per capita wine consumption in the early 1990s were still mainly the most important wine producers: France and Italy, Portugal, and Argentina. Total national wine consumption has fallen significantly in each of these countries since the early 1980s. Countries in which total national wine consumption rose significantly in the 1980s were South Africa, Japan, and the Netherlands.

The following are national annual per capita wine consumption figures in litres according to the OIV:

Country	*1991*	*1992*
France	67.00	64.50
Italy	60.28	60.28
Luxembourg	60.30	59.70
Portugal	62.00	55.00
Argentina	55.01	51.63
Switzerland	47.20	44.47
Spain	39.77	39.10
Slovenia	40.00	39.00
Austria	33.70	33.10
Greece	32.40	31.50
Hungary	30.00	30.00
Chile	29.50	29.50
Denmark	23.60	25.56
Uruguay	25.40	25.40
Germany	26.10	22.80
ex Yugoslavia	22.10	n.a.
Romania	19.30	21.30
Belgium	21.10	21.10
Australia	17.70	18.60
Netherlands	16.50	16.50
Cyprus	13.20	13.70
New Zealand	12.10	12.80
Sweden	12.78	12.78
Bulgaria	12.43	12.43
United Kingdom	10.29	12.40
Czechoslovakia	11.80	11.80
South Africa	9.06	8.90
Canada	8.28	8.28
United States	7.12	7.11
CIS	6.95	n.a.
Norway	6.90	6.90
Ireland	4.50	5.00
Finland	4.49	4.86
Israel	3.50	3.20
Tunisia	2.20	2.20
Paraguay	2.01	2.01
Poland	1.95	1.95
Brazil	1.83	1.83
Algeria	1.53	1.53
Morocco	0.99	1.36
Jordan	0.90	0.90
Japan	0.91	0.86
Turkey	0.47	0.57
Peru	0.47	0.47
Mexico	0.22	0.21
China	0.08	0.08

See HEALTH for official medical advice on safe personal consumption levels of alcoholic drinks.

CONTAINERS for wine are used at four main stages in a wine's life: during the FERMENTATION that creates it, during its

MATURATION, for its TRANSPORT, and for SERVING it. Moreover, while wine containers have changed throughout history, they have also varied through space, with each wine-making region becoming characterized by vessels of different dimensions.

History

A wide variety of materials were used for drinking and serving wine in Ancient CHINA. In prehistoric times in the eastern Mediterranean, wine was generally put in earthenware jars, or sometimes into WOODEN containers, soon after the grapes had been trodden or pressed, and this basic fermentation technology remained the norm until the 20th century, when VATS or tanks of concrete and STAINLESS STEEL were introduced. The basic receptacles used for storing and transporting wine in classical antiquity were pottery AMPHORAE which varied greatly in size and shape, but which had the important characteristic that they could be sealed, thus preventing the potentially harmful access of OXYGEN. During the 1st century BC experiments were also undertaken in transporting wine in large jars, known as *dolia*, anchored amidships, but their use did not persist. By the end of the 1st century AD amphorae seem no longer to have been used, and most wine was transported long distance in wooden BARRELS. For short distances numerous other vessels, and in particular animal skins, were also used, especially in Iberia.

Throughout the medieval period wooden barrels served as almost the only vessels used for maturing and transporting wine, and their sizes came to reflect local custom and requirements. The standard barrel size in England, for example, the BUTT or PIPE, was fixed by statute in the 15th century at 126 imperial gallons (572.8 l). However, in southern Italy at the same time, their wooden *botti* held about 454 l, while in Bruges the butt had a capacity of about 910 l; in Spain it varied from 454 to 477 litres. Meanwhile, it had been discovered in Germany that wines kept in larger barrels, providing they were not subjected to RACKING, lasted longer. This led to the construction of huge wooden tuns, containing thousands of litres, among the most famous of which were the Strasbourg Tun of 1472, and the Heidelberg Tuns of 1591 and 1663.

For serving wine small jugs made of pottery were generally used during the medieval period. However, from the 16th century glass BOTTLES became more frequently used, and by the second half of the 17th century these bottles began to be used to mature wines. Bottle shapes evolved so as to allow extended BOTTLE AGEING and thus were born VINTAGE wines, and CONNOISSEURSHIP. Moreover, the use of bottles also enabled completely new types of wine, such as CHAMPAGNE and vintage PORT, to be produced. P.T.H.U.

Modern times

For details of containers used for fermentation, see FERMENTATION VESSELS, which may be either open topped or closed, and may have a capaciity as big as 300 hl. Wines are matured prior to bottling in closed containers (to avoid OXIDATION), either in tanks made from materials such as stainless steel or concrete, or in some form of COOPERAGE, from small, new oak barrels to large, old casks, or even in some cases in ceramic TINAJAS or glass BONBONNES. Wine may be blended in even larger tanks holding up to 15,000 hl. Wine is transported either in BULK, usually in food-grade 250-hl stainless steel tankers, or, increasingly, in bottle, its final container before the wine GLASS, possibly after spending a short time in a DECANTER. Newer containers used in packaging wine include BOXES and CANS.

When transport containers are used for shipping wine in bottle, care is taken by some fine wine merchants and some fine wine producers that the wine is shipped only in temperature-controlled containers, and sometimes only during cooler times of year. This is particularly important for wines which have undergone a minimum of FILTRATION. For more details, see TRANSPORT.

Allen, H. W., *A History of Wine: Great Vintage Wines from the Homeric Age to the Present Day* (London, 1961).
Peacock, D. P. S., and Williams, D. F., *Amphorae and the Roman Economy: An Introductory Guide* (London, 1986).
Unwin, P. T. H., *Wine and the Vine: An Historical Geography of Viticulture and the Wine Trade* (London, 1992).

CONTAMINANTS, potentially harmful substances found in wine, either as a result of air or water pollution, vineyard treatment RESIDUES, poor winery HYGIENE, ignorance, or ADULTERATION and FRAUD.

Of these, ignorance is possibly the most forgivable reason for contamination since the scope of what is regarded as, and can be measured as, a contaminant grows wider with the rapid progress of science and measuring techniques. LEAD, for example, which was deliberately added to wines by the Romans, is now known to be a serious neural toxin. CARBAMATES, on the other hand, have been regarded as contaminants only since the late 1980s.

Nowadays, contamination as a result of poor winery hygiene is extremely rare. Pollution is difficult to guard against. Wine producers are increasingly wary of some AGROCHEMICALS, however. Orthene, a new fungicide used widely in the early 1980s, with no ill effects apparent during winemaking, produced a range of wines with an extremely unpleasant smell after several years' BOTTLE AGE. Many German wines made in the early to mid 1980s, particularly the 1983s, exhibited this particular contamination. The ST-ESTÈPHE property Ch Phélan-Ségur, a famous CRU BOURGEOIS, destroyed its entire 1984 and 1985 production because of Orthene contamination. And American authorities, in particular, have regularly applied stringent tests for traces of recently suspected contaminants, such as procymidone from agrochemical RESIDUES, to imported wines.

The wine trade, like every other commercial activity, has its villains, but they are increasingly rare. Fortunately, very few of the substances which the least scrupulous producers are tempted to add illegally to wine (SORBITOL and GLYCOLS, for example) are harmful—with the notable and horrifying exception of lethal doses of METHANOL added to one Italian producer's wines in 1987.

See also ADULTERATION, which sometimes involves the deliberate addition of contaminants.

For most of the last 2,000 years, the barrel was the usual **container** for storing and transporting wine, as here in 16th century Antwerp, where barrels were apparently moved from ship to merchants ashore by human treadmill.

CONTINENTAL climate is one with a high degree of **continentality**, defined for any place as the difference between the average mean temperature of its hottest month and that of its coldest month. Climates with a wide annual range are called continental; those with a narrow range, maritime. The former tend to be in the interiors of the larger continents; the latter, near oceans or other large water bodies.

The most continental viticultural climates are those of central and eastern Europe, together with inland northern America (see RUSSIA and CANADA, for example). The European west coastal and most Mediterranean viticultural regions rank as intermediate, while the most maritime viticultural climate of all is that of MADEIRA. All viticultural regions of the southern hemisphere, even those well inland, are classed (in this sense) as maritime. That is because the total land mass of the southern hemisphere is small relative to that of the oceans, which thus dominate temperatures.

The rapid autumn temperature drop in continental climates means that RIPENING can be precarious. Vintage variation therefore tends to be marked, and the effects of high YIELDS on ripening and wine quality are probably more evident than in maritime climates when autumn temperatures drop slowly, and ripening is relatively assured. Cool maritime climates, on the other hand, can result in viticultural problems due to insufficient warmth during FLOWERING and FRUIT SET.

European experience shows that ideal continental seasons can lead to superb wines when combined with appropriate cropping levels. Against that, maritime climates that are warm and sunny enough during flowering and setting can probably produce good quality more reliably, and thus have practical advantages for commercial viticulture.

See also CLIMATE AND WINE QUALITY, and MEDITERRANEAN CLIMATE. J.G. & R.E.S.

CONTINUOUS FERMENTATION or **continuous vinification**, relatively rare process of conducting white wine fermentation continuously rather than traditionally in batches. The process ideally introduces MUST at a lower section of a tank filled with grape juice undergoing FERMENTATION and withdraws wine from near the top of the tank. These tanks are usually tall in relation to their diameter to take advantage of the decrease in DENSITY when fermentation occurs. LEES are removed from the bottom of the tank and floating solids at the very top by a mechanical conveyor system. The partially fermented wine, still containing some SUGARS, that leaves the top of the tank is usually allowed to complete fermentation in a separate static tank.

This process was introduced for inexpensive white wines and is now confined almost exclusively to the production of low quality base wines for DISTILLATION in regions such as Mexico. It is practically impossible to produce good-quality wine this way because the YEAST needs access to OXYGEN in the early stages of growth, but SULPHUR DIOXIDE added to control other micro-organisms also eliminates most of the oxygen in the tank. It is also difficult to control TEMPERATURE, resulting in a cooked flavour which is exacerbated, if sulphur dioxide is not added, by off-odours resulting from BACTERIAL SPOILAGE. A.D.W.

CONTINUOUS METHOD, SPARKLING WINE-MAKING process developed in the USSR for SOVIET SPARKLING WINE and now used in Germany and Portugal. The method involves a series of usually five reticulated tanks under five atmospheres of pressure, the same FIZZINESS as in most sparkling wines. At one end base wine together with sugar and yeast (usually rehydrated dried yeast) is pumped in and the SECOND FERMENTATION crucial to virtually all methods of sparkling winemaking begins. This creates CARBON DIOXIDE, which increases the pressure in the tank but the yeast cannot grow under this pressure and so additional yeast has to be added continuously. The second and third tanks are partly filled with some material such as wood shavings, which offer a substantial total surface area on which the dead yeast cells accumulate and a certain amount of AUTOLYSIS, or at least reaction between the dead yeast cells and the wine, takes place. In the fourth and fifth tanks there are no yeast cells and the wine eventually emerges relatively clear, having spent an average of perhaps three or four weeks in the system. See also LANCERS.

CONTINUOUS STILL, a still used for DISTILLATION of liquids continuously passed through it, as opposed to batch distillation in a POT STILL. It tends to produce more neutral spirits with much lower levels of CONGENERS than those distilled in a pot still. By far the most common continuous still used for spirits is the COFFEY STILL.

The continuous still, while far more efficient than a pot still, is more brutal in its handling of the raw material. And in most continuous stills (although not in the special type used in ARMAGNAC) the hot wine is mixed with steam to help extract the alcohol, thus further coarsening the resulting spirit.

As the illustration shows, a continuous still uses two columns. In one, wine is preheated in a heat exchanger. It is then introduced at the top of a 'fractionating' column, so called because it divides the contents of the wine into fractions, by encouraging it to trickle down through a series of perforated plates. The alcohol is released when the wine hits the hot plates in a cloud of steam rising from the base of the column. The (lighter) alcohol fumes then emerge from the top of the column. The ALDEHYDES and other highly volatile elements pass to the very top of the column, while the desirable FUSEL OILS are concentrated about four plates from the top.

As can be imagined, there are numerous variants on the basic process. The most important is the number of plates in the distilling column. The more there are, the more highly purified ('rectified', in the language of distillation) is the spirit and the fewer impurities it contains. At the limit, a spirit of 100 per cent alcohol would be totally characterless. But even a spirit which emerges as 95 per cent pure alcohol has a surprising amount of character. At the other extreme, the brandies distilled to a mere 52 per cent in traditional armagnac stills retain a disproportionate percentage of the chemical ingredients, notably the congeners, in the original wine.

The actual percentage of these impurities may be very small (a maximum of two per cent of solid matter) but the difference in the character of the spirit, the extent to which it needs long maturation, and the resulting complexity of the mature spirit are striking. Inevitably complexity brings its own risks in terms of impurities, which are the more obvious and concentrated through the process of distillation. For this, the lower the percentage strength of the wine used as raw material the better, since the greater the volume of wine needed to produce a cask of spirit, the greater the volume of essential, flavour-making ingredients. N.F.

CONTROLIRAN, Bulgarian answer to France's APPELLATION CONTRÔLÉE category of superior wines. See BULGARIA.

CONTROLLED APPELLATIONS, a method of LABELLING wine and designating quality that is modelled on France's APPELLATION CONTRÔLÉE system. It embraces geographical DELIMITATION and is the principle on which QUALITY WINE schemes as the DOC of Italy and Portugal, the DO of Spain, and the AVA system of the United States are based. France has more than 400, Italy more than 200, Greece about 60, and Spain and Portugal an ever-lengthening list. Countries

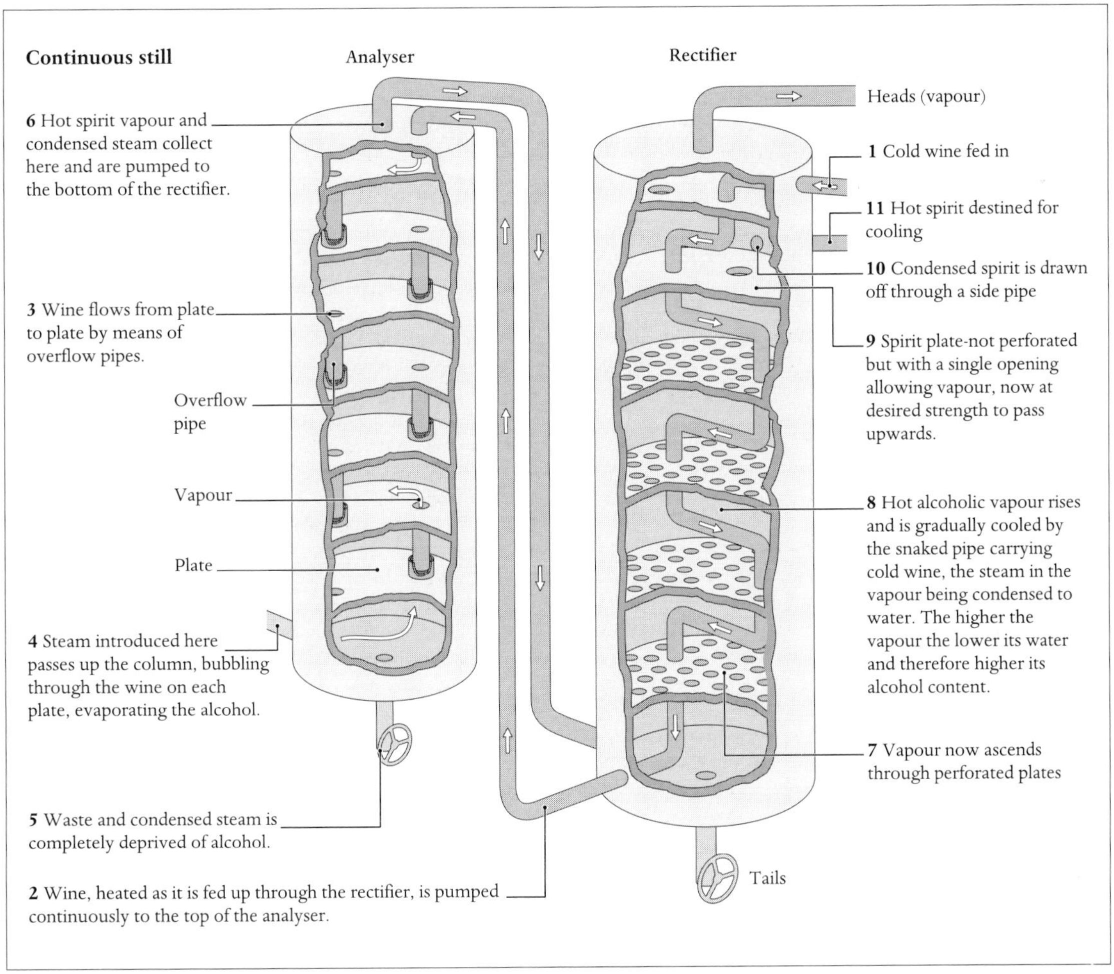
Continuous still
Analyser
Rectifier
Heads (vapour)
6 Hot spirit vapour and condensed steam collect here and are pumped to the bottom of the rectifier.
1 Cold wine fed in
11 Hot spirit destined for cooling
10 Condensed spirit is drawn off through a side pipe
3 Wine flows from plate to plate by means of overflow pipes.
9 Spirit plate-not perforated but with a single opening allowing vapour, now at desired strength to pass upwards.
Overflow pipe
Vapour
8 Hot alcoholic vapour rises and is gradually cooled by the snaked pipe carrying cold wine, the steam in the vapour being condensed to water. The higher the vapour the lower its water and therefore higher its alcohol content.
Plate
4 Steam introduced here passes up the column, bubbling through the wine on each plate, evaporating the alcohol.
7 Vapour now ascends through perforated plates
5 Waste and condensed steam is completely deprived of alcohol.
Tails
2 Wine, heated as it is fed up through the rectifier, is pumped continuously to the top of the analyser.

such as BULGARIA and HUNGARY have devised similar schemes. Controlled appellations were known even in Ancient GREECE; modern Greece has even adopted the French phrases used by the appellation contrôlée system in France for designating its better-quality wines.

COOKING WITH WINE. It is only a short step from recognizing that wine complements a meal (see FOOD AND WINE MATCHING) to using it in cooking, although often as not wine has been used as a means of disguising poor meat or poultry. The recipes of Apicius, the most famous Roman chef, show that wine was commonly used in his sauces and it has found a place in the kitchen ever since.

Wine is an essential ingredient in many dishes and can be used in every stage of cooking from the preparation and tenderizing of meat to providing the final, often sweet, finish to a dessert. It is all the more curious, therefore, that so little research has been done in to exactly what happens to wine, and food, during cooking, particularly as a result of the application of heat. Since the boiling point of ETHANOL is 78 °C/172 °F, considerably lower than that of water, however, it is reasonable to suppose that any wine used in cooking becomes progressively less alcoholic if heated to above 78 °C for any length of time. As a sauce is 'reduced' with wine, the other components in the wine such as any RESIDUAL SUGAR and, especially, its ACIDITY become even more marked. This is presumably why over-reduced sauces can taste so acid, and why they can have an almost caramelized appearance and taste. Other uses for wine in cooking do not involve changing the wine's composition by heating.

There is much debate about the necessary quality of **cooking wine**, some regarding the saucepan as the ideal repository for any wine considered too nasty to drink, others insisting that only the finest wine will do. Wine with an unpleasant flavour will not lose that flavour in the kitchen. On the other hand, the complex BALANCE and full range of volatile FLAVOUR COMPOUNDS of a great wine will not survive the application of any fierce heat.

The following are some of the most common ways in which wine is used in the kitchen.

Deglazing: pouring wine (or another liquid such as stock) into a pan in which something has been roasted or sautéed in order to dissolve the remnants of that operation in the liquid to make a sauce.

Marinade: a method of imparting extra flavour, principally to meat and game, via a mixture based on carrots, shallots, onions, pepper, salt, vinegar, garlic, and red or white wine which takes the form of cooked and uncooked marinades. Instant marinades, using brandy or madeira, are used for the ingredients of pâtés and terrines. After the meat has been removed, the marinade may be used for deglazing or for a more complicated sauce.

Stocks: wine is often used instead of, or as well as, water, to provide the essential base for soups and sauces. Red wine is used in game stock, white wine in chicken and fish stocks.

Court-bouillon: a method of cooking fish, shellfish, or white meat in which herbs and spices are infused in white wine and water in which the food is subsequently poached.

Sauces: of the many which form the basis of classic French cuisine, bordelaise comprises red wine and shallots; périgueux uses madeira, veal stock, and truffles; sauce Robert is white wine, onion, and mustard; and ravigote is made with white wine and vinegar.

Stews and casseroles: wine, preferably from the same area as the dish, is an integral part of *coq au vin*, daube of beef, fish stew, beef bourguignonne, and many more classics of *la cuisine bourgeoise*. Acidic wine will detract rather than enhance.

Desserts: wine has a surprisingly wide range of applications for sweet foods and patisserie. Red wine is used for poaching pears and macerating strawberries (a speciality of Bordeaux) while dessert wines such as Marsala and sherry are used in, respectively, zabaglione and English trifle. In Italy, strong, usually sweet wines, typically VIN SANTO, are served with dry biscuits which are moistened in them. N.L.L.

COOL CLIMATE VITICULTURE, and **warm climate viticulture**, are indefinite terms, depending on the speaker's or writer's viewpoint, but are probably applied most usefully to the coolest and warmest thirds of the climatic or geographic range used successfully for growing wine grapes. Intermediate climate viticulture (see below) lies between, while true hot climate viticulture produces mainly TABLE GRAPES and DRYING GRAPES, and cannot, in general, produce high-quality wine grapes of any kind.

Major areas of cool climate viticulture would certainly include the northern half of France (the LOIRE, CHAMPAGNE, CHABLIS, BURGUNDY, and BEAUJOLAIS): ENGLAND, LUXEMBOURG, GERMANY, SWITZERLAND, and AUSTRIA; in the USA, the Lower Columbia Valley of WASHINGTON and OREGON, and the coolest coastal strip of northern California (CARNEROS, ANDERSON VALLEY); the most southern vineyards of CHILE and SOUTH AFRICA; the South Island and southern North Island of NEW ZEALAND; and in Australia, the whole of TASMANIA, small areas of the higher Adelaide Hills in SOUTH AUSTRALIA, and Drumborg in VICTORIA. Gladstones's data (table 183) show all these to have regional average mean temperatures for the growing season (April to October inclusive in the northern hemisphere, October to April in the southern hemisphere) of below 16.0 °C/60.8 °F. Jackson and Schuster (1987) and the Oregon Wine-growers' Association (1992) deal specifically with this type of viticulture.

The distinguishing characteristic of cool viticultural climates is that they will regularly ripen only early maturing grape varieties such as CHASSELAS, MÜLLER-THURGAU, GEWÜRZTRAMINER, CHARDONNAY, PINOT NOIR, and GAMAY; and only in especially warm MESOCLIMATES can varieties such as RIESLING, which ripens early to mid season, be ripened. RIPENING also tends to take place under cool to mild conditions. The combination leads to wines which, at their best, are fresh, delicate, and aromatic. Most are white or only pale red, because full development of ANTHOCYAN pigments and TANNINS in the grape skins needs greater and more prolonged warmth than does ripening of the flesh (see PHYSIOLOGICAL RIPENESS).

Intermediate climate viticulture is that with growing seasons long and warm enough for regular ripening of mid season grape varieties such as CABERNET FRANC, MERLOT, SYRAH (or Shiraz), and SANGIOVESE, and late mid season varieties such as CABERNET SAUVIGNON and NEBBIOLO, to make mainly medium to full bodied red table wines. Typical regions are BORDEAUX and the northern RHÔNE valley in France; the RIOJA Alta in Spain; much of northern ITALY and TUSCANY; the intermediate and warmer coastal valleys of California, such as the NAPA and SONOMA valleys; the north and east coasts of the North Island of New Zealand; Margaret river and the south coast of WESTERN AUSTRALIA; the Barossa Valley and Hills, Padthaway, and Coonawarra in SOUTH AUSTRALIA; and much of central and southern VICTORIA. Average mean growing season temperatures are in the range 16.0 to 18.5 °C (60.8 to 65.2 °F).

Warm viticultural climates, if sunny enough, will ripen early and mid season grape varieties to high sugar contents and make the best sweet, fortified wines. They will also ripen late maturing grape varieties such as MOURVÈDRE (Mataro), CARIGNAN, GRENACHE, TREBBIANO, and CLAIRETTE for making table wines. Examples are the south of France; the DOURO valley of Portugal and the island of Madeira; the Adelaide district and McLaren Vale in SOUTH AUSTRALIA, the MURRAY RIVER regions of South Australia and Victoria, and the Hunter Valley and Mudgee in NEW SOUTH WALES in Australia. Corresponding average mean growing season temperatures are in the range 18.5 to 21 °C.

Typical hot climate viticultural regions are those producing table and drying grapes in GREECE and TURKEY, and the San Joaquin Valley of California. Growing season average mean temperatures are mostly 22 °C or higher. Subtropical and TROPICAL VITICULTURE for table grapes and wine, using mainly non-VINIFERA grape varieties, also falls into this temperature category.

Relationships of temperature, particularly during ripening, to wine qualities are discussed under CLIMATE AND WINE QUALITY. J.G. & R.E.S.

Casteel, E. (ed.), *Oregon Winegrapes Grower's Guide* (4th edn., Portland, Ore., 1992).
Gladstones, J., *Viticulture and Environment* (Adelaide, 1992).
Jackson, D., and Schuster, D., *The Production of Grapes and Wine in Cool Climates* (Nelson and Melbourne, 1987).

COOLERS. There are two very different types of **wine cooler**. One is a blend of usually rather ordinary wine with fruit juice, water, carbon dioxide, and/or flavourings to produce a LOW-ALCOHOL drink designed to cool the drinker, and introduce him or her gently to the taste of wine. These products, only distantly related to wine itself, enjoyed a vogue in the mid 1980s, particularly in the United States.

The other sort of wine cooler was designed to cool the wine in the days before domestic REFRIGERATION. These large and historic pieces of domestic equipment are sought after by certain collectors of wine ANTIQUES.

History

At least from the 16th century and probably earlier, it has been fashionable to serve some if not all wine chilled. Indeed 17th century tapestries depict both red and white wine being so treated in the same cistern. Until the mid 18th century wine coolers were called cisterns and were probably multi-purpose vessels. The earliest ones were faience (continental pottery); terracotta was also favoured. Silver cisterns date from the 1660s and soon after examples were also made in tinware lacquered and decorated in the prevailing oriental taste. Marble cisterns are found but these are difficult to date and to assign a country of origin accurately. It is probable that they were made throughout Europe over a long period. By the 1730s mahogany was used and was the preferred medium for the remainder of the century. Silver wine cisterns, however, became the ultimate status symbol, the grandest (now in the Hermitage Museum, St Petersburg) being 167.8 cm (5ft 6 in) long and weighing approximately 250 kg/550 lbs. It was made by Charles Kandler in 1734.

It seems that all wine coolers were oval before *c.*1740. Early ones rested on a plinth but they developed legs, the form of the first mahogany examples. A popular model of *c.*1750–70 had coopered sides (perhaps an allusion to the wine barrel) and was held secure with bands of brass. They were fitted with linings of either zinc or lead to contain the iced water necessary to cool the wine. By the 1760s they had acquired lids and the oval gave way to square, octagonal, and hexagonal shapes as the century progressed. As manufacturing techniques advanced, more fanciful shapes emerged and with the fashion for much larger dining rooms, so wine coolers tended to become larger.

The early 19th century saw the popularity of the sarcophagus-shaped cooler. Without legs, but with bun-shaped or paw feet, it sat on the floor in the space between the pedestals of the sideboard and was often made en suite. This pattern, inspired by the allusion to Nelson's victory at Aboukir bay in 1798 and consequently anything Egyptian, remained in vogue almost until the mid century, after which few wine coolers were made, as other forms of domestic refrigeration became more common.

Wine coolers were made also for cooling single bottles on the table, rather than cooling many in a piece of furniture on the floor away from it. Such an arrangement was favoured for informal gatherings and for eating in private. Few table wine coolers were made before 1700 and most afterwards were extremely grand examples of the silversmith's art. A famous pair made *c.*1700 for the duke of Marlborough are solid gold. Japanned tinware examples are delightful, if very rare. Slightly less so are those in cut glass, porcelain, and other ceramic media. The late 18th century saw a burgeoning trade in Sheffield plated coolers that lasted until the 1840s. As electroplating ousted the Sheffield technique at the end of this period, being cheaper to produce and thus to sell, they continued to be made in large numbers and in decreasing quality. R.N.H.B.

Butler, R., and Walkling, G., *The Book of Wine Antiques* (Woodbridge, 1986).
Clayton. M., *Collectors Dictionary of the Silver and Gold of Great Britain and North America* (rev. edn., Woodbridge, 1985).
Hernmarck, C., *The Art of the European Silversmith 1430–1830* (London, 1977).
Weinhold, R., *Vivat Bacchus*, trans. by N. Jones (Watford, 1978).

COONAWARRA, the most popularly revered wine region in AUSTRALIA for red wine made from the CABERNET SAUVIGNON grape grown on its famous limited strip of red TERRA ROSSA soil. For more detail see SOUTH AUSTRALIA.

COOPERAGE is a collective noun for wooden containers (as in 'small OAK cooperage') but has been more traditionally used for both the activities and workplace of **coopers**, those who make and repair small BARRELS and larger wooden VATS. At one time all wine or spirit producers of any size would have their own small cooperage, but today the craft is perpetuated almost exclusively by specialist cooperage businesses. The French term is *tonnellerie*.

History

Until relatively recently coopers played an important role not only in the wine business but in myriad aspects of daily life. Almost all containers—buckets, barrels, tanks—were made by coopers from various woods (see BARRELS, history). Barrels were made to hold salted fish, flour, gunpowder, oil, turpentine, salt, sugar, butter, and many other household commodities since they not only retain even liquids safely but also keep the elements out and are easy to manœuvre.

Coopers' guilds were already established by the end of the ninth century and, during the Middle Ages, laws relating to apprenticeships, master–apprentice relations, and guild memberships were codified throughout Europe (with nepotism already playing its part). At the end of the 18th century there were approximately 8,000 coopers in Paris alone. It is still possible to meet coopers who are the last in a line of

The **cooper's** tools and craft have hardly changed since Roman times.

craftsmen dating back to the 17th century. Such men, who can probably make barrels with handtools alone, may well have served traditional apprenticeships that often involve extensive work in different regions of their own countries as well as abroad.

As Europeans colonized the New World, they inevitably took their coopering skills with them. John Alden, one of the more famous early North American colonists of Plymouth, Massachusetts, was a master cooper and by 1648 there were enough coopers to form a guild in this New England colony. America's important export trade of staves and logs to Europe began slightly later in the 17th century when the Spanish controlled large parts of what is now the United States.

During the 19th century coopering remained an important craft, but the advent of metal (and later plastic) containers ultimately reduced coopering to an adjunct of the drinks business. More than 1 million barrels were made for salted herring in Britain in 1913, for example, but by 1953 the number had dropped to around to one-tenth of this figure and now this business is virtually extinct.

American PROHIBITION had a dramatic impact on the sale of fine wines and spirits, and in turn on the cooperage business—particularly in the United States but also in the British Isles where only those coopers working on beer barrels were unaffected. Before the Second World War most beer barrels were made of wood and many breweries had their own cooperages, but by the early 1960s wooden barrels had been replaced by metal ones. In much of the wine industry too, wood was replaced by concrete, stainless steel, and other neutral materials, particularly for larger tanks (see CONTAINERS).

Cooperage today

As wooden barrels are expensive to buy, use, and maintain, they tend to be used today only for products whose sale price can justify such a major investment or, in the case of older containers, by those who have inherited them.

Cooperages are found wherever there is a wine or spirits business that needs barrels, notably in America, Scotland, and France but also in Italy, Spain, Portugal, Ireland, Eastern Europe, Germany, Australia, and South Africa. Their activities include either or both of making new vats and barrels on the one hand (see BARREL MAKING) and repairing or maintaining older barrels and vats on the other.

Ultimate responsibility for the sale of wine barrels falls to a small but hardy band of barrel salesmen, who are required to commute between wine, spirit, and barrel production centres. They are typically required to BLIND taste a variety of experimental wines. Usually these experiments relate to different TOAST levels, WOOD TYPES, different cooperages, barrel preparation methods, and WINE-MAKING techniques. Sales are made when the representative correctly identifies the best wine as that made in his firm's barrels.

There are no serious industry analysts of the contemporary cooperage business, such as there are in the automotive or electronics industry, since it is effectively just a small part of the timber industry. Nor is there any official regulatory or inspection body as there is in the wine trade. Because of this, facts are few and rumour is rife. In the 1980s it was rumoured that oak was being shipped from Slovenia to Spain, coopered there, and shipped to unsuspecting winery owners as French oak. In the 1990s, the rumour runs the opposite way: that Limousin oak is being sawn and shipped as Slovenian oak! Naturally all coopers maintain that their oak is the best wood, entirely hand split and seasoned in the open air but that their competitors cut corners. In the absence of facts, wine-makers have to rely on results rather than rhetoric.

United States The great majority of wooden barrels traded today are made in the American Midwest for the ageing of bourbon whiskey. It is estimated that every year about 800,000 barrels are made there, made primarily by two cooperages. Only between 30,000 and 50,000 of these so-called bourbon barrels go directly to wineries.

Nearly all American logs come from privately held forests located in the eastern half of the United States, notably in Minnesota, Wisconsin, Kentucky, Arkansas, Tennessee, the Virginias, the Carolinas, and Missouri. These logs are purchased by stave mill operators, some of whom also run cooperages. Cooperage use accounts for about three per cent of all American white oak harvested every year. Most American oak is used for furniture, construction, veneer, and pulp.

The logs are cut into appropriate lengths, quarter sawn, planed, and then sold to cooperages (see BARREL MAKING). Customers for American oak staves are found not only in bourbon country, but in cooperages in California, Australia—and Spain, where American oak is used almost exclusively for wine maturation, most notably in RIOJA and JEREZ.

For whiskey to be called bourbon, it must, according to American government regulations that are a blessing to the cooperage business, be aged in a 'new, charred white oak barrel', so large quantities of used whiskey barrels are commercially available, many of them relatively new, even though distinctively charred and whiskey flavoured. An estimated 700,000 to 800,000 used bourbon barrels are sold each year to Spain, Scotland, Ireland, Japan, Thailand, India, Puerto Rico, Canada, and Taiwan, as well as to producers of other North American spirits. Most of them are used to mature spirits: various brandies, rums, and whiskies.

The Scotch whisky industry is a particularly important consumer of American oak, at any one time using as many as 13 million casks in total. In some cases American oak barrels are sent to Jerez *en route* to Scotland, where some distillers still prefer to use casks infused with sherry flavours as was the norm in the 19th century, when sherry was shipped in cask to British wine merchants, who would then pass on these casks to the Scotch whisky industry. Now that sherry is no longer shipped in cask, some Scotch whisky distillers in Scotland have their barrels 'broken in' in Jerez with sherry.

France The French cooperage business is much smaller than its American counterpart but is much more important to the wine business. Between 150,000 and 200,000 French oak barrels were produced annually in the early 1990s, primarily in BORDEAUX, BURGUNDY, and COGNAC, where most French cooperages are located. Although France remains the most important single customer for French oak barrels, slightly more than half of French annual production is exported, with the United States taking about half of all exports. The balance is shipped to 30 other countries, most notably Italy, Australia, New Zealand, South Africa, Chile, Argentina, and Germany. As well as selling to Bordeaux, Burgundy, Cognac, and Armagnac, French cooperages are also developing new 'export' markets selling to ambitious wine-makers in French regions that had abandoned new barrels. The RHÔNE, LANGUEDOC-ROUSSILLON, and SOUTH WEST FRANCE, as well as the LOIRE and to a much lesser extent ALSACE, have all become important purchasers.

In France about one-third of all forests are owned by local or national government. However, the sale of over 80 per cent of all stands, carefully delineated groups of trees, is administered by the National Forestry Office (ONF). In September and October wood auctions are held all over France. For the buyer of oak destined to be turned into barrels and tanks the most important auctions are held in Nevers, Châteauroux, and Moulins. Sales are also conducted in Blois, Beaune, Poitiers, Le Mans, Cerilly, Orléans, Epinal, Fontainebleau, Vittel, and Nancy.

A potential buyer bids on the trees in a delineated section, which should be at least 80 and preferably well over 100, sometimes 160, years old before providing suitable wood for casks. The buyer has the right to go into the forest, measure the trees, even to bore into them 30 cm/12 in to see how straight is the GRAIN. He must decide how much of each type of wood there is, how it can be used, and, of course, how much he should bid. The auction starts with a high price, which is lowered until somebody offers an acceptable bid.

As not every tree in an auction lot can be used for STAVES, French cooperages usually work with wood brokers who have other customers. The most valuable part of a tree is that with the tightest and straightest grains which can be used for panelling. The furniture and construction industries are important customers.

French barrels cost at least double those made of American oak. French logs are much more expensive because they must be hand-split rather than machine sawn and demand more expensive drying methods. French cooperages also tend to be smaller and less automated than their American counterparts. But the special qualities of French oak ensure that it is the most sought after by modern wine-makers and well able to command a considerable premium.

As the use of French oak has become more widespread, staves are now shipped all over the world, notably to Australia, Italy, South America, South Africa, America, Spain, and Portugal, where they may be made up locally into barrels.

No system of APPELLATION CONTRÔLÉE limits the period of time French oak barrels may be used for any wine or spirit. Consequently the sale of used French oak barrels is not as organized as that for American barrels. Cognac barrels may be used for more than 20 years. In Burgundy, producers often use their new barrels for their grandest appellations and then use them for progressively lower-ranking wines. In Bordeaux, one proprietor will often own several châteaux and will treat his most prestigious property to the luxury of new oak before passing the barrels down the chain to a lowlier property. Alternatively, used barrels are sold to wineries unable to command the sort of price that can support expensive new barrels, or where wine-makers do not want the taste of new oak. In the New World used barrels are often traded between wineries. Relatively young ones, especially those used for white wine, are highly valued, but barrels more than 10 years old are usually sold to be cut in half for flower planters.

Italy In Italy a relatively small but lively cooperage industry makes barrels and vats primarily with oak imported from France and Slovenia.

Spain Barrels have been consistently important to the Spanish wine and sherry industries for centuries and the cooper's craft is sustained there. In Jerez new barrels are spurned for the maturation of fine SHERRY and will probably be used at least three times for FERMENTATION before being used to mature a top-quality OLOROSO. The older a cask, the more expensive it is, and some bodegas boast casks (or butts as they are usually called here) that are more than 200 years old.

Portugal The demands of the port industry have kept the cooper's craft alive in northern Portugal so that French coopers have even imported Portuguese craftsmen. M.K.

Kilby, K., *The Cooper and his Trade* (London, 1971).
Taransaud, J., *Le Livre de la tonnellerie* (Paris, 1976).

CO-OPERATIVES, ventures owned jointly by a number of different members, are extremely important as wine producers and have the advantage for their members of pooling wine-making and marketing costs. Collectively, they usually have access to a broad range of financial advantages, including subsidies in the EUROPEAN UNION, over individual producers. In most countries they also enjoy the commercial advantage of being able to describe their wines as bottled by the producer, using such reassuring phrases as MIS EN BOUTEILLE *à la propriété* and ERZEUGERABFÜLLUNG more usually associated with much smaller, individually managed wine enterprises. The better co-operatives are becoming increasingly skilled not just at wine-making but also at marketing specific bottlings designed to look and taste every bit as distinctive as the individually produced competition. The worst co-operatives play almost exclusively with subsidies and politics. Co-operatives are at their strongest in areas where wine's selling price is relatively low and where the average size of individual holdings is low, although co-operatives are quite significant in CHAMPAGNE and there are several in the MÉDOC, for example. The majority of wine co-operatives were formed in the early 1930s in the immediate aftermath of the Depression.

France

Since 1975 more than half of the wine produced in France, for example, has been produced by co-operatives, and the total area of vineyard owned by their members is also more than half the French total. The number of members, or *adhérents*, of France's *caves coopératives* (often referred to locally simply as *la cave*) represented 47 per cent of all French vine-growers in 1993, but the average number of members of each co-operative is declining (down from 240 in the 1960s to 160 in the 1990s) as holdings are amalgamated and members are encouraged to grub up less suitable vineyards by EU subsidies. The total number of French co-operatives is declining too, although there were over 1,000 in the early 1990s. They are a particularly strong force in the LANGUEDOC-ROUSSILLON, the greater RHÔNE valley, PROVENCE, and CORSICA, where *la cave* can dominate local economic life. Although the co-operatives are being restructured and amalgamated, it is by no means unusual for a single village in the Languedoc-Roussillon to boast two *caves coopératives*, typically distinguished by political orientation.

The co-operatives produce an impressive quantity of APPELLATION CONTRÔLÉE wine, nearly half of the country's total, and those which have established a reputation for particularly sound AC wines outside their own region include La Chablisienne of CHABLIS, the co-operative at Tain l'HERMITAGE, and a number of ALSACE co-operatives, notably at Turckheim. The co-operatives' speciality, however, is VINS DE PAYS. Their combined output of these intensely local wines represents three-quarters of the national total, and is considerably more than their (declining) combined total output of wine at its most basic, VIN DE TABLE. Scores of co-operatives in the Languedoc-Roussillon have established a reputation abroad for their vins de pays, as has the Plaimont co-operative organization in GASCONY and the Haut POITOU co-operative in west central France.

Although by the early 1990s the French co-operatives were not as strong on export markets as their individual producer (*cave particulier*) and wine merchant (NÉGOCIANT) counterparts, they were actively forming partnerships with specific négociants in an attempt to target specific markets with co-operatively produced products. The co-operatives themselves have also been prime targets for FLYING WINE-MAKERS.

Germany

In GERMANY, co-operatives (which may be called a *Winzergenossenschaft*, *Winzerverein*, *Winzervereinigung*, and in Württemberg *Weingärtnergenossenchaft*) have played an increasingly significant role since 1869, when the first German wine co-operative was formally established in the AHR, where the great majority of the region's output is still processed by co-operatives. As outlined in GERMAN HISTORY, co-operatives offered smallholders the chance to compete in the newly quality-conscious German wine market of the late 19th and early 20th centuries.

Three in every four German vine-growers today belongs to the local co-operative, although their vineyards are often a small, part-time activity which therefore, cumulatively, represent less than 40 per cent of the total German area under vine. Many of the 13 wine regions of Germany have a central co-operative cellar, or ZENTRALKELLEREI, which is fed grapes, wine, or must by more localized co-operatives. In 1993 there were 300 co-operatives in Germany, of which 171 made wine on the premises.

The co-operative movement is particularly strong, and particularly successful, in the most southerly region of BADEN where about 85 per cent of all wine produced is sold under the auspices of the giant central Badischer Winzerkeller at Breisach, which processes up to 45 per cent of Baden's total output through 119 co-operatives. This vast enterprise can today store 160 million l/42 million gal, and is therefore larger than any winery in France. The Badische co-operatives have been particularly active in transcending the co-operative image of quantity over quality by developing superior, small volume bottlings of distinctive wines. Co-operatives are also extremely important in the WÜRTTEMBERG region, where there are 90 co-operatives whose central cellar is at Möglingen, and in PFALZ. In the MOSEL-SAAR-RUWER region, the central co-operative cellar, Moselland of Bernkastel, processes about 40 per cent of the region's output, but in the other classic wine region, the RHEINGAU, the role of co-operative cellars is very much less significant.

Italy

In Italy, the *cantina sociale* is no less important, particularly in the south where EU policies can be interpreted most profitably and co-operatives dominate production. One of the most respected Italian co-operatives is in the far north west, however, the Produttori del BARBARESCO whose origins are 19th century and which has a direct counterpart in the Terre del BAROLO. The influence of the *cantina sociale*, or *Kellereigenossenschaft* in German, is particularly strong in TRENTINO-ALTO ADIGE, where Cavit is perhaps the most exported name. The distinction of the Colli Berici co-operative in the VENETO, however, which is in fact two co-operatives amalgamated, is its size. Total production is 75 million/19.8 million gal a year from 4,000 ha/9,900 acres, according to Anderson, almost three times as much as is produced at one of the largest French co-operatives in the Languedoc.

The co-operative best known outside Italy is Riunite of EMILIA-ROMAGNA, famous in the early 1980s for engulfing the United States, and other markets, in a tidal wave of LAMBRUSCO. Tollo co-operative is the star of ABRUZZO and TUSCANY's co-operatives tend to be well focused on quality with the largest, drawing on 1,500 ha of vineyards, being that at Pitigliano in the Maremma. South of here quantity, and not necessarily quality, is the chief characteristic of the co-operatives that proliferate practically wherever the vine is grown. The Copertino co-operative in APULIA makes a good job of its eponymous red. The islands SARDINIA and SICILY are dominated by co-operatives, of which Settesoli in Sicily and several ambitious Sardinian co-operatives export with zeal.

Spain and Portugal

As in Italy, co-operatives are extremely important in Iberia where grapes are so often grown alongside other crops. According to Metcalfe and McWhirter, more than 60 per cent of each vintage is delivered to one of Spain's 1,000 wine co-operatives or Portugal's 300 (see PORTUGAL, history). Although the movement began in the early years of the 20th century, it substantially increased in importance in the 1950s, when the wine market was relatively depressed. One of the earliest wine co-operatives was in Olite in NAVARRE, where the movement is particularly powerful and where it can absorb as much as 90 per cent of grape production, although here, as elsewhere, links are being forged with individual producers to increase overall quality and technical expertise. It was only in the 1980s that many Iberian co-operatives even began to consider bottling wine, so much of their produce was sold off either for DISTILLATION or as BULK WINE.

Co-operatives are important in most Spanish wine regions (although in famed RIOJA they process only about 40 per cent of the region's grapes). In the vineyard vastness of La MANCHA there are about 100 co-operatives of very varied quality, while YECLA and JUMILLA have export-minded co-operatives whose level of modern equipment and expertise is considerably above average. In the fortified wine regions of JEREZ, much of the rest of ANDALUCÍA, and the DOURO, co-operatives are less important than the long-standing links between vine-growers and individual wine producers. The 20th century Portuguese table wine industry was revolutionized by the government's formation of co-operatives, however.

Rest of the world

Practically wherever wine is made, co-operatives thrive, although the movement is not particularly strong in the UNITED STATES and has had its own variants in eastern Europe. Co-operatives have played a particularly important role in the development of the wine industry in SOUTH AFRICA (see also KWV). In the RIVERLAND of AUSTRALIA, the co-operative origins of Berri Renmano, now merged with the large family-owned producer Hardy's and one of the country's largest wine companies, date back to the 1920s.

Anderson, B., *The Wine Atlas of Italy* (London and New York, 1990).
Metcalfe, C., and McWhirter, K., *The Wines of Spain & Portugal* (London and New York, 1988).

COPERTINO, DOC for robust red wine made mainly from NEGROAMARO grapes in south east Italy. For more details see APULIA.

COPITA, special glass in which SHERRY is customarily served in Spain. It is designed to maximize the AROMA and larger sizes can be used as a glass for general wine TASTING. See GLASSES.

COPPER, a trace element required in very small concentrations for healthy vine growth. Copper is toxic to plants except in very dilute concentrations. Reports of copper deficiencies in vineyards are rare, probably because of the very small requirements by the vines, but also because of the widespread use of FUNGICIDES containing copper. In acid soils, the copper from fungicide sprays can actually reach toxic levels and some parts of the MÉDOC have been affected by copper toxicity. After the annual application of several kg of copper per ha, as in BORDEAUX MIXTURE, for about a century, the level of copper in the soil can be toxic and the vine growth became severely stunted. Generous applications of humus and lime will neutralize the effects of excess copper. Curiously, the use of Bordeaux mixture is permitted by most guidelines for ORGANIC VITICULTURE. R.E.S.

CORBIÈRES, the most important appellation in the LANGUEDOC region of southern France producing some excitingly dense, lively red wines, a small amount of rosé, and a little increasingly well-made white wine from nearly 12,000 ha/29,600 acres of vineyard. The terrain here in the Pyrenean foothills (see map of Languedoc on p. 552) is extremely varied, and so hilly that it is difficult to generalize about soil types and TOPOGRAPHY. In recognition of this the appellation has been subdivided into 11 so-called TERROIRS, although not without a certain amount of local dissent. The basic distinctions in this southernmost corner of the Aude *département* are between coastal zones influenced by the Mediterranean, the northern strip on the Montagne d'Alaric (some of which has more in common with MINERVOIS), the westernmost vineyards which are cooled by both Atlantic influence and by ALTITUDE, and the rugged, mountainous terrain in the south and centre in which the FITOU appellation forms two enclaves.

Vineyards in the south west of the appellation, the so-called Terroir du Termenès, are as high as 300 to 450 m (980–1,500 ft) above sea level, and HARVEST may not take place until well into October, while those in the Sigean area are right on the coast and can vary enormously in altitude but find that the high average temperatures and very low annual rainfall are partly compensated for by the marine influence. One of the most admired terroirs is that of Boutenac, which has particularly poor soils on a LIMESTONE base.

The local details of the precise proportions of vine varieties allowed within each terroir were under review in the mid 1990s (along with a proposal for the suffix Grand Cru, or even Grand Cru Vinum, to denote superior bottlings). Carignan is still very much the dominant variety, representing well over half of all vines planted. The appellation regulations specified local maxima of between 50 and 70 per cent depending on location and proportion of Syrah grown, and these proportions were expected to decrease further, to the dismay of those who value the spice and concentration of wine from old vines. Warmer parts of Corbières offer good possibilities to ripen Mourvèdre on a regular basis (like Spain not far to the south). Plantings of Cinsaut, useful along with Syrah for rosé, are strictly limited. Grenache, its relative Lladoner Pelut, Picpoul Noir, Terret, and the local white grape varieties are also allowed in red and rosé Corbières.

White Corbières, a rare but often refreshing dry wine, is made principally from Bourboulenc, Maccabéo, and Grenache Blanc but Clairette, Muscat (sometimes vinified alone to make a dry wine), Picpoul, Terret, Marsanne, Roussanne, and Rolle or Vermentino are all also allowed, providing an interesting aromatic palette for those producers prepared to experiment with white wine-making.

CO-OPERATIVES, some of them particularly quality conscious, dominate the region, but there are many seriously ambitious individual estates too.

Simms, P. and S., *The Wines of Corbières & Fitou* (Toulouse, 1991).

CORDIER, a major owner of estates and one of the largest NÉGOCIANTS in BORDEAUX, owned since 1985 by a large French merchant bank. Désiré Cordier started his wine business in 1877 in TOUL in north east France. The First World War made the company's fortune (Cordier secured the contract to supply the French army with wines and spirits) as well as prompting its move to Bordeaux, for fear of invasion. By 1918 the family had purchased Ch Talbot in ST-JULIEN and had begun the acquisition of its flagship property in the same commune, the second growth Ch Gruaud-Larose. Cordier properties also include Chx Meyney in the MÉDOC, Lafaurie-Peyraguey in SAUTERNES, Clos des Jacobins in ST-ÉMILION, and Domaine de la Poussie in SANCERRE. Gruaud-Larose was sold in 1991, although Cordier continue to make and market the wine, something they also do for fifth growth Ch Cantemerle in the Haut-Médoc. Over half Établissement Cordier's business is export, and the quality of the wines improved noticeably after the technical director Georges Pauli took sole charge of wine-making in 1978. Gruaud-Larose, Talbot, and Lafaurie-Peyraguey in particular made exceptional wines throughout the 1980s. Pauli also heads Cordier's consultancy business, advising on wine-making to properties in France as well as abroad; notably to Montana in NEW ZEALAND, and to Domain Cordier in TEXAS, where the French company built and own the winery. M.W.E.S.

CORDON, part of the vine's woody framework, arising from the top of the trunk and on which arms are borne (see diagram on p. 918). Cordons can be at any angle but are generally trained along horizontal wires, or shallowly sloped wires as in some TENDONE trellises. The most common arrangement is a bilateral cordon in which two horizontal cordons are arranged in opposite directions from the top of the trunk, but any number of arrangements are possible. Usually the cordon is trained to its permanent position and remains there, but if there is a need for it to be flexible it is kept long and curved, or overlapped with other cordons. See vine-TRAINING SYSTEMS. B.G.C.

CORDON DE ROYAT, an old form of CORDON TRAINING used in France for wine grapes since the end of the 19th century. The system was proposed by Lefebvre, director of the French agricultural school of Royat. The classic form is a unilateral CORDON on a short trunk (about 30 to 50 cm (12–20 in)), the term unilateral meaning that the cordon is trained only to one side of the trunk. The cordon extends mostly from one vine to another. The vines are normally SPUR PRUNED to two bud spurs. The number of spurs is limited for each variety under APPELLATION laws: in Burgundy, for example, to four spurs each for Pinot Noir and Chardonnay vines, and to eight for Gamay. R.E.S.

CORDON TRAINING, a form of VINE TRAINING in which the trunk terminates in a CORDON, and the vine is then typically subjected to SPUR PRUNING. The alternative is HEAD TRAINING, both of these being essentially Californian terms. The cordon is normally horizontal and can be unilateral (trained only to one side of the trunk) or bilateral (to both sides). See also CORDON DE ROYAT and PRUNING. R.E.S.

CORKAGE, charge customarily levied in a restaurant for each bottle of wine brought in and consumed on the premises instead of buying wine from the restaurant's own selection (although see also BYO). The term is derived from the fact that the number of corks pulled represents the number of bottles consumed. There is considerable variation in the amount charged, and the grace with which the practice is accepted.

CORKED, pejorative tasting term for a wine spoiled by a contaminated cork stopper. This is one of the most serious wine FAULTS as in most cases it irrevocably imbues the wine with such a powerfully offputting smell that it cannot be drunk with any enjoyment. The unpleasantly, almost mould-like, chemical smell is occasionally present in smaller doses that may initially be noticed only by noses particularly sensitive to it, but it is difficult for tasters to enjoy a wine once their attention has been drawn to this fault.

The bark stripped from the cork oak is boiled, and cut into strips from which corks are punched. Corks are normally bleached in a strong chlorine solution prior to washing and drying. Research work in the 1980s, particularly in Australia, demonstrated that this chlorine treatment could inadvertently produce the chemical compound TRICHLORANISOLE, or TCA, which can be smelt at concentrations of just a few parts per trillion. The cork reacts with PHENOL in the cork to form trichlorophenol, which is converted to TCA by moulds growing on the cork, the germination and growth of these moulds being favoured by moist conditions. TCA appears to be at least part of the explanation for the condition known as **corkiness** in corked wines. The cork industry is therefore replacing chlorine bleaching with other processes (see CORKS).

This may not provide a complete solution to the problem, however, as moulds growing on unbleached corks can still generate a corked aroma and taste which are due to compounds other than TCA. Corks, even though cut from boiled and probably sterile cork bark, can be recontaminated with mould spores at any point during the preparation process. Corks can furthermore pick up off-flavours that migrate from other surfaces, even the floor boards in shipping containers, or as a result of poor storage conditions at the winery.

The problem of corkiness was perceived by the wine industry to have increased during the 1980s, at the end of which estimates of the proportion of corked wine bottles varied from less than two to more than five per cent of the total. This soured relations between the wine industry and the cork industry and led to increased pressure to find and use suitable alternative STOPPERS.

It is commonly, but erroneously, believed that a wine with small fragments of cork floating in it is 'corked'. This may be a SERVING fault but is certainly not a wine fault.

T.H.L. & J.Ro.

Lee, T. H., and Simpson, R. F., 'Microbiology and chemistry of cork taints in wine', in G. H. Fleet (ed.), *Wine Microbiology and Biotechnology* (Chur, 1993).

CORKS, wine bottle stoppers, without which the appreciation of fine wine, and in particular BOTTLE AGEING, might never have evolved. Cork's unique combination of qualities have made it by far the most popular stopper for wine, but in the late 20th century the science of wine production bounded ahead of the science of cork production, to the detriment of relations between the two industries.

History

See STOPPERS.

The cork tree

The cork tree, *Quercus suber*, is a relatively young species of OAK and is unusual in that its bark is so thick and resistant that it can be stripped from the trunk and large branches without hurting the tree.

It grows in sandy soils free of chalk and prefers annual rainfalls between 400 and 800 mm (15–30 in), temperatures which never fall below −5 °C/23 °F, and an altitude between 100 and 300 m (330–1,000 ft). This effectively restricts cork oaks to the coast of the western Mediterranean, particularly Spain, and much of Portugal, where cork plays a significant role in the economy. The cork industry was born in Catalonia but was disrupted by the Spanish Civil War. The commercial stability of ALGERIA, another prime source of cork, was called into question in the 1960s, so that, in the late 20th century, Portugal is the centre of the world's cork business and cork is an important contributor to the Portuguese economy. Portugal's cork forests are today the most extensive, their 670,000 ha/1.6 million acres representing about 30 per cent of the world's cork trees, significantly assisted in the late 1980s by EUROPEAN UNION grants.

Spain has the next largest total area planted with cork oaks, about 480,000 ha, most of them now in the south and west of the country, from which a high proportion of the cork is shipped across the border for processing in Portugal's more temperate climate (although, in the north east, Catalonia is still an important supplier of corks, especially to France and particularly to Champagne). So entrenched is the modern cork industry in Portugal—many of the processing centres are located just south of Oporto and therefore close to the PORT trade—that it produces more than half of the world's total output of cork, helped by imports not just from Spain but also from North Africa. Algeria and Morocco each have almost as big an area of cork forest as Spain, and there are a further 100,000 ha/250,000 acres in Tunisia. As with wine, each cork region produces cork with different characteristics, although forestry management is the key to quality. Portugal's most prized cork region is Evora.

Cork trees, if not a cork industry, also flourish along the

west coast of Italy, in Sicily, Sardinia, and Corsica, and along the Mediterranean coast of France, particularly in Provence, but little is made of these plantations commercially. There have also been trial plantings of cork trees in countries such as the United States and Japan.

The bark of the cork tree is sufficiently thick to yield commercially useful cork in its 25th year, and cork trees are regularly stripped during the summer months, no more than every nine years by Portuguese law. On average modern husbandry means that each hectare of cork forest yields 230 kg/500 lbs of cork; the older the tree the more cork it will yield. Although the average life expectancy of a cork tree is about 170 years, there is one 200-year-old tree in the Montijo region south east of Portugal's capital Lisbon which has yielded 1,200 kg of cork from a single stripping. Cork farming, an activity often administered by the state, is an even longer-term undertaking than growing vines, which have an active wine-producing life of around 30 years.

The bark micro-structure is unique in that it consists of very small, closely packed, usually 14-sided cells which render it light, elastic, inert, and impermeable to gases and most liquids except particularly strong acids or bases. These qualities and its low conductivity make cork a useful and versatile commodity as an insulator, particularly for the automotive and construction industries, but the principal use for cork is still cork stoppers and, in particular, wine corks.

Cork processing

The modern cork processing operation has changed remarkably little over the past century. The strips of cork bark yielded by the annual stripping are stacked and left outside for seasoning (just as other woods are in BARREL MANUFACTURE) for at least six months. Still in large strips, the cork is then boiled for about 90 minutes, both to make it more flexible and in an effort to kill off any moulds and other contaminants. The planks are then left to rest in the warehouse of the cork processing plant for three weeks before being sorted by hand and cut into strips as wide as the length of the final cork stopper. Corks are then punched out of these strips, usually by hand-operated punches but using an increasing degree of mechanization. Maximizing yield is a significant factor since only about 40 per cent of all the commercially interesting cork harvested is suitable for stoppers.

Corks are deliberately punched at right angles to the growth of the cork tree, so that any lenticels, occasional knots in the wood, remain transverse and the risk of possible leakage due to lenticels is minimized. The ends of the cork stoppers are then polished to present a smooth surface to the wine.

There then follow various treatments with the twin aims of cosmetics and hygiene. Bleaching, which has traditionally been done by immersing the corks in a bath of chlorine solution, makes the corks look less irregularly marked and also acts as a form of disinfectant. Unfortunately, however, there is some evidence that this chlorine increases the likelihood of TRICHLORANISOLE formation, and therefore the incidence of CORKED wines. Hydrogen peroxide treatments have been offered as an option to chlorine bleaching by most cork processors since the mid 1980s but research work is now focused on other alternatives such as moisture-saturated heat treatments to destroy moulds and BACTERIA, but not cork's natural flexibility.

Corks are then graded (the fewer markings the higher the grade), branded (most corks today are marked not only with the branding specified by the wine bottler, but also with an indication of the cork supplier), and often coated with some paraffin or silicon-based product that increases their extractability and, in many cases, eases their passage through high-speed BOTTLING lines.

Finally corks are sealed into large plastic bags, typically with SULPHUR DIOXIDE as a disinfectant, although irradiation and simple holes for aeration are used as respectively more and less sophisticated alternatives. Subsequent storage conditions are important to minimize possible contamination. Corks should ideally be stored in a ventilated, odour-free environment at a temperature between 15 and 20 °C (59–68 °F) in a humidity of 50 to 70 per cent. Poor cork storage conditions can dramatically increase the incidence of corked wines.

The range available

Although the first cork stoppers were tapered, the development of CORKSCREWS made tightly fitting cylindrical corks the norm. Modern corks are available in varying lengths, from 25 to as much as 60 mm (1–2.3 in), according to the bottle ageing aspirations, or extravagant exhibitionism, of the wine producer. (GAJA of Barbaresco, for example, perhaps the most ambitious cork buyer, personally selects his 60 mm corks from a supplier in Sardinia.) The longer the cork, the longer it is likely to remain an intact and viable stopper (see RECORKING), although some oenologists argue that longer corks result in lower FILL LEVELS, which may prejudice WINE AGEING. There is much less variation in diameter, however, with 24 mm being the norm, although corks 21 and 26 mm wide are not unknown, depending on the inside width of the necks of BOTTLES used.

The quality of the cork material itself also determines the price and potential life of the stopper, and corks may be graded into eight different quality levels. The cheapest form of cork, developed in 1891 by an American businessman, John Smith, is cork agglomerate, occasionally called 'agglo', reassembled crumbs of cork which can offer some of the benefits of intact cork itself. A more recent development is a cork of intermediate quality that looks considerably more natural than agglomerate, made from cork dust. Agglomerate corks with disks of natural cork at each end are also produced. The best-quality cork is that with the least markings. The longest, finest cork can cost five times as much as the cheapest, shortest agglomerate cork.

Stopper corks with plastic tops are used for some wines, particularly FORTIFIED wines and some SWEET WINES, a single bottle of which may be consumed over an extended period.

Corks for SPARKLING wines, commonly known, with scant regard for appellation laws, as champagne corks, have to be made to very particular specifications. Initially cylindrical, they are much wider than normal corks, about 30 mm, and have to be (half) driven into the bottle-neck, forcing them into a mushroom shape. Champagne corks are held in place, against the force of the pressure of undissolved gas inside the bottle, by a wire muzzle. Because such corks are too wide to be punched whole from the bark of most cork oaks, and to moderate the cost of such a large cork, champagne corks are usually made from cork agglomerate with one, two, or occasionally three discs of natural cork stuck on to the end which goes into the bottle-neck and is in contact with the wine.

Clues from the cork

In general, the narrower and more misshapen a cork extracted from a bottle, the longer it has been there. This is a particularly useful clue to the likely age of a non-vintage sparkling wine, or at least to the time that has elapsed since DISGORGEMENT. It can also provide a clue to the likely age of any other non-vintage wine, or fine wine which has lost its label or, perhaps in the case of vintage PORT, never had one (although see also RECORKING).

Most corks are branded with the code of the cork producer. Most fine wine corks are emblazoned with the name of the wine producer (if not the wine itself) and, often, the vintage. Different countries adopt different conventions. Italian corks, which fit particularly tightly into their narrow bottle-necks, are often marked with a two-letter regional code (UD for Udine on many FRIULI wine corks, for example). Most British wine bottlers brand their corks with a W followed by their own numerical code. The regular French message is simply MIS EN BOUTEILLE *à la propriété*.

A short agglomerate cork suggests that the bottler had little regard for the ageing ability of this wine, while a particularly long cork is indicative at least of ambition or optimism. New World bottlers seem to favour smoother corks with more obvious cork coatings than their Old World counterparts.

If a cork has crystals on the end that has been in contact with the wine (white in the case of a white wine and dyed red by a red wine) these are harmless TARTRATES. If a cork seems damp or mouldy at either end, this is not necessarily a sign of any wine fault. Some wine waiters are taught to smell the cork and present it to the customer as an essential part of wine SERVICE, but the state of a cork is no sure guide to the state of the wine it stoppered.

For alternatives to corks, see STOPPERS.

CORKSCREWS, wide range of devices for extracting CORKS from the necks of wine BOTTLES.

It might be thought that cork extraction would prove an easy matter with any simple screw device, given the relatively soft, resilient nature of the stopper. However, there have been many hundreds of inventions since the middle of the 18th century with the aim of producing a better, more efficient corkscrew, and as yet none has been accepted as the perfect instrument. In particular no corkscrew has yet been shown to be infallible with old PORT corks and PORT TONGS are sometimes employed instead. The extraction operation can vary considerably. Corks vary in length and, as they accommodate to the shape of the bottle-neck, they can also vary in shape. Furthermore, cork undergoes ageing in old bottles and may partially disintegrate on extraction. The necks of old port bottles, for example, usually have a slightly bulbous form, so that the lower part of the cylindrical cork is weakened where it ballooned out and became cone shaped. Italian wine bottles tend to be narrow at the neck, tightly compressing corks and making them relatively difficult to penetrate. Their removal may also be hampered by the amount of force required to overcome the initial frictional inertia between the glass and the cork.

History

The free-blown, onion-shaped wine bottles (see BOTTLES, history) of the 17th century did not have a standard size of neck. Under these circumstances, tapered corks made a satisfactory stopper, especially as a portion remained proud of the bottle top, facilitating manual removal. The mould-made cylindrical glass bottle which evolved in the 18th century could be binned horizontally to keep the cork moist and at the same time to save space. This necessitated a driven cylindrical cork of standard diameter and the removal of such a cork required a special tool.

Men were adept at broaching casks with gimlet-like tools, known as frets, and it would not have taken much inventive power to devise another tool of spiral form which would pierce the cork in a bottle and enable it to be removed. Furthermore, other single and double helices had been used for withdrawing wad and unspent bullets from the barrels of muskets and pistols in England from at least the early 1630s. These worms are mentioned in a Commission of 1631 drawn up under King Charles I. It is likely that the corkscrew is an English invention owing to the traditional importance of beer and cider and the need to close-cork the bottles containing them. J. Worlidge's *Treatise on Cider* in 1676 describes the binning of tightly corked cider bottles on their sides. However, the earliest actual references to a corkscrew is in 1681: 'a steel worm used for the drawing of Corks out of Bottles.'

Simple corkscrews leave the operator to do the work of screwing in the worm and pulling out the cork unassisted. Various modifications of handle, shaft, and worm can increase the efficiency of these manœuvres: the handle should be formed to give a good pulling grip; the shaft can be fitted with a metal disc, or button, to obtain more complete contact with the cork; and the worm should be a steel helix 6.35 cm/2.5 in long, of good open pitch, and have an outer diameter of between 0.8 and 1 cm. In cross-section the worm should be slim but rounded, or it can be somewhat flattened with a blunt outer edge. No other design has been found to be as efficient as the helix, which gives a maximum hold on the cork with the minimum of disruption of its internal structure. There have, of course, been various other modifications of the helix. It can be left-handed or double, planed or sharpened to give a ciphered or feather edge, or it can be grooved and is then described as a thread or fluted helix.

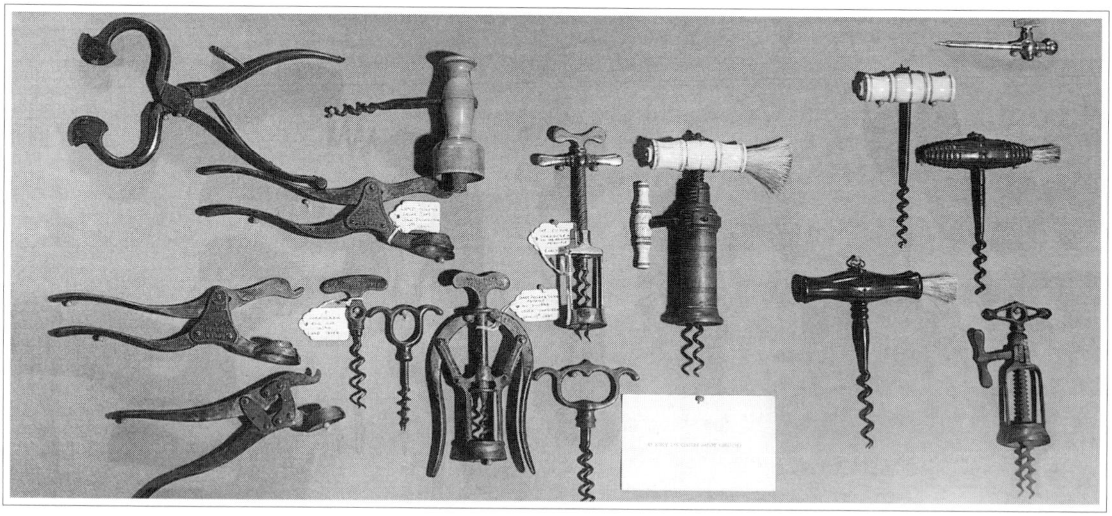

A selection of 19th century **corkscrews** from Harveys Wine Museum in Bristol, England. Note in most cases the well-formed helix, although that in the bottom right-hand corner is more likely to bore a hole through a cork.

The French favoured the Archimedean worm in which there is a central shaft overlaid by a quick-pitched, spiral screw which may have a fairly wide blade.

The auger type is similar but the spirals are more tightly packed or slow pitched, looking more like a wood screw. The centre worm, French worm, or solid cut has a central shaft which has been encroached on to a greater or lesser extent, depending on the depth of cutting on the lathe of a cylindrical rod; it can be very steep pitched or slow pitched, depending on the angle of the cutting during manufacture.

Mechanical corkscrews are designed to reduce the amount of physical effort required during the three manœuvres of piercing, pulling, and disposing of the cork. Mechanical hand-held corkscrews can never be used with the rapidity of an efficient wall- or bar-mounted mechanical instrument, although the modern hand-held **Lever Pull**, really a miniature bar-screw in concept, can be used at remarkable speed. Corkscrew inventors have employed a vast range of devices in an attempt to increase the mechanical advantage. These include levers, fulcrums, springs, racks, wheels, pulleys, ratchets, gearing, clutches, and teflon-coated worms. There are different types of left- and right-hand threaded shafts designed to work in the collar at the top of the barrel or frame, or to screw up through the handle itself, or through a wingnut on the shaft. Cotterill's registered corkscrew of 1842 has a shaft with both left- and right-hand threads combined as a crossover mechanism; the later German version is aptly named the **Perpetual** as the processes of entering the cork and extraction follow one another as the operator turns the handle clockwise.

The earliest dated corkscrew of 1685, a French *à cage* example, is a relatively complicated conception and it is likely to have evolved over a number of years from a basic design of worm, shaft, and handle. It is quite probable that simple corkscrews were in use by the middle of the 17th century in England and possibly also in France (although bottle AGEING has never been as popular a practice in the latter country).

The earliest English documentary corkscrew is a silver pocket example dated 1702 with 'BC' as the maker's mark. English patented corkscrews, on the other hand, did not appear until late in the 18th century, although this was some years before other countries followed the lead. The commencing dates for patents were: England, 1795; France, 1828; United States, 1860; Germany, 1877; Canada, 1882. Between 1795 and the first decade of this century there were nearly 350 British patents for corkscrews; the main inventive period being post-1860, possibly as a result of competition from America and the Continent. There were also English registered designs, the first being in 1840, with over 70 such entries by 1884.

The first English patented example of 1795 was invented by Samuel Henshall, the incumbent of Christchurch Spitalfields, and manufactured by Matthew Boulton, who also made other corkscrews and exported them to France.

Samuel Henshall's corkscrew is a simple one with a button on the shaft to assist in drawing the cork but making firm contact with it. The polished rounded helix has a good open pitch and an outer diameter, which varies with different examples, from 0.7 to 1 cm. The best modern claret corks measure up to 5.8 cm (2.3 in) in length and a satisfactory helix must be a little longer than that in order to pierce the cork from end to end and support it from below. The Henshall helix is only 5.4 cm in length, but 200 years ago corks were shorter and that length would have proved quite adequate. As a design for a simple corkscrew the Henshall patent has stood the test of time and even now there are few, if any, that can better it.

The second English patented corkscrew, of 1802, was the

masterpiece of Sir Edward Thomason (1769–1849). His famous corkscrew is a mechanical one of great ingenuity, which, like the slightly earlier Henshall–Boulton example, has also stood the test of time and remained top of its class with many of them still in regular use. The **Vulcan** is a recent fairly successful attempt to copy the mechanism.

According to Thomason's memoirs:

> at this period, 1801, it was a kind of fashion for persons to draw the corks of the wine even at their own table, and which not only required some strength and skill, but was sometimes attended with accident, by the breaking of the neck of the bottle, and, furthermore, it was next to an impossibility to take the cork from the worm without soiling the fingers. To avert these two inconveniences, I directed my improvements, and I produced a combination of the three screws working together, and following each other, so that, on piercing the cork with the point of the worm, and continuing to turn the handle, the cork was discharged from the worm, and fell into the finger-glass. I obtained His Majesty's Royal Letters Patent for this invention, under the name of the Patent-ne-plus-ultra Corkscrew . . . In 1801 the shopkeepers in London sold them at one guinea each, but in the course of 10 years they sold at the low price of 4s. [about a third of a guinea], which rendered the price to be within the reach of all classes.
>
> The Earl of Mountnorris (then Lord Valentia), on returning home from his celebrated travels in India, was so kind as to relate to me an anecdote which occurred at some small city on the borders of the Red Sea, during his short stay there for refreshment. He heard the native servant call out, 'Bring me the Thomason.' His Lordship enquired if a person of that name was there, when his lordship was answered, 'The man was only asking for the machine to draw the cork.' Thus do the Birmingham manufacturers find their way into the remotest corners of the globe. Mr James Watt, the celebrated engineer, paid me a high compliment for this novel mode of applying the three screws.

National characteristics

Until fairly recently the best corkscrews from the points of view of function, design, and quality of workmanship were made in Britain. This was probably due to the fact that, not being a wine-producing area, they had a wide choice of such beverages from abroad and, in particular, developed a taste for ageing fine vintage wines (see ANTIQUES).

Other countries mostly developed corkscrews which were very adequate for pulling young corks where the design of the worm was not as crucial as it is when dealing with older corks. Indeed there are characteristic national features to be discerned in corkscrew design. The two-lever Italian corkscrew with a gimlet-like worm overcame the erstwhile problem of their short, tight corks.

The Germans rarely used other than the centre worm and often combined this with an inventive use of springs and ball bearings. In 1882 Karl Wienke of Rostock, Mecklenburg, conceived of using a knife-like handle as a lever; he put a spring-folding fulcrum at the other end and a variably spring-folding corkscrew in the middle and thus brought into being one of the world's most popular corkscrews. This was patented in Germany, England, and America and known affectionately as the **waiter's friend**. It is still the essential tool of a SOMMELIER world-wide.

The French were keen on nickel plating, contrasting with the bronzed finish of English pieces; well demonstrated by the lazy tongs models of both countries.

Americans printed the wooden handles with advertisements and became largely preoccupied with self-pullers and other models which used the frame of the corkscrew as a fulcrum and derived from the French *à cage* principal. **Screwpull**, invented in the 1970s by Herbert Allen, is the culmination of applying this principle using strong modern plastics and a teflon-coated helix.

A two-pronged extractor became jokingly known as the **butler's friend**, as it enabled the cork to be extracted and replaced without evident damage and, possibly, the wine to be replaced with one less fine. Lucian Mumford of San Francisco is credited with first patenting this device in 1879 with an improvement in 1892, although it has subsequently been discovered that a more complex German two-blader was patented 15 years previously. Further patents followed, including a French one early in this century, and in fact this type of extractor became more popular in France than in America.

Special corkscrews

One particular group of corkscrews associated with CHAMPAGNE was in vogue in the 19th and first quarter of this century both in Europe and America. At the far end of these instruments is a screw or a sharp point for piercing right through the cork. Perforations lead into a hollow stem which is controlled by a tap permitting small quantities of champagne to be withdrawn from the inverted bottle without the remainder losing its sparkle. Early champagne corks had no metal cap, which enabled the champagne screw to be used without difficulty and even the first metal caps, fitted when wire replaced the twine, had a hole in the centre. At a later date, a special steel gimlet was sometimes provided to penetrate the more modern tin cap *in situ*. The earliest known **champagne tap** is a fairly massive steel and silver piece made by Phipps & Robinson in 1807 during the reign of George III. It bears the crest of Charles, earl of Stanhope, FRS, the famous inventor. The first patented tap originated from France 21 years later.

During the 18th century there appeared a whole range of remarkably decorative corkscrews made of silver, or gold, or chased and damascened steel. The French examples, typically with chalcedony handles and shagreen cases, are of the very finest workmanship. The Dutch specialized in ornate silver corkscrews with handles in the form of lions, parrots, or fish, etc., and the screws enclosed in a sheath. English and Irish silver examples are less exotic but exhibit pleasing proportions that stem from good design and craftsmanship; they were sometimes combined with nutmeg graters, seals, and pipe tampers.

Modern corkscrews

The variety of corkscrews available on the market today may easily confuse the wine drinker who just needs to open bottles with speed and efficiency. Corkscrews with poorly finished or blunt worms should be rejected and the two-armed Italian examples are best avoided as they usually have a solid core to the worm which tends to destroy the cork of an aged bordeaux or port rather than extract it; not surprisingly, such corkscrews are better adapted to the tightly compressed, almost wood-hand, corks found in bottles of Italian wine. The so-called waiter's friend, the folding lever, can have a well-formed helix but there is a danger of breaking the bottle rim during extraction unless the knack of applying the correct leverage has been acquired.

The most reliable worm is an open, smooth helix or spiral at least 5.7 cm/2.2 in long. This may be fitted with a simple wooden T-piece handle or given useful mechanical advantage by being, for example, coated with teflon and built into a modern high-tensile plastic frame. The American 'Screwpull' was the first of these efficient mechanisms to be marketed and was followed by modifications of the same theme from Holland and elsewhere. B.M.W.

D'Allemagne, Henry René, *Decorative Antique Ironwork* (New York, 1968).
de Sanctis, Paolo, and Fantoni, Maurizio, *The Corkscrew: A Thing of Beauty* (Milan, 1990).
Dipple, Horst, *Korken Zieher* (Hamburg, 1988).
Fredericksen, Paul, 'Corkscrews that Work', *Wine Review* (May 1946).
Heckmann, Manfred, *Korkenzieher Einfuhrung in den hoheren Genuss* (Berlin, 1979).
Perry, Evan, *Corkscrews and Bottle Openers* (Bucks, 1980).
Watney, Bernard M., and Babbidge, Homer D., *Corkscrews for Collectors* (London, 1981).

CORKY is another word for CORKED. A corky or corked wine is said to suffer from **corkiness.**

CORKY BARK, virus-like disease and one of the few which can kill vines. It is related to the disease LEGNO RICCIO found in Italy. Symptoms of the disease resemble another one of the VIRUS DISEASES, LEAFROLL VIRUS, in that, during autumn, leaves turn red or yellow and roll downwards. A particular symptom is that vines infected with corky bark retain their leaves after they would naturally have fallen to the ground. Many VITIS VINIFERA varieties which carry the disease do not show symptoms until they are grafted on to American ROOTSTOCKS. An incompatibility develops at the graft union and the variety slowly dies. Often the rootstock survives and this effect can sometimes be seen in old vineyards of the Napa and Sonoma valleys of CALIFORNIA. The disease is usually spread by taking cuttings from infected vines. In Aguascalientes state in MEXICO the disease is spread naturally, possibly by an insect. There is no control for infected vineyards. The disease is detected by grafting to the indicator variety LN-33 (see INDEXING). R.E.S.

Bovey, R., *et al.*, *Virus and Virus-like Diseases of Vines: Colour Atlas of Symptoms* (Lausanne, 1980).
Pearson, R. C., and Goheen, A. C., *Compendium of Grape Diseases* (St Paul, Minn., 1988).

CORNAS, underestimated red wine appellation in the northern RHÔNE with the potential to provide dense, long-lived serious challengers to HERMITAGE on the opposite bank to the north.

Cornas was renowned in the era of CHARLEMAGNE, and in the 18th century, but many of the terraced vineyards on its steep south-facing granite slopes fell into decline in the early 20th century. The appellation experienced a revival of interest in the late 1980s with the arrival of ambitious newcomers prepared to re-establish the TERRACES needed for high-quality vineyards, so that by 1990 there were 76 ha/190 acres of vineyards in production. The apparently ubiquitous consultant OENOLOGIST Jean-Luc Colombo in particular has established a base here and is making wine not only for himself, but also for the likes of Lionnet, employing such imports as new OAK and DESTEMMING, an anathema to Clape, the standard bearer during the lean years of the 1970s.

Many of the best slopes such as Les Renards in the south are well sheltered from the cold north winds and enjoy some of the best positions in the northern Rhône. It is not surprising therefore that Cornas, which is made exclusively from SYRAH, can be one of the valley's finest wines. What is surprising is that so many of the wines are still made for mandatory extended BOTTLE AGEING. For those who can afford the time, Cornas can provide some of the most satisfying red wine drinking, and offers a much more uniform and dependable quality level than the elastic ST-JOSEPH appellation to the immediate north. Clape Cornas admiration has become something of a cult.

See map on p. 796.

CORSE is the French, and therefore Corsican, name for CORSICA.

CORSICA, mountainous Mediterranean island under French jurisdiction, situated on the 42nd parallel and actually much closer to Italy (83 km/50 miles) than to France (170 km/100 miles). The island, about 180 km long and 80 km wide, comprises a series of mountains around which runs a perimeter of capes, gulfs, and sandy beaches. The average altitude is 586 m/1,900 ft. Corsica produces many different types and styles of wine: red, white, rosé; still, sparkling; dry, sweet; APPELLATION CONTRÔLÉE, VIN DE PAYS, and VIN DE TABLE. The great majority of these are of relatively ordinary quality and are sold only on the island. Its most exported product is its single vin de pays, Vin de Pays de l'Île de Beauté.

History

The history of the island is closely related to that of Italy and this is reflected in the viticulture. Evidence suggests that vines were indigenous to the island and that their cultivation by man is one of the oldest in Europe, dating back to PHOENICIAN times and the settlement in 570 BC at Aleria on the east coast. Under Genoese rule in the 16th century, laws were enacted to control the harvest and tasting of wines; the export of Corsican wines to destinations other than the republic of GENOA was banned. The English diarist James Boswell wrote in 1769, only a year after the Genoese ceded the island to France, of the excellence and diversity of Corsican wines. Napoleon was born in Ajaccio and Napoleonic laws still entitle the island to sell duty-free wines and tobacco.

The wine industry was revolutionized in the 1960s with

the repatriation of many French *pieds noirs* from ALGERIA. Between 1960 and 1976 they imported and planted their own productive and often undistinguished vine varieties (see below) with such determination that the total vineyard area increased fourfold. MECHANICAL HARVESTERS were introduced to flatter vineyards to supplement more traditional methods and further the cause of quantity at the expense of quality.

In 1980, however, as EUROPEAN UNION subsidies favoured uprooting vines rather than producing yet more liquid to be poured into the European WINE LAKE, Corsican vineyards began to be restructured, with a more determined emphasis on quality. The total area under vine dropped by two-thirds to about 9,100 ha/22,500 acres in 1991. Simultaneously, the highly productive varieties began to be replaced by nobler vines, both imported and Corsican.

Geography and climate

Four main soil types are present in Corsica: granite on the west side; schist in the north and the Cap Corse, the mountainous finger of land pointing Francewards in the far north; chalk and clay in Patrimonio immediately south of it; and marly sand and alluvial soils from Solenzara to Bastia on the east coast.

Corsica is sunnier than anywhere in mainland France with an annual average of 2,750 hours, and very little rain falls in the months of August and September. Due to the mountainous nature of Corsica, a jigsaw of MESOCLIMATES exists. The effects of ALTITUDE, latitude, maritime influence, and the winds vary considerably between vineyards. The average temperature is higher in the north of the island than in the south. The sea, by absorbing heat during the day and radiating it at night, plays a major role in diminishing the day–night temperature variation.

Viticulture

Vines are cultivated up to 300 m/1,000 ft in altitude. Traditionally vines were pruned in GOBELET form but pruning and training methods such as CORDON DE ROYAT and single GUYOT became more widespread with mechanization. The most common ROOTSTOCK is R110. The strong winds help to keep the vines free of disease, the main viticultural concerns being DOWNY MILDEW, POWDERY MILDEW, and FLAVESCENCE DORÉE provoked by cicadelle attack. Irrigation is prohibited, and VINE DENSITY is an average 2,500 vines per ha (1,000 per acre).

Vine varieties

According to the French agricultural census of 1988, more than half of all vines planted on Corsica were still the varieties CINSAUT, CARIGNAN, GRENACHE, and the particularly undistinguished ALICANTE BOUSCHET imported in the 1960s. Other notable imports include UGNI BLANC and SYRAH, of which there were about 200 ha/500 acres apiece in 1988, and MOURVÈDRE, all of which are sanctioned by the appellation laws. These have since been supplemented by the likes of CABERNET SAUVIGNON, CHARDONNAY, VIOGNIER, MERLOT, and PINOT NOIR, from which vins de pays and table wines are produced.

A host of much more traditional Corsican varieties exist but few are planted in any significant quantity. CIVAM (Centre d'Information et de Vulgarisation pour l'Agriculture et le Milieu Rural de la Région Corse) is charged with researching and selecting Corsican varieties.

NIELLUCCIO is the most widely planted (even if its origins are probably Italian rather than Corsican), particularly in the north of the island, where it thrives on the chalky clay soils of Patrimonio. Nielluccio may be vinified as either a rosé or, if well vinified, an intensely coloured red with good, structured tannins and a balanced acidity. There is only about a third as much SCIACARELLO, which is unique to Corsica, where it is most successful on the granitic south west coast between Ajaccio and Sartène, producing relatively crisp, peppery reds and rosés, light in colour but high in alcohol. It is often blended with Nielluccio or Grenache. The only significant white native grape variety is also the best travelled. VERMENTINO, also known as Malvoisie on Corsica, and as Rolle by the host of growers planting it all over the south of France, is grown all over the island but performs best in the far north. It produces wines ranging from a pale, crisp version to a full bodied golden wine with a ripe fruit flavour, depending on when it is picked. Although many of the wines are dry, sweet Vermentino wines are also produced. Codivarta, a white grape grown on the Cap Corse, is the only other uniquely Corsican variety. The deep pink-skinned BARBAROSSA, the Barbaroux of Provence, is grown to a limited extent.

Vinification

Almost 70 per cent of all Corsican wine is made by CO-OPERATIVES, which, like some of the smaller wineries, have taken advantage of EUROPEAN UNION grants available for the installation of modern STAINLESS STEEL vats and REFRIGERATION equipment. White wines are usually therefore fermented at between 18 and 20 °C (64–8 °F), and clean-tasting rosés are made by SAIGNÉE and cool fermentation. MALOLACTIC FERMENTATION is usually suppressed for whites and rosés. Red wine-making is relatively traditional with fermentation temperatures regularly rising to 30 °C, followed by malolactic fermentation. The use of OAK was still extremely limited in the mid 1990s, although a Vermentino subjected to BARREL FERMENTATION and LEES STIRRING had yielded good results, and wines such as the Cuvée des Gouverneurs from Orenga de Gaffory and Clos du Cardinal from Domaine Peraldi showed respectively that Nielluccio and Sciacarello responded well to ageing in oak.

The wines produced

Rosé is as important in Corsica as it is in its nearest mainland wine region PROVENCE, representing about 30 per cent of total production. White wine accounts for an increasing proportion of all wine produced but it is still only about 10 per cent.

More than half of the wine produced in Corsica qualifies as no more than basic vin de table. Vins de pays represent around a third of the total and are cleverly labelled as Vin de Pays de l'Île de Beauté (Island of Beauty). AC wines therefore represent a relatively small proportion of the island's total output (less than 15 per cent in 1993), although eight different appellations exist: Patrimonio, Ajaccio, Vin de Corse (Corsican wine), and Vin de Corse followed by either Coteaux du Cap Corse, Calvi, Sartène, Figari, or Porto Vecchio, the last four of these being specific towns or villages still in the process of establishing their own viticultural identity.

Patrimonio Patrimonio was the first region in Corsica to gain AC status in 1968. Red, rosé, and white wines are produced and YIELDS are restricted to 50 hl/ha (2.8 tons/acre). In the past, the wines of Patrimonio often included a mix of different imported grape varieties, notably Grenache, but by the year 2000 Nielluccio must account for 95 per cent of the blend in red wines and Vermentino for 100 per cent in the white. This has caused considerable controversy amongst the growers. Clos de Bernardi, one of the oldest estates reputed for its red, is situated in Patrimonio. Other growers such as Orenga de Gaffory, Gentile, Leccia, and Arena have also invested much time and money to make dramatic improvements in quality.

Ajaccio Ajaccio was given AC status in 1984. Some of Corsica's highest vineyards are in this area, which produces mainly red and rosé wines with a little white. Sciacarello is the grape variety typical of the appellation and yields are set at 45 hl/ha. Domaine Peraldi, which overlooks the bay of Ajaccio, is one of the best producers.

Vin de Corse - Coteaux du Cap Corse The most northerly tip of the island, the Cap Corse, is renowned for its sweet Muscat and Rappu (a sweet MUSCAT-style red wine made from the ALEATICO vine variety). Some of Corsica's best dry white wines, such as Clos Nicrosi, are produced here.

Muscat du Cap Corse This VIN DOUX NATUREL was elevated to full AC status in 1993. It is made from MUSCAT BLANC À PETITS GRAINS grapes which were originally picked and left to dry in the sun in order to concentrate the sugars. Today they are picked at between 14 and 15 per cent POTENTIAL ALCOHOL and made, by the addition of alcohol at an early stage of fermentation, into a relatively elegant vin doux naturel.

Vin de Corse Most wine labelled simply Vin de Corse without any suffix comes from the eastern plain where the largest estates were established in the 1960s to produce large quantities of wines with little or no character. These tend to be Corsica's least distinguished AC wines, although Nielluccio, Sciacarello, and Grenache must represent at least 50 per cent of any red or rosé, while whites must be at least 75 per cent Vermentino. J.K.

Dovaz, M., *Encyclopédie des vins de Corse* (Paris, 1990).
Mercurey, F.-N., *Vignes, vins et vignerons de Corse* (Ajaccio, 1991).

CORTESE, Italian white grape variety most closely associated with south east PIEDMONT, where it was known even in the 18th century. The AMPELOGRAPHY text of P. Demaria and G. Leardi published in 1870 testifies: 'Cortese is the white vine variety most widely cultivated in the province of Alessandria . . . where it is esteemed not only for its robustness and fertility but also for the exquisite excellence of its product.' Its most highly regarded wine is GAVI, produced initially to serve the fish restaurants of Genoa and the Ligurian coast not far to the south. The Cortese dell'Alto Monferrato a few miles west, like the Cortese grown on the Colli Tortonese, rarely achieves the ripeness, or wine-making proficiency, of Gavi.

Cortese is also grown in OLTREPÒ PAVESE in Lombardy and may be part of the blend in the Veneto's Bianco di CUSTOZA. The wine produced is rarely complex and can be ineffably bland (unlike Piedmont's white ARNEIS and FAVORITA grapes) but sustains a good level of acidity through to full ripeness. Total plantings fell by a quarter in the 1980s to a total of fewer than 3,000 ha/7,400 acres. D.T.

CORTON and **Corton-Charlemagne**, respectively the great red and white GRANDS CRUS in ALOXE-CORTON in Burgundy's Côte d'Or.

CORVINA, or **Corvina Veronese**, the dominant and best grape variety of VALPOLICELLA and BARDOLINO in north east Italy, producing relatively light, fruity, red wines with a certain almond quality. Valpolicella DOC regulations which stipulate that the relatively bland Rondinella, and some of the tart Molinara, must constitute a combined total of at least 30 per cent of the blend are criticized for diluting the most characterful of the permitted grape varieties. This, sometimes called Cruina, is the variety most prized in the making of such DRIED GRAPE WINES as RECIOTO and AMARONE. Italy's total plantings of the Corvina Veronese vine variety were nearly 4,500 ha/11,000 acres in the early 1990s.

COSECHA is Spanish for VINTAGE year.

COSSART GORDON, the oldest company to trade in MADEIRA wine. Cossart Gordon was established in 1745 by two Scotsmen, Francis Newton and William Gordon, who fled their homeland following the failure of the Stuart cause with which they sympathized. In 1808 William Cossart, an Irishman of Huguenot descent, joined the firm. Cossart Gordon flourished on trade with the American colonies, at the time the most important market for Madeira. Until the 1950s Cossart Gordon workers wore a distinctive uniform of blue drill suits with a bright red cap. The Cossart family has been among the most influential on the island for nearly two centuries. In 1953 Cossart, Gordon & Co. Ltd. became a partner in the important Madeira Wine Association, which had its origins in a 1913 and which has since changed its name to the Madeira Wine Company Limited (see MADEIRA for more details). Today the BLANDY and SYMINGTON families together own more than 90 per cent of the company. S.A.

Cossart, N., *Madeira: The Island Vineyard* (London, 1984).

COSTERS DEL SEGRE, small wine zone in north east Spain in semi-DESERT near the Catalan city of Lerida (see map on p. 907). The climate is severe. The thermometer often dips below freezing point in winter and exceeds 35 °C in high summer. RAINFALL barely reaches 400 mm/15 in in a year.

The river Segre, a tributary of the Ebro after which this fragmented DO is named, is little more than a seasonal stream.

The history of Costers del Segre is really the history of one estate: Raimat, which covers 3,200 ha/7,900 acres of arid country 15 km/9 miles north west of Lerida. When Manuel Raventos, owner of CAVA producer CODORNÍU, first visited the property in 1914, he found infertile salt plains abandoned by farmers. An IRRIGATION artery, the Canal de Aragón y Cataluña, has since transformed the estate into an oasis but it took over 50 years of planting cattle fodder, pine trees, and cereals before the soil was fit for vines. Today the Raimat vineyard covers 1,250 ha, which amounts to a third of the Costers del Segre DO. A labrynthine irrigation system (in order to circumvent the EUROPEAN UNION law which forbids vineyard irrigation in Spain, Raimat qualifies for 'experimental status') starts automatically whenever the temperature rises above 35 °C/95 °F, and provides FROST protection when the thermometer falls below 1 °C. As a result, imported vine varieties such as CABERNET SAUVIGNON, MERLOT, PINOT NOIR, and CHARDONNAY flourish alongside indigenous vines such as TEMPRANILLO, PARELLADA, and MACABEO. Elsewhere in the region, which splits into four separate subzones, there are few quality producers. For the moment, Costers del Segre is synonymous with Raimat.

R.J.M.

COSTIÈRES DE NÎMES, easternmost appellation of the LANGUEDOC in southern France, known as **Costières du Gard** until 1989 but changed in case of confusion with the local VIN DE PAYS du Gard. It was elevated from VDQS to AC status in 1986. It is effectively part of the RHÔNE since the climate, soil, and topography are so similar to those just over the river in the southern Côtes-du-Rhône vineyards. The relatively uniform soils are marked by large pebbles on gentle, typically south-facing slopes. A total of 25,000 ha/62,000 acres of land could qualify to produce wine for this appellation, but in the early 1990s only just over 3,000 ha were dedicated to the production of appellation wine, about three-quarters of it red, and only a very small amount white. This is an important zone for the production of vin de pays. As in the nearby southern Rhône, Grenache is an important vine variety here, and must represent at least 25 per cent of any red; while Carignan is slowly being removed, it may still make up 40 per cent. This is an appellation in transition, not just geographically between the Languedoc and the Rhône, but temporally between a bulk wine producer and a source of genuinely characterful, well-made wines. CO-OPERATIVES are less important here than in most of the Languedoc and most of the development and experimentation is taking place on smaller estates.

CÔT or **Cot** is an important synonym for the black grape variety of French origin also known as MALBEC and, in Cahors, Auxerrois.

CÔTE means literally slope or hill in French, **Côtes** is the plural, while **Coteau** (of which **Coteaux** is the plural) means much the same thing but possibly on a smaller scale. Since French vine-growers are great believers in the viticultural merits of HILLSIDES, all of these make suitable wine names. Thus, any index of French wine names contains long lists of Côte, Côtes, and Coteaux de, du, de la, and des various place-names, suggesting, often with reason, that the wine comes from the slopes above these places. Some of these prefixes are eventually dropped, however. Côtes de Buzet, for example, was renamed plain BUZET in the late 1980s, just as Côtes de Blaye in the Bordeaux region has become BLAYE.

For this reason, and to save readers having to remember whether a wine is, for example, a Coteaux de or a Coteaux du Somewhere, such an entry would be listed under S for Somewhere, rather than under Coteaux. Their Côte and Côtes counterparts are listed similarly. The only exceptions to this are names in which the Côte, Côtes, or Coteaux are integral. They follow.

CÔTE DES BLANCS, area of CHAMPAGNE on east-facing slopes south of Épernay noted for the quality of its Chardonnay grapes.

CÔTE D'OR, the heart of the BURGUNDY wine region in eastern France in the form of an escarpment supporting a narrow band of vineyards for nearly 50 km/30 miles southwards (and a touch west) from Dijon, capital of the *département* of the same name. Although the name Côte d'Or apparently translates directly as 'golden slope', evoking its autumnal aspect, it is in fact an abbreviation of Côte d'Orient, a reference to the fact that the escarpment on which the vines flourish faces east. Viticulturally it is divided into two sectors, the Côte de NUITS, in which great red wines are made from the Pinot Noir vine, and the Côte de BEAUNE, where the reds are joined by the finest white wines made from Chardonnay. (See the map on p. 163.)

The Côte d'Or represents the fault line separating the hills of the Morvan from the plain of the Saône, which, in the Jurassic period 195 to 135 million years ago, was an inland sea. The predominant rock is Jurassic LIMESTONE, which favours both Chardonnay and Pinot Noir vine varieties. However, the escarpment features many differing forms of límestone and other rocks. Oolitic limestone, which originated as a precipitation around marine debris of carbonate of lime from the seawater, is usefully porous, and provides good DRAINAGE compared to marlstone, which is made up of clay, sand, gravel, and marl, the result of decomposition of older mountains such as the Ardennes.

The escarpment is also broken up by streams—the Vouge in Vougeot, the Meuzin in Nuits-St-Georges, the Rhoin in Savigny, the Dheune and Avant-Dheune further south—running down from the hills eventually to join the Saone, and by dry valleys (*combes*) such as the Combe de Lavaux in Gevrey-Chambertin. These breaks vary the orientation of the vineyards: thus Clos-St-Jacques and Corton are both exposed more to the south than east while much of Corton-Charlemagne actually faces south west.

A cross-section of the Côte reveals topsoil too sparse on the hilltop and too fertile pin the plain to produce wine of

GRANDS CRUS OF THE CÔTE D'OR
(listed from north to south; red wine unless stated otherwise)

Village	Grand Cru
Côte de Nuits	
Gevrey-Chambertin	CHAMBERTIN
	CHAMBERTIN-CLOS-DE-BÈZE
	CHARMES-CHAMBERTIN
	CHAPELLE-CHAMBERTIN
	GRIOTTE-CHAMBERTIN
	LATRICIÈRES-CHAMBERTIN
	MAZIS-CHAMBERTIN
	RUCHOTTES-CHAMBERTIN
Morey-St-Denis	BONNES MARES (part)
	CLOS DES LAMBRAYS
	CLOS-ST-DENIS
	CLOS DE LA ROCHE
	CLOS DE TART
Chambolle-Musigny	LE MUSIGNY
	BONNES MARES (part)
Vougeot	CLOS DE VOUGEOT
Vosne-Romanée	LA ROMANÉE
	ROMANÉE-CONTI
	ROMANÉE-ST-VIVANT
	RICHEBOURG
	LA TÂCHE
	LA GRANDE RUE
Flagey-Échezeaux	GRANDS-ÉCHEZEAUX
	ÉCHEZEAUX
Côte de Beaune	
Aloxe-Corton	LE CORTON (red and a little white)
	CORTON-CHARLEMAGNE (white)
	CHARLEMAGNE (white, but usually sold as CORTON-CHARLEMAGNE)
Puligny-Montrachet	LE MONTRACHET (white, part)
	CHEVALIER-MONTRACHET (white)
	BÂTARD-MONTRACHET (white, part)
	BIENVENUES-BÂTARD-MONTRACHET (white)
Chassagne-Montrachet	LE MONTRACHET (white part)
	BÂTARD-MONTRACHET (white, part)
	CRIOTS-BÂTARD-MONTRACHET (white)

any quality. The vineyard area begins to the west of the Dijon–Lyons railway line but only the most basic wines made from Aligoté and Gamay are produced here. Approaching the main Dijon–Chagny road, the RN74, the vineyards are still on flat, fertile lane but Pinot Noir and Chardonnay are planted to produce BOURGOGNE Rouge and Bourgogne Blanc. These in turn give way to village APPELLATION vineyards; as the ground starts to slope upwards, drainage improves, and the soil is less fertile.

Where the slope becomes more pronounced and clay gives way to stonier topsoil, the vineyards are designated PREMIERS CRUS, reflecting the potential quality of the wines from land which drains well and enjoys greater exposure to the sun. The finest of these vineyards, in certain villages only, are classified as GRANDS CRUS. (See CLASSIFICATION for a list of Burgundy's grands crus.) The premier and grand cru vineyards are mainly at elevations between 250 and 300 m (800–1,000 ft) above sea level. Near the top of the slope, where the soil is almost too poor, there is usually a narrow band of village appellation vineyards providing fine but light wines.

Viticultural practices are relatively constant for both major grape varieties throughout the Côte d'Or. VINE DENSITY is notably high—about 10,000 vines per ha (4,000 per acre)—and vines are trained and pruned chiefly according to the single GUYOT system (although some villages on the Côte de Beaune favour the CORDON DE ROYAT). Harvesting is still mostly manual, especially for Pinot Noir. Maximum yields are officially set at 40 hl/ha (2.3 tons/acre) for red wines at village and premier cru level, 45 hl/ha for whites. Maximum permitted yields for grands crus are mostly at 35 hl/ha for reds and 40 hl/ha for whites. In many of the vintages of the 1980s, however, a supplementary allowance (called PLC, *plafond limite de classement*) was allowed.

There are no set rules for the production of great red burgundy, and every domaine or NÉGOCIANT house revels in its own idiosyncrasies. Principal options include DESTEMMING of the grapes (wholly, partly, or not at all); MACERATION period; fermentation TEMPERATURE; length of BARREL MATURATION; type of OAK barrels; FINING regime; and the extent to which FILTRATION is practised. In the second half of the 1980s, as promulgated by the oenologist Guy ACCAD, a period of cold maceration before fermentation became popular as a method of extracting colour and fruit. The better wines of the Côte d'Or are all matured for at least a year, more often 18 months, in 228-l (59-gal) oak BARRELS, a proportion of which are usually new. Before bottling some producers fine the wine and filter it; others prefer one treatment to the other; a few use neither in the belief that the wine thereby has more depth of flavour and capacity to evolve, even though it is less stable.

The qualities of great red burgundy are not easy to judge young, especially since the wine tends to be less deeply coloured than equivalent wines from Bordeaux or the Rhône. When young a fine burgundy should show a bouquet of soft red fruit, ranging from cherries to plums depending on the vineyard and vigneron; complexity comes with maturity, the fresh fruit components giving way to more vegetal aromas, often redolent of truffles or undergrowth (*sousbois*, according to French palates).

Some wines are weighty, others intensely elegant, but all should have concentration. Style depends in part on the character of the village: GEVREY-CHAMBERTIN, VOUGEOT, NUITS-ST-GEORGES, CORTON, and POMMARD tend to produce robust, long-lived wines; CHAMBOLLE-MUSIGNY, VOSNE-ROMANÉE, and VOLNAY epitomize finesse and elegance. Within each village different vineyards display their individual characteristics according to the exact SOIL STRUCTURE, ELEVATION, and TOPOGRAPHY.

Differences in annual WEATHER patterns are crucial in determining quality in the region. Burgundy is at a climatic crossroads, experiencing Atlantic, Mediterranean, and Baltic weather systems. A cool breeze from the north (*la bise*) is ideal to temper anticyclonic conditions in the summer; a southern wind brings heat but also danger; HAIL and thunder often result when the warm wind swings round to the west, the wettest direction. There is probably greater vintage variation in Burgundy than in any other wine region.

In some VINTAGES—1972, 1980, 1984, 1987, for instance—most Pinot Noir grapes do not fully ripen, although growers who conscientiously restrict yields often produce excellent wines. In other years excessive rainfall can either swell the crop to produce dilute wines (as in 1982) or encourage ROT (as in 1986). Most difficult to judge are the hot vintages in which the fruit in the wine is either supported, or sometimes overwhelmed, by TANNINS (as in 1976 and 1983). Certain vintages, such as 1985 and 1989, produce fully ripe grapes and wines which are attractive to taste throughout their lives.

Great white burgundy is produced in the Côte de Beaune, notably in the villages of MEURSAULT, PULIGNY-MONTRACHET, and CHASSAGNE-MONTRACHET, along with a small enclave further north yielding the grand cru Corton-Charlemagne (see ALOXE-CORTON). The soils suited to Chardonnay production tend to be paler in colour than the iron-rich, redder soils on which the Pinot Noir thrives (see SOIL COLOUR). The Chardonnay vine is hardier than the Pinot, the grapes ripen more easily, and the wines require less delicate handling. It is easier to make good white burgundy than red but very little great white burgundy is made.

The grapes are pressed, usually without SKIN CONTACT, left to settle, then fermented in oak casks for up to a year (see BARREL FERMENTATION), although those with suitable cellars prefer to keep the wine for a second winter in wood. After the alcoholic FERMENTATION the wines are racked into another set of barrels to remove the major deposits, the 'gross lees', but left on their fine LEES which are regularly stirred up to nourish the wine (see LEES STIRRING).

Fine white burgundy, when young, is more likely to show the character of the oak in which it has been vinified than the grapes from which it came. Hallmarks of quality are fullness of BODY, balance of ACIDITY, and persistence of flavour. Only after two or more years of bottle age will a fine Meursault or Puligny-Montrachet start to show the quality of the fruit. This will deepen with age and, while vegetal tones will appear, they should not overwhelm the natural elegance of the wine. A village appellation wine should be at its best between three and five years old, a premier cru from five to ten years, while a grand cru worthy of its status needs a full decade of BOTTLE AGEING.

For more detail, see under names of individual villages or appellations. See BEAUNE, CÔTE DE and NUITS, CÔTE DE for a full list of the villages in each. To most of the villages and towns in the Côte d'Or was appended the name of their most famous vineyard, typically in the late 19th century. Thus, for example, Vosne became Vosne-Romanée and Puligny became Puligny-Montrachet. J.T.C.M.

Hanson, A. D., *Burgundy* (2nd edn., London, 1994).
Norman, R. H., *The Great Domaines of Burgundy* (London, 1992).
Pitiot, S., and Servant, J.-C., *Les Vins de Bourgogne* (11th edn. of P. Poupon's original, Paris, 1992).

CÔTE-RÔTIE, one of the most exciting red wine appellations in France, in the far north of the northern RHÔNE (see map on p. 796). In the 1970s the area and its wines was somewhat moribund, a rather isolated outpost well north of Tain where the major NÉGOCIANTS and the famous HERMITAGE vineyard are situated. One man, Marcel GUIGAL, is chiefly responsible for the recent renaissance of this zone (helped by the adulation of another, the American wine critic Robert PARKER).

Côte-Rôtie may be the site where the vine was first cultivated in GAUL, and vineyards have been sculpted from these, some of the steepest slopes of viticultural France, since at least the time when nearby Vienne was an important Roman settlement. The vines then grown were identified with the local tribe, the Allobroges (see RHÔNE, history).

Vine-growing brought so little reward in the 1960s and 1970s that total plantings were only about 70 ha/175 acres in the early 1970s; by the mid 1990s, however, plantings had reached 150 ha (rather less than the extent of the single biggest wine château in the MÉDOC). Guigal's single vineyard bottlings of La Mouline, La Landonne, and, later, La Turque reminded the wine-buying world of the potential majesty of wines hewn from the Côte-Rôtie, or 'roasted slope'. Even today, however, many of the meticulous small-scale producers such as Champet and Jasmin depend more on farming other fruits such as apricots than on their wines for income.

Because of the turn of the river here, the vineyards banked up the SCHIST behind the unremarkable town of Ampuis face directly south east, and are angled so as to maximize the ripening effect of any SUNLIGHT, while being sheltered from the cold winds. The slopes have traditionally been distinguished, with associated legend, either as Côte Blonde, supposedly producing alluring wines for relatively early consumption (often as a result of blending up to the permitted maximum of 20 per cent scented white VIOGNIER in with the mandatory SYRAH grape), or Côte Brune, associated with firmer, more durable, all-Syrah wines. The finest Côte-Rôtie, local lore had it, was a blend of the two. More recently, the fame, and record prices, of wines flaunting specific vineyard sites has rather put paid to this theory, and the appellation is a hotbed of activity and ambition.

Syrah is trained particularly distinctively on these slopes (so steep in parts that winches have to be used, as illustrated opposite p. 465), single GUYOT on single or double stakes. TERRACES are essential here, where they are known as *cheys* and have been in place for centuries. The theoretical minimum potential alcohol of these wines is 10 per cent, but most growers manage to achieve considerably more ripeness than this, and wines are made, with more or less new OAK (more *chez* Guigal), with considerable EXTRACTION and ambition, producing deep coloured, relatively tannic, savoury wines which take 10 years or more to develop one of the more rewarding BOUQUETS of the wine world, all undergrowth and ripe black fruits.

COTNARI, once-famous sweet white wine produced in wild, hilly countryside in the north Romanian Moldavia (see ROMANIA for geographical details). At one time it rivalled Hungarian TOKAY as an elixir of FASHION sought after in the courts of northern Europe. It was still fashionable in Paris at the end of the 19th century, and it is clear that NOBLE ROT has played an important role here for several centuries, and continues to do so every three or four years today.

The wine is made from a blend of white grape varieties of which GRASĂ (whose very name means 'fat') provides the body and sugar, TĂMÎIOASĂ Românească provides its 'frankincense' nerve (and sugar without losing acidity in the Cotnari MESOCLIMATE), Frîncusă the acidity (it must make up at least 30 per cent of the blend, although it can suffer from poor FRUIT SET), and Fetească Albă the aroma. Grasă ripens so dramatically that in 1958, for example, Grasă de Cotnari grapes reached a sugar level of 520 g/l. Cotnari the finished wine usually has at least 60 g/l RESIDUAL SUGAR and an alcoholic strength of at least 12 per cent. Unlike Tokay, it is aged in WOOD for no more than a year, and is carefully protected from oxygen. Although golden, it retains a greenish tinge after many years in bottle.

COUDERC NOIR, a HYBRID of a dark-berried RUPESTRIS *Lincecumii* and VINIFERA, is one of several productive but undistinguished hybrids that proliferated in the MIDI in the early 20th century (see BACO, CHAMBOURCIN, PLANTET, SEIBEL, SEYVE-VILLARD, VILLARD). Although not as popular as Villard once was, Couderc Noir was so widely planted that France's total area of Cabernet Sauvignon did not overtake that of Couderc Noir until well into the 1970s. By this time vigorous steps were being taken to eradicate this embarrassing legacy of another viticultural era, and the 1988 agricultural census found only about 2,500 ha/6,200 acres of each of Couderc Noir, Villard Noir, and the various Seyve-Villard varieties. Couderc, which does not even offer particularly good resistance to PHYLLOXERA unless grafted on to a vigorous ROOTSTOCK, needs a hot climate because it ripens so late and has always been most popular in the eastern Languedoc and the southern Rhône. It ripens too late to be of any use to the eastern states of North America. The wine produced can be aggressively non-*vinifera* in taste.

COULANGES-LA-VINEUSE, commune just west of Chablis. See AUXERRE for more information.

COULURE, French term, commonly used by English speakers too, for one form of poor FRUIT SET in grapes in which, soon after FLOWERING, the small berries, less than 5 mm/0.2 in across, fall off. To a great extent, coulure is a natural and necessary phenomenon, since the vine cannot possibly ripen all the grapes which would be present if all flowers remained as berries. However, for some varieties in some years, coulure can be excessive and YIELD drastically reduced. Excessive coulure can have a disastrous effect on grape-growers' incomes, and can also affect grape supply and wine prices in certain years. GRENACHE vines are particularly susceptible to coulure, as are MALBEC, MUSCAT OTTONEL, and certain clones of MERLOT.

Coulure is caused by an imbalance in the levels of CARBOHYDRATES in vine tissue. Where these drop too low, the very small berries fall off because their stems shrivel. Weather conditions which reduce PHOTOSYNTHESIS will cause coulure, and thus periods of cloudy, cold, and wet weather around flowering can have devastating effects on yield for some varieties. This is known in France as **coulure climatique**. Coulure also happens where the total leaf area, and thus photosynthesis, is limited and unable to provide sufficient sugar levels for the vine tissue. Low plant sugar levels can also be due to excessively vigorous shoot growth, combined with warm temperatures which favour RESPIRATION. There are several known causes of this phenomenon, including very fertile soils, excessive application of FERTILIZERS, especially those high in NITROGEN, vigorous ROOTSTOCKS, and PRUNING too severely (see BALANCED PRUNING).

There is little growers can do to prevent coulure. It is not always possible to grow varieties which are not susceptible, as particular varieties may be required for a certain style or blend. CLONAL SELECTION can be effective in reducing susceptibility for some varieties, as for example with Merlot and Malbec. TRIMMING shoots, or more precisely the tips of shoots at exactly the right stage, will reduce coulure by stopping competition for sugars between actively growing shoot tips and very small berries. Later pruning may also help because a delayed BUDBREAK will increase the possibility of warmer weather at flowering. Some chemical GROWTH REGULATORS can reduce coulure by inhibiting shoot growth. R.E.S.

Galet, P., *Précis de viticulture* (4th edn., Montpellier, 1983).
Huglin, P., *Biologie et écologie de la vigne* (Paris, 1986).

COUNOISE is one of the more rarefied ingredients in red CHÂTEAUNEUF-DU-PAPE, easily confused in the vineyard with the much lesser southern Rhône variety AUBUN with which it may sometimes be mingled in older vineyards. It is authorized as a supplementary ingredient for most red wine appellations around the southern Rhône, including Coteaux du LANGUEDOC, but is not widely grown outside Châteauneuf-du-Pape, although total French plantings increased in the 1980s to around 900 ha/2,200 acres.

As a vine, it leafs and ripens late and yields conservatively. As a wine, it is not particularly deeply coloured or alcoholic but adds a peppery note and lively acidity to a blend. Properties such as Ch de Beaucastel typically use about five per cent of Counoise in their red Châteauneuf-du-Pape.

COUPAGE, French and EUROPEAN UNION term for BLENDING. It means literally 'cutting' and retains a slightly pejorative overtone, tending to be reserved for wine blending at its least glamorous while the word ASSEMBLAGE is more commonly used for blending different lots of a fine wine. EU regulations prohibit the coupage of all sorts of different wines, including EU with non-EU wines, TABLE WINES with QUALITY WINES and different types of quality wines.

COURBU, vine variety native to SOUTH WEST FRANCE. See PETIT COURBU.

COURT-NOUÉ, common French term for the virus disease of the vine, FANLEAF DEGENERATION.

COURVOISIER, one of the major COGNAC firms, but which has always been the odd man out. It has never been truly native, never owning vines, distilleries, or indeed, stocks. It was founded by Emmanuel Courvoisier, who came from the Jura, and made his name supplying cognac to the court of the Emperor Napoleon I—even though his main business interests were in his warehouses at Bercy, on the river Seine east of Paris. The imperial connection continued when, shortly after the death of Emmanuel Courvoisier's son Felix, the firm was appointed suppliers to the court of Napoleon III.

Felix Courvoisier left the business to two nephews, the Curlier brothers, the only owners of the firm ever to live in the Cognac region. But in 1909 they sold it to the Simons, Anglo-French brothers with major wine businesses in both Paris and London, and it was they who exploited the imperial connection. The shadow of Napoleon I they used on Courvoisier bottles was cognac's most recognizable trade mark during the years immediately after the PHYLLOXERA epidemic when the market was flooded with imitations.

The firm was confiscated by the Germans during the Second World War and resurrected by the late Christian Braastad, a member of a remarkable Norwegian family which had settled in Cognac, and for a time was the biggest firm in the region. But cash, and stocks, ran short at a time of rising prices and rising demand and in 1964 Courvoisier was sold to the Canadian firm of Hiram Walker, which in turn was absorbed by the English liquor and food conglomerate Allied-Lyons, in 1986. Courvoisier's brandies have always been, and remain, rather richer than those of their major rivals, though Allied-Lyons (now Allied-Domecq) did much to improve the quality of what had been somewhat coarse products. N.F.

COVER CROP, a crop of plants other than vines established in the vineyard, typically between the rows, generally for the benefit of the vineyard soil. Alternatively known as a sward, or sod culture, it is an alternative to bare soil on the vineyard floor created by cultivation. Typical cover crops are grasses and legumes, and normally they are present for only part of the growing season. The grasses used may be native to the area or specially introduced species such as rye grass, fescue, or bent grasses, although sometimes cereals such as barley or oats are used. Legumes planted as cover crops include clovers, medicks, peas, and beans.

A common reason for sowing cover crops is to increase the ORGANIC MATTER in the soil and hence improve its structure and capacity to hold water. When this is the aim, the species sown should, like cereals, peas, and beans, grow quickly and produce plenty of bulk which can then be incorporated into the soil by shallow ploughing. Mustard cover crops are grown in Switzerland since they are deep rooting and reduce the likelihood of waterlogged subsoil in spring.

Cover crops are also commonly planted to stop SOIL EROSION. In areas with summer storms liable to wash away valuable topsoil if the soil surface is bare and especially if freshly cultivated, the roots of the cover crop bind the soil and resist the flowing water. Cover crops are also used to combat wind erosion, which can cause severe damage to young plants and the soil. Cereal rye, which has a strong straw, is often used.

But perhaps the most important use of cover crops is to encourage earlier RIPENING and improve wine quality. Slight WATER STRESS hastens the ripening process, so cover crops, which compete with the vines for water and nutrients, especially NITROGEN, can help to generate this stress in areas of high summer rainfall. Apparently weedy vineyards should not necessarily be dismissed as untidy; they may represent a deliberate ploy to improve wine quality. Deep-rooting crops such as mustard and chicory can be particularly useful to use up subsoil water which shallow-rooted grasses cannot reach.

Cover crops should be grown with caution during the vine's growing season. In spring they make the vineyard more prone to FROST than if the soil is bare. In summer the cover crop can use too much water or nitrogen and the vines can suffer as a result. Because of competition with vines for nitrogen, the use of cover crops can also cause STUCK FERMENTATIONS. These effects can be offset by close mowing or by killing the cover crop by ploughing or herbicides. Cover crops reduce the problems caused by dust from traffic on bare soil alleyways in the vineyard; dust can encourage MITES and can also adversely affect TABLE GRAPES particularly.

R.E.S.

CRATER, big, deep bowl with a wide mouth used in Ancient GREECE for mixing wine, most often with water. Crater is the Roman form of the Greek word *krater*. It was an essential piece of equipment for the Greek SYMPOSIUM, where the rule was that the wine was mixed with water in proportions agreed among the participants. To judge from the scenes of drinking painted on Greek vessels, the crater stood on the floor beside the couches on which the drinkers reclined. The crater was characteristically 12 to 18 in (30–45 cm) high. It could be either painted pottery or made of bronze. Exceptionally large vessels were probably prestige gifts, rather than of any practical use; the most remarkable example is the huge bronze crater, over 5 ft/1.5 m high, probably of Spartan manufacture, which was found at Vix in France (see CELTS). J.J.P.

CREAM, the sweetest, darkest style of SHERRY created expressly for the sweet-toothed British market by HARVEYS of Bristol. Bristol Milk was a style of sweet sherry sold successfully in the early 19th century by both AVERYS and Harveys. The story goes that a lady visitor to the cellars in 1882, on tasting Harveys' new, as yet unnamed, BRAND of sweet sherry observed, 'If that is Milk, then this is Cream.' Harveys Bristol Cream was thus named, and has become the most successful branded sherry in the world. This sweet style of sherry is eschewed by the Spaniards, for it is essentially the product of BLENDING not necessarily very distinguished sherries with sweetening and colouring wines. **Pale Cream** was another highly successful sherry style launched by CROFT in the 1970s. Most Pale Cream is essentially the same as Cream but with the colour removed, by CHARCOAL or other treatments, although it may also be sweetened FINO. Cream sherries generally have a RESIDUAL SUGAR content that is the equivalent of 4.5 to 6.5° BAUMÉ.

CRÉMANT, term used as France's shorthand for the country's finest dry sparkling wines made outside Champagne using the champagne method of SPARKLING WINE-MAKING. The term was adopted in the late 1980s when the expression *méthode champenoise* was outlawed by the EUROPEAN UNION. The principal provenances of modern Crémants, in declining order of importance, are Alsace, Die, Bourgogne (Burgundy), Loire, Limoux, and Bordeaux, although others, such as Gaillac, are aniticipated. The best sparkling wines of LUXEMBOURG are also called Crémant.

Crémant had previously been used to describe slightly less fizzy champagnes, with a pressure of two to three atmospheres rather than the normal five to six. KRUG, for example, produced a Crémant in the late 1970s.

Crémant de Saumur and Crémant de Vouvray had been the first non-champagne sparkling wines to use the term, and in the mid 1970s the Crémant de Loire appellation was born, soon followed by Alsace and Bourgogne in the 1970s. Bordeaux and Limoux joined the official Crémant appellations, created under INAO authority, in 1990, and were followed by Die in 1993.

Although grape varieties and TERROIRS vary from region to region, certain strict sparkling wine-making rules are imposed, including WHOLE BUNCH PRESSING; a maximum yield of 100 l per 150 kg of grapes (the same as CHAMPAGNE prior to 1993); a maximum SULPHUR DIOXIDE content of 150 mg/l; a minimum of nine months' TIRAGE on the lees; and a compulsory tasting control.

Crémant d'Alsace

Sparkling wine-making using the champagne method in Alsace dates from the late 19th century and in the 1980s became an important commercial activity, representing about 10 per cent of the region's output. Only the grape varieties Pinots Blanc, Noir, and Gris, together with the related Auxerrois, and Riesling and such Chardonnay as is planted in Alsace, may be used (i.e. no Gewürztraminer or Chasselas), to a maximum yield of 80 hl/ha (4.5 tons/acre) (rather more restrictive than that allowed in Champagne). The wines are well made, tend to have a particularly fine mousse, high acidity, and to be relatively light in BODY. Only if substantial proportions of Riesling are used do they acquire strong flavour. Production is in the hands of nearly 500 different small-scale producers whose blending capability is usually limited.

Crémant de Bordeaux

A small amount of sparkling wine has been made in the BORDEAUX region since the end of the 19th century. Today production is controlled by several companies who in 1992 used the production of less than 200 ha/500 acres to produce Crémant de Bordeaux either Blanc de Blancs from Sémillon, Sauvignon, and Muscadelle grapes, Rosé from Bordeaux's red grape varieties, or Blanc from any combination of red or white grapes. Maximum yields were limited to 65 hl/ha (3.7 tons/acre). A considerable increase in this field of commercial activity is predicted but the wines have yet to establish a clear style or identity.

Crémant de Bourgogne

This appellation, created in 1975, has replaced that of Bourgogne Mousseux, under which name Sparkling Burgundy of all colours enjoyed considerable commercial success in the 1950s and 1960s. In the mid 1990s there were just over 100 producers of Crémant de Bourgogne. All grape varieties grown in BURGUNDY are allowed into Crémant, although Gamay may not consititute more than a fifth of the blend. Yields are limited to about 65 hl/ha. RULLY in the Côte Chalonnaise and AUXERROIS in the far north of Burgundy are the principal sources of Crémant de Bourgogne (CÔTE D'OR grapes being in general worth considerably more when sold as still wine), and there can be considerable stylistic differences between their produce. Crémant from southern Burgundy can be full and soft, a good-value alternative to bigger styles of champagne, while Crémant made in the north is usually much lighter and crisper.

Crémant de Die

Crémant de Die is replacing the appellation Clairette de Die Brut, which will be outlawed from 1999. From then on, Crémant de Die will be a dry wine made exclusively from CLAIRETTE grapes, while Clairette de Die Tradition will be the arguably more distinctive sweet sparkling wine made principally from MUSCAT BLANC. Maximum permitted yields are about 50 hl/ha (2.8 tons/acre). See CLAIRETTE DE DIE for more details.

Crémant de Limoux

This appellation represents the increasing champenization of the ancient sparkling wines of LIMOUX in a particularly cool high corner of the southern Languedoc. In 1990 Blanquette de

Limoux became an appellation reserved for sparkling wines made principally from the MAUZAC grape grown traditionally in the region, while Crémant de Limoux contains a decreasing proportion of Mauzac (70 per cent in 1993), together with Chenin Blanc and Chardonnay (neither of these representing more than 20 per cent in 1993). The result is refined, racy wines which exhibit some of Mauzac's apple skin flavour and acidity. A very high proportion is made by the CO-OPERATIVE, although the produce of nearly 300 growers is used to make this most southerly Crémant. Yields are restricted to 50 hl/ha.

Crémant de Loire

Crémant de Loire was created in 1975 and encompasses the Anjou, Saumur, and Touraine regions. Most of the Loire's wide palette of grape varieties may be used to produce Crémant, with the notable and sensible exception of Sauvignon Blanc, whose aroma has yet to prove itself an attractive sparkling wine ingredient. GROLLEAU grapes may not represent more than 30 per cent of any blend, and in practice Chenin Blanc is the most common dominant component, clearly distinguishing the flavour of most Crémant de Loire from Crémants made from Pinots and Chardonnay to the east. Yields are limited to 50 hl/ha. Levels of wine-making are generally high among the nearly 200 producers (including four co-operatives and several important NÉGOCIANTS) and an increasing level of complexity in the bottle is evident. Some producers are Loire offshoots of Champagne houses, notably Langlois Château of BOLLINGER, Gratien & Meyer of Alfred Gratien, and the ambitious Bouvet-Ladubay of Taittinger.

Crémant de Luxembourg

Luxembourg has a long tradition of sparkling wine-making, and its particularly acid wines were at one time valued as base wines for SEKT. The Crémant de Luxembourg appellation was created in 1991, following the INAO rules laid down for French wines. Permitted grape varieties are Elbling, Pinot Blanc, and Riesling for white wines, Pinot Noir for rosé.

CRÈME DE TÊTE, French phrase occasionally found on wine labels, notably white BORDEAUX, denoting special, superior bottlings.

CRÉPY, wine appellation within the eastern French region of SAVOIE on the south eastern shore of Lake Geneva producing light, dry white wines from the CHASSELAS grape which would be difficult to discern from their Swiss neighbours in a BLIND TASTING. About 70 ha/172 acres of vines were in production in the early 1990s, and most of the wine is drunk locally.

CRETE, large island to the south of GREECE famous for the Minoan civilization (*c.*2000–1400 BC). Its wines were most famous in the Middle Ages when the island was known as Candia. See GENOA, MALVASIA, MALMSEY, NAPLES, VENICE.

CRIANZA, Spanish term used both to describe the process of AGEING a wine and also for the youngest officially recognized category of a wood-matured wine. A crianza wine may not be sold until its third year, and must have spent a minimum of six months in 225-l/59-gal oak *barricas* (BARRIQUES). In RIOJA and other regions such as RIBERA DEL DUERO, where the term is most commonly used, the wine must have spent at least 12 months in oak casks. A wine described as **sin crianza** should be a fruity young wine bottled without any CASK AGEING.

CRIMEA, peninsula off southern UKRAINE surrounded by the Black Sea, whose south coast became an important holiday region for Russian aristocrats in the 19th century and centre for sanatoriums in the 20th century. Cyrus REDDING noted in 1833 that 'the Crimea wines are thought the best in the empire'. The wine-loving Count Mikhail Vorontsov, governor-general of that part of Russia which then included the Crimea, began to build the Alupka Palace and associated winery in the 1820s which still produces FORTIFIED wines in quantity, and also laid the foundations for the MAGARATCH Insitute for research into wine-making and viticulture. Vorontsov imported a wide range of grape varieties from Europe, but suffered many early wine-making failures, as did his successor as principal Crimean wine innovator, Prince Golitzin, in the early 1880s at his Novy Svet winery. Modern wine production on the south coast is chiefly under the control of the MASSANDRA central winery on the outskirts of Yalta. Average July temperatures of 24 °C/75 °F and annual sunshine of 2,250 hours at Yalta result in extremely ripe grapes best suited to the production of strong, sweet wines, most of them made like VINS DOUX NATURELS.

CRIOLLA CHICA is the Argentine name for the PAIS of Chile, the MISSION of California, and the Negra Corriente of PERU. It is thought to be descended from the seeds of grapes, presumably well raisined after their voyage under sail across the Atlantic, imported by the Spanish conquistadores, possibly as early as the 16th century. Although Criolla Chica is much less common in Argentina than the other pink-skinned grape varieties CRIOLLA GRANDE and CEREZA, it is more common in La Rioja province than Criolla Grande.

CRIOLLA GRANDE, the most important vine variety in ARGENTINA in quantitative, if not qualitative, terms. Although the area planted with this coarse, pink-skinned grape is declining, it was nearly 37,000 ha/91,000 acres in 1990, which may have been enough for its inclusion in the world's top 20 vine varieties by area planted. Most Criolla Grande is in Mendoza province, where it is the most planted vine variety by far (covering three times the area of the red wine grape MALBEC, for example).

Criolla Grande is a low-quality VINIFERA variety that was probably one of the first vines cultivated in the Americas, and is much deeper skinned than CRIOLLA CHICA. The two Criollas, along with CEREZA and Moscatel Rosada, form the basis of Argentina's declining trade in basic deep coloured white wine sold very cheaply in litre bottles or cardboard cartons. Pink wine can also be made from Criolla Grande.

CRIOTS-BÂTARD-MONTRACHET, great white GRAND CRU in Burgundy's CÔTE D'OR. For more details, see MONTRACHET.

CROATIA, northern state in what was YUGOSLAVIA, is like its northern neighbour SLOVENIA in having two very different regions split by the ranges of hills which follow the coast. The area of Kontinentalna Hrvatska (inland Croatia) runs south and east from the eastern tip of Austria along the Drava tributary of the Danube which marks the Hungarian border down to the ill-fated town of Vukovar. Like Slovenia the area produces mostly whites from its 35,000 ha/86,000 acres of vines and Laski Rizling or WELSCHRIESLING (here known by the more graceful name of Graševina) is the predominant grape variety. Other varieties planted include GEWÜRZTRAMINER, PINOT BLANC, RIESLING, SAUVIGNON Blanc, and some SÉMILLON. The wines are generally riper and more earthy in style than their Slovenian counterparts.

The gorgeous coast, including Dalmatia, islands, and, Primorska Hrvatska, producing both reds and whites, runs from the Istrian peninsula down past Split to Dubrovnik hard by BOSNIA HERCEGOVINA. Istria has its fair share of both Bordelais red grapes such as CABERNET SAUVIGNON and MERLOT and Italian varieties such as Teran (REFOSCO) as well as MALVASIA, GAMAY, and PINOT NOIR, but most of the rest of the coast boasts a whole selection of grapes which appear to be native to this region. The PLAVAC MALI grape is responsible for two potentially excellent red wines, Dingač and Postup, both of which tend to be heavy and very ripe, with a natural ALCOHOLIC STRENGTH of 15 per cent being perfectly possible for a Dingač. Babić is another good red grape. White grapes include Pošip, Grk, Vugava, and Marastina. The last named can produce wines that are fresh, quite light, and herbal. The other three which all come from separate islands are heavier, deeper coloured, often rather MADERIZED, and too old-fashioned to travel well.

This coastal region stretches over 36,000 ha of vines.

A.H.M.

CROATINA, red grape variety from the borders of the PIEDMONT and LOMBARDY regions of northern Italy. The vine buds and ripens late but yields good quantities of fruity wine with a certain bite, designed to be drunk relatively young. Its common synonym is Bonarda, under which name it has a VARIETAL appetizing red DOC in the OLTREPÒ PAVESE zone of south west Lombardy. The variety is quite distinct from BONARDA Piemontese. Total plantings of Croatina declined from 5,500 to 4,500 ha (13,600–11,100 acres) in the 1980s.

CROFT, port and sherry shippers originally established as Phayre and Bradley in 1678. The first Croft, from York, became a partner in 1736 and since 1769, after several name changes, the company has been known as Croft and Co. Croft's main property in the DOURO valley is Quinta da Roêda near Pinhão, which produces the backbone for their vintage blends. In 1911 the firm was taken over by Gilbey's, and the majority shareholding eventually passed into the hands of the multinational corporation Grand Metropolitan. No members of the Croft family are involved today with the company, which also ships the wines of Morgan Brothers which they acquired in 1952.

Croft expanded into the sherry business in the difficult era of the early 1970s. Croft invaded Jerez with energy and one novel idea: they launched an entirely new style of sherry, Pale CREAM, which could offer the beguiling combination of a pale, sophisticated appearance with the reassuring sweetness of a cream. It was an enormous and much-imitated success, necessitating almost immediate expansion for Croft Jerez, in the form of Rancho Croft, a series of ultra modern bodegas an unparalleled 200 m/650 ft long.

CROP THINNING, viticultural practice designed to improve wine quality by encouraging fruit RIPENING, known as *éclaircissage* or *vendange vert* (green harvest) in French. Simply, some bunches are removed from the vine and those remaining ripen more quickly. Crop thinning is necessarily carried out by hand, and is therefore expensive. The YIELD is reduced more or less proportionately to the bunches removed, which means that only those growers able to guarantee top prices for their produce can afford the operation. The technique became common in the early 1990s among the better wine producers in Bordeaux, where it had been practised at Ch PÉTRUS since 1973. MECHANICAL HARVESTERS can be used to thin crops, but here individual berries or parts of bunches are removed. This practice is not widespread.

Bunches can be removed before FLOWERING, or after FRUIT SET. Early bunch removal (before flowering) of 50 per cent of the crop will cause less than a 50 per cent crop loss, as the remaining bunches will set better and berries grow larger, which is the principle of compensation common to many plants. One danger of thinning too early, however, is that, because berry size is increased so much, bunches may become so tight that they are prone to BOTRYTIS BUNCH ROT. Later bunch removal has more impact on yield, and earlier removal on fruit ripening.

Thinning is also appropriate when it is obvious that the vintage will be late, decreasing the chance of ripening a large crop.

The theory of crop thinning is that the remaining fruit ripens earlier, and so has better levels of SUGARS and ANTHOCYANS for red varieties. However, many studies have shown that these benefits are small in magnitude, and that crop levels need to be greatly reduced for a small change in GRAPE COMPOSITION. For many vineyards where the yield is in BALANCE with shoot growth, and the leaves and fruit are well exposed, then there will be little benefit from crop thinning.

In vineyards for TABLE GRAPES, thinning is more common since large berry size is important, and some growers even thin individual berries so that the ripe bunch looks attractive and appeals to the consumer. R.E.S.

Reynier, A., *Manuel de viticulture* (4th edn., Paris, 1986).

Dramatic illustration of the results (below) of **crop thinning** of Merlot vines in Pomerol.

CROSS or **crossing**, the result of breeding a new variety by crossing two VINE VARIETIES of the same species, usually the European VINIFERA species. Thus MÜLLER-THURGAU, for example, is a cross. **Crosses** are different from HYBRIDS, sometimes called **interspecific crosses**, which contain the genes of more than one species of the VITIS genus.

CROUCHEN or **Cruchen**, white grape variety producing neutral wines in both South Africa and Australia. It originated in the western Pyrenees of France but is no longer grown there in any quantity, thanks to its sensitivity to FUNGAL DISEASES. There are records of its shipment to Clare Valley in SOUTH AUSTRALIA in 1850 and for long it was confused with Semillon, which Australians were wont to call Riesling. It was therefore known principally as Clare Riesling in Australia until 1976 when AMPELOGRAPHER Paul Truel identified it as this relatively obscure French variety. There were still 420 ha/1,000 acres planted in Australia in the early 1990s but the wine produced is generally used as gently aromatic blending material. The South Africans had 3,500 ha of the variety they call Cape Riesling and occasionally South African Riesling and Paarl Riesling, and the variety is still increasingly popular with grape-growers. It may be sold simply as Riesling within South Africa (where true Riesling is known as White or Weisser Riesling) and shares with that much greater German grape variety the ability to benefit from BOTTLE AGEING.

CROWN GALL, BACTERIAL DISEASE which occurs on over 600 plant species, including vines, particularly when grown where winters are so cold that vines can be damaged (see WINTER FREEZE). High incidence of the disease can make vineyards uneconomic. All Vitis VINIFERA varieties are susceptible, but some VITIS *labruscana* varieties are more tolerant.

The disease is caused by *Agrobacterium tumefaciens*. The major symptom is the growth of fleshy galls (tumours) on the lower trunk which can girdle the trunk and portions of the vine above may die. At one time it was believed that the bacterium lived in the soil like its relative that causes galls on other plants. However, crown gall of vines lives inside the vine itself and so is spread at planting. Control of crown gall is difficult. Biological control on some plants is achieved with a related species of *Agrobacterium* which produces an antibiotic; unfortunately this is not active against the strain most common in vines. Eradicant chemicals such as kerosene can kill galls but new galls frequently develop. Research in the early 1990s suggests that hot water treatment of dormant cuttings (50 °C/122 °F for 30 minutes) reduces the bacterium, and TISSUE CULTURE offers total elimination by producing nursery stock free of crown gall. Avoiding the disease can also help to reduce winter freeze injury to trunks. Covering trunks with soil was a common practice but its effectiveness has been questioned. In the north eastern UNITED STATES the growers train the vines with up to five trunks so that there is always a young healthy trunk to replace dead or dying ones. See TRAINING SYSTEMS.

In recent years the crown gall bacterium has been the focus of intense research due to its application in GENETIC ENGINEERING in a wide range of plants other than vines. *Agrobacterium* has the ability to incorporate its own DNA (the genetic code) into the plant where it is combined with that of the host, and can thus be used to transfer new genes into the plant. Many new plants being created by modern plant scientists owe their origin to this otherwise harmful organism! R.E.S.

Pearson, R. C., and Goheen, A. C., *Compendium of Grape Diseases* (St Paul, Minn., 1988).

CROZES-HERMITAGE, the north RHÔNE's biggest appellation, regularly producing almost 10 times as much wine than the much more distinguished vineyards of HERMITAGE which it surrounds, and more than twice as much as the similarly-priced, and similarly extended, appellation of ST-JOSEPH across the river. Like both these appellations, Crozes-Hermitage is usually red and made exclusively of the SYRAH grape, although a certain proportion, just over a tenth, of full bodied dry white wine is made from the MARSANNE grape supplemented by ROUSSANNE. Up to 15 per cent of white grapes may be added at the time of FERMENTATION to red Crozes, although rarely to much effect. Although some bottlers have treated the appellation with little respect for quality, a nucleus of excitingly ambitious producers such as Belle, Combier, Graillot, Pochon, and Tardy et Ange emerged in the late 1980s to provide thoughtfully made Crozes-Hermitage of real distinction and mass. The best reds are rather softer and fruitier than Hermitage because the soils are richer (and because it is more difficult to justify BARREL MATURATION at Crozes prices), but they tend to share more of Hermitage's solidity than average St-Joseph. A more typical red Crozes, however, exhibits the burnt runner smell and sinewy build of overstretched Syrah, although the co-operative in the town of Tain l'Hermitage, two-thirds of whose production is Crozes-Hermitage, should not be underestimated. Les Chassis, between France's chief north–south *autoroute* south of Tain and the river, provides some of the finest red Crozes, including Jaboulet's Domaine de Thalabert, which was for long the appellation's principal standard-bearer. Parts of Gervan just north of Tain enjoy a MESOCLIMATE very much closer to that of Hermitage than the flatter vineyards to the east, which are some of the few in the northern Rhône which can be harvested by machine. The clay-limestone alluvial soils of Crozes-Hermitage seem generally less well suited to white wine production, although there are some successful vineyards around Mercurol. The appellation, which dates from 1937, takes its name from a small village just north of Tain without any particular vinous claim. Total vineyard area in production had reached 1,000 ha/2,500 acres by 1990. The best reds can be kept for five years or more (and in good years can happily survive for 10) but the average Crozes, red or white, is probably at its best drunk young.

CRU, French specialist term for a vineyard, usually reserved for those officially recognized as of superior quality. Such recognition was already known in Ancient ROME.

In English the word is often translated as 'growth'. PREMIERS CRUS, for example, are called FIRST GROWTHS in BORDEAUX, according to one of their official CLASSIFICATIONS. A cru that has been 'classified' is a **cru classé**, or CLASSED GROWTH. GRANDS CRUS can also have a very specific meaning, notably in BURGUNDY and ALSACE.

The top-ranked communes in BEAUJOLAIS are called crus, and their produce is Cru Beaujolais.

In SWITZERLAND, the first two vineyards to be officially awarded cru status were the neighbouring Dézaley and Calamin in the Vaud.

In Italy there have been some attempts to define various superior vineyards as crus. The local dialect for such a site in PIEDMONT is SORI.

When Lodovico **Antinori** decided to create his own winery near Bolgheri to produce Ornellaia in the mid 1980s, he relied less on his family's six centuries of experience in the wine business than on the advice of outsiders such as consultant André **Tchelistcheff** of California and Hungarian wine-maker Tibor Gál (shown here).

CRU ARTISAN, a category of Médoc wine estate in Bordeaux more humble than the CRU BOURGEOIS. It includes much of the produce of the CO-OPERATIVES there.

CRU BOURGEOIS, a typical invention for the MÉDOC district of Bordeaux, a category of red wine properties, or CRUS, designated bourgeois, or a social stratum below the supposedly aristocratic crus classés. While the crus classés represent about 25 per cent of the Médoc's total wine production from about 60 estates, the crus bourgeois represent a further 40 per cent, mainly from much smaller properties. These can vary, however, from simple smallholdings to properties such as Ch Larose-Trintaudon, the largest estate in the Médoc with its own vast château buildings, or Ch Clarke of Listrac, on which Baron Edmond de ROTHSCHILD has lavished a large fortune.

In terms of wine quality, there is wide variation in quality between the best and worst of the crus bourgeois. The best are producing wine that is seriously better, and occasionally more expensive, than that of the under-performing crus classés, while the worst make wine that is just slightly more exciting than red BORDEAUX AC. In general, however, this category can offer some of Bordeaux's best value. They are made mainly from Cabernet Sauvignon grapes but often contain quite a high proportion of Merlot, usually supplemented by some Cabernet Franc. Some BARREL MATURATION is usually involved in the making of the most highly priced crus bourgeois, even if only a small proportion of new OAK is lavished on this wine category. The wines are generally ready to drink at between four and eight years old.

The crus bourgeois (like so many wine CO-OPERATIVES) were born as a desperate response to the dire state of the international wine market at the end of the 1920s. A first CLASSIFICATION of the crus bourgeois of the Médoc was drawn up in 1932, and one can only imagine the difficulties of bestowing this supposed commercial advantage, ranked into three different classes, on a few hundred Médoc wine farmers. Thirty years later, when the Syndicate of Crus Bourgeois set about revitalizing itself, it was discovered that, of the 444 members registered in 1932, more than 300 had been absorbed into other estates, or converted their land from viticulture to another crop such as pines instead.

The Syndicate, with Jean Miailhe as president, has been much revamped and by the early 1990s had nearly 300 members, farming a total of about 6,000 ha/15,000 acres of vines. The Syndicate has grouped the poroperties into **Crus Bourgeois Exceptionnels, Crus Grands Bourgeois,** and **Crus Bourgeois**, but EUROPEAN UNION authorities would grant use only of the term Cru Bourgeois.

The crus bourgeois are particularly important in MOULIS and LISTRAC, where they represent 85 and 66 per cent of these appellations' total production. In PAUILLAC and ST-JULIEN, on the other hand, the crus classés are much more important and the crus bourgeois represent just 10 and 15 per cent of total production.

Dovaz, M., *Encyclopédie des crus bourgeois du Bordelais* (Paris, 1988).

CRUESS, WILLIAM VERE (1886–1968), biochemist, teacher, and author, was the link between work in wine research and teaching of the pre-PROHIBITION and post-Repeal eras in CALIFORNIA. Professor of Food Technology at the University of California at Berkeley, Cruess had done research on FERMENTATION before Prohibition. In the 'dry years' he studied such things as the production of grape syrup and other VINE PRODUCTS. Immediately upon Repeal he undertook to re-establish viticultural and oenological research at the University of California at DAVIS and did so with remarkable speed and efficiency. His *Principles and Practices of Wine Making* (1934) was the first work for the guidance of commercial wine-making published after Repeal. Many of the young scientists at the University after Repeal were hired or directed by Cruess, who thus had a central role in the restoration of the the California wine industry. T.P.

CRUET, named CRU south east of the vermouth town of CHAMBÉRY whose name may be added to the eastern French appellation Vin de SAVOIE. Cruet is dominated by its CO-OPERATIVE, which makes a range of wines from such grape varieties as Gamay and the local Jacquère and Roussette.

CRUSADES, the series of attempts by western European Christians to wrest the Holy Land from ISLAMIC control, often overestimated for their vinous consequences. Pope Urban V preached the First Crusade at Clermont in 1095 when he proposed to liberate the Holy Land from the infidel. Although the First Crusade established Christian states in Palestine and Syria, these were lost to Saladin a century later in the Third Crusade. The sack of Constantinople in 1204, during the Fourth Crusade, was one of the most disgraceful episodes in the history of Latin Christendom. When Pope Pius II proclaimed the last crusade in 1460, the Turks were threatening to cross the Danube. In military terms the Crusades were a failure.

Yet it has often been said that the Crusades brought the west into close contact with the civilizations of the eastern Mediterranean and that Latin Christendom was the richer for it. This is misleading. The Crusaders were not the west's only contact with Islam, or the earliest or the most important. At the time of the First Crusade the west was becoming acquainted with Muslim science (including the art of DISTILLATION), philosophy, and architecture (the first two often originally Greek, translated into Arabic) in Moorish SPAIN, while SICILY offered not only Arabic but also Greek culture. The Holy Land itself had no intellectual influence on the Christian conquerors. The Crusades had little effect on western trade beyond increasing its volume.

The reason for this is that the Crusades were, in one sense, the result of the economic expansion of western Europe which started in the late 11th century, for without rapid economic growth it would not have been possible to fund the First Crusade and send more than 100,000 men overseas in 1099. Trade with the east was growing as part of this

The Quinta do Bomretiro comprises some of the best **port** vineyards in the world. It is owned partly by shippers Ramos Pinto and partly by the Serodio family who sell grapes to the **Symington** group for Warre's ports.

economic expansion. This was the age of the town and its rising middle class, first on the Flemish coast (Ghent and Bruges) and the city states of northern Italy. Amalfi, Pisa, GENOA, and VENICE had had trading posts in the Byzantine empire in the two centuries before the Crusades and had had to fight against the Saracen sea power; from the late 11th century onwards their trade with Byzantium increased further and further, and in the case of Venice turned into colonization. This is how the Venetian and Genoese galleys introduced the strong sweet wines of the AEGEAN ISLANDS and the Peloponnese in southern Greece first to northern Italy, then to all of western Europe (see MALMSEY).

Being opportunists, the merchants of northern Italy did of course manage to profit from the Crusades. The Latin kings of Jerusalem were dependent on Venetian, Genoese, and Pisan sea power, and so they granted these cities trading areas in the Holy Land's ports. Yet although Genoa's interests centred on the crusading states, most of Venice's trade was still with the Near East.

The Muslims had had vineyards in Syria and Palestine, which they used mainly to produce TABLE GRAPES and DRYING GRAPES (as today); the Christian settlers increased viticulture. Around 1220 they cultivated many vineyards around Tyre, which was owned by the Venetians for most of the 13th century. The wine of Tyre was so strong that it was said to have caused death among the sick who drank it at the siege of Acre (1189–91). The fall of Acre meant the end of the crusading states, but a record survives in Genoa of a single ship carrying 10 tuns of Tripolitan wine to that city. The fall of Acre brought the military orders of the Templars and the Hospitallers to CYPRUS (see also COMMANDARIA). They grew wine there: the Saxon Ludolphus of Suchen, who went on a pilgrimage to the Holy Land in 1336, describes a vineyard near Paphos in Cyprus. Its crop is so abundant that he calls it Engaddi (after Song of Songs 1. 14, which in the Vulgate has, 'My beloved is as a cluster of Cyprus grapes in the vineyards of Engaddi'), and a hundred Muslim slaves labour in it. It used to be owned by the Templars (suppressed in 1312) and is now the property of the Hospitallers. But their contribution merely added a little to the large and highly profitable wine production of Cyprus. The Crusades are only a very marginal part of the history of viticulture and the wine trade.

H.M.W.

K. M. Setton (ed.), *A History of the Crusades*, 6 vols. (Madison, Milwaukee, Wis., and London, 1969–89).

Runciman, Steven, *A History of the Crusades*, 3 vols. (Cambridge, 1954).

CRUSE, the most patrician and numerous of the merchant families who occupied the Quai des Chartons, playing an important part in the BORDEAUX TRADE in wine. They originated in Schleswig-Holstein before the Prussians took it from the Danes in 1864. Hermann Cruse, born in 1790, came to Bordeaux in 1819 and opened his office in the Chartrons. As Cruse & Hirschfield, the firm did considerable business with north Germany. The family's fortune was made in 1848 and 1849, when Cruse made a vast speculation on the 1847 vintage, described by the BROKERS Tastet & Lawton as 'very abundant, exquisite but not big'. Since 1848 was the year of revolution in France when Louis-Philippe fled to England, and revolutions broke out in Germany, wine prices slumped. Cruse bought no fewer than 13,650 TONNEAUX from 130 CRUS, nearly all MÉDOC and particularly CRUS BOURGEOIS for the German market.

In 1850 the firm was changed to Cruse et Fils Frères, and two years later Hermann Cruse bought Ch Laujac in the Bas-Médoc, still owned by the family. In 1865 he bought his biggest property, the first in a series of CLASSED GROWTH acquisitions, Ch Pontet-Canet in PAUILLAC. In the same year Edouard Cruse acquired Ch Giscours in MARGAUX, which they resold in 1913. In 1903 Frédéric Cruse inherited Ch Rausan-Ségla in Margaux from his clergyman father-in-law, and this was sold in 1956. In 1945 Emmanuel Cruse purchased Ch d'Issan in a semi-derelict condition. It took many years to restore this fine, moated 17th century château and its cellars.

Emmanuel Cruse was one of three brothers who ran the firm in the major part of the 20th century. They divided the world between them. Christian Cruse concentrated on Russia before the Revolution, and Britain, which he visited for 50 years after 1912. His son Édouard developed a considerable connection with ST-ÉMILION and POMEROL, previously not greatly exported to Britain.

After the beginning of the 1970s, wine prices in Bordeaux rose sharply and by 1973 had reached a point for generic red BORDEAUX AC that made it impossible for merchants to fulfil their contracts without substantial loss. A disreputable broker persuaded Cruse, then chiefly run by the younger generation headed by Yvan and Lionel, son of Emmanuel, to buy TABLE WINE for resale as APPELLATION CONTRÔLÉE Bordeaux. No doubt other firms were involved, and certainly five were subsequently fined but their names were not published (a common practice in French wine fraud cases in order to avoid wholesale discredit to the wine region involved). Cruse was the most prominent merchant of Bordeaux at this time, however, and the authorities were refused entry to their premises in order to make a detailed inspection. Accordingly, a much-publicized trial took place in 1974. The broker was sent to prison, and the Cruses received a suspended sentence together with a huge fine, substantially reduced on appeal. The firm never recovered from this and in 1979 was sold to a big group. In 1975 Ch Pontet-Canet was bought by Guy Tesseron, Emmanuel Cruse's son-in-law and a COGNAC merchant who already owned Ch Lafon-Rochet. Ch d'Issan is still owned by the Cruse family and run by Lionel Cruse. The affair broadly coincided with the decline and sale, mostly to foreign concerns, of those houses that had formed the core of the BORDEAUX wine TRADE, among whom the Cruses were for long the leaders.

E.P.-R.

Faith, N., *The Winemasters* (London, 1978).

Penning-Rowsell, E., *The Wines of Bordeaux* (6th edn., London, 1989).

CRUSH, mainly American term for the whole HARVEST season, named after one of the first processes in the winery (CRUSHING) rather than what happens in the vineyard.

CRUSHER-DESTEMMER, common combination of wine-making equipment which carries out the operations of both CRUSHING and DESTEMMING.

CRUSHING (*foulage* in French), wine-making operation of breaking open the grape berry so that the juice is more readily available to the YEAST for FERMENTATION. It is only modern winery equipment that has permitted crushing sufficiently thoroughly that the onset and completion of fermentation are effectively speeded. The additional advantages of this are that the rapid accumulation of alcohol discourages any activity on the part of wild yeast and BACTERIA. The principal result is that an overwhelming proportion of grapes finish as attractive and balanced wines rather than as VINEGAR or unacceptably faulty wines.

Crushing was traditionally done by foot, by treading grapes thinly spread on a crushing floor slanted towards a drain and bounded by low walls to prevent the loss of juice. Foot treading is a relatively inefficient method of crushing, however, and extremely expensive in areas where labour costs are more than minimal—which is why it persisted in the production of PORT in the DOURO.

Modern **crushers** operate on one of two general principles. One type uses intermeshed counter-rotating corrugated rollers spaced far enough apart to pass grape seeds (which exude bitter TANNINS and rancid oils if smashed) but smash anything larger. Such machines generally incorporate a stem-separating unit (see DESTEMMING) and are therefore known as CRUSHER-DESTEMMERS, **crusher-stemmers** in the United States, *fouloir-égrappoirs* in France. The other general type also incorporates a destemmer but crushes the clusters by impacting them with paddles on a more rapidly rotating concentric shaft. Some machines are roller destemmers, while others are destemmer rollers, and many modern machines are sufficiently flexible for either the rollers or the destemmers to be left out.

It is to minimize the period over which grapes are crushed that the HARVEST is increasingly transported from vineyard to winery in shallow containers, ideally no more than 20 to 60 cm (8–23 in) deep, and why pressing stations are increasingly located close to the vineyard. A.D.W.

CRUST, name for the SEDIMENT that forms in bottle-aged PORT, consisting of molecules that have become too heavy to stay in solution. **Crusted port** is a style of port created by British shippers in order to provide some of the qualities of vintage port in a shorter time, and therefore at a lower price.

CRYOEXTRACTION (**cryo** referring to very low temperatures), French term for freeze CONCENTRATION, the controversial wine-making practice of artificially replicating the natural conditions necessary to produce sweet white ICE WINE. Since the late 1980s the practice has been adopted by some SAUTERNES properties (notably Ch d'YQUEM) and has been used with increasing confidence there for less successful vintages. Freshly picked grapes are held overnight in a special cold room at sub-zero temperatures, −5 or −6 °C (21 °F) for example, and then pressed immediately. The freezing point of grape must depends on its concentration of sugars, so only the less ripe grapes freeze. PRESSING the grapes straight out of the cold room therefore yields only the juice of the non-frozen, ripest grapes, whose chemical composition remains unchanged. The colder the grapes are kept, the less but richer juice is obtained, and vice versa. The wine producer can therefore manipulate how much wine of what quality is made (unlike ice wine, which is entirely dictated by natural conditions). The technique is particularly useful in wet vintages in which the health and ripeness of individual berries may vary, such as 1987 in Sauternes.

Tartrate **crystals** on a cork that has spent years in contact with a fine wine which has not been subject to tartrate stabilization.

CRYSTALS in a bottle of white wine, on the underside of a cork, or on the inside of a vat, are harmless deposits. See TARTRATES for a full explanation.

CULTIVAR, term developed by professional botanists to mean a cultivated variety. In a strict sense, VINE VARIETIES are cultivars, but the term does not have a wide following outside professional botanists and horticulturists, except in South Africa, where it is widely and generally used. It has a major deficiency in that it has no adjectival form, and therefore no counterpart to VARIETAL. R.E.S.

CULTIVATION, the vineyard process of ploughing the soil, normally to kill weeds. The type of cultivation and its frequency vary from region to region around the world. Initially cultivation was by hand-held hoes. Animals were subsequently used to pull ploughs. For modern vineyards, tractor-mounted discs or tines disturb the topsoil and kill weeds. Cultivation within the vine row requires a special plough that will avoid trunks. Initially these were manually operated to dodge in and out, but now touch or electronic sensors are used to activate a hydraulic mechanism. Because of root and trunk damage this practice has now been replaced in many vineyards by the use of undervine HERBICIDES.

Cultivation of the soil to control weed growth is particularly common in regions with irrigation or summer rainfall. A fastidiously cultivated vineyard is still regarded as a sign of good husbandry in some regions, but there is a growing recognition for many vineyards that cultivation damages SOIL STRUCTURE and can lead, for example, to problems of water infiltration. The planting of COVER CROPS or allowing volunteer plants to grow is becoming more common. R.E.S.

Winkler, A. J., *et al.*, *General Viticulture* (2nd edn., Berkeley, Calif., 1974).

CURRANTS, small, dark DRYING GRAPES made from the vine variety **Zante Currant** (in Australia) or Black Corinth (in California). This dark-skinned variety originated in Greece, which is where most of the world's currants are produced, and takes its name from a corruption of the word Corinth. The bunches are long and cylindrical, and the berries very small and black with no seeds. FRUIT SET is poor without CINCTURING or the use of GROWTH REGULATORS. It is also occasionally used for wine-making in Australia, where a variant on it, **Carina**, was bred in the 1960s (see TARRANGO). R.E.S.

CUSTOZA, BIANCO DI, straightforward dry white wine produced in the VENETO region of north east Italy in a wide stretch of territory extending south westward from the city of Verona to the BARDOLINO zone on the shores of Lake Garda and the countryside immediately to the south of the lake. More than 850 ha/2,100 acres produce about 70,000 hl/1.8 million gal of wine each year. The substantial presence of TREBBIANO Toscano grapes (constituting 20 to 45 per cent of the blend), along with GARGANEGA (20 to 40 per cent), TOCAI Friuliano (five to 30 per cent) and a variety of other grapes (Riesling Italico or WELSCHRIESLING, PINOT BLANC, CHARDONNAY, MALVASIA Toscana), tends to yield a rather colourless, neutral wine. The greater fame and availability of wines from nearby SOAVE have created severe price constraints for Bianco di Custoza, particularly in its home markets of the Veneto, further reducing its potential to produce wines of real character and quality. D.T.

CUTTINGS, cut lengths of canes used for vine PROPAGATION. Rooted cuttings are the basis of propagation for commercial grape production, whether as own-rooted plants (see ROOTLINGS), or as scion varieties for GRAFTING on to rooted cuttings. Both methods are representative of asexual or vegetative propagation and, unless they mutate, the progeny are considered as CLONES of the source vines. In commerce, cuttings are cut from dormant vines in lengths of 30 to 45 cm (12–18 in). Long cuttings are needed for sandy soils. Dense and well-ripened wood is preferred. Once made, the cuttings are kept moist and planted in a nursery in spring for roots to form at the base, and a shoot to grow from the top bud. Treatments are available to improve the rooting percentage of difficult-to-root varieties. The rootling is lifted from the nursery and planted in its vineyard position the following year. Given the right conditions, a cutting of one node can produce a satisfactory rootling, a technique that is useful in increasing vine numbers from scarce bud supplies. B.G.C.

Vine **cuttings** are planted out in sterilized soil at the Ernita nursery in the Nederburg estate, Cape Province, South Africa.

CUTWORMS, the larvae of several species of moths, are one of the most serious pests of all sorts of crops world-wide. They hide in the soil or under the vine's bark during the day and emerge to feed and cause damage at night. Young vines are particularly prone to damage from cutworms. A number of species of cutworm attack grapes, and identification is important in control because of differences in activity. They attack grapevines between the time buds begin to swell and when shoots are several inches long. When cultural practices, natural enemies, and climatic factors do not keep cutworms to tolerable levels, there are highly effective chemical agents which can prevent major losses. DDT was once used, but there are now effective contact insecticides. M.J.E.

CUVE is French for a vat or tank. Thus, a **cuverie** is the vat hall, typically where fermentation takes place. *Cuves* may be made of any material: wood, concrete, or, most likely, stainless steel.

CUVE CLOSE, French for sealed tank, and a name for a bulk sparkling wine-making process (sometimes called Charmat) which involves provoking a second fermentation in wine stored in a pressure tank. For more details see SPARKLING WINE-MAKING.

CUVÉE, French wine term derived from CUVE, with many different meanings in different contexts. In general terms it can be used to mean any container-full, or lot, of wine and therefore wine labels often carry relatively meaningless descriptions incorporating the word cuvée. **Tête de cuvée**, on the other hand, is occasionally used for the top bottling of a French wine producer, particularly in Sauternes.

In CHAMPAGNE and other environments in which champagne method sparkling wines are made, cuvée is a name for the first and best juice to flow from the press (see SPARKLING WINE-MAKING). The blend of base wines assembled for second fermentation in bottle is also known as the cuvée. Thus the term is often used in many champagne and sparkling wine names.

Elsewhere, particularly in German-speaking wine regions oddly enough, cuvée may be used to describe any ambitious blend, particularly of different vine varieties.

CYPRUS, eastern Mediterranean island less than 100 km/60 miles from Syria to the east and Turkey to the north. The medieval Cyprus wine industry was commercially the most important in the Middle East, but in the 20th century Cyprus wine has languished in terms of quality. A substantial improvement in production techniques was precipitated in the 1990s by the collapse of communism.

History

Because of its position in the eastern Mediterranean, closer to the Middle East than to GREECE, Cyprus has changed hands many times. In antiquity, domination by various foreign powers alternated with brief periods of independence, and in 58 BC Cyprus became part of the Roman province of Cilicia in Asia Minor. Strabo (*Geography*, 7 BC) and PLINY mention the wine of Cyprus approvingly but it was not particularly famous. In AD 668 Cyprus was occupied by Arabs; when they were finally expelled in 965 Cyprus became an advance base of the Greek navy. In 1191, in the course of the Third CRUSADE, Richard I, king of England, conquered Cyprus and sold it to the Templars, who soon gave it back to him, whereupon he presented it to the rejected king of Jerusalem, Guy de Lusignan. Guy de Lusignan imposed a feudal system on Cyprus and governed the island as a separate kingdom, which it remained until it became a colony of the then powerful VENICE in 1489.

The Crusaders and Venetian expansionism made the island part of the Latin west, which soon became fond of its wines. The earliest record of Cyprus wine being drunk in the west is dated 1178 when Count Baldwin of Guines offered it to the archbishop of Rheims. The wine is clearly a rare luxury, designed to impress an ecclesiastical magnate. In the next century it became more widely available. The Old French poem *La Bataille des vins* (see MEDIEVAL LITERATURE) awards the palm to *chypre*, Cyprus wine, because it is stronger and sweeter than any wine that is to be had in western Europe (FORTIFICATION and MUTAGE were as yet unknown). We do not know when the wines of Cyprus first reached the English market, but in the 13th and 14th centuries they, along with other sweet wines from the east and from Italy (see ENGLAND), fetched higher prices than the wines of GASCONY and LA ROCHELLE. The Venetians shipped them from Cyprus to Venice in their galleys, and from Venice they distributed them all over Europe.

A modern Cyprus wine, COMMANDARIA, preserves in its name a piece of crusading history. When the fall of Acre, in 1281, ended the Latin Christian presence in Palestine and Syria, the Knights Hospitallers moved their headquarters from Acre to Cyprus and thence to Rhodes. Like all religious orders, the Knights Hospitallers (or Knights of St John) acquired land on a large scale and grew wine. Their organization was strictly hierarchical, into priorates, then bailiwicks and lastly commanderies. A commandery was a manor or group of manors under the authority of a commendator. Each commandery had its vineyard or vineyards: hence the name of the modern dessert wine from Cyprus. H.M.W.

Modern history

Ottoman rule (1571–1878) brought a steep decline in wine production, and in the importance of the wine industry, which remained in an underdeveloped state until the middle of the 19th century, the first of the modern wineries, Haggipavlu, not being founded until 1844. British administration of the island (1878–1960) saw a further revitalization of the industry, with Cyprus sherry becoming an important product for the first time. In 1974 northern Cyprus was invaded by the Turks and the island was partitioned. Today, wine continues to play an important role in the agricultural economy of the Greek Cypriot, southern Republic of Cyprus.

Climate and geography

Commercial wine-growing is confined to the southern foothills and slopes of the Troodos mountain range at altitudes varying from 250 m to 1,500 m (800–4,900 ft) above sea level. The vineyard area is divided into six regions: Pitsilia (the highest), Marathasa, Commandaria, Troodhos South, Troodos East, and Troodhos North. Three of the regions contain designated subregions: Madhari in the region of Pitsilia; Afames and Laona in Troodhos South; and Ambelitis, Vouni tis Panayias, and Laona Kathikas all within Troodhos East. Pitsilia and the northern (higher altitude) half of Commanderia have igneous soil and subsoil. Elsewhere soils are of sedimentary LIMESTONES with a particularly high free lime content.

The climate is typically MEDITERRANEAN: mild winters and hot summers with precipitation confined to the winter months. Rainfall is low: 500 mm/19 in per annum is the mean for the lower altitude vineyards and 900 mm/35 in for the higher. IRRIGATION is not permitted.

Mean temperatures vary with altitude as illustrated in the table overleaf.

	High (°C/°F)	Low (°C/°F)
Summer		
Mean max. temp.	25/77	35/95
Mean min. temp.	9/48	20/68
Winter		
Mean max. temp.	10/50	16/61
Mean min. temp.	2/36	7/47

The great variation in temperatures between low- and high-altitude vineyards results in one of the most extended vintage periods in the world. Picking usually starts in mid-July and continues until early November.

Climatic hazards are restricted to HAIL and, at higher-altitude vineyards, spring and autumn FROST. The lack of humidity means that downy mildew is unknown but growers regularly spray against POWDERY MILDEW. BOTRYTIS is found only in grape bunches that have previously been attacted by eudemis MOTHS or other INSECTS. Since PHYLLOXERA has never reached Cyprus, vines are ungrafted. Almost all vines are BUSH trained, the exceptions being non-indigenous varieties where bud fertility near the trunk is poor, necessitating long fruiting canes supported by TRELLISING systems.

Vine varieties

The vast majority, almost three-quarters, of the Cyprus vineyard area is planted with the indigenous Mavro (black) grape variety. Only when cultivated at altitudes above 1,000 m/3,300 ft, where yields can be as low as 25 hl/ha (1.4 tons/acre), such as Laona, is Mavro capable of producing wine of quality and character. Elsewhere it gives high yields of very large grapes; 200 hl/ha (11 tons/acre) is by no means unknown. With its high skin to juice ratio, Mavro has a tendency to give pale, unattractive colours when vinified as a red wine. To counteract this problem wine-makers often remove up to 40 per cent of the juice prior to fermentation. The juice removed has commonly been used for Cyprus sherry, whilst the remaining pulp has a much better juice to skin ratio for the production of red table wines.

At its best, Mavro gives wine with a cherry or blackcurrant candy character when young, developing vegetal characteristics with three to five years' age. The wine rarely loses its faint iodine background flavour but is often high in alcohol.

The second most planted wine grape is the indigenous white grape Xynisteri, which, if picked before overripe and carefully vinified, has the ability to produce aromatic wines with a good balance between sugar, alcohol, and acids, and a tendency towards earthiness of flavour. In the better-quality wines, Xynisteri may be supplemented by PALOMINO, a variety imported with a view to improving Cyprus sherry, and MALVASIA Grossa.

Fear of phylloxera has made the island's authorities particularly cautious about the introduction of non-indigenous grape varieties and heavy QUARANTINE regulations have been enforced, even if only in the southern part of the island. It was as recently as 1958 that the Ministry of Agriculture first imported new varieties for experimental purposes. Over the following 10 years a series of trials was conducted to discover the varieties best suited to Cypriot conditions. In 1964 a further programme of experiments began aimed at finding the best MESOCLIMATE for each of the new varieties. The trials were completed in 1990 and, of imported varieties, CARIGNAN and GRENACHE have been most widely planted, with some CABERNET SAUVIGNON as well as some surprisingly successful RIESLING, some WELSCHRIESLING, and a small amount of CHARDONNAY also grown. Since then vine cuttings have been made available to growers in those areas identified as most suitable for imported varieties.

During this time there also developed a renewed interest in the island's lesser planted indigenous varieties, thanks to researches conducted by the French ampelographer GALET at the invitation of one large Cypriot wine producer. Many of these traditional varieties have much greater quality potential than Mavro, but were less popular with growers because of cultivation difficulties. Promara can produce good-quality white wine when grown at high altitudes, Opthalmo produces red wines with better acidity than Mavro, but the native vine with perhaps the greatest potential for quality is the red Maratheftico, however unpopular it is with growers because of its sensitivity to powdery mildew. The vine is difficult to grow commercially since it is one of the wine world's few non-hermaphrodite vines, and must be planted in vineyards of mixed varieties to ensure good POLLINATION. It is known as Pambakina or Pambakada in the Pitsilia region.

Commercial wineries are divided in their opinions on the value of new as opposed to native grape varieties. In one camp are companies that see no future for the native grapes other than as the source of bulk wine, Cyprus sherry, and concentrated must. These firms believe that the new varieties, which include Cabernet Sauvignon and Riesling, not only produce better wine than indigenous varieties but also give a product which is easier to market internationally at realistic prices. Wineries taking the opposite view hold that the best indigenous grape varieties, when carefully cultivated on suitable sites and vinified using modern techniques, give wine that is equal in quality to that made from imported vine varieties, but with the unique selling point of a more distinctive local character.

With the exception of a very few estates owned by the commercial wineries or the Ministry of Agriculture, Cyprus vineyards are divided into thousands of smallholdings. Typically, the land is worked by the older generation. Children and grandchildren may be employed in the local tourist industry but are more likely to have moved to the towns to work in Cyprus's service and manufacturing industries, thus creating rural depopulation serious enough to be a significant social problem.

Wine-making

In the island's wineries, at least until the early 1990s, almost all fermentation and storage was in concrete vats, which, in some wineries, were poorly maintained, with damaged or missing epoxy linings, thereby exposing the wine to the bare concrete. Limited use was made of STAINLESS STEEL vats and

REFRIGERATION but only for relatively small volumes of better-quality white wines. Better red wines, again a limited proportion of total red production, were matured in bottle in underground cellars. CASK AGEING of light wines was virtually unknown. A small number of more modern, necessarily experimental wineries began operation only in the late 1980s or early 1990s, and they consciously try to avoid OXIDATION, the most common Cyprus wine fault.

Organization of trade

Almost all Cypriot wine is made by four large firms—SODAP, KEO, ETKO, and Loel—all based far from the vineyards but close to the docks in Limassol, with SODAP having a second plant in Paphos. SODAP is a CO-OPERATIVE while the others are public companies, with a substantial proportion of their shareholding owned by vine-growers. The minimum grape price paid to growers by the wineries is set annually by the wine authorities, the Vine Products Commission, and from 1993 was set according to area of vineyard rather than by MUST WEIGHT and weight of grapes.

Wineries rely on exports for the majority of their sales since per capita wine consumption in Cyprus is extremely small. Beer, ouzo, and brandy are the principal alcoholic beverages drunk by Cypriots.

Since the end of the Second World War, the majority of the island's wine exports have fallen into four categories:

1. Large volumes of basic wine for which the USSR (now CIS) and other eastern European countries were the principal customers. The quality of the wine was not particularly important.

2. Wine intended for industrial uses such as the basis of VERMOUTH, SANGRÍA, or, in German-speaking countries, commercially prepared GLÜHWEIN.

3. GRAPE CONCENTRATE for use, after reconstitution, in making ersatz products such as BRITISH WINE. Although concentrated must can be reconstituted to make pure grape juice, the 'made wine' producers of the United Kingdom, Japan, and central and eastern Europe were the main customers until the early 1990s.

4. Cyprus sherry: good-quality dry Cyprus sherries that can stand comparison with some of the products of JEREZ are produced, having been matured for a legally specified minimum of two years in a SOLERA system under a layer of FLOR yeast. But the majority of Cyprus sherry is sweet, less distinguished wine, matured for a year in casks stored outside. Sweetness is obtained by arresting the natural FERMENTATION with spirit at 40 g/l sugar (and therefore by mutage, a method closer to that used in the production of PORT than true SHERRY). Before bottling, the sweetness of the wine is increased by adding concentrated must. The principal market for Cyprus sherry is the United Kingdom.

This reliance on products where the quality of the base wine was not of great importance meant that, during the period from the end of the Second World War to the collapse of the eastern bloc, the Cypriot wine industry had little incentive to exploit the island's quality potential. At harvest most grapes were transported in large, open lorries. Because picking took place in the morning, the movement of the grapes would start in the afternoon, at the hottest time of the day. Further problems resulted from the rural labour shortage, which could mean that it took two days or more to fill one of the lorries, which would be parked in the open air, exposed to sun and heat. The small size of holdings, and the near universal use of bush training, make MECHANICAL HARVESTING almost impossible.

The early 1990s brought grave problems to the Cypriot wine industry. The collapse of communism meant that the eastern bloc market almost totally disappeared. Demand for Cyprus sherry was in steady decline. Spanish protection of the name 'sherry' through the EUROPEAN UNION threatened sales of what had been known as 'British sherry', the production of which had been such a significant outlet for Cypriot concentrated must. Lastly, the island was finding it increasingly difficult to compete on price with the basic wines of France, Italy, and, especially, Spain.

The cost of supporting this ailing wine industry is an increasingly embarrassing problem for the Cypriot government. In 1992 a fine four-point plan to improve vine varieties and wine-making practices and to pull up vineyards in least favoured sites was issued by the government, but its implementation is likely to be extremely costly and to meet opposition from many vine-growers. The ambitious plan incorporated the establishment of 'designation of origin' legislation, with Commandaria being the first candidate. In the mid 1990s, only (a polished version of) Commandaria seemed to have any potential in an industry which was facing considerable competition, not only from the traditional wine-producing countries, but also from the New World and the eastern European countries—some of which once bought huge volumes of Cypriot wine but were then, as radically but as relatively late as Cyprus, reorganizing their own wine industries.

See also COMMANDARIA and Cyprus BRANDY. G.J.L.

Dion, Roger, *Histoire de la vigne et du vin en France* (Paris, 1959).
Simon, A. L., *The History of the Wine Trade in England*, 3 vols. (London, 1906–9).

CYTOKININS, natural HORMONES in vines produced in the root tips and affecting the growth of other parts of the plant. Cytokinins favour cell multiplication and affect growth and development of shoots and inflorescences. Fewer cytokinins are produced in dry soils, and also in cold and wet soils, and this appears to be critical for BUDBREAK and early shoot growth.

CZECHOSLOVAKIA in the early 1990s became two eastern European wine-producing countries rather than one: the **Czech Republic** in the west, consisting of Bohemia around Prague in the north and Moravia in the south; and **Slovakia** in the eastern half of the country. Apart from a few very small vineyard areas around the town of Melnik, Bohemia is rightly far better known for its beer production (and production of glasses) than for its wines.

Under the communist rule that left erstwhile Czechoslovakia almost exclusively introspective, land use was very well documented. In 1990 just after this system broke down, the country declared 47,000 ha/116,000 acres of vineyard of which 36,000 were in production, yielding a total of about 1.6 million hl/42 million gal of wine (about the same as Switzerland for example, from more than twice as much land, and less than half the total wine production of AUSTRIA to the immediate south).

Czechoslovakia had expanded its production 20 per cent in 15 years in response to its own consumption requirements. Very little, if any, attempt was made to export and any natural shortfall in the vintage against national consumption projections was made up by buying in and vinifying must from HUNGARY for use in the cheapest blends.

The use of Hungarian must to complement home production made sense as the Moravian and Slovakian vineyards lie close to their southern borders on land which drains into the Danube and immediate tributaries. They share a common history and viticultural heritage with Austria and Hungary. In the furthest south eastern corner of Slovakia the famous TOKAY vineyards extend over the border from Hungary. A symptom of the isolationist view which the Czechoslovakians had of the world was the fact that they cheerfully traded away their right to the Tokay appellation beyond their own borders in return for a 25-year contract to export beer in bulk to Hungary. This deal has now been rescinded.

Slovakia has around 25,000 ha/62,000 acres of vineyards in total. As in Moravia, the vast majority of these were rationalized under the communist regime from individual smallholdings with the patchwork quality of a Burgundian hillside to holdings of more than 1,000 ha/2,500 acres with long rows of vines that could easily have been adapted to mechanical cultivation.

About two-fifths of the vineyards lie on gentle slopes, usually topped by woodland, while the rest are on undulating plains which fall away to the flatter Danube basin. The lower reaches tend towards clay and sand but the major influences on these vineyards are the relatively low altitude (much of the vineyard is between 100 and 250 m (330–820 ft) above sea level) and the continental climate. Rainfall here is relatively low, on average between a half and two-thirds of the annual rainfall in French vineyards on an equivalent latitude (BURGUNDY and ALSACE).

Because of their position north of the Danube, most of the slopes face between south west and south east and are very protected by higher land in the north. The vines are trained like those of Germany and Austria. Latterly the LENZ MOSER system has been widely adopted for the increased YIELDS that it gives. Unfortunately it also affects ripening and can retard the vintage date by between two and three weeks. A problem here can be harvesting so late, sometimes as late as the end of November, that the crop gets frostbite.

Under the old, state-run system, the vintage was graded first by grape variety. Only Cabernet Sauvignon, Pinot Noir, Sauvignon, Gewürztraminer (often known as Traminer or Tramin), (Rhine) Riesling, and, sometimes, Pinots Blanc and Gris could qualify in the top grade. A ripeness level, or MUST WEIGHT, of 16° BRIX was required to qualify for top grape prices. Most of these varieties are not widely planted as they did not reward Czechoslovakia's rather careless viticultural practices with generous yields. Apart from Riesling and Pinot

Blanc, Rizling Vlassky (WELSCHRIESLING), MÜLLER-THURGAU, Veltlin Zelene (GRÜNER VELTLINER), and Silvaner are the major white wine varieties, together with the Muscat-scented Irsay Oliver. Frankovka (BLAUFRÄNKISCH) and Vavrinecke, or Svatovavrinecke (ST LAURENT) are the principal red wine varieties, which probably total no more than 35 per cent of the two nations' vineyard.

Between 1950 and 1990, country dwellers were allowed 10 acres (0.1 ha) of private holdings per adult. The rest of the agricultural land was nationalized. Farms which included the big vineyards usually also included other forms of agriculture. The state-owned wineries, which made more than 80 per cent of Czechoslovakian wine, were allocated farms to buy from but few of them owned any of the vineyards which supplied them.

Both Moravia and Slovakia had a state winery office which consolidated and ran the major CO-OPERATIVES in each region or state. Within each system, following the standard eastern European model (as in RUSSIA, UKRAINE, MOLDOVA, BULGARIA, HUNGARY, ROMANIA) were several centralized bottling plants, each of which had its own wine production as well as satellite vinification centres. Privatizing this system since the fall of communism has not been without its complications.

Horizontal presses with very limited capacity are almost universally used, after crushing and destalking. Often the press capacity is inadequate to meet the quantity of the incoming harvest. When this happens the crushed, destalked grapes are held in hoppers where, inadvertently but often beneficially, some useful SKIN CONTACT takes place.

CHAPTALIZATION is allowed and frequently practised. MALOLACTIC FERMENTATION was still being mastered in the mid 1990s. Other more technical forms of DEACIDIFICATION are beyond the capabilities of most wineries.

A small amount of wine is both made and aged in old oak casks holding between 20 and 100 hl (528–2,600 gal). Most of the wine is made in tanks, however, usually metal lined with enamel, sometimes cement lined with food-grade paint, and occasionally fibreglass. Even in the early 1990s FERMENTATION temperatures were rarely controlled, although the lateness of the harvest usually keeps them below danger level. Red wines are usually fermented in small closed steel tanks with an internal paddle system. Colour and tannin EXTRACTION can thus be very well done.

The wines show very good intrinsic fruit character, although this may be masked by sloppy wine-making practices such as late RACKING. Identification of the best individual sites and MESOCLIMATES is so far in its infancy, but injection of technical knowledge and capital investment are expected to help both Moravia and Slovakia produce some wines of distinctly fine quality. A.H.M.

CZECH REPUBLIC, western part of what was CZECHOSLOVAKIA comprising Bohemia and Moravia. Now an independent state whose viticultural identity is still being forged.

D

DÃO, wine region in north central PORTUGAL with the reputation of producing some of the country's best red wines (see map on p. 750). There is no doubt that the region has great potential. Locked in on three sides by high, granite mountains and sheltered from the Atlantic, Dão benefits from long, warm summers and abundant winter rainfall. The sandy soils are well drained and the vineyards are stocked with a wealth of indigenous grape varieties. In modern times, however, the wines have rarely lived up to expectations.

Dão became a REGIÃO DEMARCADA in 1908 but since the 1940s it has suffered from heavy-handed government intervention. In a laudable attempt to impose some form of organization on the highly fragmented, largely subsistence economy in the north of Portugal, the Salazar government introduced a programme of co-operativization. Ten CO-OPERATIVES were built in Dão between 1954 and 1971 to much the same design. In order to make the programme work, the authorities passed legislation giving co-operatives the exclusive right to buy grapes. Private firms were effectively restricted to purchasing ready-made wine. The system served Dão badly. Wines became ever more standardized and, as co-operatives paid scant attention to HYGIENE, standards fell. This monopolistic legislation was felt to be incompatible with Portugal's membership of the European Union and the law institutionalizing Dão's co-operatives was overturned in 1989. But in spite of some enterprising initiatives from one or two private companies with cellars in the region, Dão wines continued to suffer from the co-operative legacy well into the 1990s.

Over two-thirds of Dão wines are red and made from anything up to nine different authorized grapes. TOURIGA NACIONAL, one of the main PORT grapes, is accepted as the best in the region and must now account for at least 20 per cent of any one wine. The other grapes permitted to make up the remainder are BASTARDO, JAEN, TINTA PINHEIRA, ALFROCHEIRO PRETO, and another port grape, Tinta Roriz, alias Spain's TEMPRANILLO. Red Dão tends to be firm and tannic but the wines are often astringent from prolonged post-fermentation maceration in contact with the stalks. Added to this disadvantage, few wines are bottled sufficiently early and the healthy fruit present in many young wines tends to fade with protracted ageing in old casks or cement tanks.

White wines also suffer from being aged for too long and often taste flat and OXIDIZED by the time they are drunk. Younger, fresher wines are beginning to appear from modern, private wineries. ENCRUZADO, the best grape for white Dão, produces some crisp, fragrant wines but all too often it is blended with other less successful varieties such as Assario Branco and Borrado das Moscas ('fly droppings'), the obscure local name for the BICAL of Bairrada.

In line with Portugal's other Regiões Demarcadas (RD), Dão became a Denominacão de Origem Controlada (DOC) in 1990. R.J.M.

Mayson, R., *Portugal's Wines & Wine Makers* (London, 1992).
Metcalfe, C., and McWhirter, K., *The Wines of Spain & Portugal* (London, 1988).

DAVIS, the usual abbreviation in the wine world for the influential wine-related faculties of the University of California at Davis, a small city at the northern end of California's Central Valley. The city came to be known throughout the world as a centre for research and instruction in all aspects of agriculture because it was the home of the University Farm established in 1906.

Until the late 19th century grape-growing and wine-making in California had been relatively haphazard, with numerous problems generally unrecognized. An act of state legislature in 1880 directed the nascent University of California to start research and instruction in VITICULTURE and OENOLOGY. The fact that Berkeley, the original site of the university, was too cold and foggy for grape-growing encouraged the establishment of the farm in the warm, inland climate of Davis.

The then Professor of Agriculture, Eugene Hilgard, soon recognized that grafting VINIFERA scions on to hybrid ROOTSTOCKS was the only practical solution to the world's PHYLLOXERA epidemic. He also recognized the importance of matching vine variety to soil and climate for fine wine production. Hilgard established early co-operation between ACADEME and practitioners.

PROHIBITION brought a temporary hiatus in Davis's wine-related activities, including the work of William V. CRUESS, who was obliged to switch from researching the effects of SULPHUR DIOXIDE and TEMPERATURE CONTROL on FERMENTATION, to increasing the appeal of fresh and dried fruits to consumers. The Second World War subsequently closed the campus, effectively postponing the flowering of a newly organized research and teaching group until the late 1940s.

This powerful group included the late Albert J. WINKLER, famous for his DEGREE DAY/heat summation method of CLIMATE CLASSIFICATION; Harold P. Olmo, breeder of NEW VARIETIES, whose international consultancy work has borne fruit, quite literally, around the world; oenologist Maynard A. AMERINE, who applied statistics to wine tasting and published numerous wine books; Vernon Singleton, who researched some of the complex processes involved in wine maturation; Cornelius Ough, who was at the forefront of wine analytical methods and cellar technolgy; A. D. Webb, who identified several of the pigments and flavour substances of grape and wines; and many others who made significant contributions to viticulture and oenology. The late 1980s and early 1990s saw the retirement of most of the large group of academics recruited before or soon after the Second World War, and their replacement with younger specialists perforce more aware of the necessary mechanics of funding by industry/budgetary constraints.

During the century since California's legislature mandating the university's attention to grape-growing and wine-making problems, most of the most obvious difficulties have been resolved by research which has often demonstrated our ignorance of the fundamentals underlying the problem. Detailed study of these fundamentals makes up the core of current research activity.

Davis has continued to be the principal centre for teaching viticulture and oenology in the Americas and has been responsible for the training of the majority of technicians in California's wine industry. It has become synonymous with a wholly scientific approach to wine production, as opposed to one informed by TRADITION, or even experimentation.

A.D.W. & J.Ro.

California Agriculture, 34/7 (California, July 1980).

DEACIDIFICATION, wine-making process of decreasing the excessive ACIDITY of grape juice or wine made in cold wine regions or, in particularly cool years, in temperate wine regions. A number of techniques for making excessively acid wines more palatable have been developed and are usually strictly governed by local regulations.

Because poor summers result in low SUGARS as well as high ACIDS, the most common permitted correction is adding water to dilute the acidity and, simultaneously, enough sugar to give a balanced wine after fermentation, effectively a combination of dilution and ENRICHMENT. MALOLACTIC FERMENTATION is another way of lowering acidity, but it is difficult to persuade LACTIC BACTERIA to work in very acid conditions.

Most other forms of deacidification rely on chemical processes, notably adding chemicals to MUST or wine that will precipitate significant amounts of acidity as insoluble solids that can be filtered or settle out. Calcium carbonate, or chalk, is the most satisfactory of these, since its addition results in insoluble calcium TARTRATES and the liberation of harmless CARBON DIOXIDE. Sodium and potassium carbonates and hydroxides affect flavour adversely. In theory, ION EXCHANGE can be used for deacidification, but the alterations to other wine constituents that accompany its use make it generally unacceptable.

Deacidifications are most effective after fermentation, partly because alcohol decreases the solubility of cream of tartar, thereby reducing some of the must acidity, and fermentation itself produces a better mix of flavour by-products in the more acid solution.

Deacidification is not the commonplace procedure that ACIDIFICATION is in warmer regions. It is practised in northern Germany, Luxembourg, the United Kingdom, Canada, New York state, Tasmania, and New Zealand's South Island in certain years. EUROPEAN UNION law will not normally sanction as high a reduction in acidity by deacidification as it does an increase by acidification.

A.D.W.

DEAD ARM, one of the FUNGAL DISEASES affecting vines, called excoriose in Europe and dead arm in America. It is widespread, especially where the weather around BUDBREAK is wet. Symptoms are brown to black spots on leaves, PETIOLES, shoot bases, and bunchstems. Where there are numerous infections on bunchstems they can become brittle and break, reducing the eventual crop. The causal fungus is *Phomopsis viticola*, which survives over winter in the bark. The spores germinate over a wide temperature range; rain or nearly 100 per cent humidity are required. Young tissue is most prone to infection, and cool, wet weather in spring can lead to an epidemic. The disease is controlled by removing and destroying as much diseased wood as possible during winter pruning, by eradicant sprays just before budbreak, and by protective sprays the first few weeks after budbreak. There are no resistant varieties, but some such as Aramon, Grenache, Chasselas, Sultana, and Müller-Thurgau are particularly susceptible.

R.E.S.

Emmett, R. W., Harris, A. R., Taylor, R. H., and McGechan, J. K., 'Grape diseases and vineyard protection', in B. G. Coombe and P. R. Dry (eds.), *Viticulture, ii: Practices* (Adelaide, 1992).

Pearson, R. C., and Goheen, A. C., *Compendium of Grape Diseases* (St Paul, Minn., 1988).

DEALCOHOLIZED WINE is increasingly popular as wine drinkers search for a drink that tastes like wine but has none of the implications for HEALTH or subsequent activity such as driving. Such wines also have fewer calories than regular wine, fewer than 150 calories per bottle in many cases. They may broadly be divided into 'no alcohol wines', with an ALCOHOLIC STRENGTH of less than one or at the most two per cent, and 'low alcohol wines' with between two and 5.5 per cent alcohol.

Wine may be dealcoholized in several ways, all of which involve removing ALCOHOL from normally fermented wine, using either thermal or membrane techniques, yet retaining all other components. (See also REDUCED ALCOHOL WINES, which are low alcohol wines made by either dilution or partial fermentation.)

One method, particularly common in Germany, is a process of vacuum distillation, whereby wine, at extremely low pressures at normal room temperatures, is separated into various fractions in a tall column. Under vacuum conditions the boiling point of alcohol is reduced and it literally 'boils' away at room temperature. The non-volatile wine compounds such as MINERALS, ACIDS, PHENOLICS, SUGARS, and VITAMINS are fully preserved. By avoiding high temperatures, there is no risk of 'cooked' flavours.

Another similar method, pioneered in France by

UCCOAR, the large co-operative based in the Côtes de la MALEPÈRE region, working in conjunction with researchers at the local INRA station, and launched in 1988, involves evaporation under vacuum at low temperatures and under INERT GAS. The resulting wine has the colour and most of the taste characteristics of the original wine, but an alcoholic strength of less than 0.5 per cent.

Reverse osmosis can also be used, using osmotic pressure to separate, through an impermeable membrane, a solution of low concentration from one of higher concentration. This is the only method which eliminates alcohol while remaining in its liquid state.

INRA at Narbonne have also developed another method of dealcoholizing wine called pervaporation. It depends on dense silicone membranes which at about 30 °C are particularly efficient at separating alcohol from water. A system involving a spinning disc can also be used, which effectively spins out the alcohol using a principle similar to CENTRIFUGATION.

Taking the alcohol out of wine leaves it much less stable, so even higher standards of HYGIENE and STERILE BOTTLING conditions are necessary.

All of these methods of removing alcohol to produce no alcohol or low alcohol wines are expensive, however, relative to the methods of simply reducing alcohol.

By 1993 about a dozen companies in France, Germany, Australia, and the UNITED STATES were producing dealcoholized wine.

Escudier, J.-L., 'Les Nouveaux Produits de la vigne', *Bulletin de l'O.I.V.*, May–June (1993).

DEBINA, the sprightly white grape variety that is responsible for the lightly sparkling white wines of Zitsa in Epirus high in north west GREECE near the Albanian border. It seems likely that the variety is also cultivated in Albania. At these altitudes acidity levels remain high, and a tendency to OXIDATION has largely been checked by improved vinification methods.

DÉBOURBAGE, French term for SETTLING out solids from must or wine.

DECANTER LABELS, part of the wine ANTIQUES repertoire and, typically, silver labels hung round the necks of DECANTERS.

Today most wine is poured straight from the bottle into the glass. At dinner parties, and on formal occasions, decanters are often used, particularly if the wine has thrown a sediment, but the person doing the DECANTING will know the contents and the need for a label is slight. However, if more than one wine is decanted, and formerly when it was done by servants, it was necessary to indicate the contents of each decanter. In the 18th century the indicator was called a bottle ticket; today it is called a wine label.

Most wine labels were made of silver in small geometrical shapes (rectangles, crescents, etc.) although some were heraldic, asymmetrical, or of cartouche outline. Usually they were suspended around the decanter neck by a thin chain. The first were made in the 1730s, often by the inappropriately named craftsman Sandilands Drinkwater. They have been made ever since, although the few that have been made since 1880 have mostly been commemorative.

Ivory and mother-of-pearl were used for inexpensive versions and some very attractive examples were enamelled in polychrome on copper—particularly in continental Europe where porcelain can also be found. In colonial India there was a mid 19th century fashion for silver filigree-mounted tiger claw labels and for mounted boar tusks. The finest labels were produced at the beginning of the 19th century, heavily cast in silver and usually gilt; these are formed as lion pelts, shells, or fruiting vines and often in sets of many labels, the names tellingly indicative of wine preferences current when the labels were made. They particularly show the effect of the Methuen Treaty in the paucity of French wines in the 18th century. These wine labels are plentiful and have long been collected. The principal forum for enthusiasts is the Wine Label Circle (founded in 1952) based in London.

R.N.H.B.

Butler, R., and Walkling, G., *The Book of Wine Antiques* (Woodbridge, 1986).

Clayton, M., *Collectors' Dictionary of the Silver and Gold of Great Britain and North America* (rev. edn., Woodbridge, 1985).

Penzer, N. M., *The Book of the Wine Label* (London, 1974).

DECANTERS, vessels, usually glass and stoppered, into which wine is poured during DECANTING. Older examples constitute some of the most obvious wine ANTIQUES.

The decanter as we know it today has changed form very little in the last 250 years, in that it is a handleless clear glass bottle with a capacity of about 1 l and, normally, a stopper. The shape and the decoration have changed in line with fashion and as technology has allowed. Since the capacity is noticeably more than that of a standard 75-cl/27-fl oz bottle, it allows the wine to 'breathe' and develop (see AERATION).

History

The decanter's origins lie with the Roman serving bottle, which was typically square. It was the Romans who first utilized the technique of blowing glass on a widespread scale and they perfected other facets of glass technology to a high degree (see GLASS, history). Some Roman glass bottles may have been used for serving wine, but the Romans also used silver. After the collapse of the Roman empire glass production went into a sharp decline and, although it never completely ceased, it continued on a very small scale until the revival of the glass trade in Renaissance Italy. By the 16th century Venice had emerged as the principal centre of glass-making and the output included flasks, BOTTLES, ewers, and jugs, although these accounted for a small percentage of the total compared to drinking glasses, *tazze*, and bowls.

Despite harsh endeavours to contain glass technology within the city, knowledge of Venetian products and their manufacture spread across Europe, with copies being made

A set of seven **decanter labels** made in London in the early 1790s. Shrub was a common cordial made usually of citrus fruit juice laced with rum.

particularly in Germany and the Netherlands. These copies were sometimes of very high quality, being almost indistinguishable from the originals; they are known as *façon de Venise*.

While the glass trade was expanding, other developments were afoot. Popular throughout northern Europe during the 16th and early 17th centuries were bulbous earthenware jugs with flat, small handles and short, narrow necks. Many had a moulded decoration near the neck of a bearded mask—an allusion to Cardinal Roberto Bellarmino, a universally hated figure in the Reformationist north; they are known as bellarmines. Sometimes the glaze was a blueish grey and consequently those are called grey-beards, but most were a dark brown.

A more sophisticated finish, sometimes employed, was a saltglaze which produced a textured surface not unlike an orange peel. Saltglaze jugs were sometimes off-white, while others are a mottled brown and known as tigerware (surely a misnomer, but nobody talks of leopardware). In addition, Chinese porcelain jugs were being imported for the most sophisticated of tastes, while some preferred their wine served in carved rock crystal. Whether the jug was saltglaze, tigerware, porcelain, or crystal, all the better-quality pieces were given silver or silver-gilt mounts. For the grandest, gold was used.

Throughout the medieval period and well beyond, pouring vessels were also made in bronze and silver, but these media often gave way to glass once a centre of production became established in a country. The new glass serving vessels represented the latest in fashion and technology and were quickly adopted by society. For almost a century, England, which was an important wine market and was to become an even more important market for serving and drinking vessels, had had a very limited supply of home-produced glass, and relied on imports until George Ravenscroft started producing glass using lead oxide as a flux in the 1670s. This, together with his flint glass, allowed the production of usable jugs and glasses. His developments gave Britain a lead that lasted for about 100 years.

Ravenscroft's and others' wine jugs (they are often referred to as **decanter jugs**) had wide, almost cylindrical bodies, pronounced shoulders, and narrow necks that broadened out at the rim to form an in-built funnel (see diagram 1). They had handles and were decorated with trailed glass, moulded ribs, or were pincered to give a lattice effect—a form of decoration known as 'nipt diamond waies', from a contemporary description. They were also fitted with hollow, loosely fitting, pear-shaped stoppers, although few of these survive.

Contemporary with the jug, decanters were also made which took the same form as bottles. They had more or less compressed globular bodies and tall narrow necks. Some had 'nipt diamond waies' decoration, some were coloured, but all are distinguished from BOTTLES by a much greater sophistication of material, decoration, and workmanship. Decanters made before about 1720 are now very rare.

The 'shaft and globe' shape (see diagram 3) continued to be made (although the proportions changed) until the mid century, earlier examples sometimes having handles. During the 1720s there was a fashion for decanters with a cruciform plan (see diagram 2). It may be that such a shape allowed wine to be cooled more quickly because of its greater surface area. Many were made in the ensuing decade or so.

The evolution of decanter design can be a confusing subject for study because more than one shape may be associated with a given date. During the period 1745–75 the 'mallet' (see diagram 4) and the 'shoulder' (see diagram 5) decanter dominated. Both had approximately cylindrical bodies and slightly tapering necks above rounded shoulders. With the 'shoulder' the body tapered inwards towards the base, while the mallet tapered outwards. The body was about twice the height of the neck and the rim was plain.

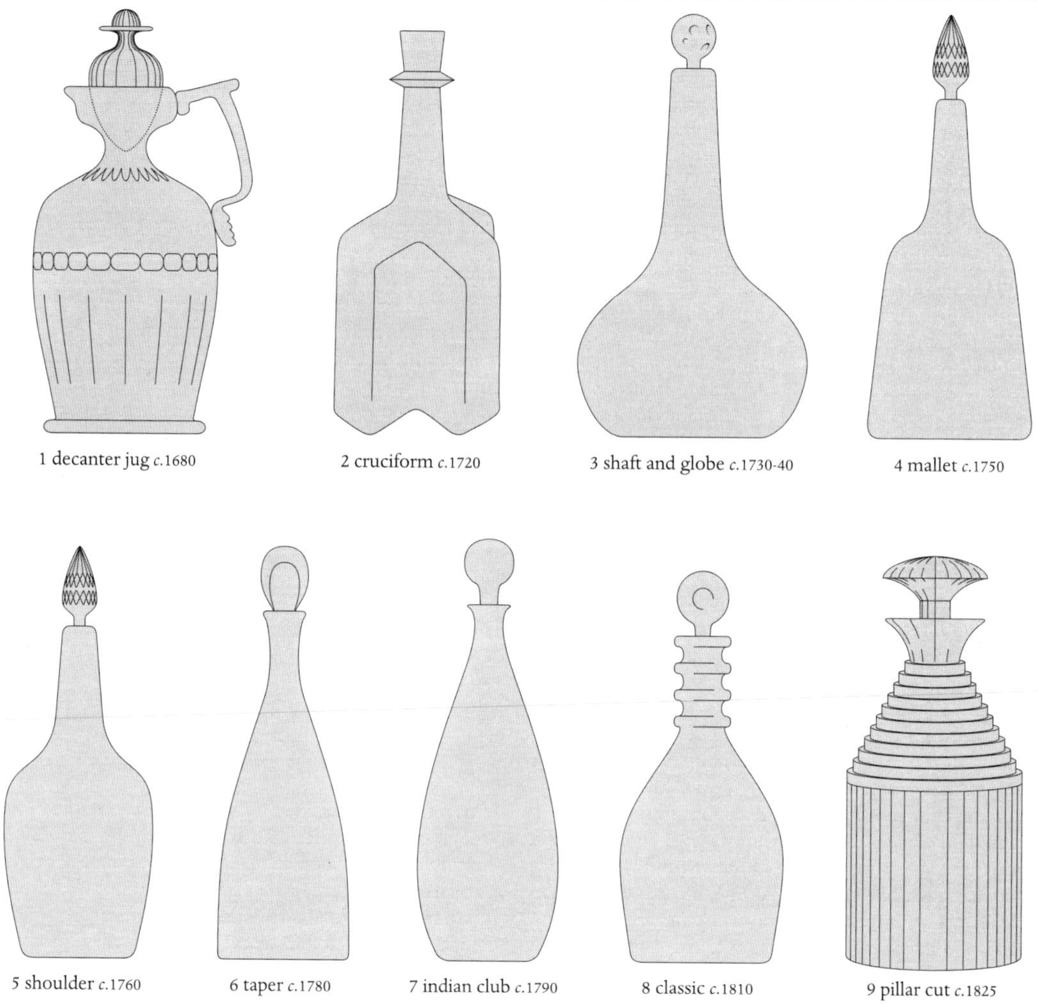

Decanters

With the exception of very early decanter jugs, decanters first acquired stoppers in the 1730s. These were globular and often had a series of air bubbles within. This form was superseded by the 'spire'—which was faceted and tapered to a point. It was the standard fitment to the shoulder and mallet decanters.

The 'taper' decanter (see diagram 6) came next and is little more than a development of the mallet but the crucial difference was the lack of any shoulder that made the body and neck separate elements. Concurrent with the 'taper' is the 'Indian club' (see diagram 7), which is very similar to the taper but has a body that curves inwards for the lower third of its height. Both the taper and the Indian club usually had flat stoppers with bevelled edges but they were made in a variety of shapes and some were cut to decorative effect.

'Mallet' and 'shoulder' decanters tend to be heavier than their later cousins. Some were decorated with facet cutting all over while others were engraved with the name of the contents—Claret or Port for example—within a decorative cartouche. By the last quarter of the century some decanters were cut or wheel engraved, but most decoration was of a light, repetitive nature in a more or less debased neo-classical style. Coloured decanters were introduced but these were generally designed for spirits.

A useful dating feature (for collectors of wine antiques) developed towards the end of the 18th century. The rim of the neck became everted at first and, within a decade, had become a wide flange. At about the same time neck rings appeared, at first cut from the neck but soon made from rings of glass applied during the making. The 'bull's eye' stopper matched the design of the three-ring neck and the body shape reverted to the shoulder form, although by this time, with its different beck and stopper, it looked quite different (see diagram 8).

At this point, *c.*1810–20, the introduction of steam-driven cutting tools produced a fashion for profusely cut decanters which were made thick and heavy so that they could withstand the deeply cut decoration often performed to cover the entire surface to brilliant effect. The preferred stopper was the star-cut mushroom shape. By the 1820s decanter design was degenerating, the now-cylindrical bodies often cut with heavy pillars and panels and with abruptly squared shoulders (see diagram 9).

The 1840s saw the return of the shaft and globe that had been popular a century before. This time it was usually cut with panels and often had a star-cut base. This form continued in fashion until the 20th century, gradually changing in proportion and weight of cutting. This period also saw acid-etched decoration of machine precision and other applications of mechanical and chemical technology which enabled decanters to be made in a variety of complex patterns. Some decanters from this time were raised on a foot, a new idea that remained popular for the remainder of the century.

Decanters were not the only vessels from which wine was served. Jugs were made in silver throughout the 18th century. The plain baluster forms of the early to mid century are usually called beer jugs but it seems likely they were used for wine too. By the 1770s jugs of neo-classical form and decoration are known as claret jugs and continued to be made until the turn of the century. Glass claret jugs were made during the 19th century and followed the pattern of decanters, the only difference being the addition of a handle and a modified rim to form a pouring lip.

Claret jugs of glass mounted with silver, silver plate, or gilt became popular in the 1850s. One favoured design, incorporating a globular body with a wide neck, closely imitated the jugs of the late 16th century. Like its tigerware predecessor, the new version had a silver neck mount to which a lid was hinged and from which a handle hung. The mounts were profusely decorated with neo-Elizabethan motifs while the glass bodies sometimes bore engraved decoration.

The Arts and Crafts movement influenced some designs for claret jugs, as did art nouveau and late 19th century interest in Japanese forms. Novelty jugs would also be made in the form of a duck, walrus, seal, or some other animal, with the body in glass and the head in silver or silver plate. All these forms were prevalent in the closing 30 years of the 19th century.

While it is not possible to describe every sort of decanter, there is one type which should not pass unmentioned. It has a conical body giving it a very wide base and it usually has neck rings. Many are plain but some have cut decoration. Their name may well be disputed because who in their right mind would take a decanter in a sailing ship? Nevertheless they are ship's decanters. At least 90 per cent of them are modern copies but period ones do exist.

See also DECANTER LABELS. R.N.H.B.

Butler, R., and Walkling, G., *The Book of Wine Antiques* (Woodbridge, 1986).
Charleston, R. J., *English Glass* (London, 1984).
Johnson, H., Janson, D. J., and McFadden, D. R., *Wine Celebration & Ceremony* (New York, 1985).
Klein, D., and Lloyd, W., *The History of Glass* (London, 1984).
Tait, H., *The Golden Age of Venetian Glass* (London, 1979).
Warren, P., *Irish Glass* (London, 1970).
Westropp, D., *Irish Glass* (rev. edn., Dublin, 1978).

Modern decanters

Any container can be used as a vessel for wine, so long as it is made of an inert material and can hold at least the contents of a bottle while, ideally, leaving a considerable surface area in contact with air. Some decanters, notably one designed by the Ch LATOUR management, are shaped so that a bottle exactly fills them to their maximum width, thereby maximizing the potential for aeration. Some decanters are designed specifically for magnums, or double-sized bottles. Others have handles, all manner of different shapes, engravings, shadings, and designs, including one to ensure circulation with a spherical base that cannot be laid to rest other than in a special cradle by the host's elbow (see PASSING THE PORT). Wine need not be served from clear glass, or even glass at all, but most wine's COLOUR (whites every bit as much as reds) can give great aesthetic and anticipatory pleasure.

See LEAD for details of the limited extent to which this toxic element may be leached from different sorts of decanters.

DECANTING, optional and controversial step in SERVING wine, involving pouring wine out of its bottle into another container called a DECANTER.

Reasons for decanting

The most obvious reason for decanting a wine is to separate it from any SEDIMENT that has formed in the bottle which not only looks unappetizing in the glass, but usually tastes bitter and/or astringent. Before wine-makers mastered the art of CLARIFICATION this was necessary for all wines. Today such a justification of the decanting process effectively limits it to those wines outlined in AGEING as capable of development in bottle, in most of which some solids are precipitated as part of the maturation process. Vintage and crusted PORTS in particular always throw a heavy deposit (since they are bottled so early in their evolution), as do red wines, particularly Rhônes it would seem, made with no or minimal FILTRATION. It is rare for inexpensive, everyday TABLE WINES to throw a deposit, and most supermarkets insist on such heavy filtration that a deposit is unlikely (although not unknown in older, higher-quality reds). To check whether a wine bottle contains any sediment it should be stood upright for at least 24 hours and then carefully held up to the light for inspection at the base (although some BOTTLES are too dark for this exercise to be effective).

Another, traditional but disputed, reason for decanting is to promote AERATION and therefore encourage the development of the wine's BOUQUET. Authorities as scientifically respectable as Professor Émile PEYNAUD argue that this is OENOLOGICALLY indefensible: that the action of OXYGEN dissolved in a sound wine is usually detrimental and that the longer it is prolonged—i.e. the longer before serving a wine is decanted—the more diffuse its aroma and the less marked its sensory attributes. His advice is to decant only wines with a sediment, and then only just before serving. If they need aeration because of some wine FAULT such as REDUCTION or MERCAPTANS, then the taster can simply aerate the wine by agitating it in the glass. His argument is that from the moment the wine is fully exposed to air (which happens when it is poured, but not to any significant extent during so-called 'BREATHING') some of its sensory impressions may be lost, and that decanting immediately before serving gives the taster maximum control.

It is certainly wise advice to decant fully mature wines only just before serving, since some are so fragile that they can withstand oxygen for only a few minutes before succumbing to OXIDATION. And it is also true that the aeration process of an individual glass of wine can be controlled by the person drinking out of it—and that there are certain types of wines, BAROLO most obviously, which may not have been included in Professor Peynaud's experiments with decanting regimes, which can be so concentrated and tannic in youth that to lose some of their initial sensory impressions is a positive benefit.

There is also the very practical fact that many hosts find it more convenient to decant before a meal is served rather than in the middle of it. There are also people who enjoy the sight of (perhaps both red and white) wine in a decanter so much that they are prepared to sacrifice the potential reduction in gustatory impact.

How to decant

The ideal method is to stand the bottle upright for at least 24 hours before opening, preferably longer with wines which have a great deal of sediment. Ensure that the decanter looks and smells absolutely clean, and find a strong light source against which the bottle can be held (a candle, flashlight, desk light, or unshaded table lamp will do). After opening the bottle, as gently as possible, and wiping the lip of the bottle clean, steadily pour the contents of the bottle into the decanter watching the lower shoulder of the bottle with the light source behind it. The sediment should eventually collect in the shoulder and the pouring action can be halted as soon as any sediment starts to spill into the bottle-neck.

To extract maximum volume of liquid from a bottle with sediment, or if there is no time to let all the sediment fall to the bottom of the bottle, or if a cork collapses into fragments in the bottle during extraction, the wine can be filtered into the decanter through clean fabric such as muslin, or a paper coffee filter, with no perceptible harmful effects.

Conclusion and guide-lines

In sum, of course, decanting is a personal choice, but the following are suggested guiding principles:

- decant, or pour extremely carefully, wines with a sediment;
- decant old wines, say more than 20 to 30 years old depending on their concentration, only immediately before serving.

Peynaud, É., *The Taste of Wine* (London, 1987).

Decanting cradles are of prime interest to mechanical engineers and vintage port addicts.

DECANTING CRADLES, bottle carriers, usually made of wicker or metal, which keep the bottle at a perpetually inclined angle so that, in theory anyway, any SEDIMENT remains in the base while wine is poured off, either into a glass or decanter.

Special **decanting machines** have also been constructed, designed to invert a bottle mechanically and smoothly as its contents are poured into a DECANTER.

DEER, a vineyard pest in some areas of the United States, See ANIMALS.

DEFOLIATION, loss of leaves, of a vine can be caused by various agents. If extensive and badly timed, it inevitably adversely affects fruit RIPENING and wine quality, although the precise effects depend on the time of the year. Defoliation is, of course, a natural process and happens at the end of each growing season in the autumn. Normally it is caused by the first frost, but it may also be through mechanical damage or merely senescence. By this time the vines have lost most of the green colour from their leaves anyway and they are no longer effective at PHOTOSYNTHESIS. Providing the vine's reserves of CARBOHYDRATES are topped up by late season photosynthesis, there is no negative effect of defoliation and indeed it is the normal conclusion to the growing season.

However, defoliation can occur at any time of the growing season due to climate, disease, or pests. FROSTS at any time in the growing season can partially or totally defoliate vines, but they typically remove the outermost leaf layers of a thick CANOPY. HAIL can also defoliate vines. A mild hailstorm may simply tear some leaves, but a severe hailstorm will rip off all the leaves, and cut shoots back to their thick stubs. FUNGAL DISEASES such as DOWNY MILDEW can also cause defoliation if left unchecked. Similarly, insect pests such as the western grapeleaf skeletonizer and GRASSHOPPERS can defoliate entire vines unless checked.

The vine responds to defoliation by producing new leaves on lateral shoots. However, this new growth will depend on stored carbohydrate reserves of the vine for a month or so, and so will weaken the vine until the new leaves are able to produce carbohydrates and build up reserves again. While vigorous vines may be able to recover from a single defoliation, repeated defoliation can weaken the vine to the point of death.

Obviously, defoliation will have an impact on fruit growth and ripening. A low LEAF TO FRUIT RATIO causes a reduction in levels of fruit sugars (see SUGAR IN GRAPES), as well as in PHENOLICS, with an adverse effect on colour and flavour of the resultant wine. Note, however, that the vine can compensate for a lower than ideal leaf area by automatically increasing the rate of photosynthesis, so that practices such as LEAF REMOVAL and TRIMMING do not normally cause negative effects, as might be imagined. Good-quality wine can be made only from vines with a good area of well-exposed, healthy leaves. R.E.S.

DÉGORGEMENT, French term for the DISGORGEMENT operations at the end of the champagne method of SPARKLING WINE-MAKING.

DEGREE, or **degré** in French, the ALCOHOLIC STRENGTH of a wine, and identical to the wine's percentage of ETHANOL by volume. This has traditionally been regarded as the most vital statistic of all for everyday French VIN DE TABLE, whose price was traditionally quoted per *degré/hecto*, as though its only important characteristics were its potency and volume (although, at this quality level, wines with low alcohol levels tend to have been over-produced and to be vapid and low in fruit and concentration).

DEGREE DAYS. Unit devised to measure climate. See CLIMATE CLASSIFICATION for more details.

DEHYDRATION, wine-making process used in the production of DRIED GRAPE WINES. The dehydration process transforms grapes into RAISINS and has to be arrested before completion if appetizing wines are to be made from the results.

DEINHARD, family-owned German company of wine producers, merchants, and estate owners, founded in 1794 and based in Koblenz, MOSEL. The firm has a long exporting tradition, particularly to Britain where its London office was opened in 1835. Deinhard Koblenz and its independent sister company based in London are still run by the Wegeler and Hasslacher families, each with direct links to the founder Johann Friedrich Deinhard. Deinhard is one of the largest private vineyard owners in Germany, making stylish estate wines under the Wegeler-Deinhard label from over 100 ha/250 acres of prime sites in the RHEINGAU, PFALZ, and Mosel, its most famous holding being 1.1 ha/2.7 acres of the Bernkasteler Doktor vineyard. It is also one of Germany's largest producers of premium sparkling wine, Deutscher SEKT, which accounts for nearly three-quarters of its production. In the 1970s and 1980s the firm was one of the leaders in the move towards making and marketing drier styles of German wine; but just as Deinhard's great rival, the family company SICHEL, is best known for its Blue Nun LIEBFRAUMILCH, so Deinhard's best-known product is its Green Label, the world's largest selling Mosel BRAND. M.W.E.S.

Bruce, G., *A Wine Day's Work* (London, 1985).

DEKKERA, the sporulating form of the yeast genus BRETTANOMYCES which can cause off-flavours in wines, often described as 'mousy'. Like *Brettanomyces*, Dekkera is very sensitive to SULPHUR DIOXIDE. In practice, Dekkera is used as a European, particularly French, synonym for *Brettanomyces*.

DELAWARE, dark pink-skinned VITIS *labruscana* vine variety that is quite popular in NEW YORK and, for reasons that are now obscure, is the most widely planted in JAPAN. Its early ripening is presumably an advantage in Japan's damp autumns. The wine is not as markedly FOXY as that of its great New York rival CONCORD. It was first propagated in Delaware, Ohio, in 1849.

DELIMITATION, GEOGRAPHICAL. The central purpose of geographical delimitation of a wine area, typically into a CONTROLLED APPELLATION, is to establish a distinctive identity for the wines produced within it, and provide a means whereby the provenance of those wines can be guaranteed. It is based primarily upon the assumption that different environments give rise to wines of different character (see TERROIR).

Although since classical antiquity wines from certain regions tended to be called after the area of their production, with many gaining particularly high reputations (FALERNIAN, for example), the first legal vineyard delimitation is that introduced in the DOURO valley of northern Portugal in 1756 associated with the establishment of the Companhia Geral da Agricultura das Vinhas do Alto Douro. During the 18th century there had been many disputes over the sources and qualities of wines exported from Oporto (see PORT), as well as conflicts between foreign wine shippers and the Portuguese growers, and the formation of the Companhia Geral with strictly defined areas of operation was designed to remedy the situation. At the heart of this legislation was the establishment of a specific area in the upper Douro valley from which farmers were able to obtain higher prices for their wines compared to those produced elsewhere.

During the 18th century in other parts of Europe, CLASSIFICATIONS of the different qualities of wine were becoming increasingly common, with Thomas JEFFERSON, for example, commenting on the various categories of wines from Bordeaux and Burgundy in 1787. In the 19th century more formal classifications emerged, with the most famous of these being the classification of the wines of the Médoc, and Lavalle's classification of the wines of the Côte d'Or, both of which date from 1855. By the early 20th century, in the wake of the devastation caused by POWDERY MILDEW and PHYLLOXERA, there were two fundamental problems facing the wine industry: ADULTERATION AND FRAUD. Many wines contained a range of additives designed to mask their flavour; and wine purporting to come from a respected source frequently contained wines from elsewhere. In order to overcome these problems, some groups of growers, such as those in Chablis and Bordeaux, decided to form their own associations designed to guarantee the origin of their wines. National governments then began to concern themselves more formally with the geographical delimitation of areas of wine production, with the French taking a first step in 1905 towards the creation of a national system of wine control based on the delimitation of areas of origin. Through further laws, most notably those of 1919 and 1927, this eventually culminated in 1935 in the law creating the Appellations d'Origine Contrôlées, today's APPELLATION CONTRÔLÉE system.

A GERMAN WINE LAW was also developed, notably that of 1930, but although this included the use of vineyard names, the perceived quality of Germany's wines has never been based primarily on geography but on MUST WEIGHTS. Even as early as the 1830s (see GERMAN HISTORY), this was the accepted basis of measuring wine quality.

Italian wine laws also include an element of geographical delimitation, as represented in the creation of the Denominazione di Origine Controllata (DOC) system in 1963 and most recently in the 1992 legislation with its specific reference to Indicazione Geografica Tipica (IGT).

The precise practical methods of geographical demarcation vary from country to country, but are usually based on the compilation of a detailed vineayrd register and include varying degrees of political intrigue (see, for example, ALBANA DI ROMAGNA). Producers wishing to gain a certain status must satisfy regional and national committees of both the quality, origin, and distinction of their wines. One of the most rigorous systems of geographical delimitation is that adopted in France under INAO auspices. This requires that commissions of inquiry examine the relationships between such factors as GEOLOGY, SOILS, TOPOGRAPHY, DRAINAGE, slope, exposure, and wine quality. In BURGUNDY, for example, the geological origin of the soils is a determining factor in differentiating the GRANDS CRUS.

The central feature of geographical delimitation as it applies to wine is not just that it usually leads to an improvement in wine quality, thus enabling the wines to be sold at a higher price, but also that it is a legislative procedure whereby a privileged monopolistic position is created for producers within a demarcated area. Whether a given vineyard falls within or outside the legal boundary of a delimited wine region can have important commercial consequences, which is why the much more recent demarcation of America's AVAS can be such a contentious process. P.T.H.U.

Francis, A. D., *The Wine Trade* (London, 1972).

Fregoni, M., 'Changes to Italy's wine legislation: the *Nuova Disciplina delle Denominazione d'Origine Vini*', *Journal of Wine Research*, 3/2 (1992), 123–36.

Hallgarten, F., *Wine Scandal* (London, 1987).

Pomerol, C. (ed.), *The Wines and Winelands of France: Geological Journeys* (London, 1989).

Unwin, T., *Wine and the Vine: An Historical Geography of Viticulture and the Wine Trade* (London, 1991).

DEMI-SEC, French term meaning medium dry. See SWEETNESS. In practice the term is used particularly for Chenin Blanc wines in the ANJOU, SAUMUR, and TOURAINE as well as for some SPARKLING WINES (see DOSAGE).

DENOMINAÇÃO DE ORIGEM CONTROLADA, the name of a controlled appellation in PORTUGAL, which replaced the earlier REGIÃO DEMARCADA when Portuguese wine laws were revised for EUROPEAN UNION entry. For more details, see DOC.

DENOMINACIÓN DE ORIGEN, Spanish controlled appellation. See DO.

DENOMINACIÓN DE ORIGEN CALIFICADA, Spain's superior controlled appellation. RIOJA was the first DO to be promoted to this status. See DOCA.

DENSITY, a measurement of the concentration of matter in units of mass per unit volume. In wine it is usually expressed as g/cc, and occasionally as g/ml, at 20 °C/68 °F (which must be specified since wine's mass per unit volume decreases with temperature). Wine is an interesting mixture because it contains dissolved solids (SUGARS, ACIDS, PHENOLICS, and MINERAL salts) which increase its density above that of pure water, but it also contains ALCOHOL, which is less dense than water. The result is that very dry wines can have densities near 0.8 g/cc while very sweet wines that are low in alcohol (such as some Italian MOSCATO, for example) can have densities around 1.03 g/cc.

A term closely related to density, and used in technical wine analysis, is **specific gravity**. The specific gravity is the ratio of the weight or mass of a volume of a liquid to the weight of an equal volume of water. It is thus a pure or unitless number which differs only slightly from density, according to temperature (since the density of water is only exactly 1 g/cc at a temperature of 3.98 °C).

Wine densities are also frequently reported in terms of one of the traditional scales used for measuring the sugar solution concentrations (see BALLING, BAUMÉ, BRIX, OECHSLE) which also measure wine density but in units other than g/cc. These scales all use different scales (see MUST WEIGHT for equivalencies) from each other, with Oechsle bearing the most obvious relationship to specific gravity: a must with the specific gravity of 1.070, for example, is said to measure 70° Oechsle. A.D.W.

DEPOSIT. See SEDIMENT.

DESERT, an arid, treeless region. True deserts are not conducive to growing grapes for wine, even where IRRIGATION water is available. Low HUMIDITY and extreme temperature ranges place stresses on the vine which usually preclude good grape quality. In those desert climates warm enough for spring frosts not to be a problem, conditions are inevitably hot during ripening. With irrigation they can still be very suitable for TABLE GRAPES, especially early maturing varieties, and for DRYING GRAPES, but wine grapes seldom rise above mediocre quality. See CLIMATE AND WINE QUALITY.

Some near-desert regions used extensively for viticulture include the SAN JOAQUIN VALLEY of California; the Bekaa Valley of LEBANON; parts of ISRAEL; AZERBAIJAN on the west coast of the Caspian Sea; the lower Murray Valley of SOUTH AUSTRALIA and VICTORIA; and the Little Karoo of SOUTH AFRICA. MEDITERRANEAN CLIMATES (by no means all of which are in the Mediterranean) have desert rainfall conditions in summer, but their best wine areas benefit from reliable winter–spring rainfall, and mild, humid afternoon sea breezes throughout summer and early autumn.

Traditional desert life-styles are in general inimical to wine, which is a beverage of settled, agricultural communities. When desert dwellers use alcohol it is mostly in the form of concentrated spirits, such as ARAK, which are easily transported and not affected by extreme storage conditions; or else desert nomads use fermented milk products from their own mares or herds, as in the case of koumiss. J.G.

DESIGNATIONS. Within the EUROPEAN UNION wine is broadly designated either a QUALITY WINE or a TABLE WINE. Within these broad categories there are more precise designations, usually CONTROLLED APPELLATIONS or categories such as VIN DE PAYS, IGT, LANDWEIN, or VINO DE LA TIERRA.

DESSERT WINES. See SWEET WINES and FORTIFIED WINES.

DESTALKING. See DESTEMMING.

DESTEMMING, the wine-making process of removing the STEMS, or stalks, from clusters of grape berries. Known as *égrappage* or *éraflage* in French, it usually takes place immediately after and combined with the CRUSHING operation. Grape stems, and the attached BRUSH of pulp, contain TANNINS. If they are crushed or broken these can be leached into the wine during FERMENTATION, making the wine taste bitter and astringent. Destemming also very slightly increases the resultant COLOUR and ALCOHOLIC STRENGTH because stems, if included, have a dilution effect. Fermentation is also likely to be slightly slower and cooler since including stems increases the interfaces between the fermenting must and air, or OXYGEN.

Although historically all wines were made without either crushing or stem removal, most white and the majority of black grapes are destemmed today. The exceptions are those white grapes subjected to WHOLE BUNCH PRESSING and black grapes used for CARBONIC MACERATION and those few employed in WHOLE BUNCH FERMENTATION. Some producers, notably in BURGUNDY and parts of the RHÔNE, believe in retaining a certain proportion of the stems to add structure, colour, and to ease the drainage of the juice through the CAP during MACERATION of red wines and during PRESSING of white wines. Other, more primitive, wine producers simply lack the resources to buy a destemming machine.

Modern destemming machines, or **destemmers**, are usually based on the principle of straining or sieving larger stems from the crushed grape mixture which is fed into a

Labour-intensive precursor of the **destemming** machine in 19th century Burgundy.

rotating perforated cylinder. As the mass is tumbled, the juice, skins, and seeds pass through the perforations into a collector. The stems, which are long enough to bridge across the perforations, are carried to the open exit end where they are collected in a separate receiver. Stem fragments small enough to fall through the perforations in the cylinder go into the juice, which means that they remain in contact with the juice until after FERMENTATION in the case of red wines but are removed along with the skins and seeds before fermentation in the case of white wines (see WINE-MAKING).

DESUCKERING, the viticultural practice of removing unwanted young shoots. Known in most parts of France as *épamprage*, or *bonne œuvre* in the MIDI, the practice is common to most vineyards of the world. Typically, the shoots removed are either on the TRUNK or in the HEAD of the vine, and grow from buds surviving in the old wood. These shoots are termed WATER SHOOTS and for the majority of vine varieties have no bunches of grapes. They can therefore be removed with no effect on YIELD. Varieties differ in their production of water shoots; GEWÜRZTRAMINER, for example, produces many, while others produce few. The operation is carried out in spring, several weeks after BUDBREAK, when the water shoots are 10 to 15 cm (4 to 6 in) long. The work is relatively tiresome, as for many vineyards the shoots can be near the ground, although shoots can be removed from trunks mechanically with no damage to the trunk by mounting a rotating cylinder with rubber straps attached on the front of a tractor.

In California, desuckering is also carried out on CORDON trained vines and so can alternatively be termed SHOOT THINNING. R.E.S.

DEUTSCHE means literally 'German', thus the **Deutsche Weinstrasse** is a particularly famous route through the vineyards of the PFALZ region in Germany; **Deutscher Sekt** is that rarity, a SEKT or sparkling wine made in Germany that is actually made of German wine; and **Deutscher Tafelwein**, or DTW, means literally German TABLE WINE and is distinct from EU TABLE WINE in that it is made exclusively from German grapes, such grapes failing to qualify for either QBA or QMP wine.

The **Deutscher Weinsiegel**, or German Wine Seal, is a significant award made to superior bottlings assessed by BLIND TASTING panels whose standards are more exacting than those which award the official AP NUMBER. Award-winning bottles can be identified by a large, round paper seal on the bottleneck: a yellow seal for dry wines, green for medium dry, and red for other styles. These awards, and a national competition, are held under the auspices of the **Deutscher Landwirtschaft Gesellschaft**, or DLG, an agricultural society formed in the late 19th century to encourage quality and agricultural expertise. Prize-winning bottles carry gold, silver, or bronze strips across the neck.

DEW, water which condenses on objects, such as leaves, when the air in immediate contact with them is cooled below dew point, the temperature at which the air becomes fully saturated by its current content of water vapour (see HUMIDITY). Like condensation in free air to form mist or fog, dew contributes little directly to the water supply of the vine. However, the latent heat of vaporization that is released during condensation plays a positive role by slowing nighttime temperature drop. The risk of FROST is appreciably reduced when the air contains enough water vapour to result in dew or other condensation at above freezing point.

Dew has a major (mostly unfavourable) impact on the incidence of VINE DISEASES. It provides the necessary conditions for spore germination and the establishment of several fungal disease organisms, most notably those for DOWNY MILDEW (*Plasmopara viticola*), BLACK ROT (*Guignardia bidwellii*), and the malevolent form of botrytis bunch rot, GREY ROT (*Botrytis cinerea*), even in the absence of wetting rain.

Bunch infection by the last of these after (but only after) maturity has been reached constitutes the benevolent form, NOBLE ROT, which is responsible for most of the world's greatest SWEET WINES. Dewy and misty mornings, regularly followed by mild, sunny autumn days, are essential for its development, but timing is critical. It is also worth noting that such conditions occur most reliably on land that is fairly flat or only gently undulating, or on the lowest slopes and floors of valleys or basins (often near water), thus providing a part exception to the general rule that the best wines come from HILLSIDE VINEYARDS (see CLIMATE AND WINE QUALITY and TOPOGRAPHY). J.G.

DIAMMONIUM PHOSPHATE, common YEAST nutrient added during FERMENTATION.

DIE, town between the RHÔNE valley and the alps (see map on p. 399) whose name features in the Clairette de Die and Crémant de Die appellations. According to PLINY, the local tribe in Roman times, the Voconces, made a sparkling sweet wine, and practised an early form of TEMPERATURE CONTROL by plunging barrels full of fermenting must in the river. Most wines are sparkling and many of them are sweet and grapey. The inhabitants and products of the region are described as **Diois**. For more information, see CLAIRETTE DE DIE, CRÉMANT, and CHÂTILLON-EN-DIOIS.

DIET, WINE AS PART OF. Today few consumers would claim to drink wine for dietary reasons (although one French doctor, E. Maury, devoted an entire book to prescribing different wines for various ailments). Wine contains various VITAMINS and MINERALS but in such small concentrations that, for them to make any sufficient contribution to the human diet, excessive amounts of ALCOHOL would also have to be ingested. 'Moderate' wine consumption can have a beneficial effect for some medical conditions, however, and wine consumption clearly plays a part in the much-vaunted **Mediterranean diet** (see HEALTH AND WINE).

No wine is 'slimming', but dry **dealcoholized wine** is usually lower in calories than most.

History

In Mediterranean countries it has always been natural to drink wine because it is abundant and relatively cheap. But wine forms part of our diet for reasons beyond necessity or ease of access.

Traditionally societies have wanted to drink wine because it tastes good, with or without food, and is sometimes used to cook food. It was popular not least because of the dangers associated with drinking unclean water. Wine has also long been recognized as an important element in a healthy diet.

The concept of maintaining good health through diet can be traced back to Ancient GREECE and the Greek Hippocrates, in particular, although wine was included in the dietary laws of Moses 1,000 years earlier. It was at the medical school established in 11th century Salerno, Italy, that wine's importance in diet was most influentially codified. Here classical and Arab scholarship fused to form the basis of European medicine. The Salerno Regimen—which specified different wines for different constitutions and 'humours', as had Hippocrates—was disseminated through Europe by CRUSADING knights and travellers treated at the school.

As late as the 1860s doctors were still matching wines to life-styles, as they would be termed today. For example Dr Robert Druitt suggested CLARET 'for children, for literary persons, and for all those whose occupations are chiefly carried on indoors'. The fuller bodied wines of BURGUNDY, the MIDI, and GREECE he considered better suited to manual workers. H.B.

André, J., *L'Alimentation et la cuisine à Rome* (Paris, 1961).
Johnson, H., *The Story of Wine* (London and New York, 1989).
Tannahill, R., *Food in History* (2nd edn., London, 1988).

DIETHYLENE GLYCOL. Notorious, illegal, mild chemical compound which can add apparent BODY to a wine. When found in a significant number of Austrian and German wines in 1985 (see ADULTERATION), it was popularly called antifreeze because of its nominal similarity to ethylene glycol, which is a common antifreeze additive.

DIJON, town in northern BURGUNDY and the focus of the region's vinous ACADEME, the Université de Bourgogne (formerly the **Université de Dijon**). For some time OENOLOGY was taught by the charismatic vigneron René Engel, who was also a leading light in the Chevaliers de Tastevin, but Dijon was able to offer graduate diplomas in oenology from 1947. The course was further refined in 1955 when a viticultural research station and experimental winery were established in nearby MARSANNAY. Since then the station has worked in close collaboration with INRA.

From 1982 Dijon offered the four-year Diplôme National d'Oenologue. Research has concentrated on three major areas: improved mastery of alcoholic FERMENTATION and MALOLACTIC FERMENTATION; improved knowledge of both Chardonnay and Pinot Noir vines, particularly with regard to their PHENOLIC composition, varietal AROMA, and individual TERROIRS; and study of wine-making techniques such as TEMPERATURE CONTROL, membrane FILTRATION, and BARREL MATURATION.

Professor of Oenology is Michel Feuillat.

DIMIAT, Bulgaria's most planted indigenous white grape variety although it may not cover as much ground as RKATSITELI. It is grown mainly in the east and south of Bulgaria where it is regarded as a producer of perfumed everyday whites of varying levels of sweetness but usefully dependable quality. The vines yield copper-coloured grapes in great quantity. The wines should be consumed young and cool. Dimiat is also a parent, with Riesling, of Bulgaria's MISKET.

DINING CLUBS, private societies of like-minded individuals who meet over meals. A high proportion of what are called dining clubs are in fact wining clubs devoted to the consumption and discussion of fine wines. They may be small groups of friends or professional fellow enthusiasts, or many-tentacled professionally run organizations. Some of the more internationally famous of these are the Beefsteak and Burgundy Club, the SAINTSBURY CLUB, and the INTERNATIONAL WINE & FOOD SOCIETY.

DINKA, very ordinary but widely planted white grape variety in HUNGARY and VOJVODINA. It is also known as Kövidinka and Kevedinka.

DIOIS, COTEAUX. Appellation created in 1993 for the still wines produced around Die on the Drôme tributary of the RHÔNE. For more details of likely grape varieties, see CLAIRETTE DE DIE and CRÉMANT.

DIONYSUS, the classical god of wine, for whom Bacchus was the more common name among the Romans. However, grapes and vines are not his only attributes, and neither is wine the only aspect of his cult.

Although some scholars have argued that wine is a secondary element in his cult and the god Dionysus was a late importation from the east, he is a wine god, an Olympian, and an important influence on Ancient GREECE. In classical times his most famous festival at Athens was the City Dionysia, when tragedy and comedy were performed in the gods' theatre. The earliest festival known to be devoted to Dionysus, the three-day feast of the Anthesteria, is a wine festival. It takes its name from the spring month of Anthesterion and celebrates the broaching of the new wine (the wine of the most recent vintage, which was always kept until the next spring). The Anthesteria are common to Athens and Asia Minor so they must predate the Ionian migrations to the west coast of modern TURKEY, which took place in the 10th century BC. Clay tablets dating from the late Bronze Age (*c.*1200 BC), inscribed in Linear B (a script used to record Mycenaean, an early form of Greek), connect Dionysus with wine, and thus provide further evidence for the early cult of Dionysus as a wine god.

Dionysus has been taken to be a non-Greek because he is a god of epiphanies. He appears suddenly, from outside, to strike people with madness. In Euripides' tragedy *The Bacchae* (probably written shortly after 408 BC), the most famous representation of Bacchic madness, Dionysus introduces

Dionysus being supported in his drunkenness, from a fourth-century mosaic, Antioch, Turkey.

himself as a Lydian, and as such he is literally a foreigner. But, more importantly, he is an intruder because he brings madness and loss of control into the previously well-ordered existence of the people of Thebes. Dionysus' coming from abroad is a metaphor for the threat that he forms to reason and civilization. And yet Dionysus is also something within human beings themselves, the animal part of our nature, for an entirely rational being would not be vulnerable to attacks of insanity.

The Bacchae is about Dionysiac frenzy and, although the play praises Dionysus for his gift of wine which lessens the cares of mortals, the madness that he brings is not the result of excessive consumption of wine. The maenads, female followers of Bacchus, are explicitly said not to be drunk, and the preparations Pentheus, king of Thebes, makes in order to accompany Dionysus to spy on the maenads include dressing up as a female bacchant, but not drinking wine. Pentheus tries to resist the god, and as a punishment Dionysus sends him mad; the maenads, too, are mad. Pentheus, male intruder upon the secret Dionysiac revels, which take place in the mountains and which, unlike the Anthesteria, are confined to women, is torn apart by his own mother. He has become the victim of *sparagmos* (also called *omophagia*), in which the maenads tear animals limb from limb and eat their flesh raw.

The essence of the cult of Dionysus is the surrender of personal identity. Hence one of Dionysus' symbols is the mask, and he is often depicted in VASE PAINTINGS of drinking ceremonies as a mask set up on a column draped in cloth. His other attributes are the thyrsus, a tall stick with a bunch of ivy leaves on top—ivy because it is evergreen and it produces its berries in the winter when the mountain ritual takes place and the vine is bare. He is also depicted with grapes or a wine cup, and often has an effeminate appearance with long flowing locks. The bull is sacred to him, as are pine trees and the fig. He is also associated with wild animals, the leopard, the lion, and the panther. His following is made up of satyrs and sileni (amoral woodland creatures, basically human but with some animal characteristics) and maenads, who seem possessed or intoxicated. Myths about him relate how with this irregular army of votaries he conquers Asia Minor and India, subduing all who try to resist him when he attacks them with his madness. He is frequently equated (especially by HERODOTUS in the 5th century BC) with the Egyptian god Osiris.

One well-known myth about Dionysus concerns the invention of wine. Dionysus discloses the secret of wine-making to the peasant Icarius and his daughter Erigone, with whom he had lodged as a guest, in return for their hospitality. Obedient to the god's command to teach the art to other people, Icarius shares his wine with a group of shepherds. At first they enjoy this delicious new drink, but as the unaccustomed wine overwhelms them they begin to suspect Icarius of having poisoned them. So they turn on him and batter him to death with their clubs. For a time his body cannot be found, but eventually Icarius' faithful dog Moera leads Erigone to the spot where he lies buried. Erigone hangs herself in despair. However, in death they receive their due rewards: Icarius becomes the star Boötes, his daughter the constellation Virgo, and Moera becomes Canis, or Sirius, the dog star. Boötes, also known in Greek as 'the grape-gatherer', rises in the autumn, at the time of the vintage, and in the warm climate of Greece the vintage may well have taken place some time before the autumnal equinox, still under the constellation of Virgo. It is also interesting to note that PLINY the Elder recommends the rising of the dog star, 2 August, as the day when wine jars should receive their inside coating of RESIN to make them airtight in readiness for the vintage.

Dionysus, then, is a god who strives against reason, calm and order. As such he is a god of the people, dangerous and subversive to those in authority. His cult attracts further suspicion because it is surrounded by secrecy. Maenadism excludes men, and there seem to have been other, secret, groups which held out the promise of eternal life to initiates. Probably initiation into the cult involved the drinking of wine, but we know little about this.

Gradually Dionysiac orgies appear to have become orgies in the modern sense, and among the Romans the cult of Dionysus was a disreputable affair. Livy gives a lurid account of the banning of the Bacchanalia, now open to men and the occasion of unspeakable acts, but it should not be forgotten that Livy was a historian of conservative tendencies, an admirer of Augustus, who lamented what he considered to be the recent slide into luxury and immorality. Bacchus certainly played little part in the official religion of Ancient ROME; he was too dangerous a god. Among the Romans he survives in a sanitized version, jolly Bacchus the wine god, giver of wine and bringer of joy, who makes sorrow bearable. Satyrs and nymphs gambol about him harmlessly, and Silenus is a cheerful old soak. This is the Bacchus that survived into the Renaissance, familiar from the pictures of Titian and his contemporaries. The Romans reduced the complex god of the Greeks to little more than wine personified. H.M.W.

Burkert, W., *Greek Religion*, trans. by John Raffan (Oxford, 1985).

Carpenter, T. H., *Dionysian Imagery in Archaic Greek Art* (Oxford, 1986).

Otto, W. F., *Dionysus: Myth and Cult*, trans. by Robert B. Palmer (Bloomington, Ind., and London, 1965).

DIRECT PRODUCER, term used for a group of vines, also known as FRENCH HYBRIDS, bred from the late 19th century onwards in an effort to combine pest and disease resistance of AMERICAN VINE SPECIES with the desirable fruit characters of the European VINIFERA species. They are called direct producers, and sometimes hybrid direct producers, or HDPs, because, unlike *vinifera* VINE VARIETIES, they do not need GRAFTING on to PHYLLOXERA-tolerant ROOTSTOCKS. They are not all sufficiently phylloxera tolerant, however, and added soil stresses such as drought or weeds can see them weakened by phylloxera. R.E.S.

DISEASES, VINE. See VINE DISEASES and individual diseases.

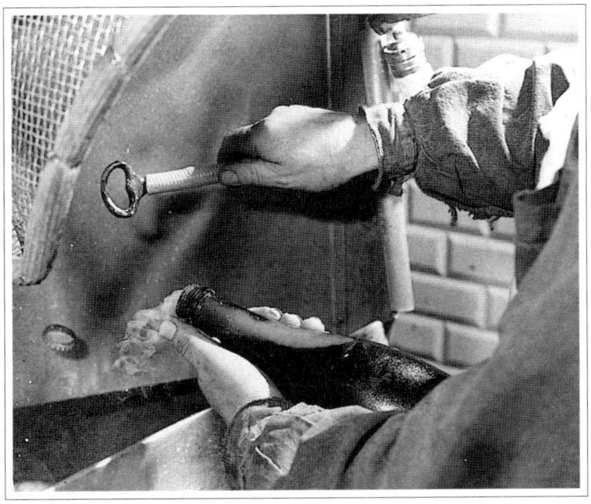

Traditional manual **disgorgement**. The frozen deposit from most bottle-fermented sparkling wines is removed mechanically today.

DISGORGEMENT, or *dégorgement* in French, an integral stage in the traditional champagne method of SPARKLING WINE-MAKING. It entails the removal of a pellet of frozen sediment from the neck of each bottle and does nothing to improve the quality of the wine. Modern alternative techniques may eventually render this cumbersome process superfluous.

DISTILLATION, the separation of the constituents of a liquid mixture by partial vaporization of the mixture and the separate recovery of the vapour and the residue. When applied to wine, or any other fermented liquid, the result is a considerably stronger alcoholic liquid: brandy in the case of wine and other fermented fruit juices, calvados in the case of certain apples from northern France, whisky in the case of fermented barley.

History

The processes which preceded the distillation of alcohol were the practices of medieval alchemists which reduced solids to fine powders. The Arabs recognized and refined these processes in the early Middle Ages, using them to make elixirs, perfumes, and medicines by extracting the essences from fruits and flowers. The distillation of drugs was already known in the Arab world of the 10th century. As a result, we still use words of Arabic origin for the still and distillate: ALEMBIC (*al-anbiq*) and ALCOHOL (*al-kuhl*) respectively.

It is unlikely, however, that the Arabs used it as a method to isolate the alcohol in grape wine. The earliest documentary sources describing the practice of distilling wine originate from Italy and date from the 12th century. Stills used before this time left too much water in the wine. The use of more sophisticated equipment eventually enabled alchemists to produce *aqua ardens*, 'burning water', or an alcohol and water compound that would burn, and *aqua vitae*, 'water of life', or alcohol. Alcohol was also known as 'quintessence', the fifth element.

Initially distillation was practised almost exclusively by alchemists, doctors, and apothecaries. Alcohol was prized for its medicinal qualities as the writings of ARNALDUS DE VILLANOVA (13th century) and other famous doctors attest: 'It prolongs life, clears away ill humours, revives the heart, and maintains youth.'

During the course of the Middle Ages alcohol distilled from wine developed a wide popularity and its manufacture passed increasingly into the hands of specialist 'water-burners' and vintners. It was recognized as a beverage, particularly in Germany, where it was known as *Gebrandtwein* or 'burnt wine', a term adapted by the Dutch into BRANDEWIJN (subsequently corrupted into the English BRANDY).

Grains were distilled later than wine, and in any case brandy was perceived as superior. This did not mean that good-quality wines were used. For centuries distillation was seen primarily as a means of using up old wines, or a too-abundant harvest. Pressed or trodden grape skins and LEES were also conveniently distilled to produce POMACE BRANDY.

The turning point in the history of distilled wine came in the late 17th century, when it was recognized that the wines of the COGNAC region of western France produced a better-tasting brandy, particularly when aged. During the course of the following century the cognac industry developed as price differentials between specific areas became apparent and merchants committed themselves to greater investment. H.B.

Enjalbert, H., 'Aux origines du Cognac', in A. Heutz de Lemps and P. Roudié (eds.), *Eaux-de-vie et spiritueux* (Paris, 1985).

Forbes, R. J., *Short History of the Art of Distillation* (Leiden, 1948).

Sigerist, H. E., *The Earliest Printed Book on Wine* (New York, 1943) (contains Villanova's *Tractatus vinis*).

Modern wine distillation

However distillation is carried out, it remains essentially a simple process, physical rather than chemical, separating the alcohol and other impurities in the wine (or other ferment) from the water which forms its bulk. The principle is simplicity itself: alcohol, and many other impurities, boil at lower temperatures than water. In particular, ETHANOL, or ethyl alcohol, boils at a 78.3 °C/173 °F, considerably cooler than the 100 °C boiling point of water. Distillation consists merely of heating the wine, or any other fermented liquid, and then capturing the fumes. Of course an infinite number of slightly different forms of distillation have emerged in the course of history. These have something to do with the type of still—the traditional POT STILL or the more industrial CONTINUOUS STILL—which themselves entail innumerable complexities.

The variation in character between the host of wine-based spirits such as ARMAGNAC, COGNAC, and the very different sorts of BRANDY are in part a reflection of differences in distillation techniques.

It gradually emerged that there was a crucial balance to be observed: the more complete and thus theoretically efficient the distillation process, the less interesting the resultant distillate since, by definition, it contained fewer of the impurities which alone give spirits their character. Indeed cognac's fame came about because the grapes grown on the slopes round the town had only to be distilled twice to produce a wholesome and drinkable spirit, whereas those from rival French wine regions had to be distilled six or more times. In the process of losing their unpleasant (or simply poisonous) impurities, they also lost almost all their original character.

At the (relatively) low strengths at which brandy is distilled in Cognac (up to 70 per cent alcohol) or Armagnac (where it can be as low as 52 per cent) the concentration which is at the heart of the process uncovers all the features of the original raw material. (Most brandies, like most other spirits, are 'broken down' by the addition of water to the more palatable alcoholic strength of 40 per cent before bottling.) The 'impurities' include hundreds of different ingredients, and the use of chromatography has revealed not only their number, but the very different relative importance they can enjoy—a high concentration of one substance need not change the perceived taste or aromas of the brandy, while a minuscule amount of another can have the most extraordinary effects, for good or ill.

The speed of distillation is also important, and brandies distilled in a pot still enjoy an enormous advantage, since, by varying the rate at which the wine is heated, the distiller can maximize the length of time required and thus extract the greatest possible proportion of the desirable ingredients in the wine. In that sense distillation is like stewing fruit, where the longer and slower the cooking process, the more concentrated and flavourful the final product. Pot stills also enable the distiller to control the process more accurately.

But choice of raw material is also crucial. Grapes are complex fruits, and brandies can be made either from the wine or from the pomace. A wide variety of grape detritus can be employed effectively for POMACE BRANDIES, including black grape skins, whereas the wine suitable for distillation has to fall within certain clearly defined parameters, largely because the wine should be relatively acid. Ideally the acidity should be balanced—as it is with the FOLLE BLANCHE grape—by a certain concentration of fruit. Nevertheless modern cognac is almost invariably distilled from the UGNI BLANC, one of the most neutral of all white grape varieties. None the less it contains enough CONGENERS, fatty acids, and other impurities to produce the finest of all brandies.

But of course distillation is only the first stage in the production of a fine spirit (as opposed to an industrially produced alcohol such as gin, vodka, or grain whisky). The more interesting, chemical reactions occur when the raw spirit is matured in wood. See OAK AND BRANDY. N.F.

DISTILLATION, COMPULSORY. In an effort to curb, and dispose of, SURPLUS wine production, the EUROPEAN UNION authorities instituted a system in 1982 whereby any wine produced over a certain limit should theoretically be compulsorily bought, at a standard and not too attractive price, and distilled into industrial ALCOHOL (which policy resulted, perhaps inevitably, in an alcohol surplus). Average quantities distilled under this scheme in the 1980s were well over 30 million hl/790 million gal, or about a fifth of total European production. In 1993 the European Commission admitted that the scheme had done little to curb over-production, and announced stricter measures designed to offer less financial support to over-producers, and to curb abuse of the system more effectively.

DIVIDED CANOPY, group of vine-TRAINING SYSTEMS which involve separation of a leaf CANOPY into two or more sub-canopies, sometimes called curtains. The expression was popularized by Professor Nelson Shaulis in the 1960s and 1970s as part of his pioneering promotion of CANOPY MANAGEMENT. One of the most important divided canopy training systems is the GENEVA DOUBLE CURTAIN developed by Shaulis. The LYRE is a more recent development. The advantage of canopy division is that it increases the surface area of the canopy that is exposed to sunlight, while reducing canopy SHADE. Both yield and wine quality can increase as a result. R.E.S.

DLG, source of German wine awards. See DEUTSCHE.

DNA 'FINGERPRINTING', more formally **DNA typing**, a development of modern technology allowing the potential and unequivocal identification of all living material from small samples of tissue. First suggested for human identification in 1985, the technique has been applied to the identification of different VINE VARIETIES and, possibly, CLONES. Complementing the science of AMPELOGRAPHY, it provides a means of identifying a vine variety without the disadvantages of an observer's subjectivity or the influence of such external factors as drought or disease.

Leaves and shoot tips are most commonly used to provide vine tissue whose DNA is then purified and subjected to a series of biochemical manipulations to produce a pattern of bands looking remarkably like a supermarket bar code, and which as such can be read and stored in a computer.

Varieties can easily be distinguished one from another, and the chance of any two vine varieties having the same patterns has been calculated as being one in 6 million by Carole Meredith of the University of California at DAVIS. Since the total number of vine varieties is probably no more than 10,000, varieties should be easily identified.

One of the Davis team's first significant results in the early 1990s was to establish that ZINFANDEL and PRIMITIVO (or at least the Davis vines thus labelled) have identical DNA patterns and can therefore, after years of speculation, be regarded as identical. The technique was also applied to ROOTSTOCKS, particularly important in the wake of California's PHYLLOXERA outbreak, and found marked differences in DNA pattern between rootstocks such as SO 4 and 5 C which look very similar to the human eye.

The technique was initially relatively crude and unable to distinguish between different mutations or clones of the same variety but is being refined. Australia's Commonwealth Scientific and Industrial Research Organization (CSIRO) scientists DNA typed clones of Pinot Noir, Cabernet Sauvignon, and Sultana. They found a DNA difference for only one clone of Cabernet Sauvignon, but many differences in virus content between the other clones. These results suggest that differences between these clones at least are more likely to be due to virus diseases than mutation. It is also hoped that similarities of DNA patterns will shed light on the geographical origins of various varieties (see PROLES). R.E.S.

Bowers, J. E., Bandman, E. B., and Meredith, C. P., 'DNA fingerprint characterization of some wine grape cultivars', *American Journal of Enology and Viticulture*, 44/3 (1993) 266–74.

DO stands for Denominación de Origen, a Spanish controlled appellation and the mainstay of SPAIN's wine quality control system. Each region awarded DO status is governed by a Consejo Regulador made up of representatives of the Ministry of Agriculture and vine-growers, wine-makers, and merchants who earn their livelihoods in the region. The Consejo, in conjunction with the regional government and INDO (Instituto Nacional de Denominaciones de Origen, the Spanish equivalent of France's INAO) in Madrid decides on the boundaries of the region, permitted VINE VARIETIES, maximum YIELDS, limits of ALCOHOLIC STRENGTH, and any other limitations pertaining to the zone. Back labels or neck seals are granted by the Consejo to certify that a wine meets the standards laid out in the DO regulations. A Denominación de Origen Provisional (DOP) may be awarded to regions on their way to becoming full DOs. A superior category, Denominación de Origen Calificada (see DOCA), was created in 1991.

Rioja (which was promoted to DOCa status in 1991) became Spain's first DO in 1926 when its own Consejo Regulador was established. Jerez and Málaga had joined the ranks by the end of the 1930s and they were joined by several other regions immediately after the Civil War. In the 1970s there was a move to centralize power but Spain has reverted to federal administration.

Spanish wine law has been subject to some criticism as the list of regions promoted to DO status continues to lengthen (see also PORTUGAL). With so many obscure regions joining the ranks, the DO has become an increasingly bureaucratic concept and has ceased to act as a reliable guarantee of superior quality. DOs have been awarded to regions with little or no historical tradition of quality wine production, while Consejos Reguladores continue to uphold certain local quirks which may sometimes stifle enterprise and initiative among growers and wine-makers.

See also VINO DE MESA and VINO DE LA TIERRA.

DOBLE PASTA, dark, full bodied Spanish wine produced by running off a proportion of fermenting must after two days and adding more crushed grapes to refill the vat. The ratio of skin to pulp is effectively doubled, producing wines with a deep, black colour and very high levels of TANNIN. Doble pasta wines have traditionally been made in JUMILLA, YECLA, UTIEL-REQUENA, and ALÍCANTE, where they are used for blending but they are being superseded by GRAPE CONCENTRATE. R.J.M.

DOC, initials which stand for Denominação de Origem Controlada in PORTUGAL and Denominazione di Origine Controllata in ITALY, those countries' much more embryonic counterparts of the French APPELLATION CONTRÔLÉE system of controlled appellations. In both countries, DOC wines represent those regarded as QUALITY WINES by European wine law. A DOC system is also evolving in ARGENTINA.

Denominação de Origem Controlada

In Portugal DOC stands for Denominação de Origem Controlada. On joining the EUROPEAN UNION in 1986, Portugal undertook revision of its wine laws to bring them into line with other European countries, most notably those of France. Each of the nine regions which had already been designated a REGIÃO DEMARCADA (RD) in earlier legislation was renamed as a DOC. The laws controlling grape varieties, yields, alcoholic strength, and maturation times remained largely the same. Both Região Demarcãda and Denominação de Origem Controlada could be found on labels well into the 1990s.

Portugal's wine laws are a bureaucrat's dream and a winemaker's nightmare, stifling initiative in a number of wine regions (see DÃO and COLARES). Many of Portugal's best wines have traditionally been blends from more than one region (see GARRAFEIRA) and these fall outside the DOC legislation. A second tier of delimited regions, Indicação de Proveniencia Regulamentada (see IPR), was also introduced following Portugal's entry into the EU, along with a third catch-all category named Vinho Regional, roughly equivalent to France's VIN DE PAYS. R.J.M.

Denominazione di Origine Controllata

Italy's viticultural production was given its first systematic regulation in 1963. A chosen few of its most famous wines had already been given legal recognition and protection during the 1930s when the Italian parliament approved a framework law for the entire country and established a nation-wide system of controlled appellations or denominazioni; DOC is simply the abbreviation of Denominazione di Origine Controllata, a direct translation of the French Appellation d'Origine Contrôlée. Also in 1963 legislators added another higher category, DOCG (Denominazione di Origine Controllata e Garantita) which added 'guaranteed' to 'controlled', a category which was intended to be reserved for the country's élite wines. The law, universally referred to in Italy as '930' (its number on the legislative calendar that year) was ostensibly inspired by French legislation and the French appellation system: individual production zones were mapped out and delimited; the VINE VARIETIES to be cultivated and fermented were defined (often in strict percentages); levels of ALCOHOL, TOTAL ACIDITY, and EXTRACT were established; ceilings placed on YIELDS; viticultural and wine-making practices regulated (although often in the haziest of terms: as in 'in conformity with existing practices' or 'so as to not change the nature of the wine' are frequent phrases in the rules of individual DOCs).

As the legal framework was fleshed out by the establishment of the various zones and the overall system of regulation went into effect, it became increasingly obvious that the Italian system bore only a superficial resemblance to the French one and was not succeeding in its fundamental purpose of guaranteeing wines of quality to the consuming public, a fact that the public itself was not slow in realizing. Statistics bear eloquent and incontrovertible testimony to this fact: only 13.5 per cent of the country's viticultural production is classified as DOC or DOCG, which means that, within the EU, only GREECE has a lower proportion of QUALITY WINE. (The French percentage is about 40 per cent, the Portuguese and Spanish ones well over 25 per cent.) The 8.5 million hl / 224 million gal DOC wine produced in an average Italian vintage are a mere third of the potential production of the existing DOC vineyard, confirming that producers in many DOC zones see no advantage in attaching the DOC name to their wines and deliberately choose not to label the wines as such.

Although over 250 separate DOC zones have been established and more than 700 DOC wines theoretically exist, only a small percentage of these wines have any real commercial vitality: 20 DOCs account for close to 45 per cent of the country's total DOC production, and 100 DOCs account for 80 per cent of the overall total; 300 DOC wines are produced in quantities less than 1,000 hl per year. The situation is particularly critical in Italy's south, which can be said to have collectively turned its back on the DOC system. In 1990, for example, the DOC production of the six regions of Italy's south represented just three per cent of total wine production.

If producers have been sceptical of the advantages that DOC recognition would bring and reluctant to classify their wines as DOC products, consumer disenchantment with the general quality of these wines has been even more accentuated and Italian consumers in particular, unlike their French counterparts, have refused to pay substantially higher prices for DOC wines than for non-DOC wines. From 1975 on, in fact, an opposite phenomenon began to manifest itself and has become even stronger over the years: a refusal on the part of ambitious producers to label their best wines DOC and a policy of higher prices for many a VINO DA TAVOLA than for the DOC production of the same zones. The phenomenon began with the SUPERTUSCANS of TUSCANY but spread to EMILIA-ROMAGNA, FRIULI, PIEDMONT, and SICILY, and the apparent paradox of vini da tavola universally recognized as the best products of famous zones worthy of the highest prices threatens to become generalized.

What went wrong Various causes have been adduced for the general failure of law 930 to meet its expressed purposes, but the most common criticism has been of the overly strict and precise regulations established in the individual DOCs. While it is true that requirements of excessively long CASK AGEING have not been helpful to wines such as BRUNELLO DI MONTALCINO and BAROLO, it is also true that these have none the less been two of Italy's finest wines and that these zones have not witnessed defections from the DOC. And while it is true that the extremely exact percentages of individual grapes allowed in the final blend of various DOC wines may seem a misguided attempt to establish the methodology of pharmacists or cookbook authors as standard operating procedure for cellar work, it is also true that authorities have done little to enforce these regulations. The very first Supertuscan, Tignanello 1970 (see VINO DA TAVOLA), was in fact released as a CHIANTI CLASSICO despite its thoroughly illegal mere three per cent of white grapes, and even now many a prominent producer of Chianti Classico or VINO NOBILE DI MONTEPULCIANO has no qualms in publicly declaring that his wine is a far from orthodox 100 per cent SANGIOVESE.

The two major defects of the individual DOCs, in reality, were the extremely generous yields allowed, a generosity which was inconsistent with any serious attempt to produce wines of quality, and the equally generous definition of the territorial limits of the denominations which frequently lumped in peripheral, or not even peripheral, zones with the historic areas which had given their names to the wines themselves, the division of DOC into a CLASSICO and nonclassic zone being only one variation of this tactic.

The coexistence of a superficially formal attempt at rigour with a *laissez-faire* approach to actual practice is a product of a national political culture whose improvisatory style to a certain extent reflects centuries of foreign domination. But law 930 principally reflects the period in which it was drafted, a period in which Italian producers, with little knowledge of the wines outside of their own regions and with virtually no knowledge of the wines of other countries, had no other reference points for their regulations than the established practices of their own zones. It also reflects the conviction of the time that the natural market for Italian wines was in the lower–medium price range (Italy, in 1963, was the poorest member of a Common Market which had not yet admitted Spain, Portugal, or Greece) and that high-volume production was a necessity for economic survival. In this context it was probably inevitable that only those DOC wines with an established name, history, and reputation would draw any real benefits from law 930 and that the hundreds of 'invented' DOC wines, many of which were devised for political reasons and to satisfy local chauvinism, would attain no real public recognition and find few customers.

An attempt at reform Law 930 was modified by law 164 of December 1992, and the new legislation was drafted with the express purpose of giving Italy's DOC system a credibility which, by unanimous agreement, it had not succeeded in obtaining. Its principal innovation was to introduce the principle of territorial subdivision by allowing larger DOC zones to be broken down into subzones, townships, hamlets, microzones, individual estates, and vineyards, and to give the entire structure a vertical and hierarchical basis: the new and smaller units more specific than DOC or DOCG zones will be required to have stricter production limits and criteria. Producers who wish to use a single vineyard name for their DOC or DOCG wines will have to register their vineyard and define its extension with the authorities, a reform aimed at curbing the multiplication of invented single-vineyard names (following the Italian FASHION for individual CRUS) with no real territorial basis.

Various DOCs or DOCGs may now cover the same geographical limits, and producers will have the option of declassifying their wines from a more restricted (and thus in a certain sense 'higher') to a more extended (and thus in a certain sense 'lower') DOC. Quality will thereby be given a geographical basis by anchoring it in smaller, homogeneous areas with a real and proven aptitude for producing fine wines, instead of attaching to definitions such as SUPERIORE or RISERVA which attempted, and failed, to link better quality with higher levels of alcohol and/or longer periods of ageing. All DOCG and DOC wines will now be required to undergo and pass ANALYSIS and tasting panels. And a new category of wines called IGT (Indicazione Geografica Tipica), intended as the approximate equivalent of the French VIN DE PAYS and German LANDWEIN, has been created in an attempt to bring all the renowned and high-quality wines selling as vino da tavola into the overall DOC system.

While many of these reforms are sensible and well intentioned, there is good reason to doubt that they will achieve their stated purposes, and the loopholes in the legislation are only too obvious. Nothing has been done to curb the excessively generous yields of existing DOCs, the chief reason for extremely modest quality levels in the past. The subdivision of the territory and a hierarchical system of denominazioni on the French model is commendable in its purported goals, but there are significant differences between current French practice and the text of law 164. The exclusion of certain less-favoured parts of a given village's vineyards from the village appellation in BURGUNDY, for example, an exclusion aimed at reserving the village name for the better part of a commune's *vignoble*, could not be in starker contrast to the Italian principle of conceding the use of the village name to all of the vineyards within the village limits, a principle inconsistent with real quality distinctions in hillside viticulture with varied ELEVATIONS and TOPOGRAPHY.

The new IGT category will permit some of Italy's finest wines to shed the vino da tavola designation, although this has so far done little to harm their commercial viability, and the IGT category is theoretically a lower one than DOCG or DOC, creating the anomaly of some of Italy's most acclaimed and expensive wines being in a legally lower classification than many a mediocre, mass-produced DOC wine.

Chemical analysis and tasting panels may lead to a better overall quality level, but the tasting panels currently operating for Italy's DOCG wines have been notorious for their lack of rigour and reluctance to disqualify poorly made wines. And early signs were that the new law was more likely to spawn an increasing number of individual DOCs rather than simplify the system.

Perhaps the inevitable conclusion is that a wine industry interested only relatively recently in high quality is not currently suited for an appellation system like that of France, established to ratify, certify, and protect a long and settled tradition of fine wines, and not to create them from scratch. Italian wine production of the 1990s, marked by creative ferment and constant experimentation, seems particularly ill suited to a system of simple and stable rules.

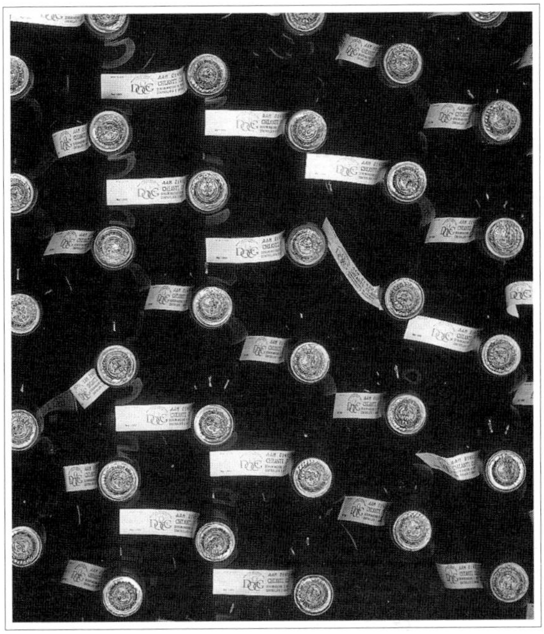

Bottles accorded **DOCG** status are decorated with special seals, as in this stock of Riecine Chianti Classico.

Italy's current, apparently chaotic vinicultural façade unquestionably creates multiple problems for consumers attempting to understand the often incomprehensible variety of labels on the market, but some consolation may be found in the fact that behind the chaos are at least two decades of serious commitment to quality which has changed the country's wines for the better. D.T.

DOCA, Denominación de Origen Calificada, is the highest category in Spanish wine law, reserved for regions complying with certain conditions including above-average grape prices, and particularly stringent quality controls. RIOJA was the first Spanish region to be awarded DOCa status, in 1991. R.J.M.

DOCE, Portuguese for sweet. See SWEETNESS.

DOCG (Denominazione di Origine Controllata e Garantita), is a legal category established in ITALY for its highest-quality wines in 1963, at the same time as its DOC was created as an Italian version of the French APPELLATION CONTRÔLÉE system by law 930. The express purpose of this category was to identify and reward the finest Italian wines, which were to be 'guaranteed' (the G), and not merely 'controlled' (C). If the DOC system did not enjoy general credibility because it was applied liberally and with little rigour, the DOCG title, in contrast, was conferred with admirable parsimony in its first years of existence. It was not even used until 1980, and by 1992, when the system was overhauled by law 164, only 11 wines had been deemed worthy of receiving the honour, and the first five DOCGs to be conferred—

BAROLO, BARBARESCO, CHIANTI, BRUNELLO DI MONTALCINO, and VINO NOBILE DI MONTEPULCIANO—are likely to be on everyone's short list of Italy's most important wines. The awarding of DOCG status to the undistinguished ALBANA DI ROMAGNA in 1986, however, widely regarded as political in inspiration and a violation both of the letter and the spirit of law 930 and, as such, a threat to the viability of the DOCG category itself, met such criticism that it may well have prevented repetition of such an episode. Eight further DOCGs have been approved since 1986—TORGIANO, CARMIGNANO, GATTINARA, SAGRANTINO di Montefalco, TAURASI Riserva, VERNACCIA DI SAN GIMIGNANO, ASTI SPUMANTE, and MOSCATO D'ASTI—and, if the wines do not have the unquestioned distinction of the first five, they are undoubtedly valid products and are all (something which could not be said of Albana di Romagna) well known in national and international markets.

The greatest single success of the DOCG, however, was unquestionably the revision of Chianti regulations when it was promoted from DOC to DOCG in 1984. Permitted YIELDS were lowered from 80.5 to 52.5 hl/ha (3 tons/acre); minimum EXTRACT levels were substantially raised, and the percentage of white grapes in the blend drastically lowered. See CHIANTI for more details of the beneficial effects of these new rules.

There is every sign that the DOCG category will be truly representative of quality. D.T.

DOCTORS of medicine through the ages have displayed an uncommon affection for wine, and not just because of wine's uses as a MEDICINE and beneficial effects on HEALTH. Doctors have long been enthusiastic wine consumers (see Alexander HENDERSON, for example) and, more recently, producers. The WINE SOCIETY, an important wine-buying group founded in London in the late 19th century, regularly surveys the occupations of its members and the largest group is always made up of members of the medical profession, as are a number of the world's most serious wine COLLECTORS. There are numerous examples of vineyard owners who combine viticulture with practising medicine. Docteur Peste's slice of the CORTON vineyard is sold each year in the HOSPICES DE BEAUNE auction, itself a medical charity, for example. The MOSEL-SAAR-RUWER of Germany has an example of what might be called double-doctoring, in that the producer Dr Thanisch owns a portion of the world-famous Doctor, or Doktor, vineyard of Bernkastel. Particularly strong medical connections can be traced in the history of AUSTRALIAN wine, however. One Sydney general practitioner counted more than 135 doctors who had established vineyards in Australia (including those that gave rise to the substantial wine concerns PENFOLDS, Lindemans, Angove, Houghton, and HARDY'S) and reminds us that 'Australia was founded in the rum age, developed in the beer age, and is now maturing in the wine age'. See also AUSTRALIAN INFLUENCE and LITERATURE OF WINE.

DOLCE, Italian for sweet. See SWEETNESS.

DOLCEACQUA, or **Rossese di Dolceacqua**, wine from the north western coast of Italy. For more details, see LIGURIA.

DOLCETTO, an early ripening, low-acid red grape variety cultivated almost exclusively in the provinces of Cuneo and Alessandria in the north west Italian region of PIEDMONT. The wines produced are soft, round, fruity, and fragrant with flavours of liquorice and almonds and most are designed to be drunk in their first two or three years. Dolcetto therefore plays an important role in the economy of various estates, providing a product which can be marketed early while the wines based on BARBERA or, particularly, NEBBIOLO grapes demand extended ageing in cask and bottle. Unlike Barbera, it is rarely blended with other varieties, chiefly because it is so rarely planted outside VARIETALLY minded Piedmont.

As a precocious ripener, ripening up to four weeks before the majestic Nebbiolo, Dolcetto also permits growers to exploit either higher or less favourably exposed vineyard sites and thus maximize the return on their holdings. In the precious BAROLO and BARBARESCO zones, for example, Dolcetto is rarely planted on a south-facing site unless the vineyard is too high to ripen Nebbiolo reliably. And in the zones of Dogliani, Diano d'Alba, and Ovada, Dolcetto is planted where other varieties may not ripen at all. There is a consensus amongst growers in the Dolcetto d'Alba DOC, source of much of the finest Dolcetto, that the variety prefers the characteristic white marls of the right bank of the Tanaro and cannot give maximum results in heavier soils.

If the grape is relatively easy to cultivate, apart from its susceptibility to FUNGAL DISEASES and a tendency to drop its bunches in the cold mornings of late September, it is far from easy to vinify. While low in ACIDITY, relative to Barbera at least, and therefore 'dolce' (sweet) to the Piedmontese palate, Dolcetto (little sweet one) does have significant TANNINS, which producers have learned to soften with shorter fermentations. So rich are the skins of Dolcetto in ANTHOCYANS that even the shortest fermentation rarely compromises the deep ruby and purple tones of the wine. Less easy to solve have been the aromatic problems caused by the heavy SEDIMENT thrown by many young wines which frequently leads to unattractive MERCAPTANS. Careful attention to the evolving wine and early and punctual RACKING are the sole solution to these problems, which were aggravated in the late 1980s by early bottling in misguided attempts to imitate BEAUJOLAIS.

There are seven Dolcetto DOCs in Piedmont: Acqui; Alba; Asti (where little is planted, GRIGNOLINO being the young wine of choice); Diano d'Alba; Dogliani; Langhe Monregalesi; and Ovada. Alba, Ovada, and Dogliani are quantitatively the most significant, while the Langhe Monregalesi is a barely extant curiosity. Alba is generally considered to produce the finest quality, with good quality also being produced in what are virtually satellite appellations in Diano and Dogliani.

Ormeasco is LIGURIA'S version of Dolcetto and is therefore the southernmost extent of Dolcetto territory in Italy. It grows just on the Ligurian side of the mountains that separate Piedmont from Liguria.

GALET contends that Dolcetto is one and the same as the Douce Noire of SAVOIE, over the alps from Piedmont in France, one of whose synonyms is Charbonneau, and that this is the variety known as CHARBONO in California. It would certainly be logical for the Barbera so enthusiastically imported into California by immigrants from Piedmont to have been accompanied by Dolcetto, although it is a mystery why it should have been called by an obscure French synonym. A variety known as Dolcetto is known in Argentina but it is grown on an extremely limited scale, whereas some Argentine authorities contend that their dominant 'Bonarda' is in fact Charbon. D.T. & J.Ro.

Galet, P., *Cépages et vignobles de France* (2nd edn., Montpellier, 1990).

DÔLE, red wine made from mainly Pinot Noir with Gamay grapes grown in the Valais of SWITZERLAND. A high proportion of Dôle lacks real interest and concentration but exceptions exist. **Dôle Blanche** is a lightly pressed, pale pink version. See also BOURGOGNE PASSETOUTGRAINS.

DOLIUM, a large earthenware vessel used in the Ancient Roman period. Sometimes with a capacity of several thousand litres, they were often partly buried in the floor of a barn to act as a FERMENTATION VESSEL and provide storage for wine until it was transferred to AMPHORAE. In the late 20th century a number of Roman wrecks have been discovered off the south coast of France in which the cargo space has largely been taken up by up to 14 *dolia*, thus creating the ancient equivalent of a tanker for the transport of wine in bulk. While the ratio of wine to weight of container was more favourable than a hold full of amphorae, a vessel loaded thus must have been potentially highly unstable. J.J.P.

DOMAINE, French word for an estate, typically a vine-growing and wine-making estate in BURGUNDY.

DOMAINE BOTTLING, the relatively recent practice of BOTTLING the produce of a DOMAINE on the property which produced it. Such wines are described as **domaine bottled**, or *mis(e) en bouteille au domaine* in French. The term is the BURGUNDY equivalent of Bordeaux's CHÂTEAU BOTTLING, whose history is mirrored by the practice of domaine bottling. Domaine bottling was even later and less common, however, since burgundy is generally produced in very much smaller quantities than bordeaux. Even today a high proportion of all burgundy is still sold in bulk to be blended for the NÉGOCIANTS' own labels. It was not until energetic wine merchants such as Frank SCHOONMAKER and Alexis LICHINE visited Burgundy in the second half of the 20th century that the better individual producers were encouraged, and in many cases subsidized, to bottle their own production, typically with the help of mobile BOTTLING lines. Poor standards of HYGIENE, and even faults in basic WINE-MAKING, still dog some domaines and it is by no means the case that all domaine bottled burgundy is necessarily superior to any burgundy bottled at a larger enterprise. A domaine bottled wine should, however, lack bland anonymity, and any Burgundian prepared to bottle his own wine shows signs of ambition.

See also ESTATE BOTTLED.

DOMAINE DE LA ROMANÉE-CONTI, the most prestigious wine estate in Burgundy, based in Vosne-Romanée. 'The Domaine', as it is frequently called, is co-owned by the de Villaine and Leroy families and produces only GRAND CRU wines: one white, Le MONTRACHET, and six reds: Romanée-Conti and La Tâche, both monopolies of the domaine, Richebourg, Romanée-St-Vivant, Échezeaux, and Grands Échezeaux. For more details of individual wines, see VOSNE-ROMANÉE and ÉCHEZEAUX. The Domaine is the exception to the law by which no estate in Burgundy may be named after a specific vineyard. Its wines are notable for their richness and longevity.

History

What is now Romanée-Conti was identified by the monks of St-Vivant as Le Cloux des Cinq Journaux in 1512 and sold off, as Le Cros de Cloux, in 1584 to Claude Cousin. His nephew and heir Germain Danton sold again to Jacques Vénot in 1621. Vénot's daughter married a Croonembourg, which family retained the vineyard, now known as La Romanée (first mentioned in 1651), for four generations until it was sold to the Prince de Conti in 1760. The title Romanée-Conti was not used, however, until after dispossession by the revolutionaries and its sale by auction in 1794.

Romanée-Conti was bought by Julien Ouvard in 1819 and sold by his heirs to Jacques-Marie Duvault-Blochet 50 years later. Duvault-Blochet's eventual heirs were the de Villaine family. In 1911 Edmond Guidon de Villaine became director of what was now known as the Domaine de la Romanée-Conti, selling a half-share in 1942 to his friend Henri Leroy.

Over the years Duvault-Blochet built up major vineyard ownership including part of Échezeaux, Grands Échezeaux, Richebourg, and the section of La Tâche known as Les Gaudichots. In 1933 the rest of La Tâche was bought from the Liger-Belair family, making a monopoly, and a small holding of Le Montrachet (0.67 ha / 1.6 acres) was added in three slices between 1963 and 1980. The Domaine entered into a long-term contract to farm and produce the wines of Domaine Marey-Monge's holding of Romanée-St-Vivant before eventually buying the land in 1988. This necessitated selling part of their Échezeaux vineyards and a slice of Grands Échezeaux, although they continue to farm the land and bottle the wines. Further vineyards owned by the Domaine in Vosne-Romanée and Bâtard-Montrachet are sold in bulk.

J.T.C.M.

The de Villaine-Leroy era

Henri Leroy provided the financial means, and the determination, firmly to cement DRC's position as the finest domaine in Burgundy, but its joint ownership and direction was a source of conflict for several decades. Henri Leroy's NÉGOCIANT business, Société Leroy, was granted the valuable exclusive distribution rights to DRC wines in all markets other than the USA and UK, but the de Villaine family at times expressed distaste for or resentment of this arrangement. Henri de Villaine, who had succeeded his father in 1950, was in particular critical of some of the comparative tasting activities of Henri Leroy's daughter 'Lalou' Bize-

Leroy. In 1975 Lalou and Henri's son Aubert were appointed co-directors of this most famous estate, each representing the interests of their respective families. When Henri Leroy died in 1980, Lalou and her sister Pauline Roch-Leroy each had a 25 per cent share in the Domaine, while the de Villaine half was shared between about 10 different family members.

Lalou's passion is tasting and wine-making, and she worked closely with the Domaine's cellarmasters, first André Noblet and then his son Bernard, to maximize the quality of DRC's wines which were released, at the most robust prices, even in mediocre vintages. Lalou's control of Société Leroy gave her power over both production and sales, but resulted in her dismissal as co-director of the Domaine in 1993, when Aubert de Villaine and her sister Pauline decided to replace her with Pauline's son Charles Roch (soon to be killed in a motor accident and succeeded by his brother Henri Roch). The Leroy way of selling DRC wines in lots of one bottle of the sought-after Romanée-Conti itself packaged with 11 less glamorous bottles had resulted in serious marketing problems in the early 1990s, thanks to speculation by Japanese and European investors.

From the 1989 vintage, adjustments were made to price individual wines closer to their market value. The 1990 Romanée-Conti was released at a record $US900 a bottle.

See also LEROY.

Mansson, P.-H., 'Behind the breakup at Domaine de la Romanée-Conti', *Wine Spectator* (15 Feb. 1993) 20–7.
Olney, R., *Romanée-Conti* (Paris, 1991).

DOMÄNE is the German word for domaine but has the additional significance among the wine estates of GERMANY of distinguishing those in the hands of aristocratic families, which may be described as a Domänenweingut, or those in the hands of the state, which may be described as a Weinbaudomäne. Many of the former are members of the VDP organization of family-run estates, and many of the latter have some quasi-academic role, whether in teaching or research. If the word Domäne appears on a wine label, the wine should have been produced entirely on the estate.

Don José Ignacio, the most famous **Domecq**, known as 'The Nose' for his sherry tasting skills.

DOMECQ, JEREZ-based, famous for its SHERRY and a pioneer of Spanish BRANDY. The firm's origins date back to the 1730s, when farmer Patrick Murphy came to Spain from Ireland and teamed up with Juan Haurie to manage vineyards. When Murphy died in 1762, Haurie took over the estates, by now well established in the finest sherry vineyards of Macharnudo and Carrascal. The company's rise to fame and fortune started in the early 19th century when the firm of Ruskin, Telford and Domecq dominated the British sherry trade. Ruskin's son John preferred to write on art and architecture and it was left to another partner, Pedro Domecq Lembaye (a relative of the Haurie family which had owned the firm since 1791), to develop the business.

In 1816 Pedro Domecq returned to Jerez. He quarrelled with the Haurie family, bought the business, and renamed it after himself. When he died in 1839 he was succeeded by his brother Juan Pedro, who bought the Palacio de Aladro, which remained in the family for more than a century.

Juan Pedro died childless in 1869 and left the firm to his adopted son, also called Juan Pedro. A relative, Pedro Domecq Lustau, who was born near Cognac, was responsible for pioneering the sale of 'Brandy de Jerez'. The family had been distilling it in small quantities for some time but it was Pedro Domecq who launched the Fundador brand in 1874, five years before the arrival of the PHYLLOXERA louse interrupted the supply of cognac in the Charentes and gave the Jerezanos a chance to supply world markets with their brandy. Until recently Fundador was the biggest single brand of Spanish brandy, and it remains synonymous with the type in Anglo-Saxon eyes.

The Domecqs also pioneered the production of Spanish-style brandy in Latin America. Indeed the Presidente brand, distilled in MEXICO, is one of the world's largest selling spirits, with sales of more than 4 million cases a year. Domecq sells a total of about 7 million cases of wines and spirits in Mexico each year, which presumably helped to offset the impact of the sherry slump of the early 1980s.

Domecq owns about 1,000 ha/2,500 acres of vineyards in Jerez Superior. Its best-known sherry brands are the FINO La Ina and the Double Century range. Domecq controls the sherry firms of Blazquez and de la Riva.

The firm continued in family ownership until 1994, when it became part of Allied-Domecq. N.F. & S.A.

DOMESTIC WINE PRODUCTION. See HOME WINE-MAKING.

DOMINA is a modern red vine CROSSING that has had a certain success in Germany's cooler sites such as the Ahr and Franken so that there were a total of 65 ha/160 acres planted by 1990. Its parents are Portugieser × Spätburgunder (Pinot Noir) and it combines the productivity of the first with the ripeness, tannins, and colour of the second but not its finesse and fruit.

DOMITIAN, Roman emperor (AD 81–96) who, in the words of the eulogy by the contemporary poet Statius (*Silvae* 4. 3. 11–12), restored 'to chaste Ceres the acres which had so long been denied her and lands made sober'. By a famous edict, possibly from AD 92, Domitian banned the planting of new vineyards in Italy and ordered the destruction of at least half of the vineyards in the provinces (Suetonius, *Domitian* 7). He may also have sought to ban the planting within cities of small vineyards, of the sort which have been found at POMPEII. His purpose was not, as some have supposed, an attempt to protect the price of Italian wine at a time of general over-production, but a heavy-handed attempt to divert investment into the production of cereals, the supply of which was a perennial problem for the large cities of the Roman empire. There was no way that Domitian could enforce such a ban and, following the protests which we know came from Asia, he did not persist with the measure. Hence the much later efforts of the Emperor Probus (AD 276–282) to encourage the planting of vineyards should not be taken as a sign that the ban lasted for centuries, as has often been thought. J.J.P.

DOM PÉRIGNON. See **Pérignon, Dom**.

DONNAZ, red wine based on NEBBIOLO grapes made in Italy's Valle d'AOSTA.

DOP, meaning 'drink' in Afrikaans, gave its name to the notorious 'dop system' in SOUTH AFRICA of giving wine to Cape Coloured vineyard workers partly in lieu of wages. The wine was usually inferior, unstabilized, and rough and was given daily, and often several times daily, beginning at dawn. The custom was much criticized by anti-apartheid campaigners as the means by which white landowners obtained cheap labour from an under-educated Coloured community ravaged by rampant alcoholism. (As a result, the Afrikaans language is particularly rich in expressions of intemperance and drunkenness: more than 150 words and phrases.) Since the mid 1980s the dop system has been officially discouraged. Most Cape growers had abandoned the practice by the mid 1990s. J.P.

Opperman, D. J., *et al.*, *Spirit of the Vine* (Cape Town, 1968).

DORADILLO, white grape variety, probably of Spanish origin, but known today only in AUSTRALIA. It produces handsome quantities of entirely unremarkable wine more suitable for DISTILLATION or basic FORTIFIED wines than for bottling as a table wine. In the early 1990s there were still about 850 ha/2,100 acres of Doradillo planted, mainly in the hot, irrigated RIVERLAND of South Australia. In its time it has erroneously been called Blanquette and considered identical to the JAEN of Spain.

DORDOGNE, river in SOUTH WEST FRANCE which rises on the Massif Central south west of Clermont-Ferrand, flows through the Corrèze *département* (whence the merchants of LIBOURNE came), flows through BERGERAC and related appellations, and in to form the more northerly of the two 'seas' referred to in the name of ENTRE-DEUX-MERS, with ST-ÉMILION, POMEROL, FRONSAC, and finally BOURG on its right bank. VIN DE PAYS de la Dordogne, typically a dry white wine made from Bordeaux grape varieties, may come from anywhere within the *département* named Dordogne, of which Périgord is the principal town.

DORMANCY, sleep, the normal state of vines in winter. This period nominally starts with autumn LEAF FALL, although buds are in a state of so-called organic dormancy from VERAISON onwards. The period of dormancy ends with BUDBREAK in the spring. Pruning is carried out when the vines are dormant, and buds and cuttings taken from the vines at this time are used in PROPAGATION. Tests on vines in winter show they are literally asleep or dormant, with minimal metabolic activity. R.E.S.

DORNFELDER is increasingly appreciated as Germany's most successful red wine vine crossing, bred in 1956 by August Herold, who had unwisely already assigned his name to one of its parents, the lesser HEROLDREBE, and so Dornfelder owes its name to the 19th century founder of the Württemberg viticultural school. A HELFENSTEINER × Heroldrebe cross, Dornfelder incorporates every important red wine vine grown in Germany somewhere in its genealogy and happily seems to have inherited many more of their good points than their bad.

The wine is notable for its depth of colour (useful in a country where pigments are at a premium), its good acidity but attractively aromatic fruit, and, in some cases, its ability to benefit from BARRIQUE ageing and even to develop in bottle. It can often provide more drinking pleasure than a Spätburgunder, perhaps because its producer's ambitions are more limited. In the vineyard, the vine is easier to grow than Spätburgunder (Pinot Noir), has much better resistance to rot than Portugieser, stronger stalks than Trollinger, better ripeness levels than either, earlier ripening than Limberger (Blaufränkisch), and a yield that can easily reach 120 hl/ha (6.8 tons/acre) (although quality-conscious producers are careful to restrict productivity). It is hardly surprising that it continues to gain ground in most German wine regions, especially Rheinhessen and Pfalz, where results are particularly appetizing. Germany's total plantings rose steadily throughout the 1980s to reach a total of more than 1,200 ha/2,960 acres by the end of the decade.

The best bottles of this variety, usually sold as a varietal rather than blended, demonstrate the point of VINE BREEDING.

DOSAGE, the final addition to a SPARKLING WINE which may top up a bottle in the case of champagne method wines, and also determines the sweetness, or RESIDUAL SUGAR, of the finished wine. In French this addition is sometimes called the *liqueur d'expédition* and, in champagne method wines, usually comprises a mixture of wine and sugar syrup. Champagne is naturally so high in ACIDITY that even wines with relatively high RESIDUAL SUGAR can taste bone dry. BOTTLE AGE or extended AUTOLYSIS are excellent substitutes for dosage, however, and, in general, the older the wine, the lower the necessary dosage to produce a BALANCED wine, and vice versa. Some champagnes are made with no, or zero, dosage. The table gives the legal limits within Europe.

Description	g/l additional sugar
Extra brut	less than 6
Brut	less than 15
Extra dry	12–20
Sec	17–35
Demi-sec	33–50
Rich or doux	more than 50

DOUBLE PRUNING, a viticultural technique in which the vines are pruned twice, which alters the timing of vine development (see PHENOLOGY). Double pruning can be carried out in two ways: to delay BUDBREAK and hence reduce frost hazard in cool climates: or to delay harvest and hence potentially increase wine quality in hot regions.

Since early winter pruning encourages earlier budbreak, frost injury risks to young shoots can be increased. Pruning lightly in the beginning of the winter delays budbreak of basal buds; a second or double pruning can be done after the danger of frost is passed.

The related technique of double pruning in hot climates for quality improvement was developed by R. E. Smart and P. R. Dry at ROSEWORTHY in South Australia in the 1970s to delay fruit ripening from the heat of midsummer to cooler conditions of autumn. The vines are pruned normally in winter and then again in early summer just after flowering. Yields are reduced by this process but wine quality is much improved. The process has limited commercial application.

R.E.S.

Baskets of grapes destined for port in the **Douro** valley.

DOURO, river which rises, as the **Duero**, in the hills far upstream of RIBERA DEL DUERO and flows for more than half its course in Spain until it turns south to form the frontier with PORTUGAL before turning west towards the Atlantic coast to cut a cleft through the hard, granite mountains of northern Portugal (see maps on pp. 750 and 907). The Douro valley is most famous as the source of the famous fortified wine port, although the Douro DOC is increasingly well known for the production of unfortified table wine.

The Douro valley was demarcated in 1756, making it one of the oldest delimited wine regions in the world (see DELIMITATION and PORTUGAL, history). The boundaries have since been modified but the irregular outline corresponds closely with an outcrop of pre-Cambrian SCHIST. Hemmed in by GRANITE, this schist runs either side of the river for nearly 100 km/63 miles from the Spanish frontier in the east to the village of Barqueiros in the west. For over two centuries the demarcation applied only to the fortified wine port, but in 1979 it was extended to cover table wine as well. Depending on the year, around half the Douro's total wine production is not FORTIFIED but fermented out to make table wine, the proportion of the crop used to make port being increased only in years when grapes are in short supply.

Under a complicated classification system, individual port vineyards are graded A to F (for more detail, see PORT). Properties in the Baixo Corgo (the most westerly and therefore the coolest and wettest subregion) as well as those in the hills close to the Douro's 650-m boundary are considered to be less suitable for making port than vineyards located in the heart of the region. Outlying farms, or QUINTAS, therefore qualify for lower grades. Under the system of licences handed out annually by the Casa do Douro, the organization representing the Douro vine-growers, they are not permitted to fortify as much of their must to make port as those whose vineyards qualify for higher grades.

Table wines are not new to the Douro. Until the early part of the 18th century, most of the wine exported from the

Gamay grapes arrive at the **Fleurie** co-operative, one of the most admired in France, in **Beaujolais**, an exceptional example of a one-grape wine region.

region was fermented dry and shipped without the addition of spirit. At that time, however, the quality of many of these wines was so poor that merchants added BRANDY in order to stabilize them during shipment. Port, the sweet, fortified wine that we know today, only evolved at the end of the 17th century, when shippers learned to arrest the fermentation leaving RESIDUAL SUGAR. Since then, table wines were for long largely neglected in favour of port, but Douro table wines have slowly been receiving more attention ever since the 1950s, when port shippers FERREIRA launched Barca Velha, a red wine made from grapes grown in the upper reaches of the Douro which has established itself as one of Portugal's finest and most admired wines. Early experiments with making other Douro table wines were often hampered by a lack of technology, but an increasing number of wine-makers are now investing in the skills and equipment that are necessary to make table wine in the extreme Douro climate.

The grape varieties used in making Douro table wines are similar to those used to produce port, more than 90 different grapes being permitted, of which TOURIGA NACIONAL and Tinta Roriz (TEMPRANILLO) are widely accepted as the best for red wines, many of which share the ripe, spicy, tannic character of a young ruby port. Gouveio (thought to be VERDELHO), Malvasia Fina, and Viosinho are the favoured white grapes although in the mid 1990s most Douro white table wines still suffered from poor handling. R.J.M.

Douro bake, traditional expression for the character imparted to wines, especially PORT, matured in the hot, dry climate of the DOURO valley (rather than the much cooler, damper atmosphere of VILA NOVA DE GAIA, where port has traditionally been matured by the shippers). Some wines matured in the Douro seem to develop faster, losing colour, browning, and sometimes acquiring a slightly sweet, caramelized flavour—although poor and often unhygienic storage conditions often have a greater impact on wine quality than the climate, and many reputable shippers successfully age large stocks of port in the Douro. R.J.M.

doux, French for sweet, may be applied to still wines with a RESIDUAL SUGAR of 20–30 g/l (and therefore less sweet than MOELLEUX and LIQUOREUX). See SWEETNESS AND DOSAGE.

Dow, Graham, Warre, important port shipper's. See SYMINGTONS.

downy mildew, one of the most economically significant FUNGAL DISEASES affecting vines, often called peronospera in parts of Europe. It is a particular problem in regions with warm, humid summers such as many wine regions in northern Europe. The disease is caused by the organism *Plasmopara viticola*. This fungus is indigenous to eastern North America, and so some species of native AMERICAN VINES such as *Vitis cordifolia*, *Vitis rupestris*, and *Vitis rotundifolia* are relatively resistant. Commercially important varieties of VITIS VINIFERA, however, are highly susceptible.

The fungus caused havoc in the vineyards of Europe when it was accidentally introduced before 1878, probably on American vines imported as grafting stock to combat PHYLLOXERA. By 1882 the disease had spread to all of France. The famous BORDEAUX MIXTURE was first used as a preventive spray to control this disease.

The disease is now widespread around the world, but a few areas with low spring and summer rainfall are free of it. These include Afghanistan, California, northern Chile, Egypt, and Western Australia. Downy mildew attacks all green parts of the vine and young leaves are particularly susceptible. When severely affected, leaves will drop off. The loss of leaves reduces PHOTOSYNTHESIS and thus causes delays in fruit ripening and, typically, levels of fruit SUGARS, vine reserves of CARBOHYDRATES, and ANTHOCYANS are depressed. BUDBREAK and early shoot growth can be delayed the following spring. Severe infections result in pale, puny reds and weak whites. In regions with severe winter cold, the loss of leaf area reduces the ability of the vine to withstand this stress, since the vines are low in reserves of carbohydrates.

The symptoms of the disease are described quite aptly by the name. Leaves show patches of dense, white cottony growth on the undersurface. This is the sporulating stage of the fungus. The earliest stage of the fungus is the so-called 'oil spot', easily seen on the upper leaf surface when it is held up against the light. PETIOLES, TENDRILS, young inflorescences, and developing berries are also affected. The fungus spends the winter in fallen leaves and can sometimes survive in the buds. Spores germinate in the spring when temperatures reach 11 °C/52 °F and they are spread to the vine by rainsplash from the soil. Spores are further spread and germinated with high humidity (95 to 100 per cent relative humidity), warm temperatures (18 to 22 °C), and moisture. The most severe epidemics of the disease occur with frequent rainstorms and warm weather. The low yields of the French vintages of 1886, 1910, 1915, 1930, 1932, 1948, 1957, and 1969, all of them produced after wet growing seasons, are probably due to downy mildew.

The sources of downy mildew infection cannot be effectively removed from the vineyard. There are two principal protection approaches. The first and most common is to use protective sprays which are often based on COPPER. However, the protection lasts for only 10 days or so, especially when the shoots are growing rapidly in early spring. Curative fungicides which act against established infections became available in the early 1990s. An alternative approach to the control of this disease is to breed resistant varieties (see NEW VARIETIES). European vine breeders, especially at GEISENHEIM and GEILWEILERHOF in Germany, have been particularly successful in developing varieties which require no, or less, spraying against downy mildew, with native American vines contributing the resistant genes. Increased environmental

Mustard, seen here in flower in early springtime, forms part of a deliberate **cover crop** between vine rows in **Carneros**, northern California. The result is soil better equipped to retain California's precious **rainfall**.

awareness may encourage their use, but there is some consumer resistance to new varieties. R.E.S.

Emmett, R. W., Harris, A. R., Taylor, R. H., and McGechan, J. K., 'Grape diseases and vineyard protection', in B. G. Coombe and P. R. Dry (eds.), *Viticulture, ii: Practices* (Adelaide, 1992).
Galet, P., *Précis de viticulture* (Montpellier, 1983).
Pearson, R. C., and Goheen, A. C., *Compendium of Grape Diseases* (St Paul, Minn., 1988).

DRAINAGE, free movement of water through the SOIL profile or across the land surface; or alternatively, the removal of surplus water by artificial means. The importance of good soil drainage for viticulture and wine quality cannot be overstated. For a detailed discussion, see Seguin. See also TERROIR and SOIL AND WINE QUALITY.

All good vineyard soils are well drained, whether naturally or by artificial drainage. Any prolonged waterlogging after the start of spring growth is lethal to vine roots. Even marginal waterlogging can be deleterious, by causing restriction of root and soil microbial activity, and consequent starvation of the vine for nutrients and root-produced growth substances (see CYTOKININ). Soils that are cold and wet at the time of FLOWERING are a major factor in poor berry setting, or COULURE.

Waterlogging confined to the SUBSOIL can still be a serious disadvantage, through killing or inactivation of the deeper roots. This can result in a vine with only a shallow effective root system, readily subject both to later DROUGHT after the surface moisture has evaporated or been used, and to excessive water uptake following rains during ripening. Seguin argues that such irregularity in the supply of SOIL WATER can be seriously detrimental to wine quality. Subsoils that are regularly waterlogged can be identified by their bleached, white or grey colour (see SOIL COLOUR). Well-drained subsoils, by contrast, are usually yellow to reddish. Mottled subsoils indicate intermittent waterlogging, and a likely need for artificial drainage.

As a broad rule light-textured and stony soils drain freely, while tight or heavy clay soils (see SOIL TEXTURE) have restricted drainage. Subsoils composed of the latter type can result in water-tables 'perched' on top of them. These develop most commonly on gradients, where seepage of water down the slope through the surface soil is interrupted by barriers of rock, or of clay reaching or approaching the surface.

However, even heavy soils and subsoils can drain adequately if they have good crumb structure (see SOIL STRUCTURE). This depends on their chemical nature, including sufficient contents of CALCIUM and, in the upper layers, ORGANIC MATTER. Unstructured soils can easily pack down to form impermeable hardpans below the surface when subjected to trampling or wheeled traffic. Some sandy soils have natural subsurface hardpans which need to be broken up before vine planting.

Several other management factors can influence soil drainage. Deeply tap-rooted green manuring or COVER CROPS, such as mustard or lupins, can help to create and maintain vertical channels which allow water to infiltrate freely into the deeper soil layers. The maintenance of an organic surface MULCH, whether applied or originating naturally from cover crops, attains the same effect through encouraging earthworm activity. These useful creatures also help to distribute surface organic matter and nutrients through the soil profile. Finally, the application of LIME or gypsum can help on some acid soils, by improving their crumb structure and permeability. This should be considered part of SOIL PREPARATION before vine planting, because both lime and gypsum are largely immobile in the soil, and therefore need to be incorporated thoroughly and to depth.

Artificial drainage, where required, can be of several types according to situation and need. Webber and Jones describe them in detail.

All forms of artificial soil drainage are expensive, but, on otherwise valuable land for producing high-value grapes, they can be essential. Drainage did, after all, transform the Médoc from a marsh to one of the world's most admired wine regions (see BORDEAUX, history). J.G.

Seguin, G., ' "Terroirs" and pedology of wine growing', *Experientia*, 42 (1986), 861–72.
Webber, R. T. J., and Jones, L. D., 'Drainage and soil salinity', in B. G. Coombe and P. R. Dry (eds.), *Viticulture, ii: Practices* (Adelaide, 1992).

DRAINING (*égouttage* in French). In WHITE WINE- MAKING the operation usually takes place just after CRUSHING. Any juice run off without pressing is called drainings. The FREE-RUN juice is drained off the grape skins in a **draining tank** or **draining vat**, many of which incorporate special design features to assist the separation of liquids from solids. Similarly, in red wine fermentation, the red wine run off the skins may also be called drainings.

DRC, famous initials in the world of fine wine, standing for the DOMAINE DE LA ROMANÉE-CONTI.

DRIED GRAPE WINES, varied category of generally intense, complex wines made from partially raisined grapes. The production technique, involving either leaving the grapes to raisin on the vine or picking and then drying them (on mats of straw or reed, racks of bamboo, or strung in bunches under the rafters), is associated with most of the celebrated wines of antiquity. This early CONCENTRATION technique continues one of the oldest traditions in the gastronomic world.

In the classical world this wine-making style may well have evolved because of problems of wine conservation, particularly for wines traded and consumed outside their area of origin, semi-dried grapes naturally resulting in sweeter, stronger and therefore more stable wines. (BOTRYTIZED wines and the technique of FORTIFICATION were developed many centuries later.) The dried grape tradition has proved particularly resilient close to its origins, notably in Italy.

Dried grape wines: Drying racks of healthy grapes for Amarone and Recioto at Masi' property near Negrar in the Veneto.

Ancient history

The technique of twisting the stems of grape bunches to deprive them of sap, and leaving them to raisin on the vine, may have originated in CRETE, but vinification techniques for dried grapes were perfected in Ancient GREECE. The Ancient Greeks also learned from other inhabitants of the eastern Mediterranean, particularly the Hittites of Anatolia (see ASIA MINOR). The first description of how to make wine from dried grapes is provided by HESIOD, in the 8th century BC. His *Works and Days* describes how grapes should be dried in the sun 'for ten days and nights' and then in the shade for a further five, before fermenting the wine in jars.

Such methods were responsible for the famous wines of the islands (Chios, Lesbos, and Thasos) which were so highly prized by Homer and succeeding writers. These wines were often noted as being at their best after many years' maturation, when they had 'lost their teeth': clear evidence of the longevity which only dried grape wines could provide before the invention of stoppered bottles. Sealed AMPHORAE may have been relatively airtight containers but long journeys in Mediterranean heat demanded exceptionally robust wines.

Coincidental with the rise of the Greek city states was the emergence of the most adventurous traders of the Mediterranean, those of PHOENICIA. They exported the wines of Lebanon (and the wine-making practices of CANAAN) along the littorals of North Africa and to Spain, Sardinia, and Sicily. One of their colonies was CARTHAGE, founded in 814 BC, where in about 500 BC Mago wrote his seminal work on agriculture, now known only in the extensive quotations which survive in the works of succeeding classical authors, notably the Roman COLUMELLA. Redding quotes Mago in the following passage which summarizes the Graeco-Roman understanding of dried grape vinification:

> Let the bunches of grapes quite ripe, and scorched or shrivelled in the sun, when the bad and faulty ones are picked out, be spread upon a frame resting on stakes or forks and covered with a layer of reeds. Place them in the sun but protect them from the dew at night. When they are dry (sufficiently shrivelled) pluck the grapes from the stalks, throw them into a cask and make the first must. If they have been well drained, put them, at the end of six days, into a vessel, and press them for the first wine. A second time let them be pounded (or trodden) and pressed, adding cold must to the pressing. This second wine is to be placed in a pitched vessel, lest it become sour. After it has remained twenty or thirty days, and fermented, rack it into another vessel and stopping it close immediately, cover it with a skin.

Other writers in Ancient ROME such as CATO, PLINY, HORACE, and VIRGIL add other details (such as storing these wines in the rafters, as with modern Tuscan VIN SANTO), but in general repeat the principles laid down by their Mediterranean forebears.

The Romans, like the Greeks, planted vineyards wherever they went—in Spain, France, Germany, and central Europe, perhaps even in England. Only in the latter would the climate have been too austere for the production of *passum* (PASSITO) wines; elsewhere the practice became embedded in the complex strata of vinicultural history, a rich seam of vinous tradition to be mined in later centuries, after the long upheavals which followed the collapse of the Roman empire.

Evolution since the Middle Ages

Italy The *vinum reticum* of Verona praised by Pliny was presumably the ancestor of today's RECIOTO and AMARONE. It was relatively common for wines to be made from grapes dried on the vine cut off from the flow of sap by having their stems twisted, or *torcolato* (the name of a modern VENETO white Recioto made by Maculan from partially dried, though not in fact twisted, VESPAIOLO grapes). The dried grape tradition was presumably enhanced in 1204 when Venice conquered Crete, the stronghold of this classical heritage. The result seems to have been a revival of dried grape wine-making throughout the growing Venetian empire, not just in the Veneto but on the islands and coast of what is now SLOVENIA and CROATIA. Hugh Johnson lists Grk, Vugava, Dingač, Postup, and Prošek as examples of these 'Greek' wines.

In early 14th century PIEDMONT, such wines were in great demand and are mentioned again in the mid 17th century, but the tradition survives only as a curiosity today.

In TUSCANY, however, VIN SANTO survives as an apparently unbroken tradition, practised by most of the best estates. Versions exist in other parts of Italy, notably in TRENTINO. Other survivals include the VERDUZZO of Ramandolo, the generally overrated PICOLIT of FRIULI, the remarkable Rosenmuskateller of TRENTINO-ALTO ADIGE, SFORZATO or SFURSAT of VALTELLINA, ALBANA passito from Romagna, and Sagrantino passito from UMBRIA. In the south and islands examples of this renascent tradition are too numerous to mention in detail but include a range of wines based on raisined MOSCATO, ALEATICO, MALVASIA, and Nasco grapes, not to mention Vecchio Samperi, the rare unfortified wine in the style of MARSALA from de Bartoli.

Elsewhere It is clear from REDDING that dried grape wines were much more common in early 19th century France than today. He mentions the VIN DE PAILLE of Alsace, two types from Argentac in the Corrèze (way up river of modern BERGERAC), one of them slightly sparkling, and what sounds like a magnificent example from the Sciacarello grape made at Sartène in CORSICA. He also makes clear that Muscat de RIVESALTES was then a true raisin wine, often the result of twisting grape stems on the vine, and not, as now, a fortified blend. In contemporary France the tradition survives only in the vins de paille of HERMITAGE and the JURA, made as curiosities by two or three producers in each region, in quantities so tiny that they scarcely ever reach the market.

In Spain the classical traditions continued in muted form through the Muslim occupation and were revived thereafter. The most notable surviving derivatives are the Andalucian specialities SHERRY, MONTILLA, and MALAGA, whose richer styles have always been made with semi-dried grapes, but these are not pure dried grape wines because most are now fortified. Elsewhere in Spain the tradition is almost extinct. In RIOJA there is evidence of an ancient local habit of using dried Moscatel or Malvasia grapes to produce wines which were variously described as *supurado, tostadillo, vino de paja*, or *vino dorado* (suppurating, toasted, straw wine, golden wine).

Surprisingly few dried grape wines can be found in modern Greece. The rich wines of Samos date from the replanting of the island's vineyards in the 16th century but those of Santorini (Thíra of the ancients) are debased descendants of the classical prototypes, as is the now fortified COMMANDARIA of Cyprus.

There are records of straw wine being made in FRANKEN in Germany; a rich red dried grape wine just over the border in Switzerland from Italy's VALTELLINA; a 'green' wine of remarkable strength produced near Cotnar on the borders of Moldova and Romania (see COTNARI); and of course the rather special case of TOKAY in Hungary. The latter survives; most of the others have vanished. The only notable additions to the once splendid roll-call of wines from the old Austro-Hungarian empire are a few straw wines and reed wines from AUSTRIA.

Redding mentions Shahoni, the 'royal grape' of the province of Cashbin in Persia, claiming that 'the grapes are kept over the winter, and remain on the vine a good deal of the time in linen bags', and also lists from Argentina a 'sweet wine, resembling Malaga, made at Mendoza at the foot of the Andes, on their eastern side' and the famous CONSTANTIA from South Africa, now being revived. In modern times there have also been tentative experiments with dried grape wines in California and South Australia.

Modern production techniques

Grapes with maximum EXTRACT and SUGARS are required, which normally entails restricting YIELDS. Such grapes may be picked either before, at, or after full RIPENESS. Twisting the stalk was once practised in the Veneto but most growers now prefer to dry their grapes off the vine.

Those who pick slightly before full maturation claim there is less risk of ROT, thicker skins, enhanced resistance during drying, and higher acidity, all of which favour aroma, freshness, balance, and longevity—and concentrate the grapes which remain on the vine.

Only the ripest, healthiest grapes are generally picked, which today means a pre-selection by experienced pickers (although see RECIOTO). Healthy grapes are vital since any incipient mould or rot soon spreads during the drying process. Skins must remain intact, to which end the grapes may well be laid in small trays for transport to the winery. The bunches should be *spargolo*, loose rather than compact, so that air circulates around the individual berries during the all-important drying process.

Sun drying is still practised in places such as the Sicilian island of PANTELLERIA off Tunisia, and the Greek island of Santorini. It can be three or four times as fast as drying under cover, but this can result in excessive colour, caramelized flavours, and loss of aroma, bypassing some of the microbiological transformations which are the essence of fine dried grape wine. For the same reason, purists reject the use of drying ovens.

Most grape drying for commercial purposes happens in a winery loft, where windows may be opened to let in plenty of air (essential against the development of rot and mould). Bunches are hung up vertically (on hooks, or on long strings), or laid out horizontally on neutral, bone dry materials. Straw is rarely used because of its attractions for mice, while oak slats can be expensive. Wire mesh, nylon nets, and fruit boxes are 20th century developments; cane and rush mats and bamboo racks remain popular in much of Italy.

The duration of the drying process is dictated by the grape variety, the type of wine required, and microclimatic conditions during drying. Sugar-rich Greek grape varieties such as Muscat, Aleatico, and Malvasia require less time than more northern varieties. Three weeks may suffice for a Muscat whereas a Veronese variety such as GARGANEGA for a white Recioto or CORVINA for a red Recioto or Amarone will need three to four months. Ideal conditions include considerable currents of dry air, and humidity is such a problem in some valley sites that drying facilities are being moved to higher altitudes. Excessive heat is generally regarded as negative, as is excessive cold.

The main effect of drying grapes is loss of water and the consequent concentration of sugars. The relationship between water loss and sugar gain is relatively direct so that a water loss of a third from grapes picked at 12° BAUMÉ would result in a wine of 16 per cent alcohol (if all the sugar were fermented out). Depending on the wine style desired, the loss of grape weight by evaporation varies between 10 and 60 per cent, with the norm for a PASSITO wine being somewhere in the region of 35 to 40 per cent, so the potential alcohol is raised by just over a third.

Other components behave less predictably. The TOTAL ACIDITY in grapes undergoing a 40 per cent dehydration rises not by 40 per cent but by around 25 per cent. These and other organic substances undergo various transformations, and there may be development of certain aromas and loss of others in the process. The longer the drying period, the greater the biological change of organic substances and resultant wine quality.

NOBLE ROT may develop on the grapes during dehydration but it is not desired by most practitioners, particularly those making the drier styles of dried grape wines such as AMARONE. A further problem is insect infestation, particularly of bees, wasps, and hornets.

Crushing or pressing should ideally be as gentle as possible. Gravity, but certainly not CENTRIFUGATION, may be used to clarify white must, while in the case of red wines, stems may be totally or only partially removed.

The must of raisined grapes is so concentrated that it slows FERMENTATION, an effect accentuated in cooler climates, especially where the long drying period may mean that the grapes are crushed in midwinter and the ambient temperature is naturally low. In Italy, fermentation may therefore safely take place in wood, and may need to be started by heating and/or adding specially cultured local YEAST. In traditional areas the right yeasts have been in the atmosphere for centuries. *Saccharomyces uvarum* begins the job in Valpolicella, according to Masi, while *Saccharomyces bayanus* is able to work at higher temperatures and at the ALCOHOLIC STRENGTH of 16 per cent or more that is necessary for many Amarones.

Some producers allow the fermentation to stop and start for months or even, as in the case of Guiseppe Quintarelli, two to three years, and allow Nature to decide how sweet the final wine will be. Most, however, use RACKING and, increasingly, REFRIGERATION to stop fermentation.

The wine is then generally racked off its LEES and the lees sometimes used to enrich normal VALPOLICELLA with the process called RIPASSO. In CHIANTI, dried grapes may be added intact to a finished wine to achieve a similar effect, the so-called GOVERNO process.

Dried grape wines tend to be particularly high in VOLATILE ACIDS, a direct result of high sugar levels (accentuated if any BOTRYTIZED grapes have been included). The ACETIC ACID of such a wine may well exceed legal levels, sometimes entailing unacceptably high SULPHUR DIOXIDE additions. Many argue that high levels of volatile acidity are essential to the quality of such wines, and some maintain that false passito wines can be exposed precisely by improbably low levels of acetic acid.

Dried grape wines may be divided into two categories: those in which the fresh primary AROMAS are retained and those in which primary aromas are sacrificed to the development of a more complex BOUQUET. The former include most wines based on aromatic varieties such as Muscat, Brachetto, Aleatico, and Riesling, as well as sweet whites where the emphasis is on fruit, such as Recioto di Soave. These are subjected as far as possible to REDUCTIVE wine-making techniques in which MACERATION, AGEING, and exposure to oxygen are minimized. (Although, since the grapes are subject to OXIDATION during the drying stage, no dried grape wine can be purely reductive.)

The latter include vin de paille, Vin Santo, Amarone, and Recioto della Valpolicella of the traditional type. They are treated oxidatively, the aim being to incorporate in the final organoleptic experience an evolution of aromas due in some measure to exposure to oxygen. They are, typically, the result of prolonged maceration, deliberately frequent racking, and ageing for years in large, old barrels. Strong, dry Valpolicella Amarone is a notable example, as is Vin Santo with the RANCIO character encouraged by traditionalists. Since the 1980s there has been a movement away from such classic styles, however.

In the early 1990s an accelerated Euro-technique was authorized experimentally by EUROPEAN UNION authorities, involving drying bunches in a single layer at between 30 and 35 °C (86–95 °F) under a current of warm air. Early results suggested an increase of one per cent POTENTIAL ALCOHOL in the first 12 hours. S.P.D.L. & N.J.B.

Johnson, H., *The Story of Wine* (London and New York, 1989).
Loftus, S., and Belfrage, N., *Dried Grapes* (Southwold, 1992).
Masi, Grupo Technico, *Amarone and Recioto; Historical and Technical Notes* (private communication, Verona, 1990).
Redding, C., *The History and Description of Modern Wines* (London, 1833).
Tachis, G., *Il Libro del Vin Santo* (Florence, 1988).

DRINKING VESSELS. Before the development of glass-making enabled the production of GLASSES (the most common modern wine drinking vessels), a wide variety of drinking vessels were used for wine. Pottery cups were commonplace, and goblets made of a variety of metals, but even earlier than this wine was sucked through a reed, either from a bowl such as a CRATER, or possibly from a hollowed-out gourd or similar vessel provided by Nature. See Ancient EGYPT, INDIA, and ARMENIA.

Modern history

The majority of drinking vessels are glass but despite its use for thousands of years, glass has not always been available. In such times the principal alternative has been silver. There are other occasions when glass has been too fragile for a particular environment. Clear drinking glasses were an expensive commodity beyond the means of most people in the 18th century, but then so was wine—at least in countries where wine was not produced.

Silver was most commonly used for wine drinking vessels until the Venetian glass industry burgeoned in the 16th century. Although glass became preferred, trade in it was limited and, but for exceptional grand occasions and settings, in each country wine was usually consumed from indigenous vessels.

The social history of drinking and eating habits and customs has inevitably played an important part in the history of drinking vessels. Today a wine connoisseur will buy a specific shape and size of glass for each different wine type, a custom which has obtained for over a century. But FASHIONS change and a plain tall narrow glass is now preferred for champagne over the cut saucer-bowl version that was in vogue earlier in the century. The first introduction of suites of glasses in limited sizes was in the late 18th century but the designated use for each size can only be conjectural. Glass collectors (see ANTIQUES) give names to differing forms of 18th century drinking glasses but not all these names were applied at the time of manufacture. Tall, narrow glasses are called flutes and they may be decorated with hops, apples, or grapes, and sometimes all three, which clearly indicates that they were not restricted to wine consumption. Very narrow flutes are called ratafias—after RATAFIA, a concoction popular in the mid 18th century.

There is no specific division between a wine glass and a goblet except that the latter is larger, but a very small glass is called a cordial. The term 'mead glass' for a cup-bowl goblet is a modern and meaningless one.

It is often observed that many 18th century drinking glasses are small, but they have to be considered in context. They were not placed on the table for the diner to quaff at will. Rather, they were brought by the footman to each diner when requested and were taken after each draught to await another request. It may be speculated that the larger goblets were used by gentlemen after the servants had been dismissed towards the end of the meal.

By the mid 19th century service *à la russe* had become fashionable, with its place settings of cutlery and glasses with which a diner today would be familiar. The 'new' arrangement dispensed with the need for a footman for each diner and it was the cause of the widespread use of long sets of glasses with each diner having up to six glasses for different wines, not to mention tumblers and finger bowls.

Glass Drinking vessels in both silver and glass were made by the Romans. The glass-making craft went into decline after the collapse of the Roman empire and, although glass was made in small quantities, it was not until the Renaissance that glass-making gained a prominent place in the decorative arts in Venice. By the 16th century Venice was producing fine and elegant drinking glasses. The soda glass was almost colourless and very thin. The often-decorated baluster stems had elements of very narrow section.

Draconian attempts to prevent the secrets of glass-making from leaving VENICE were put in place in order that the city should retain its supremacy. However, a few of those with the knowledge left and small factories sprang up all over Europe in consequence. To raise revenue, the English monarch granted glass-making monopolies on payment of a fee and in 1574 Elizabeth I let a lapsed monopoly fall to Giacomo Verzelini. A few of his glasses, closely following Venetian models, sometimes dated, and usually engraved, survive. As explained under ANTIQUES, England and subsequently Britain became the dominant production centre.

In the early 17th century, wood-fired furnaces were outlawed in England, hence the setting up of glass houses in coal-producing areas—Newcastle, Stourbridge, and Bristol. As described in DECANTERS a major advance in glass technology was made in the 1670s by George Ravenscroft with the introduction of lead and flint glass and it was this which enabled British glass-makers to hold world supremacy for the ensuing hundred years. However, drinking glasses were still being made in Italy and in large numbers in what is now Germany and the Netherlands throughout the 17th century.

The earliest lead glass was frequently unstable and soon after manufacturers developed crizzling: a myriad of short cracks within the glass that gave it a milky effect. Ravenscroft soon improved the recipe and technique, enabling him to produce glasses of a rich weight and colour, quite unlike the light, pale products of Venice. The soda glass of Venice lent itself to thin and elegant shapes, often embellished with lattice designs in opaque white glass within the form or with coloured elements. The English lead glass, by contrast, was heavy and dark, capable of being drawn into bold plastic forms. Ravenscroft's early work emulated Venetian patterns—not surprisingly, as he had worked there for many years—but soon his products developed into the recognizably solid English style.

The drinking glass can be divided into three parts: the bowl, stem, and foot. Made separately, the parts were put together during the final stages of production. The bowl can take a variety of shapes, each with a name recognized in the large glass-collecting fraternity. Trumpet, ovoid, bell, and bucket are obvious shapes, but rounded funnel, ogee, cup, and pan-top are also illustrated opposite.

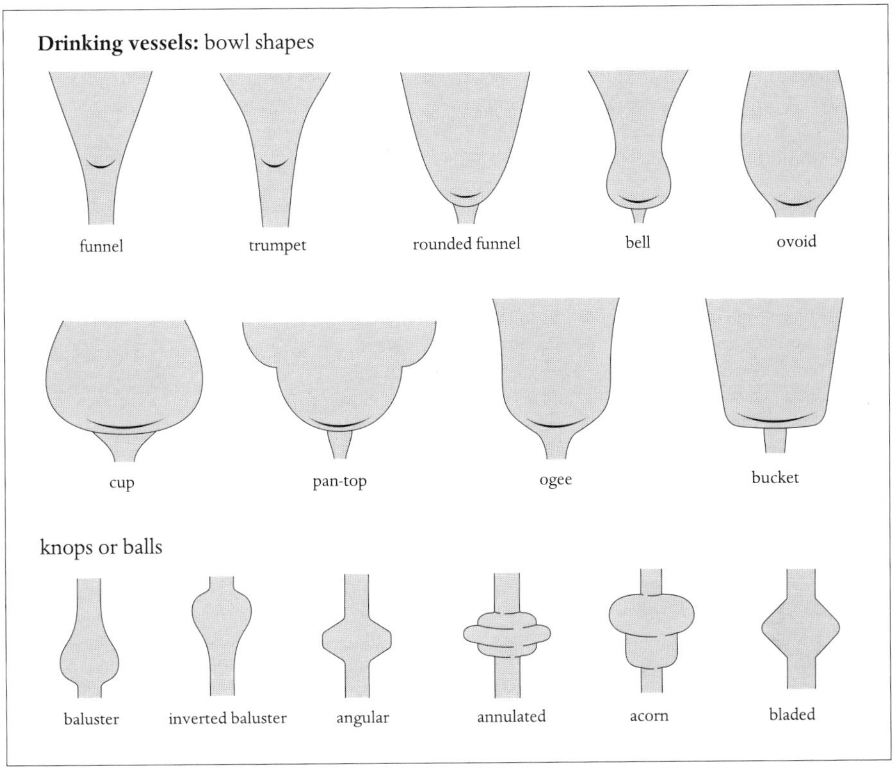

The stem of a wine glass is perhaps the element offering most opportunity for decorative treatment. The stem may be straight or with swellings called knops. The early examples were generally heavily knopped, the main element of the stem often of baluster outline but with other swellings above, or below, or both. The knops, like the bowls, have names such as acorn, bladed, baluster, annulated, and ball, all of which are more or less self-descriptive (see illustration).

Beneath the stem is the foot. Most wine glasses have a foot of a flattish conical section, some raising the stem 5 mm (0.25 in) or more away from the table, others by three times as much. Most glasses before the mid 18th century have an additional feature called a folded foot. Long before English glass became pre-eminent it was realized that if, when the foot was made, the rim was folded underneath (very rarely on top of) itself, a much sturdier glass was the result. Some glasses have a domed or tiered foot rather than a conical one.

During the 1670s and 1680s wine glasses followed the Venetian forms, some of which had changed little over 100 years. By the 1690s the particular qualities of lead-glass began to be appreciated and resulted in the manufacture of glasses of substantial weight and a solid form quite distinct from the Venetian tradition. Over the next 20 years, designs were refined to what many consider the zenith of glass-making, characterized by bold, pure, unadorned form. Many glasses were lightened by air bubbles or tears being blown within the stem and occasionally at the base of the bowl but the form remained substantial. These glasses are referred to as heavy balusters.

The heavy balusters became lighter as time progressed, partly perhaps because of taxation on the weight of glass. The bold designs became more fussy, with increased numbers of elements in the stem, and the stem itself became thinner. The heavy balusters had given way to light balusters and balustroids by the 1730s and 1740s. Some glasses had stems moulded of polygonal section; these are known as Silesian stems. During the 1740s and 1750s many glasses had stems that had inserted in them a series of small bubbles. When twisted and stretched these formed helices of air within the stem, or air twists. By this time, too, it was becoming fashionable for the stems to be straight sided and folded feet were at the end of their span.

A popular form in the 1760s was the result of twisting opaque white or coloured glass into the stem, instead of air bubbles. Opaque twist stems, rarely in colour, were made in large numbers and are highly collectable. There were numerous patterns in the twists and just occasionally a single glass with both air and opaque twists may be found.

The next phase of glass-making was the facet stem—quite simply the cutting of the stem with shield, diamond, or hexagonal facets. Traditionally air twists have been dated in the 1750s, opaque twists in the 1760s, and facet stems in the 1770s. It seems far more likely in view of the general shape and proportion of these styles that they were made more or less concurrently but, whatever the truth, it marked the final act of British supremacy in glass manufacture. Facet stems continued to be made to the end of the century, with the stems becoming shorter and the overall proportion degenerating.

During the 18th century there were forms of embellishment other than pure shape. Wheel-engraving produced fine decoration in the 1730s and 1740s, sometimes being delicate bands of flowers and scrolls around the rim, while glasses engraved with Jacobite and Williamite symbolism had their enthusiastic followers. In the 1760s the enamelled decoration of William and Mary Beilby of Newcastle enjoyed royal and other esteemed patronage while in the following decade the gilt decoration of James Giles drew its admirers, as did the stipple engraving of David Wolff.

The 19th century saw the fast decline of design, with many drinking glasses cut to match the cut decanters of the period. At this time, too, the idea of having glasses in different sizes and shapes for different drinks was becoming widespread, although this idea was not unknown in the 1780s. By the mid century glasses could be ordered in large suites with sizes from goblet to liqueur matching the decanters, claret jugs, and finger bowls. Decoration was either cut or acid etched and in a variety of patterned styles.

The 20th century saw an interest in antiques and a large quantity of glass was made, much of it in the Georgian style. For the amateur it can be difficult to distinguish between a Georgian decanter of, say, 1815 and a copy made 100 years later. Descriptions of the distinctions can be found in reference books (see below), or professional antique dealers may help. Wine glasses with green and cranberry-coloured bowls on clear stems also became popular at this time.

Silver During the 16th century and before, glass was a very highly prized commodity and wine would normally have been consumed from silver or silver gilt goblets. Early wine cups—often with a cover—were invariably heavily decorated and were considered status symbols. Many that remain are so large that their use must have been communal. Smaller cups for individual use date back to the Middle Ages but by the 1570s a standard pattern of a wide, shallow bowl on a baluster stem emerged. By 1610 it had changed dramatically to being narrow and tall and usually much decorated, but by 1630 wine cups were plain and had assumed a proportion normal for a drinking glass. The 1650s saw the return to simple decoration, often in panels, of a bucket-shaped bowl resting not on a stem but directly on a high trumpet foot. At this point the making of silver drinking cups appears to have almost stopped, probably due to the impact of Venetian glass and the subsequent burgeoning of glass-making in England.

There was a revival of silver drinking goblets in the 1780s which lasted for some 25 years. These were usually quite large, having ovoid bowls often made in prevailing styles during the 19th century in small numbers.

Many other drinking vessels have been made in silver. The beaker has been made throughout Europe at least since the beginning of the 15th century, being particularly popular in Scandinavia, the Netherlands, and Germany. Whether or not these beakers were used for wine is doubtful but 18th century French beakers with their characteristic plinth feet may well have been. Round-bottomed tumbler cups were favoured in Britain and America and may have been used for wine. They were made from *c.*1660 but were probably intended for punch or wassail like their treen (wooden) counterparts.

Other materials Drinking vessels were made in a variety of other media. Before long-distance maritime trade became frequent, ostrich eggs and coconuts were particularly prized for their exotic rarity and were mounted in silver as cups. At a more basic level, the horns of various animals were used for drinking, and wood was lathe-turned into cups and goblets. Antique cups of pottery and earthenware are also occasionally found. R.N.H.B.

Bickerton, L. M., *18th Century Drinking Glasses* (2nd edn., Woodbridge, 1986).
Butler, R., and Walkling, G., *The Book of Wine Antiques* (Woodbridge, 1986).
Charleston, R. J., *English Glass* (London, 1984).
Clayton, M., *Collectors' Dictionary of the Silver and Gold of Great Britain and North America* (2nd edn., Woodbridge, 1985).
Tait, H., *The Golden Age of Venetian Glass* (London, 1979).

DRIP IRRIGATION, a form of IRRIGATION in which water is applied literally as drops to each vine from a pressure-reducing plastic device (the dripper) attached to a plastic pipe.

Drip irrigation system installed for new vines at Wyndham's estate at Cowra, New South Wales.

DROSOPHILA, an insect pest. See FRUIT FLY.

DROUGHT, a severe and prolonged deficit of RAINFALL, compared with that normally received. Its implications for viticulture depend on the region and its normal climate. In cool and wet viticultural regions drought years often produce the best vintages, especially of red wines. This is because excessive vegetative growth, excess VIGOUR, is arrested; YIELDS are limited; BERRY SIZE remains small with a high ratio of the colour- and flavour-containing skin to juice; and sunshine and warmth are greater than average.

Such beneficial effects nevertheless depend on the drought's not being too extreme. Severe WATER STRESS is almost always detrimental to wine quality, especially if it occurs during ripening. Penning-Rowsell discusses the impacts of individual Bordeaux seasons in some detail.

Most dry viticultural climates are regularly warm and sunny enough, and drought is nearly always detrimental: whether directly, in the case of DRYLAND VITICULTURE, or indirectly via a lack and/or reduced quality of IRRIGATION water. Drought in such climates drastically reduces growth and yield, and if very severe through ripening can disrupt the RIPENING process and flavour development more or less completely.

See also CLIMATE AND WINE QUALITY. J.G. & R.E.S.

Penning-Rowsell, E., *The Wines of Bordeaux* (6th edn., London, 1989).

DROUHIN, JOSEPH, one of the most respected NÉGOCIANTS and wine-makers in Burgundy. Founded in 1880, the firm is based above historic cellars in the city of Beaune, dating from the 13th century. Joseph's son Maurice, who took over control of the firm in 1918, built up the firm's reputation for quality and acquired a number of important vineyard holdings, including Drouhin's exclusivity, the Clos des Mouches (see BEAUNE). After the Second World War, exports of Joseph Drouhin wines increased considerably.

Robert Drouhin took over control of the house in 1957 and made many significant vineyard acquisitions, particularly on the CÔTE DE NUITS, including Musigny, Griotte-Chambertin, Bonnes Mares, and Grands Échezeaux. In 1968 an outpost in CHABLIS was established so that, of all Beaune merchants, Drouhin is the best placed in this northerly region with holdings in several grands crus and premiers crus. The firm's holdings totalled about 60 ha/150 acres in 1993, when it sold the merchant house of Jaffelin, which it had acquired in 1969. The firm also makes and sells the Marquis de Laguiche MONTRACHET.

The firm has its own NURSERY and practises deliberate LEAF REMOVAL. Drouhin's wine-making facilities were some of the first to investigate and embrace the fundamentals of modern wine-making, although many traditional techniques are also used. Oenologist Laurence Jobard has been responsible for a succession of clean, rigorous wines that are never among Burgundy's richest but are serious expressions of each appellation.

Somewhat ironically in view of Maurice's stated aim that Joseph Drouhin should concentrate on burgundy exclusively, Robert Drouhin was the first Burgundian to make a significant investment in a wine region outside France. **Domaine Drouhin**, established in 1988, owns significant land in OREGON and 1989 was its first commercial vintage of Pinot Noir, made from bought-in fruit. Domaine Drouhin is managed by Robert's daughter Véronique, while his son Philippe manages the vineyards and supervises grape purchases in both the Côte d'Or and Chablis.

DRUMBORG, particularly cool wine region in the state of VICTORIA in AUSTRALIA much used as a source of grapes for sparkling wines. For more detail see VICTORIA.

DRUNKENNESS and its history is inextricably entwined with that of wine, since one of the chief reasons wine has been cherished, and prohibited, is its property to intoxicate. Excessive wine drinking has therefore always had moral or religious connotations, beginning with the 'shameful' intoxication of Noah after the Flood (see BIBLE).

Varying definitions of what constitutes excessive drinking have prevailed at different times and in different societies, with opinions sometimes diverging within that same society. It is also important to note that drinking has always accompanied festivity and ritual, and that societies have developed rules to contain it. The fear that these rules may be violated and society threatened is therefore apparent at almost every stage in the history of drunkenness.

Wine drinking is first documented in the ancient civilizations of the Middle East; the same is true of drunkenness (see SUMER and Ancient EGYPT). An early Mesopotamian tablet describes a man drunk from strong wine: 'he forgets his words and his speech becomes confused, his mind wanders and his eyes have a set expression.' The suggested hangover cure includes liquorice, beans, and wine, to be administered before sunrise and before he has been kissed. The request of an Egyptian woman living in the 17th Dynasty may have been typical: 'Give me 18 cups of wine, behold I should love drunkenness.' Other races were quick to point the finger of over-indulgence at the Egyptians. (See Ancient EGYPT.)

Sources show that drunkenness was both tolerated and at times denounced in these ancient civilizations. Although wine played a part in all their religions the voice of disapproval most frequently heard was clerical. The Ancient Jews also displayed a somewhat equivocal attitude towards wine drinking. The Old Testament contains many warnings against drunkenness alongside the positive benefits of temperate wine drinking. Some Jewish religious sects, such as the Nazarenes, chose to abstain altogether.

Society in Ancient GREECE also showed a marked ambiguity in attitudes towards wine drinking. On the one hand strict guide-lines were laid down to curb any excess. Plato advised no wine before the age of 18 and moderation until 30. The all-male drinking party known as the SYMPOSIUM was, when properly observed, a strictly controlled ritual of drinking combined with poetry, entertainment, and debate. The aim

Admonitory picture of 'the **drunkard** who terrorizes his family' in a 1900 booklet on the dangers of alcohol.

was pleasant intoxication without loss of reason. See HERODOTUS for some more details.

On the other hand some Greek wine drinkers drank specifically to lose their reason. The worshippers of the wine god DIONYSUS deliberately became intoxicated and indeed this was, in their eyes, a fundamental point of their religion. The authorities took fright at their wild behaviour, identifying drunkenness with a breakdown in social order. Despite attempts to ban the cult its popularity continued into Roman times. The historian Livy was appalled by the licentious and threatening behaviour of the worshippers 'when wine had inflamed their minds'.

Stories of Roman drunkenness have passed into folklore but not all are exaggerations, as contemporary observers such as PLINY the Elder show. Drunkenness in classical Rome deserves its own special note below.

Attitudes toward drunkenness shifted somewhat after the Roman era. The Christian Church, whilst hallowing wine as a sacrament (see EUCHARIST), sought to dissociate itself from the riotous habits and heavy drinking of earlier religions. Behaviour reminiscent of the Dionysiac cult was met with excommunication. When St Bernard developed the Cistercian order in Burgundy he originally intended abstinence for his brethren; this was soon dropped. Monks earned a reputation for excessive drinking in the Middle Ages but this reflected their dominance in wine-growing as much as in wine consumption (see MONKS AND MONASTERIES).

There were periods in Ancient INDIA where drunkenness was considered a desirable state. Drunkards in the Middle East faced a formidable obstacle, however, in Muhammad's total prohibition on wine (see ISLAM). Wine drinking did not cease because of it, but had to be covert. Drinking among the upper classes of Persian society, for example, took place at secret parties reminiscent of Greek symposia with their strictly ritualized etiquette and emphasis on poetry and discussion (see ARAB POETS. Drunkenness was a welcome state at such occasions and could hardly be avoided when parties lasted several days, although the penalty and shame were severe.

Meanwhile in Europe the scope for drunkenness was considerably increased with the discovery of DISTILLATION in the 12th century. Intoxication reached new heights as demand for this new liquor spread across the continent. The Dutch and Germans gained reputations throughout Europe for their drunkenness. In 17th century Holland drinking hours were applied to keep drinking in check. In Britain, too, drunkenness on the streets was increasingly blamed on spirits. By the 18th century wine was relatively expensive and only the middle and upper classes could afford this route to drunkenness.

The Victorians were not the first to confront the problem of drunkenness, but they put it on a new footing. Alcoholism was defined as a disease in the mid 19th century and came to be identified with degeneracy of race. In Britain wine was not seen as the main culprit—indeed it was seen by many, including Prime Minister Gladstone, as the remedy against drunkenness. The new catchword was 'temperance', and, whilst in the minds of some this meant the encouragement of moderate wine drinking to combat the medical and social ills of addiction to spirits, to a growing band of (often religiously inspired) campaigners it denoted complete abstinence. The governments of Britain and the United States adopted differing interpretations. Gladstone lowered the duty on light table wines to improve the health and morals of the British whilst American states gradually voted themselves 'dry', culminating in full-blown PROHIBITION in 1918. H.B.

Lucia, S. P. (ed.), *Alcohol and Civilization* (New York, 1963).
Sournia, A., *Histoire de l'alcoolisme* (Paris, 1986), trans. by N. Hindley as *A History of Alcoholism* (Oxford, 1990).
Vickers, M., *Greek Symposia* (London, 1978).

Roman drunkenness

Wine's power to intoxicate evoked forceful, and often contradictory, responses in the classical world, as in every society. The beneficial effects of wine were certainly not ignored. Indeed, a passage in Aristophanes' play *The Knights* deserves to rank alongside Falstaff's great eulogy of sherry ('Nothing is so conducive to living an effective life as wine. Do you not see? It is wine-drinkers who make money, clinch their business deals, win their legal cases, become happy, and help their friends', Shakespeare, 1 *Henry IV*). People of all ages have taken to heart the practice ascribed to both the Persians and the Germans of considering serious decisions first when drunk, then the next day again when sober, and only acting on those that still seem right (Herodotus, *Histories* 1. 133, and Tacitus, *Germania* 22). Total abstention could be a source of criticism; Demosthenes' water drinking was derided by his political opponents. Further, the idea of 'in vino veritas' had a long history in the ancient world. Plato argued that drink could be a good test of a man's character, and ancient biographers were fascinated by the drinking habits of their subjects, believing that their true nature was revealed in their cups.

On the other hand, the bad effects of drink were also a ready subject for moralists. Undisciplined drinking, which flouted the conventions, was the core of the criticisms. It was not primarily how much you drank; indeed, a distinguished magistrate of the 1st century AD seemed proud of his nickname Tricongius, or Ten-Litre Man, and, when political opponents criticized the Younger CATO's habit of drinking all night, his admirers pointed to the fact that it never affected his ability to carry out his public duties in the morning. The real issues were how and when you drank. First and foremost mixing wine with water was an essential mark of civilized behaviour. Only barbarians, Scythians, and Germans drank wine neat. Unmixed wine was supposed to have a deleterious effect on both physical and mental health. Even a half and half mix of wine and water was considered a heady brew. A sure sign of declining standards in ROME, according to many contemporary Jeremiahs, was the practice of beginning dinner and drinking ever earlier in the day and carrying on late into the night (see e.g. Suetonius, *Nero* 27). Pubs and snack-bars were open in the mornings; but no respectable person could afford to be seen staggering out of a bar at 11 a.m., as Cicero reminds his political enemy L. Piso—not even if your excuse was that you needed a drink as a medicinal pick-me-up (Cicero, *Against Piso* 13).

It is no accident that so many of Cicero's opponents are alleged to have been drunks. Rhetoric both in the courts and in the political arena frequently resorted to character assassination, concentrating on drink and sex to as great a degree as any modern tabloid journalist. Cicero claimed that his great enemy Mark Antony had a riotous home life, where drinking began by 9 a.m., and he never let anyone forget the unfortunate occasion when Antony threw up over the benches of the senate. Antony consistently denied the charges; but the mud stuck to such a degree that he was forced to publish a pamphlet *De ebrietate mea* ('Concerning my Drunkenness'), which Pliny wittily took to be his claim to the world drinking championship.

Whole peoples—normally those beyond the frontiers of the civilized Mediterranean world—could gain reputations for drunkenness. The Gauls' alleged passion for wine and their drunkennness was a theme to be found in writers from early to late antiquity. It was reinforced and renewed by Christian bishops and writers from the region, who came to count drunkenness alongside other sins. As Jerome said of one unfortunate, 'Sodom did not do him in, but the wine did.'

J.J.P.

Pliny the Elder, *Natural History* trans. by H. Rackham (London, 1938), 14. 137 ff.
Athenaeus, *Deipnosophistae* 2. 35 ff.

DRUPEGGIO, name for the light-berried CANAIOLO Bianco that adds interest to Trebbiano grapes, along with Grechetto, Malvasia, and Verdello, in the ORVIETO wine of central Italy.

DRY, adjective often applied to wines, usually to describe those in which there is no perceptible SWEETNESS. Such wines may have as many as 10 g/l RESIDUAL SUGAR, or even more in wines with particularly high ACIDITY (which tends to counterbalance sweetness. In this sense virtually all red wines are dry, while white, rosé, sparkling, and fortified wines can vary considerably between **bone dry**, **dry**, **medium dry**, medium sweet, and sweet.

Some wines, particularly reds, are said to have a 'dry finish' if they are especially bitter or astringent.

DRY CREEK VALLEY, California wine region and AVA. See SONOMA.

DRY EXTRACT. See EXTRACT.

DRYING GRAPES, which become **dried grapes**, second most common commercial use for viticulture, less important than wine but more important than TABLE GRAPES. Drying is a means of preserving grapes for eating (and precedes fermentation in the production of DRIED GRAPE WINES). Dried grapes are an ancient food supply. The low moisture content of the dried grape (10 to 15 per cent) and high sugar concentration (70 to 80 per cent) make the product relatively unsuitable for survival of food spoilage organisms.

Grapes have been dried since antiquity. Records of grape drying found in Egypt date back to 3000 BC, and records of dried grapes are found in biblical times. Aristotle in 360 BC referred to the seedless character of the Black Corinth grape, today's currant. Legend has it that Hannibal fed his troops with raisins during the crossing of the alps in 218 BC.

The common English name raisin comes from the French *raisin sec*, or dry grape. Three varieties dominate world trade in drying grapes: SULTANA (also known as Thompson Seedless in America, and Kishmish or Sultanina in Asia and the Near East); Zante CURRANT or Black Corinth (California); and MUSCAT OF ALEXANDRIA (Gordo Blanco in Australia and White Hanepoot in South Africa).

Major dried grape-producing countries are the USA (by far the dominant producer), Turkey, Greece, Australia, Iran, and Afghanistan, and world production is around 1 million dried tonnes. Climate is a major factor determining where grapes are grown for drying. Temperatures should be high and there should be plenty of sunshine, while humidity and rainfall should be low. In such conditions the evaporation rate is reliably high, but this usually means that the vineyards need IRRIGATION. Rainfall prior to harvest or during drying has catastrophic results.

Harvested grapes are placed outside on wooden or paper

trays, or concrete or clay slabs. After about 10 to 14 days, the bunches must be turned over to dry the other side. Grapes dried by this method are known as 'naturals'. An alternative method widely used is to dip the grapes in solutions to speed their drying. A mixture of wood ash and olive oil was used in classical times, and some modern dips are of similar composition, containing vegetable oils and potassium carbonate. Raisins produced this way have a more golden brown colour than the dark purple brown colour of the naturals. In Australia and South Africa special drying racks with roofs are used. These can help reduce rain damage, and allow drying solutions to be sprayed on the fruit.

Alternative methods of drying fruit on the vines have been developed in Australia and California. The canes supporting the bunches are cut at the base, but left on the trellis wires. The vines can be sprayed with the drying emulsion, and then mechanically harvested when dried. Dried grapes should not be packed with more than 13 per cent moisture, and sometimes grapes dried in the field need to be dried further.

Quality factors in raisins are size, hue, and uniformity of colour, surface condition, texture of both skin and pulp, and lack of any contamination. The highest-quality raisins are produced from the ripest fruit. See also CURRANTS, LEXIAS, MUSCATELS, SULTANAS, and RAISINS for specific sorts of dried grape. R.E.S.

Whiting, J. R., 'Harvesting and drying of grapes', in B. G. Coombe and P. R. Dry (eds.), *Viticulture, ii: Practices* (Adelaide, 1992).
Winkler, A. J., *et al.*, *General Viticulture* (2nd edn., Berkeley, Calif., 1974).

DRYLAND VITICULTURE, viticulture relying entirely on natural RAINFALL, and a term used only in regions where IRRIGATION is common.

In its commonly visualized form, irrigation is carried out in hot, arid regions, and employs heavy furrow or sprinkler irrigation to maximize yield for TABLE GRAPES, DRYING GRAPES, and bulk wines. That is the background for the widely held view, especially in France, that only dryland viticulture can produce outstanding wines, and that irrigation inevitably reduces quality.

Widespread adoption of trickle irrigation since the 1960s has now greatly blurred the distinction. Although originally developed for and used in true arid climates, such as in ISRAEL, the technique has found its major viticultural use for supplementary watering. That is, the vineyards rely mainly on natural rainfall, and irrigation is used to make up small to moderate deficits which occur either irregularly or at particular times of year. It is extensively used in MEDITERRANEAN CLIMATES and their like which mostly have good winter–spring rainfalls, but are regularly dry during the critical ripening period; or else in climates with more uniform rainfall but which might periodically suffer from DROUGHT at any time of year. In both of these climates the capacity to avoid severe WATER STRESS potentially improves grape and wine quality, provided that irrigation does not excessively stimulate vine growth and yield. Indeed, by allowing viticulture for quality wine-making to extend further into areas with reliable warmth and sunshine during ripening, and on to soils and MESOCLIMATES more favourable for wine quality within them, the capacity to produce high-quality wines regularly is considerably enhanced. See also SOIL AND WINE QUALITY; SOIL WATER.

There can be little doubt that some European areas with both uniform rainfall and mediterranean climates, now practising fully dryland viticulture, could improve their wine quality if limited irrigation were possible. Excessive water stress causes loss of PHOTOSYNTHESIS and eventually of the leaves themselves, and can seriously prejudice normal RIPENING.

Whether viticulture which employs limited watering still qualifies as 'dryland' is increasingly an academic question. The term is obsolescent, and will in time probably disappear. J.G. & R.E.S.

DTW, DEUTSCHER Tafelwein.

DUBŒUF, GEORGES (1933–), important producer and indefatigable promoter of BEAUJOLAIS, controlling more than 10 per cent of the wine produced in the region, with considerable interests outside it. Brought up in a wine-making family that has lived in the MÂCONNAIS since the 15th century, Dubœuf originally studied physical education in Paris, returning to POUILLY-FUISSÉ in 1953. He started selling to restaurants in the region, and subsequently became a contract bottler. In 1957 he grouped together 45 growers from the region under the title L'Écrin du Beaujolais (the Beaujolais Casket), but when the group fell apart three years later he branched out alone, taking some growers with him and establishing a base in Romanèche-Thorins. The Beaujolais boom, led by the Beaujolais Nouveau craze, is in no small part due to Dubœuf, who encouraged temperature-controlled fermentation and mastered CARBONIC MACERATION, leading to a reliable, particularly fruity style of wine. In the 1990s he works with 20 CO-OPERATIVES and over 400 growers, and virtually owns the village of Romanèche-Thorins. His company has an annual production of 20 million bottles, and although the famous floral Dubœuf label goes on bottles containing many styles of wine, it is Beaujolais, and white Mâconnais, for which he is best known. More than 4 million bottles of his production each year are Beaujolais Nouveau alone. Indeed, the Dubœuf name appears on the label of more than 15 per cent of all the Beaujolais sold anywhere. His early contacts in the important local restaurant trade have stood him in good stead, and Dubœuf now counts many Michelin-starred establishments among his best clients. A venture in California's Napa Valley in the 1980s failed to get off the ground, but in the late 1980s Dubœuf had more success within France, expanding outside the Beaujolais region to sell wines from the ARDÈCHE and the Rhône. A huge museum of wine in Romanèche-Thorins is another achievement. Dubœuf's son Franck is closely involved with the family business. S.A.

Dubœuf, G., and Elwing, H., *Beaujolais, vin du citoyen* (Poitiers, 1989).

Georges **Dubœuf**, 'the prince of Beaujolais'.

DUBOURDIEU, a father and son of particular importance in the history of white wine-making in BORDEAUX. The father Pierre (1923–), owner of Ch Doisy-Daëne in BARSAC, produced the first dry white wine in the SAUTERNES area and it is still made today. He was also instrumental in helping the Vaslin company improve the action of their grape PRESSES and he has clearly been an inspiration to his son Denis, with whom he has worked on many experiments.

Denis Dubourdieu (1949–) is a research scientist at BORDEAUX UNIVERSITY, and owner and wine-maker at Ch Reynon in the PREMIÈRES CÔTES DE BORDEAUX. He and his research team have been a significant influence on white wine-making, not just in Bordeaux but throughout France and abroad. His early areas of research were into the nature of *Botrytis cinerea,* and in particular NOBLE ROT; earlier picking dates to enhance the BOUQUET of wines made from aromatic white grape varieties; and the influence of fermentation TEMPERATURES and selected YEAST on white wines. More recently he investigated individual molecules of aroma in grape skins, identification of which can assist in the matching of vine varieties to soils, and in aspects of vinification strategy such as picking dates, fermentation temperatures, and—a favourite research area of his—the extent of prefermentation maceration (see SKIN CONTACT). He has also clarified the significant reductive and FINING properties of yeast LEES during BARREL FERMENTATION and BARREL MATURATION, rationalizing the ancient practice of BÂTONNAGE and also explaining why white wines fermented and aged in barrel are less oaky and astringent than those put into barrel only after fermentation and without lees. Most importantly to wine enthusiasts, his explanations of many of the phenomena of vinification have helped wine-makers exploit them on a practical level. M.W.E.S.

Dubourdieu, D., 'Vinification des vins blancs secs en barriques', *Le Bois et la qualité des vins et eaux-de-vie* (Bordeaux, 1992).

DUCELLIER, name associated with a special fermentation vat designed to extract, without electricity, maximum colour and tannins even in short fermentation periods. The system was devised for wine-making in ALGERIA but is now most commonly used to make PORT. See AUTOVINIFICATION.

DULCE, Spanish for sweet. See SWEETNESS.

DUNKELFELDER is a black German grape variety notable mainly for the depth of its colour, a useful commodity in Germany's blending vats. Plantings totalled rather more than 100 ha/250 acres in the early 1990s, mainly in the Pfalz and Baden.

DURAS is perhaps the oldest vine variety still used in the once-famous red wines of GAILLAC. Its presence distinguishes them from the complex mosaic of other blending permutations that comprise the reds of SOUTH WEST FRANCE. It is not grown in the Côtes de Duras, nor anywhere else in any significant amount outside the Tarn *département*, where Gaillac is the chief appellation. In the Tarn, however, it has steadily gained ground, thanks to Gaillac's powerful internal lobby against incoming INTERNATIONAL VARIETIES, so that it was the most commonly planted of all Duras's traditional dark-berried grape varieties by the end of the 1980s, with more than 800 ha/2,000 acres in total. Duras, Fer, and Syrah are regarded as the principal red wine varieties and Gaillac growers are preparing to increase the proportion of Fer and Duras in their reds as the parvenu Gamay is gradually sent packing. The wine is deeply coloured, full bodied, and lively. Varietal Duras produced in Gaillac eloquently demonstrate a marriage of cépage to TERROIR well worth defending.

The vine buds inconveniently early but gives wines of particularly good structure and acidity. As Gaillac's producers turn increasingly from slightly fizzy white wines to solid red ones that express their rich varietal heritage, Duras is expected to be a beneficiary, replacing either MAUZAC or the popular non-appellation red wine varieties such as JURANÇON Noir and PORTUGAIS.

DURAS, CÔTES DE, red and white wine appellation on the north eastern fringe of BORDEAUX which is regarded as one of the wine districts of SOUTH WEST FRANCE. It is bounded by Côtes du MARMANDAIS to the south, BERGERAC to the north, and ENTRE-DEUX-MERS and Ste-Foy-Bordeaux to the west. The town of Duras, with its impressive castle, marks the eastern extremity of the Entre-Deux-Mers plateau and the 1,600 ha/3,950 acres of vines are planted either on limestone hill-tops, mainly for white wine grapes, or on slightly more sheltered limestone and clay slopes for red wine grapes. The vine varieties are essentially those of Bordeaux, and a specifically Duras character in the red wines is certainly difficult to discern (although more luxurious wine-making techniques such as BARREL MATURATION are increasingly employed). White Côtes de Duras can display originality, however, especially in the sweet or MOELLEUX wines sometimes produced from the Bordeaux grape varieties Sémillon, Sauvignon Blanc, and Muscadelle together with the south western specialities ONDENC and MAUZAC. Some Chenin Blanc has also been imported from the Loire. Red wine production was slightly greater than white wine production in the early 1990s, and some imported talent (see FLYING WINE-MAKERS) had demonstrated that the appellation was capable of producing good quality at sensible prices. Historically, the region was commercially penalized by the Bordelais as part of the HAUT PAYS, but the Huguenots who fled to the NETHERLANDS remained faithful to its wines.

DURIF is a relatively undistinguished black grape variety, a selection of another variety, Peloursin. It was propagated eponymously by a Dr Durif in south eastern France in the 1880s, useful for its resistance to DOWNY MILDEW but unable to produce wines of high quality. It was tolerated but not encouraged by the French authorities in such regions as Isère and the Ardèche in the mid 20th century.

Today it has all but disappeared from France but has for long been thought to be the same as the variety known in both North and South America as PETITE SIRAH, although DNA 'FINGERPRINTING' has since cast doubt on this hypothesis. Small plantings of Peloursin, and some Durif, have been identified in north east Victoria in Australia too.

DUSTING, a vineyard practice designed to apply AGROCHEMICALS in dry powder form. Typical of such operations is the application of finely ground elemental SULPHUR dust to control the fungal disease POWDERY MILDEW. Most vineyard agrochemicals are applied as a liquid formulation with water as the carrier, and applied by SPRAYING. R.E.S.

DUTCH EAST INDIA COMPANY, powerful trading organization which played a seminal part in the wine history of SOUTH AFRICA. Founded in March 1602 by the amalgamation of four Holland and two Zeeland companies which had been set up between 1596 and 1602 to conduct trade in East Asia, the General United Chartered East-India Company in the United Netherlands (Vereenigde Oost-Indische Compagnie: VOC) dominated European trade with the Orient for the rest of the 17th century, with counters and outposts strung out along the extended sea routes which linked the Netherlands with southern Africa, India, Ceylon, Sumatra, Java, Borneo, and Japan. Apart from its participation in the bulk transport of fortified wines such as MADEIRA and spirits to the ends of its seaborne empire, it played a vital part in the Dutch penetration of southern Africa and in the establishment of viticulture on the Cape of Good Hope. It was one of its agents, Jan van Riebeeck, who founded the first Cape colony in 1657 and planted cuttings from European vines at the foot of Tagelberg mountain. Less than two years later, his diary triumphantly proclaimed the first pressing of Cape wine on 2 February 1659. Twenty-five years later Simon van der Stel, governor of Cape Province, planted the Groot Constantia, destined to be the most famous vineyard in Africa, producing the renowned CONSTANTIA or Constance, a fine dessert wine which was exported throughout the Dutch empire and later graced the tables of Napoleon Bonaparte. (See also SOUTH AFRICA, history.) A.J.D.

Boxer, C. R., *The Dutch Seaborne Empire 1600–1800* (London, 1965, 1977).

Glamann, K., *Dutch–Asiatic Trade 1620–1740* (Copenhagen and The Hague, 1958).

Israel, J. I., *Dutch Primacy in World Trade 1585–1740* (Oxford, 1989).

DUTCHESS, white grape variety grown with limited success in NEW YORK state. It is a VITIS *labruscana* variety.

DUTCH WINE TRADE, a major influence on the history of international trade in wine. By the middle years of the 17th century the Dutch republic had achieved a dominant position in the world trade in wines and spirits (and much else besides), greater, even, than that of ENGLAND, whose Navigation Acts in the 1650s were directed specifically at Dutch freight. John Locke recorded in 1678 that the Dutch conducted more trade through BORDEAUX than England. Amsterdam, Rotterdam, and Dordrecht were world emporia. Its geographical position, at the estuaries of three great RIVERS, Schelde (Scheldt), Maas (Meuse), and Rhine, made it a natural point of convergence for river-based traffic; its wealthy bourgeoisie created a consumer demand distributed throughout the region, in addition to that of the nobility; and, lastly, its relative proximity to long-established and highly productive wine-producing areas enabled it to become a major conduit for the highly prized wines of the Rhineland and Alsace (see GERMAN HISTORY).

The RHINE (and its distributaries Waal and Lek) was virtually a wine highway, linking Cologne with Dordrecht and Rotterdam. Moreover, Middelburg in Zeeland, on the island of Walcheren at the estuary of the Schelde, had been the principal port of call for a centuries-old and highly lucrative seaborne traffic which linked the Atlantic seaboard with Scandinavia and the lands of the Baltic; formerly the principal staple (official market) for the whole of the Netherlands and earlier still the out-port serving the Flemish and Brabançon cities of Bruges, Ghent, and Antwerp, it had been secured for the independent Netherlands after the rising against Spain in 1568.

Hanseatic League

Although merchants from the region had been handling wine from very early times—one of the oldest surviving trade agreements in European history (between Kings Offa of Mercia and CHARLEMAGNE in 796) concerned commerce between Frisia and England, which included the importation of wine from the Rhineland—it was not until the late 13th century that the Dutch, principally Hollanders and Zeelanders, entered the thriving maritime commerce which linked the countries of the Atlantic seaboard with the Baltic, as associates of the German Hansa (the Hanseatic League). This powerful alliance of about 80 merchant towns had by that time established a virtual monopoly of Baltic and Scandinavian trade by organizing large fleets of merchant vessels to transport basic commodities in bulk: salt from Lüneburg (on a tributary of the Elbe); herring from Denmark, cod from Bergen in Norway; grain, timber, wax, and furs from Baltic lands. From 1237 they began to acquire rights in English markets; and from 1252 they acquired trading privileges in Flanders, with reduced customs in Bruges and its out-port Damme, then the leading staple in Flanders.

Thus they gained access to the Atlantic trade and the estuaries of the 'wine rivers' of Europe; Adour, Lot-Tarn-GARONNE, LOIRE, Seine, Schelde (Scheldt), Maas (Meuse), and Rhine-MOSEL, to which would later be added the Guadalquivir, for SHERRY, and the DOURO for PORT, or at least its prototypes. French wines, chiefly from Gascony and Poitou, French salt from the bay of Bourgneuf, English wool, and Flemish cloth constituted the major commodities traded for the produce of the northern lands. This was the commerce which enriched the cities of Ghent, Bruges, Ypres, Antwerp, and many others. Wine consumption was a mark of wealth in northern lands. At a time when a wage-earning man might have to spend a third of his income on bread, noble households devoted more than a third of their expenditure to wine, although cheap wine was readily available in taverns and inns, where it had to compete with locally brewed BEER and ale.

Led by the merchantmen of Stavoren and Kampen on the Zuiderzee (Ijsselmeer), Zeelanders and Hollanders played an increasing role in the transportation of wines from Bordeaux and LA ROCHELLE to England, Flanders, and the Baltic from the last quarter of the 13th century onwards, gradually supplanting the Flemings and Brabançons, and they were joined in the course of the 14th century by mariners and traders from Dordrecht (already the major market for Rhine wines, with a privileged staple granted by the count of Holland in 1299), Zierikzee, and Middelburg. In the first quarter of the 14th century, wine represented respectively 31 per cent and 25 per cent of imports into England and the Low Countries (Flanders, Zeeland), although this very high proportion was never equalled again. Much of this wine was re-exported: Gascon wine from England; Poitevin, Loire, and Rhine wines from Flanders and Zeeland.

The Dutch dominated the Bourgneuf salt trade during the 15th century, acquired a large share in the export of CLAIRET from Bordeaux and of the cheaper, white Poitevin wines from La Rochelle, and established a direct trade between Bourgneuf and the Baltic, carrying principally salt and wine, and returning to the Low Countries with fish, furs, and grain. The chief commercial centre was the thriving port of Middelburg, which had superseded Damme and L'Écluse (formerly out-ports, now silted up, for Bruges in Flanders) as the preferred entrepôt (recognized by the Habsburg government in 1523 as the official French-wine staple for the whole of the Netherlands), where merchant ships of all countries transported their wares.

After England's loss of Gascony in 1453, before which wine was exported from Bordeaux to England and then re-exported by licence, the Dutch secured the lion's share of the direct trade out of Bordeaux so that Hanseatic and Dutch vessels shipped huge quantities of wine to Middelburg. The western French wines of Poitou, Saintonge, and Aunis were transported in Dutch and Breton ships. Expensive sweet Mediterranean wines (from the Peloponnese, Crete, Cyprus, and Rhodes) were carried by ships from GENOA and VENICE. Some Rhine wines also found their way to Middelburg, but the bulk of these highly favoured wines travelled down the Rhine by barge to Dordrecht. From Middelburg and Dordrecht wines could radiate by sea or pass by river to Antwerp, and thence to the rest of the region and beyond. The Dutch employed fleets of full-rigged ships of relatively large tonnage (up to 200 tons), which enabled them to undercut the freight charges of their competitors by a significant margin. In 1438, for example, one Dutch merchant fleet comprised 104 ships.

Expansion outside Europe

During the 16th century three major changes, economic, religious, and political, contributed to the further expansion of Dutch commerce. The first was the fragmentation of the Hanseatic League itself, of which the Dutch were major beneficiaries and agents, and which enabled them to establish a virtual monopoly of Scandinavian and Baltic trade, The second, and much more dramatic, event was the undermining of Antwerp's commercial dominance by Spanish attempts to retain control of the Netherlands during the last third of the 16th century. The third was the declaration of independence from Spain made in 1581 by the seven northern provinces (Holland, Zeeland, Utrecht, Gelderland, Groningen, Friesland, Overijssel). Although the United Provinces did not secure final international recognition until the treaty of Westphalia in 1648, they were from the 1580s a formidable maritime force, opposed to Spanish hegemony on religious (they had embraced Calvinism) and political grounds. After Antwerp's capture by Spanish forces in 1585, the United Provinces blocked the entry to the river Schelde and so cut the principal artery which linked Antwerp to Middelburg and the North Sea. The Dutch economy was thus for the first time decisively detached from the rest of the Netherlands in terms of capital, shipping, and the expertise of refugee Jews, who had earlier fled Spain and Portugal and migrated north with their commercial knowledge and connections to Amsterdam, which grew to become the major commercial, maritime, and banking centre of the western world for the next century or so. Amsterdam, in north Holland, became heir to the Hanseatic League's Baltic trade and to Antwerp's international banking and commerce.

By the end of the 16th century, the Dutch fleet equalled the combined commercial fleets of Spain and Portugal, and far outstripped those of France and England. It was thus able to take advantage of Iberian colonial expansion in the Americas and participate in south east Asian commercial colonialism. The DUTCH EAST INDIA COMPANY was founded in 1602; the West India Company in 1621. These major enterprises, which transformed the Netherlands into a colonial power and a major competitor of the English, French, and Portuguese, were driven not by wine but by the desire to control as much as possible of the commerce of the New World and Asia: sugar, tobacco, calico, spices, and their manufactured products. But the handling of wine remained a significant part of the commercial interests of the independent Netherlands, whose fleets competed for markets around the globe. Wine, brandy, and vinegar constituted nearly 40 per cent of Dutch imports from France in 1645; most of the 224 ships which loaded wine at Bordeaux in 1682 were Dutch; and wines, fortified wines, and spirits, especially the latter two, were carried to the furthest corners of their trading empire, to North America, Surinam, the Caribbean islands, South Africa, Ceylon, and the Malay archipelago (Sumatra, Java, Borneo).

Influence on wine styles

Dutch interest in the transport of and trade in wines helped shape the evolution of wine production according to the dictates of changing taste and the requirements of the long-distance transportation of a perishable product by sea. Until the end of the 17th century most wines could not survive from one vintage to the next, and many were spoiled and undrinkable within six months of the vintage, partly because they were transported in large oak casks, 'tuns' of 900 l weighing 1,000 kg, inclusive of the wood, which constituted the units of freight. Even before the creation of overseas colonies, wine destined for the Baltic had to overwinter at some convenient point. The grape harvest occurred too late in the year to permit immediate transportation to the northern lands, since the Baltic and White Seas often became impassable from November onwards. To overcome these disadvantages the Dutch popularized *mistelles*, wines fortified by the addition of brandy to stop fermentation and prolong the life of the wine, and *vins pourris*, made from overripened grapes. They also introduced the French to the stabilizing effects of SULPHUR candles (known in French as *allumettes hollandaises* for many years), and encouraged the production of distilled liquors, based on both grain and grape. Amsterdam and Rotterdam became the principal international markets for wines and brandy (see BRANDEWIJN and Spanish BRANDY) in the 17th century, sustained by regular and reliable supplies, bulk storage, and an international network of merchants. One effect was the increase in planting white grape varieties in western France, to satisfy the tastes of the Dutch market.

At the same time, they practised BLENDING wines from different areas to increase the bulk of more popular varieties, to improve the taste or increase the BODY of inferior wines, or simply to make them conform to the changing palates of consumers. From the 15th century, for example, the English came to prefer stronger and sweeter wines than formerly. Thus the weak *clairet* of Gascony was 'strengthened' by blending with CAHORS or Portuguese wines. When in the 16th century the English developed a liking for SACK, the white wines of southern Spain (exported through Seville and Cádiz), and when at about the same time the Canary islands and MADEIRA began producing sweet wines (malmseys and madeiras) from the MALVASIA grape (introduced from Crete), the Dutch entered that trade too, and made significant inroads into the rapidly growing trade in Portuguese wines (via Lisbon, Lamego, and Oporto). And, of course, it was the Dutch who had the technical skills with which to drain the marshes of the MÉDOC in the mid 17th century, thereby enabling production of what were to be recognized as some of the finest red wines in the world.

Dutch prominence in the wine trade in the 16th and 17th centuries was merely one aspect of their general primacy in all aspects of international commerce during that period. They were principally merchants and shippers, controlling all aspects of trade, purchase, transport, storage, and sale to local merchants and retailers. Their purchasing power enabled them often to dictate advantageous terms to the producers and the large tonnage of their ships enabled them to transport their wares at relatively low cost. Such was their access to the wine-producing areas of Europe that they were able to circumvent the English embargo on all French wines during the Anglo-French war of 1690–6 by passing them off as Spanish, Portuguese, or even Rhenish, and transporting them in the appropriate casks.

By the 1690s, however, this dominance was being seriously undermined by an aggressive trade war with England, culminating in the Franco-Dutch war of 1692–4, in which Holland's commercial enemies conspired with France against her. A combination of protectionist legislation in England, widespread piracy, the successful French invasion of 1692, and the rapid rise of English seaborne trade (especially from Bristol and London) marked the end of the Dutch supremacy, though not of Dutch involvement in the world trade in wines and spirits.

The Dutch also played the crucial role in the emergence of the Médoc as a fine wine area (see BORDEAUX, history), and in dictating the style of modern MUSCADET. A.J.D.

Craeybeckx, J., *Un grand commerce d'importation: les vins de France aux anciens Pays-Bas (xiii–xvi siècle)*, École Pratique des hautes Études, section VI, Centre des Recherches Historiques (Paris, 1958).

Israel, J. I., *Dutch Primacy in World Trade 1585–1740* (Oxford, 1989).

James, M. K., *Studies in the Medieval Wine Trade* (London, 1971).

DUTY is levied on wine importation and movement into circulation from bond in many countries at an extremely variable level. In general, countries in which viticulture is an economically (and therefore politically) important activity, such as France and Italy, tend to have extremely low duties, while almost non-producing countries, such as Great Britain, and/or those with restrictive policies on the sale of alcoholic drinks, such as Norway, tend to have high duties.

Wine is rarely a good buy in so-called **duty-free** shops, however, as profit margins are rarely low enough to warrant the weight and breakability of wine bottles. In 1993 the relaxation of duty-free allowances when crossing borders within the EUROPEAN UNION led to widespread loss of trade to British wine merchants as consumers crossed the English Channel to take advantage of bulk buying in France.

DYING ARM, vine disease. See EUTYPA DIEBACK.

E

EATING GRAPES. See TABLE GRAPES.

EAU-DE-VIE, French for brandy or other distilled spirit, meaning literally 'water of life'. For details of a more precise official definition, see BRANDY AND THE EUROPEAN UNION.

EC stood for European Community. **EEC** stood for European Economic Community. In November 1993 they were replaced by EU, which stands for EUROPEAN UNION, the international economic and political association of the major countries of Europe, the world's centre of wine production and consumption.

ÉCHANTILLON, French for a sample. See SAMPLING.

ÉCHEZEAUX, GRAND CRU of the village of Flagey-Échezeaux in Burgundy's Côte de Nuits, producing red wines from Pinot Noir grapes. While wines of VILLAGE or PREMIER CRU status in Flagey-Échezeaux are sold under the name of neighbouring VOSNE-ROMANÉE, the majority of the commune's vineyard land is shared between the two grands crus Échezeaux and Grands Échezeaux.

Échezeaux is perhaps fortunate to be rated grand cru, certainly in its entirety (37.6 ha/92.9 acres), as many of its wines are disturbingly light. The vineyard is made up of 11 lieux dits (see LIE) ranging from Les Treux, which has a deep clay soil with indifferent drainage, to Les Échezeaux du Dessus, where the soil is shallower and chalkier and the wine correspondingly finer. It is not the equal, however, of neighbouring Grands Échezeaux (9 ha), which also abuts CLOS DE VOUGEOT.

There are 21 owners of Grands Échezeaux and over 80 of Échezeaux. Proprietors of both include DOMAINE DE LA ROMANÉE-CONTI, Domaine René Engel, and Domaine Mongeard-Mugneret.

See also CÔTE D'OR and its map. J.T.C.M.

Special **échantillon**, or sample, label for this fifth growth Pauillac.

ÉCLAIRCISSAGE. See CROP THINNING.

ECOLOGICAL VITICULTURE. See ORGANIC VITICULTURE.

ECUADOR bottles a considerable quantity of wine (including a SCHEUREBE), but the extent of its vineyards is considerably more limited. Historically Ecuador was ruled by PERU and its viticulture followed a similar pattern, although concentrated on the coast and decidedly TROPICAL. Wine production was revitalized in 1982 when 200 ha of vines were planted, mainly in the mountain provinces of Imbabura, Pinchincha, Cotopaxi, Tungurahua, Canar Azuay, and Loja which are cool enough to permit vine DORMANCY and produce one vintage a year. The 50 ha planted on the coast produce three vintages a year. Principal vines planted are native varieties called Nacional Negra, and Moscatel Morado.

EDEL means 'noble' in German and thus **Edelfäule** is German for NOBLE ROT, **Edelkeur** is the brand name of one of the most successful sweet wines of SOUTH AFRICA and **Edelzwicker** is the name chosen to add lustre to a not particularly noble blend in ALSACE. Similarly, Gutedel is the German synonym for the not particularly noble CHASSELAS grape.

EDELKEUR, a celebrated South African BOTRYTIZED sweet white, probably its best-known wine in the 1970s. Officially designated noble late harvest or NLH (Edel Laat Oes in Afrikaans), it was introduced in 1969 by Günter Brözel, a German immigrant wine-maker at Nederburg Wines, Paarl, who labelled it Edelkeur ('noble choice' in Afrikaans). Initially it was made from CHENIN BLANC grapes. Nederburg now makes Noble Late Harvest wines from other grape varieties, including Rhine RIESLING, SAUVIGNON Blanc, and even CHARDONNAY. These are labelled Noble Late Harvest rather than Edelkeur, which is a Nederburg trade mark. Scores of the other producers have since made botrytized wines. The very high sugar content (250 g/l RESIDUAL SUGAR or more) of the first Edelkeur and NLH vintages has been reduced steadily; now sugars of 80 and 90 g/l are more common. By law, natural sugar content must exceed 50 g/l and the wine cannot be sweetened by GRAPE CONCENTRATE. J.P.

EDELZWICKER, Alsace term, originally German, for what is usually a relatively basic blend. See ALSACE.

EDEN VALLEY, wine region near the important Barossa Valley in AUSTRALIA with a particularly fine reputation for white RIESLING. For more detail see SOUTH AUSTRALIA.

EDNA VALLEY, California wine region and AVA. See SAN LUIS OBISPO.

EDUCATION, WINE. Education plays an important part in the production, sale, and enjoyment of a product as complex and, in many countries, as foreign as wine. Detailed knowledge of wine involves an appreciation of history, geography (inevitably including a host of foreign names), science, and technology, quite apart from the development of practical tasting skills.

Education for wine-producing professionals is discussed under ACADEME and is, naturally, concentrated in the world's wine regions. Some universities, such as BORDEAUX UNIVERSITY, offer courses, especially in tasting, that are open to wine merchants and the general public. There is even more overlap between wine trade education, courses designed specifically for the wholesale and retail trade, and consumer education; the most enthusiastic wine consumers may well want to know more about wine than the less academically inclined wine traders. The Institute of MASTERS OF WINE, for example, the leading international wine trade educational body which opened its notoriously stiff series of trade examinations to those unconnected with the wine trade in the early 1990s, admitted its first non-trade 'MW', a Hollywood lawyer, in 1993.

While trade education is usually undertaken by this sort of professional body (the United States has its Society of Wine Educators), consumer education may be undertaken by professional lecturers and wine merchants. This can take the form of TASTINGS so informal as to constitute a party, tutored tastings, BLIND TASTINGS, or some form of wine TOURISM.

Other forms of wine education include wine articles, books (see the LITERATURE OF WINE), and various forms of audio-visual instruction such as television programmes, and computer software. Interactive wine tasting is a way of combining the practical with the theoretical.

EFFEUILLAGE. See LEAF REMOVAL.

EGER, much-disputed town in north east HUNGARY whose wines have been exported with success since the 13th century, although various Turkish incursions interrupted this trade. Eger's most famous siege was during the Ottoman occupation of the 16th century when, according to legend, the defenders of Eger were so dramatically fortified by a red liquid which stained their beards and armour that the Turks retreated, believing their opponents to have drunk Bikavér, or bull's blood. The vine-growers of Eger have since been further encouraged to believe in the potency of their red wine, particularly during the 1970s, when BULL'S BLOOD was one of the most successful wine BRANDS produced by the state-owned Egervin monopoly.

The town gives its name to a wine region on the foothills of the volcanic Bükk mountains where rainfall is low and spring tends to come late. As well as producing Egri Bikavér, or Bull's Blood, in huge quantities, the region produces white wines, notably from LEÁNYKA grapes.

EGG-WHITES play a surprisingly important part in the production of fine red wines. Their particular albumin content makes them highly desirable FINING agents for red wines because they are a relatively gentle fining agent which tends to adsorb harsh and bitter TANNINS in preference to the softer tannins. Five egg-whites are usually sufficient to fine excess COLLOIDS from a 225-l/59-gal barrel of young red wine. The separation of yolks from egg-whites can form an important part of CELLAR WORK in some seasons (and egg-yolks can be a significant waste product of wine-making).

ÉGRAPPAGE, French term for DESTEMMING grapes meaning literally 'debunching'.

EGYPT, North African country which continues to make a small quantities of wine, about 20,000 hl/528,000 gal a year (slightly more than ENGLAND produces, for example) from its less than 40,000 ha/98,840 acres of vineyard, which are mainly devoted to producing TABLE GRAPES. The Ancient Egyptians provide us with some of the oldest depictions of wine-making techniques, however.

Ancient Egypt

Remains of grapes have been found at First Dynasty (*c.*3100–2890 BC) and even prehistoric sites, but the vine is not part of the native flora of the country, and was probably introduced from CANAAN in Predynastic times, despite HERODOTUS' false claim (*Histories* 2. 77) that there were no vines in Egypt. The best grapes were considered to come from the Nile delta; only in the Ptolemaic Period (after 323 BC) was the vine taken further south. Vines, irrigated, and manured with pigeon droppings, were grown in walled gardens (where children acted as scarecrows), sometimes amongst other fruits such as olives, and trained over pergolas (see TENDONE) or allowed to form a natural canopy propped up by poles.

As in Ancient GREECE and Ancient ROME, there were two distinct wine-making operations: treading, or CRUSHING, to yield some FREE-RUN juice, and PRESSING the remainder with a sack-press. When harvested, grapes were trodden by foot by men who could hang on to overhead supports, or suspended ropes. The vat was deliberately shielded from the heat, and an offering of the must was made to the goddess Renenutet. Tomb paintings illustrate wine production amply, although the precise details are not always clear. After treading, the pressing was often carried out in a special sack-press with a pole fixed in a loop at either end of what was effectively a giant jelly bag. This was then twisted by several men in opposite directions and the liquid was collected in a vessel beneath. The liquid flowing out of the sack-press is always depicted as red, which suggests that the pressing took place only after some form of FERMENTATION. In Old Kingdom times (*c*.2686–2181 BC) the wine was transferred to AMPHORAE, which in this period were almost always vessels with spouts.

In scenes dating from the New Kingdom (*c*.1552–1070 BC), must flows from the trough along a small conduit into a receptacle. In the sack-press apparently only the skins would have been pressed. Probably the free-run juice and the PRESS WINE were fermented together, since differentiation of quality can hardly have been possible. Depictions show only the transfer of the must from the press into amphorae. In one illustration the contents of the press are transferred to large fermentation vats, then pressed in the sack-press and transferred into amphorae.

The actual alcoholic fermentation took place in the amphorae, from which the Ancient Egyptians would then deliberately exclude air, just like modern wine-makers. The filled amphorae were covered with cloth or leather lids, smeared with Nile mud, and then sealed. Small holes to allow the continuing escape of CARBON DIOXIDE were later blocked up.

There is no evidence of white wine before the Graeco-Roman period, nor of the resination of wine jars to produce RESINATED WINES. Wine was also drunk for medicinal purposes, when it was sometimes flavoured with *kyphi*, a mixture of gums, resins, herbs, spices, and possibly other less pleasant ingredients such as the dungs of various animals and birds, and asses' hair.

Ancient **Egyptians** in Thebes tread grapes, strap-hanging for security. The free-run juice (bottom left) is already run off separately.

Wine trade organization It is clear from the seals on amphorae and from the titles of certain officials that the manufacture and delivery of wine were already organized at royal level in the earliest periods. Wine is often shown in scenes on wall paintings. Lists from the Fifth Dynasty distinguish six types of wine according to its origin. 'Wine from Asia' and Canaan is also mentioned, and Canaanite wine amphorae are found in the New Kingdom. Inscriptions on amphorae of that period usually indicate year, vineyard site, owner, and chief wine-maker (rather more information than is given on most modern wine labels). Most but not all centres of wine production lay on the western arm of the Nile delta.

Wine drinking Wine was drunk by gods, kings, and nobles, especially at feasts, and seems to have enjoyed a higher social cachet than BEER. Amphorae, often painted with vine leaves, are depicted on tables or resting on stands. The wine was sieved as it was poured out. Servants would fill small beakers for serving, sometimes carrying a second small jug (possibly containing water to dilute the wine). The wine was drunk, occasionally through a reed-straw, from bowls or cups (which sometimes rested on stands). The king and his family are shown drinking at the royal capital Tell-el-Amarna (14th century BC). Priests received wine as part of their daily rations, likewise army officers and foreign mercenaries; but the workmen of Amarna received none, an indication of its value.

Religion and wine Wine is said to be the drink of gods, and also of the dead (along with milk). Thus it was important in cult and is frequently mentioned in lists of offerings, sometimes several sorts together. It was frequently offered as nourishment to deities by the king or private persons, also symbolizing purification. LIBATIONS of wine and water were made.

The goddess Hathor was the protectress of an important wine-producing area, and myths linked her to wine and DRUNKENNESS. When she was brought back to Egypt from the Nubian desert by command of Re (the sun god), she was still violent and savage in nature, and had to be appeased by music, dance, and the offering of wine. Wine was offered to her at the Feast of Drunkenness, and was interpreted as a symbol of the blood of the enemies of the enraged goddess.

Classical authors identified Osiris as the benefactor who bestowed wine on mankind, comparing him in this respect with the Greek god DIONYSUS. The grape certainly became a symbol of the dying and rising god. Vines depicted in tomb paintings symbolized the deceased's hope for resurrection. Other texts refer to wine as the perspiration of Re or as the eyes of the god Horus. His pupils are said to be grapes through which wine flows. In the later periods the term 'Green Eye of Horus' was used to refer to wine.

The god Thoth of Pnubs was the 'lord of wine, who drinks much', and the annual inundation, the beginning of which fell during the month named after him, led to a comparison between wine and the reddish colour of the Nile at that season. J.A.B.

See articles 'Wein', 'Weinkrug', 'Weinopfer', and 'Weintrauben', in *Lexikon der Ägyptologie* (Wiesbaden, 1975–86), cols. 1169–92 (the standard scholarly reference work on the subject).

EHRENFELSER is one of the finest of Germany's new generation of 20th century CROSSINGS of *vinifera* vine varieties, a Riesling × Silvaner developed at GEISENHEIM in 1929. In this case the aim of producing a super-Riesling that will ripen in a wider range of sites was achieved and the crossing's only inherent disadvantages are that the wine is slightly too low in acidity for long-term ageing and that it cannot be called Riesling. Ehrenfelser, named after the Rheingau ruin of Schloss Ehrenfels, regularly ripens better and more productively than Riesling but is not nearly as versatile in terms of site as the more recently developed KERNER, which became a more obvious choice as a flexible Riesling susbtitute. Total plantings of Ehrenfelser fell in the late 1980s to less than 500 ha/1,235 acres, with the largest areas in the vine variety patchworks of Pfalz and Rheinhessen. See GERMAN CROSSINGS.

EINZELLAGE, literally 'individual site' in the wine regions of GERMANY. Almost all of Germany's vineyards are officially registered as one of these approximately 2,600 **Einzellagen**, which can vary in size from a fraction of 1 ha to more than 200 ha/494 acres. The average size of an Einzellage is about 38 ha, about the same size as a typical BORDEAUX estate. As in BURGUNDY, for example, the vines may be divided among many different owners, who are allowed to put the name of the Einzellage only on QBA and QMP wines. Such names must usually be preceded by the name of the village in which they were produced; thus a wine from the Mandelring vineyard in the village of Haardt is called Haardter Mandelring. In the case of estates such as SCHLOSS JOHANNISBERG and Schloss Vollrads in the RHEINGAU, the name of the property itself suffices as provenance, and Scharzhofberger in the SAAR is considered so important that it dispenses with the prefix Wiltinger, but these cases are rare.

Producers whose output includes a range of bottlings of varying quality have tended to reserve their finest grapes for wines labelled thus, although this, as so much in German wine marketing, is currently in flux. A wine labelled with the name of an Einzellage is likely to be superior to, and certainly more characterful than, one labelled with the name of a GROSSLAGE, a collection of individual Einzellagen for long used as a difficult-to-distinguish commercial entity for labelling purposes. It was proposed that from the 1994 vintage, however, the words Einzellage and Grosslage should appear on wine labels as appropriate.

See also the Austrian term RIED.

Johnson, H., *The Atlas of German Wines* (London and New York, 1986).

Ripe grapes frozen on the vine into **Eiswein** ingredients.

EIRE. See IRELAND.

EISACKTALER, German for Valle Isarco, pure, dry white wines from the ALTO ADIGE.

EISENBERG, famous wine town in the Burgenland region of AUSTRIA, now part of the Südburgenland district.

EISWEIN, German for ICE WINE and a special Prädikat within the QMP quality wine category defined by the GERMAN WINE LAW. Eisweine are very high in sugar and very high in acidity (like BOTRYTIZED wines), except that in this case the concentration is a direct result of the grapes freezing on the vine. They are then picked and pressed immediately so that water crystals are left in the press and only the sweetest juice, which has a lower freezing point than water, runs from the press. Temperatures of at least −8 °C/18 °F in the vineyard are required, so picking of Eisweine usually takes place very early in the morning. The grapes have to be left on the vine at least until November and often until the following calendar year (the process may not be artificially created in Germany, as in the CRYOEXTRACTION process used in less successful vintages in SAUTERNES or the ice wine production techniques allowed in some countries). The resulting wines lack NOBLE ROT, or *Edelfäule*, character, which makes them easier to drink when young, and their high acidity makes them extremely refreshing. Eisweine are a relatively new German wine phenomenon and it is difficult to say how their evolution compares with that of a BEERENAUSLESE (which must reach the same MUST WEIGHT) since very old examples are rare. The 1962 vintage was the first famous Eiswein vintage in Germany.

Since a market for Eiswein has been established, an increasing number of growers choose not to engage in a time-consuming and expensive gathering of grapes with noble rot for AUSLESE wine (apart from exceptionally ripe vintages such as 1976). Instead they leave part of the crop of healthy grapes on the vine (perhaps not in their best site), in the hope of the necessary low temperatures for Eiswein production. The costs of harvesting an Eiswein are less than that of picking individual bunches of grapes for Auslese wine; the must weight of an Eiswein is increased by the elimination of some of the water in the grape by freezing; and the market price of Eiswein is much greater than that of an Auslese.

See also AUSTRIA.

EIXIMENIS, FRANCISC (?1340–?1409), Catalan Franciscan friar and author of *Lo Crestià* ('The Christian'), an encyclopedia of the Christian life. Thirteen books were planned but only four were finished. It is aimed at a popular, not a learned, audience, and hence it is written not in Latin but in the vernacular, Catalan. As a result it has had no influence on other European authors of the Middle Ages (see LITERATURE OF WINE).

Its third book, *Lo terç del Crestià*, dated 1384, is concerned with sin. The section on gluttony deals with DRUNKENNESS (chs. 350–9) and the etiquette of wine drinking (chs. 362–7, 393–5). Eiximenis is aware of the medical properties of wine, but his interest is in the moral aspects of drinking. Drunkenness, he says, leads to every conceivable vice, but, taken in moderation, wine is a good thing. All other nations, except perhaps the Italians, drink too much: only the Catalans have the art of sensible drinking. This means three cups at dinner, three at supper: one should never have more than four, and there is to be no drinking between meals. Although he disapproves of the fastidious habits of connoisseurs, he does tell where the best wines are to be found. They are the strong, sweet wines of the Mediterranean, particularly MALMSEY (Malvasia), the Cretan Candia, and Picapoll from Mallorca (Majorca). He ranks Italian wines above French wines, and insists that strong wines (these do not include the wines of France) should be mixed with water, the stronger the wine the more water. H.M.W.

Gracia, Jorge J. E., 'Rules and regulations for drinking wine in Francisc Eiximenis' *Terç del Crestià* (1384),' *Traditio*, 32 (1976), 369–85.

—— 'Francisc Eiximenis' *Terç del Crestià*: edition and study of sources, chs. 359–436' (Ph.D. thesis, University of Toronto, 1971).

ELBA, Mediterranean island off TUSCANY. Viticulture played an important role in the economy of the island in the ancient world, and PLINY described Elba as 'insula vini ferax' (an island with abundant production of wine). This continued until the late 19th and early 20th centuries, when a quarter of the cultivated surface was occupied by vines. Emigration from the island and the increasing attractions of the booming tourist industry have drastically reduced the role of wine in the overall economic picture, however, to the point where little more than 200 ha/490 acres of the Elba DOC are in production, with an annual yield of only 4,500 hl/118,800 gal, three-quarters of it white wine. The wines themselves are standard Tuscan products: SANGIOVESE with CANAIOLO and/or white grapes for the reds: TREBBIANO (known locally as Procanico) for the whites. Elba's wines are correct but hardly inspiring, and rarely seen outside Tuscany. D.T.

ELBLING is an ancient, and some would say outdated, vine variety that has been cultivated in the valley of the MOSELLE since Roman times. At one time it was effectively the only variety planted in LUXEMBOURG and dominated the extensive vineyards of medieval Germany (see GERMAN HISTORY). Today it is far less important than Rivaner (MÜLLER-THURGAU) in Luxembourg but retains a fairly constant 1,100 ha/2,720 acres of vineyard in Germany, most of it in the upper reaches of the MOSEL-SAAR-RUWER above Trier where chalk dominates slate and Riesling has difficulty ripening. Much of the Elbling grown here is used for SEKT and its naturally high acidity is certainly mitigated by the addition of carbon dioxide. While the vine is distinguished for its antiquity and productivity, its wines are distinguished by their often searing acidity and their relatively low alcohol, making it an even tarter, lighter version of SILVANER. (Weisser Silvaner is one of Elbling's German synonyms.) MUST WEIGHTS are typically only about 60° Oechsle, about 10° lower than Riesling. In the vineyard Elbling can produce up to 200 hl/ha (11.4 tons/acre) but its productivity is prone to variation as the vine is prone to COULURE. Only the most dedicated wine-maker can extract any suggestion of Elbling's evanescent flavour of just-ripe apricots but this is a wine to appeal to viticultural archivists.

Often grown as a vineyard mixture of Elbling Rouge and Elbling Blanc, the variety is called Räifrench in Luxembourg.

ÉLEVAGE, French word that describes an important aspect of wine-making that has no direct equivalent in English (other than the Anglicization 'elevage'). *Élevage* means literally 'rearing', 'breeding', or 'raising' and is commonly applied to livestock, or humans as in *bien élevé* for 'well brought up'. When applied to wines it means the series of cellar operations that take place between FERMENTATION and BOTTLING, suggesting that the wine-maker's role is rather like that of a loving parent who guides, disciplines, and civilizes the raw young wine that emerges from the FERMENTATION VESSEL. The word élevage implies that all this effort is worth it, and is therefore normally applied only above a certain level of wine quality.

In WHITE WINE-MAKING the first stage of élevage is rough CLARIFICATION to remove the gross LEES, most of the dead yeast cells, and fragments of grape skins, stems, and seeds from the new wine. The next step in warmer climates might be ACIDIFICATION before preliminary BLENDING to optimize flavour and character and to ensure that the wine conforms to legal specifications. The wine is then aged, either in WOOD or other material, in BARREL (see below) or much larger CON-

TAINER. During this ageing, which might last for as long as two years, the wine should mature into something less raw and more complex. The ageing phase might be followed by final blending and any final cellar treatments needed.

RED WINE-MAKING differs only in that most fine young red wine needs wood ageing, often in labour-intensive small oak barrels. BARREL MATURATION demands regular monitoring, TOPPING UP as a result of evaporation, and a certain amount of FINING and RACKING wine from one barrel to another. MALOLACTIC FERMENTATION is also much more likely to be encouraged to reduce acidity and final filtrations may be much less severe since deposits are more popularly acceptable in fine red wines than whites. Reds are also much more likely to be given a period of ageing in bottle before being released, such an activity being considered by some to be part of what constitutes élevage. A.D.W.

ELEVATION, the height either above sea level or above some local base altitude, such as that of a valley floor. Local elevation of vineyards above valley floors or flat land determines their air drainage and temperature relations, including TEMPERATURE VARIABILITY and liability to FROST (see also TOPOGRAPHY; MESOCLIMATE; CLIMATE AND WINE QUALITY). Beyond such topographical effects are those of altitude *per se*. With comparable topography, average temperature falls by about 0.6 °C/1.1 °F for every 100 m/330 ft greater height. For more details, see ALTITUDE.

ELGIN, cool wine region in SOUTH AFRICA.

ELISA, acronym for enzyme-linked immunosorbent assay, a serological test which can also be used to detect vine pathogens. First used in plant pathology in the mid 1970s, the technique is now used routinely to determine the presence of a wide range of vine pathogens, and test kits are available commercially. R.E.S.

EMBOTELLADO is Spanish for bottled.

EMERALD RIESLING, one of the earliest of vine varieties developed at the University of California (see DAVIS) by Dr H. P. Olmo to emerge in VARIETAL (white) wine. It is a Muscadelle × Riesling cross and had its heyday in the late 1960s and early 1970s before slumping towards oblivion. Although just over 1,000 acres/400 ha remained in the early 1990s, mainly in the very south of the SAN JOAQUIN VALLEY, nearly all of the grapes disappear into generic blends. The purpose of the variety was to permit light, crisply acidic wines to be grown in warm inland climates. In spite of the aim it performs its best in the coastal counties, especially MONTEREY. It has also been tried with a certain degree of success in SOUTH AFRICA.

EMILIA. Western part of EMILIA-ROMAGNA.

EMILIA-ROMAGNA, Italian wine region which stretches across north central Italy from the eastern Adriatic coast to include vast tracts of inland Emilia in the west, which is quite distinct from coastal Romagna in the east. Much of the region lies in the deep, alluvial plain of the Po river, and contains some of Italy's most fertile agricultural land. Its abundant agricultural output has created Italy's richest cuisine and a race of hearty eaters. It is no surprise, therefore, that the region's viticulture also produces abundantly, more than 8 million hl/211 million gal a year, about the same amount as Italy's other most prolific wine regions APULIA, SICILY, and the VENETO.

Quantity, however, is in inverse proportion to quality in the case of Emilia-Romagna: only 12 to 13 per cent of the region's total output is DOC wine, and many of the DOC wines—TREBBIANO DI ROMAGNA and Emilia's LAMBRUSCO in particular—are hardly names to conjure with, falling more into the quaffing than the quality category. The region's inhabitants seem content to view wine merely as lubrication for their copious repasts and, at least in Emilia, are firm believers in the diuretic qualities of sparkling wine, both white and red; not only Lambrusco, but also the local MALVASIA, BARBERA, BONARDA, and the non-VARIETAL Gutturnio are as likely as not to be served foaming in the glass rather than as still wines.

The potential for good wine does exist, none the less, in the sub-Apennine strip on the region's southern border. Sangiovese has a long history in Romagna and certain areas to the south of Faenza and Forlì have demonstrated over the past decades that reasonable yields and careful vinification can give SANGIOVESE DI ROMAGNA wines that can compete with good, if not yet the best, Tuscan Sangiovese.

The hills to the south west of Bologna, a DOC zone known as Colli Bolognesi or Monte San Pietro, have given good results with the Bordeaux grapes SAUVIGNON Blanc and CABERNET SAUVIGNON, although the quantities made are small; the total DOC zone, in fact, produces less than 15,000 hl.

The Colli Piacentini at the western edge of Emilia-Romagna are geologically and climatically similar to the contiguous OLTREPÒ PAVESE of Lombardy. Its best-known wine, Gutturnio, made from Barbera and CROATINA grapes, can reach the level of a good Oltrepò Rosso and has shown a certain affinity for wood ageing, including small BARREL MATURATION. In addition, the zone produces varietal Barbera, Bonarda (made from the Croatina grape), and refreshing white wines from Malvasia and Sauvignon Blanc grapes. The area's most interesting recent developments, however, have come from the subzone of Riverargo-Vigolzone, where important, age-worthy wines from CHARDONNAY, PINOT NOIR, and, especially, Cabernet Sauvignon indicate that the real potential of the Colli Piacentini, despite the significant size of its productions (over 150,000 hl per year), is yet to be discovered. These superior wines, just as in the case of the best Sangiovese of Romagna, have generally been marketed as VINO DA TAVOLA, indicating that the DOC label in Emilia-Romagna carries few, if any, connotations of quality or character. D.T.

Anderson, B., *The Wine Atlas of Italy* (London and New York, 1990).
Gleave, D., *The Wines of Italy* (London and New York, 1989).

ENCÉPAGEMENT, widely used French term for the mix of *cépages*, or VINE VARIETIES, planted on a particular property.

Detail from the Bayeux Tapestry showing how the Normans regarded wine as just as important a provision as arms for their invasion of medieval **England**.

These proportions (typically for a MÉDOC estate, for example, Cabernet Sauvignon 60 per cent, Cabernet Franc 20 per cent, and Merlot 20 per cent) do not necessarily correspond to the proportions of each grape in a given wine, partly because different varieties vary generally in terms of productivity, but also because the FLOWERING for each variety may well take place at different times and therefore in different meteorological conditions, which can dramatically affect that particular year's yield from that variety.

ENCOSTAS D'AIRE, an IPR in western Portugal. See OESTE for more details.

ENCRUZADO, Portuguese white grape variety most commonly planted in DÃO. It can yield quite respectable wine.

ENGARRAFADO, Portuguese for bottled.

ENGLAND, the largest and warmest country in the British Isles, Great BRITAIN, and the United Kingdom and the only one which produces wine in any quantity, albeit minuscule relative to most European wine-producing countries.

History

Perhaps the Romans introduced viticulture to England, but, whether they did or not, they cannot be held responsible for introducing the grapevine itself, because archaeologists have found prehistoric remains of the pollen of VINIFERA vines at Marks Tey in Essex, as well as seed at Hoxne in Suffolk (see PALAEOETHNOBOTANY). Both these finds go back to the Hoxnian Interglacial, i.e. the period between the Second and Third Ice Ages, when summers were warmer than they are now. Grape seeds dating from the Hoxnian have also been found in the NETHERLANDS, north GERMANY, Denmark, and Poland. Since the British Isles were still part of the Continent at the time (they did not become separated until after the Fourth Ice Age), this shows that VITIS *vinifera* had spread to regions of northern Europe which are now too cold for grapes. The seeds and pollen found in East Anglia are not accompanied by remains of cereals or other signs of agriculture.

Seeds have been found at Roman sites in London, Bermondsey, Silchester in Hampshire, and Gloucester, and stalks at a Roman villa near Boxmoor in Hertfordshire, but all without any evidence of cultivation, so these may be the remains of imported raisins. And even if grapes were grown in England, we cannot prove that they were made into wine. Wine was certainly imported from Italy, even before the Roman invasion of AD 43: remains of AMPHORAE testify to that. (See CELTS for evidence that a small quantity of wine was carried by Breton sailors to Hengistbury Head, overlooking Christchurch Harbour in Hampshire, at the end of the 2nd century BC.) The earliest wine drinkers in Britain were the Belgae, a Celtic tribe that had invaded Britain in two waves, the first in 75 BC and the second in 20 BC, after the Romans had put down the Belgic rebellion in Gaul. The British Belgae kept in close contact with their kinsmen in Gaul, who were prodigious drinkers of Italian wine. In the reign of Cymbeline (Cunobelin), AD 10–40, galleys came up the river Colne to Camulodunum (one mile from Colchester in Essex).

Consumption of wine probably increased after the Roman invasion of Britain, for remains of amphorae and pottery drinking cups are common finds on the sites of Roman towns and country houses. Recent finds show that amphorae were manufactured at Brockley Hill, Middlesex, which appears to have been an important pottery centre, and also at other London sites. They are of a type that, according to archaeological evidence from southern France, were used as containers for locally produced wine; the London amphorae were probably the work of immigrant potters from France. The amphorae all date from AD 70–100: perhaps this short period could be explained by the edict issued by the Roman emperor DOMITIAN, which, by reducing the number of vineyards in the provinces, put a stop to the Romano-British wine industry. Remains of imported amphorae are rare after AD

300: does this mean that the Romano-British were now producing enough wine to meet their own needs? It seems unlikely. In any case, from the 3rd century onwards wine began increasingly to be transported not in amphorae but in wooden BARRELS, which are perishable, so one would not expect to find many amphorae dating from the 4th century AD and certainly no wooden casks.

Our earliest conclusive evidence for wine-growing in Britain, then, must be Bede's *Ecclesiastical History*, which he finished in 731. It opens with a general description of Britain and Ireland, including geography, climate, agriculture, animals, nations, and languages. 'Britain', Bede says, 'is rich in grain and timber; it has good pasturage for cattle and draught animals, and wines are cultivated in various localities' (Book 1, ch. 1). Unfortunately, that is all he tells us about Anglo-Saxon viticulture, and what other information we have is scanty. As well as growing their own, the Anglo-Saxons certainly bought wine from the Franks. In the 8th and 9th centuries Southampton was one of the largest ports of northern Europe and well placed for trade with northern France, especially Rouen (see PARIS). In return for animal hides, the merchants of Southampton obtained gold, silver, glassware, and wine. However, as Viking pirates began to capture more and more ships, overseas trade was disrupted, and if imported wine was available at all it must have been a rare luxury item.

The Anglo-Saxons' daily drink was BEER, but they needed wine for the EUCHARIST: supply being erratic, it made sense for monasteries to have their own vineyards, as some had probably been doing since Bede's day (See MONKS AND MONASTERIES). A charter, dated 955, of King Edwy, great-grandson of King Alfred, grants a vineyard at Pethanesburgh, Somerset, to the monks of Glastonbury Abbey. But not all vineyards were owned by monks. The Laws of King Alfred regard viticulture as important enough to make it an offence for anyone to destroy a vineyard; no mention is made of monasteries here. An 11th century document lists looking after the vineyard as one of the duties of the manager of a secular estate and, out of the 38 vineyards named in Domesday Book, only 12 were monastic. More importantly, if the figure is accurate—and William the Conqueror's surveyors did their work thoroughly—38 vineyards cannot possibly have produced a plentiful supply of wine for the whole of England. (According to the Bayeux Tapestry's depiction of William's invasion of England in 1066, he judged it as important to take wine as arms with him. See picture on p. 360.)

Wine continued to be grown in England during the 12th and 13th centuries. There were vineyards as far north as south Yorkshire, and the praise lavished on the wines of Gloucestershire by the 12th century chronicler William of Malmesbury demonstrates that English wine was no thin, sour plonk. Worcestershire, too, was renowned for its wine. This golden age of English viticulture was the result of a long period of warm summer weather, which started in the mid 11th century (see CLIMATE CHANGE). It ended abruptly in the 14th century, when the ocean currents changed and summers became wet and cloudy. Moreover, when on his marriage to Eleanor of Aquitaine Henry II acquired Gascony, and when King John (1199–1216) granted the citizens of BORDEAUX numerous privileges in order to win their favour, Gascon wine became cheaper to buy for the English than any other wine, imported or home produced. Around 1,300 commercial vineyards were grubbed up all over England, and grapes made way for more profitable crops: this is how the Vale of Evesham, still famous for its plums and apples, came to be planted with fruit trees. Monastic viticulture continued for longer, but between 1348 and 1370 the Black Death carried off a third or more of the population, lay and ecclesiastic alike. Not only did many monks die, but the ensuing shortage of labour deprived the monasteries of their unsalaried work-force, the lay brothers. English viticulture did not cease altogether, but it was no longer commercially viable, even for the monks.

But with a wine-drinking Norman aristocracy domestic production could never have satisfied demand. Via Rouen, then governed by the king of England, who was also duke of Normandy (until John lost Normandy), the English had ready access to the wines of the Île-de-France (see PARIS), which in 1200 were the most expensive on the English market, although people bought more of the wines of Poitou (see LA ROCHELLE) and Anjou (see LOIRE), and probably with reason, for they must have been less acidic. With the rise of Bordeaux this changed, and until the end of the HUNDRED YEARS WAR the English bought more wine from Gascony than from anywhere else, with wine being second only to wool in importance for English trade at this time. Wine was shipped to England, principally to the port of Southampton, twice a year from Bordeaux, in the autumn and in the spring. Even if the vintage had been early, the new wine did not usually reach England before November; the wines that arrived in the spring were the wines 'of rack', so called because they were not racked off their LEES until the spring. The wines, 'of rack', an early form of SUR LIE, fetched higher prices. Since there was nothing better in which to keep the wine than wooden casks, OXIDATION was the norm and wine did not keep from one year to the next. The wine of the previous year was therefore sold off cheaply at AUCTION as soon as the new vintage appeared on the market in England. White wine was more expensive than red.

French wines were not the only wines to be drunk in 14th century London. From the 1350s onwards, sweet wines from southern Europe began to be introduced (see VENICE, NAPLES, and GENOA), and they became the most expensive available. The most highly prized of these was 'vernage', the Italian VERNACCIA. Another favourite was 'malvesye', or MALMSEY. The name is a corruption of Monemvasia (in the south west corner of the Peloponnese; see GREECE), the port from which the wine was shipped: it was produced all over the eastern Mediterranean, but the chief suppliers were Cyprus and Crete. Because of their additional strength and sweetness, these wines lasted longer than the thinner, drier wines that the English had been used to and were greatly prized. The wines of Alsace and the Rhine were highly valued because they were so brilliantly clear. Spanish wine, which was higher in alcohol than other wines, was regarded mainly as cheaper heady plonk, and better, more expensive, wines were often cut with it (see SPAIN, history).

Attempts were made to protect the consumer from ADULTERATION AND FRAUD, but their frequency suggests that they were not always successful. In 1321 a proclamation was made that in London all wines should be graded 'good' or 'ordinary' and the casks marked; everyone would have the right to see his wine drawn and maximum prices were fixed. Merchants and innkeepers refused to co-operate and were promptly fined. The marking of casks was probably abandoned, but the right to see one's wine being drawn is reiterated from one writ and proclamation to the next, and one even says that taverners should keep red wines and white in different cellars: a note of desperation is clearly creeping in. A London proclamation of 1371 makes clear what the unfortunate drinker was subjected to: overcharging, adulteration, and wine that was off. It makes one grateful for clearly labelled, tamper-free modern packaging: the glass BOTTLE and the CORK have improved the wine drinker's life almost beyond imagination. H.M.W.

Dion, Roger, *Histoire de la vigne et du vin en France* (Paris, 1959).
James, M. K., *Studies in the Medieval Wine Trade* (Oxford, 1971).
Simon, A. L., *The History of the Wine Trade in England*, 3 vols. (London, 1906–9).

Modern English wine

English wine is an increasingly respectable drink, despite being produced at relatively high LATITUDES. Almost as much as the weather, nomenclature has dogged the fortunes of English wine (a term used collectively for wine made in England, Wales, and the Channel Islands). Too few consumers realize that English wine is quite distinct from BRITISH WINE; that it is the produce of freshly picked grapes grown in England and Wales, rather than of reconstituted, imported, grape concentrate. The British government did little to encourage 20th century English viticulture, for many years charging a lower excise duty on British wine than on the indigenous product.

It is clear that English viticulture did not cease entirely after the Middle Ages. Samuel Pepys's diaries of life in late 17th century London record his consumption of wines made from vineyards around the city at Hatfield, Walthamstow, Greenwich, and Audley End. And, as outlined in the LITERATURE OF WINE, a number of 18th century English publications referred to domestic vine-growing. William Speechly, gardener to the duke of Portland, wrote a *Treatise on the Culture of the Vine* (1790) which discussed both hothouse vines and vineyards, and the wines they produced. England's vines, however, remained only as specialities of well-tended aristocratic estates (such as the Great Vine of the royal palace at Hampton Court, for example).

Major-General Sir Guy Salisbury-Jones established England's first commercial vineyard since the Middle Ages in the early 1950s at Hambledon in Hampshire, and over the next three decades was followed by a number of others, typically retired gentlefolk with little experience of viticulture or OENOLOGY. Since the early 1980s, however, the industry has become increasingly professional in its methods, and the total area under vine increased from about 400 ha/988 acres in the early 1980s to about 1,000 ha in the early 1990s.

Vineyards are concentrated in the warmest southern counties of Kent and Sussex, although there are about 400 vineyards all over southern England, and nearly 20 on the southern coast of Wales. Vineyards are planted in all but six counties of England, and the most northerly vineyard in the world is planted in Durham, near the 55th latitude.

The maritime influence and the Gulf Stream help to moderate the climate, but grape RIPENING so far from the equator is still hazardous, and grapes may remain on the vine until late October or even November. VINEYARD SITE SELECTION is critical in such a climate. The ideal site is a south-facing slope, with good DRAINAGE, protected from both FROST and WIND, with annual RAINFALL below 30 in/800 mm and an ALTITUDE of less than 350 ft/110 m above sea level. Spring frosts and ROT are constant problems in England's cool, wet climate. Only relatively early ripening varieties are suitable, and good resistance to FUNGAL DISEASES is a great advantage.

The most planted variety is MÜLLER-THURGAU, followed by SEYVAL BLANC, whose HYBRID status has been a major stumbling block to introducing a QUALITY WINE scheme that meets with EUROPEAN UNION approval. REICHENSTEINER is the only other variety planted on more than 100 ha in the mid 1990s, with the remaining 60 per cent of English vineyard a patchwork of dozens of other varieties, typically white GERMAN CROSSINGS, representing the frustrations of a nascent industry trying to coax RIPENESS from the English climate.

Total wine production can vary considerably, according to VINTAGE. In 1988, for example, only 4,000 hl/105,600 gal of English wine were produced, while 21,000 hl were made the following year. Average yields are about 35 hl/ha (2 tons/acre) in a good year. A little rosé and a minuscule amount of red wine (the colour sometimes the result of plastic tunnels; see PROTECTED VITICULTURE) is produced. English wine's hallmark, high acidity, is useful for the increasing proportion of traditional method English sparkling wine, but increasingly sophisticated wine-making techniques are being introduced such as MALOLACTIC FERMENTATION, BARREL MATURATION, and even some BOTRYTIZED WINE.

In the 1980s a high proportion of English wine was sweetened using (often imported) SWEET RESERVE, but a more typical current style is dry, aromatic, its acidity balanced by a certain amount of BODY, even if considerably assisted by ENRICHMENT.

The average vineyard is hardly more than 2 ha in size, and often lacks marketing skills, relying heavily on tourist traffic (not unlike the other far northern wine industries of CANADA and upstate NEW YORK, with which England shares many features, although not their extremely low winter temperatures).

ENGLISH LITERATURE, WINE IN. References to specific wines in English literature are relatively common, and provide a useful record of FASHIONS in wine styles and the history of wine imports to the British Isles, from the time

English literature: Johnson and Boswell—'filling the interval between lunch and dinner'?

of Chaucer to the present day. Literary references to wine drinking are legion, presumably because it encouraged conversation, civilized, bawdy, or sometimes nonsensical. Generic 'wine' is mentioned too often to report, and more detailed and revealing references specifying wine type or provenance are scarce in English literature before the 17th century.

The first English writer to demonstrate a serious interest in wine was Geoffrey Chaucer (1345–1400), himself the son and grandson of a vintner. *The Canterbury Tales* are dotted with references to specific wines (see CONDADO DE HUELVA, for example). The Prologue details contemporary eating and drinking habits, while the 60-year-old knight in 'The Merchant's Tale' drank spiced wine in the form of 'ypocras, clarree, and vernage' (see VERNACCIA) for 'courage' in the bedchamber.

BORDEAUX was England's chief medieval wine supplier and it dominates wine references in the literature until long after Aquitaine was ceded to France. William Shakespeare's (1564–1616) 'good familiar creature' in *Othello* would undoubtedly have been bordeaux, although 'sherris SACK' was Falstaff's favoured drink in *Henry IV, Part I* and Sir Toby Belch's call for 'a cup of CANARY' in *Twelfth Night* also demonstrates the increasing importance of Spanish wines. Shakespeare's contemporaries Robert Herrick, John Webster, and Burton certainly refer to wine, but only Robert Burton (1577–1640) mentions the evocative names of Alicant, Rumney, and Brown Bastard (respectively, wines from ALICANTE, sweet wines made in the Greek style, and a sweet blend from Portugal).

Samuel Pepys's (1633–1703) life seems to have been a succession of drinks if his diary provides an accurate record, with references to TENT, Canary, Rhenish (wine from the RHINE), and English wine from vineyards around London (see ENGLAND). Pepys also famously provides the first reference to New French CLARETS, and in particular that of 'Ho Bryan' (HAUT-BRION). Pepys mentions champagne, as does the comic playwright Sir George Etherege (?1634–91), who qualifies the reference with 'sparkling'. These, together with a brief note from Dean Swift (1667–1745), are the earliest mentions of what must have been a very new product (see CHAMPAGNE, history). Edward Ravenscroft (*fl.* 1671–97), the relatively obscure author of a rollicking farce *The London Cuckolds* (1682), which was for long performed in the City of London each year on Lord Mayor's Day, is very forthcoming, with sack and PORT mentioned almost as many times as pretty women. John Gay (1685–1732) even published in 1708 a rather indifferent poem entitled 'Wine' which mentions the mysterious drink 'Golorence'.

In the 18th century the number of references to wine by English dramatists, novelists, and poets rises dramatically. R. B. Sheridan (1751–1816) insists about claret in *School for Scandal* that 'women give headaches, this don't', and champagne appears more than once in his *Paris Sketchbook*. David Garrick (1716–79) provides one of the first mentions of burgundy in English: 'rich Burgundy with a ruby tint.' As today, however, opinions about the relative merits of various wine regions are divided. The observation of Tobias Smollett (1721–77) in his *Travels through France and Italy* that 'the Wine known as Burgundy is so weak and thin' is a useful indication of the general derision of any wine region other than Bordeaux. Even Hermitage is described as a small wine, and his hero *Humphrey Clinker* estimated that 'Life would stink if he did not steep it in Claret.'

In the 18th century Samuel Johnson (1709–84) and Parson Woodforde (1740–1803) both give disquieting insight into the prodigious quantity of both food and drink which then customarily appeared at table. Boswell reports Johnson's observation that 'few people had intellectual resources sufficient to forgo the pleasures of wine. They could not otherwise contrive how to fill the interval between lunch and dinner.' And during travels in Germany, 'I drank too much Moselle, imagining it to be a mere diuretic.' The next day he 'was uneasy from the Moselle'. There is a disparaging reference to Florence wine which 'neither pleases the taste nor exhilarates the Spirits'.

Jane Austen (1775–1817) admits to some of her characters drinking wine, although only in appropriate quantities of course. Among very few references to specific wines, the treasured South African CONSTANTIA is considered a suitable restorative for a young lady in *Sense and Sensibility.* Keats refers to claret frequently in correspondence but his most famous vinous reference is in 'Ode to a Nightingale' ('O, for a draught of vintage!' etc.). George Crabbe (1754–1832), whose works illustrate his somewhat grim sense of humour, describes the sorts and conditions of men who drink various wines in 'Champagne the courtier drinks the spleen to chase, the Colonel Burgundy, Port His Grace . . .' Crabbe's approver Lord Byron (1788–1824) is entertaining on the subject of wine and DRUNKENNESS, and recommends 'hock and soda-water' as a hangover remedy: the relief it brings is so profound as to surpass even burgundy 'after long travel'. He also turned wines into verbs, as in 'We clareted and champagned till two' in a letter to Thomas Moore. In his *Don Juan* VI. 607–8, one of the most misquoted pieces of literature (often confused with Keats), Byron eventually declares, 'If Britain mourn her bleakness we can tell her, the very best of vineyards is the cellar,' an admirable sentiment.

The 19th century writers indicate the increasing range of wines imported to the British Isles, and the widening appreciation and understanding of them. In *Melincourt* Thomas Love Peacock (1785–1866) describes wine as both 'a hierarchical and episcopal fluid' and 'the elixir of life', and further references appear in *Crotchet Castle.* Peacock was clearly a burgundy *aficionado*, daring to suggest that 'an aged Burgundy runs an ageless Port'. George Meredith (1828–1909), who married the widowed daughter of Peacock, shares his interest in burgundy; precise references to Musigny and Romanée appear in *The Egoist* and *One of our Conquerors.* R. S. Surtees (1805–64), the master of comic fox-hunting novels, brings port, champagne, and 'tolerable St Julien doing duty for Ch Margaux' into such pieces as *Handley Cross* and *Mr Sponge's Sporting Tour.* He sagely advises against the excesses of the previous century, 'no side dishes, no liqueurs, only two or three wines'.

At a somewhat more elevated level, William Thackeray (1811–63) names Beaune and Chambertin and also refers to claret, sherry, and madeira, and comments, 'if there is to be Champagne have no stint of it . . . save on your hocks, sauternes, and moselles, which count for nothing'. This last quotation is from *Pendennis,* in which appears the character Captain Shandon, heavily based on William Maginn (1793–1842), who wrote under the pseudonym Sir Morgan O'Doherty, Bt. As a regular contributor to *Blackwoods Edinburgh Magazine* Maginn wrote many wonderful 'Maxims', many of which refer to or include wine and food: they are well worth searching out, as is the 'Spectator ab extra' of A. H. Clough (1819–61), an entire poem devoted to food and drink of which the first stanza has particular appeal for this writer:

> Pass the bottle and damn the expense
> I've heard it said by a man of sense
> That the labouring classes could scarce live a day
> If people like us didn't eat, drink and pay.

Henry James (1843–1916) is particularly descriptive about Burgundy and its vineyard in *A Little Tour of France.* Robert Louis Stevenson (1850–94) also enthuses over Burgundy in *Travels with a Donkey in the Cévennes.* His ill health led to frequent foreign journeys even as far afield as California: *The Silverado Squatters* is the first literary work to include reference to the vineyards there.

Other serious 19th century writers who regularly included comments on wine are Robert Browning (1812–89), who clearly enjoyed Chablis; Charles Dickens (1812–70), whose novels, as one might imagine, mention punch more often than wine; and, most amusingly, Saki, or H. H. Munro (1870–1916), who delights in his many comments on wines and the manners of those who serve it, such as 'the conscious air of defiance that a waiter adopts in announcing that the cheapest Claret on the list is no more'. Finally, Edward Fitzgerald (1809–83), the erudite translator of the 11th century ARAB POEM *The Rubáiyát of Omar Khayyám*, must be cited, as one particular passage has cut wine merchants to the quick ever since publication: 'I often wonder what the Vintners buy, one half so precious as the goods they sell.'

The 20th century sees further geographical extension of the wine regions mentioned in English literature, and a greater awareness of the variety and quality of the products available. Hilaire Belloc (1870–1953) wrote much in praise of all sorts of drink, notably 'Advice' full of vinous references, and his 'Heroic Poem in Praise of Wine', which expresses the sentiment, 'Dead Lucre: burnt Ambition: Wine is best.' The *Forsyte Saga* of John Galsworthy (1867–1933) abounds with references to hock, especially Steinberger. Aldous Huxley offers the somewhat jaded assessment that 'Champagne has the taste of an apple peeled with a steel knife,' while Eric Newby in *Love and War in the Apennines* also paints a grim picture of the wine 'the Italians call *vini lavatori*'. But the balance is redressed by P. G. Wodehouse, whose characters' 'form' can often be restored by various vinous substances. Evelyn Waugh's diaries and letters inform us of his own serious wine-drinking habits, although only *Brideshead Revisited* among his works contains many specific wine references. He wrote a monograph *Wine in Peace and War* for wine merchants Saccone & Speed and was paid, according to his son Auberon, at the rate of a dozen bottles of champagne per thousand words. More recent novelists whose work displays a deep understanding of wine include Sybille Bedford, and Dick Francis, who in one of his novels treats good wine extensively. Wine is one of the alcoholic drinks to figure so largely in Kingsley Amis's work.

Are spy stories literature? Ian Fleming's James Bond has rather common tastes in champagne, and more than once Fleming mentions a vintage of Taittinger or Dom Pérignon which was never made. This usefully illustrates the way in which wine, mentioned by authors throughout the history of literature, is used more for illustrative purposes than anything else. In ingested form, however, wine has probably offered writers more inspiration than opium, and their references to it have helped us better understand the chronology of importation and imbibing of wine through the ages. H.G.B.

ENOLOGIST is the American and South African spelling of OENOLOGIST, just as **enology** is the alternative spelling of OENOLOGY, the study of wine and, especially, wine-making.

ENOTECA, term used frequently in Italy for a wine shop with a significant range of high-quality wines, opposed to a *bottiglieria*, a shop with a more pedestrian selection, and a *vinaio*, more of a tavern, in which wine is sold by the glass as well as by the bottle. Various **enoteche** in Italy offer tasting facilities and some serve food to accompany the wines—from the mere appetite-stimulating to the most ambitious *haute cuisine*. Regional *enoteche* and *enoteche* of a single DOC, both organized to show off the local wine production, are variations on the theme which have developed since the DOC system came into effect. The word comes from the same root as OENOTRIA, the Ancient Greeks' name for Italy, and *theke*, Greek for a case or receptacle and found in *biblioteca* or *bibliothèque*, Italian and French respectively for 'library'. D.T.

ENOTRIA, corruption of the Ancient Greek name for what is now Italy. See OENOTRIA.

EN PRIMEUR, wine trade term, French in origin, for wine sold as FUTURES before being bottled. It comes from the word PRIMEUR, or early producer. En primeur sales are a speciality, but not exclusivity, of CLASSED GROWTHS by the BORDEAUX TRADE. Cask SAMPLES of wines have customarily been shown in the spring following the vintage and sales solicited, through BROKERS and NÉGOCIANTS, almost immediately. A particular property often releases only a certain proportion, or *tranche*, of its total production, depending on its need for cash and reading of the market.

This form of early sale has long been available to the wine trade, but was undertaken by wine consumers only in the late 20th century. It has been most popular in times of frenetic demand such as in the very early 1970s (when some wine was even sold *sur souche*, or on the vine before the grapes were picked) and throughout the 1980s, when a succession of good VINTAGES coincided with widespread economic prosperity and the accessibility of early VINTAGE ASSESSMENTS from the wine trade and press. The consumer pays the opening price as soon as the offer is made and then up to two years later, having paid the additional shipping costs and DUTY, takes delivery of the wine after it has been bottled and shipped. The theory is that, by buying wine early, the consumer not only secures sought-after wines, he or she also pays less. This is by no means invariably the case, however, as outlined in INVESTMENT in wine.

En primeur purchases have many disadvantages in periods of economic recession. Not only do prices stagnate or even fall, but there is a much higher risk that one of the many commercial concerns in the chain between wine producer and wine consumer will fail, leaving the consumer with the possibility of having paid for the wine without any prospect of receiving it. There is also the important fact that en primeur purchases inevitably mean investing in an embryonic product. A third party's assessment of a single cask sample taken at six months is a poor justification for financial outlay on a liquid that is bottled only a year later (and is particularly hazardous for a wine as notoriously transient as red BURGUNDY), unless the wine market is extremely buoyant.

Buying en primeur may make financial sense only for the most authoritatively lauded vintages and the most sought-after wines, although it can of course give a great deal of pleasure to those with a strong wine-COLLECTING instinct.

ENRICHMENT (*amélioration* in French,. *Anreicherung* in German), wine-making operation whereby the fermentable sugars of grape juice or must are increased in order to increase the ALCOHOLIC STRENGTH of the resultant wine. This is traditionally and habitually done to compensate for natural underripeness in cool regions or after particularly cool summers in warmer regions. The original process, often called CHAPTALIZATION after its French promulgator CHAPTAL, involves adding sugar, whereas the wider term enrichment encompasses the addition of sugar, grape must, concentrated grape must, and rectified concentrated grape must, or RCGM, and is the term favoured in official EUROPEAN UNION terminology.

Enrichment is the wine-making counterpoint to ACIDIFICATION, which is the norm in hot wine regions. Most regions' wine regulations set limits for these processes and most of them, as in Bordeaux and Burgundy, for example, forbid the enrichment and acidification of the same batch of wine.

Geography

Enrichment is the norm in climates which cannot be relied upon to bring grapes to full ripeness every season: throughout northern Europe, for example, in the north eastern wine regions of the UNITED STATES, throughout CANADA, BRAZIL, in JAPAN, and in much of NEW ZEALAND, especially for red wines.

At the coolest limits of vine cultivation it is a prerequisite of wine production. The poorest summers in the United Kingdom, for example, yield grape sugar levels in some varieties that have difficulty reaching the legal minimum potential alcohol level of five per cent. In regions as cool as England and Luxembourg, the so-called Zone A of the EU, musts may be enriched to a maximum increase in alcoholic strength of 3.5 per cent (4.5 per cent in particularly unripe years) for white wines, and an additional 0.5 per cent for red wines.

Many Burgundian wine-makers, in Europe's Zone C where potential alcoholic strength may be raised by up to two per cent, and with a particularly variable climate, accustomed themselves to automatic enrichment, regardless of the characteristics of the growing season and ripeness of the grapes. This resulted in some unbalanced, excessively alcoholic wines in ripe vintages such as 1983 and 1989.

In Bordeaux, also in Zone C, chaptalization has also been the norm historically, and is thought to provide 'support' for wine's flavour, but some producers are developing alternative techniques for juice CONCENTRATION, a practice increasingly used elsewhere.

In principle, enrichment is forbidden for TABLE WINE produced within the EU, although there are local exceptions.

Enrichment is also much relied upon, especially for more commercial wines, in eastern Europe, Switzerland, Austria, and Germany. Indeed the major distinction between Germany's better-quality wine classified as QMP and ordinary QBA wine is that QmP wines may not be enriched by added sugar (although they may include SÜSSRESERVE of comparable ripeness for sweetening purposes). Similarly in AUSTRIA, sugar may not be added to wines of Kabinett quality or above.

In southern France, notably Languedoc-Roussillon, the southern Rhône, Provence, and Corsica, and throughout the rest of the south of the EU, chaptalization is expressly forbidden, but enrichment using concentrated must of various sorts is often permitted, and even encouraged, depending on the quality level of the wine and the characteristics of the VINTAGE. This sort of enrichment by adding concentrated must is commonplace in northern Italy, and provides an end use for vast quantities of otherwise SURPLUS wine made in southern Italy (see Materials below).

Wine-makers prohibited from practising enrichment tend to scorn the practice as artificial and manipulative (just as those in cooler regions, prohibited from adding acid, are wary of the practice of ACIDIFICATION).

There are wine regions, however, such as TASMANIA, the recently planted vineyards on the southern tip of SOUTH AFRICA, and even some of the higher vineyards of northern Italy, in which chaptalization is prohibited, to the detriment of wine quality in many seasons, simply because they belong to a political unit whose other wine regions are too hot to need it.

Materials

SUCROSE is the usual enrichment material used. In northern Europe this has normally been refined sugar beet, or occasionally cane sugar.

In an effort to help drain Europe's WINE LAKE, however, EU authorities have been trying to encourage the use of high-strength grape sugar syrups made from surplus wine, especially in Italy and southern France (see GRAPE CONCENTRATE and RECTIFIED GRAPE MUST for more details). Enrichment using grape concentrate is also permitted in Australia, where sugar may be added only to induce the second fermentation for sparkling wines.

Adding grape concentrate rather than sugar, however, has the effect of diluting flavour, as those determined to make only the very best German wines are well aware.

Technique

The enrichment material may be added before and/or during FERMENTATION. Both sugar and acid tend to inhibit yeast growth, however. Adding the enriching sugar when fermentation is already fully under way avoids the delay which could ensue if it were added to the original must.

About 1.8 kg/4 lb of sugar is needed to raise the alcoholic strength of 1 hl of wine by one per cent (slightly less for less dense white and rosé wine musts), which means that stacks of sugar sacks can be a regular sight in many large and not-so-large French wine cellars.

When conducted properly, enrichment increases the volume of the wine negligibly, has no tastable effect on the wine, and merely compensates for Nature's deficiencies in a particular growing season. Enriched wines certainly should not taste sweet, since all of the fermentable SUGARS should have been fermented into ALCOHOL; the wine should merely have more BODY and BALANCE than it would otherwise have done.

The non-wine-making observer may wonder, however, why in an age in which many consumers wish to curb their consumption of alcohol, and there is a global wine SURPLUS, the wine industry systematically and deliberately increases the alcohol content of so many of its products, in many cases to compensate for overcropped vines (see YIELD).

ENTRAYGUES, or **Entraygues et du Fel, Vins d'**, miniature VDQS in SOUTH WEST FRANCE. Fewer than 10 ha/25 acres of vines around Entraygues on the river Lot in the Aveyron *département* were dedicated to the production of this wine in the early 1990s. Reds can be made from a wide range of south western vine varieties while the even rarer whites are made from Chenin Blanc and Mauzac.

ENTRE-DEUX-MERS, large area of the BORDEAUX wine region between the rivers DORDOGNE and GARONNE; hence a name which means 'between two seas'. A high proportion of the vineyard land in this pretty, green region (which has much in common with BERGERAC to its immediate east) is light red, often slightly austere wine made from MERLOT and CABERNET grapes and sold as BORDEAUX AC. Indeed, since vine-growers converted their white wine vineyards to red varieties in the 1960s and 1970s, the Entre-Deux-Mers district has become the chief source of red Bordeaux AC. The Entre-Deux-Mers region contains a number of other appellations, some of them enclaves such as GRAVES DE VAYRES, STE-FOY, Bordeaux-Haut-

Benauge (dry white wines which may also be sold as Entre-Deux-Mers-Haut-Benauge). The PREMIÈRES CÔTES DE BORDEAUX and its sweet white wine-making enclave lie between the Entre-Deux-Mers appellation and the river Garonne. Wines sold as Entre-Deux-Mers are dry whites made, with degrees of wine-making skill which vary from minimal to dazzling, from SAUVIGNON, SÉMILLON, MUSCADELLE, and UGNI BLANC grapes. After Bordeaux AC, this is the biggest dry white wine appellation in the Bordeaux region, producing well over 150,000 hl/3.96 million gal in an average year. Clay and sandy clay predominate and this is one of the few French wine districts to have adopted the LENZ MOSER system of high vine TRELLISING to any great extent. Most Entre-Deux-Mers should be drunk as young as possible.

Matthews, T., *Village in the Vineyards* (New York, 1993).

ENZYMES, large molecules containing a PROTEIN segment which functions in all living systems to catalyse reactions which would otherwise be extremely slow. Enzymes, named using the suffix 'ase', are characterized by both their substrate and the reaction which they catalyse.

Enzymes are very sensitive to their environment, functioning poorly at particularly high and low temperatures, which is one reason why vines show low rates of PHOTOSYNTHESIS at high and low temperatures. INVERTASE, for example, aids photosynthesis in vine leaves, combining carbon dioxide and water into sugar by converting SUCROSE to the invert sugars FRUCTOSE and GLUCOSE. Invertase also converts the non-fermentable sugar sucrose into fermentable sugars during CHAPTALIZATION.

The PECTINS in grape must may slow the rate at which solids settle, and so pectolitic enzymes (pectinoses) are often added to break up pectins, decrease the VISCOSITY of the juice, and speed SETTLING, especially after cool growing seasons.

Proteases split proteins into polypeptides and AMINO ACIDS which are more readily used by yeasts and bacteria and thus promote both alcoholic FERMENTATION and MALOLACTIC FERMENTATION.

Grapes affected by BOTRYTIS BUNCH ROT contain high concentrations of the enzyme laccase, which promotes very rapid OXIDATION and browning of the juice and young wine. At the end of fermentation the combination of higher ALCOHOLIC STRENGTH, the TANNINS, and added SULPHUR DIOXIDE reduce the enzyme activity, thereby making the wine stable to laccase-catalysed oxidation.

Special enzymes have been developed for particularly aromatic wines such as those based on Gewürztraminer and Riesling grapes, which, if added after fermentation, are able to free the terpene FLAVOUR COMPOUNDS that are bound in a non-aromatic, polymeric form, thereby substantially increasing the AROMA of the resulting wine.

During wine AGEING, various oxidase enzymes may play a role in hastening the oxidation of PHENOLICS. A.D.W. & T.J.

ÉPAMPRAGE. See DESUCKERING.

ÉPINEUIL, commune just west of Chablis. See Côtes d'AUXERRE for more information.

ÉRAFLAGE, French term for DESTEMMING grapes meaning literally 'scratching'.

ERBALUCE, white grape variety, speciality of Caluso in the north of the PIEDMONT region of north west Italy. Most dry Erbaluce is relatively light bodied and acidic, although there are some fine examples. Erbaluce's most famous, if rare, manifestation is the golden sweet Caluso PASSITO.

ERINOSE MITE. The grapevine is the only known host in the plant kingdom to the grape erineum mite, *Colomerus vitis*, sometimes called grape leaf blister mite. The mite is widely distributed, but usually only causes minor damage in commercial vineyards. The damage first appears as pinkish or reddish swellings or galls on the upper surfaces of the leaves. Beneath the gall, the concave portion of the leaf is lined with a felty mass of plant hairs or 'erinea'. The erinea later turn yellow, and then brown. This is one of the most unsightly grape pest problems, yet it has negligible effects on vine performance. In addition to the leaf galling form of this insect there also exists a strain which, although indistinguishable from the erinose mite, inhabits the buds and feeds on the tissues in the dormant buds and also the shoots as the buds break. Control is usually by preventive applications of SULPHUR dust, and, as this is often applied to control POWDERY MILDEW, these mites are often incidentally controlled. M.J.E.

Buchanan, G. A., and Amos, T. G., 'Grape pests', in B. G. Coombe and P. R. Dry (eds.), *Viticulture, ii: Practices* (Adelaide, 1992).

ERMITAGE, alternative and historic name for HERMITAGE in the northern Rhône.

EROSION. See SOIL EROSION, a severe problem in some steeply sloping vineyards.

ERYTHORBIC ACID, alternative antioxidant to ASCORBIC ACID.

ERZEUGERABFÜLLUNG, German word meaning literally 'producer bottled'. In theory this word should indicate quality, and certainly all the finest wines of Germany qualify as Erzeugerabfüllung, but, as in France (see MIS EN BOUTEILLE), the term may be used by CO-OPERATIVES to describe blends of wines from many different member-producers over whose viticultural techniques the bottler exercises no control. One useful aspect of the term, however, in a country where wine label obfuscation is rife, is that it cannot be used by the giant mass market bottlers (see GERMANY and, particularly, MOSEL-SAAR-RUWER), except for those vineyards they themselves own. GUTSABFÜLLUNG is a more exclusive term.

ESCA, one of the earliest vine FUNGAL DISEASES ever described, with records dating from Roman times. It is a problem in warm regions, but is not present all over the world. The disease is due to wood-rotting fungi but the causal agent is not definitely known. Esca, or the vine apoplexy of Europe, is probably the same vine disease as California's black measles. Affected leaves have a burn between the veins, typically in midsummer, and may fall off. Affected berries may fail to size or develop violet patches, hence the name measles. Infected vines may suddenly die, especially in hot weather. In California the disease typically causes loss of leaves. Cutting the arms or trunk shows dead zones of wood. The fungus probably gains entrance through large wounds made at pruning so these should be avoided. Sprays of sodium arsenite in winter after pruning provide control. Ten- to 15-year-old vineyards are more susceptible than young vineyards, probably because they have accumulated more pruning wounds. R.E.S.

Pearson, R. C., and Goheen, A. C., *Compendium of Grape Diseases* (St Paul, Minn., 1988).

ESGANA and **Esgana Cão**, synonyms for the Portuguese white grape variety known on the island of Madeira as SERCIAL. Its full name on the mainland means 'dog strangler', presumably a reference to its notably high acidity. It can be found as an ingredient in VINHO VERDE, BUCELAS, and white PORT.

ESPADEIRO, red grape variety known, although not widely grown, in both the RIAS BAIXAS zone of Galicia and Portugal's VINHO VERDE country. It can produce quite heavily and rarely reaches high sugar levels.

ESPALIER, a relatively unusual TRAINING SYSTEM for vines or other fruit trees, by which the plant is trained to grow in a single plane to form a flat shape, for example against a wall (see diagram). Espalier training leaves a trunk and one or two arms with several canes which are trained in the same plane with a trellis or wire for support. Different vines are trained to different heights in the French Espalier de Thoméry. R.E.S.

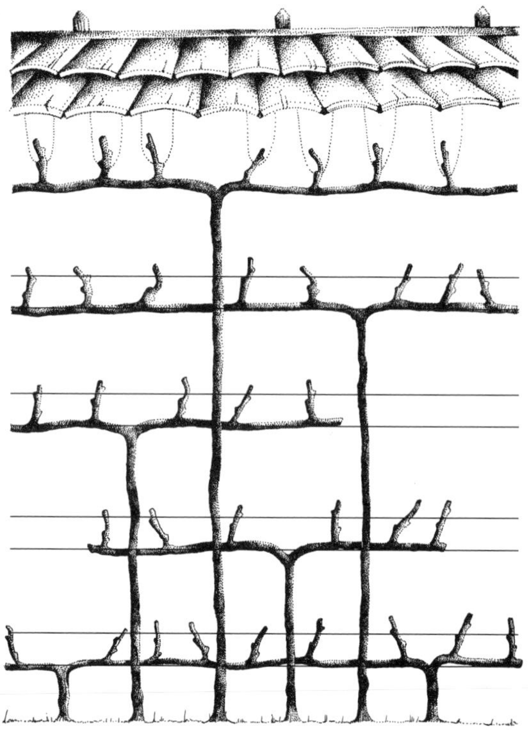

Espalier

ESPUMOSO, Spanish for sparkling (although Spanish sparkling wine that is exported is more likely to be labelled CAVA).

ESTAING, VINS D', miniature VDQS in SOUTH WEST FRANCE. Fewer than 10 ha/25 acres of vines around Estaing up the river Lot from ENTRAYGUES in the Aveyron *département* were dedicated to the production of this wine in the early 1990s. Reds can be made from a wide range of south western vine varieties. A very small quantity of white wine is made from Chenin Blanc and Mauzac. The climate here makes MARCILLAC look positively balmy.

ESTATE BOTTLED, term used on labels which has a very specific meaning in the United States, where an estate bottled wine must come from the winery's own vineyards or those on which the winery has a long lease; both vineyards and winery must be in the geographical area specified on the label. This is the American counterpart of CHATEAU BOTTLED or DOMAINE BOTTLED.

ESTER, name now used by chemists for the compounds formed by reaction of organic ACIDS with ALCOHOLS. Originated by the German chemist L. Gmelin and published in his 1842 handbook, the designation for these compounds is now universally accepted by scientists. The two most common forms of esters in wine are FERMENTATION esters, commonly found in the aroma of young white wine (sometimes called biochemical esters), and esters that are chemically formed during AGEING (sometimes called chemical esters).

The fresh, fruity aroma of young wines derives in large part from the presence of the mixture of esters produced during fermentation, which is why it is usually called fermentation AROMA. The precise nature of esters formed during fermentation is strongly influenced by the fermentation temperature. For more details, see TEMPERATURE.

Other natural organic compounds of grapes and from fermentation are of many chemical classes other than esters and it is the smell of these compounds, when mixed with the general fruitiness, that provides the nuances of aroma that permit varietal and regional identification (as in BLIND TASTING).

Since wines contain much more ETHANOL than any other alcohol, and since the most common volatile organic acid is ACETIC ACID, it is not surprising that the most common ester in wine is ETHYL ACETATE, but many more combinations are possible, and help to explain why wines differ so greatly in their aroma and, after years in bottle, BOUQUET.

A number of esters that are not particularly odoriferous are also present in wines. Among these are those resulting from reaction of the ethyl alcohol produced by fermentation with TARTARIC, MALIC, SUCCINIC, and other acids of the grape and wine, and such acids may yield a series of compounds, depending on how many of the acid functions are **esterified**. In certain young wines, for instance, a significant proportion of the acid taste can be the result of these partially esterified acids.

Further **esterification**, as occurs after many years, reduces the tart taste as the second acid function is esterified. This is one reason why most wines, and red wines in particular, tend to taste smoother or softer with age (although in some the acid seems more prominent as they age—presumably because the fruitiness and TANNINS diminish at a faster rate than the tartness).

Esters are among the many compounds involved in plant metabolic processes and therefore appear frequently in fermenting systems such as bread and wine. Although yeast and bacteria may contain the ENZYMES for production of esters within their cells, such esters are normally of much less importance than those produced by reactions catalysed by hydrogen ions between acids and alcohols in the wine medium.

When an acid reacts with an alcohol, water is produced in addition to the ester. This reaction is assisted or catalysed by the hydrogen ion, a substance plentiful in acid (low PH) solutions such as wines. Hydrogen ions not only catalyse the formation of esters from acids and alcohols, they also function as catalysts for the splitting of esters into their acid and alcohol segments. The result of these two tendencies, formation and splitting, is that wines contain mixtures of the four participants in the reactions: organic acids, alcohols, the several esters from the possible combinations, and water. The relative amounts of the four participants in the two reactions is governed by their concentrations and the reaction rates for formation and splitting. Given enough time, a state will be reached in which the net formation of esters just balances the splitting of them. This is known as the equilibrium state and describes what could be reached if a wine were aged long enough. In practice, the equilibrium state in wines is not reached but merely approached, because the formation rates for some esters are extremely slow under wine storage conditions.

The fact that esters are formed at different rates, some of them reaching equilibrium only after decades, helps to explain the changes in wine aroma and bouquet as wine ages.

Esters frequently reveal themselves in the odours of household materials such as nail polish remover. A.D.W.

ESTUFA, Portuguese word meaning hothouse or stove, also applied to the tanks used to heat wine on the island of MADEIRA, thereby accelerating its development and maturation. The heating process itself is called **estufagem**. *Estufas* simulate the effects of the long tropical sea voyages in the 18th and 19th centuries when madeira (and SETÚBAL) was, at first accidentally and then deliberately, stowed in the hold of a ship to age prematurely as a result of the temperature changes involved in a round trip, or *torna viagem*, across the tropics. R.J.M.

ETHANOL, scientific name for ethyl alcohol, the most potable of the ALCOHOLS and an important, intoxicating constituent of wine and all other alcoholic drinks. Ethanol, often called simply 'alcohol', is colourless and odourless but can have considerable impact on how a liquid tastes. Wines relatively high in alcohol—over 13 per cent for example (see ALCOHOLIC STRENGTH)—can taste sweet even if they contain practically no RESIDUAL SUGAR. Wines whose alcohol level robs them of their BALANCE may 'burn' or taste 'hot', especially in the after-taste. Alcohol makes an important contribution to VISCOSITY so that, as a general rule, wines described as full bodied, or having considerable BODY, are high in alcohol while wines that are low in viscosity and body are low in alcohol. Alcohol may also play a role in wine conservation since low alcohol wines may be prey to BACTERIAL attack. See ALCOHOLIC STRENGTH for ways in which the alcohol level may be manipulated.

Ethanol is produced in two ways, the most traditional and natural of which is by the FERMENTATION of solutions that contain SUGARS by YEAST, such as that involved in wine production. It is required in huge volumes by industry, however, as a solvent for perfumes and as a raw material for the synthesis of products such as drugs, plastics, lacquers, polishes, plasticizers, and cosmetics. Most of the ethanol used by industry, other than that produced by distilling the European wine surplus, is produced in factories by hydrating ethylene, a component of petroleum. When petroleum is treated with the proper catalyst, a molecule of water combines with the ethylene to yield ethanol, which is then separated and purified by DISTILLATION in large CONTINUOUS STILLS. A.D.W.

ETHYL ACETATE, the most common ESTER in wine, and a natural organic compound present in most fruits, berries, other foods, and alcoholic drinks. Ethyl acetate is present in much higher concentrations than any other ester because it is formed by the reaction of the most common volatile organic acid in young wine, ACETIC ACID, with the most common alcohol produced by FERMENTATION, ETHANOL.

Ethyl acetate dominates the aroma of young wines, modified and varied by the different combinations of other chemical compounds present. Grape variety, weather, soil, and wine-making practices govern the types and concentrations of these other compounds and thus the AROMA and BOUQUET of the resultant wine. Present in moderate concentrations, ethyl acetate is perceived as contributing to the generally

The traditional **estufa** entailed simply storing madeira in the heat immediately under the roof.

fruity character—although people vary in their sensitivity to the compound.

At higher concentrations, however, ethyl acetate can become unacceptably dominant and increasingly impart the character described as VOLATILE and, eventually, vinegary. (Wine VINEGAR, on the other hand, with its even higher concentration of ethyl acetate, is in equilibrium, with correspondingly high concentrations of acetic acid.) In wine, the concentration of ethyl acetate is governed or limited by a relatively low concentration of acetic acid. In wine vinegar, the much higher concentration of acetic acid equilibrates with the higher ethyl acetate concentration.

Wines exposed to oxygen first lose their fresh fruitiness and become vapid in smell and taste because of the ACETALDEHYDE resulting from the oxidation of ethanol. The OXIDATION goes further to yield acetic acid from the acetaldehyde intermediate and then, when some of this acetic acid reacts with ethanol, ethyl acetate is produced. By the time this stage is reached the wine is no longer wine but wine vinegar which combines the sharp, acid taste of acetic acid with the odour of ethyl acetate. A.D.W.

ETHYL ALCOHOL, traditional, non-scientific name for ETHANOL, the alcohol most commonly encountered in wine and other alcoholic drinks.

ÉTOILE, L'. See L'ÉTOILE

ETRUSCANS. The origins of viticulture in TUSCANY are as problematic as the origins of the Etruscan peoples who flourished in central north Italy from the 8th century BC until being absorbed by the Romans from the 3rd century onwards. However, at its height Etruscan society was heavily influenced by the culture of the Greek colonies of southern Italy. They imported fine Greek pottery for use in the SYMPOSIUM and made their own copies. The dinner and drinking party was a favourite theme in the lavish paintings which adorned their tombs. Indeed, the Etruscans became a byword among Greek and Roman moralists for luxurious living and eccentric customs, such as allowing wives to participate in banquets. There are literary references to Etruscan wine from the late 3rd century BC, but much earlier, from the late 7th century, the wine was exported in a distinctive type of AMPHORA well beyond Italy to southern France. Various wines are attested throughout the region in the classical period, although none was universally recognized as of the highest class. J.J.P.

Bouloumie, B., 'Le Vin etrusque', *Quaderni della scuola di specializzazione in viticoltura e enologia* (Turin), 7 (1983), 165–88.
Cerchiai, C., *L'alimentazione nel mondo antico: gli Etruschi* (Rome, 1987).
Heurgon, J., *Daily Life of the Etruscans* (London, 1964).

EU stands for EUROPEAN UNION.

EUCHARIST, WINE IN THE. The significance of wine in the Christian sacrament of Eucharist derives from the meanings of wine in the BIBLE and from the purposes of a variety of religious rituals. Metaphors of the vine, the vineyard, wine bottling, and wine-making show that wine was as important then as now in the Mediterranean region for rejoicing and happiness. God's generous love of his people is symbolized by his gift of 'the fermented blood of the grape for drink' (Deut. 32. 14). The contrast of old wine and new wine is often used, new wine bursting its container, a proof of exuberance.

In Jewish sacrifices, wine to signify well-being and abundance, and animal blood to signify life itself, were both offered by being poured out, and so given back to God, in acts of thanksgiving, worship, and atonement for sin. Neither was consumed by the participants. Indeed, uniquely among contemporary cults of the Near East, the Jews were forbidden to consume blood because 'the life of the creature is in the blood and I have given it to you for performing the rite of expiation on the altar for your lives, for blood is what expiates for a life' (Lev 17. 11). Instead, the wine was emptied out in libation, and blood was sprinkled on altar and people, sealing the covenant between God and his people. In the celebration of the annual Passover supper, wine was drunk in joyful commemoration of the deliverance (redemption) by God of the whole people from enslavement to the Egyptians. In that original act of liberation, the Jewish first-born were preserved from death by the sprinkling of the blood of a sacrificial lamb upon the doorways of their houses.

On the dark side, red wine is often compared with bloodshed. Contact with blood could be a defilement. Lapses into pagan ritual sacrifices involving human blood earned God's particular condemnation. Drinking from a cup and especially drinking it to the dregs was an expression indicating deep suffering rather than rejoicing, and the CRUSHING of grapes in the wine PRESS was a metaphor for the punishment of God. When Christ in spiritual agony in the garden of Gethsemane, anticipating his betrayal and death, prays for 'this cup' to be taken away from him (Matt. 26. 39–42), there is an echo of

Eucharist: the Mass of St Gregory by Maître de la Flemalle, Brussels.

Isaiah's 'the stupefying cup', the cup of God's wrath (Isa. 51. 22), and Ezekiel's 'cup of affliction and devastation' that has to be drunk (Ezek. 23. 33).

In the light of this tradition, the words of Christ to his disciples would have been mysterious, even scandalous, yet evocative: 'If you do not eat the flesh of the Son of Man and drink his blood you have no life in you . . . for my flesh is real food and my blood is real drink. Whoever eats my flesh and drinks my blood lives in me and I live in that person' (John 6. 53–6). At his last supper before his crucifixion, Christ takes the cup and says, 'Drink from this all of you, for this is my blood, the blood of the new covenant poured out for many for the forgiveness of sins' (Matt. 26. 28). It was wine, so it should have been for rejoicing, but drinking from a cup could have the connotations of the cup of suffering, and as for drinking blood, that would be an inconceivable abomination. Yet his next words, 'From now on . . . I shall never again drink wine until the day I drink the new wine with you in the kingdom of my father' (Matt. 26. 29), suggest his joyful renewed presence with his followers at the messianic banquet that the Old Testament prophet Isaiah described when in the last times God would make for his people a feast of good things, including wine (Isa. 25. 6). Finally Christ commands his Church do this in memory of me.

So, the Eucharist of the risen Christ becomes the principal act of Christian faithfulness. In it the participants share in the redemptive death and resurrection of Christ through sacramental communion with his body and blood, signified by consuming consecrated bread and wine. By his blood shed on the cross the Eucharist has power to give peace and unity and continuously makes the Church into a unified, living body. It is called eucharist or thanksgiving since, at his last supper with his disciples, Christ pronounced over the wine (and bread) the traditional thansksgiving to God when he inaugurated a new covenant between God and his people in his own blood to be poured out in the sacrifice of the cross. Wine, in particular, would recall the blood shed by Christ whom some contemporaries greeted as the Lamb of God.

Controversy

Rites intended for unity tend paradoxically to be the focus of disunity, and the Eucharist is no exception. The eucharistic wine challenges the Old Testament tradition from which it originates. For the Jews, blood shed in animal sacrifice reconciled God and humans—it made atonement, literally, putting man and God 'at one'. Christ puts his own death in the place of that of the sacrificial animal. The Christian doctrine of drinking wine that has (sacramentally) become blood, even the blood of Christ the son of God, would be rejected as scandalous by Jews. Conversely, the Christian sacrifice of bread and wine in the Eucharist is a rejection of the shedding of blood in animal sacrifice.

After the Reformation, seemingly irreconcilable views about the Eucharist separated Protestants and Roman Catholics, notably about the exact meaning of the Eucharist as a 'memorial' of Christ's death and as a sacrifice, and about the sense in which the wine (and bread) become the body and blood of Christ. After the disputes of the Reformation there are now welcome signs of a reconvergence of views in which the emphasis is placed on the real presence of Christ in the Eucharist as a sacramental sign of his redemptive death.

A lesser controversy concerns receiving communion in the form of both bread and wine. In the course of centuries the Church had developed the practice of allowing the laity to take communion only under the form of bread, reserving communion under both species for the celebrant. The Church maintained, that since Christ is fully present under both species, this was only a matter of Church discipline and practical convenience—problems of hygiene with the cup and so on. All the great Reformers—Wyclif, John Huss, Luther, Calvin—campaigned for the restoration of communion wine for the laity, wishing to reduce the distinction between the celebrant and the congregation, and this has become universal in the Reformed tradition. In the 1960s the Second Vatican Council allowed, subject to the local bishop's permission, communion under both kinds for the Catholic laity.

Sacramental signs are supposed to be 'natural', that is, unmistakable and able to be specified unambiguously. So the sacramental wine has to be fermented juice of the grape: it should not be turned to VINEGAR, nor heavily diluted with water; it must be real wine. But tradition fixes what the sacramental signs are and tradition varies. The fermented juice of the grape is what has always been meant by 'wine' in those parts of the world where Christianity arose. However, in spreading over the globe, Christianity encounters regions where the grapevine has never grown and where there never has been wine of the grape. The question arises in the world of MISSIONARIES whether the tradition could be modified to include rice 'wine', for example, or palm 'wine'.

There are other pastoral issues for sacramental wine. Christian missions among the urban poor in the 19th century were sensitive to the dangers of alcoholism. Was it right to put temptation in people's way? Was it even right to accord high ritual status to alcohol? John Wesley, the father of the Methodist tradition, took it for granted that the Eucharist should be celebrated with wine. In the second half of the 19th century, the alternative of celebrating with grape juice ('unfermented wine') gradually became common in the Methodist Church, under the influence of 'temperance' movements in both Britain and the United States.

A similar question was raised in relation to alcoholic priests in the Catholic Church. In 1974 bishops were authorized to grant to priests who had been treated for alcoholism permission to drink the unfermented juice of the grape instead of wine at the Eucharist. This authorization was revoked in 1983: in the Roman Catholic Church the symbolism of wine is recognized to be so central that even alcoholic priests are not now dispensed from taking at least a trace of wine when celebrating the Eucharist (by 'intinction', dipping the bread in the consecrated wine).

See also RELIGION and MONKS AND MONASTERIES. J. & M.D.

Albert, J.-P., 'Le Vin sans ivresse: remarques sur la liturgie eucharistique', in D. Fournier and S. d'Onofrio (eds.), *Le Ferment divin* (Paris, 1992).
Jeremias, J., *Die Abendmahlsworte Jesu* (3rd edn., Göttingen, 1960), trans. as *The Eucharistic Words of Jesus* (London, 1966).
Tillard, J. M. R., *The Eucharist. Paths of God's People* (New York, 1967).

EUDEMIS, a flying insect which can damage vines. See MOTHS.

EUROPEAN UNION (EU), known as the **European Community** (EC) before the Maastricht Treaty came into force in November 1993, a group of advanced western industrialized countries co-operating on both economic and political fronts. Of its 12 member countries in the mid 1990s, eight produce wine, yielding a total which represents about 60 per cent of the world's wine production.

About 3.5 million ha/8.5 million acres within the Union were planted with vines at the end of 1993, representing about 42 per cent of the total global vineyard area (a significant proportion of Asian vines produce DRYING GRAPES and TABLE GRAPES rather than wine). Spain has the most extensive area under vines in Europe, and indeed the world, although France and Italy produce substantially more wine than Spain and indeed than any other country. The other EU wine-producing countries are, in descending order, Portugal, Germany, Greece, Luxembourg, and the United Kingdom. Although the EU includes some of the most industrialized nations of the world, it is in Europe that wine is of greatest social and economic importance. Vines are planted on five per cent of the Union's agricultural land and employ 10 per cent of its agricultural work-force.

Wine produced within the EU is designated either TABLE WINE or QUALITY WINE, each country having its own precise system. Wine imported into the EU, known as 'third country wine', must conform to European wine law and may not be blended with wine made within the EU.

The EU is an important net exporter of wine, but within the EU both France and Germany import considerable quantities of wine from Italy.

The EU represents the world's most important market for wine, accounting for almost half of global consumption, although average per capita consumption varies considerably bewteen countries. The 345 million people in the European Union are tending to drink less, but better wine, especially in richer northern countries. Consumption is plummeting at a rate of 2 million hl a year, especially in the southern wine-producing countries. Production, meanwhile, is still potentially rising. The market for table wine has been shrinking fastest, but even that for quality wines seems saturated.

The European Commission, the Union's Brussels-based executive, estimates that if current trends continue, production will stand at around 178 million hl by the year 2000, with a SURPLUS of around 39 million hl, or nearly 22 per cent of European production.

Mindful of its many vine-growing and wine-producing inhabitants, the Union has tried to curb output via its Common Agricultural Policy. In 1982 it imposed compulsory distillation on over-producers (see DISTILLATION, COMPULSORY). In 1984 it made these provisions even stricter. In 1988 it offered premiums to producers grubbing up vines (see VINE PULL SCHEMES) so that more than 320,000 ha were grubbed up between 1988 and 1993, notably in Spain. No new planting is allowed without special authorization (indeed some CLASSED GROWTH proprietors in the Médoc were asked to pull up some particularly expensive, but unauthorized, new vines in 1993). This wine policy accounts for between three and five per cent of total EU farm spending, and cost over 1.6 billion European Currency Units in 1993.

In July 1993, the Commission, which proposes legislation on which member states decide, signalled that tougher measures would have to be introduced to achieve balance in the market by the year 2000. It acknowledges that the effect of the compulsory distillation scheme has been to transform, at considerable cost, a wine surplus into an ALCOHOL surplus, and admits that there are profitable outlets for less than half of this output on the alcohol market. 'The trend will be towards production of wine in smaller quantities, but of better quality,' the Commission says in a paper for EU agriculture ministers.

The Commission proposes:

- Asking the regions producing wine to draft plans for reducing areas under vine and controlling YIELDS, even of quality wines. There would be EU aid for growers complying.
- Curbing wine-making practices, particularly ENRICHMENT, that encourage production.
- Reforming the compulsory distillation system by cutting prices to over-producers.
- Policing the compulsory distillation system effectively to curb ADULTERATION AND FRAUD.

The EU has specific LABELLING requirements, although individual EU countries may have national legislation on labelling that goes beyond these requirements.

The Commission negotiates accords on trade in wine on behalf of EU member states with other countries. In 1993 it concluded agreements with Australia, Bulgaria, Hungary, and Romania, and started negotiations with New Zealand, while plans for a new accord with the United States were in the pipeline. Accords cover reciprocal protection and control of wine denominations, and tariff quotas. Australia has, for instance, agreed to phase out use of French names such as Champagne and Chablis, while France and Italy have agreed to stop using the term Tokay. E.K.

The Agricultural Situation in the Community 1992: Report (European Commission, 1992).
Cahiers de la PAC 1993: Vin (European Commission, 1993).
'Commission Communication to the Council: Development and Future of Wine Sector Policy,' COM (93) 380.
'Proposals for Council Decisions on wine accords with Bulgaria, Hungary, Romania,' COM (93) 358–9.

EUROPEAN VINES, much-used description for varieties of the common vine species VINIFERA of the VITIS genus, as opposed to AMERICAN VINE SPECIES and Asian vine species.

EUSKADI. See BASQUE.

EU TABLE WINE, for long called **EC table wine**, is wine at its most basically European, a blend of TABLE WINES from more than one country in the European Union, until 1993 known as the European Community. The constituents of an EU table wine tend to vary with the vagaries of the bottom layer of the European wine market. One of the most common blends, however, has been cheap white VINO DA TAVOLA from Italy, neutralized by extensive FILTRATION, CENTRIFUGATION, and, sometimes, CHARCOAL treatment, 'Germanized' by the addition of some German TAFELWEIN made from a heavily aromatic variety such as MORIO-MUSKAT, and sold as EWG TAFELWEIN. In France, EU table wine blends have included blends of French red VIN DE TABLE and much deeper coloured vino da tavola from southern Italy, and blends of French white vin de table with the much cheaper Spanish white VINO DE MESA.

EUTYPA DIEBACK, one of the FUNGAL DISEASES which, by rotting the wood, can be very destructive and cause whole vineyards to be replanted. Sometimes it is known as dying arm, and is called **eutypiose** in France. Distribution is world wide, over a wide range of climates. It is especially common in MEDITERRANEAN climates such as California, south eastern Australia, south west France, and South Africa. The disease became more widespread in southern France in the 1980s. Eutypa is caused by the fungus *Eutypa lata*, synonymous with the fungus *Eutypa armeniacae*. Many other plants are attacked by the fungus and it is a major disease of apricots. Symptoms rarely show in vineyards less than eight years old, but this can be several years after infection has occurred. In the mid 1990s there was concern in France, for example, that the disease had spread beyond the COGNAC region which had most obviously been attacked. Young shoots are stunted and yellow with cupped leaves, thought due to a toxin produced in the infected trunks or arms. Old wood cut open reveals dead sapwood extending from an old pruning wound which was the point of entry of the fungus. No vine variety is immune, but some such as Cabernet Sauvignon, Sauvignon Blanc, Ugni Blanc, and Grenache are more susceptible. Infection takes place with mild temperatures following rain. Pruning wounds less than four weeks old can be infected. It is difficult to control the disease by removing infected vine parts as spores may blow in from other host plants. Studies in California suggest that spores may travel betweeen 50 and 100 km (30–60 miles). Painting the fresh pruning wound with a paste of the FUNGICIDE Benlate is very effective in stopping infection. R.E.S.

Emmett, R. W., Harris, A. R., Taylor, R. H., and McGechan, J. K., 'Grape diseases and vineyard protection', in B. G. Coombe and P. R. Dry (eds.), *Viticulture ii: Practices* (Adelaide, 1992).

Pearson, R. C., and Goheen, A. C., *Compendium of Grape Diseases* (St Paul, Minn., 1988).

EUVITIS, considered by many botanists to be one of two sections of the genus VITIS (see BOTANICAL CLASSIFICATION), the other being MUSCADINIA. These two are considered to be two separate genera by others, since *Euvitis* and *Muscadinia* vines differ in chromosome number and in appearance. All of the commercially important wine, table, and drying grapes belong to the genus *Euvitis*. R.E.S.

Mullins, M. G., Bouquet, A., and Williams, L., *Biology of the Grapevine* (Cambridge, 1992).

EVANS, LEN (1930–), promoter, taster, judge, consumer, teacher, and maker of wine who has done more to advance the cause of wine in AUSTRALIA than any other individual. Born in Felixstowe, England, he is an architect *manqué*, like his friend Michael BROADBENT, but in Evans's case the distraction was professional golf rather than wine. He emigrated to New Zealand in 1953 and arrived in Sydney, Australia, two years later, where his stepping stone into what was to become a lifetime's immersion in wine was working for the new Chevron Hilton Hotel. His energetic enthusiasm for wine was such that by 1965 he was the first National Promotions Executive for the Australian Wine Board. Evans was one of the few to see that the future lay in table wine rather than in the sweet fortified drinks in which Australia then specialized. A natural performer and publicist, Evans caused such a stir that Australians were apparently convinced that real men could indeed drink table wine, and since then table wine has become increasingly important to Australia's social life, and indeed economy.

By 1969 he was writing books and articles on wine, had left the Wine Board, and was starting up the Rothbury Estate in the HUNTER VALLEY and establishing his own restaurant-cum-dining club at Bulletin Place by Sydney Harbour. He collected people, preferably famous, with as much enthusiasm as seriously fine wine, but distinguished himself in his practical relish of both. He did not just raise BLIND TASTING to an art form, but even oversaw the creation of a game predicated on it, the OPTIONS GAME which has since been put to work raising substantial sums for charity under Evans's direction.

In the late 1970s it seemed as though Evans, by now an intimate of the great and the good of the wine world, was about to take it over. Financed by a tax lawyer friend Peter Fox, he acquired properties in GRAVES, SAUTERNES, and the NAPA Valley, with plans to staff them using an early version of the FLYING WINE-MAKER concept. His exceptional tasting skills had also been recognized by his numerous invitations to judge at Australia's important wine COMPETITIONS, and by his appointment as chairman of judges (the first of many) at the Royal Sydney Show.

In 1981 Peter Fox was killed in a crash and the Evans Wine Company was thrown into turmoil. From the remains, Rothbury eventually survived, as did the Petaluma winery in the ADELAIDE HILLS, with which Evans was involved from the start. Evans attempted to rusticate himself at his much embellished mud hut 'Loggerheads' overlooking Rothbury.

The ebullient Len **Evans**.

Since then he has continued to write, broadcast, and keep tables or halls full of people entertained, while reminding them that wine is for drinking. He has been awarded an Order of the British Empire for services to wine and the community, as well as numerous wine industry distinctions.

EVAPORATION, conversion of water (or other liquids) from the liquid to the gaseous or vapour state, brought about by the input and absorption of heat energy. It has important implications for both growing vines and maturing wines and spirits.

Viticulture

Evaporation from vineyard soils can affect grape and wine quality.

The power of the atmosphere to evaporate water is related inversely to its HUMIDITY and directly to its temperature. Unfortunately the direct climatic records of evaporation, or potential evaporation, are sparse. The records are further confused by the fact that different countries use different instruments for measurement. Nevertheless broad averages for regions can be estimated with fair accuracy.

Such figures are still not uniformly applicable to vineyards, however. Evaporation varies among sites within regions due to wind, depending in turn on TOPOGRAPHY, WINDBREAKS, and, within the vineyard, CANOPY MANAGEMENT. For these and other reasons most viticultural scientists continue to use the more commonly available statistic of relative humidity, which, considered together with temperature, provides an accurate enough indicator of potential evaporation.

Evaporation out of grapevine leaves (a process known as TRANSPIRATION) takes place mainly through pores, or STOMATA, which form openings in the waxy leaf surface. It is regulated by opening and closing of the stomata, with closure taking place regularly at night. Transpiration from individual leaves is increased by their direct exposure to sunlight, which provides the energy needed for evaporation.

On the other hand stress, whether due to lack of water available to the vine roots, atmospheric heat and aridity, or strong wind—or any combination of these—can close stomata during the day. But in saving itself from moisture loss under these conditions, the vine also shuts off entry of CARBON DIOXIDE into the leaves, and therefore reduces potential growth and yield. Under conditions of very high evaporation, this can occur even when the soil is quite wet (see WATER STRESS). Thus the potential yield of irrigated vines in arid areas can often be less than that of adequately watered vines in more humid climates, assuming that they receive about the same amount of SUNLIGHT. This is additional to the likely adverse effects on grape and wine quality of low relative humidities and high evaporation rates described in CLIMATE AND WINE QUALITY.

Inadequate evaporation from wet leaves and bunches is, of course, a factor in FUNGAL DISEASE infection. Vine-growers in many climates deliberately trim vines and remove leaves from the vicinity of the bunches, partly to allow in more light, but partly also to encourage evaporation, and thus avoid diseases like BOTRYTIS BUNCH ROT (see CANOPY MANAGEMENT).

J.G. & R.E.S.

Maturation

Evaporation also causes a loss of liquid stored in tight wooden containers, such as wine or brandy undergoing BARREL MATURATION. WATER, the principal component in wines, diffuses through small pores of OAK, eventually reaching the outer surface of the stave where it evaporates into the atmosphere. ALCOHOL also diffuses through the stave, but at a rate considerably slower than that of water.

The atmosphere in contact with the barrel STAVE contains many molecules of water vapour (more when humidity is high, fewer in dry conditions) but relatively few molecules of alcohol. Water vapour molecules which hit the stave may stick and thus create a thin film of water on the staves' outer surface which slows the net transfer of water from the barrel interior to the atmosphere. Since there are relatively few alcohol molecules in the atmosphere, no film of alcohol accumulates on the staves' outer surface and the rate of evaporation is not slowed. To summarize, wine or brandy subjected to barrel maturation in a high-humidity storage cellar will decrease in ALCOHOLIC STRENGTH, while that stored in a dry cellar will increase.

This is why COGNAC matured in barrels stored in the damp British climate, sometimes described as 'early landed', is quite different from that matured in the warmer, drier climate of western France. It also explains why, in the low-humidity SHERRY bodegas of JEREZ, it is common practice to sprinkle water on the earth floors to raise the relative humidity and therefore prevent the alcoholic strength of the wine under FLOR film yeast from increasing to the point at which the yeast would be killed.

Evaporation is almost negligible in new, tight barrels that are stoppered with a new bung, but some air will seep into any older or poorly made wooden container around the bung and badly fitting joints between staves and tank heads. In such cases, regular TOPPING UP is essential.

The space left by this evaporation is called the ULLAGE, while the liquid lost is sometimes called the 'angels' share' and is particularly financially significant in the production of older cognac and armagnac. A.D.W.

EVAPOTRANSPIRATION, total loss of water from a vineyard. See EVAPORATION and TRANSPIRATION.

EWG TAFELWEIN, basic wine blended from the produce of more than one European Union country. For more details see EU TABLE WINE and TAFELWEIN.

EXCORIOSE. Vine disease. See DEAD ARM.

EXTRACT, or **dry extract**, the sum of the non-volatile solids of a wine: the SUGARS, non-volatile ACIDS, MINERALS, PHENOLICS, GLYCEROL, glycols, and traces of other substances such as PROTEINS, PECTINS, and gums. Sometimes sugars are deliberately excluded to give sugar-free extract. Wines' extract, including sugars, usually starts at between 17 and 30 g/l but can vary considerably depending on the wine's SWEETNESS, COLOUR (red wines usually having a higher extract than whites, thanks to their greater phenolic content), and age, since some extract is precipitated as SEDIMENT over the years.

Historically, extract was determined by the simple expedient of evaporating a measured quantity of wine and weighing the residue, but this method is imprecise and has been replaced by techniques involving the measurement of ALCOHOLIC STRENGTH, the DENSITY, and the RESIDUAL SUGAR (if sugar-free extract is required).

To be high in extract, a wine does not necessarily have to be high in alcohol or BODY. Many fine German wines are high in extract, and yet are low in alcohol and are light bodied, especially low yield Rieslings after dry summers.

Determinations of sugar-free extract have been useful in detecting fraud and ADULTERATION in wine. Although they do not constitute proof, abnormally high or low extract values are reason to suspect fraudulent manipulation. Fraud is much less prevalent than in the era immediately post-PHYLLOXERA in the late 19th and early 20th centuries so that determinations of extract value are now less frequent in wine analyses.

A.D.W.

EXTRACTION in a wine context usually refers to the extraction of desirable PHENOLICS from grape solids during and after FERMENTATION. See MACERATION for more details.

EXTREMADURA, one of the 17 autonomous regions in SPAIN and, surprisingly, the country's fourth most important producer of wine. Spain's wild west is hardly ideal for growing grapes. Sheep are reputed to outnumber people in this semi-arid upland area between CASTILE-LA MANCHA and PORTUGAL (see map on p. 907). Most of the wine is sold in bulk for DISTILLATION, and local names rarely appear on labels, but one small zone on the Portuguese border is helping to drag Extremadura from vinous obscurity. Tierra de Barros, meaning land of clay, earned a provisional denomination in 1979 and has been struggling for promotion to full DO status ever since. Its reputation rests with one producer, Bodegas Inviosa, who are making solid, if slightly rustic, reds from their own Cencibel (TEMPRANILLO) and GARNACHA grapes. Some CABERNET SAUVIGNON has also been planted. Other growers earn a living from productive white grapes such as the CAYETANA and Pardina, which are generally vinified in poorly equipped wineries. Much of the wine ends up as BRANDY de Jerez. CORK is an important crop here. R.J.M.

EZERJÓ, white grape variety widely planted in HUNGARY but scarcely known outside it. Most of the wine produced is relatively anodyne, but Móri Ezerjó produced from the vineyards near the town of Mór enjoys a certain following as a light, crisp, refreshing drink, and the Ezerjó grown, in quantity, in the far north west of Hungary can also yield lively dry whites for early consumption. Ezerjó means 'a thousand boons'.

F

FABER, or **Faberrebe**, like SCHEUREBE, a German vine crossing bred by Dr Scheu at Alzey in the Rheinhessen in the early 20th century. This crossing of Weissburgunder (Pinot Blanc) and Müller-Thurgau emerged in 1929. Faber, which will ripen easily in sites unsuitable for Riesling, has been particularly popular with growers in the Rheinhessen where three-quarters of Germany's total of 2,000 ha/5,000 acres were grown in 1990, although total plantings are declining after a peak in the mid 1980s. Germans see Faber as a 'traditional' variety in that it shows some of the raciness of Riesling and has markedly more acidity than Müller-Thurgau. Acidity levels are even higher than those of Silvaner which adds considerably to its appeal although the wines are not intensely flavoured, are not designed to age, and are generally more useful for blending than for VARIETAL wines. Faber can easily be persuaded to reach the must weights that qualify for SPÄTLESE status if picked after Müller-Thurgau in a fine autumn. Like the even more popular BACCHUS, Faber suffers from stalk NECROSIS and, like the most popular modern crossing KERNER, needs careful trimming during the growing season.

FACTORY HOUSE, handsome Georgian monument on a patch of British soil in OPORTO to the power of the British in the port wine trade. The only surviving example of any Factory House, it is possibly the only actual building constructed as a meeting place for a 'factory', a body of traders or 'factors' buying and selling any commodity in a foreign country. The Portuguese were probably the first to establish such a factory, which they called a *feitoria*, in one of their earliest West African settlements. The first British factory was established by the East India Company near Bombay in 1613. By the beginning of the 18th century British factories had been established in all major Portuguese ports, including of course Oporto, from which wine was an important export (see PORTUGAL). The Factory House, probably the first and only permanent meeting place for the Oporto factory, was begun in 1786 and finished, under the supervision of the consul John Whitehead, four years later.

The British factory's enjoyment of their grand, and determinedly exclusive, new clubhouse was cut short by the French invasion of Portugal in 1807. The official reopening of the Factory House took place at a dinner based on the number 11 on 11 November 1811. The factory itself was abolished and replaced by the British Association in Oporto in 1814 after British port traders had trickled back to enjoy a period of unparalleled prosperity and privilege.

The British Association (which still boasts its own Cricket and Lawn Tennis Club) is made up exclusively of members drawn from the British port shippers. So firmly are these British port shippers entrenched in Oporto and, especially, Vila Nova de Gaia immediately across the Douro from the city, that the most exciting event in the Factory House's subsequent history was the granting of a perpetual lease by King Don Miguel in 1832.

The Factory House continues to be maintained for the exclusive use of the British port shippers, whose directors (many of them related) meet for lunch at the Factory House every Wednesday according to strict rules: no women, no smoking before 2 p.m., napkins taken from dining room to the same place in the near-identical dessert room next door where the shipper and year of the vintage port served are to be guessed at. Relations between the Factory House and the Portuguese-run Instituto do Vinho do Porto nearby are understandably delicate.

Delaforce, J., *The Factory House at Oporto* (London, 1983).

FALERNIAN or **Falernum** was the most famous and most highly prized wine of Italy in the Roman period. It was produced on the southern slopes of Monte Massico, the range of hills which runs down to the west coast of Italy in northern CAMPANIA. With a precision which was unusual for the Romans, three distinct zones, or CRUS, were distinguished: Caucinian on the hilltops, Faustian on the slopes (probably in the region of present-day Falciano), and Falernian proper at the edge of the plain. Recent archaeological survey has revealed numerous Roman farms in this region and part of a vineyard of Roman date has been excavated. The vines were trained up trees and also on trellises on poles of willow.

Falernian was a white wine of at least two types, one relatively dry, the other sweeter. As with other Roman fine wines such as CAECUBAN and MASSIC, it was normal to age it considerably. It was considered drinkable between 10 and 20 years. Its distinctive colour, deep amber, was probably the result of MADERIZATION, which may also explain the references to 'dark' Falernian in one source. The frequent descriptions of the wine's 'strength' and 'heat' suggest a high ALCOHOLIC STRENGTH. One curious claim was that it was the only wine which could be set alight! Despite the concern of PLINY in the second half of the 1st century AD that the reputation of Falernian was being endangered by a commitment to quantity rather than quality, the wine remained in the front rank until at least the 4th century AD.

The contemporary revival is Falerno del Massico, produced in white, blended red, and all-PRIMITIVO grape versions in modern CAMPANIA. J.J.P.

FALKENSTEIN, important wine centre in lower AUSTRIA, now part of the Weinviertel district.

FANLEAF DEGENERATION, sometimes called **fanleaf virus**, one of the oldest known VIRUS DISEASES affecting vines. Records of it date back some 200 years in Europe and there are indications that it may have existed in the Mediterranean and Near East since grape culture began. Rather than being a single disease, it is in fact a complex of related diseases which include forms known as yellow mosaic and vein-banding. Shoot growth is typically malformed, leaves are distorted and asymmetric, and teeth along the edge are elongated. Shoots show abnormal branching with double nodes, short internodes, and zigzag growth. Leaves on infected plants look fanlike—hence the name. Bunches are smaller than normal, with poor FRUIT SET and many 'shot' (seedless) berries. Sensitive varieties such as Cabernet Sauvignon can lose up to 80 per cent of potential yield and have a shortened productive life.

The disease can be detected by INDEXING using varieties of other species of VITIS such as Rupestris St George, or with other plants such as Chenopodium, or by serological tests using ELISA. The virus can be spread by infected planting material, and this reached widespread proportions in the late 1880s with the adoption of grafting vines on to ROOTSTOCKS resistant to PHYLLOXERA. A second means of spread was discovered in California in 1958. The NEMATODE *Xiphinema index* spreads the disease within a vineyard by feeding on the roots of infected plants and then healthy ones. Thus the symptoms of the disease spread slowly around an original infected plant.

There is no control for an infected vineyard and it must be removed. The virus particle can survive in root pieces for over six years. Nematode populations can be reduced by FUMIGATION. Current research aims to develop resistant rootstocks for planting in infested vineyards. The most successful method is to plant virus-free vines in a nematode-free soil. Fanleaf-free planting material is readily obtained by THERMOTHERAPY or TISSUE CULTURE. (See also NEPOVIRUSES.) R.E.S.

Bovey, R., *et al.*, *Virus and Virus-Like Diseases of Vines: Colour Atlas of Symptoms* (Lausanne, 1980).

Pearson, R. C., and Goheen, A. C., *Compendium of Grape Diseases* (St Paul, Minn., 1988).

FARA, small red wine DOC in the Novara hills of eastern PIEDMONT in north west Italy. The wines are made from the NEBBIOLO grape. For more details, see SPANNA, the local name for Nebbiolo.

FASCIATION, a growth abnormality, of shoots in particular, in which growth is broadened and flattened as though there were several shoots fused side by side. It is relatively rare in grapevines, although some varieties seem to be prone. The cause is unknown but it is a common symptom of FANLEAF DEGENERATION infection. B.G.C.

Perfectly preserved Victorian kitchen in Oporto's **Factory House** with knife sharpener in the foreground.

FASHION has played a part in wine consumption, and therefore eventually wine production, for at least two millennia. The wine drinkers of Ancient ROME favoured white wines, preferably old, sweet white wines (see FALERNIAN, for example). Indeed throughout much of the modern age sweet, heady wines have been prized above all others. In the early Middle Ages the wine drinkers of northern Europe had to drink the thin, tart, sometimes spiced ferments of local vineyards because TRANSPORT was so rudimentary, and RHINE wines were considered the height of fashion. But when these consumers were introduced to such syrupy Mediterranean potions as the wines of CYPRUS and MALMSEY, wines traded so energetically by the merchants of, for instance, VENICE, a fashion for this richer style of wine was established. By the 16th century, for example, light, white ALSACE wine was regarded as unfashionable by the German wine drinker (see GERMAN HISTORY), who was beginning to favour red wines. Many fashions were restricted to one particular district or region, particularly before the age of modern communications. It is clear that the wines favoured by the French court in the medieval period, for example, were considerably influenced by fashion, and, possibly, more pragmatically political considerations (see MEDIEVAL LITERATURE and ST-POURÇAIN).

Towards the end of the Middle Ages, fashion seems to have begun to favour not just RESIDUAL SUGAR, but ALCOHOLIC STRENGTH too. Such wines as SACK and TENT from southern Spain were valued for their potency, although by the end of the 17th century seafaring and exploration brought a new range of drinks to the trendsetters of northern Europe (see COFFEE HOUSES) which were very much more fashionable than any form of wine.

A new age demanded new products, and the most durable of these were the so-called New French Clarets (see CLARET and BORDEAUX, history), whose initial success was largely due to fashion. In the 18th century, however, no wines were more fashionable than a clutch of what a modern salesperson might call 'speciality items': Hungarian TOKAY, South African CONSTANTIA, and Moldavian COTNARI. These were available in necessarily very limited quantities, but the wine styles created during or soon after this period illustrate the wine qualities regarded as fashionable then: PORT, MADEIRA, MÁLAGA, and MARSALA are all remarkable for their colour, alcohol, and often sweetness.

By the 19th century much more detailed evidence of the wines then considered most fashionable is available, not just in the form of CLASSIFICATIONS and a number of books specifically comparing different wines (see LITERATURE OF WINE), but also in the form of price lists—for wine PRICES have reflected fashions in wine throughout history. It would surprise the modern wine drinker, for example, to see the high prices fetched by German wines compared with the classified growths of Bordeaux in the late 19th and early 20th centuries. The late 19th century was also a time in which CHAMPAGNE was considered exceptionally modish in northern Europe, notably in St Petersburg.

In the 1920s and 1930s, wine in almost any form was extremely unfashionable. This was the age of the cocktail on one side of the Atlantic and of PROHIBITION on the other. These phenomena, together with the marked decline of traditional markets and a world-wide economic depression, threatened many small-scale vine-growers with penury (this was the era during which so many wine CO-OPERATIVES were established).

It was not until well after the Second World War, when some measure of real economic recovery and stability had returned, that wine slowly re-established itself as a fashionable drink (although of course it had long been a drink of necessity in wine-producing areas). As foreign travel became an economic possibility for the majority of northern Europeans, consumers in non-producing countries began to link wine with a way of life they associated with leisure, the exotic, and warmer, wine-producing countries.

By the late 1970s wine CONNOISSEURSHIP itself was beginning to be fashionable, and the economic boom of the 1980s provided the means for a new generation of COLLECTORS. This led inevitably to a fashion for marathon 'horizontal' and 'vertical' TASTINGS of scores of bottles at a time. Buying wine EN PRIMEUR was particularly fashionable in this decade of superlative VINTAGES.

What has been most remarkable about fashions in wine consumption in the late 20th century, however, has been how rapidly wine production has reacted to them, and in some cases created them (see wine BRANDS, pale cream SHERRY, LOW ALCOHOL wine, and wine BOXES among others). The speed of producer reaction is doubtless related to the development of wine criticism, and its publication in the more immediate media of newspapers, newsletters, magazines, radio, and television, rather than books.

Perhaps the most significant fashion has been for VARIETAL wines, especially but by no means exclusively in the NEW WORLD. This has led to a dramatic increase in the area planted with INTERNATIONAL VARIETIES—Chardonnay, and to a lesser extent Cabernet Sauvignon, in particular. During a single decade, the 1980s, the world's total area planted with Chardonnay vines quadrupled, to nearly 100,000 ha/247,000 acres. There is hardly a country in which wine is produced that does not at least try to produce commercially acceptable Chardonnay in marketable quantities.

On a much more limited scale, the development of a cult following for the distinctive wines of CONDRIEU in the northern Rhône has meant that VIOGNIER, the vine variety from which it is made, was introduced to wine regions as far afield as ROUSSILLON, South Australia, and several parts of California in the late 1980s and early 1990s.

Such versatility in a crop which usually takes at least three years to establish, and is expected to last about 20 years once planted, has been greatly encouraged by the practice of TOP WORKING, or field grafting.

There have inevitably been casualties among unfashionable vine varieties. Many workhorse varieties have lost ground, which is no great shame, but so has an often rich diversity of indigenous varieties, which is surely regrettable. Outside Germany and Austria, the Riesling vine was one of the most significant varieties to have suffered a sad contraction of influence during the 1980s.

In the vineyard, there has been a fashion for seeking not just RIPENESS, but PHYSIOLOGICAL RIPENESS (and 'soft' rather than 'hard' TANNINS), even if viticultural ACADEME denied all knowledge of the concepts.

Another viticultural fashion in evidence around the world has been the long overdue acceptance of the now much-vaunted maxim that 'wine is made in the vineyard not the winery'. But if WINE-MAKERS were so much more fashionable than VITICULTURISTS in the 1980s, some of what they did seemed heavily influenced by fashion. The flavour of new OAK, particularly French oak, became extremely fashionable in the 1980s, as to a lesser extent did the practice of MALOLACTIC FERMENTATION, together in some quarters with an overstatement of the flavours associated with it.

Of course fashions change rapidly, and what is fashionable in southern England, for example, may not be fashionable in Sydney or San Francisco. But for certain periods there are wine types and whole wine regions which can be said to be generally out of fashion outside their region or country of production. Obvious examples early in 1994 included most German wines, Beaujolais, and sherry, although by the end of 1994 at least one of these could once again find itself under the fickle spotlight of fashion.

FATS, see LIPIDS.

FATTORIA, Italian for a farm, also used for a wine estate. A *fattoria* is generally bigger than a PODERE.

FAUGÈRES, red wine appellation in the LANGUEDOC in southern France. About 1,500 ha/3,705 acres of vineyard, mainly at relatively high altitudes (about 250 m/820 ft) on schistous foothills of the Cévennes, look down on the plains around Béziers where vines are dedicated to VINS DE PAYS and VIN DE TABLE. The Faugères appellation vineyards are planted with quintessentially Mediterranean grape varieties to produce big, southern reds that taste like a cross between the spice of the southern RHÔNE and wild, rustic CORBIÈRES to the south west. Faugères graduated from VDQS to AC status in 1982. When the Coteaux du Languedoc appellation was created in 1985, Faugères was grafted on to it, given the status of special CRU, like neighbouring ST-CHINIAN. The ubiquitous Carignan is gradually being replaced by Syrah, Grenache, and Mourvèdre (each of them mandatory in Faugères), and Cinsaut is still grown for fruit and rosés. As Carignan declines in importance, so CARBONIC MACERATION is expected to be replaced by more traditional vinification techniques. From 1997 Carignan may represent no more than 40 per cent of the

One of Emilia-Romagna's more delightfully named **fattorie**.

blend. Top-quality producers such as Alquier eschew carbonic maceration, and have been experimenting with BARREL MATURATION and refinements thereof since the mid 1980s.

FAULTS IN WINES vary, of course, according to the taste of the consumer. Some diners will quite wrongly 'send back' a wine (see SERVING WINE and SOMMELIER) simply because they find it is not to their taste. Taste varies not only according to individuals but also according to nationality. Italians are generally more tolerant of bitterness, Americans of SWEETNESS, Germans of SULPHUR DIOXIDE, the French of TANNINS, and the British of decrepitude (see MATURITY) in their wines, while Australians tend to be particularly sensitive to MERCAPTANS. To wine-makers, however, wine faults are specific departures from an acceptable norm, the least quantifiable of which may be a lack of TYPICALITY.

Visible faults

Faults in a wine's appearance are generally either hazes, clouds, or precipitates in the bottle, all of which hazards STABILIZATION is designed to avoid. (In the past, BACTERIA sometimes affected a wine's VISCOSITY, but this problem is rare today.) Haze and cloud in bottled wines can have a variety of causes, of which the most common today is the growth of the micro-organisms YEAST or bacteria. Mycoderma is a yeast-related fault which forms a film on the wine's surface (and so may be visible to wine-makers, if not wine consumers). Clouds from heat-unstable PROTEINS and from heavy metal contamination do occur but they are much less frequent than they were in the era of copper and brass pipes and taps.

Precipitates, especially crystalline ones, are found from time to time and are usually the harmless result of excess potassium or calcium TARTRATES finally coming out of solution. (Tartrate stabilization usually guards against this.) From white wines, these may form as needle-like colourless or white crystals on the end of the cork in contact with the wine or in the bottom of the bottle where they look misleadingly like shards of glass. From red wine, tartrate crystals are usually dyed red or brown from the adsorbed PHENOLICS. See SEDIMENT.

Visible bubbles in a supposedly still wine are frequently viewed as a fault. Some wines, particularly off-dry whites, are deliberately bottled with a trace of CARBON DIOXIDE gas to make them taste more refreshing. Bubbles in a bottle of older wine, particularly a red wine, usually indicate unintentional FERMENTATION IN BOTTLE, however, and are definitely a fault.

While most consumers would agree that cloudy wines are faulty, there is much less agreement about COLOUR. Some wine judges in COMPETITIONS automatically disqualify rosé wines with a hint of amber, even though it is almost impossible to make a pure pink wine out of the GRENACHE grape variety, for example—and wines of all sorts and hues turn amber with age.

OXIDATION, which can brown wines prematurely, is a fault in young table wines but is best confirmed by the nose.

Smellable faults

Off-odours can vary considerably. Oxidized wines (see above) smell flat and ALDEHYDIC. VINEGARY wines indicate the presence of ACETIC ACID due to microbiological activity by bacteria and yeast. ETHYL ACETATE, HYDROGEN SULPHIDE, mercaptans, excess sulphur dioxide, and the smellable compounds generated by some bacteria all can be reasons for judging a wine faulty. The picture is complicated, however, by the fact that we all vary in our sensitivities to most of these compounds (see TASTING), and some of them may be more acceptable in some sorts of wine than others. Acetaldehyde, for example, is the principal odorant of FINO sherries, but definitely indicates over-oxidation in white wines, and makes red wines taste vapid and flat. Although the average palate should not detect acetic acid on a fault-free wine, there are some much-admired, full bodied red wines (such as some PORT, PENFOLDS Grange and VEGA SICILIA) whose VOLATILITY is much higher than the norm. Many fine German wine-makers at one time deliberately used relatively high concentrations of sulphur dioxide to preserve some of their best wines for a long life in bottle.

A wine may not smell clean because of the influence of one or several CONTAMINANTS such as agrochemical RESIDUES. If it smells of geranium leaves, there has probably been some bacterial degradation of SORBIC ACID, although this can easily be controlled by adding sulphur dioxide at the same time.

A wine may smell MOULDY either because of BACTERIAL SPOILAGE, or because it has taken on the smell of a less-than-clean container. A wine tainted by waterlogged COOPERAGE may be described as STAGNANT.

Another much-discussed microbiological fault, which can cause a wine to smell mousy, may be caused by yeasts of the BRETTANOMYCES genus, closely related to DEKKERA. It can be a symptom of other bacterial and yeast activity and cannot normally be smelled in wine unless it is alkalinized or rubbed in the palm of the hand (an action which neutralizes wine acidity). This mousy flavour is volatile only at neutral or high PH, which explains why it is not immediately apparent but builds up in the back of the mouth once a wine has been swallowed or expectorated, as the palate slowly returns to neutral PH through the buffering action of saliva.

Some wines smell so stale and unpleasant that the taster is unwilling even to taste them. The most likely explanation for this is a mouldy cork causing cork taint. Such a wine is said to be CORKED, but a wine served with small pieces of cork floating in it indicates a fault in the SERVICE of the wine rather than a fault in the wine. Contact with fragments of sound cork does not harm wine.

Tastable faults

Most faults are already obvious to the nose and need only confirmation on the palate (which is why in a restaurant it is, strictly speaking, necessary only to smell a sample of wine offered by the waiter). Some contaminations, notably from metal, are easier to taste than smell, however, and a wine that is excessively tannic or bitter (see BALANCE) will not display this fault to the eye or nose. A.D.W.

Amerine, M. A., and Roessler, E. B., *Wines: Their Sensory Evaluation* (San Francisco, 1976).
Peynaud, É., *The Taste of Wine* (London, 1987).

FAVORITA, white grape of PIEDMONT in north west Italy, often considered a relation of VERMENTINO because of the resemblance between the bunches of the two varieties, is cultivated near ALBA, both on the left bank of the Tanaro in the ROERO zone, and on the right bank in the LANGHE hills. Native to Piedmont, Favorita was not widely planted in the mid 1990s, having lost ground to ARNEIS in the Roero and to the newly popular CHARDONNAY in the Langhe; annual production was little over 700,000 bottles per year. The wine itself has a pleasant citric tang, and its higher ACIDITY seems to permit longer AGEING potential than Arneis has thus far demonstrated, but it has no very marked personality. Experiments with small BARREL MATURATION have added more aromatic qualities, as have blends with more characterful grape varieties, Chardonnay in particular. Favorita may have more of a future as the base wine of a blend than as a VARIETAL wine. D.T.

Anderson, B., *The Wine Atlas of Italy* (London and New York, 1990).
Gleave, D., *The Wines of Italy* (London and New York, 1989).

FENDANT, Valais name for the most planted grape variety in SWITZERLAND, the productive CHASSELAS. Fendant is therefore one of the most common Swiss VARIETAL wines, although the finest examples of Valais wines made from this grape variety tend to have some geographical designation on the label.

FER, alias **Fer Servadou** (and many other aliases), is a black grape variety traditionally encouraged in a wide variety of the sturdy red wines of SOUTH WEST FRANCE. In MADIRAN, often called Pinenc, it is a distinctly minor ingredient, alongside Tannat and the two Cabernets. In GAILLAC, called Brocol or Braucol, it has also lost ground. It is technically allowed into wines as far north as Bergerac, but today it is most important to the red wines of the Aveyron *département*, ENTRAYGUES, ESTAING, and the defiantly smoky, rustic MARCILLAC. The iron-hardness of the name refers to the vine's wood rather than the resulting wine, although it is well coloured, concentrated, and interestingly scented. Fer has also been invited to join the already crowded party of varieties permitted in CABARDÈS.

The variety called Fer of which there are about 1,500 ha/3,200 acres in Argentina is apparently a clone of MALBEC.

FÉRET. See COCKS ET FÉRET.

FERMENTATION, as it applies to wine, is the process of converting SUGAR to ETHANOL (ethyl alcohol) and CARBON DIOXIDE effected by the anaerobic (oxygen-free) metabolism of YEAST. It comes from the Latin word *fervere*, to boil, and any mass containing sugar that has been infused with yeast certainly looks as though it is boiling, as it exudes carbon dioxide bubbles.

History

Before yeast's metabolic processes were properly understood, the word fermentation was also used to describe a much wider range of chemical changes that resulted in the appearance of boiling and in some of which carbon dioxide evolved. These have included the leavening of bread, the production of cheese, and the tumultuous reactions of acids with alkalis. Today such changes involving the intervention of yeast or BACTERIA in aerobic processes are not usually considered true fermentations.

By the middle of the 19th century, our understanding of science was such that opinions were divided about the nature of 'organized ferments' as opposed to 'unorganized ferments' in fermentation. Thanks to Louis PASTEUR, we now know that it is the organized ferments, the yeasts and bacteria, that are primarily responsible. They act through their internal ENZYMES, the unorganized ferments which, functioning as catalysts, mediate the series of reactions involved in the conversion of sugar into alcohol and carbon dioxide.

The net change during fermentation of one glucose molecule giving two alcohol and two carbon dioxide molecules expressed as a chemical equation is:

$$C_6H_{12}O_6 \rightarrow 2C_2H_5OH + 2CO_2$$

Many years and the research talents of several scientists, notably Embden, Meyerhof, and Parnas, have elucidated the successive steps in the apparently simple conversion of sugars to the metabolic end products, alcohol and carbon dioxide.

The complex process

The first steps in the process attach phosphate groups to the sugars. Next comes a series of steps in which the six-carbon sugar is split into two three-carbon pieces, one of which is then rearranged into the structure of the other. After some further rearrangements this three-carbon molecule loses its terminal carboxylic carbon atom in the form of carbon dioxide gas. The residual part is the two-carbon compound ACETALDEHYDE, which goes next to alcohol if oxygen is lacking, or into another multi-step series of reactions eventually yielding energy, water, and more carbon dioxide if generous amounts of oxygen are available.

The net change when oxygen is present in excess is one glucose plus six oxygen molecules giving six carbon dioxide and six water molecules, as shown by this chemical equation:

$$C_6H_{12}O_6 + 6O_2 \rightarrow 6CO_2 + 6H_2O$$

Ideally for the yeast, therefore, the process should be carried out with generous quantities of oxygen available, for then much more cell-building energy is produced. For wine-making man, however, it is important that this process can be modified by limitation of the oxygen supply because then alcohol, rather than water, is produced along with carbon dioxide. Without the alcohol there would be no wine.

(It is interesting that this same series of steps in decomposition of sugar is employed by man during muscular activity, another form of fermentation. In man, and other mammals, the three-carbon compound PYRUVATE is converted to LACTIC ACID and supplies energy for muscular action.)

A number of intermediate compounds are involved. The biochemical reactions converting one compound into its successor in this series are not 100 per cent efficient, with the result that small amounts of certain of the intermediate compounds accumulate in the wine. These compounds and their reaction products with other substances in the mixture contribute to what is known as fermentation, or secondary AROMAS. Included among these compounds are ACETALDEHYDE, ETHYL ACETATE, and numerous other ESTERS, FUSEL OILS, and ACETALS.

Physical chemistry tells us that the reaction of six-carbon sugar to ethanol and carbon dioxide yields generous amounts of energy. A significant portion of this energy is captured during the process and used by the yeast for its own purposes. Another major portion of the energy, however, is not captured but appears as waste heat. Unless this waste heat is removed from the fermenting mass, its temperature will rise, reaching levels which damage or kill the yeast cells and stop the reaction, resulting in a 'stuck fermentation' which can be very difficult to restart. Heat removal is not a major problem when fermentations are conducted in a small FERMENTATION VESSEL because the greater ratio of surface to volume furnishes sufficient radiation and conduction surfaces from which the heat can be dissipated. In a large container, however, the amount of heat liberated may be so large that it cannot all be radiated or conducted away and in such cases some REFRIGERATION system is needed.

Monitoring fermentation

Progress of a fermentation can be monitored in several ways. The most obvious is by simply observing activity in the fermentation vessel. As long as carbon dioxide is vigorously given off, the yeast are still working. Laboratory fermentations are sometimes followed by weighing the fermentation vessel at frequent intervals, thus obtaining a record of the weight of carbon dioxide gas lost and therefore, by calculation, the amount of sugar remaining. Chemical analyses of the unfermented sugar remaining, or of the alcohol produced, are accurate measures of the course of fermentation but are seldom used as they are complex and time consuming. The technique most commonly used in the operating cellar is a measurement of the DENSITY of a sample of fermenting juice.

Density can be determined quickly and with reasonable accuracy by floating a calibrated HYDROMETER in the juice. Although most hydrometers are calibrated to read the remaining sugar's percentage in weight, it must be remembered that this calibration is for a sugar in water solution. When alcohol, less dense than water, is added to the solution during fermentation, the hydrometer reading no longer gives a true reading of the sugar remaining. Indeed, when all of the fermentable sugar has been converted into alcohol, these hydrometers will give the apparently ridiculous reading of less than no sugar. The problem of deciding when the fermentation is complete matters because the presence of small amounts of sugar renders the wine susceptible to bacterial attack and necessitates different treatment after fermentation. Today there are quick, simple paper strips which can reliably detect the presence of even very small amounts of fermentable sugars.

Factors affecting fermentation

The time required for complete fermentation of white grape juice or crushed red grapes varies greatly. The TEMPERATURE maintained in the fermenting mass is the principal factor, affecting duration of fermentation (as well as resultant character of the wine) more even than the initial sugar concentration (see MUST WEIGHT), YEAST type, the aeration of the MUST, and the quantity of micro-nutrients in the juice. In general, red wine fermentations are complete within four to seven days but white wines, which are frequently fermented at much lower temperatures, may require several weeks, occasionally months and sometimes years in the case of extremely sweet musts.

Other factors which influence the course of a fermentation include agrochemical RESIDUES, ROT, and various chemical additions such as SULPHUR DIOXIDE. In the most commercially minded wineries, fermentations may be deliberately hastened so that a single fermentation vessel may be used twice or even three or more times a season.

Styles of wines in the making of which the fermentation

may be arrested deliberately include PORT, VIN DOUX NATUREL, and other VINS DE LIQUEUR in which yeast is overpowered by the addition of alcohol, usually GRAPE SPIRIT.

For dry white wines, free of fermentable sugars, the next step is usually the immediate separation of the liquid that is now wine from the LEES, the residue of dead yeast, pulp, stem fragments, and seeds, although some white wines, such as Muscadet SUR LIE, are deliberately left for some months to take on additional flavour from the lees. Red wines, on the other hand, are usually left to macerate with the skins and lees for some time after fermentation is complete, extraction having been encouraged during fermentation by REMONTAGE. (See also WINE-MAKING.)

The above is an outline of the most usual sorts of fermentation but there are many variants, including BARREL FERMENTATION, CARBONIC MACERATION, CONTINUOUS FERMENTATION, ROSÉ WINE-MAKING, and, quite distinct from the first, alcoholic fermentation, FERMENTATION IN BOTTLE, MALOLACTIC FERMENTATION, and SECONDARY FERMENTATION.

See also MACERATION, the process that inevitably accompanies red wine fermentation, and also RED WINE-MAKING, WHITE WINE-MAKING, and SPARKLING WINE-MAKING.

A.D.W.

Halliday, J., and Johnson, H., *The Art and Science of Wine* (London and New York, 1992).

FERMENTATION IN BOTTLE plays an important part in SPARKLING WINE-MAKING. In most still wines, however, it is one of the wine FAULTS most feared by wine-makers. It usually results from the presence of some RESIDUAL SUGAR together with live cells of either YEAST or BACTERIA under conditions which favour their growth. (High ALCOHOLIC STRENGTH and high levels of SULPHUR DIOXIDE inhibit the growth of such micro-organisms.) It is also possible that a completely dry wine will start to ferment in bottle if it contains a high concentration of MALIC ACID since live LACTIC BACTERIA may metabolize the malic acid causing a MALOLACTIC FERMENTATION in bottle.

The implications of a fermentation in bottle for the wine consumer can range from an inconsequential level of carbon dioxide in the wine to the generation of such large quantities of the gas that it explodes. This latter, potentially dangerous, occurrence is most likely if the wine contains significant amounts of fermentable sugar and is kept at warm room temperatures. If the fermentation is bacterial rather than by yeast, gas is usually produced, together with off-flavours, cloud, or haze (see BACTERIAL SPOILAGE).

A low level of gas in a wine, particularly a young white wine, is by no means necessarily a sign of unwanted fermentation in bottle. Many wine-makers deliberately incorporate a low level of CARBON DIOXIDE to enliven some wines.

A.D.W.

FERMENTATION VESSEL. The container in which FERMENTATION, and MACERATION in the case of red wines, take place can vary enormously in size, material, and design: from a small plastic bucket (in the case of some HOME WINE-MAKING) to an oak BARREL (in the case of white wines undergoing BARREL FERMENTATION) to what is effectively a vast, computerized STAINLESS STEEL tower (for high-volume everyday wines). Stainless steel has the advantage that both cleaning and TEMPERATURE CONTROL are much easier than for wooden or concrete fermentation vessels and most modern white and rosé wines, and many reds, are fermented in stainless steel tanks.

Wooden fermentation vessels are still used by many wine-makers, however. Traditional wine producers in Germany, Alsace, and the Loire may well use large, old, wooden CASKS which offer natural STABILIZATION and CLARIFICATION. Unless scrupulous attention is paid to cellar HYGIENE, however, harmful bacteria can linger in the staves of wooden casks.

Red wine may be fermented either in large wooden casks or open-topped wooden vats. An open top requires constant surveillance since BACTERIA can attack the floating CAP of skins, which will dry out and fail to achieve proper MACERATION without REMONTAGE or PIGEAGE. The cap may alternatively be kept submerged with a headboard or some other design feature.

Wooden fermentation vessels are particularly treasured by some traditionalists for red wine maceration, however, as they retain heat especially well, which favours the extraction process, and tend to have a much higher diameter to height ratio than stainless steel tanks, which favour the contact between wine and solids.

Modern stainless steel tanks, and design modifications of them such as various autovinifiers (see AUTOVINIFICATION), computer-controlled fermentation vessels, self-draining vessels, and such modifications as the Vinomatic automatic vinifier, are closed at the top and automatically offer a high degree of hygiene.

Lined cement vats are also widely used for fermentation, even at such highly respected properties as Ch PÉTRUS in Pomerol, Bordeaux's most expensive wine.

FERMENTED IN BOTTLE, legitimate description of a SPARKLING WINE made by the champagne, transversage, or transfer methods described in SPARKLING WINE-MAKING. Only champagne method wines could claim to be **fermented in this bottle**, however.

FERNÃO PIRES, versatile and widely planted Portuguese white grape variety. Its distinctive aroma can be somewhat reminiscent of boiled cabbage. It is planted all over Portugal, notably in RIBATEJO and, as Maria Gomes, is the most common white grape variety in BAIRRADA. The variety has also been planted experimentally in South Africa.

FERREIRA, one of the leading Portuguese port shippers, established in 1715. Dona António Adelaide Ferreira, the *grande dame* of the DOURO valley, was perhaps one of the most dedicated personalities in the PORT industry in the latter half of the 19th century. Born in 1810 in Régua, Dona António devoted her life to the Douro, ruling her vast estates as a benevolent dictator. She invested much of her considerable fortune in planting and improving her properties throughout this harsh terrain. Her first husband, António Bernardo Ferreira, founded one of the largest and most stately quintas in the Douro, the Quinta do Vesúvio, which the family owned until its sale in 1989 to the SYMINGTONS. Today Ferreira own three properties in the Douro: Quinta do Seixo and Quinta do Porto near Pinhão and Quinta da Leda high up in the Douro, as well as buying in wine from other properties owned by the family. In the 1980s the properties were the subject of considerable research and investment, with the company pioneering the vertical system of planting whereby vine rows are aligned uphill rather than along contours. Until 1987 Ferreira was owned by descendants of Dona António, but the company now belongs to Sogrape, producers of MATEUS Rosé, although one or two members of the Ferreira family are still involved in the company.

FERTIGATION, the viticultural practice of mixing FERTILIZERS with IRRIGATION water for direct application to vines. The technique is most often used with drip irrigation systems, for which each vine has a water outlet. Fertilizers are placed in a tank through which the irrigation water passes, and so the vine is fed with appropriate amounts of water and nutrients as the growth proceeds. Such a process is more suited to vineyards for TABLE GRAPES than premium-quality wine grape vineyards. Some nutrients such as NITROGEN are readily available in a soluble form (urea); others such as PHOSPHORUS require a relatively expensive formulation to render them immediately soluble. R.E.S.

FERTILITY, viticultural term for the FRUITFULNESS of buds or shoots, and also of vineyard soils, see SOIL FERTILITY.

FERTILIZERS. Vines, in common with other plants, may require additions of fertilizers to overcome the deficiency in the soil of a particular nutrient (see SOIL NUTRIENTS). However, grapevines are less demanding of fertile soils than many other crops. Indeed, the vineyards most highly regarded in terms of the quality of wine they produce are often those with relatively infertile soils. While a modicum of nutrient stress may be prescribed to enhance quality, this is not to suggest that the fewer the soil nutrients the greater the wine quality. For example, a severe NITROGEN deficiency will cause a STUCK FERMENTATION and poor wine quality.

Fertilizers are commercial formulations which are rich in plant nutrients. Typically they are manufactured (for example, superphosphate) but may be a mined natural product (for example, rock phosphate). Compost is not commonly used in commercial vineyards because of its lack of cost effectiveness, but its use is encouraged from an ecological point of view (see ORGANIC VITICULTURE). Animal manures are more widely used, but again, unless they are readily and cheaply available (as from the cattle deliberately kept at Ch MARGAUX, for example), then their use is restricted because of the relatively high cost of applying sufficient nutrients in this form.

The mineral elements most likely to be deficient in vineyards are nitrogen, POTASSIUM, PHOSPHORUS, ZINC, BORON, IRON, MANGANESE, and MAGNESIUM. The fertilizers commonly used to overcome some of these deficiencies are therefore urea; potassium or ammonium nitrate; potassium chloride or potassium sulphate; superphosphate; zinc sulphate; boric acid or borate; and magnesium sulphate. For the major nutrients of nitrogen, phosphorus and potassium, where up to several hundred kilograms per hectare may be required, fertilizers are commonly spread on the ground. Typical application rates of the three elements are respectively 20–100, 20–30, and 50–150 kg/ha. The so-called minor or trace elements are required in small amounts only, typically a few kilograms per hectare. Thus fertilizers compensating for deficiencies of the micro-nutrients zinc, boron, iron, and magnesium can be applied either mixed with other fertilizers to the ground, or sprayed on to the leaves.

The efficiency of fertilization varies with the type of fertilizer and the soil. For example, phosphate fertilizers are not readily available to plants grown in acid soils, so LIMING might increase growth because it makes more phosphorus available to the vine. Similarly, with high rainfall or irrigation, the nitrate form of nitrogen is leached so easily that it is lost to the vine roots unless they are very deep. The nitrate may end up contaminating groundwater, as has been the case in some parts of Germany, making fertilizer use in viticulture (and other forms of agriculture) the subject of scrutiny from environmentalists. R.E.S.

Coombe, B. G., and Dry, P. R. (eds.), *Viticulture, ii: Practices* (Adelaide, 1992).

Winkler, A. J., Cook, J. A., Kliewer, W. M., and Lider, L. A., *General Viticulture* (2nd edn., Berkeley, Calif., 1974).

FETEASCA, Fetiaska, or **Feteaska**, scented white grape variety grown widely in eastern Europe. ROMANIA, where the variety is the most widely grown vine by far, has two subvarieties, respectively white and royal: **Fetească Albă** and the exclusively Romanian **Fetească Regală** which is a crossing of the GRASĂ of Cotnari and Fetească Albă developed in Daneş in Transylvania in the 1930s. There is also a dark-skinned variant, **Fetească Neagră**, whose red wines show potential when well vinified. Feteasca is made into peachy, aromatic, almost MUSCAT-like wines with definite if varying degrees of RESIDUAL SUGAR and, often, slightly too little ACIDITY. Fetească Regală was Romania's most planted grape variety in the early 1990s with more than 17,000 ha/42,000 acres, when Fetească Albă was planted on more than 15,000 ha and Fetească Neagră plantings totalled only about 1,000 ha.

The vine is also important in HUNGARY, where it is known as Leányka, in BULGARIA, MOLDOVA, and UKRAINE. When cited on a label for export to Germany, the grape's name is often directly translated as Mädchentraube, or Maiden's grape. (In Romanian, Fetească meaning young girl's grape contrasts directly with Băbească, grandmother's grape.)

FIANO, white grape variety responsible for the flavourful Fiano di Avellino. For more details, see CAMPANIA.

FIDDLETOWN, town in the SIERRA FOOTHILLS, California wine region and AVA.

FIÉ, occasionally written **Fiét**, old Loire white grape variety that is thought to be an ancestor of SAUVIGNON Blanc. The variety has largely been abandoned because of its remarkably low yield, but producers such as Jacky Preys of Touraine pride themselves on their richer versions of Sauvignon made from particularly old Fié vines.

FIEFS VENDÉENS, small, oceanic VDQS zone south of Nantes near the mouth of the Loire. Most wines are red, from Gamay and Cabernet, but there are rosés, and some whites made from varying combinations of Loire grapes, including Chenin Blanc, Sauvignon Blanc, and Grolleau Gris.

FIELD BUDDING AND GRAFTING, viticultural operation of planting grafted ROOTSTOCK rootlings in their vineyard position and inserting SCION buds during the first growing season. Many types of insertion may be used but CHIP BUDDING is common. The success rate can be erratic, and careful attention is needed to watering, nutrition, and the tending of each vine. This method is therefore most suitable for small vineyards with good soils and a well-trained work-force.

(See TOP WORKING for details of the viticultural operation of changing VINE VARIETY in an established vineyard.) B.G.C.

FIGHTING VARIETAL, term coined in CALIFORNIA in the late 1980s for relatively inexpensive VARIETAL wines. As varietal names gained currency in the US market, producers of low-priced wines began bottling Cabernet Sauvignon, Chardonnay, and other sought-after varieties from places where they could be assured of large crops at low prices, and thus was born a replacement class of wines for old-fashioned GENERIC jug wines. Fighting varietals, though far from grand, improve upon what went before.

FILL LEVEL, an aspect of individual bottles of wine which can be closely related to the condition of the wine. The lower the fill level when a wine is bottled, the more the space between the top of the wine and the bottom of the cork (the so-called ULLAGE) in which OXYGEN may be trapped in the bottle and may hasten the AGEING process. Most bottlers try to ensure that there is minimal ullage space in the bottle immediately after BOTTLING, perhaps a depth of 1 mm/0.04 in. Subsequent reductions in temperature cause a reduction in the wine's volume, thereby apparently lowering the fill level. For wines designed for early consumption, this is unlikely to make much difference, but fill levels are important indicators of the condition of a fine and, especially, mature wine, so that fill levels should always be specified by the AUCTION houses and other fine wine traders. The lower the fill level, the more likely a harmful level of OXIDATION and therefore the lower should be the selling price. (Some sorts of wine seem more resilient to low fill levels than others—vintage port and Sauternes are examples—and a low fill level can apparently, sometimes usefully, hasten the ageing process of an extremely TANNIC wine.)

During long-term BOTTLE AGEING some wine is likely to be absorbed by the CORK, resulting in a drop in fill level of perhaps 7 mm after 10 years. (To reduce this absorption effect, Ch MOUTON-ROTHSCHILD adopted a policy of using shorter corks from the 1991 vintage.) Some wine may also evaporate from the top of the bottle during this time, especially if some were trapped between the cork and the inside of the bottle-neck during bottling. Other reasons for a low fill level include poor control during bottling, wine being bottled at too high a temperature, and a faulty cork. In any event, it is always wise policy to pick bottles with the highest fill levels off the shelf, and to drink bottles of wine from the same case from lowest to highest fill level since the wine in bottles with the lowest fill level is likely to be the most evolved.

Note that the fill level in wine GLASSES should ideally be less than half the height of the glass and never more than two-thirds, in order to provide somewhere for the AROMA to collect.

Léon, P., 'On the level', *Decanter* (Nov. 1993).

FILM-FORMING YEASTS, sometimes called **film yeasts**, comprise a large group of several genera and many species of wild YEASTS, all of which require OXYGEN for their metabolism. For this reason they appear on the surface of wine in barrels or vats that are not kept completely filled. Some of them such as FLOR can add desirable aromas and flavours, others produce off-flavours, while others are essentially inert.

Pichia, *Hansenula*, and *Candida*, and other yeast genera are also film formers with characteristics unfavourable to good wine quality. These yeasts are widely dispersed in vineyard regions and are among the types encountered in spontaneous or wild yeast fermentations. When sugar is present, they are producers of alcohol and carbon dioxide, but have a low level of alcohol tolerance. Thus, while they are active in early stages of spontaneous fermentations, they are usually crowded out by the more alcohol-tolerant *Saccharomyces* yeast which finish the sugar conversion. These genera of yeasts in general form more ESTERS and ALDEHYDES than do *Saccharomyces*, which probably explains the fact that some wine-makers favour their use in spontaneous fermentations.

Candida mycoderma, previously called *Mycoderma vini*, is another yeast that is responsible for the thin films that will form on top of wines in tanks or barrels that are not completely full. This yeast requires oxygen for film formation and thus acts as a signal to the wine-maker that a more frequent TOPPING UP regime is required. For white wines the ACETALDEHYDE produced is a negative factor, but for red wines, short exposure to a film of *mycoderma* does little damage.

Film-forming yeasts perform a vital function in the production of wines such as FLOR sherry, TOKAY, and VIN JAUNE.

A.D.W.

FILTRATION, much-discussed wine-making process whereby solid particles are strained out of the wine with various sorts of filter. Filtration is a physical alternative to natural SETTLING and, like CENTRIFUGATION, requires more expensive equipment but much less patience. Basically, filtration speeds the wine-making process and allows better control, thereby lowering production costs.

There are two general types of filtration. **Depth filtration** (or **sheet filtration**) involves use of a relatively thick layer of a finely divided material such as cellulose powder, diatomaceous earth, or perlite. As the cloudy wine passes through the layer, small particles are trapped in the tortuous channels and clear liquid passes through. **Surface filtration** (or **membrane filtration**), on the other hand, depends upon a thin film of plastic polymer material having uniformly sized holes which are smaller than the particles being removed from the solution.

After FERMENTATION as much as possible of the new wine is drained away from the solids and held in a settling tank. Soon afterwards, the wine is separated from the solids at the bottom of the tank by RACKING. At this point the new wine is often given a rough filtration as a start of the clarification and STABILIZATION process. Depth filtration, usually with a particularly porous form of silica called diatomaceous earth forming the layer through which the cloudy wine is passed, is commonly used for this early rough filtration. Subsequent depth filtrations use finer-meshed diatomaceous earth, cellulose, or thick paper pads to catch ever smaller particles.

Finally, just before bottling, the apparently clear wine may be passed through a synthetic polymer sheet which has holes of uniform size smaller than the cells of potentially hazardous YEAST or BACTERIA. This surface filtration should render the wine sterile and is called a **sterile filtration** but can only be done once a rougher filtration has cleared the wine of particles that would otherwise plug the holes in the plastic membrane. Sterile filtration is simple in comparison with the subsequent problem of getting the sterile wine into a stoppered bottle without any possible contamination from the atmosphere and bottling equipment. Only mastery of sterile filtration and STERILE BOTTLING has permitted the modern phenomenon of stable young white wines containing significant fermentable sugars (although added SORBIC ACID and SULPHUR DIOXIDE can assist in controlling micro-organisms).

Carefully made fine red wine which has benefited from extended BARREL MATURATION should not need filtration. Indeed many wine-makers believe that even an early rough diatomaceous earth filtration should be avoided because all solids can contribute to flavour and that wine should be 'dirty' when it begins its maturation, even in small BARRELS. After months in wood a wine should be stable against any problems caused by PROTEINS, TARTRATES, and malates (MALIC ACID salts)—which is one of the great advantages of wood maturation. It is also likely that yeast and bacteria populations are negligible.

Filtration of fine wines is a controversial issue. While it may be a necessity for ordinary commercial wines, too heavy a filtration can indeed rob a fine wine of some of its complexity and capacity to age, not to mention some loss of colour, particularly a red wine as subtle as some fine red BURGUNDY. Some commentators and wine-makers claim that filtration of any sort is harmful, and some labels trumpet 'unfiltered' as an attribute. Even though examples of unstable wines spoilt by less than perfect storage or transport conditions are not rare, some producers and consumers feel this is a risk worth taking, and are prepared for the added inconvenience and cost involved in shipping such wines in temperature-controlled conditions. An unfiltered wine throws a much heavier crust, or SEDIMENT, than one that has been filtered.

Other specific filters or pieces of equipment used to separate solids from liquid include a **centrifuge decanter**, a **pressure leaf filter**, and a ROTARY DRUM VACUUM FILTER, which is an earth filter designed specifically for liquids with a very high proportion of solids such as LEES.

See also FINING, another method of clarification which involves less capital expenditure than filtration but probably has much the same effect on the colour and health of a wine.

A.D.W.

FINDLING is a mutation of the German vine crossing MÜLLER-THURGAU grown to a limited extent in the MOSEL-SAAR-RUWER, where its higher must weights are treasured, even if its tendency to rot is not.

FINE, a French term for a BRANDY made by distilling wine, as distinct from MARC, which is a POMACE BRANDY made from grape pomace. *Fine* is made in small quantities in many French wine regions, most notably in Burgundy where it is called **Fine de Bourgogne**.

When applied to COGNAC the term is much abused, and really rather meaningless. Legally *fine* is an abbreviation of Fine Champagne, which denotes a cognac from the Champagne districts of the Cognac region of which at least half comes from the Grande Champagne.

FINE WINE is a nebulous term, much used by the AUCTION houses to describe the sort of wines they sell (which roughly coincide with those described in INVESTMENT): from the classic regions of Europe generally and, in Bordeaux for example, of CRU BOURGEOIS or ideally CLASSED GROWTH level. The extent to which this category of wine coincides with the best wine the world produces has declined slowly but steadily since the 1970s. Buying from, selling to, and in many cases in direct competition with the auction houses are the **fine wine traders**, a small group of wine merchants who specialize in servicing the needs of COLLECTORS and the like.

FINING, wine-making process with the aim of CLARIFICATION and stabilization of a wine whereby a **fining agent**, one of a range of special materials, is added to coagulate or adsorb and precipitate quickly the COLLOIDS suspended in it. Fining (*collage*, or 'sticking', in French) is important because, by encouraging these microscopic particles to fall out of the wine, the wine is less likely to become hazy or cloudy.

Traditional egg-white **fining** at Ch Langoa-Barton in St-Julien.

Most young wines, if left long enough under good conditions, would eventually reach the same state of clarity as fining can achieve within months, but fining saves money for the producer and therefore eventually the consumer. Fining is most effective in removing molecules of colloidal size, which include polymerized TANNINS, ANTHOCYANS, PIGMENTS, other PHENOLICS, and heat-unstable PROTEINS. (Other reasons for clouds, hazes, and deposits in bottled wines include TARTRATES and BACTERIA. See STABILIZATION for details of other methods of removing them.)

Over the centuries a wide range of fining agents have doubtless been essayed, but scientific and technical advances have eliminated those (such as dried blood powder) that are dangerous to health and those (such as various gums) that are less than fully effective in improving the wine. Many fining agents, deriving variously from EGG-WHITES, milk, fish bladders, and American BENTONITE clay deposits, may strike consumers as curious wine-making tools but it should be recognized that only insignificant traces, at most, of the fining agent remain in the treated wine. (Research by Cornelius Ough of DAVIS shows that very low levels of some of the proteinaceous fining agents such as egg-whites may remain, but that when bentonite is used nothing remains.)

Today two general classes of fining agents are used: pulverized solid or mineral materials, and complex organic compounds. Bentonite, an unusual form of clay, is particularly effective in adsorbing certain proteins and, to a limited extent, bacteria. SILICA functions similarly but somewhat less effectively. Kaolin, another type of clay, is even less effective than silica. Activated carbon (CHARCOAL) has been used to remove brown colours and is also effective in removing some off-odours. Potassium ferrocyanide may still be used as a fining agent in some very old wineries where copper and iron equipment has yet to be replaced (see BLUE FINING). All of these fining agents are inorganic chemicals.

Organic compounds used as fining agents include proteins such as the CASEIN from milk, albumin from egg-whites, ISINGLASS, and GELATIN, which form insoluble complexes with the unstable pigments and tannins. These complex colloids become so large that they fall out of the solution.

Everyday wines, both white and red, are normally fined earlier and to a greater extent than finer wines. Given the extra time accorded the making of finer wines, many of the potentially unstable components polymerize earlier and deposit without assistance from man. In general, white wines need fining to preserve their lighter colour and to prevent heat-unstable proteins forming a cloud, while red wines need it for a reduction of astringent and bitter tannins. The fining operation removes components that are soluble but potentially subject to polymerization and cloud, or may precipitate with time.

See also FILTRATION, which cannot remove these soluble substances and acts only on particulates. A.D.W.

FINO, Spanish word with two related meanings in the SHERRY-making process. *Fino* is one of two types of wine made naturally in the sherry bodega (*oloroso* being the other). Fino is a style of sherry, the commercial result of filtering and bottling a *fino*, the palest, lightest, and driest apart from MANZANILLA, and quintessentially the product of the *fino* type of sherry preserved and influenced by the film-forming yeast FLOR. It may be made in any of the three sherry towns, although Fino de Jerez is by far the most common, and that made in Puerto de Santa María is known as Puerto Fino. Most Fino sold in Spain has an alcoholic strength of about 15.5 per cent and is bone dry, but commercial export brands are often shipped at about 17 per cent and some are slightly sweetened. A freshly opened bottle of true, dry, light Fino is one of the most appetizing wines in the world, but the wine in an opened bottle loses its freshness and appeal as though it were a fragile low-strength wine. For more details, see SHERRY.

FIRST GROWTHS is a direct translation of the French PREMIERS CRUS but its meaning tends to be limited to those BORDEAUX wine properties judged in the top rank according to the various CLASSIFICATIONS: Chx LAFITE, LATOUR, MARGAUX, HAUT-BRION, MOUTON-ROTHSCHILD, CHEVAL BLANC, AUSONE, together often with the unclassified but generally acknowledged star of POMEROL, Ch PÉTRUS. Just below these red bordeaux in terms of status are the so-called SUPER SECONDS.

FITOU, large red wine appellation in the LANGUEDOC in two enclaves in the CORBIÈRES where it meets ROUSSILLON (see map on p. 552). When the boundaries of this, the first wine appellation of Languedoc, were drawn up in the late 1940s, local politics prevailed and Fitou has remained with, apparently, a great tract of Corbières bisecting it. The clay limestone soils of coastal Fitou are quite different from the mountainous schists of the other Fitou 30 minutes' drive inland. The low-yielding vines on the 2,500 ha/6,175 acres of poor soils in these Pyrenean foothills should be capable of great expression, but this was rare in the 1970s and 1980s when the name Fitou was cleverly marketed and there seemed little incentive to improve quality. The region is even more in the grip of CO-OPERATIVES than its northern neighbour and it was not until the early 1990s that seriously ambitious bottlings began to emerge from the likes of the Caves de Mont Tauch at Tuchan and the Cave Pilote at Villeneuve-lès-Corbières, both well inland. The dominant vine variety is Carignan but it is allowed in diminishing proportions, supplemented by increasing amounts of Grenache, its relative Lladoner Pelut, Mourvèdre, and Syrah. The wine clearly responds well to OAK AGEING but too high a proportion of it is made as an ordinary commercial blend without too many distinguishing marks.

The territory demarcated for Fitou may also produce RIVESALTES.

Simms, P. and S., *The Wines of Corbières & Fitou* (Toulouse, 1991).

FIXED ACIDS, those organic ACIDS of wines whose volatilities are so low that they cannot be separated from wine by DISTILLATION. The two main fixed acids of wine are TARTARIC ACID and MALIC ACID, but several other non-volatile acids are present in small amounts. Unfortunately, the distinction between fixed and volatile acids is not precise because there are some acids which have intermediate volatilities. Among these are LACTIC ACID and SUCCINIC ACID, both found in wine. The fixed acids are important in wines because they are the acids that give wine its refreshing tartness, as well as its natural resistance to bacterial attack. VOLATILE ACIDS, on the other hand, are more obviously smelly than fixed acids and generally produce fruity or, when present in excess, vinegary aromas. TOTAL ACIDITY, a standard wine measurement, is the sum of the fixed acids and volatile acids. A.D.W.

FIXIN, appellation abutting Gevrey-Chambertin in the Côte de Nuits district of Burgundy, producing red wines of a similar style to its neighbour, though currently of lesser fame. Fixin wines have a similar sturdiness to Gevrey but have less powerful fruit and fragrance.

There are five PREMIER CRU vineyards: Les Arvelets and Les Hervelets (seemingly interchangeable; certainly wine grown in the former may be labelled the latter), Clos de la Perrière, Clos Napoléon, and Clos du Chapître. Dr Lavalle, writing in 1855, noted Le Chapître, Les Arvelets, and Clos Napoléon but he singled out Clos de la Perrière for special praise since at that time the Marquis de Montmort sold it at the same price as his Chambertin.

See also CÔTE D'OR and its map. J.T.C.M.

Fizziness

FIZZINESS, the property of a SPARKLING WINE to bubble, which may be measured as the pressure inside the stoppered bottle. A wine bubbles when the bottle is opened because the dissolved CARBON DIOXIDE in the wine moves from a stable to a meta-stable state once the pressure is reduced on opening. In a meta-stable state, the carbon dioxide comes out of solution in the form of bubbles, provided there are nucleation sites on the glass. Nucleation sites are pits, scratches naturally occurring in bottles or glasses. Carbon dioxide cannot simply leap out of the wine; it has to diffuse to a nucleation site and find a bubble that can then lift off from the glass and rise to the surface. A bottle of gently bubbling sparkling wine will take several hours to go flat, for all the carbon dioxide to be released in this way.

In a stoppered bottle, the cork maintains a pressure in the bottle so that there is an equilibrium between the dissolved carbon dioxide and the carbon dioxide above the wine. When the bottle is opened, the pressure above the wine drops to normal atmospheric pressure, one so-called atmosphere (the pressure at sea level at 20 °C/68 °F), and the wine is in the meta-stable state described above.

Most fully sparkling wines such as CHAMPAGNE have a little pressure during DISGORGEMENT and are sold with a pressure of between five and six atmospheres, about three times that inside a tyre, which is the pressure which a normal champagne cork and bottle can withstand without undue risk. Such wines may be described as mousseux or CRÉMANT in French, espumoso in Spanish, SPUMANTE in Italian, and SEKT in German.

Many wines are somewhere between still and this level of fizziness, however. Such wines may be described as PÉTILLANT in French, FRIZZANTE in Italian, and SPRITZIG in German, although many variations in nomenclature exist. European wine law defines a sparkling wine as any wine with an excess pressure of more than three atmospheres, while a semi-sparkling wine has a pressure of between one and 2.5 atmospheres.

The amount of pressure can be controlled by the wine-maker by varying the amount of sugar added during the TIRAGE stage in order to provoke the second fermentation or, in the case of carbonation, simply by controlling the amount of gas dissolved in the wine. J.Ro. & T.J.

Jordan, A. D., and Napper, D. H., 'Some aspects of the physical chemistry of bubble and foam phenomena in sparkling wine', *Proceedings of the Sixth Australian Wine Industry Technical Conference* (1986).

FLAME SEEDLESS, black grape variety grown for TABLE GRAPES but occasionally used by wine-makers in Australia.

FLAVESCENCE DORÉE, a MYCOPLASMA DISEASE of the vine which has the potential to threaten many of the world's vineyards. It first appeared in the Armagnac region in south west France on the vine variety BACO 22A in 1949. A similar disease has been described in Germany, Switzerland, Romania, Israel, Chile, Italy, and Australia. Shoots on infected vines stop growing while leaves yellow and curl downwards. Later in the season shoots droop as though made of rubber. When affected early in the season, bunches fall off. Otherwise, the berries shrivel and are bitter. At first this disease was thought to be a virus but now mycoplasma-like organisms (MLO) are suspected (see MYCOPLASMA DISEASES). The disease is transmitted in the field by the LEAF HOPPER insect *Scaphoideus titanus*. Originally native to the eastern United States and Canada, this insect was apparently introduced to Europe after the Second World War.

Disease epidemics in France and Italy are associated with the leaf hopper presence. In Europe it is expected that the leaf hopper can spread further. When the leaf hopper and the disease organism are both introduced to a new region then a potential for disease spread exists. Insecticide sprays can reduce the leaf hopper populations and reduce the spread of the disease. Chardonnay and Riesling are among the most susceptible VINIFERA varieties. Some American species are tolerant. R.E.S.

Bovey, R., *et al.*, *Virus and Virus-Like Diseases of Vines: Colour Atlas of Symptoms* (Lausanne, 1980).
Pearson, R. C., and Goheen, A. C., *Compendium of Grape Diseases* (St Paul, Minn., 1988).

FLAVOUR, arguably a wine's most important distinguishing mark. As outlined in TASTING, most of what is commonly described as wine's flavour is in fact its AROMA (or alternatively, in the case of older wines, its BOUQUET). This, the 'smell' of a wine, may be its greatest sensory characteristic, but is also the most difficult of its attributes to measure and describe. A wine's flavour could, in its widest sense, be said to be the overall sensory impression of both aroma (as sensed both by the nose and from the mouth), and the taste components, and may therefore incorporate the other, more measurable aspects of ACIDITY, SWEETNESS, ALCOHOLIC STRENGTH, FIZZINESS, and astringency and bitterness (closely related to level of TANNINS). In this book, however, the word flavour is used interchangeably with aroma.

FLAVOUR COMPOUNDS, imprecise and inclusive term for substances in wines that can be smelled or tasted (see TASTING), sometimes called aroma compounds. The term flavour compounds is used more particularly for the volatile compounds which are sensed olfactorily, by the nose, and which contribute to both AROMA and, later, BOUQUET, the flavour changing rapidly and markedly during the first few months of a wine's life and then more and more slowly as it matures. Certain compounds are associated with particular VINE VARIETIES although the exact chemical nature of compounds associated with varietal flavours was still being studied in the early 1990s.

These volatile aroma compounds are in vastly smaller concentrations than those of the non-volatile taste compounds such as GLYCEROL or various ACIDS, some little more than one part per trillion. The flavour differences between varieties arises mainly from the differences in the types and amounts of volatile aroma compounds in their berries. It is commonly stated that these occur in the skins, but grape juice also contains significant amounts, and sometimes in different proportions from those found in the same grapes' skin.

Hardie and O'Brien present the novel proposal that flavour compounds may be present in grapes because they fulfilled an evolutionary role in attracting insects to assist POLLINATION, defending the developing berry flesh against attack from insects and microbes, attracting birds and animals which would eat grapes and so disperse the seeds, repelling disturbers of dispersed plants, and inhibiting germination of competitive plant species. In accordance with selection theory, the variation in flavour and aroma compounds between different VITIS groups of diverse origin is considered to reflect the range of ecological conditions existing during evolution.

The study of grape aroma has attracted scientific attention because of its importance in wine quality, long appreciated but methodologically difficult because of the abundance of candidate compounds, every one of which is potent but scarce. Research quickened in the 1980s as better measuring techniques emerged, notably gas chromatograph-mass spectrometers.

Some of the types of compounds so far identified among the aroma volatiles in the grape are as follows: *monoterpenes*, e.g. linalool, nerol, geraniol, found in floral grapes such as Muscat, Gewürztraminer, and Riesling; *norisoprenoids*, CAROTENOID derived, e.g. damascenone (rose oil), megastigmatrienone (tobacco, spice), found in Chardonnay; *shikimate-derived*, e.g. raspberry ketone, vanillin, zingerone, found in Syrah/Shiraz; *nitrogen-containing*, e.g. methoxypyrazine (grassy), found in Cabernet Sauvignon and Sauvignon Blanc; *aliphatics*, some gamma lactones, an important component of OAK flavour.

A large proportion of these compounds occur in grapes combined with SUGARS (glycosides) and as such are odourless. They revert to their aromatic form after hydrolysis of the glycoside by the action of ENZYMES or acids, a process that is undoubtedly important in wine ageing.

There is no doubt that increasing knowledge about flavour compounds, and their manipulation in the vineyard and winery (as, for example, by the addition of selected enzymes), represent the most important likely technological advances in the wine industry at the end of the 20th century. As emphasized above, our knowledge of this area is constantly expanding, especially as new measuring techniques are being developed.

While it is misleading to imply that the chemical characterization of VARIETAL FLAVOURS is imminent, it is instructive to consider the example of the methoxypyrazines studied by Allen *et al.* These remarkable compounds, associated with the 'green', herbaceous, or vegetative aromas in Cabernet Sauvignon and Sauvignon Blanc grapes, can be detected at one part per trillion in water (the equivalent of one grape berry in a million tons of grapes). Three methoxypyrazines have been identified for these varieties, commonly known as MIBP, MIPP, and a third, present only in trace amounts. Sensory evaluation has confirmed the contribution of MIBP to the aroma described as characteristic of capsicum or bell pepper and green gooseberries. MIPP, on the other hand, has a more earthy aroma, characteristic of cooked or canned asparagus.

Related studies have demonstrated that the levels of these two compounds in grape berries matches what is known commercially about the HERBACEOUS wine character. First, the berry concentrations of MIBP drop during ripening, as does the herbaceous character. Secondly, concentrations of MIBP are higher for grapes grown in cooler as opposed to hotter climates; Australian samples have been found to have much lower levels of MIBP than French or New Zealand samples, for example. MIBP is generally higher in Cabernet Sauvignon than in Sauvignon Blanc, suggesting that other compounds may play a part in contributing to the complex Cabernet Sauvignon flavour, masking the methoxypyrazine flavour to a certain extent.

Studies of flavour compounds in the early 1990s were beginning to provide important links between viticulture and wine quality such as the relationship between CANOPY MICROCLIMATE and the development of flavour compounds, which Allen *et al.* in Australia found can be increased tenfold using appropriate vineyard practices.

The above examples indicate the enormous effect that flavour chemistry is likely to have on our understanding and manipulation of wine quality, although it also raises the more sinister possibility of 'manufacturing' wines by the addition of traces of flavour compounds to neutral, low-quality wines.

See PHENOLICS, AGEING, and BOTTLE AGEING.

R.E.S. & B.G.C.

Allen, M. S., *et al.*, 'Contribution of methoxypyrazines to the flavour of Cabernet Sauvignon and Sauvignon Blanc', in P. J. Williams *et al.* (eds.), *Proceedings of the Seventh Australian Wine Industry Technical Conference* (Adelaide, 1990).

Hardie, W. J., and O'Brien, T. P., 'Some considerations of the biological significance of some volatile constituents of grape (*Vitis* spp)', *Australian Journal of Botany*, 36 (1988), 107–17.

FLAVOURED WINES, somewhat amorphous category of wines whose basic wine grape flavour is modified by the addition of other flavouring materials. VERMOUTH is a flavoured FORTIFIED wine, while the Greek RETSINA is perhaps the most strikingly flavoured unfortified wine.

History

Spices have traditionally been added to wine (as they have to food) to provide some variety in taste, or, more likely, to hide any imperfections of taste. A wine that tasted like VINEGAR would have been much improved.

The ancient cultures of the Mediterranean added spices, herbs, and honey (and also drugs or resins such as myrrh) to their grape and date wines. Descriptions and recipes abound in ancient texts from MESOPOTAMIA to Ancient ROME. (See also Ancient EGYPT and Ancient GREECE.) The Greeks were reputed by the Romans almost never to drink their wines straight, and PLINY lists virtually everything from pepper to absinthe as wine flavourings.

Flavourings such as herbs and honey would not only cover off-flavours but would give appeal to light bodied wines (see GERMAN HISTORY). There have long been local specialities of wines flavoured with herbs, spices, flowers, or nuts.

In medieval times wine usually needed some improvement within a few months when it began to turn sour. This was often done at home and the most popular recipe was for 'hippocras', made with red or white wine. Sugar, honey, cinnamon, ginger, and pepper were the usual ingredients, and the name came from Hippocrates' sleeve, a reference to the muslin bag through which the infused wine was strained. Hippocras remained popular in England well into the 17th century, when it was enjoyed by Pepys, undergoing various changes of name and composition to emerge as punch, so beloved by the Victorians.

Meanwhile in Europe spiced wines, often fortified with alcohol, evolved into the vermouths we know today. H.B.

Pliny the Elder, *Natural History*, trans. by H. Rackham (London, 1938), Book 14.

Younger, W., *Gods, Men and Wine* (London, 1966).

Modern variations

The category has been much expanded in recent years, however, by the emergence of flavoured, often low alcohol, wines such as those marketed as COOLERS, an attempt to persuade those who do not see themselves as wine drinkers to buy wine diluted and disguised as something else. They come in all degrees of alcoholic strength, sweetness, and fizziness and are popularly flavoured with such fruits as strawberry, peach, mango, and so on. Such products should be distinguished from FRUIT WINES, whose alcohol derives from the sugars of the (non-grape) fruit itself. A.D.W.

Fleurie's most famous character, Mlle Chabert, head of the local wine co-operative.

FLAVOURINGS are available to wine producers, and are used, illegally, to an unknown extent. Of the three sorts of flavourings available to the beverage industry—natural, nature-identical, and artificial—the latter can be discounted because they are easily detectable, and natural and nature-identical flavourings are readily available, no more expensive, and extremely difficult to detect. Natural and nature-identical flavourings which impose the characteristics of a range of noble grape varieties such as CABERNET SAUVIGNON and SAUVIGNON Blanc are marketed. Because they are natural or nature-identical, their use is extremely difficult to detect, especially since they are now usually based on ETHANOL rather than isopropanol, which used to be a useful indicator of flavourings use. In time, a combination of the powerful NUCLEAR MAGNETIC RESONANCE technique and isotope ratio mass spectrometry (see ANALYSIS) should be able to indicate the use of flavourings. Since these flavourings are so intense, they can be effective at concentrations as low as 0.001 per cent and the addition of, for example, 100 ml/3.6 fl oz of essence to a 100-hl/2,640-gal vat is an operation which can be performed easily and discreetly. As with one of the most obvious wine flavourings OAK ESSENCE, however, the apparent benefits of these flavourings are relatively short lived and they should be of interest to only the most cynical wine producer.
G.T.

FLÉTRI, French term used to described grapes which have been dried, or partially dried, before fermentation to increase the sugar content. It is used most commonly in SWITZERLAND and occasionally in the Valle d'AOSTA. See also PASSITO for the Italian counterpart.

FLEURAISON or **floraison**, French terms for FLOWERING.

FLEURIE, one of the 10 BEAUJOLAIS Crus, and surely the appellation with the prettiest name in France. Fleurie includes about 800 ha/1,976 acres of vines, has a particularly efficacious CO-OPERATIVE, and produces wines which, it is easy to believe, have a particularly floral perfume. Partly because of its name perhaps, Fleurie is one of the most expensive Beaujolais.

FLEURIEU PENINSULA, up and coming wine region in AUSTRALIA. For more detail see SOUTH AUSTRALIA.

FLOC DE GASCOGNE is the ARMAGNAC region's answer to the PINEAU DES CHARENTES of cognac. This strong, sweet VIN DE LIQUEUR, awarded APPELLATION CONTRÔLÉE status in 1990, is made by arresting the fermentation of local grape juice at an early stage by adding young armagnac, which in this case must have been produced by the same enterprise. The resulting liquid, of which about 17 per cent is alcohol, is aged for at least nine months (although not necessarily in wood, as for Pineau). It is usually drunk as an aperitif but is also much used by Gascony's famously resourceful chefs. A *pousse-rapière* (or rapier-pusher) is a blend of sparkling wine and Floc de Gascogne.

FLOODING of vineyards might at first sight seem an unmitigated disaster but is not necessarily so. Flooding (where feasible and controlled) was at one time one of the measures deliberately used in France, Argentina, and elsewhere to prevent or to minimize the effects of PHYLLOXERA, the root louse that devastated many of the world's vineyards in the late 19th century. Flooding when the vines are dormant can drown the lice but leave the vines unharmed, if not prolong their life expectancy. Unfortunately this treatment was also a factor in the abandonment of many of France's good HILLSIDE VINEYARDS, and replanting on flatland where the MESOCLIMATE and soils are inferior for wine quality (see LANGUEDOC in particular).

Natural winter flooding was used for vineyard IRRIGATION in antiquity, and is still so employed at Langhorne Creek in SOUTH AUSTRALIA where the annual flood waters of the Bremer river are diverted across the vineyards each winter, bringing rich silt which tops up the soil fertility, and water to recharge the reserve of moisture held throughout the deep, water-retentive soil profile. This gives the vines enough moisture to carry them right through the summer and results in high YIELDS, despite a summer-dry climate with only 500 mm/20 in of annual RAINFALL. Watering in this way can only be done safely during the winter DORMANT period for vines are readily damaged if flooding occurs after BUDBREAK.

J.G. & R.E.S.

FLOOD IRRIGATION. See IRRIGATION.

FLOR, or **flor yeasts**, are benevolent FILM-FORMING YEASTS which are able to form a film of yeast cells which floats on the surface of a wine. Flor yeasts are typified by those native to the JEREZ region of southern Spain which produce Fino and Manzanilla SHERRY. Although these yeasts have been assigned many names by different microbiologists over the years, in the 1990s they are known as *Saccharomyces bayanus*, *Saccharomyces capensis*, and *Saccharomyces fermentati*.

This unusual growth of **flor** yeast in glass carboys exhibits its strange bready texture more effectively than the usual sherry butt.

The *bayanus*, *capensis*, and *fermentati* species of flor yeasts are all capable of fermenting sugar in an anaerobic phase of their metabolism. In Jerez they are the active sugar-fermenting yeast. When all fermentable sugar has been consumed, these yeasts have the capacity to switch to another metabolic phase in which they use alcohol and oxygen from the atmosphere to produce a waxy or fatty coating on the cells' exterior which permits them to float on the wine's surface. The flor yeasts begin to form as small white curds on the surface of the wine, typically in the spring after fermentation as the ambient temperature begins to rise. These increase in size until the surface is completely covered by a thin white film which gradually thickens and browns. They also produce ACETALDEHYDE and other products which characterize the aroma of film or flor sherries.

Many studies have shown that these desirable yeasts will form films only in the narrow ALCOHOLIC STRENGTH range of 14.5 to 16.0 per cent. Below 14.5 the usual result is VINEGAR; above 16.0 the yeast struggles and dies, resulting in an *oloroso* style of sherry. Film sherry cannot be made in STAINLESS STEEL tanks because the yeast use so much alcohol that the wine becomes watery and eventually acetifies. In wooden barrels such as the BUTTS of Jerez, in the area's low-humidity cellars, there is enough preferential EVAPORATION of water through the wood that the water loss just balances the alcohol used by the yeast, the end result being sherry.

Flor yeasts have been studied in detail by Fornachon in Australia, by Niehaus in South Africa, and by CRUESS in California, all regions hospitable to the flor yeast strains and the PALOMINO grape used for sherry, and where wines similar to sherry have been produced (although see also CYPRUS).

Flor or a similar film-forming yeast has been observed on wines in many and varied parts of the world, both ancient and modern.

Flor wines are made in MONTILLA, RUEDA, and Huelva (see CONDADO DE HUELVA) in Spain, and the ALGARVE in southern Portugal, where flor is also used to make a rather crude aperitif wine. See also JURA, whose VIN JAUNE is very similar to sherry, as well as TOKAY and ROMANIA.

A.D.W.

FLORA, CALIFORNIA aromatic white vine crossing. Perhaps the most delicately aromatic of Dr H. P. Olmo's DAVIS creations (see also CARNELIAN, EMERALD RIESLING, RUBY CABERNET, SYMPHONY), Flora deserves a rather better fate than it had endured by the early 1990s when acreage was too small for official statistics and Flora rarely appeared as varietal wine. The easiest place to find it is in Schramsberg Crémant sparkling wine. A result of Gewürztraminer × Sémillon, it appears to take after Gewürztraminer in cooler climates, Sémillon in warmer ones.

FLORENCE. See TUSCANY.

FLOTATION. See CLARIFICATION.

FLOWER CAP of the vine is known as the CALYPTRA.

FLOWERING, important event in the annual growth cycle of vines, the process preceding the fertilization of vine flowers and their subsequent development into berries. The sequence of events includes the opening of individual flowers, with the calyptra being shed, pollen being liberated, and ovules becoming fertilized. Fertilization leads to berries being set, the stage following flowering. Compared with many other plants, the vine has unattractive small green flowers, and the flowering process in the vineyard is so notably unspectacular that it is likely to be missed by the casual observer. The vine-grower, however, is aware that this process is particularly important in the chain of events that leads up to harvest, and, with some varieties and some weather conditions, a poor flowering can mean financial disaster for the vineyard owner.

Flowering, or bloom, takes place about six to 13 weeks after budbreak, the period being shorter for warm climates and early varieties. The vine flower usually contains both male parts (stamens) and female parts (a pistil-containing ovary). Unlike those of most other flowers, the petals of vine flowers are joined at the top, forming a cap, or calyptra. The flowering process begins as this cap falls away, exposing the stamens. Pollination is the process whereby pollen grains are shed and land on the moistened stigma surface where they germinate. They then penetrate the style and fertilize the ovary, leading to fruit set and the creation of a berry. The fertilized ovaries form seeds, with up to four per berry. The flower wall enlarges to form the skin and pulp of the grape berry. See diagram.

Most wine grape varieties have perfect, or hermaphroditic, flowers, that is with well-developed and functional male and female parts. Some varieties such as currant, sultana, and Perlette, more suitable for drying grapes and table grapes, have non-functional or defective female parts. Berries from such varieties are typically seedless or have small, poorly developed seeds, and therefore tend to be small because of a lack of hormones produced by normal seeds.

Cold, wet, and windy weather at flowering has a bad effect on flowering and fruit set. Studies in Europe (in Champagne, for example) have shown that regional vineyard yield can be correlated with the concentration of pollen in the lower atmosphere, which in turn can also be correlated with weather conditions. Many studies have shown that the vine flower is probably self-pollinated, with insects and wind making little contribution; even flowers surrounded by a bag tend to set perfectly (although cross-pollination between flowers is possible). However, grape flowers do release a pungent odour, from odour glands at the base of the pistil, which is known to attract insects. R.E.S.

Winkler, A. J., *et al.*, *General Viticulture* (2nd edn., Berkeley, Calif., 1974).

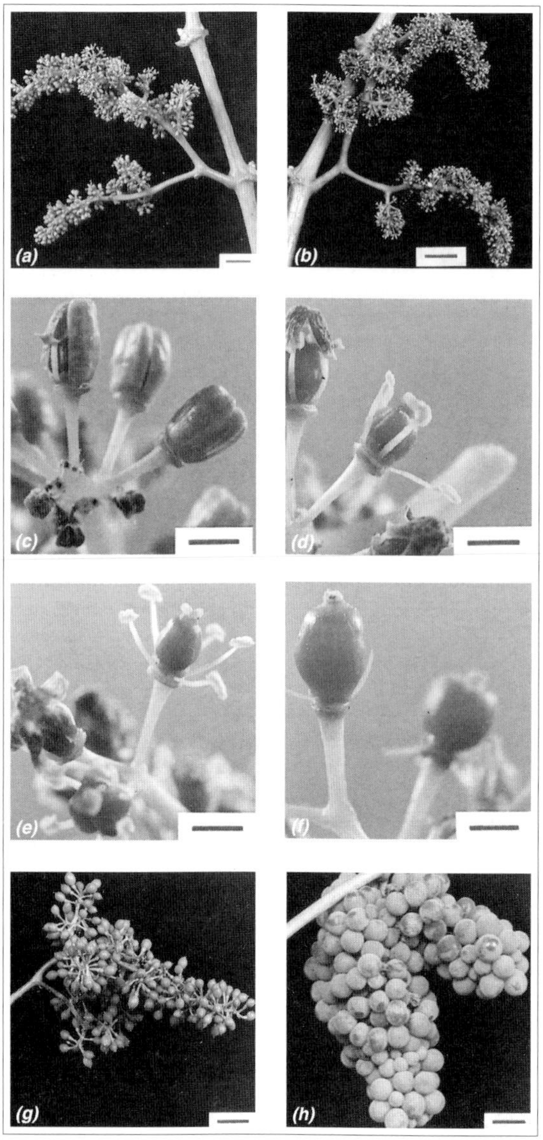

From **flowering** to harvest:
(*a*) at the beginning of flowering, when about 20 per cent of the caps, or calyptrae, have fallen, the stamens are visible;
(*b*) towards the end of flowering, with about 80 per cent cap fall;
(*c*) and (*d*) close-ups of caps falling off and stamens;
(*e*) a single flower showing five stamens and the stigma on the top of the pistil;
(*f*) and (*g*) the first stages of berry development following fruit set;
(*h*) a mature bunch of grapes.

FLOWERS, VINE. The grapevine flower is not showy, and has little attraction for birds, but it has the normal complement of sepals and petals surrounding the sexual parts: the male in the stamens and the female in the pistil. Flowers are grouped together on an inflorescence (see bunch). The five petals are locked together to form a cap or calyptra and, at flowering, they fall off, usually as a unit joined at the base; this is called 'capfall'. Once the caps are off, the stamens expand to their full length and the inflorescence begins to

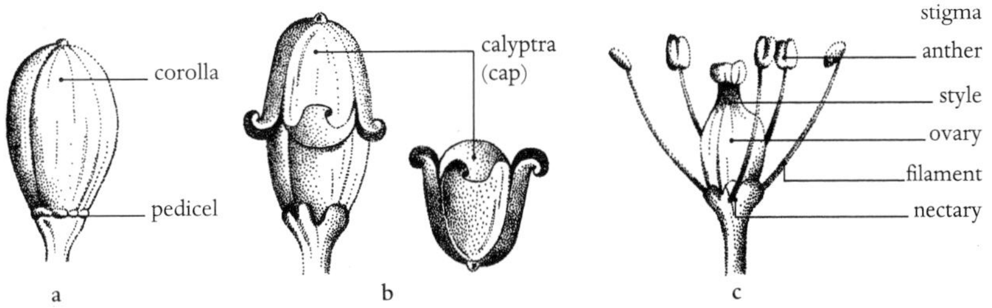

Bloom sequence of grape **flower**: (a) calyptra attached, (b) calyptra separating, and (c) open flower.

look fluffy. A wet, glistening coating covers the stigma at the top of the pistil when it is ready to receive large numbers of POLLEN grains lodged on this surface.

Different species and varieties of grapevine have one of three types of flower. The most common, and most FRUITFUL, are those with bisexual or hermaphrodite flowers, whose pistil and stamens are both functional. Some vine varieties (such as Ohanez) may have female or pistillate flowers, with a well-developed, functional pistil but with reflexed stamens which contain usually sterile pollen; with cross-pollination, using fertile pollen, these varieties become fruitful. And other varieties, particularly ROOTSTOCKS, may have male or staminate flowers (with functional stamens but no pistil) and therefore do not bear fruit. Most species of VITIS, in their native habitats, have male and female flowers on separate vines, which ensures cross-pollination and hence genetic diversity among the seedling progeny (see SEXUAL PROPAGATION). Commercial VINE VARIETIES are almost invariably bisexual and self-fruitful, and genetic diversity is avoided by VEGETATIVE PROPAGATION.

Flowering occurs in late spring when shoots have developed 17 to 20 visible internodes. This is a crucial stage in the reproductive development of the grape since a host of mishaps may lead to unsuccessful pollination or failure to develop into a berry (see FRUIT SET). B.G.C.

Mullins, M. G., Bouquet, A., and Williams, L. E., *Biology of the Grapevine* (Cambridge, 1992).

Pratt, C., 'Reproductive anatomy in cultivated grapes: a review', *American Journal of Enology and Viticulture*, 22 (1971), 92–109.

FLOWERS IN VINEYARDS may be deliberately planted at row ends or even between rows as COVER CROPS. Rose bushes at row ends are commonplace in the Médoc and, increasingly, elsewhere, either for aesthetic reasons or because they may act as early indicators of a POWDERY MILDEW attack. Tulips may be cultivated between rows in parts of the Loire.

FLURBEREINIGUNG, a word of great significance to the landscape of GERMANY's wine regions meaning 'restructuring', a programme undertaken in the second half of the 20th century. Many of the slopes on which some of Germany's finest wines have been produced were relatively inaccessible, uneconomically steep, often terraced, vineyards and so, with national and local government assistance, more than half the landscape devoted to viticulture in western Germany has been physically reshaped, with improvements to access, drainage, and workability. In some cases land has also been reallocated between individual owners to lower their production costs. Outsiders can only guess at the number of parochial man-hours put into the organization of this substantial operation.

FLYING WINE-MAKERS, term coined by English wine merchant Tony Laithwaite for a team of young Australian wine-makers he hired to work the 1987 vintage in French CO-OPERATIVE wineries. The idea was to apply Australian hard work and technological expertise to inexpensive grapes, thereby producing a unique range of wines for his mail order wine business. The concept was such a success that it has since been much imitated and developed into a phenomenon with a long-term impact on wine-making techniques and wine styles in wine regions all over the world.

The scheme originally depended on the fact that AUSTRALIA has a substantial number of talented wine-makers who are relatively idle during HARVEST time in the northern hemisphere, where most of the world's wine is made. (Miguel TORRES had already capitalized on transhemispherical possibilities by investing in Chile from his base in Spain in 1978, about the same time as the Australian Len EVANS was investigating the possibilities of investment of capital and wine-making expertise in Bordeaux and California.) During the late 1980s an increasing number of antipodeans were to be found using record amounts of WATER and working record hours in various European wineries. These co-operating wineries had to be open to outside OENOLOGICAL influence (which therefore excluded almost any wine producer with a reputation for its own products).

The scheme has since been developed into the creation of the flying wine-maker, or rather 'international wine-maker', since Laithwaite has registered his original name, as a long-term vocation. By the early 1990s Australian-trained individuals such as Jacques LURTON and Hugh Ryman, son of an English Monbazillac producer, were running teams of wine-makers around the globe, from MOLDOVA to Mendoza, often creating special wines or wine styles specifically to order from potential customers in northern Europe. This sort of

Hugh Ryman—one of the more celebrated **flying wine-makers**—travels the world from his base in Bordeaux.

bought-in OENOLOGY works best in areas with a considerable quantity of relatively inexpensive grapes but whose technical potential is yet to be realized. This necessarily excludes the classic wine regions and much of the NEW WORLD but has included southern France, much of Italy and Iberia, eastern Europe, some of the more open South African wineries, and South America.

The flying wine-makers are almost invariably Australian trained if not actually Australian. They often have to import materials such as ENZYMES and sometimes mobile BOTTLING equipment, but their most notable import has often been human energy.

See also AUSTRALIAN INFLUENCE.

FOIL, alternative name for the CAPSULE which covers the cork and neck of a wine bottle. The term is most commonly used for bottles of sparkling wine because in this case it is almost invariably made of metal foil, whereas the 'foil' covering tops of bottles of still wine may be made from a wide range of materials. LEAD was once common but was prohibited in the USA and the EU in 1993 because of both health and ecological concerns. Various plastics and tin are used, as is, increasingly, paper. The foil is there largely for aesthetic reasons since the CORK should provide an airtight seal and only a faulty one will allow any seepage of wine. Very occasionally, in the case of an oversight during bottling, a wine may be bottled with a foil but no cork; a tight foil has been observed to act as an effective bottle stopper in at least one case. The length and design of a foil is another purely aesthetic matter, although some clear identification on the top of the foil can be very useful in a CELLAR full of bottles on wine racks.

FOIL CUTTER, gadget for SERVING wine which helps cut the FOIL neatly just below the lip of the bottle with the advantages that this avoids unsightly and possibly dangerous torn metal edges, and that there is no likelihood of the wine's being poured over a foil which might taint it. Some foil cutters are blades incorporated into CORKSCREWS; others are separate prongs which are rotated after cutting the foil in several places. Life without a foil cutter is quite feasible; living without one after being introduced to it is not.

FOLLE BLANCHE, white grape variety once grown in profusion along the Atlantic seaboard of western France, providing very acidic but otherwise neutral base wine for distillation by the largely DUTCH WINE TRADE. It never regained its position after PHYLLOXERA ravaged the vineyards of Europe in the late 19th century and France's total plantings of Folle Blanche continue to decline: from 12,000 ha/29,640 acres in 1968 to 3,500 ha 20 years later, mainly for *Gros Plant* production. It has also been grown to a very limited extent in California.

FOLLE NOIRE is another name for the rather ordinary dark-berried grape variety called JURANÇON.

FONSECA, common Portuguese surname associated with three important wine producers in PORTUGAL, only two of which are related.

Fonseca, or **Fonseca Guimarãens**, are PORT shippers founded by a Portuguese gentleman, Manual Pedro Guimarãens, who acquired Fonseca, Monteiro and Co. in 1822 and proceeded to place the company on a commercial footing. The Guimarãens took the original firm's name of Fonseca as their label and still ship all their vintage and other ports under this name. Bruce Guimarãens, the fourth generation to work at Fonseca, is the wine-maker and vice-president of the company. His son David worked in Australia before returning to Oporto in the early 1990s. He is also estates manager for both Fonseca Guimarãens and TAYLOR, Fladgate and Yeatman, which acquired Fonseca in 1948. The two houses maintain separate identities and styles of port, however. Fonseca owns two main QUINTAS, Cruziero and Santo António, located in the Val de Mendiz above Pinhão. The 20 ha/49 acres of vineyards on these properties produce 80 per cent of the blend for Fonseca's particularly rich vintage ports. In 1978 they acquired Quinta do Panasçal, on the south side of the Douro, which was still being replanted in the mid 1990s. It should count as one of the best Douro quintas when finished and will add another 27 ha to the firm's vineyards.

Fonseca's best-known wine is the superior ruby port Bin 27; they also produce some excellent aged tawnies and Fonseca vintage ports which, in blind tastings, can rank above all others. Fonseca-Guimarãens is effectively used as a second label for their vintage ports, although their quality can be excellent.

José Maria da Fonseca Successores is based in the south of the country at Azeitão in ARRÁBIDA on the Setúbal peninsula. Originally a producer of rich, fortified SETÚBAL, it is now more important as a producer of a wide range of unfortified Portuguese wines, notably Periquita, designed for the international market from grapes bought widely, from Arrábida, neighbouring PALMELA, and beyond.

J. M. da Fonseca Internacional, or 'Internacional' as it is called by the locals, is also based in Azeitão, although it is now quite separate from the original family company above. It is best known in the United States for its high-volume LANCERS branded rosé, supplied by the João Pires winery, whose Australian- trained wine-maker also produces a range of extremely modern wines from both Portuguese and imported grape varieties grown all over southern Portugal.

FOOD, WINE AS. See DIET.

FOOD AND WINE MATCHING is either an extremely complex, detailed subject, a set of rules embedded in one's national culture, or an activity only for gastro-bores, according to one's point of view. To the French, not surprisingly, wine is simply part of *gastronomie* in general, and few Frenchmen would dream of describing a wine without suggesting which dish or dishes it should be served with. France has traditionally looked to its chefs for expertise in tasting and selecting wine, and it was only in the late 1980s that wine began to be viewed as a distinct subject in its own right. In the United States food and wine matching became a subject of intense scrutiny in the 1980s as wine producers, under pressure from so-called neo-Prohibitionists, sought to distance wine from drinks consumed principally for their alcohol content by putting it firmly on the dining table. For some of the most fanatical wine enthusiasts, food is an obstacle between palate and wine glass, whose flavours and aromas can get in the way of a decent wine-TASTING session.

It is certainly true that it is perfectly physically possible to drink any sort of wine with any sort of food. It is also true that 'white wine with fish and red wine with meat' is an absurd generalization built on a couple of sound maxims. There are also certain foods which have very specific effects on wine, and others which distort the PALATE to such an extent that wine tastes very odd or downright nasty in their wake.

Some specific reactions

The wine merchant's maxim 'buy on an apple and sell on cheese' has a sound basis in gustatory fact. Fresh, uncooked apples, like most fruits high in acidity, make many wines taste thin and metallic; any wine that impressed when tasted with an apple must have been seriously good. Hard cheese such as cheddar, on the other hand, tends to make wines taste softer and fuller. Strongly acidic foods such as dishes containing lemon juice and VINEGAR were for long cast as villains in terms of serving with food, but can make a slightly too acid wine taste fuller and more agreeable (while reacting badly with top-quality wines). Raw garlic can react with water to produce a burning sensation in many palates, while an acidic drink such as wine (Provençal rosé with *aïoli*) neutralizes the garlic and refreshes the palate. Hanni has demonstrated that, to the majority of palates, freshly ground pepper is a sensitizing element that may ruin the nuances of a fine, old wine, but can flatter a young, light bodied wine by making it taste stronger, fuller, and more complex.

Some wine-unfriendly foods

Globe artichokes and asparagus. A significant proportion of the population are sensitive to a substance in artichokes which has been dubbed 'cynarin' and which has the effect on them of making water taste sweet, and making wine taste metallic. McGee reports the evidence for this. A similar effect has been observed with fresh asparagus.

Some forms of chocolate are not only so sweet that it is difficult to find a wine sweeter than they are, they also coat the inside of the mouth. In this case a very strong, very sweet wine will overcome these disadvantages; lively young port, Australian Liqueur Muscat or Tokay, and Malaga, seem to manage.

Some general rules

White wines generally (although not universally) taste more acid than red wines, so it makes sense to serve them with simple fish dishes which would normally call for the sort of acidity in lemon juice or vinegar.

Red wines high in TANNINS taste less tannic if served with heavily textured foods, so it can make sense to partner a steak with a young wine based on Cabernet Sauvignon, Syrah, Nebbiolo, or Sangiovese.

Many cheeses are too pungent or greasy textured for very fine or mature red wine. Sweet wines, whether fortified or not, can be more flattered by the savoury, salty nature of cheese, and are less overwhelmed by it than, say, a mature red bordeaux.

All dry wines taste horrible with sweet foods which seem to emphasize their acidity. Even quite sweet wines can taste very thin and nasty if served with dishes that are sweeter than they are themselves. It is therefore advisable to choose only relatively sweet, full bodied wines with the sweet course. Germany's delicious sweet AUSLESEN are best sipped without food.

Clever use of lemon juice, vinegar, fresh pepper, and chewy meats can compensate for the shortcomings of ordinary wines. With very fine wine, however, it is probably safest to serve relatively neutral foods.

Some particularly successful combinations

Riesling and smoked salmon or other smoked fish.

Riesling (even medium sweet Riesling) with onion tart.

Chablis with oysters.

Cru Beaujolais with charcuterie, particularly *rosette de Lyon*.
Red bordeaux and lamb.
Red burgundy with feathered game.
Sauternes and Roquefort or other blue cheese.
See also ORDER OF WINES.

Hanni, T., *The Cause and Effect of Wine and Food* (St Helena, 1991).
McGee, H., *On Food and Cooking* (New York, 1984).

FOOT TREADING, almost extinct wine-making process now superseded by mechanical CRUSHING, even in most of the DOURO.

FORESTS, by supplying wood of a certain sort, have an important impact on the character and flavour of wine made using COOPERAGE made from that wood. See WOOD TYPES and, particularly, OAK for details of individual forest locations.

Forez, Côtes du. A range of hills between the upper reaches of the Loire and Lyons in eastern France give their name to light, vigorous red and rosé wines made, like BEAUJOLAIS, from the GAMAY grape. The wines, designed for early drinking, may taste reminiscent of those of the Côtes ROANNAISES to the north. Both regions, part-granitic, have known greater glory. Both were awarded VDQS status in the mid 1950s. The more southerly of the pair is higher, has a slightly less dependable climate, and has taken an almost exclusively CO-OPERATIVE route (rather like another pair of small, struggling wine regions to the south west, CABARDÈS and Côtes de la MALEPÈRE). The Vignerons Foréziens co-operative is based in Boën-sur-Lignon and has won acclaim for its policy of developing quality through a series of different cuvées.

FORTIFICATION, the practice of adding spirits, usually GRAPE SPIRIT, containing ALCOHOL to wine to ensure microbiological stability, thereby adding ALCOHOLIC STRENGTH and precluding any further FERMENTATION.

After fortification, wines become **fortified wines**, of which the most common are those made in the style of PORT, SHERRY, and VERMOUTH. Others whose final alcoholic strength is usually around 18 per cent include MADEIRA, MÁLAGA, MARSALA, as well as the Australian LIQUEUR MUSCAT and Liqueur Tokay of north east Victoria. Producing slightly less potent liquids, fortification also plays a vital role in the production of France's VIN DOUX NATUREL, VIN DE LIQUEUR, and similar mixtures of grape juice and alcohol made elsewhere.

The principle behind this addition of alcohol is that most BACTERIA and strains of YEAST are rendered impotent, unable to react with sugar or other wine constituents, in solutions containing more than 16 to 18 per cent alcohol, depending on the strain of yeast.

The stage at which spirit is added has enormous implications for the style of fortified wine produced. The earlier it is added in the fermentation process, the sweeter the resulting wine will be. Vins de liqueur such as PINEAU DES CHARENTES, for example, are simply blends of sweet, hardly fermented grape juice with grape spirit. An even stronger charge of alcohol is added before fermentation to a significant proportion of the rich grape juice used in the production of Australia's Liqueur Muscats and Tokays. For most port style wines (including the sweeter styles of madeira) and for all vins doux naturels, fortification takes place during fermentation. Much of the natural grape sugar is retained by arresting fermentation before its completion, thereby boosting alcoholic strength to a pre-ordained level: usually between 18 and 20 per cent in port but between 15 and 16 per cent in most vins doux naturels. Spirit is added only at the end of fermentation, to dry, fully fermented wine, in the making of sherry, similar wines such as VIN JAUNE, and the drier styles of madeira. Any sweetness in such wines is usually due to a pre-bottling addition of sweetening agent, often itself a mixture of grape juice and spirit (see MISTELA, PX).

The spirit used for fortification comes from a variety of different sources and could be based on grapes, sugar beet, cane sugar, agricultural by-products, or even petroleum. Local regulations specify the types of spirit allowed for a given fortified wine and only grape spirit is allowed for fortified wines of any quality. The spirit used for fortifying port, however, is supplied by the Portuguese monopoly which has, in its time, been unable to provide grape spirit, without any perceptible damage to the final quality of the wines. Carbon dating usefully allows the immediate detection of petroleum-based spirit in any wine, however.

The method of DISTILLATION of the spirit plays a part possibly even more important than its source. The most neutral spirits are the products of a CONTINUOUS STILL which contain a minimum of flavour CONGENERS and tend to be used in the fortification of wines that are designed for early consumption and deliberately exhibit the characteristics of the base wine (the MUSCATS of southern France, for example). Spirits produced by POT STILL distillation on the other hand are much more violently flavoured and are rarely added to fortified wines. A.D.W.

FOULAGE, French for the wine-making operation of CRUSHING grapes.

FOXY, usually deeply pejorative tasting term for the peculiar flavour of many wines, particularly red wines, made from HYBRIDS, vine varieties developed from both American and European species of the VITIS genus, particularly *Vitis labrusca* and *Vitis labruscana*. (Wines made from many other hybrids (SEYVAL, for example) are completely free of **foxiness**.) The CONCORD grape, widely planted in NEW YORK state, is one of the most heavily scented, reeking of something closer to animal fur than fruit, flowers, or any other aroma associated with fine wine, although the 'candy'-like aroma is, incidentally, quite close to that of the tiny French fruit *fraise des bois*. It has long been considered that the juice component reponsible is methyl anthranilate, but now there is another contender, o-amino acetophenone.

It has been discovered that earlier harvesting or long CASK AGEING reduces some of Concord's foxy characteristics. Aged New York sherry style wines are a good example of wines that have Concord that is virtually undetectable in their blends. Ironically, while often shunned at home, Concord grapes have delighted some California wine-makers with their perfume, and some *labruscana* varieties have been distilled into some exceptionally aromatic BRANDIES.

H.L. & B.G.C.

FRACTIONAL BLENDING, prosaic English name for the labour-intensive SOLERA system of maintaining consistency of a blended wine, particularly SHERRY, over many years.

FRANCE, the country that produces more fine wine (and BRANDY) than any other, and in which wine is firmly embedded in the culture. Although wine consumption, and to a lesser extent production, has fallen in the late 20th century, the total quantity of wine produced in most French vintages has been over 65 million hl/1,716 million gal, more than in any country other than Italy. This level of production has been maintained, as in Italy, despite a considerable decrease in the total area planted with vines (see EUROPEAN UNION and its efforts to encourage RIPPING OUT of large tracts of less promising vines): down from 1.23 million ha/3.04 million acres in the late 1970s to a total of 0.93 million ha (including some vines dedicated to TABLE GRAPES) in the early 1990s.

There are few wine producers anywhere who would not freely admit that they have been influenced by the great wines of BORDEAUX, BURGUNDY, CHAMPAGNE, or possibly the RHÔNE (see map on p. 399). Other qualitatively significant wine regions, perhaps better appreciated within France than abroad, include ALSACE (for historical details of which see GERMAN HISTORY), BEAUJOLAIS, CHABLIS, JURA, LOIRE, PROVENCE, SAVOIE, and SOUTH WEST FRANCE. France's most important wine region by far in terms of quantity, however, is the LANGUEDOC, and ROUSSILLON to the immediate south, whose remorseless output of VIN DE TABLE continues to make a major contribution to the European WINE LAKE, but whose better-quality wines provide some of the world's best wine value. The Mediterranean island of CORSICA is also under French jurisdiction, although it shares many characteristics with the Italian island of SARDINIA.

Although the first instance of geographical DELIMITATION was in Portugal's DOURO valley, France is the birthplace of the widespread application of the notion that geography, or TERROIR, is fundamental in shaping the character and quality of a wine. This resulted in the early 20th century in the much-copied APPELLATION CONTRÔLÉE system. Its governing body is INAO. Appellation contrôlée, or AC, wines represent the wines of which France has traditionally been most proud, sold under the geographical name of the appellation rather than by VINE VARIETY, as the substantially VARIETAL wines of the NEW WORLD have been. AC wines represent an increasing proportion of all wine produced in France, more than 40 per cent since the late 1980s. Vins Délimités de Qualité Supérieure, or VDQS wines, represent a small fraction of French wine production judged not (yet) up to AC standard. An increasingly significant category of French wine (and another that has been much copied elsewhere in Europe) is that represented by the VINS DE PAYS, or country wines. Rules governing vins de pays are much less constricting than the AC regulations: higher YIELDS and a wider range of vine varieties are generally allowed, and varietal vins de pays are common. By 1992 vins de pays constituted nearly 20 per cent of all French wine produced and the long-term aim is to upgrade even more of the production of the vast Languedoc-Roussillon regions from vin de table to vin de pays.

Curiously, and perhaps because wine is so deeply entrenched in French history and culture, wine CONNOISSEURSHIP and to a certain extent the wine TRADE are not as evolved in France as, for example, in Australia, Belgium, Great Britain, Switzerland, and the United States. Although things are slowly changing, the average French citizen has bought and drunk little other than the wine produced closest to him, whether geographically or by virtue of human connections. This has tended to stifle the development of wine retailing, although the number of specialist wine MERCHANTS, known here as *cavistes*, has increased significantly since the early 1980s. As might be expected in a country associated with so many forms of gastronomic excellence, wine appreciation in France is closely tethered to the table. Wine is rarely drunk without food, and France's chefs and SOMMELIERS have been regarded as the rightful repositories of wine knowledge.

Although France is rivalled only by Italy as the world's principal wine exporter, it is also an important importer of wine. Wine has been imported ever since Massilia was settled by the Greeks (see below), but it was the development of the Languedoc as a virtual factory for particularly light red wines at the end of the 19th century and the beginning of the 20th that meant vast quantities of strong, deep coloured red wines had to be imported for BLENDING (*coupage* in French), from North African colonies initially and subsequently from southern Italy and, to an increasing extent, Spain.

France is so important as a role model to the world of wine that many terms used internationally are French in origin (BLANC DE BLANCS, PIGEAGE, and VERAISON are just three varied examples). France is recognized the world over as a centre of wine research and ACADEME and has benefited ever since the time of Colbert in the late 17th century from the country's ability to identify and solve potential problems on a national level (see OAK). The OENOLOGICAL and viticultural faculties of the universities of BORDEAUX and MONTPELLIER have long enjoyed international prestige, and considerable viticultural research emanates from INRA stations.

One of France's great commercial strengths in recent years has been that it is the world's prime source of oak for top-quality wine and brandy COOPERAGE. France is an important exporter of barrels, notably but not exclusively to the United States.

History

Around 600 BC Greek immigrants arrived from Phocaea in ASIA MINOR and founded Massalia (Marseilles) as a Greek city (see Ancient GREECE). One of the colonists' importations was viticulture. In the 2nd century BC the settlement, now known as Massilia, had become vital to the Romans, now a major power (see Ancient ROME), if they were to safeguard their trading route with Saguntum (modern Sagunto, near Valencia in Spain). When Massilia was attacked first by the Ligurians and then by the Celtic tribes of the Allobroges and the Arverni (of modern AUVERGNE), self-interest made the Romans take on the defence of the city. As a result they gained a new province, named at first Provincia (modern PROVENCE) and later, with the foundation of the Roman city of Narbo (modern Narbonne) in 118 BC, Gallia Narbonensis. Massilia remained Greek until 49 BC.

In the eyes of the Greek colonists, vines grew where olives and figs grew: the commercial exploitation of the three together had long been characteristic of Mediterranean agriculture, so it did not occur to a Mediterranean people that the vine could be cultivated further north than the olive and the fig. The wines of Massilia were available in Rome, but they were cheap and nasty. Even before Caesar's conquest of Gaul in 51 BC, the Gauls had consumed Italian wine in prodigious quantities, as the evidence from AMPHORAE found in France shows. The Greek geographer Strabo, who finished his *Geography* in 7 BC, said that Massilia and Narbo produced the same fruits as Italy, but that the rest of Gaul was too far north for the olive, the fig, and the vine (4. 2. 1). His statement may have been too sweeping, however, and in the 1st century AD good wine certainly did come from Gaul. PLINY tells us in his *Natural History* that in Vienna (modern Vienne in the RHÔNE valley) the Allobroges produced RESINATED WINES which were a source of national pride and for which they charged high prices (14. 57). For more details, see GAUL.

Thus the first French wine of note was a Rhône wine. Yet at the same time or earlier the inhabitants of Gallia Narbonensis may themselves have taken the vine beyond the familiar territory of the olive and the fig, to GAILLAC in modern SOUTH WEST FRANCE. Archaeological evidence shows that in the second half of the reign of the Emperor Augustus (he was Imperator from 27 BC to AD 14) amphorae were being made in large numbers in workshops near Gaillac, and near Béziers in the LANGUEDOC. This suggests that they were needed for wine that was grown there and not imported. The RIVERS Tarn and GARONNE would have provided convenient transport to the Atlantic coast, where BORDEAUX was already a trading post. Since these wines are not mentioned by any classical author, they probably did not reach Rome, unlike the wines of Vienne.

Gaillac and Vienne are beyond the northern limit for olive trees, but they do sustain another tree that is considered characteristic of Mediterranean vegetation, the evergreen oak, QUERCUS *ilex*. Where the evergreen oak grows, the climate is hot enough to produce a good grape harvest every year, without fail. Yet viticulture advanced further north, away from the evergreen oak, to where the success of the vintage is no longer guaranteed. Bordeaux and BURGUNDY were next in line; by the 3rd century AD wine was grown in both regions, despite the possibility of cold, wet summers when the grapes might not ripen fully. Yet even if the harvest failed occasionally, the demand for wine was such that the expansion of viticulture made economic sense.

The Romans had regarded the CELTS as drunks, and hence a source of great profit, immoderate fools who drank wine unmixed with water until they fell into a stupor, but when the drunken Celts started growing their own wine, its reputation was soon to surpass that of the Italian wines that they had once imported. After Bordeaux and Burgundy came the LOIRE and the Île-de-France (the PARIS basin including CHAMPAGNE). By the 6th century AD even the west of Brittany had vines, and wine was grown further north than it is now, well north of Paris.

As the Roman empire disintegrated, Gaul ceased to be a Roman province and was overrun by Germanic invaders. The Visigoths, the Burgundians, and the Franks established kingdoms in Gaul; eventually, Aquitaine and Burgundy were subjected to Frankish rule. Under the Romans the Gauls had been governed from the south; the Franks had come from the north, and Clovis, the first of the Merovingian kings (481–511), established Paris as the capital city of a kingdom that hardly extended further than the Île-de-France. Under CHARLEMAGNE and his heirs, the royal court's principal seats were Aachen (Aix-la-Chapelle) and Paris. Hence political power, and the wealth that went with it, were concentrated in the north. In the Mediterranean wine was part of everyday life, but in Paris and Aachen, on the northernmost limits of viticulture, wine was a luxury item, and from a luxury item it became a status symbol. Also, because Gaul was largely Christian by the 6th century, the Church's requirements added impetus to northern viticulture (see EUCHARIST). Monasteries and churches needed wine; local magnates, both lay and spiritual, wanted good wine.

Monastic influence

Monasteries had their own vineyards (see MONKS AND MONASTERIES and BURGUNDY), and so, often, did cathedrals. From the Carolingian era onwards, lay viticulture generally used the system of 'complant', which meant that a wine-grower would approach an owner of uncultivated land with an offer to plant it for him. Since it takes about five years for new vines to start yielding sufficient fruit, the grower would be given that length of time to work the vineyard; after that, half the land would revert to the owner, while the vines on the other half would become the possession of the grower, on condition that part of the harvest, or sometimes a monetary payment, be given every year in perpetuity. The Loire wine QUART DE CHAUME, for instance, owes its name to the complant mode of ownership and production: the 'quart', or fourth, being the share the vigneron owed the landowner (in 1440, the Abbey of Ronceray d'Angers); 'chaume' meaning an uncultivated plot that is to be planted with vines. As labour grew more expensive, the conditions became more favourable to the grower: in the course of the 13th century, the owner would often no longer reclaim the half of his property, but the grower, and his children and his children's children after him, would continue to make their annual payments in wine or money. The system made it possible for wild country to be colonized and cultivated at no expense to the landowner: in this way, the new wine-growing region of Poitou (see LA ROCHELLE) was planted so efficiently in the 12th and 13th centuries. The advantage to the grower was that he was not a serf, tied to the land, but a free man, entitled to a large share of what he produced. It was therefore in his interest to make wine for which he could get a good price; nevertheless the owner exercised ultimate control, for the decision how and with what grapes to plant the vineyard was his, and he had the right to terminate the contract and evict the vigneron if the wine was not good enough.

In the Middle Ages wine was France's chief export product, and the reasons why certain nations drink some wines in preference to others go back to this period. The English drink CLARET because BORDEAUX was at one time governed by the English crown and later remained the largest supplier of wine to England. The Scots drink claret because of the Auld

Alliance with France against England. The Flemish and the Dutch have traditionally bought wines of Burgundy because Flanders and the southern part of the Netherlands were part of the dukedom of Burgundy and Burgundy's trade routes were mostly overland to the north. But transporting wooden BARRELS of wine along bumpy roads was difficult and expensive: whether a region exported a large share of its wine or produced wine mainly for its own consumption depended on its proximity to navigable RIVERS rather than on the quality of its wines. Apart from its trade with the north, which did not develop until the 15th century, Burgundy did not export much wine, whereas regions accessible by water, such as the LOIRE, the Île-de-France around PARIS, and GASCONY, did. The chief ports were Bordeaux, Rouen, and La Rochelle. Bordeaux served the Bordeaux area and the HAUT PAYS; Rouen served the Île-de-France; and La Rochelle served Poitou.

The ships used to transport wine before the 12th century were longboats like the Viking ships. But in the 12th century the new ports of La Rochelle and Gravelines (on the English Channel near St-Omer), as well as the new Flemish ports of Nieuwpoort (near Ypres) and Damme (near Bruges), adopted a new type of ship, the cog. The cog was a broadly built ship, with a roundish prow and stern, more manœuvrable than the old kind and specifically designed for carrying freight. Its capacity was far larger than that of the old longboat, and soon all other ports started using it as a more efficient way of transporting wine. The cog doubled up as a warship if need arose.

The unit in which wine was measured, the TONNEAU, derived from Bordeaux. A tonneau, or wooden barrel, could hold 252 old wine gallons, or 900 l/238 US gal. A Paris tonneau was 800 l, but, because of the prominence of Gascon merchants in London and English merchants in Bordeaux, the Bordeaux measure became the standard. Many cogs could hold as many as 200 tonneaux; in practice, a barrel containing 900 l was too heavy to handle, and casks half or a quarter the size were used. Such was the importance of the medieval wine trade that, from being the space occupied by a tun of wine, a tonneau, or ton in English, became the unit in measuring the carrying capacity of any ship, whatever its load. H.M.W.

Dion, Roger, *Histoire de la vigne et du vin en France* (Paris, 1959).
Duby, Georges (ed.), *Histoire de la France rurale*, i (Paris, 1975).
Lachiver, M., *Vins, vignes, vignerons* (Paris, 1988).

Modern history

The social turmoil of the French Revolution at the end of the 18th century made few important changes to the patterns of wine production (although it did engender an entirely new class of consumers, and new styles of *restauration* for them). Until the middle of the 19th century the vine was cultivated much more widely in France than it is today, and such abandoned areas as, for example, the Côtes d'AUVERGNE on the Massif Central, PARIS, and the MOSELLE were flourishing wine regions. As communications improved, the patterns of the wine trade changed, although Bordeaux continued to operate with a certain degree of autonomy, thanks to its geographical position and long-established trading links with northern Europe, first ENGLAND and then the DUTCH WINE TRADE. The 17th and 18th centuries saw an explosion of interest in wine production in the Gironde, and by the mid 19th century, when the world's most famous wine CLASSIFICATION was formalized at a magnificent exhibition in Paris, the great CHÂTEAUX of the MÉDOC were enjoying a period of prosperity that would not be rivalled until the 1980s. Wine continued to be important to the Burgundian economy, and French wine was recognized throughout the civilized world as one of the corner-stones of civilization itelf. CHAPTAL had devised ways of improving overall wine quality (for the incidence of ADULTERATION AND FRAUD was high in the immediate aftermath of the Revolution), and France was beginning to produce its own wine experts such as the widely travelled and independently minded JULLIEN. A historian might say that a catastrophe to end this golden age was inevitable.

In fact there was a series of catastrophes, all viticultural, which had devastating effects on both the quantity and quality of wine produced. Oidium, or POWDERY MILDEW, was the first of a series of disastrous imports from North America, presumably the result of the 19th century passion for collecting botanical specimens. Unlike European vines, most American vines are resistant to this FUNGAL DISEASE and so it was not until it had been imported to Europe that its effects, of reducing quantity, quality, and colour, were noted, in 1852. The 1854 vintage in France was disastrous, the smallest for more than 60 years. French vineyards were just returning to health, thanks to the development of SULPHUR dusting, when another curious vine condition was noted: inexplicable debilitation and, eventually, death. The cause was a tiny louse, PHYLLOXERA, which was to ravage the vineyards of the world, but affected southern France first, causing the greatest commercial havoc there while a remedy was sought. Since phylloxera affects only the roots of vines, the only effective solution was eventually found to be to graft European vines on to resistant American ROOTSTOCKS. But the renewed importation of North American plant material seems to have brought with it two more deadly American fungal diseases, DOWNY MILDEW, whose effects on wine quality and quantity were first noted in 1878 and lasted until well into the 20th century, and BLACK ROT, which was evident from the mid 1880s.

It is hardly surprising therefore that French vignerons saw their salvation in planting HYBRIDS, vines with at least some American genes to provide a defence against these completely new and unforeseen hazards to one of France's greatest glories. First, after considerable debate, AMERICAN HYBRIDS were planted and then, in the early 20th century, so-called FRENCH HYBRIDS were developed which tasted more like the European VINIFERA vines' produce.

There was such a crisis in wine quality in the late 19th century that the great scientist PASTEUR was asked to look into the matter, and the result was a giant step forward for the science of wine-making, in which France has long been at the forefront of research (see BORDEAUX UNIVERSITY in particular).

By the turn of the century the plains of the LANGUEDOC had been transformed into a great factory producing light red for drinkers in northern France, now commercially accessible thanks to the development of the RAILWAYS. These light wines were given weight, alcohol, and colour by the produce of new vineyards in ALGERIA and the economy of this North African colony was transformed.

Two World Wars left France's wine business in serious need of reorganization, and from the mid 20th century it has certainly been the world's most thoroughly and harmoniously organized, with the development of the powers of the INAO and increasing emphasis on the importance of the APPELLATION CONTRÔLÉE system for which it is responsible. Vigorous, and successful, efforts have been made to uproot hybrids from France's vineyards, to ensure that a sound standard of scientific training is available to France's thousands of vine-growers and wine-makers, and that a thorough programme of research is dedicated to the concept of wine quality.

Geography and climate

France does not have the monopoly on fine wine production, but its geographical position is exceptionally favoured for growing a wide range of different styles of grapes with a good balance of sugar and acidity. With wine regions lying between LATITUDES 42 degrees and 49.5 degrees, France can provide the two most suitable environments identified in CLIMATE AND WINE QUALITY for growing grapes. In the south the MEDITERRANEAN CLIMATE can be depended upon to ripen grapes fully, but not so fast that they do not have time to develop an interesting array of FLAVOUR COMPOUNDS and PHENOLICS. In the west, relatively high latitudes are tempered by the influence of the Atlantic's Gulf Stream. In the east, centuries of viticultural tradition have established what seem to be potentially perfect marriages between grape variety and particularly favoured TERROIR in the more CONTINENTAL CLIMATE of Burgundy, Alsace, and Champagne, France's most northerly wine region where, over the centuries, the perfect wine style has evolved to take advantage of the area's climate and special geology.

France also has a wide variety of SOIL TYPES, much charted and revered (although see GEOLOGY and SOIL AND WINE QUALITY for a discussion of the limited extent to which they may affect wine quality).

Vine-growing in modern France is concentrated in the south but there are vineyards in all regions other than the most mountainous and the most cloudy, which excludes most of the Massif Central, the high-altitude mass in the middle of the country, most of the alpine region on the south east, and the flat north western sector closest to Great Britain. See map.

Vine varieties

France conducts a full agricultural census only every 10 years, the most recent one being dated 1988, when the total area of vines dedicated to wine production was nearly 900,000 ha / 2.2 million acres, of which more than two-thirds were planted with dark-skinned grape varieties. Between 1988 and 1993 more than 70,000 ha of vines were ripped out, mainly in the Languedoc-Roussillon, under the auspices of the European Union's VINE PULL SCHEME, and other vineyards were also abandoned, but France still has more land under vine than any country other than Spain and Italy.

CARIGNAN has been France's most planted vine variety for many decades, thanks to its ubiquity in France's largest wine region, the Languedoc-Roussillon. For the same reasons ARAMON was important in the mid 20th century but is now France's seventh most planted variety. Second most planted variety is UGNI BLANC, the white grape which provides so much base wine for COGNAC. Other important red wine grape varieties were, in decreasing order of total area planted, GRENACHE, MERLOT, CINSAUT, and CABERNET SAUVIGNON, Merlot and Cabernet having increased considerably in popularity. No light-skinned grape variety other than Ugni Blanc is planted to anything like the extent of these red wine grapes, but CHARDONNAY has become increasingly popular, as elsewhere, in Burgundy, Champagne, and throughout France, so that it had become the second most planted white grape variety in France, overtaking SÉMILLON, in the 1980s.

One of France's strengths is her treasury of traditional local varieties, either imported as a result of shifting political power (most of France's most planted red varieties were originally Spanish), or the apparently indigenous likes of those still to be found in limited quantity in SOUTH WEST FRANCE. More than 100 different varieties are still planted to a significant extent, even though the trend has been towards increasing reliance on what are now known as INTERNATIONAL VARIETIES (most of them apparently French in origin).

Viticulture

Most vineyards in France are immediately recognizably French. With its reliable RAINFALL and supply of soil water, northern France has the highest VINE DENSITY in the world, with up to 13,000 plants per ha, and the vines are typically planted in neat, low-trained rows, often using GUYOT systems of pruning and training (typically dictated by the detail of APPELLATION CONTRÔLÉE regulations). LEAF TRIMMING during the growing season is common. French vignerons have in general had centuries to match cultural practices to local conditions, although in the early 20th century many less suitable terrains were planted in an extension of classic zones. IRRIGATION is usually unnecessary in northern and western France, and strictly, if theoretically, controlled in the south. The relatively humid climate of western France means, however, that frequent SPRAYING against FUNGAL DISEASES is often necessary. In the early 1990s, concern was increasingly expressed at the use of AGROCHEMICALS in many French wine regions. Other common viticultural hazards are FROST in the north, HAIL in Burgundy, and DROUGHT in the south. Crop levels can vary considerably since the weather during FLOWERING is by no means predictably fine, WINTER FREEZE may kill vines, as in 1956, and spring frosts can seriously affect total national production, as in 1991.

French viticultural research is of a high level, and co-ordinated nationally under the auspices of INRA which has stations all over the country. Many of the world's vine-growers regard French NURSERIES as their prime source of planting material, and there has been considerable work on CLONAL SELECTION.

France's vine-growers are probably the most regulated in the world. For all wines other than VIN DE TABLE, dates of HARVEST are limited by regional annual decree, and YIELDS are minutely regulated. A low yield is generally regarded as the safest prerequisite for wine quality, but in the 1980s the maximum basic yield allowed by appellation contrôlée regulations was routinely increased by the 20 per cent so-called *plafond limite de classement*, or PLC, supplement. Towards the end of the 1980s, CROP THINNING was increasingly practised in the better-quality wine regions.

Wine-making

In many wine regions TRADITION is as important as SCIENCE in determining wine-making techniques, although France's wine-makers can and do draw on many centres of OENOLOGICAL academe for instruction and research (of which only BORDEAUX UNIVERSITY, DIJON, and MONTPELLIER are described in any detail in this book).

Techniques vary enormously in France's hundreds of thousands of *caves* but in general, and in sharp contrast to the New World, PROTECTIVE JUICE HANDLING and an obsession with winery HYGIENE are relatively rare. Mastery of MALOLACTIC FERMENTATION and OAK AGEING, on the other hand, are taken for granted, much to the frustrated amusement of wine-makers elsewhere, who regularly make pilgrimages to study the minutiae of wine-making operations in some of France's most revered wine regions in an effort to learn the 'tricks' involved in the production of great wine.

Part of French wine-makers' easy relationship with BARREL MATURATION comes from the fact that France is the centre of the world's COOPERAGE industry, or at least that part of it of interest to wine-makers. French OAK is revered the world over, and one of the major investments of many a non-French wine producer is in shipping quantities of new BARRELS from France.

France is also the birthplace of CHAPTALIZATION, and a high proportion of her wines depend on some degree of ENRICHMENT (although the EUROPEAN UNION has announced its intention to control this practice of increasing ALCOHOLIC STRENGTH by adding sugar to the fermentation vat).

Wine in France is red. Less than a quarter of all wine consumed in France is white, and in the hot summers of the south of France rosé is more likely to be consumed than white, as a sort of red for high temperatures. Wine consumption, which used to be one of the highest in the world, has been falling rapidly in France. In 1980 the average per capita wine consumption was 91 l/24 gal a year but this is expected to fall to 68 l by 1995. The average quality of wine drunk in France has been increasing substantially, however.

Wine quality categories

Of the average French harvest, wines from the most revered quality wine category APPELLATION CONTRÔLÉE now represent the most significant proportion, about 36 per cent in the early 1990s, while the most basic wine for direct consumption, that classified as VIN DE TABLE, is made in ever-decreasing quantities and, in 1992, for example, represented just 23 per cent. The VIN DE PAYS category, distinctly superior to table wine, represented nearly 20 per cent, while the VDQS wines waiting in the wings for promotion to full AC status represented about one per cent. The remaining 20 per cent of an average year's French wine production is designed for DISTILLATION into brandy. France dominates the production not just of fine wine but also of fine brandy (see ARMAGNAC, COGNAC, EAU-DE-VIE, and MARC).

For details of the history, climate, geography, vine varieties planted, and wines produced, see under regional, or even more geographically specific, names. For individual regions, see also ALSACE, BEAUJOLAIS, BORDEAUX, BUGEY, BURGUNDY, CHABLIS, CHAMPAGNE, CORSICA, JURA, LANGUEDOC-ROUSSILLON, LOIRE, PROVENCE, SAVOIE, RHÔNE, and SOUTH WEST FRANCE. See also VIN and immediately following entries, as well as CRÉMANT for some of France's better-quality sparkling wines.

Johnson, H., *The Story of Wine* (London and New York, 1989).
—— *The World Atlas of Wine* (4th edn., London and New York, 1994).
Le Guide Hachette des Vins (Paris, annually).

FRANCIACORTA, one of ITALY's newest areas for the production of high-quality red, white, and sparkling wines, extends across the hills of a series of townships to the south of Lake Iseo in the province of Brescia in LOMBARDY. Although the zone presents a certain number of indisputable natural advantages—a mineral-rich soil of morainic origin, warm days and cool evenings in the summer, the latter assisted by the moderating influences of the lake—the wine had only a local reputation until the 1960s when the SPUMANTE house of Berlucchi launched the first Franciacorta sparkling wines. The ensuing demand for the wines of this house gave national prominence to Franciacorta, a prominence which was rapidly exploited by a series of able entrepreneurs from Milan and Brescia.

Sparkling wine, made by the classic method of CHAMPAGNE and from CHARDONNAY, PINOT BLANC, PINOT NOIR, and PINOT GRIS grapes, still represents nearly half of the Franciacorta DOC production, but there was a significant development of French-style still wines in the 1980s, made at least partially from the classic red grapes of BORDEAUX and the red and white grapes of BURGUNDY, frequently given a full-blown international treatment including lavish amounts of new OAK ageing. A certain number of the best still wines, however, are currently being marketed as a VINO DA TAVOLA, which means that the DOC itself risks becoming a category to which the least interesting wines of the zone are relegated. The DOC rules themselves are at least partly at fault: in the mid 1990s permitted yields were excessive (84 hl/ha (5 tons/acre)) and the obligatory percentages of BARBERA (20–30 per cent), NEBBIOLO (15–25 per cent), and CABERNET FRANC (40–50 per cent) tend to crowd out the CABERNET SAUVIGNON and MERLOT grapes of Bordeaux (neither of which may constitute more than 15 per cent of a Franciacorta DOC wine). Pinot Noir of

Burgundy is only permitted in the zone's sparkling wines. More ambitious products are thus virtually compelled to refuse DOC status.

The producer's consortium adopted an admirable code of self-regulation while the DOC regulations are being revised, with a gradual reduction of yields (to 10 tons/ha); elimination of Pinot Gris; a minimum VINE DENSITY of 4,000 vines per ha; outlawing of TENDONE and GENEVA DOUBLE CURTAIN training systems; and fractional PRESSING of musts. Although Franciacorta made great progress in the 1970s and 1980s, the zone still suffers from an excessive variation in quality between the excellent products of such vanguard estates as Cà del Bosco and Bellavista and the more pedestrian efforts of younger houses, many of whose owners have invested more capital and enthusiasm than a specific technical competence in the production process. The area under vines grew rapidly in the decade after the mid 1980s to reach its almost 1,000 ha/2,500 acres by the mid 1990s, producing over 44,000 hl/1.16 million gal of white wine (60 per cent of which is sparkling wine) and over 13,000 hl of red wine. D.T.

Anderson, B., *The Wine Atlas of Italy* (London and New York, 1990).
Gleave, D., *The Wines of Italy* (London and New York, 1989).

FRANCONIA, alternative English name for the German wine region FRANKEN.

FRANCS, village which gives its name to the small BORDEAUX CÔTES appellation **Côtes de Francs**, or **Bordeaux Côtes de Francs**, just north of CÔTES de CASTILLON between ST-ÉMILION and BERGERAC. The original settlement took its name from a detachment of Franks sent there by Clovis after defeating the Visigoths (see FRANCE, history). The Côtes de Francs wine region has considerably more personality than regular BORDEAUX AC and its revival in the 1980s owed much to the Belgian Thienpont family (also associated with Ch Le Pin, Vieux-Ch-Certan, and Ch Labegorce-Zédé). About 300 ha/740 acres of vines are on high clay-limestone slopes, many of which enjoy a favourable west south west exposure. Almost all of the wine produced is well-structured red from CABERNET and MERLOT grapes, but a little sweet white is made in memory of a style once traditional for this area. For more detail see BORDEAUX.

FRANKEN, known in English as **Franconia**, distinctive wine region in central GERMANY. Until reunification in 1990, Franken's 5,250 ha/12,940 acres formed the country's most eastern wine region. The sometimes severe winters and the risks of autumn and spring FROSTS have largely decided where vines should now be grown. Since the 1960s the area under vine has doubled, and old vineyards have been rebuilt and modernized (see FLURBEREINIGUNG). In some cases the advantages of having more economically worked vineyards have been won by an increased risk of damage from cold winds, no longer filtered by trees or hedges (see WINDBREAKS). No other region based on the Rhine or its tributaries has such wide variations in the size of its harvest, as was emphasized

The famous Bocksbeutel in which all fine **Franken** wine is sold.

in 1985. In February, warm sunny days in the best south-facing sites above the Main were followed by temperatures down to −25 °C/−13 °F at night, with catastrophic results for the vineyard owners. The average yield in the following autumn was no more than 13 hl/ha (0.7 tons/acre). The dead vines had to be replaced, according to Bavarian regulations, by vines grown within the region, and three years were to pass before the NURSERIES could satisfy all the demands on their stocks.

Hard frosts are all too frequent in some villages, including Hammelburg on the river Saale, 51 km/32 miles north of Würzburg. When weather permits, Hammelburger Silvaner is a lively wine with high acidity, and elegance, presumably from the limestone soil. During the first half of this century SILVANER was the most widely grown vine in Franken. By 1964 it still covered over 50 per cent of the vineyard area and by 1990 its share had settled at around 20 per cent. As the wood of the vine is not very resistant to extremes of cold in winter, Silvaner needs to grow in the top-quality sites. It does well in the famous Würzburger Stein vineyard and on the slopes of the Steigerwald near Castell in the east of the region. MÜLLER-THURGAU grows in nearly half of the region's vineyards and besides the 520 ha of BACCHUS, there are also more than 100 ha each of KERNER, RIESLING, and SCHEUREBE. Those producers who sell their wine in bottle directly to the consumer often like to have a range based on different vine varieties, particularly if their vineyard holding is in only one site. The range of VINE VARIETIES planted is great and probably larger than necessary.

Although red and rosé wine represents only three per cent of the region's production, interest is growing in red wines for drinking with food. The retail price of a bottle of QBA Spätburgunder (PINOT NOIR) may be 30 per cent more than that of a Riesling of equivalent quality, but sales are not deterred, and 17 per cent of the small 247 ha Bereich Mainviereck is now planted in Spätburgunder.

The best QUALITÄTSWEIN of Franken are sold in the flagon-shaped BOCKSBEUTEL, as are those of a few villages in neighbouring north BADEN. Its use within Germany is protected by law. Most Franken wines come from a single vine variety. Because of their rather different structure, sweetness suits the cheaper versions less well than it does those from the northern Rhine regions. In fact 42 per cent or so of the volume of Franken quality wine is *fränkisch* TROCKEN (dry), with a RESIDUAL SUGAR content of less than 4 g/l. A further 11 per cent has between 4 and 9 g/l residual sugar and therefore falls below the upper limit of the official EUROPEAN UNION definition of what qualifies as dry. Müller-Thurgau from a restricted yield with adequate acidity can produce solid, concentrated wine which improves with age. It does very well in the Bereich Steigerwald. With Würzburg, it is also a source of Silvaner, which appears confidently in all the quality categories and can fulfil expectations of a fine German wine.

In 1806 Johann Wolfgang von Goethe wrote to his wife 'send me some Würzburger wine, for no other really pleases me'. Certainly, as a capital of a wine region, Würzburg is incomparable, in spite of air raid damage in 1945 which left the majority of the city in ruins. It has three large, fine estates with top-quality vineyard sites within the city boundaries, as well as many holdings scattered throughout the region.

Riesling does not play a leading role in Franken but the quality of its best wine from good estates is excellent and the style unique to the region. The Rieslings of the Stein and Innere Leiste vineyards at Würzburg, of Randersackerer Pfülben, Escherndorfer Lump, Iphöfer Julius-Echter-Berg, and of the, in part, somewhat run down and almost 70 per cent steep Homburger Kallmuth, can be quite splendid. Much cheap Franken wine is overpriced compared to wines from the PFALZ, but the best, although expensive, is good value.

The crossing BACCHUS produces surprisingly elegant wine from the Steigerwald, when the yield is restricted to 60 or 70 hl/ha, reminding some of SAUVIGNON BLANC. The RIESLANER, a Silvaner × Riesling crossing from Würzburg, produces wines with high acidity, but not the quality of Riesling. They can, nevertheless, be very impressive at AUSLESE level or above.

The CO-OPERATIVE movement in Franken achieves on average some of the highest wine prices per litre of any co-operative cellars in Germany. The large cellar at Kitzingen receives the crop from over a quarter of the region's vines, and smaller co-operatives account for another 15 per cent. Most of the regional co-operative's customers are in south Germany and the quantities exported are small. The strong local market, in which much wine is sold through supermarkets, and the clear identity of Franken wine emphasized by the Bocksbeutel, have meant that sales outside Bavaria have not been needed. In the 1990s some of the larger estates are showing more interest in exporting. I.J.

Breider, H., *Das Buch vom Frankenwein* (Würzburg, 1974).

FRANKLAND, relatively cool, promising vineyard area in the Lower Great Southern region of the state of WESTERN AUSTRALIA.

FRANKOVKA, synonym for the red BLAUFRÄNKISCH grape used in Slovakia and Vojvodina.

FRAPPATO, lesser Sicilian red grape variety.

FRASCATI is both the most famous and quantitatively the most important of the CASTELLI ROMANI wines. Close to 300,000 hl/7.9 million gal of Frascati are produced in favourable vintages from 2,800 ha/6,920 acres of vineyards. Its fame is less by virtue of its intrinsic quality—it differs little from the wines of its neighbouring DOC zones—than by virtue of its constant citation in the literature of Italy and in the accounts of the countless foreign visitors to Rome. The charms of the town of Frascati, with its beautiful villas, gardens, fountains, and cypress-lined boulevards, have doubtlessly contributed to the wine's cachet, as has the town's geographical proximity to Rome, a mere 24 km/15 miles away. Weekend and summer visitors from Rome have long been a significant factor in the town's economy, and Frascati had 1,022 taverns as long ago as 1450. The wine itself, the standard blend of Malvasia with Trebbiano of the Castelli Romani, is a sound, if rarely exciting, commercial product. A lightly sweet or AMABILE version with up to 10 g/l of RESIDUAL SUGAR also exists, as does a sweet DOLCE or *cannellino* version with 10 to 30 g/l. This latter wine is, at least in theory, obtained from grapes affected by NOBLE ROT, but any significant presence of BOTRYTIS fungus in the vineyards would result in much sweeter wines than these. D.T.

FRAUD, WINE. See ADULTERATION AND FRAUD.

FREE-RUN is the name used by wine-makers for the juice or wine that will drain without pressing from a mass of freshly crushed grapes or from a FERMENTATION VESSEL. Depending on the type of vessel used for DRAINING, it constitutes between 60 and 70 per cent of the total juice available and is generally superior to, and much lower in TANNINS than, juice or wine whose extraction depends on PRESSING. Most modern white wine is made from grapes that pass through a CRUSHER-DESTEMMER before going into a draining tank with a perforated bottom through which the free-run juice passes to the FERMENTATION VESSEL. In some wineries, free-run juice is collected by draining through specially designed, perforated-bottom screw or drag-link transfer conveyors which move the MUST directly from the crusher-destemmer to the PRESS, bypassing draining tanks completely. Many wine-makers boast of using only free-run juice in the production of fine white wines, but PRESS WINE, the wine produced by pressing what is left, can always be useful as a BLENDING element.

In RED WINE-MAKING, the free-run wine is that which, after SETTLING, is drained or racked (see RACKING) away from the LEES. In some wineries, free-run red wine is also recovered from specially designed transfer conveyors. Whatever remains goes into the press to yield PRESS WINE, which can be even more useful for its tannin concentration when making up blends of red wines. A.D.W.

FREEZE CONCENTRATION. See CONCENTRATION.

FREISA is a light red grape variety indigenous to the PIEDMONT region of north west Italy and, more specifically, to the provinces of Asti, Alessandria, and Cuneo in scattered vineyards which reach almost to the gates of the city of Turin.

The vine was known in Piedmont in 1799 and at least two clones have been identified, the smalled-berried Freisa Piccola generally being planted on hillier sites and the larger-berried Freisa Grossa producing less lively wines on flatter vineyards. Freisa musts can be quite high in both ACIDITY and TANNINS even if relatively light coloured for the region.

The wine exists as a VARIETAL in a range of styles, but the predominant one is slightly frothy from a SECONDARY FERMENTATION in bottle which retains some unfermented RESIDUAL SUGAR which serves to balance the slight bitterness from the LEES. Freisa's decisively purple colour and aromas of raspberries and violets tend to find favour much more readily than its flavours, which, with their combination of the bitter and the sweet, seem to arouse widely divergent reactions: from Hugh JOHNSON's 'immensely appetizing' to Robert PARKER's 'totally repugnant wine'.

Two DOCS exist for Freisa, in both dry and sweet (amabile) form: the larger Freisa d'Asti and the minuscule Freisa di Chieri, 18 km/11 miles from the boundaries of Turin. These are dwarfed, however, by the 3 million bottles produced each year of the regional VINO DA TAVOLA Freisa del Piedmonte, which encompasses some of the best Freisa from the zones of BAROLO and BARBARESCO.

Modern technology, in the form of pressurized tanks, now permits producers better control of both the residual sugar level and the amount of CARBON DIOXIDE in the wine, and this type of Freisa, which does not undergo a secondary fermentation in the bottle, tends to be distinctively drier and almost imperceptibly fizzy. Some producers are experimenting with a more age-worthy, completely dry, and completely still type of Freisa such as Aldo Vajra's version aged in BOTTE, and by the mid 1990s there were even some attempts to age the wine in small oak barrels. Italy's total plantings of Freisa fell by a third to 2,000 ha/5,000 acres in 1990.

A vine variety called Freisa is quite widely grown in Argentina, although total plantings are no more than a few hundred hectares. D.T.

FREISAMER is a 20th century German vine crossing (SILVANER × Ruländer or PINOT GRIS), originally called Freiburger after its birthplace. It reached a peak of popularity in the German wine region of Baden in the early 1970s but is declining in popularity, a casualty of KERNER's success perhaps. It is still grown today in a number of north and central cantons in SWITZERLAND, and sweeter versions are a speciality of the Herrschaft in Graubünden.

FREIXENET, the largest exporter of CAVA in the world, although not as strong on the domestic Spanish market as CODORNÍU. The brand was born at the beginning of the 20th century when Pedro Ferrer Bosch and his wife Dolores Sala Vivé decided to concentrate on sparkling wines. The company was named after an estate in Mediona, PENEDÈS, which had been in Pedro Ferrer's family since the 13th century, known as La Freixeneda, meaning a plantation of ash trees. His wife's grandfather founded the former Sala company, which started exporting wines to the USA in the second half of the 19th century. The company was initially keen to establish export markets, a policy which has paid off in the latter half of this century. It now has six production centres in San Sadurni de Noya, including Segura Viudas SA, Castellblanch SA, and René Barbier SA, as well as the original Freixenet base. The combined total production of the six operations is 86 million bottles per year, and work in progress in the early 1990s was expected to raise this figure to 100 million. The best-known brands are the medium dry Carta Nevada, launched in 1951, and Cordon Negro, a brut Cava in a distinctive black bottle. Freixenet's overseas interests are: the Freixenet Sonoma Caves in the CARNEROS district of California which produce the sparkling wine Gloria Ferrer; a 50-ha/124-acre estate in Mexico where the sparkling brand is called Sala Vivé; and ownership of the Champagne house Henri Abelé. All three investments took place during the 1980s, and Freixenet has expressed an interest in establishing joint ventures for sparkling wine production in both the ex-Soviet republic of GEORGIA and CHINA. S.A.

FRENCH-AMERICAN HYBRIDS. See FRENCH HYBRIDS.

FRENCH COLOMBARD, common California name for one of the state's most planted grape varieties, the French white COLOMBARD, now much more widely planted in California than in France. Originally brought from Cognac and throughout the 1980s California's most planted wine grape variety, Colombard is no longer often seen as a varietal wine. Most of it grows in the SAN JOAQUIN VALLEY for JUG whites and CHARMAT sparklers. A small and shrinking acreage remains in the coastal counties where—especially along the Russian river from Healdsburg (Sonoma County) north to Ukiah (Mendocino County)—it makes an off-dry white of greater interest and better balance than most Chenin Blanc, if harvested while still crisply acidic and before its perfumes coarsen.

During the 1970s it became the state's most planted wine grape variety, a position it retained until 1991 when it was usurped by the market's apparently insatiable demand for something richer, more expensive, and called Chardonnay.

FRENCH HYBRIDS, group of vine HYBRIDS bred in France in the late 19th and early 20th centuries, usually by crossing or hybridizing AMERICAN VINE SPECIES with a European VINIFERA variety (see VINE BREEDING). These are also known as direct producers, hybrid direct producers, HDPs, or, in French, *hybrides producteurs directs*. One early response to the invasion of the American PHYLLOXERA louse in Europe was to plant American varieties, once it was known that most had developed phylloxera tolerance. In Europe they proved to be both hardy and resistant to a wide range of diseases, but, because of the strange, often FOXY, flavour of the wine they produced, it has been illegal to plant ISABELLA, Clinton, NOAH, Othello, Black Spanish (Jacquez), and Herbemont in France since 1934.

The aim of the early hybridizers was to combine the pest and disease resistance of the American species with the accepted wine quality of the European wine species *vinifera*. A group of French breeders such as François Baco, Castel, Georges Couderc, Ferdinand Gaillard, Ganzin, Millardet, Oberlin, Albert Seibel, Bertille Seyve, and Victor Villard, and, more recently, Joanny Burdin, Galibert, Eugene Kuhlmann, Pierre Landot, Ravat, Jean-François Seyve's sons Joannes and Bertille (who married Villard's daughter and developed the important Seyve–Villard series of hybrids), and Jean-Louis Vidal, produced thousands of new hybrid varieties with such aims in mind. They used AMERICAN HYBRIDS as parents as well as American vine species. VITIS *aestivalis, rupestris, riparia*, and *berlandieri* were common parents because of their excellent disease and pest resistance, and a reduction in the strong fruit flavour associated with *labrusca*. Some of the rootstocks used today were bred by these hybridizers, particularly Castel, Couderc, Ganzin, and Millardet. Active hybridizers in other countries included the Italians Bruni, Paulsen, Pirovani, and Prosperi.

These hybrids were widely favoured because of disease resistance and high productivity, so by 1958 about 400,000 ha/988,000 acres of French hybrids were planted in France, or about one-third of the total vineyard area. Wine quality was, however, often inferior, especially from the earlier French hybrids. With continued crossing and back crossing, the objectionable features in the taste of the wine could be reduced (see diagram for NEW VARIETIES). French planting regulations since 1955 have deliberately discouraged vine varieties associated with poor wine quality, however, both hybrids and *vinifera*, and so by 1988 there were fewer than 20,000 ha of hybrids. With the exception of BACO 22A, which may be used for ARMAGNAC, hybrids are being systematically phased out of French wine and brandy production, even though there were still sizeable plantings of COUDERC Noir, various SEYVE–VILLARD hybrids, VILLARD Noir, CHAMBOURCIN, PLANTET, and SEIBEL for red wines and Villard Blanc and SEYVAL BLANC for white wines, according to the French vineyard census of 1988. Other hybrid varieties that are authorized, if not actually encouraged, in France include Baco 1, Chancellor, Garonnet, Oberlin Noir, and Varousset for red wine and Rayon d'Or for white wine. The pedigree of many modern hybrids is much more complex than that of the early French hybrids.

The French hybrids have been planted outside France and have made significant contributions at some time or other to the wine industries of the eastern UNITED STATES (see NEW YORK in particular), CANADA, ENGLAND, and New Zealand, where French hybrids were planted in the majority of vineyards into the 1960s, and used for FORTIFIED WINES. R.E.S.

Galet, P., *Précis de viticulture* (4th edn., Montpellier, 1983).
—— and Morton, L. T., *A Practical Ampelography* (Ithaca, NY, and London, 1979).

FRENCH PARADOX, term coined in the United States in 1991 to express the infuriating fact that the French apparently eat and drink themselves silly with no apparent ill effects on their coronary health. Immediately after this thesis was aired on prime time television, and red wine consumption cited as a possible factor in reducing the risk of heart disease, sales of red wine in the United States quadrupled and GALLO had to put their leading branded GENERIC Hearty Burgundy on allocation. For more details, see HEALTH.

FRESCOBALDI, one of Florence's most prominent noble families since the 13th century, are among the largest landholders in the central Italian region of TUSCANY with interests in a wide range of agricultural acitivities. Of their 4,200 ha (10,370 acres), 725 are under vine, which makes them the largest private owners of vineyards in the region (more important than, for example, the ANTINORI). The Frescobaldi holdings can be divided into three distinct blocks: the first, to the south west of Florence, produces light and refreshing white and red wines; the second, to the east of Florence, produces classic CHIANTI Rufina from the Nipozzano estate and the distinctive red and white wines of Pomino, a high-altitude property with vineyards that rise to 700 m/2,300 ft above sea level; the third block is Castelgiocondo in MONTALCINO, with 210 ha of vineyards in all, of which 150 is Brunello di Montalcino, its acquisition in the late 1980s having made the Frescobaldi the largest potential producer of Brunello.

Although the house's fame was created by its Nipozzano and Pomino wines, these two estates have belonged to the Frescobaldi for a relatively short time, having been acquired by marriage with the Albizi family in the late 19th century. The last of the Albizi, Vittorio, born into the French branch of the family near AUXERRE, had a profound knowledge of the French viticulture of his time and rapidly decided, after returning to Tuscany in the mid 19th century, that the higher portions of the Pomino estate could not ripen SANGIOVESE vines. He accordingly planted PINOT BLANC, CHARDONNAY, PINOT NOIR, CABERNET, and MERLOT vines, a decision which he explained and defended in the numerous writings and speeches that marked his career. His ideas were too far ahead of his time, however, and had no influence on his era. The Frescobaldi were, none the less, the first Italian producers of a BARRIQUE-aged white wine, beginning in the mid 1970s with the grapes from their Benefizio vineyard at Pomino. Their single vineyard Chianti Rufina, Montesodi, was also among the first superior all-Sangiovese wines aged in small barrels. The house currently produces approximately 5.5 million bottles of wine each year. D.T.

FRESH GRAPES. See TABLE GRAPES.

FRIULI, or **Friuli-Venezia Giulia**, the north easternmost region of ITALY, borders both on Austria to the north and on SLOVENIA to the east and has long been a confluence of three distinct peoples and cultures: Italian, Germanic, and Slavic. (See map on p. 517.) Despite endorsements of local wines by the usual succession of popes, emperors, princes, and princelings, Friuli had little commercial history of distinctive wines until the late 1960s, when the introduction both of German wine-making philosophy and of cold fermentation technology (see TEMPERATURE CONTROL)—innovations usually credited to wine-maker Mario Schiopetto—produced Italy's first truly clean, fresh, fruity white wines. This created a FASHION which has lasted to this day. This style of (predominantly white) WINE-MAKING is one of the characterizing features of the region's production; the other is the large number of wines produced by each single estate, a fact which can be attributed both to the lack of a stable viticultural tradition linking specific varieties to specific locations, and to the market-driven approach to product development of what was, in effect, a very young production structure.

Friuli's geographical position on land successively disputed by Romans, Byzantines, Venetians, and Habsburgs, ensured that a large number of varieties would be available for planting. TOCAI Friulano, RIBOLLA, MALVASIA di Istria, VERDUZZO, PICOLIT, REFOSCO, SCHIOPETTINO, PIGNOLO, and the acidic red wine grape Tazzelenghe are considered indigenous (although see ROBOLA, for example). RIESLING, WELSCHRIESLING (here called Riesling Italico), TRAMINER, MÜLLER-THURGAU, and BLAUFRÄNKISCH (locally called Franconia) are imports from Austria. The French varieties PINOT BIANCO, PINOT GRIGIO, CHARDONNAY, SAUVIGNON, CABERNET, MERLOT, PINOT NERO were introduced during the 19th century Habsburg domination (and greatly expanded during the replanting of Friuli's vineyards after the ravages of PHYLLOXERA), a domination which lasted until 1918 in the case of the province of Gorizia.

The result has been the multiplicity of single VARIETAL wines in each DOC: 17 for the 2,100 ha/5,200 acres of the COLLI ORIENTALI, 17 for the 1,500 ha of COLLIO. If the proliferation of DOC wines with varietal names attached to specific zones has created some confusion amongst consumers, the geography of Friuli's DOC structure is actually fairly easy to understand. Udine marks the northern border beyond which low temperatures make viticulture an impractical proposition in most cases: to the south of Udine exist two distinct bands of territory for the growing of grapes: the two hillside DOCs of Colli Orientali and Collio with calcareous MARL soils, and the ALLUVIAL plain with plentiful quantities of sand, pebbles, and rocks deposited by the various rivers—the Tagliamento, the Natisone, the Judrio, the Isonzo—which criss-cross the plain. These flatlands are divided into five DOCs, moving from west to east: LISON-PRAMAGGIORE, LATISANA, GRAVE DEL FRIULI, AQUILEIA, and ISONZO. The HILLSIDE VINEYARDS give wines of much the greater personality, with Collio generally offering more delicacy and bouquet, Colli Orientali much body and length. The white, and red, wines of this latter zone have shown a real suitability for small BARREL MATURATION, a phenomenon much less widespread in Collio.

The region's overall production averages a bit over 1 million hl/26.4 million gal per year, modest by Italian standards, but the percentage of DOC production, approaching 45 per cent, is one of Italy's highest, surpassed only by that in the TRENTINO-ALTO ADIGE.

Although Friuli enjoyed almost uninterrupted commercial success and expansion throughout the 1970s and 1980s, the formula of crisp and refreshing technologically sound wines is not difficult to copy, and the early 1990s saw increased competition and price pressure from other areas of Italy, particularly from the Trentino-Alto Adige, where similar INTERNATIONAL VARIETIES—CHARDONNAY, SAUVIGNON, PINOT GRIGIO, PINOT BIANCO—are cultivated and now fermented in a style similar to Friuli's.

For more details of notable specific wines, see also AQUILEIA, CARSO, COLLI ORIENTALI, COLLIO, GRAVE DEL FRIULI, ISONZO, LATISANA, LISON-PRAMAGGIORE, and see specific grape varieties PICOLIT, PIGNOLO, REFOSCO, RIBOLLA, SCHIOPPETTINO, TOCAI, and VERDUZZO. D.T.

FRIZZANTE, Italian wine term for semi-sparkling wine (as opposed to SPUMANTE, which is used for fully sparkling wines). Frizzante wines generally owe their bubbles to a partial second fermentation in tank, a sort of interrupted CHARMAT process sparkling wine.

FROMENTEAU, name for several grape varieties, most importantly the medieval name for a Burgundian variety which had pale red berries and white juice, and is probably the ancestor of PINOT GRIS. It is also used as a synonym for both the ROUSSANNE of the Rhône and SAVAGNIN of the Jura.

FRONSAC, small but once famed red wine appellation in the Bordeaux region just west of the town of Libourne on the RIGHT BANK of the river DORDOGNE (see map on p. 124). The wooded low hills of Fronsac, and **Canon-Fronsac**, the even smaller and more famous appellation to the immediate south, constitute Bordeaux's prettiest countryside, and the region's altitude, unusual so close to the Gironde estuary, gave it great strategic importance. Fronsac was the site of a Roman temple, and then of a fortress built by CHARLEMAGNE, who is locally supposed to have taken a particular interest in this wine. The wine benefited further in the mid 17th century when the Duc de Richelieu, also Duc de Fronsac and a man of considerable influence, replaced the fortress with a villa at which he entertained frequently. According to Enjalbert, the first great right bank wines were produced, around 1730, in Canon-Fronsac. Even well into the 19th century, the wines of

Fronsac were much more famous than those of POMEROL on the other side of Libourne.

The low-lying land beside the river and any ALLUVIAL soils further inland from the Dordogne and its tributary the Isle are entitled only the BORDEAUX AC, while the Fronsac and Canon-Fronsac appellations are concentrated on the higher land where LIMESTONE predominates and SANDSTONE is also characteristic. Merlot and Cabernet Franc (Bouchet) are the dominant grape varieties, supplemented by Malbec and, where it will ripen, Cabernet Sauvignon, densely planted on about 4,320 ha / 1,750 acres of land entitled to the Fronsac appellation and 1,850 ha / 750 acres, mainly around the villages of St-Michel-de-Fronsac and Fronsac itself, being entitled to the supposedly superior Canon-Fronsac appellation.

Wines made in the 1960s and 1970s often suffered from less conscientious wine-making than producers in the more reputable appellations of Pomerol and St-Émilion could afford, and the result was wines which could offer concentration, but were often both austere and slightly rustic. The 1980s saw considerable refinement of techniques, and investment in wine-making equipment, notably some new barrels, so that Fronsac is now both supple and dense. It does not have the lush character of Pomerol but can offer a keenly priced alternative to more famous red bordeaux, with the juicy fruit of a St-Émilion and the ageing potential of a Médoc. The interest shown in the region by the likes of the MOUEIX family, who since the 1980s have owned Chx Canon-Moueix, La Dauphine, and Canon de Brem, as well as distributing several others, has indubitably injected confidence into the region. The largest and most picturesque property on the entire right bank is Ch de la Rivière.

Enjalbert, H., *Great Bordeaux Wines: St Émilion, Pomerol, Fronsac* (Paris, 1983; Eng. trans. 1985).

FRONTIGNAC is used as a name for grapey, sweet wines, particularly in South Africa. It derives from the Languedoc town of FRONTIGNAN, once famous for its Muscat. Frontignac is also a common Australian synonym for MUSCAT BLANC À PETITS GRAINS, the finest Muscat grape variety of all.

FRONTIGNAN is the name of the wine for long called Muscat de Frontignan, the most important of the Languedoc's four Muscats. Now a distinctly unglamorous town on the semi-industrial lagoon between Montpellier and Sète, Frontignan was famous for the quality of its MUSCAT for centuries. It was probably one of France's earliest vineyard sites, being close to the saltmarshes around Narbonne. Pliny the Younger singled out this particular 'bees' wine' for mention in his letters. ARNALDUS DE VILLANOVA, who is credited with the discovery of the process by which Muscat de Frontignan is made today (see VIN DOUX NATUREL), claimed that his daily ration of the wine, as advised by the then all-powerful Aragon monarch, made him feel years younger. It was popular in both Paris and London in the 17th and 18th centuries, doubtless with wider appeal then than the dry reds of south west France that were also shipped north. 'Frontiniac' was specifically praised by the philosopher John Locke in 1676, while both Voltaire and, even further afield, Thomas JEFFERSON were well-documented and enthusiastic purchasers. In the 18th and 19th centuries Frontignan clearly made red as well as white wines which were compared with those of that other favourite of our sweet-toothed ancestors, CONSTANTIA.

Muscat de Frontignan, despite being one of the first appellations, and certainly the first vin doux naturel appellation, to be officially recognized, fell into decline for much of the 20th century. Only the rather lighter Muscat de BEAUMES-DE-VENISE somehow escaped the malaise that affected the market for France's sweeter wines, until the 1980s, when the winemakers of Frontignan awoke as if from a deep sleep and started to produce a much higher proportion of more delicate, more refreshing, yet more characterful golden Muscats (although some dark, turgid, raisiny Frontignan can still be found). As in all Languedoc Muscats (see LUNEL, MIREVAL, and ST-JEAN-DE-MINERVOIS), only the finest Muscat variety, MUSCAT BLANC À PETITS GRAINS, should be used and the final wine must be at least 15 per cent alcohol with a sugar content of at least 125 g/l (sweeter than Beaumes-de-Venise's 110 g/l minimum). Cheaper Muscats made well outside the region but marketed vigorously to tourists do nothing for the image of this once-great appellation. Co-operatives dominate output, but Ch de la Peyrade can take much of the credit for revitalizing wine-making in Frontignan whose seaside vineyards may not be the Mediterranean's most picturesque but are at least reliably warm enough to maximize Muscat Blanc's potential.

A small proportion of Muscat de Frontignan is fortified so early it qualifies as a VIN DE LIQUEUR.

George, R., *French Country Wines* (London, 1990).

FRONTONNAIS, CÔTES DU, about 1,700 ha / 4,200 acres of vines just north of Toulouse in SOUTH WEST FRANCE distinguished by its local red grape variety the NÉGRETTE, which must constitute 50 to 70 per cent of the appellation's reds, plus some rosés. Complementary grape varieties are usually Fer, Syrah, and the Cabernets and the character of the wines can vary considerably according to the exact TERROIR and ENCÉPAGEMENT. Soils on the gravelly terraces of the Tarn are particularly poor. The CO-OPERATIVE is an important producer (of table wine too) but there is considerable experimentation on the part of some relative newcomers to the region, although a high proportion of the wine is drunk without ceremony in Toulouse. When the appellation was created in 1975, it incorporated the VDQS Villaudric as well as the VDQS Fronton, these two villages having for centuries been intense rivals. Fronton has been producing wine since before the time of CHARLEMAGNE and in the 12th century the vineyard was already associated with 'négret'. The local VIN DE PAYS, used for white wines, is Vin de Pays du Comté Tolosan.

FROST, the ice crystals formed by freezing of water vapour on objects which have cooled below 0 °C/32 °F. Such frosts are known as white frosts, or hoar frosts. Black frosts cause freezing and extensive killing of plant tissue itself, without any necessary hoar formation (see FROST DAMAGE).

Frost frequencies are, in many studies, imputed arbitrarily from weather records. Temperatures as recorded in the standard Stevenson screen used by meteorologists, at 1.25 m/4.1 ft above the ground, are always higher than at ground level. A screen temperature of 2.2 °C/36 °F is normally assumed to indicate a light ground frost, and one of 0 °C a heavy ground frost. Temperatures at vine height of −1 °C or lower after BUDBREAK in spring will usually cause serious injury to the young shoots. Even 'light' frosts can often cause damage somewhere in the vineyard, because their incidence tends to be patchy, depending on TOPOGRAPHY. Geiger covers this aspect in detail.

Two main causes, or types, of frost are distinguished: radiation and advection. Radiation frost occurs typically on still, dry, cloudless nights. Without cloud, mist, or much water vapour to absorb and trap heat radiated from the ground and plant tissues, heat escapes freely to space and rapid surface cooling results. Air in immediate contact with these surfaces then becomes cooled. The coldest air, being densest, remains or collects close to the ground and in hollows. Lowest air temperatures in the early morning on flat land are at 5 to 15 cm/2–5 in above ground, rising with height to a relatively warm 'inversion' layer, commonly some 15 to 30 m above, beyond which temperatures gradually fall again with altitude. This pool of cold, dense air close to the ground is stable unless dispersed by wind, or unless it can flow away by gravity to still lower regions (as in HILLSIDE VINEYARDS).

Advective frosts result from such flows of already chilled air from elsewhere. They can originate locally, or arrive from up to several hundred kilometres away, following valleys or other natural courses of air drainage. Periodic severe frosts on the inland slopes of the Australian alps, at Milawa in Victoria, for example, can be of the advective type.

The origins of frost point to logical methods of avoiding it. The first is to plant on hill slopes from which surface-chilled air can drain away freely. Free-standing and projecting hills are best, because they have no external sources of chilled air and what slips away must be replaced from the warmer atmosphere above (see TOPOGRAPHY). Above all it is necessary, in frost-prone regions, to avoid hollows and the floors of valleys that are the natural courses of reservoirs for advective cold air coming off plateaux or snowfields, which can be sites of intense and anomalous cooling.

A second method, on flat land subject to radiation frosts, is to use high TRELLIS SYSTEMS so that the main vine growth stands above the coldest air layer that settles close to the ground on still nights. Plant cover between the rows also needs to be slashed by the time of budbreak, so as to lower the effective cooling surface. The soil should preferably be firmed so that it most readily absorbs day heat to depth and reradiates it continuously through the night. STONES AND ROCKS in the soil surface assist in this. WIND MACHINES are sometimes employed to break up the sedentary cold air layer and mix in warm upper air. SMUDGE POTS and other burners create limited local heating which may help to promote convectional mixing of upper and lower air, together with smoke (by-laws permitting) which reduces further radiative heat loss from the soil. In vineyards with sprinkler IRRIGATION, the SPRINKLERS can be turned on when temperatures fall to danger levels. This 'aspersion' technique both warms the vines and soil directly, and (if the soil was previously dry) improves its heat conductivity so that more warmth comes up from below. McCarthy *et al.* give more detail of the various measures that can be used. Note, however, that none of them is greatly effective against advective frosts.

Spring frost damage to vines is by no means confined to cool viticultural climates. In fact it is not necessarily most characteristic of them. That is because the VINE GROWTH CYCLE is adapted to the general run of temperatures experienced, with spring budbreak delayed in cool climates until the average mean temperature reaches about 10 °C, as described under CLIMATE CLASSIFICATION. More damaging is short-term TEMPERATURE VARIABILITY, such that an early spring warm enough to induce budbreak may frequently be followed by a return to killing frosts after growth has started. Paradoxically, such events are most common in certain subtropical vineyard regions, such as TEXAS. This is because their early spring weather is often very dry and cloudless, and the temperature variability around budbreak can be extreme.

Planting on frost-prone sites is normally confined to grape varieties with naturally late budbreak, such as (where the growing season is long enough) CABERNET SAUVIGNON, CARIGNAN, MOURVÈDRE, CLAIRETTE, and TREBBIANO. RIESLING, SYLVANER, MÜLLER-THURGAU, and SAUVIGNON Blanc are classed as having mid season budbreak. Unfortunately some of the prime-quality varieties grown in COOL CLIMATES, such as PINOT NOIR and CHARDONNAY, burst early and are very vulnerable to spring frosts (see CHABLIS, for instance). The selection of individual sites with minimal frost risk is crucial for such varieties. The risk in any situation can be reduced to a small extent by late pruning, but this can only delay the effective time of budbreak by up to about a week or, at the most, 10 days.

See also FROST DAMAGE. J.G.

Geiger, R., *Das Klima der bodennahen Luftschicht* (4th edn., Brunswick, 1961), trans. by Scripta Technicha, Inc., as *Climate near the Ground* (Cambridge, Mass., 1966).

McCarthy, M. G., Dry, P. R., Hayes, P. F., and Davidson, D. M., 'Soil management and frost control', in B. G. Coombe and P. R. Dry (eds.), *Viticulture, ii: Practices* (Adelaide, 1992).

FROST DAMAGE occurs in vineyards mostly in spring but also in autumn and occasionally summer, when the air temperature drops below freezing (see also FROST). Temperatures of −0.5 °C/31 °F cause mild frost damage, although high TRAINING SYSTEMS may avoid cold temperatures which occur closer to the ground. Ice may form in the plant tissue of buds which have begun to break, young shoots, leaves, and inflorescences, which may subsequently turn brown and die. The vine can respond by growing more shoots from BASE BUDS, but these are typically less fruitful and the crop is

Stoves lit in vineyards near Aÿ in Champagne to protect vines from **frost damage**.

reduced. Frost in the autumn causes DEFOLIATION, which is no hazard if the ripe fruit is harvested and the vine's reserves of CARBOHYDRATES have been restored.

Frost damage prevention can be difficult and expensive. VINEYARD SITE SELECTION is important, as is use of late bursting varieties. Late PRUNING can also delay BUDBREAK. Maintaining the soil as a firm, moist, weed-free surface helps encourage soil warming and nocturnal back radiation which will to some extent counter cold air temperatures. WIND MACHINES, helicopters, heaters, and fog-creating machines can all be used to circulate the cold air just above ground level and to minimize frost damage. Another common form of frost control is by sprinkling, or aspersion, of water over the vines. The release of latent heat as the water freezes on the vines protects the vine tissue from injury. Sprinkler IRRIGATION systems are ideal for this.

Several important wine regions such as CHABLIS and CHAMPAGNE are particularly prone to spring frost, and in 1991 frost damage was so great in western France, particularly for the earlier budding white grape varieties, that total French wine production, usually more than 65 million hl, was less than 43 million hl/1,135 million gal.

See also WINTER FREEZE, a related but different vine injury.

R.E.S.

Winkler, A. J., *et al.*, *General Viticulture* (2nd edn., Berkeley, Calif., 1974).

FRUCTOSE, also known as levulose, is with GLUCOSE one of the two principal SUGARS of the grape and sweet wines. It is a six-carbon atom sugar, or a hexose. Common table sugar, SUCROSE, is made up of one molecule of fructose and one of glucose.

The grapevine leaf in the presence of sunlight, water, and carbon dioxide makes sucrose by a complicated series of steps called collectively PHOTOSYNTHESIS. The sucrose is transferred in the plant sap from the leaf to the grape berry. There the sucrose is split into fructose and glucose, the forms in which it is stored in the berry. The vine is unusual among fruiting plants in the extent to which it is capable of concentrating the two sugars fructose and glucose in its berries; sugars routinely represent between 18 and 25 per cent of grape juice weight, while 12 per cent is the norm in apple and pear juice.

Fructose accumulates in the grape berry along with glucose but at lower concentrations during the early stages. However, at RIPENESS, and especially when grapes are overripe, fructose levels often exceed glucose. This is important because fructose is remarkable in that it has between 1.3 and 1.8 times the sweetening power of either glucose or sucrose (which has led to its manufacture in large quantities for use in so-called diet foods).

During FERMENTATION of grape juice, both fructose and glucose are consumed. Furthermore, in the acid and enzymic environment of grape juice, any sucrose present is split into its constituent parts, fructose and glucose, and will consequently be fermented. With selected strains of wine yeasts, nearly all the fructose and glucose are converted to alcohol and carbon dioxide, leaving the wine with only traces of fermentable sugars. A.D.W. & B.G.C.

FRÜH is German for 'early'. Thus, for example, Früher Roter Malvasier is early red MALVASIA.

FRÜHBURGUNDER, BLAUER, is an early ripening strain Spätburgunder (Pinot Noir) grown to a very limited extent in Württemberg. It tastes like a paler, leaner version of the lightest red burgundy.

FRÜHROTER VELTLINER, or **Früher Roter Veltliner**, early ripening red-skinned VELTLINER, is a white wine grape variety most commonly encountered in Austria where there were still about 800 ha/1,980 acres planted in the late 1980s, mainly in the Weinviertel district of lower Austria. The wine produced is often less distinguished than that made from Austria's most common grape variety GRÜNER VELTLINER, being notably lower in acidity in many cases. Yields are also lower.

In 1990 there were still 10 ha of this variety, known as **Frühroter Malvasier** or occasionally Roter Malvasier in the Rheinhessen region of Germany. Small plots may still be encountered in older vineyards of ALTO ADIGE in Italy (where it is known as Veltliner) and SAVOIE (where it may be known as Malvoisie Rouge d'Italie).

FRUIT. To a VITICULTURIST, fruit is a synonym for GRAPE, and details of grape ripening are to be found under RIPENING. To an OENOLOGIST or wine taster, fruit is a perceptible element essential to a young wine. Young wines should taste fruity, although not necessarily of grapes, or any particular grape variety. During BOTTLE AGEING, the fruity FLAVOUR COMPOUNDS in a good wine evolve into more complex elements which are described as BOUQUET; in a less good wine the fruit simply dissipates to leave a non-fruity wine sometimes described as 'hollow'. The word **fruity** is sometimes used in wine descriptions concocted for marketing purposes as a euphemism for 'sweet'.

FRUIT FLY, vinegar fly, and pomace fly are all names applied to various species of *Drosophila*, in particular *Drosophila melanogaster*. *Drosophila* feed and reproduce in fermenting fruits of all kinds and can frequently be found in the domestic fruit bowl. The major damage they cause in grapes, with a drastic reduction in wine quality, is the spread of BUNCH ROTS. *Drosophila* multiply rapidly—with a period of only six to eight days from egg to egg in hot climates—which explains why this fly has been used so much for the study of genetics. They are also a common problem in wineries during vintage, when insects can contaminate wine by spreading harmful BACTERIA. Control is difficult, and includes destruction of breeding places, such as piles of rejected fruit and POMACE.

Mediterranean fruit fly, *Caratitis capitata*, can be a grape pest in some areas such as parts of Australia and South Africa. Infestations of grapes are often due to a buildup in other soft fruits such as figs, apricots, peaches, nectarines, or citrus. Where Mediterranean fruit fly is a potential problem, bait should be laid six weeks before picking. M.J.E.

Buchanan, G. A., and Amos, T. G., 'Grape pests', in B. G. Coombe and P. R. Dry (eds.), *Viticulture, ii: Practices* (Adelaide, 1992).

FRUITFULNESS, viticultural term describing the number of bunches of grapes on each shoot. It can also be used to describe the potential productivity of buds. A shoot of low fruitfulness will have zero or one bunch only, while a **fruitful** one may have two or three or, very rarely, four. Some varieties are known to be very fruitful, an example being the so-called FRENCH HYBRIDS, no doubt due to their American parentage. At the other end of the fruitfulness spectrum is SULTANA, which has notoriously low fertility of buds at the base of canes. Many of the commercially important wine grape varieties fall between these two extremes. Where fruitfulness is low, the vine-grower must prune to CANES as opposed to SPURS, as shoots which arise from short spurs will typically be of lower fruitfulness, arising as they do from BASE BUDS.

Interestingly, potential fruitfulness is determined at about the time the vines flower, before the bunches are evident on the shoots, as the buds are developing on the growing shoot. This process is known as INITIATION and is encouraged by warm, sunny weather and an open CANOPY that allows the sunlight to penetrate to the developing buds and adjacent leaves. By late summer it is usually possible to estimate the potential number of bunches which will be produced the following year by dissection and microscopic examination of the buds. The vine-grower anxiously assesses fruitfulness just as soon as the small bunches are evident on the developing shoots in spring. Normally, the higher the bunch number the higher is the potential yield of that season, although of course there are many other critical stages, especially FRUIT SET, before the harvest is brought in. R.E.S.

Winkler, A. J., *et al.*, *General Viticulture* (2nd edn., Berkeley, Calif., 1974).

FRUIT SET, an important stage of the vine's development which marks the transition from flower to grape berry. Only 'set' or fertilized flowers grow into the berries from which wine is made; the others fail to grow and eventually fall off. Fruit set occurs immediately after FLOWERING, and is the result of successful pollination achieving fertilization and the development of seeds. Not all flowers set, or form berries, and normally only about 30 per cent of flowers become berries, although the range can be from almost zero to 60 per cent. Those flowers that do not set fall from the bunch in a process called 'shatter' in English.

The grape SEED contains an embryo, formed by the union of the sperm cells from the POLLEN and the egg cell of the OVARY. Most wine grape varieties contain some, up to four, seeds. The more seeds there are, the larger is the berry. Fruit set is affected by the environment. At one extreme common in interior desert regions, both high temperatures and WATER STRESS can reduce fruit set. On the other hand, cold and rainy weather at flowering in the classical, cooler wine regions commonly reduces fruit set, and such conditions can cause widespread yield losses.

There are various forms of abnormal fruit set. MILLERANDAGE is when a high proportion of berries have no seeds and so remain small while normal-sized grapes grow on the same bunch. COULURE on the other hand leaves few berries per bunch, and much of the bunch stem is empty. This can be due to the variety, vine VIGOUR, climatic conditions, or disease. In any case, poor fruit set can have significant effects on YIELDS, and vine-growers are always relieved when the flowering period coincides with good weather and the developing bunches have set many berries.

See also SETTING. R.E.S.

Huglin, P., *Biologie et écologie de la vigne* (Paris, 1986).
Winkler, A. J., *et al.*, *General Viticulture* (2nd edn., Berkeley, Calif., 1974).

FRUIT WINES, made by the FERMENTATION of fruits other than grapes, include cider and perry, but not beer or sake, since they derive their fermentable sugars from hydrolized starch.

A wine-like beverage can be made from almost any fruit, berry, or other plant material containing sugar. Most of these sources contain so little fermentable sugar, however, that it is usually necessary to add sugar from another source (a form of ENRICHMENT) to obtain sufficient ALCOHOL for stability (see STABILIZATION). Table sugar, or SUCROSE, is usually used, and most fruits other than grapes have excessive concentrations of ACIDS that split the sucrose into fermentable GLUCOSE and FRUCTOSE. Yeasts also contain a natural ENZYME which will convert sucrose to its component glucose and fructose.

In most cases acid levels are so high that it is necessary to dilute the crushed fruit to reduce any resulting wine's tartness. In most fruits other than grapes, much of the acid mixture is CITRIC ACID (which predominates in the citrus fruits), although in apples and a few others it is MALIC ACID. (Grapes are distinguished by their high levels of TARTARIC ACID which is more resistant to attack by BACTERIA.)

Lack of YEAST nutrients is a further problem in persuading fruits other than grapes to ferment. Commercial preparations made from autolysed yeast together with sufficient nitrogen, phosphorus, and potassium to make up the fruit's natural deficiency are commonly available to those who practise HOME WINE-MAKING on various fruits.

Very few fruit wines improve with BOTTLE AGE in the way of which fine grape wine is capable. Characteristic fruit flavours fade very rapidly and most are best consumed well within a year of bottling. A.D.W.

FUDER, German for large wooden BARREL, typically one with a capacity of 1,000 l/264 gal used in the MOSEL-SAAR-RUWER region. (The STÜCK is more commonly used in Rhein regions.) A **Halbfuder**, longer than a Halbstück, contains 500 l and was traditionally used for transporting wine from the Mosel.

FULL. A wine is described as full, or **full bodied**, if it is high, but not excessively high, in ALCOHOL and VISCOSITY. See BODY for more details.

FUMÉ BLANC is the curious descendant of the Loire synonym BLANC FUMÉ for the white grape variety Sauvignon Blanc. In the early 1970s California's famous ideas man Robert MONDAVI had one of his most famous ideas, that of renaming his unfashionable Sauvignon Blanc, Fumé Blanc, thereby imbuing it with some of the glamour of imported French Pouilly-Fumé. He also gave it some oak ageing and a dark green bordeaux-shaped BOTTLE, both entirely alien to Pouilly-Fumé, but this less-than-authentic formula proved a runaway success and Fumé Blanc became the highly successful name of a wine type in America, New Zealand, and elsewhere, even if there is little agreement about what exactly that wine type is. Most, but not all, producers who release both a Sauvignon Blanc and a Fumé Blanc tend to give the Fumé Blanc some oak ageing and, possibly, some added Semillon so that, ironically, the Sauvignon Blanc is more Loire-like and the Fumé Blanc in fact more Bordelais.

FUMIGATION, the viticultural practice of fumigating vineyard soils with the aim of killing soil-borne VINE PESTS or VINE DISEASES. It is usually carried out before planting. The earliest example of viticultural fumigation was the use of carbon bisulphide in France to combat PHYLLOXERA in the 1880s. Approximately 68,000 ha/167,960 acres were treated, requiring the painstaking insertion of about 30,000 holes per ha (12,000 per acre). Phylloxera is now controlled by GRAFTING, and today fumigation is used primarily to control the NEMATODE vector *Xiphenema index* of the virus disease FANLEAF DEGENERATION, but also for ARMILLARIA ROOT ROT, CROWN GALL, and occasionally squirrels and gophers.

Fumigation is difficult since it requires deep injection and a volatile chemical or gas which will permeate every pore to kill effectively. The exercise is most effective if the soil is porous and is not too wet. Newly fumigated vineyards in environmentally conscious areas such as California may be covered with a large plastic sheet to prevent the fumigant being lost to the atmosphere. Some fumigants were banned in the early 1990s since they were found to contaminate groundwater. R.E.S.

FUNGAL DISEASES, very large group of vine diseases which are caused by small, mostly microscopic, and filament-shaped organisms. Since fungi lack chlorophyll they need to live on other organisms to obtain nourishment. Fungal diseases have been of major significance in affecting grape production over centuries, with important consequences for both quantity and quality. Today they receive little public attention since they can successfully be controlled by a wide range of agricultural chemicals. In fact the famous fungicide

BORDEAUX MIXTURE was used commercially to control DOWNY MILDEW in 1885 and for 50 years was the most important control of fungal and bacterial diseases. Fungal disease epidemics are commonly related to weather conditions; examples are downy mildew and BOTRYTIS BUNCH ROT, both of which are favoured by warm, wet or humid weather, while POWDERY MILDEW is favoured by overcast weather.

Many of the economically important fungal diseases originated in America and therefore common varieties of the European *Vitis* VINIFERA species have no resistance. Thus, when powdery mildew was introduced in 1847, and then downy mildew in 1878, French *vinifera* vineyards were devastated. Fungal diseases can attack shoots and leaves but also developing bunches and ripe fruit. Some fungi such as Armillaria and Verticillium attack roots.

Botrytis is the fungus with which wine consumers are probably most familiar. In its benevolent form (see NOBLE ROT), it contributes to a high proportion of the most famous SWEET WINES. The more common malevolent form (see GREY ROT) causes substantial yield and quality losses, on the other hand.

Common fungal diseases are ANTHRACNOSE, ARMILLARIA ROOT ROT, BLACK ROT, BOTRYTIS BUNCH ROT, BUNCH ROTS, COLLAR ROT, DEAD ARM, DOWNY MILDEW, ESCA, EUTYPA DIEBACK, POWDERY MILDEW, TEXAS ROOT ROT, VERTICILLIUM WILT, WHITE ROT.

Other groups of vine diseases include BACTERIAL DISEASES, MYCOPLASMA DISEASES, and VIRUS DISEASES. R.E.S.

Emmett, R. W., Harris, A. R., Taylor, R. H., and McGechan, J. K., 'Grape diseases and vineyard protection', in B. G. Coombe and P. R. Dry (eds.), *Viticulture, ii: Practices* (Adelaide, 1992).

Pearson, R. C., and Goheen, A. C., *Compendium of Grape Diseases* (St Paul, Minn., 1988).

FUNGI, a group of small and often microscopic multicellular or filamentous organisms which derive their energy living as saprophytes on dead plant or animal tissue, or as pathogens on living tissue. Fungi include YEASTS important in fermentation and many organisms causing vine FUNGAL DISEASES.

FUNGICIDE, type of pesticide that is effective against FUNGAL DISEASES in vineyards. The first of the modern fungicides used for any crop was the BORDEAUX MIXTURE used on grapevines against DOWNY MILDEW in 1885. Fungicides are applied by SPRAYING at times which are deemed effective to control the fungal disease. Fungicides are generally classified as protectants, eradicants, or systemics. Protectant fungicides are applied before the fungus infects the vines and they prevent infection by inhibiting fungal development on the plant surface. For example, copper atoms (from copper oxychloride) are toxic to the zoospores of grapevine downy mildew, thus preventing infection. Most protectant fungicides are non-specific, and are effective against a number of fungal diseases. Examples used in viticulture include copper compounds (such as copper oxychloride, Bordeaux mixture), dithiocarbamates (such as mancozeb), and SULPHUR preparations.

Eradicant fungicides are effective when applied after the infection has occurred. They can either inhibit or kill fungi present on or in the vine, thus preventing these fungi from further disease development. A significant characteristic of eradicants is their ability to penetrate plant tissues, most being systemic (see later). Some eradicant fungicides can be applied one week or more after infection and still be very effective.

Systemic fungicides have the ability to infiltrate and move within plants. Movement may be relatively localized, such as from one side of a leaf to the other, or extensive, via the vine's vascular system. In the latter case the movement may be mono-directional, only towards shoot tips, for example. Systemic fungicides used in viticulture include the benzimidazoles (benomyl, for example), acylanilides (metalaxyl), dicarboximides (procymidone), and sterol inhibitors (fenarimol).

Mixtures of active ingredients may be used in formulations for different purposes, and may take advantage of synergistic effects: copper oxychloride and zineb mixtures, for example, or to create mixtures of protectant and eradicant fungicides, or copper oxychloride and metalaxyl. Some fungicides may be used against more than one fungal pathogen: mancozeb is effective against both downy mildew and ANTHRACNOSE, for instance, whereas others have a narrow range of action.

It is important to keep levels of fungicide RESIDUES below limits specified for toxicological reasons. For wine grapes, there is an additional consideration: residues of some fungicides will inhibit yeast activity, thus affecting fermentation and resultant wine quality. The use of fungicides such as chlorothalonil, therefore, must cease well before harvest.

As with other pesticides, the potential for development of resistance to fungicides varies according to the type of fungicide. Fungicides can be grouped according to their mode of action as either multi-site or specific-site inhibitors. Multi-site inhibitors are potentially toxic to all fungal cells and the chance of developing resistant strains by mutation is therefore low. This group includes the protectant fungicides, which have been widely used in viticulture for decades without any significant decrease in efficacy. Specific-site inhibitors have more specific toxicity and, because they only inhibit one or a few steps in fungal metabolism, the chance of resistant strains arising is much greater. Most of the newer, systemic fungicides fall into this group. Strategies that delay or prevent the development of resistant strains include restrained use, the use of mixtures of multi- and specific-site inhibitor fungicides, and alternation of multi- and specific-site inhibitors during the season.

See also AGROCHEMICALS. P.R.D.

Emmett, R. W., Harris, A. R., Taylor, R. H., and McGechan, J. K., 'Grape diseases and vineyard protection', in B. G. Coombe and P. R. Dry (eds.), *Viticulture, ii: Practices* (Adelaide, 1992).

FUNNELS used for pouring wine from one container into another with a narrow neck should be clean and made from

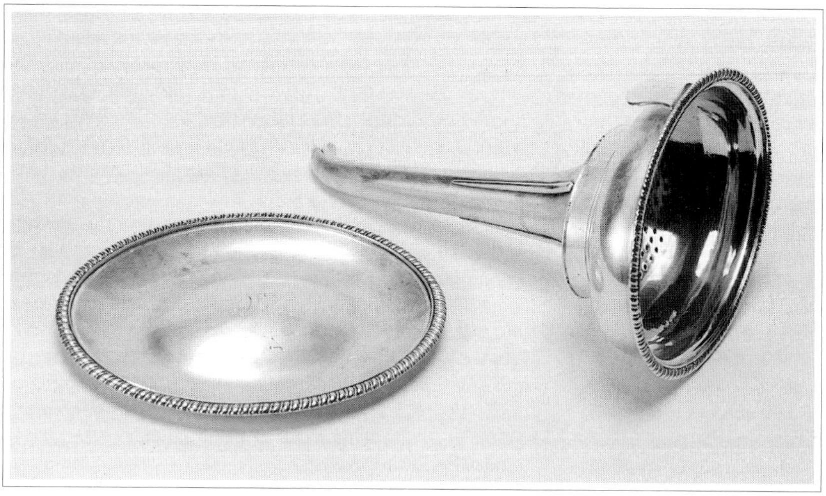

This unusual oval **funnel** and stand were made about 1810 in Edinburgh.

a material that will not taint the wine. Collectors of wine ANTIQUES seek out early examples of funnels made expressly for wine.

With the invention of binning cylindrical BOTTLES (*c*.1730) and the burgeoning use of DECANTERS after *c*.1750, it is not surprising that a specially designed funnel was invented to ease the passage of the wine from one to the other. Such a funnel has a cranked spout that deflects the wine down the wall of the decanter. Wine funnels have strainers perforated in geometrical patterns and come apart for ease of cleaning. Those made before about 1800 separate at the union of the bowl and spout, while after that date the strainer lifts out of the bowl. Wine funnels had a perforated interior ring on to which muslin could be sewn for fine filtration, but in many cases this ring has been lost.

The earliest wine funnels were made in the 1760s. Earlier funnels do exist but their straight spouts suggest they were for general use and not made exclusively for wine. Most appear to date from *c*.1780–1825 and few were made after *c*.1840. As with wine tasters (see TASTEVINS), glass examples exist, as do porcelain ones, but neither are common.

R.N.H.B.

Butler, R., and Walkling, G., *The Book of Wine Antiques* (Woodbridge, 1986).

Clayton, M., *Collectors Dictionary of the Silver and Gold of Great Britain and North America* (rev. edn., Woodbridge, 1985).

Hernmarck, C., *The Art of the European Silversmith 1430–1830* (London, 1977).

Johnson, H., Janson, D. J., and McFadden, D. R., *Wine Celebration and Ceremony* (New York, 1985).

FURMINT, fine, fiery white grape variety grown most widely in HUNGARY, but is also grown, as Sipon, in SLOVENIA. It is probably the same as the Pošip of CROATIA and some have argued it is identical to the Grasă of ROMANIA. There are even suggestions that the ROUSSETTE of Savoie is Furmint.

Furmint is the principal ingredient in TOKAY, one of the world's most famous dessert wines, and the variety is therefore grown not only in Hungary but also just over the border with SLOVAKIA. The grapes are particularly sensitive to NOBLE ROT, yet the wine is characterized by very high acidity, which endows the wine with long ageing potential, high sugar levels, and rich, fiery flavours. In Tokay it is usually blended with up to half as much of the more aromatic grape variety HÁRSLEVELŰ, and some Muscat (Blanc à Petits Grains) is also sometimes included in the blend.

Furmint can easily produce wines with an ALCOHOLIC STRENGTH as high as 14 per cent, and sturdy, characterful dry Furmint can be a delicious wine, even when drunk very young. Furmint is planted quite widely in Hungary but is most common in the Tokaj-Hegyalja region. The vine buds early but ripening slows towards the end of the season and the botrytized (*aszú*) grapes may not be picked until well into November in some years.

The vine is so well established in Hungary that there is little concrete evidence for its geographical origins. It may have been brought by the wine-making immigrants encouraged by King Bela IV in the 13th century (see HUNGARY, history). Some posit a relationship between its name and FROMENTEAU, possibly an ancestor of PINOT GRIS, but there is little obvious relationship between modern Pinot Gris and Furmint—whereas Pinot Gris is identical to the quite distinct Hungarian grape variety Szűrkebarát.

Furmint is known, at least historically, in AUSTRIA, particularly just over the border from Hungary's Sopron in Burgenland, where it was habitually used for AUSBRUCH wines until more commercially reliable varieties such as WELSCHRIESLING were introduced in the late 19th and early 20th centuries.

The variety was also grown in CRIMEA when Tokay found such favour at the imperial court that the tsars wished to make their own version, and it is still grown to a limited extent in South Africa where it was also imported in tandem with the other Tokay grape Hárslevelű.

FUSEL OILS, a general collective term for the complex, unpleasant-smelling, and varied mixtures of natural organic chemicals that are separable from one of the plates below the product withdrawal plate as wine is distilled into BRANDY in a CONTINUOUS STILL. The point of continuous distillation of brandy is to remove these fusel oils. Wine is fed in a third of the way up the column. HEADS are taken from the top plate, brandy from a few plates below, and the tails, slop, or stillage comes from the very bottom. Fusel oils are removed from a plate below the production plate, but above the wine feed plate.

Fusel oils, of much more significance to distillers than to wine-makers, are predominantly higher ALCOHOLS but they also contain smaller amounts of ESTERS and traces of other substances. The mixture that remains in a POT STILL after the DISTILLATION of brandy from wine is also sometimes said to contain fusel oils, although the significant differences between the two methods of distillation result in differences between these two sorts of fusel oils. Fusel oils belong to that hangover-inducing group called CONGENERS. Some distillers, notably in California, deliberately try to minimize the fusel oils and make a light style of brandy by using carefully cleaned wine with no SKIN CONTACT. Others cherish the fusel oils because in time, during brandy maturation in cask, they change into the desirable compounds known as esters. A brandy with too high a proportion of fusel oils, however, will taste disagreeably tarry and rasping.

The word fusel probably comes from Old German for bad brandy and, occasionally, bad tobacco, derived from the verb *fuseln*, to bungle. That the general smell of fusel oils is unattractive is indisputable. The main component, isoamyl alcohol, can be oppressively cough-provoking.

Analysis of a fusel oil mixture typical of those left after distilling brandy from wines of the San Joaquin Valley in CALIFORNIA showed that isoamyl alcohol constituted 54 per cent by weight, while other constituents from the alcohols group included 18.3 per cent isobutyl alcohol, 9.6 per cent active-amyl alcohol, 4.9 per cent secondary butyl alcohol, 4.1 per cent propyl alcohol, 1.5 per cent hexanol, together with smaller amounts off many VOLATILE ACIDS, ACETALS, and esters. It should be emphasized, however, that individual fusel oils differ greatly, influenced by the characteristics of the grapes, how they were fermented, how the ferment was distilled, and how the still was operated.

Fusel oils are of only minor importance to the wine drinker since they represent such a small proportion of wine, except in the case of some red wines made from Cabernet Sauvignon and Zinfandel grapes in which a hint of isoamyl alcohol can sometimes be detected. The amyl alcohols can also frequently be detected in pot still brandies, the malt whiskies of Scotland, and in some drinks to which pot still brandy is added.

The fusel oil alcohols are predominantly by-products of the nitrogen metabolism of the yeast cells living in grape juice as it becomes wine. The yeast obtain the nitrogen they need for their various living processes from the grape juice's AMINO ACIDS. Humans cannot synthesize many of the amino acids within themselves but the yeast cells can.

Fusel oils have enjoyed an evil reputation for many years. Not only do they smell bad but the individual alcohols became increasingly intoxicating with increasing molecular weight. There can be little doubt that high fusel oil concentrations are likely to correlate with headaches on the morning after consumption. N.F. & A.D.W.

FUTURES in wine, wine bought before it is bottled. See EN PRIMEUR.

G

GAGLIOPPO, predominant red grape variety in CALABRIA in the far south of Italy. Possibly of Greek origin, it thrives in dry conditions and reaches high sugar levels which result in robust, if rarely subtle, wines. It is also grown in Abruzzi, Marches, and Umbria and Italy's total plantings of the variety were about 7,000 ha/17,300 acres in 1990.

GAILLAC, wine district in SOUTH WEST FRANCE of considerable historic importance. As outlined in the history of FRANCE, archaeological evidence suggests that Gaillac may have been one of the first viticultural centres of ancient GAUL, with wine production well established in the early years of the 1st century AD, probably after the Romans established the first vineyards of the LANGUEDOC around Narbonne, but possibly before then if those who contend that vine-growing pre-dated Roman conquest are correct.

Gaillac certainly seems to have been producing wine long before BORDEAUX, the port through which its wines would have been shipped after being transported down the RIVERS Tarn and GARONNE. Barbarian invasions then curbed wine production until it was revived by MONKS at the Abbey of St-Michel-de-Gaillac in the 10th century and Gaillac wines were highly prized both locally and in northern Europe, especially ENGLAND, in the Middle Ages. Gaillac's export trade was thwarted, however, by the merchants of Bordeaux, who imposed stiff tariffs and conditions on the more robust wines of Gaillac and other 'high country' or HAUT PAYS wines made in the warmer, more dependable climate up river.

The wines may be called Gaillac after the small town at the centre of the production zone, but the most important settlement in the region by far is Albi just up river, with its extraordinary brick cathedral, a monument to the strength of religious belief. The Albigensian Crusade and the religious wars of the 12th and 13th centuries inevitably disrupted trade, although there is evidence that the English were once more buying Gaillac with enthusiasm in the 16th century, and the region, along with 'Limouth' (LIMOUX), was already associated with SPARKLING WINE production in 1680 (about the same time as CHAMPAGNE).

The powerful, deeply coloured red wines of Gaillac continued to be prized by blenders in the early 19th century when ADULTERATION AND FRAUD were rife, but the arrival of the PHYLLOXERA louse towards the end of the century drove many local farmers to exploit crops other than the vine.

Today Gaillac's rolling fields are put to many uses, and in the whole region only about 100,000 hl/2.6 million gal of wine is produced from about 1,600 ha/3,900 acres of vines in an average year, a fraction of mid 19th century output. But the district is distinguished by its rich heritage of local VINE VARIETIES, and by its unusual diversity of wine styles.

The most distinctive local white grape variety is MAUZAC (which is also characteristic of Limoux), whose wines have a strong apple peel aroma and sometimes a certain astringency. LEN DE L'EL is another strictly local variety whose wine can lack acidity; appellation regulations insist on at least 15 per cent of Len de l'El and/or SAUVIGNON Blanc (although iconoclasts such as Robert Plageoles happily ignore these and produce a range of VARIETAL Gaillacs in an extraordinary range of styles). The other two white Bordeaux varieties SÉMILLON and MUSCADELLE are also grown but the indigenous ONDENC is also being revived, notably for sweet wines.

Red wine is Gaillac's most important product today, however, and, among red wine varieties, DURAS is the intriguing local speciality (it has no connection with the Côtes de Duras appellation to the north west). Its combination of colour, fruit, and BODY suggests that it may well have been largely responsible for Gaillac red wines' past reputation. FER, called locally Braucol, may also have added structure in the form of TANNINS, and the mandatory proportion of these two varieties in red Gaillac is being increased. A relatively recent arrival GAMAY, imported to provide Gaillac vignerons with income from PRIMEUR wines (in the style of BEAUJOLAIS), is, judiciously, being written out of the regulations and Gaillac's history. SYRAH, however, is encouraged to add its concentration to that of the local varieties, while the Cabernets and Merlot of Bordeaux are tolerated minor ingredients. The APPELLATION CONTRÔLÉE regulations of Gaillac hint at thousands of man-hours of local political manœuvre.

Red Gaillac, made from a high proportion of the local varieties and a low proportion of Gamay, can be an exciting wine, with the structure of a good bordeaux but more spicy flavours. Some well-made Sauvignon is produced among dry whites, and the quality of still Mauzac has improved greatly. About a third of all white grapes, and much of the Mauzac, is vinified as a slightly sparkling wine sold as Gaillac Perlé, most notably by one of the two important CO-OPERATIVES in the region. More interesting and artisanal, however, are the medium sweet, lightly sparkling wines made by the *méthode gaillacoise*, a close relation of the *méthode ancestrale* (see SPARKLING WINE-MAKING) sold by some with the sediment still in bottle.

Plageoles specializes in sweet wines matured in small barrels (like the best SAUTERNES), made from Mauzac, Muscadelle and recently resurrected Ondenc. Others make slightly less ambitious sweet white Gaillac, either DOUX or MOELLEUX. Plageoles also makes a VIN JAUNE style of wine sold as Vin de Voile, the *voile* or veil being that of the FILM-FORMING YEAST responsible.

GAJA, the most renowned producer of high-quality, estate bottled wines in PIEDMONT, traces its origins to 1856 when the Gaja family opened a tavern in its home town of BARBARESCO and began serving its own wines to accompany the food. By the end of the 19th century the wines were already being bottled and supplied to the Italian army in Abyssinia, a highly unusual development in their home district of the Langhe, where a tradition of bottled wine assumed real significance only from the 1960s. The firm became an important force after the Second World War under the direction of Giovanni Gaja, who began an important series of vineyard purchases in what is now the Barbaresco DOC zone, a strategy that has given the house an important dimension both in terms of total vineyard area (currently 81 ha/200 acres, dwarfing all other Barbaresco houses) and an excellent selection of superior vineyard positions in the zone. Another significant influence on the firm's activities was that of Clotilda Rey, the mother of Giovanni Gaja, educated at Chambéry in French SAVOIE and a firm believer both in high quality to attract a selected clientele and in high prices to ensure that the house's efforts and philosophy were concretely reflected in a form that would further increase the prestige of the wines.

Angelo **Gaja**.

Gaja wines have gained world-wide recognition under Giovanni's son Angelo Gaja, who took over the direction of activities in the late 1960s; trained at the oenological school of Alba and at MONTPELLIER, an indefatigable traveller in the world's major viticultural areas, and a tireless and charismatic champion of his native region and its wines, he has given a new international perspective and a new elegance to the traditionally robust and powerful Piedmontese red wines, pioneering small BARREL MATURATION of both Barbaresco and BARBERA, and introducing international grape varieties—CABERNET SAUVIGNON, CHARDONNAY, and SAUVIGNON Blanc—to the vineyards of Piedmont (his Cabernet Sauvignon is called Darmagi, Piedmontese for 'what a shame', supposedly his father's reaction). He also acquired land in nearby BAROLO, with the 1988 Barolo Sperss marking a return to the zone from which the Gaja family made a wine from purchased grapes until 1961. D.T.

Steinberg, E., *The Vines of San Lorenzo* (New York, 1992).

GALEN, Greek physician whose work in the 2nd century AD was influential in Greece, Rome, and beyond. He identified the antiseptic properties of wine. See MEDICINE.

GALESTRO, the Italian name for the MARL-like soil that characterizes many of the best vineyard sites in CHIANTI CLASSICO, and also the name with which a Tuscan white wine based on TREBBIANO grapes was baptized when it was born at the end of the 1970s. The wine must contain from 60 to 85 per cent Trebbiano Toscano from central Tuscany, together with a number of other varieties, both local and international: MALVASIA, VERNACCIA di San Gimignano, CHARDONNAY, PINOT BLANC, and RIESLING. Like any Italian VINO DA TAVOLA with a specific geographical indication, Galestro can contain up to 15 per cent of wine from outside its specific production zone and the Chardonnay, Pinot Blanc, and Riesling tend to be purchased from more northerly zones of Italy, in particular from the TRENTINO-ALTO ADIGE. Galestro is regulated and heavily promoted by a consortium founded in the late 1970s by the dominant NÉGOCIANT houses of Tuscany—ANTINORI, FRESCOBALDI, RICASOLI, Ruffino—which had admitted 14 members by 1993. The wine was produced to specifications aimed at creating a light and fresh thirst-quencher (with rules forbidding an ALCOHOLIC STRENGTH of more than 10.5 per cent and an ACIDITY of less than 6 g/l) and was an immediate commercial success in Italy, followed by Germany, with total sales rising from 350,000 bottles in 1980 to over 8 million in 1991. More importantly, by providing an important commercial outlet for the large quantities of Trebbiano and Malvasia grapes grown in Tuscany, it enormously facilitated the task of modifying the DOC regulations for Chianti Classico: when this latter DOC was promoted to DOCG in 1984 the minimum percentage of white grapes in the Chianti Classico blend was lowered from 10 to two per cent without a hint of opposition. D.T.

GALET, PIERRE (1921–), father of modern AMPELOGRAPHY based in MONTPELLIER. Galet was born in Monaco and his upbringing in the mediterranean climate of southern France undoubtedly helped to prepare him for a working life spent outside surrounded by vines. Galet's working life has been devoted to the science of describing and identifying VINE VARIETIES on the basis of minute botanical observation. After a conventional academic training he succeeded Branas in the Chair of Viticulture at Montpellier and presided over what came to be regarded as a national, if not international, centre of viticultural ACADEME. He taught thousands, including Paul Truel, whose own work based at Montpellier has been of world-wide significance, and Jean-Michel Boursiquot, who has succeeded him. Other accolytes include Lucie T. Morton, who translated some of his work into English for successful publication in the United States, Umberto Camargo in Brazil, Erika Dettweiller in Germany, and Anna Schneider in Italy.

His most tangible achievements, however, have been as author (and publisher, he has consistently published and sold his own books). His four-volume *Cépages et vignobles de France* came out between 1956 and 1964, and battered copies are still circulated although he has since updated it to include handsome separate volumes with colour illustrations on American and French varieties, published in 1988 and 1991 respectively. His two-volume work on *Maladies et parasites de la vigne* came out in 1977 and 1982, while the fifth edition of his invaluable handbook *Précis de viticulture* appeared in 1988. In the early 1990s he was working on an international dictionary of vine variety names and their synonyms.

Much of his work involved not teaching but vine identification for the practical purpose of, for example, settling a legal dispute, or advising a wine region on which varieties were actually growing in some of its old vineyards. This sort of work took him all over the Americas, North Africa, Cyprus, Afghanistan, Nepal, Thailand, and South Korea (Truel inspected the vineyards of Australia and Portugal). Able to identify scores, perhaps hundreds of vine varieties at a single glance, he was made an Officier de l'Ordre du Mérite Agricole and won many important awards, including a prize in 1983 from the OIV for the entirety of his published work. Few individuals embody such concentrated expertise. The reprint pamphlet cited below gives some of the flavour of this expert who has little patience with those not prepared to get their shoes dirty.

Galet, P., 'La Culture de la vigne aux États-Unis et au Canada', *France viticole* (Sept.–Oct. 1980 and Jan.–Feb. 1981).

GALICIA, Spain's wet, Atlantic north west and one of the country's 17 autonomous regions encompassing the DO wine regions of RIAS BAIXAS, RIBEIRO, and VALDEORRAS. Separated by mountains from CASTILE-LEÓN, Galicia has developed in isolation from the rest of Spain, the region being geographically and culturally closer to northern Portugal than to Madrid (see map on p. 907). The locals, many of whom are of Celtic descent, speak Gallego, a hybrid of Castilian Spanish and Portuguese. The wines also share an affinity with the light, acidic VINHO VERDE produced south of the Miño (Minho in Portuguese), the river that divides this part of Spain from Portugal.

Wines were exported from Galicia as early as the 14th century, but northern European merchants quickly moved on in search of fuller bodied wines from the DOURO in northern Portugal. The progressive fragmentation of agricultural holdings left the region with a subsistence economy and in the 19th century the countryside suffered from depopulation as people moved away to find work. Many of the magnificent TERRACES in the PORT vineyards of the Douro were constructed by itinerant labour from Galicia. Since Spain joined the European Union in 1986, however, Galicia has benefited from a massive injection of funds which has transformed its wine industry and by the early 1990s Galician ALBARIÑO had become extremely fashionable in Spain.

Galicia is one of the wettest parts of Iberia. On the coast, RAINFALL averaging more than 1,300 mm/50 in a year is compensated by an annual average of over 2,000 hours of sunshine. Vines flourish in these humid conditions and YIELDS of up to 100 hl/ha (5.7 tons/acre) are unequalled anywhere else in Spain. Most of the vineyards are to be found towards the south in the provinces of Orense and Pontevedra. Valdeorras, the DO furthest from the coast, remains the most backward in terms of wine production. Ribeiro, a DO spanning the Miño valley downstream from Orense, has made more progress, but it is in Rias Baixas on the coast where the transformation has been most startling. Albariño, a long-neglected white grape variety native to Galicia and north west Portugal, has gained cult status and some Galician wines are now able to command a high price all over Spain and in some foreign markets. R.J.M.

GALLO winery of Modesto, CALIFORNIA, the largest single wine-making establishment in the world, was developed by the brothers Ernest (1909–) and Julio (1910–93) from the vineyards of their father, who shipped grapes for HOME WINEMAKING during PROHIBITION. On the eve of Repeal in 1933 the brothers obtained a licence to manufacture and store wine, and on the demise of Prohibition at the end of that year began the rapid expansion of their business. The received story is that they had only a couple of pamphlets published before Prohibition to guide their first wine-making efforts, but their father and uncle had been associated with the wine business before Prohibition, and wine-making in some form went on in the CENTRAL VALLEY, where the Gallos lived and grew grapes, throughout Prohibition. They perhaps knew more than a good story later would allow for.

Julio's special charge was production; Ernest's was sales. By 1935, just two years after Repeal, the winery was producing 350,000 gal/13,300 hl of wine, and in 1936 the brothers built a new facility with a capacity of 1.5 million gal. The new winery's design showed their concern for the highest level of technical efficiency, as its capacity showed their determination in pursuing new and larger markets. In common with most large California wineries, the Gallos at first sold largely in bulk to bottlers; in 1937 they began to promote their own label and to devise their own marketing methods. The development of the firm thereafter was as a completely self-contained enterprise: it either owned its own vineyards or signed growers to long-term contracts; it built its own glass factory, maintained its own sales force, acquired control over distributorships, operated its own research department, its own print shop, and its own transport company.

By 1950 Gallo had the largest wine-production capacity in the United States. By 1967 it held first position in sales, and has continued to do so. Storage capacity at its four wine producing facilities in 1992 was 330 million gal/12.5 million hl, many times more than that of Europe's largest wineries. In the process of its growth, Gallo has encouraged the planting of superior vine varieties, the use of modern crop management methods, and the best available wine-making technology. It has thus been involved in improving the basic standards of the California wine industry. It has also been accused of a domineering influence, through its sheer size, over the rest of the industry, particularly in the councils of the trade organization the Wine Institute.

Known from the beginning for sound, inexpensive wines of every kind, including FLAVOURED WINES, wine COOLERS and FRUIT WINES, BRANDY, and bulk process SPARKLING WINES, Gallo has inevitably become synonymous with 'pop' wine and JUG WINE, i.e. PLONK. Since 1977 Gallo has made a determined effort to associate its name with premium wines, in the USA understood to be VARIETAL wines sold in bottles stoppered with a CORK. To supply these, Gallo has become the largest vineyard owner in SONOMA County. Its current policy reserves the **E. & J. Gallo** name for its more expensive wines, the less expensive being sold under other Gallo brands such as Carlo Rossi and Livingston Cellars. The firm is wholly owned by the family and discloses little information about its operations.

The Gallo brothers became as jealous of their own name as producers in the CHAMPAGNE region, prohibiting CHIANTI CLASSICO producers from using their age-old symbol of the black cockerel, or Gallo Nero, and even preventing their own younger brother Joseph from using his own name on the cheese he produced.

Hawkes, E., *Blood & Wine: The Unauthorized Story of the Gallo Wine Empire* (New York, 1993).
Shanken, M. R., 'Gallo's dramatic shift to fine varietals', *Wine Spectator*, 16/10 (1991), 20–9.

GAMAY, the French red grape variety solely responsible for the distinctive wines of BEAUJOLAIS. Galet cites scores of different Gamays, many quite unrelated to the Beaujolais archetype, many of them particular clonal selections of it, and many more of them red-fleshed TEINTURIERS once widely used to add colour to vapid blends. Even as recently as the 1980s, more than 1,000 ha/2,500 acres of Gamay Teinturiers were planted in France, and the vine can still be found in the Mâconnais and the Touraine. The 'real' Gamay is officially known as Gamay Noir à Jus Blanc to draw attention to its noble white flesh.

The introduction of Gamay to the vineyards of the CÔTE D'OR in the late 14th century was viewed as scandalous by those whose livelihood did not personally depend on rearing productive vines, and great efforts were made to retain PINOT NOIR at the expense of the less noble newcomer.

The vine is a hasty one, budding, flowering, and ripening early, which makes it prone to spring frosts but means that it can flourish in regions as cool as much of the Loire. It can easily produce too generously and the traditional GOBELET method of training is designed to match this aptitude to the granitic soils of the better Beaujolais vineyards.

Gamay juice also tends to be vinified in a hurry, not least because of market pressure for Beaujolais NOUVEAU, and if Gamay-based wines are cellared for more than two or three years it is usually by mistake. As a wine Gamay tends to be paler and bluer than most other reds, with relatively high acidity and a simple but vivacious aroma of freshly picked red fruits, often overlaid by the less subtle smells associated with rapid, anaerated fermentation such as bananas, boiled sweets, and acetone. In France and Switzerland it is often blended with Pinot Noir, endowing the nobler grape with some precocity, but often blurring the very distinct attributes of each. Gamay fruit is naturally low in potential alcohol, and for many Gamay's charm lies in its refreshing lightness, but prevailing perceptions equating weight with worth encouraged many wine-makers towards over-CHAPTALIZATION. Beaujolais regulations stipulated a maximum ALCOHOLIC STRENGTH of 13 per cent from 1985, as well they might.

Gamay and Beaujolais are entirely interdependent. No wine region is so determinedly *monocépagiste* as Beaujolais, which has just a few Chardonnay vines for Beaujolais Blanc to prove the rule, while 33,600 ha/83,000 acres in 1988, well over half of the world's total Gamay plantings, are in this single region. Vinification techniques vary but most common is a local variant on CARBONIC MACERATION. Similar, often lighter and arguably truer, wines are made from the Gamay grown in the small wine regions of central France, particularly those around Lyons and in the upper reaches of the Loire such as CHÂTEAUMEILLANT, Coteaux du LYONNAIS, COTEAUX DU GIENNOIS, CÔTES D'AUVERGNE, Côtes du FOREZ, Côtes ROANNAISES, and ST-POURÇAIN.

Outside Beaujolais, and perhaps because its wines have been seen as too different from the intense, tannic, fashionable norm, the Gamay vine has been losing ground. In the Côte Chalonnaise and the Mâconnais between Beaujolais and the Côte d'Or the Gamay was displaced as principal grape variety by Chardonnay during the 1980s, and the unexcitingly muddy quality of Gamays made here is expected to continue this trend. Gamay still took up 400 ha/990 acres of the Côte d'Or's valuable vineyard in 1988 but is fast being supplanted by more rewarding varieties.

Gamay is grown all over the Loire but is not glorified by any of the Loire's greatest appellations. Gamay de Touraine can provide a light, sometimes acid, but usually cheaper alternative to Beaujolais, but it is most widely grown west of the Touraine, alongside Sauvignon, for such light, lesser-known names as CHEVERNY and Coteaux du VENDÔMOIS. Gamay also provides about 40 per cent of all of the Loire's important generic Vin de Pays du Jardin de la France.

Outside France there is even less incentive to develop this under-appreciated variety although a few California growers have bothered to import and vinify true Gamay as opposed to the less distinguished vine known there as **Napa Gamay** (see VALDIGUIÉ) or the variety called **Gamay Beaujolais**, which is probably a lesser clone of Pinot Noir. It is also grown in minute quantities in Canada and is confused on a grand scale with Blauer LIMBERGER throughout eastern Europe. It is grown to a certain extent in Italy, and plays a relatively important role in the vineyards of what was YUGOSLAVIA, notably in CROATIA, SERBIA, KOSOVO, and, to least effect, in MACEDONIA.

It is chiefly valued, however, outside Beaujolais, by the Swiss, who grow it widely and, often blending with Pinot Noir, take it seriously—although they too are apt to chaptalize the life out of it.

Galet, P., *Cépages et vignobles de France* (2nd edn., Montpellier, 1990).

GAMBELLARA, dry white wine from the VENETO region of north east Italy. Based on GARGANEGA grapes (a minimum of 80 per cent, with 20 per cent of TREBBIANO di Soave or Trebbbiano Toscano permitted in the blend), it is produced in the townships of Gambellara, Montebello Vicentino, Montorso, and Zermeghedo, only a short distance from SOAVE but in the neighbouring province of Vicenza rather than that of Verona. The wines, made from the same exaggerated yields as their neighbour (98 hl/ha (5 tons/acre) is quite legal), share the blandness of the vast majority of Soave, without sharing the reputation or the instant consumer recognition that Soave enjoys. In the mid 1990s the zone was still to attract quality-minded pioneer producers to demonstrate the potential of Garganega in this particular zone. D.T.

GAMZA, red grape variety in BULGARIA.

GANCIA, large Italian wine merchant house headquartered in Canelli in the heart of the production zone of MOSCATO D'ASTI, has played a leading role in the development of SPARKLING WINE in Italy since the 1850s. Carlo Gancia, founder of a house of wines and liqueurs in 1850, returned to Italy from a period of study in CHAMPAGNE and began to apply the techniques he had learned in France. Commercial production of dry sparkling wine from PINOT NOIR and CHARDONNAY grapes began around 1865 (one of the suppliers of Pinot Noir grapes being the Marquis Incisa della Rocchetta, an ancestor of the inventor of SASSICAIA) and has continued to this day. The house's fortunes, however, were built on its pioneering 'Moscato Spumante', whose production began in the early 1870s. It was Camillo Gancia, the son of Carlo Gancia, who succeeded in obtaining a consensus of the Asti producers and renamed the wine ASTI SPUMANTE around 1910. Gancia purchased an important estate in APULIA in 1983, the Tenuta Torrebianco in Minervino Murge, with the express purpose of developing a line of still wines; CHARDONNAY and SAUVIGNON Blanc have dominated the first plantings. Current production of the house is approximately 1.5 million cases. D.T.

GARGANEGA, vigorous, productive, often over-productive white grape variety of the VENETO region in north east Italy. Its most famous incarnation is SOAVE in which it may constitute anything from 70 to 100 per cent of the blend, often sharpened up by the addition of TREBBIANO di Soave, but increasingly plumped up by CHARDONNAY and other imports. In the Soave CLASSICO zone, with yields kept well in check, it can produce the fine, delicate whites redolent of lemon and almonds which give Soave a good name. The vine is also responsible for GAMBELLARA—indeed Garganega di Gambellara is its most important subvariety—but Garganega has such a long history in the Veneto that it has developed myriad, if rarely particularly interesting, strains, clones, and subvarieties. Other wines in which it plays a major part include Bianco di CUSTOZA, Colli Berici, Colli Euganei, and it is also grown to a more limited extent in both FRIULI and UMBRIA. It is Italy's fifth most important white grape variety, planted on more than 13,000 ha/32,000 acres in 1990.

GARNACHA is the Spanish, and therefore original, name for the grape known in France and elsewhere as Grenache. Its most common and noblest form is the black-berried and white-fleshed Garnacha Tinta, sometimes known as Garnacho Tinto. **Garnacha Tintorera**, on the other hand, is a synonym for the red-fleshed ALICANTE BOUSCHET, Tintorera being Spanish for TEINTURIER. Garnacha Blanca is the light-berried Grenache Blanc (see GRENACHE).

GARONNE, river that rises south of Toulouse in SOUTH WEST FRANCE and flows north west towards the Atlantic, on which the city of BORDEAUX is situated. The confluence of the Garonne and the DORDOGNE, between MARGAUX and BOURG, marks the southern end of the GIRONDE estuary. The Garonne was an important trade route through south west GAUL in the era of Ancient ROME and continued to play a vital role in the medieval wine trade, where there was particular commercial rivalry between the wines produced up river in the HAUT PAYS, either on the Garonne or on its tributaries the Lot and the Tarn, and those produced in the immediate vicinity of Bordeaux.

Today the Garonne links the isolated but promising VIN DE PAYS de la **Haute-Garonne** (represented by the ambitious and internationally targeted vins de pays of Domaine de Ribonnet) with, travelling north west down river, the Côtes du FRONTONNAIS, LAVILLEDIEU, Côtes du BRULHOIS, BUZET, Côtes du MARMANDAIS, GRAVES, PREMIÈRES CÔTES DE BORDEAUX, and Bordeaux's sweet white wine areas SAUTERNES, BARSAC.

GARRAFEIRA, word used by wine-makers, wine bottlers, and wine collectors in PORTUGAL meaning a private wine cellar or reserve. The term is used on wine labels to denote a red wine from an exceptional year that has aged in bulk for at least two years prior to bottling and then aged a further year in bottle before sale. White garrafeira wines must be aged for at least six months in bulk followed by six months in bottle to qualify. The law states that both red and white DOC wines must have an ALCOHOLIC STRENGTH at least 0.5 per cent above the legal minimum for the DOC region, although in practice most garrafeiras are blends of wines from different parts of the country, labelled with the name of the merchant who bottled them. R.J.M.

GARRUT is a Catalonian black grape variety producing aromatic wines reminiscent of liquorice that are high in tannins.

GASCONY, proud region in SOUTH WEST FRANCE which today comprises ARMAGNAC country and such wines as MADIRAN and JURANÇON. Its name appears on labels of VIN DE PAYS des Côtes de Gascogne. In the Middle Ages it was incorporated into Aquitaine and was therefore, like BORDEAUX, under English rule for nearly 300 years from the middle of the 12th century.

GATTINARA, historically the most celebrated, and certainly the most focally situated, of the sometimes intense red wines based on NEBBIOLO grapes, here known as Spanna, in the cluster of hills which span Vercelli and Novara provinces in the PIEDMONT region of north west Italy. The Vercelli hills on the west bank of the Sesia river and Novara hills on the east are capable of producing some of the most serious rivals to the great BAROLO and BARBARESCO, and there have been times in Piedmontese history when Gattinara has been more admired, particularly for its longevity, than Barolo. It is traditional here to add a small softening portion of local BONARDA and/or VESPOLINA grapes, a ploy needed particularly in less ripe vintages when Nebbiolo grown this high can seem austere rather than majestic. Of the seven Spanna DOCS, Gattinara should produce the most long-lived wines and the most substantial are given extended ageing in cask.

For more detail, see SPANNA.

See also LESSONA and BRAMATERRA, also in Vercelli, and, in declining order of potential longevity, BOCA, GHEMME, SIZZANO, and FARA in Novara across the river Sesia.

GAUL, part of western Europe closely approximating to modern France which existed before the rise of classical ROME. The élites of the CELTIC communities beyond the alps were large-scale consumers of wine, long before they were producers. The accoutrements of the Greek and Roman dinner party are frequently found amid the grave goods of Celtic chieftains. Their passion for wine was even claimed as the motive for the Gallic invasions of the Mediterranean world from the 4th century BC onwards (see e.g. Livy, 5. 33). The widespread ready market in Gaul for wine, as well as the slaves who were offered in exchange, was a major stimulus for exports from Italy, particularly in the last century BC (Diodorus, 5. 26). The cultivation of vines arrived with Greek settlers at Massilia (Marseilles) about 600 BC. From them the Gauls 'got used to living by the rule of law, and to pruning the vine, and planting the olive' (Justin, 43. 4. 1). But the real impetus came with the arrival of Roman settlers from the end of the 2nd century BC. By the end of the 1st century BC southern France and the RHÔNE valley (Gallia Narbonensis) was planted with all the fruit that Mediterranean visitors expected. But beyond the Cévennes was a world where 'no vine, olive, or fruit grew', as the great scholar VARRO (*De re rustica*, 1. 7. 8) noticed while on campaign there. The reasons for this were part sociological and part ecological. Some tribes banned the drinking of wine and even massacred traders, in the belief that it undermined their manliness and was the explanation of their defeats by Julius Caesar's armies. More significant was the need for vines which were resistant to FROST. The 1st century AD was a time of considerable development in the south, including wines from Baeterrae (Béziers) and around Vienne (see CÔTE-RÔTIE), where the Allobrogica vine was noted for producing a wine with a natural resinated taste. Wines from this region competed in the markets of Italy and the western Mediterranean, as the finds of the distinctive local AMPHORAE confirm. Elsewhere in Gaul it is more difficult to trace the introduction of viticulture. The GARONNE was an important trade route from an early date; so it is highly likely that the BORDEAUX region was developed in the 1st century AD. On the other hand, the first references to vineyards in BURGUNDY, on the MOSELLE, and in the area of PARIS belong to the 4th century AD. However, recent archaeological finds suggest that viticulture may have developed considerably earlier in many regions than the inadequate literary sources suggest. For example, the discovery of kilns producing amphorae for wine from the late 1st century AD onwards on the LOIRE and its tributaries is testimony to the presence of viticulture in an area for which there is no other evidence. The scale of production should not be exaggerated. The modern map of wine production in France owes less to the Romans than to the Christian Church in the post-Roman period (see CHARLEMAGNE and MONKS AND MONASTERIES). J.J.P.

Dion, R., *Histoire de la vigne et du vin en France des origines au XIXe siècle* (Paris, 1959).

Ferdière, A., *Les Campagnes en Gaule romaine*, ii (Paris, 1988).

GAVI, fashionable Italian dry white and the most interesting expression of the CORTESE grape in PIEDMONT. It is produced around the town of Gavi in a strip of land 15 km/9 miles long and no more than 5.5 km wide in the south east of the province of Alessandria (thus some bottles may be labelled Cortese di Gavi and others, made close to the town, Gavi di Gavi). Cortese appears to be indigenous to this province and the variety has certainly been prized there for over a century, although the red DOLCETTO grape predominated here until PHYLLOXERA devastated the vineyards. Cortese was then planted principally to satisfy the demand for white wine from Genoa and the Ligurian coast, less than 64 km/40 miles away to the south, whose leading families are still an important presence in the zone and the owners of many of the leading estates.

At its best, Gavi is fruity and aromatic, occasionally with mineral notes and a tangy, citric finish; comparisons to white burgundy on the part of its more fervent admirers seem far-fetched. Thanks partly to the high quality achieved by the pioneering La Scolca estate in Rovereto di Gavi, the wine enjoyed great commercial success in the 1960s and the early 1970s, first in the Italian market and subsequently abroad, before the emergence of FRIULI as an important source of fresh white Italian wine. Total production more than tripled in the 20 years since approval of DOC status in 1974, to more than 35,000 hl/924,000 gal per year.

Increasing competition in its category from the TRENTINO, and the ALTO ADIGE, as well as from Friuli, has subsequently put Gavi under a certain commercial pressure as a wine that had reached significant price levels, and estates in the zone seem uncertain as to where to position their production: as a medium-quality, medium-priced wine or as a wine with higher quality and price aspirations. The abundant yields (over 75 hl/ha (4.3 tons/acre)) permitted by the DOC regulations, coupled with possibly over-enthusiastic adoption of cold fermentation technology in the zone, have led to the production of a certain amount of bland Gavi, which has not helped the wine's image, although good bottles of Gavi are by no means difficult to find. Experiments to mate the wine with new OAK have begun and, when done with discretion and tact, have given pleasing results, although it seems unlikely that Gavi subjected to small BARREL MATURATION will be an important phenomenon in the near future. D.T.

GDC, vine-TRAINING SYSTEM. See GENEVA DOUBLE CURTAIN.

GEELONG, one of the many relatively small, relatively isolated wine regions of the state of VICTORIA in AUSTRALIA.

GEILWEILERHOF, viticultural research station at Siebeldingen in the Pfalz region of GERMANY specializing in breeding vine varieties which combine resistance to FUNGAL DISEASES with superior wine quality. As early as 1930 Professor Husfeld was working on combining the desirable characteristics of AMERICAN VINE SPECIES with the wine quality produced by VINIFERA varieties. Today some Asian species of the genus VITIS are also explored. Much of the focus of research is on improving vine-breeding efficiency, with particular reference to frost and drought resistance, pest and disease resistance, eventual wine constituents (particularly aroma and phenolic compounds), the genetic resources of *Vitis*, and biotechnology, including genetic engineering. Some of the most famous varieties for which Geilweilerhof holds the plant breeding licence are MORIO-MUSKAT, BACCHUS, OPTIMA, and DOMINA. A Bacchus-like variety, Phoenix, was released in 1992, and a host of other fungus-resistant new varieties such as Sirius, Orion, and Regent were set to follow. Geilweilerhof is particularly concerned with long-term storage of genetic material and maintains germplasm of more than 15,000 varieties and species. The institute has experimental stations in the Pfalz, Rheingau, and Franken which cover a total vineyard area of 165 ha/407 acres. The journal *VITIS* has been published by the institute since 1957.

See also GEISENHEIM.

GEISENHEIM, viticultural research institute named after the small town in the Rheingau region of Germany where it is sited. It was founded in 1872 by the king of Prussia to improve the science of growing fruit, particularly apples, and has continued a tradition of combining education with applied research ever since then. In 1876 Professor Müller-Thurgau joined Geisenheim as a biologist and in 1882 crossed Riesling × Silvaner to produce the MÜLLER-THURGAU variety, which later became the most planted in Germany. In 1890 the Geisenheim Institute for Grapevine Grafting and Breeding was founded as a direct consequence of the PHYLLOXERA invasion of Germany and since then has continued to be a leading European VINE-BREEDING research centre.

Today the focus of research work is on minimizing chemical inputs in the cellar and, particularly, vineyard, and on creating a sound ecological base for viticulture. ROOTSTOCKS with a notably efficient uptake of SOIL NUTRIENTS and good tolerance to such adverse conditions as SALINITY and DROUGHT and resistance to PHYLLOXERA and NEMATODES have accordingly been developed. Further research programmes have been designed to minimize the use of FERTILIZERS and PESTICIDES. Most problems are expected to be overcome using specially bred NEW VARIETIES which combine these useful resistances with the wine quality associated with traditional varieties. Much of the work of Professor Helmut BECKER, who was at Geisenheim from 1964 until 1989, made particular progress in this area. He was succeeded as director of Grapevine Breeding and Grafting by Professor Ernst Rühl.

Wine-making research is equally concerned with minimizing technical inputs (see ORGANIC WINE) and in 1989 a system of wine-making which did not involve any additions of SULPHUR DIOXIDE was introduced, with considerable success. Other areas of activity include describing and detecting objective parameters for wine quality.

See also GEILWEILERHOF, although Geisenheim is the only German establishment to award the highest educational degree in wine-making.

GELATIN, the gel familiar in jelly and jello, used by winemakers as a FINING agent. This animal product (of which very small traces, unfortunately, remain in the wine after the fining operation) is particularly useful for precipitating excess TANNINS as large insoluble molecules which can be removed by FILTRATION. Gelatin is deliberately avoided by those making vegan wines.

GENERIC wine, one named after a wine type (and usually borrowed European place-name) as opposed to a VARIETAL named after the grape variety from which the wine was made. The term has been used particularly in AUSTRALIA and the UNITED STATES. Under American law, wines labelled as generics may be made from any grape variety or blend of varieties, and called either after their colour (red, white, rosé) or after places. With nothing else to call their results, early CALIFORNIA wineries borrowed European place-names shamelessly. Before PROHIBITION one could buy, not just St-Julien and Margaux made in the state, but wines named after particular châteaux. After Prohibition, tightened laws limited the borrowings to a handful of names, most commonly Burgundy, Chablis, Champagne, Chianti, Rhine, Sauterne (*sic*), Sherry, and Port, but did nothing to demand even the faintest approximations of the original in terms of grape varieties or style. Chablis could and can be just as sickly sweet as Rhine, and both can be made from THOMPSON SEEDLESS or any other white grape. Burgundy, Chianti, and Claret could all come from the same tank, and admittedly have done. Towards the end of the 1980s, Red Table Wine, White Table Wine, and Rosé began to replace place-names on many of the more reputable labels. However, Chablis, Burgundy, and other borrowed names remain in widespread use by a number of large-volume producers, giants GALLO foremost among them.

Generic names can still be found on many wine labels, particularly in non-exporting or developing wine regions. No third-country wine entering the EUROPEAN UNION may carry a geographical name recognized by European wine officials. Thus, for example, the Australian company PENFOLDS had to change the name of their most famous wine from Penfolds Grange Hermitage to Penfolds Grange.

Outside Europe, CHAMPAGNE is still widely used as a generic name for SPARKLING WINE, although not usually for the best-quality products.

GENEROSO is a Spanish and Portuguese term for a FORTIFIED wine.

GENETIC ENGINEERING, the modern approach to VINE BREEDING which involves transfer of genes between organisms. A proposed benefit of genetic engineering is to insert foreign genes, carrying a particular desirable characteristic, into the genetic material of traditional VINE VARIETIES such as Cabernet Sauvignon, without altering the genes concerned with their other characteristics. There are hopes of introducing resistance to VIRUS DISEASES as well as to INSECT PESTS by the use of this technique, as well as improving specific quality factors of berries and wine. The problems potentially involved in naming these new varieties are as yet untested. Investigations in gene transfer use the bacterium *Agrobacterium* (see CROWN GALL) and also particle acceleration. Grapevines have proved relatively difficult to manipulate, but genetically transformed apples and walnuts have been produced.

See also TISSUE CULTURE. R.E.S.

Mullins, M. G., Bouquet, A., and Williams, L., *Biology of the Grapevine* (Cambridge, 1992).

GENEVA DOUBLE CURTAIN, often abbreviated to GDC, a vine-TRAINING SYSTEM whereby the CANOPY is divided into two pendant curtains, trained downwards from high CORDONS or CANES. The system was developed by Professor Nelson Shaulis of Geneva Experiment Station in upstate New York in the early 1960s. The vines are planted in about 3-m / 10-ft rows and the trunk divided at about 1.5 m height to form two parallel cordons about 1.3 m apart. The foliage is trained downwards from these cordons, forming the so-called double curtains. This training system was one of the first examples of a DIVIDED CANOPY developed in the New World and, by reducing shade, it increases both yield and grape quality (see CANOPY MICROCLIMATE). While initially developed for the American variety CONCORD, the system has been applied to VINIFERA wine grapes, especially in Italy. It is one of a number of TRELLIS SYSTEMS advocated as part of CANOPY MANAGEMENT in the 1990s. The GDC system is particularly useful for wide row spacing vineyards of high VIGOUR. While most wine grape varieties have more erect shoots than the American vines it was developed with, it has been found suitable for use in many vineyards, and some notable increases in yield and wine quality have resulted from use of the system. R.E.S.

Smart, R. E., and Robinson, M., *Sunlight into Wine: A Handbook for Winegrape Canopy Management* (Adelaide, 1991).

GENOA, north west Italian port and the principal city of the LIGURIA region. After the fall of Ancient ROME and the barbarian invasions, Genoa was occupied by the Lombards, a Germanic tribe, in 642. Under the Lombards the region disintegrated economically, and the old Roman highways across the Apennines and along the coast were not maintained. It took Genoa until the early 11th century fully to recover from the effects of Lombard rule.

Genoa was therefore initially at a grave disadvantage compared to the city that was to become its deadly rival, VENICE. The Genoese navy had fought to protect its ships from Saracen sea power in the two centuries before the CRUSADES, together with Amalfi, Pisa, and Venice, and Genoa had established trading posts in the Byzantine empire, although it was nowhere near as successful in this as Venice. Nevertheless Genoa's rise, like Venice's, was at first based on its eastern trade, and by the time of the Crusades it was battling with Venice, and occasionally Pisa, for economic control of the eastern Mediterranean. The Latin kings of Jerusalem were dependent on Venetian, Genoese, and Pisan naval power for their protection, and so they granted these cities trading areas in their ports. Whereas Venice continued to trade mostly with Constantinople and the Near East, Genoa's interests centred largely on Palestine and Syria. Along with sugar, glass, and textiles, it shipped wine from vineyards there, many of which had been planted by Christian settlers, to Italy, where these strong, sweet wines were accounted a luxury and bought by rich merchants for their own consumption.

Along with luxury goods acquired in the East, Genoa also began to export cheap bulky goods such as grain, salt, oil, alum (for dying woollen cloth), and wine to western and northern Europe. The overland route was prohibitively expensive, and so from the 13th century onwards Genoa organized regular sailings to Bruges and Southampton in galleys, which used their oars to get into and out of ports swiftly, regardless of the prevailing winds. The voyage still took several months, and only strong, sweet wines such as VERNACCIA ('vernage'), produced mainly in Liguria, and the MALMSEYS of the Aegean had any chance of arriving in drinkable condition. The Venetians did not follow the Genoese galleys until 40 years later. In the late 14th century Genoa abandoned its galleys in favour of the much larger cogs, which had a capacity of 700 to 800 tons and could travel from Genoa to Southampton with only one stop on the way, at Cádiz (see SPAIN).

See also NAPLES and ITALY. H.M.W.

Lopez, R. S., 'The trade of mediaeval Europe: the South', *The Cambridge Economic History of Europe*, 7 vols. ii: *Trade and Industry in the Middle Ages* (Cambridge, 1987).

Melis, Frederigo, 'Produzione e commercio dei vini italiani nei secoli XIII–XVIII', *Annales cisalpines d'histoire sociale*, 1/3 (1972), 107–33.

Porosity = space occupied by air and water.
Matrix-permeability = ease of movement of air and water between sand grains.
Mass-permeability = ease of movement of air and water along cracks within the ground + the matrix permeability.

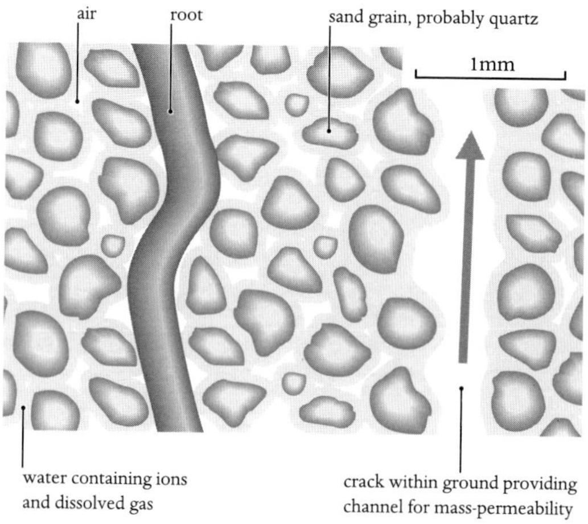

Geology: cross-section within moist sandy ground with the small root of a vine.

GEOLOGY, mainly the study of the Earth's crust, has probably been overestimated in its importance in shaping wine quality and flavour, and some geological remarks in popular wine books are nonsense. In its potential influence on wine, geology includes not only the ROCKS underlying vineyards, but the SOILS at the surface and variations in the slopes on which many vineyards grow (see TOPOGRAPHY). Some wine flavours are given names which may sound geological, such as 'earthy' or 'flinty', but these bear no relation at all to the associated geology. In fact, the influence of geology on a wine is much less than that of weather, vine variety, viticultural methods, and wine-making technique (see CLIMATE AND WINE QUALITY, VINE VARIETIES, VITICULTURE, and WINE-MAKING).

Geology is, however, of importance to the vine-grower because it affects the growth of vines and their production of suitable grapes in ways that are similar for many other long-lived plants: influences on the air temperature around the vines; controls on supplies of water to the roots; and provision of soil nutrients. See SOIL AND WINE QUALITY for more detail than appears below.

It is in any case difficult to establish the precise geology of a vineyard. The most widely available geological maps chart the geological system of the region (Devonian or Miocene, for example), but not the lithology, the actual sort of rock and its mineral composition, for which geological maps at a scale of 100,000 or greater are needed. Small-scale maps show only the 'solid' geology, above which there may be superficial sediments of another composition, possibly several metres thick, and on top of this a layer of soil. The soil, at least, will reflect the composition of the underlying geology, but its all-important DRAINAGE structure may be very different.

The classification of SOILS, meaningless not only to the general public but also to scientists who do not work on soils, is based mainly on a combination of climate and associated natural vegetation, together with a physical analysis of the soils themselves. The names used—gley podsol, for example—are not in common use and are difficult to define in a few words.

It is therefore more common for vineyard soils to be classified in terms of their texture (see SOIL TEXTURE). All soils considered as sediments are clastic, that is, composed of fragments. If the majority of fragments are pebbles (more than a few millimetres across), the sediment is a conglomerate (which is more common in vineyards than in the countryside in general). If the majority of the soil particles are between 0.02 and 2 mm (0.08 in), then it is SAND; particles between 0.02 and 0.002 mm make up SILT; and particles less than 0.002 mm across constitute CLAY (although many soils described as clay are actually relatively rich in silt). LOAM is a mixture of clay, silt, and sand.

The above classification seems unrelated to the soil's mineral composition, but in general 'clay' as sediment is dominated by clay minerals which have strong powers to absorb water and metallic ions, or charged atoms, the charge allowing metals to go into solution in water (K^+ for POTASSIUM and Ca^{++} for CALCIUM, for example). Silts and sands are usually dominated by the mineral quartz, which is chemically largely inert. Some sandstones contain significant quantities of feldspars (see Effect on vine nutrition below). The pebbles in conglomerates may also be of quartz, as they are in Châteauneuf-du-Pape, but in vineyards are often lumps of the underlying hard rock such as the limestone in Chablis.

LIMESTONES, in vineyard terms, may be normal rocky limestones or chalk, the first being much more common and its drainage properties rather variable. CHALK is much softer and has better drainage properties, but is rare in vineyards outside CHAMPAGNE and parts of southern ENGLAND. If a soil contains a substantial quantity of fragmented limestone, it can be described as calcareous, or *calcaire* in French, which has often been wrongly translated as chalk in English wine literature. Similarly, the French word *schiste* means SLATE as well as schist, and is sometimes used loosely to mean SHALE, and its direct translation as schist has caused further confusion. (The word 'limy' is sometimes used by writers instead of calcareous, but should more properly be limited to those soils whose PH is greater than about 7.6.)

Effect on temperature

General air temperatures around vines are modified by the TOPOGRAPHY, itself largely a product of geology, in two ways: by controlling the amount of radiant heat from the sun which reaches the grapes; and by varying the quantity of heat reradiated from the ground on to the vines and grapes. The physiological significance of the latter is discussed in CLIMATE AND WINE QUALITY.

In vineyards in which the ground is kept clear of WEEDS and COVER CROPS, the effects of reradiation can be considered in terms of bare soils. The albedos (the diffuse reflectivity) of most soils and rocks are in the range of 0.1 to 0.3. In other words, 10 to 30 per cent of radiation from the sun is reflected back. Sandy soils have higher albedos than clays; dry ground has a higher albedo than damp. Hence a dry, sandy soil reflects back about twice as much radiation as a damp clay.

Effect on water balance

A balanced supply of water to the vines' roots is needed to produce high-quality wine grapes. The capacities of soils to supply this are discussed under SOIL WATER and SOIL AND WINE QUALITY. Underlying rocks can also play a significant role in vine-water relations because of the exceptional length of vine roots.

The ideal ground (soil and bedrock) for water balance has a high porosity for storing water; a sufficiently low matrix-permeability to stop it draining away too fast; but a high mass-permeability to ensure good drainage. Permeability is a measure of the ease with which a liquid passes through a sediment. The passage of water from one microscopic pore to another between the particles is known as the matrix-permeability. Most rocks and soils are traversed by cracks along which water can flow much more easily. The total possible rate of flow is known as the mass-permeability (see diagram).

Some examples of common vineyard rock types are given in the table, together with very approximate typical values of porosity in percentages, and permeabilities in millidarcys in fresh rock.

Of the rocks listed in the table, the ideal is chalk. The values given in this table are for fresh rock; in many vineyards there may be a thick cover of weathered and broken-up rock which, for water balance, behaves as an unconsolidated sediment. On the GRANITES of Beaujolais, for example, there are often several metres of material that behave like an unconsolidated sand in terms of both porosity and permeability. And regions which are indicated as limestone on a simple geological map, may actually have sufficient clay interbedded with the limestone or along joint planes to hold adequate supplies of water. Sandstones and conglomerates, which dry out easily, may have lenticular patches out of sight below the surface, with much lower matrix-permeabilities which can hold reserves of water during periods of DROUGHT. Examples include the finer sand with its low matrix-permeability in the Méric conglomerate of the Médoc, lenticles of silt beneath the conglomerates of the central Torres vineyards in Penedès. Very approximately, permeabilities increase with the square of the grain size, but the subject as a whole is complicated.

Rock type	Porosity %	Matrix-permeability (mD)	Mass-permeability (mD)
Sandstone and conglomerate	20–40 seldom below 5	35–400	50–3,000
Clay and shale	8–20	0.05–0.3	10–10,000
Limestone:			
Regular	less than 5; occasionally up to 25	typically under 0.1	100 but very variable
Chalk	30–45	2–3	30–3,000
Granite	very low	very low	high

Effect on vine nutrition

Even in vineyards with some soil, vine roots usually extend below it into the underlying rock. The mineral composition of the rock as well as the soil affects the nourishment of the vine. Vines do best with the slow but regular supply of potassium ions from the breakdown by weathering of primary potassium-bearing minerals.

A significant proportion of the world's famous wines are from vineyards whose underlying rock contains potassium feldspar (a group of minerals), or is rich in illite (a clay mineral visible only with an electron microscope). Examples include the feldspar and illite-bearing Méric conglomerate of the Médoc; the potassium feldspar in the granites beneath Beaujolais and Hermitage; the illitic clays within the limestones of the Côte d'Or; the feldspathic sandstones of the Rotliegend formation west of Nierstein in the Rheinhessen and some of the grands crus vineyards in Alsace; the muscovite-illite rich phyllites of parts of the Upper Mosel; the feldspar porphyry of Schlossböckelheim in the Nahe; and the alluvial sediments in the Napa Valley derived from volcanic and pyroclastic rocks lining the sides of the valley.

For more detail, see SOIL, SOIL AND WINE QUALITY, ROCK, TOPOGRAPHY, TERROIR, and for details of specific soil and rock types, see under their individual names. J.M.H.

Bibliographical note: There is little general literature on the relationships between geology and wine. A pioneering work was by P. Wallace, *International Geological Congress 24* (Canada, 1972) 6, 359–65. A more recent and lavishly illustrated book is C. Pomerol (ed.), *Terroirs et vins de France* (Paris, 1984–6), trans. as

The Wines and Winelands of France (London, 1989), but, apart from the chapters on Burgundy and Jura, it lacks critical information on geological controls. Much more informative, albeit brief and modestly claimed to be no more than a discussion paper, is E. Berry, 'The importance of soil in fine wine production', *Journal of Wine Research*, 1/2 (1990), 179–94. A book with considerable geological detail is H. Enjalbert, *Les Grands Vins de St-Émilion, Pomerol et Fronsac* (Paris, 1983) trans. as *Great Bordeaux Wines* (Paris, 1985).

An introduction to general geology is H. H. Read and J. Watson, *Introduction to Geology*, i (2nd edn., London, 1970). Simple geological maps are available from national surveys of wine-producing countries.

GEOPONIKA, a compilation of advice on agriculture put together about AD 950 at the behest of the scholarly Byzantine Emperor Constantine VII Porphyrogenitus, as part of a grand scheme of digests of knowledge. It may have been based on a compilation of some three centuries earlier by Cassianus Bassus. Of the 20 books the largest section, Books 4–8, consisted of a long list of precepts on viticulture and winemaking. It survives in part. The information is of variable quality. Much can be traced back to the Roman AGRICULTURAL TREATISES but it includes material from authors, particularly of the hellenistic period, whose work is otherwise unknown to us. J.J.P.

GEORGIA, independent ex-member of the SOVIET UNION immediately north east of TURKEY between the Black Sea and the High Caucasus. The capital is Tbilisi and the region, one of the world's great and historic centres of both wild and cultivated vines, contains the Republics of Abkhazia, Adzharia, and South Ossetia. Within the CIS only RUSSIA, UKRAINE, and MOLDOVA produce more wine.

History

See ARMENIA for the important role played by this part of the world in the ORIGINS of viticulture. Archaeology provides ample evidence that viticulture was long an important occupation of the Georgian people and wine drinking an integral part of their culture. Grape seeds, special knives for vine pruning, stone presses, crushers, clay and metallic vessels for wine, and jewellery depicting grape bunches and leaves dating back to between 3000 and 2000 BC have all been unearthed in Mukheta, Trialeti, Pitsunda, and in the Alazan valley. Rich ornaments of fruited vines are found on the walls of ancient temples in Samtavisi, Ikalto, Zarmza, Gelati, Nikortsminda, and Vardzia. According to a poem by Apollonius Rhodius (3rd century BC) the Argonauts, having arrived in the capital of Colchis, saw twining vines at the entrance to the king's palace and a fountain of wine in the shade of the trees.

Georgian legends and folklore bear witness to that people's love of the grapevine. Georgia adopted Christianity in the 4th century, and the first cross was made of vines to show that the Christian faith and the vine were the most sacred treasures of the nation.

For many centuries, viticulture was of prime agricultural and economic importance to Georgia. In the second half of the 19th century vineyards covered 71,200 ha/176,000 acres, but FUNGAL DISEASES and PHYLLOXERA had reduced the total vineyard area to 37,400 ha by the beginning of the 20th century. In order to restore vineyards destroyed by phylloxera, the country had to import phylloxera-resistant ROOTSTOCKS and there are more than 100,000 ha of vineyard today.

WILD VINES are widely distributed in Georgia, where *Vitis vinifera silvestris* can still be seen. By both natural and artificial selection, they have given rise to more than 500 identifiable indigenous grape varieties. The most famous vine nursery is at Sakar in western Georgia.

Viticulture

Vines in Georgia (unlike Russia) do not need WINTER PROTECTION, and new vineyards are planted to grafted seedlings. Vineyards mostly use TRELLIS SYSTEMS and various TRAINING SYSTEMS such as cordon systems, fan-shaped systems with numerous canes, Georgian systems with canes trained in one or two directions, and pergola forms. Vines are planted at a 1.5 × 2 m and 2 × 3 m vine and row spacing, with the trunk's height at 0.6–1.2 m (2–4 ft). Zones with frequent hailstorms use special reticular shelters. The total vineyard area in 1990 was 113,000 ha/279,000 acres.

Climate and geography

Georgia's topography is complex. Mountains of the High Caucasus in the north account for about 30 per cent of its total area. The peculiarities of the relief determine a great diversity in the country's soil and climatic conditions, which, in turn, influence grape culture. The climate varies from moderate to subtropical. The annual rainfall is 300 to 600 mm (23 in) in the east and 1,000 to 4,000 mm (156 in) in the west. A great diversity of soils are found in the country.

Georgia has five viticultural zones: Kakheti, Kartli, Imereti, Racha-Lechkhumi, and the humid subtropical zone.

Kakheti, which grows 70 per cent of Georgia's wine and brandy grapes, is in the south east of the country in the Alazani and Iori valleys. The climate here is moderate, with an active temperature summation of 3,800 to 4,000 °C and an annual rainfall of 400 to 800 mm. Cinnamonic forest and calcareous soils, some of them alluvial, are found in the zone.

In terms of mesoclimatic conditions and types of wines produced, Kakheti can be subdivided into three macroregions and more than 25 microregions (Tsinandali, Kvarelo-Kindzmarauli, Manavi, Napareuli, Akhmeta, etc.). These regions produce the distinctive Kakhetian wines, made peculiarly tannic by FERMENTATION in special earthenware jars (*kvevri*) (not unlike the *tinajas* of VALDEPEÑAS) followed by an extended MACERATION of three or four months, very much as wines were made thousands of years BC.

Kartli occupies a vast territory in the Kura valley, the Gori and Mukhran lowlands included. These wines are most European and the region produces materials for sparkling wines (especially) and brandy that account for 15 per cent of Georgia's wine and brandy production. The zone is moderately warm, with hot and dry summers; vineyards have to be irrigated because of the small amount of rainfall (350 to 500 mm (19 in) per year). The capital of Georgia, Tbilisi, where wineries producing sparkling wines and brandy are located, is in this zone. Tbilisi's oldest winery, founded in 1897, has a unique wine collection of about 1,600 brands of wine (up to 150,000 bottles) including old foreign wines such as Hungarian Tokay (1846), Spanish Malaga (1820) and sherry (1848), Italian Marsala and Portuguese madeira (1822), and French cognac (1811).

Imereti is in the east part of west Georgia, in the basins and in the gullies of Rioni, Kvirila, and other rivers. Imereti also uses an original wine-production method, similar to Kakheti's except that grape skins are *added* to the clay jars during fermentation, a little like Italy's GOVERNO, and this is followed by a maceration of six to eight weeks. The vine variety particular to this region is Tzitzka.

Racha-Lechkhumi is north of Imereti, on the banks of the Rioni and Tskhenistskali rivers. Moderate rainfall (1,000 to 1,300 mm (50 in) a year), southern exposed soils, and the assortment of local grape varieties encourage grapes with a sugar content as high as 30 per cent.

The Khvanchkara microregion is famous for its semi-sweet Ehvanchkara wine, often made from Alexandrouli and Mujuretuli vine varieties. The **humid subtropical zone** contains Abkhazia, Adzharia, Guria, and Megrelia, which are also noted for their sweet wines.

Vine varieties

Thirty-eight grape varieties are officially allowed for commercial viticulture in Georgia. Wine varieties include RKATSITELI, Tsolikouri, Tsitska, Chinuri, SAPERAVI, Goruli Mtsvane, Mtsvane Kakhetinski, Ojaleshi, Aladasturi, Khikhvi, Chkhaveri, Dzvelshvari Obchuri, ALIGOTÉ, PINOT NOIR, CHARDONNAY, and CABERNET SAUVIGNON. V.R.

Chkhartishvili, N. S., and Darakhvelidze, O. K., 'The Soviet Socialist Republic of Georgia' (Russian), in A. I. Timush (ed.), *Encyclopaedia of Viticulture* (Kishinev, 1986).

Geguadze, N. N., 'Prospects of the development of viticulture in Kakhetia' (Russian), *Vinogradarstvo i vinodelie SSSR*, 3 (1980), 61–2.

Loladze, G. (ed.), *Georgian Wine* (Russian) (Tbilisi, 1989).

Modebadze, K. V., 'The beginning of viticulture and enology of Georgia' (Russian), *Vinogradarstvo i vinodelie SSSR* 4 (1948), 43–6.

GERANIUM, pejorative tasting term for the smell of crushed geranium leaves that is given off by wines in which LACTIC BACTERIA have reacted with the fungistat SORBIC ACID. This geranium smell, which occurs in very varied concentrations and for which the compound 2-ethoxyhexa-3, 5-diene is responsible, first appeared in wines during the 1970s, when sorbic acid use became common. Its formation can be prevented by adding SULPHUR DIOXIDE at the same time as the sorbic acid to prevent the growth and acitivity of the lactic bacteria responsible. A.D.W.

GERMAN CROSSINGS, an important group of VINE VARIETIES that are the result of VINE BREEDING, an activity that was particularly vigorous in the first half of the 20th century but which continues to this day, most notably at GEISENHEIM. Because of EUROPEAN UNION law, only CROSSINGS containing exclusively VINIFERA genes have so far been released.

The man who bred Germany's first commercially successful modern crossing was in fact Swiss, Dr Hermann MÜLLER-THURGAU, whose eponymous vine variety was to become the most planted in Germany in the second half of the 20th century, almost 100 years after it was developed. A succession of new crossings followed in the 20th century, notably from research institutes at Geisenheim, GEILWEILERHOF, Alzey, Würzburg and Freiburg, producing a large number of NEW VARIETIES usually designed to achieve the high MUST WEIGHTS encouraged by the GERMAN WINE LAW. The most successful white wine varieties, in descending order of area planted in Germany in the early 1990s, are KERNER, SCHEUREBE, BACCHUS, FABER(REBE), MORIO-MUSKAT, HUXELREBE, ORTEGA, EHRENFELSER, OPTIMA, REICHENSTEINER, PERLE, SIEGERREBE, REGNER, NOBLING, WÜRZER, KANZLER, SCHÖNBURGER, FREISAMER, FINDLING, RIESLANER, JUWEL, ALBALONGA, and, more popular in England than Germany, GUTENBORNER. Few of these crossings make distinctive, attractive and characterful wines, although Kerner, Ehrenfelser and, particularly, Scheurebe and Rieslaner can make fine wines if sufficiently ripe. More typically, the vines have been planted to yield good quantities of high must weight wines.

Successful German crossings for red wine include DORNFELDER, HEROLDREBE, and HELFENSTEINER, bred by Dr August Herold in the 1950s, as well as a host of others bred usually for their COLOUR, often using red-fleshed TEINTURIERS, including DOMINA, Deckrot, Rotberger, Carmina, Sulmer, and Kolor.

GERMAN HISTORY. This article encompasses the history of wine production not just in GERMANY but also in ALSACE.

The origins of viticulture to AD 800

Although the wild vine *Vitis vinifera silvestris* may be traced back to prehistoric times on the upper Rhine, the cultivated, wine-yielding vine species *Vitis vinifera*—and with it viticulture in Germany— almost certainly owe their origins to the Romans (see Ancient ROME).

Archaeological discoveries have unearthed curved pruning knives near the sites of Roman garrisons on the left bank of the Rhine which can be dated to the 1st century AD. These finds relegate the importance of the much-cited decrees of Emperor PROBUS (276–82), traditionally regarded as the founder of viticulture in Germany. Firm literary evidence for viticulture only occurs with the tract *Mosella*, written around 370 by the Roman author Ausonius of Bordeaux, who lyrically describes the steep vineyards on the banks of the river. It is likely that Roman viticulture in large measure withstood the waves of subsequent Germanic invasions, for around 570 the north Italian poet Venantius Fortunatus could describe vines on the river MOSEL at Metz and Trier, as well as on the Rhine at Andernach. Interestingly, he mentions the existence of red wines, which were apparently common in Germany in Roman times.

Continuity of viticulture is also suggested by the use of

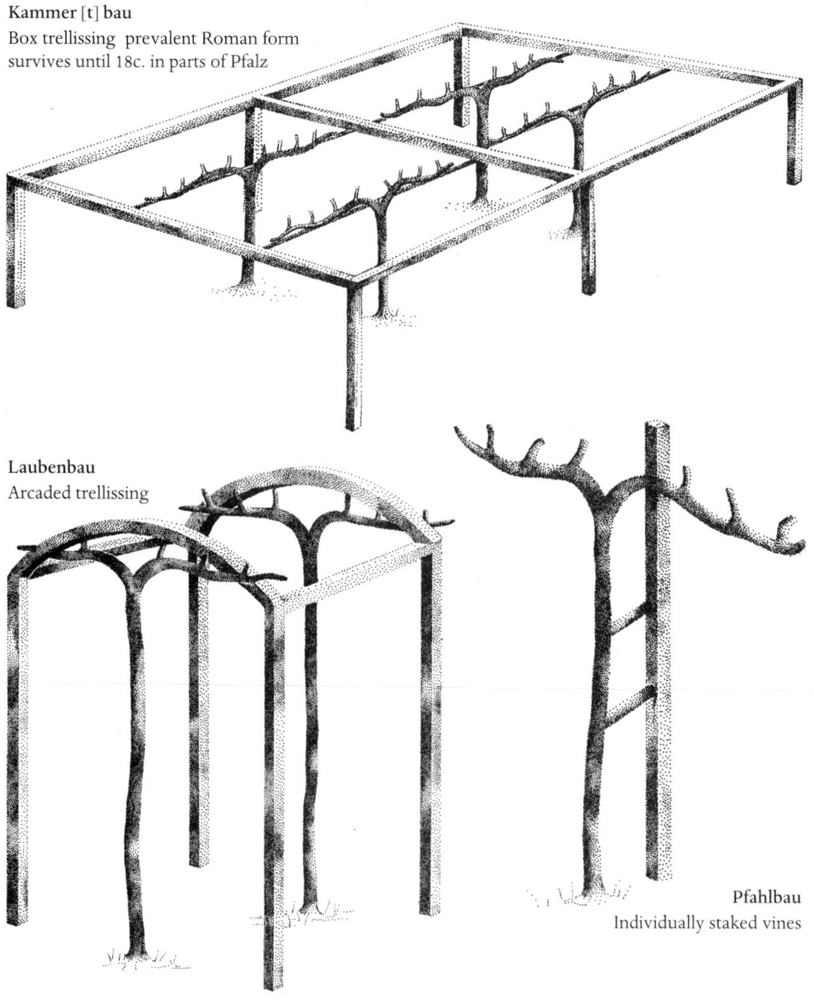

German history

typically Roman forms of TRELLIS SYSTEMS on low and high frames (*Kammer(t)*-, and *Lauben*- or *Rahmenbau*), which survived in parts of the PALATINATE as late as the 18th century (see diagram). Evidence of wine-growing under the Merovingians can be seen in the pious donations of their kings: Dagobert I (622–88) gave vineyards at Ladenburg on the Neckar (in what is now the most northerly, Oberrhein district of BADEN) to the church of St Peter in Worms. This grant is especially significant, since it offers one of the earliest pointers to vines on the right bank of the Rhine, although some modest viticulture has been conjectured for Baden from the 2nd century AD under the influence of the extensive vineyards of Alsace.

Until the era of CHARLEMAGNE, nevertheless, wine-growing was concentrated west of the Rhine: from Alsace down river into the Palatinate (the modern German wine regions of PFALZ and RHEINHESSEN), and thence downstream along the middle Rhine as far as Koblenz. Wine-growing extended up three left bank tributaries: the NAHE valley down to Bingen, where wine-growing is securely documented from 750; the Mosel (with its own tributaries, the SAAR and RUWER), where the tradition of Roman viticulture was vigorously maintained by monastic foundations such as St Maximin and St Martin in Trier; and the most northerly European wine-growing district, the AHR valley south of Bonn, where vines had been planted on sheltered slopes from at least the 3rd century AD.

East of the Rhine, in the districts beyond the frontier of Roman occupation, the spread of viticulture went hand in hand with the missions of Christian monks. Wine-growing was introduced into FRANKEN in the late 7th century by St Kilian (*fl.* 700), while St Columban of Freising (*c.*545–615) was responsible for promoting viticulture in Bavaria, whose vineyards covered a sizeable area throughout the Middle Ages.

Apart from the existence of red wines, next to nothing is known about grape varieties and the quality of wine in this period. Earliest references distinguish only between 'frens' (*fränkisch*, or Frankish) and 'heunisch' or 'hünsch' (Hunnish?) varieties, the former already regarded as superior to the latter. Whether any of these grapes came from Italy or Gaul, or if they were crossings of imported with local (wild) grapes, cannot be determined. T.S.

Bibliographical note. There is no reliable survey in English. Readers of German may consult F. von Bassermann-Jordan, *Geschichte des Weinbaus*, 3 vols. in 2 (4th edn., Landau, 1991); and H. Hahn, *Die deutschen Weinbaugebiete*, Bonner Geographische Abhandlungen, 18 (Bonn, 1956).

Viticulture's importance in the Middle Ages

From the foundation of the Carolingian empire, the history of German wine can be traced with greater confidence. CHARLEMAGNE's numerous capitularies (law codes, relating particularly to landholding) contain instructions to his officials to plant vines and demands for renders of saplings. His true significance, however, lay in the support he gave to the spread of Christianity, for churches and convents were the principal cultivators and consumers of quality wine (see MONKS AND MONASTERIES). The nature of impersonal ownership and the right to demand labour and services from the dependent peasantry ensured continuity of planting and production by ecclesiastical institutions.

Many vineyards still famous today originate in monastic settlements of the High Middle Ages. In the RHEINGAU, Archbishop Ruthard of Mainz (1088–1109) founded a Benedictine

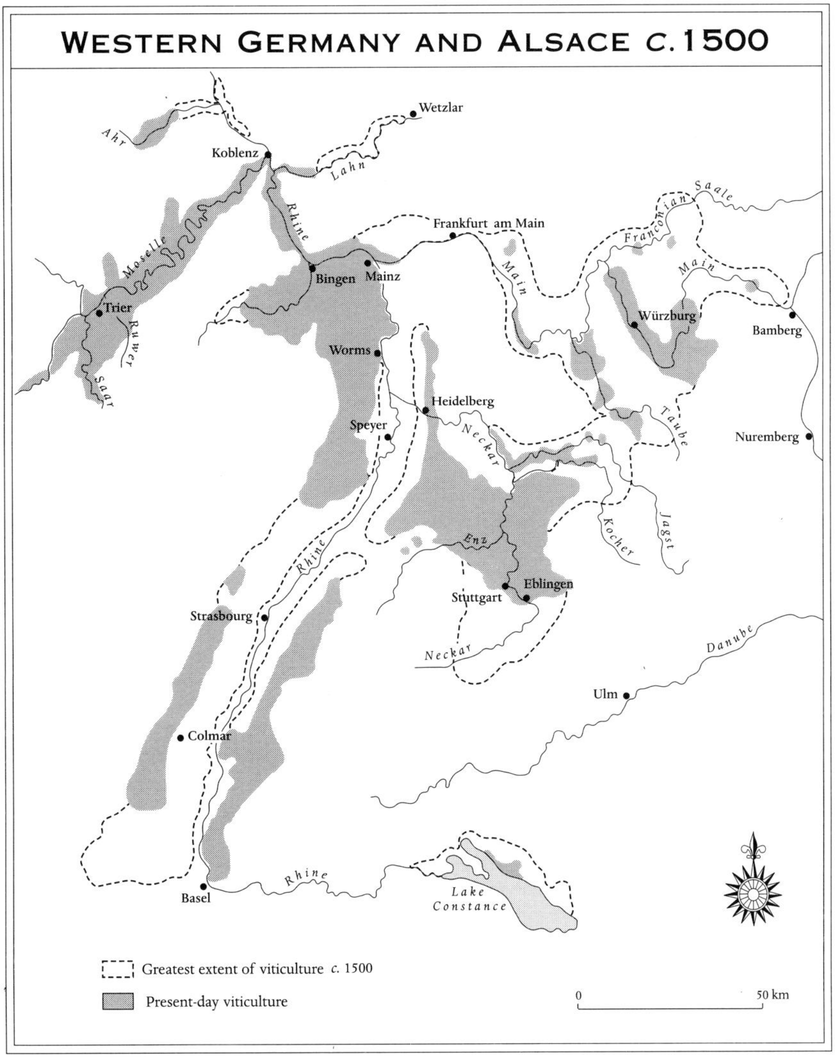

abbey on the slopes above Geisenheim, the Johannisberg, later known as SCHLOSS JOHANNISBERG. In 1135 his successor, Archbishop Adalbert, gave the Steinberg vineyard above Hattenheim to the Cistercians, whose abbey of Eberbach (KLOSTER EBERBACH) remains the informal headquarters of the German wine industry to the present. On the river MOSEL, Archbishop Baldwin of Trier founded the Carthusian priory of St Alban in 1335, which was endowed with vineyards at Eitelsbach on the RUWER, the Karthäuser Hofberg. In FRANKEN (Franconia) too, the bishops of Würzburg actively encouraged viticulture along the river Main.

Elsewhere, secular princes played a leading part, especially in the PALATINATE, where the count-electors had promoted Bacharach on the Rhine as the entrepôt for wine from their many territories on both banks of the river. The medieval Palatinate was indeed a highly fragmented principality, and several of the best wine-producing villages in the middle and upper Haardt (in what is now the PFALZ region) belonged to other lords: Deidesheim, Forst, and Ruppertsberg were part of the secular territory of the bishops of Speyer; the counts of Leiningen controlled Kallstadt, Ungstein, and Dürkheim; only Wachenheim was palatine. On the Rhine the electors palatine owned Oppenheim and Nierstein, as well as Bacharach, but the archbishop of Mainz was lord of Bingen.

Although viticulture was dominated by the Church and the aristocracy, bourgeois ownership of vineyards was common, too, either corporately by city councils or by individual merchants and investors. The vineyards of the city hospital (Bürgerspital) of Würzburg, founded in 1319 by a patrician family, can be traced, for example, from the early 15th century. Merchants from as far afield as Cologne (Köln) bought vineyards in ALSACE: in 1473 Johann Kremer, called 'up den Berge', invested in vineyards in Ribeauvillé and in Hohwiller south of Wissembourg, doubtless in part to ensure continuity of supply.

The rapid expansion of viticulture after the millennium, which only came to a halt in the 16th century, can largely be attributed to the recovery in population and the rise of towns as centres of consumption and exchange: 'a wine landscape is an urban landscape' ran the medieval tag. But the spread of vineyards into the higher valleys, often far from urban centres, can only be explained by the foundation of the new ascetic religious orders, Cistercians and Carthusians, who established their houses from the 12th century at a deliberate distance from civilization. In Alsace, for example, vineyards followed convents into the remote valleys of the Vosges: at Orbey above Kaysersberg, around Münster in the valley of the Fecht, or at Lièpvre in the Liepvrette valley west of Sélestat; even in the 18th century 15 villages in the Val du Villé still retained their medieval viticulture. Apart from the heartlands of medieval viticulture in Alsace, the Palatinate, and the Mosel valley, all of which witnessed the further intake of land for vineyards up to 1500, wine-growing had spread by 1300 to the Rheingau, and throughout BADEN (with vineyards on Lake Constance from the 8th century), WÜRTTEMBERG, and Franken.

By 1500 even the rolling uplands of Swabia and the heavily afforested valleys of northern Franken had been cleared for vines. There viticulture reached its greatest extent in the 15th century, covering perhaps four times the area under vines today (see map on p. 431, and CLIMATE CHANGE for the possible role played by northern Europe's warmer weather during this period). In the less suitable districts, however, vines were never the principal crop: in much of Franken they took second place to grain tillage. Even in the Palatinate many wine-growing villages practised a mixed agricultural economy. In western Germany vines spread into districts which have long lost any trace of viticulture: the lower Rhine beyond Bonn, the Lahn valley as far as Wetzlar, the foothills of the Taunus mountains, northern Hesse, and Westphalia on church estates south of Münster, in the Sauerland, and along the Ruhr.

In eastern Germany the Ottonian emperors promoted viticulture in their Saxon dynastic lands from the late 9th century. The sees which they founded in Meissen, Magdeburg, and Merseburg all became major vineyard owners. Vines were planted on the Elbe around Dresden and Meissen, and on the Saale and Unstrut, especially around Freyburg (see SAALE-UNSTRUT). There were further pockets of viticulture on the sandy-gravelly soils on the banks of the Neisse at Guben and on the Oder into Silesia around the German settlement of Grünberg (Zielona Góra). Thuringia, too, had extensive viticulture, with its leading cities—Erfurt, Rudolstadt, Arnstadt, and Jena—all engaged in a regional export trade in wine. Even in Brandenburg around Berlin and Jessen, east of Wittenberg, vines were grown on a commercial basis from the 14th to the 16th centuries.

The sites chosen for planting were by no means those on which wines still thrive today. Low-lying level sites were preferred; in Alsace, acknowledged as producing the best wines of medieval Germany, vineyards stretched across the plains from the Ried down to Mulhouse. From the 10th century vines were at last being planted on slopes in TERRACES, with low walls to prevent SOIL EROSION. The famous slopes of the Rheingau were initially planted in the 11th century: first the Rüdesheimer Berg, then in the 12th century the Johannisberg and Steinberg, with the slopes of Rauenthal not planted until the 13th. Even on slopes with better exposure vines of greater and lesser quality continued to be grown side by side. Although yields were low—20 hl/ha at best (hardly more than 1 ton/acre)—quantity still came before quality.

Vine varieties Workaday wine was made everywhere from the ELBLING grape, by far the commonest medieval variety, with RÄUSCHLING widely planted in Baden. SILVANER, too, was extensively grown, but rarely as a high-quality grape in its own right: before 1800 it was normally blended with other varieties. Of the better grapes, MUSCAT (red and white) was grown on the Rhine and in Alsace, TRAMINER chiefly in the

Bottles of **Roederer's** famous **prestige cuvée** champagne, Cristal, during **remuage**, which literally 'shakes' the sediment from the second fermentation in bottle on to the stopper so it will be expelled during **disgorgement**. New techniques may eventually replace this cumbersome process (see **sparkling wine-making**).

latter. Riesling is first documented at Rüsselheim on the river Main just east of the modern RHEINGAU in 1435. It is also documented in the late 15th century near Worms, and in the mid 16th at Trittenheim on the Mosel. Although the view that Riesling and Traminer derive from crossings of imported noble varieties with local wild grapes in Carolingian times can be discounted, there is every likelihood that Riesling had been established and recognized as a high-quality grape much earlier than the sources suggest, for in 1477 Duke René of Lorraine, in praising the red and white wines of Alsace, mentioned in particular its Riesling.

In the Middle Ages many Alsace wines were fortified (see FORTIFICATION) or spiced (see FLAVOURED WINES) in order to compete with the fuller bodied Mediterranean wines such as SACK and MALMSEY. Red wine was made from the Blauburgunder (PINOT NOIR) grape on the upper Rhine in Alsace and Baden (where Affental had already acquired a reputation by 1330). The Pinot Noir was also planted in the less favourable latitudes of Saxony and Thuringia, having been imported from BOHEMIA in the 14th century. In Württemberg, by contrast, where much of the production, then as now, consisted of light red wines, the TROLLINGER grape predominated. The Ahr valley may have been planted with red grapes, but they cannot have included the Pinot Noir, which was not introduced there until the 18th century.

By the end of the Middle Ages population pressure made more intensive land use an urgent necessity. Viticulture, which required up to eight times as much labour as arable agriculture, but which could yield a good return at market, seemed to provide the answer in terms of employment and income. Yet the hypertrophic expansion of the later Middle Ages was to plunge viticulture into a severe crisis in the 16th century. T.S.

Bibliographical note: There is no reliable survey in English. Readers of German may consult, in addition to the works previously cited, M. Barth, *Der Rebbau des Elsass und die Absatzgebiete seiner Weine* (Strasbourg and Paris, 1958).

The wine trade in the Middle Ages

Although the quantity of wine harvested in medieval Germany never approached that of France, Italy, or the Iberian peninsula, production in the main growing regions on the left bank of the Rhine always exceeded local consumption, so that commerce in wine became an economic necessity. Until the rise of towns, the wine trade was largely in the hands of the Church, although the term 'trade' often simply meant the transport of wine by convents and foundations, sometimes hundreds of miles distant, from their estates in the wine-growing areas, as with St Gallen in eastern Switzerland, which had extensive holdings on the Upper Rhine.

Thereafter the volume of trade grew rapidly, although the total naturally included imports, chiefly of sweet and red wines from southern Europe, as well as exports of German wine. Because the best vineyards lay along the Rhine and its tributaries, shipments of wine could pass easily down one of the great arteries of European trade to northern Germany, the LOW COUNTRIES, Scandinavia, and England. The earliest centres of the wine trade were all inland ports on or near the Rhine: Colmar and Strasbourg in ALSACE; Speyer (which handled much of the production of the middle Haardt in the modern PFALZ region), Worms and Mainz in the PALATINATE; Frankfurt on the Main; and the Lower Rhine outlets of Bacharach and, above all others, Cologne (Köln).

Ease of transport, however, was offset by the numerous tolls which local lords levied on cargoes shipped down the Rhine. From Strasbourg to the Dutch border 31 toll stations survived from the Middle Ages to the 18th century, the majority concentrated between Mainz and Cologne. The harm inflicted on wine exports by these added costs is very hard to determine: the wines of Alsace, after all, had to pass the most customs posts, yet were still the most sought after in overseas markets.

Cologne and Frankfurt dominated Germany's medieval wine trade, a point tellingly illustrated by the decision of KLOSTER EBERBACH, the important abbey in the rural depths of the RHEINGAU, to acquire its own cellars in Cologne in 1162 and in Frankfurt 50 years later. But their pattern of trade differed. Cologne is first mentioned trading with England in the 10th century, although the notion that German wine was regularly sold in England in the reign of Ethelred the Unready (978–1016) may be dismissed as fanciful. None the less, it was Cologne merchants who obtained the franchise from King Henry II (r. 1154–89) in 1157 to sell their German wines in England at the same price as French wines (such as those now being produced under the British crown throughout Aquitaine, see BORDEAUX).

Throughout the Middle Ages, Cologne's trade with the Baltic, Scandinavia, and England was far more extensive than Frankfurt's. As the chief commercial rival within the Hanseatic League of north German mercantile cities to Lübeck, Cologne's fortunes depended upon its pre-eminence in northern Europe. The city's wine trade reached its peak in the late 14th and early 15th centuries: in 1380 its merchants were handling around 120,000 hl/3.1 million gal per annum, but by the end of the 15th century that figure had been halved. See also DUTCH WINE TRADE.

Cologne continued to play a major role in the export of the best German wines, but its trading area was increasingly exposed to the rise of BEER as the everyday drink of northern Germany. Cologne's merchants are recorded as exporting 'Rhenish wine', but that term undoubtedly embraced the wines of Alsace as well. However, it was Frankfurt's merchants who increasingly specialized in Alsace wines, although their popularity was challenged during the 15th century by wines from the Palatinate and the Rheingau. Just as Cologne traded Rhine and Mosel wines to the Baltic and the Low Countries in exchange for herrings and stockfish, Frankfurt did the same with Alsace wines. Within northern Germany, indeed, competition between the two cities led to accusations

Barrel maturation and **bottle ageing** are two quite different, but often complementary processes. The typical **Jerez** bodega (top) belongs to **Domecq**, of sherry and brandy fame, while the bottles in the **bins** below contain burgundy, in the cellars of **négociant** Prosper Maufoux.

German history: Wine was an important commodity for the merchants of the Hanseatic League, such as these pictured at Hamburg in 1487.

at the diet of the Hanseatic League in 1417 that Frankfurt was supplying poorer-quality 'niderländisch' (RHINE) wines under the pretext of better-quality 'oberländisch' (Alsace) wines to Lower Saxony.

Although German wines were firmly established in northern Europe during the Middle Ages, there were limits to their share of the market. In the southern Low Countries 'Rhine wine' was consumed, but it had to compete with the heavier wines of Burgundy, Auxerre, and also Bordeaux. In England, too, German wines faced a stiff challenge from France, as the trade with Gascony flourished from the 12th century. It is true that in England there are frequent references to the wines of 'Aussay' (or 'Osoye', 'Osey'), which in the French and Lorraine sources certainly means Alsace, but since the English documents invariably mention 'Aussay' in the same breath as Gascon and Spanish wines, it must be assumed that in the English context this was indeed a southern wine, perhaps from Portugal.

But German wine was not confined to northern markets. Alsace wines were extensively exported to southern Germany, Switzerland, and central Europe. By 1500 Ulm in Swabia had become the largest wine market in southern Germany, outstripping Esslingen and Heilbronn. Its merchants exported Alsace and Rhine wines alongside local WÜRTTEMBERG wines down the Danube to Bavaria and Austria, with Regensburg as an important staging post. Wine was the duchy of Württemberg's most valuable export at the end of the Middle Ages, and some of its production may even have reached the Low Countries and England. Nuremberg, the most powerful commercial metropolis in Germany by 1500, was also a major entrepôt for wine, although its function lay principally in the distribution of South Tyrolean, Italian, and Spanish imports (mostly of red wine) to the rest of Germany, rather than in handling exports of German wine.

T.S.

Bibliographical note: There is no reliable survey in English. Readers of German may consult, in addition to the works previously cited, H. Ammann, 'Von der Wirtschaftsgeltung des Elsaß im Mittelalter', *Alemannisches Jahrbuch* (1955), 11–63.

Crisis and decline, 1500–1650

The Thirty Years War, which ravaged Germany in the early 17th century, left few viticultural regions unscathed, although in general the districts flanking the Rhine were worse hit than FRANKEN, where the Taubergrund bordering BADEN may even have escaped altogether. Everywhere vineyards were laid waste and cellars plundered, but the real problem arose from the loss of manpower through the casualties of war: labour to work the vineyards was either no longer available, or else not at affordable wages.

The signs of crisis were already apparent in the early 16th century, however. The decline in exports of ALSACE wines is symptomatic of the difficulties. Wine consumption was dictated by FASHION, and by 1500 taste was moving away from the often spiced (see FLAVOURED WINES) white wines of Alsace towards those of the PALATINATE and the RHEINGAU, as well as to the lighter wines of Franken. At the same time, demand for heavier red wines was increasing, so that Alsace found itself having to plant more PINOT NOIR vines together with 'Lampersch' (a red wine variety from Lombardy in Italy) to compete with imports from France and the Mediterranean. Alsace was also the victim of its own success: its penetration of the Swiss market had prompted Zurich in the 15th century to ban imports in order to stimulate its own local wine industry, and it was followed in the 16th by Berne, anxious to protect the vineyards of its newly acquired territory of the Vaud on Lake Geneva. Moreover, Strasbourg's insistence later in the century on making Alsace wines a staple item of commerce and levying customs duties before onward shipment further diminished their competitiveness.

Some authorities have sought to explain the general crisis of German viticulture by vague allusions to adulteration, increases in tolls and excises, the advent of a cooler climate after 1550, and, above all, to the impact of the Reformation, which led to the dissolution of many religious houses in the Protestant territories of the empire. The underlying truth is more prosaic. The excessive expansion of vineyards up to 1500 brought about a slump in the land market by 1540, with a consequent collapse in the price of wine, much of it in any case of dismal quality, having been grown on sites quite unsuitable for viticulture.

It is no coincidence that the widespread agrarian rebellion of 1525 known as the German Peasants' War was concentrated in the wine-growing areas, where the peasantry had been exposed to the fluctuations of the market, demands by lords for higher taxes on its crop, and the need to subdivide holdings into unprofitably small parcels by the laws of partible inheritance (see BURGUNDY, history), and yet was compelled to cling to its foothold in commercialized viticulture for want of alternative employment.

Throughout the century viticulture retreated from the cooler, more remote valleys; poor-quality vineyards in the plains were abandoned in favour of slopes with better exposure and drainage. In Alsace, for example, only the vineyards along the foothills of the Vosges from Thann to Marlenheim survived, still the core of viticulture today. All the same, the decline was gradual—and the survivors on the better sites may have prospered. The peripheral vineyards in Hesse, the Swabian uplands, Upper Franken, and Bavaria disappeared around 1600, some not until the Thirty Years War itself, although vineyards in the Lahn valley well to the north of Frankfurt survived into the 18th century. In 1600 there were still 432 identifiable wine-producing villages in Thuringia in eastern Germany.

As the century wore on, however, the demand for grain for bread and brewing swelled, so that corn prices outstripped wine prices, and much land reverted to tillage. Nevertheless, on the eve of the Thirty Years War around 350,000 ha / 865,000 acres of land in Germany were still under vines, over four times the extent of viticulture today.

The picture of unrelieved gloom, therefore, needs to be qualified. Certain wine-growing regions were actually flourishing in the 16th century. In WÜRTTEMBERG, most strikingly, 13,500 ha / 33,000 acres of new vineyards were planted between 1514 and 1568, more than twice the present total area of viticulture. Its ruler, Duke Christopher (1550–68), even planned to make the upper reaches of the Neckar navigable in order to promote exports. Moreover, Württemberg's achievements were emulated elsewhere. In the early 17th century the SACHSEN vineyards were rearranged 'in the manner of Württemberg', which seems to have implied terracing, and the planting of vines in rows of unmixed vine varieties. The Saxon prince-electors hired Swabian vignerons to advise on planting—one was sent from Bad Cannstatt just outside Stuttgart in 1623—and cuttings from Württemberg vines were also imported. This at least raises the possibility that Saxony was intent upon making red wine in significant quantities. More generally, the 16th century witnessed the rediscovery and printing of CLASSICAL TEXTS on horticulture and agriculture. How widely their precepts were applied is hard to say, but by 1600 the three basic stages of vineyard work—pruning, binding, and weeding—had been commonly elaborated into as many as 10 stages, with particular attention paid to TRELLIS SYSTEMS and CANOPY MANAGEMENT.

A first classification Although the use of individual site names to distinguish quality (as opposed merely to identifying different vineyards) was largely unknown before 1800, there is one striking instance of ranking by quality in this period. In 1644 the council of Würzburg in Franken classified the city's vineyards into four groups. In the first class were included steeply sloping sites such as Abtsleite, (Innere)

German history: Four methods of vine training in early 16th century Alsace: up a tree (front left), in a tunnel shape (centre), on a horizontal overhead trellis (front right), and up a stake (background).

Leiste, and Stein, which are still among the premier vineyards today, whereas the low-lying vineyards by the river Main were assigned without exception to the third and fourth classes.

The improvement of Franconian viticulture owed much to the great Counter-Reformation bishop of Würzburg Julius Echter von Mespelbrunn (r. 1573–1617), who founded the city's Juliusspital in 1576 and endowed it with top-class vineyards. After him is named the eponymous Julius-Echter-Berg site in Ipfhofen, whose planting he promoted. The 16th century also saw greater emphasis on better-quality white varieties. As Hieronymus Bock's *Kräuterbuch* (Herbal) noted in 1551, the great RIESLING vine was planted throughout the RHINE and MOSEL, and in Alsace; MUSCAT vines were likewise widely grown, and in Alsace itself the TRAMINER was joined by several varieties of KLEVNER, corresponding to PINOT BLANC and Pinot AUXERROIS. The CHASSELAS grape, known in German as Gutedel, also made its first appearance in the 16th century. Together, these plantings helped to reduce reliance on the poor-quality ELBLING. Red wine, too, remained common: the Italian writer on viticulture Andrea Bacci at the end of the 16th century noted red wines in the Palatinate (in the Speyergau and Wormsgau), while the mild red wines of Marlenheim, Ottrott, and St Hippolyte in Alsace enjoyed a high reputation. T.S.

Bibliographical note: There is no reliable survey in English. Readers of German may consult, in addition to Bassermann-Jordan and Hahn, cited above, W. Lutz, 'Die Geschichte des Weinbaus in Würzburg im Mittelalter und in der Neuzeit bis 1800', *Mainfränkische Hefte*, 43 (Würzburg, 1965); R. Weinhold, 'Winzerarbeit an Elbe, Saale und Unstrut', *Akademie der Wissenschaften der DDR. Zentralinstitut für Geschichte: Veröffentlichungen zur Volkskunde und Kulturgeschichte*, 55 (Berlin, 1973); K. H. Schröder, 'Weinbau und Siedlung in Württemberg', *Forschungen dur deutschen Landerkunde*, 73 (Remagen, 1953).

Recovery and improvement, 1650–1800

The recovery of German viticulture after the depredations of the Thirty Years War was slow and painful. Only FRANKEN (Franconia), which had been the scene of fierce fighting in the 1630s, experienced a swift recuperation in vineyards and wine prices in the 1650s. In the PALATINATE viticulture was not fully restored until the 1710s. There many growers, despairing of making a decent living, emigrated to America in the mid 17th century. The region was further afflicted by the wars of Louis XIV of France from 1674 to 1700, as indeed were districts on the left bank of the Rhine as a whole, including the MOSEL.

Only with the dynastic union of the two Wittelsbach lines in 1777, thereby uniting the Palatinate with Bavaria, did its wines find a ready export market in its sister territory. The vineyards of BADEN and WÜRTTEMBERG, which had suffered least the previous century, may have declined by as much as 80 per cent by the end of the 18th century. In ALSACE, however, the loss of manpower was partly compensated by policies to encourage immigration from France, Lorraine, and Switzerland. The ceding of Alsace to France by the Peace of Westphalia in 1648 and the subsequent loss of Strasbourg in 1681 had no significant impact on the region's viticulture, since the customs frontier remained the crest of the Vosges rather than the Rhine until the French Revolution.

Efforts to improve viticulture from the late 17th century onwards pursued a double strategy: to encourage the planting of better-quality grape varieties, often on selected new sites, while at the same time prohibiting the clearing of land for vines where only poor quality could be expected. In what is now the MOSEL-SAAR-RUWER, for instance, the Abbey of St Maximin had been replanting at Grünhaus on the RUWER since 1695; as many as 100,000 new cuttings, it has been reckoned, were put down. But at the other end of the scale, more land was constantly being taken in by small growers, so that the prince-archbishops of Trier issued an edict in 1720 banning the clearing of forest for new vineyards.

In 1750 another decree enjoined the production of natural, unsugared ('naturrein') wines, and in 1786 the last archbishop-elector, Clemens Wenceslas (r. 1768–1801), a keen champion of viticulture, ordered that inferior grapes be grubbed up and replaced with the RIESLING vine. Thirteen years earlier he had endowed the diocesan seminary (Priesterseminar) with vineyards, which, together with the bishop's hostel (Bischöfliches Konvikt), founded in 1653, and the chapter of Trier cathedral (Hohe Domkirche), made up a trio of charitable owners whose estates on the Mosel achieved worldwide renown. At Bingen, the archbishop of Mainz decreed in 1697 that the famous Scharlachberg ('scarlet slope', perhaps because it once grew red wines) be planted exclusively with Riesling.

Likewise in the Rheingau, Constantine, prince-abbot of the ancient Hessian convent of Fulda, which had acquired the site and castle of Johannisberg (see SCHLOSS JOHANNISBERG), ordered the replanting of the vineyards with Riesling and Orléans (probably PINOT NOIR) vines in the 1760s. In this period the sources begin to distinguish the quality of Rhine wines according to village or, on occasion, site. Johann Valentin Kauppers in his *De natura . . . vini Rhenani* of 1703 gave pride of place to the RHEINGAU, with Rüdesheim as the best commune, but he also praised the wines of Oppenheim and Pfeddersheim in the modern region of RHEINHESSEN. The vineyards adjacent to the church of St Mary's at Worms, the Liebfrauenstift, from which the name LIEBFRAUMILCH is taken, are also mentioned by several authors.

In southern Germany several more famous Franken vineyards, for example in Escherndorf, came to prominence in the 18th century. The appeal of Franconian wine was undoubtedly heightened from this period by its being bottled in distinctive round flat flagons, known as BOCKSBEUTEL. In Baden, Margrave Karl Friedrich (1746–1811) strove energetically to improve viticulture in his territories. Local vignerons were sent to learn new techniques both in Germany, in the Rheingau and on the Mosel, and abroad, in Burgundy and Champagne. As well as promulgating a law against the adulteration of wine in 1752, he experimented with Riesling on the Klingelberg below his castle of Staufenberg by Baden-Baden (hence the name 'Klingelberger' for Riesling in the Ortenau). He also promoted TRAMINER (confusingly called Klevener in Baden), and brought in Gutedel, or CHASSELAS, cuttings from Lake Geneva.

Vine varieties In Alsace improvement owed nothing to the French crown, everything to local initiatives by institutions such as the Jesuit College at Sélestat, which began to plant Riesling in 1756 in place of lesser vines. Alsace saw the development of two new varieties in the 18th century. In 1756 Johann Michael Ortlieb of Riquewihr pioneered an early ripening clone of RÄUSCHLING, the Kleiner (small) Räuschling (also known as Ortlieber or, in Alsace, as KNIPPERLÉ). In 1740 the mayor of Heiligenstein by Barr, Erhard Wantz, introduced a new variety under the name of Klevener (already a common vine name in Alsace) which appears to have been a red TRAMINER grape producing white wines, probably the non-aromatic form of GEWÜRZTRAMINER (see also SAVAGNIN). To this day 'Clevner de Heiligenstein', or Klevener de Heiligenstein, is found uniquely in Alsace and is locally adapted Traminer.

In much of southern Germany Silvaner was displacing ELBLING, but the real innovation was the development of PINOT GRIS by Johann Seger Ruland in Speyer around 1711. This grape, called in Germany Ruländer after its propagator, was known—mysteriously—in Alsace as Tokay. It has nothing to do with the Hungarian wine TOKAY, or with Emperor Charles V's commander, Lazarus von Schwendi, who is alleged to have brought the vine back from his campaigns in Hungary to his estates in Alsace. However, the name Tokay was used from the mid 18th century in Baden and Württemberg to denote the low-quality Hungarian varietal Putschera, which has long since vanished from Germany. Although it spread quickly, the Ruländer suffered a rapid decline because its early ripening meant that its harvest could not be held back until the later maturing Riesling, so that peasant growers preferred to let it rot rather than gather it early only to have to deliver up a fine wine as a tithe to their feudal lords. Not until tithing was abolished in the wake of the French Revolution did Ruländer establish its rightful place among German wines of distinction.

The 17th and 18th centuries also saw the first attempts

to make specially selected or late-picked wines. The term CABINET to indicate a wine of reserve quality is first encountered at KLOSTER EBERBACH in the Rheingau in 1712. The picking of individual ripe berries off the stalks (*Abrappen*) was also deployed, particularly with Traminer grapes, to make what were in effect AUSLESEN, although the wines were relatively short lived. Nevertheless, the potential of picking grapes affected by NOBLE ROT was well recognized by the early 18th century.

Despite these advances, the period up to 1800 was a troubled one for German wine in export markets. Cologne and Frankfurt maintained their leading role in overseas trade, and the 18th century witnessed the first wine auctions of quality wines. Cologne's merchants were proud of their adherence to the oenological equivalent of the brewing purity laws (Reinheitsgebot), which forbade blending Rhine wines with those from the south, especially France and Italy. Yet their stranglehold on the market in Rhenish wines was challenged in the 1670s when English merchants began to buy at source. Even so, England was a languishing market for German wine in the 18th century, although Alsace succeeded in recapturing much of its market in Switzerland. T.S.

Bibliographical note: There is no reliable survey in English. For readers of German, Bassermann-Jordan, cited above, remains an indispensable guide but some information may be gleaned from O. W. Loeb and T. Prittie, *Moselle* (London, 1972).

The rise of modern viticulture, 1800–1900

The French Revolution and its aftermath wrought profound changes in German viticulture. During the Revolution itself the PALATINATE was invaded—Landau in the heart of today's southern PFALZ was besieged five times—and occupied, although in the succeeding Napoleonic Wars it was barely affected. At the Congress of Rastatt in 1797, whose decisions were ratified by the Treaty of Lunéville four years later, the whole of Germany on the left bank of the Rhine was ceded to France, which proceeded to reorganize the region's administration into four departments.

The patchwork of diminutive principalities was swept away: in 1792 the Palatinate had been split among 44 territorial lords. Though the Rhine tolls were retained in a much rationalized form by the French state, land tolls were altogether abolished (thereby foreshadowing the free trade of the league of Rhenish states in the Rheinbund era from 1806 to 1813), as were tithes, which gave peasant growers an incentive to plant good-quality vine varieties. On the MOSEL these political upheavals led to around one-fifth of the vineyards, many of them owned by the Church, changing hands, and once the estates of the empire had agreed upon the abolition of all ecclesiastical principalities at the diet of Regensburg in 1803, another 25 per cent came under new ownership.

Although after the fall of Napoleon the Church regained some of its estates, a new and substantial class of peasant and bourgeois vineyard proprietors had been created. On the right bank of the Rhine in the RHEINGAU, Johannisberg (see SCHLOSS JOHANNISBERG) passed through several hands, including Napoleon's general Marshal Kellermann, before it fell to Austria at the Congress of Vienna in 1815 and was bestowed upon the then Foreign Minister Prince Metternich, in whose family it still remains. On the Main, the estates of the prince-bishops of Würzburg in FRANKEN, or Franconia, were acquired after a short interlude by the Bavarian crown in 1816.

In ALSACE, however, the repercussions of the Revolution were quite different. Once it had become part of the French customs area, growers hastened to increase production in order to capitalize upon a huge internal market. The result was the renewed planting of inferior vine varieties on low-lying sites: in 1848 vineyards were once again in evidence at Huningue, Landser, Mulhouse, Andolsheim, and Neuf-Brisach. Moreover, the imposition by France of tolls on foreign wines hurt Alsace in particular, since it elicited reprisals from Baden, Württemberg, and Switzerland, all still important customers for Alsace wines.

At the Congress of Vienna the political map of Germany was redrawn. The Mosel became a province of Prussia; RHEINHESSEN (west of the Rhine) was absorbed into the grand duchy of Hesse-Darmstadt; the Rheingau fell to the dukes of Nassau; and what remained of the Palatinate, the Pfalz proper, was reunited with Bavaria. From 1805/6 Saxony (see SACHSEN) and WÜRTTEMBERG had been elevated to kingdoms, BADEN to a grand duchy. The regulation of customs dues between these independent states became a matter of urgent necessity. The wines of the Mosel enjoyed a short-lived preference in the markets of northern Germany, but, once Prussia had concluded a bilateral customs union with Hesse-Darmstadt in 1828, they faced competition from Rheinhessen wines.

When Bavaria and Württemberg joined Prussia to create the general customs union (Zollverein) of 1834, followed by Baden and Hesse-Darmstadt the next year, all the major wine-growing districts were in open competition with each other. As a result, the better wines prevailed, and the market in lesser wines collapsed, although at least the Zollverein enabled German wines to compete on more favourable terms in the domestic market with French wines, especially those from BORDEAUX, which had begun to reach the north German cities in huge quantities in the 1820s. Baden and Württemberg were the worst hit by the new competition. In Baden the tithe was abolished in 1833, but the area under cultivation constantly receded, and many vignerons emigrated to Algeria or Venezuela.

The development of the transport network, above all the railways, allowed rapid and easy distribution of the better wines from the more favoured regions, so that Württemberg's production declined by 40 per cent in the 19th century. Franken, too, suffered because of Bavaria's link with the Palatinate; the area under vines shrank by 60 per cent between 1850 and 1900. Franconian farmers switched to other crops, chiefly clover and hops, hence the irresistible rise of the Franconian brewing industry in this period.

Only the foundation of the German empire in 1871, however, put an end to all internal customs barriers. Yet the reabsorption of Alsace and Lorraine (see MOSELLE) in that year brought little relief to wine-growers there. Alsace may have constituted 26 per cent of German vineyards yielding 39 per cent of production after 1871, but its wines were threatened by imports of cheap wines from France, sweetened wines from across the Rhine, and preferential trade treaties signed by Germany with Austria and Italy in 1891 and with Spain in 1893.

Quality in the ascendant Quality of production became the central concern of German vine-growers and administrators after 1800. The beginnings of QUALITY DELIMITATION can be traced to the 1830s; the Palatinate, for example, instituted a highly unwieldy system which embraced 65 classes of quality, although elsewhere the categories were fewer and simpler. Wine ordinances in the German states began to prescribe that grapes of different levels of ripeness should be harvested separately. Their measurement was greatly facilitated by systems for weighing the must to achieve a specific MUST WEIGHT, developed first by the Württemberg scientist J. J. Reuss, but much refined in the 1830s by the Pforzheim physicist Ferdinand OECHSLE, whose system is still in use today.

Growers' associations for the improvement of wines and viticulture were founded in many German territories. Some of the earliest, strikingly enough, were not in the main growing areas but in eastern Germany in SACHSEN or Saxony (1799–1801) and at Jena in Thuringia (1829). In 1825 an association for the whole of Württemberg was set up, followed by similar societies in the 1830s in Franken and for the MOSEL-SAAR-RUWER. A general German Wine-Growers' Association, however, had to wait until 1874.

The state authorities, moreover, played a vital role by establishing schools of viticultural research and teaching. Württemberg was the pioneer in 1860 with its academy at Weinsberg, followed by Prussia's establishment of the institute at GEISENHEIM in 1870, after it had annexed the Rheingau from Nassau in 1867. The Hessian wine academy at Oppenheim dates from 1885; in 1899 citizens of Neustadt an der Weinstrasse founded a wine school to serve the Palatinate; and the Nahe acquired a Prussian academy in 1902. These endeavours were underpinned by the creation of state domains (see DOMÄNE), committed to the highest standards of viticulture. The earliest was set up by Baden at Meersburg on Lake Constance in 1802, followed shortly thereafter by the Bavarian state domain in Würzburg. After its acquisition of Nassau, Prussia formed a state domain at Eberbach, the KLOSTER EBERBACH, from its abbatial estates throughout the Rheingau. At the end of the century Prussia established further state domains: on the Moselle at Avelsbach in 1896, with estates on the Saar at Ockfen, and on the Nahe at Niederhausen in 1902.

The emphasis on quality, however, placed the smaller peasant growers in a quandary. Without the capital to invest in better vines and wine-making equipment, they were left with inferior grape varieties on poorer sites in a shrinking market. The only solution, albeit imperfect, was to seek safety in numbers by banding together in CO-OPERATIVES. The first such growers' union was formally established on the river AHR in 1869; similar attempts in the 1850s on the Mosel only bore fruit in 1896 with the co-operative at Gonsdorf, followed by Trier in 1897. By then the co-operative movement had spread to Baden, where three associations were set up between 1881 and 1897 on Lake Constance. Other parts of Germany were quick to follow suit. The greater financial and marketing power which collective vinification, storage, and distribution permitted tided many small growers over in the crisis years of the early 20th century, when the bulk of modern co-operatives were founded.

For viticulture in general, however, the century did not end on a confident note. Structurally, viticulture fell victim to Germany's late industrialization, which sucked labour into the cities; wages rose in what was already a labour-intensive industry, and the hardest hit were the producers of better-quality wines, for their vineyards were usually the most arduous to work. In terms of marketing, the industry was torn between the lure of the controlled addition of sugar, pioneered by the chemist Ludwig Gall (the German counterpart to Jean CHAPTAL in France), which helped to make thin, sour wines from sun-starved soils saleable (see CHAPTALIZATION), and the reputation which attached to untreated, 'naturrein' wines. The first national Wine Law of 1892 had permitted controlled sugaring, but the Imperial Wine Law of 1909 restricted sugaring to 20 per cent of the undiluted wine.

One answer was to turn the more acidic vintages into sparkling wine, known in German as SEKT, which by the 1840s was being produced as far afield as the Rhine, Mosel, Württemberg, and Saxony. With some good vintages in the 1860s, Sekt had become a highly popular drink in Germany by the late 19th century.

The true threat to German viticulture, however, lay in VINE PESTS and VINE DISEASES. The commonest fungal disease, DOWNY MILDEW, was able to flourish because the chemicals to combat it had not yet been discovered. Most ominous of all, the PHYLLOXERA louse (*Reblaus* in German) first appeared in German vineyards in the Ahr valley in 1881, spreading continuously thereafter to all wine regions. Only recently has it been fully eradicated. T.S.

The 20th century wine industry

The first half of the 20th century was a period of deep recession in the German wine industry. The area under vines shrank still further, from around 90,000 ha/220,000 acres in 1914 to less than 50,000 ha/123,000 acres in 1945. Both World Wars placed severe strains on Germany's domestic economy and caused considerable dislocation in its export markets. Exports had reached a peak of 190,000 hl/5 million gal by 1914, but in the aftermath of the First World War the situation was bleak.

The major growing regions on the left bank of the Rhine were occupied by France until 1929. In the PFALZ region, moreover, the activities of separatist groups severely disrupted civilian life up to 1924, which hit the wine industry in particular. The raging inflation of the Weimar period brought economic hardship to many growers, especially the smaller proprietors. In addition, growers had to face unprecedented competition under the terms of the Versailles Treaty, which obliged Germany to allow 260,000 hl/6.8 million gal of French wine to enter the country each year duty free; it also imposed a further duty-free quota for LUXEMBOURG wines, as compensation for her withdrawal from the German Customs Union in 1918. The flood of imports undercut the prices which German producers could charge; many growers faced bankruptcy, and by 1928 exports had collapsed to no more than 39,000 hl/1 million gal per annum.

The Nazi era helped to revive domestic consumption of German wine, but the National Socialist policy of subordinating all private associations to state control (*Gleichschaltung*) meant, for the wine industry, that all independent professional bodies of brokers, merchants, and growers were abolished and replaced by a single Union of Viticulture under one president, thereby destroying the enterprise and initiative of individual growers and regional wine associations. The end of the Second World War heralded the return of some of the consequences of the First. German growers faced a shortage of labour but an abundance of cheap imports from France, Algeria, and Hungary. In their zone of occupation in the Pfalz, the French requisitioned wine on a grand scale, either without compensation or at knock-down prices, through their economic administration in Bingen, Officomex. Although Officomex was disbanded in 1949, the French retained control of the Saar until it was returned to Germany by plebiscite in 1956.

Those German growers and merchants who survived the grim decades after 1900 did so because they had learned from the advances of the late 19th century. These years were the heyday of the co-operative movement, which saved many small growers from extinction. By 1900 there were already over 100 CO-OPERATIVES in Germany, and that figure had risen by 1950 to 483, embracing over 35,000 growers. In Baden, for instance, a region dominated by co-operatives, what was then the largest ZENTRALKELLEREI in Europe, already with a capacity of 120,000 hl/3 million gal, was opened at Breisach in 1952.

Individual growers, too, had long banded together to promote the quality and reputation of their own districts. In the Palatinate, the largest estates of the middle Haardt agreed in 1904 to use the term 'Naturwein' for unsweetened wine: from that accord sprang four years later the Association of Unsugared Wine Auctioneers of the Rheinpfalz. It was followed in 1910 by a similar union of growers of the MOSEL-SAAR-RUWER, who conducted AUCTIONS as the 'Great Circle' (GROSSER RING), selling only 'natur' wines from a delimited quality area stretching from Trittenheim to Erden. Shortly thereafter the national Association of Unsugared Wine Auctioneers (Verband Deutscher Naturweinversteigerer) was formed. The provincial authorities of the wine-producing states remained committed to quality in adverse circumstances. Both the Franconian Viticultural Research Institute at Veitshöchheim in FRANKEN and the Wine Academy at Ahrweiler in the AHR (for the Rhine Province of Prussia) were founded in 1902, followed by the BADEN State Institute of Viticulture at Freiburg in 1920. In 1950 the Academy of the Oenological Research Station of the Ortenau was founded at Schloss Ortenberg in Baden.

By contrast, the parlous state of exports in the 1930s persuaded some merchants, principally those trading to the United Kingdom, to try to increase sales by marketing BRANDS, which could contain more than one grape variety, were sourced from more than one region of production, and were usually sweetened. This is the origin of LIEBFRAUMILCH. With these wines the aim was to achieve a commercially acceptable wine, rather than one which conformed to strictly defined criteria of quality and authenticity. Despite the success of brands such as SICHEL's Blue Nun in certain foreign markets, they are rarely seen within Germany itself.

Undoubtedly the most significant step forward for German viticulture in the first half of the century was the Wine Law of 1930, which went far towards rectifying the deficiencies of the 1909 law. It provided a clear definition of what constituted a natural, as opposed to a sweetened, wine, forbade the blending of red and white, and of German and foreign, wines, and outlawed the planting and sale of wines made from hybrids of American and European vine varieties. Notwithstanding frequent amendments, the 1930 Wine Law remained the legal basis of German wine-growing until the major GERMAN WINE LAW of 1971, which brought Germany into alignment with other member states of the EUROPEAN UNION.

Viticulture Between 1950 and 1990 German viticulture underwent a dramatic transformation. The area under vine once again expanded steadily, and in 1990 was more than 81,000 ha/over 200,000 acres, although the figure is unlikely to rise much further unless it is decided to restore the vineyards of eastern Germany in the SACHSEN and SAALE-UNSTRUT regions which were marginalized during the German Democratic Republic's 40 years of existence.

But the most startling development was the increase in YIELDS. At the beginning of the century the average of 20 hl/ha (1.1 tons/per acre) was no more than what might have been expected of an abundant vintage in any preceding century. By 1950 that had doubled to 40 hl/ha, and by the advent of the Wine Law of 1971 the yields had doubled again, and by the 1980s frequently exceeded 100 hl/ha (5.7 tons/acre), although more discriminating growers crop less heavily.

These results were achieved in three main ways: by more efficient vineyard techniques, including the use of FUNGICIDES and PESTICIDES; by selecting disease-resistant and better-cropping vine CLONES; and by developing new vine varieties which will ripen (and can therefore be harvested) earlier, or else which are more resistant to FROST (see GERMAN CROSSINGS).

These viticultural innovations have been accompanied from the 1950s by a radical restructuring of German vineyards, known as FLURBEREINIGUNG, whereby the myriad diminutive and often barely accessible plots of vines have been rationalized into larger, consolidated sites with better drainage and access routes. The number of individual sites has been substantially pruned, and since the German Wine Law of 1971 a new vineyard register has been compiled, listing and delimiting each individual site (EINZELLAGE) and each grouped or collective site (GROSSLAGE) within defined districts (BEREICHE) of larger regions of production (ANBAUGEBIETE).

Despite these advances, the outlook for German wines is uncertain. The industry remains uneasily poised between what one might call the quantity-directed and quality-directed sectors. The quantity sector is dominated by merchants and shippers, catering for a largely foreign market in inexpensive and undistinguished white wines made from high-yielding varieties, while the quality sector, upheld by the leading private estates, emphasizes the subtlety and individuality which can be achieved on the best sites from noble varieties, particularly RIESLING. German wines are at present out of fashion among wine-lovers; if they are to come back into favour, it is reasonable to assume that quality rather than quantity will restore their reputation. T.S.

Hallgarten, S. F., *German Wine* (London, 1976).
Langenbach, A., *German Wines and Vines* (London, 1962).
Loeb, O. W., and Prittie, T., *Moselle* (London, 1972).

GERMAN WINE LAW has until recently been a source of pride for German wine producers. In its fifth generation, however, it was an animal bred with particular care in 1971 but which grew fairly rapidly into a monster which many of the best wine producers in GERMANY have since done their best to amend or ignore. The German Wine Law of 1971 substantially updated the 1930 Wine Law (see GERMAN HISTORY), particularly in vineyard rationalization, and was precipitated by the demands of the EUROPEAN UNION wine regime. Compared to the anarchic chaos of Italy's wine-labelling habits, and the convoluted geography of France's APPELLATION CONTRÔLÉE (AC) system, the German Wine Law of 1971 was a marvel of precision. Each vineyard is delineated and registered (see EINZELLAGE) and its produce can be used to make wine at any quality level, depending not at all on YIELDS but on the ripeness, or MUST WEIGHT, of the grapes.

The least ripe grapes qualify as Deutscher TAFELWEIN, or table wine, which represents less than five per cent of all wine produced in a typical German vintage (and less than one per cent in the period 1988–90). All the rest is graded as QUALITY WINE according to the generous terms of the German Wine Law, and in EU terms is therefore seen as the equal of France's AC wine. German officials make much of the fact that every quality wine is analysed and tasted and has to earn its AP NUMBER, but the failure rate is so low as to cast doubt on this highly bureaucratic 'control'.

The bottom layer of Germany's quality wine is made from grapes whose ripeness qualifies for QBA status, a 'quality wine from a specified region'. This is the main category under which most German wine is sold. Wines made from riper grapes, however, are qualified as QMP, 'quality wine with distinction': the riper the grapes, the higher the official Prädikat or distinction (and selling price), rising from KABINETT through SPÄTLESE, AUSLESE, BEERENAUSLESE, TROCKENBEERENAUSLESE, to EISWEIN. This category accounts for between seven per cent (of the 1984 vintage) and 83 per cent (of the entire 1976 vintage). This emphasis on must weights was understandable in a country where the perennial challenge is to ripen grapes fully, but did little to encourage real quality and harmony in Germany's wines (see GERMANY and GERMAN HISTORY). Many quality-conscious producers themselves declassify wines from one Prädikat to a lower one, from QmP to QbA, because the wine does not reach their own personal evaluation of what constitutes, say, an Auslese.

The German Wine Law has been substantially amended since 1971. The little-used LANDWEIN category was introduced in 1982 as a German answer to France's VIN DE PAYS, and at about the same time Eiswein, with its entirely different production technique, was admitted as a Prädikat in its own right alongside Beerenauslese and Trockenbeerenauslese.

And in 1989 the German parliament agreed to comply with EU regulations to limit yields, but a measure of how much progress was still to be made was that the maximum yield proposed for the noble RIESLING vine in the supposedly noble wine region MOSEL-SAAR-RUWER was 120 hl/ha (6.8 tons/acre) (more for other grape varieties).

During 1993 much more stringent amendments were proposed, for enactment in time for the 1994 vintage. The maximum permitted yields are to be calculated for each grower strictly on the basis of the actual area in production rather than, as in the past in some regions, on the basis of the area owned, and were instituted for QbA wines at no more than average production for the previous 10 years. There are additional controls on SURPLUS wine and greater enforcement of compulsory DISTILLATION, although individual growers can elect to produce nothing but Deutscher Tafelwein, in which case there are no yield controls other than those imposed directly by EU authorities.

More significantly, the minimum MUST WEIGHTS required for various Prädikats in Ahr, Mittelrhein, Mosel-Saar-Ruwer, Saale-Unstrut, and Sachsen were raised, and there were moves to substitute a much clearer labelling system whereby the consumer could tell at a glance whether a wine comes from a single site or Einzellage, or a collective site signalled on the label either as one of the old GROSSLAGE, or as one of the newer URSPRUNGSLAGEN.

GERMANY. Grape growing in Germany is a small but prestigious part of the whole country's farming industry. The financial turnover represented by wine is a little greater than that of cut flowers or eggs, but considerably less than the figure for sugar beet. Whilst a small part of the grape harvest results in wines of exquisite finesse, unique in style to Germany, over half the crop is sold on price, and not on quality. There are individual vineyard sites, EINZELLAGEN, in part or all of which superior grapes can be harvested nearly every year, but the trail that leads to the best German wines is discovered most easily through the name of the producer. Only a little skill is needed to make acceptable wines in a warm MEDITERRANEAN CLIMATE in which grapes will always fully ripen. In the cooler weather of northern Europe (see CONTINENTALITY) the cheapest wines can also be made according to a more or less unchanging recipe, but producing fine

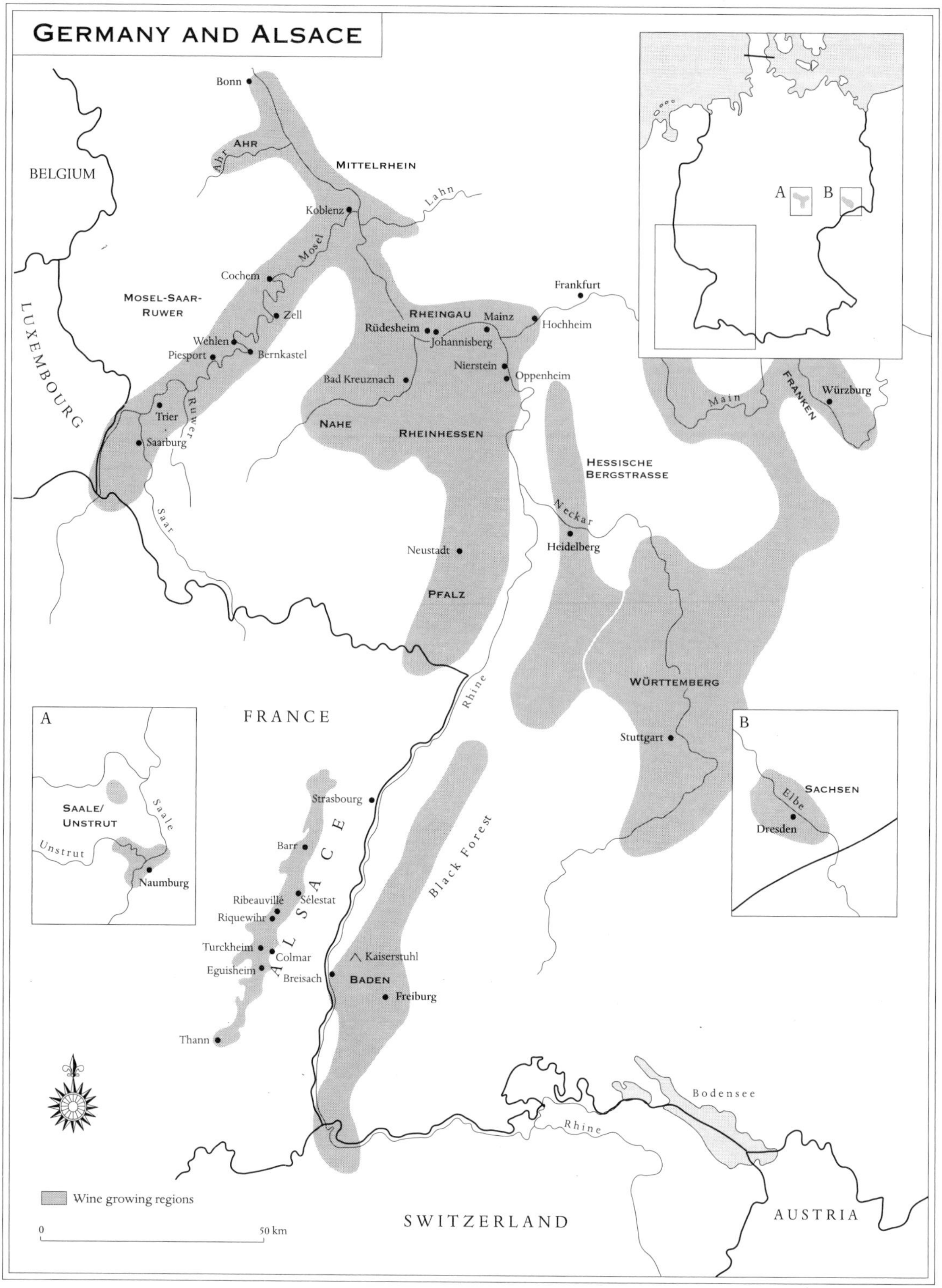
GERMANY AND ALSACE
Bonn
AHR
Ahr
MITTELRHEIN
BELGIUM
Lahn
Koblenz
Mosel
Cochem
MOSEL-SAAR-
RUWER
LUXEMBOURG
Zell
Wehlen
Piesport
Bernkastel
Trier
Ruwer
Saarburg
Saar
RHEINGAU
Rüdesheim
Johannisberg
Mainz
Hochheim
Frankfurt
Bad Kreuznach
Nierstein
Oppenheim
NAHE
RHEINHESSEN
HESSISCHE
BERGSTRASSE
Neckar
Heidelberg
Neustadt
PFALZ
Main
FRANKEN
Würzburg
WÜRTTEMBERG
Stuttgart
A
B
FRANCE
Rhine
SAALE/
UNSTRUT
Saale
Unstrut
Naumburg
SACHSEN
Elbe
Dresden
Strasbourg
ALSACE
Barr
Ribeauvillé
Sélestat
Riquewihr
Turckheim
Colmar
Eguisheim
Breisach
Thann
Black Forest
Kaiserstuhl
BADEN
Freiburg
Bodensee
Rhine
Wine growing regions
0
50 km
SWITZERLAND
AUSTRIA

wines in Germany requires not only technical ability, but imagination and a dedication to excellence. It is upon the lustre and prestige of the names associated with the best wines, both geographical and qualitative, that many cheaper versions have been allowed to draw since the 1970s, devaluing the official quality system in Germany in the process.

History

See GERMAN HISTORY.

Geography and climate

Over the centuries the German vineyard has expanded and contracted, often in response to the price and availability of corn. See GERMAN HISTORY and map on p. 431. Many of Germany's best vineyards are on the steepest slopes, quite unsuited to anything other than the vine. Overlooking the rivers RHINE, Neckar, Main, Nahe, Ahr, MOSEL and its tributaries, their high cost of cultivation is justified only by the quality of the wine they can produce. In the steep vineyards three times as many man-hours are spent tending the vine as is the case on flat or rolling terrain, where the natural position of the vine-grower is on the seat of a tractor.

Several other factors limit MECHANIZATION in the vineyards, amongst which are the smallness of the holdings and the principle of grape selection. Vine-growing in Germany was once the work of peasants, controlled by the Church and the nobility. Statistically, it has now become a mainly female, mainly part-time occupation, based on an average holding of a little over a hectare (2.47 acres), or a quarter of the equivalent figure for France. Nearly two-thirds of the working German population are entitled to a minimum of six weeks' annual holiday, a proportion of which for most part-time vineyard owners is likely to be absorbed by the lengthy grape HARVEST. The majority do not make wine but supply grapes to merchants or, more likely, to the CO-OPERATIVE cellars which receive the crop from 37 per cent of the total German vineyard of about 100,000 ha/247,000 acres. Contrary to the situation in France and Italy, Germany's wine production and consumption are more or less in balance. She is by far the largest importer of wine in the European Union and yet, having deducted consumption and exports of wine from the amounts that she produced and imports, the surplus remaining is in most years only about two per cent of her own annual harvest. (In France and Italy, the main contributors to the European WINE LAKE, excess wine amounts to more than a quarter of the total production.)

For more geographical detail, see map on p. 442 and see entries under the names of individual wine regions which are, in declining area of total vineyard, RHEINHESSEN, PFALZ, BADEN, MOSEL-SAAR-RUWER, WÜRTTEMBERG, FRANKEN, NAHE, RHEINGAU, MITTELRHEIN, AHR, HESSISCHE BERGSTRASSE, SACHSEN, and SAALE-UNSTRUT. Most German wine labels carry the name of the region in which the wine was produced.

Viticulture

The vine-growing regions of the EUROPEAN UNION are divided into climatically different zones. In Germany, Baden shares Zone B with a number of French regions including Alsace, Champagne, and the Loire valley. Although the remaining German regions are all in Zone A, their MACROCLIMATES and MESOCLIMATES are perhaps the most varied of all the world's vineyards. Even within one single site or Einzellage, variations of the mesoclimate can produce a difference in ALCOHOLIC STRENGTH of over 1.5 per cent in wine of the same vine variety, harvested at the same time in different parts of the vineyard. According to research at GEISENHEIM, the average alcohol content of wine of the same vineyard can vary from one vintage to another by over six per cent. The degree of LATITUDE, TOPOGRAPHICAL features such as a favourable exposition to the sun, no danger from frequent cold winds or damaging frosts, and the ALTITUDE are some of the factors which in Germany's position in northern Europe influence the quality of its viticulture.

Some seven per cent of Germany's vines are individually supported by POSTS, a system followed mainly in the Mosel-Saar-Ruwer region. Elsewhere, they are trained on WIRES in rows, of which over half are under 1.8 m/6 ft apart. Nearly five per cent of all vines grow on their own roots, without having been grafted on to resistant ROOTSTOCKS. Partly through the replanting involved in modernization programmes (see FLURBEREINIGUNG), only 18 per cent of the vines at the start of the 1990s were over 20 years old. Among growers whose aim is to produce top-quality fruit, PRUNING is usually to six to eight buds per square metre, depending on the variety. To produce a more concentrated must, excess bunches of grapes are removed in the months following the FLOWERING in June (see CROP THINNING). The aim in VINE TRAINING in the 1990s is not just to harvest healthy grapes, but sometimes also to reduce costs by facilitating MECHANICAL PRUNING and MECHANICAL HARVESTING. Many estates now claim to gather their grapes not according to their ripeness as expressed by their sugar content but according to their TOTAL ACIDITY. The Germans like high acidity, with a substantial amount of TARTARIC ACID being particularly welcome.

It is only following really hot summers in Germany that most of the crop will be fully ripe. Usually, at the time of picking on one bunch there will be grapes in varying states of ripeness, from relatively immature to very sweet. For some 200 years, it has often been the practice to pick bunches, or even individual grapes, at the moment when they have reached a particular level of sweetness. This process of selection cannot be other than the most manual of labour, quite beyond the scope of a mechanical harvester. On a good estate, wines from these chosen grapes are individually vinified, matured, and bottled, to form the aristocracy of the wine offered. In talking to his customers the German wine-maker likes to have a theme which he feels expresses his own personal attitude to standard wine-making practices. An ecologically aware approach to both vineyard and cellar (see ORGANIC VITICULTURE) is much discussed in the 1990s and more emphasis is now put on the quality and condition of grapes than was generally the case in the early 1980s. An expression of this is the gathering of rotten grapes before the main harvest. Here, the aim is to allow those that are left behind to ripen further without any trace of ROT, so as to produce a totally clean tasting must. This applies especially, but not exclusively, to dry white wine-making, and to modern red wines where a depth of colour is expected which rotten grapes would damage.

Wine-making

The aim of good, modern German WINE-MAKING is wine that is true to its region and vine variety. It must be clean and fruity, the result of physics rather than chemistry. On estates of not more than about 50 ha/123 acres, more care and individual attention can be given to wine-making than is possible in much larger establishments. PRESSES are set to work at not more than two atmospheres and must SETTLING in many cellars is left to the gentle force of gravity. Temperature during the white wine FERMENTATION of about eight to 10 days is kept below 20 °C/68 °F. Only the better red wines are fermented with the skins of the grapes present. In the large merchant or co-operative cellar, red wine must is often briefly heated to a high temperature to produce a light, fruity, but relatively short-lived wine (see THERMOVINIFICATION).

The use of SÜSSRESERVE or unfermented grape juice to sweeten wine is no longer so common in the cellars of private estates. If their wines have a little RESIDUAL SUGAR it is often the result of low cellar temperatures and STERILE BOTTLING FILTRATION. Great sweetness and finesse combine in AUSLESE and TROCKENBEERENAUSLESE wines produced from grapes that have been attacked by *Botrytis cinerea* that has developed into NOBLE ROT. Such grapes may be gathered at any time during the harvest. (In 1989, the PFALZ estate of Bürklin-Wolf gathered a Riesling Trockenbeerenauslese as early as 27 September.) A similar sweetness, but without the flavour or complexity of noble rot, is achieved by gathering grapes when they are frozen on the vine, to produce EISWEIN. The artificial refrigeration of grapes or wine (for example, the CRYOEXTRACTION employed on some Sauternes estates) is not allowed in Germany.

CHAPTALIZATION, or the adding of sugar to increase ALCOHOLIC STRENGTH, is permitted for TAFELWEIN and QBA but is specifically prohibited for QMP wines. DEACIDIFICATION is allowed but only in exceptionally poor vintages. ACIDIFICATION is not allowed, although it would rarely be advisable. The somewhat experimental BARREL MATURATION of white and red wine, from vine varieties which do not have the firm structure of Riesling, is common. Some regard it as an equalizer of flavour and BOUQUET. Liveliness, some CARBON DIOXIDE in white wine, is widely admired but the controversial wine-making techniques of must CONCENTRATION and deliberate OXIDATION have yet to be invited into the German cellar on any wide scale.

As a general statement it is true that difficult trading conditions since 1985, helped by some outstanding vintages such as 1989 and 1990, have improved the quality of producer-bottled wines (labelled Erzeugerabfüllung, or Gutsabfüllung, if estate bottled). Without a veil of sweetness the flavour of a wine is more clearly exposed, and the new preference for drier wines labelled TROCKEN and HALBTROCKEN, especially marked within Germany, has meant a readjustment of the way in which German white wine is popularly assessed. Sweeter wines are less fashionable and producers in the northern regions of the Rhine and Nahe are more likely to be judged by their drier Spätlese trocken, for example, which are destined to be drunk with food, than by their declining output of sweet or medium sweet wines. This change in taste has also completely revitalized the German red wine market. If the rate of progress of the late 1980s is maintained throughout the 1990s the German Spätburgunder (PINOT NOIR) could be compared to all but the best of BURGUNDY by the year 2000, assuming the Burgundians do not improve greatly on their present performance. PINOT wines, both red and white (as Weissburgunder and Grauburgunder), could well add the singularly under-represented name of BADEN to wine lists abroad in the 1990s. Of all the 13 wine-producing regions, Baden has a climate which results most easily in dry wine with a structure and a balance of acidity which, although still recognizably Germanic, resembles that of neighbouring countries. The good German red wine-maker, with few laurels to rest upon from the past, seems to have a greater experience and knowledge of what is offered on the international wine market than many of his counterparts in France. The German viticultural institutes (see GEISENHEIM, GEILWEILERHOF) have helped the wine industries of Australia, New Zealand, South Africa, and North America, and German producers have learnt from their visits to and work in the NEW WORLD.

Vine varieties and yield

As most vine varieties approach the outer edge of their climatically possible growing area there is a steep decline in the qualities that make their wine worthwhile. With RIESLING, the classic German wine, matters run differently. Near the northern edge of the vineyards in the Mosel-Saar-Ruwer, Rheingau, and Nahe, Riesling sheds all unnecessary fat. What remains is style, and structure—the analogy to an elegant, slim fashion model may be banal but it is accurate. Before the concept of quality in wine started to spread from the estates of the Church and the nobility in the 18th century, different vine varieties were not grown separately in the vineyard but mixed together in the hope that at least some would produce a crop. In these circumstances the question of grape RIPENESS was less important and, until the early 19th century, many harvests were gathered before their time, to avoid the risk of uncontrollable ROT. The attraction of Riesling was its performance in the vineyard rather than its wine. Amidst the chaos and competition of a mixed plantation, Riesling made a mark, sufficient for large estates to start growing it as a single vine. As the value of late harvesting became understood, the reputation of Riesling wine rose above that of all other white grape varieties.

If the German wine on offer until the 1960s was largely decided by the way the vine grew in the vineyard, the more ephemeral wishes of the consumer in the mass market took over thereafter, with results from which few have gained any lasting good. Difficult-to-define levels of quality have been defined in law, based purely on MUST WEIGHT, the concentration of SUGARS in the grape juice measured in degrees OECHSLE. The system is valid when applied to a single vine variety growing in a narrowly defined area but, given a broader application, it becomes increasingly unreliable, as the consumer has discovered. Public opinion and taste can change swiftly in Germany, and among many wine producers in the Rheinhessen and the Pfalz there is the feeling that the whims of the market in the last 20 years were followed too closely. Responding to this sentiment, those who sell their wine in bottle and not in the cheap, bulk wine market are showing the confidence of formal training and international experience. They are concentrating on the vine varieties that have been known in Germany for several centuries, and, where growing conditions permit, their choice will always include Riesling. In the early 1970s a producer would have spoken first of the sweetness of his grapes as shown by the must weights, but his son now talks of the amount of ACIDITY in his wine, and the modesty of the YIELD. This last risks being somewhat overdone as an indication of seriousness or purpose, for 70 hl/ha (4 tons/acre) does not automatically produce a better wine than a yield of 80 hl/ha. Some German wine producers who play mainly to a local audience susceptible to seemingly unequivocal data persuade their customers weaned on Oechsle readings that once again wine can be judged by numbers. If it were true, how handy it would be but, unfortunately, it is not—as those who make wine are perfectly well aware.

Eighty-five per cent of Germany's vineyard is planted in white vine varieties with Riesling and its offspring, MÜLLER-THURGAU together occupying 45 per cent of the total area under vine. Red vine varieties, particularly Spätburgunder, PORTUGIESER, and DORNFELDER, are spreading at the expense of some of the white wine varieties, including the less fashionable GERMAN CROSSINGS and the sadly declining SILVANER.

After the name of the producer, that of the vine variety is probably the next most important fact about a German wine. No one region has a monopoly of fine wine but there are more top producers of Germany's best-known Riesling wine in the Rheingau and the Mosel-Saar-Ruwer than anywhere else.

Wine labelling

The official EUROPEAN UNION-recognized category of table wine is TAFELWEIN and quality wine is QUALITÄTSWEIN. The latter is subdivided into simple quality wine QBA, and quality wine with distinction QMP, which embraces Kabinett, Spätlese, Auslese, Beerenauslese, and Trockenbeerenauslese wines, as well as Eiswein. Each of these 'predicates' represents very approximate differences in style and total alcohol content, rather than in true quality. Within the range offered by one producer, a Spätlese wine would normally be superior to a Kabinett wine, and be priced accordingly. However, a QbA from a top estate at DM8 per bottle will be a far better wine than a Spätlese bottled for a supermarket and sold at less than half the price. All German quality wines (some 95 per cent of the annual harvest throughout the 1980s!) are analysed by officially approved laboratories and tasted without having the name of their bottler revealed. Any serious technical faults, or deviation from the regional style, obvious at the time of examination will prevent a wine from receiving a control number (see AP NUMBER) and being sold as quality wine. The system may be open to criticism for being too lenient in its judgements, but there is no other member of the EU which has anything much better to offer on a national scale.

The Germans are a well-trained people, accustomed to dealing with experts with formal qualifications, which are often mentioned in conversation and correspondence. In the past they have grown to like their wines, other than the cheapest, to be similarly characterized. The climate may have encouraged selective grape-picking and the creation of individual wines, ostensibly with unique qualities. The result is that an estate of 10 ha/25 acres, producing about 7,000 dozen bottles annually, may well have a list of 30 or more different wines, mainly of the last two vintages to have been bottled. This multiplicity of bottlings, combined with the divided ownership of individual sites, has made it very difficult for vineyard names (other than those of a few hundred or so) to have any widely recognized meaning in terms of flavour, bouquet, or style. Reacting to this, some bottlers have abandoned the use of the names of individual sites of no particular merit. They have created their own categories of quality based, perhaps, on the age of the vine or the size or type of cask in which the wine was fermented or, more likely, matured. The range of German wine on offer is particularly complicated in the 1990s, as it includes the notions of nomenclature and quality categories of the past as well as the latest innovations based on different standards.

A CLASSIFICATION of German estates similar to that of the Médoc has been suggested by commentators and those who believe it would be to their advantage. Whereas the Bordelais in their 1855 classification were concerned with one wine only per château per year, the huge number of German estate bottlings, with their many varieties, makes a true and correct estate classification seem almost impossible. Were such a classification to be attempted, it might be an aid to sales in Germany, but beyond that its value would be questionable. Equally meaningless, other than in a few instances, would be a classification of the present individual vineyards. The variations in quality within any one site are considerable, and the worst part of a top site is often not as good as the best part of a more ordinary vineyard.

The German wine producers are faced with the fact that, if a special characteristic of a wine is individuality, by definition, the quantity available is strictly limited. Marketing efforts therefore have to be concentrated not on specific wines but on the name of the producer. German wine is better today than it has ever been before, even if finding the ideal name under which it can be sold sometimes causes difficulties. Well-known and ancient estates are expected to produce top-quality wine, but many are now willing to experiment in a limited way, while still making their classic Rieslings. Wine lovers will also be pleased by the rise of a number of relatively unknown private estates, particularly in the Pfalz.

Here, and in Baden, the new drier wines sold under a vine variety name by co-operative cellars at a fair, but not ultra-cheap, price are a good starting-point for understanding serious German wine. For most producers, marketing and not wine-making is the problem.

See also RHEINHESSEN, PFALZ, BADEN, MOSEL-SAAR-RUWER, WÜRTTEMBERG, FRANKEN, NAHE, RHEINGAU, MITTELRHEIN, AHR, HESSISCHE-BERGSTRASSE, SACHSEN, SAALE-UNSTRUT, and German BRANDY. I.J.

Bassermann-Jordan, F. von, *Geschichte des Weinbaus* ('History of viticulture') (Frankfurt, 1907).
Becker, H., *et al.*, *Der deutsche Wein* (Munich, 1978).
Hallgarten, S. F., *Rhineland Wineland* (London, 1965).
Jamieson, I., *German Wines* (London, 1991).
Pigott, S., *Life beyond Liebfraumilch* (London, 1988).

GEVREY-CHAMBERTIN, small town in the Côte de Nuits producing some of Burgundy's most famous red wines from Pinot Noir grapes. With over 500 ha / 1,200 acres under vine, including an overflow of vineyards into neighbouring Brochon, which does not have its own APPELLATION, this is the largest viticultural source in the Côte d'Or. In 1847 Gevrey annexed the name of its finest vineyard, Chambertin, somewhat tediously dubbed the king of wines and wine of kings (although it was in fact the Emperor Napoleon's favourite wine).

Gevrey-Chambertin wines are typically deeper in colour and firmer than their rivals from Vosne-Romanée and Chambolle-Musigny. Good examples may take time to develop into perhaps the richest and most complete wines of the Côte d'Or. Sadly, due to the ease with which a famous name sells, there are too many underachievers, both at VILLAGE WINE level and amongst the GRANDS CRUS.

In all Gevrey boasts eight grands crus, the pick of which are Chambertin and Chambertin Clos de Bèze. The latter, comprising 15.4 ha / 38 acres, may equally be sold as Le Chambertin. It is hard to differentiate between the two qualitatively although Clos de Bèze is slightly further up the hill than Chambertin, with a less deep soil, giving wines which are fractionally less powerful but full of sensual charm.

Le Chambertin, 12.9 ha (plus the 15.4 of Clos de Bèze), is the flagship. Theoretically the most powerful vineyard of them all, Chambertin has tended to suffer from over-production since the appellation commands such a high price. None the less, Chambertin has always been regarded as the most complete vineyard of the Côte d'Or: if not quite as sumptuous as Musigny or Richebourg, or as divinely elegant as La Tâche or Romanée-St-Vivant, Chambertin is matched only by Romanée-Conti (see VOSNE-ROMANÉE) for its completeness and its intensity.

Two other grand cru vineyards, Mazis-Chambertin and Latricières-Chambertin, lie on the same level as Chambertin and Clos de Bèze; one, Ruchottes-Chambertin, is to be found a little higher up the slope, while Charmes-Chambertin, Griotte-Chambertin, and Chapelle-Chambertin are further downhill.

Mazis-Chambertin (12.59 ha), also written Mazy-, is usually regarded as being next in quality to Chambertin and Clos de Bèze. The flavours are just as intense, the structure perhaps just a little less firm. Latricières (6.94 ha) is less powerful, although the wines are explosively fruity when young, with an entrancingly silky texture. Ruchottes (3.50 ha), thanks to a particularly thin chalky soil, is lighter in colour, angular in style, but again impressively intense. The wines are finer than those of Chapelle-Chambertin (5.39 ha), which also tends to lightness of colour.

Griotte-Chambertin (5.48 ha), which owes its name to the grill-pan shape of the vineyard rather than the griottes cherry aromas which the wine seems to have, produces wines which are better than those of neighbouring Chapelle- or Charmes-Chambertin. The latter, at 31.6 ha, is the largest grand cru in the village and, as with Clos de Vougeot and Échezeaux, its size precludes homogeneous quality. Some of the vineyard, such as the part stretching down to the main road, the RN74, should perhaps not be classified as grand cru, although a good Charmes is one of Gevrey-Chambertin's most seductive, fragrant wines when young.

Some of the grand crus are matched, if not surpassed, by the best of the premier cru vineyards, especially those with an ideal south eastern exposition such as Les Cazetiers and Clos St Jacques. Indeed Domaine Armand Rousseau, the famous name in Gevrey thanks to the eponymous Armand's pioneering DOMAINE BOTTLING in the 1930s, charges significantly more for Clos St Jacques than for several grand crus in an impressive range of wines.

See also CÔTE D'OR and its map. J.T.C.M.

GEWÜRZTRAMINER, often written **Gewurztraminer,** pink-skinned grape variety responsible for particularly pungent, full bodied white wines. Gewürztraminer may not be easy to spell, even for wine merchants, but is blissfully easy to recognize—indeed many wine drinkers find it is the first, possibly only, grape variety they are able to recognize from the wine's heady perfume alone. Deeply coloured, opulently aromatic, and fuller bodied than almost any other white wine, Gewürztraminer's faults are only in having too much of everything. It is easy to tire of its weight and its exotic flavour of lychees and heavily scented roses, although ALSACE's finest Gewürztraminers are extremely serious wines, capable of at least medium-term ageing.

This by now internationally famous vine variety's genealogy is both ramified and fascinating. Traminer, like Gewürztraminer but with pale green berries and much less scent, is the original variety, first noted in the village of Tramin or Termeno in what is now the Italian Tyrol (see ALTO ADIGE) around AD 1000. It was popular here until the 16th century, when the much more ordinary, but more prolific VERNATSCH or Schiava supplanted it.

Traminer has also been known in Alsace since the Middle Ages (see GERMAN HISTORY), although it is said to be cuttings imported much more recently from the PFALZ, the German wine region in which it was widely grown and prized for its richness, that encouraged its spread in Alsace. Today, according to GALET, the SAVAGNIN so vital to the VIN JAUNE of the

JURA is none other than Traminer, both varieties famous for their ripeness levels, depth of flavour, and ability to age.

Traminer, like PINOT, mutates easily, however, and Gewürztraminer is the name adopted in the late 19th century for the dark pink-berried MUSQUÉ mutation of Traminer (and adopted as its official name in Alsace in 1973). Although much has been read into the direct German translation of *gewürz* as 'spiced', in this context it simply means 'perfumed'. Traminer Musqué, Traminer Parfumé, and Traminer Aromatique were all at one time French synonyms for Gewürztraminer. As early as 1909 the AMPELOGRAPHER Viala acknowledged Gewürztraminer as an accepted synonym for SAVAGNIN Rosé, and this aromatic, dark-berried version is known as Roter Traminer in German and Traminer or Termeno Aromatico, Traminer Rosé, or Rosso in Italy. Its long history in Alsace means that it is occasionally known as some sort of KLEVNER, particularly in this case Rotclevner.

Gewürztraminer has become by far the most planted variant of Traminer. The grapes are certainly notable at harvest for their variegated but incontravertibly pink colour, which is translated into very deep golden wines, sometimes with a slight coppery tinge. Wine-makers unfamiliar with the variety have been known to be panicked into extracting colour and flavour. Gewürztraminers also attain higher alcohol levels than most white wines, with over 13 per cent being by no means uncommon, and acidities can correspondingly be precariously low. MALOLACTIC FERMENTATION is almost invariably suppressed for Gewürztraminer and steps must be taken to avoid OXIDATION.

If all goes well the result is deep golden, full bodied wines with a substantial spine and concentrated heady aromas whose acidity level will preserve them while those aromas unfurl. In a lesser year or too hot a climate the result is either an early-picked, neutral wine or an oppressively oily, flabby one that can easily taste bitter to boot.

Viticulturally, Gewürztraminer is not exactly a dream to grow. Relative to the varieties with which it is commonly planted, it has small bunches and is not particularly productive, although the Germans have predictably selected some high-yielding CLONES. Its early budding leaves it prey to spring frosts and it is particularly prone to VIRUS DISEASES, although the viticultural station at Colmar has developed such virus-free clones as those numbered 47, 48, and 643.

Since Gewürztraminer has been seen as a second-rank variety in terms of international popularity and saleability (perhaps because of its associations with the unfashionable RIESLING), few wine-makers outside Alsace have expended real energy on making great Gewurz. By the early 1990s the finest examples still came almost exclusively from this region in eastern France, where Gewürztraminer, Riesling, and PINOT GRIS are considered the only 'noble' grape varieties.

Of these three, Gewürztraminer was the second most planted in Alsace as a whole, and the most widely planted in the more famous vineyards of the Haut-Rhin *département*, with a total of 2,500 ha/6,100 acres in 1989. It is particularly successful on the richer clay soils of the Haut-Rhin and has inspired a raft of late harvest examples labelled VENDANGE TARDIVE or even Sélection de Grains Nobles in the sunnier harvests of the 1980s and 1990s. The variety easily attains must weights well in excess of Riesling at comparable ripeness levels and regulations take account of this. Such late harvest Gewürztraminers may not last the same number of decades as their Riesling counterparts but many last longer than their first decade.

Earlier-picked Alsace Gewürztraminer should be intriguingly aromatic yet dry and sturdy enough to accompany savoury food but too many examples are simply scented fly-by-nights, lightweight wines produced from heavily cropped vines that taste as though they have been aromatized by a drop of MUSCAT OTTONEL. In these lower ranks, it can be difficult to distinguish a poor Alsace wine labelled Gewürztraminer from one labelled Muscat. Producers with a particularly fine reputation for their Gewürztraminer include Léon Beyer of the bigger houses and Zind-Humbrecht and Cattin among the grower/bottlers.

Germany relegates its (Roter) Traminer to a very minor rank, well behind Riesling, with much less than 1,000 ha in total, including some plantings of the non-aromatic sort which is very occasionally bottled separately. The variety needs relatively warm sites to avoid spring frost damage and to assure good FRUIT SET so that in northern Germany Riesling is usually a more profitable choice. More than half of Germany's Traminer is planted in Baden and Pfalz, where it can produce wines of discernible character but is too often associated with somewhat oily sickliness.

There is almost as much Traminer planted in AUSTRIA as in Germany but here too it has been consigned to the non-modish wilderness, even though some examples, particularly later-picked sweet wines from Styria, can exhibit an exciting blend of race and aroma and can develop for a few years in bottle.

The variety is grown, in no great quantity but usually distinctively, throughout eastern Europe, called Tramini in Hungary; Traminac in Slovenia; Drumin, Pinat Cervena, or Liwora in what was Czechoslovakia; occasionally just Rusa in Romania; and Mala Dinka in Bulgaria. Most of the vines are the aromatic mutation and demonstrate some of Gewürztraminer's distinctive perfume but often in extremely dilute, and often sullied, form, typically overlaying a relatively sweet, lightish white. Hungarians are particularly proud of their Tramini grown on the rich shores of Lake Balaton. It is grown by the Romanians in Transylvania, by the Bulgarians in the south and east, and also, as Traminer, in Russia, Moldova, and Ukraine, where it is sometimes used to perfume Soviet sparkling wine.

It is grown in small quantities, sometimes called Haiden or Heida, in Switzerland and in ever smaller quantity in Luxembourg. In Iberia Torres grow it in the High PENEDÈS for their Viña Esmeralda and it is essentially a mountain grape even in Italy, where Traminer Aromatico is grown almost exclusively, and decreasingly, in its seat, ALTO ADIGE. The less scented and less interesting Traminer is also grown to a limited extent, and Italian wine-making together with vineyard altitude do nothing to emphasize Gewürztraminer characteristics in the resulting wines, although the international nature of the variety may encourage a small renaissance of popularity.

In the New World Gewürztraminer presents a challenge. Many wine regions are simply too warm to produce wine with sufficient acidity, unless the grapes are picked so early (see HARVEST, timing), as in some of Australia's irrigated vineyards, that they have developed little Gewürztraminer character. Australia's 'Traminer' vine population, concentrated in some of the less exciting corners of South Australia and New South Wales, had fallen to 600 ha / 1,500 acres by 1991, much of it used to perfume and sweeten Riesling in commercial blends.

The variety has been more obviously successful in the cooler climate of New Zealand, although even here total plantings are falling, to 200 ha in 1990, the most lively wines coming from Gisborne on the east coast of the North Island. This, curiously, was one of the earliest identifications of varietal / geographical matching in the southern hemisphere.

Another happy home for Gewürztraminer is in the Pacific Northwest of America, particularly in Washington and Oregon, although even here the variety has been losing ground to the inevitable Chardonnay. Washington had 330 acres in 1991 but could demonstrate some appetizing life in several well-vinified examples, even if too many were too sweet. In Oregon too the smoky fume of Alsace is apparent in some bottlings, although rot can be a problem in this wetter climate.

Gewürztraminer remains a relatively minor variety in California, however, whose 690 ha / 1,700 acres, almost half of them in Monterey, too often bring forth oil rather than aroma (see CALIFORNIA for more on the wines). There are a few hectares of Traminer in Argentina but generally South America relies on TORRONTÉS and MOSCATEL to provide aromatic whites. Limited plantings in South Africa have so far yielded sweet wines but some of the right aromas.

It seems likely that serious Gewürztraminer will remain an Alsace speciality for some years yet.

Galet, P., *Cépages et vignobles de France* (2nd edn., Montpellier, 1990).

GHEMME, red wine DOC high up in the subalpine Novara hills in the north of the PIEDMONT region of north west Italy. Like GATTINARA across the river Seisa in the Vercelli hills with its satellites LESSONA and BRAMATERRA, Ghemme is made from the NEBBIOLO grape leavened with BONARDA and VESPOLINA. Other Novara DOCs are BOCA to the north and the rather lighter SIZZANO and FARA to the south. For more details, see SPANNA, the local name for Nebbiolo.

GIBBERELLINS, naturally occurring plant HORMONES which regulate vine growth as for other plants. Isolated in 1941 from a rice fungus, they have been much studied since. In the vine they are formed in growing tissue in the leaves, roots, and berries. Many thousands of hectares of Thompson Seedless (SULTANA) vines are treated by spraying with gibberellins during FLOWERING and shortly afterwards, and this results in larger berries suitable as TABLE GRAPES. Other seedless varieties respond similarly to this treatment (seeds release hormones themselves). R.E.S.

Winkler, A. J., *et al.*, *General Viticulture* (2nd edn., Berkeley, Calif., 1974).

GIENNOIS, COTEAUX DU, once known as **Côtes de Gien**, zone which extends on both banks of the Loire to the north of POUILLY-FUMÉ in the upper Loire to the town of Gien. Although the zone is quite extensive, and encompasses both calcareous and flint soils, it includes only about 30 ha / 74 acres of white grape vines and 70 ha of red. Most of the wines are light reds made from Gamay, and occasionally Pinot Noir grapes, while crisp pale whites may be Sauvignon or, theoretically, Chenin Blanc. Joseph Balland-Chapuis is one of the most dedicated producers in this region, where spring FROSTS are a perennial threat.

See also LOIRE and map on pp. 576–7.

GIGONDAS, potentially excellent-value red and rosé wine appellation in the southern RHÔNE. From about a third of the total area, the best wines are remarkably similar to good red CHÂTEAUNEUF-DU-PAPE, and overall wine standards are high, even if Gigondas wine-making is more rustic than high-tech. Gigondas can taste delightfully untamed (even if inappropriate in the heat of a typical Gigondas summer's day). Gigondas shares Châteauneuf's low maximum YIELD, 35 hl/ha (2 tons/acre); high minimum natural ALCOHOLIC STRENGTH, 12.5 per cent; and a compulsory TRIAGE to eliminate imperfect grapes.

The total *vignoble* is about 1,000 ha / 2,500 acres of rugged, herb-scented vineyard just below the much-painted rocks, the Dentelles de Montmirail. For red wines, Grenache grapes must account for no more than 80 per cent of the total blend, while Syrah and / or Mourvèdre make up at least 15 per cent. The varieties permitted for Côtes-du-RHÔNE, except Carignan, may be used for the rest. Neither Syrah nor Mourvèdre are mandatory in the rosés, however.

The district has been noted for its wine since Roman times. Later a significant proportion of the land under vine formed part of the estates of the princes of Orange. In the 20th century, however, lacking a Baron Le Roy of its own (see CHÂTEAUNEUF-DU-PAPE), it laboured under the commercial disadvantage of qualifying merely for the Côtes-du-Rhône appellation for several decades. In 1966 it was elevated to Côtes-du-Rhône-Villages, and in 1971 finally won its own appellation. The best wines can repay BOTTLE AGEING for a decade or more.

GIRASOL, name for GYROPALETTE, the mechanized riddling crate used in CATALONIA, where they were invented in the 1970s. *Girasol* is Spanish for sunflower, which also turns during a 24-hour period.

GIRDLING, making an incision round a vine trunk, cane, or shoot, usually to improve fruit set. For more details, see CINCTURING.

Glass, history: The Victorians further developed the notion of complete ranges of matching glasses, including finger bowls, so that by 1902 this was a typical page in London's Army & Navy store's catalogue.

		Montrose.	Edinburgh.	No. 270.	No. 462.	No. 1008.	No. 1422.	No. 1866.	No. 25681.
12 Sherries	per doz.	5/9	15/0	6/3	10/0	6/0	7/3	6/3	10/6
12 Ports	"	5/9	15/0	6/3	10/0	6/0	7/3	6/3	10/6
12 Clarets	"	8/3	18/0	8/9	12/0	7/6	8/9	8/9	13/0
12 Champagnes	"	10/9	21/0	11/3	15/9	10/9	12/3	11/6	17/6
6 Liqueurs	"	5/6	13/0	5/9	9/6	5/6	6/9	5/9	10/0
12 Tumblers (half pints)	"	7/0	14/6	8/9	11/3	7/6	10/3	10/3	9/9
12 Finger Glasses	"	12/9	23/6	15/0	15/0	17/0	22/6	21/9	13/0
2 Caraffes and Tumblers	each	3/0	5/6	3/9	3/6	2/9	3/9	5/0	6/0
2 Decanters (quarts)	"	3/9	9/6	5/9	8/3	6/1	7/6	6/9	7/3
2 " (pints)	"	3/0	7/6	3/9	7/0	4/9	5/6	5/0	5/3
1 Claret Jug	"	5/3	13/3	8/3	12/0	8/9	10/9	10/3	11/0
The Suite of **87 Pieces**, as above		**77/9**	**173/3**	**93/11**	**128/3**	**93/8**	**118/11**	**111/8**	**127/3**
Soda Tumblers to match	per doz.	13/9	22/9	15/0	15/0	11/6	16/3	15/3	14/6
Ice Plates "	"	16/3	26/3	15/0	12/6	19/9	25/9	21/9	13/0
Jelly Glasses "	"	8/3	18/0	8/9	12/0	7/6	8/9	7/6	8/0
Custard Glasses "	"	8/9	18/0	8/9	12,0	7/6	8/9	7/6	8/6

Any portion can be purchased at the above price.

GIRONDE, the estuary which separates the MÉDOC from BLAYE and the south western extreme of COGNAC country gives its name to the *département* in which the city of Bordeaux and the BORDEAUX wine region is to be found. The rivers DORDOGNE and GARONNE flow into the Gironde (see map on p. 124).

GIVRY, famous as the preferred wine of King Henri IV, produces mostly red wine in the Côte CHALONNAISE district of Burgundy. The rare white wines, a tenth of the total production, are often particularly interesting with a soft bouquet reminiscent of liquorice. The reds have more structure and ability to age than those of neighbouring RULLY, but less depth than Mercurey. About one-sixth of the vineyard area is designated PREMIER CRU, including Clos Marceaux and Clos Salomon.

J.T.C.M.

GLASS, HISTORY OF. For more than 3,000 years glass has played a unique role in the history of wine, in terms of both serving (GLASSES and DECANTERS) and storage (BOTTLES).

Glass vessels were known in the Ancient world (first appearing in EGYPT *c.*1500 BC) and became common during Roman times when, the techniques of glass-blowing spread throughout the Roman empire. Wine was sometimes drunk from glass tumblers and surviving examples show astonishingly intricate craftsmanship. Glass bottles were used as DECANTERS for carrying wine to table, but not for storage because they were too fragile.

Glass-making continued after the collapse of Roman power and was certainly known, for example, in 9th century Arabia (see ARAB POETS). By the time of the Renaissance, VENICE had become the centre of luxury production. Venetian glassware was exported throughout the known world and Italian craftsmen settled across Europe setting up new workshops. In Tudor England aristocrats preferred Venetian-style glasses to silver (which was considered too common) but glass was so expensive that several diners were expected to share each beaker.

Glass bottles at this time were used by apothecaries rather than wine merchants, although the wines produced around Florence were sometimes transported in *fiaschi* wrapped in straw. The problem with glass was that it was too light and therefore too fragile to withstand either transport or storage. The most common CONTAINERS for wine were BARRELS for bulk, and leather, tin, or stoneware bottles.

A turning-point in the history of glass (and the history of wine) came early in the 17th century, when a timber shortage led to the introduction of coal-fired furnaces in England. Hotter furnaces made possible the production of bottles that were not only darker and heavier, but stronger. At first these dark, onion-shaped bottles were used mainly as decanters and for personal use, but by the beginning of the 18th century they were used for the long-distance transport of wine. Initially the French had to rely on English imports, but during the course of the century bottle factories sprang up in France. By 1790 there were five factories around Bordeaux (still an important centre of glass production) producing 400,000 English-style bottles; there had been none in 1700.

This development was revolutionary because it made possible the ageing of wine. The necessary corollary was the CORK, whose use became common at this time. The advantages of BOTTLE AGEING were most noticeable in PORT, a staple drink in Georgian England. As the practice of BINNING wine became more common, the shape of wine bottles evolved towards the taller cylindrical shape (*c.*1760) we know today.

Meanwhile a revolution in drinking glasses had emanated from the two southern English workshops of George Ravenscroft, who in 1675 had discovered how to make LEAD crystal. This gave rise to a whole new style of English glassware quite distinct from intricate Venetian fashions. Increasingly, different glasses were designed and produced to be used specifically for certain wines, and by the end of the 18th century the concept of a uniformly decorated glass service was well established throughout Europe. See also DRINKING VESSELS. H.B.

Charleston, R. J., *English Glass and the Glass Used in England circa 400–1940* (London, 1984).

Harden, D. B., 'Glasses and glazes', in C. Singer (ed.), *A History of Technology*, ii (Oxford, 1956).

Klein, D., and Lloyd, W., *The History of Glass* (London, 1984).

GLASSES, not just the final CONTAINER for wine but an important instrument for communicating it to the human senses (see TASTING). Wine can be drunk from any DRINKING VESSEL but clean (and only clean) GLASS has the advantage of being completely inert and, if it is clear, of allowing the taster the pleasure (or in the case of BLIND TASTING the clues) afforded by the wine's appearance: colour, clarity, and so on.

A small selection from Riedel's Sommelier range of **glasses**, designed specifically for (left to right), Chardonnay, vintage champagne, Cabernet Sauvignon, Pinot Noir, and Riesling.

For this reason, wine professionals and keen amateurs prefer completely plain, uncoloured, unengraved, uncut glass, preferably as thin as is practicable to allow the palate to commune as closely as possible with the liquid. Thin-rimmed glasses are particularly highly valued.

The ideal wine glass also has a stem—indeed Americans call wine glasses 'stemware'—so that the wine taster can hold the glass without necessarily affecting the wine's TEMPERATURE (a critical element in wine tasting). The stem also enables a glass to be rotated easily (although it takes a certain knack); rotation, as explained in TASTING, is essential for maximizing AROMA. This rotation process also means that the ideal wine glass narrows towards the rim, to minimize the chance of spillage during rotation, and to encourage the volatile FLAVOUR COMPOUNDS to collect in the space between the surface of the wine and the rim of the glass.

Individuals will have their own aesthetic preferences, but any glass which fits the above criteria will serve as a wine glass, including some relatively inexpensive examples. There is a sensual thrill to be had, however, in really thin crystal. This is usually expensive, although central Europe, and BOHEMIA in particular, has a long tradition of producing fine glasses at good prices.

For many households, a single wine glass model will do, perhaps supplemented by smaller glasses for FORTIFIED wines and an elongated one for SPARKLING WINES (see below). Purists, however, use slightly different glasses for different sorts of wine, conventionally (although not particularly logically) a smaller glass for white wines, and traditionally Germanic shapes for German and Alsace wines, as shown below.

In this respect there is no greater purist than Georg Riedel, an Austrian glass-maker who is unusual for his wine CONNOISSEURSHIP and has designed a series of different glasses not just for young red bordeaux and mature red bordeaux, but also, for example, different glasses for vintage port and tawny port, and for Brunello di Montalcino and for Chianti. These designs are all based purely on analysing how different taste characteristics are optimized on the nose and palate by minute variations in glass design. Those determined to take full advantage of all Riedel permutations may need to give up a room or two to accommodate the necessary number of glasses, however, and in practice most people content themselves with just two or three possible glass types, often chosen as much on appearance as on efficacy.

Special glass types

Over the centuries various specific glasses have come to be associated with different wine types.

CHAMPAGNE and other sparkling wines were for long drunk in a flat, saucer-like glass called a **coupe**, but this has been abandoned in favour of the tall **flute** which preserves the wine's MOUSSE. This has evolved into a slightly more bulbous **tulipe** which combines height with narrowing towards the rim.

In Spain SHERRY has traditionally been served in the **copita**, and tastes infinitely better in a part-filled glass in this elongated tulip shape than it does brimming over a cut glass thimble as it is so often served elsewhere.

The ideal PORT glass is not so very different from the copita, although it is often rather bigger in order to allow maximum appreciation of the complex BOUQUET of a vintage port. Glasses like this are ideal for almost all fortified wines, which, for obvious reasons, are served in smaller quantities than table wines.

BURGUNDY, particularly red burgundy, has come to be served in glass balloons so large as to resemble fish-bowls in some cases. The idea, apart from lusty exhibitionism, is that a good burgundy can offer such a rich panoply of aromas that they should be given every chance to escape the wine and titillate the taster. Most wine connoisseurs use the shape on a reduced scale.

The wines of ALSACE and GERMANY are sometimes served in particular forms of glass such as the Rohmer, often with green or brown glass stems, mainly for traditional reasons. There are still those who teach wine SERVING who regard serving these wines in standard white wine glasses as an intolerable aberration.

BRANDY is another drink for which the acceptable glass has changed since the end of the 19th century. The size of the brandy *ballon* has shrunk considerably, and with good reason. See TASTING BRANDY for more details.

See also SERVING WINE.

GLUCOSE is with fructose one of the two principal SUGARS of the grape and of sweet wines. Like fructose, it is a six-carbon atom sugar, or a hexose. In solution, it rotates polarized light to the right, hence the original name dextrose and its correct name, D(+)-glucose.

The two major sugars that accumulate in grapes occur in about equal amounts; at the beginning of RIPENING glucose exceeds fructose (up to fivefold), but in overripe grapes there is less glucose than fructose. Glucose also serves a very important function as the major sugar used by the vine for forming glycosides (see FLAVOUR COMPOUNDS).

Common table sugar, sucrose, is made up of one molecule of glucose and one of fructose. See FRUCTOSE for details of the unusual relationship between these sugars and the grape.

B.G.C. & A.D.W.

GLÜHWEIN, German for 'glow wine', seems a particularly apt name for the MULLED WINE that has cheered many an alpine skier. Pre-mixed wine, sugar, and spices are also available under this name.

GLYCEROL, or **glycerine**, member of the chemical class of polyols and a minor product of alcoholic fermentation. The name derives from the Greek word for sweet and glycerol does indeed taste slightly sweet, as well as oily and heavy. It is present in most wines in concentrations ranging from about 5 to 12 g/l, although BOTRYTIZED wines frequently have concentrations up to 25 g/l.

Glycerol does have a slight effect on the apparent sweetness of a wine but, contrary to popular conception, glycerol makes only a very minor contribution to the apparent VISCOSITY of a wine, and bears no relation to the TEARS observed on the inside of many a wine glass. Whereas sensory tests have demonstrated that glycerol imparts sweetness at a threshold of about 5.2 g/l in white wine, a level of more than 28 g/l would be needed before any difference in viscosity were noted. A.D.W. & T.H.L.

GLYCOLOSIS. See YEAST.

GOBELET, or **goblet**, a form of vine-TRAINING SYSTEM, used since Roman times, whereby the spurs are arranged on short arms in an approximate circle at the top of a short trunk, making the vine look something like a goblet drinking vessel. The vines are free standing and the system is best suited to low-VIGOUR vineyards in drier climates. This is a form of HEAD TRAINING and is generally subject to SPUR PRUNING. The trunk is short, typically 30 to 50 cm (12–19 in), and this training system uses no support for the foliage.

The gobelet is widespread in France, from Beaujolais southwards, and, according to Galet in 1983, was used on more than 500,000 ha/1.2 million acres of vineyard. The traditional spacing was 1.5 by 1.5 m (5 ft), but the distance has been increased to allow tractor access. Sometimes the vines are trained with several trunks. With low-vigour vineyards the foliage can be relatively erect, but shoots may trail on the ground in high-vigour vineyards, and there can be substantial SHADE. Grape yield and quality may suffer as a result. The system is used widely in many Mediterranean countries and is most suited to low vigour vineyards. In Italy the system is called *alberelli a vaso*, in Spain *en vaso*, and in Portugal *en taça*. In many New World countries such as Australia, South Africa, and California, the traditional and low-vigour gobelet-trained vineyards were often called bush vines; they have increasingly been replaced by vines with some form of trellising to accommodate the improved vigour of newer vineyards. R.E.S.

Galet, P., *Précis de viticulture* (4th edn., Montpellier, 1983).

GOBLETS. See DRINKING VESSELS.

GODELLO, fine white grape variety native to Galicia and most successful in VALDEORRAS, where plantings are increasing once more.

GOLDBURGER, Austrian gold-skinned grape variety, a crossing of WELSCHRIESLING and Orangetraube. In the late 1980s there were 500 ha/1,200 acres of this vine, almost all of them in BURGENLAND, where it reaches high MUST WEIGHTS but rarely produces exciting wines. Austria's answer to many GERMAN CROSSINGS.

GOLDKAPSEL. Some producers in GERMANY deliberately give their finest bottlings a gold CAPSULE over the cork, rather as some SAUTERNES producers in France make a wine labelled CRÈME DE TÊTE or TÊTE DE CUVÉE in particularly successful vintages. Goldkapsel bottlings are usually available in very small quantity and invariably command a considerable premium, although there are no legal controls over the use of Goldkapsels. The VDP group of top estates reserve Goldkapsel for particularly good SPÄTLESE or AUSLESE wines (presumably on the basis that wines richer than this have no difficulty in fetching high prices). The position is further complicated (or enriched, depending on your budget) by the fact that some producers use gold capsules of two different lengths, thus their very finest bottlings qualify as **lange Goldkapsel**.

GOLD RUSHES have had a considerable effect on wine history, having played a significant role in the development of New World wine production through their influence both on demand for alcoholic beverages and also on labour supply. In CALIFORNIA, commercial viticulture had emerged during the 1830s, and with the discovery of gold in 1848 there was a massive increase in demand for all types of alcohol in the gold-mining counties of Amador, Calaveras, El Dorado, Nevada, Placer, and Tuolumne. However, by the 1850s, once the first flush of gold fever was over, a number of the immigrants, seeking to profit from the rising price of wine, turned to grape-growing and wine-making as a more reliable source of income. By 1857 it is estimated that there were some 1.5 million vines in California, and only three years later, after the enactment of legislation in 1859 which exempted vineyards from taxation, this total had risen to some 6 million.

Viticulture had been introduced into AUSTRALIA on the establishment of the new colony in New South Wales in 1788. Its subsequent spread followed the increasing pace of colonization and settlement, with new vines being planted almost as soon as each new colony was founded. During the first half of the 19th century, however, despite the activities of proponents such as James BUSBY, wine-making remained a minority interest. The gold rush of 1851 changed this by attracting numerous immigrants to VICTORIA, with large numbers coming from France, Switzerland, Italy, and Germany, countries which had long traditions of viticulture and wine-making. Many, failing to make a success of prospecting, turned to farming, and in particular to viticulture, with the result that the pattern of vineyards in Victoria closely reflected the scattered distribution of the gold. In particular, during the 1870s and 1880s, the gold-mining areas of Ballarat, Bendigo, Great Western, and the Murray river all became important wine regions. P.T.H.U.

Halliday, J., *The Australian Wine Compendium* (London, 1985).
Pinney, T., *A History of Wine in America: From the Beginnings to Prohibition* (Berkeley, Calif., 1989).

GONZALEZ BYASS, the world's largest producer of sherry, still run by the family that founded the house. In 1835, 23-year-old Manuel María González Angel set up business as a shipper in JEREZ in southern Spain, selling just 10 BUTTS of sherry in the first year. Within months he had joined forces with D. Juan Dubosc to make their first large shipment to London: 48 hogsheads and a quarter cask, sent to Robert

Gold rushes: A 'digger's wedding' in late 19th century Melbourne, complete with local wine.

Blake Byass, who was to become their UK agent. In 1844 the company purchased its first vineyards, and in 1846 the first wines were bottled in Jerez. The FINO brand Tio Pepe was born in 1849, named after Manuel's uncle José de la Pena (*tío* being Spanish for uncle), who helped his nephew establish the SOLERA. In 1855 Robert Blake Byass became a shareholder in the business, but it was not until his sons and the sons of the founder entered the firm that it became Gonzalez Byass & Co. The company remained in the hands of the two families until, in 1988, the González family financed the purchase of the 45 per cent of shares held by the Byass family, later placing most of these with IDV, the British drinks subsidiary of the conglomerate Grand Metropolitan. The present chairman is Mauricio González Gordon, from the fourth generation of the family to work in the company. There are several fifth generation members of the family in the company, including Mauricio González Gordon Jr., whose wife Cristina is a member of the DOMECQ family. The company is now the world's largest producer of sherry, and consistently wins awards for the quality of its wines. The company owns 550 ha/1,300 acres of vineyards, and controls a further 450 ha owned by independent farmers. Its top sherry brands are Tio Pepe, the world's best-selling sherry, and Elegante, a less expensive (and less fine) version of Tio Pepe. The company also produces BRANDY, including the labels Lepanto and Soberano; a good quality RIOJA at Bodegas Beronia; CAVA at Castel de Villernau/Jean Perico; and spirits and liqueurs under the name Alcoholera de Chinchon. The UK remains the company's most important export market. S.A.

González Gordon, M., *Sherry: The Noble Wine* (3rd edn., London, 1990).

GOPHERS, rodents which can damage vines in parts of North America. See ANIMALS.

GOULBURN VALLEY, relatively sprawling wine region in the state of VICTORIA in AUSTRALIA.

GOÛT, French noun for TASTE in all its senses. Some wines, particularly old CHAMPAGNES, are described as suiting the **goût anglais**, or English taste (supposedly for wine necrophilia). Sweet champagne was described as to the **goût russe** in the days of the imperial court. A wine made from fruit adversely affected by HAIL, for example, might be described in French as having a **goût de grêle**. Another much discussed and loosely applied tasting term is **goût de terroir**, sometimes used synonymously with the term 'earthy'. (It has no connection with the concept of TERROIR.)

Gonzalez Byass have preserved the tasting and blending room of Tio Pepe's creator, Manuel María González Angel, just as he left it when he died in 1887.

(The late 19th century Champenois defined champagne sweetened to satisfy the *goût russe* as one with 273 to 330 g/l of RESIDUAL SUGAR, as opposed to the *goût anglais* of 22 to 66 g/l for the English.)

GOUVEIO, synonym for the Portuguese white grape variety VERDELHO, used particularly in the DOURO.

GOVERNO, also known as *governo alla toscana*, since it is most closely associated with TUSCANY, is a wine-making technique once widely used in the various CHIANTI production zones, and occasionally in UMBRIA and the MARCHES. The technique consisted of setting aside and drying grapes from the September and October harvest, pressing them in mid to late November, and reintroducing the resulting unfermented grape juice into young wines which had just completed their alcoholic FERMENTATION. This practice led to a slight increase in the ALCOHOLIC STRENGTH of the wines, but its principal and most desirable effect was to encourage the MALOLACTIC FERMENTATION, which was not always easy in the cold cellars of the past, with wines made from a grape as high in ACIDITY as SANGIOVESE. A side-effect was to increase the level of CARBON DIOXIDE in the wine, some of which inevitably remained in young Chianti, bottled and marketed in the spring after the harvest.

Today *governo* is much less widely used as producers have striven to transform Chianti's image from quaffing wine to a serious candidate for BOTTLE AGEING. The technique was also used in the VERDICCHIO production zone in the Marches, to add fizz and a slight sweetness—from the high sugar content of the dried grapes—to counteract Verdicchio's occasionally bitter finish. It has virtually disappeared here now. D.T.

GRACIANO, sometimes called **Graciana**, is a richly coloured, perfumed black grape variety once widely grown in Rioja in northern Spain. It has fallen from favour because of its inconveniently low yields, thereby depriving modern Rioja of an important flavour ingredient. It is still planted in a handful of Rioja vineyards and is being encouraged in Navarre.

The vine buds very late and is prone to downy mildew but can produce wine of great character and extract, albeit quite tannic in youth. Known as Morrastel in France, it was popular in the Midi until the middle of the 19th century, when Henri BOUSCHET stepped in to provide growers with a more productive, more disease-resistant, but wildly inferior crossing of Morrastel with Petit Bouschet, the Morrastel-Bouschet which in time virtually replaced all of the original Morrastel in French vineyards. True Morrastel, or Graciano, is still grown in southern France in minute quantities but Languedoc's viticultural archivists have recently shown interest in it. Morrastel-Bouschet, on the other hand, still covered 1,600 ha/4,000 acres of the Midi in 1979 but is rapidly being pulled up.

There is ample possibility for confusion since the Spaniards use the name Morrastel as a synonym for their very different, and widely planted, variety Monastrell (MOURVÈDRE). Even today in North Africa the name Morrastel is used for both Graciano and Mourvèdre.

The variety known as Xeres in California, which has also been planted on a similarly limited scale in Australia, is probably Graciano, as is Graciana, the variety of which there were 144 ha/356 acres recorded in Mendoza in 1989. Argentina therefore has the distinction of being home to the world's largest plantation of this interesting grape variety.

Galet, P., *Cépages et vignobles de France* (2nd edn., Montpellier, 1990).

GRAFTING, the connection of two pieces of living plant tissue so that they unite and grow as one plant, has been a particularly important element in growing vines since the end of the 19th century, when it was discovered that grafting on to resistant ROOTSTOCKS was the only effective weapon against the PHYLLOXERA louse. If the SCION material contains just one bud, the operation is called budding.

History

The grafting of vines as a means of PROPAGATION was well known in Ancient ROME, and it is referred to as early as the 2nd century BC by CATO in his treatise *De agri cultura*. Knowledge of grafting survived through the medieval period, but it was in the 19th century that it came into particular prominence as the only method of satisfactorily ensuring the continued production of wine in the face of the threat posed by phylloxera. European varieties of VITIS VINIFERA had little resistance to phylloxera, and it was only through the grafting of *vinifera* cuttings on to American species of *Vitis*, which had some phylloxera resistance, that wine with the commercially acceptable taste of the traditional European varieties could continue to be made. Early experiments to counter phylloxera had generally centred on chemical treatments or flooding, but during the 1870s those, such as Laliman, who had been advocating the use of AMERICAN VINE SPECIES gained increasing support. Eventually, at the 1881 International Phylloxera Congress in Bordeaux, it became generally accepted

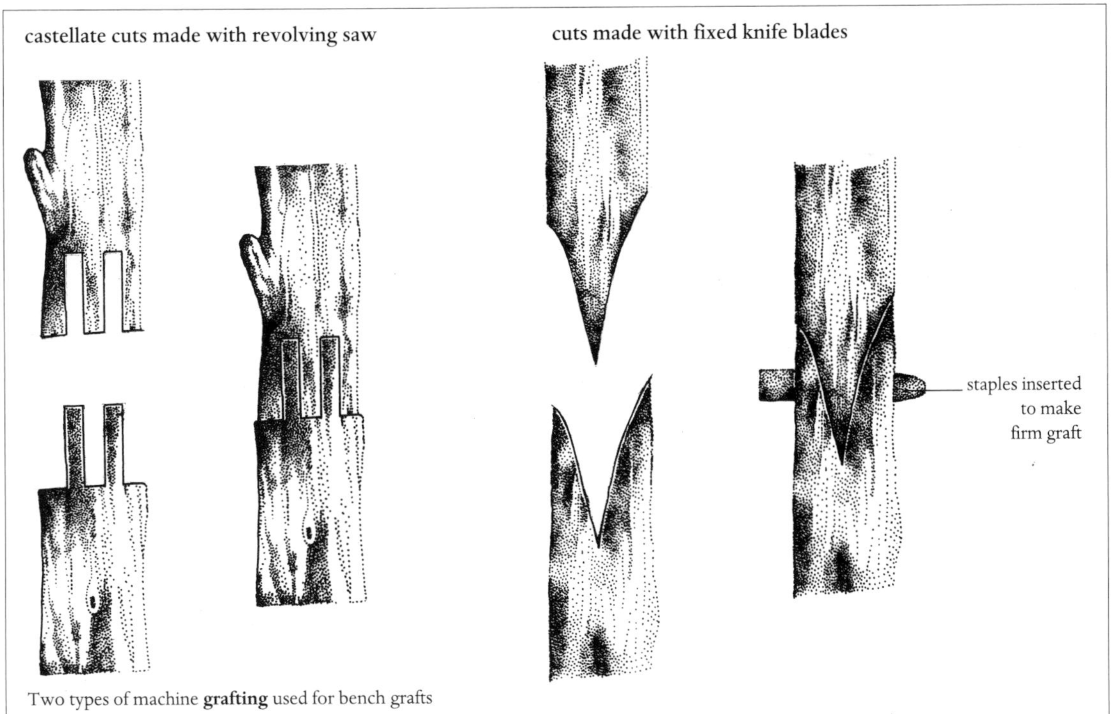

Two types of machine **grafting** used for bench grafts

The **grafting** of Pinot Noir vines on to American rootstock shows the callus that has formed around the graft.

that grafting of French scions on to American rootstock was the best solution, and this led to much experimentation to identify the best rootstocks for particular soil types. On a regional scale, however, widespread adoption of grafting awaited the efforts of people such as Gustave Foëx, director of the agricultural school at MONTPELLIER, who in 1882 produced a small booklet recommending the use of American vines, written in a clear style specifically designed for the small wine producers of the Languedoc. Traditionally grafting was done by hand, either in the field (FIELD BUDDING) or indoors (BENCH GRAFTING), using such techniques as the whip and tongue method. Today, however, most grafting is done by machines which join together scion and rootstock, usually in an omega-shaped cut. P.T.H.U.

Foëx, G., *Instruction sur l'emploi des vignes américaines à la reconstruction du vignoble de l'Hérault* (Montpellier, 1882).
Laliman, L., *Études sur les divers travaux phylloxériques et les vignes américaines* (Paris, 1879).
Ordish, G., *The Great Wine Blight* (London, 1972).
Winkler, A. J., *et al.*, *General Viticulture* (Berkeley, Calif., 1974).

Modern viticultural practices

Vines are grafted or budded to take advantage of the desirable properties of the rootstock variety. Foremost is resistance or tolerance to soil-borne pests and diseases, especially phylloxera and NEMATODES. Other properties are tolerance to soil SALINITY, to high LIME levels, to SOIL WATER logging or deficiency, and an ability to modify VIGOUR or to hasten or delay RIPENING. If conducted in the vineyard, as FIELD BUDDING AND GRAFTING, the practice offers a method of changing a VINE VARIETY. If conducted indoors, before planting, it is called BENCH GRAFTING, which may in warm climates be complemented by NURSERY grafting.

The uniting of the SCION with the rootstock is achieved by a slow growth process: a mass of undifferentiated cells, the CALLUS, develops at each cut edge of the respective CAMBIUMS (zones of dividing cells), so it is important to position the two cambiums opposite each other and close together. Once the callus is well established, a plane of cells develops between the cambiums of the scion and the rootstock as a new, linking cambium. The new continuous cambium then cuts off new PHLOEM cells on the outside, adding to the bark, and new XYLEM cells on the inside, adding to the wood. Thereafter, the scion piece is part of the whole plant vascular system.

A number of factors determine success or failure in grafting, in addition to the skill involved in cutting and matching of cambiums. The first is that the graft needs specific environmental conditions such as warm temperatures (24–30 °C/75–86 °F) and high humidities (90–100 per cent) around the union. The second is the compatibility of the scion/stock combination. The third, and probably the most serious, is that some rootstocks are difficult to root (see ROOTLING).

Particular forms of graft include CLEFT GRAFTING, NOTCH GRAFTING, WHIP GRAFT. See also GREEN GRAFTING. B.G.C.

GRAFTING MACHINE, a device which facilitates the viticultural operation of GRAFTING by making cuts through the vine rootstock and scion pieces with mirror-image shapes that permit snug fitting. Shapes used include castellate and omega. Grafting machines are an essential part of the factory-like methods used for BENCH GRAFTING, but innovative growers have used modified machines for NURSERY grafting and FIELD (BUDDING AND) GRAFTING. B.G.C.

GRAIN, an important aspect of any wood, particularly OAK, used for wine COOPERAGE. French oak is classified by wine-makers and coopers as either tight grained or wide grained. STAVES used in BARREL MAKING are essentially cuts of wood fashioned from transversal sections of the tree. The ends of each stave therefore reveal growth rings from the life of the tree. Tight grained, less porous wood can be separated from wide grained wood by a glance at the end of the stave.

The slower the growth of the tree, the tighter the grain of the wood. Alternating bands of dark and light wood reveal spring and summer growth. Growth in spring, the most important growing season for oak, is often rapid and is marked by large XYLEM vessels, cells with large openings for conducting water. Much smaller vessels mark growth in the summer. Of course, as with grapes, trees reflect soil and climate conditions, as well as the differences between species. For example, within the same region, minor differences in soil and climate may mean that one stand (delineated grouping) of trees grows straight and tall, and therefore has tight grains, while a few kilometres away another stand of trees may grow out, with wider grains. Within a single tree, the side of a tree furthest from the equator grows slightly slower than its opposite. Trees on the edge of a forest will also tend to grow out rather than up, while the reverse is generally true of trees growing in the depths of a forest.

Quercus robur (see OAK) usually gives wide-grained staves, which is to say that there are at least 3 mm/0.1 in between growth rings. Between the growth rings a gradual shift from spring to summer growth can be seen. For *Quercus robur* spring growth is usually more than a quarter of the total annual growth. *Quercus sessiliflora* on the other hand usually provides wood with less than 3 mm between the growth rings between which a sharp division between spring and summer growth can be seen. With *Quercus sessiliflora* spring growth usually amounts to less than a quarter of the total annual growth. There is considerable cross-fertilization between species, however.

Limousin oak tends to be wide grained. In the Limousin forests trees are wider apart than they are in the forests of central France, where trees must grow up, rather than out, for sunlight. Furthermore the Limousin forest appears to be dominated by *Quercus robur*. Consequently Limousin staves reveal greater spring growth and hence, more annual growth. Because of the greater percentage of large xylem vessels these oaks are more porous.

Wider-grained wood tends to be more tannic than tight-grained wood because of the larger vessels. Analytically wide-grained wood is about 10 per cent TANNINS; tight grained around seven per cent. Thus wide-grained wood needs longer air drying (see BARREL MAKING) lest the wine aged in it be too bitter.

Although most coopers divide wood by forest so that tight- and wide-grained woods are worked together, others may divide wood into tight- and wide-grained woods.

See also WOOD INFLUENCE. M.K.

GRAISSE, also known as Plant de Graisse, is a minor white grape variety grown increasingly rarely in ARMAGNAC country where, unusually, it is capable of producing wine quite drinkable in pre-distilled form. The grape pulp is unusually viscous, however, and only a small area remains.

GRANDE RUE, LA, red burgundy GRAND CRU vineyard in VOSNE-ROMANÉE.

GRANDES MARQUES, SYNDICAT DES. This grouping of some of the major firms or BRANDS of CHAMPAGNE was founded in 1882 by three firms, who were joined by 19 others within the year, representing virtually the whole champagne trade at the time. In 1945 the Syndicat merged with a rival body. In 1993 the Syndicat was reorganized to ensure that only firms conforming to certain minimum standards were included. The term *grande marque* is French for 'big brand'.

N.F.

GRAND NOIR DE LA CALMETTE hardly deserves a name that suggests it is the great black grape variety of the BOUSCHET experimental vine-breeding station, Domaine de la Calmette. At least ALICANTE BOUSCHET had the relatively noble Grenache as a parent while 'Grand' Noir was bred from Petit Bouschet and the common Aramon. Not surprisingly it has a very high yield and, from its TEINTURIER parent, red flesh (although not as red as Alicante Bouschet's).

Often known simply as Grand Noir, it was widely planted in France until the 1920s, when its susceptibility to powdery mildew and winter cold precipitated a decline in its fortunes. Although 2,000 ha/5,000 acres remained in France at the beginning of the 1980s, there were fewer than 400 ha/1,000 acres by the 1990s, mainly in the Midi but also in COGNAC country, which are systematically being pulled up. It is still grown to a very limited extent in north-east Victoria in Australia.

GRAND ROUSSILLON, an appellation that effectively encompasses Greater ROUSSILLON, is a rarely used VIN DOUX NATUREL appellation less stringent than that for RIVESALTES.

GRANDS CRUS, French for great growths, are those CRUS judged superior in some way. In BURGUNDY and ALSACE the grands crus are a very specific group of superior vineyards.

GRANDS ÉCHEZEAUX, red GRAND CRU in Burgundy's CÔTE D'OR. For more details, see ÉCHEZEAUX.

GRAND VIN, name current in BORDEAUX for the main wine produced by a CHÂTEAU (as opposed to a SECOND WINE).

GRANITE, a coarse-grained, visibly crystalline plutonic rock, composed of QUARTZ and feldspar as well as other minerals. Bereich Ortenau, a subregion of BADEN in south west Germany, has soils composed mainly of crumbled granite.

The MOULIN-À-VENT vineyards of Beaujolais in France are made from grapes grown on shallow soils of decomposed granite, and granite is the dominant element in the soils of the northern RHÔNE to the immediate south. Many of the vineyards of SARDINIA are on granite soils, as are the vines producing the table wines of the lower DOURO and neighbouring DÃO (but not the vineyards producing PORT). Granitic soils are often of low fertility and this fact combined with typical rapid DRAINAGE makes such soils favoured for viticulture. See entries prefixed SOIL. M.J.E.

GRANITE BELT, the most northerly wine region in AUSTRALIA. For more details see QUEENSLAND.

GRANJA, town in southern Portugal whose co-operative is establishing a certain reputation for its wines. See ALENTEJO for more details.

GRAN RESERVA, Spanish term for a wine supposedly from an outstanding VINTAGE which has been subject to lengthy AGEING before release. Red wines must spend a minimum of two years in BARRIQUES, and another three years in tank or bottle. The wine may not leave the BODEGA until the sixth year after the vintage. White wines must spend a total of at least four years in cask and bottle, including at least six months' CASK AGEING, to qualify.

See also RESERVA. R.J.M.

GRANVAS, Spanish term for sparkling wine made by the tank or Charmat SPARKLING WINE-MAKING method.

GRAPE, the berry or fruit of the grapevine, or VINE, whose juice is the essential ingredient in WINE. A grape is *raisin* in French, *uva* in Italian, *Rebe* in German. The grapes produced by commercial viticulture are sold either as TABLE GRAPES or DRYING GRAPES, or crushed and processed into wine or GRAPE JUICE, GRAPE CONCENTRATE, RECTIFIED GRAPE MUST. Wine production is, however, the most important use, accounting for some 80 per cent of the world's grape production. The solids, including stems, skins, seeds, and pulp, left after these juicing processes are called grape POMACE. There are several hundred grapes to a BUNCH for wine grape varieties, and berries are individually relatively small.

The form and appearance of grape berries varies hugely between VINE VARIETIES. Their shape varies from flattened, through spherical and oval, to elongated and finger-like; colour from green to yellow, pink, crimson, dark blue, and black; and size from as small as a pea (as in CURRANT, for example) to the huge, egg-like berries of some recently bred table grape varieties which may weigh as much as 15 g/0.5 oz each. The majority of wine grapes, however, are spherical to short oval, 1–2 g in weight, and are coloured yellow (called WHITE by vine-growers) or dark blue (called 'black' or 'red').

Grape berries are borne on the end of a stalk, the PEDICEL, which in turn is borne on the BUNCHSTEM, or peduncle. At the end opposite the pedicel is a small stub of dead tissue which is the remnant of the style and stigma (see FLOWER). Some varieties, for example Riesling, have corky lenticels scattered over the skin. When cut open (see diagram) the grape is seen to have two units (carpels) side by side, each enclosing a space (a locule) in which are the seeds. When the berry enlarges, the space becomes compressed by encroaching flesh. The significant parts of a berry are the flesh, skin, and seeds.

Flesh or pulp

The flesh or pulp (*pulpe* in French) is the bulk of the berry or PERICARP. A section across the flesh shows that there are about 40 large parenchyma cells from beneath the skin to the single cell layer that is the inner lining. A central core of vascular strands connects to a mesh of veins that encircles the outer edge of the flesh like a chicken-wire cage and provides the vascular connection with the rest of the vine; the veins contain the XYLEM, which transports water and minerals from roots, and PHLOEM, which is the all-important pathway for sugar from the leaves. The inner flesh cells are elongated radially and are the largest, giving this section a more fragile texture. Another zone with a different texture is the so-called BRUSH, which is the lighter coloured part of the flesh near the junction with the pedicel.

The pulp and the juice are the most important part of the grape to the wine-maker, and the wine drinker, for they contain the main components of the finished wine. Because the juice of all grapes (apart from the specialist TEINTURIER varieties) is a pale grey, whatever the colour of the grape's skin, white wine can be made from grapes of all colours, so long as the juice is not left in contact with dark skins. Red wines can be made only by leaching colour from such skins, while pink wines can be made either from short contact with dark skins or more prolonged contact with pink or red skins.

Skin

The grape's skin (*pellicule* in French) is the tough, enveloping layer around the grape that holds it together. The outside layer, or bloom, consists of wax plates and cutin, both of which resist water diffusion and hence water loss from the berry. They also impede penetration of fungal spore growths and other biological infections. This waxy layer forms the grape's typically whitish surface, called the BLOOM. The fatty acids and sterols from the bloom supply important nutrients for the growth of YEAST, either added or ambient yeast in the atmosphere, during FERMENTATION.

Below the wax and cutin are the cell layers that form the skin; the first is the true epidermis, below this are about seven cell layers forming the hypodermis in which are concentrated most of the berry PIGMENTS, yellow CAROTENOIDS, and xanthophylls, and the red and blue ANTHOCYANS important in the making of red wine. As well as some TANNINS, a significant amount of a grape's FLAVOUR COMPOUNDS are also associated with the skin layers. There may well be differences in the precise locations of the PHENOLICS (pigments, tannins, and flavour compounds). Those compounds located closest to the pulp are presumably extracted first.

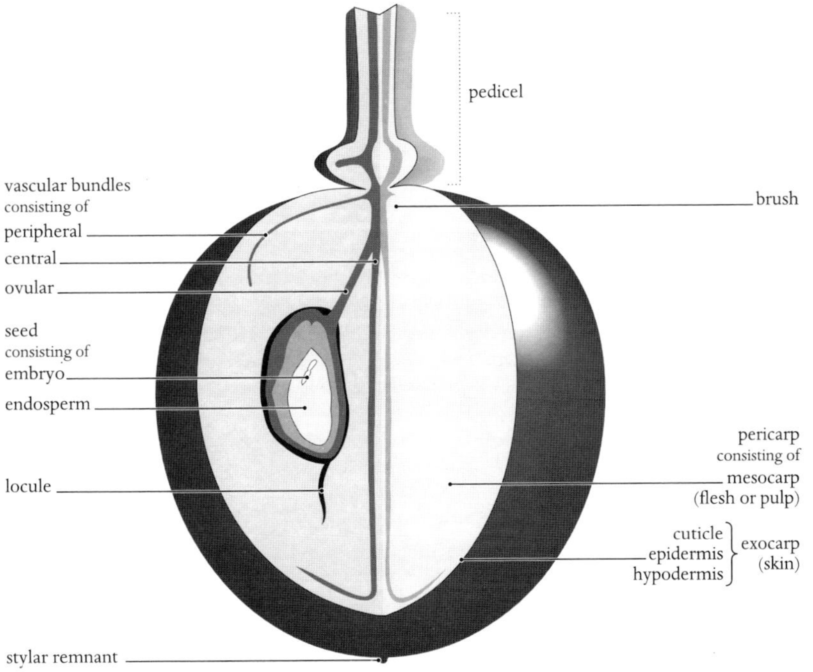

Grape berry

There are other differences in the chemical composition of skin compared with the underlying flesh: besides phenolics, they are rich in POTASSIUM. Skins constitute between five and 12 per cent by weight of a mature grape berry, depending on the vine variety. The thickness of grape skin can vary from about 3 to 8 μm.

Seeds

Seeds, *pepins* in French, of grapes vary in size and shape between varieties; for example, those in MUSCAT BLANC À PETITS GRAINS are about 5 mm long while those in the table grape Waltham Cross are nearly 10 mm. Their number per berry tends to be a characteristic for each variety with one or two predominating. Four is possible since each carpel bears two ovules; however, some freak Ribier berries with double the number of carpels may have eight seeds. Often, incompletely developed seed structures occur, called stenospermic (thin-seeded), alongside fully developed seeds. In fact so-called seedless berries usually have stenospermic seeds in them; these may be soft (unlignified) as in the important raisin and table grape variety SULTANA (also known as THOMPSON SEEDLESS) or have a lightly hardened seedcoat but be empty inside. The greater the number and amount of seed development, the larger the berry; this relationship is largely a reflection of differences in the amount of cell division in the pericarp. The berry-enlarging effect of seeds is overridden by the plant hormone GIBBERELLIN, which may be used to override the berry-enlarging effect of seeds, as it is when Sultana is grown for the table, for example.

Seeds are only of minor importance in wine-making although if they are crushed, as those who eat seeded grapes know, the bitter tannins they contain are released. Unlike the stems, which are relatively easy to separate from the berries, seeds always accompany the juice and skins into the draining tanks or press for white wines, or into the fermentation vessel for red wines. In WHITE WINE-MAKING the contact time between juice and seeds and absorption of tannins from the seeds is minimal. In RED WINE-MAKING, on the other hand, the prolonged contact between the seeds and an increasingly alcoholic solution means that tannins are very likely to be dissolved. Grape seeds have served as a source of edible or industrial oil.

Other parts of the grape include BRUSH, PERICARP, PEDICEL, peduncle (see BUNCH STEM). See also GRAPE COMPOSITION AND WINE QUALITY, GRAPE QUALITY ASSESSMENT, and RIPENING. (For other parts of the vine plant, see VINE MORPHOLOGY.)

B.G.C. & A.D.W.

Coombe, B. G. 'Research on development and ripening of the grape berry', *American Journal of Enology & Viticulture*, 43 (1992), 101–10.

GRAPE BRANDY, a spirit made by distilling wine. In Europe at least this should have become a tautology since the introduction of regulations governing use of the word BRANDY (see BRANDY AND THE EUROPEAN UNION). Nevertheless the term is still used for a number of 'brandies' made by adding flavourings to neutral GRAPE SPIRIT.

GRAPE COMPOSITION AND WINE QUALITY. Grape composition is the essential basis of wine quality, and knowledge of grape composition is critical for those wine-makers interested in making the best wine possible. The concentrations of all component chemical groups play a part. Grape SUGARS, for example (see MUST WEIGHT), determine the possible potential ALCOHOLIC STRENGTH of the wine. ACIDS and nitrogenous compounds (see NITROGEN) affect the course of FERMENTATION and exert their own effects on flavour. POTASSIUM salts have effects on PH and thus on microbiological activity and oxidative STABILITY. PHENOLICS contribute to levels of COLOUR and TANNINS. A multitude of volatile compounds alter aroma (see ACIDITY, AMINO ACIDS, FLAVOUR COMPOUNDS, SUGARS). Some values of concentrations of selected components of FREE-RUN juice from ripe grapes are given below in GRAPE JUICE COMPOSITION.

Grape composition is constantly changing during RIPENING. A central factor in grape ripening is the steady increase in sugar concentration after sugar accumulation has been triggered at VERAISON. Assessment of the timing and rate of sugar increase indicates the general timing of ripening. It also serves as an index of the changes in other components of grapes. Another feature is that acidity declines, due mainly to the RESPIRATION of malate but also to dilution by berry growth and the formation of salts, especially with potassium, which increases concurrently with sugar. Colour and tannins increase in skins early during ripening. Less is known about the timing of the increase in aroma compounds because of the difficulty of measurement, but in some varieties intensity appears to develop late in the ripening process, after sugar concentration has levelled (see GRAPE QUALITY ASSESSMENT). Quality epitomizes the integration of these chemical groups in such a way that there is a balance between individual components, coupled with an intensity of VARIETAL character. B.G.C.

GRAPE CONCENTRATE is what is left when the volatile elements are removed from fresh grape juice. Rarely used to produce really fine wine, it can provide a useful supply of grape SOLUBLE SOLIDS for use long after the HARVEST. Grape concentrate is the main ingredient, for example, in so-called MADE WINES produced without the benefit of freshly picked grapes (see BRITISH WINES and HOME WINE-MAKING). Grape concentrate can also be used in BLENDING and BACK BLENDING to soften and sweeten dry wines of everyday commercial standard made in cooler regions. It is widely used in Germany, for example, where it is called *Süssreserve*. For more details of grape concentrate used for sweetening purposes, see SWEET RESERVE. Grape concentrate is also in some circumstances used for ENRICHMENT, increasing the eventual alcohol content of a wine (it is a permitted prefermentation additive in Australia, for instance, although sugar is not). It is also used to sweeten some other fruit juices and foodstuffs, and is sometimes used as an alternative to honey.

Historically, wine-makers made a form of grape concentrate by simply boiling grape juice until the volume was reduced by at least one-half. This resulted in a liquid with a strong cooked, caramel flavour, however, and such an additive is used exclusively for sweet, dark, strong wines such as rich SHERRY, MÁLAGA, and MARSALA. In Spain it is known as *arrope*.

Today, the caramelizing effect is avoided by CONCENTRATION of the grape juice under very low temperatures in vacuum evaporators. Modern low pressure concentrators represent a heavy investment for a single winery and they tend to be operated by specialists who may use them to concentrate other fruit juices at other times of year. Most grape juice is subject to CLARIFICATION and is reduced in TARTRATES before concentration so that the solids precipitated are minimal when water is removed.

Red grape concentrate may be made by first heating the grapes to extract PIGMENTS into the juice before concentration. Alternatively, red grape concentrate can be made by high SULPHUR DIOXIDE extraction. A.D.W.

GRAPE JUICE is a sweet, clear, non-alcoholic liquid. Wine-makers generally use the term to refer to MUST that has undergone CLARIFICATION and STABILIZATION. Preserved by holding at temperatures so low that any YEAST or BACTERIA are inhibited, such juice was often used in commercial wine-making to soften or sweeten new, dry wines. Since the development of efficient juice concentrators, however, it has generally been supplanted in wine-making by GRAPE CONCENTRATE which can be stored much more cheaply, is inherently stable against microbiological attack, and dilutes the wine much less.

A certain amount of grape juice is bottled and sold as a drink, however, although grape juice is a minor beverage compared to juices of other fruits such as citrus and apple. Since it so readily ferments, it needs to be protected from yeast contamination. This is usually done by PASTEURIZATION and/or ultra-FILTRATION and heavy additions of SULPHUR. Many VINIFERA varieties lose their pleasant, fresh taste after pasteurization, and the American grape juice industry uses the non-*vinifera* CONCORD variety. The juice from grapes harvested at optimum ripeness for wine has a rather cloying sweetness which can overshadow the refreshing ACIDITY. Interestingly, it is very difficult to distinguish VARIETAL character in most grape juices, other than such conspicuous flavours as those associated with MUSCAT and Concord grapes. Wine drinkers generally find grape juice bears disappointingly little relation to wine. A.D.W.

GRAPE JUICE COMPOSITION. Most of the sugary solution that results when grapes are squeezed or crushed derives from the contents of the vacuoles of the cells of the pulp or flesh, although heavy crushing and pressing adds further solution from vacuoles of the skin and vascular strands, thereby mixing many different compounds into the must. Thus the composition of the juice that issues when berries are crushed changes with the pressure and time of crushing; the first, FREE-RUN juice has fewest suspended solids and skin extracts; further pressing yields juice with more PHENOLICS and POTASSIUM salts, and hence lower TOTAL ACIDITY.

Fermentation of juice with skins present, as in red wine-making, yields still more FLAVOUR COMPOUNDS and PIGMENTS that are enriched in the cells of the skin. See GRAPE.

See also ACIDITY, AMINO ACIDS, ANTHOCYANS, ASCORBIC ACID, CAROTENOIDS, CITRIC ACID, FRUCTOSE, GLUCOSE, LIPIDS, MALIC ACID, MINERALS, PECTINS, PROTEINS, SOLUBLE SOLIDS, STARCH, SUCROSE, TANNINS, TERPENOIDS, VARIETAL character, VITAMINS, and the all-important SUGAR IN GRAPES. B.G.C.

GRAPE QUALITY ASSESSMENT is needed by wine-makers for long-term strategic planning and, in the short term, for the planning of each vintage, especially in fixing HARVEST dates. Assessment is often a matter of combined judgement by grape-growers and wine-makers, using experience of the performance of previous vintages as the main guide, supplemented by tasting of berries and by measurements of GRAPE COMPOSITION (see SAMPLING). In some regions, sugar content (see MUST WEIGHT) is sufficient to indicate forthcoming wine quality, especially in cool regions (unless, of course, major catastrophes such as disease intervene). In warm to hot regions, sugar alone is an unreliable guide to quality and additional measurements are needed: TOTAL ACIDITY and PH of the juice are useful, as well as some measure of the colour of skins in some red grapes. The importance of aroma is increasingly recognized, but it is difficult to measure. Valuable information can be obtained by collecting and storing juice samples at intervals during grape development and running comparative 'sniffing tests', but these are costly and difficult. It is hoped that techniques of grape analysis will eventually be found to supplement these methods. One suggestion is to measure the total glycoside concentration in grapes since this correlates with total AROMA COMPOUNDS.

Many other characteristics of the harvest contribute to the assessment of its quality. Foremost is the amount and type of berry ROT. Other factors are the presence of broken skins due to heavy RAINFALL, HAIL, or physical damage. The extent of berry shrivel, evenness of ripening, contamination with leaves, clods, and other non-grape material, and BERRY SIZE are other important factors. Careful vine-growers will also take account of the appearance of the vineyard, the state of the CANOPY, condition of the leaves, and the general vineyard management.

See also ACIDITY, ANTHOCYANS, FLAVOUR COMPOUNDS, GRAPE COMPOSITION AND WINE QUALITY, PHENOLICS, SUGARS. B.G.C.

GRAPE SORTING. See TRIAGE.

GRAPE SPIRIT, term sometimes used for the neutral alcoholic spirit of vinous origin used in FORTIFICATION, or as a base for grape-flavoured spirits such as the Greek branded spirit Metaxa. It should now be used only as exactly defined in BRANDY AND THE EUROPEAN UNION.

GRAPE VARIETIES. This term is often used interchangeably with vine varieties since different varieties of vine have predictably different grapes or berries. Different varieties of vine produce grapes with very different and distinct characteristics (many of them outlined under the names of individual varieties). The terms grape variety and vine variety are therefore used almost interchangeably both in this book and generally. Wines made predominantly from a single grape variety, usually specified on the label, are called VARIETAL wines. The wine consumer is thus familiar with the names of many popular varieties such as CHARDONNAY, CABERNET SAUVIGNON, MERLOT, PINOT NOIR, RIESLING, and SAUVIGNON Blanc.

See VINE VARIETIES and under the names of individual varieties. Specialized varieties are listed for both TABLE GRAPES and DRYING GRAPES.

GRAPEVINE, an alternative name for the plant on which most of the world's wine trade depends. It is known by most wine producers and consumers as the VINE.

GRAPPA, Italian POMACE BRANDY, the equivalent of France's MARC. Until the early 1990s grappa was unjustly despised by most non-Italian drinkers, who were acquainted only with the fiery and unremarkable grappas mass produced by firms such as Nardini, but even some of these are perfectly agreeable, if a little petrolly, once they have been aged in wood for a year or two (see OAK AND BRANDY).

Of much greater interest are the hundreds of grappas marketed by individual producers who have reverted to the spirit's origins as a prudent avoidance of waste by peasant wine-makers. Like their forebears, they employ the skins and pips of the grapes from which they have made their wines. To retain their freshness and fruitiness these grappas are not generally matured in wood but stored in glass containers.

Inevitably, given the sheer number of firms and families involved, a significant number of grappas on the market are rather muddy, heavy, and badly made. But there are also dozens of serious interest, particularly those made from a single VINE VARIETY that more or less accurately reflect the qualities of that variety. Some varieties such as MOSCATO may be too strong and obvious for the DISTILLATION process, which inevitably concentrates a grape's characteristics. But grape varieties such as BRACHETTO and NEBBIOLO seem to adapt well to the process, providing rich yet delicate brandies now being more properly appreciated, and not only in Italy. Indeed, by the mid 1990s VARIETAL grappas, sometimes in extremely elegant and expensive bottles, had become the height of FASHION among cognoscenti.

See also Italian BRANDY. N.F.

GRAPPUT is a synonym for the rapidly declining French grape variety BOUCHALÈS.

GRASĂ, the 'fat' white grape of COTNARI in ROMANIA, where it is grown exclusively, on a total of about 850 ha / 2,000 acres of vineyard in the early 1990s. It can reach extremely high MUST WEIGHTS but needs the balancing acidity of grapes such as TĂMAÎOASĂ Romanească in a blend. In 1958 Grasă grapes in Cotnari reached a sugar concentration of 520 g / l. The vine is usefully sensitive to NOBLE ROT and is said to have been grown in this part of western Moldavia since the 15th century. A few authorities believe that this is the same variety as the FURMINT of Tokay.

GRASSHOPPERS, insects of the families *Acrididae* and *Tettigoniidae* which are typically terrestrial and plant feeding. Reductions in vineyard leaf area impair grape RIPENING, with potentially severe effects on wine quality. Many different species can cause damage in vineyards by feeding on the foliage and on young shoots and bark of young vines. In California, for example, the devastating grasshopper (*Melanoplus devastator Scudder*) is particularly harmful to vineyards, causing damage by defoliation, usually in mid to late summer. In eastern Australia the Australian plague locust (*Chortoicetes terminifera*) can be a major pest. Dense swarms can build up in pasture areas, and descend very quickly on vineyard areas, especially when pastures dry out. Control where necessary is usually by insecticides. M.J.E.

Buchanan, G. A., and Amos, T. G., 'Grape pests', in B. G. Coombe and P. R. Dry (eds.), *Viticulture ii, Practices* (Adelaide, 1992).

GRASSY, tasting term usually used synonymously with HERBACEOUS.

GRAUBURGUNDER, German synonym for PINOT GRIS used by many, particularly in BADEN and the PFALZ, to designate a crisp, dry style of wine as opposed to sweeter wines normally labelled with the variety's more common German synonym RULÄNDER.

GRAVE DEL FRIULI, vast DOC zone in the FRIULI region of north east Italy which sprawls across the southern portion of the provinces of Pordenone and Udine (with the largest portion in the former). This is flatland whose gravel- and sand-based soil has been deposited over the millennia by the many rivers and streams that cross the territory before adding their waters to the Adriatic. It owes its name to the same root as the gravelly GRAVES region of Bordeaux in France.

Over 6,500 ha / 16,000 acres of vineyards produce light, fruity reds and fresh, aromatic whites. MERLOT, with more than 2,500 ha / 6,100 acres, is the dominant vine variety here, as in the neighbouring LISON-PRAMAGGIORE DOC to the west. Various CABERNETS (close to 700 ha) and REFOSCO dal Peduncolo Rosso (over 200 ha), plus minuscule quantities of PINOT NERO, bring the total area of red varieties to virtually 3,500 ha, more than half the total, making this, the largest DOC, something of an anomaly in Friuli.

As elsewhere in the region, TOCAI Friulano dominates among the white varieties with close to 1,000 ha, although there are significant plantings of PINOT BIANCO (some 475 ha), PINOT GRIGIO (over 750 ha), SAUVIGNON Blanc (more than 300 ha), and VERDUZZO (325 ha). Sauvignons of marked character are produced here, with an aromatic intensity that appeals to lovers of the powerfully herbaceous. Some attempts—often unconvinced and unconvincing—at more structured reds have been made since the mid 1980s but the Merlots and Cabernets of Grave del Friuli seem intrinsically lighter than the better reds from the COLLI ORIENTALI, Friuli's second most important DOC. D.T.

GRAVEL, a soil or unconsolidated rock in which pebbles are the most obvious component, known in French as *graves*, from which the two appellations below, and the DOC above, take their names. Gravel is the most distinctive soil type of Bordeaux's so-called LEFT BANK wine regions. It is said that glaciers, slowly moving down to the Atlantic coast from the distant Pyrenees, followed the course of the nearby river, pushing back its high right bank. When glaciers melted, the pebbles remained near the surface. These pebbles give the soils of the MÉDOC their special virtue of holding the sun's heat during the day and reradiating it back to the low trained grapes at night. The vineyards of the GRAVES are, not surprisingly, characterized by their gravelly surface and gravel is nowhere so prevalent as at Ch HAUT-BRION, where in places it is 16 to 20 m / 50–65 ft deep. The porous soil, with its pebbles holding the heat from the sun, is said to be the factor that enables the two Haut-Brion properties, and Ch LATOUR, to produce high-quality wine even in lesser VINTAGES. Water drains away quickly giving the vine the slight WATER STRESS favoured for wine quality. See VINE PHYSIOLOGY and SOIL AND WINE QUALITY.

Gravel soils are also highly prized for quality wine production on the plateau of ST-ÉMILION, in CHÂTEAUNEUF-DU-PAPE, and in the Gimblett Road region of Hawkes Bay in NEW ZEALAND. However, many gravel areas may well be used for viticulture simply because they are too difficult to work and too infertile for any other form of agriculture. It is notable that Chx Haut-Brion and La Mission-Haut-Brion are now viticultural oases in the southern suburbs of Bordeaux, indicating that the land is more valuable for housing than for vines.

See entries prefixed SOIL. M.J.E., R.E.S., & J.M.H.

Enjalbert. H., *Great Bordeaux Wines: St Émilion, Pomerol, Fronsac* (Paris, 1983: Eng. trans. 1985).

GRAVES, French for gravelly terrain, and a term at one time used for many of Bordeaux's wine districts, but now the name of one particular large region extending 50 km / 30 miles south east of the city along the left bank of the river GARONNE (see map on p. 124). Graves is Bordeaux's only region famous for both its red and white wines, although its aristocratic, mineral-scented, Cabernet-dominated red wines are made in much greater quantity than its dry whites. In the early 1990s, about 1,800 ha / 4,500 acres were planted with red wine grapes, while about 950 ha produced dry white Graves. **Graves**

Supérieur is a declining appellation reserved for sweet wines to which about 400 ha were dedicated in the early 1990s, producing wines very similar to, but often coarser than, those from the enclave entitled to the CÉRONS appellation.

The Graves, and in particular the outskirts of Bordeaux, the Grabas de Burdeus, is the birthplace of CLARET. In the Middle Ages, much of the light CLAIRET dispatched in such quantity to England was grown in these vineyards within easy distance of the quayside; the Médoc was largely marshland (see BORDEAUX, history). Ch Pape-Clément is Bordeaux's first named château, while HAUT-BRION was the first New French Claret noted in London, by Samuel Pepys, in 1663. Thomas JEFFERSON noted that in the late 18th century 'Grave' wines were considered the finest Bordeaux had to offer. It was presumably this historic fame which had Ch Haut-Brion, Graves's most famous property, included with the finest Médoc châteaux in the famous CLASSIFICATION in 1855.

For centuries Graves encompassed all the vineyards south of the border with the MÉDOC in a great sweep around the city and upstream along the Garonne as far as Langon, with the exception of the enclaves for sweet white wine appellations BARSAC, Cérons, and SAUTERNES. In 1987, the separate appellation of Pessac-Léognan was formed, a slice of the original Graves appellation which includes all of its most famous properties, and the southern suburbs of Bordeaux itself. For more details of the wines produced there today, see PESSAC-LÉOGNAN.

The creation of this new premium appellation has had the effect of somewhat declassifying the historic name Graves, although some excellent wines are conscientiously made within the modern Graves appellation on the varied GRAVEL terraces which have been deposited there over the millennia. Comparison of annual average yields usually shows a lower figure in Graves, for both red and white wines, than in Pessac-Léognan. The reds, which can truly taste like country cousins of their more urbane neighbours in Pessac-Léognan, can often be good value, and mature earlier than their Médoc counterparts. It is in this area that some serious barrel-fermented, or at least oak-aged, dry whites are made, from Sauvignon and Sémillon grapes in varying proportions, at properties such as Clos Floridène and Chx Chantegrive and La Grave (although better value can sometimes be found on the opposite bank of the Garonne; see PREMIÈRES CÔTES DE BORDEAUX and ENTRE-DEUX-MERS).

Parker, R., *Bordeaux* (2nd edn., New York, 1991).
Penning-Rowsell, E., *The Wines of Bordeaux* (6th edn., London, 1989).
Peppercorn, D., *Bordeaux* (2nd edn., London, 1991).
Vandyke Price, P., *Wines of the Graves* (London, 1988).

GRAVES DE VAYRES, a small BORDEAUX district, named after the historic town of Vayres, which has nothing to do with GRAVES but is just across the river DORDOGNE from the town of Libourne. From more than 500 ha / 1,200 acres of, not surprisingly, gravelly soil, with patches of sand, the appellation produces mainly light red wines made substantially from MERLOT grapes, although many of them are sold under the simple BORDEAUX AC. White wines, both sweet and dry, were once more important. Today the white is usually dry, occasionally given BARREL MATURATION, and constitutes the minority of wine sold as Graves de Vayres.

GRAY RIESLING, California name for a pale grape variety that has nothing to do with Riesling and is a light-berried mutation of TROUSSEAU, Trousseau Gris. It makes pale hued, pale flavoured varietal white wines of pleasant but resolutely small character. Such wines, usually made off-dry, were once popular but the variety covered fewer than 300 acres / 120 ha of California in the early 1990s.

GREAT SOUTHERN, wine region in the extreme south west of the state of WESTERN AUSTRALIA comprising Frankland, Albany, Denmark, Mount Barker, and Porongurup.

GREAT WESTERN, small, isolated but historic wine region in the state of VICTORIA in Australia.

GRECANICO DORATO, Sicilian white grape variety whose total vineyard area increased from less than 3,000 ha to more than 4,500 ha / 11,000 acres in the 1980s.

GRECHETTO, characterful central Italian white grape variety most closely associated with UMBRIA. It is an ingredient in ORVIETO and in the whites of TORGIANO. The vine has good resistance to DOWNY MILDEW and is sufficiently sturdy to make good VIN SANTO. It is typically blended with TREBBIANO, VERDELLO, and MALVASIA, although in ANTINORI's most admired white wine Cervaro it has played a supporting role to CHARDONNAY. Occasionally called Greco Spoletino or Greco Bianco di Perugia, it is by no means identical to GRECO (although it may well share its Greek origins).

GRECO, name of one or perhaps several, usually noble, white grape varieties of Greek origin currently grown in southern Italy, although, according to the 1990 vineyard survey, the most widely planted Greco vine variety is **Greco Nero**, of which there were 3,200 ha / 7,900 acres, while **Greco Bianco** plantings totalled less than 1,000 ha.

In CAMPANIA it produces the respected full bodied dry white **Greco di Tufo** around the village of Tufo, while, blended with Falanghina and Biancolella grapes, it makes a contribution to the inconsequential dry whites of the island of Capri.

Perhaps the finest Greco-based wine is the sweet **Greco di Bianco** made from semi-dried grapes grown around the town of Bianco on the south coast of CALABRIA.

GREECE, Mediterranean country with a particularly rich history of wine production and consumption in classical times from the 7th century BC and on in the Roman era (see Ancient ROME). Early Greek colonization led to the vine being taken to all parts of the Mediterranean, thus laying the foundations for viticulture and the whole later development of wine in this area. In modern Greece about 150,000 ha / 370,000 acres are devoted to vines, only about half of them producing grapes for wine, DRYING GRAPES and TABLE GRAPES being important to the agricultural economy. About 60 per cent of the annual wine production of between 4.5 and 5.0 million hl (132 million gal) is of white, often sweet, wine.

Ancient Greece

Origins Wine was important in Greek society from the earliest times, forming part of the Greek cultural identity. The Ancient Greeks were aware that other societies, such as the Babylonians in MESOPOTAMIA and the inhabitants of Ancient EGYPT, made and drank wine, but for them it was a luxury, and they normally drank BEER (a drink disparaged by Greek writers as inferior and fit only for foreigners) or else 'wine' made from dates or lotus. Complete ignorance of viticulture was the mark of savages; so too was the drinking of undiluted wine, which was associated with northern barbarians such as the Scythians (in modern CRIMEA).

Although evidence remains scanty, it is very likely that wine was part of the culture of Minoan CRETE in the 2nd millennium BC: remains of grapes and of what are probably wine presses have been found by archaeologists at palaces and villas, and it is quite possible that some of the large storage jars found in the palace complexes contained wine rather than olive oil; an ideogram for 'wine' has been identified in the early script Linear A, and artistic evidence suggests the use of wine in religious rituals. Given the links between Crete and Egypt in this period, the Minoans might be expected both to have learned viticulture from their neighbours and to have exported to supply the demand there and elsewhere in the Near East. In turn, Crete will have influenced contemporary Thíra (modern SANTORINI), where vines and grapes are depicted on painted pottery.

Mycenae There is no doubt of the importance of wine in Mycenaean culture (*c.*1600–1150 BC) which followed and developed on the mainland from Minoan culture: evidence from Mycenae, Tiryns, and Sparta includes grape pips and residues of wine, as well as the seal of a jar bearing the impression of vine leaves, while the palaces have revealed many storage jars, including a complete cellar at Pílos which contained at least 35 large jars, some labelled as containing wine. The evidence of the Linear B script, preserved on clay tablets fired hard in the destruction of the palaces, confirms that wine was important: the palace records contain many references to it, and include words for 'wine', 'vineyard', and, apparently, 'wine merchant', not to mention allusions to the god DIONYSUS. Finds of Mycenaean pottery abroad imply that they were exporting wine and oil to Syria, Palestine, Egypt, Cyprus, Sicily, and southern Italy, while the discovery of a few small CANAANITE jars (the earliest AMPHORAE) at Mycenae suggests that connoisseurs were also importing foreign wines.

Early Greek literature In the poetry of HOMER and HESIOD, the earliest Greek literature, wine is an essential part of life. It is naturally drunk by Greek and Trojan heroes at their feasts, but also used in the rituals of sacrifice, prayer, and burial, to solemnize agreements, and for therapeutic purposes; it is also the human drink, whereas gods drink nectar. A depiction of the vintage, in an enclosed vineyard, is part of the encapsulation of human life on the shield which Hephaestus makes for Achilles (*Iliad* 18. 561 f.). Wine is the touchstone of civilization: even the Cyclopes in the *Odyssey* drink it, but without cultivating the vine, unlike the pleasure-loving Phaeacians, and, when offered the fine wine of Maron, Polyphemus swigs it neat until he falls into a stupor. Homer implies that the vine was widespread in Greece in his time, describing a number of places as 'rich in vines' (including Phrygia: in this as in other respects the Trojans are as civilized as the Greeks), and he gives us our earliest reference to specific wines, Pramnian and Ismarian, while Hesiod mentions Bibline. Advice on viticulture forms part of Hesiod's *Works and Days*: he mentions pruning and the harvest, including drying the grapes before vinification to make early forms of DRIED GRAPE WINES.

The extent of viticulture In the classical period, vines were grown throughout Greece, and, through colonization, the Greeks carried viticulture to Sicily and southern Italy (which the Greeks called OENOTRIA, 'land of trained vines'), southern France, and the Black Sea. Some producers operated on a large scale, with extensive estates: we can infer the existence of vineyards of 8 to 10 ha and 30 ha/74 acres on the island of Thásos in the northern Aegean in the late 5th century BC and of one of about 12 ha in Attica in the middle of the 4th century, and Diodorus records a cellar at Acragas in Sicily with a storage capacity of 12,000 hl/317,000 gal and a vat holding 400 hl/10,500 gal (*Library of History* 13. 83). However, most viticulture was probably on a small scale, part of the normal peasant system of polyculture, which in Greece was founded on grain, vines, and olives; vines require more labour than cereals, but wine and grapes clearly played an important part in the Greek diet.

Trade Viticulture was also important to the economy of many cities, as is shown by the number of states whose coinage bears wine-related designs. Greek wine was traded within Greece, with Athens, the largest and richest city, offering the best market, and exported throughout the Mediterranean world, especially to Egypt, the Black Sea, Scythia, and Etruria (modern TUSCANY). Soon the colonial cities began to produce and export their own wine. (See CELTS for archaeological evidence of the geographical extent to which Greek wine and drinking rituals were adopted.) Amphorae from Marseilles are found along the southern coast of France and up the RHÔNE valley, while in the CRIMEA archaeology has revealed extensive estates, their vineyards protected from the prevailing winds by low walls and planted with indigenous grapes which were gradually domesticated, rather than with imported varieties.

Grapes losing moisture in a well-ventilated attic. Masi use one of the simplest ways of concentrating sugars to produce their **Amarone**, a **dried grape wine** which, unusually, tastes dry rather than sweet.

Galegati

The scale of the Greek wine trade can be inferred from the widespread finds of amphorae and the seals which indicate their origin. The richest evidence is from the island of Thásos, which took elaborate precautions to regulate its wine trade, both to maximize tax revenues and to prevent fraud which would damage its reputation; amphorae were required to be of standard sizes and were sealed with the name of an annual magistrate, which acted as a guarantee of authenticity; other states also used this system. Thásos also protected her commerce by forbidding her citizens to import foreign wine.

Viticultural practices No vine grown today can be confidently traced back to any Ancient Greek variety, although we know the names of 50 or more, some of which were cultivated in Italy in Roman times, and names such as GRECO, GRECHETTO, and AGLIANICO (i.e. Helleniko) reflect popular traditions of continuity. Roman writers noted that the YIELDS of Greek varieties were low, although their quality was good. In the 4th century BC the botanically expert THEOPHRASTUS was aware of the need to match varieties to soil type and MESOCLIMATE, and recommended PROPAGATION by cuttings or suckering. A variety of TRAINING regimes was used: often vines were supported by forked props or trained up trees, but a few varieties naturally formed bushes, and sometimes plants were simply left to trail on the ground; training on trees meant climbing up, or using trestles, to pick the grapes. PRUNING was known to have an important effect on yields and quality, and land leases sometimes specify that the lessors be allowed to oversee it towards the end of a lease, as well as regulating the use of manure as fertilizer.

Vinification The HARVEST was, as in modern Greece, early by European standards: Hesiod recommends early September. Vase paintings suggest that, in many cases, pressing took place near the vineyard: the grapes were trodden inside a handled wicker basket which in turn stood in a wooden trough with low legs, from which the juice ran through a spout into an earthenware vat sunk in a hole in the ground; sometimes a sieve was placed over the mouth of the vat. As pickers brought grapes in, they were added to the basket, while the treader held on to the basket handles or a ring or rope overhead (or a convenient vine) to keep his balance, and worked at CRUSHING in time to a flute. There are also scenes of treading in the vat itself, in which case the skins and pips will not have been strained out, and the wine will have taken colour from the skins, an early form of PIGEAGE. In either case, the vats will then have been covered and the juice taken for FERMENTATION in jars of larger capacity (*pithoi*); these could be 3 m / 10 ft high, with a mouth a metre across. Larger and more specialized establishments had permanent stone treading floors rather than wooden ones, but otherwise the process was the same; although the beam PRESS was normally used for olives, there is no firm evidence for its use in wine production in classical Greece, and the screw press probably only appeared in Roman republican times.

References to the drying of grapes in Hesiod and the *Odyssey* (see DRIED GRAPE WINES) suggest that this was the early norm, but in later times practices varied: a Lesbian wine, protropon, was made from FREE-RUN juice, while in other cases grapes were deliberately harvested unripe to produce a wine with high ACIDITY (Omphakias); fresh MUST itself was sometimes drunk, as was boiled must. Finally, the solids left after treading could be moistened with water and trodden again to yield a low-quality PIQUETTE called Deuterias or Stemphulites.

Although wine was often transferred from the fermentation vessels once fermentation was over, it is clear that it had not been subjected to proper RACKING or FINING since a sieve or strainer through which to pour the wine is a standard feature of the SYMPOSIUM, and although Theophrastus may refer to the addition of gypsum, which was later used for the purposes of both CLARIFICATION and ACIDIFICATION, he describes this as an Italian practice. References to 'strained wine' suggest that it was unusual, and the straining may have been done at the point of sale, rather than during production.

Common additives The basic wine could be 'improved' by various additives: the use of a small percentage of seawater or brine seems to have begun in the 4th century BC, apparently as a flavouring, although it probably also had preservative qualities, and the technique was associated with particular areas of production, notably the island of Kós. We also hear of the addition of aromatic herbs, to produce a sort of VERMOUTH, and of perfume being added both in production and by the consumer, as well as of the use of boiled must and, on Thásos, of the addition of a mixture of dough and honey to produce a special CUVÉE for consumption on state occasions. BLENDING of different wines was also practised: Theophrastus gives one example, a mixture of hard but aromatic wine from Heraclea with soft Erythraean (a salted wine) which lacks BOUQUET, and says that there are many other blends known to experts (see TASTING, ancient history).

Containers for wine Finished wine was normally stored in AMPHORAE lined with resin or pitch (see RESINATED WINES) to limit porosity, which will have affected the taste to some extent, and pitch was also used to secure the stopper, which was usually of pottery, although the use of cork was known. Amphorae of the classical period held between 20 and 75 l (5–20 gal), depending on their origin, and added 5–15 kg (11–33 lbs) to the total load. These commercial amphorae are, of course, to be distinguished from the much smaller painted pots, also called amphorae, which were used to present the wine when it was drunk. In the *Odyssey* (2. 340 f.), Telemachus had wine drawn off from the big *pithoi* in which it had been ageing into amphorae for his journey abroad. Homer also refers quite frequently to wine kept in wineskins, but in classical times skin bags were probably mainly filled for rapid consumption; despite being lighter and, perhaps, less fragile, they will have flavoured the wine, being usually made from the skin of a sheep or goat.

Steep vineyards such as those of **Guigal** in **Côte-Rôtie** produce great wine, but **mechanization** is physically impossible. Each full hod (remarkably like those depicted on the Cluny tapestry opposite p. 80) weighs between 35 and 40 kg.

Part of a vase dating from 480 BC depicting boys serving wine in **Ancient Greece**.

Selling wine At Athens, wine was mainly bought from wine sellers for immediate consumption: after the purchaser had sampled the wine, the required amount was ladled or siphoned from the amphora into a jug or small amphora which the purchaser usually provided: wealthier customers, however, and those holding parties, will have bought an amphora at a time. Evidence on price is scanty, but for imported wine of good quality, such as Chian or Mendean, at Athens in the 4th century BC a *chous* of about 3.25 l cost between a quarter of a drachma and 2 drachmas (a drachma being a day's wage for a craftsman). Of course, these were luxury wines, with prices to match: one Athenian, urged to improve his morals by the Areopagus, the Council of Elders, cited drinking Chian, along with keeping a mistress, as evidence of a life of blameless hedonism appropriate to a gentleman. See also MERCHANTS, ancient history.

Specific wines Some idea of the leading wines of classical Greece can be obtained from references in literature, particularly lyric poetry and the Athenian comic poets; these make it clear that in Athens, at least, there was a degree of CONNOISSEURSHIP, different poets singing the praises of different wines while disparaging their rivals. The most frequently praised wines are those of Thásos, Lésvos, Mende, and Khíos (especially one called Ariousian), while those of Ismaros (in Thrace), Náxos, Peparethos (modern Skópelos), Acanthos and, from the 4th century, Kós were also admired.

This makes it clear that, although other areas had their admirers, the regions which produced the best wines were, by general consent, the AEGEAN ISLANDS, particularly to the east, and Chalkidike (modern Khalkhidhikhi near Ch Carras, see below) and Thrace on the northern mainland.

Two other much-praised wines, Pramnian and Bibline, are problematic. Pramnian, whose name goes back to Homer, is associated with a number of places—Lésvos, Smyrna, and the island of Ikaros (modern Ikaría, in the Dodecanese)—and indeed, according to ATHENAEUS, some considered it a generic name for dark wine, or long-lived wine; however, there was also a vine variety called Pramnian, and it seems most likely that Pramnian, which perhaps originated on Ikaría, came to be used as the name of wine of the style of the original, 'neither sweet nor rich, but dry, hard and unusually strong', whether or not made from the original vine.

In the case of Bibline, the problem is a confusion of names, since there was also Bybline wine, from Byblos in PHOENICIA, which is highly praised for fragrance by the 4th century BC gastronome Archestratus; Bibline, however, took its name from a region in Thrace where it originated, and came from a vine called Bibline, which was apparently subsequently introduced elsewhere. Since scribes were prone to confuse the two, allusions cannot always be reliably attributed to one or the other, but it is plain that both had excellent reputations. On these interpretations, both Pramnian and Bibline will also fall within the top zone outlined above. In all cases, wines are praised in terms of their origins; we never hear of particular estates or producers as being superior.

What was Greek wine like? First, it could be of three colours, white, black or red, and tawny, the last being less frequently mentioned; Homer's wine is always dark. Greeks were sensitive to aromas, and often speak of wines being fragrant; more specifically, they refer to wine as 'smelling of flowers', an expression often almost equivalent to our BOUQUET, although the way in which the comic poet Hermippus talks of a mature wine 'smelling of violets, roses and hyacinth' shows that it was not always metaphorical; the same passage attributes a scent of apples to Thasian wine. The sweetest wines were said to lack bouquet, which could, according to Theophrastus, be supplied by blending, spicing, or perfuming.

In taste, wine is often praised as sweet, honeyed, ripe, and soft, and this must have appealed to the Greek palate, to judge from the production of PASSITO, or dried grape wines, and even sweet wine further concentrated by boiling. Given the likely ripeness of the grapes, the limitations of natural YEASTS, and, perhaps, the risk of STUCK FERMENTATION without TEMPERATURE CONTROL, sweetness must have been the most frequent outcome. However, this was not always the case: as noted earlier, grapes were sometimes picked unripe, and some varieties, like Pramnian, were naturally more austere; one vine was allegedly called 'smoky' because the wine was so sharp as to bring tears to the eyes, like smoke. Medical writers discussing the qualities of wines class them as dry or sweet white; and dry, sweet, or medium red/black, so there was obviously a wide range of styles.

Wine ageing Given the vagaries of vinification, much Greek wine will not have lasted long, succumbing either to OXIDATION, which medical and scientific writers noticed and discussed as a form of decomposition, or to spoilage due to inadequate storage, the risk of which was noted by Aristotle. It is not surprising that the people of Thásos traded in VINEGAR as well as wine, and that sour wine was a regular cheap drink, especially since the risk of oxidation must have increased as a large jar was emptied.

Nevertheless, some wines clearly aged, since old wine was highly regarded by the Greeks: 'praise old wine, but the flowers of new songs,' said the poet Pindar, and comic poets noted that women preferred old wine but young men. The old wine praised by Hermippus (above) was described as *sapros*: literally, 'rotten' or 'decomposed', but obviously referring in the case of wine to the production of secondary flavours through AGEING; older wine was also described as having 'lost its bite'. We never find discussion of particular VINTAGES (unlike Roman wines and specific vintages such as OPIMIAN wine mentioned by Roman writers), and there is little reliable evidence as to how long good wine might keep: Theocritus speaks of drinking four-year-old wine, perhaps from Kós, in the early 3rd century BC, and in the same era Peparethian wine was regarded as a slow developer in requiring six years to reach maturity, while the elder PLINY (in the 1st century AD) considered all foreign wines middle-aged at seven years old; comparisons with the wines of Ancient ROME, which evidently matured more slowly, might allow one to guess that few Greek wines lasted more than 10 years, a good age for a wine in the heroic age (*Odyssey* 3. 390–2), but not a very long time by modern standards, especially when we remember that the CONTAINERS were very much larger than modern ones, so that the rate of development should have been proportionately reduced.

The uses of wine Wine had many uses for the Greeks. It was of course important as a food and drink (it was doubtless often safer than water), and the SYMPOSIUM, which centred around the drinking of wine, was one of the most important Greek social forms. Wine was almost always drunk diluted with water: the ratio varied, normally ranging between 2 : 3 and 1 : 3, which would give a range in ALCOHOLIC STRENGTH of about three to eight per cent (roughly the same as British draught beer). Weaker mixtures are disparaged in comedy (and even 1 : 3 called for a good wine), but 1 : 1 was considered by some dangerous to the health, and the regular drinking of unmixed wine, a habit confined to barbarians, was believed by some Spartans to have caused the insanity and death of their King Cleomenes. The mixed wine was also normally cooled, sometimes in special pottery coolers; the very rich added snow.

The medical uses of wine were numerous, and much discussed by medical writers. Its advantages as a pick-me-up, tonic, and analgesic were obvious, and by experience it became clear that certain wines were nourishing, diuretic, good for the digestion, and so on, but the qualities of different types were also discussed in terms of the four essential qualities (hot, cold, wet, dry) in order to decide how they should be used to correct imbalances in the bodily humours.

There are occasional references to procedures for making wine-based medicines, either by adding drugs to the wine or by treating the vines with an appropriate agent, although these usually seem to be closer to folklore than science; certain wines also had the reputation of producing medical side-effects: those of Troizen (just across the Saronic Gulf from Athens), for example, were said to render the drinker sterile. The Greeks were also well aware of the hazards of consuming wine to excess, and Athenaeus mentions popular remedies for a hangover.

After social aspects, however, the most important aspect of wine was its place in religion. A LIBATION (*sponde*) of wine was offered whenever wine was drunk as a sort of first fruit (at the symposium different gods were invoked for each bowlful) and drink offerings were part of the formula for prayers; hence treaties and truces were referred to as *spondai*, because they were sanctified by prayers and libations. Wine was used to quench the burning offerings on the altar at a sacrifice, and was one of the liquids poured on the ground as an offering to the dead.

More than this, however, wine was directly associated with a particularly divinity: DIONYSUS was the patron god and the symbol of wine, as Demeter was of cereals, and one of the 12 major divinities (a further indication of the basic importance of wine to the Greeks). R.B.

Wine festivals

For the Athenian of the 5th century BC, festival days in honour of the gods at set times of year gave the sort of relaxation now provided by weekends. Many of them were associated with wine drinking, vine-growing, and the HARVEST. The most important of these, the Anthesteria, was in honour of DIONYSUS, celebrated in February the opening of wine jars to test the new wine. It included processions and ritual wine drinking contests and was probably closest to the modern idea of a wine festival. None the less, at the heart of the festival was the serious business of the dedication of the new wine to Dionysus.

Other festivals included the Oschophoria, a vintage celebration in September which seems to have been restricted to aristocratic families: two young men led a procession carrying vine branches with the grapes still on them (*oschoi*) in honour of Dionysus. The Apatouria in the same month was the festival when young males were registered in their *phratries*, or clans, and there was much associated pouring of wine. The last day of this festival was called Epildon and came to mean 'the morning after'. Strangely, there does not seem to have been a particularly important festival at the time of the grape harvest. At the country Dionysia celebrated in the country around Athens, a jar of wine and a vine headed the procession.

The great festivals of Athens, the Panathenaia and the City Dionysia, were dominated by the vine (perhaps because they were held further from the vineyards) but there is no doubt that wine was enjoyed at them. H.H.A.

Bibliographical note: There is no modern book on Greek wine, works on ancient wine (cited under Ancient ROME) tend to pass rapidly on to Rome, where the evidence is much fuller; however, Roman sources are not necessarily reliable evidence for Greek practice 500 years earlier. Of the ancient sources, ATHENAEUS' *Deipnosophistae* collects much classical literary material (especially Books 1–2, 25e–40f) and Theophrastus' *Enquiry into Plants and On the Causes of Plants* (especially 3. 11–16) contain a lot of botanical lore; all are accessible in translation in the Loeb Classical Library, the first two with good indexes. Modern research has tended to concentrate on details, especially AMPHORAE: V. Grace, *Amphoras and the Ancient Wine Trade* (2nd edn., Princeton, NJ, 1979) is a good general introduction to this area, while F. Salviat, 'Le Vin de Thasos', *Bulletin de correspondance hellénique supplément*, 13 (1986), 145–95, collects the evidence for the best-documented region. B. A. Sparkes, 'Treading the Grapes', *Bulletin Antieke Beschaving*, 51 (1976), 47–64 collects and discusses the pictorial evidence for the vintage.

Medieval history

In the medieval Greece that was part of the Byzantine empire wine was grown by private individuals and by monasteries (see MONKS AND MONASTERIES). Monasteries were foremost among the great landowners because, as in western Europe, they received donations and bequests from the laity. In the 8th and 9th centuries agriculture was exceptionally profitable; its chief products were wine and fruits and also cotton and medicinal herbs. As in antiquity, the best wines came from the AEGEAN ISLANDS, Khíos first of all, and Thásos and Crete. The wines of Thrace and ASIA MINOR (Cappadocia in particular) were ranked second to these. Evidence from shipwrecks shows that wine was still transported in amphorae in the 7th century, whereas wooden BARRELS were commonly used in western Europe from the 3rd century AD. After the 7th century the Greeks, too, started using wooden casks, which are lighter and easier to handle than amphorae.

In the 12th century Constantinople (on the site of modern Istanbul) was the centre of the Byzantine empire's wine trade. Wines were shipped to Constantinople from the Aegean islands, from Thebes, and also from near Monemvasia, a port on the southern Peloponnese, which gave its name to MALVASIA and its English corruption MALMSEY. Monasteries were exempted from customs duties and were therefore at an advantage compared to private growers and traders: the monasteries of Patmos and Mount Áthos, for instance, made large profits from selling their wines in Constantinople.

But the private growers and wine merchants of Greece faced a much greater problem than unfair competition from monks. In 1082 the Emperor Alexius I Comnenus had granted VENICE trading facilities at Constantinople and in 32 towns without payment of taxes of any kind. As a result so much money disappeared to the west that Byzantium was economically ruined. Wine producers and wine merchants suffered badly. With no duties to pay, the Venetians were able to sell wine much more cheaply than any Greek could. Often this was imported Italian wine, but most of the wine came from Crete, known then as Candia, which was a colony of Venice (and which was to remain one until the mid 17th century). Worse still, many taverns in Constantinople were owned by Venetians so, in Constantinople at least, they controlled the retail trade as well.

It took until the middle of the 14th century for the Byzantine government at least to try to protect the empire's own trade. After earlier failed attempts, the Venetians agreed in 1361 to accept a distinction between wholesale and retail trade and to impose a tax on their own, with the proceeds of course going to Venice, on taverns run by Venetians. In the 15th century tax was finally levied on wine imported by Venetians, but by then it was too late, for Byzantium's wine trade was no longer viable. Crete and CYPRUS, under Venetian ownership, continued to produce the strong, sweet wines that were capable of surviving the long sea voyage to western Europe, but the harbour of Monemvasia, close to Byzantium's own supply of Malvasia wines, was now too small to take the larger ships that the west had increasingly come to adopt. Monemvasia had been an entrepôt for ships from Cyprus and Crete bound for the west; from the late 14th century onwards it lost out to Cyprus and Crete as a port and the south west Peloponnese declined as a producer of export-quality wine. All trade in Greek wine ceased in the late 15th century, when, after the fall of Byzantium, the Ottoman Turks occupied the Peloponnesian shore and drove out its inhabitants. H.M.W.

Kazhdan, A. P. (ed.), *The Oxford Dictionary of Byzantium*, 3 vols. (Oxford, 1988).
Lambert-Gócs, Miles, *The Wines of Greece* (London, 1990).
Nicol, Donald M., *Byzantium and Venice* (Cambridge, 1988).

Modern history

The centuries of domination by the Ottoman Turks were to blight Greek viticulture and wine-making until well into the 20th century. Wine-making was not normally forbidden to the Christian population, but communication difficulties resulted in a localized peasant industry viewed by the Turkish rulers as a useful means of raising revenue through TAXATION. Thus, while FRANCE, for example, was developing fine wine regions and their markets, Greece remained in what might be termed the vinous Dark Ages.

The battle for independence was prolonged and tortuous, and the exhausted and impoverished modern Greek state, founded in 1913, had preoccupations more important than the creation of a fine wine industry. It was not until well after the two World Wars and the subsequent bitter civil war that Greece began to modernize its fragmented wine industry, widely regarded as a source of cheap, often poorly made wines suitable only for the domestic market.

The Wine Institute of Athens, which experiments with wine-making techniques and advises wine-makers, was in fact founded in 1937, and some of the major modern wine companies had been established in the late 19th century, but were then chiefly concerned with DISTILLATION, bulk wine sales being a subsequent addition. Only in the 1960s was any significant proportion of Greek wine sold in bottle rather than directly from the barrel.

Since the 1960s, however, there has been considerable investment in modern technology, and its results have been evident since the early 1980s with the emergence of Greece's first generation of trained OENOLOGISTS (although it is to the Greek language that we owe the very term OENOLOGY). Such is their enthusiasm that, although in strict commercial terms the big companies Achaia Clauss, Boutari, Kourtakis, and Tsantalis still dominate the market, an increasing number of small, quality-minded estates is emerging. Most modern Greek wine finds a ready market within Greece, where the appreciation of good wine has increased considerably, but some Greek wine, notably that of Domaine Carras, is also exported.

Geography and climate

There are vineyards in all parts of Greece. At latitudes of between 33 and 41 degrees north, they constitute some of the world's hotter wine regions, although some vines are deliberately planted at relatively high ALTITUDES.

The climate is generally predictably MEDITERRANEAN, with short winters and very hot summers in which DROUGHT can be a serious threat in some years, particularly in the south. There can be considerable variation between the cooler vineyards in the mountains, whether on the plateau of Mantinia in the Peloponnese or in Epirus and Macedonia, where grapes may not even reach full RIPENESS, and the intense heat of Pátras or islands such as Crete and Rhodes on which some grapes may be picked in July.

Most of the vineyards are sufficiently close to the sea for maritime breezes to moderate temperatures, but lack of water, particularly on the islands and in the south, is a major problem. Although some rain does fall in the autumn, the first three months of the year are generally the wet months, and many wine areas have no rain at all for six months, which can make the establishment of young vines extremely difficult. IRRIGATION is not generally permitted but may be used to establish new vineyards.

Most of Greece is extremely mountainous. Vines can be found growing on flat land near sea level, such as at Ankhialos; on foothills as at Rapsani on the lower slopes of Mount Olympus; and at altitudes as high as 800 m/2,600 ft on the highest slopes in Neméa. Vines are often planted on north-facing slopes in the hottest areas in order to slow ripening.

There are many soil types in Greece but the soil is generally of low fertility. Subsoils on the mainland tend to be limestone, while on the islands they are mainly volcanic. Clay, loam, schist, and marl are all found, as well as sandy clay and chalk.

Viticulture

The Greek land tenure system means that much of the vineyard area is in the hands of smallholders. Little by little, the large companies which buy in the great majority of their grapes have been working more closely with these vine-growers and spreading more modern viticultural techniques. Grape PRICES were for long determined by sugar levels, which too often resulted in dangerously low levels of ACIDITY, but these problems have been largely resolved by the big commercial concerns, the more modern CO-OPERATIVES, and the more ambitious of the small estates.

Traditionally most vines were left to grow as BUSH VINES, but almost all new vineyards have been designed with TRELLIS SYSTEMS on wires, except for those on very windy sites such as are common on the island of SANTORINI. CORDON systems of pruning and training are more common than GUYOT.

Viticultural knowledge lags behind wine-making practice and the small Vine Institute in Athens for some time concentrated its work on varieties suited to TABLE GRAPES and DRYING GRAPES. VIRUS DISEASES of the vine are common in some vineyards, and the wine industry might profit from research into improving ROOTSTOCKS, particularly for hotter areas. The most common rootstocks are 110 R or 41 B.

Vine varieties

Greece is a still underdeveloped source of indigenous, ancient grape varieties of which more than 300 have been identified. Many of them are used solely for the important table grape or dried fruit industries, however, and many others are used in tiny quantities on a purely local basis. There is still considerable work to be undertaken in vine identification, not just in rediscovering classical varieties, but in discovering the relationships between Greek varieties and those grown elsewhere, in ITALY, CYPRUS, TURKEY, ALBANIA, MONTENEGRO, KOSOVO, CROATIA, and MACEDONIA in particular.

The specifically Greek wine grape varieties can offer unique characters and flavours. Although, for example, Debina remained a speciality of Epirus in the north west, and Xynomavro of Macedonia in the north east, Greek vine-growers are increasingly experimenting with varieties in areas far from their traditional homes as their value in blends is being recognized.

The most important Greek white grape varieties are ASSYRTIKO, RHODITIS, ROBOLA, SAVATIANO, MOSCOPHILERO, VILANA, DEBINA, and both MUSCAT BLANC À PETITS GRAINS and the slightly less important MUSCAT OF ALEXANDRIA. The Greek port of Monemvasia also gave its name to the MALVASIA grape. Among Greek red grape varieties, the most important to the modern Greek wine industry have been AGIORGITIKO, LIMNIO, MANDELARIA, and XYNOMAVRO. See regional details below for more local grape varieties.

In addition to these native varieties, a number have been imported, particularly from France. These include Chardonnay, Sauvignon Blanc, and Ugni Blanc among whites and both Cabernet Sauvignon (thought by some to have been grown in northern Greece since Roman times) and Cabernet Franc, a little Merlot, Grenache, Cinsaut, and Syrah among red grape varieties. Some wines, particularly from the newer, small estates, may be made exclusively from one of these imported varieties: the early 1990s saw one Greek Chardonnay, a Merlot, and a number of Cabernet Sauvignons, but it is far more usual to find these foreign varieties playing a minor role in blends with Greek varieties. Indeed there is a strong lobby within Greece which argues that Greek wine should not be made from imported varieties, and any new wine applying for appellation status is likely to encounter difficulties if the principal grapes used are not Greek in origin.

Wine-making

Since the mid 1980s, almost all Greek wineries have had some sort of REFRIGERATION and the sort of HYGIENE afforded by the use of STAINLESS STEEL vats. Only the oldest co-operatives had yet to make such investments in the mid 1990s.

As in other Mediterranean areas, early picking and cool fermentations enabled by temperature control resulted in clean but characterless white wines of about 11.5 per cent alcohol. Such techniques as SKIN CONTACT, slightly later picking, and deliberate OXIDATION of the must prior to fermentation were used from the early 1990s to develop more interesting wines.

Better-quality red wines have traditionally been matured in large, old casks, but imported French BARRIQUES are increasingly used for the BARREL MATURATION of reds and even some whites.

Wine laws

Greek wine laws were drawn up in the early 1970s and refined in the early 1980s as Greece prepared to join the EUROPEAN UNION. It is hardly surprising, therefore, that the laws conform strictly to EU guide-lines, often even employing the use on the label of the French terms Appellation d'Origine Contrôlée and VIN DE PAYS (for which, as in France, a wider variety of grape varieties may be used than for full APPELLATION CONTRÔLÉE wines).

Wines which qualify as QUALITY WINES according to EU law are either sweet wines, from Mavrodaphne or Muscat grapes, described as Controlled Appellation of Origin (OPE) with a blue seal over the cork, or dry wines described as Appellation of Superior Quality (OPAP) with a pink seal. The words Réserve or Grande Réserve indicate superior wines with extended AGEING.

Vins de pays may be made in a wide variety of specified areas, nearly always from a range of vine varieties which includes both Greek and foreign grape varieties. Commercially the most important vin de pays areas are Attica, Drama, Thívai (or Thebes), Crete, Macedonia, and the Peloponnese.

The large TABLE WINE category includes wine BRANDS that were Greece's most successful wines, as well as some more interesting wines made outside the appellation regulations. The Greeks have also used the term CAVA to indicate high-quality table wine which is made only in small quantities and which has been subject to prolonged ageing.

The official list of Greek wine appellations was drawn up in the 1950s, although some more recent wine areas, such as the Côtes de Meliton on the Khalkhidhikhi peninsula (see Ancient history above), were subsequently grafted on to the official list. Of the 27 appellations in Greece's widely differing regions, some are produced only in tiny quantities. Some are in danger of extinction and one, Kantza, is no longer made at all. Many are seen rarely outside their area of origin while some are well known and thriving.

Wine regions

Wine is made all over Greece, often on a very small, traditional scale. The following includes those quality wine regions which have established their own identity within Greece and sometimes abroad. See map on p. 471.

Northern Greece The regions of Macedonia and Thrace are noted mainly for their red wines, although wines of all hues are made there today. Náoussa, home of red wine from Xynomavro grapes, is on the south eastern slopes of Mount Vermio, at altitudes of between 200 and 350 m (660–1,150 ft), where there is usually no serious lack of rain and winters are cool enough for vine dormancy. Náoussa must be aged for at least a year in OAK, traditionally in old wooden casks, but there has been considerable experimentation with new, small barriques. A system of defining the better slopes and awarding them GRAND CRU status was also being studied in the early 1990s.

Xynomavro is also grown in this area to produce Goumenissa, where it is blended with Negoska grapes, and to make Akmindeo, which lies on the opposite, north western slopes of Mount Vermio from Náoussa but at altitudes as high as 650 m / 2,100 ft. Sparkling rosé is made here as well as red wine.

Perhaps the most famous appellation in northern Greece is its most recent, the Côtes de Meliton on the slopes of Mount Meliton in Sithoniá. This is the appellation specially created by Domaine Carras, a wine estate developed with the well publicized assistance of Professor Émile PEYNAUD of Bordeaux. Here both white and red wines are made with a mixture of Greek and French vine varieties, notably Cabernet Sauvignon. It is significant, however, that, as the domaine extends its vineyards, many of the new vines planted are Greek varieties, including the recently rediscovered and elegant indigenous white Malagousia.

Also in Thrace is an area around Drama where some good

quality vins de pays are made from a mixture of Greek and French grape varieties.

Central Greece Not far from the town of Ioánnina and near the border with ALBANIA lies Zitsa, which produces a dry or medium lightly sparkling white wine from the local Debina grape variety. To the immediate south west, in the mountains round Ioánnina, are Greece's highest vineyards at Métsovon, which have no appellation but yield the popular and superior table wine Katoi from locally grown Cabernet Sauvignon grapes blended with Agiorgitiko grapes grown in Neméa.

On the east coast in Thessaly Rapsani is produced on the foothills of Mount Olympus from Xynomavro (here grown at its most southerly point) blended with Krassato and Stavroto grapes and given extended CASK AGEING. This appellation is undergoing much-needed revival but old vintages suggest that the potential for long-lived, concentrated reds is there. Thessaly's other appellation is Ankhíalos, a dry white wine made from Rhoditis with some Savatiano grapes grown near Vólos at sea level.

Peloponnese This dramatically formed, large southern peninsula has the greatest number of Greek wine appellations, as well as some interesting vins de pays and table wines. On the plateau of Mantinia in Arcadia, at altitudes of about 600 m/2,000 ft, the Moscophilero grape produces a fresh, dry, aromatic, slightly spicy white appellation, while the same grape can be vinified, with extended MACERATION, to yield a simple but fruity rosé.

At Neméa, not far from the Corinth canal which separates the Peloponnese from mainland Greece, the Agiorgitiko grape is grown on deep red soil to produce intense red wine from three different zones whose altitude varies between 250 and 800 m. Grapes from the lowest vineyards frequently lack acidity and can be used to make a sweet wine, but the finest, dry wine is said to come from vineyards between 450 and 640 m above sea level. As in Náoussa (see below) barriques are increasingly used for the maturation, and SEMI-CARBONIC MACERATION has even been used to make a sort of Neméa NOUVEAU.

The vineyards around Pátras on the north coast are responsible for four different appellations. Pátras itself is a dry white wine made from Rhoditis grapes grown on the slopes around the town. Muscat of Pátras is a dessert wine made strong and sweet like a VIN DOUX NATUREL from Muscat Blanc à Petits Grains grapes, as is Rion of Pátras, which is almost extinct owing to the encroachment of buildings on the vineyard area. Mavrodaphne of Pátras is a very popular appellation, on the other hand, consisting of a blend in which Mavrodaphne makes up the majority but may be supplemented by the locally grown Korinthiaki (Corinth or CURRANT) grape grown mainly for DRYING GRAPES. Fermentation is arrested when alcoholic strength has reached about four per cent (as in making PORT) and the wine, like tawny port, is then aged in wood. Examples aged for ten to twelve years in cask can be delicious.

The islands Among the Ionian islands off the west coast, Cephalonia is best known for its wine, particularly the powerful dry white Robola, made from grapes of the same name, which is almost certainly the same variety as the RIBOLLA of north east Italy. Vines here were individually trained on high, stony land, and mainly ungrafted (although PHYLLOXERA'S arrival in the late 1980s presumably signals an end to this). Mavrodaphne and Muscat dessert wines, similar to those of Pátras, are also produced on the island.

From the Cyclades come the wines of Páros and SANTORINI. Páros is a powerful, quite tannic red made from a curious blend of grapes in which the deep colour of the Mandelaria is lightened by the addition of half as much of the white grape called Monemvasia (see MALVASIA). Rainfall is low but the maritime location helps raise humidity. Vines are trained on low bushes as protection against the strong winds. Strong winds are also a characteristic of Santorini. Rainfall on this volcanic island is also very low, but the porosity of the chalk subsoil helps to retain overnight humidity. The Santorini appellation is for a dry white made from Assyrtiko grapes blended with a little Athiri and Aedani, but a sweet DRIED GRAPE WINE, Vissanto, is also made.

The island of Rhodes has been an important producer of wine since classical times. Today there are three appellations: one for a sweet Muscat made in very limited quantities, one for a dry white from Athiri grapes, and another for a red from the Mandelaria, here known as Amorgiano. Only grapes grown on the higher reaches of the north or north eastern slopes qualify for appellation wines. The Rhodes co-operative, the CAIR, also makes a considerable quantity of improving sparkling wine.

Two of Greece's most famous wines are made among the Aegean islands. Lemnos was the original home of the Limnio grape which is still grown there, but the appellation wines are both Muscats. The dry version is rarely seen off the island, but the VIN DE LIQUEUR Muscat of Lemnos is widely admired, being surprisingly delicate.

Muscat of Sámos can claim to be Greece's most famous wine (after retsina). Muscat Blanc à Petits Grains is grown up to 800 m/2,600 ft above sea level, often on TERRACES on the island's steep hillsides, and the vintage can last a full two months, depending on vineyard altitude. Muscat of Sámos comes in several forms: Sámos Doux is a vin de liqueur, while Sámos Vin Doux Naturel is made by stopping the fermentation even earlier. Potentially finest of all, however, is Sámos Nectar, a dried grape wine made from grapes dried in the sun so that they are capable of being fermented into a wine of 15 per cent alcohol, which is then given prolonged cask maturation.

The last of the appellation wines of any commercial importance comes from Crete from a variety of grape varieties unique to the island, together with Mandelaria. The red Liatiko reaches high alcohol levels and ripens very early, sometimes as early as July, while the powerful, deep coloured Kotsifali produces particularly robust red wines. The most important local white grape is Vilana. Local red wine appellations for dry and sometimes sweet wines are Archanes, Daphnes, and Siteaia, while Peza, the most common wine appellation on the island, may be either dry red or white. The vineyards, which tend to be on the north of the island, protected from the hot winds from North Africa by the mountain range, are in the process of being replanted after phylloxera was discovered on the island in the late 1970s.

See also RETSINA, a FLAVOURED WINE speciality of Greece which can claim direct descent from the RESINATED WINES of later classical times. M.McN.

Lambert-Gócs, M., *The Wines of Greece* (London, 1990).

GREEN GRAFTING, viticultural term for BUDDING and GRAFTING in the vineyard or nursery using green stem tissue. Green grafting offers less flexibility in timing than CHIP BUDDING and T-BUDDING because the ROOTSTOCK shoots must be green, and so it must take place in late spring or early summer. As with T-budding, the SCION pieces to be inserted may be from stored winter cuttings or the current season's green shoots. Green grafting is not widely used commercially but is useful for researchers with mist equipment for extending the time and extent of grafting, especially with scarce plant material. B.G.C.

GREENHOUSE EFFECT and viticulture. See CLIMATE CHANGE.

GREEN HUNGARIAN, undistinguished CALIFORNIA white grape variety. 'The best Green Hungarian is the one with the least Green Hungarian in it,' said an early producer of varietal white wine from this bland, obscure grape. The roster of producers dwindles; those who persist rely on RESIDUAL SUGAR for allure. GALET claims that the variety is indeed Hungarian in origin and that it has been known and grown in both Alsace and the Gers as Putzscheere, a German name that refers to the beauty and abundance of its grapes (which have good rot resistance, according to Galet).

Galet, P., 'La Culture de la vigne aux États-Unis et au Canada', *France viticole* (Sept.–Oct. 1980 and Jan.– Feb. 1981).

GRENACHE, the world's second most widely planted grape variety sprawling, in several hues, all over Spain and southern France. It probably owes its early dispersal around the western Mediterranean to the strength and extent of the ARAGON kingdom, but it would make a rewarding subject for an AMPELOGRAPHICAL sleuth. It has been widely accepted that, as Garnacha, it originated in Spain in the northern province of Aragon and then spread to Rioja and Navarre before colonizing extensive vineyard land both north and south of the Pyrenees, notably in Roussillon, which was ruled by Spain, and more particularly by the kingdom of Aragon, for four centuries until 1659. From here, it is assumed, Grenache made its way east and was certainly well established in the southern Rhône by the 19th century. Grenache is undoubtedly, however, the same grape variety as Sardinia's CANNONAU, which the Sardinians claim as their own, advancing the theory that the variety made its way from this island off Italy to Spain when Sardinia was under Aragon rule, from 1297 until 1713.

Whatever its origins, Grenache covers more vine-dedicated ground than any grape variety other than AIRÉN, most commonly encountered in its darkest-berried form as Garnacha Tinta. It is Spain's most planted black grape variety with more than 170,000 ha/420,000 acres and the French census of 1988 demonstrated Grenache Noir's continued advance on the Midi with a total of 87,000 ha by then. For a variety that covers so much terrain, it is remarkably rarely encountered by name by the wine drinker, much of it being blended with other varieties higher in colour and tannin.

With its strong wood and upright growth, Grenache Noir is well suited to traditional bush-like viticulture in hot, dry, windy vineyards. It buds early and, in regions allowing a relatively long growing cycle, can achieve heady sugar levels. The wine produced is, typically, paler than most reds (although low yields tend to concentrate the pigments in Spain), with a tendency to oxidize early, a certain rusticity, and more than a hint of sweetness. If the vine is irrigated, as it has tended to be in the New World, it may lose even these taste characteristics. If, however, as by the most punctilious Châteauneuf-du-Pape producers, it is pruned severely on the poorest of soils and allowed to reach full maturity of both vine and grape, it can produce excitingly dense reds that demand several decades' cellaring. The rediscovery of Rhône reds in the late 1980s encouraged some New World producers to invest more effort in their own Grenache, even though its sturdy trunk has made it less widely popular in the modern era of MECHANICAL HARVESTING.

In Spain Garnacha Tinta is grown extensively, particularly in north and east, being an important variety in such wine regions as Rioja, Navarre, Ampurdán-Costa Brava, Campo de Borja, Cariñena, Costers del Segre, Madrid, La Mancha, Méntrida, Penedès, Priorato, Somontano, Tarragona, Terra Alta, Utiel-Requena, and Valdeorras. In Rioja it provides stuffing and immediate charm when blended with the more austere TEMPRANILLO. The cooler, higher vineyards of Rioja Alta are reserved for Tempranillo while Garnacha is the most common grape variety of the warm eastern Rioja Baja region where the vines can enjoy a long ripening season. The juiciness apparent in these early maturing Riojas can be tasted in a host of other Spanish reds and, especially, rosados. Grenache has been adopted with particular enthusiasm in Navarre, where it is by far the dominant grape variety and dictates a lighter, more obviously fruity style of red and *rosado* than in Rioja. The authorities, anxious to modernize Navarre's image, have been positively discouraging new plantings of Garnacha, however.

Perhaps the most distinctive Spanish wine based on Garnacha Tinta (often incorporating some Garnacha Peluda, otherwise known as LLADONER PELUT) is PRIORATO, the naturally heady wine reminiscent of Roussillon's COLLIOURE made just over the frontier with France, along with exceptional Grenache-based age-worthy VINS DOUX NATURELS such as BANYULS, RIVESALTES, and MAURY. Such wines are further proof that Grenache is capable of producing great wine, albeit a very particular sort of wine.

In France, the great majority of Grenache's extensive vineyards are in the windswept southern Rhône, where seas of Côtes-du-Rhône of varying degrees of distinction are produced alongside smaller quantities of Châteauneuf-du-Pape (and the isolated vin doux naturel RASTEAU). It is undoubtedly the Grenache ingredient that determined Châteauneuf-du-Pape's unusual official requirement of a minimum alcoholic strength (of 12.5°). Although blending has been the watchword here, notably with the more structured Syrah, such monoliths as the famously concentrated Châteauneuf-du-Pape Ch Rayas show what can be done by Grenache and determination alone. Grenache is also responsible for much of southern France's rosé, most obviously and traditionally in Tavel and in neighbouring Lirac but also much further eastwards into Provence proper. In the Midi Grenache plays an unsung supporting role except in Roussillon, where it is the vital ingredient in such distinctive vins doux naturels as BANYULS.

Grenache Noir is being uprooted in Corsica but in Sardinia, as Cannonau, it plays a dominant role in the island's reds, which can achieve daunting levels of natural ripeness, whether in deep, dark dry reds which may have as many as 15° of natural alcohol or dessert wines. The vine is also grown in Calabria and Sicily.

Grenache's ability to withstand drought and heat made it a popular choice with New World growers when FASHION

A bunch of Sémillon grapes at Domaine de Chevalier in the Graves before and after fruit affected by harmful **grey rot** has been cut out.

had little effect on market forces. Thanks to extensive historic acreage in the central San Joaquin Valley, and some in Mendocino, it was still California's third most planted black grape variety after Zinfandel and Cabernet Sauvignon, with a total of 13,000 acres/5,200 ha in 1991 but declining fast. Not even California's RHÔNE RANGERS were expected to reverse this downward trend, although dry-farmed, short-pruned fruit from old vines has been sought out by some wine producers. Grenache has consistently been difficult to ripen in coastal counties and so its primary contributions have been in the form of sweetish rosés and tawny port style wines made from Central Valley fruit. Its fortunes suffered a brief reprise in the late 1980s when White Grenache (made to BLUSH from black grapes) was developed as the natural alternative to WHITE ZINFANDEL when cheap Zinfandel grapes were in short supply.

Grenache was Australia's most planted black grape variety until the mid 1960s. Shiraz (Syrah) overtook it in the late 1970s but it was not until the early 1990s that Australia's Cabernet Sauvignon output overtook that of Grenache. The variety has been shamelessly degraded and milked in the heavily irrigated, undistinguished vineyards in which it has been expected to produce large quantities of wine for basic blends. Only a handful of producers, mainly in the Barossa Valley, take it seriously enough to emulate Châteauneuf-du-Pape.

Grenache Noir is also grown in Israel, where it was exported at the end of the 19th century, to a very limited degree in South Africa, and still, to a much greater extent, in North Africa, where it was once an important element in the usefully soupy reds of Algeria and in some fine Moroccan rosés.

In its white-berried form, **Grenache Blanc**, the variety is discreetly important in France, where it was overtaken by Sauvignon Blanc as fourth most planted white grape variety (after Ugni Blanc, Chardonnay, and Sémillon) as recently as the late 1980s. Although in decline, the variety is much planted in Roussillon, where it produces fat, soft white wines and can be an important ingredient in the paler Rivesaltes. Grenache Blanc is also often encountered in the blended white wines of the Languedoc, to which it can add supple fruit if not longevity. It need not necessarily be consigned to the blending vat, however. If carefully pruned and vinified, it can produce richly flavoured, full bodied varietals that share some characteristics with MARSANNE and can even be worthy of ageing in small oak barrels.

As Garnacha Blanca, it plays a role in north eastern Spanish whites such as those of Alella, Priorato, Tarragona, Rioja, and Navarre.

Grenache Rose and **Grenache Gris** are also commonly encountered in southern French whites and some pale rosés.

Galet, P., *Cépages et vignobles de France* (2nd edn., Montpellier, 1990).
MacDonogh, G., *Syrah, Grenache and Mourvèdre* (London, 1992).

GREY ROT, sometimes known as **grey mould** and sometimes just **rot**, the malevolent form of BOTRYTIS BUNCH ROT and one of the most harmful of the FUNGAL DISEASES that attack vines. In this undesirable bunch rot form, the *Botrytis cinerea* fungus rapidly spreads throughout the berry flesh and the skin breaks down. Other fungi and bacteria then also invade the berry and the grapes become rotten. Badly infected fruit develops off-flavours; badly infected vineyards themselves have a characteristic mouldy and often vinegary smell. Wines produced from such fruit smell mouldy and red wines look pale and grey-brown. When the *Botrytis cinerea* fungus attacks healthy, ripe, white wine grapes and the weather conditions are favourable, it results in so-called NOBLE ROT, which can produce some of the world's finest sweet wines. If the grapes are dark-skinned, unripe, or damaged, or the weather is unremittingly humid, the fungus wreaks so much damage that it is called grey rot.

GRIGNOLINO, a very localized grape variety of the PIEDMONT region in north west Italy sold almost invariably as a pale red VARIETAL wine with an almost alpine scent and a tangy ACIDITY. Grignolino is a native of the Monferrato hills between Asti and Casale and serves the same function as DOLCETTO in the province of Cuneo: that of providing a wine that can be drunk young with pleasure while the brawnier wines of the zone are shedding their youthful asperity—although Grignolino is more difficult to match with food than the fuller Dolcetto. The light colour and relatively low alcohol (11 to 12°) can be deceptive; the wine draws significant TANNINS from the abundant pips of the Grignolino grape and, in fact, takes its name from *grignole*, the dialect name for pips in the province of Asti.

Although Piedmont's producers have been regularly predicting a breakthrough for Grignolino that would transform it into Italy's answer to BEAUJOLAIS, the wine remains an unquestionably local taste and, with its rather odd combination of pale colour, perceptible acidity, and tannins, somewhat *sui generis*. The two DOC areas, Asti and Monferrato Casalese, are rather large, the former having been extended to the south and the latter to the north of the historic areas of Grignolino cultivation, but they produce only 2 million bottles a year between them. Grignolino del Piemonte, a blander VINO DA TAVOLA version, accounts for another 6 million bottles. The substantial variation from producer to producer, a variation which is as much in character as in quality, can be accounted for both by substantial variation in CLONES between different vineyards and by the variety's sensitivity to particular soils. Grignolino seems to show a decided preference for dry, loose soils but is more frequently planted in heavier, moister ones.

The future of the vine appears uncertain, partly because of its extreme susceptibility to disease and, perhaps even more importantly, because of its tendency to ripen late and unevenly. This means that it requires the best sites and exposures, which, in its home base of the Monferrato, are increasingly being reserved for BARBERA or, in the case of the highest vineyards, for international white varieties such as CHARDONNAY. A 1990 survey found only 1,350 ha/3,330 acres of Grignolino, although this represented a small increase on the 1982 area.

Grignolino is also grown in California, thanks to the high proportion of Italians among early grape-growers. Winemaker Joe Heitz is a particular fan, producing some pink wines and, most unusually, a 'Grignolino Port' in 1989. D.T.

GRILLET, CHÂTEAU-. See CHÂTEAU-GRILLET.

GRILLO, Sicilian white grape variety which may have potential but of which plantings halved in the 1980s so that there were hardly more than 2,000 ha/5,500 acres in 1990. See SICILY for more details.

GROLLEAU or **Groslot**, is the Loire's everyday red grape variety. It produces extremely high yields of relatively thin, acid wine and it is to the benefit of wine drinkers that it is so systematically being replaced with Gamay and, more recently, Cabernet Franc. Total French plantings are falling steadily but were still nearly 4,000 ha/9,800 acres in 1988. The status of the variety is such that it is allowed into the rosé but not red versions of APPELLATION CONTRÔLÉE wines such as ANJOU, SAUMUR, and TOURAINE. It has played a major part only in Rosé d'Anjou, in which it is commonly blended with Gamay, which ripens just before it.

Grolleau Gris produces innocuous white wines which may form part of the blend for the Loire's hugely successful VIN DE PAYS du Jardin de la France, although if yields are restricted (which can be very difficult) it can produce wines of real character.

GROPPELLO, red grape variety grown to a limited extent in the Italian wine region of Lombardy.

GROSLOT is a common synonym for the Loire's rather commonplace red vine variety GROLLEAU. Both names are of course identical in pronunciation.

GROS MANSENG is the lesser form of MANSENG.

GROS PLANT, or, to give it a name that is more of a mouthful than the wine usually is, **Gros Plant du Pays Nantais**, is the country cousin of MUSCADET. Made from FOLLE BLANCHE vines, called Gros Plant here, grown in a wide arc east but mainly south of the city of Nantes on the Loire, Gros Plant is one of the most acidic-tasting wines made anywhere. The wines of ENGLAND, LUXEMBOURG, and parts of GERMANY may reach similar levels of acidity, but Gros Plant's aggressively dry style serves only to accentuate its inherent tartness. The Folle Blanche vine was introduced to this region by the DUTCH WINE TRADE, and outnumbered the Muscadet vine until the ravages of PHYLLOXERA in the late 19th century. Gros Plant qualifies as a VDQS and about a third as much Gros Plant is made as Muscadet, although a much smaller proportion ever manages to leave the region. A small amount of sparkling Gros Plant is also made.

GROSSER RING, or, to give it its full name, **Der Grosser Ring der Prädikatsweinversteigerer von Mosel, Saar und Ruwer**, German organization to which only the finest estates in the MOSEL-SAAR-RUWER region of GERMANY may belong. Founded in 1908 by the mayor of Trier, and still based in that Roman city in the upper Mosel, it was initially based on the owners of the best sites who voluntarily agreed to sell, at an annual auction in Trier, only what was then called NATURREIN, or wine that owed nothing to the process of CHAPTALIZATION. The Grosser Ring formed the basis for, and is still a member section of, the national VDP organization. The Grosser Ring is axiomatically devoted to the RIESLING grape by virtue of its location, and is distinguished by its willingness to expel under-performing members. Trier auctions continue, but are usually restricted to the rarest bottles.

GROSSLAGE, literally a 'large site' in GERMANY, is in wine terms a collection of individual sites (EINZELLAGEN) and a somewhat opportunistic geographical device which has enabled some very ordinary wines to be labelled as though they were from a single vineyard. About 150 Grosslagen were created by the GERMAN WINE LAW of 1971, each of them given a popular name. The average size of a Grosslage is about 600 ha / 1,500 acres, while the average size of an Einzellage is just 38 ha. Wines produced anywhere within the Grosslage, all of which fall within individual wine regions, may use the Grosslage name. Thus in RHEINHESSEN, for example, the Krötenbrunnen Grosslage covers 1,800 ha of flat land which includes 28 individual vineyards or Einzellagen in 13 different villages. Since the name of one of these villages, Oppenheim, is the most famous, wine from anywhere in the Grosslage area may be sold as Oppenheimer Krötenbrunnen. Lawmakers may know that there is at the very least a quantitative difference between an Oppenheimer Krötenbrunnen and, for example, an Oppenheimer Kreuz from a single vineyard on the elevated RHEINTERRASSE, capable of producing really concentrated wines of distinction, but the average consumer does not.

Some of the most commonly exported combinations of village name and Grosslage name (a village name must always be prefixed) are in the MOSEL-SAAR-RUWER Zeller Schwarze Katz, Kröver Nacktarsch, Bernkasteler Badstube, Bernkasteler Kurfürstlay, Piesporter Michelsberg, Klüsserather St Michael, Wiltinger Scharzberg; in NAHE Binger Schlosskapelle, Rüdesheimer Rosengarten; in Rheinhessen Niersteiner Gutes Domtal, Oppenheimer Krötenbrunnen; and in PFALZ Forster Mariengarten.

In 1993 there were moves to abandon Grosslagen altogether and replace them with more rigorously defined URSPRUNGSLAGEN. This was fiercely resisted by those merchants who find Grosslagen so commercially convenient.

The wine regions of AUSTRIA have also been divided into Grosslagen, or collective sites. Some of them, such as Retzer Weinberge in the Weinviertel, encompass a vast vineyard area, but none of them has any reputation outside Austria.

Johnson, H., *Atlas of German Wines* (London and New York, 1986).

GROWER, the all-important producer of the raw material for wine-making. This individual may be called a grape-grower, more precisely a vine-grower, possibly even a wine-grower if he or she also vinifies. Terms in other languages include *vigneron* and *viticulteur* in French, and *vignaiolo* in Italian. Wine producers who grow their own grapes and vinify them into wine but on a limited scale are often referred to somewhat carelessly and often inaccurately as **small growers**. A significant proportion of all vine-growers produce only grapes, however, which they sell to CO-OPERATIVES, merchant-bottlers, or larger wineries.

GROWTH CYCLE of the vine. See VINE GROWTH CYCLE.

GROWTH REGULATORS, synthetic substances which act on vines like HORMONES to regulate their growth and development. A synthetic AUXIN, 4-CPA, has for example been used to improve FRUIT SET, as has the growth retardant CCC (2-chloroethyl trimethylammonium chloride). Synthetic GIBBERELLINS have been used to increase berry size, especially for the seedless SULTANA, and a synthetic ethylene-releasing compound termed ethephon can be used to hasten grape maturity and enhance coloration in particularly cool climates. More recently applied to viticulture, hydrogen cyanamide encourages early and complete BUDBREAK, which can be useful for TROPICAL VITICULTURE. These chemicals are mostly used for TABLE GRAPES and their application to both table grapes and wine grapes is regulated by rules governing the use of AGROCHEMICALS. R.E.S.

GRUMELLO, subzone of VALTELLINA in the far north of Italy.

GRÜNER VELTLINER, the most commonly planted vine variety in AUSTRIA and grown elsewhere in eastern Europe. In 1992 this well-adapted variety was planted on more than a third of Austria's 58,000 ha / 143,000 acres of vineyard, particularly in lower Austria, where it represents more than half of total white grape production, and in the Vienna region, where it comprises about a third and plays an important part in HEURIGE wine.

The vine is productive and relatively hardy, but ripens too late for much of northern Europe, for example. Yields of 100 hl/ha (5.7 tons/acre) are often achieved, almost invariably using the LENZ MOSER system of vine training, in the least distinguished vineyards of the Weinviertel in lower Austria and the resulting wine is inoffensive if unexciting. At its best, arguably in the Wachau and in the hands of some of the most ambitious growers in Vienna, Grüner Veltliner can produce wines which combine both perfume and substance, not unlike some ALSACE in style. The wine is typically dry, peppery, or spicy, and best drunk in its youth, but, even if they do not actually improve with time, better examples do not deteriorate fast either.

The variety is also grown just over lower Austria's northern border in CZECHOSLOVAKIA, where it is known as Veltlin Zelene or Veltlinske Zelené and in the Sopron vineyards of HUNGARY as Zöldveltelini. The detailed German vine census of 1990 counted just 1 ha of this variety, in the Rheinhessen region.

Roter Veltliner (once planted in California) and, less importantly, **Brauner Veltliner** are grown to a much more limited extent in lower Austria. The combined plantings of both of these dark-skinned mutations of Grüner Veltliner totalled not much more than 200 ha/500 acres, or one per cent of the area planted with Grüner Veltliner, in the early 1990s. See also FRÜHROTER VELTLINER, however.

GUENOC VALLEY, CALIFORNIA wine region and AVA. See LAKE COUNTY.

GUIGAL, family-owned merchant-grower based at Ampuis, CÔTE-RÔTIE, in the northern RHÔNE. Although established as recently as 1946 by Étienne Guigal, Établissements Guigal is the most famous of any of the Rhône valley's merchants or growers. This is very largely due to the efforts of its manager since 1971, Étienne's only son Marcel, a man of exceptional modesty and a gifted, meticulous wine-maker. Guigal owns 12 ha/30 acres of prime vineyard in Côte-Rôtie, and it was the wines made from three of its best parcels, extravagantly praised by influential American wine writer Robert PARKER in the early to mid 1980s, that first drew international attention to Marcel Guigal. It would be fair to say that the quality of Guigal's top wines, along with Parker's persistent enthusiasm for them among many other Rhône wines, spearheaded a resurgence of interest in the whole region.

Guigal's so-called CRU wines (La Mouline, La Landonne, and La Turque) are dark, dramatic, mouth-fillingly rich and oaky expressions of the SYRAH grape; made from low yields of very ripe, late-picked fruit aged for three and a half years in 100 per cent new oak, and bottled without FINING or FILTRATION. They are particularly impressive when young and their quality is beyond question, but opinions are divided about their style; purists in particular feel that their Syrah character is masked by excessive oak. Reputation and rarity combined (only 400 to 700 cases of each are made each year) have also made them extremely expensive and therefore game for criticism, fair or not. Because of the ballyhoo over his top wines, it is easy to overlook the fact that Guigal's NÉGOCIANT wines, made substantially from bought-in grapes, are also very good and deservedly popular.

In 1984 Guigal bought and revitalized the firm of Vidal Fleury, the company where Étienne Guigal worked for 15 years before founding his own. Vidal Fleury is run quite independently of Guigal although Marcel makes its Côte Rôtie wines. M.W.E.S.

Livingstone-Learmonth, J., *The Wines of the Rhône* (3rd edn., London, 1992).

GUMPOLDSKIRCHEN, wine centre in lower AUSTRIA famous for its fiery, full bodied whites made from ZIERFANDLER (or Spätrot) and ROTGIPFLER grapes. Now part of the district known as Thermenregion.

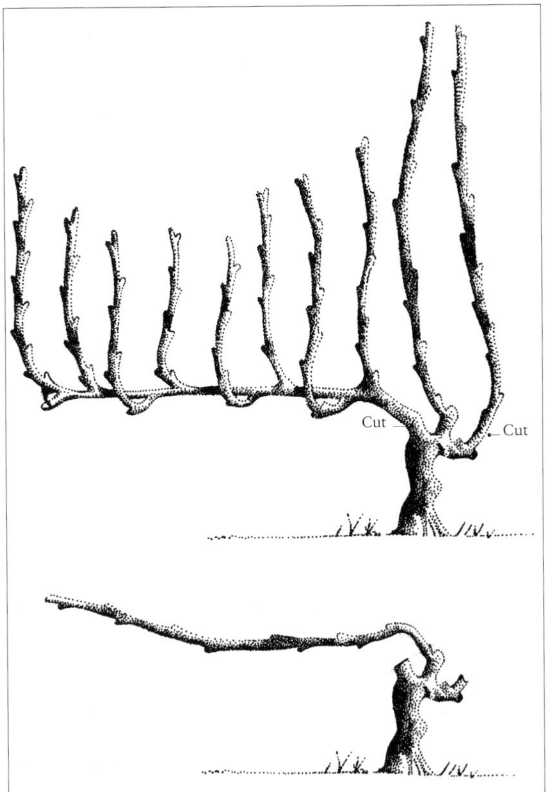

Simple single **Guyot** pruning

GUTEDEL, meaning 'good and noble' in German, is not the most obvious synonym for CHASSELAS today but Germany still grows more than 1,300 ha/3,200 acres of Weisser Gutedel, almost all of them in the Markgräflerland region of BADEN where it continues to be popular with growers. A dark-berried form, Roter Gutedel, is also known here.

GUTENBORNER is a very minor white-berried German vine crossing bred from Müller-Thurgau × Chasselas Napoleon which has had some success in sheltered sites of GREAT BRITAIN and, unusually for a modern crossing, the Rheingau and Mosel-Saar-Ruwer in Germany, where total plantings had fallen to just 10 ha/25 acres by 1990. Its main attribute is its ability to ripen in cool climates.

GUTSABFÜLLUNG, term found on wine labels in GERMANY meaning 'estate bottled'. The wine must be bottled by the cellar which harvested the grapes and made the wine. The bottler must have cultivated the vineyard for at least

Gyropalettes—the late 20th century alternative to manual *remuage*.

three years and must have kept records for tax purposes. The wine-maker must have some professional training in OENOLOGY. This is therefore a much more exclusive term than ERZEUGERABFÜLLUNG.

GUTTATION, botanical term applied to vines losing water through small pores at the leaf margin due to root pressure. It can be seen early in the morning for vines in wet soil under cool conditions. See also BLEEDING. R.E.S.

GUTTURNIO, red wine from EMILIA-ROMAGNA in Italy.

GUYOT, JULES, respected 19th century French scientist with a particular interest in viticulture and wine-making whose name lives on in the system of CANE PRUNING which he promulgated. His practical treatises on growing vines and making wine were translated into English in the second half of the 19th century and enthusiastically followed by NEW WORLD vignerons.

Although cane pruning had been used in France for a very long period, it was enthusiastically proposed and made common by Dr Guyot in 1860. The basic principal of Guyot pruning is to leave six- to ten-bud canes and a single two-bud spur at the base; shoots from this spur form the cane the following year (see PRUNING). The Guyot simple form, also known as single Guyot, has one cane and one spur. The length of the cane (in French *long bois* or *aste*), or at least the number of buds thereon, may be fixed by APPELLATION laws. Double Guyot, the most common vine-TRAINING SYSTEM in Bordeaux, has two canes and two spurs, and the canes are trained to each side. Sometimes the canes are arched, as in the Jura. Galet lists regional variations of the Guyot.
R.E.S.

Galet, P., *Précis de viticulture* (4th edn., Montpellier, 1983).

GYROPALETTE or **girasol**, special metal crate holding many dozen bottles of champagne method sparkling wine in a remote controlled, movable frame. This is the mechanized form of RIDDLING and was developed in Catalonia in the 1970s. For more details, see SPARKLING WINE-MAKING.

H

HAIL, frozen raindrops or ice bodies built up by accretion, typically falling in thunderstorms. To the normal ill effects of heavy summer RAINFALL is added direct physical damage to the vines and fruit. That to the vines ranges from ripping and stripping of the leaves to bruising and breaking of the young stems: effects which can carry over to the following season or even much longer. Damage to young bunches reduces the crop, although compensatory growth of the remaining berries may minimize the effects on final YIELD if damage is limited, and the remainder of the season is kind. Hail damage while berries are ripening, on the other hand, is invariably a disaster. Smashed berries are prey to ROT and ferment on the vine, rendering even undamaged parts of the bunches unusable. BURGUNDY is particularly prone to hail damage.

Hailstorms characteristically follow irregular but well-defined pathways through an area, sometimes devastating parts of a vineyard but leaving other parts untouched, before wandering off to wreak ruin on the next unlucky recipient. Local TOPOGRAPHY may result in a tendency for the storms to follow preferred pathways, but largely their incidence is unpredictable. Various devices have been tried for warding them off, such as explosive rockets fired into thunderclouds, or towers charged with static electricity to divert them. The technologies can hardly be described as proven, but have found supporters among vine-growers understandably desperate to protect their hard-won crops. J.G.

HAIL DISEASE. See WHITE ROT.

HALBSÜSS, literally 'half sweet' in German. Used on labels in AUSTRIA to designate wines whose RESIDUAL SUGAR is between 9 and 18 g/l.

HALBTROCKEN, German for 'half dry' and an intermediate wine style between the sweet wines so popular in GERMANY throughout the 1970s and early 1980s and the dry TROCKEN wines so popular with Germans from the early 1980s. The RESIDUAL SUGAR should be less than 18 g/l and not more than 10 g/l greater than the TOTAL ACIDITY. In the early 1990s, over 20 per cent of German wine was officially described as halbtrocken. Less than two-thirds of total German still wine production was medium sweet, containing between 18 and 45 g/l residual sugar, the best known of which abroad were the likes of LIEBFRAUMILCH and Niersteiner Gutes Domtal. However, dryness and sweetness do not of themselves determine quality. Under EUROPEAN UNION law, the use of the term halbtrocken is optional and, with the general move to a lower sugar content in all German wines, many bottlings are halbtrocken or indeed trocken without this being indicated on the label.

A sparkling wine produced within the EU can be described as halbtrocken if it contains between 33 and 50 g/l residual sugar and, therefore, tastes perceptibly sweet.

In AUSTRIA halbtrocken signified a residual sugar level of between 4 and 9 g/l until 1994 when it followed the German model.

See also SWEETNESS.

HAMMURABI (end of 18th century BC), king of BABYLONIA responsible for uniting MESOPOTAMIA with its capital Babylon. His law code survives on baked clay tablets and contains the earliest references to wine shops and wine sellers.

HANEPOOT, traditional Afrikaans name meaning literally 'honey pot', for SOUTH AFRICA's most planted Muscat vine variety, MUSCAT OF ALEXANDRIA. A few commercial, low-priced wines are sold under this name.

HARASZTHY, AGOSTON (1812–69), early CALIFORNIA wine-grower and promoter, frequently but wrongly identified as the 'father of California wine'. Born in Austro-Hungary, he went to the United States in 1842 and to California in 1849, where he engaged in multifarious activities, including politics, horticulture, and gold-refining. In 1856 he bought a SONOMA County vineyard and established the Buena Vista winery, still extant today. In 1861, as a member of the state commission on viticulture, he travelled to Europe and sent back many thousands of vine cuttings to California. His account of this trip and of his work as a wine-grower in California, *Grape Culture, Wines, and Wine-Making* (1862), first brought California as a wine state to the attention of the nation and is Haraszthy's main claim to importance in the history of wine in America.

After losing control of the Buena Vista winery he migrated to Nicaragua, where he died in mysterious circumstances, perhaps devoured by an alligator. In the years after his death it came to be believed that Haraszthy was the first to show the possibilities of wine-growing in the state, the first to introduce superior grape varieties into California, and in particular the first to introduce the ZINFANDEL vine. None of this is true, but the story has become legendary and difficult to dislodge. T.P.

Pinney, T., *A History of Wine in America* (Berkeley, Calif., 1989).

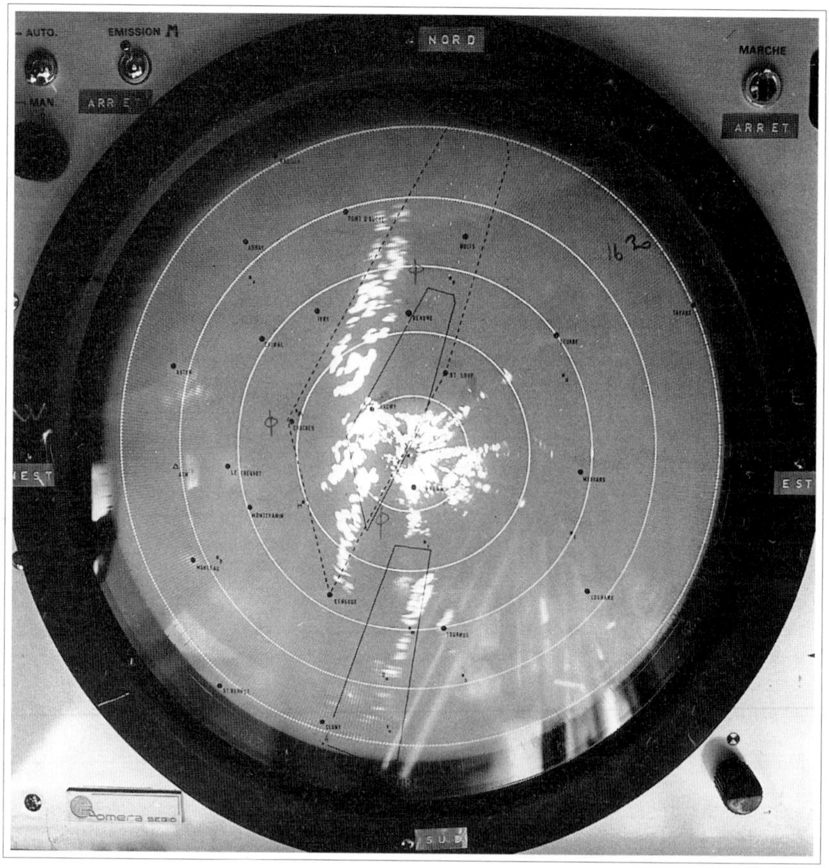

Potentially catastrophic **hail** clouds identified on a radar screen in Chalons, southern Burgundy.

HARD, tasting term applied to wine that is high in tannins and apparently lacking in fruit.

HARDY'S, or **Thomas Hardy & Co.**, important wine company in Australia which also controls Houghton of Western Australia. In the early 1990s they diversified into the Languedoc and, for a short time, owned the Ricasoli property in central Italy. This resulted in the amalgamation of this venerable, still family-run company with the Riverland Berri-Renmano co-operative to become **BRL Hardy**.

HARES can damage vineyards. See animals.

HÁRSLEVELŰ, white grape variety most widely grown in Hungary, where it produces characteristically spicy, aromatic white wines. This is the variety which brings perfume to the furmint grapes which make up the majority of the blend for the famous dessert wine Tokay, although it is widely planted elsewhere in Hungary and produces a range of varietal wines which vary considerably in quality and provenance. Good Hárslevelű is typically a deep green-gold, very viscous, full, and powerfully flavoured.

The variety, whose name means 'linden leaf', makes particularly full bodied wines in Villány in the far south of Hungary and is popularly associated with the village of Debrő in the Mátra Foothills (although much of the wine sold as Debrői Hárslevelű has been a much less specific and less distinguished off-dry blend).

The variety is also grown over the border from Hungary's Tokay region in Slovakia and is even more widely grown in South Africa than Furmint.

HARVEST, both the process of picking ripe grapes from the vine and transferring them to the winery (or field pressing station), and its festive, if frenetic, duration. This transition period in the wine-making cycle from vineyard to cellar is also known as vintage (crush in the United States), and récolte or *vendange* in France, *vendemmia* in Italy, *Ernte* in Germany, *cosecha* in Spain, and *vindima* in the Douro and *colheita* in the rest of Portugal.

Timing

The single most critical aspect of harvest is its timing, choosing that point during the grape ripening process when the grape is physiologically mature and the balance between its natural accumulation of SUGARS and its decreasing tally of natural plant ACIDS is optimal (see SAMPLING, grapes).

Typically this is a frenzied period, especially in hotter climates where warm, dry weather can rapidly accelerate ripening, sometimes putting pressure on available FERMENTATION VESSEL space. In cooler climates the threat of humid weather and possible ROT, heavy RAINFALL making vineyard access difficult, HAIL damage, or even FROST can also put unwelcome pressure on picking schedules. ACIDIFICATION and ENRICHMENT are respectively the most common rescue operations in the case of grapes picked slightly after or before ideal maturity.

Timing of harvest is additionally complicated by the fact that the fruit in different parts of a single vineyard may vary in ripeness, and the picking of a single plot may take several days. In hot weather, sugar concentration may well vary substantially between the start and finish of picking of a single vineyard.

Although the timing of harvest depends on fruit RIPENESS, it also depends on the region, the grape variety, and the type of wine required (Pinot Noir grapes destined for sparkling white wine are invariably picked much earlier than they would be for a still, red wine, for example). Harvest typically takes place in autumn: September and October in the northern hemisphere and March and April in the southern hemisphere. In very hot climates harvest may start in midsummer, however, while at the coolest limits of vine cultivation grapes may be picked when all the leaves have fallen from the vine and there is snow on the ground.

Harvest can, at least theoretically, take place somewhere in the world in every month of the year. Some German EISWEIN is not picked until the January following the official year of harvest (which it must by law carry on the label, no matter when it was picked). The hotter southern hemisphere regions such as Australia's HUNTER VALLEY regularly begin to pick in January or February, with the common vintage period for most regions being March and April. In very cool southern hemisphere vineyards such as Central Otago in NEW ZEALAND, grapes may remain on the vine until early June.

By July the harvest has usually begun in the earliest regions of the northern hemisphere, the warmest vineyards of CYPRUS, for example. In August grapes for the production of California sparkling wine are usually picked. For the majority of wine regions in the northern hemisphere, September and October are the harvest months, with the cooler and later regions and varieties extending into November. Northern hemisphere fruit may still be on the vine in December, particularly for Eiswein production. Very hot southern hemisphere vineyards have been known to pick particularly precocious grapes before the end of December.

Manual harvesting

The traditional method of harvesting, by hand, consists of cutting the stem of individual bunches (peduncle) and putting the bunches into a suitable container. This method, as opposed to MECHANICAL HARVESTING, can be employed regardless of terrain, row spacing (see VINE DENSITY), and precise vine-TRAINING SYSTEM. It also allows pickers to select

The grape **harvest** in Champagne.

individual bunches according to their ripeness and to eliminate unhealthy fruit affected by ROT OR DISEASE.

Occasionally individual berries are harvested, in the case of bunches affected by BOTRYTIS, an operation that is possible only with a high LABOUR input. This is most famously practised at Ch d'YQUEM and in other vineyards specializing in sweet wines in SAUTERNES and in Germany (see AUSLESE, BEERENAUSLESE, and TROCKENBEERENAUSLESE) but the technique may also be employed in the production of (necessarily expensive) dry wines when the vineyard has been attacked by less noble rot.

A competent picker picks up to a ton of grapes in a day if the crop is reasonably heavy. The cost of manual harvesting increases dramatically for light crops, either in terms of grapes per bunch or bunches per vine, for particularly widely spaced vines, or on particularly steep vineyards as in the MOSEL.

The efficiency of hand picking, as opposed to mechanical harvesting (see below), depends on vineyard conditions. If the fruit is at a convenient height and the crop heavy, an experienced picker can harvest up to 2 tons a day. Output is reduced by worker fatigue, or in regions where the fruit is at a less convenient height: close to the ground as in traditional Bordeaux vineyards, for example; or grapes trained on the overhead TRELLIS SYSTEMS of southern Italy, northern Portugal, Argentina, and Chile. Light crops are also particularly expensive to pick by hand, where bunches are small because of the grape variety (GEWÜRZTRAMINER, for example) or because of poor fruit set (see COULURE). In such circumstances, even an experienced picker may have only 500 kg/1,100 lb to show for a day's work.

Manual harvesting requires little equipment. The stems are cut by small scissors or hooked-tip knives. The fruit is put into a small container holding perhaps 5 or 10 kg of fruit. This was traditionally, and still is in parts of Europe, a wooden trug, cane basket, or leather hod strapped on to the pickers' backs, but nowadays it is most likely to be an unromantic but lighter and easier-to-clean plastic container emptied at intervals into a larger container for transport to the winery, or field pressing station, typically by tractor. These larger containers, often called 'gondolas' in the New World, holding between 500 kg and 2 tons, are passed down the row before being towed to the winery. In many vineyards the fruit is simply emptied into the back of a trailer, although the shallower the depth of fruit, the less damage it will suffer, and so containers full of grapes are increasingly stacked on trailers for transport to the grape reception area.

The harvest work-force varies from region to region. In much of Europe picking teams include both experienced locals and casual workers, often students and itinerant workers. Iberia traditionally supplied picking teams that would systematically work their way northwards through Europe from region to region as they successively reached ripeness. Similarly, Australian vineyards were traditionally picked by the large numbers of itinerants who moved between the sugar-cane-fields of northern Australia and the vineyards of the south. But increased mechanization in the sugar-cane industry has necessitated increased mechanization of the Australian wine industry. In the western United States the typical grape-picker is Mexican. Wine farms in South Africa for long had a considerable labour input, with a resident team of under-rewarded coloured workers. When in the late 1980s the Iron Curtain was torn down and EUROPEAN UNION membership raised wages in Spain and Portugal, eastern Europe became an important source of itinerant labour for vineyard owners in northern Europe.

Providing this annual influx with accommodation, sustenance and, often, transport is an increasingly onerous task each harvest. It is said that in many wine regions mechanical harvesting is the direct result of protest by the wives of vineyard owners, to whom much of this annual work-load has traditionally fallen.

Mechanical harvesting

See MECHANICAL HARVESTING. R.E.S. & A.D.W.

Coombe, B. G., and Dry, P. R. (eds.), *Viticulture, ii: Practices* (Adelaide, 1992).

Loftus, S., *Puligny-Montrachet: Journal of a Village in Burgundy* (London, 1992).

HARVEST TRADITIONS celebrate the culmination of a year's hard work in the vineyard and, in areas which have not yet succumbed to MECHANIZATION, encourage the pickers in their back-breaking task.

France

Harvest traditions are at their strongest in France, where they have evolved from the uninterrupted centuries of wine HARVEST.

The church plays a role in many European villages, where a symbolic bunch of grapes is blessed before the harvest and a thanksgiving service held at the end (see also RELIGION). (New World producers such as Robert MONDAVI of California have emulated this tradition.)

Vineyard owners and other members of their families try to be present for the harvest even if they usually work in a distant city. Some may welcome assembling pickers, many of whom return year after year, with an APERITIF of the estate's own wine. At the end of the harvest a certain amount of horseplay almost inevitably accompanies the picking of the last rows, and one or two pickers end up being thrown into the sticky mass of grapes (a tradition endangered by the increasing use of shallow plastic containers to transport grapes to the cellar).

Traditionally, the tractor pulling the final load is decorated with flowers before it drives, horn blaring, to the cellar. On some estates the pickers still offer a bouquet of flowers to the owner and speeches are made. Large or small, almost all estates celebrate the end of harvest with a party and some regions have their own name for this: *la paulée* in BURGUNDY, *la gerbebaude* in BORDEAUX, and *le cochelet* in CHAMPAGNE.

Most harvest traditions are gastronomic, however, and the major events in a picker's day are the three meals which punctuate it (or four if the *casse-croute*, a second breakfast normally taken in the vines, is counted). In France, the women who run the kitchens during the harvest are usually part of a family team, helped by local women who may work in the vines during the rest of the year. For 11 months these women cook only for their families and friends, but for one month they must turn themselves into restaurateurs of a special kind. Working in often rudimentary kitchens, they must feed demanding pickers both well and economically. Soups, rabbit dishes, and dishes such as *pot-au-feu*, *coq au vin*, and *blanquettes* are often requested by pickers nostalgic for an era when long, slow cooking was the norm. A harvest would not be a harvest in Burgundy without a *bœuf bourguignonne*, for example, and in Bordeaux the bonfires of *sarments* or vine shoots, on which are grilled steaks and sausages, may be kept blazing to form the focus of informal dancing and singing after dinner.

The harvest cook's work is regularly interrupted to administer first aid—pickers gash fingers with secateurs, suffer from hangovers, sunstroke, and gastric problems—and when the cook's long day ends, she is likely to be kept awake by pickers at play. Small wonder that there is something of a revolt among the younger generation of vine-growers' wives, who may anyway have full-time jobs elsewhere. Caterers are increasingly used, and high unemployment has in some cases substituted for students in search of a good time local people who would rather increase their earnings by forgoing lunch. These developments, together with an increase in the paperwork involved in being even a temporary employer, have contributed substantially to the substitution of MECHANICAL HARVESTERS for human pickers, and therefore to the death of harvest traditions.

The menus for each day, handwritten in notebooks every year, enlivened by remarks about weather conditions, the picking teams, and the cost of ingredients, are kept by many of the cooks and handed on from generation to generation. Eventually they, together with the photograph albums kept on many estates, may be the only record of harvest traditions. R.R.

Rest of Europe

Harvest traditions are most likely to survive where vineyards are picked by approximately the same people each year, which is why few survive in Italy and Germany, where grapes are increasingly picked by immigrants with no tradition of grape-picking in their families. As mechanization invades a wine region, so harvest traditions retreat, presumably until revived as a public relations exercise. This means that harvest traditions are more likely to survive where LABOUR costs are relatively low.

A prime example of this has been the DOURO valley, where PORT is made, although even here a labour shortage caused by war in Portugal's African colonies made significant changes in the 1960s, and increasing urbanization and EUROPEAN UNION membership in 1986 will probably make even more. Even in the mid 1990s, however, it was possible to associate a genuine sense of folk tradition and celebration with the harvest, as some local pickers invaded the QUINTAS at which they and their families had traditionally worked every September for decades. The increasingly depopulated TRÁS-OS-MONTES region has supplied many of the teams, or *rogas*, of pickers who brought noise, chatter, and traffic to a region marked by its silence the rest of the year.

At a few properties in the Douro, pickers' feet were still expected to provide a more bucolic, gentler, and more effective alternative to the mechanical CRUSHER, or the AUTOVINIFICATION vat. The *roga*, or sometimes only its male members, is expected not only to pick the grapes, but to make the wine as well. Donning shorts, and with their arms around each others' shoulders, they march methodically backwards and forwards across the granite LAGARES, often thigh high in sticky purple grapes, to a chant or beat of a drum. Once a floating CAP of skins has visibly been separated from the juice beneath, *liberdade* (liberty) is declared and the march evolves into dancing, traditionally to the sound of an accordion but nowadays, more often than not, to recorded music from a stereo system.

Traditionally the leader of the *roga* would present the owner of the farm or winery, the *patrão*, with a decorated vine branch at a final celebratory vintage feast.

New World

Such traditions as have evolved around the harvest, or crush, in the New World tend to be the direct result of having large numbers of people, often from very different backgrounds, doing work unfamilar to many of them, in the open air. The weather conditions, especially the temperature and sunshine, have greatest effect on worker comfort, and indirectly on the development of traditions. In many parts of the New World, harvest can be a time of heavy physical work for moderately low pay under trying conditions. Where the weather is hot, the harvest can start early in the morning, and meal breaks are short as there is often little opportunity to relax in a hot, dusty, vineyard with little available shade.

Many of the social aspects of harvest are changing with use of the mechanical harvester. One harvester and operator can pick as much in three shifts during the 24 hours as could hundreds of human pickers during the day.

HARVEYS OF BRISTOL, a powerful force in the British retail wine trade in the mid 20th century and owners of the world's most significant brand of sherry, Harveys Bristol Cream, and thereby creators of an entire style of sherry (see CREAM). In 1822 the first in a long line of John Harveys entered the wine trade, working with his uncle in wine cellars in Denmark Street in the west of England port of Bristol. (The date 1796, used by the company, is the date of establishment of these wine cellars, still owned by Harveys.) The third John Harvey pioneered the use of advertising by the wine trade in the early 20th century. It was only in the 1930s, after the Repeal of PROHIBITION in the USA, that the company's sales of sherry outstripped its port business. By the 1950s Jack Harvey built up an export business for Harveys' sherries, particularly in North America (although the firm had no production base in Spain). The new young chairman, George McWatters, a member of the Harvey family, had master-

The naming of **Harveys** Bristol Cream: 'If that is milk, then this is cream.'

minded advertising and marketing campaigns so memorable that when the company went public in 1959 (just as they had entered into an association with the ill-fated Ruiz-Mateos group; see SHERRY, history) the share issue was 39 times over-subscribed.

In 1946 the firm had taken on Harry WAUGH, a talented wine buyer, salesman, and teacher, to vitalize Harveys' fine wine business, and to rival that of their neighbours AVERYS. During the 20 years that Waugh and McWatters were there, Harveys was to take the wine trade lead in training, in sponsorship of the arts and other activities, and in presentation of its wares to an increasingly discerning public. Wine merchants who spent their formative years *chez* Harvey include, among many others, Michael BROADBENT and a significant proportion of the early MASTERS OF WINE. Harveys instituted the annual Oxford v. Cambridge university wine-tasting match in 1953, for example, and continues to own one of Britain's finest collections of wine-related ANTIQUES at Harveys Wine Museum in the old Denmark Street cellars. Harveys' wine lists and other publications were famous for their aesthetically high standards, with work commissioned from such artists as David Gentleman and Edward Ardizzone.

In 1960 Harveys acquired the port shippers COCKBURN, and its ports became as internationally successful as Harveys' sherries; so successful in fact that, after a fierce take-over battle, the firm was acquired by the Showerings group, famous for cider, perry, and BRITISH WINE, in 1966. Two years later Showerings merged with the giant Allied Breweries Group (later to become Allied-Lyons) and in 1970 Harveys acquired their first ever production base in JEREZ in the form of shippers Mackenzie & Co. Two years later, significant investments were made in sherry vineyards and, in the post-Rumasa era (see SHERRY, history), the important Jerez businesses of de Terry and Palomino y Vergara were acquired from the Spanish government in 1985. Harveys developed their substantial new footholds in Jerez and Puerto de Santa María so that, from 1989, all Harveys sherries were, for the first time, bottled in Jerez. A decline in the sherry market forced substantial rationalization so that by the early 1990s Harveys were concentrating on their fortified wine BRANDS Harveys Bristol Cream and Cockburn's Special Reserve.

These activities were run in parallel with, but at an increasing distance from, Harveys' fine wine business, which declined considerably in prestige after the Showerings take-over, even though in 1963 the firm had acquired a quarter share in the Bordeaux first growth Ch LATOUR. The parent company Allied-Lyons acquired a majority holding before selling it in 1993, taking over the sherry firm DOMECQ the following year.

HAUT-BRION, CHÂTEAU, the most famous property in the GRAVES district in BORDEAUX producing both red and white wines. Haut-Brion has a special reputation as the first of the wines which were designated PREMIERS CRUS in the famous 1855 CLASSIFICATION of Bordeaux wines to be mentioned and praised by Samuel Pepys. The London diarist recorded for 10 April 1663 that he 'drank a sort of French wine called Ho Bryen that hath a good and most particular taste I never met with'. It was also praised by Thomas JEFFERSON when, as American minister in France, he visited Bordeaux in 1787. The property was then owned by the Pontac family, very rich members of the *noblesse de la robe*, and prominent in the Parlement of Bordeaux. But when in 1694 François-Auguste de Pontac died childless, the estate was divided between two of his family, and the two parts were not reunited until 1840, by the latest of a number of owners, Eugène Larrieu, whose family held it until after the First World War. After a further series of not very successful owners in a very difficult time, the château was bought in 1935 by Mr Clarence Dillon, an American banker. It is now run by his grand daughter Joan, married to the Duc de Mouchy. The RÉGISSEUR is Jean-Bernard Delmas, who has both established an important vine NURSERY and effected considerable changes in wine-making equipment and design.

Partly, no doubt, owing to its historic reputation Haut-Brion was the only non-MÉDOC to be included in the famous 1855 classification of the wines of Bordeaux. Enclosed in the Bordeaux suburb of Pessac, the château building dates from the 16th century, and the 53 ha/130 acres of vineyards are composed of 55 per cent CABERNET SAUVIGNON vines, 22 per cent CABERNET FRANC, and 23 per cent MERLOT. Average production is 13,000 cases, including a SECOND WINE, **Ch Bahans-Haut-Brion**, since 1976 sold with a vintage date. About 10 TONNEAUX a year of the property's rare dry white wine, **Haut-Brion Blanc**, is made from almost equal parts of SÉMILLON and SAUVIGNON vines planted on 2.5 ha. E.P.-R.

For many years Haut-Brion was in fierce competition with its neighbour **Ch La Mission-Haut-Brion**, where a second red wine **Ch La Tour-Haut-Brion** and a full, waxy white wine **Ch Laville-Haut-Brion** are also made. La Mission itself usually contains considerably more Merlot than Haut-Brion, and very much more than La Tour-Haut-Brion. The property was revitalized by the Woltner family, who acquired it in 1919 and in many subsequent vintages managed to make even more concentrated, long-lived wines than their FIRST GROWTH neighbour, typically fermented at much lower temperatures than Ch Haut-Brion. In 1983, however, La Mission was sold to the Dillons, so that both these famous estates, the flagships of the newer PESSAC-LÉOGNAN appellation (although much of La Mission is in fact in the Bordeaux suburb of Talence rather than Pessac), are run, retaining their quite distinct premises and characters, by the same team. Of the varied total vineyard, 16.6 ha is classified as La Mission, about 4 ha as La Tour, and 5 ha is planted with slightly more Sémillon grapes than Sauvignon to produce Laville. J.Ro.

HAUTES CÔTES DE BEAUNE and **Hautes Côtes de Nuits**, sometimes known collectively as the **Hautes Côtes**, vineyards dispersed in the hills above the escarpment of the Côte d'Or in Burgundy. Most of the production is red wine from Pinot Noir, with some white wine made from Chardonnay or occasionally Pinot Blanc or Pinot Gris, but at ALTITUDES reaching 500 m/1,640 ft the grapes do not ripen easily. This is also suitable ground for BOURGOGNE ALIGOTÉ, especially as the blackcurrant bushes needed for the production of CASSIS can often be seen growing alongside.

Forty-seven communes are included in the Hautes Côtes appellations. The most prolific villages include Meloisey, Nantoux, and Échevronne above the Côte de Beaune and Villars-Fontaine, Magny-lès-Villars, and Marey-lès-Fussey above the Côte de Nuits. There is a good CO-OPERATIVE for the Hautes Côtes wines located just outside Beaune and an enjoyable restaurant and tasting area, the Maison des Hautes Côtes, at Marey-lès-Fussey.

See also CÔTE D'OR and its map. J.T.C.M.

HAUT-MÉDOC, the higher, southern part of the Médoc district of Bordeaux which includes the world-famous communes of MARGAUX, PAUILLAC, ST-ESTÈPHE, and ST-JULIEN, as well as the less glamorous ones of LISTRAC and MOULIS. Red wines made here outside one of these appellations usually qualify for the appellation of Haut-Médoc. For more details, see MÉDOC.

HAUT PAYS, French term meaning 'high country' which was used in the Middle Ages to describe the area upstream of BORDEAUX which produced wines (and presumably had done for longer than Bordeaux since at the beginning of the Christian era wine-making seems to have spread north west from Narbonne towards the Atlantic). This included GAILLAC, BERGERAC, Quercy (modern CAHORS), and Nérac (BUZET). Their more dependable climate often produced wines stronger than the light, thin wines then made in the Bordeaux region itself and were seen as a serious commercial threat. The port of Bordeaux penalized them by taxing them heavily and barring them from the port until the region had exported its own wines. See also HUNDRED YEARS WAR.

HAUT-POITOU. See POITOU.

HAWAII, chain of islands in the Pacific Ocean, outside the continental USA, but one of the 50 UNITED STATES. It produces mainly FRUIT WINES, notably a sparkling pineapple wine, as well as some grape wines, on the island of Maui.

HEAD, or crown, of a vine is the top of the TRUNK where cordons branch, or where a group of arms are placed for new canes in cane pruning.

HEADS, known as *têtes* in French, the first spirit to flow from the POT STILL during DISTILLATION. In practice it is generally discarded, or simply redistilled, because it is too high in alcohol and thus too neutral. This first fraction can, however, be useful in a year when the base wine is too alcoholic, lacks acid, and is liable to produce brandies which are bland and characterless. N.F.

Although wines used for distillation are in general low in alcohol and high in acidity, they contain the normal complement of ALDEHYDES, ESTERS, and other compounds produced during alcoholic FERMENTATION. Several of these compounds boil at lower temperatures than either water or alcohol, and many of the substances in wines when mixed together combine to form an AZEOTROPE. ACETALDEHYDE, ACETIC ACID, ETHYL ACETATE and the FUSEL OILS all tend to form azeotropic mixtures with the water and ETHANOL of the wine. The heads, or low-boiling first distillate, contain these compounds and others in various proportions, together with higher molecular weight aldehydes and compounds with particularly low boiling points such as SULPHUR DIOXIDE and HYDROGEN SULPHIDE.

Both the CONTINUOUS STILL and the pot still produce heads, but they can be very different in character. When the most basic wine is distilled in a continuous still, the heads fraction contains many more decidedly unattractive components, particularly aldehydes and low-boiling esters, than are found in pot still heads fractions. The former should certainly be discarded rather than added back for redistillation, as it can be with the very different heads produced by a pot still.

A.D.W.

HEAD SPACE, that space in a container holding a liquid that is not taken up by that liquid. In wine containers it is often called the ULLAGE, or ullage space. In large, modern wineries, the head space of stainless steel tanks is often deliberately filled by an INERT GAS as a preservative measure.

HEAD TRAINING, a form of VINE TRAINING whereby the trunk has a definite head, or knob, consisting of old wood rather than arms of a CORDON. Head trained vines are normally subject to CANE PRUNING, but may, after SPUR PRUNING, be described as GOBELET. The head may be from 40 cm to 1 m/3.3 ft from the ground. The GUYOT system is a common cane-pruned form of head training. R.E.S.

HEALTH, EFFECTS OF WINE CONSUMPTION ON. Until the 18th century wine played a central role in medical practice, not least because it was a safer drink than most available drinking WATER, as outlined in MEDICINE. Because of its ALCOHOL and ACID content, wine inhibits the growth of all micro-organisms pathogenic to man. No special cellar treatment is required since any micro-organism dangerous to man will die in wine.

In the 1970s and early 1980s wine drinking, like any form of alcohol consumption, was targeted by some health campaigners, and warning labels proliferated on wine bottles (see LABELLING). Since the late 1980s, however, medical science has reported some rather better news for wine drinkers, in particular some suggestions that moderate consumption of red wine may reduce the risk of heart disease. Moderate wine drinking can have social as well as coronary aspects, and some research suggests that it can be appropriate in the management of stress. The prudent wine drinker, however, keeps a sufficient eye on what and how he or she drinks to ensure that the benefits exceed the risks.

Wine as alcoholic drink

Because wine contains alcohol and alcohol is a poison, it is wise to monitor personal wine consumption. Alcohol's contribution to liver damage, dementia, and accidents is well known. Less well known is that the incidence of cancer of the mouth and larynx, nerve and muscle wasting, blood disorders, strokes, raised blood pressure, skin infections, psoriasis, and infertility increases with alcohol intake, and the babies of mothers who drink excessively during pregnancy may have abnormal facial features and low intelligence.

How much is safe is not universally agreed. Average levels officially recommended as safe limits by British medical bodies are cautious: 21 'units' of alcohol per week for men and 14 for women, spread over the week, a unit containing 8 g of alcohol. A 75-cl/27-fl oz wine bottle may contain anything from seven to 12 units, depending on ALCOHOLIC STRENGTH. According to this official counsel, healthy, white, middle-aged males are almost certainly safe when consuming a level they report as 21 units per week, but for others the official limits are lower. Sex, age, build, genetic make-up, ill health, and drinking habits affect the degree to which alcohol is concentrated in sensitive tissues and the rate at which it is detoxified by the liver. Furthermore, the tissues of some people are more resistant to damage than others.

There is some evidence that moderate consumption of any form of alcoholic drink is better than total abstinence. A Danish survey of more than 13,000 men and women, begun in 1976 and published in 1994, found that those who drank between one and six units a week had the longest life expectancy, that life expectancy fell dramatically only among those who drank more than 70 units a week.

Migraine

Some migraine sufferers identify red wines as a trigger. Their downfall is likely to be in the PHENOLICS; in the test tube these liberate from cells the chemical messenger 5-hydroxytryptamine which plays a part in the initiation of migraine.

Asthma

Some asthmatics experience a reaction to wine, and in particular to those containing a high level of SULPHUR compounds (although these levels are being reduced). For this reason some countries insist that wine labels state that wine contains sulphites, or a code indicating the presence of a sulphur compound.

Bones

The toxic effect of alcohol and the unhealthy life-style of most heavy drinkers are responsible for their weak bones. However, modest drinking is associated with some protection from osteoporosis. If this finding reflects cause and effect, it is of particular interest to women, whose bones become significantly weakened by osteoporosis after the menopause.

Health: French anti-liquor propaganda from about 1900. On the right is all that is wrong with spirits based on beetroot and potato. On the left the more benign effects on the guinea pig of wine and similar ferments.

Coronary heart disease

Coronary heart disease is the deposition of plaques of cholesterol in the arteries supplying the heart muscle. It leads to angina and heart attacks and is the western world's major killer. Yet those who drink moderately are less likely to die from coronary heart disease than both those who drink heavily and those who abstain. Why?

Heavy drinkers develop raised blood pressure, weakened heart muscle, increased blood fat levels, and a susceptibility to potentially fatal abnormal heart rhythms, and some of the teetotallers are converts who gave up drinking because of ill health. However, other abstainers are healthy and do not appear to have any other habit which might explain their increased risk, and it is now widely accepted that moderate drinking offers some protection against coronary heart disease. How?

The so-called FRENCH PARADOX has suggested clues. In most industrialized countries, death from coronary heart disease is directly proportional to dietary fat intake: both are low in Japan, high in Finland. However, southern France has an unexpectedly low death rate. Garlic, a preference for olive oil rather than dairy fats, or an active life-style could explain the paradox, or perhaps it is simply that the French have in fact increased their fat intake recently and their coronary statistics reflect a healthier diet of 30 years ago. All are possible explanations, but the best case for resolving the paradox has been made for red wine. Coronary arteries which are furred up with cholesterol cannot supply the heart muscle with enough oxygen. The result is the pain of angina. In the laboratory phenolics from red wine chemically modify the lipoproteins, the fraction of the blood fats which determines the development of coronary artery disease. If phenolics do the same in the body, they should reduce the amount of cholesterol deposited in the arteries. The deposits in the arteries disturb the blood flow making it liable to form a clot, causing a sudden total blockage—a coronary thrombosis or heart attack. The blood of red wine drinkers appears to clot less readily than that of those who drink white wine or other alcoholic drinks and both alcohol and some phenolics reduce blood coagulability in the test tube. Thus there is evidence for mechanisms by which moderate red wine consumption could be beneficial in reducing both the fixed narrowing of arteries and the sudden blockage by blood clots.

See also ALLERGIES, DIET, DOCTORS, HISTAMINE, MEDICINE, PHYTOALEXINS, VITAMINS. J.H.H.

Doll, R., 'Good news that complicates health education', *Alcoholism* (Newsletter from the Medical Council on Alcoholism), 3 (1993), 1–2.

Frankel, E. N., *et al.*, 'Inhibition of oxidation of human low-density lipoprotein by phenolic substances in red wine', *Lancet*, 341 (1993).

Grønbæk, M., *et al.*, 'Influence of sex, age, body mass index, and smoking on alcohol intake and mortality', *British Medical Journal*, 308 (1994).

Renaud, S., and de Lorgeril, M., 'Wine, alcohol, platelets, and the French paradox for coronary heart disease', *Lancet*, 339 (1992), 1523–6.

In 1987 a **helicopter** was used to try to dry the grapes at Ch Pétrus in Pomerol.

HEAT STRESS affects vines when air temperatures are high. Very high daytime temperatures, of more than 40 °C/ 104 °F, cause the vine to 'shut down', or virtually cease PHOTOSYNTHESIS, as the enzymes responsible can no longer work. High temperatures also lead to WATER STRESS, especially when occurring with bright sunshine and strong, dry winds. High temperatures cause fast RESPIRATION in vines and this leads to, for example, low levels of MALIC ACID in mature fruit in hot regions. Very high temperatures are not associated with superior-quality table wine production, and it is normally early maturing table grapes which are grown in very hot regions. R.E.S.

HEAT SUMMATION, a computation that forms part of many systems of CLIMATE CLASSIFICATION.

HEAT TREATED VINES, vines which have undergone **heat treatment**, or THERMOTHERAPY.

HELFENSTEINER is famous principally as a parent of the successful German red wine crossing DORNFELDER. It is itself a crossing of FRÜHBURGUNDER × TROLLINGER and is essentially a product of Württemberg, where its ability to ripen earlier than Trollinger is valued but its susceptibility to COULURE is causing its decline from a small flurry of popularity in the early 1970s.

HELICOPTERS have several uses in viticulture. They are particularly useful for crop SPRAYING (although there are the usual problems where individual landholdings are small). They may be used as airborne WIND MACHINES to stir up cold, dense air just above the vineyard surface with warmer air above to prevent spring FROST damage. On occasion they have been used in an attempt to dry excess moisture off vine leaves and bunches immediately after heavy RAINFALL at HARVEST.

HENDERSON, DR ALEXANDER (1780–1863), Scotsman who qualified as a doctor and then moved to London and contributed to a wide range of publications, including the *Encyclopaedia Britannica*. After visiting the wine regions of France, Germany, and Italy, he wrote *The History of Ancient and Modern Wines*, which was published in 1824 (eight years after JULLIEN but nine years before REDDING). Some of the most useful aspects of his book perhaps reflect some aspects of his medical training: his observations on the art of wine TASTING.

HENNESSY has been one of the dominant forces in COGNAC since the business was founded in 1756 by Richard Hennessy, an officer in the French army of Irish Catholic *émigré* stock. Hennessy flourished during the French Revolution, emerging as 'Citizen Hennessy', and it was during this period that his family established the duopolistic control of the market which they shared with MARTELL, which was usually a rival, sometimes an ally, often connected by marriage.

The Hennessys remained true to their rather careless, Irish, aristocratic background, relying largely on the English—and Irish—markets and ignoring French buyers. They also failed to patent their ideas; they pioneered the use of three stars to identify the cheapest brandy in their range, and were the first to call their better brandy 'XO'.

At the beginning of the 20th century James Hennessy, disheartened by his wife's death, moved to Paris and the firm lost momentum. In 1922 his son Maurice, a friend of the Firino-Martell family, engineered a 25-year pact between them. They already set the price for young brandies, and they set about dividing the world, with Martell taking England, while the Hennessys took the United States and the Far East.

In the long run this benefited the Hennessys, as these latter two markets proved to have the greatest potential after the Second World War when the pact ended. The firm has remained dominated by the family even though it merged with MOËT & CHANDON in 1971 and became part of the giant LVMH-Moët Hennessy group in the late 1980s.

For the past 200 years the firm's brandies have been blended by successive generations of the Fillioux family, who have maintained the same style, round and fruity, helped by the firm's tradition of owning the biggest stocks of old cognac in the business.

Hennessy also owns the thriving COOPERAGE business Taransaud, which prides itself on its stocks of mature French OAK. N.F.

HERBACEOUS, tasting term for the leafy or grassy aroma of crushed green leaves or freshly cut grass. **Herbaceousness** is considered a defect only when present in excess. Wines made from the produce of SAUVIGNON Blanc, SÉMILLON, CABERNET SAUVIGNON, CABERNET FRANC, or MERLOT vines which failed to ripen fully are often excessively herbaceous. In general, the younger the vines, the greater their VIGOUR, and the earlier the grapes are picked, the more pronounced the herbaceousness.

This herbaceousness is due to leaf aldehydes, six-carbon atom ALDEHYDES. Numerous investigations have shown that they, and the corresponding six-carbon atom ALCOHOLS, derive from two of the higher molecular weight fatty acids found in plant leaves and in the fruit. Linoleic and linolenic acid decompose rapidly once the grape berry is crushed to yield hexanal, hexenal, and the related unsaturated alcohols, all six-carbon atom compounds which can react further during FERMENTATION to produced a wide range of flavour compounds which are responsible for the aroma called herbaceous.

Another reason why a wine may taste herbaceous is from vine leaves inadvertently picked with the grapes. Early MECHANICAL HARVESTERS were particularly prone to do this, and the grapes were often so mangled that it was impossible to separate the wet leaves from them. Wines made from such a blend would also not surprisingly be high in leaf aldehydes and taste distinctly leafy or herbaceous, a problem accentuated when such mechanical harvesters are used on relatively young vineyards. More sophisticated machine harvesters have reduced leaf contamination considerably. A.D.W.

HERBICIDES, chemicals applied to vineyards to control the growth of WEEDS. They may be either pre-emergent (or residual) or post-emergent (knockdown). The latter group comprises two types, contact and systemic herbicides. Residual herbicides act against germinating seedlings of the weeds, while post-emergent herbicides damage live plant tissue. Typically, herbicides are applied only to the strip of ground directly under the vine, and weeds growing between the rows are controlled by cultivation or mowing. Herbicides are increasingly used even between rows in some vineyard regions, however, though there can be risks of soil erosion or loss of water infiltration without the organic matter produced by plant growth in this zone.

In areas of winter rainfall, a contact or systemic spray is typically used in late autumn to early winter, followed by a pre-emergent herbicide in the early spring. In regions with summer rainfall, or irrigated areas, further contact or systemic sprays may be needed to control weeds that grow during the growing season. Most herbicides used in vineyards are low-hazard chemicals which present no danger to the operator (see AGROCHEMICALS). Many of the knockdown chemicals are inactivated by soil, and so leave no soil residues.

Continued use of some herbicides leads to the increased presence of so-called 'escape' weeds, however, which were previously suppressed by competition from other weeds. Varying the type of herbicides used can sometimes control these, otherwise mechanical removal is essential. Some herbicides can even damage vines, either by wetting vine leaves inadvertently, or when herbicides are leached into the root zone, as can happen with young vines, sandy soils, and irrigation.

Concern about environmental pollution as a result of herbicide use has been increasing (see ORGANIC VITICULTURE), and an increasing number of vine-growers are substituting undervine ploughing for herbicide use. See WEED CONTROL. R.E.S.

HERCEGOVINA. See BOSNIA HERCEGOVINA.

HERMITAGE, the most famous northern RHÔNE appellation of all, producing extremely limited quantities of seriously long-lived reds and about a third as much full bodied dry white wine. Although the appellation is only the size of a large Bordeaux estate, Hermitage was one of France's most famous wines in the 18th and 19th centuries when the name alone was sufficient to justify prices higher than any wine

The harvest by the famous Chapelle near the summit of the hill of **Hermitage**.

other than a FIRST GROWTH bordeaux (which were sometimes strengthened by the addition of some Hermitage until the mid 19th century). The origin of the name Hermitage is not so much shrouded in mystery as obscured by many conflicting legends, most of them concerning a hermit, *ermite* in French. Not least of the puzzles is how and when Ermitage acquired its H, although there was no shortage of English-speaking enthusiasts of the wine in the 18th century (including Thomas JEFFERSON). The first recorded mention of Hermitage in English was in Thomas Shadwell's 1680 play *The Woman-Captain*, 'Vin de Bon, Vin Celestine, and Hermitage, and all the Wines upon the fruitful Rhône'. These 'manly' wines were also a great favourite with the Russian imperial court, but the economic upheavals of the first half of the 20th century affected Hermitage as much as any Rhône appellation.

The wine comes from an almost unenlargeable 126 ha/311 acres of particularly well-favoured vines on the extraordinary hill of Hermitage, a south-facing bank of granite, thinly covered with extremely varied and well-charted soil types, which almost pushes the town of Tain l'Hermitage into the river Rhône just as it turns sharp left (see map on p. 796). Wines produced here in the Roman town of Tegna were already known to writers such as PLINY and MARTIAL.

The combination of heat-retaining granite and a reasonably steep southern exposition do much to encourage grape RIPENING here. It is not surprising that such a celebrated vineyard has been for long divided into various CLIMATS, each with their own soil types and reputations for wine types. Professor Pierre Mandier, a geologist at Lyons, has charted the hillside in considerable detail. The most famous *climats* are at the western end of the hill, which benefits from the highest temperatures. Les Bessards has a topsoil of sandy gravel on granite and produces some of the sturdiest wines. Le Méal produces more aromatic wines from a soil with more limestone, and bigger stones towards the top of the slope, where l'Hermite is crowned with a small stone chapel owned by Paul JABOULET Aîné and has more sand and fine LOESS. Clay predominates in the lower *climats* of Les Gréffieux and Les Diognières. Other famous *climats* include Beaume(s), Maison Blanche, Péléat, Les Murets, Rocoule, La Croix, and Les Signeaux in the extreme east. Although white and red grapes are planted all over the hill, some of the finest white Hermitage comes from the higher vineyards, and clay-limestone soils are considered the best suited.

Producers such as Gérard Chave, the modest master of Hermitage, delight in blending the produce of holdings all over the hill to produce a complex, well-balanced expression of each vintage. Producers with less diversified holdings may produce much simpler wines.

Red Hermitage is made from the SYRAH vine alone, indeed Hermitage has laid claim to be the cradle of Syrah, while white Hermitage may be made from the robust MARSANNE or the nervier, and less common, ROUSSANNE.

SOIL EROSION is a frequent problem here, the result as much of exposure as of gradient, although the hill is steep enough in parts for TERRACES to be necessary, and some retaining walls are used as advertising sites for the merchant houses of CHAPOUTIER and Jaboulet, based in and near Tain respectively.

Wine-making philosophies vary here, but are essentially traditional. Red wines are the result of relatively hot FERMENTATIONS matured in often quite old COOPERAGE of varied capacity, often according to vintage characteristics. Red Hermitage should be very deeply coloured and headily perfumed. They can evolve for two or three decades after which they may be mistaken for great red bordeaux.

White wines are possibly even more varied, according to blend of grape varieties used, RIPENESS, whether MALOLACTIC FERMENTATION has taken place, and whether WOOD is used for fermentation and/or AGEING. Almost all white Hermitage is notably full in BODY, and some of the more serious examples such as Chave's and Chapoutier's Chante Alouette are among the longest-living dry white wines of France.

In very ripe years some of Hermitage's white grapes are transformed into VIN DE PAILLE, delicious but all too rare.

Hermitage has also been used as a synonym for SHIRAZ in Australia, where, for example, PENFOLDS Grange was originally called Penfolds Grange Hermitage.

Livingstone-Learmonth, J., *The Wines of the Rhône* (3rd edn., London, 1992).

HERODOTUS, prolific Ancient Greek writer. The *Histories* of Herodotus (490/480–425 BC), a native of Halicarnassus in Asia Minor, are not a history in the modern sense: the Greek word *historia* means 'an investigation'. Herodotus' main subject is the conflict between the Greeks and the Persians, and as such his book is history; but it is also an investigation into the geography and anthropology of the east in Herodotus' own day, for as a young man he had travelled widely in the Greek-speaking world and in Egypt and Africa.

Forming part of Herodotus' descriptions of the customs of foreign nations are some intriguing observations about wine and DRUNKENNESS. He says that the Assyrians use palm-wood casks to transport wine, in boats built in Armenia, down the Euphrates (1. 194). In fact, Herodotus' curiosity concerns the construction of the boats: their cargo is mentioned in an aside and he expresses no surprise at the Assyrians' use of palm-wood BARRELS instead of AMPHORAE. He has just told us that the date palm supplies the people with food, honey, and wine and that Assyria is the world's largest producer of grain. The country does not grow vines (1. 193) but, as we know from other sources, Babylon imported wine from ARMENIA. This is probably what the casks contained: with date palms growing all around, transporting fermented date juice would not have made sense. See also MESOPOTAMIA.

All of Book 2 and the beginning of Book 3 are taken up with Herodotus' description of Egypt before he goes on to relate the Persian conquest of that country. He states that the Egyptians have no wine but drink a wine made from barley (2. 81). This cannot be true, for we know that the vine was grown there in the 5th century BC. Egyptian wine may have been too scarce, however, for Herodotus to have come across it on his travels. Egypt certainly imported wine from Greece and PHOENICIA, as Herodotus mentions (3. 8). He says that it came in earthenware jars, and that when the wine had been finished the mayor of the town had to collect the empty jars and send them to Memphis, where they would be filled with water and sent to the Syrian desert. This system was devised by the Persians immediately after they had conquered Egypt so that they could reach Egypt through the Syrian desert without risking death through thirst.

When the Persians have subjugated the Egyptians, the king, the megalomaniac Cambyses, marches against the Ethiopians. The expedition is a disaster, and the Ethiopians recognize the Persians' superiority in one respect only: they have wine, and that is the reason for their longevity (3. 23). But Cambyses is too fond of it, and when he is told so by a court official he wrongly deduces that the Persians regard this as the cause of his madness (3. 35). His madness and cruelty seem to have been congenital (3. 38). Wine can cause madness, though: Cleomenes, king of Sparta, went mad and died as a result of drinking wine unmixed with WATER, a nasty habit he had picked up from those notorious drunkards the Scythians (6. 85). Only a barbarian would drink unmixed wine. The Persians are all great drinkers of wine, and their frequent drunkenness explains one of the strangest of their customs. The sensible part is that any decision they take when they are drunk they reconsider when they are sober. But the opposite also holds: any decision taken when they are sober has to be reconsidered when they are drunk (1. 135). Far from regarding drunkenness as undesirable and immoderate behaviour, the Persians, if Herodotus is to be trusted, view it as an altered state of consciousness that is as valuable as sobriety. H.M.W.

Herodotus, *The Histories*, trans. Aubrey de Sélincourt, rev. A. R. Burn (Harmondsworth, 1972).

HEROLDREBE is the marginal black German vine crossing to which the prolific breeder August Herold of the Weinsberg in Württemberg put his name. This PORTUGIESER × LIMBERGER crossing yields regularly and prolifically, about 140 hl/ha (8 tons/acre), but it ripens so late that it is suitable only for Germany's warmer regions, particularly the Pfalz where two-thirds of its German total of 220 ha/540 acres were planted in 1991 and are better at providing pink than red wine. Its most useful function was that, like Herold's even less popular HELFENSTEINER, it spawned the promising DORNFELDER.

HESIOD (*c.*700 BC), the earliest agricultural writer of Ancient GREECE, wrote *Works and Days*. Most of this is homely advice for the farmer: 'Be sparing of the middle of the cask, but when you open it, and at the end drink all you want; it's not worth saving dregs.' He is the first writer to tell of simple rustic pleasures: 'I love a shady rock and Bibline wine [from BYBLOS] wine, a cake of cheese, and goat's milk, and some meat of heifers pastured in the woods, uncalved, of first-born kids. Then I may sit in the shade and drink the shining wine, and eat my fill, and turn my face to meet the fresh west wind, and pour three times an offering from the spring which always flows, unmuddied, streaming down, and make my fourth LIBATION one of wine.' Hesiod gives the time for the grape HARVEST as 'when Orion and the dog star [Sirius] move into the mid sky'. H.H.A.

HESSISCHE BERGSTRASSE, one of the smallest wine regions in GERMANY (see map on p. 442). The northern vineyards on the western slopes of Germany's Odenwald have formed a separate region since 1971. They cover 390 ha/964 acres of which 53 per cent is planted in RIESLING, the best of which produces distinguished wine, comparable to that of the RHEINGAU. Of the 900 or so growers, approximately 620 deliver their grapes to a large regional CO-OPERATIVE cellar at Heppenheim, which sells 90 per cent of its stock in litre bottles within the region. Only a small and decreasing amount of the co-operative's wine is sold by supermarkets, and sales directly to the consumer and to the wine trade are increasing (although Hessische Bergstrasse wines are rarely seen outside Germany). The state of Hesse is the largest vineyard owner with 38 ha/94 acres under vine, based on Bensheim. It is particularly well known for its Riesling EISWEINE, but the wines from other vine varieties are also very elegant, and compare well with those from elsewhere in Germany. A good 60 per cent of Hessische Bergstrasse wines are dry: TROCKEN, or HALBTROCKEN. I.J.

HEURIGE is an Austrian wine speciality. Heurige means both wine from the most recent vintage and the place where the wine is offered for consumption by its producer. A winemaker's right effectively to set up his own wine bar was established in the time of CHARLEMAGNE, officially recognized by Emperor Josef II in 1784, and has continued as a tradition throughout AUSTRIA. Heurigen, these small, often family-run wine taverns, are most numerous in the suburbs of VIENNA, where they are a popular tourist attraction. Food is usually served alongside the owner's wine, usually crackling new Heurige wine but sometimes supplemented by old, or Alte, wines. The wine of the new vintage officially becomes Heurige on St Martin's Day, 11 November. Before that it may have been sold at the unfermented MUST (Most) stage, as partially fermented Sturm, or as still cloudy new wine (Staubiger). Local by-laws determine when a Heurige may sell its new wine, which period it signals by hanging out a bush of pine twigs above the entrance. See also PRIMEUR, the French counterpart, minus the hospitality.

HIGHER ALCOHOLS. See FUSEL OILS.

HILLSIDE VINEYARDS. Even in Ancient ROME it was said *Bacchus amat colles*, or BACCHUS loves the hills, suggesting that hillside vineyards have long been regarded as a source of high-quality wine.

This is partly because hillside soils are typically shallow, so that vineyard VIGOUR is relatively low, a factor commonly associated with high wine quality. Over millions of years soil tends to be washed down the hillsides and accumulates in the valley floors. Vines planted there will typically be more vigorous as the roots will be able to reach more water and nutrients.

Hillside vineyards: the warmth received by direct radiation on the vineyard depends on the elevation of the sun combined with the inclination of the vineyard towards the sun. In simplistic terms the two angles can be added together, but the elevation of the sun controls the thickness of the atmosphere (an absorbing medium) through which the radiation passes. The inclination of the vineyard is independent of this variation.

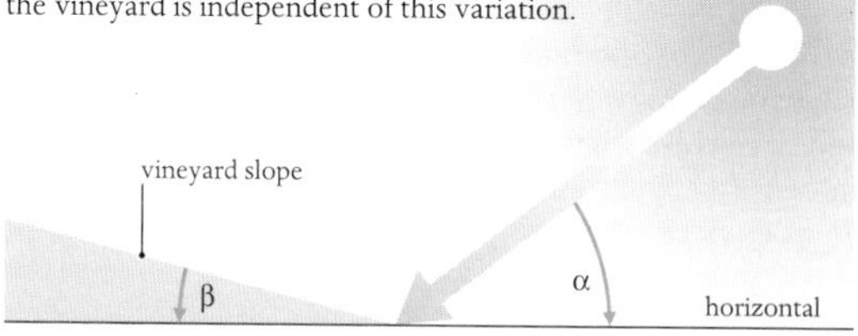

$I = k \sin \alpha + q \sin \beta$

Where I = Intensity of radiation received in vineyard
k and q = constants
α = angular elevation of sun
β = angle of inclination of the vineyard to the horizontal along a meridian

Vines may also be planted on hillsides for reasons of MESOCLIMATE, as hillsides are less prone to FROST because cold air can drain freely away at night. If the slopes face the equator, they receive more sunshine during the day and can reradiate the heat absorbed during the day at night or during cloudy weather. In warmer regions some vineyards may be planted on hillsides to take advantage of cooler temperatures. At higher ELEVATIONS the air temperature drops about 0.6 °C/1 °F for each 100 m/330 ft, and so elevated vineyards are cooler, and the growing season is extended. Since the early 1980s there has been an increasing tendency to plant elevated sites in Australia and California, for example, in order to produce a more COOL CLIMATE style of table wine.

Hillside vineyard sites have their drawbacks. SOIL EROSION is an obvious example, as are greatly increased costs of vineyard management. Working on steep slopes is particularly tiring and productivity is affected. Machines which have to be tracked rather than wheeled are more expensive. In most vineyards of the world, rows run up and down the slopes. Where the slopes are too steep for tractors, as in parts of the MOSEL valley and SWITZERLAND, everything must be done by hand, or by machines winched down into the vineyards. Where rows run across the slopes, the vineyard is normally laid out in TERRACES, as in Portugal's DOURO valley or France's hill of HERMITAGE. R.E.S.

HIPPOCRAS, popular medieval FLAVOURED WINE.

HISTAMINE, the amine involved in a range of allergic reactions in humans, was once thought the cause of some people's allergy to red wine. Improved methods of wine ANALYSIS, however, have demonstrated that the amounts of histamine in wine are at least an order of magnitude below that required to cause an allergic reaction in the great majority of people. One ADELAIDE research project found levels of between 2 and 9.9 mg/l of histamines in wine, while another at DAVIS found an average of 1.8 mg/l in 253 California wines, with higher concentrations in fortified wines. A.D.W.

HOCHGEWÄCHS, one of a number of label clues to one of GERMANY's better wines launched to supplement those provided by the GERMAN WINE LAW. A wine labelled Riesling-Hochgewächs is a QBA which has reached much higher MUST WEIGHT and overall quality than the legal minimum.

HOCK, generic term for (white) Rhenish wines, from the RHINE regions of GERMANY, sometimes for the wines of Germany in general. A contraction of hockamore, an English rendering of the adjective Hochheimer, denoting wines from Hochheim on the river Main just west of Frankfurt (see RHEINGAU).

The earliest firm reference in English occurs in Thomas D'Urfey's play *Madam Fickle; or, The Witty False One* in 1676: 'Here's a glass of excellent old Hock.' The *Oxford English Dictionary* gives a first reference in 1625 in John Fletcher's play *The Chances*, but this depends on a corrupt reading of hock for hollock, a light red wine. However, it is likely that the term was already current in England by the 17th century, for its use is closely linked to the growth in popularity of Rhenish and Main wines, which began to supplant the wines of ALSACE in export markets after 1500 (see GERMAN HISTORY). The former were traded principally by Frankfurt merchants, Hochheimer exclusively so.

At the outset, hock appears to have described only wines from the middle Rhine: in an address to the Royal Society in 1680 Anthony van Leeuwenhoeck, the inventor of the microscope, spoke of 'vinum Mosellanicum, vinum Rijnco-viense and vinum Rhenanum, quod vulgo hogmer dicitur' (called 'hogmer' in the vernacular). In 1703 Johann Valentin Kauppers in his *De natura . . . vini Rhenani* could still distinguish between 'Rhine wines' and wines from the Rheingau, but in the course of the 18th century hock became the general designation of German wines sold in Britain.

The prestige of wines from the commune of Hochheim itself was enhanced after Queen Victoria had observed the vintage there in 1850, for the owner of one of the lesser sites, Pabstmann, gained royal permission to rename his vineyard after her. Since that time it has been known as Königin-Viktoria-Berg. T.S.

In modern commerce, a wine labelled 'Hock' is likely to be a simple QBA wine from a German Rhine wine region such as RHEINHESSEN or possibly PFALZ. It has been by no means uncommon for the same wine to be offered as Hock to a gentlemen's club and LIEBFRAUMILCH to a supermarket buyer. Hock has also occasionally been used outside Germany as a GENERIC term.

HOLLAND, the heartland of the small north European country now called the Netherlands, has had considerable influence on the wine and, particularly, spirit industry, thanks to Dutch naval power in the late Middle Ages (see DUTCH WINE TRADE). Derivations of the word Holland live on in the names of various spirits (see *holandas* in BRANDY, Spanish). For an outline of the small 20th century Dutch wine industry, see NETHERLANDS.

HOMER, writer(s) in Ancient GREECE of the two epic poems: the *Iliad* (telling the story of Achilles and the Trojan wars) and the *Odyssey* (the return of Odysseus from Troy to his home, Ithaca, and his adventures on the way). Homeric poems are usually dated to the 8th century BC and wine features regularly in both books. See also CLASSICAL TEXTS.

HOME WINE-MAKING, popular hobby for individuals who make wine in their own homes, either for fun, to save money, or both. Because such wine attracts no DUTY, it has great appeal in countries like Great Britain where wine duties are relatively high. It also enjoyed enormous popularity in the United States during PROHIBITION, when vinifying an annual allowance of 200 gal/7.5 hl of fruit juice (a limit that still applies in the USA) was the only legal way the average American household could procure alcoholic drink. The boom in home wine-making between 1919 and 1926 was so great that California's vine acreage almost doubled, as the craft spread from those brought up to make wine at home because of their southern European origins, to hundreds of thousands of others prepared to risk exploding bottles in their homes. In 1992 it was estimated that a total of 400,000 Americans make the equivalent of a total of 2.5 million cases of wine a year from grapes (and another 500,000 cases of non-grape FRUIT WINES). Most of them buy fresh, American-grown grapes, mainly from California which has a long tradition of shipping grapes by rail to Midwest and East Coast cities. Others buy juice or GRAPE CONCENTRATE. British home wine-makers determined to make wine based on grapes rather than other fruits, flowers, or vegetables (parsnip has its devotees) tend to use grape concentrate as their raw material, so that their produce is technically MADE WINE and lacks the fresh fruitiness of wine made from the juice of freshly picked grapes. Some individuals in Britain, and other countries not famed for their supply of domestically grown grapes, buy imported wine grapes from wholesale fruit markets for home wine-making purposes—the truly dedicated may even collect them direct from a reputable wine region. Most home wine-makers use cultured yeasts. The greatest financial outlay required is on equipment, which may include small-scale

CRUSHER-DESTEMMER, PRESS, and an adequate supply of FERMENTATION VESSELS, which allow the CARBON DIOXIDE to escape without accident.

Heimoff, S., *et al.*, 'Army of amateurs', *Wine Spectator*, 17/8 (31 July 1992).

HORACE (Quintus Horatius Flaccus) (65–8 BC), the Latin poet, did not write a systematic guide to viticulture but wine does figure prominently in his work, and reflects his Epicurean philosophy of enjoying its pleasures in moderation. He tells us that at the Sabine farm which his patron Maecenas gave him he does not grow wine (*Epistles* 1. 14), but as a token of his gratitude he serves Maecenas the local wine, laid down by the poet himself in the year that his patron had recovered from a serious illness (*Odes* 1. 20). This matching of the wine to the guest and the occasion is a constant feature of Horace's invitation poems, and other poems about drinking: see also *Odes* 1. 9 and 4. 2 (simple wines for intimate occasions), 3. 21 (a wine from the year of the poet's birth for an honoured guest), 1. 37 (a grand old CAECUBAN to celebrate the defeat of the monstrous Cleopatra), 3. 14 (a wine that goes back to the Social War, 91–88 BC, to celebrate Augustus' return), 3. 28 (Caecuban of Bibulus' consular year, 59 BC, in honour of Neptune), and so on.

Horace cannot afford the very best wine, old FALERNIAN: to spend a feast day drinking that would be the greatest happiness (*Odes* 2. 3). Note that to Horace good wine is always old wine: the Romans (and the Greeks) preferred old wine to the wine of the current vintage. *Epistles* 1. 19 is Horace's contribution to the debate about poetic inspiration. Callimachus (*c*.310/05–*c*.240 BC) first raised the question of whether water, symbol of the purity of poetic labour, or wine, which brings poetic frenzy, is the better drink for a poet. On the authority of Cratinus (*c*.520–*c*.423 BC) Horace sides with the wine drinkers, for were not Homer and Ennius (see Ancient GREECE), the fathers of Greek and Latin epic respectively, wine bibbers? 'Laudibus arguitur vini vinosus Homerus', Horace asserts: 'in his praises of wine, winebibbing Homer betrays himself.' To the modern reader Horace seems to have more in common with today's civilized wine enthusiast than any other classical writer. H.M.W.

Commager, S., 'The function of wine in Horace's Odes', *Transactions of the American Philological Association*, 88 (1957), 68–80.
Griffin, J., *Latin Literature and Roman Life* (London, 1985).

HORIZONTAL TRELLIS. See TENDONE system of VINE TRAINING.

HORMONES, natural substances present in trace concentrations in vines and other plants which carry messages from one organ or part of the plant to another to regulate growth and development. Synthetic GROWTH REGULATORS may have similar chemical structures, and a similar mode of action. There are three groups of hormones which promote growth, these being AUXINS, GIBBERELLINS, and CYTOKININS, and two groups which inhibit growth, ABSCISIC ACID and ethylene. R.E.S.

HOSPICES DE BEAUNE, charity auction which has taken place in BEAUNE annually since 1851 on the third Sunday in November, a key feature of the Burgundian calendar. The beneficiaries are the combined charitable organizations of the Hôtel Dieu, founded in 1443 by Nicolas Rolin, chancellor of the duchy of Burgundy, and the Hôpital de la Charité.

The produce of vineyard holdings donated by benefactors over the centuries is auctioned at prices usually well in excess of current commercial values. Nevertheless the results serve as a signal to indicate the trend for bulk wine prices in the region for the new vintage.

The cuvées sold are named to commemorate original benefactors such as Nicolas Rolin and his wife Guigone de Salins or more recent ones such as de Bagèzre de Lanlay, an inspector of aerial telegraphs. The Hospices de Beaune also provides the occasion for 'Les Trois Glorieuses', the three great feasts held over the weekend at CLOS DE VOUGEOT on Saturday night, in Beaune on Sunday night, and in MEURSAULT for the extended lunchtime bottle party that is the Paulée de Meursault on Monday.

The Hospices de Nuits also holds a charity wine auction; see NUITS-ST-GEORGES. See also AUCTIONS. J.T.C.M.

HOT BOTTLING. See PASTEURIZATION.

HOT PRESSING. See THERMOVINIFICATION.

HOWELL MOUNTAIN, California wine region and AVA. See NAPA Valley.

HUGEL, one of the best-known and oldest wine producers in Alsace, having been established in 1639. The family business is run today by the 12th and 13th generations. The Hugels, based in Riquewihr, make fine wines from their own 26 ha/65 acres of vineyard around the village planted mainly with Riesling and Gewürztraminer, together with a little Pinot Gris and Pinot Noir. Their Cuvée Tradition range can be excitingly full and the Jubilee range masterful. The Hugel family also pioneered the resurrection of Alsace's late harvest wines and were instrumental in drawing up the rigorous requirements for these VENDANGE TARDIVE and Sélection de Grains Nobles wines. They are arch exponents of these styles themselves, and produce them, and the Jubilee range, exclusively from their own ALSACE GRAND CRU vineyards. The Hugel family, of which six family members worked in the Riquewihr wine business in the mid 1990s, have long been champions of maximizing quality in Alsace's finest wines, and were for long vociferous opponents of the Alsace Grand Cru appellation. The Hugels buy in grapes, not wine, for their less exciting generic range of wines from about 120 ha/300 acres of vineyard under contract from more than 300 growers.

HUMIDITY, or moisture content, of the atmosphere has considerable implications both for vine growth and for the STORAGE of barrels and wine, whether in bulk or bottle. Humidity is normally measured as per cent relative humidity

(% RH): the amount of water (in true gaseous, or uncondensed form) a given volume of air holds, as a percentage of the maximum it could hold without condensation at the same temperature. (The latter amount increases with temperature, so the RH of air containing a constant amount of water vapour falls as temperature rises, and vice versa.) The difference between a given air body's water vapour content and what it could hold when saturated at the same temperature is called its saturation deficit, which is a direct measure of evaporative power. Actual EVAPORATION is further influenced by WIND and SUNLIGHT.

Relative humidity follows a regular daily cycle, normally being highest in the early morning, when temperature is lowest, and lowest in the early to mid afternoon when temperature is highest. Broadly speaking high humidity is conducive to the spread of FUNGAL DISEASES, especially when combined with high temperatures. The early morning figure is more critical for certain fungal diseases, however, which need water condensation on the vine or fruit for their spore germination and growth (see DEW). The afternoon figures, together with temperature and wind, dominate in determining evaporation, and therefore moisture demands on the vine. The contrast between morning and afternoon relative humidities tends to be greatest inland, and least near coasts which have alternating dry morning winds from the land and humid afternoon breezes from the sea (see WIND).

In all viticultural climates there is a seasonal trend opposite to that of temperature: relative humidities are highest in winter and lowest in summer. The contrast between seasons is greatest for the afternoon relative humidities.

Whereas high relative humidities encourage fungal diseases, Gladstones argues that they are also conducive to high yields and wine quality, provided that there is enough sunlight and diseases are absent or controlled. The critical humidities in this respect are those in the afternoon. Where the vines suffer little WATER STRESS, PHOTOSYNTHESIS is relatively continuous and there is maximum production of SUGAR IN GRAPES and its derivatives in the form of berry colour, flavour, and aroma. Moreover, because the yields are attained with least TRANSPIRATION (water throughput and evaporation), there will be less uptake of certain minerals into the vines and fruit, including POTASSIUM. Must and natural wine PH should therefore be lower, with benefits for brightness of wine COLOUR, freshness of wine flavour and aroma, and greater resistance to OXIDATION and BACTERIAL SPOILAGE.

Viticultural regions of the world with high afternoon relative humidities during the fruiting period include all those of Germany, Switzerland, Austria, and Hungary; Burgundy, Alsace, Champagne, the Loire valley, Bordeaux, and the Mediterranean coastal strip of France; marginally central and northern Italy, and the upper Rioja region of Spain; Madeira and some exposed coastal areas of Portugal; most of the coolest parts (Region I: see CLIMATE CLASSIFICATION) of the coastal valleys of California, Oregon, and Washington; the Cape Town/Constantia area in South Africa; Margaret River and the south coast of Western Australia; Geelong, the Mornington peninsula, and Gippsland in Victoria; and all of Tasmania and New Zealand.

Typical intermediate areas include the southern Rhône valley of France; most inland table wine-producing areas of Portugal, such as Dão, and of Spain; Bulgaria; intermediate and warmer parts of the coastal valleys of California, such as the Napa and Santa Clara valleys; probably Stellenbosch and Paarl in South Africa; the Western Australian west coast and hills; the Barossa and Adelaide hills, Langhorne Creek and Coonawarra in South Australia; Great Western and other parts of the Great Dividing Range in Victoria; and the Hunter Valley and marginally Mudgee in New South Wales.

Viticultural regions with low afternoon relative humidities are nearly all hot as well, and tend to have high TEMPERATURE VARIABILITY. Such regions include the middle and upper Douro valley of Portugal (to a moderate degree); the Central Valley of California; the Little Karoo in South Africa; and the Murray and Murrumbidgee valley areas of South Australia, northern Victoria, and southern New South Wales.

For details of humidity and barrels, see EVAPORATION. For details of humidity and wine storage, see STORING WINE. J.G.

Gladstones, J., *Viticulture and Environment* (Adelaide, 1992).

HUNDRED YEARS WAR. The sporadic fighting between the kings of England and France known as the Hundred Years War (1337–1453) changed both the political map of Europe and the nature and volume of the medieval wine trade. Both crowns claimed ownership of the wine regions of western France which, through the wealthy port of BORDEAUX, supplied England with almost all her wine.

The hostilities themselves had a marked effect on the wine trade. First the large and commercially successful vineyards of the HAUT PAYS, or 'high country', upstream from Bordeaux (GAILLAC, BERGERAC, BUZET, CAHORS) were for the most part under French control. This increased English reliance on the lesser vineyards of Bordeaux and its environs, encouraging their expansion.

Secondly the ships carrying wine back to England faced the risk of greater piracy. Convoys organized for their protection proved expensive. Reduced supplies and greater freight costs led to a dramatic rise in the price of wine in England.

After Bordeaux's surrender at CASTILLON in 1453 England remained a major market for her wines, although the overall volume of this trade was not to reach the pre-war peak for many centuries. English merchants became more willing to look beyond western France for their wine imports while Bordeaux attracted a wider clientele of merchants from northern Europe.

See also BORDEAUX, history. H.B.

Dion, R., *Histoire de la vigne et du vin en France* (Paris, 1959).
James, M. K., *Studies in the Medieval Wine Trade* (Oxford, 1971).
Renouard, Y., *Études d'histoire médiévale* (Paris, 1968).

HUNGARY, important eastern European wine-producing country with its own particularly distinctive range of vine varieties and wines. Hungary usually produces less wine than its eastern neighbour Romania, but considerably more than, for example, Austria and Bulgaria. About 110,000 ha/271,700 acres were devoted to vines in the early 1990s, and about 70 per cent of them produced white wines. Total Hungarian wine production has varied between 4.0 and 5.5 million hl (105–145 million gal) a year.

History

Vine-growing and wine-making have been practised in what is modern Hungary since at least Roman times, when it was part of the Roman province of Pannonia. The Magyar tribes who arrived here at the end of the 9th century found flourishing vineyards and familiarity with wine-making techniques. Under Bela IV (1235–70), the king who rebuilt Hungary after the Mongol invasion of 1241, wine production was given such priority that immigrants from areas with particular expertise in vine-growing and wine-making were deliberately invited to rebuild the devastated areas, and by the end of his reign wines from the two towns of SOPRON and EGER were being exported in relatively large quantities. Hungary's most famous wine, Tokay, is first mentioned in records in the late 15th century, although it was almost certainly dry at this time.

Following the defeat and death of Louis II at the battle of Mohács in 1514, much of the country was under Muslim rule for a century and a half, during which wine production survived, but did not thrive (see ISLAM).

The most important development in the 17th century was the emergence of especially rich Tokay Aszú. As early as 1641 a Vine Law for the entire Tokaj-Hegyalja district was drawn up which regulated VINEYARD SITE SELECTION, the construction of TERRACES, IRRIGATION, manuring, and hoeing (which had to be done for the last time on 20 August before the official harvest date of 28 October). By 1660 NOBLE ROT was recognized, and the laws for Aszú formulated. For more details, see TOKAY.

In 1686 the city of Buda was liberated from the Turks, followed within the next few years by all of the rest of Hungary, which then became part of the vast Habsburg empire. A bid for independence led by Ferenc Rákóczi failed in 1711, but had the effect of spreading the fame of Tokay wines to the court of the French king, Louis XIV, to whom Rákóczi had wisely sent sample bottles as gifts. This was the beginning of Tokay's formidable international reputation.

PHYLLOXERA struck Hungary in the 1870s, devastating the southern vineyards at Pancsova initially but eventually spreading to the Northern Massif and Tokaj-Hegyalja. Replanting on phylloxera-resistant ROOTSTOCKS began in 1881, but scientific proof that the phylloxera louse could not thrive in sandy soils had just been published, encouraging the planting of new vineyards in the Great Plain, where vines were also discovered to be particularly suitable plants for stabilizing the shifting sands.

In 1947 the National Association of Hungarian Vine-Growers, Wine Trades and Wine-Growing Communities, which had originally been founded in 1830 to promote co-operation and study for the benefit of all in the wine industry, was forced to suspend its activities when the communist state monopoly took control. An era of state farms and state wineries followed, during which all wine exports were funnelled through the state-controlled trading company Monimpex (and half of all production at one point handled by just two state wineries designed to export huge quantities of very ordinary wine to the USSR). Unlike the similarly organized BULGARIAN wine industry, that of Hungary suffered a period of stagnation and generally low technology during this era, which stultified the development of Hungarian wine until the somewhat complicated return of a free market economy and private enterprise in the late 1980s. A considerable proportion of all Hungarian vines had remained in private hands in the communist era, which may help to explain why average YIELDS were rather higher than in other Comecon wine-producing countries.

In the post-communist division of vinicultural spoils (see below), there was no shortage of western interest in the unique Tokay wines, and technology in other areas benefited from temporary invasion by foreign—typically antipodean (see AUSTRALIAN INFLUENCE)—wine-makers.

Geography

Hungary, which lies between the latitudes 45 and 50 degrees north, is land-locked but includes Europe's largest lake, Balaton. The river Danube (called Duna in Hungary) flows through it from north to south, dividing the country in almost equal halves. To the west lies Transdanubia, while to the immediate east of the river is the Great Plain. North east of the capital Budapest are the volcanic hills which constitute the Northern Massif, whose south-facing slopes are particularly well suited to vine-growing. In the extreme north east of the country is the Tokaj-Hegyalja region, which borders SLOVAKIA. See TOKAY for more details.

Soils are very varied. The Great Plain is mainly sand, while the area around Lake Balaton is of basalt volcanic rock with clay, sandstone, and loess. Other soils include limestone and slate, particularly around Balatonfüred. In Tokaj-Hegyalja the soils are volcanic with a topsoil of decayed lava.

See below for details of individual wine regions.

Climate

Hungary's climate is essentially continental and central European, involving fairly predictably cold winters and hot summers (see CONTINENTALITY). The sun shines for a high average of about 2,000 hours a year, and the total heat summation during the vegetative ripening period is approximately 2,500 °C. Prolonged, sunny autumns which favour the development of noble rot are by no means rare, however.

Vine varieties

Wine labelling in Hungary is largely VARIETAL so that wine producers and consumers have a keen appreciation of specific vine varieties. Hungary had a particularly rich selection of indigenous vine varieties, many of which were largely abandoned when phylloxera invaded the country's vineyards in the late 19th century. A potentially exciting selection of localized white grape varieties can still be found, although some such as KÉKNYELŰ, found almost exclusively in Badacsony on

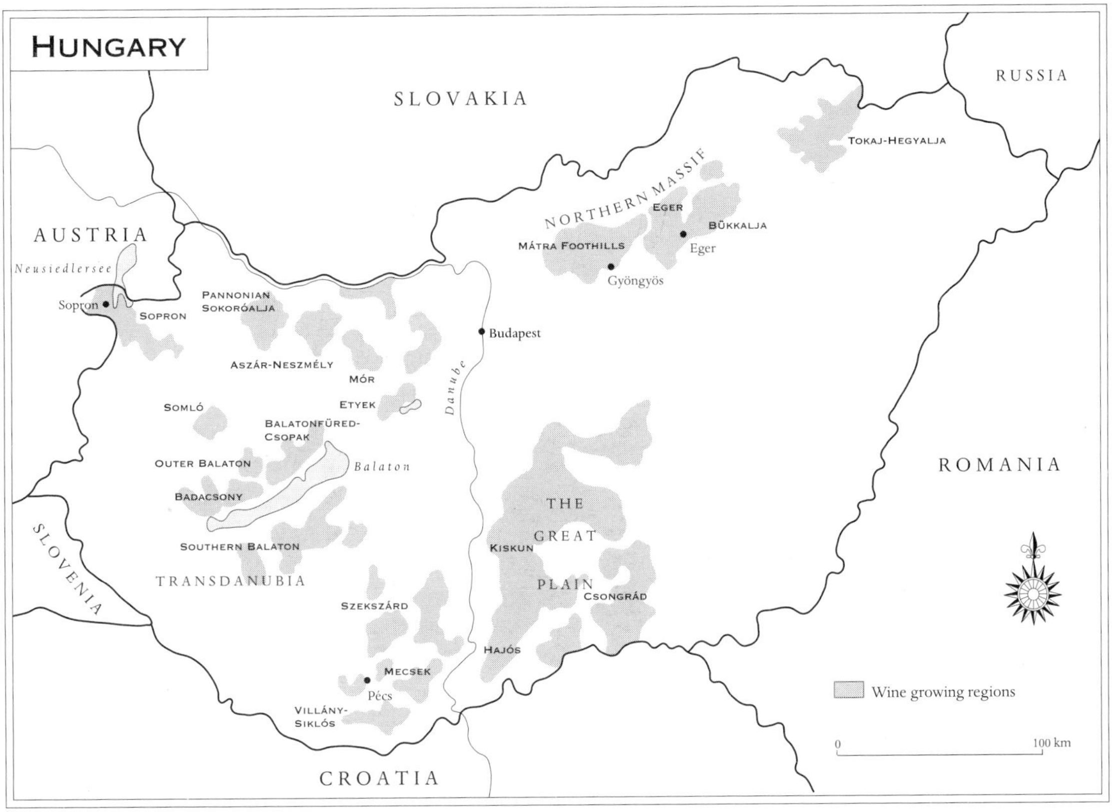

the north shore of Lake Balaton, and JUHFARK, known mainly in Somló, are dangerously close to extinction. The aromatic Sárfehér of Somló is also valued as a TABLE GRAPE.

Indigenous varieties which are relatively widely planted include the EZERJÓ, a light speciality of the Mór region west of Budapest; FURMINT, which is widely grown but is the most characteristic ingredient of Tokay; HÁRSLEVELŰ, which is usually a lesser Tokay ingredient and is also widely grown throughout Hungary; and MEZESFEHÉR is widely planted and used for sweet wine, particularly in Eger and Gyöngyös. Kövidinka, or DINKA, produces ordinary wines in quantity on the Great Plain, as it does across the southern border with VOJVODINA. Hungary's most characteristic red grape variety is KADARKA, although KÉKOPORTO also shows promise.

The usual range of central European vine varieties is grown: Olaszrizling (the Hungarian name for WELSCHRIESLING), Leányka (the FETEASCA of Romania), Zöldveltelini (Austria's GRÜNER VELTLINER), Cirfandli (Austria's ZIERFANDLER, a speciality of Pécs); and, for red wine production, KÉKFRANKOS (along with Nagyburgundi the Hungarian name for BLAUFRÄNKISCH), and Austria's ZWEIGELT.

A wide range of vine varieties have been imported into Hungary from western Europe, however, including Chardonnay, Sauvignon, Sémillon, Riesling (sometimes called Rajnai Rizling or Rheinriesling), Gewürztraminer (Tramini), Muscat Ottonel and Gold Muscat, the deeper hued Muscat Blanc à Petits Grains (both of which are sometimes called Muskotály), Silvaner (Zöldszilváni), Müller-Thurgau (Riesling Silvaner or Rizlingszilváni), and Pinot Gris, whose distinctively Hungarian synonym is Szürkebarát. Red wine varieties imported from the west include both Cabernet Sauvignon and Cabernet Franc (although the vague term Cabernet is more usual on a label), Merlot (sometimes perversely called Médoc Noir), and Pinot Noir.

Wine regions

According to Hungarian law, the official Hungarian wine regions are the 20 areas shown on the map above, but the following may be considered pre-eminent today: Badacsony, Balaton, EGER, the Mátra Foothills, Szekszárd, Villány-Siklós, and Tokaj-Hegyalja (for details of which see TOKAY). See also SOPRON for more information about this historic area. Names such as Mór and Gyöngyös may also be familiar from export labels. The wine regions fall into four major geographical groups as outlined below.

The Great Plain This vast, flat expanse (known as Alföld in Hungary) south of Budapest and between the Danube and Hungary's second river the Tisza accounts for nearly half the country's vineyards. The plain was heavily planted after the phylloxera invasion because of phylloxera's intolerance of sandy soils, and because vines were better than the fruit trees planted earlier at stabilizing the soil. MECHANIZATION is easy on this flat land, but the DROUGHT in summer and FROST in both late spring and early autumn are a perennial threat, and the combination of sandy soil and high summer temperatures means that soil temperatures can be very high indeed.

Most of the wide variety of vines planted here are the western, 'international' varieties or Olaszrizling, although some Kadarka and a little Ezerjó are planted.

The three official wine regions of the Great Plain are Csongrád, Hajós-Vaskút, which is best known for red wines, and Kiskun.

Transdanubia This western part of Hungary, between the Austrian border and the Danube, contains 13 of the designated wine regions and is effectively split into two parts by Lake Balaton.

Traditionally the northern side of the lake was the vine-growing area, with the famous Badacsony area on the volcanic slopes at the south west end. The surface area of water in the lake has a considerable ameliorating effect on the MESOCLIMATE (see TOPOGRAPHY) and the wines tend to be full and powerful. This is home to the ancient Kéknyelű, but also makes fine Szürkebarát, as well as Olaszrizling. Balatonfüred-Csopak also lies on the northern shore, on slate, and produces a range of western varieties and Olaszrizling.

On the slopes of an extinct volcano north west of Lake Balaton is the once historic wine region of Somló, whose oxidized, wood-aged, blended wines once enjoyed a similar reputation to those of Tokay. Juhfark was once prized here, along with Furmint, but today Riesling, Olaszrizling, and Traminer are in the ascendant.

On the south shore of the lake is a relatively new area, southern Balaton or Balatonboglári, where the fertile soils include sand and loess. Important grapes grown here are Merlot, Pinot Noir, Chardonnay, Muscat, and Sémillon.

The most westerly wine region of northern Transdanubia is Sopron, effectively a continuation of Neusiedlersee-Hügelland, AUSTRIA's most revered source of sweet white wine. Today Sopron is mainly a red wine region and the principal vine varieties are Cabernet Sauvignon, Cabernet Franc, Merlot, and Pinot Noir.

Mór, between Sopron and Budapest, is best known for its Ezerjó, while Etyek to the east of Mór produces a wide range of exportable varietal wines.

Southern Transdanubia has three important wine regions close together in the far south of the country just west of the Danube. Villány-Siklós is made up of the red wine vineyards on the limestone Villány hills and mainly white wine vineyards of Siklós. A wide range of red wine grapes is grown here on numerous smallholdings, including Kékoporto, which arguably performs better here than anywhere else, as well as Pinot Noir and Kékfrankos (both of which have in their time been bottled as Nagyburgundi), and Cabernet, Merlot, and Zweigelt. The most common white wine grapes of the region are Olaszrizling, Chardonnay, Tramini, and a particularly full bodied Hárslevelű.

Szekszárd has traditionally been associated with Kadarka, which it has managed to ripen more healthily than most regions, owing to its long, warm summers. A BOTRYTIZED sweet version was even sold, as Nemes Kadar. This native red variety has been supplanted, however, by vigorous Kékfrankos, Merlot, and Cabernet.

The Mecsek Hills is a wine region better known by the name of its principal town Pécs and, as Hungary's warmest wine region, is at constant risk of drought. A wide range of vine varieties is cultivated here, often on very small estates. They include Olaszrizling, Chardonnay, Kadarka, Cabernet, Merlot, and Pinot Noir.

The Northern Massif This range of hills running north east from Budapest along the border with Slovakia contains three wine regions, the Mátra Foothills (or Mátraalja), Eger, and Tokaj-Hegyalja (for details of which, see TOKAY).

In the foothills of the Mátra mountains the soils are mainly volcanic and most of the wine produced is white. Muscat, Olaszrizling, and Kadarka predominate, and within Hungary the area is associated with Debrői Hárslevelű, once a noble cask-aged sweet white but now a commercial blend. In western Europe at least, this wine region is better known for the Gyöngyös Estate on which modern Chardonnay, Sauvignon Blanc, and Sémillon have been made for export, with other wine styles projected.

Just to the east of the Mátra Foothills, in the foothills of the Bükk mountains, is the wine region named after the historic town of EGER. Spring often comes late here and the rainfall is low. Some white wines are made, principally from Leányka, but the region is best known for age-worthy red wine, notably Egri Bikavér or, on export markets, BULL'S BLOOD. Once one of the most famous wine BRANDS, this blend represented a triumph of marketing on behalf of Monimpex and the state-owned Egervin wine complex. At one time the blend depended heavily on Kadarka, but as elsewhere this troublesome native variety was replaced by Kékfrankos, supplemented by Cabernet, Merlot, and Kékoporto.

Only Tokay, made even further east, rivals Bull's Blood for recognition outside Hungary, although the situation has been changing rapidly as wine-making and exporting skills have passed into private, and often non-Hungarian, hands.

Structure of the trade

Prior to the reintroduction of a capitalist system in the early 1990s, the Hungarian wine industry was under the control of the state. AGKER controlled 125 large state farms. Hungarovin was the state-owned wine trust which had its own vineyards, vinified a significant proportion of the state farms' grapes, and oversaw wine sales from the co-operatives and many smaller wine farms. All wine exports were under the control of the state trading organization Monimpex.

In the early 1980s Hungary was the principal eastern European wine exporter, shipping out more than 3 million hl/79 million gal, or 60 per cent of production, notably very ordinary quality wine in bulk to the USSR and East Germany. These markets shrank abruptly at the end of the 1980s, leading to sudden over-supply and extreme uncertainty among vine-growers and wine-makers.

In 1989 the national association of these two parties, which had been dissolved in 1947, was effectively re-formed, as the Federation of Hungarian Grape and Wine Producers, with the aim of rebuilding the image of Hungarian wine. The Association of Hungarian Wine Merchants acts primarily on export control. Per capita wine consumption within Hungary rose markedly in the early 1990s, when the official target was to export about one-third of all wine production.

Under government policy, the state farms and state wineries were offered for sale, often in a state of perilous financial health. Foreign investment was actively sought, with some degree of success, particularly in Tokaj-Hegyalja, where the famous name of Tokay attracted buyers from France, Spain, Germany, Britain, and the Netherlands. The monolithic Hungarovin organization was sold to the German SEKT giant Henkell and the famous Italian firm of ANTINORI, for example, made an investment in the Szekszárd region.

Uncertainty over property rights, exact boundaries, and land ownership dogged many proposals, however, and would-be investors on occasion lost confidence in what exactly they were buying. Moreover, not only the state farms but also many of the state wineries were in poor condition, which at least depressed selling prices, thereby enabling local investment. Some of those made redundant by the introduction of a capitalist system are investing in vineyards, making wine, and acting as consultants and educators.

In the mid 1990s the entire Hungarian wine industry was in a state of flux. The wine laws of 1970 which controlled every aspect were replaced in 1990 with laws more like those of the EUROPEAN UNION, quality wines being labelled Minöségi Bor, but even these have been subject to a regular barrage of amendments. A register of vineyards and wine cellars has been created and a host of new companies of varied sizes and structures has emerged and, once a period of commercial and legal stability returns, there is every reason to believe that Hungary will be a source of distinctive and varied wines.

M.McN.

Halasz, Z., *The Book of Hungarian Wines* (19th century).

Katona, J., *A Guide to Hungarian Wine*, trans Z. Béres (Budapest, 1990).

HUNTER VALLEY, relatively small but keenly promoted wine region in AUSTRALIA made up of two very distinct subregions, the **Lower Hunter** and the more recently developed **Upper Hunter**. For more detail see NEW SOUTH WALES.

HUXELREBE is an early 20th century German vine crossing that has enjoyed some popularity both in Germany and, on a much smaller scale, in ENGLAND. Although like SCHEUREBE and FABER it was actually bred by Dr Georg Scheu at Alzey, this crossing takes its name from its chief propagator, nurseryman Fritz Huxel. It was bred in 1927 from GUTEDEL (Chasselas) and Courtillier Musqué (which is also an ante cedent of the popular hybrid MARÉCHAL FOCH). The crossing is capable of producing enormous quantities of rather ordinary wine—so enormous in fact that the vines can collapse under the strain. If pruned carefully, however, and planted on an average to good site, it can easily reach Auslese MUST WEIGHTS even in an ordinary year and produce a fulsome if not exactly subtle wine for reasonably early consumption. Huxelrebe's flavours are more reminiscent of Muscat than Riesling and in England its ripeness is a useful counterbalance to naturally high acidity. In Germany it is grown almost exclusively in the Pfalz and Rheinhessen and, although it is slowly losing ground, there were still more than 1,500 ha/3,705 acres in 1990.

HYBRIDS, in common viticultural terms, the offspring of two varieties of different species, as distinct from a CROSS between two varieties of the same species. (See VITIS for details of the various species of the vine genus.) EUROPEAN UNION authorities prefer the somewhat cumbersome term 'interspecific cross' to the word hybrid, which has pejorative connotations within Europe.

Hybrids can occur naturally by cross-pollination, as happened, for example, in early American viticulture (see AMERICAN HYBRIDS). More commonly, however, hybrids have been deliberately produced by man (see NEW VARIETIES and VINE BREEDING) to combine in the progeny some of the desirable characteristics of the parents. This viticultural activity was particularly important in the late 19th century when European, and especially French, breeders tried to combine the desirable wine quality of European VINIFERA varieties with AMERICAN VINE SPECIES' resistance to introduced American pests and diseases, especially the PHYLLOXERA louse, which was devastating European vineyards (see FRENCH HYBRIDS).

Grafting European vines on to American ROOTSTOCKS proved the eventual solution, and many of today's commercially important rootstocks are hybrids. Early rootstocks were often pure varieties of a single American vine species chosen for their resistance to phylloxera. It was subsequently found, however, that hybrid rootstocks with combinations of genes from several American vine species allowed tolerance of various soil conditions and diseases, are were more successful in the nursery.

Different species of *Vitis* contain genes with natural tolerance or resistance to winter cold, lime CHLOROSIS, SALINITY, DOWNY MILDEW, POWDERY MILDEW, BOTRYTIS BUNCH ROT, CROWN GALL, PIERCE'S DISEASE, NEMATODES, WINTER FREEZE injury, and phylloxera. It is logical, therefore, to explore the possibilities of new hybrid varieties for wine production in an age of increasing concern about the AGROCHEMICALS which are used to control some of these. Vine breeders such as Professor Alleweldt and his colleagues at GEILWEILERHOF have proved that new hybrids may, without recourse to agrochemicals, produce useful quantities of wine which cannot be distinguished from that of their pure *vinifera* counterparts in controlled tests. Their acceptance is hampered, however, by an EU ban on hybrids and a widespread suspicion of hybrids in general, fuelled by the poor wine quality associated with the early French hybrids, and by the problem of nomenclature. The pedigree of many modern hybrids can involve seven or eight generations of crosses so that their ancestry is typically complex and includes *vinifera*, American varieties, possibly Asian varieties, and also early released French hybrids.

Although hybrids are forbidden by EU authorities in the production of QUALITY WINE, not all of these varieties are inherently inferior in all circumstances and SEYVAL BLANC has yielded good results in the cool climate of ENGLAND, for example. Another example of the successful modern use of a disease-tolerant hybrid is that of CHAMBOURCIN in summer rainfall areas of Australia, such as parts of NEW SOUTH WALES. Vine-growers in NEW YORK and CANADA use modern hybrids claimed by their breeders to have flavours that are not discernibly different from those of *vinifera*.

See also AMERICAN HYBRIDS, FRENCH HYBRIDS. R.E.S.

Galet, P., and Morton, L. T., *A Practical Ampelography* (Ithaca, NY, and London, 1979).
Huglin, P., *Biologie et écologie de la vigne* (Paris, 1986).
Mullins, M. G., Bouquet, A., and Williams, L., *Biology of the Grapevine* (Cambridge, 1992).

HYDROGEN SULPHIDE, or H_2S, is the foul-smelling gas, reminiscent of rotten eggs, which can form during FERMENTATION, either in the active phase or towards the end. The formation of H_2S during the active phase is associated with a deficiency in the amount of NITROGEN in grape must or juice. This problem can usually be suppressed by the addition of nitrogen, typically in the form of diammonium phosphate. Some varieties, depending on soil type and vintage conditions, tend to have a low nitrogen content. Riesling, Chardonnay, and Syrah are examples. The amount of H_2S produced can also be affected by the addition of a high level of SULPHUR DIOXIDE to the must shortly before inoculating with YEAST, and by the strain of yeast involved. Certain yeasts more readily reduce sulphate, especially sulphur dioxide, to H_2S when deprived of nitrogen, in a futile attempt to make sulphur-containing AMINO ACIDS needed for cell growth. The addition of diammonium phosphate stops H_2S accumulating in the wine, not by stopping its formation but by enabling the yeast to make amino acid precursor compounds which react with the H_2S to form sulphur-amino acids. Hot climate reds, which are prone to rapid fermentations in higher TEMPERATURES, use more nitrogen and tend to develop sulphidic smells.

Small amounts of SULPHUR used as vineyard fungicide can easily be reduced to H_2S by the highly REDUCTIVE conditions generated by yeast. Reducing or eliminating sulphur residues by ceasing sulphur applications several weeks before HARVEST can help. Recent research suggests that the role of sulphur residues as a source of H_2S in wine is overstated. In rare instances, usually when the juice has been stored for some time, a deficiency of VITAMINS can also cause H_2S to be formed.

Even traces of hydrogen sulphide can spoil a wine's aroma. Fortunately, however, hydrogen sulphide is very volatile and can usually be removed by the stripping action of CARBON DIOXIDE produced during fermentation. However, H_2S formed towards the end of fermentation or, worse still, after fermentation is completed is of greater concern to the winemaker. If allowed to remain in the wine, it is thought to react with other wine components to form MERCAPTANS, thiols, and disulphides (see SULPHIDES), which have pungent garlic/onion/rubber aromas. The smell of rotten eggs is always a FAULT in a finished wine but acceptance of the presence of trace amounts of mercaptans and disulphides is more controversial. Hydrogen sulphide and thiols can usually be removed from the new wine by a small addition of copper sulphate, or in the case of robust wines (especially reds) by AERATION, traditionally achieved by simple stirring, or by RACKING. A.D.W.

The **hydrometer**, seen here measuring the all-important ripeness of port grapes at Quinta do Bomfim in the Douro.

Henschke, P. A., and Jiranek, V., 'Hydrogen sulfide formation during fermentation: effect of nitrogen composition in model grape must', in J. M. Rantz (ed.), 'Nitrogen in Grapes and Wine', Proc. Int. Symposium, Seattle, June 1991, *American Journal of Enology and Viticulture* (1991), 172–84.
Rauhut, D., 'Yeasts: production of sulfur compounds', in G. H. Fleet (ed.), *Wine Microbiology and Biotechnology* (Chur, 1993).

HYDROMETER, an instrument used for measuring the soluble solids, sugar content, or MUST WEIGHT of juice and wine, consisting of a closed glass tube with a bulbous base, weighted so that it floats upright. The floating depth is proportional to the DENSITY of the solution and is read by matching the bottom of the meniscus against a scale within the stem. This scale may be calibrated as for BAUMÉ, BRIX/Balling, or OECHSLE. As with all such density measurements, correction for the TEMPERATURE of the solution is necessary. B.G.C.

HYGIENE, an essential discipline in modern cellar management, involving cleanliness of wine-making premises and equipment, and a great deal of WATER.

History

Winery hygiene was clearly already regarded as important in Ancient ROME, as suggested by writers such as CATO and references in classical literature to SULPHUR.

At the heart of the transformation from traditional mouldy cellars to their spotlessly clean counterparts has been a desire by wine-makers to obtain much greater control over the processes of vinification and the maturation of wine, primarily through an emphasis on hygiene. While the pace of scientific research on the microbiology and biochemistry of wine-making has quickened appreciably since 1945, its origins lie in the middle of the 19th century with the experimental work of Louis PASTEUR. Until then, the precise reasons why pressed grapes would ferment into wine, and would then become unpalatable if left open to the air for any length of time, were unknown. Practical experience had convinced Roman wine-makers of the need to use chemicals such as sulphur to help prevent spoilage, and by the late 15th century in Germany it was recognized that wine kept in large barrels that were subjected to regular TOPPING UP would last longer than wine kept in small barrels which was left on ULLAGE. However, it was Pasteur who first reported that wine deteriorated mainly as a result of the actions of micro-organisms, and that these could be killed by heating the wine in the absence of oxygen.

Much of the impetus for the recent changes in winery hygiene has come from the New World, and in particular from institutions such as the Department of Viticulture and Enology at the University of California, DAVIS, where the driving mentality during the 1950s and 1960s was towards the eradication of poor-quality wine. This, it was argued, could best be achieved through tight control of the fermentation process, excluding the chance interference of a range of micro-organisms. Above all, greater hygiene has enabled the adverse effects of ACETOBACTER and other spoilage micro-organisms to be avoided. P.T.H.U.

Current practice

Hygiene is regarded as vital by modern wine-makers (although it is still ignored by many traditional or peasant wine-makers, some of whom somehow manage to produce top-quality wine). Old cellars, while usually more picturesque, are almost impossible to keep clean and free of BACTERIA and wild YEASTS. Most modern wineries, on the other hand, are designed with sanitation and hygiene in mind. STAINLESS STEEL tanks can be easily cleaned and sanitized; hard floors are designed to drain dry; and all equipment is sited and mounted so that it can be cleaned thoroughly around, above, and below the unit. Vast quantities of water are used, together with non-foaming detergents and sterilizing agents, by carefully trained staff. In many wineries, all places where finished wine is exposed to the atmosphere are in separate, essentially sterile rooms, and care is taken particularly during BOTTLING, to its limit in STERILE BOTTLING.

Local wine-making traditions which supposedly rely on cellar moulds (see TOKAY in Hungary, for example) rarely stand up to something as unromantic as scientific scrutiny.

Hygiene, or **sanitation**, is also important where the grapes are received, as overripe and damaged fruit can easily attract insects, particularly FRUIT FLIES *Drosophila melanogaster*. Piles of POMACE and stems should also be distanced from the winery as these can also become a breeding ground for insects. A.D.W.

Amerine, M. A., 'The fermentation industries after Pasteur', *Food Technology*, 19/5 (1965), 75–90.

Winkler, A. J., *Viticultural Research at University of California, Davis, 1921–1971* (Davis, Calif., 1973).

I

ICE WINE, direct Anglicization of the German EISWEIN, wine made from ripe grapes picked when frozen on the vine and pressed so that water crystals remain in the press and the sugar content of the resulting wine is increased. This sort of true ice wine is a speciality of CANADA, although the term has also been used in other English-speaking, wine-producing countries for wines made by artificial freeze CONCENTRATION, or CRYOEXTRACTION.

IDAHO, state in the PACIFIC NORTHWEST of the UNITED STATES which, as a wine region, may have more in common with its neighbour eastern WASHINGTON than with western OREGON. With vineyards at an altitude of around 2,500 ft/762 m, however, it is close to if not beyond the normal viticultural fringe. Its climate contrasts high daytime temperatures with cool nights (as does Washington's), but to an almost exaggerated degree with the effect of a paradoxical combination in grapes of high acid and high sugar. This poses interesting challenges for both grape-grower and wine-maker (usually part of the same enterprise) and the responses often prove unconventional. Contrary to some tenets, high YIELDS can be the answer to quality here in order to dilute excess acidity and alcohol. Marginality here is not about ripening but about sheer survival, for Idaho winters are bitterly cold and only the hardier VINIFERA varieties are likely to tolerate them. (WINTER PROTECTION of vines is frequently necessary.) It is thus no surprise to find RIESLING vines, which produce very successful sweet white wines in which the sugar is well balanced by natural acidity. CHARDONNAY too can be a polished performer, whether austere or buttery. CABERNET SAUVIGNON may succeed if it does not find the growing season here too short (harvest is usually in September). The industry has been dominated by Ste Chapelle winery, one of the Northwest's larger and more successful wineries situated in the Snake River valley to the west of Boise, in an area renowned for its cherries, apples, and peaches, always an indication of wine grape potential. There is substantial cross-border traffic in wine between Idaho and Washington. M.S.

Clark, C., *American Wines of the Northwest* (New York, 1989).
Hill, C., *The Northwest Winery Guide* (Seattle, 1988).
Meredith, T. J., *Northwest Wine* (Kirkland, Wash., 1990).

IGT, (*Indicazione Geografica Tipica*), a category of wines created in ITALY by law 164 in 1992 as an approximate equivalent of the French VIN DE PAYS or German LANDWEIN. It was also designed to include Italy's myriad esteemed, and often extremely expensive, wines selling as a VINO DA TAVOLA outside the much-criticized DOC system. It seems unlikely, however, that the many wines which have a won a loyal following on their own as vini da tavola, and have no difficulty in being sold at very remunerative prices, will hasten to change their classification. D.T.

ÎLE DE BEAUTÉ is VIN DE PAYS language for CORSICA and, along with the Loire's similar denomination as 'Jardin de la France', one of the most alluring vin de pays names.

IMBOTTIGLIATO is Italian for bottled.

INAO, the **Institut National des Appellations d'Origine**, is the organization in charge of administering, regulating, and granting the French APPELLATIONS CONTRÔLÉES, not just for about 400 different wines and spirits, but for more than 30 different cheeses and a range of other foods. As such, and since VIN DE TABLE production is slowly declining, it controls an increasing proportion of all French wine, more than 40 per cent by the mid 1990s. Nearly 100,000 vine-growers therefore depend on its rules, its protection, and its efforts to strengthen France's reliance on geographically based wine names. The organization, whose annual budget was well over FF70 million in the mid 1990s, is based in Paris but run by regional committees and administrative centres.

INAO was founded in 1935 and, since for much of the 20th century France's leading role in the world of wine was undisputed, it provided a role model for the administration of more embryonic CONTROLLED APPELLATION schemes in other countries. During the 1980s, however, commercial competition from non-French wines, and even from some French VINS DE PAYS on export markets, encouraged a re-examination of the role of INAO in the late 20th century. The result was an even stronger INAO, given additional powers in 1990, fiercely dedicated to the notion of controlled, geographically determined appellations, empowered to protect them against imitation both in France and abroad, and determined that France's viticultural future in particular depended on her ability to trade on her uniquely well-established wine names.

In 1990 the INAO stated as a possibility its eventual aim to remove all VINE VARIETY names from wine labels, on the premiss that French wines express TERROIR rather than mere fruit flavour. (Certain vin de pays producers positively relish their freedom to sell VARIETAL wines, or *vins de cépages* as they are known, and often despised, within France.) A policy of specifying appellations but not varieties may not help the

Indian vines trained into an arbour to protect them from sunburn.

consumer in the short term—see TOURAINE, for example—but it may well help France in the long term by distancing French wines from direct comparison with foreign wines. The re-evaluation of 1990 also stressed INAO's determination to award ACs in order to preserve France's agricultural heritage, and its willingness to grant suitably formulated appellations to 'all agricultural and alimentary products', envisaging a distant era in which vins de table and vins de pays could almost be extinct.

Any group of wine producers can apply to INAO to establish an appellation, possibly of VDQS status initially. They have to prepare a dossier by giving reasons for the request, proof of the traditional use of the name of the proposed appellation, full details of the terroir and how it affects production, and economic details concerning markets, sales, prices, and comparative prices of similar products.

INCROCIO, Italian for vine CROSSING. A wine made from **Incrocio Manzoni** grapes, for example, is made from one of Signor Manzoni's many crossings of one VINIFERA variety with another. His Incrocio Manzoni 6.0.13, Riesling × Pinot Blanc, is the most widely planted, particularly in north east Italy. Incrocio Manzoni 2.15 is Prosecco × Cabernet Sauvignon.

Anderson, B., *The Wine Atlas of Italy* (London and New York, 1990).

INDEXING, method of testing vines for VIRUS DISEASES and MYCOPLASMA DISEASES and their like. Sap from the plant to be tested is exposed to so-called indicator plants which show typical symptoms if the virus is present. Sap from the two plants can be mixed by abrading leaves or by grafting. Cabernet Franc, for example, is used as an indicator vine variety to test for LEAFROLL VIRUS. R.E.S.

INDIA, large Asian country in much of which alcoholic drinks are frowned upon and the climate is too hot for successful commercial wine production.

History

The vine was probably introduced into north west India from Persia as early as the 4th millennium BC, during the Indus civilization, but wine may not have been made from its fruit for many centuries. The gradual invasion of Aryan tribes from central Asia during the 2nd millennium BC produced the Vedic period (broadly *c.*2000–800 BC), a blossoming of culture in north west India. The Aryans enjoyed gambling, music, and intoxicating drink and in the four Vedas, the world's oldest religious texts, two drinks are mentioned: *soma*, a milky drink ceremoniously prepared immediately before a sacrifice and probably containing hallucinatory hemp; and *sura*, a potent secular drink made from either barley or paddy (rice) fermented with honey.

While praising the favourite Aryan god, the rowdy and hard-drinking warrior Indra, the Vedas clearly condemn the effects of drinking. Later Hindu, Buddhist, and Jain texts reveal similar dichotomies. While the fifth of the Ten Precepts of Buddhism forbade alcoholic drinks, the Buddha (d. 483 BC) himself is said to have regarded alcohol as less reprehensible, merely an 'opening for the swallowing up of wealth'. The remarkable Kautilya, chief minister under the Mauryan King Chandragupta (ruled *c*.324–300 BC), partly or wholly wrote the Arthasastra, a text on statecraft in which he condemns alcohol and yet chronicles the king's drinking bouts and mentions *madhu* (wine) of various varieties and qualities, some home produced. This is the first documentation of wine made from grapes in India.

Down the centuries wine has maintained its status in India as a drink of the Ksatriya caste of aristocrats and warriors rather than of the masses, who have preferred more potent alcohol prepared from the staple local agricultural crops of what and barley in the north, paddy in irrigated areas, and millet in dry zones.

The contradictory attitudes towards intoxicating drinks continue into modern times. The Muslim (see ISLAM) Mughal emperors' royal vineyards were in the Deccan; the alcoholic emperor Jehangir (who ruled 1605–27) would drink himself insensible on double- and triple-distilled wine (BRANDY), violating the Qur'ān's command not to lose one's sensibilities through intoxication.

Secular independent India's Constitution, adopted on 26 January 1950, states as one of its aims total prohibition of alcohol. In the 1990s, while orthodox Indians of all faiths and especially Hindu brahmins continue to abstain, and while Gujarat state enforces total prohibition, alcohol is made under government licence in most states.

Furthermore, since Independence in 1947, wine production has been slowly increasing despite the long-term investment required and the lack of a substantial local market. The Indian government has begun to promote wine-growing as an agro-processing industry but, although there are a few CO-OPERATIVES, it remains almost entirely private. The fortified wines of Goa, introduced by the Portuguese in the 16th century, have remained a low-quality local industry fashioned in the image of Portugal's most famous wine, PORT.

Under the influence of Victorian Britain, whose upper classes expected to consume wines of all sorts in quantity, Indian viticulture was encouraged in the 19th century. Vineyards were established in Kashmīr and at Bārāmati. A number of Indian wines were exhibited at the Great Calcutta Exhibition of 1884 and elicited favourable comment. But in the 1890s Indian vineyards, like their European counterparts, succumbed to PHYLLOXERA. L.N.

Prakash, O., *Food and Drinks in Ancient India* (Delhi, 1961).

Modern India

Almost 70 per cent of India's 50,000 ha/12,500 acres of vineyards lie in western Mahārāshtra. Cultivation is concentrated around Poona, Nāsik, and Kolhāpur, on the west of the Deccan Plateau, 200–300 km/125–85 miles inland from Bombay. The remainder of India's plantings are at Surat in Gujarāt; Bangalore in Karnataka; Hyderābād in Andhra Pradesh; and Tamil Nadu. In the north, grapes are grown in the Punjab, on the border with Pakistan near Amritsar and Gurdāspur and in the Hunza valley in Kashmir bordering CHINA and AFGHANISTAN. No more than five per cent of India's grapes are used for wine, however, most of the rest being TABLE GRAPES.

Plantings range from altitudes of 300 m/984 ft in Mahārāshtra and Karnataka to 600–780 m on slopes of the Sahyadri mountains, but are rarely higher than 1,000 m except on terraced vineyards in Kashmir. With India's hot monsoon climate, temperatures in growing areas range from 8 °C/46 °F in winter to 45 °C in summer, with 300–700 mm/12–27 in of rain falling between June and August depending on the region. There is little unseasonal rain. Humidity levels are high particularly in the spring post-monsoon, moderated only by the afternoon winds. Eastern regions suffer most from humidity and extreme heat.

Indigenous table grapes such as Arkawati, Arka Shyam, and Anab e Shahi are grown for the local market on small 1-ha holdings. Native Bangalore Purple, imported THOMPSON SEEDLESS, and Selection Seven vine varieties flourish on clay and sand, increasingly used for low-quality sweet wines for the domestic market.

In the 1980s UGNI BLANC, CHARDONNAY, PINOT BLANC, COLOMBARD, PINOT NOIR, CABERNET SAUVIGNON, MERLOT, and SYRAH were planted on lime/chalk-based soils near Nārāyangaon on south east-facing slopes of the Sahyadri Mountains at 780 m. Ugni Blanc, with Chardonnay, is used for good-quality sparkling wines, and in combination with Thompson Seedless for BRANDY production.

High-culture trellising (see LENZ MOSER) on galvanized wire and bamboo with wide row spacing is used to maintain soil moisture, prevent scorching, control sugar levels, and maximize aeration of the vines to prevent disease. POWDERY MILDEW and BOTRYTIS BUNCH ROT are prevalent. SO4 ROOTSTOCKS imported from France are increasingly used as protection from PHYLLOXERA and to increase YIELDS; 35 hl/ha (2 tons/acre) was the norm in the early 1990s. Drip IRRIGATION is used throughout the growing season. PRUNING takes place twice yearly in October and April, with harvesting in January–February for the best acid–alcohol balance. In warmer regions in Andhra Pradesh, vines are evergreen, growth retardents may be used, and there are two to three harvests per year (see TROPICAL VITICULTURE). All vineyard activities are done manually.

Modern technology and temperature control are limited in co-operative wineries, but improving gradually. Small village operations use traditional methods to produce sweet, MADERIZED wines. The desire for sweet, high alcohol wines for the domestic market has meant that wines are typically coarse, aromatic, and potent, lacking balance and finesse.

The most sophisticated winery is at Nārāyangaon, 150 km from Poona. It was set up in 1982 with imported French equipment and consultants from CHAMPAGNE. The result is a dry, fragrant sparkling wine called Omar Khayyám, and one with higher DOSAGE known as Marquise de Pompadour. Both are widely exported and their quality should improve as further plantings of Chardonnay mature. Italian VERMOUTH producers Cinzano have an interest in Bārāmati Grape Industries, also near Poona. R.M.B. & J.V.P.

Murray Brown, R., 'Order in the wilderness', *Wine* (Dec. 1992), 40–2.

Indicação de Proveniencia Regulamentada, the second tier of designated wine regions in PORTUGAL. For more information, see IPR.

Indicator. See INDEXING.

Inert gas, any gas other than the highly reactive gas OXYGEN. NITROGEN is one of the most commonly used in wine-making to protect wine from OXIDATION.

Inert gas mixture, mixture of gases that does not include OXYGEN. Usually produced by some purification of combustion gases, such mixtures are composed mainly of nitrogen, carbon dioxide, and traces of several other gases. They are used in industrial processes in lieu of NITROGEN, which is more expensive, in cases where the presence of carbon dioxide and minor impurities is not troublesome. Inert gas mixtures are not used in wine-making as often as nitrogen because the carbon dioxide fraction dissolves in wine and because some of the minor components may be detrimental to flavour. A.D.W.

Inferno, subzone of VALTELLINA in the far north of Italy.

Inflorescence, the structure that bears the flowers (see BUNCH for more details). At FLOWERING the grape flower becomes a berry and the inflorescence a bunch.

Initiation, botanical term for the start of the vine's fruiting when the first signs of bunches are evident as small pieces of tissue in the developing bud. These buds are themselves developing beside the leaf stalk on the shoots as they grow in spring. Initiation happens during the FLOWERING stage of the growing season. Warm, sunny weather conditions at this time favour initiation, with one, two, occasionally three, or very rarely four bunches initiated. When this shoot bursts the following year, it will be termed FRUITFUL.

Part of the annual variation in vineyard YIELD is thus due to weather conditions affecting initiation during the year previous to the crop being harvested. The time when the vines are flowering is the most critical period for bunch initiation. To most vine-growers a 'light crop year' refers in an oblique way to weather conditions which affected initiation a little over 12 months previously. R.E.S.

Huglin, P., *Biologie et écologie de la vigne* (Paris, 1986).
Winkler, A. J., *et al.*, *General Viticulture* (2nd edn., Berkeley, Calif., 1974).

Injection, alternative name for CARBONIZATION, the cheapest and least effective method of SPARKLING WINE-MAKING involving the simple pumping of CARBON DIOXIDE into a tank of wine.

INRA (l'Institut National de Recherche Agronomique), the French specialist organization for agronomic research. Founded just after the Second World War in 1946, it is funded by the government, a larger proportion of its budget coming from the Ministry for Scientific Research than from the Ministry of Agriculture. It employs about 8,500 people in all.

There are 22 separate research centres in France, those in Montpellier and Bordeaux specializing in viticulture and effectively constituting a viticultural counterpart to the OENOLOGICAL research centres of the universities there (see MONTPELLIER and BORDEAUX UNIVERSITY respectively).

Advances in viticulture since its creation have been enormous. The Institut's most significant contribution has been the introduction of CLONAL SELECTION in France. As a result of the monocultural use of the land in many French wine regions, VIRUS DISEASES had reduced YIELDS to uneconomic levels by the end of the Second World War, and the development of virus-resistant CLONES was essential to maintain economically viable wine production in France.

More recent research has yielded new clones of ROOTSTOCKS developed to suit specific SOIL TYPES, such as Fercal for chalk and Gravesac for sandy, acidic soils.

There has also been successful research on the best ways of using FERTILIZERS on high-quality vineyards.

Current research is focused on reducing the use of FUNGICIDES, whose extravagant use in the 1970s and 1980s has led to an urgent need for more sophisticated control regimes. This development, known as La Lutte Raisonnée (the rational struggle) in France, aims at the minimal, and only carefully considered, use of products conducive to sound viticultural aims as opposed to the predetermined programme which was previously used. As the ill effects of the last generation of AGROCHEMICALS become clearer, particularly in respect of COPPER toxicity, this is expected to become the area of greatest viticultural change.

More basic research is concentrated on the exact nature of grape RIPENING, which is still not fully understood.

The importance for eventual wine quality of the grapes' condition at HARVEST has long been realized by viticulturists as well as by oenologists, and INRA is also studying the effects on wine quality of various vine-TRAINING SYSTEMS.

In 1991 the Institut d'Oenologie de Bordeaux (see BORDEAUX UNIVERSITY) and INRA, Bordeaux, formed a Pôle de Recherche Scientifique sur la Vigne et le Vin with a view to working more closely together in the two areas in which scientific research can improve the quality of wine. W.B.

INSECTICIDES. See PESTICIDES.

INSECT PESTS. A wide variety of insects attack grapevines. Injury may occur as a result of direct feeding action, where reductions in leaf amount or leaf health can delay RIPENING with serious implications for wine quality, or by carrying (vectoring) a particular VIRUS DISEASE. Alternatively the vine root system can be attacked, which leads to development of WATER STRESS and restricted VINE NUTRITION. While a minor stress may enhance wine quality (see VINE PHYSIOLOGY), the more likely outcome of root damage by insects such as PHYLLOXERA is severe stress or vine death. Some insect pests, such as phylloxera, attack only grapevines, while many attack a range of different plants.

The root-feeding aphid phylloxera is undoubtedly the most destructive of the insect pests which attack grapevines: it laid waste much of the European wine industry in the late 19th century and destroyed a significant proportion of vineyards in northern California in the late 20th century.

However, serious damage is not inflicted by all insect pests. Different insect pests attack grapes and vines in different parts of the world, and in different districts, and what may be an important pest in one area may be unimportant or non-existent in another. The most important insect pests in European vineyards are the BEETLES *écrivain* and *cigarier* and the MOTHS pyrale, cochylis, eudemis, and eulia, and MITES. Mediterranean FRUIT FLY can be a pest in some areas of Australia, but is not present in the United States, while LEAF HOPPERS are serious pests in California but not Australia. Other insects, such as CUTWORM and GRASSHOPPERS, are general agricultural pests world-wide.

Insect pests which affect only the appearance of grapes concern growers of TABLE GRAPES but not wine grape-growers, who are more likely to be concerned with effects on YIELD or wine quality. Grape RIPENING can be seriously delayed, for example, when the WESTERN GRAPELEAF SKELETONIZER reduces leaf area and thus reduces PHOTOSYNTHESIS; vineyards can be destroyed as young plantings by cutworms, or when mature by MARGARODES and phylloxera. Perhaps more insidiously, insects such as fruit fly can carry spores associated with BUNCH ROTS, and MEALY BUG can transmit LEAF ROLL virus. Leafhoppers spread the serious FLAVESCENCE DORÉE and PIERCE'S DISEASE.

In general insect pests are relatively easy to control in vineyards, although insecticides (see PESTICIDES) are among the more dangerous AGROCHEMICALS for operators to apply. Modern approaches to viticulture are more environmentally aware than previously, and so persistent chemicals such as DDT are no longer used and INTEGRATED PEST MANAGEMENT, designed to reduce insecticide use, is becoming increasingly common (see also ORGANIC VITICULTURE). For example, predatory mites are encouraged, to control levels of damaging mites.

See also entries for the specific pests APHIDS, BEETLES, BORERS, CUTWORMS, ERINOSE MITE, FRUIT FLY, GRASSHOPPERS, LEAF HOPPERS, LEAF ROLLERS, LOCUSTS, MARGARODES, MEALY BUGS, MITES, MOTHS, PHYLLOXERA, SCALE, THRIPS, WESTERN GRAPELEAF SKELETONIZER. M.J.E. & R.E.S.

Buchanan, G. A., and Amos, T. G., 'Grape pests', in B. G. Coombe and P. R. Dry (eds.), *Viticulture Vol. ii: Practices* (Adelaide, 1992).
Flaherty, D. L., *et al.* (eds), *Grape Pest Management* (2nd edn., Oakland, Calif., 1992).

INTEGRATED PEST MANAGEMENT, or IPM, may be defined as the use of all available control technologies to maintain populations of INSECTS below a damaging level. Similar principles can be extended to VINE DISEASES and WEEDS. This has the potential result of increasing economic returns for the grower and improving environmental and human safety. Philosophically it is not dissimilar to ORGANIC VITICULTURE although the judicious use of AGROCHEMICALS is allowed under IPM. IPM is not an easy option. It is complex, involving many interactions, requiring a greater level of grower education than that required merely to operate a sprayer of agrochemicals, the alternative approach.

IPM is a system that takes account of the environment, particularly weather phenomena, the occurrence and life cycles of pests, their growth patterns, and the incidence of natural enemies and alternative host plants. It requires a knowledge of the biology of the pest, the monitoring of the occurrences of the pest and any natural predators, the recording of the environmental conditions, and the integration of all these into a decision-making process. A basic aim of IPM is to reduce pesticide use, with potential benefit to the environment and economics of viticulture.

A number of VINE PESTS and diseases have been studied under the aegis of IPM philosophy. For example, the European grape berry MOTHS *Lobesia botrana* and *Eupoecilia ambiguella* can cause extensive damage, and studies have shown that their population levels can be limited naturally by VIRUS DISEASES and protozoan diseases. Similarly, MITES which can cause damage to vines can be controlled by other species of predatory mites, and sometimes this effect can be limited by the application of PESTICIDES, in particular some FUNGICIDES. Indeed, the increased use of some agrochemicals has altered the balance of predator to pest mites. The fungus *Trichoderma* is known to be antagonistic to BOTRYTIS BUNCH ROT, but as yet this has not been developed into an effective control. The light brown apple moth is a native Australian insect which can be controlled commercially by application of a spray of antagonistic bacteria, *Bacillus thuringiensis*.

There is no doubt that pest and disease control in the vineyards of the future will rely less on calendar-based sprays of agrochemicals and more on timely application of remedies which are based on more thorough knowledge of the biology of the pest to be controlled. M.J.E. & R.E.S.

Cavalloro, R., *Integrated Pest Control in Viticulture* (Rotterdam, 1987).

INTERNATIONAL VARIETIES, loose term for those VINE VARIETIES with an international reputation for their VARIETAL wines. They are planted in almost every major wine region in which they stand a chance of ripening. Foremost among them are the red wine variety CABERNET SAUVIGNON and the white wine variety CHARDONNAY (which many consumers take to be either a place or, more usually, a BRAND). Other strong candidates as international varieties are MERLOT, PINOT NOIR, and possibly SYRAH/Shiraz among reds and SAUVIGNON Blanc, RIESLING, MUSCAT, and possibly CHENIN Blanc, COLOMBARD, and SÉMILLON among whites. As wine-makers and wine consumers constantly search for new excitement, the list of possibilities grows longer.

INTERNATIONAL WINE & FOOD SOCIETY, the oldest and most cosmopolitan of the gastronomic societies for consumers rather than professionals. Initially simply the Wine & Food Society, it was founded in London in 1933 by André SIMON and like-minded friends. Its aim, other than providing a readership for a journal *Wine and Food* which Simon planned to edit, was to promote the highest quality of raw materials and an appreciation of how they could best be served and consumed. An early motto was 'Not much, but the best'. Launched in full economic depression (partly as a reaction to the culinary decline which resulted from it) the society attracted its fair share of criticism initially, and might well have withered had not the Repeal of PROHIBITION opened up North America to the proselytizing of M. Simon. Soon there were branches all over the United States and today over half the membership is based in North and South America and the Caribbean. Although the IWFS remains based in London, fewer than a quarter of its members live in Britain. There are 150 branches in 30 countries, all organizing their own programmes of lunches, dinners, tastings, lectures, and gastronomic tourism depending on the inclinations and aspirations of local branch members. The Society, now much imitated, is a non-profit-making concern and has always taken a particular interest in wine. André Simon and his early colleague A. J. A. Symons launched the first pocket VINTAGE CHART in 1935 and it is annually revised by a special committee of the IWFS to this day, providing useful income through sales to publishers of diaries and the like. The journal *Wine and Food* has been published regularly since 1934 and was at one stage edited by Hugh JOHNSON.

INTERNODE, the part of the stem between NODES. The internode length in vines varies between different VINE VARIETIES and with growing conditions. It is inhibited by weak roots, low temperatures, water stress, mineral deficiencies (especially of NITROGEN), and the position along the shoot (with the nodes closest together at the base and the tip). Shoots on vigorous vines have long internodes, and are large in diameter. Measured lengths vary from about 1 mm to 350 mm/13.6 in but commercially used cuttings usually have internode lengths between 50 and 150 mm. B.G.C.

INTERSPECIFIC HYBRID denotes the result of sexually crossing more than one grapevine species, while a CROSS of varieties of the same species is **intraspecific**. See HYBRID and VITIS for some background.

INVECCHIATO, Italian for aged.

INVERTASE, an important ENZYME in the vine for converting the larger molecule SUCROSE to its constituent molecules of GLUCOSE and FRUCTOSE in the ripening fruit so that sugar develops (see SUGAR IN GRAPES). The enzyme was first discovered in yeast in 1846, and is sometimes also called saccharase, sucrase, and Beta-fructosidase. The name invertase comes from the so-called 'invert' sugars of glucose and fructose. The reaction of this enzyme differs from that of other enzymes in that it is not reversible. This is one of the most widespread enzymes in the plant kingdom, and indeed one of the most efficient. It can metabolize 1 million times its own weight of sucrose with no loss of activity. The enzyme is located in the vacuole of berry cells, where it functions readily in the acidic environment. R.E.S.

INVESTMENT IN WINE is the acquisition of wine for gain, whether as a means of making money or financing consumption or a combination of the two.

'This crisis is perfectly rational. It was even foreseeable. The day I saw in *Time* magazine a photograph of a bank vault with a bottle of Lafite in it, I assembled my staff and told them: "the crisis has started". Indeed from the moment when you start to think of wine as an investment and not as something to be drunk, that's the end' (Baron Elie de ROTHSCHILD of Ch LAFITE-Rothschild, quoted in *The Winemasters* by Nicholas Faith).

The principal object of wine investment is to make a profit on wine which has increased in value as it matures. The essential premise on which wine investment is based is that demand for the wine in question exceeds supply, a premise that is often hard to gauge accurately. Such investment may be made purely for financial gain or to purchase wines with a view to financing consumption. In the latter instance, the investor's prime objective is to secure wines of limited availability or high fashion that may not appear again on the market.

Wine investment is not an activity confined to private individuals or investment companies outside the wine trade. Indeed, historically, the wine trade itself, with its inside knowledge, has been known to 'take a position' on a vintage, buying grapes on a speculative hunch. This practice, known as buying *sur souches*, i.e. while the grapes are still on the vine, was referred to in Roman times by Pliny the Younger (8. 2) and became part of the folklore of the BORDEAUX TRADE, as discussed below.

Speculation and buying for consumption need not be mutually exclusive. Indeed, spreading the risk by buying mixed portfolios of wine with both disposal and consumption in mind makes sound sense and is normally advised by companies dealing in wine investment. The benefits can make wine investment an attractive proposition. As a wasting asset with a life expectancy for tax purposes of less than 50 years, wine does not generally attract Capital Gains Tax. There may, however, be circumstances in which tax officials would regard wine investment as a business and tax it accordingly. Vintage

PORT, in particular, with a life expectancy of 50 years or more, is liable not to be regarded as a wasting asset for tax purposes.

But wine investment is inevitably a gamble, especially for anyone under the mistaken impression that making money from it is simply a question of holding on long enough to one's stock. Speculation in wine tends to be especially risky because wine is subject to both the vagaries of the weather and the unpredictable fluctuations of market forces. Buyers' and sellers' markets come and go and wine PRICES are as liable to go down as up. BORDEAUX, for reasons discussed below, is the principal medium of wine investment. The name Bordeaux is virtually synonymous with wine investment and its turbulent past bears witness to fortunes made and unmade in the name of wine.

Bordeaux: cyclical history

The first great boom in Bordeaux resulted from a period of prosperity which coincided with shortages caused by POWDERY MILDEW, or oidium, in the 1850s. The canny merchant Hermann CRUSE had struck the first speculative blow already, when, in 1848, he had bought up vast quantities of the 1847 vintage, only to release his hoard at undisclosed prices following Napoleon III's imperial accession. British Prime Minister Gladstone's reduction of duty on French wine following the 1860 Anglo-French Commercial Treaty and the Single Bottle Act of 1861 (which paved the way for the off-licence, and thus a retail trade in alcoholic drinks) further fuelled demand for red bordeaux.

Following the fine vintages of 1864 and 1865, prices doubled. Two successive lean years then led to speculative buying of the hard and slow-maturing 1868 vintage, *sur souches*. Chx Lafite and Margaux offered their 1868 to the Bordeaux market, achieving record prices which were not to be surpassed for another 58 years. But this was already the beginning of the end. The Bordeaux merchant Edouard Kressmann mirrored Hermann Cruse's earlier coup with his successful speculative purchase of the fine 1870 vintage harvested during the Franco-Prussian War. The 1875 vintage marked the end of this first golden era, however, as the imminent plagues of DOWNY MILDEW and PHYLLOXERA cast a blight over the the vineyards of Bordeaux (see BORDEAUX, history).

History was to repeat itself nearly a century later. During the post-war period of economic regeneration, the turning-point came in 1959 when, following two devaluations of the French franc, the Americans first decisively entered the market for fine Bordeaux wines. The 1959 vintage was hailed as the vintage of the century, a term which subsequently came to be applied *ad nauseam* to almost any vintage of note (usually revealing more about the ability of the Bordelais to feed speculation than about the quality of the vintage at issue). The clamour increased for the small but spectacular vintage of 1961. Between 1958 and 1961, the prices of the FIRST GROWTHS, on which most of the speculative activity was focused, more than quadrupled. By 1961, they had widened the gap between themselves and the other CLASSED GROWTHS to such an extent that their reputation as blue chip investment wines became even more firmly established.

Towards the end of the decade, the devaluation of the French franc in 1969 and the rivalry between Ch LAFITE and Ch MOUTON-ROTHSCHILD contributed to a fresh climate of speculation that was to grip Bordeaux in the early 1970s. An opening price battle between the first growths heralded the start of a boom, underpinned by a widespread feeling that demand would outstrip supply for the foreseeable future. A flood of foreign investment capital washed into Bordeaux to lap up the 1970 and 1971 vintages. Extortionate prices were asked—and paid—for the 1972 vintage, even though it turned out to be lean and mean.

A market develops

As inflation soared, red bordeaux became an investors' haven. The AUCTION houses Christie's and Sotheby's, whose new wine departments were established in, respectively, 1966 and 1970, provided the ideal forum for acquisitions and disposals. During the same period, numerous investment schemes were established to attract corporate finance, while wine merchants such as Justerini & Brooks set up their own schemes to cater for the speculative appetites of consumers. (Such schemes were to be the precursors of the government-backed Business Expansion Schemes set up in the British economic boom of the mid 1980s in the wake of a fresh outbreak of speculation fever.)

Rising oil prices and the collapse of American financial hegemony already signalled impending disaster by the spring of 1973. Tastings of the 1972 vintage coincided with the prospect of a large 1973 vintage, which turned out to be unexceptional in quality. An East Anglian wine merchant, writer Simon Loftus, was offered—and refused—£1 million by a respectable City finance house to buy 1972 vintage wines. Circumstances were aggravated by a scandal in which the Bordeaux house of CRUSE was charged with—and subsequently convicted of—fraud. By 1975, Chx Lafite and Mouton-Rothschild buried the hatchet and offered surplus stocks through Christie's.

Speculation fever was rekindled by the *annus mirabilis* of 1982, when an exceptional red Bordeaux vintage coincided with a relatively weak French franc and a strong American dollar. Opening prices of the first growths, FF170, were more than double those of the 1980s. The fashion for buying EN PRIMEUR, boosted by the superb 1982 vintage, created a new wave of populist investment fervour. The momentum for this new form of speculative buying was buoyed by a succession of fine vintages during the 1980s, and by, for the first time, accessible press comment on the relative merits of individual, if embryonic, wine samples. A typical good investment from the 1982 vintage would have been a case of the ST-ESTÈPHE Ch Cos d'Estournel 1982, which could be bought for less than £100 in the spring of 1983 and was fetching £385 at auction 10 years later.

But by the mid 1980s, despite particularly fine crops in 1985, 1986, and 1989, the market began slowly to deflate, largely because the unfulfilled promise of increasing consumption was further aggravated by an embarrassing surplus of fine bordeaux. A case of the PAUILLAC Ch Grand Puy Lacoste 1986 offered in June 1987 for £118 excluding all duty and taxes could be bought at auction seven years later for £130, excluding buyer's premium.

How to minimize the risks

The lessons of the 1980s and the earlier booms demonstrate that, in order to fulfil the promise of any investment, timing, knowledge, and skill (not to mention a measure of luck) are all essential preconditions for would-be investors, whether individuals or companies. Timing requires knowledge both of market conditions and of the potential of a wine for maturing. The finer the wine, generally speaking, the longer it takes to reach its peak, and the longer it remains on a plateau of maturity. It takes knowledge and skill to be aware of and interpret the likely future trends of individual properties and vintages, taking into account their real and perceived qualities. (One of the best ways to acquire such knowledge is to keep abreast of the pronouncements of the most influential WINE WRITERS. It is not easy to gauge precisely to what extent their opinions affect FASHION and therefore price, but there is undoubtedly a relationship.)

At the same time, investors need to be aware of less immediately obvious features of wine investment such as the importance of optimum STORAGE conditions, the costs involved, and the disposal options. The better the guarantee of storage in ideal conditions, the more attractive the proposition for the vendor. At the commercial auction rooms of Christie's and Sotheby's in London, the vendor can expect to receive the current auction market price on disposal. At the same time, vendors should be aware of the requirement to pay a vendor's premium, or, if a disposal is effected through a specialist wine BROKER or fine wine MERCHANT, of commission on the disposal.

Investors need also to take full account of the buying options. If the conditions are right, the simplest and most attractive method of purchasing is buying en primeur, as buying futures is known in the French wine trade. Buying en primeur involves buying wine which is offered by specialist wine merchants immediately following the vintage when it is still in cask. If the merchant's offer is accepted and the asking price paid, this leaves a subsequent payment of excise duty, any further sales taxes, and any shipping or delivery costs. The attraction to investors is the advantageous terms offered for buying before the wine is bottled and shipped. The corresponding disadvantages are the element of risk attached to buying an unfinished product sight unseen and the burden of financing the stock in optimum conditions during the period for which it is held.

Wine may also be bought at auction, in which case care should be taken to ensure that the wine has been properly stored and that the initial outlay is not prohibitive. For both reasons, any such purchase should be made at a commercial auction house holding regular, professionally run sales, such as Christie's or Sotheby's in London. (And wine should ideally be bought in complete, original CASES offered in BOND, to avoid the additional expenses of paying duty and value added tax.) Buying through an investment company or wine merchant is a less attractive alternative, particularly since it adds administration costs to the investor's burden. The failure of the Business Expansion Schemes is a case in point.

These companies attracted millions of pounds of British investors' money in the 1980s on the basis of highly optimistic claims by offering five years' tax-free investment in new business ventures. The schemes, in fact designed to stimulate economic growth, were touted by some simply as a tax-free means of investing in wine. By 1985, when many of these schemes started up, the market had already caught a chill. Crippled by establishment and administration costs and unable to offer their shareholders an escape route, most of them sank without trace, leaving shareholders with their investment either significantly reduced in value or virtually worthless. A handful of companies rose from the ashes, offering mixed portfolios of wine for investment and long-term consumption.

Some British specialist wine merchants offer investment schemes but, due in part to the speculation fall-out of the 1980s, most such schemes are specifically designed with consumption in mind.

Suitable wines for investment

The factors that make wine a worthwhile investment are numerous and complex. For one thing, political and economic auguries, specific market conditions, and likely future trends need all to be taken into account. Purchasing is always best made in a buyer's market when conditions allow investors to take advantage of low prices such as occurred in the mid 1970s following the Bordeaux crisis, or during a glut as occurred at the end of the 1980s. A period of relatively high inflation too, in contributing towards the creation of demand and putting pressure on supplies, such as occurred at the end of the 1960s and early 1980s, may also help bring about the desired preconditions for investing in wine.

Wine purchased for investment must be capable of being purchased at a price attractive enough, after a reasonable period of holding on to stock, to give the purchaser a return on his or her initial outlay that is at least comparable with other forms of investment. It follows that the type and format of wine chosen must be intrinsically capable of increasing sufficiently in value over a period of time. Generally speaking, investment wines should be capable of ageing for a good 20 years or longer so that investors are able to hold on to the wines and sell when the market is right. Investment wines must either have an established reputation or, where the investor is in a position to evaluate likely trends, be lesser-known wines with the potential to gain in value. And, where appropriate, wines should come from a good, preferably great, vintage and should be capable of being easily traded. Account should be taken of the fact that magnums and larger sizes (see BOTTLE SIZE) are popular with COLLECTORS.

Only a handful of wines fulfil these limited but strict criteria. On the basis of their pedigree and availability for purchase en primeur, the soundest wines for investment are the very top Bordeaux châteaux. In the case of Bordeaux, the 1855 CLASSIFICATION of Bordeaux provides an essential starting-point for wines of investment potential. Since it was based on historic prices, it has by and large stood the test of time, despite the fact that the composition of many of the properties in the 1855 classification has changed.

The endurance of this, wine's most famous classification, and the confidence that familiarity with it engenders have done much to reinforce the prestige of the leading group within it, the FIRST GROWTHS Chx LAFITE, LATOUR, MARGAUX, MOUTON-ROTHSCHILD, and HAUT-BRION. Within the top five, Ch Mouton-Rothschild is a particular favourite among investors thanks to Baron Philippe de ROTHSCHILD's policy, initiated for the 1945 vintage, of commissioning important contemporary artists to illustrate the label with an original work. To this illustrious group of five can be added St-Émilion's two top classified châteaux, AUSONE and CHEVAL BLANC, and Pomerol's unclassified Ch PÉTRUS. These are Bordeaux's blue chips, a first growth élite, which transcends the narrow confines of the world of wine itself.

As long as the right conditions obtain, the élite are safe investments because their track record shows that there will always be a demand for them. They may not always be the most exciting investments, however, because their reputation attracts a premium which makes the initial outlay generally twice the price or more of the properties ranking immediately beneath them. This is irrespective of whether the quality of the wines of the lower-ranking properties is equal or almost equal to that of the first growths.

If the first growths provide a yardstick for stability and safe investment, there is a second group of properties whose performance may be equally if not more attractive to investors because their consistency is linked in certain instances to a capacity to gain in value. This second group of estates, commonly referred to as SUPER SECONDS, is more elastic in its composition. Its basis is a core of châteaux which, thanks to a policy of rigorous selection for their GRAND VIN since the 1960s, have developed a sufficiently impressive track record of their own to entitle them to consideration as wines with investment potential. The group comprises Chx La Mission Haut-Brion in PESSAC-LÉOGNAN; four 1855 second growths Chx Léoville Las Cases and Ducru-Beaucaillou in ST-JULIEN, Pichon Longueville Comtesse de Lalande in PAUILLAC, and Cos d'Estournel in ST-ESTÈPHE; and one third growth, Ch Palmer in Margaux. On the fringes of the group are such properties as Ch Pichon Longueville Baron also in Pauillac; Domaine de Chevalier in Pessac-Léognan; Chx Figeac and Canon in ST-ÉMILION; and Vieux Ch Certan in POMEROL.

Yet another separate group exists of a number of relatively tiny properties, such as the Pomerol properties Chx Trotanoy, Lafleur, and Le Pin, which, as much by their size as anything, have gained substantially in value from their endorsement by influential commentators, in particular the American writer Robert PARKER.

Vintage PORTS have also traditionally been regarded as investment potential because of their long history and the management of vintage declarations, which conveniently limits their availability. TAYLOR, FONSECA, Graham, Warre, Dow, CROFT, COCKBURN, and Quinta do NOVAL are all regarded by Christie's as 'sound investment houses'. With the fashion for vintage ports waning in the 1990s, however, it remains to be seen whether vintage port will maintain its reputation in the 21st century as automatically sound investment material. Outside Bordeaux and vintage port, most wine regions lack either the necessary track record or the simplicity of structure to inspire the confidence which is an essential precondition of wine investment.

A tiny handful of fine wines from BURGUNDY, SAUTERNES, CHAMPAGNE, and the RHÔNE, however, have shown sufficient consistency and appreciation in value over a period of time to warrant consideration for investment purposes. In Burgundy, the red GRANDS CRUS of the DOMAINE DE LA ROMANÉE-CONTI, particularly Romanée-Conti itself and La Tâche, have the best track record, with de Vogüé's Musigny Vieilles Vignes and a number of Chambertin producers in the second rank. The grand cru Montrachets of Domaine de la Romanée-Conti, Domaine Ramonet, and the Marquis de Laguiche, and Domaine Leflaive's Chevalier-Montrachet, usually fetch the highest white burgundy prices. In the Rhône, JABOULET's Hermitage la Chapelle, Chave's Hermitage, and GUIGAL's single-vineyard Côte-Rôties, La Mouline, La Landonne, and La Turque have proved successful investments.

Ch d'YQUEM in Sauternes, the sole 'grand premier cru' at the head of the 1855 classification of Sauternes, is the safest of all sweet white bordeaux investments, while the pedigree of Chx Climens and Rieussec puts them at the head of the Sauternes premiers crus. In Champagne, such wines as KRUG, ROEDERER Cristal, and the de luxe Dom Pérignon cuvée from MOËT & CHANDON all have a certain limited investment potential. The wines of the New World have yet to inspire wholesale confidence in their ageing capacity, but wines such as PENFOLDS Grange from Australia and California's Opus One (see MONDAVI and MOUTON-ROTHSCHILD) have the potential to become investment stars of the future. Catering for the largely American appetite for wines which are 'hot', specific vintages of wines scoring a rare 100 out of 100 mark (see NUMBERS) in Robert Parker's *Wine Advocate* have been eagerly snapped up by speculators. Beyond wines with established reputations, however, the market for investment becomes too highly specialized for any but the best-informed insiders to dabble in with any degree of confidence or measure of success.

'At one moment the example of a fashionable person will make a wine held in very little estimation before and perhaps worthless in reality the prime wine of a table for a season. In England it is the fashion, or accident, which frequently makes the demand considerable for a particular species' (Cyrus Redding).

See also AUCTIONS, EN PRIMEUR, PRICE. A.H.L.R.

Broadbent, M. (ed.), *Christie's Price Index of Vintage Wine* (London, 1989).

Faith, N., *The Winemasters* (London, 1978).

Penning-Rowsell, E., *The Wines of Bordeaux* (6th edn., London, 1989).

Redding, C., *A History and Description of Modern Wines* (3rd edn., London, 1851).

INZOLIA, white grape variety grown mainly in Sicily and to a much more limited extent in Tuscany. It is also known as Ansonica or Anzonica. It was planted on a total of nearly 13,000 ha/32,100 acres of vineyard in the early 1990s, although total plantings were declining. It is grown mainly in western Sicily, where it is valued as a relatively aromatic ingredient, often with the much more common CATARRATTO, in dry white table wines. It may also be used for less noble purposes. See SICILY for more details.

ION EXCHANGE, chemical process used in, for example, water softening which was once thought to have useful applications in wine-making. Ion exchange can indeed reduce excessive ACIDITY or can be used to increase the acidity. Its main use was to ensure the stability of TARTRATES in wines by replacing some of the potassium ions with sodium ions. This has the serious disadvantage of increasing the sodium content of wine, which is one of the few foods that is naturally low in sodium. Successive ion exchange treatments to remove all positive ions and then all negative ions would reduce the MINERAL content of the wine to essentially zero. However, ion exchangers also alter the taste and aroma of wines so much that the practice is banned in the EUROPEAN UNION and many other wine regions. A.D.W.

IPR stands for Indicação de Proveniencia Regulamentada, a second-tier designated wine region in PORTUGAL. In theory, all are candidates for promotion to full DOC status but few of the 28 regions delimited in 1989/90 are likely to make the grade. Portugal's IPRs are an approximate, if proportionately more important, counterpart of the VDQS wines of FRANCE with specified grape varieties, minimum alcohol content, and maximum yields. Several years after the legislation, however, the laws remained confused, and many of Portugal's wine producers were either ignoring them or labelling their wines VQPRD, standing for Vinho de Qualidade Produzido em Região Determinada but also the standard European Union abbreviation for quality wine produced in a specific region. R.J.M.

IRAN, large country in the Near East once known as PERSIA, under which title details of Iran's important vinous history are to be found. Alcoholic drinks of all sorts are officially prohibited in modern Iran (see ISLAM). According to OIV statistics, there were 220,000 ha/543,400 acres of vines in Iran in 1991, with Iran being the second most important Asian producer of DRYING GRAPES, after Turkey.

IRANCY, town near Chablis country whose light red Pinot Noir has a certain reputation. See Côtes d'AUXERRE for more information.

IRAQ, Middle Eastern country with about 45,000 ha/111,150 acres of vines planted in the early 1990s grown chiefly for DRYING GRAPES and TABLE GRAPES. In ancient times it was part of MESOPOTAMIA, where there was a thriving trade in wine. See also BAGHDAD for evidence of early medieval viticulture, and ISLAM for an explanation of Iraq's modern relationship with wine.

IRELAND, or **Irish Republic**, country with several small vineyards (not dissimilar to those of ENGLAND). Ireland may well have been a more faithful customer of GASCON wines than England. Several Irishmen have played a part in the history of Bordeaux wine: the BARTONS provide one example, and the Lynch of PAUILLAC's Ch Lynch-Bages was also Irish.

IRON, a mineral element essential for healthy vine growth in trace amounts. Normally enough iron is taken up from the soil to meet the plant's needs, but iron deficiency in leaves can cause lime-induced CHLOROSIS, the well-known disorder of the vine when it is grown on wet, alkaline soils. Leaves turn yellow; this occurs because iron is unavailable for the manufacture of chlorophyll. In alkaline soils (rich in LIMESTONE), iron is in a chemical form which makes it unavailable to the vine roots. Soils can be measured for their ability to provide sufficient iron to the vine (see SOIL ALKALINITY).

Fertilizer containing iron cannot simply be added to the soil as it will in turn be made unavailable by the soil alkalinity; the answer is to add iron in a protected form, such as a chelate, a form in which iron is bound in an organic complex preventing it from oxidation. Although expensive, such chelate forms can be both applied to the soil and sprayed on the leaves.

Most commonly, however, lime-induced chlorosis is overcome by using a suitable ROOTSTOCK. R.E.S.

Champagnol, F., *Éléments de physiologie de la vigne et de viticulture générale* (St-Gely-du-Fesc, 1984).

IROULÉGUY, unique and isolated French wine appellation in BASQUE country in the extreme south west of the country fuelled almost entirely by national pride. The language and lettering used on labels here are distinctively Basque, with a heavy sprinkling of Xs. These vineyards of lower NAVARRE and the Spanish CHACOLÍ DE GUETARIA are the last officially recognized vestiges of what was once a thriving wine industry (which can now be traced as far as URUGUAY). Although there were 470 ha/1,160 acres of vines in 1906, vines were almost abandoned until the late 20th century. An APPELLATION CONTRÔLÉE was granted in 1970, and by the early 1990s the vineyard area was once again expanding. About 100 ha of vineyards are now cultivated by about 60 vine-growers, many of them on TERRACES cut painstakingly from steep, south-facing slopes in the Pyrenees, up to more than 400 m/1,300 ft above sea level, under heavy Atlantic climatic influence in the west. The vines are protected from north winds and enjoy more sunshine than most French wine regions. The local Tannat grape must be blended with at least as much Cabernet Sauvignon or Cabernet Franc and much of the wine produced is a fragrant, relatively substantial rosé although an increasing amount of red wine is made and Domaine Brana, one of the few wine producers outside the CO-OPERATIVE, also makes a little distinctive white wine from Courbu and Manseng.

Sprinkler **irrigation** in Napa Valley vineyards, California.

IRRIGATION, the application of water to growing plants such as vines, effectively a man-made simulation of RAINFALL which can be useful in drier regions. Few vineyard practices are more maligned than irrigation. The origin of this phobia is France, where irrigation is banned with a few minor exceptions, but anti-irrigation sentiments have been exported even as far as parts of the New World.

Irrigation is one of the oldest agricultural and viticultural techniques and was clearly practised, for example, in Ancient EGYPT, and in Ancient ARMENIA too. The need for irrigation depends entirely on CLIMATE. Where EVAPORATION is high and rainfall low, vines suffer WATER STRESS. Many of the world's vineyards are in MEDITERRANEAN CLIMATES where the rain falls mostly over the winter, and the summers are dry and hot. Water stress in the vineyard during the summer depends on how much of the winter rain can be stored in the soil. Soils such as sand and gravel can hold only limited amounts of water, silts and clays much more. Vines with only shallow roots because of restricting soil conditions also experience water stress. On the other hand, some soils are able to store so much water that vines can grow without significant water stress, despite long periods without any rain. Typically these are deep loamy or silt soils, and are commonly found on valley floors. Some of the deeper soils of California's Napa Valley are representative, and these may be found side by side with shallower soils where there is a need to irrigate.

While a modicum of water stress is desirable to encourage fruit RIPENING and enhance wine quality, excessive water stress has serious implications. In the worst situation the plant can become so stressed that it ruins the potential wine. Leaves are shed and the grape berries are exposed to the sun's rays without relief and may burn. Without leaves the vine cannot ripen fruit properly (see PHOTOSYNTHESIS). The berries are often so small that the amount of juice available for wine-making is restricted, and its constituents are out of balance. In these circumstances irrigation, when applied in a restricted fashion to relieve severe water stress, can actually improve quality.

It is easy to understand irrigation's notoriety, however. When vines have access to generous supplies of water they grow rapidly, producing long shoots, big leaves, big berries, and where YIELD is increased, then ripening is delayed. All of these are features of vineyards which produce poor-quality wine grapes. Yield is also greatly increased; depending on the severity of the water stress, irrigation may improve yield by 300 per cent or more.

Irrigation is widely practised in the New World but less frequently in the Old (although irrigation is commonplace in some of the oldest vineyards in the world in the Near East and central Asia). In principle it is banned in much of the EUROPEAN UNION other than for young vines, such a ban being incorporated into the accession treaties of both Spain and Portugal, but this is a restriction which is easy, if initially quite expensive, to flout. While some still believe that irrigation is intrinsically inimical to wine quality, and there are many examples of deliberate over-irrigation within Europe, some of those who deliberately install irrigation systems in southern Europe are motivated by the desire to make better wine (see COSTERS DEL SEGRE, for example). The modern view is that excessive water stress can be as damaging to quality as can excessive irrigation and that in drier regions carefully controlled irrigation can be a useful technique for maximizing yield and/or quality.

The mechanics

Soils vary in their ability to store water. The 'field capacity' is the maximum amount of water a thoroughly, deeply wetted soil will retain after normal drainage. The driest moisture content at which vines can extract water from the soil is called the 'permanent wilting point'. At this point, the plant will not recover if water is applied. Between these two limits is the amount of available water in a soil. The ability to store water is highest for silt soils and lowest for coarse sands and gravels. The latter soils are preferred for fine wine production as there is less likelihood of excessive water supplies to the vine following rainfall.

The irrigation strategy employed by a vine-grower depends on his or her ambitions for quality and yield. For maximum yields the vines are not allowed to experience water stress at any stage of the growth cycle, and vines are irrigated to maintain moisture levels near field capacity. Such strategies are common for bulk wine production, which is often undertaken in hot, dry climates. Irrigation amount is measured as a depth of water applied: for unrestricted irrigation in a hot climate, up to 800 mm/31 in of water can be applied during the growing season. Smaller quantities of water are applied to vines producing better-quality wine. The regions in which they are grown are typically cooler and more humid, so the evaporation is less, and also the rainfall is often higher. Further, it is desirable to have the vines experience a little water stress, so application amounts can be as low as 100 mm/4 in, or in some years even zero, depending on the weather.

There are several ways of deciding when to irrigate. In desert regions where the climate is relatively constant, such as much of Argentina, California, and inland Australia, irrigation is generally done by the calendar. The interval between irrigations can be longer in the early spring and late autumn, but the vineyards are irrigated most often in midsummer, when evaporation is highest. In areas with more rainfall, and especially where it is irregular, irrigation has to be much more carefully timed according to measurements of either the soil moisture or, less frequently, the plant water stress.

Soil moisture can be measured in several ways. The appearance and feel of the soil can be a useful guide, but while the surface is dry the subsoil can be still wet. Tensiometers are ceramic cups connected to a water column which creates a vacuum as water is extracted into the dry soil. Gypsum blocks contain an electrode; as the soil dries the electrical resistance changes. Neutron moisture meters are a recent irrigation aid by which an aluminium tube is placed permanently in the soil, and a neutron source lowered into it. The meter measures the spread of neutrons from a source, which depends on soil moisture.

Plant stress can be measured by the experienced viticulturist observing stress symptoms such as drooping shoot tips, tendrils, and leaves. Leaf temperature can also provide a guide since, as vines become water stressed, leaves facing the sun are heated significantly above air temperature. This temperature difference can be determined by feel, or by a remote sensor which can measure routinely and non-destructively, but not in wind or cloud.

The amount of water applied depends on many factors. Water supplies are limited in many vineyard areas, so water is used sparingly and only to avoid the worst effects of severe water stress. Where water is not limited and maximum yield is the aim, then sufficient water should be applied to bring the vine root system back to field capacity. This can be calculated by measuring either evaporation or soil moisture. Much more difficult is to apply a limited amount of water so that a desired level of vine water stress is maintained to promote ripening and improve quality. However, this is the common aim of vine-growers interested to maximize wine quality.

Methods of irrigation vary considerably. The ancient method, still used in some desert areas for bulk wine production, is **flood irrigation**. Water fed from a supply canal is run down the rows and is soaked up by the dry ground. For this to work the vineyard floor must be flat and the rows not too long. More recent developments have been **sprinkler** and **drip** (or **trickle**) **irrigation**. Sprinklers are typically about 20 m/65 ft apart and span several rows. Dripper supply lines, usually long plastic tubes, are placed down each row, usually with one dripper at each vine. Both sprinkler and drip irrigation are capable of delivering exact amounts of water fairly uniformly over a vineyard. Even a well-operated flood system is less accurate. R.E.S.

Coombe, B. G., and Dry, P. R. (eds.), *Viticulture ii: Practices* (Adelaide, 1992).

Winkler, A. J., *et al.*, *General Viticulture* (2nd edn., Berkeley, Calif., 1974).

IRSAY OLIVER, aromatic, relatively recent white vine crossing grown in SLOVAKIA and also known in HUNGARY as **Irsai Olivér**. This eastern European cross of Pozsony × Pearl of Csaba was originally developed in the 1930s as a table grape. It ripens extremely early and reliably (although it is prone to POWDERY MILDEW) and produces relatively heavy, but intensely aromatic, wines strongly reminiscent of MUSCAT.

ISABELLA, widely planted VITIS *labruscana* vine variety grown to a limited extent in NEW YORK state, and also in parts of the CIS. It is a LABRUSCA × VINIFERA cross of unknown origin. It is said to have been named after a Mrs Isabella Gibbs, in honour of her beauty, and to have been developed in South Carolina in 1816.

ISCHIA, an island in the bay of Naples in the Italian region of CAMPANIA (see map on p. 517), is best known as a vacation spot and spa, but has managed to preserve a small part of the vineyards which once covered a significant part of the island. The DOC Ischia wine, produced from 165 ha/407 acres of vineyards, exists in both red and white versions: the former from Guarnaccia grapes plus some PIEDIROSSO and a little BARBERA, the latter from Forastera with Biancolella and others. A Bianco Superiore, with at least 50 per cent Biancolella, is also produced with both lower yields and more alcohol. The DOC wines do not tell the entire story, however, as d'Ambra, the island's principal wine merchant, also produces 100 per cent VARIETAL wines from Forastera, Biancolella, and Piedirosso (the last of which is called by its dialectical name Per'e Palummo). Each marketed as VINO DA TAVOLA, they have shown marked improvement in the 1980s and indicate that Biancolella and Piedirosso have an interesting future as varieties. D.T.

ISINGLASS, a particularly pure PROTEIN obtained from the bladders of sturgeon and other freshwater fish that has been used for FINING wine for centuries. As early as 1660, King Charles II of England regulated the use of isinglass by merchant VINTNERS.

Like gelatin, isinglass reacts with the excess TANNINS in harsh young red wines. Although expensive, and difficult to prepare, isinglass is also occasionally used in the CLARIFICATION of white wines to be bottled without a final polish FILTRATION, as it has about the same clarifying property.

A.D.W.

ISLAM, the Muslim religion founded by the Prophet Muhammad (spelt variously Mohammed, Mohamet, etc.) in the 7th century AD, has had, and continues to have, the most profound effect on the history of wine. The consumption of any alcoholic drink was prohibited by Muhammad so that wine is neither officially consumed nor enthusiastically produced in most of the Near and Middle East, North Africa, and parts of Asia. Wine is therefore no longer produced in much of the land most closely associated with the ORIGINS OF VITICULTURE, and the rise of Islamic fundamentalism in the late 20th century represents a considerable constraint on the world's wine consumption.

Muhammad's prohibition

Wine (in Arabic *khamr*) was not prohibited from the outset of the Prophet Muhammad's preaching (between 610 and 632). Islam, both dogma and practice, emerged initially as the product of continuous revelation (the Qur'ān, often spelt Koran) during the Prophet's lifetime and his responses to the vicissitudes of the early Islamic community (these are recorded in the *hadīth* literature and constitute the second most substantive source of Islamic law). There are four verses in the Qur'ān which refer to wine; the first is quite positive: (*Sūra* 16, verse 69): 'We give you the fruit of the palm and the vine from which you derive intoxicants and wholesome food.' The following two verses are cautionary but are not considered by Muslim jurists to enjoin abstinence from alcohol: (Sura 2, verse 216, and Sura 4, verse 46): 'They will ask you concerning wine and gambling. Answer, in both there is great sin and also some things of use unto men, but their sinfulness is greater than their use.' 'Believers do not approach your prayers when you are drunk, but wait till you can grasp the meaning of your words; nor when you are polluted—unless you are travelling the road—until you have washed yourself.'

There is consensus amongst medieval Muslim jurists, however, that the fourth verse, which came in response to disturbances in the community, was tantamount to an injunction (although it is not couched in the same language as the prohibition on other dietary items, such as pork) (Sura 5, verse 92) 'Believers, wine and games of chance, idols and divining arrows are abominations devised by Satan. Avoid them so that you may prosper. Satan seeks to stir up emnity and hatred among you by means of wine and gambling and to keep you from the Remembrance of Allah and from your prayers.'

Although this verse was understood universally to articulate prohibition, there was dissension when it came to establishing the precise nature of forbidden wine. *Khamr*, the word used in the Qur'ānic verses, is the Arabic generic term for wine. There were, however, many types of fermented beverages known to pre-Islamic and later Arabs. The second caliph, 'Umar ibn al-Khattāb, is reported in the *hadīth* literature to have settled the question: 'Wine has been prohibited by the Qur'ān; it comes from five kinds of fruits: from grapes, from dates, from honey, from wheat and from barley; wine is what obscures the intellect.' The issue remained whether beverages prepared in a way different from wine were prohibited. For example *tilā'* appears to have been allowed by 'Umar; this was a kind of syrup made from grape juice which was cooked until two-thirds of it evaporated. However, the same source relates that 'Umar punished a man who became drunk on this concoction.

Another tradition quotes the Prophet stipulating the kinds of vessels in which fruit juice beverages could be made or stored: '. . . I forbid four things: *dubbā'* (a gourd), *hantam* (glazed wine jars), *muzaffat* (a vessel smeared with pitch) and *naqīr*.' When asked about the nature of *naqīr* he answered: 'It is a palmtrunk which you hollow out; then you pour small dates into it and upon them water. When the process of fermentation has finished, you drink it with the effect that a man hits his cousin with the sword.' The community was, therefore, enjoined to store fruit beverages in leather skins that prevented fermentation.

Nabīdh, date wine, is the drink about which there has been the most controversy. Several traditions state that this beverage was amongst the drinks prepared by Muhammad's wives and drunk by him: 'Aisha said: 'We used to prepare *nabīdh* . . . in a skin; we took a handful of dates or a handful of raisins, cast it into the skin and poured water upon it. The *nabīdh* we prepared in this way in the morning was drunk by him in the evening; and when we prepared it in the evening he drank it the next morning.' Despite this, three of the four Sunni schools of law as well as the Shiah prohibit *nabīdh*. The Hanafi school allows it when used in moderation, although intoxication is still prohibited.

Most jurists now consider discussions about types of wine to be secondary casuistry. What is deemed crucial, on the basis of *hadīth*, is that any beverage which intoxicates should not be consumed.

Despite the Qur'ānic injunction, even those types of wine recognized to be *harām* continued to be imbibed in many periods of Islamic history; this is best reflected in the rich tradition of Bacchic poetry which had its roots in pre-Islamic Arabia but flowered as a poetic genre in the early Abbasid period (see ARAB POETS). This canon of literature is largely mimetic and most certainly reflects the drinking habits of a significant sector of the Islamic community, notably—in some cases—the caliph and his entourage.

The wines consumed

Both Arabic poetry and other sources such as agricultural works tell us much about wine as a product. Although wine was produced in al-Tā'if in the Hijaz (1,560 km/975 miles south east of Mecca) from pre-Islamic times, it was imported mainly by Jewish and Christian merchants from SYRIA and MESOPOTAMIA. With the expansion of Islam, Arabs were introduced to finer wines grown mostly in the Christian monasteries of Iraq. 'Ana in upper Mesopotamia is only one of many areas that were known for viticulture. It was in the taverns around monasteries and in the monasteries themselves that most wine was consumed, as well as some of the outlying towns of Baghdad, districts of Baghdad itself (especially al-Karkh), and not infrequently in the caliphal court at the very heart of the Islamic community.

The most lauded of beverages were four types of wine—white, yellow, red, and black—made from both red and white grapes, from a variety of vine varieties whose names are preserved in medieval agricultural books (Heine gives details of 21 of them, including Kišmiš. In poetry, the date wine *nabīdh* was despised (cf. above). Grape wine was always mixed with water before drinking (one-third wine to two-thirds water, about the same dilution as in Ancient GREECE). The poets were fascinated by the bubbles which this mixing produced; although wine was celebrated as an ancient product ('It has aged since the time of Adam'), it may be that it was often very young and thus still fermenting when consumed. There were three classes of age: young wine, which was less than a year old, low in alcohol, and had little bouquet; middle-aged, which was a year old; and old wine, which one source claims was usually sour. P.K.

Heine, P., *Weinstudien, Untersuchungen zu Anbau, Produktion und Konsums des Weins im arabisch-islamischen Mittelalter* (Wiesbaden, 1982).

'Khamr', *The Encyclopaedia of Islam*, vol. iv (new edn., Leiden, 1978).

Effect of Islam on wine history

In the Middle Ages Muslim conquest by no means outlawed wine production, however. Muhammad's caliph successors were based in Damascus and, subsequently, in BAGHDAD, which had its own local wine industry. Wine production continued in Moorish Spain (the Alhambra built by the Moors in 14th century Granada has its Puerta del Vino), Portugal, North Africa, Sicily, Sardinia, Corsica, Greece, Crete, and other eastern Mediterranean islands, usually under the heavily taxed auspices of Jews or Christians, even though they were ruled by Muslims. The Ottoman Turks made repeated raids on various eastern European wine regions in the Middle Ages, and, if the TOKAY legend is based on fact, could therefore be said to have been indirectly responsible for the discovery of BOTRYTIZED WINES. For some more details, see SPAIN, GREECE, CYPRUS, and the CRUSADES.

It is because of the dissemination of Muslim techniques associated with alchemy that the art of DISTILLATION is said to have spread through western Europe. Indeed the words ALCOHOL and ALEMBIC are of Arab origin.

ISOAMYL ALCOHOL. See FUSEL OILS.

ISONZO, small DOC in the extreme north east of Italy in the FRIULI region. The plain to the south of the COLLIO hills formed by the Isonzo river on its way to the Adriatic can be considered, from a geological point of view, an extension of the GRAVE DEL FRIULI into the province of Gorizia. The soil, like that of the Grave, is a mixture of gravel and soil formed by fluvial and glacial deposits. The zone produces, with the aid of cold technology, the fruity reds and the aromatic whites which typify the wines of Friuli. TOCAI Friulano (275 ha/679 acres in 1993), PINOT GRIGIO (140 ha), SAUVIGNON Blanc (125 ha), and PINOT BIANCO (110 ha) are the significant white varieties; MERLOT (220 ha) and CABERNET (100 ha, with a dominance of CABERNET FRANC) are the important red grapes planted.

The wines have been slower to emerge and find their place in the market than those of Collio and the COLLI ORIENTALI. This lesser reputation, coupled with higher yields (91 hl/ha/5 tons/acre is the permitted maximum for the whites, against 77 hl/ha for Collio and the Colli Orientali), has resulted in lower prices and some spotty quality, although the best producers of the Isonzo have demonstrated that, with the requisite commitment to quality, the wines can compete with the better products of their neighbours to the north. D.T.

ISRAEL, the biblical land of milk and honey (see CANAAN), lays claim to being the cradle of the world's wine industry, yet has leapt to international prominence only since new, cooler vineyards were planted in the Golan Heights in the early 1980s.

History

The fruit of the vine was economically important in the Holy Land and was designated one of the seven blessed species of fruit specified in the book of Deuteronomy (see BIBLE). The dangers of immoderate wine consumption were fully recognized, and excess was strictly forbidden. Vine-growing continued under Christian rule, even after the destruction of the Second Temple in Jerusalem, until AD 636, when Muslim fanaticism brought about the destruction of the vineyards (see ISLAM). The CRUSADERS temporarily restored wine production between AD 1100 and 1300, but with the exile of the Jews, vine-growing ceased.

At the end of the 19th century, Jews returned to the Holy Land from the Diaspora, and in 1882 the first vineyards were replanted at Rishon Le Zion. The first few settlers were poor, inexperienced, and unable to cope with the terrible problems of creating vineyards in difficult conditions.

In 1882 a massive benefaction of 60 million gold francs from Baron Edmond de ROTHSCHILD (many times more than his father James had paid for Ch LAFITE in 1868) made viticulture an important part of the agricultural resettlement programmes. French experts selected vine stock, mainly from the Rhône valley and Midi, which were regarded as of equivalent climate, and instructed the 'new' farmers in all necessary techniques for wine-making. The industry grew and thrived, exporting KOSHER wine to Jewish communities throughout the world, until the 1948 War of Independence, when important sales to Arab countries ceased overnight. Since the 1967 war, the Golan Heights, at an altitude of 1,000 to 1,200 m/3,280–3,940 ft, and with appropriate volcanic soils, have also become an important viticulture area.

Climate

The vine thrives in Israel's conditions. The seasons divide in two: the winter with rain from October to March, and the summer almost totally dry from April to October. IRRIGATION is essential to nourish the vines, which are pruned to provide maximum shade for the grapes from the harsh sunlight. Much harvesting is mechanical, the white varieties being picked mainly at night to minimize temperatures.

Geography

In the early 1990s there were 2,200 ha/5,434 acres under vine for wine production, and 2,600 ha producing TABLE GRAPES.

Israel's viticulture is divided into five regions: Galilee (Galil in Hebrew) northern Israel, including the Lake Galilee area and the Golan Heights; Samaria (Shomron), upper central Israel, including the Haifa area and Mount Carmel; Samson (Shimshon), lower coastal Israel between the Judean Mountains and the coastal plain; the Judean Hills (Harey Yehuda) including the hill vineyards of Jerusalem and the West Bank; and Negev, southern, desert Israel.

The following are subregions, some of them EUROPEAN UNION registered: Galilee (Canaan-Meron, Golan Heights, Naftali, Nazareth-Cana, Tabor); Samaria (Mt Carmel, Sharon); Samson (Adulam, Dan, Latroun); Judean Hills (Beth-El, Bethlehem, Hebron, Jerusalem); Negev (Beersheva, Ramat Arad).

Vine varieties

Descendants of the original cuttings imported from France, CARIGNAN, GRENACHE, ALICANTE BOUSCHET, SÉMILLON, CHENIN Blanc, and MUSCAT OF ALEXANDRIA are still widely planted. In the more recently planted vineyards, however, particularly those in the cooler areas of Galilee, varieties such as CABERNET SAUVIGNON, MERLOT, SAUVIGNON Blanc, RIESLING, and CHARDONNAY (the latter used for sparkling as well as still wines) have been planted with considerable success. The high-altitude vineyards tend to produce much more elegant wines than those made in the coastal areas, where acid levels tend to be low.

Modern wine production

In the early 1990s Israel's total annual production of a wide range of wine types was between 130,000 and 160,000 hl/3.4–4.5 million gal, of which only about 15 per cent was exported. Most vineyards are owned either by kibbutzim or moshavim, collective farms, although there are some private owners.

The dominant, and oldest, producer is the co-operative based at Rishon Le Zion, which accounts for as much as 60 per cent of the domestic market and exports typically rather sweet, heady wines under the brand name Carmel. There are nearly 20 other producers however, including the monastery Latroun, the Canadian-owned Eliaz Benyamina, and Baron Cellars and Golan Heights winery, both of which were founded in the early 1980s.

Modern wine-making techniques are most apparent at the newer wineries, Baron and Golan Heights, where picking at optimum ripeness, TEMPERATURE CONTROL, and the use of new OAK barrels resulted in a dramatic improvement in wine quality. Golan Heights sell under the names, in declining order of price, Yarden, Gamla, Golan, and Mount Hermon.

See also KOSHER (although not all Israel's wine is kosher) and Israeli BRANDY. P.A.H.

ITALIAN RIESLING, or **Italian Rizling**; sometimes **Italianski Rizling**. White grape variety. See RIESLING ITALICO and WELSCHRIESLING.

ITALY, with FRANCE one of the world's two mammoth wine producers, producing annual volumes of wine which regularly exceed 60 million hl/1,584 million gal. Italy has more land under vine, close to 1.4 million ha/3.4 million acres in the early 1990s, than any other country with the exception of Spain. Unlike either France or Spain, however, the vine is cultivated virtually everywhere in the Italian peninsula, from the alps in the north to islands that are closer to the coast of North Africa than to the Italian mainland (see map opposite). Viticulture impinges on the national consciousness, on the national imagination, and on daily life in a way that is hardly conceivable to those not accustomed to the Mediterranean

ITALY
SWITZERLAND
AUSTRIA
HUNGARY
FRANCE
SLOVENIA
CROATIA
BOSNIA-HERCEGOVINA
TUNISIA
Alps
Alps
TRENTINO
Bolzano
ALTO-ADIGE
Trento
FRIULI
Gorizia
VALLE D'AOSTA
Novara
Vercelli
LOMBARDY
Milan
VENETO
Verona
Venice
Trieste
Turin
Pavia
Asti
Alba
PIEDMONT
Po
Piacenza
LIGURIA
Genoa
EMILIA ROMAGNA
Bologna
SAN MARINO
Ligurian Sea
Florence
Apennines
TUSCANY
THE MARCHES
Ancona
Adriatic Sea
Bolgheri
Siena
Montalcino
Perugia
UMBRIA
Orvieto
Elba
CORSICA
LATIUM
Rome
Frascati
ABRUZZI
MOLISE
SARDINIA
Oristano
Cagliari
Naples
Ischia
CAMPANIA
Capri
Bari
APULIA
BASILICATA
Taranto
Tyrrhenian Sea
CALABRIA
Lipari
Mediterranean Sea
Palermo
Marsala
SICILY
Pantelleria
0
200 km

way of life and its dietary trinity of bread, olive oil, and wine; until the late 1980s it was unthinkable for Italians to sit down and eat without wine on the table.

The Italian's relationship to wine is not necessarily a hedonistic one. The average Italian is far from a connoisseur of fine bottles, but is rather the heir of thousands of years of vineyard cultivation and wine-making. There are few Italians without some conception—though the conception itself may be naïve, foolish, banal, or simply wrong-headed—of how grapes are grown and transformed into wine.

The result is what might be called the Italian paradox: a country with a plurimillennial tradition of wine, a country whose Roman legions spread viticulture to a large part of western Europe, a country where wine is omnipresent in the nation's life and customs, is also a country where wine is, for the most part, taken for granted in the national consciousness. While France and Germany played a major role from the beginning of the age of modern wine—an era in which wine circulates in bottles with labels which identify both its provenance and its maker—wine in most of Italy, with the exception of Tuscany and a few other scattered areas, was sold in bulk until well after Second World War. Little of the country's better wine was exported until the 1970s, and a significant part of the export trade was in important volumes of wine for the large colonies of Italian emigrants in northern Europe, in the United States, and in South America (Argentina, for example, was a major market for Barolo immediately after the Second World War). Knowledge of non-Italian viticulture and OENOLOGY was virtually nonexistent in Italy, and circulation of foreign wines was confined to a tiny élite in the country's major cities. Luigi VERONELLI's book at the end of the 1950s was the first general treatment of Italian wines in over 350 years, since Andrea Bacci's opus of 1595. And even in the early 1990s wine appreciation was an activity of very little significance to Italians.

To consider the history of wine in Italy is to consider the history of Italy itself, however; wine and Italian civilization are virtually synonymous. The Ancient Greek name for much of Italy already acknowledged the importance of viticulture to the peninsula: OENOTRIA, or 'land of trained vines'. D.T.

Italy, Magna Graecia, and Roman Italy

The pastoral past of the tribes of Italy may be reflected in the use of milk in LIBATIONS rather than wine (see PLINY *Natural History*, 14. 88), but viticulture and wine will have made an early impact as part of GREEK and ETRUSCAN culture (see ORIGINS OF VITICULTURE for more details). SICILY may have played a key role in the development of viticulture on the mainland. The Sicilian Murgentina grape, which flourished in volcanic soils, was successfully transplanted near POMPEII on the slopes of Vesuvius, where it was called locally the Pompeian grape. This in turn was introduced further north around Clusium (Chiusi) in Etruria, where it proved particularly prolific. Again, the Eugenia, the high-quality grape from Tauromenium (Taormina in Sicily), successfully found a home in the Colli ALBANI south of Rome, but was a failure elsewhere.

Grape treading as depicted in an **Italian** fresco.

Incidental mentions by the historians suggest that by the time that Hannibal invaded Italy in the late 3rd century BC, vines could be found throughout the peninsula, from beyond the Po valley, down the Adriatic coast, and in CAMPANIA; but little wine was of particular note before the middle of the 2nd century BC according to Pliny (*Natural History* 14. 87). It was Pliny, too, who in a key passage (*Natural History* 14. 94 ff.) made a very acute observation. He noted that OPIMIAN wine of the year when Opimius was consul (121 BC) was accepted as one of the greatest vintages, but that this applied generally to wine in that year, not to any particular CRUS. An edict of the censors of 89 BC imposing a price limit on costly wines refers only to wine made from the Aminnean grape (see ANCIENT VINE VARIETIES), not to any estates.

The creation of the grands crus of Roman Italy belongs to the 1st centuries BC and AD. This fact is more or less confirmed by ARCHAEOLOGY. The expansion of villas connected with wine production and overseas trade, as evidenced by the AMPHORAE, may have begun in the late 3rd or 2nd centuries, but the real growth is later. Three factors were involved in this development. First there was the exceptional growth of the city of ROME, which created a huge market for wine. Secondly there was the opening up of trade routes to GAUL and SPAIN, which stimulated the growth of vineyards in the areas immediately behind ports; and finally there was the interest of the Roman aristocracy with an ever-increasing level of wealth to invest. So it is no accident that the areas in which the great wines of Roman Italy developed were LATIUM and Campania, regions within easy reach of the Roman market and where the Roman élites had their country homes. In the Colli Albani the mainly sweet wines of Alba itself were highly prized, as were those of Velletri. The Emperor Augustus gave a boost to the wines of Setia (Sezze) by favouring them above all others. Beyond Terracina, CAECUBAN, produced in the marshes around the Lago di Fondi, was in the very front rank of wines. The wines from the slopes of Monte Massico, particularly the various types of FALERNIAN, long remained the most favoured. In northern and central Campania, the wines of Cales, along with Gauranum (from Monte Barbaro, overlooking the northern end of the bay of Naples) had reputations which were close to that of Falernian. Then on the bay of Naples itself were the noted vineyards of Pompeii and the Sorrento peninsula. The very light, white wine of this region, SURRENTINUM, made from the Aminnean Germana Minor grape, enjoyed very high status in the 1st century AD, although it did not win universal approval ('high-quality vinegar' was the view of the Emperor Tiberius).

Few wines outside Latium and Campania ever approached their status and none exceeded it. On the north western side of Italy Etruria (TUSCANY) had a great variety of wines, but only those of Luni and Genoa in Liguria made much impact. In Magna Graecia (southern Italy) a number of areas produced wines of some note, including Tarentine (from Taranto). The Adriatic coast of Italy presents an interesting test case. It would be difficult to guess at the importance of the wines of this area simply from the rather limited literary evidence. But the evidence of amphorae shows that APULIA and Ancient Calabria and, perhaps, areas further up the east coast exported wine to all the countries round the Adriatic and to the Greek world from the 2nd century. Brindisi certainly was the focus for a flourishing export trade. Further north, Hadrianum, the wine of Atri, and the adjoining Praetuttian vineyards (roughly the northern area of Montepulciano d'ABRUZZO) achieved a high reputation in the 1st century AD. A significant development is to be associated with the time of the first Roman emperor, Augustus (31 BC–AD 14); this was the increasing prominence of northern wines from the Po valley and beyond. The distinctive type of amphora which carried the wines of this region was sometimes stamped with the names of men who rose to prominence in the entourage of Augustus and had estates in the region. These amphorae doubtless carried Praetuttian, the wines of Ancona, of Ravenna, and of the towns along the Via Aemilia. VIRGIL, Augustus' court poet, reflected the emperor's liking for the wines of Verona (see VENETO), made from the Rhaetic grape (although, because of its distance from the sea, it is unlikely this area's wines achieved more than a passing prominence). Augustus' wife Livia did her bit to promote the wines of the FRIULI region, by publicly ascribing her longevity to an exclusive diet of the wine of Pucinum, beyond Aquileia.

Archaeology has combined with history to give us this picture of viticulture in Roman Italy, which differed in significant ways from the current scene. It should always be remembered that, as now, there would be an enormous consumption of undistinguished, local wines, which never travelled, and are rarely to be identified in the historical record. J.J.P.

Pliny, *Natural History*, trans. by H. Rackham (Loeb Classical Library, 1945), Book 14.

Tchernia, A., *Le Vin de l'Italie romaine* (Rome, 1986).

Medieval history

The fall of the Roman empire did not put an end to viticulture in Italy, but barbarization and economic collapse meant the disappearance of the market for fine wines. With Goths, then Lombards, in Rome and most of the north, and the remains of the empire administered precariously from Ravenna, Falernian and Caecuban had become distant memories. Yet the Italian diet remained based on bread, olives, and wine, and so wine continued to be grown as one of the necessities of Mediterranean life.

The Dark Ages were a period of economic stagnation; except for the importation of luxury goods from the Near East, trade was local. We know little about the wine that was grown until the 11th century, when population, production, and exchange increased, and Italy, particularly northern Italy, became politically and economically the most important part of Europe (see GENOA and VENICE). Between the 11th and the 14th centuries the population of Italy doubled to between 7 and 9 million inhabitants. People of all social classes migrated to the towns, including members of the nobility. As a result, urban communes came to govern the countryside. South of Tuscany, however, the aristocracy lived near the land and the feudal system, with its lack of distinction between trade and agriculture persisted.

One of the reasons for the strength of the Italian economy was that it had monopolized the trade in luxury items and their distribution throughout Europe. These included the strong, sweet wines of Crete, Cyprus, and other parts of the Aegean (see MALMSEY), but also goods produced in Italy itself, such as high-quality wool and silk (from Lucca and Florence). When it became possible to transfer credit throughout the Mediterranean and western Europe (instead of having to carry and exchange actual coins), Florence became the banking capital of Europe. The Florentine house of ANTINORI is a good example of several of these developments. The Antinoris were, and still are, a noble Tuscan family that moved from the country to the city; having made their money in banking, they diversified into selling wine and also used their capital to buy up land to grow their own wine.

The rich merchants of the cities became a new market for fine wines. Good wine became a sign of affluence and a source of profit: it is no coincidence that the merchant dynasties of Bardi and FRESCOBALDI should have gone into winegrowing, buying up land for the purpose. All over Italy the usual way to improve land was to deforest it and plant it with vines. When there was enough moisture, the vines were raised on trees, stakes, or trellises (see TENDONE), in the Roman way, to increase yields by exposing the grapes to the sun. Thus sown and planted crops could be raised in the same fields. In the drier regions, particularly in the south (with the exception of CAMPANIA), the vines were left to grow unsupported, as BUSH VINES, or left to trail on the ground in vineyards or at least in separate plots.

Vine-growing as well as wine-making in medieval Italy were much as they had been in the days of the classical writers on agriculture, and in one crucial respect things were worse: since AMPHORAE and other impermeable earthenware vessels were no longer available, wine was kept in wooden BARRELS, which were hard to clean and were not airtight. Unless a vine contained high proportions of two natural preservatives, sugar and alcohol, it would not last out the year.

The Roman VINE VARIETIES seem to have disappeared. In his treatise on agriculture (1303) PETRUS DE CRESCENTIIS, who had read the classical authorities and often repeats their advice, does not mention any of the famous Roman CÉPAGES. He lists some 37 contemporary Italian varieties, but he makes no attempt to relate those to the grapes he encountered in his classical predecessors. The list he gives is mostly concerned with the northern half of Italy, and especially his own city of Bologna. The list is not a great help to the modern scholar, because his descriptions are too brief for identification and most of the names are unrecognizable. 'Sclaua' is the variety he praises most highly; in the Middle Ages it was grown in the Po valley. This must be the same name as modern SCHIAVA, except that the modern variety is red, whereas Petrus' is white. Other varieties with recognizable names are 'graeca' (like the modern GRECO) and 'uernacia' (VERNACCIA), both of which Petrus says make good wines but have low yields, and 'muscatellus' (MUSCAT), which is better for eating. 'Tribiana' (TREBBIANO?) has small berries, takes long to start producing, and makes good wine that keeps well. 'Albana', a white grape that is characteristic of Romagna, may well be the parent of the modern grape of that area (see ALBANA). However, a familiar name is no guarantee of identity. Modern Trebbiano (Ugni Blanc) is also sometimes known as Greco, so Petrus' 'graeca' and his 'tribiana' may in fact be the same grape. 'Graeca' is unlikely to be Greco di Tufo, which is now grown in Campania and may well be a genuine and very ancient Greek import. Also, since the grapevine mutates relatively easily, modern grape varieties may be very different from their medieval ancestors. None of Petrus' 17 red varieties has a familiar name, and Petrus does not devote much space to them. Like most medieval drinkers, he preferred white wines to red.

From the 13th century onwards wine was medieval Italy's most profitable cash crop. Share-cropping was traditional throughout the country, with the land owner taking half the wine or more if production was high. Sometimes a contract was drawn up for a longer period at a fixed rent. Smallholders survived in the highlands, but in Tuscany and the northern plain they could not afford to stay on the better land. Peasants occasionally retailed their wine, but usually the landowners regulated sales to the towns. Consumption was high (the figure for Florence, *c.*1338, is a gallon a week for every man, woman, and child, but estimates for Milan and Venice are very much higher), yet production more than met demand, particularly in Campania.

Italy is mountainous and has few navigable rivers, which made internal transport costly and difficult before the coming of the RAILWAYS. Also, because Italy was not a political unity, there were obstacles in the form of tolls, duties, and differences in coinage, weights, and measures. Transport by sea was cheap and export to other countries no more laborious than much internal trade, so merchants in northern Italy or near the sea readily turned to foreign markets. The northern districts sold wine in Switzerland and Germany, the MARCHES exported to the Levant via Venice, which enjoyed tax privileges in Constantinople, and Genoese ships took the wines of LIGURIA to Spain, Flanders, and England. Nevertheless the volume of Italy's international wine trade was merely the surplus production of a fertile vine-growing country. The Italians could afford not to deprive themselves of any of the *vin ordinaire* or fine wine they wanted to drink and still make money out of what remained.

See also GENOA, NAPLES, VENICE, and TUSCANY. H.M.W.

Jones, Philip, 'Italy', in *The Cambridge Economic History of Europe*, 7 vols., i: *The Agrarian Life of the Middle Ages* (Cambridge, 1966).

Marescalchi, A., and Dalmasso, G. (eds.), *Storia della vite e del vino in Italia*, 3 vols. (Milan, 1993).

Modern history

That the revival of Europe's trade in the early Middle Ages began in the Mediterranean is by now universally accepted. It is therefore no surprise that specific references to what were to become some of Italy's most important grapes and wines can be found as early as the late 13th and early 14th centuries. Barbera was already mentioned during this period, and Nebbiolo, Trebbiano, and Garganega were specifically named by PETRUS DE CRESCENTIIS in his *Liber ruralium commodorum* of 1304. The country's chronicles, both civic and monastic, of the 14th and 15th centuries abound with descriptions of the leading wines of their day—at times identified by grape variety, at times identified by their production zone. Many of them coincide, at least nominally, with the current wines of these same zones.

English records seem to indicate that wines such as Vernaccia, Trebbiano, and Greco were all known as such at this time. Sante Lancerio, cellarmaster to Pope Paul III, recounted the wines of his day in an account of papal travels in 1536, describing, criticizing, and praising the prominent products of his epoch, amongst which we find Aglianico, Aleatico, and Greco from the south, Vino Nobile di Montepulciano, Trebbiano di Romagna, Sangiovese di Romagna from the centre, and Cinqueterre from the north. And in Andrea Bacci's work we find a full-fledged treatise on Italy's wines, an attempt to deal with and describe the country's viticultural production on a national basis and in a national context, a surprising phenomenon inasmuch as Italy was far from being a nation in the modern sense in the late 16th century.

But it was precisely at this time—in the 17th, and then in the 18th, centuries—that the development of Italian viticulture and wines began to diverge from those of her neighbours. This critical period, which saw the rise of modern wine in BOTTLES stoppered with CORK and from specific producers, left Italy virtually untouched. Old bottles from this period are non-existent, nor is there any evidence of a long history of bottled wine from individual properties. Although some of Tuscany's leading NÉGOCIANT houses trace their history back to the Middle Ages (see ANTINORI and FRESCOBALDI), they, and the few Piedmontese houses which can trace their history to the late 18th century, sold bulk rather than either bottled wine or estate wines until relatively recently.

Any overall evaluation of the quality of Italian wine in the 18th century is impossible, but signs of deterioration do exist. The 'Florence' wines so greatly appreciated in the late 17th and early 18th centuries by Lady Sandwich, by Swift, and by Bolingbroke are described as 'disagreeably rough' by Sir Edward Barry in 1775, and there is good reason not to dismiss his words as a mere subjective reaction. Pietro Leopoldo, grand duke of Tuscany, during an inspection tour of his realm in 1773, reported a significant loss of viticultural commerce with England due to the lessened quality of the wines of Chianti. More importantly, Italy's wines, including many of its most famous ones, did not assume their current form until quite recently: Barolo and Barbaresco were sweet wines until the middle and end of the 19th century, respectively; Chianti did not become a predominantly Sangiovese wine until well into the 19th century; Brunello di Montalcino did not even exist as a wine until the end of the 19th century; Orvieto and Cinqueterre were predominantly sweet wines until the modern epoch; the best-known wines of central Italy such as

Orvieto, Verdicchio, Frascati, and the other white wines of the Castelli Romani were regularly fermented on their skins until the 1970s. The INTERNATIONAL VARIETIES which today play so important a role in the viticulture of Italy's north east—Trentino-Alto Adige, Veneto, and Friuli—began to assume a significant role only after the replanting of the country's vineyards in the wake of the ravages of PHYLLOXERA in the early 20th century. The crisp and refreshing white wines of Friuli are entirely a post-Second World War phenomenon; Sicily's first dry table wines, in contrast to the better-known sweet wines or blending wines of the island, were created only in 1824, by Duke Edoardo di Salaparuta.

Cyrus REDDING's observation that 'Italian wines have stood still and remained without improvement, while those of France and Spain . . . have kept pace to a certain extent with agricultural improvement and the increasing foreign demand' testifies to two and half centuries of marking time, of neglect, and probably of deterioration of quality.

The reasons for this period of stagnation, which in Italian historical literature is often called the period of Italy's *decadenza*, are not difficult to determine. The country experienced an extended domination by foreign powers, first by the Spanish Habsburgs both in the north and the south, then by Spanish Bourbons in the south and Austrian Habsburgs in the north. Meanwhile the increased influence—both temporal and spiritual—of Counter-Reformation Catholicism effectively removed the country's destiny from its own hands. Even more significant was the general shift of trade and commerce from south to north, from the Mediterranean to the Atlantic, which transformed Italy's geographical position for the first time in two millennia from that of a central to that of a peripheral power. Italy was on the fringes of a Europe in which the most prosperous and progressive areas, the northern markets, were virtually inaccessible to her, and were increasingly dominated by the fine wines of France and Germany.

The unification of Italy in 1861, and a slow but steady period of economic growth, did much to reverse the decline of the previous two and a half centuries, although economic growth and modernization were neither unfaltering nor swift. It was only the economic boom after the Second World War which allowed the Italians to attain a truly European standard of living. It also created a class of consumers with both an interest in wine and the means to purchase it, which gave Italian wine producers the essential confidence in their own capacities and their own products which are the only real basis for making good quality wine. Thus wine began to be transformed from a daily beverage and a source of calories (see DIET) to a source of pleasure based on the concept of choice. Even in the Italy of the 1990s, these two conceptions of wine survive in an uneasy state of coexistence.

Major developments in the recent history of Italian wine are described under DOC, DOCG, IGT, and VINO DA TAVOLA.

Geography and climate

Generalizations about a peninsula 1,200 km/750 miles long extending through about 10 degrees of LATITUDE are not easy. The dominant geographical feature of 'the boot' is the Apennines, which begin close to the border with France and then form the central ridge, the national spinal column, down the peninsula to the 'toe' in Calabria. In the far north are the alps; in Sicily, the Madonie form yet another chain of central mountains. Good-quality viticulture is almost entirely a HILLSIDE phenomenon in Italy; there are no Italian equivalents of the *vignoble* of Bordeaux, and the Grave del Friuli and other flat viticultural areas of Friuli do not produce wine at the same quality level as the higher nearby districts of Collio and Colli Orientali. Unlike that of France, Italian agriculture has always been organized vertically instead of horizontally: instead of growing grapes in certain given areas and other crops in different areas, Italians have used the richer soils of the valley floors for the cultivation of grain and vegetables and for the grazing of cattle, reserving the hills of the same areas for the cultivation of the vine and the olive.

A significant number of the country's most admired wines come from CALCAREOUS soils. Piedmont, Tuscany, the hillside zones of Friuli, and the Salento in Apulia all provide examples of this. The other dominant soil type is VOLCANIC, present in such zones as Soave, the Castelli Romani to the south west of Rome, the interior of Campania and Basilicata, and Sicily.

Climate is inevitably affected by ALTITUDE. Latitude is not a sure guide to temperature and further south is not always synonymous with hotter temperatures. Altitude, exposure, wind currents, TOPOGRAPHY, soil composition, and proximity to the sea are other relevant factors. If Cabernet Sauvignon can be grown at 46 degrees 30 minutes of latitude (north of Bordeaux), it is due to the narrow, heat-trapping alpine valleys of Alto Adige. Umbria is generally cooler than Tuscany albeit further to the south; a wide span of central Italy—Umbria, the Marches, Latium—is more renowned for its white wines than for its reds, while Piedmont, in the far north on the French and Swiss border, is principally a producer of dense red wines. Even Sicily confirms the rule that, in the case of Italy, geography is not destiny: the island as a whole produces considerably more white wine than red, and the western part of the island, in particular the province of Trapani in the extreme south west of the island, produces almost exclusively white wine.

The climate of northern Italy, where most of the country's most famous and most exported wines are produced, is CONTINENTAL rather than MEDITERRANEAN. In his work comparing the climates of the world's wine regions, Gladstones points out that the total number of hours of SUNLIGHT here is 'less than might be imagined', and that TEMPERATURE VARIABILITY is extremely low. Climatological analysis of the most famous Italian wine regions alone suggests that they would produce wines with only moderate amounts of BODY, ACIDITY, TANNINS, and COLOUR, but Italians have in general chosen to offset this by growing vine varieties which are naturally high in these elements (see below). Italy's indigenous red grape varieties—with the exception of Dolcetto—are almost invariably later ripeners. Nebbiolo, Barbera, Refosco, Corvina, Sangiovese, Sagrantino, Aglianico, Negroamaro, and Nero d'Avola all require sustained heat throughout the summer and early autumn to ripen properly and lose their tannic and acidic asperity, and successful ripening is therefore far from automatic. Poor VINTAGES are by no means a strange or inexplicable phenomenon in Italy, and in a typical decade there are usually at least two vintages of unacceptable quality.

Gladstones, J., *Viticulture and Environment* (Adelaide, 1992).

Viticulture

Two distinguishing features mark Italian viticulture: first, the late development of vineyards as such and a significant presence until relatively recently of polyculture in grape-growing areas; second, the current dominance of vine-TRAINING SYSTEMS created expressly for high YIELDS and easy MECHANIZATION. Polyculture was a common phenomenon throughout Europe at one time. What is distinctive about Italy is the extent to which this practice lasted into the modern epoch. Grain was planted between rows of vines even in Barolo and Barbaresco until the 1950s, and central Italy was dominated by an almost standard type of mixed culture in which vines, planted amidst olive groves and rows of grains, were trained up trees to prevent the grapes from being eaten by the animals allowed to roam freely in the fields. Some modern vineyards, planted exclusively with vines in regular rows, did exist, particularly in Italy's north west, but viticulture in general was merely part of a general system of agriculture, one cash crop among many. It is no surprise, therefore, that when Italy's vineyards were replanted in the 1960s and 1970s, frequently with the assistance of EUROPEAN UNION funds, vineyards were generally adapted to the new exigencies of mechanization and productivity. Whereas in France the practicalities of mechanization were adapted to the existing low trained vines and high VINE DENSITY with their proven ability to give high-quality grapes, Italian vineyards were redesigned when they were replanted, in a way that would make them compatible with the new large TRACTORS and other machines which were then becoming generally available. The result was spacings of up to 3 m/10 ft between the rows and high training systems. This low-density viticulture, with an average of between 2,500 and 3,300 vines per ha, coupled with the large yields that were common in the initial period of Italy's DOC epoch (roughly 1965–80), had as their inevitable result the very high yields per vine, often as much as 5 kg/11 lb of grapes, and a reduction in vine longevity.

The higher training systems, while offering improved protection against FUNGAL DISEASES, reduced the amounts of reradiated heat and often resulted in less ripe grapes with higher acidity, rougher tannins, and lower levels of EXTRACT. In the 1980s there was renewed interest in higher density vineyards and lower yields per vine, and it seems inevitable that vineyards will be planted more densely and trained lower in the coming decades, although VINE DENSITIES are unlikely to match those of 7,000 to 10,000 vines per ha in the best vineyards of Bordeaux and Burgundy, where prices can justify this density.

Expansive vine-training systems such as TENDONE or even more extreme horizontal systems such as Sylvoz, Casarsa, and other accentuatedly productive CORDON systems are no longer as popular, and there is a visible return to more quality-orientated systems, GUYOT or CORDON DE ROYAT in particular.

CLONAL SELECTION aimed at identifying and reproducing qualitatively superior clones of native vine varieties and the most appropriate ROOTSTOCKS to graft them on to is a relatively recent activity, although important research programmes were already under way for Sangiovese, Nebbiolo, and other indigenous varieties by the early 1990s.

Wine-making

If Italian viticulture has tended to follow its own course, with little attention paid to the practices of other countries, the same cannot be said of its OENOLOGY and wine-making practices. Indeed, substantial investments in cellar equipment have made Italian wine-making facilities some of the most modern in Europe, and Italians make equipment such as bottling lines that is some of the best, and most exported, in the world.

Wooden FERMENTING VESSELS have, for better or for worse, been eliminated and, although cement vats and tanks are still widely in use both for fermentation and for storage, stainless steel tanks are very much more common. TEMPERATURE CONTROL is widely accepted, for the production of both red wines and white wines, and the PUNCHING DOWN of the cap of red wines has been generally replaced by regular PUMPING OVER during the period of fermentation. The lengthy fermentations and MACERATIONS of the past have been substantially abbreviated, although avant-garde producers seeking the highest quality in their wines are extending some fermentations, even if the six-week periods of the past seem irrevocably gone. DESTEMMING has long been an integral part of modern Italian wine-making since the vigorous tannins of most of Italy's major red varieties make fermenting with the stems far from advisable.

WHITE WINE-MAKING techniques, on the other hand, changed drastically in the 1970s and 1980s, with the introduction of cool fermentations, FILTERS, and CENTRIFUGES. The most fundamental change of all, however, has been the end of the practice of fermenting white wines on their skins, which was once widely practised in Friuli and throughout central Italy. Gains in lightness and freshness have been obvious, even if at the price of a certain standardization. Producing white wines of more character without sacrificing the newly achieved crispness and cleanliness is the current challenge for Italian white wine-making.

Fermentation may have evolved considerably in the second half of the 20th century, but ÉLEVAGE has undergone more profound modifications during the same period. Large casks, usually oval rather than upright, have always been the preferred containers for AGEING red wine in Italian cellars; long ageing periods, particularly for what were considered the grandest wines, was an almost unvarying rule; wood of a certain age was generally preferred to new wood (although this may often have been for financial rather than qualitative reasons). Current practice favours smaller casks, with 15- to 50-hl (395- to 1,300-gal) containers replacing the 100- to 150-hl sizes of the past; ageing periods have been diminished, but many of Italy's most renowned red wines have tannins which need a considerable time in cask to soften and round, and periods of two years in cask (for Chianti Classico Riserva, Barolo, and Vino Nobile di Montepulciano), or even three years in cask (for Brunello di Montalcino and Barolo Riserva), are by no means uncommon, even though only Brunello is still legally obliged to age for a full three years; regular replacement of excessively old wood has been accepted as an integral part of correct cellar techniques.

OAK has generally been the preferred wood for casks, much of it from Slovenia or elsewhere in central Europe. In the south of Italy in areas such as the Basilicata and Sicily, where chestnut forests abound and there are no local sources of oak, the traditional chestnut cooperage is gradually being replaced by oak casks to achieve a more international style. French oak became increasingly popular in the 1980s, most notably in the form of BARRIQUES, which were first used for Italian wine in the late 1960s but became general, if controversial, only in the 1980s. Sangiovese and Barbera were the first varieties to be widely paired with new oak in small barrels, and the generally positive results have led to widespread use of barrique maturation in many zones of Italy, albeit only by the most ambitious producers. Their use for such international varieties as Cabernet, Merlot, Pinot Noir, Chardonnay, and Sauvignon Blanc is also a recent phenomenon which has yielded both excellent results and some heavily over-oaked wines.

General inexperience in modern wine-making techniques is a chronic problem in Italy, where fine wine is such a recent phenomenon. This led to a major boom, particularly in the 1980s, in the employment of consulting OENOLOGISTS in Tuscany, Piedmont, and Friuli, the three most important fine wine regions. Press coverage of the exploits of individual consultants threatened to overshadow the significance both of specific estates and of individual TERROIRS (increasingly acknowledged within Italy). Italy's training institutes in oenology and viticulture are still woefully inadequate to its future needs (although see CONEGLIANO and SAN MICHELE ALL'ADIGE), with tertiary educational faculties of agriculture devoting little time and few resources to sound, professional oenological training. This suggests that the authorities have yet to realize the enormous economic potential of Italy's myriad distinctive grape varieties and viticultural environments.

Vine varieties

Despite the recent appearance of widely acclaimed wines from international varieties, Italian viticulture as a whole still remains firmly wedded to her traditional, indigenous varieties, whose number has been estimated as over 2,000. Of the country's 20 most widely planted grapes, a group which includes all varieties with over 10,000 ha / 24,700 acres planted, only Merlot, with some 48,000 ha, is an obvious import. According to an agricultural census conducted in 1990, Sangiovese was by far the most planted variety in Italy with 86,000 ha planted (albeit in strains of varying distinction), followed by the Sicilian white grape Catarratto, the central Italian white Trebbiano Toscano, Piedmont's Barbera, Merlot, Apulia's Negroamaro, the central and southern red Montepulciano, Trebbiano Romagnolo, Primitivo of the south, and white Malvasia. See articles on individual regions and zones for the names of other Italian vine varieties.

Large-scale plantings of international varieties—principally French, although there is also some Riesling and Gewürztraminer—are on the whole confined to the country's north east (which, in many cases, was under either direct Austrian rule or strong Austrian influence until 1919). They are planted in an arc stretching from Franciacorta, in the eastern part of Lombardy, through the Trentino-Alto Adige, the northern part of the Veneto (the provinces of Vicenza and Treviso), and Friuli. Scattered plantings of international varieties exist throughout the rest of the country, but had not established significant toeholds in any one zone or subzone by the mid 1990s. There was little generally accepted identification of variety with terroir, and even in the Alto Adige and Friuli, no single international variety dominated, with Schiava by far the most significant vine planted in the former, Tocai in the latter.

Plantings of international varieties have tended to follow international FASHION: various members of the Pinot family in the 1970s; Chardonnay, Sauvignon Blanc, and Cabernet in the 1980s. Central Italy, with only the late ripening Sangiovese an important red grape and with the relatively uninteresting Trebbiano as its major white grape, is likely to see expanded plantings of international varieties in the coming decades; the high costs of viticulture in its important hillside zones make it imperative to obtain a higher return from the vineyards, an objective which may be realizable only with non-native varieties.

Organization of trade

Italy's wine trade resembles those of its European neighbours in terms of a division of labour between individual properties, commercial and NÉGOCIANT houses, and CO-OPERATIVE wineries. What distinguishes Italy is the overwhelming importance of the latter two categories, a dominance which is the direct result of the extreme fractioning of vineyard property. Close to 40 per cent of the country's agricultural properties grow grapes and the average size of their 'vineyards' is 0.8 ha. Middlemen for the marketing of the wines, be they négociants or co-operatives, are thus indispensable links in the distribution chain which connects growers to consumers. Private estates of a certain size are an important reality only in Tuscany and, to a lesser extent, in Friuli, while the recent development of a significant number of prestigious small 'domaines' in the finest zones of Piedmont might be considered a miniature, but embryonic, version of Burgundy. It is no coincidence that these are the three regions currently producing Italy's best wines.

Large commercial houses were a relatively late development in Italy, virtually all of them having been founded after the unification of the country in 1861 and thus being a century younger than comparable houses in France, Spain, and Portugal. The reasons for their late foundation and slow growth are far from mysterious: Italy was not a country prior to her unification and the movement of merchandise across the borders of the many small states which existed in the peninsula was a costly and cumbersome procedure. REDDING cites 'a vexatious system of imposts' as a major cause of Italian viticultural backwardness in the 19th century, a backwardness which was commercially, as well as technically, penalizing. There was very little in the way of a national market, and little knowledge of even the finest products outside of their specific production zones. Even today négociant houses are a major presence only in Tuscany, the Veneto, and Sicily, while co-operative wineries play a more significant role in other Italian regions.

Co-operatives have become the dominant force in the production and distribution of Italian wine in the late 20th century, a logical development considering the political dominance of the Christian Democratic party in the country's various governments and the favour shown to co-operative movements in the social doctrine of the Roman Catholic church. Income maintenance has been as significant a concern as the products themselves, an objective which, in concrete terms, has entailed large volumes which, thanks to ample subsidies, could be marketed at low prices. Quality has not always been the strong point of the resulting wines, although individual co-operatives, particularly in the north, have always been responsive to the market and conscious of the need to create products that would please consumer palates. Italy enjoyed particular, but short-lived, success in the 1970s and 1980s with its exports to the USA, notably of LAMBRUSCO.

As EUROPEAN UNION and national subsidies are reduced, Italian wines will have to respond more readily to free market economics. The creation of the European Economic Community and the opening of neighbouring markets to large quantities of low-priced Italian wine can be seen as merely postponing the day of reckoning. Rapidly falling wine consumption (in Italy alone, per capita consumption fell more than 50 per cent between 1960 and 1990) signals that a fundamental modification of Italy's production philosophy is only a matter of time.

Cyril RAY, writing in 1966 in the early days of the Common Market and shortly after the approval of Italy's first DOC law, foresaw a new golden age for Italian wine. If the subsequent period turned to more of an age of brass or, at best, silver, there can be few doubts that Italy's new prosperity and the world-wide popularity of the 'Mediterranean diet' (a shorthand, in most cases, for Italian cooking) have changed prospects and possibilities for Italian wine and created a new viewpoint amongst the country's producers. And there can be even fewer doubts that admirers and enthusiasts of Italian wine have never had such an embarrassment of riches as they have at the end of the 2nd millennium AD.

For details of individual regions see ABRUZZI, ALTO ADIGE, APULIA, BASILICATA, CALABRIA, CAMPANIA, EMILIA-ROMAGNA, FRIULI, LATIUM, LIGURIA, LOMBARDY, MARCHES, MOLISE, PIEDMONT, SARDINIA, SICILY, TRENTINO, TUSCANY, UMBRIA, Valle d'AOSTA, and the VENETO.

For details of terms to be found on Italian wine labels, see CLASSICO, DOC, DOCG, IGT, RISERVA, and VINO DA TAVOLA. D.T.

Anderson, B., *The Wine Atlas of Italy* (London and New York, 1990).
Gleave, D., *The Wines of Italy* (London and New York, 1989).

IWO. See OIV.

J

JABOULET AÎNÉ, PAUL, important RHÔNE valley merchant and wine producer, whose most famous wine is Hermitage la Chapelle. The house was founded in the early 19th century by Antoine Jaboulet and takes its name from the older of his twin sons. In the mid 1990s six Jaboulets from two generations were involved with the firm, of which Gérard, one of the wine world's most energetic travellers, had been at the helm since 1976. His younger brother Jacques was in charge of wine-making and buying the substantial quantities of wine and grapes needed for the firm's annual sales of up to 200,000 cases. Jaboulet's own vineyard holdings totalled about 72 ha / 178 acres, mainly in the northern Rhône, in the early 1980s, and this was being steadily increased to include, for example, some land in the Condrieu appellation. Of the raw materials bought in, from 150 growers the length of the Rhône valley, two-thirds is wine rather than grapes. The firm occupied premises in Tain l'Hermitage from 1834, until 1984 when a modern winery and warehouse was built in La Roche de Glun just south of the town. Jaboulet sell a range of more than 20 different wines, most of them in the firm's own deep-PUNTED bottle, and the best are their own special cuvées, usually historically named. Their CROZES-HERMITAGE, Domaine de Thalabert, was some of the earliest proof offered to wine drinkers outside France that this appellation could produce serious, age-worthy wine. Some vintages of their CHÂTEAUNEUF-DU-PAPE, Les Cèdres, and CÔTE-RÔTIE, Les Jumelles, have been exemplars of those appellations. Other blends can be less distinctive, but Jaboulet's red and white HERMITAGE, La Chapelle and Chevalier de Stérimberg respectively, are extremely fine wines. La Chapelle 1961 is an acknowledged classic, and Chevalier de Stérimberg demonstrates Gérard Jaboulet's admiration for the ROUSSANNE grape.

Livingstone-Learmonth, J., *The Wines of the Rhône* (3rd edn., London, 1992).

JACQUÈRE is the common white grape variety in SAVOIE, where it produces high yields of lightly scented, essentially alpine dry white. Plantings once again increased in the 1980s so that there were 1,000 ha / 2,470 acres by 1990.

JADOT, LOUIS, merchant-grower based in BEAUNE, dealing exclusively in Burgundy and owners of some 37 ha / 91 acres of vineyards in the CÔTE D'OR; owned by its American importer Kobrand since 1985. Founded in 1859 by the eponymous Louis Jadot, the company was run from 1962 to 1992 by André Gagey, who joined the firm as an assistant in 1954. When Louis-Alain Jadot, last of the family line, died prematurely in 1968 Gagey was asked by the family to become general manager, and he has now been succeeded by his son Pierre-Henry. Jadot's success has been very much due to the combined talents of Gagey and wine-maker Jacques Lardière. Both red and white NÉGOCIANT wines, made from bought-in fruit, are thoroughly reliable, but the firm's reputation is based on the high quality of its domain wines. Vineyard holdings were substantially increased in 1985 with the acquisition of the Clair Dau holdings of 17 ha, and in 1989 Jadot acquired both cellars and vineyards of the Maison Champy. Among the reds the Côte de Beaune wines stand out, with the MONOPOLES Beaune, Clos des Ursules, being especially fine. The domain whites are wines of concentration, class, and distinction. Never over-oaked, they are a clear expression of their TERROIR and wines such as their Puligny-Montrachet, Les Folatières; Corton-Charlemagne; and Chevalier-Montrachet, Les Demoiselles, are regularly among the best bottles of white burgundy to be had. M.W.E.S.

Hanson, A., *Burgundy* (2nd edn., London, 1994).
Parker, R., *Burgundy* (New York, 1990).

JAEN, workhorse red grape variety commonly planted in central Spain. The name is also used for an undistinguished dark-skinned grape variety in Portugal's Dão region.

Jaen Blanco is light skinned and is said to be the AVESSO of Portugal.

JAHRGANG, German for VINTAGE (as in the year rather than the HARVEST process, for which the word is *Ernte*).

JAPAN. Grape-growing and, to a lesser extent, wine production have a long history in this Far Eastern country, even though wine drinking on any appreciable scale is a very recent phenomenon. In 1992, the Japanese were still drinking an average of little more than a bottle (0.9 l) per person per year, and the typical wine made from Japanese grapes (as opposed to the typical Japanese wine) was sweetish, white, and noticeably light.

History

Legend has it that grape-growing began at Katsunuma, in Yamanashi Prefecture of central Honshu. As the story goes, in the year 718 the Buddha Nyorai passed vines to a holy man by the name of Gyoki, who planted the vines at Katsunuma, where he built the Daizenji Temple.

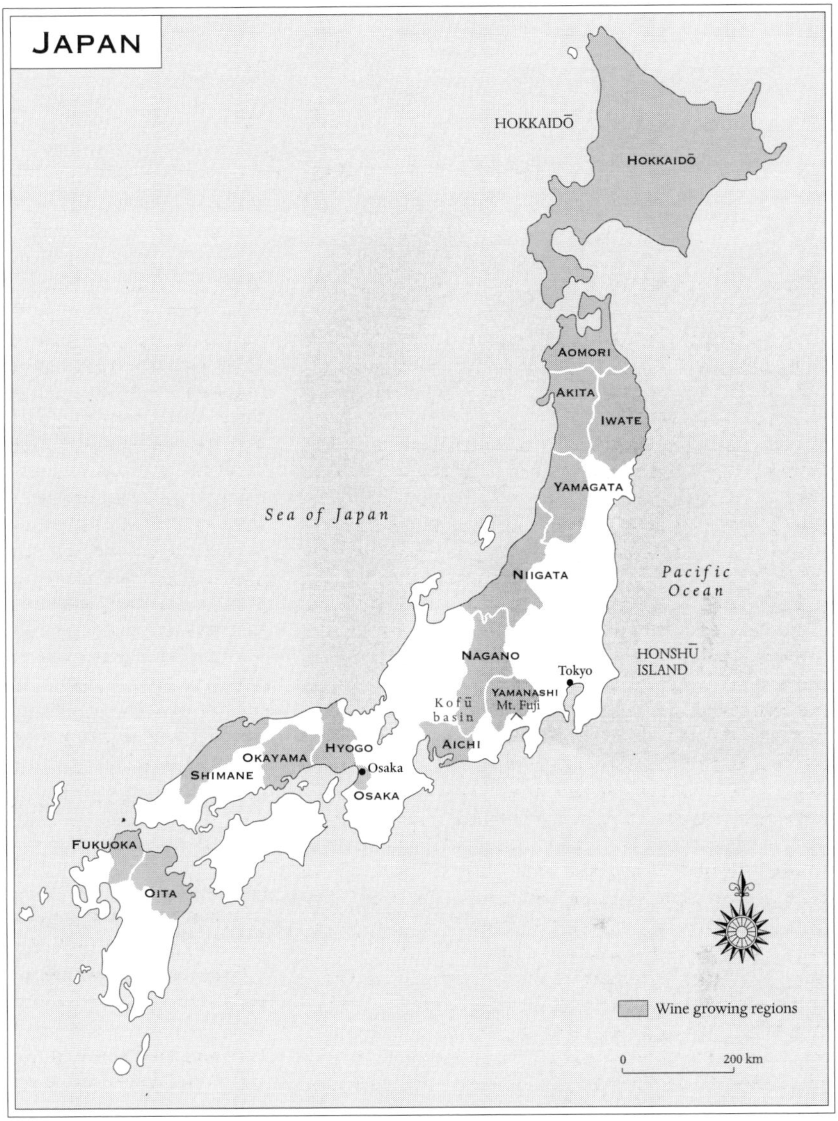

It was the grape itself, rather than wine, in which the Japanese were initially interested. The monks taught that grapes had medicinal value. The statue of Nyorai, which Gyoki had carved in his honour and which is still housed in the Temple today, was named Budo Yakushi (*budo* meaning grape; and *yakushi* meaning teacher of medicine) by pilgrims to the Temple.

Wine may, perhaps, have been made from local grapes in Katsunuma in earlier times but wine consumption in Japan had not been documented until the arrival of Portuguese MISSIONARIES in the 16th century. The Jesuit missionary St Francis Xavier carried wine as gifts for the feudal lords of Kyūshū in southern Japan whom he visited in 1545. Others who followed him continued the practice so that the locals acquired a taste for wine and began to import it regularly.

They called the wine *tintashu*, combining the Japanese word for sake (*shu*) with a derivative of the Portuguese word for red (TINTO). (The word lives on today, incidentally, as the brand name for a port style wine produced by Suntory, the brewing and whisky giant.)

During the Tokugawa shogunate of the 17th century the missionaries were expelled, Christians persecuted, and practices associated with Christianity, such as drinking wine, condemned. Ironically, however, the choice of Edo as the Tokugawa capital (on the site of modern Tokyo) was a boost for the farmers of nearby Yamanashi: their grapes

Thinning bunches of Suntory's Kofu vineyards in anticipation of **Japan**'s summer rains.

quickly came to be prized for the tables of the shogun's court.

Eventually, in 1875, the first attempts at commercial wine-making were undertaken in Yamanashi, where grape-growing had begun over a millennium before. An enterprising merchant who had seen foreigners at the port of Yokohama drinking wine set out to make a substitute from local grapes. The early product was not good, but the effort was enough to convince local authorities to permit the import of European VINIFERA and AMERICAN VINES as the basis for a new industry.

Today, the viticultural industry is small, but entrenched—and still focused mostly on producing TABLE GRAPES, rather than on providing top-quality raw material for WINE-MAKING.

Geography and climate

Grapes are now grown in 46 of the 47 provinces, the exception being tropical Okinawa.

Three provinces (Yamanashi, Yamagata, and Nagano) on the main island, Honshū, however, account for 40 per cent of the 26,000 ha/64,220 acres under vine throughout Japan.

Production is in the order of 270,000 tonnes of grapes per year, although only one-tenth of these grapes are used for wine-making. The bulk of the production is for the table and the grape varieties under cultivation and viticultural practices reflect this.

Japan's climate is not naturally suited to viticulture and successful grape-growing has always been a struggle.

In Yamanashi Prefecture, where 27 per cent of Japan's grapes are grown and around two-thirds of the wine is made, a monsoonal climate presents a serious problem of excess water and HUMIDITY. Here, and in most of the prefectures of Honshu, vines traditionally have been trained on to overhead wires or platforms (*budodana*) so that the bunches will hang lower than the foliage and be more freely exposed to circulating air. This TENDONE method of cultivation, known as *tanazukuri*, was developed as a defence against FUNGAL DISEASES and has been reasonably effective. VINE DENSITY is notoriously low: in some places there may be only two or three vines generating foliage to cover 100 sq m/120 sq yds. The demands made on the vine to support this practice, combined with the excess RAINFALL and the tendency of growers to maximize YIELDS in any case, robs the grape of the character necessary for robust wines.

Grapes from the district of Katsunuma, with about 15 per cent of the Prefecture's vines, are those generally preferred by wine-makers. Katsunuma fares considerably better climatically than districts lower down in the Kōfu basin. Rainfall is lower, it has better DRAINAGE because of its higher ELEVATION, gets a refreshing breeze which helps control rot and mildew, has a wider day–night temperature range, and better ripening conditions for wine grapes generally.

Yamagata and Nagano prefectures do better again but conditions are still far from ideal.

In the 1960s a second frontier of the modern Japanese industry was opened up in an even more unlikely location, in central Hokkaidō, Japan's northernmost island. This is an extremely cold environment for grape-growing. Average temperatures rise only to about 23 °C/73 °F in July, August, and the early part of September. By the end of September, average temperatures are about 15 °C and, by October, below 10 °C. Vineyards are covered in deep snow for most of the winter and vines are given WINTER PROTECTION by being buried in heaped soil to avoid damage. In Hokkaidō, canes are trained low along horizontal wires, in contrast to the *tanazukuri* technique.

Japanese vineyard soils are in general very acid.

Vine varieties

History, the dominant demand for TABLE GRAPES, and the climatic vagaries with which growers have had to contend over the years, have combined to result in the rather exotic range of grape varieties which form the basis of viticulture in Japan.

Strictly speaking, there are no vines native to Japan. There are several introduced vines which have evolved here uniquely, however, and these are now regarded justifiably as Japanese varieties.

The most significant of these, and the undoubted sentimental favourite of the Japanese, is the Koshu. This is the descendant of the vines carried along the Silk Road to Japan

1,200 years ago and, in the public eye at least, is virtually synonymous with the industry of Katsunuma.

Koshu has survived as an important variety because it has adapted to the difficult growing conditions in Yamanashi Prefecture and because it is supported by long tradition. It is a heavy-bearing vine producing big, round, pink-tinged berries. It is most suitable as a table grape, but is also used to make a wine which is almost colourless and, as might be expected, without a great deal of BODY.

Koshu is the most visible of the modest *Vitis vinifera* presence in the Japanese viticulture. Neo-Muscat, a variety developed from a crossing of Koshu Sanjaku with MUSCAT OF ALEXANDRIA, is also *vinifera* and is now, in fact, more widely planted than Koshu, but is less well known. Another Koshu cousin, Ryugan (also known as Senkoji, and probably the same as the Longyan of CHINA), is grown only in tiny quantities, chiefly in Nagano Prefecture in central Honshū. As with Koshu, Neo-Muscat and Ryugan produce grapes which are best suited to the table, but which are also made into light and generally sweetish wine.

In Hokkaidō, a vine growing wild in the region for centuries and known locally as *yamabudo* (literally, mountain grape) has been the subject of a great deal of research and genetic development since the 1960s. The variety has been identified as belonging to the oriental, cold-resistant *amurensis* species of VITIS originating along the Amur river which forms the border between China and Siberia.

The only wine of this variety is produced in small quantities by the large Tokachi winery at Ikeda, in central Hokkaidō, from grapes picked in the wild by local townsfolk. The small black berries make an interesting, although unconventional, red wine with a distinctive gamey bouquet and an austere, earthy palate. It is labelled, simply, Amurensis.

Drawing on earlier work on the species done at a research station in Kharbarovsk in the former Soviet Union, the Ikeda Viticulture and Enology Experimental Station has sought to adapt and cross this local vine to breed NEW VARIETIES which are a match for the extreme climatic conditions of Hokkaidō and are more suitable for commercial viticulture and wine-making.

A crossing of the vine with a SEIBEL hybrid is the most successful product of this work so far. The new variety, named Kiyomi, produces berries which are larger than the wild *amurensis* vine, and more regular in shape and general appearance. The wine is more conventional and has some of the characteristics of Pinot Noir, although it is considerably lighter in body.

However, the vines which are by far the most widely planted throughout Japan, accounting for almost 80 per cent of the total area under vine, are HYBRIDS based on *Vitis labrusca*, most of which were introduced directly from the United States.

They have generally performed well in the difficult local growing conditions and, most importantly, have provided the best commercial results for growers attuned primarily to the table grape market. In particular, as the highest prices are attracted by the first fruit on to the market each season, the fact that many of them are early ripening varieties has been very attractive to growers.

DELAWARE is most popular, comprising around a third of the total vineyard area. Campbell's Early was once a clear second, but has been quite rapidly overtaken by Kyoho, a local hybrid of the American variety CONCORD and the Persian *vinifera* white grape variety Rosaki. Kyoho has been further bred to produce a rash of minor varieties aimed at achieving better-quality table grapes, including Pione, which produces quite creditable VARIETAL rosé. Another popular hybrid is Muscat Bailey A.

All of these varieties find their way into wine, even though the vines were not bred originally, nor are grown specifically in modern Japan, for this purpose. Grapes which for some reason fail to satisfy requirements as table grapes, or those which ripen late in the season, end up at the wineries.

Industry organization

Since the wine boom of the 1980s (per capita consumption doubled between 1981 and 1992) many of the larger Japanese wine producers have sought to improve the quality of the wine they have been making.

Initially they had focused on investment in modern wine-making equipment and on training their wine-makers in the methods used in the major wine-producing nations (Suntory even went so far as to buy the ST-JULIEN classed growth Ch Lagrange, and the 1980s saw several substantial Japanese investments in the California wine industry). They had hoped that this, along with various practices in the winery aimed at extracting more flavour and body from the flimsy local fruit base, would be sufficient to match the competition from the foreign producers whose attention to the Japanese market had been attracted by its rapid growth, by the potential associated with 123 million affluent people, by favourable exchange rates, and by the relaxation of import barriers.

The domestic industry has also tried to hold its ground by using imported bulk wine, GRAPE CONCENTRATE, MUST, and even imported grapes to extend the quantity and improve the quality of its own base material (see ARGENTINA, for instance). Labelling laws had allowed considerable leeway for producers in this regard and some 'domestic' wines were known to contain the barest minimum of genuine domestic material. (In 1990, for example, according to OIV statistics, Japan produced 583,000 hl/15.4 million gal of wine and imported 935,000 hl.)

But the increasing sophistication of the Japanese consumer and the persistence of the European and New World producers has seen, nevertheless, major inroads into the domestic industry's hold on the market. In 1982 domestic producers were accounting for three-quarters of the bottled wine market in Japan; by 1992 this share had fallen to just over half.

Furthermore, the extent to which even this reduced market share depends on imported product is now more readily evident because of a voluntary labelling code, adopted by the Japan Wineries Association under pressure from the Ministry of Finance, which has removed much of the ambiguity regarding the origin of wine bottled under domestic labels.

Wine bottled under domestic labels must now be declared either as *kokunai san* (domestic wine) or *yunyu san* (imported bulk wine). If these two entities are blended, then the exact proportions of each have to be shown on the label, with the majority portion written first. To be called *kokunai san*, the wine has to have been wholly fermented in Japan, although it is still permitted to use imported grape must or imported whole grapes in a ferment. Genuine domestic wine can command a price premium. Recognizing this, the winemakers of Katsunuma have taken the new labelling code a step further and have adopted a Certificate of Origin seal for the district's top wines. On these wines the label carries a declaration of the grapes used, where they were grown, where and when the wine was made, and the total number of bottles produced. Bottles carrying the seal are usually individually numbered. Belatedly, therefore, wine-makers have come to accept that if they are to retain their relevance in the domestic wine market they will have to do it with inherent quality.

In turn, this will require major alterations to vineyard practices. If the existing vine varieties are to continue to be the basis of the wine-makers' raw material then, at the very least, yields must be substantially reduced and grapes should be grown specifically for wine-making.

But the structure of the industry militates against rapid progress. There are an estimated 80,000 grape-growers. The average vineyard size is around 0.25 ha in Yamanashi, and not much bigger elsewhere. Even in Hokkaidō, where the scale of viticulture is greatest, the average vineyard is only slightly more than 0.5 ha.

Price maximization is essential to maintain a viable income for small grape-growers and, when table grapes can command a price four or five times the price wine-makers are prepared to pay, it is hard to imagine that the bulk of the existing growers will change their ways. Vineyards dedicated solely to producing wine grapes are the answer but there were very few of them in the mid 1990s.

The large domestic wine producers rely overwhelmingly on bought-in grapes. Most of them do also have vineyards, but these are small and primarily for experimental purposes. They are testing new varieties of wine grapes, new approaches to SOIL MANAGEMENT and DRAINAGE, different methods of PRUNING and TRAINING SYSTEMS, new approaches to leaf and CANOPY MANAGEMENT, and alternative ways of treating the fruit. The fruit from these experimental vineyards is, of course, made into wine and some of it is very good, but it is generally not available in sufficient quantities to make any appreciable difference to the quality of their major labels, or even to enter the mainstream market as individual bottlings.

The small number of growers who also make and sell their own wine, therefore, may represent some of the most interesting possibilities for Japanese wine quality, at least in the short term. Some have been responsible for serious attempts to improve the quality of wine and, as small-scale operations, their outcomes are more readily discernible.

Both large and small producers have accelerated their efforts recently to expand the small area of land planted to superior European *vinifera* varieties. Cabernet Sauvignon and Cabernet Franc have been planted in the west of Yamanashi Prefecture with some reasonable results; Chardonnay and Merlot look reasonably suited to Nagano; and northern European varieties such as Müller-Thurgau and Zweigelt have done well in Hokkaidō.

Together, however, the European varieties comprised little more than five per cent of the total area under vine in the mid 1990s and, with the exception of a few hectares of Cabernet Sauvignon, almost all had been planted since the 1970s.

In contrast to the fragmentation of the grape-growing industry, wine-making is extraordinarily concentrated. Only holders of licences issued by the Ministry of Finance are permitted to make wine. There are over 400 such licences current, although at least 100 of these make wine from fruit other than grapes and at least 100 make wine only occasionally. Industry sources put the number of active makers of wine from grapes variously at between 60 and 160. However, all major wine-makers are members of the Japan Winery Association, of which there are only 30 members.

Five giant, diversified beverage conglomerates account for three-quarters of the total production of wine (including *kokunai san, yunyu san*, and blends). Suntory and Sanraku (who sell under the Mercian label) vie for top position with between a fifth and a quarter of total production each. They are followed by Manns Wine (subsidiary of soy sauce maker Kikkoman) and Sapporo (Polaire label) with around 10 per cent each, and Kyowa Hakko Kogyo (Ste Neige label) with about eight per cent of total production. The largest of the remainder are the Tokachi winery in Hokkaidō, owned by the city of Ikeda, several other city-owned wineries throughout Japan, and a number of smaller, family-owned and operated wineries such as the Marufuji winery, whose Rubaiyat label is one of the best-selling small producer labels in speciality wine outlets, the Shirayuri winery (L'Orient label), and Ch Lumière. D.G.

JARDIN DE LA FRANCE is the cleverly evocative name devised for the Loire, 'garden of France', as a vast VIN DE PAYS regional entity. It has been one of the most successful vins de pays, typically a red made from Gamay and Grolleau, although one bottle in every three is a white which may be made from Sauvignon Blanc, Chardonnay, and/or Chenin Blanc. Gamays and even Sauvignons are sometimes sold as PRIMEUR wines.

JASNIÈRES, small but revived white wine appellation in an enclave within the less favourably exposed Coteaux du LOIR district in the northern Loire. The appellation all but expired in the 1950s but Joël Gigou at Domaine de la Charrière and others have injected new passion into the making of these traditionally dry wines from the Chenin Blanc grape. Locals see Jasnières as 'the SAVENNIÈRES of Touraine', so dry and steely are these traditional wines in their youth, and so well do they respond to BOTTLE AGEING. In particularly ripe

Monticello, **Jefferson's** home in Virginia, where he undertook considerable, if unsuccessful, experimentation with domestic and imported wines.

vintages since the late 1980s, however, extraordinarily rich, appley, BOTRYTIZED wines have been fashioned, either dry or sweet according to the extent of NOBLE ROT infection. The soils are characterized by their high flint content, on the south south-east-facing slopes on the north bank of the Loir. Annual production of Jasnières is about double that of white Coteaux du Loir.

The local VDQS is Coteaux du VENDÔMOIS. See also LOIRE and map on pp. 576–7.

JEFFERSON, THOMAS (1743–1826), third president of the United States, a wine lover whose interest in wine and hopes for American wine-growing typified the early Republic. As a Virginia farmer, Jefferson grew grapes from all sources, native (see VITIS, AMERICAN VINE SPECIES) and VINIFERA, at his estate Monticello for 50 years with uniform unsuccess: no Monticello wine ever materialized, but the hope never died. His vineyard at Monticello has now been restored to the form it had in 1807.

As ambassador to France (1784–89), Jefferson made himself expert in wine, travelling to all the major French wine regions as well as to those of Germany and Italy. He tasted, discussed, and bought largely, and acted also as agent and adviser for his friends in the selection and purchase of wines. The record of this activity contained in his papers is a small encyclopedia of pre-Revolutionary wine and wine production. As president (1801–9), Jefferson was celebrated for the variety and excellence of his cellar at the White House in Washington, which abounded in CHAMBERTIN, MARGAUX, HERMITAGE, YQUEM, and TOKAY. Bottles of late 18th century wines such as Ch LAFITE, supposedly ordered by Jefferson (and in some cases engraved with the initials Th.J.), have in the late 20th century fetched record-breaking prices at AUCTION.

After his retirement from public life, living on a much-reduced scale, Jefferson turned to the wines of the south: the reds of BELLET and MONTEPULCIANO, for example, and the Muscat of RIVESALTES. He spared no effort to ensure a good supply from good sources. At all times, Jefferson was eager to assist the many efforts to solve the riddle of successful wine-growing in America: he gave land next to his Virginia estate to support Philip Mazzei's Italian Vineyard Society, an ambitious effort to grow wine by importing Italian vines and vineyard workers; he encouraged such neighbours as James Madison and James Monroe in their viticultural experiments; it was in his administration that land on the river Ohio in Indiana was granted to Swiss-born J. J. Dufour for the enterprise that resulted in the first successful commercial wine production in the UNITED STATES.

By such assistance, and by keeping taxes on wine low, Jefferson hoped to make the USA a wine-drinking country. He could be extravagant in his optimism: a wine from the native Alexander grape he called equal to Chambertin; a sweet SCUPPERNONG from North Carolina he thought would be 'distinguished on the best tables of Europe'. The USA, he affirmed, could 'make as great a variety of wines as are made in Europe, not exactly of the same kind, but doubtless as good', even though his own experience contradicted the proposition.

Jefferson's personal pleasure in wine was clear: 'Good wine is a daily necessity for me,' he wrote. He also saw wine as an element in his vision of a nation of independent yeomen: 'no nation is drunken where wine is cheap,' hence wine should

Typical backstreet in **Jerez** de la Frontera.

be the nation's drink. Despite his failures in practical vine-growing, Jefferson is the great patron of the idea that the USA should be a wine-growing nation. T.P.

de Treville Lawrence, R. (ed.), *Jefferson and Wine* (2nd edn., The Plains, Va., 1989).

JEREPIGO or **jerepiko**, unfermented dessert 'wines' in South Africa, the Cape's version of VIN DOUX NATUREL produced by adding alcohol before fermentation to ripe, very sweet grape juice, usually MUSCADEL. Such products are often labelled Muskadel or Muscadel Jerepigo. Usually about 17 per cent alcohol, often with intense ripe fig and muscat flavours, these traditional, warming wines, popular in South African winters, probably derive their name from the Portuguese term JEROPIGA. J.P.

JEREZ, or **Jerez de la Frontera**, city in ANDALUCÍA, south west Spain, that is the centre of the sherry industry. Jerez is also the name of the DO which produces sherry. In Spain the wine is known as *vino de Jerez* (or simply *Jerez*), and sherry is an English corruption of the Spanish word (while in France the town and drink are known respectively as Xérès and *xérès*). The town owes its full name to the fact that in the Middle Ages it was on the frontier between Christian and Moorish Spain. For more details of Jerez's history and organization, see SHERRY.

JEROPIGA, Portuguese term for grape must prevented from fermenting by the addition of spirit or AGUARDENTE. *Jeropiga* is often used to sweeten FORTIFIED wines. (*Vinho abafado* on the other hand is partially fermented before spirit is added; see CARCAVELOS.)

JOHANNISBERG, Valais name for fuller-than-average dry white wine made from SILVANER grapes in SWITZERLAND.

JOHANNISBERG RIESLING, sometimes abbreviated simply to **JR**, common synonym for the great white RIESLING grape variety of Germany, notably in California. There is no direct connection with the famous SCHLOSS JOHANNISBERG in Germany's RHEINGAU region except that both the famous castle and the region's reputations are founded on the Riesling grape.

JOHNSON, HUGH (1939–), world's best-selling wine author. Johnson's passion for wine began when he was at Cambridge University, where he read English. One of the great stylists of the LITERATURE OF WINE, he was immediately taken on as a feature writer for Condé Nast magazines on graduation. As a result of his close friendship with André SIMON, the founder of the International Wine & Food Society, he became General Secretary of the society and succeeded the legendary gastronome as editor of its magazine *Wine and Food*. At the same time he became wine correspondent of *The Sunday Times* and embarked on his first book *Wine*, whose publication in 1966 established him as one of the foremost English gastronomic writers of the time. More than 750,000 copies have been printed, in seven languages.

His next book was even more successful, even though it allowed only limited scope for Johnson's matchless prose. *The World Atlas of Wine* represented the first serious attempt to map the world's wine regions, and first appeared in 1971. More than 2.5 million copies have been sold of this, and subsequent editions in 1977 and 1985, in a total of 13 languages. The director of the INAO, at a time when the French were generally slow to acknowledge British connoisseurship, described this book as 'un événement majeur de la littérature vinicole'.

Pausing only to write a best-selling book on trees, *The International Book of Trees*, inspired by his acquisition of an Elizabethan house in 12 acres of Essex countryside, he went on to devise and write a best-selling annual wine guide, *The Pocket Wine Book*, which has sold more than 3.5 million copies in 13 languages since its first edition in 1977.

The more expansive *Hugh Johnson's Wine Companion* followed in 1983, revised in 1987, which sold widely in the USA as *Hugh Johnson's Modern Encyclopedia of Wine* and in France as *Le Guide mondiale du connaisseur de vin*. This prolific output, encouraged by Johnson's publishers Mitchell Beazley, was supplemented by *The Principles of Gardening*, another best seller, and a succession of co-authored and less serious wine books (including even a 'pop-up' version).

Johnson's most durable and greatest work, however, did not appear until 1989. *The Story of Wine* is a *tour de force*, a single-volume sweep through the history of wine in which Johnson's literary skills and breadth of vision are headily combined. The book was written to coincide with an ambitiously international 13-part television series, *Vintage: A History of Wine*, which has been transmitted in the UK, USA, Japan, and France, written and presented by Johnson himself.

Schloss **Johannisberg** commands a view of vineyards leading down to the Rhine.

SENSORIAL ANALYSIS TASTING SHEET FOR WINE JUDGING COMPETITIONS STILL WINES

OCCASION

commission n°	sample n°	vintage	name of wine	presentation category
date	time			

test

		EXCELLENT	VERY GOOD	GOOD	FAIR	UNSATISFACTORY	POOR	NEGATIVE	NON CORRESPONDENCE (DEFECT)	EXCESS (DEFECT)	LACK (DEFECT)	IMBALANCE (DEFECT)
SIGHT	LIMPIDITY	6	5	4	3	2	1	0	■	■		■
	COLOUR HUE	6	5	4	3	2	1	0		■	■	■
	COLOUR INTENSITY	6	5	4	3	2	1	0				■
BOUQUET	GENUINENESS	6	5	4	3	2	1	0	■	■		■
	INTENSITY	8	7	6	5	4	2	0		■		■
	REFINEMENT	8	7	6	5	4	2	0		■		■
	HARMONY	8	7	6	5	4	2	0	■	■	■	
TASTE FLAVOUR	GENUINENESS	6	5	4	3	2	1	0	■	■		■
	INTENSITY	8	7	6	5	4	2	0		■		■
	BODY	8	7	6	5	4	2	0				■
	HARMONY	8	7	6	5	4	2	0	■	■	■	
	PERSISTENCE	8	7	6	5	4	2	0	■	■		■
	AFTER TASTE	6	5	4	3	2	1	0		■	■	
OVERALL JUDGEMENT		8	7	6	5	4	2	0		■	■	
partial TOTALS	tens								TOTAL			
	units											

NATURE OF DEFECTS

biological ☐

chemical physical ☐

accidental ☐

congenital ☐

remarks

member/s of committee | signature/s

METHODE OF THE "UNION INTERNATIONALE DES OENOLOGUES"

Judging wine often entails awarding marks to specific attributes.

In 1986 Johnson started the Hugh Johnson Collection Ltd., which sells glassware and other wine-related artefacts, with notable success in Japan, where he is a consultant to Jardines Wines and Spirits and honorary chairman of Wine Japan, an annual wine show. He has also served on the administrative council of first growth Ch LATOUR, as a consultant to British Airways, and has been president of the Sunday Times Wine Club since its inception in 1973. Other activities include regular journalism on gardening and the maintenance of arboreta at his English house and at his French house on the edge of the TRONÇAIS forest.

Johnson is one of the most vocal opponents of SCORING wine, and his writing has been characterized more by a sensual enthusiasm for wine in all its variety than by the critical analysis of individual wines which characterizes writers such as the American Robert PARKER.

JONGIEUX, named CRU in the upper Rhône valley just north of Chambéry whose name may be added to the French appellation Vin de SAVOIE. Vineyards allowed this special appellation produce a range of still wines from such varieties as Mondeuse, Pinot Noir, Gamay, Jacquère, and Chardonnay.

JORDAN, Middle Eastern country which produces about 10,000 hl/264,000 gal of wine a year from a total vineyard area of about 13,000 ha which is mainly dedicated to TABLE GRAPES.

JOVEN, Spanish for young. Some wines destined for early consumption are sometimes sold as a Vino Joven.

JUDGING WINE, an activity that most wine drinkers undertake every time they open a new bottle, but also a serious business on which the commercial future of some wine producers may to a certain extent depend. For details of domestic wine judging, see TASTING.

The judging process at a more professional level can vary from a gathering of a few friends, a few bottles, and much hot air to an event in which wines have been carefully categorized by wine type, style, and possibly price and are tasted BLIND, in ideal conditions, without any consultation until a possible final discussion of controversial wines. Back-up bottles are always needed in case of CORKED bottles, and to verify whether any other FAULT is confined to a single bottle. SCORING systems vary but usually involve awarding a specific allocation of points for various different aspects such as appearance, nose, palate, perhaps TYPICITY, and overall quality. MEDALS are often awarded as a result. Wine 'shows' are particularly important in Australia where to be invited to act as a judge, or even associate judge, is a great honour. For more details of professional wine judging, see COMPETITIONS.

JUGS for serving wine. See DECANTERS.

JUG WINE, term current in CALIFORNIA for the most basic sort of wine, an American counterpart to VIN ordinaire or PLONK. After PROHIBITION was repealed in 1933, most inexpensive California GENERIC table wine was bottled in half-gallon and gallon (1.9–3.9-l) glass jugs or flagons to satisfy a demand largely made up of thirsty immigrant labourers from the Mediterranean and eastern Europe. As this market segment has aged and died without direct replacement, newer generations turned to FIGHTING VARIETALS bottled in magnums, and jug wines have faded.

JUHFARK, distinctive but almost extinct white grape variety once widely grown in HUNGARY. After the PHYLLOXERA invasion it never regained its importance and is today found almost exclusively in the Somló region, where it can produce wine usefully high in acidity which ages well. It is usually blended in with the more widely planted FURMINT and RIESLING. The vine, whose name means 'ewe's tail', is inconveniently sensitive to both frost and mildew.

JULIÉNAS, one of the 10 BEAUJOLAIS Crus in the far north of the region. Its 560 ha/1,383 acres of vines can produce wines with real backbone, although most should be drunk within two or three years of the vintage.

JULLIEN, ANDRÉ (1766–1832), seminal wine writer, Parisian wine merchant, and one of the first explorers of the *world* of wine, venturing even as far as 'Chinese Tartary' in order to discover and assess all international wine regions and their produce. His was an extraordinary outlook, and it must have been a demanding journey, in an era when his peers barely ventured beyond the threshold of their wine shops. He had clearly read the contemporary literature of wine, which, until that point, concerned itself almost entirely with the details of how to grow vines and how to make wine (see CHAPTAL, for example). His aim was to discover and categorize the characteristics of as many different CRUS as he could find, travelling throughout eastern Europe, along the Silk Road to Asia, as well as discovering the vineyards of Africa. There can be few contemporary wine writers who are as well travelled. The result was the publication in Paris in 1816 of *Topographie de tous les vignobles connus*, a substantial volume full of useful detail which includes the most comprehensive wine CLASSIFICATION (into five classes according to quality) ever undertaken. Much of it was translated into English and published, in abridged form as 'a manual and guide to all importers and purchasers in the choice of wines' in London in 1824. In effect Jullien's work set the style for a high proportion of modern wine writing.

For more details of Jullien's classification, see the LITERATURE OF WINE.

JUMILLA, denominated wine region in the LEVANTE north of Murcia in central, southern Spain (see map on p. 907) producing mainly strong, often coarse, red wines. The climate is arid, with RAINFALL amounting to just 300 mm/11.7 in a year. The principal grape variety in this DO is the red (MOURVÈDRE), which ripens in the summer temperatures of around 40 °C/104 °F to produce wines that can reach a natural ALCOHOLIC STRENGTH of 18 per cent. Average YIELDS of 12 to 15 hl/ha (0.7–0.8 tons/acre) have been uneconomically low, but more recent planting of GRAFTED wines has improved prospects.

Much of the wine from Jumilla was traditionally produced by the DOBLE PASTA method and used for blending with lighter wines from other parts of Spain. The vast San Isidro CO-OPERATIVE dominates the region's production, although since the mid 1980s a number of smaller, private producers have been striving, with some success, to tame Monastrell and produce lighter, more approachable red and rosé wines for export. The Merseguera grape produces rather fat, bland, hot country white wine. R.J.M.

JURA, far eastern French wine region, between Burgundy and Switzerland, that is sufficiently isolated to have retained TRADITION, some unique grape varieties, and such unusual wine types as VIN JAUNE and the occasional VIN DE PAILLE, as well as the local VIN DE LIQUEUR, Macvin du Jura, and a certain amount of MARC du Jura.

Although this was once an important wine region, with nearly 20,000 ha/49,400 acres planted in the early 19th century, there are only about 1,500 ha of vineyards today, on slopes mainly at ALTITUDES of between 250 and 400 m/820–1,310 ft on the first upland between the Bresse plain and the Jura mountains. The chief town is Lons-le-Saunier, although Arbois, L'Étoile, and Ch-Chalon are more famous for their wines. The lower land may be flat CLAY while there is LIMESTONE on higher ground (mirroring that of the CÔTE D'OR on the other side of the Saône). Some slopes are steep enough for SOIL EROSION to require annual treatment. Vines have to be trained high, usually in double GUYOT, in order to avoid autumn frosts, for the harvest here can continue until well into November, so late do some varieties ripen. The climate here is even more CONTINENTAL than in Burgundy and winters can be very cold.

Five grape varieties are of importance in modern Jura (although more than 40 played a role at the end of the 19th century). PINOT NOIR and CHARDONNAY, often known here proprietorially as Melon d'Arbois, have been borrowed from Burgundy, although they have been grown in the Jura vineyards since the Middle Ages. Chardonnay has been increasing in importance here as elsewhere, and had reached 45 per cent of total plantings by the late 1980s. Its early ripening and good sugar levels make it popular with growers, even if it can

Sorting grapes in the vineyard in the **Jura**.

hardly be said to provide the definitive expression of the region. Pinot Noir is valued because it can add useful colour and sometimes structure to the local POULSARD, which is grown chiefly in the north of the region and makes deep coloured rosés, often with an orange tint, sometimes described as *corail*. Poulsard may account for as much as 20 per cent of total vine plantings in Jura. Another local red wine grape variety is TROUSSEAU, now extremely rare. It needs the additional warmth of gravelly soils to ripen and Pinot Noir has largely replaced it, but some producers are capable of fashioning it into a deep flavoured VARIETAL wine.

Jura's really distinctive grape variety, however, is the white SAVAGNIN, also caled Naturé here, which is probably an antecedent of TRAMINER and hence GEWÜRZTRAMINER. Grown to a limited extent all over the region, it is a permitted ingredient in all of its white wines but in practice is chiefly used to produce the extraordinary, nutty, long-lived *vin jaune*, sold in the distinctive *clavelin* squat bottle. (Other Jura wines are mainly sold in another specially shaped bottle with the word Jura stamped on the shoulder.) See CHÂTEAU-CHALON and L'ÉTOILE, which specialize in this unusual drink, France's answer to top-quality dry SHERRY.

See also the more varied appellation ARBOIS. Most Jura appellations produced both sparkling and still wines, and vin de paille may be produced anywhere.

Wine-making techniques are generally traditional, and CHAPTALIZATION is as common as one would expect of a region sited between Burgundy and Switzerland. All grapes must have a POTENTIAL ALCOHOL of 10 per cent (much more for *vin jaune* and vin de paille), and may be chaptalized up to a final ALCOHOLIC STRENGTH of 13.5 per cent.

The wines are distinctive, particularly those which contain the local grape varieties. At their worst they taste like thin burgundy; at their best they are particularly good candidates for FOOD AND WINE MATCHING.

Côtes du Jura is the region's second most important appellation, after Arbois, includes about 630 ha of vines grown in 12 communes, and wines may be red, white, or dark pink; still or sparkling; vinified normally or matured slowly into *vin jaune*. About a fifth of the wine produced is still red or pink. Ch d'Arlay, whose history testifies to Jura's varied past under Burgundy and Spanish domination, is one of the appellation's most notable producers. An increasing proportion of varietal wines are made, whether Chardonnay, Poulsard, Pinot Noir, or even Trousseau. **Côtes du Jura Mousseux** is generally dry white and must be made by the champagne method (see SPARKLING WINE-MAKING).

JURANÇON is a name closely associated with SOUTH WEST FRANCE, of a distinguished white wine both dry and sweet, of a relatively important, if undistinguished, dark-berried vine variety, and of an entirely unimportant light-berried vine.

The wine

This tangy, distinctive white wine has been celebrated and fiercely protected since the Middle Ages, and Jurançon was one of France's earliest APPELLATION CONTRÔLÉES. In the 14th century the princes of BÉARN and the parliament of NAVARRE introduced the concept of a CRU by identifying and valuing specific favoured vineyard sites. Locals claim this as France's first attempt at vineyard CLASSIFICATION, just as they claim the drop of Jurançon with which the infant Henri IV's lips were rubbed at his baptism in 1553 was responsible for most of his subsequent achievements. The Dutch were great enthusiasts for this wine and there was also a flourishing export trade across the Atlantic until PHYLLOXERA almost destroyed the wine. Jurançon's reputation was further advanced in the early 20th century by the enthusiasm of the French writer Colette.

Petit Manseng, Gros Manseng, and a few of the local Courbu, Camaralet, and Lauzet vines are grown on more than 600 ha/1,482 acres of vineyards in this hilly, relatively cool corner of southern France near Pau at the relatively high average ALTITUDE of 300 m/984 ft. Spring FROSTS are such a threat that vines are ESPALIER trained, but the Atlantic influence ensures sufficient RAINFALL.

Gros MANSENG is chiefly responsible for Jurançon Sec, the more common dry but strongly flavoured version of this wine, but Petit Manseng, with its small, thick-skinned berries, is ideal for the production of Jurançon's real speciality, sweet Jurançon made from grapes partially dried on the vine (see PASSERILLÉ). These wines, whose green tinge seems to deepen with age, serve well as aperitifs and with a wide range of foods. This is one of France's best-value SWEET WINES.

The vine varieties

Jurançon vines have in their time been cultivated in practically every region of South West France, other than Jurançon itself. The black- or red-berried version was once the high-yielding ARAMON-like workhorse of this part of France and nearly 4,000 ha were still in production in 1988. This was more than France's total area planted with the much more noble south western red wine vine TANNAT when Jurançon Noir, for example, was by far the most planted dark grape variety in the region producing GAILLAC, even though this Jurançon Noir could only be sold as VIN DE PAYS. Some south western appellations still sanction Jurançon Noir in their red wines, but its inclusion is today usually theoretical. Jurançon Blanc was once quite widely planted in Gascony but is nearly extinct.

JUWEL, white grape variety and one of the GERMAN CROSSINGS. Only about 30 ha/74 acres were planted in Germany in the early 1990s, mainly in the RHEINHESSEN.

K

KABINETT, the most basic Prädikat in the QMP quality wine category defined by the GERMAN WINE LAW. Specific minimum MUST WEIGHTS are laid down for each combination of vine variety and region and are being increased. Because CHAPTALIZATION of QmP wines is not allowed, Kabinett wines are usually the lightest German wines and can make excellent APERITIFS. Their lack of BODY makes them generally less appropriate candidates for TROCKEN wine-making than SPÄTLESE, the next ripest Prädikat. The term used for these distinctly superior and usefully pure wines was once CABINET.

See also AUSTRIA.

KADARKA is the most famous red wine grape of HUNGARY, largely because of the important role it once played in BULL'S BLOOD, but the variety is in marked decline and has been substantially replaced by the viticulturally sturdier KÉKFRANKOS, and KÉKOPORTO in Villány. It is still cultivated on the Great Plain and in the Szekszárd wine region just across the Danube to the west but its tendency to GREY ROT and its habit of ripening riskily late limit it to certain favoured sites. The vine is also naturally highly productive and needs careful control in order to produce truly concentrated wines. Fully ripened Szekszárdi Kadarka can be a fine, tannic, full bodied wine worthy of ageing but is produced in minuscule quantities. Kadarka is too often over-produced and picked when still low in colour and flavour and is no longer the backbone of Hungary's red wine production.

Kadarka's origins are obscure, but some believe it is related to the variety known as Skadarsko, from Lake Scutari, which forms the frontier between ALBANIA and MONTENEGRO.

Today the variety is cultivated on a very limited scale over the eastern border in Burgenland in Austria, over the southern border in VOJVODINA in what was Yugoslavia and in ROMANIA, where it is called Cadarca, and, most importantly, in BULGARIA, where it is called Gamza and is widely planted in the north, where it can produce wines of interest in long growing seasons if yields are restricted.

Because of its, largely historic, fame, this is a variety which is often included in any large NURSERY collection of vine varieties.

KALTERER or **Kalterersee**, German for the TRENTINO and ALTO ADIGE zone known as Caldaro or Lago di Caldaro in Italian.

KANGAROOS can occasionally cause real damage to young vineyards in Australia. See ANIMALS.

KANZLER is a modern German vine crossing already falling from grace. A Müller-Thurgau × Silvaner cross bred at Alzey in 1927 and always essentially a Rheinhessen variety, it reaches high MUST WEIGHTS but needs a good site and, most fatally, does not yield well.

KAZAKHSTAN, independent central Asian republic, member of the CIS. This large area south of RUSSIA and bordering CHINA is subject to great extremes of climate. Its capital in the far south east is Alma-Ata. Less than four per cent of Kazakhstan offers favourable soil and climatic conditions for commercial grape culture.

Australian vine-growers view **kangaroos** as pests.

History

Evidence of grape culture in Kazakhstan dates back to the 7th century AD. The Turkestan area of the Chimkent region (where the grapevine was imported from the Samarkand and the Fergana regions of UZBEKISTAN) and the Panfilov area of the Taldy-Kurgan region (where grapevines are popularly believed to have come from China's western Xinjiang province) are the country's most ancient viticultural areas.

At the end of the 19th century grapes were grown on a small scale by private farms. The development of commercial grape culture began in the 1930s when the first fruit- and wine-growing state farms such as Issyk in the Alma-Ata region, Uch-Bulak in the Dzhambul region, and Juvaly and Kaplanbek in the Chimkent region were established. In 1940 Kazakhstan had 1,700 ha / 4,200 acres of vineyards, the bearing area accounting for only 500 ha, producing just 8,000 hl / 211,200 gal of wine. Viticulture developed rapidly after 1957. Vineyards occupied 4,997 ha in 1958, 16,604 ha in 1966, and 22,311 ha in 1976. Twenty-six specialized fruit- and wine-growing state farms in the south and south east of the country owned 85 per cent of the total vineyard area with the rest divided between collective farms and individuals.

Modern viticulture

The climate of the country is very CONTINENTAL. The active temperature summation varies from 1,800° in the north east to 4,500° in the south, and winters can be very cold indeed with between −30° and −55 °C (−22 and −67 °F) in some areas of the Chimkent region. The average January temperature is −3 °C in the south to −18 °C in the north, while that of July is 28 and 19 °C, respectively. The annual rainfall is 700 to 1,000 mm / 27–39 in in the Zaili and Talas Alatau but is as little as 100 to 150 mm in some areas of the Gur'yev and the Aktyubinsk regions.

Commercial vine culture is principally located in the Chimkent, the Alma-Ata, the Dzhambul, the Kzyl-Ordin, and the Taldy-Kurgan regions. IRRIGATION is the norm, and most vineyards also need WINTER PROTECTION (vines are covered with soil in winter). Vines cultivated in the premountainous zones of the Chimkent and the Alma-Ata regions are laid flat during winter. Vine-TRAINING SYSTEMS include trunkless (see TRUNKED), fan-shaped forms with numerous canes trained in one direction.

At present, 43 grape varieties are allowed for commercial culture, of which 24 are for TABLE GRAPES, an important crop here. Wine varieties include RKATSITELI, RIESLING, PINOT NOIR, SAPERAVI, ALIGOTÉ, ALEATICO, Bayan Shirey, Kuljinski, Maiski Cherny, CABERNET FRANC, CABERNET SAUVIGNON, Rubinovy Magaratcha, Hungarian Muscat (probably MUSCAT OTTONEL), and Muscat Rosé.

The areas best suited for the production of high-quality table wines and sparkling wines are the foothills of the Dzhambul, the Alma-Ata, and the Chimkent regions. Lower and more southern vineyards specialize in dessert wines. In 1990 Kazakhstan's 26,000 ha of vineyard produced a total of 660,000 hl of wine.

Kazakhstan has the potential to become one of the main suppliers of wines and especially grapes to eastern portions of Russia. V.R.

Jangamiyev, A. D., Ponomarchuk, V. P., and Tekhneriadnova, R. T., *Grape Varieties of Kazakhstan* (Russian) (Alma-Ata, 1967).

Jerembayev, E. I., *The Intensification of Kazakhstan's Viticulture* (Russian) (Alma-Ata, 1979).

Madenov, E. D., and Beketayeva, L. I., 'The Soviet Socialist Republic of Kazakhstan' (Russian), in A. I. Timush (ed.), *Encyclopaedia of Viticulture* (Kishinëv, 1986).

Ponomarchuk, V. P., Tekhneriadnova, R. T., Bogdanova, V. S., Bachevski, Y. T., and Madenov, E. D., *Grapes of Kazakhstan* (Russian) (Alma-Ata, 1976).

KÉK means blue in Hungarian and, as such, can be a direct equivalent of BLAU in German or even Noir in French.

KÉKFRANKOS, Hungarian name for the red grape variety known in Austria as BLAUFRÄNKISCH (of which it is a direct translation). This useful variety, which produces lively, juicy, peppery, well-coloured reds for relatively early consumption, is grown widely in HUNGARY. It is most successful in Sopron near the Austrian border although it can also produce full bodied wines in Villány. On the Great Plain its wines can be relatively heavy.

KÉKNYELŰ, revered but rare white grape variety grown in HUNGARY and named after its 'blue' stalk. Once widely planted, it was becoming rare even in its last stronghold Badacsony on the north shore of Lake Balaton in the mid 1990s. The vine itself is so sensitive that yields are extremely low and so it fell from favour in the 1970s and 1980s when wine-making philosophy in Hungary was to produce large quantities of ordinary wine for export to other Comecon countries. True, well-made Kéknyelű can be aromatic and exciting, but some very ordinary blends have been labelled Badacsony Kéknyelű.

KÉKOPORTO, sometimes written **Kékoportó**, useful red grape variety of unknown origins grown in HUNGARY. It produces well-coloured lively red wine not unlike that of KÉKFRANKOS but with a little more body and possibly a better aptitude for cask ageing. It is grown in the red wine region of Villány where it can yield wines of real concentration, is an ingredient in BULL'S BLOOD, and is also grown, with slightly less success, on the Great Plain. It is often called simply Oporto (*kék* means blue) and its name suggests a relationship with the variety known in German as PORTUGIESER; it may even be identical. It is also grown in ROMANIA.

KELLER is German for a cellar, even a small domestic cellar, while **Kellerei** is used in much the same way as the word CAVE in French, for any sort of wine-producing premises whether above or below ground. A German wine specifying a Keller rather than a WEINGUT on the label is usually the produce of a merchant rather than an estate. In ALTO ADIGE, the Italian Tyrol, **Kellereigenossenschaft** is a common name for one of the many wine CO-OPERATIVES. **Kellermeister** is German for cellarmaster, a position very similar to MAÎTRE-DE-CHAI in France.

KENYA. Very limited production of wines from this African country virtually on the equator. Since the mid 1980s *vinifera* vines have been cultivated and have been harvested every eight months, providing three vintages every two years, chiefly from vineyards around Lake Naivasha. Rainy seasons are March to May and October to December and some producers may revert to one growing season from June to September. Best white wines have been made from Sauvignon Blanc grapes together with some experimental Chardonnay, Colombard, and Chenin Blanc, while some decent red wine has been made from Ruby Cabernet with some Carnelian. The pioneer growers were John and Guy d'Olier of Lake Naivasha Vineyards. Until the early 1990s wine was bottled and marketed exclusively by the Kenya government. J.P.

KERNER is the great success story of modern German vine breeding. Bred only in 1969, four or five decades after crossings such as SCHEUREBE, FABER, and HUXELREBE, Kerner had almost overtaken the ancient SILVANER to become Germany's third most planted vine by 1990, presumably because it ripens so reliably almost anywhere. As with most 20th century crossings, the bulk of Germany's 8,000 ha/19,760 acres of Kerner are planted in the Rheinhessen and Pfalz but it is still popular in Württemberg, where it was bred from a red parent TROLLINGER (Schiava Grossa) × Riesling. The large white berries produce wines commendably close to Riesling in flavour except with their own leafy aroma and very slightly coarser texture. It is a crossing which does not need to be subsumed in the blending vat but can well produce fine varietal wines, up to quite high PRÄDIKAT levels, on its own account. Of the 20th century *vinifera* crossings, only the more capricious EHRENFELSER is as Riesling-like, both crossings having the ability to age thanks to their high acidity. Kerner is popular with growers as well as wine drinkers because of its late budding and therefore good frost resistance. It is so vigorous, however, that it needs careful summer trimming. It ripens slightly later than Müller-Thurgau, about the same time as Silvaner, but can be planted in almost any vineyard site and regularly achieves MUST WEIGHTS and acidity levels 10 to 20 per cent above the dreary Müller-Thurgau.

Kerner, which takes its name not from any vine breeder but from a local 19th century writer of drinking songs, has also been planted in South Africa but it seems unlikely that there is a long future for it there.

The variety is planted to a limited extent in ENGLAND.

KEVEDINKA, ordinary white eastern European grape variety. See DINKA.

KIR, alternative name for a *vin blanc cassis*, dry white wine and blackcurrant liqueur, named after a hero of the Burgundian resistance movement during the Second World War, Canon Kir who was also mayor of Dijon. The CÔTE D'OR is an important grower of blackcurrants and most of the best-quality blackcurrant liqueurs, or *eaux-de-vie de cassis*, are made here. The typical base wine is the relatively acid Bourgogne ALIGOTÉ and to most palates a dash of full-strength liqueur is all that is needed. In France, however, the *cassis* may make up to a fifth of the mix.

KLEIN KAROO, inland wine region in SOUTH AFRICA.

KLEVNER, like CLEVNER, is, and more particularly was, used fairly indiscriminately in Alsace and other German-speaking wine regions for various vine varieties, notably but not exclusively for CHARDONNAY and various members of the PINOT family. References to Klevner or **Klevener** in Alsace in the mid 16th century are common.

Klevner or **Klevener de Heiligenstein** is an Alsace oddity, wine made in the village of Heiligenstein from the particular strain of the related SAVAGNIN Rose and GEWÜRZTRAMINER introduced to the village (see GERMAN HISTORY), probably from Chiavenna in the Italian alps. It has been a speciality for at least two centuries, although barely 20 ha/49 acres are planted today.

KLÖCH, wine centre in Styria in AUSTRIA, now part of the Süd-Oststeiermark district.

KLOSTER EBERBACH, monastery in the RHEINGAU region of Germany with a tradition of viticulture; now seen as the cultural wine centre of the Rheingau. Kloster Eberbach was founded in 1135 by Bernard of Clairvaux. Throughout the Middle Ages Cistercian monks produced wine at the monastery, and made its name as one of the most important wine estates of its time. Through viticultural enterprise, the monastery became extremely powerful, owning a fleet of ships which sailed the Rhine.

Kloster Eberbach is now the home of the educational organization the German Wine Academy and the Rheingau Wine Society. It also provides a regional centre for wine auctions, trade fairs, and seminars. The Lay Brothers' Refectory houses a collection of historic wine presses, dating back to 1668. The Steinberg vineyard, planted by monks 700 years ago next to the monastery, is still producing highly rated wines.

See also MONKS AND MONASTERIES. S.A.

KLOSTERNEUBURG, city on the Danube west of Vienna in AUSTRIA whose Augustinian monastery has since the 11th century been a substantial vineyard owner and wine producer and has, since 1860, been the country's centre for viticultural and OENOLOGICAL research. Austria's standard measurement of grape ripeness or MUST WEIGHT is the KMW, or Klosterneuburger Mostwage, which is equivalent to 5° OECHSLE. Klosterneuburg's total vineyard holdings, spread over the districts of Vienna, Thermenregion to the immediate south of the capital, and Donauland-Carnuntum, of which the abbey is in effect the wine capital, constitute the country's largest estate with more than 100 ha/247 acres. Klosterneuburg wines are made by a company owned by the monastic order,

The original Cabinet Keller at **Kloster Eberbach** where once the monastery's finest wines, including the famous Steinberger, were matured in cask for up to 28 years.

and are bottled in their own special squat bottle. The cellars also house the Austrian State Wine Archive and there is both a quality control centre and an oenological school. Research activity is wide ranging but centred on developing vine crossings as well as pest control and general oenological and viticultural matters. In the 1920s Dr Zweigelt developed several successful vine variety crossings at Klosterneuburg which are widely planted in modern Austria (see ZWEIGELT).

KMW, measure of MUST WEIGHT in AUSTRIA. See KLOSTERNEUBURG.

KNIGHTS VALLEY, California wine region and AVA. See SONOMA.

KNIPPERLÉ is now almost a relic, a dark-berried vine once much more popular as the base of light white wine in Alsace. This early ripening subvariety of RÄUSCHLING was introduced in 1756 by Johann Michael Ortlieb and it was therefore alternatively known as Ortlieber (see GERMAN HISTORY). Occasional bottles can still be found but this variety, relatively popular as a high yielder and early ripener at the end of the 19th century, is too prone to rot to be of more than historical interest.

KOSHER wine satisfies the strict rabbinical production criteria that make it suitable for consumption by religious Jews. Wine has always played an important part in Jewish ritual, is mentioned frequently in the BIBLE, and was produced in Palestine, as attested by archeological excavations, until the Muslim conquest of AD 636, when all alcoholic beverages were banned (see ISLAM).

The rabbis on the other hand encouraged moderate wine consumption as good for HEALTH. Wine was the constant thread through Jewish festivals since it is sipped as the sabbath starts (Kiddush) and again when it ends (Havdala) with the blessing: 'Blessed are You, Lord our God, king of the universe, who creates the fruit of the vine.' Because wine has been used by numerous cults associated with idol worship, Jews insisted that wines destined for sacramental use should be made exclusively by religious Jews, to avoid contamination by non-believers.

These 'kosher' (meaning literally 'right' or 'correct') wines are produced under strict supervision of the rabbinate, and only sabbath-observing, strictly orthodox Jews are allowed involvement with the production and bottling processes. Some rabbis insist on the wine's being 'boiled' (subjected to PASTEURIZATION) so that non-Jews, heathens, would no longer recognize it as wine and there would be no danger of their using it for their religious rites. The treated wine, 'meshuval', regrettably loses most of its qualities, even if modern flash-pasteurization techniques are used.

Wines described as 'kosher for Passover' have not come into contact with bread, dough, or leavened dough.

Kosher wine produced in ISRAEL must conform to the following strict dietary laws:

1. No wine may be produced from a vine until its fourth year.
2. The vineyard, if within the biblical lands, must be left fallow every seven years.
3. Only vines may be grown in vineyards.
4. From arrival at the winery, the grapes and resulting wine may only be handled by strictly sabbath-observing Jews, and only 100 per cent kosher materials may be used in the wine-making, maturation, and bottling processes.

Of these laws, the second is the most expensive to keep and is sometimes circumnavigated by temporary sale of the vineyard to a Gentile for the relevant year, followed by repurchase. The vines have to be tended every year to keep the vineyard in good condition.

In practice, kosher winery employees include many non-sabbath-observing Jews who may be allowed to handle freshly picked grapes but not must or wine. Wine technologists or oenologists who are not themselves sabbath-observing may instruct observant Jews to carry out the necessary physical operations in the winery.

Any winery outside Israel can make kosher wine provided that the fourth law is strictly observed. Good kosher wines are made each year in various parts of France, Italy, South Africa, Morocco, Australia, and the United States, and some kosher wine for local consumption is made in most wine-producing countries. P.A.H.

KOSOVO, small south central republic in what was YUGOSLAVIA between MACEDONIA, SERBIA, and ALBANIA. Its 10,000 ha/24,700 acres of vineyards in spectacular inland mountain and valley settings are largely devoted to the production of Amselfelder branded wine for sale in Germany. Trainloads of light red are sent in bulk to Belgrade for STABILIZATION, sweetening, and shipment. The light aromatic fruit of the PINOT NOIR was certainly the inspiration behind this brand. CABERNET FRANC, MERLOT, PROKUPAC, and GAMAY are also part of the region's production.

Kosovo is a poor region and throughout the 1980s was heavily dependent on its exports of the Amselfelder range. This dependence became a serious liability when Yugoslav turmoil made the German importers realize how easily other eastern European vineyard areas could copy the style.

A.H.M.

KÖVIDINKA, ordinary white eastern European grape variety. See DINKA.

KRATER. See CRATER.

KREMS, important wine town in lower AUSTRIA, now part of the Kamptal-Donauland district.

KRUG, small but important Champagne house founded in Rheims in 1843 by Johann-Joseph Krug, who was born in Mainz, Germany, in 1830. By 1893 the firm occupied its current modest cellars, around whose courtyard the Krug family still live. Krug does not make an ordinary NON-VINTAGE champagne, but sells its non-dated Grande Cuvée at the same price as other houses' PRESTIGE CUVÉES, and at almost the same price as its own vintage-dated champagne. Consistently producing champagne that is among the most admired in its region of origin, Krug is the only house to persist in BARREL FERMENTATION of its entire production of base wine, in old 205-l/54-gal casks. Wines from at least six and sometimes nine different vintages make up the blend for Grande Cuvée, one of the most distinctive and long lived of champagnes. Grande Cuvée, with new packaging and a special bottle, succeeded the rather fuller bodied Private Cuvée as Krug's most important product in 1979. In 1971 Krug acquired and replanted the Clos de Mesnil, a walled vineyard of less than 2 ha/5 acres. Its Chardonnay grapes provide one of Champagne's very few single-vineyard, or CRU, wines of which the 1979 vintage was the first. Although the firm is run by members of the fifth and sixth generation of champagne-making Krugs, the majority of the shares are now held by Rémy-Cointreau, which also owns RÉMY MARTIN cognac.

Arlott, J., *Krug: House of Champagne* (London, 1976).

KRUG, CHARLES (1825–92), German-born American wine producer, came to San Francisco in 1852 as a newspaper editor. After vineyard ventures in San Mateo and SONOMA, perhaps at the urging of HARASZTHY, Krug settled in the NAPA Valley in 1860. He had been employed as a seasonal wine-maker there since 1858. In 1861 he founded a winery near St Helena and operated it with great success until his death, although in the crash of 1885 he was forced to file for bankruptcy. Krug was not the first Napa Valley wine-maker but he soon became the most eminent of his day and inevitably came to be called the 'father of Napa wine'. His success came in part because he understood public relations and because he developed his own sales organization. His winery was technically advanced, and he seems to have made good wine. Krug was also prominent in industry affairs as an original member of the Board of State Viticultural Commissioners. The winery he founded was acquired by the MONDAVI family in 1943 and is still notable among Napa Valley establishments, although Robert Mondavi has not worked there since an acrimonious dispute with his brother Peter in 1965.

Although Charles Krug did not come from a German wine region (he was born near Kassel), he exemplifies the important contribution to pioneer wine-growing made by Germans in all parts of the USA where the vine was successfully cultivated. T.P.

Henri **Krug** blending up to 50 different wines for a single cuvée.

KWV, the South African Co-operative Winegrowers Association, or Ko-operatiewe Wijnbowers Vereniging van Zuid Afrika, is the 4,900-grower body which, uniquely, has combined the functions of producer, marketing bódy, and statutory government control board, only gradually releasing its tight grip on the country's wine industry in the early 1990s. It was established in 1918 after years of glut and grower bankruptcy and enforced production quota limits to prevent unmanageable surpluses. It also fixed annual minimum wine prices.

These powers—weighted in favour of producers rather than consumers and often oblivious to market forces—were criticized by free-marketeers and some producers themselves who, even if non-members, were subject by law to KWV regulations. The KWV argues it spared government the embarrassment of the direct grower subsidies.

Grower subsidies, however, have been indirect. Wine co-operatives and farmers enjoyed Land Bank credit terms well below commercial interest rates. These were not available to non-whites and land ownership was opened to all races only in 1991. Wine, alone among alcoholic drinks in South Africa, was exempt until 1991 from excise duty.

The industry's structure was the subject of close scrutiny as the country moved deeper into its post-apartheid phase; the new authorities inevitably wish to erode many of the powers and privileges previously enjoyed by the all-white grower body.

Meanwhile, less than half the annual harvest of about 1 million tons becomes table wine. The KWV's 70 co-operative wineries produce 85 per cent of each vintage, with two-thirds of this total consigned to the production of BRANDY and other distilled products as well as GRAPE CONCENTRATE which in 1993 accounted for most of the wine industry's exports by volume. The KWV exports a wide range of table wines, including blends such as as Roodeberg (made up of Cabernet Sauvignon, Shiraz, Pinotage, and Tinta Barocca), and has a wide range of FORTIFIED WINES made in the image of port and sherry.

Most top-quality South African table wine, however, comes from private producers, a few wholesaler-producers, and individual estates which make wine as well as grow their own grapes (fewer than 80 in the early 1990s). The biggest wholesalers, Stellenbosch Farmers' Winery (SFW) and Distillers Corporation (selling under the name Bergkelder, or 'mountain cellar'), together with the KWV, have controlled the great majority of South Africa's vine-related alcohol products since 1979.

The KWV's functions include research, vine propagation, advisory services, administrating the WINE OF ORIGIN system, wine education, and marketing campaigns. These activities are co-ordinated from the KWV's 22 ha/55 acres depot at Paarl, 60 km/37 miles north of Cape Town. J.P.

Fridjhon, M., and Murray, A., *Conspiracy of Giants* (Johannesburg, 1986).
KWV, *South African Wine Industry Statistics* (Paarl, 1992).

KYRGYZSTAN, mountainous central Asian republic of the CIS on the border between KAZAKHSTAN and China. Kyrgyzstan, whose capital is Bishkek, has extremely varied topography, soil, and climatic conditions. The country has a continental climate and Kyrgyzstan has three zones favourable for viticulture: the Chuia and the Talas valleys, the south of the country, and the Issyk-Kul depression. Commercial viticulture is developed in the first two zones. Depending on altitude, the average January temperature in the Chuia valley is −6 to 7 °C/21–45 °F and the average July temperature is 23 to 25 °C, while in the south of the country (the Osh region) the average January and July temperatures are −3 to 6 °C and 24 to 25 °C, respectively. The active temperature summation is 3,300 to 3,500 °C. The annual rainfall in the north is 250 to 550 mm/10–21 in and 270 to 600 mm in the south. The climate of the Chuia and the Talas valleys is hot and continental yet more moderate than in the south. Vineyards are located at an altitude of 600 to 1,100 m/1,970–3,610 ft.

The country's grape and wine industry specializes in the production of TABLE GRAPES and DRYING GRAPES although more than 150,000 hl/3.9 million gal of wine, mostly strong and sweet, was produced from the country's 9,000 ha/22,230 acres of vineyard in 1990.

In the south of Kyrgyzstan (the Dzhalal-Abad and Osh regions) vineyards may bear as high as 2,000 m above sea level while grapes are mostly cultivated at an altitude of 500 to 750 m. This area produces central Asian varieties destined for drying or the production of sweet, heavy wine.

The Issyk-Kul depression is at an altitude of 1,600 to 1,800 m, around Lake Issyk-Kul. This viticultural region does not experience large temperature fluctuations. Because the July average daily temperature is 18 °C and that of January is 3 °C, no WINTER PROTECTION is needed. The central part of this region, on the south and north banks of Lake Issyk-Kul, is particularly favourable for viticulture and the production of dessert wines and base materials for sparkling wines (see also CHINA).

By the beginning of the 20th century, the north portion of Kyrgyzstan had only 13 farms with more than 5 ha of vineyard. Development of the grape and wine industry came in the 1940s. In 1940, the total vineyard area was 300 ha. Vine varieties PINOT NOIR, Tavkveri, ALIGOTÉ, and RIESLING occupied 15 ha and the rest was planted to table grapes. Between 1942 and 1950, the first state farms specializing in wine production were established. In 1949 vineyards occupied 1,100 ha; in 1960 the total vineyard area was 3,500 ha; and in 1966 it was 6,100 ha.

Practically all vineyards in Kyrgyzstan have some form of IRRIGATION, depending on the zone of cultivation, and are given winter protection. Vineyards use trellises (trunkless FAN-shaped and semi-fan-shaped forms and oblique CORDON systems are especially widely used) as well as the goblet-shaped head type forms used in MOLDOVA, spread forms (without posts), and some vines are even grown up trees. Wine varieties account for up to 85 per cent of the gross yield of grapes.

Forty-five grape varieties are recognized, including 23 wine varieties such as RKATSITELI, PINOT NOIR, Bayan Shirey, Kuljinski, CABERNET SAUVIGNON, RIESLING, SAPERAVI, Budeshiru Tetri, Mairam, Mourvèdre Kirghizski, Hungarian Muscat, and Black Muscat. Table varieties include CINSAUT, and MADELEINE ANGEVINE. V.R.

Gareyev, E. Z. (ed.), *The Principles of Fruit Growing and Viticulture* (Russian) (Frunze, 1966).
Kazanski, S. L., 'The Soviet Socialist Republic of Kirghizia' (Russian), *Vinodelie i vinogradarstvo SSSR*, 6 (1967), 45–6.
Sosina, E. I., 'The Soviet Socialist Republic of Kirghizia' (Russian), in A. I. Timush (ed.), *Encyclopaedia of Viticulture* (Kishinev, 1986).
Yanpolskaya, M. A., 'Viticulture and enology of Kirghizia' (Russian), *Vinodelie i vinogradarstvo SSSR*, 6 (1962), 54–7.

L

LABEL, the principal means by which a wine producer or bottler can communicate with a potential customer and consumer (although see also BOTTLE, CASE, FOIL).

Wine labels are a relatively recent development, which awaited the widespread sale of bottled wine, and use of glues strong enough to stick to glass in about 1860. Before then wines were sold unlabelled and stacked in BINS, and served in decanters, so BIN LABELS and DECANTER LABELS are the precursors of today's wine bottle label. For many years wines were identified by branded CORKS rather than by paper labels, as vintage PORT may still be today.

Every wine in commercial circulation has to have a main label, as its passport quite apart from its function as a sales aid. Many wines also have a **neck label**, typically carrying the VINTAGE year so that the producer need not have new main labels printed for each new vintage (although labelling requirements can change so rapidly that in practice this sometimes seems necessary). See LABELLING INFORMATION for details of the information available on a main label. As wine consumers have become ever more sophisticated and curious, however, an increasing proportion of bottles carry a **back label** giving additional background information. This can vary from a genuinely useful outline of grape varieties used, vintage conditions, approximate SWEETNESS level, and serving advice, to a collection of fine-sounding words involving the 'finest' grape varieties picked at 'perfect ripeness' in 'optimum conditions' and vinified according to the 'highest standards', but which contain no genuine information whatsoever. Now that the amount of mandatory information required on wine labels is so considerable, some design-conscious bottlers try to beat the system by conveying all of this detail on what is obviously meant to be the back label, while applying a dramatic design statement without all the clutter of the mandatory information which the retailer, but not the labelling inspector, is meant to treat as the main label.

Labels matter to lawyers and officials, and they matter enormously to the retail wine trade, in which they communicate far more effectively with many consumers than any recommendation or award, but they are relatively unimportant to wine sales from a list, such as by mail or in the hotel and restaurant industry. The efforts of some new wine producers to design a really distinctive label may often be wasted, although they may be appreciated. The Italians have been as innovative in label design as in that of bottles, and some NEW WORLD designs can be arresting, effective, innovative, and sometimes all three. ARTISTS' LABELS have a certain following. Producers of established wines have usually inherited a label and rarely do anything more than slightly modify it (although even most of the established Bordeaux CLASSED GROWTHS have incorporated some design modification into their labels in the last 10 years). The fact that the label of Ch PÉTRUS would win no design award seems to do little to hinder sales. The label design of wine BRANDS, however, is an extremely important factor in their success. One of the most evocative labels is that used for MATEUS Rosé, depicting a beautiful palace in northern Portugal which has nothing whatever to do with the wine. The owner, who was offered the choice of a one-off payment or a royalty per label printed, was unwise enough to choose the former.

Labels are usually, but not always, applied straight after BOTTLING as part of the same mechanized process. Some small-scale producers still apply their labels by hand with pots of glue. Producers of champagne and other sparkling wines take particular care to use strong, water-resistant adhesive in applying their labels since their bottles are likely to spend their last hours in public circulation immersed in a bucket of water.

Wine labels have such a fascination of their own, and can help recollection of the circumstances of their consumption, that wine **label collecting** is a recognized activity. Some of those who practise it call themselves vintitulists.

Butler, R., *The Book of Wine Antiques* (Woodbridge, 1986).
Joseph, R., *The Art of the Wine Label* (London, 1987).

LABELLING INFORMATION. The amount of information required on wine LABELS seems to increase dramatically each year. The following are the main categories of usually mandatory information, with national or international minimum criteria (which may be stricter on a local or regional basis).

Wine designation: wines made within the European Union have to be identified as to whether they qualify as TABLE WINE, QUALITY WINE, or one of several specific intermediate categories such as France's VIN DE PAYS or Germany's LANDWEIN. They will accordingly carry one of the descriptions listed under these headings (Appellation Contrôlée, or Vino de Mesa, for example). Labels on wines made outside the European Union have to carry the tell-tale word 'wine' when travelling within Europe. In the United States, wines are usually identified as 'table wine'. See DESIGNATION.

Geographical reference: this may take the form of the name of a country (as in Greek table wine, for example), or the name of an AVA or any other state or smaller region in the

① RHEINPFALZ
② 1988
③ Winzerdorfer Rebberg
④ Riesling, Halbtrocken ⑤
⑥ Qualitätswein b. A.
⑦ A.P.-Nr. 516 987 89
Alc. 10,5% vol.
0,75 l. ℮
⑧ Erzeugerabfüllung Winzer Bacchus, Winzerdorf

Geographic origin, grape variety, the degree of ripeness at harvest and the wine maker's individual style determine a wine's taste. And German wine labels provide all the information you need to select the right wine.

Example of a German Wine Label:

① The specific growing region: one of the eleven designated regions in Germany.

② The year in which the grapes were harvested.

③ The town and the vineyard from which the grapes come. (In this case a hypothetical example.)

④ The grape variety.

⑤ The taste or style of the wine. In this case, medium-dry.

⑥ The quality level of the wine, indicating ripeness of the grapes at harvest.

⑦ The official testing number: proof that the wine has passed analytical and sensoric testing required for all German Quality Wines.

⑧ Wines bottled and produced by the grower or a cooperative of growers may be labeled "Erzeugerabfüllung" (estate-bottled). Other wineries and bottlers are identified as "Abfüller".

Labelling information the German way.

United States, or could be the name of a tiny controlled appellation (such as BOCA in north west Italy, for example). In France this is often written Appellation X Contrôlée, where X is the name of the geographical reference, or even Appellation d'Origine X Contrôlée. Within Europe, if a geographical zone is cited on the label, all the wine should come from this zone. In the United States, if an AVA is stated on the label, then 85 per cent should come from that area. Eighty-five per cent of an Australian wine must also come from the region specified. Exported wine has to carry the name of the country of origin.

Volume of wine: this is most likely to be 75 cl/27 fl oz but must, quite rightly, be stated on all labels. See BOTTLE SIZES and BOXES.

Alcoholic strength: this is usually stated as a percentage followed by '% vol' but may be expressed in degrees (°) or, in Italy in particular, as 'gradi'. See ALCOHOLIC STRENGTH.

Vintage year: within Europe, a vintage may not be stated for a TABLE WINE, and, wherever it is stated, at least 85 per cent of the wine should be the produce of that year. See VINTAGE and NON-VINTAGE.

Name and address of producer or bottler: this is usually provided in a fairly straightforward fashion, although, within Europe, an address which happens to incorporate the name of a controlled appellation cannot be used on the label of a table wine, or even a vin de pays, so some sort of postal code has to be substituted.

Bottling information: the relationship between the source of the grapes and the producer or bottler is indicated by exactly how this is expressed. See BOTTLING INFORMATION for more details.

On a CHAMPAGNE label, the following codes printed next to the registered number of the bottler are useful:

NM: *négociant-manipulant*, one of the big houses/firms/négociants;
RM: *récoltant-manipulant*, a grower who makes his own wine;
CM: *coopérative de manipulation*, one of the co-operatives;
RC: *récoltant-coopérateur*, grower selling wine made by a co-op;
MA: *marque d'acheteur*, buyer's own brand;
SR: *société de récoltant*, a small family company (rare);
R: *récoltant*, very small-scale growers (very rare).

Varietal information: this is entirely optional, but, if a variety is specified on a label of wine in Europe, then it must comprise at least 85 per cent of the wine. In the United States it must comprise at least 75 per cent (or 51 per cent in the case of some particularly FOXY native varieties: see NEW YORK). In Australia it must comprise at least 85 per cent of the stated variety.

Gratuitous government interference: in some countries wine labels have to carry 'warnings', usually as a result of some scientifically vague but much-publicized connection between wine and ill HEALTH. In the United States labels on all wine have to warn that pregnant women and those in charge of heavy machinery are ill advised to consume any or much of it. In several countries, including the UNITED STATES, all wine labels must warn 'contains sulfites'. In Australia all additives must be mentioned, so a label may say 'contains antioxidant (300) and preservative (220)', 300 and 220 being the respective numerical codes for ERYTHORBIC ACID and SULPHUR DIOXIDE. Sulphur dioxide is used to a certain extent in the making of virtually all wine, therefore virtually all wine contains sulfites, or SULPHITES. Wine labels all over the world have had to be redesigned because, unfortunately, severe asthmatics can suffer if they consume excessive amounts of sulphites (which are present, in much higher concentrations, in a wide range of other products such as fruit juices).

Sweetness: see SWEETNESS.

Fizziness: see FIZZINESS.

Colour: see COLOUR.

LABOUR. Viticulture, unlike wine-making, has long required a substantial input of labour. The Romans used slaves while MONKS AND MONASTERIES played an important part in medieval vine-growing. A peasant class was long necessary to maintain viticulture in Europe, and increasingly vineyard labour was paid for by leasing part of the vineyard to the labourer, share-cropping or, in French, *métayage*. The close association between vine-growing and humans began to alter as the closing decade of the 20th century approached, however, mainly because of changes in technology.

There have traditionally been three levels of labour input to viticulture: man alone, man plus draught animal, and man plus machines. In ancient vineyards all work was done by man, which consisted of digging WEEDS, PRUNING, TRIMMING, DESUCKERING, LAYERING, HARVESTING. The labour input was high, and vineyards on the plains required between 70 and 80 man-days per hectare per year. This means that any one person might tend about 3 ha, with due allowance for using other labour at times of peak demand such as harvesting and pruning. The YIELD from such vineyards was not high compared to modern standards. A generous 33.5 hl/ha (2 tons/acre) meant that one man's labour might produce a maximum of about 15 tonnes of grapes. For HILLSIDE VINEYARDS one man might tend only about 100 sq m of vineyard, although this was not necessarily full-time work, with a likely output of tens of kilograms of grapes per person per year. Such vineyards relying totally on manual labour are increasingly rare, as the price of labour has increased much more than the price of wine, but some may be found all around the Mediterranean.

Intensive labour input continued for many vineyards up until the mid to late 19th century, when the invasion of POWDERY MILDEW, DOWNY MILDEW, and PHYLLOXERA led to the need for SPRAYING, and rootstocks. Previously many vineyards had been planted haphazardly without rows, and with high density, almost like a field of wheat. As need be, unhealthy vines were replaced by LAYERING from adjacent vines. With the need to spray, and also for ploughing, draught animals became more common, not only horses but also mules and oxen. Indeed milk cows were also used; in France's Auvergne, for example, cows provided meat, milk, and labour. Vines then needed to be planted in rows to make easy the passage of the animal, and there were typically many fewer plants per hectare because of the cost of GRAFTING plants on rootstocks. One horse was able to work 7 ha, and one man was needed for every 3 ha. A typical family farm consisted of about 7 ha of vines, one horse with two drivers, and one labourer.

Since the Second World War the pattern of viticulture has changed in France and elsewhere with the widespread introduction of MECHANIZATION. This was no simple matter, as there were conflicts between generations of farmers about replacing horses with tractors, and substantial changes in the support services in rural villages. Mechanics and fuel salesmen replaced blacksmiths and fodder merchants. In the end economic necessity determined the future; one man and a tractor was now able to tend 30 ha of vineyards, although with manual labour including pruning, trimming, and harvesting, 1 ha still required 43 days' work throughout the year.

In the 1960s, the mechanization revolution intensified. Ploughing had been largely replaced by HERBICIDES, and then there was the introduction of MECHANICAL HARVESTING followed by MECHANICAL PRUNING. Some sprays were even applied from the air, using aeroplanes or HELICOPTERS. There are some vineyards in south eastern Australia where in the 1990s the total annual labour input is less than 50 man-hours per hectare: all operations are carried out mechanically including harvesting and pruning; spraying is conducted from the air; and weed control is by herbicides. On large estates, one worker is required for each 30 ha with this degree of mechanization, and the output can be more than 500 tonnes of wine grapes. This figure, compared with less than 15 tonnes per person about a century earlier, demonstrates how productivity has increased through mechanization.

Future trends are not obvious. It is unlikely that robots will replace vineyard labour to any significant extent, although a robot capable of pruning vineyards was developed in France in the 1980s. The variability of vineyards, of terrain, and of the weather make the task of robot development more difficult than for the factory floor.

It seems likely however that an increasing proportion of vineyard tasks will be mechanized, even in countries where labour resources are not necessarily limiting or expensive. Mechanization is seen to offer benefits of timeliness as well as of economics which encourage its further adoption.

Once the grapes have been delivered to the winery, wine-making requires relatively little labour. A WINE-MAKER is required to make decisions and, increasingly, program a computer which may control such operations as TEMPERATURE CONTROL and RACKING wine from one container to another.

Only BARREL MATURATION and, especially, LEES STIRRING require much manual labour (see CELLAR WORK). Otherwise, cleaning is the chief operation. R.E.S.

Coombe, B. G., and Dry, P. R. (eds.), *Viticulture, ii: Practices* (Adelaide, 1992).

Galet, P., *Précis de viticulture* (4th edn., Montpellier, 1983).

LABRUSCA, species of the *Vitis* genus native to North America. The juice of its grapes, and wine made from them, usually have a pronounced flavour described as FOXY. See VITIS for more details.

LABRUSCANA, North American term for a native vine variety with at least one *Vitis* LABRUSCA parent, whose grapes have a FOXY flavour. *Labruscanas* may be either a HYBRID, incorporating genes from another species, or a CROSS with two *Vitis labrusca* parents. For more details see VITIS, UNITED STATES, and NEW YORK.

LACCASE, a powerful oxidative ENZYME particularly associated with BOTRYTIS BUNCH ROT.

LA CLAPE. See CLAPE.

LACTIC ACID, one of the milder ACIDS in wine, present in much lower concentrations than either MALIC ACID or TARTARIC ACID. Lactic acid, named after *lactis*, Latin for milk, is most frequently encountered as the principal acid in yoghurt, sour milk, pickled cucumbers, and sauerkraut. Lactic acid is a common participant in both plant and animal metabolic processes. It is the end-product of intense muscular activity in animals (see ACIDS); a by-product of the alcoholic FERMENTATION process in wines and beers; and the end-product of the metabolic action of the many LACTIC BACTERIA.

In wine, lactic acid can be produced by bacteria both from traces of sugar and from malic acid. The function of the second MALOLACTIC FERMENTATION which a high proportion of red wines and some white wines undergo is to transform harsh malic acid into the much milder lactic acid.

The lactic acid used in commerce is almost invariably produced synthetically, and is used as an acidulant in food and drink production (in cases where tartaric or CITRIC ACID would be considered too tart) as well as in many industrial processes. A.D.W.

LACTIC BACTERIA, an abbreviation of **lactic acid producing bacteria**, known by some wine-makers simply as **lactics**, are some of the few BACTERIA that can survive in such an acidic solution as wine. They all produce LACTIC ACID and can be subdivided into the three genera *Lactobacillus*, *Leuconostoc oenos*, and *Pediococcus*. They are involved in the production of pickles, sauerkraut, and yoghurt as well as being the agents of MALOLACTIC FERMENTATION in wines, by which the harsh MALIC ACID is effectively decomposed into the milder lactic acid.

Lactic bacteria function best in environments that contain very small amounts of OXYGEN, which is why their growth in grapes is limited. Lactic bacteria inhabit wooden vats and barrels in traditional wineries and can be so deeply embedded in the wood fibres that even the highest standards of HYGIENE are unable to remove them. They can have the positive effect of precipitating malolactic fermentation in wines with an excess of malic acid. In newer wineries lactic bacteria may need to be deliberately introduced to achieve this effect. Unfortunately, however, many strains of lactic bacteria can generate off-flavours and turbidity in wines. This is most likely to happen when traces of sugar remain as nutrients in the wine.

Fortunately, however, lactic bacteria are very sensitive to SULPHUR DIOXIDE and are much easier to control than ACETOBACTER, the other group of bacteria of wine-making importance. Lactic bacteria grow best in very weakly acidic solutions and at temperatures near those of the human body. Bacteriologists regard them as 'fastidious' in that they require a wide range of micro-nutrients. They are also intolerant of high concentrations of ETHANOL.

Their effect on new wine can therefore be limited by sulphur dioxide, low temperatures, and frequent RACKING so as to eliminate the possibility of providing micro-nutrients from the YEAST decomposition products in the LEES. A.D.W.

LADOIX, the appellation from the village of **Ladoix-Serrigny** in the Côte de Beaune district of Burgundy's Côte d'Or producing mostly red wines from Pinot Noir grapes. They are more frequently sold as Côte de Beaune Villages (see BEAUNE, CÔTE DE). Although there are 14 ha/34 acres of Ladoix PREMIERS CRUS, a further 8 ha of the best-placed vineyards are sold as Aloxe-Corton premier cru. Furthermore, 6 ha of Corton-Charlemagne and 22 ha (out of 160) of Le Corton, including part of Le Rognet and Les Vergennes, are actually sited in Ladoix (see ALOXE-CORTON for more details).

As well as the Corton-Charlemagne, a tiny amount of white Ladoix-Serrigny is made from Chardonnay or Pinot Blanc.

See also CÔTE D'OR and its map. J.T.C.M.

LAFITE, CHÂTEAU, subsequently **Ch Lafite-Rothschild**, FIRST GROWTH in the MÉDOC region of BORDEAUX. The vineyard, to the north of the small town of PAUILLAC and adjoining Ch MOUTON-ROTHSCHILD, was probably planted in the last third of the 17th century. Inherited in 1716 by the SÉGURS, who also owned Ch LATOUR, it was sold in 1784 to Pierre de Pichard, an extremely rich president of the Bordeaux Parlement who perished on the scaffold. The estate was confiscated and sold as public property in 1799 to a Dutch consortium which in 1803 resold it to a Dutch grain merchant and supplier to Napoleon's armies, Ignace-Joseph Vanlerberghe. When he fell on hard times, he resold it to his former wife in order to avoid its falling into a creditor's hands. Perhaps for the same reason, or to avoid splitting it up under French inheritance laws, in 1821 she apparently sold it to a London banker, Sir Samuel Scott, for 1 million francs. He and then his son were the nominal owners for over 40 years. But when the real proprietor Aimé Vanlerberghe died without issue in 1866, the family decided to sell it and pay up the fines due owing to the concealment. In 1868, after a stiff contest with a Bordeaux syndicate, it was knocked down to Baron James de ROTHSCHILD of the Paris bank, for 4.4 million francs, including part of the Carruades vineyard. Baron James died in the same year and the château has remained in the family ever since. Baron Eric de Rothschild took over direction of the property from his uncle Baron Élie in 1977. In the famous 1855 CLASSIFICATION Lafite was placed first of the premiers crus, although there is controversy as to whether the order was alphabetical or by rank. Yet, as Christie's AUCTIONS in the 1960s and 1970s of 19th century British country mansion cellars showed, in Britain Lafite was nearly always the favoured first growth, and at auction now it usually secures the highest price of the Médoc first growths.

The château itself is a 16th century manor. The vineyard, one of the largest in the Haut-Médoc, was 90 ha/222 acres in 1993 with an ENCÉPAGEMENT of 70 per cent CABERNET SAUVIGNON, 13 per cent CABERNET FRANC, 15 per cent MERLOT, and two per cent PETIT VERDOT. Annual production is about 35,000 cases, of which about a third may be the SECOND WINE, called Carruades de Lafite but not restricted to wine produced on the plateau in the vineyard known as Les Carruades. E.P.-R.

Ray, C., *Lafite* (2nd edn., London and New York, 1971).

LAGAR, term used in PORTUGAL for a low-sided stone trough where grapes are trodden and fermented. Most have now been replaced by conventional fermentation vats except in the DOURO valley, where some of the best PORTS continue to be foot trodden in *lagares*.

LAGREIN, red grape variety grown in TRENTINO-ALTO ADIGE. Although often over-produced, it can produce **Lagrein Scuro** or **Lagrein Dunkel**, velvety reds of real character, as well as fragrant yet sturdy rosés called **Lagrein Rosato** or **Lagrein Kretzer**. According to Burton Anderson, this variety, whose name suggests origins in the Lagarina valley of Trentino, was mentioned as early as the 17th century in the records of the Muri Benedictine monastery near Bolzano in Alto Adige.

Anderson, B., *The Wine Atlas of Italy* (London and New York, 1990).

LAIRÉN, southern Spanish name for the white grape variety AIRÉN.

LAKE COUNTY, smallest viticultural district among CALIFORNIA'S NORTH COAST counties and also the least understood. A vigorous but short-lived 19th century industry died out with PROHIBITION, leaving scant historic guidance to the growers who restored vineyards to the region during the 1970s. The county's 3,000 acres/1,214 ha of vines and its small population of wineries are concentrated in the eponymous Clear Lake AVA. A much smaller AVA is further south in the Guenoc Valley.

Clear Lake AVA

Nearly all of the AVA's vineyards nestle between steep hills to the west and the lake, California's largest, to the east. By the early 1990s the district, north of NAPA and east of MENDOCINO, has grown some excellent Sauvignon Blanc and pleasant, early maturing Cabernet Sauvignon. Zinfandel may be well adapted, although evidence remains scant. Although several wineries (especially Konocti and Kendall-Jackson) are located near the town of Lakeport, a fair proportion of the region's grapes go to wineries in Mendocino and SONOMA counties.

Guenoc Valley AVA

A one-owner AVA in the south of the county, near its boundary with Napa County, Guenoc Valley was first planted before Prohibition by the legendary actress Lillie Langtry. Revived only in the mid 1970s, her old property has yet to show which varieties it favours most, though Petite Sirah, Zinfandel, and Sauvignon Blanc are in the running.

The circular second year *chai* at Ch **Lafite**, constructed, like so much else in the Médoc, in the late 1980s.

LOVELY WOMAN IN THE LAGAR.

Lagar: From Vizetelly's *Facts about Madeira and Port* (1880).

LALANDE-DE-POMEROL, appellation to the immediate north of Pomerol that is very much in the shadow of this great red wine district of Bordeaux. It includes the communes of Lalande-de-Pomerol and Néac and produces lush, Merlot-dominated wines which can offer a suggestion, sometimes a slightly rustic suggestion, of the concentration available in a bottle of fine Pomerol at a fraction of the price. Including nearly 900 ha/2,223 acres of vineyards, the Lalande-de-Pomerol appellation is bigger than that of Pomerol, and its soils are composed of well-drained gravels, particularly in the south, where it is divided from the Pomerol appellation only by the Barbanne river. At one time, the Barbanne separated that part of France which said *oc* for yes (see LANGUEDOC) from the *langue d'oil* where they said *oil*.

See also POMEROL.

LA MANCHA. See MANCHA.

LAMBRUSCO, central Italian VARIETAL wine based on the eponymous red grape variety which is cultivated principally in the three central provinces of EMILIA—Modena, Parma, and Reggio nell'Emilia—although significant plantings can be found across the river Po in the province of Mantova, and occasional plantings can be found as far afield as PIEDMONT, the TRENTINO, and even BASILICATA. This robust variety, of which there are at least 60 known subvarieties, has long been known for its exceptional productivity, and CATO described it as *trecenarie* by virtue of the 300 AMPHORAE that each *jugero* (two-thirds of an acre) yielded.

Modern Lambrusco, a frothing, fruity, typically red wine meant to be drunk young, is produced principally by the CO-OPERATIVES of Emilia in four separate DOCS: **Lambrusco di Sorbara** (from the subvarieties Lambrusco di Sorbara and, the most planted, Lambrusco Salamino); **Lambrusco Grasparossa di Castelvetro** (85 per cent of which must come from the clone of the same name); **Lambrusco Reggiano** (produced principally from the Lambrusco Marani and Lambrusco Salamino clones, with Lambrusco Maestri and Lambrusco Montericco permitted although they are gradually disappearing); and **Lambrusco Salamino di Santa Croce** (which should include 90 per cent of the synonymous clone whose small bunches are thought to resemble a 'small salami'). The Lambrusco Grasparossa, Sorbara, and Salamino tend to be dry or off-dry wines with a pronounced ACIDITY which, together with its bubbles, are reputed to assist the digestion of Emilia's hearty cuisine.

Lambrusco Reggiano, on the other hand, tends to be AMABILE or slightly sweet, the sweetness generally being supplied by the partially fermented must of the Ancellotta grape, which DOC rules permit (up to a maximum of 15 per cent) in the blend. (It is notable that, according the Italian agricultural census of 1990, total plantings of Ancellotta were 4,700 ha, more than of any single Lambrusco subvariety.) This is the wine that took America by storm in the late 1970s and early

1980s when the Cantine Riunite of Reggio nell'Emilia, a consortium of co-operatives, succeeded in exporting up to 3 million cases per year to the UNITED STATES. So successful has Lambrusco been on export markets that special white, pink, and light (LOW ALCOHOL) versions have perversely been created, the colour and alcohol often being deliberately removed.

Most Lambrusco made today is a fairly anonymous, standardized product made in industrial quantities by co-operatives or large commercial wineries using the Charmat BULK process, together with heavy FILTRATION, STABILIZATION, and, frequently, PASTEURIZATION. 'Proper' Lambrusco, whose SECONDARY FERMENTATION takes place in the bottle, has become something of a relic of the past, although occasional artisan Lambruscos of this type can be found in the production zones themselves. The distinctive qualities of the different clones and different zones have tended to disappear with large quantities and industrial techniques. Although it is still possible to find good bottles of Lambrusco from small producers in the various DOC zones, conferring a generalized superiority on a given zone or a given type would be risky business indeed in current circumstances. Lambrusco Reggiano, with an annual production of about 250,000 hl/6.6 million gal, is the most common, followed by Lambrusco di Sorbara with 115,000 hl, Lambrusco Grasparossa with 65,000 hl, and Lambrusco Salamino with 55,000 hl.

There are also several hundred hectares of a red grape variety known as Lambrusco Maesini in Argentina. D.T.

Anderson, B., *The Wine Atlas of Italy* (London and New York, 1990).
Gleave, D., *The Wines of Italy* (London and New York, 1989).

LANCERS, BRAND of medium sweet, lightly sparkling wine made by the firm of J. M. da FONSECA Internacional at Azeitão, near SETÚBAL in PORTUGAL. The brand was created in 1944, when Vintage Wines of New York saw that American veterans of the Second World War were returning home from Europe with a taste for wine. With most European countries engaged in the war, and Spain in disarray after its own civil war, neutral Portugal was an obvious source for the wine. Lancers, initially sold in a stone crock, continues to be hugely successful in the United States, whereas MATEUS Rosé, created two years earlier, tends to be better known in Europe. A sparkling Lancers, made by the CONTINUOUS METHOD, was introduced in the late 1980s. Lancers rosé has since been made using a modification of this method so that it is naturally sparkling. R.J.M.

LANDWEIN, superior category of dry or medium dry table wine, or TAFELWEIN, in German-speaking countries. In GERMANY Landwein must have an ALCOHOLIC STRENGTH of at least half a per cent more than the minimum level for German table wine. Although all the German wine regions contain Landwein areas, their names are not widely used. Since an average of 95 per cent of each German vintage has been classified as QUALITÄTSWEIN, or quality wine, much of it sold at a very low price, the scope for Landwein is small. It does not enjoy the reputation of its French equivalent VIN DE PAYS, which is so successful on the German market. I.J.

In AUSTRIA, Landwein is slightly more common but must be bottled either in bottles of 25 cl/9 fl oz or less, or in 1-l or 2-l ('Doppler') bottles. It must be dry, with no more than 6 g/l RESIDUAL SUGAR, and reach at least 68° OECHSLE (considerably riper than the German minimum, reflecting the warmer climate).

LANGENLOIS, important wine town in lower AUSTRIA, now part of the Kamptal-Donauland district.

LANGHE, plural of **Langa**, name given to the hills to the north and south of the city of Alba in the province of Cuneo. The soils, composed of clay marls, are the classic ones for the NEBBIOLO grape, and produce notably the Langhe's most famous wines BAROLO and BARBARESCO, although they can also yield BARBERA and DOLCETTO of excellent quality. The hills gradually rise in altitude to the south of Monforte d'Alba, creating a climatic limit to the cultivation of Nebbiolo; to the south of Dogliani, where altitudes of over 600 m/1,970 ft are reached, the cultivation of grapes of any sort virtually ceases. D.T.

LANGHORNE CREEK, wine region in AUSTRALIA. For more detail see SOUTH AUSTRALIA.

LANGUEDOC, the single most important French wine region, in terms of volume of wine produced, and in terms of the importance of viticulture to the region's economy. The Languedoc takes its name from a time when its inhabitants spoke Occitan, the language in which *oc* is the word for 'yes' hence *langue d'oc*. It comprises the three central southern *départements* of the Aude, Hérault, and Gard, a sea of little other than vines just inland from the beaches of the Mediterranean (see map on p. 552 and FRANCE). Between them they had a total of nearly 300,000 ha/741,000 acres of vineyard at the beginning of the 1990s—about a third of all French vines, or more than the total area of the United States under vine. This was despite 10 years' strenuous EUROPEAN UNION-inspired initiatives to encourage widespread RIPPING OUT of vines in an effort to reduce Europe's wine SURPLUS. The Languedoc is often bracketed with the region to its immediate south, as in LANGUEDOC-ROUSSILLON, although the ROUSSILLON has a perceptibly different character, and is better equipped to replace vines with the other fruit crops it has for long cultivated.

Despite its quantitative importance, the Languedoc produces only just over 10 per cent of France's AC wines. For many years its only appellation was Fitou, but in 1985 Corbières, Minervois, and the catch-all appellation Coteaux du Languedoc were elevated from VDQS to AC status. A high proportion of the vast area technically included in these AC zones is dedicated to non-appellation wine, however, either because the ENCÉPAGEMENT is outside the appellation specifications, or because the vigneron is more interested in quantity than quality. The Languedoc is still by far the principal

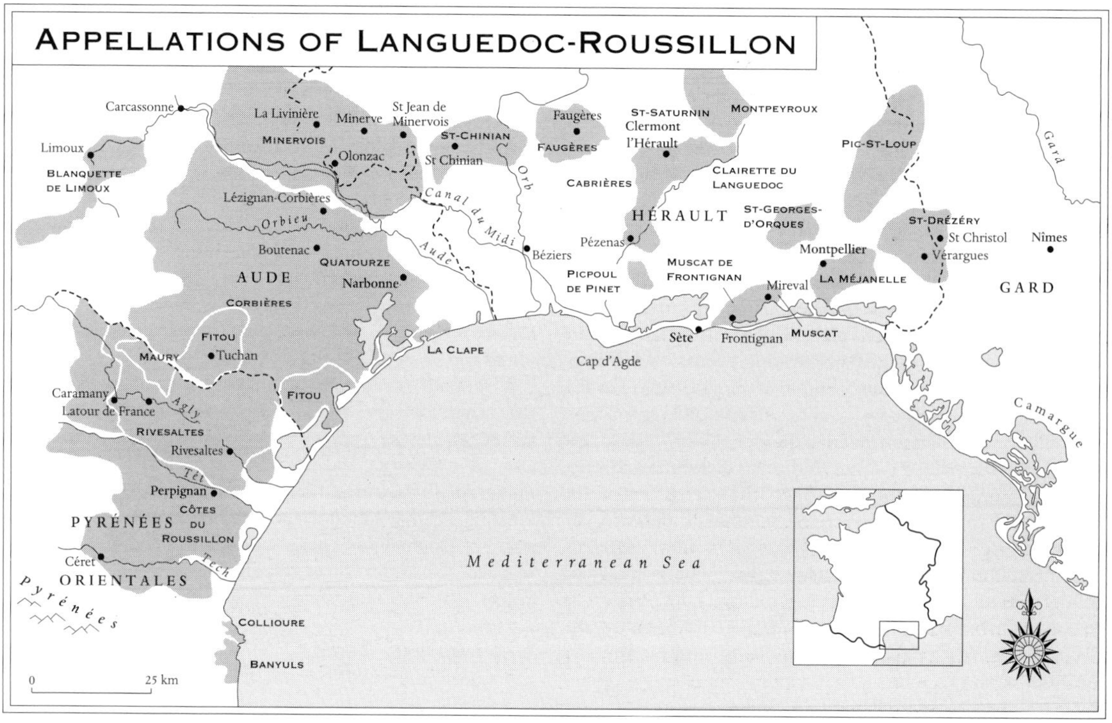

producer of VIN DE TABLE, as well as producing more than 80 per cent of France's intermediate category VIN DE PAYS, much of it labelled regionally as Vin de Pays d'Oc. A much wider range of VINE VARIETIES is usually allowed for vin de pays than for appellation wines. In a very real sense the Languedoc is France's most anarchic wine region. Not only is it the only one in which vignerons still take direct and often violent action in protest at the organization of their sector of the wine business, it is also the one in which wine producers are most obviously dissatisfied with the detail of the, admittedly relatively recent, appellation laws. Some important producers ignore the AC system completely and put most of their effort into making high-quality vins de pays.

Less than 10 per cent of the region's wine output was white in the early 1990s, but this is increasing, and great efforts are being made to refine white wine-making. The small proportion of dry rosé is mainly for local consumption. A substantial quantity of VIN DOUX NATUREL is made (see MUSCAT), and LIMOUX is the Languedoc's centre of SPARKLING WINE-MAKING. The Languedoc is still principally a source of red wine, however, which varies from pale remnants of the region's past as a bulk wine supplier to dense, exciting, good-value souvenirs of some of France's wildest countryside.

History

There is some debate about whether the CELTS cultivated vines before the Roman, or even Greek, invasions of GAUL, but the first French vineyards about which all historians can agree were planted around 125 BC on the hills near the Roman colony of Narbo, modern Narbonne, which today produce Corbières, Minervois, and Coteaux du Languedoc. Narbonne was then an important Roman port, protected by what was then the island of La Clape. Cargoes would be taken up river as far as Carcassonne and then transported overland to join the GARONNE and thence to the Roman legions in Aquitaine. The hinterland of Narbonne and Béziers came to produce so much wine that it was exported to Ancient ROME, although the edict of DOMITIAN was designed to put a stop to this.

It was not until the Middle Ages, under the auspices of the Languedoc's MONKS AND MONASTERIES, that viticulture once again thrived (although today only the Abbaye de Valmagne retains its wine-producing role). Already the University of MONTPELLIER was established and ARNALDUS DE VILLANOVA oversaw several important developments for wine and spirit production there. The development of greatest potential significance for the Languedoc and its wines was the late 17th century construction of the Canal du Midi, which connected the Mediterranean with the Atlantic. The Bordelais were by now so experienced at protectionism, however (see HAUT PAYS, for example), that the wine producers of the Languedoc failed to benefit substantially from this new distribution network until the end of the 18th century.

Much more profitable were the efforts of the DUTCH WINE TRADE in the late 17th century to develop northern European markets for *picardan*, a sweet white wine made from Clairette and Picpoul grapes that was well known in Holland by 1680, and subsequently for eaux-de-vie (BRANDY). The port of Sète was established in 1666 and became particularly important for exports to ENGLAND and the NETHERLANDS, Narbonne having long since silted up. Sweet wines were also produced, notably a DRIED GRAPE WINE made from Muscat grown at FRONTIGNAN, whose inhabitants insist that it was as a result of a visit by a Marquis de Lur-Saluces to Frontignan after the great frost of 1709 that Ch d'YQUEM became a sweet wine property, and that their straight-sided bottle was adopted for bordeaux.

By the mid 19th century the vineyards of the Languedoc could be divided into the HILLSIDE VINEYARDS, vines planted on gravelly terraces at mid altitude (these two roughly approximating to the modern Languedoc appellations), and vines, mainly Aramon and Terret grapes, planted on the plains for DISTILLATION into brandy.

In 1855 the Languedoc's fortunes were to change forever, as a result of its first RAILWAY connection, via Lyons, with the important centres of population in the north. A link via Bordeaux was opened the next year. Between 1850 and 1869, average annual wine production nearly quadrupled in the Hérault. The arrival of PHYLLOXERA could hardly have been worse timed, but, thanks to feverish experimentation and the eventual adoption of GRAFTING, as well as HYBRIDS and some of the new BOUSCHET crossings, the Languedoc vineyard was the first to be reconstituted after the devastations of this American louse. By the end of the 19th century, the Languedoc became France's principal wine supplier, producing 44 per cent of the entire French wine production, from 23 per cent of the country's total *vignoble*.

This superficial success was at some cost, however. Dr GUYOT had in 1867 warned against the increasing influence of VINE VARIETIES and practices designed to produce quantity rather than quality, and against the over-industrialization of the Languedoc wine trade. By the turn of the century, the plains of the Languedoc, the Hérault particularly, were being milked of thin, light, pale red that needed blending with the much more robust produce of new colonial vineyards in ALGERIA to yield a commercially acceptable drink. France had sown the seeds of her (continued) dependence on wine imports. Such was the extent of commercial interference in the French table wine market, including widespread ADULTERATION AND FRAUD, that prices plummeted and France's social crisis of 1907 provoked what were merely the first in a long series of wine-related riots.

Since then the vignerons of the Languedoc, most of them members of one of the region's 500 CO-OPERATIVES, many of them formed in the 1930s, have been some of the world's most politicized. Their sheer number has given them political power, but the fall in demand for VIN DE TABLE has led to an increasing frustration of it.

Geography and climate

The great majority of the Languedoc's vines are planted on flat, low-lying alluvial plain, particularly in the southern Hérault and Gard. In the northern Hérault and western Aude, vines may be planted several hundred metres above sea level, in the foothills of the Cévennes and the Corbières Pyrenean foothills respectively, sometimes at quite an angle and on very varied soils which can include gravels and limestone.

The climate in all but the far western limits of the Languedoc (where some definite Atlantic influence is apparent) is definitively MEDITERRANEAN and one of the major viticultural hazards is DROUGHT. Annual rainfall can be as little as 400 mm / 15.6 in by the coast. July and August temperatures often exceed 30 °C / 86 °F; such rain as does fall tends to fall in the form of localized deluges. WIND is common throughout the growing season, with the *tramontane* bringing cool air from the mountains.

Viticulture

The Languedoc is the land of the proud peasant farmer. The size of the average holding is small, and usually much divided between parcels inherited from various different branches of the family. Basic, straggling BUSH VINES still predominated in the early 1990s, although an increasing proportion of vines, especially the newer vine varieties, were being trained on WIRES. IRRIGATION is theoretically permitted only within strictly specified limits, and in practice only the best and the worst producers tend to have any form of available irrigation system. The flatter, larger vineyards lend themselves to MECHANICAL HARVESTING but their parcellation has slowed the inevitable invasion. The region is by no means free of FUNGAL DISEASES and some sprayings are usually necessary.

Vine varieties

The dominant vine variety of the Hérault and Gard was ARAMON, until the 1970s, when CARIGNAN took its place. At the end of the 1980s Carignan accounted for more than half of all vines in the Aude, nearly 40 per cent of all vines in Hérault, and a quarter of all vines in Gard, but there were considerable incentives to plant better-quality varieties, known as *cépages améliorateurs*, such as GRENACHE, SYRAH, CINSAUT, and MOURVÈDRE. Old Carignan vines, planted in suitably infertile locations, have their devotees. Other varieties have made substantial inroads in the region since the mid 1980s. Between 1983 and 1993, almost 35,000 ha were replanted with new, 'improved' varieties, many of which are outlawed for the production of APPELLATION CONTRÔLÉE wines and are used to produce VIN DE PAYS, about 70 per cent of which are VARIETAL wines. These include such obvious candidates as Merlot and Cabernet Sauvignon, but also Sauvignon Blanc, Rolle, Marsanne, Viognier, and of course Chardonnay (although this is most common around LIMOUX in the Aude). Other 'traditional' (pre-phylloxera) Languedoc vine varieties included Aspiran, Bourboulenc, Clairette, Picpoul, Maccabéo, and Œillade.

Wine-making

Winery equipment and techniques are still relatively unsophisticated in the Languedoc, where selling prices have rarely been high enough to justify major investment. DESTEMMING equipment, for example, is widely regarded as a luxury, new oak BARRELS beyond the wildest dreams of most producers. The great majority of Languedoc wine is made in one of the co-operative cellars whose will to make good-quality wine varies considerably. Fermentation and élevage typically take place in large concrete *cuves*, although stainless steel is slowly invading the region. Partly in an effort to tame the natural astringency of Carignan, full or partial carbonic maceration is the most common red wine-making technique. bottling usually takes place at a merchant's cellar rather than on the premises where the wine was made. The wine container most frequently seen by the consumer in the region is probably the road tanker (a high proportion of the locals buy their wine in bulk rather than bottle).

For more specific information see the individual appellations clairette de bellegarde, clairette de languedoc, corbières, costières de nîmes, faugères, fitou, limoux, minervois, st-chinian, and Coteaux du languedoc. See the vdqs wines cabardès and Côtes de la malepère and also the vin de liqueur cartagène, and various muscat vins doux naturels, plus frontignan.

Berry, E., *The Wines of Languedoc-Roussillon* (London, 1992).
Clavel, J., and Baillaud, R., *Histoire et avenir des vins en Languedoc* (Toulouse, 1985).

Languedoc, Coteaux du, extensive appellation whose zone includes most suitable vine-growing land above the plain in a swathe through the Hérault *département* from Narbonne towards Nîmes. This territory was once known as Septimanie and is in effect a giant south-facing amphitheatre, although of course there are many local variations in topography. As elsewhere in the Languedoc, much of the land technically included within the appellation is used for other purposes, so the total vineyard area dedicated to producing Coteaux du Languedoc in the early 1990s, for example, was just 6,500 ha / 16,055 acres.

Although much of the zone qualifies for the basic Coteaux du Languedoc appellation, a number of subappellations, crus, or specific terroirs have been identified and are allowed to append their own name to that of the appellation on labels. Of these clairette du languedoc, faugères, and st-chinian have already managed to break free and establish their own independent identity. Others waiting with particular impatience in the wings are La clape, picpoul de pinet, pic-st-loup, montpeyroux, and st-saturnin. Others, some of which produce relatively little wine of distinction, are cabrières, méjanelle, quatourze, st-christol, st-drézéry, the historically celebrated St-Georges-d'Orques, and vérargues. With the exception of Picpoul de Pinet and Clairette de Languedoc, which are white wines, most of the wine produced under these names is a full bodied blend of southern red wine grape varieties, or crisp, light rosé.

On the schists of the highest sites such as St-Saturnin and Montpeyroux, yields are particularly low but the wines can be powerful, concentrated, long-lived essences of the Languedoc. Well-drained gravelly limestone can yield more forward, fruity wines. La Clape, on the other hand, produces wines from vineyards heavily influenced by the Mediterranean.

The appellation regulations have been concerned to diminish the proportion of Carignan and Cinsaut permitted for red wines; it was reduced to 40 per cent with the 1992 vintage. Grenache, its relative Lladoner Pelut, Syrah, and Mourvèdre are the principal varieties that are encouraged for the appellation's red wines. Grenache Blanc, Clairette, and Bourboulenc are the principal white grape varieties.

For more information, see under individual subappellation names. This appellation is probably too big and varied for its own good.

George, R., *French Country Wines* (London, 1990).

Languedoc-Roussillon, common name for the wide sweep of varied vineyards from Marseilles around the Mediterranean coast of the south of France to the Spanish border, incorporating both languedoc and the contiguous roussillon region.

Lanuvini, Colli, white wines from the hills south east of Rome. For more information see castelli romani.

La Rochelle, port on the Atlantic coast about 160 km / 100 miles north of bordeaux in the *département* of charente-Maritime. In the Middle Ages La Rochelle was a New Town, having been founded in 1130, in an age of economic expansion. The climate at La Rochelle is hot and dry enough for the winning of sea salt. Salt was once vital as a preservative and hence much more valuable than it is now; initially, salt was the basis of La Rochelle's economy. Merchants came from the north to buy salt, but they also wanted wine, and it was in response to that demand that the people of La Rochelle turned to viticulture. Because of its favourable climate, poitou, as the region comprising the bishoprics of Poitiers and Saintes was called, was a more reliable producer than the Seine basin (see paris), Rheims (see champagne), burgundy, or the rhine. Hence the English and the Flemish turned more readily to the wines of Poitou, all the more so because these wines were less acidic than those of Rheims and Paris. La Rochelle also exported its wines to Normandy, Scotland, Ireland, and even Denmark and Norway. In 1199 Poitou was the wine the royal household bought most of, with the wines of anjou and the Île-de-France coming second and third. But in 1224, when La Rochelle fell to the French, it had to cede its position of best-selling wine to Bordeaux, although the wines of La Rochelle remained popular with the English in the 14th and 15th centuries.

The grape varieties were probably those of Burgundy and the Paris region: morillon, which was an early form of pinot noir, and Fromenteau, thought to be the ancestor of pinot gris. In documents of the 13th and 14th centuries a third cépage appears: it is called Chemère, Chemière, Chenère, or Chenère Blanche, and it is likely to have been the parent of chenin blanc. In accordance with medieval preference, most of the wines that Poitou made were white.

See also dutch wine trade. H.M.W.

Dion, Roger, *Histoire de la vigne et du vin en France* (Paris, 1959).

LASKI RIZLING, the name current in SLOVENIA, VOJVODINA, and some other parts of what was YUGOSLAVIA for the white grape variety known in Austria as WELSCHRIESLING (under which name more details appear). The vine is cultivated widely in Yugoslavia, but most successfully in the higher vineyards of Slovenia (just over the border from the spirited Welschrieslings of STYRIA), and Fruška Gora in Vojvodina, where it can produce equally crisp and delicately aromatic wines. Few of these have been exported, however, and most of the large bottling enterprises have been hampered by poor equipment and importers who have been more concerned with quantity than quality. For decades a Slovenian BRAND, Lutomer Riesling (eventually renamed Lutomer Laski Rizling after German lobbying), was the best-selling white wine in the UK, its heavily sweetened style conveying little of the intrinsic character of the variety. The Rizling Vlassky is the variant known in CZECHOSLOVAKIA.

LATERAL SHOOT, sometimes called simply a **lateral**, secondary shoot that grows from the axil of a leaf on the main shoot. Its origin on grapevines is linked with the complex development of the BUD. At most nodes, especially on weak vines, the lateral shoot is short (less than 20 mm/0.8 in), fails to become woody, and drops off in autumn leaving a prominent scar at the side of the bud. But on more vigorous shoots, especially at the middle nodes or at the end where vigorous shoots have been topped or trimmed, the lateral shoot grows in the same way as a primary shoot producing hardened permanent wood. Sometimes, lateral shoots are fruitful (see SECOND CROP). Laterals that develop on secondary shoots are called tertiaries; quaternaries have even been seen on extremely vigorous vines. B.G.C.

LATIN AMERICA. See SOUTH AMERICA and MEXICO.

LATISANA, a DOC of the FRIULI region in north east Italy whose unchallenging wines are rarely exported.

LATITUDE, angular distance north or south of the equator, measured in degrees and minutes. The main northern hemisphere viticultural regions extend between 32 and 51 degrees north, and most of those in the southern hemisphere between 28 and 42 degrees south. Extreme poleward limits are at about 52 degrees north in ENGLAND (and Ireland), and just over 46 degrees south in Otago, NEW ZEALAND. Some vines are also cultivated for wine production in tropical highlands close to the equator in MEXICO, BOLIVIA, PERU, BRAZIL, and KENYA. See also TROPICAL VITICULTURE.

Comparisons between hemispheres based purely on latitude are misleading. Northern hemisphere vineyards are on average warmer during the growing season at given latitudes, a fact partly related to their greater CONTINENTALITY. But even over the whole year, the northern hemisphere is on average warmer than the southern hemisphere at similar latitudes, partly because of the greater land mass and its disposition around the North Pole, and partly (in the case of western Europe) because of warming by the Gulf Stream.

When wine regions with equal average mean temperatures during the growing season, or equal temperature summations (see CLIMATE CLASSIFICATION), are compared, grapes tend to ripen more fully when grown at high latitudes, i.e. further from the equator. Alternatively, later maturing grapes varieties can be ripened. The reasons for this phenomenon of great significance for wine quality remain unproven, but two main mechanisms have been proposed.

First, compared with low latitudes, the summers at high latitudes have longer days, with given totals of SUNLIGHT hours more spread through them. One can argue, on physiological grounds, that this should be used more efficiently for PHOTOSYNTHESIS and sugar production than the same sunlight duration concentrated in a shorter day. In the latter case the rate the vines can use the sugar, or transport it away from the leaves, may itself become a limitation to further photosynthesis. Also, it seems likely that the high-latitude summer and autumn days will have more hours of weak sunlight, not intense enough to register as bright sunlight by the standard recording methods, but still intense enough to support photosynthesis. Huglin and earlier European researchers favour these explanations.

The second (and probably complementary) explanation is that the conventionally used monthly average mean temperatures (i.e. for each month, the average of its maximum temperatures plus that of its minima, divided by two) do not accurately reflect the actual average temperatures experienced by the vines (McIntyre *et al.*). Where summer days are longer, it seems likely that a greater proportion of the 24 hours is in the upper half of the temperature range. The day's mean, which is strictly half-way between its maximum and minimum temperatures, then underestimates its true average. With shorter summer days at low latitudes this is less marked, so that higher mean temperatures are needed to achieve the same temperature averages and rates of vine and fruit development; and thence earliness and completeness of PHYSIOLOGICAL RIPENING, or flavour ripening. (Accumulation of SUGAR IN GRAPES, on the other hand, could be expected to be more directly related to effective sunlight duration, as described above.) Further, in high-latitude continental climates, calculation from monthly average mean temperatures close to or below 10 °C/50 °F at the beginning and end of the vine-growing season fails to credit up to several weeks of true growing conditions above 10 °C in the warmer parts of those months. Gladstones explains these distortions more fully, and proposes ways to compensate for them when estimating effective viticultural climates.

Finally, it can be noted that high-latitude viticultural climates tend to have higher relative HUMIDITIES and less day-to-day TEMPERATURE VARIABILITY during the growing season than those at low latitudes (apart from where the latter are coastal). Both factors have likely implications for ripening and for grape and wine quality. See CLIMATE AND WINE QUALITY, HUMIDITY, TEMPERATURE VARIABILITY, and map p. 1076. J.G.

Gladstones, J., *Viticulture and Environment* (Adelaide, 1992).

Ch **Latour's** trade-mark tower, although one quite unlike that depicted on the label.

Huglin, P., 'Possibilités d'appréciation objective du milieu viticole (Possibilities of objective evaluation of the viticultural environment)', *Bulletin de l'OIV*, 56 (1983), 823–33.

McIntyre, G. N., Kliewer, W. M., and Lider, L. A., 'Some limitations of the degree day system as used in viticulture in California', *American Journal of Enology and Viticulture*, 38 (1987), 128–32.

LATIUM, known as **Lazio** in Italy itself, is the ancient homeland of the Latins (see ITALY, history), and the seat of Italy's government and administration in the capital, Rome (see map on p. 517). The region also has a significant viticultural production, its approximately 100,000 ha/247,000 acres of vineyards yielding annual totals of between 4 and 5 million hl/132 million gal of wine, fifth among Italy's regions behind SICILY, APULIA, VENETO, and EMILIA-ROMAGNA. About 17 per cent of the total Latium vineyard is dedicated to the production of DOC wine. White wines, almost exclusively from MALVASIA and TREBBIANO grapes, represent over 85 per cent of the total DOC production, with the wines of the CASTELLI ROMANI representing by far the majority. Malvasia and Trebbiano blends are also produced in some quantities in the DOC zones of Cerveteri, Est!Est!!Est!!!, and in that small portion of the ORVIETO zone which spills over the Umbrian border into Latium. Lazio has no significant red DOCs although an occasional CABERNET/MERLOT blend of significant quality—from the Boncompagni Ludovisi estate near Rome and from the Di Mauro estate in Marino, for example—suggests that the soil and climate are well suited to red wine production, even if no real tradition exists in the region. Merlot was planted this century in the DOC zone of Aprilia by the settlers from the Veneto who drained the Pontine marshes, but the 14 tons/ha allowed by the DOC rules are hardly compatible with quality. The CESANESE grape has its proponents in its home province of Frosinone, but most Cesanese is neither well made nor interesting (despite the example set by a blend of Cesanese, Merlot, and Cabernet produced at the Colacicchi estate in Agnani during the 1960s and 1970s). D.T.

LATOUR, CHÂTEAU, FIRST GROWTH in the MÉDOC region of BORDEAUX. The originally square tower from which the château takes its name was one of a defensive line against ocean-going pirates. Vines were already planted here in the late 14th century and at least a quarter of the land was vineyard by 1600. At the end of the 17th century a number of smallholdings were accumulated into one ownership under the de Mullet family. The New French Clarets they produced made their first publicized appearances in AUCTIONS in London COFFEE HOUSES early in the 18th century. Owned from 1677 by the Clauzel family, it passed by marriage to the powerful SÉGURS, who also owned Lafite, MOUTON, and Calon-Ségur. On the death in 1755 of the Marquis Nicolas-Alexandre de Ségur, 'Le Prince des Vignes', his properties passed to his four daughters, three of whom in 1760 acquired Latour. Their male descendants owned the château, which in 1842 became a private company, until its purchase by the British Pearson family in 1963, with 25 per cent acquired by HARVEYS of Bristol, and a diminishing minority remaining in the hands of the French families. The property was greatly improved, with STAINLESS STEEL tanks controversially installed as FERMENTATION VESSELS in time for the 1964 vintage, partly on the advice of director Harry WAUGH. In 1989 the estate was sold to multinational corporation Allied-Lyons, already owners of Harveys, for the equivalent of £110 million. Allied-Lyons sold their 93 per cent share of the property to French businessman François Pinault in 1993, when the complete property was valued at £86 million.

The estate of 59 ha/142 acres of vineyard in 1993 consisted of 80 per cent CABERNET SAUVIGNON vines, 15 per cent MERLOT, 3.5 per cent CABERNET FRANC, and 1.5 per cent PETIT VERDOT, with an average annual production of 29,000 cases of the three wines made there. In 1966 was first produced a SECOND WINE, Les Forts de Latour, made from the young vines and from three small plots on the other side of the St-Julien–Pauillac road. A third wine is also bottled and sold as Pauillac. A dry white BORDEAUX AC Blanc de Pauillac, was made from 1992. The red wines of Latour generally require much longer to develop than those of the other first growths, and they often have greater longevity. Latour is also known for its ability to produce good wines in lesser vintages.

It also possesses better archives, back to the 14th century, than any other wine estate in Bordeaux and so has spawned an unusual and useful array of monographs. E.P.-R.

Faith, N., *Latour* (London, 1991).
Higounet, C. (ed.), *La Seigneurie et le vignoble de Château Latour* (Bordeaux, 1974).
Penning-Rowsell, E., *Château Latour: A History of a Great Vineyard 1331–1992* (London, 1993).

LATOUR, LOUIS, one of Burgundy's most commercially astute, and oldest, merchants. Jean Latour first planted vines in Aloxe-Corton, then called simply Aloxe, in 1768; his family had grown vines on the plain to the east of Beaune since the 16th century. Jean's son was the first in a long line of Louis Latours and enlarged the domaine considerably and it was not until the late 19th century that the family added wine brokering to their vine-growing activities.

With an eye to the developing export markets, the third Louis Latour bought the Lamarosse family's NÉGOCIANT business in Beaune's historic Rue des Tonneliers in 1867, and was so successful that in 1891 he was able to buy Ch Corton-Grancey in Aloxe-Corton. With this acquisition came one of the most handsome, and most photographed, houses in the Côte d'Or, together with extensive wine-making premises, and some notable vineyards around the hill of Corton to add to the Latour family holdings, which already included some Chambertin; Romanée-St-Vivant, Les Quatre Journaux; and Chevalier-Montrachet, Les Demoiselles.

It was the third Louis Latour who is reputed to have realized the hill of Corton's potential for great white wine when he replanted some of the hill now designated Corton-Charlemagne with Chardonnay vines after PHYLLOXERA had laid waste vineyards originally planted with Pinot Noir and Aligoté.

Innovations of succeeding Louis Latours include a succession of 'new' and increasingly daring white wines. What was then known as Grand Pouilly, and subsequently became known as Pouilly-Fuissé, was introduced to the United States in the 1930s, immediately after the Repeal of PROHIBITION. A wine known as MÂCON-Lugny was introduced as a respectable alternative to CÔTE D'OR white wines. And, continuing this tradition of close co-operation with a wine CO-OPERATIVE, Louis Latour pioneered the planting of Chardonnay vines in the relatively unknown ARDÈCHE, in the early 1980s.

The house enjoys a solid reputation for its white wines, but has incited controversy over its endorsement of PASTEURIZATION of even its finest red wines.

LATOUR-DE-FRANCE, like CARAMANY, is a small village singled out for special mention as a suffix to the appellation Cotes du Roussillon Villages. It may have been accorded this distinction less because of the superior quality of the wine than because the name had been successfully promoted to the French wine consumer by wine merchants Nicolas who once bought the majority of production. For more details see ROUSSILLON.

LAVILLEDIEU, VINS DE, almost extinct VDQS in SOUTH WEST FRANCE on terraces between the GARONNE and Tarn rivers. Lavilledieu has a long history, dating back to the pre-Christian era and revived by monks (see MONKS AND MONASTERIES) who cleared the forest of Agre and replaced trees with vines in the 12th century, but its wine production today is minuscule. In 1990 just 842 hl/22,230 gal of red and rosé wine was produced, all by the local CO-OPERATIVE. A wide variety of south western vine varieties are allowed (notably the NÉGRETTE of the Côtes du FRONTONNAIS): one for every 50 hl of wine produced today!

LAW impinges on wine principally in the areas of penalizing ADULTERATION AND FRAUD of all sorts; regulating wine DESIGNATIONS, CONTROLLED APPELLATIONS, and LABELLING INFORMATION; and controlling the sale and service of any alcoholic drink as, for example, in state liquor laws or licensing laws.

LAYERING, an ancient method of vine PROPAGATION which involves taking a long cane from one vine and training it down to the soil, and burying a section to normal planting depth but with the end bent up and emerging in a desired position. The French term for the practice is *marcottage*. This is a useful method of filling empty spaces in established vineyards, a task that is difficult by normal planting methods, but only if the new roots survive in that soil, and so only in areas without PHYLLOXERA, NEMATODES, and other soil-borne pathogens (such as BOLLINGER's Vieilles Vignes vineyard, the Nacional vineyard at QUINTA DO NOVAL or COLARES in Portugal, and much of Australia and Chile). The foster vine may be left connected to the parent or may be separated after it has reached normal size. B.G.C.

LAYING DOWN wine is an English expression for holding wine as it undergoes BOTTLE AGEING. Thus most people lay down wine in their (however notional) CELLARS. Considerable quantities of red bordeaux of vintages in the 1980s have been **laid down** by COLLECTORS all over the globe, for example.

LAYON, COTEAUX DU, large appellation, for generally medium sweet white wine made from the Chenin Blanc grape, in the Anjou district of the Loire. Until 1950, these wines were sold as ANJOU Blanc. Two small areas within the area produce wines of such quality that they have earned their own appellations, BONNEZEAUX and QUARTS DE CHAUME. They, and most of the best vineyards of the Coteaux du Layon, are on the steep slopes on the right bank of the Layon tributary of the Loire. TERROIR is all here, for Coteaux du Layon should be an intense wine made ideally from several TRIS through the vineyard, selecting BOTRYTIZED grapes, or those that have begun to raisin on the vine. Producers such as Claude Papin of Ch Pierre Bise vinify grapes picked on slate, schist, clay, and sandstone separately to demonstrate the variation in style and potential longevity. Yields vary enormously according to the conditions of the vintage, but are officially limited to 30 hl/ha (1.7 tons/acre), and 25 hl/ha for wines produced in the clay soils around Chaume and sold as **Coteaux du Layon-Chaume**. The villages Beaulieu-sur-

Layon, Faye d'Anjou, Rablay-sur-Layon, Rochefort-sur-Loire, St-Aubin-de-Luigné, and St-Lambert-du-Lattay can append their name to that of Coteaux du Layon, or sell it as **Coteaux du Layon-Villages**, provided the wines have a POTENTIAL ALCOHOL of 13 per cent, and an actual ALCOHOLIC STRENGTH of 12 per cent rather than the 11 per cent minimum demanded of the rest of Coteaux du Layon. In favourable vintages some great wine is produced in this appellation, but producers are dogged by the depressing effect on selling prices of a substantial quantity of extremely ordinary just-sweet wine sold under the name Coteaux du Layon. Wines may be sold as DEMI-SEC, MOELLEUX, and, sweetest of all, LIQUOREUX.

See also LOIRE and map on pp. 576–7.

LAZIO, Italian for the region of LATIUM.

LEAD, one of the familiar and widely dispersed heavy metals which occurs naturally in trace amounts in all plants, therefore in grapes, and therefore, usually in microgram per litre quantities only, in wines. This ubiquitous element, which has no known biological function in plants or animals, is now known to be a neural toxin of particular danger to children. This has resulted in the reformulation of many products, particularly petroleum products, so as to exclude lead.

History

Lead has been associated with wine since the time of Ancient ROME. The Romans recognized that lead not only prevented wines from turning sour (and rescued those that already had) but also made them taste sweeter (see PLINY). What they did not know, however, is that, even when taken in only very small quantities over a long period, lead is a poison.

Its dangers were understood from the end of the 17th century when a German doctor, Eberhard Gockel of Ulm in Württemberg, noticed that the symptoms suffered by some of his wine-drinking patients matched those observed in lead miners. Gradually legislation was passed in Europe banning the use of lead in wine but the practice continued. At last, in 1820, the campaigner Frederick Accum complained that 'the merchant or dealer who practises this dangerous sophistication, adds the crime of murder to that of fraud'. British Food and Drugs Acts from the 1960s onwards finally eradicated this danger in Britain.

Poisoning could result not only from the wilful addition of lead to wine. The Romans heated grape juice in lead vessels in order to produce *sapa*, a sweet concentrate used as a wine additive and in cooking, and even in the 19th century wine BOTTLES were cleaned with lead shot, thereby contaminating the wine. H.B.

Viticultural aspects

Grapes containing lead may produce wine containing lead. Recent health concerns about lead in wine have led to studies of lead in grapes. There are two principal sources of lead. One is from lead-rich automobile exhaust particles settling on both grapes and soil. This is a problem for roadside vineyards in particular, but one which will decline as the use of unleaded fuels increases. The other source is from prior use of the now-banned chemical insecticide lead arsenate, which has contaminated many vineyard soils, especially where SOIL ACIDITY is high. R.E.S.

Lead in modern wine

Most of the traces of lead from grapes are precipitated out during wine-making with the LEES. However, as analytical methods continue to improve, microgram quantities per litre are likely to be found in most wines.

The equipment used in modern wineries should not result in any lead contamination. The few wines which contain lead in milligram per litre concentrations derive it principally from capsules or FOILS which contain lead, or from lead crystal DECANTERS. (Modern bottles are made of lead-free glass.) Seepage of wine around the cork can corrode the foil and, if the lip of the bottle is not thoroughly cleaned before pouring, the wine may be contaminated by some of the lead salt. To protect those who do not clean obvious lead salts from a bottle lip before pouring, however, the use of lead capsules or foils is now declining or prohibited in many regions.

Lengthy storage of wines in lead crystal decanters provides time for the wine acids to leach some lead from the glass, but keeping a wine in a lead crystal glass or decanter for the usual period of no more than a few hours is too short for dangerous amounts of lead contamination. One study found a lead concentration of around 5 mg/l in port left in a lead crystal decanter for four months, so that 10 l of it would have to be consumed in a short time for a potentially toxic human intake of lead! The amount of lead leached from glassware is determined by the raw materials used to make it and research reported in the *Lancet* suggests that lead concentrations in wine increased by 50 per cent after one hour in a low-quality Yugoslavian decanter, but by only 15 per cent after three hours in better-quality decanters.

Analyses of thousands of representative samples of wine suggest that the lead content of wines is decreasing in general but in the early 1990s ranged from 0 to 1.26 mg/l, with the average lead content being 0.13 mg/l, values well below any legal maximum. A.D.W.

Accum, F., *Treatise on Adulteration of Food, and Culinary Poisons* (London, 1820).

Eisinger, J., 'Early consumer protection legislation: a 17th century law prohibiting lead adulteration of wines', *Interdisciplinary Science Reviews*, 16/1 (1991), 61–8.

McWhirter, K., 'Lead-Free Lessons', *Wine & Spirit* (Nov. 1993).

Pliny the Elder, *Natural History*, trans. by H. Rackham (London, 1938), Book 14.

LEAF (*feuille* in French). Vine leaves range in size up to that of a dinner plate but are normally the area of a human hand (100 to 200 cm^2). Their individual area correlates with shoot VIGOUR and also varies with vine variety (Merlot has large leaves, for example, while Gewürztraminer has small leaves.) The vine is a leafy plant with several hectares of total leaf area per hectare of vineyard. A proportion of these leaves will be shaded and therefore not PHOTOSYNTHETIC. The total leaf and shoot system of a vine is known as the CANOPY.

The green, flat zone of the leaf connected to the stem by the PETIOLE is known as the leaf blade, or lamina. The lamina of a grape leaf expands to nearly its full area in six or more weeks, growing to a shape and form characteristic for each VINE VARIETY. The arrangement of the five lobes, the shape of the 'teeth' at the edge of the leaf, the size and shape of the sinuses, and especially the angle and lengths of the main veins are features that are measured (ampelometry) for vine variety identification by AMPELOGRAPHERS.

Leaf colour is responsive to VINE NUTRITION, becoming yellow all over with deficiencies of nitrogen and phosphorus, or patterned with yellow and/or dead zones with most other deficiencies. Similarly, yellow and dead areas on leaves occur with some virus infections and as a result of herbicide contamination, although usually in different patterns. With the onset of autumn, leaf colour changes naturally from green to yellow or red, depending on the vine species and the presence of certain VIRUS DISEASES. B.G.C.

LEAF ALDEHYDES make wines taste HERBACEOUS.

LEAF FALL, the process which occurs naturally in autumn, often after the first frost, which marks the end of the VINE GROWTH CYCLE. Ideally this is some time after HARVEST, so that the vine has been able to build up its reserves of the CARBOHYDRATES important for growth the following spring. See also DEFOLIATION. R.E.S.

LEAF HOPPERS, members of the insect family *Cicadellidae* which can cause both direct and indirect damage to vineyards. In California both the grape leaf hopper, *Erythroneura elegantula*, and the very similar variegated leaf hopper, *Erythroneura variabilis*, cause damage to grapes. They begin to feed on grapevine foliage as soon as it appears in spring, and do so by sucking out the liquid contents. As injury progresses, heavily damaged leaves lose their green colour and PHOTOSYNTHESIS is much reduced. TABLE GRAPES are spoilt by spots of leaf hopper excrement. The damage caused is in direct proportion to the numbers.

There are a number of natural enemies of leaf hoppers, however, the most important being a tiny wasp, *Anagrus epos*. Low leaf hopper populations do not need treatment, especially if this parasite is found to be active.

Leaf hoppers not only cause direct damage, but they are responsible for the spread of important diseases. PIERCE'S DISEASE of the Americas is spread by so-called sharpshooter leaf hoppers and FLAVESCENCE DORÉE by the leaf hopper *Scaphoideus littoralis*. The mechanisms by which the insects act as vectors for the spread of some diseases are not well understood. Leaf hoppers appear quickly to develop immunity or resistance to insecticides, so it is necessary to change these every few years. M.J.E. & R.E.S.

Flaherty, D. L., *et al.* (eds.), *Grape Pest Management* (2nd edn., Oakland, Calif., 1992).

Pearson, R. C., and Goheen, A. C., *Compendium of Grape Diseases* (St Paul, Minn., 1988).

LEAF REMOVAL, vineyard practice aimed at helping to control BOTRYTIS BUNCH ROT and other BUNCH ROTS, and at improving GRAPE COMPOSITION and therefore wine quality. Typically the leaves are removed around the bunches to increase exposure to the sun and wind. The bunches dry out more quickly after dew and rain so that moulds are less likely to develop. Increased exposure to sunlight helps the berries produce more of the PHENOLICS important in wine quality. Grape SUGARS are also increased and MALIC ACID reduced, both of which contribute to improved wine quality.

For optimal effects on wine quality, leaves should be removed several weeks before VERAISON, although it is more usual to remove them at its onset. Leaf removal is also used to improve the colour of black and red TABLE GRAPES. Traditionally leaf removal has been done by hand, requiring about 50 hours of labour per hectare (2.5 acres). Machines which take less than five hours per hectare to remove leaves by suction and/or cutting were developed in the late 1980s, however.

Decreasing dependence on AGROCHEMICALS in the vineyard has led to renewed interest in leaf removal in both Old and New Worlds. As well as making the fruit less prone to FUNGAL DISEASES by improving aeration, leaf removal can also increase the effectiveness of such chemicals as may be applied to protect the fruit. R.E.S.

Smart, R. E., and Robinson, M., *Sunlight into Wine* (Adelaide, 1991).

LEAF ROLLERS, also called **leaf folders**, insects which cause damage to vines at the caterpillar stage (and nothing whatever to do with LEAFROLL VIRUS disease). As the name suggests, they form the leaf into a roll, and feed on the edge of the leaf inside the roll. The roll restricts the exposed leaf surface, and the feeding reduces the leaf area. In California both the grape leaf roller (*Desmia funeralis*) and the omnivorous leaf roller (*Platynota stultana*) are serious vineyard pests. In Australia a native leaf roller, light brown apple moth (*Epiphyas postvittana*), is the country's most serious insect pest, feeding on a wide range of native and imported plants, including grapevines. As well as feeding on young shoots, the larvae cause damage by feeding on berries, resulting in yield reductions of up to 10 per cent, and allowing the entry of BOTRYTIS and other BUNCH ROTS. Control of leaf rollers can be by selective or by broad spectrum insecticides, but some predators are active against some species, which can help to control low populations.

See also BEETLES for a European insect which causes leaf rolling. M.J.E.

Buchanan, G. A., and Amos, T. G., 'Grape pests', in B. G. Coombe and P. R. Dry (eds.), *Viticulture, ii: Practices* (Adelaide, 1992).

Flaherty, D. L., *et al.* (eds.), *Grape Pest Management* (2nd edn., Oakland, Calif., 1992).

LEAFROLL VIRUS, virus disease that is widespread in all countries where grapes are grown. The disease is now thought to be due to a complex of different viruses which can be differentiated. Of all the VIRUS DISEASES of vines, it can have the most serious effects on wine quality. These dramatic effects are not understood by the many appreciative tourists of wine regions who marvel at the attractive autumnal colours of vineyards. Few realize that these colours often indicate the presence of a serious disease, although other factors may contribute to autumnal colours. Leafroll virus causes yield to be reduced by as much as 50 per cent. Wine quality is also affected because of delayed RIPENING. Thus wines from infected vines are lower in alcohol, colour, flavour, and body. The disease does not kill vines, so they are infrequently removed. Yet removal is the only known treatment to overcome the effects of the virus.

Leafroll probably originated in the Near East along with VITIS VINIFERA and was carried along with grape cuttings. The disease is spread chiefly by man, using cuttings or buds from infected vines. Once infected planting material is used then the new vineyard is immediately infected, and will perform at below its potential for its lifetime.

Characteristic symptoms are downwards rolling of the leaf blade in autumn. The area between the leaf veins turns red for black-fruited varieties, and yellow for white-fruited varieties—hence the attractive autumn colours at the end of the season. Some varieties such as Cabernet Franc and Chardonnay show the classic symptoms; others such as Riesling and most ROOTSTOCKS show no symptoms at all. Infected vines may be stunted but this is hardly sufficient for diagnosis.

There are a few recorded instances where natural spread of the virus has been confirmed, including New Zealand and South Africa. An insect vector (MEALY BUG) is implicated. The virus is spread most commonly, however, by man using poor nursery practices and taking cuttings from infected vines. Cuttings for budwood are taken when the vines are dormant and of course no leaves are present to show symptoms, so it is impossible to distinguish healthy from infected plants.

This virus disease, like many others, has become more widespread as GRAFTING on to PHYLLOXERA-resistant rootstocks has become more commonplace because grafting increases the chances of using infected material. Thus, many Old World vineyards planted early in the 1900s show the virus. Some tasters believed that grafting to phylloxera-resistant rootstocks from the 1880s onwards led directly to a decline in wine quality. In fact this supposed drop in quality may have been an effect of increased spread of leafroll virus due to grafting.

Because there is no control for this disease, growers should ensure that they plant only material that is tested free of the virus. The University of California at DAVIS led the world in developing a 'clean stock' programme, with the result that vineyards planted in California since the early 1960s are generally virus free. In addition, this virus-tested planting stock has been exported and, for example, many of the vineyards of Australia and New Zealand are planted with such material. The virus is detected by INDEXING, or by using immunoassays such as ELISA, or by electron microscope searches for the virus particles. Healthy planting material is produced by eliminating viruses using THERMOTHERAPY or heat treatment or, more reliably, by TISSUE CULTURE. Propagation is recommended from these 'clean' mother plants. R.E.S.

Emmett, R. W., Harris, A. R., Taylor, R. H., and McGechan, J. K., 'Grape diseases and vineyard protection', in B. G. Coombe and P. R. Dry (eds.), *Viticulture, ii: Practices* (Adelaide, 1992).

Pearson, R. C., and Goheen, A. C., *Compendium of Grape Diseases* (St Paul, Minn., 1988).

LEAF TO FRUIT RATIO, viticultural measurement which indicates the capacity of a vine to ripen grapes. The ratio of vine leaf area to fruit (grape) weight determines just how well a vine can mature grapes and how suitable they will be for wine-making. Although it is less understood and discussed, it can have an even more important effect on wine quality than YIELD.

This ratio indicates the vine's ability to manufacture compounds important for grape RIPENING. If most leaves are exposed to the sun, then the leaf area is proportional to the ability of the vine to make SUGARS by PHOTOSYNTHESIS. Against this should be set the weight of grapes to be ripened. Some studies, however, show that photosynthetic rate can somewhat adjust to a low leaf to fruit ratio, and so the effect of over-severe LEAF REMOVAL in the fruit zone, for instance, may not be as detrimental to ripening as anticipated.

A low value of leaf to fruit ratio, for example 5 sq cm per g grape weight, indicates that the fruit will ripen sluggishly, and so levels of SUGAR IN GRAPES will increase slowly along with PHENOLICS and flavour, but PH will be relatively high for the corresponding sugar level. The other extreme of, say, 30 sq cm per g grape weight suggests a very leafy vine with a small crop of grapes, but one which will ripen quickly and completely, and so produce better wine quality than for the low leaf to fruit ratio. Such low yields, however, may be uneconomic, and so most vine-growers would aim to manage their vineyards with a sufficient but not excessive leaf to fruit ratio. A value of between 10 and 15 sq cm per g grape weight is considered adequate for ripening of most vine varieties, although higher values are considered necessary by some for PINOT NOIR and perhaps MERLOT. Also, high leaf to fruit ratios must be carefully managed in the vineyard, so as to avoid any negative effects on wine quality due to canopy SHADE. R.E.S.

Champagnol, F., *Éléments de physiologie de la vigne et de viticulture générale* (St-Gely-du-Fesc, 1984).

LEAFY, tasting term usually used synonymously with HERBACEOUS.

LEÁNYKA, Hungarian name for the white grape variety called FETEASCA in Romania. A varietal Leányka has long been produced in Eger, source of Bull's Blood. It can produce good-quality wine if yields are restricted, and a particularly aromatic strain is grown on the south shore of Lake Balaton. For more details see HUNGARY.

Within Europe, **Spain** was unusual in the extent of Islamic influence, although, as this page from the 'Beatus' of King Ferdinand and King Sancho shows, the grape harvest was as culturally important as the grain harvest even under the Moors.

UBI METENT MESSEM TERRE
CIUITAS
UBI CALCATUM EST TORCULAR
EXTRA CIUITATE. ET EXIIT SANGUIS
DE TORCULARI USQUE AD FRENOS
EQUORUM

2

LEBANON, one of the oldest sites of wine production, incorporating some of the ancient eastern Mediterranean land of CANAAN and, subsequently, most of PHOENICIA. In Baalbek, the ancient Greek city in the Bekaa valley which is the vine-growing centre of Lebanon, is the Temple of BACCHUS, built in the middle of the 2nd century AD and excavated, displaying much of its former glory, in the early 20th century.

In the Middle Ages, the rich wines of Tyre and Sidon were particularly treasured in Europe, and were traded by the merchants of VENICE, to whom they belonged for much of the 13th century.

Apart from some vineyards in the Lebanese mountains, most vines are grown in the wide Bekaa Valley, where an altitude of around 1,000 m/3,280 ft and mountain ranges on either side provide cool nights and rainfall respectively so that the grapes rarely ripen before the middle of September (considerably later than some southern French vineyards, for example). Minimal vineyard treatments are needed, and most vines still sprawl in vigorous bush form, although a small but increasing proportion is being trained on wires.

One of the less serious effects of the war that devastated the country's capital Beirut in the 1980s was to diminish local demand for wine, and to reduce statistical records. Of the 29,000 ha/71,600 acres of Lebanese vines reported to the OIV in 1990, the great majority are used to produce either DRYING GRAPES or TABLE GRAPES. Only about 3,000 ha were believed to be cultivated for the production of table wine in 1992, and an increasing proportion of grapes were used for the DISTILLATION of ARAK as demand for this popular anise-flavoured spirit grew at the expense of demand for wine.

French influence on the country is still apparent in the grape varieties most commonly planted—CINSAUT, CARIGNAN, ARAMON, ALICANTE—the varieties also planted under French influence in North Africa in the mid 20th century. A little Cabernet Sauvignon and Syrah are also planted. Ch Musar, the country's innovative producer of good-quality wines, has a long track record of intense red wine made from 50 to 80 per cent Cabernet Sauvignon fleshed out with Cinsaut. Following lessons learned from the BARTON family of Bordeaux in the 1950s, Ch Musar introduced DESTEMMING and BARREL MATURATION in new French OAK. The result, sold only after the second of three years' ageing in bulk has been spent in NEVERS oak, and perhaps as many as four years in bottle, is a heady, rich, powerful red that invites comparisons with PENFOLDS Grange of Australia or FERREIRA's Barca Velha but has a character that is entirely its own. Ch Musar also produces small quantities of an equally full bodied, oak-aged white, primarily from the indigenous white grape variety Obaideh, thought by some to be identical to CHARDONNAY, as well as some relatively hard indigenous Meroué, or Merweh. Ch Musar exports 95 per cent of production to markets including the UK, USA, Sweden, and, more recently, France. Lebanon's other important wineries, Kefraya and Ksara, are close to the vineyards of the Bekaa valley, while Ch Musar's grapes have to be trucked over the mountains to the winery in Ghazir just north of Beirut. No wine was made in 1976, and the 1984 vintage was the only one, miraculously, to fall prey to the effects of the conflict of the 1980s.

Jefford, A., 'War and Peace', *Wine* (Aug.–Sept. 1993).

LEES, old English word for the dregs or sediment that settles at the bottom of a container such as a FERMENTATION VESSEL. Wine lees are made up of dead YEAST cells, grape seeds, pulp, stem and skin fragments, and insoluble TARTRATES that are deposited during the making and ageing of wine.

In the production of everyday wines, clear wine is separated from the lees as soon as possible after FERMENTATION, to ensure that yeast AUTOLYSIS is avoided and to begin clarification and stabilization. Some wines, both red and, especially, white, may be deliberately left on some of their lees, the so-called **fine lees** (as opposed to the coarser **gross lees**, from the French *grosses lies*, off which most wines are racked early in their life if greater complexity and reduction of MALIC ACID is desired), for some months in order to gain greater complexity of flavour. This is called LEES CONTACT. Lees contact also encourages the second, softening MALOLACTIC FERMENTATION because the LACTIC BACTERIA necessary for malolactic fermentation feed on micro-nutrients in the lees.

Fine wines left on lees for a considerable time usually require much less drastic processing than more ordinary wines that were separated early from the lees, because the semi-stable colloidal PHENOLICS and tartrates gradually precipitate during this AGEING period.

Deposits of FINING agents used in CLARIFICATION such as bentonite, silicic acid, and casein are also referred to as lees. They are usually simply settled to permit the recovery of as much wine as possible, but in some large wineries are processed by ROTARY DRUM VACUUM FILTRATION to salvage a bit more wine with a strong lees flavour.

Once the maximum amount of good wine has been recovered, usually by RACKING after prolonged SETTLING, or by the harsher process of FILTRATION, the lees are valuable only for their potassium acid tartrate (cream of tartar) and small amounts of alcohol. After the recovery of tartrates and alcohol, lees are usually returned to the vineyard, where they serve to add some NITROGEN to the soil. Care should be taken when otherwise disposing of lees as they contain organic matter which may rot and cause environmental pollution.

A.D.W.

LEES CONTACT, increasingly popular and currently fashionable wine-making practice known to the Ancient Romans (see CATO) whereby newly fermented wine is left in contact with the LEES. This period of lees contact may take place in any container, from a bottle (as in the making of any BOTTLE-FERMENTED sparkling wine where yeast AUTOLYSIS produces desirable flavour compounds) to a large tank or

By no means all of Turkey's vineyards are devoted to **table grapes** and **drying grapes**, as is evident in this press house near İzmir, although most Turks consume their wine in distilled forms such as **brandy** and raki.

vat—although a small oak BARREL is the most common location for lees contact. It may take place for anything between a few weeks and, in the special case of some sparkling wines, several years. Most commonly, however, lees contact is prolonged for less than a year after the completion of FERMENTATION.

Lees contact has the effect of encouraging MALOLACTIC FERMENTATION and of adding complexity to the resultant wine's flavour. Many producers, particularly those of white BURGUNDY and other wines based on CHARDONNAY grapes, try to increase the influence of the lees on flavour by LEES STIRRING, or *bâtonnage*, as this practice is known in French.

White wines made with deliberate lees contact are sometimes described as SUR LIE, a description commonly used to differentiate one type of MUSCADET from another, although in this case small barrels rarely play a part in the process. Lees contact even in BULK STORAGE is increasingly used as a way of increasing flavour in everyday white wines.

Red wines, with their more robust flavours, gain less benefit from lees contact, but, for many red wines, the added complexity of the malolactic fermentation, which is encouraged by lees contact, is very valuable.

Wines left in contact with a layer of lees more than 10 cm/4 in thick for more than a week or so, however, are very likely to develop HYDROGEN SULPHIDE, disulphide, or MERCAPTAN odours. This is because, as the YEASTS start to autolyse, or digest themselves, they produce strongly REDUCING CONDITIONS. Any fungicide residues of SULPHUR, SULPHUR DIOXIDE, or even the sulphur-containing amino acids of the yeasts, are likely to be reduced to the foul-smelling SULPHIDES. This is why it is important to rack new wine from its gross lees (see LEES) so that the lees level does not become too thick.

LEES STIRRING, or *bâtonnage*, as it is called in French, is the wine-making operation of mixing up the LEES in a barrel, cask, tank, or vat with the wine resting on them. It is an optional addition to the process of LEES CONTACT and is often employed, particularly for whites which have undergone BARREL FERMENTATION. As the French name suggests, such stirring is usually done with a stick.

Lees stirring is done partly to avoid the development of malodorous HYDROGEN SULPHIDE. Unless a thick layer of lees is stirred, oxygen does not reach the bottom layer and strong enough REDUCING conditions develop to change any small amounts of SULPHUR into hydrogen sulphide.

Stirring up the lees in the barrel also affects WOOD FLAVOUR, however. If the lees are stirred, they act as an even more effective buffer between the wine and the wood, limiting the extent to which wood TANNINS and PIGMENTS are extracted into the wine. Wines subjected to lees stirring therefore tend to be much paler and less tannic than those whose lees are not stirred.

LEFT BANK, an expression for that part of the BORDEAUX wine region that is on the left bank of the river GARONNE. It includes, travelling down river, GRAVES, SAUTERNES, BARSAC, PESSAC-LÉOGNAN, MÉDOC, and all the appellations of the Médoc. The most obvious characteristic shared by the red wines of these appellations, and distinct from RIGHT BANK appellations, is that the dominant grape variety is Cabernet Sauvignon rather than Merlot and Cabernet Franc, although there are many other distinctions. The land between the left and right banks is said to be 'between the two seas', or ENTRE-DEUX-MERS.

LEFTOVER WINE in an opened container such as a half-empty bottle is prey to OXIDATION and steps must be taken in order to prevent it turning to VINEGAR—which could happen within hours or even minutes for a very old wine, within days for most young table wines, within a few weeks for a robust vintage character PORT or OLOROSO sherry, or within months for most MADEIRA.

Because OXYGEN is the villain in this piece, the easiest way to avoid spoilage of leftover wine is to decant it into a smaller container, perhaps a half-bottle. There are also patent devices for filling the ULLAGE in a bottle or decanter with INERT GAS, by pumping or spraying, or an attempt can be made to create a vacuum with a pump device.

The most satisfactory way of disposing of wine leftovers is surely to drink them and the leftovers of some wines, particularly concentrated young red wines, can taste better, and certainly softer, after a day or even two on ullage (see AERATION and DECANTING).

Leftover wine can also be used quite satisfactorily as COOKING wine and can also be used quite deliberately to make vinegar.

LEGNO RICCIO, one of the vine VIRUS DISEASES and recognized in Italy. It seems related to CORKY BARK, and reduces growth and yield.

LEGS, tasting term and alternative name for the TEARS left on the inside of a glass by some wines, giving rise to various dubious jokes among male wine tasters.

LEMBERGER. See LIMBERGER.

LEN DE L'EL and **Len de l'Elh** has, like MANSENG, been a beneficiary of proud regionalism in SOUTH WEST FRANCE. It was once a major and is now a compulsory minor ingredient in the white wines of GAILLAC. The wine is powerful, characterful, but can be flabby. Its name is local dialect for *loin de l'œil*, or 'far from sight'. This vigorous vine needs a well-ventilated, well-drained site if it is to escape rot in lesser years.

LENGTH or persistence of flavour is an important indicator of wine quality. See the tasting term LONG.

LENZ MOSER, important wine producer in AUSTRIA which can trace its history back to the 12th century. In the 1920s Dr Lenz Moser III experimented with a new way of training vines (see below) which revolutionized Austrian viticulture, making it feasible despite high labour costs. The company was taken over in 1986 by a large Austrian drinks company and Lenz Moser V has channelled considerable investments into renewing vineyards and into the winery at Rohrendorf in Kamptal-Donauland, concentrating increasingly on ORGANIC VITICULTURE and innovations such as paper (as opposed to lead) CAPSULES. The company has managed the Malteser (Knights of Malta) wine estate at Mailberg near the Czech border since 1969 and has here pioneered both BARRIQUE maturation for red wines and the Cabernet Sauvignon grape in lower Austria. In 1988 Lenz Moser acquired the Klosterkeller Siegendorf in Burgenland and is developing Pinot Blanc here.

LENZ MOSER VINES. The name Lenz Moser is known by the world's viticulturists because of the popular and eponymous vine-TRAINING SYSTEM. The system employed wider rows (about 3.5 m/11.5 ft) and higher trunks (1.3 m) than had previously been the norm, thereby reducing VINE DENSITY. This system found favour in parts of Europe in the mid 20th century because it decreases LABOUR and therefore production costs, without any need for special machinery. French and German studies found reductions in fruit quality, however, probably because of SHADE in the fruit zone. For long it has been the dominant vine-training system in Austria but is becoming less common. It is also known as high culture, or *Hochkultur* in German. R.E.S.

LEÓN, wine zone in north west Spain. See CASTILE-LEÓN.

LEROY, famous name in French wine, not just because **Baron le Roy** of CHÂTEAUNEUF-DU-PAPE was instrumental in the development of the APPELLATION CONTRÔLÉE system, but also in the CÔTE D'OR. The NÉGOCIANT house **Maison Leroy** was founded in the small village of Auxey-Duresses in 1868 and its extensive warehouses there still house substantial stocks of fine, mature burgundy. Henri Leroy joined the family firm in 1919 and made his fortune exporting fortified wine from the Charentes to Germany between the two World Wars. This enabled him to buy a half share in the world-famous DOMAINE DE LA ROMANÉE-CONTI, a share inherited equally by his two daughters Pauline Roch-Leroy and **Lalou Bize-Leroy** on his death in 1980.

Lalou, a prodigious taster, rock climber, and keen follower of *haute couture*, had been co-director of the Domaine since 1975 and contributed considerably to its wine-making policy of quality above all. She also ran Maison Leroy, but Burgundy's steady move towards DOMAINE BOTTLING made her job of buying the finest raw materials for her négociant skills of ÉLEVAGE increasingly difficult. In 1988, helped by an £8 million investment from her Japanese importers Takashimaya, she succeeded in buying the Domaine Noëllat of VOSNE-ROMANÉE, an already fine canvas on which to paint her vision of the perfect domaine, soon renamed **Domaine Leroy**. This domaine now comprises more than 22 ha/54 acres of some of the Côte d'Or's finest vineyards, including a total of more than 6 ha in nine different GRANDS CRUS.

This effectively entailed setting up in competition with DRC, since the Domaine Leroy is based in the same village and also has holdings in the grand cru RICHEBOURG. Unfettered by the commercial considerations of the dozen or so shareholders in DRC, Lalou was able to institute fully BIODYNAMIC VITICULTURE, almost uneconomically low YIELDS, and to invest in every possible wine-making luxury. The wines, which come from a much broader range of (mainly red wine) appellations than those of DRC, are extremely concentrated, expressing as definitively as possible their exact geographical provenance.

A sales company, **Société Leroy**, enjoyed the exclusive distribution rights to DRC wines, some of the most highly priced in the world, in all markets except the USA and UK until a bitter dispute in 1993 which ousted Lalou from co-directorship of DRC. Today, only Domaine Leroy prices rival those of DRC.

Mansson, P.-H., 'Behind the breakup at Domaine de la Romanée-Conti', *Wine Spectator* (15 Feb. 1993), 20–7.

LES BAUX. See BAUX.

LESSONA, small but historically important red wine district in the Vercelli hills in the subalpine north of the PIEDMONT region of north west Italy. NEBBIOLO grapes, here called Spanna, make up the majority of the wine although some BONARDA or VESPOLINA may be added to produce a slightly less austere wine. Sella is the only producer of note. See SPANNA for more details.

See also the nearby BRAMATERRA also in Vercelli and BOCA, GHEMME, SIZZANO, and FARA in Novara.

L'ÉTOILE, small appellation in the JURA region of eastern France, dominated by the CO-OPERATIVE, which specializes in the production of the extraordinarily nutty VIN JAUNE which is sold in the 62-cl/22-fl oz *clavelin* bottle like the more famous CH-CHALON made nearby. L'Étoile also produces sweet white VIN DE PAILLE in some years, and regular light, dry whites from Chardonnay and the region's SAVAGNIN grape. **L'Étoile Mousseux** is also made, using the champagne method of SPARKLING WINE-MAKING. In 1990 there were just over 70 ha/173 acres in production.

LEVANTE, the collective name for four Mediterranean provinces of SPAIN forming two autonomous regions officially known as Comunidad Valenciana and Murcia (see map on p. 907). The Levante encompasses five DO wine zones: ALICANTE, UTIEL-REQUENA, VALENCIA in the Valencian autonomy; and JUMILLA and YECLA in Murcia. There are also numerous smaller wine-producing zones such as Bullas, Cartagena, and Castellón. Cheste, which once had its own DO, has now been absorbed into DO Valencia. The climate becomes progressively extreme away from the coast with summer TEMPERATURES reaching 45 °C/113 °F in places and annual RAINFALL amounting to less than 300 mm/12 in. Most of the wines are correspondingly coarse but progress has been made in Jumilla, Yecla, and Valencia. The port of Valencia itself is one of the largest wine entrepôts in the world with five huge

Silver bowl designed for **libations** in southern Italy in about 300 BC.

firms handling millions of litres of bulk wine from all over south and central Spain, although by the early 1990s this trade was declining. R.J.M.

LEVERANO, DOC for robust red wine made mainly from NEGROAMARO grapes in south east Italy. For more details see APULIA.

LEXIAS, DRYING GRAPES produced principally from the MUSCAT OF ALEXANDRIA variety in Australia, named after a contraction of Alexandria. A similar product, which also requires deseeding, is called valencias in Spain.

LIBATION, the pouring out of wine (occasionally other liquids: water, oil, honey) as a religious act. The practice of offering a libation to a god was universal in the Greek and Roman world. Whenever wine was drunk in formal gatherings, such as symposia, a libation was poured while a prayer was said to invoke a chosen god. Libations also regularly accompanied prayers and sacrifices on all sorts of occasions.

The origins of the practice are to be found in the offering of the first fruits to gods; but libation should also be seen in the context of the way in which social intercourse between humans (and by analogy between humans and gods) was maintained by the mutual exchange of gifts. Libations poured on the ground were also specifically seen as a gift for the dead. 'The souls are nourished by libations', as Lucian says.

J.J.P.

Burkert, W., *Greek Religion* (Oxford, 1985).

LIBOURNE, small port on the RIGHT BANK of the Dordogne in the Bordeaux region. It is now the commercial centre for the right bank appellations, although it was established in the 13th century, much later than ST-ÉMILION's port Pierrefitte, and was at the time considered a parvenu in comparison with FRONSAC. In modern history its wine trade is much more recent than the Chartronnais of the BORDEAUX TRADE in the great city across the Garonne, and its more modest traders concentrated initially on selling in northern mainland Europe rather than in the British Isles. Of merchants based here on the banks of the river Dordogne, J. P. MOUEIX is the most important. For more details, see POMEROL, the wine region on the eastern outskirts of the town.

The wines St-Émilion, Pomerol, and Fronsac are sometimes referred to collectively as **Libournais**.

LICHINE, ALEXIS (1913–89), was born in Russia but, unlike André TCHELISTCHEFF, another Russian who was to shape the American wine industry, he and his family left before the Revolution, and he was educated in France.

After the Repeal of PROHIBITION, Lichine sold wines, first in a shop in New York and subsequently for the gifted American wine importer Frank SCHOONMAKER. After the Second World War, in which he served with distinction, he returned to finding French and German wines from individual estates and selling them in an America where wine was all but unknown.

His success in doing this was considerable and came from a flair for seeing and recounting the romantic side of wine and wine-making, as well as appreciating the pleasures wine can bring.

During the 1950s he became a major figure in the French wine world, setting up his own company, Alexis Lichine & Co., to sell only CHÂTEAU BOTTLED and ESTATE BOTTLED wines, for the most part from major properties. He sold this company to British brewers Bass-Charrington in 1964, and gradually left the commercial world to make wine and write books.

His first book, *The Wines of France*, was an excellent primer to the subject and his second, the ambitious *Alexis Lichine's Encyclopedia of Wines and Spirits*, was a great success with enthusiasts anxious to learn.

Lichine assembled a group of investors to buy and renovate the MARGAUX second growth Ch Lascombes in 1952, and ran the property with great success before selling it, also to Bass-Charrington, in 1971.

He also bought in 1951 the fourth growth Ch Prieuré at Cantenac just outside Margaux. He officially renamed this property, based on an old Benedictine priory, Ch Prieuré-Lichine in 1953 and it was at this property, typically one of the first to welcome passing visitors, that he died in 1989. W.B.

Alexis **Lichine** in front of his base in Margaux, Ch Prieuré-Lichine.

Lichine, A., *Alexis Lichine's Encyclopedia of Wines and Spirits* (2nd edn., New York, 1980).

LICOROSO, Portuguese sweet FORTIFIED WINE (as opposed to a GENEROSO which may be dry or sweet).

LIE or **lies**, French for LEES.

LIEBFRAUMILCH, medium dry white wine from GERMANY known almost exclusively in export markets. As defined by law, it is a QBA from any one of the following regions: RHEINHESSEN, PFALZ, NAHE, and RHEINGAU, of which the first two account for some 55 and 42 per cent of the total production respectively. Liebfraumilch must contain not less than 18 g/l RESIDUAL SUGAR and contain at least 70 per cent of RIESLING, SILVANER, MÜLLER-THURGAU, and KERNER grapes, although in practice Müller-Thurgau usually dominates the blend. Until the early 19th century Liebfraumilch (or **Liebfrauenmilch**) was the name given to the wine (principally from Riesling) of the vineyard in Worms in the Rheinhessen by the collegiate church of Our Lady, the Liebfrauenstiftskirche. In 1989, well over a million hl (26.4 million gal) of Liebfraumilch was authorized—an amount which corresponded almost exactly to the quantity exported that year. Consumed within 18 months of the vintage, most Liebfraumilch is fresh, low in alcohol, agreeably sweet, and deliberately designed to wean newcomers to wine off soft drinks. Well-known BRANDS include BLUE NUN and Black Tower. I.J.

LIECHTENSTEIN. The principality's 15 ha/37 acres of vineyard are concentrated on the capital Vaduz, above and at some distance from the river RHINE, where the climate is strongly influenced by the warming föhn effect of the wind from the south. The largest vineyard owners, the domain of the Fürst von und zu Liechtenstein, produces good-quality wine in the style of eastern SWITZERLAND, from Blauburgunder (PINOT NOIR) and from a small plantation of CHARDONNAY. Seventy per cent is sold directly to the consumer. I.J.

LIGHT. A wine is described by wine tasters as light, or **light bodied**, if it is low in ALCOHOL and VISCOSITY. See BODY for more details.

LIGHTNING, a climatic phenomenon which may strike a vineyard and, by travelling along a wire, damage vines around the point of contact. Because of the high voltage and ensuing heat, any shoots touching the wire are damaged and effectively girdled (see CINCTURING), but normally the effect is extended over only a few vines because the current runs to ground through the trunks. Lightning damage is to be expected in regions with summer storms, and a sign that lightning is to blame is that the damage is restricted to a few otherwise quite healthy vines in a single row. Closer examination will indicate burns on the vine shoots touching wires, or sometimes shattered vine stakes or posts. R.E.S.

LIGURIA, the crescent-shaped strip that runs along Italy's Mediterranean coast from the French border to the edge of Tuscany, is Italy's third smallest region after the Valle d'Aosta and Molise. See map on p. 517, and see GENOA, VERNACCIA, and ITALY for some historical detail. The extremely rugged terrain—the Apennines descend virtually all the way to the sea—combined with the microscopic size of individual properties make agriculture in general and viticulture in particular a marginal activity, and the greater economic possibilities offered by the thriving tourist industry, commercial flower-growing, and olive-growing have drained manpower from the region's vineyards at a steady pace ever since the Second World War. Total Ligurian wine production is less than 300,000 hl/7.9 milion gal, and DOC wines represent just six per cent of this figure.

A crossroads of trade and traffic between Italy, France, and Spain, with a rich history described under GENOA, Liguria has long cultivated a multitude of different vine varieties, and a census of the province of Imperia in 1970 revealed no fewer than 123. Many of these have since been abandoned, however, and, although the undistinguished Albarola is the region's most planted variety, the region is concentrating its efforts on three white varieties (VERMENTINO, PIGATO, and the less characterful Bosco) and three red varieties (ROSSESE, SANGIOVESE, and DOLCETTO, the last of these called Ormeasco in Liguria). Ormeasco, Pigato, Rossese, and Vermentino each have their own DOC within the Riviera di Ponente zone, a wide stretch of territory between Genoa and the French border.

Liguria's most renowned wine, the white Cinqueterre, is perhaps most famous for its vertigo-inducing vineyards perched on TERRACES sculpted into cliffsides high above the Tyrrhenian Sea. The wine itself, made from Bosco plus Albarola and/or Vermentino, rarely rises above the thirst-quenching level. The once-renowned Sciacchetrà, a sweet Cinqueterre made from raisined grapes, has virtually disappeared.

Production of Vermentino is concentrated in Castelnuovo Magra, to the south of La Spezia (where the wine is not a DOC), and in Diano Castello and Imperia in the province of Imperia. Good bottles of Vermentino can be delicate and floral, although they cannot be compared to a fine BELLET made across the French border from the same grape variety. Pigato, a fleshier wine with more intense flavours, is potentially more interesting than Vermentino, although well-made bottles are more difficult to find; production of the wine is concentrated in Ranzo and Pieve di Teco, to the north of the city of Imperia. Ormeasco is produced almost exclusively in Pornassio and Pieve di Teco. With an average production of under 700 hl/17,780 gal annually, it is more a curiosity than a real commercial proposition, but good Ormeasco has an unmistakable Dolcetto character. The Rossese grape, of minor significance in the Riviera di Ponente DOC, has its own DOC near Ventimiglia, Rossese di Dolceacqua or simply Dolceacqua. The wine has its fanatical admirers who have found in it blackcurrants and roses, power and delicacy, and cite Napoleon's admiration for Dolceacqua (although the terms of the praise—a comparison to CH-CHALON—are peculiar in and of themselves). Since an annual production that rarely exceeds 2,000 hl is divided between 100 growers, finding a representative bottle of wine that could serve as a yardstick of quality is no easy task. D.T.

LIMBERGER, also known as **Blauer Limberger** or **Lemberger**, is the German name for the black grape variety much more widely grown in Austria as BLAUFRÄNKISCH. Germany has only about a quarter as much of the variety planted, nearly 700 ha/1,730 acres in the early 1990s, almost exclusively in WÜRTTEMBERG, where both climate and consumers are tolerant of pale reds made from late ripening vines (see TROLLINGER). The wine, often blended with Trollinger to produce a light red suitable for early drinking, has a better colour than that of most Germanic red wine varieties and has a good bite, notably of acidity. WASHINGTON state, curiously, has sizeable plantings of this variety, known there as Lemberger.

LIME, in the forms of slaked lime (calcium hydroxide) or ground limestone (calcium carbonate), is sometimes added to soils to neutralize SOIL ACIDITY. It is fairly immobile in the soil, except in light sands, and must therefore be incorporated deeply and thoroughly to be fully effective. **Liming** is therefore most appropriately used, if likely to be needed, before vine PLANTING. The CALCIUM in lime or limestone also helps to give the soil greater crumb structure and friability (see SOIL STRUCTURE). Gypsum (calcium sulphate) can be used for the latter purpose on soils where acidity is unlikely to become excessive. J.G.

LIME KILN VALLEY, small California wine region and AVA in SAN BENITO County.

LIMESTONE, a rock made of the mineral calcite (calcium carbonate); in dolomitic limestone there is some admixture of calcium-magnesium carbonate. Limestone is *calcaire* in French.

Common limestones differ from CHALK (a special type of limestone) in being hard and not readily penetrated by plant roots, except through cracks. The soils formed over limestones are often much richer in clay than the underlying limestone, although pebbles of the limestone may be common in the vineyard, especially on slopes. Some limestone soils, such as the Mediterranean TERRA ROSSA, are red-brown in colour; these are moderately alkaline and have a good clay-loam texture and structure. Leaching of the calcium carbonate from sandy limestones will leave the soil relatively sandy.

Some limestone soils overlie substantial reservoirs of SOIL WATER, of high quality for IRRIGATION. The longer roots of well-established vines may be able to reach these reservoirs, especially if deep RIPPING to shatter and crack the hard limestone has been carried out before planting. Limestone-derived soils are in general valued most highly in cool viticultural regions. The great wines of BURGUNDY come from vines grown on head, sediment which has slipped down a slope and deposited on its lower reaches, generally mixed with limestone pebbles.

The red limestone-derived terra rossa of Coonawarra in SOUTH AUSTRALIA similarly produces some of Australia's best red wines from Cabernet Sauvignon and Shiraz, both vine varieties being close to the cool limit for their reliable ripening.

In warm climates, however, such as those of the south of France, and the Riverland of South Australia, limestone soils are not regarded as superior, or even necessarily as suitable for viticulture (see SOIL AND WINE QUALITY).

J.G., R.E.S., & J.M.H.

LIMNIO, dark grape variety native to the island of Lemnos in GREECE, where it can still be found. It has also transferred successfully to Khalkhidhikhi in north east Greece, however, where it produces a full bodied wine with a good level of acidity. It is thought that this is the variety which Aristotle called Lemnia.

LIMOUSIN, old French province centred on the town of Limoges, and a term encountered most frequently in the wine world as a term for the region's OAK.

LIMOUX, small town in the eastern Pyrenean foothills in southern France. For centuries it has been devoted to the production of white wines that would sparkle naturally after a second fermentation during the spring. They became known as Blanquette de Limoux, Blanquette meaning simply 'white' in Occitan. Locals claim that fermentation in bottle was developed here long before it was consciously practised in CHAMPAGNE, dating the production of cork-stoppered sparkling wines at the Abbey of St-Hilaire from 1531. (Limoux is just north of CATALONIA, a natural home of the CORK oak.)

The region's vineyards are so much higher, cooler, and further from Mediterranean influence than any other Languedoc appellation (even Côtes de la MALEPÈRE to its immediate north) that the INAO authorities classify it as part of the Atlantic-influenced SOUTH WEST FRANCE rather than as part of LANGUEDOC-ROUSSILLON. Within the region there are distinctly different zones, according to factors such as altitude, soil types, and the influence of the Atlantic or Mediterranean.

The grape used traditionally was the MAUZAC, called locally Blanquette, but increasing amounts of Chardonnay and, to a lesser extent, CHENIN BLANC have been planted so that in the 1980s the Limoux vineyards were much valued as one of southern France's very few sources of CHARDONNAY grapes from mature vines. Still wines made from them were therefore in great demand, especially for export markets. This international success was cleverly capitalized upon by Toques et Clochers, an annual charity auction of different Chardonnay barrel samples, inspired by the famous HOSPICES DE BEAUNE auction but embellished by the involvement of some of France's most famous chefs. These often lean, oak-aged Chardonnays regularly fetch prices far in excess of their official classification as VINS DE PAYS.

The Limoux appellation drawn up in 1993 applies to still whites made mainly from Chardonnay, with, unusually, compulsory BARREL FERMENTATION and LEES STIRRING. This activity, together with light Cabernet and Merlot reds sold as Vins de Pays de la Haute Vallée de l'Aude, supplements Limoux's sparkling wine business, dominated by the dynamic local CO-OPERATIVE, which sells a range of bottlings under such names as Aimery and Sieur d'Arques.

A new appellation CRÉMANT de Limoux was devised in 1990 for less rustic, more internationally designed sparkling wines made from a maximum of 70 per cent Mauzac together with Chardonnay and/or Chenin. From the 1990 vintage the Blanquette de Limoux appellation was reserved for wines containing at least 90 per cent of Mauzac and will presumably be increasingly marginalized in favour of Limoux's Crémant, a more obvious and good-value alternative to CHAMPAGNE.

Traditionalists may content themselves however with

Limoux's distinctly marginal speciality, Blanquette Méthode Ancestrale (see SPARKLING WINE-MAKING), a sweeter, often slightly cloudy, less fizzy sparkling wine made exclusively from Mauzac left to ferment a second time in bottle without subsequent disgorgement of the resultant sediment. Like the GAILLAC Mousseux made from Mauzac by the *méthode gaillacoise* with similar regard for tradition and disdain for technology, these hand-crafted wines are low in alcohol, high in Mauzac's old apple peel flavours, and can taste remarkably like a superior sweet cider.

LIPIDS, a group of chemicals that includes oils, fats, and waxes. Lipids are distinctive in plants because, despite the plant's watery environment, they are not soluble in water, which is also the basis of their important roles. They make up the membranes of plant CELLS which keep apart entirely different zones of metabolic activity, often with large differences in ACIDITY on either side of the membrane. They make energy-rich reserves of food as in seeds, grapeseed oil being a good example. Also they coat the surface of the plant with a water-impermeable layer of waxy cutin which stops desiccation. Many lipids are ESTERS formed from the combination of fatty acids, such as oleic acid, and various alcohols, such as GLYCEROL, which gives a triglyceride. The special structural components of membranes include phospholipids and glycolipids. A host of other compounds have lipid-like structures, including important plant pigments such as chlorophyll and CAROTENOIDS. B.G.C.

Mick Morris—a life dedicated to **Liqueur Muscat** and other Australian 'stickies'.

LIQUEUR MUSCAT and **Liqueur Tokay** are two of AUSTRALIA's great gifts to the world: sumptuously hedonistic dark, sweet, alcoholic liquids that taste something like a cross between madeira and Malaga. They are made from, respectively, a very dark-skinned strain of MUSCAT BLANC À PETITS GRAINS, called here Brown Muscat, and MUSCADELLE, traditionally known as Tokay in Australia. The centre of production is a hot north western corner of the state of Victoria around the town of RUTHERGLEN. Grapes are semi-raisined on the vine, partially fermented, and then FORTIFIED with grape spirit before being subjected to an unusual wood ageing programme that resembles a cross between a sherry SOLERA and, under many a hot tin roof, a Madeira ESTUFAGEM. The results can be uncannily fine quality, although they are best enjoyed in a much cooler climate.

LIQUOREUX, French term meaning syrupy sweet, used for very rich, often BOTRYTIZED wines that are markedly sweeter than those described as MOELLEUX.

LIQUOROSO, Italian for a strong, usually FORTIFIED wine.

LIRAC, large appellation on the right bank of the southern RHÔNE producing mainly full bodied reds and rosés, and a small amount of sometimes heavy white wine. The rosés can offer good-value alternatives to nearby TAVEL, made in very similar conditions and from the same sort of grape varieties, while the reds resemble a particularly soft, earlier maturing Côte-du-Rhône Villages. The appellation includes three communes other than Lirac, of which Roquemaure was an important port in the 16th century from which wines would be shipped as far north as England and Holland (see RIVERS). In the 18th century Roquemaure was a much more important wine centre than CHÂTEAUNEUF-DU-PAPE just across the river.

Modern red and rosé Lirac is quite different from that nearby appellation in that it may contain no more than 40 per cent Grenache, while white wines must contain at least a third of Clairette, supplemented by a range of other southern white grapes and Ugni Blanc. The official maximum yield is 35 hl/ha (2 tons/acre), notably lower than Tavel, although this is regularly increased to 42 hl/ha.

In one sense the appellations Lirac and Tavel have more in common with the LANGUEDOC, which they abut, than with the Rhône. See map on page 796.

LISON-PRAMAGGIORE, DOC mainly in the VENETO region of north east Italy created in 1986 by the fusion of two previous DOCs, the CABERNET di Pramaggiore and TOCAI di Lison. Other grapes are grown in the zone, however, and each of CHARDONNAY, PINOT GRIGIO, Riesling Italico or WELSCHRIESLING, SAUVIGNON Blanc, VERDUZZO, MERLOT, and

REFOSCO is entitled to DOC status as a VARIETAL wine. Tocai is the workhorse grape amongst the white, with close to 8,000 hl/211,200 gal produced each year, but Merlot, with an annual production of more than 18,000 hl, has surpassed Cabernet (predominantly Franc rather than Sauvignon) amongst the red wine varieties.

The vineyards themselves are in the wide plain created by the Piave river as it descends from the hills of Conegliano and Montello towards the Adriatic and, as such, can be considered an eastward continuation of the PIAVE DOC zone, extending into the Pordenone province of FRIULI. The wines are fresh and pleasurable, if not memorable, with Cabernet regularly giving the most interesting results, in warm years approaching the level of a medium-quality CHINON or BOURGUEIL from France's Loire valley. Cooler vintages, together with the high percentage of Cabernet Franc and high yields in the vineyards (84 hl/ha), tend to bring out an aggressive herbaceousness which is perhaps more appealing to local markets than to international ones. D.T.

LISTÁN, synonym for PALOMINO, the white grape variety that can produce superb sherry around JEREZ, but results in dull, flabby white table wines almost everywhere else. Listán is the name by which the variety is known in much of Spain and in France. There are still several hundred hectares of it in the western Languedoc and in armagnac country but it is being systematically grubbed up.

LISTRAC, or **Listrac-Médoc**, one of the six communal appellations of the Haut-Médoc district of Bordeaux. Of the six (MARGAUX, ST-JULIEN, PAUILLAC, ST-ESTÈPHE, and even MOULIS, with which it is often compared) Listrac seems the least well favoured. It is, just, furthest of them all from the Gironde estuary and the vineyards are planted on 700 ha/1,730 acres or so of mainly clay-limestone on a gentle rise which, at an altitude of about 40 m/131 ft, constitutes some of the highest land in the Médoc. Although the Merlot grape is increasingly widely planted, the wines can be relatively austere in youth and their chief characteristic is their reliable density even in lighter vintages. The most cosseted property is probably Baron Edmond de ROTHSCHILD's Ch Clarke, while the similarly renovated Ch Fourcas-Hosten has a reputation as solid as its wines. Yields of 45 hl/ha (2.6 tons/acre) are officially tolerated here, whereas the limit is 40 hl/ha in Moulis and other Haut-Médoc village appellations.

For more information see MÉDOC and BORDEAUX.

Parker, R., *Bordeaux* (2nd edn., New York, 1991).
Penning-Rowsell, E., *The Wines of Bordeaux* (6th edn., London, 1989).
Peppercorn, D., *Bordeaux* (2nd edn., London, 1991).

LITERATURE OF WINE. The literature that concerns wine specifically, as opposed to references to wine in more general writing (for which see ENGLISH LITERATURE), is a complicated tapestry that has been woven from a broad variety of strands from classical times to the present day. Most writers concern themselves with how and where grapes are grown, how and where wine is made, and how individual wines taste, but their methods vary considerably and there are works on wine which are also works on travel, on history, on medicine, on agricultural matters, and on gastronomy.

Early works and agriculture

Many early works are richer in references to the effects of drinking wine (see DRUNKENNESS) than to the wine itself. CLASSICAL TEXTS constitute the earliest known literature of wine (although see also Ancient MESOPOTAMIA). While Mago of CARTHAGE clearly inspired many subsequent writers, his text does not survive and the first known classical writers to concentrate on wine and wine-making were probably CATO (234–119 BC) and VARRO (116–27 BC). Cato, particularly, was keen on the profit motive in wine-making and his instructions appear mainly to have been aimed at quantity rather than quality, even suggesting, at one point, how Coan wine (from Kós, one of the AEGEAN ISLANDS) could be faked from Italian grapes.

Much more modern in his outlook towards the production of wine was COLUMELLA (2 BC–AD 65), whose family, based near Cádiz in southern Spain, may well have owned vineyards. His *De re rustica* gives detailed advice on such matters as CLONAL SELECTION, the planting of vineyards, and the need for wines to be as natural as possible. 'The wine is clearly the best which can solely give pleasure by its own nature.' PLINY the Elder (AD 23–79) was the last great classical writer on wine and wine-making, although he was clearly influenced by Varro. The works of all these three, and the more derivative PALLADIUS in particular, were translated and used as textbooks throughout Europe until the end of the 16th century.

In these books, viticulture was treated merely as a part, albeit a major part, of the broader subject of agriculture. This tradition was continued by such writers as PETRUS DE CRESCENTIIS (1230–1310), an Italian lawyer who was forced to leave his own country and spent 30 years in exile in Spain and France. One volume of his monumental *Liber ruralium commodorum* dealt specifically with wine-growing and making. The work was translated into French on the instructions of Charles V.

The first French writer to attempt to classify wines in any way was Charles Étienne (1504–64). His *Vinetum . . .* first appeared in Lyons in 1536. This was subsequently translated into French and incorporated in *L'Agriculture et maison rustique des maistres Charles Étienne et Jean Liebault*, 1564 (Liebault was Étienne's son-in-law). This was a best seller and was followed in due course by the *Nouvelle Maison rustique* by Louis Liger of AUXERRE, which appeared in many editions throughout the 18th and early 19th centuries. While this book deals with a broad selection of rural topics, the sector on wine is particularly fascinating with its details of the then popular wines of Orléans, Burgundy, and Champagne. The characteristics are also given of 50 different VINE VARIETIES grown in France both as table grapes and for wine-making, of which 'morillon noir' is today's PINOT and 'gamet' is today's GAMAY. More than 15 varieties of MUSCAT are mentioned, but CABERNET SAUVIGNON is notably absent.

In some ways an English equivalent was Philip Miller's *Gardeners' Dictionary*, which first appeared in 1731. Here, under the headings Vitis and Wine, are detailed articles on such subjects as grape varieties, Burgundy, Champagne, and English vineyards, although he says of these last, 'There have of late years been but very few vineyards in England, tho' they were formerly very common.'

As wine was the everyday drink throughout much of Europe, in parallel with the books on the agricultural aspects of wine there were others devoted, perhaps only in part, to its keeping and serving. In England the anonymously written *Mystery of Vintners* appeared in 1692 and *L'Art d'améliorer et de conserver les vins* was published in Paris in 1781, with editions coming out in Liège and Turin within the following four years. The information they gave was often plagiarized and adapted to appear in such general books as *The Laboratory*, or *School of Arts* (1799).

Wine as medicine

The role of wine in the world of MEDICINE had been important from the earliest of times. It was used widely as a medium for the infusion of medicinal herbs and many wine-based remedies were given in such books as *The Secrets of Alexis of Piedmont*, which appeared in a number of languages from 1555 onwards.

Indeed the first book specifically on wines in English, *A New Book of Wines* (1568), was written by William Turner, who studied medicine at Cambridge. He warned of the danger of drinking the sweet, heavy wines of the Mediterranean as opposed to the healthy, light wines of the Rhine.

This medicinal tradition was adapted by the wine merchant Duncan M'Bride in his *Choice of Wines . . .* (1793) which included general discussion about the wines that were available at the time and their potential application for various medical conditions. Particularly recommended was Toc-kay de Espagne (*sic*), of which only M'Bride knew the source.

A much later sequel is *Wine is the Best Medicine* (1974, updated 1992) by the Frenchman Dr E. A. Maury. This has a more rational approach to the subject, with a variety of individual French wines being recommended for everything from flatulence to cystitis.

DOCTORS have always had a major role to play in English wine literature. Sir Edward Barry was a Bath physician whose *History of Classical Wines* appeared in 1775. He has been criticized for relying too closely on the work of the 16th century papal medical adviser Barrius, but he also includes an appendix on modern wines and viticulture in England.

Doctors were also responsible for the first two 'modern' books to deal with wine in depth. Whilst the title of *A Practical Treatise on Brewing, Distilling and Rectification*, by R. Shannon, MD (1805), might put off the oenophile there is 'A Copius Appendix on . . . Foreign Wines, Brandies and Vinegars'. This work is particularly strong on the wines of Portugal and Spain, but does not hesitate to lift, unattributed, from Miller on the wines of Burgundy.

Dr Alexander HENDERSON's *The History of Ancient and Modern Wines* (1824) is perhaps the first book in English to attempt to give descriptions of a broad range of wines, based upon his own travels to France, Germany, and Italy. It is also the first book to try to analyse the science of tasting.

The golden age

In the number of wines it talks about, Henderson's book is overwhelmed by what must be the most remarkable book on wine ever published, the *Topographie de tous les vignobles connus* (1816) by André JULLIEN, a Parisian wine merchant who was born in Burgundy. In this are rated all the wines, not just of France, but of all known wine regions of the time including California, South America, South Africa's Cape, and 'Chinese Tartary'! He forecasts (or perhaps helps to shape) the 1855 CLASSIFICATION in Bordeaux by rating as first-class wines Lafitte (*sic*), Latour, Ch-Margaux, and Haut-Brion.

Outside Europe, his favourites all seem to be dessert wines, including TOKAY, CONSTANTIA, COMMANDARIA, and COTNARI. Both his first-hand experience and his reading must have been gargantuan for him to compile such a work of reference. Cavoleau's *Oenologie française* was a similar work, but limited to French wines, which came from the same publisher 11 years later.

The 19th century was a golden age for wine writing in Britain. Shannon and Henderson were followed by Cyrus REDDING (1785–1870), a journalist whose interest in wine was stimulated during five years based in Paris. An avid traveller, he wrote *A History and Description of Modern Wines* (1833) as a result of first-hand observation of the ADULTERATION AND FRAUD which were then prevalent in the wine trade.

Many of the books were written by wine merchants, often criticizing the practices of their colleagues, or vaunting their own specialities. Perhaps the most enjoyable to read is Thomas Shaw, whose *Wine, the Vine and the Cellar* (1863) is an agreeable blend of reminiscences, knowledge, and simple advice. He was convinced even then that 'in wine tasting and wine talk there is an enormous amount of humbug'. Another of his campaigns was against excessive DUTIES on wine and this led to the famous Gladstone budget in 1862 in which they were considerably reduced.

Charles Tovey was a wine merchant in Bristol in south west England and in the introduction to *Wine and Wine Countries* (1862) he says that 'there can be no question that the Wine Trade is losing its position by the introduction into it of unscrupulous traders'. He drew heavily upon his 50 years' experience in denouncing and describing their deceits.

This same theme was continued by his London colleague James L. Denman, who wrote copiously on wine adulteration. His more particular interest, however, both commercial and literary, was the wines of Greece.

Another doctor to write on wines was John Thudichum, who had come to London from Germany, where his father had written technical books on wine. One of his particular hobby-horses was the adding of gypsum to SHERRY, but his credibility within the trade was compromised by extensive research that he had carried out in Jerez, trying to produce AMONTILLADO by purely chemical means. His *Treatise on Wines* (1872), written with another doctor, A. Dupré, does, however, give a clear picture of viticulture and vinification at that time.

Specialist books

While all these books give a general idea of the wines of Europe and, in some cases, the world, some specialist books on individual regions had also begun to appear. One of the first of these was published in London as early as 1728. This was the *Dissertation sur la situation de Bourgogne* by the French tutor to the son of a Mr Freeman. Arnoux, in this brief book, describes the various wines of Burgundy and how they are made. He also makes a plea for them to be imported into England in bottle rather than in cask. This book must have met with some success, for it was soon translated into English and was subsequently used by Philip Miller in his *Gardeners' Dictionary* and by Robert Shannon.

It was more than a century until the next two classic books on the vineyards of Burgundy appeared and coincidentally it was in the same year, 1831. Morelot's *Statistique de la vigne dans le département de la Côte d'Or* is largely what its title suggests, although the second half of the book deals with both viticulture and vinification in the region. The *Histoire et statistique de la vigne et des grands vins de la Côte d'Or* by Lavalle is a more readable book, for it gives many historical details concerning Burgundy and its wines, as well as more details of the characteristics of the wines from the various villages and ownership of the vineyards. Later editions have etchings of vineyard scenes.

In Bordeaux, the first book of significance was the *Variétés bordelaises of Abbé Beaurein* (1784–5), which noted that the English were at last showing interest in the wines of the Médoc. The first major book dealing solely with the wines of Bordeaux, however, was the *Traité sur les vins du Médoc* of William Franck (1824) which ran into several editions. In many ways this was the forerunner of Charles Cocks's book *Bordeaux, its Wines and the Claret Country* (1846), which was translated into French four years later and became the classic reference work on Bordeaux wines, known after its original authors as COCKS ET FÉRET, now sadly neglecting its English roots and published simply as *Féret*. An interesting independent view of the region is also given by the Paris merchant Charles Pierre de Saint in *Le Vin de Bordeaux* (1855).

Writing on Portuguese wines was dominated by the English. In 1787 John CROFT wrote *A Treatise of the Wines of Portugal* and this was followed by the many works of James Forrester (1809–61), who, from his position in the trade, took a strong position against the many adulterations that were taking place.

The 19th century saw the rapid expansion of vineyards in the New World and guidance was sought in Europe as to how to make the finest wines. From this came two interesting works. The first was the *Journal of a Tour through some of the Vineyards of Spain and France* by James BUSBY, which was published in Sydney in 1833. This is a fascinating account of a three-month trip, mainly by stage-coach, to find the right vine varieties for planting in Australia. The interpretation of what he learned appeared in two further books. The journey, almost 30 years later, by Agoston HARASZTHY, one of the pioneers of California viticulture, was largely by train. Perhaps because of his origins, he spent more of his time in the various states of Germany and none at all in France. His *Grape Culture, Wines and Wine-Making*, a journal of this tour, appeared in New York in 1862 and did much to establish the reputations of both Haraszthy and California wine.

A third, and earlier, New World traveller to have left his memories of vineyard visiting is Thomas JEFFERSON, later to become president of the United States. During his five years as minister to France (1784–9) he took advantage of his situation to visit many of the vineyards of Europe, and his diaries leave a fascinating picture of a layman's perception of the world of wine as it then was.

One final wine writer of Victorian times was the journalist and publisher Henry VIZETELLY. His books on champagne, port, and sherry are notable for their many illustrations. These works, with their beautiful engravings, many used by modern publishers, are the forebears of the lavishly illustrated wine books published today.

Technical literature

Parallel with this growth in books on the vineyard regions and their wines, there was a considerable body of work on VITICULTURE and WINE-MAKING. In France at the end of the 18th century the Burgundian Béguillet and Maupin, from Paris, both wrote detailed works which were widely read.

In England, William Speechly, gardener to the duke of Portland, wrote a *Treatise on the Culture of the Vine* (1790) which went into three editions. This dealt with both hothouse and open-air vines in ENGLAND and discusses some of the vineyards which were then planted there and the wines they produced.

Three French writers of the 19th century whose names live on in the world of wine are Jean-Antoine CHAPTAL (1756–1832), Dr Jules GUYOT, and Louis PASTEUR (1822–95). Chaptal was the essential polymath, rising from humble beginnings to become Minister of the Interior under Napoleon. In 1799 he wrote the article on wine for the monumental *Dictionnaire d'agriculture* of the Abbé Rozier, but is better known for his *L'Art de faire le vin* (1807) and his support for the concept of increasing the alcohol strength of wine by adding sugar to the must, the procedure now known as CHAPTALIZATION.

Jules Guyot was instructed under the Second Empire to carry out a survey of the vineyards of France and to make recommendations as to how viticulture might be improved. His three works on viticulture in north and central France (1860), the east (1863), and the west (1866) give a vital picture of France before the arrival of PHYLLOXERA. His name lives on as a method of vine TRAINING. It is largely to him that we owe the parade-ground look of today's vineyards in place of the rabble-like appearance of vines subjected to the traditional practice of LAYERING.

Louis Pasteur's *Études sur le vin* (1866) deal with the question of vinification and particularly the advantages of the heat treatment, or PASTEURIZATION, of wine. His is also the first detailed work on the role that YEASTS have to play in

FERMENTATION. Another important work on the techniques of vinification was *Le Vin* (1867), by the Burgundian Comte de Vergnette-Lamotte.

Modern wine writing

The 20th century has seen a great resurgence in wine writing, particularly in Britain. Much of the credit has been laid at the door of Professor George SAINTSBURY, whose vinous reminiscences, *Notes on a Cellar-Book* (1920), were written when he was 75 years old. While this erudite miscellany of thoughts is an enjoyable read, there are many who consider it overrated despite its commercial success. (It was reprinted twice within four months and has run through many editions since.)

What it did prove, however, was that there was a demand for books on wine and authors soon appeared to satisfy that demand. In the main, they fall into two fields, the reminiscent and the relevant. One of the finest of the former is H. Warner Allen, a journalist with a deep love for wine and its history. Much of his work is memories of bottles of vintages long past. His *A History of Wine* (1961) is, however, necessary reading for any wine enthusiast. Others who might be said to be in this group were Maurice Healy and Stephen Gwynn. All of them were highly educated men, for whom drinking fine wines was a part of everyday life.

The relevant school was nobly fronted by André SIMON (1877–1970), even if much of his work is also reminiscent. Born in Paris, he came to Britain as the agent for a leading champagne house in 1902. His early writings were largely on the history of the wine trade and he was, all his life, passionately interested in wine books, compiling a number of bibliographies on food and drink (see below). As a member of the wine trade, he introduced a degree of accuracy to his work that is missing from some of the 'gentlemen' wine writers cited above. In all he wrote more than 100 works in which his knowledge is matched by his readability.

Contemporary wine writing in Britain continues this parallel, with works coming from writers who have taken to wine and wine professionals who have taken to writing. While the choice might seem to be between elegance and erudition, the distinction is not always so straightforward.

From the British wine trade have come such as Tommy Layton, a prolific writer on the wines of Loire, Alsace, Spain, and Italy; his one-time office boy Michael BROADBENT, whose *Great Vintage Wine Book* is an unrivalled reference work with tasting notes on more than 6,000 wines going back to the 17th century; Clive Coates on the wines of Bordeaux; Anthony Hanson on Burgundy; Serena Sutcliffe on Champagne; Gerald Asher, now based in the United States; Steven Spurrier; and many others.

Representing the world of the professional writer are the biographer and founder of the Good Food Club, Raymond Postgate, whose *The Plain Man's Guide to Wine* proved so successful that it went through 16 editions in 26 years; Edmund PENNING-ROWSELL, whose book on the wines of Bordeaux is a masterpiece of research; the polished journalist Cyril RAY; John Arlott, whose enjoyment of wine and the pleasure it brings shines through his writing; Julian Jeffs, the genial patent lawyer; and Pamela VANDYKE PRICE, particularly strong on the wines of France.

Recently there has sprung up something new in the world of wine books: writers who are deliberately writing for their customer, the reader, rather than for their own pleasure. The most successful and innovative of these has undoubtedly been Hugh JOHNSON, with *Wine*, *The World Atlas of Wine*, and *The Story of Wine*. That there is a broader demand for wine knowledge is borne out by the interest shown in the subject by other media such as television. This has undoubtedly widened the market for such writers as Jancis Robinson and Oz Clarke.

In the rest of Europe, much of the wine literature was originally written in English, although the Dutch writer Hubrecht Duijker, with a series of heavily illustrated and highly instructive works on Bordeaux, Burgundy, Rioja, and other wine regions, has achieved a broad international readership. Few French writers are read outside France, although each region has its specialized writers such as Pierre Poupon and Pierre Forgeot in Burgundy, René Pijassou in Bordeaux, and there is also the eclectic Bernard Ginestet. An exception, for the technically minded, is Pierre GALET's work on AMPELOGRAPHY, which is a worthy successor to the larger book on the same subject by Pierre Viala. The works of Émile PEYNAUD on wine-making and wine tasting have also been widely read outside France.

In the United States wine writing became a boom industry in the late 20th century. This was led by Alexis LICHINE, who before the Second World War joined the wine trade with Frank SCHOONMAKER, himself a successful writer on wine. During the war he served as social aide-de-camp to General Eisenhower and afterwards bought vineyards in Bordeaux and Burgundy, eventually writing two highly successful and informative books, *Wines of France* and *Alexis Lichine's Encyclopedia of Wines and Spirits*.

Other effective writers on wine in America include Alexis Bespaloff, who worked for the Alexis Lichine wine company, the journalist Robert Balzer, and the lawyer Robert PARKER, whose personal system of SCORING WINE out of 100 points has won him both followers and critics. The mainly technical works coming from the wine faculty of the University of California at DAVIS, particularly those of Maynard AMERINE, have also played a major role in the education not just of the American wine-maker, but also of the American consumer. The American journalist Burton Anderson, who has lived in Italy for more than 20 years, has written a number of books on the wines of that country.

Wine writing in Australasia has been led by Len EVANS (*Australian and New Zealand Complete Book of Wines*, 1973) and James Halliday (*The Australian Wine Compendium*, 1985 and, with Hugh Johnson, *The Vintner's Art/The Art and Science of Wine*, 1992). Both of these writers are also vineyard owners and speak with authority on their subjects.

The 20th century has seen a dramatic increase in interest in wine, which has led to a corresponding increase in the number of wine books available. It is easy to chart through wine literature the change in public perception of wine, from élitist to populist, a move encouraged by wider travel and higher disposable incomes. A book on wine is less often now a literary work than a work of instruction or, increasingly, a buyer's guide. Illustrations, too, tend to play a larger part. Even supermarket chains have commissioned their own books on wine to satisfy the demands of their customers, often new wine drinkers.

The literature of wine is infinite and, as appreciation of wine spreads around the world, so will the demand for books on wine. From Cato the Censor to Oz Clarke is a long road, but the road is far from being at its end. C.C.F.

Useful bibliographies:
Gabler, J. M., *Wine into Words: A History and Bibliography of Wine Books in the English Language* (Baltimore, 1985).
Simon, A., *Bibliotheca vinaria* (London, 1913, and facsimile: London, 1979).
Vicaire, G., *Bibliographie gastronomique* (Paris, 1890, and facsimile: London, 1978).

LITTLE LEAF, a symptom of ZINC deficiency of vines. An associated symptom is a PETIOLAR sinus that is wider than normal.

LIVERMORE VALLEY, California wine region and AVA. If the gods had got it all right, Sauvignon Blanc and Semillon would dominate the 1,400 acres/566 ha planted to vines in Livermore Valley in the early 1990s, for no other grape does half so well in this small bowl in Alameda County east of San Francisco Bay. Those two grape varieties, linked by their history in Bordeaux, first came with French emigrants during Livermore's first great blossoming in the 1870s and 1880s (see CALIFORNIA, history). Presumably the pioneer growers believed the virtues in its stonier-than-GRAVES soils outweighed the perils of its heat. Eventually they left the field to Germans and Italo-Irishmen, but Sauvignon Blanc and Semillon stayed on, now as then the most praiseworthy grape varieties in an always small acreage.

Although that acreage recently has been pinched harder and harder by expanding suburban housing, since 1980 several small wineries have joined the two larger old-timers, Wente Bros. and Concannon. The newcomers have done little to increase the focus on Sauvignon and Semillon, but rather have helped maintain a long-standing dispersion of plantings across a dozen or more varieties.

A small bulge within a long, narrow trough that parallels San Francisco Bay for most of its length, Livermore hides behind hills high enough to screen out nearly all of the sea fogs common on the bay proper, hence its signature extra degree of heat.

LLADONER PELUT is a black grape variety also known as GRENACHE Poilu or Velu in the south of France. Both vine and wine closely resemble Grenache Noir except that the underside of the leaves of the Lladoner Pelut are downier. It is officially and widely sanctioned in the Languedoc-Roussillon, often being specified alongside Grenache, and has the advantage of being less susceptible to rot. In practice it is declining in popularity but in the early 1990s there were more than 150 ha/370 acres planted with the variety in the Aude and Pyrénées Orientales as well as some plantings in Spain around Tarragona.

Galet, P., *Cépages et vignobles de France* (2nd edn., Montpellier, 1990).

LLEDONER. See LLADONER.

LOAM, the ideal soil for the growth of most plants, consisting of a balanced mixture of clay, silt, and sand (see SOIL TEXTURE). With enough ORGANIC MATTER, loams have a friable, crumby structure (see SOIL STRUCTURE). These desirable characteristics are enhanced where CALCIUM is prominent among the ions bonded to the clay particles and organic matter, i.e. where the soil is not acid. A good loam has a high capacity to store water and plant nutrients but, unlike stiff clay, is not close textured enough to impede the free drainage of water. Rich, loamy soils can encourage excessive VIGOUR in vines, however, particularly in cool to mild climates with ample RAINFALL, so loams (which exist in almost all regions) are not always the best for viticulture. J.G.

LOCUSTS can damage vines. See GRASSHOPPERS for more detail.

LODGE, term used by British shippers of PORT and MADEIRA for a building where wine is stored and matured, especially in Vila Nova de Gaia in OPORTO and Funchal in MADEIRA respectively. It is derived from the Portuguese word *loja* meaning shop or warehouse. The Portuguese themselves tend to use the term ARMAZÉM. R.J.M.

LODI, town in the SAN JOAQUIN VALLEY of California that also gives its name to an AVA.

LOESS, a light coloured, fine-grained accumulation of CLAY and SILT particles that have been deposited by the wind. An essentially unconsolidated, unstratified CALCAREOUS silt, it is usually homogeneous, permeable, and buff to grey in colour, containing calcareous concretions and fossils. It is found particularly in some vineyards in AUSTRIA and GERMANY.

LOIR, COTEAUX DU, northerly wine outpost of the greater Loire region on the confusingly named Loir tributary about 40 km/25 miles north of Tours in the Sarthe *département*. Viticulture seriously declined here, but enthusiasts such as Joël Gigou at Domaine de la Charrière are investing in a bright future for the varied wines of this small area, of which JASNIÈRES is the most famous appellation. Bright reds, occasionally the product of BARREL MATURATION, are being made from Gamay, which does well on the clay-limestone sectors of the appellation. In ripe years such as 1990 Pineau d'Aunis can be good enough to shine in a VARIETAL wine. Cabernet Franc and Cot (Malbec) are also allowed for reds, and Grolleau may be used in its light, dry rosés. Dry white

L B V
1987
22025
646

wines are made from Chenin Blanc, but red wine production predominates.

The local VDQS is Coteaux du VENDÔMOIS. See also LOIRE and map on pp. 576–7.

LOIRE, France's most famous river and name of one of its most varied wine regions whose wines are greatly appreciated locally and in Paris, but—with the famous exceptions of Sancerre and Pouilly-Fumé—are widely underrated outside France. This may be partly because the Loire's best red wines are distinguished by their delicacy rather than by their weight and longevity, and because so many of its finest white wines are made solely from Chenin Blanc, a grape variety associated with very ordinary wine outside the middle Loire: Anjou, Saumur, and Touraine.

History

We know little about the early history of viticulture in the Loire valley, but recent archaeological discoveries suggest that it was extant at least in the upper Loire in the 1st century AD (see GAUL), and it was certainly well established by the 5th century. In a letter to a friend, probably prepared for publication *c.*469, Sidonius Apollinaris (*c.*430–*c.*480), who was born in Lyons but spent a large part of his life in the Auvergne, praises the country of the Arverni (the Auvergne) for its landscape, its fertile fields, and its vineyards. During Sidonius Apollinaris' lifetime, in the year 475, ROME was forced to cede the Auvergne to the Visigoths, but the depredations of the barbarians left vine-growing safe.

In the next century Gregory of Tours (*c.*539–94) makes frequent mention, in his History of the Franks, of viticulture in the Loire region. As bishop of Tours, he took a great interest in the wine of his diocese (modern TOURAINE). He tells us that, in 591, drought was followed by rain so that the grain harvest was ruined but the vines yielded abundantly. He also tells in detail of the Bretons' often successful attempts to seize the vineyards and/or grapes of the Nantes region (modern MUSCADET) in the 6th century.

The wines of the Loire continued to be held in high regard, and not only by the Bretons, who gave up plundering and bought the wines they wanted. The inhabitants of west Brittany had grown some wine themselves, but in the 13th century they gave up viticulture in favour of growing grain and instead purchased their wines from Nantes. Like Nantes, Touraine produced wine of export quality, and by the end of the 11th century the wine of SANCERRE was already well reputed. In the 12th century it was exported to Flanders and sold via Orléans.

From the late 11th century onwards, the aspiring bourgeoisie of the newly rich Flemish cities wanted more and more of its chief status symbol, which was wine (see DUTCH WINE TRADE). With its excellent river connections, the Loire region was especially well placed to meet this growing demand. Some of its wine was shipped to Flanders, or further north, or to England: some of it was carried to PARIS by river to be consumed there or sold on. Angers in particular grew rich on the Flemish guildsmen's desire for social advancement, and vines were planted even just outside its city walls. The count of ANJOU granted Angers the monopoly of carrying wine on the rivers Maine and Loire as far as the Breton port of Ingrandes; in addition, merchants could not buy their wines direct from the vineyards but had to buy them at Angers. These two privileges put the producers of SAUMUR at a disadvantage. The wines of Saumur were not fashionable in France, and Saumur was badly placed for overseas trade. In England in the late 12th century, before the rise of BORDEAUX, Anjou was the only wine to rival Poitou, shipped from LA ROCHELLE, in popularity. Anjou remained highly esteemed in England throughout the Middle Ages.

In France itself the Loire wine that was most prized was one that has now all but disappeared from public regard: ST-POURÇAIN, made on the river Sioule in the Loire basin. King Louis IX served it at a banquet in Saumur to celebrate his brother Alphonse's 21st birthday. St-Pourçain fetched high prices during the 14th century and was a favourite with the papal court at Avignon. The wines of the Coteaux de LAYON did not become famous until the 15th century.

For more historical detail, see entries under individual wine names. H.M.W.

Dion, Roger, *Histoire de la vigne et du vin en France* (Paris, 1959).

Geography and climate

So long is the extent of the viticultural Loire that generalizations are impossible. The Loire's vineyards vary from the continental climate which produces Sancerre and Pouilly-Fumé, to the Muscadet region warmed by the Gulf Stream. Loire wine regions represent today, however, the north western limit of vine cultivation in Europe (with the exception of ENGLAND'S vineyards). Spring FROST can be a serious problem, as it was in 1991, when it destroyed up to 70 per cent of the crop in some of the Loire's wine regions. The character of Loire wines can vary considerably from VINTAGE to vintage, since in a cool summer the grapes may struggle to reach full RIPENESS, while a particularly hot year such as 1989 and 1990 may result in some exceptional sweet white wines, some of them BOTRYTIZED in the middle Loire, but can rob the Loire's many dry white Sauvignons of their nerve, and leave Muscadet dangerously limp. The region is sufficiently far from the equator, however, that few of its red wines can be accused of being TANNIC, and the naturally high acidity associated with these latitudes, and some of its grape varieties, make much of the Loire's produce ideal base wine for sparkling wines.

Viticulture

The Loire is essentially a region of small family holdings; vines are often just one of several crops cultivated. In the middle Loire, rainfall is relatively low, but SPRAYING against FUNGAL DISEASES can be a frequent activity elsewhere, and even in the middle Loire in some years. VINE DENSITY is relatively high, between 4,000 and 5,000 plants per ha (1,600–

The **lodge** of port shippers Smith Woodhouse in Vila Nova de Gaia.

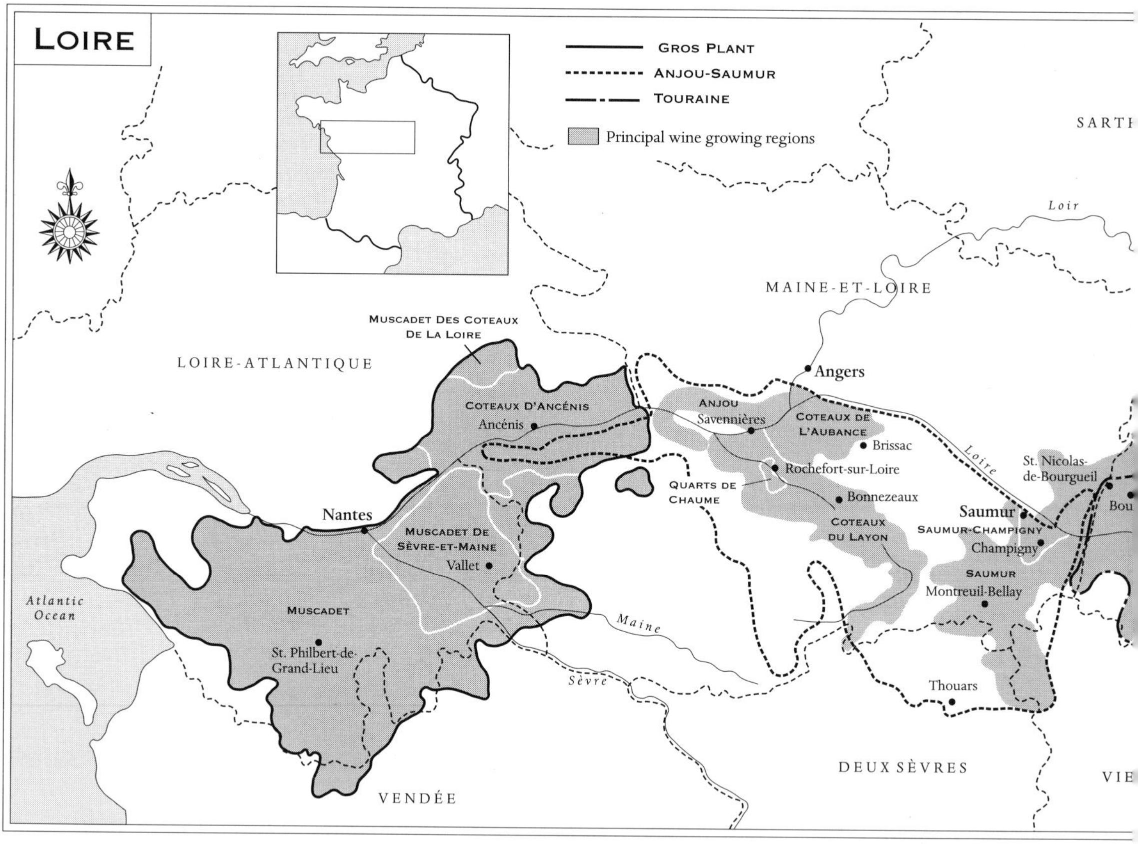

2,000 per acre) on average. Excess VIGOUR was a problem in the late 1980s and early 1990s, and resulted in HERBACEOUS flavours in many of the red wines. COVER CROPS have long been the norm, and CROP THINNING was introduced in the early 1990s. MECHANICAL HARVESTING is relatively common, but cannot be used for the sweet white wines of the middle Loire, where successive TRIS through the vineyards are needed to select only the ripest grapes.

Wine-making

White wine-makers of the Loire have traditionally followed very similar principles to their counterparts in Germany, assiduously avoiding MALOLACTIC FERMENTATION and any new OAK influence, preferring instead to ferment and store wines in inert containers, and to bottle wines early, possibly after some LEES CONTACT in the case of Muscadet. For years, Loire reds suffered from a lack of EXTRACTION.

The result of the particularly competitive wine market of the 1980s, however, was to stimulate a rash of experimentation in cellars along the length of the Loire. BARREL MATURATION and in some cases BARREL FERMENTATION were introduced for reds and whites. Some producers encouraged their white wines to go through malolactic fermentation, while red wine-makers worked hard to extract greater colour and TANNINS from their red wine musts, by the use of prolonged SKIN CONTACT, TEMPERATURE CONTROL, and PUMPING OVER regimes. (It should be said that, in many a Loire autumn and winter, temperature control is just as likely to include heating the must as cooling it.) SKIN CONTACT prior to fermentation was also introduced for some white wines, especially Sauvignons.

CHAPTALIZATION is the norm in the Loire, for both reds and whites, and is usually done to a maximum of an additional 2.5 per cent ALCOHOLIC STRENGTH of the finished wine.

Vine varieties

At the mouth of the Loire MELON de Bourgogne and FOLLE BLANCHE predominate. The upper Loire is, in the late 20th century anyway, the terrain of Sauvignon Blanc for white wines and Pinot Noir for reds and rosés. The majority of the most successful sites in the middle Loire have proved themselves suitable for either CABERNET FRANC or CHENIN BLANC, but in the thousands of hectares of vineyard planted around them, there is a greater diversity of vine varieties than anywhere else in France, including a mix of CABERNET SAUVIGNON, MALBEC, GAMAY, MEUNIER, PINOT GRIS, CHARDONNAY, and of course seas of Sauvignon and Pinot Noir. This is usually explained in terms of spheres of Bordeaux and

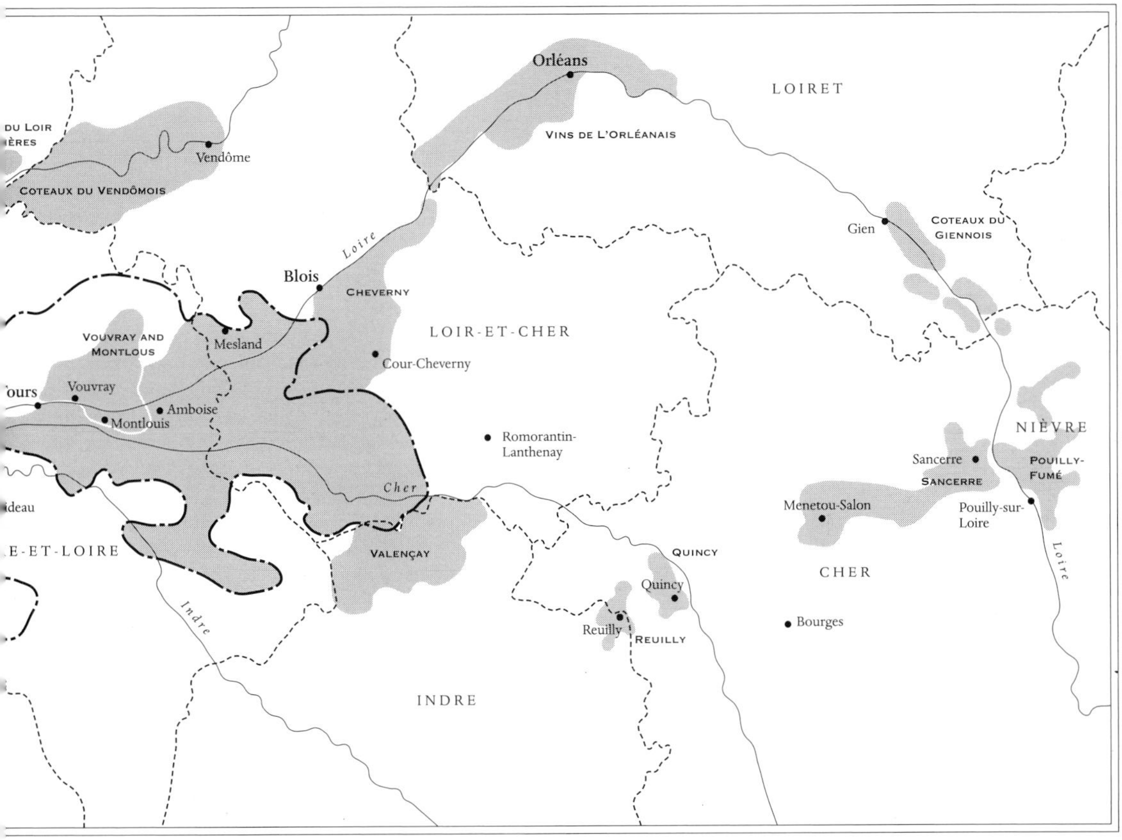

Burgundy influence, but it indicates that, outside its most famous appellations, the regions of the Loire have been searching for their own wine identities. The vineyards of the Loire were particularly badly hit by PHYLLOXERA. The heavily limestone soils in many regions meant that CHLOROSIS was a common problem when vines were replanted grafted on to resistant ROOTSTOCKS. The Loire, with its relatively cool climate, persisted with a higher proportion of HYBRIDS than any other French wine region. The maximum proportion of 20 per cent Chardonnay written into the rules of so many Loire appellations shows that the authorities at least are aware of the danger of the Loire losing its own identity. Those varieties that are exclusive to the Loire such as PINEAU D'AUNIS, GROLLEAU, ARBOIS, ROMORANTIN, and Meslier-St-François are all in retreat.

Wines produced

Of all French wine regions, the Loire produces the greatest diversity of wine styles: from still through all types of sparkling wine, including the generic CRÉMANT de Loire; from bone dry and searingly tart to unctuous LIQUOREUX (although still with a high degree of acidity); and all hues from water white to (quite) deep purple. Rosés are a speciality of the Loire, whether the various VINS GRIS made well upstream, the famous Rosé d'Anjou, various pink Cabernets, or the generic ROSÉ DE LOIRE.

Travelling upstream the major districts, with each appellation for which there is a separate entry, are (see map):

Pays Nantais: MUSCADET; GROS PLANT du Pays Nantais; Coteaux d'ANCENIS; FIEFS VENDÉENS.

ANJOU: SAVENNIÈRES; Coteaux du LAYON; QUARTS DE CHAUME; BONNEZEAUX; Coteaux de l'AUBANCE.

SAUMUR.

TOURAINE: CHINON; BOURGUEIL; VOUVRAY, MONTLOUIS, CHEVERNY, VALENÇAY.

Upper Loire: REUILLY, QUINCY, MENETOU-SALON, SANCERRE, POUILLY-FUMÉ.

Northern outposts: Coteaux du LOIR; JASNIÈRES; Coteaux du VENDÔMOIS.

On the bend: Vins de l'ORLÉANAIS; Coteaux du GIENNOIS.

Southern outposts: Vin du THOUARSAIS; Haut-POITOU; CHÂTEAUMEILLANT; ST-POURÇAIN; Côtes d'AUVERGNE; Côtes ROANNAISES; Côtes du FOREZ (although some of these are very far from the Loire and its climatic influence).

Duijker, H., *The Loire, Alsace and Champagne* (London, 1983).

Ribéreau-Gayon, P. (ed.), *The Wines and Vineyards of France* (London and New York, 1990).

LOMBARDY, or **Lombardia** in Italian, the largest and most populous region of ITALY, and the driving force behind the country's post-Second World War economic boom, the dynamo which has given Milan and its hinterland one of Europe's highest standards of living. Visitors driving across the great Lombard plain of northern Italy between the Ticino of southern SWITZERLAND and the river Po (see map on p. 517) get little sense of a thriving agriculture, but the region is a viticultural centre of some importance: its annual production of over 1.6 million hl/42.2 million gal (with DOC wines accounting for more than a third of the total) is larger than that of such famous wine regions as FRIULI, TRENTINO-ALTO ADIGE, UMBRIA, or the MARCHES, areas whose more bucolic landscapes suggest a greater significance for the vine.

Lombardy's centres of viticulture are off-centre geographically—in the far north, in the far south, and in the far east—all well off the region's main axis of communication. And the fact that each of Lombardy's three major viticultural areas cultivates different grapes and makes wine in a completely different style from the others does little to clarify the image of Lombardy wine: the region has neither a key grape nor a key wine to make it better known, and its sheer size and disparity are marketing handicaps. Good wine is none the less produced in the Valtellina, Oltrepò Pavese, and Franciacorta.

Valtellina is the northernmost outpost of the NEBBIOLO vine and its wines—often labelled with the subzones INFERNO, GRUMELLO, SASSELLA, VALGELLA—are the most widely known in national and international markets. The Oltrepò Pavese, by far the largest DOC of Lombardy, supplies sturdy red wines from BARBERA, Croatina, and UVA RARA grapes (either singly or as blends), everyday dry SPUMANTE, and innocuous white from RIESLING ITALICO, and is largely dependent on the local market of Milan; price cutting and over-production have left the area performing well below its potential. Franciacorta is the youngest and most dynamic of the three major DOC zones, the new centre for high-quality spumante production in Italy, and an interesting source of ambitious CHARDONNAY, Bordeaux-style red CABERNET/MERLOT blends, and PINOT NOIR.

Other DOCs include Lugana, whose Trebbiano-based white wines are produced to the south of Lake Garda. Botticino and Cellatica are red blends (the former with a slight suggestion of sweetness) from SCHIAVA, BARBERA, and MARZEMINO grapes grown in the province of Brescia and served with the local versions of *pot-au-feu* or wine-laced stews. Riviera del Garda are light red and rosé wines produced on the western shore of Lake Garda in the image of BARDOLINO across the lake as it were, although the grapes (Groppello, Sangiovese, Barbera, and Marzemino) could not be more different.

For more detail on specific notable wines see BONARDA, CROATINA, FRANCIACORTA, LUGANA, OLTREPÒ PAVESE, VALTELLINA, as well as Colli BOLOGNESI and Colli PIACENTINI. D.T.

LONG is a much-derided tasting term for wines whose impact on the PALATE is particularly persistent. A wine that is long is usually of high quality. For more details see TASTING.

LOS CARNEROS. See CARNEROS, wine region and AVA of California.

LOT MARKING, a requirement within the European Union since the early 1990s that all packaged wine should be marked with a lot number so that the packaging circumstances can be identified in the event of any complaint or recall. The mark is usually an L followed by a coded date of packaging (usually BOTTLING date) and may appear on the label, on the bottle itself, or on the foil.

LOUPIAC, sweet white wine appellation on the right bank of the GARONNE in the BORDEAUX region sandwiched between CADILLAC and STE-CROIX-DU-MONT. The wines of Loupiac were first cited in the 13th century (the Loupiac region was once much bigger), although in much of the 20th century the wines failed to fetch the prices necessary to justify truly meticulous wine-making. The best vineyards are on clay-limestone slopes overlooking the river and are well situated to benefit from NOBLE ROT, provided producers are prepared to take the necessary risks. Good Loupiac such as that produced at Domaine du Noble and Ch Loupiac-Gaudiet is generally deeply coloured and noticeably full bodied; the use of new OAK became gradually more common from the late 1980s (see SAUTERNES for more details).

LOUREIRO, fine white grape variety grown in VINHO VERDE country in northern Portugal and also, increasingly, as **Loureira** in GALICIA in north west Spain. It has often been blended with TRAJADURA but can also be found as an aromatic VARIETAL wine. It can yield quite productively in the north of the Vinho Verde region.

LOW ALCOHOL WINE, is usually REDUCED ALCOHOL WINE but may also be, like NO ALCOHOL WINE, regular wine from which alcohol has been deliberately removed, usually but not necessarily with harmful effects on flavour and quality. Such wines are usually reduced to an ALCOHOLIC STRENGTH which excludes them from DUTY, lessening the amount to be paid. See also WINE COOLERS, and DEALCOHOLIZED WINE.

LOW COUNTRIES, historical region of north west Europe including the NETHERLANDS, BELGIUM, and LUXEMBOURG, which once played an important part in the wine and spirit trade. See DUTCH WINE TRADE.

LOWER GREAT SOUTHERN. See GREAT SOUTHERN in western Australia.

LOW INPUT VITICULTURE, an alternative to conventional viticulture with the aim of minimizing all inputs to the vineyard. This may be of AGROCHEMICALS with the aim of improving the environment (see ORGANIC VITICULTURE), or of inputs such as LABOUR with the aim of improving the vineyard's profitability.

LUBÉRON, CÔTES DU, wines made on the fashionable slopes of the Lubéron, where vineyards add colour and bucolic allure to one of the more sought-after corners of Provence. The appellation, which comprised nearly 3,000 ha/7,410 acres of vineyard in the early 1990s, is a sort of buffer state between the RHÔNE and PROVENCE, or more precisely between the Côtes du VENTOUX appellation and that of Coteaux d'AIX-EN-PROVENCE.

The appellation was created only in 1988 and produces significant quantities of all three colours of wine, although single VARIETAL wines must be sold as VINS DE PAYS du Vaucluse. All reds contain some Syrah, augmented by Grenache, possibly Mourvèdre and Cinsaut, and no more than 20 per cent Carignan. Those who try hard, such as old-timers Chx de Mille and de l'Isolette and the relatively recently arrived Chancel family at Ch Val Joanis, can produce herb-scented reds with real concentration and ageing potential. Whites are made from Grenache, Clairette, Bourboulenc, possibly some Marsanne and Roussanne, and no more than 50 per cent Ugni Blanc. The region's rather cooler nights (and winters) than in most Côtes-du-Rhône vineyards help to produce some of the crisper, more interesting white wines of the southern Rhône. Rosés may incorporate up to 20 per cent of white grapes, and have particular allure when drunk locally to the sound of cicadas.

LUGANA, dry white Italian wine based on the TREBBIANO grape (in this case the Trebbiano di Lugana or Trebbiano Veronese) produced to the south and south west of Lake Garda in the province of Brescia, straddling the provinces of Lombardy and Veneto. Over 700 ha/1,730 acres produce more than 40,000 hl/1 million gal of wine per year. The wine, most of which is fairly anonymous, demonstrates the limits of its variety, and also of the DOC rules, which permit yields of 85 hl/ha (4.8 tons/acre), but an occasional Lugana with more developed aromas and the refreshing tang of Trebbiano's high ACIDITY can provide an enjoyable bottle for summer quaffing. Local *aficionados* insist that it is the perfect accompaniment for Garda fish, a claim that can be verified only on the spot.
D.T.

LUNEL is the centre of the Muscat de Lunel appellation for sweet golden VIN DOUX NATUREL made from MUSCAT BLANC À PETITS GRAINS grapes grown on potentially interesting infertile inland soils between Montpellier and Nîmes. Yields are low and vinification techniques improving although many local vine-growers have been more interested in developing lower alcohol, dry vins de CÉPAGE or wines that qualify as COTEAUX DU LANGUEDOC. A single CO-OPERATIVE is responsible for almost all the wine produced, which, as any geographer might suspect, tastes like a cross between the Muscats of FRONTIGNAN and ST-JEAN-DE-MINERVOIS. Lunel's historical claim to fame is less convincing than Frontignan's: its Muscat was dispatched to console Napoléon on the island of St Helena. The town does call itself the Cité du Muscat, however.

LUNGAROTTI, owners of an eponymous estate in UMBRIA in central Italy. The 250 ha/617 acres, plus 40 ha leased, is in the village of Torgiano Perugia. An old family estate, it was developed in the 1950s by Giorgio Lungarotti, and incorporated as Cantina Lungarotti in 1962, to become within 20 years the leading vineyard property in the region, with an annual output of about 2 million bottles. Beginning with Torgiano Rosso 'Rubesco' (SANGIOVESE grapes with CANAIOLO) and Torgiano Bianco 'Torre di Giano' (TREBBIANO with GRECHETTO), Torgiano was awarded the DOC in 1968, and the exceptional Rubesco Riserva from the Vigna Montichio vineyard the DOCG in 1990. Fourteen other wines are produced including large quantities of Chardonnay dell'Umbria, Pinot Grigio dell'Umbria, Cabernet Sauvignon di Miralduolo, as well as VIN SANTO and Metodo Classico Lungarotti Brut sparkling wine. Almost half of all wine is exported. The OENOLOGIST is Teresa Severini Lungarotti, daughter of Signor Giorgio's wife Maria Grazia. In 1974 the latter opened a remarkable Wine Museum in the village, containing exhibits from the 3rd millennium BC to the Renaissance. Adjoining this is the family-owned Tre Vaselle hotel, restaurant, and conference centre.
E.P.-R.

LURTONS, ramified family of property owners and winemakers in BORDEAUX, owning more wine estates in the Bordeaux region than any other single family. The original Lurton property is the modest Ch Bonnet in the ENTRE-DEUX-MERS which belonged to Léonce Recapet, François Lurton's father-in-law. Although he and François acquired Ch Brane-Cantenac in MARGAUX in 1925, the current extent of the Lurton empire is largely due to the efforts of the brothers André and Lucien, both of whom bought numerous properties during the 1960s and 1970s. The elder brother André, who now owns Ch Bonnet and whose estates are mainly in the GRAVES (Chx La Louvière, Couhins, Rochemorin, Cruzeau), was a particularly potent force in the renaissance of the Graves region during the 1980s. A man of vision, energy, and a flair for promotion, he led the campaign for the new appellation of PESSAC-LÉOGNAN and became the first president of its Syndicat Viticole. He led by example, reconstituting the vineyards of the properties he bought and considerably improving the standards of both red and white wine-making.

The younger brother Lucien was the owner of 10 properties (among them Chx Brane-Cantenac, Durfort-Vivens, and Desmirail in Margaux, Bouscaut in Graves, and Climens in BARSAC) before passing them on to his 10 children. He too did much to improve the estates he owned, but, in marked contrast to André, Lucien did very little in the way of public relations. If his red wines were often thought to be not quite up to the potential of their vineyards, Ch Climens has been, year in, year out, one of the finest Barsacs. The younger generation of Lurtons seem likely to continue to be a significant presence in Bordeaux and beyond: André's sons

Jacques and François started a world-wide wine-making service in 1988, advising in France, Spain, Italy, Moldova, South America, and South Australia, and in 1991 Pierre Lurton (son of André and Lucien's brother Dominique) became the estate manager at Ch CHEVAL BLANC, the St-Émilion first growth. M.W.E.S.

LUSSAC ST-ÉMILION, satellite appellation of ST-ÉMILION in Bordeaux.

LUTOMER, known as **Ljutomer** in SLOVENIA, small town in the far east of the country which lends its name to a popular British BRAND, most famously of LASKI RIZLING.

LUXEMBOURG, or **Luxemburg**, was for long the European Union's smallest and coolest wine producer before being rivalled in both respects by GREAT BRITAIN. Wines produced are relatively dry and somewhere between those of Alsace and England in style. Except for a few pale rosés made from Pinot Noir, all wines made on the western, Luxembourg bank of the river MOSELLE are white, and most are noticeably high in acidity and made from vines expected to yield as much as those planted down river in Germany. The average yield can be more than 150 hl/ha (8.5 tons/acre). In 1991 there were 1,345 ha/3,322 acres of vineyard—roughly the same as in England but producing in some vintages ten times as much wine. Except in very ripe years such as 1990 and 1991, CHAPTALIZATION is a necessity here, a typical wine being boosted from perhaps 8.5 to 11 per cent alcohol.

History
The German Mosel, below Trier, and the Luxembourg Moselle above it, had to surmount the same problems for centuries but since the First World War the two regions have adopted different solutions. After the war, during which the grand duchy remained neutral, Luxembourg was required to break the free tariff agreement that had been made with Prussia in 1842. Thus a ready market for Luxembourg's sharp whites made from the ELBLING grape evaporated and Germany looked elsewhere for base wines for SEKT and suitable blending material for the Rheinpfalz's flabbiest wines. Certain Champagne houses, including Mercier, opened up offshoots in Luxembourg in the late 19th century. A new economic agreement with Belgium signed in 1921 did little to soak up the surplus; Belgian taste is for the richness of Pomerol, the vinous antithesis of Elbling. Thus Elbling has been replaced by nobler, or at least softer, varieties.

Geography and climate
Luxembourg's vineyards are in two of the grand duchy's eastern cantons, Remich and Grevenmacher. On the alluvial plain of Remich the heavier soils tend to produce less aromatic, heavier, earlier maturing wines from such villages as Remich, Wintrange, and Schengen. Parts of the narrower valley of Grevenmacher to the north have been reshaped by terracing, as in the Mosel across the German border, but yields are lower, calcareous soils predominate, and wines such as the village of Ahn's fine Rieslings are particularly slow maturing.

Luxembourg, at the northern limit of vine cultivation in Europe, suffers a wide range of cool climate problems such as spring frosts, hail, and COULURE, so that yields can vary substantially.

Vine varieties
Most Luxembourg still wines are varietal wines and are almost invariably labelled as such.

Rivaner This, Luxembourg's own strain of Müller-Thurgau, so effectively replaced Elbling in the 20th century that by the early 1980s it covered as much as half of the grand duchy's total vineyard, being relatively easy to ripen whatever the local conditions. Its ability to yield obligingly high quantities was so abused by many growers, however, that it became synonymous with mediocrity and is now in decline—although in the early 1990s it was still the country's most planted vine by far.

Elbling This was still Luxembourg's second most planted variety in the early 1990s, having been a Luxembourg speciality since Roman times. Consumers increasingly exposed to wines softer, fuller, and more aromatic than ELBLING can produce have hastened its replacement with the varieties below.

Riesling This has been falling from favour, however noble. It demands time, that most expensive of commodities, before showing its best in bottle. In 1991 Riesling still represented one-eighth of Luxembourg's vineyards but here, as elsewhere, did not enjoy the public esteem of those listed below.

Auxerrois This enjoys higher status in Luxembourg than anywhere else in the world (and certainly higher than in Alsace, where 10 times as much is planted). Its low acidity is a positive attribute this far from the equator and when yields are curbed it can produce smoky, full bodied wines worth ageing. See AUXERROIS.

Other varieties Pinot Gris is also highly regarded in Luxembourg, again for its low acidity and its weight as, for much the same reasons, are Pinot Blanc and Gewürztraminer, which is still relatively rare. Pinot Gris in particular has won acclaim in international comparative tastings.

Appellations
Luxembourg's answer to the APPELLATION CONTRÔLÉE system of France is highly individual and would be difficult to apply to a bigger wine industry. There is just one appellation, Moselle Luxembourgeoise, which is allowed to practically all wines, both still and sparkling, although they are all submitted to analysis and a tasting. Superior wines may be ranked as Vins Classés, Premiers Crus, or even Grands Premiers Crus. This generous system, which ignores geographical differences and the influence of TERROIR, has attracted some criticism and a rival organization in the form of Domaine et Tradition, which encourages local variation and expression

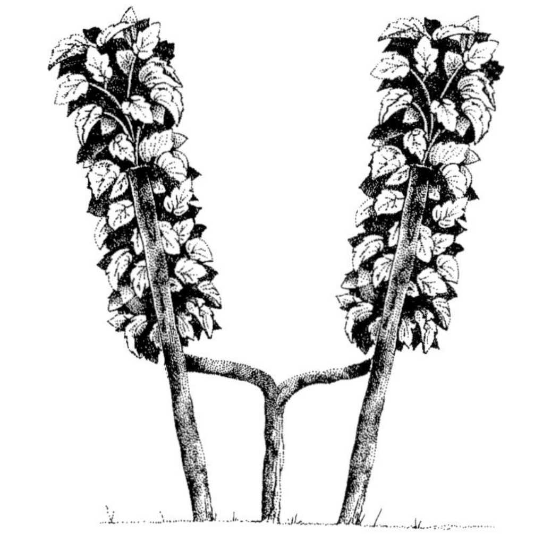

Cross-section of **lyre**-trained vines during the growing season.

Vine training to the **lyre** system showing spur pruning (cane pruning can also be used).

and imposes a maximum yield of 85 hl/ha (4.8 tons/acre). (The maximum yield allowed on the French MOSELLE is 60 hl/ha.)

For details of Luxembourg's appellation for champagne method sparkling wines, see CRÉMANT de Luxembourg.

Industry organization

As in the German Mosel, the average vine-holding is extremely small—less than 2 ha. This fragmentation, together with the economic problems of the 1920s and 1930s, encouraged the formation of five wine CO-OPERATIVES which together function as Vinsmoselle and represent more than 70 per cent of the grand duchy's wine production. There are perhaps only 50 independent producers who vinify their grapes themselves.

LVMH, scrupulously even-handed acronym for Moët Hennessy-Louis Vuitton, the French luxury goods conglomerate which has a dominant interest in the CHAMPAGNE industry, not least through its subsidiaries, which include MOËT & CHANDON and VEUVE CLICQUOT, and a substantial position in COGNAC, and the COOPERAGE business, through HENNESSY. Its distribution, and production, companies throughout the world play an important part in the international wine and spirits trade. In 1987 LVMH acquired a 12 per cent stake in the Guinness Group, which rose to a 24 per cent stake in 1990. Moët Hennessy and the United Distillers Group/Guinness have an agreement to develop joint venture distribution companies in the USA, Japan, the Far East, China, and France.

LYONNAIS, COTEAUX DU. Light red wines made chiefly from Gamay grapes grown in the hills both north and south west of the city of Lyons, and drunk mainly by its inhabitants. The red wines can be every bit as good as nearby BEAUJOLAIS, although the appellation was granted only in 1984. A small proportion of whites from Chardonnay and Aligoté is also made. The CO-OPERATIVE at Saint-Bel vinifies a high proportion of production.

LYRE, a vine-TRAINING SYSTEM whereby the CANOPY is divided horizontally into two curtains of upward-pointing shoots and which resembles a lyre in shape. The system was developed by Dr Alain Carbonneau of the French INRA viticultural research station at Bordeaux in the early 1980s, under the influence of the pioneering studies of Nelson Shaulis of New York state in CANOPY MANAGEMENT. The lyre system improves the CANOPY MICROCLIMATE and leads to improvement in yield and wine quality because of better leaf and fruit exposure. Either SPUR PRUNING or CANE PRUNING can be used, and the mechanization of both pruning and harvesting is being developed. The system is being adopted in New World vineyards in particular, in California, Australia, New Zealand, and Chile, for example.

The lyre system is essentially an inverted GENEVA DOUBLE CURTAIN, with the two adjacent curtains of foliage trained upwards rather than downwards. Both systems are used to reduce the shading of dense canopies. The lyre system is typically recommended for medium-vigour vines, whereas the GDC can harness higher vine vigour. R.E.S.

Smart, R. E., and Robinson, M., *Sunlight into Wine: A Handbook for Winegrape Canopy Management* (Adelaide, 1991).

LYRIC POETRY. There are many references to wine in the lyric poets of Ancient GREECE. Archilochos, writing in the middle of the 7th century BC, describes the comfort brought by wine on a long sea journey:

Along the rowers' benches bring your cup
And lift the lids of the big wine jars up
And drain the good red wine: we can't, 'tis clear
Be sober all the time we're watching here.

Fifty years later Alkaios of Lesbos (who knew and admired the poetess Sappho) has many references to wine, often in vigorous verse: 'Wet your lungs with wine; for the dog star is coming round, and everything is thirsty with heat.' In an early variant of not waiting for the sun to be over the yard-arm, he writes: 'Drink! Why wait for the lamps? The day is almost done!'

The curmudgeonly Theognis, writing at the same time, probably from Megara on the isthmus of Corinth, extols the value of wine and the dangers of DRUNKENNESS. 'Stand by ready to pour for those who want to drink. We cannot have a party every night. Still because I am moderate in my use of honeyed wine, I reach my house before I think of soothing sleep, and I make clear how divine a beverage for man is wine.' H.H.A.

M

MACABEO is northern Spain's most planted white grape variety and, as **Maccabéo** or **Maccabeu**, has become so popular in ROUSSILLON that it was France's eighth most planted white grape variety by the end of the 1980s.

Macabeo spread to southern France from Spain but Odart claims that its origins are Middle Eastern. It is a vigorous vine that buds conveniently late for regions prone to spring frosts and can be quite productive so long as autumns are dry and the possibility of rot is minimized. Well established at one time in North Africa, the vine can tolerate hot, dry conditions.

The wine produced tends to have a vaguely floral character and relatively low acidity unless the grapes are picked so early that the floral character is even more difficult to discern, but it has the advantage, unlike other, more traditional RIOJA varieties, of withstanding OXIDATION well.

Perhaps this is one of the reasons why it has been so enthusiastically embraced by the growers of Rioja, where, as Viura, it has all but displaced Malvasia and Garnacha Blanca to represent more than 90 per cent of all white varieties planted. The fact that it is so much better suited to making light whites for early consumption than heavy, oak-aged wines for the long term may help explain the stylistic evolution of white Rioja.

It is also grown widely in Penedès and, especially, Conca de Barberá, where, with Parellada and Xarel-lo, it makes-up the triumverate of CAVA varieties as well as being found throughout north eastern Spain as far south as Tarragona.

Odart, A., *Traité des cépages* (3rd edn., Paris, 1854).

MACCABÉO or **Maccabeu** is what the French call the common white grape variety of northern Spain, MACABEO. Between 1968 and 1988 it rose from 15th to eighth most popular French white variety, thanks largely to its importance in ROUSSILLON, where it is commonly used, in early-picked form, in Côtes du Roussillon either as a fairly characterless white, a useful ingredient in rosé, or, as in Spain, as a common lightener of potent reds in which it is officially sanctioned up to 10 per cent of the total blend. Later picked, it may be an ingredient in, or even sole constituent of, one of Roussillon's distinctive VINS DOUX NATURELS. It is also common in the LANGUEDOC. In the white wines of Minervois and Corbières it is regarded as a principal ingredient, often blended with BOURBOULENC, GRENACHE BLANC, and a host of other southern white varieties.

MACEDON, small but varied wine region in the state of Victoria in AUSTRALIA. For more detail see VICTORIA.

MACEDONIA, state to the north of Ancient GREECE famous as the home of Alexander the Great and his father Philip, who had conquered Greece by 346 BC. Alexander went on to defeat all the empires of the east before his early death aged 33 in 323 BC. In 167 BC Macedonia collapsed and became part of the Roman empire. The members of the Macedonian royal family were notorious as heavy drinkers of wine. Macedonia is now split: half in what was YUGOSLAVIA and half a province of modern GREECE.

Ex-Yugoslavian republic

Squeezed into an enclave surrounded by BULGARIA, SERBIA, KOSOVO, ALBANIA, and Greece, the republic is hot and mountainous and is also prone to earthquakes. The climate here is extremely favourable to vine cultivation and its 35,000 ha/ 86,450 acres of vineyards produce TABLE GRAPES, red wine in great quantity, and a little white.

Macedonia has some good, modern vineyards planted with the most famous French grape varieties including, unfortunately, far too much GAMAY, which here produces notoriously stewed, short-lived wines. VRANAC also flourishes here but is yet to produce wines of the quality seen in MONTENEGRO to the north west; technology and suitable storage conditions may prove the answer.

Other local grapes include the PROKUPAC of SERBIA, which is plentiful, and the less well-known red Kratosija (often blended with Vranac), as well as the white ZILAVKA from BOSNIA HERCEGOVINA. A.H.M.

MACERATION, ancient word for steeping a material in liquid with or without a kneading action to separate the softened parts of the material from the harder ones. This important process in RED WINE-MAKING involves dissolving of the PHENOLICS (TANNINS, colouring materials or ANTHOCYANS, and phenol-based FLAVOUR COMPOUNDS) from the grape skins, seeds, and stem fragments into the juice or new wine. Some maceration inevitably takes place in the FERMENTATION VESSEL. It is governed by TEMPERATURE, contact between the solids and liquid and the degree of agitation, time, and by the composition of the extracting liquid, in this case the grape juice as it becomes wine. Although everyday red wines are made simply by a rapid fermentation lasting just two or three days, many wine-makers encourage an additional maceration period after fermentation has been completed, particularly for long-lived wines made in cooler regions such as red BORDEAUX.

The maceration process can never extract all of the phenolics from red grapes, however, because the enclosed membranes of individual CELLS within the skin layer containing the phenolics are not broken by the CRUSHING operation that breaks open the berry. The diffusion of anthocyans through these membranes is a slow process and one limited by the size of the diffusing molecules. The process is further complicated by the fact that reactions can occur among the compounds newly released from their confining cells which decompose the extracted materials and produce altogether newer ones. Wine-makers must use trial and error, often over many years, to decide which are the optimum maceration conditions for each grape variety and season. Rapid laboratory analyses can help to estimate colour and tannins (and Ferré has shown in his *Traité d'œnologie bourguignonne* that extraction reaches a maximum of 80 per cent of the grapes' available colouring matter on the sixth day of maceration), but the wine-maker's eye and palate often prove surer guides.

Both heat and alcohol encourage the extraction of desirable compounds, which is fortunate since both are produced by fermentation. As fermentation continues, heat is produced and the increasingly alcoholic liquid becomes a better and better solvent for the organic compounds to be extracted. But the grape solids (mainly skins) have to be encouraged to make sufficient contact with the liquid for optimal extraction. Air entrained with grape skins in the crushing operation tends to make them float to the surface in the fermentation vessel to form a layer known as a CAP. This tendency is accentuated by the bubbles of CARBON DIOXIDE gas generated by fermentation within the lower liquid layers. Without human intervention, a thick and drying layer of grape skins will be buoyed up by this stream of carbon dioxide and the extraction of desirable skin components will cease. For generations wine-making ingenuity has been harnessed to devising methods of breaking up and submerging the cap and keeping the skins mixed with the fermenting liquid.

Keeping skins and liquid in contact is relatively simple with small batches of fermenting grapes. In tanks filled to a depth of 1–1.5 m/3–4 ft a man can physically mix the floating solids into the fermenting grape juice using a wooden punch (known as punching down the cap or, in French, PIGEAGE), or even his feet. Some wineries use mechanical alternatives to this ancient human operation. With larger batches, a system of either grids or coarse mesh screens must be devised to keep the cap submerged, or liquid from the bottom of the tank must be pumped to the top and sprayed over the skins (known as **pumping over** or, in French, REMONTAGE.) Several proprietary systems have been devised to extract the desirable organic compounds from the grape skins into the fermenting wine. Some of these use a quick high-temperature phase to kill the cells containing anthocyans and liberate the desirable organic compounds (see THERMOVINIFICATION); others use mechanical stirrers or rotating tanks (see ROTOFERMENTERS) which keep the skins and liquid in contact; or some form of AUTOVINIFICATION. In general, heat and mechanical agitation systems are used for ordinary wines, while the more sensitive techniques of punching down or pumping over, between one and three times a day depending on the fermentation rate, are preferred for finer wines, although care must be taken that any pumps used are relatively gentle.

Along with temperature, liquid composition, and intimacy of contact, the fourth factor influencing colour, tannin, and flavour extraction is time of contact, a factor, albeit less than perfectly understood, over which wine-makers can have total control (provided they have access to sufficient vat space). In general the longer the solids and liquids are in contact, the greater the degree of extraction. It has been shown, however, that the extraction of the desirable compounds slows down considerably after the new wine approaches 10 per cent alcohol and is at its height during the earlier phases of fermentation. The total maceration time varies according to the phenolic content of the skins (itself a function of grape variety and weather) and according to the desired style of wine. Within certain limits, the greater the degree of extraction, the longer the life expectancy of a wine—although care must be taken to avoid extracting the harshest phenolics. In red wine-making maceration has to last at least as long as fermentation does, but may be prolonged for a further week to three or even four weeks afterwards. Some musts, naturally low in tannins, may be heated after the completion of fermentation to encourage the extraction of phenolics.

Some wine producers favour a prefermentation **cold maceration** of red grapes rather than maceration of skins in an alcoholic liquid. The practice when applied to red Pinot Noir grapes in Burgundy is famously a policy of consultant OENOLOGIST Guy ACCAD. This optional wine-making operation involves the maceration of grape skins with juice while the mass is held at a low temperature. In theory each of the extractable compounds in the skins has its own temperature coefficient governing the extraction rate, and the theory of cold maceration is that a more favourable combination of phenolics is dissolved and extracted by water and added SULPHUR DIOXIDE than is dissolved in an alcoholic solution.

See also BARREL FERMENTATION for an outline of a red wine-making option which dispenses with post-fermentation maceration altogether.

In WHITE WINE-MAKING maceration is usually actively discouraged by separating the juice from the skins as soon as possible in order to avoid extraction of tannins, since no colouring matter is required and the resultant astringency is viewed as a fault in white wines. Some wine-makers deliberately allow a certain period of SKIN CONTACT for white grapes before they are crushed, however, and in the late 1980s this technique (known as **macération pelliculaire** in French) was encouraged by Denis DUBOURDIEU among others in order to produce more flavourful dry white bordeaux. Sauvignon and, particularly, Sémillon grapes are held for between four and eight hours at about 18 °C/64 °F, resulting in juice higher in flavour compounds, tannins, POTASSIUM salts, and polysaccharides, and wines with more BODY and a slightly higher PH.

A quite different red wine-making technique is CARBONIC

MACERATION, practised particularly in Beaujolais and for other red wines designed for early consumption.

Maceration is also important in the production of fruit-flavoured spirits such as the *crème de cassis* used in making a *vin blanc cassis* or KIR which is the aromatic and deeply coloured product of blackcurrants macerated in alcohol. A.D.W.

MACÉRATION CARBONIQUE. French term for CARBONIC MACERATION.

MACÉRATION PRÉFERMENTAIRE. French term for the prefermentation maceration of white grapes described in MACERATION and known elsewhere as SKIN CONTACT.

MCLAREN VALE, wine region in AUSTRALIA. For more detail see SOUTH AUSTRALIA.

MÂCON, important commercial centre on the river Saône and capital of the **Mâconnais** district of BURGUNDY which produces considerable quantities of white wine and some red. Unlike in the Côte d'Or to the north (see map on p. 399), vineyards on the rolling limestone hills of the Mâconnais are interspersed with land dedicated to livestock and arable farming.

The climate and ambience of the region differ from the Côte d'Or: southern tiles are used for roofs, cicadas can be heard in summer, and the vineyards benefit from more sun, less rain, and little risk of frost. BEAUJOLAIS is to the immediate south of the Mâconnais.

Viticultural practices are broadly similar to those in the CÔTE D'OR, although yields may be a little higher, up to a permitted 55 hl/ha (3 tons/acre). Vinification is sometimes carried out in barrels, although only the best producers use new OAK. Bottling normally takes place in the summer before the next vintage.

The appellations of the Mâconnais, in approximately ascending order of quality are, for white wines made from Chardonnay: **Mâcon Supérieur**; **Mâcon Villages** or **Mâcon** followed by a particular village name (for more details of which see MÂCON VILLAGES); ST-VÉRAN; Pouilly-Vinzelles, Pouilly-Loché, and Pouilly-Fuissé (for more details of which see POUILLY-FUISSÉ). Red wine appellations are **Mâcon**, **Mâcon Supérieur**, and **Mâcon** followed by a particular village name. Almost all these red wines are made from the Gamay grape since, although Pinot Noir is permitted, such wines may be sold as BOURGOGNE Rouge at a higher price than Mâcon fetches. J.T.C.M.

MÂCON VILLAGES, appellation covering the great majority of the white wines of MÂCON. The wines may be sold either as Mâcon Villages or as Mâcon followed by the name of the particular village. Viré and Lugny have been the best known by virtue of their CO-OPERATIVES. The full list of 43 villages with the right to the appellation is: Azé, Berzé-la-Ville, Berzé-le-Châtel, Bissy-la-Mâconnaise, Burgy, Bussières, Chaintré, Chânes, La Chapelle-de-Guinchay, Chardonnay (whence the grape may have taken its name), Charnay-lès-Mâcon, Chasselas, Chevagny-lès-Chevrières, Clessé, Crèches-sur-Saône, Cruzilles, Davayé, Fuissé, Grévilly, Hurigny, Igé, Leynes, Loché, Lugny, Milly-Lamartine, Montbellet, Péronne, Pierreclos, Prissé, Pruzilly, La Roche-Vineuse, Romanèche-Thorins, St-Amour-Bellevue, St-Gengoux-de-Scissé, St-Symphorien-d'Ancelles, St-Vérand, Sologny, Solutré-Pouilly, Vergisson, Verzé, Vinzelles, Viré, and Uchizy.

Most Mâconnais wines are vinified in stainless steel or glass-lined concrete vats for early bottling and consumption within a year or two of the vintage. A handful of growers are producing significantly finer wines through low yields followed by BARREL FERMENTATION and BARREL MATURATION. Jean Thévenet has also made a speciality of an extraordinary late-picked and sometimes BOTRYTIZED sweet white Mâcon. J.T.C.M.

MACROCLIMATE, also called regional climate, means a climate broadly representing an area or region on a scale of tens to hundreds of kilometres (Dry and Smart). Unlike the more precise terms MICROCLIMATE and MESOCLIMATE, macroclimate approximates to what is normally meant by the word 'climate'. It is usually taken from a long-established recording station within the region. While easy enough to define, the concept is subject to problems in practice, however. Most climate-recording stations with long enough histories to be reliable over time are sited in towns and cities; they therefore potentially suffer from two defects. First, urban growth around them has in many cases led to a spurious warming trend in the records; mainly in the minimum temperatures, due to retention of the day's heat by roads and buildings, and by industrial and domestic energy input. Secondly, the sites are likely to be disproportionately on flat land or in valleys. They therefore tend to be unrepresentative, not only of the landscape as a whole, but even more so of the better vineyard sites.

Clearly the accepted macroclimatic data have to be used with caution when applied to viticulture. Informed adjustments are often needed for urban warming, and then nearly always for differences in ALTITUDE, LATITUDE, slope, aspect, and even SOIL type, before worthwhile estimates can be made for the mesoclimates of actual vineyards. This is especially so in cool regions, where small differences in effective temperature can make big differences in time and completeness of RIPENING, and in the maturity gradings of the grape varieties that can be ripened. J.G.

Dry, P. R., and Smart, R. E., 'Vineyard site selection', in B. G. Coombe and P. R. Dry (eds.), *Viticulture, i: Resources* (Adelaide, 1988).

MACVIN DU JURA, powerful VIN DE LIQUEUR made in the JURA in eastern France by arresting the fermentation of Jura GRAPE JUICE by adding local MARC. This sweet but curiously earthy drink should be served cool as an APERITIF or with sweet dishes. It has been made since at least the 14th century and was awarded its own APPELLATION CONTRÔLÉE, the 400th created by the official INAO organization, in 1991.

MADAGASCAR, large tropical island off the east African coast which was a French colony between 1896 and 1960. The French introduced viticulture to the plateau land of the Fianarantsoa area south of the capital, and the island produces about 88,000 hl / 2.3 million gal of wine a year (about as much as LUXEMBOURG) from about 2,000 ha / 4,940 acres of vines. See TROPICAL VITICULTURE.

MADEIRA, Atlantic island belonging to Portugal, nearly 1,000 km / 625 miles from the Portuguese mainland and 750 km off the coast of North Africa, formerly a REGIÃO DEMARCADA (RD), now a DOC producing **madeira**, a FORTIFIED wine that is probably the world's most resilient and longest living. This volcanic island rising steeply from the ocean is an unlikely place to find such an exciting and individual wine. But Madeira flies in the face of generally accepted wine-making norms.

History

Like PORT, madeira seems to have begun as a strong, unfortified wine. There are few early records but Madeira's strategic position in the middle of the Atlantic put the island at an advantage and the island's capital Funchal became a natural port of call for ships *en route* to Africa, Asia, and South America. By the end of the 16th century (less than 200 years after the discovery of the island) there is firm evidence that Madeira's wine industry was well established. However, the early madeira wines were unstable and many deteriorated long before they reached their destination. Alcohol (probably distilled from cane sugar) was therefore added to some wines in order to help them survive a long sea voyage, although FORTIFICATION did not become general practice until the middle of the 18th century.

In the second half of the 17th century, ships *en route* to India (including many of the DUTCH EAST INDIA COMPANY fleet) called regularly at Funchal to pick up casks of wine termed pipas or PIPES. It was soon found that madeira somehow tasted better after pitching and rolling across the tropics in the hull of a ship. With this came a fashion for *vinho da roda*, wines that had benefited from a round trip, as opposed to *vinho canteiro*, wine which matured on the island, called after the trestles (*canteiros*) on which the pipes rested in the madeira LODGES. Wines continued to undergo long, tropical sea journeys to induce this special flavour until the 1900s, when the practice became too expensive. Over the preceding century most shippers turned to using ESTUFAS, rooms or tanks in which the wine could be artificially heated to simulate the rapid maturation brought about by a long sea journey—although the finest madeiras continue to be aged naturally on *canteiros* (see Wine-making below).

With the colonization of North America in the 17th century, Madeira established an important export market on the east coast. By the end of the 18th century the new North American colonies were buying a quarter of all the wine produced on the island. Madeira was held in such high esteem that it was used to toast the Declaration of Independence in 1776. Colonial troops returning to Britain opened up a new market for madeira there, but high-quality madeira is still much appreciated in the United States. The Madeira Club of Savannah survived PROHIBITION and continues to meet regularly over a quarter of a millennium after the first pipes of madeira were landed on the coast of Georgia. See MADEIRA PARTIES for more details.

As well as being extremely fashionable in Britain and the United States, the drink was also popular with Portuguese settlers in Africa, and in Brazil, and demand began to outstrip supply.

In 1851, however, the first of a series of crises struck the island's wine industry. Oidium or POWDERY MILDEW reached the island (in the same year as it was first identified in BORDEAUX) and quickly spread through the dense vineyards, almost wiping out production in just three years.

The industry revived after it was found that oidium could be controlled by dusting the vine leaves with SULPHUR but shortly afterwards the PHYLLOXERA louse struck, leaving the island's wine-based economy in ruins. From the mid 1870s, vines all over the island were uprooted and replaced by sugar cane. Wine shippers abandoned Madeira and many vineyards were never replanted.

Phylloxera-resistant AMERICAN VINE SPECIES were introduced a decade or so later but many farmers, seeking a rapid return to prosperity, cultivated VITIS *labrusca*, *riparia*, and *rupestris* vines rather than use them merely as ROOTSTOCKS on to which Madeira's traditional Vitis VINIFERA varieties could be grafted. (Many of these high-yielding, ungrafted varieties remain in the island's vineyards today, although grapes from such 'direct producers' as Jacquet and Cunningham may no longer be used for madeira wine.)

Madeira's wine industry returned to normal levels of production at the beginning of the 20th century and shipments to traditional markets were restored. But the island's economy was dealt another blow, first by the Russian Revolution in 1917, and immediately thereafter by the introduction of Prohibition, in the United States. Many firms were forced to close, but a number chose to amalgamate to form the Madeira Wine Association, renamed as the Madeira Wine Company in 1981.

Although at the end of the 17th century there were about 30 wine shippers operating on Madeira, by the mid 1990s there were just eight exporters of madeira, of which the Madeira Wine Company is now much the largest wine producer on the island, comprising BLANDY, COSSART GORDON, Leacock, Rutherford & Miles, and more than 20 other brand names. In 1988 the SYMINGTON family of OPORTO took a stake in the company, which subsequently became a controlling interest, and thoroughly overhauled the wine-making practices and equipment.

France, Germany, and the Benelux countries are the largest markets for modern madeira, although most of the wine destined for these countries is of very basic quality and bought

Vine terraces on the volcanic island of **Madeira**.

for cooking rather than drinking. The United States, Japan, and the United Kingdom are the main markets for better-quality madeira.

Viticulture

Madeira is a difficult place to grow grapes. Nearly all the island's vineyards are planted on tiny step-like terraces called *poios*, carved from the red or grey basalt bedrock. Most vineyards are planted on trellises similar to those of the VINHO VERDE region on the Portuguese mainland which raise the CANOPY well above the ground, making the grapes less vulnerable to the FUNGAL DISEASES that thrive in this damp, subtropical climate. With a mean annual temperature of 19 °C/ 66 °F and high rainfall, powdery mildew and BOTRYTIS BUNCH ROT are constant threats.

Viticulture at this latitude is only made possible by altitude. Madeira rises to over 1,800 m/5,900 ft and the mountains are almost perpetually covered in cloud as moisture in the warm oceanic air is forced to condense. Annual rainfall on the island's summit reaches nearly 3,000 mm/117 in, over three times the total in the island's capital Funchal on the south coast, where EVAPORATION is high. The network of IRRIGATION channels called *levadas* now extends to over 2,000 km/1,200 miles, supplying the 4,000 growers farming around 1,800 ha/4,500 acres of piecemeal vineyard. MECHANIZATION is rendered impossible by both the terracing and the small size of the vineyard plots. As a result, cultivation costs are rising.

Vine varieties

The most planted variety by far is the red-skinned Tinta Negra Mole, which has been the principal *vinifera* variety on the island since phylloxera arrived at the end of the 19th century. Its name means 'black, soft' and it is often denigrated, somewhat unfairly in view of its versatility. It can make good madeira, but wines based on Negra Mole rarely have the keeping qualities of those based on the nobler varieties. Plantings of the traditional varieties SERCIAL, VERDELHO, BUAL, and MALVASIA are slowly increasing once again since their rout as a result of phylloxera. Other varieties planted are principally disease-resistant AMERICAN HYBRIDS such as Cunningham and Jacquet, although they are no longer permitted as ingredients in madeira and should be used exclusively in the production of the island's rustic table wine.

Wine-making

Madeira is made in a number of different ways and methods of production vary enormously according to the market and the price that the wine commands. Production revolves around the use of the ESTUFA system and its natural alternatives. There are two main types of *estufa* in which the finished wine is effectively artificially aged.

Lined concrete tanks (*cubas de calor*) ranging in size between 20,000 and 50,000 l/13,200 gal are the most widely used for large-volume production. Hot water circulates through a stainless steel coil in the middle of the tank, heating the wine to a temperature between 40 °C and 50 °C/122 °F for a minimum of three months. The process is carefully monitored by the wine industry's controlling body, the Instituto do Vinho da Madeira (Madeira Wine Institute, or IVM), although bulk *estufagem* followed by rapid cooling tends to produce wines that taste stewed and are often flawed by excess VOLATILE ACIDITY.

A second type of *estufagem* takes place in 600-l wooden casks or lodge pipes which are stored in warm rooms (*armazens de calor*) heated by the nearby tanks or by steam-filled hot water pipes. Temperatures usually range between 30 °C and 40 °C and the wines develop over a longer period, usually six months to a year. This is a gentler process than the bulk method generally used, and is used for wines destined to make higher-quality five- and 10-year- old Reserve and Special Reserve blends (see below).

The very finest madeiras are produced without any artificial heating at all. Some of the smaller shippers and stockholders (*armazenistas*) refuse to resort to the *estufa* to age their wines. These madeiras are left to age naturally in 600-l pipes stowed under the eaves of lodges in Funchal, heated only by the sun. These *vinhos de canteiro* mature in cask for at least 20 years, although some may remain in this state for a century or more before bottling, and are usually destined for vintage lots.

One of Madeira's most pressing problems is a lack of good-quality base wine caused by a shortage of grapes from *vinifera* vine varieties. The white Sercial, Verdelho, Bual, and Malvasia varieties which are classified as 'noble' by the ruling Madeira Wine Institute are in short supply (see below). Most madeira is therefore made from the versatile Tinta Negra Mole.

Traditionally, shippers bought unfermented MUST direct from the growers, who trod the grapes by foot in stone LAGARES. Today few wine-makers use *lagares* and the main shippers buy grapes rather than must, from farmers all over the island. Most firms ferment in 25,000-l vats made of wood or lined cement although one major shipper (which in the 1960s mistakenly built AUTOVINIFICATION vats like those used for port) is now installing stainless steel. The noble varieties are usually pressed and fermented separately from Tinta Negra Mole, often in lodge pipes. Malvasia and Bual are traditionally fermented on their skins while Sercial and Verdelho musts are separated from the grape skins before fermentation.

Higher-quality wines (usually those made with a high percentage of the more expensive noble grapes) are made by arresting the fermentation with 95 per cent strength grape spirit, or AGUARDENTE, to produce a wine with an ALCOHOLIC STRENGTH of between 17 and 18 per cent. Wines made from Malvasia and Bual are fortified early in the FERMENTATION process, leaving up to 7° Baumé (see MUST WEIGHT for conversions into other scales of measurement) of RESIDUAL SUGAR in the wine. Verdelho and Sercial are fermented until they are practically dry, although they may be sweetened at a later stage with either *vinho surdo* or *abafado*. *Surdo* is an intensely sweet MISTELA fortified to an alcoholic strength of 20 per cent, often before fermentation has begun, while *abafado* is a drier wine arrested at a later stage.

Producers of bulk wines, on the other hand, prefer to ferment all wines dry, leaving the fortification until after the wines have passed through the *estufa*. This saves on the cost of valuable alcohol, a few degrees of which are lost through evaporation during *estufagem*. The wines are sweetened after fortification according to style and are often adjusted with caramel.

The wines' age is counted from the point at which *estufagem* has been completed. The most basic wines are generally shipped in bulk (*granel*) after spending between 18 months and three years in BULK STORAGE. Better-quality wines are set aside for blending into one of the styles and qualities outlined below.

Styles of madeira

Madeira varies greatly in quality. Inexpensive wines tend to smell cooked and taste coarse and stewed. Finer wines are distinguished by their high-toned RANCIO aromas and searing ACIDITY. Madeira varies in colour from orange-amber to deep brown with a yellow-green tinge appearing on the rim of well-aged examples.

Standard blends Madeira's wines have traditionally been named Sercial, Verdelho, Bual (or Boal), and Malvasia (or MALMSEY) after the principal noble grape varieties grown on the island, these names denoting increasingly sweet styles of madeira. But since phylloxera destroyed many of Madeira's best vineyards at the end of the 19th century, much of the island's wine has in reality been made from either AMERICAN HYBRIDS or the basic local *vinifera* variety Tinta Negra Mole. The use of American hybrids has technically been illegal since 1979. From the beginning of 1993 Madeira has been made to conform to the EUROPEAN UNION requirement that a VARIETALLY named wine must contain at least 85 per cent of wine made from the specified grape variety. Insufficient quantities of the noble varieties resulted in renaming most standard blends simply 'Dry', 'Medium Dry', 'Medium Sweet', and 'Rich' or 'Sweet'.

Sercial Among the noble grapes, Sercial is usually grown in the coolest vineyards, at heights of up to 1,000 m/3,300 ft or on the north side of the island. Many growers erroneously believe that the variety is related to Germany's RIESLING grape but it is in fact the same as the ESGANA Cão (meaning dog strangler) which grows on the Portuguese mainland, the grapes exhibiting the same ferocious levels of ACIDITY. At high altitudes Sercial ripens with difficulty to make an 11° base wine which is dry, tart, and astringent when young. With fortification and 10 or more years' ageing in cask, a good Sercial wine develops high-toned, almond-like aromas with a nervy character and a searing dry finish. The Sercial wines range in residual sugar from 0.5° to 1.5° Baumé.

Verdelho Verdelho, which is also planted on the cooler north side of the island, ripens more easily than Sercial and therefore lends itself to producing a medium dry wine with Baumé readings of between 1.5° and 2.5° after fortification. With age the wines develop an extraordinary smoky complexity while retaining their characteristic tang of acidity.

Bual Bual, or Boal in Portuguese, is grown in warmer locations on the south side of Madeira. It ripens to achieve higher sugar levels than either Sercial or Verdelho and, after fortification to arrest the fermentation, Bual wines range from 2.5° to 3.5° Baumé. These dark, medium rich, raisiny wines retain their acidic verve with age.

Malmsey The MALVASIA grapes which produce malmsey are usually grown in the warmest locations at low altitudes on the south coast, especially around Câmara de Lobos. Two types of Malvasia grape, Malvasia Candida and Malvasia Babosa, ripen to produce the very sweetest madeira wines, which gain in richness and concentration with time in cask. Sugar readings in a malmsey range between 3.5° and 6.5° Baumé, but the wines are rarely cloying as the sweetness is balanced by characteristically high levels of acidity. Like all high-quality madeira made from noble varieties, malmseys are some of the most resilient in the world and will keep in cask and bottle for a century or more.

Historic styles Madeira's unparalleled ability to age means that styles of wine long abandoned by the island's wine shippers may still be found, and enjoyed. Rainwater is a light, medium dry style of madeira named after wine which was supposedly diluted by rain during shipment to the United States. Rainwater madeira is still made in small quantities, although the law is vague on what exactly constitutes the style. Two other styles of madeira based on the noble Terrantez and BASTARDO grapes are no longer made, since both varieties are almost extinct on the island, although older bottles may be found. Intensely sweet wines made from three types of Moscatel (MUSCAT) grape, usually produced for blending, are occasionally bottled on their own.

Qualities of madeira

A generally accepted hierarchy (from the youngest and most basic to the oldest and most distinguished) parallels the different styles of madeira as follows.

Bulk wine *Granel*, meaning 'bulk', accounts for between 30 and 40 per cent of the island's production. After rapid *estufagem* in tank, the wine is aged for about 18 months before being shipped in bulk, often having been coloured and sweetened with caramel.

Finest 'Finest' in the context of madeira means a blended three-year-old wine, bottled after *estufagem* and ageing in tank, rarely in wood.

Reserve 'Reserve' madeira is a blended five-year-old wine, some or all of which will have undergone *estufagem* in tank. A proportion of the blend will have been aged in cask.

Special Reserve 'Special Reserve' madeira is a wine where the youngest component in the blend will be around ten years old, having aged in cask, usually without recourse to *estufa* tanks. These wines are mostly made from the noble grape varieties and labelled accordingly.

Extra Reserve 'Extra Reserve' is a category of madeira which is rarely seen but the term denotes a blended, 15-year-old wine.

Solera The SOLERA system more commonly associated with SHERRY has been used for blending madeira since the 19th century but this category is currently being abandoned on Madeira in favour of dated blends. Many madeira labels have specified completely fictitious soleras on their labels.

Vintage Vintage madeira is a wine from a single year which, unlike vintage PORT, must age in cask for a minimum of 20 years followed by a further two years in bottle before shipment. Most wines spend considerably more time in wood than the legal minimum and are sometimes aged in 20-l/5-gal glass carboys, or *garrafoes*, before bottling. The wines are extremely resistant to OXIDATION and may be kept in bottle for many years. Vintage madeira, especially Sercial, is capable of many decades' BOTTLE AGEING. Shippers carrying stocks of old vintages are so confident of madeira's ability to withstand oxidation that they keep the bottles standing upright so that there is no risk of a poor or tainted cork spoiling the wine.

Serving madeira

Madeira is probably the most robust wine in the world. Little can harm the wine after it has suffered the indignity of the *estufa*, or been aged for twenty or more years in cask. Most shippers storing bottles upright RECORK their most venerable vintages, say, once every 20 years. All wines tend to throw a deposit with age, but madeira throws less than most. Decanting is therefore recommended for older, vintage wines but is not always necessary. Such wines should be left to breathe for a short time before serving simply to allow any BOTTLE SICKNESS to dissipate. Drier Sercial and Verdelho styles benefit from being served 'cellar cool' rather than iced. Sweeter buals and malmseys should be served at room temperature. Once opened, a bottle of madeira has the advantage of lasting almost indefinitely. R.J.M.

Cossart, N., *Madeira the Island Vineyard* (London, 1984).
Huetz de Lemps, A., *Le Vin de Madère* (Grenoble, 1989).
Mayson, R., *Portugal's Wines and Wine Makers* (London, 1992).

MADEIRA PARTIES. Such was the popularity of MADEIRA in the 19th century, particularly in the United States, that whole gatherings were devoted to the drink and the custom has occasionally been revived, thanks to such associations as the Madeira Club of Savannah, Georgia. Standard late 19th century practice was to assemble eight men round a table and circulate decanters of five or six different and increasingly rich madeiras clockwise to the accompaniment of biscuits, nuts, cigars, and discussion. Thus, claims Cossart, 'madeira is the only wine whose strict devotees allow smoking'.

Cossart, N., *Madeira the Island Vineyard* (London, 1984).

MADELEINE ANGEVINE, relatively very early ripening vine variety used for TABLE GRAPES and for wine production in ENGLAND and KYRGYZSTAN.

MADERA, town and county in the SAN JOAQUIN VALLEY of California that is also the name of an AVA.

MADERIZATION, occasionally **madeirization**, is the process by which a wine is made to taste like MADEIRA, involving mild OXIDATION over a long period and, usually, heat. Such a wine is said to be **maderized**. Although this tasting term is occasionally applied to any sort of wine as though it meant the same as oxidized, it should properly be applied only to wines with a high enough ALCOHOLIC STRENGTH to inhibit the action of ACETOBACTER, which would otherwise transform the wine into VINEGAR.

Very few maderized wines are made today by simply ageing the wine at cellar temperature (although this was once a technique practised for making fuller sherry styles outside Jerez); the oxidation process is instead hastened by heating or 'baking' the wine as on the island of Madeira. Oxidation reactions, like most organic chemical reactions, can be roughly doubled in speed by a temperature rise of 10 °C/18 °F. For example, a wine requiring 10 years at a cellar temperature of 20 °C to develop a maderized character could manifest approximately, although not exactly, the same character after about two and a half years at 40 °C or 15 months at 50 °C.

Maderized wines are normally amber to brown in colour and have a distinctive cooked or mildly caramelized flavour. Wines processed at excessively high temperatures may taste burnt and harsh. Most such wines and especially those made from AMERICAN VINES or AMERICAN HYBRIDS are fortified and sweetened before being marketed. Madeira and similar wines such as early sherry style wines made in California were particularly popular in the 18th and early 19th centuries but have since fallen from favour somewhat.

See also RANCIO wines. A.D.W.

MADE WINE, somewhat inelegant name for wine made not from freshly picked grapes but from reconstituted GRAPE CONCENTRATE. The advantages for producers are that it can be made throughout the year, and that grapes can be sourced wherever they happen to be cheapest. CYPRUS has been an important source. BRITISH WINE is one of the most commercially successful made wines, but made wines have been produced in Japan and eastern Europe. The produce of many HOME WINE-MAKERS is made wine.

MADIRAN, important red wine appellation in SOUTH WEST FRANCE in the throes of remodelling its concentrated, traditionally tannic wines.

There are said to have been vineyards here in Gallo-Roman times, and certainly the wines of Madiran were appreciated in the Middle Ages by pilgrims *en route* for Santiago de Compostela. More than 1,000 ha/2,500 acres, mainly clay and limestone, in the south of the ARMAGNAC region produce GASCONY's signature red wine (just as JURANÇON to the south is its most famous white). The climate in Madiran is softened, and often moistened, by the Atlantic to the west, but autumn is usually dry.

The traditional grape variety is TANNAT, its very name hinting at the naturally astringent character of its high TANNIN level. The proportion of Tannat allowed to add local flavour to Cabernet Sauvignon and Cabernet Franc was adjusted during the 1970s so that it may now constitute anything between 40 and 60 per cent of the blend. A little FER (Pinenc) is also grown. The wine traditionally needed long BOTTLE AGEING but some of Madiran's most dynamic wine-makers have been experimenting with ways of softening the impact of Tannat and producing wines which have density, potential for ageing, but considerable charm in youth. Madiran can taste like a classed growth claret given the sort of Gascon twist needed to cope with *magret de canard*.

The Madiran region also produces some fine white wine under the name PACHERENC DU VIC-BILH.

MADRID, VINOS DE. The Spanish capital Madrid, strategically placed at the heart of the country by Philip II, is much less well known as the name of a wine denomination. The DO Vinos de Madrid forms a semicircle around the southern suburbs. Of the three officially recognized subzones, the most important is round the town of Arganda del Rey to the east of Madrid. White wines are made from the Malvar, which is also eaten in the capital as a table grape, and AIRÉN. Reds are produced from Tinto Fino (TEMPRANILLO), also known as Tinta Madrid, and Garnacha (GRENACHE). Few wines stray further than city bars and cafés. R.J.M.

MAGARATCH, wine research institute at Yalta in the CRIMEA, the most important centre of wine ACADEME in the Soviet Union, now CIS. The Institute Magaratch was founded in 1828, more than 50 years before DAVIS or the Institute of Oenology at BORDEAUX UNIVERSITY. Although its activities have been unusually wide ranging (including some innovative by-product recycling), the Institute Magaratch has been particularly distinguished in developing CROSSINGS and special vinification techniques.

Its three experimental vineyards cover nearly 2,000 ha/5,000 acres and include one of the largest collections of vines, with more than 3,000 varieties, in the CIS. Some of the most successful of 30 vine varieties designed to combine quantity with quality are Magaratch Ruby or Roubinovyi Magaratcha (CABERNET SAUVIGNON × SAPERAVI), Magaratch Bastardo or Bastardo Magaratchski (BASTARDO × Saperavi), and Ranni Magaratcha. A newer generation of varieties has since been developed with specific resistances to various pests and diseases.

At one time much of Magaratch's effort was directed towards producing convincing copies of various classic wine styles (Magaratch Malmsey, for example). The institute's own cellar harbours nearly 20,000 sample bottles, some of them containing wine from the mid 19th century.

Specific research avenues have included a refinement of

CONTINUOUS FERMENTATION techniques and tend to have a particularly practical aspect, involving hundreds of patents.

MAGNESIUM, mineral element essential for healthy vine growth. Magnesium is an essential element in the chlorophyll molecule, and so CHLOROSIS is a common symptom of magnesium deficiency. The most conspicuous symptom is chlorosis between the main veins of the leaf, which becomes particularly noticeable around VERAISON. This zone is yellow for white varieties, and red for dark fruit varieties. This deficiency can be severe in some situations, reducing YIELDS, and slowing fruit ripening because magnesium is essential for PHOTOSYNTHESIS to proceed. Magnesium deficiency may be associated with the disorder of SHANKING, in which the bunch stems and berries shrivel before ripening. Maturity is affected and wine quality suffers.

Soils high in POTASSIUM encourage magnesium deficiency. Similarly, some ROOTSTOCKS such as SO4 and Fercal are incapable of taking up sufficient magnesium and commonly show deficiency symptoms. Magnesium deficiencies with such rootstocks as 140 Ru and 1103 P are very rare, on the other hand. R.E.S.

Champagnol, F., *Éléments de physiologie de la vigne et de viticulture générale* (St-Gely-du-Fesc, 1984).

MAGNUM, large BOTTLE SIZE containing 1.5 l/54 fl oz, or the equivalent of two bottles. It is widely regarded as being the ideal size for BOTTLE AGEING fine wine, being large enough to slow the AGEING process, but not so big as to be unwieldy, or unthinkably expensive (unlike some other 'large formats').

MAGO, influential classical writer on agricultural, including viticultural, matters. See CARTHAGE for more details.

MAÎTRE-DE-CHAI, term often used in France, particularly in Bordeaux, for the cellarmaster, as opposed to the RÉGISSEUR, who might manage the whole estate, or certainly the vineyards. It means literally master of the CHAI. As SCIENCE and ACADEME invade wine-making, the wine-making decisions are increasingly made by an OENOLOGIST.

MAJORCA, known as **Mallorca** in Catalan, Spanish Balearic island in the north west Mediterranean which was once the seat of the kings of ARAGON. In the 19th century the island was famous for its sweet MALVASIA wines, which all but disappeared when the vineyards fell victim to PHYLLOXERA. Of the 2,500 ha/6,175 acres of vines currently in production on the island, 400 belong to the BINISSALEM, Spain's first offshore DO wine region on the island's central plateau, with good, original reds from the local Manto Negro grape made by J. L. Ferrer.

MÁLAGA, city and Mediterranean port in ANDALUCÍA, southern Spain (see map on p. 907), which lends its name to a denominated wine zone producing rich, raisiny FORTIFIED wines. Since the 1960s Málaga has become more famous as the tourist gateway to the Costa del Sol, but its wine industry has a long and distinguished history dating back to around 600 BC, when the Greeks first planted vines in the area. The Moors continued to make wine, calling it *xarab al Malaqui*, or Málaga syrup, probably to remove any reference to alcohol but also evoking the extraordinary sweetness of the grapes growing in the hills above the city. In the 17th and 18th centuries Malaga was exported world-wide and by the mid 19th century there were over 100,000 ha/247,000 acres of vineyard, making Málaga Spain's second largest wine region. Exports of Mountain, as the wine became known in Great Britain and North America, totalled between 30,000 and 40,000 BUTTS (as much as 220,000 hl/5.8 million gal) a year.

In the mid 19th century Málaga was dealt a double blow, first by POWDERY MILDEW, then, in 1876, by the arrival of PHYLLOXERA. Málaga was the first wine region in Spain to be affected by the louse and its effect on the local economy was devastating. The terraced vineyards to the north and east of the city were abandoned and many families emigrated to South America. Málaga never really recovered until well after the Spanish Civil War, in the 1960s, when tourism became Málaga's major industry. From a peak immediately prior to the arrival of phylloxera of 113,000 ha, the region's vineyard area had declined to 900 ha by the early 1990s, making Málaga one of Spain's smallest Denominaciones de Origen, or DO. Where there were once over 100 BODEGAS near the port in the centre of the city, in the 1990s there are just three producers located on modern industrial estates on the edge of Málaga.

Málaga's vineyards are still split into four zones, the most important of which is the Antequera plateau 50 km/30 miles north of the city of Málaga itself. The principal grape variety is the PEDRO XIMÉNEZ which gives high sugar levels in the hot, dry climate (although considerable amounts of the more productive AIRÉN vine were also planted in the 1980s). In the cooler mountain zone immediately north of the city Moscatel de Alejandria (MUSCAT OF ALEXANDRIA) is the dominant vine, which is grown mainly for the production of RAISINS in the two coastal zones to the east and west of Málaga. In order to compensate for the lack of grapes in the region, Pedro Ximénez may temporarily be imported from MONTILLA-MORILES, which abuts Málaga to the north, although it may not exceed 10 per cent of the volume.

Traditionally, Malaga was a DRIED GRAPE WINE made by leaving the grapes in the sun on grass mats for between seven and 20 days to concentrate the natural sugars. Today the wines are made in larger, central bodegas using a number of different methods. The sweetness is normally obtained by arresting the fermentation with grape spirit (as for VIN DOUX NATUREL in France), although some grapes are still dried and can be fermented to 18 per cent alcohol leaving considerable RESIDUAL SUGAR. A third way of adjusting the sweetness is with *arrope*, unfermented grape must that has been boiled down to 30 per cent of its normal volume. This may be added either before or after fermentation.

Wherever the grapes are grown, Málaga wines must be aged in the city of Málaga itself to qualify for the DO. The wines mature in different sizes of oak COOPERAGE arranged into SOLERAS. The Consejo Regulador recognizes 16 different types of wine ranging from sweet to dry with an ALCOHOLIC STRENGTH between 15 and 23 per cent. Most wines are deep brown, intensely sweet, and raisiny, some tasting slightly burnt through the addition of too much *arrope*. Dry wines are paler with a rather undistinguished nutty character. The most common styles are as follows:

Lágrima: intensely sweet wine made from FREE-RUN juice without any mechanical pressing.
Moscatel: sweet, aromatic wine made exclusively from Moscatel de Alejandria grapes.
Pedro Ximénez (occasionally labelled Pedro Ximen): sweet wine made exclusively from Pedro Ximénez grapes.
Solera: sweet wine from a dated solera (Scholtz Hermanos Solera 1885, for example, which is one of the best-known Malagas).

R.J.M.

Duijker, H., *The Wine Atlas of Spain* (London, 1992).
Metcalfe, C., and McWhirter, K., *The Wines of Spain & Portugal* (London, 1988).
Read, J., *The Wines of Spain* (London, 1986).

MALAGOUSSIA, elegant grape variety rediscovered and identified only recently in modern GREECE. It has already yielded interesting results at Domaine Carras in the north east.

MALBEC, black grape variety once popular in Bordeaux but now more readily associated with ARGENTINA and CAHORS, in both of which it is one of the most planted vines. It has many synonyms, of which Galet cites as the true name Côt, or Cot as it is known in much of western France, including the Loire where it is quite widely grown. In Argentina it is often called Malbeck, in the Libournais Pressac, and in Cahors, suggesting origins in northern Burgundy, Auxerrois. Galet's complete list of synonyms runs to nearly 400 words, however, for the variety has at one time been grown in 30 different *départements*.

Malbec has been declining in popularity in France for it has many of the disadvantages of Merlot (sensitivity to COULURE, frost, DOWNY MILDEW, and rot) without as much obvious fruit quality. Indeed it can taste like a rather rustic, even shorter-lived version of Merlot, although when grown on the least fertile, high, rugged limestone vineyards of Cahors it can occasionally remind us why the English used to refer to Cahors as 'the black wine'. Cahors APPELLATION CONTRÔLÉE regulations stipulate that 'Cot' must constitute at least 70 per cent of the wine. Other appellations of SOUTH WEST FRANCE in which Malbec may play a (smaller) part are Bergerac, Buzet, Côtes de Duras, Côtes du Frontonnais, Côtes du Marmandais, Pécharmant, and Côtes du Brulhois. It is also theoretically allowed into the Midi threshold appellations of Cabardès and Côtes de la Malepère but is rarely found this far from Atlantic influence.

At one time, especially before the predations of the 1956 frosts, Malbec was quite popular in Bordeaux and is still permitted by all major red bordeaux appellations, but total Bordeaux plantings fell from 4,900 ha/12,100 acres in 1968 to 1,500 ha in 1988. It persists most obviously in Bourg, Blaye, and the Entre-Deux-Mers region but is being systematically replaced with varieties whose wines are more durable.

Blended with Cabernet and Gamay, it is also theoretically allowed in a wide range of mid Loire appellations—Anjou, Coteaux du Loir, Touraines of various sorts, and even sparkling Saumur—but has largely been replaced by Cabernets Franc and Sauvignon.

It is in Argentina that Malbec really holds sway, covering 10,000 ha/24,700 acres of vineyard (more than any other red wine grape until recently) in most of Argentina's wine regions. Varietal Argentinian Malbecs have some perceptibly Bordelais characteristics, of flavour rather than structure. The wines can be ripe and lush and capable of extended AGEING here. Malbec, usually spelt without a k but sometimes called Cot, is Chile's third most important black grape variety after Pais and Cabernet Sauvignon and there were about 4,000 ha of it planted in the early 1990s. Chile's version tends to be more tannic than those raised across the Andes and is often blended with Merlot and (Petit) Verdot.

Australians have no great respect for their Malbec and have been uprooting it systematically but still had 250 ha in 1990. Californians had got their total, significant before PROHIBITION, down to about the same level, but who knows when this may be driven up by a desire to replicate, for example, the country wines of France? Most of today's California Malbec is dutifully added to MERITAGE style bordeaux blends.

A small amount of Malbec, Malbech, or Malbeck is also planted in north east Italy.

Galet, P., *Cépages et vignobles de France* (2nd edn., Montpellier, 1990).

MALEPÈRE, CÔTES DE LA, shares many of the wine characteristics of CABARDÈS, another small wine region where the Midi and Aquitaine meet near Carcassonne in the south west of France. The wines, mainly red, are made up of a blend of Bordeaux and Languedoc varieties but in the case of Malepère, with its wetter, more Atlantic climate, it is the Bordeaux varieties of Merlot and Cot (Malbec)—together with Cinsaut in the east of the region—that predominate. Secondary varieties, all of these tested and developed at the region's important viticultural research station at Alaigne, include Cabernet Franc, Cabernet Sauvignon, Grenache, and Syrah. In contrast to Cabardès, Carignan is not allowed. The region, awarded VDQS status relatively late, in 1983, is working actively towards full APPELLATION CONTRÔLÉE recognition just like its counterpart to the north, Cabardès, although it belongs climatically even more definitively to South West France than to the LANGUEDOC, from which it is geographically protected by the Hautes Corbières peaks. The vineyards, mainly clay and limestone, are immediately north

Pruning, the vine-grower's winter communion with his plants/charges, a particularly arduous task in the harsh winters of **Champagne**, such as here below the windmill of Verzenay on the Montagne de Reims. Burning cuttings minimizes the clearing up, and helps mitigate the cold. On the surface of the vineyard are specks of Parisian rubbish, habitually used as **fertilizer** in Champagne.

ENTRANCE
PARKING

of those responsible for Blanquette de LIMOUX. Wine production is dominated by several large co-operatives, of which the determinedly *océanique* Cave du Razès alone is responsible for almost two-thirds of the region's entire production.

MALIC ACID, one of the two principal organic acids of grapes and wines (see also TARTARIC ACID). Its name comes from *malum*, Latin for apple, the fruit in which it was first identified by early scientists. Present in nearly all fruits and berries, malic acid is now known to be one of the compounds involved in the complicated cycles of reactions by which plants and animals obtain the energy necessary for life. One of these cycles of reactions is known as the citric acid, Krebs, or tricarboxylic acid cycle and its elucidation was one of the outstanding triumphs of biochemistry.

Another, which comes into play during the final stages of ripening in many fruits, including grapes, causes the decomposition of malic acid. When all of the malic acid has been used up in this latter series of reactions, the fruit becomes overripe, or senescent. The malic acid decomposing reaction is much more rapid in hot summer temperatures, probably because of the more rapid RESPIRATION of malate in the berry (in fact, it has been suggested that this takes place particularly in the berry's vascular bundles). This is, at least in part, one reason for the lower total acid concentrations in grapes grown in warmer regions. It accumulates in young grape berries reaching high levels at about VERAISON—sometimes as high as 20 g/l—but, as ripening progresses, the level of malate declines to concentrations of between 1 and 9 g/l when the grapes are ripe. This large range in ripe grapes is an important source of variation in quality.

Tartaric acid, the other main grape acid, does not participate in several of the reaction pathways in which malic acid is an essential component, which is why the hotter the summer, the lower the likely proportion of malic acid in the grapes. Malic acid's different chemical structure allows it to participate in many more of the enzymatic reactions involved in living systems than tartaric acid because it can be pumped across plant membranes serving as a transportable energy source. Because the concentrations of tartaric acid are relatively and desirably stable, attention is given to the tartrate/malate (T/M) ratio which varies from about 1 to 6 and is characteristic for each grape variety. High malate varieties, with a low ratio, are desirable for hot districts and examples are SYLVANER, COLOMBARD, BARBERA, and CARIGNAN.

Malic acid is lost not just through the citric acid cycle, and through other reaction cycles during grape ripening, but also in many cases as a result of MALOLACTIC FERMENTATION of wines either during or after alcoholic FERMENTATION. Just as high temperatures favour the loss of malic acid in grapes, they encourage the lactic organisms responsible for malolactic fermentation. The wine-maker can exercise some control over this loss of malic acid if necessary, however, since the growth and activity of these organisms can be slowed or inhibited by moderate concentrations of SULPHUR DIOXIDE. In addition, since the LACTIC BACTERIA responsible for malolactic fermentation require many micro-nutrients (vitamins, growth factors, nitrogenous compounds), early and thorough separation of the new wine from its LEES can inhibit bacterial activity and preserve malic acid.

Malic acid is available commercially for use in acidifying foods and beverages and in numerous industrial processes. At one time it was isolated from fruits and other plant tissues but is more usually synthesized from another organic acid today. A.D.W. & B.G.C.

MALMSEY, English corruption of the word MALVASIA, derived from the port of Monemvasia which was important in Ancient GREECE. The word was first used for (probably a wide range of) the unusually sweet, rich wines of Greece and the islands of the eastern Mediterranean, particularly Crete, then called Candia (see GREECE, medieval history). Sweet white wines were particularly prized in the Middle Ages, particularly but not exclusively by northern Europeans, who regarded their own wines as thin, and admired the longevity of these liquids, very possibly DRIED GRAPE WINES, so sturdily high in sugar and alcohol. The acute merchants of GENOA, NAPLES, and VENICE were able profitably to capitalize on this stability in their trading links between east and west.

As European temperatures fell as a result of CLIMATE CHANGE, these richer wines held even more allure. Venetians in particular created a demand for malmsey in 15th century England. George, duke of Clarence and younger brother of England's King Edward IV was popularly believed to have been drowned in a BUTT of malmsey in the Tower of London in 1478.

Malvasia vines came to be planted all round the western Mediterranean (even today Malvasia and MALVOISIE are two of the most commonly used synonyms for various, often quite unrelated, VINE VARIETIES). Malmsey, which originally denoted any strong, sweet wine, was eventually used specifically for the sweetest style of MADEIRA, particularly that made from Malvasia grapes.

See also MALVASIA.

MALOLACTIC FERMENTATION, occasionally abbreviated to **MLF** or, in French, 'le **malo**', conversion of stronger MALIC ACID naturally present in new wine into weaker LACTIC ACID and CARBON DIOXIDE. Malic acid has two acid groups whereas lactic acid has only one. It is accomplished by LACTIC BACTERIA, which are naturally present in most established wineries but may have to be cultured and carefully introduced in newer establishments where malolactic fermentation is desired. This process is unrelated to and almost never precedes the alcoholic FERMENTATION, for which reason it is sometimes called a SECONDARY FERMENTATION. One sign of this process, as of alcoholic fermentation, is that carbon

Two expressions of opulent capital investment in wine: second growth Ch Pichon Longueville Comtesse de Lalande in **Pauillac** (top) built during the Médoc's 19th century golden age and, all decked out to receive visitors, Clos Pegase winery near Calistoga in the **Napa** Valley, a direct result of **California's** 20th century wine boom, and a national architectural competition.

dioxide bubbles escape from the wine. It is written chemically thus:

$$COOH\text{-}CHOH\text{-}CH_2\text{-}COOH \rightarrow COOH\text{-}CHOH\text{-}CH_3 + CO_2$$

malic acid — lactic acid — carbon dioxide

Malolactic fermentation is desirable in wines which have excessive ACIDITY, particularly red wines produced in cooler climates. Malolactic fermentation can also add flavour and complexity to both red and white wines, as well as rendering the wine impervious to the danger of malolactic fermentation in bottle. Recognition and mastery of malolactic fermentation (which would traditionally happen as if by accident when temperatures rose in the spring) was one of the key developments in wine-making in France and elsewhere in the mid 20th century. By the early 1990s most fine red wines, many sparkling wines, and a small but increasing proportion of the world's white wines involved full or partial malolactic fermentation. In hotter climates or warmer years in cooler areas, some wine-makers deliberately suppress malolactic fermentation in some or all batches of a wine in order to maintain the wine's acidity. Some grape varieties seem to have a greater affinity with malolactic fermentation than others. Of white grapes Chardonnay, for example, is a generally successful candidate for the process, while most producers of Riesling and Chenin Blanc deliberately avoid the process, despite the high natural acidity in these latter two.

Malolactic fermentation may reduce the acidity of a particularly ripe wine unduly, and care must be taken that the amount of the buttery-smelling diacetyl produced by the process is not unpleasantly excessive, as it has tended to be in early experiments with malolactic fermentation in some white wines.

Malolactic fermentation's effect on decreasing TOTAL ACIDITY is often most marked on those wines which were highest in malic acid before it took place, that is the products of particularly cool growing seasons. In some cases the wine-maker may even have to ACIDIFY after malolactic fermentation.

Like most BACTERIA, lactic bacteria grow best in very weakly acidic solutions and at temperatures near those of the human body (which is why malolactic fermentations traditionally took place without encouragement as temperatures rose in the spring, especially if cellar doors were opened). Malolactic fermentation is therefore strongly influenced by the wine's PH: if it is less than 3.1 it is practically impossible, if more than 4.5, considerably retarded. Bacteriologists regard lactic bacteria as 'fastidious' in that they require a wide range of micro-nutrients. They are also intolerant of even moderate concentrations of SULPHUR DIOXIDE and high concentrations of ETHANOL.

Malolactic fermentation can therefore be encouraged by adding lactic bacteria to the MUST soon after alcoholic fermentation has started. At this point conditions are ideal for the lactic bacteria—the solution is warm, its alcohol content is low, the sulphur dioxide added before fermentation has already been volatilized, and the dying yeast cells, or LEES, provide the necessary micro-nutrients. Alternatively, immediately after alcoholic fermentation has been completed, the new wine can be transferred to an old wooden vat in which successful malolactic fermentations have already been completed and in which there will almost always be a sufficient population of lactic bacteria. Or it can be transferred to an inert tank or vat, or to small barrels, and inoculated with lactic bacteria. In general old wooden COOPERAGE will carry a heavy enough population of bacteria so that no inoculation is needed. The wine-maker must be careful to discard cooperage harbouring any undesirable bacteria, but save those casks with a good record for malolactic fermentation. A malolactic fermentation which occurs during alcoholic fermentation is particularly efficient since it advances the wine-making schedule and because it is easier to start when the alcohol level is lower than after full alcoholic fermentation has been completed.

Malolactic fermentation may well be regarded as undesirable in wines to be bottled and sold young, most white wines, mass market bottlings of any hue, for example, together with light reds such as Beaujolais and Dolcetto. In this case, care is taken to avoid any contact with vats infected with lactic bacteria and to rack the new wine off the lees and their micro-nutrients quickly. SULPHUR DIOXIDE additions and cool cellar temperatures can also stun any lactic bacteria into inactivity. Such techniques as sterile FILTRATION, STERILE BOTTLING, and PASTEURIZATION can insure against the commercial embarrassment of malolactic fermentation's taking place in bottle. If a bottled still wine starts to fizz, this is the most likely cause and is most commonly encouraged by the combination of heat and residual lactic bacteria. See FAULTS IN WINE for more. A.D.W.

McWhirter, K., 'Flavour Enhancement', *Wine & Spirit* (Sept. 1988), 63.

MALTA, the central Mediterranean island, has a small wine industry that can trace its history back to Phoenician times. In the early 1990s just under 1,000 ha/2,500 acres of vineyard were mainly in the hands of relatively unskilled, part-time farmers. The majority of vines planted were TABLE GRAPE varieties which produced wines so low in sugar and acid that considerable adjustments were needed in wineries rarely equipped for high-quality wine production. Demand for wine on this tourist island is such that local grapes are supplemented by grapes imported from Italy. Most common grape varieties are the local specialities, Gellewza for red wine and Ghirghentina and Gennarua for white wine. Experiments suggest that imported noble grape varieties together with French and Italian technological support may result in some very much finer wine. The most successful vineyards are in the north and north west of the island. The Italian producer ANTINORI is involved in an ambitious new wine estate near Mdina. M.M.-F.

MALVASIA, name used widely, especially in Iberia and Italy, for a complex web of grape varieties, typically ancient and of Greek origin and producing characterful wines high in alcohol and, often, RESIDUAL SUGAR. Most are deeply coloured whites but some are, usually light, reds. Malvasia is widely disseminated, even if it not grown in enormous quantity anywhere nowadays.

Malvasia is the Italian corruption of Monemvasia, the southern Greek port which, in the Middle Ages, was a busy and natural entrepôt for the rich and highly prized dessert wines of the eastern Mediterranean, notably those of Crete, or Candia (see GREECE, history). **Malvasia di Candia** is today one distinctive subvariety of Malvasia, which, like the somewhat similar MUSCAT, exists in many guises and hues. So important was Malvasia during the time of the Venetian republic that wine shops in VENICE were called *malvasie*.

The French corruption of Malvasia has been used particularly loosely; for more details see MALVOISIE. The word was also corrupted into MALMSEY in English, which continues to be an important style of MADEIRA, traditionally based on the Malvasia grape. The Germans call their various though rare forms of Malvasia **Malvasier** and occasionally early, or *früh*, VELTLINER in various colours of berry.

Malvasia, in its various forms—white and red, dry and sweet—is one of Italy's most widely planted grapes, with close to 50,000 ha / 123,500 acres being cultivated in the early 1990s in regions as distant and disparate as the Basilicata and Piedmont. White **Malvasia Bianca**, the larger part of the production, is widely used throughout Latium, Umbria, and Tuscany, frequently in combination with various types of Trebbiano, forming what might be called the standard central Italian white blend. This type of wine has lost considerable ground in Tuscany, and then Umbria, since the 1970s, however, as producers replaced both Malvasia and Trebbiano with more strongly characterized INTERNATIONAL VINE VARIETIES. Monovarietal Malvasia wines are rare in central Italy, but pioneering efforts began to appear in the Castelli Romani zone in the early 1990s.

The finest dry white VARIETAL Malvasia is made in Friuli, where two DOCs—COLLIO and ISONZO—cultivate what is called locally **Malvasia Istriana** and which, according to local tradition, was carried to these vineyards from Greece by the fleets of Venice. Substantial quantities, about 35,000 hl / 924,000 gal annually, are also produced as a DOC wine in the Colli PIACENTINI, where a slight sparkle is quite common. Lightly sparkling dry to demi-sec Malvasia is frequently encountered in Emilia, where it is referred to as *champagnino* or 'little champagne', and where local trenchermen consider it the perfect accompaniment and *digestif* for the rich local fare.

Sweet white Malvasia, normally a PASSITO and once considered one of Italy's finest dessert wines, underwent a major loss of consumer favour and an even more significant contraction in acreage after the Second World War, so that its very existence seemed threatened. Latium's **Malvasia di Grottaferrata** and Sardinia's **Malvasia di Bosa** and **Malvasia di Planurgia** have, in fact, become so rare that they can be said no longer to exist in commercial terms, although an occasional bottle can still be found in the production zones themselves. **Malvasia delle Lipari**, which seemed destined to share their fate, was revived in the 1980s and the survival of this distinctive sweet orange relic from the volcanic island of Lipari off SICILY seems assured, at least in the short run, although current quantities are a mere fraction of the more than 100,000 hl / 2.6 million gal produced annually before the arrival of PHYLLOXERA. The Basilicata has its own version of sweet Malvasia, produced in the same zone as Aglianico del Vulture, and local producers, buoyed by the new interest in their red wine, are attempting to capture the market's favour with their Malvasia, which also exists in dry and spumante versions.

Red Malvasia, also known as **Malvasia Nera**, is most commonly used in conjunction with other grapes: as the minority partner of Negroamaro in the standard red blend of the provinces of Lecce and Brindisi in Apulia, and as a useful supplement to Sangiovese in Tuscany, where it adds both colour and perfume. The introduction of the even more aromatic and deeply coloured Cabernet Sauvignon to Sangiovese-based Tuscan blends in the 1970s and 1980s (see TUSCANY) has led to a distinct loss of favour for Malvasia Nera and uncertain long-term prospects.

Piedmont is the only significant producer of varietal Malvasia Nera wines, with two DOC zones: **Malvasia di Casorzo**, in both a dry and sweet version, and **Malvasia di Castelnuovo Don Bosco**. Total area planted is less than 100 ha / 250 acres, however, and total annual production less than 4,000 hl / 105,600 gal.

On the French island of CORSICA most growers believe that their Malvoisie is identical to VERMENTINO, which may be related to the greater Malvasia family.

Malvasia is planted to a declining extent in northern Spain, notably in RIOJA and NAVARRA, although the less interesting VIURA has been gaining ground. Malvasia is also planted on the CANARY ISLANDS.

Further into the Atlantic, **Malvasia di Candia** in particular is beginning to gain ground once more in the vineyards of MADEIRA, where it was traditionally the variety used to produce Malmsey, before the advent of phylloxera. Myriad Malvasias are also grown on the mainland in PORTUGAL, making a contribution to such varied wines as Buçaco and COLARES, and, as the distinctly ordinary **Malvasia Rei** (also known as Seminario), it is an ingredient in white PORT.

In California there are more than 2,000 acres / 800 ha of Malvasia Bianca, the most substantial plantings being in Tulare County at the very southern end of the SAN JOAQUIN VALLEY. D.T. & J.Ro.

MALVOISIE is one of France's most confusing vine names, perhaps because, like Pineau, the term was once used widely as a general term for superior wines, notably those whose origins were supposed to be Greek. There is no single variety whose principal name is Malvoisie, but it has been used as a synonym for a wide range of, usually white-berried, grape varieties producing full bodied, aromatic whites. Despite the etymological similarity, Malvoisie has rarely been a synonym for the famous MALVASIA of Greece and Madeira. Malvoisie is today found on the labels of some Loire and Savoie wines made from such plantings of PINOT GRIS as remain, as Malvoisie du Valais is a common synonym for Pinot Gris in Switzerland. It is also sometimes used for BOURBOULENC in the Languedoc, and occasionally for MACCABÉO in the Aude, for CLAIRETTE in Bordeaux, and for TORBATO in Roussillon. VERMENTINO, which may in fact belong to the Malvasia family, is sometimes called Malvoisie in Iberia and is known as Malvoisie de Corse in Corsica.

Malvoisie Rose and **Malvoisie Rouge** are occasionally used as synonyms for FRÜHROTER VELTLINER in Savoie and northern Italy, while the **Malvoisie Noire** of the Lot in south west France may be TROUSSEAU.

Galet, P., *Cépages et vignobles de France* (2nd edn., Montpellier, 1990).

MAMMOLO, heavily perfumed red grape variety producing wines which supposedly smell of violets, or *mammole*, in central Italy. This, a permitted ingredient in CHIANTI, is relatively rare today, although a small amount is also grown in the VINO NOBILE DI MONTEPULCIANO zone. Its significance, as an often theoretical seasoning to the blend, may be compared to that of PETIT VERDOT in the classic MÉDOC of Bordeaux.

MANCHA, LA. Europe's largest single demarcated wine region in the heart of Spain (see map on p. 907). The vineyards of the DO La Mancha cover 170,000 ha/419,900 acres of arid table land from the satellite towns north of Madrid to the hills beyond VALDEPEÑAS nearly 200 km/125 miles to the south. The Moors christened it Manxa, meaning 'parched earth', and that is an apt description of the growing conditions in southern Castile, CASTILE-LA MANCHA. RAINFALL is unreliable with annual totals averaging between 300 and 400 mm/16 in. Summers are hot with temperatures rising to over 40 °C/104 °F, while winters are bitterly cold with prolonged FROSTS.

The doughty AIRÉN vine seems to be well suited to these extreme conditions and is therefore popular among La Mancha's 18,000 smallholders. It takes up over three-quarters of the total vineyard area, planted at the remarkably low VINE DENSITY of between 1,200 and 1,600 vines per hectare (485–650 per acre) because of the very dry climate. FUNGAL DISEASES are almost unknown in La Mancha's dry growing season and cultivation is therefore relatively easy. YIELDS of between 20 and 25 hl/ha (1.4 tons/acre) seem puny by international standards, and, despite limited MECHANIZATION, production costs remain low. LABOUR costs were low in central Spain, but vineyard workers began to be recruited from Morocco in the early 1990s.

Traditionally the grapes were picked late in the season and fermented rapidly without TEMPERATURE CONTROL in earthenware TINAJAS. As a result, Manchegan wine was coarse and alcoholic. Much was distilled or sold in bulk, and most wines were brown and OXIDIZED by the time they reached consumers. During the 1980s, however, a sea change took place in La Mancha. In an effort to make the wines more appealing to the changing tastes of both domestic and international

La Mancha's famous seventeenth-century literary hero Don Quixote is seen here returning from the inn.

customers, producers began to pick their grapes up to a month earlier and vinify them at low temperatures in STAINLESS STEEL.

Technological development has given La Mancha a new lease of life and opened new and more discerning markets for the region's fresh, inexpensive, if rather neutral dry white wines. Red wines, made increasingly from Cencibel (TEMPRANILLO) grapes, have also improved enormously and a number of enterprising growers are experimenting with other grape varieties, including CABERNET SAUVIGNON and CHARDONNAY. Of the 2 million hl/53 million gal produced annually, a large part is distilled into industrial alcohol or sent to JEREZ to make BRANDY de Jerez. In the early 1990s only 30 per cent of the region's production was sold in bottle, but with modernization taking place in all but the most hidebound CO-OPERATIVES, this proportion was expected to increase and La Mancha's prospects had never looked better. R.J.M.

MANDELARIA, dark-skinned grape variety planted widely on the islands of GREECE, notably on Paros, Crete, SANTORINI, and Rhodes, where it is known as Amorgiano. It tends to produce wines relatively light in alcohol, although not in colour. Blended with more substantial grapes, it can produce harmonious dry reds such as Peza, or even sweet reds.

MANGANESE, a soil nutrient essential for vine growth but in very low quantities. Manganese deficiency causes leaf yellowing, and is found most commonly on alkaline soils high in LIMESTONE. Acid soils (see SOIL ACIDITY) which are poorly drained and high in manganese can cause toxicity, reducing both vine growth and YIELD. R.E.S.

MANSENG in both Gros Manseng and, even finer, Petit Manseng forms is the Basque vine variety responsible for the exceptional tangy rich white wines of JURANÇON in the western foothills of the French Pyrenees. It is also grown in nearby Gascony for the somewhat similar PACHERENC DU VIC-BILH and can be found in some of the rare white wines of BÉARN. Such has been Jurançon's return to public favour, and corresponding Gascon enthusiasm for Pacherenc, that Manseng was one of the few grape varieties to have increased its hold on French viticulture in recent years. According to official statistics, France's total area planted with Manseng rose from just 90 ha in 1968 to 1,152 ha / 2,845 acres two decades later, almost half of this total being in the Gascon Gers *département* (although this apparent increase may be due more to Gascony's recent viticultural archive work than to new plantings).

Petit Manseng has particularly small, thick-skinned berries which yield very little juice (sometimes less than 15 hl/ha, although up to 40 hl/ha (2.3 tons/acre) is allowed for both Jurançon and Pacherenc) but can well withstand lingering on the vine until well into autumn so that the sugar is concentrated by the shrivelling process known as PASSERILLAGE. The variety is however sensitive to both sorts of mildew.

Gros Manseng is more widely planted, has bigger berries than Petit Manseng, and usually has slightly different leaves. In practice the two Mansengs are usually cultivated together and the richer, more concentrated juice of the Petit Manseng particularly prized for sweet wines, while Gros Manseng usually dominates the blends for the dry Jurançon Sec appellation (in which there may well be some Courbu too).

Manseng, usually Petit Manseng, can also be found in Uruguay, where it, like TANNAT, was taken by Basque settlers in 19th century.

There are signs that Petit Manseng may follow VIOGNIER in terms of popularity with those groups who follow vine variety FASHION.

MANZANILLA, a special style of SHERRY that is made quite naturally in the seaside sherry town of SANLÚCAR DE BARRAMEDA. Like FINO, it is a very pale, light, dry style of wine that is heavily influenced by FLOR yeast, but *manzanilla* is made in the particularly humid, maritime air of Sanlúcar which tends to result in a thicker layer of flor, a slower maturation process, lower alcohol content, and slightly higher acidity—especially since grapes are often picked slightly less ripe than for *fino*. As the wine matures, and the flor dies, a *manzanilla* may develop into a **Manzanilla Olorosa** and then a **Manzanilla Pasada**, which is a Sanlúcar equivalent of a *fino amontillado*. Although most natural *manzanilla* is barely 15 per cent alcohol, most producers ship commercial Manzanillas to export markets at about 17 per cent in order to ensure stability. For more details, see SHERRY.

MARANGES, the southernmost VILLAGE WINE appellation in the Côte de Beaune district of Burgundy, produces medium bodied red wines of some charm when young but of unproven distinction in the long term. The vineyard stretches across the three villages of Cheilly, Dezize, and Sampigny, each of which takes Les Maranges as a suffix. Formerly the wines were sold either under the village name or, much more frequently, as Côte de Beaune Villages. Since 1988 such wines may be called Maranges or Maranges Côte de Beaune. White wines are permitted but are scarcely made.

See also CÔTE D'OR and its map. J.T.C.M.

MARC, the general French term both for grape POMACE and, more widely, for POMACE BRANDY. It used to distinguish the product from a FINE which may be made by distilling local wine. Most traditional wine regions make marc from the pomace, grape skins, and pips left after pressing. This was rarely for financial gain but often because peasant winegrowers hate to see anything they have grown go to waste.

The biggest distillery making marc is owned by the firm of Jean Goyard in Champagne, which takes in the pomace from all the region's wines. It distils the marcs using a system of small, steam-heated vats (see CALANDRE). The marcs are then aged by individual champagne houses who sell them under their own names. **Marc de Champagne** is far more aromatic than most of the **Marc de Bourgogne** made in Burgundy, since the pomace from the grapes which have been pressed whole, as for CHAMPAGNE, contains high levels of sugar and virtually no alcohol, in marked contrast to typical BURGUNDY pomace, which is what is left after destalking and fermentation.

The production of Marc de Bourgogne is in the hands of two specialist distillers as well as a number of mobile stills. A handful of NÉGOCIANTS and individual estates proudly offer their own oak-aged marcs that are aromatic, rich, powerful, and the ideal conclusion to a gigantic Burgundian repast for gourmands not overly interested in extending their lifespan. The only other French region offering marcs in any quantity is Alsace, where the merchants and CO-OPERATIVES sell **Marc d'Alsace** alongside their equally potent and delicious eaux-de-vies, brandies made by distilling the fermented juice of other fruits. Marcs are also a by-product in other wine regions, notably Jura (where they also make BRANDY) and Provence.

In Italy such brandies are called GRAPPA, in Portugal BAGACEIRA. N.F.

MARCHES or, in Italian, **Marche**, the easternmost region in the central belt of Italy stretching from TUSCANY through UMBRIA to the Adriatic coast (see map on p. 517). It shares a variety of characteristics with these neighbours to the west: a TOPOGRAPHY shaped by land rising from the coastal plains to rolling hills and, westward, to the central spine of the

Apennines; Mediterranean vegetation of cypress, umbrella pine, olive, and vine; and a TEMPERATE climate marked by hot, dry summers. Viticultural characteristics are also shared: CALCAREOUS soils from the sea which once covered an important part of central Italy; HILLSIDE VINEYARDS; and a preponderance of SANGIOVESE and TREBBIANO vines. The Marches has been the last of the three regions to realize its potential for good-quality wines, however, partly because the region is off Italy's main commercial axis of Milan–Bologna–Florence–Rome–Naples, and partly because of the lack of any urban centre more important than Ancona. The region experienced remarkable economic growth between 1960 and 1990, but was relatively impoverished before the Second World War and the lack of a discerning local clientele has been an undoubted handicap in the improvement of wine quality.

The **marc**, press cake, pressed into shape for Marc de Bourgogne by Louis Latour's basket press.

(Cesare MONDAVI, who laid the foundations of one of the most famous wine producers in the world, emigrated from this region in the early 20th century.)

Total current production of wine averages over 1,600,000 hl/42.2 million gal per year, with about 17 per cent qualifying for a regional DOC, of which there are 10. VERDICCHIO in its two versions—from the Castelli di Jesi and from Matelica—dominates this DOC production with close to 200,000 hl produced in an average year. Bianchello del Metauro, Falerio dei Colli Ascolani, and Bianco dei Colli Maceratesi are bland and anonymous white wines, the first from the local Bianchello grape variety, the latter two based on Trebbiano.

The greatest potential in the region, however, is represented by its two outstanding red varieties, Sangiovese and MONTEPULCIANO D'ABRUZZO, far superior to any of the local white varieties grown. Both of the major red DOCs, Rosso Conero and Rosso Piceno, employ these two red varieties. Rosso Conero, taking its name from Monte Conero, which towers over the city of Ancona to the south, is produced from Montepulciano along with a maximum 15 per cent of Sangiovese, while Rosso Piceno is produced from a minimum of 60 per cent Sangiovese and a maximum of 40 per cent Montepulciano in a large part of the region's hill country outside the Rosso Conero zone. A Rosso Piceno CLASSICO heartland does exist in the province of Ascoli Piceno, but does not constitute a real guarantee of superior quality and is virtually irrelevant in terms of labels on the market. Maximum permitted YIELDS, at close to 100 hl/ha (5.7 tons/acre) in both DOCs, are excessively generous; winemaking is frequently slipshod and haphazard, and it is far easier to find a poor bottle of Rosso Conero or Rosso Piceno than a genuinely interesting one. An occasional excellent wine only confirms that great potential is only sporadically realized, although it is true that seriously good red wines from this region face stiff competition from the better-known products of Tuscany and Umbria, a fact which acts as a brake on investment and commitment to quality. The data concerning the Rosso Piceno DOC are starkly illustrative of the region's commercial problems: of the annual potential of 465,000 hl, from 4,800 ha/11,860 acres of vineyard, less than 30,000 hl are declared most years.

See also VERDICCHIO. D.T.

MARCILLAC, isolated small red wine region in SOUTH WEST FRANCE whose vigorous red wines can have real character. This is the liveliest wine district of the Aveyron *département* (although see also the Vins d'ENTRAYGUES and d'ESTAING), but it will be hard to preserve the viticultural tradition here in the harsh climate of the Massif Central at altitudes up to 600 m/2,000 ft. Perhaps Marcillac was granted a promotion to AC status in 1990 partly to encourage an endangered but worthwhile species of wine. Although there were several thousand ha of vines here in the late 19th century, only about 100 ha/250 acres of VINIFERA vines survive (many growers responded to the PHYLLOXERA crisis by planting HYBRIDS). Marcillac, usually red and sometimes rosé, must be made of at least 90 per cent FER, here often called Mansois, a hard-wooded vine capable of making peppery, aromatic mountain wines with good structure. BARREL MATURATION has been introduced and the wines of Marcillac are, unlike many of the Bordeaux duplicates produced in the south west, worthy of attention and encouragement. The local CO-OPERATIVE at Valady is an important producer.

MARCOTTAGE, French term for the LAYERING method of vine propagation in the vineyard.

MARÉCHAL FOCH, red wine grape variety named after a famous French First World War general. This FRENCH HYBRID was bred by Eugene Kuhlmann of Alsace, who cited the VINIFERA variety Goldriesling as one parent. It has good winter hardiness and ripens very early. It was once widely cultivated in the Loire and is still popular in CANADA and NEW YORK, where it is spelt **Marechal Foch** and may be vinified using CARBONIC MACERATION.

MARGARET RIVER, small, self-conscious, and successful wine region in the state of WESTERN AUSTRALIA.

MARGARODES, otherwise known as ground pearls, are a serious insect pest in some vineyards, although they are, fortunately, found only in some areas. Margarodes weaken and kill vines with a similar action to PHYLLOXERA, and afflicted vines normally die about four years after a decline in VIGOUR is noted.

While many species of margarodes occur on a wide range of host plants world-wide, the most damaging to vines is the *Margarodes vitis* of South America. There are 10 species of margarodes in South Africa, five of which infest vine roots, with *Margarodes prieskaensis* being one of the most damaging. The pre-adult insect is a round cyst which attaches itself to the roots, and is covered by a hard, waxy covering. The insects are conspicuous by their foul odour.

The mature cysts can remain inactive in the soil for many years. Winged male and female forms mate above the soil surface and eggs are laid in the vicinity of vine roots in early summer. There are no sources of resistance to ground pearls within the VITIS genus which includes vines, so control by grafting on to resistant ROOTSTOCKS seems unlikely. Many attempts to control margarodes with chemicals have failed, but recent studies in South Africa with hexachlorobutadiene have been successful. R.E.S.

de Klerk, C. A., 'Chemical control of *Margarodes prieskaensis (Jakubski) Coccoidea: Margarodidae* on grape-vines', *South African Journal for Enology and Viticulture*, 8 (1987), 11–15.

Winkler, A. J., *et al.*, *General Viticulture* (2nd edn., Berkeley, Calif., 1974).

MARGAUX, one of the potentially most seductive communal appellations of the Haut-Médoc district of Bordeaux. At their stereotypical best, the wines of Margaux combine the deep ruby colour, structure, and concentration of any top-quality Médoc with a seductive perfume and a silkier texture than is found to the north in ST-JULIEN, PAUILLAC, and ST-ESTÈPHE. Mid 20th century vintages from its two finest properties Ch Margaux (see below) and Ch Palmer certainly demonstrated this and helped to develop a cliché conception of Margaux that can be of little help in BLIND TASTING vintages of the 1980s, when so many wines up and down the Médoc seemed to be designed to maximize BODY and EXTRACT, often at the expense of intercommunal distinctions.

Margaux is the most southerly, most isolated, and most extensive of the Médoc's communal appellations (see map on p. 124). Although it is made of several non-contiguous parcels of the best portions of vineyard land, inferior parcels qualifying merely as Haut-Médoc, the appellation takes in not just the substantial village of Margaux, (with one of the few serious hotel-restaurants of the Médoc), but also the neighbouring communities of Cantenac, Soussans, Labarde, and Arsac.

In total more than 1,300 ha/3,210 acres qualified for the Margaux appellation in the mid 1990s, and within its boundaries there are inevitably considerable variations in both topography and soil type. Within the apellation is limestone, chalk, clay, and sand, but most of the finest wines should come from gentle outcrops, or *croupes*, where gravel predominates and DRAINAGE is good—although properties here are particularly parcellated and intermingled with one estate often comprising very different, and often distant, plots of land. Ch Margaux, for example, has vineyards in both Cantenac and Soussans.

Margaux has in the past enjoyed enormous *réclame*, and more Margaux properties were included in the 1855 CLASSIFICATION of the Médoc and Graves (more than 20) than from any other appellation. The appellation clearly still has great potential, but in the 1970s and much of the 1980s a curious number of châteaux failed to keep pace with the substantial improvements in wine quality achieved in the other three major appellations of the Médoc.

Ch Margaux itself, the FIRST GROWTH standard-bearer as well as name-bearer for the appellation, was revived only in 1978 after more than a decade of disappointing vintages (see below for more details). The five second growths within the appellation, Chx Rausan-Ségla, Rauzan-Gassies, Durfort-Vivens, Lascombes, and Brane-Cantenac, included some of the most notable under-performers in the whole Médoc, while, among the original 10 third growths, Desmirail, Ferrière, and, especially, Dubignon-Talbot had been practically abandoned. Only Ch Palmer, officially a third growth, could be said to have represented the appellation with any glory and consistency in the second half of the 20th century. Ch Palmer, part owned and managed by Peter A. SICHEL, produced a wine that could without hyperbole be described as legendary in 1961.

Rausan-Ségla and Rauzan-Gassies were originally one estate and, according to Penning-Rowsell, probably the first other than the first growths to establish a reputation abroad. Rausan-Ségla, the larger part, or rather many different parts, was for long owned by the CRUSES and has since then passed through several corporate hands, but not without experiencing a dramatic increase in quality, largely thanks to new wine-making equipment, in the mid 1980s. This policy revision, which included declassifying the entire 1987 vintage into a SECOND WINE, resulted in one of the most marked, and welcome, improvements of the decade. By the mid 1990s, a similar miracle was yet to be effected at Rauzan-Gassies and Durfort-Vivens (see LURTON).

Ch Lascombes passed from Alexis LICHINE to a British brewer in 1971 and, after considerable land acquisitions, took more than a decade to hit form, while the large Ch Brane-Cantenac estate, also owned by a Lurton, has been producing lighter wines than its status in the 1855 classification suggests.

Of Margaux's many third growths other than Palmer, Kirwan can lack concentration; moated Issan is more famous for its romantic moated château than its modern wines (see CRUSE); Giscours and Cantenac-Brown can please in a rich, rather obvious way (although the latter was taken in hand in the late 1980s); Malescot St-Exupéry, originally called St-Exupéry, is taking on welcome flesh; Boyd-Cantenac is too often dull; while Marquis d'Alesme-Becker, originally called Becker, can be uncomfortably lean.

Thanks to the efforts of Alexis Lichine, more care has been lavished on Ch Prieuré-Lichine (one of the Médoc's first châteaux ever to welcome tourists) than on Margaux's other fourth growths Chx Pouget and Marquis de Terme, although the latter is much improved since the mid 1980s. Chx Dauzac and du Tertre are Margaux's fifth growths, but such unclassified growths as Chx d'Angludet (Peter Sichel's home), La Gurgue, Labégorce-Zédé, and Monbrison can often provide more excitement and wine-making integrity, particularly in terms of value.

One of the Médoc's most famous white wines is made here, even though it qualifies only as BORDEAUX AC (see below).

For more information see MÉDOC, BORDEAUX, and MARGAUX, CH.

Ginestet, B., *Margaux* (Paris, 1984).
Parker, R., *Bordeaux* (2nd edn., New York, 1991).
Penning-Rowsell, E., *The Wines of Bordeaux* (6th edn., London, 1989).
Peppercorn, D., *Bordeaux* (2nd edn., London, 1991).

MARGAUX, CHÂTEAU, exceptional building and the most important wine estate in the village of MARGAUX in the Bordeaux wine region, and a FIRST GROWTH in the 1855 CLASSIFICATION. There is much potential for confusion since both Ch Margaux and GENERIC wine from the commune of Margaux are colloquially referred to as 'Margaux', but the former is likely to cost several times the latter.

Ch Margaux was one of the four New French Clarets captured in the Anglo-French wars at the beginning of the 18th century, and sold in the COFFEE HOUSES of the City of London (see BORDEAUX, history). Thomas JEFFERSON on his visit to Bordeaux in 1787 picked it out as one of the 'four vineyards of first quality'. Sequestered in the French Revolution after the execution of the owner, it was bought by the Marquis de la Colonilla in 1804 and rebuilt in the First Empire style, by J. Combes, as we know it today—the grandest CHÂTEAU of the Haut-MÉDOC. After passing through several hands, shares were bought by a Bordeaux wine merchant, Fernand Ginestet, in 1925, and the family share was slowly increased to give his son Pierre Ginestet complete ownership in 1949. Also a merchant, he was badly hit by the 'energy crisis' in the early 1970s and had to seek a buyer. The French government refused to allow the American conglomerate National Distillers to buy it, but in December 1976 the château was acquired by the French grocery and finance group Félix Potin, headed by the Greek André Mentzelopoulos, domiciled in France. A great deal of money was spent on restoring the neglected vineyard, *chais*, and mansion and Émile PEYNAUD was taken on as consultant. André Mentzelopoulos suddenly died in December 1980, and first his wife Laura and then his daughter Corinne took over control, assisted by Paul Pontallier, the young director who joined the estate in 1983. In 1992, in a complicated international deal involving Perrier mineral water, the Italian Agnelli family of Fiat motor cars became involved in ownership of the estate, but Corinne Mentzelopoulos remained in charge and took a personal stake in the property.

Corinne Mentzelopoulos of Ch **Margaux**.

The 78 ha/192 acres of dark grape varieties is planted with 75 per cent CABERNET SAUVIGNON grapes, 20 per cent MERLOT, and five per cent of CABERNET FRANC and PETIT VERDOT. Average output is about 30,000 cases, of which the resurrected Pavillon Rouge de Ch Margaux is the excellent SECOND WINE. A hitherto somewhat uninspiring white wine Pavillon Blanc was transformed, and, made in a new and separate temperature-controlled cellar, is an ambitious dry wine made, with BARREL FERMENTATION, exclusively from SAUVIGNON Blanc grapes planted on 12 ha of separate vineyard. Ch Margaux, unusually, still has its own COOPERAGE. E.P.R.

Coates, C., *The Great Wines of Bordeaux* (London, 1994).
Faith, N., *Château Margaux* (London, 1980).

MARIA GOMES, Bairrada synonym for the Portuguese white grape variety FERNÃO PIRES.

MARIGNAN and **Marin** are both named CRUS on the south eastern shore of Lake Geneva whose name may be added to the French appellation Vin de SAVOIE. The wine is typically a light, dry white made from the Chasselas grape.

MARINO. See CASTELLI ROMANI.

MARITIME CLIMATE, the opposite of a continental climate, one with a low degree of CONTINENTALITY, or a relatively narrow annual range of temperatures. Places with a maritime climate tend to be near oceans or other large bodies of water.

MARL, the crumbly combination of LIMESTONE and CLAY which is often added to soils lacking limestone (see LIME). Whitish marl is found naturally to some extent in the vineyards of BEAUNE and POMMARD. It assumes more importance in MEURSAULT, where it forms the best soil for grapes grown for white wines. There is pebbly marl in the JURA region of France, and TAVEL in the southern RHÔNE has soils which are predominantly Cretaceous marl. In the German region of RHEINHESSEN the soil is partly derived from marl. Many of the finest wines of the CÔTE D'OR are from grapes grown on predominantly CALCAREOUS marl with some limestone. See entries prefixed SOIL. M.J.E.

MARMANDAIS, CÔTES DU, wine district in SOUTH WEST FRANCE that is on either side of the river GARONNE just outside the Bordeaux region. The town of Marmande, on the Garonne, gave it its name and provided a ready means of transporting the wines to Bordeaux and then to northern Europe, especially the NETHERLANDS, from the Middle Ages until the early 19th century. The arrival of the PHYLLOXERA louse caused many farmers to abandon viticulutre, however, and vines are just one of many crops in these gentle Marmandais hills, whose average altitude is about 50 m/164 ft. Geographically the region is simply an extension of eastern GRAVES in the south and ENTRE-DEUX-MERS in the north. Bordeaux grape varieties CABERNET SAUVIGNON, CABERNET FRANC, and MERLOT predominate, and the cooler climate here up river tends to result in light versions of red, and some rosé, bordeaux. But these varieties may not exceed three-quarters of production, and Côtes du Marmandais's distinction is in the local variety ABOURIOU, which, with FER, GAMAY, and SYRAH, must make up the rest. About 1,100 ha/2,717 acres of land were planted with vines in the early 1990s, only a small proportion of it with the white wine varieties SÉMILLON, UGNI BLANC, and, increasingly, SAUVIGNON Blanc, which is the principal white variety. All but a tiny proportion of the wine is made by one of two CO-OPERATIVES and, although in 1990 the wine was elevated from VDQS to full AC status, truly first-class wine was still to emerge from this Bordeaux satellite.

MARQUE. French for BRAND.

MARSALA, town in western SICILY and the FORTIFIED wine produced around it. For over 200 years one of Sicily's, and Italy's, most famous products, Marsala has fallen on hard times as declining quality, evaporating markets, and plunging production levels have called into question the very survival of the wine, or at least of its better types.

History

Although the province of Trapani, where the wine is produced, has always been a centre of Sicilian viticulture, Marsala can said to have been born with the arrival in Marsala in 1770 of John Woodhouse, an English merchant and connoisseur of PORT, SHERRY, and MADEIRA, who noted a striking similarity between the wines of the subzone of Birgi and these fortified wines of Spain and Portugal, a similarity which undoubtedly reflected a comparably arid climate and scorching summer temperatures. Woodhouse 'invented' Marsala in 1773 by adding 8 1/2 gal of GRAPE SPIRIT to each of the 400-l/105-gal barrels which he shipped to England, and proceeded to open a warehouse and cellars in the township of Marsala in 1796. The victualling of Nelson's fleet in 1798 doubtlessly assisted in spreading the name of the wine, and Woodhouse was followed by another Englishman, Benjamin Ingham, who founded a Marsala firm in 1812 and contributed greatly to improving the area's viticulture. The largest Marsala house, Florio, was founded by Vincenzo Florio from CALABRIA in 1832, and the size of the enterprise gives some idea of the importance of Marsala at that date: the firm's cellars and warehouses occupied a full kilometre of sea front. As for port, Marsala's production and marketing has always been dominated by large commercial houses, although there has been little continuity over time. These three pioneering houses failed to survive the 1920s and were absorbed by the vermouth house of Cinzano in 1929, and of the various Italian houses founded in the 19th century only Rallo and Pellegrino remain today.

Wine-making and viticulture

Marsala has always been a fortified wine, but production techniques have changed over the decades and modern Marsala, as codified in the DOC regulations of 1969, can be fortified not only by alcohol but also by must which has been concentrated by heating (*mosto cotto*) and by a *muté* (see MUTAGE) called *sifone* created by adding 20 to 25 per cent of pure alcohol to a must of late-picked, overripe grapes. The viticulture of the zone has been considerably modified. Vines are trained on either WIRES or TENDONE systems rather than the traditional GOBELET. This and enthusiastic IRRIGATION has led to significant increases in the production per hectare (the DOC rules allow an excessively generous 10 tons) and a corresponding drop in the grapes' sugar levels. All these factors have led to systematic use of all three systems of fortification of the wine (Marsala Fine must have 17 per cent of alcohol, while Marsala Superiore and Marsala Vergine must have 18) and a loss of the intrinsic character of the base wine itself.

It should be mentioned that, while GRILLO is considered the quality grape for Marsala Oro or Marsala Ambra, the DOC regulations also permit the less suitable CATARRATTO and the quite unsuitable Damaschino. As for Marsala Rubino, it bears the same resemblance to the historic Marsala as white port bears to vintage port. The ageing of the better categories of Marsala (Superiore and Vergine) in ancient and poorly maintained casks has done little for the quality of these wines, which, in theory, should be the standard-bearers of the zone. What has been most damaging to Marsala, however, has been the multiplication of the types produced, which tended to obscure the fact that Marsala Superiore and Marsala Vergine (also called Solera and produced with the same sort of SOLERA system used for sherry) are the only true descendants of the historic tradition of Marsala.

Modern Marsala now comes in three different colours—Oro (golden), Ambra (amber), and Rubino (ruby)—and each colour comes in a Secco (a maximum of 40 g/l of RESIDUAL SUGAR), a Semisecco (40 to 100 g/l), and a sweet (over 100 g/l) version. There are, in addition, five further types, depending on the CASK AGEING that the wines receive: one year for Fine, two years for Superiore, four years for Superiore Riserva, five years for Vergine, ten years for the Stravecchio version of Vergine. Consumers in the past were just as likely to encounter Marsala in its various *speciale* forms, sweet, cloying, and flavoured with coffee, chocolate, strawberries, almonds, eggs, all of which enjoyed a DOC status equal to the real wine from 1969 to 1984 and which doubtlessly helped to create the impression that Marsala was, at best, a product for the kitchen, more appropriate for cooking a scallop of veal or for preparing a zabaglione than drinking. The revision of the DOC in 1984 banned the use of the name Marsala for these *speciale* forms, and also banned the use of *mosto cotto* in the preparation of Marsala Oro and Marsala Rubino. *Mosto cotto* is regrettably still required for Marsala Ambra, and represents a foolish attempt to create the impression of a cask-aged wine by deepening its colour with concentrate. The Vergine version, however, the purest and most interesting type of all, cannot be made with concentrate, a lesson which seems to have been lost on the zone, which produces a minute, and decreasing, proportion of Vergine.

Production figures show a wine virtually on its deathbed: from production levels that approached 600,000 hl/15.8 million gal in 1979, total Marsala production in 1991 was just 109,500 hl, and the common types of Marsala represented over two-thirds (81,000 hl) of this latter total. Marsala Superiore amounted to a mere 16,000 hl, while Marsala Vergine, the only product with serious prospects in quality markets, amounted to a near invisible 800 hl. It is hardly an encouraging sign that Marco de Bartoli, the most innovative producer in the zone, makes no reference to Marsala on the label of his Vecchio Samperi, a prototypical and high-quality Marsala Vergine in its production techniques which prefers to hide its origins and call itself a VINO DA TAVOLA. D.T.

MARSANNAY, northernmost appellation of the Côte de Nuits district of the Côte d'Or. It is unique in Burgundy for having APPELLATION CONTRÔLÉE status for red, white, and pink wines. The vineyards of Couchey and Chenove are included with those of Marsannay. Prior to 1987 the wines were sold as generic BOURGOGNE followed by the specification Marsannay or Rosé de Marsannay. The latter style of wine is a speciality of the village pioneered in 1919 by Joseph Clair and taken up by the local CO-OPERATIVE.

The small white wine production has yet to show particular character. The red wines are attractive and fruity, if lighter than those of neighbouring FIXIN. There are no PREMIER CRU vineyards.

See also CÔTE D'OR and its map. J.T.C.M.

MARSANNE is an increasingly popular white grape variety probably originating in the northern RHÔNE, where it has all but taken over from its traditional blending partner ROUSSANNE in such appellations as ST-JOSEPH, ST-PÉRAY, CROZES-HERMITAGE, and, to a slightly lesser extent, HERMITAGE itself. The vine's relative productivity has doubtless been a factor in its popularity, and modern wine-making techniques have helped mitigate Marsanne's tendency to flab. It is increasingly planted in the Midi, where, as well as being embraced as an ingredient in most appellations, it is earning itself a reputation as a full bodied, characterful varietal, or a blending partner for more aromatic, acid varieties such as Roussanne, VIOGNIER, and Rolle (VERMENTINO). The wine is particularly deep coloured, full bodied with a heady, if often heavy, aroma of glue verging occasionally on almonds. It is not one of the chosen varieties for Châteauneuf-du-Pape, in which CLAIRETTE shares many of Marsanne's characteristics.

California's RHÔNE RANGERS are generating interest in the variety. Australia has some of the world's oldest Marsanne vineyards, notably in the state of Victoria, and a fine tradition of valuing this Rhône import and the hefty wines it produces, which can brown relatively fast in bottle. In Switzerland, as Ermitage Blanc, it produces a lighter wine that is nevertheless one of the Valais's heaviest.

MARTELL, the oldest of the major COGNAC firms. Indeed its origins date back to the very first brandy merchant in the town of Cognac, Jacques Roux, since his descendant, Rachel Lallemand, was the second wife of the firm's founder Jean Martell, who had come to Cognac in 1815 from the Channel Islands, then a major entrepôt for smuggling brandy into Britain.

Despite its British origins the firm emerged as one of the dominant forces in Cognac, together with HENNESSY, during the French Revolution and received a boost in the middle of the 19th century, when control passed to the Firinos, who had married into the Martell family and adopted the name of

Martell's head blender Pierre Frugier in the 'paradis' where the choicest cognacs are kept.

Firino-Martell. They built a complex of stills, warehouses, bottling plants, and offices that almost constituted a town-within-a-town and was regarded as one of the industrial marvels of late 19th century France.

But the PHYLLOXERA epidemic so damaged the cognac trade that in 1922 Maurice Hennessy, a friend of the Firino-Martell family, engineered a 25-year pact between the two firms. They already set the price for young brandies, and they set about dividing the world's markets, with Martell taking England, while the Hennessys took the United States and the Far East.

Partly as a result, the Martells gradually lost market share after the Second World War and in 1986 sold their firm to the giant Canadian liquor firm Seagram. Although some of their newer brandies are rich, bland, and well suited to and specifically aimed at the increasingly important oriental palate, most of their classic brandies retain the traditional house style. The Martell style is relatively dry and nutty, helped by the presence of a lot of brandy from the Borderies district, and by the use of tight-grained oak (see GRAIN) from the Tronçais forests. This allows Martell cognacs, which are distilled rather dry and strong, to mature relatively slowly. N.F.

MARTIAL (Marcus Valerius Martialis) (*c.*AD 40–103/4), born in Bilbilis, in Spain; he was poor and wrote Latin poetry for a living. In his *Epigrams*, in 15 books, more than 1,500 short poems in all, he writes about the vices he sees around him in Ancient ROME but he prudently uses pseudonyms to disguise the names of those he satirizes: e.g. 'Hesterno fetere mero qui credit Acerram, fallitur in lucem semper Acerra bibit' (1. 28). ('He who thinks that Acerra reeks of yesterday's wine is wrong. Acerra always drinks until daybreak.') Since snobbery and pretentiousness are two of his main targets, he often mentions wine. Misers and the *nouveaux riches* drink OPIMIAN wine (1. 26, 3. 82, 9. 87, 10. 49), and when Martial satirizes the classical cult of old wine (old wine was always preferred to new and was known by its consular year), he invents a wine that has not even got a consular year, because it was laid down before the Republic (13. 111). He generally presumes detailed knowledge about wine on the reader's part, as for instance in 2. 53, 4. 49, 3. 49. The reader needs to know which wines were good and which were not in order to get the point of the epigram. At the end of Book 13 (106–25) is a series of epigrams listing 21 types of wine. Martial expresses his opinions of certain wines tersely, as in the following (13. 122), 'Acetum' (Vinegar):

> Amphora Nilliaci non sit tibi vilis aceti
> esset cum vinum, vilior illa fuit.

(Don't think an amphora of Egyptian vinegar is mean stuff. When it was wine, it was meaner still.)

H.M.W.

Griffin, J., *Latin Literature and Roman Life* (London, 1985).

MARTINI & ROSSI was officially founded in Turin in 1863, although in reality it continued the work of a pre-existing distillery which had been founded in 1847. Although VERMOUTH and other drinks based on grape spirit were and are the basis of its work, the company has documents dating from the end of the 19th century which indicate that at that time it was already producing Moscato Champagne, the former name of ASTI SPUMANTE (the first official production of wines called Asti Spumante dates from the 1930s). SPUMANTE made in the style of CHAMPAGNE from PINOT grapes has been produced since the 1920s and a sparkling Riesling (from Riesling Italico (WELSCHRIESLING) from the OLTREPÒ PAVESE) has been produced since 1983. Current production of wine (other than vermouth, of which it is the world's leading producer) is over 21 million bottles per year, with Asti Spumante representing close to 90 per cent of the overall total. The company owns no vineyards, preferring to purchase its grapes from selected growers, over 400 in the case of the Moscato grapes for its Asti Spumante. D.T.

MARZEMINO, interesting, late ripening red grape variety grown to a strictly limited extent in northern Italy. Once much more famous than now, it does not have particularly good resistance to FUNGAL DISEASES, and is often allowed to over-produce, but it can yield lively wines, some of them lightly sparkling. For more details see TRENTINO and LOMBARDY.

MAS, southern French term for a domaine. The most famous wine-producing *mas* is **Mas de Daumas Gassac**, established by outsiders to the world of wine just south east

The **Massandra** winery in the Crimea built between 1894 and 1897 to provide fine wines for the Russian imperial court.

of MONTPEYROUX in the Languedoc in the 1970s. Aimé Guibert has proved that a French non-appellation wine, labelled merely VIN DE PAYS de l'Hérault, can be an extremely serious, long-living red which can easily fetch the same sort of prices as a Bordeaux CLASSED GROWTH. Some ambitious whites and unusual rosés are also made at the Mas de Daumas Gassac.

MASSANDRA, winery built to extremely high specifications on the outskirts of Yalta in the CRIMEA in the 1890s to supply Livadia, the tsars' summer palace. Miners had to be imported from GEORGIA to tunnel into the rock to excavate three layers of cool, damp cellars. Prince Golitzin (see CRIMEA) was the first wine-maker and was succeeded by the first of the Yegorov family, members of which made wine at Massandra for almost a century from 1898. The most successful wines are strong and sweet, many of them VINS DOUX NATURELS as well as FORTIFIED. The modern installation at Massandra is used not for wine-making, but for AGEING and BOTTLING. Massandra staff oversee production in a number of satellite wineries from the 2,500 ha/6,175 acres of vines under Massandra control. Grapes grown on the southern hillsides and in mountain valleys are responsible for such unique dessert wines as White Muscat of the Red Stone, White Muscat Livadia, Rosé Muscat Yuzhnoberezhny, Black Muscat Massandra, Tocay Yuzhnoberezhny, Pinot Ai-Danil, and Kokur Surozh.

The **Massandra Collection** was begun by Prince Golitzin and its oldest member is an 18th century SHERRY, but it is today made up substantially of the best Crimean wines. Approximately 10,000 bottles are added each year and some wines in the collection are decades old. The Collection was carefully evacuated during the German occupation of Yalta 1941–4, some as far as to Georgia, but was back in place in time for the historic Yalta peace conference in 1945. Sotheby's offered two consignments of strong, very sweet, durable wines from the Massandra Collection at AUCTION in London in 1990 and 1991 as part of the auctioneers' trading arrangements with the disintegrating Soviet Union.

MASSIC, a white wine which was among the most famous wines of Roman Italy and was much praised by the Roman poets. The type of grape is unknown. The wine was produced on Monte Massico, the line of hills which runs down to the sea on the west coast of Italy between the rivers Garigliano and Volturno. This zone is adjacent to the territory which produced FALERNIAN and some writers treat Massic as a subtype of that famous wine. The wine was transported to Sinuessa on the coast, where there were numerous kilns producing the AMPHORAE in which the wine was exported.

J.J.P.

MASS SELECTION, a viticultural technique used to provide large quantities of buds for the propagation of vines. Field vine selection can be either by mass selection or by selecting individual mother vines, as in CLONAL SELECTION. Mass selection is normally done when a large quantity of buds for propagation is required, and the identity of individual vines is not maintained.

Mass selection can be called either negative or positive. If negative, then undesirable vines in a vineyard are marked so that cuttings are not taken from them. These vines might include those with low yield, poor fruit maturity, virus disease symptoms, higher than average incidence of fungal diseases, or off-types (MUTATIONS). Negative mass selection is also a good opportunity to mark 'rogue vines' (those of another variety) to ensure that mixed plantings do not occur in the future. Positive selection identifies the best vines, for example those with good fruit set, larger and looser bunches, good fruit maturity, and so on. Vineyards planted from mass-selected material can be considered to consist of many different unidentified CLONES.

Usually the vineyard assessment is made at several times over the season. For example, rogue vines and NEPOVIRUS symptoms are easier to pick out in the spring, whereas differences in grape ripening are obviously best determined just before harvest. Vines are commonly marked by paint on the trunk. In winter, cuttings are taken from marked vines in positive mass selection, whereas marked vines are avoided in negative mass selection.

Mass selection is normally carried out over one or two seasons only. Since there is not the same detailed recording and selection of individual vines, the gains in yield or quality from mass selection are typically less than for clonal selection. The benefits to be had from mass selection will depend on how heterogeneous was the field from which the selection is made. Obviously there will be little benefit of mass selection if the vineyard is quite uniform, but if there is a high proportion of rogue vines, off-types, or virus diseases, then the nurseryman might expect substantial benefits.

Unfortunately, in many viticultural regions of the world cuttings are taken in winter from vineyards which have not benefited from even the most cursory inspection in the preceding summer. In the winter all vines appear similar, and so mistakes of mixed plantings, off-types, and virus diseases are spread unwittingly from one vineyard to the next generation by propagation. R.E.S.

Coombe, B. G., and Dry, P. R., *Viticulture, i: Resources in Australia* (Adelaide, 1988).
Galet, P., *Précis de viticulture* (4th edn., Montpellier, 1983).

MASTERS OF WINE, those who have passed the examinations held every May by the **Institute of Masters of Wine**, the wine trade's most famous and most demanding professional qualification. The Institute had its origins in the British wine trade in the early 1950s when a counterpart to the qualifying examinations for other professions was devised by a group of wine merchants in conjunction with the VINTNERS' COMPANY. The first examination was held in London in 1953 and six of the 21 candidates were deemed to have qualified as Masters of Wine. The Institute of Masters of Wine was formed in 1955. Then as now the examinations consisted of five written papers and three 'practical' (i.e. wine tasting) tests. The examinations are distinguished by the breadth of their scope. University courses (see ACADEME) offer more detailed instruction in the OENOLOGY or VITICULTURE of a particular country or region, while the 'MW' examinations test knowledge of both subjects on a world-wide basis, as well as of such varied subjects as ÉLEVAGE, BOTTLING, transport, QUALITY CONTROL, marketing, commercial aspects of the wine trade, and general wine knowledge. Each tasting paper requires candidates to describe, assess, and, often, identify up to 12 wines served BLIND. These wines may come from anywhere in the world.

Despite a notoriously low pass rate (although candidates have always been allowed to pass practical and theoretical parts in separate years), by 1978 the number of Masters of Wine reached 100, including two women. In 1982 the Institute held its first, relatively academic, symposium, at Oxford, but also lost four of its members and realized that some expansion would be necessary for its survival (it had no executives and no premises until 1987). In 1983 it relaxed its entry requirements and allowed candidates from the fringes of the wine trade, such as wine writers, to take the examinations. In 1987 the examinations were opened up to those outside the United Kingdom and the next year the first overseas candidate, an Australian, passed the examinations, at this stage still held in London. In 1990 two Americans qualified as Masters of Wine and in 1991 examinations were held, on the same dates, in London, Sydney, and New York. By 1993 there were 179 Masters of Wine, including 27 women, 23 non-Britons, and the first MW from far outside the wine trade, a Hollywood lawyer.

Numbers of candidates have increased just as markedly as numbers of Masters of Wine. The examinations are increasingly demanding as the wine world expands, although the standard of preparation offered by the Institute's Education Committee was raised considerably in the early 1990s.

The aims of the Institute have always been less clear than the status of its members, and for many years it offered examinations but remarkably little education. A Mission Statement issued by the Institute in 1992 accorded pride of place to the promotion of excellence in wine, closely followed by 'education at the highest level'. Soon afterwards the Institute launched its Seal of Excellence scheme.

MASTROBERARDINO, the most important producer of TAURASI in the southern Italian region of CAMPANIA.

MATARO is one of the many synonyms of MOURVÈDRE used primarily in Australia, sometimes in Roussillon, and, by those who do not realize how fashionable Mourvèdre has become, in California (see RHÔNE RANGERS). It is almost invariably the case that someone who refers to Mourvèdre as Mataro does not have a particularly high opinion of it.

MATEUS. The Palace of Mateus near Vila Real just north of the DOURO valley in northern Portugal lent its name to **Mateus Rosé**, a medium sweet, sparkling rosé that has become one of the world's most famous wine BRANDS. It was created in 1942 by Fernando van Zeller Guedes, whose family owned a property producing VINHO VERDE. Inspired by these naturally pétillant red and white wines which were already popular in Portugal and Brazil, Guedes produced a sparkling rosé which was sweetened to make it more appealing to the developing North American and northern European markets. Production began at the end of the Second World War (at very much the same time as that of its rival LANCERS) in a winery built close to the Mateus Palace. The property did not belong to the Guedes family and its owners opted for a single payment in return for the use of the name and a picture of the palace on the label, rather than a royalty on each bottle sold.

In the 1950s and 1960s sales grew rapidly and by the late 1980s Mateus, by then supplemented by a white version, accounted for over 40 per cent of Portugal's total table wine exports with world-wide sales amounting to 3.25 million cases. A small quantity of Mateus Rosé is still made at Vila Real but most of the wine is produced at Anadia in BAIRRADA. Faced with falling sales of Mateus in the early 1990s, Sogrape, the Guedes family firm which owns the Mateus brand and is the largest wine producer in Portugal, has diversified into other areas of the Portuguese wine industry. R.J.M.

MATINO, DOC for robust red wine made mainly from NEGROAMARO grapes in south east Italy. For more details see APULIA.

MATURATION of wine. See AGEING.

MATURE, tasting term for a fine wine that seems to have enjoyed sufficient AGEING for it to have reached the peak of its potential. In practice it is also used by the most polite, or determinedly optimistic, tasters to describe wines that are past that point. Any hint of yellow at the rim of a red wine suggests **maturity**.

MATURITY, desirable state in a wine when it is consumed. In a sense the most basic wine designed for early drinking is mature almost as soon as it is bottled, but mature when applied to a wine carries with it the implication that the maturity is the result of a certain amount of BOTTLE AGEING. Such a (red) wine is deemed fully mature when it has dispensed with its uncomfortably harsh TANNINS and acquired maximum complexity of flavour (sometimes described as BOUQUET) without starting to decay. The period of maturity varies considerably with wine type, but is probably longer than most wine consumers believe. A wine that has been followed since its youth and begins to taste mature may continue to delight, and possibly evolve for the better, for a decade or more. For more details of the process, and of the difference between individual wine types, see AGEING.

Robinson, J., *Vintage Timecharts* (London and New York, 1989).

MAURY, is one of ROUSSILLON's famous VINS DOUX NATURELS, a cousin from the hilly hinterland of seaside BANYULS. Like Banyuls it is produced predominantly from Grenache Noir with a maximum yield of 30 hl/ha (1.7 tons/acre) and is almost invariably strong, sweet, red, and possibly RANCIO, having been aged in a variety of containers (cement, wood, glass) in a variety of conditions (hot, cold, humid or not). Maury is as small an appellation as Banyuls but is on high inland schist at the northern limit of the Côtes du Roussillon Villages area in the Agly valley. Table wines produced here qualify as Côtes du Roussillon Villages (just as those produced in the Banyuls area belong to the COLLIOURE appellation). The ruins of the Cathar castle of Quéribus, a constant reminder of the area's harsh natural environment, dominate the village of Maury. The wines are particularly tannic in youth and often have a deeper colour than Banyuls. The CO-OPERATIVE, Les Vignerons du Maury, dominates production but other producers manage to surface too, notably Mas Amiel. The wines serve much the same purpose as Banyuls but more insistently demand ageing.

MAUZAC, or more properly **Mauzac Blanc**, is a declining but still surprisingly important white grape in SOUTH WEST FRANCE, especially in GAILLAC and LIMOUX, where it is the traditional and still principal vine variety. It produces relatively aromatic wines which are usually blended, with Len de l'El around Gaillac and with Chenin and Chardonnay in Limoux.

In the Tarn *département*, whose chief wine appellation is Gaillac, Mauzac Blanc still covered 3,300 ha/8,150 of vineyard in 1988, which was half of total plantings 20 years earlier but still made it far more important that the region's second vine variety JURANÇON NOIR. Thanks to energetic wine-makers such as Robert Plageoles, since the late 1980s there has been a revival of interest in Gaillac's Mauzac, which comes in several different hues, sweetness levels, and degrees of fizziness. During the 1970s and 1980s in Limoux, however, total plantings of Mauzac rose from 900 to 2,300 ha, thanks to demand for the sparkling Blanquette de Limoux in which it is the dominant ingredient, although the region is fast being invaded by Chardonnay.

The vine, whose yields can vary enormously according to site, buds and ripens late and grapes were traditionally picked well into autumn so that musts fermented slowly and gently in the cool Limoux winters, ready to referment in bottle in the spring. Today Mauzac tends to be picked much earlier, preserving its naturally high acidity but sacrificing much of its particular flavour reminiscent of the skin of shrivelled apples, before being subjected to the usual champagne-making technique. Some gently sparkling Gaillacs are still made by the traditional *méthode gaillacoise*, however, just as a small portion of Limoux's Blanquette is made by the *méthode ancestrale*.

MAVRODAPHNE, dark skinned grape variety grown particularly round Pátras in the Peloponnese in GREECE where it is the foundation of a port-like dessert wine, **Mavrodaphne of Pátras** which responds well to extended CASK AGEING. This aromatic, powerful variety, also grown to a much more limited extent on the island of Cephalonia, is occasionally vinified dry but only for use as a blending component. Various relationships with the similarly named Mavro of CYPRUS and

MAVRUD of Bulgaria have been posited but Mavro is simply Greek for black, and Mavrodaphne means 'black laurel'.

MAVRUD, indigenous Balkan grape variety most closely associated with BULGARIA capable of producing intense, tannic wine if allowed to ripen fully. Grown exclusively in central southern Bulgaria and a speciality of Assenovgrad near Plovdiv, it is small berried and low yielding and is usually grown in untidily straggling bushes. The robust wine produced responds well to oak ageing, although it tends to age rather faster than Bulgaria's other noble indigenous vine MELNIK. Mavrud is also grown in ALBANIA.

MEAD, a fermented alcoholic drink made from honey. A concentrated, impure GLUCOSE solution, it has much in common with FRUIT WINES.

MEALY BUGS, small, white insects of the family *Cicadellidae* which suck vine sap. They live beneath the vine bark, in cracks of trellis posts, or among weeds during winter. Young mealy bugs infect new growth in the spring, typically the undersurface of leaves at the base of the shoot. They become mature and reproduce in early summer, and there can be three generations a year. Mealy bugs prefer a humid environment, and so are mostly found in a dense vine CANOPY.

Mealy bugs do not cause significant commercial damage by their sap-sucking action alone, but there can be two indirect effects. First, they produce copious quantities of a sugary, sticky liquid called honeydew which collects over the bunches and foliage, and on which fungus grows, often giving it a sooty appearance. Grapes affected with mealy bugs impart a distinctive and undesirable taste to wine, and the fruit may be fit only for DISTILLATION. Mealy bugs of the genera *Planococcus* and *Pseudococcus* have been implicated in the spread of LEAFROLL VIRUS, which has serious implications for the loss of vineyard yield and grape quality. Mealy bugs have been confirmed as spreading leafroll virus in South Africa and Israel, and are implicated in New Zealand.

A number of predators, including wasps and ladybirds, attack mealy bugs and assist in their biological control. Sometimes the predator populations are affected by broad-spectrum insecticides. Where mealy bug infestations are serious, a schedule of preventive sprays is necessary, but the waxy covering of the insect and the sheltered locations make control difficult. M.J.E. & R.E.S.

Buchanan, G. A., and Amos, T. G., 'Grape pests', in B. G. Coombe and P. R. Dry (eds.), *Viticulture, ii: Practices* (Adelaide, 1992).

MEASLES, as it affects vines, see ESCA.

MECHANICAL HARVESTING, harvesting by machine in place of the traditional manual HARVEST. Undoubtedly one of the greatest changes from ancient to modern vineyards has been the adoption of machine harvesting, which was first introduced commercially in the 1960s. Whereas manual grape harvesting required literally hordes of pickers to descend on vineyards and complete the harvest, now the vintage may be completed by just one harvester driver, perhaps with a supporting driver and vehicle to receive the harvested grapes. Depending on the YIELD and vineyard topography, to harvest a vineyard by hand requires between one and 10 man-days per hectare, as opposed to less than five man-hours per hectare by machine.

Mechanical harvesting has been adopted for different reasons in different parts of the world. In NEW YORK state, scene of some of the earliest developments in the 1960s, a major consideration was potential cost savings. In Australia

Mechanical harvesting: Ripe grapes are literally beaten off the vine and collected on moving belts which transfer them to a tractor-drawn hopper.

the availability of labour was important, and welfare payments were another factor. In France, according to GALET, the fixing of the date of return to school as 15 September precluded students from participating in vintage, as compulsory holidays in August precluded others. The net effect was that seasonal workers were more difficult to find, demanded higher wages, and were also perhaps less reliable, all of these factors promoting machines over man at vintage time. Machine harvesting may have been developed in the United States, but the technology was rapidly refined in France.

History

Mechanical harvesting can either increase the efficiency of manual labour, or virtually replace it. Early attempts at mechanization emphasized the first approach, with mobile picking platforms both to convey the workers and also to catch the cut bunches. Developments in Crimea and California saw hand-harvested bunches deposited on a paper band which could be mechanically picked up, which was particularly useful for DRYING GRAPES. Similarly, conveyor systems which deposited harvested grapes in bins for transport to the winery were developed in many countries. However, it has been the second approach which has been the more successful, developing machines which essentially replace most of the manual operations.

Many forms of integrated machine harvesters have been developed and evaluated, although by the mid 1990s most machines worked by striking the CANOPY to remove fruit and catching it with horizontal conveyor belts. Again, early developments were semi-automatic machines, with, for example, hand-held suction devices which were positioned on the bunches. Cutter bars were evaluated in California, Italy, and eastern Europe but these were found to leave too much fruit, even after expensive hand-positioning of the bunches. A German suction machine was found to harvest too slowly and cause excessive OXIDATION, especially of white wines. An early French machine removed berries singly by means of 3,200 thin plastic rods mounted on four panels. Also evaluated were spinning discs and compressed air to remove fruit, but these attempts were unsuccessful. The early New York development was the 'vertical impactor', which used a metal finger to strike the vine cordon and the shock dislodged the berries. However, the most common form of harvesting now is the 'horizontal slapper' which uses fibreglass rods to strike the foliage and dislodge the fruit, sometimes as single berries, sometimes as bunches.

Effect on wine quality

The effect of machine harvesting on wine quality has been the subject of much scientific study and commercial experience. The majority of studies have shown that sophisticated mechanical harvesting has no negative effect on wine quality, and some have even argued that there is a positive effect. Certainly most forms of machine harvesting damage some grapes so that parts of berries and bunches are mixed with the juice of broken berries. However, the juice can be protected from OXIDATION by SULPHUR DIOXIDE, if moved quickly in a closed container to the winery. This problem can be minimized by harvesting at night; a practice widely adopted in hotter wine regions where grapes harvested by day can arrive at the winery at over 40 °C / 104 °F.

Another disadvantage of machine harvesting is that there can be excessive SKIN CONTACT, which can lead to white wines becoming too high in PHENOLICS. Long distances between the winery and vineyard may make mechanically harvested delicate white wines an impossibility.

Despite much evidence in favour of machine harvesting, some producers will remain with hand harvesting. The gentler nature of hand harvesting is preferable for many top-quality wines, especially sparkling wines, for which whole bunches may be pressed without first crushing. R.E.S.

Coombe, B. G., and Dry, P. R. (eds.), *Viticulture, ii: Practices* (Adelaide, 1992).
Galet, P., *Précis de viticulture* (4th edn., Montpellier, 1983).

MECHANICAL PRUNING involves using machines for PRUNING vines in winter. Viticulture is a very traditional form of agriculture and many who tend the vines regard the annual winter pruning as their prime opportunity to interact physically with each vine. Because of this, and because they feel that mechanical pruning cannot offer the precision of manual pruning, many vine-growers oppose mechanical pruning, even at the expense of hours of back-breaking labour in cold and sometimes wet weather.

Early experiments in mechanical pruning were carried out in Australia and New York state in the mid 1970s. The machinery was not as elaborate as that for MECHANICAL HARVESTING, which was undergoing simultaneous development. The pruning machines were simply reciprocating cutters or flails mounted on a tractor. In Australia circular saws were widely used, and sometimes these were mounted on a machine harvester with the picking head removed.

Machine pruning is simple in the extreme, as the vine canes are trimmed back leaving typically a SPUR with two or more buds. Of course not all shoots are cut uniformly. Early commercial experiments followed mechanical pruning with hand pruning to tidy the vines' appearance, by thinning out spur numbers and cutting them to a uniform two-bud length. Even this semi-mechanical technique cut pruning time by half. Encouraged by early experiments in Australia, however, most vines have since been left untended after machine pruning. Although they look ugly in late winter, soon after BUDBREAK they cannot be distinguished from hand-pruned vines. Because more buds are left on the vine (up to fivefold) the YIELD usually increases for the first year or so, but many studies show no significant effect on wine quality.

Mechanical pruning is now widespread in Australia, and Italian research has also been important in the adoption of machine pruning. Other parts of the world have been much slower to embrace mechanical pruning, however. In California the great majority of vineyards are pruned by Mexican labour. Mechanical pre-pruning is becoming more wide-

Mechanical pruning of Frontonnais vines in summer.

spread for the extensive vineyards of southern France. In cooler regions such as northern Europe, mechanical pruning is less useful because of the extra buds left after machine pruning which can increase the resultant yield to the extent that it leads to inadequate RIPENING. In countries such as parts of South America and South Africa, labour is so plentiful that there is no need for mechanical pruning.

The 150 hours per hectare required for hand pruning can be reduced to less than 10 hours per hectare with mechanical pruning. Some of the substantial cost savings associated with this reduction may be lost if too extensive hand pruning follows. The logical extension of mechanical pruning is not to prune at all, so called MINIMAL PRUNING. R.E.S.

Coombe, B. G., and Dry, P. R. (eds.), *Viticulture, ii: Practices* (Adelaide, 1992).

Winkler, A. J., *et al.*, *General Viticulture* (2nd edn., Berkeley, Calif., 1974).

MECHANIZATION. Most WINE-MAKING operations other than tasting are fully mechanized, but mechanization has been much slower to invade the vineyard. For more details of viticultural mechanization see MECHANICAL HARVESTING, MECHANICAL PRUNING, and, most importantly, LABOUR.

MEDALS from wine COMPETITIONS and other JUDGINGS are coveted by many wine producers. There is a certain hierarchy of medals, however. States and national wine shows are important to the Australian wine trade, but a Hobart gold medal may be reckoned less glamorous than a Canberra silver. In France, medals awarded by the fairs in Paris and Mâcon are usually indications of real quality, as are those awarded in Germany by the Deutscher Landwirtschaft Gesellschaft, or DLG.

MEDICAL ASPECTS OF WINE CONSUMPTION. See HEALTH.

MEDICAL PROFESSION. See DOCTORS.

MEDICINE, WINE IN. From ancient times to the 18th century, wine enjoyed a central role in medicine. The earliest practitioners of medicine were magicians and priests who used wine for healing as well as religious purposes (see RELIGION). Receipts for wine-based medicines appear in papyri of Ancient EGYPT and the tablets of SUMER.

The beginnings of systematized medicine are commonly attributed to the Greek Hippocrates (*c.*450 BC), who recommended the use of wine as a disinfectant, a medicine, a vehicle for other drugs, and as part of a healthy DIET. He experimented with different wines in order to discover how each might be most appropriately used to cure a specific ailment, from lethargy or diarrhoea to easing difficult childbirth.

The most famous physician of Ancient ROME was GALEN (2nd century AD), whose medical experience was shaped by treating injured gladiators in Asia Minor. He learned (like the Good Samaritan of the BIBLE) that wine was the most effective means of disinfecting wounds. His post as imperial physician involved tasting the emperor's wines in order to select the best and most healthy.

Ancient Jewish civilization prized wine for its medicinal properties. In the Talmud it is stated that: 'Wine is the foremost of all medicines: wherever wine is lacking, medicines become necessary.'

Similarly many Arab doctors such as Avicenna (11th century AD) recognized the importance of wine in healing, but found themselves in a difficult position because of the prohibition of alcohol throughout the world of ISLAM. Arabs studied medicine from Greek sources then transmitted it back, slightly amended, to the west. The works of Galen, for example, reached medieval Europe via the great medical school of Salerno in Italy, where they were translated from Arabic to Latin. It was here that the notion of wine as an essential element in a healthy diet gained ground.

The medicinal use of wine continued throughout the Middle Ages, in monasteries, hospitals, and universities. The earliest printed book on wine was written by a doctor, one ARNALDUS DE VILLANOVA of the University of MONTPELLIER, at the beginning of the 14th century. Building on the observations of his classical forebears, he offered not only remedies for curing human ailments with appropriate wines, but also recipes for curing 'sick' or bad wines too.

A new dimension was added to the role of wine in medicine with the invention of distilled spirits in the 12th century (see DISTILLATION). Hieronymus Brunschwig, the German pharmacologist, wrote in the 15th century that *'Aqua vitae* [the water of life, or alcohol] is commonly called the mistress of all medicines', but warned, 'it is to be drunk by reason and measure'.

Medicinal attitudes towards wine began to change in the latter half of the 19th century. Alcoholism was defined as a disease and the injurious side-effects of excessive drinking studied. The appearance of temperance societies, sometimes supported by the medical establishment, caused many to re-evaluate the role of wine in diet and medicine, although strong, sweet wines such as PORT were still being prescribed as aids to recuperation in the early 20th century.

One further aspect of the conjunction of wine and medicine is the great influence that DOCTORS have had since ancient times, not just as wine consumers (and producers) but also in promoting or damaging the commercial potential of certain wines. Undoubtedly Roman connoisseurs took note of the recommendations of Galen and others, while in 17th century France the commercial battle between wine regions reached new heights when Louis XIV's physician prescribed burgundy in preference to champagne. Other examples of vinous prescriptions abound.

For a modern view of the medical effects of wine consumption, see HEALTH. H.B.

Darby, W. J., 'Wine and medical wisdom through the ages', in *Wine, Health and Society* (San Francisco, 1982).
Lucia, S. P., *A History of Wine as Therapy* (New York, 1963).
Sigerist, H. E., *The Earliest Printed Book on Wine* (New York, 1943) (contains Villanova's *Tractatus de vinis*).

MEDIEVAL LITERATURE. The only medieval successor to the Roman AGRICULTURAL TREATISES is PETRUS DE CRESCENTIIS' *Liber commodorum ruralium* of 1303; otherwise there are few medieval authors who wrote specifically on wine.

One of these is Henri d'Andely, whose *Bataille des vins* dates from just after 1223. It belongs to the genre of the medieval debate poem. The king of France, Philip Augustus, wants to know which is the best wine: his preference is for whites. Some 70 wines are tasted. The judge is an English priest, who promptly excommunicates wines that are too acidic and bad for one's health, such as the north eastern wines of Beauvais, Argences, Rennes, and Tours (as outlined in CLIMATE CHANGE, warmer weather permitted viticulture in these northern districts then). The wines of the south present their strength as their claim to victory; the northern wines object that they may not be as strong but that they are delicately flavoured. Yet the crown of victory passes all the French wines by, for it goes to the wine of CYPRUS. The priest goes to sleep for three days and three nights, and the poet tells us that if we drink good wine we will not be ill until the day we die. A charming thought.

Another Old French poem about wine is *La Disputoison de vin et de l'iaue* ('The Debate between Wine and Water'), written some time between 1305 and 1377, when the papal court was at Avignon. Unlike the usual wine and water debate, in which the wine is described no further and always wins, this poem is a contest between different kinds of wine as well as between wine and water and there is no winner. The debate reflects the changing FASHIONS of the time. The sudden rise to prominence of the wines of BEAUNE was the result of the papal court's move to Avignon: 'The Pope loves me', Beaune asserts. And Beaune boasts of being red, when previously the fashion had been for white wines. St-Jean-d'Angely (near La Rochelle) objects that it is better to be a white wine, because one keeps one's colour. GASCONY comes in either colour and adds strength to the wines. LA ROCHELLE observes that since we taste with our mouths and not with our eyes all that matters is that wine should not be hard, which is a dig against the tannic wines of Gascony, and that it should not cause headaches. ST-POURÇAIN-SUR-SIOULE in the Loire basin is a favourite of both pope and king. St-Pourçain brags of its colour, which is neither white nor red but 'œil de perdris', an expression that is still used (see ŒIL DE PERDRIX). This wine was indeed much in vogue in the 14th century. 'Vin francois', the wine made around PARIS in the Île-de-France, protests: *vin francois* is light and well balanced and gives health, peace, and joy. Oh no, Water says: wine makes people behave badly. Then the God of Love, who is the judge, announces his decision: all wines are good, and they differ according to region, but water is the same everywhere. So let there be no winner, and no quarrel.

Of the Middle English poets, Chaucer is the one who displays most knowledge of wine, although he tends to mention different wines only briefly. Chaucer's father and grandfather were among the most important VINTNERS in London and held the office of deputy to the king's butler, who was the person responsible for the collection of taxes on imported wines. Jugs of MALMSEY ('malvasye') and vernaccis or VERNACCIA ('vernage') are the extravagant presents that the monk in 'The Shipman's Tale' gives his friend the merchant, whom he is about to cuckold. In the Prologue to his own Tale the hypocritical Pardoner warns against the white wine 'of Lepe', in southern Spain, on the coast between Jerez and the Algarve (see CONDADO DE HUELVA). It is exceptionally strong, and unscrupulous innkeepers often used it for the ADULTERATION of the more expensive wines of Bordeaux and La Rochelle. Yet as a seller of fake relics the Pardoner is every bit as avaricious as the innkeepers, and they do not preach sermons against the sin of covetousness.

The Pardoner's warning is part of a tirade against DRUNKENNESS, but preachers and moralists do not usually bother to specify those kinds of wine that are particularly dangerous: too much wine makes one drunk, and drunkenness is a branch of the deadly sin of gluttony. Moreover, drunkenness is the cause of other sins such as lechery. Wine is just wine in the medieval drinking songs, too. There is a large number of them, most of them in Latin, and they are not so much in praise of drinking as of getting drunk. The 9th century poem about Adam, abbot of Angers, for example, has an address to BACCHUS as its refrain. Adam was drunk day and night, and when he died his body was so saturated with wine that it was incorruptible—a witty allusion to one of the traditional manifestations of sainthood, the undecayed corpse. One of the *Carmina Burana*, 'Potatores exquisiti' (*CB* 179), asks all

The vintner's son of English **medieval literature**—Geoffrey Chaucer.

serious topers to banish moderate drinkers from parties and to drink until speech becomes impaired and walking impossible. Even when one is on one's own, the object of drinking should be inebriation.

The moralists may have inveighed against drinking to excess, but they had no intention of making medieval Europe give up wine, because through the miracle of the EUCHARIST wine became the body of Christ. Wine and even drunkenness are frequent images in medieval hymns and other religious poems. Christ's sacrifice of his own life is re-enacted in the offering up of bread and wine in the Eucharist, when to drink the wine that is Christ's blood is to be drunk with his love.

H.M.W.

Hanford, J. H., 'The mediaeval debate between wine and water', *Publications of the Modern Language Academy of America*, 28 (1913), 315–67.

Raby, F. J. E., *The Oxford Book of Medieval Latin Verse* (Oxford, 1959).

Waddell, H., *Medieval Latin Lyrics* (London, 1933).

MEDITERRANEAN, famous sea, climate, diet, and many other things besides. By classical times vines were grown for wine in almost all the countries bordering the Mediterranean Sea and on many of the islands; from Spain in the west to Byblos in the east, from northern Italy to Egypt, the vine made inexorable progress, with AMPHORAE of wine traversing the sea regularly. Historically, the Mediterranean was the focus of viticulture, and most wine was produced in MEDITERRANEAN CLIMATES. In the Middle Ages, particularly when temperatures rose overall (see CLIMATE CHANGE) and when consumers were accustomed to very light, acid wines, viticulture spread much further north than the shores of the Mediterranean (see PARIS, ENGLAND, and GERMAN HISTORY, for example).

MEDITERRANEAN CLIMATE, a climate type characterized by warm, dry, sunny summers and mostly mild, wet winters. It occurs throughout the Mediterranean basin, on the west coast of the United States, in Chile, southern and south western Australia, and the Cape Province of South Africa. The autumn and spring seasons range from mostly dry on the hot, equatorial fringes bordering deserts, to wet at the poleward fringes, where mediterranean climates merge into those with a more or less uniform rainfall distribution as in central and western Europe.

It was in the Mediterranean region that viticulture and wine-making developed, as an adjunct (some might say, an essential component) to western civilization as we know it. Yet the Mediterranean is no longer the place most readily associated with fine wine. Why is this so?

The most famed and esteemed wines of classical times were undoubtedly sweet and strong: made from very ripe grapes, fermented to the limit of natural fermentation, and then left with considerable RESIDUAL SUGAR. The warm, sunny climates typical of the Mediterranean are well suited to this style of wine, but late 20th century consumers are more likely to seek wines that are fruity, dry, and not too high in alcohol. These are the natural characteristics of wines made in cooler and perhaps less sunny climates, where grapes ripen at lower sugar levels and with higher ACIDITY (see CLIMATE AND WINE QUALITY and COOL CLIMATE VITICULTURE).

For all that, a renaissance is now taking place in mediterranean climate viticulture around the world. With appropriate SITE SELECTION, mediterranean climates have some distinct advantages for viticulture over uniform or summer-rainfall climates, provided that supplementary IRRIGATION can be given as needed. Sunshine is mostly more reliable and generous. There is less risk of excessive rainfall during ripening. As a result of both, the risk of FUNGAL DISEASES is generally lower. And to the extent that many mediterranean climates have the disadvantages of low HUMIDITY and high temperatures during the ripening period, precise VINEYARD site selection can help to minimize these disadvantages, by seeking out coastal or high-altitude sites, for example.

Further favouring mediterranean climates is the fact that some of the main advances in both vineyard management and wine-making technology have particular application there. Drip irrigation in a summer-dry climate allows a degree of control over SOIL WATER availability and vine VIGOUR, and permits the use of MESOCLIMATES and soils (see SOIL AND WINE QUALITY) that have quality advantages but were not commercially exploitable before. Improved CANOPY MANAGEMENT has at least as great an application as in other climates.

In the winery, control of TEMPERATURE and BACTERIA, YEAST

nutrition, and careful ACIDIFICATION now make it possible to use fully ripe grapes more safely than under previous, more primitive wine-making regimes, and thereby to capture regularly the attractive fullness of fruit flavour that ripening under warm, sunny conditions can give.

Finally, it has been suggested that rising atmospheric concentrations of CARBON DIOXIDE will have their greatest advantage, for both vine yields and for grape and wine quality, in climates with warm, sunny growing and ripening seasons (see CLIMATE CHANGE). J.G. & R.E.S.

MÉDOC, the most famous red wine district in Bordeaux, and possibly the world. The Médoc stretches north west from the city of Bordeaux along the left bank of the Gironde estuary, a virtually monocultural strip of flat, unremarkable land sandwiched between the *palus*, or coastal marshes, and the pine forests which extend for miles south into the Landes. The vineyard strip is about 5 to 12 km/3 to 8 miles wide, and runs northwards, with various intermissions for scrub, pasture, polder, and riverbank, more than 70 km/50 miles from the northern suburbs of Bordeaux to the marshes of the lower, more northerly part of the Médoc, the so-called Bas-Médoc (see map on p. 124). Wines produced in the Bas-Médoc may use the **Médoc** appellation, while those on the higher ground are entitled to the **Haut-Médoc** appellation, although many of them qualify for the smarter individual village, or communal, appellations. From south to north, these are MARGAUX, MOULIS, LISTRAC, ST-JULIEN, PAUILLAC, and ST-ESTÈPHE.

As outlined in BORDEAUX, history, the Médoc is a relatively recent wine region. Before the Dutch diligently applied their drainage technology to the polders of the Médoc in the mid 17th century, the region was salt-marsh, of interest for grazing rather than vine-growing. The ditches were so effective, and Bordeaux merchants so keen to supply vinous rivals to GRAVES and the powerful Portuguese wines that had been shipped in great quantity to the important British market, that New French Clarets were born, and great estates established in the Médoc on the back of their commercial success. In the mid 19th century, the Médoc enjoyed a period of prosperity unparalleled until the 1980s.

The climate on this peninsula is Bordeaux's mildest, moderated both by the estuary and the Atlantic Ocean just over the pines. These forests protect the vineyard strip from strong winds off the ocean, and help to moderate summer temperatures, but it is only in the Médoc and the GRAVES district further south that Bordeaux vignerons are confident of ripening Cabernet Sauvignon grapes with any frequency. The Médoc is also Bordeaux's wettest region, which makes ROT a constant threat and SPRAYING a habit.

A typical estate, or château, in the greater Médoc district hedges its viticultural bets and grows at least three different grape varieties: a majority of Cabernet Sauvignon, supplemented principally by Merlot, together with some Cabernet Franc with, perhaps, a little late ripening Petit Verdot and occasionally some Malbec. However, Merlot often predominates in the damper, cooler soils of the Bas-Médoc as it is easier to ripen in lesser vintages, and by the early 1990s Cabernet Sauvignon comprised just over 50 per cent of all the vines planted in the district.

While the Médoc possesses few distinctive geographical features, many man-hours have been spent charting the subterranean Médoc. It has long been argued that its great distinction is its soil, in particular its GRAVEL. Many a geological theory has been employed to explain exactly how, and whence, these gravel deposits arrived in the Médoc, and efforts have been made to correlate exact soil and rock types with the quality of wine produced from vines grown on them. The work of Dr Gérard Seguin of BORDEAUX UNIVERSITY, however, indicates that the soil's physical attributes may well be very much more important than its mineral composition, and that one of the most important soil attributes is good DRAINAGE (see SOIL AND WINE QUALITY). The gravels of the Médoc are ideal in this respect, and are particularly important in such a damp climate—although in hotter vintages mature vines can benefit from the extensive root systems encouraged by the gravel. The gravels of the Médoc are also good at storing valuable heat, thereby promoting RIPENING.

It is traditionally said that the best vines of the Médoc are those which grow within sight of the Gironde, and certainly this is true of all the district's FIRST GROWTHS. Some argue that this is because the gravels deposited here are younger and more effective for vine maturation, others that the MESOCLIMATES of coastal vineyards tend to be slightly warmer, others that vines on higher ground have to establish more complex root systems.

A total of about 1,500 vine-growers farm this land, about a quarter of which forms part of one of the classed growths ranked in the famous 1855 CLASSIFICATION of the Médoc (and Graves).

The Haut-Médoc appellation

The landscape of the Haut-Médoc may not be remarkable but it is peppered with grandiose château buildings erected and embellished with the money to be made from selling CLASSED GROWTH red bordeaux. Certainly the Haut-Médoc today is nothing if not stratified, thanks largely to the effects of the 1855 classification of its most famous estates, which recognized scores of them as first, second, third, fourth, and fifth growths, commercial and social positions from which none but Ch MOUTON-ROTHSCHILD has so far been able to escape.

Most of these classed growths are entitled to a village appellation such as Pauillac or Margaux (see p. 124), but five of them are in communes without their own appellations and qualify merely as Haut-Médoc. The most highly ranked of these is the third growth Ch La Lagune in Ludon just outside the city, a property which has retained its reputation for robust, concentrated wines, and some of the first in the Médoc to be made by a woman. Just north of this well-run property is the fifth growth Ch Cantemerle, renovated in the 1980s by a group including the firm of CORDIER. The commune of St-Laurent, inland from ST-JULIEN on the main road through the forests of the Médoc, boasts the under-performing fourth growth Ch La Tour-Carnet and two improving fifth growths, Chx Belgrave and Camensac.

Vineyards qualifying for the Haut-Médoc appellation totalled about 3,800 ha / 9,400 acres in the early 1990s and many of them are CRUS BOURGEOIS offering some of the best value to be found in Bordeaux (indeed there is a sense in which the recent history of the Médoc is told by the fortunes of these crus bourgeois). The best wines share the deep colour, concentration, tannins, and ageing potential of the classed growths, and are made in a very similar fashion except that the basic YIELD allowed is 43 hl / ha (2.4 tons / acre) rather than the 40 hl / ha permitted for the Médoc's four important village or communal appellations and the selling prices hardly justify the use of new BARRELS. Some of the most ambitious properties include Chx Citran, Coufran, Sociando-Mallet, Lamothe-Bergeron, Lanessan, Liversan, Moulin Rouge, Sénéjac, and Tour du Haut-Moulin.

The appellation Médoc

The total area of Bas-Médoc planted with vines, which reached 4,000 ha / 9,900 acres in 1990, exceeds that of the finer Haut-Médoc. The basic limit to yields is 45 hl / ha, and a high proportion of the wines are dominated by Merlot. Much of the wine produced on these lower, less well-drained, heavier soils is solid if uninspiring claret sold in bulk to CO-OPERATIVES or to the BORDEAUX TRADE for blending into GENERIC Médoc. Estates on which an effort is made to produce something more distinctive than this, usually by restricting yields, include Chx La Gorre, La Tour de By, Loudenne, Patache d'Aux, Potensac (run in tandem with Ch Léoville-Las-Cases of ST-JULIEN), Tour Haut-Caussan (one of Bordeaux's rare ORGANIC WINES), and Vieux Robin.

For more details, see BORDEAUX.

Parker, R., *Bordeaux* (2nd edn., New York, 1991).
Penning-Rowsell, E., *The Wines of Bordeaux* (6th edn., London, 1989).
Peppercorn, D., *Bordeaux* (2nd edn., London, 1991).

MÉJANELLE, sometimes called **Coteaux de la Méjanelle**, named TERROIR within the Coteaux du LANGUEDOC in southern France, just outside the city of MONTPELLIER. Unlike the rest of the Coteaux du Languedoc, this is a historic zone of individual estates, most notably Ch de Flaugergues. Syrah, Grenache, and Mourvèdre dominate in these particularly Mediterranean vineyards, at a much lower altitude than much of the rest of the Coteaux du Languedoc.

MELNIK, powerful indigenous Bulgarian red grape variety that is grown exclusively around the ancient town of Melnik close to the Greek border in what was Thrace. It may therefore have been cultivated here for many centuries (see GREECE, Ancient) and its wines certainly taste more Greek in their extract, tannin, and alcohol than typical of modern Bulgaria. Its full name is Shiroka Melnishka Losa, or 'broad-leaved vine of Melnik', and its berries are notably small with thick, blue skins. Some wines have the aroma of tobacco leaves, another local crop. Oak ageing and several years bring out a warmth and powerful subtlety not unlike a CHÂTEAUNEUF-DU-PAPE. This is probably the Bulgarian wine with the greatest longevity, but see also MAVRUD.

MELON, or **Melon de Bourgogne**, French white grape variety, is famous in only one respect and one region, MUSCADET. As its full name suggests, its origins are Burgundian, Melon having been outlawed just like Gamay at various times during the 16th and 17th centuries. Unlike its fellow white burgundian Chardonnay, several of whose synonyms include the word Melon, it is not a noble grape variety but it does resist cold well and produces quite regularly and generously. It had spread as far as Anjou in the Middle Ages according to Bouchard and so it was natural that the vine-growers of the Muscadet region to the west might try it. It became the dominant vine variety of the Loire-Atlantique in the 17th century, when DUTCH traders encouraged production of high volumes of relatively neutral white wine, in place of the thin reds for which the region had previously been known, as base wines for Holland's enthusiastic distillers.

Melon's increasing importance today rests solely on the mysteriously popular Muscadet, whose main attribute could be said to be that it has so few distinguishing features. Among France's six most planted white grape varieties, only Chardonnay, Sauvignon, and Melon increased their total area in the surplus-conscious 1980s, to more than 11,000 ha / 27,170 acres in the case of Melon, exclusively around the mouth of the Loire.

Many of the older cuttings of the variety called PINOT BLANC in California are in fact Melon.

Bouchard, A., 'Notes ampelographiques rétrospectives sur les cépages de la généralité de Dijon', *Bulletin de la Société des Viticulteurs de France* (1899).
Galet, P., *Cépages et vignobles de France* (2nd edn., Montpellier, 1990).

MENCÍA, red grape variety grown quite widely in north west Spain. It produces light, relatively fragrant red wines in such zones as BIERZO, RIAS BAIXAS, VALDEORRAS, and LEÓN. So strong is the prevailing belief that this vine is related to Cabernet Franc that Cabernet is a local synonym.

MENDOCINO, one of CALIFORNIA's largest and climatically most diverse counties. All of its 11,000 acres / 4,400 ha of vineyards are in the southern half. Even there, the meteorological range between the coastal Anderson Valley AVA and the interior McDowell Valley AVA beggars the imagination.

Isolation from San Francisco kept its 19th century vineyards small, and delayed their impact outside the county. The same isolation kept vines growing there throughout PROHIBITION. Most of the plantings flank the town of Ukiah, at the headwaters of the Russian river. Although the districts of Redwood Valley, Ukiah, and Hopland are fairly well defined, they were slow to seek individual AVA status, contenting themselves with a blanket Mendocino AVA.

Mendocino AVA

The coverall AVA in Mendocino County includes the more specific Anderson Valley, McDowell Valley, and Potter Valley AVAs, as well as the county's most substantial vineyard plantings along the Russian river course from Redwood Valley southward through Ukiah to Hopland and beyond. Cabernet Sauvignon, Petite Sirah, Zinfandel, and Sauvignon Blanc have been reliable in the large zone along the Russian river. Chardonnay from a few vineyards has been surprisingly fine. Fetzer is the dominant winery by size; Jepson, Parducci, and Husch are others of commercial importance.

Anderson Valley AVA

Scouts for Louis Roederer of CHAMPAGNE say they hunted in California until they found somewhere with weather as bleak as this part of north eastern France, and that Mendocino County's coast-hugging Anderson Valley fitted their requirement perfectly. Visually, scores of scenes sluiced out by a short, swift river, the Navarro, make landscape painters lunge for canvas and brushes. Close framed by steep hills, the valley has only a couple of patches that might pass for floor and, unusually for California's valley vineyards, only one or two of the 20 or so are flat. Anderson Valley is hardly 10 miles end to end, but a steady rise in elevation combines with a rising wall of hills to make the inland end at Boonville warmer and sunnier than the oft-befogged area between Philo and Navarro, where most of the vines grow.

Sheep and apples reigned hereabouts until grapes came, a little wave of them in the 1970s, a bigger one in the 1980s. America's grandest Gewürztraminers have come from it. Some of its Rieslings and Chardonnays have been memorable. Ridgetops to the west have yielded a succession of wonderfully oak-ribbed Zinfandels from a scattering of tiny patches. Greenwood Ridge, Handley, Husch, Lazy Creek, and Navarro vineyards are the mainstay wineries for table wine production. However, since 1984, first Roederer then Scharffenberger have thrown the region's weight behind classic method sparkling wines from Chardonnay and Pinot Noir.

McDowell Valley AVA

In practice this is a one-winery AVA located in a small, upland valley east of the town of Hopland in southern Mendocino County. It has been of interest primarily for Grenache, Syrah, and Zinfandel first planted before the turn of the century.

Potter Valley AVA

Without a winery of its own, the upland district in eastern Mendocino County is seldom identified on labels. Sauvignon Blanc has been its premier achievement to date. Planting began in the 1970s.

MENDOZA. See ARGENTINA.

MENETOU-SALON, just west of the much more famous SANCERRE, near the city of Bourges, producing a not dissimilar range of red, white, and rosé wines which can often offer better value. Sauvignon Blanc grown here is capable of making wines every bit as refreshingly aromatic as Sancerre. Soils in the appellation are mainly LIMESTONE and can be very similar to those in the more famous zone to the east, especially in its best zone around the village of Morogues, a name used on the labels of producers such as Henry Pellé. The village of Parassy also has a high concentration of vineyards. Sauvignon represents about 60 per cent of the appellation's total production, while Pinot Noir grapes are responsible for scented, light reds and pinks for early consumption—more evidence of the similarity between Sancerre and Menetou-Salon.

See also LOIRE and map on pp. 576–7.

MÉNTRIDA, Spanish town and wine zone south west of Madrid in CASTILE-LA MANCHA (see map on p. 907) producing robust red wines from GARNACHA grapes. It is by no means clear what the wine-makers in the hills around the town have done to deserve DO status. Most of the wines are hefty reds made in old-fashioned, often unhygienic CO-OPERATIVES that travel no further than the bars in nearby Madrid. The one producer who is making high-quality wine in this part of Spain, Marqués de Griñon, has CABERNET SAUVIGNON, CHARDONNAY, SYRAH, and PETIT VERDOT vines growing in his vineyard at Malpica de Tajo just outside the denomination. He has to be content with the category VINO DE MESA de Toledo, even though the quality of his wine is far above anything from DO Méntrida. R.J.M.

MERANESE, or **Meraner** in German, red wines from around the town of Merano in the ALTO ADIGE.

MERCAPTANS, a group of foul-smelling chemical compounds in which one of the hydrogen atoms of HYDROGEN SULPHIDE has been replaced by an alkyl group, a chain of carbon atoms with hydrogen atoms attached at all vacant sites. Mercaptans, which smell uncomfortably skunk-like, are formed by YEAST after the primary alcoholic FERMENTATION reacting with SULPHUR in the LEES. If not removed from the new wine (which can usually be achieved by simple AERATION, by prompt RACKING, for example), less volatile and even more unpleasant compounds tend to be formed.

MERCHANTS are almost as important to the wine world as producers and consumers, and may have been for at least four millennia (see MESOPOTAMIA, for example). Three very different types of wine merchant are considered below, but they share a dependence on the vine and the attractions its produce has for the consumer.

Ancient Greece

As outlined in the ancient history of TASTING, specialized wine merchants already existed as a class in Ancient GREECE. They developed the art of wine tasting which, with cunning, could be applied to the art of selling wine, as recorded in detail by the 3rd century AD writer Florentinus (preserved in the *Geoponica* 7. 7):

> Purchasers of wine should be offered a taste when the north wind blows [when, as he has already explained, wines taste at their best].

The Ch de **Menetou-Salon**.

Some people try to trick their customers by using an empty cup which they have dipped in very good wine with a great aroma. The quality of the wine leaves its trace for some time, so that the bouquet seems to belong to the wine now poured in the cup, and in this way they deceive the customer. More unscrupulous dealers put out cheese and nuts in the shop, so as to tempt the customers who come in to eat something; the aim is to prevent them from tasting accurately. I record this not as a suggestion for us to follow, but so that we shall not suffer from these practices. The farmer will often need to taste the wine, both new and old, to detect wine which is about to deteriorate.

N.G.W.

Modern Britain

The British wine merchant is, almost necessarily, an importer, or customer of one. Wine merchants were important in medieval England and Gascony, when they were known as VINTNERS in English. Even today, a wine merchant in Britain enjoys a certain social standing perceptibly higher than that of, for example, a grocer. This is somewhat ironic since the majority of the wine sold in Britain has been sold by grocers, as opposed to specialists, since at least 1987. This was largely due to the efforts of the licensed supermarkets to improve the range and quality of wines they sell, although it is also simply a function of the fact that so many Britons pass through a supermarket at some point every week. The independent specialist wine merchant has to struggle to compete with the low margins funded by the sheer quantity of wine a chain of supermarkets can sell. They do so by offering personal service, advice, sale or return facilities, credit, mail order, glass loan, and so on, with the supermarkets and specialist chains hot on their heels.

France

The French term most often translated as merchant is *négociant*, most often a producer/bottler rather than a specialist retailer (who is known as a *caviste* in French) and is still a relatively rare phenomenon, since so many wine purchases in France have been made direct from the producer (*vente directe*) or, increasingly, at the supermarket (*grande surface*). See NÉGOCIANT and BORDEAUX TRADE for more details.

See also wine TRADE.

MERCUREY, most important village in the Côte CHALONNAISE district of Burgundy. While most of the production is in red wines made from Pinot Noir, a small quantity of unusually scented white wine from Chardonnay is also made. With 522 ha/1,358 acres under vine, Mercurey produces almost as much wine as the other Côte Chalonnaise appellations Givry, Rully, and Montagny combined. The appellation, including the commune of St-Martin-sous-Montaigu, includes 29 PREMIER CRU vineyards making up 20 per cent of the total.

The red wines tend to be deeper in colour, fuller in body, more capable of ageing, and half as expensive again as those of the neighbouring villages. Maximum yields for Mercurey are the same as those for VILLAGE WINES in the CÔTE D'OR, whereas the other appellations of the Côte Chalonnaise may produce an additional 5 hl/ha (0.3 tons/acre).

Mercurey is said to have been the favourite wine of Gabrielle d'Estrées, although her lover Henry IV preferred neighbouring Givry. J.T.C.M.

MERILLE was once widely planted in the Garonne vineyards but produces undistinguished red wine not permitted by any local appellation such as Buzet or Côtes du Marmandais.

MERITAGE, trade-marked name for American wines made from a blend of grape varieties in the image of MÉDOC and GRAVES, devised to distinguish these wines from VARIETAL Cabernet Sauvignon, Merlot, etc., most usefully on wine lists. The name is available only to American wineries that agree to join an association and uphold the following requirements of the wine labelled Meritage: made exclusively from Cabernet Sauvignon, Cabernet Franc, Merlot, Malbec, Petit Verdot grapes for red wines and Sauvignon Blanc, Semillon, and Muscadelle for whites; produced in quantities of no more than 25,000 cases a year; one of the two most expensive wines produced by the winery.

Nearly but not all of the members are in CALIFORNIA (and only wineries there have track records long enough to permit even hazy judgement). A few whites might challenge dry Graves on quality though their precise characters have been pure California. Meritage reds were meant to challenge some of the finest wines of BORDEAUX, although early Meritages tended to be slightly or markedly less distinct counterparts to full blooded Cabernet Sauvignons from the same vineyards or districts. As (or is it if?) growers find patches where Merlot and Cabernet Franc improve on Cabernet Sauvignon, the breed may improve. The finest few give hope.

One of the problems of the association is that it came long after leaders among its member wineries had coined fantasy names for their bordeaux-style blends, and so Meritage nomenclature is sometimes convoluted beyond explanation.

MERLOT Noir, the black grape variety popularly associated with the great wines of St-Émilion and Pomerol, is Bordeaux's most planted black grape variety, and has been enjoying unaccustomed popularity elsewhere. It has no direct relationship to the much less distinguished white-berried Merlot Blanc which has also been cultivated, on a much smaller and decreasing scale, in Bordeaux.

Throughout south west France and, increasingly, much of the rest of the world, Merlot plays the role of constant companion to the more austere, aristocratic, long-living Cabernet Sauvignon. Its early maturing, plump, lush fruitiness provides a more obvious complement to Cabernet Sauvignon's attributes than the CABERNET FRANC that often makes up the third ingredient in the common 'Bordelais' blend. It also provides good viticultural insurance in more marginal climates as it buds, flowers, and ripens at least a week before Cabernet Sauvignon (although this makes Merlot more sensitive to frost, as was shown dramatically in both 1956 and 1991). Its early flowering makes it particularly sensitive to COULURE, which weaker ROOTSTOCKS can help to prevent. Merlot is not quite so vigorous as Cabernet Sauvignon but its looser bunches of larger, notably thinner-skinned grapes are much more prone to rot. It is also more sensitive to DOWNY MILDEW. (Spraying can be a particularly frequent phenomenon in the vineyards of Bordeaux.) Merlot responds much better than Cabernet Sauvignon to damp, cool soils, such as those of St-Émilion and Pomerol, that retain their moisture well and allow the grapes to reach full size. In very well-drained soils, dry summers can leave the grapes undeveloped.

For the vine-grower in anything cooler than a warm or hot climate, Merlot is much easier to ripen than Cabernet Sauvignon, and has the further advantage of yielding a little higher to boot. It is not surprising therefore that, in France and northern Italy, total Merlot plantings have for long been greatly superior to those of Cabernet Sauvignon.

This is particularly marked in Bordeaux where Cabernet Sauvignon dominates Merlot only in the famously well-drained soils of the Médoc and Graves. Elsewhere, not just in St-Émilion and Pomerol but also in Bourg, Blaye, Fronsac, and, importantly, those areas qualifying for basic Bordeaux or the rest of the so-called BORDEAUX CÔTES appellation, Merlot predominates. Throughout the 1970s and 1980s it, with Cabernet Sauvignon where it would ripen, was the popular choice for land that was previously dedicated to the less fashionable, and lucrative, white varieties Sémillon, Colombard, Muscadelle, Ugni Blanc, and the other hotchpotch of varieties still thriving even less gloriously in the Gironde.

According to the 1988 census, Merlot represented more than half of all black vine varieties in the Gironde while Cabernet Sauvignon covered only 28 per cent of vineyard dedicated to red wine. Even in the Médoc, however, where one vine in two was Cabernet Sauvignon, Merlot plantings outnumbered those of Cabernet Franc by nearly seven to one. And in the greater St-Émilion and Pomerol area known as the Libournais, Merlot represented more than two vines in every three.

It was already documented as a good-quality vine variety in the Libournais in 1784 according to the historian Enjalbert, and in 1868 was noted by A. Petit-Laffitte as the Médoc's premier variety for blending with Cabernet Sauvignon. But it is clearly in St-Émilion and, especially, the clay soils of Pomerol that the variety produces its more glorious wines (see under ST-ÉMILION and POMEROL for more detail). Even here, however, except for notable exceptions such as Ch PÉTRUS, Merlot produces wines perceptibly lower in colour, acid, and, especially, tannin than left bank red bordeaux dominated by the thicker-skinned Cabernet Sauvignon. The relatively early maturing, easy-to-appreciate Merlot is a wine with distinct advantages over Cabernet Sauvignon in times of inflation.

Such was the increase in popularity of Merlot with the vine-growers of Bordeaux, Bergerac, and Languedoc-Roussillon in the 1980s that Merlot was France's third most planted black grape variety, after Carignan and Grenache, by 1988. France's Merlot plantings totalled 60,000 ha/148,200 acres, as opposed to Cabernet Sauvignon's 36,500 ha. Merlot is more widely planted than either sort of Cabernet, not just in Bordeaux but also in the rest of SOUTH WEST FRANCE. Wherever in this quarter of France the APPELLATION CONTRÔLÉE regulations sanction Cabernet Sauvignon (see CABERNET SAUVIGNON for details), they also sanction Merlot, although the latter is favoured in the Dordogne while the Cabernets are preferred in Gascony.

With Syrah, Merlot has been a major beneficiary of the Midi's turn towards 'improving' grape varieties. There were nearly 4,000 ha in each of the Aude and Hérault *départements* by 1988 and 400 ha in Roussillon. Much of this has been blended with more traditional varieties, notably the tough Carignan, to add fruit and appeal. The only appellations of the Midi to sanction Merlot within their regulations are CABARDÈS and Côtes de la MALEPÈRE but much of it is made into light, fruity varietal VIN DE PAYS wines whose quality is usually in inverse proportion to yield.

Merlot is also extremely important in Italy, where there were more than 30,000 ha in 1990. The variety is grown particularly in the north east, often alongside Cabernet Franc, where output of the wine called there 'Merlott' can be easily 100,000 hl/2.6 million gal a year from the plains of both GRAVE DEL FRIULI and PIAVE, even if better, more concentrated wines come in smaller quantities from higher vineyards. In FRIULI indeed, where Merlot performs perceptibly better than most CABERNET, there is even a Strada del Merlot, a tourist route along the Isonzo river. Individual denominations for Merlot abound in Friuli, the VENETO, and TRENTINO-ALTO ADIGE. Merlot is also planted on the Colli BOLOGNESI in Emilia-Romagna. The variety is planted in 14 of Italy's 20 regions. In general, little is expected from or delivered by the sea of light, vaguely fruity Merlot from northern Italy, which makes it all the more remarkable that the variety is being taken seriously by a handful of producers in Tuscany and Umbria. Lodovico Antinori at Ornellaia and the Fattoria de Ama were the first to show that Italy could provide something more in the mould of serious Pomerol.

The variety is vital to the wine industry of Italian SWITZERLAND and is made at a wide range of quality levels.

Merlot has also been popular over Italy's north eastern border in SLOVENIA and all down the Dalmatian coast, where it can be attractively plummy when yields are restricted. As 'Médoc Noir' it is also known in HUNGARY, notably around Eger in the north east and Villány in the south. It is also the most widely planted red wine variety in ROMANIA where there may be as much as 10,000 ha/25,000 acres, and is the second most planted variety in BULGARIA after Cabernet Sauvignon, with which it is often blended. It is also planted in RUSSIA and, particularly, MOLDOVA.

Outside these traditional strongholds, Merlot has been taken up much more slowly than the world-famous Cabernet Sauvignon. The fact that it is slightly lower in acidity as well as international *réclame* may have hindered its progress in some warmer climates such as Iberia and most of the eastern Mediterranean, where it was still relatively rare in the early 1990s (although the mid-Portuguese Ma Partilha already showed promise).

A lift in Merlot's reputation was already apparent, however, by 1990, most obviously in North America. Merlot was suddenly regarded as 'the hot varietal' in the Cabernet-soaked state of California, and demonstrated decisively that it had a particular affinity with the conditions of Washington State and possibly even of those of Long Island in the State of NEW YORK.

Although in 1985 California had a total of hardly 2,000 acres/800 ha of Merlot, this had already risen to about 8,000 acres by 1992 and the variety was in great demand both for blending with other Bordeaux varieties for MERITAGE and the like, and for varietal reds that were softer and milder than the state's Cabernet Sauvignons. See CALIFORNIA for more detail of the wine style.

Merlot has had little success in Oregon's vineyards, where the much cooler climate makes coulure too grave a problem, but in Washington's sunny inland Columbia basin Merlot has produced consistently fine, fruity, well-structured reds about which there are more details under WASHINGTON. Merlot is the state's most popular black grape variety with over 1,500 acres by 1991, an increase of more than 100 per cent in just three years. Merlot is also grown increasingly in other North American states.

In South America Merlot is important to the wine industry of ARGENTINA, where its 2,500 ha/6,200 acres of Merlot in 1989, mostly in Mendoza, was only slightly less than the country's total area of Cabernet Sauvignon, and very much less than that of Malbec. Merlot is also planted to a more limited extent in CHILE, URUGUAY, BRAZIL, and BOLIVIA.

California's relatively late enthusiasm for Merlot was mirrored in Australia, where, of the 500 ha planted in 1990, only 300 were old enough to bear fruit. There is great potential for Merlot in selected spots there but the prevailing tradition has been to soften Cabernet Sauvignon (inasmuch as ultra-ripe Australian Cabernet needs ripening) with Shiraz rather than Merlot.

Merlot clearly has great potential in New Zealand too and there were 150 ha planted, mainly for filling in the flavour holes of the more angular Cabernet Sauvignon, in 1992. South Africa has produced some interesting varietal Merlots as well as using it to good effect in Bordeaux blends but the variety has yet to establish a distinct identity for itself on the Cape.

As the world's wine consumers search for yet more fine red wine that offers an alternative to the unfashionably rigorous charms of Cabernet Sauvignon, it seems likely that Merlot will become increasingly important in countries other than France.

Enjalbert, H., *Les Grands Vins de St-Émilion, Pomerol et Fronsac* (Paris, 1983).

MERSEGUERA, Spanish white grape variety that is widely grown in ALICANTE, JUMILLA, and VALENCIA but produces little wine of any distinction. The vine ripens relatively early and has compact bunches of large grapes.

MESLIER ST-FRANÇOIS is, like ARBOIS, a white grape variety that is a local speciality of the Loir-et-Cher *département* in the westward bend of the Loire but has been disappearing at an even faster rate. At one time it was used for producing cognac and, especially, armagnac.

MESOCLIMATE, a term of climatic scale, intermediate between regional climate or MACROCLIMATE, and the very small scale MICROCLIMATE. It encompasses the more specific terms TOPOCLIMATE and SITE CLIMATE, and has largely replaced both in common usage (although the word microclimate is widely and incorrectly used by non-specialists for mesoclimate). The usual scale of a mesoclimate is in tens or hundreds of metres, so one speaks correctly of the mesoclimate of a particular vineyard or potential vineyard site.

The full definition of a mesoclimate (or site climate) requires detailed on-the-spot records, but these are seldom available over the long periods (conventionally 30 years or more) needed to iron out short-term climatic fluctuations, and thus to be fully representative. The process can be considerably shortened if site records can be calibrated continuously against those of a nearby and reasonably comparable older station. The differences, once established as consistent over a number of seasons, can be applied to the longer-term records of the latter.

In the absence of any local temperature measurements it is still possible to make fair estimates by interpolating within known regional trends, and then allowing for differences in altitude at the rate of 0.6 °C/1.1 °F per 100 m/330 ft. Following that, individual mesoclimates can be approximated more closely still by allowing for features of TOPOGRAPHY such as slope and aspect, and even soil type, as discussed in general terms by Geiger.

Gladstones has suggested effective temperature adjustments (for predicting vine development and RIPENING) as for vineyard topographies in mid latitudes, as compared with nearby flat recording locations with non-stony and non-calcareous soils:

Terrain	Adjustment to: Max. temp.	Min. temp.
Moderate slopes in undulating terrain	−0.5 °C (0.9 °F)	+1.0 °C (1.8 °F)
Steep slopes, or moderate and steeper slopes of free-standing hills	−0.5 °C	+1.5 °C
Slopes directly facing the midday sun	+0.25 °C	+0.75 °C
Slopes directly facing away from the midday sun	−0.25 °C	−0.75 °C
Slopes facing east or west	no change	no change
Markedly stony, rocky, limestone, or chalk-based soils	−0.5 °C	+1.0 °C

Reduced adjustments apply to lesser topographical or soil contrasts. All individual adjustments are additive. J.G.

Geiger, R., *Das Klima der bodennahen Luftschicht* (4th edn., Brunswick, 1961), trans. by Scripta Technica, Inc., as *Climate near the Ground* (Cambridge, Mass., 1966).
Gladstones, J., *Viticulture and Environment* (Adelaide, 1992).

MESOPOTAMIA. In ancient Mesopotamia, which lay in the fertile land between the rivers Tigris and Euphrates and is often thought of as the cradle of civilization, the most widely consumed alcoholic drink at all periods was probably BEER. It was available in numerous different varieties and strengths, and there is much ancient information about beer. However, grape wine is already mentioned in cuneiform texts preserved on clay tablets from Ur dating to approximately 2750 BC. A drinking song of Ancient SUMER (*c*.2000 BC) lists all the implements required for making beer and wine; both drinks are included. Wine and beer were often served together. A wine was also made from dates. Vines do not grow so well in the low-lying and humid south of Mesopotamia, and wine seems to have been imported from the more mountainous north. This is probably the origin of the poetic Mesopotamian name for wine, 'liquor of the mountains'.

By the first millennium BC wine was as widely used as beer, at least in privileged circles. Unfortunately, little information is available about the methods of production. Designations of wine suggest that a great variety of types was available: 'new', 'old', 'mature', 'strong', 'very sweet', 'clear', 'red', 'ox-eye (coloured)', 'good-tasting'. One sort is even called 'drink of the king'. Some wines, such as the so-called 'bitter wine' of Tupliash, an area lying to the east of the river Tigris, seem to have been drunk FLAVOURED with herbs. Wine was also sometimes drunk mixed with honey.

But from the beginning of the first millennium BC, it appears that wines were more commonly identified by their place of origin than by their type. These are mostly regions in the north or north west of Mesopotamia, (in modern northern Iraq and northern Syria), but also including Suhu (a region in modern Iraq on the middle course of the river Euphrates, downstream from the modern Syrian border). In an inscription detailing offerings made to the god Marduk in his temple at Babylon, King Nebuchadnezzar II (r. 604–563 BC) mentions 'liquor of the mountains', 'clear wine', and the wines of eight different named regions.

A few documents (in the form of clay tablets) survive from the early 8th century BC from the Assyrian capital Kalhu (modern Nimrud). These are the remnants of a once vast archive detailing the administration of wine rations to the 6,000-strong palace household, from the king and queen down to assistant cooks and shepherd boys. The wine magazines were lined with great wine jars and archaeologists have estimated that one magazine stored at least 151 hl/4,000 gal. The basic daily ration was quite modest: 0.184 l, with 0.306 l for a skilled craftsman. Nobles received considerably more.

Wine and beer were frequently offered, among many other foods and drinks, to deities as part of the cult, and the practice of LIBATION was widespread in temple ritual.

Among the Babylonians and Assyrians wine was widely used, as was beer, for medicinal purposes (see MEDICINE), especially as a vehicle for various concoctions often of rather dubious, if not frankly revolting, ingredients.

See also Ancient SUMER, and see HERODOTUS for details of the earliest recorded mention of the use of BARRELS for transporting wine, down the Euphrates. J.A.B.

Bottéro, J., 'Getränke' ('Drinks'), *Reallexikon der Assyriologie und vorderasiatischen Archäologie* (the standard reference work on the subject, 1st pub. in Berlin, 1928, and still being completed).

Kinnier Wilson, J. V., *The Nimrud Wine Lists* (London, 1972).

METABISULPHATE, often added to freshly picked grapes to prevent OXIDATION of the must. See SULPHUR DIOXIDE.

METALS. See MINERALS.

METHANOL, another name for **methyl alcohol**, **methylated spirits**, or '**meths**', also known as wood alcohol, is the member of the chemical series of common ALCOHOLS with the lowest molecular weight. Methanol, which is moderately toxic, has unfortunately been confused with ETHANOL on occasion, with serious results to the health and even life of the unwary consumer. The immediate risk of ingesting any quantity of methanol is blindness, but consumption of between 25 and 100 ml/4 fl oz can be fatal. As recently as the mid 1980s, some Italian wines were found to have been deliberately contaminated with methanol (see ADULTERATION).

Wines naturally contain very small quantities of methanol: about 0.1 g/l, or less than one-hundredth of the normal concentration of ethanol. Some methanol is naturally present in grapes and further traces are formed during FERMENTATION but most is formed by demethylating the pectin materials that are naturally present in the grape (see ENZYMES). Red wines, and particularly those subjected to prolonged MACERATION, are likely to have higher methanol concentrations than average. BRANDY in general has rather higher levels of methanol than wine because the DISTILLATION process concentrates it. And wines and brandies made from fruits other than grapes tend to have higher methanol concentrations because grapes have fewer pectins than most other fruits. It would be impossible to ingest a dangerous level of methanol from such drinks, however, without ingesting a fatal amount of ethanol long beforehand.

Methanol is often encountered in everyday life because it is a common solvent for household products as well as being used as fuel for chafing dishes. A.D.W.

MÉTHODE ANCESTRALE, sometimes called **méthode artisanale** or **méthode rurale**, very traditional SPARKLING WINE-MAKING method used chiefly in Limoux, resulting in a lightly sparkling, medium sweet wine, sometimes complete with sediment.

MÉTHODE CHAMPENOISE, French term for the champagne method described in detail in SPARKLING WINE-MAKING. This description was once a valuable aid to the consumer in distinguishing the most meticulously made sparkling wines from those made by less complicated methods. From 1994 this description was outlawed by EUROPEAN UNION authorities, however, in favour of one of the following: 'fermentation en bouteille selon la méthode champenoise'; 'méthode traditionnelle'; 'méthode classique'; 'méthode traditionnelle classique'. An English-language equivalent is 'fermented in this bottle'.

MÉTHODE CLASSIQUE, term for the champagne method of SPARKLING WINE-MAKING approved by the EUROPEAN UNION.

MÉTHODE DIOISE, SPARKLING WINE-MAKING process used for CLAIRETTE DE DIE.

MÉTHODE GAILLACOISE, GAILLAC's version of the MÉTHODE ANCESTRALE. See SPARKLING WINE-MAKING.

MÉTHODE TRADITIONNELLE and **méthode traditionnelle classique**, alternative terms for the champagne method of SPARKLING WINE-MAKING that are approved by the EUROPEAN UNION.

METHUEN TREATY, accord signed between Britain and Portugal in 1703 which gave Portuguese goods preferential treatment in Britain and encouraged the imports of Portuguese wine, at the expense of wine from the rest of Europe, notably France, at a time when PORT was evolving into the strong, sweet drink we know today.

METODO CLASSICO and **metodo tradizionale**, Italian terms for SPARKLING WINES made by the champagne method.

MEUNIER is one of France's dozen most planted black grape varieties but neither it nor its common synonym **Pinot Meunier** are often encountered on a wine label. Meunier was probably an early, particularly downy, MUTATION of the famously mutable PINOT NOIR. It earns its name (*meunier* is French for miller) because the underside of its downy leaves can look as though they have been dusted with flour. In Germany it is known as Müllerrebe (miller's grape) as well as Schwarzriesling.

Meunier is treasured in Champagne, as it was in the once-extensive vineyards of northern France, because it buds later and ripens earlier than the inconveniently early budding Pinot Noir and is therefore much less prone to COULURE and more dependably productive. Acid levels are slightly higher although alcohol levels are by no means necessarily lower than those of Pinot Noir. Meunier is therefore the popular choice for Champagne's growers, especially those in cooler north-facing vineyards, in the damp, frost-prone Vallée de la Marne, and in the cold valleys of the Aisne *département*. In fact, so commercially reliable is Meunier for Champagne's powerful vine-growers that it is Champagne's most popular variety by far, covering 11,000 ha/27,170 acres, or more than 40 per cent of the region's vineyards. Plantings of Pinot Noir and Chardonnay increased at a greater rate than those of Meunier in the 1980s, partly because of premiums paid for these 'nobler' varieties, but Meunier will remain the region's principal variety in terms of quantity for many years to come.

Common wisdom has it that, as an ingredient in the traditional three-variety champagne blend, Meunier contributes youthful fruitiness to complement Pinot Noir's weight and Chardonnay's finesse. Few producers boast of their Meunier, however (with the honorable exception of *Krug*), and few preponderantly Meunier growers' champagnes have great weight or staying power. Meunier is generally lower in pigments than Pinot Noir, and one of its common French synonyms is Gris Meunier.

It has largely disappeared elsewhere in northern France although it is still technically allowed into the rosés and light reds of Côtes de TOUL, wines of MOSELLE, and, in the Loire, TOURAINE and wines of the ORLÉANAIS.

As Müllerrebe or Schwarzriesling, a selection of Meunier is relatively, and increasingly, popular in Germany, where the majority of its nearly 2,000 ha/5,000 acres are grown in the WÜRTTEMBERG region. It is also grown in German-speaking SWITZERLAND, and to a much lesser extent in Austria and Yugoslavia.

Curiously, in Australia Meunier has a longer documented history as a still red varietal wine (at one time called Miller's Burgundy) than Pinot Noir, notably at Great Western in VICTORIA. New-found enthusiasm for authentic replicas of champagne saved the variety from extinction in Australia where some new plantings in cooler spots boosted what had been the nation's declining total to 38 ha in 1991.

It was also with an eye to producing 'genuine' replicas of champagne that growers in California sought Meunier cuttings in the 1980s so that the state's total acreage of the variety was 275 by 1992, almost exclusively in CARNEROS.

MEURSAULT, large and prosperous village in the Côte de Beaune district of Burgundy's Côte d'Or producing mostly white wines from the Chardonnay grape. Although Meursault contains no GRAND CRU vineyards, the quality of white burgundy from Meursault's best PREMIERS CRUS is rarely surpassed.

The finest vineyards are Les Perrières, Les Genevrières, and Les Charmes. Between them and the village of Meursault are three more premiers crus, Le Poruzot, Les Bouchères, and La Goutte d'Or. Another group by the hamlet of BLAGNY are sold as Meursault-Blagny if white or Blagny premier cru if red while, at the other end of the village, Les Santenots is sold as Meursault Santenots if white and Volnay Santenots if red, as it usually is. Apart from Les Santenots, and the lean but fine red wines of Blagny, the other red wines of Meursault tend to be grown low on the slope and do not feature among the best of the Côte de Beaune.

Les Perrières was cited as a 'tête de cuvée' vineyard in the original CLASSIFICATION of 1861 and might well have been classified as a grand cru. Its character derives from the quantity of stones, after which the vineyard is named, which reflect the sun back on to the vines. If Les Perrières is regularly the richest wine in Meursault, Les Genevrières comes close, producing particularly elegant wines. Les Charmes is the biggest of the three major vineyards and produces the most forward wines, seductive even in their youth.

Meursault also enjoys a wealth of good wines from other named vineyards such as Chevalières, Tessons, Clos de la Barre, Luchets, Narvaux, and Tillets. These are frequently more interesting than the village wines of PULIGNY-MONTRACHET, where the water-table is higher. Furthermore, it is possible to dig cellars significantly deeper in Meursault, which enables many growers to prolong BARREL MATURATION through a second winter, which improves the depth, stability, and ageing potential of the wines.

Meursault also hosts one of the three glorious feasts of Burgundy during the third weekend in November (see TROIS GLORIEUSES). On the Monday after the HOSPICES DE BEAUNE sale some 600 local growers and guests gather at noon for the Paulée de Meursault, an end-of-harvest feast revived in the 1920s by Comte Jules Lafon. Everybody brings their own bottles to share with other tables. The occasion slightly belies the local proverb that he who drinks only Meursault will never be a drunkard.

See also CÔTE D'OR and its map. J.T.C.M.

MEXICO, the Americas' oldest wine-producing country, had more than 40,000 ha/98,800 acres under vine in 1992, almost two-thirds as much as Australia, for example, although only a small fraction of this land is designed to produce wine, and an even smaller percentage of that is exported. TABLE

Picking **Meursault's** precious grapes, in plastic boxes so as to minimize damage to the fruit.

GRAPES and, to a lesser extent, DRYING GRAPES are important products in Mexico, but much of the modern vineyard was planted after the early 1960s in response to huge domestic demand for BRANDY and cheap, often sweet, still and sparkling wine. This demand was fuelled by protectionist import taxes on both wines and spirits, which also encouraged foreign investment from the likes of MARTELL and DOMECQ, brandy producers who have done much to develop modern wine-making methods in the country. (For more details, see Latin American BRANDY.) The Spanish sparkling wine producer FREIXENET has also made important investments in Mexico.

Mexico's history of wine production dates from 1521, just a year after the arrival of the Spanish conquistadores, who had no intention of forswearing wine in this new continent (see SOUTH AMERICA, history). Cortés issued an edict three years later ordering all new Spanish settlers to plant vines on the land they had been granted, which made the country self-sufficient in wine (and curbed exports from Andalucía) by the end of the 16th century. Marqués de Aguayo at Parras in the north east of the country lays claim to being the oldest winery in the Americas, having been founded in 1593, although by the 1980s it was distilling its entire production into brandy. Father Juan Ugarte is credited with spreading viticulture northwards into what is now the state of CALIFORNIA.

Mexico's vineyard was but a few hundred hectares at the beginning of the 20th century and a fragile domestic market for wine began to develop only in the 1960s. The country's total vineyard area doubled in the 1970s, although there is enormous variation in characteristics between the various vineyard regions. Average annual wine production was about 2 million cases in the 1980s but, thanks to a 1989 free trade agreement with the EUROPEAN UNION and a flood of cheap imports from Germany, had dropped considerably by 1992, of which Domecq, L. A. Cetto, and Santo Tomas were the important producers, Monte Xanic, San Antonio, and Valmar smaller enterprises of interest.

The majority of vineyards are in the north of the country in the states of Sonora, associated with brandy production, and, the most significant producer of better-quality wines, Baja California between California and the Tropic of Cancer. Here IRRIGATION is practised wherever possible, and low rainfall is Mexico's greatest viticultural disadvantage. Other vineyards are further south where the heat is mitigated by altitude (up to 2,100 m / 7,000 ft) on the plateaux of Aguascalientes and Zacatecas, for example, where the contrast between day and night temperatures can be dramatic. Potential seems particularly good in Zacatecas and in the new area of Querétaro.

By no means all vines are grafted against the predations of PHYLLOXERA, even though only the sandy soils of Sonora are likely to remain free of this damaging insect pest. VINE DENSITY can vary from a very Spanish 1,250 SULTANA plants per hectare in parts of Sonora to 3,500 for better-quality varieties in areas with lower fertility such as the valley of Guadalupe in Baja California and parts of Zacatecas and Querétaro. The great majority of vineyards are planted to an ESPALIER training system.

Vine varieties planted include the historic MISSION grape, whose ancestors were planted by the early Spanish settlers, as well as a wide range of European red wine varieties such as CABERNET SAUVIGNON, MERLOT, MALBEC, NEBBIOLO, GRENACHE, and CARIGNAN, supplemented by varieties more common in California such as ZINFANDEL, PETITE SIRAH, and RUBY CABERNET. A wide range of European light-skinned grape varieties are also planted, including brandy grapes such as TREBBIANO, COLOMBARD, and PALOMINO as well as CHENIN BLANC.

Mexico is the fourth most important wine producer in Latin America after ARGENTINA, BRAZIL, and CHILE. Of all Latin American wine producers, Mexico is probably most strongly influenced by California and there has been a certain influx of expertise in vineyard and cellar assimilated at the University of California at DAVIS.

Mexico's own influence on New World wine has also been considerable, if indirect. Without Mexicans as the prime LABOUR source for vineyard work, California's late 20th century wine industry might have developed quite differently.

Walker, L., 'Going Native', *Wine & Spirit*, May 1994.

MEZESFEHÉR, white grape variety grown widely in HUNGARY, where its soft, usually sweet, white wines are much admired. Such wines are rarely exported to western markets, however. Its name means 'white honey' and it is perhaps most successful around Eger and Gyöngyös.

MIA or **Murrumbidgee Irrigation Area**, one of the irrigated wine regions of AUSTRALIA associated mainly with inexpensive wine for blending. For more detail see NEW SOUTH WALES.

MICE can cause vine damage. See ANIMALS.

MICROBES, or **micro-organisms**, extremely small living beings, a few of which are capable of causing VINE DISEASES and FERMENTATION. Those affecting wines and vines are usually referred to as YEASTS and BACTERIA. **Microbiology** is the study of such micro-organisms, which need **micro-nutrients** as well as nutrients for growth.

MICROCLIMATE, widely misused term meaning the climate within a defined and usually very restricted space or position. In viticulture it might be at specified positions between rows of vines, or distances above the ground. CANOPY MICROCLIMATE is that within and immediately surrounding the vine canopy, or green parts of the vine. There are microclimates on or close to the surfaces of individual leaves, grape bunches, or even berries. Microclimates exist at various positions or depths within the soil. All these distinctions are important in understanding vine responses to environment.

Microclimate is potentially influenced by management practices, such as vine TRELLISING, VINE TRAINING, and TRIMMING; vine VIGOUR and the factors affecting it; and SOIL MANAGEMENT and mulching. In this respect it differs in important ways from climatic definitions of wider embrace, such as MACROCLIMATE and MESOCLIMATE, which are wholly or largely uninfluenced by management.

Common use of the term microclimate to describe the climate of a vineyard site, hillside, or valley is clearly wrong and should be deplored. The correct term for these is usually mesoclimate, or possibly SITE CLIMATE or TOPOCLIMATE.

Microclimate distances are normally measured in millimetres to a maximum of a few metres; those of mesoclimate, in tens or hundreds of metres. J.G. & R.E.S.

MIDI, common name for the south of France. Like 'Mezzogiorno' in Italy it means literally 'midday' and refers to regions where midday is a time of extreme heat and inactivity, at least in summer. Midi is often used synonymously with LANGUEDOC-ROUSSILLON, although strictly speaking the Midi encompasses PROVENCE as well.

MILAWA, significant Australian wine region in north east VICTORIA. Brown Brothers is the best-known producer.

MILDEW. See DOWNY MILDEW and POWDERY MILDEW.

MILLAU, CÔTES DE, promoted to VDQS status in 1993.

MILLERANDAGE, abnormal FRUIT SET in the vine which is shown by the joint presence of large and small berries in the same bunch. This mixed berry size is due to differences in seed number, with the small berries being seedless. They may be known as 'hen and chicken' or 'pumpkins and peas'. The condition is due either to inclement weather at FLOWERING, which affects some varieties, Gewürztraminer, for example, more than others, or alternatively to BORON deficiency, or FANLEAF DEGENERATION. The cause of millerandage is poor fertilization of the ovary by pollen.

Millerandage can cause a major loss of YIELD, especially where the proportion of small berries is high. Wine-makers have, however, been known to welcome the condition, as there is a widely held view that small BERRY SIZE makes better-quality wine. A common New World example of this belief is the Chardonnay CLONE developed at DAVIS which is known as both 1A and Mendoza. This clone is subject to millerandage with cool flowering, but is appreciated for its beneficial effect on wine quality by some wine-makers in New Zealand, Australia, and California. R.E.S.

Galet, P., *Précis de viticulture* (4th edn., Montpellier, 1983).

MILLÉSIME is French for VINTAGE. A vintage-dated wine is therefore said to be **millésimé**.

MINERALS and **mineral elements**, the dissolved non-organic salts in grapes and wine. Many are elements essential for vine growth. These can vary enormously between different vineyards and production methods but in grapes would typically include—in addition to the elements carbon, hydrogen, and OXYGEN which are essential for growth—in declining concentrations, POTASSIUM, NITROGEN, PHOSPHORUS, SULPHUR, MAGNESIUM, CALCIUM (as 200 to 2,000 mg/l in grape juice), followed by BORON, MANGANESE, IRON at 20 to 50 mg/l, and then COPPER, ZINC, and molybdenum at less than 5 mg/l. Analyses also show the presence of many other elements—sodium, chloride, rubidium, silicon, cobalt, LEAD, arsenic, and others—each with unknown or nil function. (Notable is wine's high ratio of potassium to sodium, as advocated for cardiac patients' diets, and the relatively low concentration of iron, despite the traditional view that wine is an important source of this particular mineral.)

Concentrations of minerals in wine can vary between low parts per million to fractions of parts per billion and may reflect the substances present in the soils, whether naturally or as a result of FERTILIZERS or PESTICIDES (although see VINE NUTRITION and SOIL AND WINE QUALITY for more detail of the relationship between minerals in soil and minerals in wine).

The mineral content of wine was once determined by drying and then ashing a given quantity of liquid and finally weighing the residue. Today there are instruments and techniques which can measure quantities in fractional parts per billion, a capability that has resulted in the establishment of legal limits for components that were undetectable as recently as the 1970s. Carbon dating and NUCLEAR MAGNETIC RESONANCE are just two of the powerful analytical tools which may be applied to wine and involve measuring mineral content. A.D.W. & B.G.C.

MINERAL VINE NUTRITION. See VINE NUTRITION.

MINERVOIS, western LANGUEDOC appellation for some lush reds, together with some rosé and white, produced on nearly 4,000 ha/9,880 acres of varied inland terrain in the Aude and eastern Hérault *départements* (see map on p. 552). The appellation takes its name from the village of Minerve, scene of one of the bloodiest sieges of the Cathar sect in the 13th century. There is considerable archaeological evidence that the Romans practised viticulture here. Cicero records the dispatch of wine to Rome from the *pagus minerbensis* and La Livinière, the Minervois village with the most reasonable claim to its own appellation, is said to take its name from *cella vinaria*, Latin for 'wine cellar'. More recently, the vineyards of Minervois were invaded first by PHYLLOXERA and then by the CARIGNAN vine, whose influence is being successively reduced.

Since 1985, when Minervois was granted APPELLATION CONTRÔLÉE status, strenuous efforts have been made to upgrade overall quality, and a number of both CO-OPERATIVES and individual wine producers have made considerable investments both in winery equipment and in planting better vine varieties. By 1999 Carignan must account for no more than 40 per cent of the blend, with Grenache, Syrah, and Mourvèdre accounting for at least 60 per cent (although other traditional Languedoc varieties are also allowed). Various combinations of Bourboulenc, Rolle (Vermentino), Maccabéo, Roussanne, Marsanne, and Grenache Blanc are responsible for the varied quality and character of white Minervois, the first two being best suited to the south eastern part of the appellation closest to the Mediterranean, while the last two perform best in western, Atlantic-influenced sites. White Minervois is increasingly aromatic. Experiments with BARREL MATURATION began in the late 1980s, and there are even attempts to revive an ancient SHERRY-like style once called Vin Noble du Minervois.

For red wines most Carignan is vinified using full or partial CARBONIC MACERATION for five to 12 days, while other red wine varieties are given longer in the fermentation vat, with frequent pumping over or punching down to encourage EXTRACTION of PHENOLICS. DESTEMMING is slowly being introduced for these varieties, and red wines have traditionally been given at least a year in cement tanks or large old casks. Small barrel maturation is slowly becoming more common, but there are constraints on investment in a region whose selling prices have been relatively low.

Many other vine varieties are being planted in the varied soils of the region—only about 5,000 ha of the total 18,000 classified as Minervois produce wine that is declared as appellation wine; much of the rest produces VINS DE PAYS. The official maximum yield for Minervois is 50 hl/ha (2.8 tons/acre) for red wine and 60 hl/ha for white, while yields can rise to 90 hl/ha for most vins de pays.

In the north of the region at higher ALTITUDE, Minervois's

lowest-yielding vineyards are to be found on the south-facing flanks of the Cévennes, and in the extreme north east of the region some of France's rarest, and possibly most delicate, VIN DOUX NATUREL is produced: MUSCAT DE ST-JEAN-DE-MINERVOIS.

MINHO, province in northern PORTUGAL, named after the river (called Mino in Spanish) which forms its boundary with Spain (see map on p. 750). The VINHO VERDE region includes the Minho and much of the Douro Litoral province.

MINIMAL PRUNING, also known as zero pruning, viticultural technique developed by the Commonwealth Scientific and Industrial Research Organization (CSIRO) in Australia whereby the vines are essentially left without any form of PRUNING from one year to the next, other than a trim underneath typically. The technique has particular application to higher-yielding, low-cost vineyards in warmer areas but is also being evaluated in some cooler regions producing high-quality wines, especially Australia's COONAWARRA region.

The technique was developed and popularized in the late 1970s and 1980s but its scientific interest can be traced back to a difference of opinion between two eminent viticultural scientists in the late 1960s. When Professor Nelson Shaulis of Cornell University in New York state was visiting the CSIRO at Merbein in Victoria, Australia, he debated with Dr Allan Antcliff whether an unpruned vine might die. A SULTANA (Thompson Seedless) vine was left unpruned and produced a large crop which ripened satisfactorily. At this time there was interest in MECHANICAL PRUNING, and in many ways minimal pruning is a natural extension of that method. The technique has been extensively evaluated for vine varieties for both wine production and DRYING GRAPES and in both hot and cooler climates.

One might imagine that an unpruned plant would exhaust itself and die if its growth and cropping were not controlled by pruning. Interestingly, the opposite is true. Although vines are not killed by pruning, it has been shown to have a weakening effect on them. Furthermore, zero winter pruning is what vines experience in their natural state, and primitive vines survived in the wild for millennia before they were first cultivated by man and pruned. A feature of unpruned, or minimally pruned, vines is that there are many short shoots, whereas a pruned vine has fewer shoots which in turn grow more vigorously. A minimally pruned vine typically produces more fruit than one conventionally pruned, especially in the first year or so of minimal pruning. Ripening of this increased crop can be delayed, and if RIPENING is inadequate, due to cool weather for example, then wine quality can be reduced. In hot regions a harvest delay of a week or so is of little consequence, but in cooler climates the delay may be disastrous.

Minimally pruned vines look extremely wild and untidy compared to vines pruned by hand. After several years old wood builds up in the centre of the thicket that is an unpruned vine, and this can exacerbate the threat of pests such as MEALY BUG and diseases such as POWDERY MILDEW. During the growing season, however, the vine's appearance may not be too different from that of normally pruned vines. Where minimal pruning is practised in hotter, dry climates, shoots stop growing quite early in the summer because there are so many shoots relative to the amount of root CARBOHYDRATE reserves and soil water supply, and so the CANOPY can be relatively open with good fruit exposure. Where the climate is cooler and more humid and the vines are growing in fertile, moist soil, however, shoots may continue to grow, and the bunches of grapes may effectively be buried under several layers of leaves. This shaded CANOPY MICROCLIMATE may then result in reduced colour and flavour in the grapes and eventual wine. R.E.S.

Coombe, B. G., and Dry, P. R. (eds.), *Viticulture, ii: Practices* (Adelaide, 1992).

MIREVAL is the large village that gives its name to Muscat de Mireval, the sweet golden VIN DOUX NATUREL appellation that adjoins and is somewhat overshadowed by FRONTIGNAN to the west of it. Production has been almost exclusively in the hands of the CO-OPERATIVE, called La Cave de Rabelais in honour of the only well-known writer to have mentioned it. The wine is virtually indistinguishable from Frontignan and to those who live outside Mireval there seems little justification for Muscat de Mireval's independent existence, although soils here may be a little more calcareous than those of Frontignan.

MIS(E) EN BOUTEILLE is French for bottled. A wine that is **mis(e) en bouteille au château** is CHÂTEAU BOTTLED, while **mis(e) en bouteille au domaine** is DOMAINE BOTTLED. **Mis(e) en bouteille du château/domaine** is a term used by CO-OPERATIVES for their bottlings of wines they vinified from the grapes of individual properties. The BOTTLING operation is often referred to as **la mise**.

MISKET, Bulgarian grape-scented white grape variety that, despite its name, has no member of the MUSCAT family in its antecedents. It is a crossing of the native DIMIAT with Riesling and is a speciality of the sub-Balkan region (see BULGARIA). **Red Misket**, also used for perfumed white wines, is probably a pink-berried mutant of Misket and is relatively well established in Bulgaria with numerous local subvarieties such as **Sliven Misket** and **Varna Misket**. Misket is a speciality of the Sungurlare region.

MISSION, the original black grape variety planted for sacramental purposes by Franciscan MISSIONARIES in MEXICO, the south west of the UNITED STATES, and CALIFORNIA in the 17th and 18th centuries. Mission was presumably of Spanish origin, imported to America by the conquistadores, and is important as a survivor from the earliest VINIFERA vine varieties to be cultivated in the Americas. It is identical to the PAIS of Chile, is a darker-skinned version of the CRIOLLA CHICA of Argentina, and is thought by some to be the same as the MONICA of Spain and Sardinia. It was an important variety in California until the spread of PHYLLOXERA in the 1880s and there were still more than 1,000 acres/405 ha grown in the early 1990s, mainly in the south of the state, and used for sweet wines. The wine made from Mission is not particularly distinguished but the variety has enormous historical significance.

Pinney, T., *A History of Wine in America* (Berkeley, Calif., 1989).

MISSIONARIES have doubtless played a role in the establishment of viticulture all over the world and, particularly, in documenting these achievements. Missions and missionaries had a particularly profound effect, however, on the history of wine production in much of Latin America, in California, in New Zealand, and, to a certain extent, in Japan.

Soon after European colonization of South and Central America, missionaries, particularly Jesuit missionaries, established missions alongside more commercial ventures and, whatever the commercial interest in establishing viticulture, the missionaries grew vines to provide some wine for the EUCHARIST (although see SOUTH AMERICA, history). Both Argentina and Chile date their wine industries from the first successful attempts to cultivate the vine at missions in the foothills on either side of the Andes in the late 16th century, and by the 17th century Peru's viticulture, which probably pre-dated that of both Chile and Argentina, was concentrated around Jesuit missions in coastal valleys. Mexico, however, is the Americas' oldest wine-producing country, and grape seeds were planted almost as soon as Cortés had landed there. Jesuit missionaries are believed to have been the first to cultivate vines for the specific purpose of wine-making in Baja California (northern Mexico) in the 1670s. It was not until the late 18th century that they established their series of missions up the west coast of what is now the American state of CALIFORNIA, and brought with them the so-called MISSION grape from Mexico.

Two centuries earlier, in 1545, Portuguese Jesuit missionaries had introduced wine to the feudal lords of southern JAPAN, who developed a taste for wine and continued to import it. Much more recently, it was Jesuit missionaries who sowed the seeds of the modern wine industry in CHINA.

At much the same time or even earlier, in the early 19th century, French Marist missionaries played a significant role in New Zealand's wine history by introducing vine cuttings from Europe, brought expressly to provide sacramental wine. The first Catholic bishop of the South Pacific, from Lyons, arrived with cuttings in 1838 and by 1842 they were reported to be performing well. The Mission winery in Hawkes Bay, founded by Catholic priests in 1851, is still in production and run as an adjunct to a Marist seminary.

See also RELIGION and MONKS AND MONASTERIES.

Cooper, M., *The Wine and Vineyards of New Zealand* (Auckland, 1984).
Seward, D., *Monks and Wine* (London, 1979).

MISTELA is the Spanish term and **mistelle** the French for a mixture of grape juice and alcohol. The FERMENTATION process is arrested by the addition of alcohol, leaving a sweet, stable, alcoholic liquid arguably less complex than an equivalent wine that owes its alcohol content to fermentation. It was the commercially vigorous and adaptable Dutch who developed this sort of drink, so much more stable over long journeys than wine (see DUTCH WINE TRADE). In Spain such usefully stable sweetening agents are used in blending wines such as SHERRY and MÁLAGA, but are also sometimes sold, like France's PINEAU DES CHARENTES, for drinking as aperitif. Other examples of wines that either comprise or may include mistelle are all those that qualify as VIN DE LIQUEUR, some VIN DOUX NATUREL, Australia's LIQUEUR MUSCAT, and Liqueur Tokay.

MITES, minute insects which feed on leaf surface cells and which can be an important grapevine pest world-wide. Those that feed on the leaves include grape (or grapeleaf) rust mite (*Calepitrimerus vitis*); Pacific spider mite (*Tetranychus pacificus*), which is the most destructive; two-spotted spider mite, which is only occasionally found on grapes; and Willamette mite (*Eotetranychus willametti*). Mite feeding slows PHOTOSYNTHESIS and can reduce grape RIPENING. Bunch mite (*Brevipalpus californicus* and *Brevipalpus lewisi*) causes black scars on bunch and berry stems, thereby spoiling TABLE GRAPES in California.

In Europe red mite (*Panonychus ulmi*) and two types of yellow mite (*Eotetranychus carpini* and *Tetranychus urticae*) cause the most damage. They feed on green parts of the vine and can affect FRUIT SET and CANE RIPENING, as well as reducing leaf health.

Predatory mites often keep these mites sufficiently under control, although it is important not to destroy them with other sprays. Sulphur sprays applied for erinose or POWDERY MILDEW are effective on some types of mite. White oil applied before BUDBREAK or miticides during summer can control mites. See also ERINOSE MITE. M.J.E.

MITTELRHEIN, small wine region in GERMANY of predominantly local interest. Most of the vines of Germany's 730-ha/1,800-acre Mittelrhein region grow within sight of the river RHINE, often looking down upon it from a considerable height (see map on p. 442). The first commercial vineyards start about 8 km/5 miles south of Bonn and none is found on the west bank of the river until Koblenz is reached, 58 km/36 miles upstream. Thereafter, they climb both sides of the Rhine gorge, wherever site, the MESOCLIMATE, and much hard work make vine-growing a more or less viable exercise. The temperature is raised by the large volume of water in the Rhine (see TOPOGRAPHY), and in summer there is usually enough rain to maintain the health and strength of the vines on their porous, steep, slate-covered slopes. Most winters are mild and spring, arriving early, starts a growing season which, for the RIESLING vine, lasts into late autumn.

Riesling covers 75 per cent of the area under vine. At its best, the wine is characterized by ripe, firm ACIDITY, and at least a quarter is dry (TROCKEN or HALBTROCKEN). The greatest amount of good wine comes from south of Koblenz, at Spay,

Boppard, and at Bacharach, a small town once famous as a market for wine destined to be shipped down the Rhine to northern Europe and beyond. Riesling from the vineyards near Bacharach has a strong, attractive taste from the soil, and in its simplest form converts well into good sparkling wine. MÜLLER-THURGAU wine made from a low yield is often more concentrated in flavour than it is in the RHEINHESSEN or in the south of the PFALZ.

The Mittelrhein vineyard is slowly shrinking, giving way in the north of the region to urban development and in the south to easier and more lucrative ways of earning a living. Little wine is exported, or even leaves the region, but there are a few private estates which are of sufficient standing to be members of the prestigious VDP association of German high-quality estates. About a quarter of the harvest is processed by co-operative cellars at Bacharach and Oberwesel, and grape-growing is very much a part-time occupation, or simply a weekend hobby. Costs are most likely to be covered if the producer sells directly to tourists. The Rhine gorge is spectacular in parts, and deeply involved in the story of Germany, both mythical and real. Its admirers keep the local wine industry in business. I.J.

MOELLEUX, French term meaning literally like (bone) marrow, or mellow. Wines described as *moelleux* are usually medium sweet rather than the very rich BOTRYTIZED wines which may be described as LIQUOREUX.

MOËT & CHANDON, Champagne house producing the single most important champagne BRAND in the world, and part of the vast LVMH group. The Champagne house was founded by Claude Moët, born in 1683 to a family which had settled in the Champagne district during the 14th century. He inherited vineyards and became a wine merchant, establishing his own firm in 1743. He was succeeded by his son Claude-Louis Nicolas and his grandson Jean-Rémy Moët, who used his impressive connections to open up international markets for his wine. Jean-Rémy was a close personal friend of Napoleon Bonaparte, and was awarded the cross of the Légion d'Honneur in the final years of the emperor's rule. In 1832 Jean-Rémy handed over the firm to his son Victor and his son-in-law Pierre-Gabriel Chandon. At the same time, the company acquired the Abbey of Hautvillers and its vineyards. In 1962, Moët & Chandon's shares were quoted for the first time on the Paris Stock Exchange, leading to a period of considerable expansion. First, Moët bought shares in Ruinart Père et Fils, the oldest Champagne house, in 1963. Five years later, it acquired a 34 per cent stake in Parfums Christian Dior, increasing this to a 50 per cent stake shortly afterwards. In 1970 Moët took control of Champagne Mercier, a popular brand in France, and capped it all by buying out Dior and merging with HENNESSY in 1971 to form the holding company Moët-Hennessy. The acquisitions continued unabated, including, in 1981, a stake in the American importers Schieffelin which incorporated a 49 per cent share in H. SICHEL Söhne in Germany, producers of BLUE NUN, until the Sichel family bought it back in 1992. This American investment also involves the Simi winery in Sonoma, Moët having established Domaine Chandon, a seminal sparkling California winemaking establishment in the Napa Valley, in 1973.

This was by no means the company's first venture into the New World. Bodegas Chandon was established in Argentina in 1960, and Provifin followed in Brazil in 1974, both companies making considerable amounts of wine for the domestic market, much of it sparkling. In Germany too, a SEKT business had been established in the form of Chandon GmbH in 1968. In 1985 the group founded Domaine Chandon, Australia, to make a premium sparkling wine sold as Domaine Chandon in Australia and Green Point in the UK, and in 1987 established a company in Spain for the production of a CAVA called Cava Chandon (Torre del Gall outside Spain).

In 1987 Moët-Hennessy merged with the Louis Vuitton Group, makers of luxury leather goods and owners of Champagne houses VEUVE CLICQUOT, Canard-Duchêne, and Henriot, and Givenchy perfumes. By 1993 the LVMH group owned seven Champagne houses: Moët & Chandon, Mercier, Ruinart, Veuve Clicquot, Canard-Duchêne, Henriot, and Pommery (having briefly bought Lanson and stripped it of its extensive vineyard holdings before selling it on). Of these, Moët & Chandon and Mercier are run most closely in tandem.

Moët, the brand, continues to sell at over twice the rate of its nearest competitors and claims that one in four bottles of Champagne exported comes from the house. It is the leading brand of champagne in most world markets with a share of the champagne market in the United States that can be as high as 50 per cent. Non-vintage blends have been inconsistent, but at their best are fine, well-balanced champagnes. In 1994 an innovative and informative back label was introduced for non-vintage Brut impérial. The house prestige cuvée is named after Dom PÉRIGNON, the legendary figure of the Abbey of Hautvillers, and broke new ground in terms of packaging, pricing, and qualitative ambitions when it was launched in 1936. S.A.

MOLDAVIA. Important wine-producing member of the CIS now known as MOLDOVA.

MOLDOVA, one of the smallest members of the CIS but possibly the one with the greatest potential for wine quality and range, thanks to its extensive vineyards, temperate continental climate, and gently undulating landscape sandwiched between eastern ROMANIA and the UKRAINE. Moldova, the Romanian name for what was known as Moldavia when it was part of the Soviet Union, was the name adopted on independence in 1991 since Romanians constitute 65 per cent of the population, and Romanian is the national language in the republic. Moldova is more 'European', and has more land planted to vines (some of them European varieties introduced by French colonists at the end of the 19th century), than any other CIS member. Ten per cent of the country is vineyard, although grape products other than wine are also produced.

History

Archaeological evidence confirms that this area, Bessarabia, has been growing vines for at least 4,000 or 5,000 years. Grape seeds dating back to 2800 BC have been found, as well as AMPHORAE, and the well-documented voyages to this region by the Greeks and then Romans can only have encouraged this particular branch of agriculture. HERODOTUS visited the colonies of Ancient GREECE at the mouth of the rivers Dnepr and Dnestr in the middle of the 5th century BC and reported that wine drinking was already common there.

After the feudal state of Moldova was formed in the second half of the 14th century AD, trade was established with RUSSIA, UKRAINE, and Poland, and Moldovan viticulture developed rapidly.

The Turkish occupation of Bessarabia (or Bogdan as it was known in the Ottoman empire) was a severe blow to Moldovan wine production (see ISLAM), and it was only after the country was annexed to Russia in 1812 that the industry was revived. By 1837 vineyards totalled 13,000 ha/32,110 acres and total wine production was 100,000 hl/2.6 million gal. Moldova, with neighbouring Walachia, formed the basis for independent Romania in the middle of the 19th century. In 1891 Moldova's vineyard totalled 107,000 ha but was severely ravaged by PHYLLOXERA and OIDIUM until GRAFTING was adopted in 1906. The tsars provided incentives to grow European vine varieties which still predominate. In 1940 the country was annexed by Russia and the vineyards were once again devastated by the effects of the Second World War. Energetic centralization and reconstruction had restored the country's vineyard total to 190,000 ha by 1958.

Climate and geography

Much of Moldova is low and hilly, rarely rising above 350 m/1,150 ft above sea level and with a gradual descent towards the Black Sea in the south. The climate is ideal for viticulture, with average summer temperatures of around 20 °C/68 °F. Spring (and occasionally winter) FROST can be a problem but the active temperature summation is between 2,700 °C in the north and 3,400 °C in the south. Annual rainfall is between 400 and 600 mm/23 in. The main rivers are the Dnestr, Prut, and Reut.

More than 90 per cent of vineyards are in southern or central Moldova, more than half the total area belonging to the state farms, with vineyards representing about a third of the land under their control. The remainder of the vineyards belong to individuals or collective farms, in the throes of sometimes painful and complex privatization.

Viticulture

Unlike the wine regions of Russia to the north east, Moldova is able to grow the great majority of its vines, 70 per cent, without WINTER PROTECTION against frost damage and most vines are trained high. Fewer than two per cent of Moldova's 182,000 ha of vines (in the early 1990s) are irrigated and there is a high level of MECHANIZATION, reflecting grapes' importance to the Moldovan agricultural economy. Most vines are grafted, with the most common ROOTSTOCK being SO4.

Vine varieties

Moldova has a more European range of grape varieties than any other ex-Soviet republic. In the early 1990s it included ALIGOTÉ, FETEASCA, RKATSITELI, SAUVIGNON BLANC, MUSCAT OTTONEL, CHARDONNAY, PINOT GRIS, RIESLING, and GEWÜRZTRAMINER among grape varieties for white wine and CABERNET SAUVIGNON, GAMAY, Fréaux (a red-fleshed TEINTURIER), SAPERAVI, MERLOT, PINOT NOIR, and Black Sereksia for red wines, as well as a range of varieties for TABLE GRAPES. There were also a number of new varieties specially bred for their resistance to pests and diseases: Viorica, Doina, Negru de Yaloven, white Sukhomlinski, and Golubok. Indigenous varieties include PLAVAI, also known as Belan and Plakun.

Wines produced

Acid levels are good to high, ENRICHMENT rare, MALOLACTIC FERMENTATION haphazard, and winery hardware and hygiene lag many years behind what the west has come to regard as the norm. PASTEURIZATION has been regarded as a panacea. In 1992 there were only two westernized bottling lines, for example, and wine FAULTS were commonplace. Potential is exciting, however, especially since commercially popular vine varieties are in place. The republic's total wine production was more than 1 million hl/26.4 million gal in 1990, very approximately the same quantity as GEORGIA and ARMENIA but with much more European styles and structure. Sparkling wine production is important, particularly at Cricova, while sherry styles are a promising speciality of the Yaloveni winery. The Moldovan range also includes answers to Australia's LIQUEUR MUSCAT. Most saleable of Moldova's wines, however, are probably those based on Chardonnay, Sauvignon Blanc, and Cabernet Sauvignon. Reds made in the early 1960s such as Negru de Purkar and Roshu de Purkar were exported to and acclaimed in Britain as the Soviet Union was breaking up. Pucar in the east of the country is a source of fine, age-worthy red wines. Tarakliya in the south, almost on the border with Ukraine, is a source of fruity Cabernet Sauvignon from old vines.

Industry organization

Moldova has been less damaged than most eastern European wine producers by the disappearance of the centralized Soviet wine market. Its wines are highly prized within the CIS and are customarily bartered with fellow republics, notably with Ukraine for grain. Since independence, some Moldovan wineries have wooed outside expertise and the Australian firm PENFOLDS invested in Moldova in 1993. This is archetypal FLYING WINE-MAKER territory. Moldova is in a state of gradual privatization and particularly frenetic reconstruction. There are plans for increased vine plantings, and for some sort of controlled APPELLATION system. V.R.

Godelman, Y. M., *Ecology of Moldavia's Viticulture* (Russian) (Kishinev, 1990).

Lupashcu, M. F., 'The Soviet Socialist Republic of Moldavia' (Russian), in A. I. Timush (ed.), *Encyclopaedia of Viticulture* (Kishinev, 1986).

Makarenko, P. P., 'The principal stages of the development of Moldavia's viticulture' (Russian), *Sadovodstvo i vinogradarstvo Moldavii*, 5 (1987), 21–5.

MOLETTE is a common white grape variety used particularly for the sparkling wines of SEYSSEL in SAVOIE. The base wine produced is neutral and much improved by the addition of some ROUSSETTE.

MOLINARA, red grape variety grown in the Veneto region of north east Italy, particularly for VALPOLICELLA. Its wines tend to be high in acidity and it is considerably less planted than the more substantial CORVINA.

MOLISE, after the Valle d'AOSTA Italy's smallest and least populated region, is a poor and mountainous area situated south of the ABRUZZI in the south east of Italy. Poor, and further impoverished by a continuous emigration of manpower for almost a century, the region has only 9,500 ha/23,465 acres of vineyards with an annual production of 500,000 hl/13.2 million gal, a mere twentieth of the production of neighbouring APULIA. The production is almost entirely in the hands of CO-OPERATIVE wineries, which sell virtually all of the wine in bulk, bottling only a small fraction of what they produce.

The proximity of the Abruzzi—to which the Molise was joined administratively until the 1960s—has left its mark on Molise's viticulture with the two predominant vine varieties now being MONTEPULCIANO d'Abruzzo and TREBBIANO D'ABRUZZO. There are attempts to diversify, however, with the planting of grape varieties from southern Italy such as FIANO and GRECO DI TUFO and of more international varieties such as CHARDONNAY, RIESLING, SYLVANER, and PINOT BLANC. Specific wine objectives—whether to produce sparkling wine, DOC wines, pétillant, or sweet table wines—are few, however. The only DOC of any significance is Biferno, which may be red, rosé, and white, and is produced in the uplands of the regional capital of Campobasso. Reds and pinks are based on Montepulciano grapes with some red AGLIANICO and white TREBBIANO TOSCANO; Biferno Bianco is based on Trebbiano Toscano, with additions of BOMBINO and MALVASIA.

The best wines of the region, produced by the De Majo Norante winery, have chosen the VINO DA TAVOLA route in response to the world's lack of interest in Molise's DOCs.

D.T.

Anderson, B., *The Wine Atlas of Italy* (London and New York, 1990).
Gleave, D., *The Wines of Italy* (London and New York, 1989).

MONASTERIES. See MONKS AND MONASTERIES.

MONASTRELL is the main Spanish name for the black grape variety known in France as Mourvèdre and also as Mataro. See MOURVÈDRE for more details.

MONBAZILLAC, potentially serious sweet white wine appellation within the BERGERAC district in South West France immediately south of the town of Bergerac on the left bank of the DORDOGNE. Monbazillac has a long history of sweet wine production, which here seems to pre-date the influence of the DUTCH WINE TRADE (one property's label still boasts 'Reputé en Hollande depuis 1513').

Like SAUTERNES it is made from Sémillon, Sauvignon, and Muscadelle grapes and the vineyards lie on the left bank of an important river close to its confluence with a small tributary, in this case the Gardonette. This environment favours autumn morning mists and the development of NOBLE ROT but, as was the case in much of the 1960s and 1970s in Sauternes, only a few producers are willing or able to take the risks involved in trying to produce fully BOTRYTIZED wines. In a determined quest for quality MECHANICAL HARVESTING was banned from 1993 and a minimum of TRIS through the vineyard insisted upon. The exceptional VINTAGE of 1990 had already inspired some producers to make top-quality botrytized wines which offer exceptional value. Official statistics suggest that in this vintage average YIELDS were less than 20 hl/ha (1.1 tons/acre) (markedly less than in Sauternes, although the declaration of some wines as Côtes de Bergerac may have artificially depressed the Monbazillac figure). Basic maximum permitted yields here are 40 hl/ha, as opposed to the 25 hl/ha in Sauternes. About 2,500 ha/6,170 acres of vineyard are dedicated to Monbazillac, almost twice the area of the Sauternes appellation.

The POTENTIAL ALCOHOL must be at least 14.5 per cent. The most conscientious producers have quite rightly relied on nature for the richness of their often markedly orange-tinged wines. Too much Monbazillac, however, has been simply a sweetened, heavy wine, sometimes redolent of SULPHUR DIOXIDE, blended and bottled by a NÉGOCIANT who has little passion for the possibilities that exist within this region. From 1993 there should be a clear distinction between serious sweet Monbazillac and early-picked dry white wine which may be sold as Bergerac Sec.

Brook, S., *Liquid Gold* (London, 1987).

MONDAVI, important family in the recent history of CALIFORNIA wine, with Robert Mondavi (1913–) in particular doing more than anyone to raise international awareness of California as a source of top-quality wine.

Robert's father Cesare came to the USA in 1906 from the MARCHES on Italy's east coast. He and his Italian wife Rosa ran a boarding house for miners in Minnesota before moving to Lodi in California's SAN JOAQUIN VALLEY in 1922 whence, throughout PROHIBITION, they shipped grapes back east to America's temporarily swollen band of HOME WINE-MAKERS. Immediately after Repeal Cesare turned to wine-making and was joined in the late 1930s by his sons Robert and Peter.

As early as 1936 the Mondavis made their crucial move out of the hot Central Valley (leaving GALLO to build up the world's largest winery there) into the cooler NAPA Valley where they were determined to make table wines, rather than the then much more popular dessert wines. After rapid expansion from their base at the Sunny St Helena winery, they acquired the nearby Charles KRUG winery in 1943. Robert

Robert **Mondavi**—with the Napa Valley at his feet.

Mondavi's obsession with constant fine tuning of wine quality grew here, inspired by old bottles from the Inglenook winery, and guided by oenologist André TCHELISTCHEFF. During the 1950s he became increasingly fascinated by the CABERNET SAUVIGNON grape and in 1962 visited BORDEAUX for the first time, a seminal visit which was to convince him of the necessary conjunction between fine wine and gracious living.

This led to disputes with his younger brother Peter which were exacerbated by Cesare's death in 1959 so that by 1965 Robert was excluded from the Charles Krug winery, where Peter remained, and won compensation only after a long and bitter lawsuit. The opening of the Robert Mondavi winery on the Oakville highway in 1966, strikingly Californian thanks to architect Cliff May, marked the beginning of a new chapter not just for the Mondavis but for California wine. Just as Baron Philippe de ROTHSCHILD had signalled a new era for Bordeaux when he took over at Ch MOUTON-ROTHSCHILD in the 1920s, so the Robert Mondavi winery was at the forefront of developing VARIETAL wines based on Europe's most famous vine varieties (each, innovatively, made differently); continual experimentation with different BARRELS, TOAST, FINING, and FILTRATION regimes; special Reserve bottlings; comparative tastings with France's most famous wines; wine TOURISM; and cultural events associated with the winery and its wines.

It was therefore no surprise when in 1979 (the same year that a winery in Woodbridge, back in the Central Valley, was acquired for a high-volume, lower-priced range) a joint venture was announced between Robert Mondavi and Baron Philippe; Opus One, with its own lavish winery since 1992, is a Napa Valley Cabernet-based wine made jointly by Tim Mondavi and Mouton's wine-maker. During the 1980s Robert Mondavi tried to extricate himself from day-to-day operations, which now also include the separate Vichon and Byron wineries, as well as a range of Robert Mondavi CARNEROS wines made using more ORGANIC VITICULTURE methods. His children Michael, Tim, and Marcia divided up responsibilities and left him more time for an itinerary of tireless evangelism on behalf of California wine, and for fighting, with some success, the force described as neo-Prohibitionist in the late 1980s and early 1990s. The Mondavi Mission subsidized academic research into wine's place in society and history.

Although the Robert Mondavi winery had considerable assets in the form of 1,500 acres/607 ha of prime Napa Valley vineyard, and produced 700,000 cases of Napa Valley wine a year in the early 1990s (more than any other producer), borrowings forced this family-owned winery to make a public share issue in 1993.

Laube, J., 'Robert Mondavi: scenes from a life in wine', *Wine Spectator*, 18/3 (1993), 16–27.
Ray, C., *Robert Mondavi of the Napa Valley* (London, 1984).

MONDEUSE NOIRE, one of the oldest and most distinctive red grape varieties of SAVOIE, bringing an Italianate depth of colour and bite to the region in contrast to the softer reds produced by the Gamay imported only after PHYLLOXERA. The juicy, peppery wines are powerfully flavoured and coloured and are some of Savoie's few to respond well to careful small oak ageing (although when grown prolifically on Savoie's more fertile, lower sites Mondeuse can easily be a dull wine too, which may explain why the variety has been underrated). Some authorities argue that Mondeuse is identical to the REFOSCO of FRIULI. The wines are certainly extremely similar and the extent of the House of Savoy in the 16th century would provide an explanation, but several respected Italian ampelographers dispute this theory.

Total French plantings of Mondeuse Noire fell sharply in the 1970s, from nearly 1,000 ha/2,470 acres to under 200 ha but it is to be hoped that there will be a local renaissance in this characterful variety, much of whose produce is sold as a varietal Vin de Savoie unusually capable of ageing. It may also be blended with Pinot Noir and Gamay in BUGEY.

A **Mondeuse Blanche** can occasionally be found in Savoie, and Bugey, where it may be called Dongine.

MONICA, red grape variety grown in great quantity on SARDINIA, where some varietal Monica di Sardegna is thus labelled. The Italian vineyard census of 1990 found more than 6,000 ha/14,820 acres of Monica in 1990, but nearly 4,000 ha had been pulled out since 1982. It is thought to have originated in Spain (although it is not known in modern Spain) and some ampelographers think it may be identical to the historic MISSION of California. Its wines are undistinguished and should be drunk young.

MONKS AND MONASTERIES. Wine has always had spiritual and religious significance (see RELIGION AND WINE), and just as wine is an integral part of monastic life, so monks and monasteries have long been regarded as playing a crucial part in wine history.

While wine and the vine played a prominent role in most religions of the eastern Mediterranean during antiquity, it was in Christian religious symbolism and practice that it achieved particular significance, as an essential element of

Monks and wine, a well-established combination by the late 18th century.

the EUCHARIST. Such Christian imagery undoubtedly built on earlier Jewish symbolism, in which the vine or vineyard was used as one of the favourite symbols for the nation of ISRAEL in the Old Testament. The adoption of Christianity as the state religion of the Roman Empire during the 4th century AD (see Ancient ROME) meant that wine was to attain a position of the utmost ideological prominence in European society. This religious significance of wine is widely regarded as of particular importance at two stages in its history: first, in ensuring the survival of viticulture following the collapse of the Western Roman Empire; and secondly in the introduction of viticulture and wine-making to the NEW WORLD.

It has generally been argued that Christian communities' need for grape-based wine with which to celebrate the Eucharist was one of the main factors enabling viticulture and wine-making to survive in western Europe following the fall of Rome in AD 476. It is assumed that when transport was difficult, it was easier for isolated Christian communities in northern Europe to cultivate their own vines rather than import wine. Moreover, monks, with their literacy, their continuity of land ownership, and the time for experimentation, are widely regarded as the only individuals capable of nurturing viticultural and wine-making traditions.

There is, however, little firm evidence for this hypothesis. The Germanic tribes which overran the western Roman Empire were known to be fond of wine, and there is little reason to suppose that they consciously destroyed vast expanses of European vineyards. This is supported by the evidence of surviving elements of the Gallo-Roman aristocracy, who recorded the continued cultivation of vines during the second half of the fifth century in areas of GAUL such as Clermont-Ferrand. Bishops and monks certainly did own vineyards and organized the production of wine throughout the period from the sixth to the 10th century, but it is significant that in most instances they appear to have gained their vineyards mainly as grants from royalty or the secular nobility. This implies that substantial non-monastic vineyards survived and were developed in the aftermath of the Germanic invasions of the 5th century. The real role of monasteries therefore seems not so much to have been in the preservation of a tradition of viticulture following the collapse of Rome, but rather in building up substantial holdings of vineyards, and thus in being among the most important wine-makers of medieval Europe (see also CHARLEMAGNE).

During the Middle Ages monastic houses came to possess some of the most renowned vineyards of Europe. The Benedictines (who, like the Carthusians, are now popularly associated with a high quality liqueur based on distilled wine) thus owned extensive vineyards. In BURGUNDY the monks of Cluny owned most of the vines in what is now GEVREY-CHAMBERTIN, while the abbey of St Vivant owned vineyards in what is now called VOSNE-ROMANÉE. Along the Loire, the Benedictine abbey of St Nicolas held vineyards in what is now ANJOU, and Benedictine monasteries at BOURGUEIL and La Charité also produced quantities of wine. Further south, the Benedictine abbey at ST-POURÇAIN produced what was one of the most renowned wines in medieval France. In CHAMPAGNE the Benedictines held six monasteries in the diocese of Rheims, while in the RHÔNE they held vineyards at both CORNAS and ST PÉRAY. In BORDEAUX they owned such properties as Ch Prieuré in Cantenac (now carrying the suffix of a more recent owner, Alexis LICHINE) and Ch Carbonnieux in GRAVES. In Germany, the abbey at St Maximin in the RUWER was producing about 9,000 l of wine a year towards the end of the 8th century. Although they also owned many German vineyards, especially in RHEINHESSEN and FRANKEN, the Benedictines' best known German wine estate was SCHLOSS JOHANNISBERG in the RHEINGAU.

The more ascetic Cistercians likewise owned numerous important vineyards throughout Europe. The abbey of Clairvaux had extensive vineyards in CHAMPAGNE, and the Cistercians of Pontigny are reputed to have been the first to plant the CHARDONNAY vine in CHABLIS. Their most famous vineyard, however, was the extensive, walled CLOS DE VOUGEOT, and their other holdings in Burgundy included vineyards in MEURSAULT, BEAUNE, and POMMARD. Cistercians also produced fine wines in SANCERRE and PROVENCE. Their most important wine-producing abbey in Germany was KLOSTER EBERBACH in the RHEINGAU, but there were many others, notably at Himmerod and Machern in the MOSEL and Maulbronn in WÜRTTEMBERG. As major landowners throughout Europe, other monastic orders also owned extensive vineyards with, for example, the Carthusians having particular interests in CAHORS, SWITZERLAND, and Trier in the Upper Mosel. See also PRIORATO in north east Spain.

The second main viticultural role widely attributed to the monks was their influence on the development of vineyards in the Americas. In the 17th century, the Jesuits were major wine producers on the coastal plain of PERU, and in the 18th century with the expansion of Spanish interests in CALIFORNIA, the Franciscans, particularly under the leadership of Júnipero Serra, played an important part in introducing viticulture and wine-making to Alta California. Most of the missions established in California during the 1770s and 1780s thus cultivated vines and made wine, with the Mission of San Gabriel becoming particularly famous for its wines, although the majority of mission vineyards nevertheless remained very small.

In the 20th century monastic wine-making continues, despite the earlier effects of the Reformation in northern Europe. Benedictine monks at the abbeys of Gottweig in AUSTRIA, St Hildegard above Rüdesheim in the German Rheingau, and Muri-Gries near Bolzano in ALTO ADIGE in Italy are all currently producing wine, as are Cistercian monks at Heiligenkreuz in Austria and in Spain's NAVARRE, and the Augustinian canons at KLOSTERNEUBURG, also in Austria.

Specific examples

Quite apart from the general role played by monastic orders in the history of wine, certain individual monks and monasteries enjoy vinous fame on their own account. The classic example of this is the work of Dom PÉRIGNON in improving the quality of the wines of Hautvillers in CHAMPAGNE at the end of the 17th century. Three centuries later, Brother Timothy was a renowned wine-making monk for the Christian Brothers in California's NAPA Valley.

See also MISSIONARIES. P.T.H.U.

Cushner, N. P., *Lords of the land: sugar, wine and Jesuit estates of colonial Peru, 1600–1767* (Albany, 1980).

Goodenough, E. R., *Jewish symbols in the Greco-Roman period*, vols. 5 & 6 (New York, 1956).

Seward, D., *Monks and wine* (London, 1979).

Unwin, T., *Wine and the vine: an historical geography of viticulture and the wine trade* (London, 1991).

MONOPOLE, Burgundian term for wholly-owned vineyard or CLIMAT.

MONOPOLIES. State, province, or national exclusive controls over the sale, and occasionally production, of all alcoholic drinks have a long history. In INDIA the manufacture of the sort of wine drunk in the immediately pre-Christian era was a state monopoly. The administrators of many ancient civilizations saw the economic and social advantages of exercising a monopoly over the distribution of wine and beer (the only alcoholic drinks known in antiquity). State monopolies on selling alcoholic drinks have been features in many Scandinavian countries and parts of Canada, although some of these monopolies were, in theory at least, being broken in the 1990s. The disadvantage for consumers can be a restriction of choice, and in many cases severe restrictions on places and conditions of sale whereby wine is sold with all the safeguards and ignominy associated with the distribution of dangerous drugs. The advantage for producers can be that a sale to a monopoly represents a relatively high-volume order. Bulk sale to the Swedish monopoly, for example, was for long an important factor in the export business of PENFOLDS and other Australian companies.

MONOTERPENES. See terpenoids in FLAVOUR COMPOUNDS.

MONTAGNE DE REIMS, the 'mountain of Rheims', or the forested high ground between the CHAMPAGNE towns of Rheims and Épernay. Its lower slopes are famed for the quality of PINOT NOIR base wine they produce.

MONTAGNE ST-ÉMILION, satellite appellation of ST-ÉMILION in Bordeaux.

MONTAGNY, the appellation for white burgundy produced in the communes of Montagny-lès-Buxy, Jully-lès-Buxy, Buxy, and St-Vallerin in the Côte CHALONNAISE. The wines have a little more body and more acidity than other whites from this region. Uniquely, all vineyards may be designated as PREMIER CRU on condition that the wine has an ALCOHOLIC STRENGTH of 11.5 per cent. Much of the production passes through the excellent CO-OPERATIVE founded in 1929 at Buxy which boasts the motto 'with the good wines of Buxy everyone sings and everyone laughs'. J.T.C.M.

MONTALCINO, town in TUSCANY in central Italy famous for its long-lived red BRUNELLO DI MONTALCINO.

MONTECARLO, zone near Lucca in north west TUSCANY which was one of the first to produce modern dry white wines, blending the ubiquitous TREBBIANO with a host of more interesting grape varieties. Reds are made too.

MONTENEGRO, comparatively small southern coastal region of what was YUGOSLAVIA, immediately north of ALBANIA. Montenegro, with 4,000 low-yielding ha/9,880 acres of vineyard, has been most famous for VRANAC, a red grape which gives intense, deeply coloured VARIETAL wine capable of developing a really velvety texture if aged correctly for three or four years in bulk and then bottle. The main producer here was in the early 1990s beginning to use an element of young oak which lent a fashionably soft, spicy edge to the wines. This could allow them to be among the first Yugoslavian wines to break through a price barrier which acted as a powerful disincentive to outside investment even before the outbreak of civil war. A.H.M.

MONTEPULCIANO, name of a vigorous red grape variety planted over much of central Italy (31,000 ha/76,570 acres in 1990), and the name of a town in TUSCANY in central Italy at the centre of the zone producing the highly ranked red wine VINO NOBILE DI MONTEPULCIANO (which is not made from this grape variety, but around the town of the same name).

The grape variety is recommended for 20 of Italy's 95 provinces but is most widely planted in the ABRUZZI, where it is responsible for the often excellent value Montepulciano d'Abruzzo, and in the MARCHES, where it is a principal ingredient in such reds as Rosso Conero and Rosso Piceno. It is also grown in MOLISE and APULIA.

The variety ripens too late to be planted much further north but can yield dependable quantities of deep coloured, well-ripened grapes with good levels of alcohol and extract. It is sometimes called Cordisco, Morellone, Primaticcio, and Uva Abruzzi.

MONTEREY, one of the major agricultural counties south of San Francisco in CALIFORNIA. As a wine region it has its drawbacks. Monterey is so lacking rainfall that grapes cannot be grown there without IRRIGATION. Its large Salinas valley is also so open to the Pacific Ocean that sea fogs cool and darken its northern end so that few or no grape varieties will ripen there. Into this contradictory situation came an army of would-be growers who, between 1968 and 1975, took Monterey from one isolated vineyard to the most heavily planted county on the American west coast, with a peak 37,000 acres/14,980 ha. Nearly every year since 1975 has seen another step in a steady retreat of vines southward into the warmest and sunniest parts of the Salinas valley. The original locus at Soledad has now shifted well southward to King City. That fact notwithstanding, the first Monterey wine successes came from near the towns of Soledad and Greenfield and that area, now the Arroyo Seco AVA, remains at the forefront, save for two tiny exceptions, Chalone AVA and Carmel Valley AVA. Santa Lucia Highlands is a more recent AVA that flanks Arroyo Seco and reaches further north.

Monterey AVA
The blanket AVA for Monterey County encompasses Arroyo Seco AVA, Carmel Valley AVA, San Lucas AVA, and all other vineyards not included in these more specific regions. The San Lucas AVA was sponsored by the vast Almaden Vineyards when it owned large acreages in them; it has not been actively used on labels since Almaden left the region although it contains a hefty percentage of Monterey's total acreage in vines.

Arroyo Seco AVA
The most coherent district within the vastnesses of Monterey County's Salinas valley has its anchor point at the scruffy farm town of Greenfield. Most of its vineyards lie to the west of that town, on either bank of the dry wash for which it is named in Spanish, but some range east and north to the even scruffier precincts of Soledad. Chardonnay is the mainstay for most of the wineries who draw upon it, but some cleave resolutely to Cabernet Sauvignon. Its Rieslings can be of some interest. The earliest plantings here came in the early 1960s. Given the scarcity of local wineries—Jekel is the only established cellar inside its boundaries—many of the grapes go elsewhere.

Carmel Valley AVA
The only seaward-facing wine district in Monterey County has a handful of small wineries and vineyards draped across steep slopes towards the upper end of the Carmel River drainage, 10 to 12 miles/19 km inland from Carmel Bay. Durney vineyards is the oldest and best known of its estates.

Chalone AVA
For all practical purposes Chalone is a one-winery AVA set high in the Gavilan Mountains, on the east side of Monterey's Salinas valley, and that namesake winery has given it a remarkable degree of fame for Chardonnay, Pinot Blanc, and Pinot Noir. Although Chalone looks directly down to the Arroyo Seco AVA, it remains worlds apart in climate (for being above the fog) and soils, which for Chalone are crystal laden and CALCAREOUS.

MONTHÉLIE, a village producing red and occasionally white wine in the Côte de Beaune district of Burgundy's Côte d'Or. It is so dominated by wine production that local saying has it that a chicken in Monthélie is likely to die of hunger at harvest time.

The wines resemble those of VOLNAY but are neither quite as rich nor as elegant, although they age well and are more powerful than those of AUXEY-DURESSES, the neighbouring appellation to the south with which the PREMIER CRU vineyard Les Duresses is shared. The other premier cru vineyards of Monthélie such as Meix Bataille and Champs Fulliot lie adjacent to Volnay. Some Chardonnay was planted in the 1980s, for Monthélie also borders the white wine village of MEURSAULT.

See also CÔTE D'OR and its map. J.T.C.M.

MONTILLA-MORILES, southern Spanish denominated wine zone in ANDALUCÍA, 40 km/25 miles south of Cordoba (see map on p. 907), producing both FORTIFIED and unfortified wines in the style of SHERRY, usually known simply as **Montilla**. For many years wine from the country around the towns of Montilla and Moriles found its way into sherry SOLERAS. The practice largely ceased in 1945 when the area was awarded a separate DO, although small quantities of wine made from the PEDRO XIMÉNEZ grape are still legally exported to JEREZ and neighbouring MÁLAGA for blending. Since it became a region in its own right, Montilla has had to contend with a popular image as an inferior, cheap alternative to sherry.

The soils in the centre of the region associated with lower YIELDS and better wines resemble the chalky ALBARIZA of Jerez, although most of Montilla-Moriles is SANDY and parched. The climate is relatively harsh with summer temperatures rising to 45 °C/113 °F and short, cold winters. The Pedro Ximénez vine which accounts for over 70 per cent of production seems to thrive in the hot conditions, yielding extremely sweet grapes. The wines therefore achieve ALCOHOLIC STRENGTHS between 14 and 16 per cent without FORTIFICATION. Other grape varieties include the Lairén (AIRÉN) and MUSCAT DE ALEXANDRIA, which tend to produce lighter wines for blending. The PALOMINO vine which is the basis for most sherry has not been successful in Montilla.

Wine-making practices in Montilla parallel those for sherry. Pale, dry FINO and AMONTILLADO style wines are made from FREE-RUN juice, while heavier styles similar to OLOROSO are made from the subsequent pressings. (The terms Fino, Amontillado, and Oloroso are permitted on Montilla labels within Spain but may not be used in other European Union

Fermenting **Montilla** in stone tinajas.

countries, where they are restricted to sherry. Pale Dry, Medium Dry, Pale Cream, and Cream are the styles most commonly found on labels outside Spain.)

Pale Dry Montilla matures under a film of FLOR, initially in cement or earthenware TINAJAS, then in a solera similar to Jerez. However, in the hot climate of Montilla-Moriles, far removed from the cooling winds of the Atlantic, the flor is usually less thick than in Jerez and the wines tend to have less finesse as a result (see SHERRY). Heavier oloroso styles are fortified and aged for longer in soleras, where they become dark and pungent. Around half the region's wines are not fortified, which puts them at an advantage in certain markets where duties are levied on alcoholic strength. These usually disappear into inexpensive commercial blends, many of which are heavily sweetened with concentrated must for export. R.J.M.

MONTLOUIS, overshadowed white wine appellation in the TOURAINE district of the Loire that exists across the river from the much larger and more famous VOUVRAY, although it has its own characteristics. As in Vouvray, the CHENIN BLANC grape is grown exclusively for Montlouis, which is made in all degrees of sweetness, according to the weather.

Although TUFFEAU also forms a base from which many a house and cellar is hewn, topsoils here on the south bank just downstream of Touraine-Amboise are lighter and sandier than in Vouvray, and the wines are less sharply defined, tending to mature considerably earlier (which can be a great advantage). About 40 per cent of the wine produced from Montlouis's 250 ha/617 acres of Chenin Blanc is the usefully sturdy and characterful **Montlouis Mousseux**.

MONTMÉLIAN, named CRU just south of Chambéry whose name may be added to the eastern French appellation Vin de SAVOIE. It is dominated by a CO-OPERATIVE and most wine is light white from the JACQUÈRE grape.

MONTPELLIER, UNIVERSITY OF. L'École Nationale Supérieure Agronomique was created in 1872 as a response to the viticultural crises caused by POWDERY MILDEW, DOWNY MILDEW, and PHYLLOXERA in southern FRANCE.

The first Professor of Viticulture was Gustave Foëx, who established the first important NURSERY collection of French and American vine varieties and it remains the world's most comprehensive, with more than 3,000 in total. He experimented with phylloxera-resistant ROOTSTOCKS and published a guide to American vines which went into six editions. Ever since the Foëx era, AMPELOGRAPHY has been a speciality of Montpellier.

Pierre Viala was Professor of Viticulture at the end of the 1880s when he went to the United States expressly to collect vine varieties suitable for CALCAREOUS soils. Thanks to his efforts, VITIS *berlandieri* crossed with Chasselas yielded the rootstock 41B, which allowed the replanting of the Cognac and Champagne regions. From 1890 Viala worked at the Institut National Agronomique in Paris, where he published a treatise on vine diseases and then, with Vermorel, the classic seven-volume *Ampélographie* between 1902 and 1910.

Viala's successor in Montpellier was Louis Ravaz, who had created Cognac's viticultural research station and specialized in research into BLACK ROT and downy mildew. He also published an important work on American vines, extended Montpellier's vine collection to 3,500 varieties, and was to become the first vine physiologist. With Viala, he founded the *Revue de viticulture*, which appeared from 1894 to 1949, and also helped to create the magazine *Progrès agricole et viticole*.

From 1930 Jean Branas occupied the Chair of Viticulture and was particularly interested in VIRUS DISEASES. Together with certain ex-pupils, he undertook control of French vine nurseries and began a CLONAL SELECTION programme in the sandy, NEMATODE-free soils of Grau du Roi on the nearby Mediterranean coast.

Since 1946 INRA has provided the financial support as well as the personnel needed to develop viticultural research at Montpellier. Branas had the vine collection transferred to the Domaine de Vassal, also on the Mediterranean coast, where the soils are free of both PHYLLOXERA and the nematode *Xiphinema index*. This viticultural station has become a refuge for both VINIFERA vine varieties and HYBRIDS. Some NEW VARIETIES, CHASAN for example, have also been developed here and, thanks to the work of AMPELOGRAPHERS such as Paul Truel, Domaine de Vassal has become a world-wide focus for vine identification.

Pierre GALET succeeded Branas in the Chair of Viticulture and has published numerous works on viticulture and, especially, ampelography. Galet's direct ampelographical successor is Jean-Michel Boursiquot but he was succeeded as Professor of Viticulture by Professor Denis Boubals in 1975. His work has been much concerned with the causes and heredity of resistance to powdery and downy mildews, to phylloxera, and to *Xiphinema index*. He created the experimental Domaine du Chapître at Villeneuve-lès-Maguelonne with the vine physiologist François Champagnol.

Montpellier has also been associated with a number of OENOLOGISTS but it is for its viticultural expertise that it is world renowned.

MONTPEYROUX, the highest named CRU within the Coteaux du LANGUEDOC in southern France producing mainly red wine (much of it VIN DE PAYS and VIN DE TABLE). Carignan is still the dominant vine variety but is slowly giving way to Syrah, Grenache, and Cinsaut. DROUGHT is a common summer problem and yields on these rocky slopes are notably low. Production is still dominated by the CO-OPERATIVE in this, the frontier village between the Coteaux du Languedoc and the Massif Central, the mountain heart of France, but individuals at Domaines such as d'Aupilhac and Aiguelière are doing much for the zone's reputation.

MONTRACHET, or **Le Montrachet**, the most famous GRAND CRU white burgundy, the apogee of the Chardonnay grape produced from a single vineyard in the Côte de Beaune district of the CÔTE D'OR. Claude Arnoux, writing in 1728, could find no words in either French or Latin to describe its qualities, though he noted that it was very expensive and that you needed to reserve the wine a year in advance. Dr Lavalle's view (see BURGUNDY, history), expressed in 1855 and not necessarily valid today, was that whatever the price for a good vintage of Le Montrachet, you would not have paid too much.

Le Montrachet covers a whisker under 8 ha / 20 acres straddling the borders of Puligny and Chassagne, two communes which have annexed the famous name to their own (see PULIGNY-MONTRACHET and CHASSAGNE-MONTRACHET). Part of the secret lies in the LIMESTONE, part in its perfect south east exposition, which keeps the sun from dawn till dusk. Curiously, the vines in the Puligny half of the vineyard run in east–west rows, those in Chassagne north–south, reflecting the contours of the land.

The principal owners and producers of Le Montrachet are the Marquis de Laguiche, Baron Thénard, DOMAINE DE LA ROMANÉE-CONTI, BOUCHARD PÈRE ET FILS, Domaines Lafon and Prieur in Meursault, and Domaines Ramonet, Colin, and Amiot-Bonfils in Chassagne. In 1991 Domaine Leflaive of Puligny purchased a smallholding. The largest slices belong to the Marquis de Laguiche, whose wine is made by Joseph DROUHIN, and Baron Thénard, whose wine is made by the NÉGOCIANT Remoissenet.

Four more grands crus are associated with Le Montrachet: Chevalier-Montrachet, Bâtard-Montrachet, Bienvenues-Bâtard-Montrachet, and Criots-Bâtard-Montrachet.

Chevalier-Montrachet (7.36 ha) is situated directly above the Puligny section of Le Montrachet, on thin, stony soil giving wines which are not quite as rich as the latter. Particularly sought after are the Chevalier-Montrachet, Les Demoiselles, from Louis LATOUR and Louis JADOT, emanating from a section of the vineyard which was incorporated from what was previously the premier cru Les Demoiselles.

Bâtard-Montrachet, 11.86 ha on the slope beneath Le Montrachet, also spans the two communes, producing rich and heady wines not quite as elegant as a Chevalier-Montrachet. The vineyard covers the slope just below Le Montrachet itself. In the Puligny section of Bâtard is a separate enclave, **Bienvenues-Bâtard-Montrachet** (3.68 ha), while an extension of the Chassagne section is the rarely seen **Criots-Bâtard-Montrachet** (1.57 ha).

See CÔTE D'OR for details of viticulture and wine-making.

J.T.C.M.

Arnoux, C., *Dissertation sur la situation de Bourgogne* (Dijon, 1728).
Ginestet, B., *Montrachet* (Paris, 1988).
Loftus, S., *Puligny-Montrachet* (London, 1992).

MONTRAVEL, mainly dry white wine appellation in the extreme west of the BERGERAC district in SOUTH WEST FRANCE just over the boundary of the GIRONDE *département* with the DORDOGNE, and thus close to Bordeaux's Côtes de FRANCS, which also has a tradition of sweet white wine-making. The main grape variety is Sémillon and overall quality of these dry wines had increased considerably in the late 1980s, with a certain amount of BARREL MATURATION having been introduced.

The appellations **Côtes de Montravel** and **Haut-Montravel** are used for small quantities of sweet wines, with the former generally denoting a MOELLEUX and the latter, a description rarely used, for an even sweeter version.

MORAVIA, that part of the Czech Republic in the west of what was CZECHOSLOVAKIA best known for its wine production, just north of the Weinviertel of AUSTRIA.

MORETO, undistinguished red grape variety that is widely planted in Portugal, notably but not exclusively in Alentejo.

MOREY-ST-DENIS, important village in the Côte de Nuits district of Burgundy producing red wines from Pinot Noir grapes. Morey suffers, perhaps unfairly, in comparison with its neighbours Chambolle-Musigny and Gevrey-Chambertin because its wines are usually described as being lighter versions of Gevrey or firmer than Chambolle, according to which side of the village they are located. Indeed in the past the wines were often sold under those names. Geologically there is no need for Morey-St-Denis to feel inferior as the same stratum of hard LIMESTONE runs from the Combe de Lavaux in Gevrey through Morey to the Combe d'Antin in Chambolle.

There are four GRAND CRU vineyards, moving southwards from the border with Gevrey-Chambertin: Clos de la Roche (16.9 ha / 42 acres), Clos St-Denis (6.6 ha), Clos des Lambrays (8.8 ha), Clos de Tart (7.5 ha), plus a small segment of Bonnes Mares overlapping from Chambolle.

Although Morey chose to append St-Denis to its name in 1927, de la Roche is probably the finest vineyard. The soil is rich in MARL giving greater depth, body, and ageing ability than most other vineyards.

Clos St-Denis, sandwiched between Clos de la Roche and the village itself, may be the quintessential wine of Morey-St-Denis—a touch lighter than Clos de la Roche, with a trace of austerity, but the pinnacle of finesse.

Excellent examples of both Clos de la Roche and Clos St-Denis have been made by Domaine Ponsot, Domaine Dujac, and the Lignier brothers. While the Domaine Ponsot was one of the first to bottle their own wines in Burgundy, Domaine Dujac is the comparatively recent creation (since 1968) of Jacques Seysses, an inspirational grower whose example significantly influenced the generation taking over their family domaines in the 1980s.

Clos des Lambrays is all but a monopoly of the Saier brothers, who bought the run-down vineyard and winery from the Cosson family in 1979. At that time Clos des Lambrays was classified as PREMIER CRU but the Saiers won promotion to grand cru on grounds of the vineyard's potential, as indicated by its TOPOGRAPHY and GEOLOGY. As yet, despite major renovation and great attention to detail, it is not certain that wines comparable to Clos St-Denis or Clos de la Roche are being made.

Clos de Tart has always been a monopoly: founded by the

Cistercian sisters of Notre Dame de Genlis in 1250, it remained in their hands until the French Revolution, when it was auctioned in one piece. In 1932 one of the Marey-Monge family sold it to the current owner, Mommessin. Clos de Tart makes a fine, silky wine which does not always seem to have quite the power and concentration expected of a grand cru—although Dr Lavalle singled it out in 1855 as the only 'tête de cuvée' vineyard in Morey.

Successful premier cru vineyards in Morey-St-Denis include Les Ruchots, Clos de la Bussière (monopoly of Domaine Georges Roumier), Les Millandes, Clos des Ormes, and Les Monts Luisants. Domaine Ponsot also produces a rare and curious white wine from the latter, a proportion of which is made from Pinot Noir vines which have mutated into a type of Pinot Blanc.

See also CÔTE D'OR and its map. J.T.C.M.

MORGON, important BEAUJOLAIS Cru which encompasses about 1,100 ha/2,717 acres of vines around the commune of Villié-Morgon. The wines produced are considered notably denser and longer lived than most Cru Beaujolais and the appellation has even been used as a verb, as in describing the process by which a young Beaujolais becomes more like a Pinot Noir-dominated red burgundy with time in bottle: *il morgonne*. Soils here are more weathered and the total ripeness is likely to be greater than in most Crus, although some consider that only the wines made on the slope known as Côte de Py just south of Villié-Morgon have the real depth traditionally associated with Morgon.

MORILLON is an old north eastern French name for PINOT NOIR and is still a common name for the powerfully aromatic CHARDONNAY of STYRIA in southern Austria. It was a widely used Burgundian vine variety name in the Middle Ages and was, for example, an old name for Chardonnay in Chablis country.

MORIO-MUSKAT is Germany's most popular MUSCAT-like vine variety by far, although it is quite unrelated to any Muscat. Somehow Peter Morio's Silvaner × Weissburgunder (Pinot Blanc) crossing is almost overwhelmingly endowed with sickly grapiness that recalls some of Muscat's more obvious characteristics, even though its parents are two of the more aromatically restrained varieties. It was particularly popular with the eager blenders of the PFALZ and RHEINHESSEN in the late 1970s, when its total German area reached 3,000 ha/7,410 acres, and demand for LIEBFRAUMILCH was high: a drop of Morio-Muskat in a neutral blend of Müller-Thurgau and Silvaner can cheaply Germanize it. Total plantings fell to below 2,000 ha by 1990 and there are signs that this aggressively blowsy crossing may have had its day. If allowed to ripen fully, it can produce reasonably respectable VARIETAL wines but this is not one of Germany's finest specialities and it needs at least as good a site as Silvaner to achieve this. MUST WEIGHTS of Morio-Muskat are naturally low, although acidity is medium to high. The grapes can rot easily and ripen a week after Müller-Thurgau, which means that BACCHUS is a better alternative for Germany's cooler northern wine regions.

MORNINGTON PENINSULA, emerging small wine region south east of Melbourne, the capital of Victoria in AUSTRALIA. For more detail see VICTORIA.

MOROCCO played a significant part in the world's wine trade in the 1950s and 1960s, although it never produced as much sheer quantity as neighbouring ALGERIA. Hot, dry Morocco had 55,000 ha/135,850 acres of carefully husbanded vineyard in among its vast stretches of desert in 1956. In 1972 Morocco produced about 3 million hl/79.2 million gal of wine a year. By the early 1990s, only about 13,000 ha of the nation's 40,000 ha of vines were planted with wine grapes. The average production was just 350,000 hl—the exceptionally low average yield of well under 30 hl/ha (1.7 tons/acre) betraying a certain carelessness in viticulture.

Morocco's independence in 1956 signalled the start of a steady decline in the country's wine industry. A loss of confidence among vine-growers brought a virtual halt to new plantings so that in 1990 more than 50 per cent of Morocco's vines, many of them virused, were more than 30 years old (and therefore uneconomically unproductive). Between 1973 and 1984 the great majority of vineyards were taken over by the state, which by 1984 had also established a firm grip on the sale of wine, including grape price-fixing regardless of quality. The state has since gradually loosened its hold, but on a fragmented industry that is still suffering the effects of a lack of investment in both vineyards and cellars. The Moroccan wine trade is dominated by a state-owned company controlling a wide range of brand names and perhaps as much as 80 per cent of the market, and by the private, and much more innovative, Celliers de Meknès.

Vine-growers and wine-makers have traditionally been quite distinct, the latter sometimes buying table grapes in order to satisfy demand. Les Celliers de Meknès have invested heavily in vineyards, however, as well as in the REFRIGERATION necessary for temperature control. In the early 1990s some relatively archaic equipment was still used in some Moroccan cellars, though. The hefty sulphuring and very short fermentations traditionally employed to maximize acidity in such a hot climate can leave some wines bereft of much colour or extract.

The uninspiring Carignan dominated the Moroccan *vignoble* historically although there was a later wave of planting Cinsaut which can produce agreeable VIN GRIS, the pale pink wine which accounts for about 10 per cent of total wine production. Grenache is also important but the proportion of 'improving' grape varietes such as Cabernet Sauvignon, Syrah, Merlot, and Mourvèdre, while increasing rapidly, is still low. White grape varieties such as Clairette and Muscat tend to produce heavy, often musty, non-aromatic white wines which in 1990 comprised barely five per cent of total production. There have been experiments with July-picked, cool-fermented Chenin Blanc and, inevitably, Chardonnay.

Morocco has its own appellation system modelled on the

French APPELLATION CONTRÔLÉE and called Appellation d'Origine Garantie, or AOG. It has yet to achieve any real significance in terms of guaranteeing quality but the following zones have at least the stamp of official recognition by the EUROPEAN UNION authorities if not by the consumer.

The East: Berkane / Angad
Meknès / Fès: Guerrouane, Beni M'tir, Saiss, Beni Sadden, Zerhoune
Gharb: Gharb, Zemmour
Rabat: Chellah, Zaër
Casablanca: Zenata.

Of these Meknès / Fès, where vines are planted at an altitude of around 600 m / 1,968 ft, and Berkane have traditionally enjoyed the finest reputation.

Although rainfall between May and October is very low, a greater problem can be the strength of the prevailing winds from the Atlantic Ocean, frequently subjecting vines to 65 km / 40 miles per hour gusts. Vine TRELLISING, and careful row orientation, is a relatively recent phenomenon. Irrigation is permitted by the AOG rules, but is rarely practised.

With major investment, replanting, modernization of cellars, closer links between vine-growers, wine-makers, and wine-bottlers, and an influx of foreign expertise, Morocco certainly has the potential to produce reliable quantities of ripe, sometimes interesting wines, including such VINS DOUX NATURELS as its once-famous Muscat de Berkane. The local market for wine is buoyed by strong demand from the developing tourist industry (and high prices for imported wines) and in the early 1990s there were signs of some foreign interest in Moroccan viniculture.

See also CORKS, of which Morocco is a relatively important producer.

MORPHOLOGY. See VINE MORPHOLOGY.

MORRASTEL is the main French synonym for Rioja's GRACIANO. It is also, confusingly, one of Spain's synonyms for MOURVÈDRE, although Monastrell is the more common Spanish name for Mourvèdre. Morrastel is the name used for the Graciano still grown in the central Asian republic of UZBEKISTAN.

Morrastel-Bouschet, a much lesser crossing, is sometimes called simply Morrastel in southern France, where it was grown in considerable quantity in the mid 20th century, most notably in the Aude and Hérault *départements*. See GRACIANO for more details.

MOSCADELLO, sometimes **Moscadelleto**, local variety of the MOSCATO grape in and around MONTALCINO in central Italy. The firm Villa Banfi made an important investment in selling this sweet grapey white wine in the 1980s, and other producers of BRUNELLO DI MONTALCINO followed their lead. There is a fortified LIQUOROSO version.

MOSCATEL, Spanish and Portuguese for MUSCAT. The term may be applied to both grape varieties and wines. Thus **Moscatel de Grano Menudo** is none other than MUSCAT BLANC À PETITS GRAINS, while **Moscatel de Alejandria** and **Moscatel Romano** are MUSCAT OF ALEXANDRIA. **Moscatel Rosado** on the other hand may be a South American speciality (it is certainly widely grown in both Chile and Argentina). **Moscatel de Málaga** has been identified as a local speciality of southern Spain. Most of the vines known simply as Moscatel in Spanish- and Portuguese-speaking countries are Muscat of Alexandria, although Spain has some of the superior small seeded variety.

Inexpensive wines called simply Moscatel abound in Iberia and are in general simply sweet and grapey.

MOSCATEL DE ALEJANDRIA, Spanish name for MUSCAT OF ALEXANDRIA.

MOSCATEL DE AUSTRIA, the principal grape variety used in the production of PISCO, Chile's aromatic brandy, and almost certainly the same as Argentina's TORRONTÉS Sanjuanino. It was introduced to the pisco production zone as recently as the early 1960s and found favour more on account of its uniformly high yields than the quality of wine produced. Other forms of Moscatel grape varieties are capable of imbuing the resultant spirit with a finer, more intense aroma but Moscatel de Austria provides abundant quantities of neutral blending material. Moscatel de Austria has compact bunches of large, thin-skinned, russet coloured, neutrally flavoured grapes. It needs a hot climate to ripen properly and in damp weather is very susceptible to ROT because of its compact bunches and thin-skinned grapes.

MOSCATO, Italian for MUSCAT.

Moscato Bianco, sometimes called **Moscato di Canelli**, is the finest Muscat grape variety MUSCAT BLANC À PETITS GRAINS and is that most commonly encountered in Italy, making it the country's fourth most planted white grape variety with more than 13,000 ha / 32,110 acres planted in 1990, cited in 17 DOCS. **Moscato Giallo** and **Moscato Rosa** (both found in ALTO ADIGE, often called Goldmuskateller and Rosenmuskateller respectively) are mutations with deeper coloured berries. **Moscato di Alexandria** is the Italian synonym for the lesser white grape variety MUSCAT OF ALEXANDRIA.

Like MALVASIA, Moscato Bianco is ancient, versatile, and enjoys a geographical distribution that covers virtually the entire peninsula. Wines called Moscato are produced all over the country and are usually made from Moscato Bianco grapes. In the south and, especially, the islands, they are typically golden and sweet.

Few of Italy's regions do not have their own Moscato-based wines, and Luigi VERONELLI's *Reportorio dei vini italiani*, published in 1990, listed over 50 different types of Moscato. The majority of these are low in alcohol and at least lightly sweet, ideal accompaniments to fruit and fruit-based desserts. The best known and most widely popular of these wines—almost the national prototype for Moscato—is the Moscato planted in the Asti region in its two different forms: the sparkling ASTI SPUMANTE version and the more lightly fizzy and less alcoholic MOSCATO D'ASTI. Wines that are comparable, in style if not in quality, are also produced in significant quantities in the OLTREPÒ PAVESE and Colli Euganei DOC zones, while attempts to launch—or, perhaps more accurately, revive—the production of Moscato in the Brunello di Montalcino zone (as MOSCADELLO di Montalcino) has proven to be a commercial fiasco. A drier, crisper, but still aromatic style of Moscato is produced in the TRENTINO, and the better bottles can approach the quality of an average ALSACE Muscat.

Italy's south, in particular SICILY, was once renowned for its Moscato wines, including the mythical Moscato di Siracusa and Moscato di Noto, which by now have vanished into the land of legend. Small quantities of Moscato-based wines are still produced in SARDINIA (**Moscato di Cagliari, Moscato di Sorso Sennori**), in the BASILICATA (**Moscato del Vulture**), and in Apulia (**Moscato di Trani**), but the most significant southern Moscato is **Moscato di Pantelleria**, a PASSITO wine from the Muscat of Alexandria grape, considerably more alcoholic and more lusciously sweet than the better-known Moscato d'Asti. The revived popularity of Moscato di Pantelleria in the 1980s has coincided with, and perhaps influenced, new attempts to achieve a more luscious style of Moscato in Piedmont, and a new category of passito wines, far sweeter than Moscato d'Asti and frequently given BARREL MATURATION, began to emerge in the late 1980s. Small quantities of Moscato passito have long been made in the Valle d'AOSTA, principally near the township of Chambave.

Moscato wines come in colours other than white in Italy: a pink Moscato Rosa, redolent of roses, is produced in the Alto Adige and, to a much lesser extent, in the Trentino and Friuli, while red Moscato, aromatic to the point of decadence but not always particularly well made, is produced near Bergamo in the **Moscato di Scanzo** DOC zone. D.T.

MOSCATO D'ASTI, fragrant and lightly sweet, gently fizzy, dessert wine made in the PIEDMONT region of north west Italy. It is produced from MOSCATO BIANCO, Italy's version of the aristocratic MUSCAT BLANC À PETITS GRAINS, whose production in and around the town of Asti increased sixty-fold in the 20th century. A mere 15,000 tons of Moscato Bianco were harvested in an average late 19th century vintage, but this was before the establishment of the ASTI SPUMANTE sparkling wine industry headquartered in Canelli. Santo Stefano Belbo is considered the cradle of Moscato in Piedmont, and at the end of the 19th century almost 80 per cent of all Moscato was grown in the chalk-rich soils of Canelli, Santo Stefano Belbo, Calosso, Castiglione Tinella, and Cassinasco. Strevi, Riccaldone, and Acqui Terme in the province of Alessandria, then and now a source of excellent Moscato, produced another five per cent of the total. These are still considered the classic zones for fine Moscato, although the later expansion of the growing areas has revealed a real vocation for Moscato on the slopes of Cossano Belbo, Mango, Neviglie, and Trezzo Tinella. Moscato d'Asti is therefore something of a misnomer, since an important part of the production is not in the province of ASTI at all but in the province of Cuneo, and a significant part is in the province of Alessandria.

As a wine Moscato d'Asti is often lumped together with Asti Spumante, although the two wines are, in fact, quite different above and beyond the fact that, as a wine chiefly created by individual small producers, Moscato d'Asti is more personal and characterized than Asti Spumante, which is usually a blended wine of many provenances. With a maximum of one atmosphere of pressure in the bottle, a quarter that of Asti Spumante, Moscato d'Asti is only slightly frothy. Its ALCOHOLIC STRENGTH is considerably lower (5.5 per cent as opposed to Asti Spumante's 7–9.5), the less powerful aromas and flavour of Asti Spumante frequently give a sweeter sensation on the palate even if the RESIDUAL SUGAR level is normally slightly lower than those of Moscato d'Asti.

A vanguard minority of producers has begun to press in recent years for a lowering of the minimum alcohol requirement from its present level of 5.5°, claiming that the wine would become both more fragrant and, as a slightly sweeter wine, a more suitable accompaniment to desserts. The refusal of their requests has seen the beginning of a movement to abandon DOC status and label the wines simply VINO DA TAVOLA. Moscato d'Asti will never be a classic dessert wine, however, its chief virtues being its delicacy, its intensely musky aromas, a sweetness that is as much suggested as forthrightly declared; its definition as 'the perfect breakfast wine' contains a nugget of jocular truth. It is best served with fruit and fruit-based desserts rather than with heavier dessert offerings.

If Moscato d'Asti remains a relative drop in the overall scheme of things (3 million bottles compared to the 75 million bottles of Asti Spumante) and has known a significant commercial development only in the 1970s and 1980s as small producers who had previously sold either grapes or wine to the larger Asti Spumante houses began to bottle Moscato d'Asti under their own name, it has by now gained a secure niche as a classic and unusually refreshing expression of one of the world's most important and popular grape varieties. D.T.

MOSCATO DI SARDEGNA, relatively new and as yet relatively unrealized DOC for light, frothy, sweet white wines made in SARDINIA in the image of ASTI SPUMANTE

MOSCATO DI STREVI, fine, lightly fizzy MUSCAT made in the hills around Strevi in the east of the ASTI SPUMANTE zone. The most impressive wines by far, however, are the PASSITO versions made by Ivaldi.

MOSCATO SPUMANTE, the most basic form of light, fizzy, Italian white wine made in the style of ASTI SPUMANTE but usually with the most basic, industrial ingredients. Not to be confused with the infinitely superior MOSCATO D'ASTI.

MOSCOPHILERO, vine variety with deep pink-skinned grapes used to make strongly perfumed white wine in GREECE, particularly on the high plateau of Mantinia in the

Peloponnese where conditions are sufficiently cool that harvest is often delayed until well into October. Its name, like that of Italy's VESPAIOLO, indicates the extent to which insects are drawn to these ripe grapes. There are strong flavour similarities with fine MUSCAT but the origins of this distinct vine variety are as yet obscure. Small quantities of fruity light pink wine are also made from this spicy variety, which is also increasingly used as a blending ingredient in other parts of Greece.

MOSEL and **Moselle**, the German and French names respectively for the river which rises in the Vosges mountains of France, forms the border between LUXEMBOURG (in which it plays a key part in wine production) and Germany, and joins the river Rhein or Rhine at Koblenz in Germany, 545 km/340 miles later.

France

The name Moselle is still part of today's French wine nomenclature in the VDQS **Vins de Moselle**, which, together with Côtes de TOUL, constitute what the French call their 'vins de l'est' or wines of the east, the last remnants of what was once an important and flourishing Lorraine wine industry. Extensive vineyards around Metz supplied PINOT NOIR grapes to Champagne in the 19th century and subsequently provided base wine for SEKT when the region became German after the Franco-Prussian war of 1870. PHYLLOXERA arrived late here and the region was relatively unaffected until 1910. The poor-quality HYBRIDS chosen for replanting, together with increasing industrialization (see RAILWAYS) and the proximity of the First World War battlefields, hastened the decline of this wine region which has much in common with Luxembourg in terms of climate, soil types, and vine varieties—although the INAO authorities impose a more Gallic view of acceptable YIELDS. White Auxerrois and Müller-Thurgau are the two most common vine varieties and most wines are light, crisp, white, and aromatic, a small proportion being made sparkling.

George, R., *French Country Wines* (London, 1990).

Germany

It is the Mosel's journey of 242 km/150 miles through Germany that takes it by wine villages of world class, through one of Germany's most famous quality wine regions the MOSEL-SAAR-RUWER. In Germany 'Mosel' describes a sub-district for table wine (see TAFELWEIN) within the Mosel-Saar-Ruwer region but excluding the vineyards of the SAAR and RUWER. The name also forms part of an even bigger table wine district, Rhein-Mosel. Colloquially, apart from indicating the river and the valley, Mosel describes the wine from the whole of the Mosel-Saar-Ruwer region, regardless of quality; it is often used in this way by the world's wine trade.

As a result of its success in the English-speaking world, Moselle became a GENERIC name for any light, medium dry, faintly aromatic wine. Some traditionally minded members of the British wine trade still divide the wines of Germany into RHINE and Moselle (thereby ignoring several significant regions producing wines which have been less energetically exported). In the middle of the 19th century, Sparkling Moselle was a popular partner to Sparkling Hock (see HOCK).

MOSEL-SAAR-RUWER, the official name of GERMANY'S best-known wine region which appends to the name of the river known in Germany as MOSEL and in France as MOSELLE the names of two of its viticulturally important tributaries (see map on p. 442). It covers 12,760 ha/31,530 acres, of which over half are on slopes whose angle of inclination is more than 26 per cent. Many vineyards rise almost immediately from the banks of the Mosel or, less directly, from those of the SAAR and RUWER. A few make excursions up the smaller side valleys which feed the larger river with water from the Hunsrück plateau or the volcanic hills of the Eifel. Just downstream of Trier are the Mosel's first, steep vineyards which continue with little interruption, on one bank or the other, all the way to Koblenz. As the river twists and sometimes retraces its route, the vineyards are at their steepest on the outer edge of the curve. Those on the flatter inner edge are frequently planted in land more suited to agriculture than to viticulture. TOPOGRAPHY is all important here.

Downstream from Cochem the Mosel straightens out but, for much of the way, it still flows through a gorge, deep below the surrounding countryside. SLATE has been used in the region for hundreds of years as a building material, and where it has not been present in sufficient quantity in the soil it has been added to feed the vine with minerals and to retain warmth. Some of the vineyards between the almost vertical spurs of rock could only be created, as far back as the 16th century, with the aid of explosives, a dangerous operation when there was a wine village below. Vineyards have been modernized but to a much lesser extent than in the regions of BADEN or WÜRTTEMBERG (see FLURBEREINIGUNG). Production costs in the steep Mosel vineyards remain among the highest in Germany.

The Mosel-Saar-Ruwer normally has a warm but by no means hot summer with an average temperature in the hottest month of July of 18 °C (64 °F). The MESOCLIMATE is of rather more significance and here there are considerable variations. In some Saar and Obermosel (upstream from Trier) vineyards there is a risk of FROST damage particularly in spring, but also in late autumn and winter. Even in relatively gentle winters there are usually a few very cold nights to make possible the gathering of frozen RIESLING grapes for EISWEIN.

The Mosel-Saar-Ruwer region is divided into five districts, or Bereiche, of which the Bereich Bernkastel is the only one whose name appears with any frequency on bottles sold outside Germany. Over half of the region's production is offered under GROSSLAGE, collective site names, such as Piesporter Michelsberg, Klüsserather St Michael, Zeller Schwarze Katz, or Bernkasteler Kurfürstlay. There are some 500 or more single-vineyard (EINZELLAGE) names, of which only 60 or so have real significance in terms of the quality of wine they produce. Too often with the simple QBA quality wines, vineyard characteristics are so diluted by over-production, and hidden by added sweetness in the form of SÜSSRESERVE, that the vineyard name loses its meaning.

In the 18th century many villages produced red wine, particularly those in what we now know as the Bereich Zell (see GERMAN HISTORY). By the early 19th century white wine had taken the lead and the ELBING vine covered nearly two-thirds of the vineyard area. It still predominates in the Bereich Obermosel where, as in LUXEMBOURG across the Mosel, it supplies a clean, fresh, rather rustic wine from a yield in copious vintages as high as 220 hl/ha (12.5 tons/acre) or more. Riesling is the most widely grown vine in the region and, having reached a spread of over 90 per cent of all vineyards in 1954, it now occupies a little more than half of an enlarged, planted area. In the 1960s and 1970s MÜLLER-THURGAU was increasingly grown in what had previously been farmland. It was also planted in vineyards where the chances of Riesling ripening consistently to the level required by the GERMAN WINE LAW of 1971 were doubtful. Unlike Riesling and Elbling, Müller-Thurgau and other GERMAN CROSSINGS which were introduced in the 1960s have not produced wines with pronounced regional characteristics. Therefore, they do little to improve the image of Mosel wine, either in Germany or abroad. To emphasize their differentiation from other modern Mosel wines, producers began to put the name Riesling on the label in the 1970s, and today this is the first clue in finding a good wine from the Mosel-Saar-Ruwer.

The greater amount of alcohol in wines from warmer climates can hide a fundamental weakness. With a cheap Mosel, RESIDUAL SUGAR in the bottled wine can have a similar effect. Higher up the quality scale, these wines, usually so light in alcohol, have to be made with particular care if their lack of BODY is not to count against them. The key to a fine Mosel-Saar-Ruwer Riesling is its backbone of fruity-tasting TARTARIC ACID, but even wines which are not dry (TROCKEN) or medium dry (HALBTROCKEN) are being sold in the 1990s with less residual sugar than they were in the 1970s. Their structure is nowadays strengthened by more alcohol. The difference between a dry and a medium sweet Mosel AUSLESE may well be over two per cent of actual alcohol, and so it is wrong to assume that all Mosels are light. Nevertheless, even if some Auslese Trocken is sold with over 12 per cent of natural alcohol, the quintessential Mosel remains for many non-Germans the delicate, fresh Kabinett wine, only slightly stronger in ALCOHOLIC STRENGTH, about nine per cent, than a dark, double bock beer from Munich. Mosel Kabinett at its best is unique, and one of the glories of the world of wine. Perhaps its only rival is a wine of similar quality from the NAHE.

Upstream from Koblenz

The district with the highest percentage of Riesling vines on the river starts at Koblenz and continues upstream until shortly after the narrow town of Zell, from which the Bereich Zell takes its name. It has many small, steep vineyards which can be maintained only by hand, and the lowest percentage of flat or gently sloping sites workable by tractor. The individual holdings are not as large as those of the Bereich Bernkastel and practically every comparable vineyard statistic, not to mention the structure of the local trade, places the Bereich Zell at a disadvantage. It is, therefore, all the more pleasant to record the success of a producers' association in the district, the Erzeugergemeinschaft Deutsches Eck, devoted exclusively to the Riesling grape and a rigid, maximum allowable yield of 80 hl/ha (4.5 tons/acre)—much less than that permitted by law. The Rieslings of the Bereich Zell are generally less refined than the best of the Bereich Bernkastel but their agreeable, solid, true-to-type wines in the middle price range are as good as any that the Mosel can offer. They are steely and positive in flavour, and the wines from the vineyards near Koblenz have a not surprising affinity with those of the nearby MITTELRHEIN.

The better-known villages of the Bereich Zell start with Winningen, where average MUST WEIGHTS in the Weinhex collective site reach one degree of potential alcohol more than those of the well-known Piesporter Michelsberg. Up river from Winningen, in Kobern, Lehmen, and Pommern, private estates sell good Riesling wines directly to the consumer, and upstream of the busy but attractive Cochem, the villages of Edig and Eller are important wine producers. At Bremm the terraced Calmont rises 200 m/656 ft from the river and, with a 65 per cent incline, it is one of the steepest vineyards in Germany. After Neef and Bullay, the Mosel forms a characteristic oxbow, passing the town of Zell and leading into the Bereich Bernkastel.

Other than at Trier and Koblenz, with 99,000 and 177,000 inhabitants respectively, the Mosel-Saar-Ruwer and its surrounding countryside are lightly peopled. This has obliged many producers to find markets outside the region to supplement sales to tourists. In the absence of alternative jobs, much of the local population earns a living or a part-time income from wine. Nearly three times as many hours are spent per hectare per annum in the steep Mosel vineyards as are necessary in the more easily worked land of the PFALZ region. Unfortunately, the difference in price in the Mosel bulk wine market between high-yielding Müller-Thurgau from a second-rate site, and a Riesling from a good vineyard, does not encourage the production of less and better wine. For fine Riesling from the Bereich Bernkastel one should turn to the very large number of private estate bottlers who sell their wine directly to the consumer, to the wine trade, and to the restaurant business. They are a surer guide to a good Mosel than are the names of the famous villages, or of the best-known single-vineyard sites. Even that of a vineyard as prestigious as the Wehlener Sonnenuhr is not a guarantee of a high-quality wine, unless it originates from a good estate. Wines from the relatively inferior parts of a renowned vineyard, bottled by wine merchants, should still be of good quality but they will not compare with the best of estate bottlings, labelled GUTSABFÜLLUNG.

Of the approximately 60 vineyards of outstanding merit on the Mosel-Saar-Ruwer, over half are in the Bereich Bernkastel. Travelling upstream the first division individual sites start with the Prälat and Treppchen at Erden, and move on to Uerzig (Würzgarten); Zeltingen, Wehlen (Sonnenuhr);

Graach, Bernkastel (Doctor and Graben); Brauneberg (Juffer); Piesport (Goldtröpfchen); Dhron; and Trittenheim. In hot summers with insufficient rain, estate owners sometimes report that wines from their less good sites have been more successful than those from the best vineyards, where intense heat and a WATER STRESS can slow down the accumulation of SUGAR IN GRAPES. The result of this seemingly anarchic situation is that fine Mosel is a highly individual wine, which is never available in large quantities. To meet the needs of supermarkets and chain stores for large volumes of inexpensive labels, much ordinary wine, almost certainly not from Riesling, is sold under collective site (Grosslage) names. These include the names of famous villages such as Piesport or Bernkastel.

Saar and Ruwer

The vineyards of the Saar and Ruwer rivers form a single district occupying 13 per cent of the Mosel-Saar-Ruwer region. As every additional 100 m/328 ft above sea level results in a drop in average temperature of over 0.5 °C/0.9 °F, the extra height of the Bereich Saar-Ruwer and the upper reaches of the Mosel means that they are cooler than the Bereich Bernkastel. In good vintages the wines are a joy to taste with an abundance of flavour and wonderful acidity, but it can be difficult for the grapes to reach RIPENESS in poor years.

The main Ruwer vineyards begin near the village of the same name, and end some 10 km/6 miles upstream. Sole ownership of the Eitelsbacher Karthäuserhofberg and of the Maximin Grünhaus vineyards by two outstanding estates ensures that only top-quality wines reach the market. Leading Mosel producers also have holdings at Eitelsbach and Kasel.

The vineyards of the Saar form the Grosslage Scharzberg, whereas the most famous single vineyard is the Scharzhofberg at Wiltingen. There are a number of estates with holdings in the Scharzhofberg but, as in the Wehlener Sonnenuhr, not all of the vineyard is of the same high standard. Among other leading Saar wine villages and towns are Wawern, Ayl, Ockfen, Saarburg, and Serrig—the last two a source of uniquely steely Riesling wine.

Above Trier, and upstream of the confluence with the Saar at Konz, the character of the Mosel changes, becoming entirely rural again. The pretty rolling vineyards face those of LUXEMBOURG, a few hundred metres across the river. They form the Bereich Obermosel, in the state of Rheinland-Pfalz (along with the rest of the Mosel-Saar-Ruwer), and the tiny Bereich Moseltor in the Saarland. Much of the harvest is handled by Moselland, the central CO-OPERATIVE cellar at Bernkastel. There are a few estate bottlers and, although the local Elbing wine is fairly simple, it can be made into an attractive sparkling wine. Perhaps this will become its main role in the future.

The Mosel and commerce

Moselland processes about a quarter of the average Mosel-Saar-Ruwer harvest and exports some 40 per cent of its production, of which half is shipped to the United Kingdom. It has subsidiary cellars at various villages on the Mosel and Saar, and a number of pressing stations and reception points for grapes throughout the region. In Germany, it sells wine in bottle to the large supermarkets and in bulk to the wine trade. There are some 11,100 grape-growers in the region and, significantly, only 130 or so own more than 5 ha/12 acres of vineyard. Five ha is probably the absolute minimum amount of land from which it is possible for a small estate to provide an adequate, sole source of income for its owner.

Of the region's wine sold in bottle, about 20 per cent comes from the co-operative cellars, 30 per cent from estates, and some 50 per cent is bottled by wine merchants. These last, although they are customers of the co-operative cellars for bulk wine, are also their competitors, as they share the same supermarket customers.

The large turnover of the German supermarkets and grocery chains, increased by commercial concentration in the 1980s, has given them enormous strength and buying power. To serve their needs, merchants' cellars were built in the area of Trier in the 1960s. Their continued existence depends on a large output, but with a minute percentage of profit. These cellars also export their bottlings, of which three-quarters are either from regions other than the Mosel-Saar-Ruwer or imports from Italy and eastern Europe, for example. By the late 1980s, bulk prices on the Mosel were indirectly dictated by the supermarkets at a level at which quality is irrelevant.

As an escape from the difficulties of the cheap wine market, SPARKLING WINE can be an interesting alternative. The Sekterzeugergemeinschaft Saar-Mosel (a producers' association) concentrates on sparkling wines based on Riesling from the Mosel and Saar, and Elbling from the Obermosel. Some are offered with a vintage and the name of the vineyard or origin (see SEKT).

While the standing of Mosel wine in Germany has been debased, there remains a small upper tier of excellent estate bottled wine, no shortage of cheap and often dull wine with few of the better regional characteristics, and very little in the interesting middle price range. I.J.

MOSSEL BAY, southern Cape wine region in SOUTH AFRICA.

MOTHER VINE, an identified, preferred individual vine from which CUTTINGS or other vegetative propagation materials are taken. They can be labelled as CLONES which are the basis of CLONAL SELECTION and VINE IMPROVEMENT programmes. B.G.C.

MOTHS, flying insects which damage grapevines in the larval stages. The four most important types in France are pyrale (*Sparganothis pilleriana*), cochylis (*Eupoecilia ambiguella*), eudemis or European grape moth (*Lobesia botrana*), and eulia (*Argyrotaenia pulchellana*). The pyrale larvae attack young leaves and grapes, whereas the cochylis, eudemis, and eulia develop several generations in the grape bunch after the initial invasion from which grubs attack the developing grapes and encourage BOTRYTIS BUNCH ROT. Control of these pests is difficult because the attacks, which

Madame et Monsieur Jean-Pierre **Moueix**, at home in Libourne in the early 1980s.

may be severe, are irregular. INSECTICIDES can be used, as can feeding traps and pheromones; such pests are also the subject of INTEGRATED PEST MANAGEMENT strategies using natural predators.

The grape berry moth (*Polychrosis viteana*) causes damage to developing bunches in many parts of America but not California. The Orange Tortrix moth (*Argyrotaenia citrana*) damages buds, leaves, and bunches in California. In Australia and New Zealand the grapevine moth (*Phalaenoides glycine*) feeds on a range of plants, and the caterpillars do most damage to the leaves. It is controlled by insecticides and also a predatory shield bug. See also LEAF ROLLERS. R.E.S.

Winkler, A. J., *et al.*, *General Viticulture* (2nd edn., Berkeley, Calif., 1974).

MOUEIX, important family in the BORDEAUX TRADE, notably, but by no means exclusively, in ST-ÉMILION and POMEROL. The Moueix family came from the Corrèze, a severe district in central France, noted for its hard-headed men. Jean Moueix (1882–1957) bought Ch Fonroque in St-Émilion in 1930, and his son Jean-Pierre (b. 1913) joined him that year, with the purpose of selling only the hitherto somewhat neglected wines, nearly all red, produced on the RIGHT BANK of the Dordogne, from the Côtes de CASTILLON downstream to BLAYE. In 1937 Jean-Pierre formed Établissements Jean-Pierre Moueix on the quay in Libourne, the largest town on the right bank. Increasingly successful in the post-war period, it became from 1970 the major NÉGOCIANT there selling the finer châteaux wines, at a time when the traditional merchants were failing, and now no longer exist in their old form. In 1956 the 70-year-old firm of Duclot in the city of Bordeaux was acquired to deal mainly with the 'left bank' districts (MÉDOC, GRAVES, and so on), as well as selling direct to private customers in France. As Bordeaux Millésimes it is prominent in the export trade. Since 1968 both were headed by Jean-Pierre's elder son Jean-François (b. 1945). Fonroque was inherited by Jean-Antoine Moueix (1908–57), and then by his son Jean-Jacques (b. 1935), a director of the Libourne firm.

In 1970 the younger son, Christian (b. 1946), became a director, with special responsibilities, along with the firm's OENOLOGIST Jean-Claude Berrouet, for the 20 estates owned or farmed by the firm. In 1982 Christian started a joint venture in Yountville, CALIFORNIA, with two daughters of John Daniel, former owner of Inglenook. In a 50-ha/123-acre vineyard a Bordeaux-style wine named Dominus is produced. He now runs the Libourne négociant.

In the 1950s Jean-Pierre Moueix began to acquire châteaux in St-Émilion and Pomerol: Trotanoy (1953), La Fleur-Pétrus (1953), Lagrange (1959), and, by Christian Moueix, La Grave Trigant de Boisset (1971) in Pomerol; and Magdelaine (1954) in St-Émilion. In the 1970s and 1980s the firm expanded into FRONSAC, acquiring Canon, Canon de Brem, and Canon-Moueix in the superior Canon-Fronsac appellation and La Dauphine in Fronsac.

A number of other properties are farmed on behalf of their owners, including Ch La Clotte in St-Émilion, and Lafleur, Feytit-Clinet, Lafleur-Gazin, and Latour-à-Pomerol in Pomerol. However, much the most important acquisition was a half-share of Ch PÉTRUS in 1964. Moueix had had the exclusive selling rights since 1945, and when the owner, Mme Loubat, died in 1961 she left it to her nephew and niece and the former sold his share to M. Moueix.

Jean-Pierre Moueix, a man of great probity and courtesy, is a notable collector of art and books, and the château in which he lives beside the river DORDOGNE on the edge of Libourne is full of the works of such leading modern artists as Picasso and Francis Bacon. E.P.-R.

MOULDY, pejorative wine-tasting term used for wine spoiled by the growth of minute fungi on grapes or winery equipment. Many different types of mould grow on grapes in the vineyard, depending on region and vintage conditions. ROT is the most common, but for more details, see FUNGAL DISEASES.

Mouldy COOPERAGE can also cause this sort of aroma. Empty barrels are difficult to keep clean and free of mould for the humid conditions inside them are ideal for the growth of these organisms. Gaseous SULPHUR DIOXIDE can keep the inside of a barrel or vat free of mould for a short time, but then the absorbed sulphur dioxide has to be washed out thoroughly before the vessel can be used for wine. Once spores of mould become embedded in the pores of a wooden vessel, it is almost impossible to remove them completely. See BARREL MAINTENANCE. A.D.W.

MOULIN-À-VENT means windmill in French and is the name of one of the most famous of the BEAUJOLAIS Crus, being named after a local windmill. The area includes delimited vineyards within Chénas and Romanèche-Thorins. Of all the wine produced in the Beaujolais region, Moulin-à-Vent is expected to last the longest, taste most concentrated, and therefore, in a way, to be the least typical. With time, the wines begin to taste more like old Pinot Noir than Gamay, and some 50-year-old Moulin-à-Vent can be quite a satisfying drink, even if a dissatisfying Beaujolais. It has also generally been the most expensive. The area planted has been steadily increasing and was nearly 670 ha/1,655 acres in 1990.

MOULIS, or **Moulis-en-Médoc**, smallest of the six communal appellations of the Haut-Médoc district of Bordeaux (the others being MARGAUX, ST-JULIEN, PAUILLAC, ST-ESTÈPHE, and neighbouring LISTRAC). Although it includes only about 500 ha/1,235 acres of vineyards, there is considerable diversity TERROIR in Moulis, in terms of both topography and soil composition. Countryside that is positively rolling by Médoc standards, and soils that include various gravels, clays, and limestone, result in wines as varied as the occasionally brilliant Ch Chasse-Spleen, the good-value Ch Maucaillou, and a host of properties whose names include the word Poujeaux. The finest of these is usually long-lived Ch Poujeaux itself. As in Listrac, this is not CLASSED GROWTH country. Perhaps because of this, the best Moulis wines can offer good value, being as well structured as any Haut-Médoc, often with some of the perfume of Margaux to the east. Yields are more restricted in Moulis than in Listrac.

For more information see MÉDOC and BORDEAUX.

Parker, R., *Bordeaux* (2nd edn., New York, 1991).
Penning-Rowsell, E., *The Wines of Bordeaux* (6th edn., London, 1989).
Peppercorn, D., *Bordeaux* (2nd edn., London, 1991).

MOUNTAIN, 19th century English term for MÁLAGA. The name is no longer used but is commonly found on DECANTER LABELS produced before PHYLLOXERA devastated the Málaga region in 1876.

MOUNT BARKER, relatively cool, promising vineyard area in the Lower Great Southern region of the state of WESTERN AUSTRALIA.

MOUNT VEEDER, California wine region and AVA. See NAPA Valley.

MOURISCO TINTO, lesser PORT grape variety which produces red wines relatively light in colour in northern Portugal.

MOURVÈDRE, Spain's second most important black grape variety after Garnacha (Grenache) and was once Provence's most important vine. The Spaniards call it Monastrell (and occasionally Morrastel or Morastell although it has nothing to do with GRACIANO which is known as Morrastel in France). Mourvèdre is enjoying a resurgence of popularity, especially in southern France and, to a more limited extent, in California. In the New World it is often called Mataro.

The origins of the variety are almost certainly Spanish. Murviedro is a town near Valencia (Mataro is another near Barcelona). It is certainly easier to grow in Spain than in the cooler reaches of southern France for it buds and ripens extremely late, a week later even than Carignan according to Galet. Provided the climate is warm, the upright, vigorous Monastrell adapts well to a wide range of soils and recovers well from spring frost. (It is sensitive to low winter temperatures, however.) It is suspectible to both DOWNY and

POWDERY MILDEWS, which is of course much less of a problem in hot Spanish vineyards than in much of France.

The wine produced from Monastrell's small, sweet, thick-skinned berries tends to be heady stuff, high in alcohol, tannins, and a somewhat gamey flavour when young and well capable of ageing provided OXIDATION is carefully avoided in the winery. Its vineyards cover well over 100,000 ha/247,000 acres in Spain, especially in the Murcia, Alicante, Albacete, and Valencia regions and all over the LEVANTE. It is the principal black grape variety in such DOS as ALICANTE, ALMANSA, JUMILLA, VALENCIA, and YECLA.

Mourvèdre needs France's warmest summers to ripen fully. (Its position in the south could be compared with what was once Petit Verdot's in Bordeaux.) It dominated Provence until the arrival of PHYLLOXERA and the search for productive vines to supply the burgeoning market for cheap table wine. For many decades it marked time in its French enclave BANDOL but is now regarded as an extremely modish and desirable 'improving variety' throughout the Languedoc-Roussillon, especially now that clones have been selected that no longer display the inconveniently variable yields that once resulted from degenerated vine stock. Between 1968 and 1988 total French plantings increased from 900 to 5,600 ha, spread between Provence, the southern Rhône, the Languedoc, and Roussillon.

In southern France Mourvèdre produces wines considered useful for their structure, intense fruit, and, in good years, perfume often redolent of blackberries. The structure in particular can be a useful foil for Grenache in Provence and Cinsaut further west. In Bandol it is typically blended with both of these, and the statutory minimum for Mourvèdre is now 50 per cent. Mourvèdre is condoned in a host of APPELLATION CONTRÔLÉE regulations all over the south of France from Coteaux du Tricastin to Collioure. Although it usually plays a useful supporting role, being fleshier than Syrah, tauter than Grenache and Cinsaut, and infinitely more charming than Carignan, varietal Mourvèdres from the Languedoc have met with great commercial success.

This success has been slow to raise the reputation of Australia's Mataro (also known as Esparte), of which more than 600 ha were yet to be ripped out in 1990. Although varietal versions would not survive the market-place and encounters with unblended Australian Mataro are rare, the Barossa Valley location of most of it suggests that the wine resembles the Spanish rather than the French version.

Although grown at least since the 1870s, California's unfashionable Mataro was fast disappearing until the RHÔNE RANGERS made the connection with Mourvèdre and pushed up demand for wine from these historic stumps, notably in Contra Costa County between San Francisco and the Central Valley, where there were considerable new plantings in the early 1990s thanks to demand from the likes of Bonny Doon and Cline Cellars. By 1992 the state's total plantings were nearly 300 acres.

Galet notes that there may be some Mourvèdre in Azerbaijan, although that is not what it is called.

Galet, P., *Cépages et vignobles de France* (2nd edn., Montpellier, 1990).

MacDonogh, G., *Syrah, Grenache and Mourvèdre* (London, 1992).

MOUSSE. French term for FIZZINESS.

MOUSSEUX, French for sparkling. Some Mousseux are made by the traditional method (see SPARKLING WINE-MAKING) while others may be made by the much less painstaking CHARMAT process.

MOUSY, TASTING TERM commonly associated with the wine FAULT caused by BRETTANOMYCES. Mousiness is usually apparent only after a wine has been swallowed or expectorated.

MOUTON CADET, the most successful Bordeaux BRAND, began life in 1927, a poor vintage in which Baron Philippe de ROTHSCHILD created what was effectively a SECOND WINE called Carruades de Mouton for Ch MOUTON-ROTHSCHILD. Penning-Rowsell notes that it was not a success, and its successor in 1930 was named Mouton-Cadet, since Philippe was the *cadet*, the youngest, of the family. Eventually, as Mouton Cadet, it developed a prosperous life of its own, and demand was so great that the flexibility of the BORDEAUX AC appellation was needed. Today Mouton Cadet is available in red, white, and rosé versions and is blended, relying heavily on the ENTRE-DEUX-MERS, from wines produced all over Bordeaux. The red version is much the most interesting version.

MOUTON-ROTHSCHILD, CHÂTEAU, important wine estate in PAUILLAC in the BORDEAUX wine region and the only one ever to have been promoted within the 1855 CLASSIFICATION, to FIRST GROWTH.

Originally part of the LAFITE estate with which it is intermingled, it became in the middle of the 18th century a separate entity, owned by the de Brane family. In the first half of the following century Baron Hector de Brane (or Branne) became known as 'the Napoleon of the vines' for his work in developing the Médoc vineyards, and, in company with his neighbour Armand d'Armailhacq, in supposedly introducing the CABERNET SAUVIGNON vine. In 1830 he sold Mouton to a M. Thuret and retired to his Ch Brane-Cantenac in the commune of MARGAUX. At this time Mouton had little international repute, and the first entry in a Christie's AUCTIONS catalogue was in 1834. In 1853 Thuret sold it to Baron Nathaniel de ROTHSCHILD, of the English branch of the family, two years before the 1855 classification which placed Mouton-Rothschild at the top of the second growths, a position unsatisfactory to the family, but not seriously contested until Baron Philippe de Rothschild took over the running of it from his father in 1922. He startled Bordeaux by employing a poster artist, Carlu, to design an art deco label, including the Rothschild arrows, for the 1924 vintage, and then proposing CHÂTEAU BOTTLING of all the first growths (and Mouton-Rothschild). He also instigated what was initially a SECOND WINE, called MOUTON CADET.

On his return in 1945 after the Second World War Baron Philippe initiated the series of labels, each year designed by a well-known artist, including Cocteau, Braque, Dali, and

Ch **Mouton-Rothschild's** exceptional wine museum is perhaps the estate's most exciting building.

Henry Moore. He also began a campaign to elevate Mouton to first growth status, which he achieved in 1973. He and his American wife Pauline created a magnificent Musée du Vin, or wine museum, filled with *objets d'art* and open to the public since 1962 on application.

The 72-ha/178-acre vineyard is planted with 87 per cent CABERNET SAUVIGNON grapes, eight per cent CABERNET FRANC, and the balance MERLOT and PETIT VERDOT. Average production is about 20,000 cases. The wine is famously concentrated and intensely aromatic in good vintages. E.P.-R.

Coates, C., *The Great Wines of Bordeaux* (London, 1994).
Penning-Rowsell, E., *The Wines of Bordeaux* (6th edn., London, 1989).
Ray, C., *Mouton-Rothschild* (London, 1974).

MUDGEE, relatively isolated and well-defined wine region in AUSTRALIA. For more detail see NEW SOUTH WALES.

MULCH, materials put on the vineyard soil surface to assist vine growth. Mulch is useful because it keeps soil damp and also stops it getting too hot. Mulches also hinder the growth of weeds, and those composed of ORGANIC MATTER provide nutrients for the vine's growth as the mulch decomposes.

Animal manure and straw were common mulches of the past but in many modern vineyards these have been replaced with thin plastic film. The plastic strip is often about a metre wide and is rolled out behind a tractor with the edges being buried under soil. Young vines are planted through holes in the plastic. The response of young vine growth to plastic is often remarkable, especially for vineyards which rely on rainfall rather than IRRIGATION for their water. The film stops water evaporating from the soil surface and in spring it warms the soil, promoting root growth. Both of these factors cause young vines to grow more quickly and evenly, and the vineyard begins to bear fruit quickly. Another important advantage of plastic mulches around young vines is that they stop weeds which are normally difficult to control. Despite these important advantages, plastic film has disadvantages, other than cost. If the plastic is torn, then weeds proliferate in the hole. In mature vineyards with the normal passage of implements, the (non-biodegradable) film becomes damaged and strips can blow around the vineyard in the wind making a mess. Lastly, the appearance of a vineyard with plastic film under the vines does not please all wine tourists, nor those who favour more 'natural' means of vine establishment.

A major disadvantage to straw mulch has been the cost of placing a sufficiently deep mat below each vine. This cost can be reduced by modern techniques of mechanically unrolling bales of hay, or alternatively throwing the straw under the vine as the COVER CROP is mown.

So-called organic vineyards use mulches of living plants as well as dead material. The main disadvantage of living mulches for the young vines is that there may be too much competition for water and nutrients, and so the living mulch may need to be killed off. However, when a thick plant mulch breaks down, then nutrients are released and the soil is improved. Either living or dead organic mulches can cause problems because of insects and fungi which can be harboured in the litter around the vine trunk. R.E.S.

MULLED WINE is wine that has been heated with sugar and spices and also, sometimes, slices of fruit and even brandy. This was a particularly common way of serving wine in the Middle Ages, since honey and spices helped to compensate for any shortcomings in wine quality (which were likely to be considerable as the months since the HARVEST wore on in this age when wine was served directly from the barrel). The verb 'mull' was current at least from the beginning of the 17th century. Recipes vary and quantities are not critical. Red wine is almost invariably used, and cinnamon and cloves are common. Slow simmering retains the ALCOHOL; fast boiling dissipates it. Sugar or honey should be added to taste, and citrus fruit peel can impart bitterness. Whole oranges stuck with cloves are often used. It is far less difficult to make good mulled wine than to find DRINKING VESSELS that retain the heat but are not uncomfortably hot to hold. See also GLÜHWEIN.

MÜLLERREBE, which translates from German as 'miller's grape', is the common, and logical, name for Germany's increasingly planted selection of Pinot MEUNIER. (Schwarzriesling is another German synonym.) It is most common in WÜRTTEMBERG, which has its own low-yielding mutation called Samtrot, literally 'red velvet', of which nearly 100 ha/250 acres were planted in 1990.

MÜLLER-THURGAU, white grape variety which could fairly be said to have been the bane of German wine production. This mediocre crossing was developed in 1882 for entirely expedient reasons by a Dr Hermann Müller, born in the Swiss canton of Thurgau but then working at the German viticultural station at GEISENHEIM. His understandable aim was to combine the quality of the great RIESLING grape with the viticultural reliability, particularly the early ripening, of the SILVANER. Most of the variety's synonyms (Rivaner in Luxembourg and Slovenia, Riesling-Sylvaner in New Zealand and Switzerland, Rizlingszilvani in Hungary) reflect this combination. Since then some authorities have argued that he actually crossed two strains of Riesling rather than, as he thought, Riesling with Silvaner, but whatever the ingredients the recipe resulted in a variety all too short on Riesling characteristics (indeed much shorter on such elegant raciness than the more recent crossings EHRENFELSER, FABER, KERNER, and well-ripened SCHEUREBE).

The vine certainly ripens early, even earlier than Silvaner. Unlike Riesling it can be grown anywhere, producing prodigious quantities (sometimes double Riesling's common yield range of 80 to 110 hl/ha (4.6–6.3 tons/acre) of extremely dull, flabby wine. Müller-Thurgau usually has some vaguely aromatic quality, but the aroma can often be unattractively mousy in Germany's high-yielding vineyards and is more reliably clean and pure in the variety's other spheres of influence NEW ZEALAND and ALTO ADIGE, where growers are less demanding in terms of quantity.

Müller-Thurgau was not embraced by Germany's growers until after the Second World War, when the need to rebuild the industry fast presumably gave this productive, easily grown vine allure. In the early 1970s it even overtook the great Riesling in total area planted (having for some time produced far more wine in total) and remained in that position throughout the 1980s, although by the end of that decade there were already signs of disaffection with the grape on which the great LIEBFRAUMILCH industry was commercially based. Occasionally a German Müller-Thurgau could be said to express something—usually something territorial rather than anything inherent in the grape—but this bland vehicle for quantity above quality was substantially responsible for the decline in Germany's reputation as a wine producer in the 1970s and early 1980s. Typically blended with a little of a more aromatic variety such as MORIO-MUSKAT and with a great deal of SÜSSRESERVE, Müller-Thurgau was transformed into oceans of QBA sugarwater labelled either LIEBFRAUMILCH or one of the internationally recognized names such as Niersteiner, Bernkasteler, or Piesporter (see GROSSLAGE). In 1990 it still occupied nearly a quarter of Germany's vineyards, a third of all Baden plantings, nearly half (and still increasing) of those in Franken, but also nearly a quarter of the Mosel-Saar-Ruwer and Nahe regions.

The wood is much softer than Riesling's and can easily be damaged by hard winters. The grapes rot easily (as can be tasted in a number of examples from less successful years), and the vine is susceptible to DOWNY MILDEW, BLACK ROT, and, its own bane, ROTBRENNER, but it will continue to flourish while there is a market for cheap German wine.

Outside Germany it can taste quite palatable, if rarely exciting. A handful of Italians manage it in the Alto Adige where high altitudes keep the grapes on the vine for long enough for them to retain acidity while developing some perceptible fruit flavours. It is also increasingly planted in FRIULI and is grown as far south as EMILIA-ROMAGNA. This foreign-sounding variety, sometimes called Riesling-Sylvaner, has its followers among Italy's fashion-conscious connoisseurs.

The variety thrives all over central and eastern Europe. It is planted, appropriately enough, in SWITZERLAND, playing an increasingly important role in the vineyards of the German-speaking area in the north and east. Only the native GRÜNER VELTLINER is more important in AUSTRIA, where it still comprises nearly one vine in every ten but is rarely responsible for wines of much intrinsic interest. Across Austria's southern border, it is also grown in SLOVENIA and is even more important to the east and north of Austria in CZECHOSLOVAKIA and, particularly, HUNGARY, which is probably the world's second most important grower of this uninspiring grape. As Rizlingszilvani, it covers thousands of hectares of vineyard around Lake Balaton and produces lakesful of flabby Badacsonyi Rizlingszilvani.

Müller-Thurgau was planted enthusiastically by New Zealand grape growers on the recommendation of visiting

German experts as a preferable substitution for the hybrids that were all too prevalent in the country's nascent wine industry of the 1950s and 1960s. Chardonnay overtook the crossing's total area (1,300 ha / 3,210 acres) in 1992, however, as it is a far more valuable crop. It would be difficult to argue that New Zealand's 'Riesling-Sylvaner' is ever a very complex wine but it does usually display a freshness lacking in German examples, despite its customary similar reliance on Süssreserve or SWEET RESERVE.

Elsewhere in the New World, most growers are not driven by the need for early ripening varieties (and would find the flab in the resultant wine a distinct disadvantage), although some Oregon growers have experimented successfully with it, and fine examples have been produced in the Puget Sound vineyards of western Washington state.

Northern Europe's two smallest and coolest wine producers, ENGLAND and LUXEMBOURG, depend heavily on Müller-Thurgau, which (called Rivaner in Luxembourg) is the most planted variety in each country. Luxembourg's 580 ha represented more than 40 per cent of all plantings in 1992, while England's 200 ha made it the single most important grape variety in this far northern wine industry.

Müller-Thurgau has not had quite such a disastrous effect on German wine industry in the late 20th century as Aramon and the hybrids did on France's table wine production in the first half of the century but it is to be hoped that Müller-Thurgau's decline in Germany will be as swift.

MURRAY RIVER, mighty river that meanders through south east AUSTRALIA. Thanks to a grand and historic IRRIGATION scheme, the arid riverbanks have been transformed into green arable land, also called the **Riverland** or **Riverlands,** planted with a variety of crops, including grapes. The giant wine region straddles the states of SOUTH AUSTRALIA, VICTORIA, and NEW SOUTH WALES and produces about a third of all Australian wine. See SOUTH AUSTRALIA for more detail.

MURRUMBIDGEE IRRIGATION AREA, or MIA, one of the irrigated wine regions of AUSTRALIA associated mainly with inexpensive wine for blending. For more detail see NEW SOUTH WALES.

MUSCADEL or **Muskadel**, along with Muscat of Frontignan, is the name by which MUSCAT BLANC À PETITS GRAINS, the finest Muscat vine variety, is known in South Africa. Unrelated and distinctly superior to Bordeaux's MUSCADELLE, Muscadel as a white grape variety and its darker-berried mutation was chiefly responsible for the famous 18th century CONSTANTIA dessert wine, and is now used largely for fortified dessert wines, for JEREPIGO, and to add perfume and spice to many blends.

The total area planted in South Africa, about 1,000 ha / 2,470 acres, much of it in the inland regions of Robertson and Worcester (see SOUTH AFRICA, regions), has remained surprisingly constant since the wines it produces are not the most fashionable. J.P.

MUSCADELLE is the famous also-ran third grape variety responsible, with SÉMILLON and SAUVIGNON BLANC, for the sweet white (and duller dry white) wines of Bordeaux and Bergerac. Like all of Bordeaux's white grape varieties except for Sauvignon, its star is waning, but not nearly so rapidly as that of UGNI BLANC or COLOMBARD. Four out of every five Muscadelle vines grown in Bordeaux are not in the great sweet white wine areas of SAUTERNES, but in the unfashionable and vast ENTRE-DEUX-MERS, including such lesser sweet white appellations as PREMIÈRES CÔTES DE BORDEAUX, CADILLAC, LOUPIAC, and STE-CROIX-DU-MONT. Muscadelle is also being pulled up at quite a rate in the vineyards of the Dordogne *département*, including such appellations as MONBAZILLAC, but it is still relatively more important to Bergerac than to Bordeaux.

The variety, unrelated to any member of the MUSCAT family, shares a vaguely grapey aroma with them but has its origins in Bordeaux. The usefully productive Muscadelle leafs late and ripens early and has never demonstrated great subtlety in the wines it produces. The occasional VARIETAL Moscadelle can demonstrate a certain tang but its use is almost exclusively in blends, adding the same sort of youthful fruitiness to south western sweet whites as MEUNIER does to the north east sparkling whites called champagne.

The variety is grown widely but not importantly in eastern Europe but in only one obscure corner of the wine world does Muscadelle produce sensational varietal wine, the LIQUEUR TOKAY of AUSTRALIA. For years Australians thought the grape they called Tokay, that produced these dark, syrupy, wood-matured concentrates for after-dinner drinking, was the Hungarian HÁRSLEVELŰ but the French AMPELOGRAPHER Paul Truel identified it as Muscadelle in 1976. There were 400 ha / 990 acres of Muscadelle in Australia in 1990, (almost exactly the same area as was planted with the 'Frontignac' MUSCAT from which LIQUEUR MUSCAT is made). Much of this Muscadelle is grown in South Australia but there are plantings in the RUTHERGLEN district famous for Australian specialities too.

On the same vine classification mission to Australia, Truel also identified as Muscadelle vines imported from California as 'Sauvignon Vert' and it is probable that California's minuscule plantings of the variety known there as Sauvignon Vert (a total of less than 100 acres / 40 ha in 1991) are in fact of the third Bordeaux variety rather than Sauvignon Vert (or TOCAI Friulano).

MUSCADET, one of France's dry white commodity wines which is generally underrated outside France. The Muscadet region extends mainly south east of Nantes near the mouth of the Loire, on about 11,000 ha / 27,170 acres of gently rolling, Atlantic-dominated countryside where hundreds of wine farmers maintain small family vine holdings devoted to one grape variety. The white MELON de Bourgogne, a reliable but relatively neutral variety, was introduced to the region in the 17th century by the DUTCH WINE TRADE who were in need of distilling material for their BRANDEWIJN and had the means to transport it. The terrible winter of 1709 killed a high proportion of the red wine grapes previously grown here and transformed it into a predominantly white wine region.

The most significant, and varied, appellation by far, representing four in every five bottles, is **Muscadet de Sèvre-et-Maine**, named after two small rivers which flow through this, the most monocultural part of the Pays Nantais south and east of the city. Indeed more Muscadet de Sèvre-et-Maine is produced every year than in any other Loire appellation. Particularly ambitious wines are made on the clay soils of Vallet, while those from the sandier soils of St-Fiacre are also much admired, although schist underlies most of the best terrain here. The appellations known as **Muscadet des Coteaux de la Loire** and, simply, **Muscadet** are generally less exciting and much less common.

A high proportion, almost half, of Muscadet labels trumpet the fact that the wine was matured *sur lie*, its flavour at least theoretically enriched by LEES CONTACT. So neutral is the Melon grape that Muscadet producers have long been able to store their wines over the winter without RACKING them off the lees, and without the risk of picking up off-flavours. This left the wines with a little more flavour and a small amount of CARBON DIOXIDE when they came to be bottled the following spring. The modern, usually NÉGOCIANT, alternative has been to inject some carbon dioxide into a blended wine before bottling, and the expression *sur lie* has come to mean very little in the Muscadet region (although the best producers and négociants still use the old method).

At its worst Muscadet is an anodyne, watery, dry white with or without a little sparkle, but at its best it captures the essence of France's north Atlantic coast and provides an authentic, light, tangy, almost salty foil for its seafood. (It is the only French unfortified wine for which the authorities specify a maximum ALCOHOLIC STRENGTH, 12.3 per cent.) Since the mid 1980s, producers have been experimenting with such techniques as BARREL FERMENTATION and LEES STIRRING. Muscadet can no longer be dismissed as a simple, homogeneous wine.

Other wines produced in the Pays Nantais are GROS PLANT, Coteaux d'ANCENIS, and FIEFS VENDÉENS.

See also LOIRE and map on pp. 576–7.

MUSCADINIA, a section of the botanical genus VITIS. *Muscadinia* includes the three genera *rotundifolia*, *munsonia*, and *popenoei*, according to Galet. The other section *Vitis* contains the true grapevine, as outlined in BOTANICAL CLASSIFICATION. (Some botanists have more recently suggested that *Vitis* and *Muscadinia* be considered separate genera rather than sections of *Vitis*.) *Muscadinia* and *Vitis* differ in chromosome number and morphology.

Members of the *Muscadiniae* occur only in the south eastern United States and Mexico, but seem related to *Vitis ludwigii* found as fossil seeds in Tertiary sediments of northern Europe. There is speculation that *Muscadinia* can be regarded as transitional between the temperate genus *Vitis* and *Ampelocissus*, which is adapted to tropical climates. Species of the three genera have similar characteristics.

The Muscadines, as they are called, typically have large berries with thick skins which occur in small bunches. The three species included in Muscadinia are found in America and Mexico. The best known is *Vitis rotundifolia* of which a number of varieties, most notably SCUPPERNONG, are grown commercially. The very thick skins and musky flavour of Muscadines produce fruit and wine quite different from that of European VINIFERA vines. The most famous variety of Muscadine is Scuppernong, whose cluster has only a few berries which ripen unevenly and drop off when ripe. The large berries have a thick, slippery pulp that is difficult to press and excessive pressure brings bitterness from the skins. Muscadines are typically low in sugar concentration, and require additional sugar at fermentation for the purposes of ENRICHMENT.

A few thousand hectares of Muscadine grapes are grown in the cotton belt in the south eastern United States. According to Pinney, Paul Garrett (1863–1940) made a Scuppernong wine named Virginia Dare after the first child born to English settlers in the United States. This North Carolina wine became the most popular of the American wines after 1900, and Garrett was obliged to increase the volume with wine shipped from California.

According to the Institute MAGARATCH, there is a significant proportion of Muscadine vines in the UKRAINE.

The Muscadines have natural resistance to PIERCE'S DISEASE and can therefore be planted in some areas unsuitable for VITIS species and HYBRIDS of them. They are also usefully resistant to PHYLLOXERA, NEMATODES, DOWNY MILDEW, and POWDERY MILDEW, which makes Muscadine germplasm valuable in VINE BREEDING. For long the different chromosome numbers of *Vitis* (2n = 38) and Muscadines (2n = 40) proved a barrier to breeding, since progeny were typically infertile. However, recent advances have allowed *Muscadine* germplasm to be incorporated into VINE IMPROVEMENT programmes. R.E.S.

Galet, P., *Précis de Viticulture* (4th edn., Montpellier, 1983).

Mullins, M. G., Bouquet, A., and Williams, L., *Biology of the Grapevine* (Cambridge, 1992).

Pinney, T., *A History of Wine in America from the Beginnings to Prohibition* (Berkeley, Calif., 1989).

MUSCARDIN, light red grape variety allowed in to CHÂTEAUNEUF-DU-PAPE.

MUSCAT, one of the world's great and historic names, of both grapes and wines. Indeed Muscat grapes—and there are at least four principal varieties of Muscat, in several hues of berry—are some of the very few which produce wines that actually taste of grapes. MUSCAT HAMBURG and MUSCAT OF ALEXANDRIA are raised as both wine grapes and TABLE GRAPES (although it has to be said that Hamburg is much better in the second role). MUSCAT BLANC À PETITS GRAINS is the oldest and finest, producing wines of the greatest intensity, while MUSCAT OTTONEL, paler in every way, is a relative parvenu.

Muscat grapes were probably the first to be distinguished

and identified and have grown around the Mediterranean for many, many centuries. With such strongly perfumed grapes, described in French as MUSQUÉ as though they were actually impregnated with musk, Muscat grapes have always been attractive to bees and it was almost certainly Muscat grapes that the Greeks described as *anathelicon moschaton*, and PLINY the Elder as *uva apiana*, 'grape of the bees'. Some even theorize that Muscat derives its name from *musca*, the Latin for flies, also attracted to these scented grapes.

Muscat wines, carrying many different labels including Moscato (in Italy) and Moscatel (in Iberia), can vary from the refreshingly low alcohol, sweet and frothy ASTI SPUMANTE, through Muscat d'ALSACE and its fashionable bone dry mimics made from a Muscat surplus resulting from the world's worship of the light and dry, to sweet wines with alcohol levels between 15 and 20 per cent, usually by MUTAGE (as in the VINS DOUX NATURELS of southern France) and Greece. Since a high proportion of the world's Muscat is dark-berried, and since a wide variety of wood ageing techniques are used, such wines can vary in colour from palest gold (as in some of the more determinedly modern Muscats de FRONTIGNAN) to deepest brown (as in some of Australia's LIQUEUR MUSCATS).

Most Muscat vines need relatively hot climates (although see MUSCAT OTTONEL and GERMAN HISTORY in which the medieval cultivation of both light- and dark-berried Muscat vines is documented). There either are or have been many famous Muscats around the Mediterranean. See MOROCCO, GREECE, SICILY, SARDINIA.

Muscat Blanc à Petits Grains is the full name of the oldest and noblest variety of Muscat with the greatest concentration of fine grape flavour, hinting at orange-flowers and spice. Its berries are, as its name suggests, particularly small, and they are round as opposed to the oval berries of MUSCAT OF ALEXANDRIA—in fact another synonym for this superior variety is Muscat à Petits Grains Ronds. But its berries are not, as its principal AMPELOGRAPHICAL name suggests, invariably white. In fact there are pink-, red-, and black-berried versions (although the dark berries are not so deeply pigmented that they can produce a proper red wine) and some vines produce berries whose colour varies considerably from vintage to vintage. Many synonyms for the variety include reference to the yellow or golden (*gallego*, *giallo*, *gelber*) colour of its berries. And Brown Muscat is one of Australia's names for a Muscat population that is more dark than light, and resembles South Africa's Muskadel in that respect (thereby providing more evidence of early viticultural links between these two southern hemisphere producers). Other names for the variety in its many different habitats include Muscat of Frontignan, Frontignac, Muscat Blanc, Muscat d'Alsace, Muskateller, Moscato Bianco, Moscato d'Asti, Moscato di Canelli, Moscatel de Grano Menudo, Moscatel de Frontignan, Muscatel Branco, White Muscat, Muscat Canelli, and Muskadel (in South Africa). Any Muscat with the words Alexandria, Gordo, Romain, Hamburg, or Ottonel in its name is *not* this superior variety.

This particular Muscat may very well be the oldest known wine grape variety, and the oldest cultivated in France, having been established in Gaul around Narbonne, notably at FRONTIGNAN, by the Romans—and possibly even before then brought to the Marseille region by the Greeks. Muscat Blanc has clearly been established for many centuries round the Mediterranean, where its early budding poses few problems. It was certainly already widely esteemed in the vineyards of ROUSSILLON by the 14th century, and dominated them until the 19th century (apparently pre-dating the arrival of MALVASIA from the east). It is Piedmont's oldest documented variety. That it is recorded as growing in Germany, as Muskateller, as early as the 12th century, and is the first documented variety grown in Alsace, in the 16th century, suggests that spring frosts may have been less common then, for the variety has now been replaced by the more accommodating Muscat Ottonel in Alsace and has all but disappeared from a Germany apparently in thrall to the flashily ersatz MORIO-MUSKAT crossing (there were just 50 ha/124 acres of Gelber MUSKATELLER in 1990).

Muscat Blanc also yields more conservatively than other Muscats and is sensitive to a wide range of diseases, which has naturally limited its cultivation—although it has travelled for so long and so widely that it is, according to Galet, the world's twelfth most planted variety (covering slightly more territory than Muscat of Alexandria). This is largely thanks to plantings on a vast scale in the hot, dry vineyards of Argentina, Spain, and the warmer vineyards of the CIS. The Argentine grape census of 1989 noted just under 20,000 ha of Moscatel Rosado, making this darker-berried version of Muscat Blanc the most planted European variety other than PEDRO XIMÉNEZ, as well as another 1,300 ha of Moscato d'Asti. Muscat of Alexandria is identified separately. See ARGENTINA for details of Muscat wines produced.

As Moscatel de Grano Menudo it is still grown in Spain but to a limited extent. Most Spanish wines labelled Moscatel are made from Muscat of Alexandria.

Muscats of various sorts are grown widely in the CIS, particularly MUSCAT OTTONEL and the variety decribed as Muscat Rosé, the pink-skinned form of Muscat Blanc. Muscat of some sort is grown in RUSSIA, UKRAINE, MOLDOVA, KAZAKHSTAN, UZBEKISTAN, TAJIKISTAN, and TURKMENISTAN. Early 20th century bottles labelled White Muscat and Pink Muscat from the extraordinary MASSANDRA Collection, produced in the CRIMEA, have demonstrated the potential for great sweet wines made here.

Muscat Blanc is also grown in ROMANIA, where it is known as TĂMÎIOASĂ Alba, and in BULGARIA where it may simply be called Misket. In Russia it is known as Tamyanka.

In the heart of Habsburg country, Muscat Ottonel has held sway until recently. In the early 1980s Austrians realized the greater potential inherent in their small plantings of Muskateller. Recently, dry, racy Muskatellers from Styria and occasionally the Wachau have been some of the country's most sought after and plantings are increasing.

In Hungary too Ottonel, simply known as Muskotaly, dominates except in the TOKAY district, where Muscat Blanc, there called Lunel or Sargamuskotaly (Yellow Muscat) is grown. Some varietal Muscats of sweet Aszú quality are made from the few hundred hectares that supplement the Furmint and Hárslevelű that are the main ingredients in this extraordinary wine.

If anywhere could be said to be Muscat's homeland it is Greece and here, although it is today grown alongside Muscat of Alexandria (which is the prime Cypriot Muscat), Muscat Blanc à Petits Grains is accorded the honour of being the only variety allowed in Greece's most rigidly controlled Muscats such as those of Samos, Pátrai, and Kefallinía. For the moment Greek Muscat, like its many variations on the MALVASIA theme, is almost invariably sweet, alcoholic, and redolent of history, but drier versions more suited to drinking with food are expected. See GREECE for more details.

This is the Muscat that, as MOSCATO, predominates in Italy, which grows an estimated 13,000 ha of it, most profitably as underpinning for the sweet sparkling wine industry. The light, frothy ASTI SPUMANTE, the subtler MOSCATO D'ASTI, and other spumante and frizzante all over north western Italy demonstrate another facet of the variety's character. Various forms of MOSCATO can be found throughout Italy but most of its produce in the south and islands belongs to the richer, Mediterranean school of wines.

This school represents the traditional face of Muscat Blanc in France but, contrary to almost all other white grape varieties, this Muscat has been gaining ground, chiefly because of the development of less traditional forms of Muscat wine. France's total plantings of Muscat Blanc have been steadily increasing, thanks to the development of a virtually CLAIRETTE-free grapey (Tradition) version of the Rhône's fizzy CLAIRETTE DE DIE.

Muscat Blanc has also been supplanting the still more widely planted Muscat of Alexandria in Roussillon, however, where it is the superior Muscat ingredient in the many and various north Catalonian VINS DOUX NATURELS such as MUSCAT DE RIVESALTES. In the Languedoc and southern Rhône too its increasing area of vineyard reflects increased demand for the golden sweet Muscats of BEAUMES-DE-VENISE, FRONTIGNAN, LUNEL, MIREVAL, and ST-JEAN-DE-MINERVOIS, in which it is the exclusive ingredient. But Muscat has been enjoying a new lease of life in the Midi vinified dry, without the addition of grape spirit to preserve its natural sweetness and add extra alcohol. Such wines with an easily recognizable aroma all too rare in southern French whites, together with their fashionably dry, light impact on the palate, have provided popular inexpensive alternatives to the dry Muscat (usually Ottonel) of Alsace.

In the New World the variety grows, as Brown Muscat and Frontignac with all manner of colour of grape skins, in Australia, where it is capable of the great LIQUEUR MUSCATS, as well as in South Africa, where the wines it produces are known as both Frontignac and MUSCADEL. The 1,000 acres of Muscat used for California wine production are mainly in the central SAN JOAQUIN VALLEY, and almost all of this superior Muscat variety, once variously called Muscat Frontignan and Muscat Canelli and now officially separated into Muscat Blanc and a little Orange Muscat, the Quady winery having based its fortunes on making a sweet wine from the latter. Madera County in the Central Valley is an important source of richer Muscat Blanc, while Paso Robles in SAN LUIS OBISPO has also proved a congenial home.

Galet, P., *Cépages et vignobles de France* (2nd edn., Montpellier, 1990).

MUSCAT D'ALSACE is an Alsace synonym for the vine variety MUSCAT BLANC À PETITS GRAINS. For more details of what to expect of a wine labelled Muscat d'Alsace, see ALSACE.

MUSCAT DE BEAUMES-DE-VENISE is the often delicate VIN DOUX NATUREL from the southern Rhône village of BEAUMES-DE-VENISE.

MUSCAT DE FRONTIGNAN is the old name for the once internationally famous wine of FRONTIGNAN. It is also a French synonym for the grape variety solely responsible for it, MUSCAT BLANC À PETITS GRAINS.

MUSCAT DE LUNEL. See LUNEL for details of this southern Languedoc VIN DOUX NATUREL. It is yet another synonym for the grape variety solely responsible for it, MUSCAT BLANC À PETITS GRAINS.

MUSCAT DE MIREVAL. See MIREVAL for details of this relatively unimportant southern Languedoc VIN DOUX NATUREL.

MUSCAT DE RIVESALTES is the most important appellation of the RIVESALTES region in Roussillon and is by far the biggest Muscat appellation in France. Unlike the four Muscat VINS DOUX NATURELS listed above, and the one listed below, it is made from MUSCAT OF ALEXANDRIA as well as MUSCAT BLANC À PETITS GRAINS.

MUSCAT DE ST-JEAN-DE-MINERVOIS is the golden VIN DOUX NATUREL speciality of ST-JEAN-DE-MINERVOIS in the northern Languedoc and is produced in very limited quantities.

MUSCAT DU CAP CORSE, Corsican VIN DOUX NATUREL. See CORSICA.

MUSCAT HAMBURG is the lowest of the wine-producing Muscats. It comes exclusively in black-berried form and is far more common as a TABLE GRAPE than a wine grape. Its chief attribute is the consistency of its plump and shiny dark blue grapes, which can well withstand long journeys to reach consumers who like black-skinned Muscat-flavoured grapes. In France it is the second most important table grape after Chasselas and it is also relatively important as a table grape in Greece, in eastern Europe, and Australia. It was extremely popular as a greenhouse grape in Victorian England, where it occasionally took the name of Snow or Venn, two of its more successful propagators.

In the world of wine production its importance is limited

but it does produce a fair quantity of light, grapey red throughout eastern Europe, and in CHINA, crossed with the indigenous VITIS AMURENSIS, it has spawned a generation of varieties adapted for wine production.

MUSCAT OF ALEXANDRIA is a Muscat almost as ancient as MUSCAT BLANC À PETITS GRAINS but its wine is distinctly inferior. In hot climates it can thrive and produce a good yield of extremely ripe grapes but their chief attribute is sweetness. (In cooler climates its output can be seriously affected by COULURE, MILLERANDAGE, and a range of fungal diseases.) Wines made from this sort of Muscat tend to be strong, sweet, and unsubtle. The aroma is vaguely grapey but can have slightly feline overtones of geranium rather than the more lingering bouquet of Muscat Blanc.

Some indication of its lack of finesse as a wine producer is the fact that a considerable proportion of the Muscat of Alexandria grown today is destined for uses other than wine. California for example uses its 5,000 acres/2,020 ha for RAISINS. Chile distils most of its Muscat of Alexandria to make PISCO. The variety is even grown under glass in climates as inimical as the Dutch and British to provide grapes for the fruit bowl.

As its name suggests, Muscat of Alexandria is thought to have originated in Egypt and was disseminated around the Mediterranean by the Romans, hence its common synonym Muscat Romain. Its southern Italian synonym is Zibibbo.

Today it is most important to wine industries in that old arc of maritime history Iberia, South Africa, and Australia, where its chief respective names are Moscatel, Hanepoot, and Muscat Gordo Blanco or Lexia, a particularly Australian contraction of the North African port.

Spain, as so often, has the biggest area planted with the variety, perhaps as much as 40,000 ha, but only about half of this serves the wine industry, typically with sweet MOSCATELS of various sticky sorts. Muscat of Alexandria's various Spanish synonyms include Moscatel de España, Moscatel Gordo (Blanco), and most importantly Moscatel de MÁLAGA, which may be a close relative.

In Portugal its most famous incarnation is Moscatel de SETÚBAL but Portugal's Muscat of Alexandria grapes have also been harnessed to produce aromatic, dry, much lower alcohol Muscats whose prototype João Pires was developed, significantly, by an Australian wine-maker who knew well how to transform one of Australia's most planted grape varieties into an early picked, crisp, technically perfect table wine (see FONSECA). This is the fate of the majority of Australia's more than 3,500 ha of Gordo Blanco, once used mainly for fortified wines, although from cooler vineyards it can produce sound, unfortified wines that are sweet because late picked too. With SULTANA, Muscat Gordo Blanco is a mainstay of Australia's hot, irrigated vineyards and the proportion vinified as opposed to dried varies with the dominant market forces of each year. A much higher proportion, almost always the majority, of Muscat Gordo Blanco is made into wine than of Sultana. The wine produced is typically used for blending with, and often softening, more glamorous grape varieties.

Muscat of Alexandria is the dominant Muscat in South Africa and, although it is losing ground, it was still the country's sixth most planted variety in the early 1990s, covering well over twice as much ground as Cabernet Sauvignon, for example. For years it provided sticky, raisiny wines for fortification, as well as everything from grape syrup to raisins. Today some drier, lighter wines are also made from it. See SOUTH AFRICA and HANEPOOT, its traditional Afrikaans name, for more details.

Moscatel de Alejandría was much more important in Chile before the variety there called MOSCATEL DE AUSTRIA supplanted it as chief ingredient in PISCO. Total plantings were well below 2,000 ha by the early 1990s. It is also grown to a relatively limited extent in Argentina, Peru, Colombia, Ecuador, and even Japan.

Although Muscat Blanc is more important in GREECE, Muscat of Alexandria is grown widely there and is the Muscat that predominates in TURKEY, ISRAEL, and TUNISIA, although in much of the Near East nowadays these grapes are eaten rather than drunk. The rich, dark Moscato di Pantelleria is geographically closer to Tunisia than SICILY which administers it and is made from Muscat of Alexandria, or Zibibbo, as it is known in much of Italy. In fact this is the only wine with even a modicum of international renown that is made remotely near to the variety's eponym.

Italy as a whole probably grows about a third as much of this lesser Muscat as of the true Moscato Bianco that predominates in the north but its perceptible influence on the wine industry is negligible. See ZIBIBBO for more details.

In France total plantings of Muscat d'Alexandrie, or Muscat Romain, have remained at about the same level as Italy's, just over 3,000 ha almost exclusively in Roussillon, since the 1960s. Although Muscat Blanc is catching up, it is still the dominant Muscat in this most Spanish corner of France, where at one time its grapes were left to raisin on the vine before adding their distinctive flavour to the highly prized local wines. It is most obvious in Muscat de RIVESALTES but is also blended into other varieties, chiefly GRENACHE of all hues, to produce the *département*'s other VINS DOUX NATURELS. It was the stagnation of sales of such wines in the late 1970s that provided a catalyst for today's southern French dry Muscats (see also MUSCAT BLANC À PETITS GRAINS). The important Roussillon producers Cazes Frères of Rivesaltes began to make dry and off-dry VIN DE PAYS from Muscat grapes surplus to requirements for VIN DOUX NATUREL in the early 1980s and such wines have clearly established themselves despite a subsequent revival of interest in wines such as BANYULS, in which both Muscat of Alexandria (Muscat Romain) and Muscat Blanc are allowed. The latter Muscat predominates in both sweet and dry Muscats of the Languedoc.

MUSCAT OF FRONTIGNAN is a common synonym for MUSCAT BLANC À PETITS GRAINS and this is the Muscat variety that is solely responsible for the VIN DOUX NATUREL of the same name. See also FRONTIGNAN for details of the wine that justifies this synonym.

MUSCAT OTTONEL is the palest of all the Muscats both in terms of the colour of wine produced and in terms of its character. Its aroma is altogether more vapid than the powerful grapey perfumes associated with MUSCAT BLANC À PETITS GRAINS and MUSCAT OF ALEXANDRIA. It was bred as recently as 1852 in the Loire, probably as a table grape from CHASSELAS and the distinctly ordinary Muscat de Saumur, according to Galet.

Its tendency to ripen earlier than these other two Muscats has made it much easier to cultivate in cooler climates and nowadays Muscat Ottonel is the dominant Muscat cultivated in ALSACE. This low-vigour vine, which does best in deep, damp soils, is also grown in eastern Europe, notably in AUSTRIA, where there are still substantial plantings. Until the 1980s it was revered to the exclusion of true Muscat Blanc, or Muskateller, particularly for its rich BOTRYTIZED wines in the Neusiedlersee region, which can be very fine. It may well be that it is at its best as a late harvest wine, for there are some fine, apparently long-living examples from both HUNGARY and ROMANIA (where the variety is often known, respectively, as Muskotaly and TĂMAÎIOASĂ Ottonel. Romania had 6,000 ha / 14,820 acres of Muscat Ottonel in the early 1990s. In Alsace however, VENDANGE TARDIVE Muscat tends to remain a theoretical possibility. One of the most widely planted Muscats in the CIS is Ottonel, often known as Hungarian Muscat. It is planted in RUSSIA, UKRAINE, MOLDOVA, KAZAKHSTAN, UZBEKISTAN, TAJIKISTAN, and TURKMENISTAN.

Galet, P., *Cépages et vignobles de France* (2nd edn., Montpellier, 1990).

MUSCAT ROMAIN, or Roman Muscat, is a common name for MUSCAT OF ALEXANDRIA in Roussillon, where it has for long been the most commonly planted Muscat. It is thought to have been particularly widely dispersed around the Mediterranean by the Romans.

MUSCATELS are DRYING GRAPES produced by sun drying large-berried, seeded grape varieties, usually MUSCAT OF ALEXANDRIA.

MUSHROOM ROOT ROT, vine disease. See ARMILLARIA ROOT ROT.

MUSIGNY, LE, great red GRAND CRU in Burgundy's CÔTE D'OR. For more details see CHAMBOLLE-MUSIGNY.

MUSKATELLER, German for MUSCAT, almost invariably the superior MUSCAT BLANC, or some mutation of it. **Gelber Muskateller**, for example, is the gold-skinned version which is increasingly recognized as superior to MUSCAT OTTONEL in Austria where it is particularly popular in STYRIA. In Germany, homeland of MORIO-MUSKAT, Gelber Muskateller is a distinctly minority interest, and there is even less of the red skinned **Roter Muskateller**.

MUSKAT-OTTONEL is what Germans call their minuscule plantings of MUSCAT OTTONEL.

MUSKAT-SILVANER or **Muskat-Sylvaner** is, tellingly, the common German language synonym for SAUVIGNON Blanc and is used in Germany and Austria to a very limited but increasing extent, notably in STYRIA where the wine is more likely to be called Sauvignon Blanc.

MUSKOTÁLY, name used in HUNGARY for Muscat, usually MUSCAT OTTONEL but also occasionally a yellow-berried form of MUSCAT BLANC À PETITS GRAINS, here called Muscat Lunel.

MUSLIM, sometimes spelt **Moslem**, religion officially foreswearing the consumption of alcohol. See ISLAM.

MUSQUÉ is a French term meaning both perfumed, as in musky, and muscat-like. Many vine varieties, including CHARDONNAY, have a Musqué mutation which is particularly aromatic and may add to the variety's own characteristics a grapey scent reminiscent of MUSCAT.

MUST is the name used by wine-makers for a thick liquid that is neither GRAPE JUICE nor WINE but the intermediate, a mixture of grape juice, stem fragments, grape skins, seeds, and pulp that comes from the CRUSHER-DESTEMMER that smashes grapes at the start of the wine-making process. The French equivalent is *moût*, the Italian and Spanish is *mosto*, and the German is *Most*, but the word 'must' has been used in English for at least 1,000 years with several small nuances of specific meaning. All refer to the mixture of crushed, chopped, or smashed fruit being prepared for, or undergoing, FERMENTATION. A.D.W.

MUST CHILLING, important white wine-making operation, particularly in the NEW WORLD, which delays the onset of fermentation until after pressing, and helps prevent OXIDATION. See REFRIGERATION and TEMPERATURE. France's first MUST CHILLER was installed, by Australians, in the Languedoc, in the early 1990s.

MUST WEIGHT, important measure of grape RIPENESS, indicated by the concentration of dissolved compounds in grape juice or must. Since about 90 per cent of all the dissolved solids in grape juice are the fermentable SUGARS (the rest being acids, ions, and a host of other solutes), any measurement of these solids gives a reliable indication of the grapes' ripeness, and therefore the POTENTIAL ALCOHOL of wine made from them (see FERMENTATION).

Must weight may be measured approximately in the vineyard before harvest using a REFRACTOMETER or in the winery, using a refractometer or a HYDROMETER, calibrated according to one of several different scales for measuring the concentration of dissolved solids used in different parts of the world. This variation is not so surprising when one considers how crucial this statistic is to the wine-making process and therefore how early in the evolution of each country's wine industry a scale will have been adopted. Each scale merely requires a different calibration of the hydrometer, usually with a reading of zero indicating that the density of a solution is exactly one, as in pure water.

BAUMÉ is the scale most commonly used in much of Europe, including France, and Australia. The number of degrees Baumé indicates the concentration of dissolved compounds in a solution calibrated so that it indicates, usefully, the potential ALCOHOLIC STRENGTH of a wine made by fermenting the must to dryness. A must of 11° Baumé, for example, will yield a dry wine with an alcohol content of 11 per cent.

In the United States, and increasingly in Australia, ripeness is most commonly measured in degrees BRIX, also sometimes called Balling, both terms borrowed from the sugar-refining industry. The Brix reading simply indicates the percentage of solids (of which about 90 per cent are SUGARS) by weight.

Wine-makers in Germany most commonly use the OECHSLE scale which simply indicates the DENSITY of the juice, in that a grape juice whose specific gravity is 1.085 is said to be 85° Oechsle. This scale is much discussed since the GERMAN WINE LAW has tended to equate quality with degrees Oechsle. Austria has its own, similar scale, devised at KLOSTERNEUBURG, which measures ripeness in degrees KMW.

Since it takes about 16.5 g/0.6 oz of sugar to produce one per cent alcohol by fermentation, it is possible to calculate the potential alcohol using any of these scales. All of these must weight measurements can be approximately converted among themselves, with Baumé values about five-ninths of Brix/Balling values, and 14.7° Brix/Balling = 60° Oechsle. Some equivalences are outlined in the table, although, according to published scales, the relationship between the different measurements is not a strict one. See nomograms in Hamilton and Coombe.

Baumé (degrees)	Brix/Balling (degrees)	Oechsle (degrees)	Potential alcohol (% vol)
10	18.0	75	10
11	19.8	84	11
12	21.7	93	12
13	23.5	101	13
14	25.3	110	14
15	27.1	119	15

A typical dry wine is made from grapes which measure between 11.1° and 13.3° Baumé, between 20° and 24° Brix or Balling, and between 83° and 104° Oechsle. Grapes grown in ENGLAND in particularly cool years, however, may reach a natural must weight of less than 50° Oechsle, while some grape varieties in the SAN JOAQUIN VALLEY of California can easily reach 30° Brix, as they gradually dehydrate under the intense heat. One German wine harvested at Nussdorf in the PFALZ in 1971 was picked at 326° Oechsle and in 1993 was still fermenting, having reached just 4.5 per cent alcohol.

B.G.C. & A.D.W.

Hamilton, R. P., and Coombe, B., 'Harvesting of winegrapes', in B. G. Coombe, and P. R. Dry (eds.), *Viticulture, ii: Practices* (Adelaide, 1992).

MUTAGE is the process of stopping a MUST (*moût* in French) from fermenting, sometimes by adding SULPHUR DIOXIDE but usually by adding alcohol, thereby creating an environment in which yeasts can no longer work. Mutage transforms fermenting must into a **vin muté** such as a VIN DE LIQUEUR or a VIN DOUX NATUREL. The alcohol may be added before or after the grape juice has been separated from the skins. Mutage plays a crucial part in making PORT, although the term is not used.

MUTATION, spontaneous change to genetic material occurring during cell division in organisms such as grapevines. Since so many VINE VARIETIES are of ancient origin, they have accumulated a substantial load of mutations. Generally mutations are deleterious, but man has had many centuries in which deliberately to select those vines which perform best (a process now formalized as CLONAL SELECTION), so beneficial mutations have been maintained.

Mutation is particularly common among certain black-berried vine varieties that degenerate easily such as PINOT NOIR, CARIGNAN, ASPIRAN, GRENACHE, and TERRET. Most of these have forms called variously Noir (black), Gris (grey), Blanc (white), Rose (pink), Vert (green), Rouge (red), and sometimes more.

Galet lists the types of mutations commonly seen in vines, which include leaf and berry colour, including albinism, absence of hairs on shoots and leaves, deeply lobed leaves, cauliflower-like growths on shoots, fasciations on shoots, very large inflorescences, and absence of inflorescences. Mutation can also cause polyploidy (multiple sets of chromosomes), which leads to 'giant' plants and berries. The table grape Muscat Cannon Hall was thought a polyploid mutant of MUSCAT OF ALEXANDRIA (although this is disputed by Antcliff of Australia). The two Gamay TEINTURIERS, Gamay Fréaux and Gamay de Chaudenay, are thought to be mutations of Gamay de Bouze. A mixture of normal and mutant tisue is known as a chimera, and the varieties Pinot Noir and (Pinot) Meunier are partners in a so-called periclinal chimera. Such plants are essentially composed of a mutant 'skin' enclosing a 'normal' interior. Meunier is essentially similar to Pinot Noir, with the exception of white hairs on the shoot tip and young leaves.

Mutation can be induced by chemicals such as colchicine and by ionizing radiation. A form of genetic variation known as somaclonal mutation is induced during TISSUE CULTURE, and it is thought that this will be a useful means of increasing clonal variation among existing varieties. R.E.S. & J.Ro.

Galet, P., *Cépages et vignobles de France* (2nd edn., Montpellier, 1990).
—— *Précis de viticulture* (4th edn., Montpellier, 1983).
Mullins, M. G., Bouquet, A., and Williams, L., *Biology of the Grapevine* (Cambridge, 1992).

MUZZLE, the wire which holds a SPARKLING WINE cork in place.

MW, abbreviation for MASTER OF WINE.

MYCODERMA. See FILM-FORMING YEASTS.

MYCOPLASMA, small and sometimes submicroscopic organisms similar to BACTERIA. They are associated with vine diseases of the PHLOEM, and are transmitted by insects and grafting. See also FLAVESCENCE DORÉE.

MYCOPLASMA DISEASES, group of diseases which result from mycoplasma-like organisms and can affect vines. These organisms are like BACTERIA but smaller. They can be deadly to vines and are often spread by insects. (See also FLAVESCENCE DORÉE.) R.E.S.

Pearson, R. C., and Goheen, A. C., *Compendium of Grape Diseases* (St Paul, Minn., 1988).

N

NAGYBURGUNDI is Hungarian for BLAUFRÄNKISCH.

NAHE, wine region in GERMANY of 4,580 ha/11,318 acres of vines, scattered over a wide area on either side of the river Nahe (see map on p. 442). Vineyards begin upstream at Martinstein, with Monzingen being the first famous and ancient wine village, mentioned as early as 778. Good-quality wine is produced in many parts of the region but the greatest concentration of fine vineyards is in three main areas. First there is the pretty stretch of the river between Schloss Böckelheim and Bad Münster am Stein-Ebernburg, covering Niederhausen, Norheim, and Traisen. Here the vineyards have been modernized and reconstructed where necessary and practical (see FLURBEREINIGUNG), to produce world-class RIESLING wines from volcanic and in some places, porphyritic soil. The DOMÄNE Niederhausen, owned by the state of Rheinland-Pfalz, is one of the most respected producers in this part of the region, and in the Nahe valley as a whole. The second outstanding area, also famous for its Rieslings, lies on the northern outskirts of Bad Kreuznach, immediately adjacent to the town. The third is near the confluence with the Rhine at Bingen, 116 km/72 miles from the source of the Nahe. Outside these three main areas vines are found where local growing conditions are favourable and viticulture is economically sensible.

The climate of the Nahe is dry, with the annual rainfall dropping to 500 mm/20 in between Bad Kreuznach and Bingen. The rain is at its heaviest in August, when it swells the ripening grapes, but the autumn HARVEST season is usually dry. Only a little over a quarter of the area under vine is on flat land, and the warmer MESOCLIMATE of sloping terrain (see HILLSIDE VINEYARDS) is as important here as it is on the MOSEL. MÜLLER-THURGAU has long been the most widely grown vine variety, but during the 1980s its area decreased by over nine per cent. Thus Müller-Thurgau has been used chiefly as part of a blend sold under a GROSSLAGE collective site name (Rüdesheimer Rosengarten, for example,) although as a VARIETAL wine from the upper end of the region at Meddersheim, it can surprise with its firm and lively character. With RIESLING and SILVANER, Müller-Thurgau is also a constituent of the medium dry Nahesteiner, a blend produced by co-operative cellars and producers' associations, Erzeugergemeinschaften, and sold in litre bottles, mainly in Germany. Some three per cent or so of LIEBFRAUMILCH originates in the Nahe, and here too Müller-Thurgau plays a role.

Among the best producers, Riesling represents about 65 to 75 per cent of their vines and by the mid 1990s it was for the first time grown more widely in the region than any other vine variety. Its current share of 23 per cent of the region's total vineyard area has varied little in the last 15 years, which suggests that any site offering good conditions for Riesling already has the vine growing in it.

In 1960 Silvaner covered over half of the region but today it accounts for only 12 per cent, and its share continues to dwindle. Silvaner is a reliable vine whose wine in the Nahe is sound, solid, and usually unremarkable. If it becomes more profitable for growers to produce fewer but better grapes, Silvaner may retrieve some of the land lost to Müller-Thurgau.

Most inexpensive Nahe wine is blended to suit the needs of German supermarkets and grocery chains, where large bottlings of one type of wine are required. Such wines do not normally show much regional character but they are often a little more robust in flavour than similar wines from the neighbouring RHEINHESSEN.

For wines of finesse one must turn to the private and state-owned properties. At its best, Nahe Riesling shows vineyard style well, and, as an increasing proportion of wine is bottled with less residual sugar, other flavours also become more pronounced. In recent years the region has seen experiments with BARRIQUES, but it is a treatment which seems better suited to wines made from PINOT than Riesling. Cool cellar fermentation has long been practised to retain freshness of flavour, and CASK AGEING in large old wooden ovals, from which all oak flavours have long dispersed, is usual for Riesling on good estates. Bottlers on the Nahe are as keen as anyone in Germany to see their wines married to food, and, probably with this in mind, nearly a quarter of the region's quality wine is now dry (TROCKEN) or medium dry (HALBTROCKEN). On some estates a high level of ACIDITY is considered almost more important than a good MUST WEIGHT. Acid cannot be added to German wine, but an addition of sugar is allowed for ENRICHMENT purposes, sometimes even to potential SPÄTLESE and AUSLESE musts. The resulting wines must then be downgraded (since QMP wines cannot be legally enriched) and sold on their perceived merits as table wine TAFELWEIN or simple quality wine QBA at a relatively high price. The modern growers on the Nahe are energetic in their search for new styles of wine but, for most, these remain a sideline. Perhaps because of the region's geographical position, its wines are often likened by commentators to a cross between those of the MOSEL and those of the Rheinhessen. The comparison is fair, if a little superficial.

There are two main co-operative cellars which sell their

wine in bottle, and handle about a quarter of the region's harvest. The wines of the first, the Nahe-Winzer-Kellereien, come from a wide catchment area, and are sold mainly on the export market, or in the supermarkets and grocery chains of Germany. More than half the grapes received by the co-operative cellar at Meddersheim are Riesling, which rightly suggests wine of above average quality. All is sold in bottle (as opposed to in bulk), much to the wholesale trade and the consumer.

Good Nahe wine at all quality levels is underpriced in Germany. The leading estates are aiming to improve their position in the market by the end of the 1990s, and hope to obtain prices on a level with those of the Rheingau. Their main customers are the wine trade in Germany, the export market, industry, the consumer, and, for some, the restaurant trade. I.J.

NAPA, small town north of San Francisco in CALIFORNIA that gives its name to **Napa County** and, California's most famous wine region and now an AVA, the **Napa Valley**. Although Napa was one of the last of California's coastal counties to receive the vine, the Napa Valley has earned the state's wine most of its fame both inside and outside the UNITED STATES in both the 19th and 20th centuries. In America if not the wine world, 'the Valley' is Napa Valley (just as Burgundy's DOMAINE DE LA ROMANÉE-CONTI is 'the Domaine').

Napa landmark—the Robert Mondavi winery at Oakville.

Something about the place has attracted, not just willing investors, but owners and wine-makers with aggressive desires to make names for themselves and their properties. The first generation of them outstripped all competitors between 1880 and 1919. The third kept Napa out in front of the pack during the boom times between 1966 and the early 1990s. But it was an undervalued interim group that kept the flame alive through the lean years between 1933 and 1966, when California wine was at its ebb. Six companies, Beaulieu Vineyard, Beringer Vineyards, the Christian Brothers, Inglenook Vineyards, Charles Krug, and Louis M. Martini, pursued fine wine under their own labels when most districts sold commodity products in bulk (see CALIFORNIA, history). Their vineyards provided the models that attracted the dizzying investments of the 1970s and 1980s, when vineyard acreage tripled and the number of Napa wineries shot from fewer than 20 to more than 200, including such now prominent wineries as Heitz Cellars, Robert MONDAVI winery, Stag's Leap Wine Cellars, and Sterling Vineyards.

The Napa Valley proper is a long, lazy arc with its foot in San Francisco Bay and its head on the shoulder of Mount St Helena. Like most of the north–south valleys around San Francisco Bay, it has a cool end at the bay and a warm one away from it, although it is barely more than 20 miles/32 km end to end, and sometimes less than a mile wide. With more than 30,000 acres/12,000 ha of vineyard in the Napa Valley AVA, the main valley has little more land to plant, although a succession of smaller valleys in hills to the east such as Chiles and Pope valleys offer some room for expansion.

Napa's diversity of exposure, climate, and soil has led to several sub-AVAs within the generously drawn main AVA. Several old-timers resisted dilution of the identity when the AVA boundaries were being decided, and distinctions among the wines makes even greater refinement of internal boundaries seem inevitable. With or without diversity, Napa has been such a congenial home to Chardonnay and Cabernet Sauvignon that one could argue a case for Napa's having caused their popularity, not the other way around. Versatile growing conditions give Napa growers Sauvignon Blanc, Zinfandel, and several other varieties as options should the markets for Chardonnay and Cabernet Sauvignon falter.

Howell Mountain AVA
Howell Mountain won its pre-PROHIBITION fame for Zinfandel, but the current generation of growers and wine-makers, led by Dunn Vineyards and La Jota, has turned sharply towards Cabernet Sauvignon as the variety of choice. The district ranges upward from 1,400 ft/430 m elevation in Napa's east hills, and has as its anchor the Seventh Day Adventist community of Angwin.

Mount Veeder AVA
A sub-AVA stretches out along ridgetops that separate the Napa and SONOMA valleys, and is centred on the peak from which its name comes. Its oldest winery is Mayacamas, its largest the Hess Collection. Most of the plantings in it are Cabernet Sauvignon and Chardonnay.

Oakville
AVA that is part of a grower plan to divide the Napa Valley floor into communes much as the Haut MÉDOC is divided. If the scheme succeeds, the sub-AVAs from south to north would be Napa, Yountville, Oakville, Rutherford, St Helena, and Calistoga. By 1994 only Oakville and Rutherford had been authorized.

Rutherford
With Oakville, the name of Rutherford was put before BATF during 1991 as part of the grower plan to divide all of the Napa Valley into community-based sub-AVAs. The original petition would have further divided Rutherford into Rutherford and Rutherford Bench, but that refinement was dropped before hearings began. Before AVAs, Rutherford Bench was an innocently coined name meant to distinguish the long, snaky alluvial band stretching along the Napa Valley's west side, from St Helena down to Yountville, from the valley floor closer to the Napa river. Rutherford Bench has become a source of equal parts of humour and ire in Napa. It ain't a bench, it ain't only at Rutherford because it extends through Oakville, it shuts out too much good vineyard, say the wrathful. Whatever, the west side of this middle stretch of valley holds many of California's premier patches of Cabernet Sauvignon, including Beaulieu Vineyard Nos. 1 and 2, Inglenook, Martha's Vineyard, Bella Oaks, Bosche, Sycamore, Mondavi's To Kalon, and more.

Stags Leap District AVA
A sub-AVA, Stags Leap District (shunning the apostrophe) celebrates Cabernet Sauvignon and Merlot, and virtually nothing else. All of its fame rests on varietals from those grapes. Other varieties grow well, but not with enough regional distinctiveness to call attention to themselves. The hallmarks of its Cabernets are a greater emphasis on berry flavours—or a lesser emphasis on herbs—than counterparts from other parts of Napa, and suppler TANNINS. Curiously, it was little planted to Cabernet before 1970. It takes its name from a palisade north east of Napa City, under the towering wall of which its vineyards lie. Clos du Val and Stag's Leap Wine Cellars were the pioneers, since joined by Chimney Rock, Pine Ridge, Shafer, Silverado Vineyards, and others.

Wild Horse Valley AVA
Wild Horse is an appellation east of the city of Napa. Most lies in the south eastern corner of Napa County and within the Napa Valley AVA; a small bit spills into Solano County to the east. The track record is too short and narrow to be characterized. Most of the grapes go into wines with Napa Valley appellations.

See also CALIFORNIA and map on page 178.

Conaway, J., *Napa: The Story of an American Eden* (Boston, 1990).

NAPLES, large south Italian port and capital of the CAMPANIA region. The area around Naples had once produced all the greatest wines of Ancient ROME, not only FALERNIAN, but also CAECUBAN, MASSIC, and SURRENTINE, but in viticultural terms it was never to be that famous again. With the fall of the Roman empire and the economic decline of Italy, the market for fine wines collapsed. Because the Lombards failed to take the whole of Italy in 586, Naples remained part of the empire, which had Ravenna as its capital. Until the 11th century the political situation was confused and Naples, although nominally part of the Byzantine empire, was in fact an independent city state, which prospered from its trade with the East. When the Normans had driven the Saracens out of SICILY, Naples, along with southern Italy, came under Norman rule. Naples ceased to rely mostly on its eastern trade, and under Robert Guiscard and King Roger II of Sicily turned to Sicily instead. Like Palermo and Messina, Naples grew rich as an exporter of grain. In 1194 the kingdom passed to the Hohenstaufen emperor and was afterwards, in 1266, conquered by Charles, count of Anjou. In 1282 the revolt against the harsh Charles of Anjou split the kingdom of Sicily in two. The richer part, Sicily itself, was annexed by the king of Aragon, and Naples became a separate kingdom consisting of southern Italy as far north as the ABRUZZI.

Its oriental trade, which dates from Naples's period under Byzantine rule, included the strong sweet MALMSEY of Crete, but APULIA produced similar wines itself, mostly for consumption in southern Italy. Naples also traded in the VERNACCIA of Liguria, which it sold to Sicily, Majorca, and PARIS. These wines were known collectively as *vini grechi*, because like the wines imported from the Aegean they were high-quality sweet wines, capable of surviving a long sea voyage. The wines of Campania, which were not in the Greek style but dry, were called *vini latini*. They were considered inferior and were not long lived enough to be sent overseas to northern Europe. The highest regarded of the *vini latini* were those of Mount Vesuvius, which were sold to other parts of Italy by the merchants of Naples and Salerno. In addition, Naples sold CALABRIAN wines to Aragon and the Balearic islands.

All this made Naples the most important Mediterranean wine-trading port in the 14th century, yet, because of its many changes of regime and its severance from Sicily in 1282, Naples never became a political or economic power to match the northern city states. Geographically it was far better placed than VENICE and GENOA to conduct the lucrative trade in Aegean wines and other luxury goods with northern Europe, but by the late 13th century, when Genoa began to send its galleys to Southampton and Bruges, Naples was no longer in a position to compete.

See ITALY. H.M.W.

Lopez, R. S., 'The trade of mediaeval Europe: the South', in *The Cambridge Economic History of Europe*, 7 vols., ii: *Trade and Industry in the Middle Ages* (Cambridge, 1987).

Melis, Frederigo, 'Produzione e commercio dei vini italiani nei secoli XIII–XVIII', Annales cisalpines d'histoire sociale, 1/3 (1972), 107–33.

NARDO, DOC for robust red wine made mainly from NEGROAMARO grapes in south east Italy. For more details see APULIA.

NATURE when applied to a French wine usually means still.

NATURREIN, term used in mid 20th century GERMANY to describe **Naturwein**, wine to which no sugar had been added for the purposes of ENRICHMENT of its alcoholic strength. The term was abolished by the 1971 GERMAN WINE LAW, which established as QMP all wine which would have qualified as Naturwein. See GERMAN HISTORY.

NAVARRE, known in Spanish as **Navarra**, autonomous region in north east SPAIN which also lends its name to a denominated wine zone. The kingdom of Navarre once stretched from BORDEAUX to Barcelona but today this extensive denomination is overshadowed by the neighbouring DO zone RIOJA, a small part of which extends into the province of Navarre (see map on p. 907). The wines share a common history.

Pilgrims *en route* to Santiago de Compostela fuelled the demand for wine in the Middle Ages. Later, in the mid 19th century, both Rioja and Navarre benefited greatly from their proximity to France after the arrival of the PHYLLOXERA louse. Because northern Spain was affected considerably later than south west France, vineyards here were expanded and large quantities of Navarran wine were sold to producers in France until phylloxera arrived in Navarre itself in 1892. The region recovered fairly quickly but the area under vine in 1990 was less than a third of that a century before.

The region splits into five subzones according to climate, from the cooler slopes of the Baja Montaña close to the Pyrenean foothills and the slightly warmer Valdizarbe and Tierra Estella districts in the north of Navarre, to Ribera Alta in the centre of the region, and Ribera Baja round the city of Tudela in the south. Rainfall totals range between 600 mm (23 in) in the north and 400 mm in the south and east, while summer temperatures become correspondingly warmer. With over 30 per cent of Navarre's vineyards, Ribera Baja has traditionally been the most important of the five subzones, although most of the new planting in the late 1980s and early 1990s took place in the cooler north.

The GARNACHA grape dominates Navarre's vineyards and accounted for over 80 per cent of total production in the early 1990s, with TEMPRANILLO coming a poor second. Garnacha lends itself to good, dry rosé which Navarre continues to make in large quantities. Its red wines can be rather clumsy and coarse unless wine-making is carefully controlled, when Garnacha can produce light, fruity reds for early drinking. White wines account for less than 10 per cent of the region's production and have traditionally been made from the neutral Viura, or MACABEO, grape. In 1981 the Consejo Regulador set up an impressive oenological research station at Olite to experiment with different VINE VARIETIES, and the imported French vines CABERNET SAUVIGNON, MERLOT, and CHARDONNAY have since been recognized and encouraged under the local regulations.

One of the first wine CO-OPERATIVES in Spain was established here in 1911, and most of the region's wines continue to be produced in large, often rather moribund, co-operative

BODEGAS. The oenological station EVENA is working closely with the co-operatives, but most of the innovation is taking place among a handful of private producers. The intensive replanting programme currently under way should help to carve a distinctive niche for Navarre's wines in future.

R.J.M.

NEBBIOLO, great black grape variety responsible for some of the finest and longest lived wines in Italy. It is native, and almost confined, to the PIEDMONT region in the north west, and is its most distinctive and distinguished vine.

Italian Nebbiolo

It has been hypothesized that PLINY the Elder's citation of Pollenzo (just north west of the current Barolo zone) as a source of outstanding wine referred to wines made from this grape. Documents from the castle of Rivoli dating from 1235 have also been taken as a description of Nebbiolo. Canale d'Alba in the Roero district provides the first unmistakable historical reference in 1303: 'une carrata [barrel] de bono puro vino nebiolo'. PETRUS DE CRESCENTIIS' *Liber ruralium commodorum* in 1304 made an unambiguous link between the 'Nubiola' grape, which he termed 'delightful', and 'excellent wine'. He described it as much sought after in Asti and its environs. The communal statutes of La Morra of 1431 furnish further evidence that the variety's exceptional qualities were understood and appreciated at an early date: substantial fines were levied against those guilty of cutting down a Nebbiolo vine, and recidivists could be punished with the loss of their right hand or even hanging. Some have postulated that the name derives from *nobile*, or noble, but a more likely derivation is from *nebbia*, or fog, a frequent phenomenon in Piedmont in October when the grape is harvested.

Modern Piedmont has shown its respect for Nebbiolo in a more concrete, if less poetic, way by restricting its planting to a few selected areas: the total production of wines from the grape rarely exceeds 125,000 hl/3.3 million gal, or just three per cent of the region's production, less than a fifteenth of the annual production of BARBERA. Nebbiolo is always a late ripener, with harvests that regularly last well past the middle of October, and the variety is accordingly granted the most favourable HILLSIDE exposures, south to south west being generally considered the most desirable. Perhaps as important as the vineyard site, however, are the soils in which the variety is planted: Nebbiolo has shown itself to be extremely fussy and has given best results only in the calcareous marls to the north and south of Alba on the right bank of the Tanaro in the DOCG zones of BARBARESCO and BAROLO respectively. Here Nebbiolo-based wines reach their maximum aromatic complexity, and express a fullness of flavour which balances the relatively high ACIDITY and substantial TANNINS which are invariably present.

Good Nebbiolo wines are also produced in varying soil types in the hills on the left and right banks of the Sesia river in the provinces of Novara (see BOCA, GHEMME, SIZZANO, FARA) and Vercelli (see LESSONA, BRAMATERRA, GATTINARA). Here Nebbiolo is called SPANNA and is usually blended with softer VESPOLINA and/or BONARDA grapes.

NEBBIOLO D'ALBA, a tamer, less savage version of the grape, only suggests the heights which the variety can gain in more choice positions. The ROERO district on the left bank of the Tanaro has predominantly sandy soils which give a lighter and softer version of Nebbiolo, but with its unmistakable aromas of tar and roses.

Nebbiolo, often called Picutener, also plays the leading role in the postage stamp-size DOC of CAREMA on the border of the Valle d'Aosta, in the neighbouring and equally Lilliputian DOC of Donnaz in the Valle d'AOSTA itself, and in Lombardy in the VALTELLINA, where it is known as Chiavennasca—the only sizeable zone where Nebbiolo is cultivated outside Piedmont. The latter three areas, subalpine in latitude and definitely cool during the growing season, produce a medium bodied style of Nebbiolo in which the fruit must frequently struggle against the grape's tannic asperity and acidic sharpness; the added ripeness of warmer vintages is even more valuable here.

These zones apart, Nebbiolo is hardly known in Italy, although it is an ingredient in the FRANCIACORTA cocktail, and the innovative VENETO wine-maker Giuseppe Quintarelli makes a RECIOTO version of Nebbiolo, a modern reminder of what may have been Piedmont's legion of DRIED GRAPE WINES.

Three principal CLONES of Nebbiolo are conventionally identified: Lampia, Michet, and Rosé. The last of these is disappearing because of the pale colour of its wines, while Michet is Lampia afflicted with a virus which causes the vine's canes to fork. More importantly, however, this clone, while producing smaller YIELDS and particularly intense aromas and flavours, does not adapt itself to all soils. Most producers, mindful of the relatively embryonic state of clonal research, prefer to rely on a careful MASS SELECTION in their vineyards rather than staking their future on a single clone.

The total area planted with Nebbiolo declined in the 1980s, to about 5,200 ha/13,000 acres in 1990—about half the area planted with Piedmont's Dolcetto, and about a tenth the total area of Italian vineyard planted with Barbera. D.T.

Outside Italy

The quality of Barolo and Barbaresco has inspired vine-growers all over the world to experiment with Nebbiolo, but the resulting wines have so far lacked most of the variety's best qualities on home ground. Nebbiolo has somewhat reluctantly accompanied Barbera to both North and South America. Few California examples have so far demonstrated much of the grape's instrinsic worth, although some are hard at work on it, and high yields tend to subsume the variety's quality in South America. The few hundred hectares planted in Argentina are mainly in San Juan province.

NEBBIOLO D'ALBA is an Italian DOC red produced from NEBBIOLO grapes grown in 32 townships surrounding the city of Alba in the PIEDMONT region and is, to all extents and purposes, a satellite appellation to BAROLO and BARBARESCO. Seven of the townships are partially inside the Barolo DOCG

Even in a lighter vintage such as 1987, **Nebbiolo** produces particularly deeply coloured wine, as here from Aldo Conterno's stainless steel fermentation tank.

zone, although the areas which can produce Nebbiolo d'Alba—the southern sections of Monforte d'Alba and Novello, the north eastern tip of La Morra, all but a western slice of Diano d'Alba, the northern parts of Verduno, Grinzano Cavour, and Roddi—have been carefully and intelligently excluded from the Barolo zone. The wines are, in fact, softer, less intense, and faster maturing than a Barolo or a Barbaresco, more generically 'Nebbiolo' and less pointedly characterful. D.T.

NEBBIOLO DELLE LANGHE, a VINO DA TAVOLA of the PIEDMONT region in north west Italy. It should be noted that the great DOCG red BAROLO cannot be declassified into the DOC wine NEBBIOLO D'ALBA; producers in the Barolo zone can only declassify their less successful efforts into the vino da tavola Nebbiolo delle Langhe, which is usually a particularly light version of this usually intense grape.

A few leading Barolo producers—Aldo Conterno and Elio Altare in particular—have begun to prepare special CUVÉES for small oak BARREL MATURATION, however. These wines, which command a much higher price and enjoy an entirely different prestige from the average Nebbiolo delle Langhe, carry the same classification on the label. Although the number of these wines will inevitably grow, they represent only a tiny fraction of the total Nebbiolo delle Langhe production. D.T.

NECROSIS, a term used to describe death of tissue. For example, necrotic spots of leaf tissue caused by DOWNY MILDEW appear blackish brown among the healthy tissue. For many vine foliar diseases and disorders, the yellowing of leaf sections, or CHLOROSIS, precedes necrosis.

NÉGOCIANT, French term for a MERCHANT and one used particularly of wine merchants who buy in grapes or wine, blend different lots of wine within an APPELLATION, and bottle the result under their own label. Making a perfectly balanced blend from a number of imperfect parts is a potentially noble calling, but one that once provided so many opportunities for ADULTERATION AND FRAUD that it brought the entire profession into question, if not ill repute.

The role of the négociant is particularly worthwhile in Burgundy, where the négociants are concentrated in Beaune, and where so many individual growers produce tiny quantities from each of a number of different appellations. The selling of the DOMAINE BOTTLED concept by the likes of Frank Schoonmaker and Alexis Lichine was so successful that it cast a slur on the work of the négociants by imputation. This was unfortunate, but the likes of DROUHIN and JADOT have worked hard to prove how they can be a source of more reliable wine-making skills than all but the top one per cent of grower wine-makers. The Burgundy négociants have been acquiring increasingly significant vineyard holdings of their own, so that BOUCHARD PÈRE ET FILS in Beaune and Faiveley of Nuits-St-Georges, for example, are two of the CÔTE D'OR's most subtantial vineyard owners. The term **négociant-éleveur** implies that the négociant oversees the ÉLEVAGE of the wine it sells.

Bordeaux also has a great concentration of négociants, many of which own CHÂTEAUX (while some of the FIRST GROWTH châteaux also now own a négociant business). For more details, see BORDEAUX TRADE.

NEGRA MOLE and **Negramoll**, Iberian dark-skinned grape variety. See TINTA NEGRA MOLE.

NÉGRETTE is the black grape variety special to the vineyards north of Toulouse. In Côtes du FRONTONNAIS it must dominate the blend and in Vins de LAVILLEDIEU it must constitute at least 35 per cent. Wine made from Négrette is more supple, perfumed, and flirtatious than the more famous south western black grape variety TANNAT can provide, and is best drunk young, with its fruit, sometimes described as having a slightly animal flavour, unsuppressed by heavy oak ageing. As a vine, the variety is inconveniently prone to POWDERY MILDEW and BOTRYTIS BUNCH ROT and is therefore better suited to the hot, dry climate of Toulouse than to many other wine regions. The variety sold as Pinot St George in California in the 1960s and 1970s was thought to be none other than Négrette by French ampelographer GALET on his 1980 tour of American vineyards.

Galet, P., 'La Culture de la vigne aux États-Unis et au Canada', *France viticole* (Sept.–Oct. 1980 and Jan.–Feb. 1981).

NEGROAMARO, or **Negro Amaro**, dark-skinned southern Italian grape variety that is the country's sixth most planted variety with a total of 31,000 ha/76,500 acres in 1990. The variety, whose name means 'black, bitter', is most common in Apulia and is particularly associated with Salento. Although it has traditionally been used for blending, it can produce vigorous red wines worthy of ageing as well as some lively rosé. For more details, see APULIA.

NEMATODES, microscopic roundworms generally found in soil which can seriously harm vines. Some feed on bacteria or fungi and are part of the normal vineyard ecosystem. Others, however, feed on grapevine roots and thus reduce both the size and efficiency of the root system. Although the vines do not necessarily die, they suffer WATER STRESS and deficiencies in VINE NUTRITION and may grow so poorly as to be uneconomic. Some species of nematodes, called NEPO-VIRUSES, are important because they transmit VIRUS DISEASES. The virus can be spread throughout the vineyard from just one infected plant by nematode feeding.

The fact that nematodes damage vines was established only in about 1930, in California. Because of characteristic and visually striking root damage, the root knot nematode, *Meloidogyne* species, was considered most important. However, in 1958 it was discovered that FANLEAF DEGENERATION was spread by nematodes of the species *Xiphenema index*. This milestone discovery in plant pathology was made by Hewitt and colleagues of the University of California at DAVIS. It had been established in France as long ago as 1883 that fanleaf degeneration spread through the soil, and some French authorities believed until the 1950s that the PHYLLOXERA louse was responsible for the spread.

Root knot nematodes occur mainly in sandy soil. Their presence is visible to the naked eye since the knots (swollen tissue or galls) formed in response to their feeding resemble a string of beads on the roots. One female can lay up to 1,000 eggs, and there can be up to 10 generations a year in warm climates. The root lesion nematode *Pratylenchus* also damages vines by feeding on their roots.

The so-called dagger nematode, *Xiphenema index*, is especially important in spreading a number of virus diseases (see FANLEAF DEGENERATION). Other *Xiphenema* species spread other virus diseases. Virus particles can survive for many years in root fragments after an infected vineyard is removed. Replanting a new, 'virus-free' vineyard can lead to disappointment, as reinfection with nematode feeding can follow.

A vineyard in which nematodes were previously present may be subjected to FUMIGATION with injected chemicals before planting. The nematicide DBCP was considered to control all nematodes but is now banned. Methyl bromide and 1,3-dichloropropene are highly effective and can kill nematodes surviving on old root pieces. Ethylene dibromide is less useful for replanting since it does not penetrate roots. Vineyards are temporarily covered with plastic sheeting after injection of the chemical.

Nematode diseases are often spread on infected planting material or by the movement of infected soil on cultivation implements or by irrigation water. Infected nursery plants can be freed of nematodes by dipping them in hot water. Biological control using ROOTSTOCKS is possible and generally preferred. Some VITIS species (*solonis*, *champini*, and *doaniana*) show resistance to nematodes. Among the most nematode-resistant rootstocks are Couderc 1613, Ramsey, Schwarzmann, Harmony, and Dog Ridge. R.E.S.

Hardie, W. J., and Cirami, R. M., 'Grapevine rootstocks', in B. G.

The **Netherlands** have long been an important market for cognac and the wines of western France.

Coombe and P. R. Dry (eds.), *Viticulture, i: Resources in Australia* (Adelaide, 1988).
Winkler, A. J., *et al.* (eds.), *General Viticulture* (2nd edn., Berkeley, Calif., 1974).

NEPOVIRUSES, group of VIRUS DISEASES which are spread from plant to plant by the feeding of NEMATODES (microscopic worms) on roots. Such diseases can be very destructive and almost impossible to control. This is because the virus can survive for years in nematodes and root fragments even after all infected vines have been removed. So, even if a new, supposedly virus-free vineyard is planted, it will quickly become infected by the nematode feeding. Among the important virus diseases in this group are FANLEAF DEGENERATION, tomato ringspot, and tobacco ringspot. R.E.S.

Pearson, R. C., and Goheen, A. C., *Compendium of Grape Diseases* (St Paul, Minn., 1988).

NERELLO, important Sicilian red grape variety. **Nerello Mascalese** is more widely planted than **Nerello Cappuccio** and is concentrated in the north east of the island. The wines produced tend to lack the concentration of NERO D'AVOLA although they are usually high in alcohol. Most of the wine is used for blending. Total plantings of the two varieties together were about 18,000 ha / 44,500 acres in 1990. For more information, see SICILY.

NERO D'AVOLA, red grape variety that is one of the best in Sicily and is also known as Calabrese, suggesting origins in Calabria on the mainland. Total plantings of the variety fell by a third in the 1980s to about 14,000 ha / 34,600 acres in 1990 (only a fraction of Sicily's vineyard devoted to the white CATARRATTO grape), but quality-minded producers on the island value the body and ageing potential which Nero d'Avola can bring to a blend. VARIETAL Nero d'Avola has shown itelf a fine candidate for BARREL MATURATION. For more information, see SICILY.

NETHERLANDS, small north European country incorporating Holland, whose inhabitants are known as the Dutch and in the 17th century played a dominant role in the world's wine and spirit trade (see DUTCH WINE TRADE). They are now serious drinkers of dry and medium sherry, constituting one of the most important export markets for JEREZ in terms of quantity, if not necessarily value. The country also has its own small indigenous wine industry with an impressive history, despite the coolness of the climate. There are records of wine-producing vines growing in Limburg in southern Holland in 1324 and vine-growing around Maastricht ceased only in the early years of the 19th century, discouraged by a series of cold summers and the economic turbulence of the Napoleonic era.

It was not until 1967 that the Netherlands became a wine producer once more when Frits Bosch planted less than a hectare with Müller-Thurgau and Riesling in the far south of the country, resulting in a new dry Dutch wine called Slavante. Others followed, but generally on a very small scale. Only one of the six vineyards registered with the official Dutch Wine Information Centre in 1992, Apostelhoeve near Maastricht, was more than 1 ha in area. Müller-Thurgau, Auxerrois, Riesling, and some of the Pinots are, as in nearby BELGIUM and LUXEMBOURG, the most popular varieties. Wines tend to be light, dry whites of around 10 per cent alcohol, depending heavily on CHAPTALIZATION. See also GREAT BRITAIN for wines produced in a similar climate.

NETS can literally save a grape crop. See BIRDS.

NEUBURGER, sometimes distinguished white grape variety grown almost exclusively in AUSTRIA, where it was the fifth most common white wine grape in 1993. It is a crossing, quite possibly an accidental crossing, of Weissburgunder (PINOT BLANC) × SYLVANER which makes wine that tastes like an even fuller bodied Weissburgunder. It ripens relatively early and achieves a higher MUST WEIGHT than GRÜNER

VELTLINER, Austria's most popular vine. It is grown in most of Austria's wine districts, other than Styria, and in Transylvania in ROMANIA.

NEUSIEDLERSEE, shallow lake in the Burgenland region in the far east of AUSTRIA around which most of the country's best sweet white and red wines are made.

NEVERS is the town that gives its name to the central French *département* of Nièvre, most famous in the wine world for the wines of POUILLY-FUMÉ and for its OAK.

NEW SOUTH WALES, AUSTRALIA's most populous state, consumes far more wine than it produces, although the **Hunter Valley**, 130 km/80 miles north of Sydney, has always had a special hold on the affections (and palates) of Sydneysiders. It is also one of the internationally known regions, notwithstanding its relatively small contribution (less than four per cent) to the country's total crush, and its perverse climate. That climate is abnormally hot for a fine wine district, although the heat is partially offset by high HUMIDITY, by afternoon cloud cover, and by substantial rainfall during the growing season—less beneficially in the years in which most of the rain falls during harvest.

Out of this climatic witches' brew comes exceptionally long-lived dry SEMILLON, the best peaking somewhere between 10 and 20 years of age and assuming a honeyed, buttery, nutty flavour, and texture which suggests it has been fermented or matured in oak, when (traditionally) none was used. Most remarkable is the ALCOHOLIC STRENGTH, often as low as 10 per cent. Since 1970, CHARDONNAY also has proved its worth: Australia's first Chardonnays of note were made in the Hunter Valley by Tyrrells. Here the lifespan is usually much shorter, but there are exceptions. Whether young or old, Hunter Chardonnays are generous and soft, with peachy fruit and considerable VISCOSITY.

SHIRAZ was the traditional red counterpart to Semillon in the Hunter, making extremely distinctive, moderately tannic, and long-lived wines with earth and tar overtones, sometimes described as having the aroma of a sweaty saddle after a hard day's ride. At 20 to 30 years of age, the best acquire a silky sheen to their texture and move eerily close to wines of similar age from the RHÔNE valley in south east France.

CABERNET SAUVIGNON is another relatively new arrival, planted for the first time this century at Lake's Folly winery in 1963. By and large, Hunter Valley wines tend to be more regional than varietal in their statement, a tendency which becomes more marked with age.

Different coloured, but equally vital, **nets** on this bird-prone vineyard.

Riesling, Sauvignon Blanc, and Pinot Noir are among prominent varieties which have been tried and found unsuited to the climate and TERROIR. Small but increasing quantities of VERDELHO and MERLOT offer the most potential outside the principal four varieties, but will never assume the same importance.

Overall, the Hunter Valley produces better white wines than it does red, with Semillon its one unique contribution. If one is to differentiate the **upper Hunter**, a separate viticultural region well to the north, from the **lower Hunter**, the bias towards white wine becomes more acute in the former. Rosemount have enjoyed wide acclaim for their Chardonnay, although the Semillon in particular lacks the concentration and longevity of its lower Hunter Valley counterpart. Hunter Valley wineries regularly buy the exuberant fruit from **Cowra**. **Orange** is a new, much cooler NSW vineyard region.

Mudgee, due west of the Hunter Valley on the inland side of the Great Dividing Range, is first and foremost red wine country, however well the ubiquitous Chardonnay does here. Indeed, Mudgee was the source of a precious virus-free clone of Chardonnay almost certainly brought to Australia in the early 19th century. As with the Hunter Valley, Mudgee has never been attacked by PHYLLOXERA, and has remained continuously in production since 1858.

The climate is as hot as that of the Hunter Valley, but the summer rainfall is significantly lower, and it is rare for harvest rain seriously to interrupt proceedings. The red wines—Shiraz and Cabernet Sauvignon—are deeply coloured and intensely flavoured, and are ideal blend components for the products of the Hunter Valley's frequent wet vintages. Only a small proportion of the grapes growing in Mudgee end up in wines bearing the Mudgee Appellation of Origin insignia (it has its own self-administered CONTROLLED APPELLATION scheme).

The **Murrumbidgee Irrigation Area**, **MIA**, or **Riverina**, centred around Griffith 450 km/275 miles south west of Sydney, produces around 65 per cent of the state's wine. With the notable exception of BOTRYTIZED Semillon (made in a SAUTERNES style), the wines are on a par with those produced along the irrigated RIVERLANDS of the Murray River spanning New South Wales, VICTORIA, and SOUTH AUSTRALIA. The emphasis is on white varieties and on high yields (averaging 17 tonnes/ha or 115 hl/ha (6.5 tons/acre)). Almost 75 per cent of the crush is of white grapes, with Semillon, TREBBIANO, and Muscat Gordo Blanco (MUSCAT OF ALEXANDRIA) in turn accounting for 50 per cent of the total. For its part, Shiraz utterly dominates red grape plantings (60 per cent of the total), Cabernet Sauvignon having been tried and found wanting.

The wines reflect the very warm climate and the quasi-hydroponic growing regimes. The technical excellence of the wineries assures clean, fault-free, mildly fruity wines well suited to the drinker of cask wine (in BOXES), and to the requirements of overseas bulk markets such as Sweden and the own brands of the British retail chains.

The **Canberra district** is home to almost 20 wineries grouped in a ring outside the borders of the Australian Capital Territory. All are small, and rely heavily on cellar door sales to Canberrans and tourists. The few wine-makers with technical skills (or consultants) produce good-quality wines across a broad range of styles in a continental climate characterized by hot days, cold nights, and a dry summer. J.H.

NEW VARIETIES, somewhat loose and relative term used to describe VINE VARIETIES specifically and deliberately developed by man, which effectively means developed since the late 19th century (although it is sometimes used parochially to describe varieties new to a region).

There is interest in producing new varieties because of the possibility of breeding varieties which are resistant, for example, to environmental stresses, fungal and bacterial diseases, and nematodes and insects (see VINE BREEDING). Of these, the major goals are varieties tolerant to the fungal diseases DOWNY MILDEW, POWDERY MILDEW, and BOTRYTIS BUNCH ROT. Unfortunately, new varieties, especially HYBRIDS but even some CROSSES, suffer from the stigma of the poor wine quality of the early French hybrids. The uptake of newly developed grape varieties has been further hindered by consumer preference for traditional varieties, a consequence in part of VARIETAL labelling.

The early French hybridizers mentioned in FRENCH HYBRIDS, were not the only French vine breeders to have developed new varieties. Louis BOUSCHET and his son Henri used controlled pollination from 1824 to create a range of seedlings which after selection became known as the Bouschet crosses. Of these the TEINTURIER variety ALICANTE BOUSCHET is the most important and indeed is the only one to be officially recommended for planting in France. Another early and successful VINIFERA vine breeder was MÜLLER-THURGAU, whose eponymous vine variety was to become the most planted in Germany. A succession of new GERMAN CROSSINGS followed, notably from research institutes at GEISENHEIM, GEILWEILERHOF, Alzey, Würzburg, and Freiburg, producing a large number of new varieties such as, in descending order of the area planted in Germany in the early 1990s, KERNER, SCHEUREBE, BACCHUS, FABER(REBE), MORIO-MUSKAT, HUXELREBE, ORTEGA, DORNFELDER, EHRENFELSER, OPTIMA, REICHENSTEINER, PERLE, HEROLDREBE, SIEGERREBE, REGNER, NOBLING, WÜRZER, DOMINA, KANZLER, SCHÖNBURGER, FREISAMER, FINDLING, RIESLANER, HELFENSTEINER, JUWEL, ALBALONGA, RIESLANER, and, more popular in England than in Germany, GUTENBORNER.

Other new varieties such as Zweigelt, Blauburger, and Neuburger were bred in Austria, the first two at KLOSTERNEUBURG. The emphasis in RUSSIA has been on breeding varieties with cold tolerance as well as disease tolerance, and there are substantial areas, not just in Russia but in other parts of the CIS, planted with varieties such as Saperavi Severny, Stepniak, Fioletovy Ranni, and Cabernet Severny. In NEW YORK state and CANADA the emphasis also has been on developing varieties with cold and disease tolerance, often relying on the French hybrids for resistant genes. Recent releases such as Cayuga White, Melody, and Chardonel are becoming more widely planted.

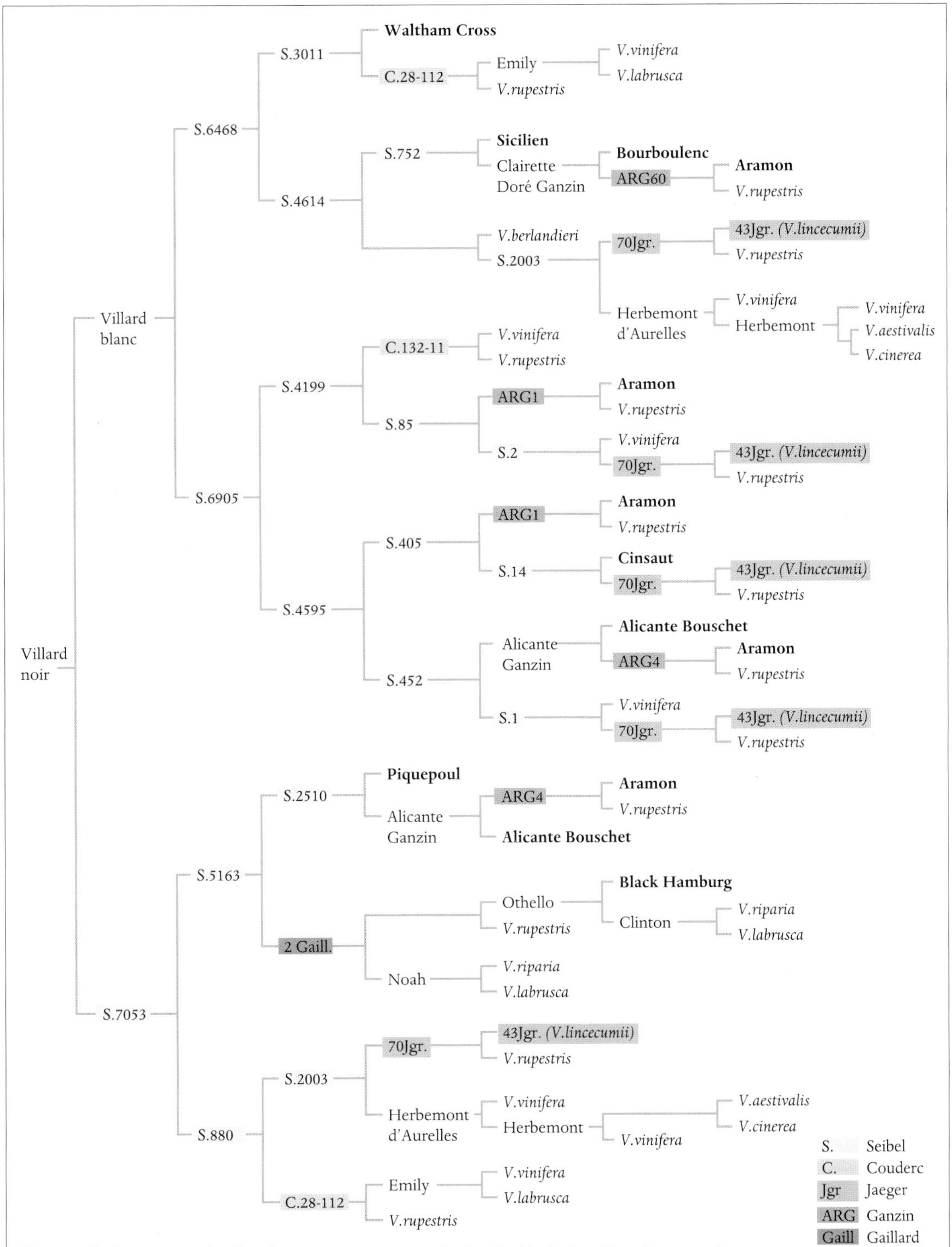

New varieties: an example of just how many varieties may be involved in the breeding of a new variety: pedigree of the French hybrid variety Villard noir.

New varieties in France, most of them developed in association with the University of MONTPELLIER, have been *vinifera* crosses such as PORTAN, CALADOC, Chenanson, Ganson, Gramon, Monerac, CHASAN, Arriloba, Odola, and Perdea. In France new varieties must first be registered with the Comité Technique Permanent de la Sélection des Plantes Cultivées (CTPS) as a prelude to their recognition in the EUROPEAN UNION.

Australia has a vine-breeding programme designed to produce varieties suitable for hot climates, and Goyura, TARRANGO, Tullilah, and Taminga have all been released. In California the varieties CARNELIAN, RUBY CABERNET, EMERALD RIESLING, and FLORA have been established, along with the Teinturiers RUBIRED and ROYALTY.

New varieties of particular interest today are interspecific hybrids because of the opportunities they offer for natural disease resistance with much reduced use of AGROCHEMICALS. These varieties have complex genealogies which may include, not just *vinifera* genes, but also those of various AMERICAN VINE SPECIES, French hybrids, and even Asian vine species. The emphasis is now on wine quality, although these new varieties are by no means officially accepted (see HYBRIDS).

A full account of vine breeding and the inheritance of characteristics is given by Huglin.

See also VINE BREEDING. R.E.S.

Huglin, P., *Biologie et écologie de la vigne* (Paris, 1986).
Mullins, M. G., Bouquet, A., and Williams, L., *Biology of the Grapevine* (Cambridge, 1992).

NEW WORLD, term much used in the wine world, initially somewhat patronizingly but with increasing admiration, to distinguish the colonies established as a result of European exploration which began with some of the longer voyages in the 15th century. As such it contrasts with the OLD WORLD of Europe and the other Mediterranean countries. The vine was widely established in the Old World by the 4th century, but was not planted in the most recent New World country to produce wine, New Zealand, until the 19th century.

History

The new colonists needed wine for religious reasons (see EUCHARIST), and the planting of the vine was a matter of high priority when the conquistadores invaded South America. Cortés was already arranging to plant vines in MEXICO by 1522. By 1530 vines were cultivated in both Mexico and JAPAN, and by the 1550s in PERU, followed soon after by CHILE.

The European settlement of SOUTH AFRICA followed a decision by the DUTCH EAST INDIA COMPANY soon after 1640 to establish a victualling post at the Cape of Good Hope, to serve the growing Batavia trade. Dutch settlement began in 1652 and the first vines were planted in 1655.

British settlers planted the first vines in the UNITED STATES of America in Virginia in 1619; thus began a series of unsuccessful attempts to establish European or VINIFERA vine varieties on the east coast of America. Settlers there were dismayed that they could not cultivate the introduced vine when local wild vines, AMERICAN VINES, grew in profusion in the forests. At that time they were not to know the nature of the pest and disease scourges which were attacking their plantations, and were subsequently to invade Europe (see DOWNY MILDEW, POWDERY MILDEW, and PHYLLOXERA). PIERCE'S DISEASE presumably also played a role in the devastation of these European vines on some sites. Added to these problems were those of much colder winters than *vinifera* varieties can withstand.

There were not the same problems in Baja California where Spanish-Mexican Jesuit MISSIONARIES established vineyards in the 1670s. Although prone to summer drought, this region was free of both FUNGAL DISEASES and PHYLLOXERA and European vines flourished here. Gradually plantings were made further north—in Los Angeles in the 1820s and the NAPA and SONOMA in the 1850s (see CALIFORNIA, history).

Vines were introduced to AUSTRALIA by Captain Arthur Phillip in 1788 as part of the first British colony at Sydney. As this large country was invaded by the British, so the culture of the vine spread also. Viticulture was well established in all modern wine-producing states by the 1850s. Samuel Marsden, a missionary from Australia, is acknowledged as bringing the first vines to NEW ZEALAND in 1819.

Viticulture

New World viticulture is a phrase used to differentiate the viticultural practices in the New World from those of the Old World. It is difficult but not impossible to generalize about the diverse viticultural practices of countries such as the United States, Australia, New Zealand, South Africa, and the countries of South America as opposed to those more usual in Europe.

A common difference is in planting distances, or VINE DENSITY, with a particularly marked contrast between the 1 m by 1 m (3 ft × 3ft) high-density planting of the MÉDOC and the 4 m by 2 m planting pattern common in California and Australia. But no difference is absolute or constant. In some parts of the Old World there is a trend towards wider spacings for reasons of economy, while some growers in the New World are planting more densely in search of higher quality.

The VINE VARIETIES planted in the New and Old Worlds are increasingly similar, as are the ROOTSTOCKS on to which they are grafted. Old World methods are more traditional, many aspects of modern viticultural technology having been developed and first used in the New World. MECHANICAL HARVESTING and MECHANICAL PRUNING, for example, were first developed in America, but by the early 1990s there was a high degree of acceptance, of the former at least, in Europe. Some vineyard sites in the Old World have been used for viticulture for hundreds of years, but there are still potential new vineyard regions to be discovered in the New World.

Technological advance is by no means the sole prerogative of the New World, however. The development and application of new technology in Europe is the equal of anywhere in the world. R.E.S.

Wines

If New World wines can be said to have a style of their own it is that they are much more likely to be VARIETAL both in how they are described on the label and in how they taste. Only a small, but increasing, proportion of New World wines are made with the clear intention of expressing their geographical provenance, but the great majority seen on export markets at least are designed to express the fruit of the vine varieties from which they are made, together perhaps with some WOOD FLAVOUR. 'Fruit driven' is an essentially New World wine description.

New World wine-making, particularly in CALIFORNIA, has been subject to more rapid changes of direction and swings of FASHION than its Old World counterpart. This has been possible because both viticulturists and wine-makers in the New World are much more willing, and much freer, to experiment. (Those in the Old World are more likely to be restrained by local regulations such as the APPELLATION CONTRÔLÉE laws.)

In the Old World, with its centuries of wine-making tradition, Nature is generally regarded as the determining, guiding force. In much of the New World, however, it is regarded with suspicion, as an enemy to be subdued, controlled, and mastered in all its detail, thanks to the insights provided by SCIENCE. (Most of the world's best wines are made by those who incorporate aspects of both these approaches, although some are made almost by benevolent accident by Old World wine-makers whose grasp of scientific principles is meagre.)

New World wine-makers differ from their Old World counterparts from the moment grapes are picked during HARVEST. They are more likely to adopt PROTECTIVE WINE-MAKING methods, attempting to shield grapes, juice, must, and wine from OXYGEN throughout the wine-making process, especially for white wines and light reds. This may involve BLANKETING and MUST CHILLING, using only fully enclosed PRESSES, and careful use of INERT GAS. (By the mid 1990s, however, many New World wine-makers were adopting the Old World technique of deliberately exposing some juice to oxygen before fermentation, particularly for fuller bodied white wines, in an effort to obtain more character.)

Obsession with HYGIENE is generally more marked in the New World than the Old, with the consequence that WATER use is much higher. Rubber boots are not essential for most Old World wine-makers.

In general, target TEMPERATURES throughout wine-making are lower in the New World than in the Old. This is especially true for FERMENTATION. Use of wild, natural, or ambient YEASTS is extremely rare in the New World (although it is gradually becoming rarer in the Old World).

The Old World red wine-making practice of following fermentation with an extended MACERATION in the fermentation vessel is increasingly replaced in the New World by RACKING some red wines into barrel before they have completed their fermentation, in the belief that this results in a softer, fuller, earlier maturing wine.

ENZYMES, both for settling and for releasing flavours, are a much more common wine-making addition in parts of the New World than in the Old.

NEW YORK, north eastern state of the UNITED STATES of America, between the Atlantic and the Great Lakes, historically an important source of wine and still second only to CALIFORNIA as a US wine-producing state. Its inland wine regions share some characteristics with those of Ontario across the CANADA border, particularly those from south and east of Ontario. The market for wine in New York City is one of the world's most competitive and demanding.

History

After unsuccessful trials with VINIFERA around Manhattan Island in the first days of settlement, nothing more is heard of viticulture in New York until the early 19th century. Vine-growing then developed in three regions across the state. The work with native grapes (see AMERICAN VINE SPECIES) of the Long Island nurseryman William Robert Prince led to plantings along the Hudson river from which wine was produced in small quantities by the 1840s.

The second region was the Finger Lakes district of central New York, where significant plantings of native AMERICAN HYBRIDS began in the 1850s. From these a large industry developed, centred on the towns of Hammondsport, Penn Yan, and Naples, and specializing in white wines, both still and sparkling. By the end of the 19th century there were 24,000 acres/9,700 ha of vines in the Finger Lakes region.

In western New York, along the Lake Erie shore, a 'grape belt' developed after the Civil War. A part of the region's grapes went into wine, but the vineyards were increasingly planted to the CONCORD grape, destined for grape juice.

After PROHIBITION, vine-growing in New York was dominated by a few large wineries in the Finger Lakes, which continued the traditional trade in still and sparkling white wines from native grapes, but also used large quantities of neutral blending wine from California. A special trade in New York is the production of sweet KOSHER wine from the Concord grape.

The new interest in wine that emerged in the 1970s in the UNITED STATES had important results in New York. The Farm Winery Act of 1976 made it economically feasible to own and operate a small winery and allowed direct sales to consumers. FRENCH HYBRIDS, then VINIFERA varieties, began to be planted more and more widely; new wineries, mostly small, grew up; one entirely new region, the eastern end of Long Island, was successfully developed; the large established wineries of the Finger Lakes passed through repeated changes of ownership, saw their traditional markets shrink under new competition, and fell into decline. By 1993, New York had 97 wineries, 73 of them established since the Farm Winery Act, and produced 25 million gal/950,000 hl of wine. T.P.

Geography and climate

New York's grape and wine industry preserves about 30,000 acres/12,000 ha of vineyards, and is a significant part of the state's agricultural economy. The industry provides thousands of jobs, generates millions of dollars in sales,

contributes millions of dollars in taxes, and attracts over 500,000 tourists each year. About 45 per cent of all grapes grown in the state are destined for wine production, while the majority are used for GRAPE JUICE and some for TABLE GRAPES.

New York state has four distinct wine regions which, with some subdividing in the 1980s, have become six American Viticultural Areas, or AVAS. The regions are Finger Lakes in the central part of the state; Lake Erie at the western border; Hudson Valley, which begins about 40 miles/64 km north of New York City; and Long Island, about 90 miles east of NYC. New York is the most northerly eastern American state that can grow and ripen a wide variety of grapes. In spite of frequent low winter temperatures, the growing season has from 2,000 to 2,700 DEGREE DAYS. Its glacier-altered topography, strategic bodies of water, and deep, well-drained soils also encourage viticulture. The greatest viticultural hazard is sudden temperature changes; on Christmas Day 1980, for example, temperatures dropped 50 °F/28 °C, killing many vines (see WINTER FREEZE).

Finger Lakes The picturesque Finger Lakes district is the oldest, and has been the centre of the New York wine industry, with grape-growing and wine production dating back to the 1820s. While Finger Lakes is the second largest grape-growing area in the state, 90 per cent of the state's wine is produced there in 45 bonded wineries. The narrow, deep lakes, so named because they look like the fingers of a hand, were carved by Ice Age glaciers, which deposited shallow topsoil on sloping shale beds above the lakes. This combination of steep slopes and deep lakes provides good DRAINAGE of both water and cold air, and fewer extremes of temperature in winter and summer. Since the lakes retain their summer warmth in winter, any cold air sliding down the steep slopes is warmed by the lake and rises, permitting more cold air to drain from the HILLSIDE. Conversely, in spring, the now cold water of the lakes retards budding until the danger of FROST is past.

The lakes significant to the wine industry are Canandaigua, Keuka, Seneca, and Cayuga, which are big enough to moderate the climate. The official Finger Lakes AVA was established in 1982, with Cayuga Lake being granted its own AVA in 1988, since local wineries could demonstrate that its lower altitude and greater lake depth created a MESOCLIMATE suitable for the VINIFERA varieties most recently planted there. The area now has eight bonded wineries.

Lake Erie Lake Erie is the Great Lake that provides the most protection against extremes of weather to western New York, since it is lower in latitude and downwind from the arctic air masses that prevail over Lakes Superior and Huron. (Lake Michigan provides similar benefits to the states around its southern tip; see UNITED STATES.) Furthermore, besides the beneficial effects of the lake itself, the three-mile wide Allegheny Plateau which runs parallel to Lake Erie extends the lake's moderating influence. The Lake Erie AVA was established in 1983, and includes three states: New York around Chautauqua, Pennsylvania, and Ohio, with counties that border on the lake. About 20,000 acres/8,100 ha are planted, giving Lake Erie the largest acreage in NY, but it has only eight wineries to date since most of the grapes planted in the region are for GRAPE JUICE and TABLE GRAPES—a result of pressure from Prohibitionists in the early 19th century. In the 1970s and 1980s, however, many vineyard sites have been cleared and replanted with wine grape varieties.

Hudson River Wine has been made in the Hudson River region continuously for the past 300 years, and it contains the oldest winery in the United States still in operation: Brotherhood America's Oldest Winery, Ltd. established in 1839. Hudson River became an AVA in 1982. There are wineries on both sides of the Hudson river, but the moderating effects of the river on the local climate are seen as less important than the steep palisaded valley which acts as a conduit for maritime air and weather generated by the Atlantic Ocean. Glaciers have deposited shale, slate, schist, and limestone throughout the region.

Long Island The eastern Long Island region has been split into two AVAs: The Hamptons, Long Island, in 1985, with three bonded wineries and fewer than 100 acres of vines in the mid 1990s; and North Fork of Long Island in 1986 with 14 and 1,200 acres. North Fork of Long Island is a peninsula surrounded by Long Island Sound on the north, Peconic Bay to the south, and the Atlantic Ocean to the east. These bodies of water make the area temperate, sending breezes that moderate heat and cold, extending the periods where frost is not a threat, reducing daily temperature swings, and increasing winter precipitation. Long Island's greatest viticultural hazard, however (apart from BIRDS), is the threat of ocean hurricanes, and some vineyards on the South Fork shore have been washed by salt water (see SALINITY). The growing season is at least three weeks longer than other wine regions in New York state, which means that dark-skinned *vinifera* varieties predominate here for they may be ripened fully almost every year. The first pioneers to buy potato fields and replant them with vines were Alex and Luisa Hargrave, who started the first commercial *vinifera* vineyard on Long Island in 1973. Local growers feel that the Atlantic's maritime influence is similar to its influence on BORDEAUX, and Bordelais grape varieties predominate. The North Fork soils have less silt and loam than those on the South Fork, and require IRRIGATION due to their reduced water-holding capacity.

The Hamptons is also a peninsula, south of North Fork of Long Island. Thus, Peconic Bay now forms the northern edge, and the Atlantic Ocean washes the east and south. The Atlantic Ocean provides the same benefits to this area as it does to North Fork. Spring fogs keep the area cool and prevent premature BUDBREAK. The soils are deep and have a higher percentage of silt and loam, which makes for better water-holding capacity, with less irrigation needed.

Vine varieties and wines

New York has more vinous diversity than any other US state because it grows three distinct categories of VITIS vine genus. There are native varieties and all-AMERICAN HYBRIDS of the American vine species; FRENCH HYBRIDS of both European and American species; and more internationally familiar varieties of the European VINIFERA species.

American vines The indigenous vines were originally termed *Vitis labrusca* (see AMERICAN VINE SPECIES) and were valued for their resistance to PHYLLOXERA and harsh winters, although the early settlers found the grapes quite different in flavour from those of their European homelands. These native vines often hybridized by chance with other *labruscas* or even other American vine species, and produced a second generation of native grapes commonly grown today, called *Vitis labruscana*, of which the blue-black skinned CONCORD is the most planted variety. These formed the backbone of the early New York wine industry, although they are often derided today for their FOXY flavour. (So pronounced is this flavour that native *labruscana* varieties were exempted when the US laws on VARIETAL labelling increased the minimum permitted percentage of the cited grape variety from 51 to 75 per cent.)

The major red-pink native varieties are CATAWBA and DELAWARE, both of which are winter hardy and vigorous. Since Catawba has been used in wine COOLERS and bulk-process sparkling wines (see CHARMAT), it is often 'hot pressed' (see THERMOVINIFICATION), or given limited SKIN CONTACT to yield pink juice. Delaware, on the other hand, is prized for use in fine sparkling wines, and it is fermented cold in stainless steel tanks without skin contact. It has higher SUGARS and lower ACIDS than Catawba. Both grow in the Finger Lakes and Lake Erie regions.

The white native varieties currently grown include Niagara, Elvira, Dutchess, and Moore's Diamond, but only

Niagara has a bright future in New York state. The others are declining due to such reasons as susceptibility to disease, poorer tolerance to cold temperatures, limited use for table grapes, grape juice, and wine, and low grape prices. Any remaining acreage of these is in the Finger Lakes. Niagara, however, is vigorous, winter hardy, and productive, and has a large following among those who enjoy its decidedly foxy flavour. It is grown mostly in Lake Erie and the Finger Lakes, but there is also a little in the Hudson Valley. It is fermented cold, and finished with some RESIDUAL SUGAR to balance its intense aroma.

Of dark-skinned native varieties, Concord is widely planted, being grown in every area of New York except Long Island, and highly productive. It has low sugars and high acids, and the wine is invariably sweetened, resulting in residual sugar ranging from one per cent for table wines to more than 10 per cent for dessert wines. Thermovinification is used to extract colour for sweet, red wines, or grapes may be pressed without skin contact when used in sparkling wines. Other red grapes include Fredonia, which was developed in the early 1900s at the viticultural research station at Geneva (which gave its name to the GENEVA DOUBLE CURTAIN system of vine training; see TRAINING SYSTEMS). Fredonia is similar to Concord, but ripens a useful two weeks earlier. Today it is planted mostly in Lake Erie, and used as a table grape or for juice. Ives is used similarly to Concord, and is planted mostly in the Finger Lakes. ISABELLA, which used to be very popular, has been largely replaced by other varieties.

Traditional vine spacing for native varieties is 10 ft × 6 ft (3 × 2 m) with vines trained to wires for maximum sunlight interception. William Kniffen developed the widely used umbrella, four-cane, and double Kniffen vine-training systems in the 1850s. ENRICHMENT by adding sugar is permitted and is usually necessary here, while ACIDIFICATION is forbidden and usually unnecessary. DEACIDIFICATION is often practised, and MALOLACTIC FERMENTATION is increasingly encouraged.

French hybrids FRENCH HYBRIDS represent the majority of acreage devoted to dry table wines. Most were developed to create new varieties that were hardy and disease- and pest-resistant by French hybridizers, working intensively from 1880 to 1950. Newer HYBRIDS have been created at Geneva Experiment Station (see above). Besides hybrids, which combine the resistance of American species and the flavour characteristics of *vinifera* species, the hybridizers also created crosses which combine the desired characteristics of different varieties in the same species. Hybrids are numbered until they become commercially acceptable. Once in general use, they are named. The most important white hybrid is SEYVAL BLANC, which grows in every New York wine region and which, much to the confusion of some consumers, can either be made clean and fruity in STAINLESS STEEL, or can be the much more complex result of BARREL FERMENTATION and malolactic fermentation. VIDAL and, particularly, Vignoles (Ravat 51) by J. F. Ravat both lend themselves to making late harvest, dessert wines, Vignoles sometimes being beneficially affected by NOBLE ROT. Aurore (Seibel 5279), created by Albert Seibel, has been the most widely planted white hybrid grape in New York but is giving way to the prestige of Seyval Blanc. Since its flavour varies from neutral to fruity, it is mostly used in inexpensive generic wines. Two New York white hybrids, developed at the Geneva Experiment Station and released commercially in 1982, are Cayuga GW3 and Melody. Both of these are vigorous, resistant, and productive, and make fruity off-dry wines. Melody has PINOT BLANC as one of its parents, and the wine is reminiscent of a fruity Pinot Blanc. The red French hybrids have not fared as well as the whites, and are declining in acreage. While they answered a need early in the 20th century, their flavours are by no means as popular as the *vinifera* varieties which may now be cultivated thanks to increased viticultural knowledge of ROOTSTOCKS, PESTICIDES, and FUNGICIDES. The most famous hybrids are BACO Noir which is now used for NOUVEAU style wines; MARÉCHAL FOCH, which also makes a good nouveau using CARBONIC MACERATION; DeChaunac (Seibel 9549) and CHANCELLOR (Seibel 7053), which need some OAK ageing to add complexity; and Chelois (Seibel 10878), which works well in blends, especially with Baco Noir.

Vinifera In the 1950s, Charles Fournier, Finger Lakes winemaker at Gold Seal winery and former wine-maker at Veuve Clicquot in CHAMPAGNE, hired Dr Konstantin Frank, a *vinifera* expert from the UKRAINE, to make experimental plantings of rootstocks and *vinifera* varieties in a cold climate. By the early 1960s they had produced commercial *vinifera* wines. The most adaptable varieties were brought from Europe and, in descending order of total acreage in the mid 1990s, the state's white *vinifera* varieties are CHARDONNAY, RIESLING, GEWÜRZTRAMINER, PINOT BLANC, and SAUVIGNON Blanc. The first four are grown successfully, some in limited amounts, in all of New York's regions, but Sauvignon Blanc grows well only on Long Island, where the growing season is long enough to ripen it. Of the red *vinifera* varieties grown in New York—CABERNET SAUVIGNON, MERLOT, PINOT NOIR, and CABERNET FRANC—Merlot shows the most promise. It ripens earlier, and gives greater YIELDS than Cabernet Sauvignon. Cabernet Sauvignon does best on Long Island, needing its long growing season to ripen. Cabernet Franc, which ripens earlier, will most likely increase in acreage, as it is adaptable to different soil types, and can make fine wines on its own as well as blending well with other red Bordeaux varieties. Only Pinot Noir does not do well in the maritime climate of Long Island, which is too moist and warm. It performs better in the warmer areas of the Hudson Valley and Finger Lakes, although yields are very low and viticultural requirements high.

Vinifera plantings are increasing, as is narrow vine spacing and increased VINE DENSITY, sometimes as close as 3 ft × 5 ft. On the warmer Long Island region, the open LYRE training system is gaining favour. In colder areas, especially the Finger Lakes, a multi-trunk fan system is preferred (see WINTER PROTECTION. The multiple trunks (CANES) provide adequate budwood in case of WINTER FREEZE damage. Grafts are hilled up with soil to protect them against winter freezes, using a hydraulic grape hoe, which also removes the excess soil in the spring. H.L.

Finger, P., and Trezise, J., *New York Wine Country* (Stillwater, Minn., 1994).
Hedricks, U. P., *The Grapes of New York* (Albany, NY, 1908).
Miller, M., *Wine: A Gentleman's Game* (New York, 1984).

NEW ZEALAND, southern Pacific islands 1,000 miles away from the nearest land mass, AUSTRALIA, has an agricultural economy that is far more dependent on sheep and dairy products than it is on wine. Vines were first planted in 1819 but it took more than 150 years for New Zealanders to discover that their country's cool, maritime climate was suitable for high-quality wine production. Although production is small by world standards (one-tenth of Australia's relatively small wine output) vines are now grown in nine regions spanning 1,200 km/720 miles, almost the full length of the country's North and South Islands.

History

MISSIONARIES were responsible for New Zealand's first grapevines, planted by an Englishman, the Reverend Samuel Marsden, at Kerikeri on the far north east coast of the North Island in 1819. There is no record of Marsden making wine. That honour belongs to the first British resident, James BUSBY, who established a vineyard at nearby Waitangi in 1836 and subsequently sold his wine to the British troops.

New Zealand's early English working-class settlers preferred BEER to wine, their thirst founding and sustaining a substantial brewing industry. (The country's annual per capita consumption of beer still exceeds 100 l/26 gal per capita, while that of wine is well below 20 l.)

The wine industry has experienced a roller-coaster ride during its relatively brief history. Nature has played a part in its fortunes, thanks to pests such as PHYLLOXERA and diseases such as POWDERY MILDEW, but government policy has had by far the most significant impact. Economic peaks include the growth years 1890–1910, when New Zealand wine managed to capture 25 per cent of the country's total wine consumption (imports, especially from Australia, have long dominated); the Second World War years when visiting American troops offered a new and affluent market; and the period ever since 1958 after the government raised the duty on beer, spirits, and imported wine and restricted the importation of wine.

Significant developments in wine quality include the era of New Zealand's first government viticulturist, Romeo Bragato, who made significant improvements between 1895 and 1909 despite the ravages of phylloxera; the gradual replacement of AMERICAN HYBRIDS with European VINIFERA varieties from the late 1960s; the first vines planted in the Marlborough region in 1973; the founding of the official trade body the Wine Institute of New Zealand in 1975; the prohibition of wine dilution (as recently as 1983); and the Closer Economic Relations agreement with Australia which, from 1990, forced New Zealand wine-makers to compete against wines imported from Australia without the protection of tariffs.

Troughs in the economic fortunes of the wine industry are as common as peaks. Low points have included the damaging effect of the temperance movement between 1910 and 1919. New Zealand voted for national PROHIBITION by a narrow margin in 1919 but the votes of returning servicemen tipped the balance. The post-war economic depression had a predictably adverse affect on the wine industry. As one wine-maker put it, 'We had to sell the grapes to get the money to buy the sugar to make the wine' (see CHAPTALIZATION). During the post-war era of 1945 to 1958 a flood of imports severely affected the viability of local wine-making and encouraged the industry to band together and lobby the government for relief, a move which ultimately resulted in significant protection. The rapid expansion of vineyards and a large harvest in 1983 led to a wine surplus, and heavy discounting in 1985 and 1986. The government intervened with a sponsored VINE PULL scheme in 1986 which meant that one-quarter of of the country's vines were uprooted.

Troughs in national wine quality occurred after powdery mildew (oidium) first appeared in 1876, and after the identification of phylloxera in 1895. In most of the rest of the world vine-growers chose immunity from this voracious root louse by grafting European grape varieties on to American phylloxera-resistant ROOTSTOCKS. Their counterparts in New Zealand chose a second option: they simply planted phylloxera-resistant American hybrids. In 1960 the American ISABELLA vine, nicknamed Albany Surprise, was New Zealand's most widely planted grape variety.

Until 1881 wineries were not able to sell wine directly to the public but had to channel their produce through hotels, the country's only liquor outlets. Both hotels and wineries had to sell a minimum of 9 l/2.4 gal to every customer. From 1955 specialist wine shops were allowed to sell single bottles of New Zealand table wine, although the allocation of licences was carefully controlled. In 1960 restaurants were allowed to sell wine. A BYO licence was introduced in 1976 to allow diners to take their own wine to restaurants. Supermarkets were granted a licence to sell local and imported wine (but not beer or spirits) from 1990.

Geography and climate

New Zealand grows the world's most southerly grapes and, less significantly, the world's most westerly, thanks to an adjacent dateline. A parallel is sometimes made between the southern latitudes of New Zealand's wine regions and those of famous European regions. If New Zealand were in the northern hemisphere the country would stretch from North Africa to Paris but the moderating influence of the Gulf Stream on European vineyards results in hotter growing conditions than in the vineyards of equivalent southern latitudes.

A broad climatic distinction can be made between the warmer North Island regions and those in the cooler South Island, although significant climatic differences exist within the five to six degree latitude span of each island. Under the imperfect HEAT SUMMATION measure of the daily average

temperature above 10 °C/50 °F during the vine-growing season, New Zealand qualifies as Region I (along with BORDEAUX and BURGUNDY). This system ignores diurnal and seasonal swings of temperature, however, and the largely MARITIME climate of New Zealand is very different from the CONTINENTAL climate of Burgundy. Bordeaux, with its proximity to the sea, is a closer match, in climate at least, to the North Island region of Hawkes Bay which happens to produce New Zealand's finest CABERNET SAUVIGNON.

New Zealand is a green and pleasant land thanks to an abundant RAINFALL throughout most of the country. Plentiful rain promotes good pastures but it can have a negative effect on wine quality, particularly during the critical ripening period. Excessive moisture, through poorly drained soils or heavy rainfall, encourages leaf and shoot growth. Dense vine CANOPIES tend to shade innermost leaves and grape bunches to produce green, HERBACEOUS flavours, to delay RIPENING, and to promote FUNGAL DISEASES. Excessive vine VIGOUR was one of New Zealand's major viticultural hindrances until Dr Richard Smart preached the gospel of CANOPY MANAGEMENT during his tenure as government viticulturist between 1982 and 1990. As a result, many wine-makers with vines that had produced excessively vegetal Cabernet Sauvignon reds and SAUVIGNON Blanc whites were able to make higher-quality wines within a single vintage of applying canopy management techniques. Some growers in the Marlborough region claimed that their HARVEST had been advanced by as much as seven days. Dr Smart's canopy management techniques made by far the greatest contribution to improved New Zealand wine quality during the 1980s.

Chief preoccupation of New Zealand vine-growers in the 1990s appears to be VINEYARD SITE SELECTION. New Zealand viticulture was for many years centred on the principal city of Auckland, an important market with one-third of the country's population. Between 1960 and 1983 wine production rose from 4.1 million l to 57.7 million l (15.2 million gal). New Zealand, it was claimed, had the fastest growing wine production in the world. In the late 1960s and early 1970s the flat, fertile Gisborne river valley usurped Auckland's status as New Zealand's largest wine region. High yields of often relatively lowly grapes such as MÜLLER-THURGAU helped satisfy the nation's thirst for fresh, fruity, and slightly sweet table wine. Later, as PHYLLOXERA devastated Gisborne's grape crop and as demand for higher-quality wines increased, Hawkes Bay became the country's leading wine region. In 1990 Marlborough overtook Hawkes Bay and has since widened its lead as New Zealand's largest region.

Viticulture

New Zealand's remote location has not, as it has done in CHILE, provided a barrier against the importation of vineyard pests and diseases. Phylloxera continues to threaten nearly half the country's vines which are planted on their own, ungrafted rootstock while FANLEAF DEGENERATION and LEAF-ROLL VIRUSES have a detrimental effect on both the quality and quantity of the country's grape crop. Both are symptoms of an industry which has grown faster than the availability of grafted rootstock and virus-indexed vines. Strict QUARANTINE is of course enforced, and easily enforceable, on imported plant material.

As explained above, New Zealand has come to be regarded as a cradle of knowledge about canopy management techniques, and New Zealand VITICULTURISTS, like their wine-making colleagues, are able usefully to spend the New Zealand winter in northern hemisphere wine regions. New Zealand's harvest generally takes place from February to May (and sometimes as late as June in parts of Central Otago).

New Zealand's vine-growers are free to irrigate and there

The **New Zealand** wine industry's most distinctive building, the owner's house overlooking the Coleraine vineyard at Te Mata, Hawkes Bay.

are no restrictions on PRUNING or YIELDS, which average about 90 hl/ha (5 tons/acre) nationally.

Much of the viticultural equipment has to be imported from Australia, but New Zealand technicians have even developed their own specialist equipment such as the Gallagher leaf-plucking machine (see LEAF REMOVAL). As increasing attention is paid to the selection of vineyard sites (and land in New Zealand is relatively inexpensive), the wine industry may begin to reach its full potential. Flatlands viticulture is the norm in a country where land is plentiful and wine prices do not yet justify the additional expense and trouble involved in planting vines on anything but gently rolling hills. New Zealand vine-growers regard the vineyards of the MOSEL-SAAR-RUWER or DOURO valleys with awe and disbelief.

Vine varieties

Although Sauvignon Blanc is the variety for which New Zealand established an international reputation, total plantings of Chardonnay are nearly twice as extensive and the white burgundy grape overtook Müller-Thurgau as the country's most planted variety with a substantial increase in plantings in 1992. If Sauvignon Blanc is the country's third most planted variety, it is still very much more common than Cabernet Sauvignon and Pinot Noir, New Zealand's most planted red wine varieties. Plantings of Riesling, the sixth most planted variety, are expected to increase as the quality of New Zealand's versions of German classics is increasingly appreciated. Other varieties which covered more than 100 ha/250 acres in 1994 were Muscat Dr Hogg (a bulk grape used to give extra fruitiness to basic Müller-Thurgau), Chenin Blanc, Merlot, Gewürztraminer, and Semillon. All vine materials are screened for VIRUS DISEASES by an official government-run agency, and the number of CLONES available from the country's nurseries is considerably more limited than, for example, in Europe.

Wine-making

The youthful and dynamic New Zealand wine industry has been greatly influenced by Australia's ADELAIDE University (formerly ROSEWORTHY Agricultural College), which provided training, and personnel, for many New Zealand wine-makers. Traditional wine-making techniques from benchmark European wine regions have also been adopted, however. The country's southern hemisphere location has had a positive effect on the development of wine styles and wine-making techniques. Many young New Zealand wine-makers choose to work a second annual vintage in Europe and gain a wider perspective on the world of wine. A reverse migration of mostly young French wine-makers has a similar effect.

The country's isolation does have disadvantages, however, such as adding to the cost of importing highly fashionable new oak BARRIQUES from France (or at the very least from the nearest cooperage in Australia). An efficient domestic STAINLESS STEEL industry, however, developed to serve New Zealand's dairy industry, has provided economy and ingenuity in winery tank design.

Wine-makers in New Zealand operate relatively free from regulatory constraint, with ACIDIFICATION, DEACIDIFICATION, and ENRICHMENT all permitted, and BACK BLENDING a traditional speciality. It is a remarkable tribute to the ambitions of the industry, especially abroad, that overall wine quality is as high as it is.

New Zealanders tend to worship the wine-maker rather than the vineyard. This NEW WORLD phenomenon is in direct contrast to the French view of the primacy of TERROIR. A century or two will no doubt reveal the ephemeral nature of wine-makers and permanence of geography, but until that time New Zealand wine-makers will continue to be revered by an adoring domestic public.

Industry organization

The industry is dominated by wine producers Montana, Corbans (who own Cooks), and the Villa Maria/Vidals/Esk Valley group. Only the smaller wineries do not rely on fruit bought in from the country's grape-growers.

As in other New World wine-producing countries such as ARGENTINA and AUSTRALIA, wineries have traditionally been located far from vineyards, and the development of South Island wine regions, separated from many winery headquarters by the treacherous Cook Strait, has only exacerbated this phenomenon in New Zealand. Increasing attention to field CRUSHING facilities, and the construction of wineries, or at least PRESSING stations, closer to the vineyards, is an obvious development for the 1990s.

Every winery must belong to the Wine Institute of New Zealand, a statutory body formed in 1975 which collects a production-based fee from its members. WINZ has had an enormous influence on the development of the image and quality of local wine and has overseen New Zealand's substantial export attack on the United Kingdom, which imports more than two-thirds of all the wine exported from New Zealand.

Wine regions

See map on p. 672.

Gisborne This east coast North Island region based on the town of the same name is beginning to shake off its image as a 'bulk wine' region and has largely recovered from phylloxera with massive replantings. In 1994 85 per cent of Gisborne vines were grafted on to phylloxera-resistant ROOTSTOCKS (while only 55 per cent of Hawkes Bay vines and only 25 per cent of Marlborough vines enjoyed the protection of having been grafted). Replanting also improved the mix of varieties in Gisborne. Müller-Thurgau is still the dominant grape variety but Chardonnay is in second place. Gisborne vine-growers and wine-makers have given their region the rather contentious title Chardonnay Capital of New Zealand. Gisborne Chardonnay is certainly the country's most distinctive regional example of the variety with soft and charming fruit flavours that often resemble ripe peach and melon. Gewürztraminer is Gisborne's other claim to vinous fame. Gisborne's wine-makers include the big two companies Montana and Corbans, which jointly produce about 80 per cent of the country's wine. Both companies have established large wineries in Gisborne, chiefly to process grapes for BAG-IN-BOX packaged blends, which accounted for two-thirds of the nation's wine sales in the mid 1990s. Nestled within the large-scale, high-tech production facilities of Montana and Corbans are the small batch presses and BARRIQUES used to make limited edition, premium Chardonnay. At the other end of the production scale are many small 'life-style wineries' that make only premium bottled table wine or traditional method sparkling wines. They include Millton Vineyards, New Zealand's first certified ORGANIC winery, which produces grapes and wine according to the Rudolph Steiner principles of BIODYNAMISM. Most Gisborne grapes are grown by farmers who sell the grapes to wineries under long-term contract, or to the highest bidder. Several Auckland wineries regularly buy Gisborne grapes which are mechanically harvested before being transported for nine hours by road in covered dump trucks. Varieties of grapes that are low in PHENOLICS, such as Müller-Thurgau, appear to suffer few ill effects and may even gain flavour from this period of compulsory SKIN CONTACT, but Sauvignon Blanc and Gewürztraminer can suffer as a result.

Hawkes Bay Hawkes Bay, around the town of Napier, is one of New Zealand's older wine regions and certainly one of the best. Complex soil patterns and MESOCLIMATES make it difficult to generalize about the wines of such a diverse region, particularly when they are made by such an eclectic group of wine-makers. Situated on the east coast of the North Island, 215 km/130 miles south of Gisborne and 323 km/194 miles north of Wellington, Hawkes Bay frequently records the country's highest sunshine hours. The terrain varies from coastal ranges that rise to 1600 m/5,300 ft to wide, fertile plains consisting of alluvial and gravelly soils. A high water-table and fertile soils can result in excessive vine vigour over much of the plains. In other parts of the region, deep well-drained gravel soils encourage WATER STRESS and the vines may even require IRRIGATION during long, dry periods. Over 10 per cent of vineyards in Hawkes Bay are irrigated. In pursuit of wine quality vineyards were, at least from the mid 1980s, established on free-draining soils of lower fertility. For ease of cultivation vines have been almost exclusively planted on flat land, despite the allure of nearby limestone hills which may offer superior aspect and DRAINAGE. In 1994 Chardonnay represented by far the most important vine variety in Hawkes Bay with a declining Müller-Thurgau in second place and Cabernet Sauvignon a comfortable third. Sauvignon Blanc and Merlot were fourth and fifth respectively. The best Hawkes Bay reds are Cabernet Sauvignon or a blend of Cabernet Sauvignon and occasionally Cabernet Franc. They have intense berry and cassis flavours, often with a gently herbaceous reminder of their moderately COOL CLIMATE origin and, sometimes, strong OAK influence from up to two years' maturation in new French BARRIQUES. Hawkes Bay Chardonnay may lack the seductive charm of the Gisborne equivalent but the best have intense citrus flavours and a brooding elegance that are seldom matched by the wines of other regions. Hawkes Bay Sauvignon Blanc is a softer, fleshier wine than the better known Marlborough Sauvignon Blanc. It often has a nectarine or stone fruit character, a useful indicator of regional identity.

Marlborough Marlborough is the biggest of New Zealand's big three wine regions, at least in terms of vineyard acreage. Industry giant Montana planted the first vines in Marlborough when it established the South Island's first commercial vineyard in 1973. At the time it seemed an enormous gamble but after the vines reached full production Montana's investment returned a handsome dividend in terms of quality and profit. Other producers soon followed to establish wineries in the region or to secure a supply of grapes for the 18-hour journey north to Auckland or Gisborne. The single wine that put Marlborough Sauvignon Blanc on the international map was CLOUDY BAY, in 1985. Since 1989 out-of-region wine-makers have been able to use the services of Vintech, a contract wine-making specialist, to process grapes into juice or wine which can then be transported in bulk with less risk of extracting astringent PHENOLS from grape skins. The availability of contract wine-making facilities has encouraged an increasing number of vine-growers to process part or all of their crop into wine for sale under their own label.

Marlborough, at the north eastern tip of the South Island, consists of a large, flat, river valley with deep deposits of silt and gravel. A number of soil patterns are found throughout the valley and even within single vineyards, leading to significant variations in quality and style depending on the grape source. Shallow, stony soils, which aid drainage and limit fertility, are favoured for high-quality wine production. Surface boulders help reflect the sun's rays and retain warmth during Marlborough's cool, clear, summer nights. Irrigation is widely used throughout the valley to establish vines in the sometimes arid, free-draining soils and to relieve vine stress during the typically dry Marlborough summer. Many of Marlborough's best wines are made from irrigated grapes which, it is claimed, would have suffered a loss in quality if the vines were forced to rely on a natural supply of ground water. Since the temptation to over-irrigate is greater for contract grape-growers who are paid by the ton than for wine-makers whose reputation relies on the quality of their wines, most wine producers try to build quality incentives into grape payments (see PRICE), but they acknowledge the difficulty involved in assessing grape quality. Grape SUGARS, ACIDS, and even dry EXTRACT levels can be quantified, but all fail to distinguish grapes that can make good wine from those that have the potential to make truly great wine. It is an undeniable fact that many of New Zealand's best wines are made from grapes that are grown in winery-owned vineyards where the wine-maker assumes total responsibility for wine quality.

Sauvignon Blanc is Marlborough's best-known and most planted variety. These pungent, aromatic wines that blend tropical fruit flavours with gooseberry and capsicum herbaceousness are probably the closest thing that New Zealand has to a national wine style (however much the country's wine-makers would prefer to build their international reputation on more prestigious wines, such as Chardonnay or Pinot Noir). Marlborough Chardonnay is the region's second most planted grape variety, producing a wide range of styles usually due more to wine-maker intervention than to TERROIR. A small but growing proportion of the Marlborough Chardonnay crop is used in traditional method SPARKLING WINE production. Riesling is another very successful Marlborough vine variety which reaches its apogee as a sweet, luscious botrytis-affected dessert wine. BOTRYTIZED wines can be produced here most years although the results vary considerably with vintage conditions.

Northland Northland, at the very northern tip of the country, was the birthplace of New Zealand wine. The region's warm, wet, temperate climate discouraged the commercial production of good-quality wine until the late 1980s when a vineyard was established at Kaitaia. Others are prospecting for suitable mesoclimates in an area well served by domestic consumers and visiting tourists.

Auckland Auckland, the largest city, gives its name to the one New Zealand wine region where winery visitors can be assured of finding wines made from grapes grown as far south as Canterbury in the South Island, and are more likely to be offered wine from Marlborough and Hawkes Bay than the product of a local vineyard. Auckland viticulture declined during the rapid growth of Gisborne, Hawkes Bay, and Marlborough through the 1970s and 1980s but began to grow in the 1990s as grape-growers adopted canopy-thinning techniques to correct vine vigour. New subregions, including Waiheke Island and Matakana, are now producing high-quality and highly fashionable reds which have helped raise Auckland's profile and esteem as a wine region.

Wairarapa Wairarapa, which includes the Martinborough region, is at the southern end of the North Island about one hour's drive from the nation's capital, Wellington. In 1994 Wairarapa had just three per cent of the country's vines but 13 per cent of its wine-makers. They are typically small-scale, 'life-style' producers with a quality-at-all-costs attitude to wine-making and a passionate faith in their region's potential. Wairarapa wine-makers argue over whether the region is more suitable for Pinot Noir or Cabernet Sauvignon, but there is ample evidence that both varieties perform well. In their quest to make great wine most producers crop their vines so that YIELDS are considerably below the national average, a significant factor in the region's success. In terms of topography, climate, and soils Wairarapa might easily be considered a miniature Marlborough, if it were not for the region's ability to make top-quality reds on a regular basis.

Nelson Nelson is the South Island's most northerly wine region, nearly two hours' drive across high ranges from Marlborough. The rolling hills of Nelson rise from a scenic coastline to form a beautiful setting for the region's seven wineries. Chardonnay is the main grape variety, with Riesling and Sauvignon Blanc a long way behind. The varied topography of Nelson makes it difficult to generalize about weather and soils, although records show that the region is slightly cooler and wetter than the Marlborough average.

Canterbury Canterbury, around Christchurch on the central east coast of the South Island, has three subregions: Waipara in North Canterbury; the plains west of Christchurch; and Banks Peninsula to the east of the city. The region is cool and dry with a moderate risk of October and April FROSTS. Low rainfall and light soils of moderate fertility help control vine vigour and canopy here. Viticultural research at the local Lincoln College has had a considerable influence on selecting suitable vine varieties for the local growing conditions and in assisting local growers with viticultural technique. It is no surprise, given Canterbury's cool climate, that Pinot Noir and Chardonnay are the region's most planted varieties, with Riesling in third place and Sauvignon Blanc fourth.

Central Otago Central Otago grows New Zealand's, and the world's, most southerly grapevines, some of them cultivated south of the 45th parallel. It is New Zealand's only wine region with a CONTINENTAL climate providing greater diurnal and seasonal TEMPERATURE VARIATION than any other. Most Central Otago vines are planted on HILLSIDE VINEYARDS to give better sun exposure and reduce frost risk. In 1994 Central Otago had less than one per cent of the national vineyard with seven small but enthusiastic wine producers. Yields are small but, perhaps as a result, the best Central Otago wines show impressive concentration. Pinot Noir, the region's most popular variety, has so far shown the most potential, with gentle, stylish wines. Gewürztraminer is the second most planted variety. R.F.C.

Campell, B., *New Zealand Wine Annual* (Auckland, annually).
Cooper, M., *The Wines & Vineyards of New Zealand* (4th edn., Auckland, 1993).
Williams, V., *The Penguin Good New Zealand Wine Guide* (Auckland, 1993).

NIAGARA, white grape variety grown successfully in NEW YORK state. This VITIS *labruscana* variety is vigorous, productive, and withstands low temperatures well. Its wines have a strong FOXY flavour. One of its parents is CONCORD, the other a VINIFERA variety. It was created in Niagara, New York in 1872.

NIEDERÖSTERREICH, the most important wine region in AUSTRIA, lower Austria, in the far north east of the country.

NIELLUCCIO is CORSICA's most planted indigenous grape variety, although it was probably brought there from the Italian mainland, presumably by the GENOESE who ruled the island until the late 18th century, as it is ampelographically identical to the SANGIOVESE of Tuscany. It represented only 14 per cent of all Corsican vines in 1988, however, thanks to the domination of the coarser varieties imported by French immigrants from North Africa in the 1960s and 1970s. Often blended with the, arguably more interesting, other major indigenous red wine variety SCIACARELLO, it constitutes an increasing proportion of the island's APPELLATION CONTRÔLÉE reds and, particularly, rosés for which it is particularly suitable. It is the principal ingredient in Patrimonio, on whose clay-limestone soils it thrives. It buds early and ripens late and is therefore susceptible to late frosts in spring and rot during the harvest.

NITROGEN, mineral element and inert colourless, odourless, tasteless gas that is extremely useful in both grape-growing and wine-making. Nitrogen makes up 78 per cent of air and, as an inert constituent, it dilutes air's highly reactive constituent OXYGEN, thereby moderating the rate at which RESPIRATION and burning occur. In its combined forms, nitrogen is an essential element in AMINO ACIDS, PROTEINS, and ENZYMES, without which life as we know it could not exist. In its combination with hydrogen as ammonia, nitrogen is the essential element in most FERTILIZERS, without which plants could not grow.

Viticulture

Nitrogen has a major impact on vineyard VIGOUR, and potentially on wine quality. Nitrogen is essential for vine growth and is one of the three major elements, along with POTASSIUM and PHOSPHORUS, commonly deficient in plants. Nitrogen is an important component of proteins, and also of chlorophyll. The most common symptoms of nitrogen deficiency are reduced vigour and pale green or yellow leaves. Nitrogen deficiency can be expected on sandy soils low in organic matter. Soil and plant tests can be used as a guide to the use of nitrogen fertilizers.

Much more caution is needed with vines than most other plants in applying nitrogen fertilizers, or large amounts of manure, or planting in soils naturally rich in nitrogen. COVER CROPS containing clover should also be monitored carefully as they might add excessive nitrogen to the vineyard soil. Whatever the origin, too much nitrogen in a vineyard results in vigorous vegetative vine growth. Such vineyards typically show reduced YIELD and quality owing to the SHADE effects of high VIGOUR. CANOPY MANAGEMENT procedures may be used to overcome some of these effects, but will not eliminate them completely. Vineyards with excessive nitrogen supplies are also prone to poor FRUIT SET (COULURE, for example) and are more susceptible to BOTRYTIS BUNCH ROT. Excessive nitrogen is also considered to have a direct and negative effect on wine quality, reducing SUGARS, colour, and PHENOLICS, and increasing ACIDITY. High nitrogen levels in the soil also lead to increased wine levels of urea, ethyl CARBAMATES, and HISTAMINES. In some parts of Europe such as Germany, excessive nitrogen fertilization of vineyards has led to pollution of water supplies with nitrates which pose hazards to human health.

A feature of vineyards producing high fruit quality is that they have a restricted supply of nitrogen. Along with WATER STRESS, this is one of two important checks on vine growth which result in the vine BALANCE that is essential for premium wine quality. On the other hand, severe nitrogen deficiency is equally disadvantageous to quality. Fruit from nitrogen-deficient vineyards can be lower in fermentable SUGARS and may also result in STUCK FERMENTATIONS, with the concomitant risk of forming SULPHIDES. R.E.S.

Wine-making

In combination with phosphorus and potassium nitrogen can serve as a critical factor in YEAST growth and therefore FERMENTATION, notably in HOME WINE-MAKING of FRUIT WINES. Nitrogen can also affect wine composition. In high concentrations it is associated with intensified AROMAS, while low concentrations favour the formation of HYDROGEN SULPHIDE.

Obtained by fractional DISTILLATION of liquid air, nitrogen in both gaseous and liquid forms is a major commercial product used in a wide range of industrial activities. As ammonia, it is the starting material for most fertilizer mixtures. In liquid form it has myriad uses in REFRIGERATION. In pure gas form it is used to prevent a wide range of sensitive products from coming into contact with oxygen. Wine is just one of these.

Nitrogen as an inert gas is extremely useful to the wine-maker in filling the head space in closed stainless steel tanks and bottles (see SPARGING and LEFTOVER WINE). It is more expensive but more effective than INERT GAS MIXTURE at preserving wine from potential harmful contact with oxygen.

A.D.W.

Champagnol, F., *Éléments de physiologie de la vigne et de viticulture générale* (St-Gely-du-Fesc, 1984).

Rantz, J. M. (ed)., 'Nitrogen in Grapes and Wine', Proc. Int. Symposium, Seattle, June 1991, *Amer. Soc. for Enol. and Vitic.* (Davis, Calif., 1991).

Winkler, A. J., *et al.* (eds.), *General Viticulture* (2nd edn., Berkeley, Calif., 1974).

NMR, see NUCLEAR MAGNETIC RESONANCE.

NOAH, seminal figure in the history of wine according to the BIBLE. See also ORIGINS OF VITICULTURE.

Noah is also the name of a relatively undistinguished AMERICAN HYBRID white grape variety first propagated in 1869 in Illinois. It is particularly hardy and has been widely grown in France and eastern Europe but is of declining importance.

NO ALCOHOL WINE is a term sometimes used for wine with an ALCOHOLIC STRENGTH of less than one or two per cent. For more details, see DEALCOHOLIZED WINE.

NOBLE ROT, also known as *pourriture noble* in French, *Edelfäule* in German, *muffa* in Italian, and sometimes simply as botrytis, is the benevolent form of BOTRYTIS BUNCH ROT in which the *Botrytis cinerea* fungus attacks ripe, undamaged white wine grapes and, given the right weather, can result in extremely sweet grapes which may look disgusting but have undergone such a complex transformation that they are capable of producing probably the world's finest, and certainly the longest-living, sweet wines. Indeed, the defining factor of a great VINTAGE for sweet white wine in areas specializing in its production is the incidence of noble rot. The malevolent form, which results if the grapes are damaged, unripe, or conditions are unfavourable, is known as GREY ROT.

Ideal conditions for the development of noble rot are a TEMPERATE CLIMATE in which the humidity associated with early morning mists that favour the development of the fungus is followed by warm, sunny autumn afternoons in which the grapes are dried and the progress of the fungus is restrained. In cloudy conditions in which the humidity is unchecked, the fungus may spread so rapidly that the grape skins split and the grapes succumb to grey rot. If, however, the weather is unremittingly hot and dry, then the fungus will not develop at all and the grapes will simply accumulate sugar rather than undergoing the chemical transformations associated with noble rot, so the result is less complex SWEET WINES.

In favourable conditions the botrytis fungus *Botrytis cinerea* spreads unpredictably from grape to grape and bunch to bunch in different parts of the vineyard, penetrating the skins of whole, ripe grapes with filaments which leave minute brown spots on the skin but leave the skin impenetrable by other, harmful micro-organisms. As shown in the illustration opposite page 976, the grapes turn golden, then pink or purple, and then, when they are in a severely dehydrated state, they turn brown, shrivel to a sort of moist raisin, and may seem to be covered with a fine grey powder that looks like ash (to which the word *cinerea* refers). It is almost incredible that such unappetizing-looking grapes can produce such sublime wine, and there have been many instances in which nobly rotten grapes have been discarded, or at least unrecognized, in wine regions unfamiliar with the phenomenon.

These visible changes are an outward sign of the extraordinary changes that occur inside the grape. More than half of the grape's water content is lost due either directly to the action of the fungus or to loss by evaporation as the skins eventually deteriorate. Meanwhile, *Botrytis cinerea* consumes both the SUGAR IN GRAPES and, especially, ACIDS, so that the overall effect is to increase the sugar concentration, or MUST WEIGHT, considerably in an ever-decreasing quantity of juice. The fungus typically reduces a grape's sugar concentration by a third, but reduces the TARTARIC ACID by five-sixths and the usually less important MALIC ACID by a third.

While it metabolizes these sugars and acids, the fungus forms a wide range of chemical compounds in the grape juice, including GLYCEROL (quite apart from that formed by alcoholic fermentation), ACETIC ACID, gluconic acid, various ENZYMES especially LACCASE, as well as a useful, if still mysterious, antibiotic substance dubbed 'botryticine'. The PHENOLICS in the grape skins are also broken down by the fungus, and the TANNINS released into the juice. In sum, botrytized grape juice is very different from regular grape juice, and not just because of its intense levels of sugar.

It is unusual for all grapes on a vine, or even on a single bunch, to be affected in exactly the same way, to exactly the same effect, and at exactly the same speed, which is why the HARVEST of botrytis-affected vineyard can necessitate several passages, or TRIS, during which individual bunches, or parts of them, are picked at optimum infection level, and grapes affected by grey rot may have to be eliminated.

Weather conditions other than alternating early mists and warm afternoons can result in a satisfactory noble rot infection. In cold, wet weather, noble rot may form at a reasonable rate on fully ripe grapes, and grey rot be kept at bay. Wind can help to dehydrate the grapes and concentrate the sugars.

See SAUTERNES for details of common weather patterns there. See BOTRYTIZED WINES for details of where and how they are made, and their history.

Olney, R., *Yquem* (London, 1986).

NOBLING is a 1939 crossing of Silvaner × Gutedel (Chasselas) that is declining in importance even in Baden, where there were more than 100 ha/250 acres in the late 1970s. It can achieve good MUST WEIGHTS and yet retain acidity but it needs a relatively good site that can be used more profitably for more fashionable or productive varieties.

NODE, the part of a plant's stem at which a leaf is attached. In the grapevine this zone is swollen and bears the leaf winter BUD and LATERAL SHOOT. TENDRILS or INFLORESCENCES are borne at nodes on the side opposite to the bud. B.G.C.

NOILLY PRAT, not a wine at all but a dry white French VERMOUTH particularly useful for cooking. Of the huge volume of vermouth produced and assiduously marketed each year, Noilly Prat has sufficient character to appeal to the wine drinker (although see also CHAMBÉRY).

NOIRIEN is, most commonly, the name given to the PINOT family of grape varieties found primarily in eastern France that are related to or closely associated with Pinot Noir: Pinot Gris, Pinot Blanc, Auxerrois, and (although it is not related) Chardonnay. In addition, Noirien is a synonym for Pinot Noir and, more misleadingly, Noirien Blanc is used as a synonym for Chardonnay.

NON-VINTAGE, often abbreviated to NV, a blended wine, particularly champagne or sparkling wine, which may contain the produce of several different VINTAGES, although in champagne-making practice it is usually substantially based on the most recent vintage, to which some additional ingredients from older years, often called 'reserve wines', may be added.

Within the EUROPEAN UNION, basic TABLE WINE may not be sold with a vintage year on it and is in practice often a blend made throughout the year so that the first blend of the winter season, typically, may contain a mixture of wine from both the new and last year's vintages.

NORTH COAST, general CALIFORNIA umbrella region and AVA for north of San Francisco. It includes all vineyards in LAKE, MENDOCINO, NAPA, and SONOMA counties and has rather more homogeneous growing conditions than many suspect. The name appears on some relatively prestigious wines assembled from, especially, Napa and Sonoma and also on some pretty ordinary blends.

NORTH YUBA, one-winery AVA in the northern Sierra Nevada Mountain foothills of Yuba County, CALIFORNIA. The warm, sunny site was first planted, more in hopes than expectation, to such as Riesling and Petite Sirah. More recent introductions include Cabernet Sauvignon.

NOSE, the most sensitive form of TASTING equipment so far encountered, the sense of TASTE being so inextricably linked with the sense of smell. When the nose is blocked, whether by a cold or by mechanical means, the ability to taste either food or drink is seriously impaired—so much so that cold sufferers have to resort to decongestants if the need for their tasting skills is serious.

Nose is also a synonym for the smell, AROMA, or BOUQUET of a wine, as in wines having 'a nose of raspberries', 'a raspberry nose', or even 'raspberries on the nose'.

This versatile word is also used as a verb by (particularly British) wine tasters who talk about 'nosing' wines when they smell them.

NOSIOLA, a white wine from the TRENTINO region in northern Italy made from the grape of the same name. It is produced principally between Lavis, Faedo, and SAN MICHELE ALL'ADIGE in the northern part of the region, and in the Valle dei Laghi to the west of Trento. Two DOCs share the production of the grape: Nosiola (3,000 hl/79,200 gal annually) and Sorni Bianco (a mere 300 hl). In this latter DOC 70 per cent of Nosiola is blended with 30 per cent of either MÜLLER-THURGAU, PINOT BLANC, or SYLVANER. The wines have more aroma than body, and the flavours finish with a slight bitterness; they might well be fuller and more interesting if yields were lower than the current generous limit of 98 hl/ha (5.5 tons/acre). D.T.

NOTCH GRAFTING, a method of GRAFTING vines that resembles CLEFT GRAFTING. It differs in that the cut trunk is not split across, but instead the scion pieces are cut to fit a V-shaped notch made on either side of the trunk to a length of about 3 cm/1 in. The scion pieces are often tacked into place. Notch grafts are not as secure as cleft grafts. A related method is the bark graft done later in spring when the bark lifts freely, but again the union is sometimes weak. B.G.C.

NOUVEAU, French for 'new', and a specific style of wine designed to be drunk only weeks rather than months or years after the HARVEST. The most famous and successful nouveau is BEAUJOLAIS Nouveau, which at its peak, in 1988, accounted for more than 800,000 hl/21 million gal, or 60 per cent of all Beaujolais produced. The Beaujolais producers themselves are keen to point out that their Nouveaux are not simply 'un phénomène "marketing"', but that they owe their origins to the 19th century, when the year's wine would complete its fermentation in cask while *en route* to nearby Lyons, where the new wine provided a direct link with village life in the Beaujolais hills. The phenomenon originated in a group of villages just west of Villefranche whose wines seemed to mature earliest. After the constraints of the Second World War, the Beaujolais producers were gradually allowed to release an increasing proportion of new wine. The original term was PRIMEUR, meaning young produce, and from 1951 the Beaujolais producers were allowed to release their primeurs from 15 December. These young, refreshing wines enjoyed great success in the bistros of Paris in the 1950s and 1960s, and by the end of the 1960s the phrase *'Le Beaujolais Nouveau est arrivé'* had been coined. (One British wine merchant was already importing Beaujolais Nouveau in barrel in the early 1960s.) In the 1970s the phenomenon spread outside France, thanks to energetic work on the part of producers such as Georges DUBŒUF and his agents around the world, and Alexis LICHINE in the United States. By the end of 1974 Beaujolais Nouveau had reached Great Britain to such an extent that the first Beaujolais Nouveau race (of bottles of purple ink to London) had been run. Eventually the Nouveau was flown, with inexplicable haste and brouhaha, to markets around the world: the craze reaching Australia in 1982 and Japan and Italy in 1985. Initially the release date was fixed at 15 November, but was eventually changed to the third Thursday in November, for the convenience of the wine trade and the media, who, for much of the late 1970s and 1980s were apparently fascinated by this event.

The immense commercial success of Beaujolais Nouveau inevitably spawned other Nouveaux—infant wines from other regions of France, notably Gamays made in TOURAINE and the ARDÈCHE, a range of wines made in LANGUEDOC-ROUSSILLON, and many VINS DE PAYS, particularly Côtes de Gascogne. Vin de pays Primeur or Nouveau may be released on the third Thursday of October following the harvest, a full month before Beaujolais Nouveau.

Italy produces a range of similar wines, described as **novello**, and even ENGLAND produces some nouveau. Many southern hemisphere producers have tried to sell their own early releases as 'Nouveau' because they carry the same year on the label and are available many months before the appearance of Beaujolais Nouveau (which has somewhat diluted the novelty that used to attach to bottles carrying the current vintage year).

Wine-making techniques have to be adapted to produce wines that are ready to drink so early. The majority of Nouveau wines are red and many of them are produced, like Beaujolais, by CARBONIC MACERATION or SEMI-CARBONIC MACERATION, which yields particularly fruity, soft, aromatic red wines suitable for drinking young and slightly cool, typically involving a fermentation of only about four days, and fairly brutal STABILIZATION. Those wine-makers who do not or cannot practise any form of carbonic maceration may ferment the grapes traditionally but at lower temperatures than usual (in the low 20s °C (*c.*70 °F)) and allow only the briefest of MACERATIONS. White grapes, for which carbonic maceration is not suitable, are generally fermented very cool, at 15 to 20 °C, and boiled sweet aromas typically result.

The great attraction of nouveau wines for producers is that they produce a financial return so quickly. As one taster remarked, their characteristic aroma is the scent of cash flow. Their appeal for the wine drinker is that they are a refreshing and stimulating reminder of the passing of the seasons, a sort of liquid harvest festival. Nouveau wines do not deteriorate in bottle substantially more rapidly than non-nouveau wines, but their lifespan is inevitably shorter. A well-made nouveau from a good vintage can be opened two or even three years after the harvest without too much trepidation, although, like all nouveau wines, it should be drunk cool and without too much deliberation.

NOVELLO, Italian for new, and therefore a name applied to Italian NOUVEAU wine, sold only a few weeks after harvest.

NUCLEAR MAGNETIC RESONANCE, NMR, or, more specifically, Site Specific Natural Isotope Fractionation by Nuclear Magnetic Resonance (SNIF-NMR), was in the mid 1990s the most powerful analytical tool for the authentication of alcoholic drinks. It is therefore an important modern weapon, and deterrent, against ADULTERATION AND FRAUD.

It was developed during the 1980s by Professor Gérard Martin of Nantes University (in the MUSCADET region of north west France) and is officially approved as an analytical method both by the EUROPEAN UNION and, more internationally, by the OIV. This powerful research aid has been patented and marketed on a world-wide basis by the EU-funded Eurofins enterprise.

Its strength is that it can examine the precise structure of the ETHANOL molecule in such a way that it drastically reduces the potential for fraud. The principle is based on deuterium, the stable natural isotope of hydrogen, and its distribution in the ethanol molecule. There are three distinct sites of deuterium and NMR can differentiate between these sites, showing the abundance of deuterium in each of them.

The isotopic content of each site is linked to both the origin of the molecule and the conditions prior to the production of alcohol, i.e. FERMENTATION showing the degree of CHAPTALIZATION (where the wine was enriched with sugar cane, sugar beet, or GRAPE CONCENTRATE, for example).

One obvious application is proving chaptalization in excess of legal limits. Another, much more far-reaching long-term application depends on establishing data-banks based on the analysis of representative sample wines from each wine area. (This is already well advanced for many European wine areas.) This application, based on each region's unique deuterium ratios, should be able to provide an absolute guarantee of geographical authenticity. While it may never be sufficiently detailed to distinguish a Ch LAFITE from a Ch LATOUR, it can easily distinguish between a BORDEAUX and a BERGERAC.

In 1993 it could not yet identify specific grape varieties and their proportions, but this is a possibility in the long term.

G.T.

NUITS, CÔTE DE. The Côte de Nuits, named after the principal town of Nuits-St-Georges, is the northern half of the escarpment of the CÔTE D'OR, producing the greatest red wines of Burgundy, from the Pinot Noir grape, and very occasional white wines. The principal villages, from north to south, are GEVREY-CHAMBERTIN, MOREY-ST-DENIS, CHAMBOLLE-MUSIGNY, VOUGEOT, VOSNE-ROMANÉE, Flagey-ÉCHEZEAUX, and NUITS-ST-GEORGES. See also MARSANNAY. The soils on the lower part of the slope tend to be much more fertile than the main parent rock because more immature soil has been incorporated.

Wines from FIXIN, Brochon, Prémeaux, Comblanchien, and Corgoloin may be sold as **Côte de Nuits Villages**. These are usually but not exclusively red wines.

See also BEAUNE, CÔTE DE and the map on p. 163.

J.T.C.M. & J.M.H.

NUITS-ST-GEORGES, small market town in Burgundy giving its name to the Côte de Nuits, the northern half of the Côte d'Or. Nuits-St-Georges has remained fully independent of BEAUNE to the south and Dijon to the north, with numerous NÉGOCIANTS making their headquarters here. The town also boasts its own charity auction, the Hospices de Nuits, held in March, when the wines can be better judged than those of the HOSPICES DE BEAUNE in November.

The appellation Nuits-St-Georges lies both sides of the town which straddles the small river Meuzin and incorporates the vineyards of neighbouring Prémeaux-Prissey to the south. While all the wines of Nuits-St-Georges are sturdy and long lived, those abutting Vosne-Romanée to the north show the most fruit and elegance. The finest wines are normally held to come from the vineyards south of the Meuzin, where the ground is stonier and the wines are the fullest and longest lived of them all. There is more clay in the soil of the Prémeaux vineyards, making wines which are fat but a touch less fine.

Whereas the Intendant Bouchu noted in 1666 a preference for Nuits, 'where the wine is excellent', over Prémeaux, 'where the wine is of good quality', the king of Saxony specifically ordered in 1780 'the wine of Prémeaux, the colour of the stained glass windows of La Sainte Chapelle'.

Nuits boasts 27 PREMIER CRU vineyards but no GRANDS CRUS, perhaps because the town's leading vigneron, Henri Gouges, was too modest when the CLASSIFICATIONS were agreed in the 1930s. However, the eponymous Les St-Georges vineyard, first singled out as early as the 11th century, has always been cited as of the highest quality. Also particularly fine in the southern Nuits-St-Georges sector are Les Cailles and Les Vaucrains, both adjacent to Les St-Georges, while Les Murgers and Les Boudots on the Vosne-Romanée side and Les Argillières, Clos l'Arlot, and Clos de la Maréchale in Prémeaux have good reputations.

Some white wine is also made from the Chardonnay grape, most notably in the Clos l'Arlot and by Domaine Gouges in the premier cru Les Perrières.

See also CÔTE D'OR and its map. J.T.C.M.

NUMBERS AND WINE, a combination that has assumed increasing importance as WINE-MAKING has become more scientific, and as consumers, faced with a bewildering choice of wines, need easily appreciated assessments of wine quality. As recently as the 1970s, wine-makers had only the vaguest grasp of their wines' vital statistics; and the only numbers of significance to most wine drinkers were those of VINTAGE, PRICE, and, among more sophisticated connoisseurs of bordeaux, the numerical rankings associated with wine CLASSIFICATION.

Numbers are increasingly used for identification, however. Australian wine producers such as PENFOLDS have for decades exhibited a penchant for incorporating BIN numbers into the names of their wines. Individual CLONES of various VINE VARIETIES can be so numerous that they are often identified by individual numbers, as are CASKS and individual BARRELS in some larger wineries.

As the growing of grapes and the making of wine becomes more scientific, however, numbers as measurements play a key role, as they do in all scientific thinking. Consumers, as well as producers, have an interest in measurements taken at all stages of wine production, from SOIL to finished liquid. These measurements, such as PH, level of TANNINS, or the ALCOHOLIC STRENGTH which appears on most wine labels, cannot be used on their own as a measure of how a wine will taste. Scores attempt to measure quality, however, whether in the vineyard or tasting room.

Viticultural scoring

In various parts of the world there have been attempts to classify individual VINEYARD sites numerically. The DOURO valley of northern Portugal has its own system for the production of PORT whereby existing vineyards are awarded a number of points, from plus 1,680 for the most promising, to minus 3,340 for the least favoured, taking into account not just TERROIR but the vines planted. The CHAMPAGNE region of north east France has a similar, if considerably less precise, system whereby whole COMMUNES are given a percentage rating, between 80 and 100.

The introduction of CANOPY MANAGEMENT techniques has led to vineyard scoring in even more detail, as individual CANOPY MICROCLIMATES may be measured and assigned precise scores.

Wine scoring

Here we are primarily concerned with number as a measurement of the quality of a wine. When tasting wine, the nuances of COLOUR, AROMA, FLAVOUR, and taste, the interplay of ALCOHOL, ALDEHYDES, ESTERS, and ACIDS, the location, temperature, even one's companions, have such complicated effects that, whilst providing much of the enjoyment of wine, they make the idea of describing a wine numerically seem over-simplified at best, ridiculous at worst. Yet we all accept the numerical description that is price. Reputation, age, and availability, apart from the quality of the wine, all play a part; nevertheless, price gives some indication of quality.

Respected attempts have been made by experts to provide numerical measures of quality, free from the other factors that influence price. Robert PARKER, in the United States, uses a scale from 50 to 100. Michael BROADBENT in Britain uses one from 0 to 5, expressed in stars rather than numbers. Many tastings described in the press report numerically, sometimes just describing quality, sometimes rating value. In many countries, professional wine judges (see JUDGING) employ a 20-point system, typically with three points being given for appearance, five for aroma or bouquet, nine for flavour, and three for overall quality.

There are two reasons for wanting to apply numbers to wine. First, a number is precise: the number 17 means the same to everyone, whereas words used by tasters, such as 'earthy', although very useful, are difficult to recognize or describe. Secondly, and more importantly, numbers combine easily. For example, we can take the average of the numerical values given to a wine by several tasters to obtain an improved measure. More complicated combinations can be devised to extract further information from a tasting (see Amerine and Roessler). Much criticism of numerical measures derives from the critic's inability to understand how to use the numbers, rather than from the numbers themselves; whereas words are more familiar. A similar deficiency rests with the consumer, who is misled by the precision of number to think that a wine rated 91 by Parker must be obviously better than a 90, whereas, for a reason outlined below, it need not be.

Ideally a numerical measure of a wine's quality should be reproducible. If a desk is measured to be 1 m long, then any trained person will reproduce 'one metre' on measuring it. Ideally, when Parker quotes 85, others should agree. Unfortunately they do not. The evaluation of wine is too subjective, and the wine itself too variable, for this to be possible. This does not rule out the usefulness of numerical measures, but it means that one has to be more careful in using them. For example, if all trained tasters gave wine A a mark in the 80s, and wine B one in the 70s, it is clear, despite the variability within the decades, that wine A is better than wine B.

There are many factors that may affect the variability. There may be variation from bottle to bottle, or case to case, especially with older wines stored in different conditions. Tasting conditions, particularly TEMPERATURE and exposure to air, influence the judgement. The tasting of one wine may be affected by the immediately previous tasting of another, with a carry-over effect from one experience to the next. There are obvious differences between judges' abilities and partialities. Judges tire easily and many cannot fairly assess more than 20 wines in a single session. These difficulties are not insuperable. A preliminary tasting to disqualify poor judges is a fine idea, if understandably unpopular, especially when it happens that some tasters are good with some wines, but inexperienced with others. A careful design of the tasting, accompanied by a rigorous analysis of the results, can produce judgements of real value. It may often be necessary to provide two numbers, one of which acts like a Parker–Broadbent value, the other providing a measure of variability. Thus two wines may be reported as (75 ± 2) and (75 ± 5) respectively, indicating that both were rated 75 on average, but that the latter produced more disagreement than the former. The first was rather consistent, whereas the second was more variable. A more sophisticated approach can use two numbers that characterize two different aspects of the wine's quality. The main difficulty with tasting lies in the lack of reproducibility. Whilst it is hard to make general

Vine **nursery** near Chablis.

statements about tastings, evidence suggests that, when experienced tasters work on a 0–20 scale, they can, about half the time, be out by as much as 2 and not infrequently by as much as 4. In the tasting mentioned below, one wine, on a scale from 0 to 20, was rated 2 by one experienced taster, and 16.5 by another; with an average over 11 tasters of 10.5. Some tastings reported in the wine press may be misleading, either because the tasting has not been performed with sufficient care, or because the results have not been analysed competently. It is rare for the press report of a tasting to contain enough information for a reader to assess the value of the tasting, despite the abundance of words of doubtful precision.

Numbers are also useful in the investigation of claims made by wine tasters. For example, it is often held that wines of one region are different in style from those of another. Yet in one of the most carefully controlled and analysed tastings on record, reported in the *Underground Wine Journal* for July 1976, experienced French tasters had great difficulty in distinguishing their own red Bordeaux wines from California Cabernets. Writings on wine abound in a mixture of myth and fact, in which it is hard to separate one from the other.

Much of the joy of wine comes from its enormous variety. Numbers will not destroy this variety nor lessen the appreciation, merely help to put it on a firmer basis. To do this requires more carefully organized, comparative wine-TASTINGS, and better analyses of the data obtained from them.

D.V.L.

Amerine, M. A., and Roessler, E. B., *Wines: Their Sensory Evaluation* (Davis, Calif., 1983).

Ashenfelter, O., *Liquid Assets* (Princeton, NJ, various issues).

NURAGUS, white grape variety grown principally to produce the unremarkable varietal Nuragus di Cagliari on the island of SARDINIA. Total plantings halved during the 1980s to a total of about 8,700 ha/21,500 acres in 1990.

NURSERY in viticultural terms is either a place set aside for nurturing young vines, or a name for a GRAFTING establishment. Open-ground vine nurseries are where CUTTINGS are planted to develop roots and become ROOTLINGS. Cuttings are taken in winter, stored in a cold room, then CALLUSED by burying them in moist sand until young roots form at the base (after six to eight weeks). In spring they are planted in rows in the nursery where the first-year shoots develop. Nursery soils need to be deep, friable, and well drained, free of pathogens and with a good water supply. In the following winter or spring, they are lifted, shoots and roots are trimmed, and the vines planted out in the vineyard. For grafted vines, the products of BENCH GRAFTING are callused in a humid room before planting in a nursery. B.G.C.

NURSERY BUDDING and **nursery grafting**, methods for the PROPAGATION of grafted vines that complement BENCH GRAFTING, used in warm climates. Great flexibility is possible in the type of SCION wood used and in the timing of grafting. Inserted scions are tied tightly with budding tape and, after the inserted bud has started to grow, the rootstock foliage is shortened back and later removed. B.G.C.

NUTRIENTS. All living things, including vines and yeasts, need NITROGEN, PHOSPHORUS, and POTASSIUM, along with carbon, hydrogen, and OXYGEN as nutrients.

For more details of **nutrition** of the vine, see VINE NUTRITION.

NV. See NON-VINTAGE.

O

OAK is a hard, supple, and watertight WOOD, which has the simple advantage over other WOOD TYPES used for COOPERAGE of displaying a natural affinity with wine, imparting qualities and flavours that today's consumers appreciate as enhancing or complementing those of many wines. Oak in general is one of the strongest of the common hardwoods of the temperate northern hemisphere. As well as being particularly good at holding liquids, oak is also physically easy to work, encouraging clarity and stability in red wines and adding new layers of complexity to many whites.

There are hundreds of species of oak, all of which can be broadly separated into two categories, red and white. The red oaks are porous and cannot therefore be relied upon for watertight cooperage. For wine, three sorts of white oak are most important, one American and two European, all of them belonging to the botanical genus QUERCUS:

1. *Quercus alba*, also known as American white oak. This general name is also applied to the American oak species *Quercus bicolor*, swamp white oak; *Quercus lyrata*, overcup oak; *Quercus durandii*, Durand oak; *Quercus michauxii*, swamp chestnut oak; and *Quercus prinus*, chestnut oak. Some of these species can hybridize with each other.
2. *Quercus sessiliflora*, also known as sessile oak, *Quercus rouvre*, or *Quercus petraea*.
3. *Quercus robur*, also called pedunculate or variously English, French, and Russian oak.

The anatomy of different oaks has implications for barrel making. A trunk can be thought of as a bundle of tubes or vessels and fibres running parallel to the trunk with groups of fibres called rays running radially from the outside towards the center of the trunk. Oak is non-storeyed; the longitudinal tubes and fibres overlap so as to give strength. (In a soft wood such as pine, the tubes and fibres are stacked, making the wood much less resistant to pressure.) It is also ring-porous; there are distinct bands of large and small pores or tubes laid down at different times of the year (see GRAIN).

Oak is rich in tyloses, which are structures that plug the tubes. This is what makes it particularly good for holding liquids, as the path of the liquid through the wood is blocked by these tyloses. American white oaks, *Quercus alba*, are the richest in these tyloses, which is why American barrel STAVES can be sawn into shape without risk of leakage. With European oaks there are fewer tyloses so the wood is more porous and must be split to follow the tubes and then bent so that all the tubes are parallel to the stave, thus minimizing leakage.

American oak generally has a much more obvious flavour, vanillin in character, and can be more astringent than the smoother, subtler oaks of Europe. Vital to barrel quality is not just the source of the oak, however, but its seasoning (see BARREL MAKING for more details). There has been a tendency to season American oak more crudely than European oak, although this is changing.

World oak resources

All statistics regarding the amount of standing timber in a given country should be read with some caution, but the figures in the table, many of them based on a report of the United Nations Economic Commission for Europe, were assembled in the mid to late 1980s and appear in Chang:

Country (excluding CIS)	Growing stock (cu m)
United States	693.8
France	422.7
Yugoslavia	178.0
Hungary	104.6
Bulgaria	79.4
Turkey	75.2
Germany (eastern)	72.0
Poland	64.4
Czechoslovakia	55.6
Portugal	52.4
Japan	47.4
Great Britain	33.6
Greece	21.3
Sweden	16.5
Switzerland	5.1
Netherlands	2.6
Ireland	1.9
Israel	0.2
Total	1,926.7

According to the same UN report, a little over half of Portuguese oak is CORK oak (*Quercus suber*), but the statistics are clearly incomplete as no oak was recorded as growing in Spain.

Ages of the oak forests are given but not species. In Poland, for example, approximately 75 per cent of the stands are less than 80 years old, as they are in Hungary. Cooperage-quality oak should be at least 80 years old and preferably much older.

According to research done by Backman and Waggener of

the University of Washington (USA) in 1988, the erstwhile Soviet Union (now CIS) had approximately 9.7 million ha/24 million acres of oak, of which around 3.1 million are located in the far eastern region, close to the Pacific Ocean. This is *Quercus mongolica*, not a species used for cooperage. About 1.7 million ha are in the Ukraine and are said to add up to around 233 million cu m. Most of the balance, about 4.7 million ha with 763 million cu m/8,180 million cu ft of oak, is in European Russia, where the North Caucasus, the Urals, and Povolzhsk regions have the highest proportions of oak in their forests. If these estimates are correct, the CIS has the greatest oak resources in the world, even though they may have suffered from poor forestry management for many decades (see below). According to some estimates, Romania also has substantial, if poorly managed, oak forests.

American oaks

In 1987, according to a report published by the US Forestry Service in 1989, there were 24,497 million cu ft/698 million cu m of commercially important selected white oaks in the eastern United States, although only a certain proportion of this would be suitable for cooperage, where the quality criteria are much higher than for pulp and veneer. *Quercus alba* covers most of the eastern United States, extending east from Minnesota, Iowa, Missouri, and Arkansas, north of Mexico, and south of Canada and Maine.

There is no general agreement as to which American regions provide the best oak for wine or whiskey barrels. Some people feel that oak from Minnesota and Wisconsin is best for wine barrels; others feel that it is too tannic. Wood from the more southerly parts of the USA is condemned by some for being too sappy. Oregon white oak, *Quercus garryana*, which grows about 50 to 90 ft tall, and around 24 to 40 in in diameter, has also been used experimentally for wine barrels. There are approximately 6,000 million cu ft of various species of oak in California, Oregon, and Washington, but, other than Oregon oak, little is suitable for barrels.

American oak is used widely by the wine industries of Spain, North and South America, and Australia. Because American oak generally has a more powerful flavour than European oak, it is usually used mainly for relatively powerful red wines such as RIOJA, and other Spanish reds, Australian SHIRAZ, and warm-climate CABERNET SAUVIGNON. See COOPERAGE, history.

European oaks

These oaks grow throughout Europe, as far east as the Urals, as far south as Sicily, as far west as Ireland, France, and Portugal, and as far north as southern Norway.

Quercus sessiliflora can reach a height of 25 m/82 ft and can live over 300 years. Branches form high up the relatively straight trunk. Wood from this tree is usually tight grained (see GRAIN). This species grows well in sandy, silty soil with good drainage, but thrives in a variety of soils. In Europe it is found throughout the United Kingdom and from France east to Poland and the Baltic states and as far south as Italy and Yugoslavia.

Quercus robur, thought of as English or French oak, also grows to over 25 m in height and can live over 300 years. Its branches spread out to provide more shade than *Quercus sessiliflora* and it tends to produce wide-grained wood. It prefers fertile soils where there is plenty of water. As *Quercus robur* tolerates a wider range of growing conditions, it is more widespread in Europe than *Quercus sessiliflora*. It extends further north into the Scandinavian countries, further south into Turkey, Georgia, and Portugal, and east as far as the Urals. Although wood from this species tends to have wider grains than *Quercus sessiliflora*, the two species can be positively distinguished only by examination of leaves and acorns. The acorn of *Quercus robur* is attached via a long PEDUNCLE whereas that of *Quercus sessiliflora* is attached directly to the twig. There is so much cross-fertilization that there are many hybrids of these two species, however.

Coopers do not usually distinguish the two species in their workshops. Like wine-makers, they tend to pay more attention to geographical provenance and grain size than oak species. And, as wine-makers increasingly understand, details of BARREL MAKING can have an even more significant effect on wine quality than exact forest location.

France Although Baltic and Slovenian oak were the most admired oaks in the 19th century, French oak has since become the standard by which all other oaks are judged. Thanks to sound forestry management, French oak is available in viable commercial quantities and can add to wine flavours that appeal to modern consumers.

Almost a quarter of France, or nearly 14 million ha/34 million acres, is forest, constituting more than 40 per cent of all forest in the European Union. About one-third of this forest land is oak. There are 2.6 million ha of *Quercus sessiliflora* and *Quercus robur*, the two species of oak of interest to the cooper, of which at least 2 million ha are located in the regions discussed below. France is the world's major source of European oak, by quite a margin. In 1991, for example, a total of 3.15 million cu m of oak were harvested, of which about 150,000 cu m was used for COOPERAGE, enough to make approximately 250,000 barrels.

Since 1947 around 2 million ha of France have been reforested. Unlike other countries, where ancient stands of hemlock, spruce, and fir have been cut down to make toilet paper and diapers (nappies), France has done a good job of managing its forests since the Second World War. Supplies of French oak—barring unusual circumstances such as dramatic climate change—should remain abundant.

Concern about the condition of the French forests dates back to at least 1291, when scholars note the mention of 'maistre des fôrets' in the Royal Ordinances. The most famous of these Ordinances was written during the regime of Colbert in 1669. Colbert is commemorated in the Tronçais forest, where he ordered systematic replanting of oak trees for use in shipbuilding.

Sylviculture is actively practised in France so that trees in government-owned forests are not allowed to grow wild, but are carefully farmed to yield suitable wood, just like any other crop. Trees are encouraged to grow tall and straight yielding grains appropriate for barrel making, for example, by a variety of physical techniques.

The following forests all over northern France provide oak for wine and brandy barrels:

Western Loire and Sarthe: woods from forests in the western LOIRE, from the *départements* of Indre, Cher, and Indre-et-Loire, and in the Sarthe near Le Mans, have tight grains and are highly prized.

Limousin: woods from the following regions in France are usually called Limousin: the eastern part of the *département* of Deux-Sèvres, Vienne, Hautes de Vienne, the northern part of the Corrèze, the Creuze, the eastern part of the Charente and the southern part of the Indre, the northern part of the Dordogne. These oaks tend to have wide grains and are usually grouped together as Limousin. Soils here tend to clay-limestone or granite. These woods are more tannic than the tight-grained woods and are most popular with brandy makers.

Nièvre and Allier: woods from these two central *départements* just south of SANCERRE go by many names. Sometimes this wood is sold under the name of the specific forest. Tronçais, for example, is a government-owned forest north of Moulins, while Bertranges is a forest near Nevers. This sort of oak may also be sold under the name of the region, such as Allier and Nevers. To many French wine-makers, however, all of this wood is regarded simply as 'bois de centre', wood from the centre of France. However these forests are named, the wood is usually tight grained and is popular for both brandy and wine. Soil here tends to silica and clay. As stands are planted with close spacing the trees tend to grow up, rather than out; hence the tighter grains.

Vosges: wood from the Vosges forests west of ALSACE became popular with wine-makers outside the region in the early 1980s. This wood is usually tight grained and resembles the oak from Nièvre and Allier. Oak experts say they can identify this wood by its 'clear' or 'white' colour. The character of Vosges woods varies according the altitude of the stand.

Jura and Bourgogne: just to the east of BURGUNDY are forests which traditionally supplied Burgundy with oak. These forests are still important and supply wood mainly to Burgundian wine producers.

Argonne: located near CHAMPAGNE, this forest provides a small amount of oak for the cooperage business, principally for those few champagne producers who still ferment in barrel. Sometimes the wood is sold as Vosges.

There is no APPELLATION CONTRÔLÉE but much confusion of nomenclature in the world of oak. This means not only that wine-makers are suspicious about proclaimed wood origins but that people use different definitions for the same name. Some would include wood from the western Loire in the category of 'bois de centre' while others would exclude anything but Nevers and Allier. Others will classify wood around Nevers with wood from the Yonne and CÔTE D'OR as 'Bourgogne'.

Eastern Europe Historically, the forests of eastern Europe were extremely important sources of oak, mainly *Quercus robur* and *Quercus sessiliflora*. Before the Second World War Polish, Russian, and Baltic oaks were important in both the beer and wine industries and in the 1990s coopers have been scouting east keenly in search of good-quality wood that can be bought more cheaply than French oak. Political changes in eastern Europe in the late 1980s immediately resulted in Hungarian and Moravian oak being offered to wine-makers in the west. It may be, however, that the flavours derived from these woods are too neutral for modern use.

SLOVENIA, BOSNIA HERCEGOVINA, and SERBIA have been a useful source of oak for the large casks and oval vats used by Italy's wine producers (who often called them simply Yugoslavian, or Slavonian). It is said these oaks are too tannic for French grape varieties but work well with Italy's NEBBIOLO and SANGIOVESE, but this could be a reflection of wood preparation or TERROIR. Much of this wood was sawn, rather than hand split (see BARREL MAKING) and the result was porous barrels that provided astringent flavours. These forests have been managed poorly, too many trees have been cut down, and access to these woods has been restricted for internal political reasons.

Although in the 19th century Baltic oaks were prized by the French and British, it is not known how much oak suitable for cooperage is left in Lithuania, Latvia, and Estonia. In the 1980s the then Soviet Union exchanged trade credits for thousands of oak barrels from cooperages in Cognac for use in its brandy industry, which suggests that throughout much of the 20th century Soviet forestry management may have been less than perfect. It is possible that much of the million ha of 'mature and fully mature' oak growing in Russia according to Soviet statistics is low quality.

Portuguese oak Oak grown in the far north of Portugal can, if well seasoned, be of use to Portugal's wine-makers, being more subtle than the locally used chestnut and much cheaper than oak imported from France.

For oak flavour, see WOOD FLAVOUR. For oak influence, see WOOD INFLUENCE. See also BARRELS, BARREL FERMENTATION, BARREL MAINTENANCE, BARREL MATURATION, BARREL TYPES, and OAK CHIPS and OAK ESSENCES. M.K.

Backman, C. A., and Waggener, T. R., *Soviet Timber Resources and Utilization: An Interpretation of the 1988 National Inventory* (Seattle, 1991).

Burns, R. M., and Honkala, B. H. (eds.), *Silvics of North America*, ii: *Hardwoods* (Washington, DC, 1990).

Chang, S. J., 'The demand and supply situation of the world's oak timber', *International Oak Symposium Proceedings* (San Francisco, 1993).

Waddell, K. L., Oswald, D. C., and Powell, D. L. (eds.), *Forest Statistics of the United States 1987* (US Dept. of Agriculture, 1980).

OAK AGED is a term often applied to wine. It can mean that the wine was matured in some form of oak BARREL or larger CASK, or it can mean that it was exposed to OAK CHIPS. Proper oak ageing in oak cooperage inevitably increases the price of a wine by a considerable margin, whereas oak chips are relatively inexpensive.

OAK AGEING, the process of AGEING a wine in contact with OAK. This typically involves BARREL MATURATION, ageing the wine in a relatively small oak container, although the phrase may also be used for CASK AGEING in a larger oak container, and can even be used for wines exposed to the influence of OAK CHIPS. Wines thus treated may be described as **oaked**. (**Oaky** is a tasting term usually applied to wines too heavily influenced by WOOD FLAVOUR, which smell and taste more of wood than fruit, and may be aggressively tannic and dry.)

OAK AND BRANDY. Ageing in OAK, while optional in the production of many fine wines, is a crucial element in the production of fine French BRANDY, and brandies made similarly elsewhere. Although oak was used originally for purely practical reasons (oak being the most impermeable wood grown near the COGNAC and ARMAGNAC regions), it remains the ideal container for maturing spirits. As for wine, oak not only imparts some specific qualities as extractable substances (see WOOD FLAVOUR), it also allows slow oxygenation of the spirit (see WOOD INFLUENCE). Indeed the balance between the original spirit and the qualities imparted by the oak is important in determining the quality of the final product. The balance is a delicate one: obviously, the newer the wood in which the spirit is stored and the longer it remains in wood, the greater its influence. To maximize the wood's influence on the spirit, most serious brandies are matured in relatively small oak casks. Typical cognac casks, for example, hold 350 l/92 gal.

To achieve a balanced result, young French brandy is typically, although not invariably, put into new oak for up to a year immediately after DISTILLATION. During that time it will absorb the oak's extractable substances. It is then transferred to older casks for the rest of its maturation process during which the character of slow OXIDATION may eventually dominate the extractable substances. This period of oak maturation can vary in total from two years for the youngest armagnacs (three for cognac) to ten times as long for the finest brandies.

Oak is valued, as it is in wine production, because it is hard, supple, and watertight—thus making it suitable for storage and transportation. It is particularly useful for the maturation of spirits because its density allows only a slow evaporation, which ensures that none of the precious aromatic qualities in the spirit are lost in the process. French oak, especially LIMOUSIN, TRONÇAIS, and other oaks from central France, is particularly popular for brandy maturation. American oak has too obvious a flavour and can impart bitter tastes, to cognac anyway, while Slovenian or 'Trieste oak' can be too hard.

But inevitably the EVAPORATION involves the loss of spirit. In dry cellars more liquid is lost than ALCOHOLIC STRENGTH. In damper, more desirable cellars the reverse is the case—although after 15 years in cask even in a damp cellar over half the original volume (and a mere six to seven per cent of the original alcoholic strength) is lost.

The focus of research into oak constituents and oak maturation for the brandy business differs from the wine-maker's view of oak because fine brandies are kept in cask many years longer than wine. Experiments with brandy as well as wine, however, demonstrate the superiority of air-dried over kiln-dried wood for barrel staves. During proper seasoning in the open air, most aggressive elements are leached out. (See BARREL MAKING.)

Oak's PHENOLIC compounds, of which TANNINS are the best known, are important in brandy maturation. Although they rarely comprise more than 10 per cent of oak by weight, they are easily absorbed by spirits. The phenolics impart colour to spirit which was colourless when it emerged from the still, and at first they increase its bitterness, but after a few years the molecules agglomerate and the flavour mellows (see POLYMERIZATION).

Lignin, which comprises between 25 and 30 per cent of oak, is also believed to play a part in brandy maturation, even though the spirit absorbs a much lower proportion of it than of oak's available phenolic compounds. The process of heating the staves (see TOAST) is thought to break down these lignins. Their first impact is to bring an aroma of balsam wood, but when they break down they create the lovely vanilla and cinnamon overtones detectable in some brandies (see WOOD FLAVOUR).

Even the supposedly neutral cellulose, which is oak's major constituent, is useful. As it gradually dissolves in the maturing spirit it imparts the agreeable sweetness found in older brandies.

The processes are slow, in cognac especially. The tannins only really start to build up after eight or more years, and although the brandy has absorbed the vanillins within a few years, it takes 30 years for the ALDEHYDES to reach their peak and for all the tannins and lignins to have been absorbed. The VOLATILE ACIDS build up over the full 50 years that the best brandies remain in cask. N.F.

OAK CHIPS, useful if ersatz wine-making tool, an inexpensive alternative to top-quality BARREL MATURATION. Oak chips vary considerably both in the provenance of the OAK (from subtle Limousin to harsher American oak) and in the size of the chip (from pencil shaving to the more common cashew nut size). Oak chips, just like BARRELS, are also subjected to different degrees of TOAST.

Oak chips, or *Quercus fragmentus* as some wags refer to them, are used either instead of barrel maturation or to supplement the oak flavour imparted by a used barrel. The average dose of chips is about 1 g/l, typically added prior to fermentation. Chips offer considerable savings over new COOPERAGE: a sufficient quantity of American oak chips to impart some degree of oak flavour could cost less than a twentieth of the cost of a new American oak barrel (and an even smaller fraction of the cost of a new French barrel). They are most effective when added during FERMENTATION, when presumably a combination of heat and enzymatic activity combine to generate the most favourable flavour EXTRACTION. Such wines often have such an overpoweringly oak flavour that they must undergo BACK BLENDING with unoaked wine.

It is now possible to buy oak chips impregnated with LACTIC BACTERIA immobilized at the stage immediately prior to exponential growth so that they can be used to encourage MALOLACTIC FERMENTATION.

Oak chip use has the potential disadvantage of producing very high levels of VOLATILE ACIDS which can make the treated wines appealing to some tasters in the short term, but drastically reduces their potential for BOTTLE AGEING.

Few wine producers admit to using oak chips although, unlike OAK ESSENCE, oak chips may be used perfectly legally in many wine regions. A wine description which mentions 'oak maturation' or 'oak influence' without actually mentioning any form of cooperage is a good clue.

The **oak shavings** which can result from reconditioning used barrels (see BARREL MAKING) may similarly be used.

See also COGNAC for regular oak chip use there. G.T.

OAK ESSENCES or **oak extract**, usually illegal wine-making additive (unlike OAK CHIPS) which can inexpensively substitute, at least in the short term, for some of the flavours imparted by BARREL MATURATION in expensive new oak. Various powders and liquids are marketed based on extractions from different woods. In some cases specific TANNINS are targeted and extracted so as to add structure as well as flavour to a wine.

Doses of powdered oak extracts can vary between 5 and 20 g/hl but powders are more difficult to use than liquids because of potential problems with CLARIFICATION. The usual dose of a liquid extract is about 0.01 per cent and, since most liquids are based on ETHANOL or BRANDY, they can be extremely difficult to detect analytically. However, their ability to sustain a wine through BOTTLE AGEING is questionable and they should not be of interest to any serious wine producer. G.T.

OAK INFLUENCE. See WOOD INFLUENCE.

OAK ROOT ROT, vine disease. See ARMILLARIA ROOT ROT.

OAKVILLE. Important centre of wine production in the NAPA Valley of California.

OBIDOS, an IPR in western Portugal. See OESTE for more details.

OECHSLE, scale of measuring grape sugars, and therefore grape RIPENESS, based on the DENSITY of grape juice. Grape juice with a specific gravity of 1.075 is said to be 75° Oechsle. This is the system used in Germany and it has its origins in a system of weighing grape must developed first by the Württemberg scientist J. J. Reuss, but much refined in the 1830s by the Pforzheim physicist Ferdinand Oechsle (see GERMAN HISTORY).

Like other scales used elsewhere (see BAUMÉ and BRIX), it can be measured with a suitably calibrated REFRACTOMETER or HYDROMETER. A similar scale, devised at KLOSTERNEUBURG, is used in Austria.

Each scale of sugar measurement relates to the others. For example, a grape juice of 14.7° Brix has a specific gravity of 1.06 and an Oechsle value of $(1.06 - 1.0) \times 1000 = 60$. According to published scales, these relationships are not strict ones; see nomograms in Hamilton and Coombe.

For more details, see MUST WEIGHT. B.G.C.

Hamilton, R. P., and Coombe, B. G., 'Harvesting of winegrapes', in B. G. Coombe and P. R. Dry (eds.), *Viticulture, ii: Practices* (Adelaide, 1992).

ŒIL-DE-PERDRIX, French for 'partridge's eye', used as a name and tasting term for pale pink wines, especially in the Neuchâtel canton of SWITZERLAND.

OENOLOGIST, or, in the United States and South Africa, **enologist**, one who practises OENOLOGY. A consultant oenologist is likely to concentrate on the activities traditionally considered WINE-MAKING but increasingly concerns himself or herself with what happens in the vineyard as well as the cellar. In general usage an oenologist is either a scientifically qualified employee or a roving consultant, as opposed to a fully employed practitioner who may or may not have scientific training, the WINE-MAKER.

OENOLOGY, or **enology**, the knowledge or study of wine, derived from the Greek *oinos* meaning wine. The French and Italian terms are, respectively, *oenologie* and *enologia*. Oenology has been used as synonymous with WINE-MAKING and distinct from VITICULTURE, which is concerned with vines. There is a general tendency towards including the study of viticulture as well as wine production in the term, however, as more people accept that wine is made to a great extent in the vineyard. See also OENOLOGIST.

Navarre, C., *L'Œnologie* (Paris, 1988).

OENOTRIA, name current in Ancient GREECE for what is now Italy. It derives from the Dorian word *oenotron* for the STAKE against which a vine is trained, and thus Oenotria meant, literally, 'land of trained vines', suggesting that there were already geographical differences in viticultural techniques. (The Dorians were originally northern Greeks who were to colonize the southern Italian town of Taranto.)

OESTE, Portuguese for west, is used as a collective name for a group of six wine regions north of Lisbon on the west coast of PORTUGAL: Encostas d'Aire, Alcobaca, Óbidos, Alenquer, Torres (also known as Torres Vedras), and Arruda were elevated to IPR status in 1989 (see map on p. 750). Few con-

An atmospheric example of the arbour, or **tendone**, method of **vine training** on the Greek island of Crete. The puddles of powerful Mediterranean light suggest the rationale—although the method usually works better for **table grapes** than for wine quality.

sumers have heard of them and there are few wines of any real quality, yet the Oeste produces more wine than any other part of Portugal. Henry VIZETELLY writing in 1880 reported that the 'neutral-tasting red wines' from the Oeste were exported in large quantities to France for mixing with the pale and poorer growths of the northern wine-growing departments. The rest was either drunk in Lisbon or distilled to make the grape spirit used to fortify PORT. Some wine continues to be sold for the manufacture of Portugal's national brands of VERMOUTH. Most of the wine from the Oeste's productive, maritime vineyards is sold in returnable 5-l/1.6-gal flagons known as *garrafoes* that are to be found in taverns and restaurants all over the Portugese-speaking world.

The region is dominated by 15 large CO-OPERATIVES, all of which are now included in the Oeste's six IPRs. Most growers have put quantity before quality in order to maximize returns from their tiny plots of land and so vine varieties have been chosen for their yield and resistance to disease in the warm, humid Atlantic climate. As many as 30 different varieties are officially permitted and, with a tradition of making wine for distillation, white grapes outnumber red. Wine-making in the Oeste is starting to improve. With financial help from the EUROPEAN UNION, co-operatives are installing more modern equipment and a number of single estates are producing more individual wines. With the exception of Arruda and Alenquer, where most of the progress has taken place, names from Portugal's Oeste are unlikely to make any significant impact abroad in the foreseeable future. R.J.M.

Vizetelly, H., *Facts about Port and Madeira* (London, 1880).

OIDIUM, much-used French name for POWDERY MILDEW.

OIV stands for **Office International de la Vigne et du Vin**, the Paris-based intergovernmental body which represents the interests of vine-growers, and the wine, DRYING GRAPE, and TABLE GRAPE industries of its members, about 40 different countries, including all the important wine producers. It was established in 1924, during PROHIBITION in the United States, charged with demonstrating the beneficial effects of wine consumption, as well as co-ordinating research and nomenclature and upholding high standards of production. It continued its work, with the benefit of diplomatic immunity, uninterrupted during the Second World War. Today it is more concerned with the wide spectrum of scientific, technical, economical, and social problems involving the vine and all its products. Co-ordination and harmonization are particular responsibilities. The OIV co-ordinates research, gathers statistics, publishes books, papers, and journals, including the important *Bulletin de l'OIV*, not just on VITICULTURAL and OENOLOGICAL matters, but also on legal and economic aspects of wine production. The OIV also co-ordinates conferences at which the issues regarded as most pressing by the world's wine producers are discussed. In the late 1980s and early 1990s they included the possibility of increasing commercial controls as an indirect result of HEALTH concerns, and the increasing importance of ecological concerns.

The organization is sometimes Anglicized as IWO, or International Vine and Wine Office.

OJO DE LIEBRE, meaning 'hare's eye', is a synonym for TEMPRANILLO in Catalonia.

OLASZ RIZLING or **Olaszrizling**, once **Olasz riesling** and still occasionally **Olasz Riesling**, is the most common name in HUNGARY for the white grape variety known in Austria as WELSCHRIESLING (under which more details appear). The variety is popular in Hungary, although introduced less than 100 years ago, and only the rather ordinary DINKA is more widely planted. The Olasz Rizling produced around Lake Balaton is particularly prized and, in general, the warmer climate imbues Hungarian versions of this variety with more weight than their counterparts across the Austrian border known as Welschriesling, or those across the border with what was YUGOSLAVIA, where it is commonly known as LASKI RIZLING, from the same root as Olasz, possibly meaning Vlach, or from Wallachia in ROMANIA. See also RIESLING ITALICO.

OLD WINE. See AGEING and MATURITY.

OLD WORLD is Europe and the rest of the Mediterranean basin such as the Near East and North Africa. The term is used solely in contrast to the New World, the Old World having little sense of homogeneity. In very general terms Old World techniques in vineyard and cellar rely more on TRADITION and less on SCIENCE than in the New World. The notion of TERROIR is an important and well-established one in much of the Old World, especially France, Germany, and Italy. To most Old World producers, geography is considerably more important than technique.

For more details of what characterizes the Old World, see NEW WORLD.

OLIFANTSRIVER, wine region in SOUTH AFRICA.

OLOROSO, Spanish word with two related meanings in the sherry-making process, *oloroso* being the stronger, richer type of wine made in the bodega (as opposed to *fino*), Oloroso being one of the commercial styles of sherry. Pure Oloroso is a dry, dark, nutty wine that is basically bottled *oloroso*, and is often labelled Dry Oloroso. More commonly, however, the term Oloroso is applied to any commercial sweet, dark blend of basic sherry plus colouring and sweetening wine, that falls somewhere between AMONTILLADO and CREAM. Oloroso may have an alcoholic strength anywhere between about 18 and more than 20 per cent. See SHERRY for more details.

Both vine and wine have played an important part in the practice and symbolism of **religion**. The vine and doves symbol of the Resurrection of Christ is still clearly visible in this 6th century mosaic in San Vitale, Ravenna, in Emilia-Romagna.

OLTREPÒ PAVESE, LOMBARDY's most sizeable viticultural area, extends across the hills of a series of townships in the province of Pavia south of the Po river where the land begins to rise towards the Ligurian Apennines (the name means 'beyond the Po, in the Pavia region'). Over 16,000 ha/39,520 acres of vineyards, with a potential production of approximately 1.2 million hl/31.6 million gal of DOC wines, are currently planted in the mid 1990s, although annual production is less than 450,000 hl. This apparent discrepancy is partly explained by the significant quantities of grapes, PINOT NOIR in particular, that are sold to be vinified outside the production zone: the large SPUMANTE houses of PIEDMONT—Cinzano, GANCIA, MARTINI & ROSSI, and Riccadonna—have long relied on this neighbouring zone of Lombardy (administratively part of Piedmont from 1741 to 1859) for useful varieties not cultivated in their own region. Significant amounts of bulk wine have always been sold in nearby Milan, a practice which has encouraged abundant production at extremely low prices; the quality of Oltrepò wines has thus gained little from its proximity to Italy's largest and most affluent urban market. The small size of the properties (1.8 ha per grower) and the significant role played by CO-OPERATIVES have also tended to reward quantity over quality.

If the vast majority of the Oltrepò's production is not particularly interesting, there is no doubt that good, and occasionally very good, wine can be made in this zone. The most interesting is the blended red Oltrepò Rosso, which is based on BARBERA grapes to which CROATINA adds spice (it can sometimes have a RHÔNE-like pepperiness) and UVA RARA gives body and sweetness. Regrettably this blend accounts for less than five per cent of the total DOC production. Barbera (frequently sharply acidic and not helped by the generous yields of 12 tons/ha permitted by the DOC rules) is more than five times as common, and Bonarda, produced from the Croatina grape and less interesting on its own than when combined with other varieties, is more than three times as common. The bland Riesling Italico (see WELSCHRIESLING) is the most significant white grape, accounting for over 15 per cent of total production. Oltrepò MOSCATO, which bears little resemblance to the elegant and perfumed wines produced in the bordering Piedmontese province of Alessandria, supplies another eight to nine per cent of the total. Pinot Noir is principally used for spumante, most of whose production is controlled by the CO-OPERATIVES and most of which is correct but hardly inspiring. An occasional good bottle of Oltrepò spumante and an occasional bottle of still Pinot Noir, given a Burgundian treatment and aged in OAK, indicate that the variety has real, if as yet unrealized, potential in the zone.

D.T.

Anderson, B., *The Wine Atlas of Italy* (London and New York, 1990).
Gleave, D., *The Wines of Italy* (London and New York, 1989).

OMAR KHAYYÁM (d. AD 1132) was a Persian poet, made famous in the English-speaking world by Edward Fitzgerald's translation (and adaptation) of the *Rubáiyát* ('Quatrains') in 1859 (2nd edn., 1868). In his own life he was known as a philosopher and a scientist, and was remembered for a long time, both in the Middle East and Europe, as one of the greatest mathematicians of medieval times. His quatrains would scarcely have been deemed original in his own society (see ARAB POETS). In a time of strict orthodoxy this genre of occasional verse, which was popular in PERSIA in the 11th and 12th centuries, was the best medium for expressing dangerous personal doubts to a close circle of friends.

Khayyám's own quatrains are the outpourings of a nonconformist intellectual who was opposed to religious fanaticism; they range from a pious outlook to the extremes of scepticism. Wine is an important theme in this poetry. Given the ISLAMIC prohibition against wine, many of the *rubáiyát* may seem heretical; however, the defiant anti-Islamic stance of Bacchism in the 8th and 9th centuries had by the 12th century been transformed in significance by Sufism (Islamic mysticism). Some commentators have, therefore, viewed the *rubáiyát* as a mystical genre, with wine forming part of a sensitive allegory. More recently it has been accepted that wine merely serves to express religious scepticism and provides solace from existential anguish; Omar Khayyám sought to drown the world's sorrows in wine and thus rejected 'the hope of a diviner drink' offered by Islam. Khayyám's was a humanist protest that scorned sectarianism and intolerance: 'If I'm drunk on forbidden wine, so I am! | And if I'm a pagan or idolater, so I am! | Every sect has its own suspicions of me, | I myself am just what I am . . . To be free from belief and unbelief is my religion.'

Although Persian wine poetry (especially that which had a genuine mystical input) was largely influenced by Arabic poetry, the range of Bacchic expression in the *rubáiyát* themselves is far more limited than what we find in the detailed, sometimes exuberant, descriptions of wine amongst the earlier Arab poets.

See also PERSIA and ENGLISH LITERATURE, WINE IN. P.K.

Avery, P., and Heath-Stubbs, J. (trans.), *The Ruba'iyat of Omar Khayyam* (London, 1979).

ONDENC was once an important variety in GAILLAC and all over SOUTH WEST FRANCE but has fallen from favour because it yields poorly and is prone to rot. During the 19th century, when it was much more popular in the greater Bordeaux region, Ondenc must have been taken to Australia, where it was identified, called Irvine's White at Great Western and Sercial in South Australia, by visiting French AMPELOGRAPHER Paul Truel in 1976. Since then it has all but disappeared from Australian vineyards too, although rot is much less of a problem here.

OPENING THE BOTTLE is an important and potentially difficult operation for corked bottles. A wide range of corkscrews are available for opening bottles of still wine. See modern CORKSCREWS for details of the most efficient models and designs. Pulling a cork seems all the more futile and hazardous when one considers that for most wine bottles it is a highly inappropriate STOPPER used only for cosmetic reasons.

If the cork proves too recalcitrant for a corkscrew, the cork should simply be pushed in, if possible, and the wine poured out of the bottle, possibly into a jug, while the cork is held down with a long, thin instrument of some sort. See PORT TONGS for one way of opening bottles with very old corks.

But before the cork can be extracted any FOIL or wax seal has to be broached. A knife or foil cutter is the simplest way to cut a foil neatly, just below the lip of the bottle, which should be completely untainted by any foil, especially if it is an old one and contains LEAD. The lip of older bottles often needs to be wiped with a damp cloth. Wax seals are more difficult to penetrate and call for a sharp knife and tolerance of a certain amount of mess.

Opening a bottle of SPARKLING WINE is potentially extremely hazardous, as the pressure inside the bottle can expel a cork so fast that it can inflict grave injury. The bottle should be held at 45 degrees (to maximize the wine's surface area) with the cork pointing in the least dangerous direction (and certainly not at anyone, or at anything particularly precious or fragile). The wire MUZZLE should be untwisted and discarded, while holding the cork in the bottle, usually with the top of the thumb. The bottle should then be very gently screwed off the cork with one hand while the cork is held in place with the other. The cork should be allowed to escape the bottle very slowly and the wine poured from the 45-degree angle, perhaps with a thumb in the punt (see BOTTLES). The racing driver technique of giving champagne a good shake and prising off the cork with two thumbs is about as dangerous as motor racing.

See SERVING wine for the timing of opening a bottle.

OPIMIAN wine is the wine of the consular year of Lucius Opimius, 121 BC. It owes its fame to the conjunction of an exceptionally hot summer and a momentous historical event, the assassination of C. Gracchus, which temporarily ended the movement for social reform, the senatorial class maintaining its lands and privileged position.

Writing in 46 BC, Cicero states that the Opimian vintage is already too old to drink (*Brutus* 287), and PLINY the Elder describes it as 'reduced to a kind of bitter honey' but still recognizably wine and exorbitantly expensive (*Natural History* 14. 55–7). Petronius (*Satyricon* 36) and MARTIAL (*Epigrams* 1. 26, 3. 82, 10. 49, etc.) treat Opimian as a literary commonplace rather than a real wine: drinking Opimian in large quantities is what the *nouveaux riches* do to flaunt their wealth, but this is satire, not fact.

To have lasted this long, the wines were almost certainly DRIED GRAPE WINES. H.M.W.

OPORTO, Portugal's second city and the commercial centre, known in Portuguese as Porto, which gave its name to PORT. Grapes grown in the harsh conditions up river of Oporto in the DOURO valley would be crushed and vinified before being shipped to port shippers' LODGES across the Douro from Oporto in the suburb known as VILA NOVA DE GAIA. Oporto has long had a substantial population of British merchants, whose meeting place the FACTORY HOUSE survives to this day.

Oporto is also the name of a red grape variety (see PORTUGIESER) grown in HUNGARY but which EUROPEAN UNION authorities are anxious to rename KÉKOPORTO, or Blue Oporto.

OPTIMA is a relatively recent (1970) German *vinifera* crossing, of a Silvaner × Riesling with Müller-Thurgau. It ripens very early indeed, sometimes more than 10 days before Müller-Thurgau, and can notch up impressive ripeness readings, even if the wines themselves are flabby and undistinguished. It will grow on some of the poorest of sites and is therefore used, mainly in the Mosel and Rheinhessen, as a useful but ignoble booster of PRÄDIKAT level in a blend, like the more widely planted ORTEGA. Its late budding makes it popular in the Mosel-Saar-Ruwer and it is also grown in the Rheinhessen. Germany's plantings of Optima totalled 420 ha / 1,037 acres in 1990 but are not expected to increase.

OPTIONS GAME, BLIND TASTING game which in practice allows novice tasters almost as great a chance of winning as professionals. Developed by Australian Len EVANS, it requires an informed quiz-master who presents players with a series of increasingly precise options for the identity of the wine. A typical series of options might be: 'Australia, California, or Bordeaux?', 'left or right bank?', 'St-Estèphe, Pauillac, St-Julien, or Margaux?', 'pre-1980 or post-1979?' 'first or fifth growth?', 'Latour, Lafite, or Mouton?'. Players remain in the game only by choosing the correct successive options.

ORANGE RIVER, wine region in SOUTH AFRICA.

ORDER OF WINES TO BE SERVED. This can affect how individual wines taste quite considerably. The general convention is a wise one for maximizing pleasure: dry before sweet, young before old, ordinary before fine.

A sweet wine can make dry wines taste very acidic and unpleasant if they are tasted afterwards, so it makes sense to serve wines in an increasingly sweet sequence (which matches the usual sequence of foods during a meal, although serving sweets before cheese can upset things).

Old wines are generally more complex than callow young ones and so it generally flatters all wines if the oldest in the sequence are served last. This is not infallible, however. Sometimes young wines are so overwhelmingly robust in comparison to a delicate old wine that they may overpower it. Many tasters approach large tastings of PORT, especially vintage port, from the oldest to the youngest wine. And those planning particularly generous meals may find that the nuances of the oldest, finest wine they serve last may be lost on some palates already soaked in too many younger wines.

Similar considerations apply to serving wines in an upward sequence of quality.

Oporto, or Porto, which lends its name to port, viewed across the river Douro from Vila Nova de Gaia.

OREGON, one of the UNITED STATES and part of the PACIFIC NORTHWEST. Oregon lies between CALIFORNIA and WASHINGTON state but is markedly different from both. Its propensity for ripening grapes is the most marginal of the three, significant to those who hold that grapes which struggle to ripen achieve greater complexity, and fundamental therefore to the view that it may be from the Northwest that the best wines of the USA will ultimately emerge. While Oregonian viticulture can be traced back for five generations, the growth of its wine industry has been a much more discreet affair than that of California and can hardly yet be considered mature. Underfunded and somewhat shy by instinct, the Oregon wine industry has yet to find a native, high-profile spokesperson to project it on the wide international screen. There has been no GALLO, no MONDAVI, as in California to the south, to demand that the market-place takes notice. Instead, with a degree of self-conscious pride, Oregon has cultivated an image of rustic charm and natural simplicity as opposed to glamour or sophistication, although its producers are stubborn individualists rather than simple peasants.

History

VINIFERA vine varieties arrived in the late 19th century. A census of 1860 revealed Oregon's wine production was some 2,600 gal/98 hl. Twenty years later, Jackson County alone was producing 15,000 gal and a post-PROHIBITION boom saw 28 wineries making a million gal by 1938, even if much of that was FRUIT WINE. Little progress was made in the next 25 years as California dominated the market.

Oregon's modern era dates from 1961, when Hillcrest Vineyard was established near Roseburg (well south of today's concentration of grape-growing) by Richard Sommer, a refugee from the University of California at DAVIS, where he had been firmly advised that *vinifera* grapes could not be grown in Oregon. Charles Coury, another Davis graduate, started planting vines near Forest Grove in the north of the Willamette Valley (see below). Other 1960s pioneers included Dick Erath of Knudsen-Erath and David Lett of the Eyrie Vineyard, all three of whom had done time in California before deciding that it was the wrong sort of place for their preferred style of wine.

Lett was to make the breakthrough that proved Davis wrong. It was his 1975 Eyrie Vineyard Pinot Noir that put Oregon under the spotlight with an eye-catching performance in a French-sponsored 1979 tasting comparing top French wines with their New World emulators. Beaune merchant Robert DROUHIN staged a follow-up which served only to confirm the result and the message was clearly not lost on him. He eloquently endorsed it by purchasing land within a stone's throw of Lett's own vineyard in the Dundee Hills (see below).

By the late 1980s over 5,000 acres/2,024 ha of vines were planted and around 70 wineries were in production. In vineyard and volume terms, Oregon remains significantly smaller than Washington to its immediate north, but it achieved a good deal more publicity throughout the 1980s—almost certainly because the state focused its attention on PINOT NOIR, the red grape variety that had proved so difficult to please outside BURGUNDY.

Geography and climate

While almost all Washington state vines are planted in the rain shadow and semi-desert east of the Cascade Mountains, most Oregon vines are directly exposed to the marine airflow of the Pacific Ocean, giving milder winters but cooler and wetter summers than WASHINGTON. Oregon is notoriously wet, yet in most years the majority of the rain falls between November and April, not during the crucial part of the growing season. In a late ripening year, however, rain during HARVEST can cause ROT and dilution, while flocks of migrating BIRDS can ravage a vineyard within hours.

Promoters of Northwest wine are fond of pointing to the similarities in LATITUDE between this area and Bordeaux and Burgundy. Such a comparison can be misleading, however, since it takes no account of the influence of TOPOGRAPHY. Where latitude does have an important influence on the resultant wine is in the annual ration of SUNLIGHT, vital for PHOTOSYNTHESIS, but often overlooked by those preoccupied by temperature (see DEGREE DAYS).

In any marginal ripening climate, the choice of VINE VARIETY and selection of growing site take on added importance. Oregon's best-known wine district to date is the **Willamette Valley** (pronounced with the emphasis on the *a*) which stretches 150 miles/240 km from Portland in the north to Eugene in the south. Its vineyards lie on the foothills of the Coast Range that forms the western edge of this broad valley, specifically in the Red Hills of Dundee, so called for their ruddy-coloured clay-like Jory loam soils. Similar sites and soils, equally promising, can be found in the Eola Hills between McMinnville and Salem, and it is reasonable to assume the existence of at least equal potential in many hitherto unexploited areas.

Contrary to common belief, Oregon vineyard soils owe little to volcanic origins and are not exceptionally fertile. Even as recently as the early 1990s, however, most vines were planted on their own roots, leaving them prey to PHYLLOXERA (although its spread should be slowed by the scattered distribution of the state's vineyards). Vineyard elevations are commonly between 250 and 750 ft/110–330 m. Frost is rarely a problem. Summer temperatures show little consistency, and harvest dates can vary from early September to late November. Wine characteristics differ accordingly. Pinot Noir ripened well in most of the 1980s vintages but, as in Burgundy, individual skill, or lack of it, has often been the greater influence on final wine quality.

There are also significant wine districts south of the Willamette Valley: the **Umpqua Valley**, the **Rogue River**, the warmer and drier **Applegate Valley**, and the **Illinois Valley** just north of the California border and cooler and wetter by virtue of its proximity to the Pacific. The potential of south

David Lett of Eyrie Vineyards, a founding father of the **Oregon** wine industry.

west Oregon is interesting and underdeveloped. Its main drawback may be commercial rather than climatic, for it lacks a major population centre.

The economies of scale necessary for the production of cheap wine are not a feature of the Oregonian wine industry, which is therefore motivated by a need for quality rather than quantity. Crop YIELDS are small and the vines are mostly CANE pruned rather than CORDON pruned, thus demanding more time, care, and skill from the grower.

Grape varieties

Pinot Noir has passed the test with many wines of commendable depth and complexity. PINOT GRIS followed, achieving growing popularity in a crisp, dry style of characterful white. CHARDONNAY, while widely planted, has with notable exceptions proved a harder challenge than expected. RIESLING is commercially useful, although it is not fashionable to say so, while GEWÜRZTRAMINER works but is hard to grow and even harder to sell.

Among red wine grapes other than Pinot Noir, MERLOT is rare since it usually fails to set fruit, while CABERNET SAUVIGNON finds most of Oregon too cool, although fine examples are certainly a possibility in the south of the state.

Wine-making today

Oregon is a sympathetic home for the vine which does not like too much heat (although Pinot Noir grapes which ripen too fast may have to be picked before they reach full maturity in a particularly hot year). Its production is best suited to quality rather than quantity. Increasingly mature vineyards and greater experience will reveal the extent to which the pioneers are justified in their hopes.

A typical Oregon winery both owns vineyards and buys in fruit from specialist growers. Most wineries are relatively small, with an annual production of between 5,000 and 15,000 cases the norm. Most are proud to be run personally and relatively idiosyncratically. ACIDIFICATION is rarely necessary; and although ENRICHMENT may be practised, wines with a natural ALCOHOLIC STRENGTH of at least 11 per cent are achieved without difficulty most years. M.S.

Clark, C., *American Wines of the Northwest* (New York, 1989).
Hill, C., *The Northwest Winery Guide* (Seattle, 1988).
Meredith, T. J., *Northwest Wine* (Kirkland, Wash., 1990).

ORGANIC MATTER, the CARBON-containing matter left in the SOIL from the rotting of plant, animal, and microbial residues.

Normally most organic matter is the top 20 cm / 8 in of the soil, with some deeper as a result of deeply penetrating ROOTS and distribution by earthworms and other burrowing animals. On undisturbed soils much of the store of readily available plant nutrients is associated with the surface layer and its organic matter, having been extracted from the SUBSOIL over the millennia and deposited at the surface in plant residues and those of grazing animals. This applies especially to the less soluble nutrients such as PHOSPHORUS and most of the trace elements, which do not appreciably leach down the profile except in very sandy soils.

Fresh organic matter reflects the composition of the plant and animal materials from which it was formed but, as decomposition proceeds, the more soluble elements are progressively leached away, unless quickly taken up again by plant roots. The end point of decomposition is a largely inert organic material called humus. Although fairly low in NITROGEN, this is still very important in helping to give the soil a desirable crumb structure and friability (see SOIL STRUCTURE). It also provides a framework for the absorption and further storage of both water and free nutrients, in states of varying bondage and accessibility to plant roots.

The total result in undisturbed soils is a constant recycling of nutrients and their steady availability to plants. Importantly, it is at rates which broadly match the favourability of conditions for plant growth, and therefore of plant nutrient requirements. Sound viticulture aims, if necessary, first to build up soil organic matter content and that of associated mineral nutrients, and then to maintain them at a level just high enough to ensure soil health and a steady supply of nutrients appropriate to the needs of the vines. On initially infertile soils this may necessitate a substantial use of FERTILIZERS or, in the case of ORGANIC VITICULTURE, of imported plant materials or animal wastes to make good any mineral element deficiencies. Only then is it possible to ensure vigorous growth of the green manure and COVER CROPS needed for the buildup or permanent maintenance of organic matter. At all stages the increase or maintenance of soil organic matter demands that cultivation, if any, be kept to an absolute minimum.

Viticulture for high-quality wine-making nevertheless demands that soil organic matter content and fertility only be high enough to ensure a suitable balance between fruiting and moderate vegetative growth (see vine BALANCE). Higher levels tend to be associated with excessive vegetative vigour and poor CANOPY MICROCLIMATES. Seguin discusses organic matter levels in relation to the top CRUS of Bordeaux. J.G.

Seguin, G., '"Terroirs" and pedology of wine growing', *Experientia*, 42 (1986), 861–72.

ORGANIC VITICULTURE, a system of grape-growing which is based not on the plant but on an attempt at rational management of the living part of the SOIL—regarded as a complex, living environment interacting closely with the flora and fauna which inhabit it—while respecting biological cycles and the environment. It contrasts with 'conventional', sometimes even called 'industrialized', viticulture.

There is considerable confusion about what exactly constitutes organic viticulture, involving a wide variety of organizations around the world with different motivations and operating principles. Even the term 'organic viticulture' has its opponents, as it can be truthfully stated that all forms of existing viticulture are organic in the sense that grapevines are living organisms. An 'inorganic vineyard' is an impossibility. Related concepts are ALTERNATIVE VITICULTURE, BIODYNAMIC VITICULTURE, and SUSTAINABLE VITICULTURE.

Under pressure from organic farmers and consumer

organizations in France, 'organic farming' (*agriculture biologique*) was legally defined in 1981 as 'farming which uses no synthetic chemical products'. This prohibition of a wide range of PESTICIDES, FUNGICIDES, and FERTILIZERS seems easy to understand and apply. However, even here contradictions creep in, as for example such a definition allows use of natural fertilizers sodium nitrate and potassium chloride, which are mined in Chile but banned in that country. A similar contradiction exists relating to the use of pheromones, which are synthetic products used in vineyards to cause sexual confusion of insect pests (see INTEGRATED PEST MANAGEMENT).

There are, however, several basic concepts which unite the above approaches to viticulture. A primary concern is for the soil; the organic viticulturist's preoccupation is to increase soil microbial activity, and to avoid adding to the soil any substances which are not derived directly from nature. The organic viticulturist therefore adds COMPOST and manure in preference to what he regards as sudden injections of chemicals. The implication is that 'industrial' products are 'poisonous' to the soil, and such sentiments find wide support in an increasingly chemophobic population. Some adherents to organic principles also believe that, because chemical fertilizers provide the same mix of nutrients to all vineyards, they can reduce the importance of site and TERROIR.

A second and related basic tenet is that of protecting the natural environment, for example to avoid SOIL EROSION, the pollution of water-tables by pesticides or fertilizers, etc.

The emphasis in organic viticulture is to transform the vineyard ecosystem from monoculture (towards which modern vineyards tend) towards polyculture. The biological diversity of the vineyard ecosystem is encouraged rather than discouraged, as is the case with conventional viticulture.

Most supporters of organic viticulture are also driven by respect for consumers' health, in particular by the desire to avoid any pesticide RESIDUES in wine. Similarly, aware of growing chemophobia on the part of the electorate, governments around the world are increasingly stringent about the testing and indiscriminate use of AGROCHEMICALS.

Organic viticulture became increasingly popular during the 1980s. However, it remains a system which, by and large, appeals to those with a certain philosophical outlook. These people have moved towards organic viticulture out of concern for the environment and concerns about the possibility of pesticide RESIDUES in wine. They draw some satisfaction from the number of conventional mainstream grape-growers who have moved towards environmentally friendly methods in recent years (see below); but this trend, acknowledged by the official INRA and OIV organizations, should not be seen as a whole-hearted endorsement of organic methods.

Organic production's viability depends to a great extent on climatic conditions. While organic wines are produced in most major wine regions, it is only those areas with a warm, dry climate that can hope to produce commercial quantities of high-quality grapes on a regular basis. A number of growers in regions with a suitable warm, dry climate have adopted chemical-free growing programmes for no reason other than that they are not seriously troubled by disease. Similarly, recent developments in CANOPY MANAGEMENT have lessened the need for sprays against FUNGAL DISEASES. By utilizing vine-training systems which result in a well-ventilated canopy, growers can reproduce conditions which are not conducive to the growth of fungi.

The scientist's response

From a modern viticultural scientist's point of view, many organic viticultural practices seem commendable, although some of the regulations seem arbitrary. Scientists have long recognized the need to reduce excessive vineyard cultivation and to grow COVER CROPS, for example, which provide the soil with ORGANIC MATTER and help retain SOIL STRUCTURE and water infiltration. In a similar fashion, there are increasing controls on the use of agricultural chemicals, and the modern tendency is to reduce their use by development of strategies such as integrated pest management. Governments take great pains to ensure that agrochemicals properly applied should not harm the environment or the health of consumers. It is incongruous, therefore, that the organic certifying organizations permit the use of BORDEAUX MIXTURE in viticulture, and yet the long-term application of this nominally benign chemical has led to COPPER toxicity in the soils around Bordeaux and elsewhere; copper is a very toxic element to plants, yeasts, and animals including man. Another example is the use of ROOTSTOCKS to control PHYLLOXERA and other soil-borne pests, which is one of the oldest and environmentally safest forms of biological control practised in agriculture, yet this application is frowned on by some in the organic movement. CLONAL SELECTION is also frowned on by some biodynamic vine-growers.

In a similar spirit, plant physiologists would see no need to differentiate between the nitrate form of NITROGEN taken up by the grapevine from microbial processes in the soil and the direct application of fertilizer, yet such distinctions are made by organic viticulturists. Most modern viticulturists would want to follow the principles of 'sustainable viticulture', which endeavour to maintain a rational and limited use of agricultural chemicals but in a way which is entirely consistent with maintenance of the vineyard and its immediate environment. They would want to avoid any degradation to the health of the vineyard ecosystem, vineyard workers, or the consumers.

Organic vineyards tend to yield less than conventionally managed ones, because of reduced vigour resulting from the vines' competition for water and nutrients with the cover crop, and also from reduced efficacy of pest and disease control methods. This may be one reason why organic wines tend to be more expensive than others.

Administration

The French government acted early to recognize organic farming, and such rules have now become a model for the EUROPEAN UNION's regulations. There is an organic farming logo, and a set of minimum general standards which organic farmers must follow. Various bodies are entitled to supervise organic farming by way of unannounced farm visits, analysis of samples, and checking of accounts. The EU regulations came into force on 1 July 1991, and contain three basic elements: the policies are voluntary and can be administered by a number of registered bodies; organic farming is defined by standards of production; and label granting must be verified by a third, independent body. All of the world's organic farming organizations are federated within the International Federation of Organic Agriculture Movements (IFOAM). Conversion from 'conventional' to 'organic' viticulture is overseen and can take several years.

Although the basic tenets of organic viticulture are quite simple and well defined, there are subtle variations in practices between the various monitoring organizations which oversee organic production and issue rules as to the correct farming procedures.

The most extreme of the organic creeds is biodynamics (*biodynamie* in French). Based on the teaching of Rudolf Steiner, the theory of biodynamics revolves around the belief that plants respond not only to nutrition, but also to various forces of nature. Hence biodynamic farmers plan their activities according to the positions of the moon and stars. Certain times of year are considered propitious for certain tasks, and as the moon passes through different constellations it produces four recurring types of influence which favour the growth of either leaves, roots, flowers, or fruit. They claim that by following these rhythms of nature, healthier plants are produced and ultimately better wines will result. Some excellent wines are produced by such converts to biodynamics as Domaine LEROY in Vosne-Romanée, Nicolas Joly in SAVENNIÈRES, and the Millton Vineyard in NEW ZEALAND.

The variations in standards between the many monitoring organizations have meant that only the broadest definition of the term organic is possible, although in 1993 EU authorities were still trying, with considerable difficulty, to devise a workable legal definition of the term 'organic'. The organizations have a poor track record of monitoring farming practices, and a history of both internal and external disagreements. Some of them are commercial operations which both recommend and market certain herbal treatments, thereby calling their objectivity into question. In many cases these groups seem to attract the more extreme practitioners of organic methods, who can alienate individual producers unwilling to join radical monitoring sects.

The eventual effect of trying to legislate organic viticulture may be to marginalize it, but its influence is likely to continue as the wine industry places increasing emphasis on the vineyard rather than the winery. As viticulturists attempt to make up for the great technological progress made in the 1970s and 1980s in wine-making and pursue ways of improving the quality of vineyard produce, organic viticultural practices are likely to remain a topic of great interest.

See also ORGANIC WINE. R.E.S. & A.G.W.

Dutel, G. H., 'The viticultural and oenological aspects of organic wine production', *Journal of Wine Research*, 1/3 (1990), 225–30.

George, R., 'Greener than thou', *Wine* (Aug. 1989), 72–3.

Rousseau, J., 'Wines from organic farming', *Journal of Wine Research*, 3/2 (1992), 105–21.

ORGANIC WINE, imprecise term for wine made from grapes produced by ORGANIC VITICULTURE using a minimum of chemicals during wine-making. There is little agreement between those who produce wines sold as 'organic' about the term, and indeed there is a sense in which all wines are organic. Certainly, wine-makers who espouse the organic cause are likely to prefer ambient, or 'wild', YEASTS to cultured yeast additions, for example.

The monitoring organizations which set and enforce standards for organic production forbid the use of most chemical additives, allowing only a minimal amount of SULPHUR DIOXIDE for use as an antioxidant. Many FINING agents are also forbidden, and physical treatments (such as FILTRATION) are kept to a minimum. Unfortunately, there is a lack of scientific rationale for some of the strictures applied by the monitoring organizations, at least one of which prohibits the use of TARTARIC ACID for ACIDIFICATION, but permits the addition of lemon juice, provided it comes from organically grown lemons, even though tartaric acid, and not the citric acid of lemon juice, is the predominant acid naturally present in wine.

Similarly, some organizations ban some physical treatments for no apparent reason. Under organic rules CENTRIFUGATION is forbidden. This may be laudable on grounds of wine quality, but it can have no relevance to whether or not a wine is organic.

Of course organic wine is not a new phenomenon, and it is 'conventional' agriculture using chemical FERTILIZERS and systemic SPRAYS that replaced it as recently as the second half of the 20th century. Since the early 1970s, however, an increasing number of vine-growers have reverted to the old ways, either for ecological reasons or, in some cases, as part of a deliberate marketing strategy.

By 1990 organic wine producers had begun to be taken seriously and by 1992 there were more than 400 producers world-wide registered with one of the monitoring organizations, while many others preferred not to belong to any association.

France remains the home of organic wine, often called *vin biologique*, with over half of the world's registered vine-growers, notably in the warm, dry climate of the south. FUNGAL DISEASES rarely affect vines in PROVENCE and LANGUEDOC-ROUSSILLON, minimizing the need for chemical sprays, but there are organic wine producers in all the classic French wine regions. Organic wine production in France is overseen by a plethora of monitoring organizations such as Nature et Progrès and Lemaire Boucher, which regulate viticultural practices and analyse soils and wine in order to guarantee that wines are truly organic. Some producers, such as the much-admired Ch de Beaucastel of CHÂTEAUNEUF-DU-PAPE, MAS de Daumas Gassac of the Languedoc, and Domaine de Trevallon of Provence, prefer to follow organic principles outside any formal organization.

Germany saw the greatest increase in organic wine production in the 1980s, and the approximately 150 registered vine-growers are administered by several different monitoring organizations. Ernst Loosen of the MOSEL-SAAR-RUWER is one of the more prominent growers to have adopted organic practices outside any association. In 1991 the VDP association of top German wine producers declared its intention to move towards more ecologically sound systems of production, indicating the extent to which the German consumer is concerned about pesticide sprays and high nitrate levels in water supplies.

Surprisingly, FASHION-conscious CALIFORNIA was slow to embrace organic wine production. The state has its own monitoring organization, which oversees a small number of organic vine-growers, not including the Fetzer wine company of MENDOCINO, who were organic wine pioneers in the late 1980s, or the giant GALLO, who were applying 'sustainable viticultural practices' to about 7,000 acres/2,830 ha of vineyard in 1993. Companies such as Wente Bros., Buena Vista, and Robert MONDAVI have also incorporated elements of organic production into their vineyards and wineries.

Like the Californians, the Australians have been slow to investigate the possibilities of organic wine production, even though the climate in most Australian wine regions is perfectly suited to organic viticulture. For many years, Gil Wahlquist of Botobolar, MUDGEE, was the lone Australian organic wine producer but he has been joined by an increasing number of others, including the giant PENFOLDS.

Organic production methods are generally very LABOUR intensive, and most organic wine is produced on a relatively small scale, but the interest shown by some of the wine industry's larger companies indicates that this is a subject which cannot be ignored. A.G.W.

ORIGINS OF VITICULTURE. Unlike brewing, WINE-MAKING is a natural process which does not strictly require any human intervention—in fact, apes often seek out fermenting fruits. To make wine, all that is needed is for the juice of a ripe grape to come into contact with airborne YEAST. Wine-making, then, was not 'invented' by man: humanity's role is a more modest one, to refine and guide.

Grape juice ferments quickly, so as long as grapes are available, from WILD VINES, wine can be made in little more than a day or so. Agriculture is therefore not a precondition of wine production. Nomadic tribes, who do not grow grain or pulses because they do not spend enough time in one place, can make wine. This makes it impossible to date the beginning of wine-making, and the only safe assumption is that, given the behaviour of apes, wine-making is at least as old as humanity itself, provided that man had access to grapes.

But what kind of grapes? Modern wine is commonly made from VINIFERA grapes, but other species of vine are capable of producing wine as well. From prehistoric times onwards, wine could be made wherever people and grapes coincided. Yet there is little doubt that, of all the VITIS species, *Vitis vinifera* is the most suitable for wine, since it has the largest and sweetest berries. *Vitis vinifera* is believed to have originated south of the Black Sea in Transcaucasia, now the disputed territories of GEORGIA and ARMENIA, since this is the area that had the greatest variability of human population at the time and was therefore where humans were most likely to have started using it.

It is remarkable how close to this region is Mount Ararat, where, according to the mythical account in the BIBLE, the Ark landed after the Flood and Noah planted the first vineyard and became the first wine-maker. The details of the biblical account cannot be right. Just as wine-making was not the invention of a single person, it was unnecessary to plant a vineyard in order to make wine. Planting a vineyard presupposes a fully sedentary way of life, which is a far more advanced state of civilization than that of the nomadic tribes or even of the earliest farmers, who were no more than subsistence farmers: sheep and goats require little care, and grain and pulses, which in the Near East can be harvested a few months after sowing, are not labour-intensive crops. After the harvest the farmer can move on with his animals. Archaeologists assume that by 7000 BC previously nomadic farmers in the Near East had taken up grain-farming and stock-breeding.

Domesticating fruit trees involves a different kind of existence. The first wild fruits to be domesticated in the Near East were the fig, the date, the olive, and the vine. Fruit trees have to be planted, grafted, and pruned, and they take years to reach maturity. The vine and the fig start producing fruit after three years, the date after five, and the olive tree needs five or six years to start producing but 25 to come into full bearing. Unlike grain and pulses, orchard crops will benefit generations of farmers living on the same land. Deliberate cultivation of fruit trees such as the vine therefore presupposes a fully sedentary way of life and a complex social and economic system, with one generation leaving property to the next. This stage was probably reached in the 4th millennium BC or possibly the 5th.

While collecting berries from the wild and making wine out of them is a casual activity, systematic viticulture demands time, careful thought, and technical skill. In order to produce good wine, and lots of it, the farmer presumably wanted the highest-yielding vines with the largest, sweetest berries. In the wild, fruit trees are raised from seed, but when they are domesticated they need to be propagated by taking CUTTINGS and GRAFTING. Wild populations are allogamous, that is to say, they need other members of the same species in order to reproduce. As a result, their progeny varies, and this variation is not desirable for the fruit grower, who wants grapes (or olives or figs or dates) of a consistent size and taste. Hence CLONAL SELECTION and propagation, which allows the farmer to select the kind of fruit he wants, and to continue producing from his preferred type.

This is the reason why *Vitis vinifera* in its cultivated form has uniformly shaped large grapes which are high in sugar, but all cultivated vines will revert to their wild type as soon as the grower ceases to control their mode of reproduction by taking cuttings and grafting. The feral grape, which botanists now generally class as a subspecies, *sylvestris*, of *Vitis vinifera*, has smaller, more acid berries. *Sylvestris* grapes also differ from cultivated grapes in the shape of their pips, which tend to be more globular than those of cultivated grapes. They are also smaller and have a stalk or beak at the attachment to the main body of the pip (see PALAEOETHNOBOTANY). These differences have enabled archaeologists who study plant remains to determine whether a population is wild or cultivated. But the evidence needs to be treated with caution, because the differences are slight and because *sylvestris* grapes in Europe, for example, are escapees from cultivation rather than genuinely wild grapes. But when remains can be identified beyond reasonable doubt as exclusively *vinifera* we can conclude that the people in the area were orchard farmers who cultivated the grapevine and did not just gather berries from the wild.

Unfortunately not many remains have been found, but carbon dating of those that we have suggests that *Vitis vinifera* was cultivated in the 4th millennium BC; there is no physical evidence of earlier cultivation. These finds are from Ancient EGYPT (Omari) and Syria (Hama) in what was then MESOPOTAMIA. The earliest remains of *vinifera* found around the Aegean Sea (Ancient GREECE and the islands) have been dated *c.*2500 BC.

However, cultivation of *Vitis vinifera* is not necessarily the same thing as wine-making. The olive and the grape can be eaten as whole fruits; they can also be pressed. Grape juice can be made into wine, and olive oil can be used for cooking and bathing and in oil lamps. Archaeologists have found remains of PRESSES dating from the Bronze Age (i.e. *c.*3000 to 1050 BC). Finds of empty grape skins together with pips and stalks at Myrtos, Crete, from the early Minoan period (i.e. *c.*3000 BC) are proof of wine-making as opposed to the production of table grapes.

Yet the earliest piece of evidence is not a grape skin or a stalk or a pip at all: it is a wine stain. In the 1970s a Persian AMPHORA dating from 3500 BC was found at Godin Tepe, IRAN. Recent chemical analysis of the red stain inside has shown that it contains both TANNINS and TARTARIC ACID, suggesting that the amphora must have had wine in it.

Taken together, all these diverse pieces of evidence show that the vine was domesticated for the purpose of producing wine first in the region between and to the south of the Black Sea and the Caspian Sea at least as early as the 4th millennium BC and that subsequently cultivation spread west in the following millennium to Egypt and the Aegean belt. Less evidence for the prehistoric period is available west of here: there are remains of *Vitis vinifera* but none that suggest viticulture. The exception is southern Spain: finds include vine stem cuttings (from the Cueva del Monte de la Barsella north of ALICANTE) which point to cuttings as a method of propagation in the 3rd millennium BC. At other sites, fragments of stem and pips go back to the 4th millennium BC. Whether the early development of viticulture in southern Spain was a consequence of contact with the Levant we do not know.

Archaeological research in the early 1990s finally proved that viticulture was not introduced to Italy by the Greeks. The ETRUSCANS, who occupied the western half of central Italy between the Arno and the Tiber and whose civilization flourished from the 8th century BC until they were conquered by the Romans in the 4th century BC, cultivated *Vitis vinifera* which had been growing wild in Italy for thousands of years. This does not rule out the possibility that Greek VINE VARIETIES were introduced at various stages of Italy's history. In the south and in SICILY Greek varieties came over with the Greek colonists (from the 8th century BC onwards), but they may also have used wild specimens of *vinifera* which they found in their new territories. The Roman authors of AGRICULTURAL TREATISES testify, from the 1st century BC onwards, that Greek vine varieties were imported into Italy by Roman farmers, presumably because they wanted to improve their wines by experimenting with the new cépages.

As for France, the Greek colonists who founded Massilia (modern Marseilles) around 600 BC introduced viticulture there. Like their counterparts in Italy, they probably brought their own vine cuttings over with them, but they may have used vines growing wild in Massilia as well.

Viticulture was subsequently spread throughout much of Europe from Ancient ROME (see also CELTS), within Gaul from Massilia and Narbo (Narbonne) in the 1st and 2nd centuries BC. See FRANCE for more details.

See also PALAEOETHNOBOTANY AND THE ARCHAEOLOGY OF WINE. H.M.W.

Negrul, A. M., 'Evolution of cultivated forms of grapes', *Comptes rendus (Doklady) de l'Académie des Sciences de l'URSS* (1938), 585–8.

Nuñez, D. R., and Walker, M. J., 'A review of palaeobotanical findings of early *Vitis* in the Mediterranean and of the origins of cultivated grape-vines', *Review of Palaeobotany and Palynology*, 61 (1989), 205–37.

Renfrew, J., *Palaeoethnobotany: The Prehistoric Food Plants of the Near East and Europe* (London, 1973).

Vavilov, N. I., *Origin and Geography of Cultivated Plants* (Cambridge, 1992).

Zohary, D., and Hopf, M., *Domestication of Plants in the Old World* (Oxford, 1988).

ORLÉANAIS, VINS DE L', VDQS wines produced around the city of Orléans where the river Loire turns west, and Burgundian influence is evident in the choice of grape varieties. These 100 ha/250 acres of vineyards are all too close to Paris to be of much practical interest to wine drinkers outside France, for the pale and fragrant reds, and rosés, made from MEUNIER grapes, here called Gris Meunier, have many devotees in the French capital. Reds and rosés may also be made from Cabernet or Pinot Noir. Light white wines, which are very much in the minority, are made from Chardonnay and Pinot Gris, here called Auvernat Blanc and Gris respectively. About 10,000 cases of wine are made each year.

See also LOIRE and map on pp. 576–7.

ORMEASCO, local name for DOLCETTO on the north western coast of Italy. For more details, see LIGURIA.

ORTEGA is popular as an OECHSLE booster in German wines, especially with the blenders of the Rheinhessen. This CROSSING of Müller-Thurgau and Siegerrebe produces extremely full flavoured wines that often lack acidity but can reach high must weights, if not quite as high as the equally early ripening but less widely planted OPTIMA. Varietal wines are made, and QMP Ortega is a distinct possibility even in less good vintages, but a little goes a long way. The vine does not have good disease resistance, however, and its susceptibility to COULURE leaves Optima the more obvious choice for the Mosel-Saar-Ruwer. Germany's total plantings were around 1,200 ha/2,960 acres in the late 1980s and early 1990s, half of them in the Rheinhessen. The variety is also quite popular in ENGLAND.

ORVIETO, dry, medium dry, and sometimes sweet white wine produced near the medieval hill city of the same name, an important artistic centre during the late Middle Ages and Renaissance, is one of Italy's historically renowned white wines and by far the most important DOC in UMBRIA. The production zone is divided into a CLASSICO zone of over 1,500 ha/3,900 acres, extended by 800 ha of regular Orvieto. Production figures reflect the relative size of these zones, with Orvieto Classico accounting for around two-thirds of the 140,000 hl/3.7 million gal produced in an average year.

The historic Orvieto, described by Gabriele d'Annunzio as 'the sun of Italy in a bottle', was a lightly sweet wine, often concentrated by some NOBLE ROT obtained by storing the harvested grapes in the humid caves and grottoes that dot the TUFFEAU soil of the zone. Modern Orvieto is based on 50 to 65 per cent of TREBBIANO grapes with additions of VERDELLO, GRECHETTO, DRUPEGGIO, and MALVASIA. It is overwhelmingly a dry wine, the sweet or amabile version accounting for less than five per cent of total production. Like most blends with a Trebbiano base produced in substantial quantities—YIELDS of up to 10 tons/ha are permitted by the DOC rules—dry Orvieto tends to be a bland, pedestrian product. The 1980s saw attempts to develop a richer, more luscious style of sweet Orvieto, obtained with a significant amount of noble rot developed on the berries before harvesting. Some interesting wines resulted but they had to be marketed as VINO DA TAVOLA since the DOC rules for Orvieto, which did not foresee this development, do not allow this type of wine. D.T.

OSMOSIS. See CONCENTRATION.

OTTAVIANELLO, Apulian name for the French red grape variety CINSAUT.

OUILLAGE, French word meaning both ULLAGE and TOPPING UP.

OVARY, the ovule-containing part of the pistil of a FLOWER which, in the grapevine, develops into the grape berry. After FLOWERING, the ovary becomes a berry and the ovules become seeds (see GRAPE). B.G.C.

OVERCROPPING, a vine condition which reduces grape RIPENING and wine quality. It is associated with low LEAF TO FRUIT RATIOS. Overcropping can be due to PRUNING to many buds with some fruitful varieties, or to a loss of leaf area as a result of INSECT pests or FUNGAL DISEASES. If climatic conditions are limiting for PHOTOSYNTHESIS, as with low temperatures or very limited sunlight, then vines may be considered overcropped. The grapes of overcropped vines are typically lower in sugar, colour, and flavour, and have an increased PH.

Overcropping is a term which is also used emotively in arguments against high vineyard yields. Provided that the vine is in BALANCE and good health, even high yields can be properly ripened with good weather. See also YIELD. R.E.S.

O.W.C. stands for 'original wooden case' and is frequently used as a description in the sale of FINE WINE. See CASE.

OXIDATION, wine fault resulting from excessive exposure to OXYGEN (as opposed to AERATION which is deliberate, controlled exposure to oxygen). Wines spoiled by oxidation are said to be **oxidized**.

In a broader context oxidation is the chemical reaction of oxygen with another chemical entity, whether it be the browning of a cut apple or the blue-green acquired by copper left out in the elements. (Another example of oxidation is the reaction between gaseous hydrogen and oxygen to produce water and an enormous amount of heat, as exemplified in the engines which propel space shuttles from the earth's surface.)

Oxidation is a threat as soon as the grape is crushed, which is why high-quality grapes are transported to the winery as fast as possible in shallow containers, and why field pressing stations sited as close as possible to the vineyard are increasingly common. When the grape is crushed, unless special precautions are taken to exclude oxygen, it immediately starts to react with the liberated juice compounds. The most obvious change is the browning of the juice resulting from the oxidation of PHENOLICS (which is why oxidation is a much greater danger to white wines than to reds), but oxidation of linoleic and linolenic acids to yield LEAF ALDEHYDES and leaf alcohol can also make the juice taste more HERBACEOUS. The presence of moulds associated with ROT on the grapes introduces enzymes which accelerate reactions with oxygen, especially those involved with browning. Small amounts of SULPHUR DIOXIDE are therefore usually added at the time of crushing to inactivate enzymes and counter the oxidation of phenolics. See PROTECTIVE JUICE HANDLING for the techniques involved in minimizing the risk of oxidation.

Some wine-makers, however, deliberately encourage a certain amount of prefermentation oxidation of grape varieties such as Chardonnay in order to develop a range of flavours other than those associated with primary fruit AROMA. See WHITE WINE-MAKING for more details.

The last step of FERMENTATION, the REDUCTION of ACETALDEHYDE to ETHANOL, is coupled with the oxidation of the co-enzyme NADH, as shown in this equation:

$$CH_3CHO + NADH + H^+ \rightarrow CH_3CH_2OH + NAD^+$$

Note that no new oxygen is involved in this reaction, but that the essence of the reduction is the transfer of electrons from the co-enzyme to the acetaldehyde. Most oxidation-reduction reactions involved in growing grapes and making wine are of this type.

In wine itself, however, exposure to oxygen in the presence of an organism such as ACETOBACTER could result in a reversal of the above reaction with alcohol being oxidized to acetaldehyde. The NADH produced by oxidizing alcohol is, in turn, oxidized by oxygen from the air. When this happens, the wine loses its fresh, fruity aroma and becomes vapid and flat smelling. Further exposure to oxygen converts the acetaldehyde to ACETIC ACID, the acidic component of wine VINEGAR, the wine-maker's *bête noire*.

Oxygen reacts with the phenolics in both white and red wines. In whites, the COLOUR changes from light yellow to an amber or brownish colour, while in reds, with their greater complement of phenolics (ANTHOCYANS and TANNINS), the colour change is much less apparent.

To produce table wines attractive in aroma and colour, and certainly those designed to be drunk young, the wine-maker generally restricts the exposure of must and wine to oxygen as much as is technically feasible (see PROTECTIVE WINE-MAKING for more details).

Some wines, however, such as *oloroso* SHERRY, tawny PORT, and MADEIRA, owe their character to deliberate exposure to oxygen. And those who make wines of all sorts are constantly experimenting with various aspects of controlled oxidation, often motivated by the role played by oxygen in AGEING.

The term MADERIZATION is sometimes used interchangeably with oxidation, although it should theoretically also involve excessive exposure to heat.

See also OXYGEN. A.D.W.

OXYGEN, colourless, odourless, tasteless gas that makes up nearly 21 per cent of the atmosphere. It is essential to all animal life forms and for many other living systems. Oxygen constitutes nearly half of the weight of the earth's crust in its various combined forms: WATER (oxygen combined with hydrogen); CARBON DIOXIDE (oxygen with carbon); sand (oxygen with silica); and LIMESTONE (oxygen with carbon and calcium). Oxygen is the third most abundant element in the sun and a key substance in the carbon–nitrogen cycle, the nuclear reaction which supplies the energy for most of the living processes on earth. Unlike NITROGEN, which makes up a much higher proportion of air and is inert, oxygen is highly reactive. Oxygen interacts with grape juice or must and wine in both good ways (see AERATION) and bad ways (see OXIDATION).

Handling juice

A small amount of oxygen (about as much as dissolves in must as it comes from the CRUSHER) is required for the multiplication of the YEAST that will conduct the alcoholic FERMENTATION. Larger amounts may well be detrimental by oxidizing PHENOLICS. The aim of PROTECTIVE JUICE HANDLING is to minimize oxidation.

Making wine

During fermentation, the CARBON DIOXIDE given off by the nascent wine prevents exposure to oxygen, but, when fermentation ceases, the wine must be protected from access to oxygen if it is to remain wine. Early wine-makers learned that, with very few exceptions, wines had to be kept in full containers at all times lest they change into VINEGAR.

Modern wine-makers have equipment which allows most steps in making wine to exclude oxygen. One of the most effective has been the STAINLESS STEEL tank in which ULLAGE space can be filled with INERT GAS to exclude oxygen. Wooden vats, casks, and barrels are not sufficiently impervious for this blanketing technique. In older wineries the oxidation of wine was minimized by frequent small additions of SULPHUR DIOXIDE, which reacts preferentially with any oxygen absorbed. (While sulphur dioxide is less frequently needed as an antioxidant today, it is still used to inhibit microbial activity.) ASCORBIC ACID has also been used to a certain extent as an antioxidant, but its cost and the fact that it participates in an auto-oxidative reaction with sulphur dioxide limit its value (see ERYTHORBIC ACID too). REFRIGERATION of wine in storage slows all reactions, including oxidation, but it has the danger that oxygen solubility increases at low temperatures. The aim of PROTECTIVE WINE-MAKING is to minimize oxidation.

Oxygen plays a positive role during BARREL MATURATION, however, when the small doses of oxygen which the wine receives during the inevitable operations of filling, RACKING, and TOPPING UP deepen and stabilize COLOUR, soften and intensify flavour, and assist natural STABILIZATION and CLARIFICATION by encouraging the precipitation of the less stable PHENOLICS.

See also OXIDATION, AERATION, and SERVING wine. A.D.W.

OZONE is a form of OXYGEN having three instead of the usual two oxygen atoms per molecule. It is formed in the upper atmosphere by the action of ultraviolet light on normal oxygen; and, by being opaque to further incoming ultraviolet light, happily prevents most of the potentially very damaging ultraviolet wavelengths from reaching the earth's surface.

Some man-made molecules such as the chlorofluorocarbons, used in REFRIGERATION, can add to the effects of natural gases from volcanoes, etc. to destroy ozone if released into the atmosphere. This occurs only at very low temperatures, such as occur over the poles in winter, but is nevertheless a matter of concern. It has little or nothing to do with the so-called 'greenhouse effect' (see CLIMATE CHANGE).

Some ozone is also released into the lower atmosphere as an industrial pollutant, and can cause a recognizable 'stippling' of vine leaves close to industrialized areas. Its significance to viticulture has been studied in California and New York state, but the economic effects remain uncertain.

J.G.

P

PAARL, important wine region in SOUTH AFRICA.

PAARL RIESLING. See CAPE RIESLING.

PACHERENC DU VIC-BILH, defiantly Gascon name for white wines made in the MADIRAN region from a mixture of intensely local grape varieties and some imports: the local RUFFIAT (Arrufiac) and Petit Courbu; Gros MANSENG from JURANÇON; and Sémillon and Sauvignon from Bordeaux. The deep yellow wine can be either dry or sweet, depending on the VINTAGE, and can taste very similar to Jurançon which is made further south, from a slightly different range of grape varieties. Only 100 ha/250 acres (a tenth as much as the area devoted to red Madiran) are dedicated to this keenly priced wine, which may be picked very late in the season. These sweet wines, made from PASSERILLÉ grapes, can last 10 years or so in bottle.

PACIFIC NORTHWEST, self-conscious region in the far north west of the UNITED STATES. A beautiful and unspoilt

Pacific Northwest wine scene—in Oregon's Red Hills of Dundee.

Lindemans vineyard at **Padthaway**, one of Australia's cooler wine areas.

landscape and some fine regional products, including food and wine, have brought a sense of pride to the states of WASHINGTON, OREGON, and IDAHO. Comparisons with CALIFORNIA, the state to the immediate south, are habitually made.

PACKAGING of wine most often involves BOTTLING, but alternative packages for wine include BOXES, CANS, and CARTONS.

PADTHAWAY, one of the cooler and more productive wine regions in AUSTRALIA, developed particularly by Lindemans. For more detail see SOUTH AUSTRALIA.

PAGADEBIT, light white grape of Romagna in central Italy. This may be the same prolific grape variety as the BOMBINO BIANCO of Apulia.

PAGO, Spanish term for a vineyard or group of similar vineyards, used particularly in JEREZ and PENEDÈS.

PAICINES, small California wine region and AVA in SAN BENITO County.

PAIS, the most common grape variety in CHILE identical to the MISSION grape of CALIFORNIA and MEXICO and a darker-skinned version of the CRIOLLA Chica of ARGENTINA. In Chile, where it is most common in the southern regions of Maule and Bío-Bío, it is also sometimes known as Negra Peruana. It may be the same as MONICA of Spain and Sardinia.

PAKISTAN. In the early 1990s the OIV recorded only 3,000 ha/7,400 acres of vines in this Asian ISLAMIC republic. They are dedicated to the production of TABLE GRAPES and DRYING GRAPES, but VINIFERA wine may occasionally be made from WILD VINES growing in the high valleys along the Silk Road, where one of the richest resources of ancient, genetically-varied plant material may still be found.

PALAEOETHNOBOTANY AND THE ARCHAEOLOGY OF WINE. The study of the botanical remains of grapes and wine residues found in archaeological excavations is something of a detective story in which small pieces of evidence are put together to build up a picture of the development of man's use of and, later, domestication of grapes.

The botanical evidence consists of the remains of vine stalks, LEAVES, BERRIES, STEMS, and SEEDS or pips which in certain circumstances may be recovered from archaeological deposits: sometimes even the roots, or the hollows left by them, may survive too. All these fragments survive accidentally and they may be preserved in different ways. Their recovery is the result of painstaking examination of archaeological deposits for botanical remains, especially of cultivated plants used for food or otherwise contributing to the basic economy of the site and past community being studied. Usually the finds of grape remains form a very small proportion of the total botanical material recovered, the bulk of which is usually the seeds of annual crops such as cereals, pulses, and oilseeds.

The most common remains of grapes found are grape pips and they usually survive because they have become charred at the time of deposition. Once converted to charcoal they will survive in recognizable form for many thousands of years buried in the ground. On other archaeological sites they may be preserved in damp or wet soils in a waterlogged condition. Elsewhere, where the conditions have a high concentration of calcium in the ground water, they may become mineralized or semi-fossilized. In other circumstances, where handmade clay pots were being fashioned, stray pips become incorporated in the clay and when the pot is fired they burn out leaving a small hole the exact size and shape of the pip.

Occasionally, as when grapes were thrown on to a funeral pyre as part of the ritual, complete fruits survive in charred form, as at Salamis and Athens. Exceptionally, finds of skins of fruits (possibly remains of pressings) survive, for example at early Minoan Myrtos, Crete (see Ancient GREECE).

Finds of burnt fruit stalks (PEDICELS) are exceptional but can be taken to indicate the presence of domesticated vines (the stems of bunches of WILD VINES are very strong and robust and do not come away with the fruit in the way that those of cultivated vines do). They have been recovered from the Greek prehistoric sites of Sitafroi and Lyrtos.

The Greek prehistoric potters of the early Bronze Age developed the habit of standing their pots on upturned vine leaves to dry in the sun before firing. This resulted in very fine impressions of the veins on the underside of these leaves being impressed and then baked on the bases of these pots. In some places—the Cyclades, for example—these are the only evidence that grapes were present on these islands at that time. Vine leaves were also used on clay sealings of Bronze Age pots, such as at Menelaion near Sparta. If vine leaves were being used in these ways by the Bronze Age Greeks, one might be forgiven for assuming that they may also have been used for cooking, as they are in Greece today.

The critical question in examining all this palaeoethnobotanical material is how can one tell whether it is derived from wild or cultivated sources. Apart from the fruit stalks, just discussed, it is the size and shape of the pips which give us the clue (see illustration). The pips of wild grapes are

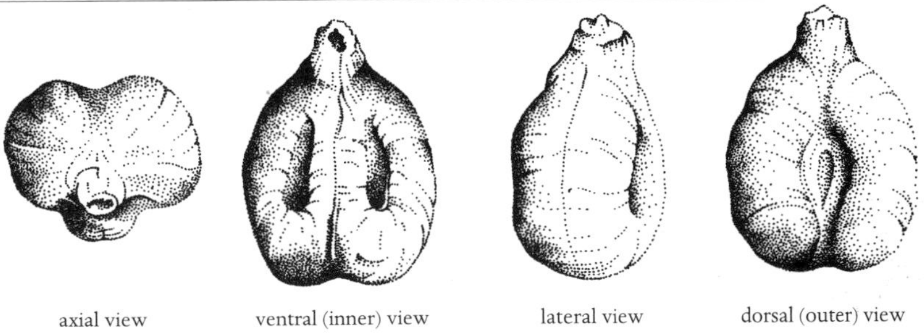

Fig 1. seed (pip) of wild vine *Vitis silvestris*

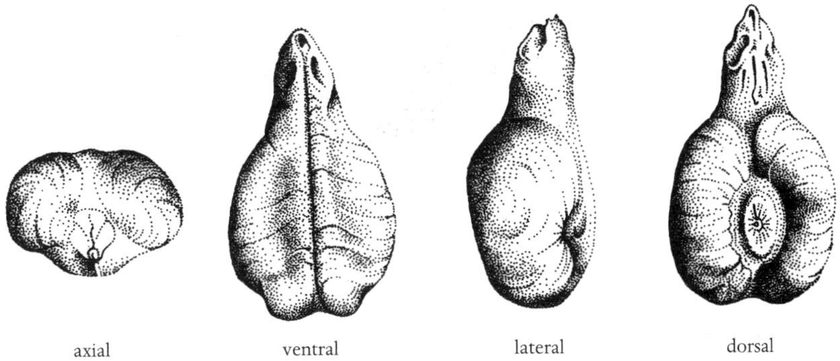

Fig 2. seed of cultivated vine *Vitis vinifera*

Palaeoethnobotony

spherical with a short stalk or beak and a small, round chalazal scar on one side, and two divergent grooves on the other side of the pip. The pips of cultivated grapes are usually larger than those of the wild form and pear shaped. The stalk is usually longer, the chalazal scar larger and often oval in outline, and the grooves on the back of the pip parallel to each other. These features can be seen on the archaeological material, however it is preserved.

The domestication of grapes seems to have first taken place probably around 4000 BC in the region between the Black and Caspian Seas. The domesticated grapevine provides fresh fruit, dried raisins, sultanas and currants (according to the VINE VARIETY); wine, vinegar, grape juice, and a light salad oil obtained by crushing the pips. The most significant product, however, was wine, which was greatly valued.

It is not essential that vines were domesticated before WINE-MAKING was invented. What appears to be necessary is having a suitable container in which to store the wine during and after the FERMENTATION process. All the ingredients—the sweet, juicy fruit, and airborne YEAST—are available for wild fruits. Thus, it is possible that the finds from palaeolithic sites (Old Stone Age) in the Mediterranean region of wild grape pips could indicate that wine-making had begun using leather bags even before the beginnings of agriculture. (One has only to observe the antics of BIRDS in a vineyard at harvest time to see the intoxicating effect of overripe grapes.) The finds of grape remains such as pips, stalks, and skins in circumstances suggesting wine production are rare. In prehistoric GREECE they occur associated with spouted vessels on the early Bronze Age sites of Áyios Kosmas, Attica, and Myrtos in Crete. Remains of wine presses also occur occasionally as at Vathypetro in Crete, and there are a great number of drinking vessels made from exotic materials from Bronze Age sites suggesting that drinking wine was a special activity.

The actual residues in the bases of pithoi of wine have not been found very often (partly because the analysis of residues found in pottery vessels is still comparatively new in archaeology). The earliest find dates back to 3500 BC at Godin Tepe, IRAN, where a reddish deposit turned out to be formed from TARTRATE crystals (similar to those which form on the bottom of wine corks today). Other residues of wine are known from 7th century BC CYPRUS, and from the contents of AMPHORAE in a Roman shipwreck off the southern coast of France, near Marseilles. There is a Roman glass BOTTLE containing what is claimed to be Roman wine in the museum in Speyer, Germany.

Thus the study of the finds of grapes—seeds, skins, stems, leaves, and so on—can lead to understanding when and where man first exploited wild vines (*c.*350000 BC at Terra Arnasta in southern France) and when and where vines were domesticated; was it a single event or did it happen in several places independently? Many different sorts of evidence have to be combined to elicit the answers as to where wine was first made and when the earliest wine trade became established. From apparently insignificant remains of grape pips found by chance to survive in sediments on archaeological sites, and extracted with painstaking care, it is possible to begin to understand the ORIGINS OF VITICULTURE and its development.

J.M.R.

Renfrew, J., *Palaeoethnobotany: The Prehistoric Food Plants of the Near East and Europe* (London, 1973).

PALATE, term used when describing TASTING as a process and an ability. It is generally used to describe the combined human tasting faculties in the mouth. The impact of a wine on the mouth may be divided chronologically, and somewhat loosely, into its impact on the front, middle, and back palate. The word may also be used more generally as in describing a good taster as 'having a fine palate'.

PALATINATE, originally territory under the jurisdiction of a local authority with sovereign powers, the term came to be used for that part of Germany which today includes both the RHEINHESSEN and PFALZ wine regions. It has since been used as an alternative English name for the German wine region Pfalz. See also GERMAN HISTORY

PALETTE, miniature appellation of barely 20 ha/50 acres in PROVENCE in the hills east of Aix-en-Provence. A single property, Ch Simone, produces four bottles in every five, and for many years has been responsible for all the most serious wine of the appellation. The appellation is a relatively old one, created in 1948 in recognition of a distinctive LIMESTONE outcrop here. For seven generations Ch Simone has been in the Rougier family, who continue to respect the traditional wine-making techniques, involving very old vines, prolonged fermentation, and BARREL MATURATION using very little new wood. Varieties are mixed in the vineyard, and include not just Mourvèdre, Grenache, Syrah, and Cinsaut for reds and rosés and Grenache Blanc, Ugni Blanc, Picpoul, and Muscat for white, but also a number of ancient Provençal varieties. The result is extremely dense, long-lived whites, uniquely full bodied rosés, and white wines which belie modern white wine-making philosophy.

George, R., *French Country Wines* (London, 1990).

PALISSAGE, French term for VINE TRAINING.

PALLADIUS (4th century AD). Next to nothing is known about the life of this agrarian writer of Ancient ROME. He is the author of a treatise called, like Varro's earlier work, *De re rustica*, in 15 books. The first book is a general introduction to farming; the last two comprise a guide to veterinary medicine and an account of GRAFTING. The remaining 12 books deal with the tasks to be carried out throughout the agricultural year, one book for each month; Palladius has more to say about the vine than about any other crop. What he says, however, is sound but not original: he relies heavily on earlier authors, especially COLUMELLA (and, to a lesser extent, PLINY and VARRO). Unlike CATO, Varro, and Columella he was well known in the Middle Ages and in the early Renaissance: he is quoted by Albertus Magnus, Vincent of Beauvais, and PETRUS

DE CRESCENTIIS, and an anonymous Middle English translation of his work, connected with Humphrey, duke of Gloucester, survives. There is no direct evidence for his influence on medieval English wine producers, however. H.M.W.

PALMELA, the larger of the two distinct wine regions into which the SETÚBAL peninsula between the Tagus and Sado estuaries on the Atlantic coast of PORTUGAL divides naturally (see map on p. 750). Low-yielding vineyards on the north-facing clay and limestone slopes of the Serra da ARRÁBIDA have traditionally produced the best wines while those on the fertile, sandy plain extending eastwards from the fortress town of Palmela have always been more productive. The most important grape of the Palmela region is the versatile red CASTELÃO FRANCES (usually called Periquita here) which is used to make red, rosé, and sparkling wines.

Although there are many individual vine-growers, wine production is concentrated in the hands of four large wine-makers: the Palmela co-operative, João Pires in Pinhal Novo in Palmela, José Maria da Fonseca Successores in Azeitão, and J. M. da Fonseca Internacional, also in Azeitão in the adjoining Arrábida region (see FONSECA for details of how the last three companies relate to each other). Other wines made from grapes grown in the Palmela region include a hugely successful dry Muscat called João Pires and a sparkling wine made by an adaptation of the CONTINUOUS METHOD. Palmela was granted IPR status in 1990, but most producers continue to sell wines under their own well-established brand names such as Periquita, Quinta de Camarate, and Quinta da Bacalhôa. R.J.M.

PALO CORTADO, a traditional and fully natural style of sherry based on a fluke of nature, a sherry that runs out of FLOR yeast and develops somewhere in between a *fino* and an *oloroso* so that it tastes like an intermediate style between Amontillado and Oloroso. For more details, see SHERRY.

PALOMINO, white grape variety most closely associated with the making of SHERRY around JEREZ in southern Spain. It is almost certainly of Andalucian origin, supposedly named after one of King Alfonso X's knights. Palomino Fino, which once grew exclusively around Sanlúcar de Barrameda (see MANZANILLA), has been adopted as the most suitable variety for sherry production, as distinct from the lowlier Palomino Basto or Palomino de Jerez once widely used.

The vine is relatively susceptible to DOWNY MILDEW and ANTHRACNOSE and responds best in warm, dry soils. Its loose, generous bunches of large grapes make it suitable for TABLE GRAPES as well as wine. Its yield is relatively high and regular, about 80 hl/ha (4.5 tons/acre) without irrigation, and the wine produced is, typically, low in both ACIDITY (as low as 3.5 g/l expressed in tartaric acid) and fermentable SUGARS. This suits sherry producers who pick Palomino grapes at about 19° Brix (see MUST WEIGHT) and find Palomino must's tendency to oxidize no inconvenience, but for this very reason the variety tends to make rather flabby, vapid table wines, unless substantially assisted by ACIDIFICATION.

Of Spain's 30,000 ha/72,000 acres or so of Palomino Fino, the great majority are in sherry country around Jerez but it is also being planted in CONDADO DE HUELVA, where it is edging out the Zalema grape variety, and has been planted in GALICIA. Outside sherry country, as in France, it is often known as Listán, or Listán de Jerez. See LISTÁN for details of the declining fortunes of this variety in France. It is commonly thought to be the Perrum of the Alentejo in southern Portugal.

The country with the most Palomino planted outside Spain is SOUTH AFRICA, where the variety is the country's second most planted, even if its 9,000 ha were a long way behind Chenin Blanc's 29,000 ha in 1990. Much South African Palomino is distilled or used for blending into basic table wines and there is some attempt to increase sugar levels using CANOPY MANAGEMENT techniques.

California's acreage of the variety once wrongly identified as Golden Chasselas there remains steady at just over 1,000 acres, almost all of them in the SAN JOAQUIN VALLEY, where the wine produced is used chiefly for blending. Argentina has limited planting of the variety but PEDRO GIMÉNEZ, predominates. In Australia the two varieties are not effectively distinguished and their combined total area was about 1,200 ha in 1990, much of it grown in SOUTH AUSTRALIA and used for making sherry style FORTIFIED wines. New Zealand also grows a small amount of Palomino in its hardly ideal climate. CYPRUS has imported the Palomino vine because of its dependence on producing inexpensive copies of sherry.

PAMID, Bulgaria's most widely planted and least interesting indigenous grape variety producing rather thin, early maturing red wines with few distinguishing marks other than a certain sweetness. It does not play a major role in bottles bound for export.

PANSÁ BLANCA, synonym for the Spanish white grape variety XAREL-LO, used particularly in ALELLA.

PANTELLERIA, VOLCANIC island at the extreme southern limit of Italy and closer in fact to Cape Bon in TUNISIA than to the southern coast of SICILY, to which it belongs administratively. Moscato di Pantelleria is one of Italy's finest dessert wines, made from the ZIBIBBO member of the MUSCAT family. The wine has enjoyed a certain reputation since the 1880s, when the MARSALA house of Rallo began to market it, and it was awarded a medal at the Paris Exhibition of 1900. It was placed on the official list of Italy's 'typical' wines in 1936 and the accompanying description, with due allowance for hyperbole, has an undeniable correspondance to a good bottle of Moscato di Pantelleria today: 'velvety, sweet, caressing, and generous'. The viticulture of the island is unusual: vines are GOBELET trained but buried in a hole (called a 'crater' by local growers) to protect them from the fierce winds that sweep across the island.

Moscato di Pantelleria comes in two different versions. The first is the regular Moscato, with a minimum alcohol level of eight per cent and 40 g/l of RESIDUAL SUGAR, although many of the better producers raisin the grapes for 10 to 12 days to achieve a higher total alcohol level and a greater quantity of residual sugar (see DRIED GRAPE WINES); wines with a POTENTIAL ALCOHOL of 17.5 per cent can be called *vino naturalmente dolce*. The second version is lusher and richer and is true dessert style, which made the wine's reputation. This Moscato Passito di Pantelleria must have at least 14 per cent alcohol and 110 g/l residual sugar, although a current trend is to seek a more decadently sweet style, raisining the grapes for up to 30 days and arriving at close to 140 g/l of residual sugar. A PASSITO with a potential alcohol of 23.5 per cent and one year of ageing can theoretically be called Extra, although the term is rarely encountered on labels.

After a period of neglect and decline, Moscato di Pantelleria seemed in the early 1990s to be entering a new period of revived popularity and recognition in Italy, with an undeniable increase in the overall quality level and a new interest in the product on the part of the commercial houses of Marsala, who have begun to market the wine once again. D.T.

PARELLADA, Catalan white grape variety widely used, with MACABEO and XAREL-LO, for the production of CAVA. It is the least planted of these three varieties in the Penedès region most closely associated with these Spanish sparkling wines, but became increasingly popular with vine-growers in the 1960s, when Cava producers paid a premium for it. Parellada can produce a fine, high-quality wine when grown in relatively poor soil and in cooler conditions, but has a tendency to over-produce lower-quality wine in fertile soils. It has large, loose bunches of large grapes which have good resistance to BOTRYTIS BUNCH ROT. It is an important variety in CARIÑENA, COSTERS DEL SEGRE, and PENEDÈS.

PARIS, capital of FRANCE, once the centre of a thriving wine region and still one of the few capital cities in which vineyards of any size may be found (although see also VIENNA). Today there are several suburban vineyards, and even a small vineyard in Montmartre whose meagre produce is auctioned off for charity.

History

Wine was grown around Paris in the 4th century, and its fame as a wine-growing area dates from long after the Roman empire. Clovis, king of the Franks 481–511, made Paris the capital of his kingdom and from the 8th century onwards Frisian, Saxon, and English merchants sailed up the river Seine to Paris to buy wine. Under the Merovingians and the Carolingians Paris was an important centre of trade, and much of the wine sold there would have been produced locally.

A document surviving from the beginning of the 9th century shows that viticulture was a major part of the local economy. The Roll of Irminon, named after the abbot of St-Germain-des-Prés who instigated this survey of his monastery's lands, is the only document of its kind dating back to the time of CHARLEMAGNE. Vineyards at Rambouillet, Dreux, Fontainebleau, Sceaux, and Versailles were cultivated not only by monks but also by laymen, and it is clear from the amounts produced that there must have been a surplus to sell on the open market. Documents from the Abbey of St-Denis, near Paris, show that St-Germain-des-Prés was not unique in this respect. In the 9th century St-Denis had vineyards in the abbey precincts and possessed wine-growing estates in the Île-de-France, as the Paris basin was known; many smaller monasteries in the area also produced wine for sale (see MONKS AND MONASTERIES).

In the 10th century Paris was well established as a centre of the wine trade. The main trade route was down the Seine to Rouen (today an important wine BOTTLING centre for northern European markets) and thence overseas. In the late 10th century merchants from England, Ireland, Flanders, and Picardy visited Rouen, and later Henry II (king of England, including Normandy, 1154–89) gave Rouen the monopoly of transporting wine to England. The other, later (from the 13th century onwards), trade route from Paris was down the Seine or up the Oise as far as Compiègne, where the wine would be loaded on to carts and carried to Flanders by road. By then the merchants of Paris had managed to acquire for themselves privileges similar to those of their Gascon counterparts (see BORDEAUX). In an edict of 1190 Philip Augustus, king of France, declared that only the merchants of Paris, who were themselves usually wine producers as well (see CLIMATE CHANGE for details of the warmer macroclimate prevailing then), had the right to sell wine in Paris. They were able to prevent the sale of any wine they wished: thus they regulated the import of wines from outside the region and they controlled the quality of the wines sold as 'vins de France'. The wines of AUXERRE, CHABLIS, and Tonnerre had to pass through Paris before they were permitted to be transported further, and wines from other regions were not to be offered for sale before the 'vins de France' had all been sold. The wines of the LOIRE were also put on the market in Paris.

The 'vins de France' included not only the wines of Paris up to Vernon in Normandy but also those of CHAMPAGNE (Rheims, Épernay, Châlons-sur-Marne): this usage continued among wine producers until just after the French Revolution. The Capetian kings of France, who reigned from 987 to 1498, were particularly fond of the wines of Paris, but some of what they drank must have been from Champagne, since no distinction was made. In those days the region grew more than it could drink. Some of it was sold to the neighbouring areas of Normandy, Picardy, and Artois; the principal foreign export markets in the Middle Ages were England and Flanders. The 'vins de France' were highly esteemed both at home and abroad: in 1200 they fetched higher prices in London than the wines of ANJOU. H.M.W.

Atkin, T., 'City Vines', *WINE*, March (1994).
Dion, Roger, *Histoire de la vigne et du vin en France* (Paris, 1959).
Lachiver, M., *Vins, vignes et vignerons* (Paris, 1988).

PARKER, ROBERT M., JR. (1947–), influential American wine critic whose most obvious contribution to the LITERATURE OF WINE has been the concept of applying NUMBERS to wine. Robert Parker was born in Baltimore and both trained and worked as a lawyer there. He discovered wine at the age of 20 on a trip to Alsace in north east France. By the mid 1970s, at the height of active consumerism, Parker became frustrated by the lack of truly independent and reliable wine criticism, and began to think about launching his own consumer's guide to wine buying.

The first, complimentary issue of his bi-monthly newsletter the *Wine Advocate* appeared in 1978, and by 1984 he felt confident enough of its success to retire from the law and concentrate on the travel and punishing schedule of tastings on which it is based. By then he had made a name for himself with his enthusiastic, and unusually detailed, endorsement of the 1982 vintage in Bordeaux, and subscriptions grew rapidly with the American market for wine FUTURES. By 1993 the *Wine Advocate* had more than 28,000 subscribers, mainly in the United States but in more than 35 other countries. There are no advertisements and little synthesis, but hundreds of tasting notes and assessments of individual, usually fine, wines. His judgements have been known to have a significant effect on market demand and the commercial future of some producers.

Parker's was by no means the first American consumer wine newsletter, but it was the first to use scores between 50 and 100 for individual wines quite so obviously. This system was easily and delightedly grasped by Americans familiar with high school grades, even though Parker himself urges caution, asking readers to use the numerical ratings 'only to enhance and complement the thorough tasting notes, which are my primary means of communicating my judgments to you'. Wine retailers were less circumspect and used Parker's ratings mercilessly in their merchandising, while the notion of scoring wine at all came under attack from some other wine authorities, notably Hugh JOHNSON, whose view is that wines themselves vary with time and conditions of tasting, and that wine tasting is an intrinsically subjective process in any case. Parker's own view, stated on the cover of every issue of the *Advocate*, is that 'wine is no different from any consumer product. There are specific standards of quality that full-time wine professionals recognize.'

Parker's diligence in recording the impressions of his hard-worked palate (he regularly tastes more than 100 wines a day) has provided the ingredients for several lengthy books, and not just the *Wine Buyer's Guides*, which are essentially *Advocate* compendia. *Bordeaux* (originally subtitled 'The Definitive Guide to the Wines Produced since 1961') first appeared in 1985 and enjoyed considerable success in the United States, in Britain in 1987, and in France in 1989. A revised, more modestly titled edition appeared in 1991. *The Wines of the Rhône Valley and Provence*, which appeared in 1987, reflected Parker's other great passion (he was instrumental in establishing the reputation and ambitious pricing policy of Côte-Rôtie's GUIGAL). *Burgundy* (1990), with its complex mosaic of appellations, producers, and vintages, and its less predictable wines, succumbed less easily to being 'Parkerized'. A book on California is yet to emerge, as is Parker's enthusiasm for the region as a whole.

Parker is recognized as a fervent, if critical, admirer of French wines. He was the first non-Frenchman to write a wine column for *L'Express* magazine, and was made a particularly emotional Chevalier de l'Ordre du Mérite National in 1992.

PASO ROBLES, California wine region and AVA. See SAN LUIS OBISPO.

PASSERILLÉ, French adjective for grapes that dry, or raisin, on the vine. For details of some of the wines made from those deliberately thus left to shrivel, see DRIED GRAPE WINES.

PASSETOUTGRAINS. See BOURGOGNE PASSETOUTGRAINS.

PASSING THE PORT. One of the wine trade's most cherished traditions is the rule that PORT, particularly a decanter of vintage port, must be passed round a table from the right to the left of diners. No single satisfactory explanation has ever been advanced, although so fiercely held is the custom that a miniature railway was constructed to transport decanters across an inconvenient fireplace in the Senior Common Room of New College Oxford.

Howkins, B., *Rich, Rare & Red* (London, 1982).

PASSITO, Italian term for DRIED GRAPE WINE.

PASTEUR, LOUIS (1822–95), a scientific genius and gifted scholar, has left a body of work which impinges on physics, chemistry, microbiology, agronomy, and medicine. On the centenary of his birth in 1922 the Institut Pasteur in Paris published a monograph on his principal discoveries listed under the following headings:

1847: Molecular disymmetry
1857: Fermentations
1862: Supposedly spontaneous generations
1863: Study of wines
1865: Silkworm diseases
1871: Study of beers
1877: Virus diseases
1880: Viral vaccines
1885: Rabies protection

Pasteur's original work on what were supposedly spontaneous generations, or transformations, led him to interpret the process of alcoholic FERMENTATION and to demonstrate that this, far from being spontaneous, was the result of intervention by living cells, YEAST, using sugar for their own nutrition and transforming it into ALCOHOL and CARBON DIOXIDE. 'The chemical act of fermentation is essentially a phenomenon which correlates to a vital act . . . Now what for me constitutes this chemical division of sugar (into alcohol and carbonic gas), and what causes it? I admit that I have no idea' (*Œuvres de Pasteur*, ii. 77). With something approaching genius, Pasteur understood the phenomenon without being able to provide a precise explanation; contemporary biochemistry was able to explain in detail the different stages of the chemical fermentation mechanism only in the first half of the 20th century.

During his career as a scientist, Pasteur must have devoted only three or four years to the study of wine. Yet in this time he achieved as much as a good specialist researcher would have been delighted to achieve in an entire lifetime. Not only did he apply his theories to fermentation and ensure the mastery of the basics of vinification and conservation of wines, he also perfected the art of adding TARTARIC ACID, demonstrated the presence of SUCCINIC ACID and GLYCEROL, and made valuable suggestions about the role of OXYGEN in wine AGEING.

But it was above all in the field of microbiological diseases of wine that Pasteur's work has been most valued. One of the early problems assigned to Pasteur was to explain and prevent the vinegar spoilage of red wines shipped in barrel from Burgundy to England, as well as to try to explain some of the many FAULTS in French wine which had become apparent at the time. He identified the following transformations in various wine constituents:

mannitic acid: degradation of sugars
'tourne': degradation of tartaric acid
bitterness: degradation of glycerol
'graisse': production of a polysaccharide

From his discovery of the various micro-organisms which caused different wine maladies, such as the ACETOBACTER which turn wine into vinegar, came the whole science of bacteriology. He suggested that the application of heat (now called PASTEURIZATION) would destroy these micro-organisms and prevent microbial development, with beneficial effects on the quality of wine. The demonstration of the existence of these BACTERIAL DISEASES was extremely fruitful for the science of OENOLOGY; it resulted in the progressive reduction in VOLATILE ACIDS in wine which was an important factor in raising overall quality. Pasteurization has not been embraced by wine-makers as one might have thought it would be, and today PASTEURIZATION is the only use of heat in wine-making which has been adopted on an industrial scale.

But Pasteur's research work on wine, and beer, gave rise to his remarkable studies on the cause and prevention of infectious diseases in humans and animals.

From a drop of faulty wine, characterized by the presence of micro-organisms which could be seen with the aid of a microscope and by faults which could be tasted, Pasteur could contaminate a perfectly healthy wine. He expressed his thoughts thus: 'When one observes beer and wine experiencing fundamental changes because these liquids have given asylum to microscopic organisms which were introduced invisibly and fortuitously to them, where they since proliferated, how could one not be obsessed by the thought that similar things can and must sometimes happen to humans and animals?' (1866)

Whatever the undoubted merits of Pasteur's work, to which we owe the basis of wine microbiology, with all its practical consequences for vinification and wine conservation, it should be noted that he did not understand the positive role that LACTIC BACTERIA could have in degrading MALIC ACID. Because of this it was particularly difficult to grasp the principles of MALOLACTIC FERMENTATION which, in 1930, Jean RIBÉREAU-GAYON elucidated as a bacterial transformation which could be of great benefit to a wide range of wines. It was not until the 1970s that the rest of the wine world was convinced. Not without reason, Émile PEYNAUD has written, 'the evolution of oenology would certainly have been very different if Pasteur, instead of leaving us the basis of a perfect method of adding tartaric acid, had taught us to add malic acid'.

For Pasteur 'yeast make wine, bacteria destroy it'.

Pasteur truly created the science of wine-making; if today oenology is a discipline in so many universities throughout the world, it is to Pasteur that we owe this achievement.

P.R.-G.

PASTEURIZATION, process of heating foods, including wines, to a temperature high enough to kill all micro-organisms such as YEAST and BACTERIA. It is named after Louis PASTEUR, the French scientist who discovered that micro-organisms were alive and the cause of much wine spoilage.

Heat sterilization techniques have improved greatly since the early versions of pasteurization, which often resulted in burnt or cooked flavours in wines treated, particularly those that had not been subjected to complete CLARIFICATION. Wines are pasteurized by rapid heating to about 85 °C/ 185 °F for one minute, quick cooling, and return to storage tank or bottling line. Keeping the wine longer, for up to three days, at about 50 °C/122 °F is used to coagulate heat-unstable proteins and to speed ageing in low-quality red dessert wines. **Flash pasteurization** may also be effected by heating to temperatures as high as 95 °C for a few seconds, followed by rapid cooling. Some wine is **hot bottled** (at about 55 °C) and allowed to cool slowly or, for utmost effectiveness, closed bottles of wine are occasionally heated to about 55 °C and cooled to room temperature under a water spray. These techniques are relatively brutal, however, and are used only on ordinary wines which have no potential for improvement after BOTTLE AGEING. A.D.W.

PAUILLAC, small port and communal appellation in the Médoc district of Bordeaux which has the unparalleled distinction of boasting three of the five first growths ranked in Bordeaux's most famous CLASSIFICATION within its boundaries—Chx LAFITE, LATOUR, and MOUTON-ROTHSCHILD—as well as a bevy of other CLASSED GROWTHS rivalling them (and each other) with increasing insistence. For all the importance of its wines, Pauillac gives the impression of being the only settlement in the Haut-Médoc to have an existence independent of wine—an impression reinforced by its size and nearby industrial installations.

This, however, is Cabernet Sauvignon country *par excellence*, and while there is considerable variation between different properties' TERROIRS and wine-making policies and capabilities, certain expressions recur in Pauillac tasting notes: cassis (blackcurrant), cedar, and cigar box (the last two sometimes a reflection of the top-quality French oak cooperage which the selling prices of Pauillac permit). A high proportion of the Médoc's most concentrated wines are produced here.

More than 1,000 ha/2,500 acres of vines are planted in an almost continuous strip between Pauillac's boundary with ST-JULIEN to the south and ST-ESTÈPHE to the north, separated from the waters of the Gironde estuary by only a few hundred metres of *palus* too marshy for serious viticulture (although very suitable for grazing Pauillac's famous *agneaux présalés*, saltmarsh lamb). This strip of vines, 3 km/2 miles wide and more than 6 km long, dedicated to the production of the world's most famously long-lived red wine, is divided into two by the small river Gaet, whose banks are also unsuitable for vines. As elsewhere in the Médoc, the layers of GRAVEL here provide the key to wine quality, offering excellent DRAINAGE, aided by the almost imperceptibly undulating topography and a series of *jalles* or streams running water off the gravelly plateau and into the Gironde.

The stars of the northern sector of Pauillac are undoubtedly the two ROTHSCHILD properties Chx Lafite and Mouton-Rothschild, whose plots of vineyard are intermingled on the plateau of Le Pouyalet, reaching the considerable (for the Médoc) altitude of 30 m/100 ft at its highest point. Clustered around them are their satellite properties, whose wines benefit from the first-class wine-making ability of their owners. Ch Duhart-Milon-Rothschild is Lafite's fourth growth, made in the town of Pauillac. The fifth growths Ch Clerc-Milon and Ch Mouton d'Armailhac (called Ch Mouton Baron Philippe and then Ch Mouton Baronne Philippe between 1956 and 1989) are made, to an often very high standard, close to Mouton itself. Other classed growths on this plateau just a stream away from St-Estèphe are the fifth growths Chx Pontet-Canet and the generally much less exciting Pédesclaux.

Throughout the 1970s much was made of the inter-Rothschild rivalry in the northern half of Pauillac. In the mid 1980s and early 1990s, the extreme south of the appellation around the village of St-Lambert has been a battleground for wine supremacy, between first growth Ch Latour and, particularly, its near neighbours the two Pichons. All three of these made considerable investments in their vineyards, *chais*, and more cosmetic aspects of their property, and the Pichons have demonstrated that, just like first growth Latour, they are capable of making sublime wine at the St-Julien end of Pauillac. The Pichon-Longueville estate was originally one, but had already been divided into a smaller 'Baron' portion and a larger Contesse de Lalande portion by the time the 1855 classification ranked them the bottom half of the second growths (a much lower position than they merit today). In the early 20th century Pichon-Baron, as it was known, was highly regarded. By the early 1980s, Pichon-Longueville-Lalande had decisively overtaken it in reputation. By the early 1990s, however, Pichon-Baron had been lavishly renovated and renamed, confusingly, Pichon-Longueville by Jean-Michel Cazes of Ch Lynch-Bages, and the AXA insurance group, and offered a perennial challenge to its neighbours.

In the hinterland of this southern extreme of Pauillac are neighbouring fifth growths Chx Batailley and Haut-Batailley, whose wines can challenge those of fifth growth Ch Grand-Puy-Lacoste to the immediate north, which is run impeccably by the Borie family and can offer some of Pauillac's best value. A dozen of the 18 fifth growths are in Pauillac, and none has been more successful than the Cazes family's flamboyantly styled Ch Lynch-Bages (the name betraying the original Irish connection), whose standing and fame suggest a considerably higher ranking. Chx Lynch-Moussas, Croizet-Bages, and Grand-Puy-Ducasse have rarely merited the limelight, although Grand-Puy-Ducasse was extensively renovated in the 1980s. Ch Haut-Bages-Libéral, between Chx Latour and Lynch-Bages, produced fine wines in the 1980s.

Two of Pauillac's most distinctive products do not feature in the 1855 classification. Les Forts de Latour, the SECOND WINE of Ch Latour, is regularly one of its most successful wines (and it is priced as such), while the co-operative at Pauillac is a particularly important one, selling some of its considerable produce under the name La Rose Pauillac.

For more information see MÉDOC and BORDEAUX.

Parker, R., *Bordeaux* (2nd edn., New York, 1991).

Penning-Rowsell, E., *The Wines of Bordeaux* (6th edn., London, 1989).

Peppercorn, D., *Bordeaux* (2nd edn., London, 1991).

PAYS. French for country. See VIN DE PAYS.

PEARLS or **pearl glands**, small, spherical nodules that develop on the surface of vine stems, PETIOLES, and the underside of leaves along the large veins. They form under warm humid conditions, such as in a glasshouse, and when the vine's growth is exuberant. They are a multicellular outgrowth of the epidermis, even to the extent of an occasional STOMA, but collapse to a rusty colour and disappear when the humidity drops. B.G.C.

PÉCHARMANT, red wine appellation within the BERGERAC district in SOUTH WEST FRANCE. About 180 ha/450 acres of vines on gravelly, south-facing slopes just east of the town of Bergerac produce some of Périgord's longest-lived red wines, made from Bordeaux grape varieties, especially MERLOT. Little of it escapes the region, with the exception of Ch Tiregand, owned, like a property in La CLAPE, by the St-Exupéry family.

Within the region some sweet white wine may occasionally be produced under the almost extinct ROSETTE appellation.

PECTINS, carbohydrate polymers made up of galacturonic acid units (some being methylated) which have the important function of 'gumming' plant cells together. The group is diverse and includes pectic acid, hemicelluloses, and gums; the associated sugars are galactose, mannose, and arabinose. The pectin content of grapes increases steadily throughout ripening, reaching levels of about 1 g/l. Pectin is an important contributor to COLLOIDS. B.G.C.

PEDICEL, the stalk of an individual flower which, on a bunch of grapes, becomes the short stem bearing each berry. Its length varies with vine variety, from 5 to 15 mm (0.5 in), and its diameter varies with variety and BERRY SIZE. After FLOWERING, pedicels are liable to develop a separation layer at their base causing the flower to drop; the remainder adhere and can develop into berries (as in FRUIT SET). When berries of certain vine varieties ripen, the pedicels may develop a corky abscission at their top, at the junction with the berry. If this does not happen, then pulling off the berry tears the skin and leaves behind a chunk of pulp on the end of the pedicel that is called the BRUSH. B.G.C.

PEDRO GIMÉNEZ, important white grape variety in ARGENTINA, where it is the country's most planted vine variety other than the coarse and declining CRIOLLA and CEREZA. There were 22,600 ha/55,800 acres of Pedro Giménez in 1989, almost three-quarters of them in Mendoza province. This is the variety that underpins Argentina's white wine production and it is also found in Chile's PISCO region. AMPELOGRAPHERS in Argentina believe there is no connection between this variety and the PEDRO XIMÉNEZ of Spain.

PEDRO XIMÉNEZ, Pedro Jiménez, Pedro Jiménez, Pedro, or **Pedro Ximénez**, white grape variety traditionally associated with ANDALUCÍA in southern Spain but now much less common than the PALOMINO Fino in the JEREZ region for sherry production. Palomino Fino is more productive and less disease-prone than Pedro Ximénez. Pedro Ximénez covers almost as much ground, however, perhaps 27,000 ha/66,700 acres, and is found all over Andalucía, VALENCIA, and EXTREMADURA. Because it is capable of producing very ripe grapes, it is particularly popular with MÁLAGA producers, some of whom depend on grapes from the MONTILLA-MORILES region, where it is by far the dominant grape variety for the sherry-like wines produced there. The other common fate of these thin-skinned grapes, which were traditionally dried in the sun to produce wines to sweeten fortified blends, is to produce somewhat flabby, neutral-flavoured dry table wines, although some rich, raisiny, sweet fortified wine called Pedro Ximénez, or simply 'PX', is bottled. The variety is also grown on Spain's CANARY ISLANDS off the Atlantic coast.

In Australia, Pedro Ximénez is not distinguished from the more popular Palomino for the purposes of vineyard censuses, but the variety has been known to shine, most particularly in BOTRYTIZED form to produce the rich, deep golden McWilliam's Pedro Sauterne (*sic*) made in irrigated vineyards near Griffith in NEW SOUTH WALES. The variety was once confused with another Australian import from Jerez, but such Cañocazo as remains is now known as False Pedro in Australia. The vine called False Pedro by South Africa is the Andalucian variety Pedro Luis, however. California has all but dispensed with Pedro Ximénez.

A vine called PEDRO GIMÉNEZ, is extremely important in ARGENTINA but AMPELOGRAPHERS believe that it is not the Pedro Ximénez of Spain.

PEDUNCLE. See BUNCHSTEM.

PENEDÈS, often spelt **Penedés**, the largest and most important denominated wine zone in CATALONIA in north east Spain (see map on p. 907), producing an innovative range of wines. With its proximity to Barcelona, Penedès has always had a ready outlet for its wines. In the 19th century, it was one of the first regions in Spain to begin mass production and France, stricken by PHYLLOXERA, became an important market. The phylloxera louse reached Penedès in 1887, by which time José Raventos had laid the foundations of CODORNÍU and the CAVA industry. Vineyards that had once produced strong, semi-fortified reds were uprooted in favour of white grapes for sparkling wine. Cava has subsequently developed a separate nationally organized DO.

Penedès underwent a second radical transformation in the 1960s and 1970s largely because of Miguel Torres Carbo and his son Miguel A. TORRES, wine (and BRANDY) producers in the heart of the region at Vilafranca del Penedès. They were among the first in Spain to install TEMPERATURE CONTROL and STAINLESS STEEL tanks. Miguel Torres, Jr. (as he was known to distinguish him from his late father), who studied OENOLOGY in France, also imported and experimented with such revolutionary vine varieties as CABERNET SAUVIGNON, PINOT NOIR, CHARDONNAY, SAUVIGNON BLANC, RIESLING, and GEWÜRZTRAMINER, which were planted alongside and blended with native varieties. Torres made a detailed study of the climate and soil types in Penedès to choose suitable vine varieties and to ensure that vineyards were planted in the optimum conditions. Other growers have followed in the Torres family footsteps and Penedès continues to be one of the most dynamic and varied wine regions in Spain.

Penedès rises from the Mediterranean like a series of steps and divides into three distinct zones. Bajo, or Low, Penedès reaches altitudes of 250 m/825 ft away from the tourist resorts of the Costa Dorada. This is the warmest part of the region which traditionally grew MALVASIA and Moscatel de Alejandria (MUSCAT OF ALEXANDRIA) grapes for sweet FORTIFIED wines. With the expansion of the resort towns and declining sales of such wines, these vineyards have either been abandoned or replanted with GARNACHA, CARIÑENA, or MONASTRELL making sturdy reds. The second zone, Medio Penedès, is a broad valley 500 m above sea level, separated from the coast by a ridge of hills. This is the most productive part of the region providing much of the base wine for the sparkling wine industry at San Sadurni de Noya (see CAVA for more details). MACABEO, XAREL-LO, and PARELLADA are grown for Cava, together with increasing quantities of Chardonnay and red varieties such as TEMPRANILLO (often called here by its Catalan name Ull de Llebre) and Cabernet Sauvignon. Penedès Superior, between 500 and 800 m above the coast on the foothills of Spain's central plateau, is the coolest part of

The original Grange cottage at Magill in South Australia which lends its name to **Penfolds'** most famous wine.

the region where some of the best white grapes are grown. The native Parellada is the most important variety here, but Riesling, Muscat of Alexandria, Gewürztraminer, and Chardonnay are also successful. Some producers would like to enlarge Penedès Superior through federation with the promising nearby DO CONCA DE BARBERÁ. R.J.M.

PENFOLDS, the premium range of wines within the **Penfolds Wine Group**, the dominant wine producer and vineyard owner in Australia whose output represents one in every three bottles of Australian wine. Penfolds' first vineyard was founded in 1844 at Magill, South Australia, by Dr Christopher Rawson Penfold. For more than 100 years Penfolds, in common with most Australian wineries, concentrated on producing FORTIFIED wines and brandy, much of which was exported to the UK. In 1950, Max Schubert, then chief wine-maker, visited Europe, making an extensive tour of the Bordeaux region. On his return, he pioneered the Bordeaux wine-making techniques he had observed in Australia, thus making a valuable contribution to the development of fine Australian table wines, particularly reds. Schubert's ambition was to create a red that would rival the finest wines of Bordeaux for both quality and the potential to improve with age. This he achieved with **Penfolds Grange** (known as Penfolds Grange Hermitage until EUROPEAN UNION authorities objected to this misappropriation of a French place-name), now widely acknowledged to be Australia's greatest wine. Grange, named after Dr Penfold's cottage in Magill, was first produced in 1952; all early vintages were made from Shiraz grapes grown at Magill and Morphett Vale, Adelaide, and the wine was matured in new American oak for 12 months. The intense fruit character combined with excellent use of wood gave Grange great potential as an ageing wine, but the first vintages were rejected as maverick 'dry port'. In 1957 Schubert was ordered to cease production of Grange; instead he took the operation underground, emerging three years later when maturing vintages began to fulfil their promise. In fact, fine vintages of Grange improve for up to 30 years and beyond, and the wine has become the most decorated in Australian history. Fruit from Kalimna in the Barossa Valley was introduced in 1961, boosted by grapes from the Clare and Koonunga Hill vineyards. Small amounts of Cabernet Sauvignon are included in some vintages of Grange, and the wood ageing period has been lengthened to between 18 and 20 months. The wine is not released for at least four years after the vintage. A string of award-winning red wines from Penfolds followed, many identified by 'bin' numbers which originated in the winery stock-keeping system. Of particular note is Bin 707 Cabernet Sauvignon. Since the late

1980s Penfolds has concentrated on developing a white wine portfolio, with emphasis on Chardonnay and Chardonnay/Semillon blends. Fruit comes from cooler climate areas such as Coonawarra and Padthaway in the south together with the premium fruit-growing areas of the Barossa Valley, McLaren Vale, and the Southern Vales near Adelaide. Penfolds' headquarters are at Nuriootpa in the Barossa. In 1990 Penfolds had acquired its greatest rival, Lindemans, long associated with fine white wines and the Hunter Valley. In 1990 Penfolds, along with Lindemans, was acquired by South Australian Brewing Holdings, which formed the Penfolds Wine Group as its wine subsidiary. Other Australian wineries under the PWG banner are Leo Buring, Hungerford Hill, Killawarra, Kaiser Stuhl, Matthew Lang, Rouge Homme, Seaview, Seppelt, Tollana, Tulloch, Woodley, and Wynns Coonawarra Estate. In the early 1990s the PWG began a programme of expansion outside Australia which initially included investments in California and MOLDOVA. In 1993 Penfolds Wine Group was renamed Southcorp Wines Pty. in an attempt to treat all subsidiary companies more equably. S.A.

Evans, L., *Complete Book of Australian Wine* (3rd edn., Adelaide, 1990).
Halliday, J., *The Australian Wine Compendium* (Sydney, 1985).

PENICILLIUM, vine disease, one of a group of fungi commonly found on rotten grapes. See BUNCH ROTS.

PENNING-ROWSELL, EDMUND (1913–), English wine writer with a scholarly interest in the history and wines of Bordeaux in particular. Educated at Marlborough College and a lifelong socialist, he was a journalist on the *Morning Post* from 1930 until 1935, when he began a career of almost 30 years as a book publisher. He was introduced to the pleasures of wine when his wife's employer at the BBC gave her as a leaving present (only unmarried females were then regarded as suitable employees) some non-vintage Moulin-à-Vent. Correspondence and eventual friendship with Bristol wine merchant Ronald AVERY was another formative influence. (During the Second World War he would visit Bristol for trade union meetings, for which he was eventually fired from his job in an aircraft factory.) It was during this period that he laid the modest foundations of one of the finest cellars ever assembled by one individual.

The traditional but non-profit-making ethos of the co-operative buying group the WINE SOCIETY suited him perfectly and he joined the Society soon after his marriage in 1937, becoming the energetic honorary secretary of its Dining Club in 1950. In 1959 he was elected to the Society's Management Committee and served as its chairman from 1964 until 1987, a record length of time.

In 1949 he had reviewed wine books for the *Times Literary Supplement* and in 1954 wrote his first wine article for the magazine *Country Life*. Since 1964, soon after his publishing career came to an end, he has been wine correspondent of the *Financial Times*, scrupulously refusing to mention the Wine Society during his chairmanship, no matter how inconvenient. His wine primer *Red, White and Rosé* was published in 1967, and a second edition appeared in 1973, but his great gift to the LITERATURE OF WINE is *The Wines of Bordeaux*, which was first published in 1969 and whose sixth edition appeared 20 years later. Penning-Rowsell's publishing background made him wary of the more ephemeral wine books which burgeoned, for a single edition, in the 1980s. His primary concern has always been to record the facts rather than to make an effect or a profit.

Edmund **Penning-Rowsell**.

The facts of his remarkable cellar have also been meticulously recorded, in a series of cellar books and, typically, in his characteristic green ink. This unique archive includes details of every purchase, every souvenir from his punishing annual round of visits to the wine regions (continued into his ninth decade), and impressions of every bottle sampled.

A perennial figure in Bordeaux at vintage time and at the HOSPICES DE BEAUNE auction, Penning-Rowsell was made a Chevalier de l'Ordre du Mérite Agricole in 1971 and a Chevalier de l'Ordre du Mérite National in 1981.

Loftus, S., 'Purple prose: the wine writers', in *Anatomy of the Wine Trade* (London, 1985).

PEPPER, a tasting term for two very different aromas commonly found in red wines. **Bell peppers**, or **green peppers**, is used characteristically of red wines made from CABERNET SAUVIGNON grapes grown in parts of CALIFORNIA—most notably those made from young vines planted in the MONTEREY part of the Salinas Valley in the 1970s. A freshly sliced green pepper or capsicum liberates the chemical compound 2-methoxy-3-isobutylpyrazine, a vegetable-like aroma to which most tasters have a very low threshold (see FLAVOUR COMPOUNDS). Young wines made from the SYRAH grape, on the other hand, particularly if it does not reach full maturity, can smell of **black peppercorns**.

PERGOLA, a form of overhead VINE TRAINING. Where the canopy is horizontal the pergola can alternatively be called TENDONE. Pergola trellises can be either one or two armed, depending on whether the vines are trained on one or both sides of the row. If the trellis is joined overhead it is called a closed pergola.

The pergola is widely used in Italy, where the canopies vary but are often inclined rather than horizontal (in Trentino, for example, the slope is 20 to 30 degrees. In Emilia-Romagna the **pergoletta** system is used, while the **pergoletta Capucci** was developed by the eponymous Bologna professor. The **pergoletta a Valenzano** is very similar to the GENEVA DOUBLE CURTAIN. The term pergola is often used to describe overhead trellis systems in gardens. R.E.S.

Le Petit Journal
ADMINISTRATION
5 CENT.
SUPPLÉMENT ILLUSTRÉ
5 CENT.
ABONNEMENTS
Numéro 1.230
DIMANCHE 14 JUIN 1914
UN BICENTENAIRE
Il y a exactement deux cents ans que Dom Pérignon, moine bénédictin de Hautvillers, découvrit l'art de faire mousser le vin de Champagne

The folkloric image of Dom **Pérignon** 'discovering' champagne.

PERICARP, the 'fruit wall' forming the bulk of a plant's ovary, consisting of sugary flesh and highly coloured skin attractive to animals, especially BIRDS, with the result that the SEEDS are spread. In the grape berry, the whole fruit except for the seeds (both the skin and the flesh) constitutes the pericarp. See GRAPE for more details.

PÉRIGNON, DOM (1639–1715), Benedictine monk who has gone down in history as 'the man who invented champagne'. The title is the stuff of fairy-tales: the transition from still to sparkling wine was an evolutionary process rather than a dramatic discovery on the part of one man. The life of Dom Pérignon was in fact devoted to improving the still wines of Champagne, and he deserves his place in the history books for that reason. Brother Pierre Pérignon arrived at the Abbey of Hautvillers, north of Épernay, in 1668. His role was that of treasurer, and in the 17th century that meant being in charge of the cellars. He collected tithes from surrounding villages in the form of grapes and wine, fermenting and blending until he created wines that sold for twice as much as those of the abbey's rivals. Dom Pérignon introduced many practices that survive in the process of modern wine production, among them severe pruning, low yields, and careful harvesting. He also experimented to a great extent with the BLENDING process, and was one of the first to blend the produce of many different vineyards. Dom Pérignon produced still white and red wines, favouring black grapes because a SECONDARY FERMENTATION was less likely. Ironically, he was often thwarted in his endeavours by the refermentation process, which produced the style of wine that was eventually to prove so popular. His fame as the 'inventor' of champagne probably spread after his death, embellished by Dom Grossard, the last treasurer of the abbey, which closed at the time of the French Revolution. More modern champagne producers have jumped on the bandwagon, promoting the idea of a founder figure. Eugene Mercier registered the brand name Dom Pérignon before MOËT & CHANDON acquired it and used it to launch the first champagne marketed as a PRESTIGE CUVÉE in 1937.

See also CHAMPAGNE. S.A.

Faith, N., *The Story of Champagne* (London, 1988).
Johnson, H., *The Story of Wine* (London, 1989).

PERIQUITA, Portuguese name for a parakeet given to both a usefully versatile red grape variety grown all over southern Portugal (see CASTELÃO FRANCES) and a branded red wine from José Maria da FONSECA Successores.

PERLANT, French term for a wine that is only slightly SPARKLING. **Perlwein** is the German equivalent. See FIZZINESS.

PERLE is, like WÜRZER, a modern German vine crossing of Gewürztraminer and Müller-Thurgau; in this case Gewürztraminer's rosy-hued grapes have been inherited but its extravagant perfume is more muted. It is particularly useful in Franken since its late budding protects it from spring frost damage and nearly half of the 1990 German total of just over 200 ha/500 acres of Perle were planted in this eastern region. The wine produced is flowery but the vine's compact bunches make it an easy target for GREY ROT, which may account for the apparent decline in popularity during the 1980s.

PERNAND-VERGELESSES, village in the Côte de Beaune district of Burgundy's Côte d'Or producing red and white wines. The former, made from Pinot Noir, are somewhat angular in style and do not always appear fully ripe as Pernand is set back from the main sweep of the Côte and many of its vineyards have a westerly, even north western exposition, which can retard RIPENING.

Pernand chose to suffix the name of its best red wine vineyard, east-facing Les Vergelesses, which it shares with neighbouring Savigny-lès-Beaune, although the most sought-after wines are the whites on the Pernard side of the hill of Corton (see ALOXE-CORTON). Seventeen of the 72 ha/178 acres entitled to the GRAND CRU appellation Corton-Charlemagne lie within Pernand-Vergelesses. White Pernand wines have a hard but attractive flinty character which develops well. BOURGOGNE ALIGOTÉ from this area is said to resemble white Pernand-Vergelesses as it ages; and white Pernand to approach the quality of Corton-Charlemagne.

See also CÔTE D'OR and its map. J.T.C.M.

PERONOSPERA, European name for the vine disease DOWNY MILDEW.

PERRICONE, SICILIAN red grape variety planted on hardly more than 1,000 ha/2,500 acres of the island. Soft varietal wines are sometimes called by its synonym Pignatello.

PERSIA, Near Eastern country officially known as IRAN since 1935, which has known the consumption of wine since ancient times.

Ancient Persia

Much of this area was also known as MESOPOTAMIA in classical times. There had been vines in the area from earliest times, but it was only from 550 BC that Cyrus the Great and Darius extended Persia's power to cover all the lands from the west end of the Mediterranean to the river Indus in the east, incorporating the old empires of BABYLONIA and ASSYRIA, which were overwhelmed and extended.

Persia may be the site of one of the earliest ever wine-related archaeological discoveries (see ORIGINS and PALAEOETHNOBOTANY). A large earthenware jar stored on its side in a room at the archaeological site of Godin Tepe (dated to about 3500 BC) in central western Iran was found to have a dark stain inside, closely akin to TARTARIC ACID, which occurs at high levels in wine.

More detailed evidence is available from the era of the Achaemenid Dynasty, which ruled Ancient Iran from *c.*559 to *c.*331 BC. Dating from the period just before Persia and Greece became embroiled in the Persian Wars, an enormous archive of documents written on clay tablets in the Elamite language preserves detailed records of the administration of the Achaemenid royal capital Persepolis from 509 to 494 BC. Here there are records concerning the distribution of large quantities of (grape) wine and *sawur*, another (probably weaker) sort of wine. Sometimes the wine was stored at, or issued from, the ancient city of SHIRAZ, whose name is now associated with so many wines. Wine was normally released in monthly amounts, although in certain cases the issue was daily. One *marrish* (a measure of 10 quarts) of wine was valued at one shekel.

Such 'rations' often amounted to far more than one person could consume: perhaps they would be better described as salaries. Some were given to important women with households of their own to support: these received 30 quarts per month. King Darius writes in one order that 100 sheep and 500 gal of wine should be issued for the royal princess Artystone, no doubt in order for her to give a lavish banquet at her own court. Persian royal ladies were very independent and maintained their own establishments and dependants.

Generally wine was not given to boy and girl workers (who did, however, receive other rations including sometimes beer), except according to one document where some boys received one-third of a quart daily for 156 days. Otherwise the general allowance was 10 or 20 quarts monthly for men and 10 for women. Some labourers received as little as half a quart per month over a three-month period.

Presumably in an effort to increase the proletarian population available for large-scale labour, special wine rations were provided under the Achaemenid dynasty as a reward for women labourers who had just given birth to children: women who bore sons received 10 quarts, and those who bore daughters 5 quarts. The issue was sometimes spread out over the entire subsequent year.

Important caravans of diplomatic visitors accompanied by élite guides travelled from as far afield as Kandahar, India, Sardis, and Egypt. Those due to arrive at the capital Persepolis during the cooler months of the year (November to May), when the king and his entourage were in residence, were issued with travel rations to ease their arduous journey at the various stations at which they put up on the Royal Road. The records indicate that these, naturally, included generous amounts of wine.

On occasions wine was issued, along with grain and beer, for the benefit of the royal horses, perhaps when they were used for long journeys. The amounts issued varied from half a pint to 10 pints per animal per month. *Sawur* wine was even made available to the king's camels as an occasional concession.

In the 5th century BC HERODOTUS noted that the Achaemenids would make important decisions in a drunken state, then confirm these decisions when sober, and vice versa.

The Persian empire was finally split up after the death of Alexander the Great in 323 BC. J.A.B.

Hallock, R. T., *Persepolis Fortification Tablets* (Chicago, 1969).

Shiraz as wine capital

The consumption of wine survived through the Sassanian Period, from the 3rd to the 7th centuries AD influenced in part by Zoroastrian rite, and continued after the subsequent ISLAMIC conquest of the country.

Shiraz, a city rebuilt 50 km/30 miles from the site of Persepolis by the Arabs in the 8th century and the home town of Hāfiz, Persia's most famous mystic Bacchic poet (see ARAB POETS), had acquired a reputation by the 9th century for producing the finest wines in the Near East.

Thanks principally to the work of Edward Fitzgerald in the 19th century, the medieval polymath and poet OMAR KHAYYÁM has become famous in the west for poetry in which wine plays an important part.

From the diaries of 17th century English and French travellers and especially the writings of C. J. Wills in the 19th century, we gain a picture of the excellence of some (although by no means all) Persian wines. Tavernier (17th century) wrote: 'the wine of Shiraz has by far the greatest foreign as well as native celebrity, being of the quality of an old sherry and constitutes an excellent beverage.' In the same century Thomas Herbert commented: 'No part of the world has wine better than Shiraz.'

The wine most often described and praised was white, made from thick-skinned, pip-filled grapes grown on terraces round the village of Khoullar, four days' camel ride away from Shiraz (those grown in the immediate vicinity of the city produced watery wine, thanks to excessive IRRIGATION). C. J. Wills describes a 19th century replication of the traditional Shiraz wine-making process in some detail. The wine, fermented on the skins with regular PUNCHING DOWN, was made either sweet and fruity for long keeping, the stems being removed immediately after fermentation in used jars, or dry and rich in PHENOLICS for drinking in its first year or so. A form of FILTRATION through coarse canvas bags was practised. Wills describes the wine as 'like a light **bucellas**' when young, to be avoided on account of the headaches it induces. After five years, however, it attains a 'fine aroma and bouquet' and 'nutty flavour'.

See also DRIED GRAPE WINES, for the Persians were certainly in the habit of drying their grapes. P.K.

Hugh Johnson paints a fascinating and vivid picture of the export of wine from Shiraz to India by European merchants, in 1677 (already in BOTTLES 'wrapped in straw and packed in cases . . . swaying down to the Gulf Coast on mule back. There is scarcely any earlier instance of the regular use of bottles for shipping wine.' Tavernier notes that the 1666 vintage was so bountiful that the Persian king gave permission to export as much wine to the French, English, Dutch, and Portuguese trading companies as was retained by himself and his court. Wine was measured in 'mans', units of weight rather than volume.

For an outline of modern viticulture, see IRAN.

Johnson, H., *The Story of Wine* (London and New York, 1989).
Planhol, X., 'Une rencontre de l'Europe et de l'Iran: le vin de Shiraz', in D. Boidanovic and J. L. Bacque-Grammont (eds.), *Iran* (Paris, 1972).
Tavernier, J.-B., *Voyages en Perse* (Geneva, 1970).
Wills, C. J., *The Land of the Lion and the Sun* (London, 1891).
—— *Persia as it is* (London, 1886).

PERU, the first country in SOUTH AMERICA to have encouraged systematic viticulture. Under orders from the famous conquistador Francisco Pizarro, the first Peruvian vineyard was planted in about 1547. Specific VINE VARIETIES were imported from Spain and by the 1560s Peru is thought to have had 40,000 ha/99,000 acres under vine, producing so much wine that it was exported to other South American countries and even, according to one document, as far as Spain. One of the several ways by which viticulture spread to Argentina was from Peru, with Nuñez de Prado, in 1550.

The arrival of the PHYLLOXERA louse in 1888 heralded the start of a serious decline in Peruvian viticulture which was halted as recently as 1960. Only in the 1970s was progress made on establishing suitable planting material and there are now NURSERIES at Ica, Chincha, Moquegua, and Tacna, as well as a national wine research centre.

The Peruvian national drink is PISCO, an aromatic grape brandy which probably evolved to solve the problem of transporting the produce of Peru's vineyards to the markets of Lima and Cuzco. It is also made in Chile to the south and takes its name from the Peruvian river and town of the same name.

Today about 11,000 ha/27,000 acres of Peru is planted with vines, almost all of it on the central coast around Pisco and, particularly, Ica to the south, where wine-making and distillation investment is concentrated. (Elsewhere, both techniques and equipment tend to be extremely primitive.) Winter temperatures are so high that full vine DORMANCY is usually impossible, and two crops a year can be harvested from the same plant (see TROPICAL VITICULTURE). Summer temperatures are also high, between 24 and 33 °C (75–91 °F) in the hottest month, and rainfall is low, but IRRIGATION water is readily available from the Andes. Yields often reach 20 tons per ha (8 tons/acre).

Vine varieties planted include ALBILLO, ALICANTE BOUSCHET, BARBERA, CABERNET SAUVIGNON, GRENACHE, MALBEC, MOSCATEL, SAUVIGNON BLANC, TORONTEL, as well as the TABLE GRAPE Italia, Negra Corriente, thought to have been imported from the Canary islands in the 17th century and possibly identical to MISSION, Quebranta, and a variety called Borgoña which is in fact ISABELLA.

Some of the less 'international' vine varieties are also planted along the coast to the north and south, in the mountains up to an altitude of 1,500 m/5,000 ft, in the dry, temperature climate of the valleys of Ayacucho, Hunaca, and Abancay.

PESSAC-LÉOGNAN, important Bordeaux red and dry white wine appellation created in 1987 for the most celebrated part of the GRAVES district immediately south of the city. It takes its name from its two vinously most important communes, although it includes all of the properties named in the 1959 CLASSIFICATION of Graves, and many other fine châteaux too. This is Bordeaux's most urban wine area—indeed the vineyards of its most famous property Ch Haut-Brion and its neighbour Ch La Mission-Haut-Brion are today surrounded by suburban development, including the campus of BORDEAUX UNIVERSITY, on the boundary of the suburbs of Pessac and Talence. It is hardly surprising that Bordeaux's earliest wine estates were developed here, although the wines of Chx Haut-Brion, La Mission-Haut-Brion, and Pape-Clément justify the properties' existence on grounds far more solid than mere geographical convenience. Further from the city, vineyards are carved out of the pine forests which extend south west into the Landes. In all, about 880 ha / 2,200 acres of vineyard within Pessac-Léognan produce red wine, and the total area devoted to white wine grapes had reached 250 ha in the early 1990s.

Soils here have particularly good DRAINAGE, being made up of gravel terraces of very different eras, and have managed to produce wines with more consistency in different VINTAGES than most other Bordeaux districts. The ENCÉPAGEMENT for red wines is very similar to that of the MÉDOC to the immediate north, being mainly Cabernet Sauvignon grapes with some Merlot and Cabernet Franc, but the wines can be quite different. It is not fanciful to imagine that the best wines of Pessac-Léognan have a distinct aroma that reminds some tasters of minerals, some of smoke, others even of warm bricks. Ch Haut-Brion is the most obvious exponent of this genre (see HAUT-BRION for details of the red and white wines of this property and those of La Mission-Haut-Brion).

White wines made here can be some of the most characterful dry white wines in the world, made from Sauvignon and Sémillon grapes grown generally on the lighter, sandier parts of the vineyard, and often produced with considerable recourse to BARREL FERMENTATION and BARREL MATURATION. The most admired, Domaine de Chevalier and Chx Haut-Brion and Laville-Haut-Brion, can develop in bottle over decades, and the dry white wines of Ch Malartic-Lagravière, for example, demand a decade in bottle at the very least. More recent, and more modern, fine white wines are made at Ch Couhins-LURTON.

For more details, see BORDEAUX.

Parker, R., *Bordeaux* (2nd edn., New York, 1991).
Penning-Rowsell, E., *The Wines of Bordeaux* (6th edn., London, 1989).
Peppercorn, D., *Bordeaux* (2nd edn., London, 1991).
Vandyke Price, P., *Wines of the Graves* (London, 1988).

PESTICIDES, substances or mixtures of substances applied to vineyards which are used to prevent, destroy, repel, or reduce the harmful effects of fungi, BACTERIA, INSECTS, NEMATODES, or other undesirable organisms regarded as VINE PESTS. Pesticides are made up of AGROCHEMICALS and are usually classified according to their principal use as, for example, fungicides, bactericides, insecticides, nematicides, miticides, etc. Many pesticides have more than one mode of action and may be effective against more than one type of pest. For example, SULPHUR is both a fungicide and a miticide in vineyards.

Most pesticides consist of an active chemical constituent in a concentrated form that is suitable for use after mixing with a diluent (water or oil). Less often, pesticides are formulated as dusts, granules, or fumigants and require DUSTING rather than SPRAYING. Mixtures of active ingredients may be used to create formulations with greater efficacy or versatility: two chemicals may be mixed, for example, to produce a DOWNY MILDEW fungicide with both protectant and eradicant properties. For convenience two or more pesticides may be combined in a spray mixture. However, problems due to chemical incompatibility may arise when different pesticides are mixed.

Pesticides are toxic chemicals (although the pesticides used on grapevines vary considerably with respect to their toxicity), and their potentially harmful effects on humans, other animals, and non-target organisms in the environment must be recognized. See also RESIDUES.

The following factors should be taken into consideration when developing strategies for pesticide use in vineyards: use patterns, rates, the potential development of pesticide resistance, and potential effects on non-target organisms. Use patterns may involve routine application schedules or more flexible strategies that rely on pest warning services and / or the monitoring of pest activity, as in INTEGRATED PEST MANAGEMENT. The latter are often adopted to minimize pesticide use.

The continuous use of some pesticides may result in a dramatic increase in the proportion of individuals in a pest population that are able to survive exposure to the pesticide. An example has been the development of resistance by the BOTRYTIS fungus to the fungicide Benomyl. A serious outcome of the development of pest resistance is the so-called 'treadmill effect': as resistance to a pesticide increases, the pesticide is used in increased dosages or more frequently, until such time that pesticide treatment becomes ineffective or uneconomic. Even more serious is the development of resistance to a group of related (cross-resistance) or dissimilar (multiple-resistance) chemicals. Pesticides which use strategies that delay or prevent the development of pest resistance are designed to avoid long-term exposure of the pest to a single pesticide or group of pesticides with similar mode of action.

See also FUNGICIDES and INSECTICIDES. P.R.D.

Emmett, R. W., Harris, A. R., Taylor, R. H., and McGechan, J. K., 'Grape diseases and vineyard protection', in B. G. Coombe and P. R. Dry (eds.), *Viticulture, ii: Practices* (Adelaide, 1992).

PESTS of vineyards. See VINE PESTS.

PÉTILLANT, French term for a lightly sparkling wine, somewhere between PERLANT and MOUSSEUX.

PETIOLE, the stalk of a plant's leaf which supports the leaf blade or lamina. Petioles are stem tissue and branch from the main stem of the shoot having similar anatomical features. At both ends of the petiole are swellings (pulvini) that alter the position of the leaf blade according to such stimuli as water stress and low light. Samples of petioles taken at FLOWERING are used as a basis for assessing a vine's status in terms of VINE NUTRITION.

The characteristics of petioles vary with vine variety and growing conditions, being longer on vigorous vines. Between varieties, petiole length varies from 5 to 20 cm (2–8 in), petiole colour varies from green to red, and petioles may vary from smooth to hairy. These features help in the identification of varieties (see AMPELOGRAPHY). B.G.C.

PETIT COURBU, ancient white grape variety of GASCONY found in BÉARN, IROULÉGUY, JURANÇON, and PACHERENC wines.

PETITE SIRAH, almost certainly an invented name, is the common name in both North and South America for a black grape variety that is less noble than and probably unrelated to the true SYRAH (of which some French growers distinguish a small-berried subvariety they call **Petite Syrah**, which is how, confusingly, some American producers also spell this, quite different, variety).

Petite Sirah is relatively important in a wide range of warm wine regions, especially in both California and South America. In California, where there were still 2,900 acres / 1,200 ha in 1992 notably in Monterey, it has been valued as a relatively tannic, well coloured blending partner for blowsier Zinfandels, but its star waned somewhat as more North Americans saw the worth of California's new toy, true Syrah. Almost all Petite Sirah vines in California are much older than the state average.

The hardy Petite Sirah has carved out a place for itself in California, for it makes dark, well-balanced, sturdily tannic red wine of agreeable if not highly distinctive flavour. As such it has been essential as a backbone for some everyday red blends: useful when rain-weakened Cabernet Sauvignon needed shoring up, or Pinot Noir went too pale and soft in a sunny vintage. Sonoma and Mendocino counties seem to grow Petite Sirah best, especially within the Russian river drainage from Redwood Valley down to Healdsburg or beyond. Louis J. Foppiano, Louis M. Martini, and Parducci Cellars produce the most polished, supple varietal examples. Even these benefit from a few years' bottle age. Ridge and Stag's Leap Winery take the varietal wine to its dark, tannic limits. Acreage is eroding everywhere, in part because Petite Sirah-based everyday red blends are fading from the market.

In 1990 Argentina had about the same area of Petite Sirah planted as California, more than 1,400 ha / 3,500 acres, often misleadingly calling it Sirah. It is also well known in Brazil's semi-tropical climate as Petite Sirah or Petite Syrah and has produced respectable sturdy red in Mexico.

During the 1980s Petite Sirah was thought to be identical to the DURIF, sometimes spelt Duriff, a nearly extinct French vine variety, but early DNA FINGERPRINTING suggested otherwise. Petite Sirah was first mentioned in California wine literature in the early 1880s, which also suggests that it cannot be identical to Durif, which had hardly been propagated in France then. PHYLLOXERA took its toll on early plantings of the mysterious Petite Sirah, which may at that stage have been Syrah. It has been suggested that in the early 20th century, and therefore subsequently, the name Petite Sirah was applied to a mixture, sometimes in the same vineyard, of grape varieties producing long-lived, deep coloured red wines.

PETIT MANSENG is the superior form of MANSENG.

PETIT RHIN, synonym for the great RIESLING grape of Germany used mainly in Switzerland.

PETITS CHÂTEAUX, the French term meaning literally 'small castles', has a very specific meaning in the BORDEAUX wine region. These thousands of properties are modest not so much in their extent as in their reputation and price. A CLASSED GROWTH is emphatically not a petit château, no matter how few hectares it encompasses. The greatest concentration of petits châteaux is in the appellations BORDEAUX AC, BOURG, and BLAYE, although they are found throughout the region. Some of Bordeaux's best wine value is to be found at the most conscientious petits châteaux.

See also CHÂTEAU.

PETIT VERDOT is one of Bordeaux's classic black grape varieties, no longer planted in any great quantity but enjoying a small revival in some quality-conscious vineyards. The vine ripens even later than Cabernet Sauvignon and is equally resistant to rot. It shares Cabernet Sauvignon's thick skins and is also capable of yielding concentrated, tannic wines rich in colour. When it ripens fully, which in most Bordeaux properties happens only in riper vintages, its rich, age-worthy wines can make a valuable contribution to some of the best wines of the Médoc. Its inconveniently late ripening encouraged many producers to abandon it in the 1960s and 1970s so that total French plantings were just over 300 ha / 740 acres in 1988. But, as its qualities are recognized, there has been a limited revival—not just in Bordeaux but in California too, where there were 100 acres / 40 ha (a third of them too young to bear fruit) of Petite Verdot (*sic*) in 1991, mainly in Napa.

The variety known as Verdot in Chile, where there were a few hundred hectares in 1991, is probably Petit Verdot, but the Verdot of which there were 100 ha in Argentina's Mendoza in 1989 may well be the coarser, probably unrelated, Gros Verdot variety.

PÉTRUS, CHÂTEAU, the most famous wine of POMEROL, and today the most expensive in BORDEAUX.

In the heart of the small Pomerol plateau, Pétrus was partly bought in 1925, by Mme Loubat, wife of the owner of the Hotel Loubat in Libourne, but not totally acquired until 1949, when it consisted of 6.5 ha planted with 70 per cent MERLOT vines and 30 per cent CABERNET FRANC. In 1969 5 ha were purchased from the adjoining Ch Gazin, and gradually the balance between the two vine varieties was altered until by

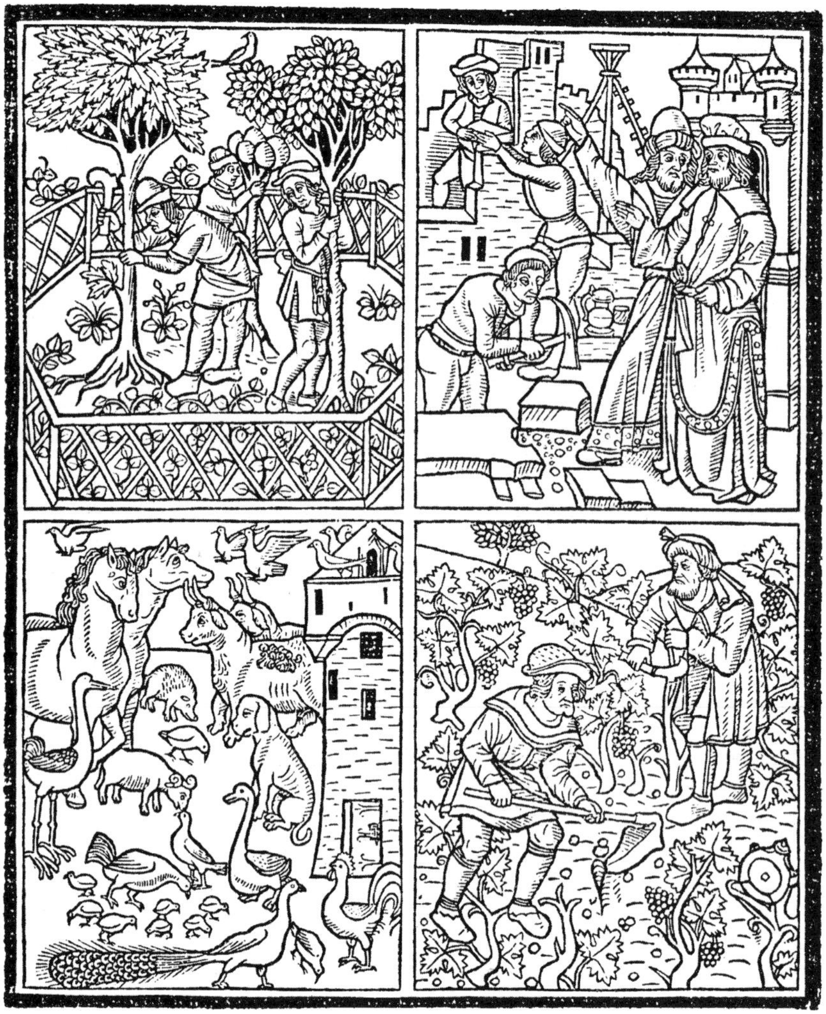

Illustration from an early 16th century edition of **Petrus de Crescentiis'** *Liber commodorum ruralium*, just one of many that were keenly followed in much of Europe in the 15th and 16th centuries.

1977 it was 95 per cent Merlot and 5 per cent Cabernet Franc.

Although it won a gold medal at the 1878 Paris International Exhibition, and the London-based WINE SOCIETY listed the 1893, Pétrus received little international attention until the remarkable, tiny crop of 1945, and the much more widely distributed 1947. Its exceptional concentration of colour, bouquet, and richness of flavour derives from a pocket of clay in the middle of the vineyard and the subsoil which affords exceptionally good DRAINAGE. Average production is 3,500 to 4,000 cases.

However, its fame is largely owing to M. Jean-Pierre MOUEIX of the Libourne merchants, who started his business before the Second World War. He took over the sole distribution of Pétrus in 1945, and, when Mme Loubat died in 1961, he acquired 50 per cent of the shareholding, while Mme Loubat's niece Mme Lily Lacoste inherited the other 50 per cent. The property is managed by Jean-Pierre Moueix's son Christian, assisted by the distinguished OENOLOGIST Jean-Claude Berrouet. The limited size of the property, and the availability of the Moueix team of pickers, mean that all the grapes can be harvested, at optimum ripeness, in half a day. FERMENTATION VESSELS are neither wood nor stainless steel, but mundane cement.

There is no official CLASSIFICATION of Pomerol, but Pétrus is unofficially recognized as a PREMIER CRU, and is distributed only through Moueix, with exclusive agents in the UK and restricted ones in the USA. It fetches a much higher price than any other red bordeaux, and at AUCTION achieves even higher prices relative to the rest. E.P.-R.

Coates, C., 'Ch Pétrus', *The Vine*, 31 (1987).

PETRUS DE CRESCENTIIS (1230–1310), Italian author whose writings on wine were much read in the Middle Ages (see LITERATURE OF WINE). Petrus de Crescentiis finished his *Liber commodorum ruralium* ('Book on agriculture') in 1303. Only part of his book, Book 4, is concerned with wine. He knows and quotes from the classical writers on agriculture (mainly PLINY, COLUMELLA, and VARRO) but he is no mere slavish follower of his authorities, for he has a great deal to say about medieval WINE-MAKING practice and his advice is reliable.

The ancients loved old wine, but Petrus knew that medieval wine was a different matter; if wine was kept in a wooden BARREL instead of an impermeable earthenware AMPHORA, it would not last long. Most medieval wine was drunk within a year of the vintage, but sweet or highly alcoholic wines, as some Mediterranean wines were, kept longer. Petrus divides wines into three categories: new (under a year); old (four years); and between new and old. New wine, he says, has no digestive or diuretic properties but inflates the belly. Old wine is bitter and can be off; unless it is mixed with water, it goes to the head. Two-year-old wine is best. Petrus also points out that TOPPING UP casks of wine is essential in order to stop the wine turning into vinegar; alternatively, a layer of olive oil can be floated on the surface of the wine. He also explains how to achieve the RACKING of a wine from one cask into another.

Given the soundness of his advice and the clarity of his prose style, it is not surprising that Petrus' book should have been popular. It survives in many manuscripts and early printed editions. By the end of the 15th century it had been translated into German, French, and Italian. H.M.W.

Marescalchi, A., and Dalmasso, G. (eds.), *Storia della vite e del vino in Italia*, 3 vols. (Milan, 1933).
Savastano, L. G., *Contribute allo studio critico degli scrittori agrari italici* (Acireale, 1922).

PEYNAUD, ÉMILE (1912–), Bordeaux oenologist whose work had a profound and world-wide impact on wine-making and wine appreciation in the second half of the 20th century. After the Second World War Peynaud worked with Jean RIBÉREAU-GAYON ('the father of modern wine science'), before joining him at BORDEAUX UNIVERSITY Institut d'Oenologie, while employed by the house of Calvet. It was here, in the late 1940s, that he began to advise numerous BORDEAUX châteaux on their wine-making. Because this consultancy work was the activity for which he later became best known, it is perhaps easy to forget his achievements as a taster, scientist, and teacher.

Peynaud wanted to understand the detail of the wine-making process, to eliminate its hitherto haphazard nature, and to produce consistently clean-tasting and healthy wines. Many of the practices that now seem unexceptional in wine-making were by no means axiomatic in the 1950s, and they are rooted in changes resulting from his wide-ranging scientific research. Among these were the complete control of MALOLACTIC FERMENTATION, the understanding that quality starts in the vineyard with good-quality grapes, that red grapes should be fully ripe when picked, that dark grapes' skins (containing the PHENOLICS so crucial to red wine aromas and textures) should be treated more gently with softer CRUSHING, better-controlled fermentation temperatures, shorter MACERATION, and more moderate PRESSING of the skins for the PRESS WINE. Each technique aimed at improving the flavour and texture of the resulting finished wine.

Taste became the arbiter in wine-making decisions, and it underlay the other cardinal principle of his: selection. Select only healthy grapes when picking, vinify the produce of plots of vines of markedly different age or quality separately, choose only the best vats to be incorporated in the principal wine, and so on. Peynaud himself describes his method as 'monitoring the whole process of wine-making from grape to bottle' and this is the subject of his first book, *Connaissance et travail du vin*.

Peynaud considered the ability to taste accurately as essential to good wine-making as a thorough grasp of OENOLOGY. He says in his second book, *Le Goût du vin*, 'I am not sure whether I have contributed most by making tasting an introduction to oenology or oenology an introduction to tasting.' *Le Goût du vin* is as comprehensive and lucid on tasting wine as his first book was on making wine. It aimed to educate the palates not only of wine-makers but of wine drinkers too. He was acutely aware of their symbiotic relationship.

Critics used to complain that his wine-making methods so marked the wines that they were losing their individuality, a criticism based largely on cask tastings where the wines were notable for their emphatic ripe fruit allied to supple textures. Mature bottles, however, though approachable earlier, age well too, with both distinction and individuality. Peynaud would have left his mark on the wine world had his gifts been limited to scientist, technician, and possessor of a refined palate; that his influence has been so widespread is due to his additional great gift as a teacher and communicator.

M.W.E.S.

Parnell, C., 'Émile Peynaud, Man of the Year', *Decanter* (Mar. 1990), 36–40.
Peynaud, É., *Connaissance et travail du vin* (Paris, 1981).
—— *The Taste of Wine* (London, 1987).
Suckling, J., and Matthews, T., 'Émile Peynaud', *Wine Spectator* (31 Aug. 1989), 89–93.

PFALZ, until recently known as **Rheinpfalz**, is an important wine region in southern GERMANY in terms of both quantity and quality. The 22,630 ha/55,920 acres of vineyard follow the eastern edge of the high lying woods of the Pfalz Forest for a distance of about 80 km/50 miles. See map on p. 442. Away from the trees, and viewed from a satellite, they would seem to reach in finger-like strips 8 km or so into the plain, which stretches a further 12 km to the Rhine. In some of the villages of the district in the southern half, the Bereich Südliche Weinstrasse, vines occupy as much as 93 per cent of the available land. Only parts of valleys at risk from cold air remain unplanted, and in this Bereich viticulture has expanded greatly in the last 25 years. To the north of Neustadt in the Bereich Mittelhaardt/Deutsche Weinstrasse, there are vineyards with internationally known names, thanks to wine estates with such historic reputations as Bassermann-Jordan,

Bürklin-Wolf, and von Buhl, but the quality of some of the wine-making elsewhere in the Rheinpfalz is so high that Ruppertsberg, Forst, Deidesheim, Wachenheim, Bad Dürkheim, and Kallstadt no longer have a monopoly of the best wines. The Pfalz has become one of the most exciting regions for the wine lover to visit.

The Deutsche Weinstrasse, the German wine route, was set up in 1935 to link some 40 villages on a north–south axis, and to strengthen the regional identity. The July temperature easily exceeds the average of 18 °C / 64 °F which is considered essential by local growers for growing vines in Germany, and it is characteristic of the general climate of the region that spring sets in early. Summers are long and warm, clouds are held back by the forest, and, in the north of the region in particular, rainfall is light.

The Bereich Südliche Weinstrasse has a reputation for being dedicated to a high yield of indifferent-quality grapes. This still applies to producers who supply the market for cheap wine in bulk, but it is no longer true for the district as a whole. Some 38 per cent of Pfalz wines are bottled by merchants outside the region who supply basic wine to supermarkets at home and abroad, and much of this wine originates in the Bereich Südliche Weinstrasse. Where there are high yields in Germany there are MÜLLER-THURGAU vines and in the Bereich Südliche Weinstrasse this variety covers 28 per cent of the vineyards in production. KERNER accounts for 14 per cent and MORIO-MUSKAT, a vine with a high yield, and the classic RIESLING each occupy about nine per cent. There is also a wide range of the GERMAN CROSSINGS introduced in the 1960s and 1970s.

On the best estates in the Bereich Mittelhaardt / Deutsche Weinstrasse, Riesling plays an important part, sometimes as the only vine. The Riesling area is increasing and may well reach 5,000 ha / 12,300 acres by the middle of the 1990s. The SCHEUREBE vine reaches a peak of quality in this northern district of the Pfalz that is seldom matched elsewhere in the world, and in response to a strong demand on the home market for red wine, Spätburgunder (PINOT NOIR) is rapidly expanding its 630 ha / 1,600 acres.

Traminer (see GEWÜRZTRAMINER) was regarded as a speciality of the Pfalz in the early 19th century and although the annual production of Forster Traminer scarcely exceeded 2,200 dozen bottles, the wine appeared on practically all wine lists, according to the historian Bassermann-Jordan. Nowadays there are some 330 ha of Traminer but the wine's strong aroma seems to have limited its appeal. Even Pfalz Riesling had a more pronounced flavour in the late 1970s, with a quite unmistakable taste of the soil. The full, slightly oxidized style (see OXIDATION) has been largely replaced by a more elegant, almost RHEINGAU-like balance. The acidity is higher than in the past, the flavour is long, and, of course, many of the best Pfalz Rieslings are dry. Across the region, over a quarter of all wines are now dry (TROCKEN), with less than 9 g / l RESIDUAL SUGAR. Rheinpfalz wines have the advantage to a non-German palate of more BODY than most dry wines from the northern regions, and more alcohol. Because of its climate the Pfalz is ideally placed to produce the types of wine which the market needs. On the one hand there are stylish Rieslings and Scheurebes with high ACIDITY, and on the other an increasing supply of interesting wines from the Burgunder, or PINOT, family. On some estates the Ruländer (PINOT GRIS) grapes are placed in two buckets at the harvest. Those grapes showing signs of NOBLE ROT produce a full, slightly dark coloured, deep flavoured wine, and from the non-BOTRYTIZED grapes placed in a separate bucket a lighter, lively, clean dry wine is made and sold under the name Grauburgunder. In a vintage with no BOTRYTIS BUNCH ROT this process is unnecessary, and Grauburgunder wines with a high alcohol content can be produced from ripe but healthy grapes.

Good Rheinpfalz Spätburgunders resemble a cross between the soft wines of the past with low TANNINS and a red BURGUNDY. Their yields (60 to 80 hl / ha (3.5–4.5 tons / acre)) are higher than those of Burgundy but many of the vines are young and at their most productive phase. This may account for a certain lack of complexity. A natural ALCOHOLIC STRENGTH of over 13 per cent is not unusual, and if the structure of the wine often betrays the cooler climate in which the grapes are grown, perhaps this is the start of a modern Pfalz style of Spätburgunder. It is based on a clean, dry, fruity flavour without any of the farmyard smells that can come from partially rotten grapes. Extreme oaky flavours from new wood, which mask the individuality of wine, are being muted as BARREL MATURATION is mastered; in some cases it has been replaced by storage in larger casks treated in the traditional way to eliminate any WOOD FLAVOUR.

The older style of light Pfalz red wine, sometimes a little sweet, is still widely represented by PORTUGIESER which covered 2,000 ha / 4,942 acres, and thus about nine per cent of the region in 1990. This undemanding vine is normally allowed to produce a high yield of reddish wine, but, on the rare occasions when the crop is limited, the improvement in concentration and quality is considerable, even if, unfortunately, less profitable. The DORNFELDER crossing is successful on good estates where it has something of the charm of the good BEAUJOLAIS without the same length of flavour.

The substantial houses in the villages between Bad Dürkheim and Neustadt show the relative prosperity and, therefore quality of the wine-making over the last 200 years. Many of the best sites on gently sloping ground at Deidesheim and Forst have been modernized and rebuilt in the 1980s (see FLURBEREINIGUNG), so that the mainly Riesling vines are still young. Quality is expected to rise during the 1990s. There is a handful of 20 or 25 outstanding good sites, but of the 359 individual vineyards in the Pfalz, many have no distinguishing characteristics and therefore hardly justify the use of their name on wine labels. As some of the co-operative cellars admit, differences of flavour in their cheaper wines derive more from the grape variety than the vineyard. Where some hitherto little-known villages are becoming more familiar, it is through the achievements of individual wine-makers.

Mechanical harvesting is rapidly becoming the norm, even in such a traditional **Old World** region as Bordeaux. Here in the Côtes de **Castillon** the labour savings are sufficient to have resulted in higher, more widely spaced vine rows; only the grander estates of the **Médoc** on the other side of the **Gironde** claim they will never succumb.

Amongst the up and coming village names, judged in this way, are Laumersheim, Grosskarlbach, Freinsheim, and Herxheim in the north of the region, and Burrweiler, Siebeldingen, Birkweiler, and Leinsweiler in the south.

An increasing amount of Pfalz wine is being made into sparkling wine in the 1990s (see SEKT). Technical specifications have been set high by an association of producers, with much attention being paid to the quality of the base wine, either from Riesling, Weissburgunder (PINOT BLANC), or Spätburgunder. Only the FREE-RUN juice from unpressed grapes and that which flows from the first pressing is used. Others may work to less exacting standards (see SPARKLING WINE-MAKING).

Of the 11,500 vine-growers in the region, about two-thirds deliver their grapes to co-operative cellars, producers' associations, or merchants' cellars. Some growers own small parcels of land in the best-known sites of the Bereich Mittelhaardt / Deutsche Weinstrasse where the standards and reputation of the local CO-OPERATIVES are high. In the Bereich Südliche Weinstrasse the co-operative cellars are known for their pleasant, true-to-type, medium-price, drier wines, sold under grape names. This is the style of wine for those who wish to progress from LIEBFRAUMILCH and yet know not where to go. An indication of the success of the best co-operative cellars is the growing percentages of wine that they sell in bottle, rather than on the depressed bulk wine market.

About 4,500 growers, owning nearly 60 per cent of the region's vineyard, make wine which they sell in bulk to the trade. A further 650 growers estate bottle their own wine. The attraction of the wooded hills of the Pfalz Forest, which rise to over 680 m / 2,231 ft in parts, draws many visitors from the towns along the Rhine, and so much wine is sold directly to the consumer. I.J.

PH, a scale of measurement of the concentration of the effective, active ACIDITY in a solution and an important statistic, of relevance to how vines grow, how grapes ripen, and how wine tastes, looks, and lasts. (The technical definition is that pH is the negative logarithm of the all-important hydrogen ion activity or concentration.) Low values of pH indicate high concentrations of acidity and the tart or sour taste that occurs in lemon juice, for example. Values near 7 are effectively neutral; drinking waters have pH values near 7. Values between 7 and 14 are found in basic or alkaline solutions such as caustic or washing soda. Grape must and wine are acidic, with pHs generally between 3 and 4. The scale is logarithmic so a solution with a pH value of 3 has 10 times as much hydrogen ion activity as one whose pH value is 4.

Soils

The pH of soils is relevant to the resultant wine. Soils high in POTASSIUM, as in some dry areas where there was once an inland sea (such as inland Australia), produce wines with moderate to high pH values because of the high levels of potassium in the grape skins. Soils high in LIMESTONE tend to have high pH values, between 8 and 9, and in general limit plant growth, although the grapevine is one of the domesticated plants most tolerant of such inhospitable soils. Poorly drained soils high in ORGANIC MATTER tend to have acid pH values, between 5 and 6, which are also unfavourable to vine growth. IRRIGATION and soils high in NITROGEN encourage vines to produce excessively large crops and can yield grapes with lower concentrations of organic acids and therefore higher pH values. See also SOIL ACIDITY.

Grapes

The pH of grapes as well as wines can vary enormously since TEMPERATURE, RAINFALL, SOIL TYPE, viticultural practices, and VINE VARIETIES can all influence the different natural organic acids and minerals of mature grapes. In general, cool regions produce wines with low pH and hot regions produce wines with high pH. Part of the reason why white wines generally have a lower pH than red wines is that there is a greater concentration in the red wines of potassium, which is extracted from the grape skin, where this ion is concentrated. See also GRAPE and ACIDITY.

Wines

The pH range of most wines is between 2.9 and 4.2 (which incidentally, since the pH of the normal stomach is about 2, means that wines are 10 to 100 times less concentrated in the acid hydrogen ion than is the stomach interior). Wines with low pHs taste very tart while those with high pHs taste flat, or 'flabby'. Wines whose pH is between 3.2 and 3.5 not only tend to taste refreshingly rather than piercingly acid, they are also more resistant to harmful BACTERIA, age better, and have a clearer, brighter colour (see below). Wines with pH values higher than this suffer from tasting flat, looking dull, and also from being more susceptible to bacterial attack.

While it is possible to manipulate pH values, with grapes and wines it is impractical because of the wine's high buffer capacity. Resistance to pH change during wine-making is measured by what chemists called buffer capacity, which roughly correlates with total acidity. The pH can be increased by decreasing the concentration of hydrogen ions, however, and vice versa. (See ACIDIFICATION and DEACIDIFICATION for discussion of the legal and practical aspects of these operations.)

The wine-maker is interested in both the pH and the TOTAL ACIDITY (both the fixed and volatile acids) of both the grape juice and the resultant wine for several reasons. What one tastes in wines as the tart or sour sensation is influenced both by the total amount of acids present and by the concentration of hydrogen ions in the solution. Different YEASTS and bacteria have varying tolerances for hydrogen ion concentration and for the nature and concentration of the acid. Finally, the resistance of the wine to changes of effective acidity (hydrogen ion concentration) during processing and STABILIZATION depends mainly on the total acid concentration.

The **colour** of wine can provide valuable clues in **blind tasting**. Whatever its initial hue, wine becomes browner with age, while deeper colours are associated with very ripe grapes and / or youth in the case of red wines. The top row (left to right) demonstrates a very young Mosel, a young Loire, a two- and then 10-year-old white burgundy. The bottom row (left to right) shows a very young and then 10-year-old good-quality Cabernet Sauvignon, an ordinary commercial red table wine designed to be drunk at this early point in its evolution, and an example of the sort of tawny colour eventually acquired by very old wines, both red and white initially, after a century or more in bottle.

Keeping wine pH values low is of further importance because the hydrogen ion concentration of the wine controls the effectiveness of SULPHUR DIOXIDE. Sulphur dioxide gas, when dissolved in wine, reacts with the water in the wine to form sulphurous acid, the form of the compound that is best at inhibiting bacteria and wild yeasts and countering OXIDATION. Sulphurous acid breaks down partially into hydrogen ions and bisulphite ions, a form having little effect on micro-organisms such as bacteria and wild yeasts. High hydrogen ion concentrations (low pH values) in the wine tend to combine with the bisulphite ions and thus keep more of the sulphur dioxide in the effective, anti-microbial form.

pH is also important in wine-making because the ANTHOCYANS that colour red wines exist in several forms of different colours. At low pH values, the high concentration of hydrogen ions forces the pigment molecule into a form with a positive charge and a bright red colour. As pH increases (and hydrogen ion concentration decreases), the pigment molecule tends more and more to change to a colourless form and eventually into a bluish or greyish form. The net result in the several pigments of red wine is a passage from bright to purplish red and finally to a dull brownish red as pH increases.

Measurement of pH is a familiar operation to those who maintain a garden, swimming pool, or aquarium. Probably the earliest measurement technique was the use of indicator solutions or papers dependent on the fact that many dyes change molecular form and colour as the hydrogen ion concentration, or pH, changes. More precise laboratory measurements use glass electrodes. A.D.W. & B.G.C.

PHENOLICS, sometimes called **polyphenolics** or **polyphenols**, very large group of highly reactive chemical compounds of which **phenol** (C_6H_5OH) is the basic building block. These include many natural colour pigments such as the ANTHOCYANS of fruit and dark-skinned grapes, most natural vegetable TANNINS such as occur in grapes, and many FLAVOUR COMPOUNDS.

In grapes

These compounds, made of benzene-OH units, occur in great profusion in grapes. They are particularly rich in stems, seeds and skins but also occur in juice and pulp. Phenols are more abundant in dark-skinned grapes than in white wine grapes, the anthocyan PIGMENTS being built from simpler molecules during RIPENING, from the stage known as VERAISON. The concentration of phenolics in grape skins increases if the berries are exposed to sunlight (see CANOPY MANAGEMENT).

Literally thousands of compounds belong to the phenolic category, and they can initially be classified as either non-flavonoid or flavonoid. The former are simpler and derived from cinnamic and benzoic acids; one of the most abundant in grape juice is caftaric acid, the tartrate ESTER of caffeic acid (esters between TARTARIC ACID and phenolic acids are common). Flavonoids encompass catechins, flavonols, and anthocyans. Many of these compounds belong to the general group known as secondary metabolites, meaning that they are not involved in the primary metabolism of the plant. They are highly water soluble and are secreted into the BERRY vacuole as a sort of waste product. Most have a sugar added, which increases their water solubility and incidentally changes their properties as, for instance, the aroma of FLAVOUR COMPOUNDS is removed. Catechins and other flavonoids also make up the structures called TANNINS which are an essential part of the taste and flavour of grapes and other fruits. B.G.C.

In wines

During wine-making, when the ripe grape is crushed, the skin cells containing pigments begin to lose these pigments to the acidic grape juice. Alcohol, produced by FERMENTATION, greatly speeds up this extraction process. Finally, during the MACERATION phase, equilibrium between the pigment in the skin cells and in the new wine is approached.

Anthocyan pigments in the young wine are not stable, however. They react rapidly with molecules of another phenolic type, the tannins, to form the complex pigments of a maturing red wine. Tannin polymers (see POLYMERIZATION) of moderate size taste bitter, while larger ones are responsible for the mouth-puckering astringency in young wines and stewed tea.

As the wine ages, the pigment complex forms larger and larger polymers which eventually exceed their solubility in the wine and precipitate as SEDIMENT. During BOTTLE AGEING, it is presumed (but not yet proven) that red wines undergo further slow reactions which gradually change the hue and intensity of the colour, and aroma and flavour become more complex, so that bottle BOUQUET may develop.

A significant number of flavour compounds also have the phenol structure as a basic part of a more complicated molecule. Notable among these are vanillin, the key aroma compound of the vanilla bean, and cinnamaldehyde, the impact compound of cinnamon bark. An ESTER, methyl salicylate, familiar as oil of wintergreen, is also a phenolic compound. These and many others are either grape constituents or are produced as trace components during alcoholic fermentation and the subsequent processing and ageing phases.

See also WOOD FLAVOUR for details of the part played by the phenolics in new OAK. A.D.W.

As a tasting term

Phenolic is also sometimes used, imprecisely, as a pejorative tasting term, to describe (usually white) wines which display an excess of phenolics by tasting astringent or bitter.

As health benefit

It is in its high phenolics content that red wine is distinguished from white, and it is thought that it may well be the anti-oxidative properties of phenolics which reduce the incidence of heart disease among those who consume moderate amounts of red wine. Research suggests that some phenolic compounds in red wines inhibit the oxidation of low-density lipoproteins, which are thought to be a major factor in building up potentially harmful levels of cholesterol in the arteries. See HEALTH, EFFECTS OF WINE CONSUMPTION ON.

Frankel, E. N., *et al.*, 'Inhibition of oxidation of human low-density lipoprotein by phenolic substances in red wine', *Lancet*, 341 (1993), 454–7.

Somers, T. C., and Verette, E., 'Phenolic composition of natural wine types', in H. F. Linskens and J. F. Jackson (eds.), *Wine Analysis*, Modern Methods of Plant Analysis, NS 6 (Berlin, 1988).

PHENOLOGY, the study of the sequence of plant development (see p. 724). As applied to vines, it records the timing of specific stages such as BUDBREAK, FLOWERING, VERAISON, and LEAF FALL. Such studies indicate the suitability of VINE VARIETIES to certain climatic zones. See VINE GROWTH CYCLE.

PHLOEM, the principal food-conducting tissue of the vine and other vascular plants. Phloem is composed of a strange mix of CELL types which lie alongside the XYLEM, the water-conducting tissue, and the combination makes up a system of veins or vascular bundles. Despite their proximity, phloem and xylem are entirely different: phloem has thin-walled tubes containing a strongly sugared sap under positive pressure which moves along from areas of strong to weak concentrations, while xylem consists of large, strong-walled tubes through which a dilute mineral solution moves under negative pressure (tension) by forces generated by TRANSPIRATION. During the thickening of woody parts, the CAMBIUM produces cells on the outside that become the new season's phloem; in later years these cells are added to the bark of the vine. Phloem of grapevine wood has the characteristic, unusual among deciduous trees, of reactivation after the next BUDBREAK and can remain functional for three to four years.

The vascular system permeates throughout the plant, but bundles of veins are particularly dense in the LEAF blade, as can be seen by holding it up to the light. This high density facilitates the loading of newly photosynthesized SUCROSE into the phloem tubes for its movement out of the leaf (see TRANSLOCATION). B.G.C.

PHOENICIA, ancient mercantile state covering modern LEBANON, extending slightly further north and slightly further south to encompass the cities of Ruad, Byblos, Beirut, Sidon, and Tyre. Vines and olives were grown on the rockier terrain, while the alluvial valleys were given over to grain. Independent Phoenician culture lasted from about 1400 BC to 322 (when Alexander the Great captured Tyre), but their greatest colony, CARTHAGE in modern Tunisia, survived until destroyed by the Romans in 146 BC.

Evidently the Phoenician colonists found in North Africa a fertile region ideal for viticultural development. The Graeco-Roman historian Diodorus Siculus describes the Carthaginian countryside as being (in the 4th century BC) full of vines, olives, and cattle, especially in the Bagradas valley and in southern Tunisia. The Carthaginian author Mago left an extensive treatise on agriculture, including instructions on viticulture. Unfortunately his work does not survive, but some citations from the Latin translation made by the Romans in 146 BC are preserved. The Roman agricultural writer COLUMELLA (1st century BC) quotes a recipe of Mago's for a DRIED GRAPE WINE or *passum* which he describes as *optimum* 'excellent—I myself have made it' (*De re rustica* 12. 39. 1). J.A.B.

Harden, D., *The Phoenicians* (London, 1962).

PHOMOPSIS, vine disease. See DEAD ARM.

PHOSPHORUS, one of the most important mineral elements required for vine growth, yet the amounts required are so small that for most vineyards, the supply from the soil is sufficient. There is only about 0.6 kg of phosphorus in a tonne of grapes (0.3 lb per ton). Phosphorus in the vine is an essential component of compounds involved in PHOTOSYNTHESIS and sugar–starch transformations as well as the transfer of energy. Phosphorus deficiency is rare, and found mostly on acid soils, but its symptoms are a gradual loss of VIGOUR and sometimes some red spots on the leaves. R.E.S.

PHOTOSYNTHESIS, a biochemical reaction which combines water and atmospheric CARBON DIOXIDE using the energy of the sun to form SUGARS in plants, including vines. Important in this process are the green chlorophyll pigments in leaves which capture the sun's energy. Photosynthesis is the essential first step in the wine-making process, as the sugars formed in photosynthesis, along with other chemical products derived from sugar, are transported to grape berries (see SUGAR IN GRAPES), and eventually fermented into ETHANOL to produce wine. (According to the neat laws of nature, humans eventually metabolize wine's ethanol back to carbon dioxide and water; see CARBON.)

Photosynthesis can be summarized by this chemical equation:

$$6\,CO_2 + 6\,H_2O + \text{light energy} = C_6H_{12}O_6 + 6\,O_2$$

carbon dioxide + water + sunlight = sugar + oxygen

The process of photosynthesis maintains atmospheric supplies of OXYGEN, essential for animal life on earth. Since these reactions take place inside the vine leaf, carbon dioxide must be able to diffuse in and oxygen out. This takes place through minute pores called STOMATA on the underside of vine leaves.

Photosynthesis is affected by environmental and plant factors, all of which have an effect on grape RIPENING and hence wine quality. Light, temperature, and WATER STRESS are the three most important climatic controls. Photosynthesis is limited by low light levels, as, for example, under overcast conditions or for shaded leaves away from the canopy surface. Light levels of about one per cent of full sunlight are too low for photosynthesis. Photosynthesis increases almost linearly with light up to about one-third full sunlight, and then is said to be light saturated, in that any further increase in sunlight intensity will not increase photosynthesis. So outside leaves on vine canopies are often light saturated in sunny conditions, and some sunlight is wasted.

Photosynthesis is highest with leaf temperatures from about 15 to 30 °C (59–86 °F), with a slight peak at about

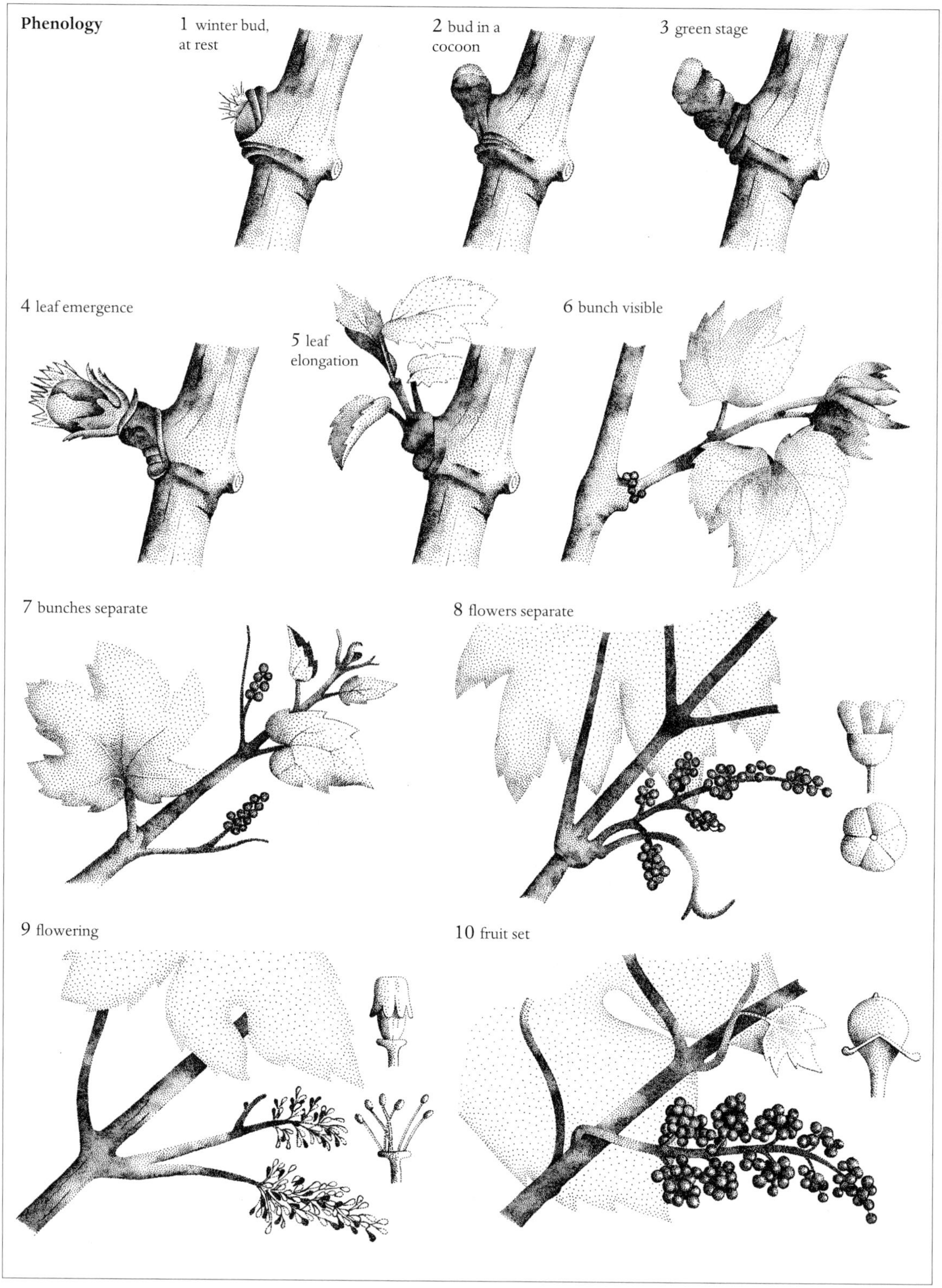
Phenology
1 winter bud, at rest
2 bud in a cocoon
3 green stage
4 leaf emergence
5 leaf elongation
6 bunch visible
7 bunches separate
8 flowers separate
9 flowering
10 fruit set

25 °C. Photosynthesis is severely inhibited for temperatures below 15 °C and above 30 °C. During one day in hot DESERT regions, vine leaf photosynthesis can be inhibited by both low temperatures in the morning and high temperatures in the afternoon. Low temperatures limit photosynthesis and hence grape ripening in cool climate wine regions such as those of northern Europe. High-quality vintages there are warm, sunny years when photosynthesis is highest.

Dry soil conditions will cause STOMATA to close, thus interfering with photosynthesis, but saving the vine from further desiccation. Such an effect of water stress on photosynthesis and grape ripening can be seen in many of the world's wine regions, typically in MEDITERRANEAN CLIMATES. The vine can, however, tolerate a mild water stress with no negative effect on wine quality, indeed it may even be enhanced. Wind also can cause stomata to close and interfere with grape ripening, as is common in MONTEREY in California, for example.

A general rule, then, is that photosynthesis is enhanced by sunny conditions and mild temperatures. These are the conditions which are known to give maximal sugar concentration in grapes and, conventionally, the best wine quality. R.E.S.

Champagnol, F., *Éléments de physiologie de la vigne et de viticulture générale* (St-Gely-du-Fesc, 1984).

Mullins, M. G., Bouquet, A., and Williams, L., *Biology of the Vine* (Cambridge, 1992).

Winkler, A. J., *et al.*, *General Viticulture* (2nd edn., Berkeley, Calif., 1974).

PHYLLOXERA. This small yellow root-feeding aphid has probably had a more damaging impact on wine production than any other VINE PEST, or any VINE DISEASE. It attacks only grapevines, and kills vines by attacking their roots. For many years there was no known cure.

The effects of phylloxera were first noted in France in 1863 (see below), just as Europe was recovering from another great scourge of 19th century European viticulture: oidium, or POWDERY MILDEW, which was first noted in 1847. Like powdery mildew, and the other FUNGAL DISEASES yet to arrive (DOWNY MILDEW in 1878 and BLACK ROT in 1885), the phylloxera louse was an unwelcome import from America which devastated European vineyards until appropriate control measures were found. In the history of agriculture it rivals the potato blight of Ireland as a plant disease with widespread social effects. In France, for example, almost 2.5 million ha/6.2 million acres of vineyards were destroyed, the aphid making no distinction between the vineyards of the most famous châteaux and those of humble peasants. For individual French vine-growers from the late 1860s, the sight of their vineyards dying literally before their eyes was particularly traumatic, although the epidemic soon spread elsewhere. Phylloxera invasion had a major social and economic impact, involving national governments and local committees, and requiring international scientific collaboration. For a while the very existence of the French wine industry was threatened.

Phylloxera has had several scientific names. Initially called *Phylloxera vastatrix* (the devastator) by the French scientist J.-E. Planchon, and also *Phylloxera vitifoliae* (A. Fitch), it is now more correctly known as *Dactylasphaera vitifoliae* (H. Shimer). See below for more detail.

Biology

The female phylloxera is yellow coloured and about 1 mm/0.039 in long. Surrounded by masses of eggs, it is barely visible to the naked eye as it feeds on the roots. There are four to seven generations in the summer, each producing females capable of laying more eggs. As the eggs hatch, so-called 'crawlers' move to other roots of the vine, and some climb the trunk and can spread to other vines, or even vineyards, by the action of wind or machinery dislodging them from the foliage. Because of the movement of the crawlers through soil cracks, phylloxera tends to spread in a circle from the original infected vine. Wind-blown crawlers create secondary infections downwind.

It has a complex life cycle, existing in both root-living and leaf-living forms, and causes damage to vines by injecting saliva to produce galls, by feeding on the sap, and by causing root deformities.

In humid regions there is also an associated life cycle whereby the root-hatched nymph produces a winged form which can travel longer distances, and which lays male and female eggs. The hatching female in turn lays a winter egg which develops into the stem mother or fundatrix, which lays eggs in a leaf gall (these galls typically being produced only on the leaves of American vines). Nymphs hatching from leaf galls can begin new infections as egg-laying females on roots.

The principal agent for the spread of phylloxera is man. It is most commonly transported from one vineyard to another on the roots of ROOTLINGS (one-year-old dormant plants). However, phylloxera is easily moved in the soil that sticks to implements, and by irrigation water. Recent research in New Zealand has shown that crawlers present in the vine foliage lead to secondary spread over considerable distances; they are moved by machines such as foliage trimmers and harvesters which brush against foliage, and also by wind.

Phylloxera is native to the east coast of the United States, and so native AMERICAN VINE SPECIES have generally evolved with resistance. Studies have shown that the basis of resistance is the development of cork layers beneath the wound made by phylloxera feeding on the root. This stops the invasion of other microbes (bacteria and fungi) which eventually rot the root and kill non-resistant vines.

Phylloxera kills vines which have not developed this resistance, such as the European VINIFERA vine species from which most wine is made, by destroying the root system. When first present, the phylloxera numbers build up quickly on roots and there is little apparent root damage. After a few years the root rot affects the top growth, shoot growth is stunted, and leaves lose their healthy green colour. Normally a vine dies within several years of the first infection. Vines which are struggling for other reasons are the more susceptible to phylloxera and succumb quickly. Those growing on deep, fertile soil can continue to produce economic crops for many years after phylloxera attack. Phylloxera does not

Life cycle of **phylloxera** (*Dactylasphaera vitifoliae*)

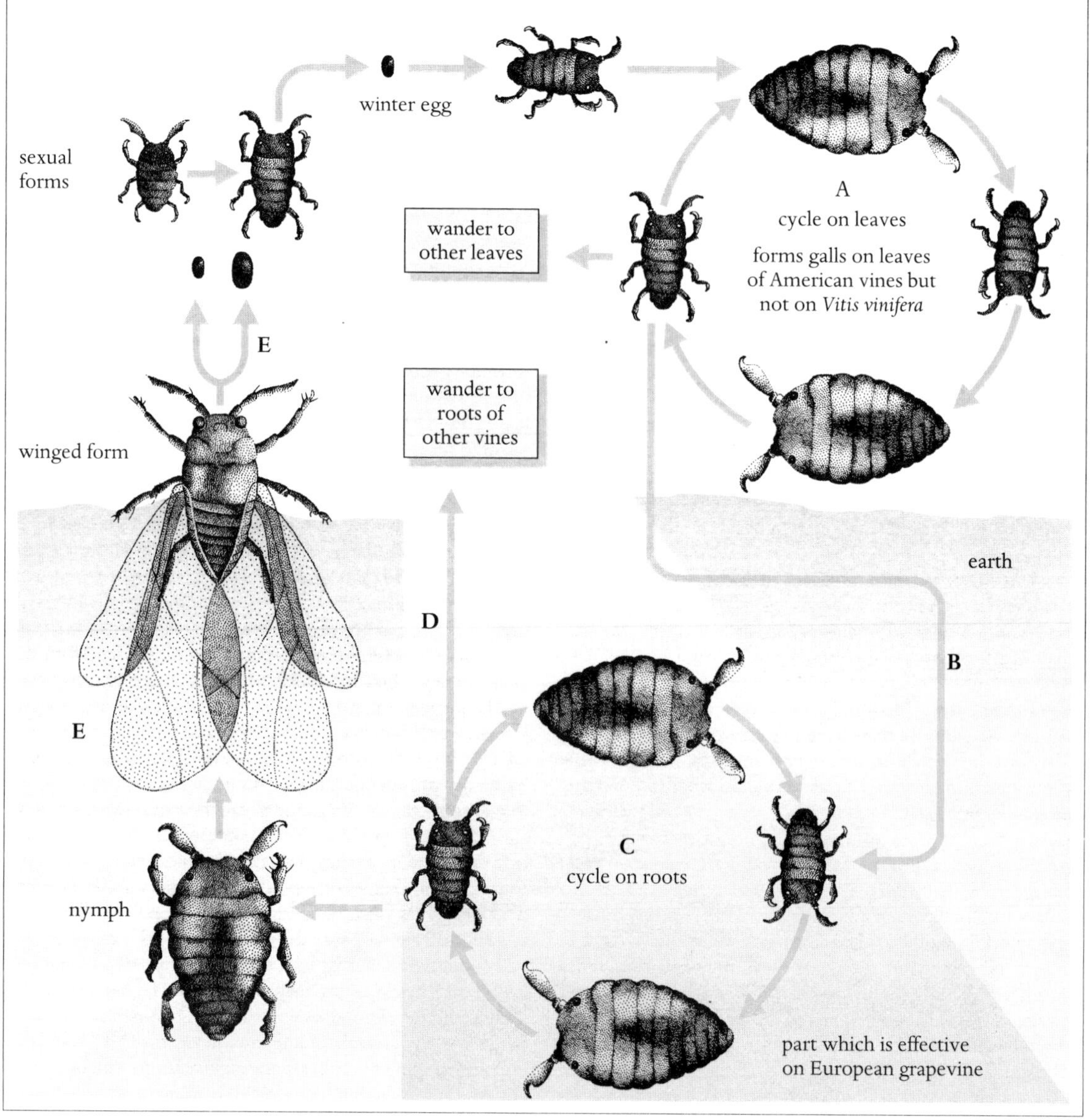

survive well in sandy soil, so vines planted in sand (such as on the Great Plain of HUNGARY, those planted by Listel on the French Mediterranean coast, or COLARES in Portugal) are immune from attack.

History

Attempts by early European colonists in North America to establish imported *vinifera* vines met with disaster, presumably substantially because of phylloxera, to which they had no resistance—although at this time phylloxera had yet to be identified, and other American vine diseases such as PIERCE'S DISEASE in Florida, downy and powdery mildew in all regions, and the very cold winters doubtless played a part. See UNITED STATES, history, for more details.

How did phylloxera come to Europe? In the mid 19th century there was a considerable importation of living plants into Europe. This trade was supported by wealthy people who could afford elaborate gardens, greenhouses, and conservatories, and encouraged by the Victorians' keen interest in botany. Plants could be imported dormant, or kept alive and protected from salt spray by the ingenious Ward case, a closed glass container mounted on the deck of the ship and not unlike today's terrariums. In 1865 alone, 460 tons of plants worth 230,000 francs were imported into France, and this trade had grown to 2,000 tons by the 1890s. In 1875 50 tons were imported from the USA and much of this was vines. Jules Planchon, Professor of Pharmacy at MONTPELLIER University, noted that rooted American vines were imported in particularly significant quantities between 1858 and 1862, and sent to parts of Europe as far apart as Bordeaux, England, Ireland, Alsace, Germany, and Portugal. No doubt phylloxera was an unsuspected passenger on vine roots at the same time.

Just like the fungal disease powdery mildew, the first reporting of phylloxera was in England, in 1863, when Professor J. O. Westwood, a famous entomologist at Oxford University, received insect samples from a greenhouse in Hammersmith, a London suburb. Since the insects were in a leaf gall, the vine species was probably American, and these plants may even have been a source of introduction of the pest to England. In 1863 an unknown vine disease in France was being talked about, with two vineyards in the southern Rhône affected. The first printed report in France was a letter written by a veterinarian in 1867 about a vineyard planted in 1863 at St-Martin-de-Crau (only about 30 km / 20 miles north east of the University of Montpellier's modern phylloxera-free domaines on the Mediterranean coast, ironically), which developed unhealthy vines in summer 1866, failing to grow the following spring. It is likely that infection occurred several years beforehand. There were other reports from Narbonne in the Languedoc, and the Gard and Vaucluse *départements* in the southern Rhône in 1867, and from Bordeaux in 1869. (It was usually several years after the initial sighting that the louse's predations had a serious effect; the Médoc, for example, was not commercially compromised until the late 1870s.)

The first of many committees formed to resolve the phylloxera question was a Commission instigated by the Vaucluse Agricultural Society. On 15 July 1868 it began its investigation of affected vineyards in the southern Rhône. One member of the Commission was Jules Planchon, who had good training to work on phylloxera. He had spent a period at Kew Botanical Gardens in England, and subsequently became the brother-in-law of J. Lichtenstein, an amateur entomologist. Planchon noticed that dying vines had small yellow insects on their roots and noted the resemblance to an aphid *Phylloxera quercus* living on oak trees. He named the insect believed to be ravaging vineyards *Phylloxera vastatrix*. The form previously described by A. Fitch as living in the leaf galls of American vines was established by Planchon to be the same insect and therefore, according to the rules of priority, it became known as *Phylloxera vitifolii* (Fitch).

The Hérault Commission made its findings public in August 1868 but these caused little interest in any but the local newspapers. There was a marked reluctance to accept that this little yellow insect could be causing such devastation. Other explanations current at the time were over-production, winter cold and other bad weather, weakening of the vineyards as a result of continued vegetative reproduction, soil exhaustion, and also God's wrath at contemporary vices (which may sound familiar to modern readers). Even eminent scientists of the time misdiagnosed the problem. The distinguished entomologist V. Signoret thought phylloxera was an effect not the cause, and Dr GUYOT thought its presence was due to over-severe pruning (the opposite of overcropping)! The debate was ended by the 1869 Commission of the Société des Agriculteurs de France headed by L. Vialla, who gently but firmly debunked all false theories.

Total French wine production fell from a peak of 84.5 million hl / 2,200 million gal in 1875 to a mere 23.4 million hl in 1889. But even by June 1873 the French government was sufficiently alarmed by the spread of phylloxera to offer a large prize (300,000 francs) for a remedy, which was to be verified by experimentation carried out by the School of Agriculture at Montpellier. Up to October 1876, 696 suggestions were forwarded to Professors Durand and Jeannenot at Montpellier and between 1872 and 1876 1,044 treatments were evaluated. Among the deluge of suggestions submitted were those verging on the ridiculous, which included burying a living toad under the vine to draw the poison, and irrigating the vines with white wine. Entries were received from other countries as different as Denmark and Singapore. All of this work, however, produced little benefit, as only two treatments based on the chemical application of various forms of SULPHIDES appeared to show much advantage. Surprisingly, carbon bisulphide failed in the evaluation even though it was later used extensively.

Early attempts at commercial control of phylloxera included FLOODING, which was studied by the Commission in 1873. It was found that flooding in winter for weeks on end controlled the pest, but of course few vineyards were near enough to water supplies or sufficiently flat for this to be a widespread solution (although it is still used in parts of Argentina). Vineyards on sandy soils were noted to be immune, although this offered no control. The injection of the liquid carbon bisulphide was to become widespread, so that by 1888 some 68,000 ha / 168,000 acres had been treated. The insecticidal properties of carbon bisulphide were found in 1854 on grain weevils, and Baron Paul Thénard evaluated it in Bordeaux in 1869. The first experiments used too high a dose, severely affecting the vines, but subsequently the practice of injecting it, mixed with water, into the soil, using about 30,000 holes per ha, became widespread.

By the time of the International Phylloxera Congress at Bordeaux in 1881 two distinct schools of thought on how the industry might be saved had emerged. The chemists considered salvation lay in carbon bisulphide or related chemicals, or in flooding. In opposition were the 'Americanists', who advocated grafting desired varieties on to American vine species used as ROOTSTOCKS. Gaston Bazille had suggested GRAFTING in 1869 and Leo Laliman of Bordeaux drew early attention to the resistance of these species to the phylloxera. Laliman had studied the resistance of American species to powdery mildew in a collection in his vineyards since 1840. (He subsequently tried to claim the prize for controlling phylloxera.)

Following successful demonstrations of the ability of American vines to withstand phylloxera, and the visit of Planchon to America in 1873 where his study was guided by the noted scientist C. V. Riley, the use of grafted vines began, rising from 2,500 ha in 1880 to 45,000 ha in 1885. All was not plain sailing, however. Many American species could not tolerate the calcareous soils of France (see CHLOROSIS), the amount of grafting to be done was almost overwhelming, and also there was a concern that the use of these foreign rootstocks (whose own wine is so often reviled for its FOXY flavour) might affect wine quality. The latter objection is voiced by the uneducated even today, and in Burgundy the importation of American vines was prohibited until 1887, although the clandestine activities of growers anxious to save their vineyards forced its repeal.

Eventually rootstock use became the established method for the control of phylloxera and this has had a dramatic effect on vine NURSERY operations world-wide. There was a period in the late 19th century, however, when it was thought that breeding HYBRIDS of European with American vine varieties might produce vines with sufficient phylloxera resistance not to need grafting, whose wines were not marked by the undesirable foxy flavour of some American grapes. The class of varieties so created is loosely termed FRENCH HYBRIDS or DIRECT PRODUCERS. These efforts were generally unsuccessful, however, in that the vines had inadequate phylloxera tolerance and produced lower-quality wine, although they became popular with growers because of their high yields and their tolerance of FUNGAL DISEASES. Nevertheless, many of the rootstocks used today (see ROOTSTOCKS for a detailed list) were bred in this period—although hybrids with *vinifera* as one parent have been generally found to have insufficient tolerance to phylloxera (see below).

Geography

Phylloxera is now widespread around the world, having been found in California (1873), Portugal (1871), Turkey (1871), Austria (1872), Switzerland (1874), Italy (1875), Australia (1877), Spain (1878), Algeria (1885), South Africa (1885), New Zealand (1885), and Greece (1898). There are few parts of the world free from the pest, although these include parts of Australia (on which a strict QUARANTINE is imposed), parts of China, Chile, Argentina, India, Pakistan, and Afghanistan, and some Mediterranean islands such as Crete, Cyprus, and Rhodes.

There are also small sandy vineyards in otherwise affected wine regions (see BOLLINGER and COLARES) which have never been affected by phylloxera either because of isolation or because of the soil composition.

For much of the late 20th century phylloxera has not been regarded as a serious problem, either because it was not known in a region, or because a wide range of rootstocks are available which are suited to different varieties, soil, and climate conditions along with tolerance to other pests such as NEMATODES. About 85 per cent of all the world's vineyards were estimated in 1990 to be grafted on to rootstocks presumed to be resistant to phylloxera.

Phylloxera has been noted in the 1980s, however, on ungrafted vines in parts of Greece, England, New Zealand, Australia, Oregon, and, most dramatically, on grafted vines in California where the so-called 'biotype B' strain of phylloxera has been identified. The widely used rootstock AXR1 (see ROOTSTOCKS for details) was found to offer insufficient phylloxera tolerance, and a significant proportion of grafted vineyards in Napa and Sonoma succumbed to phylloxera and are being replanted in the 1990s.

Phylloxera is known to occur naturally as a number of related strains or 'biotypes'. King and Rilling exchanged phylloxera and vine cuttings between New Zealand and Germany, and confirmed evidence of the biotype differences between the two countries. Interestingly, the AXR1 rootstock was found not to be affected by phylloxera found in New Zealand, but it was affected by German phylloxera. New Zealand probably obtained phylloxera from California since the industry has used DAVIS as a prime source of planting material.

No doubt one of the most important effects of the phylloxera invasion of the world's vineyards was the inadvertent spread of VIRUS DISEASES. As grafting became widespread towards the end of the 19th century, virus diseases were also spread as a common result of grafting, because virus-infected cuttings were used in grafting. A virus originally present only in the rootstock would spread to the fruiting *vinifera* variety after grafting. Rootstocks do not show virus symptoms, and virology in viticulture was not well understood until the 1950s. With known effects on fruit ripening, perhaps it was virus diseases more than grafting which led to the debate as to the relative merits of 'PRE-PHYLLOXERA' and 'post-phylloxera' wines. R.E.S.

Boubals, D., 'La Realité internationale relative au phylloxera', *Progrès agricole et viticole*, 108 (1991), 494–6.

Buchanan, G. A., and Amos, T. G., 'Grape pests', in B. G. Coombe and P. R. Dry (eds.), *Viticulture, ii: Practices* (Adelaide, 1992).

King, P. D., and Rilling, G., 'Further evidence of phylloxera biotypes: variations in the tolerance of mature grapevine roots related to the geographical origin of the insect', *Vitis*, 30 (1991), 233–44.

Ordish, G., *The Great Wine Blight* (2nd edn., London, 1987).

Winkler, A. J., *et al.*, *General Viticulture* (2nd edn., Berkeley, Calif., 1974).

PHYSIOLOGICAL RIPENESS, or sometimes **physiological maturity**, terms loosely used by some New World wine-makers to contrast with RIPENESS measured by the normal analytical measures of MUST WEIGHT, ACIDITY, and PH. The terminology is imprecise because all grapes undergo physiological ripening irrespective of how it is assessed.

The concept of physiological ripening arises out of a distrust that these chemical measures can best predict optimum HARVEST date from a wine quality point of view. In its simplest form, the concept includes aspects of the berry's maturation which are not measured (but could often be) and which describe changes in a ripening grape berry important to eventual quality. These include skin colour, berry texture including skin and pulp texture, seed colour and ripening, flavour, and phenolic changes. There is a notion that great wines are made when the harvest date coincides with the near optimum values of many of these parameters. Similarly, wines of lesser distinction arise when only a few parameters are at optimal value when the fruit is harvested; factors such as weather conditions, site, and viticultural technique can unbalance these relationships. A common example is the relatively faster rate of sugar increase in warm to hot climates compared to flavour increase and acid decrease. The resulting wines tend to be high in alcohol without necessarily being accompanied by ripe fruit aromas. On the other hand, VARIETAL flavour appears to increase more quickly relative to sugar in cooler climates.

A likely important aspect of physiological ripeness which is overlooked in conventional RIPENING considerations is that of the condition of the grape skin. There is empirical evidence that wine quality can be affected, even though other aspects of fruit condition seem similar.

As analytical techniques improve, along with better understanding of the fruit ripening process and controlling factors, then the concept of physiological ripening may drop from terminology. For the moment, however, it does serve to remind us that there is more to determine when grapes are ready to be harvested than simply measuring sugar. Z.L.

PHYSIOLOGY OF THE VINE. See VINE PHYSIOLOGY.

PHYTOALEXINS, a group of plant chemicals whose accumulation in plants is initiated by interaction of the plant with micro-organisms, and which is part of the plant's possible defence mechanisms against invasion. Phytoalexins are produced in leaves in response to infection by DOWNY MILDEW and BOTRYTIS. Resveratrol, discovered in vines in 1976, is one such compound, produced in grape skins by the enzyme stilbene synthase in response to botrytis infection and other stresses such as ultraviolet irradiation. A related compound, viniferin, was discovered in 1977. This phytoalexin was studied with renewed interest when it was discovered also to be a constituent of the Asian medicinal herb *Polygonum cuspidatum*. Resveratrol has the ability to reduce blood platelet aggregation, and this is thought to be related to the ability of red wines to reduce cardiac disease in moderate drinkers (see HEALTH). Resveratrol is known to exist in wines, and the concentration is affected by geographical origin, variety, growing methods, and wine-making procedure. R.E.S.

Langcake, P., 'Disease resistance of Vitis spp. and the production of the stress metabolites resveratrol, e-viniferin, d-viniferin and pterostilbene', *Physiological Plant Pathology*, 18 (1981), 213–26.

Siemann, E. H., and Creasy, L. L., 'Concentration of the phytoalexin Resveratrol in wine', *American Journal of Enology and Viticulture*, 43 (1992), 49–52.

PIACENTINI, COLLI, diverse DOC zone centred on the hills of Piacenza in Emilia in north central Italy. See EMILIA-ROMAGNA for more details.

PIAVE, mainly red wine DOC in the hinterland of Venice in north east Italy. Like the neighbouring LISON-PRAMAGGIORE, the Piave DOC embraces vineyards in the plain of the Piave river, and is demarcated by the Conegliano and Montello hills to the north and the flatlands of the river's Adriatic delta to the south. Unlike Lison-Pramaggiore, however, which embraces a part of the province of Pordenone in FRIULI, the Piave DOC is entirely in provinces of Venezia and Treviso in the VENETO region. This is overwhelmingly MERLOT territory (107,000 hl of varietal Merlot out of the zone's average 175,000 hl/4.6 million gal total vintage), with CABERNET (principally Franc) accounting for an additional 24,000 hl/634,000 gal; VERDUZZO (24,000 hl) and TOCAI (14,000 hl) account for the bulk of the white wine production. The wines, at their best, are fruity, fresh, and unpretentiously appealing; with yields of 90 hl/ha (5 tons/acre) for Merlot and close to 80 hl/ha for Cabernet and Tocai, they seem destined to remain that way. See also RABOSO, another local vine variety and varietal DOC. D.T.

PICARDAN, white wine, often sweet, developed from LANGUEDOC raw materials by the DUTCH WINE TRADE in the late 17th and 18th centuries, a relatively early example of a wine created expressly for a market. It was usually made from a blend of CLAIRETTE and PICPOUL. Picardan is also the name of one of the most neutral white grape varieties allowed in CHÂTEAUNEUF-DU-PAPE.

PICKING grapes is apparently romantic but in practice back-breaking work for humans. For more details of the picking season, see HARVEST. For more details of grape-**pickers**, see LABOUR.

PICOLIT, also written **Piccolit** and **Piccolito** in the past, fashionable and audaciously priced sweet white VARIETAL wine made in the FRIULI region of north east Italy, one of the more commercially successful of the DRIED GRAPE WINES. The grape variety derives its name from the small, or *piccolo*, quantity of grapes it produces, thanks to its exceptionally poor pollination rate in the vineyard.

The wine was already famous in the 18th century when Count Fabio Asquini, with a sizeable production of over 100,000 bottles, exported Picolit to the courts of England, France, Austria, Holland, Russia, Saxony, and Tuscany. A letter of Monsignor Giuseppe de Rinaldis of 1765 indicates that it was greatly appreciated by the papal court as well. Antonio Zanon (1767) described the wine as 'delighting the tables of Europe'.

Rosazzo in the COLLI ORIENTALI appears to be the variety's original home, and it is certain that Picolit owes its survival to the efforts of the Perusini family of the Rocca Bernarda of Ipplis, which laboured thoughout the 20th century first to identify and then to reproduce hardier CLONES with a reduced failure rate.

Better estates still make the wine much as it was in the past—Fabio Asquini left copious notes on his working methods—with the bunches, harvested late in mid-October, left to dry and raisin on mats before pressing. Other producers have opted for a late harvest style, with the grapes left even longer in the vineyard, picked with higher MUST WEIGHTS, but not raisined after picking. The use of small oak BARREL MATURATION is an innovation introduced in the mid 1980s. Although Picolit is generally considered a dessert wine (both the count of Polcenigo and Carlo Goldoni, playwright and Italian tutor to the daughters of Louis XVI, compared it to the great TOKAY of Hungary), it is not a dessert wine of the luscious sort and is best considered a VINO DA MEDITAZIONE, a wine to be sipped alone in order to appreciate its delicate floral aromas and its light sweetness which suggests peaches and apricots.

The wine became the object of a cult enthusiasm in Italy in the late 1960s and 1970s, fetching extremely high prices that non-Italian connoisseurs find difficult to understand or justify; the Picolit boom has also resulted in frequent and illegal blending of the wine with the more neutral VERDUZZO, which has stretched the quantities available but has done no service to the wine's reputation. D.T.

PICPOUL or **Piquepoul** is an ancient Languedoc grape variety that is commonly encountered in Blanc, Noir, and Gris versions with the white being the most planted today, although they have frequently been mixed in the vineyard in their long history in the Midi. Piquepoul meaning 'lip-stinger', signifying the high acidity of its must, was cited as a producer of good-quality wine as early as the beginning of the 17th century and, with CLAIRETTE, formed the basis of the enormously popular PICARDAN that was exported northwards from the Languedoc in vast quantites in the 17th and 18th centuries. Its susceptibility to FUNGAL DISEASES, however, together with its unremarkable yield, reduced its popularity considerably after PHYLLOXERA arrived. In the early 20th century, the variety's good tolerance of sand made it a popular choice for the coastal vineyards that serviced the then flourishing vermouth industry. Today those vineyards are campsites and vermouth is an Italian phenomenon.

Picpoul Noir produces alcoholic, richly scented, but almost colourless wine that is best drunk young. Although it is allowed as a minor ingredient in CHÂTEAUNEUF-DU-PAPE and Coteaux du LANGUEDOC, there were only 200 ha/500 acres left in all of France by the end of the 1980s.

Picpoul Blanc on the other hand, of which 500 ha remained then, has been experiencing a small revival of interest. It can provide usefully crisp blending material in the Languedoc but it is most commonly encountered as PICPOUL DE PINET.

PICPOUL DE PINET, one of the named CRUS, of sub-appellations of Coteaux du LANGUEDOC. This curious white wine speciality in the deep south of France has in the post-modern age of vinification attracted some new interest. Millions of tourists each summer see the well-signposted CO-OPERATIVE at Pinet, the most important producer of this distinctive wine and clearly visible from the main *autoroute* along the Mediterranean coast. The co-operative at Pomerols and some individual domains have usually managed to coax a more interesting green-gold, lemon-flavoured wine out of the grape than this particular production centre, however.

PIC-ST-LOUP, one of the more promising named CRUS within the Coteaux du LANGUEDOC in southern France. The zone includes 12 communes around the eponymous peak north of Montpellier (including one called Claret—although the robust red wines made here much more closely resemble southern Rhône than any bordeaux). About 5,000 ha/12,300 acres of vineyard could in theory produce appellation wine, but well under 1,000 are planted with the right vine varieties and dedicated to producing wines at the required basic yield of less than 50 hl/ha (2.8 tons/acre). Much of the wine produced within the zone is VIN DE PAYS or VIN DE TABLE. Carignan is still the dominant vine variety but may comprise no more than 40 per cent of the blend so is slowly giving way to Syrah, Grenache, Cinsaut, and Mourvèdre, the latter most successfully grown in the amphitheatre of Domaine l'Hortus at Valflaunes.

PIÈCE, size and shape of barrel conventionally used in Burgundy. See BARREL TYPES for more details.

PIEDIROSSO, Italian red grape variety planted in CAMPANIA, particularly on the islands of ISCHIA and Capri. It is also known as Per'e Palummo. Plantings halved during the 1980s so that there were hardly more than 1,000 ha/2,500 acres left by 1990.

PIEDMONT, or **Piemonte** in Italian, qualitatively very important wine region in north west ITALY whose principal city is Turin (see map on p. 517). This subalpine part (its name means 'at the foot of the mountains') of the former kingdom of Savoy was the driving force behind Italian reunification in the 19th century and the leader of the initial phases of Italy's industrial revolution. Its geographical position both isolated and protected it during the period of Habsburg, Bourbon, and papal domination which marked Italian life between 1550 and 1860, while its proximity, both geographical and cultural, to France (the kingdom's court and nobility were Francophone until well into the 19th century) gave it both an openness to the new ideas of the European enlightenment and relative prosperity—in stark contrast to the poverty of much of the rest of the peninsula. It is no surprise, therefore, that Piedmont's viticulture is the most stable and most evolved in Italy and has made the greatest progress both in identifying the proper areas for growing its own individual VINE VARIETIES and in the proper techniques for fermenting and ageing them. In 1993, the region had 42 defined and functioning DOC names and zones, easily the largest number of any of Italy's regions. Total annual wine production averaged close to 3.5 million hl/92 million gal, with 40 per cent at DOC level, almost all of it made from a single grape variety and much of it labelled as a VARIETAL wine.

NEBBIOLO is Piedmont's noblest grape and is, with the Sangiovese of Tuscany, the grape which has given the largest number of distinguished wines to Italy. Although there are 12 Nebbiolo-based DOCs or DOCGS, only the famous BAROLO and BARBARESCO supply significant amounts of wine. GATTINARA, for example, which is the largest of the Nebbiolo DOCs outside the LANGHE hills, encompasses a mere 102 ha / 250 acres. Piedmont's workhorse grape, supplying the region's everyday red wines, is BARBERA, grown virtually everywhere there are vineyards in the provinces of Alba, Asti, and Alessandria. Robust and warming, if at times rather rustic and sharply acidic, it has suffered in the past from overcropping and indifferent wine-making, but the 1980s saw notable progress and significant improvement in the overall quality level. Luxury cuvées of Barbera, aged in new oak, now challenge the price levels of fine Barolo and Barbaresco. DOLCETTO, Piedmont's fruity red wine for young drinking, also demonstrated major improvement in the 1980s as more careful vinification mitigated its inherent bitterness, and more careful AGEING reduced, if not entirely eliminated, the problems of REDUCTION and off-odours.

White grapes, with the exception of the MOSCATO used extensively for various SPUMANTE and FRIZZANTE (most notably ASTI SPUMANTE), used to be a virtual afterthought in Piedmont, but the region's production of white wine rose from a mere 10 per cent of the regional total to 25 per cent during the 1980s. Part of this surge is due to the increasing popularity and commercial success of Asti Spumante and the emergence of MOSCATO D'ASTI as a significant wine in its own right, but wines based on CORTESE such as GAVI and those from the Colli Tortonesi and Alto Monferrato have also become increasingly popular. Native Piedmontese varieties such as ARNEIS and FAVORITA, mere curiosities in the early 1980s, were planted on 400 and 100 ha of vineyards respectively by the early 1990s. But perhaps the most surprising development of the 1980s was the arrival and rapid acceptance in Piedmont of CHARDONNAY. Over 500 ha / 1,200 acres had been planted by 1993, and further expansion seems a virtual certainty. The better Langhe Chardonnay products of BARREL FERMENTATION and BARREL MATURATION have drawn increasing attention for their high quality relatively swiftly. Younger wine producers are also showing interest in CABERNET SAUVIGNON, PINOT NOIR, and SAUVIGNON, but these other INTERNATIONAL VARIETIES have yet to establish a real toehold in Piedmont.

Vines are planted at altitudes which can vary from about 150 m to above 350 m (490–1150 ft), with the best, south-facing sites typically devoted to Nebbiolo, while the coolest positions are planted with Dolcetto (or Moscato in the zones in which it is grown). Barbera is widely planted in between. Average summer temperatures and rainfall are very similar to those in Bordeaux, for example.

For more details of individual wines, see ALBA, ARNEIS, ASTI,

Pièces, or burgundy barrels in a typically vaulted, low-ceilinged cellar that is large by Burgundian standards.

Fontanafredda's estate is unusually large for **Piemonte**.

BARBARESCO, BARBERA, BAROLO, BRACHETTO, CAREMA, CORTESE, DOLCETTO, ERBALUCE, FAVORITA, FREISA, GATTINARA, GAVI, GRIGNOLINO, LANGHE, MOSCATO, NEBBIOLO, ROERO, RUCHÈ, SPANNA.

D.T.

Anderson, B., *The Wine Atlas of Italy* (London and New York, 1990).
Garner, M., and Merritt, P., *Barolo: Tar and Roses* (London, 1990).
Gleave, D., *The Wines of Italy* (London and New York, 1989).

PIEMONTE, Italian name for the PIEDMONT wine region.

PIERCE'S DISEASE, one of the vine BACTERIAL DISEASES most feared around the world as it can quickly kill vineyards and there is no cure. The disease, along with FLAVESCENCE DORÉE, is a principal reason for QUARANTINE restrictions on the movement of grape cuttings and other plants between countries. In common with many other economically significant vine diseases, it originates on the American continent. The disease is a principal factor limiting grape-growing in the gulf coastal plains of the UNITED STATES and southern CALIFORNIA. The disease was first described in 1892 at Anaheim in California, and was originally known as Anaheim disease, but was later named after the Californian researcher Pierce. By 1906 the disease had destroyed 16,000 ha/39,500 acres of vines, and there was another epidemic in the 1930s. The disease is today found in the south eastern United States, Mexico, Costa Rica, and Venezuela and probably occurs in other parts of Central and South America. There are isolated hot spots of the disease in NAPA and SONOMA in northern California.

Leaves develop dead spots which enlarge and the leaves fall, leaving the PETIOLE attached. Vines die within one to five years after infection. Originally believed to be a virus, the disease is known now to be caused by a bacterium named *Xylella fastidiosa*. This bacterium lives in a wide range of host plants, and causes damage also to almonds and alfalfa (lucerne). The disease is spread by small insects called sharpshooters (see LEAF HOPPERS), which transmit the disease from host plants to the vineyards during feeding. Thus, in California, one typically sees infected vines within 100 m/330 ft of a vineyard edge, especially where the vineyard borders a stream, as many host plants, especially sedges, grow along the banks.

There are no resistant VITIS VINIFERA varieties, and Chardonnay and Pinot Noir are especially sensitive. Varieties developed from MUSCADINE grapes have natural resistance and are the only ones to be grown where the disease is endemic. In California growers are advised to avoid planting near hot spots. There is no satisfactory chemical control of either the bacterium or sharpshooters. Since sharpshooters capable of transmitting the disease are already established in Europe and elsewhere, there remains the possibility that the disease may spread significantly beyond America. R.E.S.

Pearson, R. C., and Goheen, A. C., *Compendium of Grape Diseases* (St Paul, Minn., 1988).

PIEROTH, commercially important German-based company specializing in selling a wide range of wines, usually with exclusive labels so that price comparisons are difficult, and often in customers' homes, all over the world.

PIERREVERT, COTEAUX DE, small VDQS in the alpine foothills of northern PROVENCE. The area extends over a large area east of the Côtes du LUBÉRON but includes only about 260 ha/640 acres of some of the highest vineyards in France. Wines of all three colours are produced and, thanks to the relative harshness of the climate, they are usually marked more by acidity than body. There is no restriction on the proportion of Carignan which may be included in reds and rosés, although the better producers rely more heavily on Grenache and Syrah. Tourism in the Hautes Alpes de Provence is such that there has been little need to seek export markets.

PIGATO, characterful white grape variety producing distinctively flavoured varietal wines in the north west Italian region of LIGURIA. The variety has a long history in the region and some believe it to be of Greek origin.

PIGEAGE, French term for the action of punching down the CAP of grape skins and other solids to stop the cap from drying out, to encourage the EXTRACTION of colour and TANNINS, and to encourage useful AERATION in the making of a deeply coloured red wine. The cap may be punched down by sticks, paddles, or special metal devices, either by man or mechanically.

For more details, see MACERATION.

PIGMENTS, an inclusive name for the compounds which impart colour. Young red wines get their colour from the ANTHOCYANS in grape skins, while the yellow to amber colours of white wines come mainly from other PHENOLICS present in these grapes, and the important plant pigments CAROTENOIDS. As wine ages, pigments may become more complex compounds incorporating both anthocyans and TANNINS. See AGEING and COLOUR.

PIGNATELLO, synonym for the Sicilian red grape variety PERRICONE.

PIGNOLO, promising red grape variety native to the FRIULI region of north east Italy, probably first cultivated in the hills of Rosazzo in the COLLI ORIENTALI. It is mentioned by the Abbot Giobatta Michieli in his 'Bacchus in Friuli' in the late 17th century, and its 'excellent black wine' was appreciated by the monks of the Abbadia di Rosazzo a century later. The variety, whose Italian name means fussy, is a very shy bearer and it was generally ignored by local growers who preferred other, more productive grape varieties until, like SCHIOPPETTINO, it was given a new lease of life by a EUROPEAN UNION decree of 1978 authorizing its use in the province of Udine. Production is still on a very small scale but the results suggest encouragingly high quality. The rich, full, deep coloured wines have shown a real affinity for BARRIQUE ageing.

Pignola is a white grape variety grown in VALTELLINA.

D.T.

PINEAU, a word widely used in France as a synonym for the PINOT family of grape varieties. It seems to have been a portmanteau word for any better-quality vine in medieval France (probably a reference to the pine-cone shape of so many bunches of grapes) but is today a word associated primarily with the Loire. It is today the first word of a wide range of vine synonyms, sometimes various forms of Pinot but often CHENIN, most notably as Pineau de la Loire.

PINEAU D'AUNIS, sometimes called Chenin Noir, is a variety that is neither a Pinot nor a CHENIN according to Galet, but a distinct black-berried Loire vine variety associated since the Middle Ages with the Prieuré d'Aunis near Saumur. (Earlier authorities, including Viala, maintained that Chenin is a white-berried mutation of Pineau d'Aunis.) It is systematically being pulled up in favour of more fashionable or longer-living vines such as Cabernet Franc but there were still nearly 500 ha/1,200 acres of it planted in the eastern Loire and a substantial presence in Anjou-Saumur at the end of the 1980s. The variety is one of the many sanctioned for the red and rosé appellations of Touraine and Anjou but is used only to a limited extent, mainly to bring peppery liveliness and fruit to rosés, although in ripe years it can yield a fine red too. See Coteaux du LOIR and Coteaux du VENDÔMOIS in particular.

Galet, P., *Cépages et vignobles de France* (2nd edn., Montpellier, 1990).

PINEAU DES CHARENTES or **Pineau Charentais** is the VIN DE LIQUEUR of the COGNAC region and has enjoyed some *réclame* in France as a strong, sweet aperitif more likely to be the product of an artisan than of big business. It is made by adding at least year-old cognac, which in practice usually means year-old cognac, straight from the cask to must that is just about to ferment, thereby producing what is effectively a mixture of grape juice and brandy. These somewhat disparate elements must then be matured together in cask at least until the July following the harvest, although anything labelled Vieux Pineau should have spent at least five years in cask. The final alcohol level is usually between 17 and 18 per cent (about the same as VERMOUTH). This alternative use for the many superfluous vines of the two Charentes *départements* has been most useful, and the authorities have been careful to control quality with tasting panels and specially numbered paper seals on every bottle. The product has been embraced by French *restauration* in all its glory and much effort expended on the essential business of matching various dishes to various styles of Pineau. The style most often encountered outside France is pale gold, decidedly sweet, and with young spirit much in evidence but there are many subtler examples, including soft, fruity rosé styles made from the same grapes as red BORDEAUX. See also FLOC DE GASCOGNE.

PINENC, local name for the FER Servadou red wine grape variety in Gascony, SOUTH WEST FRANCE.

PINOT is the first word of many a French vine variety name and is thought to refer to the shape of Pinot grape bunches, in the form of a pine (*pin*) cone. Galet cites no fewer than 100 different sorts of Pinot, although most of them are synonyms. The principal true members of the Pinot family are PINOT BLANC, AUXERROIS, PINOT GRIS, MEUNIER, and PINOT NOIR, all of them related. Chardonnay is still occasionally but misleadingly called PINOT CHARDONNAY.

In Germany members of the Pinot family frequently have the word Burgunder in their German names (see SPÄTBURGUNDER, Weissburgunder, and GRAUBURGUNDER). There was a marked increase in the popularity of these grape varieties throughout the 1980s as tastes changed in favour of drier, fuller German wines.

Galet, P., *Cépages et vignobles de France* (2nd edn., Montpellier, 1990).

PINOTAGE, hardy red grape variety that is South Africa's curious contribution to the history of the VINIFERA vine. In 1925 Stellenbosch University Professor A. I. Perold crossed Pinot Noir and Cinsaut, then commonly and still sometimes called Hermitage in South Africa, hence the contraction Pinotage. In vineyard and bottle, this crossing disguises its parentage well. Not until 1961 did a Pinotage label appear in South Africa, on a 1959 Lanzerac. Although often scorned, even in the Cape, as a coarse red with a flamboyantly sweetish paint-like pungency (from ISOAMYL ACETATE), it has also produced rich, long-lasting, deep coloured wines whose wild fruitiness has been tamed by time and good oak.

Pinotage is a good vineyard performer, with intensely coloured grapes, easily attained ripeness by mid-vintage, and good fixed acidity. It is a substantial bearer, yielding between 84 and 126 hl/ha (4.8–7.2 tons/acre), so that Pinotage is often attractively priced. By the 1990s, a few producers began treating Pinotage more carefully, and expensively, ignoring the generalization that Pinotage should be made to be drunk young. Cold fermentation tended to retain the volatile esters which characterized the wine. Harvesting sooner to avoid excessive alcohol, fermenting at higher, more traditional temperatures, and then maturing in new French barrels has produced Pinotages with more finesse, some classic sweet berry flavours and tannic length. Although occasionally blended, it retains such a distinctive flavour that it usually dominates anyway. Its novelty appeals to many foreign visitors to the Cape and its popularity in export markets grows.

South Africa's Pinotage plantings fell during the 1980s so that by the early 1990s the crossing occupied about two per cent of Cape vineyards and was also grown, to a much more limited extent, in ZIMBABWE. J.P.

PINOT BIANCO is the common Italian name for the white PINOT BLANC grape of French origin. It is so widely grown in Italy that more wine may well be sold under this synonym than the total amount of wine labelled Pinot Blanc. In 1990 nearly 7,000 ha/17,300 acres of Pinot Bianco were counted (compared with 6,000 ha of Chardonnay and 3,400 ha of Pinot Grigio).

It is grown particularly in TRENTINO-ALTO ADIGE, VENETO, FRIULI, and LOMBARDY although, as in Alsace but not in Germany or Austria, Pinot Gris enjoys higher esteem here. It was first noted in Italy in Piedmont in the early 19th century and until the mid 1980s the name Pinot Bianco was used to describe Pinot Blanc, Chardonnay, or a blend of the two. Even today there are vineyards in which both varieties grow side by side. Italians generally vinify Pinot Blanc as a high-acid, slightly SPRITZ, non-aromatic white for early consumption, and often coax generous yields from the vine. In Lombardy the high acid and low aroma are particularly prized by the SPUMANTE industry.

PINOT BLANC, French white vine variety, is a widely planted white mutation, first observed in Burgundy at the end of the 19th century, of PINOT GRIS, which is itself a lighter-berried version of PINOT NOIR. Although its base is Burgundian, today its stronghold is in central Europe. For many years no distinction was made between Pinot Blanc and CHARDONNAY since the two varieties can look very similar to all but the keenest AMPELOGRAPHERS. The most famous of these, Galet, identifies the distinction and cites three different strains of the variety. True Pinot Blanc is low in both vigour and productivity, while the Pinot Blanc selected for and now widely cultivated in Alsace, called Gros Pinot Blanc by Galet, is much more vigorous and productive. There is also a selection of the variety that ripens two weeks early.

No Pinot Blanc is notable for its piercing aroma; its scent arrives in a cloud. Most wines based on Pinot Blanc are also relatively full bodied, which has undoubtedly helped reinforce the confusion with Chardonnay, not only in Burgundy but also in north east Italy. Although Chardonnay dominates white burgundy, Pinot Blanc is technically allowed into wines labelled BOURGOGNE Blanc and into some white MÂCON, but is no longer grown in any quantity in Burgundy.

It is Alsace that is Pinot Blanc's French stronghold, although even here it is less important in terms of total area planted than Riesling, Gewürztraminer, Silvaner, or even the white AUXERROIS with which it is customarily blended in Alsace, to be sold as 'Pinot Blanc'. In LUXEMBOURG, on the other hand, the higher acidity of Pinot Blanc makes it much less highly regarded than Auxerrois.

While in Alsace it is regarded as something of a workhorse (and sometimes called Clevner or Klevner), it has been generally held in higher esteem by the Germans, who have rather greater area planted (although much less in total than they have of the Pinot Gris they call Ruländer) and call it Weissburgunder or Weisser Burgunder. They have valued it for its apparent similarity to the world-famous Chardonnay and its ability to reach quite high MUST WEIGHTS even at relatively high yields. Planted mainly but not exclusively in eastern Germany, PFALZ, and BADEN, it is a popular vehicle for fuller, drier wine styles designed to be drunk with food and has been keenly adopted as a suitable vehicle for BARRIQUE ageing.

As PINOT BIANCO it is a popular dry white in Italy but it is in Austria that, as Weissburgunder, the variety reaches its greatest heights, and certainly its greatest must weights. Accounting for almost four per cent of the country's total vineyards, it is grown in all regions, although Riesling is more prized in the Wachau. As a dry white varietal, Weissburgunder is associated with an almond-like scent, relatively high alcohol, and an ability to age, but it has achieved its greatest glory in Austria in ultra-rich, botrytized TROCKENBEERENAUSLESE form.

Pinot Blanc is widely disseminated over eastern Europe. In SLOVENIA, CROATIA, and VOJVODINA it is widely grown and may be called Beli (White) Pinot. It is also grown in CZECHOSLOVAKIA and is widely used in Hungary to produce full bodied, rather anodyne dry whites more suitable for export than indigenous vine varieties.

Vine-growers in the New World recognize that Pinot Blanc has lacked Chardonnay's glamour but there are well over 1,000 acres/400 ha of a variety called Pinot Blanc in California, mainly in Monterey, where it is sometimes treated to barrel ageing and the full range of Chardonnay wine-making tricks, to creditable effect. Older vines bearing this name are almost certainly not Pinot Blanc but the Muscadet grape MELON. The fact that within California no great distinction has been noticed between the wines made from true Pinot Blanc and Melon adds further weight to the thesis that Melon is a Burgundian variety.

Elsewhere in the New World, Pinot Blanc is largely ignored in favour of the most famous white wine grape.

Galet, P., *Cépages et vignobles de France* (2nd edn., Montpellier, 1990).

PINOT CHARDONNAY is a somewhat misleading synonym for CHARDONNAY, the classic white grape of Burgundy. It was adopted at a time when Chardonnay was believed to be a white mutation of PINOT NOIR. Pinot-Chardonnay Mâcon ihas been an appellation recognized by INAO as virtually interchangeable with MÂCON Blanc but is not often seen.

PINOT GRIGIO is the common Italian name for the French vine variety PINOT GRIS and, as such, is probably the name by which the variety is best known to many wine drinkers. There were about 3,500 ha/8,600 acres of Pinot Grigio vineyard in Italy in 1990 (much less than the area planted with PINOT BIANCO, for example). Most of these plantings were in the north east and specifically in Friuli, where it produces some of the most admired wines of COLLIO as well as a sea of reasonably undistinguished dry white with low aroma and probably the most noticeable acidity of any of the world's Pinot Gris. The Italian tendency is to pick the grapes before the variety's characteristically rapid loss of nerve at full ripening. The variety is also grown widely in LOMBARDY although there is less fastidiousness here about distinguishing it from other hues of PINOT, especially when supplying grapes for the sparkling wine industry. The variety can also be found as far south as EMILIA-ROMAGNA and is planted in ALTO ADIGE—although here, as in all Germanic areas, PINOT BIANCO is favoured.

PINOT GRIS is a widely disseminated vine variety that can produce soft, gently perfumed wines with more substance and colour than most whites, which is what one might expect of a variety that is one of the best-known mutations of PINOT NOIR. If Pinot Noir berries are purplish blue and the berries of the related PINOT BLANC are greenish yellow, Pinot Gris grapes are anything between greyish blue and brownish pink—sometimes on the same bunch. In the vineyard this vine can easily be taken for Pinot Noir for the leaves are identical and, especially late in a ripe year, the berries can look remarkably similar. At one time Pinot Gris habitually grew in among the Pinot Noir of many Burgundian vineyards, adding softness and sometimes acidity to its red wine. Even today, as PINOT Beurot, it is sanctioned as an ingredient in most of Burgundy's red wine appellations and the occasional vine can still be found in some of the region's famous red wine vineyards. It was traditionally prized for its ability to soften Pinot Noir musts but older CLONES have a tendency to yield very irregularly.

There also remain small pockets of the variety in the Loire, where it is often known as Malvoisie (although even in such a small appellation as Coteaux d'ANCENIS both Malvoisie and Pinot Beurot are officially allowed as a suffix). It can produce perfumed, substantial wines in a wide range of different sweetness levels. It is also known as Malvoisie in the Valais in SWITZERLAND, where it can also produce full, perfumed, rich whites.

But, within France, Alsace is where Pinot Gris (here traditionally but mysteriously known as Tokay—see GERMAN HISTORY) is most revered, and with good reason. It may be less commonly planted than the other members of Alsace's noble triumvirate, Riesling and Gewürztraminer, but it fulfils a unique function as provider of super-rich, usually dry, wines that can be partnered with food without the distraction of too much aroma. For more on the wines see ALSACE.

As with Pinot Blanc, however, much more Pinot Gris is planted in both Germany and Italy than in France. (See PINOT GRIGIO for details of Italian Pinot Gris.) In Germany it is usually known as RULÄNDER (or occasionally Grauer Riesling, Grauer Burgunder, or even Grauklevner), under which name are more details on German, and Austrian, wines made from this variety.

The variety, like Pinot Blanc, is widely planted not just in Austria but in Slovenia, Moravia, and particularly ROMANIA, where, on 1,600 ha/3,900 acres of vineyard, it is known both as Pinot Gris and Ruländer. In Hungary it is revered as SZÜRKEBARÁT. Within the CIS, Pinot Gris is grown in both Russia and Moldova.

Pinot Gris's impact on the New World is distinctly limited although improved clonal selection has precipitated a renewal of enthusiasm in the South Island of New Zealand, albeit on a small scale.

The variety is also much admired for its weight and relatively low acidity in LUXEMBOURG.

PINOT MEUNIER. See MEUNIER.

PINOT NERO is Italian for PINOT NOIR. The variety is quite widely planted in the north east of the country and in Lombardy, and it doubled its area to a total of about 3,500 ha/8,600 ha in the 1980s, but few examples show great intensity of flavour. Much of the Pinot Nero planted is used by the upper reaches of the SPUMANTE industry.

PINOT NOIR is the grape variety wholly responsible for red burgundy and gives its name to the NOIRIEN family of grape varieties. Unlike Cabernet Sauvignon, which can be grown in all but the coolest conditions and can be economically viable as an inexpensive but recognizably Cabernet wine, Pinot Noir demands much of both vine-grower and wine-maker. It is a tribute to the unparalleled level of physical excitement generated by tasting one of Burgundy's better reds (and it is generally agreed that the Burgundians' success rate has been dispiritingly low) that such a high proportion of the world's most ambitious wine producers want to try their hand with this capricious vine. Although there is little consistency in its performance in its homeland, Pinot Noir has been transplanted to almost every one of the world's wine regions, except the very hottest, where it can so easily turn from essence to jam.

While Cabernet Sauvignon has recognizable characteristics and quality wherever it is planted, Pinot Noir is much less recognizable and dependable. If Cabernet produces wines to appeal to the head, Pinot's charms are decidedly more sensual and more transparent. The Burgundians themselves refute the allegation that they produce Pinot Noir; they merely use Pinot Noir as the vehicle for communicating local geography, the characteristics of the individual site on which it was planted. Perhaps the only characteristics that the Pinot Noirs of the world could be said to share would be a certain sweet fruitiness and, in general, lower levels of tannins and pigments than the other 'great' French red varieties Cabernet Sauvignon and Syrah. The wines are decidedly more charming in youth and evolve more rapidly, although the decline of the very best is slow.

Part of the reason for the wide variation in Pinot Noir's performance lies in its genetic make-up. It is a particularly old vine variety, in all probability a selection from wild vines made by man at least two millennia ago. There is some evidence that Pinot existed in Burgundy in the 4th century AD. Although Morillon Noir was the common name for early Pinot, a vine called Pinot was already described in records of Burgundy in the 14th century and its fortunes were inextricably linked with those of the powerful medieval monasteries of eastern France and Germany (see BURGUNDY and GERMAN HISTORY).

Clearly Pinot Noir has for long been grown in Burgundy but it is particularly prone both to mutate (as witness PINOT BLANC, PINOT GRIS, and PINOT MEUNIER) and degenerate, as witness the multiplicity of Pinot Noir CLONES available even within France.

Galet notes that no fewer than 46 Pinot Noir clones (as opposed to 34 of the much more widely planted Cabernet Sauvignon) are officially recognized within France—and that in the 1980s only Merlot cuttings were more sought after from French nurseries than those of Pinot Noir. It is thus possible to choose a clone of Pinot Noir specially for its productivity, for its resistance to rot, and/or for its likely ripeness (which can vary considerably). Most selection work has been done in Burgundy and Champagne and it has been the Champenois who have selected particularly productive clones. It is generally agreed that a major factor in the lighter colour and extract of so much red burgundy in the 1970s and 1980s was injudicious CLONAL SELECTION, resulting perhaps in higher yields but much less diversity and concentration in the final wine. The most planted clone in Burgundy is 115 but 114 is more highly regarded and the most reputable producers of all tend to have made MASS SELECTIONS from their own vine population. The clone called Pommard is well distributed in the New World, as has been one named after the Wädenswil viticultural station in Switzerland. In general the most productive clones, which have large-berried bunches, are described as Pinot Droit for the vines' upright growth, while Pinot Fin, Pinot Tordu, or Pinot Classique grows much less regularly but has smaller berries with thicker skin.

In as much as generalizations about a vine variety with so many different forms are possible, Pinot Noir tends to bud early, making it susceptible to spring frosts and COULURE. Damp, cool soils on low-lying land are therefore best avoided. Yields are theoretically low, although too many Burgundians disproved this with productive clones in the 1970s and early 1980s. The vine is also more prone than most to both sorts of mildew, rot (grape skins tend to be thinner than most), and to viruses, particularly FANLEAF and LEAFROLL. Indeed it was the prevalence of disease in Burgundian vineyards that precipitated the widespread adoption of clonal selection there in the 1970s.

Pinot Noir seems to produce the best-quality wine on LIMESTONE soils and in relatively cool climates where this early ripening vine will not rush towards maturity, losing aroma and acidity. In Burgundy, for example, where it is typically cultivated alongside the equally early ripening Chardonnay, Pinot Noir may ripen after Chardonnay in some years. There is general agreement, however, that Pinot Noir is very much more difficult to vinify than Chardonnay, needing constant monitoring and fine tuning of technique according to the demands of each particular vintage. A vogue for ROTOFERMENTERS was followed in the late 1980s by one for cold MACERATION before fermentation as a way of leaching more colour and flavour out of these relatively thin-skinned grapes.

Pinot Noir is planted throughout eastern France and has been steadily gaining ground from less noble varieties so that by 1988 its total area of French vineyard was 22,000 ha/54,000 acres, twice as big as the total area planted with Pinot Meunier but less than Syrah's total—and considerably less than the total planted with Burgundy's other red vine variety GAMAY because of the vast extent of Beaujolais in comparison with the famous Côte d'Or.

The Côte d'Or was once the wine region with the biggest single area of Pinot Noir, but the extension of the Champagne region in the 1980s meant that, by the end of this decade, more Pinot Noir went into champagne than into red burgundy. In 1988 there were 6,000 ha of Pinot Noir in the Côte d'Or. Even in the greater Burgundy region, Pinot Noir is rarely blended with any other variety, except occasionally with Gamay in a BOURGOGNE Passetoutgrains and, increasingly, to add class to a MÂCON. At one time, Pinot Gris would be planted randomly in the same vineyard as Pinot Noir and the varieties would be vinified together. The red wines of Burgundy can vary from deeply coloured, tannic, oak-aged mouthfuls that demand long bottle age to acidic dark rosés that should be drunk as young as possible. The best GRANDS CRUS are intense, fleshy, vibrant, fruity wines with structure but oak influence that is never obvious. See under individual village names specified for the CÔTE D'OR for more detail on individual wines.

Pinot Noir is also gaining ground in the Côte CHALONNAISE and, to a lesser extent, the Mâconnais, typically at the expense of Gamay, which is in decline in both of Burgundy's subregions between the Côte d'Or and Beaujolais. The 1988 census showed that total Pinot Noir plantings in the Saône-et-Loire *département* were 2,800 ha (as compared with Gamay's 3,200 ha). Pinot Noir occupied a full quarter of all Mâconnais vineyard in 1988 and the Chalonnaise reds of MERCUREY, GIVRY, and RULLY have shown that they can often deliver a more consistent level of wine-making than more expensive appellations to the north, even if the fruit quality may be slightly more rustic.

Pinot Noir is the favoured black grape variety in northern Burgundy too. In the Yonne *département*, dominated by its 3,000 ha of Chardonnay for Chablis production, there were also 450 ha of Pinot Noir by 1988 used for such AUXERRE wines as IRANCY and particularly northern versions of BOURGOGNE. It is cultivated even further north east for the light reds and VIN GRIS of Lorraine such as Côtes de TOUL and the wines of MOSELLE.

Although plantings of Pinot Noir increased throughout France (and indeed the world) in the 1980s, it was in CHAMPAGNE that the greatest increase was seen: from 4,700 ha in 1979 to 5,600 ha in 1988 in the Marne *département* alone, together with plantings of 3,000 ha in the Aube where Pinot Noir takes first rather than third place behind Pinot Meunier and Chardonnay. It is used almost exclusively in Champagne, and indeed in the production of a wide range of sparkling wines made around the world in champagne's image, as a still, very pale pink ingredient in the base blend of still wines. The grapes are pressed very gently and any remaining pigments tend to agglomerate with the dead yeast cells during the champenization process. In such a blend Pinot Noir is prized for its body and longevity, as well it might be for that small proportion of champagne made exclusively from Pinot Noir is usually memorably substantial. In Champagne, a small quantity of Pinot Noir is used for still red Coteaux CHAMPENOIS and ROSÉ DES RICEYS.

Pinot Noir is also planted, to a limited but increasing extent, in the most easterly vineyards of the Loire and its tributaries, most notably to make red and pink SANCERRE but also in MENETOU-SALON and ST-POURÇAIN, and is technically allowed in an array of the Loire's VDQS wines. It was taken to the vineyards of the JURA and SAVOIE from Burgundy centuries ago but it is usually suppressed by indigenous varieties and is rarely seen as a single varietal. It is rarely encountered in the south or west of France, the domains of Syrah and Cabernet Sauvignon, but there are limited plantings in the Languedoc with some intriguing, if atypical, results.

In Alsace, where it has been an important vine since the early 16th century (see GERMAN HISTORY), it is effectively the only black-berried vine variety planted, with a total 1,000 ha. Pinot Noir is capable of producing quite deep coloured, perfumed, sweet reds in the ripest vintages. In cooler years it produces deep pink wines, often with a similar smoky perfume to a white Pinot Blanc or Pinot Gris, that can be reminiscent of German Spätburgunders, even down to the whiff of rot in the wettest vintages. See ALSACE for more.

Germany's rediscovered interest in connoisseurship of the 1980s resulted in a marked increase in demand for the nation's noblest red so that by 1990 (Blauer) Spätburgunder was Germany's fourth most planted vine after Riesling, Müller-Thurgau, and Silvaner with more than 5,500 ha of vineyard, nearly 60 per cent more than a decade previously. An increasing proportion of German Pinot Noir is made in the image of the best Burgundian prototype to be completely dry, deep coloured, and well structured, thanks to much lower yields, longer maceration, and sometimes maturation in small oak barrels. There are ambitious producers in the Rheingau, Rheinpfalz, and Baden, where two-thirds of Germany's Pinot Noir is grown. Others, however, continue the tradition of making pale pink wines, often with notable sweetness (see WEISSHERBST). Such wines have been the traditional specialities of Assmannshausen and the AHR. (Even in 1990 the Ahr had more of this variety planted in total than the Rheingau.)

Seriously sweet Spätburgunder is occasionally made as a late-picked Beerenauslese in the Rheingau and can command the dizzy prices associated with rarities.

It is fair to say, however, that, whereas Cabernet Sauvignon is often associated with the flavours of oak, Pinot Noir is often encountered with more than its fair share of sweetness, especially in inland Europe, as though over-chaptalization had been adopted as an alternative to true ripeness. Austria's Blauer Spätburgunder, for example, can taste sweet and oddly viscous unless from one of its most skilled practitioners. Total Austrian plantings are limited, however, and the native grape ST LAURENT, sometimes confusingly called Pinot St Laurent for Pinot Noir-like soft fruitiness, is much more common.

Pinot Noir is spread widely, if not enormously, in the vineyards of eastern Europe although its name is usually some variant on the local word for Burgundian. There are plantings of Burgundac Crni in parts of CROATIA, in SERBIA, where it can be quite successful, and in much paler form in KOSOVO. It is also grown to a limited extent in CZECHOSLOVAKIA, BULGARIA, ROMANIA, and the CIS, where it is grown in MOLDOVA, GEORGIA, AZERBAIJAN, KAZAKHSTAN, and KYRGYZSTAN. In this part of the world it is most prized as Nagyburgundi in certain parts of HUNGARY, although some vines considered Pinot Noir may well be KÉKFRANKOS. Romania has its own subvariety known as Burgund Mare.

Elsewhere in Europe the finicky nature of the Pinot Noir vine has set a natural limit on its spread. Miguel TORRES has managed to coax some flavours reminiscent of red burgundy from his small Pinot Noir vineyard in Catalonia. But the vine is relatively important in SWITZERLAND, notably as Klevner around Zurich and blended with Gamay in the ubiquitous Dôle, and in some cooler Italian wine regions, where it is known as Pinot Nero or, occasionally, Pignola. See particularly AOSTA, BREGANZE, TRENTINO, ALTO ADIGE, where it is called Blauburgunder, COLLIO, and FRIULI, as well as OLTREPÒ PAVESE, where the rather neutral Pinot Noir is valued as an ingredient in classically made sparkling wine.

It was wine producers in the New World, however, who turned the full heat of their ambitious attentions on Pinot Noir in the late 1980s and early 1990s. Some even relocated their wineries many hundreds of miles in order to be closer to sources of suitably cool climate Pinot Noir fruit. Although for many years OREGON, with its often miserably cool, wet climate, was popularly supposed to provide America's answer to red burgundy, the number of seriously fine Pinot Noirs from CALIFORNIA that emerged in the late 1980s redefined the more southerly state's reputation for Pinot, especially but not exclusively in regions such as Carneros, Chalone, and the Gavilan mountains of San Benito. In 1992 there were nearly 10,000 acres/4,000 ha of Pinot Noir in California, notably in fog-cooled Carneros, where the variety is also valued as an ingredient in champagne-like sparkling wines.

The variety called Pinot St George in California, now in sharp decline, is unrelated to any known Pinot and is probably in fact NÉGRETTE, while that called Gamay Beaujolais (of which more than 1,000 acres remained in 1992) is a clone of Pinot Noir, although not one embraced by the most ambitious producers of California Pinot Noir.

Outside California and Oregon (where Pinot Noir is sometimes picked a good six weeks after it is in California), the variety has no established American outpost of great reputation. Washington state's plantings of 300 acres were in decline in the early 1990s, making way for Merlot. There are pockets of Pinot Noir in Canada's cool vineyards, however, and they are producing increasingly successful wines.

As Pinot Negro, it is known in most Argentine provinces where vines are grown but the climate is too hot and irrigation too commonplace to produce wines of real quality, as in most of the rest of South America, although Chile had a few hundred hectares planted in the early 1990s and wine-quality was improving.

Across the Atlantic in SOUTH AFRICA, on the other hand, at least one producer, Hamilton-Russell, had managed to coax convincingly burgundian flavours from Pinot Noir vines grown in a particularly cool southerly spot and this has since acted as a spur to others, even if the quantity of true Pinot Noir planted is still minute compared with the total area of South Africa's signature black grape variety PINOTAGE.

Plantings of Pinot Noir in Australia and New Zealand on the other hand rose substantially in the early 1990s as an increasing number of producers mastered the art of replicating the Pinot Noir made in both Burgundy and Champagne.

New Zealand had 275 ha/680 acres in 1992, almost double the total two years previously, with the most impressive results coming from Martinborough, Canterbury, and Central Otago. See NEW ZEALAND for more details on the wines, the least impressive of which are still over-produced from the Bachtobel clone better suited to high-volume sparkling wine production.

Total Australian plantings of Pinot Noir were 1,100 ha in 1991, of which almost a third were still too young to bear fruit—a signal in part of the success of the Australian sparkling wine industry but also of the determination of Australian wine-makers to overcome the disadvantages of their warm climate and join the world's fine wine-making club. Areas with proven success as producers of good-quality Pinot Noir as a still red varietal are Geelong, Yarra, and Mornington peninsula, all relatively cool areas around Melbourne in Victoria, as well as Tasmania. See AUSTRALIA for more details.

It should not surprise those familiar with the English climate that some growers have found success with Pinot Noir in its southern counties, although this really is a marginal exercise.

Barr A., *Pinot Noir* (London, 1992).

Galet, P., 'La Culture de la vigne aux États-Unis et au Canada', *France viticole* (Sept.–Oct. 1980 and Jan.–Feb. 1981).

—— *Cépages et vignobles de France* (2nd edn., Montpellier, 1990).

PIPE, wine trade term, adapted from the Portuguese *pipa* meaning barrel, for a large cask with tapered ends, the traditional measure of PORT as well as of MADEIRA, MARSALA, and other Portuguese wines, although the volume can vary around the country. In the DOURO valley where port is produced, the yield of each vineyard is measured in pipes of 550 l/145 gal, while downstream in VILA NOVA DE GAIA, the suburb of Oporto where port is matured, a pipe may vary in size between 580 and 630 l. For shipping purposes, however, a pipe of port is 534.24 l, divided into 21 measures of 25.44 l called *almudes*, while pipes of madeira and Marsala are 418 and 423 l respectively. Gentlemen in Victorian England traditionally laid down a pipe of port for their sons and godsons, but inflation and changing consumption patterns have altered all that.

A pipe of COGNAC was traditionally 600 l.

PIPS. See grape SEEDS.

PIQUETTE, thin, vinous liquid made by adding water to the grape POMACE. Throughout history, from the time of classical GREECE and ROME to the mid 20th century, it has been given to slaves or low-paid workers. (See ancient PRESSES for details of *lorca*, the Roman version.) In the late 20th century, with its wine SURPLUS, LABOUR shortage, and concentration on quality, few employers would dare to offer even the most lowly worker such a drink.

PISCO, aromatic BRANDY made in PERU, Chile, and Bolivia, mainly from Moscatel (MUSCAT) grapes.

Chile

Although the Spanish colonists had been making AGUARDIENTE (grape spirit) in both countries since the 16th century, the name 'pisco' was not current until the 1870s, when, according to Chileans, it was used to describe a good-quality aguardiente shipped from northern Chile to the Peruvian port of Pisco.

Production centres on the warm Andean valleys of Chile, lying between Santiago and the deserts of the north, mainly in the Coquimbo region. The most important grape variety is MOSCATEL DE AUSTRIA, together with the Moscatel Rosada (the pink-berried form of MUSCAT BLANC À PETITS GRAINS), TORONTEL, and Moscatel de Alejandria (MUSCAT OF ALEXANDRIA), which are used to a more limited extent but make the best and most aromatic pisco. PEDRO XIMÉNEZ is also used but does not make a significant contribution to pisco's distinctively fruity aroma.

The grapes are destalked and crushed, and the skins briefly macerated to preserve as much as possible of the aroma and flavour of the grapes during fermentation. Distillation of the wine is carried out in proper copper POT STILLS, the sort used for COGNAC. Only the middle fraction of the distillate is used for pisco, the HEADS and TAILS being blended with fresh wine and redistilled. The young distillate is diluted and then aged in oak or rauli (see CHILE) casks for between four and 12 months.

There are four grades of pisco: Gran Pisco at 43 per cent alcohol; Reservado at 40 per cent (the strength at which most spirits are sold in Europe); Especial at 35 per cent; and Selección at 30 per cent. The stronger the spirit, the longer it spends in wood. Selección should have a deliciously fresh aroma and a taste of Moscatel, while the stronger grades are oakier and drier with more elegance and overtones of plums and bitter almonds. All are colourless (the oak casks in which they are matured being too old to tint the spirit) and differ from cognac in their marked fruitiness. Pisco has its own CONTROLLED APPELLATION.

In Chile pisco is drunk as a liqueur after meals but a pisco sour, which is sold in bottled, pre-mixed form, can also make a refreshing APERITIF. J.R.

Peru

Pisco is the port at the mouth of the river of the same name 160 km/100 miles south of the capital Lima. The Pisco valley has a long history of grape-growing and distillation may have been an early answer to problems of transporting the produce of Pisco and other valleys to Peru's centres of population in Lima and Cuzco.

The brandy made in the Ica valley to the south, today regarded as the country's finest, was already celebrated by Franciscan MISSIONARIES as early as 1651.

Pisco is now the Peruvian national drink and, as in Chile, is produced according to strict regulations in four different grades. Pisco Fur is a single VARIETAL pisco made from Quebranta, Quebranta Mollar, or Negra Corriente grapes. Pisco Aromático is made from MOSCATEL, Torontel, ALBILLA, or Italian TABLE GRAPES. Pisco Cuivré is made mostly from Quebranta, possibly blended with other grape varieties, while Pisco Verde is made by distilling either Albilla, Moscatel, Negra Corriente, or Quebranta, but before fermentation is complete.

Bolivia

A similar aromatic spirit, high in terpenes, is made in BOLIVIA, where it is called *singani* and is made, also under a strictly controlled regime, principally from Muscat of Alexandria grapes.

PLANTET, the Loire's most popular HYBRID, has been more successfully eradicated from the French vinescape than some other hybrids (see BACO, COUDERC, VILLARD). France's total Plantet area shrank from more than 26,000 ha/63,000 acres to less than 1,000 ha between 1968 and 1988, almost all of it in the Loire, although at one point it was grown all over France's northern wine regions. Its chief attributes are its productivity and its ability to crop regardless of the severity of the winter and spring frosts (although New York state winters have proved too harsh for it). It has at least one SEIBEL parent but the obviously hybrid character of its wine can be muted by early picking.

PLANTING a vineyard ostensibly constitutes that vineyard's birth, but this viticultural operation can be undertaken only after a wide range of decisions have been taken. The potentially long process of VINEYARD SITE SELECTION is followed by SOIL PREPARATION and the choice of, and possibly choice of CLONES of, both VINE VARIETY and ROOTSTOCK. Decisions must also be made about VINE DENSITY. Following delivery from the NURSERY, the young plants must be prevented from drying out before they are finally planted.

The planting operation is normally carried out in winter or spring. It consists of simply digging a small hole sufficient to take the normal dormant ROOTLING, or occasionally a CUTTING, or even a growing plant. The hole can be dug by spade or post hole auger, but care must be taken, particularly in heavy clay soils, that holes dug by machine do not have such dense sides that roots cannot grow through them. In dry conditions a high-pressure water jet can help to create a planting hole and at the same time provide moisture to assist early growth. For large estates, a planting machine adapted from forestry can be mounted behind a tractor to allow workers to put plants into a pre-formed furrow which is then filled in as the machine passes.

A cardinal rule of establishing grapevines, as for other plants, is to press the soil firmly in around the newly planted vine to avoid air pockets. Dry soil conditions around the roots of the young plant should be avoided. R.E.S.

PLANTING DENSITY. See VINE DENSITY.

PLASTIC SHEETING in vineyards. See MULCH for more details.

PLAVAC MALI, grape variety producing dense red wines all along the Dalmatian coast and on many of the Adriatic islands in CROATIA. Mali means small and a white grape variety called simply **Plavac** is also known, and results in equally heady wines. Both varieties thrive on sandy soil. Plavac Mali produces wines high in tannins, alcohol, and colour which can, unusually for red wines from what was Yugoslavia, age well. Postup and Dingač are two of the better-known reds made from Plavac Mali.

PLAVAI, late ripening white VINIFERA grape variety native to MOLDOVA and widely planted throughout eastern Europe and the CIS. In Moldova it is also known as Belan and Plakun, in Romania it is called Plavana, in Austria Plavez Gelber, in Hungary Melvais, in the Krasnodarski region of Russia Belan or Oliver, in Ukraine Bila Muka or Ardanski, and in Central Asia Bely Krugly. It is used in Russia for both table wines and brandy.

PLC, important abbreviation for the official French *plafond limite de classement*, a mechanism whereby the maximum YIELD permitted within an APPELLATION CONTROLÉE is regularly increased by 20 per cent.

PLINY (AD 23/4–79). Gaius Plinius Secundus is known in English as 'Pliny the Elder' to distinguish him from his nephew, also a man of letters and Pliny the Elder's adoptive son. Of Pliny the Elder's many works, the only one to survive is the *Natural History*, 37 books, dedicated to the Emperor Titus and published posthumously. Book 14 is devoted exclusively to wine, while Book 17 provides important information on the techniques of viticulture, and the beginning of Book 23 is devoted to the medicinal properties of wine (see MEDICINE). Although most of the *Natural History* is based on earlier authors rather than on scientific observation, and his information, invaluable as much of it is, must be used with discrimination, the fourteenth book, on wine, seems in large part to be the product of independent enquiry. It contains practical advice as well as literary and historical learning. Its most interesting part ranks Italian wines according to quality, and sweet wines seem to be favoured (although see also ATHENAEUS). The best wine used to be CAECUBAN, but in Pliny's day it is FALERNIAN particularly Falernian of the Faustinian CLOS. Setine is also a wine of the first rank. The next best wines are Alban, SURRENTINE, and MASSIC; Pliny awards third prize to Mamertine, of Messina in Sicily. An early proponent of TERROIR, he concludes that it is the country and the soil that determine quality, and not the vine variety; in any case, people's tastes differ. Pliny died during the eruption of Vesuvius when his extraordinary curiosity got the better of his common sense. In his much-quoted writings on wine he drew on VARRO's *De re rustica*; PALLADIUS' treatise on husbandry is indebted to Pliny. H.M.W. & J.J.P.

André, J., *Pline l'Ancien: histoire naturelle, livre XIV* (Paris, 1958).
Beagon, M., *Roman Nature: The Thought of Pliny the Elder* (Oxford, 1992).
Pliny the Elder, *Natural History*, trans. by H. Rackham (London, 1945).

PLONK, vague and derogatory English term for wine of undistinguished quality, thought to have originated in Australia as an Anglicized form of (*vin*) *blanc*, French for white (wine).

PLOUGHING. See CULTIVATION.

PODERE, Italian for a farm, usually smaller than a FATTORIA.

POINTS out of 100, common method of scoring wine promoted notably by American writer Robert PARKER. For more detail, see NUMBERS.

POITOU, the north west French region around Poitiers for which the port has for centuries been LA ROCHELLE. Today its name is known to wine drinkers only for **Haut-Poitou**, a VDQS zone keenly anticipating promotion in the mid 1990's almost due south of SAUMUR in which about 700 ha/1,700 acres of vines on limestone and marl produce a range of improving VARIETAL wines, marked by clean, fruity acidity. Almost equal quantities of reds and whites are produced from the usual middle Loire range of Bordelais, Burgundian, and Loire vine varieties. SAUVIGNON and GAMAY can be particularly successful, as can CABERNET (a blend of both Sauvignon and Franc) in particularly ripe vintages. The co-operative at Neuville which dominates production has successfully experimented with OAK AGEING and champagne method sparkling wines, including an all-Chardonnay Blanc de Blancs, called Diane de Poitiers. The VDQS was once known as **Vins du Haut-Poitou**.

POLLEN, collective term for pollen grains which carry the male gametes in sexual propagation. Pollen develops within sacs of the ANTHER by a number of cell divisions leading to the pollen which has prolific cell divisions. Mature grains have a sculptured surface typical for each species. When the grains germinate, a pollen tube emerges and grows into the surface of the stigma and down the style (see FLOWERING).
B.G.C.

POLLINATION, the transfer of pollen from the anther to the receptive stigmatic surface. If the transfer is to a flower of the same genotype (regardless of its relative location) the process is called self-pollination; when to other genotypes it is called cross-pollination. Transfer may be by insects or birds (biotic), or by wind, water, or rain (abiotic). In grapevines, pollination appears to happen as a result of self-pollination of nearby flowers aided by some insects, although some pollination occurs before the CALYPTRA have fallen. Fertilization occurs two or three days after pollination depending on the ambient temperature (see FLOWERING).

See also POLLEN. B.G.C.

POLLUTION. Air pollution can damage grapevines in many parts of the world. Air pollutants arise from industrial gases and particles, exhaust gases, and agricultural chemicals. Principal pollutants are hydrogen fluoride, sulphur dioxide, and OZONE, and in restricted areas phenoxy herbicides like 2,4-D (see AUXINS) applied to nearby crops.

Ozone has been demonstrated to cause a condition referred to as oxidant stipple which shows as lesions on the upper leaf surfaces, although vine varieties vary in their sensitivity, and Carignan, Grenache, and Palomino are particularly susceptible. Hydrogen fluoride has reduced vineyard yields in many countries. While the leaves can accumulate high levels of fluoride, it is not translocated to the fruit. Mourvèdre is particularly sensitive to this type of pollution, while Carignan is tolerant. R.E.S.

Pearson, R. C., and Goheen, A. C., *Compendium of Grape Diseases* (St Paul, Minn., 1988).

POL ROGER, Champagne house founded in Épernay by Paul Roger in 1849 and still in family hands. His sons changed their surnames to Pol-Roger by deed poll, Pol being the local dialect for Paul. The wines rank high among the top champagne houses for quality, although it is one of the smaller GRANDES MARQUES. Pol Roger owns 82 ha/200 acres of vineyards on prime sites in the Vallée d'Épernay and on the Côte des Blancs. Particularly deep cellars house 7.5 million bottles, representing six years' supply. Sir Winston Churchill was a devotee of the house, even naming his racehorse 'Odette Pol-Roger' after his favourite member of the Pol Roger family. The compliment was repaid after his death, when all non-vintage labels exported to Britain were edged in black for 25 years. The Sir Winston Churchill Cuvée was launched in 1984 as Pol Roger's PRESTIGE CUVÉE. The company is now managed by the great-grandsons of the original Pol Roger, Christian Pol-Roger and Christian de Billy, and the son of the latter, Hubert de Billy. S.A.

Sutcliffe, S., *A Celebration of Champagne* (London, 1988).

POLYMERIZATION, the molecular process in which smaller molecules combine to form very large molecules. In all living material, the simple amino acids combine, or **polymerize**, in very large chains to create the PROTEINS, some of which function as enzymes. In AGEING wines, simpler PHENOLIC molecules combine to form larger TANNIN **polymers** which eventually grow so large that they fall from the solution as SEDIMENT. A.D.W.

POLYPHENOLS and **polyphenolics.** See PHENOLICS.

POLYVINYLPYRROLIDONE. See RESINS.

POMACE, a word used for centuries by English cidermakers (it comes from the Latin *pomum* meaning apple) meaning the debris of fruit processing. In WHITE WINE-MAKING the pomace is the sweet, pale brownish-green mass of grape skins, stems, seeds, and pulp left after PRESSING. In RED WINE-MAKING the pomace is a similar mass of grape debris coloured blackish red left after the FREE-RUN wine has been drained. Because red wine pomace is what is left after FERMENTATION rather than before, it also includes dead yeast cells and contains traces of alcohol rather than sugar.

In larger wineries the significant amount of sugar which remains in white grape pomace may be washed out of the solid mixture and fermented to produce material for DISTILLATION into POMACE BRANDY. Similarly, the smaller amounts of alcohol in red grape pomace may in large wineries be recovered by distillation. In some regions the solids from several wineries may be amalgamated for processing to recover TARTRATES and, occasionally, grapeseed oil.

The French call both pomace that has been drained dry and pomace brandy MARC. Some English speakers called this dry pomace the **press cake**. A.D.W.

POMACE BRANDY, spirit made by distilling grape POMACE. In a well-established example of vinous recycling, reconstituted and fermented grape skins and pips, and sometimes LEES, are distilled rather than the more usual wine. This gives a particularly distinctive flavour that is fiery and uncompromising rather than elegant, but not necessarily the worse for that. Such a brandy is called MARC in France, GRAPPA in Italy, and BAGACEIRA in Portugal.

POMEROL, small but distinctive wine region in Bordeaux producing opulent and glamorous red wines dominated by the Merlot grape. Pomerol's most successful wines are some of the world's most sought after, but the glamour attaches to the labels rather than the countryside.

Pomerol is produced from about 740 ha/1,800 acres of vineyard on a plateau immediately north east of LIBOURNE

Piles of **pomace**, from red and white grapes, at De Bortoli wines in Griffith, New South Wales.

that is as geographically unremarkable as the MÉDOC, but without even any buildings or historical landmarks of note. A confusing network of narrow lanes connects about 150 smallholdings, most of which produce only a few thousand cases of wine a year.

Vines were intermittently grown on this unhospitable, unfertile land from Roman times, but viticulture was abandoned during the HUNDRED YEARS WAR and the vineyards not re-established until the 15th and 16th centuries. For hundreds of years afterwards Pomerol was regarded merely as a satellite district of neighbouring ST-ÉMILION to the east, and it was not until the late 19th century that the wines began to be appreciated, and then only in France. In the early 20th century they became known in northern Europe, notably in BELGIUM, whose wine merchants would import the wines in bulk; Belgian bottled Pomerols of this period attract high prices at AUCTION. A succession of hard-working middlemen from the impoverished inland *département* of Corrèze made Libourne their base and developed markets for RIGHT BANK wines in such markets as Paris, Belgium, and Holland, leaving the traditional BORDEAUX TRADE to provide the British market with Médoc, Graves, and Sauternes. Such famous and well-educated British connoisseurs as George SAINTSBURY do not even mention Pomerol. It was not until the 1950s that British merchants Harry WAUGH and Ronald AVERY 'discovered' Pomerol, and its most famous property Ch PÉTRUS.

The most successful of the Libourne merchants is Jean-Pierre MOUEIX, whose fortunes have been interlinked with those of Pomerol. After establishing a reputation for the appellation, he acquired Chx Trotanoy, La Fleur-Pétrus, and Lagrange in the 1950s, and has been in control of Ch Pétrus since the 1960s, as well as running Chx Feytit-Clinet, Lafleur, Lafleur-Gazin, and Latour-à-Pomerol on behalf of their owners, and selling a significant proportion of the Pomerol made in each vintage.

The success of Ch Pétrus in particular, whose wines regularly fetch prices far above of the Médoc FIRST GROWTHS, is mirrored by world-wide demand far in excess of supply for the wines of similarly minuscule properties such as Chx Lafleur, Le Pin, and La Fleur de Gay.

Pomerol's finest wines are in general made on the highest parts of the plateau, which is predominantly gravel whose layers are interleaved with clay, becoming sandier in the west, where rather lighter wines are made. The subsoil here is distinguished by a local iron-rich clay, the so-called *crasse de fer*, of which Ch Pétrus has a stratum particularly close to the surface.

Apparently as important in fashioning wines that are plump, voluptuous, and richly fruity enough to drink at less than five years old and yet which can last for as long as many a great Médoc are VINE AGE and low yields. (At Ch Pétrus, for example, the wine produced by vines less than 12 years old is usually excluded from the ASSEMBLAGE.) Yields here are often the lowest for red bordeaux and are zealously restricted at the best properties. The early flowering of the Merlot grape, and the fact that a single vine variety accounts for about 80 per cent of plantings in the appellation, unusual in Bordeaux, means that in VINTAGES such as 1984 and 1991, the majority of the crop can be lost to, for example, poor weather at flowering or spring frosts.

Pomerol is also unusual in being the only one of Bordeaux's great wine districts to have no official CLASSIFICATION. The scores of properties are in general humble farmhouses with little to distinguish one from another, and only Ch de Sales has a building of any pretensions to grandeur, and an extent of more than 40 ha. The most sought-after wines, depending on the vintage, include Chx Pétrus, Lafleur, Le Pin, La Conseillante, Trotanoy, Certan de May, Petit Village, L'Église-Clinet, Clinet, L'Évangile, Latour-à-Pomerol, and Vieux-Ch-Certan.

See also LALANDE-DE-POMEROL.

Ginestet, B., *Pomerol* (Paris, 1984).

POMMARD, prosperous village in Burgundy producing the most powerful red wines of the Côte de Beaune district of the Côte d'Or, from the usual Pinot Noir grapes. Until the 1980s, lesser wines were often sold under this popular designation while at other times Pommard has suffered from a dearth of sufficiently conscientious producers and a perception that it offers poor value. However, a fine Pommard will be darker in colour than neighbouring Volnay, deeper in flavour, more tannic in structure, less charming when young but capable of developing into a rich, sturdy wine of great power after 10 years in bottle. Claude Arnoux noted in 1728 that Pommard lasted longer than Volnay, only in those days he meant 18 months rather than 12.

Pommard stretches from the border of Beaune to the edge of Volnay. On the Beaune side the finest vineyards are Les Pézerolles and Les Épenots, including the Clos des Épeneaux monopoly of Comte Armand. Towards Volnay the most impressive PREMIER CRU vineyards include Les Chanlins, Les Jarolières, Les Fremiers, and, in particular, Les Rugiens. The lower section of the latter, Les Rugiens Bas, has the potential to make the richest wines of all in Pommard, and is frequently mentioned as being worthy of elevation to GRAND CRU status. Clos de la Commaraine, Le Clos Blanc, and Les Arvelets have also been cited in the past as good sources for Pommard.

See also CÔTE D'OR and its map. J.T.C.M.

Arnoux, C., *Dissertation sur la situation de Bourgogne* (Dijon, 1728).

POMPEII, ancient Roman settlement at the centre of an area of thriving viticulture which stretched round the southern bay of Naples from the slopes of Vesuvius to Sorrento and at one time an important wine port. There was a Pompeian wine ('headache-inducing' according to PLINY (*Natural History* 14. 70)) and a local vine, the Holconia, which carried the name of one of the most prominent Pompeian families. The eruption of Vesuvius on 24 August AD 79 which destroyed Pompeii and its surrounding territory also preserved detailed evidence of all the processes involved in the production, sale, and consumption of wine. There are the farm-villas outside Pompeii, mainly excavated in the 19th century, which contained press rooms, and elaborate piping systems for running the must off into large DOLIA set in the ground in yards where fermentation took place. There is the more recent discovery of market vineyards within the walls of Pompeii (see ROMAN GARDENS). Then there are the incidental details: in the House of the Vettii one dining room has a painted frieze in which cherubs are engaged in what were doubtlessly the businesses of the owners, including working a wine press and the presentation of wine to be tasted by a prospective buyer. The local wine was widely exported in AMPHORAE, whose type has been identified. Finally there are the numerous inns, bars, and eating places, clustered significantly mainly around the gates of the town and in the busy public areas around the Forum. Once again our imagination can be fuelled by lively scenes of inn-life painted on their walls. J.J.P.

PONTAC, distinctive red grape variety known only in SOUTH AFRICA, probably imported to the Cape from south west France in the late 17th century. Pontac may even have been named after the de Pontac family, whose Bordeaux wines were then well known (see BORDEAUX, history). It produces wines distinguished only by deep colour and rustic flavours. Only isolated plantings remain, at Klein Constantia notably.

PORT, a FORTIFIED wine made by adding brandy to arrest fermenting grape must which results in a wine, red and sometimes white, that is both sweet and high in alcohol. Port derives its name from OPORTO (Porto), the second largest city in PORTUGAL, whence the wine has been shipped for over 300 years by English merchants. Port production varies considerably from year to year but in the early 1990s averaged about 55 million l/14 million gal, roughly two-thirds of the annual production of Spain's very different but equally famous fortified wine, SHERRY.

Port style wines are also made in places as far apart as SOUTH AFRICA, AUSTRALIA, and CALIFORNIA but, within the

Loading casks of **port** at Quinta dos Malvedos in the Douro in 1891.

EUROPEAN UNION, EU law restricts the use of the term port to wines from a closely defined area in the DOURO valley of northern Portugal (one of the first examples of geographical DELIMITATION). See map on p. 750.

History

Port originates from 17th century trade wars between the English and the French. For a time imports of French wines into England were prohibited, and then, in 1693, William III imposed punitive levels of TAXATION which drove English wine merchants to Portugal, a country with whom the English had always shared good relations. At first they settled on the northern coast but, finding the wines too thin and astringent (see VINHO VERDE), they travelled inland along the river Douro. Here merchants found wines that were the opposite of those they had left behind on the coast. Fast and furious FERMENTATION at high temperatures produced dark, astringent red wines that quickly earned them the name 'blackstrap' in London. In a determined effort to make sure that these wines arrived in good condition, merchants would add a measure of brandy to stabilize them before shipment.

The discovery of the wine-making technique which results in port is credited to an Englishman, a Liverpool wine merchant who, in 1678, sent his sons to Portugal in search of wine. At Lamego, a town in the mountains high above the Douro they found a monastery where the abbot was adding brandy to the wine during rather than after fermentation, killing off the active yeasts and so producing the sort of sweet, alcoholic red wine that port was to become.

British trade with France ceased altogether in the early 18th century with the outbreak of the War of the Spanish Succession. By this time, a number of port shippers were already well established and in 1703 England and Portugal signed the METHUEN TREATY, which laid down further tariff advantages for Portuguese wines. By the 1730s, however, the fledgeling port industry was blighted by scandal. Sugar was being added and elderberry juice being used to give colour to poor, overstretched wines. Unprincipled over-production brought about a sharp fall in prices and a slump in trade. Prompted by complaints from British wine merchants, the port shippers contacted the Portuguese prime minister of the day, the marquis of Pombal. Partly to create a lucrative Portuguese monopoly on port production, in 1756 he instituted a series of measures to regulate sales of port. A boundary was drawn around the Douro restricting the production of port to those vineyards within it. Vineyards outside the official wine region were summarily grubbed up by the authorities.

Geography and climate

Pombal's demarcation, modified a number of times since 1756 (see DOURO), corresponds closely to an area of pre-Cambrian SCHIST surrounded by granite. From the village of Barqueiros about 70 km / 40 miles upstream from Oporto, the region fans out either side of the river stretching as far as the frontier with Spain. This *terra vinhateiro* or 'wine country' is referred to by the port shippers as 'the Douro'. The vineyards are shielded from the influence of the Atlantic by the Serra do Marão, a range of mountains rising to an altitude of 1,400 m / 4,600 ft. Inland, the climate becomes progressively more extreme. Annual rainfall, which averages 1,200 mm / 47 in on the coast, rises to over 1,500 mm on the mountains and then diminishes sharply, falling to as little as 400 mm at Barca d'Alva on the Spanish border. Summer temperatures in the vineyards frequently exceed 35 °C / 95 °F. It is hard to imagine a more inhospitable place to grow grapes. The soils in this mountainous region of Portugal are shallow and stony. Over a period of 300 years, however, the land has been worked to great advantage. TERRACES hacked from the schist, often with little more than a shovel and crowbar support, give vines a metre or two of soil in which to establish a root system.

The Douro region divides into three officially recognized subzones. The Baixo (Lower) Corgo is the most westerly of the three and covers the portion of the region downstream from the river Corgo, which flows into the Douro just above the town of Régua. This is the coolest and wettest of the three zones and tends to produce the lightest wines suitable for making inexpensive ruby and tawny ports (see Styles of port below). Upstream from the river Corgo, the Cima (Higher) Corgo is the heart of the demarcated region centred on the town of Pinhão. Rainfall is significantly lower here (700 mm as opposed to 900 mm or more west of Régua) and summer temperatures are, on average, a few degrees higher. All the well-known shippers own vineyards or QUINTAS here and this is where most of the high-quality tawny, Late Bottled Vintage, and vintage port is made. The most easterly of the three regions, the Douro Superior, is pioneer country. Although it has long been a part of the demarcated zone, the country is remote and sparsely populated. It is also the most arid part of the region with average temperatures at least 3 °C higher than at Régua 50 km downstream. But rising labour costs are forcing producers to consider planting the flatter land close to the Spanish border which is more suitable for MECHANIZATION and has considerable potential for high-quality port.

Viticulture

Viticulture in the Douro altered radically in the 1970s and 1980s, perhaps more than at any time since PHYLLOXERA swept through the region at the end of the 19th century, leaving hillsides abandoned. The most noticeable change is the river itself, which was progressively dammed in the 1960s to form a string of lakes. Vineyards on or close to the narrow valley floor were submerged, provoking (unwarranted) fears among the port shippers that increased HUMIDITY would alter MESOCLIMATES.

Methods of cultivation have changed the Douro landscape. Faced with an acute shortage of labour at the end of the 1960s, along with escalating costs, growers began to look for alternatives to the tiny, step-like terraces built with high retaining walls in the 19th century. The first bulldozers arrived in the early 1970s to gouge out a new system of terraces called *patamares*. Inclined ramps bound together by seasonal vegetation replaced the costly retaining walls and, with wider spacing between the vines (resulting in a VINE DENSITY of 3,500 vines per ha (1,420 per acre) as opposed to 6,000 on some traditional terraces), small tractors can circulate in the vineyards.

At much the same time, some growers pioneered a system of planting vines in vertical lines running up and down the natural slope. This 'up and down' planting has been a qualified success, although access and SOIL EROSION are problems where the gradient exceeds 30 degrees. In the 1980s there was a flurry of new planting under a World Bank scheme which provided farmers with low-interest loans. The traditional, labour-intensive terraces, still impeccably maintained by some growers, now stand alongside the newer *patamares* and vine rows planted vertically up the hillside, both of which allow limited MECHANIZATION.

Most of the Douro's vineyards are pruned according to the French GUYOT system, and are trained on wires supported by stakes hewn from local stone. Most vines are GRAFTED *in situ* and IRRIGATION is essential for young vines. July and August are generally dry and SPRAYING against FUNGAL DISEASES is necessary only in the early summer or in exceptionally wet years. Aside from the usual vineyard PESTS, most of which can be controlled by spraying, wild boar eat grapes and occasionally wreck new vineyards.

The Douro HARVEST usually starts in late September and lasts for around three weeks. The steeply terraced vineyards come alive as gangs of pickers descend from outlying villages for the duration of the harvest (see also HARVEST TRADITIONS).

Vine varieties

More than 80 different grape varieties are authorized for the production of port but few growers have detailed knowledge of the identity of the vines growing in their vineyards. All but the most recently planted vineyards contain a mixture of grapes, often with as many as 20 or 30 different varieties intermingled in the same vineyard plot. But in recent years some of the larger shippers, notably Ramos-Pinto and COCKBURN, have conducted their own research into port grapes and identified the best varieties, which are now being planted in tracts rather than being jumbled up together. TOURIGA NACIONAL, TINTA BARROCA, TOURIGA FRANCESA, Tinta Roriz (Spain's TEMPRANILLO), and TINTÃ CÃO are the favoured five black-skinned varieties, although varieties such as SOUSÃO, TINTA AMARELA, and MOURISCO find favour with certain growers.

Gouveio (thought to be VERDELHO), Malvasia Fina, and Viosinho are generally considered among the best varieties for white port.

Port wine-making

Rapid EXTRACTION of COLOUR and TANNINS is the crux of the various vinification methods used to produce red port. Because FERMENTATION is curtailed by fortifying spirit after just two or three days, the grape juice or must spends a much shorter time in contact with the skins than in normal RED WINE-MAKING. The MACERATION process should therefore be as vigorous as possible.

Until the early 1960s all port was vinified in much the same way. Every farm had a winery equipped with LAGARES, low stone troughs, usually built from granite, in which the grapes were trodden and fermented. Some are still in use, mainly at the small, privately owned quintas, and many finest ports destined for vintage or aged tawny blends continue to be trodden in *lagares*. The human foot, for all its many unpleasant associations, is ideal for pressing grapes as it breaks up the fruit without crushing the pips that would otherwise release bitter-tasting PHENOLICS into the wine.

Grapes would usually arrive at the winery in coarse-woven baskets holding about 60 kg/130 lbs. *Lagares* would be progressively filled over the course of a day, and trodden by the pickers themselves, thigh high in purple pulp, in the evening. Most *lagares* hold between 10 and 15 PIPES (about 5,500 to 8,250 l (2,180 gal)) although a number of the larger quintas have *lagares* with a capacity of up to 30 pipes. As a rule of thumb, two people per pipe are needed to tread a *lagar*. Fermentation begins as a result of the action of indigenous YEASTS on the grapes' sugar. The alcohol produced, and the increasing TEMPERATURE of the mass of purple skins, juice, and stems, encourages the extraction of the phenolics vital for the character of port. After about two or three hours of hard, methodical treading, the CAP of skins and stalks starts to float to the surface. Regular PUNCHING DOWN of the cap was traditionally performed with long, spiked sticks from planks run across the top of the *lagares*.

After 24 to 36 hours, the level of the grape sugar in the fermenting must declines from 12 or 13° BAUMÉ to between 6 and 8° Baumé. Depending on the intended sweetness of the wine, the wine would be run off the *lagar* into a vat, already about one-fifth full with GRAPE SPIRIT, or AGUARDENTE, whose ALCOHOLIC STRENGTH is 77 per cent. As the spirit is mixed with the wine, the yeasts are killed and the fermentation is arrested. At this stage the must becomes young, sweet, fiery port with an alcohol content of 19 or 20 per cent by volume. (See HARVEST TRADITIONS for more details of the foot treading ceremony.)

In the 1960s and 1970s treading grapes in *lagares* became much less widespread. The Douro valley and the remote TRÁS-OS-MONTES region which traditionally supplied LABOUR at harvest time have suffered from marked emigration as younger people left to find more profitable work in the cities and abroad. By the mid 1960s many of the larger wine farms were unable to find the manpower necessary to tread *lagares* and the port shippers were forced to look for other, less labour-intensive, ways to make wine.

A few shippers such as Cockburn's and Sandeman adopted a system called *movimosto* specifically to help their farmers suffering from the labour shortage. Whole bunches of grapes are fed through a CRUSHER before being tipped into a *lagar* to ferment. Instead of treading, the must is pumped out of the *lagar* and sprayed over the centre of the cap. However, the force of the pump was found to be too weak for the surface area and the cap was not broken up sufficiently to ensure good extraction. Consequently many wines made by *movimosto* lacked structure and depth of colour and, in the main, the system has been abandoned.

Faced with an increasingly serious labour shortage as so many fit young men were conscripted in the late 1960s to fight in the wars in Portugal's African colonies, most port producers abandoned *lagares* altogether. Many isolated properties were without electricity and shippers set about building central wineries to which grapes from outlying farms could be delivered. Most of these were equipped with AUTOVINIFICATION tanks which have proved to be a successful alternative to treading in *lagares*, which required no external power source. The resulting wine is fortified just like foot-trodden young wines were.

Many wineries are equipped with vertical PRESSES and the mass of grape skins and stems that remains after treading or crushing is forked into a press to extract the last of the juice. This deeply coloured, astringent wine will be run off and fortified separately. It may be blended back at a later stage or used to bolster an inferior wine.

White port is made in much the same way as red with SKIN CONTACT during fermentation. White grapes used to be trodden in *lagares* but nowadays most wines are fermented on the skins in cement or stainless steel vats without recourse to autovinification. Fermentation temperatures are often high and the skins impart both colour and tannins to the wine. A few producers are now fermenting in temperature-controlled conditions, having first separated the must from the skins. This results in a cleaner, fresher, lighter, and less astringent style of white port, some of which has a lower alcoholic strength of 16.5 or 17 per cent (see below).

The fortifying grape spirit for port used to be distilled from wine made in Portugal, mainly from the OESTE region north of Lisbon, although in recent years most of the spirit has been imported, and is distilled from the EUROPEAN UNION WINE LAKE. Until 1992, this spirit had to be purchased from the Casa do Douro (see Organization of the industry, below), which set a fixed price and controlled distribution. This monopoly was broken by the EU and producers have since been free to purchase any spirit they choose provided that it complies with the 77 per cent norm of alcoholic strength.

See also VIN DOUX NATUREL for a comparison of port wine-making techniques with those in the production of French counterparts such as Banyuls.

Organization of the industry

A total of 28,000 individual growers farmed about 33,000 ha/81,000 acres of vines in the Douro in the mid 1990s, every vineyard plot being registered with the Casa do Douro, the official body set up in 1932 to represent the growers.

Vineyards in the Douro are graded according to a complicated points system and classified into six different categories rated A to F. Twelve different physical factors including site, aspect, exposure, and gradient are taken into consideration, each of which is allocated a numerical score. In theory a vineyard could score a maximum of 1,680 points but a property with more than 1,200 points is awarded an A grade. A vineyard with less than 200 points is given an F grade. On this basis the Casa do Douro distributes the annual *beneficio* authorization, the total amount of port that may be made that year. This is calculated annually by the port industry's regulating authority, the Instituto do Vinho do Porto (Port Wine Institute, or IVP).

Permits are then distributed to individual farmers detailing the amount of grape must that they may fortify to make port. The amount varies according to the year but, typically, A and B grade properties may make 550 to 600 l of port per thousand vines, while F grade properties are rarely allowed to make port at all. The surplus is usually made into table wine which has its own denomination but sells for a much lower price (see DOURO).

This quality control system, instituted in 1947, served the port industry well for four decades, but pressure for its reform intensified when in 1990 the independence of the Casa do Douro was severely compromised by its purchase of shares in Royal Oporto, one of the largest port shippers. After a period of chronic instability, efforts were made in the mid 1990s to replace the Casa do Douro–IVP duopoly with a single regulatory body representing both growers and shippers.

After vinification, the bulk of the new wine stays at the QUINTA or farm until the spring after the harvest when it is shipped downstream to the shippers' LODGES in VILA NOVA DE GAIA across the river Douro from Oporto. At one time flat-bottomed boats called *barcos rabelos* negotiated the rapids laden with PIPES of port but, since the river was dammed in the 1960s, nearly all wine has left the region by more prosaic road tanker.

Until 1986, all port destined for export had to be shipped from Vila Nova da Gaia. Although this rule has been relaxed, allowing growers to ship their own wines direct from the Douro, most shippers continue to mature their wines in Gaia, where they also have their offices. This may be partly due to inertia, but the cooler climate and markedly high humidity near the coast are thought to be beneficial for slow CASK AGEING (see DOURO BAKE for the effect on port of maturing it upstream in the Douro valley).

Just as the farmers are represented and controlled by the Casa do Douro, so the shippers in Vila Nova de Gaia have to submit to the authority of the Instituto do Vinho do Porto. This government-run body employs inspectors to check the movement of stock. It ensures that shippers adhere to the so-called *lei dos dois tercos* (law of two-thirds), which restricts shippers from selling more than a third of their stock in any one year. Shippers therefore have to keep detailed records to prove to the IVP that quantities of wine coming in accord with outgoing shipments. The IVP is also empowered to analyse and taste a sample from every port shipment before issuing the guarantee seal which is stuck to the neck of every bottle of port leaving Oporto.

The market for port has altered dramatically since the Second World War. The so-called 'Englishman's wine' that used to be drunk everywhere from gentlemen's clubs to street corner pubs became the Frenchman's wine when France's imports of *le porto* (largely inexpensive wood ports; see Styles of port below) overtook those of the United Kingdom in the early 1960s. The British market (along with that of the United States) is still highly coveted by port shippers, however, especially those of British descent such as COCKBURN, CROFT, SANDEMAN, TAYLOR and the SYMINGTONS, who control shippers such as Dow, Graham, and Warre.

Styles of port

There are two broad categories of port, fortified wines whose style is shaped by either CASK AGEING or BOTTLE AGEING. Wood-matured ports, often called simply wood ports, are aged either in wooden casks or, sometimes, cement tanks, and are ready to drink straight after FINING, FILTRATION, and BOTTLING. Ports designed to mature in bottle, however, are aged for a short time in wood and are bottled without filtration. It may then take up to 20 or 30 years before such a wine is ready to drink. Within these two general categories there are many different styles of port. The official legislation was still vague in the early 1990s (although port shippers were pressing the controlling IVP for reform of a system which allows a number of confusing, not to say misleading, terms). It permits seven loosely defined styles as well as any number of 'special designations'. Words such as 'reserva', 'superior', and 'velhissimo' (very old) are regularly found alongside brand names on port labels but are virtually meaningless.

Ruby. This is one of the simplest and least expensive styles of port. Aged in bulk for two or three years, it is bottled young while the wine retains a deep ruby colour and a strong, fiery personality. Young wines from more than one vintage are aged in all sorts of vessels (wood, cement, and occasionally stainless steel) before being blended, filtered, and bottled. PASTEURIZATION is sometimes applied to stabilize such wines and can result in 'stewed' flavours, but good ruby with its uncomplicated mulberry fruit aromas and flavours is often a good, warming drink. When the British FASHION for ruby port and lemonade faded in the 1960s, many shippers dropped the name ruby on the labels of such ports in favour of their own, self-styled brands.

Tawny. The word Tawny is applied to a confusingly wide range of very different styles of port. In theory tawny implies a wine which has been aged in wood for so much longer than a ruby that it loses colour and the wine takes on an amber-brown or tawny hue (see AGEING). In practice, however, much of the tawny port sold today is no older than the average ruby and may therefore be found at the same price. The difference between a commercial ruby and its counterpart labelled 'tawny' is that, whereas ruby is made from a blend of big, deep coloured wines, tawny is often produced from lighter wines grown in the poorer Baixo Corgo vineyards where grapes rarely ripen to give much depth or intensity of fruit. Vinification methods may also be adapted to produce paler coloured wines, and the colour of the final blend may be adjusted further by adding a proportion of white port so that the wine ends up with a pale pink hue rather than tawny brown. Many bulk tawnies are left up river for longer than other wines for the heat to speed up the maturation (see DOURO BAKE). The resulting wines often display a slight brown tinge on the rim but tend to lack the freshness and primary fruit character normally associated with young port. The French typically drink inexpensive, light, tawny-style wines as an aperitif and supplying this market has become the major commercial activity for many of the larger port shippers.

Aged tawny. Port that has been left to age in wooden casks for six or more years begins to take on a tawny colour and a soft, silky character as the PHENOLICS are polymerized (see AGEING). Most of these tawnies are bottled with an indication of age on the label. The terms 10, 20, 30, or Over 40 years old seen on labels are, however, approximations as tawny ports are blended from a number of years' produce. The legislation is deliberately vague and most aged tawnies are a blend tasted and approved by the IVP as conforming to the character expected from a wine that is the age claimed on the label. Aged tawnies are made from wines of the very highest quality: wines set aside in undeclared years that might have otherwise ended up as vintage port (see below). They mature in cask in the cool of the lodges at Gaia until the shipper considers that they are ready to blend and bottle. Labels on these wines must state that the wine has matured in wood and give the date of bottling, which is important since aged tawny port may deteriorate if it spends too long in bottle. Once the bottle has been opened, the wine oxidizes quite rapidly, losing its delicacy of fruit if it is left on ULLAGE for too long. Port shippers themselves often drink a good aged tawny, chilled in summer, in preference to any other. The delicate, nutty character of a well-aged tawny suits the climate and temperament of the Douro better than the hefty, spicy character of vintage port which is better adapted to cooler climes.

Vintage port. This, the most expensive style of port, accounts for hardly one per cent of all port sold, yet it is the wine which probably receives the most attention. British shippers, in particular, have built vintage port into a flagship wine, declared in an atmosphere of speculation when both the quality of the wine and the market are judged to be fit. But vintage port is one of the world's simplest of wines to make. Wines from a single year, or VINTAGE, are blended and bottled after spending between two and three years in wood. Thereafter, most of the wine is sold and the consumer takes over the nurturing for 15, 20, 30, or more years until the wine is ready to drink. Vintage port is also distinguished from other styles, however, by the quality of the grapes from which the wine is made. Only grapes grown in the best Cima Corgo vineyards, picked at optimum ripeness following an outstanding summer, are destined to be made into vintage port. Even then, nothing is certain until at least a year after the harvest when shippers have had time to reflect on the characteristics of the wine and the market. If, after repeated tasting, the wine-maker feels that he has sufficient quantities of high-quality wine to merit the 'declaration' of a vintage, he sends samples to the IVP in the second year after the harvest accompanied by details of just how much wine he intends to release. Only when the shipper has received approval may the vintage be 'declared'. Wine of vintage port potential is made at the best quintas in most years, but a vintage is declared only if there is sufficient quantity of top-quality wine, and if it is felt that the market is ready to support another vintage (1931 being a classic example of a qualitatively superb vintage undeclared by most shippers for entirely commercial reasons). Vintage declarations may be very irregular but very roughly three vintages have been declared in each decade. Vintage port has, not always wisely, been considered a prime wine for INVESTMENT. Because they should be bottle aged for longer than almost any other style of wine, vintage port bottles are particularly thick, dark, and sturdy. The wines, extremely high in phenolics in their youth, throw a heavy DEPOSIT and need especial care when DECANTING and SERVING.

Colheita. Meaning 'harvest' or 'crop' and therefore by extension 'vintage' in Portuguese, colheita ports are in fact very different from vintage ports. Colheitas are best understood as tawny ports from a single year, bottled with the date of the harvest on the label. The law states that colheita ports must be aged in wood for at least seven years, although most are aged for considerably longer. The wines take on all the nuances of an aged tawny but should also express the characteristics of a single year. All wines should carry the date of bottling and should usually be drunk within about a year of that date.

LBV. Late Bottled Vintage port is a wine from a single year, bottled between the fourth and sixth years after the harvest. Two different styles of LBV wines have evolved, however. First there are the so-called 'traditional' LBVs, bottled without any filtration or treatment so that, like a vintage port, they need to be decanted before serving. These wines tend to be made in good but undeclared years and are ready to drink earlier than vintage port, four to six years after bottling.

A second style of LBV is more common. These are wines which have been filtered and cold stabilized before bottling to prevent the formation of sediment. That in itself is no bad thing (decanting has always been awkward for restaurateurs) but heavy-handed filtration removes much of the character from the wine. Most filtered LBVs are therefore a poor substitute for the intensity and concentration of fruit in a traditional LBV. Some, making flagrant use of the word vintage and a date on the label, are really no better than a standard ruby. Efforts are being made to remove the word 'vintage' from the label and restrict shippers to the term Late Bottled or LB, together with the date of the harvest.

Vintage character. This is the port trade's great misnomer. The wines are not the product of a single year or vintage and few, if any, exhibit any of the character of vintage port. Again the legislation is vague but, in theory, vintage character wines are premium rubies aged in bulk, usually wood, for five to seven years before being filtered and bottled. This is a style largely aimed at the British market.

Single-quinta vintage. Just as wine-producing CHÂTEAUX evolved in France in the 18th and 19th centuries, the single, wine-making QUINTA is developing in Portugal, and many of the better-known Douro quintas belong to a particular port shipper. (TAYLOR own Quinta da Vargellas, for example, while Quinta do Bomfim is associated with Dow, Quinta da Cavadinha with Warre, and Quinta dos Malvedos with Graham.) Single-quinta ports are made in much the same way as vintage port, aged in wood for two or three years and bottled without filtration so that they throw a sediment (and should therefore be decanted before serving). A number of significant differences distinguish single-quinta vintages from declared vintage ports, however. First of all, shippers' single-quinta ports tend to be made in good (but not outstanding) years which are not declared. In years which are declared for vintage port, many of these wines will be the lots that make up the backbone of the vintage blend and are not therefore available for release as wines in their own right. Secondly many single-quinta ports are kept back by shippers and only sold when the wine is considered to be ready to drink, perhaps eight or ten years after the harvest. Single quintas or individual vineyards in the Douro were given a fillip in 1986 when the law requiring all port to be exported via VILA NOVA DE GAIA was relaxed, opening the way for a number of small vineyard owners who, in the past, had been restricted to selling their wines to large firms (although the large shippers with their established marketing networks initially had greater success in launching their own single-quinta wines).

Crusted or crusting port. This port is so called because of the 'crust' or DEPOSIT that it throws in bottle. In spite of its rather crusty, establishment name, it is the fairly recent creation of British shippers, designed to appeal to the vintage port enthusiast, even though the coveted word 'vintage' does not appear on the label (because crusting ports are not wines from a single year or vintage but blends from a number of years bottled young with little or no filtration). Like vintage port, the wines continue to develop in the bottle, throwing a sediment or crust, so that the wine needs to be decanted before it is served. Rather like traditional LBVs, many crusted or crusting ports offer an excellent alternative to vintage port, providing the port enthusiast with a dark, full bodied wine at a much lower price.

Garrafeira. The word GARRAFEIRA, meaning 'private cellar' or 'reserve', is more commonly associated with Portuguese table wines than with port. Few port shippers continue to support the tradition of garrafeira ports, wines from a single year aged for a short time in wood followed by a longer period spent in 5- or 10-l glass demijohns, or bonbonnes (like some MADEIRA). After 20, 30, or even 40 years in glass, the wine is decanted off its sediment and rebottled in conventional 75-cl bottles. The wines combine depth of fruit with the delicate, silky texture associated with tawny port. The Dutch-owned firm of Niepoort continue to support this tradition.

White port. Ernest COCKBURN remarked earlier this century that 'the first duty of port is to be red'. Nevertheless a significant proportion of white grapes grow in vineyards in the Douro and all shippers produce a certain amount of white port. White port is made in much the same way as red except that MACERATION during fermentation is much shorter or (in many instances) does not take place at all. Grape spirit is added to arrest the fermentation at about the same point as in the vinification of red port, producing a wine that is usually medium sweet with a fat, grapey character. Most white ports have a certain amount of RESIDUAL SUGAR, even those labelled 'dry' or 'extra dry'. Intensely sweet wines, made mainly for the domestic market, are labelled 'lagrima' (tears) because of their VISCOSITY (see also MÁLAGA). Another, drier style of white port, described as 'leve seco' (light dry) is made by some shippers. These are wines with an alcoholic strength of around 16.5 or 17 per cent, rather than the usual 19 to 20 per cent. Most commercial white ports are aged for no more than 18 months, generally in tanks made of cement or stainless steel. Wood ageing lends character to white port, turning it gold in colour and giving the wine an incisive, dry, nutty tang. White port is sometimes used by shippers for blending cheaper tawnies.

Moscatel. One of over 30 different grape varieties used for making white port, Moscatel is occasionally used on its own to make a sweet fortified VARIETAL white wine with the grape aroma characteristic of MUSCAT.

See also articles on DOURO, OPORTO, and VILA NOVA DE GAIA, as well as articles on individual port shippers COCKBURN, CROFT, FERREIRA, FONSECA, QUINTA DO NOVAL, SANDEMAN, SYMINGTONS, and TAYLOR. R.J.M.

Bradford, S., *The Story of Port* (2nd edn., London, 1983).
Howkins, B., *Rich, Rare & Red* (London, 1982).
Mayson, R., *Portugal's Wines & Wine Makers* (London, 1992).
Suckling, J., *Vintage Port* (New York, 1990).

PORTALEGRE, town in Portugal whose co-operative is establishing a certain reputation for its wines. See ALENTEJO.

PORTAN, like CALADOC and CHASAN, is a crossing made by French AMPELOGRAPHER Paul Truel at the INRA station at Vassal. In this case he crossed Grenache Noir and Portugais Bleu (Blauer Portugieser) to develop a Grenache-like variety that would ripen even in the Midi's cooler zones. It is grown to a strictly limited extent but is allowed into Vin de Pays d'Oc.

PORT TONGS, rare instrument for opening a bottle of vintage PORT so old that the cork is likely to crumble under the impact of a CORKSCREW. The specially shaped tongs are heated in a flame and applied to the neck of the bottle which is then immediately cooled with a cold, damp cloth. The sudden temperature change should result in a clean break. Tongs can be used on other venerable bottles.

PORTUGAIS, or **Portugais Bleu**, is the French manifestation of the more commonly Germanic black grape variety Blauer PORTUGIESER. Its influence is only slowly declining in France, where it was once one of the most planted varieties in the Tarn *département*, in some cases at the expense of the nobler varieties responsible for red GAILLAC.

PORTUGAL. Among European wine-producing nations, Portugal is something of a paradox. Sitting on the western flank of the Iberian peninsula, this seafaring nation which discovered so much of the NEW WORLD now clings firmly to the Old. Secluded both geographically and, for much of the 20th century until it joined the EUROPEAN UNION in 1986, politically as well, Portugal has developed in isolation from other countries, including neighbouring SPAIN. However, the sizeable wine industry that has grown up in this small country owes much to foreign trade. See map on p. 750.

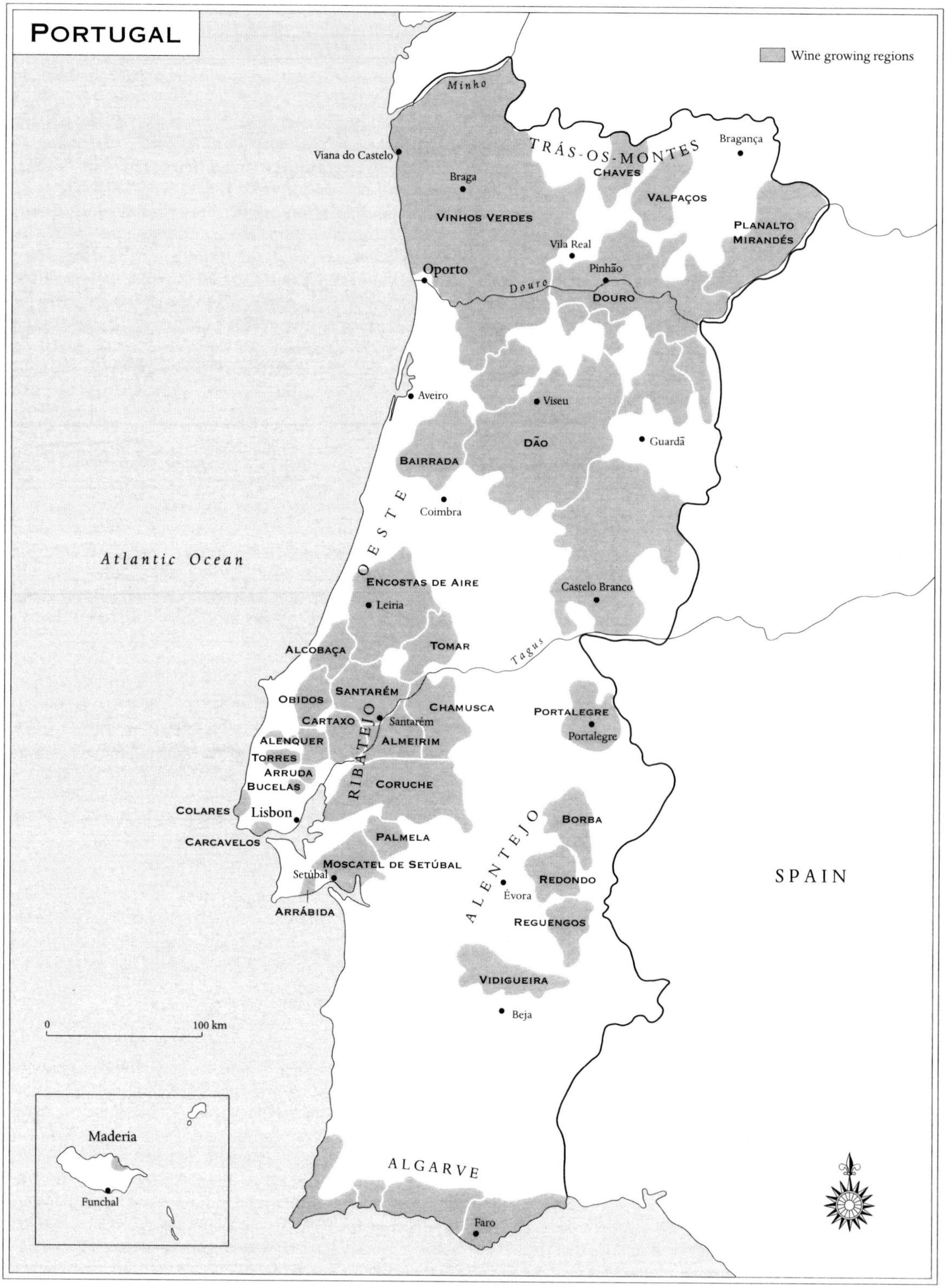
PORTUGAL
Wine growing regions
Minho
Viana do Castelo
Braga
TRÁS-OS-MONTES
Bragança
CHAVES
VALPAÇOS
VINHOS VERDES
PLANALTO MIRANDÊS
Vila Real
Oporto
Pinhão
Douro
DOURO
Aveiro
Viseu
DÃO
Guardã
BAIRRADA
Coimbra
OESTE
Atlantic Ocean
ENCOSTAS DE AIRE
Leiria
Castelo Branco
TOMAR
ALCOBAÇA
Tagus
OBIDOS
SANTARÉM
CHAMUSCA
PORTALEGRE
Portalegre
CARTAXO
Santarém
ALENQUER
ALMEIRIM
TORRES
ARRUDA
RIBATEJO
BUCELAS
CORUCHE
COLARES
Lisbon
CARCAVELOS
ALENTEJO
BORBA
PALMELA
MOSCATEL DE SETÚBAL
Setúbal
ARRÁBIDA
REDONDO
Évora
REGUENGOS
SPAIN
VIDIGUEIRA
Beja
0
100 km
Maderia
Funchal
ALGARVE
Faro

Portugal's distinctive tiles at a railway station in the Douro valley.

History

The British have always enjoyed an amicable relationship with the Portuguese. As early as the 12th century, wines were being shipped to England from the MINHO in north west Portugal. In 1386 the Treaty of Windsor set the seal on a friendship that has persisted, virtually uninterrupted, to the present day. When England went to war with France in the 17th century, Portugal was therefore the natural alternative source for wine. PORT, often called 'the Englishman's wine', originated from this conflict. By the time England and Portugal signed the METHUEN TREATY in 1703, which laid down tariff advantages for Portuguese wines, a thriving community of English and German wine shippers was already well established in OPORTO. Out in the Atlantic, the island of MADEIRA, an important trading post for passing ships, began exporting wine to the newly colonized state and yet-to-be UNITED STATES of America, an important market on the East Coast which survives to the present day. Renewed conflict between Britain and France over the French invasion of the Iberian peninsula in 1803 rekindled demand for Portuguese wines. BUCELAS, CARCAVELOS, and a red wine simply called 'Lisbon' were popular in Britain until the 1870s.

In the last 30 years of the 19th century PHYLLOXERA devastated Portuguese vineyards as severely as those elsewhere in Europe. Some Portuguese wine regions never really recovered. Many growers resorted to planting high-yielding vine HYBRIDS, which still predominate in many of the smallholdings of north and central Portugal. For much of the 20th century Portugal turned her back on the outside world. Following 20 years of political and economic turmoil, the demure son of a DÃO smallholder, Antonio de Oliveira Salazar, became prime minister in 1930. His regime, which lasted for over 40 years, fostered a corporate, one-party state. Portugal's chaotic wine industry was thoroughly reorganized. The Junta Nacional do Vinho (JNV) founded in 1937 initiated a programme of co-operativization. Over 100 winery CO-OPERATIVES were built, mostly in northern Portugal, in less than 20 years. At the time they represented a significant advance but, all too often, the system imposed by central government was too inflexible and wine-making standards deteriorated.

It is paradoxical, however, that, against this background of self-imposed seclusion, Portugal should give birth to one of the greatest international wine success stories of modern times: medium sweet, lightly sparkling rosés called MATEUS and LANCERS.

In 1974 Portugal was once again thrown into turmoil by a military-led revolution. But after two years of upheaval the soldier politicians returned to barracks and subsequent elected governments eventually returned Portugal to the European mainstream. Portugal's wine-makers benefited enormously from joining the European Union in 1986. Monopolistic legislation was overturned and, thanks to EU policies of supporting agricultural underdogs, money poured in to help update the wine industry, much of which continues to be hidebound by archaic techniques and technology.

Geography and climate

For such a small country Portugal produces a remarkable diversity of wines. Roughly rectangular in shape, it is under 600 km/360 miles long and no more than 200 km wide. The wines produced on the flat coastal littoral are strongly influenced by prevailing Atlantic westerly winds. Rainfall, which reaches 2,000 mm/78 in a year on the hills north of Oporto, diminishes sharply to less than 500 mm in some inland wine areas. The temperate maritime climate, with warm summers and cool, wet winters, becomes more extreme towards the south and east. An average annual temperature of around 10 °C/50 °F in the northern hills compares with more than 17.5 °C on the southern plains where, in summer, temperatures frequently exceed 35 °C/95 °F.

Reflecting these contrasting climatic conditions, no two wines could be more dissimilar than VINHO VERDE and PORT, which are produced in adjoining regions. There are pockets of viticulture all over Portugal. Only the very highest mountain peaks of the central and northern mountain ranges are unable to support viticulture. From the river Minho in the north to the ALGARVE in the south there are nearly 400,000 ha/988,000 acres of vines.

Vine varieties

Portugal's vineyards have evolved in isolation. Only a handful of varieties have crossed international frontiers, leaving Portugal like a viticultural island with a treasure trove of indigenous grape varieties. Since the end of the 19th century, however, little research has been undertaken, and Portugal's haphazard vineyards have remained *terra incognita*, not just to outsiders but to the vine-growers themselves. A number of studies have been undertaken since Portugal joined the EU, in order to identify the country's most promising VINE VARIETIES. Among whites, LOUREIRO and ALVARINHO (in Vinho Verde), ARINTO (in Bucelas), and FERNÃO PIRES (in Ribatejo and the south) are showing potential. Among Portugal's best red grapes are TOURIGA NACIONAL (in the Douro and Dão), TOURIGA FRANCESA, and Tinta Roriz, Spain's TEMPRANILLO (in the Douro), BAGA (in Bairrada), and CASTELÃO FRANCES (also known as Periquita where it is planted in the south). Internationally famous foreign varieties such as CABERNET SAUVIGNON and CHARDONNAY have made few inroads.

Wine laws

Portugal's wine law pre-dates that of most other European countries (although see also Tokay in HUNGARY). In 1756 the then prime minister, the marquis of Pombal, drew a boundary around the vineyards of the Douro valley to protect the authenticity of port, one of the wine world's first examples of geographical DELIMITATION. Bucelas, Colares, Carcavelos, Dão, Madeira, Setúbal, and Vinho Verde were all awarded REGIÃO DEMARCADA (demarcated region) status between 1908 and 1929, followed by Bairrada, Algarve, and Douro (for table wine) in 1979 and 1980. Since Portugal joined the European Union, the Regiões Demarcadas or RDs have been redesignated Denominação de Origem Controlada (DOC). A second tier of Indicação de Proveniencia Regulamentada (IPR) wine regions has also been introduced. This brings Portugal's wine law roughly in to line with that of other EU countries.

For details of Portugal's extremely varied viticultural techniques, wine-making practices and expertise, and individual regions, see also ALENTEJO, ALGARVE, ARRÁBIDA, BAIRRADA, BUCELAS, COLARES, CARCAVELOS, DÃO, DOURO, OESTE, PALMELA, RIBATEJO, SETÚBAL, TRÁS-OS-MONTES, VINHO VERDE, and, most importantly, PORT. The viticulturally important Atlantic island of MADEIRA is an autonomous part of Portugal.

See also Portuguese BRANDY. R.J.M.

Mayson, R., *Portugal's Wines & Wine Makers* (London, 1992).
Metcalfe, C., and McWhirter, K., *The Wines of Spain & Portugal* (London, 1988).

PORTUGIESER or **Blauer Portugieser** is a black grape variety common in both senses of that word in both Austria and Germany, its name suggesting completely unsubstantiated Portuguese origins. The vigorous, precocious vine is extremely prolific, easily producing 160 hl/ha (9 tons/acre), thanks to its good resistance to COULURE, of pale, low-acid red that, thanks to robust ENRICHMENT, can taste disconcertingly sweet to non-natives.

Blauer Portugieser is synonymous with dull, thin red in lower AUSTRIA, where it is particularly popular with growers in Pulkautal, Retz, and the Thermenregion. It covers five times as much vineyard area as Blauburgunder (Pinot Noir) and is the country's second most planted dark-berried vine variety after Blauer ZWEIGELT. Such wines are rarely exported, with good reason, and are rarely worthy of detailed study.

Germany's everyday black grape variety Portugieser was overtaken in terms of total area planted by SPÄTBURGUNDER (Pinot Noir) in the 1970s, although in the early 1990s it was enjoying a renaissance of popularity with growers determined to satisfy the German thirst for red wine regardless of its quality. In 1990 there were more than 4,000 ha/9,900 acres of Portugieser in Germany, half of them in the PFALZ, where a high proportion of Portugieser is encouraged to produce vast quantities of pink WEISSHERBST. It also plays an important role in the AHR region, famous for its reds, many of which depend on Portugieser as much as the Spätburgunder for which the region is more famous. (In 1990, the Ahr's plantings of Portugieser were nearly half those of the nobler variety.)

The variety is so easy to grow, however, that it has spread throughout central Europe and beyond (as PORTUGAIS Bleu it was once grown widely in south western France). It is ingeniously named Oporto in HUNGARY and ROMANIA and is grown in northern Croatia as Portugizac Crni, or Portugaljka.

POST, substantial support for wires and vines which is common in NEW WORLD vineyards and usually made from wood, and driven in to the ground at intervals down the row. Other materials used include concrete, steel, and plastic. Woods used for such posts are softwoods such as pine, treated to withstand insect and fungus attack, or naturally resistant hardwoods. A common spacing of about 6 m/20 ft between posts is close enough to stop the wire sagging. Smaller-diameter posts placed one beside each vine are called STAKES and these are more common for Old World vineyards. R.E.S.

POTASSIUM, one of the major elements required by the vine for healthy growth. It constitutes about three per cent of the vine's dry weight, and is an important component of grape juice. Potassium (K) deficiencies show up first in older leaves as a CHLOROSIS, which may become a marginal burn when severe. Potassium-deficient leaves are often shiny. Severe deficiencies can inhibit growth, yield, and sugar content. Potassium deficiency can be confirmed easily by analysing for potassium levels in leaves or petioles, and 1.0 to 1.5 per cent K is the optimal range. Potassium deficiency is more evident during drought or in cold soils in spring, both of which reduce the roots' uptake of potassium.

Potassium is widely regarded as the most important element affecting wine quality. This is because high potassium levels in grape juice cause high PH, which adversely affects wine quality. Juice potassium levels are influenced by soil potassium levels, although this is not always a straightforward relationship. Delas and colleagues in Bordeaux have shown positive linear correlations between plant K levels and juice K, but this was for vines with K contents up to and exceeding three times the optimal value.

ROOTSTOCKS also have an important effect on juice K, with lower-vigour rootstocks giving lower juice K. This effect has been shown both in France and Australia. Part of the explanation may be that more vigorous rootstocks tend to result in SHADE, which is known to increase both juice K and pH. In hot climates, must potassium and juice pH are high, which may be the result of the high TRANSPIRATION rate of vines growing in such an environment. It seems that distribution of potassium in the plant is important, and that shade causes accumulation in the leaves which subsequently migrates to the fruit. CANOPY MANAGEMENT techniques which reduce shade can therefore be effective in reducing must K and pH. R.E.S.

Champagnol, F., *Éléments de physiologie de la vigne et de viticulture générale* (St-Gely-du-Fesc, 1984).

Delas, J., Molot, C., and Soyer, J. P., 'Fertilisation minérale de la vigne et teneur en potassium des baies, des moûts et des vins', in P. Ribéreau-Gayon and A. Lonvaud (eds.), *Actualités oenologiques 89: comptes rendus du 4e* Symposium International d'Oenologie, Bordeaux, 15–17 juin, 1989 (Paris, 1989).

Smart, R. E., and Robinson, M., *Sunlight into Wine: A Handbook for Winegrape Canopy Management* (Adelaide, 1991).

POTENTIAL ALCOHOL, measurement of a wine or must which equates to its total ALCOHOLIC STRENGTH if all the sugar were to be fermented out to alcohol. Thus, a Sauternes might have an alcoholic strength of 13 per cent, but a potential alcohol of 20 per cent if its RESIDUAL SUGAR would ferment to a dry liquid containing 7 per cent alcohol.

POT STILL, the original form of still in which individual batches of wine or some other fermented liquid are subjected to the process of DISTILLATION, in contrast to the CONTINUOUS STILL. The pot still is an essential element in the production of COGNAC and other fine BRANDIES. It is filled with wine and then heated, relying on the simple physical fact that alcohol boils at a lower temperature than water. The alcohol fumes are then trapped at the top of the vessel and cooled. Until the development of the continuous COFFEY STILL in the 19th century, it was the only type of still available. It is less efficient than a continuous still because each batch has to be heated, thereby using far more fuel. Furthermore, the raw material has to be distilled twice to produce a properly concentrated spirit. Yet the ability to control the process and retain the CONGENERS, the precious substances which will give body and flavour to the final product, means that virtually all the world's finest spirits (apart from ARMAGNAC), including calvados and malt whisky, are produced by pot stills.

Inevitably in a piece of apparatus invented at least 700 years ago, certain elements have been standardized, while others have developed local variants. The vessels are almost invariably made of copper, which is virtually neutral (although it also helps to fix the fatty acids in the wine, as well as any sulphurous products in the alcoholic vapour that would harm the quality of the spirit). For the production of grape-based spirits, pot stills are heated from outside, although gas, which provides the desirable qualities of uniform and controllable heat, has usually replaced wood or coal as a fuel.

The differences appear most obviously in the size of the vessel and the mechanisms used to trap the fumes. The size has increased over the years—although the size of stills used in the second distillation (*deuxième chauffe* in French) in Cognac are strictly limited to 25 hl/660 gal, a tribute to the role it plays in concentrating the inherent qualities of the base wine, qualities which would be somewhat lost in a bigger vessel.

The shape of the head and the duct leading to the cooler also have a part to play. The traditional Moor's head (*tête de maure*) shape, suggestive of some sharp-beaked cartoon animal, retained more of the impurities and thus produced a richer, less uniform brandy than the modern swan's neck (*col de cygne*) shape, which provides an infinitely smoother path for the brandy than the older, more angular designs (see diagram overleaf). Control is largely exercised in the decision as to when to start to use the spirit i.e. at what point to stop discarding the relatively high-strength HEADS (*têtes*), the first drops to flow, and when to cut the TAILS (*queues*). The tails are richer and contain more of the desirable CONGENERS but, as a natural corollary, they also contain more impurities. There are many other variations. Should the wine be preheated? Should it be distilled on its lees? Modern chemistry is only now beginning to grapple with the complexities involved, thus ensuring that the personality of the product,

Pot still

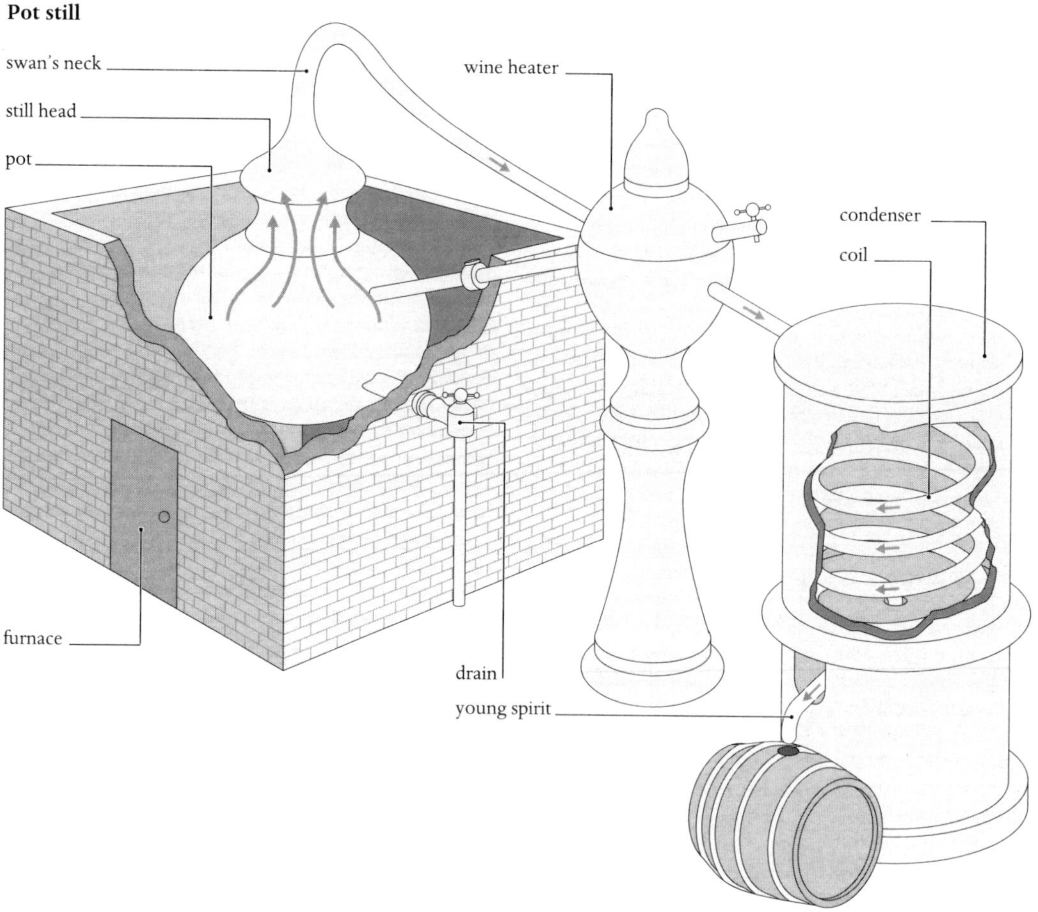

and thus of the firm selling it, is retained, a guarantee enhanced by the pot still. N.F.

POTTER VALLEY, California wine region and AVA. See MENDOCINO.

POUILLY-FUISSÉ, important white wine appellation in the MÂCONNAIS district of Burgundy. The appellation, which is restricted to the Chardonnay grape, includes 850 ha/2,100 acres in the communes of Fuissé, Solutré (which includes the hamlet of Pouilly), Vergisson, and Chaintré (see also MÂCON VILLAGES). The richest wines are said to come from Fuissé and Solutré, those of Vergisson being a little lighter but elegant. There is no concept of PREMIER CRU vineyards in this appellation but Pouilly-Fuissé may be followed by the name of a specific vineyard.

The grapes are grown in sun traps beneath the two impressive crags of Solutré and Vergisson which mark the end of the LIMESTONE plateau on which all burgundy save the Beaujolais is grown. The soil beneath the crags was supposedly enriched by the remains of animals driven from the top of the cliff by Stone Age hunters. The wines are full bodied and ripe but do not usually attain the elegance of the fine wines from the Côte de Beaune. Normally bottled after a year's BARREL MATURATION, they are capable of ageing well thereafter, particularly the wines of Ch de Fuissé and Guffens-Heynen. Prices can vary enormously depending on the demands of major export markets in a given year.

The small village of Pouilly also lends its name to two adjacent lesser appellations, **Pouilly-Vinzelles** and **Pouilly-Loché**. The latter is rarely seen, covering only 37 ha which may in any case be sold as Pouilly-Vinzelles. The local CO-OPERATIVE is the prime source for both wines. J.T.C.M.

POUILLY-FUMÉ, also known as **Pouilly Blanc Fumé** and **Blanc Fumé de Pouilly**, one of the Loire's most famous wines, perfumed dry whites that epitomize the SAUVIGNON Blanc grape, (along with nearby MENETOU-SALON, QUINCY,

REUILLY, and, most notably, SANCERRE). Sauvignon here is often called Blanc Fumé, because wines made from this variety when grown on the predominantly LIMESTONE soils, with some flint (*silex*), supposedly exhibit a 'smoky' flavour, or whiff of gunflint (*pierre à fusil*). The wines are certainly perfumed, sometimes almost acrid, and it takes extensive local knowledge reliably to distinguish Sancerres and Pouilly-Fumés in a blind tasting of both. Only about half as much Pouilly-Fumé is made as white Sancerre, and, unlike that of Sancerre, the Pouilly-Fumé appellation applies only to white wines. The best Pouilly-Fumé (such as the range produced by Didier Dageneau) is perhaps a denser, more ambitiously long-lived liquid than Sancerre, for drinking at two to six years, for example, rather than one to four (although there are, as always with wine, exceptions). At the most famous estate, de Ladoucette's magnificently turreted Ch du Nozet, are bottles which prove that Pouilly-Fumé can last for decades, although whether it actually improves is a matter of taste. Some producers began experimenting with OAK for both fermentation and maturation in the mid 1980s and the wines of the region are becoming more complex with each vintage.

The appellation takes its name from the small town of Pouilly- sur-Loire on the right bank of the Loire in the Nièvre *département*. The name **Pouilly-sur-Loire** is given to the zone's less distinguished VDQS wine, a usually thin and short-lived liquid made in very much smaller quantities from the CHASSELAS grape, grown here in the 19th century for the tables of Paris. Pouilly-sur-Loire's official minimum ALCOHOLIC STRENGTH is nine per cent, as opposed to Pouilly-Fumé's 11 per cent. In the 1970s and 1980s, Pouilly-Fumé was much favoured by FASHION, and the total area planted with Sauvignon increased considerably. Some of the finest vineyards are on the slopes above the Loire north of Pouilly between it and the village of Sancerre.

See also LOIRE and map on pp. 576–7.

POULSARD, sometimes called **Plousard** is a rare speciality of the JURA, one of the region's dark grape varieties adapted over the centuries to its very particular climate and soils. It does particularly well in the northern vineyards of the Jura. Its large, long, thin-skinned grapes give only lightly coloured wine that is distinguished by its perfume. It is so low in pigments it can make white wines, it makes particularly fine rosés which may be left on the skins for as long as a week without tainting the wine too deeply, and can add aroma to a red blended from Poulsard, TROUSSEAU, and, increasingly, Pinot Noir. It is also grown to a very limited extent in BUGEY, where it may be called Mescle.

POURRITURE, French for ROT. *Pourriture noble* is NOBLE ROT. *Pourriture grise* is GREY ROT, or malevolent BOTRYTIS BUNCH ROT.

POWDERY MILDEW, also called oidium, the first of the vine FUNGAL DISEASES to be scientifically described, in 1834 in the United States. It is native to North America, where it causes minor damage on native grapes. The fungus was given the name *Oidium tuckerii* after the gardener, a Mr Tucker, who first noted it in Europe, in Margate, England, in 1845. Today the fungus is more widely known as *Uncinula necator*. The disease was first noted in France in 1847, where it soon spread and caused widespread havoc to vineyards and wine quality. Today the disease is spread world-wide. There is a difference in susceptibility between different vine species, with many native AMERICAN VINES being very resistant. Varieties of the European vine VITIS VINIFERA are generally very susceptible, although some variation is noted. For example, Aramon, Pinot Noir, Malbec, Merlot, and Riesling of the French varieties are noticeably more tolerant than Carignan, Colombard, Chardonnay, and Cabernet Sauvignon.

All green parts of the vine are attacked. A fine, translucent, cobweb-like growth spreads around the spot where the fungus first penetrates. After one to two weeks grey-white ash-like spores are produced on short, upright stalks. The infection looks powdery, leading to the common name. Spores are spread by wind and, with favourable conditions, new infections rapidly occur. The fungus survives over winter inside buds or on the surface of the vine. If bunches are infected before flowering, then fruit set and yield may be considerably reduced. Yield can be further reduced if berries are infected before they reach full size. Surface cells are killed so that the berries never grow to full size. Fruit of coloured varieties also fails to colour properly, and wine made from affected fruit has off-flavours.

The disease develops and spreads most rapidly in warm weather, 20 to 27 °C (68–80 °F). Unlike all other fungal diseases of vines, this disease is little affected by humidity, making climate conditions which favour it different from those which favour many other fungal diseases. Powdery mildew is favoured by dense, shaded CANOPIES. In fact bright sunlight inhibits the germination of spores. Fortunately the control of this disease was discovered soon after it appeared in Europe. Mr Tucker noted the similarity between this vine disease and that affecting peach trees which could be controlled by a mixture of SULPHUR, lime, and water. Dusting with sulphur was accepted after the disastrous French vintage of 1854, the smallest since 1788. This same technique is still used today. In dry climates sulphur dust is used and wettable powders are used in higher rainfall regions. Other formulations and organic fungicides have been developed more recently. Cultural practices such as maintaining a non-shaded canopy (see CANOPY MICROCLIMATE) help prevent development of the disease. Recent developments in vine breeding have produced varieties with natural resistance and acceptable wine quality. These NEW VARIETIES use the natural tolerance of native American species somewhere in their pedigree.

R.E.S.

Galet, P., *Précis de viticulture* (Montpellier, 1983).

Ordish, G., *The Great Wine Blight* (2nd edn., London, 1987).

Pearson, R. C., and Goheen, A. C., *Compendium of Grape Diseases* (St Paul, Minn., 1988).

Winkler, A. J., *et al.*, *General Viticulture* (Berkeley, Calif., 1974).

PRÄDIKAT, in GERMANY a wine 'distinction', awarded on the basis of increasing grape ripeness or MUST WEIGHT: either KABINETT, SPÄTLESE, AUSLESE, BEERENAUSLESE, or EISWEIN, and TROCKENBEERENAUSLESE. According to the GERMAN WINE LAW, a QMP wine is a Qualitätswein mit Prädikat, or 'quality wine with distinction'.

In AUSTRIA, **Prädikatswein** excludes Kabinett wine but includes, at increasing minimum must weight levels, Spätlese, Auslese, Strohwein (or 'straw wine', see VIN DE PAILLE), Eiswein, Beerenauslese, AUSBRUCH, and Trockenbeerenauslese.

PRAMAGGIORE. See LISON-PRAMAGGIORE.

PRECIPITATES, solids which are deposited on the bottom of barrels, casks, tanks, or vats by wine stored in them.

Technically, precipitates are solids which deposit from solutions because of reactions or temperature changes, and differ from SEDIMENTS, which are suspensions of solids which settle from the mixture when agitation ceases. Technically, therefore, the stem, pulp, and skin fragments and the seeds and dead yeast cells which settle after fermentation as gross LEES are not precipitates, while subsequent deposits of TARTRATES and oxidized PHENOLICS do qualify as precipitates. Practical wine-makers, however, tend to classify both groups as precipitates, along with COLLOIDS. A.D.W.

PREDICATO, name selected in the 1980s by a group of quality-minded producers in TUSCANY in central Italy for their new range of wines made substantially or exclusively from 'international' (i.e. French) varieties, given small oak BARREL MATURATION. The Predicato designation represented an attempt to bring some order into the rapidly expanding category of high-quality wines made outside the DOC system and labelled VINO DA TAVOLA. Predicato del Selvante denoted SAUVIGNON Blanc; Predicato del Muschio is CHARDONNAY; Predicato del Cardisco is SANGIOVESE; while Predicato di Biturica originally indicated a base of CABERNET SAUVIGNON although the wines have since evolved towards a blend of Cabernet and Sangiovese.

This attempt to organize and classify the emerging vino da tavola category had little success, however, owing to the dominant role of large wineries in launching the initiative, Ruffino in particular. Few small producers, and none of the important ones in terms of quality, have been willing to join in the effort.

In 1993 the name Predicato was changed to Capitolare (chapter of classification), purportedly to give a more distinctively 'Italian' name to the wines, but also to appease some German producers who argued that Predicato was too similar to their term PRÄDIKAT. D.T.

PREMIERS CRUS, or **premiers crus classés**, are those CRUS judged of the first rank, usually according to some official CLASSIFICATION. The direct translation of the French term premiers crus, much used in the context of BORDEAUX, is FIRST GROWTHS. A **premier grand cru** (**classé**) may, as in the case of ST-ÉMILION and Ch d'YQUEM, be a rung higher even than this. In BURGUNDY, scores of vineyards are designated premiers crus, capable of producing wine distinctly superior to VILLAGE WINE but not quite so great as the produce of the GRANDS CRUS.

PREMIÈRES CÔTES DE BORDEAUX, qualitatively important member of the BORDEAUX CÔTES group of appellations. The Premières Côtes extend for 60 km/40 miles from north of the city of Bordeaux as far as Langon in a narrow strip along the south western edge of the ENTRE-DEUX-MERS appellation (although the alluvial land immediately bordering the GARONNE river qualifies only as BORDEAUX AC). The soils here are very varied, with the *coteaux* rising from the river bank offering the most valuably gravelly or calcareous terrain. Clay predominates on the plateau between the *coteaux* and the Entre-Deux-Mers boundary. About 2,200 ha/5,400 acres are planted with red grape varieties, mainly MERLOT, but the region is also the only one of the Bordeaux Côtes appellations to produce significant quantities of sweet white wines, known since 1991 as **Premières Côtes de Bordeaux Cadillac**, from SÉMILLON, SAUVIGNON Blanc, and MUSCADELLE. (This is hardly surprising since the Premières Côtes encircle the sweet white territory of the CADILLAC, CÉRONS, and STE-CROIX-DU-MONT appellations.) There is a recognizable band of seriously ambitious producers here, especially of quite concentrated red wines which may lack the ageing potential of Bordeaux's more famous examples but can offer good value for drinking at three to five years old. See BORDEAUX for more detail.

The appellation Bordeaux-St-Macaire (see BORDEAUX AC) is effectively a south eastern extension of the Premières Côtes de Bordeaux.

PRE-PHYLLOXERA, term used to differentiate European, and especially French, wines made from vines before the arrival of the devastating phylloxera louse towards the end of the 19th century from those made from the vines GRAFTED on to phylloxera-resistant American ROOTSTOCKS which replaced them. In the first half of the 20th century there was much understandable discussion about the relative merits of pre- and post-phylloxera wines with, perhaps inevitably, overall agreement that the earlier generation of wines were distinctly superior. As pointed out at the end of PHYLLOXERA, however, it was probably not the grafting itself which resulted in an apparent drop in quality, but the effects of the VIRUS DISEASES imported into European vineyards along with all this phylloxera-resistant plant material from across the Atlantic.

PRESS, in a wine context usually means **wine press**, a particularly ancient piece of wine-making equipment, used for the PRESSING operation of separating grape juice or wine from solids. Wine presses or their remains provide some of the longest-surviving evidence of the ORIGINS OF VITICULTURE. In ancient times the design of presses was varied and ingenious. See Ancient EGYPT and GREECE for more details.

Traditional, manually operated basket **press** in Champagne and a bank of computer-controlled enclosed pneumatic presses making Locorotondo in southern Italy, protecting the grapes from oxygen.

AYALA & Co

siprem
PNEUMOPRESS P.120

Ancient history

CATO (*De agri cultura* 18–19) in the 2nd century BC provided the first detailed description of a press room. He describes a beam or lever press. This would be constructed on an elevated concrete platform with a raised curb, which formed a shallow basin, which sloped gently to a run-off point. On this was constructed the press, which consisted of a long, heavy horizontal beam, which slotted into an upright at the back and ran between two uprights at the front. The front end of the beam was attached by a rope to a windlass. The grape solids were put under the beam and pressure applied by winding down the end. As the pulp compacted, so wedges were hammered into the slot at the pivot end to lower it. Over time various refinements were introduced. Most notably, according to PLINY (*Natural History* 18. 317), a 'Greek-style' press was introduced in the late republic or early empire, in which the windlass was replaced with a vertical screw thread, sometimes with a heavy counterweight. There is ample archaeological evidence from Italy, and elsewhere, for the use of presses. They are frequently found in pairs, as recommended by Pliny. All the Roman AGRICULTURAL TREATISES, apart from the writings of Palladius, assume the use of a press in their descriptions of wine-making. However, the press was an elaborate and comparatively expensive piece of equipment and its use was far from universal. Some farmsteads have large tanks for treading the grapes in, but no evidence of a press. It is not clear whether the must from the treading was always kept separate from that from the pressing. The grape pulp could be subject to a second pressing; but this was carefully kept separate. The pressed grape skins could even be soaked in water to produce *lorca*, a drink to be given to the farm hands (VARRO, *De re rustica* 1. 54), a forerunner of PIQUETTE.

J.J.P.

Rossiter, J. J., 'Wine and oil processing at Roman farms in Italy', *Phoenix*, 35 (1981), 345–61.

White, K. D., *Farm Equipment of the Roman World* (Cambridge, 1975), 112–15.

Presses today

Wine presses have evolved over the last thousand years or more into the relatively complicated machines used today. The **basket** presses used during the Middle Ages by religious orders were large devices built of wood (see illustration on p. 757, top) in which grapes were squeezed by a horizontal wooden disc which just fitted into a cylindrical basket made of wooden staves bound into the cylinder shape by encircling wooden hoops. The juice from the crushed berries escapes through the spaces between the basket staves and flows into a tray below. Some of these traditional presses, usually depending on a giant lever for pressure, still exist and are occasionally used in Burgundy and parts of Italy. Similar, usually smaller versions of the basket press reliant on hand or hydraulic power can be found in many of the Old World's less mechanized wineries today and most producers of CHAMPAGNE and SAUTERNES still rely on variations on this vertical pressing theme, demanding though they are in terms of time and manpower.

In modern **horizontal** presses the basket press principle has been turned on its side. They can be divided into either batch or continuous presses, the latter almost never used for fine wines. Most batch presses depend upon squeezing a charge of crushed grapes or POMACE against a perforated screen. Pressure may be applied by a moving press head as in the old basket press or, more gently in theory, by having an airbag, or **bladder**, expand to squeeze the pomace against the inner wall of a perforated cylinder. The firm Vaslin makes a high proportion of the horizontal basket type, while the names Willmes and Bucher are often used synonymously with the bladder type. Many of these horizontal batch presses are called **tank** presses because they are fully enclosed, in order to reduce the exposure of the pomace and juice to air.

Continuous presses are much harsher and usually worked either by a screw or a belt. The screw press usually resembles a giant domestic food chopper. The decreasing pitch of an Archimedes screw subjects the pomace to increasing pressure as it is moved along within the perforated cylindrical housing. The juice obtained, especially near the exit end, is very cloudy and rich in PHENOLICS but the juice from the crushed grape or pomace entry point is much clearer. Belt presses are much rarer and function by pressing intact clusters or a stream of pomace between two perforated moving belts arranged so that the clearance between them decreases. Juice from belt presses is much clearer and better quality than that from screw presses, but the screw press allows faster throughput and is therefore the cheapest form of press. Both screw and belt presses can also be enclosed.

Many modern presses are controlled by a computer program designed to optimize the pressing cycle for each grape variety and wine type. The screw press is the most common in large commercial wineries while some form of tank press is increasingly common for fine wine production.

A.D.W.

PRESSAC, Bordeaux RIGHT BANK name for the red grape variety Cot or MALBEC.

PRESSING, wine-making operation whereby pressure is applied, using a press, to grapes, grape clusters, or grape POMACE in order to squeeze the liquid out of the solid parts, known as *pressurage* in French. Historically, intact grape clusters were probably pressed before crushed grapes were, but it cannot have been long before someone realized that more juice could be obtained more quickly by smashing the clusters before pressing.

Timing of pressing depends on wine type. The great majority of wines today are made by CRUSHING and DESTEMMING before the pressing operation, but see also WHOLE BUNCH PRESSING whereby cooled grapes may be pressed even before crushing to avoid the extraction of unwanted PHENOLICS from the grape skins, although in some circumstances such SKIN CONTACT is considered desirable.

Grapes for red wines are usually pressed either after or during FERMENTATION, when sufficient extraction of COLOUR and TANNINS from the skins has taken place. Pressing of the sweet white grape pomace immediately after crushing is difficult because the skins are still slimy and slick, while after fermentation and maceration most of the slippery gums have been removed from the skins, making pressing much easier and quicker.

See also PRESS, PRESS WINE, and FREE-RUN. A.D.W.

PRESS WINE, dark red wine squeezed from POMACE (grape skins, stem fragments, pulp, and dead yeast) by means of a wine PRESS. Press wine is generally inferior in quality to FREE-RUN wine, and much more astringent, although some presses are capable of exerting pressure in controlled stages so that the product of the first, gentle pressing is very close to free-run in quality. Continuous screw presses in particular often exert such pressure that the product is excessively bitter and astringent. A certain proportion of press wine may be incorporated into the free-run wine, especially if it lacks TANNIN. Otherwise it is used for a lesser bottling or, traditionally, given to workers at the establishment which produced it.

All white wine except for the free-run juice is effectively press wine, although its quality and characteristics are shaped considerably by how gently the white grapes were pressed. See also the TAILLE produced in CHAMPAGNE. A.D.W.

PRESTIGE CUVÉE, one of several names given to a CHAMPAGNE house's highest-quality wine. At one time the houses saw their NON-VINTAGE wine as their greatest expression. Vintage-dated champagne was added to the range and a premium usually charged for it. ROEDERER's Cristal bottling and MOËT & CHANDON's named after Dom PÉRIGNON scaled new heights, however, and today most of the major champagne firms offer one product available, at a price and, often, in a specially created bottle, in limited quantity at the top of their range.

PRICE is probably the single most important aspect of a wine to most consumers, just as the price of grapes is one of the most important variables of the viticultural year to most grape-growers. The price of vineyard land is not directly proportional to the price fetched by grapes grown on it, however. See below.

Grape prices

Wine grapes are an important item of commerce throughout the world, and the economic fortunes of many a rural community rise and fall with wine grape prices. Although many wine consumers have the impression that most wine grapes are grown on estates which also process them into wine, nothing could be further from the truth. The majority of the world's wine grapes are sold in the form of fresh fruit, to be vinified quite independently of the grape-grower, whether by commercial wineries or CO-OPERATIVES.

The means to determine prices for wine grapes varies from region to region. Prices are normally fixed annually, taking into account supply and demand as well as individual VINTAGE characteristics. A buoyant wine market bolsters grape prices, whatever the size of the crop, with some wineries attracting fruit away from others by paying higher prices. When the market is depressed it is not unusual to see fruit left on the vine (as in Coonawarra in South Australia in 1978), since the cost of harvesting can be more than the potential income. In many areas, notably Europe and South Africa, surplus grapes are distilled into alcohol, which in turn often becomes SURPLUS to requirements (an essential element in PROTECTIVE JUICE HANDLING).

Normally grapes are bought and sold according to VINE VARIETY and sugar content. In most regions there is some sort of representative body which oversees grape prices. For example, in Bordeaux the Conseil Interprofessionnel du Vin de Bordeaux (CIVB) has a board made up of wine producers and NÉGOCIANTS which seeks to organize the market for grapes and wine. As well as documenting wine sales, the CIVB may enter the market-place in its own right and, for example, buy wine stocks for ageing in years of high supply. In Alsace there are many growers with small vineyard holdings, and the local Comité Interprofessionnel du Vin d'Alsace (CIVA) has a similar board with grower and négociant members. The CIVA sets the price for grapes, which varies with variety and sugar level. The regional organization in Champagne is the oldest of the French regional associations, and has powers and services which extend beyond grape price determination. The Comité Interprofessionnel du Vin de Champagne (CIVC) has determined grape prices by means of a relatively complex series of calculations (see CHAMPAGNE).

For many European producers, grape prices are set by co-operatives, and although the formulas may not be so rigid as those traditionally employed in Champagne, they must take into account the same factors concerning supply, demand, and intrinsic quality. In much of the New World the majority of grape-growers sell their produce to wineries. In Australia there are statutory bodies which are involved in setting minimum prices. In the United States of America, individual growers negotiate freely with individual wineries, even though they may voluntarily join an association which will set recommended prices. The US government does, however, report on prices paid after each vintage.

A basic problem in buying and selling wine grapes is that their true value is not known until they are made into wine, and indeed until that wine is sold. Concentration of SUGAR IN GRAPES is the most common measure which can be related to grape quality. This is particularly important for grapes grown in cool climates, where better-quality wines are invariably made from grapes with higher MUST WEIGHTS. However, in warm to hot climates it is not difficult to reach the desired sugar level, and other aspects of GRAPE COMPOSITION are better related to quality. Some progressive wineries have implemented grape quality assessment schemes to reward growers better for producing high-quality fruit. These schemes can be related to the vineyard site as well as to vineyard management methods, and also perhaps to a detailed chemical ANALYSIS of the fruit. Some wineries keep wine batches from different growers separate, and so are able to pay a bonus based on performance. This is the case with such leading California wineries as Robert MONDAVI and Simi, but a lack of understanding of and agreement on vineyard factors which affect wine quality is likely to delay widespread application of wine grape quality bonus systems. R.E.S.

Vineyard land prices

Wine is acknowledged as a natural product, and there is a widespread acceptance that the region or even vineyard of origin has a major effect on wine quality. The potential effect of vineyard site on wine quality is discussed elsewhere (see CLIMATE AND WINE QUALITY, SOIL AND WINE QUALITY, and VITICULTURE). Needless to say, those vineyards with a reputation for high wine quality attract high land prices. Perhaps the clearest examples are to be found in the Bordeaux region, where, thanks partly to several important CLASSIFICATIONS of individual châteaux, land prices are also clearly stratified. In 1993, for example, the price of planted vineyard entitled to the basic Bordeaux appellation was between FF100,000 and 180,000 per ha, while the renowned POMEROL property Ch Petit Village had been sold several years previously for FF10,000,000 per ha (which was widely regarded as a wild price).

In Burgundy, a region in which geographical delimitation is even more precise, land prices vary in a similar fashion. This is particularly the case where appellation boundaries are in place. For example, land within the MEURSAULT appellation in Burgundy can cost several times as much as land just over the border in ST-AUBIN. Land prices in 1993 in the NAPA Valley in California might be as high as $US50,000 per acre, or 125,000 per ha, whereas nearby land without Napa Valley's reputation might sell for well under $US20,000 per acre. In Australia, suitable vineyard land on the famous TERRA ROSSA soil of COONAWARRA was sold in 1993 at up to $A25,000 per ha, whereas the adjacent land without the terra rossa soil may sell for as little as $A2,000 per ha (as pasture).

Interestingly there are extensive tracts of land which have suitable soils and climate to grow quality grapes economically which are yet to be 'discovered' and planted to vineyards. As such, they have the value only of their existing land use. In many instances this might be low-value grazing. For example in Hawkes Bay, New Zealand, many of the vineyards are planted in soils which have alternative horticultural uses, and so are valued relatively highly, with 1993 prices at $NZ20,000 per ha. To the south are extensive areas of low fertility, stony soils which are not well regarded for grazing as they are drought prone, and yet are very well suited for viticulture. Before this became recognized in the mid 1980s, their value was as low as $NZ5,000 per ha, but the success of the few vineyards established there has pushed the value to over $NZ10,000 per ha. Similar phenomena can be observed in other countries where vineyard plantings are moving to non-traditional areas, such as Chile. R.E.S.

Wine prices

The price of a wine is a function of the price of the grapes, the price of labour, the price of a winery or the debt outstanding on it, pricing policy on the part of the producer, pricing policy on the part of any merchants involved in selling it, the cost of TRANSPORT, BOTTLING, LABELLING, and marketing, quite apart from any DUTIES and TAXATION. The interest for the wine producer must be to maximize his or her return on capital, without acquiring a reputation for profiteering.

The interesting question for the consumer, however, is the extent to which retail wine prices, which can vary more than a thousandfold, indicate wine quality. The answer is, of course, not very closely. All sorts of factors can depress the price of a wine to make it a bargain relative to the competition. Some national economies offer particularly low production costs (such as PORTUGAL in the early 1990s) when translated into the currencies of many potential importers. Currency movements in general have far more impact on wine prices than most wine drinkers realize. The enormous surge in demand for 1982 bordeaux in the United States was partly the result of the strength of the American dollar relative to the French franc in 1983 when EN PRIMEUR purchases were made. Other political events can also affect wine prices. The fall of communism in eastern Europe left SURPLUS production in countries such as BULGARIA, HUNGARY, and YUGOSLAVIA, which used to ship enormous quantities to the Soviet Union, and these emerging economies' desire for hard, western currency led them to export goods such as wine at extremely keen prices, or as part of barter deals. Specific countries may also benefit from preferential import tariffs.

Pricing policy in general may be geared to gaining a foothold in a new market, as SOUTH AFRICA needed to do after the lifting of sanctions in the early 1990s. Or it may have the result of bolstering prices in the belief that high prices automatically buy respect and prestige, a phenomenon often associated with some CALIFORNIA wines.

The above considerations relate to the prices of wine when it is first offered for sale. Serious wine COLLECTORS and those considering investing in wine are interested in what happens to the price of FINE WINE over time. As detailed in INVESTMENT and AUCTIONS, this depends on the wine and the time, and also on the rarity value of a given wine, its provenance and condition, and the general state of the market.

Most ordinary wine drinkers took a certain comfort in the story of what happened to the world's most expensive bottle of wine sold at Christie's for £105,000 in 1985: it was stood upright on display under warm lights so that, unnoticed, the cork dried out and dropped into the bottle, rendering the wine oxidized and undrinkable.

PRIMEUR, French word for young produce which has been adapted to mean young wine. The world's nouveau wines may also be known as primeurs, especially in France where at one time there was a distinction between primeurs, which could not be released until 15 December, and nouveau (usually Beaujolais), which could be released on 15 November. For more details of this style of wine, see NOUVEAU.

See also EN PRIMEUR for details of fine wine offered for sale before it is bottled.

PRIMITIVO, name of a red grape variety grown principally in APULIA in southern Italy, so extensively that its 17,000 ha/42,000 acres made it Italy's ninth most planted vine variety in 1990 (just behind Apulia's even more popular

Negroamaro). It might have remained relatively obscure had not its similarity to California's ZINFANDEL been noted, and, according to all forms of vine identification (see DNA 'FINGER PRINTING'), the two varieties do seem to be identical (to the extent that some enterprising Apulian exporters have been known to label their Primitivo as Zinfandel). There are varietal DOCs for Primitivo di Gioia, after Gioia del Colle where it was first noted, and the heady Primitivo di Manduria. Most wines labelled Primitivo are notably alcoholic and this grape was traditionally used to add weight to northern reds.

PRIORATO, one of Spain's most inspiring yet paradoxical red wines made in an isolated denominated wine zone in CATALONIA inland from TARRAGONA (see map on p. 907). Although this part of Spain is renowned for high technology and big business, the production methods for Priorato have barely altered since Carthusian MONKS first established the priory after which the wine is named in the 12th century. Priorato is one of the world's few first-class wines to be made from Garnacha (GRENACHE) and Cariñena (CARIGNAN), two grape varieties that are being replaced throughout much of Spain and southern France. The age of the vines and concomitantly low yields which average just 5 or 6 hl/ha (0.3 ton/acre) undoubtedly contribute to the intensity and strength of Priorato. Under the hot Mediterranean sun, grapes ripen to a potential alcohol as high as 18 per cent (not unlike the full dry reds of COLLIOURE over the French border in Roussillon).

Poor, stony soils derived from the underlying SLATE and QUARTZ, called locally *llicorella*, support only the most meagre of crops. MECHANIZATION is almost impossible and many steeply terraced smallholdings have been abandoned in recent years as the rural population has fled to find work in the towns and cities on the coast. A few stalwarts fight on producing big, sturdy, but extraordinarily concentrated red wines that must have a minimum ALCOHOLIC STRENGTH of 13.75 per cent to qualify for the DO.

The region is dominated by CO-OPERATIVES but there are some good, modern estates such as Scala Dei, Masia Barril. De Müller make some good *generoso*. The PENEDÈS firm of René Barbier, recognizing Priorato's potential for top quality red wines, located some particularly promising vineyard sites, or CLOS, in the 1980s. Such French vine varieties as Cabernet Sauvignon, Merlot, and Syrah were planted, and individual investment in various Clos was encouraged. By the mid 1990s Clos Dofi, Clos Martinet, Clos Mogador, and Clos de l'Obac had already released some promising wines, most of them heavily dependent on maturation in new French oak barrels. Scala Dei, which also produces dry white and rosé wines, joined in this quality drive. The wines must reach a minimum alcoholic strength of 13.5 per cent to qualify as Priorato.

R.J.M.

PROBUS, Marcus Aurelius (AD 232–82), Roman emperor (276–82) who employed troops in the planting of vineyards in GAUL and along the Danube. (See GERMAN HISTORY.) This positive encouragement of viticulture was in marked contrast to the earlier Emperor DOMITIAN.

PROCYMIDONE, a FUNGICIDE whose RESIDUES led to a US ban on certain European wine imports in the early 1990s.

PRODUCTION of a particular vineyard is normally measured as YIELD. The world's production of wine totals between 250 and 300 million hl (6,600 million–7,900 million gal) annually, with wide variation according to VINTAGE. The 1991 vintage, for example, was particularly low because in

Country	1976–80	1981–5	1986–90	1992
Italy	74,619	72,146	60,226	68,686
France	67,259	67,462	65,344	65,401
Spain	33,832	33,964	33,656	37,036
CIS	30,597	34,439	18,140	18,000
United States	16,538	17,710	17,121	15,620
Argentina	24,597	20,463	18,836	14,351
Germany	7,832	9,799	10,915	13,400
South Africa	6,297	8,649	8,572	9,998
Portugal	9,475	9,076	8,455	7,555
Romania	8,018	8,700	7,502	7,500
Australia	3,655	4,025	4,463	4,585
ex-Yugoslavia	6,694	6,125	5,887	4,562*
Greece	5,412	5,002	4,337	4,050
Hungary	5,251	4,985	4,062	3,878
Brazil	2,697	4,005	2,918	3,584
Chile	5,655	6,600	4,103	3,165
China		1,502	2,734	3,100
Austria	2,944	2,867	2,854	2,588
Mexico	147†	2,228	1,183	2,422
Bulgaria	3,740	4,361	3,261	1,966
Czechoslovakia	1,421	1,301	1,200	1,340
Switzerland	1,043	1,311	1,280	1,239
Uruguay	602	710	795	948
Slovenia				885*
Cyprus	1,000	932	667	645
Japan	244	781	542	577
Algeria	2,300	1,010	687	500
Morocco	884	392	431	435
New Zealand	363	500	464	416
Tunisia	805	578	299	412
Canada	476	470	386	378
Luxembourg	93	159	165	271
Turkey	412	390	290	264
Albania	200	220	239	158
Israel	342	190	190	124
Peru	92	90	98	100
Lebanon	40	50	82	90
Madagascar	50	50	77	87
Malta	19	19	20	29
England & Wales		7	11	26
Egypt	44	15	20	24
Bolivia	16	16	19	20
Syria	63	8	5	6
Belgium	4	3	2	2
Jordan	11	5	4	1
Other countries	253	253	235	93
World total	326,036	333,568	292,777	300,517

* Slovenia became independent from Yugoslavia in 1991
† this figure excludes wine destined for brandy production

A satirical response to **Prohibition** in 1920s USA.

many of the significant European wine regions production was seriously affected by spring FROSTS. Europe is responsible for about three-quarters of the world's production, with the Americas and then Africa being the next most important continental producers. Production is falling in Europe (see EUROPEAN UNION initiatives), North Africa, and in the Americas but is tending to rise elsewhere. The table on p. 761 gives the world's significant wine-producing countries with OIV estimates of their recent annual wine production in '000 hl.

PROHIBITION in common parlance most often means a prohibition on the consumption of alcohol (which suggests the importance generally attached to the possibility of intoxication). Prohibition has officially been in force throughout the world of ISLAM for 12 centuries, and elsewhere there have been periods throughout history (usually just after a period of particularly heavy consumption) during which the arguments for Prohibition have seemed convincing. One of these periods was the early 20th century, when Prohibition was enforced in parts of Scandinavia, was (and still is) put to a referendum in New Zealand, and was enforced most famously in the United States.

Prohibition in the USA

'Prohibition' is generally considered the period in the United States, 17 January 1920–5 December 1933, during which, according to the language of the 18th Amendment to the Constitution, the 'manufacture, sale, or transportation of intoxicating liquors' throughout the country was prohibited. The passage of the 18th Amendment crowned a movement going back to the early 19th century.

Beginning with local, voluntary organizations concerned to foster temperance in a hard-drinking country, the movement then undertook to pass restrictive legislation on a local or state basis (Maine went 'dry' in 1851). As the movement increased in vigour and confidence, total prohibition of alcohol consumption rather than temperance became the object. By the last quarter of the 19th century the aim was to secure a complete national prohibition by means of a constitutional amendment. The work of propaganda to this end was in the hands of organized reformers, especially the Woman's Christian Temperance Union (1874) and the Anti-Saloon League (1895); they had the support of many Protestant churches, especially in the south and Midwest. By the time that the 18th Amendment was passed, 33 of the then 48 states were already dry.

The working out of the amendment was provided for by the National Prohibition Act (October 1919), usually called the Volstead Act: it defined 'intoxicating liquor' as anything containing 0.5 per cent alcohol, so extinguishing the hope that wine and beer might escape under a less stern definition. Some uses of wine were, however, allowed under the act: it could be used in religious ceremonies; it could be prescribed as medicine; and it could be used as a food flavouring or in other 'non-beverage' applications. All of these provisions could be and were greatly abused, and the act had to be amended and supplemented as experience showed the problems of enforcement.

The popular conception of Prohibition is that speakeasies abounded, gangsters and bootleggers of all sorts flourished, and every American gladly flouted the law. The reality is harder to determine, but there can be no question that the consequences for the American wine industry were disastrous. A number of American wineries, by obtaining licences to manufacture wine for the permitted uses, managed to continue a restricted operation (the apparent needs of communicants, for example, soared during this period). Effectively, however, the industry was wrecked. In 1919 the production of wine in the USA was 55 million gal/2 million hl; by 1925 it had sunk to just over 3.5 million gal. Wine-makers received no compensation. Most wineries simply went out of business and their establishments were broken up.

The Volstead Act permitted the heads of households to manufacture up to 200 gal/7 hl of fruit juice annually and, by a benevolent inconsistency, this provision was construed to allow HOME WINE-MAKING. In consequence, vineyard acreage in CALIFORNIA shot up to unprecedented size to meet the national demand for fresh grapes: the 300,000 acres/121,000 ha of vineyard in 1919 had nearly doubled by 1926. Most of the new planting was in very inferior grape varieties, however (THOMPSON SEEDLESS and ALICANTE BOUSCHET, for example), and the degradation of the California vineyards thus induced by the conditions of Prohibition had seriously damaging effects on California wine long after Repeal. Nor can the quality of the average home-made wine have done much to enhance national connoisseurship.

The first efforts of the opponents of Prohibition were to achieve 'modification' of the terms of the Volstead Act. They tried for example to alter the definition of 'intoxicating liquor', or to allow individual states to make regulations different from those of the act. These efforts got nowhere; in consequence, the 'Wets' concentrated on achieving Repeal by constitutional amendment. Aided by the economic collapse of 1929 (invalidating the argument that Prohibition was economically sound) and by the adoption of Repeal as a political question (the Democratic party made Repeal a plank in its platform for the 1932 elections), the repeal movement succeeded: in December 1933 the 21st amendment, repealing the 18th, was ratified. Unfortunately, the amendment left to the separate states the entire regulation of the 'liquor traffic' within their borders, with the result that US liquor laws—including local and state prohibition—remain a crazy quilt of inconsistent and arbitrary rules, another lastingly destructive effect of national prohibition.

The forces that achieved prohibition in the USA remain potent, and protean. National prohibition in the simple terms of the 18th amendment is not likely to come again; but liquor—wine very much included—continues to be an object of punitive taxation, of moral disapproval, and of obstructive legislation in the United States today. T.P.

Asbury, H., *The Great Illusion* (New York, 1950).
Krout, J. A., *The Origins of Prohibition* (New York, 1925).
Sinclair, A., *Prohibition: The Era of Excess* (London, 1962).

PROKUPAC, red grape variety grown all over SERBIA, where the strong wine it produces is often blended with more international vine varieties. It is also grown in KOSOVO and MACEDONIA. Within its native land it is often made into a dark rosé. Its stronghold is just south of Belgrade.

PROLES, three categories of VINE VARIETIES of the VINIFERA species, grouped according to their geographical origin and, to some extent, their common end use. The classification is the work of Negrul in 1946. The differences between these groups may not only be a matter of response to environment, but also partly due to human selection for particular features related to end use, such as berry size for table grapes. Detailed observation of vine characteristics can reveal particularly close relationships which indicate that they are likely to have come from the same area. Thus are linked, for example, the CABERNET SAUVIGNON, CABERNET FRANC, MERLOT, PETIT VERDOT, and FER varieties.

Proles occidentalis: varieties native to Western Europe, which were selected mostly for wine-making use. Most of the important wine grape varieties are in this group—RIESLING, CHARDONNAY, Cabernet Sauvignon, and so on—and they have common features of small bunches with small, juicy berries.

Proles pontica: the oldest varieties, and those native to the Aegean and Black Seas, which have shoot tips and leaf undersurfaces covered with dense, white hairs. Examples of varieties in this group are CLAIRETTE, FURMINT, HÁRSLEVELŰ, and Zante CURRANT.

Proles orientalis: varieties originating in the Middle East, Iran, and Afghanistan. These varieties were selected mainly for TABLE GRAPES, and so tend to have large, oval berries in straggly bunches. The berries are often crisp, with less juice and sugar. This group of vines includes most varieties for DRYING GRAPES as well as most table grape varieties, such as SULTANA and MUSCAT OF ALEXANDRIA, but also the wine grape CINSAUT. R.E.S.

PROPAGATION, the reproduction of a plant, whether by sexual or asexual means. Sexual propagation means reproduction by seed and involves the combination of two separate sets of chromosomes, one from the male (pollen) and the other from the female (the egg cell inside the ovule); their fusion during fertilization produces an individual with a set of genes different from its two parents. Asexual or vegetative propagation means reproduction without seed, by taking vegetative bits of the parent plant and getting them to form shoots and roots; the progeny are genetically identical to the parent.

For details of micropropagation, see TISSUE CULTURE.

For more details of specific propagation methods, see SEXUAL PROPAGATION and VEGETATIVE PROPAGATION. See also LAYERING. B.G.C.

PROSECCO, late ripening white grape variety native to the FRIULI region in north east Italy. It is responsible for a popular wine of the same name, sometimes called Prosecco di Conegliano Valdobbiadene, made west of the township of Conegliano near the Piave river. Prosecco wines exist in still, but mainly fizzy and sparkling, versions. The production zone, in the province of Treviso but near the border with the alpine province of Belluno, is quite cool, and in the past the Prosecco grapes, harvested in late October or even early November, often stopped fermenting during the cold winters, leaving RESIDUAL SUGAR and, in many cases, some CARBON DIOXIDE in the wines when fermentation recommenced in the spring. Current production methods, involving the CHARMAT process of inducing a second fermentation in tank, are simply used to replicate the various types of wine that the grape and its zone produced on their own in the past. Of the 28 million bottles produced in an average year, approximately 1 million are of still wine, 7 million of FRIZZANTE or fizzy wine, and 20 million of SPUMANTE. All have the bitter finish which characterizes the grape variety. The subzone of Cartizze, even cooler than the rest of the zone, produces a spumante which, due to the traditionally high levels of residual sugar of the past, tends towards medium dry and is known as Superiore di Cartizze. A total of about 7,000 ha / 17,300 acres of Prosecco were planted in Italy in the early 1990s.

The variety is also known, to a very limited extent, in Argentina. D.T.

Propagation of popular Chardonnay vines in Marlborough, New Zealand.

PROTECTED VITICULTURE, a form of vine-growing where the vines are protected from climatological excesses to avoid stress. In a conventional agricultural sense this would involve protection from low temperatures using glass or plastic houses; such structures are rare in commercial wine grape vineyards because of the prohibitive costs although they can be seen in the cool climate of ENGLAND or even in parts of California to protect some Chardonnay vines from poor fruit set. Protected viticulture is more usual for TABLE GRAPES, as in northern Europe, Japan, and New Zealand.

Vines may also be protected from the wind by WINDBREAKS, and from frost by various techniques, and from drought by IRRIGATION. R.E.S.

PROTECTIVE JUICE HANDLING, grape and must processing techniques with the aim of minimizing exposure to OXYGEN and therefore the risk of OXIDATION. This is regarded as especially important for white wines since, once grapes are crushed and juice liberated from the berry, the PHENOLICS react rapidly with oxygen to produce amber to dark-brown polymers (see POLYMERIZATION). Some ordinary wines are made encouraging this oxidation, the brown pigments being removed subsequently by FINING. Most better-quality wines result from minimal oxygen exposure, saving the phenolics for later contribution to AROMA and BODY (although some ambitious wine-makers began experimenting with deliberate prefermentation oxidation of the must in the early 1990s). The relatively recent introduction of tank PRESSES has aided protective juice handling during the lengthy PRESSING operation enormously. Grapes for red wines are much less vulnerable to damage from oxygen since they contain much greater concentrations of TANNINS and PIGMENTS.

See also SKIN CONTACT. A.D.W.

PROTECTIVE WINE-MAKING, wine-making philosophy founded on the need to minimize exposure to OXYGEN and concomitant risk of OXIDATION. It usually incorporates PROTECTIVE JUICE HANDLING. White wines are then fermented in closed top tanks to exclude oxygen as much as possible while allowing for the escape of CARBON DIOXIDE from fermentation. All subsequent operations are then conducted as much as possible in closed equipment and small amounts of SULPHUR DIOXIDE are added if exposure to oxygen occurs. Storage and processing at low temperatures favours the retention of some of the carbon dioxide, which has the effect of sweeping out any accidentally dissolved oxygen. Red wines, because of their greater PHENOLIC content, are much less sensitive to exposure to oxygen. Indeed, if they undergo BARREL MATURATION, some exposure to oxygen during TOPPING UP contributes to the wine's maturation. See AGEING. A.D.W.

PROTEINS, very large polymers of the 20 natural AMINO ACIDS. Proteins are essential to all living beings.

In grapes

Proteins may be water soluble and function as ENZYMES, or water insoluble and function as storage reserves (as in grape seeds and vine wood). While all functions are important, the enzymatic properties of proteins are the basis of all reactions within living systems. The most abundant enzyme on earth, nicknamed 'rubisco', catalyses the trapping of carbon dioxide during PHOTOSYNTHESIS in plants. B.G.C.

In wines

Some proteins may stay in solution in white wine, notably MUSCAT, until the wine is warmed, at which point they coagulate to form a haze or cloud. These heat-unstable proteins can be removed by BENTONITE fining. The great concentration of PHENOLICS in red wines ensures that most proteins in red wines are removed in the LEES. A.D.W.

PROVENCE, region in the far south east of France (see map on p. 399) whose associations with tourism and hedonism have done little to focus outside attention on the potential of its wines, but much to maintain their relatively high prices.

The precise period during which viticulture was introduced to the region is disputed. Certainly it appears unlikely that the Phocaeans, Greeks from Asia Minor, found vines when they founded Massilia (Marseilles) in about 600 BC, and it is thought that for long the wines associated with Massilia were imported from Greek colonies in southern Italy or Sicily. It is likely, however, that the Provincia of Ancient GAUL produced its own wines under the influence of classical ROME (although it is not certain that it preceded Narbo, or Narbonne, in the LANGUEDOC as a wine producer). See FRANCE for more details.

The region was much fought over, being under the influence in successive eras of the Saracens, Carolingians (see CHARLEMAGNE), the Holy Roman Empire, the counts of Toulouse, the Catalans, René of ANJOU, and the House of SAVOY. For much of the 19th century it belonged to SARDINIA. At the end of the 19th century Provençal viticulture was nearly killed by the PHYLLOXERA louse, but was given a new lease of life by the arrival of a RAILWAY link with northern Europe.

As a result of its rich cultural heritage, Provence enjoys a particularly distinctive range of vine varieties which show various historical influences from Italy, notably Sardinia. No fewer than 13 varieties are allowed in Côtes de Provence, for example, including the most important but declining CARIGNAN, CINSAUT, GRENACHE, UGNI BLANC, and CLAIRETTE, but also MOURVÈDRE, TIBOUREN, the indigenous dark-berried Calitor (known in Provençal as Pécoui Touar), Barbaroux (Italy's BARBAROSSA), ROLLE (Vermentino), and SÉMILLON.

The climate here is France's most MEDITERRANEAN, with an average of 3,000 hours of sunshine a year, and less than 700 mm/27 in annual RAINFALL, which is concentrated in spring and autumn. Winters are mild, but usually allow full vine DORMANCY. The greatest climatological threat is WIND, in particular the famous mistral, a cold wind from the north which Stendhal is improbably quoted as describing as 'le grand drawback de Provence' (and the southern RHÔNE too).

Proximity to the sea and careful vineyard siting on southern expositions can offer some protection. It has the advantage of minimizing the risk of FUNGAL DISEASES, and Provence is particularly suitable for ORGANIC VITICULTURE.

The magic attached to such names as the Côte d'Azur, St-Tropez, and Provence in general may have increased urban development, and pushed up land prices in habitable parts of the region, but it has also attracted outsiders prepared to make significant investments in vine-growing and wine-making, thereby raising standards overall.

Côtes de Provence

This area of about 18,000 ha/44,500 acres is by far the most significant appellation in Provence, although the vineyard sites vary enormously. The appellation applies to a large part of the Var *département* (other than the enclave entitled to the Coteaux Varois appellation) from the subalpine hills above Draguignan, cooled by the influence of the mountains to the north, to the coast at St-Tropez, the epitome of a Mediterranean wine zone. But it also includes pockets of hotter terrain between Cassis and Bandol, and land immediately south and east of the Palette appellation near Aix-en-Provence. The appellation even encompasses a tiny isolated area of vines at Villars-sur-Var high up in the mountains 40 km/25 miles north of Nice in the Alpes-Maritimes.

About three-quarters of production is of pale pink dry rosé which seems to find a local market almost regardless of quality. There was renewed interest in producing 'serious' rosé in the early 1990s, however, with a distinctive new style combining flavour with a fashionably pale hue, and some producers even using a limited amount of OAK maturation. The best really do seem to have a special affinity with the garlic- and oil-based cuisine of Provence, particularly *aïoli*. Much of it is sold in a special 'skittle' bottle; all of it should be consumed as young and as cool as possible. Cinsaut and Grenache are typically used particularly for rosé, but Tibouren can add real interest to a blend.

The focus of attention for a new generation of serious wine producers in this appellation, however, is red wine, which accounts for about 35 per cent of production. In the 1980s great efforts were made to replace the prolific Carignan vine with the more recent 'improving varieties' Syrah and Cabernet Sauvignon with which to add structure to the suppler permitted ingredients in red Côtes de Provence: Grenache, Cinsaut, and Mourvèdre and Tibouren (both of which have a long history here). By 1986 no more than 40 per cent of Carignan was allowed. There is considerable experimentation with different forms of ÉLEVAGE, including the use of new OAK for some of the most ambitious cuvées, typically dominated by Cabernet Sauvignon and/or Syrah, although each of these may represent no more than 30 per cent of the total blend.

An increasing number of producers, especially in the coastal sector, are paying as much attention to their white wine output as the venerable Domaines Ott at Ch de Selle has been since the beginning of the century. Rolle in particular is enjoying renewed interest.

See also the individual Provence appellations of Coteaux d'AIX-EN-PROVENCE, BANDOL, BELLET, CASSIS, PALETTE, and Coteaux VAROIS.

McNie, M., 'The Pick of Provence', *Decanter* (Sept. 1993).
Parker, R. M., *The Wines of the Rhône Valley and Provence* (New York, 1987).

PRUNERS, devices used for winter PRUNING of grapevines. From ancient times until the 19th century a pruning hook or knife was used. In modern times pruning is normally carried out using hand-held SECATEURS. These were developed in the mid 19th century, and came into widespread use in the latter half of the century. Secateurs cut with a scissor action, and there are various forms available. Most have two sharpened blades and modern versions are ergonomically designed. Tendon fatigue is a common problem for vineyard workers engaged in prolonged pruning, especially where the vine wood is old or thick and difficult to cut. Long-handled secateurs are used for cutting thick wood and these require a two-handed action. Sometimes pruning saws may be needed to remove old CORDONS or ARMS.

Care must be taken to avoid the fungal disease EUTYPA DIEBACK infecting the pruning wounds following large cuts. Vineyard winter pruning is now being mechanized with tractor-mounted machines doing most of the cutting, as described in MECHANICAL PRUNING. R.E.S.

PRUNING of vines involves cutting off unwanted vegetative parts in the form of canes in winter. For details of cutting off unwanted vegetative growth in the form of excess SHOOTS in early spring and shoot tips in summer, see SHOOT THINNING and TRIMMING respectively. **Summer pruning** is another term for trimming.

Winter pruning is a vineyard practice developed by man primarily to produce fewer but larger bunches of riper grapes and is particularly important in cooler climates. More than 85 per cent of each year's shoot growth may be removed. There is an important relationship between vine pruning and TRAINING, as the pruning method used depends on the training system employed.

Vines growing in their natural state, as in the WILD VINES of America and the Middle East, are of course not pruned. At the top of such vines, many of which grow up trees, and on other parts of the vine exposed to the sun, are many small bunches of grapes. While the vine may have had thousands of buds present in winter which could have produced shoots and fruit, only a small proportion will burst in spring. This reduced BUDBREAK is the principal means by which unpruned vines in their natural state avoid OVERCROPPING, which may weaken the vine and shorten its life. The wild vine is much branched, with many shoots growing apparently haphazardly.

History

It is not known when man began to prune vines but vine pruning was certainly known in Ancient EGYPT and was

Pruning—a demanding winter ritual in Champagne.

already a well-established practice by the beginning of the Roman era, described in detail by such writers as PLINY and VIRGIL. There are also numerous references to vine pruning in the BIBLE. For example, 'a Sabbath of rest unto the land, a Sabbath for the Lord: thou shalt neither sow thy field, nor prune thy vineyard' (Lev. 25. 4). Vine pruning also figures in the description of the Last Days (Mic. 4. 3): 'and they shall beat their swords into ploughshares, and their spears into pruning hooks.'

Aims of pruning

Among the early aims of vine pruning as practised by the Ancient Egyptians would have been to increase the size of individual berries and bunches, an important consideration even today in the production of TABLE GRAPES. A vine which is lightly pruned has many buds and will produce numerous bunches with small berries.

Another aim of vine pruning is to establish or maintain a shape of vine which makes all other vineyard operations easier. For example, keeping vines pruned back to a more or less constant structure means they can easily be neatly trained in rows. Otherwise, vines would sprawl and quickly cover the space between rows.

But perhaps the most important aspect of pruning is that it regulates the next season's YIELD by controlling the number of buds which can burst and produce bunches of grapes.

Timing

Pruning is carried out in winter, normally once the first frost causes the leaves to fall, thereby exposing the woody CANES, but the precise timing of winter pruning is not generally critical. In most viticultural regions, however, winter pruning should be completed by the time of budbreak in spring, as the pruners can damage emerging shoots as they work. Vines also lose water (see BLEEDING) from pruning wounds just prior to budbreak, although some early-budding varieties may be pruned very late in an effort to delay budbreak and minimize FROST DAMAGE. In regions with warm winters, such as tropical and subtropical regions, the vines may not become completely dormant, and vines may have to be pruned when they are covered in leaves. See TROPICAL VITICULTURE.

Two basic options

The basic principles of pruning have changed remarkably little since classical times, although the French viticulturist GUYOT in 1860 introduced firm suggestions as to the length and position of canes, formalizing some of the old ideas.

Along the canes, which were green, soft shoots during the previous growing season, are buds which are arranged on alternate sides of the cane about 8 cm/3 in or so apart. Basically there are two types of vine pruning: either to SPURS, or to CANES.

Spur pruning

Spurs are cut to include only two buds, while canes are longer, typically with five to 15 buds. In the spring each bud on the two-bud spur normally produces one shoot. In autumn, these shoots become woody. During winter pruning the cane growing from the uppermost bud on the spur is removed, and the cane from the bottom bud is cut back to two buds, creating the new spur. The vine's physiology determines that, when a cane is cut, the last two buds will burst. This is the reason for the common two-bud spur. If spurs were left with three buds, the bottom bud would often not produce a shoot, and so the spur position would move further and further from the cordon or head as the years passed.

Spur pruning is commonly used with free-standing vines, such as are widely seen in Mediterranean wine regions. The GOBELET trained vines in the south of France are typical, the name for this training system coming from the similarity of the shape of the pruned vine to that of a goblet. Gobelet vines are free standing with short trunks rarely more than half a metre high. The spurs arise from the trunk or from short arms on the trunk.

This is of course a very simple form of vine training, requiring no supporting POSTS or WIRE; it is therefore among the oldest forms prevailing and was already known to the Roman writers COLUMELLA and PALLADIUS. This vine training is particularly common in the Old World. In southern France, for example, more than 500,000 ha/1.2 million acres of vineyards are pruned and trained in this basic way. It is common in the lower-rainfall areas of Spain, Italy, and Portugal, such vineyards being of lower VIGOUR, to which the system is best suited. Some of the older New World vineyards, for example in California, Australia, and South Africa, also have such vines, here often described as head trained.

Another spur-pruned form which is more common with higher-vigour vineyards is cordon training. Here the spurs arise from one or more horizontal arms or CORDONS. Known in France as CORDON DE ROYAT, this pruning method has been used for wine grapes since the end of the 19th century. The cordons are trained along a wire, and this method is particularly common in New World vineyards. Of all pruning methods, this one lends itself most readily to MECHANIZATION since all of the canes to be pruned are more or less in the one plane (see MECHANICAL PRUNING).

Cane pruning

Cane pruning became common after the 1860 studies of the Frenchman Dr Guyot.

In traditional French vineyards each vine is typically pruned to one cane with six to eight buds and one spur with two buds. During winter pruning the cane from the previous year is cut off and a new one laid down, using one of the canes arising from the spur. The number of buds on the cane depends on regional tradition and the small print of the APPELLATION CONTRÔLÉE laws. For example, eight buds may be left on Syrah canes in the Côtes-du-Rhône; eight on all major varieties in Burgundy; in Bordeaux seven buds is the maximum for Sémillon in Sauternes, six for Muscadelle, but eight for Merlot Blanc. These small bud numbers per cane (and hence cane length) contrast greatly with those used for wine grapes in other regions where vine vigour is higher. For example, in vigorous irrigated vineyards in Australia it is not uncommon to see up to ten canes, each with up to 15 buds, left on a single vine after winter pruning. Of course, these vines are planted further apart than their Old World counterparts as discussed in NEW WORLD.

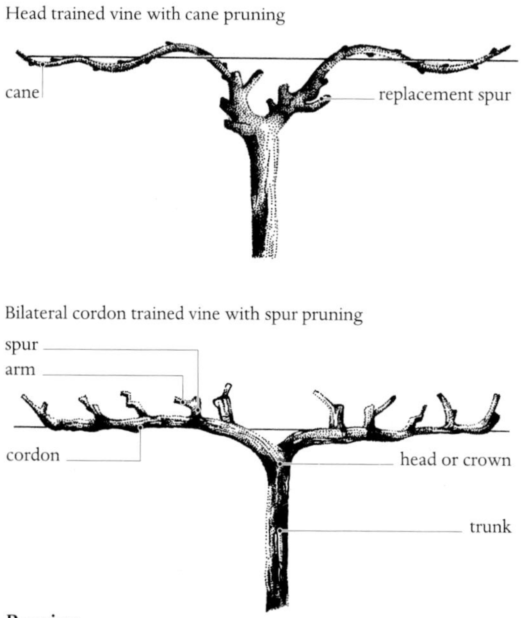

Pruning

A common observation with cane pruning is that buds in the middle of the cane often do not burst. There are often a few shoots growing near the head of the vine (at the base of the cane), and the last two shoots at the cut end of the cane will invariably grow. Where the cane was growing in shade the previous year the budburst is invariably poor, as outlined in CANOPY MICROCLIMATE.

In France, the colloquial name for canes varies regionally: *courgée* in Jura, for example, *aste* in Bordeaux, *baguette* in Burgundy, *archet* or *archelot* in Beaujolais, and, appropriately enough in view of the region's notoriously high yields, *pisse-vin* in the Languedoc.

Controlling yield

A fundamental question in relation to vine pruning is how many buds to leave on each vine at winter pruning. A corollary is, does it matter? For many vignerons in the world this is a question that is never posed, as tradition or appellation laws dictate how the vines are to be pruned. The winter pruning period can be a time when the mind is put into neutral, and the body is braced to survive long days spent outdoors, often in unpleasant and cold weather. Quite often, traditional pruning practices are followed, and vigorously defended against any suggestion of change.

When vines are pruned to just a few buds, most of them burst successfully, and the shoots will typically grow vigorously. Early shoot growth is stimulated by the vine's food reserves in the trunk and roots being spread around only a few shoots. A low-vigour vine which has limited reserves of CARBOHYDRATES must therefore be pruned more severely than a high-capacity vine.

A vine that is very lightly pruned, to scores or even hundreds of buds, will produce many more shoots and bunches of grapes. Individual shoots will be shorter, and the number and size of berries will be reduced. However, the total yield of grapes will be greater, and the grapes will take longer to ripen. This may cause no problems in warm and sunny climates, but can be disastrous in cooler climates, where it can be a struggle to ripen the grapes anyway before autumn chill and frosts stop the ripening process.

There is therefore more concern about pruning levels in cooler climates than in warmer ones. In Germany, for example, the common rule is to leave about ten buds at winter pruning for each square metre of vineyard land surface. In New York state, Professor Nelson Shaulis has developed guide-lines for pruning which rely on the vine's growth as assessed by PRUNING WEIGHT (the weight of annual growth as canes removed at pruning); about 35 buds should be retained per kg of pruning weight. Having weighed a few vines, the grower can assess the pruning weight by eye as part of his pruning decision. For more vigorous vines with higher pruning weights, more buds are retained.

For high-vigour vineyards it may not be sufficient just to prune lightly, as this will lead to crowding of shoots in the vine CANOPY. Recognition of this problem has led to the development of CANOPY MANAGEMENT strategies to avoid dense canopies for vigorous vineyards.

Mechanization

Up until the 1960s, winter pruning was labour intensive, but increases in labour costs and reductions in labour supply in Australia led to experimentation with and eventual development of MECHANICAL PRUNING, in which a machine is able to speed the laborious process of hand pruning without serious effects on wine quality in warm regions. This in turn has led to the even more iconoclastic option of MINIMAL PRUNING, or not pruning at all.

By the early 1990s, a full spectrum of vine-pruning practice was evident, from the hand pruning of a lower-vigour vine in a traditional vineyard to less than 10 buds, to one essentially unpruned following the passage of a machine, with thousands of buds remaining.

The time taken to prune a vineyard depends on how the vineyard is trained, the VINE DENSITY, and the pruning method. Pruning times can be up to 200 hours or more per ha for high-density cane-pruned vineyards. For wide-row, spur-pruned vineyards trained to cordons the figure may be as low as 50 hours per ha, and in combination with mechanical pre-pruning this may be reduced even further to less than 20 hours per ha. R.E.S.

Coombe, B. G., and Dry, P. R. (eds.), *Viticulture, ii: Practices* (Adelaide, 1992).
Galet, P., *Précis de viticulture* (4th edn., Montpellier, 1983).
Winkler, A. J., *et al.*, *General Viticulture* (2nd edn., Berkeley, Calif., 1974).

PRUNING MACHINES. See MECHANICAL PRUNING.

PRUNING WEIGHT, a measure of vine VIGOUR obtained by weighing the canes removed from a vine at winter PRUNING. The value is used to assess how many buds might be left at winter pruning to achieve the best vine performance, using concepts of BALANCED PRUNING.

PRUSSIC ACID is the common name for hydrogen cyanide, HCN, a gas which smells of bitter almonds in the pure form and is fairly soluble in water. The gas and the cyanide ion in water solution are lethal to humans at fairly low concentrations. The now rare and widely outlawed practice of BLUE FINING, carelessly undertaken, occasionally generated traces of hydrogen cyanide in wine.

PUERTO DE SANTA MARÍA, one of the three towns making and maturing SHERRY. **Puerto Fino** is the name given to a FINO matured in Puerto de Santa María.

PUGLIA, Italian name for the southern Italian region known by English speakers as APULIA.

PUISSEGUIN-ST-ÉMILION, satellite appellation of ST-ÉMILION in Bordeaux.

PULIGNY-MONTRACHET, village in the Côte de Beaune district of Burgundy's Côte d'Or producing very fine wines from CHARDONNAY and some less exalted reds. Puligny added the name of its most famous vineyard, the GRAND CRU Le Montrachet, in 1879 and has benefited from the association ever since.

Puligny contains two grand cru vineyards in their entirety, Chevalier-Montrachet and Bienvenues-Bâtard-Montrachet, and two which are shared with neighbouring Chassagne: Le Montrachet itself and Bâtard-Montrachet. Below this exalted level, yet still among the finest of all white wines of Burgundy, are the PREMIER CRU vineyards. There are at least 13 of these, more if subdivisions are counted. At the same elevation as Bâtard-Montrachet lie Les Pucelles (made famous by the

Pumping over: fermenting red wine is circulated from bottom to top of the fermentation vat where it is pumped through the cap of floating grape skins.

The traditional **pupitre** used for manual *remuage* in Champagne. See also the **gyropalette** which has superseded it.

excellence of Domaine Leflaive's version), Le Clavoillon, Les Perrières (including the Clos de la Mouchère), Les Referts, and Les Combettes, which produces the plump wines to be expected of a vineyard adjacent to Meursault-Perrières.

A little higher up the slope, at the same elevation as Le Montrachet, lie Les Demoiselles, Le Cailleret, Les Folatières (including Clos de la Garenne), and Champ Canet. Part of Les Demoiselles is classified as grand cru, Chevalier-Montrachet but a very small slice remains as premier cru being regarded, along with Le Cailleret, as the finest example.

Further up the slope, where the terrain becomes rockier and the soil almost too sparse, are Le Champ Gain, Les Truffières, Les Chalumeaux, and the vineyards attached to the hamlet of BLAGNY which are designated as Puligny-Montrachet premier cru for white wines, and Blagny premier cru for reds.

The VILLAGE WINES of Puligny-Montrachet are less impressive, perhaps because the water-table is nearer the surface here than in neighbouring MEURSAULT, for example. This phenomenon also means that the deep cellars ideal for AGEING wine are rare in Puligny, and few of the village's growers can prolong BARREL MATURATION for more than about a year. Although the Leflaive and Carillon families can both trace their origins as vignerons back to the 16th century, there are surprisingly few domaines in Puligny and a substantial proportion of its produce is contracted to the NÉGOCIANTS of Beaune.

In centuries past Puligny, though less noted than Chassagne for its red wines, grew a significant amount of Pinot Noir grapes. Little is now grown.

See also MONTRACHET, CÔTE D'OR and its map. J.T.C.M.

Loftus, S., *Puligny-Montrachet* (London, 1992).

PULP, viticulturally, the soft tissue of grape berries inside the skin (also called the flesh or PERICARP) which is the source of the juice of the grape. The word may also be used by winemakers to refer to the solid matter that settles from the juice after must SETTLING. For more detail of grape pulp, see GRAPE. B.G.C.

PUMPING OVER. Wine-making operation involving the circulation of fermenting red wine with the grape skins. The French term is REMONTAGE. For more details, see MACERATION. See also AUTOVINIFICATION.

PUMPS, mechanical devices for **pumping**, moving liquids such as wine and suspensions of solids such as grape juice from one location to another. The most traditional wineries depend on gravity, and the first generation of pumps required considerable manpower. Most modern pumps, however, are driven by electricity and come in a range of different designs and sizes which should be matched to the fluid to be moved.

MUST from the CRUSHER-DESTEMMER is usually moved to the DRAINING tank or FERMENTATION VESSEL by means of a diaphragm or off-centre helical screw type pump because this type performs particularly well with solid suspensions, including LEES. Cloudy juice from the draining tank might well be moved by means of a centrifugal pump to the fermentation tank, and most of the semi-clear and clear wines being processed are also moved using these types of pump.

Misuse of pumps can easily lead to OXIDATION, and centrifugal pumps operated at very high speeds can lead to the shearing of some of the larger COLLOIDS which results in a diminution of apparent BODY in a fine wine, but pumps have in general terms reduced wine costs and increased wine quality. Some modern pumps can move as much wine, as gently, in an hour as 100 men could do in a day, and with much less exposure to OXYGEN. A.D.W.

PUNCHING DOWN, the manual wine-making operation of breaking up and submerging the CAP of skins and other solids during red wine fermentation. The French term is PIGEAGE. For more details, see MACERATION.

PUNT, optional indentation in the bottom of wine bottles, particularly common in bottles of sparkling wine. See BOTTLES for more details.

PUPITRE, French name for a hand riddling rack, traditionally used for RIDDLING sparkling wines by hand. For more details, see SPARKLING WINE-MAKING.

PVP, or **poly(N-vinylpyrrolidinone)**, synthetic material sometimes used to remove colour from white wines or for FILTRATION. See RESINS for more detail.

PX, common abbreviation for the Spanish grape variety PEDRO XIMÉNEZ, or blending wine made from it used chiefly in SHERRY production.

PYRENEES, wine region centred on the town of Avoca in the state of VICTORIA in AUSTRALIA, named after the mountains which separate France and Spain (see BASQUE wines).

PYRUVATE, three-carbon compound formed by YEAST at a midway stage in the complex FERMENTATION process. Depending on the amount of oxygen available, it is converted either to carbon dioxide and water or, preferably for wine-making, to ACETALDEHYDE and then ETHANOL. In mammals, where it is converted to LACTIC ACID, it supplies energy for muscular action.

Q

QBA, or **Qualitätswein bestimmter Anbaugebiete**, is GERMANY's largest wine category effectively, the lower ranks of so-called QUALITÄTSWEIN, or 'quality wine'. The chief requirement of a QbA wine is that, as the direct translation suggests, all the wine in the bottle comes from only one of Germany's 13 specified wine regions (although see also LIEBFRAUMILCH). The grapes should also reach certain minimum ripeness levels in terms of MUST WEIGHT. These must weights are carefully specified for each grape variety and for each region. The classic grape variety Riesling, for example, need reach a must weight of just 57° OECHSLE (a potential alcohol of about 7.5 per cent, less than 15° Brix) in the AHR, MITTELRHEIN, MOSEL-SAAR-RUWER, WÜRTTEMBERG, and northen NAHE, while Roter TRAMINER and RULÄNDER must reach 72° Oechsle in the southernmost wine region of BADEN.

The wines also have to be made from recommended grape varieties and have to earn an AP NUMBER, but this is hardly very challenging. Unlike QMP wines, QbA wines may have their alcohol content increased by ENRICHMENT.

This category therefore includes the great majority of wines exported from Germany, all Liebfraumilch, and the sea of anonymous medium dry blends carrying such GROSSLAGE names as Piesporter Michelsberg and Niersteiner Gutes Domtal. Many top wine producers make one or several QbA blends depending on the vintage, and in particularly poor years some choose to declassify as QbA wines even those musts which technically qualify as a QmP in order to retain the prestige of their QmP labels.

The proportion of each vintage which qualifies as QbA can vary from less than 40 per cent in a very ripe VINTAGE such as 1990, to 80 per cent in the unripe year of 1984.

Few QbA wines improve with age. The exceptions are several experimental styles, notably BARRIQUE-aged wines, which may not qualify as QmP wines but need several years in bottle to show at their best.

QMP, or **Qualitätswein mit Prädikat**, is GERMANY's category of usually superior wines. It means literally 'quality wine with distinction' and the PRÄDIKAT can qualify as one of five distinct subcategories, determined by the grapes' MUST WEIGHT, as specified below. The grapes should also be picked as specified by law (see entries under each individual Prädikat name). Unlike QBA wines, a QmP wine cannot have sugar added to it for the purposes of ENRICHMENT. SÜSSRESERVE may be added to sweeten a QmP wine, on the other hand, but this practice is declining in response to demand for drier, more concentrated wines (see TROCKEN and HALBTROCKEN). In the late 1980s and early 1990s it was also common for the best producers to choose to set themselves higher minimum must weights for each Prädikat than the official minima, and even to choose to declassify wine in particularly ripe vintages such as 1990 for purely marketing reasons.

The proportion of the total German harvest which qualifies as QmP wine varies enormously with the weather conditions of each year. The cool weather of 1984 yielded a harvest of which only seven per cent qualified as QmP, while the hot 1976 summer ripened 83 per cent of the entire crop to at least Kabinett level. Most of Germany's finest wines are QmP wines, the only possible exceptions being some of the more experimental wines, notably some of those aged in BARRIQUE, which may have been refused an AP NUMBER on the ground that they lack TYPICITY, as experimental wines are wont to do.

Precise OECHSLE levels are specified by law for each combination of grape variety and region. The table gives the official minima for combinations at opposite ends of the spectrum.

Prädikat	Minimum ° Oechsle / potential percentage alcohol	
	Riesling in Mosel-Saar-Ruwer	Spätburgunder in Baden
Kabinett	67/8.6	85/11.4
Spätlese	76/10.0	95/13.0
Auslese	83/11.1	105/14.5
Beerenauslese, Eiswein	110/15.3	128/18.1
Trockenbeerenauslese	150/21.5	154/22.1

See KABINETT, SPÄTLESE, AUSLESE, BEERENAUSLESE, TROCKENBEERENAUSLESE, and EISWEIN (which has the same must weight requirements as Beerenauslese but is produced from naturally frozen grapes) for more details.

QUALITÄTSWEIN, German for 'quality wine'. In GERMANY this bloated category encompasses about 95 per cent of each German vintage, including some very ordinary blends indeed, and excludes only TAFELWEIN and LANDWEIN. GERMAN WINE LAW recognizes two sorts of Qualitätswein: Qualitätswein bestimmte Anbaugebiete or QBA, often called simply Qualitätswein, and, usually recognizably superior, Qualitätswein mit Prädikat or QMP, often called PRÄDIKATSWEIN.

In AUSTRIA Qualitätswein is the category between Landwein and Prädikatswein, and it includes not only wine officially designated Qualitätswein, but also Austria's Kabinett wine. The proportion of the total Austrian crop which qualifies as Qualitätswein varies enormously according to the character of each vintage, but can be as high as one-third.

QUALITY CONTROL, or **quality assurance**, the series of analyses and tests that verify a wine's palatability, stability (see STABILIZATION), compliance with regulations, TYPICITY, and freedom from FAULTS and CONTAMINANTS. Most large wineries maintain laboratories capable of conducting all but the most difficult of the required analyses (see ANALYSIS), while smaller wine enterprises send samples to an independent commercial laboratory. For complete quality assurance, a chemical analytical laboratory, a microbiological laboratory, and a statistically controlled taste panel are required. A.D.W.

QUALITY WINE is not only an expression widely and loosely used for any wine of good quality, it is an official wine DESIGNATION throughout the EUROPEAN UNION, and therefore throughout most of Europe. The EU recognizes quality wine as the higher of its two general categories of wine: quality wine (which must be produced in a specified region—an indicator of European reverence for geography) and TABLE WINE. In English it may be referred to as Quality Wine PSR, in French as VQPRD, or Vin de Qualité Produit dans les Régions Délimitées. Each member country has a different system to describe this designation, but most are based on a system of CONTROLLED APPELLATIONS (although the German system depends more on the level of natural, unaugmented SUGAR IN GRAPES, or ripeness and absence of CHAPTALIZATION.

Country	Quality wine
France	VDQS, APPELLATION CONTRÔLÉE*
Italy	DOC*, DOCG
Spain	DO*, DOCA
Portugal	DOC
Germany	QBA*, QMP
Greece	OPE, OPAP* (see GREECE)
United Kingdom	Quality wine (see ENGLAND)
Luxembourg	Appellation contrôlée (see LUXEMBOURG)

* indicates the more important category, in terms of the amount of wine likely to carry the designation.

The quality of the wine in each of these categories varies widely, as does the proportion of a typical vintage which qualifies as 'quality wine' in each country. Germany is notorious in classifying more than 95 per cent of every vintage as quality wine, while in France the proportion is a much more realistic 40 per cent. Like any official scheme, the above have their critics (see individual entries), but Italy, Spain, and Portugal have been particularly profligate in their creation of DOCs and DOs. Nevertheless quality wine represents just 13.5, 25, and 25 per cent respectively of the total wine production of Italy, Spain, and Portugal.

QUARANTINE of imported plant material plays an important part in international viticulture, and can put a (necessary) brake on certain aspects of its development. Like any form of agricultural quarantine, it can annoy travellers but is designed to protect farmers from the ravages which may be caused by the introduction of pests and diseases from other countries or regions (see the history of DOWNY MILDEW, POWDERY MILDEW, and PHYLLOXERA). Most of the devastating pests and diseases of the vine species used commonly for wine production, *Vitis* VINIFERA, have in fact been spread from America, AMERICAN VINE SPECIES having developed a tolerance to these diseases which the European *vinifera* lacks.

Quarantine systems for viticulture are in place at national borders, and also sometimes at regional levels. Most wine-producing countries maintain strict quarantine on vine imports in an attempt to keep out the likes of PIERCE'S DISEASE, and FLAVESCENCE DORÉE which are currently limited to certain regions. Quarantine also works to reduce the spread of other fungal, virus, and BACTERIAL DISEASES as well as insect and nematode PESTS which might not be lethal but may cause significant commercial damage. Licences issued for importation are typically restricted to a few cuttings which are subjected to disease testing. The quarantine delays can be up to two years, but new diagnostic tests such as ELISA developed in the 1980s have reduced this period. Smuggling of vines is not unknown, especially when producers believe that they are disadvantaged by not having access to better varieties or clones. In a reference to the popular luggage manufacturers, smuggled vine importations are popularly known as 'Samsonite vines' (see Chardonnay in SOUTH AFRICA).

Sometimes there are quarantine areas within national boundaries, such as those that exist in South Australia in an attempt to avoid the further spread of phylloxera. Some countries and regions are free of major pests or diseases. CHILE, for example, has remained free of phylloxera. California, Western Australia, and all but southern Chile are free of downy mildew. (It is likely, however, that the disease has inadvertently been introduced to these regions, so it may be their dry climate which prevents it from developing.) Increasing international competition in the wine market makes the possibility of sabotage from another region or nation by introduction of a pest or disease less fanciful. The economic health of many of the world's viticultural regions depends on effective vine quarantine being maintained, and continuing vigilance and community support are essential. R.E.S.

QUARTS DE CHAUME, extraordinary small enclave within the Coteaux du LAYON appellation producing, only in the best vintages and usually only as a result of NOBLE ROT infection, sweet white wines from BOTRYTIZED Chenin Blanc grapes. Total annual production can often be as little as a few thousand cases, from less than 40 ha/100 acres of vineyard, supposedly the finest quarter, or *quart*, of the Chaume part near Rochefort-sur-Loire of Coteaux du Layon (see FRANCE,

Quinta dos Malvedos in the Douro valley, northern Portugal.

history, for details). The vineyards here have the advantage of a southerly exposition within a sort of amphitheatre. The soils are distinctive, the average VINE AGE is high, since, with a maximum permitted YIELD of only 22 hl/ha (1.2 tons/acre) which is rarely achieved, few new investments are being made in this minuscule but potentially glorious appellation. The naturally high acidity of the Chenin Blanc grape endows these wines with impressive longevity.

QUARTZ, a hard glossy mineral consisting of silicon dioxide in hexagonal crystalline form, which is present in most rocks, especially sandstone and granite. Flint is a form of quartz. Predominantly quartz soils are typically infertile but often have good drainage. See GEOLOGY.

QUATOURZE, one of the named TERROIRS within the Coteaux du LANGUEDOC appellation in southern France. Production of appellation wine in this small windswept zone just west of Narbonne is so small that it seems doomed to extinction, partly because of property development.

QUEENSLAND, hot north eastern state in AUSTRALIA which produces some wine despite its latitude.

Ignoring the curious outpost at Roma in the central west (a theoretical region VIII or thereabouts—see WINKLER), where some high-quality dessert wines have been produced at a single winery for over 100 years, Queensland's viticulture is restricted to the **Granite Belt**, situated on the inland (or western) side of the Great Dividing Range just north of the NEW SOUTH WALES border. Fifteen wineries produce mainly CHARDONNAY, SÉMILLON, SHIRAZ, and CABERNET SAUVIGNON of relatively modest quality, relying almost entirely on the passing tourist trade. ELEVATION (around 800 m/2,500 ft) is the key to the otherwise subequatorial climate. Shiraz and Semillon are the wines with the greatest individuality. J.H.

QUERCETIN, also spelt **quercitin**, a yellow dyestuff originally extracted from the bark of black oak (QUERCUS), now synthesized. Quercetin is a flavonoid PHENOLIC that is commonly present in plants. It is abundant in grape leaves and its presence in wine (as a result of leaf contamination from a poorly adjusted MECHANICAL HARVESTER, for example) may lead to one type of wine haze. B.G.C.

Somers, T. C., and Ziemelis, G., 'Flavonol haze in white wines', *Vitis*, 24 (1985), 43–50.

QUERCUS is the botanical genus to which oak belongs and is therefore the most important family of plants to wine after the vine genus VITIS since it provides both CORK and wine's most classic storage material (see WOOD). It is subdivided into two subgenera, *Cyclobalanopsis*, and *Equercus*, to which all oaks used for wine containers and corks belong. The species most commonly used for BARRELS are the American white oak *Quercus alba*, and the European oaks *Quercus robur* and *Quercus sessiliflora*. For more details see OAK.

The species whose bark is stripped to provide cork is *Quercus suber.*

QUINCY, historic white wine appellation in the greater Loire region producing racy dry wines from Sauvignon Blanc grapes from about 100 ha / 250 acres of sand and gravel on the left bank of the Cher tributary. Its long history and early popularity owe much to its proximity to RIVER transport (especially in comparison with the much smaller nearby appellation REUILLY). The wines tend to be a little more rustic, less delicate, than those made in Menetou-Salon and Sancerre to the east.

See also LOIRE and map on pp. 576–7.

QUINTA, Portuguese word meaning farm, which may also refer to a wine producing estate or vineyard. Single-quinta ports are those made from a single year and from a single estate in the Douro valley; see PORT.

QUINTA DO NOVAL. Founded in 1813, Noval is the name of both the estate and the leading Portuguese PORT shipper. Quinta do Noval was owned by the firm António José da Silva, who in 1973 changed their name to Quinta do Noval-Vinhos, because Noval represented their finest wine (and they also wanted to avoid confusion with all the other da Silva companies in OPORTO). The estate of Quinta do Noval, in the Pinhão valley, was long run by the Van Zeller family. Their grandfather, Luiz Vasconcellos Porto, was the first to experiment with the new, wider, sloping vineyard TERRACES which proved so effective and are now replacing the older, narrower terraced vineyards. The firm's vineyards produce 30 per cent of their needs with the remainder being bought in from other properties in the DOURO valley. Noval's most prestigious wine is Nacional, produced from vines which have never been GRAFTED on to PHYLLOXERA-resistant American ROOTSTOCKS and are therefore 'national'. These vines yield particularly small quantities of fruit, so that a Nacional vintage port is made only in exceptional years. The wines these ancient vines produce are amongst the most concentrated of all vintage ports, however, with a deeper colour and much fuller texture than others. This results in these ports commanding high prices on the market, with the Nacional 1931 VINTAGE (which Noval was virtually alone in declaring) enjoying almost legendary status as the most expensive port ever sold. Quinta do Noval has continued to make some unusual vintage declarations, and to pursue a policy of ageing wine in the Douro valley rather than in VILA NOVA DE GAIA. In 1993 the firm was acquired by the French insurance company AXA and the Van Zeller family is no longer involved in its management.

R

RABBITS can be a serious pest in some wine regions. see ANIMALS.

RABOSO, tough red grape variety grown in the VENETO region of north east Italy, notably on the flat valley floor of PIAVE. The name is thought to derive from the Italian *rabbioso*, or angry, presumably a reference to consumer reaction to the uncompromisingly high ACIDITY and rough TANNINS which characterize the grape and its wine. This is a grape variety which has excellent resistance to disease and rot, but which makes CABERNET SAUVIGNON look rather mellow. Unfortunately Raboso is not notably high in the ALCOHOL which might compensate for its astringency and can therefore taste extremely austere in youth. Stalwart defenders of the variety insist that with prolonged FERMENTATION, oxygenated by frequent PUMPING OVER, and lengthy CASK AGEING, the grape could give distinguished wines, the Veneto's answer to the Nebbiolo of Peidmont or the Sangiovese of Tuscany. The reputation and price level of Raboso make it difficult to justify this kind of investment, however, and ambitious wines of this type are not part of the local culture. Raboso is a permitted VARIETAL of the Piave DOC but less than 1,500 hl/39,600 gal are made each year. The Italian vineyard survey of 1990 found that total plantings of the **Raboso Piave** vine had almost halved since 1982, to 2,000 ha/4,940 acres.

Raboso is also planted, to an extremely limited extent, in Argentina, presumably taken there by Italian immigrants.

D.T.

RACKING, the wine-making operation of removing clear wine from the settled SEDIMENT or LEES in the bottom of a container. The verb to **rack** has been used thus at least since the 14th century.

Racking is usually achieved by pumping or siphoning the wine away from the sediment into an empty container but special large **racking tanks** are used by some large wineries (and breweries). They are equipped with drain lines, the lower ends of which can be adjusted to just clear the sediment layer and permit more rapid and more complete wine removal from the solids. A.D.W.

Racking, or *soutirage* as it is known in French, forms an important part of the annual cycle of cellar work, or ÉLEVAGE, in the production of most fine wines matured in small BARRELS. Racking from barrel to barrel is very labour intensive and, with the cost of the barrels themselves, one of the chief economic arguments against BARREL MATURATION. Each racking inevitably involves a barrel that needs cleaning.

According to classical élevage, the first racking takes place soon after FERMENTATION and the ensuing MACERATION to separate the new wine from the gross LEES. In cooler regions the second racking typically takes place just after the first frosts of winter have precipitated some of the TARTRATES, while in many cellars there is a third in spring and a fourth before the full heat of the summer. Wines may be racked once or twice during a second year in barrel. New World wine-makers have tended to rack less frequently.

Racking is not only part of the CLARIFICATION process, it also provides AERATION and may well help the formation of FLAVOUR COMPOUNDS and the polymerization of TANNINS, meanwhile discouraging REDUCTION of any excess SULPHUR to malodorous HYDROGEN SULPHIDE.

RAILWAYS. Until the arrival of a railway in their region, wine producers were almost totally dependent on waterborne means of transport. Without access to the sea or a navigable RIVER or canal, transport was too difficult and expensive for all but the finest and rarest wines. This gave an overwhelming advantage to regions such as BORDEAUX which were served by a major port, or CHAMPAGNE, with access to the river system of northern France.

The construction of the railways enabled a number of wines previously unknown outside their region to be exported. In some cases—notably CHIANTI in central Italy and RIOJA in northern Spain—this enabled high-quality wines to achieve their deserved recognition for the first time. The construction of a railway line between the town of JEREZ and the coast in the mid 19th century, greatly encouraged exports of SHERRY.

The railways also facilitated the transport of inferior wines. They allowed the late 19th century development of the mass-production vineyards of the LANGUEDOC-ROUSSILLON in the south of France, whose rough wines were transported in vast quantities to northern France and Belgium, thus ruining such marginal northern European vineyards as those around ORLÉANS and, to a lesser extent, those of the MOSELLE. The railways in ARGENTINA were also crucial in establishing Mendoza as an important wine region so far from the capital Buenos Aires. During the 15 years of PROHIBITION in North America, efficient rail transport of fresh grapes from California to the suddenly numerous HOME WINE-MAKERS in the eastern states played a part in maintaining a wine-making tradition in the United States. The latest example of the

The labour-intensive cellar task of **racking** wine off its lees from one barrel to another.

changes wrought by railways was the opening of a line south from Tomelloso in La MANCHA in central Spain to Jerez in 1945, which enabled the Jerezanos to bring in brandy from La Mancha, store it in Jerez, and sell it as Brandy de Jerez. Their own supplies of wine, and thus brandy, were limited, so it was only the availability of La Mancha spirit which permitted the notable expansion of the Spanish brandy industry after the Second World War (see BRANDY, Spanish). N.F.

RAINFALL, a component of climate which affects grapevines in many and conflicting ways.

For vines depending directly on rainfall (see DRYLAND VITICULTURE for more details of these common, non-irrigated conditions), there needs to be enough rain, at the right times, to promote adequate growth and to avoid severe WATER STRESS during ripening. On the other hand more than enough rainfall can lead to excessive vegetation growth and a poor CANOPY MICROCLIMATE, especially on soils high in nitrogen. It can also cause waterlogging on soils prone to it (see DRAINAGE).

The effects of irregular rainfall are moderated to the extent that the soil has sufficient depth and water-holding capacity, and is well enough drained for the vine roots to survive at depth (see SOIL WATER, SOIL DEPTH, TERROIR).

Alternatively, insufficient rainfall and/or insufficient soil water-holding capacity can be overcome by IRRIGATION. This is especially important in MEDITERRANEAN CLIMATES where the summer is dry, but winter–spring rainfall is usually enough to allow surface storage and later supplementary irrigation as needed. Under all these regimes the practical minimum annual rainfall for commercially adequate yields is somewhere around 500 mm/20 in in cool viticultural climates, rising to about 600–750 mm/24–30 in in warm to hot climates.

Hot regions with full irrigation typically have 300 mm/12 in of annual rainfall or less, and mostly depend on rivers bringing fresh water from elsewhere for their supply. The normal unreliability of what rainfall they do get means that full wetting of the soil profile seldom occurs naturally, and frequent heavy watering is usually needed throughout the growing and ripening season.

No particular upper limit of rainfall is apparent for viticulture, provided that the soils are well drained, leached SOIL

Plastic sheeting used experimentally in 1992 at Ch Pétrus in Pomerol to prevent any more **rainfall** from penetrating the soil just before harvest and diluting the resultant wine.

NUTRIENTS can be replaced, SUNLIGHT is enough, and HUMIDITY is not so high that FUNGAL DISEASES cannot be controlled. Some successful viticultural areas, such as the VINHO VERDE region in northern Portugal, and parts of southern SWITZERLAND, have annual rainfall totals exceeding 1,500 mm.

Heavy rain close to and at vintage is nevertheless nearly always detrimental to wine quality, especially if it follows moisture stress. The berries than swell suddenly and often split, resulting in OXIDATION of the juice, FERMENTATION on the vine, and usually fungal and bacterial infection of the bunches. At a minimum the juice and its flavour are diluted. HAIL at this time is especially disastrous. J.G.

RAISINS, alternative generic name for DRYING GRAPES, from its direct French translation *raisins secs*, but also used specifically for relatively large, dark, dried grapes, particularly in California where raisins are as important a viticultural crop as grapes for wine.

Grapes which have dried either on the vine or have been dried after picking, to produce either dried fruit or DRIED GRAPE WINES, are often described as fully or partially **raisined**.

RAMANDOLO. See VERDUZZO.

RAMISCO, red grape variety grown exclusively in the shrinking COLARES region of Portugal and therefore probably the only VINIFERA vine variety never to have been GRAFTED. It produces wines of real character that are extremely tannic in youth.

RANCIO, imprecise tasting term used in many languages for a distinctive style of wine, often FORTIFIED WINE or VIN DOUX NATUREL, achieved by deliberately MADERIZING the wine by exposing it to OXYGEN and/or heat. The wine may be stored in barrels in hot storehouses (as for some of Australia's LIQUEUR MUSCATS and Liqueur Tokays), or immediately under the rafters in a hot climate (as for some of ROUSSILLON's vins doux naturels, or in glass BONBONNES left out of doors and subjected to the changing temperatures of night and day (as in parts of Spain). The word rancio has the same root as 'rancid' and the wines which result have an additional and powerful smell reminiscent of nuts and melted, or even rancid, butter.

Rancio is also a quality developed by brandies, most obviously by COGNAC (and hence the French term *rancio charentais*), when they have been matured in wood for twenty years or more (see OAK AND BRANDY). Chemically rancio derives from the oxidation of the fatty acids in the spirit, producing the ketones which produce the richness felt on the palate with such brandies. This is quite distinct from the artificial richness and woodiness imparted by the addition of caramel or the macerated oak chip mixture called *boisé* (see TASTING BRANDY) used to provide some artificial age to a brandy.

This richness emerges in a complex series of sensations on the nose and palate. 'Rankness, a special character of fullness and richness', was the unflattering description given by Charles Walter Berry, the wine merchant who was Britain's leading cognac connoisseur between the World Wars. This richness, allied to a certain mild cheesiness in the nose, reminds some tasters of Roquefort cheese. But the richness, depth and diversity of rancio can remind others of rich fruit cakes with their flavours of candied fruits, apricot, sultanas, almonds, and walnuts. Traditional English drinkers such as Berry and his customers rather scorned the richness of the rancio, preferring the lighter, more elegant brandies produced by firms such as Hine and Delamain. But recently even these cognacs seem to have acquired a touch of the richness and complexity which, to many modern connoisseurs, is one of the essential ingredients of a truly great cognac. N.F. & J.Ro.

RASTEAU, one of the Côtes-du-Rhône villages in the southern RHÔNE. Its heady, slightly rustic red, white, and rosé table wines are sold as Côtes-du-Rhône Villages, occasionally with the name Rasteau as a suffix. Wines sold as Appellation Rasteau Contrôlée, on the other hand, are VINS DOUX NATURELS, sweet mixtures of just-fermenting grape juice and pure grape spirit in various shades of brown and red. They are essentially alcoholic Grenache juice (90 per cent of the grapes must be GRENACHE Noir, Gris, or Blanc) treated to a range of AGEING processes which may vary from the negligible through various forms of CASK AGEING (usually in relatively ancient cooperage) to the sort of deliberate exposure to heat and oxygen that results in sticky brown liquids which can be sold as Rasteau RANCIO. Although Rasteau is the chosen name for this variable drink, the grapes may be grown anywhere in the communes of three Côtes-du-Rhône villages: Rasteau, Cairanne, and Sablet.

RATAFIA is an old, usually domestically produced wine made in the French countryside by drying grapes to a raisin-like state and then moistening and fermenting them in the spring. Ratafia de Champagne was the VIN DE LIQUEUR of Champagne, made by adding young grape spirit to hardly fermenting grape juice. Today however there are more profitable ways of selling the juice of Champagne grapes.

RATINGS, scores applied to individual wines. See SCORING and, especially, NUMBERS.

RATTI, RENATO (1934–88), industrious and dedicated wine-maker based at La Morra in BAROLO in the north west Italian region of Piedmont. He did much to revolutionize wine-making techniques to make wines from the Nebbiolo grape drinkable at a much earlier stage in their evolution. As head of the local wine-makers' association, he energetically promulgated the notion of TERROIR, and hastened the recognition of individual vineyards, or CRUS, in the LANGHE hills.

RÄUSCHLING, white grape variety today most commonly planted in German-speaking SWITZERLAND, where it can produce fine, crisp wines. In the Middle Ages it was widely cultivated in Germany, particularly Baden (see GERMAN HISTORY). The KNIPPERLÉ of ALSACE is an early ripening subvariety.

RAVAT, French vine breeder who gave his name to a number of FRENCH HYBRIDS.

RAY, CYRIL (1908–91), English war correspondent turned wine writer, famous more for his style and punctiliousness than for an obsession with wine itself. His great passion was military history and, having won scholarships both at Manchester Grammar School and at Jesus College, Oxford, he was very much a historian *manqué*. During the Second World War he was a war correspondent, receiving several commendations for his courage and scrupulous accuracy in reporting. It was his service throughout the Italian campaign that aroused his first definite interest in wine—both the ordinary peasant wines and those of the highest quality served at more aristocratic celebrations of the liberation. Subsequently he was on UNESCO missions to Italy, Greece, and Africa, where his wine experience was broadened. Later he became a member of the staff of *The Sunday Times* and was their correspondent in Moscow, being a versatile writer of wide interests.

In 1956 he edited the first of what were to be perhaps his most lasting contribution to the LITERATURE OF WINE, 16 volumes of *The Compleat Imbiber*, compilations of stories, comments, and verses, although the 'pirate' edition, produced in later years without his seeing the proofs, provoked a special outburst of his famous rage against publishers. He also became wine correspondent of the *Director* magazine, the *Observer* newspaper, *Punch* weekly magazine (where he was also a consultant to their purchases of wine), and the *Spectator*. At the same time he was producing articles and writing and editing books on many subjects other than wine. His wine columns greatly influenced sales, although he was seldom interested in tasting young wines, his preferred drink often being Guinness stout.

Cyril Ray founded the British organization the Circle of Wine Writers and was its first president. He received a succession of awards and prizes for his wine writing including Commendatore, Italian Order of Merit, 1981 and Chevalier, French Order of Merit, 1985. Among his major books, additional to the published collections of his essays and articles, and his updating and editing of the works of past wine writers, the following are of importance: *The Wines of Italy* (Bologna Trophy 1967); *Wine with Food* (together with his wife Elizabeth Ray, herself a distinguished writer on food and biographer of influential food personalities); *Cognac*; and *Vintage Tales*. He specialized in specific historical studies of individual producers, such as LAFITE-Rothschild, WARRE, BOLLINGER, MOUTON-ROTHSCHILD, Langoa-and Léoville-BARTON, Ruffino Chianti, and, one of the last, Robert MONDAVI of the Napa Valley.

Witty and precise, Cyril Ray's writings on wine were accurate to the last recorded mention and to what he could find out himself. A superb style and impeccable use of the English language drew the attention of many readers who might not otherwise have been lured to read about wine or to think of it as anything save as a drink. P.V.P.

RAYA, Spanish word meaning stripe or streak and a term for the symbol used to classify SHERRY must. A *raya* is also a coarse style of OLOROSO used in blending medium dry sherry.

REBE, German for vine. **Rebsorten** are vine varieties.

RECIOTO, distinctive category of north east Italian DRIED GRAPE WINES, a historic speciality of the VENETO. The word derives from the Italian for ear, *orecchio*, because the wine was originally produced only from the ripest grapes in the bunch, from the upper lobes, or ears, although selected whole bunches have long been substituted. The most common forms of Recioto are sweet red Recioto della VALPOLICELLA and the much rarer sweet white Recioto di SOAVE.

Recioto della Valpolicella, like its dry counterpart AMARONE, is produced from grapes which have been raisined in special drying rooms during the late autumn and winter months after the harvest; like Amarone it is produced from the same grapes as qualify for the Valpolicella DOC, which zone has been divided into a CLASSICO subzone and a larger zone whose wines are simply called Recioto. The wine is a decisively sweet one, steps being taken to prevent the conversion of its RESIDUAL SUGARS into alcohol during the period of fermentation and ageing. A certain development of NOBLE ROT is virtually inevitable, given the damp climate of Valpolicella during the months of raisining between November and March, and traditionally made wines display BOTRYTIS flavours, along with a certain OXIDIZED character. A small minority of younger producers is now seeking to avoid the imprint of botrytis and oxidation by eliminating botrytis-affected grapes and bunches prior to fermentation (as for Amarone). Some producers are also experimenting with new barrels of 400- to 500-l/132-gal capacity in place of the traditional, considerably larger casks of old Yugoslav oak.

Recioto represents a very small proportion of Valpolicella's total production: less than 4,000 hl/105,600 gal in recent years. A Recioto of white grapes—principally GARGANEGA—which resembles a Recioto di Soave is also produced in minuscule quantities in the Valpolicella zone, but qualifies only as a VINO DA TAVOLA. D.T.

RÉCOLTE, French for HARVEST. A **récoltant** is therefore a GROWER. In CHAMPAGNE a **récoltant-manipulant** (identified by 'RM' on the label) is a grower who also makes his or her own champagne, of whom there are more than 2,000 in the region, as opposed to a **récoltant-coopérateur**, who sells champagne made by a CO-OPERATIVE, of whom there are slightly fewer.

RECORKING, a hazardous exercise conducted by some top wine producers and some fine wine traders. The aim is to prolong a wine's potential longevity after extended BOTTLE AGEING may have weakened the cork. Ch LAFITE occasionally sends its MAÎTRE-DE-CHAI on recorking tours which have doubled as public relations exercises. With plenty of advance notice, bottles can be assembled from various CELLARS and COLLECTORS. He eases the old cork out and, ideally, tops up the bottle as necessary with a similar vintage of Lafite. Some documentary evidence of this operation is provided. The fine wine market became suspicious of recorking in any circumstances other than the most public in the late 1980s, however, as it potentially offers too much possibility for ADULTERATION AND FRAUD.

RECTIFIED GRAPE MUST, or RGM, is preserved GRAPE JUICE that has been rectified, processed to reduce the concentration of solids other than SUGARS. It is generally further treated by removing water to yield **rectified concentrated**

Recorking machine at Marqués de Riscal in Rioja.

grape must, or **RCGM**, which is a common commodity used principally in Europe for ENRICHMENT. The EUROPEAN UNION authorities have been keen to promote its use in place of sugar as a way of helping reduce the European WINE LAKE. Many wine-makers who need to use it in northern Europe have a natural antipathy to introducing a product made from what they view as inferior grapes. There are several major producers of rectified grape must in Europe who absorb SURPLUS grape production from areas such as the LANGUEDOC, SICILY, and APULIA. They submit it to such modern technological processes as ION EXCHANGE and reverse osmosis (see CONCENTRATION) together with super-efficient FILTRATION and evaporators to produce what is in effect a concentrated invert sugar (GLUCOSE and FRUCTOSE) solution from grape juice.

REDDING, CYRUS (1785–1870), England's answer to the great wine explorer of France, André JULLIEN. Redding came from an old Cornish family and, after publishing several biographies and histories when working as a young journalist in London, was sent to Paris in 1814, where he was based for five years. It was during this time that he was introduced to wine regions and a wine-producing culture. Jullien's book was published two years after his arrival in Paris and Redding's most important work, *A History and Description of Modern Wines*, takes full account of both Jullien and CHAPTAL's previous publications, but Redding seems to have been independently inspired by the disparity between the wines then available in the British Isles and what he tasted in cellars all over Europe (see ADULTERATION). Like Jullien, he was an intrepid traveller and his book includes observations not just on European wines but on those of Asia, Africa, and both North and South America. His emphasis on the word Modern owes much to his criticism of earlier writers such as Sir Edward Barry and Alexander HENDERSON (see LITERATURE), whose reverence for CLASSICAL WINES he felt was misplaced. The first edition of *A History and Description of Modern Wines* was written when Redding had returned to Lancing on the south coast of England in 1833 and subsequent editions appeared in 1836 and 1851; modern facsimile editions have also appeared, so useful, fresh, and unpretentious are Redding's observations to this day.

REDONDO, town in southern Portugal whose co-operative is establishing a certain reputation for its wines. See ALENTEJO for more details.

REDOX POTENTIAL, or oxidation-reduction potential, is a measure of the summation of all of a wine's components' potentials to react. Since wine is made up of components that are either oxidized or reduced (see OXIDATION and REDUCTION), it is a system composed of many joined redox pairs. Oxidation reactions are always coupled to reduction reactions. Electrons made available from an oxidation are taken up by the compound being reduced until an equilibrium is established. The reaction with the most positive value (in which electrons are most easily accepted) will occur at the expense of reactions with lower values. Thus an equilibrium is reached from all the redox pairs and a net redox potential can be determined.

Redox potentials are of only limited value to even the most scientific wine-maker, however, since they do not express how rapidly the various reactions will occur. They reveal only the potential situation that will obtain given unlimited time. A determination of the concentration of dissolved OXYGEN in a given wine can often prove to be of more value in guiding the wine-maker in his or her choice of cellar treatments.

A.D.W.

Zoecklein, B., 'Understanding oxidation: redox potential', *Vineyard & Winery Management* (Nov.–Dec. 1989), 32–3.

REDUCED ALCOHOL WINES are those with a lower than normal ALCOHOLIC STRENGTH, generally less than 5.5 per cent.

The easiest and cheapest way to produce these low alcohol products is simply to dilute wine using water (to make a SPRITZER-type drink), natural or flavoured fruit juices, or even GRAPE JUICE to make an all-vinous product. See wine COOLERS.

Another method is to arrest fermentation before it is complete by refrigeration, resulting in a sweet, low alcohol, often lightly sparkling drink. This is a particularly common technique in Italy and is conducted at all sorts of quality levels, from the finest MOSCATO D'ASTI to partial fermentation of LAMBRUSCO must stored throughout the year at low temperatures and transformed into relatively industrial 'Lambrusco Light' as required.

See also DEALCOHOLIZED WINE.

REDUCTION, chemical reaction that is in effect the complement of OXIDATION and one in which an element or compound gains electrons. The essential feature of an oxidation is that electrons are transferred from the component being oxidized to the one being **reduced**. The reaction cannot be isolated; to have a reduction, something else must be oxidized. A reduction is simply the passing of electrons from one substance to another. Common reduction reactions are those of iron ore to iron the metal, or the reduction of ACETALDEHYDE to ETHANOL as happens in the final stage of alcoholic FERMENTATION. Wine in a stoppered bottle or other airtight container is said to be in a **reductive** state because any reaction that takes place within it reduces the possibilities for further change by using up some of the available OXYGEN.

Reducing conditions such as this are desirable towards the end of fermentation (unlike at the beginning when oxidizing conditions encourage yeast growth) in order that alcohol is produced along with the carbon dioxide from the acetaldehyde. Reducing conditions continue to be generally preferable throughout ÉLEVAGE of wine in the cellar, especially for white wines, which can withstand oxidation much less well than reds with their higher content of PHENOLICS.

Wines, especially red wines held in the absence of oxygen, may suffer from excess reduction, however, as a result of the slow POLYMERIZATION of TANNINS and PIGMENTS—an oxidizing reaction requiring a coupled reduction. A wine that is reduced

Red wine-making

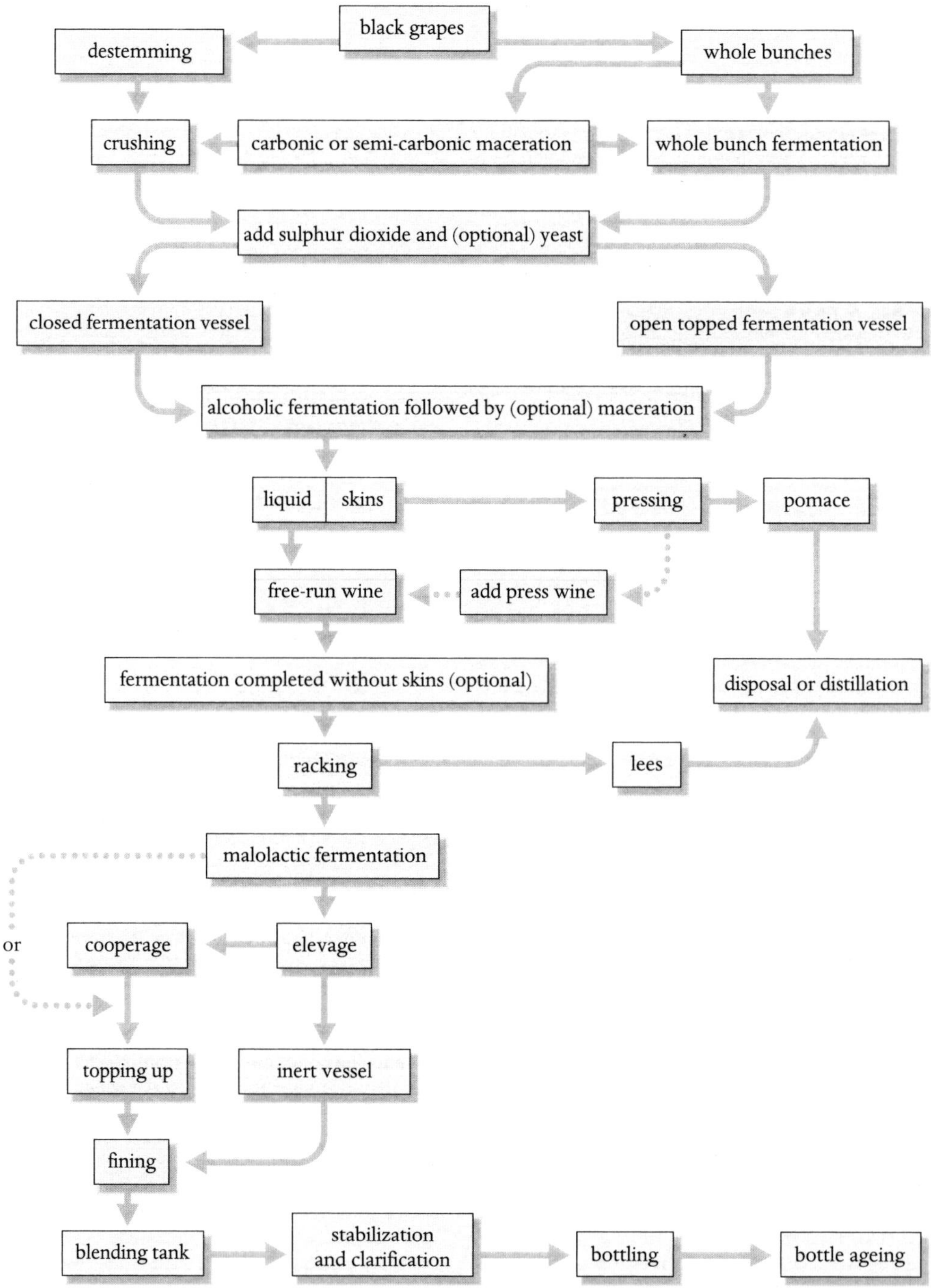

tastes dirty and frequently smells of reduced sulphur compounds such as HYDROGEN SULPHIDE and MERCAPTANS. This phenomenon can be cured by AERATION, perhaps careful RACKING, an operation which introduces some oxygen, an oxidizing agent strong enough to prevent the reduction of most sulphur compounds.

See also REDOX POTENTIAL. A.D.W.

RED WINE-MAKING, the production of wines with reddish to purple colours. The natural organic ANTHOCYAN pigments contained in darker grapes' skins are extracted into the fermenting wine by the alcohol produced by yeast during FERMENTATION and, in the presence of wine's ACIDITY, they display their red-purple COLOURS.

The great majority of red wines made today depend on CRUSHING and DESTEMMING of the grape clusters or bunches as a first step in their production (although see also WHOLE BUNCH FERMENTATION and CARBONIC MACERATION). The mixture of skins, some seeds, and stem fragments, along with the juice, then go into a FERMENTATION VESSEL, where YEAST converts SUGARS into ALCOHOL. The major exception to this prefermentation rule of crushing and destemming is the carbonic maceration alternative fermentation technique, whereby intact grape clusters are held in CARBON DIOXIDE gas. In WHITE WINE-MAKING, by contrast, the juice is separated from the skins before fermentation.

Extraction of anthocyans from skins and their dissolution into the fermenting wine is governed by several factors. Without some MACERATION of juice and skins, wine made from dark-skinned grapes is merely pink (as described in ROSÉ WINE-MAKING). Duration of this process can last anything between a simple, fast two- or three-day fermentation of an everyday wine to a week-long fermentation followed by a further week or two's maceration for fine wines designed to age.

Red wine fermentations are almost always conducted at temperatures higher than those used for white wines (see TEMPERATURE). Red wines fermented at lower temperatures tend to be lighter in colour and body and to display the fruitier range of ESTERS. There is usually some producer somewhere in the world deliberately fashioning light reds in this style to be consumed chilled.

Red wine-making differs from white-wine-making not only in terms of skin–juice contact and temperature but also because some exposure to OXYGEN is more generally desirable than with white wines, and BARREL MATURATION; or at least CASK AGEING, is also more common for red wines than white.

Because red wine-making extracts PHENOLICS from the grape skins, red wines may contain a wider range of compounds than white wines and are capable of developing a complex BOUQUET after prolonged storage in bottle. The phenolic compounds extracted from skins, seeds, and stem fragments react more or less slowly with oxygen dissolved in the wine. Some of the compounds formed contribute to the new wine's flavour. During barrel maturation, when the oxygen supply to the wine is restricted to that introduced during TOPPING UP, a new range of FLAVOUR COMPOUNDS is formed. Both the substances produced in the earlier reactions between grape phenolics and oxygen and those generated by reactions between wood phenolics with the oxygen introduced during topping up themselves interact, generating an entirely new range of flavours in the wine. For this reason, BOTTLE AGEING assumes particular importance for fine red wines. For more detail see AGEING.

See also WINE-MAKING. A.D.W.

RED WINES actually vary in colour from dark pink to almost black, with an enormous variation in the amount of blue or yellow to be seen at the rim. Their colour depends on the grape varieties used, the vintage characteristics, the health of the grapes, the wine-making methods (in particular the extent of MACERATION), the wine's PH, and the amount of time it has spent in tank, barrel, and bottle. A red wine that has suffered OXIDATION or is many decades old may be the same deep tawny colour as a very old white wine.

Red wines are produced in virtually all of the world's wine regions, although the proportion of red wines produced at the cool limit of wine production is low, since it can be difficult to develop sufficient pigmentation of most grapes' skins to produce a proper red wine.

French for red is *rouge*, Italian is *rosso*, Spanish and Portuguese more expressively *tinto*, Russian is *cherny*, and German is *rot*, which, purely coincidentally, reminds English speakers of a common hazard when growing dark-skinned grapes in a climate as potentially wet as much of Germany's.

Spain divides her red wines into those which really are *tinto* and lighter ones called CLARETE.

It has been only since the development of BOTTLES suitable for AGEING wine that red wines have been seen in any sense superior to white (see Ancient GREECE, ROME, medieval ITALY, and FASHION).

REFOSCO, red grape variety that makes usefully vigorous wine in the FRIULI region of north east Italy. The finest subvariety is known in Friuli as Refosco dal Peduncolo Rosso because of its red stem and has a long history in the area, apparently praised by PLINY the Elder and reputedly producing the favourite wine of Livia, the second wife of Augustus Caesar, cited in the *Annals of Friuli* of Francesco di Manzano in 1390.

The vine is cultivated both in hillside vineyards and in flatter parts of Friuli and gives a deeply coloured wine with plummy flavours and a hint of almonds, a medium to full body, and a rather elevated ACIDITY which can be difficult to control or moderate, the variety being a notoriously late ripener. Refosco has the advantage of good resistance to autumn rains and rot.

There was a significant return of interest in Friuli's Refosco in the 1980s, and much greater care was taken in its cultivation and vinification in an effort to improve the wine's quality, including variable experiments with small barrels. The combination of new oak and high acidity is not always successful.

The most promising zone for Refosco is COLLI ORIENTALI. Others include GRAVE DEL FRIULI, LISON-PRAMAGGIORE (outide

Friuli), Latisana, Aquileia, and Carso, where the local subvariety is known as Terrano, a reference to the variety's name Teran just across the border in SLOVENIA and CROATIA, where it produces very similar wines.

Burton Anderson cites Cagnina as its synonym in ROMAGNA, where it may have been planted by the Byzantines. Some AMPELOGRAPHERS, mainly non-Italians, believe it is identical to the MONDEUSE NOIRE of France's SAVOIE. As Refosco, the variety is grown in California to a limited extent. D.T.

Anderson, B., *The Wine Atlas of Italy* (London and New York, 1990).
Gleave, D., *The Wines of Italy* (London and New York, 1989).

REFRACTOMETER, an instrument for measuring refractive index, which is related to the amount by which the angle of a light wave is changed when passing through the boundary between two media. The amount of refraction is a convenient way to measure solute concentration of a solution and is widely used in viticulture and wine-making to follow the ripeness of grapes (by measuring MUST WEIGHT) and changes during vinification. Refractometers may be precision laboratory instruments or pocket versions that can be used in the vineyard. In either case, TEMPERATURE correction or control is important for accuracy. B.G.C.

REFRIGERATION, cooling process that has had a profound effect on how and where wine is made and how it tastes (see TEMPERATURE), enabling the wine-maker to have a much greater degree of control than was possible before mechanical refrigeration became the norm for all but the least sophisticated wineries in the second half of the 20th century. More than any other factor, refrigeration has permitted warm and hot regions to produce wine of internationally acceptable quality.

Making wine

The essence of refrigeration is the transfer of heat from the body being refrigerated to some other place. The most obvious winery application of refrigeration is in the temperature control of FERMENTATION—although refrigeration also allows wine-makers to delay the processing of freshly picked grapes or must (see MUST CHILLING) until convenient, even in hot areas. The energy generated by the conversion of sugar to alcohol, carbon dioxide, and water is only partly used by the YEAST in building cells and by-products. The rest appears as heat, which, above a certain temperature, risks killing the yeast and therefore arresting the fermentation process. The amounts of heat generated by fermentation are large. Ten hl/260 gal of grape juice containing 20 per cent sugar will generate about 3.6 million kilocalories, or enough to melt 45 tons of ice.

Not all the heat generated has to be removed by refrigeration, however. Because heat moves naturally by conduction from hotter bodies to cooler ones with which they are in contact, warm fermenting wine loses heat to the walls of the FERMENTATION VESSEL and from the wall exterior to the atmosphere. Some of the fermentation heat will be removed by radiation from the outside of the fermenting vessel too, provided its temperature is higher than that of the objects in its vicinity. Heat may also be lost by radiation if open-top fermentation vessels are used, or by volatilization of some of the water and alcohol in the wine.

All of these natural heat removal processes that function independently of refrigeration occur at the surfaces of the fermenting mass. Heat production, on the other hand, occurs throughout the entire volume of the mass. The amount of heat removed from a fermenting mass therefore depends on the surface to volume ratio of the fermentation vessel. A 225-l/59 gal BARRIQUE, for example, with a relatively high ratio of surface to volume, will probably lose enough generated heat for the temperature to remain within an acceptable range for fermentation. A typical large tank, on the other hand, which might contain several hundred hectolitres, will certainly need active heat removal to keep the temperature of the fermenting mass below danger point.

The development of mechanical refrigeration in the early 20th century at least made cooling a possibility in areas where insufficient naturally cold water was available. Early efforts to control temperature, used in France as recently as the 1970s, included the simple addition of blocks of ice to the fermenting wine (with concomitant dilution). More mechanical early systems of refrigeration cooled the wine by running cold water through metal tubes suspended in the tank. The development of more efficient PUMPS permitted systems which moved wine from the tank through coils immersed in cold water and then back into the tank.

In modern wineries, however, wines are seldom moved for cooling purposes. STAINLESS STEEL tanks with cooling devices, usually coils, incorporated in the external walls are now standard wine equipment. Temperature-sensing probes in tanks signal a computer system which controls the supply of refrigerant to the coils to a level predetermined for each tank by the wine-maker. Early refrigerants included ammonia and sulphur dioxide, but neither is desirable for food processing in the quantities required for refrigeration. Non-toxic, insoluble Freons (halogenated hydrocarbons containing fluorine or chlorine) are now used, with increasing emphasis on those with minimal effects on the OZONE layer of the stratosphere.

Refrigeration has become increasingly important in other wine-making processes, however. Some producers, notably in Australia, store grape juice in refrigerated conditions for several months before fermentation. Others prior to fermentation, notably in parts of North America, New Zealand, and SAUTERNES, may apply heavy refrigeration to emulate the conditions necessary to produce EISWEIN (see freeze CONCENTRATION). The Burgundian vogue for cold MACERATION occasionally calls for refrigeration too. In warmer wine regions some degree of refrigeration may be needed during wine maturation, and refrigerated tanks are routinely used for everyday wines to ensure that TARTRATES are not precipitated in bottle (see STABILIZATION). A.D.W.

Refrigerated tanks at Montana's winery outside Blenheim in New Zealand's South Island.

Serving wine
Refrigeration plays a part, and all too often a villainous part, in the SERVING of wine. Long before the advent of mechanical refrigeration, and its domestication, wine was deliberately chilled prior to serving (see Ancient GREECE, for example). As outlined in COOLERS, it was fashionable to chill both red and white wines before serving at least from the 16th century. A wide range of wine coolers was used to achieve this until the 20th century, when mechanical refrigeration was domestically available. The modern successors of these large containers for both ice and bottles are the single-bottle wine coolers known as ice buckets.

See also TEMPERATURE.

Região Demarcada, a demarcated region (RD) of PORTUGAL dating from the DELIMITATION of the early 20th century when boundaries were drawn around the wine regions of BUCELAS, CARCAVELOS, COLARES, DÃO, MADEIRA, SETÚBAL, and the vineyard area entitled to make VINHO VERDE. They were subsequently joined by BAIRRADA, ALGARVE, and the DOURO for table wine (PORT country having been demarcated two centuries previously). The system equates roughly with the French APPELLATION CONTRÔLÉE system and sets out permitted grape varieties, maximum yields, periods of ageing in bulk and bottle, and analytical standards for specified types of wine. Samples must be submitted to the Instituto da Vinha e do Vinho (IVV), the national authority controlling Portugal's wine industry, who grant numbered seals of origin to producers whose wines have satisfied the regulations. On joining the EUROPEAN UNION in 1986, Portugal redesignated each of its 10 RD regions Denominação de Origem Controlada (DOC), although both old and new terms could be found on labels for many years afterwards. A second tier of Indicação de Provenincia Regulamentada regions was subsequently added (see IPR). R.J.M.

Régisseur, French term used particularly of the director or manager of a Bordeaux estate.

Regner is an increasingly popular German crossing made in 1929 from a white table grape Seidentraube and Gamay. There were nearly 170 ha/420 acres planted by 1990, mainly in the Rheinhessen. Like OPTIMA and ORTEGA, it buds and ripens very early and can reach impressive must weights, even if at the expense of acidity. This is definitely not a wine to drink as a varietal (although tests in England have been successful) but is a useful Oechsle booster for blenders.

Régnié, the most recently created BEAUJOLAIS (only in 1988), is a tribute to communal spirit, or at least the spirit abroad in the neighbouring communes of Régnié-Durette and Lantignié, whose vignerons lobbied for years to be allowed to join the other nine Crus. The 650 ha/1605 acres of vines are some of the highest and most westerly of the Crus immediately east of Beaujeu. The wines are still establishing their identity.

Reguengos, or Reguengos de Monsaraz, town in Portugal whose co-operative is establishing a certain reputation for its wines. See ALENTEJO for more details.

Reichensteiner is a white grape variety whose creator Helmut BECKER maintained it was the first EUROPEAN UNION crossing, with French, Italian, and German antecedents. In 1978 he developed this crossing of Müller-Thurgau with a crossing of the French table grape MADELEINE ANGEVINE and the Italian Early Calabrese. Its antecedents are hardly noble and both wine and vine most closely resemble its undistinguished German parent, but Reichensteiner with its looser bunches is less prone to rot and well-pruned plants stand a good chance of reaching QMP must weights in good years. There were more than 300 ha/740 acres planted in Germany in 1990 with more than half, as is so often the case with the newer crossings, in Rheinhessen. The variety, named after a Rhineland castle like EHRENFELSER, has also enjoyed considerable success in ENGLAND where it is the third most planted variety.

Religion and wine. Wine is a wonder-working substance, and is therefore linked to metaphysics and to ritual. At the heart of the miraculous qualities of wine is the ALCOHOL it contains, and its capacity for quickly changing people's feelings, for better or worse. In this critical connection the wider context of wine includes all the other alcoholic drinks and, even further afield, all the various drugs which dramatically change human perceptions and experience. Thus poppies, hemp, some cacti, and some fungi share with vines a symbolic connection with the superhuman powers. The common human reaction to wine, as to these other plant substances, is that they have the power to bestow happiness, but also misery, in that their misuse can even be fatal. In these respects the substances resemble the superhuman powers themselves; they are ambiguous in character, and can cause either weal or woe.

Wine itself, however, has a quite specific history and geographical distribution. It is associated with the peoples who live round the Mediterranean Sea, in Europe, the Near East, and North Africa; and within this huge Circum-Mediterranean super-region the place of wine in the local values has been affected by the major revolution in the area whereby the old order, which was apparently partly monotheistic, partly polytheistic, and which presumably dated back into prehistory, was replaced by Christianity and ISLAM, rooted in the values of Judaic monotheism.

The different parts of the Circum-Mediterranean emerged from prehistory at different times, the western end of the Mediterranean basin far later than EGYPT and the Levant, for example, while northern and eastern Europe, outside the wine-producing area, acquired their first written records even later, and from Christian MISSIONARIES. The ORIGINS OF VITICULTURE and of wine's special place in society are obscure, however, since, by the time that written records are sufficiently detailed, the human values they reveal are already enmeshed in the dietary staples of wheat (and bread), olive oil, and wine. By the time the inhabitants of Ancient GREECE or ISRAEL become visible, they already lived in a symbolic-emotional world in which wine is taken for granted. It is quite likely that the first vines were cultivated at some time in the late prehistory of the Circum-Mediterranean, but if they were, that innovation is now lost to our view. Nevertheless it is well recorded how the peoples of that area valued their own prosperity in terms of abundant crops, as well as long life, health, and victory over enemies; and the crops regularly included vines. A careful reading of the books of the Old Testament (see BIBLE) reveals the repeated emphasis on wine as a symbol of prosperity. Indeed it is a more persistent symbol than the milk and honey of Israel's promised homeland in the Levant.

At a time when wine was so important to the prosperity of the human population, these people also saw it as a suitable offering to the superhuman authorities. Along with animal sacrifices, and offerings from other crops, LIBATIONS of wine were poured out to the gods by Italians and Greeks, and there were similar practices in the Levant. Although Israel, in the form of its remnant, the Jews, became, by reason of its monotheism, increasingly peculiar within the context of its neighbours, yet its rituals retained a mainstream familiarity. The offerings which were required in the temple in Jerusalem have been recorded, at least in part, in some of the books of the Old Testament, and they included cattle, sheep, and goats, which were ritually killed, together with cereal products, olive oil, and wine.

There was, however, another aspect to wine which probably had no Jewish counterpart, and this was obligatory, or almost obligatory, ritual DRUNKENNESS. The relevant records are not over-abundant, but in the Greek-speaking areas it was apparently normal to get drunk at the seasonal feasts of the god DIONYSUS, and his true devotees, presumably, felt bound to be drunk more often than that. In the same way, in Ancient ROME at the dark-of-the-winter festival of the Saturnalia, drunkenness was part of the general licence, and the reversal of normal sober (in every sense) behaviour. These examples emphasize the ambiguous nature of wine's effects. It can make you have a wonderful time, and it can make you dangerously irresponsible, as can the gods. (Indeed the gods themselves also get drunk—see, for example, SUMER.) Presumably, the Bacchanalia (the Roman festival of BACCHUS, the Roman name for Dionysus) and the Saturnalia were never fully respectable, but they were legal, because they emphasized the normality, and even value, of mundane daily life.

The period from prehistory to the revolution referred to above runs from *c.*3000 BC through to the opening centuries AD. The revolution itself began slowly and quietly. According to the prophetic critics of Israel, it is clear that Israel's abandonment of the various gods and spirits, most of them unrespectable (capricious, unpredictable, badly behaved), was a long, slow, bumpy, and incomplete process of conversion to the worship of God Almighty alone. However, by the time that some of them returned from the Exile in MESOPOTAMIA, in the 6th century BC, many were committed to devotional monotheism and to the sense of being the chosen people and the precious vine or vineyard of God's cultivation. This process initially made them peculiar, a minority among their neighbours, but it also led on later to the great crisis of the 1st century AD when the Jews split in two, and the Christian section set out on a world mission of evangelization.

The Christian achievement of banishing the multiplicity of gods from the Mediterranean area was reinforced by the Muslims, from the 7th century AD onward. There was a progressive impact on wine. Jews took wine for granted for secular use and for religious ritual, but rejected drunkenness as irresponsible. The early Christians accepted the Jews' position, apparently without debate, but rejected drunkenness at 'the Lord's table' as particularly disgraceful (see EUCHARIST). The Muslims rejected wine absolutely, and they still do (see ISLAM). Their response to its ambiguity has been that it is too dangerous, not worth the cost. Much later, during the modern period, some Christian groups in the northern half of Europe have independently followed the Muslims into total abstention, but they were stimulated into reaction not so much by wine as by distilled spirits. It was these various attitudes from northern as well as from southern Europe which were carried by colonists to the NEW WORLD, resulting in the most famous example of PROHIBITION, in the United States in the early 20th century.

See also MONKS AND MONASTERIES. J.D.K.

Fournier, D., and d'Onofrio, S. (eds.), *Le Ferment Divin* (Paris, 1992).

REMONTAGE, French word for various systems of **pumping over**, circulating liquid in the fermentation vessel over the CAP of grape solids during red wine fermentation. This has the important effect of AERATION, avoiding the build-up of dangerous REDUCING CONDITIONS. It also prevents drying out of the cap and encourages the EXTRACTION of the skins' valuable colouring matter and TANNINS into the wine. It may be done either in a closed top vat or, in the presence of air, in a closed tank. The mechanical systems involved include some adaptation of the AUTOVINIFICATION system, ROTOFERMENTERS, and tanks which incorporate automatic PIGEAGE. See MACERATION for more details.

The term may also be used in French for soil replacement after EROSION of vineyards.

REMUAGE is French for the RIDDLING process, an integral stage in the traditional champagne method of making SPARKLING WINES. It means literally 'shaking', a reference to the need to dislodge the deposit left in a bottle after a second fermentation has taken place inside it. Modern alternative techniques may eventually render this cumbersome process superfluous. A person or machine that performs *remuage* is a **remueur.** For more details see SPARKLING WINE-MAKING.

RÉMY MARTIN, important COGNAC house constituting the most extraordinary success story in the modern spirits industry. The firm was founded in 1724 but was virtually dormant when it was taken over exactly 200 years later by André Renaud, himself a local vine-grower who had married

The sample room at **Rémy Martin**, a historical record of production.

into the Frapin family, which owned large estates in the Champagne districts of the Cognac region.

Renaud's first success came in the 1930s through Otto Quien, a Dutch-born sales genius living in what was then the Dutch East Indies and is now Indonesia. Quien persuaded Renaud that Rémy Martin should concentrate on cognacs from the Champagne region which he sold to the quality-conscious Chinese market in the Far East. After the Second World War the firm exploited these advantages, using its much-imitated frosted bottle with a map of the Cognac districts on it, emphasizing the uniqueness of the firm's product.

In the 25 years following Renaud's death in 1965 his son-in-law André Hériard-Dubreuil exploited Renaud's initiatives to such good effect that he transformed Rémy Martin into a major force in the world drinks market. In doing so he had to fight a prolonged legal battle with his brother-in-law Max Cointreau, whose wife had inherited just under half the shares in the company (her sister, Mme Hériard-Dubreuil, had the other half). In the event Hériard-Dubreuil outmanœuvred his in-laws by setting up a separate company to distribute Rémy's brandies and thus retain much of the profits from the parent. In the last half of the 1980s he consolidated his position, merging with the Cointreau family firm (where Max had previously lost control) and adding to his portfolio of drinks companies, most notably in the CHAMPAGNE sparkling wine region of north east France, where he had bought KRUG in 1973, by acquiring Charles Heidsieck and the quite separate firm of Piper Heidsieck.

An important subsidiary and profit source for Rémy Martin has been its extensive international COOPERAGE business, Seguin Moreau.

And the brandies in all this? Rémy Martin cognacs are invariably smooth and fruity, as befits their provenance, and scrupulously made, but the younger ones in particular are not as subtle as the finest brandies. N.F.

RENDEMENT, French for YIELD, usually expressed in hl/ha.

RENDZINA, a dark, interzonal type of soil found in grassy or formerly grassy areas of moderate rainfall, on limestones, especially in chalklands. It is characterized by a brown to black, friable surface and a light grey or yellow, soft underlying horizon. Such soils are associated with TERRA ROSSA soils of Coonawarra in SOUTH AUSTRALIA. See GEOLOGY.

RESEARCH into grape-growing and wine production is officially and principally in the domain of academe, although some individual wine-makers are more prone to experimentation and subject to the rigour of SCIENCE than others. For a list of important wine research institutions, see ACADEME.

RESERVA, term used in both Spain and Portugal to distinguish wines from a supposedly good vintage. In Portugal a Reserva is a wine from a good vintage with an alcohol level at least half a per cent above the regional minimum. In Spain a red wine labelled Reserva will have had at least three years' AGEING in cask and bottle, of which a year must be in cask. The wine may not be released until the fourth year after the harvest. Spanish white wines labelled Reserva must spend a total of at least two years in cask and bottle to qualify, with at least six months of this period in OAK.

See also GRAN RESERVA. R.J.M.

RESERVE is a term liberally used by wine producers for various bottlings. It should be quite literally reserved itself, for superior wines, but, unlike RESERVA and RISERVA, the English term Reserve has few controls on its use. Some wineries release several bottlings, all of which may incorporate the word in their names (Proprietor's Reserve, Estate Reserve, Reserve Selection, Private Reserve, Vintner's Reserve, and the like). The French term is **Réserve** and there are moves to control the use of terms such as Cuvée de Réserve.

RESIDUAL SUGAR, occasionally **RS**, the total quantity of SUGARS remaining unfermented in the finished wine. This may include both fermentable sugars, mainly GLUCOSE and FRUCTOSE, which have for some reason remained unconverted to alcohol during FERMENTATION, and small amounts of those few sugars which are not readily fermented by typical wine YEAST. Some, but not necessarily all, residual sugar is tasted as SWEETNESS.

Residual sugar in wine is usually measured in grams of total sugars per litre of wine and can vary between about 1 g/l (0.1 per cent) and 25 g/l (2.5 per cent) or more. Wines with a residual sugar content of less than 2 g/l, such as the great majority of red wines and many white wines that do not taste at all sweet, are described as dry. It is rare to find a wine with much less than 1 g/l residual sugar because some sugars are almost invariably impervious to the action of the yeasts. On the other hand, many wines with a residual sugar level even as high as 25 g/l may taste dry because the sweetness is offset by high ACIDITY or possibly bitterness from TANNINS. Some ordinary wines (usually white) that are naturally high in acids may have sugars (usually the particularly sweet fructose), sweet GRAPE JUICE, or sweet RECTIFIED GRAPE MUST added deliberately to increase their palatability or commercial appeal.

Exceptionally sweet wines may be produced either in extraordinarily ripe years or by unusual wine-making techniques such as those involved in freeze CONCENTRATION, BOTRYTIZED, or DRIED GRAPE WINES. The sweetest form of the unique Hungarian sweet wine TOKAY, for example, must have a minimum residual sugar of 250 g/l—the 1947 vintage of Tokay Essencia managed 488 g/l.

Sugar levels in grapes are measured as MUST WEIGHT by various different scales, of which BAUMÉ, BRIX, and OECHSLE are the most common.

One German wine harvested at Nussdorf in the Pfalz in 1971 was picked at 326° Oechsle, or about 870 g/l sugar, and had reached only 4.5 per cent alcohol in a particularly slow fermentation 20 years later, producing a wine with about 480 g/l residual sugar.

In theory 100 g of sugar should yield 51.1 g of alcohol, but numerous practical experiments show that only 47 to 48 g of alcohol are obtained. Between 16 and 17 g of sugar are required to produce one per cent of alcohol.

There are many reasons why fermentable sugars may remain unfermented: yeasts vary enormously in their potency, especially their tolerance of higher sugar and higher alcohol concentrations; grape musts vary in their micronutrient and growth factor content; low TEMPERATURES and chemical additions can also arrest fermentation.

Residual sugar presents no great danger in a wine that is yet to be processed in bulk, but in a bottled wine the presence of such sugars may cause FERMENTATION IN BOTTLE. Small amounts of sugar are furthermore readily used by BACTERIA to produce unwanted ACETIC ACID, off-flavours, and, sometimes, CARBON DIOXIDE gas. The wine-maker therefore must ensure either that a wine is effectively free of fermentable sugars or, in the case of most sweet and medium dry wines, that the wine undergoes full STABILIZATION against the risk of further microbiological activity. This can be achieved by heavy FILTRATION followed by STERILE BOTTLING, by PASTEURIZATION, or by a technique called yeast nutrient depletion which effectively removes the micro-nutrients from the wine before bottling, but is impractical for wines aged for less than three years.

A great sweet wine such as a fine SAUTERNES or a BEERENAUSLESE remains stable because of the action of noble rot. Both the very high residual sugar and the trace materials secreted by the BOTRYTIS into the juice inhibit fermentation. Because of this, many fine sweet German wines are stable despite their high sugar levels and low alcohol levels.

A.D.W.

RESIDUES. Residues of AGROCHEMICALS, the commercial preparations used in vineyards for the control of pests, diseases, or weeds, are that portion which is found on the grapes or in wine. Residues in viticulture and wine are typically different from those in other forms of agriculture and food processing. There are usually long 'withholding periods' between application and harvest so that the agrochemical is degraded. Most of any remaining agrochemical is also likely to be eliminated with the skins after PRESSING, and more is removed during juice CLARIFICATION, FERMENTATION, and subsequent FILTRATION.

PESTICIDES may leave deposits or by-products that persist in plant or animal tissues or in soil, water, or air. Some pesticides are rapidly inactivated after application; others (or their by-products) may persist for years in a biologically active form. Such residual contamination may affect human or livestock health, subsequent crop growth, and pollute the environment. Excessive or illegal pesticide residues in wine may lead to rejection on domestic and/or international markets, perhaps as a result of the use of inappropriate pesticides, incorrect application methods, or application too close to harvest. Residue effects on non-target organisms should also be considered. Useful insects such as bees or natural parasites and predators of pests may be affected by pesticide residues.

FUNGICIDE residues may inhibit fermentation by yeast, as discussed by Lemperle, but extensive trials have shown that the proper use of fungicides has no adverse effect on the taste or smell of wines. The COPPER contained in some fungicides can even improve wine quality by reducing SULPHIDES, although residues of elemental SULPHUR used to prevent fungal disease in the vineyard can be transformed, in REDUCING CONDITIONS, into foul-smelling HYDROGEN SULPHIDE.

So-called maximum residue limits (MRLs) are established for particular agrochemicals or their metabolites (breakdown products) in particular foodstuffs by governments. Consumer health is not the only basis for such action. MRLs have, unfortunately, become important as a potential trade barrier for protectionist purposes. This can happen, for example, in cases where the importing country is free of certain vine diseases and therefore has no established MRLs for the relevant agrochemicals and can set zero MRLs for imported wines. See also AGROCHEMICALS. R.E.S. and P.R.D.

Lemperle, E., 'Fungicide residues in musts and wine' in R. E. Smart, R. J. Thornton, S. B. Rodriguez, and J. E. Young (eds.), *Proceedings of the Second International Symposium for Cool Climate Viticulture and Oenology; 11–15 January 1988 Auckland, New Zealand* (Auckland, 1988).

RESINATED WINES. Of the earthenware vessels in which the ancient Greeks and Romans kept their wines (see AMPHORAE) only the very best were perhaps airtight. Normally they were porous, and it is clear from the Roman writers on agriculture that the insides of jars were therefore coated with resin. It was therefore probably as a purely practical measure that resin was initially used. But soon people must have discovered that the wine would keep even better if they added resin to the wine itself. COLUMELLA deals at length with the different kinds of resin, some liquid, some powdered, that can be employed in this way (*De re rustica* 13. 20–14), but he emphasizes that the best wines should not have resin put into them. Yet many people came to like the taste of resin and used it not only as a preservative but also as a flavouring agent. PLINY recommends that resin should be added to the fermenting must (*Natural History* 14. 124) and he discusses which kinds of resin are best: resin from mountainous regions has a more pleasant smell than resin from low-lying areas (16. 60).

The Romans abandoned amphorae in favour of wooden casks in the 3rd century AD, because BARRELS were lighter and easier to handle. Wooden casks do not need an inside coating of resin, and this saved the wine-maker time and money. Thus the Romans ceased to make resinated wines. Wine-makers in Transalpine Gaul, most of whom did not have pine trees nearby, and those of Cisalpine Gaul, Illyria, and the alpine region, where the climate is cooler and wood does not crack so easily, had started using wooden casks in the 1st century AD. Unlike the west, however, Byzantium did not lose its taste for resin when it was no longer needed as a preservative. The pine forests of the eastern part of central Greece and of Euboea still provided the resin to enhance the flavour of some Greek wines after the 7th century.

This was very much not to the taste of one western visitor to Constantinople. In 968 Liudprand, bishop of Cremona, was sent there to arrange a marriage between the daughter of the late Emperor Romanos and the son of his own patron, Otto I, the Holy Roman Emperor. The mission was not a success. The Emperor Nicephorus treated Liudprand rudely and kept him a virtual prisoner. Liudprand's *De legatione Constantinopolitana* ('The mission to Constantinople') was his revenge. He has not a good word to say for the Byzantines in general and Nicephorus in particular. They are uncouth, their finery is threadbare, their religious ceremonial mere bombast. All heresy comes from the east, and no Greek is ever to be trusted. We are dealing with a masterpiece of invective, and since Liudprand's purpose is satirical, we should not believe his every word. But his observations on the food and wine he had are interesting. Horrified, he relates how he was given goat stuffed with onions, garlic, and leeks, swimming in fish sauce. Worst of all, and mentioned in his very first chapter, is the wine: undrinkable because it is mixed with resin, pitch, and gypsum. Like the fish sauce, not in the least remarkable to an Ancient Roman, but not a thing to serve a modern Lombard. Liudprand may have had perfectly decent, unresinated, wine at times during his enforced stay, but it would have spoilt his story to tell us about that.

For not all Greek wine was resinated in the Middle Ages. The strong, sweet wines that reached the markets of western Europe were not, but pilgrims travelling to the Holy Land say that some local wines were. The account of Pietro Casola, who sailed to Jerusalem in 1494, stopping off frequently on the way, is particularly valuable because he takes pains to describe the customs, the food, and the wines of every region. He often speaks of the excellent sweet wines in Greece, but in Modone, on the south-western tip of the Peloponnese (near Monemvasia which gave its name to MALVASIA), he is given a wine that has had resin added to it during fermentation in order, he explains, to preserve it. He objects to its strong unpleasant odour, but he goes on to describe the fine malmsey, muscatel, and rumney of Modone. Of Cyprus he says that he loves everything about it except the wine, which has resin in it. He must have been unlucky not to have tasted the famous sweet wines that Cyprus exported, but an earlier account by an anonymous French cleric, *Le Voyage de la Saincte Cyte de Hierusalem* of 1480, confirms what he observes about Cyprus and Modone.

See RETSINA for details of modern resinated wine.

H.M.W.

Newett, M. M., *Canon Casola's Pilgrimage to Jerusalem in the Year 1494* (Manchester, 1907).
The Works of Liudprand of Cremona, trans. by F. A. Wright (London, 1930).

RESINS, used in wine-making as adsorbents of colour and odour, are natural or synthetic materials usually composed of long chains of simpler organic molecules that are capable of POLYMERIZING. Examples of natural polymers derived from plants are gum arabic and starch, while protein polymers from animal sources include CASEIN from milk, GELATIN, and albumin from EGG-WHITES. Casein and gelatin function as adsorbents for PHENOLICS and can reduce a wine's excess bitterness and astringency. They may also be of use in lightening amber or brownish white wines.

Synthetic resins are made by man using modern chemical technology such as the polyethylene and polystyrene used for cosmetics, packaging, etc. The synthetic resin poly (N-vinyl-2-pyrrolidinone) (see PVP) is also used to remove amber and brown pigments when prepared in the form of small beads, and as a sterilizing filter when cast as a thin sheet on a heavier backing material (see FILTRATION). Synthetic resins capable of ION EXCHANGE have also been used in winemaking. A.D.W.

RESPIRATION, biochemical process in plants, including vines, which provides the chemical energy required for other reactions and for growth. Respiration may be considered the opposite of PHOTOSYNTHESIS in that OXYGEN is consumed and CARBON DIOXIDE and energy released, according to the following formula:

$$C_6H_{12}O_6 \text{ sugar} + 6O_2 \rightarrow 6CO_2 + 6H_2O + \text{energy.}$$

In addition to SUGARS, other compounds such as STARCH, fats, AMINO ACIDS, organic ACIDS, and other substances may be broken down to release energy. Of particular interest to wine drinkers is the respiration of MALIC ACID which takes place in the grape during RIPENING.

Temperature has a major effect on respiration rate. The rate of respiration approximately doubles for each 10 °C/18 °F increase in temperature. Young tissue which is actively growing has a higher respiration rate than older tissue. R.E.S.

Winkler, A. J., *et al.*, *General Viticulture* (2nd edn., Berkeley, Calif., 1974).

RESVERATROL, one of the PHYTOALEXINS in red wine which may play an important part in reducing the incidence of heart disease (see HEALTH).

RETSINA, modern form of RESINATED WINE that is extremely common in GREECE, and a potent catalyst of taverna nostalgia outside it. Modern retsina is made like any other white (or rosé) wine, except that small pieces of resin from the Alep pine are added to the must and left with the wine until the first RACKING separates the finished wine from all solids. Major producing areas are Attica, Euboea, and Boeotia, all in the southern part of central Greece close to Athens, but retsina is also made for local consumption all over the country. SAVATIANO is usually the principal grape, often enlivened with some RHODITIS or occasionally ASSYRTIKO, but a wide range of local grape varieties are also used, and an interesting MUSCAT retsina is made on the island of Lemnos.

Retsina is rarely made outside Greece and southern Cyprus, where local palates are accustomed to its distinctively pungent flavour, and visitors expect it. A South Australian version has been essayed. M.McN.

RETZ, important wine centre in lower AUSTRIA, now part of the Weinviertel district.

REUILLY, small French appellation so far inside the bend of the Loire that it is often described as coming from central France. Its most useful manifestation is as a less expensive and sometimes purer version of the SANCERRE appellation to the east made from Sauvignon Blanc grapes in one of the riper vintages. As much red and rosé wine is made as white, however, from Pinot Noir and a little Pinot Gris (the local Gamay is sold as VIN DE PAYS). Pale pink Reuilly has its devotees. Unlike nearby QUINCY Reuilly is not primarily a viticultural centre, but the best wines yielded by its 30 ha/74 acres of vineyards scattered on the LIMESTONE base around the village of Reuilly can be worth seeking out. This Loire appellation is not to be confused with that of RULLY in the Côte Chalonnaise.

See also LOIRE and map on pp. 576–7.

RHAMNALES, the order of the plant kingdom which includes the family *Vitaceae*, in turn including the genus VITIS, the grapevine. See BOTANICAL CLASSIFICATION.

RHEIN, German name for the river RHINE.

RHEINGAU, for generations the most economically successful wine region in GERMANY. The Church and nobility provided the discipline and organization necessary for a solid business in wine, which survived the unrest and secularization in the early 19th century (see GERMAN HISTORY). The region now covers 2,900 ha/7,166 acres, over 90 per cent of which lie on the right bank of the RHINE, between Wiesbaden and the MITTELRHEIN boundary at Lorchhausen (see map on p. 442). The remainder of the Rheingau vineyards are near Hochheim (the origin of the word HOCK) on the banks of the Main, shortly before its confluence with the Rhine at Mainz.

The vineyards at Hochheim and in the central part of the region are mostly on gently rolling or flat land, but from Rüdesheim downstream to Lorchhausen the terrain is much steeper. The Rheingau soil is very varied throughout. Downstream of Rüdesheim, dark blue slate predominates. As part of the practice of good husbandry, many Rheingauers have recorded in detail the weather conditions over the centuries. Through the telescope of hindsight, excessively cold winters seem to have been frequent, and the Rhine froze often. In spite of this and within the context of the whole of the German vineyard, the region has a favoured MESOCLIMATE. With its southern ASPECT, it is marginally warmer than much of the RHEINHESSEN to the south, and its annual RAINFALL of a little over 500 mm/20 in means that there is an adequate supply of water for the RIESLING vine to ripen its grapes long into the autumn. The vines of today can tolerate extremes of weather better than those of the past, as years of research have much improved their quality and strength.

At GEISENHEIM the Rheingau has one of the world's leading viticultural institutes, but it has not been invaded by newer GERMAN CROSSINGS to the same extent as other German regions such as RHEINHESSEN and PFALZ. The climate and exposition of its vineyards, and the structure of its trade and its traditions, have called for the RIESLING vine, which covered

82 per cent of the area under vine by 1990. To produce consistently the high-quality wine expected of Rheingau Riesling, a relatively low YIELD is considered essential. Most good Rheingau estate bottlers aim for 70 to 80 hl/ha (4–4.5 tons/acre), even if these figures will almost inevitably be exceeded in a large vintage such as 1989.

The Rheingau is principally a region for white wine, but early in its viticultural history red vine varieties are thought to have predominated, although Spätburgunder (PINOT NOIR) did not make famous the village of Assmannshausen until the middle of the 18th century. If Spätburgunder today accounts for only seven per cent of the region's vines, it is more important each year and the percentage doubled in the 1980s.

Until the end of the 18th century, the Rheingau harvest was gathered in good years during the first half of October, or even in September. As Dr Hermann MÜLLER-THURGAU (the breeder of the ubiquitous vine that bears his name) pointed out, only in poor years were the grapes left on the vine in the hope that they might ripen further. The principle of picking selected bunches of grapes AUSLESEN was understood in the 18th century, but that of the widespread picking of grapes affected by NOBLE ROT dates, in the Rheingau, from about 1820. In spite of popular beliefs to the contrary, precisely when and where vine-growers first realized the value of noble rot is not certain, although its discovery in Germany is thought to have been in the particularly suitable climate of the Rheingau. Until the development in the 20th century of filters that could eliminate yeast (see FILTRATION), most Rheingau wine was dry, and it is to this tradition of dry, or dryish, wine that the region is returning. In the early 1990s over 40 per cent of all Rheingau wine which receives a quality control AP NUMBER is dry, and it is not uncommon to find that only 20 per cent of the wines on a good estate are sweet or medium sweet. In spite of modern trends, all would probably agree that it is in rich, sweet, BOTRYTIZED wines of Auslese quality and upwards in a great vintage that Rheingau Riesling still reaches a peak of possible quality.

Other than in rare years such as 1976, an increasing number of growers choose not to engage in a time-consuming and expensive gathering of grapes with noble rot for Auslese wine. Instead they leave part of the crop of healthy grapes on the vine (perhaps not in their best site), in the hope of temperatures of −8 °C/18 °F) or lower and with them the chance to produce an EISWEIN. The costs of harvesting an

Vineyards near Schloss Vollrads in the **Rheingau**.

Eiswein are less than those of picking individual bunches of grapes for Auslese wine; the MUST WEIGHT of an Eiswein is higher through the elimination of some of the water in the grape by freezing (see freeze CONCENTRATION); and the market price of Eiswein is much greater than that of an Auslese.

German restaurants have encouraged the move to drier wines and have stimulated an interest in matching wine with appropriate food. This has led inevitably to a need for red wine, particularly from Spätburgunder. Presumably with wines of warmer climates in mind, a number of Rheingau estates are now offering fully fermented dry Spätburgunder with more TANNINS and COLOUR than was customary until the mid 1980s. Although these new wines risk being overpraised and overpriced in Germany, they are undoubtedly a most interesting development. As their rarity value declines, perhaps the cost to the consumer will also fall: they are good, but not that good.

As a further reaction to the needs of the restaurateur, the collective activity of the Association of CHARTA Estates is impressive. Nearly 50 Rheingau producers, including a CO-OPERATIVE cellar, offer Charta wines, which have passed a tasting test severe enough to fail 20 per cent or so of the candidates. The wines come exclusively from Riesling grapes with a must weight in excess of the minimum legal levels, and with a firm core of ACIDITY. They are offered in a bottle, embossed with a double romanesque arch, recalling the first full flowering of Rheingau wine in the 12th century (see GERMAN HISTORY). With such self-imposed standards and its other regulations, the Charta Association is successful in promoting the style of dry-tasting wine which the region believes it should produce in the 1990s.

In the Rheingau nine co-operative cellars receive grapes from about 440 ha/1,087 acres, or 15 per cent of the harvest. Their role is a relatively minor one, compared to that of the private and state-owned estates, of which the 12 largest have some 635 ha) under vine. Many properties date from the 18th century and a few can trace their wine-making history to a much earlier period. As everywhere in Germany part-time, or hobby, vine-growers are important and own 25 per cent of the total area under vine. About 380 growers produce and sell their wines themselves, perhaps with the assistance of a broker. Both estates and co-operative cellars often have a shop and bar where the consumer can buy their wines, and where they hold their own promotional tastings. The state of Hesse, with 136 ha of vineyard in various parts of the region, uses the 12th century Cistercian monastery KLOSTER EBERBACH for numerous wine-related functions, courses, conferences, and a famous AUCTION held each year.

Other than at the region's two famous castles, SCHLOSS JOHANNISBERG and Schloss Vollrads, most estates of some size have vineyard holdings in a number of villages. At Lorch the local wine is made mainly in the village, but upstream at Assmannshausen large estates based on the central Rheingau appear in the list of vineyard owners. The *Berg* or hill at Rüdesheim which overlooks the confluence of the Nahe and the Rhine is famous in Germany for wines that are full in flavour and often surprisingly good in poor vintages. In the villages or towns of Geisenheim, Johannisberg, Winkel, Hattenheim, and Erbach, it is not their names alone which are likely to guarantee the quality of their wine but rather that of the bottler. All are capable of producing Riesling wines of a high order, but amongst the richest and most refined will usually be found some from Erbach and Hattenheim. In hot summers the wines of Schloss Vollrads, Kiedrich, and Rauenthal, which lie on higher ground some distance from the Rhine, can be quite outstanding, with a flavour with seems to last for ever. Perhaps the fullest and most tasty Rieslings come from the deep soil of Hochheim. With skilful wine-making, they are as fine as any in the region, and, therefore, in the world. I.J.

Dahlen, H. W., *Beiträge zur Geschichte des Weinbaues und Weinhandels im Rheingau* ('Contributions to the history of viticulture and of the wine trade in the Rheingau') (Mainz, 1896).

RHEINHESSEN, large and varied wine region in GERMANY (see map on p. 442). On the eastern edge of this 24,870-ha/61,460-acre region, the red soil of sloping vineyards such as Nierstein's Roten Hang group produces wine that is internationally recognized as of the highest quality. A third of the region's stock of RIESLING vines grows in this privileged area known as the Rheinterrasse. It stretches from Bodenheim, a little south of Mainz, to Mettenheim, north of Worms. Some parts of the Rheinterrasse face due east and, as ever in Germany, MESOCLIMATE is all important. The region as a whole is protected from winds and excessive rain by the hills on its western border, which rise to over 600 m (nearly 2,000 ft). The temperature in the vineyards nearest the river RHINE is warmer throughout the year than that of the rolling country away from the river, and in severe winters they avoid the worst effects of FROST. This partly accounts for the superiority of the small collective site, or GROSSLAGE, Niersteiner Rehbach and its neighbouring single vineyard, or EINZELLAGE, in the Rheinterrasse, Nackenheimer Rothenberg.

The north of the Rheinhessen has its best vineyards at Ingelheim (known in Germany over many years for its red Spätburgunder, or PINOT NOIR, wine), and at Bingen in the Scharlachberg site. In the south of the Bereich Wonnegau, the wine villages of Westhofen, Bechtheim, and Osthofen are relatively well known in Germany, but in the central part of the region there is much mixed farming which may include viticulture. Few estates are devoted solely to the vine.

There are over 400 individual vineyard sites in the Rheinhessen, most of which have little meaning in terms of the style and quality of wine they produce. Over half of the region's wine is sold under the name of a Grosslage such as Niersteiner Gutes Domtal, Oppenheimer Krötenbrunnen, or Mainzer Domherr, the last having a good following in Germany. The Rheinhessen accounts for one-third of all German wine exports, and for more than 50 per cent of the country's LIEBFRAUMILCH.

More than in any other German wine region, the choice of vine variety and range of wines produced in Rheinhessen have been influenced by the peculiarities of the GERMAN WINE

LAW. The official wine hierarchy is founded on the idea that a heavier MUST WEIGHT (an enhanced amount of grape SUGARS) relates automatically to an improvement in the quality of the future wine. Although this is normally true of RIESLING and most other long-established vine varieties growing in Germany, it does not apply to all VINIFERA varieties. Some of the GERMAN CROSSINGS may produce grapes with a higher must weight than Riesling, but the wine is not necessarily superior, a fact which is not fully recognized by the law. Nevertheless many Rheinhessen growers planted crossings such as BACCHUS, FABER, HUXELREBE, KERNER in the 1960s and 1970s, which were grown to produce large quantities of grapes with a high must weight in almost all vintages. Their wines, often strongly scented, lacked elegance, but bottled with 35 g/l or more of RESIDUAL SUGAR they met the popular German taste of the day for sweetish wine, which was reflected in the export market. The result is that, in the 1990s, over three-quarters of the Rheinhessen's vine varieties for white wine are either new crossings or the older crossing MÜLLER-THURGAU. This has the effect of diluting any regional identity there might be in wines produced away from the best estates, or better wine villages. At the bottom end of the cheap wine market, the ultimate destiny for a large proportion of the Rheinhessen harvest, character in wine is neither required nor possible, and it is certainly not paid for.

Not all Rheinhessen wine from new crossings is inferior and, where the YIELD is restricted, Müller-Thurgau and, particularly, Scheurebe can produce wines of high quality as some estate bottlers regularly show.

The area occupied by red vine varieties is increasing although in 1992 it amounted to only eight per cent of the total Rheinhessen vineyard. The market price for basic red wine in the region is much higher than that for white and the prolific PORTUGIESER, Spätburgunder (PINOT NOIR), and the successful new crossing DORNFELDER are the most popular varieties.

The Rheinhessen is divided into three districts: the Bereich Bingen, the Bereich Nierstein, and the Bereich Wonnegau. As the Bereich Nierstein is more than three times the size of the Rheingau region, some would say that another district should be created, solely for the fine vineyards of the Rheinterrasse, which would, of course, include the 1,000 ha/2,470 acres of the town of Nierstein itself. Some would go further and have the Rheinterrasse defined as a region quite separate from the Rheinhessen. The wish to be part of such a district within the Rheinhessen is strong in Nierstein. Although it has many of the best individual vineyard sites in the Rheinterrasse, its reputation has been diminished by having its name linked to that of Gutes Domtal. This Grosslage covers 27 individual sites in 15 villages, but hardly 30 ha/74 acres actually lie within the boundary of Nierstein itself. Some of Germany's cheapest wine is sold as Niersteiner Gutes Domtal at retail prices which are less than half that of the cost to a producer of a wine from Nierstein's better, low-yielding, and expensive-to-run vineyards. Oppenheim, Nierstein's immediate neighbour, suffers similarly through its connection with the Grosslage Oppenheimer Krötenbrunnen.

The flavour from the red sandstone and slate, which is so characteristic of the northern part of the Rheinterrasse, is shown clearly and cleanly by the Rieslings from the Rothenberg site at Nackenheim and its neighbouring vineyards. They resemble a little the concentrated, firm wines grown in the porphyritic Traiser Bastei site in the NAHE, but their character is more gentle. In the varied soils of Oppenheim, where loess and loam often predominate, the Riesling wines are particularly elegant and charming, and often less full flavoured than those of Nierstein. The increasingly widespread adoption of ORGANIC VITICULTURE principles in the vineyard and cellar, lower yields, and less residual sugar in wine should all help to emphasize the regional flavour, which will be to the advantage of the embattled market for fine wines in the Rheinhessen.

Almost half of the region's wine is bottled by merchants elsewhere (many supplying the lower end of the market from cellars on the MOSEL), and a quarter is exported. Within Germany the Rheinhessen has become popularly associated with cheap SPÄTLESEN, sold at low prices in supermarkets, particularly to the middle-aged in the north of the country. The national swing to drier wines has reduced the Rheinhessen share of the market and, in response, a dry wine has been created called Rheinhessen Silvaner, often referred to simply as RS. It is bottled by over 50 producers and sold under a label common to them all. The wine has to pass an effective quality control examination and is aimed at superior wine merchants and restaurants. It is crisp, attractive, almost like a Riesling, and a serious attempt to rid the region of its lack-lustre image. Its commercial success has yet to be demonstrated.

The Rheinhessen, pleasant and peaceful though parts of it are, does not have the type of countryside to attract many visitors so that the trade with the tourist in producer-bottled (ERZEUGERABFÜLLUNG or GUTSABFÜLLUNG) wine is smaller than in most other regions. Nevertheless, many estates and co-operative cellars offer tasting facilities to the general public, and there are a number of instructional wine paths through the vineyards. Villages and towns also hold wine festivals from July to December at which it is usually easier informally to drink, than formally to taste the local wine. About 45 per cent of the owners of vineyard holdings sell grapes, or wine in bulk, at prices which for the last two decades have been forced down to an uneconomic level by the large supermarket buyers and their suppliers. The co-operative cellars are unable to influence bulk wine prices in the way their members would like. The development in the 1980s of profitable sales of SEKT sparkling wine made from Rheinhessen base wine, has therefore been welcomed in the region.

The leader in this field is a producers' association, the Erzeugergemeinschaft Winzersekt Rheinhessen, which offers sparkling wine bearing a vintage, the name of a vine variety, and sometimes that of a vineyard site. Extra dry and brut are the preferred styles, and the selling prices are comparable to those of the good-quality Riesling brands of the large manufacturers of German sparkling wine (see SEKT). The success of the Erzeugergemeinschaft Winzersekt

Rheinhessen is important to the whole of the region, as it shows there is profit to be made from Rheinhessen wine, away from the good and well-known estates. I.J.

RHEINPFALZ, German wine region. See PFALZ.

RHEIN RIESLING, or **Rheinriesling**, common synonym in German-speaking countries for the great white RIESLING grape variety of Germany.

RHEINTERRASSE, admired wine district in Germany. For more details see RHEINHESSEN.

RHENISH, description of wines in common use in the Middle Ages which usually encompassed most of the wines then produced in what is GERMANY today and also those of ALSACE.

RHINE, English name for the river known in German as the **Rhein** and French as the **Rhin** (where it lends its name to the two ALSACE *départements* Haut-Rhin and Bas-Rhin). The German 'Rhein' describes a table wine (see TAFELWEIN) sub-district identical to the quality wine regions AHR, HESSISCHE BERGSTRASSE, MITTELRHEIN, NAHE, PFALZ, RHEINGAU, and RHEINHESSEN. On some wine lists in the English-speaking world all German wines, other than those regarded as MOSEL (or often 'Moselle'), appear somewhat imprecisely under the heading 'Rhine'. A German white table wine from either Riesling or Silvaner grapes, or their derivatives (of which nearly 50 are registered varieties), entitled to bear the name 'Rhein' may also be known as HOCK. See also SWITZERLAND and LIECHTENSTEIN. 'Rhine' is used colloquially by Australians as an abbreviation for their synonym, Rhine Riesling, for the Riesling grape variety. The word Rhine has been incorporated into a host of names associated in the English-speaking world with white, usually medium, dry but not necessarily at all Germanic, wines. I.J.

RHINE RIESLING, common synonym for the great white RIESLING grape variety of Germany, colloquially abbreviated to 'Rhine' in Australia, where it is most common.

RHIZOPUS, vine disease and one of a group of fungi commonly infecting grapes with rot. See BUNCH ROTS.

RHODITIS, slightly pink-skinned grape variety traditionally grown in the Peloponnese which was much more important in the GREECE of the pre-PHYLLOXERA era. The vine is particularly sensitive to POWDERY MILDEW. It ripens relatively late and keeps its acidity quite well even in such hot climates as that of Ankhíalos in Thessaly in central Greece, although it can also ripen well in high-altitude vineyards in Greece. It is often blended with the softer SAVATIANO, particularly for RETSINA.

RHÔNE, one of the most important wine RIVERS, linking a range of vineyards as dissimilar as those of CHÂTEAUNEUF-DU-PAPE in southern France, sparkling SEYSSEL, and Fendant du Valais in SWITZERLAND.

In wine circles, however, the term Rhône usually means the wines made in the Rhône valley in south east France which themselves vary so much north and south of an almost vine-free 50-km/30-mile stretch between approximately Valence and Montélimar, that they are divided into two very distinct zones, (although the regional appellation Côtes-du-Rhône encompasses the less ambitious wines of the north as well as a large area of the south). The Rhône regularly produces more APPELLATION CONTRÔLÉE wine than any region other than Bordeaux, about 95 per cent of the more than 3 million hl/79 million gal produced each year being red and usually high in alcohol relative to other French wines.

The greater Rhône valley is divided into four wine districts of which the **southern Rhône** (Rhône Méridionale in French) is by far the most important in terms of quantity. Its own specific appellations produce a total of nearly 250,000 hl a year, and the overwhelming majority of the more than 2 million hl of wine that qualifies as **Côtes-du-Rhône** or **Côtes-du-Rhône Villages** comes from the southern part of the Rhône valley.

The most important Rhône district in terms of the prestige of its wines is the **northern Rhône** (Rhône Septentrionale in French), which includes the appellations of Hermitage and Côte-Rôtie, representing serious rivals to the great names of Bordeaux and Burgundy in the quality and, especially, longevity of their best wines. The northern Rhône is quite different from the southern Rhône in terms of climate, soils, topography, and even vine varieties.

A third small but extremely ancient district about 64 km/40 miles east of Valence up the Drôme tributary comprises the Diois appellations, named after the town of Die, of CHÂTILLON-EN-DIOIS, CLAIRETTE DE DIE, CRÉMANT de Die, and Coteaux DIOIS.

And finally there are the outlying appellations that are on the eastern borders of the southern Rhône and the northern borders of PROVENCE. See Coteaux du TRICASTIN, Côtes du LUBÉRON, Côtes du VENTOUX, and VDQS Côtes du VIVARAIS.

It should be noted that COSTIÈRES DE NÎMES for long considered part of the LANGUEDOC region, is effectively a western extension of the southern Rhône.

History

Finds of AMPHORAE show that the inhabitants of the Rhône valley drank wine from Baetica, the eastern province of Roman-occupied SPAIN, in the 1st century BC. In the 1st century AD the Romanized élite of the Rhône valley drank FALERNIAN. From the 1st century BC onwards wine was carried up the Rhône: Chalon-sur-Saône was a river port for the Gauls (see Côte CHALONNAISE). In his *Geography*, completed in AD 7, Strabo emphasized the importance of good RIVER connections for trade in Gaul. From the Mediterranean one can get to the Atlantic Ocean and the Channel by river (*Geography* 4. 1. 2).

Strabo asserted categorically that viticulture was impossible beyond the Cévennes, which was north of the territory of the evergreen oak, *Quercus ilex*, and hence too cold for the vine, which he assumed needed a MEDITERRANEAN CLIMATE. He was proved wrong by the GAULS, who even in his day had probably discovered that the Côte Rôtie and the hill of Hermitage were superb sites for vineyards. They were

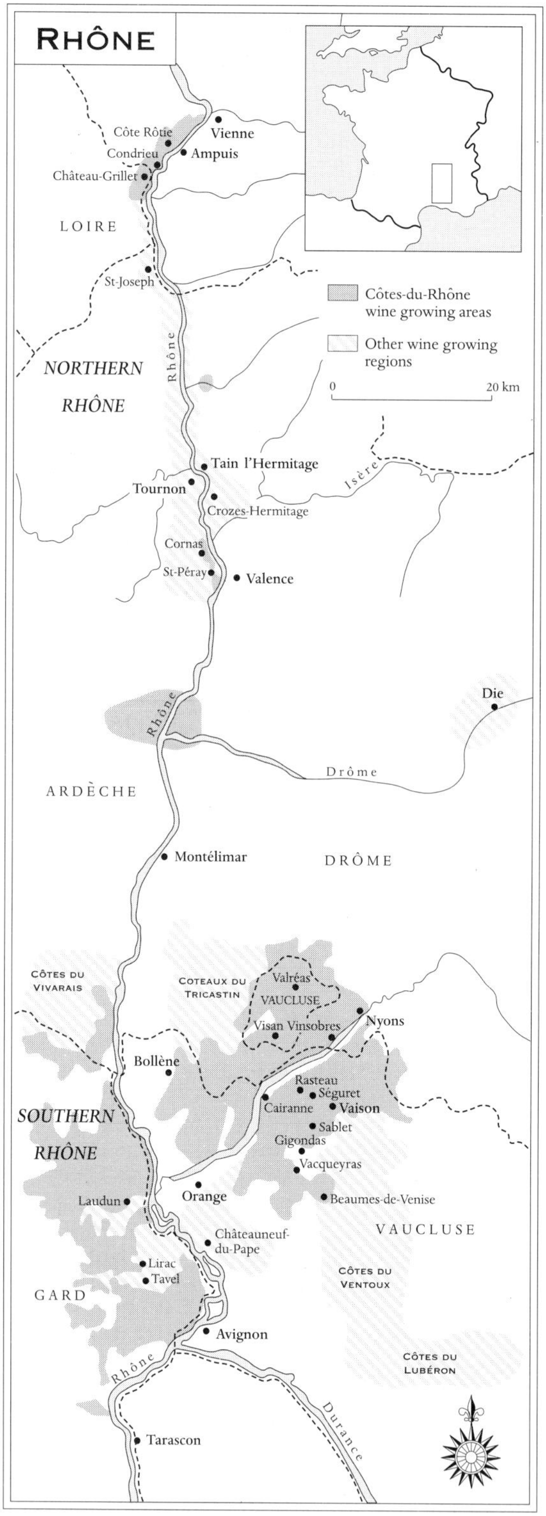

certainly making wine by AD 71, when PLINY said that in Vienne the Allobroges were producing an excellent wine, still unknown in VIRGIL's day (*Natural History* 14. 18). There were three CRUS, Taburnum, Sotanum, and Helvicum. Pliny's observation that they tasted naturally of resin cannot be correct, for wine was stored and transported in earthenware vessels which were covered with resin on their insides in order to make them impermeable, so any wine, and particularly a wine that had come from afar or was old, would have tasted of resin (see RESINATED WINES).

Pliny calls the vine that the growers of Vienne used Allobrogica. It has black grapes and is resistant to cold (*Natural History* 14. 26–7). Given the latter, Allobrogica is unlikely to be SYRAH—unless Pliny, like Strabo, thought that the Rhône valley's climate was inclement and decided therefore that any vine variety growing there must be able to withstand the cold. The Allobroges are proud of their wines, which fetch a high price (*Natural History* 14. 57). Elsewhere, Pliny remarks that the Gauls have mastered the art of grafting and improved on CATO: the Romans in turn have learned from them (*Natural History* 17. 116). The Allobroges exported their wines not only to Rome but also to Britain.

We do not know for certain where the two vine varieties that are characteristic of the Rhône, Syrah and VIOGNIER, came from. Some authors claim that the name Syrah equals Shiraz, the wine-growing city in PERSIA, and that the Phocaeans brought the vine from Persia after they had established their Greek colony at Marseilles (Massilia) around 600 BC. The vine must then have made its way up the Rhône and disappeared from the region of Marseilles. A second theory is that Syrah derives its name from Syracuse, from where the legions of the Roman Emperor PROBUS carried it to the Rhône valley after AD 280. If this is right, Pliny's allobrogica cannot be Syrah. Because there is no AMPELOGRAPHICAL evidence for either of these theories, a third one has been proposed: the Syrah vine had established itself in the Rhône valley long before the advent of systematic viticulture and grew wild there. Probus' legions have been held responsible for the introduction of Viognier as well: the hypothesis is that Probus' soldiers brought the Viognier vine with them from Dalmatia, which was a wine-growing area when it was part of the Roman empire. There is in Dalmatia (but mainly on Vis, an island off the Dalmatian coast) a vine called Vugava, which bears some resemblance to Viognier in that it produces a strong dry and highly aromatic wine. It is an appealing, but uncomfortably complicated, theory, and again we have as yet no ampelographical proof.

The people living in the Rhône valley doubtless carried on making wine after the Romans left, but we have hardly any records at all until the late Middle Ages. Medieval wine merchants eagerly bought and sold the wine of Bordeaux, Gaillac, La Rochelle, the Île-de-France, and the Loire, but there was no trade in Rhône wines until the 14th century. This cannot have been because they were bad wines, for when Pope Clement V moved the papal court to Avignon in 1305 his entourage was quick to discover the local wines (see CHÂTEAUNEUF-DU-PAPE). Some three-quarters of the wines consumed

The banks of the north **Rhône** are so steep here in Guigal's Côte-Rôtie vineyards that grapes have to be winched up the slope.

at the papal court came from the Rhône valley, although the court was fond of Burgundy, too. When Clement V went back to Rome for three years from 1367 to 1370, he had a vine from the Côtes-du-Rhône planted there.

It was his hatred of political infighting, not his love of French wines, that drove Clement back to Avignon. After his successor Gregory XI returned to Rome for good in 1377, the pope and his Roman household continued to drink the wines of the Rhône.

Châteauneuf-du-Pape owes its name to the new palace built by John XXII. The old château was the work of Urban V: the new château of his successor was a summer residence in the hills 16 km / 10 miles north of Avignon. It was destroyed by German bombers in the Second World War.

The name Hermitage La Chapelle has its origins in medieval legend. When the Crusader Gaspard de Stérimberg returned from the Holy Land, he gained the permission of Blanche of Castille, queen of France and regent during the minority of her son Louis IX (1226–70), to build a chapel and dedicate it to St Christopher; there he lived as a hermit for 30 years until he died. JABOULET's white Hermitage Chevalier de Stérimberg is named after this knightly recluse on the hill of Hermitage.

It was not only the Rhône which benefited from the extravagant habits of the papal court at Avignon: BURGUNDY, too, saw demand for its wines soar. As Burgundy became a major wine-producing region, it realized the dangers of competition from the south, especially because the wines of the Rhône were heavier than its own and hence more likely to survive transport unscathed. The duchy of Burgundy was in a powerful position, for in order to reach the markets of Paris and the north of France the wine of the Rhône had to be carried up the Saône through Burgundian territory. The solution was simple: Burgundy imposed severe restrictions on the entry and transit of all non-Burgundian wines. In 1446 the city of Dijon banned wines from Lyons, Vienne, and Tournon altogether, for the spurious reason that they were *'très petits et povres vins'*. While these measures remained in force, from the 14th to the 16th centuries, they were successful. The wines of the Rhône valley were excluded from the trade with England and the Low Countries, and they were not available in Paris until the 17th century, when transport overland had become less expensive and merchants could afford to carry their wines to the lower reaches of the Loire by ox-drawn cart and then ship them down the Loire.

H.M.W.

Dion, R., *Histoire de la vigne et du vin en France* (Paris, 1959).

Livingstone-Learmonth, J., *The Wines of the Rhône* (3rd edn., London, 1983).

Robinson, J., *Vines, Grapes, and Wines* (London, 1986).

Northern Rhône

The vineyards of the northern Rhône have probably been noticed by more tourists than any others, since so many millions of tourists are funnelled each year between northern and southern Europe down the narrow Rhône valley south of Lyons past Tain l'Hermitage. Here, high above the *autoroute du soleil*, TERRACES have been set to work as advertising hoardings for such producers as JABOULET and CHAPOUTIER. For a few seconds, the vineyards of the northern Rhône make an impression, but their produce is aimed in the main at the fine wine connoisseur rather than at the mass market. The total production of the northern Rhône is usually less than the total production of red Châteauneuf-du-Pape, a single appellation in the southern Rhône, with Crozes-Hermitage alone representing about half of all wine produced in the north.

At the southern limit of that part of Europe where CHAPTALIZATION is allowed, the northern Rhône is under the influence of a CONTINENTAL climate, with hard winters and summers whose influence on the grapes can be exaggerated by the steep slopes to which many of the better northern Rhône vineyards cling, although SOIL EROSION is a constant threat. The steep banks of this now heavily industrialized river naturally limited vine cultivation for many centuries, and the best wines are produced on inclines which are expensive to work and help to maximize the effect of the available SUNLIGHT (see TOPOGRAPHY). Since the 1980s, however, when the better wines of the Rhône were recognized as offering some of the best fine wine value (and wine-making recognized as a potentially noble way of earning a living), there has been considerable expansion, particularly on the flatter land in such appellations as St-Joseph and Crozes-Hermitage. Most appellations are based on the right bank of the river, but the left bank vineyards of Crozes-Hermitage, and especially Hermitage, are particularly well exposed to afternoon sunshine.

This is the prime territory of the SYRAH grape, which is the only red grape permitted in northern Rhône red wines. Fashionable VIOGNIER is the defining grape variety of the white wines Condrieu and Château-Grillet, while other white northern Rhône wines are made from the robust MARSANNE given nerve by the more delicate ROUSSANNE.

Most wine-making and all vine-growing is in the hands of individuals working a family holding. About half of all wines are bottled by merchants, of which Jaboulet, Chapoutier, and GUIGAL are some of the best known. Guigal's single-vineyard bottlings and distinctive, if controversial, use of new OAK did much to raise international awareness, and prices, of the northern Rhône in the 1980s. The district has benefited from an influx of wine-making perfectionists, whose hero is often Gérard Chave. There are very few CO-OPERATIVES, although the one at Tain l'Hermitage is well regarded.

For more details see the specific appellations CHÂTEAU-GRILLET, CONDRIEU, CORNAS, CÔTE-RÔTIE, CROZES-HERMITAGE, HERMITAGE, ST-JOSEPH, and ST-PÉRAY.

Southern Rhône

The southern Rhône has only the river in common with the northern Rhône. The countryside here in the flatter, southern part of the valley is definitively southern, almost Provençal, with both houses and vegetation demonstrating the influence of a MEDITERRANEAN climate. Many other fruits are grown here, and one of the chief hazards is the sometimes cold WIND that can blow down the Rhône valley. Most vines are GOBELET trained, although Syrah grapes are usually trained on wires in a single GUYOT system. If drought persists some limited IRRIGATION may be permitted.

Most wines are blends rather than made from a single vine variety. Although Syrah is increasingly widely planted to endow red wines with longevity, the main red grape variety is GRENACHE, which accounts for the great majority of vines planted in the southern Rhône. It can in theory be supplemented or seasoned by a wide range of other local varieties, but in practice only CARIGNAN, CINSAUT, MOURVÈDRE, and Syrah are planted to any extent. Similarly, UGNI BLANC is in reality the most planted white grape variety, even though it, like Carignan, may make only a limited contribution to a blend.

CO-OPERATIVES are very important in the southern Rhône, making about 70 per cent of total production. The NÉGOCIANTS of the northern Rhône also have a long tradition of buying wine here for blending and bottling *en route* to the north. But there is also a host of individual estates, especially in Châteauneuf-du-Pape, keen to etch their own stamp on a particularly accessible appellation. Wine-making techniques here are extremely varied, including everything from full-blown CARBONIC MACERATION to fly-blown ancient, open, wooden fermenting vats of uncertain age and certain lack of HYGIENE. New oak is treated with suspicion.

The southern Rhône is the only part of France other than the LANGUEDOC-ROUSSILLON to have a tradition of making sweet VIN DOUX NATUREL: a golden Muscat version, RANCIO tawny, and ruby red.

For more details, see CHÂTEAUNEUF-DU-PAPE, GIGONDAS, LIRAC, TAVEL, and VACQUEYRAS, as well as the two vin doux naturel appellations BEAUMES-DE-VENISE and RASTEAU.

Côtes-du-Rhône

This expression is sometimes used for the entire Rhône valley, but the specific appellation, granted in 1937, has almost become French for red wine. With BEAUJOLAIS and BORDEAUX AC, Côtes-du-Rhône has almost become a commodity, which must be discouraging for those seriously quality-minded producers. The great majority of Côtes-du-Rhône comes from the flatter, arid, often windswept vineyards of the southern Rhône, typically a light fruity red wine made, using full or SEMI-CARBONIC MACERATION, by one of the many co-operatives in the region.

A significant proportion of this wine is released as a PRIMEUR, in competition with Beaujolais Nouveau. There are some notable independent estates such as Ch du Grand Moulas and Domaine St-Estève (which also makes a varietal VIOGNIER), but the two most age-worthy and exceptional red Côtes-du-Rhônes available are Cru de Coudelet and the extraordinary Domaine de Fonsalette, produced respectively as adjuncts to two of the greatest estates in Châteauneuf-du-Pape, Chx de Beaucastel and Rayas. About two per cent of Côtes-du-Rhône is white, but a considerable quantity of rosé is made, specifically for summer drinking in the region.

The total area of vineyard dedicated to the appellation is about 40,000 ha / 98,800 acres, a vast proportion of viticultural France matched only by the generic Bordeaux appellation. The area which qualifies for the appellation includes the fringes of smarter northern Rhône appellations as well as huge tracts of both the left and right banks of the southern Rhône. Most of the northern Rhône NÉGOCIANTS blend and bottle their own Côtes-du-Rhône, and that of GUIGAL can show the marked Syrah character of the northern Rhône.

The great majority of grapes used for Côtes-du-Rhône, however, are southern, which means officially those allowed in CHÂTEAUNEUF-DU-PAPE plus the scented white Viognier, and Carignan, which may not exceed 30 per cent of any blend. Grenache tends to dominate.

Côtes-du-Rhône Villages

This useful appellation represents a distinct step up in quality, and often value, from generic Côtes-du-Rhône. The basic maximum permitted YIELD is 42 rather than 50 hl/ha (2.4 tons / acre), and the appellation has adopted the Châteauneuf-du-Pape's minimum alcoholic strength of 12.5 per cent for red wines. The possibility for promotion to a specific appellation exists for each named village, and first GIGONDAS then VACQUEYRAS escaped the relative anonymity of the Villages appellation. In 1993 16 villages were allowed to append their name to the appellation Côtes-du-Rhône Villages (and very cumbersome wine names some of them made too): Rochegude, St-Maurice-sur-Eygues, Vinsobres, Rousset-les-Vignes, and St-Pantaléon-les-Vignes in the Drôme *département*; Cairanne, RASTEAU, Roaix, Séguret, Valréas, Visan, Sablet, and BEAUMES-DE-VENISE in Vaucluse; and Chusclan, Laudun, and St-Gervais on the right bank of the river Rhône in the Gard. Of these, Cairanne has long been considered ripe for promotion. Many more communes, including some as far north as the ARDÈCHE, are allowed to submit wine for the appellation, though they may not append their village name. The total area of vineyard supplying wine for this appellation was nearly 5,000 ha in the mid 1990s, about an eighth of that producing generic Côtes-du-Rhône. Some of the most energetic and thoughtful wine producers of France are based within this appellation.

Livingstone-Learmonth, J., *The Wines of the Rhône* (3rd edn., London, 1992).
Parker, R. M., *The Wines of the Rhône Valley and Provence* (New York, 1987).

RHÔNE RANGERS, loose affiliation of CALIFORNIA wine producers who decided in the late 1980s to produce wines in the image of the reds and, increasingly, whites of the RHÔNE valley in France. Such wines provided a useful outlet for the produce of old GRENACHE and Mataro (MOURVÈDRE) vines which had previously languished out of favour. It also resulted in a dramatic increase in plantings of such vine varieties as SYRAH and VIOGNIER. Two-thirds of the state's total acreage of these two varieties in 1991, for example, was too young to bear fruit. Joseph Phelps of NAPA was an early exponent, Bonny Doon of SANTA CRUZ a later but noisier one. The movement was regarded by some as providing welcome alternatives to the usual California diet of unblended CABERNET SAUVIGNON and CHARDONNAY, by others as an act of treachery against the state's own wine styles and vine varieties (PETITE SIRAH was generally excluded from the Rhône Rangers' blending vats).

RIAS BAIXAS, the leading DO wine zone in GALICIA, north west Spain (see map on p. 907), producing some of the country's most sought-after dry white wines. Named after the flooded coastal valleys, or *rias*, that penetrate up to 30 km / 19 miles inland, the zone's reputation is based on the white ALBARIÑO grape, which has been accorded cult status in Spain, a country that is generally lacking in distinctive indigenous white grape varieties. Wines were exported to northern Europe in the 16th and 17th centuries but, after the ravages of PHYLLOXERA, many of the traditional vine varieties were abandoned, and by the 1900s the region's vineyards were largely planted with high-yielding HYBRIDS producing poor-quality wine. The revival began in the early 1980s, when growers were encouraged to replant higher-quality vine varieties and producers were given incentives to invest in modern wine-making equipment. The metamorphosis gathered pace with the application of EUROPEAN UNION funds following Spain's accession to the EU in 1986.

Rias Baixas splits into three separate subzones, all within the province of Pontevedra. Many of the purest Albariño wines come from Val do Salnes zone centred on the town of Cambados on the west coast. The two further subzones, O Rosal and Condado de Tea, are on the northern slopes of the river Miño facing the VINHO VERDE region in Portugal on the opposite bank. All three zones share the same GRANITE-based subsoils and a relatively cool, damp, MARITIME climate. The Atlantic influence is strongest in Val do Salnes, where annual RAINFALL averages 1,300 mm/50 in. Vines were traditionally cultivated on pergolas (see TENDONE) to protect grapes from the constant threat of FUNGAL DISEASES, although modern vineyards are planted on a more practical local variant of the GENEVA DOUBLE CURTAIN vine-training system.

Eleven different vine varieties are officially permitted in Rias Baixas although Albariño covers 90 per cent of the vineyard area. Other white grapes which may be blended with

Albariño according to local regulations include Caiña Blanca, TREIXADURA, and LOUREIRO, both of which are found in the Vinho Verde region. On its own, Albariño produces a fragrant, intensely fruity, dry white wine with a natural minimum alcohol content of just over 11 per cent. Yields are low, the wines are sought after, and are therefore correspondingly expensive. Other varieties produce lighter, more acidic wines akin to Vinho Verde. The five permitted red grapes, including MENCÍA, ESPADEIRO, and Caiño Tinto, are relatively unimportant. R.J.M.

RIBATEJO, agricultural heartland of PORTUGAL on either side of the river Tagus (Tejo) inland from the capital Lisbon (see map on p. 750). Fertile alluvial soils yield ample supplies of fruit and vegetables for the urban population around the river estuary. The Ribatejo province is therefore one of the wealthiest parts of rural Portugal, although west of the river the land tends to be divided into the smallholdings which characterize the OESTE just over the hills. The river is roughly the dividing line between these modest properties and the vast estates of southern Portugal. Vines planted on the flood plain are naturally irrigated most winters by the swollen river so that yields as high as 100 hl/ha (5.7 tons/acre) are common here. The Ribatejo is second only to the Oeste in the amount of wine it produces each year, although much of the Ribatejo wine is rough and astringent. Made in co-operatives, it is bottled in 5-l flagons and sold in bars and cafés. Ribatejo, however, is also the anonymous source of some of Portugal's best red wines, the GARRAFEIRAS set aside for at least three years and sold under the name of a merchant rather than that of the region. Two of Portugal's larger merchant firms, Carvalho, Ribeiro & Ferreira, and Caves Velhas, are based on the edge of the Ribatejo and they select and blend wines from local growers. FERNÃO PIRES, ARINTO, and Talia (the Portuguese name for UGNI BLANC) are the favoured white grapes while CASTELÃO FRANCES (sometimes called João de Santarém or Periquita) is much the most significant red grape. Ribatejo is not itself a denominated wine region, but the Ribatejo province has been divided into six Indicação de Proveniencia Regulamentada (IPR) regions: Almeirim, Cartaxo, Chamusca, Coruche, Santarém, and Tomar. Of these IPR regions, Almeirim and Cartaxo, each dominated by a large CO-OPERATIVE winery, are the most promising in terms of wine quality. R.J.M.

RIBEIRO, means riverbank or riverside in Spanish and is the name of a red and white wine zone in GALICIA, north west Spain (see map on p. 907). Ribeiro spans the valleys of the river Miño and its tributaries and Arnoya downstream from Orense. The region became a DO in 1957 but this has had little impact on exports (although in the 16th and 17th centuries wines from Ribeiro had been exported as far afield as Italy and England). PHYLLOXERA put paid to the region's prosperity at the end of the 19th century. Farmers, seeking a quick return to profit, replanted their holdings with the SHERRY grape PALOMINO. Over recent years, growers have been encouraged to uproot this productive but unsuitable variety in favour of TREIXADURA and TORRONTÉS, white grape varieties which perform well in the damp MARITIME climate of north west Iberia. Both varieties can be made into aromatic, crisp white wines. The deeply coloured, light bodied red wines, mainly from GARNACHA Tintorera grapes, rarely leave the region and are of no great interest. With help from EUROPEAN UNION funds, wineries have been updated and the traditional, labour-intensive pergolas (see TENDONE) are being replaced by lower vine-TRAINING SYSTEMS. R.J.M.

RIBERA DEL DUERO, qualitatively important wine zone in CASTILE-LEÓN in north central Spain challenging RIOJA as the leading red wine-producing region in Iberia. Ribera del Duero spans the broad valley of the river Duero (known as DOURO in Portugal) east of the city of Valladolid (see map on p. 907). The region was awarded DO status only in 1982, but Bodegas VEGA SICILIA on the western margin of the denomination has been producing one of Spain's finest wines since the last century. For 100 years or more it languished on its own among fields growing sugar beet on the banks of the Duero.

At first sight, the Duero valley is not the most congenial place to grow grapes. At between 700 and 800 m/2,624 ft above sea level, the growing season is relatively short. Temperatures which can reach nearly 40 °C/104 °F in the middle of a July day fall sharply at night. FROST, commonplace in winter, continues to be a threat well into the spring. But these diurnal extremes seem to be a positive factor when it comes to making high-quality wine. ACIDITY, so often lacking in wines from central Spain, is retained by grapes growing in Ribera del Duero's rarefied mountain air.

The potential was recognized by Alejandro Fernández, who played a key role in the considerable development of the region in the 1980s. Pesquera, his wine vinified from grapes growing around the village of Pesquera del Duero a short distance upstream from Vega Sicilia, was released in the mid 1980s to international acclaim. Other growers (many of whom had previously sold their grapes to the CO-OPERATIVES) were thereby encouraged to make and market their own wines, so giving birth to the only new wine region to challenge Rioja's traditional hegemony inside Spain. In the early 1990s consumption of top quality Ribera wines soared within Spain, denting Rioja's traditional markets and causing deepening concern in that region. Several Ribera producers attained quality levels not much below those of Vega Sicilia and Pesquera. The leading challengers included Dehesa de los Canoñigos, Ismael Arroyo, Pérez Pascvas, Félix Callejo, Señorio de Nava, Valduero, Pago de Caraovejas, and Hijos de Antonio Barceló. Several of these growers are in the east of the region, near Aranda de Duero, where a tradition of cheap rosés had previously inhibited production of top quality reds.

The region's principal vine variety, the Tinto Fino (also called Tinta del Pais), is a local variant of Rioja's TEMPRANILLO. It seems to have adapted to the Duero's climatic extremes and produces deep coloured, occasionally astringent, firm flavoured red wines without the support of any other grape variety. White wine made from the ALBILLO, a white variety enjoyed as a table grape by the locals, is not entitled to the

DO but may occasionally be blended into the intense red wine to lighten the load. CABERNET SAUVIGNON, MERLOT, and MALBEC have experimental status and are theoretically confined by law to vineyards such as those of Vega Sicilia where they were planted in the last century. GARNACHA is used in the production of rosé. R.J.M.

RIBÉREAU-GAYON, dynasty of important OENOLOGISTS closely associated with the history of the Institut d'Oenologie at BORDEAUX UNIVERSITY.

RIBOLLA, white grape variety also known as **Ribolla Gialla** to distinguish it from the less interesting **Ribolla Verde**, best known in FRIULI in north east Italy but also grown, as Rebula, in SLOVENIA, and almost certainly the Robola of the island of Cephanolia in GREECE .

Ribolla's first historically documented appearance in Friuli is in a notarial contract of 1289. The city of Udine demonstrated its respect for the wine by specifically legislating against its adulteration in 1402. That the wine had its admirers from an early date is demonstrated by Boccaccio's inclusion of Ribolla in a diatribe against the excesses of gluttony, an opinion confirmed by Antonio Musnig towards the end of the 18th century, when he rated it the finest white wine of Friuli. The grape lost ground steadily in the 19th and 20th centuries, however, in the wake of the PHYLLOXERA epidemic and Friuli's subsequent enthusiasm for non-native (French) varieties when vineyards were replanted. In the mid 1990s Ribolla accounts for less than one per cent of all the white DOC wines of Friuli. Rosazzo and Oslavia are generally considered the two classic areas for Ribolla Gialla. The wine is light in body, floral, not without delicacy, but without a particularly strong personality. Some attempts at new oak ageing have been made in recent years, particularly in Oslavia, but these wines are frequently marketed as a VINO DA TAVOLA instead of as COLLIO DOC.

Ribolla Nera is the SCHIOPPETTINO grape. D.T.

RICASOLI, one of the oldest and most powerful noble families of TUSCANY in central Italy, important landholders between Florence and Siena for over a thousand years. The vast size of their holdings led the medieval republic of Florence to bar them from holding public office lest the combination of territorial dominion and civic position create a threat to republican liberties. Bettino Ricasoli (1809–80), a dominant figure in the political life of his time and the second prime minister of the newly united Italy in 1861, a dedicated agricultural experimenter and reformer, played a fundamental role in the revitalization of the viticulture of his time and invented what came to be the standard varietal formula for the production of CHIANTI: Sangiovese and Canaiolo for wines meant to be aged; Sangiovese and Canaiolo plus Malvasia for wines to be drunk young. The formula itself was significantly modified in the 20th century with the introduction of Trebbiano into the blend and a generalized use of white grapes in all Chianti wine, without the original distinction between the different styles of Chianti.

Perhaps even more important than the formula that he promulgated were Ricasoli's efforts in organizing the production and marketing of the wines of Chianti. A firm believer in a division of labour in which the peasantry—virtually all share-croppers at the time—would grow the grapes and large commercial houses—principally controlled by the Tuscan nobility (see ANTINORI and FRESCOBALDI, for example)—would age and distribute the finished wines, he founded the Ricasoli NÉGOCIANT firm, which would assume a position of leadership in Tuscany for the better part of a century; André SIMON could still write after the Second World War that 'the most reliable brand of Chianti is that of Baron Ricasoli'. The more recent past has been less kind to the fortunes of the house: a partnership with American distillers Seagram in the négociant part of the business in the 1960s led to a large expansion of production and a general lowering of quality, and the marketing of Ricasoli wines in supermarkets and other mass distribution centres was extremely damaging to their image. More damaging yet has been the seeming obliviousness to modern ideas in Tuscan and Italian OENOLOGY, as the house missed both the trend to fruitier wines for younger drinking and fuller, more complex wines for cellaring. After a brief encounter with the Australian family wine producers Hardy's, the négociant operations were repurchased by the Ricasoli family in early 1993 with the declared intention of putting the house back on track, an uphill struggle after 30 years of marking time while the viticulture and wine-making of their region made enormous progress. D.T.

RICH is a tasting term for, generally, a red wine that gives an appealing impression of power and sweetness even though it has negligible RESIDUAL SUGAR. It may also be found as a label description on bottles of relatively sweet CHAMPAGNE (see DOSAGE).

RICHEBOURG, great red GRAND CRU in Burgundy's CÔTE D'OR. For more details, see VOSNE-ROMANÉE.

RIDDLING, an integral stage in the traditional champagne method of making SPARKLING WINES, known as *remuage* in French. It involves dislodging the deposit left in a bottle after a second fermentation has taken place inside it and shaking it into the neck of the inverted bottle. It can be achieved either by hand or, more speedily, by machine (see GYROPALETTE). Modern alternative techniques may eventually render this cumbersome process superfluous. A **riddling rack** is English for a PUPITRE. For more details see SPARKLING WINE-MAKING.

RIED, term used in AUSTRIA for single-vineyard sites.

RIESLANER is a Silvaner × Riesling crossing that is grown to a very limited extent in Germany's FRANKEN region where, provided it can reach full ripeness, it can produce wines with race and curranty fruit. Fewer than 40 ha/100 acres were planted in 1990 and its late ripening is likely to reduce this total still further.

RIESLING is the great white wine grape variety of Germany and could claim to be the finest white grape variety in the world on the basis of the longevity of its wines and their ability to transmit the characteristics of a vineyard without losing Riesling's own inimitable style. Its name has been considerably debased by being applied to a wide range of white grape varieties of varied and often doubtful quality, the ultimate backhanded compliment.

In the late 19th and early 20th centuries, German Riesling wines were prized, and priced, as highly as the great red wines of France. Connoisseurs knew that, thanks to their magical combination of ACIDITY and EXTRACT, these wines could develop for decades in bottle, regardless of ALCOHOLIC STRENGTH and RESIDUAL SUGAR. Riesling is made at all levels of sweetness, and it is indubitable that the high proportion of late 20th century German wines that have been far too low in extract and, for many consumers, too high in residual sugar has damaged Riesling's reputation. The average residual sugar of Riesling made everywhere is gradually declining, but the variety will surely always be distinguished for its ability to produce great sweet wines, whether they be the cold weather speciality EISWEIN or ICE WINE, or the late harvest, often BOTRYTIZED, Beerenauslese and Trockenbeerenauslese and their counterparts outside Germany. Riesling's high natural level of TARTARIC ACID provides it with a much more dependable counterbalance to high residual sugar than, for example, the SÉMILLON grape of SAUTERNES.

Riesling wine, wherever produced, is also notable for its powerful, rapier-like aroma variously described as flowery, steely, honeyed, and whichever blend of mineral elements is conveyed by the individual vineyard site. This distinctive aroma, usually experienced in conjunction with Riesling's natural raciness and tartness, is particularly high in monoterpenes (see FLAVOUR COMPOUNDS), 10 to 50 times higher, for instance, than WELSCHRIESLING, a less noble and unrelated white grape variety prevalent in central Europe which, much to German fury, has borrowed the word Riesling for many of its aliases (RIESLING ITALICO, for example).

Viticulturally, true Riesling (often called **White**, **Rhine**, or **Johannisberg Riesling**) is distinguished by the hardness of its wood, which helps make it a particularly cold-hardy vine, making it a possible choice for relatively cool wine regions, even if it needs the most favoured, sheltered site in order to ripen fully and yield economically. So resistant is it to FROST that winter pruning can begin earlier than with most other varieties. Its growth is vigorous and upright, and this is a top-quality variety which seems able to produce yields of 60 or 70 hl/ha (4 tons/acre), without any necessary diminution of quality. (Maximum yields allowed by the French INAO authorities are higher in Alsace, for example, than for any other

Traditional manual **riddling** of the sediment formed by fermentation in bottle during the champagne-making process. See the alternative **gyropalette**.

comparable fine wine.) Its compact bunches of small grapes make it relatively prone to BOTRYTIS and COULURE can be a problem, but its chief distinction in the vineyard is its late budding. Riesling ripens relatively early but in cool vineyards in the northern hemisphere it is often not picked until mid October or early November (and even later when sweet wines are made). Riesling whose ripening is accelerated by being grown in warmer regions can often taste dull; it seems that a long, slow ripening period suits Riesling and manages to extract maximum flavour, while maintaining acidity. Thus, many of Germany's (and therefore most of the world's) most admired Rieslings are grown on particularly favoured sites in cooler regions such as the MOSEL-SAAR-RUWER.

Germany

As outlined in GERMAN HISTORY, Riesling is by no means the oldest documented vine variety grown in Germany (including, as it did for so long, Alsace). ELBLING and SILVANER were widely grown throughout the Middle Ages, while RÄUSCHLING was the speciality of Baden in the south. An invoice dated 1435, from a castle in the extreme south east of the Rheingau on the river Main, mentions '*riesslingen in die wingarten*', presumably Rieslings in the vineyard. Early spellings of words like Riesling have to be treated with care, since the similarly named Rauschling was so much more common then than today, but 1,200 'Ruesseling reben' (*reben* being German for vines) were bought by the Jacobshospital in Trier in the upper Mosel in 1464 and 'Ruesslinge' are documented near Worms in the Rheinhessen in 1490. The Latin text of Heironymus Bock's herbal in 1552 provides the first known instance of Riesling spelt as it is today. Riesling seems to have been recognized as a top-quality variety from the late Middle Ages and was planted throughout the Rhine and Mosel from the middle of the 16th century.

Riesling is first mentioned in connection with Alsace as one of its finer products in 1477 by Duke René of Lorraine, even if we have to wait until 1628 for the first documentary evidence of its actually being planted there.

In the 18th century, various prince-bishops did their utmost to encourage Riesling plantings at the expense of other lesser varieties, notably in the Mosel. But the habit of picking grapes earlier than is today customary did the late ripening Riesling no favours and by 1930 the Rheingau region, supposedly the classic Riesling heartland, had only 57 per cent of its vineyards planted with the variety (as opposed to 80 per cent today).

This provided a stimulus to Germany's burgeoning viticultural researchers (see GEISENHEIM) to select and develop top-quality CLONES of the variety. Today, partly thanks to the efforts of a special centre for the CLONAL SELECTION of Riesling at Trier, the German vine-grower can choose from more than 60, of which one of the more controversially perfumed is the N90 used by such innovative growers in the Pfalz region as Müller Catoir and Lingenfelder. (French-certified clones of Riesling numbered precisely one, 49, in 1990, on the other hand.)

Much of the work of these viticultural institutes was also focused on developing the famous GERMAN CROSSINGS, designed to produce high yields of grapes with high MUST WEIGHTS but without the viticultural inconveniences of Riesling. One of the earliest, and certainly the most famous, of these was MÜLLER-THURGAU, whose productivity and early ripening has made it so popular with growers that, since the early 1970s, it has been Germany's most widely planted vine variety. And from the mid 1960s Riesling was also systematically displaced by many even newer, flashier crossings. By 1980, Riesling's 18,900 ha / 46,680 acres represented barely 19 per cent of all German vineyard. Since then, however, there has been some recognition of Riesling's superiority, helped by some severe winters which some Müller-Thurgau could not survive. By 1990, there were well over 21,000 ha of Riesling in about-to-be-unified Germany, which represented about 21 per cent of the total.

The exception to this trend, and indeed a brake on it, is the Riesling show-case of the northerly Mosel-Saar-Ruwer, which is the home of about a third of all Germany's Riesling. The variety represented 80 per cent of Mosel-Saar-Ruwer plantings in 1964 and only 54 per cent in 1990, presumably because of the philosophy of quantity over quality which has prevailed in the large bottling operations centred in this region. The finest estates here are without exception dedicated to Riesling and plant the variety on their finest sites to the exclusion of all else. Some would argue that Riesling finds its finest expression on the steep banks of the Mosel and its Saar and Ruwer tributaries, ideally with a 30 per cent gradient to attract maximum ripening sunlight both directly and by reflection from the river surface. For the same reason, all the best Mosel sites face south (which is why the best vineyards may be on either side of this meandering river). The site should also be sheltered from wind and its ripest grapes are likely to come from vines neither so close to the river that morning mist slows ripening, nor above about 200 m / 660 ft. The easily warmed slate soils typical of the region can also help late season ripening. The result is wines unique in the world for their combination of low alcohol (often only about eight per cent), striking aroma, high extract, and delicacy of texture. No other variety planted here can achieve as much subtlety.

The PFALZ region, on the other hand, the second most important for German Riesling, increased its plantings of Riesling dramatically during the 1980s, to 4,300 ha in 1990 from 3,000 ha in 1980. Like neighbouring Rheinhessen, this has always been a region with a particularly varied palette of vine varieties, but the gentle climate of the Mittelhaardt provides Riesling with such shelter and favourable exposition that in many years here it can ripen naturally to produce full bodied dry wines of really spicy, exuberant character, Spätlese Trocken in particular, yet still with a sufficiently extended growing season to keep both acidity and subtlety appetizingly high.

By 1990 the WÜRTTEMBERG region had (just) overtaken the Rheingau as third most important grower of German Riesling, even if most of it is for local consumption and relatively dry and full bodied. The RHEINGAU, which also had just over 2,500 ha of Riesling planted in 1990, is regarded as Riesling's traditional home and indeed the variety represents 80 per cent of all vine plantings. The best Rheingau Rieslings represent a faithful statement of their exact provenance. They are made increasingly dry and the CHARTA organization is a standard-bearer for Rheingau Riesling designed to be drunk with food. The region is also famous as the original source of Germany's BOTRYTIZED sweet wines.

Riesling is also the most planted variety in Germany's smaller Mittelrhein and Hessische Bergstrasse regions and has just reasserted itself in terms of area planted over Müller-Thurgau in the NAHE, where the upper reaches of this river yield the finest, most crackling wines. There are another 1,000 ha or so of Riesling in Baden where the warmer soils rarely show the variety at its best and tend to favour the various PINOT varieties. Riesling is not quantitatively important in the vine chequerboard that is RHEINHESSEN but the quality of some wines produced on the famous Rheinterrasse and around Bingen and Ingelheim defines the potential of those areas. Many of them are dry and exhibit a concentration that is truly thrilling. Riesling is relatively unknown in the red wine region of AHR and even in FRANKEN, which has generally remained faithful to Silvaner, but some distinguished, if earthy, dry wine is produced.

Elsewhere

For many wine drinkers, Riesling is acceptable only in its French form, a wine from ALSACE, the only part of France where this German vine is officially allowed (although several producers in such diverse appellations as Pouilly-Fumé and Barsac surreptitiously rear a row or two for fun). Alsace's plantings of the variety wine producers there view as their most noble have been increasing steadily and passed the 3,000-ha mark in the late 1980s. The great majority of Alsace Riesling is planted in the higher, finer vineyard of the Haut-Rhin, where GEWÜRZTRAMINER covers even more ground. On the flatter land of the Bas-Rhin, the soil and climate are not unlike the less interesting parts of the German Pfalz regions and the wines that result can be thin and uninteresting. What is needed to produce Alsace Riesling of real class is, as in Germany, a favoured site of real interest such as many of Alsace's famous grands crus vineyards.

The hallmark of Alsace has been dry wines from aromatic grapes such as Riesling and certainly the great majority of Alsace Rieslings follow the variety's alluring perfume with a taste that is fairly alcoholic (easily 12 per cent) and bone dry. The dry climate of Alsace minimizes the risk of rot and makes extended ripening a real possibility, however, often resulting in the prized late harvest wines which qualify as VENDANGE TARDIVE or, even sweeter, SÉLECTION DE GRAINS NOBLES the richest, most sumptuous ripeness category of ALSACE wines.

To the north, about 10 per cent of the LUXEMBOURG vineyard is planted with Riesling, which tends to produce dry, relatively full bodied (thanks to CHAPTALIZATION) wines closer to Alsace in style than to the Mosel-Saar-Ruwer, which is just over the German border.

In AUSTRIA Riesling, sometimes called **Rheinriesling** or **Weisser Riesling** to distinguish it from the more widely planted WELSCHRIESLING, is quantitatively unimportant, covering just over 1,000 ha of vineyard, but is regarded as one of the country's finest wines when made on a favoured site. The most hallowed Austrian Rieslings are dry, whistle-clean, concentrated, and aromatic, and a high proportion of them come from the terraced vineyards of the Wachau in lower Austria. Certain favoured sites in neighbouring Kamptal-Donauland such as the Zöbinger Heiligenstein vineyard near Langenlois and those just over the border from the Wachau near Krems also enjoy a high reputation for their aristocratic, whistle-clean Rieslings. Riesling is a relatively important variety in the vineyards of Vienna, especially those of Nussberg and Bisamberg.

Not surprisingly, Riesling works well in the continental climate of CZECHOSLOVAKIA to the immediate north of Austria's vineyards, where relatively light wines have real crackle and race. Most of SWITZERLAND is too cool to ripen Riesling properly, with the exception of some of the more schistous soils and warmest vineyards of the Valais around Sion.

Although practically unknown in Iberia (*pace* TORRES in Spain's high PENEDÈS), Riesling has infiltrated the far north east of Italy. It is grown with real enthusiasm in the high vineyards of ALTO ADIGE, where it produces delicate, aromatic wines quite unlike most Italian whites. It is also grown quite successfully in FRIULI, where it is known as **Riesling Renano**, and just over the border in SLOVENIA, where it may be called **Rheinriesling**. Riesling, known as Rizling Rajinski and variants thereof, is also planted southwards through what was Yugoslavia in CROATIA and, less distinctively, in VOJVODINA.

It is planted throughout the rest of eastern Europe in Hungary and Bulgaria and to a much more limited extent in Romania but in each of these countries the climate can be too warm to coax much excitement from the variety and Welschriesling tends to reign supreme.

The country which had more Riesling planted than any other, even Germany, in the mid 1980s was what was then the USSR. If official statistics were to be believed, the Soviet Union grew 25,000 ha of true Riesling before Gorbachev's VINE PULL scheme. It seems unlikely that the communist system encouraged the long wait for Riesling to ripen, so Soviet Riesling wines were presumably not the fullest, but it is easy to see why the variety would be popular in the cold winters of RUSSIA and UKRAINE, which has by far the biggest area planted with the variety. Rhine Riesling is also grown in MOLDOVA and in most of the central Asian republics: KAZAKHSTAN, UZBEKISTAN, TAJIKISTAN, KYRGYZSTAN, and TURKMENISTAN.

In the New World true Riesling is most widely grown in AUSTRALIA, where it was the most planted white wine grape variety until Chardonnay caught up with its nearly 4,000 ha in 1990. Here, known as **Rhine Riesling**, it has received little of the respect it deserves, precisely because of its ubiquity (and perhaps also because the Australians had at one time a confusing tendency to call just about any white grape variety Riesling). It is associated most intimately with the Barossa district of South Australia because of its influx of Silesian immigrants in the mid 19th century. The hot Barossa Valley floor is less suitable for this cool-climate vine, however, than in the higher, cooler reaches of the Clare Valley or Eden Valley. Australian Rhine Rieslings are necessarily much higher in body and alcohol than most, but the best have carved out their own tangy, often lime-flavoured style which can withstand the test of a decade in bottle admirably. Some late harvest styles have also been made successfully.

NEW ZEALAND began to produce convincing wines from its nearly 300 ha of Riesling in the late 1980s, notably when some producers addressed themselves to making scintillating late harvest sweet wines. New Zealand's status as a cool-climate producer is undisputed but initial vintages (Riesling was introduced in the early 1970s) were less than satisfactory. Today, the Rieslings of Marlborough, where the variety is the third most planted after Chardonnay and Sauvignon Blanc, display excellent acidity and a delicacy unknown across the Tasman Sea in Australia. Nelson has also proved an excellent source of late harvest bottlings by the Redwood Valley winery.

Riesling is cultivated far more widely in South America than one might think wise. Argentina has about 1,300 ha, mainly in the hot, irrigated vineyards of Mendoza province. Chile has 250 ha, and there are plantings all over the rest of the continent, often, although not exclusively, in vineyards which ripen far too fast.

Riesling's progress in North America has been hampered simply by consumer demand for anything *but* Riesling. California's total acreage of what is known as **Johannisberg Riesling** or **White Riesling** remained at around 4,000 throughout the 1980s (while Chardonnay plantings grew from 22,000 to 56,000 acres in the decade to 1992). The variety is rarely made bone dry in California, and can command a decent price only if very sweet and described as Select Late Harvest (the equivalent of a German BEERENAUSLESE) or somesuch. Recognition and mastery of NOBLE ROT came only in the 1970s, and in the late 1980s there were still some grapegrowers willing to sell BOTRYTIZED grapes for a song, believing them beyond redemption. Such wines have trouble hanging on to their acidity and tend to brown after five years or so in bottle, although exponents such as Joseph Phelps and Ch St Jean have had more experience than most. Riesling is planted all over the state and has enjoyed particular success in the cooler patches of SANTA BARBARA, MONTEREY and MENDOCINO.

WASHINGTON state claims a special affinity for Riesling, even organizing the world's first truly international conference on the subject, although total area planted has been declining and was only just over 2,000 acres in 1991. As in Oregon, the variety suffers from consumer passion for other varieties rather than from any inherent viticultural disadvantage; indeed, some Washington Rieslings can be delightfully delicate.

Because of its winter hardiness, Riesling tends to be treasured in the coolest wine regions of North America. In CANADA Riesling is cultivated with particular success in Ontario, just over the border from the Finger Lakes region of NEW YORK state, where it is also respected not least for its ability to yield commercially interesting EISWEIN.

Pigott, S., *Riesling* (London, 1991).
Pro Riesling Organization, *The Riesling and its Wines* (Trier, 1986).

RIESLING ITALICO, or **Riesling Italianski**, white grape variety which Germans would like to see called RIZLING Italico to distinguish it from true RIESLING known as Riesling Renano in Italy. In Austria it is called WELSCHRIESLING (under which more details can be found); in much of what was YUGOSLAVIA it is called LASKI RIZLING, in CZECHOSLOVAKIA it is called Rizling Vlassky, and in HUNGARY it is called OLASZ RIZLING. Riesling Italico (*sic*) was ROMANIA'S third most planted variety in the early 1990s, and was often blended with other varieties such as Muscat Ottonel. Within Italy it is most common in the far north east, in FRIULI just over the border from SLOVENIA. Provided its tendency to overcrop is curbed, it can produce delicate, crisp, mildly flowery wines, most in COLLIO. It is grown to a limited extent in ALTO ADIGE and, more successfully, in LOMBARDY. In 1990 there were about 2,400 ha/5,930 acres of Riesling Italico in Italy, while total plantings of true Riesling were less than 1,000 ha.

RIESLING-SYLVANER is the flattering name for MÜLLER-THURGAU, which may not actually be a crossing of Riesling and Sylvaner at all but of two strains of Riesling. This name is, curiously, preferred in SWITZERLAND, where the canton of Thurgau is to be found. It has also been widely used in NEW ZEALAND, where it has been the most planted variety, although EUROPEAN UNION authorities disapprove. (And now that the term is on the wane, the reputation of true New Zealand Riesling is in the ascendant.)

RIGHT BANK, an expression much used of that part of the BORDEAUX wine region that is on the right bank, or north, of the river DORDOGNE. It includes, travelling down river, Côtes de CASTILLON, Côtes de FRANCS, ST-ÉMILION and its satellite appellations, POMEROL and LALANDE-DE- POMEROL, FRONSAC and Canon-Fronsac, BOURG, and BLAYE. The most obvious characteristic shared by these appellations, and distinct from LEFT BANK appellations, is that the dominant grape varieties are Merlot and Cabernet Franc rather than Cabernet Sauvignon.

RIMAGE, French term sometimes given to a superior selection of wines from a particular year. It is used in BANYULS and has more recently spread to BEAUJOLAIS.

RINGING vines. See CINCTURING.

RIOJA, the leading wine region of SPAIN producing predominantly red wines in the north of the country. Named after the *rio* (river) Oja, a tributary of the river Ebro, most of the Rioja wine region lies in the province of La Rioja in north east Spain, although small parts of the zone extend into the neighbouring BASQUE country to the north west and NAVARRE to the north east. Centred on the provincial capital Logroño, Rioja divides into three zones along the axis of the river Ebro. **Rioja Alta** occupies the part of the Ebro valley west of Logroño and includes the wine-making town of Haro. **Rioja Alavesa** is the name given to the section of the zone north of the river Ebro which falls in the Basque province of Alava. **Rioja Baja** extends from the suburbs of Logroño south and east to include the towns of Calahorra and Alfaro.

Spain's vineyards, such as these in **Rioja** Alavesa, are some of the most sparsely planted in the world, typically because of lack of soil water.

History

There is archeological evidence that the Romans made wine in the upper Ebro valley (see SPAIN, history). Wine trade was tolerated rather than encouraged under the Moorish occupation of Iberia, but viticulture flourished once more in Rioja after the Christian reconquest at the end of the 15th century. The name Rioja was already in use in one of the statutes written to guarantee the rights of inhabitants of territory recaptured from the Moors. Rioja's wine industry grew around the numerous monasteries (see MONKS AND MONASTERIES) that were founded to serve pilgrims *en route* to Santiago de Compostela, and the region's first wine laws date from this period.

For centuries Rioja suffered from its physical isolation from major population centres, and the wines only found a market outside the region in the 1700s, when communications improved and Bilbao became an important trading centre. In 1850 Luciano de Murrieta (subsequently the Marqués de Murrieta) established Rioja's first commercial BODEGA in cellars belonging to the Duque de Vitoria and began exporting wines to the Spanish colonies. The Rioja region benefited unexpectedly, but substantially, from the all too obvious arrival of POWDERY MILDEW in French vineyards in the late 1840s. Bordeaux wine merchants crossed the Pyrenees in large numbers and in 1862 the Provincial Legislature in Alava employed a French adviser to help local vine-growers. Shunned by smallholders who were concerned only with the requirements of the local Basque market, Jean Pineau was finally employed by the Marqués de Riscal, who set about building a bodega at Elciego along French lines. It was finished in 1868, four years before Murrieta built its own similar installation at Ygay.

When the PHYLLOXERA louse began to devastate French vineyards in the late 1860s, yet more merchants came to Spain in search of wine. French duties were relaxed and Rioja enjoyed an unprecedented boom which lasted for nearly four decades. New bodegas were established, among them the Compañía Vinícola del Norte de España (CVNE), López de Heredia, La Rioja Alta, and Bodegas Franco-Españolas, all of which were heavily influenced by the French. During the period the 225-l/59-gal oak *barrica*, or BARRIQUE, was introduced from Bordeaux, and these influential maturation containers are still sometimes referred to as *barricas bordelesas* in Rioja (although American OAK was the popular choice). Helped by a new rail link (see RAILWAYS), Rioja sometimes exported 500,000 hl/13.2 million gal of wine a month to France in the late 19th century.

Phylloxera did not reach Rioja until 1901, by which time Bordeaux had returned to full production with vines grafted on to phylloxera-resistant ROOTSTOCKS. Spain also lost its lucrative colonial markets and Rioja's wine industry declined rapidly. A number of new bodegas were established in the period following the First World War and Spain's first Consejo Regulador was established in Rioja in 1926, but the Civil War between 1936 and 1939 and the Second World War which followed put paid to further expansion. Recovery came in the late 1960s and 1970s, when, encouraged by growing foreign markets and the construction of a motorway connecting Logroño and Bilbao, a number of new bodegas were built in the region, many with the support of multinational companies. The most ambitious of these organizations was the Spanish-owned Rumasa SHERRY and banking conglomerate, which acquired a number of large Rioja producers until the company was expropriated by the government in 1983. Sales on the domestic market continued to grow throughout the 1980s, although exports slowed when prices increased by 40 per cent between 1985 and 1989. Rioja was promoted from DO to DOCA status in 1991, current DO regulations dating from 1976.

Climate and geography
Rioja enjoys an enviable position among Spanish wine regions. Sheltered by the Sierra de Cantabria to the north and west, it is well protected from the rain-bearing Atlantic winds that drench the Basque coast immediately to the north. Yet Rioja's wine producers rarely experience the climatic extremes that burden growers in so much of central and southern Spain. It is difficult to make climatic generalizations, however, about a region that stretches about 120 km/75 miles from north west to south east. The vineyards range in ALTITUDE from 300 m/984 ft above sea level at Alfaro in the east to nearly 800 m on the slopes of the Sierra de Cantabria to the north west. Average annual RAINFALL increases correspondingly from less than 300 mm/12 in in parts of Rioja Baja to over 500 mm in the upper zones of Rioja Alta and Rioja Alavesa.

Rioja Alta and Rioja Alavesa share a similar climate and are only distinct from each other for administrative reasons. Many of the best grapes are grown here on the cooler slopes to the north west around the towns and villages of Haro, Labastida, San Vicente, Laguardia, Elciego, Fuenmayor, Cenicero, and Briones. These zones share similar CLAY soils based on LIMESTONE. Downstream to the east, the climate becomes gradually warmer with rainfall decreasing to less than 400 mm at Logroño. Where the valley broadens there is a higher incidence of fertile, ALLUVIAL soils composed chiefly of SILT. Around Calahorra and Alfaro in Rioja Baja the climate is more MEDITERRANEAN. In summer, DROUGHT is often a problem here, and temperatures frequently reach 30 to 35 °C/95 °F.

Viticulture and vine varieties
Seven grape varieties (four red, three white) qualify for Rioja's Denominación de Origen and their distribution varies in different parts of the region. The most widely planted variety is the probably indigenous, black TEMPRANILLO, which ripens well on the clay and limestone slopes of Rioja Alta and Rioja Alavesa, where it forms the basis for the region's best wines. Most Riojas are blends of more than one variety, however, and wines made from the GARNACHA vine, which seems to thrive in the hotter vineyards of Rioja Baja, are often used to add BODY to Tempranillo, which can taste thin on its own in cooler VINTAGES. On its own Garnacha produces hefty, alcoholic red wines which tend to OXIDIZE quickly and are not therefore suitable for prolonged BARREL MATURATION (see below) although Rioja, like neighbouring Navarre, produces rosé entirely from Garnacha grapes. Two further red varieties, Mazuelo (Cariñena or CARIGNAN) and GRACIANO, are of relatively minor importance. Although Mazuelo is not especially prized for quality, the indigenous Graciano has great potential, contributing to the aroma of the wine. Owing to its susceptibility to disease and its low productivity, Graciano fell from favour with Rioja's vine-growers in the second half of the 20th century and was replanted only in the early 1990s (when there were fewer than 100 ha in total). The CABERNET SAUVIGNON and MERLOT vines which arrived with the French in the 19th century are allowed by special dispensation in vineyards belonging to the Marqués de Riscal. Several other companies have experimental Cabernet Sauvignon vineyards.

Historically, Rioja's chief white grape variety was the MALVASIA. On its own it produced rich, alcoholic, dry white wines which responded well to ageing in oak. From the early 1970s, however, fresher-tasting, cool-fermented, early bottled white wines were in FASHION, and Viura (known elsewhere in Spain as MACABEO) became the most planted light-berried variety in the region. By the early 1990s most white Riojas were made exclusively from Viura, and Malvasia vines were extremely difficult to find, although one or two of the traditional oak-aged wines claim to be blends of Malvasia and Viura.

Vineyards in Rioja tend to be small, especially in Rioja Alta and Rioja Alavesa, where vines are often interspersed with other crops. Vines are free-standing BUSH VINES and trained into low goblet shapes (see GOBELET), although a few experimental vineyards are trained on WIRES for higher yields. DO regulations permitted yields of up to 60 hl/ha (3.4 tons/acre) for white wines and 50 hl/ha for red wines, although in the more arid parts of the region producers struggle to achieve yields of 30 hl/ha. In 1992 there were about 44,000 ha of authorized vineyards, producing an average of about 1.4 million hl of wine, of which about 80 per cent was red.

Wine-making
Grapes are usually delivered to large, central wineries belonging either to one of the CO-OPERATIVES or to a merchant's bodega. Most wineries in Rioja are reasonably well equipped with a modern STAINLESS STEEL plant and facilities for TEMPERATURE CONTROL. In some of the smaller, more traditional bodegas, fermentation of both red and white wines takes place in wooden vats or casks, but this is the exception rather than the rule.

Rioja wine-making is characterized not by fermentation techniques but by BARREL MATURATION, however, and the shape and size of the 225-l *barrica bordelesa* introduced by the French in the mid 19th century is laid down by law. The regulations also specify the minimum ageing period for each officially recognized category of wine. In Rioja, wines labelled CRIANZA and RESERVA must spend at least a year in oak, while a GRAN RESERVA must spend at least two years. In common with other Spanish wine regions, American OAK is the favoured WOOD TYPE for wine maturation. New American oak barrels give the soft, vanilla flavour that has become accepted as typical of Rioja, but a similar effect can also be achieved by slow, oxidative maturation in older barrels. French oak is used increasingly, however, with some bodegas specifically favouring LIMOUSIN and others preferring the finer GRAIN of NEVERES and ALLIER.

Over 40 per cent of all Rioja falls into one of the three oak-aged categories above (the rest is either white, rosé, or sold as young, unoaked JOVEN red, much of it within Spain), and the larger bodegas therefore need tens of thousands of casks. In the early 1990s the largest producer of Rioja, Bodegas Campo Viejo, maintained a stock of over 45,000 *barricas*. Most bodegas renew their *barricas* on a regular basis although, other than for certain specialized wines, new oak is not particularly prized, casks are used over and over again, and some producers even pride themselves on the age of their casks. Rioja producers are therefore the wine world's greatest specialists in BARREL MAINTENANCE.

Rioja regulations also specify the length of time that an oak-aged Rioja must spend in tank or bottle before the wine can be released. Crianzas must age for a further year in tank or bottle where Reservas must spend two further years. Gran Reservas, usually specially selected wines from the best vintages, must spend at least three years in bottle so that the wines are a minimum of five years old before they go on sale. Wines with a higher percentage of Tempranillo are selected for prolonged ageing in cask.

Since the widespread adoption of cool fermentation techniques in the 1970s, the amount of oak-aged white Rioja has progressively diminished. López de Heredia and Marqués de Murrieta continue to uphold the traditional style by ageing their white wines in oak *barricas*, however, as do a few other bodegas for some wines. For whites labelled Crianza, Reserva, or Gran Reserva, the minimum wood ageing period is just six months with a further year, two years, or four years respectively before the wines may be released for sale. The addition of TARTARIC ACID helps the wine to age for such long periods. In the mid 1990s some of the more modern producers who pioneered early bottled white Rioja in the early 1970s were experimenting with fashionable BARREL FERMENTATION for white Rioja, notably Martinez Bujanda.

Some reds as well as whites may occasionally need ACIDIFICATION. See SPAIN for more details of permitted wine-making practices.

Organization of trade

Rioja's vineyards are split among 14,000 growers, most of whom tend their plots as a sideline and have no WINE-MAKING facilities of their own. Many growers have an established contract with one of the 100 or so merchant bodegas. Others belong to one of the 30 CO-OPERATIVES that serve the region and receive around 45 per cent of the grapes. Most co-operatives sell their produce, either as must or as newly made wine, to the merchant bodegas, who blend, bottle, and market the wine under their own labels.

In the 1980s a number of bodegas bought up large tracts of land to plant their own vineyards, although few as yet have sufficient to supply their entire needs. A number of single estates, such as Contino and Remelluri, are also emerging, with the distinction in the region of growing, vinifying, and marketing their own wines.

Like other Spanish DOs, Rioja is controlled by a CONSEJO REGULADOR. Based in Logroño, the Consejo keeps a register of all vineyards and bodegas and monitors the movement of stocks from the vineyard to the bottle. The Consejo also maintains laboratories at Haro and Laguardia where tests are carried out on all wines before they are approved for export. After a long debate dating from the 1970s, Rioja was granted DOCa status in 1991. The qualifications have little to do with absolute quality, the single most important being that Rioja's grape prices are at least 200 per cent above the national average. The Consejo Regulador set itself the target of mandatory BOTTLING within the region, but was defeated in the EUROPEAN UNION court in 1992. R.J.M.

Duijker, H., *The Wines of Rioja* (London, 1987).

Metcalfe, C., and McWhirter, K., *The Wines of Spain and Portugal* (London, 1988).

Read, J., *The Wines of Rioja* (London, 1984).

RIPAILLE, named CRU on the south eastern shore of Lake Geneva whose name may be added to the French appellation Vin de SAVOIE. The wine is typically a slightly sparkling white made from the Chasselas grape.

RIPARIA, species of the VITIS genus native to North America much used in developing suitably resistant ROOTSTOCKS and HYBRIDS.

RIPASSO, Italian term meaning literally 'repassed', for the technique of adding extra flavour, and alcohol, to VALPOLICELLA by adding the unpressed skins of AMARONE wines after these DRIED GRAPE WINES have finished their fermentation in the spring. While this undoubtedly adds body and character to a ripasso Valpolicella, it may also impart some of the OXIDIZED and BOTRYTIS flavours of the Amarone as well, together with additional TANNINS. Some producers are therefore substituting grapes that have been dried, but not to the extent required for Amarone, for the fermented Amarone skins, although this technique is necessarily expensive. D.T.

RIPENESS, term used to describe that stage of the continuous process of grape RIPENING or development which is chosen by the wine-maker and/or grape processor as that desired at HARVEST. What constitutes the ideal chemical and physical composition of any fruit, including grapes, at this point is a SUBJECTIVE judgement dependent on wine style, FASHION, and many other factors, so ripeness is by no means an absolute term. It is a relative term which can have many different meanings. Grapes considered at perfect ripeness by one wine-maker for one purpose may be considered overripe or underripe in other circumstances.

Ripeness is often related to MUST WEIGHT or grape sugar concentration. Being directly related to POTENTIAL ALCOHOL, the concentration of SUGAR IN GRAPES has a major impact on wine type. The commercial table (non-fortified) wines of the world fall between two extremes, both European. VINHO VERDE grapes grown in northern Portugal are traditionally harvested early to give bottled wines that are sparkling, refreshing, and low in ALCOHOLIC STRENGTH (about 8.5 per cent). At the other extreme are the BOTRYTIZED wines of the world which contain so much sugar in their raisin-like berries that yeast cannot ferment all of the sugar. So the alcohol concentration may approach 15 per cent and yet there is also considerable RESIDUAL SUGAR in the finished wine.

Sugar levels are not the only aspect of grape composition to affect what is considered ripeness. Especially in cool climates, ACIDITY levels can be closely monitored to determine the grapes' ripeness. The acidity in grapes declines with ripening, and must be below certain values (which differ for different wine styles) so that the resultant wine will not be too tart and unpalatable. In warm to hot regions it is more common that the acidity is too low and the PH is too high once sugars have reached the desired potential alcohol level.

Measures of sugar, acidity, and pH have been commonly used around the world to define grape ripeness and optimal harvest time, but this situation is likely to change in the foreseeable future. In the search for better definitions of ripeness to improve wine quality many other analyses are being proposed and investigated. For red wine, measurements of grape PHENOLICS, including anthocyans and tannins, are proving useful. For all grapes, a measure that indicates flavour is so eagerly sought that it may be said to be the grape researcher's holy grail. This is a particularly difficult measurement because of the huge diversity of potential FLAVOUR COMPOUNDS on the one hand, and their minute concentration on the other.

Individual grapes' physical condition, especially skin thickness and integrity, is also considered as an aspect of grape ripeness relevant to wine quality.

See also PHYSIOLOGICAL RIPENESS, GRAPE COMPOSITION AND WINE QUALITY, and GRAPE JUICE COMPOSITION, R.E.S. & B.G.C.

RIPENESS MEASUREMENT. See MUST WEIGHT.

RIPENING, GRAPE. The important process of grape development which is a prelude to harvesting for winemaking. Ripening begins when the berries soften at the stage called VERAISON and is concluded normally by HARVEST, which can occur at different stages for different wine styles. Ripening can be affected by many plant, pest and disease, and environmental factors, and is in many ways the most important vine process affecting wine quality since it is so crucially related to the chemical and physical composition of the harvested fruit.

Following FRUIT SET, grape berries grow in size but are hard, green, and very acidic (see GRAPE). When almost half their final size, veraison, or the inception of ripening, occurs. The timing of this will depend on variety and climate, but it is normally 40 to 60 days after fruit set, being longer for cooler climates. The period from veraison to harvest will obviously depend on the harvest stage of ripeness required, but for grapes destined for dry table wine the period varies from about 30 days in hot regions to about 70 days in cooler regions. For early ripening varieties such as Pinot Noir and Chardonnay the ripening period is shorter than for a variety such as Cabernet Sauvignon which ripens relatively late.

Not all bunches on a vine nor berries on a bunch are at the same stage of development. Those which flower first are the first to show veraison, and these in turn are the first to mature. There is variation of over 20 days between berries on any one bunch in the time of veraison.

During the latter stages of ripening when the sugar content is about 24°BRIX the berry skin may lose some water. So for very ripe grapes the increase in concentration for some compounds in the berry is due to a loss of water rather than more movement into the berry.

It is relevant to consider the development of the various chemical compounds of most interest to the wine-maker. Sugar, or more precisely SUCROSE, is the most important. It is moved from the leaves to the berries by TRANSLOCATION, and is broken down to the constituent molecules GLUCOSE and FRUCTOSE by the enzyme INVERTASE. Sucrose may originate from current PHOTOSYNTHESIS or from stored CARBOHYDRATE reserves in the woody parts of the vine such as its trunk, arms, and roots. As these sugars accumulate in the berry their ratio one to the other changes. Before veraison, glucose predominates, but for much of the latter stage of ripening the ratio is equal, and in overripe grapes fructose exceeds glucose. Heavy crop loads slow the increase in concentration of SUGAR IN GRAPES, as also do factors slowing photosynthesis such as low or high temperatures and cloudiness. There can also be competition for the products of photosynthesis; if shoot tips are growing actively, for example, then fruit ripening is slowed.

The second major indicator of grape ripening is ACIDITY. The concentration of TARTARIC ACID falls during ripening, but this has been shown to be due to dilution effects associated with berry growth. The concentration of MALIC ACID falls more quickly than tartaric during ripening, and this is because of temperature-dependent RESPIRATION in addition to dilution. Grapes ripening in cool climates therefore tend to have higher acidity. Juice PH rises throughout ripening due to the decreases in free acids and increases in POTASSIUM. In hot regions, alarmingly high juice pH can be a factor in the timing of harvest. The most important nitrogenous compounds in grape juice are AMINO ACIDS, and these along with other organic nitrogen compounds increase markedly during ripening, while levels of ammonia nitrogen decrease.

The skin colour of red grapes is due to ANTHOCYANS; veraison is signalled as they replace the green colour of chlorophyll. Anthocyanin concentration rises during ripening and the value at harvest depends on both environmental and plant factors. Temperature and light have major effects; high temperatures and low light levels reduce skin coloration in many varieties. Grape TANNINS are distributed between the skins, seeds, and stems. They increase during ripening at a rate comparable to anthocyans.

The most abundant minerals in the grape are POTASSIUM,

CALCIUM, MAGNESIUM, and SODIUM, and they increase in concentration during ripening. Potassium is predominant and its concentration has a major effect on juice pH. Potassium is distributed between flesh and skins, and the potassium extracted from skins during fermentation is one reason why red wines have a higher pH than white wines.

Flavour compounds are all-important factors in wine quality, although as yet their measurement is many years away from becoming a universal practice. In the mid 1990s analytical techniques as well as knowledge about their role were still a developing science. Monoterpenes are a group of compounds important in Muscat flavour, for example, and they increase in concentration during ripening. Other important flavour and odour compounds are discussed under FLAVOUR COMPOUNDS.

See also GRAPE JUICE COMPOSITION, GRAPE QUALITY ASSESSMENT, RIPENESS, and PHYSIOLOGICAL RIPENESS.

R.E.S. & B.G.C.

Coombe, B. G., 'Research on development and ripening of the grape berry', *American Journal of Enology and Viticulture*, 43 (1992), 101–10.

Hamilton, R. P. and Coombe, B. G., 'Harvesting of winegrapes', in B. G. Coombe and P. R. Dry (eds.), *Viticulture ii: Practices* (Adelaide, 1992).

Winkler, A. J., *et al.*, *General Viticulture* (2nd edn., Berkeley, Calif., 1974).

RIPPING is a viticultural operation conducted in many parts of the world before PLANTING a vineyard. Normally bulldozers or heavy tractors are used, and these might pull one or two vertical tines through the soil, up to 1 m/3 ft or so deep. The aim of ripping is to break up compact soils so that water can penetrate and roots can grow to a greater depth. Sometimes large boulders can be brought to the surface, especially if, for instance, sheet limestone is broken up. In California slip ploughs rather than tines are used. Sometimes the tines are straight, and merely fracture the soil during passage. Alternatively a mouldboard plough can be used, which will turn the soil over and bring subsoil to the surface. This practice is common in South Africa.

Ripping provides the opportunity to incorporate FERTILIZERS and soil amendments (see SOIL AMELIORATION) such as phosphates, forms of potassium or lime, as they will not readily leach through the soil. The distance between rip lines and their depth will depend on the power of the bulldozer or tractor and the strength of the soil. The best time to rip is when the soil is dry, as fracture planes are created in the soil. Vineyard soils will recompact with time, and so initial benefits may be lost. Ripping can also be done after planting, but the size of the tractor, and therefore the power available, is then limited by the space between rows, so it can be difficult to reach more than about 30 cm/12 in below the surface.

Ripping dense clay soils allows roots to penetrate to greater depths and so the vines are able to access more water and nutrients. This will increase the vineyard VIGOUR and likely YIELD. There are instances in which wine quality may be reduced by ripping. Unless steps are taken to manage these more vigorous vines correctly, then SHADE may reduce both yield and quality.

R.E.S.

Coombe, B. G., and Dry, P. R. (eds.), *Viticulture, ii: Practices* (Adelaide, 1992).

RIPPING OUT vines is known as *arrachage* in France, where it has become an increasingly common practice as a result of EUROPEAN UNION subsidies offered in an effort to diminish Europe's wine SURPLUS. In the late 1980s and early 1990s, smallholders in the south of both France and Italy in particular took advantage of substantial financial inducements to abandon viticulture on all or part of their land. About 300,000 ha/741,000 acres of French vineyard and about 400,000 ha of Italian vineyard were ripped out between the late 1970s and 1991. Other parts of the world in which concerted VINE PULL SCHEMES have operated in the late 20th century include NEW ZEALAND and ARGENTINA.

The more traditional reason for ripping out a vineyard is that the VINE AGE is so high and the average YIELD so low that the vineyard is no longer economic (although the prestige associated with old vines, or VIEILLES VIGNES, has tended to retard this process).

A vineyard may also be ripped out because its owner wishes to change VINE VARIETY or CLONE, although this may be achieved by TOP WORKING, or field grafting on to, the existing trunks and root systems. Ripping out is normally necessary to change the ROOTSTOCK (although GRAFTING to another rootstock is being evaluated in California in the 1990s as a possible response to the predations of PHYLLOXERA). Vineyards are normally ripped out when invaded by a pest as deadly as phylloxera, and a disease such as LEAFROLL VIRUS may damage production to such an extent that ripping out is the only option.

If the vineyard is to be replanted, care must be taken that the soil is free of pests and disease. FUMIGATION may be necessary; see also NEMATODES.

RISERVA, Italian term usually denoting a wine given extended AGEING before release and one with a higher minimum ALCOHOLIC STRENGTH, by one or half a per cent, than the non-Riserva version. In this latter respect there is a certain overlap with the SUPERIORE designation. Some Riserva wines, unlike Superiore wines, are obliged to undergo a certain minimum ageing period in wood in order to qualify as a Riserva; the regular bottlings of such wines are not normally aged in wood at all. The Riserva bottlings of the most famous Italian wines—BARBARESCO, BAROLO, BRUNELLO DI MONTALCINO, CHIANTI CLASSICO, VINO NOBILE DI MONTEPULCIANO—are not necessarily aged for a longer period in wood, however, but are simply required to have been aged longer overall, either in wood or in bottle, before being released. (Chianti Classico Riserva, in fact, does not require any wood ageing whatsoever.) Producers are not required to declare a Riserva or set aside given quantities of wine as a Riserva before the commercial release of their production, but may simply decide which wines are Riserva on an *ad hoc* basis. This latitude has allowed a certain number of houses simply to reclassify their unsold inventory as Riserva in an

Berri estates' base in Australia's **Riverland**.

effort to obtain a higher price, prompting some calls for the abolition of the entire category. D.T.

RIVANER is the LUXEMBOURG name for MÜLLER-THURGAU, which is the country's most planted grape variety.

RIVERLAND, the most productive wine region in AUSTRALIA, a sprawl of vineyards irrigated by the river Murray mainly in the state of SOUTH AUSTRALIA, but also part of the state of VICTORIA, which may also be called the Murray River Valley. Almost all production is high-yield, technically sound material for blending, although each year a significant, if variable, proportion of the Riverland SULTANA grapes are processed for DRYING GRAPES and TABLE GRAPES. There have been plans to call the Victorian Riverland the Murray River Valley, and the vast South Australian section Murray Mallee, but wine producers are generally reticent about proclaiming these provenances. South Eastern Australia is the catch-all description usually found on labels.

RIVERS have played a fundamental role throughout the history of wine, serving both as arteries of trade and also through their action in creating valley slopes particularly well suited to the cultivation of the vine.

A river is crucial to the earliest detailed account of the wine trade. HERODOTUS, writing in the 5th century BC, records how in MESOPOTAMIA wine in palm-wood casks was loaded on to boats in the upper reaches of the river Tigris, and then sailed down to Babylon, where the boats were broken up because of the impossibility of paddling them upstream against the current.

During the Roman era rivers continued to play a critical role in the transport of bulky items such as wine. There were two main trade routes in GAUL: a western one from Narbonne to Toulouse and then along the river GARONNE to Bordeaux and the Atlantic; and a northern one up the RHÔNE to Lyons, and thence along the Saône, before cutting across country to the MOSEL and the RHINE, and eventually reaching the North Sea. These routes witnessed the transport of thousands of AMPHORAE of wine, but they also served as arteries along which the idea of vine cultivation and wine-making passed. By the 1st century AD viticulture was thus well established along the Rhône and the Garonne, and gradually through the ensuing centuries of Roman rule vineyards came to be cultivated along most of the other major river valleys of Gaul such as the LOIRE and the Seine (see PARIS).

By the year 1000, although vineyards were relatively widely established throughout southern Europe, in the north they were found most frequently in river valleys. The main reason for this was the high cost of overland transport, which gave those with easy access to the main fluvial transport routes a distinct competitive advantage. Environmental factors were also important, with the south-facing slopes of such valleys providing ideal sites because of the extra exposure to the sun that they afforded (see VINEYARD SITE SELECTION). This is particularly evident in the development of vineyards in the cool Mosel–Rhine area, where most of those established before 1050 were in close proximity to rivers.

Coastal transport became increasingly important during the later medieval period, but rivers also maintained their role as arteries of the wine trade, and, with the opening up of eastern Europe, rivers such as the Dnestr, the Vistula, and the Danube came to play as significant a role as did the Garonne, Loire, Seine, Rhône, and Rhine in the west.

In the 20th century, with the development of the RAILWAYS and, subsequently, efficient road transport, it is the environmental factors that are most important in determining the location of vineyards along the slopes of river valleys. Above all, these locations provide additional sunshine, generally alleviate the problems associated with frost and excess humidity (see HILLSIDE VINEYARDS), and frequently have soils that are particularly well suited to vine cultivation (see TOPOGRAPHY). Moreover, in some special locations, as in SAUTERNES and along the Rhine, the proximity to water provides the ideal conditions for NOBLE ROT, which can result in some of the world's greatest sweet wines. P.T.H.U.

Postan, M. M., and Miller, E. (eds.), *The Cambridge Economic History of Europe, ii: Trade and Industry in the Middle Ages* (2nd edn., Cambridge, 1987).

Pounds, N. J. G., *An Historical Geography of Europe 450 B.C.–A.D. 1330* (Cambridge, 1973).

Schenk, W., 'Viticulture in Franconia along the river Main: human and natural influences since AD 700', *Journal of Wine Research*, 3/3 (1992), 185–204.

RIVESALTES, town north of Perpignan in southern France that gives its name to two of the biggest appellations of ROUSSILLON, Rivesaltes and Muscat de Rivesaltes, both of them VINS DOUX NATURELS. Muscat de Rivesaltes, which represents about 70 per cent of France's total Muscat production, can in fact be produced throughout most of Roussillon's recognized wine-producing area, together even with some sections of the Aude *département* to the north (including much of the energetically lobbied FITOU appellation). The Rivesaltes production zone is similarly generous but specifically excludes those vineyards that produce BANYULS.

The Muscats of 'Perpinyà' and 'Clayrà' (Claira is the next town to Rivesaltes) were already sought out by 14th century wine buyers from as far away as Barcelona and Avignon. Their sweetness was originally concentrated by leaving the grapes on the vine to shrivel, as was still the custom in the 19th century (see DRIED GRAPE WINES), and may even have been enhanced by adding honey, for which the region is still famous. Today Muscat de Rivesaltes is the only Muscat vin doux naturel which may be made from MUSCAT OF ALEXANDRIA as well as the finer MUSCAT BLANC À PETITS GRAINS, which was once unpopular for its degeneration and unreliable yields; but new clones are being replanted. Average yields of these low trained vines, often on difficult-to-work dry terraces, can be as little 22 hl/ha (1.3 tons/acre). Since the 1980s more skilled vinification has helped improve quality, despite the domination of Muscat of Alexandria. Techniques include SKIN CONTACT and MUTAGE 'sur marc', on the skins. Muscat de Rivesaltes is already on sale the spring after the harvest and should be drunk as young and cool as possible, either as an aperitif or with fruit or creamy desserts.

Rivesaltes, on the other hand, has the potential to be much more complex vin doux naturel, made in all conceivable colours and styles. These sweet, heady, wines can be made from any permutation of Grenache Blanc, Noir, and Gris, Maccabéo, Torbato (here called Malvoisie du Roussillon), and the two Muscats allowed for Muscat de Rivesaltes. Varietal Rivesaltes are permitted, from a golden Maccabéo to a Grenache Noir that can be anything from crimson to deep chocolate brown, depending on its ÉLEVAGE. These tests for the food-and-wine matcher may be vinified 'en blanc', like white wines without any contact with the skins, or may be macerated for weeks in an effort to leach maximum colour, tannin, and flavour into the wine. They may be fermented in stainless steel and bottled young or fermented and aged in wooden casks of all ages and sizes, sometimes according to some sort of SOLERA. Some wines are made to taste deliberately RANCIO and, while some producers deliberately expose the maturing wine to the punishing heat and light of a Roussillon noon, others may include a period in glass BONBONNES in the ageing process. No Rivesaltes can be released until 16 months after the harvest. If the overall quality is more varied and less exciting than that of Banyuls or MAURY, it is improving, largely thanks to the efforts of Domaine Cazes. Rivesaltes may taste of raisins, coffee, chocolate, fruits, or nuts and the most concentrated can, like Banyuls, be some of the few wines that happily partner chocolate.

From 1993 the Institut de Rivesaltes granted numbered neckbands to superior wines submitted to blind tastings.

RIVIERA DI PONENTE, or **Riviera Ligure di Ponente**, wine from the north western coast of Italy. For more details, see LIGURIA.

RIZLING, term for the white grape variety known variously in central Europe as WELSCHRIESLING, OLASZ RIZLING, LASKI RIZLING, and RIESLING ITALICO. The Germans disapprove of any name for this inferior grape variety which suggests a relationship with their own noble RIESLING vine, but will accept Rizling as a suitably distinctive alternative.

RKATSITELI, Russian white grape variety which is probably planted much more extensively than most western wine drinkers realize, on as many as 260,000 ha/645,000 acres according to one official estimate. It is by far the most planted grape variety in the SOVIET UNION and may be the world's most common white wine grape. President Gorbachev's widespread uprooting of vineyards affected Rkatsiteli but it is still the most planted vine variety in the CIS, being grown in all of its wine-producing independent republics with the exception of TURKMENISTAN. It is widely grown throughout eastern Europe and there are pockets of the variety in China and the United States as well.

In RUSSIA alone, where it is well adapted to particularly cold winters, it is by far the most planted wine grape variety; there were nearly 60,000 ha/148,200 acres of Rkatsiteli in 1990. The variety was first recognized in GEORGIA but is also important in UKRAINE, MOLDOVA, AZERBAIJAN, KAZAKHSTAN, UZBEKISTAN, TAJIKISTAN, KYRGYZSTAN, and ARMENIA.

Much is demanded of this variety and it achieves much, providing a base for a wide range of wine styles, including fortified wines and brandy. The wine is distinguished by a keen level of ACIDITY, easily 9 g/l even when picked as late as October, and by good sugar levels too. The variety is also widely cultivated in BULGARIA, where it has been the country's most important white grape variety, and there are more than 500 ha of it in ROMANIA.

In CHINA it is known as Baiyu and has been an important source of neutral white wine for the nascent Chinese wine industry.

Roannaises Côtes, hand-crafted, lightish reds and some rosés made chiefly from locally adapted GAMAY grapes, called St-Romain à Jus Blanc here, using Beaujolais cellar techniques, usually SEMI-CARBONIC MACERATION. The south east-facing slopes of the upper Loire, on which vines are grown on a granitic base, are only one range of hills west of the BEAUJOLAIS region. Direct river and canal links with Paris gave the region's wines relative fame and popularity in the 19th century so that annual production was almost 800,000 hl/21.1 million gal at the beginning of the 20th century. VDQS status was granted in 1955 but production was down to 4,000 hl by the mid 1990s, when APPELLATION CONTRÔLÉE status was won. Wine quality is in the hands of more than a score of individual wine-makers (unlike Côtes du FOREZ to the south), egged on by the Troisgros family at their famous restaurant in the town of Roanne.

Robola, wine and grape variety for which the Ionian island of Cephalonia in GREECE is most famous. The distinctively powerful, lemony dry white is made exclusively from Robola grapes, which are cultivated exclusively on the island, except that the vine is almost certainly the Rebula of SLOVENIA, and the RIBOLLA which has been grown in FRIULI in north east Italy since the 13th century. The wine made from these early ripening grapes is high in both acidity and extract and is much prized within Greece.

Rochelle, La. See LA ROCHELLE.

rock. Those who study GEOLOGY take a very broad view of this word. Any of the natural solid constituents of the Earth's crust are MINERALS. Any natural assemblage of minerals is a rock (although it may also contain liquids and/or gases), whether it is hard or soft, at the surface of the Earth or far beneath it. From this it follows that 'rock' in its widest sense includes soil, and SUBSOIL. There are some geologists whose research is devoted to soils, particularly ancient ones.

For more information about rock types, see SOIL and SOIL TYPES. J.M.H.

Roederer, Louis, family-owned Champagne house known both for its early links with the Russian court and for its extensive vineyard ownership. The original company was founded by a M. Dubois around the year 1776; Louis Roederer joined in 1827, becoming owner in 1833. By the second half of the century RUSSIA had become the major market for Champagne Louis Roederer: 666,386 bottles out of a total company production of 2.5 million were exported there in 1873. In 1877 the special Cuvée Cristal Louis Roederer was commissioned by Tsar Alexander II, who wanted his champagne in clear glass crystal bottles so that it would stand out. The bottles were so strong that they did not need a PUNT. The creation of Cristal (sold in clear glass bottles without a punt to this day) strengthened links with the imperial court, but in 1917 the Russian Revolution brought an immediate 80 per cent loss of its market. Camille Orly-Roederer, widow of the great-nephew of Louis, rebuilt the company after this blow, in particular by strengthening Roederer's vineyard holdings at a time when other houses were selling, a move many later regretted. By the mid 1990s, 180 ha/444 acres supplied 80 per cent of Roederer's requirements, thereby allowing the house to remain unusually independent. Mainly thanks to these vineyard holdings, Roederer produces far more vintages of Cristal than is usual for a PRESTIGE CUVÉE. The best cuvées of almost every harvest are blended to make a vintage Cristal, except in notably poor years such as 1968 and 1972. In 1993 the house acquired 60 per cent of the capital of the holding company of Champagne Deutz. Outside France, the company owns Heemskerk Vineyards in TASMANIA (purchased in 1985), where a range of still wines are produced as well as a sparkling wine called Janz. A California CM/CV sparkling wine is also made, under the brand name Roederer Estate in the Anderson Valley, near the MENDOCINO coast. Roederer Estate was first released in 1988. Camille Orly-Roederer's grandson Jean-Claude Rouzaud runs the company today.

See also SOVIET SPARKLING WINE. S.A.

Sutcliffe, S., *A Celebration of Champagne* (London, 1988).

Roero, sandy hills on the left bank of the river Tanaro in the PIEDMONT region of north west Italy, which takes its name from the villages of Montaldo Roero, Monteu Roero, and Santo Stefano Roero to the north west of Alba. The sandy soils give a lighter character to the widely cultivated NEBBIOLO, the most popular grape of the zone; significant quantities of red BARBERA and white ARNEIS are also grown in the conical hills, whose topography is strikingly different from that of the LANGHE hills directly to the east on the right bank of the Tanaro. D.T.

Rolle, the white grape variety traditionally most closely associated with BELLET, is now increasingly grown in the Languedoc and, especially, Roussillon. It is aromatic and usefully crisp for warm wine regions and is accepted by French authorities as identical to the VERMENTINO of Corsica, Sardinia, and southern Italy and the variety sometimes called Rollo in Liguria. It may therefore be part of the widely dispersed MALVASIA story.

ROMAGNA. Eastern part of EMILIA-ROMAGNA.

ROMANÉE, Romanée-Conti, Romanée-St-Vivant, great red GRANDS CRUS, for more details of which see VOSNE-ROMANÉE. See also DOMAINE DE LA ROMANÉE-CONTI.

ROMAN GARDENS WITH VINES. The systematic work of Wilhelmina Jashemski and her team at POMPEII in the 1960s and 1970s has transformed our knowledge of Roman gardens and led to one of the most endearing publications on a subject from classical antiquity. When the trees and plants growing at the time of the eruption of Vesuvius in AD 79 died, their roots decayed, leaving cavities to be filled by the volcanic debris. Careful excavation can discover these cavities and a cast of the root system can be made. Nearly one-fifth of the town of Pompeii turns out to have been devoted to gardens, orchards, and allotments. The characteristic Pompeian house with its peristyle garden, planted with trees and shrubs, frequently had an outdoor dining area (*triclinium*), shaded by a canopy of vines. Several of the inns in the town, such as the so-called *caupona* of Euxinus, had a small back garden planted with vines, which doubtless provided some of the wine drunk in the establishment as well as the promise of 'rest for the weary self beneath the shady vine', offered by the hostess in the delightful Latin poem, the *Copa*. Most remarkable of all are the several substantial market vineyards within the walls of the town, the most noteworthy of which was the walled vineyard just across the piazza from the amphitheatre with over 2,000 trellised vines, a press room, two dining areas shaded by pergolas of vines, and a small retail outlet on the main road. These discoveries prove that the descriptions of relaxation with a drink beneath a canopy of vines to be found in the poets, as well as the paintings of vine-covered pergolas and trellises to be found on Roman walls, were not just artistic conceits, but reflected the everyday reality. J.J.P.

Grimal, P., *Les Jardins romains* (Paris, 1943).
Jashemski, W. F., *The Gardens of Pompeii* (New York, 1979).

ROMANIA, sometimes spelt **Roumania** or **Rumania**, eastern European country with the greatest acreage under vine—just under 200,000 ha/494,000 acres in 1992. In this respect it is rivalled only by neighbouring Moldova, with which Romania has powerful historical and cultural links. This latter eastern part of the old province of Moldavia, also once called Bessarabia, was annexed by Russia during the Second World War. It is now an independent, Romanian-speaking republic; see MOLDOVA.

History

The coastal region of what is now Romania (modern Dobrudja) was settled by the Ancient GREEKS in the 7th century BC and they may have introduced viticulture. Vine-growing was certainly well established in Tîrnave, Odobeşti, and Drăgăşani when this region was part of the province of Dacia in the first century AD, and some archaeological evidence suggests that Romania may have a 6,000 year-old tradition of vine-growing.

The region was overrun by successive cultural influences, including the Ottoman Turks (and, later, Russians and Austrians), but vine-growing seems to have continued without interruption. Romania's existence as a united political unit comprising the old principalities of Wallachia and Moldavia dates only from 1861, when the total vineyard area began to grow from 95,000 ha to 150,000 ha by 1884, when the PHYLLOXERA louse began its devastation of Romanian vineyards. As a result, resistant HYBRIDS dominated wine production in 1930.

Between 1947 and 1989 Romania was a socialist republic and in the 1950s and 1960s, in an effort to increase productivity, the total vineyard area was expanded, to more than 340,000 ha by 1972. Immediately prior to the revolution of December 1989 this figure had decreased, largely as a result of uprooting hybrids, to about 275,000 ha. During the communist period the state gradually increased its share of vineyard holdings to about 30 per cent of the total by the end of the 1980s. About 60 per cent was owned by CO-OPERATIVES, leaving just 10 per cent in private hands, and those of the state-funded viticultural institutes.

Romanians have always consumed their own wine more enthusiastically than other eastern bloc countries. Whereas Bulgaria and Hungary export nearly 90 and 70 per cent respectively of their total wine production, Romania exported barely 15 per cent in the early 1990s—although significant efforts to harness Romania's underdeveloped wine industry to earn foreign currency were being made in the post-communist era.

In the early 1990s the state's official exporting body became a private company incorporating western European interests and a limited number of shareholding wineries.

Geography and climate

Although there is a coastal plain on the Black Sea coast, the country is dominated by mountains, the north–south southern Carpathians and the east–west Transylvanian alps whose average altitude is about 1,000 m/3,280 ft. The Wallachian plain stretches south to the river Danube and Bulgaria, while the Pannonian plain lies between the hills and Hungary to the east. Romania's wine regions are widely dispersed thoughout the country, in a wide range of different conditions.

Romania lies on much the same latitudinal span as France, although its climate is much more extreme. The climate is CONTINENTAL although the Black Sea influence helps to moderate winter temperatures in Dobrudja by the coast. Temperatures are high but rarely excessive in the growing season, and rainfall during the harvest is unusual in most wine regions.

Viticulture

Vine-training systems used here traditionally were mainly GOBELET or single, double, or multiple bows, as in the MOSEL, and as still in Odobeşti. From the late 1950s a state plan to raise foreign currency by export-funded research has resulted in today's impressive predominance of neatly wired rows using concrete posts and mainly GUYOT, LENZ MOSER, or SYLVOZ systems. Yields are low, just 26 hl/ha (1.5 tons/acre) on average, which in some cases reflects old or badly tended vines rather than conservative pruning policy.

IRRIGATION may be used in some years, particularly in the sandy regions along the Danube, Murfatlar, Banat, and Valea lui Mihai, and to a lesser extent in Miniş and Huşi.

Winters can be very harsh in parts of Romania, although many of the longest-established wine regions have MESOCLIMATES which offer some protection. Trees may be used as WINDBREAKS in new areas such as Ştefăneşti-Argeş. Some particularly FROST-prone valley floor vineyards are being uprooted, and higher vine training systems are used to protect against frost in other areas.

Wine-making

Many co-operatives still lack full TEMPERATURE CONTROL facilities, but fully controlled stainless steel tanks are used for most quality wine production in wineries formerly owned by the state. Special ROTOFERMENTERS have been designed in conjunction with the University of Craiova, and are used for a high proportion of Romanian red wines, and also for aromatic white wines.

DESTEMMING is compulsory for better-quality wines. In the least ripe years wines other than quality wines may be CHAPTALIZED (although not sweet wines). ACIDIFICATION is allowed in some circumstances, although it is rarely needed in Transylvania and Moldavia. Indeed there has been experimentation with DEACIDIFICATION of some wines from Iaşi with TOTAL ACIDITIES of up to 15 g/l expressed as tartaric acid.

If wine is aged in oak, it is usually large, old Carpathian oak. The country had a severe shortage of modern BOTTLING facilities in the early 1990s.

Vine varieties

Romania is notable for the number and scope of its grapevine collections. It has a wide range of vine varieties, many of them purely local specialities. Romanians with an eye to export markets, however, are particularly proud of the extent of their CABERNET SAUVIGNON plantings, which totalled 7,200 ha in the early 1990s, more than any single country other than France, the United States, and Chile, and more than twice as much as Bulgaria, which has established such a successful export market for its Cabernet.

The most planted varieties by far are two FETEASCAS, Fetească Albă (White) and a 1930s crossing of it, Fetească Regală

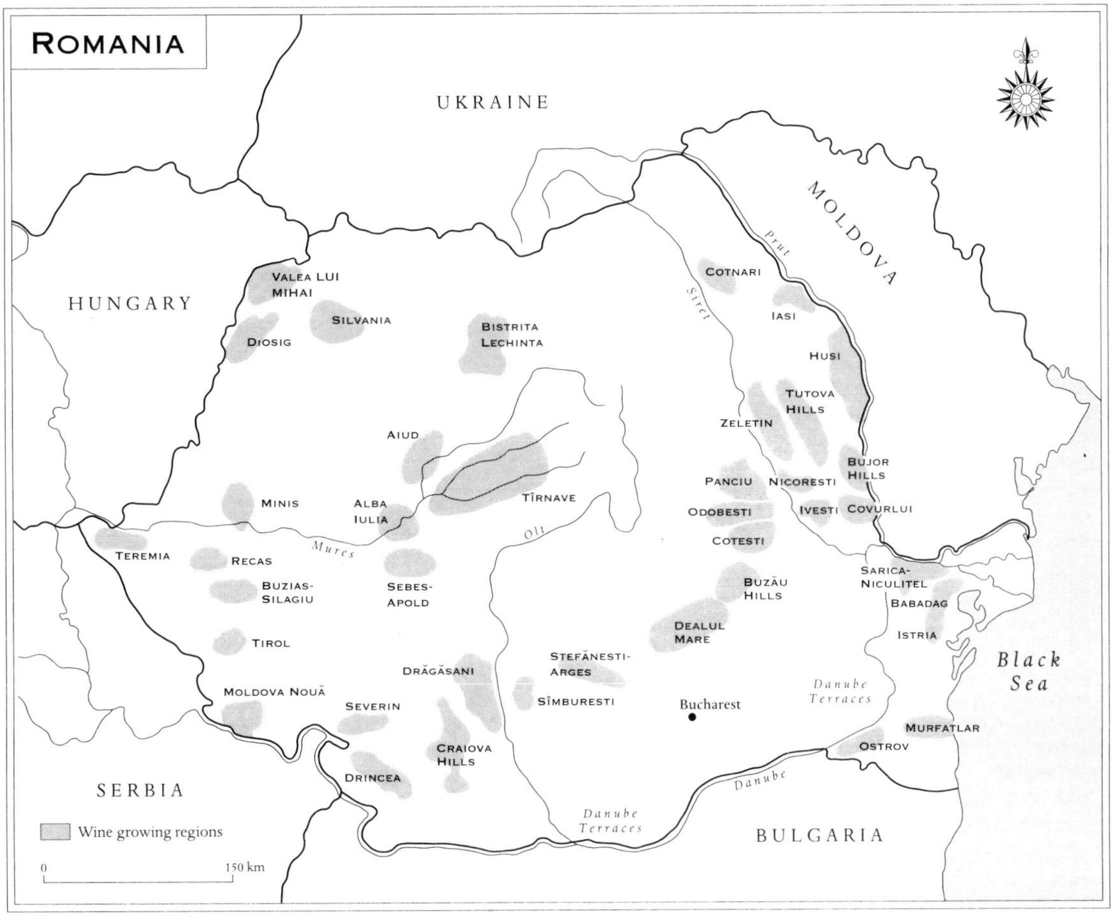

(Royal), both of which can produce perfumed white wines of varying sweetness and quality. Riesling Italico or WELSCHRIESLING is the next most planted vine variety, while the white ALIGOTÉ from Burgundy and red MERLOT from Bordeaux are also planted on more than 10,000 ha of Romanian vineyard each. Other significant international varieties include SAUVIGNON Blanc, PINOT GRIS, RKATSITELI, MUSCAT OTTONEL, and GEWÜRZTRAMINER among white wine grapes and PINOT NOIR among red wine grapes. In 1990 there were also just under 1,000 ha of CHARDONNAY.

Specifically Romanian varieties planted to a significant extent include the light berried 'fat' Grasă and the aromatic 'frankincense' TĂMÎIOASĂ Românească grapes of COTNARI, and Galbenă of Odobeşti which makes light, crisp whites with a relatively long life. Of dark-berried varieties Roşioară is relatively common for everyday wine, Băbească can produce light, fruity reds, and Fetească Neagră is capable of producing deep coloured, age-worthy red wines.

Other specifically Romanian varieties planted to a significant extent include Majarcă Albă and Steinschiller Roz (planted in Banat); Plăvaie grown in Odobeşti; Berbecel planted in Drincea, a clone of Pinot Blanc called Selection Carriere planted in Iveşti; and Crîmposie planted in Drăgăşani.

There are also limited plantings of such varieties as KÉKOPORTO (more usually called simply Oporto), and a clone of Pinot Noir called Burgund Mare ('big Burgundian'), whose produce has good colour and good rot resistance.

Romanian viticultural stations have been enthusiastic developers of vine CROSSINGS, including for example Columna, a crossing of Pinot Gris and Grasă, and the red wine grape Codană.

Wine laws

Romania has developed a relatively sophisticated wine law, predicated as in the GERMAN WINE LAW on MUST WEIGHTS. This original law was recognized by the EUROPEAN UNION in 1972 and 1975, although it was under review in the mid 1990s and may well change. *Vin de masa* is wine at its most basic, for local consumption only. VS is made from grapes a notch higher than this and must have a POTENTIAL ALCOHOL of 10.5 per cent, while VSO wines claim some denomination of origin. Specific grape varieties must be used. VSOC wines represent the top of the range and there are three quality categories: late harvest (CMD), late harvest with NOBLE ROT (CMI), and selected late harvest with noble rot (CIB, sometimes translated as Sélection de Grains Nobles) which incorporates a minimum RESIDUAL SUGAR level of 60 g/l. With minimum permitted OECHSLE levels of 95, 100, and 112° respectively, these last three categories are Romania's answer to SPÄTLESE, AUSLESE, and BEERENAUSLESE.

Wine regions

The Romanian wine regions can be divided into eight distinct zones (see map): the plateau of Transylvania in the middle of the country; the Pannonian plain on the Hungarian border in the old province of Crişana; the Moldavian hills on the eastern slopes of the Carpathians; the warm, central Muntenia region in the southern Carpathians; the Oltenia hills to the immediate west; the Banat Hills towards the border with Serbia in the former Yugoslavia; the knolls of Dobruja between the Danube and the Black Sea; and the flatter Danube terraces.

Transylvania This high central region produces almost exclusively white wines. The most important and oldest Transylvanian wine region is **Tîrnave**, also sometimes spelt **Tarnave**. These are some of Romania's coolest vineyards at ALTITUDES up to 300 m/984 ft on slopes which can approach those of the MOSEL in steepness. (The mainly white wines also have an appealing Mosel-like acidity; reflecting the medieval immigration of Saxon settlers from the Mosel valley to the region.) One of the most common varieties is Fetească Regală, often called Dănăşana here since it was developed in the Transylvanian commune of Daneş. The other Fetească, Welschriesling, Muscat Ottonel, and the Austrian NEUBURGER are also grown here. Wine styles are relatively Germanic. Some sparkling wines are also made, and Transylvanian wine was sold for more than £2 a case in London in the 1840s.

Vines are also grown on south-facing hills in the **Alba Iulia** region along the Mureş river, and benefit from the usually rather warmer autumn weather here. **Aiud** is distinguished as the site of Romania's historic school of viticulture, and has a long history of producing fine white wines. A FLOR sherry style wine is now produced.

In the far south of Transylvania are the **Sebeş** and **Apold de Sus** wine regions, where the proximity of the southern mountains lowers overall temperatures slightly. Apold's Iordană vine makes high-acid, low alcohol wine used mainly for Apold sparkling wines.

The **Bistrita-Lechinta** vineyards are Transylvania's northernmost, and dampest. SOIL EROSION can help ripening by radiation here, and some vineyards consist of TERRACES, typically on south-facing slopes.

Crişana This region is so far west that parts of it are climatologically influenced by the Adriatic. This is certainly true of **Miniş** in the south, whose wines have been renowned since the 15th century. Springs can be so mild on the south- and south west-facing slopes on the foothills of the Zarand mountains that BUDBREAK is usually earlier than in the rest of Romania. Annual rainfall is about 600 mm/23 in, but is often as little as 200 mm during the growing season. Soils vary considerably and include VOLCANIC, SHALE, LIMESTONE together with some GRAVEL, CLAY, and iron oxide. This is one of the few parts of Crişana known for its red wines, notably those made from Cadarcă (the Hungarian KADARKA). The traditional white variety in the Măderat region is Mustoasă, which makes light, crisp wine. Cabernet Sauvignon, Merlot, Welschriesling, Muscat Ottonel, and Fetească Regală are more recent imports.

Silvania includes the vineyards of Zalău, Şamşud, Şimleul

The Marlborough region of **New Zealand's** South Island, epitomized by Montana's Brancott vineyard in the Wairau valley, was created so recently, in the early 1970s, that **mechanization** was an automatic assumption.

Silvaniei, and Rătești and is further north than the Transylvanian vineyards, but the climate is moderated by the Mezeș mountains so that winters are less harsh in these gentle, and sometimes quite steeply eroded, valleys. Ardeleancă is a local vine variety, although more recent plantings have been of the two Feteascăs and Iordană. Ardeleancă is officially authorized close to the Hungarian border in the **Diosig** region although the region is best known for very basic wine and TABLE GRAPES raised on richer soils, as is **Valea lui Mihai** on the Hungarian border where sandy, loose soils are effectively a continuation of the Great Plain (see HUNGARY), where mainly basic white grapes and hybrids are planted.

Moldavia (See MOLDOVA for details of the eastern part of the old Romanian province of Moldavia.) Possibly the oldest, and certainly the most famous wine region of what is now Romania is Cotnari, whose golden nectar was at one time almost as sought after as those of TOKAY and CONSTANTIA. For more details of this specific sweet wine, see COTNARI. Vineyards are typically sited on the slopes of south- and south west-facing amphitheatres which protect the vines from the harsh north winds. Altitudes can vary from 100 to almost 400 m. The region enjoys more than 2,000 hours of sunshine in an average year, and annual rainfall is only about 550 mm. Soil types include RENDZINA, chernozem, and podsols. Grasă is the variety responsible for most of the best sweet wines, supplemented by Tămîioasă, but Muscat Ottonel is also grown, together with Fetească Albă, Frîncușa, and the related Tîrtără vines are also grown and produce dry and medium dry lesser wines.

Iași, is the historic capital of Moldavia and a major trading centre between east and west. On the surrounding hills the traditional Moldavian Fetească Albă is grown, mainly for better-quality wines, together with the more recent Fetească, Frîncușa, Welschriesling, Aligoté, and, unusually but successfully, Muscadelle. A SPUMANTE style of wine is also made here from Muscat Ottonel. A range of red varieties, including Merlot and Cabernet Sauvignon, is also cultivated around Iași, where Băbească shows perhaps its finest form.

In the nearby **Huși** vineyards sweet, scented, deep yellow wine is made from Busuioacă grapes grown at Bohotin. Another local variety is Zghihară, which is closely related to Galbenă but ripens earlier, and reaches higher sugar levels.

Odobești is one of the largest and oldest viticultural centres in Romania and may well date from the Roman era. The gentle south west-facing slopes are protected from the north by the Carpathians. Vines are traditionally supported in a horizontal star shape by up to 20 thin props. Deep, fertile soils are mainly dedicated to everyday table wine made from the local Galbenă grape, but it is sensitive to both DROUGHT and GREY ROT. Superior-quality wines are made from Fetească Albă, Welschriesling, and Șarba, a CROSSING of Welschriesling and Tămîioasă developed at the Odobești research station in 1972 which has a grapey aroma and good acidity. In **Panciu**, to the immediate north of Odobești, winters are colder, winds stronger, and HAIL more frequent, but some good still white and sparkling wines are made. **Cotești** just south of Odobești, on the other hand, is distinctly warmer and can produce some deep coloured red wines from Merlot, Cabernet Sauvignon, Fetească Neagră, and Băbească. **Nicorești**, east of Panciu, is another red wine region, particularly well known for its Băbească.

On the Bîrlad plateau is the newly recognized **Zeletin** region and the **Tutova Hills** where most of the wine produced is of table wine standard.

In Galați some promising red and white wines are made in the **Bujor Hills** in the north east and in the sand dunes of **Ivești**, while **Covurlui** makes whites of superior quality.

Muntenia On south-facing foothills of the Carpathians north of the capital Bucharest is the historic and extensive **Dealul Mare**, occasionally written Dealu Mare ('big hill'), region, best known for its red wines. Vineyards are at altitudes of between 130 and occasionally even 600 m, protected from winter freeze by TOPOGRAPHICAL quirks and special local MESOCLIMATES. This is principally a red wine district with Pinot Noir, Cabernet Sauvignon, Merlot, and Fetească Neagră grown in the Valea Călugărească, or 'valley of the monks'. Some superior white wines are also produced, however, including some late harvest wines, using the two main Cotnari varieties. Tămîioasă from Pietroasele, which may be BOTRYTIZED, has a particular reputation. Local vine specialities include Bășicată and Gordin, known respectively as Slavita and Gordan at Drăgășani in Oltenia (see below).

To the immediate east and north east the **Buzău Hills**, a continuation of Dealul Mare, produce some quality red wine from Merlot, Cabernet Sauvignon, and 'Burgund Mare' as well as whites from Welschriesling, Aligoté, and Fetească, and Muscat Ottonel.

Ștefanești-Argeș is a relatively new wine area with a MACROCLIMATE similar to that of Moldavia. Terraced vineyards, sheltered at times by new tree plantations, are situated on south east- and south west-facing slopes, and produce mainly VSO wines.

Oltenia The extensive (10,000 ha) vineyards of *Drăgășani* west of Bucharest are said to date from Roman times and stretch over 60 km in the foothills of the Transylvanian alps up to an altitude of nearly 700 m. Average rainfall is more than 700 mm and hail is a frequent hazard. The Sauvignon vine performs well here, and can produce late harvest wines, although a range of local varieties also yield a range of more basic wines. **Sîmburești** is a much smaller wine region which specializes in red wine production, as do the **Craiova Hills**, which have a certain reputation for their Cabernet Sauvignon. **Severin** is the sunniest and warmest of the southern Carpathian wine regions and concentrates on red wine production. **Drincea** is another wine region whose history dates to pre-phylloxera times. The south-facing replanted slopes of

Two faces of Italian wine-making: small **barriques** in front of a big, oval *botte* traditionally favoured for **cask ageing** wine in Italy. The d'Angelo brothers Lucio (left) and Donato taste their Canneto, one of **Basilicata's** more modern wines made from the local **Aglianico** grape.

Grape-decorated house at Hogilag in the Tirnave region of **Romania**.

Vinju Mare now produce heavy Cabernet Sauvignon, grassy Merlot, and some Pinot Noir.

Banat One of the few proper names to have reached export markets on Romanian wine labels, Banat was the name of a province on the Yugoslav border. **Teremia** is the most westerly wine region in Romania and lies between the Hungarian and VOJVODINA borders. Densely planted vineyards on sandy soil produces mainly basic table wines. In the less favourable climate of **Recaş** to the south, south-facing slopes are planted with Cabernet Sauvignon, Kadarka, and, with notable success, Burgund Mare, which also peforms well in the **Tirol** region to the south. In **Buziaş-Silagiu** the climate is milder and white wines are a speciality, particularly those made from the local Creaţa vine grown on the hillsides, where it is much less productive than on the sandy plain. The **Moldova Nouă** region by the river Danube enjoys some of Romania's mildest winters and no WINTER PROTECTION of vines is needed, even though they are planted at altitudes of about 300 m. Burgund Mare, Cabernet Sauvignon, Merlot, and Oporto are all planted here as well as Fetească Regală, Welschriesling, and Muscat Ottonel.

Dobrudja **Murfatlar** is the most important wine region on the Romanian coast. This warm region is cooled by breezes from the Black Sea, but can have as many as 300 days of sunshine each year and rainfall betwen April and October averages only 150 to 200 mm. Late harvest wines are a speciality here and the concentration of SUGAR IN GRAPES can reach 430 g/l some years. Noble rot is much rarer here than in Cotnari, however. Chardonnay was introduced here as early as 1907 in an effort to create something like champagne from the chalky soils in some parts of the region. There are also substantial plantings of Pinot Gris, Welschriesling, Muscat Ottonel, and Sauvignon. Pinot Noir and Merlot tend to be planted on north-facing slopes in an effort to prolong RIPENING, while a sweet late harvest Cabernet Sauvignon is also produced.

In **Babadag-Istria**, the climate is similar to Murfatlar and red wines from Merlot, Cabernet Sauvignon, and Burgund Mare are produced in the main, while the vineyards of **Sarica-Niculiţel**, on hills overlooking Tulcea and the Danube just before it reaches the delta, produce whites from Aligoté, Pinot Gris, Muscat Ottonel, and Rkatsiteli as well. **Ostrov** is largely devoted to TABLE GRAPE production, but some Merlot/Cabernet red wines from Lake Oltina have been exported.

Danube Terraces Most of the vines grown in the Danube Terraces are devoted to table grapes, but some wine is produced in the regions of Dacilor, Calafat, Sadova-Corabia, and Brăila. The climate is similar to that of Severin in Oltenia.

See also COTNARI.

ROME, CLASSICAL. '*Vita vinum est*' ('Wine is life'), exclaimed Trimalchio to his dinner guests (Petronius, *Satyricon* 34). Wine was deeply embedded in Roman culture at all levels; it was as much a staple for the poor as for the wealthy. So the evidence is particularly rich, detailed, and varied—as rich, indeed, as for any aspect of ancient society. There are the casual, but often illuminating, references in the poets, in letters, and even in the graffiti scatched on inn walls. All the AGRICULTURAL TREATISES, one of the largest bodies of technical literature to survive from antiquity, devote great space to detailed discussion of viticulture (see in particular CATO, *De agri cultura passim*, from the 2nd century BC, VARRO, *De re rustica* Book 1, from the end of the 1st century BC, COLUMELLA, *De re rustica*, particularly Books 3–5, 12, and the separate work 'On trees' from the mid 1st century AD, and his contemporary PLINY, *Natural History*, Books 14, 17, and 23, and PALLADIUS from late antiquity). What these reveal is a lively debate, which has its modern counterpart, about CLIMATE, VINE VARIETIES, PLANTING and PRUNING techniques, technological developments, and the economics of viticulture. A more surprising source of information is Roman law; the sale of wine, particularly wholesale, raised considerable problems for the law of sale, when there was the question of what guarantee of quality the buyer might reasonably expect. The legal texts tell us much about the details of how wine was marketed. Equally interesting material comes from medical writers. Wine played an important role in medical treatment, and much of the information about the colour, quality, and effects of particular wines owes far less to the tasting books of Roman connoisseurs than it does to the notes of the doctors (see MEDICINE). Finally there is ARCHAEOLOGY, of which the most spectacular recent achievement, inspired by the underwater excavation of Roman wrecks, has been the identification of the types of AMPHORAE used to carry the wine and the recognition of the scale and pattern of the wine trade.

Both Pliny (*Natural History* 14. 21–39) and Columella (*De re rustica* 3. 2. 7–28) offer surveys of the main ANCIENT VINE VARIETIES (any attempt to identify these with modern varieties must be largely conjectural). Columella's classification is the most revealing. His first class consists of the varieties used for the great Italian wines, most notably the types of Aminnean. His second class is high-yielding vines, which nevertheless can produce wines which can be aged successfully. The final group is those prolific vine types used largely to produce *vin ordinaire*. This reveals that wine producers were aware of the great diversity in the markets for their wines and chose their vines accordingly.

'Classic wines can only be produced from vines grown on trees,' was Pliny's verdict (*Natural History* 17. 199). Although this was disputed by some agricultural writers, the most striking fact about Roman viticulture was that the great wines—CAECUBAN, FALERNIAN, etc.—nearly all came from vineyards in which the vines were trained up trees, usually elms or poplars. However, all the normal forms of TRAINING vines were also known and described by agricultural writers, from the low, free-standing BUSH VINE to elaborate TRELLIS SYSTEMS. As in every age, the literature abounds with references to extraordinary YIELDS (for example, over 300 hl/ha (17 tons/acre), high but not unknown in modern terms); but Columella (*De re rustica* 3. 3) considers the economics of a vineyard on the basis of yields ranging from 21 to 63 hl/ha, which range may look familiar to modern vine-growers concerned with wine quality.

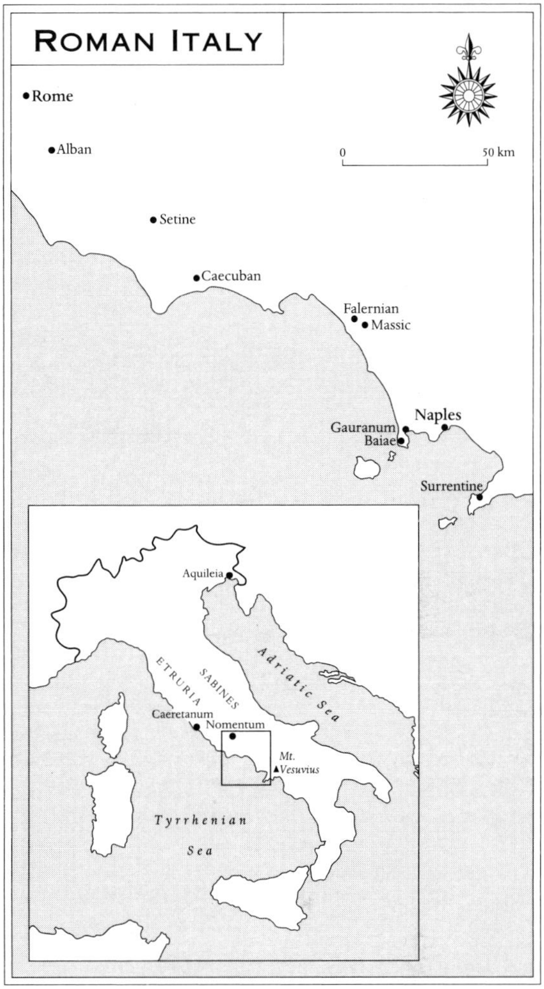

'Be the first to dig the ground . . . but the last to harvest the grapes' was the advice in VIRGIL's poem of the countryside (*Georgics* 2. 410). This is just one of many clues which suggest that the Romans sought to make their white wines—and nearly all the great wines were white—sweet.

The treading of the grapes was usually, but not invariably, followed by their PRESSING. The must obtained from the treading was sometimes kept separate, but more frequently added to that from the pressing. The grape pulp could be subject to a second pressing, or even, after being soaked for a day, a third, to produce a thin drink for slaves (see PIQUETTE). From the press room the must was run off to ferment in large DOLIA, which were frequently sunk in the ground. The wine could be racked off into amphorae at any stage from 30 days after being made, to various points through the winter and into the next spring. Many white wines of note were probably left SUR LIE, with the possible consequent enhancement of flavour and complexity. To those in the post-PASTEUR age of stainless steel vats, Roman wine-making must seem somewhat slapdash and uncertain. However, the accumulated wisdom and experience conveyed in all the AGRICULTURAL TREATISES demonstrate a commitment to care (for example, in stressing the need for cleanliness at all stages) and sophisticated observation (as in the siting of the press room and *dolia*-yard with regard to the ambient TEMPERATURE during fermentation).

'We consider the best wine is one that can be aged without any preservative; nothing must be mixed with it which might obscure its natural taste. For the most excellent wine is one which has given pleasure by its own natural qualities.' Columella's statement (*De re rustica* 12. 19) reflected current opinion. However, it is made at the beginning of a long discussion of additives for wine. Some of these are less objectionable to modern opinion than others. It was a normal practice to add boiled must to wine either during fermentation or soon after to act both as a sweetener and, so it was thought, a preservative. The addition of quantities of chalk or marble dust may be seen as attempts to modify the acidity of the wine (see DEACIDIFICATION). More surprising is the general advocacy of the addition of seawater or salt during fermentation. This was a distinctive Greek practice, taken over by the Romans. It was supposed both to 'enliven a wine's smoothness' (Pliny, *Natural History* 14. 120) (presumably increase acidity) and to prevent a mouldy taste (Columella, *De re rustica* 12. 23. 2). RESINATED WINE was common. So were FLAVOURED WINES with all kinds of herbal and plant additives, of which the primary effect was to disguise the inferior nature of the basic wine.

For Roman connoisseurs the key to a good wine was AGEING. In Roman law the distinction between 'new' wine and 'old' was that the old had been aged for at least one year. Of course, vast quantities of wine were drunk within the first year. However, a higher price could be expected if the producer could hold back even for as short a period as the summer following the vintage. As for the great wines, both white and red, their key characteristic was their capacity to be aged for considerable periods. Falernian was considered drinkable after 10 years, but at its best between 15 and 20 years; SURRENTINE, another white wine, came into its own after 25 years. It may be that being sealed in an amphora which had an impermeable coating of resin meant that the ageing process was slowed. On the other hand, CATO recommends that air space should be left when amphorae are filled, which must have led to OXIDATION on a level which would be unacceptable now. The frequent mention of the darkening of the colour of the great whites suggests that MADERIZATION was normal and, indeed, desired. The final curiosity of Roman wines was the widespread practice of storing them in lofts over hearths, where they were exposed to smoke and heat. This was seen as a means of accelerating ageing, for which the nearest modern parallel may be the process of heating which MADEIRA is subjected to.

The heyday for Roman viticulture was the 1st century BC and the 1st two centuries AD. This was the time for the recognition and development of great wines in central ITALY which could compete successfully with those from the Greek world (see GREECE). It was a period of considerable experimentation and innovation, not least in western areas such as GAUL and SPAIN, which saw the creation of their own vineyards, often by Italian settlers after the areas had become part of Rome's empire. There was clearly a massive increase in the market for wine throughout the empire. Rome itself, with a fluctuating population of a million or more, sucked in imports from Italy and the provinces, while the process of the Romanization of the provinces included the stimulation of new markets for a commodity which was at the heart of Roman culture. The market for wine was a very diverse one, ranging from the élite's desire for great wine to the mass market for wines (for which the thousands of amphorae recovered from sites throughout the empire and beyond are ample testimony). Great claims have been made for the way in which these markets may have brought about a major transformation in the agrarian economy of Italy and elsewhere. But there is need for caution. It is clear from archaeology that only vineyards within easy reach of the sea and a port could participate effectively in the international trade. Furthermore, despite the claims of the Roman agronomists, questions could be, and were, raised about viticulture. Members of the Roman élite certainly had much of their wealth tied up in land, while at the same time constantly being strapped for the considerable quantities of cash which were needed in public life in Rome. To them the high initial investment and the costs of experienced manpower and of equipment could be offputting. Columella's elaborate defence of the profitability of viticulture (*De re rustica* 3. 3), although it would not pass muster with a modern accountant, can be used to suggest a return of, perhaps, 10 per cent on investment, which compared well with most other methods of land use. J.J.P.

Billiard, R., *La Vigne dans l'antiquité* (Lyons, 1913).
Purcell, N., 'Wine and wealth in Ancient Italy', *Journal of Roman Studies*, 75 (1985), 1–25.
Tchernia, A., *Le Vin de l'Italie romaine* (Rome, 1986).

ROMORANTIN, a white, eastern Loire grape variety that is fast fading from the French *vignoble*. Cour CHEVERNY is an appellation especially created for Romorantin grown just west of Blois.

RONCO, north east Italian term derived from the verb *roncare* (to clear land, particularly land which is either wooded or overgrown with undergrowth), which has been used for over a century in a wide swathe of northern Italy to indicate a HILLSIDE VINEYARD. The first appearance on a wine label dates from the early 1970s, when it was used by Mario Pasolini in the province of Brescia in LOMBARDY for his Ronco di Mompiano, a VINO DA TAVOLA from MARZEMINO and MERLOT grapes. More or less contemporary examples can also be found from the OLTREPÒ PAVESE, frequently with the diminutive form **Ronchetto**. The widest current use is in FRIULI, where the dialect form is *ronc*. Examples can also be found in the ALTO ADIGE and in ROMAGNA.

See also COLLI. D.T.

RONDINELLA, Italian red grape variety grown in the VENETO.

ROOT, one of the three major organs of higher plants, the others being leaves and fruits/seeds. All three are completely interdependent but roots are the least studied and the least understood. Their main functions are anchorage of the plant, storage of reserves of CARBOHYDRATES, absorption of WATER and MINERALS from the soil, and synthesis of specific compounds such as reduced nitrogen compounds and CYTOKININS.

The roots of a commercial vineyard derive from the roots that develop at the base of CUTTINGS, which are more divided than the tap-root style of a SEEDLING's root system. The position and number of the main framework roots, the 'spreaders' which extend out and down, are determined during the first three years. From these, branches, or 'sinkers', continue down to an extent controlled by the overall health of each vine and the suitability of the soil (see SOIL WATER). Although most vine roots occur in the top metre of soil (less if unfavourable soil horizons impede their penetration) there are many examples where roots have penetrated to 6 m/20 ft or more; often these examples are found in dry conditions such as the DOURO valley. The root framework supports a large number of fibrous roots which, by their continuing growth, comb the soil for minerals and water. Root density, which reflects the frequency of formation of root laterals, is highest in friable soil with continuing supplies of minerals, water, and oxygen.

Vine roots are much less dense than those of many other crop plants. Different species of VITIS have different root distribution and habits, a difference that is deliberately used in the breeding of ROOTSTOCKS. B.G.C.

Van Zyl, J. L., 'The grapevine root and its environment', Republic of South Africa, Department of Agriculture and Water Supply, Technical Committee 215 (Stellenbosch, 1988).

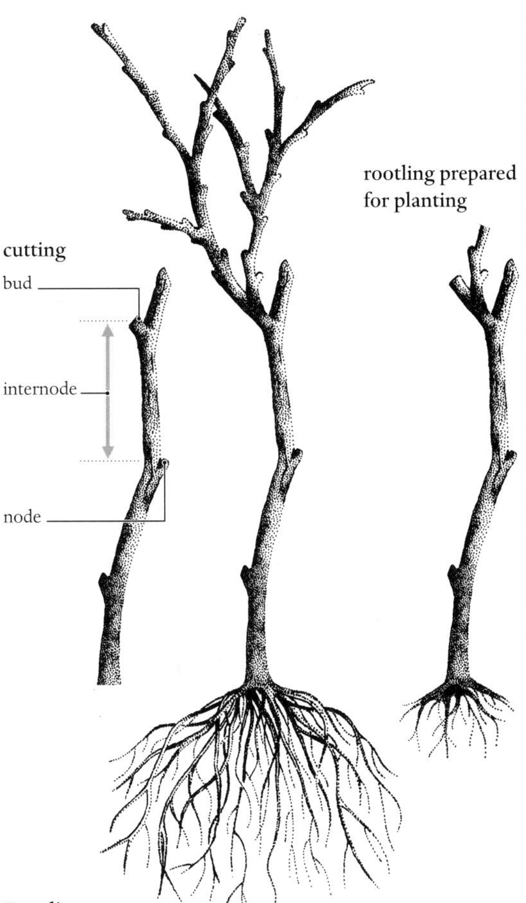

Rootling

ROOT GROWTH, that part of a vine's annual growth cycle which takes place below ground. In most fruit trees, the spring flush of root growth occurs at the same time as BUDBREAK, but for the vine it is delayed. There are two peaks of root growth during the year. The first takes place at FLOWERING of the shoots in early summer, and the second coincides with the normal HARVEST period in autumn. There is an important correlation between the size, health, and activity of the vine's root system and the growth of shoots and leaves above ground, because the roots act as storage sites for the vine's crucial reserves of CARBOHYDRATES and also the production by the roots of HORMONES such as cytokinins and gibberellins. Vines with restricted or unhealthy roots have low VIGOUR and this is the basis of the principles of BALANCED PRUNING. Root growth also varies according to VINE AGE. R.E.S.

ROOT KNOT NEMATODE. See NEMATODES.

ROOT LESION NEMATODE. See NEMATODES.

ROOTLING, a one-year-old vine grown in a NURSERY, the most common material used for planting a vineyard. Generally it is a grafted rootling, with the upper fruiting variety, or SCION, grafted on to a rootstock. Most species of the vine genus VITIS, especially VINIFERA varieties, form roots readily on their CUTTINGS, but some are difficult to root; the most difficult are rootstocks with *Vitis berlandieri* or *Vitis champini* genes. Some improvement results from soaking the rootstock cuttings in water before GRAFTING, but treating the cutting base with the AUXIN indole butyric acid (IBA) is most successful. B.G.C.

ROOTSTOCK, the plant forming the root system of a grapevine to which a fruiting variety, or SCION, is grafted. In most vineyards in the world European wine-producing VINIFERA vines are grafted on rootstocks which are, with few exceptions, either varieties of one AMERICAN VINE SPECIES or HYBRIDS of several. See VITIS for details of the different species of this genus. Rootstocks are normally used to overcome soil pests or diseases, but may also be used for special soil conditions.

The use of rootstocks for grapevines became common around 1880 in France in order to combat the devastating root louse phylloxera, which attacked the roots of the European grapevine *Vitis vinifera*, and the control of phylloxera remains a major reason why rootstocks are used—although some wine regions are free of phylloxera (see PHYLLOXERA for details).

There are parts of the world where the choice of rootstock is more debated than the choice of the fruiting variety, since the latter might well be regulated by law or tradition. Even in the traditional viticultural regions of the Old World, the choice of rootstock tends to change with time, helped by long-term experiments and commercial experience. By contrast, in some parts of the New World, the use of rootstocks is relatively new, or prior use has been restricted to only a few locally available rootstock varieties.

While phylloxera has been present in California since 1873, for example, only a few rootstock varieties were used in more recently developed vineyards. The rootstock AXR1 (alternatively ARG1 or Ganzin 1) had been found so adaptable in California it was described in Winkler's textbook as 'the nearest approach to an all-purpose rootstock', and was the majority rootstock, despite Winkler's qualifying phrase that 'resistance to phylloxera is not high'. In the 1980s AXR1 succumbed to phylloxera, and the choice of rootstocks for replanting has been largely based on guesswork, since there was only limited evaluation of other rootstocks under local conditions.

Choice of rootstock

Although at one time it was a common complaint that pre-phylloxera wines are better than those since the invasion (perhaps because early rootstocks were not always ideally matched with soil types), more recent experiments have shown that little effect on wine quality which can be attributed directly to rootstock. The effect of rootstock on wine quality is probably no greater than that of other factors such as soil, climate, fertilization, and irrigation. Certainly rootstocks can influence VIGOUR, and the high-vigour rootstocks such as Rupestris St George can produce canopies so dense that they affect wine quality (see CANOPY MANAGEMENT). Other studies indicate that the high-vigour rootstocks Harmony, Dog Ridge, Freedom, and Ramsey can result in high levels of POTASSIUM and PH in the resultant wine, but again this may be an indirect effect mediated through vigour and excessive canopy SHADE.

Any vigorous rootstock which stimulates vegetative growth late in the season will have a detrimental effect on fruit RIPENING and therefore on wine quality (see VINE PHYSIOLOGY). The use of rootstocks has also led to an increase in vine CHLOROSIS in those regions where limestone soils are common. Similarly, some rootstocks can induce MAGNESIUM deficiency which, when severe, can inhibit PHOTOSYNTHESIS and ripening. Perhaps the most significant negative effect of all has been the impact of the universal adoption of GRAFTING on the spread of VIRUS DISEASES; rootstocks do not always show virus symptoms, and it can easily be shown that the spread of virus diseases is increased by grafting. LEAFROLL VIRUS in particular delays ripening and can substantially reduce wine quality, and recent work on VINE IMPROVEMENT has concentrated on avoiding the inadvertent spread of virus diseases by grafting.

Rootstocks can have a dramatic effect on YIELD. In the absence of a rootstock, a vine grown on its own roots may not grow at all and die because of root damage from phylloxera or NEMATODES. Grafting on to a rootstock suitable to LIME conditions or DROUGHT can, on the other hand, increase yield dramatically.

Rootstock selection for any particular vineyard may be guided by known soil pests or diseases (especially nematodes and phylloxera), by suitability to the soil environment (especially lime content, fertility, drought incidence, and waterlogging), or by the effect on the performance of the scion variety that is desired, such as lower vigour or earlier ripening.

Rootstocks also differ in characteristics that are important to nurserymen. These include the ability of mother plants to produce plenty of wood, the ease with which cuttings root, and also the ease with which they can be grafted.

Rootstock characteristics

Phylloxera resistance The three most resistant AMERICAN VINE SPECIES are *V riparia*, *rupestris*, and *berlandieri*, and the most susceptible species is the European VINIFERA (see VITIS). Interspecific HYBRIDS containing genes from any of the first three species will therefore have satisfactory resistance, and those hybrids including *vinifera* will have suspect resistance. Rootstocks of *vinifera–rupestris* (including AXR1, and Couderc rootstocks 1202 and 93–5) and *vinifera–riparia* parentage should be avoided as possessing insufficient resistance to phylloxera. Interestingly, *vinifera–berlandieri* rootstocks such as 41 B and 333 EM generally have sufficient resistance. A few examples of rootstocks with high phylloxera resistance are Riparia Gloire, 101–14 Mgt, SO 4, and 5 BB.

Nematode resistance Two principal types of NEMATODES are present in vineyard soils. Vitis species having the most resistance to root knot nematodes are *V champini*, *longii*, and *cinerea*. Note that there is some confusion in the naming of some *Vitis* species, including *V champini* and *V longii*. *V longii* is sometimes called *V solonis*, and it has been suggested that, because it is such a variable species, it may be a natural hybrid of other species, including *V candicans*. Similarly, *V champini*, sometimes spelt *V champinii*, was originally described by Planchon as a separate species, but is considered by some as a natural *rupestris–candicans* hybrid, and perhaps to include *berlandieri*. Those having most resistance to the dagger nematode include *V candicans*, *longii*, and *rufotomentosa*. Vines of the MUSCADINIA section of the *Vitis* genus are resistant to both types of nematodes, which explains the interest in this group of vines for rootstock breeding. As for phylloxera, *V vinifera* is very susceptible to nematodes, so any one rootstock will not have resistance to all nematode species, nor indeed to all nematode races. Rootstocks commonly used for nematode tolerance include Ramsey, Dog Ridge, Harmony, 1613 C, 1616 C, SO 4, and Schwarzmann.

Lime tolerance Both *V. vinifera* and *V. berlandieri* contribute tolerance to the soils high in LIMESTONE common in Burgundy and Champagne. Rootstocks acknowledged to have the highest lime tolerance are 41 B, 333 EM, and the more recently bred Fercal.

Drought tolerance *Berlandieri–rupestris* hybrids are best able to tolerate drought, and these include 110 R and 140 Ru, followed by 1103 P and 99 R. *V riparia* species and hybrids have low drought tolerance.

Salt tolerance The chloride component of salty soils can be toxic (see SALINITY). The *V berlandieri* species is considered tolerant, but Australian research has found the *V champini* rootstock Ramsey to be quite tolerant. *V vinifera* is also tolerant.

Vigour The species *V champini*, *berlandieri*, and *rupestris* and their hybrids give the most vigour, and *V riparia* the least. Among the most vigorous rootstocks are therefore Rupestris St George, 99 R, and 110 R, while Riparia Gloire and 101–14 are among the least vigorous. Vigorous vines tend to delay fruit maturity and can substantially reduce red wine colour.

Some internationally important rootstocks

AXR1, otherwise called **ARG1** in France, Australia, and New Zealand, is a *vinifera–rupestris* hybrid made by Ganzin in 1879. The rootstock was initially popular in France but at the turn of the century it was found there and in South Africa to have insufficient phylloxera tolerance. It is popular with growers because the vines are vigorous and yield well, and is favoured by nurserymen because it is easy to graft. It was found satisfactory in California until the 1980s, when it succumbed to a supposed new biotype of phylloxera.

Dog Ridge is a seedling from the species *V champini* which is suggested for use on light textured soils with high nematode contents. It is only moderately resistant to phylloxera. This rootstock is extremely vigorous, so it should not be used in fertile soils, and vines need to be pruned lightly to achieve BALANCE. Although cuttings are difficult to propagate, they graft readily. The rootstock is not suggested for high-quality vineyards.

Fercal is a relatively recent rootstock bred at the Institut Nationale de Recherche Agricole (INRA) at Bordeaux and developed especially for high lime soils. It is a result of crossing a *berlandieri* × Colombard hybrid with 333 EM. It is resistant to phylloxera, and grafts readily. Fercal is of moderate vigour, and more tolerant of chlorosis and drought than 41 B.

Harmony is a hybrid of open pollinated seedlings selected from *V champini* and 1613 C. It was selected at Fresno, California, in 1966, and is quite tolerant of root knot and dagger nematodes. Phylloxera tolerance is, however, low, and vigour moderate to high.

Riparia Gloire de Montpellier is one of the oldest rootstocks used against phylloxera in France. Of the several *riparia* crosses brought in at the time of the phylloxera crisis, this proved the best. It confers excellent phylloxera tolerance and is of low vigour, providing for lower yields of improved-quality fruit and early ripening. This rootstock is suited to soils well supplied with water, but cannot tolerate lime. It is widely used throughout Europe for the production of good-quality wine.

Rupestris St George is sometimes called **Rupestris du Lot** or **Rupestris-monticola**. It was another early introduction to France to fight phylloxera, and the exact origin is unknown. This is an extremely vigorous variety with a long growing season. It has excellent resistance to phylloxera, but vines grafted to it can easily overcrop or set poor crops because of extreme vigour. The vines can be prone to drought on shallow soils. The vine grafts readily. Because of high vigour, it is not used for high-quality vineyards.

Schwarzmann, a *riparia–rupestris* hybrid with high tolerance of phylloxera and nematodes but only moderate vigour. It is suited to deep, moist soils and is not as widely used as it might be.

SO 4, a *berlandieri–riparia* hybrid, is correctly known as **Selection Oppenheim de Teleki No. 4**, from the viticulture school at Oppenheim in Germany. This popular rootstock, used widely in France and Germany, shows excellent phylloxera resistance, and tends to favour fruit set and slightly advanced maturity. Vigour is moderate, as is tolerance to nematodes. SO 4 is not, however, suited to dry conditions. This rootstock roots readily and grafts easily, but is prone to magnesium deficiency.

5 BB Kober is sometimes called **5 BB Teleki**, and is a *berlandieri–riparia*. The seedling was raised by the Hungarian Sigmund Teleki from seeds produced by a French nurseryman. In 1904 some of the most interesting plants were sent to the Austrian Franz Kober, who selected 5 BB. This is quite a vigorous rootstock which is suited to more humid, clay soils. The vines show moderate nematode tolerance, but in many situations vigour is excessive. The rootstock 5 BB is widely used in Europe, especially in Germany and Switzerland.

5 C Teleki is a *berlandieri–riparia* hybrid selected in 1922 by Andre Teleki. The rootstock is similar to 5 BB in aptitude, and is mostly used in Germany.

41 B is an old rootstock obtained by Professor Millardet in 1882 at Bordeaux, and is a hybrid between the *vinifera* variety Chasselas and *berlandieri*. This rootstock has the advantage of being highly tolerant to lime and so it is widely used in Cognac and Champagne. Its resistance to phylloxera is sufficient but not absolute. The vines establish very slowly, and sometimes cannot be field-grafted in the first year. Cuttings root poorly, which makes BENCH GRAFTING difficult. This rootstock is moderately tolerant of drought.

99 Richter is a *berlandieri–rupestris* hybrid created by Franz Richter in 1889. This vigorous rootstock should not be used in cool regions because it can delay ripening. Phylloxera resistance is high and nematode resistance moderate. Lime tolerance is reasonable but it is sensitive to salt. Wet, poorly drained soils should be avoided, and the rootstock is reasonably drought tolerant. 99 R is easy to field graft but performs poorly as a bench graft.

101–14 Millardet et de Grasset is a lower-vigour and early maturing rootstock used in some of the higher-quality vineyards in France. The vine is a *riparia–rupestris* hybrid made by Professor Millardet and the Marquis de Grasset. It has high resistance to phylloxera but moderate nematode tolerance. The vine can tolerate only low lime content and has a shallow root system.

110 R is a relatively old rootstock resulting from a *berlandieri–rupestris* cross made by Franz Richter in 1889. This rootstock is noted for its high vigour and thus tends to delay maturity, especially if planted in fertile soils. 110 R has high phylloxera tolerance but low nematode tolerance. It is moderately lime resistant and quite drought resistant, and so is widely used in MEDITERRANEAN CLIMATES. Initially it was not used extensively because of poor rooting in the nursery.

140 Ruggeri is a hybrid produced in Sicily by Ruggeri using *berlandieri* and *rupestris*. This vigorous rootstock is well suited to dry soils high in lime, and mediterranean climates. Nematode tolerance is low to moderate but phylloxera tolerance is high. This rootstock should not be planted on fertile, moist soils because of possible excess vigour.

161–49 Couderc, *riparia–berlandieri* hybrid obtained in 1888. This rootstock has high resistance to phylloxera but is susceptible to nematodes. Lime tolerance is quite high, but drought tolerance is low.

333 EM (École de Montpellier) is one of the few rootstocks used (with Fercal and 41 B) which has a *vinifera* parent. It was hybridized by Professor Foëx of MONTPELLIER by crossing Cabernet Sauvignon with *berlandieri*. Despite initial fears to the contrary, 333 EM has sufficient phylloxera tolerance. This rootstock is slightly more lime tolerant than 41 B, and is also drought tolerant. However, with some varieties it encourages COULURE. It roots readily as long as the wood is ripe, and grafts easily.

420 A Millardet et de Grasset is one of the oldest rootstocks obtained in 1887 by Professor Millardet and his assistant the Marquis de Grasset. It is a *berlandieri–riparia* hybrid and is highly regarded for good-quality vineyards, being a lower-vigour rootstock which hastens maturity. It is regarded as 'the *riparia* for chalky soils'. Phylloxera tolerance is high but nematode tolerance is low to moderate. The tolerance of limestone is quite high, but the rootstock is susceptible to waterlogging. It roots and grafts satisfactorily.

1103 Paulsen was bred by the director of an American vine nursery in Sicily by crossing *berlandieri* and *rupestris*. It is regarded as a drought-tolerant rootstock with high phylloxera tolerance and moderate nematode resistance. Lime tolerance is intermediate, and vigour moderate to high. It is welcomed by nurserymen as being easy to graft and root.

1613 Couderc is a complex hybrid between Solonis (*riparia–rupestris–candicans*) and Othello (*labrusca–riparia–vinifera*) bred by Georges Couderc in 1881. Phylloxera resistance is low to moderate, but it finds favour because of moderate to high nematode resistance. It is well suited to fertile, sandy, loam soils, and is used mainly in California.

1616 Couderc is a Solonis (*riparia–rupestris–candicans*) cross with *riparia* in 1881 to produce a low-vigour rootstock with high nematode and phylloxera tolerance. It is best suited to more humid soils, and it advances maturity. Lime tolerance is moderate, and salt tolerance good. Grafting and rooting are satisfactory.

3309 Couderc is a *riparia–rupestris* cross made in 1881. George Couderc planted 18 seeds in a row of the nursery where he had added lime; of the five which did not show chlorosis, 3309 C became the most successful. Phylloxera tolerance is high and lime tolerance medium, and it is better suited to humid than drought-prone soils. Rooting and grafting are easy, and the use of this rootstock is widespread. R.E.S.

Galet, P., and Morton, L. T., *A Practical Ampelography* (Ithaca, NY, and London, 1979).
Galet, P., *Précis de viticulture* (4th edn., Montpellier, 1983).
Hardie, W. J., and Cirami, R. M., 'Grapevine rootstocks', in B. G. Coombe and P. R. Dry (eds.) *Viticulture i: Resources in Australia* (Adelaide, 1988).
Pongracz, D., *Rootstocks for Grape-Vines* (Cape Town, 1983).
Winkler, A. J., *et al.*, *General Viticulture* (2nd edn., Berkeley, Calif., 1974).

RORIZ, or **Tinta Roriz**, is the most common of several Portuguese names for the Spanish red wine grape variety TEMPRANILLO, used particularly in the Douro valley, where it is one of the most planted varieties for the production of port. Others include Aragonez and Tinto de Santiago.

ROSADO is Spanish and Portuguese, and **rosato** is Italian, for ROSÉ. See also CLARETE.

ROSÉ DE LOIRE, general, and relatively important, appellation created in 1974 for ROSÉ WINE made from a blend of Loire red grapes (Cabernet Franc, Cabernet Sauvignon, Pineau d'Aunis, Pinot Noir, Gamay, and Grolleau), of which Cabernet constitutes at least 30 per cent. The wine may be produced anywhere within the ANJOU, SAUMUR, and TOURAINE zones and usually lies, in quality terms, somewhere between Rosé d'Anjou and Cabernet d'Anjou, with the disinction that it is always dry.

See also LOIRE.

ROSÉ DES RICEYS, rare, still, pink wine made in the commune of Riceys in the Aube *département*, the southern end of the CHAMPAGNE region. This dark, rose-coloured wine is made by only three producers, from Pinot Noir grapes, but can be one of France's most serious rosés. Like the still red wine of Champagne Bouzy Rouge (see Coteaux CHAMPENOIS), part of its appeal may be its name.

Stevenson, T., *Champagne* (London, 1986).

ROSETTE, almost extinct sweet white wine appellation in SOUTH WEST FRANCE. It includes some of the PÉCHARMANT zone and, for example, just 650 hl/17,160 acres were produced in 1990.

ROSÉ WINE-MAKING, production of wines whose colour falls somewhere in the spectrum between red and white.

Historically, rosé wines have been made by a number of different processes, but today two methods are in general use. The preferred technique is a short MACERATION of the juice with the skins (see SKIN CONTACT) of dark coloured grapes just after CRUSHING for a period long enough to extract the required amount of colour or ANTHOCYANS. The juice is then separated from the skins by DRAINING or PRESSING and FERMENTATION proceeds as in WHITE WINE-MAKING. With the red-skinned GRENACHE grape, traditionally much used for rosés partly because of its relative lack of anthocyans, a maceration of eight to 12 hours is usually sufficient. Highly pigmented grape varieties may need much less contact time, while very lightly coloured grapes may need a day or two's maceration. See also SAIGNÉE.

Many basic rosés are made by blending a small amount of finished red wine into a finished white wine. While a pinkish colour can be achieved by this process, the hue and flavour of such a wine are quite different from those of a wine made by short-term maceration. Pink wines may also be made by using CHARCOAL treatments to remove the colour from red wines which are for some reason not saleable as reds.

CHAMPAGNE is one of the few controlled appellations in which the blending method of rosé wine-making is sanctioned—and in practice rosé CHAMPAGNE is more often made by blending than by maceration.

A VIN GRIS or BLUSH wine is made as above but with no maceration. Both tend to be even paler than most rosés.

A.D.W.

ROSÉ WINES, wines coloured any shade of pink, from hardly perceptible to pale red. For some reason they are rarely known as pink wines, although the English word BLUSH has been adopted for particularly pale rosés. There was also a FASHION in California, from the late 1980s when wine had to be white to be popular, to label pale pink wines made from dark-skinned grapes White, as in WHITE ZINFANDEL (which has spawned a host of supposedly White wines made from such darkly coloured grape varieties as Cabernet, Merlot, Granache, and Barbera).

In France rosés are particularly common in warmer, southern regions where there is local demand for a dry wine refreshing enough to be drunk on a hot summer's day but which still bears some relation to the red wine so revered by the French. PROVENCE is the region most famous for its rosé, often in a strange skittle-shaped bottle, although, in the greater southern RHÔNE (especially TAVEL) and the LANGUEDOC-ROUSSILLON, rosés are at least as common as white wines. The Loire valley also produces a high proportion of rosé wine of extremely varied quality and sweetness levels, particularly around ANJOU. See also ROSÉ DE LOIRE. VIN GRIS and SAIGNÉE are French terms for particular types of rosé.

Spain also takes pink wines seriously—so seriously that it has at least two names for them, depending on the intensity of the colour. A *rosado* is light pink, while darker pink (light red) wines are labelled *clarete*. Portugal's best-known pink wines are exported, as in MATEUS and LANCERS. Pink wines are not especially popular in Italy, where the term used is usually *rosato* although *chiaretto*, meaning claret, is occasionally used for darker rosés. It is only with the greatest of difficulty than German grapes can be persuaded to yield wines that can genuinely be called red rather than rosé. Official German terms for pink wines include WEISSHERBST and, in WÜRTTEMBERG, SCHILLERWEIN. See also ŒIL DE PERDRIX.

ROSEWORTHY, town north of Adelaide in the state of SOUTH AUSTRALIA, close to the Barossa Valley, known in the wine world for the **Roseworthy Agricultural College**, which trained a high proportion of wine-makers and viticulturists in Australia and New Zealand and has contributed greatly to the technical standing of the Australian wine industry (see AUSTRALIAN INFLUENCE).

Roseworthy was Australia's first agricultural college, established in 1883 following the recommendation of a South Australian government commission on agricultural education. (This was just three years after the establishment of similar institutions in Bordeaux and California—see BORDEAUX UNIVERSITY and DAVIS.) Although the first agricultural students were taught some viticulture, instruction in both VITICULTURE and OENOLOGY developed considerably on the appointment of Arthur Perkins to the dual position of State Viticulturalist and Lecturer in Viticulture in 1892.

Perkins, a graduate of MONTPELLIER in 1890, was made Professor of Viticulture in 1895. He developed Roseworthy's vineyard and winery, still used for teaching purposes, and was responsible for the inspection and certification of wines for Australia's already flourishing wine exports to the United Kingdom.

Viticulture and oenology were taught within the Roseworthy Diploma of Agriculture, with oenology an optional third-year subject. In 1936, with encouragement from the wine industry, the College established the two-year Roseworthy Diploma in Oenology (RDOen). Four students enrolled in the first year, with Alan Hickinbotham and Jock Williams as lecturers. Hickinbotham was an excellent chemist and with his students made a significant contribution to wine research during his 18 years at Roseworthy, notably in the areas of FLOR sherry, ACIDITY, ACIDIFICATION, and MALOLACTIC FERMENTATION.

This Diploma course continued until 1978, when a three-year Bachelor of Applied Science in Oenology was introduced. A new winery was opened in 1971. The development of the Australian wine industry greatly increased the number of students. A Graduate Diploma in Wine was introduced in 1980 following the two-year Associate Diploma in Wine Marketing introduced in 1975.

In 1991 Roseworthy Agricultural College merged with the University of Adelaide and continues its work as the Department of Horticulture, Viticulture and Oenology. For more details see ADELAIDE.

T.H.L.

ROSSESE, esteemed red grape variety producing distinctively flavoured varietal wines in the north west Italian region of LIGURIA. The variety has a long history in the region and it has its own DOC in the west of the region in Dolceacqua whose wines are admired, though variable.

ROSSO CONERO, Italian red wine based on MONTEPULCIANO grapes whose full potential is yet to be realized. See MARCHES for more details.

ROSSO DI signifies a red wine from the Italian zone whose name it precedes, often a declassified version of a long- lived, more serious wine such as BRUNELLO DI MONTALCINO or VINO NOBILE DI MONTEPULCIANO.

ROSSO PICENO, Italian red wine based on SANGIOVESE with some MONTEPULCIANO grapes whose full potential is yet to be realized. See MARCHES for more details.

ROT, loose term for the decay, with microbial interference, of any part of the vine. Rot is most commonly used as synonymous with BOTRYTIS BUNCH ROT, which is the most important sort of rot for wine quality; it occurs sometimes in benevolent form as NOBLE ROT, but more commonly causes the loss of yield and quality in its malevolent form as GREY ROT. Other fruit rots include BLACK ROT, SOUR ROT, WHITE ROT, and also rots of other vine parts such as ARMILLARIA ROOT ROT and TEXAS ROOT ROT.

Rot in its common, malevolent form.

ROTARY DRUM VACUUM FILTER, specialized form of earth FILTRATION designed to cope with very dirty liquids, those which contain a high concentration of solids or particles that would rapidly block other filters. It relies on the constant regeneration of the filter medium, which is the same diatomaceous earth material used in other depth filters.

The filter comprises a slowly rotating drum, semi-immersed in the product to be filtered, covered in a fine stainless steel mesh, and fitted with an internal vacuum pump. The filtration cycle begins when a layer of cellulose pre-coating is applied to the drum. Diatomaceous earth is then applied continuously, mixed with the wine. The wine is drawn through the earth by the vacuum and collected in a tank, while the solids are retained in the matrix. The filter surface is regenerated by removing the solids and earth with a scraper knife on the other side of the drum.

These filters are normally used to clarify the products of settled grape juice or wine, such as LEES after crushing, pressing, and settling, and the residue of FININGS such as bentonite. If used carefully they can recover good-quality wine that is otherwise impossible to separate from such solids and would therefore be either discarded or sent as POMACE for distillation.

ROTBRENNER, vine FUNGAL DISEASE found in most of Europe which can cause severe crop losses. Caused by the fungus *Pseudopezicula tracheiphila*,the disease is encouraged by prolonged rainfall and attacks leaves and young bunches. Satisfactory control is obtained with fungicides applied early in the growing season. This disease also affects the grapevine's relative, the Virginia creeper *Parthenocissus quinquefolia*. (See BOTANICAL CLASSIFICATION.) R.E.S.

ROTGIPFLER, the marginally less noble of the two white wine grape varieties traditionally associated with GUMPOLDSKIRCHEN, the dramatically full bodied, long-lived spicy white wine of the Thermenregion district of AUSTRIA. (The other is ZIERFANDLER.) At the end of the 1980s there were about 200 ha/490 acres of Rotgipfler, which ripens late, but earlier than Zierfandler and whose wines are particularly high in EXTRACT, ALCOHOL, and BOUQUET.

ROTHSCHILDS AND WINE. The Rothschilds first entered the world of wine in 1853 when Baron Nathaniel (1812–70), grandson of Mayer Amschel and a member of the English branch of the family, bought Brane Mouton in 1853 and renamed it Ch MOUTON-ROTHSCHILD. This was always common practice among more important CHÂTEAU owners. It was a buyer's market in Bordeaux vineyards then devastated by oidium, or POWDERY MILDEW, and the Rothschild purchase was viewed more as a property transaction than as the acquisition of a distinguished vineyard. When the important 1855 CLASSIFICATION placed Ch Mouton-Rothschild top of the

Baron Philippe de **Rothschild** in his 'decantoir', a chamber specially designed for decanting the wines to be served at his peripatetic dining table.

second growths, however, the Rothschilds were particularly exercised by what they regarded as its unfairly low placing.

Nathaniel was succeeded by his son Baron James (1844–81) and then Baron Henri (1872–1947), who was more interested in literature than wine, and James's widow was responsible for Mouton until the arrival of Henri's younger son Philippe (1902–88) in 1922.

Baron Philippe de Rothschild was to prove one of the most influential forces in the wine business of Bordeaux and beyond. Not only did he acquire two neighbouring Pauillac fifth growth châteaux—Mouton d'Armailhacq (named at various stages Mouton-Baron-Philippe, Mouton-Baronne-Philippe, and Mouton d'Armailhac in 1933 and Clerc Milon in 1970—he established the importance of château BOTTLING, established MOUTON CADET as one of the world's most successful wine BRANDS and an important NÉGOCIANT business in the Médoc, astutely developed the concept (and value) of artist's LABELS, established the finest collection of wine-related works of art in the world, and developed a joint venture with Robert MONDAVI of California, Opus One. In 1988 he was succeeded at Mouton by his daughter Philippine.

Meanwhile, Baron James of the French family bought Ch LAFITE in 1868 in the face of local competition. He died a few months later but is said to have visited the property briefly in the spring of that year. His son Edmond (1845–1934) was to sow, and indeed provide, the seeds for the establishment of the ISRAELI wine industry by making a vast donation in 1882. James's great grandson Élie (1917–) was the family member who eventually took charge of Lafite, subsequently Lafite-Rothschild, until 1974 when his nephew Eric (1940–) became the château's head. In 1962 the fourth growth PAUILLAC Ch Duhart-Milon was acquired, as was the large Bas-MÉDOC property Ch La Cardonne in 1973, although this was exchanged in 1982 for the top POMEROL, Ch L'Évangile. Earlier, in 1984, the leading SAUTERNES property Ch Rieussec was also purchased. Since then substantial shareholdings in Los Vascos in CHILE, the American company Chalone Inc., and a property in Portugal have also been acquired by the Lafite Rothschilds.

In 1973 Baron Edmond (1926–), one of many partners in Lafite but engaged in many other affairs, bought the semi-derelict Ch Clarke of LISTRAC and in 1977 and 1978 built a very large new cuvier and *chai*. In 1979 he added Ch Malmaison in the adjoining commune of MOULIS, which was also treated to major renovation, as well as acquiring two more non-classified châteaux in the Médoc.

In 1994 the English financier Lord (Jacob) Rothschild (1936–) opened a wine museum and cellar for the display and sale of Rothschild wines at Waddesdon Manor just outside London. E.P.-R. & J.Ro.

Littlewood, J., *Milady Vine: The Autobiography of Philippe de Rothschild* (London, 1984).

ROTOFERMENTER, or **rotary fermenter**, a type of FERMENTATION VESSEL arranged so that the contents can be mixed mechanically. Designed to eliminate the need for PUNCHING DOWN or PUMPING OVER, this equipment speeds the FERMENTATION and MACERATION phases of RED WINE-MAKING. Some wine producers, notably in Burgundy, have invested in them but they are used relatively rarely. Like most mechanical systems that promote skin–juice contact, they are expensive to build and operate and are difficult to clean and tend to produce excessively astringent wines. A.D.W.

ROUCHET, Italian red grape variety. See RUCHÈ.

ROUPEIRO, Portuguese white grape variety grown particularly in the ALENTEJO producing basic white wine to be drunk as young as possible. It is known as Códega in the Douro and sometimes as Alva in Alentejo.

ROUSING, alternative term for the wine-making operation of STIRRING.

ROUSSANNE, which doubtless owes its name to the russet or *roux* colour of its grapes, is one of only two vine varieties allowed into the white versions of the northern Rhône's red wine appellations HERMITAGE, CROZES-HERMITAGE, and ST-JOSEPH and into the exclusively white but often sparkling ST-PÉRAY. In each of these appellations MARSANNE, its traditional blending partner here, is far more widely grown because, although the wine produced is not as fine, there is more of it. Roussanne's irregular yields, tendency to POWDERY MILDEW and rot, and poor wind resistance all but eradicated it from the northern Rhône until better clones were selected and even today it is preferred by a minority of producers such as Jaboulet.

Roussanne's chief attribute is its haunting aroma, something akin to a particularly refreshing herb tea, together with acidity that allows it to age much more gracefully than Marsanne, which, in blends, can lend useful body. It does need to reach full maturity, however, in order to express itself elegantly. In the southern Rhône Roussanne (but not Marsanne) is one of four grape varieties allowed into white CHÂTEAUNEUF-DU-PAPE and Ch de Beaucastel here has demonstrated that carefully grown Roussanne can respond well to oak ageing. The variety is also grown in Provence (although the more common pink-berried **Roussanne du Var** is a lesser, unrelated variety used for VINS DE PAYS and ordinary table wines) and, increasingly, in the Languedoc-Roussillon, where Roussanne's tendency to ripen late is less problematic than in the northern Rhône and where results can be impressive. Although it is usually classified with Marsanne and Vermentino in appellation regulations, it can also make a fine blending partner with the fuller bodied Chardonnay. It can suffer in drought conditions.

The variety is also beguilingly fine and aromatic at Chignin in SAVOIE, where it is known as Bergeron, but should not be confused with ROUSSETTE. It is grown to a limited extent in Liguria and Tuscany, where it is a permitted ingredient in Italy's Montecarlo Bianco, and can also be found in Australia, presumably having been taken there as a partner to the much more successful SHIRAZ.

ROUSSETTE is the most exciting white grape variety grown in the eastern French wine region of SAVOIE, and a wine carrying its name on the label is likely to be superior. Roussette is also known as Altesse, and its origins are rich in mystery and intrigue. The widespread influence of the House of Savoie in the Middle Ages was such that this corner of France has its own distinctive vine varieties with possible links beyond what is now the French border (see MONDEUSE, TROUSSEAU, SAVAGNIN, POULSARD). Altesse was for long thought to have been imported from Cyprus, but GALET reports that, grown alongside the famous FURMINT of Hungary, the Savoie variety is virtually indistinguishable.

The variety is a shy, late producer but it resists rot well and the wine produced is (like Furmint) relatively exotically perfumed, has good acidity, and is well worth ageing. In recognition of Roussette's superiority over the more common JACQUÈRE, **Roussette de Savoie** has its own appellation in four communes, Marestel, Monterminod, Monthoux, and most notably Frangy. If followed by the name of a commune on the label the wine will be made exclusively of Roussette; if not, Chardonnay may constitute up to 50 per cent of the wine. **Roussette de Seyssel** is a fine, aromatic still wine from an area most noted for its sparkling wines, in which Roussette is sometimes included to add aroma.

It is also grown in the nearby Ain *département*, where it was once responsible for **Roussette du Bugey**, a VDQS wine that is today, curiously, more likely to be made from Chardonnay. The name Roussette du BUGEY may be followed by the name of the commune in which the wine was made.

ROUSSILLON, although usually encountered by outsiders as a suffix to LANGUEDOC, has a quite distinct identity, both cultural and geographical. Its inhabitants are Catalan rather than French, with a history rich in Spanish influence, particularly between the 13th and 17th centuries, when it was ruled first from Majorca and then from Aragon. They identify closely with the inhabitants of Spabish CATALONIA just across the Pyrenees. Quite unlike the flat coastal plains of the Languedoc, Roussillon's topography can be guessed at by the fact that today it is effectively the *département* called Pyrénées-Orientales, the eastern section of the Pyrenees, a mountain range so high that much of it remains snow covered throughout the summer. Vines and olives are two of the rare agricultural crops that can thrive in the tortured, arid valleys of the Agly, Têt, and Tech—although the lower land is today an important source of soft fruit. The climate is France's sunniest, with 325 days' sunshine a year, warm winds accentuating the grape-drying process in summer. Wine styles and techniques as well as grape varieties have much in common with neighbouring Spain. Despite the prevailing temperatures Roussillon's cellars were some of France's last to install efficient temperature control, and new oak is still a rare extravagance.

Viticulture was probably introduced to the region via the Greek establishment of Marseilles in the 7th century BC and developed by the Romans. It seems highly likely that the MUSCAT vine was the first to be introduced, in an effort to ape the popular sweet wines of the AEGEAN ISLANDS. The RIVESALTES region had certainly earned an important reputation for its Muscat by the 14th century, which probably predated that of the Languedoc's FRONTIGNAN. Sweetness was often concentrated by leaving Muscat grapes to shrivel on the vine, a practice that continued at least until the late 19th century (see DRIED GRAPE WINES). Roussillon became the world's foremost producer of VINS DOUX NATURELS, with BANYULS and to a lesser extent MAURY eventually overtaking Rivesaltes in *réclame* if not volume. But this was to be its downfall for much of the 20th century when strong, sweet wines were decidedly unfashionable, and the region's table wines, rather Spanish in terms of their depth of colour and alcohol, were regarded as useful only for blending with the lighter wines of the Languedoc. Awarded APPELLATION CONTRÔLÉE status as recently as 1977, **Côtes du Roussillon** has been a name in search of an image outside the region in which it is, with the exception of COLLIOURE, the sole appellation for table wines.

Côtes du Roussillon can be white and rosé as well as red, but the **Côtes du Roussillon-Villages** appellation that officially designates the region's finest wines is only for red wines made in the northern third of the region just south of CORBIÈRES and FITOU. The best reds, as geography suggests, are like a Spanish rendering of Corbières. Roussillon's reds are typically made from Carignan (which is slowly being pulled out but in 1988 still represented one vine in every three in Roussillon) fleshed out with at least 30 per cent of Syrah and Mourvèdre together perhaps with some Grenache, Lladoner Pelut, and Cinsaut. As has been the Spanish custom, some white Maccabéo can constitute up to 10 per cent of the blend—although as Carignan's influence declines so should this practice. As in the Languedoc, CARBONIC MACERATION has been much employed to counter Carignan's inherent astringency but more 'traditional' vinification techniques are increasingly employed on the nobler varieties. The reds are robust, rarely subtle but good value. Within the northern Villages region, the small villages of CARAMANY and LATOUR-DE-FRANCE successfully lobbied to have their names allowed as suffixes to the Côtes du Roussillon-Villages appellation but it would take a skilled taster to identify either of them blind.

Whites, with their relatively low acidity, may be more difficult to make successfully, but they are also more distinctive, their full bodied fragrance shaped by Maccabéo, Malvoisie du Roussillon or Tourbat (Sardinia's TORBATO), Marsanne, Roussanne, and Vermentino. Grenache Blanc and and Carignan Blanc are also used substantially for white wines. Fewer individual domaines have yet carved out their own identities than in Corbières to the north and CO-OPERATIVES and some worthwhile NÉGOCIANTS dominate here instead.

Many producers, especially on the coastal plain around Rivesaltes, are trying their luck with such INTERNATIONAL VARIETIES as Chardonnay and Merlot, although it can be difficult to preserve acidity in the first and fruit concentration in the second. These, like some first-class whites whose alcohol content breaks the 12.5 per cent barrier imposed by the appellation contrôlée regulations, are usually labelled as local VINS DE PAYS, des Côtes Catalanes in the northern third, Catalan in the south. Idiosyncratic but virtuoso producers such as Fernand Vaquer produce miraculous wines, also outside the appellation system and therefore some of France's most expensive VINS DE TABLE, from low-yielding traditional varieties grown on higher terraced vineyards. The vine-growers of Roussillon are some of France's least content with the details of their appellation regulations. There can be considerable scepticism about a system devised as far away as Paris and administered from Brussels, especially among those who identify so closely with the inhabitants of Barcelona.

Ponsich, P., 'Histoire de la vigne et du vin en Roussillon', in Éditions Montalba, *Les Vins du Roussillon* (France, 1980).

ROW SPACING, the space between rows of vines in the vineyard. See VINE DENSITY.

ROYALTY, also known as **Royalty 1390**, CALIFORNIA hybrid vine variety with red flesh, a TEINTURIER. It was bred by crossing the progenitor of all red-fleshed Teinturiers, Alicante Ganzin, with the Jura grape variety of TROUSSEAU and was released in 1958 along with the somewhat similar but much more successful RUBIRED, in 1958. There is little regal about this particular variety which is difficult to grow, although more than 800 acres/320 ha persisted in the early 1990s, almost exclusively in the hot SAN JOAQUIN VALLEY.

RS, signature style of dry white made from SILVANER grape produced co-operatively in the German wine region RHEINHESSEN by many of the more forward-looking producers. RS is also a common abbreviation for RESIDUAL SUGAR.

RUBIRED, popular red-fleshed CALIFORNIA hybrid, the result of crossing the progenitor of all red-fleshed TEINTURIERS, Alicante Ganzin, with the port variety TINTA CÃO. It

Row spacing of 2.1 m in Petaluma's Tiers vineyard in the Adelaide Hills is the result of a precise mathematical calculation based on the ideal number of buds per acre.

was released, along with the somewhat similar but much less successful ROYALTY, in 1958. Its productivity and depth of colour have made the variety popular with blenders of wine, California port, and grape juice, so that there were still more than 6,000 acres/2,430 ha in the hot SAN JOAQUIN VALLEY in the early 1990s. Unlike Royalty, it is easy to grow and has been tested in Australia.

RUBY, style of fortified wine. See PORT.

RUBY CABERNET, once-popular red grape variety bred in and for CALIFORNIA in 1949. Dr H. P. Olmo of the University of California at DAVIS (see also EMERALD RIESLING, CARNELIAN) crossed Carignan with Cabernet Sauvignon in an attempt to combine Cabernet characteristics with Carignan productivity and heat tolerance. Ruby Cabernet had its heyday in the 1960s. Although faded as a varietal wine since then, it may deserve a better fate. Although designed to yield claret-like wines from hot regions, it has done better in cooler, coastal climates, but has not been widely tested in these precincts. Total California plantings have remained static since the 1970s at just under 7,000 acres/2,890 ha, most notably in the southern SAN JOAQUIN Valley. It is grown by several producers in South Africa, Latin America, and has also been grown to a very limited exent in Australia,.

RUCHÈ, Rouchet, or occasionally **Roche**, relatively obscure red grape variety of the PIEDMONT region in north west Italy enjoying something of a revival with its own varietal DOC around Castagnole Monferrato, occasionally labelled Rouchet. Like NEBBIOLO, the wine is headily scented and its TANNINS imbue it with an almost bitter after-taste. According to Gleave, it is locally supposed to have been brought from BURGUNDY in the 18th century.

Gleave, D., *The Wines of Italy* (London and New York, 1989).

RUEDA, historic Spanish white wine zone named after the unprepossessing town which straddles the main road from Madrid to León in CASTILE-LEÓN (see map on p. 907). In the Middle Ages vineyards flourished on this bleak Castilian plateau and cellars were hollowed out of the limestone under the town, but after PHYLLOXERA ravaged the zone, Rueda went into rapid decline. Farmers looking for a quick return planted the high-yielding PALOMINO grape and made coarse, FORTIFIED WINES in the image of SHERRY.

For much of the 20th century, the native VERDEJO grape has been Rueda's sleeping beauty. It was awoken in the 1970s, when Bodegas Marqués de Riscal of RIOJA recognized the area's potential for dry white wine and sold a fresh Rueda white alongside its Rioja reds. Rueda was awarded DO status in 1980 and the local Consejo Regulador has since been cajoling growers to plant more of the low-yielding Verdejo at the expense of Palomino. Two very different forms of Rueda currently coexist: fortified and unfortified. The fortified wines, which are sold in two styles, continue to find favour on the local market. Rueda Pálido, with a minimum ALCOHOLIC STRENGTH of 14 per cent, develops under a film of FLOR and resembles a coarse FINO sherry. Rueda Dorado has a minimum strength of 15 per cent and tastes like a cross between an AMONTILLADO sherry and a RANCIO as a result of being aged in large glass carboys exposed to the sun.

In complete contrast, modern Rueda is a light, fruity, dry white wine. It may be made from a blend of VIURA and Verdejo, the latter accounting for at least 25 per cent of the blend. Rueda Superior must contain at least 60 per cent Verdejo and, as more farmers convert their vineyards, there are ever more VARIETAL wines. SAUVIGNON Blanc is also being planted in Rueda, having been introduced by Marqués de Riscal in the early 1980s. Some fine wines have resulted.

TEMPRANILLO produces some typically firm red wine in the zone but, as this falls outside the DO regulations, the red is not permitted to bear the name Rueda. R.J.M.

RUFFIAC, also known as Arrufiat, is a historic white vine variety enjoying a modest renaissance in Gascony in SOUTH WEST FRANCE. An ingredient in PACHERENC DU VIC-BILH, indeed the ingredient that distinguishes it from the otherwise similarly constructed JURANÇON, it was rescued from obscurity in the 1980s by André Dubosc of the Plaimont CO-OPERATIVE.

RULÄNDER is the main German name for PINOT GRIS, which was propagated in the Rheinpfalz in the early years of the 18th century by wine merchant Johann Seger Ruland. Since the mid 1980s some German producers have used this synonym to differentiate sweeter styles, often made from BOTRYTIZED grapes, from a drier wine that would be labelled Grauburgunder. Ruländer needs a good site with deep, heavy soils to maximize the impressive level of extract of which it is capable. It can easily achieve much higher MUST WEIGHTS than a RIESLING on the same sort of site although it is rarely in direct competition for territory. It is planted in most of the wine regions of Germany and is quite important in eastern Germany and the south, although it is relatively rare in the Mosel. More than half of Germany's total Ruländer plantings are in the relatively warm BADEN region, although there are several hundred hectares in both RHEINHESSEN and PFALZ. Because of its inherent fatness, it can be one of Germany's more successful varieties when styled as a dry wine.

In most German-speaking wine regions—Germany, Austria, and Italy's Alto Adige—Pinot Gris is regarded as rather more ordinary than Pinot Blanc, although it can quite easily reach ripeness levels which demand a high PRÄDIKAT and therefore attention for its rich spicy character. In Austria, where its wines are typically even earthier and richer than their German counterparts, it is also commonly called Ruländer and is also much less common than Pinot Blanc, covering just one per cent of the country's vineyard, chiefly in Styria and Burgenland.

The name Ruländer is also used for some of the Pinot Gris that is widely planted in ROMANIA.

RULLY, rambling village in Burgundy's CÔTE CHALONNAISE providing approximately equal quantities of red and white wines. The wines are attractive early and rarely age well, being grown on light and sandy soil. Rully is also a good source of sparkling CRÉMANT de Bourgogne. Nineteen vineyards in the village, one-sixth of the total, are designated PREMIERS CRUS, with Grésigny, Rabourcé, and Les Cloux being the most frequently seen. J.T.C.M.

RUMANIA. See ROMANIA.

RUPESTRIS, species of the *Vitis* genus native to North America much used in developing suitably resistant ROOTSTOCKS and HYBRIDS. For more details, see VITIS.

RUSSIA, the dominant state of the CIS whose capital is Moscow. Russia may be vast but has less than favourable conditions for viticulture. The principal limiting factors are a short vegetation period, lack of water, and high summer temperatures. Russia is the CIS's fourth most important grape grower (after MOLDOVA, UKRAINE, AZERBAIJAN), but by far its major wine producer, thanks to imports. Russia's production of wine and brandy accounts for nearly 50 per cent of the total amount of wine, SOVIET SPARKLING WINE, and brandy produced by the viticultural Republics of the former Soviet Union. Total Russian wine production in 1990 was 7.5 million hl/197 million gal—a considerable reduction from the 17 million hl produced in the early 1980s before President Gorbachev tried to cut alcohol consumption.

History

South Dagestan is Russia's only ancient viticultural area. Grapes have been cultivated there for more than 2,000 years. In other regions of the North Caucasus and in the Low Volga region, viticulture was first practised in the 17th to 18th centuries. In 1613, vineyards were established in Astrakhan to supply the tsar's household with both fruit and wine. After 1660, vines were planted in Kursk, Tambov, and in the vicinities of Tula and Moscow. In 1880 PHYLLOXERA reached Russia and devastated the country's viticulture.

The first vineyards in the Anapa zone of the Krasnodar region were established in the locality of Pilenkovo and planted to RIESLING and PORTUGIESER varieties. In 1914 the Russian vineyard area averaged 50,000 ha/123,500 acres, and the gross yield of grapes was 213,000 tons. During the First World War viticulture declined in Russia, and the total vineyard area had halved by 1919. In 1940 vineyards occupied 42,000 ha. The great development of commercial vineyards came at the end of 1950.

See also CIS, history.

Climate and geography

Most commercial vineyards are in the North Caucasus. Almost all vineyards are in the valleys and on hillsides suitable for mechanical cultivation. A small proportion of grapes are also grown on steeper slopes of the Caucasus. The climate of most Russian viticultural zones is very CONTINENTAL and winters are severe, so that up to half of all vines need to be covered with soil in this period for WINTER PROTECTION. The most favourable soil and climate conditions are in the Krasnodar region and Dagestan, with active annual temperature summations of 3,600 to 4,000 °C and, even more importantly, winters warm enough to permit non-protected viticulture. F. I. Geiduk, Black Sea district agronomist, recorded in 1871 that 'of all areas of the world, the north west coast of the Caucasus is best suited for viticulture. This is a new California for wines. One could hardly find a place bearing even a faint resemblance to it. Neither Burgundy nor Champagne or Kakhetia in GEORGIA, to say nothing about the CRIMEA, can serve as a perfect model for imitation.'

The North Caucasus has more than 90 per cent of Russia's vineyards which can be subdivided into five principal zones of grape culture: the Krasnodar region, Dagestan, the Stavropol' region, Checheno-Ingushetia, and the Rostov region. Only about five per cent of Russian vineyard is in Kabardino-Balkaria and in the north Ossetia.

The important Krasnodar region can be further subdivided into three zones: the Anapa-and-Taman' zone, the Central Black Sea zone, and the South Black Sea zone. The climate of this region is mild, yet great damage can be caused by strong winds. The average annual amount of rainfall is 400 to 800 mm/31 in and the average annual temperature is 11 to 14 °C/57 °F. The absolute minimum temperature of −23 °C occurs once every three to five years. The Black Sea coast has humus carbonate (differing in depth and humus content) and cinnamonic soils and the northern slopes of the main Caucasus spine have podzolized and pre-Caucasian chernozems (loamy LOESS).

Dagestan, an even more important vineyard region, is located in the east part of the North Caucasus. It has a moderately warm, arid, and continental climate. The average January temperature is 1 to 3 °C in lower vineyards, and −5 to −11 °C in the mountains. The average July temperature is 24 °C. The duration of the frost-free period in the lower portion is 160 to 180 days in the north and 235 to 240 in the south. The annual rainfall is 300 to 600 mm. Chestnut, meadow soils and solonchaks (dry steppe soils) prevail in the premountainous portion of Dagestan and chestnut and mountain forest soils are found in the mountainous portion of the country. Vineyards are located mainly on the coast of the Caspian Sea and in the Terek river valley.

The central part of the Stavropol' region is occupied by the Stavropol' upland which turns in the valleys of rivers Terek and Kuma in the east and merges with the Kuma and Manych depression in the north. In the south west foothills, the climate of the region is continental, the active temperature summation being 2,600 to 3,300 °C. Annual rainfall is 300 to 600 mm. The low portion has chernozem and chestnut soils in the east and light chestnut soils in the north east. Vineyards are mostly winter protected and those in the river valleys are irrigated.

Checheno-Ingushetia is slightly warmer but the minimum winter temperature is 30 °C. Vineyards are established on meadow chestnut and alluvial soils and alkalized chernozems.

The Rostov region has dry, hot summers and frosty winters. The average annual amount of rainfall decreases from west (650 mm) to east (400 mm). The active temperature summation is 3,350 °C with temperatures dropping occasionally to −28 °C in winter.

Industry organization

In the late 1970s Russia had nearly 200,000 ha of vineyard but, by the end of 1990, the total vineyard area after Gorbachev's anti-alcohol drive was 54,600 ha in Dagestan, 48,800 ha in the Krasnodar region, 13,900 ha in the Stavropol' region, 12,700 ha in the Rostov region, 14,400 ha in Checheno-Ingushetia and 1,400 ha in Kabardino-Balkaria. Small vineyard areas are found in the north Ossetia, in the low and in the middle Volga regions, and on the coast.

State farms manage 90 per cent of the total vineyard area, while six per cent of the grape area belongs to collective farms and four per cent to individual households. In Russia of the mid 1990s, grapes are cultivated by 235 state farms, each having approximately 800 ha. Grapes grown in the North Caucasus are processed mainly by state wineries; 42 secondary vinification enterprises where wine is finished and bottled are located close to Russian centres of population (see CIS). Imported wine and GRAPE CONCENTRATE are processed by 50 wine enterprises of which the largest ones are in Moscow, St Petersburg, Rostov-on-Don, Krasnodar, and Stavropol'. The best dry table wines of Russia are those produced in the valley of the Don, on the Black Sea coast of the Caucasus, in South Dagestan, and in the premountainous zones of the Stavropol' region. Vine varieties ALIGOTÉ, RIESLING, and CABERNET predominate.

Dessert wines are produced in the Don and Kuban' valleys, the Stavropol' region, Dagestan, and Kabardino-Balkaria.

Sparkling wine is important to Russians. Their largest production centres for Soviet sparkling wine are in Moscow (with a capacity of 20 million bottles per year), Rostov-on-Don (16 million bottles), St Petersburg (10 million bottles), and Nizhniy Novgorod and Tsimlyansk (9 million bottles each). Soviet sparkling wine is produced by the Abrau-Durso winery by classic bottle fermentation (as for CHAMPAGNE).

Viticulture

Vine-TRAINING SYSTEMS changed enormously during the 20th century. Densely planted vineyards (5,000 to 10,000 vines per ha) with single vine supports have given way to TRELLIS SYSTEMS in wider-spaced rows. The many vineyards that need winter protection are either trained with long and medium canes left in one direction and covered with soil in winter by a vine-laying machine, or left without a trunk to be covered with a high mound of soil. Row and vine spacing is 2.5 to 3.0 m and 1.25 to 2.0 m, respectively.

In warmer, non-protected viticultural zones, there may be IRRIGATION in areas with a satisfactory water supply. The trunks of particularly vigorous vines are trained 1.2 m high, their canes being supported vertically, with free-hanging terminal shoots; such vines are planted in rows spaced between 3 and 4 m. Vineyards on non-irrigated lands have medium- and high-TRUNKED forms spaced between rows and vines at 2.5 to 3.0 m and 1.25 to 2.0 m respectively.

Vine varieties

The varietal assortment of Russia's vineyards is extremely diverse, with 100 varieties allowed for commercial cultivation in 1992. Depending on the region, 70 to 85 per cent of vineyards are planted to wine grapes, with table grapes accounting for 15 to 30 per cent of the total vineyard area. Among wine grapes cultivated in all viticultural regions of Russia, the most common is RKATSITELI, with 45 to 50 per cent. This variety allows various cultural practices and produces a range of different types of wine. Such varieties as ALIGOTÉ, RIESLING, CLAIRETTE, CABERNET SAUVIGNON, TRAMINER, MUSCATS, SILVANER, SAPERAVI, MERLOT, PINOT GRIS, and the indigenous Moldovan variety PLAVAI are also widely planted, as well as the local red Tsimlyansky.

Recently, NEW VARIETIES with improved resistance to FUNGAL DISEASES and FROST have been released by the All-Russia Potapenko Research Institute for Viticulture and Ecology. Most notable among the wine grape varieties are Saperavi Severny and CABERNET SEVERNY. They, and other new varieties such as Stepniak and Fioletovy Ranni, occupy about 10,000 ha on various Russian farms. Commercial cultivation of these new, specially bred varieties has allowed considerable expansion of non-protected viticulture.

In the early 1990s there was a substantial expansion in the total area planted to new, high-yielding wine grape varieties such as Vydvizhenets, and varieties suitable for both wine and table grapes such as Muscat Derbentski and Zala Gyöngye, as well as to indigenous varieties to be made into wine with CONTROLLED APPELLATIONS of origin such as Sibirkovy, Tsimlianski Cherny, Plechistic, Narma, and Güliabi Daghestanski.

V.R.

Negrul, A. M., *Viticulture with Basic Principles of Ampelography and Breeding* (Russian) (3rd edn., Moscow, 1959).

Shesterkina, V. N., Kolomiyets, V. A., and Rogozhine, T. P., *The Specialization of Agro-industrial Enterprises of Viticulture and Ecology* (Russian) (Moscow, 1988).

Zakharova, E. I., 'The Soviet Federative Republic of Russia' (Russian), in A. I. Timush (ed.), *Encyclopaedia of Viticulture* (Kishinev, 1987).

RUSSIAN RIVER VALLEY, high-quality California wine region and AVA. See SONOMA.

RUST, town on the western shore of the NEUSIEDLERSEE in the Burgenland region of AUSTRIA famous for the production of sweet white AUSBRUCH wines.

RUTHERFORD. Important centre of wine production in the NAPA Valley of California.

RUTHERGLEN, small town in north east VICTORIA that could be said to be AUSTRALIA'S answer to Oporto. It is the centre of production of Australia's most distinctive wines, both fortified, LIQUEUR MUSCAT and Liqueur Tokay.

RUWER, small German river, 40 km/25 miles in length, which rises in the Hunsrück and flows into the MOSEL, downstream from Trier. In recent years, some of the vineyards have been replaced by houses, and in the 1960s the area under vine did not expand as it did in the main part of the Mosel-Saar-Ruwer wine region. In steep sites (once in ecclesiastical hands) at Eitelsbach, Maximin Grünhaus, and Kasel, Rieslings from good years are among the best in Germany. They are similar in structure to those of the SAAR, but have a touch of earthiness to add individuality.

See also MOSEL-SAAR-RUWER. I.J.

S

SAALE-UNSTRUT, wine region in eastern GERMANY of terraced and sometimes isolated vineyards, starting to recover from the forlorn condition in which they were left by the former East German regime (see map on p. 442). The main producers in the 480 ha/1,190 acres under vine are the cellars at Naumburg belonging to the state of Sachsen-Anhalt, and the co-operative cellar at Freyburg. All the wines from Müller-Thurgau, Silvaner, Bacchus, Gutedel (CHASSELAS), Weissburgunder (PINOT BLANC), and other vine varieties are fully fermented, and thus completely dry. These are northern vineyards, with a CONTINENTAL climate and frequent, dangerous FROSTS. The dilapidated state of the vineyards (many vines are missing), and annual rainfall of no more than 450 mm/17.5 in, result in a small yield per hectare (30 to 35 hl/ha; 1.7–2 tons/acre). The result is wines that are naturally light in alcohol but relatively rich in extract. It is said that the chalk soil gives them added BODY, so that they can seem better balanced than many dry wines grown in the slate of the Mosel. I.J.

SAAR, river which rises in the Vosges mountains and joins the MOSEL at Konz, near Trier. Downstream from Serrig, Riesling vines grow in slate soil, resulting in steely, firm wines with a powerful aroma and long flavour. In good vintages they are amongst the most successful in the MOSEL-SAAR-RUWER wine region of GERMANY. Only top estates or, at least, growers with vines in favoured sites can produce good wines in poor vintages. For the rest, their lesser wines can be converted into sparkling wine. Within Germany, Saar Riesling SEKT has a good reputation and a long-established position in the market.

See also RUWER. I.J.

SACCHAROMYCES. See YEAST.

SACHSEN, or **Saxony** in English, the smallest wine region in GERMANY. Formerly in East Germany, it is also known colloquially as the Elbtal, and established the first German viticultural training institute in 1811–12. Some 300 ha/740 acres of vineyard follow the course of the river Elbe, from Pillnitz on the southern outskirts of Dresden, to Diesbar north of Meissen (see map on p. 442). This is the most northerly wine region in Germany. A co-operative cellar receives the grapes from 160 ha of vineyard, cultivated by 1,500 part-time growers. The state of Sachsen has a WEINGUT at Schloss Wackerbarth near Radebeul, supplied by 100 ha of mainly rented vineyards. The principal vine varieties are Müller-Thurgau, Riesling, Weissburgunder (PINOT BLANC), Traminer, and Ruländer (PINOT GRIS). Sachsen is the only German region still growing the distinguished-sounding, but somewhat indifferent, Goldriesling vine. Virtually all the wines are dry. Sachsen's financial recovery and the necessary investment in the wine industry should produce an increase in yield and an improvement in wine quality. I.J.

SACK, name for a white FORTIFIED WINE, imported from Spain or the Canary islands, which was much in vogue in England in the 16th and 17th centuries. Its most famous, fictional, consumer was Sir John Falstaff in Shakespeare's *Henry IV, Part II* (IV. iii). The etymology of sack is disputed. The *Oxford English Dictionary* derives the word from the French word *sec* meaning 'dry', but admits that it cannot produce a convincing explanation for the difference in vowels. Moreover, sack was probably sweet. It was matured in wood but not for longer than two years so it would have been like a cheap OLOROSO. Hence Julian Jeffs proposes another derivation: Spanish *sacar*, to draw out, from which *sacas* became exports of wine. Often the place of production was put before the noun, as in Canary sack, Malaga sack, Palm (= Palma de Majorca) sack, Sherris (or Sherry) sack. Sherris is JEREZ, hence the modern word SHERRY. From the end of the 17th century onwards 'sherry' began to replace 'sack' as the generic term, but sack was still used in the 18th century.

Around 1264 Jerez was at last reconquered from the Moors by Alfonso X, surnamed 'the Sage', who encouraged viticulture. Because Jerez remained at the Moorish frontier, King Juan gave it the title Jerez de la Frontera in 1380. The earliest mention of wine shipped from Jerez to England is in 1485. After the discovery of America, Sanlúcar became a port for the new American trade; it was also a convenient place for a colony of English merchants to establish itself. When Henry VIII divorced Catherine of Aragon and married Anne Boleyn, the English merchants had to do a fine balancing act to keep on the right side of the Inquisition. Life was easier under the Catholic Queen Mary, but under the Protestant Elizabeth they had to bear the full force of the Counter-Reformation. From 1585 wine could no longer be shipped direct to England so the merchants resorted to foreign ships or ships ostensibly bound for foreign ports. Sack was popular in England, even more so when in 1587 Drake raided the Spanish fleet at Cádiz and captured 2,900 PIPES (not BUTTS at this stage) of sherry intended for the Armada and made drinking sack an act of patriotism. Undoubtedly the English colony did not welcome the second raid on Cádiz in 1595; yet sack continued to be exported to England. With the accession of James I in 1603 tension eased and the merchants flourished once more. Sack appears in the works of many of the major English writers of the 17th century, and, however much the Puritans disapproved of the theatre, they did drink sack: when Cromwell paid an official visit to Bristol he was presented with a pipe of sack. H.M.W.

Jeffs, Julian, *Sherry* (4th edn., London, 1992).

Sacramental wine, saviour of some CALIFORNIA wineries during PROHIBITION. For more details of the sacramental nature of wine, see EUCHARIST.

Sacramento Valley, northern part of the vast Central Valley of CALIFORNIA from Lodi northwards, including the state capital Sacramento and the vinously important University of California at DAVIS. The Sacramento delta has been a source of distinctive Chenin Blanc grapes, and some of Contra Costa County's older vines have been a useful source of grapes for the RHÔNE RANGERS. See SAN JOAQUIN VALLEY for more details.

Sacy, the white grape variety nowadays most closely associated with the YONNE *département*, at one time threatened to usurp all manner of nobler vines in eastern France, most notably Chardonnay, from southern Burgundy in the 18th century and from the vineyards of Chablis in the early 20th century. Its productivity is the vine's chief attribute, its acidity the wine's most noticeable characteristic. This has been used to reasonable effect by the producers of such sparkling wines as Kriter and the variety, called here Tresallier, is still an important ingredient in the white wines of ST-POURÇAIN.

Sagrantino, lively, sometimes tannic red grape variety grown in UMBRIA in central Italy, particularly in the Montefalco area. **Sagrantino di Montefalco** was elevated to DOCG status in the mid 1990s. Sagrantino has been used as an ingredient in DRIED GRAPE WINES but today shows promise as a carefully vinifed dry red, sometimes blended with SANGIOVESE.

Saignée, French term meaning 'bled' for a wine-making technique which results in a ROSÉ WINE made by running off, or 'bleeding', a certain amount of FREE-RUN juice from just-crushed dark-skinned grapes after a short, prefermentation MACERATION. The aim of this may be primarily to produce a lightly pink wine, or to increase the proportion of PHENOLICS and FLAVOUR COMPOUNDS to juice, thereby effecting a form of CONCENTRATION of the red wine which results from fermentation of the rest of the juice with the skins. The second operation has often been undertaken by ambitious producers of both red bordeaux and red burgundy.

St-Amour, the most northerly of the BEAUJOLAIS Crus and an area in which a considerable amount of white Beaujolais Blanc (and ST-VÉRAN) is made. About 260 ha/640 acres of Gamay vines are planted for the production of relatively light but true red Beaujolais. The Cru was added several years after most others. One theory is that its name, which indubitably adds to its appeal, comes from a Roman soldier who celebrated a narrow escape from death in Switzerland by converting to Christianity and establishing a mission. He was later canonized as St-Amour.

St-Aubin, village in the Côte de Beaune district of Burgundy's Côte d'Or tucked out of the limelight between Meursault and Puligny-Montrachet, producing two-thirds red wine from Pinot Noir and one-third white from Chardonnay. A high proportion, two-thirds, of the vineyard area is designated PREMIER CRU, notably Les Charmois, La Chatenière, En Remilly, and Les Murgers Dents de Chien, part of a swathe of mostly south west-facing vineyards lying between the borders of Chassagne-Montrachet and Puligny-Montrachet and the hamlet of Gamay, which is included in the St-Aubin appellation. The remaining vineyards have the ideal south and south easterly exposition but are less favourably situated further up the cooler valley.

White St-Aubin has some of the character of Puligny-Montrachet, especially in the warmer vintages; the reds resemble a more supple version of red Chassagne-Montrachet.

See also CÔTE D'OR and its map. J.T.C.M.

St-Chinian, red wine appellation in the LANGUEDOC in southern France which extends over arid, spectacular, mountainous terrain in the foothills of the Cévennes between the MINERVOIS and FAUGÈRES appellations (see map on p. 552). Some fresh, dry rosé is also made. The small town of St-Chinian itself is in the middle of the zone, which extends upwards and northwards as far as Vieussan, including Berlou and its famous CO-OPERATIVE, whose wines are sometimes labelled Berloup. In the early 1990s about 2,100 ha/5,190 acres were dedicated to the production of appellation wine within the zone, which can be divided into two very different sections. In the northern zone around Berlou and Roquebrun vines at around 200 m/656 ft altitude grow on arid schists and yield low quantities of extremely sharply etched wines. In the southern zone closer to St-Chinian itself the clays and limestone, typically at about 100 m, tend to result in fuller, softer wines. Carignan vines are being gradually replaced by Syrah, Grenache, and, in warmer sites, some Mourvèdre. Cinsaut may represent no more than 30 per cent of any blend. Many producers here also grow other varieties with which to make some excellent VIN DE PAYS. St-Chinian was made a VDQS in 1945 and graduated to AC status in 1982. When the Coteaux du Languedoc appellation was created in 1985, St-Chinian was grafted on to it, given the status of special CRU, like neighbouring Faugères.

St-Christol, the easternmost named TERROIR within the Coteaux du LANGUEDOC appellation in southern France, named after a village on the eastern boundary of the Hérault *département* with Gard. Production of appellation wine is relatively low here, and is chiefly in the hands of the village CO-OPERATIVE.

STE-CROIX-DU-MONT, most important of the sweet white wine appellations on the right bank of the GARONNE in the BORDEAUX region. At their best, these wines can resemble the wines made across the river in SAUTERNES and BARSAC, being high in alcohol, sugar, and concentration. Prices are considerably lower, however. The topography and soil structure of Ste-Croix-du-Mont are generally more promising than those of its right bank neighbours LOUPIAC and CADILLAC, for some of the vineyards here are on gravel slopes well situated for the development of NOBLE ROT. An increasing number of producers are prepared to take the risks necessary to produce BOTRYTIZED wines and BARREL FERMENTATION, such as introduced for the prestige cuvées of Chx Loubens, La Rame, and du Mont, is becoming increasingly common (see SAUTERNES for details). Some very ordinary, sugary MOELLEUX is also made, however.

ST-DRÉZÉRY, the smallest named TERROIR within the Coteaux du LANGUEDOC appellation in southern France. Like neighbouring ST-CHRISTOL it is named after a village on the eastern boundary of the Hérault *département* with Gard and such appellation production as there is chiefly in the hands of the village CO-OPERATIVE.

ST-ÉMILION, important red wine district in Bordeaux producing more wine than any other RIGHT BANK appellation. It takes its name from the prettiest town in the Bordeaux region by far, and one of the few to attract tourists to whom wine is of no interest.

The town's historical importance is undisputed, and obvious to the most casual of visitors. In the 8th century it was a collection of caves hollowed out of the cliff on which a fortified medieval town was to be built. In the Middle Ages its port, Pierrefitte, played an important part in shipping wine down the DORDOGNE river, until it was overtaken by LIBOURNE a few miles downstream. It was on the pilgrim route to Santiago de Compostela, and even today its CONFRÉRIE the **Jurade de St-Émilion** prides itself on maintaining the district's reputation for hospitality. As outlined in BORDEAUX, history, St-Émilion was a wine region long before the Médoc on the left bank of the Gironde, even though for most of the 19th century it was less important commercially. In the early 20th century the wines of St-Émilion were left to the merchants of Libourne to sell in northern France and northern Europe, while the BORDEAUX TRADE concentrated on selling left bank wines. Whereas the Médoc is made up of large, grand estates, St-Émilion's 400 or so smallholders are essentially farmers, albeit dedicated to a single crop.

That crop is dominated by the MERLOT and CABERNET FRANC (here called Bouchet) vine varieties, Merlot accounting for more than 60 per cent of all vine plantings and imbuing the wines with their characteristic almost dried fruit sweetness. A little CABERNET SAUVIGNON is grown, but it can be relied upon to ripen profitably only in very selected spots in the generally cooler soils and MACROCLIMATE of the right bank, and then only if a suitable CLOVE has been planted.

Grape varieties apart, variation is the hallmark of this extensive region. The quality of its wines can vary from light, fruity, serviceable clarets to the finest FIRST GROWTHS capable of ageing for a century or more. The diversity of soils in the district is such that Bordeaux's most diligent geologist, Henri Enjalbert, was at first inspired to write his *tour de force* on the region, and then, apparently, mesmerized.

Although conventionally the St-Émilion district has been divided into two general soil types—the Côtes or hillsides, and the Graves or gravelly limestone plateau—there are inevitably myriad soil types within the 5,300/13,090 acres ha of St-Émilion. More than 3,000 ha of vineyard lie on the plain between the town and plateau and the river Dordogne. Wines made on this lower land, a mixture of gravel, sand, and alluvial soils, tend to be lighter and less long lived than the wines produced on the plateau or the hillsides, and most, but not all, of them qualify for the most basic appellation, **St-Émilion**.

But the St-Émilion district also boasts a diversity of appellations and, uniquely in France, has a CLASSIFICATION of individual properties which is regularly revised, and depends on tasting. This classification, first drawn up in 1955 and revised every 10 years since, distinguishes several hundred properties as of **St-Émilion Grand Cru** status, so that a typical vintage might produce about 100,000 hl/2.6 million gal of AC St-Émilion, and perhaps 130,000 hl of St-Émilion Grand Cru.

But the classification's most significant task is to identify which properties rank as **St-Émilion Grand Cru Classé** and which few qualify as **St-Émilion Premier Grand Cru Classé.** See CLASSIFICATION p. 248 for a listing of the 1985 classification of Grands Crus Classés and Premiers Grands Crus Classés. Ch Beauséjour-Bécot is expected to regain Premier Grand Cru Classé status in the 1995 classification, while Ch l'Angélus certainly deserves elevation, and Ch Tertre Rôtebœuf should be accorded Grand Cru Classé status.

Most of the district's most highly ranked properties are either on the steep, clay-limestone hillsides immediately below the town or on a gravelly section of the plateau 5 km/3 miles west of the town and immediately adjacent to the POMEROL appellation. Of St-Émilion's two most most highly ranked properties, Chx AUSONE and CHEVAL BLANC, the first is the archetypal Côtes property, with tiny, vertiginous vineyard, and cellars burrowed into the hillside, and the second is on particularly gravelly soils with clay and some of the iron-rich deposits characteristic of neighbouring Pomerol. The startling difference in the style of these wines, the second the only great wine to be made predominantly from Cabernet Franc grapes, is a telling demonstration of the variety that St-Émilion can offer.

Of famous St-Émilion properties, Ch Figeac, which predated and is now an effective rival of Ch Cheval Blanc, is (unusually for the appellation) attached to Cabernet Sauvignon. Since most other St-Émilions lack this tannic ingredient, the district's wines in general mature much faster than their left bank counterparts, although wine-making at some properties, notably at Ch Canon just outside the town, seems very definitely designed for the long term.

The St-Émilion co-operative, l'Union des Producteurs de St-Émilion, is one of France's most ambitious, and bottles a quarter of St-Émilion's production. The whole region is characterized by a strong sense of local identity, no doubt enhanced by the fact that, as one of Bordeaux's 'big four' red wine districts, St-Émilion lacks the fame of the Médoc and Graves, and the glamour of Pomerol.

The satellite appellations

On the outskirts are the so-called St-Émilion satellites, **Lussac St-Émilion, Montagne St-Émilion, Puisseguin St-Émilion**, and **St-Georges St-Émilion**, encircling St-Émilion proper to the north and east. On this more rolling countryside north of the Barbanne (see LALANDE-DE-POMEROL) the vine is grown alongside other crops and viticulture accounts for about half of the total area, or just over 3,000 ha. CO-OPERATIVES are important here and Montagne and Lussac St-Émilion produce significantly more wine than either Puisseguin or, especially, St-Georges, which was for many years sold exclusively as Montagne St-Émilion. The grape varieties planted are similar to those in St-Émilion proper but the standard of wine-making is generally more rudimentary. There are, nevertheless, bargains to be sought out.

The vine variety

St-Émilion is also a synonym for the widely planted white grape variety called UGNI BLANC in France and TREBBIANO in Italy. The name is used particularly in Cognac country in south west France where it is widely planted, and in California where it is not.

Enjalbert, H., *Great Bordeaux Wines: St Émilion, Pomerol, Fronsac* (Paris, 1983; English trans., 1985).
Parker, R. M., *Bordeaux* (2nd edn., New York, 1991).
Penning-Rowsell, E., *The Wines of Bordeaux* (6th edn., London, 1989).

ST-ESTÈPHE, the northernmost and most bucolic of the four important communal appellations in the Haut-Médoc district of Bordeaux. St-Estèphe is separated from the vineyards of Pauillac's Ch LAFITE only by a stream—indeed Ch Lafite owns one plot of land in the commune of St-Estèphe itself. To the immediate north of St-Estèphe, across a stretch of polder, lies the Bas-Médoc, the lower, lesser portion of this most famous region.

The soils of St-Estèphe contain their fair share of GRAVEL, but these layers of gravel are often to be found on a CLAY base. These more poorly drained soils are cooler and can slow ripening, leaving St-Estèphe grapes higher in acidity than their counterparts further south in the Médoc. In Bordeaux's low-rainfall vintages, such as 1990, St-Estèphe can be at an advantage, however.

A high proportion of St-Estèphe's 1,200 ha/2,960 acres of vines, almost a quarter, produce grapes which find their way into the vats of the village's co-operative, which often uses the name Marquis de St-Estèphe. The village may boast fewer famous names and CLASSED GROWTHS than MARGAUX, PAUILLAC, and ST-JULIEN, but its wines have a distinctive style that is deep coloured, full of extract, perhaps a little austere in youth, but very long lived. This style was perceptibly softened during the 1980s as higher proportions of Merlot grapes blurred the edges of the Cabernet, and wine-making techniques concentrated on taming some of the harsher TANNINS.

The stars of St-Estèphe are its two second growths, Ch Montrose and Cos d'Estournel, whose fortunes and reputations have alternated throughout the village's relatively recent history as a fine wine producer. Cos d'Estournel, or Cos as it has been styled on the label by the owner Bruno Prats, has the Médoc's most eye-catching architecture, in a façade of pure oriental folly beside the main road through the Médoc's wine villages. Its wines are the commune's most ambitious, styled for many decades to come, and its sister property Ch Marbuzet is in effect its respectable SECOND WINE. Ch Montrose has produced much more traditionally structured wines, in the mid 20th century somewhat reminiscent of Ch Latour for their solidity, but many of the vintages in the 1980s were noticeably lighter.

St-Estèphe's other classed growths are the sometimes excellent third growth Ch Calon-Ségur, the fourth growth Ch Lafon-Rochet, well sited between Chx Lafite and Cos, and the modest fifth growth Ch Cos-Labory. Some of the village's most conscientiously made wines, however, are such CRUS BOURGOIS as the exotic Ch Haut-Marbuzet, Ch Meyney run by CORDIER, Chx de Pez and Les-Ormes-de-Pez (the latter run in tandem with Pauillac's Ch Lynch-Bages), Ch Beau-Site, and the recently reconstructed Ch Lilian-Ladoueys.

For more information see MÉDOC and map of BORDEAUX.

Ginestet, B., *St-Julien* (Paris, 1984).
Parker, R., *Bordeaux* (2nd edn., New York, 1991).
Penning-Rowsell, E., *The Wines of Bordeaux* (6th edn., London, 1989).
Peppercorn, D., *Bordeaux* (2nd edn., London, 1991).

STE-FOY, or **Ste-Foy-Bordeaux**, district in the extreme east of the BORDEAUX region on the border with, and arguably more properly part of, BERGERAC. It is named after its principal town, just 22 km/14 miles west of the town of Bergerac. Its red wines are very similar to red Bergerac and BORDEAUX AC, while its white wines, made from just 55 ha/136 acres of vineyard, are sweet and mostly undistinguished.

ST-GEORGES ST-ÉMILION, satellite appellation of ST-ÉMILION in Bordeaux.

ST-JEAN-DE-MINERVOIS is the small mountain village in the far north east of the MINERVOIS region that gives its name to the Languedoc's most individual VIN DOUX NATUREL appellation, Muscat de St-Jean-de-Minervois. Like the other Muscats of FRONTIGNAN, LUNEL, and MIREVAL, it is made exclusively from the best Muscat variety, MUSCAT BLANC À PETITS GRAINS, to which alcohol is added half-way through fermentation to produce a wine with at least 15 per cent alcohol and 125 g/l residual sugar. Unlike these other Muscats produced closer to the Mediterranean, however, St-Jean's vineyards are hacked out of the *garrigue* 200 m/660 ft above sea level and the grapes ripen a good three weeks later. The altitude and less reliable weather can affect both quality and yields, which often have difficulty reaching the permitted maximum of 28 hl/ha (1.6 tons/acre), but the resulting wines are more reliably interesting and display more of the variety's delicate orange-flower flavours than is usually the case in Muscats other than those of BEAUMES-DE-VENISE. The wines of the co-operative improved immensely when one of the best local OENOLOGISTS was taken on in the mid 1980s although, like most vins doux naturels, the wines are rarely vintage dated.

ST-JOSEPH, ambitiously expanded north RHÔNE west bank appellation producing mainly red wines from the SYRAH grape but also some full bodied dry whites from the MARSANNE and, occasionally, ROUSSANNE grapes. The vineyard area increased sixfold during the 1970s and 1980s although a more stringent development plan was put into place in the early 1990s as the better producers realized that the reputation of this relatively new appellation (1956) would be enhanced by the produce of few of the new vineyards on the plateau. The appellation now extends from CONDRIEU in the north (where there is some overlap) to a small pocket of St-Joseph vineyards between ST-PÉRAY and the town of Valence. The heart of the region, however, is the stretch of old, terraced vineyards around the town of Tournon (including the communes of Vion, Lemps, St-Jean-de-Muzols, Tournon, Mauves, and Glun) just across the wide river Rhône from the hill of HERMITAGE. The wines are lighter and certainly faster maturing than this north Rhône archetype, not so much because the soils are very different—on the best sites granite predominates, supplemented by sand and gravel—but because St-Joseph's east-facing vineyards simply lose the sun up to two hours earlier in the crucial ripening season. For this reason, locals view St-Joseph as their answer to BEAUJOLAIS, a fruity wine for drinking in the first three years or so. Those less accustomed to the sheer weight of a good North Rhône red may prefer to drink them at between two and six years old, depending on the character of the vintage, but Gripa's VIEILLES VIGNES bottling can easily repay a decade's bottle age. Red St-Joseph can be a delightfully transparent expression of Syrah fruit, and is one of the most flattering north Rhône reds to taste young. The best should be approached in a much less reverential way than a Hermitage or a CÔTE-RÔTIE, the rest (which comprise too high a proportion of the total) can be too light and insubstantial to be worth the price premium that St-Joseph can, often inexplicably, command over the other basic north Rhône appellation CROZES-HERMITAGE. White St-Joseph represents less than 10 per cent of the appellation's total production and the best can provide lovers of white Hermitage with a good-value alternative.

ST-JULIEN, one of the most homogeneous, reliable, and underrated village appellations in the Haut-Médoc district of Bordeaux. St-Julien may suffer in popular esteem because, unlike PAUILLAC to its immediate north and MARGAUX a few miles to the south, there is no FIRST GROWTH property within its boundaries. Instead, however, it can boast five superb second growths, two excellent third growths, four well-maintained fourth growths, and, from the 1980s at least, an unrivalled consistency in wine-making skill. St-Julien is the commune for wine connoisseurs who seek subtlety, balance, and tradition in their red bordeaux. The wines may lack the vivid, sometimes almost pastiche, concentration of a Pauillac, the austerity of a ST-ESTÈPHE, or the immediate charm of a Margaux, but they embody all the virtues of fine, long-lived blends of Cabernet and Merlot grapes, being deep coloured, dry, digestible, appetizing, persistent, intriguing, and rewarding.

The appellation, the smallest of the Médoc's most famous four, included about 900 ha/2,220 acres of vineyard by the mid 1990s within the communes of St-Julien and Beychevelle to its immediate south. Both gravelly soils and subsoils here are relatively homogeneous, broken only by a narrow strip of riverbank on either side of the *jalle* that bisects the zone and flows into the Gironde north of Ch Ducru-Beaucaillou. South of St-Julien is a considerable extent of land classified merely as Haut-Médoc, but to the north the appellation is contiguous with the southern border of Pauillac, and Ch Léoville-Las-Cases in the extreme north of St-Julien shares many characteristics with some fine Pauillac wines, notably Ch LATOUR which is well within sight.

The Léoville estate, as Penning-Rowsell points out, must have been the largest in the entire Médoc in the 18th century, before it was divided into the three second growths known today as Chx Léoville-Las-Cases, Léoville-Poyferré, and Léoville-Barton. Léoville-Las-Cases is the biggest of the three by far, and is today run the most ambitiously by Michel Delon, whose policy is admirably strict in terms of wine quality and longevity, although he believes in pricing the wines accordingly. These firm, deep coloured, Cabernet-based wines are supported by a strict selection process which can make Clos du Marquis one of Bordeaux's finest SECOND WINES.

Léoville-Poyferré, which includes the original château building, enjoyed a heyday in terms of its reputation in the 1920s, but also demonstrated something of a return to form in the 1980s. Best value, and perhaps most representative of the appellation, is Léoville-Barton, run from Ch Langoa-Barton, a fine third growth, by Anthony BARTON.

Chx Gruaud-Larose and Ducru-Beaucaillou are the other two St-Julien second growths, and produce two of the Médoc's finest wines in most vintages. Gruaud-Larose is usually the richer of the two, and the property was well run for most of the 20th century by the NÉGOIANTS CORDIER, who introduced their own special bottle for this as well as their fourth growth Ch Talbot, another correct St-Julien wine. The particularly distinctive Victorian box that is Ch Ducru-Beaucaillou ('beautiful pebble') is, unusually for a Médoc château, the home of the owners, the Borie family, who produce one of the most traditionally fashioned wines of the Médoc here, as well as owning Ch Grand-Puy-Lacoste of PAUILLAC.

Second growth **St-Julien** Ch Gruaud-Larose, whose wines embody St Julien's virtues of harmony and longevity.

The third growth Ch Lagrange was much improved in the 1980s by the Japanese spirits firm Suntory, with help from Michel Delon of Léoville-Las-Cases, while fourth growths Chx St Pierre, Talbot, Branaire-Ducru, and Beychevelle are all well run.

St-Julien's classed growths account for about three-quarters of the appellation's total production, and even such unclassified properties as Chx Gloria, Hortevie, and Lalande-Borie do not believe in underpricing their admittedly admirable produce.

For more information see MÉDOC and map of BORDEAUX.

Ginestet, B., *St-Julien* (Paris, 1984).
Parker, R., *Bordeaux* (2nd edn., New York, 1991).
Penning-Rowsell, E., *The Wines of Bordeaux* (6th edn., London, 1989).
Peppercorn, D., *Bordeaux* (2nd edn., London, 1991).

ST-LAURENT,,as well as being one of the few villages of any size in the MÉDOC, is the name of a black grape variety for long thought to be related to PINOT NOIR and today most commonly encountered in lower AUSTRIA and the Austrian wine region Burgenland. It is capable of producing deep coloured, velvety reds with sufficient concentration—provided yields are limited—to merit ageing in oak and then bottle. Lesser versions can be simply and soupily sweet but the variety has been successfully blended with such fashionable varieties as CABERNET SAUVIGNON, Blauburgunder (PINOT NOIR), and also with Austria's BLAUFRÄNKISCH, notably in Austria's Neusiedlersee-Hügelland district on the west shore of the lake.

It has been known in eastern France and there were about 30 ha/74 acres in Germany, mainly Pfalz, in 1990, but this is essentially an Austrian speciality and one in which the

Austrians themselves see considerable potential. Certainly it has had several centuries to adapt itself to conditions in lower Austria and Burgenland, where its only major viticultural disadvantage, dangerously early budding, is less problematic than in Alsace, for example. It also ripens well ahead of Pinot Noir and can be cultivated on a much wider range of sites. Its thicker grape skins also help ward off rot, although COULURE can be a problem.

The variety is also cultivated in CZECHOSLOVAKIA where it is known as Vavrinecke, or Svatovavrinecke.

GALET refutes earlier ampelographers' suggestions of a genealogical link with Pinot Noir.

Galet, P., *Cépages et vignobles de France* (2nd edn., Montpellier, 1990).

ST-MACAIRE, town in the BORDEAUX region just across the river GARONNE from Langon in the GRAVES district. It lends its name to **Côtes de Bordeaux-St-Macaire**, a small, and declining, BORDEAUX AC regional appellation for sweet white wines.

ST-MONT, CÔTES DE, VDQS in the ARMAGNAC region used particularly by the dynamic Plaimont CO-OPERATIVE. The zone is effectively a northern extension of the MADIRAN area and much the same grape varieties are planted, although yields are generally higher. TANNAT must constitute at least 70 per cent of some surprisingly juicy reds, while Arrufiac (RUFFIAC), CLAIRETTE, and PETIT COURBU must constitute at least half the blend of whites, the MANSENGS making up the rest. More than 700 ha / 1,730 acres of vineyard are dedicated to this wine, about three-quarters of it to red wine production. Quality is increasing with every vintage, as is the price differential between it and the local VIN DE PAYS des Côtes de Gascogne.

ST-PÉRAY, small and shrinking appellation for white SPARKLING WINES that seem something of an anomaly in the northern RHÔNE, famous for the weight and longevity of its wines. Soils and MESOCLIMATE here are admittedly cooler than most of the rest of the Rhône, but the Marsanne and Roussanne or Roussette grapes grown here produce few wines of great finesse, despite the fact that the MÉTHODE TRADITIONELLE is employed to transform them into sparkling wine. A considerable proportion of production is given its first fermentation at the co-operative of Tain l'HERMITAGE before being made sparkling in the St-Péray co-operative cellars. A small quantity of still St-Péray is also made which is not unlike white St-Joseph.

ST-POURÇAIN, sometimes called **St-Pourçain-sur-Sioule**, small VDQS in the cereal- and OAK-producing ALLIER *département* almost precisely in the centre of France. (St-Pourçain cannot be found on maps of French wine regions; only on detailed maps of the whole *hexagone*—see FRANCE.) It was an important site in Roman times, near RIVER transport and offering suitable HILLSIDE VINEYARDS. White St-Pourçain was one of the most respected wines in France in the Middle Ages (see LOIRE, history, and MEDIEVAL LITERATURE) but is today more of a cool-climate curiosity. From fewer than 500 ha / 1,235 acres of vineyard on varied soils of limestone, granite, and gravel, a wide range of wine colours and flavours are made, being typically dry, light in body, and relatively high in acidity.

The traditional vine variety was TRESALLIER, the local variant of SACY, but modern white wines are just as likely to be made from CHARDONNAY and/or SAUVIGNON and there is a legal limit (50 per cent in 1993) on the amount of Tresallier which may be used for white wines. GAMAY is the most common grape used for pink and light red St-Pourçain, although some PINOT NOIR is also grown and individual producers as conscientious as the Domaine de Bellevue make increasingly serious red wine from it. The CO-OPERATIVE in the town of St-Pourçain-sur-Sioule itself dominates production. Promotion to APPELLATION CONTRÔLÉE status is regularly sought.

George, R., *French Country Wines* (London, 1990).

ST-ROMAIN, exquisitely pretty village perched on top of a cliff in the Côte de Beaune district of Burgundy producing red wines from Pinot Noir and white wines from Chardonnay, the former maintaining a slight majority. There are no PREMIERS CRUS in the appellation which was granted only in 1967.

The vineyards of St-Romain are situated behind those of Auxey-Duresses and at higher altitude, 300 to 400 m / 985–1,310 ft above sea level, than is usual in the Côte d'Or. In lesser vintages the grapes do not ripen as well as elsewhere but in warmer years the wines can be excellent value. St-Romain is also home to one of the region's best-known COOPERS, François Frères.

See also CÔTE D'OR and its map. J.T.C.M.

ST-SATURNIN, one of the most exciting of the named CRUS within the Coteaux du LANGUEDOC appellation in southern France named after the eponymous village but including parts of St-Guiraud, Jonquières, and Arboras. Just west of MONTPEYROUX, this zone is also in high, rugged country where little other than the vine will grow. The St-Saturnin CO-OPERATIVE is particularly dynamic, as are such individual producers as Mas Jullien, who coax maximum character out of local grape varieties grown here on the south-facing slopes of the Cévennes.

SAINTSBURY, PROFESSOR GEORGE (1845–1933). Though a distinguished man of letters in his day, Saintsbury is now principally remembered for *Notes on a Cellar-Book*, a seminal work on wine which was an immediate success and has run to many editions.

He was born on 23 October 1845 in Southampton, where his father was superintendent of the docks. The family moved to London in 1850 and Saintsbury attended King's College School, where he acquired his deep love of literature. Aged 17 he won a Postmastership to Merton College, Oxford, but to his everlasting regret he failed to win a Fellowship. For 10

Merton College, Oxford's portrait of Professor George **Saintsbury** by William Nicholson. The scholar would never have believed that his most durable work would be his cellar-book (top).

years, from the age of 21, he was a schoolmaster but eventually settled in London with his wife and two sons, becoming a journalist, and for a time was assistant editor of the *Saturday Review.*

The actual cellar book was a simple exercise book in which Saintsbury listed the contents of just two cellars, the first in his London house in West Kensington, the second in Edinburgh, where from 1895 to 1915 he held the Regius Chair of Rhetoric and English Literature at Edinburgh University. It was reported that for 18 years he started his day by reading a French novel.

In June 1915 he retired from the Chair in Edinburgh, having some 10 years previously developed gout, which prevented him from drinking red wine. He eventually retired to Bath, in an annexe to 1 Royal Crescent.

During his retirement he published 13 volumes, including *Notes on a Cellar-Book*, which first appeared in July 1920, as well as innumerable articles and pamphlets.

The SAINTSBURY CLUB was founded in 1931 but, although nominated president, the Professor, due to ill health, never attended a meeting. J.M.B.

Saintsbury, G., *Notes on a Cellar-Book* (15th edn., London, 1978).

SAINTSBURY CLUB, perhaps the most famous of all DINING CLUBS connected with wine, founded in 1931 in honour of Professor George SAINTSBURY. The Club meets twice a year, as nearly as possible on his birthday 23 October and on his name day 23 April St George's Day.

Its beginnings were unremarkable. At a luncheon given by André SIMON, J. L. Squire casually mentioned Saintsbury, old and ill in Bath. Shortly after, in May 1931, a dinner was organized, and it was at this that Maurice Healy (author of *Stay me with Flagons*) suggested that a Saintsbury Club should be founded 'to perpetuate and honour his name'. The first meeting, or dinner, was held at Vintners' Hall (see VINTNERS) on Saintsbury's 86th birthday.

The membership, limited to 50, has always comprised men of letters, wine lovers, both professional and amateurs, with a good sprinkling of DOCTORS and lawyers. The perpetual president George Saintsbury himself never attended a meeting, but his health is toasted by the members at each meeting. André Simon was, unsurprisingly, a leading light and the original cellarer and treasurer. Founder members included Sir John Squire as 'editor'; Vyvyan Holland, son of Oscar Wilde, as honorary secretary; and such luminaries as H. Warner Allen, Hilaire Belloc, Duff Cooper, Sir Gerald du Maurier, the Marquis of Hartington, Maurice Healy, A. P. Herbert, and Compton Mackenzie. Representing the wine trade were Col. Ian Campbell, John HARVEY, Francis Berry, and William Byass (of GONZALEZ BYASS). The president of Le Club des Cent in Paris is ex officio an honorary member.

Members, upon election, donate fine wine, and the Club cellar, at Vintners' Hall, is of a high order. Once a year a member of the Club is invited to give the Saintsbury 'oration', which is then privately printed for members. J.M.B.

ST-VÉRAN, appellation created in 1971 for white wines from the Chardonnay grape in southern Burgundy, between the Mâconnais and Beaujolais, to include much of the wine that was once sold as Beaujolais Blanc. St-Véran encompasses seven communes between Mâcon and Pouilly-Fuissé: St-Vérand as well as Davayé and Prissé in the north and Chânes, Chasselas, Leynes, and St-Amour in the south.

The wines frequently have more body and ageing ability than a typical MÂCON-VILLAGES without rivalling the power and persistence of the wines of POUILLY-FUISSÉ, which forms an enclave within St-Véran. J.T.C.M.

SALARY, WINE AS. The practice of paying workers in wine is an old one (and certainly older than the payments in salt from which the word 'salary' is derived). In Ancient PERSIA, for example, wine rations were strictly ordered and were often far in excess of any individual's possible personal consumption.

More recently, labourers, and in particular grape-pickers on the bigger BORDEAUX estates, would expect to receive some quantity of wine (rarely of great quality and often lowly PIQUETTE) in addition to wages.

The most notorious, and fast disappearing, instance of paying workers with deliberately stupefying quantities of wine is the DOP system once prevalent in SOUTH AFRICA.

SALICE SALENTO, DOC for robust red wine made mainly from NEGROAMARO grapes in south east Italy. For more details see APULIA.

SALINITY, the concentration of salt (sodium chloride) in soils or irrigation water. High concentrations in **saline** soils can adversely affect vines. Symptoms of salinity damage include marginal CHLOROSIS, followed by NECROSIS and then DEFOLIATION. When vines are irrigated by sprinklers with water containing excessive salt, leaves may be burnt, and in severe cases this leads to defoliation. Similar effects can occasionally be found in coastal vineyards affected by wind-borne salt. MERLOT vines are particularly susceptible. Saline soils are typically found in hot and dry climates where IRRIGATION has been introduced, such as in inland Australia. Applied irrigation water can come into contact with salty underground water, allowing salt to be brought to the surface by evaporation. The problem is also found in southern France, where there are 10,000 ha/24,700 acres or more of vineyards planted on ancient marine deposits. Salinity can be overcome by applying more irrigation water than the vines need, provided the soil has good DRAINAGE. As surplus water washes through the soil, salt is removed downwards. Some vine varieties such as COLOMBARD are tolerant to salt, and there are ROOTSTOCKS such as Dog Ridge and Ramsey which show some salt tolerance. Wine from vineyards with saline soils may contain elevated levels of salt. R.E.S.

SALT can affect vines. See SALINITY. Some, but very few, wines may taste slightly salty.

SALVADOR, CALIFORNIA red-fleshed hybrid vine variety superseded by RUBIRED and therefore in decline.

SALVAGNIN, Vaud name for a light red blend of Pinot Noir with a bit of Gamay in SWITZERLAND. Similar to but less common than the DÔLE of Valais.

SALVAGNIN (NOIR) is a Jura name for PINOT NOIR, disconcertingly similar to the name of one of the Jura's own vine varieties, SAVAGNIN.

SÄMLING 88, common Austrian synonym for the SCHEUREBE vine variety which has not shone there, although several hundred hectares are planted in the southern Austrian wine regions of Burgenland and Styria.

SAMOS, see GREECE.

SAMPLING, important part of a continuum of wine quality control procedures which begin in the vineyard and may end when a consumer picks a bottle out of a CASE in his or her CELLAR.

A very small proportion of a vineyard's fruit may be sampled to assess its chemical composition to help predict the HARVEST date, as well as to indicate likely quality and, in some cases, eventual wine style. In its simplest form, grape sampling might consist of selecting some berries haphazardly from the vineyard and expressing juice into a REFRACTOMETER to measure sugar content (see MUST WEIGHT).

The person taking the sample must be careful to avoid any bias which might affect the sampling result. Fruit must be sampled from both sides of the row, including fruit from the sunny outside of the CANOPY as well as fruit from the shaded interior. Similarly, all parts of the vineyard should be sampled, with particular attention paid to any variations in the vineyard which could affect fruit ripening. Either berries or bunches are taken, and a normal sample may weigh 300 g (10.5 oz) to several kilograms. Typically the sample is taken to the winery laboratory and crushed or pressed to obtain juice, which is then analysed for sugar and perhaps also ACIDITY and PH.

Many vineyards are harvested without a fruit sample being taken, however, particularly in more primitive traditional regions.

A second sampling is frequently made when a load of grapes is delivered to the winery, particularly if the grapes have been bought by contract, since grape PRICES are often based on sugar levels.

During FERMENTATION samples are taken at least daily to verify the regular conversion of sugars to ALCOHOL. Later, during ÉLEVAGE, regular sampling provides the wine-maker with valuable guidance. Finally, shortly before BOTTLING, samples are taken for detailed analysis to ensure that the wine meets all regulations and is free of FAULTS and CONTAMINANTS.

An important part of selling wine EN PRIMEUR is the release of **cask samples,** or *échantillons* in French, samples drawn from the containers in which the wine is still being matured, typically a BARREL, on which wine merchants and wine writers can base their assessments. Such raw wines, often roughly drawn off into small sample bottles, have not undergone STABILIZATION and can suffer OXIDATION and other faults after only a week or two. The best way to judge a young wine still in cask is sampling in the cellar or winery itself, tasting it straight from the barrel, but sampling the contents of a wide range of different barrels. R.E.S., A.D.W., & J.Ro.

SAMTROT. See MÜLLERREBE.

SAN BENITO, small CALIFORNIA county inland from Monterey County. San Benito experienced a brief flurry of growth in its vineyards during the 1970s, but has largely subsided into somnolence. The one exception to a prevailing mediocrity is a one-vineyard AVA named Mount Harlan after the limestone-rich slopes on which Calera winery's several celebrated blocks of Pinot Noir grow. The county has other AVAs (Cienega Valley, Lime Kiln Valley, Paicines) from which little is seen.

SANCERRE, dramatically situated hilltop town on the left bank of the upper Loire which lends its name to one of the Loire's most famous wines: racy, pungent, dry white Sauvignon Blanc which enjoyed enormous commercial success in the 1970s. The town's situation on such a navigable RIVER, and the favourable DRAINAGE and TOPOGRAPHY of the rolling countryside around it, assured Sancerre's long history as a wine producer; the suitability of the site for viticulture was obvious from Roman times. Until the mid 20th century, however, Sancerre produced red wines and white wines from the Chasselas table grape. Sancerre's dramatically simple, piercing Sauvignon flavours of gooseberries and nettles were initially introduced into the bistros of Paris as a sort of white wine equivalent of Beaujolais, but, by the late 1970s and early 1980s, Sancerre was regarded as the quintessential white wine for restaurants around the world.

The average altitude of the Sancerre hills is between 200 and 400 m/655–1,310 ft. The Sauvignon has adapted well to many of the varied TERROIRS around Sancerre where, in 14 different communes, vines are cultivated, particularly on south-facing slopes. There are three distinct areas: the 'white' western vineyards are made up of clay and limestone soils that produce quite powerful wines; those between here and the town of Sancerre are high in gravel as well as limestone and produce particularly delicate wines; while those close to Sancerre itself are rich in flint (*silex*) and yield longer-living, particularly perfumed wines. Comparisons with POUILLY-FUMÉ, made just a few miles upstream on the opposite bank, are inevitable, although both are relatively large, heterogeneous appellations. The total area given over to the Sancerre appellation, which had declined to about 700 ha/1,730 acres in the 1960s, was more than 2,000 ha three decades later.

A wide range of agricultural activity takes place on this terrain, and in many of the outlying villages the vine plays a subordinate role, but viticulture is particularly important in Bué (just as nearby Chavignol, where the meticulous grower Henri Bourgeois is based, is famous for its goat's cheese).

The climate here is distinctly CONTINENTAL, and the vineyards are easily subject to spring FROSTS, but the river to the east and the forests to the west moderate low temperatures. Vines are generally CORDON or single GUYOT trained. Winemaking in the 1970s and 1980s was a relatively simple affair of maximizing the fruit qualities by TEMPERATURE CONTROL and a fair amount of STAINLESS STEEL. There have since been attempts to marry Sancerre fruit with OAK, with varying degrees of success.

Sancerre's popularity has brought with it the inevitable increase in the proportion of mediocre wine produced under the appellation. In particularly cool years, even the best producers have to work hard to avoid unpleasantly HERBACEOUS aromas and a lack of fruity substance. Most Sancerre is ready for drinking almost as soon as it is bottled, and rarely improves beyond two or three years, although the best certainly keep. In years as ripe as 1989, some sweet VENDANGE TARDIVE wine was produced by the likes of Alphonse Mellot and Henri Bourgeois.

Sancerre also exists in light, often beguiling, red and rosé versions, made from Pinot Noir grapes. These wines have enjoyed a certain vogue but need very high standards of winemaking and good weather to imbue them with a good core of fruit.

See also LOIRE and map on pp. 576–7.

SAND, description of sediment or soil which is made up of relatively large particles (bigger than silt, and much bigger than clay). See SOIL TEXTURE and GEOLOGY, for more details of this particular form of soil classification. Sandy soils can be difficult to cultivate because of their poor ability to store water or nutrients, but they are notable in viticulture for providing a good measure of protection from the PHYLLOXERA louse. Vineyards dominated by sand include those of COLARES in Portugal, the Camargue in the south of France, and the Great Plain of HUNGARY.

SANDEMAN, port and sherry house with one of the most famous logos in the wine trade, the black Sandeman Don. It was founded in London by a Scotsman, George Sandeman, who in 1790 established his shipping business with a £300 loan from his father. He began by shipping sherry and moved swiftly on to port, travelling frequently to Spain and Portugal and trading in Tom's Coffee House in Cornhill, London. In 1809 George Sandeman established an office in Cádiz and shipped wines under the Sandeman name. In 1879 the company took over all the assets, vineyards, bodegas, and wine stocks of a bankrupted sherry producer. Sandeman made its headquarters in St Swithin's Lane, where it remained until 1969. The famous trade mark Sandeman Don was created in 1928. Chairman Walter Albert Sandeman pioneered advertising for his brand with great success. Sandeman became a public company in 1952, although it was increasingly vulnerable to a take-over bid. Eventually it was sold to the North American multinational corporation Seagram in 1980 for £17 million. The following decade saw an increasing emphasis on quantity rather than quality. Sandeman's Founder's Reserve is now the biggest selling BRAND of port in North

Ungrafted vines planted on their own roots are safe from phylloxera in the **sandy** soil of Colares on the Portuguese coast.

America. In 1991 George Sandeman (representing the seventh generation of the family to make port) moved to OPORTO to take control, becoming the first Sandeman to live in Portugal. The company's vineyard holdings in the DOURO are being reorganized, with the less promising land put up for sale. A 1988 single-quinta port (see PORT styles) from the highly rated Quinta do Vau was released in 1993.

Sandeman's sherry business is today equal to port, in terms of both volume and value. The company, the fourth biggest sherry producer, owns nearly 400 ha/988 acres of vineyards in the JEREZ region. S.A.

Halley, N., *Sandeman: Two Hundred Years of Port and Sherry* (London, 1990).
Mayson, R., *Portugal's Wine and Winemakers* (London, 1992).

SANDSTONE, a sedimentary rock composed of SAND-grade particles which are usually QUARTZ. The rock may be unconsolidate or the grains may be held together by another material such as calcium carbonate forming a CALCAREOUS sandstone, or the rock may be hardened by the quartz grains growing into one another. These variations mean that sandstones vary greatly in fertility and drainage. Sandstones occur in the higher alluvial ground of the river Dordogne, just below the Côtes of ST-ÉMILION, and in similar settings elsewhere. J.M.H.

SANGIOVESE, red grape variety that is Italy's most planted and is particularly common in central Italy. In 1990 almost 10 per cent of all Italian vineyards, or more than 100,000 ha/247,000 acres, were planted with some form of Sangiovese.

In its various clonal variations and names (Brunello, Prugnolo Gentile, Morellino) Sangiovese is the principal vine variety for fine red wine in TUSCANY, the sole grape permitted for BRUNELLO DI MONTALCINO, and the base of the blend for CHIANTI, VINO NOBILE DI MONTEPULCIANO, and the vast majority of SUPERTUSCANS. It is, in addition, the workhorse red grape of all of central Italy, widely planted in UMBRIA (where it gives its best results in the DOCG wines Torgiano and Montefalco), in the MARCHES (where it is the base of the Rosso Piceno and an important component of the Rosso Conero), and in LATIUM. Sangiovese can be found as far afield as Lombardy and Valpolicella to the north and Campania to the south.

The vine itself, probably indigenous to Tuscany, is of ancient origin, as the literal translation of its name ('blood of Jove') suggests, and it has been postulated that it was even known to the ETRUSCANS. The first historical mention of the variety, however, by Giocanvettorio Soderini, is relatively recent; he described it in 1722 as 'highly praised for the making of wine'. Cosimo Trinci, in 1738, observed that wines made solely from Sangiovese were somewhat hard and acid, but excellent when blended with other varieties, a judgement echoed by Giovanni Cosimo Villifranci in 1883. Bettino RICASOLI found a way to tame Sangiovese's asperity— a substantial addition of sweetening and softening CANAIOLO—which became the basis of all modern Chianti and of Vino Nobile di Montepulciano (although MAMMOLO and COLORINO as well as the white grapes MALVASIA and, especially, TREBBIANO were subsequently added to the blend). The use of small oak barrels, begun in the 1970s, can be seen as a modern solution to the same problem of excessive asperity.

Conventional ampelographical descriptions of Sangiovese, based on the pioneering work of G. Molon in 1906, divide the variety into two families: the Sangiovese Grosso, to which Brunello, Prugnolo Gentile, and the Sangiovese di Lamole (of Greve in Chianti) belong, and the Sangiovese Piccolo of other zones of Tuscany, with the implicit identification of a superior quality in the former. Current thinking is that this classification is too simplistic, that there are a large number of CLONES populating the region's vineyards, and that no specific qualitative judgements can be based on the size of either the berries or the bunches. Significant efforts are at last being made to identify and propagate superior clones; MASS SELECTION in the past sought principally to identify high-yielding clones without any regard for wine quality. The variety adapts well to a wide variety of soils, although the presence of limestone seems to exalt the elegant and forceful aromas that are perhaps the most attractive quality of the grape.

Sangiovese's principal characteristic in the vineyard is its slow and late ripening—harvests traditionally began after 29 September and even today can easily be protracted until or even beyond mid-October—which gives rich, alcoholic, and long-lived wine in hot years and creates problems of high ACIDITY and hard TANNINS in cool years. Over-production tends to accentuate the wine's acidity and lighten its colour, which can also OXIDIZE and start to brown at a relatively young age. The grape's rather thin skin creates a certain susceptibility to ROT in cool and damp years, which is a serious disadvantage in a region where rain in October is a frequent occurrence. Too often Sangiovese has been planted with scant attention to exposure and ALTITUDE in Tuscany, where the vine is often cultivated at an altitude up to or even beyond 500 m/1,640 ft. A good part of contemporary viticultural research in Tuscany—which involves increased VINE DENSITY, lower YIELDS per vine, better clones, more appropriate ROOTSTOCKS, lower vine-TRAINING SYSTEMS, small oak BARRELS, more suitable supplementary varieties for blending, different temperatures and lengths of FERMENTATION—are dedicated to resolving a single problem: how to put more meat on Sangiovese's bones, how to add flesh to its sizeable, but not always sensual, structure. D.T.

Throughout modern Tuscany, Sangiovese is now often blended with a certain proportion of the Bordeaux grape CABERNET SAUVIGNON, whether for Chianti (in which case the interloper should not exceed 10 per cent of the total) or a highly priced VINO DA TAVOLA. This highly successful blend, in which the intense fruit and colour of Cabernet marries well with the characterful native variety, was first sanctioned by the DOC authorities in CARMIGNANO.

In UMBRIA the variety dominates most of the region's best red wine, as in the Torgiano of the firm LUNGAROTTI. But in terms of quantity rather than quality, Sangiovese is most important in Romagna (see EMILIA-ROMAGNA), where SANGIOVESE DI ROMAGNA is as common as the LAMBRUSCO vine is in Emilia. Sangiovese di Romagna wine is typically light, red, ubiquitous, and destined, quite properly, for early consumption. The most widely planted Sangiovese vines planted in Romagna appear to have little in common with Tuscany's most revered selections, although there has been some careful CLONAL SELECTION in Romagna with promising results. Some Sangiovese is grown in the south of Italy, where it is usually used for blending with local grapes, and the success of Supertuscans has inevitably led to a certain amount of experimentation with the variety to the north of Tuscany too.

Outside Italy

Like other Italian grape varieties, particularly red ones, Sangiovese was taken west, to both North and South America, by Italian emigrants. In South America it is best known in Argentina, where there are several thousand hectares, mainly in Mendoza province, producing wine that few Tuscan tasters would recognize as Sangiovese.

In California, however, international recognition for the quality of Supertuscans brought a sudden increase in Sangiovese's popularity in the late 1980s and early 1990s. In 1991 its acreage was climbing towards 200, or about as much land as CABERNET SAUVIGNON had commanded in 1961. Most substantial plantings are in the NAPA Valley, but smaller patches can be found in SONOMA County, SAN LUIS OBISPO County, and the SIERRA FOOTHILLS. Early results give real hope to Californians, showing promising balance and structure. Some had the faintly floral aromas veteran drinkers of Chiantis and Brunellos would recognize as Sangiovese, although the wines were made in Californian rather than Tuscan styles. Robert Pepi and Atlas Peak, in which the Tuscan firm of

ANTINORI have an important stake, both in Napa, were the important pioneers.

Anderson, B., *The Wine Atlas of Italy* (London and New York, 1990).
Gleave, D., *The Wines of Italy* (London and New York, 1989).

SANGIOVESE DI ROMAGNA, quantitatively important VARIETAL central Italian red made from the most widely cultivated grape variety in ROMAGNA. In the DOC zone 5,500 ha / 13,585 acres were planted in the mid 1990s, with an average annual production of 170,000 hl / 4.5 million gal. The reputation of the zone has been sullied by the mediocre quality of much of the wine produced, and by the efforts of a number of Tuscan producers to blame the low quality of Tuscan wines between 1965 and 1980 on the infiltration of their vineyards by high-yielding, low-quality Sangiovese di Romagna. Just like the SANGIOVESE of Tuscany, the Sangiovese of Romagna exists in many clonal variations, some of which do indeed produce abundant quantities of indifferent wine, but the better clones of Sangiovese di Romagna are by no means inferior to those of Tuscany, and the occasional bottles of fine Sangiovese produced in Romagna give tantalizing hints of possibilities yet to be exploited.

The variety is cultivated throughout the region and, in the past, took on a distinctive personality in the various subzones in which it was planted: lighter and fruitier in the eastern and western extremes (near the border with the Marches and close to Bologna); fuller, richer, and more tannic in the central provinces of Ravenna and Forlì. Modern WINE-MAKING techniques and practices have partially flattened and standardized these differences, but there can be few doubts that the best Sangiovese di Romagna comes from the hills to the south of the ancient Via Emilia, where the terrain rises towards the Apennines. The DOC reflects this widely accepted view of the most suitable terrain, confining the territory of Sangiovese di Romagna to the eastern hills of the province of Bologna and the Apennine zones of the provinces of Ravenna and Forlì. Here the mixture of sandstone and clay in the soil and the high summer temperatures succeed in ripening Sangiovese and could, with more commitment and more professional wine-making, give products of real distinction. A tradition of CASK AGEING has long existed and, in the area extending from Marzeno to Modigliana to the west and Predappio to Meldola and Bertinoro in the east, successful experiments with small oak barrels have given results comparable to a good Tuscan VINO DA TAVOLA from Sangiovese. These superior products remain, for the moment, mere drops in the bucket: permitted yields of 11 tons/ha and the domination of the large CO-OPERATIVES have tended to reduce Sangiovese di Romagna to its lowest common denominator. Highly successful commercial fruit production in Romagna has given the paradoxical result of a high level of professional preparation and the tendency to treat grapes as a mere cash crop whose value can be assessed only by calculating the price per ton and the potential tonnage per hectare. Sixty per cent of Romagna's production is controlled by co-operatives, and another 25 per cent is controlled by large commercial wineries. The virtual elimination of the vine-grower from the process of transforming his grapes into wine continues to impede the kind of quality revolution for Sangiovese that transformed Tuscan wines between 1975 and 1990. D.T.

Anderson, B., *The Wine Atlas of Italy* (London and New York, 1990).
Gleave, D., *The Wines of Italy* (London and New York, 1989).

SANGRÍA, a mixture of red wine, lemonade, and, sometimes, spirits and fresh fruit, served typically in Spain's tourist resorts.

SANITATION. See HYGIENE.

SAN JOAQUIN VALLEY, southern half of the vast Central Valley in CALIFORNIA, and that part of the state which produces the great bulk of its wine, and its TABLE GRAPES and DRYING GRAPES. It stretches almost 400 miles/640 km from Stockton down to Bakersfield, and approaches 60 miles in width at its widest. Its great expanses of vineyard include more than 100,000 acres/40,000 ha of wine grapes. It is, in certain senses at least, California's MIDI or Mezzogiorno, its bottomless well of cheap, everyday wine. Except for the Lodi and Clarksburg AVAS at its very northern end, near the confluence of the San Joaquin and Sacramento rivers, it resists any internal dividing lines because its climate and soils are so relentlessly consistent. The dominant wine varieties in an era when white so definitively outsells red in the United States, the 1980s and early 1990s, are Chenin Blanc and Colombard.

Huge as it is, its wineries match. The immense E. & J. GALLO is unquestionably the most important firm in it, making about 55 million cases of wine a year. Heublein Inc. has a major winery at Madera producing for that firm's many labels. Bronco and the Wine Group (Franzia) are other major firms in the heart of the San Joaquin Valley. Grapes from Lodi and Clarksburg, especially, are sought after both by the big wineries of the valley and by smaller, more prestige-orientated firms in the coastal valleys. Both Robert MONDAVI of NAPA and Sebastiani of SONOMA have wineries in Lodi. Glen Ellen, J. Lohr, and others also reach into the area regularly, mainly for their FIGHTING VARIETALS.

Clarksburg AVA

Much of the AVA is composed of deep-soiled islands in the Sacramento delta from a point near Sacramento west beyond the town of Clarksburg. Though its position in the river channel leaves its vineyards open to the strongest summer sea fogs, the vast proportion of surrounding water retards overnight cooling when fogs are not afoot, so Clarksburg is far from being California's coolest vineyard district. Although a spectrum of varieties grows within the zone, only Chenin Blanc truly distinguishes itself. Indeed only here in all of California does Chenin Blanc become regionally identifiable. For all practical purposes it has swallowed up the Merritt Island AVA, which lies within its western end.

Lodi AVA
In spite of the Italian name, German settlers have historically controlled much of Lodi's grape-growing and it was they who made this California's capital of CO-OPERATIVE wineries. Of the dozen or so co-ops once in existence, only East-Side (Oak Ridge, Royal Host, Handel & Mettler labels) continues as a substantial producer of bottled wines. The AVA surrounds the town of the same name, on a deep, rich-soiled valley floor so flat that here is where the San Joaquin river begins to divide and redivide itself on the way to becoming part of the Sacramento delta system. Lodi is inland from, less watery, and thus warmer than the Clarksburg AVA to the north west, but much less warm than Madera, Fresno, and other districts further south in the San Joaquin Valley. Zinfandel and Ruby Cabernet have shown the greatest adaptability to Lodi's growing conditions, and Zinfandel commanded nearly 12,000 acres/5,000 ha. Ruby Cabernet yielded agreeable, well-balanced wines throughout the 1960s and early 1970s, but the variety has faded with expanded plantings of Cabernet Sauvignon. Zinfandels from here tend to cluster at the fleshy, plummy, ripe end of the spectrum.

Madera AVA
At the very heart of California's vast San Joaquin Valley, the viticultural area anchors itself on the town of Madera. Most of its acreage is in Madera County, but some lies across the line in Fresno County. The AVA's long-term reason for being may come to be dessert wines, especially port types and Muscats. Its table wines are for everyday.

SANLÚCAR DE BARRAMEDA, one of the three Spanish towns in which SHERRY is made and matured. MANZANILLA is a delicate, pale, dry sherry matured in Sanlúcar.

SAN LUIS OBISPO, wine-producing county in the CENTRAL COAST AVA of CALIFORNIA. Many of California's coastal counties demonstrate why the American AVA system, its embryonic answer to France's APPELLATION CONTRÔLÉE, tries to avoid political boundaries in the shaping of vineyard districts. San Luis Obispo County does so more vigorously than most. A boiling summer sun beats down on the high, sheltered plain that is the Paso Robles AVA while fogs hang over a narrow, cool coastal shelf holding the Edna Valley AVA near San Luis Obispo city. The two AVAs are fewer than 20 miles/32 km apart, and well within the same county. A third AVA, Arroyo Grande, exaggerates the situation in Edna Valley.

Arroyo Grande AVA
A long range of bare hills sloping towards Pismo Bay at the southern edge of San Luis Obispo County, Arroyo Grande has so far been viticulturally distinguished only by the painstaking decision to plant 350 ha/865 acres of it for Maison Deutz, the California arm of Champagne house Deutz. The views out to sea are splendid, if one can overlook the sprawl of coastal development that threatens to end the region's vinous career near its outset.

Edna Valley AVA
Directly south of the town of San Luis Obispo, Edna Valley won quick fame for its Chardonnays beginning in the mid 1970s. Edna Valley Vineyards is the principal winery. Gewürztraminer has also done well, but Pinot Noir has been variable. Low hills shelter the small, soup tureen-shaped valley slightly from air cooled by the Pacific Ocean, yet allow it to collect enough moisture from fog to make up, in part, for a persistent lack of rainfall.

Paso Robles AVA
An isolated upland valley about midway between Los Angeles and San Francisco, Paso Robles earned an early reputation as a place where outlaws could hole up, no questions asked. Locals still cultivate the impression that this is a haven for the wayward. From the 1880s onward, its role as a wine district was to produce the kind of sun-baked, high alcohol, fiercely tannic Zinfandels that could pull an outlaw into a saloon on the bleak, wintry nights that are almost as common hereabouts as blistering summer days. Since its confirmation as an AVA, newcomers in an expanding roster of local wineries and the southern end of the SACRAMENTO VALLEY have taken to making Cabernet Sauvignon, Sauvignon Blanc, and Chardonnay in vineyards set on a restlessly rolling plain east of Paso Robles town. Wines from these new territories can charm early, but few have shown long staying power. The Zinfandelists have stuck with their traditional haunts in high hills to the west, but now even they are joining up as growers of Cabernet and Chardonnay. Meridian, J. Lohr, and Arciero represent the new breed; Mastantuono, Pesenti, and Tobin James the old. One stubborn holdout, Martin Brothers, is trying to carve out a name with Nebbiolo and other Italian varieties.

York Mountain AVA
A small subappellation of the western edge of the larger Paso Robles AVA, York Mountain has not established itself as a source of any particular wine type although history favours Zinfandel from its mostly east-facing slopes.

SAN MARINO, tiny republic within Italy between the regions of EMILIA-ROMAGNA and the MARCHES. The quality of wine produced rose dramatically in the 1980s and is mostly 'exported', to tourist resorts on the Adriatic.

SAN MICHELE ALL'ADIGE, ISTITUTO AGRARIO DI, one of Italy's better-known wine schools and centres of ACADEME. It was founded in 1874 in what was then the Austrian South Tyrol and is now the province of Trento in the far north of the country. Its activities have always spanned both education and research, and now encompass fruit crops other than wine, and dairy farming. Its first director was Edmund Mach, highly regarded in the former Austro-Hungarian empire as an OENOLOGIST. A wide range of viticultural research is undertaken, often with other research institutes, and oenological concerns include the analysis of flavour and PHENOLICS, microbiology, and sensory analysis (see TASTING). The institute produces a range of wines under its own label.

SAN PASQUAL VALLEY, California wine region and AVA. One vineyard gave rise to the AVA but PIERCE'S DISEASE devastated that property, throwing the name into disuse. The valley stretches eastward from Escondido in San Diego County in the South Coast region.

SANTA BARBARA, southern CALIFORNIA city which gives its name to the southernmost in a string of three heavily planted wine counties on California's CENTRAL COAST (see also MONTEREY and SAN LUIS OBISPO). Its southernmost vines grow hardly more than 100 miles/160 km from downtown Los Angeles. Most of Santa Barbara has one of the dreamiest climates man could hope to find, almost rain free, and so mild that semi-tropical plants grow in lush profusion. And yet! Pinot Noir and Chardonnay are its prized varieties because most of its vineyards hug the Pacific Ocean shore north of Cape Concepcion, where nearly eternal sea fogs create conditions cooler and cloudier than either CARNEROS or much of SONOMA County's Russian River. MISSIONARIES brought vines to the region in the 1770s (see CALIFORNIA, history), and a few commercial wineries dotted the landscape during the later 19th century, but it was not until the wine boom of the 1970s that Santa Barbara began to assert any serious claims as a wine-producing area. It has only two AVAS, and they do not encompass all of its 8,000 acres/3,200 ha of vineyard, but its reliance on fog as a cooling agent gives it remarkably complex shadings.

Santa Maria Valley AVA

A flock of distinctive Pinot Noirs brought this AVA swift identity during the 1980s. It also has proven well adapted to Chardonnay in a short career that began only with the 1970s. The Santa Maria river valley is a geographic curiosity for the fact that it runs true east–west, the only one of the state's wine valleys that does, and thus is wide open to the prevailing sea fogs of the region. Much more heavily planted than the Santa Ynez Valley to the south, it has only a sparse handful of wineries. Byron and Au Bon Climat were its most prominent wineries at the outset of the 1990s. Most of its grapes go to cellars outside the county. Much of the part that stays home goes to wineries in other parts of the county.

Santa Ynez Valley AVA

Although far from being the only schizophrenic AVA in California, the Santa Ynez Valley comes close to being the extreme case. It starts as a narrow, fog-beset river course between steep east–west hills that run inland from the Pacific shore at Lompoc as far as the village of Solvang. There the main valley turns north and, sheltered from sea fogs by elevation and higher hills, grows warmer. The lower end seems best suited to Pinot Noir, Chardonnay, and, perhaps, Riesling. The upper end appears to do better by Sauvignon Blanc and, mostly in blends, Cabernet Franc, Merlot, and Cabernet Sauvignon. Judgements must remain tentative; early plantings here came only after 1970, and acreage remains small, although nearly a score of cellars call the valley home. Firestone Vineyards, Zaca Mesa, and Carey Cellars were pioneers in the 1970s. They remained prominent in the early 1990s along with the Brander Vineyard, the Gainey Vineyard, Sanford, and Babcock.

SANTA CLARA VALLEY, California wine region and AVA south of San Francisco. Its other name, Silicon Valley, explains its status in the computer industry. In spite of a long vinous history, factories, shopping malls, and homes have long since supplanted most of its vineyards. A few acres of vines persist to the west in the SANTA CRUZ MOUNTAINS and at its southern end, near the town of Gilroy in the form of the San Ysidro AVA, which is, in essence, two adjacent vineyards devoted primarily to Chardonnay.

SANTA CRUZ MOUNTAINS, diverse CALIFORNIA wine region immediately south of San Francisco and AVA. Its vineyards amount to a light dusting of freckles on a long, lopsided, bony body. In a stretch of coast ranges that begins as the ridgepole of the San Francisco peninsula and continues south as far as the city of Santa Cruz, climates and soils would be so diverse as to beggar description even if vineyards were not separated one from another by miles of forest, meadows, even towns. The most useful points to make about it are: it is one of California's cooler growing regions; Pinot Noir has the longest and richest history; Cabernet Sauvignon has won the AVA its greatest fame; and a prominent RHÔNE RANGER, Bonny Doon's Randall Grahm, thinks it offers great prospects for Marsanne, Roussanne, and Syrah. A small sub-AVA, Ben Lomond Mountain, is a first effort to refine the gross boundaries. Ridge, David Bruce, Mt Eden, and Bonny Doon were among its best-known wineries in the early 1990s.

SANTA MADDALENA, known as **St Magdelener** by the many German speakers who make and drink it, is the most famous wine of the ALTO ADIGE in north east Italy. (In an Italian government classification of 1941 it was ranked after Barolo and Barbaresco as the country's most significant wine, a rating which would be unlikely to be repeated today.) It takes its name from the hill of Santa Maddalena to the east of the city of Bolzano (Bozen), long considered a particularly suitable site for the cultivation of the SCHIAVA (Vernatsch) grape from which the wine is made. Some 400 ha/988 acres are planted in the DOC zone and produce approximately 30,000 hl/792,000 gal per year. Like other important Italian DOCs, Santa Maddalena has undergone a significant enlargement of its production zone from the original nucleus (now called Santa Maddalena CLASSICO) of the communes of Santa Maddalena, Retsch, Justina, Leitach, and St Peter. The zone with its well-known name now stretches all the way to Settequerce (Siebeneich) in the Val d'Adige to the west and to Cornedo (Karneid) in the Val d'Isarco to the east. These latter

This botanical print demonstrates clearly one of **Syrah**'s great attributes as a producer of great red wines high in **phenolics**: small **berry size**.

zones undoubtedly give a Schiava of good quality but with less personality than the Schiava of Santa Maddalena; fortunately over 85 per cent of the current production of Santa Maddalena is Santa Maddalena Classico. The wine itself is a ruby to garnet red with aromas of berries and almonds, medium bodied with pronounced almond flavours on the finish. This bitter after-taste is often due to the illegal 'correction' of Santa Maddalena with 5 to 15 per cent of LAGREIN grapes to increase COLOUR, BODY, TANNINS, and potential longevity. D.T.

SANTA MARIA VALLEY, California wine region and AVA. See SANTA BARBARA.

SANTA YNEZ VALLEY, California wine region and AVA. See SANTA BARBARA.

SANTENAY, somewhat forgotten village and spa in the Côte de Beaune district of Burgundy producing red wines from Pinot Noir and occasional whites. The soils in Santenay are a little richer than most of the Côte d'Or in MARL, producing red wines tending to the rustic more than the elegant. They are not counted among Burgundy's finest, although they are capable of ageing well. The vineyards are trained and pruned according to the CORDON DE ROYAT system in place of the usual GUYOT.

Most of the best vineyards, the PREMIERS CRUS La Comme, Clos de Tavannes, and Les Gravières, form an extension from Chassagne-Montrachet. Also reputed are La Maladière, situated behind the main village, and Clos Rousseau on the far border of Santenay, beyond the casino and thermal waters of the higher village.

See also CÔTE D'OR and its map. J.T.C.M.

SANTORINI, one of the southern Cyclades islands that are part of GREECE, known in classical times as Thíra. It is a part of the core of an ancient volcano, which erupted *c.*1500 BC (perhaps a century earlier), destroying the Minoan civilizations of Thíra and, it is thought, neighbouring Crete. A large part of Thíra became submerged, and has remained so to this day.

In antiquity the island was not especially famous for its wine, but this was to change in the Middle Ages. It belonged to the Byzantine empire until the CRUSADERS sacked Constantinople in 1203–4 and Santorini was given to one of the Venetian conquerors, remaining in his family until 1336. It then became part of the duchy of Naxos but VENICE retained a strong influence; 1479–89 was another period of direct Venetian rule. It was Venetian enterprise that made Santorini an important wine producer. The wine it exported was made from the MALVASIA grape, like that of Crete, and it was prized for its sweetness and high alcohol content. These qualities enabled it to withstand the six-month sea voyage, via Venice, to western Europe. Santorini was conquered by the Ottoman Turks in 1579, but the Turks did not discourage the production of the only cash crop that the island's volcanic soil could sustain.

Loanwords from Italian still in use in Santorini today testify to Venice's importance in its wine-making past. The local dialect word for the vintage is 'vendemma' from Italian *vendemmia*; the sweet but not highly alcoholic (about nine per cent) wine is called Vissanto, from Italian *vin santo*; while the stronger but less sweet wine is known as 'medzo', from *mezzo*, Italian for half. The traditional wine of the island, which may be red, white, or rosé, is called 'brousko', from the Italian *brusco*, meaning rough. H.M.W.

Lambert-Gócs, M., *The Wines of Greece* (London, 1990).

SAN YSIDRO, small California wine region and AVA. See SANTA CLARA VALLEY.

SAPERAVI, Russian red wine grape variety notable for the colour and ACIDITY it can bring to a blend. As a VARIETAL wine, it is capable, not to say demanding, of long BOTTLE AGEING. The flesh of this dark-skinned grape is deep pink, so that Saperavi has much in common with TEINTURIER grape varieties. It ripens late, is relatively productive. and is quite well adapted to the cold Russian winters, but not so well that the Russian Potapenko viticultural research institute has been discouraged from producing a **Saperavi Severny**, a hybrid of SEVERNY and Saperavi which was released in 1947 and incorporates not just Saperavi's VINIFERA genes, but also those of the cold-hardy VITIS *amurensis*.

Traditional Saperavi is planted throughout almost all of the wine regions of the CIS. It is an important variety in RUSSIA, UKRAINE, MOLDOVA, GEORGIA, KAZAKHSTAN, UZBEKISTAN, TAJIKISTAN, KYRGYZSTAN, and TURKMENISTAN, although in cooler areas the acidity may be too marked for any purpose other than blending, despite its relatively high sugar levels. It has also been grown in BULGARIA for some time.

See also MAGARATCH, the Crimean wine research centre which has crossed Cabernet Sauvignon and Saperavi to produce the promising Magaratch Ruby and also devised Magaratch Bastardo for FORTIFIED WINES by crossing the Portuguese BASTARDO with Saperavi.

SARDINIA, known as **Sardegna** in Italian, Mediterranean island 200 km/125 miles off the coast of Italy at its nearest point, governed by CARTHAGE before conquest by Ancient ROME, and subsequently by Byzantines, Arabs, and Catalans. (See map on p. 517.) Sardinia became an integral part of Italy only in 1726, when it was ceded to the House of Savoy. Historically, linguistically, and culturally, as well as geographically, the island seems detached from the mainstream of Italian civilization, and it is therefore no surprise that most of its significant grape varieties—VERMENTINO, CANNONAU, Carignano (CARIGNAN), Bovale—are of Spanish origin and that, due to limited local demand, and few commercial

Old vine that has split in two, the product of **head training** and **cane pruning** and such venerable **vine age** that the wine it produces is notably concentrated.

The black cliffs of **Santorini**.

contacts with the mainland, viticulture dedicated to quality has been slow to develop.

Vines in any case play only a small part in a total agricultural economy in which over 40 per cent of the land is dedicated to the grazing of animals—sheep in particular—for milk and meat. While the total area under vines and the total production of wine underwent a significant increase in the post-war period, aided by lavish subsidies both from Rome and from the regional government, the result has not been a self-sustaining wine industry. As markets for Sardinian wines have contracted and the flow of public funds to CO-OPERATIVE wineries has dwindled to a trickle, the total vineyard surface has decreased from a high of 70,000 to 40,000 ha/98,800 acres in the early 1990s and the island's total production of wine has dropped from a high of 4.5 million hl to an average of around 1 million hl/26.4 million gal (or even less in a year of low yields such as 1990).

The production of DOC wine meanwhile dropped from close to 90,000 hl in the mid 1980s to below 60,000 hl in 1990. As a percentage of the total production this is not particularly low for a region in Italy's south (see APULIA, for example). The powerfully alcoholic wines of Sardinia have long been prized more for beefing up wines produced in cooler climates to the north than for drinking on their own. The DOC structure in Sardinia, none the less, deserves to be mentioned in passing since it recapitulates and sums up the misguided Italian approach to controlled appellations that has undermined their credibility. Little has been done to match individual vine varieties to proper soils and climates; the production zones of the most popular varieties—Vermentino and Cannonau—have been extended to include the entire surface of the island; and yields have been allowed to rise to such mind-boggling levels as 105 hl/ha (6 tons/acre) for the Carignano del Sulcis DOC, 130 hl/ha for the Vermentino di Sardegna DOC, and 140 hl/ha for the Nuragus di Cagliari DOC. The result has been a general flight from DOC 'status', with several—Monica di Cagliari, Giro di Cagliari, Nasco di Cagliari—having become virtually inactive. The Arborea DOC, approved in 1987 in an attempt to launch the well-known vine varieties SANGIOVESE and TREBBIANO in a zone of commercial fruit cultivation, established 135 hl/ha as its official maximum permitted yield, and has yet to see the first producer to request DOC status for his wines.

It must also be added that the existence of four different types of wine—dry, sweet, a *liquoroso*, or higher alcohol, dry wine, and a *liquoroso* sweet wine—in many of the DOCs (Malvasia di Cagliari, Monica di Cagliari, Giro di Cagliari, Nasco di Cagliari, Cannonau di Sardegna) seems programmed to create confusion, and it is far from clear that Sardinia's powerfully alcoholic wines need to reach still higher ALCOHOLIC STRENGTHS.

If the overall picture is far from encouraging, small quantities of good wines do exist and suggest that Sardinia's soil and climate could give, with a different approach, products of a certain validity. Vernaccia di Oristano, although dwindling in quantities produced, can be a good approximation of a dry SHERRY with a clean and bitter finish, and the hard to find Malvasia di Bosa justly enjoys a certain reputation as a dessert wine. Refreshing bottles of Vermentino di Gallura, produced in the island's north, do exist and the wine would be better if its production limits were lowered from the current 98 hl/ha. An occasional good bottle of Nuragus di Cagliari only increases the regret for the DOC rules which permit 140 hl/ha (8 tons/acre) to be produced. Carignano di Sulcis has shown marked improvement in recent years, with some interesting experiments with small BARREL MATURATION currently being carried out as well; revision of the DOC would undoubtedly give a better overall level here as well.

Cannonau, thought to be a clone of GRENACHE and accounting for 20 per cent of the island's total production, has given some good wines in the province of Nuoro, particularly in the subzone of Oliena. Attempts to extend its cultivation to the provinces of Cagliari and Sassari have proven to be a fiasco from both the quantitative and the qualitative point of view, however. Although more attention to quality has now come to mark Sardinia's viticulture, the burden of the recent past is none the less a heavy one, and the lack of a reputation, coupled with geographical isolation and a lack of firms who have experience in marketing the island's wines beyond its borders, will doubtless continue to be a major handicap in the near future. D.T.

SASSELLA, subzone of VALTELLINA in the far north of Italy.

SASSICAIA, trail-blazing central Italian wine made, largely from CABERNET SAUVIGNON, originally by Mario Incisa della Rochetta at the Tenuta San Guido near BOLGHERI and one of the first Italian reds made in the image of fine red bordeaux. The first small commercial quantities were released in the mid 1970s. For more details, see VINO DA TAVOLA.

SAUMUR, town in the Loire giving its name to an extensive wine district and several appellations. Saumur is effectively a south western extension of TOURAINE, yet is more of a centre for the wine trade of Anjou–Saumur than is Anjou. The grapes grown in these latter two neighbouring regions are very similar, except that Saumur does not have Anjou's range of potentially great sweet white wines.

Saumur's most important wine (and France's most important mousseux) is **Saumur Mousseux**, a well-priced sparkling wine made from Chenin Blanc grapes with increasing amounts of Chardonnay and, usually less successful, Sauvignon Blanc. These grapes can come from an even wider area than that permitted for still Saumur, and the quality of wine-making is high among the larger houses of the town of Saumur, such as Gratien & Meyer and Bouvet Ladubay, and also at the important CO-OPERATIVE at St-Cyr-en-Bourg, with its extensive underground cellars hewn out of the local TUFFEAU. This CALCAREOUS rock predominates around Saumur, and was much quarried, both locally and abroad (according to Duijker it was used for rebuilding after the Great Fire of London, and also extensively in the Dutch city of Maastricht). This left the Saumurois with ready-made wine cellars, perfect not just for mushrooms, one of their most important products, but also for the maturation of their acidic wines which, as in CHAMPAGNE, had a natural tendency to retain some carbon dioxide in spring. Ackerman-Laurance was the first producer of sparkling Saumur, in the early 19th century. The wines have enjoyed considerable commercial success, although an increasing proportion of the base material for Saumur Mousseux is expected to be fashioned into CRÉMANT de Loire, for which the criteria are rather more rigorous: yields of 50 rather than 60 hl/ha and 12 rather than nine months' TIRAGE.

Saumur Blanc can be remarkably difficult to distinguish from Anjou Blanc, being made substantially from Chenin Blanc and being both high in acidity and potentially long lived. Only the most conscientious growers can coax much fruity charm out of them, however. The parallel between still white Saumur and the still white wines of Champagne, Coteaux CHAMPENOIS, is an apt one.

Saumur Rouge is a much more successful wine, made on soils similar to those of CHINON and BOURGUEIL. It may be made from Cabernet Franc, Cabernet Sauvignon, or Pineau d'Aunis grapes, but is usually made almost exclusively from Cabernet Franc and can be a refreshing, relatively light fruity wine. A little more Saumur Rouge is produced than Saumur Blanc, but the most significant still wine of the region is **Saumur-Champigny**, whose extraordinary expansion in the 1970s and 1980s was largely due to FASHION, and mainly Paris fashion at that. The Saumur-Champigny zone, prettily named after the village of Champigny, is on a tuffeau plateau that lends itself well to viticulture, as in neighbouring Touraine. Its high LIMESTONE content made the Chenin Blanc vine traditionally grown here prone to CHLOROSIS in the post-PHYLLOXERA era, but by 1990 more than 1,000 ha/2,470 acres of vines were producing Saumur-Champigny. It was the St-Cyr-en-Bourg co-operative in particular that encouraged the planting of Cabernet Franc vines and developed the still red wine appellation with such success. Today as much as 40 per cent of all Saumur-Champigny is produced by the co-operative. Most Saumur-Champigny is too light to be worth ageing, and in many cases its substantial premium over, for example, Anjou-Villages can be difficult to justify, although it is usefully, and quintessentially, fruity and flirtatious: the BEAUJOLAIS of the Loire.

A small amount of light rosé **Cabernet de Saumur** is made, usually considerably drier and less ambitious than Cabernet d'Anjou, while **Coteaux de Saumur** is Saumur's medium sweet white, made in very small quantities from Chenin Blanc grapes.

See also LOIRE and map on pp. 576–7.

Duijker, H., *The Wines of the Loire, Alsace and Champagne* (London, 1983).

SAUSSIGNAC, very small sweet white wine appellation in SOUTH WEST FRANCE. It lies within the BERGERAC district to the west of Monbazillac and produces sweet white wines, from mainly Sémillon grapes, although only 74 ha / 183 acres of vineyard were dedicated to this relatively obscure wine in the early 1990s.

SAUTERNE, occasionally found on labels of GENERIC sweet white wine. Real SAUTERNES always ends in s.

SAUTERNES. The special distinction of this region embedded within the Graves district south of BORDEAUX is that it is dedicated, in a way unmatched by any other wine region, to the production of unfortified, sweet, white wine. In Germany or California, say, where superlative sweet Rieslings are occasionally made, such wines are the exception rather than the rule, and emerge from vines that more usually produce drier or medium sweet wines.

In Sauternes the situation is quite different. The appellation is reserved for wines from five communes that must adhere to regulations stipulating minimum levels of ALCOHOLIC STRENGTH (13 per cent) and a tasting test that requires the wine to taste sweet. Three grape varieties are planted: Sauvignon Blanc, Sémillon, and Muscadelle. Sémillon is the principal grape, because it is especially susceptible to noble rot, and it accounts for about 80 per cent of a typical estate's ENCÉPAGEMENT. Sauvignon often attracts botrytis earlier than Sémillon, and its naturally high acidity can give the wine a freshness that balances the richer, broader flavours of Sémillon. Muscadelle's contribution is mostly aromatic, but its viticultural frailty leads many growers to find it more trouble than it is worth.

No one is exactly sure when sweet wine production became the norm here. The style was well entrenched by the

Houses cut into the tuffeau of **Saumur** to form a network of caves, many of which are used for the making and storage of wine.

late 18th century, when Thomas JEFFERSON and others were purchasing wines from the district's most famous property Ch d'YQUEM that were evidently sweet; and harvesting details from the 1660s suggest, but do not prove, that the wines made then were probably sweet.

Sauternes is the product of a specific MESOCLIMATE. The communes of Sauternes, Barsac, Preignac, Bommes, and Fargues are close to two rivers, the broad GARONNE and its small tributary, the Ciron. When, in autumn, the cool spring-fed Ciron waters flow into the warmer tidal Garonne, evening mists develop that envelop the vineyards until late morning the following day, when the sun, if it shines, burns the mist away. This moist atmosphere encourages *Botrytis cinerea*, a fungus that attacks the grapes and causes them to shrivel and rot (see BOTRYTIS BUNCH ROT). Mist activates the botrytis spores in the vineyards, and the alternating sunshine completes the process of desiccation.

The onset of botrytis is crucial to the evolution of the grapes. Without it, they may indeed ripen sufficiently to ensure that a sweet wine can be made, if fermentation ceases before all the sugar has been converted into alcohol, but the result will lack complexity. As outlined in more detail in NOBLE ROT, the overall effect of a benevolent botrytis infection is to increase dramatically the concentrations of TARTARIC ACID and SUGAR IN GRAPES; to stimulate the production of GLYCEROL that gives the wine its VISCOSITY; and to alter considerably the AROMA and flavour of the finished wine.

The essential difference between mediocre and great Sauternes hangs on the willingness of estate owners to wait until botrytis arrives. This act of patience is largely responsible for the cost of Sauternes. There are years, such as 1978 and 1985, when botrytis either fails to develop at all or arrives very late in the year. Proprietors must then decide whether to delay or to begin the harvest. Delay is a risky strategy: the chances of frost or rain, both of which can wreck the harvest, clearly increase as the autumn months wear on, but by picking too early the estate can end up with insipid sweet white wine while its more scrupulous neighbours are in a position to market great botrytis wine.

This introduces an economic issue unique to this region. Sauternes is exceptionally costly to make. There are a number of vintages each decade in which it is either impossible to make good sweet wine or in which, as in 1991, it can be produced only in minute quantities. Even in excellent VINTAGES, maximum YIELDS are restricted to 25 hl/ha (1.4 tons/acre), a quantity infrequently attained. At Yquem the average yield is a trifling 9 hl/ha, and at most conscientious estates the yields probably fluctuate between 12 and 20 hl/ha. (In the red wine districts of MÉDOC or ST-ÉMILION yields of more than 40 hl/ha are routine.)

In addition the harvest is unusually protracted. Botrytis occasionally swoops over entire vineyards, as in 1990, but this is rare. More commonly, it performs its unsightly activities patchily. A typical harvesting pattern might be as follows: an attack of botrytis on Sauvignon grapes allows half of them to be picked in late September; two weeks of drizzle follow, during which picking is suspended; finer weather resumes, grapes affected by undesirable GREY ROT are eliminated, and in late October another attack of botrytis allows the Sémillon and remaining Sauvignon grapes to be picked over a three-week period. The necessity for selective harvesting, or TRIAGE, essential for Sauternes, is expensive, as teams of pickers must be kept available for a very long period.

More than any other wine, Sauternes is made in the vineyard. Once the grapes have been picked, they are difficult to manipulate. Their MUST WEIGHT (sugar content), their PHYSIOLOGICAL RIPENESS, and the degree of botrytis infection will all determine quality before the wine-maker has got to work. None the less Sauternes calls for careful vinification. Pressing should be as gentle as possible, and some leading estates still use old-fashioned hydraulic or basket PRESSES for this purpose. Fermentation takes place in tanks or, more usually since the mid 1980s, in BARRIQUES, of which a third or more are likely to be new (see BARREL FERMENTATION). Fermentation either stops of its own accord when the wine has achieved a balance of about 14 per cent alcohol and a RESIDUAL SUGAR level that is the equivalent of a further four to seven per cent alcohol, or it is arrested with the addition of SULPHUR DIOXIDE. For more details, see BOTRYTIZED wine-making.

In weaker vintages CHAPTALIZATION may be permitted, although better estates avoid the practice, which merely adds sweetness rather than complexity and is often used to disguise lazy harvesting. The wine is usually aged in oak barrels for between 18 and 36 months (see BARREL MATURATION). The necessary investment in these barriques also contributes to the high cost of production. Some estates—Chx d'Yquem, Raymond-Lafon, La Tour Blanche—use up to 100 per cent new oak, while others, such as Chx Climens or Doisy-Daëne, prefer a lesser proportion. It is a question of style rather than quality. Less distinguished lots of wine are usually sold off to NÉGOCIANTS; in 1978 Yquem bottled only 15 per cent of the crop under its own label, and in 1987 many estates marketed no wine at all.

A technological development introduced in 1985 has stirred considerable controversy. CRYOEXTRACTION can help growers to save part of a crop that might formerly have had to be rejected. Grapes are chilled for 20 hours in a cold chamber before pressing, thus eliminating water and the least ripe grapes. Cryoextraction has no effect on chemical components of the grape and its must but it is a rescue operation only, and its major drawback is cost. None the less in damp vintages such as 1987 it came in useful for estates such as Yquem which had invested in the process.

Although the prevalence of botrytis and overall geographical location are common to all Sauternes, specific MICROCLIMATES and SOIL STRUCTURES affect the styles of the different estates. BARSAC is the most distinctive commune, and is entitled to its own appellation, although it can also be sold as Sauternes. Its proximity to the Ciron and its ALLUVIAL soil give wines that are often lighter and more elegant than its neighbours. The communes of Bommes and Sauternes itself tend to give the fattest wines, although exceptions are numerous. There are also differences in maturation dates:

the grapes at Ch Filhot, for instance, often ripen a week later than those of Barsac.

All these factors were taken into account when in 1855 the existing estates were classified. Successful candidates were ranked as either first or second growths, with Yquem rightfully given its own super-status (see CLASSIFICATION). In the 1960s especially, standards slumped. The wines were out of FASHION and there was a string of poor vintages. Only the richest estates could afford to maintain standards. Elsewhere, corners were cut, grapes were picked too early, and barriques were replaced with tanks. For two decades many classified growths produced wines that were mediocre at best, even in fine vintages. Only with the excellent 1983 vintage did matters improve. Prices rose, and wise proprietors invested in long overdue improvements, which bore fruit in the superb 1986, 1988, 1989, and 1990 vintages. The official 1855 classification is once again a reasonably reliable guide to quality, although a number of unclassified growths, such as Ch de Fargues (owned by Yquem), Gilette, and Raymond-Lafon, are often of first growth quality, and price.

After a bad patch, Sauternes is again showing the quality of which it is capable. It combines power, voluptuousness, and elegance, and good bottles can evolve and improve for up to 50 years (longer in the case of Yquem). Given the risks and costs involved in its production, it remains underpriced in relation to the enormous pleasure it brings to those growing numbers of wine lovers who find a fine Sauternes has an undeniable place on the dinner table. S.B.

Benson, J., and Mackenzie, A., *Sauternes* (2nd edn., London, 1990).
Brook, S., *Liquid Gold: Dessert Wines of the World* (London, 1987).
Olney, R., *Yquem* (London, 1986).

SAUVIGNON. Sauvignon Blanc is the vine variety solely responsible for some of the world's most popular, and most distinctive, dry white wines: Sancerre, Pouilly-Fumé, and a host of Sauvignons and Fumé Blancs from outside France. And in many great white wines both dry and sweet it also adds nerve and zest to its most common blending partner SÉMILLON. Like the famous and quite distinct black-berried vine Cabernet Sauvignon, Sauvignon Blanc seems to have its origins in Bordeaux, where it has been enjoying a revival in popularity.

The variety is often simply called **Sauvignon**, especially on wine labels, but there are **Sauvignons Jaune**, **Noir**, **Rose** (or **Gris**), and **Violet**, according to the colour of the berries. **Sauvignon Vert** is more commercially important than any of these; it is a synonym for **Sauvignonasse**, closely related to TOCAI Friulano.

Sauvignon Blanc's most recognizable characteristic is its piercing, instantly recognizable aroma. Descriptions typically include 'grassy, herbaceous, musky, green fruits' (especially gooseberries), 'nettles', and even 'tomcats'. Research into FLAVOUR COMPOUNDS suggests that methoxypyrazines play an important role in Sauvignon's aroma. Over-productive Sauvignon vines planted on heavy soils can produce wines only vaguely suggestive of this but Sauvignon cautiously cultivated in the central vineyards of the Loire, unmasked by oak, can reach the dry white apogee of Sauvignon fruit with some of the purest, most refreshingly zesty wines in the world. The best Sancerres and Pouilly-Fumés served as a model for early exponents of New World Sauvignon Blanc, although by the 1980s it was the Loire vignerons who copied their counterparts in California, Australia, and New Zealand (which achieved rapid fame with this variety) in experimenting with fermentation and maturation in oak.

Oak-aged examples usually need an additional year or two to show their best, but almost all dry, unblended Sauvignon is designed to be drunk young, although there are both Loire and Bordeaux examples that can demonstrate durability, if rarely evolution, with up to 15 years in bottle (see POUILLY-FUMÉ). As an ingredient in the great sweet white wines of SAUTERNES, on the other hand, Sauvignon plays a minor but important part in one of the world's longest-living wines.

The vine is particularly vigorous, which has caused problems in parts of the Loire and New Zealand. If the Sauvignon vine's vegetation gets out of hand, Sauvignon grapes fail to reach full maturity and the resulting wine can be aggressively HERBACEOUS, almost intrusively rank. (And underripe Sémillon can exhibit very similar characteristics—just as underripe Cabernet Sauvignon can smell like Cabernet Franc.) A low-vigour ROOTSTOCK and CANOPY MANAGEMENT can help combat this problem.

Sauvignon buds after but flowers before Sémillon, with which it is typically blended in Bordeaux and, increasingly, elsewhere. Until suitable clones such as 297 and 316 were identified, and sprays to combat Sauvignon's susceptibility to POWDERY MILDEW and BLACK ROT developed, yields were uneconomically irregular. In 1968, for example, Sauvignon was France's 13th most planted white grape variety but within 20 years it had risen to fourth place.

In Bordeaux it was not until the late 1980s that Sauvignon overtook Ugni Blanc, or TREBBIANO, as second most planted white grape variety after Sémillon, which still outnumbered Sauvignon almost three to one in terms of area planted—although the newer clones of Sauvignon are much more productive than the important but rapidly declining Sémillon. The Gironde's Sauvignon is concentrated in the Entre-Deux-Mers, Graves, and the sweet wine-producing districts in and around Sauternes. In each of these areas it is dominated by and usually blended with Sémillon, particularly in Sauternes, where the typical blend incorporates 80 per cent of the more rot-prone Sémillon together with a little Muscadelle. BORDEAUX BLANC owes much to Entre-Deux-Mers Sauvignon although low yields and, often, expensive oak ageing, as in the best dry white PESSAC-LÉOGNAN, GRAVES, and the handful of expensive Médoc whites (see BORDEAUX AC), are prerequisites for a memorable performance from Sauvignon in Bordeaux. It is perhaps no coincidence that the average Loire Sauvignon has more Sauvignon character than the average all-Sauvignon Bordeaux Blanc when the official maximum yield for the first is 10 hl/ha (0.6 tons/acre) lower than the 65 hl/ha allowed in Bordeaux.

As in red wines, the satellite areas reflect Bordeaux's spread of vine varieties and Sauvignon is often an easily perceptible ingredient in the dry whites of such areas as BERGERAC, Côtes du MARMANDAIS, and PACHERENC DU VIC-BILH.

It is in the Loire that Sauvignon is encountered in its purest, most unadulterated form. In the often limestone vineyards of SANCERRE, POUILLY-FUMÉ, and their eastern satellites QUINCY, REUILLY, and MENETOU-SALON it can demonstrate one of the most eloquent arguments for marrying variety with suitable TERROIR. The variety is often called Blanc Fumé here and has happily replaced most of the lesser varieties once common, notably much of the Chasselas in Pouilly-sur-Loire. Most of these wines are designed to be drunk, well chilled, within two years and are none the worse for that.

From this concentration of vineyards, which might well be considered the Sauvignon capital of the world (however much the inhabitants of Marlborough in NEW ZEALAND'S South Island might dispute it), Sauvignon's influence radiates outwards: north east towards Chablis in SAUVIGNON DE ST-BRIS, south to ST-POURÇAIN-sur-Sioule, and north and west to Coteaux du GIENNOIS and CHEVERNY, as well as to a substantial quantity of eastern Loire wines, typically labelled TOURAINE. Such Sauvignons tend to be light, racy, and, of course, aromatic. With Chardonnay, it has also been allowed into the vineyards of Anjou, where it is sometimes blended with the indigenous CHENIN BLANC.

Elsewhere in France Sauvignon Blanc has been an obvious, though not invariably successful, choice for those seeking to make internationally saleable wine in the Midi (yields may have been too high to extract sufficient varietal character from the vine) and small plantings of Sauvignon can be found in some of the Provençal appellations.

Across the alps, Sauvignon's most successful Italian region is the far north east in Friuli with some ALTO ADIGE and COLLIO examples exhibiting extremely fine fruit and purity of flavour. In the 1980s Italy's plantings of Sauvignon doubled to nearly 3,000 ha/7,410 acres. As wine-making skills increase in SLOVENIA, wines of similar finesse are emerging from that region, at whose north eastern limit, in Austrian STYRIA, the variety thrives, combining fruit with aroma. As 'Muskat-Silvaner' (as the variety is known in German) it is grown but rarely in Germany, where many would argue that young Riesling can provide the same sort of crisp, aromatic white. It is planted to a certain extent further east—even if the wines tend to be progressively heavier and sweeter. Parts of SERBIA, the Fruška Gora district of VOJVODINA, and some of CZECHOSLOVAKIA clearly have potential. ROMANIA had nearly 5,000 ha of Sauvignon Blanc in the early 1990s, and within the CIS only neighbouring MOLDOVA had any sizeable plantings of the variety.

Sauvignon Blanc has been imported into Iberia by only the most dedicated internationalists (TORRES, for example, although see also RUEDA), and certainly Portugal and north western Spain have no shortage of indigenous varieties (see MINHO and GALICIA) capable of reproducing similar wine styles. There is a tendency for Sauvignon Blanc to taste oily when reared in too warm a climate, as it sometimes does in Israel and other Mediterranean vineyards where those with an eye to the export market put it through its paces.

This was clearly perceptible in many of Australia's early attempts with the variety although by the early 1990s there was even keener appreciation of the need to reserve it for the country's cooler sites (see AUSTRALIA for more on the wines produced). Chardonnay plantings outnumber those of Sauvignon Blanc by more than four to one in Australia.

In New Zealand, on the other hand, Chardonnay has overtaken Sauvignon Blanc fairly recently and this relatively minute wine industry can boast almost as big an area planted with Sauvignon (800 ha in 1992) as Australia. This is the variety that introduced New Zealand wine to the world and did it by developing its own style: intensely perfumed, more obviously fruity than the Loire prototype, and with just a hint of both gas and sweetness. This style of Sauvignon can now be found in the South and the cooler areas of North America, in the south of France, and, doubtless, even further afield before long.

'Sauvignon' is the white wine most commonly exported from CHILE, but, according to official statistics in the early 1990s, Sauvignon Blanc accounted for less than 5 per cent of the country's total wine production (while Semillon accounted for more than 26 per cent). Much of Chile's Sauvignon is Sauvignon Vert, otherwise known as Sauvignonasse, although there are strenuous efforts to replace this with true Sauvignon Blanc. California clones of Sauvignon Blanc have been widely planted in Chile but tend to suffer from excessive VIGOUR. High yields also help depress the keynote aromas of Sauvignon Blanc in South American wines labelled Sauvignon, including those made from Argentina's 600 ha of Sauvignon (as opposed to 800 ha of Tocai Friulano and 2,000 ha of Semillon counted in 1989), although some attention is being focused on Sauvignon within Argentine companies keen to export. Brazil's 'Sauvignon' is usually SEYVAL, according to GALET, who also maintains that the variety called Sauvignon Vert in California is in fact the MUSCADELLE of Bordeaux.

Thanks to Robert MONDAVI, who renamed it FUMÉ BLANC, Sauvignon Blanc enjoyed enormous success in California in the 1980s and the state's total plantings were more than 13,000 acres in 1991, one-third of it in Napa, where problems of vine vigour were largely overcome by the late 1980s. See CALIFORNIA for more on the wines, which are occasionally sweet and even botrytized, a sort of Semillon-free Sauternes. There has also been an increase, as elsewhere in the New World, in blending in some Semillon to dry white Sauvignon to add weight and fruit to Sauvignon's aroma and acidity. Like California, WASHINGTON state makes both Sauvignon Blanc and Fumé Blanc from its 800 acres (in 1991) of Sauvignon, a poor third to Chardonnay and Riesling. Of other American states, TEXAS has had particular success with the variety.

But perhaps Sauvignon's real *succès fou* has been in SOUTH AFRICA, where, for want of genuine Chardonnay perhaps (see AUXERROIS), local wine drinkers fell upon the Cape's more successful early Sauvignons as a fashionable internationally recognized wine style. By 1990 there were 3,300 ha of Sauvignon Blanc to South Africa's barely 2,400 ha of Cabernet

Sauvignon, and the variety's long history on the Cape seems to be reflected in particularly vibrant, concentrated wines.

Sauvignon Gris is another name for Sauvignon Rose and has discernibly pink skins. It can produce more substantial wines than many a Sauvignon Blanc, and has a certain following in Bordeaux and the Loire. See also FIÉ.

Brook, S., *Sauvignon Blanc and Sémillon* (London, 1992).

SAUVIGNON DE ST-BRIS, VDQS created in 1974 for dry white wines made from about 60 ha/150 acres of Sauvignon grapes grown in the communes of St-Bris-le-Vineux, Chitry, Irancy, and parts of Vincelottes, Quennes, St-Cyr-les-Colons, and Cravant in the Yonne *département* south of AUXERRE and west of CHABLIS. The wine is too obscure to be made with anything other than artisan passion, but it lacks the breed and concentration of great Loire Sauvignon made in Sancerre about 96 km/60 miles to the south west, and is more of a curiosity (being technically Burgundian but made from a decidedly non-Burgundian grape) than anything else.

SAVAGNIN is a fine but curious vine variety with small, round, pale berries. In France it is as much a viticultural curiosity as the wine it alone produces, VIN JAUNE, is a winemaking oddity. Today it is cultivated almost exclusively in the JURA in eastern France, and presumably only those producers rewarded by the high prices fetched by *vin jaune* would persist with a vine that can yield so churlishly.

It is cultivated to a limited extent throughout the Jura vineyards and may be included in any of the region's white wine appellations but is usually in practice reserved for the Jura's extraordinary, sherry-like *vin jaune*. It is well adapted to the ancient, west-facing slopes of Jura but many believe it is at its finest in what remains of the vineyards of CHATEAU-CHALON, where it may sometimes be left to ripen as late as December. The resulting distinctively nutty wine is left in cask, under a FLOR-like film, for at least six years, and can continue to evolve for many years in bottle, usually the special clavelin.

Called Gringet, it is also a minor ingredient in the sparkling wines of Ayse in SAVOIE. It is also grown, at particularly high altitudes, in the Valais of SWITZERLAND, where it is called either Païen or Heida.

Galet maintains that Savagnin is identical to the TRAMINER which was once grown widely in Germany, Alsace, Hungary, and Austria, and that GEWÜRZTRAMINER is the pink-berried MUSQUÉ mutation of Savagnin. Certainly a non-Musqué Savagnin Rosé is still cultivated to a very limited extent in Alsace, where it is sometimes called KLEVNER or Klevener d'Heiligenstein. Austrian Traminer is, like Jura's Savagnin, famous for its aroma and ability to age.

Galet, P., *Cépages et vignobles de France* (2nd edn., Montpellier, 1990).

SAVATIANO, white grape variety widely planted throughout Attica and central GREECE. This vine, with its exceptionally good DROUGHT resistance, is the most common ingredient in RETSINA, although RHODITIS and ASSYRTIKO are often added to compensate for Savatiano's naturally low acidity. On particularly suitable sites, Savatiano can produce well-balanced dry white wines.

SAVENNIÈRES, distinctive and much celebrated white wine appellation in the Anjou region of the Loire, immediately south west of the town of Angers. Total production of the appellation is less than 30,000 cases in a good vintage but these examples of dry CHENIN BLANC display such an unusual combination of nerve, concentration, and longevity that they have won devotees around the world. Many producers have abandoned the south east-facing SLATE and SANDSTONE slopes on the north bank of the Loire. In its Napoleonic heyday, Savennières was a sweet wine, but today it is dry, and unusually concentrated because maximum permitted yields are relatively low. The best wines can last for several decades, and can be unappetizingly tart at less than seven years old. Within Savennières are the two subappellations **Savennières-Coulée de Serrant**, a single estate of just 7 ha/17 acres run by the Joly family on BIODYNAMIC lines, and the 33 ha of **Savennières-La Roche-aux-Moines** in which there are several different producers struggling to make a living in this frost-prone corner of the Loire valley.

Across the river to the south east are the sweet white wine appellations of Anjou: BONNEZEAUX; Chaume; Coteaux de l'AUBANCE; Coteaux du LAYON; and QUARTS DE CHAUME. See also LOIRE, and map on pp. 576–7.

SAVIGNY-LÈS-BEAUNE, a small town in BURGUNDY near Beaune, as *lès* (Old French for near) implies, with its own appellation for red wine and a little white. The reds are agreeable but lack the depth and character of wines from villages such as Pommard or Volnay more prominently sited on the LIMESTONE escarpment.

The village is divided by the river Rhoin. Those vineyards on the southern side, including PREMIERS CRUS Les Peuillets, Les Narbantons, Les Rouvrettes, and Les Marconnets, are on sandy soil and are similar to wines of Beaune, although lighter. Those on the other side of the village, towards Pernand-Vergelesses, including Les Lavières and Les Vergelesses, are on stonier soil.

An engraving dating from 1703 at the Château de Savigny describes the wines as nourishing, theological, and disease-defying—'nourrissants, théologiques et morbifuges'. A little white wine is produced from Chardonnay.

See also CÔTE D'OR and its map. J.T.C.M.

SAVOIE, eastern French alpine region on the border with Switzerland, sometimes anglicized to **Savoy** and now strictly comprising the two *départements* Savoie and Haute-Savoie. This dramatic countryside is so popular with visitors for both winter sports and summer relaxation that only a small amount of the wine ever leaves the region.

Such was the influence of the House of Savoy at one time

that Savoie and much of northern Italy were part of the same kingdom. This may help to explain Savoie's particularly distinctive family of apparently indigenous vine varieties, and in particular suggests why the variety known as MONDEUSE in Savoie may be the REFOSCO of north east Italy. Most Savoie wines are white and are sold under the much-ramified appellation **Vin de Savoie**, although CRÉPY, SEYSSEL, and ROUSSETTE de Savoie have their own appellations. Crépy and Seyssel are specific areas while Roussette, also known as Altesse, is Savoie's finest white grape variety and may be produced from anywhere in the Vin de Savoie zone.

Much of the terrain here is too mountainous for viticulture and the Savoie vineyards tend to be widely dispersed, clustered in the flatter, more sheltered parts of the region.

Many of the vineyards are on the banks of the river RHÔNE as it flows from Lake Geneva towards the wine region known as the Rhône valley. Seyssel is here as well as the communes of CHAUTAGNE and JONGIEUX, two of the 17 CRUS which can append their names to the appellation Vin de Savoie.

South of here, just south of the town of CHAMBÉRY, famous for its VERMOUTH, is a cluster of CRUS whose names may be more familiar to some wine enthusiasts than the main appellation itself: ABYMES, APREMONT, ARBIN, CHIGNIN, CRUET, and MONTMÉLIAN. A wine labelled Chignin-Bergeron must be made, unusually, from the Roussanne grape, Bergeron being a local name for it.

Further north the Chasselas grape predominates and the isolated cru of AYZE (which Michelin insists is Ayse) makes sparkling wine while a cluster of vineyards on the south eastern shores of Lake Geneva make a range of light, almost Swiss wines under the names of the crus MARIGNAN, Marin, RIPAILLE, and the appellation Crépy.

The characteristics of these Vins de Savoie and the environments in which they are produced are sufficiently different to justify their being granted separate appellations. Total vineyard area for the Vin de Savoie appellation was about 1,650 ha/4,075 acres in 1990 and about two-thirds of production is white: crisp, lightly scented, often chaptalized in the Swiss manner. The most widely planted variety is JACQUÈRE, which is increasingly popular with growers because of its productivity. Chardonnay is grown in some parts, and some producers are experimenting with BARREL MATURATION, but the finest varieties are Roussette, with its own appellation, and the occasional plantation of ROUSSANNE, or Bergeron (see CHIGNIN).

Many of Savoie's wines are VARIETAL and, among reds, Gamay and Pinot Noir imported from Beaujolais and Burgundy respectively can be perfectly respectable, if light, examplars. Most inspiring, however, is Mondeuse, with its deep colour, peppery flavour, and slight bitterness. Mondeuse grown at Arbin has a particular reputation, and such wines go well with the local cheese-dominated cuisine.

A small amount of sparkling wine may be sold as **Mousseux de Savoie** and **Pétillant de Savoie**.

See also the Vins du BUGEY made just over the border in the Ain *département*.

George, R., *French Country Wines* (London, 1990).

SCALE, types of insects which attack grapevines, comprising at least 13 different species. Some scale insects feed on more than one part of the vine, others remain in place for feeding. Scale insects feed by sucking sap, and heavy infestations can weaken vine VIGOUR. Some scale insects excrete honeydew, which can spoil any bunches close to the insect because a black, sooty mould usually grows on the honeydew. Scale insects are often controlled by natural predators including a parasitic wasp, ladybirds, and moth larvae in Australia. Ants attend the insects to feed on honeydew, and they can unfortunately deter predators. Midwinter oil sprays are also used to control scale. R.E.S.

SCANDINAVIA, part of northern Europe which includes Norway, Sweden, Denmark, Finland, and Iceland. Of these countries, only Denmark has a liberal attitude towards alcoholic drinks and their sale. Elsewhere wine has been sold by state MONOPOLIES, which has had the effect of restricting choice. High levels of TAXATION have made the lot of the Scandinavian wine drinker even harder, although Scandinavian cellars provide famously good, if slow, conditions for wine BOTTLE AGEING. The climate may be unsuitably cold for vine-growing, but can be excellent for wine tasting.

SCHEUREBE is the one early 20th century German vine crossing that deserves attention from any connoisseur, and the only one named after the prolific vine breeder Dr Georg Scheu, the original director of the viticultural institute at Alzey in the Rheinhessen. Like KERNER and EHRENFELSER, it can produce some top-quality wines. Riesling genes would seem a prerequisite for quality, and Scheurebe was a Silvaner × Riesling cross, but it is much more than a riper, more productive replica of Riesling. Provided it reaches full maturity (like such other GERMAN CROSSINGS as BACCHUS and ORTEGA it is distinctly unappetizing if picked too early), Scheurebe wines have their own exuberant, racy flavours of blackcurrants or even rich grapefruit. Some Pfalz examples have been particularly exciting and 'Scheu', as it is often called, is one of the few varietal parvenus countenanced by quality-conscious German wine producers, not just because it can easily reach high PRÄDIKAT levels of ripeness, but because these are so delicately counterbalanced with the nerve of acidity—perhaps not quite so much as in an equivalent Riesling, but enough to preserve the wine for many years in bottle.

Scheurebe can be relied upon not only to reach a good 10° Oechsle above Riesling, but also to yield considerably more wine, often 100 hl/ha (5.7 tons/acre). It is not, however, as bountiful as Kerner, Bacchus, and Morio-Muskat, and was decisively overtaken by Kerner in the 1980s, although there were still nearly 4,000 ha/9,880 acres of Scheurebe planted in Germany in 1990, mainly in Rheinhessen and, to a lesser extent, in Pfalz. It also needs a relatively good site, often one which could otherwise support the great Riesling, and young Scheurebe vines are prey to frost damage. Ambitious growers can rely on good frost resistance in mature vines and on Scheurebe's useful encouragement of NOBLE ROT in good years. The variety can produce extremely fine BEERENAUSLESE and TROCKENBEERENAUSLESE which may not last quite as many decades as their Riesling counterparts but are much less rare and therefore better value.

The variety is also grown in southern Austria where it is known as SÄMLING 88.

SCHIAVA, Italian name for the undistinguished dark-skinned grape variety known as Vernatsch by the German speakers of the Alto Adige, or Südtirol as they would call it; and as TROLLINGER in the German region of Württemberg, where it is widely grown. The name Schiava, meaning 'slave', is thought by some to indicate Slavic origins.

It is most planted in TRENTINO-ALTO ADIGE in northern Italy, where several forms are known. The most common is **Schiava Grossa** (Grossvernatsch), which is extremely productive but is not associated with wines of any real character or concentration. Total Italian plantings of Schiava Grossa declined by about a quarter in the 1980s to 3,400 ha/8,400 acres. **Schiava Gentile** (Kleinvernatsch) produces better quality, aromatic wines from smaller grapes, and total plantings had declined by 1990 to about 1,200 ha. The most celebrated, and least productive, subvariety is Tschaggele.

The grapes are found in most of the non-varietal light red wines of Trentino-Alto Adige.

SCHILLERWEIN, pink wine speciality from blending red and white wines made in the WÜRTTEMBERG region in Germany. The term is also used in German SWITZERLAND for a similar sort of wine.

SCHIOPPETTINO, red grape variety native to the FRIULI region of north east Italy. It probably originated in the border area between Prepotto and SLOVENIA, where wine made from Schioppettino is cited in a marriage ceremony in 1282. In spite of official attempts to encourage its replanting, Schioppettino was substantially neglected after the PHYLLOXERA epidemic of the late 19th century in favour of the new imports from France Merlot, Cabernet Franc, and Cabernet Sauvignon. It seemed destined to disappear until a European Union decree of 1978 authorized its cultivation in the province of Udine (see also PIGNOLO). The wine is deep in colour, medium in body, but with an attractively aromatic richness hinting at violets combined with a certain peppery quality reminiscent of the RHÔNE. Although vine plantings and therefore wine production are still limited, and concentrated in the COLLI ORIENTALI, the potential seems notable. Prepotto is considered its elective home, but quite good quality has also come from the Buttrio-Manzano area. D.T.

SCHIST, a large group of coarsely crystalline metamorphic rocks that can be split into thin layers because their micaceous minerals have become aligned. The history of the DOURO valley in northern Portugal demonstrates the role played by schist (see also DELIMITATION). The schists in this terrain split and crumble easily, and are set in the midst of a tumbled, wild country which is otherwise almost entirely GRANITE. Schist is otherwise an uncommon rock type beneath vineyards, but occurs in CÔTE-RÔTIE and in some parts of northern ALSACE. The French word *schiste* means SLATE as well as schist, and is sometimes used loosely to mean SHALE. J.M.H.

SCHLOSS JOHANNISBERG, German wine estate in the RHEINGAU with a history closely interlinked with that of the entire region. Around the year 1100, the Benedictine monks of Mainz built a monastery on the site, the first in the Rheingau. In 1130 the hill, monastery, and village were renamed Johannisberg after St John the Baptist. In 1716 the abbey was purchased by Konstantin von Buttlar, the prince-abbot of Fulda. Neglected vineyards were restored and planted, in particular with the Riesling grape, an important and innovative move which eventually led to the variety's being known in some parts of the world (notably modern California) as Johannisberg Riesling. Legend has it that Schloss Johannisberg played an important role in the discovery of BOTRYTIZED wines. Grapes affected by NOBLE ROT were first harvested at Johannisberg unwittingly, leading the administrator to record on 10 April 1776: 'I have never tasted such a wine before.' The discovery gave rise to the AUSLESE, BEERENAUSLESE, and TROCKENBEERENAUSLESE styles. In 1802 Johannisberg became secularized and the property of the prince of Orange. It was won four years later by Napoleon, who presented it to Marshal Kellerman, duke of Valmy, who owned it until 1813. From 1813 to 1815 the property was administered by the allies Russia, Prussia, and Austria; it was then given to the Habsburg Emperor Francis I of Austria at the Vienna Congress. In 1816, the emperor presented it to his State Chancellor Clemens Wenzeslaus, prince of Metternich-Winneburg, a gift which entailed an obligation to pay an annual tithe of the harvest to the Habsburgs or their legal successors. Today Schloss Johannisberg belongs to the Austrian state chancellor's great-grandson, Prince Paul Alfons of Metternich-Winneburg.

In 1811 Peter Arnold Mumm, a successful banker and wine merchant, purchased the entire Schloss Johannisberg vintage for 32,000 florins. He made a healthy profit and decided to invest in the estate. Ever since there has been a close association between the Mumm wine estate and Schloss Johannisberg and today they are run in tandem under the same ownership, with the wine of both estates made at von Mumm's cellars and the administration based at Schloss Johannisberg. Of von Mumm's 59 ha/145 acres of vineyards, 83 per cent are planted with Riesling and the remainder with Pinot Noir. Of the seven vineyard sites belonging to Johannisberg, three are almost totally owned by the von Mumm estate, Schwarzenstein, Hansenberg, and Mittelholle, while they also own a sizeable share of the remaining four: Holle, Klaus, Goldatzel, and Vogelsang. In addition, the estate owns the Berg Schlossberg, Rottland, and Roseneck vineyards in Rüdesheim; the Klauserweg in Geisenheim; and the Hollenberg, Hinterkirch, and Frankenthal in Assmannshausen. The vineyards of Schloss Johannisberg itself cover an area of 86 acres, and are planted entirely to Riesling. Wines mature in wood in cellars with a capacity of 7,500 hl/2 million gal, but were not ranked among Germany's finest in the late 1980s and early 1990s.

See also GERMAN HISTORY. S.A.

SCHÖNBURGER is a pink-berried 1979 vine crossing with Pinot Noir, Chasselas Rosé, and Muscat Hamburg among its antecedents which has been more useful to the wine industry of ENGLAND than to its native Germany. There were fewer than 60 ha/148 acres of German vineyard planted with this extremely reliable ripener in 1990, most of them in the ever-experimental Rheinhessen and Pfalz; but England's plantings of 83 ha made it the country's fifth most planted variety in 1992. It has good disease resistance, yields reasonably well, and its tendency to lack acidity is a positive advantage as far from the equator as Kent and Somerset. Its wines are white and relatively full bodied.

SCHOONMAKER, FRANK (1905–76), highly influential American wine writer and wine merchant. Born in South Dakota, he first became interested in wine when researching travel books in Europe in the late 1920s. Immediately after the Repeal of PROHIBITION he wrote a series of wine articles for the *New Yorker* which were published as *The Complete Wine Book* in 1934. Soon afterwards he founded an eponymous wine import company and travelled extensively, becoming noted for his abilities as a judge of young wines, his espousal of DOMAINE BOTTLING in Burgundy, and his expertise in German wines. An early advocate of American wines, he was highly critical of the habitual GENERIC naming of them. In the 1940s he was hired as consultant to the large California producer Almaden, for whom he created the best-selling VARIETAL Grenache Rosé, having been inspired by the French wine TAVEL. Schoonmaker employed Alexis Lichine, who was to occupy a very similar, if not more public, post immediately before the Second World War and the two men were to publish the first editions of their respective wine encyclopedias in 1964 and 1967. He published five wine books and numerous shorter works on wine.

Bespaloff, A., *The New Frank Schoonmaker Encyclopedia of Wine* (New York, 1988).

SCHWARZRIESLING, or 'black Riesling', is a German synonym for Pinot MEUNIER.

SCIACARELLO (sometimes written **Sciaccarello**) is a speciality of the French island of CORSICA. The grape variety is capable of producing deep flavoured if not necessarily deep coloured reds and fine rosés that can smell of the island's herby scrubland. The vine has good disease resistance and thrives particularly successfully on the granitic soils in the south west around Ajaccio and Sartène. It buds and ripens late and may well have been imported by the Romans but no one has yet identified its Italian cousin. Between 1979 and 1988 the island's total plantings of this characterful variety fell from more than 700 to fewer than 400 ha/9,880 acres and it is now much less important than NIELLUCCIO.

SCIENCE. For long it was maintained that WINE-MAKING was an art, but the proportion of the world's wine made by individuals with no grasp of the basic principles of OENOLOGY is shrinking rapidly. Meanwhile, the vineyards of the world are increasingly managed by individuals who have been taught at least the rudiments of the science of VITICULTURE. By the late 1980s it had even become difficult to discuss wine with many of those who grow and make it without being conversant with a wide range of scientific terms and concepts, including a host of measurements such as PH, TA, RS, and GA (for gallic acid equivalents for TANNINS). The dramatically improved overall quality of wine since ACADEME took a role in teaching and researching wine-related subjects is eloquent testimony to the beneficial effect of the increasingly scientific approach of all those involved with wine. As in all fields, however, the best scientists are often those who seek to explain rather than dominate, and in OLD WORLD regions whose wines have been admired for centuries, the best results are often obtained by those who combine scientific knowledge with a respect for TRADITION.

SCION, in viticulture, is the piece of the fruiting vine that is grafted on to the quite separate ROOTSTOCK. When grown, such a plant will have the leaves and desired fruit of one VINE VARIETY (Cabernet Sauvignon, for example), but the roots of the other, rootstock, variety (110 Richter, for example). GRAFTING is very widely used in viticulture since rootstocks are needed to combat soil-borne pests or diseases, such as PHYLLOXERA and NEMATODES. B.G.C.

SCORING individual wines, and many aspects of their production, is an increasingly popular pursuit with professionals and amateurs alike. The American writer Robert PARKER did much to promote the controversial but highly influential practice of awarding **scores** as points out of 100. For more detail, see NUMBERS.

Scoring vineyards

Vineyards may be scored to assess their suitability for producing good-quality wine grapes. The most famous system is that used in the DOURO valley of northern Portugal for PORT production. Vineyards are allocated points for YIELD, SOIL TYPE, MESOCLIMATE, vineyard maintenance, GRAPE COMPOSITION, and VINE AGE. Highly classified vineyards are entitled to produce as much wine as they are able each year, while the production from lower classifications can be restricted to meet demand.

Vineyards may also be scored for their adherence to organic growing principles as part of their accreditation (see ORGANIC VITICULTURE).

A newer system for assessing vineyards for potential wine quality was developed by this writer in New Zealand. This is based on the principles of CANOPY MANAGEMENT, but also allows for assessment of vine VIGOUR. This system, or variants of it, is being used as the basis of assessing both the quality and PRICE of grapes in Australia and New Zealand. R.E.S.

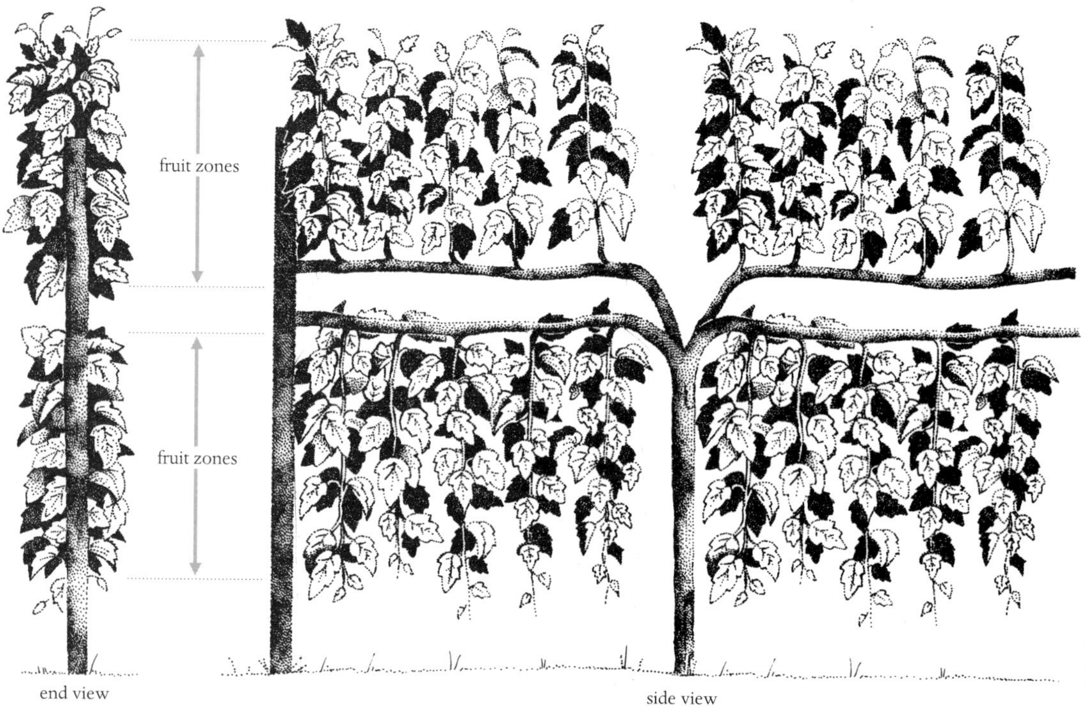

Scott Henry trellis

SCOTLAND, northern British country too cold for vine-growing but with some fine wine merchants and a long tradition of importing wine, notably from Bordeaux.

Kay, B., and Maclean, C., *Knee Deep in Claret* (Edinburgh, 1983).

SCOTT HENRY, a vine-TRAINING SYSTEM whereby the CANOPY is divided vertically and the shoots are separated and trained in two curtains vertically, upwards and downwards (see diagram). The canopy is about 2 m/6.5 ft tall, and the leaves are held in place by foliage wires. The system was developed by an Oregon vine-grower of the same name in the early 1980s when his vines were so vigorous that both yield and quality were reduced. Both CANE PRUNING and SPUR PRUNING are feasible with the Scott Henry system. The CANOPY MICROCLIMATE is improved by canopy division, and the system tends to yield about 20 per cent more than vines trained to undivided vertical canopies.

The Scott Henry system is suited to moderate-vigour vineyards with row spacing of about 2 m or more. It is becoming widely used in many New World countries in the 1990s because of its suitability for MECHANICAL HARVESTING and potential for improving wine quality. R.E.S.

Smart, R. E., and Robinson, M., *Sunlight into Wine: A Handbook for Winegrape Canopy Management* (Adelaide, 1991).

SCREWCAP. See STOPPERS for wine.

SCUPPERNONG, the best known of the vine varieties belonging to the *Vitis rotundifolia* species of the MUSCADINIA genus planted in the south east of the United States and in Mexico. It is commercially cultivated to produce musky wine that is markedly different from wine as it is best known, the product of *Vitis vinifera* varieties.

SCYTHIA, name used for different regions at different times, but for HERODOTUS Scythia was south eastern Europe between the Carpathians and the river Don, so much of modern ROMANIA and UKRAINE, including CRIMEA. The **Scythians** were nomadic, however. Writers in Ancient ROME are wont to describe all of northern Asia as Scythia.

SEC is French for DRY while **secco** is Italian and **seco** is Spanish and Portuguese for dry. See SWEETNESS.

SECATEURS, hand-held scissors used for winter PRUNING of vines. Normally the blades are curved and slide one past the other for a cutting action. Two-handled secateurs are used for cutting larger-diameter and older wood of the vine. Pruning can be faster, more effective, and less tiring with pneumatic secateurs with the pressure supplied from a portable compressor. Several pruners can operate from a single compressor, which is often powered by a tractor. R.E.S.

SÉCHERESSE, French for both DROUGHT and WATER STRESS. When the stress is mild this is a recognized contributor to wine quality.

SECONDARY FERMENTATION, a fermentation that occurs after the completion of the normal alcoholic FERMENTATION. This may be a FERMENTATION IN BOTTLE, or the evolution of carbon dioxide that accompanies a MALOLACTIC FERMENTATION, or simply a restarting in the winery of an alcoholic fermentation of a wine that still contains fermentable SUGARS. This can happen if, for example, there is a rise in TEMPERATURE or a more powerful YEAST is introduced. The GOVERNO wine-making process associated with TUSCANY in central Italy is another example of deliberate provocation of a secondary fermentation.

SECOND CROP, crop that may form after the main one on secondary LATERAL SHOOTS borne on a vine's primary SHOOTS. Lateral shoots arise in the axils of leaves in the normal course of development of the axillary bud. The amount of their growth is correlated with that of the whole shoot; on weak shoots laterals can barely be seen, while on long, strong shoots and at NODES near the cut ends of trimmed shoots laterals can grow so strongly as to resemble primary shoots. Second crop bunches are most abundant on strong laterals. In some varieties a second crop is rare, but on others, such as PINOT NOIR and many MUSCAT varieties, this crop can be large. Usually the existence of a second crop is a negative factor for wine quality since its development runs six to eight weeks behind the main crop and it competes for nutrients, as well as complicating the development and control of VINE PESTS and VINE DISEASES. Worse, it adds a proportion of immature fruit to the HARVEST (especially where MECHANICAL HARVESTERS are used) which usually adversely affects the quality of the resulting wine. B.G.C.

SECOND WINES are wines made from lots rejected as not good enough for the principal product, or *grand vin*, made at an estate. The phenomenon was born in BORDEAUX in the 18th century, and was revived in the early 20th century at Ch LAFITE but was hardly developed commercially until the 1980s, when increased competition forced ever more rigorous selection at the ASSEMBLAGE stage. Some of the more famous second wines are Ch LATOUR's Les Forts de Latour and Ch MARGAUX's Pavillon Rouge. (The branded wine MOUTON CADET began life as the second wine of Ch MOUTON-ROTHSCHILD.) Second wines are likely to contain the produce of young vines together with the least satisfactory lots. In particularly unsuccessful VINTAGES some properties make no *grand vin* at all so that the second wine is the only wine produced that year. In general, a second wine from a poor vintage (when a *grand vin* was also bottled) is rarely an exciting drink, but a second wine from a quality-conscious producer in a good vintage can represent good value—so long as it is not consumed alongside the *grand vin*. Some proprietors have even developed labels for their third wines, but this may often be closer to exhibitionism on the part of the producer than a great purchasing opportunity for the consumer.

SEDIMENT, the solid material which settles to the bottom of any wine container, whether it be a bottle or a vat, tank, cask, or barrel. This sediment is a very heterogeneous mixture which at the start of wine-making consists mainly of dead yeast cells (the gross LEES), the insoluble fragments of grape pulp and skin, and the seeds that settle out of new wine. At subsequent stages it consists of TARTRATES and, from red wines, PHENOLIC polymers, as well as any insoluble materials added to assist CLARIFICATION or to facilitate FILTRATION.

Sediments in bottled wines are relatively rare, and usually signal a fine wine that has already spent some years in bottle. So unaccustomed have modern wine consumers become to sediment that many (erroneously) view it as a fault. Most wine-makers therefore take great pains to ensure, through clarification, STABILIZATION, and filtration, that the great majority of wines made today, and virtually all of those designed to be drunk within their first few years, will remain free of sediment for at least a few years. Wines designed for long periods of BOTTLE AGEING, on the other hand, frequently deposit crystals of tartrates, white in white wines and dyed red or black in red wines. Red wines, in addition, deposit the complexes of TANNINS and ANTHOCYANS that are the result of phenolic polymerization. The heavy deposits in bottles of vintage port are a particularly dramatic example of this phenomenon. Wine-makers deliberately leave more tartrates and phenolics in wines designed for long ageing in bottle so that they are able to develop the compounds that constitute BOUQUET.

A bottle of wine containing sediment needs special care before SERVING.

Sediment from wine production presents a problem in its environmentally responsible disposal. Skins, stems, seeds, and pulp residues can be processed for the recovery of small amounts of sugar, tartaric acid, anthocyans, and grapeseed oil but, in most wine regions, the costs of recovery greatly exceed the market value of the recovered substances. The solid sediments are frequently returned to the vineyard and worked into the soil instead. A.D.W.

SEEDLING, the young plant that develops when a seed germinates. Grape seeds have tiny embryos which develop rapidly as the seed germinates, growing a freely branching tap-root and a shoot. This shoot is unusual because its first six to 12 leaves are spiral and tendrils are absent; it is taken to represent the juvenile phase of the seedling. Thereafter, leaves alternate and nodes bear tendrils as in mature clonal vines. The growth of seedlings is important in VINE BREEDING, but not otherwise in commercial viticulture (see VEGETATIVE PROPAGATION). B.G.C.

The point of decanting is to pour as much wine as possible out of the bottle and into the decanter, while leaving behind all of the **sediment**, shown here in the shoulder of the bottle.

SEEDS. For details of grape seeds, see GRAPE.

For details of the historical evidence provided by finds of ancient grape seeds (and other parts of the grape) see PALAEOETHNOBOTANY.

SÉGALIN is a recent INRA crossing of Jurançon Noir × Portugais Bleu which has good colour, structure, and flavour and is authorized in SOUTH WEST FRANCE. (See also CALADOC, CHASAN, PORTAN.)

SÉGURS, important family in the history of the BORDEAUX wine region, originally from the village of PAUILLAC. In 1670 Jacques de Ségur, a notary who was a councillor of the legal Parlement of Bordeaux, became the second husband of Jeanne de Gasq, daughter of another Parlement councillor. As a dowry she brought with her the *seigneurie* of LAFITE, to add to others he had including Calon in ST-ESTÈPHE, and an estate of about 1,000 ha/2,470 acres to the north of Pauillac. Their son Alexandre de Ségur was born in 1674. His father died in 1691, but in 1695 he married Marie-Thérèse de Clausel, the heiress of LATOUR, which gave him all the southern part of Pauillac and another very large estate. Their son, the future Marquis Nicolas-Alexandre de Ségur, was born in Bordeaux in 1697, and when his father died in 1716 he took over the very large domaine, which then included the farm of MOUTON before it passed in the 1730s to the Marquis de Branne. The marquis, a vice-president of the Bordeaux Parlement, was said to have been called 'le prince de vignes' by Louis XV. He is reputed to have said, 'I make wine at Lafite and Latour, but my heart is at Calon,' and on the label of Ch Calon Ségur there is today a large heart. When he died in Paris in 1755 he left 2 million livres (approximately the same as the later francs). He had four daughters. The eldest, Marie-Thérèse, married Alexandre de Ségur-Calon, provost of Paris, who was succeeded at Lafite by his son Nicolas-Marie Alexandre de Ségur, who, debt ridden through gambling, had to flee abroad to the Netherlands in 1784. Of the other three Ségur daughters, Angelique-Louise married the Seigneur de Maisconcel, and they had a son, Comte de Ségur-Cabanac; Marie-Antoinette-Victoire married the Comte de Miromesnil; and Charlotte-Émilie married the Comte de Coetlogon. As the last couple had no children and the second pair had two daughters who married the Comte de la Pallu and the Marquis de Beaumont, it was the Miromesnil, de la Pallu and Beaumont families whose descendants owned Ch Latour until it was acquired by HARVEYS of Bristol and, principally, 'the family interest of Lord Cowdray' (the British Pearson group) in 1962.

E.P.-R.

Penning-Rowsell, E., *The Wines of Bordeaux* (6th edn., 1989).

SEIBEL, common name for many of the FRENCH HYBRID vine varieties, most of them identified by number and many of them given a more colloquially appealing name. Seibel 5455 is more often called PLANTET, for example, while Seibel 4986 is Rayon d'Or and Seibel 9549 is DeChaunac (see NEW YORK). The variety known as CHANCELLOR in New York state but simply as Seibel in France is Seibel 7053. In the late 1960s there were more than 70,000 ha/172,900 acres of it planted in France, but it has now almost disappeared from French vineyards. Small quantities of various Seibels are planted in some cooler wine regions around the world.

SEKT, word used in German-speaking countries to describe quality SPARKLING WINE as defined by the EUROPEAN UNION. Its etymology is uncertain but is popularly said to be the result of a misunderstanding between the German classical actor Ludwig Devrient and a waiter at Lutter & Wegener's restaurant in Berlin in November 1825. Devrient, a regular customer for CHAMPAGNE, quoting from his Falstaff role, cried 'Give me a cup of sack, rogue. Is there no virtue extant?' (*Henry IV, Part I*, II. iv). He was served with his usual champagne, and a new meaning for the word Sekt had been invented, which, according to the authority on German sparkling wine, Professor Dr Helmut Arntz, had been accepted throughout Germany by 1900.

Of Germany's total annual sparkling wine production of more than 375 million bottles (a figure that steadily increases), 94 per cent can be described as Sekt, of which about 85 per cent is white. Most Sekt is inexpensive and over two-thirds of the production sells in Germany for less than DM5 per bottle, a price which includes a Sekt tax of DM2 per bottle and a value added tax.

About 90 per cent of Sekt made in Germany is based on Italian, French, or other non-German still wine, and most is sold as dry (TROCKEN) or medium dry (HALBTROCKEN). The average Sekt consumer buys a branded wine, and is interested neither in its method of production (98 per cent acquires its sparkle by the tank method; see SPARKLING WINE-MAKING), nor in the origin of the base wine.

Deutscher Sekt, however, is made solely from German-based wine, and it is in this small part of the market where there is fine, elegant sparkling wine, mainly BRUT or extra dry.

Some 84 per cent of the volume of Sekt comes from firms making in excess of 5 million bottles per year. Amongst them are names, established in 1850 or earlier, such as Deinhard, Feist Belmont, Henkell, Kupferberg, and Matheus Müller, although only Deinhard is still owned by the founding family. The most successful brands in terms of annual sales are Faber Krönung (45 million bottles), followed in order of decreasing volume by Söhnlein Brilliant, Ruttgers Club, Deinhard Cabinet, and Henkell Trocken (14 million bottles).

In the 1980s there was great growth in the number of enterprises (including producer's associations, co-operative cellars, and private estates) making Deutscher Sekt for the wine lover—as opposed to the less demanding traditional sparkling wine market. These new high-quality sparkling wines are sold under the name of a region and vineyard of origin, bearing a vintage and almost always the name of a vine variety. The acidity and finesse of RIESLING in particular make a most stylish sparkling wine, and Sekt from the PINOT family is also very successful. Sparkling wines from a private estate may be made either by a contract Sekt manufacturer or by the estate itself. Where an estate is making its own Sekt, the relatively small volume of liquid involved requires the wine to be BOTTLE FERMENTED.

Austria's Sekt producers, many of which were established during the time of the Austro-Hungarian empire, are concentrated in the Weinviertel in lower Austria on the road north out of Vienna towards Brno in Moravia. I.J.

Arntz, H., *Deutsches Sektlexikon* (Wiesbaden, 1987).
Dohm, H., *Sekt zwischen Kult und Konsum* (Neustadt, 1985).

SÉLECTION CLONALE is French for CLONAL SELECTION, while **sélection massale** is French for MASS SELECTION. The term **selection** is also used for TRIAGE or sorting of good-quality, healthy grapes from others, and for the selection process involved in choosing wines for the ASSEMBLAGE of the main wine, as opposed to a SECOND WINE.

SÉLECTION DE GRAINS NOBLES, the richest, most sumptuous ripeness category of ALSACE wines.

SELFED VINE, a plant created by one VINE VARIETY crossed to itself. This is not a very successful breeding strategy, since most varieties carry deleterious recessive genes, and there is consequently a strong inbreeding depression. This is avoided by crossing unrelated vines, which is a feature of the progeny of successful VINE BREEDING. See also NEW VARIETIES. R.E.S.

SEMI-CARBONIC MACERATION, wine-making process which involves a short CARBONIC MACERATION phase followed by a normal alcoholic FERMENTATION. The great majority of Beaujolais NOUVEAU and most other PRIMEUR wines are made in this fashion. Such wines have a very distinct aroma reminiscent of bananas or kirsch.

Before the days of mechanical CRUSHER-DESTEMMERS, most red wines would have been made by a very similar process, whereby whole grape clusters went into fermentation vessels where spontaneous FERMENTATION started in the small amount of juice liberated while the vessel was being filled. The CARBON DIOXIDE generated by the fermentation would provide the environment necessary to sustain a carbonic maceration fermentation within the intact berries at the bottom of the vessel. In shallow vessels, however, the atmosphere around the intact berries was seldom completely free of OXYGEN so that the deeper the vessel, the greater the proportion of grapes which underwent carbonic maceration. A.D.W.

SÉMILLON, often written plain **Semillon** in non-francophone countries, a golden grape variety from south west France, is one of the unsung heroes of white wine production. Blended with its traditional partner SAUVIGNON Blanc, this golden-berried vine variety is the key ingredient in SAUTERNES, arguably the world's longest-living unfortified wine, as it is in most of the great dry whites of Graves (see PESSAC-LÉOGNAN). Unblended, in Australia's HUNTER VALLEY, it is responsible for one of the most idiosyncratic and historic wine types exclusive to the New World. Thanks to its widespread establishment in Bordeaux and much of the southern hemisphere, it has been the world's most planted white grape variety capable of top-quality wine production but is not fashionable and is declining in importance.

Sémillon seems destined to play a supplementary role. The wines it produces tend to fatness and, although capable of ageing, have little aroma in youth. Sauvignon Blanc, with its internationally recognized name, strong aroma, high acidity, but slight lack of substance, fills in all obvious gaps. But if

Sémillon had traditionally been blended with Sauvignon, it has recently attracted another blend-mate, if for entirely different reasons. Sémillon does not exactly complement Chardonnay so much as provide neutral padding for it and, in a world desperate for Chardonnay, Sémillon has found itself the passive ingredient in commercially motivated blends sometimes, even, called SemChard—most notably but not exclusively in Australia. And here, as elsewhere in the New World, Sémillon's weight, and high yield, make it a popular base for commercial blends.

As a vine Sémillon is easy to cultivate. It is almost as vigorous as Sauvignon Blanc with particularly deep green leaves, but flowers slightly later and is not particularly susceptible to COULURE. Nor is it a victim of disease, apart from rot, which, in favourable conditions, is the blessed NOBLE ROT rather than the destructive GREY ROT. This makes Sémillon a particularly productive vine which was doubtless a factor in its widespread popularity.

Its greatest concentration is still in Bordeaux, where, although total plantings halved between 1968 (when it was the most planted variety of either hue) and 1988, it is still the most planted white grape variety by far with nearly 12,000 ha/29,640 acres in 1988. On the left bank of the Garonne, in the Graves, Sauternes, and its enclave BARSAC, Sémillon still outnumbers Sauvignon in almost exactly the traditional proportions of four to one, while in the ENTRE-DEUX-MERS, where most Sémillon is planted, Sauvignon (together with varieties for financially more rewarding red wine production) is fast replacing it.

In the great, long-lived dry whites of Graves and Pessac-Léognan Sémillon usually predominates and inspires rich, golden, honeyed, viscous wines quite unlike any Sémillons made elsewhere. Low yields, old vines, oak ageing, and Sauvignon all play their part. In Sauternes, Sémillon's great attribute is its proneness to noble rot. This special mould, *Botrytis cinerea*, concentrates sugars and, acids and shrinks yields so that the best of the resulting wines such as Ch d'YQUEM may continue to evolve for centuries. Again, oak ageing deepens Sémillon's already relatively deep gold (really ripe grapes may almost look pink). Thus one of Sémillon's disadvantages, a tendency to overcrop, is eliminated. Similar, but usually less exciting, sweet whites, the most ordinary made simply by stopping fermentation or adding sweet grape must, are made in the nearby appellations of CADILLAC, CÉRONS, LOUPIAC, and STE-CROIX-DU-MONT.

In quantitative terms, however, Sémillon's most common expression, other than as basic white in CHILE, is as the major ingredient in basic white bordeaux. The best are usually made exclusively of Sémillon with some of the other two 'noble' varieties Sauvignon Blanc and Muscadelle, but up to 30 per cent of the blend may technically comprise Ugni Blanc (the undistinguished TREBBIANO), Colombard, and even the much less common Merlot Blanc, Ondenc, and Mauzac. Cynically made Bordeaux Sémillon can be very dull stuff indeed, high in yield and SULPHUR content but low in interest, acidity, and flavour.

Like Sauvignon Blanc, Sémillon is allowed in many other appellations for dry and sweet whites of SOUTH WEST FRANCE but is perhaps most notable in qualitative terms in MONBAZILLAC. Thanks to its (declining) importance throughout BERGERAC Sémillon is still the most planted variety in the Dordogne, outnumbering Merlot almost two to one, and is the most planted white-berried variety in the Lot-et-Garonne *département*, although little of it finds its way into APPELLATION CONTRÔLÉE wine. It is allowed in most appellations of PROVENCE, where there were about 120 ha in 1988, but has made little impact on the vineyards of the Midi, where acidity is at a premium.

Sémillon's other great sphere of influence is South America in general and Chile in particular, where its more than 20,000 ha provide two-thirds of all white wines produced, although it is rarely seen on labels outside the country. Chilean Sémillon was for long somewhat fat and oily, and the native tendency to over-produce has so far done little to improve this except in very isolated examples of the most ambitious producers. Argentina has more than 2,000 ha of Sémillon, which makes it unimportant there relative to such white varieties as Pedro Ximénez, Torrontés, and Muscat of Alexandria. Some is used as SPARKLING WINE base in the case of vintage madeira.

In North America Sémillon is generally rather scorned, lacking the image of Sauvignon Blanc, although a significant number of producers use the former to add interest to the latter. There are just 2,000 acres of usually high-yielding Sémillon in California (where some have experimented with producing BOTRYTIZED wines in the image of Sauternes from it). It has been given a fillip by the useful part it can play in adding weight to Sauvignon in white bordeaux MERITAGE blends. Historically LIVERMORE VALLEY has produced the best fruit for dry white VARIETALS, while it can also perform well in parts of NAPA, SONOMA, and Santa Ynez Valley in SANTA BARBARA County. Sémillon also has a relatively significant presence in Washington, where it often displays grassy, Sauvignon-like aromas.

It is quite widespread, without being particularly important, throughout eastern Europe (see CROATIA), but it is in SOUTH AFRICA and AUSTRALIA where Sémillon had a particularly glorious past. In 1822 93 per cent of all South African vineyard was planted with this variety, imported from Bordeaux. So common was it then in fact that it was simply called Wyndruif, or 'wine grape'. It was subsequently called Green Grape, a reference to its abnormally green foliage, but has been declining in importance so that today the Semillion, as it is sometimes called, accounts for just one per cent of Cape vineyards.

Sémillon is still relatively widely grown in Australia, on the other hand, although it was overtaken by Chardonnay and even Sauvignon Blanc in the late 1980s. It seems to have settled in Australia's wine industry relatively early, possibly having been imported from South Africa, and is still mainly grown in NEW SOUTH WALES, making either extraordinary, age-worthy, full bodied dry whites in the Hunter Valley or more commercial liquids, together with the odd sweet marvel, in the irrigated vineyards inland. Only the best bottles from the Hunter and Bordeaux demonstrate Sémillon's ability to age and, often, its tendency to acquire an almost orange depth of colour when it does. It was not until the 1980s, however, that Sémillon was publicly revealed as the source of the Hunter's greatest. Until then the wines were usually called Hunter Riesling, and occasionally Chablis and White Burgundy, depending on slight variations in style.

In Australia's cooler sites such as Tasmania and the south of Western Australia, Sémillon often demonstrates the same sort of grassiness as in Washington state and in NEW ZEALAND, where, presumably, proximity to Australia encouraged its establishment and there are a few hundred hectares. Some interesting sweet wines have been coaxed out of Sémillon in Gisborne.

The variety was also exported to Israel to establish vineyards there at the end of the 19th century.

Brook, S., *Sauvignon Blanc and Sémillon* (London, 1992).

SEQUENCE of wines to be served. See ORDER.

SERBIA, the largest and most central republic in what was YUGOSLAVIA. Serbia, excluding VOJVODINA, produces around one-third of all ex-Yugoslavian wine, both red and white. Between the flattish countryside around Belgrade and Skopje in MACEDONIA is a series of valleys, some with easily worked, fertile, open slopes and some wilder, steeper, and more wooded. Broadly, the vineyard trail follows the Morava river from the Danube due south towards its source in the mountains of KOSOVO, leaving the border hills of BULGARIA to the east.

Immediately to the south of Belgrade in the Šumadija-Velika Morava region, the rather ordinary white grape variety SMEDEREVKA grows, around the town of Smederevo, from which it takes its name. Here too, and to the south in the Oplenac subregion, a more ambitious range of white grape varieties are now growing. SAUVIGNON Blanc with a potentially excellent intensity of flavour can be produced, but wine-making practices frequently leave much to be desired.

Serbia is at its best producing red wines. Its own PROKUPAC grape, used by itself or blended with more internationally known varieties, grows in all Serbian wine regions. It predominates in the small but ancient district of Zupa in the Zapadna Morava region not far south of Belgrade. The wines are well balanced, pleasantly coloured, and can demonstrate an easy, if sometimes light, fruit quality which can be used to bolster PINOT NOIR and GAMAY. While Pinot Noir wines can have a very true BOUQUET, occasionally more reminiscent of German than French versions, Gamay rarely shows at all true to its Beaujolais archetype, tending rather to produce a coarse, over-extracted red if it is not well handled.

Many of the most promising red wine vineyards lie in the region of Juzna Morava from around the towns of Niš, Leskovac, and Vranje towards the Bulgarian border. Healthy CABERNET and MERLOT grapes are being grown here, often in big privately owned vineyards as well as some belonging to bottler/brand owners who correctly identified the region as climatically suitable for these classic Bordeaux red wine varieties in the early 1980s; their investments should bear fruit now that the vineyards are mature.

Further east, by the Bulgarian border, Timok is also being developed as a vineyard area with similar potential for classic reds, although without a modern vinification plant, potential cannot be transferred from vineyard to bottle. A.H.M.

SERCIAL, Anglicized name for the Portuguese white grape variety CERCEAL, once quite commonly planted on the island of Madeira but subsequently used to denote style of MADEIRA rather than the grape variety from which it was made. The vine ripens particularly late and grapes retain their acidity quite notably. After PHYLLOXERA devastated the vineyards of Madeira it became easier to find the variety on the mainland, as ESGANA or Esgana Cão, than on the island, although plantings are now increasing. For more details, see MADEIRA.

Sercial is the lightest, driest, most acid and delicate style of madeira, and takes the longest, often many decades in the case of vintage madeira, to mature.

SERVICE OF WINE. See SERVING WINE and SOMMELIERS.

SERVING WINE involves a number of fairly obvious steps, but mastering each of them can maximize the pleasure given by any individual wine. See OPENING THE BOTTLE, BREATHING, DECANTING, GLASSES, FOOD AND WINE MATCHING, ORDER, and LEFTOVER WINE for details of these aspects of serving wine.

Perhaps the least obvious requirement of anyone serving wine is that they appear superficially mean, by filling glasses no more than two-thirds, and preferably less than half, full.

Temperature is a crucial element in **serving** wine. Before reliable refrigeration, glasses as well as wine were cooled, as in this Bristol blue wine glass cooler made in the first decade of the 18th century by Isaac Jacobs.

This allows energetic agitation of the glass if necessary, and enables the all-important AROMA to collect in the upper part of the bowl (see TASTING).

The factor which probably has the single greatest effect on how a wine tastes, however, is temperature, and this is a factor which can be controlled by whoever is serving. Because of the well-known general rule that white (and rosé) wines should be chilled and red wines should be served at something called room temperature, and because many refrigerators are set at relatively low temperatures, in practice many white wines are served too cool and many red wines dangerously warm. See TEMPERATURE for some guidance on specific recommended serving temperatures for certain styles of wine. Few wine drinkers have wine thermometers, however, so a certain amount of experimentation with ways of changing temperature is advisable.

Cooling wine in a refrigerator is much slower than cooling wine in a container holding water and ice (two hours rather than 30 minutes to cool an average bottle from 22 to 10 °C/ 50 °F). An ice box would do the job faster but has the serious disadvantage that the bottle will be cooled right down to icebox temperature if left there. This may well freeze the wine and push the cork out. Some main refrigerator cabinets are, furthermore, set at such low temperatures that wines may emerge simply too cool. (Note that a container full of ice cubes but no water is not a very effective cooler as it provides relatively little contact between the bottle and the cooling medium.)

It is a happy coincidence that the ideal cellar temperature, around 15 °C, is also ideal for serving a wide range of wines such as complex dry white wines and light bodied red wines, and is not so low that it takes long to warm tannic red wines to a suitable serving temperature.

In cool climates wine drinkers may have difficulty in warming bottles of red wine to suitably high temperatures for serving. This is one argument for decanting, into a decanter warmed with hot water. Direct heat should not be applied to a bottle, and even contact with a radiator can heat wine to a dangerously high temperature (above 20 °C the ALCOHOL begins to dominate and it can start to taste unbalanced).

One of the most effective ways of warming wine, whether intentionally or not, is to pour it out into glasses in a relatively warm environment. This effect is accentuated if the glasses are cupped in human hands. For this reason it is usually wise to serve wines slightly cooler than the ideal temperature at which they are best appreciated. Warming wine in microwave ovens can be effective if the oven is big enough, and if great care is taken not to overheat.

Ambient temperature, or even the precise temperature of the taster, can affect how a wine tastes: crisp, light wines taste either delightfully refreshing or disappointingly meagre when the taster is hot or cold respectively. On the other hand, in tropical climates, where both temperature and humidity are high, it can be almost impossible to find suitable conditions in which to serve even the finest red wine as, without air conditioning, drinks heat up so rapidly that a red wine has either to be served well chilled or run the risk of being almost MULLED. Light red wines with marked ACIDITY such as BEAUJOLAIS and reds from cooler climates such as the LOIRE, NEW ZEALAND, TASMANIA, NEW YORK, and WASHINGTON can taste much more appetizing in hot climates than CLASSED GROWTH red bordeaux or fine burgundy.

One final aspect of serving wine, about which the Latin poet HORACE wrote extensively, is matching wine to guest and occasion. Part of what might generally be called CONNOISSEURSHIP, this is a pleasure associated with wine which can be almost as great as drinking it.

See also TASTING for the special conditions of serving wine for this particular purpose, a very different one from actually drinking it.

SET, the process by which vine flowers become berries. See FRUIT SET.

SETTING, stage in plant development after FLOWERING when the flowers either fall off or adhere to the plant and fruits start to grow. The percentage of grapevine flowers that set can range from nil to 100 but in most seeded varieties of grape it ranges from 20 to 50 per cent, depending on vine variety and weather conditions. The setting period of about a week is a nervous one for the vine-grower, since it is a major determinant of the size of the crop, yet the grower can do little to change the course of events. Except in parthenocarpic berries (see GRAPE), poor POLLINATION and fertilization of the ovules, or non-functional ovules which preclude the development of seeds, lead to poor FRUIT SET, or COULURE.

It is not clear whether the supply of organic nutrients to the INFLORESCENCE during flowering or the activities of several types of plant HORMONES arising particularly from synthesis in the developing seed is the more important factor in successful fruit setting, but the crucial role that weather plays during this period is beyond dispute. Low temperatures, heavy cloud, prolonged rain, or hot, dry winds may each interfere with this delicate and complicated sequence of plant development, and cause poor set. Strategies for avoiding poor set include TRAINING SYSTEMS designed to open the vine CANOPY, avoiding rapid shoot growth, ensuring balanced VINE NUTRITION and water supply, TOPPING shoots during flowering, or, in extreme circumstances, CINCTURING vine trunks at flowering. Treatment with growth retardants before flowering often improves setting, but the practice has negative side-effects and is discouraged on environmental grounds. Several GROWTH REGULATORS improve the setting of seedless varieties. B.G.C.

SETTLING, the wine-making operation of holding MUST or wine in a vessel so that suspended solids fall to the bottom. The French term *débourbage* is sometimes used for the most common example of settling, to begin the CLARIFICATION of freshly drained and pressed white musts before FERMENTATION. Fermentation is delayed by adding SULPHUR DIOXIDE and by cooling before pumping to the settling vessel.

Red wines, whose skins are included in the fermentation vessel, are settled after fermentation and MACERATION when the purpose is to remove not just grape debris but also dead yeast cells, or LEES.

Settling is governed by factors which include the size of the solid particles, the difference in their DENSITY from that of the liquid, and the extent to which the liquid moves within the settling vessel. Because must and and cloudy grape juice are so much denser than wine, they are much more difficult to settle. Solids as large and dense as seeds and stem fragments settle rapidly. Finely divided pulp debris and dead yeast cells which are very small settle more slowly and are easily resuspended by currents within the settling vessel. COLLOIDS, which have dimensions of large molecular size, are very slow to settle because their movement is influenced by the smallest liquid movement within the vessel. The settling of colloids can be greatly assisted by the addition of clarifying or FINING agents such as BENTONITE, which adsorbs them and grows them into complexes large enough to settle. Settling of particularly viscous grape juice can also be encouraged by the addition of ENZYMES designed to break chains of PECTINS.

Settling may also be part of processing and finishing in wine-making. Unless time is a critical factor, settling, possibly followed by a light filtration, is preferable to the more expensive options of CENTRIFUGATION or FILTRATION. A.D.W.

SETÚBAL, an overgrown fishing port on the Sado estuary south of Lisbon, the capital of PORTUGAL, is also the name of a Portuguese FORTIFIED WINE with its own DOC region (see map on p. 750). Made predominantly from Moscatel (MUSCAT) grapes growing on the lower slopes of the Arrábida hills and the plain around the town of Palmela, the region was officially demarcated in 1907 for Moscatel de Setúbal. EUROPEAN UNION regulations, however, state that for a wine to be labelled with a variety it must be made with at least 85 per cent of the specified grape. Since local regulations allow a number of other grapes to make up 30 per cent of the blend, the word Moscatel has been omitted from the name of the wine since Portugal joined the EU in 1986. Three different varieties of Muscat are permitted: the so-called Moscatel de Setúbal, or MUSCAT OF ALEXANDRIA, which is much the most important; together with Moscatel do Douro and the rare pink-skinned Moscatel Roxo. To begin with, Setúbal is made in much the same way as many other sweet fortified wines, the FERMENTATION being arrested with GRAPE SPIRIT. After vinification, however, pungent Muscat grape skins are left to macerate in the wine for five or six months which imparts a taste of fresh dessert grapes and gives Setúbal its intense aroma and flavour. Most Setúbal is bottled after spending four or five years in large oak tanks, by which time the wine has an amber-orange colour and a spicy, raisiny character. Small quantities, however, are bottled after 20 years in cask, when the colour is deep brown and the wine has a rich, grapey intensity.

José Maria da FONSECA Successores, by fár the largest producer of Setúbal, hold stocks of wine dating back to the mid 19th century which are occasionally bottled and released for sale. A minute quantity of Setúbal is also made separately from Moscatel Roxo.

For details of the exciting range of table wines made on the Setúbal peninsula, see ARRÁBIDA and PALMELA. R.J.M.

SEVERNY, Russian vine variety developed at the All-Russia Potapenko Institute from a Malengra seedling with a member of the famously cold-hardy VITIS *amurensis* vine species native to Mongolia.

See also SAPERAVI Severny and CABERNET SEVERNY. There is small-scale experimentation with a Severny variety in CANADA, where winters are as harsh as in Russia.

SEXUAL PROPAGATION, reproduction by seed involving the union of a male gamete (POLLEN sperm) and a female gamete (the egg cell or OVARY). The important feature of this type of propagation is that the two units are genetically different, so the product of the union (zygote to embryo to seedling) is in turn genetically different from either parent. Throughout the world of nature, this is how genetic diversity is continued, permitting selection of those progeny best suited to survive. Man has circumvented this process by propagating selected, desirable individuals and propagating them vegetatively (see VEGETATIVE PROPAGATION). The varieties RIESLING and CABERNET SAUVIGNON are excellent examples of this process. Originally sexual seedlings, they have been propagated asexually for at least 1,000 years with substantially the same genetic constitution. Sexual propagation is used for VINE BREEDING throughout the world to produce NEW VARIETIES. Success depends on selecting suitable parents. B.G.C.

SEYSSEL, wine appellation within the eastern French region of SAVOIE producing light, dry white still and sparkling wines. This is one of the few Savoie wines to escape the region itself, notably in the form of sparkling Seyssel from producers Varichon et Clerc. About 55 ha/135 acres of vines were devoted to still wine and a further 16 ha to sparkling wine production in the early 1990s, concentrated on the steep slopes of the upper Rhône valley about 24 km/15 miles down river of Geneva. CHASSELAS is the dominant grape variety here although the local MOLETTE is also grown for sparkling wines and all wines must contain at least 10 per cent of the superior local variety ROUSSETTE, whose Savoyard roots are said to be here. The sparkling wines need to have a POTENTIAL ALCOHOL of just 8.5 per cent at harvest and must be BOTTLE FERMENTED in the region. They are light, refreshing, and the best can develop in bottle, but most are drunk locally.

SEYVAL BLANC, useful white grape variety that is a FRENCH HYBRID, the most widely planted Seyve-Villard hybrid, number 5276, the result of crossing two SEIBEL hybrids. It is productive, ripens early and is well suited to relatively cool climates such as that of ENGLAND where it is the most planted vine variety after MÜLLER-THERGAU. It is also popular in CANADA and, to a lesser extent, in the eastern UNITED STATES, notably in NEW YORK state. Its crisp white wines have no hint of FOXY flavour and can even benefit from BARREL MATURATION but, because it contains some non-VINIFERA genes, it is outlawed by European Union authorities for QUALITY WINE production, a bone of contention in the English wine industry.

SEYVE-VILLARD, series of about 100 FRENCH HYBRIDS developed by hybridizer Bertille Seyve and his partner and father-in-law Victor Villard. France had a total of more than 3,000 ha/7,410 acres of various Seyve-Villard hybrids, most of them making red VIN DE TABLE, planted in the late 1980s. Perhaps the most famous, however, is the white SEYVAL BLANC wine grape.

Galet, P. (trans. Morton, L. T.), *A Practical Ampelogrophy* (Ithaca, 1979).

SFORZATO, Sfursat, Sfurzat, all names for a DRIED GRAPE WINE made in the VALTELLINA zone in the far north of Italy.

SHADE, the absence of sunlight in a vine CANOPY. This is typically due to leaves blocking out sunlight, as the transmission of light through one leaf layer is less than 10 per cent of full sunlight. In most vineyards the blocking leaves are other vine leaves, but occasionally they may be the leaves of weeds or even adjacent trees, as occurs in the VINHO VERDE region of Portugal. For most vineyards in the world, shade is due to vigorous vines being trained to restrictive vine-TRAINING SYSTEMS.

Sunlight levels in the centre of dense canopies with many leaf layers can be as little as one per cent of the levels above the canopy. At this very low level of light PHOTOSYNTHESIS is almost zero, and in time the leaves turn yellow and then fall off. Leaves deep in the canopy also experience filtered sunlight with marked spectral shift, in that red light is reduced and far red light relatively enriched. The ratio of red to far red light can act as a signal system for the vine, and may play a role in the vine's response to shade.

Shade can reduce both vine YIELD and grape quality. Shade has been shown to reduce bud INITIATION, BUDBREAK, FRUIT SET, and hence berry number, as well as BERRY SIZE. So shade can reduce yield dramatically, and yields may increase up to threefold where shade has been removed by improving the training system.

Many studies around the world, for a range of vine varieties in a range of climates, have also demonstrated that shade alters must composition and reduces wine quality. Shade is known to decrease levels of SUGARS, ANTHOCYANS, PHENOLICS, TARTARIC ACID, monoterpene FLAVOUR COMPOUNDS and apparent varietal character. Other negative effects of shade on wine quality are increases in MALIC ACID, PH, POTASSIUM, and in the so-called HERBACEOUS characters. Shaded fruit is also more susceptible to BOTRYTIS BUNCH ROT and POWDERY MILDEW. CANOPY MANAGEMENT can reduce shade in the canopy and, in high-vigour vineyards, may improve yield and quality simultaneously. R.E.S.

Champagnol, F., *Éléments de physiologie de la vigne et de viticulture générale* (St-Gely-du-Fesc, 1984).
Smart, R. E., and Robinson, M., *Sunlight into Wine: A Handbook for Winegrape Canopy Management* (Adelaide, 1991).

SHALE, a dark, clay-grade sediment which splits easily into very thin layers. It is much more easily crumbled than SLATE. Both as a ROCK and in SOILS, shale behaves as a clay for cultivation. J.M.H.

SHANKING, physiological condition which causes grape bunch stems to shrivel and die during RIPENING. This condition is also known as water berry in California, *Stiellahme* in Germany, and *dessèchement de la rafle* in French. Affected berries do not ripen properly and shrivel on the bunch, although it is rare for all berries to be affected. CABERNET SAUVIGNON vines are particularly prone to shanking. Affected berries have lower SUGARS, ANTHOCYANS, and fatty acids, but higher ACIDITY. The exact cause is unknown, but factors associated with the condition are vigorous shoot growth, the weather at flowering, and levels of magnesium and ammonium in the plant tissue. There is no widely accepted control, although magnesium sprays at VERAISON have sometimes reduced shanking. R.E.S.

SHARPSHOOTERS, insects which feed on vine foliage and can carry diseases. See LEAF HOPPERS.

SHENANDOAH VALLEY is the name of two AVA wine regions. For details of the California region, see SIERRA FOOTHILLS. There is also a Shenandoah Valley in Virginia.

SHERRY, fortified wine from the region around the city of Jerez de la Frontera in ANDALUCÍA, south west Spain. The term sherry has also been used as a generic term for a wide range of FORTIFIED WINES made from white grapes, but from the mid 1990s within the EUROPEAN UNION it must be restricted to the produce of the Jerez DO. (For details of other once-prominent producers of sherry styles of wine see CYPRUS, SOUTH AFRICA, and British SHERRY.)

Sherry production was declining in the early 1990s but averaged about 750,000 hl/19.8 million gal a year, about half as much again as that of Portugal's equally famous, yet very different, fortified wine, PORT.

Sherry is the English corruption of the word Jerez, while Xérès is its French counterpart and is also the French name for sherry. The words Jerez-Xérès-Sherry appear on all bottles of sherry, on paper seals granted by the CONSEJO REGULADOR to guarantee the origin of the wine. Within the Jerez DO there are in fact three centres for sherry maturation: JEREZ DE LA FRONTERA, SANLÚCAR DE BARRAMEDA, and PUERTO DE SANTA MARÍA, each of which imparts subtle differences to the wines. Throughout this article, the types of wine made naturally in sherry BODEGAS are referred to in lower case italics, as in *oloroso*, while the sherry styles created for commercial use on the label are referred to with a capital letter, as in Oloroso.

Sherry is initially made to conform to two principal types: pale, dry *fino* (or, in Sanlúcar de Barrameda, *manzanilla)*, which ages under the influence of the film-forming yeast FLOR, and dark, full, but dry *oloroso*. All sherry styles found on labels (Manzanilla, Fino, Amontillado, Oloroso, Pale Cream, Cream, etc., in generally ascending order of BODY) are derived

The brilliant white landscape of **sherry** vineyards around Jerez in southern Spain.

from these two main types. The only exception is Palo Cortado, which is a naturally resulting intermediate type and style between Amontillado and Oloroso. Pedro Ximénez is an intensely sweet wine, usually for blending, made from the grape variety of the same name.

History

Jerez is one of the oldest wine-producing towns in Spain. It may well have been established by the PHOENICIANS who founded the nearby port of Cádiz in 1110 BC. The Phoenicians were followed by the CARTHAGINIANS, who were in turn succeeded by the ROMANS. Iberian viticulture advanced rapidly under Roman rule and Jerez has been identified as the Roman city of Ceritium. After the Romans were expelled around AD 400, southern Iberia was overrun by successive tribes of Vandals and Visigoths, who were in turn defeated by the Moors after the battle of Guadalete in 711 (see ISLAM). The Moors held sway over Andalucía for seven centuries and their influence can still be felt in many spheres of Andalucian life, not least in the architecture of Seville, Cordoba, and Granada. Under Moorish domination, Jerez grew in size and stature. The town was named 'Seris' and this later evolved into Jerez de la Frontera, when it stood on the frontier of the two warring kingdoms during Christian reconquest in the 13th century.

Viticulture, which continued despite Moorish occupation, was revitalized by the Christians, although the region around Jerez continued to be plagued by war until the 15th century. Exports began and, in spite of periodic set-backs, trade with England and France was well established by the 1490s, when it was declared that wines shipped abroad would be free from local tax. In the 'Pardoner's Tale', Chaucer mentions the wines of Lepe, a village between Ayamonte and Huelva (see CONDADO DE HUELVA), which were blended with sherry until the early years of the 20th century. In 1492 the Jews were expelled from Spain, their vineyards were confiscated, and foreigners, many of them English, took their place as merchants. Certain basic quality controls were established, including the capacity of the sherry cask or BUTT, which has not changed to this day.

At the end of the 15th century, after Christopher Columbus had discovered America from his base in Andalucía, the sherry town of Sanlúcar de Barrameda became an important port for the new transatlantic trade and in the 16th century large quantities of wine were shipped to the Americas from Jerez. In his book *Sherry* Julian Jeffs speculates that Vino de Jerez (sherry) was almost certainly the first wine to enter North America.

Relations between England and Spain began to deteriorate in the 16th century and, although trade continued, the colony of English merchants trading from Sanlúcar began to suffer privations. In 1585, after a number of raids by Sir Francis Drake and his fleet, English merchants were arrested and their possessions seized. Exports ceased. Two years later, in an attack on Cádiz, Drake both 'singed the King of Spain's beard' and captured '2,900 pipes' of wine. This plunder helped to establish sherry as a popular drink in Elizabethan England.

After the death of Elizabeth I trade became easier and 'sacke', or SACK, returned to royal circles. The English colony re-established itself and prospered, often by shipping poor-quality wines. But minor skirmishes continued and in 1625 Charles I, having been rebuffed by the infanta of Spain, sent in an expeditionary force commanded by Sir Edward Cecil to Andalucía. The manœuvre was poorly planned and Cecil's men were easily defeated when they reached a BODEGA owned by the de Soto family and literally turned to drink.

By the 17th century 'sherris-sack' was well established in England and was drunk by Samuel Pepys, who in 1662 records that he mixed sherry and MÁLAGA. Pepys visited the English colony in Sanlúcar de Barrameda in 1683. At that time, until the construction of a railway in the mid 19th century, most of the sherry bodegas were located on the coast at Sanlúcar and Puerto de Santa María, where proximity to the quays made the wine readily available for export.

The sherry industry suffered many set-backs at the beginning 18th century, when England and Spain became embroiled in a series of conflicts beginning in 1702 with the War of the Spanish Succession. The METHUEN TREATY (1703) diverted trade to Portugal and a series of restrictive measures imposed by the Gremio or Wine Growers Guild of Jerez sent merchants to Málaga in search of wine. However, the latter half of the century was an era of increasing prosperity stimulated by the arrival of a number of French and British merchants. The firms of Osborne, Duff Gordon, and Garvey date from this period.

The Peninsular Wars (1808–14) devastated Jerez. Andalucía became a battleground, occupied for a time by the French, who pillaged the sherry bodegas and forced a number of families to flee to the relative safety of the Cádiz garrison. With the defeat of the French, merchants set about rebuilding their businesses with spectacular success. Pedro DOMECQ took over the firm of Juan Haurie in 1822 and Manuel María González Angel, founder of GONZALEZ BYASS, began trading in 1835. Sherry exports rose steadily from about 8,000 butts in the early years of the century to over 70,000 butts in 1873, a figure not exceeded again until the 1950s. In the 1850s the sherry industry was greatly helped by the construction of a RAILWAY linking Jerez and Puerto de Santa María, and a number of merchants left their quayside bodegas. Many new producers took advantage of the sherry boom only to be wiped out by PHYLLOXERA and economic depression a few years later. Some survived, among them Terry, SANDEMAN, Diez Hermanos, and Williams & Humbert.

By the end of the 19th century the sherry industry was on the brink of collapse. The boom gave rise to numerous spurious 'sherries' from South Africa, Australia, France—and from Germany, where a sherry style potion was made from potato spirit. A spiral of price-cutting began and sherry was stretched with poor quality wine imported from other parts of Spain. Demand fell as Victorian society refused sherry, alarmed by scare stories that the wine was detrimental to health. The predations of the phylloxera louse from 1894 helped to stabilize the market and the shippers who survived the depression held large stocks of unsold wine to tide them through the lean years when all the vineyards were replanted. Sherry BRANDY, which grew in popularity at around the same time, also sustained some shippers during the slump. Today Brandy de Jerez is an important part of the output of many sherry companies although the base wine comes from elsewhere.

In 1910 the leading traders united to form the Sherry Shippers Association, which campaigned vigorously to restore the fortunes of the beleaguered industry. After the First World War exports returned to their late 19th century levels. In 1933 a CONSEJO REGULADOR was formed to protect and control the sherry industry and in 1935, a year before the outbreak of the Spanish Civil War, Jerez established its own DO region. The Civil War (1936–9) had little effect on sherry exports, but trade collapsed during the Second World War.

The most dramatic episode in the recent history of sherry began in 1944 when Don Zoilo Ruiz-Mateos y Camacho, mayor of the town of Rota, bought out a small sherry stockholder whose business had suffered badly during the war. In the late 1950s his son, the now legendary José María Ruiz-Mateos, secured a 99-year contract to supply the important BRAND owners HARVEYS of Bristol with all their sherry requirements. With help from the banks, he began buying up other bodegas including A. R. Ruiz, Palomino & Vergara, Bertola, Otaolaurruchi, and later Williams & Humbert, Garvey, Diez-Merito, and Terry. In 1961 they were amalgamated into a Madrid-based holding company, Ruiz-Mateos Hermanos SA, known as Rumasa. In the 1970s Ruiz-Mateos acquired substantial wine interests outside Jerez (see RIOJA), as well as in banking, construction, retailing, tourism, chemicals, and textiles. The group is said to have bought three banks in a single day. In 1977 Ruiz-Mateos founded Bodegas Internacionales, which became the largest single bodega in Jerez. Although Ruiz-Mateos contributed greatly to the modernization of the Spanish wine industry, Rumasa initiated a price-cutting spiral which continued to blight the long-term interests of sherry well into the 1990s. Ruiz Mateos's empire building came to an abrupt end in 1983 when, fearing imminent collapse, the newly elected Socialist administration of

Filipe González nationalized Rumasa, which at that point controlled about a third of the sherry industry. The government then split Rumasa into its component parts and all the firms were subsequently returned to the private sector. In the mean time the multinationals Allied-Lyons (owners of Harveys) and Grand Metropolitan (CROFT) built up substantial interests in Jerez.

Since the mid 1980s the sherry industry has been facing decline. Predictions made in 1974 that sherry would enjoy 20 years of uninterrupted growth went unfulfilled and this has been met in the early 1990s by considerable reorganization and rationalization. The total vineyard area is being reduced to under 13,000 ha / 32,110 acres; half what it was at the end of the 1970s. Plots of sunflowers and cereals are now commonplace among the vines. In the early 1990s, with a world-wide market estimated to be around 1.09 million hl / 28.7 million gal, stocks were being drastically reduced as the sherry industry attempted to bring supply and demand back into balance.

See also SPAIN, history, and SACK.

Geography and climate

The climate of the Jerez region is strongly influenced by its proximity to the Atlantic. Sea breezes from the Gulf of Cádiz alleviate extremes. The oceanic influence is strongest in the coastal towns of Sanlúcar de Barrameda and Puerto de Santa María, where temperatures in July and August may be 10 °C / 18 °F lower than in Jerez, 20 km / 12 miles inland. Winters are mild and damp with most of the region's annual average rainfall of 650 mm / 25 in falling between late autumn and spring. There is almost no rainfall between June and October. Summer temperatures often reach 30 °C inland, occasionally rising to 40 °C with the *levante*, a piercing, dry, dusty wind from the south east.

The vines are sustained during the dry summer months by the porous, white ALBARIZA soils that are at the heart of the Jerez DO. The demarcated region is roughly triangular in shape and extends from the town of Chiclana de Frontera in the south east to the river Guadalquivir in the north west, tapering inland. However, the best albariza soils cover a stretch of rolling country north of the river Guadalete between Jerez and Sanlúcar de Barrameda. These outcrops of albariza are known collectively as Jerez Superior and the majority of these vineyards are within the municipality of Jerez de la Frontera, with secondary pockets around Sanlúcar de Barrameda, Puerto de Santa María, Chipiona, and Rota.

The albariza zone is divided into subdistricts. Those with the deepest, but not necessarily the most CALCAREOUS, albariza soils like the famous Balbaina, Macharnudo, Carrascal, and Añina districts produce the most delicate wines for the finest Finos and Manzanillas (see Wine-making below). The most calcareous soils, known as *tajon*, are generally unsatisfactory for viticulture because of potential CHLOROSIS. The finest albarizas include a proportion of sand and clay and tend to vary with depth, with a limestone content of 25 per cent or more on the surface rising to 60 per cent in the rooting zone 80 to 100 cm / 39 in below the surface. In between the hills of albariza, barro soils have more clay and produce fuller, coarser wines and slightly higher yields. On the sandy soils known as arenas yields are twice as great as on the albariza but the quality of the wine is poor. Arena soils were popular with growers at the end of the 19th century as the phylloxera louse found it difficult to survive in sand. However, with the recent rationalization of the sherry industry, viticulture is increasingly concentrated on the albariza soils and over 80 per cent of the region's vineyards are situated in Jerez Superior.

Viticulture and vine varieties

In the 19th century a variety of different vines were planted around Jerez but, after phylloxera wiped out most of the vineyards in the 1890s, many varieties were never replanted. Only three varieties are now authorized for new vineyards in Jerez: PALOMINO, PEDRO XIMÉNEZ, and MUSCAT OF ALEXANDRIA. Of these, the Palomino is the most important and accounts for around 95 per cent of the total vineyard area. There are in fact two types of Palomino: Palomino Basto (also known as the Palomino de Jerez) and Palomino Fino. Palomino Basto has largely been supplanted by Palomino Fino, which provides better YIELDS and is more resistant to disease. Palomino Fino has proved to be a particularly versatile grape and is used for most types of sherry.

Moscatel Gordo Blanco (Muscat of Alexandria) represents about three per cent of the Jerez vineyard and is planted principally in the more sandy soils on the coast around Chipiona. It is mainly used for sweetening although some producers make and market their own VARIETAL Moscatel wines.

Pedro Ximénez (known for short as PX) has given ground to Palomino and currently represents less than 100 ha of vineyard. It used to be grown more widely, mainly on the lower albariza slopes, where it produced grapes that were rich in natural sugars to make intensely sweet wines for blending. However, Palomino Fino is easier to cultivate. Most sweet wine is now made from Palomino although some smaller producers still maintain small PX SOLERAS which they bottle as a varietal wine. In recent years special dispensation has been granted for the importation of PX must from MONTILLA-MORILES to compensate for the lack of PX in Jerez.

Since phylloxera swept through Jerez, all vines have been grafted on to American ROOTSTOCKS which are selected according to the soil's LIME content. In the past vines were planted in a hexagonal pattern known as *tresbolillo* but, with increasing MECHANIZATION, vineyards are planted in orderly rows at a maximum VINE DENSITY of 4,100 vines per ha (1,660 per acre). Yields from the Palomino are high, although the maximum permitted yield for the entire DO has been set at 80 hl / ha (4.5 tons / acre).

Like so much of Spain, vines used be free standing, with each plant supported on individual props or stakes. With the onset of mechanization, modern vineyards are trained on WIRES, although the PRUNING method, called *vara y pulgar*, is unchanged, and similar to the GUYOT system. A *vara* (meaning stick or branch) with seven or eight buds produces the current year's crop. The *pulgar* (meaning thumb) is a short shoot with one bud which will produce the following year's *vara*. This replacement method takes some years to achieve and, like all pruning systems, *vara y pulgar* may vary from vine to vine and grower to grower.

Wine-making

The HARVEST begins when the Palomino has reached a MUST WEIGHT of at least 11° BAUMÉ. The traditional date for the start of the harvest was 8 September but nowadays the exact date is set after monitoring the POTENTIAL ALCOHOL and ACID content of the grapes. The harvest lasts for about a month. The traditional method of drying grapes on straw mats has largely been abandoned.

Grapes are loaded into plastic crates and transported to large automated wineries, where they are destalked and pressed. Most bodegas use horizontal plate or pneumatic PRESSES to control the extraction rate, which may not legally exceed 72.5 l/19 gal of juice from 100 kg/220 lb of grapes (16 per cent higher than the extraction rate permitted for CHAMPAGNE, for instance). Others, especially the CO-OPERATIVES, use continuous de-juicers which tend to produce coarser wines with more solids and PHENOLICS. Traditionally the must would be ACIDIFIED with gypsum or *yeso*. This rather crude technique known as plastering, which led to so many unfounded health scares in the 1870s (see history above), converted natural potassium bitartrate into calcium tartrate thereby increasing levels of tartaric acid in the juice. Today acid levels are adjusted with the addition of TARTARIC ACID prior to fermentation, and cold STABILIZATION before bottling is usually essential.

After SETTLING or CENTRIFUGATION, fermentation generally takes place in temperature-controlled, stainless steel tanks, although a few shippers continue to ferment a small proportion of their wine in butt, mainly to impregnate and season new casks of American oak that are to be used for maturation. (New BARRELS are not valued in Jerez.)

The modernization of the sherry industry which began in the 1960s and continued through the 1970s and 1980s has removed much of the mysticism that once surrounded the production of sherry. Some producers continue to perpetuate the myth that the different sherry types miraculously evolve as the wine is aged in butt, but the modern reality is that the wine-maker can predetermine which of the two initial sherry types—*fino* and *oloroso*—each lot of grapes becomes.

The first selection takes place in the vineyard. Wines for the best *finos* are sourced from older vines growing on the best albariza soils while *olorosos* are made from grapes grown on the heavier clays. Elegance is crucial to *finos*, also made from the best FREE-RUN juice, which has fewer impurities than the slightly coarser and more astringent juices from the press which are set aside for *olorosos* or inferior *rayas*, particularly coarse *olorosos*.

Hygienic handling and temperature-controlled vinification have also eliminated much of the uncertainty which used to arise from foot treading and barrel fermentation. Wine destined for *fino* tends to be fermented at a lower temperature than that made for *oloroso*. Barrel-fermented wine is often too coarse and astringent for the production of *fino*.

The second selection takes place soon after the end of fermentation. Although many shippers producing table wine endeavour to persuade otherwise, Palomino-based wine is fairly flat and characterless with a natural alcohol content of 11 or 12 per cent. Depending on the style of the wine, sherry is fortified with grape spirit known as AGUARDIENTE to between 15.5 and 22 per cent. The appearance of FLOR, the veil of yeast that forms on the surface of the wine and distinguishes *fino* from other styles of sherry, is determined by the degree of fortification. Growth is inhibited by an ALCOHOLIC STRENGTH much above 16 per cent. Wines destined to develop into *finos* are therefore fortified to 15 or 15.5 per cent. *Olorosos*, which mature without flor, are fortified to a higher strength of around 18 per cent.

The sherry bodegas are teeming with the flor YEAST strains. This beneficial FILM-FORMING YEAST grows naturally on the surface of the wine, although some houses now choose to cultivate their own flor culture. Butts used for *fino* are only partially filled to around five-sixths of their 600- to 650-l (160–70-gal) capacity because flor, which both protects the wine from OXIDATION and changes its character, feeds off OXYGEN as well as alcohol.

Flor is also extremely sensitive to heat and in the warm summer months it tends to die. In Montilla, for example, flor is reduced to a scum-like film in July and August, while in the cooler Jerez region it grows all the year round. However, there are significant climatic differences within the Jerez region (see Geography above). Flor grows more thickly and evenly in the cooler, more humid coastal towns of Sanlúcar de Barrameda and Puerto de Santa María than it does in the bodegas situated in Jerez de la Frontera itself. This accounts for many of the subtle differences in style between Jerez Fino, Puerto Fino, and Manzanilla outlined below.

Left to its own devices, flor would feed on the nutrients in the wine and die before having a profound influence on the wine's character. However, flor is kept alive in casks of *fino* for six years or more by continually replenishing the butt with younger wine, and replenishing the yeast nutrients. This is the basis of the SOLERA system, a method of fractional blending which, apart from nurturing flor in *fino*, also maintains a consistent style for other sherry styles.

A sherry solera comprises a number of groups of butts each of which is known as a criadera. Wine is withdrawn from the group containing the oldest wine, which is itself called the solera. This is replenished from the butts that form the first criadera, which is in turn replenished by wine from the second criadera, a process known as 'running the scales'. Wine used to be transferred from one criadera to another by hand with pitchers but the larger bodegas now pump the wine from one scale to the next. Simple soleras are fed by three or four criaderas while more complex systems run to as many as 14. The whole system is fed with new wine from the most recent harvest. Up to 33 per cent of the wine in a solera may be withdrawn in any one year. *Fino* soleras need to be refreshed the most frequently, and by running the scales at regular intervals (usually two or three times a year) flor may be kept alive for eight to 10 years.

Derivation of **sherry** styles

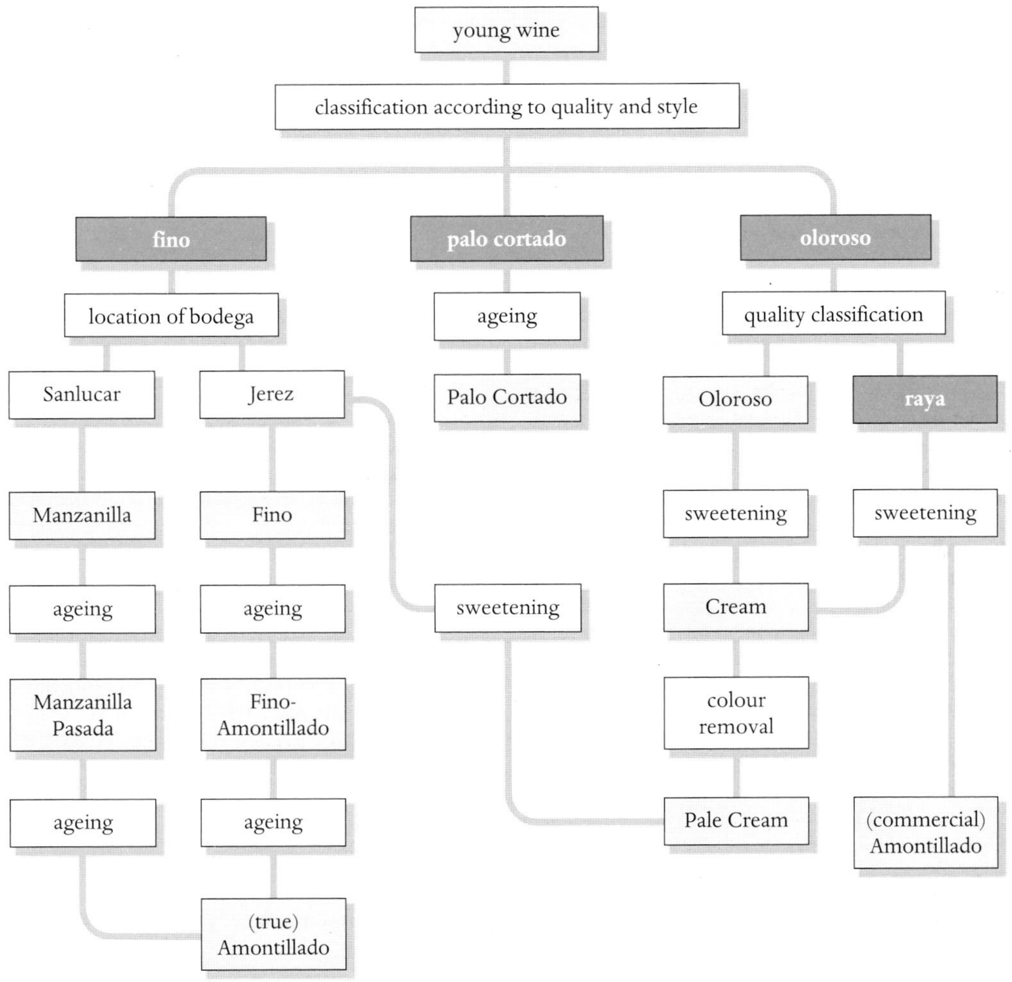

Soleras are often portrayed diagrammatically with the solera at ground level and successive criaderas stacked on top. This rarely happens and, in the case of large and complex soleras, one criadera may be housed in a completely different bodega from the next. However, a criadera may vary from just one butt to many thousands. For example GONZALEZ BYASS's entire Tio Pepe solera is made up of 30,000 butts.

Styles of sherry

The diagram shows how commercial styles of sherry are made from the types of wine naturally formed.

Before bottling as Fino or Manzanilla styles of sherry, *finos* are filtered and fortified to a minimum of 15.5 per cent. Some of the more commercial BRANDS are slightly sweetened.

Finos which lose their covering of flor become a sherry type known as *amontillados*, turning amber in colour and changing in character due to greater contact with the air. *Amontillados* evolve naturally if the flor has exhausted its supply of nutrients, or the style may be induced if the flor is killed off by fortification to 16 per cent alcohol or above. A *fino* beginning to take on the characteristic of an *amontillado* may be bottled as a *fino-amontillado* or, in the case of a wine from Sanlúcar de Barrameda, a Manzanilla Pasada. True Amontillados are completely dry and the finest examples age for many years in their own soleras. Most so-called 'Amontillados' are no more than medium dry sherries blended from inferior quality *rayas* and sweet wines, however (see AMONTILLADO).

Having been fortified to 18 per cent, *olorosos* on the other hand develop without recourse to flor. They age in greater contact with the air, turning dark brown and gaining in concentration with age. The alcoholic content increases with slow EVAPORATION such that the strength of an old *oloroso* may approach 24 per cent. In their natural state *olorosos* are dry, although old wines may taste full and concentrated. *Rayas* (inferior *olorosos* used in blending) may be aged in the open air. A certain proportion of Oloroso on the market is natural, dry OLOROSO; the majority is sweet wine of various quality levels.

Sweet sherries, most of them styled Cream, are made in a number of different ways. The finest sweet sherries such as Oloroso dulce (sweet oloroso) are produced by blending intensely sweet wines made from sun-dried Pedro Ximénez grapes. However, today Palomino grapes are frequently dried to raisins under plastic tunnels, pressed, and fortified before fermentation to make a MISTELA. This is never as sweet or as powerfully concentrated as PX, but the method is widely used for the production of more commercial sherries. Commercial Cream sherries may be very ordinary blends to which sweetening and colouring wines have been added.

The darkest sherries may be adjusted with ARROPE grape concentrate, or *vino de color*, a dark, sweet syrup that has been prepared by boiling down fresh grape must. Pale Cream sherry, typically a blend of *fino* and sweet wine, is normally adjusted with RECTIFIED CONCENTRATED MUST and fresh Palomino must, vacuum CONCENTRATED, and the colour removed with activated CHARCOAL. A few bodegas sweeten their wines with fortified Moscatel but this tends to produce a rather obvious, aromatic, grapey style of sherry.

Organization of the trade

Although few boundaries are visible, there are over 6,000 individual vineyards in Jerez farmed by over 5,000 different growers. A few sherry firms have vineyard holdings that amount to 2,000 ha but the majority of properties are small, averaging little over a hectare. The majority of growers sell their grapes either directly to a shipper or to one of seven CO-OPERATIVES. Some co-ops maintain their own soleras but most sell the wine to one of the sherry bodegas.

Four classes of sherry bodega are recognized by the Consejo Regulador:

Bodegas de Producción: wine-making bodegas which are not permitted to mature wine.

Bodegas de Elaboración: wine-making bodegas which are allowed to hold stocks of wine for a short period of time before selling it on.

Bodegas de Crianza y Almacenado: firms which mature and keep stocks of wine or ALMACENISTAS. These bodegas are required to have a minimum of 1,000 hl of which 60 per cent must be from Jerez Superior.

Bodegas de Crianza y Expedición: firms which both mature and sell wine for consumption. These bodegas are required by law to maintain a minimum stock of 12,500 hl of wine of which 60 per cent must be from Jerez Superior. Exporters of sherry must hold a government licence.

Apart from Spain, the two most important markets for sherry have been Great Britain and the Netherlands. Note the commercial importance of BRANDY de Jerez to many of these sherry bodegas.

See also individual articles on sherry shippers CROFT, DOMECQ, GONZALEZ BYASS, HARVEY, and SANDEMAN, and see specific styles of sherry: FINO, MANZANILLA, AMONTILLADO, OLOROSO, CREAM, PALO CORTADO, and PEDRO XIMÉNEZ. R.J.M.

Gonzalez Gordon, M., *Sherry: The Noble Wine* (London, 1990).
Jeffs, J., *Sherry* (4th edn., London, 1992).
Metcalfe, C., and McWhirter, K., *The Wines of Spain and Portugal* (London, 1988).
Mey, W., *Sherry* (Rhoon, 1988).
Read, J., *Sherry and the Sherry Bodegas* (London, 1988).

SHIRAZ, the Australian (and South African) name for the SYRAH grape, is a name arguably better known by consumers than its Rhône original. French wine producers are typically reticent about identifying grape varieties, however noble. Shiraz appears on possibly the majority of Australian red wine labels, either in lone varietal splendour or in conjunction with, most often, Cabernet Sauvignon—typically labelled simply Cabernet Shiraz or Shiraz Cabernet, depending on which is the dominant variety. Viticulturally Shiraz is identical with Syrah but the resulting wines taste very different with Australian versions tasting much sweeter and riper, more suggestive of chocolate than the pepper and spices often associated with Syrah in the Rhône. Shiraz is the most widely planted red wine grape in Australia with a total of more than 5,000 ha / 12,350 acres in the early 1990s and still increasing. It has had particular success in the Barossa Valley in SOUTH AUSTRALIA, the Hunter Valley in NEW SOUTH WALES, and in a number of wine areas in the state of VICTORIA. For more detail see AUSTRALIA. See also SOUTH AFRICA.

The grape variety shares a name, but little else, with the medieval capital of PERSIA, although the (white) wine of Shiraz has been enthusiastically documented.

SHOESTRING ROOT ROT, vine disease. See ARMILLARIA ROOT ROT.

SHOOT, new growth in a plant that develops from a bud and consists of a stem with lateral organs, especially leaves. Collectively, the shoots and leaves of a vine form its CANOPY. The BUDS of a grapevine, which were one of the shoot's appendages the previous growing season, burst in spring to begin a new shoot (see BUDBREAK). Shoot growth gradually accelerates to a maximum rate before FLOWERING, then slows to a stop at about VERAISON, although in humid regions shoots can continue to grow after veraison. See also WATER SHOOT, however.

VIGOUR, which effectively means shoot growth rate, varies hugely between and within vines and is apparent for each shoot well before flowering. The length of the fifth INTERNODE from the base, for example, may vary as much as threefold. A vigorous shoot is evident by its long internodes, large leaves, and long tip tendrils well before flowering; weak shoots are the opposite. Despite these differences in growth

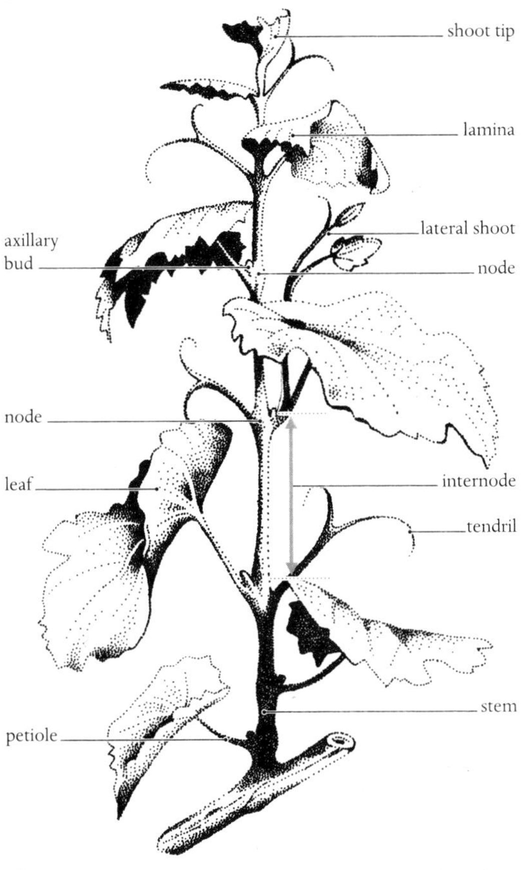

Shoot system: the axillary buds develop into summer lateral shoots, each bearing a latent bud on the over-wintering cane.

rate and length, the rate of formation of new nodes at the shoot apex is synchronized with the rate of development of the FLOWERS so that, at full bloom, shoots, whether weak or vigorous, have 17 to 20 visible internodes. Later in summer the stem of the shoot changes from green to brown and thus becomes a CANE (see CANE RIPENING).

The 1 cm/0.4 in of shoot furthest from the vine's original bud is known as the shoot tip, or shoot apex. On a vigorous shoot it may contain eight or more NODES and embryonic leaves, the largest being less than 1 cm long. This small piece of tissue is a large sink for food produced by the mature leaves, but these nutrients may be diverted by TIPPING the shoots. The balance between shoot growth and fruit growth has important effects on grape RIPENING and wine quality (see BALANCE, LEAF TO FRUIT RATIO, and VINE, PHYSIOLOGY).

B.G.C.

SHOOT POSITIONED, term used to describe vine-TRAINING SYSTEMS in a very general way. Shoot-positioned vines have shoots normally trained upwards and held between pairs of so-called foliage wires. Also the tips of the shoots are normally TRIMMED, because otherwise they can fall down the sides and cause shading. The typical vine-training system of Germany is shoot positioned, as are all VERTICAL TRELLISES. In some cases, such as with the SCOTT HENRY and GENEVA DOUBLE CURTAIN systems, the shoots can be positioned downwards. Some important examples of non-shoot-positioned canopies are the GOBELET trained vines of the Mediterranean, and also the 'drooping' canopies of vigorous vines in California and Australia.

R.E.S.

SHOOT POSITIONING, spring and summertime viticultural practice of placing vine SHOOTS in the desired position to assist in TRIMMING, LEAF REMOVAL, and HARVEST operations, and to facilitate the control of VINE DISEASES and VINE PESTS.

The practice is by no means universal but is more common in wet and humid climates with high vineyard VIGOUR and a high risk of FUNGAL DISEASES, particularly in Germany, Alsace, and New Zealand. In the drier climates of southern France, Spain, Portugal, California, and Australia, the risk of fungal diseases is much lower and shoots are not commonly positioned.

Typically the shoots are positioned upwards and are held between two pairs of so-called foliage wires, and sometimes the foliage wires themselves are moved to catch the shoots. Generally the operation is carried out manually, but a VINE FOLIAGE LIFTER may also be used. They are then trimmed to resemble a neat hedge. This then facilitates other vineyard operations such as SPRAYING and general cultivation, and enables mechanical operations such as leaf removal. For some training systems, such as GENEVA DOUBLE CURTAIN and SCOTT HENRY, shoots are positioned downwards.

R.E.S.

Smart, R. E., and Robinson, M., *Sunlight into Wine: A Handbook for Winegrape Canopy Management* (Adelaide, 1991).

SHOOT THINNING, vineyard operation normally carried out by hand in the early spring which consists of breaking off unwanted shoots arising from the vine's HEAD or CORDON. Sometimes these shoots have no bunches and are called WATER SHOOTS. The shoot-thinning operation can be done most quickly when the shoots are 20–40 cm/8–15 in long and the bunches are quite visible, which allows discrimination between fruitful and non-fruitful shoots. The aim of shoot thinning is to reduce density of the CANOPY and to avoid leaf congestion later in the season. This can help improve wine quality (see CANOPY MANAGEMENT). See also DESUCKERING.

R.E.S.

SHOWS, WINE. See JUDGING and COMPETITIONS.

SICHEL, influential wine family now made up of two very distinct branches. The family originated in Germany and was involved with wine from the middle of the 18th century. The direct descendants of the German founders established the wine and spirits distribution company H. Sichel Söhne at Mainz in Germany in 1857 and it grew to be an important commercial force. Its activities were severely curtailed during the First World War but a successful export business was developed in the 1930s, based increasingly on the branded wine BLUE NUN Liebfraumilch. Walter Sichel re-established a London office for Sichel in 1927 and had to work to overcome prejudice against all things German. In 1935 he became a naturalized British citizen, and the Sichels remaining in Germany were dispersed to Britain, France, and the United States. It was during the 1950s that Blue Nun began to establish itself as one of the world's most successful wines. It was cleverly marketed, in this era of uncertainty about wine and etiquette, as the wine to be drunk 'right through the meal', whatever was being eaten.

The fact that the quality of Blue Nun has always been vastly superior to that of the average LIEBFRAUMILCH also presumably played a part in the success of the brand, of which in the mid 1980s about 2 million cases a year were sold in 81 countries. Ronald Sichel succeeded his father Walter in London in 1988, while Peter M. F. Sichel directs the firm's fortunes from New York, widening the range of Blue Nun products in partnership with Sichel's American distributors Schieffelin Somerset, a subsidiary of LVMH.

The Anglo-French-Scandinavian branch of the Sichel family is descended from a Dane who married a Sichel of Mainz, worked for the firm and took his wife's name. He was sent to Bordeaux in 1883 to establish a Sichel & Company there. His son married another Dane, and extended the Bordeaux business into château ownership. His grandson Allan Sichel, who married a Swede, was an influential member of the British wine trade in the mid 20th century, introducing Harry WAUGH among others to the delightful, if hazardous, business of buying wine *sur place* in post-war France, and writing *The Penguin Book of Wines*, which was published in 1965. Allan's son Peter A. Sichel now lives in MARGAUX at Ch d'Angludet and runs the Bordeaux NÉGOCIANT Maison Sichel, developing a number of French wine BRANDS. He is the majority shareholder in Ch Palmer, took over the business of Pierre Coste of Langon in the GRAVES in 1992, and has invested in CORBIÈRES in the south of France. At least four of his five sons followed him into the wine business.

Peter A. **Sichel** of Bordeaux, in the *chai* at Ch Palmer.

SICILY, large, often hot, and viticulturally important island off the toe of ITALY (see map on p. 517).

Ancient history

In startling contrast to the present day, Sicily was famed throughout classical antiquity for its agricultural produce, not least its wines. The settlement of colonies of Greeks around the island in the 8th century BC was an undoubted spur to the development of viticulture. Flourishing vineyards are testified for the 5th century at the later Greek settlement Akragas (Agrigento). Sicily may have played a key role in the development of viticulture on the Italian peninsula (see ITALY, Ancient history). Vines from Morgantina and Tauromenium were transplanted to POMPEII around Vesuvius, the Colli ALBANI, and southern Etruria, where they were well established by the 2nd century BC (Pliny, *Natural History* 14. 25, 35, and 38). The most notable characteristic of Sicilian wines was their sweetness. The most famous, which could stand comparison with Italian vintages, were Mamertine, a sweet, light wine from the north east of the island around Messina, and a very similar wine from Tauromenium (Taormina); but there is evidence for wine production right down the east coast, around Etna, Catania, and in the territory of Syracuse. But much of the rest of the island had its own wines. Inland there was the Murgentina vine from Morgantina (Serra Orlando). Inscriptions on AMPHORAE testify to a so-called 'Mesopotamian' wine from the south coast near Gela. Sicilian wines were certainly exported (references to Tauromenian, for example, appear on amphorae), but the scale of the trade is difficult to judge, since the identification of Sicilian amphora types remains a tantalizing problem. J.J.P.

Wilson, R. J. A., *Sicily under the Roman Empire* (Warminster, 1990).

Medieval history

Throughout the Middle Ages Sicily's main export product was grain. It had wheat of superior quality, hard and with a high gluten content, which would not start fermenting in the hold of a ship during a long sea voyage. Its low yields made it a luxury item which found a ready market in Italy and the Levant. Sicily also produced olives, citrus fruits, and wine, but wheat has the advantage of being far less capital intensive: whereas olive trees, citrus fruit trees, and vines take years to come into full bearing, wheat can be harvested months after it has been sown. Medieval Sicily owed its wealth to grain, and wine was not its most important commercial product.

Under the Normans, who governed Sicily from 1130 to 1194, smallholders owned most of the land, and they made their living mainly by growing wheat or, in the mountainous parts of the island, keeping livestock. They grew vines as well, but the wine made in these small vineyards was usually for domestic consumption. In the course of the 14th century demand for high-quality wine rose, and vineyards spread through Sicily. Many of these vineyards, which produced wine for well-to-do Sicilians or for export, were owned by members of the feudal aristocracy or the local nobility. The principal wine-making towns were strung along the north eastern and eastern coasts: Cefalù, Patti, Aci, Catania, Augusta, and Syracuse. These not only produced large surpluses of wine, they were also able to ship their wine safely to Messina, from where it was taken to Africa and the Levant. From Patti, wine was carried to Constantinople, and Syracuse traded with nearby MALTA. Messina also imported wines from CALABRIA, which it then shipped to northern Italy; Messina and Palermo also carried Sicilian wines to the towns of northern Italy.

Palermo was Sicily's largest and most important city. In the early 14th century it had 100,000 inhabitants, as did NAPLES: in the whole of Europe, only VENICE and Milan, with populations of 200,000, were larger. Because of its size, Palermo and its surrounding countryside could never make enough wine for the city's needs, and so it imported wine from Naples and Calabria, which was cheaper than transporting wine overland from eastern Sicily. This provoked the wrath of the citizens of Catania. Palermo exported wine as well.

From the late 14th century onwards more and more vineyards around Palermo, Messina, and Catania came to be owned by members of the upper classes, and so, after 1400, did taverns. In the 15th century most of the wine continued to be made in areas near ports: Aci, Catania, Messina, Taormina, and, in the west, Trapani. But further inland, Noto and Randazzo were also important. By far the biggest exporter was Messina, but Francavilla, Patti, Trapani, and Palermo handled a lot of the foreign trade in wine, too.

The wines that Sicily exported were, for the most part, the strong, sweet wines which were capable of surviving the sea voyage, such as VERNACCIA and Muscatello. Other names of wines mentioned in documents are Mantonico (also called Mantonicato), which could be red or white; a white wine named Cuctumini; and finally Mamertino, which shares its name with the classical Mamertinum, which PLINY tells us was grown in Messina (*Natural History* 14. 66).

See NAPLES for more information about medieval Sicily.

H.M.W.

Epstein, S. R., *An Island for Itself: Economic Development and Social Change in Medieval Sicily* (Cambridge, 1992).

Matthew, D., *The Norman Kingdom of Sicily* (Cambridge, 1992).

Modern wines and other vine products

With over 200,000 ha/494,000 acres under vine and annual volumes of wine which average over 10 million hl/264 million gal per year, Sicily has been rivalled only by APULIA as the most productive wine region in a country that is often the world's most productive. The western province of Trapani alone produces close to 4.5 million hl annually, more than 16 of Italy's 20 regions. The COLOUR and ALCOHOLIC STRENGTH which can be easily and naturally obtained in such high summer temperatures provided FRANCE in particular with useful blending material for her own much lighter VIN DE TABLE, especially after the independence of ALGERIA. More recently, however, economic crisis and a fall in demand for blending wines led a severe drop in annual production to a mere (for Sicily) 7.7 million hl in 1990.

The island's geography and climate—a hilly and mountainous terrain with poor soil, intense summer heat, and low RAINFALL—make it ideal for the classic Mediterranean agriculture of grain, olive oil, and wine, and Sicily's viticulture, in fact, enjoys a series of natural advantages which have not yet been fully exploited: HILLSIDE VINEYARDS with excellent exposures, abundant SUNLIGHT, and high TEMPERATURES to ripen the grapes; excellent ELEVATION (it is by no means unusual to find a flourishing vineyard at 500 to 900 m/1,640–2,950 ft above sea level); good diurnal TEMPERATURE VARIATION; and a range of native VINE VARIETIES with real personality. The concentration on quantity over quality, systematically encouraged by the regional government's subsidies for the transformation of the traditional GOBELET training systems into more productive WIRE-trained or TENDONE systems between 1960 and 1987, and by the equally systematic use of IRRIGATION and FERTILIZERS, has done no small harm to Sicilian viticulture and has led to a chronic cycle of over-production, declining prices, and wines which are impossible to market.

YIELD statistics tell a significant story: after averaging 5 tons/ha in the early 1960s, they reached 7 tons in 1968, exceeded 9 tons in 1973, 1978, and 1980, and surpassed 10 tons as an island average in 1979. The philosophy of high production with no market in sight has encouraged a significant part of Sicily's viticulture to aim no higher than producing anonymous blending wines (although expanded production per hectare has drastically lowered the ALCOHOLIC STRENGTH of Sicilian wines: 81 per cent were between 13 and 17 per cent in 1952 but by 1975 most wines were between 10 and 15 per cent). A high proportion of Sicilian wine is also earmarked for transformation into concentrated grape must, (see GRAPE CONCENTRATE) RECTIFIED GRAPE MUST, or for compulsory DISTILLATION.

Despite all this, a significant number of quality-orientated Sicilian wine producers alse emerged in the 1970s and 1980s, and their wines have had little difficulty in establishing a place for themselves in national and international markets. DOC production is still low, usually well below five per cent of total wine production (although these statistics are heavily influenced by the declining fortunes of MARSALA, the island's only quantitatively significant DOC). It should none the less be noted that a significant number of Sicily's better producers are either voluntarily or involuntarily outside the regional DOC system. The Duca di Salaparuta winery, a large

NÉGOCIANT run by the regional government, Regaleali and Terre di Ginestra, two of the island's leading private estates, and Settesoli, Sicily's most important CO-OPERATIVE winery, are among the many examples of houses which market their wine as a VINO DA TAVOLA.

Classic accounts of Sicilian viticulture categorized the island's west as the area for white wines, its east as the area for red wine; Andrea Bacci's *Naturalis vinorum historia* of 1596 described the white wine of Palermo as 'light, white, and gracious on the palate'. Nowadays Sicily's wines are conventionally divided into seven zones, each corresponding to a dominant vine variety: the ZIBIBBO, which is the island of Pantelleria (see MOSCATO DI PANTELLERIA); the zone of white grape varieties CATARRATTO and GRILLO, which is the province of Trapani, and the DOC zones of Marsala and Alcamo in particular (although the varieties are cultivated further to the north as far as Calatafimi and Castellamare del Golfo); the zone of PERRICONE and INZOLIA, which is the province of Agrigento; the zone of NERO D'AVOLA and Frappato, which is the province of Ragusa; the zone of NERELLO Mascalese which is the province of Messina, both on the slopes of Mount Etna and in the north east of the province; and the zone of MALVASIA, which is the Aeolian islands, including Lipari. These divisions are obviously only rough ones and it is not difficult to find Inzolia cultivated in the province of Trapani; Inzolia, Nero d'Avola, and Perricone are also cultivated in the centre of the island, in the south east of the province of Palermo, and in the province of Caltanissetta.

Among white varieties (which are far more widely planted than red varieties), Inzolia (also known as Ansonica) and Catarratto are generally considered the best-quality grape varieties while the somewhat neutral Grillo is best suited to the production of Marsala. So far Inzolia has regularly given a lighter and more fragrant wine, Catarratto a fuller and spicier wine, although much remains to be learned about the proper fermentation and ageing of each. Recent experiments with Inzolia have suggested a certain affinity with new OAK and both Inzolia and Catarratto from higher, cooler sites, fermented in modern wineries with efficient REFRIGERATION, have also shown a fruity and floral quality not unlike the wines of FRIULI and the ALTO ADIGE.

Nero d'Avola is undoubtedly a red variety of very high potential, capable of giving wines of great richness, texture, and longevity, in addition to aromas of some complexity; ageing in new oak has given wines that can compete with the best southern Italian wines, such as AGLIANICO DEL VULTURE or TAURASI. Frappato can yield fruity wines with a peppery, berry character not unlike a RHÔNE wine in its classic zone of Vittoria. In combination with Nero d'Avola (the canonical blend of Cerasuolo di Vittoria) it gives a fuller wine with more ageing ability. Nerello Mascalese is also considered a red variety of some potential, but the Etna area has not participated in the general improvement of the 1980s and no wines or wineries have emerged to indicate what the grape could give at its best.

Sicily once enjoyed a great reputation for SWEET WINES, and attempts to revive the tradition are currently under way, although the once famous Moscato of Siracusa seems irremediably extinct and Moscato of Noto on the verge of becoming so. Moscato of Pantelleria returned to the market with convincing evidence of its inherent quality, and the Malvasia delle Lipari of Carlo Hauner which emerged in the 1980s has demonstrated that the reputation of this wine was not entirely mythical either. D.T.

SIEGERREBE is a modern German vine crossing grown, like certain giant vegetables, purely by exhibitionists. In Germany it can break, indeed has broken, records for its ripeness levels, but the flabby white wine it produces is so rich and oppressively flavoured that it is usually a chore to drink. It was bred from Gewürztraminer and a red table grape and has been known to reach *double* the Oechlse reading required for a TROCKENBEERENAUSLESE. It is, however, one of the very few modern German crossings that is not particularly productive ('only' 40 to 50 hl/ha (2.3–2.8 tons/acre), as it is particularly susceptible to COULURE) and is useful only as an enriching, very minor ingredient in a blend. So powerful is its heady flavour that a fine Riesling is quite overpowered by even 10 per cent of Siegerrebe. Total German plantings were still more than 200 ha/490 acres in 1990, mainly in Rheinhessen and Pfalz, but are expected to decline. The variety also can usefully bolster some blends in ENGLAND.

SIERRA FOOTHILLS, wine region in CALIFORNIA'S GOLD RUSH country and AVA. Thousands flocked here after 1849 and, miners being notoriously thirsty, the region's vineyards go back almost that far. Although there is a great deal more to the Sierra Foothills than the AVA of the same name, it blankets all of the vineyards in El Dorado and Amador counties, takes in a few others in the flanking Nevada and Calaveras counties, and, in the process, points to most of the abandoned mines still there. Shenandoah Valley-California AVA and Fiddletown AVA are AVAs within Amador County; El Dorado AVA takes in the vineyards in that county.

El Dorado AVA

Where most of Amador County's vines grow at an altitude of 600 to 800 ft/180 to 240 m, El Dorado's start close to 1,500 ft and range up toward 3,000 ft/915 m. Predictably, conditions are cooler, and the choice of varieties leans toward Cabernet Sauvignon, Merlot, Chardonnay, and Riesling, with some Syrah and other varieties thrown in. Representative, established wineries include Sierra Vista, Boeger, Lava Cap, and Madrona.

Fiddletown AVA

Fiddletown adjoins the upper, eastern end of California-Shenandoah Valley, in the Sierra Nevada Mountain foothills east of the town of Plymouth. Amid rolling meadows and patchy pine forest it grows some of the state's oldest plantings of ZINFANDEL in a region now most famous for that grape, and going back to gold rush days.

Shenandoah Valley-California AVA
California is tacked on to the end of Shenandoah Valley to distinguish this one from one in Virginia. The California model is a shallow bowl running east of the town of Plymouth, most of it in Amador County, a rump in El Dorado. It became famous for hearty Zinfandels before the turn of the century and, after a long slumber, has regained some of its old momentum since the mid or late 1970s, again with Zinfandel at the heart of the matter. Roughly a score of wineries share a modest acreage that also includes some Sauvignon Blanc and Petite Sirah. Monteviña, Shenandoah Valley, and Santino led the resurgence.

SILICA GEL and **silica sol**, amorphous forms of silicon dioxide in which there is no crystalline structure, used in wine-making as FINING agents. The elements, silicon and OXYGEN, are the two most abundant elements on earth and their compound, silica, is similarly ubiquitous. Both forms of silica are useful because of their ability to adsorb and precipitate undesirable compounds such as PROTEINS which could cause a haze in bottled wines. Silica is used almost interchangeably with BENTONITE but is used rather more often in Europe than the United States, presumably because bentonite, principally an American product, sells at higher prices which include transport. A.D.W.

SILT, description of particles of intermediate size between clay and sand. See SOIL TEXTURE and GEOLOGY for more details of this particular form of soil classification. Grains of silt dominate LOESS and are often predominant in ALLUVIAL soils. Silt is a major component of many of the soils in the Napa Valley of California.

SILVANER, or **Sylvaner**, white grape variety grown mainly in Germany and central Europe. Its very name suggests romantic woodland origins, and certainly it has a long history over much of eastern Europe, where it may indeed first have been identified growing wild. Its origins are thought to be in what is now Austria (although it is hardly grown there today) and it certainly came to Germany from the banks of the Danube (Österreicher was once a common synonym for it) although some posit Transylvanian origins. It probably invaded Germany from the east, and a vine known as Silvaner was widely grown throughout the extensive vineyards of medieval Germany. Its arrival from Austria at Castell in FRANKEN in 1659 is well documented and the variety is still the second most planted in the region. Silvaner enjoyed its greatest popularity in the first half of the 20th century, when it took over from ELBLING as Germany's most planted vine variety, before that position was taken over by the more productive and earlier ripening MÜLLER-THURGAU. In Germany it is often called Grüner Silvaner, whereas in France, especially Alsace, (as in Austria) it is known as SYLVANER.

This vigorous vine buds a few days before Germany's quintessential RIESLING, and can suffer spring frost damage. It is not notable for its disease resistance but it is productive. The chief characteristic of the wine produced is its high natural acid, generally lower than Riesling's in fact but emphasized by Silvaner's lack of body and frame. (It is significant that the German name for Sauvignon Blanc, a variety essentially notable for its aroma and high acid, is Muskat-Silvaner.) Provided yields are not too high, it can provide a suitable neutral canvas on which to display more geographically based flavour characteristics (see TERROIR) but Silvaner is not noted for either its longevity or its high must weights.

Most of Germany's finest Silvaners come from Franken, where Riesling is difficult to ripen and Silvaner has remained popular. Here the variety sometimes called Franken Riesling (in both Germany and California) is capable of tingling concentration, and even some exciting late harvest sweet wines. Elsewhere, Silvaner is being systematically replaced by more fashionable varieties. Overall it is still Germany's third most planted vine, after Müller-Thurgau and Riesling, but the 10,000 ha/24,700 acres that remained at the end of the 1970s fell by nearly a quarter during the 1980s and it may well be overtaken by Spätburgunder (Pinot Noir) during the 1990s. About half of the country's Silvaner is planted in the Rheinhessen (where there are some particularly suitable sites in the north) with much of the rest in Franken and Pfalz.

Prized for its reliable early ripening and productivity, Silvaner is a parent in a wide variety of Germany's army of modern vine crossings, including BACCHUS, EHRENFELSER, MORIO-MUSKAT, OPTIMA, RIESLANER, and SCHEUREBE. It is well adapted to the German climate but is less versatile in choice of site than Riesling, a more profitable choice in many cases. **Blauer Silvaner** is a local, dark-berried mutation that is a speciality of Württemberg.

Outside Germany Silvaner is relatively important in CZECHOSLOVAKIA, is still grown in SLOVENIA and around Lake Balaton in HUNGARY, and is prized in RUSSIA for its ability to ripen early. It is also planted in ALTO ADIGE, where it can provide light and piercing wines for youthful consumption.

In the Valais of SWITZERLAND it is called Johannisberg and seems positively lush in comparison to French Switzerland's ubiquitous CHASSELAS. Sylvaner is the second most planted grape variety in the Valais, where it is often called Rhin, or Gros Rhin (as opposed to Petit Rhin, the local synonym for RIESLING). The variety ripens later than Chasselas and, in villages as warm as Chamoson and Leytron, can result in wines with more body, character, and race.

Despite its useful acidity levels Silvaner is not widely grown in the New World, although California still grew 185 acres of Sylvaner, mainly in Monterey, in 1991 and there were nearly 120 ha/300 acres of Sylvaner grown in Australia.

SIMON, ANDRÉ LOUIS (1877–1970). A.L.S. was the charismatic leader of the English wine trade for almost all of the first half of the 20th century, and the grand old man of literate connoisseurship for a further 20 years. In 66 years of authorship he wrote 104 books. For 33 years he was one of London's leading champagne shippers; for another 33 years active president of the Wine & Food Society. Although he lived in England from the age of 25 he always remained a French citizen. He was both Officier de la Légion d'Honneur and holder of the Order of the British Empire.

A.L.S. was born in St-Germain-des-Prés, between the Brasserie Lipp and the Deux Magots (the street has since been demolished), the second of five sons of a landscape painter who died (of sunstroke, in Egypt) while they were still youths.

From the first his ambition was to be a journalist. At 17 he was sent to Southampton to learn English and met Edith Symons, whose ambition was to live in France. They married in 1902 and remained happy together for 63 years. A.L.S. was a man of judgement, single-mindedness, and devotion all his life.

He was also a man of powerful charm, the very model of his own description of the perfect champagne shipper, who 'must be a good mixer rather than a good salesman; neither a teetotaller nor a boozer, but able to drink champagne every day without letting it become a bore or a craving'.

He became a champagne shipper, the London agent of the leading house of Pommery, through his father's friendship with the Polignac family. It gave him a base in the centre of the City's wine trade, at 24 Mark Lane, for 30 years. From it he not only sold champagne; he soon made his voice heard as journalist, scholar, and teacher.

Within four years of his installation in London he was writing his first book, *The History of the Champagne Trade in England*, in instalments for the *Wine Trade Review*. A. S. Gardiner, its editor, can be credited with forming Simon's English prose style: unmistakably charming, stately, and faintly whimsical at once. He spoke English as he wrote it, with a fondness for imagery, even for little parables—but with an ineradicable French accent that was a much part of his persona as his burly frame and curly hair.

His first *History* was rapidly followed by a remarkable sequel: *The History of the Wine Trade in England from Roman Times to the End of the 17th Century*, in three volumes in 1906, 1907, and 1909—the best and most original of his total of over 100 books. None, let alone a young man working in a language not his own, had read, thought, and written so deeply on the subject before. It singled him out at once as a natural spokesman for wine, a role he pursued with maximum energy, combining with friends to found (in 1908) the Wine Trade Club, where for six years he organized tastings and gave technical lectures of a kind not seen before; the forerunner by 45 years of the Institute of MASTERS OF WINE. In 1919 he published *Bibliotheca vinaria*, a catalogue of the books he had collected for the Club. It ran to 340 pages.

The First World War ended this busy and congenial life, full of dinners, lectures, book-collecting, and amateur theatricals. Before war was declared Simon was in France as a volunteer, serving the full four years in the French Artillery, where as 'un homme de lettres' he was made regimental postman, before being moved on to liaison with the British in Flanders and on the Somme. It was in Flanders that the irrepressible scribbler wrote his best seller, *Laurie's Elementary Russian Grammar*, printed in huge numbers by the War Office in the pious hope of teaching Tommy, the British soldier, Russian.

In 1919 Simon bought the two homes he was to occupy for the rest of his life: 6 Evelyn Mansions, near Westminster Cathedral (where he attended mass daily), and Little Hedgecourt, a cottage with 28 acres beside a lake at Felbridge in Surrey. Gardening these acres, making a cricket pitch and an open-air theatre, and enlarging the cottage into a rambling country house for his family of five children were interspersed with travels all over Africa and South America to sell Pommery, until suddenly, in 1933, caught in the violent fluctuations of the franc–pound exchange rate when Britain came off the gold standard, he could no longer pay for his champagne stocks and Pommery, without compunction, ended their 33-year association.

Simon began a second life at 55: that of spokesman of wine and food in harmonious association. Already, with friends, he had founded the SAINTSBURY CLUB in memory of the crusty old author of *Notes on a Cellar-Book* (see also SAINTSBURY). With A. J. A. Symons he founded the Wine & Food Society (now INTERNATIONAL WINE & FOOD SOCIETY). Its first (Alsace) lunch at the Café Royal in London in the midst of the Depression (and for 10/6) caused a sensation. But its assured success came from the ending of PROHIBITION in America. Sponsored by the French government, Simon travelled repeatedly to the USA, founding its first Wine & Food Society branch in Boston in December 1934 and its second in San Francisco in January 1935.

Meanwhile, while working briefly for the advertising agency Mather & Crowther, he conceived the idea of *A Concise Encyclopedia of Gastronomy* to be published in instalments. It sold an unprecedented 100,000 copies. Research, writing, and editing (and finding paper to print) the *Encyclopedia* and the Society's *Quarterly* occupied him throughout the Second World War. His daughter Jeanne and her family moved into Little Hedgecourt for the war and thereafter. His son André was a wine merchant. His two other daughters and a son all retired from the world into religious communities.

Simon was a better teacher than a businessman. He was repeatedly helped out of difficulties by adoring friends. Thus the National Magazine Company gave him an office in Grosvenor Gardens in 1941, to be followed by the publisher George Rainbird, still in central London at Marble Arch. In 1962 his friend Harry Yoxall suggested that at 85, daily responsibility for the Society and its magazine was too burdensome and bought the title from him for Condé Nast Publications. But in his 90s Simon was still exceptional company at dinner and gave little picnics for friends beside his woodland lake.

His final book, *In the Twilight*, written in his last winter, 1969, recast the memoirs he had published *By Request* in 1957. On what would have been his 100th birthday, 28 February 1977, 400 guests at the Savoy Hotel in London drank to his memory in CLARET he had left for the occasion: Ch LATOUR 1945. H.J.

SIRAH is the name by which some PETITE SIRAH is known in South America. It should not be confused with the true Syrah of the northern Rhône.

SITE CLIMATE, the climate of a specified site, for instance a vineyard or part of a vineyard. The scale of definition usually falls within that of MESOCLIMATE.

SITE SELECTION. See VINEYARD SITE SELECTION.

SIZZANO, red wine DOC in the Novara hills in the subalpine north of the PIEDMONT region of north west Italy. The proportion of NEBBIOLO grapes in Sizzano is usually lower than in either Gattinara or nearby LESSONA and BRAMATERRA in the Vercelli hills across the river Sesia. Sizzano is also usually plumper and earlier maturing than its northern neighbours in the Novara hills GHEMME and BOCA, although FARA may be lighter still. For more details see SPANNA, the local name for Nebbiolo.

SKIN, GRAPE. For details of grape skins, see GRAPE.

SKIN CONTACT, *macération pelliculaire* in French, wine-making operation with the aim of extracting FLAVOUR COMPOUNDS and ANTHOCYANS from grape skins into grape juice or wine. In its widest sense it is identical to MACERATION, and some form of skin contact is essential to ROSÉ WINE-MAKING, but the term is generally used exclusively for the maceration of white grapes for about four to 24 hours before PRESSING and FERMENTATION with the aim of increasing flavour. Vine varieties frequently processed with skin contact are SÉMILLON, SAUVIGNON Blanc, MUSCAT, RIESLING, and in some wine regions CHARDONNAY (although this is rare in Burgundy and increasingly rare elsewhere since the wines' COLOUR often darkens markedly after very few years in bottle). Denis DUBOURDIEU and his team have been responsible for its application to white bordeaux since the late 1980s. It is important to arrest skin contact before excessive amounts of bitter PHENOLICS (which may also darken colour) are extracted. In some vintages and in some regions the technique simply does not work as too much undesirable material is extracted with the minimum amount of additional flavour compounds. Skin contact is usually superfluous if LEES CONTACT is to be employed since the lees flavour usually dominates any that would result from skin contact.

SLASHING, vineyard operation of mowing or cutting a COVER CROP, or cutting vine shoots in summer (see TRIMMING).

SLATE, (*schiste* in French and *Schiefer* in German), a group name for various very finely crystalline, fissile rocks derived from clay, shale, mudstone, and other fine-grained sediments, sometimes with silt, which have been metamorphosed into a moderately hard dark, slab-like rock. Some of the vineyards in southern Beaujolais are on a brown soil over weathered slates. Just north of here the vineyards of POUILLY-FUISSÉ are also partly over slates. The most celebrated vineyard occurrence of slate is the MOSEL-SAAR-RUWER region of Germany, where Riesling vines grow in slate which holds moisture and heat, and reradiates warmth at night and when the sun is in shade. Several vineyard names end in -lay or -ley, a reference to the slatiness of the soil. See entries prefixed SOIL.

M.J.E. & J.M.H.

SLOPE, or incline, an important characteristic of any vineyard site that is not completely flat. For more details, see TOPOGRAPHY.

SLOTTING, viticultural operation designed to improve SUBSOIL and developed by CSIRO in Australia in the early 1990s. The slotting machine cuts trenches 1 m/3 ft deep along the vine row, so that SOIL AMELIORANTS, mixed with finely ground soil, can be added directly to the subsoil. Slotting, still being evaluated in the mid 1990s, could be used to overcome a number of subsoil problems: SOIL ACIDITY can be treated by adding LIME; low SOIL FERTILITY by adding FERTILIZERS or ORGANIC MATTER; and poor DRAINAGE by breaking up dense layers.

R.E.S.

SLOVAKIA, the **Slovakian republic**. Eastern part of what was CZECHOSLOVAKIA and now an independent state whose viticultural identity is still being forged.

SLOVENIA, in the far north west of what was YUGOSLAVIA, was the first republic to establish its independence, in 1991. It is divided into three wine regions: the Littoral, west of the range of hills protecting the eastern Italian border, which produces about 45 per cent of Slovenian wine; the Eastern or Drava Valley (Podravski), which is responsible for about 40 per cent; and the less important Central Southern or Sava Valley (Posavski), which produces the remainder. In 1993 Slovenia had about 21,000 ha/51,870 acres of vineyards, very much less than the 50,000 ha of vines which were grown at the turn of the century when Slovenia was a major wine production area within the Austro-Hungarian empire.

The two major wine regions are heavily influenced by their neighbours. Although it produces far more red wine than white, the Littoral is effectively a continuation of COLLIO, which was reunified with Italy only after the First World War. The Drava Valley, on the other hand, is heavily influenced by Austrian practices as conducted just over the border in southern Styria, or Südsteiermark (see AUSTRIA), and can even produce interesting BEERENAUSLESE and EISWEIN. This is woody, hilly temperate land with occasionally steep, sometimes even terraced vineyards of LIMESTONE and CLAY, ideal for the production of relatively delicate, fruity white wines. The Littoral vineyard terrain varies from steeply contoured terraces on limestone around Nova Gorica to a plateau at 300 m/984 ft close to the CROATIAN border with red topsoil over the limestone.

Civil war in the early 1990s brought an end to Slovenian wine's traditional market, the Dalmatian coast's tourist trade, and new customers were urgently sought for the new republic's QUALITY WINE surplus (Slovenians themselves tending to prefer quantity, even imported, to quality).

The great majority of wine is produced in old, centralized, often poorly equipped CO-OPERATIVES, but the number of private producers, many of them ambitious, is increasing. Large casks and vats of old Slovenian oak are the norm.

The town of Lutomer in north east Slovenia lent its name to a brand of Laski Rizling (WELSCHRIESLING) which was once the best-selling wine in the UK. The area also grows GEWÜRZTRAMINER (known here as Traminec), PINOT BLANC, RIESLING, and SAUVIGNON Blanc, and Šipon (probably Hungary's FURMINT) makes locally prized dry white wine. Even the most basic dry whites from this region can be enormously fresh, tangy, and aromatic, like their fashionable Austrian neighbours. Sauvignon Blanc especially has international potential and it is to be hoped that some carefully made, young, dry Slovenian wines will reach export markets in addition to the duller, older, sweetened offerings for so long identified with the region. Some of the wineries here certainly have the means to achieve this.

Primorski, the Littoral plateau region, is better known for its red wines, especially Italianate Teran (REFOSCO) and BARBERA, which are the kind of solid, lively, tannic wines that the Italians would recognize, and CABERNET SAUVIGNON and MERLOT, probably this region's best products. Some whites are also produced. PINOT BLANC and the local Rebula (see RIBOLLA) make dry wines while dessert wines are made from MALVASIA and Yellow MUSCAT BLANC À PETITS GRAINS, as well as a limited production of PICOLIT (yet another feature shared with FRIULI just over the border).

Once wine-making techniques have improved, the wines of Slovenia will presumably be well able to compete with their immediate neighbours in Styria and Friuli which are so respected in their native markets of Austria and Italy respectively. Dedication on the part of a new generation of winemakers is certainly not lacking, and some of Slovenia's VARIETAL specialities, such as Šipon and Zelen, may also find favour in export markets. A.H.M.

SMEDEREVKA, white grape variety commonly planted and admired throughout the south of what was YUGOSLAVIA. It takes its name from the town of Smederevo south of Belgrade and is planted extensively in SERBIA and VOJVODINA. As a VARIETAL wine, it is usually dry and relatively high in both alcohol and acidity, but it is often blended with other varieties, notably LASKI RIZLING. It is also planted to a much more limited extent in HUNGARY.

SMELL. The smell of a wine is probably its single most important attribute, and may be called its AROMA, BOUQUET, odour or off-odour if it is positively unattractive, or even FLAVOUR.

The sense of smell is the most acute human tasting instrument (as witness how a blocked nose robs food and drink of any flavour) but since it is so closely related to what we call the sense of taste, it is considered in detail under TASTING.

SMUDGE POT, burner, usually fuelled with oil, lit in frost-prone parts of an orchard or vineyard on still nights when lethal frost seems imminent. Rather than by direct local heating, it acts mainly by creating air convection currents which mix relatively warm upper air with the chilled air settled at ground level. The smoke it creates also supposedly reduces further radiative heat loss from the land and vine surfaces. Since a density of some 100 pots per ha (40 per acre) is required, not to mention fuel, smoke, lost sleep, and the general inconvenience of operating such contraptions in the cold darkness of the early morning, many consider the alternative of occasional yield losses to be preferable.

Other approaches to frost avoidance are available: see FROST. J.G. & R.E.S.

SNAILS, vine pests of which at least two types can be of economic significance to wine production: the white Italian snail, *Theba pisana*, and the brown or English snail, *Helix aspersa*. They are mainly a problem in early spring, and can strip vines of young foliage if they are in large numbers, which happens particularly in wet conditions. They will contaminate fruit and wine if they are present at HARVEST time. Clean cultivation is an important preventive measure, and sprays or baits used early can also control snails. Copper-based FUNGICIDES used on vines also affect snails by repelling and killing them. Ducks and geese feed on snails, and their presence in vineyards will keep numbers down. M.J.E.

SOAVE, the most common dry white wine from the VENETO region of north east Italy. Like the neighbouring VALPOLICELLA zone, the Soave zone has expanded enormously with the creation of the Soave DOC in 1968. Nearly 5,000 ha / 12,350 acres of vineyards in the alluvial plain of the Adige river were grafted on to the CLASSICO zone, first defined and delimited in 1927 and currently comprising fewer than 1,500 ha of mostly HILLSIDE VINEYARDS on decomposed volanic rock. This disproportion is reflected in the production figures: an annual average of 180,000 hl / 4.7 million gal of Soave Classico is produced as opposed to 550,000 hl in the expanded zone.

Soave is dominated by CO-OPERATIVES, which control 85 per cent of total production and have followed a policy of high volumes at low prices. In 1988 a proposal to increase maximum permitted YIELDS to 112 hl / ha (6.4 tons / acre) (plus a possible further 20 per cent) was defeated after a heated public debate. The Soave consortium regrouped and succeeded in revising the DOC rules to supplement Soave's workhorse grape GARGANEGA with up to 30 per cent CHARDONNAY, PINOT BLANC, or TREBBIANO di Soave (which had been almost entirely replaced by the more productive, if less interesting, Trebbiano Toscano). Chardonnay, the most widely planted of the new varieties, has the ability to tame and soften some of the overtly vegetal character of overcropped Garganega, particularly by adding body to wines intended for wood ageing, but this is rarely achieved with the high yields to which the TENDONE vineyards are dedicated.

Although high-volume, mass-market Soave from areas never previously planted to vines has helped to create an image of the wine as a bland, neutral product, the wines of such small producers as Pieropan and Anselmi have demonstrated that the Garganega grape can yield wines of real character with a pungency that marries well with wood ageing. Experiments with BARRIQUES have also given positive results. These remain isolated exceptions, none the less, in a sea of mediocrity.

The 1980s saw a revival of the sweet RECIOTO di Soave, a PASSITO made from raisined Garganega grapes with a long local tradition. Extremely low production levels had restricted these wines to local and domestic consumption, but recognition of their outstanding quality, some of the finest dessert wines of Italy, has now made them a viable commercial proposition. D.T.

SODIUM, element that is not a required nutrient for vine growth. Sodium chloride (common SALT) is, however, a major hazard for vine-growers, particularly in hot, irrigated areas where ground waters are saline, or where salty irrigation water is applied to the leaves. Sodium has an unfavourable effect on soil fertility because it reduces water infiltration due to its tendency to disperse clay particles. This can be overcome by addition of CALCIUM to the soil, normally as gypsum. See also SALINITY. R.E.S.

SOGRAPE, the most important wine producer in PORTUGAL, a firm built up by the Guedes family and established largely on the success of MATEUS Rosé.

SOIL, the sediment at the surface of the Earth capable of supporting the growth of plants, including vines. There is no absolute dividing line between soil and the underlying ROCK, another term used in geology. A typical early 20th century definition of soil was 'rocks that have been reduced to small fragments and have been more or less changed chemically, together with the remains of plants or animals that live in it or on it'. For most purposes this is still a satisfactory working definition, emphasizing as it does the ORGANIC MATTER content.

For modern soil scientists this definition is inadequate, however, as it fails to include the stratification into 'horizons' which are present in all soils (in Britain, for example, eight horizons are recognized above the bedrock); it fails to bring out variations in porosity and permeability which affect plant roots; and it fails to take account of variations over the world associated with different CLIMATES and different belts of vegetation.

For vines, the problems of distinction between soils and rocks are exacerbated by the fact that many vineyards are in areas where the underlying bedrock is not a hard rock but an unconsolidated young sediment, so that the dividing line between soil and bedrock is even less obvious than normal, and by the fact that vines have ROOTS long enough to extend below the soil into the bedrock.

See GEOLOGY, SOIL ACIDITY, SOIL ALKALINITY, SOIL COLOUR, SOIL DEPTH, SOIL FERTILITY, SOIL MANAGEMENT, SOIL STRUCTURE, SOIL TESTING, SOIL TEXTURE, SOIL TYPES, SOIL WATER, STONES AND ROCKS, SUBSOIL, TERROIR, TOPOGRAPHY, and, most importantly, SOIL AND WINE QUALITY. J.M.H.

SOIL ACIDITY. The problem of high soil acidity, or low soil PH, occurs where hydrogen cations (H^+) predominate relative to those of the alkaline elements CALCIUM, POTASSIUM, and MAGNESIUM adsorbed to the fine particle surfaces of the CLAY and ORGANIC MATTER. Acidity is found mainly where the alkaline mineral elements have been leached down or out of the soil profile under heavy rainfall over long ages, and their places in the so-called 'exchange complex' on the soil particles have been taken by hydrogen ions. The process is accelerated under pines and certain other plant types by the chemical natures of their leaf litter. Any increase in soil organic matter content without a matching increase in alkaline MINERAL elements will also result in acidification of the soil. Problems of soil acidity are to be expected in most viticultural regions with high rainfall, and affect parts of Europe and the east coast of Australia.

Soils of pH below about 6 are described as acid; below 5 as highly acid; and below 4 as extremely acid. The last are clearly unsuitable for most plants, while grapevine root growth is inhibited below pH 5.5. Soils more acid than that are best avoided for viticulture; if this is not possible, then the application of LIME should at least be considered before planting. Apart from direct effects on root growth, excessive soil acidity reduces the availability of NITROGEN, PHOSPHORUS, potassium, and magnesium to the vines, and greatly increases the risk of MANGANESE and, especially, aluminium toxicity. The soil acidity of the MÉDOC in Bordeaux also promotes COPPER toxicity where there has been a buildup of copper in the topsoil from spraying vines with BORDEAUX MIXTURE.

Acidity tends to increase with the use of nitrogen FERTILIZERS and leguminous green manures; and indeed with any buildup of soil ORGANIC MATTER. It is unlikely that this effect will be noticed in vineyards unless nitrogen fertilization is heavy. However, where nitrogen is added via drip irrigation, in the system known as FERTIGATION, localized acidity problems may develop.

Soil acidity should be contrasted with SOIL ALKALINITY.

J.G. & R.E.S.

SOIL ALKALINITY. A soil is said to be alkaline when the measured PH (see SOIL ACIDITY) is above about 8.0. Above pH 8.5 usually implies a content of free lime or common salt (sodium chloride) in the soil; while many less alkaline surface soils sit above chalk or limestones, or contain limestone rocks. Saline soils should definitely be avoided for viticulture, but some of the best vineyard soils in cool climates are associated with LIMESTONE or CHALK.

Soils high in free lime can create nutritional difficulties through the reduced availability of POTASSIUM. High lime and pH can also induce deficiencies of ZINC, IRON, and MANGANESE or BORON in the vines. These can usually be controlled by spraying the leaves. Selection of particularly well-adapted varieties of ROOTSTOCK is another approach. J.G.

SOIL AMELIORATION, a viticultural practice for improving soils by the addition of so-called **soil amendments**. These can include FERTILIZERS (such as superphosphate) to overcome mineral nutrient deficiencies, LIME, which will overcome SOIL ACIDITY, and gypsum and ORGANIC MATTER, which will improve SOIL STRUCTURE. These ameliorants are spread on the soil surface, and occasionally turned in by cultivation. Where there is a need for deep placement, as in LIMING, then large and powerful bulldozers are used, normally before planting. R.E.S.

Coombe, B. G., and Dry, P. R. (eds.), *Viticulture, ii: Practices* (Adelaide, 1992).

SOIL AND WINE QUALITY. The SOIL has many attributes that can influence the vine grown in it, and thence the quality of both grapes and wine. Quite how influential these attributes are remains a matter of debate, with a fairly marked divergence of opinion between the OLD WORLD and NEW WORLD.

Old World versus New World

Old World opinion, especially in France, strongly emphasizes soil effects. It is a principal basis for the concept of TERROIR which underlies the official French system of wine appellation, the APPELLATION CONTRÔLÉE system. In Germany, by contrast, large local differences in climate associated with TOPOGRAPHY are often considered to override soil effects (see MESOCLIMATE and CLIMATE AND WINE QUALITY), although they are still regarded as an important factor governing wine quality. SOIL COLOUR can be critical at the extreme cool limit of viticulture in determining whether grapes will ripen at all. Fregoni and Berry give examples.

New World opinion has tended to minimize the role of soil, and instead to stress major differences in regional climate, or MACROCLIMATE. Amerine and Winkler's 1944 CLIMATE CLASSIFICATION of California into five temperature regions, Regions I to V, epitomizes this view.

Much of the divergence in approach can be ascribed to differences in historical, geographical, and commercial background. Traditional European vineyards were small, and the identities of their wines sometimes established over many generations. It was observed that certain sites consistently produced different and/or better wines than others, apparently regardless of VITICULTURE management and WINEMAKING practices, and sometimes in the absence of discernible differences in mesoclimate. One general observation, especially marked in Bordeaux, was that the best sites stood out most clearly in poor VINTAGE YEARS. These sites maintained a relative consistency of high quality, whereas others, superficially similar and often very close, suffered greatly diminished quality. The only possible reason seemed to lie in unalterable (and perhaps invisible) properties of the soil.

New World viticulture generally lacks this experience. Moreover, its dominant commercial organizations tend to employ extensive BLENDING of wines from different soils and regions, so that any individualities are often masked or lost. Attempts to identify wine differences that could be related to soil type, for instance that of Rankine *et al.*, have generally yielded negative results. It is therefore hardly surprising that subtle differences in wine quality due to the soil should have commanded little attention in the New World.

Despite all this, the absolute need for quality (and in some cases, wine individuality) in a now highly competitive world market means that the New World can no longer afford to neglect any avenue to excellence. The Old World meanwhile needs to identify more closely the reasons why some soils can give better wines than others, so that ways can be found to bypass the old constraints of soil and terroir, and thus to attain the best wine qualities more widely. Pre-eminent in this field has been the work of the Bordeaux researcher Dr Gérard Seguin, which forms a background to the discussion that immediately follows. Other French studies of note are of PREMIER CRU vineyards in Burgundy by Meriaux and Chrétien reported by Berry. In this account we distinguish between chemical and physical soil attributes.

Physical soil attributes

Scientific opinion now almost universally agrees with Seguin's conclusion that soil physical characteristics predominate as the main influence over grape and wine qualities other than CLIMATE; and further, that, among the physical characteristics, the most important are those which govern water supply to the vine. These and their relationship to individual soil types are discussed in some detail under TERROIR. See also SOIL WATER, SOIL TEXTURE, DRAINAGE, and VINE PHYSIOLOGY.

Here we may note briefly that the best wines come from soils that are very well drained, and furnish a steady, but only moderate, water supply to the vines. When combined with appropriate restrictive mineral VINE NUTRITION, this ensures that growth is restrained. The leaves remain relatively small, and nearly all leaves and bunches are well exposed to SUNLIGHT. The grape berries do not become over-sized (see BERRY SIZE), so their skin to pulp ratios remain high, and the PIGMENTS and FLAVOUR COMPOUNDS that reside largely in the skins are not diluted. The smaller berries are also usually less liable to congestion and compression within the bunch, and are therefore less likely to split or suffer spoilage as a result of FUNGAL DISEASES or BACTERIA. WATER STRESS needs to be just enough to attain these ends, and not enough to interfere with normal leaf functioning.

Some other physical properties of soils almost certainly influence wine qualities in subtle ways.

SOIL COLOUR affects soil temperature and that of the air immediately above. Dark coloured soils absorb and convert nearly all of the light falling on them into heat, and so are warmer than light coloured soils, and, at night and during daytime cloud cover, radiate more warmth back to the vines and bunches. This can be critical in some cold marginal viticultural climates, allowing fuller RIPENING and thus better wine quality (as in the bituminous soils of the Neckar valley in WÜRTTEMBERG or the Meuse valley of southern BELGIUM for example). More speculatively the amount and spectral quality of the light reflected back into the vine CANOPY might have effects of their own in some situations (see SUNLIGHT).

The presence of STONES AND ROCKS in the soil or on its

surface influences both water and temperature relations. A high proportion of stones throughout the soil profile is commonly associated with very good profile DRAINAGE, but at the same time reduces water-holding capacity and encourages desirably extensive ROOT GROWTH to assure its water supply. A cover, or mulch, of stones or rocks also protects against surface EVAPORATION, leading to a greater consistency of water supply. A mulch also protects against soil erosion, and allows the exploitation of MESOCLIMATES which are probably beneficial for wine quality but might otherwise be too risky. The steep, rubbly slate surfaces of many of the MOSEL-SAAR-RUWER vineyards in Germany are a good example. Stony soils, whether sloping or not, usually have the further advantage for wine quality that they are at most only moderately fertile, as discussed below.

Soils containing a large proportion of rock or stone have the additional advantage that they most readily absorb heat and transmit it to depth, because solid rock is a particularly good conductor of heat: much better than dry or loose soil. Moderately damp soil beneath surface stones is both a reasonable heat conductor and a good heat storer, because of the high heat storage capacity of its water content. It is also protected from evaporative cooling. Such soils are efficient at absorbing and storing warmth, and retransmitting it to the above-ground vine parts during cloud cover and in the evening. This may not only help to promote ripening in cool climates, but could also be more or less universally advantageous during ripening for flavour and aroma development, and therefore for wine quality. See TEMPERATURE VARIABILITY and CLIMATE AND WINE QUALITY.

Whatever the mechanisms, there can be little doubt that stony and rocky soils produce many of the world's great wines; and that, within given areas, the stoniest or rockiest usually produce the best. Typical are the coarse gravels that characterize the most eminent châteaux of the MÉDOC in Bordeaux; the large stones that completely cover the best sites of CHÂTEAUNEUF-DU-PAPE in the southern Rhône; and the coarsely stony gravels that give wines of outstanding quality in the Marlborough region of NEW ZEALAND's South Island.

Chemical attributes

The relationship between soil chemistry and wine quality is in the main very poorly understood. Soil NITROGEN is in part an exception to this. It is clear from Seguin's work, and that of other European researchers, that the optimum nitrogen supply to the vine is at most only moderate. Vines receiving much nitrogen, unless severely constrained by other factors, have vigorous and leafy growth. This leads readily to excessive SHADE within the canopy, and thence to poor fruit quality (see CANOPY MICROCLIMATE). The effects of nitrogen, water supply, and various other nutritional and environmental factors can to varying degrees reinforce or counteract each other in this regard. The best combination among them is that giving optimum vine BALANCE.

A further complication has arisen from recent research showing that low nitrogen contents in the berries can be a cause of difficulties in wine-making, leading to STUCK FERMENTATIONS and the presence of HYDROGEN SULPHIDE and its malodorous MERCAPTAN derivatives in the wine. This is especially common with fruit from warm, sunny climates. While it is now known that at least much of the problem can be overcome by adding nitrogen-based YEAST nutrients during fermentation, the problem of combining suitable nitrogen nutrition for vine balance with optimum concentrations of natural nitrogen compounds in the berries remains largely unsolved.

POTASSIUM availability is another soil factor with mixed relationships to wine quality. Deficiencies are common in cool and humid climates, where the efficiency of water use for growth and yield (see HUMIDITY and CLIMATE AND WINE QUALITY) means that potassium and some other elements are diluted in the plant. Potassium-deficient vines are more than usually susceptible to DROUGHT and VINE DISEASES, and the fruit lacks sugar (see SUGAR IN GRAPES) as well as COLOUR and flavour.

Conversely, vines in hot, atmospherically arid climates readily accumulate excess potassium in the leaves, stems, and fruit. High potassium levels in grapes can lead to high wine PH, with all its attendant quality defects. It should be stressed, however, that the problem is not necessarily correlated with high soil potassium content, nor even always with atmospheric aridity. Excessive leaf shading in a poor canopy microclimate contributes importantly in many cases, and improved CANOPY MANAGEMENT can help greatly in assuring more appropriate fruit potassium levels.

The rule for other nutrient elements appears to be that adequate supplies are needed equally for vine health and for fruit and wine quality.

Possible specific quality roles for the trace elements (COPPER, ZINC, MANGANESE, IRON, BORON, and molybdenum) remain obscure but potentially interesting. Their contents in the soil and availability to the plant vary enormously from soil to soil, and, in often disparate ways, with SOIL MANAGEMENT. Fregoni and Champagnol cite some cases where differences in wine quality or character from different soils could conceivably be associated with the amounts or balances of trace elements in the soil, vines, or grapes. At the moment, however, no trace element constituent has been shown to be a decisive factor, either in wine quality or in any particular wine characteristic.

SOIL ACIDITY and SOIL ALKALINITY are further possible influences; but again, little firm evidence exists at present. Extremes in either direction, sufficient to upset vine nutrition and health seriously, seem unlikely to improve wine quality. On the other hand vines can tolerate a fairly wide soil pH range without evident harm, while the potential trace element deficiencies that are often encountered at high pH levels can in most cases be readily overcome by spraying leaves or by judicious choice of ROOTSTOCKS. Fregoni cites examples of acclaimed wines coming from the full range of soil pH levels. Robinson gives a comprehensive account of this and other aspects of VINE NUTRITION.

The subject of ORGANIC MATTER in soils for viticulture needs careful evaluation. On the one hand, soils naturally high in organic matter tend to be too fertile, and to supply too much nitrogen and water, for good wine quality (as explained above). On the other, many respected TERROIRS that have otherwise favourable characteristics for wine quality are naturally low in organic matter, or have become so, so that both their physical condition and vine health benefit, or would benefit, from its buildup and maintenance (see ORGANIC VITICULTURE). Very sandy soils need organic matter to give them sufficient capacity to store water and nutrients. All soils benefit from having some organic matter, to give them friability (see SOIL STRUCTURE), and to encourage the activity of earthworms, which help to keep them well aerated and freely draining.

The natures and geological origins of the ROCKS or sediments from which soils are formed (see GEOLOGY) are further factors sometimes held to influence wine qualities. Soils formed from CHALK and LIMESTONE, for example, are highly valued in some cool climates, although not generally in warm regions such as the south of France (see, for instance, Champagnol). Most researchers consider this to be related to their free DRAINAGE and the ability of the SUBSOIL to store water. Certain grape varieties, particularly PINOT NOIR and CHARDONNAY, are also regarded by some as having a special requirement for chalk or limestone soils to produce their best wines; but again, this seems to be a largely northern French view. Experience elsewhere, especially in the New World, lends it little support. One universally positive role of chalk and limestone (or deliberately adding LIME) is that the resulting high level of calcium absorption to the soil clay particles helps to maintain crumbly texture in the soil, thus encouraging aeration, even at very high clay contents (see SOIL TEXTURE).

On the general role of geology we can conclude that any influence is mostly indirect, via the shaping of TOPOGRAPHY and through effects which are more properly those of the derived soil rather than of the rock or sediment. There can be some direct effects on water supply, however, where vine roots penetrate into the geological stratum underlying the soil. Chalk in Champagne (see above) and the Médoc gravel beds of Bordeaux (see SOIL WATER) have been cited in this regard. The deep, water-bearing gravel beds of Milawa and Bendigo in the Australian state of VICTORIA provide other examples.

Other factors

These relations are often obscured in practice, and great variation of soils over even short distances means that generalizations of any kind are dangerous. In some vineyards, especially those on alluvial soils, the soil type may change dramatically over a few metres, despite an apparent uniformity at the surface. For the same reason, SOIL MANAGEMENT procedures are seldom equally appropriate across an entire vineyard, let alone between different vineyards.

A second point is that, despite this, management technologies are increasingly becoming available which obviate many of the effects of this variability. This is especially so in the New World. Among the more important is adoption of drip IRRIGATION, which in climates with a dry summer can go far towards giving the vines a controlled optimum water regime that is little influenced by soil type. Similarly, techniques of soil and (especially) leaf or PETIOLE analysis are making possible a more controlled optimum vine nutritional regime, so that differences in nutrient supply by the soil are moderated, or even, potentially, eliminated. Remaining soil characteristics, for instance those influencing the vine's temperature and light microenvironments, then perhaps assume greater prominence as being more difficult to manipulate.

A third point is that most vineyards throughout the world are now grafted to PHYLLOXERA-tolerant ROOTSTOCKS. The various rootstocks differ in their ability to take up mineral elements and water, in their capacity to root to depth, and in their effects on the VIGOUR of the vines grafted on to them. It is therefore possible to compensate for and adapt to particular soils as a means of approaching an optimal combination of vigour, nutrition, and canopy management for vine balance. Any consideration of soils now has to acknowledge the role of rootstocks.

At the same time it is salutary to remember that no single rootstock variety can be identified in France which in any case distinguishes the GRAND CRU vineyards from their less celebrated neighbours; nor have vineyard reputations changed much, whereas rootstock usage has. These facts support the conclusion that the main effects of both soil and rootstock on wine quality are mediated by observable effects on the vine that can be subsequently manipulated by management, and are not due to any direct influence of the soil or rootstock itself.

Conclusions

There can be no doubt that soil characteristics do influence wine quality. However, in most situations the effects of soil are subsidiary to those of CLIMATE, VINE VARIETY, and VINE MANAGEMENT. Of the influential soil characteristics, the most important are those governing the supply of water to the vine, probably followed by those influencing temperatures in and above the soil. Soil chemistry and vine nutrition, within the bounds of normal vine health and growth, play little role that has yet been discerned, other than the role of nitrogen in vegetative vigour and berry nitrogen content, and in some situations that of excess potassium on the pH of must and wine.

Most typically, the best soils for wine quality are:

- moderately deep to deep;
- fairly light textured, often with gravel through much of the profile and at the surface;
- free draining;
- sufficiently high in organic matter to give soil friability, a healthy worm population, and adequate nutrient-holding capacity, but not, as a rule, particularly high in organic matter;
- overall, relatively infertile, supplying enough mineral elements for healthy vine growth, but only enough nitrogen early in the season to promote moderate vegetative vigour.

J.G. & R.E.S.

Berry, E., 'The importance of soil in fine wine production', *Journal of Wine Research*, 1 (1990), 179–94.
Champagnol, F., *Éléments de physiologie de la vigne et de viticulture générale* (St-Gely-du-Fesc, 1984).
Fregoni, M., 'Effects of the soil and water on the quality of the harvest', *Proceedings: International Symposium on the Quality of the Vintage* (Cape Town, 1977).
Rankine, B. C., Fornachon, J. C. M., Boehm, E. W., and Cellier, K. M., 'Influence of grape variety, climate and soil on grape composition and on the composition and quality of table wines', *Vitis*, 10 (1971), 33–50.
Robinson, J. B., 'Grapevine nutrition', in B. G. Coombe and P. R. Dry (eds.), *Viticulture ii: Practices* (Adelaide, 1992).
Seguin, G., '"Terroirs" and pedology of wine growing', *Experientia*, 42 (1986), 861–72.

SOIL COLOUR, a term normally referring to the surface colour of a soil. Viticultural folklore associates red wine with red soils, and white wines with white or grey soils. However, while the balance of circumstantial evidence does seem to support such an idea, many exceptions exist. Present explanations for the apparent correlation are largely speculative.

Colour can certainly affect soil temperature, and that of the air immediately above it. Fregoni discusses this in some detail. Dark coloured soils or rocks absorb most of the incoming light energy and convert it to heat. Therefore, whereas they reflect less light than light coloured soils, they radiate more heat at night and when the sun is shaded. In cool climates this may be especially beneficial to red grapes, which in general need more warmth than white grapes to ripen fully. Other examples of the exploitation of these thermal characteristics include the vineyards of Deidesheim in the PFALZ region of Germany, where black basalt rock is mined and spread on the vineyards to help produce wines of unusual sweetness. Fragmented dark grey SLATE helps Riesling to ripen in the otherwise very cool MOSEL-SAAR-RUWER. 'Bituminous' SCHIST soils are reportedly the only ones on which grapes can be ripened at the extreme northern limit of viticulture in BELGIUM. At the other extreme, the white ALBARIZA soils of JEREZ in southern Spain, produce the best (white) grapes for sherry in a very hot climate.

The relationships of soil colour to temperature suitability for vine-growing are far from straightforward, however. Many reddish and brown soils are still favoured for viticulture in hot regions such as the Hunter Valley of NEW SOUTH WALES and the Swan Valley of WESTERN AUSTRALIA. Presumably the greater warmth radiated during the evening and under cloud cover can still result in a net benefit for the vines and wines, despite possibly adverse effects in the heat of the day: see CLIMATE AND WINE QUALITY.

One point of potential speculation is the role of light reflected back from the soil into the vine CANOPY, and to the grape bunches. Little is known about this, but either or both of the quantity and spectral quality of light could conceivably be significant in various ways. White soils obviously reflect back most light (but radiate least heat). A red soil, on the other hand, may be fairly efficient at absorbing and radiating heat, but still reflect the light wavelengths most useful for PHOTOSYNTHESIS back into the canopy. See further discussion under SUNLIGHT.

Soil colour is in any case a useful indicator of some of its other properties. Black shows a high content of MINERALS and/or ORGANIC MATTER. Red or brown are due to the presence of oxidized IRON compounds, and normally indicate good DRAINAGE. (Under waterlogging, iron is reduced to colourless forms which, being more soluble, tend to be leached away.) A grey soil surface shows that most of the original iron compounds have been leached downwards, often to be deposited in a heavier-textured SUBSOIL.

The colour of the subsoil is a particularly important indicator of soil suitability for viticulture. Except where it consists largely of decomposing chalk or LIMESTONE, a white, grey, or mottled subsoil shows drainage that is usually too poor for viticulture; or at least, a need for artificial drainage. J.G.

Fregoni, M., 'Effects of the soil and water on the quality of the harvest', in *Proceedings, International Symposium on the Quality of the Vintage* (Cape Town, 1977).

SOIL DEPTH, a loose term for the depth to the boundary between the SOIL and its parent ROCK material; or, alternatively, the depth to which plant ROOT GROWTH is possible before reaching some impenetrable barrier. Examples of the latter include the tight and/or poorly drained subsoils of some podzolic soils; cemented ironstone, or 'coffee rock', which forms at the base of some iron-rich soils that have been subject to leaching; or layers with excessively high or low PH, or of salt or some other toxic factor which effectively prevents further root penetration.

Deep, well-drained soils are valued for viticulture to the extent that deeply penetrating root systems bestow a favourable consistency of moisture and, to a lesser extent, supply of VINE NUTRIENTS. Contemporary researchers, led by Seguin, consider that consistency of moisture supply to the vine is a major contributor to wine quality (see SOIL WATER and SOIL AND WINE QUALITY). Nevertheless deep, moisture-retentive soils can be counter-productive when they encourage strong vegetative growth into the ripening period. Shallower soils, combined with the possibility of supplementary IRRIGATION when needed, can sometimes be preferable. J.G.

Seguin, G., 'Influence des terroirs viticoles', *Bulletin de l'OIV*, 56 (1983), 3–18.
—— '"Terroirs" and pedology of wine growing', *Experientia*, 42 (1986), 861–72.

SOIL DISINFECTION. See FUMIGATION.

SOIL EROSION, shifting or removal of soil by wind or running water. Wind erosion is fairly uncommon in established vineyards, because the vines themselves constitute an effective WINDBREAK at ground level, although it can be a problem in young vineyards. Driving sand, in particular, can seriously injure young vines, and there can in addition be irreparable loss of the most valuable topsoil. The danger can be minimized by growing COVER CROPS between the vine

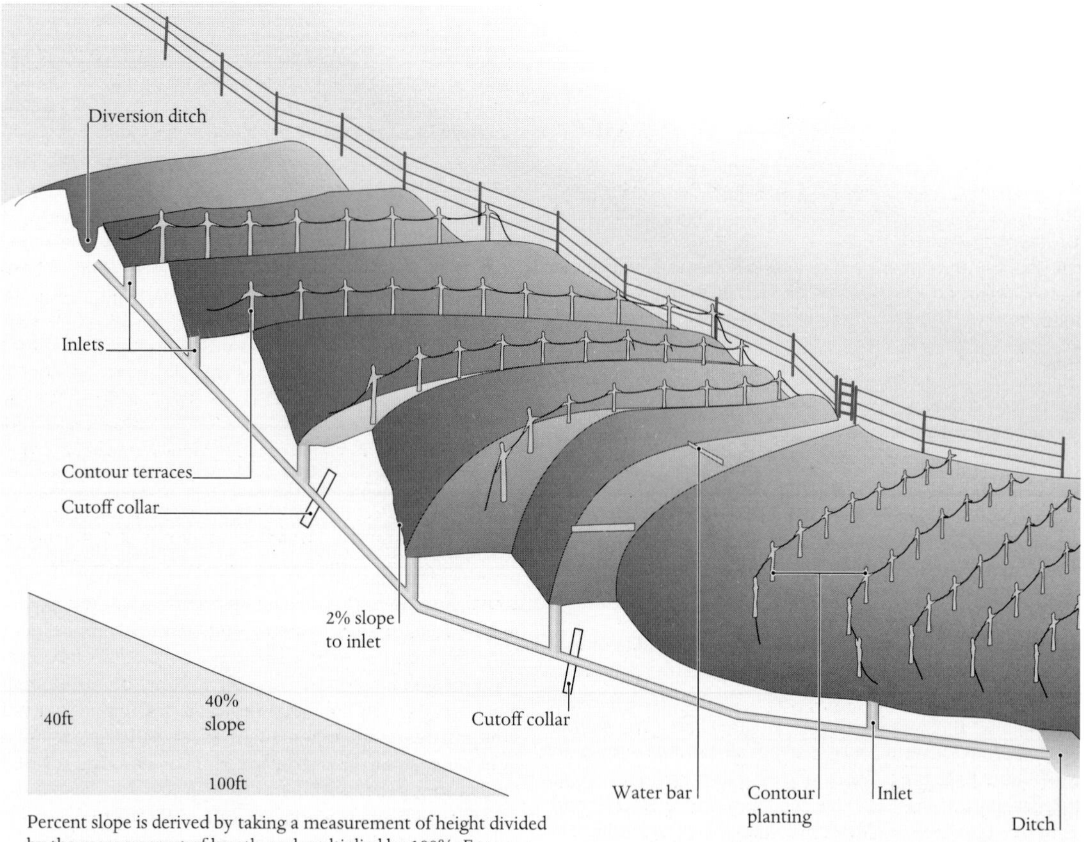

Percent slope is derived by taking a measurement of height divided by the measurement of length, and multiplied by 100%. For example, a 40% slope would have a 40 foot rise in a 100 foot length.

Soil erosion: planting along the contour of the slope minimizes soil loss by reducing runoff between vine rows. In steeper areas over 15% slope, contour terraces should be installed with a 2% slope leading to an underground pipe inlet. Pipe size and installation depth is determined by local conditions such as hydrology, drainage area, slope, etc. Terraces are backsloped to prevent uncontrolled runoff. Cutoff collars prevent movement of water along the outside of the pipe.

rows, especially tall-growing cereals such as rye, which act as windbreaks as well as directly binding the soil.

Erosion by water, on the other hand, is always a potential problem on the sloping sites that normally afford the best MESOCLIMATES for wine quality (see HILLSIDE VINEYARDS). Some steeply sloping sites, such as in the MOSEL-SAAR-RUWER region of Germany and the northern RHÔNE, necessitate a constant and laborious replacement of soil from the bottom of the slope to the top.

VINEYARD SITE SELECTION and the selection of suitable soils are important elements in the avoidance of erosion. STONES AND ROCKS of the soil surface can offer protection by breaking the flow of water across the surface, and by shielding the fine soil from direct battering and dispersion by raindrops. Plant cover and MULCHES (including vine prunings) have a similar effect. Permanent grassing between the rows is feasible in some situations, where water and NITROGEN supplies are sufficient for both grass and vines. Planting on convex hill slopes helps too, to the extent that there are no external sources of flowing water. Where occasional water flow on to or across a site cannot be avoided, it can often be made harmless by diversionary banks, directing flow into drains or permanently grassed waterways which follow the natural flow line.

Avoidance of unnecessary cultivation is essential, together with other measures which maintain the soil's ORGANIC MATTER content and physical crumb structure (see SOIL STRUCTURE and SOIL MANAGEMENT). These enable rain to be absorbed readily where it falls. Row orientation and such cultivation as is unavoidable should ideally be directed just a little off the contour, so that any water flow along furrows will be gentle and harmless, and able to spill out on to permanently grassed natural waterways. Cultivation straight up and down slopes lends itself to general erosion. Vine rows which follow the contour may successfully dam surface water following moderate rain, but break-outs following heavy rain can cause locally catastrophic erosion.

The practicalities of vineyard design often limit control over the direction and slopes of cultivation. The best control of erosion is therefore through its avoidance as far as possible, and adoption of the other planning and management measures described above. In all cases when planting a new vineyard it is essential to assess the risks beforehand, and not to plant vines where the potential for full erosion control is in doubt. J.G.

SOIL FERTILITY, the physical and chemical characteristics of a soil determining its ability to support vigorous plant growth. A fertile soil is generally understood to be one with a high content of available plant nutrients, moderate to high ORGANIC MATTER content, good SOIL STRUCTURE and DRAINAGE, and most typically a SOIL TEXTURE high in LOAM. Neither SOIL ACIDITY nor SOIL ALKALINITY will be excessive, so that the nutrient elements will all be in a favourable balance of availability for plant growth.

Highly fertile soils, especially those rich in NITROGEN, are undesirable for wine grapes because they encourage excessive vegetation and a congested CANOPY MICROCLIMATE. This in turn can reduce both YIELD and, especially, the quality of the grapes for wine-making. On the other hand, the notion that only infertile soils can make good wines is undoubtedly mistaken. CANOPY MANAGEMENT techniques can allow vigorous vines on moderately fertile soils to mimic the canopy microclimates of traditional vineyards on less fertile soils. Carbonneau and Casteran have elucidated these principles in the Bordeaux environment.

See also SOIL AND WINE QUALITY, CLIMATE AND WINE QUALITY, BALANCE. J.G. & R.E.S.

Carbonneau, A. P., and Casteran, P., 'Interactions "training system × soil × rootstock" with regard to vine ecophysiology, vigour, yield and red wine quality in the Bordeaux area', *Acta horticulturae*, 206 (1987), 119–40.

SOIL MANAGEMENT, the practices of cultivation, or non-cultivation, of soils in vineyards, including the use of COVER CROPS and MULCHES, and other measures to improve the soil's physical condition or improve SOIL FERTILITY.

In the past, and still too much in the present, soil management has consisted primarily of clean cultivation to control WEEDS. The disadvantages of this approach are increasingly recognized, however. Modern soil management seeks to conserve and, if necessary, increase the ORGANIC MATTER content; to conserve and improve SOIL STRUCTURE and porosity, and thereby improve aeration and free absorption and DRAINAGE of SOIL WATER and resistance to SOIL EROSION; and to maintain a reserve of nutrients in organic and slowly available inorganic forms to provide a steady and balanced supply of VINE NUTRIENTS matched to the plants' needs.

Measures of soil management include growing plant covers and green manure crops, with minimal cultivation for their establishment; using inorganic FERTILIZERS (as needed) mainly to grow these crops, and thence to supply the vines as far as possible from organic sources; summer mulching with the residues of the cover and green manures grown *in situ*, or with imported vegetable materials or manures; and, when essential, the use of environment-friendly herbicides to control cover crops and weeds.

Measures by which undesirable soil compaction can be reduced include the use of lighter equipment in the vineyard, and avoidance of all traffic when the soil is wet. In large vineyards it is feasible to apply some sprays from the air (see HELICOPTERS). Similarly the future greater use of biological methods for pest control (see ORGANIC VITICULTURE) should help to reduce the movement of equipment in the vineyard. The use of LIME or gypsum may be indicated for some soils. All these measures serve to improve soil physical conditions for vine ROOT GROWTH, thereby improving vine health, YIELD, and probably wine quality. J.G. & R.E.S.

McCarthy, M. G., Dry, P. R., Hayes, P. F., and Davidson, D. M., 'Soil and management and frost control', in B. G. Coombe and P. R. Dry (eds.), *Viticulture, ii: Practices* (Adelaide, 1992).

SOIL NUTRIENTS, elements occurring in the soil which are taken up by plant root systems. Soils which are rich in nutrients are often termed fertile, but such soils do not usually produce good-quality wine. The amounts of nutrients that are available to the vine depend on the soil's mineralogy, the amount and nature of ORGANIC MATTER, and also the soil PH. Soils with a long history of pasture use have high levels of surface organic matter and are typically rich in NITROGEN. Old vineyard soils on the other hand are often relatively impoverished of organic matter, but may have high levels of COPPER as a result of repeated FUNGICIDE application. Many nutrients including nitrogen and PHOSPHORUS, for example, are less available in acid soils. Others such as IRON and MANGANESE are less available in alkaline soils. Nutrient deficiencies are diagnosed by symptoms on the vines, or by plant and soil tests, and can be remedied by applying FERTILIZERS. R.E.S.

Robinson, J. B., 'Grapevine nutrition', in B. G. Coombe and P. R. Dry (eds.), *Viticulture ii: Practices* (Adelaide, 1992).

SOIL PREPARATION, the treatment of SOIL before PLANTING a vineyard, can be an important viticultural operation. Proper attention at this stage can determine the long-term success or otherwise of a VINEYARD.

Having selected the best possible site (see VINEYARD SITE SELECTION, TOPOGRAPHY, and TERROIR) and vineyard layout, and assured suitable DRAINAGE, the potential vine-grower should in most soils undertake deep RIPPING along the paths of the future vine rows. This should be done when the soil is as dry as possible, and aims to break through any pre-existing hard pans and to open up the SUBSOIL to facilitate rapid and deep penetration of the vine roots. Boehm and Coombe give greater detail in the general context of land preparation for vines. Any old roots should be cleared out, since these can carry fungal organisms which may affect the vines. On old vineyard sites the longer the fallow period before planting, the better.

If the SOIL ACIDITY is high, with a pH at a depth of 3 cm/1.2 in of less than, say, 5.5, adding LIME will probably be beneficial in the long run. SOIL TESTING should establish the suitable application of lime which should be incorporated as deeply as is feasible, particularly in the ripped area. This is also the time to incorporate a band of superphosphate (or equivalent phosphate form of FERTILIZER), plus trace elements as indicated, as deeply as possible along the rip lines. Rates as high as 2 tons/ha are used in areas with markedly phosphate-deficient soils, such as Australia, on all but the lighter sandy soils. This provides a store of phosphate which will last the vines for many years. Deep placement is especially important in MEDITERRANEAN-type climates, because summer drying of the surface soil can kill or seasonally inactivate many of the shallower roots.

Finally, WEEDS need to be controlled. In most climates it is usual to grow an autumn–winter green manure crop to add ORGANIC MATTER prior to vine planting in spring. J.G.

Boehm, E. W., and Coombe, B. G., 'Vineyard establishment', in B. G. Coombe and P. R. Dry (eds.), *Viticulture, ii: Practices* (Adelaide, 1992).

SOIL SLOTTING. See SLOTTING.

SOIL STRUCTURE, the physical structure of soils, an important vineyard characteristic, as governed by bonding of the primary particles (as described in SOIL TEXTURE) into larger aggregates. The size and stability of these aggregates help to determine the soil's friability or crumb structure, and hence its porosity for air movement, water DRAINAGE, and ROOT penetration, and its capacity to withstand the effects of cultivation and compression by vineyard machinery and the elements.

Soil structure depends on the following factors:

1. The amount and chemical nature of the clay. To have stable structure, a soil must have at least a moderate CLAY content. Montmorillonite clays, common in soils formed from ROCKS or sediments under cool, and fairly dry, conditions, have the property of swelling when wet, then shrinking and cracking into fragments when dry, leading to a desirable 'self-mulching' soil character. At the other extreme, clays formed and weathered in warm, wet climates tend to be mainly kaolin, or pipe clay, and do not have this property. Good structure is hard to build up and preserve in kaolinitic soils. Illitic clays (see GEOLOGY) are intermediate.

2. Relative contents of CALCIUM and SODIUM. Calcium helps to build up good soil structure, sodium causes breakdown and dispersion of the aggregates.

3. ORGANIC MATTER content. Humus is necessary for good structure in most soils, especially where the clay is kaolinitic. It is formed from decaying plant roots, leaves, etc. deposited at the surface, and the remains of microflora and microfauna living in the soil. Gummy substances excreted by living roots and soil organisms also play an important part in forming and preserving soil aggregates.

4. Soil disturbance by cultivation. All cultivation is destructive of soil structure, especially when the clay content is low and of unfavourable chemical nature, and the organic matter content is low.

Good SOIL MANAGEMENT aims principally to preserve and strengthen soil structure. J.G.

SOIL TESTING, or analysis by laboratory techniques, seeks to determine the concentrations of nutrient elements in the soil, and to give other information on its physical and chemical state. Soil testing still has fairly limited value in viticulture, apart from simple tests for PH (see SOIL ACIDITY, SOIL ALKALINITY) and one or two specific VINE NUTRIENTS. The supply of most nutrients to the vines depends as much on their complex forms, placement, and individual availability to the roots, and on methods of SOIL MANAGEMENT, as on their total contents or (so far) easily identifiable forms in the soil. Tissue analysis of the vines themselves usually gives a better guide to any FERTILIZER requirements than soil testing.

Soil tests nevertheless do give useful preliminary information for some nutrients. Carried out before planting, they allow the placement of any necessary nutrients such as PHOSPHORUS, POTASSIUM, CALCIUM, MAGNESIUM, and BORON below the vine rows, at depths where they will remain readily, and more or less permanently, available to the roots (see SOIL PREPARATION). Field inspection to determine SOIL TEXTURE and its natural DRAINAGE to as great a depth as possible is of course an essential preliminary to any vine planting. See also SOIL AND WINE QUALITY, TERROIR, VINEYARD SITE SELECTION. J.G. & R.E.S.

SOIL TEXTURE, the overall physical nature of the soil as determined by its proportions of constituent clay, silt, sand, STONES AND ROCKS, and ORGANIC MATTER. The individual constituents are defined below. Soils predominantly of clay are described as heavy textured. Loams are medium-textured soils, normally containing a fairly even balance of clays, silt, and sand, together with a moderately high organic matter content. Sands are light-textured soils, often loose and gritty, with at most a low clay content. Certain mineral elements, most notably CALCIUM, complement textural differences in helping to determine soil friability (see SOIL STRUCTURE).

Clay is the finest of the inorganic soil fractions, with particles conventionally set at less than 0.002 mm in diameter. If mixed in water, most of the particles remain in colloidal suspension for a long time. Because their surface areas are so large relative to their volumes, they have by far the greatest capacity for combining with, adsorbing, and holding plant nutrient elements and water. Fertile soils normally have at least a moderate proportion of clay.

Silt is an intermediate fraction, comprising the particles ranging between 0.002 and 0.02 mm in diameter. Being small enough to be carried in suspension by turbulent rivers, but large enough to settle out fairly quickly, silt particles are prominent in alluvial soils deposited by river floods.

Sand particles are the largest of those generally thought of as truly constituting soil, and range from 0.02 mm up to 2 mm in diameter. Unless mixed with a proportion of clay, sand remains loose under most conditions. In contrast to clay, the surface area of a sand particle is small relative to its volume, so it has little capacity for surface binding and storing of plant nutrients or water.

Organic matter plays an important complementary role, especially on very sandy soils where it is practically the only medium for nutrient and water storage. Organic matter also helps to make clay soils more friable.

Stones and rocks appear to have particular significance for viticulture, through their effects on TEMPERATURE both within and immediately above the soil. Stony soils are also usually well drained, while a surface layer of stones greatly enhances resistance to SOIL EROSION and reduces surface water loss by evaporation.

Commercial viticulture is carried out across a very wide range of soil textures. Clay and clay-loam soils can be suitable provided that they contain ample calcium (as in most LIMESTONE or CHALK-derived soils) and at least some organic matter. The strongest growth of vines, as with most other plants, is usually on loams and silty soils. Whether or not this is desirable depends on various other management and environmental factors, as described under SOIL FERTILITY and elsewhere. Soils in the clay to loam texture range will store in the vicinity of 15 mm / 0.6 in of RAINFALL per 10 cm / 4 in of soil depth, in forms that the vine roots can extract.

Soils consisting mostly of sand can pose problems for viticulture because of their lack of storage capacity for both water and nutrients. Typically they will hold 10 mm or less of root-available water per 10 cm of soil depth. The great depth of some sandy soils can be an offsetting factor, however, because vine roots penetrate many metres if the SUBSOIL texture and DRAINAGE permit, and can thus exploit a large enough volume to compensate. On some very sandy soils, the problems of water supply are overcome by supplying carefully controlled amounts by drip IRRIGATION. Nutrients can be supplied at the same time, in a process known as FERTIGATION.

An ideal soil for wine quality, depending on CLIMATE and the rate of EVAPORATION, together with the potential for irrigation, will balance texture against root-available depth to give an adequate storage capacity for water and nutrients, and to provide the vine with a steady moderate supply of both for BALANCED growth and fruiting. No single soil texture has a monopoly of these characteristics. Seguin notes that in the Bordeaux region the soils giving the best water regimes and producing the best wines range from the dominant deep, stony sands of the MÉDOC, to heavy (but well-structured) clays in POMEROL.

See also GEOLOGY. J.G.

Seguin, G., 'Influence des terroirs viticoles' ('Influence of viticultural terroirs'), *Bulletin de l'OIV*, 56 (1983), 3–18.

SOIL TYPES. For types of SOIL and ROCK, see individual entries on ALBARIZA, ALLUVIAL, CALCAIRE, CHALK, CLAY, GRANITE, GRAVEL, LIMESTONE, LOAM, LOESS, MARL, QUARTZ, RENDZINA, SAND, SANDSTONE, SCHIST, SHALE, SILT, SLATE, TERRA ROSSA, TUFFEAU, and VOLCANIC. See also SOIL AND WINE QUALITY and GEOLOGY, however, for evidence of soil's relatively indirect role in shaping wine and wine quality.

SOIL WATER, normally understood as being that held by the soil, within the potential rooting zone for plants, after any surplus has drained away (if it can). It exists in varying degrees of bondage to the finer soil particles (see SOIL TEXTURE) and ORGANIC MATTER, other than for surpluses in the open soil pores, which either drain away quickly (in well-drained soils) or remain in a stagnant state under waterlogging. In the last case a lack of OXYGEN quickly kills most plant roots.

Healthy vine tops need a healthy and extensive ROOT system. Regular waterlogging, even if only of the subsoil or the zone immediately overlying it, is a clear counter-indicator for vines, particularly if it occurs during the vine growing season. The effects are not merely on vine VIGOUR. Deep, healthy, and active roots are crucial to the consistency of moisture supply through the season that appears so critically to govern grape and wine quality. (See CLIMATE AND WINE QUALITY, SOIL AND WINE QUALITY, TERROIR.)

The binding capacity of the soil for the water that remains after free DRAINAGE has its own significance for vine–water relations. Some is so tightly bound to the CLAY and ORGANIC MATTER that roots cannot extract it at all, and some can only be extracted slowly. The small amount of water held in sandy soils, on the other hand, is readily and quickly available, and therefore easily exhausted.

The optimum soil water regime is thus usually found where there is an adequate depth of well-drained soil (see SOIL DEPTH), with at least moderate contents of clay and organic matter so that water can be supplied steadily from soil reserves over a long period. The less the clay and organic matter content, the deeper the soil needs to be to achieve that end. Note, however, that too much available soil water can be counter-productive in viticulture if it promotes too much vegetative vigour, or helps to prolong vegetative growth into the fruit-ripening period.

Ideally there should be ample available soil water during FLOWERING and FRUIT SET, diminishing so as to create just enough mild WATER STRESS before VERAISON to inhibit further vegetative growth. Opinions vary as to the optimum water supply between veraison and RIPENING, but most agree at least that there should be no severe stress through this period; nor should there be so much water available, especially after preceding stress, as to encourage a sudden uptake into the berries or renewed vegetative growth. Seguin notes that the soils of the best Bordeaux vineyards tend to have a water-table at some depth, but within reach of the vine roots. The water-table falls as the season progresses, but the vine roots can follow it down so as to maintain some water supply from it to the end of the season.

In MEDITERRANEAN CLIMATES with very low summer RAINFALL, soil water storage capacity needs to be high if the vines are to depend entirely on natural rainfall (as opposed to IRRIGATION). Excessive SOIL FERTILITY and water availability

A large sherry bodega such as this will house several **solera** systems.

early in the season then commonly lead to over-vigorous early growth, followed by water stress late in the season when it is least desired. In such climates, relatively shallow soils, or sandy/stony soils with limited water-holding capacity, combined with supplementary irrigation when needed, can have advantages in allowing the best control over water availability to the vines. J.G. & R.E.S.

Seguin, G., '"Terroirs" and pedology of wine growing', *Experientia*, 42 (1986), 861–73.

SOLANO-GREEN VALLEY, small CALIFORNIA wine region and AVA near the town of Fairfield in Solano County between San Francisco and Sacramento. Most of the grapes go to modest wineries selling mostly in the neighbourhood.

SOLAR, Portuguese term meaning a manor house which (like CHÂTEAU in France) may also be a wine-producing property.

SOLERA, system of fractional blending used most commonly in JEREZ for maintaining the consistency of a style of SHERRY which takes its name from those barrels closest to the *suelo*, or floor, from which the final blend was customarily drawn.

The system is designed to smooth out the differences between vintage years and is effectively a more subtle, and very much more labour-intensive, version of the BLENDING of inexpensive table wines between one vintage and another, although the solera system concerns barrel-aged liquids and is made up of several different scales. Depending on market demand, a fraction of wine is removed from the oldest scale of the solera, the so-called solera barrels themselves, and replaced (although the barrels are never filled completely) with wine from the next scale of barrels containing wine of the same type but one year younger, the so-called first criadera. They in turn are replenished from the scale two years younger (the second criadera) and so on, the youngest scale being replenished with new wine. This system is particularly useful for FLOR wines because it refreshes each barrel with younger wine and provides micro-nutrients to sustain the flor yeast for several years. It takes several years' operation for a solera to reach an equilibrium average age. Many soleras in Jerez were started decades ago and, since no barrel is ever emptied, there is always some of the oldest wine in the final blend. Fewer scales are needed to produce a consistent AMONTILLADO or OLOROSO sherry than a FINO or MANZANILLA sherry because these fuller, richer wines vary less from year to year.

Even using modern pumps, a tremendous amount of labour is needed to maintain a solera system and it is only in regions where labour costs are relatively moderate that a large solera is feasible. Another disadvantage of the system is the high inventory cost involved and the fact that the character of a blend cannot be altered quickly in response to changes in demand.

The solera system is also used for blending BRANDY, especially Brandy de Jerez, and for many other fortified wines such as MÁLAGA, MONTILLA, MADEIRA, LIQUEUR MUSCAT and Liqueur Tokay in Australia, as well as in the production of top-quality VINEGAR. If a product is labelled 'Solera 1880', for example, it should come from a solera established in 1880.

For mathematical calculations of the average age of a solera, and the time required to reach equilibrium average age, see Baker *et al.*

Baker, G. A., Amerine, M. A., and Roessler, E. B., 'Theory and application of fractional blending programs', *Hilgardia*, 21 (1952), 383–409.

SOLUBLE SOLIDS, also called **total soluble solids (TSS)** and **total dissolved solids (TDS)**, refer to the collective concentration in juice of all solutes (dissolved molecules and ions). The predominant solutes, accounting for about 90 per cent of the total, in the juice of ripe grapes are the reducing sugars GLUCOSE and FRUCTOSE; others are acids (MALIC and TARTARIC), ions (organic and inorganic), and literally hundreds of inorganic and organic molecules that together contribute to the characteristics that make grapes such an adaptable and useful product. Collective concentrations of TSS range from 5 to over 25 per cent and may be expressed in many ways, most usually either as degrees BRIX, BAUMÉ, or OECHSLE. With all such measurements, TEMPERATURE control or correction is necessary. B.G.C.

SOMMELIER, widely used French term for a specialist wine waiter or wine steward. The sommelier's job is to ensure that any wine ordered is served correctly and, ideally, to advise on the individual characteristics of every wine on the establishment's wine list and on FOOD AND WINE MATCHING. In some establishments the sommelier may also be responsible for compiling the list, buying and storing the wine, and restocking whatever passes for a CELLAR. (All too few restaurants today have their own serious collection of wines, although there are notable exceptions such as the Tour d'Argent in Paris, whose cellar is but a few feet from the river Seine, and Taillevent, whose cellar is so important that it has spawned a retail wine business.)

A sommelier should present the wine or wines ordered to the host before they are opened to ensure that there has been no misunderstanding (and so that the host can especially check that the vintages correspond to expectations). The bottle should be opened in view of the host, and, if a wine is to be DECANTED (and that is an option that any decent sommelier should be able to offer), that operation should be performed in public too.

Some sommeliers offer the cork to the host to smell, which is well meaning but is no certain guide to whether or not the wine is FAULTY. Some sublime wines come from under some rather unpleasant-smelling corks, and vice versa.

A surer guide to whether a particular bottle happens to be one of the relatively few to exhibit a fault (CORKINESS is the most common) is to examine the small tasting sample usually offered by the sommelier to the host for this very purpose. A glance will confirm that it is not cloudy, dull, or fizzing when it should not. A swift inhalation should confirm that it smells 'clean'. Few people can then resist actually tasting a mouthful, but it is generally unnecessary as the most common faults are apparent to the eye or nose.

In many countries there are official associations of sommeliers, often with a series of examinations, qualifications, or at least competitions. French, and other, sommeliers compete in these events all over the world and, such is the average French person's reverence for the wine knowledge of a sommelier, to win the title Meilleur Sommelier du Monde (Best Sommelier in the World) is henceforth to inhabit another world.

SOMONTANO, wine zone in the foothills of the central Pyrenees, in ARAGON in north east Spain (see map on p. 907). Somontano (meaning 'under the mountain') is one of the most impressive of Spain's recently designated (and often underwhelming) DO regions. In stark contrast to much of inland Spain, Somontano looks like wine-making country. The heavy winter rains are supplemented by a network of rivers and streams flowing off the mountains. Even in summer, when temperatures can easily reach 35 °C/95 °F, the fields remain green and productive.

A single huge CO-OPERATIVE produces over 80 per cent of the region's wine. Moristel (said to be related to the MONASTRELL grown in the Levante) and GARNACHA are the varieties favoured by smallholders and these two grape varieties continue to provide the backbone for traditional Somontano reds. But since the late 1980s a number of experimental vineyards have been planted with help from the Aragon regional government. Of the new varieties TEMPRANILLO is the most widely planted, but CABERNET SAUVIGNON, MERLOT, and even PINOT NOIR are now being grown in Somontano's relatively cool climate. VIURA and Alcañón, the traditional white grapes, have been joined by CHARDONNAY, CHENIN BLANC, and GEWÜRZTRAMINER. In the early 1990s, progress in the vineyards was still to be matched by investment in wine-making equipment and skill, although there were already some dazzling exceptions. R.J.M.

SONOMA, northern CALIFORNIA town and one of the state's most important wine counties. **Sonoma County** is one of the larger of northern California's coastal counties, and one of its most historic, with **Sonoma Valley** rivalling and occasionally beating nearby NAPA Valley for *réclame*. Vineyards are everywhere in the county, and have been since the last third of the 19th century. Sprawling, geologically and climatically diverse, it is the most resolutely amoebic of all the fine wine regions, having divided and redivided itself into AVAS and sub-AVAs until they run three layers deep in several places, four in a few. Growing conditions are a little more homogeneous than the welter of names suggests, but Sonoma still gives would-be gurus some of their most engaging opportunities to define subtle boundaries by taste and taste alone. The full roster follows.

Alexander Valley AVA
The largest and most fully planted of Sonoma County's many vineyard valleys, Alexander Valley takes in the Russian river watershed from the neighbourhood of Healdsburg north all the way to the Sonoma–Mendocino county line north of Cloverdale. If the general history is long, with vines dating back to the 1850s, the particular history of noble varieties is—a few rare plantings excepted—as short here as almost everywhere else in California. The valley awakened from a long drowse of mixed black grapes for bulk red only in the late 1960s and early 1970s. Simi winery started the renaissance in 1970, when a new owner breathed life into a moribund cellar. Alexander Valley Vineyards followed in 1975. Jordan Vineyards added a stamp of elegance in 1976. Growth has been steady since then.

The Alexander shares with its near neighbour, the Napa Valley, the curse of versatility. Almost every grape variety grows at least passably well and delivers at least agreeable wine. Its great vocation, on the other hand, seems reluctant to be coaxed into the open. Inevitably, it would seem, Cabernet Sauvignon and Chardonnay do well. These varieties, market driven, dominate plantings. Sauvignon Blanc and Zinfandel succeed often enough to make one wonder if they are not suited best to these particular suns and soils. Rhône varieties were introduced at the beginning of the 1990s and some dream of Sangiovese and other Italian varieties. Most of its substantial plantings are on a broad and nearly flat floor very nearly bisected by the river, but some significant ones creep into the east hills. Among the wineries that brought Alexander Valley to wide attention during the 1970s and 1980s were Jordan Vineyards, Simi, Alexander Valley Vineyards, and Geyser Peak.

Chalk Hill AVA
In essence a small sub-AVA of the Russian River Valley, Chalk Hill is at its eastern edge near the town of Windsor. It flanks the larger Alexander Valley at its southern tip. Its 800 acres/320 ha are given over almost entirely to Chardonnay and Sauvignon Blanc.

Dry Creek Valley AVA
A sparsely settled offshoot of the Russian river drainage, Dry Creek Valley has slowly emerged over the past decade as one of Sonoma County's most intriguing appellations. Among white varieties, Sauvignon Blanc stands head and shoulders above Chardonnay. Among reds, the race is more even between Zinfandel and Cabernet Sauvignon. The sad thing, from the point of view of Zinfandel fanciers, is that nowhere else does that grape grow nearly so well, while Cabernet does at least as well and perhaps better in several other zones in California. Still, current economics favour Cabernet to a degree that no farmer can ignore.

The valley heads north and west from Healdsburg, where Dry Creek flows into the Russian river. Plantings stop at Warm Springs Dam. The reservoir above drowned some good patches of Zinfandel; the hills above its shore have yet to be planted. The terrain further west is almost too wild to be cultivated. Italian immigrants planted the early vineyards. Italian names remain commonest among vineyard owners, but they are far from having a monopoly in the post-Zinfandel era. Dry Creek's most prominent wineries at the beginning of the 1990s were Dry Creek Vineyard, Ferrari-Carano, Quivira, J. Pedroncelli, and Preston Vineyards.

Knights Valley AVA
A small, handsome, upland valley in Sonoma County separates the upper end of the Napa Valley from the lower end of the Alexander Valley. It was originally developed by Beringer Vineyards, but now has several growers and one winery. The most impressive grape variety to date has been Cabernet Sauvignon. However, plantings date only from the early 1970s, and much exploratory work remains to be done.

Northern Sonoma AVA
This oddity of an AVA encompasses all of Sonoma that drains into the Pacific, which is to say all but Sonoma Valley; it was proposed and is mainly used by E. & J. GALLO, but has proven useful to a few others with scattered vineyards.

Russian River Valley AVA
Most of the Russian river's course is through other AVAs in MENDOCINO and Sonoma counties. Only when the valley widens and turns west from Healdsburg, in Sonoma County, do it and the Russian River Valley AVA become one and the same.

Cool, often foggy, it blossomed as a wine-growing region only after 1970, because Sonoma's first wave of vine-growers were Italian, and they taught their children not to plant Zinfandel, Carignane (*sic*), and Petite Sirah in wet, shadowy places. They were and are correct about those varieties, but it has taken the valley fewer than 20 years to prove itself eminently well adapted to still wines from Chardonnay and Pinot Noir as well as to sparkling wines from the same varieties. It appears to have a vocation for Gewürztraminer as well. Dehlinger, De Loach Vineyards, Iron Horse, Sonoma-

Cutrer, Rodney Strong Vineyards, and Williams & Selyem were some of the region's best-known wineries at the beginning of the 1990s.

Sonoma-Green Valley AVA
A sub-AVA of California's Russian River Valley AVA described above, Sonoma-Green Valley lies at the western edge of the larger region, and answers to all the same descriptions. Its best-known estate is Iron Horse.

Sonoma Coast AVA
This AVA stands out as a purely artifical construction. Its sponsors (including Sonoma-Cutrer) drew boundaries to include widely scattered vineyards so they could continue to describe their wines as ESTATE BOTTLED after tightened federal regulations began requiring that both winery and vineyard be within the same AVA to qualify. The AVA covers some otherwise excluded vineyards along Sonoma County's shore, but swings inland to encompass parts of the Russian river and Sonoma valleys, and Carneros.

Sonoma Mountain AVA
A sub-AVA of Sonoma Valley (see below) best known for Cabernet Sauvignon. It occupies east-facing slopes of a low, rolling range called the Sonoma Mountains above the towns of Glen Ellen and Kenwood.

Sonoma Valley AVA
For history, especially romantic history, no other AVA in California compares to the Sonoma Valley. In addition to being the seat of the first revolt against Spanish rule, it had the last of the Franciscan MISSIONARY vineyards, one of the earliest commercial vineyards north of San Francisco (General Mariano Vallejo appropriated the Franciscan plantings), and, courtesy of public relations master Agoston HARASZTHY, the first great winery name of northern California, Buena Vista. In more modern times, its Hanzell Vineyard started the rush to using French oak BARRELS to age California wines and thereby revolutionized their style, most especially Chardonnay's. The valley parallels the Napa Valley to the east, and nearly touches the Russian River Valley to the north west. Its southern tip doubles as the Sonoma portion of CARNEROS. A long, thin comma of a trough in the coast ranges, it warms markedly from south to north because San Francisco Bay's influence dwindles mile by mile. Steep hills on each side make it geologically as well as climatically complex. Some of its memorable wines portray that diversity: Zinfandel, Gewürztraminer, Pinot Noir, Chardonnay, and Cabernet Sauvignon. Sonoma Mountain (see above) is a sub-AVA. Sebastiani is the old-timer of the valley. Others of some fame during the 1980s and early 1990s included Ch St Jean, Hanzell Vineyard, Kenwood Vineyards, Landmark Vineyards, and Laurel Glen.

SOPRON, wine region in the extreme north west of HUNGARY which is geographically part of the Neusiedlersee wine regions of AUSTRIA. Its climate is much more temperate than that of most of the rest of Hungary, with cooler, wetter summers and milder winters. From the 14th century, when Hungary was recognized as a useful source of fuller, richer wines than those of northern Europe, Sopron was an important centre of the wine trade, dispatching not just its own wines but those of the rest of Hungary to Austria, Poland, and Silesia. Today Sopron produces mainly red wines, more tannic than the Hungarian norm, from grape varieties such as KÉKFRANKOS and Cabernet and Merlot.

SORBATES. See SORBIC ACID.

SORBIC ACID (2,4-hexadienoic acid), wine-making additive and preservative discovered in 1940 to inhibit the growth of YEAST and other fungi. Sorbic acid, or its salt potassium **sorbate**, is used widely in food and drink production to inhibit the growth of yeast and mould, notably in keeping cheeses and meats free of mould. It is classified as one of the safest food preservatives. Sorbic acid use has permitted the wide range of everyday commercial wines currently available which contain some RESIDUAL SUGAR but whose ALCOHOLIC STRENGTH alone is not sufficient to inhibit yeast metabolism.

There is a drawback, however. While most people detect about 135 mg/l, a small proportion of humans are sufficiently sensitive to sorbic acid to find about 50 mg/l in wines. It has a particular taste and a rancid odour to some palates, even at levels that are hardly high enough to inhibit yeast.

Sorbic acid inhibits the growth of some BACTERIA but not, unfortunately for wine-makers, the large group of LACTIC BACTERIA. SULPHUR DIOXIDE must be used together with sorbic acid in sweet wines that are low in alcohol in order to prevent the growth of lactic bacteria. Some of these lactics metabolize sorbates to produce compounds which smell of crushed geranium leaves—definitely a wine FAULT. A.D.W.

SORBITOL, one of the ALCOHOLS present in trace amounts in grapes and wines, and closely related to GLUCOSE. It has a mildly sweet taste, is very soluble in water and, when present in high concentrations, confers a sense of BODY on a liquid.

Since sorbitol can be made easily and cheaply from many agricultural raw materials, this property has been harnessed by a few unscrupulous wine bottlers to increase consumer acceptance of thin, acid, ordinary wines. Sorbitol is not harmful to humans but its use is prohibited by most wine regulations. A.D.W.

SORI is a PIEDMONTESE dialect term used for vineyard sites of the highest quality, particularly for those with an exceptional favourable southern exposure. More subtle variations also exist: a 'morning' sori (*sori de mattino*) with a south eastern exposure or an 'evening' sori (*sori de sera*) with a south western exposure. The term was first used on a wine label by Angelo GAJA for his Sori San Lorenzo Barbaresco 1967 and was widely imitated in the subsequent quarter-century. D.T.

SORTING of grapes. See TRIAGE.

SOUR ROT, a breakdown of mature grapes caused by a mixture of fungi, bacteria, and yeast which invades damaged berries. The fruit takes on the smell of vinegar, and juice from rotting berries can spread the infection, as can fruit fly. Common entry points for the mixture of microbes are bird pecks. Some organisms involved are the fungi *Aspergillus*, *Botryosphaeria*, *Cladosporium*, *Monilia*, *Penicillium*, and *Sclerotinia* and the yeast *Saccharomyces*. The rot is encouraged by rain and high humidity, and control relies on avoiding fruit damage as well as encouraging fruit aeration. R.E.S.

Pearson, R. C., and Goheen, A. C., *Compendium of Grape Diseases* (St Paul, Minn., 1988).

SOUSÃO, or **Souzão**, black grape variety widely planted in Portugal's Douro valley, where it is regarded as a useful, if slightly rustic, ingredient in PORT for its colour and obvious fruit character in youth. It has also been planted by aspirant makers of port style wines in California and Australia, with a certain degree of success.

SOUTH AFRICA, prolific southern hemisphere wine producer with a lustrous past and now bidding for fresh recognition. The famous Muscat-based dessert wines of CONSTANTIA seduced 18th century Europe at a time when names like LAFITE and Romanée-Conti (see DOMAINE DE LA ROMANÉE-CONTI) were still in the making. Then Constantias commanded fabulous prices, second only to Hungarian TOKAY. The two centuries since have, by comparison, been a disappointment, with the ordinary being too plentiful and the individual too rare, until the late 1980s, when the Cape began to shake off its political notoriety and vinous obscurity.

In one sense, the Cape (South Africa's vineyards are in the hinterland of the Cape of Good Hope) has been a vast distillery, draining a partly subsidized annual wine lake. The growers' body founded in 1918, the KWV (Co-operative Growers Association), until 1992 was legally empowered to determine quota limits, fix minimum prices, and predetermine production areas and limits—a system which tended to handicap the private wine producer and favour the bulk grape-grower. Under pressure, the KWV began to relinquish most of these powers in 1992, and set the stage for a much freer, livelier production scene in which bulk producers of low-quality wine will probably diversify into other products, while prospective new vine-growers may venture into completely new viticultural areas.

However, even more markedly than most wine industries, the Cape's can still be divided between the quantity-producing majority and the quality-conscious minority. More than half the annual harvest of about a million tons is destined for distillation or non-table wine products such as GRAPE SPIRIT and GRAPE CONCENTRATE. Grape prices have traditionally been based principally on sugar content, not instrinsic ripeness and grape condition. The focus on quantity is summed up in the old Afrikaans harvest refrain 'maak die bak vol' ('fill up the bin').

With just over one per cent of the world's vineyards, South Africa ranks about 20th in area under vines, but its annual output, at some 10 million hl/264 million gal makes it the world's eighth largest wine producer. Most vineyards are irrigated; there are no checks on yields, which rise to 20 tons/acre (about 350 hl/ha) along the Orange river (almost nine times as high as permitted for some French APPELLATION CONTRÔLÉE wines), although the national average is about 4.4 tons/acre (77 hl/ha). Of the 28 million vines, one-tenth are of the classic *vinifera* varieties; fewer than 100 of the nearly 5,000 grape-farmers produce their own wine.

The risks and discipline of cooler environments suited to classic, low-yielding varieties have been braved by those who represent the innovative side of the South African wine industry. Together with a few wholesale merchant-producers, such wine-growers began to revolutionize the Cape wine scene in the 1980s, picking up the baton dropped nearly 200 years previously at the eclipse of Constantia.

By the early 1990s South Africa produced around 3,500 wines across the style spectrum, from first-rate dry whites to deep flavoured, splendidly oaked, intense, tannic reds; feathery sparkling wines, including some made strictly in the image of champagne; and port and sherry types—all this representing a tenfold expansion of choice within a decade. It is still a chaotic renaissance on a broad scale—some call it a steeplechase into the unknown—and it flies in the face of declining consumption: a 21 per cent drop between 1970 and 1990, to 9 l per capita a year (making South Africans some of the world's less enthusiastic wine drinkers).

This scramble for excellence has confirmed the benefits of cooler sites and matching locality to grape varieties. The historic Constantia area has been rediscovered and replanted. Climatic conditions here and in newly pioneered areas such as Elgin, Walker Bay, and Mossel Bay (see below), all along the eastern seaboard, differ dramatically from those in the hot hinterland.

But Chenin Blanc, known as Steen, remains the farmers' favourite vine variety, making almost any and every style of white wine. Chenin Blanc makes up nearly one-third of all vines planted. It is the base of myriad sweetish wines locally called Stein, often sold by the 5-l BOX, a frequent fixture at barbecues.

Only 15 per cent of Cape vineyards produce red grapes, and only one bottle in eight sold is red. By the early 1990s, traditional, burly red blends featuring Cabernet Sauvignon, Shiraz, Cinsaut, Tinta Barocca, and the Cape's own crossing PINOTAGE were emphatically dethroned by scores of new, lighter, Bordeaux-style blends of Cabernet Sauvignon with Merlot and/or Cabernet Franc, the best of them beautifully oaked and packed with fruit and tannins.

A decade before, such reds were non-existent; nor had any champagne method sparkling wine or Chardonnay yet been made. By 1991 there were 33 classical sparkling wines, and the number of Chardonnays had rocketed to more than 100, an all-sorts lot ranging from the hugely alcoholic and over-oaked, to the pale and acid. But amidst this plethora were some significant hints of the Cape's potential to produce world-class Chardonnays, Sauvignon Blancs, and reds in the style of bordeaux.

Three landmark developments punctuated this comeback. First, the introduction of cold fermentation, tested as early as 1926 and put into practice in the 1950s, led to fresh, fruity, albeit still short-lived dry whites—a major quality leap from the previous stale parodies of serious table wines.

Next, in 1973, the government introduced Wine of Origin legislation, South Africa's answer to the APPELLATION CONTRÔLÉE system. Consumers quickly began to favour officially certified wines stating grape variety, vintage, region of origin.

Then in 1985 the first commercial barrel-fermented Chardonnay was made, by Backsberg Estate in Paarl. Now scores of wine-makers use French COOPERAGE for both reds and whites, and have mastered the technique of controlled MALOLACTIC FERMENTATION.

However, poor grape quality has hindered even greater progress. CANOPY MANAGEMENT, increased planting densities, and limited cropping rates are recent innovations. LEAFROLL, FANLEAF, and CORKY BARK viruses affect hundreds of vineyards (partly explaining the popularity of hardy bulk-producing grape varieties such as Cinsaut and Chenin Blanc).

While their counterparts elsewhere in the New World streaked ahead, South African government authorities were slow to release clean, virus-tested CLONES of the major classic vine varieties. Until the mid 1980s, only one, heavily diseased, Chardonnay clone was generally available; in desperation, some farmers smuggled in cuttings, some of them completely mislabelled as Chardonnay (see AUXERROIS). A government commission saw leading growers admitting guilt but defiant about their motives. The furore helped kick-start the authorities into improving their plant material programmes. But the first virus-free vineyards produced maiden wines only in the late 1980s.

A few fundamental natural handicaps exist. Apart from isolated CALCAREOUS outcrops, Cape soils tend to be excessively acid, requiring heavy LIME amendments, hefty tartaric acid adjustments to musts and wines, and severe TARTRATE removal procedures before bottling.

If great wines are made by their markets, the Cape has another disadvantage. Its core market is distant and small: 3 million whites in the Transvaal several days' drive to the north east of the Cape. Transporting wine from Cape Town 1,600 km / 1,000 miles to Johannesburg costs almost as much as container-shipping it to Europe.

The black majority, the elusive dream market of Cape wine producers, remains faithful to beer, and with an annual per capita consumption of more than 130 l is one of the world's top five beer markets, unmoved by a recent campaign for low alcohol flavoured wines. In the Cape Province, the traditional wine-drinking Coloured community is consuming less, partly due to political campaigns which condemn wine and rural alcoholism as 'enslavement', recalling the DOP system whereby workers on Cape wine farms were sometimes 'paid' in wine.

During the 1980s, anti-apartheid sanctions excluded Cape wine from most foreign markets. South African wine paid a dear price, but at least Cape growers were able to look before leaping at world-wide wine-making and marketing trends. But as sanctions were eased in the early 1990s, the industry found itself more competitive at the bottom end of the market than the top. High local inflation, an ailing rand, and the import costs of French barrels and winery and vineyard equipment, were factors, alongside the inefficiencies of years of protectionism and an under-trained, if under-paid, workforce. Denied the rigours and rewards of international competition for so long, the Cape wine industry is now sprinting to catch up with New World excellence, innovation, and aggressive marketing. In 1993 its wine exports to the UK overtook those of Chile and New Zealand.

History

The father of the South African wine industry was a 33-year-old Dutch surgeon intent on developing a cure for scurvy. Jan van Riebeeck, the Cape's first European settler, was a reluctant pioneer, and no viticulturist. But his brief was to set up a supply station for DUTCH EAST INDIA COMPANY sailors on the spice routes; and the Cape's MEDITERRANEAN CLIMATE suggested vines might well flourish.

Nine years after sailing into Table Bay on 6 April 1652, at the head of a ragtag mercenary band, he recorded: 'Today, praise be to God, wine was pressed for the first time from Cape grapes.' The cuttings came from 'somewhere in western France' according to Professor C. Orffer, South Africa's leading academic viticulturalist. Van Riebeeck's elation was understandable. The odds had been considerable. Hostile native Khoisan people torched the vineyards. Flocks of sparrows devoured the berries. Slaves were truculent. The Dutch burghers were oenologically ignorant.

The first wines were exceptionally astringent: useful only to 'irritate the bowels' wrote an early diarist. Dutch administrators in Batavia and Holland frequently rejected them. But conditions and quality improved when a new governor, Simon van der Stel, established the legendary 750-ha CONSTANTIA wine estate outside Cape Town in 1685. Three years later, 200 French Protestant Huguenot refugees—fleeing religious persecution after the revocation of the Edict of Nantes—brought welcome wine-making expertise to the Cape.

Constantia again became the focal point of the wine industry in 1778, when the estate was bought by a talented and ambitious grower, Hendrik Cloete. His Constantia dessert wines soon became the toast of European aristocracy. This heyday continued under British rule until 1861, when the Gladstone government removed empire preferential tariffs. French wines had only the Channel to cross to capture the British market; far-flung Cape colony products became uncompetitive.

PHYLLOXERA struck in 1886, adding a 20-year recuperation period to the industry's already unhealthy fortunes. Making up for lost time, growers had re-established some 80 million high-yielding vines such as Cinsaut by the early 1900s. A manageable flow swelled into a deluge; unsaleable wine was poured, literally, into local rivers.

This fuelled the formation in 1918 of the Cape Wine Growers' Co-operative (KWV), which was subsequently legally empowered to limit production and set minimum prices. Relative stability ensued, with the emphasis increasingly on BRANDY and FORTIFIED wines.

South Africa's winelands, as here at Stellenbosch, are some of the most beautiful in the world.

By the mid 1980s, regulations were eased to permit importation of improved vine cuttings, beginning the Cape's preoccupation with Chardonnays, bordeaux-style blends, and other classics. Two centuries after the golden age of Constantia, a renaissance had begun.

Burman, J., *Wine of Constantia* (Cape Town, 1979).
Leipold, C. L., *Three Hundred Years of Cape Wines* (Cape Town, 1952).
Oppermann, D. J. (ed.), *Spirit of the Vine* (Cape Town, 1968).

Climate and geography

It has been suggested that if South Africa jutted another 200 km/124 miles south into the Atlantic, the cooler climate would slow grape ripening and produce wines of greater elegance. Producers in the south of France may happily boast of their *'vins du soleil'*, but Cape growers are not keen to emphasize the intense African sunshine when describing their otherwise mediterranean climate. The Benguela current from Antactica makes the Cape cooler than its LATITUDE may suggest, however.

Long, hot summers from November to May are moderated by cold, wet, blustery winters, frequently with snowfalls on the higher mountains. Late frosts are rare; so are unseasonally heavy summer rains.

The winelands are widely dispersed throughout the Cape Province, some 700 km from north to south and 500 km across, strung between the Atlantic and Indian Oceans. Only three cellars, in the Orange Free State goldfields and the Transvaal bushveld, lie beyond. Climates and soils vary as dramatically as landscapes: mountains rear out of the sea, unfolding into lush valleys, sere drylands, and a series of inland mountain chains.

In the Stellenbosch region alone, just outside Cape Town, there are more than 50 soil types. On the hillsides, decomposing granite prevails. Soils tend to be high in acid with a predominance of clay (25 per cent and more), low in PH (4.5), but well drained and moisture retentive. The bulk of the harvest comes from hot, irrigated river valleys such as the Orange and Breede, where vineyards yield prodigiously. Around inland Robertson there are some calcareous lime-rich outcrops akin to the chalky soil of Burgundy's CÔTE D'OR. But in the cooler coastal areas, such soils must be man made with chemical additions.

Annual rainfall rises from 250 mm/9.7 in in the near-desert Little Karoo to 1,500 mm in the lee of the Worcester mountains, about 120 km inland from Cape Town. Growers supplementing this with IRRIGATION argue they merely make up the shortfall to reach the 900 mm annual rainfall of a vineyard in the Bordeaux region of France.

Average summer daily temperatures often exceed 23 °C/ 73 °F during the February and March harvest months, and maximum summer temperatures can scorch to nearly 40 °C. They tend to promote prolific crops, ripen grapes quickly, and can reduce flavour intensity. However, an increasing proportion of new, cooler vineyard sites are making this as questionable a generalization as the old belief that Cape vintage variations are insignificant.

A unique but mixed blessing is the frequent gale-force summer south easter, the 'Cape Doctor', that reduces humidity, mildew, and other FUNGUS DISEASES, but also sometimes batters vines.

Most wine regions would, according to the WINKLER scale, be classified Region III sites (as in Oakville, Napa Valley), IV (like Sydney and Florence), and some in V (Perth). But a number of areas experience cooler European (or Winkler II) conditions, especially in high-altitude or sea-cooled vineyards. New growth areas such as Walker Bay (on aerenaceous shale), Constantia (granite and sandstone), Elgin (shale), and Mossel Bay (decomposed granite 350 km north east of Cape Town, on the Indian Ocean) have stretched horizons and broadened the Cape's climatological repertoire.

Burger, J., and Deist, J., *Viticulture in South Africa* (Cape Town, 1981).

Wine regions

Constantia Fabled name in the annals of Cape wine (see CONSTANTIA), now a demarcated wine area in Cape Town's southern suburbs, on the slim peninsula pointing into the south Atlantic, cooled by the sea on two sides for relatively slow summer ripening with average daily temperatures of 18–19 °C, and very wet but moderate winters (average annual rainfall over 1,000 mm (39 in). Rich, loamy Table Mountain sandstone and decomposed granite soils nurture vigorous vines and even shy-bearing classic vines require ruthless SUMMER PRUNING and CROP THINNING. Here three vineyards have, since the mid 1980s, once again been producing classic wines from vineyards once part of the historic 750-ha Hendrik Cloete estate, since subdivided.

The government-owned Groot (Large) Constantia is the Cape's most popular historic tourist attraction, a classic example of thatched and gabled Cape Dutch architecture, with a modern winery alongside. Wine quality is improving after a run of uneven vintages and poor cooperage in the 1970s and 1980s. Two neighbours, German-owned Buitenverwachting, and Klein (Little) Constantia, both with new cellars and replanted vineyards, have spearheaded the renaissance. Klein Constantia has demonstrated its top New World calibre with showy and powerful Sauvignon Blanc, Chardonnay, and Cabernet Sauvignon. In 1991 it became the first modern Cape estate to resuscitate the ancient Constantia style with the release of a 1986 white Muscat of Frontignan (MUSCAT BLANC À PETITS GRAINS).

Stellenbosch Charming university town 45 km east of Cape Town, its Cape Dutch, Cape Georgian, and Victorian buildings shaded by ancient oaks, in the heart of the Cape winelands and traditionally home of the country's finest reds. After Constantia, it is the oldest wine region, established in 1769. The government Oenological and Viticultural Research Institute (OVRI), the STELLENBOSCH University Oenology Department, the Wine & Spirit Board, government experimental vineyards, the biggest wine wholesalers, Stellenbosch Farmers' Winery (SFW), and the Bergkelder (see above), with its 10,000-barrel maturation cellars, are all here, surrounded by valleys of vines and the soaring blue-grey mountains of Stellenbosch, Simonsberg, and Helderberg. Soils and climate vary, from sandy alluvial loam along the valley floors and river courses to deep, moisture-retaining decomposed granite on the hillsides. The climate is tempered by the Atlantic sweeping into False Bay, a 15-minute drive from the town. Average daily summer temperatures are about 20 °C.

Although best known for Cabernet Sauvignon, Merlot, Shiraz, and Pinotage, Stellenbosch produces a host of wine types including port style wines and some excellent Chardonnays and Sauvignon Blancs. Stellenbosch returns lower average yields than hotter, more extensively irrigated inland regions. It is the source of only about 13 per cent of the country's total wine production although it boasts the greatest concentration of leading estates, an extensive wine route network, and scores of restaurants. Estates and vineyards particularly famous for red wines include Rustenberg, Kanonkop, Rust-en-Vrede, Overgaauw, Le Bonheur, Uitkyk, Alto, Meerlust, Vriesenhof. Others with a wider range include Neethlingshof, Delheim, Simonsig, Thelema, Blaauwklippen. Associated with this area are the original DUTCH EAST INDIA COMPANY farms of Durbanville on the northern outskirts of Cape Town.

Paarl Paarl means pearl in Afrikaans and houses the headquarters of the South African wine industry. The Co-operative Growers' Association (KWV) handles the annual surplus, producing port-like fortified wines, brandies, and other spirits (gin, vodka) and liqueurs (including the mandarin-flavoured Van der Hum). Paarl's latitude, 33.4 degrees south—JEREZ in Spain is on a similar northern latitude—is cited as a reason for the quality of South Africa's SOLERA-system FLOR sherry style wines, first made by the KWV in the 1940s. Paarl is a warm region. A few well-known estates market a spectrum of wines, reds and whites of the classic varieties, sparkling wines, port style wines, and recently even estate-matured brandies. The region reaches north into Tulbagh (sometimes considered a separate district) and Wellington and east toward Franschhoek (meaning 'French corner'), home of the first French Huguenot settlers. The best-known estates include Backsberg, Fairview, Boschendal, L'Ormarins, La Motte, Clos Cabriere, Glen Carlou, Villiera. The biggest producer of fine wines is Nederburg, with a comprehensive range of 40 labels; it produced the Cape's first BOTRYTIZED wine, labelled Noble Late Harvest, from Chenin Blanc in 1969.

Worcester Extensive, fertile vineyard area, delivering 20 to 25 per cent of the national crop, mainly bulk varieties for

DISTILLATION OF FORTIFICATION. Generally hot, heavily irrigated, served by numerous co-operatives beyond the Du Toitskloof mountains. A number of aromatic white table wines from Colombard and Chenin Blanc are popular for everyday early drinking. The Worcester region is the home of many a national champion fortified red and white MUSCADEL and dessert HANEPOOT.

Robertson Hot, dry region of many estates and co-operatives growing almost exclusively whites, including bold Chardonnays. Most vineyards fringe the Breede river, which provides irrigation and alluvial soils. Some calcium-rich outcrops are found, which explain the region's predominance as a racehorse stud centre, the pastures being considered ideal for strong bone formation. The many enterprising, prize-winning, close-knit growers here are typically members of the Robertson Wine Trust. Lovely Muscats, including fortified Muscadels, Gewürztraminers, off-dry Colombards, and burly Chardonnays, are produced but memorable Sauvignon Blanc was slow to emerge. Best-known estates include De Wetshof, Weltevrede, Van Loveren (all whites), Graham Beck (sparkling wines), and Zandvliet (Shiraz). Robertson produces about 10 per cent of the national harvest. Average daily growing season temperatures are about 22 °C, while rainfall is less than 400 mm annually.

Olifantsriver Chiefly bulk grape-producing region among mountains and along the Atlantic western seaboard, the majority of whose growers supply large co-operatives with wine for distillation. South Africa's biggest single winery, the progressive Vredendal Co-operative, vinifies more than 40,000 tons of grapes annually.

Orange River Hottest, most northerly, and most recently established (in the 1960s) of South Africa's wine regions, producing nearly 12 per cent of the national crop. Bulk wines, huge yields—40 tons per ha or 140 hl/ha are common—thanks to irrigation schemes.

Klein Karoo Inland, semi-desert ostrich- and sheep-farming area. A few enterprising estates here such as Boplaas are making hearty port style wines and fortified Muscadels, as well as some dry table wines.

Mossel Bay Small, new area with promising cool vineyards. South Africa's most southerly wine region fronting the Indian Ocean, almost outside the MEDITERRANEAN CLIMATE area with its winter rainfall, producing individual white wines made from Sauvignon Blanc and Rhine Riesling. Pinot Noir is also planted.

Walker Bay Southerly, relatively cool maritime vineyards producing among South Africa's most promising wines made from the Burgundy grapes Chardonnay and Pinot Noir, from Hamilton Russell Vineyards and Bouchard-Finlayson, the first French–South African joint venture (in this case with Paul Bouchard of Bouchard Aîné et Fils of Burgundy).

Elgin Cool, high vineyards in apple orchard country west of Cape Town. A recently designated wine region whose early vintages of Sauvignon Blanc showed intense individuality. Hopes are also high for Pinot Noir here.

Hughes, D., and Hands, P., *Complete Book of South African Wine* (Cape Town, 1988).
Knox, G., *Estate Wines of South Africa* (Cape Town, 1982).
Platter, J., *John Platter's South African Wine Guide* (Stellenbosch, annually).

Viticulture

The stark contrast between the traditional and the progressive in South African viticulture, often visible on adjoining farms, reflects the disparate objectives of growers. The bulk grape-farmer delivering to one of the less progressive co-operatives strives for quantity; the grower bottling his own crop knows quantity can be the enemy of quality.

The tractor, trellising, wide planting spaces, and chemical pest and weed control became common features by the 1960s, but on some farms vineyard workhorses could still be seen drawing simple tilling implements between traditional, densely planted rows of untrellised BUSH VINES planted only 1.2 m/4 ft apart to a density of 7,000 vines per ha (2,800 per acre), similar to many French vineyards.

In the 1990s quality wine producers have put the horses out to pasture but are swinging back to close planting; more restrained ORGANIC and biological pest controls; careful CLONAL SELECTION; painstaking SOIL PREPARATION that can involve additions of up to 16 tons of lime per ha to achieve higher pH, calcium-balanced soils; and pruning for lower yields.

The national average crop, nearly 4.4 tons/acre (77 hl/ha), climbs to highs of 16 and 20 tons in some areas. Average planting densities are around 3,300 vines per ha. Yields in cooler, coastal climates are appreciably lower; about 2.8 or 3.2 tons/acre for Cabernet Sauvignon and Chardonnay are considered consistent with quality in Cape conditions. Yields from hundreds of virus-infected vineyards can drop to below 1.6 tons/acre.

Most vineyards (outside Paarl, Stellenbosch, and the coastal areas) are IRRIGATED in summer, with overhead sprays or fixed sprinkler systems supplying individual vines, a typical regime delivering 200 to 700 mm/7.8–27.3 in of extra moisture a year in evenly spaced intervals. Producers who do not water make a marketing feature of wines from 'dryland vineyards'.

Mechanical harvesters were introduced by some leading large growers in the late 1980s.

The most common trellising system is a simple vertical 'hedge row' developed from a split vine cordon, supported by a wire raised about 750 mm/2.4 ft for ease of pruning. The summer foliage is trained upright in a canopy held by one or more wires above the cordon. Short-SPUR PRUNING is commonly practised (eight to 10 spurs, four to five on each cordon, pruned back to two or three buds each).

Most vine diseases and pests found their way from the northern hemisphere long ago. Chemical pesticides are in wide use—the ladybird, a natural predator of the dreaded MEALY BUG, is increasingly rare—though farmers are now encouraged by the government Oenological and Viticultural Research Institute (OVRI) to experiment with INTEGRATED PEST MANAGEMENT programmes, emphasizing biological and physical measures and minimizing the use of insecticides. Baboons are also a pest in several areas.

POWDERY MILDEW, locally called 'white rust', is the most serious common disease. DOWNY MILDEW poses a seasonal threat. Both are containable by systemic fungicides. BOTRYTIS is not a serious problem most years, and is welcomed by growers specializing in dessert wines.

Cape vineyards were decimated by PHYLLOXERA from 1886 and virtually all vines are grafted on to resistant American ROOTSTOCKS, mainly Richter 99 and 110.

Virus-infected vines are widespread, shortening the productive lifespans of vineyards. Affected vines succumb to LEAFROLL, CORKY BARK, and FANLEAF, inhibiting PHOTOSYNTHESIS and ripening, diminishing yields but not improving grape quality.

From the mid 1980s, heat-treated, virus-tested plant material was more freely available, along with a greater selection of imported clones of classic varieties. Healthier vineyards are the result, but scientists warn the virus will eventually affect these too, although more slowly. Virus-free Cabernet Sauvignon vineyards planted with Schleip clone 163 ripen in mid February, four to six weeks earlier than diseased vineyards, and at higher sugar levels.

Although some smaller wineries have begun to specialize, most wine farms grow a fruit salad of grape types. Their different ripening periods conveniently space out the harvest but amaze foreign visitors, unused to encountering the whole gamut of Bordeaux, Burgundy, Alsace, Loire, and Rhône varieties on a single estate.

Developing a significant pattern of regional/varietal characteristics is Cape viticulture's current challenge.

Burger, J., and Deist, J., *Viticulture in South Africa* (Cape Town, 1981).

Wine-making

Although wine-making in South Africa remains in a state of flux and experimentation, at some point in the 1980s, almost in the twinkling of an eye, the small French BARRIQUE transformed the face and taste of top Cape wines. Stainless steel, cement, and fibreglass tank vinification still styles the vast output of wine, but the boom in Chardonnays and bordeaux-style reds reflects investments in OAK by numerous cellars, from large bulk wine co-operatives to small estate operations. French oak leads the field but American and Yugoslav barrels are used too.

Most premium-quality producers now renew their barrels regularly and BARREL FERMENTATION is increasingly common. A new confidence with LEES-enriched wines, delicately handled, minimally sulphured, lightly filtered, often with MALOLACTIC FERMENTATION completed, has become part of Cape cellar practice. Occasionally red wines are bottled without tartrate or cold STABILIZATION by those sufficiently confident, or brazen enough, to seek consumer indulgence about bottled CRYSTALS. Increasingly wine-makers are abandoning the clinical, no-risks, mass-production techniques learned at South Africa's oenological institutes, and based on the German rather than French ethos. The old cultural and linguistic imperatives have given way to a new adventurism. Afrikaans speakers who in the past furthered their studies in Germany, where the language barrier was more easily overcome, now seek inspiration from France and the New World; many spend the Cape's quiet season working in Bordeaux and Burgundy and exchange agreements with French houses have been concluded by a few Cape growers.

Gleaming giant automatic rotating tanks and presses, computer programmed to link temperatures to DENSITY levels and fermentation speeds, are now common. But fresh, fruity, cold-fermented dry whites are a relatively recent South African development. The first successful experiments with REFRIGERATION date back to the 1920s, but cold fermentation only became common in the 1960s. Though more necessary for whites, many wineries cool their reds too to hold them at 25 °C or even below during fermentation. A recent popular innovation has been the 'mash cooler', which pumps crushed grapes through cooling coils immediately after destemming, lowering temperatures by up to 10 °C (grapes are often harvested well in excess of 30 °C). A few farmers pick at night, using miners' headgear, to achieve the same objective.

But long after the advent of cold fermentation, cellar technology remained essentially geared to processing bulk wines. Completed fermentation prompted an immediate RACKING, sulphuring, and brisk clean-up, ACID ADJUSTMENT, protein and cold STABILIZATION, and sterile FILTRATION. Reds were seldom left on their skins after fermentation; the usual method was to draw off juice and press the grapes even before fermentation was complete.

Malolactic fermentation in reds was still a hit and miss affair into the 1970s; only cellars equipped with sterile filtration could guarantee 'safe' bottlings. Red wines low in extract and high in alcohol were common. By the early 1990s, however, all the better wineries were familiar with monitoring or inducing malolactic fermentation, and Chardonnay producers became adept at manipulating it to achieve individual styles. Cape wine producers benefited from California and general New World experiences, quickly passing through the phase of predominantly heavy, alcoholic, and obviously over-oaked Chardonnays and aiming at finer, fruitier, lightly wooded wines.

But in general, heavy irrigation, high yields, a hot climate, and low pH soils still produce musts that are low in ACIDITY from the majority of commercial vineyards, requiring TARTARIC ACID additions most years.

Many growers argue against the national ban on ENRICHMENT, saying sugar adjustments would result in more balanced musts and wines because grapes could be harvested earlier when in healthier condition, at lower pHs and with higher natural acids. But local authorities, mindful of export requirements and EUROPEAN UNION strictures, have remained deaf to such demands.

Platter, J., *John Platter's South African Wine Guide* (Stellenbosch, annually).

Vine varieties

In South Africa, a vine variety is known as a cultivar, and South Africa is a cultivar-conscious wine country. Regional wine characteristics are still insufficiently well defined to challenge grape variety as the determining factor for quality, style, and even labelling and marketing of a wine.

White varieties constitute some 85 per cent of Cape vineyards. Chenin Blanc, known as Steen, is the most widely planted with about 30 per cent of the total area. From the 1980s Sauvignon Blanc and Chardonnay boomed (although Sauvignon Blanc was widely planted in the 19th century), but together they made up little more than six per cent of the country's total vine plantings by 1991. Other major white grapes include, in decreasing quantity: Colombar(d), Cape Riesling (see CROUCHEN), Clairette Blanche, Sémillon, Ugni Blanc, BUKETTRAUBE, (Weisser) Riesling, Gewürztraminer, as well as various Muscats. Muscat of Alexandria, locally known as Hanepoot, doubles as a table grape. White and a mutant red MUSCADEL (Muscat Blanc à Petits Grains) remain important for fortified wines. Cape crossings Chenel and Weldra, both from Chenin Blanc and Ugni Blanc, have not caught on, producing wine so neutral it is suitable only for brandy.

Highest-priced reds are Cabernet Sauvignon and the bordeaux-styled blends including Merlot and/or Cabernet Franc which proliferated from the early 1980s. Syrah (Shiraz in South Africa) is popular, on its own and blended. Pinot Noir has been generally disappointing but new clones are being tried. Gamay has begun to make a modest impact in its Beaujolais-styled CARBONIC MACERATION mode. PINOTAGE, the Cape's own crossing of Pinot Noir and Cinsaut, has produced mostly brash, pungent reds but the grape has its enthusiasts.

For most of this century, high-yielding Cinsaut was the most widely planted red, but it is gradually declining in importance. There are small vineyards of Grenache, Carignan, Zinfandel, Ruby Cabernet, and some port varieties, most commonly Tinta Barroca, often made into a dry red. PONTAC is a South African speciality, on a minuscule scale.

Other varieties planted to a considerable extent but used principally for blending, fortified wines, distillation, or grape concentrate are all white berried and include Palomino and Sultana (of which there were more than 8,000 ha of each in 1990); an undistinguished Midi variety called Servin, Servan, or Raisin Blanc; a rot-prone South African speciality known variously as Canaan, Kanaän, or Belies; and Pedro Luis or False Pedro.

Orffer, C. J., *Wine Grape Cultivars in South Africa* (Cape Town, 1979).
Pongracz, D. P., *Practical Viticulture* (Cape Town, 1978).

Wine of Origin and labelling

Wine of Origin (WO) legislation introduced in 1973 ended decades of a labelling free-for-all in which confused South African wine nomenclature and unverified vintage and grape variety claims baffled the consumer. A wine may be 'certified' for any of the following: region or ward of origin, vintage, grape variety.

Blended wines qualify for a varietal statement provided the variety makes up at least 75 per cent of the blend; and at least 75 per cent comes from one harvest. The balance may come from the preceding or subsequent year. Blends which do not claim single varietal status may state the grape composition.

Participation is voluntary and only about 10 per cent of Cape bottled wine is certified. Non-certified wine is liable to spot-check analysis for health requirements.

Wine for certification is submitted to the government-appointed Wine & Spirit Board. The wine must pass an analytical test and is blind tasted by a panel which may reject wines judged faulty or atypical, and often does.

A controversial Superior rating, awarded if the panel scored the wine 7.5 or more out of nine, was abandoned in 1990. Superiors were allowed to flaunt gold neck seals, while regular WO sported black and white ones. Bright stripes—red for vintage, blue for area, green for variety—added to the gaudiness of what locals dub the 'bus-ticket' that decorated WO bottles. From 1993, a smaller, more discreet monochrome seal without stripes was phased in.

The designation 'Estate' is the Cape's equivalent of the French Château, or Domaine. All the wine must originate from and be fermented at a registered, demarcated estate. The definition of an estate is loose. Two vineyards owned and operated by one proprietor may be miles apart but their crops can be blended and qualify for a single estate label, provided the authorities deem the 'ecological circumstances' similar. Wine can be barrel matured and bottled at a different establishment without losing its estate status—not strictly the MIS EN BOUTEILLE *au château* idea.

Wines may state a single origin but be blends of the products of several regions. The authorities have merged, on paper, various wine-growing areas. Parts of the Coastal Region, stretching for nearly 400 km, are far from the sea. Local wags call this the Wine of Mixed Origin system.

South Africa meets requirements on prohibition of additives, and for labelling, which must state the ALCOHOLIC STRENGTH (from 1992) to within half a per cent. Champagne method Cape sparkling wine is not labelled Champagne but Méthode Cap Classique, even locally, nor is FLOR yeast fortified wine matured in a SOLERA system exported as Sherry.

Although the WO regulations borrow from France and Germany, there are no rulings on crop YIELDS, fertilizer quantities, or IRRIGATION levels. Chaptalization and all other forms of ENRICHMENT are banned. ACIDIFICATION is permitted.

See also South African BRANDY. J.P.

SOUTH AFRICAN RIESLING. See CAPE RIESLING.

SOUTH AMERICA, the world's second most important wine-producing continent, after Europe, with ARGENTINA being by far the biggest producer, followed by BRAZIL and CHILE. Other, relatively minor, wine producers are, in descending order of importance, URUGUAY, PERU, BOLIVIA, and also ECUADOR and VENEZUELA. See also the important North American wine producer MEXICO. Spain and, in some parts, Portugal were important influences in the 16th and 17th centuries, although more recently France, Italy, and the United States have helped to shape South America's wine industries.

History

The famous late 15th century European voyages of discovery, notably to the Americas, were followed by migrations of European settlers there, associated with substantial movement of animals and plants between the two continents. Although indigenous varieties of vine grew in Central America (see VITIS), there is no evidence that the Aztecs made wine from them, and it was thus with the arrival of the Spanish conquistadores in the 16th century that vine cultivation and wine-making were first introduced to the region. Mexico was the first part of the continent to witness the introduction of European VINIFERA vines, and as early as 1522 Cortés is recorded as having sent for vine cuttings from Spain. Moreover, by 1524 the planting of vines was a condition of *repartimiento* grants, through which the Spaniards were granted land and labour on the foundation of Mexico City. From Mexico, the spread of viticulture followed swiftly on the heels of Spanish conquests.

Vines were planted in Peru soon after Pizarro's defeat of the Incas between 1531 and 1534, and within 20 years Spanish commentators described vineyards producing a substantial quantity of grapes. Some of the earliest Peruvian vines appear to have been introduced from the CANARY ISLANDS, whereas others seem to have been derived from the seeds of dried grapes brought from Spain. From Peru, viticulture and wine-making then spread south to Chile and Argentina, where vines were cultivated as early as the mid 1550s, although there were even earlier experimental plantings on Argentina's coast. See also MONKS AND MONASTERIES.

The traditional explanation for the rapidity of this spread was that the Spanish conquerors required a ready supply of wine for the EUCHARIST, and that monks therefore played a central role in establishing vineyards. There is, however, little evidence to support this view, and most of the early vineyards and attempts to produce wine were on secular estates. Economic factors, such as the cost of importing wine and the difficulties of transporting it overland, meant that the early Spanish conquerors had a very real interest in establishing vineyards if they wished to continue to consume the main alcoholic beverage that they had known in Iberia. In particular, the long sea voyage across the Atlantic, followed by an overland haul across Panama, and then a further voyage down the Pacific coast, meant that most wine reaching Peru and Chile from the Iberian peninsula was likely to have been of poor quality.

By the end of the 16th century, Spanish restrictions on wine production in 'New Spain', designed to protect the metropolitan wine producers and merchants in Iberia, served to limit further secular development of viticulture in Mexico, but they also appear to have provided an incentive to Peruvian producers, who rapidly became the dominant wine suppliers to the region as a whole. Subsequently, in the 17th century, Jesuit MISSIONS along the coastal valleys of Peru became the most important centres of viticulture in the region. P.T.H.U.

Blij, H. de, *Wine Regions of the Southern Hemisphere* (Totowa, NJ, 1985).

Dickenson, J., and Unwin, T., *Viticulture in Colonial Latin America: Essays on Alcohol, the Vine and Wine in Spanish America and Brazil* (Liverpool, 1992).

Hyams, E., *Dionysus: A Social History of the Wine Vine* (London, 1965).

SOUTH AUSTRALIA, *the* wine state in AUSTRALIA.

At a little under 60 per cent, South Australia's contribution to the annual CRUSH may have fallen from its high point of 75 per cent in the 1940s and 1950s, but it still dominates the country's wine output. Vine-growing is a major contributor to South Australia's gross domestic production, yet occupies only a small percentage of the state's vast land mass. It is concentrated in the south eastern corner, much of it within an hour's drive of the capital Adelaide. The two outposts are the Riverland sprawling along the Murray river; and Coonawarra and nearby Padthaway 325 km/200 miles south east of Adelaide, not far from the border with VICTORIA.

The **Barossa Valley**, an hour north of Adelaide, vies with the Hunter Valley as Australia's best-known wine region. Italian immigrants (in the Riverlands), Dalmatians (in the Swan Valley of WESTERN AUSTRALIA), and Swiss (Yarra Valley and Geelong in Victoria) all played key roles in the establishment of viticulture elsewhere, but in the Barossa and Clare valleys it was the Germans, and to this day the Germanic influence is everywhere to be seen—in the town names, the Lutheran churches, the stone buildings, and in the names of the leading families.

It should come as no surprise to find that RIESLING should be (and always has been) the most favoured white wine grape, even if its still dominant plantings are increasingly moving from the valley floor to the hills of the **East Barossa Ranges**. This shift reflects two things: first, the warm climate of the valley floor, more suited to red wine production; second, a fundamental reappraisal of the function of the Barossa Valley proper. For decades vine plantings shrank while production soared, not because of increased yields, but because the Barossa Valley wineries process a major part of the grapes grown in the Riverland, Coonawarra, Padthaway, Southern Vales, and Langhorne Creek.

Most of Australia's largest companies are based here. The presence of PENFOLDS, and the creation of its masterwork Grange Hermitage, embody the glory of the Barossa Valley: substantial plantings of SHIRAZ dating as far back as 1860, dry farmed (no IRRIGATION) and BUSH pruned, typically yielding 0.9 tons/acre (16 hl/ha) of inky, dark purple essence. There is still twice as much Shiraz grown in the Barossa as there is CABERNET SAUVIGNON, a situation likely to continue.

While the Barossa Valley has over 40 wineries within its precincts, the **Southern Vales** (which incorporate **McLaren Vale**), 45 minutes due south of Adelaide, has a greater number still and is often called the home of the small winery. These wineries represent a mixture of the old and the new, thus reflecting the dynamics which have operated here no less than in the Barossa Valley.

At the northern end, urban sprawl has swallowed up many once-substantial vineyards, and encircles the few remaining plantings at Reynella. However, the southern end of the fashionably cool and increasingly important **Adelaide Hills** to the east, the open plains of McLaren Vale, and the hills of the **Fleurieu Peninsula** offer abundant suitable land for the continuing new plantings.

This is a strongly maritime-influenced region, with considerable variation in MESOCLIMATE. Once famous for its supposedly iron-rich red wines exported to England under the Emu and Glenloth labels and prescribed by (surely enlightened) physicians around the turn of the century as tonics, the emphasis is now as much on melon- and citrus-tinged CHARDONNAY, pungent gooseberry SAUVIGNON Blanc, full flavoured Riesling and SEMILLON, as it is on gutsy Shiraz and Cabernet Sauvignon. The high quality of the grapes, and hence the wines, is better understood by the industry than by the public, and (as with neighbour **Langhorne Creek**) much of the production ends up in regional blended wines, the labels of which may or may not show the composition of that blend.

The twins of **Coonawarra** and **Padthaway** in the far south east of the state are generally recognized as producing Australia's finest Cabernet Sauvignon (Coonawarra) and some of its best Chardonnay, Sauvignon Blanc, and Riesling. Both are cool regions (Coonawarra is the cooler of the two) with considerable LIMESTONE, and an extensive underground water-table.

While vines were first planted in Coonawarra in 1890 (by John Riddoch), for all practical purposes both regions dated from the early 1960s. This explains why both areas are exclusively planted to premium grape varieties, and why the major wine companies are the dominant landholders (there is only one small winery in Padthaway, a dozen or so in Coonawarra). It is the belief of some critics that the viticultural practices adopted by the major companies have in fact prevented either region from reaching its full potential: near total MECHANIZATION and maximum YIELDS make for attractive economics, but not for the best grapes. It is a tribute to the inherent quality of each region, and to a few winemakers and flagship brands, that the wines have such a high reputation.

The **Clare Valley**, just to the north west of the Barossa Valley, is one of the unspoilt jewels of South Australia. The narrow, twisting folds of the hills provide an intimacy in total contrast to the flat, featureless plain of Coonawarra. Like the Barossa Valley, it is steeped in history, with splendid stone buildings and wineries. For reasons unknown, its moderately warm climate produces Australia's finest Riesling (challenged only by that of the **Eden Valley** in the Barossa Ranges), a fragrant yet steely wine which ages superbly, taking on the aroma of lightly browned toast with a twist of lime as it ages.

Most of the 25 or so wineries are small; almost all produce Riesling, Shiraz, and Cabernet Sauvignon, the red wines being intensely coloured, deep flavoured, and long lived, often with a skein of eucalypt mint running through them. MALBEC also flourishes here as nowhere else, used as a blend component with Cabernet Sauvignon (sometimes with a dash of Shiraz thrown in for good measure).

Finally, there is the **Riverland**, stretching along the mighty **Murray river** from Waikerie to Renmark, producing 55 per cent of South Australia's total crush and over 30 per cent of the nation's. Most of this is of white wine destined for casks (see BOXES) or for sale in bulk to overseas markets. The Riverlands are still strongholds for Muscat (Gordo Blanco MUSCAT OF ALEXANDRIA), SULTANA, and DORADILLO, and even in Australia one cannot make silk purses out of sow's ears. J.H.

SOUTH COAST, name loosely defining vineyards close to the CALIFORNIA coast from Los Angeles southwards to the Mexican border. TEMECULA has the only substantial vineyards within the region. San Diego County's SAN PASQUAL also falls within it.

SOUTHCORP, holding company of the PENFOLDS Wine Group.

SOUTHERN RHÔNE. See RHÔNE.

SOUTHERN VALES, important wine region in AUSTRALIA. For more detail see SOUTH AUSTRALIA.

SOUTH WEST FRANCE, recognized region within FRANCE which incorporates all of the wine districts in the south western quarter of the country with the exception of BORDEAUX and COGNAC. This means in effect all of the upriver wines once regarded as serious commercial rivals by the Bordelais (most notably Bergerac, Monbazillac, Côtes de Duras, Cahors, Buzet, Côtes du Frontonnais, and Gaillac travelling away from and roughly clockwise round Bordeaux) together with those made in GASCONY and BASQUE country (Côtes de St-Mont, Madiran, Pacherenc du Vic-Bilh, Jurançon, Béarn, and Irouléguy).

Few generalizations can be made about such an extensive area, except that the climate is heavily influenced by the Atlantic.

The vine was cultivated in most of these districts in the Roman era (see FRANCE and GAUL) but wine-making was developed only under the medieval influence of MONKS AND MONASTERIES. During the CRUSADES some of these areas came under direct English protection.

The history of the first group of wines has been heavily influenced, nay hampered, by the commercial muscle of protectionist Bordeaux. The fact that these wines were made up river of but outside Bordeaux in the 'high country', or HAUT PAYS, meant that they were penalized at their exit port, and the HUNDRED YEARS WAR was to have an everlasting effect on their trading history, opening the door for the DUTCH WINE TRADE to take the place of once-powerful ENGLAND. The commercial progress of wines from the second group was long hindered by the difficulty of navigating the Adour RIVER down to the port of Bayonne, and by competition with other crops.

The grape varieties grown in the first group of wine districts is generally very similar to the ENCÉPAGEMENT of Bordeaux, while the southern districts can boast one of the most exciting collections of local vine varieties in Europe, including the likes of ABOURIOU, BAROQUE, DURAS, FER (Servadou), LEN DE L'EL, MANSENG, MAUZAC, NÉGRETTE, RUFFIAC, TANNAT, JURANÇON Noir, and PETIT COURBU. Culturally, Gascony is one of the proudest and greediest regions of France; the region needs wines to drink with *foie gras*, duck, and goose.

For more details see the individual entries for all the APPELLATION CONTRÔLÉE wines BÉARN, BERGERAC, BUZET, CAHORS, Côtes de DURAS, Côtes du FRONTONNAIS, Côtes du MARMANDAIS, GAILLAC, IROULÉGUY, JURANÇON, MADIRAN, MARCILLAC, MONBAZILLAC, PACHERENC DU VIC-BILH, PÉCHARMANT, ROSETTE, and SAUSSIGNAC. See also the VDQS wines, some of them produced in only very small quantities, Côtes de ST-MONT, Côtes du BRULHOIS, LAVILLEDIEU, TURSAN, Vins d'ENTRAYGUES, and Vins d'ESTAING. See also LIMOUX.

George, R., *French Country Wines* (London, 1990).

SOUTIRAGE, French term for RACKING, or moving clear wine off its sediment and into a clean container. It can also be used for the wine serving process of DECANTING.

SOVIET SPARKLING WINE is a specific term which, in tune with EUROPEAN UNION law, replaced the term Soviet champagne, or *champanskoe*, in the early 1990s. Although bottle-fermented sparkling wines have been made in what has variously been called Russia, the Soviet Union, and, more recently, the CIS since the 18th century, consumer demand for sparkling wine was most notably demonstrated at the end of the 19th century, when the imperial court of Tsar Nicholas II regularly imported 800,000 bottles of, usually sweet, CHAMPAGNE. (The late 19th century Champenois defined champagne sweetened to satisfy the *goût russe* as one with 273 to 330 g/l of RESIDUAL SUGAR, as opposed to the *goût anglais* of 22 to 66 g/l for the English.)

High import taxes led to the development of a domestic industry initially constructed on base wines imported from France in barrel, made sparkling according to champagne production techniques. This led to the development of vigorous sparkling wine industries based on grapes grown in the CRIMEA and around Odessa in UKRAINE, where Henri ROEDERER of Rheims established a Franco-Russian sparkling winery in 1896.

Today about 15 per cent of all Soviet sparkling wine is made by the CHAMPAGNE METHOD of provoking a second fermentation in bottle, officially followed by three years' TIRAGE. A substantial proportion is made by second fermentation in tank, the so-called CHARMAT method, while another popular method, perfected in the CIS, is the Russian CONTINUOUS METHOD, by which sparkling wine is made continuously under pressure, rather than in batches. The most important centres of production are in RUSSIA, and in Ukraine, where sparkling wines represent an even higher proportion of the republic's total wine output. Some 1993 estimates put annual production of Soviet sparkling wine at 240 million bottles a year, about the same as the total annual output of Champagne.

For more details of individual methods, see SPARKLING WINE-MAKING.

SOVIET UNION, the Union of Soviet Socialist Republics which, following the fall of communism, fragmented into its 16 constituent republics. In the early 1990s, most of them regrouped as the CIS. See also RUSSIA, MOLDOVA, UKRAINE, CRIMEA, GEORGIA, KAZAKHSTAN, AZERBAIJAN, UZBEKISTAN, ARMENIA, KYRGYZSTAN, TAJIKISTAN, and TURKMENISTAN.

SPACING of vines. See VINE DENSITY.

SPAIN, country with the most land under vine in the world (about half as much again as both France and Italy) and yet only the world's third most important producer of wine. Thanks to Spain's arid climate, and ban on IRRIGATION, about 1.4 million ha/3.5 million acres of vines yield only about 35 million hl/924 million gal of wine a year. Spain's exceptionally low average YIELDS, of about 25 hl/ha (1.4 tons/acre), reflect the extreme physical conditions in much of central Spain, where DROUGHT is a persistent problem (see below).

Spain occupies most of the Iberian peninsula and is the third largest country in Europe, extending from the Pyrenees that form the frontier with France in the north to the Strait of Gibraltar just 15 km/9 miles from Africa to the south. Spain is a diverse country with distinct regional and cultural differences. In recognition of this, the 1978 Constitution divides Spain into 16 autonomous regions and one principality (Asturias), each with their own regional seat of government. The autonomous communities are further subdivided into provinces, of which there are fifty in all. The national capital is Madrid, located roughly in the centre of the country. The principal language spoken throughout Spain is Castilian, although CATALONIA, GALICIA, and BASQUE country have their own regional tongues, which are now generally used within those regions in preference to Castilian.

The country's regional diversity is reflected in her wines, which range from light, dry whites in the cool Atlantic region of Galicia to heavy, alcoholic reds in the Levante and the Mediterranean south. ANDALUCÍA in the south west is known for the production of fortified and dessert wines, the most famous of which is SHERRY.

Spain is a significant beneficiary of recent improvements in WINE-MAKING technology. Modern production methods have been slow to reach Spain and, until the late 1970s, few winemakers had either the finance or the incentive to update traditional methods. A programme of investment which began in the early 1980s was further helped by Spain's accession to the EUROPEAN UNION in 1986.

History to Columbus

Although the wine-growing PHOENICIANS founded Cádiz *c.*1100 BC on the coast of southern Spain, they did not introduce viticulture to the Iberian peninsula, for the vine had been cultivated in Spain since between 4000 and 3000 BC. Grapes, found in Spain from the close of the Tertiary era onwards, pre-date *Homo sapiens* by millions of years.

Cádiz, gateway to the Atlantic, was an important Phoenician trading post. After the Phoenicians came the Carthaginians, themselves inhabitants of a city, CARTHAGE, founded by Phoenicians. The Carthaginians grew wine in Spain; more importantly, they were a threat to the emerging republic of Ancient ROME. The First Punic War (264–240 BC) had driven the Carthaginians out of Sicily and Sardinia: their reaction was to extend their settlements in Spain into an empire. Rome, too, had possessions in Spain to the east of the river Ebro (Latin *Iberus*); Hannibal's attack on Saguntum in 219 was the start of the Second Punic War, which ended in 202, Rome having taken possession of Carthaginian Spain in 206 BC. By winning the First and Second Punic Wars, the Romans had achieved their aim of hegemony in the Mediterranean, but once it had paid Rome its indemnity, Carthage rose again as an economic power. This, combined with a lingering fear of its old enemy, led Rome, on the urging of CATO the Censor, to declare the Third Punic War in 149 BC, destroying Carthage in 146. The source of Carthage's wealth was agriculture: it had grown rich on its corn exports and was to do so again under the emperors.

The 2nd century BC was a time of much unrest under Roman rule in Spain, and no systematic colonization was attempted until Rome finally 'pacified' the whole of the pen-

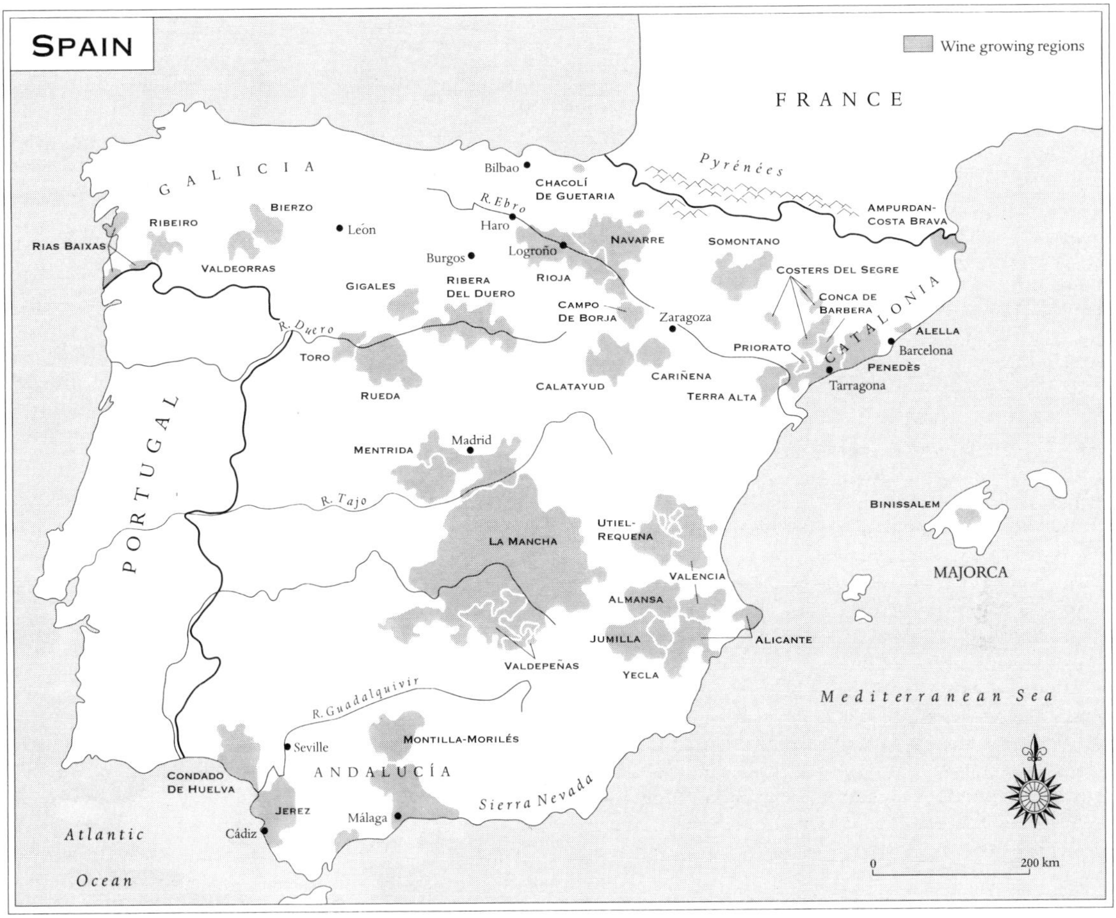

insula under Augustus. Political stability furthered trade: as the evidence from AMPHORAE shows, a great deal of wine from Baetica (which approximated to ANDALUCÍA) and Terraconensis (TARRAGONA) was sold in Rome, and Spanish imports far exceeded exports of Italian wine to Aquitaine and south eastern GAUL via Bordeaux. Spanish wine reached the Loire valley, Brittany, Normandy, and England, and it was given to the troops guarding the Roman frontier with Germany. Literary evidence confirms the discoveries of archaeology. Strabo says in his *Geography* (completed AD 9) that, since the fall of Carthage, Baetica has been famous for the beauty of its many vineyards (and if he is quoting from Posidonius, as has been claimed, this statement goes back to *c.*70 BC). COLUMELLA, a native of Cádiz (Latin *Gades*) in Baetica, sees the wine imports from Baetica and Gaul as symptomatic of the decline of Roman agriculture (1, *Praefatio*. 20).

Most of the Spanish wines, and particularly that of Saguntum, sold in Rome appear to have been PLONK: perfect for getting the porter of one's mistress drunk on, is Ovid's advice (*Ars amatoria* 3. 645–6). Some wines earn praise, however: PLINY says that Terraconensis is good (*Natural History* 14. 71) and so repeatedly does MARTIAL, himself a native of Spain.

Spain was no mere outpost of empire. It was the birthplace of other Roman authors besides Martial and Columella: Seneca, Lucan, and Quintilian. The emperors Hadrian and Marcus Aurelius came from Spanish families. When the Roman empire disintegrated, Spain was invaded by barbarians, first by the Suevi and then by the Visigoths, officially allies of Rome, who defeated the Suevi and established a kingdom in Spain. Although we know about the intellectuals that Spain continued to produce under the Visigoths, such as Isidore of Seville, we do not know what happened to viticulture and the wine trade: presumably it continued.

The overthrow of the Visigoths by the Moors in 711 did not mean the end of viticulture, for the ISLAMIC conquerors were enlightened rulers, who did not impose their own way of life on their subjects. Better still, many of them liked wine themselves. The Moorish position with regard to wine was ambiguous. Although the Prophet forbade the use of wine, the emirs and caliphs of Spain grew wine; although its sale was illegal, it was subject to excise (see TAXATION). By the time ENGLAND was importing considerable quantities of wine from Spain, the mid 13th century, the Christians had largely succeeded in their reconquest. In the 12th century Navarre, León and Castile, Aragon, and Barcelona were under Christian rule, and Portugal became a kingdom in 1134. By 1300, only the province of Granada remained in Moorish hands.

Around 1250, wine was regularly shipped from Bilbao to the English ports of Bristol, Southampton, and London. Names of Spanish merchants were inscribed in the Guildhall Letter Books of the 1350s, which shows that the wine trade with Spain was well established by then. The quality of the wines varied. The best wines were very good indeed: when Edward III fixed maximum prices for wines in 1364, a cask of the best Spanish wine was to cost as much as a cask of the best GASCON, which fetched more than wine from LA ROCHELLE. Spanish wines were popular because being from a hot climate they were high in alcohol and therefore kept better than French or German wines. But some of these wines were just high in alcohol, and that was their only merit. Hence they were often used to ADULTERATE more expensive and weaker wines. Laws forbidding this practice were widely disregarded. The wine of Lepe (a village between JEREZ and the Algarve) was infamous in this respect. Chaucer mentions it in his 'Pardoner's Tale'. It was white and very strong. An illegal mixture, commonly to be had in London taverns, of this with Gascon or La Rochelle must have been a prize recipe for speedy inebriation followed by a long-lasting hangover.

See also SACK, and ARNALDUS DE VILLANOVA and EIXIMENIS, two important medieval commentators on aspects of wine who were Catalan by birth. H.M.W.

Blazquez, J. M., 'La economía de la Hispania Romana', in A. Montenegro *et al.* (eds.), *Historia de España: España romana*, (Madrid, 1982).
Curchin, L. A., *Roman Spain* (London, 1991).
Jeffs, Julian, *Sherry* (4th edn., London, 1992).
Keay, S. J., *Roman Spain* (London, 1988).
Tchernia, André, *Les Vins de l'Italie romaine* (Paris, 1986).

History from Columbus

Spain emerged as a united, Christian country under a single crown in January 1492 following the final defeat of the Moors at Granada. Christopher Columbus discovered the West Indies in October of the same year, opening up a whole NEW WORLD to Spanish trade. This was recognized by the Treaty of Tordesillas in 1494, which, under the arbitration of Pope Alexander VI, divided the world between Spain and Portugal. All newly discovered territory to the west of a line of longitude 370 leagues west of the Cape Verde islands were to be Spanish. Everything to the east would be Portuguese. The treaty gave Spain most of Latin America with the exception of Brazil, which became Portuguese. The expulsion from Spain of all Jews who refused to be baptized commenced in 1492, creating opportunities for foreign merchants, many of whom began trading in wine.

The wine regions around Cádiz and MÁLAGA, both important Spanish ports, were the first to attract the attention of foreign traders and SHERRY, often called SACK, became a popular drink at the English court. Foreign traders in the sherry town of SANLÚCAR DE BARRAMEDA were granted special privileges by the duke of Medina Sidonia in 1517 and an English church was built to encourage more merchants. But relations between England and Spain began to deteriorate in the 1520s and after Henry VIII's divorce from Catherine of Aragon in 1533 brought English merchants into direct conflict with the Spanish. In the latter part of the century, war erupted between the two countries. English settlers fled fearing the Spanish Inquisition and trade between the two nations diminished. A new business was established in JEREZ: the production of ship's biscuits for the Armada.

The English defeat of the Armada in 1588 destroyed Spain as a seafaring power and, on the death of Philip II ten years later, the country was left with a crippling debt despite its immense colonial wealth. Trade in wine soon resumed and, after the death of Elizabeth I, sack became a favoured drink in the court of James I. But 17th century trade was sporadic. Peace did not last long and in 1625 the English attacked Cádiz under the ill-fated command of Sir Edward Cecil. In 1655 the English captured Jamaica. Spain retaliated a year later by declaring war and seizing English ships in Spanish ports. Even

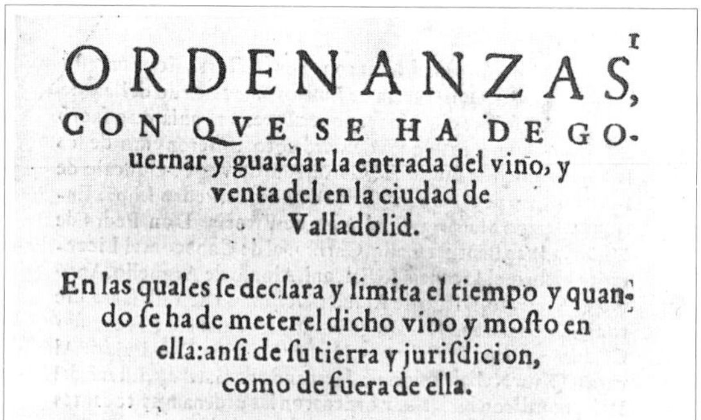
I

ORDENANZAS,
CON QVE SE HA DE GO-
uernar y guardar la entrada del vino, y
venta del en la ciudad de
Valladolid.

En las quales ſe declara y limita el tiempo y quando ſe ha de meter el dicho vino y moſto en ella: anſi de ſu tierra y juriſdicion, como de fuera de ella.

IMPRESSAS POR MANDADO DE
Valladolid, En caſa de Andres de Merchan Impreſſor
de Libros, Año de Mil y Quinientos
y Nouenta y Siete.

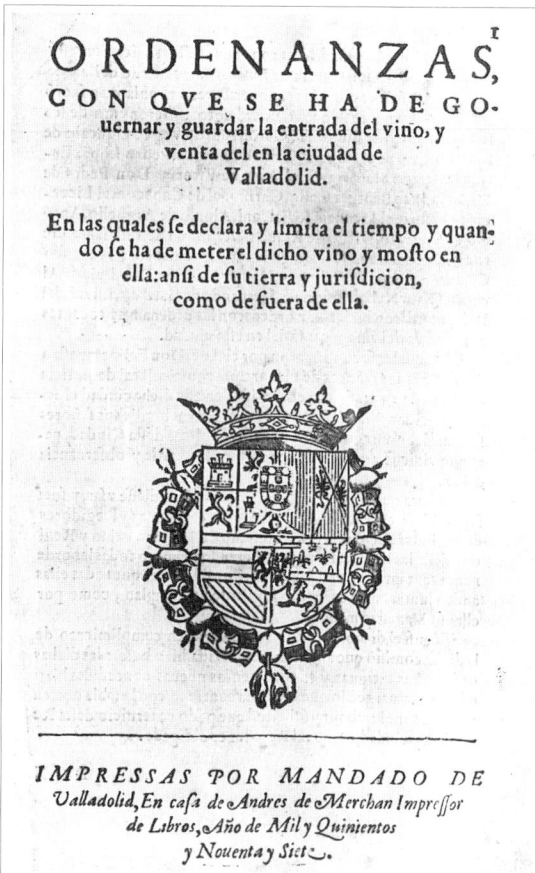

Spain: Title-page of the regulations governing the sale of wine in the Spanish town of Valladolid in 1596.

after the war, the trouble continued and trade in Spanish wines was blighted by excessive English import duties. Not surprisingly, the Spanish fostered markets elsewhere in Europe and the New World. A century of war combined with the preferential rates of duty for Portuguese wines as set out in the METHUEN TREATY of 1703 were a severe set-back for the sherry industry. By 1754 there were only nine shippers left in Jerez owing to the poor state of trade. But in the second half of the 18th century prosperity returned to the region and trade resumed. A generation of foreign merchants, among them an Englishman, Sir James Duff, and an Irishman, William Garvey, heralded a new era of prosperity for Jerez. This was interrupted by the Peninsular Wars, which began in 1808 and left Jerez in a state of ruin. But by 1820 merchants had returned to pick up the pieces and in the mid 19th century men such as Pedro DOMECQ, Manuel GONZALEZ, and Robert Blake Byass initiated an unprecedented sherry boom.

At the same time, Málaga also enjoyed a spectacular increase in popularity, producing an estimated 35,000 BUTTS of wine in 1829, equivalent to 175,000 hl. 'Mountain', as the wine was popularly known in its 19th century heyday, sat alongside PORT, MADEIRA, and sherry as one of the world's great FORTIFIED wines.

By all accounts there was little wine of exportable quality from the rest of Spain. Even RIOJA, already Spain's leading table wine at the turn of the 19th century, found few markets other than neighbouring Basque country and South America. The chronicler Richard Ford writing in 1846 notes that Spanish 'wine continues to be made in an unscientific and careless manner'. Cyrus REDDING writing in the 1851 edition of the *History and Description of Modern Wines* observes 'the rude treatment of the grape' in Spain. It seems that outside Jerez and Málaga little had changed since Roman times. In central and southern Spain, wines continued to be made in crude earthernware TINAJAS, while to the north wooden casks were used. Wine was frequently stored in *cueros*, pigskins lined with pitch or resin which tainted the wine. Richard Ford describes the commonplace *cuero* as a 'tanned and manufactured article [which] preserves the form of the pig, feet and all, with the exception of one . . . turned inside out so the hairy coat lines the interior, which is carefully pitched like a ships bottom'. These were the same imaginary 'big-bellied monsters' attacked by Don Quixote two centuries before. Wine-making progressed slowly in Spain.

From the middle of the 19th century wholesale change was forced on the Spanish wine industry, first by POWDERY MILDEW, which was found in Catalonia in the 1850s, and then much later by PHYLLOXERA. This devastating aphid was to arrive in Málaga in 1878, where it destroyed the livelihoods of thousands of vine-growers, many of whom left to establish a new life in South America, and Málaga's wine industry never fully recovered. But phylloxera spread relatively late and slowly through Spain, partly because of the long distances between the various Spanish wine regions, and in the 1860s the French, who had also suffered powdery mildew (oidium) for 10 years, had crossed the Pyrenees to compensate for the shortfall in French wine. Rioja and NAVARRE, the closest wine regions to BORDEAUX, benefited most from France's misfortune, and the resulting influx of French influence and expertise.

The BARRICA (225-l/59-gal oak cask) which is now used throughout Spain was introduced from Bordeaux and wine-making was refined along the Bordelais lines (although American OAK continued to be preferred, for the reasons outlined in COOPERAGE, history). Rioja BODEGAS belonging to Marqués de Murrieta, Marqués de Riscal, López de Heredia, and CVNE date back to this period when up to 500,000 hl of wine a month were shipped across the Pyrenees to France.

Phylloxera took hold in Jerez in 1894 and reached Rioja in 1901, by which time the epidemic had been controlled by grafting European vines on to resistant American ROOTSTOCKS. Vineyards were replanted throughout the country but many traditional, indigenous VINE VARIETIES in such regions as Galicia and Catalonia were rendered virtually extinct. In Catalonia, the post-phylloxera period coincided with the development of the sparkling wine industry which is today one of the largest in the world. Following a visit to the Champagne region, José Raventos introduced the CHAMPAGNE METHOD for the production of sparkling wine to the family firm of Codorníu in 1872. The wine, originally christened *champaña*, was a success, and vineyards around the town of San Sadurni de Noya were replanted with the trio of white grapes that now produce over a million hl of CAVA annually.

The first half of the 20th century was a turbulent era for Spain. Political infighting led to the abdication of Alfonso XIII in 1931 and the proclamation of a republic. However, one of the lasting measures introduced by the monarchist dictator General Primo de Rivera was the DO system of controlled appellations administered by a CONSEJO REGULADOR, which was first established in Rioja in 1926. Jerez and Málaga followed suit respectively in 1933 and 1937.

In June 1936, following the election victory of the Popular Front, Spain erupted into civil war. For three years sentiment ran high and Spain tore itself apart, often along regional, separatist lines. Some parts of the country, notably Catalonia and VALENCIA, were affected more than others but throughout the country vineyards were neglected and wineries were destroyed. The Nationalist victory in 1939 brought political stability to Spain under General Franco but economic recovery was hampered by the Second World War, which effectively closed European markets to Spanish exports.

In the 1950s the wine industry began to revive, helped by the nation-wide construction of large CO-OPERATIVE wineries which had begun some years earlier. This turned Spain, with its vast area of vineyard, into a natural source for inexpensive bulk wine either sold under proprietary BRAND names, or labelled with spurious GENERIC names such as Spanish Chablis or Spanish Sauternes, subsequently outlawed by European Union authorities. Since the early 1960s the Spanish government has exercised increasing control over wine producers with the proliferation of DOs (see Spanish wine law below).

The post-war history of the Spanish wine industry is overshadowed by the Rumasa saga, outlined under SHERRY. But

Rumasa's horizons ran far beyond Jerez (where it took over, among others, the bodegas of Palomino y Vergara, Bertola, Williams & Humbert, Garvey, and Terry) and Ruiz-Mateos accumulated substantial holdings in Rioja, Catalonia, MONTILLA, and La MANCHA. Rumasa also bought up banks, hotels, construction firms, department stores, factories, and shipyards, so that by the late 1970s José María Ruiz-Mateos seemed to control Spain. Ruiz-Mateos contributed greatly to the much-needed modernization of the Spanish wine industry but by the early 1980s there were signs that the empire was in trouble. In 1983 the newly elected Socialist government stepped in and expropriated Rumasa, promising to split up the unwieldy conglomerate and return it to private ownership. The government's actions were vehemently contested by Ruiz-Mateos and the Rumasa saga came to an end only with the sale of Williams & Humbert in 1989.

The 1960s sherry boom was accompanied by the emergence of Rioja as one of Spain's best-known wines. In the 1970s and 1980s the family firm of TORRES wrought a single-handed transformation of the wines of PENEDÈS. The death of General Franco in 1975 and the restoration of the monarchy set the foundations for a modern, multi-party democracy in Spain. Greater economic freedom has led to the growth of an urban middle class which has in turn stimulated a new interest in high-quality wine. Economically deprived rural regions such as La Mancha and Galicia have further benefited from EU finance, which is helping to change the face of the Spanish wine industry. However, as in neighbouring PORTUGAL, there is still a shortage of skilled WINE-MAKERS in Spain. With the exception of certain notable examples, in the early 1990s the transformation of the Spanish wine industry was still painfully slow.

Spanish wine law

Since joining the EU, Spain has brought her wine law into line with that of other European countries. There is now a five-tier system administered by INDO, acronym for the Madrid-based Instituto Nacional de Denominaciones de Origen.

VINO DE MESA (VdM) at the bottom of the pyramid includes all the wine made from unclassified vineyards or wine that has been declassified by blending. This is Spain's equivalent of the EU category TABLE WINE.

Vino Comarcal (VC) gives regional status to certain producers of table wine who fall outside a DO, or Denominación de Origen: Vino de Mesa de Toledo for the wines of Marqués de Griñon, for example.

VINO DE LA TIERRA (VdlT) covers wine from a specific, but usually large, region provided producers conform to certain local norms. This is Spain's counterpart to France's VIN DE PAYS.

Denominación de Origen, or DO, regions are the mainstay of the system, each with their own Consejo Regulador who regulate the growing, making, and marketing of wines, ensuring that they comply with specified regional standards. However, as they proliferate, the significance of the DO is debased. At the end of 1993 there were 39 DO regions covering nearly half the total vineyard area of Spain. As if to rectify this INDO has introduced a new category:

Denominación de Origen Calificada (DOCA) equates with Italy's DOCG. Rioja was the first region to be awarded DOCa status in 1991.

Geography and climate

Around much of Spain the land rises steeply from the coast reaching a maximum altitude of 3,482 m / 11,420 ft at Mulhacén in the Sierra Nevada just 50 km/30 miles from the Mediterranean. Iberia's dominant feature is the vast plateau that takes up much of central Spain. Known as the *meseta*, this undulating table land ranges in altitude from 600 to 1,000 m, tilting slightly towards the west. Four of Iberia's five major rivers (the Duero, Tajo, Guadiana, and Guadalquivir) drain westwards into the Atlantic, with the Ebro flowing south east to the Mediterranean. Other rivers are seasonal, many drying up completely in the summer months.

Great mountain ranges known as *cordilleras* divide Spain into distinct natural regions. The north coast, from Galicia to the Pyrenees, is relatively cool and humid with few extremes. Annual RAINFALL in this part of Spain ranges from 1,000 mm/39 in on the coast to over 2,000 mm on the mountain peaks inland. Galicia, Asturias, and BASQUE country are intensively cultivated and densely populated.

The Cantabrian Cordillera, a westerly spur of the Pyrenees which rises to over 2,600 m in the Picos de Europa, protects the main body of Spain from cool, rain-bearing north westerlies. Rioja in the upper Ebro valley is therefore shielded from the Bay of Biscay so that, although annual rainfall reaches around 1,500 mm on the Basque coast, it declines sharply to the east and is just 450 mm at Haro, the wine-making capital of Rioja, only 100 km inland.

The Spanish climate becomes more extreme towards the centre of the central plateau. Winters are long and cold with temperatures falling well below freezing point (the lowest recorded temperature is −22 °C/−7.6 °F in Albacete). Summers here can be blisteringly hot with daytime temperatures sometimes rising above 40 °C. Little rain falls in the summer months and DROUGHT is a constant problem. Agriculture has adapted to the lack of rainfall which struggles to reach 300 mm in places. Much of this comes in sudden downpours in spring and autumn which sometimes cause devastating flash floods.

South and east from the central plateau the climate is increasingly influenced by proximity to the Mediterranean. The climate on the narrow coastal littoral is equable with long, warm summers giving way to mild winters. These are Spain's holiday Costas, but there are lush market gardens producing rice and citrus fruit around Valencia, and, on the mountain slopes inland, olives, almonds, and TABLE GRAPES are important crops. The hottest part of Spain is the broad Guadalquivir valley in Andalucía, north of the Sierra Nevada where summer temperatures rise to 45 °C. The south west corner of Andalucía has a climate of its own, strongly influenced by the Gulf of Cádiz and the Atlantic (see SHERRY).

Viticulture

Throughout much of Spain, YIELDS are notably low. In most of central and southern Spain vines are widely spaced to survive the summer drought with VINE DENSITIES ranging from 1,200 to 1,600 vines per ha (480–650 per acre) according to the amount of water available (less than an eighth of the vine density in some MÉDOC or CÔTE D'OR vineyards, for example). Growers have adopted a system of planting known as the *marco real* with 2.5 m between each vine in all directions. In all but the most modern vineyards (which tend to be planted with increasing MECHANIZATION in mind), vines tend to be free standing, BUSH trained, and pruned according to the GOBELET method known as *en vaso* in Spain. Yields from these vineyards, many of which are over 40 years old, are frequently less than 20 hl/ha (1.1 tons/acre). The records for the DO of JUMILLA, for example, show average yields of just 10 to 12 hl/ha (less than a tenth of customary yields in many an Italian DOC).

However, one considerable advantage that accompanies a dry climate is the lack of FUNGAL DISEASES. POWDERY MILDEW, DOWNY MILDEW, and BOTRYTIS BUNCH ROT are virtually unknown in central Spain.

IRRIGATION, which would undoubtedly help to increase yields, is technically forbidden by Spain's accession treaty to the European Union. In the more arid regions of Spain there is a strong case for allowing irrigation provided it is carefully controlled. A number of properties, the most notable of which is the Raimat estate in COSTERS DEL SEGRE, have been granted experimental status for irrigation enabling them to sidestep EU law. Judicious use of water has transformed an otherwise semi-arid waste into a productive vineyard with yields approaching those of other European countries.

Viticultural practices vary sharply from one part of Spain to another. In areas like Rioja and Penedès, where more systematic replanting is taking place, vines are more densely planted (up to 5,000 vines per ha) and are increasingly trained on WIRES. Here yields may reach 50 or 60 hl/ha. In Galicia, vines were traditionally trained on pergolas (see TENDONE), both to make maximum use of the limited space in this densely populated part of Spain and to lessen the risk of fungal diseases in this humid climate. Newer vineyards are planted on lower vine-TRAINING SYSTEMS to ease cultivation but have to be regularly sprayed to combat disease. Yields are frequently high, reaching 90 hl/ha in RIBEIRO.

Harvesting is mostly carried out by hand and grapes frequently arrive at co-operative wineries already starting to ferment, having been squashed when loaded into large trailers. The more quality-conscious bodegas provide growers with stackable plastic containers to keep the grapes whole during transportation (see HARVEST). Some firms also set out a harvest regime refusing grapes delivered after midday, when they have been heated by the sun. MECHANICAL HARVESTERS are few and far between and their use is limited to vineyards supported on wires.

Vine varieties

The Spanish claim to have up to 600 different grape varieties, although 80 per cent of the country's vineyards are planted with just over 20 of them. Since the arrival of phylloxera at the end of the 19th century, farmers have tended to favour varieties that are well adapted to local climatic conditions. The drought-resistant white AIRÉN is planted throughout central Spain, occupying almost three times as much land as any other variety. Airén traditionally produced base wines for Spain's important BRANDY industry and oxidized, alcoholic white wines for local bars and cafés but with careful handling and improved vinification (see below) it is capable of producing some simple, refreshing dry wines. Dark-skinned GARNACHA is the second most widely planted variety with 170,000 ha, principally in the north of the country. It flourishes in windy, arid conditions, especially Navarre, Rioja Baja, Aragon, and parts of Catalonia, where Garnacha makes rather clumsy reds and some fresh, fruity rosés.

BOBAL and Monastrell (the MOURVÈDRE of France) perform Garnacha's role in the Levante, where they each cover around 100,000 ha. Both varieties yield dark, alcoholic reds and the occasional dry rosé.

TEMPRANILLO is Spain's most widely planted vine variety associated with quality wine, planted on more than 33,000 ha, under such aliases as Cencibel, Ull de Llebre, and Tinto Fino in different parts of the country.

Other white varieties which are also important in Spain are the sherry grapes PALOMINO (planted in Jerez, RUEDA, and parts of Galicia) and PEDRO XIMÉNEZ (Montilla-Moriles and Málaga). The white MACABEO (also called Viura) is widely planted in Rioja and Catalonia, especially Penedès, where, along with Parellada and Xarel-lo, it is grown for Cava sparkling wine. High-quality white varieties which are gaining ground include ALBARIÑO (Galicia) and VERDEJO (Rueda), while other promising grapes which are making a more limited come-back include the white LOUREIRA and GODELLO (both in Galicia) and the red GRACIANO (Rioja).

Foreign varieties are making significant inroads in some parts of Spain. CABERNET SAUVIGNON, MERLOT, and CHARDONNAY are increasingly important in Catalonia and Navarre.

Wine-making

Spanish wine-making has changed radically since the 1960s. Stainless steel, once a rarity, is now commonplace and most bodegas have the means of TEMPERATURE CONTROL for fermentation. These improvements transformed Spanish wines, especially in La Mancha and the Levante, where temperature control is essential to preserve the primary fruit character in both red and white wine. Some producers in central and southern Spain continue to use TINAJAS for both fermentation and storage. Originally made from clay, now cast in concrete, *tinajas* are probably a Roman legacy. They are difficult to clean and even more difficult to cool. Montilla is now the only region continuing to use *tinajas* with any success. The epoxy-lined concrete tanks still to be found in some of the less punctilious co-operative wineries are little better.

With the gradual introduction of stainless steel technology, an increasing number of white wines are being bottled young without any further ageing. With the notable exception of sherry, a few traditional white Riojas, and some wines from Catalonia's more avant-garde wine-makers, Spanish wood-matured whites have tended to taste flat and OXIDIZED.

Spain continues to foster the long-established tradition of ageing red wines in OAK. The use of wooden BARRELS as vessels for fermentation and storage dates back many centuries but in the second half of the 19th century the French introduced the 225-l BARRIQUE (*barrica*) to Rioja, and its use has subsequently spread throughout the country. Unlike the French, however, most Spanish wine-makers use American oak, which is not only considerably cheaper than French oak, it can also impart a stronger flavour to the wine. The Tempranillo grape in particular seems to produce wine that responds to maturation in new oak. Spanish oak-aged reds are usually denoted by the words CRIANZA, RESERVA, or GRAN RESERVA, which are enshrined in local legislation. The wines often share a pungent, vanilla character which is sometimes simulated in inexpensive red, and occasionally white, wines by short maceration with OAK CHIPS.

Most Spanish DOs also stipulate minimum bottle age and few wines are ever released before they are ready to drink.

For specific wine regions see ANDALUCÍA, ARAGON, BASQUE, CASTILE-LA MANCHA, CASTILE-LEÓN, CATALONIA, GALICIA, LEVANTE, NAVARRE, and RIOJA.

See also SHERRY and Spanish BRANDY, an important wine-based product in Spain. R.J.M.

Duijker, H., *The Wine Atlas of Spain* (London, 1992).
Jeffs, J., *Sherry* (London, 1982).
Metcalfe, C., and McWhirter, K., *The Wines of Spain and Portugal* (London, 1988).
Radford, J., *Guide to the Wines from Spain* (London, 1993).
Read, J., *Wines of the Rioja* (London, 1984).
—— *The Wines of Spain* (London, 1986).

SPANNA, local name for the NEBBIOLO grape in eastern PIEDMONT in north west Italy, particularly around GATTINARA in the hills of the Vercelli and Novara provinces. This just may be the 'uva spinea' mentioned by PLINY, who added that this is the variety 'quae sola alitur nebulis'. Nebbiolo, a very late maturing vine variety, may well be said to 'breathe the fog' of the Piedmont autumn. Seven DOC wines are made either wholly or in part from Spanna, three in the province of Vercelli (BOCA, GATTINARA, LESSONA) and four in the province of Novara (BRAMATERRA, FARA, GHEMME, and SIZZANO). Only Gattinara and Ghemme, with 100 and 85 ha (250 and 210 acres) planted, have a significant production, and several of the others are virtually of postage stamp size (Boca is 15 ha, Lessona 6.5 ha). The wines display strong Nebbiolo personality, although only Lessona can be 100 per cent Spanna, the other DOCs requiring blending with the less interesting VESPOLINA and BONARDA Novarese grapes. All-Spanna wines are increasingly common, however, even if they may be marketed only as a VINO DA TAVOLA. Spanna wines had an excellent reputation before the Second World War and were quite popular in the major market of nearby Milan, but the post-war period has seen a definite loss of ground to the richer and more professionally made Nebbiolo wines of the Langhe; the combination of excessive CASK AGEING in old casks, and imperfectly executed or non-existent MALOLACTIC FERMENTATIONS have not been helpful to the reputation of these wines. The extreme fragmentation of vineyard property and an elderly work-force have also been handicaps, but there were significant improvements in the wines in the 1980s, and a general sense that Spanna—or at least Gattinara and Ghemme—may have turned the corner in terms of quality and of recognition. D.T.

Anderson, B., *The Wine Atlas of Italy* (London and New York, 1990).
Gleave, D., *The Wines of Italy* (London and New York, 1989).
Wasserman, S., *Italy's Noble Red Wines* (New York, 1985).

SPARGING a wine means stripping it of OXYGEN or CARBON DIOXIDE by purging it with fine bubbles of an INERT GAS, usually NITROGEN. The technique is not widely used because it removes not only oxygen but also significant amounts of volatile FLAVOUR COMPOUNDS. A tank or bottle may also be sparged with an INERT GAS, for example. A.D.W.

SPARKLING WINE, wine which bubbles when poured into a glass, an important and growing category of wine. The bubbles form because a certain amount of CARBON DIOXIDE has been held under pressure dissolved in the wine until the bottle is unstoppered, in which case the wine is transformed from the stable to the meta-stable state described under FIZZINESS.

Sparkling wine may vary in as many respects as still wine: it can be any wine COLOUR (although it is usually white); it can be any degree of SWEETNESS (although a high proportion tastes bone dry and may be labelled BRUT, while Italians specialize in medium sweet SPUMANTE); it can vary in ALCOHOLIC STRENGTH (although in practice most dry sparkling wines are about 12 per cent, while the sweeter, lighter Spumante are between 5.5 and eight per cent); and it can come from anywhere in the world where wine is produced.

Unlike still wines, however, sparkling wines vary in fizziness, not just in the actual pressure under which the gas is dissolved in the wine, but also apparently in the character of the foam. Some sparkling wines froth aggressively in the mouth while others bubble subtly. The average size, consistency, and persistence of the bubbles also vary considerably. Study of foam and foaminess, along with research into YEASTS, are two of the few areas which unite the (sparkling) wine industry with the BEER industry.

To the wine-maker, however, the most obvious way in which sparkling wines differ is in how the gas came to be trapped in solution in the wine: champagne method, transversage, transfer, Charmat, or carbonation, in declining order of cost, complication, and likely quality of sparkling wine, together with the rarer *méthode ancestrale* and *méthode dioise*. (See SPARKLING WINE-MAKING for details of each method.)

The most famous sparkling wine of all is CHAMPAGNE, the archetypal sparkling wine made in north eastern France, which represents about eight per cent of global sparkling wine production. A significant proportion of all sparkling wine is made using the same basic champagne method, much of it from the same grape varieties Pinot Noir, Chardonnay, and, to a lesser extent outside Champagne, Meunier, even though different wine regions often stamp their own style on the resulting sparkling wine. Examples of such wines were made with ever-increasing frequency in the 1980s and early 1990s in CALIFORNIA, AUSTRALIA, and ITALY particularly.

A host of fine, very individual sparkling wines is made using the champagne method but with non-champagne grapes, however. The most prodigious example of this is CAVA, the sparkling wine so popular with the Spanish. The LOIRE region of France also produces champagne method sparkling wine in great quantity, notably under the SAUMUR Mousseux appellation. All of France's new CRÉMANTS also use the champagne method. In almost every wine region in the world with aspirations to quality, some champagne method wine has been made. Wines made by this, the most meticulous method, may be described on the label within Europe as *méthode traditionnelle*, *méthode classique*, or *méthode traditionnelle classique*. Other descriptions include bottle fermented (although strictly speakling wines made by the transfer method, described below, may be labelled 'bottle fermented', while only those made by the champagne method can be labelled 'fermented in *this* bottle').

Similarly, in almost every wine region in the world, Charmat process sparkling wine is made in considerable quantity, often for specific local BRANDS, especially for SEKT in Germany and a host of wines such as LAMBRUSCO and ASTI SPUMANTE in Italy. The country which has been an enthusiastic market for sparkling wines is RUSSIA, ever since the imperial court imported such vast quantities of champagne (and base wine to make sparkling) at the end of the 19th century. Today SOVIET SPARKLING WINE is still made in enormous quantity in both Russia and UKRAINE, much of it using the so-called continous method. ASTI SPUMANTE and a number of other low alcohol, sweet Italian, or Italianate, sparkling wines are made using a variation of the Charmat process.

The transfer method is used for some better-quality branded wines, particularly in Germany and the United States (giving rise to the defiant description on some American sparkling wine labels 'Fermented in *This* Bottle').

Some characterful sparkling wines are made eschewing DISGORGEMENT and selling the part-fermented, still sweet wine together with the LEES of its second fermentation in bottle. These include some GAILLAC, LIMOUX, and CLAIRETTE DE DIE made by the *méthode ancestrale*.

See also specific information under OPENING THE BOTTLE, LABELLING INFORMATION, and DOSAGE.

SPARKLING WINE-MAKING, making SPARKLING WINES, most obviously involves the accumulation of gas under pressure in what was initially a still 'base wine' or, ideally, blend of base wines. The most common methods of achieving this are discussed below—champagne method, transversage, transfer method, continuous method, Charmat process, carbonation, *méthode ancestrale*, and *méthode dioise*—but these are matters of technique rather than substance. Almost all of them depend on initiating a second FERMENTATION, which inevitably produces CARBON DIOXIDE, and most of them incorporate some way of keeping that gas dissolved under pressure in the wine, while separating it from the inconvenient by-product of fermentation, the LEES. What matters most to the quality of a sparkling wine, however, is the quality and character of the blended base wines.

Making and blending the base wine

Wines that are good raw material for the sparkling wine-making process are not usually much fun to drink in their still state. Rather like the most suitable wines for DISTILLATION into a fine brandy, they are typically high in acidity and unobtrusively flavoured (although they should in general have more interesting fruit characters than wines destined for the still). There is a school of thought that the austerity of the still wine of the CHAMPAGNE region, Coteaux CHAMPENOIS, is the most eloquent argument of all in favour of champagne's carbon dioxide content.

It is not just in Champagne, however, that sparkling wine-makers argue that BALANCE is the key to assembling a base wine to make sparkling, and that the best sparkling wines are therefore essentially blended wines. Some fine VARIETAL sparkling wines exist (some of the best BLANC DE BLANCS champagnes, for example), but a great sparkling wine never tastes just like the still wine version plus gas; the very nature of sparkling wine-making is to try to make a sum that is greater than the parts (although this may not be achieved, or even attempted, for cheaper wines). Those who aspire to make good sparkling wine are acutely aware that any minor fault in a base wine may be amplified by the sparkling wine-making process.

Accordingly, for better sparkling wines, grapes had invariably been hand picked up to the early 1990s since WHOLE BUNCH PRESSINGS was the norm, and such MECHANICAL HARVESTERS as had been tested by then risked splitting berries and extracting harsh PHENOLICS into the grape juice which could cause astringent, coarse characteristics which would be magnified by the pressure of bubbles. It is possible that gentler mechanical picking machines will change this, although it is essential to press grapes as soon as possible after picking. Press houses in the vineyards have long been *de rigueur* in Champagne and are increasingly common for other top-quality sparkling wines.

Grapes destined for sparkling wines are usually picked at lower MUST WEIGHTS than the same varieties would be if they were to be sold as a still wine. In very general terms, average YIELDS can be higher for sparkling wines than still wines (see below), partly because there is no imperative to achieve high sugar levels. In California, for example, HARVEST begins in mid, or sometimes early, August for Pinot Noir and Chardonnay destined for one of their 'CMCV' sparkling wines. In Australia, the aim is to pick such varieties just as HERBACEOUS characters have been lost when ripe fruit FLAVOUR COMPOUNDS are beginning to develop, which in practice tends to mean at about 17 to 20° BRIX in Australia's cooler areas.

PRESSING is an important stage in sparkling wine-making, particularly in Champagne, where black grapes are used, as it is essential that the concentration of phenolics, both astringency and colour, is kept to a minimum. There has been much experimentation with horizontal presses of various types, and modern airbag or tank presses can certainly offer a reliably high standard of HYGIENE, but modern technology has found it difficult to improve upon the traditional vertical presses of Champagne, although they are LABOUR intensive. So-called 'thin layer' presses which minimize pressure, and therefore the extraction of phenolics by pressing a layer of grapes no more than 70 cm/27 in thick are used increasingly.

The wine-maker can then make the usual still white wine choices concerning OXIDATIVE versus PROTECTIVE JUICE HANDLING; juice CLARIFICATION; choice of YEAST strain and FERMENTATION rate; protein STABILIZATION; and MALOLACTIC FERMENTATION (sparkling wines made from wines which have not undergone malolactic fermentation may be simpler and fruitier in youth).

Then comes the crucial blending stage, the true art of making sparkling wine, and one in which experience is as important as SCIENCE. A large champagne house such as MOËT & CHANDON may be able to use several hundred base wines in order to achieve the house style in its basic expression, that year's NON-VINTAGE blend. A small, independent concern, especially outside Champagne, may have access to only a very limited range of base wines a disadvantage in a poor vintage, although not necessarily in a good one. And a producer of the most basic Charmat process wine may simply blend the cheapest vaguely suitable ingredients available in the market-place.

Champagne method

This method, known variously as traditional method, classic method, *méthode traditionnelle*, and *méthode classique*, is the most meticulous way of making wine sparkle; the raw ingredients vary considerably but the basic techniques do not.

Pressing and yield Pressing is the first operation defined in detail by the champagne method, which understandably differentiates rigorously between the fractions of juice from each press load, for the first juice to emerge from the press is highest in sugar and acidity and lowest in phenolics, including pigments. A maximum extraction rate is usually defined in any regulations concerning sparkling wine production (such as those for France's CRÉMANTS, for example). Those who produce champagne method sparkling wine acknowledge that the first juice to emerge from the press is generally the best, even if there is a certain amount of vintage variation. From 1992 the permitted extraction rate for champagne was reduced so that 160 kg (350 lb) of grapes rather than 150 kg of grapes were required to produce 100 l (26.4 gal) of wine, about the same extraction rate as that used by producers of top-quality sparkling wine anywhere in the world. (This compares with an approximate average extraction rate of 100 l of wine from about 130 kg of grapes for still red wines; see YIELD.)

Base wines After the making of the base wines (described above), which usually takes place over the winter following the harvest, the final blend is made after extensive tasting, assessment, and BENCH BLENDING. There is extreme flexibility in blending a non-dated wine and a high proportion of 'reserve wine' made in previous years may be used. Some champagne houses include up to 45 per cent of reserve wines in their NON-VINTAGE blend. (KRUG indulge in the luxury of using base wines from up to six different vintages being held in reserve.) The ingredients in a vintage-dated sparkling wine are more limited (often by necessity for those new to sparkling wine-making, by law in Champagne). Many of the base wines made from dark-berried grapes, however lightly pressed, may have a light pink tinge at this stage, although the pigments are precipitated during *tirage*, the crucial next stage during which the blended wine rests on the lees of a second fermentation in bottle. As soon as the new blend has been made in bulk blending tanks, it usually undergoes cold STABILIZATION in order to prevent subsequent formation of TARTRATES in bottle.

Second fermentation This new blend then has a mixture of sugar and yeast added to it before bottling in particularly strong, dark BOTTLES, usually STOPPERED with a crown cork, so that a second fermentation will occur in bottle, creating the all-important fizz. Conventionally, an addition or *tirage* of about 24 g/l of sugar is made. This creates an additional 1.2 to 1.3 per cent ALCOHOLIC STRENGTH and sufficient carbon dioxide to create a pressure inside the bottle of five to six atmospheres after disgorgement (see below), which is roughly the FIZZINESS expected of a sparkling wine, and one which can safely be contained by a wired champagne cork. During this second fermentation, known as *prise de mousse* in French, the bottles are normally stored horizontally at about 12 °C/54 °F and the fermentation has produced the required pressure and bubbles after four to eight weeks.

Special types of YEAST culture which help sparkling wine-makers have been developed (and are much used for still wines too). Such yeasts are particularly good at flocculating, and produce a granular deposit that is easy to riddle, or shake, to the neck of the bottle for extraction.

At this stage, sometimes called *tirage* in French, RIDDLING agents are increasingly added with the yeast and sugar. Made of some combination of TANNINS, BENTONITES, gelatines, or alginates, they help to produce a uniform skin-like yeast deposit that does not stick to the glass but slips easily down it during the riddling process. The development of smoother glass bottles has also helped.

Ageing on lees Timing of the riddling process after the second fermentation is a key element in quality and style of a champagne method sparkling wine, the second most important factor affecting quality after blending the base wine. The

Sparkling wine-making

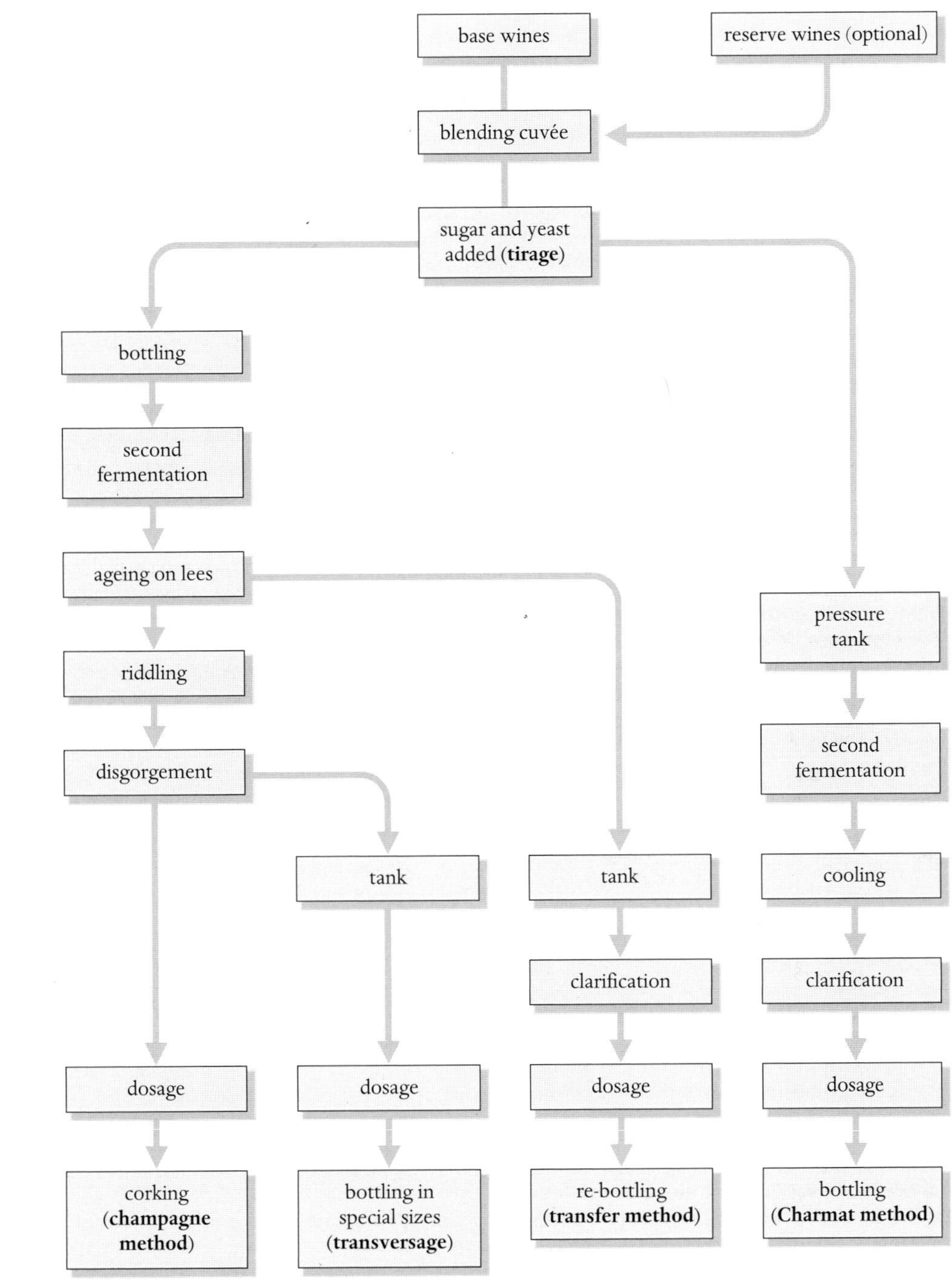

longer a wine rests on the lees of the second fermentation in bottle, the more chance it has of picking up flavour from the dead yeast cells, a process known as yeast AUTOLYSIS.

Most regulations for champagne method sparkling wines specify at least nine months ageing on lees, and the minimum period for non-vintage champagne was increased to 15 months in the early 1990s (vintage champagnes are usually aged for several years). During the bottle ageing process the yeast cells autolyse, releasing increasingly complex flavour compounds. The chemistry of autolysis is not fully understood, but it seems that autolysis has significant effects only after about 18 months on the lees, and that the most obvious changes occur after five to 10 years of lees contact, which inevitably increases production costs considerably. It may be that compulsory periods of lees contact in bottle of only a few months have less effect on quality than has been imagined.

Riddling The riddling process, known as *remuage* or shaking in French, is one of the most cumbersome (and most publicized) parts of the champagne method, but it is undertaken for cosmetic rather than oenological reasons: to remove the deposit that would otherwise make the wine cloudy (as it does in the *méthode ancestrale* described below).

Traditionally bottles were gradually moved from the horizontal to an inverted vertical by hand, by human *remueurs* or riddlers who would shake them and the deposit every time they moved them towards the inverted vertical position in special *pupitres* or riddling racks. This was a slow and extremely labour-intensive way of moving the deposit *en masse* from the belly of the bottle to its neck. The CAVA industry based in Catalonia developed an automatic alternative in the 1970s, the *girasol* or GYROPALETTE, which has since been widely adopted for champagne method sparkling wine-making the world over. The bottles are stacked, 50 or 400 dozen at a time, in large metal crates, and their orientation changed at regular intervals (including night time, unlike the manual method), with accompanying shake, from the horizontal to inverted vertical by remote control. Using riddling agents, well-adapted yeasts, and gyropalettes, bottles may now be riddled in as little as three days, as opposed to the six weeks or more needed for hand *remuage* without riddling agents.

Disgorgement and dosage The final stage in a sometimes short (but inevitably complicated) production process compared, say, with a fine oak-aged red is to remove the deposit now in the neck of an inverted bottle. The conventional way of achieving this is to freeze the bottle neck and deposit by plunging the necks of the inverted bottles into a tray of freezing solution. The bottles are then upended, opened, and the deposit flies out as a solid pellet of ice. Bottles are then topped up with a mixture of wine and sugar syrup, the so-called DOSAGE, stoppered with a proper champagne CORK held on with a wire MUZZLE, and prepared for labelling. Most dry sparkling wine is sweetened so that it contains between 5 and 12 g/l RESIDUAL SUGAR, and the further from the equator the grapes are grown, the more dosage is generally required to counterbalance high natural ACIDITY, although the longer a wine is aged on lees, the less dosage it needs.

Alternative methods Riddling and disgorgement are unwieldy processes which contribute nothing to the innate quality of the sparkling wine. It is not surprising therefore that, in the 1980s, as labour costs spiralled, there was considerable research into alternative methods of expelling the sediment.

One of the most successful has been the development of encapsulated yeast. Yeast can be trapped in a 'bead' made of calcium alginate. Such beads are about a few millimetres in diameter and are able to hold the yeast trapped in their interior while having big enough pores to admit sugar and nutrients into the bead so that a full second fermentation can proceed as normal. The great advantage is that the riddling stage takes seconds as the beads simply drop into the neck of the inverted bottle. The only brake on the adoption of encapsulated yeasts has been the development of reliable machinery which will dispense beads into bottles without shearing them.

Another possible method is to insert a membrane cartridge into the neck of the bottle. Yeast is dispensed into it and it is then plugged before the bottle is stoppered with the usual crown cap. Like the beads, the cartridge allows ingress of sugar and nutrients for fermentation to take place there, as well as allowing the carbon dioxide gas out. In this case there is no need at all for riddling, and disgorgement simply entails taking off the crown cap and allowing the pressure inside the bottle to expel the cartridge. This particular alternative could be particularly useful to small wineries for whom the investment in riddling and disgorgement equipment has been prohibitive.

Transversage

Transversage is an occasional twist on the champagne method whereby, immediately after disgorgement, the contents of bottles of sparkling wine made by the champagne method are transferred into a pressure tank to which the dosage is added before the wine is bottled, typically in another (often small) size of bottle, under pressure. This is how many half-bottles, all airline 'splits' or quarter-bottles, and virtually all BOTTLE SIZES above a jeroboam of champagne are filled.

Transfer method

The transfer method, known as *transvasement* (decanting) in French and Carstens in the United States, also depends on inducing a second fermentation by adding sugar and yeast to a blend of base wines and then bottling the result. It differs from the champagne method, however, in that riddling and disgorgement are dispensed with and, after a period of lees contact, the bottles are chilled, and their contents transferred to a bulk pressure tank where the sediment is removed by clarification, usually FILTRATION. A suitable dosage is then added and the result is once again bottled, using a counter pressure filler, before being corked and wired. Such wines can demonstrate many but not all of the qualities of a champagne method wine but the transfer method is likely to be abandoned in the long term when encapsulated yeast and membrane cartridge systems are adopted.

Continuous method
A process developed in the USSR for SOVIET SPARKLING WINE and now used in Germany and Portugal. The method involves a series of usually five reticulated tanks under five atmospheres of pressure, the same FIZZINESS as in most sparkling wines. At one end base wine together with sugar and yeast (usually rehydrated dried yeast) is pumped in and the SECOND FERMENTATION crucial to virtually all methods of sparkling wine-making begins. This creates CARBON DIOXIDE which increases the pressure in the tank, but the yeast cannot grow under this pressure and so further yeast has to be added continuously. The second and third tanks are partly filled with some material such as wood shavings, which offer a substantial total surface area on which the dead yeast cells accumulate and a certain amount of AUTOLYSIS, or at least reaction between the dead yeast cells and the wine, takes place. In the fourth and fifth tanks there are no yeast cells and the wine eventually emerges relatively clear, having spent an average of perhaps three or four weeks in the system. See also LANCERS.

Charmat process or tank method
This very common method, also called *cuve close* (French for sealed tank), tank, or bulk method, *granvas* in Spanish, *autoclave* in Italian was developed by Eugene Charmat in the early years of the 20th century in Bordeaux. Its advantages are that it is very much cheaper, faster, and less labour intensive than the above processes, and is better suited to base wines which lack much capacity for AGEING. A second fermentation is provoked by yeast and sugar added to base wine held in bulk in a pressure tank and, after a rapid fermentation, the fermentation is typically arrested by cooling the wine to −5 °C when a pressure of about five atmospheres has been reached. The result is clarified, a dosage is added and the resulting sparkling wine is bottled using a counter pressure filler. This style of sparkling wine is the most likely to taste like still wine with bubbles in it, rather than to have any of the additional attributes which can result from fermentation in bottle.

Carbonation
Also known as the injection, or simply the 'bicycle pump', method, carbonation of wine is achieved in much the same way as carbonation of fizzy, soft drinks: carbon dioxide gas is pumped from cylinders into a tank of wine which is then bottled under pressure, or very occasionally it is pumped into bottles. Fizziness must by law be at least three atmospheres in Europe. The result is a wine which has many, and large, bubbles when the bottle is first opened, but whose mousse rapidly fades. This is the cheapest, least critical, and least durable way of making wine sparkle and is used for perhaps the cheapest 10 per cent of all sparkling wines.

Méthode ancestrale or **méthode rurale**
This method is rarely used and results in a lightly sparkling, medium sweet wine, often with some deposit, but it most closely parallels how wines were originally made sparkling. It involves bottling young wines before all the RESIDUAL SUGAR has been fermented into alcohol. Fermentation continues in bottle and gives off carbon dioxide. Variants on this theme are still made in Gaillac, where the method is sometimes known as the *méthode gaillaçoise*, from BLANQUETTE in Limoux, and may still occasionally be found in SAVOIE. The wine is designed to be sweeter and less fizzy than a champagne method sparkling wine and no dosage is allowed. The wine may in some cases be decanted off the deposit and rebottled under pressure in a form of transfer method.

Méthode dioise
This is an unusual variation on the *méthode ancestrale* above and the transfer method, producing wines similar to ASTI SPUMANTE. It is used for the sweet wine CLAIRETTE DE DIE, most of which is made by the local CO-OPERATIVE. The base wines are fermented in stainless steel tanks at very low temperatures over several months. The wine is then filtered, bottled, and fermentation continues in bottle until an alcoholic strength of about 7.5 per cent has been reached. The wine is disgorged six to 12 months after bottling (by inserting a pipe through the crown cap and sucking out the clear wine under pressure) before being filtered again and immediately transferred to new bottles.

SPÄTBURGUNDER is the chief synonym in GERMANY for PINOT NOIR.

SPÄTLESE, one of the PRÄDIKATS in the QMP quality wine category defined by the GERMAN WINE LAW. Spätlese means literally 'late harvest' and the grapes should have been picked at least a week after a preliminary picking of less ripe grapes (until the 1994 vintage Spätlese was the only Prädikat for which this was explicitly required). Specific minimum MUST WEIGHTS are laid down for each combination of vine variety and region and some were reduced for the 1994 vintage. These wines' additional ripeness, and therefore POTENTIAL ALCOHOL, make them excellent candidates for TROCKEN winemaking, especially in the PFALZ, RHEINHESSEN, and BADEN regions. Spätlese trocken wines can go well with all sorts of savoury foods, while sweeter Spätlesen are usually better drunk on their own, as they often lack the BODY necessary to accompany sweet foods and yet their sweetness can taste strange with many savoury dishes. (AUSLESE, the next ripest Prädikat, is usually better dedicated to SWEET WINES as the alcohol can be so high as to be out of BALANCE.)

See also AUSTRIA.

The term Spatlese, usually without the umlaut, was once widely used outside Europe, notably in Australia.

SPECIFIC GRAVITY. See DENSITY.

SPICED WINES. See FLAVOURED WINES and MULLED WINE.

SPITTING is an essential practice at professional TASTINGS where several dozen, often more than 100, wines are regularly offered at the same time. Members of the wine trade, and wine writers, rapidly lose any inhibitions about spitting in public. Since there are no taste receptors in the throat, spitting allows the taster to form a full impression of each wine, while minimizing the blunting effects of ALCOHOL. It does not, unfortunately, leave the taster completely unaffected by alcohol. Some ethanol is vaporized and absorbed on the palate, and, no matter how assiduous the taster, it is extremely difficult to prevent any liquid from dribbling down the throat. According to the estimates of this writer, tasting 30 wines involves ingesting approximately a glass of wine.

Whatever tasters spit into is a **spittoon**. These can vary from specially designed giant metal funnels, through wooden CASES filled with sawdust, to ice buckets, jugs, or, particularly convenient at a seated tasting, personal plastic or cardboard beakers. Most professional tasting rooms are equipped with channels, or sinks with running water designed to drain away expectorated wine.

SPRAYING, a vineyard practice of applying AGROCHEMICALS to control pests, diseases, and weeds. Late last century vineyard sprayers were often drawn by draught animals and operated with manual pumps; nowadays they are mounted on tractors or drawn by them. Agrochemicals in dry powder form are applied by a process known as DUSTING.

The aim of economically and environmentally sound spraying is to achieve maximum coverage of the 'target' (leaves, bunches, or weeds) by applying minimum amounts of the appropriate agrochemical. There should be ideally no chemical lost to the surrounding environment as 'spray drift'. Good coverage depends on having very small droplets, although these are more readily blown off target by wind than large drops.

There are several ways of spraying a vineyard from the ground, including boom sprayers, Controlled Droplet Application (CDA), and air blast sprayers.

Vineyards can also be sprayed from the air, using fixed wing aircraft or HELICOPTERS. Ideal spraying height is 1.5 to 3 m/5–10 ft above the vines, sufficiently low to give the pilot and spectators a thrill, especially if there are trees or other obstacles near the vineyard. Costs can be lower, but coverage is typically not as good as for ground spraying. Low wind conditions are required, and spraying from the air is typically done soon after dawn. Aerial spraying can be used when ground conditions are unsuited for tractors, such as following heavy rain.

Relatively few vineyards are now sprayed from containers strapped on workers' backs, although this is still done in Portugal's DOURO valley and on one-man properties. The costs of such spraying operations are of course very high, and generally not sustainable for most commercial vineyards.

R.E.S.

Coombe, B. G., and Dry, P. R. (eds.), *Viticulture, ii: Practices* (Adelaide, 1992).

SPRINKLERS are used in some vineyards to control FROST. Where sprinklers are used for IRRIGATION, it is a simple matter to use them also for frost prevention. Sprinkling is effective not only by directly warming the vines during frost; wetting the surface soil with (relatively) warm water also temporarily slows its cooling and, by increasing heat conductivity, facilitates the radiation of soil-stored warmth to the vines. Normally much less water is used than when irrigating. It is important to avoid waterlogging, which can readily cause injury to the newly growing roots. J.G. & R.E.S.

SPRITZER, common name for a mixture of white wine and fizzy water that is usually drunk as an APERITIF.

SPRITZIG, German term for semi-SPARKLING, applied widely to wines which are not meant to be particularly fizzy but which have a small but attractive concentration of CARBON DIOXIDE in solution such that there is a slight prickle on the tongue when they are tasted. **Spritz** has become an international tasting term, perhaps for onomatopoeic reasons.

SPUMANTE, Italian word for sparkling wine from the verb *spumare*, to foam or froth. The most important of these is ASTI SPUMANTE, made from the MOSCATO BIANCO grape cultivated in the provinces of Asti, Cuneo, and Alessandria, of which 80 million bottles may be made in an average year.

Significant quantities of sparkling wines from CHARDONNAY and PINOT NOIR, the classic grapes of CHAMPAGNE, are also produced in Italy, principally from three areas: the TRENTINO-ALTO ADIGE, the OLTREPÒ PAVESE, and FRANCIACORTA. The Italians, unlike the Champagne houses, also employ PINOT BLANC and PINOT GRIS in their blends. Some of these wines are produced using the CHARMAT process, but the majority are fermented in bottle like champagne and are labelled 'metodo classico'.

A vast number of other types of sparkling wine are made in Italy from a bewildering range of grape varieties, in a dazzling array of colours, ALCOHOLIC STRENGTHS, and RESIDUAL SUGAR levels. Over 30 DOCS allow sparkling wine made to be made: Bianco di CUSTOZA, Colli Albani, Colli Euganei, Colli Piacentini, Colli Tortonesi, CORTESE dell'Alto Monferrato, FRASCATI, GAVI, GRECO DI TUFO, Locorotondo, Marino, Roero ARNEIS, TREBBIANO di Romagna, Velletri, and VERDICCHIO dei Castelli di Jesi are some of the more significant white sparklers. Red sparkling wines are permitted within the AGLIANICO, BRACHETTO, Cesanese di Olevano Romano, Elba Rosso, FREISA, and LISON-PRAMAGGIORE (from MERLOT, CABERNET, or REFOSCO) DOCs. In addition to these there are myriad sparkling wines made and sold as a VINO DA TAVOLA: from VERNACCIA di San Gimignano, from Trebbiano grown in ORVIETO and many, many more.

One can conclude that Italians simply like CARBON DIOXIDE in their wine and do not, unlike the French perhaps, require that it resembles a single paradigm.

See also FRIZZANTE. D.T.

Sprinkler system in Chablis designed to protect the vines from frost.

SPUR, a viticultural term for a shortened grapevine cane. A spur is a stub formed by shortening the CANE to between one and four NODES, usually two. Spurs are used to provide the next season's fruiting SHOOTS. Of all PRUNING systems, SPUR PRUNING is the most severe since over 90 per cent of the previous year's cane growth is removed. Spurs are also left on cane-pruned vines to augment replacement canes at next pruning. B.G.C.

SPUR PRUNING, a form of winter vine PRUNING whereby the canes are cut back to two bud SPURS (see diagram p. 920). Normally the spurs are spaced along a CORDON and point upwards. There are several advantages to spur pruning, in that it takes less time to prune by hand and the operation can also be mechanized easily using pre-PRUNING MACHINES. Also, setting the spur spacing results in the correct shoot spacing in the canopy, which in turn leads to well-exposed leaves and fruit (see CANOPY MICROCLIMATE). Spur pruning is not particularly well suited to very vigorous vineyards, however, as excessive SHADE can lead to the loss of both yield and quality. The other main form of vine pruning is CANE PRUNING. See also CORDON TRAINING. R.E.S.

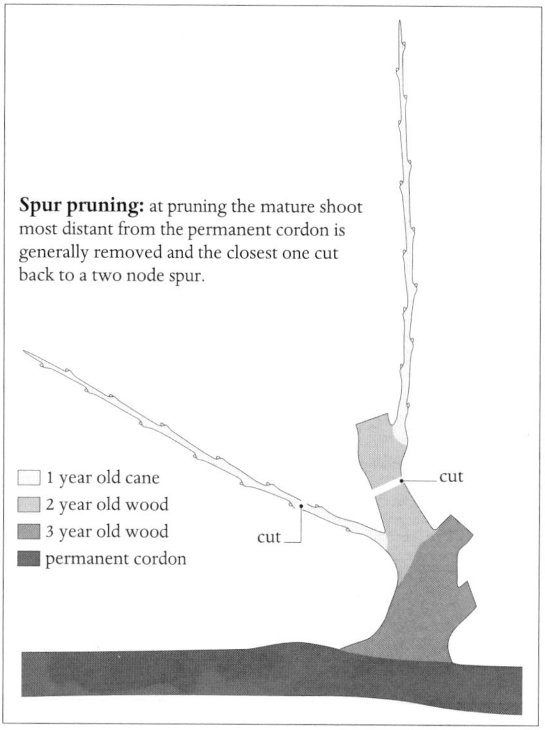

Spur pruning: at pruning the mature shoot most distant from the permanent cordon is generally removed and the closest one cut back to a two node spur.

SQUINZANO, DOC for robust red wine made mainly from NEGROAMARO grapes in south east Italy. For more details see APULIA.

SQUIRRELS can sometimes damage vines. See ANIMALS.

STABILIZATION, group of wine-processing operations undertaken to ensure that the wine, once bottled, has **stability** and will remain essentially **stable** or unchanged. A stable wine is one that will not form hazes, clouds, or unwanted deposits; become gassy; or undergo rapid deterioration of flavour after BOTTLING. A quick recovery from BOTTLE SICKNESS and subtle changes in flavour that occur with lengthy AGEING are considered normal in a stable wine.

Everyday wines are usually more thoroughly stabilized than fine wines since consumers have come to expect them to be crystal clear. Fine wines are normally less drastically stabilized since those who buy them are expected to understand about TARTRATES and the slow throwing of a SEDIMENT, and also because it is believed that the less stable constituents contribute to the ageing process. (The fine wine process of BARREL MATURATION has the effect of stabilizing a wine naturally in any case.)

Stabilization includes two sorts of operations: one to counter physical and chemical changes and another to counter microbiological changes.

Physical and chemical stability

Young wines are supersaturated in tartrates; REFRIGERATION and cold FILTRATION will reduce the concentration of tartrates below the level that would subsequently form crystals in the bottle.

Young white wines often contain high concentrations of rapidly browning PHENOLICS which, if left in the wine, will cause undue darkening of the wine after bottling. Selective FINING can remove the offending type of phenolic and ensure longer light colour in young white wines. Young red wines may also contain excessive amounts of TANNINS which taste bitter and astringent unless allowed to POLYMERIZE during extended bottle ageing. Red wines designed to be drunk young can be fined to remove some of these tannins.

Some varieties of white grape such as MUSCAT contain large amounts of heat-unstable PROTEINS which can coagulate and appear as a haze in the bottle unless it is kept at a constant, low temperature. These proteins can be removed by fining with BENTONITE or, less effectively, some other fining agents.

Microbiological stability

Measures to ensure microbiological stability have to counter the growth of either YEAST or BACTERIA. The simplest way to avoid yeast growth, which could result in a SECONDARY FERMENTATION, is to ensure that the wine is free of fermentable sugar, and its RESIDUAL SUGAR is negligible. If some residual sugar is necessary to balance, say, high ACIDITY in the wine, then sterile filtration and STERILE BOTTLING are the surest way of guaranteeing stability. Failing the necessary equipment and trained personnel, additions of SULPHUR DIOXIDE and SORBIC ACID will sufficiently inhibit most yeast growth, at some marginal depreciation of wine quality.

Stabilization of wine against bacterial attack is not so much of a problem in clean, modern wineries where the level of HYGIENE is high. The most harmful bacteria, those which turn wine into vinegar, ACETOBACTER, can operate only in the presence of OXYGEN and so stability can be assured by protecting the wine from air. Furthermore, sulphur dioxide which is invariably used by wine-makers, helps by suppressing the growth of acetobacter, and that of LACTIC BACTERIA. Lactic bacteria can also be inhibited by removing all fermentable sugars and all of the MALIC ACID (by MALOLACTIC FERMENTATION), two substrates for growth of some lactics.

No cellar treatments are needed against micro-organisms harmful to man since wine's high levels of acidity and alcohol naturally inhibit their growth. A.D.W.

STAGNANT, pejorative tasting term used principally by American professionals for the comparatively rare cases of sound wine stored in wooden COOPERAGE that contained water for an extended period. The odour differs from most of those smells described as MOULDY and is immediately recognizable to those who have smelled an old rain barrel. Many

The modern wine industry is heavily dependent on **stainless steel**, as here at Domaine Chandon in Australia's Yarra Valley (where wood is used complementarily).

organisms grow in water held in cooperage and most of them produce unpleasant-smelling compounds. It is to avoid these odours that most wine-makers try to keep their cooperage in good condition by keeping barrels full of wine. See BARREL MAINTENANCE. A.D.W.

STAGS LEAP DISTRICT, California wine region and AVA. See NAPA.

STAINLESS STEEL is widely used for holding wine, both for AGEING and, especially, for FERMENTATION. For wines made PROTECTIVELY it has the great advantage over wood that it is easy to clean and OXYGEN can be completely excluded from it, by the use of INERT GAS to fill head space if necessary. It has the advantage over concrete, still much used (including at Ch PÉTRUS), that TEMPERATURE CONTROL is even easier, especially with refrigerated jacketing and cooling/warming coils, and any TARTRATES can be hosed out rather than having to be chipped off the concrete walls. For some wines its exclusion of oxygen can be a disadvantage, however. There is no possibility of the gradual CLARIFICATION and STABILIZATION process that is possible in wooden containers.

STAKE. The simplest form of vine support is a stake driven into the ground beside the vine. A stake supports an individual vine, whereas POSTS, which are usually thicker than stakes, support several vines from suspended wires. Stakes are a very traditional form of vine support, having been used for centuries. Vines trained to stakes are most common in the OLD WORLD, although the vineyards of California are a significant exception. Since vines are climbing plants, they are unable to support themselves unless specially trained with a short trunk as for GOBELET vines.

Materials used for stakes vary enormously between different wine regions, reflecting local availability. Most common is WOOD, which has been used for centuries, although it is only recently that timber has been treated chemically, preventing softwoods from rotting in the ground. Sometimes stakes are made from round timber, as in much of Europe, or from sawn timber as in California. They can also be made from stone (slaty schist) as in the Douro valley of Portugal, or from cement as in parts of Italy. Stakes made from steel, plastic, or fibreglass have become more common in recent times and can be installed already notched and punched for wires.

See also POST. R.E.S.

STALK. For information about the stalk of an individual grape or berry, see PEDICEL. For information about the stalk of a bunch of grapes, see BUNCHSTEM. See also STEM.

STAMEN, pollen-bearing part of a flower that consists generally of an ANTHER borne on a filament. A grapevine flower is small and has five erect stamens that become evident after the CALYPTRA or cap has fallen off at FLOWERING. B.G.C.

STARCH, VINE, an insoluble carbohydrate polymer composed of GLUCOSE residues. It is non-osmotic and is the principal storage substance in plants, forming as starch grains. Starch grains occur in the leaf and in cells of storage tissue in stems and roots of the vine. During daylight hours, when SUCROSE levels rise in leaves due to PHOTOSYNTHESIS, starch grains build up. At night they are metabolized to provide the sugar needed for RESPIRATION (this is also their fate in the human gut). Starch (and arginine) storage reserves are remobilized when buds burst and shoots begin to grow. Unlike many fruits, grape berries do not contain much starch, which is one reason why grapes do not ripen after picking. Starch is the principal CARBOHYDRATE reserve of vines. B.G.C.

STATE WINE-MAKING has been important, not just in eastern Europe during the communist era when all activity took place under the auspices of the state, but also in Germany, where the state owns a number of important vineyards and cellars, including KLOSTER EBERBACH.

STAVES are the shaped wooden planks that are cut and formed into BARRELS. See BARREL MAKING for more details.

STEEN, South Africa's most common name for CHENIN BLANC, the Cape's most common white vine variety grown in all wine regions. Steen is also South Africa's most versatile grape producing an astonishing spectrum of wine styles: dry, sweet, BOTRYTIZED, sparkling, brandy, and sherry types. Confusingly, wines are labelled either Chenin Blanc or Steen at the whim of the producer, while Steen is the major and often sole grape in local wines labelled **Stein** denoting not grape variety but an off-dry to semi-sweet white, the country's biggest-selling wine category. Vinified by cold fermentation, the wine can show lively fruity appeal for a year or two but this attraction tends to fade in dry Cape Steens. J.P.

STEIERMARK, wine region in AUSTRIA known in English as STYRIA.

STELLENBOSCH, important wine region in South Africa, famously beautiful town within it, and the name of the only university in South Africa where both VITICULTURE and OENOLOGY may be studied. Informal teaching in these two subjects started in 1889 but the Department of Viticulture and Oenology was formally opened only in 1917, with Professor A. I. Perold as director.

As elsewhere (see BORDEAUX, DAVIS, GEISENHEIM, for example), the PHYLLOXERA crisis was a powerful motivation for viticultural research, and from 1890 until about 1920 most of Stellenbosch's work was concentrated on re-establishing the phylloxera-devastated vineyards of the Cape. This research was concentrated on the selection of suitable phylloxera-resistant ROOTSTOCKS and on refining GRAFTING techniques.

During the 1920s, considerable effort was expended on improving the quality of fruit-bearing vine SCIONS, a range that was naturally restricted by strict QUARANTINE regulations. This involved VINE BREEDING which led to NEW VARIETIES, of which PINOTAGE has been the most widely acclaimed. The programme, of breeding both rootstocks and wine grape varieties, was successfully continued by Professor Orffer. Professor Perold and his successors also devoted considerable efforts to improving PRUNING and TRELLISING techniques.

Under the guidance of Stellenbosch oenologists, South Africa was one of the first wine-producing countries to apply widespread TEMPERATURE CONTROL to fermentations. Stellenbosch graduates also played a major part in forming South Africa's WINE OF ORIGIN legislation in 1973.

Current research in viticulture is concerned particularly with VINE DENSITY, CANOPY MANAGEMENT, and TISSUE CULTURE of vine plant material to improve wine quality. The elimination of harmful vine VIRUS DISEASES by such GENETIC ENGINEERING techniques has received international acclaim. Oenological research is mainly concerned with aroma and flavour compounds of particular significance to wine.

See SOUTH AFRICA for more detail of the Stellenbosch wine region.

STEM. The terms stem and stalk tend to be used somewhat carelessly by wine-makers, if not by viticulturists. For information about the stem of an individual grape or berry, see PEDICEL. For information about the stem of a bunch of grapes, see BUNCHSTEM. For information about the stem of a vine plant, see SHOOT. See also DESTEMMING.

STEMMING, paradoxically alternative term for DESTEMMING grapes.

STEM PITTING, vine disease. See LEGNO RICCIO.

STEMWARE, see GLASSES.

STERILE BOTTLING, or **aseptic bottling**, the technique of getting wine into a closed bottle without incorporating any micro-organisms (notably YEAST and harmful BACTERIA). Borrowed from the pharmaceutical packaging industry, this technique does the job of PASTEURIZATION without producing cooked or burnt flavours. It involves the highest level of HYGIENE but the necessary equipment is also considerably more expensive than that for regular BOTTLING, which is why it is justified primarily for high-volume, relatively low alcohol wines containing some RESIDUAL SUGAR which could suffer SECONDARY FERMENTATION if yeast cells are allowed into the bottle, typically LIEBFRAUMILCH and other mass-market German blends.

An aseptic bottling line involves the creation of a germ-free room, modifying the usual equipment so that it may be sterilized easily. The room is kept under a slight positive pressure of sterilized air and entry, through a double door system, is restricted to the few specially trained and clothed personnel required. Micro-organisms are removed from the wine by depth membrane sterile FILTRATION and the corks are sterilized by gaseous SULPHUR DIOXIDE or other chemical sterilizing agents. The bottling and corking machines are usually sterilized by steam, or by chemical sterilants. Frequent sample bottles are removed at random for

Stellenbosch—the Cape's topography is some of the wine world's most distinctive.

Young Rolle vines establishing an existence in the **stones and rocks** of Domaine Rimauresq in Côtes de Provence.

microbiological analysis, and each bottling run is held in storage until it is certain that no organisms are growing.

A.D.W.

STEWARD, WINE. See SOMMELIER.

STIGMA. See vine FLOWER.

STIRRING, wine-making term which may be used as a synonym for LEES STIRRING or may refer to the important operation of stirring, usually in much larger containers, when blending disparate components in a blend. This is particularly necessary when GRAPE SPIRIT is added to wine, as during FORTIFICATION, since the spirit, with its lower DENSITY, tends to float on top of the wine.

STOMA (plural **stomata**), minute opening on the surface of leaves bordered by two guard cells which open and close, thus regulating the exchange of gases between the atmosphere and the air chambers inside the leaf, especially of water out and carbon dioxide in (see RESPIRATION and TRANSPIRATION). The stomata of the grapevine occur only on the underside of each leaf blade.

B.G.C.

STONES AND ROCKS, as visible constituents of the soil or its surface (cf. the underlying ROCK), loom large in the folklore of wine quality. They figure prominently in the older French concepts of TERROIR. Nineteenth century French writers such as Rendu and Petit-Lafitte laid particular emphasis on the proportions of stone or gravel in the soils of the best vineyards. The stonier the soil, they said, the better in general is the wine quality.

Present thinking broadly supports the old ideas. Rocky and stony soils are usually well drained, but at the same time not too fertile. A high proportion of stones also reduces water-holding capacity per unit of soil volume (see SOIL WATER). Both factors are significant in climates and management systems where excessive vine VIGOUR, leading to unsatisfactory CANOPY MICROCLIMATES, is a threat. Forcing the vine to develop a sparse, but extensive, ROOT system also helps to buffer it against sudden changes in nutrition or water supply. Beyond that, a rocky or stony soil is thought to help by efficiently absorbing heat during sunshine and reradiating it during the evening and cloudy periods—thereby perhaps affording the ripening fruit a better temperature regime for flavour RIPENING (see CLIMATE AND WINE QUALITY). Verbrugghe *et al.* document the temperature effects on ripening grapes of the famously large stones of CHÂTEAUNEUF-DU-PAPE in the southern Rhône. Stones and rocks also form an efficient mulch against surface evaporation, and offer protection against SOIL EROSION.

See also SOIL AND WINE QUALITY.

J.G.

Petit-Lafitte, A., *La Vigne dans le Bordelais* ('The vine in the Bordeaux region') (Paris, 1868).

Rendu, V., *Ampélographie française* ('Ampelography of France') (Paris, 1857).

Verbrugghe, M., Guyot, G., Hanocq, J. F., and Ripoche, D., 'Influence de différents types de sol de la basse vallée du Rhône sur les températures de surface de raisins et de feuilles de Vitis vinifera' ('Influence of different soil types of the lower Rhône valley on the temperatures of the berry surface and leaves of *Vitis vinifera*'), *Revue française d'œnologie*, 128 (1991), 14–20.

STOPPERS for wine containers are necessary to avoid harmful contact with OXYGEN and have changed remarkably little. CORKS are still the principal closures used for wine BOTTLES, just as they were more than two centuries ago and probably long before that.

History

Cork was certainly known in Ancient GREECE, where, as in Ancient EGYPT, great care was taken to provide AMPHORAE with a wide variety of airtight stoppers. Roman authors such as CATO, writing in the 2nd century BC, refer to the need to seal jars with cork and pitch when the fermentation was complete. However, this use of cork does not appear to have continued into the early medieval period, possibly because the main potential supply of European cork was in southern Iberia, which had been conquered by the Moors in the 8th century. Medieval illuminations illustrate barrels generally sealed by wooden stoppers, with cloth frequently placed between the barrel and the stopper to provide a more airtight seal. Pitch and wax were also sometimes used to provide additional protection. In the long period during which wine was mainly stored in and served from the BARREL, the most common stopper was some form of BUNG.

With the development of glass bottles during the 17th century, it was necessary to devise new methods of stoppering. Glass stoppers, ground to fit individual bottles and tied to them with thread, were therefore introduced, and survived well into the 19th century. Indeed, as they are found in DECANTERS, they remain in use to this day. However, such stoppers were expensive, and gradually from the beginning of the 17th century cork became the most frequent substance used to seal bottles. The use of corks also required the invention of another piece of equipment, the corkscrew or, as it was first called, the bottlescrew. The earliest corks were not pressed completely into the bottles, and so could be pulled out without excessive difficulty. However, by the end of the 17th century the introduction of CORKSCREWS enabled corks fully to be inserted into the necks of bottles. P.T.H.U.

Johnson, H., *The Story of Wine* (London, 1989).
Simon, A. L., *Bottlescrew Days: Wine Drinking in England during the 18th Century* (London, 1926).

Modern stoppers

Modern technology offers a range of alternatives to the traditional cork, and every CORKED bottle increases interest in them, particularly since most are cheaper than corks. They have to offer a reliable seal, an inert substance to the wine, be easily removable, and be capable of being produced at a relatively low cost. Few have proved as successful as cork for long-term BOTTLE AGEING, however, and there is still considerable attachment on the part of many wine drinkers to the ritual of pulling a cork.

The synthetic **plastic 'cork'** is designed to satisfy the wine drinker's need to wrestle with corkscrews while using a man-made material without the fine pores which can harbour moulds. Its disadvantage is that it can be even more difficult to extract than the traditional cork and that it is not yet proven as a suitable stopper for the long term.

The **screwcap**, sometimes known as an ROPP (roll-on, pilfer-proof), is a usefully inexpensive closure for the short and medium term. During the roll-on process the unthreaded cap is compressed from the exterior so that threads are formed exactly matching those of the particular bottle. Pressure on the top seats the cap lining firmly against the bottle lip so that the seal is reasonably gas-tight. Made of non-corroding metal, usually an alloy of aluminium, the screwcap is lined with moulded cork and an inert film in contact with the wine. It also has the great advantage of requiring no equipment to remove it and being extremely easy to replace. However, unlike cork, screwcaps cannot compensate for bottle-necks whose glass finish is not completely smooth. The screwcap itself can last many years (and has kept white wines fresh for at least 10 years) but has yet to prove itself the equal of cork for extended bottle ageing in the eyes of traditionalists. Unlike cork, screwcaps cannot compensate for bottle lips that are not perfectly flat, although the Australian Wine Research Institute of ADELAIDE conducted extensive tests in the mid 1970s on the Stelvin closure, which performed well.

The **crown cap**, the small metal cap used on beer and soda bottles, has proved the most reliable stopper for long-term wine bottle storage (see Helmut BECKER of Geisenheim) and provides an extremely cheap and efficient stopper for any sort of wine, but many wine drinkers find its association with what they regard as less sophisticated drinks unacceptable, particularly when it comes to wine SERVICE in a smart restaurant. The crown cap is also used nearly universally for closing SPARKLING WINE bottles during the TIRAGE process; DISGORGING is much more difficult if a cork has to be extracted.

There has been experimentation with a wide range of other stoppers, but the field is open to more acceptable alternatives to a piece of bark.

See also CAPSULES.

STORING WINE is an important aspect of wine consumption, since wine is one of the very few consumer products that can improve with age (although see AGEING for details of how few, and which, wines this applies to). Until the era of inflation, the wine trade regarded storing and ageing wine as part of their business, but since the 1960s they have steadily relinquished this role. The development of the EN PRIMEUR market and the increase in the number of wine COLLECTORS leaves many more ordinary wine drinkers with the problem of how to store wine over long periods, often a decade or two.

There are two basic choices: to consign the bottles to professional storage and/or to establish some form of domestic cellar. If wine is put in storage it is vital that a specialist in wine storage is found, since wine is a much more fragile commodity than most things kept in warehouses, and needs specialist treatment and conditions. It is important that the wine storage specialist is in sound financial health itself, it understands the detail of storage conditions needed, and that it provides some facility for marking individual CASES with some identification of their owner. In the case of business failure this can make the difference between establishing possession and not.

For more details of how to identify and, if necessary, convert part of a home into a suitable place to store wine, see CELLAR.

Storage conditions

Even in Ancient GREECE there was some appreciation of the importance of storage conditions on the evolution and health of wine. The key factors are TEMPERATURE, light, HUMIDITY, peace, and security.

If wine is kept too hot, or exposed to strong sunlight, it rapidly deteriorates. If it is kept too cold, it can freeze, expand, and push out the stopper of whatever container it is held in.

For bottles stored for a few weeks, the primary concern is to keep them from strong direct light (white wines in colourless glass are most at risk) and to ensure that they do not reach temperatures more than about 25 °C/77 °F, at which point the wine may be spoilt and forever afterwards taste cooked.

Bottles to be stored for more than a few weeks, however, should be stored so that the cork is kept damp and there is no possibility of its drying out and allowing in the enemy, OXYGEN. This usually entails storing the bottles horizontally, ideally in a wine rack so that individual bottles can easily be extracted, or in a BIN full of wines of the same sort. Many wine producers deliberately mark their cases in an effort to keep bottles upside down, and corks damp, during shipment. Wine in an inverted bottle comes to no harm, although if it is kept in this position for many years the SEDIMENT may stick to the inside of the neck of the bottle, which will be inconvenient when SERVING.

A fairly wide range of temperatures is suitable for wine storage, although, in general, the lower the storage temperature, the slower and possibly more complex the wine maturation. Dramatic temperature swings should be avoided and an average temperature somewhere in the range 10 to 15 °C is considered suitable (see TEMPERATURE for more details).

Some degree of humidity is beneficial, to ensure that the exposed end of the cork does not dry out and allow in oxygen. A level of 75 per cent relative humidity is usually cited, although this, like so many aspects of wine consumption rather than production, suffers from a lack of scientific research. The disadvantage of very damp cellars is that damp labels eventually deteriorate and make identification difficult.

If a maturing wine is agitated it may disturb the sediment and therefore the AGEING process (although this is unproven hypothesis). Many cellars are specifically designed with rubber racks for bottles in order to avoid any risk of vibration. The need for a secure storage space is obvious, especially since bottles of alcoholic drink seem to be widely regarded as common currency rather than private property.

It is also important that there are no strong, persistent smells in a long-term wine storage area.

See also BULK STORAGE.

STRAW WINES, see VIN DE PAILLE and DRIED GRAPE WINES.

STÜCK, German term for a large wooden BARREL, typically one with a capacity of 1,200 l/317 gal used in RHINE regions of GERMANY. (In the MOSEL-SAAR-RUWER region the FUDER is more common.) A **Halbstück** contains 600 l, and was commonly used for transporting wine in the pre-tanker era, while a **Doppelstück** contains 2,400 l.

STUCK FERMENTATION, wine-maker's nightmare involving an alcoholic FERMENTATION which ceases before completion. Such fermentations are notoriously difficult to restart and the wine is at risk of spoilage from OXIDATION and BACTERIAL DISEASE. Before cooling equipment was commonplace, fermentation TEMPERATURES could reach a dangerously high level, often in excess of 35 °C/95 °F. In extreme cases, with temperatures nearing the range at which YEASTS are killed, over 40 °C, the yeast cells release compounds which inhibit future yeast growth, thereby making it difficult or impossible to restart such fermentations, even after cooling.

Stuck fermentation has many documented causes, with the most common being a deficiency of NITROGEN. Grapes, particularly the varieties Riesling and Chardonnay which come from vineyards deficient in nitrogen, yield fruit with a low ratio of nitrogen to sugar. This limits the development of yeast cells, and fermentation activity is not sustained after the yeasts become starved of nitrogen. This problem is exacerbated in the fermentation of white grape varieties where, in an attempt to produce a wine with clean, pronounced VARIETAL character, the must is kept highly protected from air and with a very low level of grape solids. In the absence of air these grape solids, which contain LIPIDS, are essential for strong yeast growth and for sustaining high yeast cell viability during the critical final stage of fermentation. This problem can be controlled either by increasing the level of grape solids, or aerating the yeast culture (when not using commercial dried yeast), or exposing the fermentation to a small amount of air once the yeast is active. The latter is most simply achieved by stirring or PUMPING OVER.

Failure of the added wine yeast to dominate the wild yeasts that are invariably present in grape must can result in a stuck fermentation if these yeasts have a lower tolerance to alcohol. Wild yeasts, which produce the 'killer toxin' (zymocidal yeasts), can be especially aggressive by actively eliminating the sensitive wine yeast. This problem is diminished considerably by using highly active preparations of dried yeasts, inoculating with wine yeast that is resistant to killer toxin, and by any method that reduces the number of wild yeasts present in the must. Cool harvesting and processing conditions, and FILTRATION, CENTRIFUGATION, or PASTEURIZATION are usually effective.

Henschke, P. A., and Jiranek, V., 'Yeasts: metabolism of nitrogen compounds', in G. H. Fleet (ed.), *Wine Microbiology and Biotechnology* (Chur, 1993).

Kunkee, R. E., 'Relationship between nitrogen content of must and sluggish fermentation', in J. M. Rantz (ed.), *Proceedings of the International Symposium on Nitrogen in Grapes and Wine* (Seattle, 1991) *American Journal of Enology and Viticulture* (1991) 148–55.

STYRIA, small but fashionable wine region in the far south east of AUSTRIA, most famous for aromatic, lively dry whites.

SUBJECTIVITY plays an unavoidable part in wine TASTING. Personal preferences inevitably play some role in wine assessment.

SUBSOIL, the usually heavier-textured layer of a SOIL which underlies the main zone containing ROOTS and ORGANIC MATTER. It overlies the native ROCK or sediments from which the soil is formed. The contrast in texture between surface soil and subsoil is greatest in ancient soils and in forest (especially pine forest) regions, due to the progressive downward leaching of the heavier minerals and fine CLAY particles. Such subsoils are, however, typically depleted of many of the important nutrient elements, because roots have continuously extracted them from depth and deposited them at the surface in leaf litter and derived organic matter.

A fairly heavy-textured subsoil, provided that it drains freely enough, can have advantages for viticulture because it provides a good store of moisture that is well protected against direct EVAPORATION and exploitation by shallow-rooted WEEDS. The usual relative sparseness of vine roots in the subsoil, together with the strength with which clay particles hold water (see SOIL WATER and SOIL TEXTURE), ensures that the stored water can be used only at a limited rate. Seguin cites the clay soils of POMEROL as an example of this. It helps to provide the vine with the consistent regime of water supply that Seguin believes to be important for wine quality. See also TERROIR and SOIL AND WINE QUALITY.

On the other hand, many heavy subsoils impede DRAINAGE, particularly those formed from acid rock materials. These can be detrimental to viticulture, unless carefully drained and, possibly, LIMED to overcome SOIL ACIDITY and improve the SOIL STRUCTURE. J.G.

Seguin, G., 'Influence des terroirs viticoles', *Bulletin de l'OIV*, 56 (1983), 3–18.

—— '"Terroirs" and pedology of wine growing,' *Experientia*, 42 (1986), 861–72.

SUBSOILING, vineyard practice normally conducted before PLANTING that is designed to break up SUBSOIL, removing barriers to root growth and improving water infiltration. Subsoiling is synonymous with RIPPING. R.E.S.

SUCCINIC ACID, an acid found to a limited extent in both grapes and wine. Present in low concentrations in ripe grapes, it is a contributor to the fresh or tart taste of the fruit, albeit to a much lesser extent than TARTARIC ACID or MALIC ACID. Like these two principal grape acids, pure succinic acid is a white crystalline solid that is very soluble in water and alcoholic water solutions such as wine.

Succinic acid concentrations tend to be much higher in wine than grapes because the acid is a by-product of the complex nitrogen metabolic processes involved in YEAST growth during FERMENTATION. In some wines a considerable proportion of the succinic acid reacts with one molecule of ETHANOL to form an ESTER, mono-ethyl succinate, which has a very mild, fruity aroma somewhat reminiscent of wines. Very small amounts of the compounds resulting from the reaction of both acid groups of succinic acid with ethanol are also found but these are non-odoriferous. A.D.W.

SUCKERING. See DESUCKERING.

SUCROSE, cane sugar, the most common of the SUGARS, is ubiquitous in plants because it is the preferred compound for PHLOEM translocation of energy and carbon around the plant (although sorbitol serves this function in some *Prunus* species). Sucrose, a disaccharide, is a non-reducing compound and consists of a GLUCOSE joined to a FRUCTOSE (both of which are reducing). Breakdown (hydrolysis) of sucrose is achieved readily by the enzyme INVERTASE, which 'inverts' it to these hexoses. Invertase in the vine occurs in CELL wall spaces but not in those of the leaf, which is why sucrose is confined in vines mainly to leaves and phloem tubes. Invertase is abundant in grape berries both in the cell walls and in the vacuoles; hence the sugars that accumulate in berries are mainly glucose and fructose. B.G.C.

SÜDTIROL, or South Tyrol. See ALTO ADIGE.

SUGAR ADDITION, wine-making practice more usually called CHAPTALIZATION or, in European Union parlance, ENRICHMENT.

SUGAR CONCENTRATION in grapes. See MUST WEIGHT.

SUGARING, term occasionally used for the wine-making operation of CHAPTALIZATION.

SUGAR IN GRAPES, the *raison d'être* of VITICULTURE (an exaggeration which can be used equally for sugar cane and any other crop in which free sugar is the predominant accumulated compound). The central role of sugar in the utility of grapes for wine, TABLE GRAPES, DRYING GRAPES, and other viticultural products cannot be over-emphasized. SUGARS produce SWEETNESS and ferment to produce ETHANOL, both of which are valued by humans. However, of all sugary plant produce, none yields a commodity as highly valued or widely grown as grape wine.

The free sugar that accumulates in grapes, GLUCOSE and FRUCTOSE, is the result of translocation of SUCROSE photosynthesized in leaves and moved via PHLOEM tubes into grape berries during RIPENING, where it is inverted (hydrolysed) by the enzyme INVERTASE. The astonishing feature of grapes is that this accumulation occurs at the same time as water is accumulating in the berry, yet concentration is also increasing; in other words, sugar is increasing proportionately more than water. The mechanism of this process is not known. Other phloem-provided sucrose moves throughout the vine dispensing energy and the carbon skeletons for all organic molecules throughout the vine. Additionally, sugar is used for carbon storage, as STARCH in wood, and for the formation of glycosides in the storage of secondary metabolites in vacuoles of cells (see FLAVOUR COMPOUNDS).

While total sugar content (see MUST WEIGHT) is a key factor in determining optimum RIPENESS of grapes for wine, sugar–acid balance is equally important; hence the use of sugar–acid ratio as a guide to the date of harvest (see GRAPE QUALITY ASSESSMENT). B.G.C.

Winkler, A. J., *et al.*, *General Viticulture* (2nd edn., Berkeley, Calif., 1974).

SUGARS, simpler members of the large group of natural organic chemical compounds called CARBOHYDRATES. The sugar of common parlance, SUCROSE, comes from either sugar cane or sugar beet plants and is a major international commodity. To scientists, sucrose is a molecule made up of one unit of each of GLUCOSE and FRUCTOSE linked together with the elimination of a molecule of water.

Plants produce sucrose by PHOTOSYNTHESIS, many of them accumulating sucrose within their cells but others, such as the common wine vine *Vitis* VINIFERA, breaking this sucrose down into its two simpler constituent parts, glucose and fructose, which are stored in the berries. AMERICAN VINES store small amounts of sucrose in the fruit along with the two simpler forms. Over the millennia during which man has selected grape vines, he has chosen those capable of photosynthesizing an excess of sugars and storing them in berries. For more detail, see SUGAR IN GRAPES.

Although the amounts of sugars other than glucose and fructose detected in grape must are very small, the process of photosynthesis involves sugars with three, four, five, and seven carbon atoms as well as the six-carbon glucose and fructose. It would be surprising, therefore, if traces of some of these were not identified in grape juice, and in wines some dozen different residual sugars have been reported.

Sucrose, usually in the form of sugar beet concentrate or some form of GRAPE CONCENTRATE, may be added to some grape musts before fermentation in order to increase the ALCOHOLIC STRENGTH of the resultant wine (see ENRICHMENT).

The total amount of sugars left in a finished wine is called its RESIDUAL SUGAR.

Some of the sucrose resulting from photosynthesis, stored in the berries as glucose and fructose before grape harvest, is converted into STARCH and stored in the vine's trunk and larger arms and roots during winter DORMANCY until spring temperatures begin the annual cycle of leaf and fruit production once more, and the starch is remobilized to soluble sugars, mainly glucose.

See also MUST WEIGHT. A.D.W.

SUISUN VALLEY, small CALIFORNIA wine region and AVA flanking SOLANO-GREEN VALLEY between San Francisco and Sacramento. Suisun Valley has only a sparse scattering of vineyards and a few modest, primarily local wineries. No particular wine type has pushed itself forward.

SULFATE, sulfide, sulfite, and **sulfur**, the American spellings of SULPHATE, SULPHIDE, SULPHITE, and SULPHUR respectively. Even some non-Americans argue that the word's etymology suggests that sulfur is the correct spelling.

SULPHIDES and **disulphides** are the compounds of SULPHUR with hydrogen or metallic elements in which the sulphur atom exists in its most reduced state, that is having gained two electrons from the other element or elements in the compound (see REDUCTION).

Sulphides occur naturally during wine-making. As FERMENTATION nears completion, the REDOX POTENTIAL can fall so low that elemental sulphur residues on the grapes from fungicides, and even SULPHUR DIOXIDE itself, can be reduced to HYDROGEN SULPHIDE. The wine-maker can detect this problem easily because hydrogen sulphide has an intense smell of bad eggs. Fortunately, the compound is very volatile and can usually be removed by simple AERATION.

In a wine-making context any reference to 'sulphide' or 'sulphides' is invariably a criticism and usually means hydrogen sulphide. Sulphides should not be confused with SULPHITES, however.

In the 19th and early 20th centuries, copper and bronze were commonly used for winery equipment and small amounts of copper would dissolve in the wine. If traces of hydrogen sulphide were present, copper sulphide, one of the least soluble of all compounds, would be formed. Later, after bottling, the colloidal copper sulphide would form a cloud or haze with some of the wine proteins. This problem has been averted by the use of STAINLESS STEEL. A.D.W.

SULPHITES and **bisulphites**, the negatively charged ions liberated when sulphurous acid dissociates, as shown below:

$$\underset{\text{sulphurous acid}}{H_2SO_3} \rightleftarrows \underset{\text{hydrogen ion}}{H^+} + \underset{\text{bisulphite ion}}{HSO_3^-}$$

$$\underset{\text{bisulphite ion}}{HSO_3^-} \rightarrow \underset{\text{hydrogen ion}}{H^+} + \underset{\text{sulphite ion}}{SO_3^{--}}$$

The analytical method usually used for the measurement of sulphites determines all of the various forms which are active in terms of smell, effect on YEAST and BACTERIA, and potential danger to asthmatics (see SULPHUR DIOXIDE). The term sulphites, or sulfites in the United States, is therefore used on wine labels (as in 'Contains sulphites') as an inclusive term for free sulphur dioxide, sulphurous acid (hydrated sulphur dioxide), bisulphite ion, sulphite ion, and some forms of complexed sulphites. See LABELLING INFORMATION. A.D.W.

SULPHUR, an element that constitutes about 0.5 per cent of the weight of the Earth's crust and one of the more important elements for mankind. It is extremely important in wine production because of the wide-ranging uses of SULPHUR DIOXIDE. A pale yellow, brittle, solid substance at room temperature, it was already known to the speakers of Ancient Sanskrit as *sulvere*. The book of Genesis in the Bible refers to sulphur as brimstone. In its combined form as sulphuric acid, sulphur is used in so many manufacturing processes that the tonnage consumed by a nation can be taken as an indication of the health of its economy.

History

Sulphur has been used as a cleansing agent and wine preservative since antiquity. Among the various substances, such as pitch and resin, used by the Romans to prepare vessels in which wine was stored and to assist in the preservation of wines, authors such as CATO and PLINY also mention the use of sulphur. It seems probable that the pungent smells given off when ores containing sulphur were burned led to their association with a cleansing action, and experimentation would then have revealed the most efficacious methods of use. In the late 15th century a German decree specifically refers to the use of sulphur, with wood shavings, powdered sulphur, herbs, and incense being burned in barrels before they were filled. By the 18th century, sulphur wicks were being regularly used to sterilize barrels in the best châteaux of Bordeaux (having been introduced by the DUTCH), and advances in chemistry had also led to the synthesis of derivatives of elemental sulphur, thus enabling inorganic salts containing sulphur to become widely used in wine-making. Sulphur dioxide is today used in the production of virtually all wines. In the vineyard, sulphur products are widely used to protect vines against both POWDERY MILDEW and DOWNY MILDEW. P.T.H.U.

Johnson, H., *The Story of Wine* (London, 1989).

Viticulture

Sulphur is essential for vine nutrition, although sulphur deficiency in vineyards is very rare. Vines usually obtain sufficient quantities from soil supplies, or from FUNGICIDES. Continued application of sulphur to vineyards to control powdery mildew for over a century has led to excess SOIL ACIDITY in France. Carbon bisulphide was injected into vineyard soils in the late 19th century to control PHYLLOXERA, although the practice was replaced by the use of resistant rootstocks. See also SULPHIDES. R.E.S.

Wine-making

Sulphur is most familiar to wine-makers as sulphur dioxide (although it can also react with oxygen to form sulphur trioxide, implicated in the problem of acid rain).

Residues of elemental sulphur used in the vineyard can combine with hydrogen in new wine to produce HYDROGEN SULPHIDE, the compound responsible for the foul smell of bad eggs. See also MERCAPTANS.

Everyday wines to which high sulphur additions have been made for particular operations, or for transport, may be **desulphured**.

See also SULPHITES. A.D.W.

SULPHUR DIOXIDE, or SO_2, formed when elemental sulphur is burned in air, is the chemical compound most widely used by the wine-maker, principally as a preservative and a disinfectant. Sulphur dioxide, as fumes from burning sulphur, has been used since antiquity to preserve and disinfect during the production and storage of foods (see SULPHUR for more historical detail).

It reacts so readily with oxygen that it precludes OXIDATION, or the reaction of OXYGEN with any other constituents of grape juice or wine with undesirable effects on colour and flavour. It is often added to freshly picked grapes in the form of metabisulphate. (The compound is therefore widely, often more liberally, used in the preparation of other foods and drinks, particularly fruit juices and dried fruits.) Sulphur dioxide has the further property, of particular value to the wine-maker, of inhibiting or killing BACTERIA or wild YEAST, and of encouraging a rapid and clean FERMENTATION. Other less important reasons for using sulphur dioxide in wine-making are that it helps brighten the colour of red wines and encourages the extraction of compounds from the grape skins during MACERATION. Sulphur dioxide's efficacy is influenced by the wine's PH.

At room temperatures and normal atmospheric pressures the compound exists as a colourless gas with a pungent, choking aroma similar to that of a struck match or burnt coke. (It reacts readily with oxygen to form sulphur trioxide which, in turn, reacts with water to yield sulphuric acid, the principal acid of 'acid rain'.)

The disadvantage of using sulphur dioxide (which all but a fraction of one per cent of wine-makers do) is that its aroma can be quite unpleasant even at fairly low concentrations, especially to some particularly sensitive tasters (who are likely to find it most noticeably on sweet Loire, sweet bordeaux, and German wines). Tests using both experienced and inexperienced wine tasters have shown that concentrations of 11 mg/l of sulphur dioxide in water are just detectable. In wines the threshold is much higher, partly because the acid-tasting effect of sulphur dioxide which is so obvious in pure water is overwhelmed by the acids naturally present in wine. The minimum detectable sulphur dioxide concentration in white wines for most people is just over 200 mg/l in white wines and 100 mg/l in reds, although palates can vary considerably in their sensitivity.

The threshold at which sulphur dioxide can be detected also varies with wine type, because sulphur dioxide reacts or combines to form 'bound' sulphur dioxide with up to 50 other wine constituents which interferes with sulphur dioxide perception. Only 'free', or uncombined, sulphur dioxide is active in terms of its effect on aroma, yeast, bacteria, or potential oxidation, although regulations about maximum permitted sulphur levels tend to concern the total amount of sulphur dioxide, both free and bound. Free sulphur dioxide can be difficult to measure in red wines.

During the latter half of the 20th century, maximum levels of sulphur dioxide permitted by law have been systematically reduced. From permitted levels of up to 500 parts per million (ppm) in 1910, they were no more than 200 ppm by the early 1990s. (Sweet wines need higher levels of sulphur dioxide to inhibit possible fermentation of the RESIDUAL SUGAR.) These reductions have been made partly because the smell of sulphur dioxide is undesirable, but they are also a response to lobbyists, especially in the United States, concerned about the effect of high doses of sulphur (more than any single bottle of wine contains) on asthmatics. This latter force has resulted in compulsory LABELLING INFORMATION in various countries. In the United States, for example, all wines carry the legend 'Contains sulfites' (see SULPHITES), while Australian labels must admit that sulphur dioxide, or 'Preservative (220)', has been added. Within the EUROPEAN UNION, sulphur dioxide is known as E220, but this need not be specified on wine labels.

Within the EU maximum permitted levels of total sulphur dioxide in 1993 were 160 mg/l in dry red wines, 210 mg/l in dry white, dry rosé, and sweet red wines, and 260 mg/l in sweet white and rosé wines. Certain very sweet wines could contain up to 400 mg/l, however, including all sweet white bordeaux, Jurançon, and a number of sweet white Loire wines, Beerenauslese, Trockenbeerenauslese, and Ausbruch wines. In 1993 the Australian maximum level, in any sort of wine, was 300 mg/l, although there was some pressure to reduce this to 250 mg/l.

There have been attempts to produce wines without any addition of sulphur dioxide (see GEISENHEIM, for example). Such wines are particularly prone to oxidation and the off-flavours generated by wild yeast and bacteria and need careful handling and possibly even PASTEURIZATION. It would be impossible to produce an entirely sulphur-free wine since a small amount of sulphur dioxide is one of the by-products of the metabolic action of yeast during fermentation when the material being fermented contains sulphate salts. Since sulphate salts are natural components of such fermentable materials as dough and fruit juices, it is normal to encounter small amounts of sulphur dioxide in such fermented products as bread and wine. A.D.W.

Rose, A. H., 'Sulphur dioxide and other preservatives', *Journal of Wine Research*, 4 (1993), 43–7.

SULTANA, the most important white grape variety used to produce the pale brown particular DRYING GRAPES sometimes called SULTANAS. The fruit of the Sultana vine, called Thompson Seedless in California, is remarkable for its versatility. As well as being dried, it can be vinified into a neutral white wine and, especially after treatment with GIBBERELLIN growth regulators to increase BERRY SIZE, is a much sought-after crisp, green, seedless TABLE GRAPE. In some viticultural regions, such as Australia's RIVERLAND and California's CENTRAL VALLEY, the Sultana harvest can be diverted to whatever happens to be the most profitable end use, including wine.

It is originally from the eastern Mediterranean where it may be known as Sultanine, Sultanina, variants on Kismis in the CIS and eastern Europe, and Cekizdecsis in Turkey. It is still much grown and used both for dried fruit and table grapes in countries such as AZERBAIJAN and ARMENIA. This variety, producing thin-skinned, seedless grapes, is too susceptible to a variety of FUNGAL DISEASES, and needs too hot a climate, to be grown in most of western Europe, but it can be very productive in hot, dry conditions. In widely varying locations, it provides base material for some, usually undistinguished, wines. As Thompson Seedless it is the most widely planted grape variety in California by far, as it is in Australia, where there was a total of nearly 16,000 ha/39,520 acres of Sultana planted in 1990. Sultana and Muscat Gordo Blanco (MUSCAT OF ALEXANDRIA) are two much-planted grape varieties in Australia used by both the wine and dried fruit industries, in proportions annually dictated by market forces. Most of Australia's Sultana is planted in the hot irrigated Riverland vineyards, particularly those on the Murray river in the states of Victoria and South Australia. In South Africa, plantings of Sultana increased steadily throughout the 1980s so that they totalled 8,000 ha in 1990, making it the country's third most planted grape variety after Chenin Blanc and Palomino. Much of the wine produced is distilled or made into basic FORTIFIED WINES. See also THOMPSON SEEDLESS.

SULTANAS, pale brown DRYING GRAPES made, often by dipping, from the SULTANA grape variety, also known as THOMPSON SEEDLESS.

SUMER. In Ancient Sumer (3500–1900 BC), the earliest literate civilization of southern MESOPOTAMIA, wine and BEER were both widely consumed, and are often mentioned as being drunk on the same occasion. 'Wine' almost certainly refers to grape wine in most contexts, although date wine was also prepared by the Sumerians.

At the sacred city of Nippur, just downstream from Babylon, which stood on an important branch of the river Euphrates, the principal quay of the temple was known as the 'Quay of the Vine', although it is not clear if this refers to an original commercial activity or is simply an ornate epithet of the sort beloved of Sumerian poets. In praise poetry addressed to King Shulgi, who was deified in his own lifetime (*c*.22nd century BC), the king's martial prowess with the double-edged axe is eulogized with the image of him 'spilling his enemies' blood on the mountain-side like the contents of a smashed wine jug'.

DRUNKENNESS seems to have carried no stigma of disapprobation. In a number of Sumerian literary works, the gods get drunk on wine and beer in circumstances which are not merely amusing but are dramatically important. The ambitious goddess Inana, for example, plies her father Enki with sweet wine and beer to the point where he agrees formally to bestow on her the *me*, or divine powers of the universe. He is devastated, when the effect of the drink wears off, to discover what he has done and tries all sorts of tricks to get the powers back. (The end of the story is not preserved.)

In another myth, when Enki and his mother the goddess

Nammu create mankind, the goddess Ninmah acts as midwife. Afterwards, at a celebratory banquet, the deities drink too much and become merry. Having been obliged to play a subsidiary role in creation, Ninmah now boasts to Enki that, however well or ill favoured the bodily form of individual humans may be, she herself has the power to direct their destiny in a benign or malign way as she chooses. Accepting the challenge, Enki says, 'If the fate you choose is bad, I will improve it.' In the first round of the drunken gambling game which follows, to a man blind from birth Enki gives the gift of song; a congenital idiot he appoints to high bureaucratic office. Four other clever solutions follow, and Ninmah becomes incensed by Enki's success. They then reverse roles, and soon he creates a creature so sick or weak in every part of its body that Ninmah cannot devise any useful function for it at all. Victory is assigned to Enki. J.A.B.

Bottéro, J., 'Getränke', *Reallexikon der Assyriologie und vorderasiatischen Archäologie* (the standard reference work) (Berlin, 1928–).

Kinnier Wilson, J. V., *The Nimrud Wine Lists* (London, 1972).

SUMMER PRUNING, optional vineyard operation designed to sacrifice quantity for quality. See PRUNING and CROP THINNING.

SUNBURN can damage grapes and is a viticultural term used loosely for a range of conditions. Classical sunburn produces a round halo of burnt skin on the side of the berry facing the sun. Such sunburn is due to a combination of bright sunshine, high air temperatures, and low winds, and the so-called 'hot spot' can be up to 12 °C/54 °F above air temperature. The injured tissue becomes dead and sunken, and in California this is known as 'Almeria spot' after damage to the heat-sensitive table grape variety. Berries which were previously shaded from the sun are most sensitive, as their skins become conditioned by exposure. Sunburn sensitivity is higher for vineyards suffering WATER STRESS. A combination of very high air temperatures and sunlight can make grapes, particularly those most exposed, collapse and shrivel. This may be the result of water stress due to high atmospheric evaporation.

The condition in which grapes develop pigmentation in response to sun exposure is also loosely called sunburn. This is particularly obvious with some white varieties, and the skin can develop deep yellow or even brown colours. Whether such exposure is harmful to the berry is arguable. Such berries may be smaller, and exposed fruit has been shown to produce better-quality table wine (see CANOPY MICROCLIMATE). R.E.S.

Winkler, A. J., *et al.*, *General Viticulture* (2nd edn., Berkeley, Calif., 1974).

SUNLIGHT, the ultimate energy source of all life, and of wine itself. Through a process known as PHOTOSYNTHESIS, part of its energy is used by plants to combine CARBON DIOXIDE from the air with WATER taken up from the soil, to form SUGAR IN GRAPES. This is the building block for other plant products, as well as being the immediate source of energy for all of a plant's biochemical processes, via its RESPIRATION back to carbon dioxide and water.

In climatology, the traditional measurement of sunlight is by means of a glass sphere which acts as a magnifying glass, focusing the light on to a strip of paper below. The length of burnt strip traced on the paper, as the sun moves across the sky, indicates the duration of 'bright sunlight' received. Such measurements of hours of bright sunshine have limitations when applied to the study of climatology of grapevines. When continuously illuminated, the leaves become saturated with light at only about one-third of average sunlight intensity, at which point other plant processes or environmental factors become more directly limiting to plant growth and RIPENING, the most important in cool climates being TEMPERATURE.

Moreover, sunlight can still support photosynthesis, albeit at diminishing rates, down to quite low intensities. This means that significant amounts of usable sunlight are not registered by these standard bright sunlight measurements. Useful sunlight and potential photosynthesis can therefore be seriously underestimated in climates where there is considerable light cloud or haze, and at high LATITUDES, where the sun is lowest over the horizon and there are often long periods of weak or diffused sunlight.

More recently electronic sensors have been used in climate recording networks which give readings of total energy, rather than of bright sunlight only.

Some implications follow for the CANOPY MICROCLIMATE and CANOPY MANAGEMENT of grapevines. If it is accepted that potential vine growth and grape production depend on the total leaf area that can be directly exposed to sunlight, then greatest efficiency (especially in regions of mostly bright sunlight) is when the leaves are obliquely angled to the sun, so that their surfaces receive just enough intensity for a maximum or near-maximum photosynthetic rate, but cast least shadow on the leaves underneath. For the same reasons lateral exposure to sunlight, such as in the early morning and late afternoon, and as predominates at high latitudes, can be more photosynthetically effective than that of the leaves directly facing for example the overhead sun. This is especially so for vines with a VERTICAL TRELLIS, and also in hot climates, where midday photosynthesis may be reduced anyway because of excessive temperatures and WATER STRESS. Finally, leaves that are only partly or intermittently illuminated by direct sunlight use what energy they get with an enhanced efficiency.

Another important role of sunlight in viticulture is that of heating the vines and the soil. Grape berries for example may be heated up to 15 °C above air temperature for black berries exposed to bright sunlight in low wind conditions. Leaves are heated less when exposed to sunlight, as they are evaporatively cooled by the process of TRANSPIRATION. Berry temperatures are of considerable importance in affecting the chemical make-up of the grapes. Similarly, leaf temperatures have important effects on photosynthesis and respiration and this also directly affects GRAPE COMPOSITION AND WINE QUALITY.

Soil temperature depends on the reflectivity to sunlight of the soil surface; thus dark soils absorb more sunlight and are warmer than white or light coloured soils (see SOIL COLOUR). The total amount of sunlight energy over all of the spectrum is important in heating vines and soils.

The intensity of sunlight is not its only characteristic of importance to grapevines. Another is spectral quality or the proportion of sunlight at different wavelengths. This does not vary greatly from region to region, or under full sunlight versus cloud; but it does vary enormously within the vine CANOPY. It also varies to a smaller, but perhaps still significant, extent in the spaces between and below the vine rows.

The total spectrum of solar radiation comprises ultraviolet radiations, visible light, and infra-red (heat) radiations, in order of increasing electromagnetic wavelengths. Visible light is in the wavelength range 400 to 760 nanometres (nm) (1 nm is a millionth of a millimetre). Within that range, in order of increasing wavelength, are the component colours of the visible light spectrum: violet, indigo, blue, green, yellow, orange, and red.

Most of the wavelengths between 400 and 700 nm are absorbed by leaves, and are used to varying degrees for photosynthesis. Those absorbed and used most efficiently are in the blue and (especially) red parts of the spectrum, centred around 440 and 660 nm respectively. It is the partial reflection of the intermediate wavelengths, by the photosynthetically active pigment chlorophyll, that gives plant leaves their characteristic green colour. Thus shade light, as well as being much less intense that full sunlight, is still more impoverished of its photosynthetically useful wavelengths. If overall light intensity is reduced eight- or tenfold, that of red light around 660 nm can be reduced a hundredfold in deep canopy shade.

Also important physiologically are the barely visible 'far red' wavelengths, between 700 and 760 nm. These and the adjacent infra-red wavelengths are hardly absorbed at all, being either reflected or transmitted through the leaves. Canopy shade light is therefore relatively rich in them. The ratio of normal red to far red wavelengths (measured as 10-nm-width bands centred around 660 and 730 nm, and known as the R : FR ratio) is between 1.0 and 1.2 in the open, whereas in deep canopy shade it can be 0.1 or less.

It is the R : FR ratio, rather than light intensity as such, that appears to govern many plant reactions to shading within the canopy, probably through the action of a wavelength-sensitive pigment known as phytochrome. A low R : FR ratio, characteristic of deep canopy shade, promotes rapid spindly stem growth (trying to reach the light); sparse leaves and light green colour; sparse lateral branching; and poor bud FRUITFULNESS. Conversely, a high R : FR ratio, as in normal external light, promotes stocky growth, with strong lateral branching; deep green leaf colour; and good bud fruitfulness. Direct exposure of the bunches to such light also promotes the formation of ANTHOCYAN pigments in the berry skins of red wine grape varieties, and appears to be associated with superior flavour and potential wine quality. The practice of LEAF REMOVAL around the bunches is in part a response to this.

The fact that such wavelength discrimination can still occur at quite low light intensities raises further interesting questions on which, at present, there is little direct information for grapevines. They include the effects of height, orientation, and distance between rows on the quality of the light reaching the lower canopy and bunches; also those of different soil colours, MULCHES, or COVER CROPS on the intensity and spectral quality of light reflected back to the lower canopy and bunches.

Smart reviews general aspects or light-quality effects on grapevine growth and fruit composition. He also deals comprehensively with sunlight relations in the context of vine canopy microclimate, canopy management, and wine quality.

See also VINE PHYSIOLOGY. J.G. & R.E.S.

Smart, R. E., 'Principles of grapevine canopy microclimate manipulation with implications for yield and quality', *American Journal of Enology and Viticulture*, 35 (1985), 230–9.

—— 'Influence of light on composition and quality of grapes' *Acta horticulturae*, 206 (1987), 37–47.

—— 'Canopy management', in B. G. Coombe and P. R. Dry (eds.), *Viticulture ii: Practices* (Adelaide, 1992).

SUPÉRIEUR, Supérieure, or **Supérieures** may be found suffixed to the name of an APPELLATION CONTRÔLÉE on French wine labels. The regulations for a Supérieur wine usually demand a slightly higher minimum ALCOHOLIC STRENGTH (typically by half a per cent). The term is often optional and Quelquechose Supérieure is by no means infallibly superior to plain Quelquechose.

SUPERIORE, Italian term applied to DOC wines which are deemed superior because of their higher minimum ALCOHOLIC STRENGTH, usually by a half or one per cent, and a longer period of AGEING before commercial release. Among the more significant wines which fall into this category are the three BARBERA DOCs of PIEDMONT (Alba, Asti, Monferrato), BARDOLINO, CALDARO, GRAVE DEL FRIULI, SOAVE, VALPOLICELLA, and VALTELLINA (where the use of the word Superiore is strictly linked to the sub-denominations of Grumello, Inferno, Sassella, and Valgella and indicates to all effects and purposes the CLASSICO zone of the Valtellina). Both Barbera d'Alba Superiore and Barbera d'Asti Superiore must be aged in wood for at least one year, in addition to the requirement of an extra half a per cent of alcohol compared to the regular Barbera bottlings of the two zones. D.T.

SUPER SECOND, a specialist term in the market for CLASSED GROWTH wines from BORDEAUX to denote the best-performing wines ranked as second growths in the 1855 CLASSIFICATION of the Médoc and Graves. There is no absolute agreement about which properties qualify as super seconds but Chx Pichon-Longueville-Lalande, and more recently Pichon-Longueville (Baron), in PAUILLAC, Cos d'Estournel in ST-ESTÈPHE, and Léoville-Las-Cases and Ducru-Beaucaillou in ST-JULIEN have all been nominated at one time or another. Other strong candidates (although not second growths) include Ch Palmer in MARGAUX, and Ch La Mission-Haut-Brion and Domaine de Chevalier in PESSAC-LÉOGNAN, as well as Chx Figeac and Canon in ST-ÉMILION

SUPERTUSCAN, term sometimes used by English speakers to describe the new class of superior wines labelled VINO DA TAVOLA made in the central Italian region of Tuscan. Prototype Supertuscans were Tignanello and Sassicaia, both initially marketed by ANTINORI. For more details, see TUSCANY.

SUR LIE, French term meaning 'on the lees', customarily applied to white wines whose principal deviation from everyday WHITE WINE-MAKING techniques was some form of LEES CONTACT. The term has been used most commonly for the French dry white MUSCADET to differentiate those wines which remained on their lees after fermentation, usually in tank, in an effort to increase flavour. The practice, and term, has since spread south to the LANGUEDOC and beyond and has proved a useful way of adding flavour and value to the produce of relatively neutral grapes.

SURPLUS PRODUCTION has for years been the single greatest problem facing the world's wine industry, aggravated by improved efficiency in the vineyard and falling consumption in most important wine markets. In the early and mid 1990s there was over-production in all continents except the Americas, but most especially in Europe.

Even in the late 1950s, the world produced almost 15 per cent more wine than it consumed, but wine consumption was rising rapidly, and it was assumed that it would catch up. By the late 1970s average YIELDS began to increase substantially. This was largely the result of increased proficiency, but also reflected the availability of particularly productive CLONES of established vine varieties, as well as the more widespread use of AGROCHEMICALS to combat VINE DISEASES, and FERTILIZERS. Just at this point, consumption began to decline, especially markedly in the principal wine-producing countries (which had been the principal wine markets): France, Italy, USSR, Spain, and Argentina.

The exceptionally large European harvests of 1979 and 1980 plunged what is now the European Union into crisis and forced measures which included compulsory DISTILLATION of about a fifth of total production (only of the lowest-quality wine), a VINE PULL SCHEME, and a somewhat fruitless attempt to control yields, which continued to rise by an average of about 0.5 per cent a year. By the late 1980s the world was producing 18 per cent more than it could consume, with particularly marked surpluses in France, Italy, and Spain, and a marked surplus of industrial ALCOHOL as a result of compulsory distillation.

The breakup of the Soviet Union, for long a net wine importer, and the introduction of free market economies within the CIS meanwhile deprived many eastern European wine producers of their traditional, and none too fastidious market, creating fresh pressure on the world's wine suppliers.

Surpluses on a smaller scale, sometimes simply of the wrong type of wine, have resulted in national vine pull schemes such as that enacted in NEW ZEALAND in the late 1980s.

For more details of European efforts to curb surplus wine production, see EUROPEAN UNION.

SURRENTINE wine from vineyards on the slopes of the Sorrento peninsula in southern Italy achieved prominence from the latter half of the reign of Augustus in the first decade of the 1st century AD. It ranked high in Classical ROME, but behind CAECUBAN and FALERNIAN, in PLINY'S assessment. It was produced from the vine known as the Aminnea Gemina Minor, which, unusually for one of the classic wines, was trellised rather than grown up trees. The wine itself was a rather thin white wine, which nevertheless could be described as 'strong'. It may well have had a high acidity. There are recommendations to age it for 20 to 25 years. It never won universal approval—'a high class vinegar' was the opinion of both the emperors Tiberius and Caligula, and there are some signs that its MEDICINAL properties were among its most important selling points. J.J.P.

Pliny the Elder, *Natural History*, trans. by H. Rackham (London, 1945), Book 14.

SUR SOUCHE, French expression meaning 'on the stump' or, in the context of a purchase of a future vintage of wine, 'on the vine'. Such advance purchases of promising vintages have sometimes been made by the BORDEAUX TRADE, at times of particularly buoyant sales.

SÜSS, literally 'sweet' in German. Used on labels in AUSTRIA to designate wines whose RESIDUAL SUGAR is more than 18 g/l.

SÜSSRESERVE, German term for SWEET RESERVE, the sweetening agent much used, especially in the 1970s and 1980s, for all but the finest or driest German wines. Its use is declining as GERMANY makes an increasing proportion of dry wines, however (see TROCKEN and HALBTROCKEN).

SUSTAINABLE VITICULTURE, a form of viticultural practice which aims to avoid any environmental degradation. The term became popular in the 1990s especially in California, and the approach is seen to be more rational than that followed in so-called ORGANIC VITICULTURE. One of the earliest examples of sustainable viticulture to achieve recognition is Fetzer Vineyards Redwood Valley home ranch in Mendocino County in California. The vineyard was certified 'organic' in 1989, and by 1991 405 acres/165 ha of vineyard were conducted as sustainable viticulture.

The system encourages ecological diversity in the vineyard and shuns the more traditional monocultural approach. An attempt is made to reduce inputs of extraneous substances, especially of AGROCHEMICALS, although there are no strict rules governing which chemicals may or may not be used. Enhancing soil fertility is fundamental, and so green COVER CROPS are used, as is undervine ploughing rather than HERBICIDES. Ploughing is kept to a minimum, as is driving heavy tractors and implements on wet soils, which causes compaction and loss of structure. Copper and sulphur sprays are used as FUNGICIDES, and soap sprays and natural oils are used to control insects. Insect predators of other pests are of course encouraged. BOTRYTIS BUNCH ROT is reduced by LEAF REMOVAL.

The acronym LISA stands for Low Input Sustainable Agriculture, which is a related approach. R.E.S.

Ingels, C., 'Sustainable agriculture and grape production', *American Journal of Enology and Viticulture* 43 (1992), 296–8.

SWAN VALLEY, the hot vine heartland of the state of WESTERN AUSTRALIA.

SWARD. See COVER CROP.

SWEETNESS. Wines taste sweet mainly because of the amount of RESIDUAL SUGAR, or RS, they contain (although the impact of this on the palate is greatly influenced by factors such as the levels of ACIDITY, TANNINS, and CARBON DIOXIDE in the wine as well as by the serving TEMPERATURE). ETHANOL, or alcohol, can also taste sweet, as can GLYCEROL and a high level of PECTINS. A dry wine with a residual sugar of less than 2 g/l that is relatively high in alcohol, such as many a Chardonnay for example, can taste quite sweet. A sweet VOUVRAY, on the other hand, made in a cool region from the naturally acidic grape variety CHENIN BLANC, may contain well over 30 g/l residual sugar, but in youth can taste dry.

A wide variety of different terms in different languages are used to describe sweetness, although they invariably relate strictly to the RESIDUAL SUGAR rather than to the taste impression. The table gives a very approximate indication of equivalences.

RS g/l	English	French	German	Italian	Spanish
<5	Bone dry	Brut			
<10	Dry	Sec	Trocken	Secco	Seco
10–20	Medium dry	Demi-sec	Halbtrocken	Abboccato	Semi-seco
20–30	Medium sweet	Doux	Mild	Amabile	Dulce
30–40	Sweet	Moelleux	Lieblich	Dolce	
>40/45		Liquoreux	Süss		

See also the specific terminology for the DOSAGE of sparkling wines.

Some wine drinkers have been conditioned to be suspicious of any sweetness in a wine, perhaps because neophytes generally prefer some residual sugar (which is why so many wine BRANDS contain some) and sweetness is therefore associated with a lack of sophistication. Some of the greatest wines of the world are sweet, however. So long as there is sufficient ACIDITY to balance the sweetness, a sweet wine is by no means cloying. Indeed a comparative tasting of great young sweet wines is more likely to leave the taster with the impression of excess acidity than excess sugar.

See SWEET WINES and SWEET WINE-MAKING for more details of sweeter wines.

SWEET RESERVE, preserved GRAPE JUICE held for BLENDING purposes, usually to sweeten, or at least soften, wines high in ACIDITY. The unfermented grape SUGARS counterbalance the tart flavours of wines produced from grapes grown in cool regions such as much of GERMANY (where it is known as *Süssreserve*) or grapes naturally high in acidity such as UGNI BLANC and COLOMBARD.

Historically grape juice was preserved simply by adding offensively high doses of SULPHUR DIOXIDE. Modern REFRIGERATION and near-sterile FILTRATION enable the production of sweet reserve that does not reek of sulphur dioxide. The sweet juice usually undergoes CLARIFICATION and REFRIGERATION so as to precipitate any TARTRATES and can be stored at very low temperatures for up to 12 months.

In many wine regions sweet reserve is being replaced by GRAPE CONCENTRATE or RECTIFIED GRAPE MUST. Grape concentrate is cheaper to store because it is much richer in sugar, which also prevents the growth of micro-organisms so that it can be stored without recourse to expensive REFRIGERATION. Rectified grape must is preferred simply because it more closely resembles a solution of sugar and water than does preserved juice. A.D.W.

SWEET WINE-MAKING, the production of wines with noticeable amounts of RESIDUAL SUGAR which may vary considerably in ALCOHOLIC STRENGTH and production techniques. Local regulations differ considerably but, with a few exceptions, non-grape sugar may be added only for the purposes of CHAPTALIZATION, to increase the final alcoholic strength, and not to add sweetness after fermentation. The most common method of sweetening basic wine is the addition of some form of sweet grape juice followed by STABILIZATION (for any wine containing sugar is theoretically susceptible to SECONDARY FERMENTATION).

The finest sweet wines are made by concentrating the SUGAR IN GRAPES, however, and the combined effect of the alcohol produced and the residual sugar tends to inhibit further YEAST activity. The three common ways of doing this are by the benevolent NOBLE ROT effect of the botrytis fungus on the vine as it nears maturity in perfect conditions (see BOTRYTIZED WINES); by processing frozen grape clusters (see EISWEIN); or by drying mature grapes either on the vine or after picking (see DRIED GRAPE WINES). Many sweet wines are made by simply leaving the grapes on the vine for as long as possible in order to concentrate the grape sugars. If BOTRYTIS BUNCH ROT fails to materialize, the grapes simply start to raisin or shrivel, a condition known in French as *passerillé*. Such wines, sweet JURANÇON, for example, described as *moelleux* in French, can be extremely rich and satisfying, but are typically less complex and less long-lived wines than those made from grapes transformed by the action of noble rot.

Many everyday sweet wines are made nowadays, however, simply by fermenting the wine out to dryness and subsequently adding GRAPE CONCENTRATE or RECTIFIED GRAPE MUST just before a sterilizing membrane FILTRATION and sterile BOTTLING. These wines owe their stability not to their composition but to the fact that all micro-organisms have been filtered out. They are best drunk within a year of bottling and within a day or two of opening the bottle. Most sweet German wines of QBA level, such as LIEBFRAUMILCH, are examples of this type of wine, and the sweetening agent is called SÜSSRESERVE in German.

Another technique, commonly employed for inexpensive sweet white French wines, is to ferment a must relatively high in sugars, between 200 and 250 g/l, until the alcohol level has reached about 11 or 12 per cent, and then add a substantial dose of SULPHUR DIOXIDE.

One quite different way of transforming grapes into a liquid that is both sweet and stable is to add spirit to grape juice either before fermentation (see VIN DE LIQUEUR) or during it (see VIN DOUX NATUREL). Such liquids are usually more than 15 per cent alcohol, much stronger than most wines.

Many FORTIFIED WINES are sweet. See also WHITE WINE-MAKING, RED WINE-MAKING, ROSÉ WINE-MAKING, and, particularly, BOTRYTIZED WINES, DRIED GRAPE WINES, and EISWEIN for details of how these particularly fine sweet wines are made.

SWEET WINES, wines that are noticeably sweet. Sweet wines have been popular since ancient times; indeed most of the most admired wines of classical ROME were sweet and white, many of them DRIED GRAPE WINES made by deliberate raisining to concentrate the sugars. In the Middle Ages the great city states of Italy such as VENICE and GENOA profited from the popularity of wines made so much sweeter than northern European wines by the Mediterranean climate. And by the late 17th century the DUTCH WINE TRADE was energetically profiting from the sweet wines of western France.

For specific modern sweet wines see AUSLESE, BANYULS, BARSAC, BEERENAUSLESE, BONNEZEAUX, BOTRYTIZED WINES, CADILLAC, CÉRONS, CLAIRETTE DE DIE, LAYON, EISWEIN, JURANÇON, LATE HARVEST, LOUPIAC, MAURY, MOELLEUX, MONBAZILLAC, MONTLOUIS, various MOSCATELS, MOSCATO, MUSCAT, PICOLIT, QUARTS DE CHAUME, RASTEAU, RECIOTO, RIVESALTES, SÉLECTION DES GRAINS NOBLES, STE-CROIX-DU-MONT, SAUTERNES, TROCKENBEERENAUSLESE, VENDANGE TARDIVE, VIN DE PAILLE, VIN SANTO, and VOUVRAY.

See SWEETNESS for details of sweet wine descriptions in various languages and what they entail.

See also DRIED GRAPE WINES, ICE WINE, VINS DE LIQUEUR, and VINS DOUX NATURELS, most of which are sweet wines.

SWITZERLAND, small, alpine country in central Europe with a steady annual wine production of more than a million hl/26.4 million gal from less than 15,000 ha/37,050 acres of often spectacular vineyards. The majority of these are in the western French-speaking part of the country, Suisse romande. There are also extensive vineyards all over eastern, German-speaking Switzerland (or Ostschweiz), and many vineyards in Ticino, the Italian-speaking south of Switzerland (or Svizzera). See map p. 936. The country is divided into 24 cantons, of which all produce some wine. For many years Swiss wine labelling lacked the discipline applied to the north in Germany or the controls imposed to the west in France, but from the early 1990s an APPELLATION CONTRÔLÉE system has been applied with increasing rigour, initially in French-speaking Switzerland. Most Swiss wine is light, white, and relatively neutral, but an increasing proportion of it is seriously good. CHASSELAS is the principal grape variety and, when well vinifed, it can express well the country's diversity of soils and climates.

History

Grape seeds of the neolithic age, between 3000 and 1800 BC, have been found at St-Blaise in Neuchâtel, and the Romans (see Ancient ROME) certainly cultivated the vine in most modern Swiss wine regions. In the Middle Ages, vine-growing spread under monastic influence, notably that of the Cistercians (see MONKS AND MONASTERIES), who created the abbey at Dézaley. As elsewhere, medieval wines were thin, acid, and often helped by the addition of honey and other flavourings. In the 17th century Swiss vignerons were already feeling the effects of wine imports from hotter climes, notably from further down the RHÔNE valley.

Switzerland was far more seriously affected by the viticultural catastrophes of the late 19th century (DOWNY MILDEW, PHYLLOXERA, POWDERY MILDEW) than most other wine-producing countries. Between 1877 and 1957 the total Swiss vineyard declined by 60 per cent from 33,000 to 12,500 ha, a decrease encouraged by competition from cheaper imported wines, increasing industrialization, and development of the all-important lakesides. In the mid 20th century CLONAL SELECTION and FERTILIZERS were harnessed with particular enthusiasm in attempts to increase productivity from Switzerland's relatively inconvenient, expensive-to-work vineyards. More recent developments in both vineyard and cellar are concerned with quality.

(The earliest successful commercial wine venture in the UNITED STATES was undertaken in the early 19th century by Swiss-born J. J. Dufour, as outlined in JEFFERSON. And another Swiss was the leading light in the important Australian wine industry in late 19th century VICTORIA.)

Climate

Although Switzerland is on a particularly suitable latitude for wine production, between 45 and 47 degrees, a high proportion of the country is simply too high. However, the country's lakes and the föhn, a local wind which warms up sizeable portions of the south of the country, particularly Graubünden in the upper Rhine Valley, enable full grape ripening to take place in many valleys and on lakesides. And in the Valais in the south west, the upper Rhône valley, sunshine is so dependable (an average of more than 2,000 hours a year, rising sometimes to more than 2,500 hours) that vineyards can be as high as 750 m/2,460 ft and one, at Visperteminen, is 1,100 m above sea level. The Valais is sheltered by the alps and, like south east Switzerland, benefits particularly from the föhn, but it can be dry and IRRIGATION with mountain water is sometimes necessary. The slope of some vineyards is as steep as 90 per cent. Most Swiss wine regions have an annual rainfall of between 500 and 1,800 mm/19.5–70 in a year, the wettest region being Ticino, which suffers violent but short storms and is also the hottest with average July temperatures of more than 21 °C/70 °F. Elsewhere, average July temperatures are between 17.5 and 20 °C, there is good day–night temperature variation, and winter temperatures in the vineyards rarely fall below danger level for vines. The Valais is most at risk.

Viticulture

The slope and, in some regions, rainfall make SOIL EROSION many Swiss vine-growers' prime concern. REMONTAGE and TERRACES are common in Switzerland's steep vineyards, and COVER CROPS are increasingly common. Sophisticated MECHANIZATION is possible only on some of the flatter vineyards on the plain, or on some of the terraces of eastern Switzerland. A wide variety of training methods are used, including CORDON, GOBELET, GUYOT, TENDONE (in Ticino), and the Swiss German speciality *taille à l'onglet* designed to protect the vines against spring frost danger there. Elaborate monorail systems may be used to transport equipment and, at harvest, grapes.

Many vine-growers sell their grapes direct to NÉGOCIANTS or CO-OPERATIVES but an increasing number make and sell their own wine. YIELDS are nationally restricted, according to Switzerland's somewhat microscopic unit of measurement, to 1.4 kg/sq m for Chasselas grapes and 1.2 kg/sq m for red and superior white grapes, the equivalent of more than 105 hl/ha (6 tons/acre) and 84 hl/ha respectively. Some cantons, such as those of eastern Switzerland and Geneva, Neuchâtel, and Valais, apply their own stricter limits, however, and the national average yield in 1991 was 71 hl/ha, an approximate annual average for France.

The most common viticultural problems are downy mildew, powdery mildew, BOTRYTIS BUNCH ROT, SOIL EROSION, and occasional spring FROST in the east of the country.

Switzerland's most famous viticultural research stations are at WÄDENSWIL in German-speaking Switzerland and CHANGINS at Nyon in Suisse romande.

Wine-making

ENRICHMENT, increasing potential alcohol by adding sugar, has been almost *de rigueur* for many Swiss wines, although the practice is unnecessary in much of the Valais and the Rhine valley, and is declining elsewhere. Ordinary wines may have their alcohol content increased by up to three per cent, although Swiss consumers are increasingly favouring lighter, drier wines.

Swiss presses, made by Bucher and Sutter, are known throughout the wine-making world, and are put to particularly effective work in their native land, where the aim is to extract as much juice as possible from the country's precious grapes with only the gentlest of pressure from an inflatable membrane.

DESTEMMING and MALOLACTIC FERMENTATION are the norm, indispensable for Chasselas, and common for other white

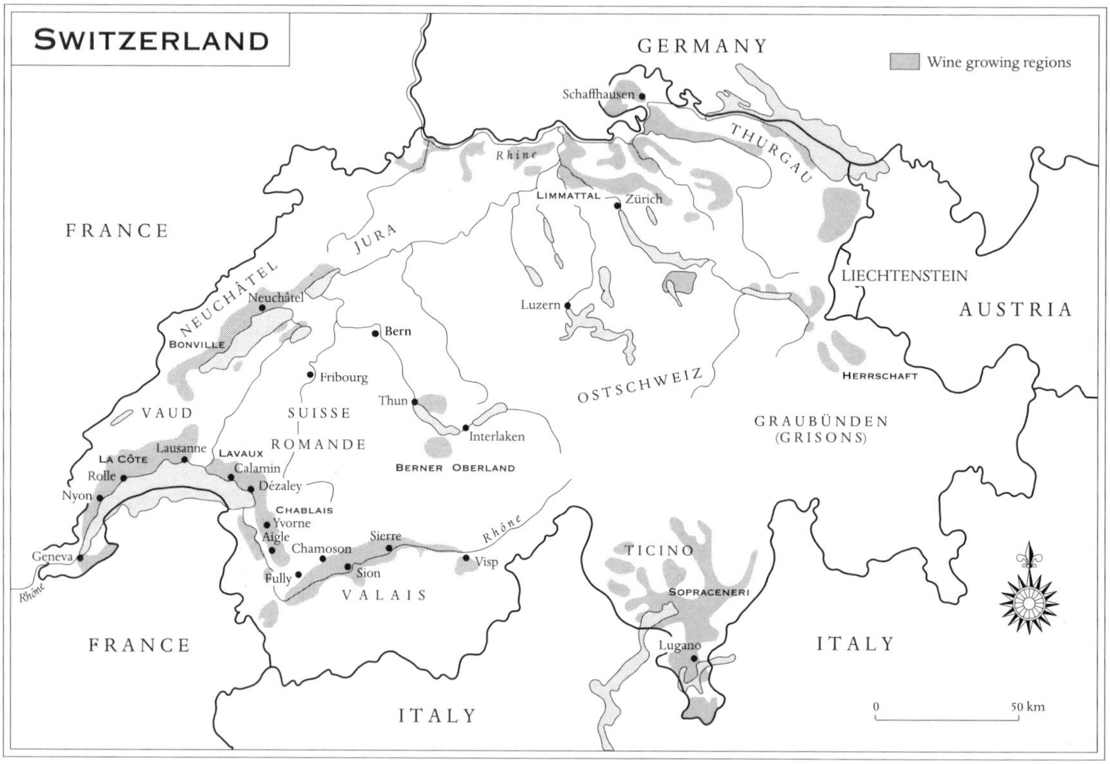

Vineyards in **Switzerland** overlooking Lake Geneva.

wines (the latter marking the essential difference in style between Swiss wines on the one hand and Austrian and German on the other). For red wines in German Switzerland, some form of CARBONIC MACERATION may be employed. Other Swiss reds are made more traditionally with frequent REMONTAGE and TEMPERATURE CONTROL. As elsewhere BARREL MATURATION has become increasingly popular, for red wines at least. Few Swiss white wines have the structure to withstand the impact of OAK although some of the fuller bodied grape varieties, including the indigenous Petite Arvine and Amigne, may yield good results.

Switzerland has several pink wine specialities: white wines made from Pinot Noir and/or Gamay grapes such as the Valais's DÔLE Blanche. ŒIL-DE-PERDRIX, 'partridge eye', is made only from Pinot Noir in Neuchâtel, while Gamay provides rosé. Federweisser or WEISSHERBST is a product of German Switzerland where SCHILLERWEIN, made from a mixture of both red and white grapes, often Pinot Noir and Pinot Gris, is also made.

BLENDING has played an important part in the Swiss wine industry for decades. As Switzerland is a non-member of the EUROPEAN UNION, Swiss wine merchants are unencumbered by the mass of regulations which protect wines within EU countries and have long depended on imported wines, particularly deeply coloured red ones, to add bulk to many of their less expensive blends. (In 1991, for example, Switzerland imported 1.6 million hl, considerably more wine than she produced, and exported less than a hundredth as much.) Such blending is now under the supervision of the Ordonnance sur les Denrées Alimentaires (ODA), which forbids the blending of Swiss white wines with imported wines, and permits only small additions of superior, foreign wines to Swiss reds.

The introduction of a full APPELLATION CONTRÔLÉE system within Switzerland, however, is focusing attention on authentic domaine bottled all-Swiss products.

Vine varieties

Switzerland's most planted variety, covering 45 per cent of the country's vineyard land and responsible for a remarkable 60 per cent of the country's total wine production, is CHASSELAS, or Gutedel as it is known by German speakers. In the Valais it is called Fendant, while in the Vaud, where it may locally be called Dorin, wines are sold under their geographical appellation names. In the Valais the second most important variety is SYLVANER, whose wines, fuller bodied than Chasselas, are sold as Johannisberg. Petit Rhin (RIESLING) is relatively rare and can be reliably ripened only on the schists around Sion in the Valais.

The conveniently early ripening MÜLLER-THURGAU, in its native land curiously known as Riesling–Sylvaner, is the most common grape variety in German Switzerland, having substantially replaced the historic RÄUSCHLING vine, particularly around Zurich just south of the German border. There are signs of a revival of interest in the more distinctive variety, however.

Other white grape varieties include PINOT GRIS, sometimes called Malvoisie du Valais; PINOT BLANC; a little GEWÜRZTRAMINER; CHARDONNAY, which can be elegant in the cantons of Neuchâtel and Geneva, and richer in Vaud and Valais; and ALIGOTÉ, COMPLETER, SAUVIGNON Blanc, KERNER, and SÉMILLON.

PINOT NOIR, called Blauburgunder in German, is Switzerland's most widely planted red grape variety by far, although the productive GAMAY is more important in the Vaud and Geneva, and MERLOT reigns in Ticino to such an extent that it accounts for three-quarters of production. Bondola is a local red grape of Ticino, and SYRAH can produce a respectably ripe wine in sheltered parts of the Valais such as Leytron and Chamoson.

A number of crossings have been developed as suitable for Switzerland's very particular growing conditions: FREISAMER, Charmont (Chasselas × Chardonnay), Gamaret and Granoir (both Gamay × REICHENSTEINER), and, a Valais speciality, Diolinoir (Rouge du Diolly × Pinot Noir).

But of most interest to students of AMPELOGRAPHY is the Valais's rich collection of about 40 ancient indigenous varieties, each with substantial body, ageing potential, and its own whiff of history: the Amigne of Vétroz; the elegant Petite Arvine of Fully (now planted at MAS de Daumas Gassac in southern France); the powerfully scented Humagne Blanc; the almost extinct Rèze which made VIN DES GLACIERS, or glacier wine, in the valley of Anniviers; and, among dark-skinned varieties, the noble Cornalin and the powerful Humagne Rouge, which may well be more closely related to the Oriou vine of AOSTA over the Italian border than to Humagne Blanc. MARSANNE Blanche, also known as Ermitage, Muscat du Valais (MUSCAT BLANC À PETITS GRAINS), MUSCAT OTTONEL, and Païen or Heida (SAVAGNIN Blanc) are also grown in the Valais, the latter up to 1,100 m altitude at Visperterminen.

The wine regions

The country's emerging appellation contrôlée system is applied by each canton individually.

Valais The 5,200 ha of productive vineyards of this south western canton produce 40 per cent of every Swiss vintage. Concentrated on the south-facing slopes of the sunny upper Rhône valley, the region is known as 'the California of Switzerland'. Many of these beautiful vineyards are terraced, some into so-called *tablars*, horizontal slices of vineyard cut into the mountainside, farmed as a part-time activity by 22,000 smallholders. Typical of what they produce is the ubiquitous FENDANT (made from the Chasselas grapes which cover nearly half the *vignoble*), and medium-weight reds labelled either Pinot Noir or DÔLE, a blend in which Pinot Noir must dominate the Gamay element. (Dôle Blanche is made from a blend of Pinot Noir and Gamay grapes vinified as a white wine.)

Some of the most concentrated Sylvaners, sold here as JOHANNISBERG, come from particularly well-favoured sites at Chamoson. Petite Arvine of Fully is accorded the greatest respect, however, for its exotic intensity, while Cornalin and Humagne make some of Switzerland's most seriously age-worthy reds. Fine, sweet, late harvest wines, made from Johannisberg (Sylvaner), Amigne, Ermitage (Marsanne), Malvoisie (Pinot Gris), and Petite Arvine picked in November and December, can easily reach 20 per cent potential alcohol. They may be described as *flétri*, or withered, a reference to parital raisining on the vine. Wines made from such indigenous varieties as Gwäss, Lafnetscha, Himbertscha, or Rèze are curiosities. VIN DES GLACIERS from the Val d'Anniviers above Sierre is another local rarity with a long tradition.

Vaud Switzerland's second most important wine canton is also in French Switzerland, round the northern shore of Lake Geneva, or Lac Léman (almost everything has at least two names in Switzerland). The canton's five wine regions are northern Vaud, La Côte, Lavaux, Dézaley, and Chablais. Here Chasselas accounts for 80 per cent of the production from 3,700 ha, although, under the influence of the Vaud's varied soils, its character can vary from almost insultingly innocuous to an almost POUILLY-FUMÉ-like steeliness. In La Côte the aromatic floral notes of the variety itself tend to dominate the wines. In Yvorne, Aigle, Bonvillars, and Calamin the mineral character of individual soils can easily dominate this fruit, while in Dézaley and St-Saphorin these two aspects are probably balanced most harmoniously.

A little Chardonnay and Pinot Gris are also grown here. Red wines, especially Gamay, are a speciality of La Côte. Salvagnin approximates to a Vaud version of Valais' Dôle, although Pinot Noir need not be the dominant ingredient. Terravin is a locally guaranteed white wine. Many of Switzerland's largest NÉGOCIANTS are based here.

Geneva The 1,500 ha of vineyards around the city at the south western end of the lake are much flatter than those of the Valais and Vaud and benefit from good sunlight, those next to the lake often escaping spring frost danger. Chasselas dominates, Riesling–Sylvaner is on the wane, while all manner of newcomers, including Chardonnay, Aligoté, Sauvignon, Sémillon, Kerner, Freisamer, Merlot, and even Cabernet Sauvignon are increasingly popular with growers and consumers alike. Gamay is particularly successful here, whether as a well-structured red, a PRIMEUR, or a rosé. This was the birthplace of Switzerland's burgeoning appellation contrôlée laws.

Neuchâtel Only 600 ha of the ancient CALCAREOUS soils, on the well-situated south-facing slopes above Lake Neuchâtel, grow vines, but with characterful results. Chasselas as usual predominates, but Chardonnay and Pinot Noir are also important, just as they are over the French border in the JURA. The pale pink Pinot Œil-de-Perdrix is a Neuchâtel invention. This was the first canton to restrict yields.

Eastern cantons In the 17 German-speaking cantons of Switzerland are 2,330 ha of vines, ranging from 0.2 ha in Nidwald to more than 600 ha in the canton of Zürich. Schaffhausen, effectively an outcrop into south BADEN in Germany, has nearly 500 ha of vines. Here in eastern Switzerland nearly 70 per cent of production is red wine, particularly rot-resistant Mariafeld and 2–45 clones of Blauburgunder (Pinot Noir) and, to a lesser extent, the crossings Gamaret and Granoir developed locally at the CHANGINS viticultural research station. Räuschling is once again gaining ground in Limmatal and on the shores of the lake south of Zürich, where Blauburgunder is often labelled Clevner. Riesling–Sylvaner (Müller-Thurgau) is the dominant white grape variety of eastern Switzerland, while Completer is a local speciality of Herrschaft near the border with Austria and Liechtenstein in Graubünden, where a small quantity of sweet Freisamer and serious red wine is also produced.

Italian-speaking Switzerland There are 1,200 ha of vineyard in the southern canton of Ticino, and barely 50 ha over the border with Graubünden in the Italian-speaking Mesolcina valley. This makes Ticino Switzerland's fourth most important wine canton, and nearly 90 per cent of its production is of the Bordeaux red variety Merlot, imported in the first half of the 20th century. Here, vineyards lower than 450 m are sunny enough to ripen this variety, although higher vineyards may have to concentrate on Pinot Noir. Merlot del Ticino can be relatively light or, from well-sited vineyards and carefully vinified, often using new oak, can be a serious challenge for fine red bordeaux. Most of the best red Merlots carry the VITI seal, for which they must be tasted and assessed, while pale pink Merlot Bianco is increasingly popular. Sopraceneri, north of Mont Ceneri, is an important wine region of which the local red grape variety Bondola is a speciality. It tends to be included in the rustic local version of 'house wine' called Nostrano, or 'ours', from which the HYBRIDS and AMERICAN VINES still representing seven per cent of total production here are excluded. GRAPPA, distilled substantially from AMERICAN VINE SPECIES, is another local speciality to which the VITI qualification is applied.

Other cantons The German-speaking but central canton of Berne has more than 200 ha of vines, mainly on the north shore of Lake Bienne, although there are some vines on the Thunersee west of Interlaken. On the southern shores of Lake Neuchâtel are 100 ha of mainly Chasselas and Pinot Noir in the canton of Fribourg, most of them on the north shore of Lake Morat. The Swiss canton of Jura also has a few hectares of vines.

Joris, D., *Connaissance des vins suisses* (Geneva, 1992).
Koblet, W., *Reben und Wein in der Schweiz* (Wädenswil, 1992).

SWIZZLE STICK, curious wine-related artefact (see ANTIQUES AND ARTEFACTS) which was particularly fashionable in certain circles in the first decade of the 20th century. A stick with spokes which opened out rather like an umbrella frame, its purpose is disputed. Some people used a swizzle stick to 'swizzle' out of sparkling wine the gas that had so painstakingly been trapped in solution in it, while others, perhaps later, used it to froth up sparkling wine that had gone flat, notably by being served in saucer-shaped *coupes*. In terms of design, its inspiration may have been the veined clubs used to stir early 18th century chocolate pots. Much larger versions were also used in the Caribbean for putting gas into rum punches. A mosser, a small blunt wooden implement used to decarbonate sparkling wine, was also used, particularly in the United States, in the early and mid 20th century.

SYLVANER is the French name for the eastern European variety known in German as Silvaner (under which name details of all non-French plantings appear). In France it is practically unknown outside ALSACE, where it is still the most planted vine in the lower, flatter, more fertile vineyards of the Bas-Rhin (although Riesling and to a lesser extent Gewürztraminer are catching up fast). The total area planted with Sylvaner, about 2,700 ha, has been one of the few constants in Alsace in the late 20th century.

Sylvaner may be an old vine and, at one time, an extremely important one in Germany at least, but as a wine producer it can be decidedly dull. Its wines can be quite full bodied and display sufficient acidity (often more appetizing acidity levels than the PINOT BLANC which is Alsace's other important non-noble varietal) but even the most ingenious taster can be hard pressed to find adjectives to describe the quintessential *flavour* of Sylvaner. Indeed the Sylvaners of Alsace provide one of the most convincing arguments for the influence of TERROIR on flavour, since they do exhibit the broad, smoky perfume characteristics that are typical of Alsace wines made from any variety.

Sylvaner represents one vine in every five in Alsace and has only recently fallen behind Riesling as the region's most planted vine. It provides typically bland varietal whites at the bottom of the price range, usefully crisp blending material for Alsace's widely planted but rarely vaunted AUXERROIS, but is worth ageing only when made in the sharpest of styles such as that of Trimbach.

See SILVANER for more details.

SYLVOZ, a vine-TRAINING SYSTEM developed by the Italian grower Carlo Sylvoz in which canes of up to, say, 10 buds in length are tied to a wire below a high CORDON. The vines can be trained with a high cordon, about 2 m/6.5 ft, or a mid height cordon at about 1 m. Depending on the number of buds retained, the system can be very high yielding. A variation of the Sylvoz is the Casarsa system common in northern Italy, where the canes are not tied below the cordon, but fall downward as a result of their own weight. The Sylvoz system is suited to vines of high vigour where it is necessary to minimize pruning labour. R.E.S.

Eynard, I., and Dalmasso, G., *Viticoltura moderna: manuale pratico* (Milan, 1990).

SYMINGTONS, family of port wine shippers for four generations whose group of port companies includes W. & J. Graham, Warre, Dow's Port (Silva & Cosens), Quarles Harris, and Smith Woodhouse. The family is therefore an extremely important force in OPORTO. Founder of the family firm was Andrew James Symington, who arrived in Oporto from Glasgow in 1882 at the age of 19. Originally he joined the firm of Warre & Co., rising to become a partner. At the time George Warre was senior partner in Dow's, and in 1912 a swap took place whereby Symington took a share in Dow's while Warre regained a part of the firm that his family had founded. The Symingtons ran production and the vineyards for the two firms while the Warre family ran sales and marketing in London. The Warre family sold their remaining shareholding to the Symingtons in 1961. W. & J. Graham & Co. was purchased from the Graham family in 1970 along with the smaller sister company of Smith Woodhouse. The family owns Quinta do Bomfim near Pinhão, which provides much of the fruit for Dow's. It also owns Warre's Quinta da Cavadinha in the Pinhão valley and Graham's Quinta dos Malvedos at Tua. The group was instrumental in reviving interest in single-quinta ports in the late 1980s (see PORT, styles). In 1989 the Symingtons acquired Quinta do Vesúvio, a 400-ha/990-acre estate widely regarded as one of the finest vineyard sites in the Douro, but in need of some restoration (see FERREIRA). The vineyards have been extended and improved and, from 1992, Quinta do Vesúvio was marketed as a brand in its own right. In 1988 the extensive Quinta do Marco plant in VILA NOVA DE GAIA was opened and it bottles more than 1 million cases of port annually. Despite this integration, each company within the group has its own separate stocks and the group maintains a full range of vintage and wood ports for each company. Ninety-six per cent of total activity is in wood ports and the opening of Quinta do Marco saw a great enlargement in storage capacity. The group holds total stocks of about 35 million l/9.2 million gal of port.

In 1988, the BLANDY family approached the Symingtons and offered a partnership in their MADEIRA business, hoping to reverse a general decline in sales of madeira. The Symingtons have since acquired a controlling interest in the Madeira Wine Company, the dominant producer of island bottled madeira. Madeira brands held by the Blandy and Symington families include BLANDY'S, COSSART GORDON, Leacock, and Rutherford & Miles. The Symingtons have established their own import companies in Britain and the USA.

Andrew James Symington eventually passed the company on to his three sons Maurice, John, and Ronald. Michael Symington, Maurice's elder son, who joined the company in 1947, was chairman for much of the late 20th century, his cousin James Symington (Ronald's elder son) is responsible for Graham's Port, while Ian (John's eldest son) looks after Warre's and Smith Woodhouse. Peter Symington, brother of Ian, is responsible for all the blending and wine-making in the group. Amyas, the third brother, is based at Vila Nova de Gaia, while the fourth generation is represented by Michael's son Paul, in charge of European export sales, Ian's son Johnny, and James's son Rupert. S.A.

The **Symington** tentacles reach deep into the port industry, including the cellars of the Factory House in Oporto, where each member provides a parcel of vintage port.

SYMPHONY, white-berried vine crossing of Grenache Gris and Muscat of Alexandria developed in CALIFORNIA at DAVIS by Dr H. P. Olmo. It lives the tenuous existence of all crossings, especially ones that make powerfully aromatic wines, although in the early 1990s it enjoyed a small vogue as an off-dry table wine something like a MALVASIA Bianca and, as a sparkling wine, nothing at all like an Asti Spumante. Of the state total of more than 200 acres/80 ha, the most successful plantings have been in Sonoma County (Chateau de Baun, Sebastiani). Lodi has also grown the grape well (Las Vinas).

SYMPOSIUM (meaning 'drinking together') was one of the most important social forms in the world of Ancient Greece, and was a considerably less cerebral affair than its 20th century counterpart. From Greece it spread to Etruria and the rest of Italy and flourished until the end of antiquity. Symposia were usually intimate gatherings: the room normally held seven or 11 couches, on each of which two men reclined on their left side, a custom adopted from oriental feasting; respectable women did not take part, and the servants and entertainers were mostly handsome slaves, both male and female. As part of the life-style of the leisured class, symposia were lavish affairs: in the richest households, the vessels for the mixing and drinking of wine would have been of gold or silver, although most will have been content with fine painted pottery. Both the shapes and the decoration of Greek pottery bear witness to the strong influence of the symposium.

The drinking of wine at the symposium followed the meal and was distinct from it, although a dessert of nuts, fruit, cakes, and the like often accompanied the wine. The end of the meal proper was marked by the drinking of a small amount of neat wine in honour of the 'Good Daemon' as a 'demonstration of the power of the good god', after which the tables were removed and the guests washed their hands and were offered garlands and perfumes. The wine was then

Greek pottery from 380–360 BC bearing witness to the strong influence of the **symposium** in Ancient Greece.

mixed with water in a *krater* (mixing bowl; see CRATER) according to one of the numerous possible ratios (as detailed under Ancient GREECE). From each bowl, a LIBATION was first offered together with a prayer (the god or gods invoked seem to have varied), and the Paean, a hymn of praise to Apollo, was also sung at the beginning of the proceedings by the whole company. A standard *krater* had a capacity of 14 l/3.7 gal, and various ancient writers indicate that three *kraters* would be emptied at a temperate symposium, so, although the alcoholic strength of the mixture was not high, the amount consumed must have been considerable (42 l for 14 or 22 people, apparently). The ratio for the dilution of the wine was determined by a *symposiarch* or master of ceremonies, chosen from the company, who also regulated the progress of the drinking: he could propose toasts, and order any member of the company to drink more, the aim being to maintain a level of pleasurable but controlled intoxication. However, since the drinking involved an element of competition, and since the proceedings might last all night, the outcome was often outright DRUNKENNESS, as VASE PAINTINGS and literary evidence make clear.

The most basic forms of entertainment arose out of the drinking itself: there were various drinking challenges with forfeits, and the heeltaps of wine were used to play the game of *kottabos*, in which each drinker would shoot the last drops of wine from his cup with a flick of the wrist at the target, which was usually a light bronze disk, balanced on top of a stand or tripod; when hit, it would fall into the basin beneath with a satisfying clatter. There was a variation in which the targets were small pottery cups floating in a basin, the aim being to sink them.

Music and poetry played an important part in the entertainment (and were linked together, since poetry was normally sung to a musical accompaniment): most, if not all, of the LYRIC POETRY of archaic Greece is now thought to have had its origins in the symposium, with its preoccupations of warfare and politics, wine and feasting, and love. Some extemporized poetry was no doubt sung at classical symposia, but it was more normal to perform existing poems, which often celebrated the great men and deeds of the past: the collection of Athenian songs of this type (*skolia*) preserved in ATHENAEUS' *Deipnosophistae* (694–96) offers a sample of the traditional songs of one city.

Like the drinking, the singing was both communal and competitive: a branch of myrtle was passed round, and each man as he received it had to sing, sometimes picking up the song from the last singer, although good singers might be called on for a 'party piece'. Singers often accompanied themselves on the lyre, but slave girls were also hired to play the flute to entertain the company, to accompany singers, and to provide music for dancing, and professional dancers, acrobats, and mimes might also perform. Flute players would also be expected to provide sexual services at the end of the evening if required (hence the assumption that any women present at a symposium were not respectable).

Urbane and cultured conversation was also an essential feature; at times this might be structured, and given a competitive aspect, by the posing of riddles or the exchange of witty (and often abusive) comparisons applied to fellow guests. This too might be stimulated by professional help: the career of the parasite who pays for his dinner with his jokes and clowning can be traced back to HOMER. The genre of the literary symposium, a gathering of learned figures conversing on literary or philosophic issues, as in Plato's *Symposium* (whence the modern use of 'symposium'), may give a misleadingly high-minded impression of the average Greek symposium, but such discussion clearly had its place, albeit at a less rarefied level.

Finally, those revellers still awake might go out into the street as a *komos*, a mobile party with wine and music, calling on other symposia or making rowdy attempts to rouse those now asleep. R.B.

Bibliographical note: O. Murray, 'The Greek Symposium in History', in E. Gabba (ed.), *Tria corda: scritti in onore di Arnaldo Momigliano* (Como, 1983) discusses historical and political aspects; O. Murray (ed.), *Sympotica* (Oxford, 1990) is a collection of essays on particular aspects, with very full bibliographies. Athenaeus' *Deipnosophistae* collects many stories of symposia, while XENOPHON'S *Symposium* gives the flavour of a classical symposium better than the more famous one of Plato; both are accessible in translation in the Loeb Classical Library.

SYRAH, one of the noblest black grape varieties, if nobility is bestowed by an ability to produce serious red wines capable of ageing majestically for decades. Indeed, so valued was the durability of France's HERMITAGE, arguably Syrah's finest manifestation, that many red bordeaux were in the 18th and 19th centuries '*hermitagé*' (see ADULTERATION).

Syrah's origins are the subject of much debate and hypothesis, its name conveniently suggesting some relationship to either Syracuse in SICILY or the Shiraz of Ancient PERSIA, whence the Crusaders could have brought it back in their saddle bags. A more recent theory is that Syrah is indigenous, a direct descendant of the vine family VITIS *allobrogica* recognized as producing fine wine in the Rhône since Roman times. Evinced as evidence for this is that Syrah can vary enormously even in the relatively limited vineyards of the northern Rhône and that the varieties of this sector of France, including those up river in Savoie, are very particular. Some see strong similarities between Syrah and MONDEUSE, and argue that Mondeuse could also be a local selection of *Vitis allobrogica*. See RHÔNE, history.

The vine is relatively productive and disease resistant, sensitive to COULURE but conveniently late budding and not too late ripening. Care has to be taken with rootstocks because it is sensitive to CHLOROSIS. Its deep, dark, dense qualities are much reduced once the yield is allowed to rise and it has a tendency to lose aroma and acidity rapidly if left too long on the vine.

Many vignerons in the northern Rhône distinguish between a small-berried, superior version of Syrah, which they call Petite Syrah (although there is no relation between Syrah and the variety known in North and South America as PETITE SIRAH), and the larger-berried Grosse Syrah, which produces wines with a lower concentration of PHENOLICS. AMPELOGRAPHERS reject this distinction, although connoisseurs have reason to be grateful for it. The total ANTHOCYANS in Syrah can be up to 40 per cent higher than those in the tough, dark Carignan, which makes it, typically, a wine for the long term that responds well to OAK maturation, even new oak at its ripest.

The most famous prototype Syrahs—Hermitage and more recently CÔTE-RÔTIE—are distinguished by their longevity or, in the case of newer producers, ambition. Only ST-JOSEPH and that paler shadow CROZES-HERMITAGE can sensibly be broached within their first five years. And the better wines of CORNAS repay bottle maturation even more handsomely than some Hermitages. Syrah that has not reached full maturation can be simply mean and astringent, with more than a whiff of burnt rubber. When planted on the fringes of the Rhône such as in the ARDÈCHE, Syrah may avoid this fate only in the ripest vintages.

Until the 1970s French Syrah plantings were almost exclusively in and around the very limited vineyards of the northern Rhône valley and were dwarfed in area by total Syrah plantings in the vine's other major colony, Australia, where it is known as Shiraz and has been that country's major black grape variety for decades (see below).

Since then, however, Syrah has enjoyed an extraordinary surge in popularity throughout southern France so that total French plantings rose from 2,700 ha/6,670 acres in 1968 to exactly ten times that 20 years later. The increases were noticeable throughout the southern Rhône, particularly in Châteauneuf-du-Pape country, where Syrah has been increasingly valued as endowing Grenache with life expectancy, but have been most spectacular to the west in the Languedoc, especially in the Gard and the Hérault, where Syrah has been most enthusiastically adopted as an officially approved 'improving variety' that has added structure to wines both APPELLATION CONTRÔLÉE and VIN DE PAYS. By 1993 there were 24,000 ha in the Languedoc-Roussillon alone, and Syrah has frequently been responsible for the Midi's most successful varietal wines, usually labelled Vin de Pays d'Oc. Yields very much in excess of the low yields that characterize the arid hill of Hermitage have somewhat diluted its north Rhône characteristics, however. In the north Rhône it is rarely blended, except perhaps with a little Viognier, while in the south it is typically blended with Grenache and perhaps Mourvèdre and Cinsaut. In Provence the very Australian blend of Syrah and Cabernet Sauvignon is becoming more common and Syrah is one of the most successful noble vine imports to Corsica, where there are more than 200 ha in production.

The ubiquity of Shiraz in Australia, whose 5,000 ha in 1990 still represented well over a quarter of the nation's total black grape vineyard, has done little to imbue Syrah with the respect it commands in its homeland and there were signs that it would be overtaken by the more highly regarded Cabernet Sauvignon. For long Australian grape-growers regarded Shiraz as their workhorse and expected it to produce far too great a quantity of inevitably undistinguished wine (Syrah does not respond well to high yields), but Australia is producing an increasing proportion of top-quality, concentrated Shiraz, notably from old Barossa Valley vines.

Shiraz, then known as Scyras, was probably taken to Australia, possibly from Montpellier, in 1832 by James BUSBY. It flourished so obviously that it was rapidly adopted by New South Wales and spread therefrom. Today Australian Shiraz can vary from a brown, baked, dilute everyday red to the glorious, almost porty concentration of Australia's most famous wine, Penfolds Grange.

Another unexpectedly successful site for mature, concentrated Syrah is the Valais in Switzerland, particularly around the suntrap village of Chamoson on the upper reaches of the Rhône valley. Here classic north Rhône techniques are employed, sometimes to great effect. Italy too is flirting with Syrah, most successfully so far at Isola e Elena in Tuscany. The variety was initially introduced from MONTPELLIER, in 1899 in Piedmont.

To ripen fully Syrah demands a warm climate, which naturally limits its spread, but some plantings in California have been very successful. Californians were slow to distinguish between true Syrah and Petite Sirah and even slower to import suitable plant material so that, despite a modishness achieved thanks to the RHÔNE RANGERS, there were still barely 400 acres of it in the state in 1992 but the total was rising rapidly, as nurserymen reported Syrah their most sought-after cutting in Napa and Sonoma. Although there are pre-PROHIBITION remnants in McDowell Valley in MENDOCINO and a Napa Valley planting that dates from the 1950s, the most substantial Syrah plantings have been in the 1990s and in Mendocino and Sonoma. Effective early practitioners were McDowell Valley Vineyards, Joseph Phelps, Meridian, and Qupé.

South Africa's total, usually called Shiraz, had reached nearly 900 ha by 1992, most of it in Paarl and Stellenbosch, and the results are promising in those who manage to restrict yields. A small amount is also grown with some success in Argentina, where it was known until identified in 1968 as Balsamina, not a bad synonym for this headily scented grape variety.

MacDonogh, G., *Syrah, Grenache and Mourvèdre* (London, 1992).
(La Syrah', supplement to *Le Vigneron des Côtes-du-Rhône et du Sud-Est* (1992) 341.

SYRIA, country in the Middle East with more than 100,000 ha / 247,000 acres of vineyards, most of which have been dedicated to the production of TABLE GRAPES and DRYING GRAPES rather than wine since the rise of Islamic fundamentalism in the late 1970s (see ISLAM). Average annual wine production in the late 1970s was 63,000 hl / 1.6 million gal but fell to 8,000 hl in the early 1980s and is still declining.

Syria has a particularly long history of wine production (see ORIGINS OF VITICULTURE). See also MESOPOTAMIA.

SZÜRKEBARÁT, Hungarian name for PINOT GRIS which is quite widely planted there; but its naturally low acidity can result in slightly flabby wines, particularly on the Great Plain. It is most revered within HUNGARY as Badacsonyi Szürkebarát, a rich, heavy wine from the north shore of Lake Balaton. It can yield livelier wines from the Mátra Foothills.

T

TA. See TOTAL ACIDITY.

TABLE GRAPES, the common term for those grapes specially grown to be eaten as fresh fruit. Of the grapes grown world-wide, table grapes represent the third most frequent use, following wine and dried grapes. About 10 million tonnes are grown each year. The most important producing countries are Turkey, Italy, the former Soviet Union, Spain, Portugal, USA, Japan, Greece, Brazil, Chile, and to a lesser extent France. The fruit is consumed primarily within the producing country because it is relatively low in value and perishable. However, with refrigeration the opportunities for export are increasing. Grapes represent less than five per cent of the annual fresh fruit consumption of Europe and North America.

The varieties of grapes for fresh consumption are usually specialized and different from those for wine and drying. They should taste good, have a reasonably consistent BERRY SIZE, bright colour, firm flesh texture, not too many seeds, and skins tough enough to withstand storage and transport. Recently developed seedless varieties are now very important in the table grape market. Some important table grape varieties are Barlinka, Calmeria, Cardinal, CHASSELAS, Dattier, Emperor, Flame Seedless, Gros Vert, Italia, MUSCAT OF ALEXANDRIA, MUSCAT HAMBURG, Perlette, Ruby Seedless, Ribier, and SULTANA (or Thompson Seedless).

Table grapes are typically grown in warm to hot regions to encourage early maturity and freedom from any ROT brought on by rain. Low night temperatures assist the colour development of some varieties, while both very high and very low day temperatures may inhibit colour development. Many of the table grape regions of the world are inland desert areas.

There are some important differences between table grape and wine grape vineyard management. For table grapes, the aim is generally to produce maximum berry size, and so IRRIGATION and FERTILIZERS are used more liberally than for wine grapes. Excessive use of NITROGEN fertilizers, however, can reduce the fruit's colour. TRAINING SYSTEMS should be designed so that the fruit hangs free from surrounding foliage; this makes easy any hand work and also reduces blemishes to the fruit. Sloping and overhead trellis systems such as the pergola and TENDONE are common, where the shoots and leaves form a canopy over the fruit, avoiding excessive and direct sun exposure.

Because they are worth more than most wine grapes (although see Ch d'YQUEM, MONTRACHET, and DOMAINE DE LA ROMANÉE-CONTI), table grapes typically require more manual vineyard work. This can include SHOOT THINNING and CROP THINNING, which can be done by removing whole inflorescences before flowering or after fruit set. Sometimes part of the bunch is removed, and sometimes even individual berries thinned. These practices lead to larger berries which ripen early. GROWTH REGULATORS are also commonly used to thin flowers, but more particularly to increase berry size of seedless varieties such as Sultana. CINCTURING or girdling can also be used to hasten ripening. Plastic covers or even glass-houses can be used to encourage early maturity and give rain protection, or where the climate is too cold for outside culture. However, such production methods are expensive, and normally only high-quality or highly priced fruit can be produced in this way.

Table grapes are harvested earlier than wine grapes as a lower sugar level and higher acidity make them taste more refreshing, in the range of 15 to 18° BRIX (whereas wine grapes would preferably be harvested for dry wines at about 22° Brix). Harvesting should ideally be carried out in the cool of the morning. Each bunch is inspected and immature, misshapen, diseased, undersized, or split berries are carefully removed. The bunches can be packed in the field or taken in bulk to a packing shed. They are normally packed in a cardboard box holding about 10 kg of grapes. It is important in extending shelf life that the grapes are immediately cooled, especially if they are to be transported long distances. Cooling, preferably to 0–2 °C/36 °F reduces RESPIRATION rates as well as inhibiting the growth of any fungal spores and the loss of moisture from the bunches.

Some table grape varieties can be kept in cool stores for up to 20 weeks, although eight to 12 weeks is more common. Long storage life is promoted by low temperatures such as −1 °C (at which the sugar content stops them freezing), a relative humidity of about 96 per cent, and SULPHUR DIOXIDE fumigation for mould control. R.E.S.

TABLE WINE, term often used to distinguish wines of average ALCOHOLIC STRENGTH from FORTIFIED WINES which have been strengthened by the addition of alcohol and are usually more than 15 per cent alcohol. In this context, 'table wines' rely solely on FERMENTATION for their alcoholic strength which tends to be between nine and 15 per cent.

The term 'table wine' has a specific meaning within the

Chapoutier of Tain l'Hermitage persisted with **crushing** grapes by foot rather than machine longer than most. Tradition is yet to be replaced by science and expediency in much of the northern **Rhône**.

EUROPEAN UNION, however, and is applied to all wine produced within it that does not qualify as superior QUALITY WINE. Table wine is therefore the EU's principal wine product.

Within France table wine is known as VIN DE TABLE. The distinct and superior category is VIN DE PAYS.

Within Italy the situation is rather different. Although all of Italy's most basic wine (and there is a great deal of it) is designated vino da tavola, that designation has also been chosen, confusingly, by a considerable number of the best producers for some of their best wines, whose production does not happen to conform to any rule for Italian quality wine, DOC and DOCG (see VINO DA TAVOLA for more details). Italy also has an embryonic counterpart to France's vin de pays, IGT, but by far the majority of Italian wine is designated vino da tavola.

The reverse is the case in Germany where less than five per cent of total production is deemed to be Deutscher TAFELWEIN or its superior category LANDWEIN. See below, however.

Spain's table wine is called VINO DE MESA, and Spain also has a small superior category, VINO DE LA TIERRA.

Portugal's table wine is known as VINHO de mesa and its even more nascent superior subcategory is IPR.

Greek table wine is called 'epitrapezios oinos' within Greece and is rarely exported.

Most of Luxembourg's wine qualifies as quality wine, and the rest is called vin de table.

The minuscule English wine industry was still establishing its quality wine scheme in the mid 1990s so that most English wine has been sold as table wine.

Within the EU, however, table wines from different countries may be freely blended to produced **European table wine**. This is particularly common in Germany, where it may be called EWG Tafelwein, or simply Tafelwein. Within France, however, a significant proportion of France's considerable imports from Italy and, more recently, Spain, are blended with French vin de table to produce a Vin de Table des Pays Différentes de l'EU.

TÂCHE, LA, great red GRAND CRU in Burgundy's CÔTE D'OR. For more details see VOSNE-ROMANÉE and DOMAINE DE LA ROMANÉE-CONTI.

TACORONTE-ACENTEJO, DO wine region on the west-facing slopes in the north east of the volcanic island of Tenerife in the CANARY ISLANDS. Tacoronte-Acentjo produces fairly inconsequential red wines made predominantly from the dark-berried LISTÁN Negro and Negramoll grapes. Production methods are improving but the wine finds favour only with the locals and large numbers of tourists. R.J.M.

TAFELWEIN, German for TABLE WINE, the most basic official category of wine recognized within Europe. A wine bottled in Germany and labelled simply as Tafelwein, or **Tafelwein aus Ländern EWG**, will contain wine from EUROPEAN UNION (EWG in German) countries other than Germany (normally inexpensive Italian white). A wine labelled **Deutscher Tafelwein** should contain only German wine, albeit made from grapes so unripe that they failed to achieve the MUST WEIGHT necessary to qualify as a QBA. LANDWEIN is a subcategory of Deutscher Tafelwein which is Germany's answer to France's VIN DE PAYS. Neither Deutscher Tafelwein, nor Tafelwein, needs to be submitted to the control of AP NUMBER testing, so some producers deliberately declassify their most unconventional bottlings (BARRIQUE-aged Rieslings, for example) to Deutscher Tafelwein status in order to bypass the prejudices of the tasting panel at the AP control stations.

TAILLE, French term for PRUNING and also, by extension, for vine-TRAINING SYSTEM. The name is also used in CHAMPAGNE and sometimes elsewhere for the coarser, later juice which flows from the press in the champagne method of SPARKLING WINE-MAKING.

TAILS, or *queues* in French, the end of the run of spirit through a POT STILL. The lower the strength of the final spirit, the richer it is in CONGENERS and other aromatic but sometimes undesirable elements. Distillers wanting a richer final product have to risk these impurities in order to preserve as much of the characterful aromatic matter as possible. N.F.

TAIWAN, island republic off, and independent of, CHINA which is experimenting with vines imported from DAVIS for wine production.

TAJIKISTAN, mountainous central Asian republic of the CIS between UZBEKISTAN and CHINA. Lowlands, plateaux, foothills, and mountain slopes suitable for viticulture occupy only seven per cent of Tajikistan's area. The climate of the country is continental. In the lowlands and valleys at 900 m/2,950 ft above sea level, the average January temperature is 2 to −3 °C/27 °F and the average July temperature is 26 to 31 °C, while the annual rainfall is 150 to 600 mm/23 in. On the foothills, at an altitude of 1,000 to 1,500 m, the average January temperature varies from 0 to −5 °C, that of July is 23 to 25 °C and the annual rainfall is 350 to 850 mm.

Viticulture and wine-making were developed in Tajikistan even before the military campaigns of Alexander the Great in the 4th century BC. Ancient documents testify to the cultivation of numerous VINE VARIETIES in the country, which were made into wine, vinegar, and *bekmes* (CONCENTRATED GRAPE MUST), as well as being traded as TABLE GRAPES and RAISINS. Viticulture was highly developed in Osrushan in Ura-Tyube, Fergana, and in the Zeravshan river valley.

The adoption of ISLAM in the north prohibited the consumption of wine and changed the country's range of grape varieties. Wine varieties were grubbed up and table and raisin varieties were planted in their place. Central, south, and south eastern parts of the country were also affected by this trend but to a lesser extent. In the 1920s, small private vineyards were amalgamated to form large farms, and the total vine-

Harvest at Ch Palmer, one of the most admired properties in **Margaux**. Picking the low-trained vines of **Bordeaux** can be particularly back-breaking work.

Picking **table grapes** in Israel near Jerusalem.

yard area continued to increase in order to meet the needs of commercial wine production. The first state farms specializing in viticulture were established and wineries in the towns of Ura-Tyube, Leninabad, and Pendzhikent were built.

In 1940, the total vineyard area was 8,200 ha/20,250 acres, with the gross yield of grapes being 49,000 tons and the grape wine production accounting for 27,900 hl/736,500 gal. Thereafter, the raw material base of the industry and grape-processing facilities continued to increase.

Tajikistan can be divided into three viticultural zones: the Leninabad region in the north, the Ghissar valley in the centre, and the Vakhsh valley together with the Kuliab regions in the south. Although most vines are trained into fan shaped TRAINING SYSTEMS with numerous canes on vertical trellises and high-trunked forms, several areas still have vines trained to horizontal trellises. Most vineyards need WINTER PROTECTION, and irrigated vineyards account for 75 per cent of the total.

In 1992 25 grape varieties were in commercial cultivation, with 10 wine varieties such as RKATSITELI, SAPERAVI, CABERNET SAUVIGNON, RIESLING, Tagobi, Bayan Shirey, and Muscat Rosé. In 1990 vineyards occupied 37,000 ha, with wine grapes accounting for 65 per cent of the total grape area, providing 150,000 hl.

The 20 wineries of Tajikistan (including four secondary vinification enterprises—see CIS) produce more than 50 brands of wine, most of them strong and sweet. V.R.

Kirillov, I. F., Brodnikovski, M. I., Savchenko, A. D., Podkolzin, I. V., *Viticulture of Tajikistan* (Russian) (Dushanbe, 1969).

Kiselev, N. A., *Viticultural Regions and Wines of Tajikistan* (Russian) (Moscow, 1967).

Savchenko, A. D., 'The Soviet Socialist Republic of Tajikistan' (Russian), in A. I. Timush (ed.), *Encyclopaedia of Viticulture* (Kishinëv, 1986).

TALIA. Portuguese white grape variety. See THALIA.

TĂMÎIOASĂ name for MUSCAT grape or wine in ROMANIA. Thus **Tămîioasă Alba** is Romanian for MUSCAT BLANC À PETITS GRAINS, **Tămîioasă Hamburg** or **Tămîioasă Neagră** is MUSCAT HAMBURG, **Tămîioasă Ottonel** is MUSCAT OTTONEL.

Tămîioasă Românească is an old Romanian variety, and there were more than 1,000 ha/2,500 acres planted in Romania in the early 1990s. It is a very powerfully, aristocratically scented grape variety well suited to producing sweet white wines of real distinction. The latter is also grown in Bulgaria as Tamianka. In Germany it is known tellingly as the Weihrauchtraube, or 'frankincense grape'.

TAMINGA, grape variety bred specifically for AUSTRALIAN conditions (see also TARRANGO) by A. J. Antcliff. Taminga is capable of ripening and producing white wine of fair quality in a wide variety of different sites with an average yield of 90 hl/ha (5 tons/acre).

TANK METHOD, alternative name for a bulk SPARKLING WINE-MAKING process which involves provoking a second fermentation in wine stored in a pressure tank. Other names include Charmat process and *cuve close*.

TANKS. See CONTAINERS.

TANNAT is a tough, black-berried vine variety most famous as principal ingredient in MADIRAN, where its inherent astringence is mitigated by blending with Cabernet Franc, some Cabernet Sauvignon, and FER, and wood ageing for at least 20 months. Young Tannat can be so deeply coloured and tannic than it recalls NEBBIOLO. If Madiran is Tannat's noblest manifestation, slightly more approachable, if more rustic, wines are made to much the same recipe for Côtes de ST-MONT, as well as for the distinctively hard reds and rosés of IROULÉGUY and the rare reds and pinks labelled TURSAN and BÉARN.

Although it can also be found as a minor ingredient in such wines as Côtes du BRULHOIS, overall plantings in France have been declining so that there were fewer than 3,000 ha/7,400 acres by 1988. Although it may owe its French name to its high tannin content, the vine is almost certainly Basque in origin and, like MANSENG, was taken to URUGUAY by Basque settlers in the 19th century. There are still several thousand hectares there where it is called Harriague, presumably after its original promulgator. From here it spread to Argentina, where it is still grown to a very limited extent.

TANNINS, a group of chemicals that occur in the bark of many trees and in fruits, including the grape, conferring astringency to their taste. Tannins are derived from flavonoids (see PHENOLICS) by condensing together two or more structures of the flavonol type, including catechin and pro-anthocyanidins. Tannins play an important role in the AGEING of wine, particularly red wine, and need careful mastery during wine-making as they can taste bitter and astringent. Handling tannins is one of the most critical steps in optimizing the quality and character of a red wine. Tannins in wine come from the grapes, and the WOOD in which it was aged.

Tannins are very similar in structure to ANTHOCYANS, natural colouring matter, except that in tannins the development of red colours is precluded and, in solution, they are usually light yellow to amber, although they can react with iron to take on a blue-black colour.

Tannins are most frequently encountered by the human palate in over-steeped tea and in young red wines designed for a long life in bottle. They are one of the few wine constituents which cannot be sensed by the NOSE but produce a physical sensation, bitterness and an uncomfortable 'drying', in the mouth, particularly on the inside of the cheeks. Medium-sized POLYMERIZED tannins interact with the proteins of taste buds sensitive to bitterness, while larger ones function as tanning agents (tannins also have the property of interacting with the protein collagen to convert animal hides to leather), actually forming a bit of leather with the proteins on the tongue and insides of the cheek.

Tannins in wines come principally from grape SKINS, SEEDS, and STEMS. The amount of tannins in grape pulp is relatively insignificant. Thus, the more skins, seeds, and stems are involved in the wine-making process, the higher the possible resultant level of tannins. Tannin levels in white and rosé wines, which are made largely by excluding or minimizing these grape components, are therefore lower than in reds. Tannins are measured by a particular method and reported as if they were all gallic acid. Gallic acid, or GA, equivalent concentration averages about 300 mg/l in white wines, but 1,800 mg/l in reds.

The tannin types and their extraction rates vary considerably with VINE VARIETY and WINE-MAKING methods. Varieties notably high in tannins include CABERNET SAUVIGNON, NEBBIOLO, SYRAH, TANNAT. Much RED WINE-MAKING experimentation and research work in the late 1980s and early 1990s was concerned with minimizing the bitter and astringent impression made by tannins on the palate, while retaining tannins' preservative properties. This included more detailed considerations of the precise nature of grape RIPENESS and refinement of MACERATION techniques. Some wine-makers have also experimented with deliberately controlled exposure to OXYGEN at various points during the wine-making process.

Different WOOD TYPES contain different sorts of tannins, but these have most effect on wine when the COOPERAGE is new. OAK is by far the most common sort of new wood used for BARREL MATURATION. The tannins of the various species and varieties of oak vary among themselves, and according to how the oak was seasoned (see BARREL MAKING), and differ in significant ways from the tannins of grapes. For more details see WOOD FLAVOUR.

Wine consumers have come to expect a certain amount of wood flavour in some immature wines, both red and white, whether the result of genuine barrel maturation or the use of OAK CHIPS (or even, although it is illegal in most countries, OAK ESSENCE). They are therefore often exposed to the effects of tannin on the palate, which can be considerably mitigated by the right choice of accompanying FOOD. It is not unknown for wine-makers to add tannins.

Excessively high tannin levels can be adjusted by FINING with casein, gelatin, or albumin. Given a sufficient amount of time, tannins are removed naturally, however, during wine maturation. The tannins agglomerate and polymerize so that eventually those molecules above a certain size precipitate as SEDIMENT and no longer have any bitter or astringent effect on the palate. For more details see AGEING. A.D.W. & J.Ro.

Somers, T. C., and Verette, E., 'Phenolic composition of natural wine types', in H. F. Linskens and J. F. Jackson (eds.), *Wine Analysis* (Modern Methods of Plant Analysis, NS 6) (Berlin, 1988).

TARRAGONA, Mediterranean port in Spanish CATALONIA which has played an important part in a flourishing wine industry since Roman times (see map on p. 907 and SPAIN, history). Until the 1960s wines called Tarragona were predominantly sweet, red, fortified, and drunk as a cheap alternative to PORT. Tarragona, awarded DO status in 1976, continues to ship communion wine all over the Christian world (see EUCHARIST). Over 70 per cent of Tarragona's wine production today is white, however, a large proportion of which is sold to the CAVA houses in PENEDÈS. The red wines, made from GARNACHA and Cariñena (CARIGNAN), are mostly sold in bulk for BLENDING, which is why the name Tarragona is seldom seen on a bottle of wine. R.J.M.

TARRANGO, red wine grape variety developed at Merbein in AUSTRALIA in 1965. The aim of this TOURIGA × SULTANA crossing was to provide a slow-ripening variety suitable for the production of light bodied wines with low TANNINS and relatively high ACIDITY. As a result, some Australian wines have been fashioned in the image of BEAUJOLAIS but the variety will ripen satisfactorily only in the hot irrigated wine regions of Australia such as the RIVERLAND. Brown Brothers of Milawa have been particularly persistent with this variety. Other varieties developed by A. J. Antcliff specifically for Australian conditions included Carina and Merbein Seedless for drying and Tulillah, Goyura, and TAMINGA for white wines.

TARTARIC ACID, the most important of the ACIDS found in grapes and wine. This chemically interesting substance is also notable because, of all the natural organic acids found in plants, it is one of the rarer. Tartaric acid is not widespread in plants. The grape is the only fruit of significance that is a tartrate accumulator, and yet it is of critical importance to the wine-maker because of the major part it plays in the taste of the wine. Furthermore, because tartaric acid exists in wine partially as the intact acid and partially as the acid tartrate, or bitartrate ion, it is the principal component of the mixture of acids and salts that constitutes wine's all-important buffer system and maintains the stability of its ACIDITY and COLOUR.

Tartaric acid is of even further interest because its potassium acid salt, potassium tartrate or cream of tartar, while being moderately soluble in grape juice, is only partially soluble in alcoholic solutions such as wine. Most wine-makers therefore try to ensure that no excess tartrates remain in the wine when it is bottled lest these crystals frighten less sophisticated consumers by their resemblance to glass shards. See TARTRATES for more on this important by-product of the wine-making process.

Grapes and the resultant wines vary considerably in their concentrations of tartaric acid. Among the thousands of cultivated VINE VARIETIES, some are noted for their high concentrations of tartaric acid, while others are remarkably bland. In general, wine grapes have higher concentrations of acids than table grapes. Among wine grape varieties, however, there is considerable variation in concentrations of the two principal acids tartaric acid and MALIC ACID. Palomino, the sherry grape, for example, is particularly high in tartaric acid, while the Pinot Noir of Burgundy and Malbec, or Cot, are relatively low in tartaric.

The relative amounts of these two acids that are present in grapes do not necessarily govern the relative amounts in wines, however. Precipitation of potassium acid tartrate, as outlined above, limits total tartaric acid concentration, while malic acid is frequently decomposed by MALOLACTIC FERMENTATION. Wines that have not undergone this secondary fermentation generally have slightly more tartaric acid than malic acid, while those which have undergone this 'softening' process usually have many more times tartaric than malic acid.

Weather and soil, as well as grape variety, affect the amounts of different acids in the grape and wine. Cooler climates in general favour higher concentrations of acids and lower levels of POTASSIUM in the grape skins. Malic acid is much more effectively decomposed by excessive heat during the grape ripening period than is tartaric acid. Soils deficient in potassium, or potash, may result in grapes of high acid concentration and low PH because low potassium levels allow greater concentrations of acid tartrate ion to stay in solution. Another curious difference is that tartrate levels are very high in grape flowers. Tartaric acid is not respired during ripening, meaning that its amount per berry stays relatively constant during berry RIPENING. More than half of the tartrate in ripe berries can be present as a salt. The proportion of free to salt form varies with variety and the concentration of metal cations in the juice; potassium is by far the most abundant.

A.D.W. & B.G.C.

TARTRATES, the general term used by wine-makers to describe the harmless crystalline deposits that separate from wines during FERMENTATION and AGEING. In English the substances are also called argols, in French *tartres* and in German *Weinstein* or 'wine stones'. The principal component of this deposit is potassium acid tartrate, the potassium salt of TARTARIC ACID, which has therefore given rise to the name. Small amounts of pulp debris, dead yeast cells, precipitated phenolic materials such as TANNINS and ANTHOCYANS, and traces of other materials make up the impurities contaminating the potassium acid tartrate (see SEDIMENT).

The LEES, the thick layer of dead yeast and grape skins, seeds, and pulp fragments that sinks to the bottom of the FERMENTATION VESSEL during the later stages of fermentation as deposit, contains lower concentrations of tartrates than do the crystalline deposits that form on the walls of the vessel. Lees are a commercial source of tartrates, but extraction and purification of potassium acid tartrate from lees is much more expensive and time consuming than from the crystalline deposits on walls, the preferred source for commercial tartrates.

The main forms of tartrates used commercially are pure crystalline tartaric acid used as an acidulant in non-alcoholic drinks and foods; cream of tartar (pure potassium acid tartrate) used in baking; and Rochelle salt (potassium sodium tartrate) used mainly in electroplating solutions. The wine industry is the only source of tartrates available to commerce and the crystalline encrustations left inside fermentation vessels are therefore regularly scraped off for eventual commercial use after purification.

Tartrates separate from new wines because potassium acid tartrate is less soluble in solutions of alcohol and water such as wine than it is in plain water, or grape juice. The exact

Hacking **tartrates** off the inside of a barrel in Gaja's cellars in Barbaresco, Piedmont.

figures for wines vary slightly according to grape variety and region, but experience shows that about a half of the tartrate soluble in grape juice is insoluble in wine. The problem is that the tartrate may remain in a supersaturated state in the complex wine mixture only to crystallize at some unpredictable later time.

Only the most informed consumers appreciate the harmlessness of tartrate crystals in bottle. Although tartrates precipitated in red wines usually take on some red or brown colouring from adsorbed wine pigments and are commonly regarded as mere sediment, in white wines they can look alarmingly like shards of glass to the uninitiated. The modern wine industry has in the main decided that tartrate STABILIZATION is preferable to consumer education.

Tartrate instability was recognized as a problem only in the 19th century when, with greater wine production and standardization of BOTTLE production, bottle-aged wines first became common. Previously wines were not expected to be perfectly clear and many would routinely be strained, but producers of most modern wines, and all inexpensive white wines, believe that their customers expect a brilliantly clear liquid to emerge from the bottle, no matter how long it has been there.

With the efficient degrees of FILTRATION possible today, it is relatively easy to ensure perfect clarity immediately prior to BOTTLING. The problem is to ensure that the wine will remain clear. Historically, wines were stabilized against tartrate precipitation by letting the cellar cool to temperatures near or below freezing during the winter. Low temperatures for three to four months would usually remove so much potassium acid tartrate that further precipitation was unlikely. The modern equivalent is to use REFRIGERATION to chill the wine before bottling to between −5 and −10 °C/24 to 14 °F for two to three weeks. Precipitated tartrate crystals are then filtered from the cold wine before it is warmed back to cellar temperature. Sometimes small amounts of finely divided CHARCOAL or BENTONITE clay are mixed into the wine to be chilled to act as nucleation centres for the supersaturated potassium acid tartrate and therefore induce crystal formation. A more recent and faster technique involves the stirring up of finely ground potassium acid tartrate in the wine, which is then cooled to a low temperature and the cold wine and crystal mixture immediately filtered. This method depends on the rapid crystallization of tartrates from the wine on the millions of fine crystals added that act as nucleation centres. This newer method saves both time and power. A technique involving ION EXCHANGE which lowered wine's naturally high potassium content and increased its naturally low sodium content was used in the 1940s and 1950s but was abandoned, primarily for health reasons.

Some everyday wines produced in large quantities contain enough calcium to cause precipitation of calcium tartrate during bottle ageing, although this was most common in the era of the concrete tank. When the concrete tanks were new, or had had their protective coating of tartrates removed, wine dissolved enough calcium carbonate from the concrete surface to cause subsequent calcium tartrate instability. Stainless steel tanks, or lined concrete ones, have overcome the problem of calcium tartrate instability.

Tartrates are most commonly encountered in bottles of German wine because, coming from a relatively cool region, they have the greatest concentration of tartaric acid. In white wines colourless, perfectly shaped crystals of potassium acid tartrate are found. In red wines there are usually sufficient adsorbed TANNINS and ANTHOCYANS to colour the crystals reddish brown and to ensure that they are small and irregular in shape. A.D.W.

TASMANIA, small island state to the cool south of AUSTRALIA, with most of its vineyards clustered round Launceston in the north or Hobart in the south of the island.

In volume terms the Tasmanian wine industry is as tiny as its potential is large. It crushed a total of 629 tonnes of grapes in 1992, while Lindeman's winery at Karadoc in VICTORIA routinely processes 1,500 tonnes of grapes a day.

Outside observers not only habitually exaggerate the extent of Tasmania's viticulture, but are oblivious to the diversity of TERROIR and climate in the island's extremely complex geography. There are sites which are both warmer and very much drier than in southern Victoria (for example the **Coal River** region in the east of Hobart, and, in terms of warmth, the **Tamar River** south of Launceston) and there are sites cooler and wetter (for example **Pipers Brook**, east of Launceston).

ZINFANDEL was once grown successfully at the Coal River; the colour and extract of the Tamar River red wines is extraordinary, hinting misleadingly at a warm to very warm climate. The island's big three wineries—Pipers Brook Winery, Moorilla Estate, and Heemskerk—have hitched their future to such cool climate vine varieties as RIESLING, CHARDONNAY, and PINOT NOIR (with Heemskerk now firmly wedded to ROEDERER of Champagne for the production of sparkling wine).

Although the climate does not necessarily dictate this, whether Tasmania realizes part or all of its potential may well rest with sparkling wine—sparkling wine produced not in Tasmania but on the mainland (as MOËT & CHANDON already does). If the larger Australia wineries decided that the quality and style of Tasmanian grapes produced a base wine which added significant complexity to their premium wines, there would have to be an exponential increase in Tasmania's vine plantings.

Tasmania has its own CONTROLLED APPELLATIONS system. J.H.

TASTE. What we call the sense of taste is to a very great extent the sense of smell. See TASTING for more details.

TASTEVINS, or, wine tasters as they are known by collectors of wine ANTIQUES, are shallow, often dimpled, saucers used for TASTING by professionals (and occasional self-conscious amateurs). They were therefore seldom made for domestic use. Because they were usually used in a cellar, or on purchasing journeys where robust construction was essential, they were almost invariably made of silver. The earliest English references to tasters date from the 14th century but only a single extant example pre-dates 1600. British tasters mostly copy the BORDEAUX model, being 65–110 mm (2.5–4.5 in) in diameter with sloping sides, a domed base, and lacking a handle. They are often engraved with the owner's name and sometimes the date. Very few were made after 1800. Extremely rare tasters were made of glass or porcelain, usually Worcester.

Tastevins are far more plentiful in France than elsewhere and follow set regional patterns varying little from one century to the next. Most have a single handle and a slightly domed base. Many are decorated with a different pattern on either side of the handle, usually gadrooning on one side and repeated circular dimples on the other. Like their English counterparts many are engraved, although often in an

Tastevins: An English wine taster made during the reign of King Charles I in 1647, the fourth earliest recorded fully marked example.

amateur hand, with the owner's name. Late 19th and 20th century examples are often plated. R.N.H.B.

Some BURGUNDY producers still use tastevins in their own cellars, where they can be useful to demonstrate hue and clarity even in a dim light. For actual tasting, GLASSES are much better, even if more fragile and less easily portable. Their contemporary manufacture is sustained by many CONFRÉRIES, most obviously the Burgundian Chevaliers du Tastevin.

Butler, R., and Walkling, G., *The Book of Wine Antiques* (Woodbridge, 1986).

Clayton, M., *Collectors Dictionary of the Silver and Gold of Great Britain and North America* (rev. edn., Woodbridge, 1985).

Goldsmith's Company, *Goldsmith and the Grape* (London, 1983).

Johnson, H., Janson, D. J., and McFadden, D. R., *Wine Celebration and Ceremony* (New York, 1985).

Mazenot, R., *Le Tastevin à travers les siècles* (Grenoble, 1973).

TASTING, the act of consciously assessing a wine's quality, or identity (see BLIND TASTING). It is certainly not synonymous with, nor necessarily contemporaneous with nor accompanied by, the act of drinking it. The ideal conditions for the act of tasting, and the organization and classification of formal wine tastings, is outlined under TASTINGS. This article is concerned with the activities and mechanisms involved in consciously receiving the sensory impressions a wine can stimulate.

Ancient Greek tasters

The existence of an organized trade in wine in Ancient GREECE must have created a class of specialized MERCHANTS. Both for them and for discerning members of the public, skill in tasting was necessary, and the Greeks had a word for the wine taster and his art: *oinogeustes/-geustikē*. The first attestation of this activity is through the cognate verb meaning 'to taste wine', found as early as the 4th century BC.

References to the professionals are extremely rare; one is found in a document of the 3rd century AD from Roman Egypt (*Oxyrhynchus Papyrus* 3517), where it is said, 'The wine taster has declared the Euboean wine to be unsuitable.'

The most enlightening ancient text is by Florentinus, a writer of the early 3rd century AD, who gives the following advice (preserved in the *Geoponica* 7. 7).

> When and how to taste wine. From Florentinus. Some people taste wines when the wind is in the north, because then the wines remain unchanged and undisturbed. Experienced drinkers prefer to taste when the wind is from the south, because this has the most effect on the wine and reveals its nature. One should not taste when hungry, because the sense of taste is blunted, nor after heavy drinking or a large meal. The person tasting should not do so after consumption of food with a sharp or very salty taste, or anything which affects the sense of taste strongly, but should have eaten as lightly as possible and be free from indigestion.

See the ancient history of MERCHANTS for a continuation of this advice, as applied to the art of selling wine. N.G.W.

How we taste

Most of what is commonly called the sense of taste is in fact the sense of SMELL. To verify this it is enough to eat or drink something with the nose pinched shut, or to consider the extent to which we 'lose our appetite' when we have a head cold which blocks the nose. The human brain senses what we call flavours and aromas in the olfactory bulb, which is reached via perhaps a thousand different receptors, each sensitive to a small group of different aromas, located in the nose. These are reached mainly by the nostrils, and also by a channel at the back of the mouth called the retronasal passage (which is why most healthy people can still perceive some flavour even with the nose pinched shut). The human olfactory sense is extremely acute (although not as acute as some animals'). Concentrations of some compounds of one part per 10,000 can be sensed, recognized, and remembered by the average person. A single whiff can transport us immediately to a remembered scene many years before. Our high number of receptors helps us recognize all the 10,000 or so aromas that humans are capable of smelling.

The tasting capacity of the mouth is much more limited. Our tactile sense can register FIZZINESS, TEMPERATURE, VISCOSITY, and the sensation induced by TANNINS of drying out the sides of the mouth. The tongue also has certain taste receptors we called taste buds, which can sense the four 'primary tastes' of sweetness, acidity, bitterness, and saltiness. In very general terms these taste buds have different sensitivities so that those at the front of the tongue are usually particularly sensitive to sweetness, those on the edges of the tongue are particularly sensitive to acidity, those at the back of the tongue are particularly sensitive to bitterness, and those at the front edges are particularly sensitive to saltiness (although this can vary considerably from person to person). Although most wines contain MINERAL salts, very few wines taste salty because these salts are present in much lower concentrations than SWEETNESS and ACIDITY, two of the most important measurements of a wine. During tasting, therefore, the front of the tongue can usually detect the apparent sweetness of a wine (which is not necessarily the same as its RESIDUAL SUGAR). The sides of the tongue react quite markedly in most people to acidity; so markedly that a smell of a particularly acid wine is enough to make the sides of the tongue tingle in anticipation in an experienced taster. Some wines taste quite bitter (bitterness often accompanies astringency and tannins) and this bitterness is most commonly sensed on the flat rear portion of the tongue.

So the mouth's tasting ability, apart from being usefully linked to the olfactory bulb by the retronasal passage, is limited to *measuring* the wine, assessing its dimensions of sweetness, acidity, bitterness, fizziness, temperature, viscosity, and tannins, rather than actually *tasting* it, or sensing what we call its flavour.

Just as what is commonly called the sense of taste is really the sense of smell, so what is commonly called flavour is really AROMA. The word FLAVOUR can be used to incorporate all the measurements sensed by the mouth, but the essential character or distinguishing marks of any wine (or any food or drink, since they are always transformed into a liquid and then into a vapour so that they can be sensed by the olfactory bulb) are in its smell: its aroma, which in mature wines may be described as BOUQUET. This aroma is made up of hundreds, probably thousands of different FLAVOUR COMPOUNDS, present in widely varying permutations and concentrations in different wines.

What is commonly called tasting therefore involves persuading as many of these flavour compounds as possible to reach the olfactory bulb, while ensuring that contact is made between the wine and all of the inside of the mouth for 'measuring' purposes.

How to taste

The operation of tasting is generally divided into three stages involving sequentially the eye, the nose, and the mouth (although, as outlined above, this is not the same as the simple sequential application of the senses of sight, smell, and taste).

Eye The job of the eye in wine tasting is mainly to assess clarity and colour, as well as to monitor the presence of CARBON DIOXIDE and ALCOHOL (the former indicated by bubbles, the latter by any TEARS of the wine that may form on the inside of the glass when it is rotated).

The clarity of a wine is an indication, hardly surprisingly, of the extent to which CLARIFICATION has been carried out, but also of the wine's condition. Many wine FAULTS result in a haze of some sort. A wine with particles floating in it, however, may simply be an innocent casualty of poor SERVING technique. Experienced tasters can sometimes discern quality simply by looking at a wine's luminescent clarity and subtle range of hues.

The colour of a wine, both its intensity and its hue, is one of the potentially most valuable clues to any BLIND TASTER. Intensity of colour is best judged by looking straight through a glass of wine from directly above (preferably against a plain white background). Different grape varieties tend to make deeper or lighter coloured wines (Cabernet Sauvignon, Syrah, and Nebbiolo make particularly deep red wines; Gewürztraminer and Pinot Gris are examples of varieties which make particularly deep white wines). A deep colour also indicates youth, long MACERATION, and thick-skinned grapes in a red wine; sometimes age, some OXIDATION, BARREL MATURATION, although not if preceded by BARREL FERMENTATION in white wines.

The actual hue can also provide clues, and can be best assessed by tilting the glass away at an angle so that the different shadings of colour at the rim can be seen, again preferably against a plain white background. A blueish tinge in a red wine indicates youth, while orange/yellow indicates AGE (or OXIDATION). Very pale green in a white wine may indicate Riesling, while a pink tinge suggests that the wine was made from pink-skinned grapes such as Gewürztraminer and Pinot Gris. For more information see COLOUR.

This stage in tasting for any purpose other than identification is usually very short, and it is rare, if tasters are scoring various aspects of a wine, for a wine not to gain maximum points for its appearance.

Nose As demonstrated above, this is the single most important stage in wine tasting. The trick is to persuade as many flavour compounds as possible to vaporize and come into contact with the olfactory bulb (although what we smell is in fact an AZEOTROPIC mixture of many, rather than isolated, individual, flavour compounds). It is then necessary, of course, to be in a suitable frame of mind to interpret the messages received by the olfactory bulb, which is why the act of tasting requires concentration.

The simplest way to maximize the evaporation of a wine's volatile elements is by the judicious use of TEMPERATURE and agitation. Higher temperatures encourage any sort of evaporation so ideal tasting temperatures tend to be slightly higher than ideal SERVING temperatures. It is unwise to taste wines so hot that the alcohol starts to evaporate at such a rate that it dominates the flavour, however, so an ideal tasting temperature for wines, red or white, is somewhere between 15 and 20 °C/59–68 °F. At these relatively elevated temperatures, faults as well as attributes should be perfectly apparent. What is lost is the refreshment factor, but then the point of tasting rather than drinking is analysis rather than pleasure. Sparkling wines tend to be tasted slightly cooler to retain the carbon dioxide.

A further increase in the number of molecules liberated by a wine can be achieved by agitating the wine and increasing its surface area, preferably rotating it in a bowl-shaped glass with a stem (see GLASSES) so that no wine is lost.

As soon as the wine has been agitated, the aroma collects in the bowl of the partly filled glass above the wine and can be transmitted to the olfactory bulb up the nostrils with one thoughtful inhalation. (Concentration is vital to serious tasting.)

The taster monitors first whether the wine smells fresh and clean, or whether any off-odours indicate the presence of a wine FAULT. The next basic measurement might well be of the intensity of the aroma (if it is an attractive smell, then intensity is preferable). And then comes the complex part of the operation which is much more difficult to describe: the sensation and attempt at description of the individual components that make up the aroma, or 'bouquet' as it is called if it has taken on the complexities associated with AGEING. For a discussion of this, see TASTING TERMS.

Quite apart from those components which result from the grapes themselves, the aroma can provide certain overall hints about viticulture and wine-making techniques. LEAF ALDEHYDES suggest that the grapes were less than fully ripe. Oak ageing may be betrayed by a certain amount of WOOD FLAVOUR; scents of spices and toast can be the result of the degree of TOAST which the barrels received. Tropical fruit aromas suggest that the fermentation was particularly long and cool. Diacetyl, which can smell like butter and other dairy products, is a particularly obvious sign of MALOLACTIC FERMENTATION. The subject is too complex for more than the most cursory treatment here, but the three books cited below are well worth studying.

As a wine undergoes gentle AERATION in the glass, it may well begin to give off other compounds with time. World-famous taster Michael BROADBENT, for example, keeps a series of records of how a single glass of wine tastes, marked according to how long after pouring each note was made. Most good wines seem to get better with time and then to start to deteriorate. In blind tasting, however, a taster's first impressions are usually the most accurate, and insights are rarely provided by constant repetition of the 'nosing' process.

Mouth In terms of aroma, 'flavour' in its narrow sense, the mouth, or palate as it is sometimes called, usually merely confirms the impressions already apparent to the nose when some vapour escapes the mouth and reaches the olfactory bulb via the retronasal passage. Many tasters take in a certain amount of air over their mouthful of wine to encourage this process (and are often mocked for the accompanying noise).

The main function of the mouth in the tasting process is to measure the dimensions rather than the character of a wine by assessing sweetness, acidity, bitterness, viscosity, and tannin level. Monitoring of the combination of sweetness, viscosity, and any sensation of 'heat' gives a good indication of the likely alcohol content of any individual wine, ETHANOL tending to leave a burning sensation in the mouth. For this reason it is a good idea to rinse the mouth thoroughly with wine so that all possible taste receptors may come into contact with it—another reason why wine tasting looks both ridiculous and disgusting to outsiders.

After rinsing a wine around their mouths, and noting the impressions given by the vapour rising up the restronasal passage, most professional tasters then demonstrate their devotion to duty rather than alcohol by SPITTING. There are no taste receptors in the throat. The taster then notes how LONG the impressions given by the wine seem to persist after spitting, or swallowing.

Conclusions Perhaps the most important stage, however, is a fourth stage of analysis, in which all previous impressions are considered. This includes most particularly considering whether the measurements taken by the mouth suggest that the wine is in BALANCE, and monitoring the persistence of LENGTH of the after-taste, these last two factors being important indicators of quality. A fine wine should also continue to make favourable sensory impressions throughout the entire tasting process.

Experience is necessary to judge balance. A significant, if decreasing, proportion of young red wines designed for long term evolution, for example, are not by any objective criterion in balance. Their tannins may still be very marked and make the wine an unpleasantly astringent drink, even if they suggest that the wine will keep well. (Making red wines with less obvious tannins so that they can be both aged and drunk in their youth is one of the prime current preoccupations of wine-makers.) Similarly, the acidity in a young German wine may be aggressively dominant, but experience shows that it is essential to preserve a top-quality Riesling, for example for the 10 or 20 years' bottle ageing it may deserve. (Some would also argue that a perceptible level of SULPHUR DIOXIDE was also acceptable in such a wine.)

Professional tasting usually involves making **tasting notes**, typically under the four headings noted above. It may also involve scoring by allotting NUMBERS to different elements according to a carefully predetermined scale, especially if wine JUDGING is involved.

Tasting for pleasure, which is what most wine drinkers do every time they open a bottle, requires nothing more complicated than a moment's concentration and an open mind.

Broadbent, M., *Wine Tasting* (9th edn., London, 1992).
Peynaud, É., *The Taste of Wine* (London, 1987).
Rankine, B., *Tasting and Enjoying Wine* (Adelaide, 1990).

TASTING BRANDY. A proper appreciation of a spirit depends very much more on the nose than on the palate. This is just as well considering the average ALCOHOLIC STRENGTH of 40 per cent in most BRANDIES in commercial circulation and up to 70 per cent in cask samples of some young COGNACS.

Only a few professional tasters can actually taste, in the sense of rinse the palate with, more than half a dozen spirits at any one go. The others need a break between flights, accompanied by copious draughts of water and black coffee, and even then can manage only three flights of five or six samples in a morning. That said, the tasting of spirits can be a most satisfying business since a fine brandy will have considerable depths to be plumbed, if only because its constituents are so concentrated—distilled in the popular as well as the technical meaning of the term.

In the past the tasting of brandy was bedevilled by the mystique of the enormous balloon-shaped *ballon* glasses traditionally used. These were disastrous: socially because they lent an air of absurdity and snobbery to the drinking of fine brandy; and technically because their very size precluded proper appreciation of the aromas. Large glasses mean large surfaces and considerable evaporation, which emphasizes the alcohol at the expense of the brandy's fruit. Professional and modern specialist brandy glasses have tulip-shaped bowls rarely more than 10 cm/4 in deep. This allows the aromas to expand in the glass—albeit far less than in the traditional *ballon*—before being concentrated in the neck, where the human nose can best appreciate them.

The appreciation is greatest if the brandy is the right TEMPERATURE, about 18 °C/64 °F, since too warm a brandy evaporates too quickly, and thus tastes too alcoholic. Indeed it is not a bad idea to start with a cold brandy (and a cold glass) and allow the warmth of the taster's hands to bring the spirit slowly up to the right temperature. (And if the brandy is already at the right temperature it is better to hold the glass by the foot or stem to avoid overheating.)

With brandy, as with wine, an amateur's tasting process usually starts with colour appreciation. Professional brandy drinkers know, however, that this can be deceptive, so they often use blue glasses to prevent a brandy's appearance from influencing their judgement of it. Although in theory the darker and more viscous the spirit, the more richly mature it will be, even the most reputable houses unsettle this general rule by adding a neutral-tasting colorant to standardize the colour of their blends. Nevertheless all the finest brandies, however old, have a certain golden luminosity, and a lack of the treacly viscosity that is a sure sign that *boisé*, the macerated

A tutored wine **tasting**—a serious business.

OAK CHIPS additive, or too much caramel, has been added to the brandy.

The nosing of a brandy, as with a wine, should be done in two stages to try and separate the more volatile constituents from the heavier ones. So the brandy should first be smelled without swirling the glass and with the nose slowly approaching the rim of the glass, which should then be rotated slowly rather than swirled, to capture the variety of aromas which should be emanating from the spirit. After a short pause, the nose should enter the glass in order to capture the less volatile, more alcoholic components. Only then should the brandy be tasted, after another swirl, to check the same aspects as in a wine: the fruit, the balance, and the after-taste, which, thanks to the higher alcohol level, is usually much more persistent than that of a wine. Indeed the aromas of the best brandies can linger for days, leaving a magical sweetness in the glass. N.F.

TASTINGS, events at which wines are tasted. Informal tastings take place every time a bottle of wine is opened by a wine enthusiast. The most common sort of formal tasting is one held for the purposes of wine assessment, typically by a wine MERCHANT keen to sell his wares, sometimes by a generic body keen to promote wines of a particular style or provenance. Formal tastings are also held by wine clubs and societies for less commercial purposes: EDUCATION or simple pleasure perhaps.

A **horizontal tasting** is one in which a number of different wines of the same VINTAGE are compared, while a **vertical tasting** is a comparison of different vintages of the same wine, most commonly the same Bordeaux CHÂTEAU. George SAINTSBURY is credited with the first recorded use of these expressions.

A BLIND TASTING is one whose purpose is that the taster identifies unknown wines as closely as possible.

Equipment

The only essential equipment for a wine tasting, apart from the wine, is suitable GLASSES and a CORKSCREW, but it is almost impossible to hold a tasting without a substantial area of flat surface on which to put bottles and glasses safely, usually in the form of a table to which there is good access. Next most useful objects are undoubtedly spittoons (see SPITTING), and something in which to pour away leftover wine from a tasting sample (bottles plus funnels are customary although spittoons can also be used for this purpose). The thoughtful organizer ensures that there is some plain white surface against which to hold a glassful of wine (see TASTING). This typically involves lining up bottles on a table with a white surface or covering such as a tablecloth or sheet. A truly assiduous host provides tasters with a tasting sheet on which is a full and accurate list of wines to be tasted, in the correct order, with appropriate space for tasting notes. Water and some completely neutral-tasting food for 'cleaning the palate' can be helpful too. Cheese is usually too strong (see FOOD AND WINE MATCHING); dry biscuits are generally preferred by professionals.

Conditions
Ideal conditions include a strong natural light, ambient temperature between 15 and 18 °C/59–64 °F, and an absence of any extraneous smells. (It is clear therefore that tasting in most cellars, even those of the finest wine-makers, is far from ideal.) In practice, a tasting that involves many people inevitably generates its own heat and smell, so it is wise to begin at a lower ambient temperature and not to be too exercised about a whiff of aftershave or polish, to which an individual taster soon becomes accustomed.

Organization
One glass per taster usually suffices, and no more than a fifteenth or even twentieth of a bottle is needed to give someone a decent tasting sample. Ensuring that tasters are served rather than serving themselves can limit wine consumption.

A suitable number of different wines to be shown at a single tasting is controversial. Some tasters claim to be able to assess up to 200 wines in a day at JUDGING sessions such as the Australian wine shows, while the most experienced professionals in CHAMPAGNE deliberately limit themselves to no more than a dozen wines at a time. A novice taster should probably start with no more than four wines while a professional might feel a tasting which offered only 15 was hardly worth the detour.

What is clear is that it is difficult to *enjoy* more than a dozen wines at a time, and that the ORDER in which any selection is served is vital to the impression they give.

Broadbent, M., *Wine Tasting* (9th edn., London, 1992).
Peynaud, É., *The Taste of Wine* (London, 1987).
Rankine, B., *Tasting and Enjoying Wine* (Adelaide, 1990).

TASTING TERMS, the myriad and oft-mocked words used by tasters in an often vain attempt to describe sensory impressions received during TASTING.

The difference between a taster and a social drinker is this need to describe, to attempt the difficult task of applying words to individual, invisible sensations. The sense of smell is an exceptionally private one, for which there is no common public domain which can be codified. The best we can do is describe aromas by other aromas of which they remind us. Hence 'blackcurrant' or CASSIS, frequently for Cabernet Sauvignon; 'strawberry' or 'raspberry' for Pinot Noir; 'vanilla' for OAK.

There is as yet no official wine-tasting language, although there have been many valiant attempts at establishing one and, particularly as research on FLAVOUR COMPOUNDS continues apace, this is becoming an increasingly attainable goal. The Scottish doctor Alexander HENDERSON was one of the first to attempt it in the English language in *The History of Ancient and Modern Wines* in 1824, CHAPTAL having applied about 60 French terms in his *L'Art de faire le vin* in 1807. These early tasting vocabularies tended to concentrate on the dimensions of a wine rather than its character or aroma, and applied words such as 'acidic, sweet, bitter, light'.

Terms used for mouth sensations
The most straightforward of these 'dimensional terms', which describe what is sensed in the mouth (and the even more public and obvious visual impressions), are still in use today and, since they describe what is measurable, are useful and indisputable. Inevitably, some jargon has evolved, of which the following are the most obvious examples.

Body—a noun; see BODY.
Big—high in alcohol.
Crisp—attractively high in ACIDITY.
Fat—full bodied and viscous.
Flabby—lacking in ACIDITY.
Finish—a noun for after-taste.
Full—of BODY.
Green—too acid.
Hard—too much TANNIN and too little fruit.
Heavy—too alcoholic; too much EXTRACT.
Hot—too alcoholic.
Legs—see TEARS.
Light—agreeably light in BODY.
Long—impressively persistent after-taste; see LONG.
Short—opposite of LONG.
Tears—a noun; see TEARS.
Well balanced—having good BALANCE.

Terms used for aroma
It is in their attempts to find 'character terms' to apply to these more subtle, more private olfactory sensations that wine tasters seem so foolish.

Some 'idioterms' are just plain fanciful, descriptions obviously applied in sheer desperation at the apparent impossibility of the task. In this category come the 'fading but well-mannered old lady'—and who can forget James Thurber's 'naive domestic burgundy but I think you'll be amused by its presumption'?

Other sorts of terms, 'simile terms', are applied in a serious attempt to recall palpable objects which give rise to similar aromas: the fruits, flowers, and vegetable descriptors.

And there is another category of 'derivative terms' which must once have been coined by an authority and continue to be widely used even though they are literally inaccurate. So many wine tasters have been taught to describe the powerful and characteristic smell of GEWÜRZTRAMINER as 'spicy', for example (perhaps because *gewürz* is German for 'spiced'), that this is the most common tasting term for the aroma, even though it does not smell like any particular spice at all (much more like lychees, in fact).

It will be of the 'simile terms' that a common tasting vocabulary is finally composed—although there is the obstacle of many different languages and national conventions to be overcome first. Max Leglise, a researcher in Burgundy has attempted to concoct essences of each of his approved terms so that there is an objective standard for them. (Unfortunately, synthetic flavourings deteriorate.) Professor Ann C. Noble at DAVIS, clearly frustrated by the looseness with which tasting terms are applied, has done sterling work with her AROMA WHEEL. This corresponds sufficiently closely with the tasting terms suggested by Professor Émile PEYNAUD, Bordeaux's tasting guru, to give us all hope that soon an international tasting language that is no more ambiguous than any other will be available to the world's wine tasters.

See also AROMA WHEEL.

Broadbent, M., *Wine Tasting* (9th edn., London, 1992).
Peynaud, É., *The Taste of Wine* (London, 1987).
Rankine, B., *Tasting and Enjoying Wine* (Adelaide, 1990).

TAURASI, the outstanding wine of the CAMPANIA region and indeed of the whole of southern Italy since the 1970s, is produced from the AGLIANICO grape in a zone north east of the city of Avellino. The village of Taurasi is a mere 64km / 40 miles from Barile, the centre of the AGLIANICO DEL VULTURE production zone, and, like the most famous wine of BASILICATA, Taurasi demonstrates the heights which Aglianico can reach in the volcanic soil which it prefers. Although there are 158 producers and over 220 ha / 540 acres in the Taurasi DOC zone, the firm of Mastroberardino has been until recently virtually the only label on the market and still controls over 90 per cent of the total production of Taurasi which, despite a maximum potential of 17,000 hl / 450,000 gal per year, does not reach 1,000 hl in a normal vintage. DOC regulations require three years of ageing, one of which must be in wood, and RISERVA bottlings must be aged for four years. The permitted production zone sprawls over a large and heterogeneous area, with little regard for the fact that Aglianico gives its best results only at a certain altitude (Mastroberardino considers 400 m / 1,300 ft as the minimum altitiude for fine Taurasi). Little has been proposed or done in terms of subdivision of the zone, although the Riserva bottlings of Mastroberardino, in any case, have always included Aglianico from the Castelfranci, Jampenne, and Torre vineyards in Montemarano. The house's single-vineyard bottling, called Radice, comes exclusively from the subzone of Lapio. Taurasi Riserva was granted DOCG status in 1993. D.T.

Anderson, B., *The Wine Atlas of Italy* (London and New York, 1990).
Gleave, D., *The Wines of Italy* (London and New York, 1989).

TAVEL, right bank rosé appellation in the southern RHÔNE whose historic reputation is still sufficient to justify a sometimes unwarranted price premium over other rosés, although Tavel at its best manages to combine refreshment with interest and concentration of flavour. Tavel was already favoured by Louis XIV in the 13th century, and writers Balzac and Mistral continued to promulgate its superiority. Today its superiority is often more likely to be in weight than in quality; the grapes can reach such levels of RIPENESS here that the appellation enforces a maximum ALCOHOLIC STRENGTH of 13.5 per cent.

The wine is always bone dry, but the Grenache and Cinsaut grapes give the blend a certain apparent sweetness. Chilling is essential, and the wine should be drunk young, as an alternative to red wine in hot weather. Grenache is the dominant grape variety, as throughout the southern Rhône, but may not exceed 60 per cent of the blend.

Such was demand for the wine in the 1950s that the area was considerably extended, by clearing *garrigue*. About 900 ha / 2,220 acres of sand and clay is shared mainly by members of the Tavel CO-OPERATIVE, although there are some quality-minded estates. The village of Tavel itself makes the most of the promotional opportunities available to a famous wine village.

TAWNY, style of FORTIFIED wines usually associated with extended CASK AGEING. See PORT, for example.

TAXATION. Wine has attracted the attention of the taxman since ancient times. Its production, sale, and distribution have been so closely regulated by the authorities for one simple reason: revenue. The civilizations of the ancient Middle East (see Ancient EGYPT and MESOPOTAMIA) were the first to recognize this useful attribute. It was carefully regulated in parts of Ancient GREECE, but it was the Romans who, in this as in many other aspects of wine history, helped realize its potential.

In Ancient ROME tax was paid from the moment the grape appeared on the vine (Roman vine-growers paid a vineyard tax calculated on the quality of the land) to when it was consumed. It was paid either in kind or in cash and represented a huge proportion of state income. Some areas in the empire, CALABRIA, then the heel of Italy, for example, paid their entire tax to Rome in wine, which was then sold or distributed free to the urban masses.

Medieval kings found wine taxation fabulously lucrative. During England's occupation of western France, for example, the crown benefited doubly by receiving duties paid on wine exported from BORDEAUX, and then again on the same wine as customs when it entered London. During the early part of the 14th century, when this trade was at its peak, wine duties collected in Bordeaux surpassed the king's total tax revenue in England.

Not surprisingly, taxes on wine have been perceived as a fast, easy way of raising cash and the state has shown no scruples in doubling or tripling them at times of emergency—often to pay for wars such as the HUNDRED YEARS WAR, the English Civil War, and the Napoleonic Wars.

Although they may complain, in certain circumstances wine merchants have been happy to pay tax because it legitimizes their business. Wine merchants within the Islamic empire of the caliphs (usually Jewish or Christians) viewed their payments as a kind of insurance policy; the state would not outlaw their activities, despite the Koranic ban on alcohol, because the income was so useful (see ISLAM).

Wine taxation has uses beyond mere revenue. Different levels can be used to reward or punish trading partners. For example throughout the 18th century French wines attracted twice as much duty as Portuguese wines (see METHUEN TREATY). Not surprisingly trade in French wines suffered and port became the staple English wine (see WAR).

Differential taxation has also been used to manipulate consumer tastes for reasons of health or morality. Gladstone's Act of 1860 reduced the duty on light, less alcoholic wines in an attempt to switch the British palate away from the heavy, fortified wines and spirits that earlier taxation had favoured.

Taxation has at times had indirect consequences. During the 18th century, when duties were high and complicated (French wines were subject to 15 separate duties), ADULTERATION AND FRAUD and smuggling increased in England. Grievances against excessive taxation of wines entering Paris have been recognized as one of the sparks that lit the fire of revolution in 1789.

It was inevitable that, as soon as wine was taxed, certain parties should be exempt. Traditionally these have included the crown, the Church, and sections of the nobility; such exemptions go back at least as far as Ancient EGYPT. This privilege has been extended in modern times (so far as customs duties go) to all travellers via the system of duty-free allowances. H.B.

Briggs, A., *Wine for Sale: Victoria Wine and the Liquor Trade 1860–1984* (London, 1985).
Francis, A. D., *The Wine Trade* (London, 1972).
Hyams, E., *Dionysus: A Social History of the Vine* (London, 1965).

TAYLOR'S, important independent PORT shipper known in full as **Taylor, Fladgate & Yeatman**. The original firm of port shippers was established in 1692 by Job Bearsley, and between then and 1844 there were no fewer than 21 name changes. However, with the arrival of Joseph Taylor in 1816, John Fladgate in 1837, and Morgan Yeatman in 1844, the company assumed its present full name, and Taylor's for short. In 1744 Job Bearsley's son Bartholomew bought Casa dos Alambiques at Salgueiral near Régua, the first known British port shipper's property in the DOURO valley. Salgueiral is still the company's main vinification centre.

In 1808 a new partner, Joseph Camo, arrived, the first American to be admitted into partnership in a port company and until recently the only non-British shipper ever to be allowed into meetings of the British Association at the FACTORY HOUSE. As an American Camo remained neutral during the Peninsular Wars, and was important in keeping export routes open in the face of French invaders.

Taylor's best-known property, Quinta da Vargellas high up in the Douro, was acquired in 1893, when it was still suffering from the ravages of PHYLLOXERA. This acquisition marked the start of Taylor's now considerable landowning and farming activities. In 1948 Taylor's bought FONSECA Guimarãens, with its three quintas: Panasçal, Cruzeiro, and Santo António. Quinta da Terra Feita, which had been supplying port to Taylor's since at least 1903, was bought in 1974, adding a further 37 ha/91 acres of well-placed vines. In 1990 Terra Feita de Cima was added.

Taylor's vintage port is consistently one of the most admired and longest lived of the year, and its Quinta de Vargellas single quinta bottling can often be almost as concentrated.

The principal shareholder is now a nephew of Mrs Dick Yeatman, Alistair Robertson, who took over the firm in 1967 since when the firm has been one of the most successful companies in VILA NOVA DE GAIA, doing much to revitalize the selling and marketing of port, notably by introducing the LBV, or 'late bottled vintage', style.

Foulkes. C. (ed.), *A Celebration of Taylor's Port* (London, 1992).

T-BUDDING, a BUDDING method used extensively in woody horticultural plants, including the grapevine. The method entails making two T-shaped cuts in the bark of the ROOTSTOCK, when the bark is slipping, then lifting back the flaps to permit insertion of a shield-shaped piece cut from the scion with a bud on it. After insertion, the bud is wrapped tightly with budding tape to ensure close contact of the tissues and high humidity around the cuts. T-budding can be done when the bark of the stock lifts freely, during two to three months over midsummer. Scion buds may be taken from stored winter cuttings or green current shoots. As with CHIP BUDDING, T-budding may be used for TOP WORKING. B.G.C.

TCA, or **2,4,6-trichloranisole**, the unpleasant-smelling compound associated with CORKED wine. See TRICHLOROANISOLE.

TCHECHOSLOVAKIA. See CZECHOSLOVAKIA.

TCHELISTCHEFF, ANDRÉ (1901–94), consultant oenologist and founding father of the modern California wine industry. Tchelistcheff was born in Moscow, the sickly son of a Russian professor of law. He came close to death once more while in the White Russian army but survived to continue his education, training for five years as an engineer-agronomist in Brno, Czechoslovakia.

Only when he was 36 did he decide to study VITICULTURE and OENOLOGY in more detail, in Paris. While working on a farm near Versailles, he became a graduate assistant to the director of the department of viticulture at the National Institute of Agronomy as well as taking a course in wine microbiology at the Institut PASTEUR. An obviously talented student, who combined intellectual rigour with a philosophical bent, he worked briefly at MOËT & CHANDON and had already been offered jobs in Chile and China before being introduced to his future employer. Georges de Latour was a Frenchman who had established himself as a highly successful businessman and owner of Beaulieu Vineyard in the Napa Valley but was anxious to import a French-trained wine-maker for the post-PROHIBITION era.

During his 35-year career at Beaulieu, Tchelistcheff introduced the principles of winery HYGIENE as well as pioneering temperature-controlled FERMENTATION, mastery of MALOLACTIC FERMENTATION, and frost damage prevention techniques such as the orchard heaters and WIND MACHINES which dominate Napa Valley to this day. He also made considerable progress in the prevention of various VINE DISEASES and established a reputation as both wine and vineyard consultant.

From his first years in California, Tchelistcheff established an identity independent of Beaulieu, with his own small laboratory in St Helena advising other Napa and Sonoma wineries and training a younger generation of wine-makers such as the young MONDAVI brothers. He was a consultant to Buena Vista winery, for example (see HARASZTHY), since 1948, and in 1967 began a long association with Ch Ste Michelle in WASHINGTON state. He was also one of the first to recognize the viticultural potential of the CARNEROS district of northern California. Although he retired from Beaulieu in 1973, four years after it was sold to the Heublein corporation, he continued to be an active consultant to a host of California wineries as well as to Ornellaia of BOLGHERI in Italy. In 1991, however, he was wooed back to Beaulieu by the multinational corporation which by then owned it.

Tchelistcheff was a charter member of the American Society of Enologists and was made a Chevalier de l'Ordre du Mérite Agricole by the French government as long ago as 1954, being promoted to Officier in 1979. Tchelistcheff was unique in the wine world for the geographical breadth and historical depth of his singularly acute views on the contemporary wine scene.

Conaway, J., *Napa: The Story of an American Eden* (Boston, 1990).
Lord, T., 'André Tchelistcheff', *Decanter* (Mar. 1992).

TEARS, (to rhyme with 'ears'), tasting term used to describe the behaviour of the surface liquid layer that is observable in a glass of relatively strong wine. The wine wets the inside of a clean glass and climbs up a few millimetres. At the upper edge of the thin layer on the inside wall patches of the film thicken, become more drop-like, and eventually roll back down the inside wall to the liquid surface. These traces of what look like particularly viscous droplets are also sometimes called 'legs', and give some indication of a wine's ALCOHOLIC STRENGTH.

James Thomson, a British physicist and engineer, observed and correctly explained in 1855 what he called 'tears of strong wine'. Unfortunately his work was overlooked and the explanation for the action is usually credited to Marangoni who published in 1871.

Four physical relationships are involved in producing tears. The attractive forces between molecules in a liquid are called surface tension forces and are what hold the liquid together. The same type of force also acts between a liquid molecule and the molecules of a solid surface, but is called interfacial tension. If the interfacial tension between a liquid and a glass is a bit greater than the surface tension, then molecules of liquid will adhere to the glass and wet areas higher and higher above the liquid surface. A point is reached at which the weight of the liquid clinging to the wall just balances the force trying to lift more liquid up the wall surface. If the liquid is a pure single substance, action stops at this point and no tears are observed.

Wine is not a single component substance, however, but is mainly a solution of alcohol and water. While the thin film of wine climbs up the inner wall of the glass, another physical action occurs: the alcohol evaporates faster than the water from the film surface. This changes the composition of the film, increasing its concentration of water and thereby increasing its surface tension and index of refraction. This increase in surface tension of an area of film depleted in alcohol causes the film to assume a drop-like form and to grow at the expense of the surrounding film. Eventually the drop becomes so heavy that interfacial tension can no longer hold it to the glass surface. It then runs down the wall, forming a tear or leg. The change of refractive index makes the boundary between the water-rich drop and the alcohol-rich film clearly visible.

Dubious readers can convince themselves of this somewhat complicated explanation of an apparently simple phenomenon by observing the lack of tears in glasses of pure water (or pure alcohol). That evaporation is necessary can be demonstrated by simply covering a glass that previously demonstrated **tearing**. Tearing ceases, and will resume upon removal of the cover.

It is often thought that tears are the result of GLYCEROL but in fact entirely unrelated phenomena are responsible. The small changes in VISCOSITY and index of refraction make the drop contrast with the liquid film on the glass surface. Tears are *not* a measure of viscosity.

Although the tears phenomenon occurs in any multi-component liquid mixture, it is most obvious in wines above about 12 per cent ALCOHOLIC STRENGTH because the higher alcohol evaporates faster. A.D.W.

TEINTURIER literally means 'dyer' in French, which is the function for which these vines with their red-fleshed grapes are grown, notably in the Midi to add at least apparent depth to the pale wines of the dominant ARAMON in the early years of the 20th century. The original variety called **Teinturier**, or sometimes Teinturier du Cher, was probably extremely ancient, possibly a selection of WILD VINES, and was first noted around Orléans in the 17th and 18th centuries, where it imbued the pale pink wines of the region with valuable colour.

As long ago as 1824 the Frenchman Louis BOUSCHET decided to try to breed vines with coloured flesh, and the 1828 crossing of Aramon × Teinturier du Cher resulted in the popular Petit Bouschet. Henri Bouschet, Louis's son, crossed Petit Bouschet with Grenache to produce the very popular ALICANTE BOUSCHET, a deeply coloured teinturier, known as Garnacha Tintorera in Spain, *tintorera* being Spanish for teinturier. Other red-fleshed varieties bred by the Bouschet family and used for their 'dyeing' properties at one time include Morrastel Bouschet, Carignan Bouschet, and GRAND NOIR DE LA CALMETTE.

Red-fleshed versions of the lightly coloured GAMAY grape

have been widely grown, not just in the Loire but outside France. The Gamay Teinturiers include Gamay Fréaux, Gamay de Bouze, and Gamay de Chaudenay. Gamay Fréaux and Gamay de Chaudenay are said to be mutants of Gamay de Bouze. Colobel (Seibel 8357) is a Teinturier FRENCH HYBRID which was the only such variety to be authorized in France.

Germany's useful red-fleshed varieties include Carmina, Deckrot, DUNKELFELDER, Kolor, and SULMER. ROYALTY 1390, RUBIRED, and SALVADOR are all California creations while the important Russian Teinturier is SAPERAVI which is, if not red fleshed, then certainly pink fleshed. R.E.S. & M.J.E.

Galet, P., *Cépages et vignobles de France* (2nd edn., Montpellier, 1990).
Robinson, J., *Vines, Grapes and Wines* (London, 1986).

TEMECULA, CALIFORNIA wine region and AVA south of Los Angeles. Temecula is the viticultural aspect of a mixed-use residential and industrial development called Rancho California. Beginning in the late 1960s, the founders used vineyards as part of their sales pitch to the urban-weary Los Angelenos who were their prime customers. Vineyards came swiftly to rolling hills at the southern edge of Riverside County, between the towns of Riverside to the north and Escondido to the south. Houses followed right behind. Within 20 years grape-growers began to find themselves squeezed between rows of residences. However, enough vines still exist to satisfy more than a dozen small wineries and one fairly good-sized one, Callaway. White varieties have succeeded best. Sauvignon Blanc ranks foremost among them, with Chardonnay not too far behind. The odd patch of Sémillon has also done well. Some growers are still making brave tries with, especially, Cabernet Sauvignon, Petite Sirah, and Zinfandel. While Callaway has been the dominant force since the outset, other firms of substance in the early 1990s included Culbertson, Mount Palomar, and Maurice Car'rie.

TEMPERATE, a broad class of climates, usually taken to include those with an annual average temperature of less than 20 °C/68 °F, but a warmest month average temperature greater than 10 °C/50 °F, the latter being the approximate poleward limit of tree growth.

Just as wine is a beverage of temperate people, so the grapevine is a plant of temperate climates. It is specially so when the grapes are to be used for WINE-MAKING, and still more so for table wines. Excessive heat during ripening leads to a loss of the more delicate fruit aromas and flavours from the grapes, and therefore from the wines. Insufficient warmth leads to incomplete RIPENING in which FLAVOUR COMPOUNDS, which become manifest only late in the ripening process, are lacking regardless of berry sugar content (see SUGAR IN GRAPES). (The gross geographical limits for commercial viticulture resulting from temperature constraints are noted under LATITUDE.)

At a more detailed level may be added the further relevant concept of 'equability', or lack of extreme variation about given average temperatures through the vine growing and ripening seasons.

See TEMPERATURE VARIABILITY and CLIMATE AND WINE QUALITY. J.G.

TEMPERATURE is critically important to VITICULTURE, WINE-MAKING, wine MATURATION, and wine SERVICE, each in very different ways.

Climate, viticulture, and temperature

Temperature, along with SUNLIGHT, RAINFALL, HUMIDITY, WIND, and the concentration of CARBON DIOXIDE in the air, is one of the major environmental factors governing vine growth and grape RIPENING. Coombe and Gladstones comprehensively review the role of temperature in viticulture.

Vines in cool climates start growing in the spring at about the time when the mean air temperature reaches 10 °C/50 °F. The rate of vine growth and development then increases to a maximum at about 22 to 25 °C, before falling away at even higher temperatures. Temperature is often discussed in viticulture as mean temperature, that is maximum plus minimum temperatures divided by two. These facts underlie the traditional methods for viticultural CLIMATE CLASSIFICATION, which are based on excesses of monthly average mean temperatures over 10 °C. Such classifications can at best be only approximate, however, if only because mean temperatures seldom truly reflect the real average temperatures as they might be measured continuously throughout the 24 hours, and as experienced by the vine (McIntyre *et al.*). Nor do established long-term temperature recording sites, from which most of the available data come, often truly represent existing or potential vineyard sites (see TOPOGRAPHY, MESOCLIMATE, CLIMATE CHANGE).

Prescott proposed that viticultural climates could be characterized just as accurately as by any other existing method, by the average mean temperature of their warmest month. Smart and Dry adapted this for use in Australia as mean January temperature (MJT): an index now quite widely used for approximate comparisons of viticultural climates, although July should be substituted for January in the northern hemisphere. Average mean temperatures for the full growing season can also be a reasonable basis for broad comparisons (see COOL CLIMATE VITICULTURE).

The risk of killing dormant vines in winter is a second basis for defining climatic suitability for viticulture, being the main limiting factor in cool climates with marked CONTINENTALITY. Most fully dormant VINIFERA vines with well-matured canes can withstand air temperatures down to about −15 °C. Native AMERICAN VINE SPECIES are in general hardier, and AMERICAN HYBRIDS, their hybrids with European varieties, intermediate. However, there is considerable variation among VINE VARIETIES within each group.

The winter hardiness of RIESLING, for instance, is almost certainly one of the reasons for its historical success in Germany. See also WINTER FREEZE.

The chance of winter killing of vines in Europe increases from south west to north east (see RUSSIA, for example). Extensive commercial viticulture without WINTER PROTECTION reaches its limit where the average mean temperature of the coldest month falls below about −1 °C (Prescott).

Air temperature is not the only kind governing vine growth and fruiting, however. Vines and soils are warmed by SUNLIGHT, which has major effects on grape berry temperature, leaf temperature, grape composition, and hence wine quality (see VINE PHYSIOLOGY). Some evidence now confirms the old belief that soil temperature is also important. This control appears to be mediated by the root-produced hormone CYTOKININ, although soil temperature can also affect vine temperature, especially at night. The composition of the soil, its colour, drainage, and duration and angle of exposure to the sun are all important factors in this respect. See SOIL COLOUR, STONES AND ROCKS, TOPOGRAPHY, MESOCLIMATE.

Soil and air temperatures at particular stages of vine growth or during ripening can have specific effects. Winter and early spring temperatures govern BUDBREAK in spring. Air TEMPERATURE VARIABILITY largely determines the risk of FROST damage after budbreak. Temperatures around FLOWERING contribute to differences in FRUIT SET (by influencing COULURE, most notably) and to the FRUITFULNESS of the developing new buds which form shoots and bunches the following year. Both fruit set and bud fruitfulness are favoured by moderately high temperatures. Finally, both average temperature and temperature variability during ripening can have a direct influence on fruit and wine qualities, as discussed under CLIMATE AND WINE QUALITY. J.G.

Coombe, B. G., 'Influence of temperature on composition and quality of grapes', *Acta horticulturae*, 206 (1987), 23–35.

Gladstones, J., *Viticulture and Environment* (Adelaide, 1992).

McIntyre, G. N., Kliewer, W. M., and Lider, L. A., 'Some limitations of the degree day system as used in viticulture in California', *American Journal of Enology and Viticulture*, 38 (1987), 128–32.

Prescott, J. A., The climatology of the vine (*Vitis vinifera*): 3. A comparison of France and Australia on the basis of the warmest month', *Transactions of the Royal Society of South Australia*, 93 (1969), 7–15.

Smart, R. E., and Dry, P. R., 'A climatic classification for Australian viticultural regions', *Australian Grapegrower and Winemaker*, 196 (1980), 8, 10, 16.

Wine-making and temperature

Temperature and **temperature control** are of critical importance in making good-quality wine (although great wine may have been made fortuitously long before the theory of temperature control was understood and temperature was deliberately manipulated). Temperature has direct effects on the rates of the biochemical reactions involved in FERMENTATION, and on the slower reactions involved in CLARIFICATION and STABILIZATION of wine. Years of experiment and calculation have demonstrated that most chemical reactions happen about twice as fast if the temperature is raised by 10 °C (18 °F)—and it is for this reason that REFRIGERATION slows down the reactions of harmful BACTERIA, as well as the reactions involved in AGEING.

In warm regions, therefore, care should be taken to ensure that grapes arrive at the winery in a cool, and relatively undamaged, condition. The harmful effects of ACETOBACTER and wild YEAST are encouraged by high temperatures. Low temperatures are vital if there is any interval between HARVEST and CRUSHING; the potential quality of white wines in particular can be lost through carelessness at this early phase of wine-making. During DESTEMMING and crushing, when the PHENOLICS in grape juice are in direct contact with oxygen, OXIDATION begins at a rate proportional to the temperature. To slow browning of white grape juice, therefore, care is usually taken to keep temperatures as low as possible (see MUST CHILLING). SULPHUR DIOXIDE may also be added. Oxidation of red grape juice is less of a problem because its higher phenolic content, including the red colour compounds, can conceal small amounts of amber or brown, although lower temperatures during prefermentation processes are in general desirable whatever the colour of the grape skins.

If temperature control is desirable prior to fermentation, it is critical during it. At temperatures below 10 °C (50 °F) most yeasts will act prohibitively slowly or not at all, while at temperatures above 45 °C (113 °F) they are damaged and finally killed. Secondly, higher fermentation temperatures speed up some reactions so that undesirable flavour compounds become apparent. Thirdly, at higher temperatures, some of the desirable FLAVOUR COMPOUNDS are volatilized in the rapidly evolving stream of carbon dioxide, literally 'boiled off'. The result of this is a wine low in fruit and marked by 'hot' fermentation characteristics. In the extreme case of temperatures nearing the range at which yeasts are killed, the yeast cells secrete compounds which inhibit future yeast growth, thereby making it difficult or impossible to restart this STUCK FERMENTATION even after cooling.

There are yeast strains which grow and ferment very slowly at very low temperatures, only just above freezing. Such strains are particularly useful in cool wine regions such as Switzerland and parts of Germany but fermentation rates are so slow that a single FERMENTATION VESSEL can be used only once after each harvest, which therefore affects the capital cost of production, as it does at the most ambitious wineries elsewhere where there has been investment in fermentation capacity for any year's total production.

White wines are in general fermented at lower temperatures than red, partly in order to conserve the primary grape AROMAS, partly because there is no MACERATION for which heat may be useful in encouraging the extraction of phenolics and other flavour compounds from the grape skins. White wine temperatures between 12 and 17 °C are common for fermentation in the New World to yield fruity, well-balanced, light coloured wines quickly enough that the fermentation vessel can be used two or three times in a season (although see also BARREL FERMENTATION). Grape varieties such as Sauvignon Blanc, Riesling, and Muscat tend to be fermented at the lower end of this temperature range, whereas more neutral varieties, with a less complex blend of grape flavours to be conserved, may be fermented at the upper end and rely on the accumulation of secondary fermentation aromas. Old World white wine fermentation temperatures are likely to be closer to 18 to 20 °C. The techniques of barrel fermentation and LEES CONTACT, such as are often applied to Chardonnay grapes, often involve slightly higher fermentation temperatures too, although the small size of the barrel (in comparison with the normal stainless steel tank) helps to control temperature.

Temperature control is also extremely important during red wine-making. The main concern here is the extraction of sufficient TANNINS, ANTHOCYANS, and flavour compounds from the grape skins. Temperature is one of the factors governing this extraction, agitation and time being the others. Fermentation temperatures between 25 and 30 °C generally produce the best flavour and extraction in red wines, provided other conditions (and grape variety, agitation, and time all play a part interlinked to temperature in the maceration process) are optimal. Temperatures higher than this threaten the yeast activity while temperatures below it inhibit extraction. Temperature continues to be an important factor in wine production long after the fermentation phase. Oxidation and loss of fruitiness in white wines can be discouraged by low temperatures, while the bacterial activity that stimulates MALOLACTIC FERMENTATION can be positively encouraged by storing the newly fermented wine between 25 and 30 °C until this secondary fermentation is completed.

Fermentation temperatures govern the types of ESTERS that are formed and accumulate in the wine. Lower temperatures (10 to 15 °C) favour both the production and retention of the fruity esters, which have lower molecular weights. Among these are nearly all of those possible by reactions between ACETIC, propionic, isobutyric, and isovaleric acids with ETHANOL, propy, isobutyl, and FUSEL OILS. These are the esters which give tropical fruits their characteristic flavours (isoamyl acetate, for example, is the flavour material of ripe bananas), which is why cool-fermented wines so often taste of tropical fruits. The aroma compounds of each grape variety are also better retained at these lower temperatures.

Higher fermentation temperatures (20 to 25 °C) favour heady, heavier esters and, at the same time, destroy more of the VARIETAL character of the grape. Temperatures of 30 °C and higher result in the loss of much of the fruity ester complex through hydrolysis and volatilization and its replacement by substances which smell 'cooked'. A.D.W.

Storage temperature

In the same way that it affects the reactions involved in wine-making, temperature becomes the governing factor in the much slower reactions in bottle that constitute wine AGEING. Interactions among the thousands of natural organic chemicals in the wine during this important phase of its maturation are directly affected by temperature. Applying the general scientific formula for temperature's effect on chemical reactions, a CELLAR temperature of 30 °C should in theory mature a wine twice as fast as storage at 20 °C—except that at such a high temperature compounds with a cooked or jammy note are formed and may well dominate the more desirable compounds. A cellar temperature of 10 °C should in theory age wine at half the speed of a 20 °C cellar, which is to say very slowly, although not quite so slowly as a cellar kept at 0 °C, which would also result in extremely high deposits of TARTRATES and PHENOLICS. In practice, a reasonable cellar temperature for ageing wines to be drunk within one's own lifetime is somewhere between 10 and 15 °C. (The cellars of the Swedish state MONOPOLY were said to have been so cold that any fine, old wine bought in Sweden would taste markedly different from the same wine aged in France, for example.)

Even lower down the temperature scale, wine freezes at a temperature below 0 °C roughly half its ALCOHOLIC STRENGTH, so usually somewhere between −4 and −8 °C. For this reason, in cool climates care should be taken to insulate wine stored in places such as garden sheds or garages where winter temperatures are not maintained at a level acceptable to humans.

Serving temperature

The temperature at which a wine is served has a profound effect on how it smells and tastes. Different styles of wine deserve to be served at different temperatures to enhance their good points and try to mask any faults. The following are some general observations, with suggested guide-lines in italics.

The higher the temperature, the more easily the volatile FLAVOUR COMPOUNDS evaporate from the surface of wine in a glass. So, to maximize the impact of a wine's AROMA or BOUQUET, it is sensible to serve it relatively warm, say between 16 and 18 °C (at temperatures over 20 °C the ALCOHOL can begin to evaporate so markedly that it unbalances the wine). *Serve complex and mature wines relatively warm.*

Conversely, the lower the temperature, the fewer volatiles will evaporate and, at a serving temperature of about 8 °C, all but the most aromatic wines appear to have no smell whatsoever. *The gustatory faults of a low-quality wine can be masked by serving it very cool.*

The higher the temperature, the more sensitive is the PALATE to sweetness, so it makes sense to serve sweet wines which may not have quite enough ACIDITY to counterbalance the sweetness quite cool, say at about 12 °C. For the same reason, medium dry wines served with savoury food will probably taste dry if served well chilled. *In general, chill sweet wines.*

The lower the temperature, the more sensitive the palate to TANNINS and bitterness. Peynaud points out that the same red wine will taste 'hot and thin at 22 °C, supple and fluid at 18 °C, full and astringent at 10 °C'. *Tannic or bitter wines such as many Italian red wines and any young red designed for ageing should be served relatively warm.*

The effect of temperature on apparent acidity is more widely disputed by scientists, but it is generally observable that flabby wines can seem more refreshing if they are served cold, say at 10 °C. (This may be related to the effect of temperature on sweetness described above.) *To increase the refreshment factor of a wine, serve it cool.*

Temperature also has an observable effect on wines containing CARBON DIOXIDE. The higher the temperature, the more gas is released, which means that fizzy wines can be unpleasantly frothy at about 18 °C. *Sparkling and lightly sparkling wines are generally best served well chilled.* Since very few wines with a complex bouquet ever have any perceptible gas, this is no great limitation (those who make Australia's extraordinary Sparkling Shiraz claim it is best served at room temperature, but these sparkling wines are not particularly fizzy).

General rules are therefore:

Serve tannic red wines relatively warm, 15–18 °C.
Serve complex dry white wines relatively warm, 12–16 °C.
Serve soft, lighter red wines for refreshment at 10–12 °C.
Cool sweet, sparkling, flabby white and rosé wines, and those with any off-odour, to 6–10 °C.

Of course wine tends to warm up to match the ambient temperature, so initial serving temperatures at the bottom end of these brackets are no bad thing, especially in warmer environments. For more details, see SERVING WINE.

See also TASTING for its different requirements of wine temperature.

Peynaud, E., *The Taste of Wine* (London, 1987).

TEMPERATURE CONTROL during WINE-MAKING is crucially important, as outlined in TEMPERATURE. Although it has been widely and systematically practised only since the 1960s and 1970s, its efficacy was appreciated as long ago as Roman times (see DIE). See REFRIGERATION for details of how wine may be cooled at various points in its life. In cool wine regions or particularly cool years, a FERMENTATION VESSEL may need to be heated to encourage alcoholic FERMENTATION, most easily by circulating warm water in equipment also designed to carry cooling cold water or, in smaller cellars, simply by closing doors and installing a heater or two. Some form of heating may also be required to encourage both alcoholic fermentation and MALOLACTIC FERMENTATION.

TEMPERATURE VARIABILITY, a characteristic of climates referring to the short-term variability of temperature between night and day, and from day to day. It is unrelated to annual temperature range, as described under CONTINENTALITY, and clearly distinct in its VITICULTURAL and OENOLOGICAL implications. Temperature variability plays an important role in determining the risks of FROST damage to dormant vines in winter, and of HEAT STRESS and direct heat damage to the vines and fruit in summer. There is a more speculative suggestion (see CLIMATE AND WINE QUALITY) that it also influences the formation of PIGMENT, aroma and FLAVOUR in the vines and ripening berries: these processes being favoured, relative to the mere accumulation of SUGAR IN GRAPES, by a narrow daily temperature range and minimal temperature fluctuations from day to day. (Wine producers in some regions boast of their wide temperature variability between night and day, but this is not a scientifically proven benefit in terms of wine quality—although cool nights may indeed seem a blessing in particular regions which are hot by day.)

The concept of temperature variability as a partial basis for evaluating viticultural climates was developed and extensively used by Gladstones. His suggested Temperature Variability Index (TVI) for any month is the sum of the range between its average daily maximum and minimum temperatures, and that between its average highest maximum and lowest minimum temperatures. A low index is suggested to be conducive to wine quality (particularly in table wines) and general climatic suitability for viticulture, given appropriate totals of growing season heat and sunlight. The index is influenced in predictable ways by local TOPOGRAPHY and to some extent soil type (see SOIL COLOUR and STONES AND ROCKS), but for given topographies and soils, it is substantially consistent within geographic regions. J.G.

Gladstones, J., *Viticulture and Environment* (Adelaide, 1992).

TEMPRANILLA is how the Spanish black grape variety TEMPRANILLO is more commonly known in Argentina.

TEMPRANILLO is Spain's answer to Cabernet Sauvignon, the vine variety that puts the spine into a high proportion of Spain's most respected red wines. Its grapes are thick skinned and capable of making deep coloured, long-lasting wines that are not, unusually for Spain, notably high in alcohol.

Temprano means early in Spanish and Tempranillo probably earns its name from its propensity to ripen early, certainly up to two weeks before the Garnacha (GRENACHE) with which it is almost invariably blended to make its most important wine, RIOJA. This relatively short growing cycle (Tempranillo buds neither early nor late) enables it to thrive in the often harsh climate of Rioja's higher, more Atlantic-influenced zones Rioja Alta and Rioja Alavesa, where it constitutes up to 70 per cent of all vines planted. Tempranillo has traditionally been grown in widely spaced bushes here, but this relatively vigorous, upright vine has responded well to recent efforts to train it with more rigour on wires.

Wine made from Tempranillo grown in relatively cool conditions, where its tendency to produce musts slightly low in acidity is a positive advantage, can last well but the variety does not have a particularly strong flavour identity. Some find strawberries, others spice and leather, but determining a constant aroma attributable to the grape rather than the oak in which it was aged in all-Tempranillo wines can be a fruitless task. It is easy to see why such a high proportion of Tempranillo is blended with other juicier, more perfumed varieties.

In Rioja these are Garnacha, Mazuelo (Carignan), Graciano, and Viura. In Penedès, where it is known as Ull de Llebre and Ojo de Liebre in Catalonian and Spanish respectively, Tempranillo stiffens and darkens the local Monastrell. In VALDEPEÑAS, where, as Cencibel, Tempranillo is the dominant black grape, white grapes are commonly added to soften the wine. The variety is ideally suited to the cool conditions of Ribera del Duero where, as Tinto Fino, it is by far the principal grape variety, but the seasoning of varieties imported from Bordeaux is an important ingredient in that high plateau's

Tendone vines trained high off the ground in Bardolino.

most successful wine Vega Sicilia, while Pesquera benefits from the flesh of its Garnacha.

It is also grown in La Mancha, Costers del Segre, Utiel-Requena, and increasingly in Navarre and Somontano. The variety is so well entrenched in northern and central Spain that Spain's total Tempranillo plantings were well over 33,000 ha / 81,510 acres in 1990, making it one of the country's most important black grape varieties quantitatively as well as qualitatively.

Vine growers over the Pyrenees have been taking note and Tempranillo cuttings have been in demand in the Midi, where Tempranillo is officially recommended (though not for APPELLATION CONTRÔLÉE wines) and there were already nearly 2,500 ha in the late 1980s, most notably in the Aude.

Tempranillo is one of the very few Spanish varieties to have been adopted in any quantity in Portugal, where it is known as (Tinta) Roriz and is a valued, if not particularly emphatic, ingredient in port blends. Also in the Douro, downstream of Ribera del Duero, it has demonstrated its strength for table wines as the major ingredient in Ferreira's famous red Barca Velha. Tinta Roriz, also known mysteriously as Tinta Aragonez, is also grown increasingly in Dão.

As Tempranilla and making rather light, possibly over-irrigated reds, it has been important in Argentina's wine industry but is losing ground to more marketable grape varieties and in 1990 covered 7,500 ha, mainly in Mendoza.

Tempranillo is almost certainly the true identity of the unfashionable low-acid variety known in California as Valdepeñas, of which 500 acres remained, mainly in the Central Valley, in 1992.

On the other hand, Tempranillo's starring role in one of the world's most famous and distinctive wines, Rioja, makes it a likely ingredient in any of the world's many experimental vine nurseries.

TENDONE, the Italian name for the overhead vine-TRAINING SYSTEM widely used in southern Italy. The system is also common in in South America, where it is used for both TABLE GRAPES and wine grapes, and is called *parral* (Argentina) or *parron* (Chile). English terms used include both arbour and pergola, although the system is little used in English-speaking countries.

The vines are normally trained with trunks about 2 m / 6.5 ft high and a system of wooden frames and cross wires supports the foliage and fruit. Arbours are normally high enough from the ground to allow tractors and implements to pass underneath, but not so high as to make hand work difficult. The vines are pruned to either canes or spurs (see PRUNING). The overhead arbour can be a very productive training system, producing 30 to 70 tonnes of grapes per hectare in high rainfall regions.

Such training systems are limited in use because of the

expense of their construction and the high cost of labour required to manage them. Worker productivity is lower because of fatigue, and, where the vines are vigorous, the leaves form a very dense canopy on top and so the fruit and lower leaves are heavily shaded (see shade and colour plate opposite page 688). This reduces both yield and quality, and increases the risk of powdery mildew. Furthermore, the ventilation under such canopies is very restricted and the buildup of humidity favours botrytis bunch rot. The arbour system is used for table grapes in many parts of the world, and has the advantage that the fruit hangs freely and makes access easy. Inclined overhead trellis systems which do not completely cover the ground are often used for table grapes, as in South Africa (where it may be called the verandah system), and around the borders of fields in the vinho verde region of Portugal. R.E.S.

TENDRIL, coiling, clasping organ that enables the stems of plants to climb. In many plants these organs are modifications of stems, leaves, or leaflets, but in the grapevine they are modified inflorescences, developing at two of every three consecutive nodes. Tendrils are sensitive to touch; when sufficiently elongated, they react to pressure on their surface by coiling around the touched object, be it a wire, a part of the vine, or any other adjacent material. Once coiled, the tendrils become lignified and very tough. Young tendrils at the shoot tip are a sensitive indicator of the growth rate of the shoot: very active shoot tips have tendrils considerably extended beyond the end of the stem; decline in the rate of shoot extension is indicated by a matching decline in the extent of growth of the tendrils near the tip. B.G.C.

TENT, medieval term for strong red wine from Iberia, mainly Spain (notably deeper in colour that the clairet then still associated with Bordeaux). It is merely an Anglicized version of the word tinto, Spanish and Portuguese for red.

TENUTA, Italian word for an agricultural holding or estate.

TERAN, Terrano, names for subvarieties of the red friuli grape variety refosco used, respectively, in slovenia and the Carso DOC in the extreme east of Friuli.

TERLANO, or **Terlaner** in German, white wines from around the town of Terlano in the alto adige.

TERMITES, can be pests in older vineyards, where they tunnel old wood and can weaken it so much that the vine may collapse. Occasionally newly planted cuttings are attacked where growing conditions are poor. M.J.E.

TEROLDEGO ROTALIANO, the red Teroldego grape, makes lively wines for early drinking in north east Italy. For more details see trentino.

TERPENES, distinctive flavour compounds associated with the floral aromas found in wines made from such varieties as Muscat, Gewürztraminer, and Riesling. They are also found in oak, particularly American oak (see wood flavour).

TERPENOIDS, an important group of plant chemicals including many essential oils, carotenoids, plant hormones, sterols, and rubber. They contribute much to the unique qualities of the vine. Chemically, they are multiples of branched, five-carbon (isoprene) units yielding a variety of compounds with diverse properties: the C10 monoterpenes make an important contribution to floral aromas (see flavour compounds); the C15 sesquiterpenoids include the non-isoprenoid compounds that play a large part in non-floral aroma of grapes, and sterols and the hormone abscisic acid also derive from sesquiterpenoids; the C20 diterpenes include the gibberellin hormones and, when doubled, the carotenoids. B.G.C.

TERRA ALTA, Spanish for 'high land', is the highest of the do wine zones in Spanish catalonia (see map on p. 907). Its recent development parallels that of tarragona, which adjoins Terra Alta to the east. With the decline in popularity of sweet, fortified wines, the garnacha Blanca grape is slowly being replaced by macabeo in order to provide lighter styles of wine for the local market. R.J.M.

TERRACES make work in vineyards planted across sloping land considerably easier, and can also help combat soil erosion. Terraces more or less follow the contours of the land, and so row spacing is not necessarily as constant as it is for vineyards on flat land. Terraces are created when the hillside is re-formed into a series of horizontal steps between the rows. The world's most famous vineyard terraces are those of the port wine region of the douro valley in northern Portugal, although they are common in much of switzerland, the northern rhône, and elsewhere.

In centuries past such terraces were laboriously constructed by hand and supported by stone walls. For modern vineyards the cost of laying stones by hand can be prohibitive, and so most modern terraces are formed by bulldozers. Terraces are expensive to create, and are therefore justified only for expensive wines. There is a modern tendency to avoid planting vineyards on such slopes.

An alternative to creating terraces is to plant hillsides up and down the slopes, as in Germany and other parts of northern Europe. This practice avoids the expense of forming terraces but can lead to soil erosion and worker fatigue, and some slopes are too steep for tractors. See also hillside vineyards. R.E.S.

TERRA ROSSA, red brown loam or clay directly over well-drained limestone found typically in regions with a mediterranean climate. Such soils are found in southern

The port vineyards of the Douro valley have long depended on **terraces** such as these modernized ones near Croft's Quinta do Roeda.

Europe, North Africa, and parts of Australia. The quality of many wines made from Cabernet Sauvignon and Shiraz grapes grown at Coonawarra in SOUTH AUSTRALIA is said to owe much to the terra rossa soils there. See entries prefixed SOIL. M.J.E.

TERRET is one of the Languedoc's oldest vine varieties and, like PINOT, has had plenty of time to mutate into different shades of grape which may even be found on the same plant. Indeed Galet claims to have seen different-coloured grapes in the same bunch. **Terret Gris** is by far the most planted white wine variety in the Languedoc, even if it is concentrated in the Hérault *département* where there were well over 5,000 ha/12,350 acres planted in 1988 (as compared with the Aude's 2,200 ha of Mauzac and the Gard's 1,500 of Ugni Blanc). It can be made into a relatively full bodied but naturally crisp varietal white, but as a name Terret lacks the magic of internationally known varieties. **Terret Blanc** was once grown near Sète expressly for the local brandy and vermouth industry (it too was prized for its acidity). Although light-berried Terrets (rarely distinguished by officialdom) are in decline, combined they represented France's ninth most planted white wine variety at the end of the 1980s. They are allowed into the white wines of Minervois, Corbières, and, to a decreasing extent, Coteaux du Languedoc.

Terret Noir is the dark-berried version which is grown on a much more limited scale (hardly 800 ha remained in 1988) but is one of the permitted varieties in red CHÂTEAUNEUF-DU-PAPE to which it can add useful structure and interest. All Terrets bud usefully late and keep their acidity well.

Galet, P., *Cépages et vignobles de France* (2nd edn., Montpellier, 1990).

TERROIR, much-discussed term for the total natural environment of any viticultural site. No precise English equivalent exists for this quintessentially French term and concept. Dubos and Laville describe it fully, and how it underlies and defines the French APPELLATION CONTRÔLÉE system. See also Halliday and Johnson.

Major components of terroir are SOIL (as the word suggests) and local TOPOGRAPHY, together with their interactions with each other and with MACROCLIMATE to determine MESOCLIMATE and vine MICROCLIMATE. The holistic combination of all these is held to give each site its own unique terroir, which is reflected in its wines more or less consistently from year to year, to some degree regardless of variations in methods of VITICULTURE and WINE-MAKING. Thus every small plot, and in generic terms every larger area, and ultimately region, may have distinctive wine-style characteristics which cannot be precisely duplicated elsewhere. The extent to which terroir effects are unique is, however, debatable, and of course commercially important, which makes the subject controversial.

Opinions have differed greatly on the reality and, if real, the importance of terroir in determining wine qualities. Major regional classifications of European vineyards have been largely based on the concepts of terroir. NEW WORLD viticulturists and researchers, on the other hand, have tended to dismiss it as a product of mysticism and established commercial interest. Dickenson canvasses the issues in detail, and is likewise mostly sceptical. But against these views it might also be justly charged that 'newer' viticulture has notoriously attempted to imitate the products of the great vineyards without regard to terroir, and therefore has a commercial reason for belittling its potential contribution.

It can certainly be argued that modern improvements in vineyard and winery technology, by raising and unifying standards of wine quality, have to some extent obscured differences in both style and quality of wines that in the past were (sometimes wrongly) attributed to terroir in its true sense. But paradoxically, the same improvements can serve to unmask genuine differences due to terroir. By eliminating extraneous odours and tastes derived from faulty wine-making, they allow the fuller expression of intrinsic grape qualities, which can be related to site.

Laville lists the following factors (components) as determining terroir:

- Climate, as measured by TEMPERATURE and RAINFALL.
- Sunlight energy, or insolation, received per unit of land surface area (see SUNLIGHT).
- Relief (or TOPOGRAPHY, or geomorphology), comprising altitude, slope, and aspect.
- Geology and pedology, determining the soil's basic physical and chemical characteristics (see GEOLOGY).
- Hydrology, or SOIL WATER relations.

An essential notion of terroir is that all its components are natural, and that they cannot be significantly influenced by management.

The main emphasis in nearly all recent French writings is on the soil, and especially its role and interactions with other elements of the environment in governing water supply to the vine. The most important evidence for this comes from the studies of Dr Gérard Seguin, of BORDEAUX UNIVERSITY. He found that, while many of the acknowledged best Bordeaux vineyards are on the Quaternary (recently laid down) gravelly sands, by no means all are. Neither geological origin nor SOIL TEXTURE could explain the region's best terroirs, as judged by the wines they produce. The best in fact covered extremely diverse soil textures, ranging from heavy CLAYS, as in Pomerol, through CALCAREOUS brown soils, to sandy LOAMS and SANDS over clay (podzols), to the deep, gravelly sands most typical of the Médoc. An analysis of the soils' chemical properties showed them also to be extremely variable.

Two unifying themes did, however, emerge among the top CRUS. First, none of their soils was very fertile, but then none of the vines showed mineral element deficiencies either (see VINE NUTRITION). Secondly, their soils regulated water supply to the vines in such a way that it was nearly always just moderately sufficient, without extremes in either direction. DRAINAGE was always excellent, so that both water-logging and sudden increases in water supply to the vines were avoided no matter how much the rainfall. In the case of clay soils, this depended on their having fairly high ORGANIC

MATTER and/or CALCIUM contents, so that they maintained friability and an open pore structure through which water could move readily (see SOIL STRUCTURE).

At the same time the capacity to store soil water within a SOIL DEPTH accessible to the vine ROOTS was great enough to ensure supply through prolonged rainfall deficits. This might be achieved either by great soil depth and a deep, sparse root system, in the case of sandy soils with little water storage capacity per unit volume; or a lesser depth in heavier soils, combined with a capacity of the clay and organic matter to hold some of the water tightly enough that it is only slowly available to the roots. The deep, gravelly sands of the MÉDOC exemplified the former situation, the heavy clays of POMEROL, the latter. This explained why the best terroirs maintain their wine quality notably better in poor seasons than the rest, a consistency which has always been one of the most striking features of the Bordeaux CLASSED GROWTHS.

Studies of terroir in Burgundy, cited and illustrated by Johnson, and by Halliday and Johnson, have led to similar conclusions. There the best wines are from stony clay loam soils, formed on the middle slopes from MARL (a clay and soft limestone mixture) mixed with SILT and rubble from outcropping hard LIMESTONE further up. These soils combine good drainage with just the right capacity to store and supply water to the vines.

Extensive studies by Carbonneau and colleagues in the Bordeaux region, and by Smart and colleagues in Australia and New Zealand, have revealed a further common feature of vineyards producing the best wines. All have a high degree of leaf and bunch exposure to direct sunlight, with little complete shading of internal and lower leaves (see further discussion under SUNLIGHT, CANOPY MICROCLIMATE, and CANOPY MANAGEMENT). Variation in this respect is explained by differences in vegetative VIGOUR and vine BALANCE. Best quality is associated with only moderate vigour, which typically results from a somewhat restricted water supply, limited NITROGEN, and (in some cases) appropriate TRAINING SYSTEMS. These studies suggest that soil effects on wine quality are indirect; that is soil conditions regulating water and nitrogen supply to the vine affect vine vigour, which in turn affects fruit and leaf exposure to sunlight, which in turn affects wine quality. While the latter two are amenable to management control on soils that are not too fertile, the first, in the absence of IRRIGATION, is very largely not. It is therefore the prime contributor, together with local TOPOGRAPHY to the immutable influence of terroir.

An implication is that GEOLOGY, often cited as a basis of terroir, has in general no more than an indirect role. To varying degrees parent ROCK materials do contribute to the natures of the soils derived from them; they also shape local topography and therefore MESOCLIMATE. Occasionally the parent materials contribute directly because vine roots can penetrate them, as in the cases of CHALK subsoils and the recent ALLUVIAL deposits of the Médoc. In the broad sense, however, it remains the soil itself, and its water relations, that play the decisive role. The study of terroir is one of soil and mesoclimate, not of geology.

An international concept?

The question remains as to how far the French concept of terroir, with its primary emphasis on soil, is relevant to other regions and viticultural systems. An overriding influence of soil and its water relations can be easily enough understood in the Bordeaux environment, with its relatively flat topography and, as a consequence, few really major differences in mesoclimate. The situation is clearly different in areas such as Germany's MOSEL-SAAR-RUWER region at the cold limit of commercial viticulture. The topographic differences between individual sites decide whether grapes, in particular the high-quality varieties such as RIESLING, will ripen fully at all. Topography and mesoclimate are inescapably major components of terroir (or its German equivalent).

Moreover, it has been argued that mesoclimatic differences may not merely govern the degree of ripeness attained. Some believe that they could also affect more subtle grape and wine qualities of the kinds commonly attributed to terroir; see CLIMATE AND WINE QUALITY and TEMPERATURE VARIABILITY. Soil might similarly influence grape and wine qualities through its effect on MICROCLIMATE; see STONES AND ROCKS, SOIL COLOUR, and SOIL AND WINE QUALITY.

Any such effects serve, of course, to underline terroir as a real concept, and not something expressed merely through the relationships between vine vigour, balance, and the vine canopy. The distinction is critical because, to the extent that the latter is true, other approaches are often available to achieve the same end. Two stand out in importance.

1. The use of larger or more complex vine-TRAINING SYSTEMS, such as Carbonneau's LYRE trellis, making it possible to maintain good leaf and fruit exposure on larger and more productive vines. This in turn allows the exploitation of moister, and possibly more fertile, soils, giving higher yields without any necessary loss of fruit and wine quality.

2. In regions with dry summers, the use of controlled IRRIGATION, especially that made possible by drip irrigation. This allows vegetative vigour to be held at appropriate levels for the available trellising, but water to be supplied during ripening as needed. It is an important advance in regions of MEDITERRANEAN CLIMATE, giving them scope to duplicate many of the terroir characteristics of the long-established best table wine areas, but with fewer climatic risks.

It seems inconceivable, however, that these developments will ever totally eliminate the regional and local differences in wine qualities that have been traditionally ascribed to terroir. Differences in MACROCLIMATE, MESOCLIMATE, and soil MICROCLIMATE remain, while there are many conceivable avenues by which differences in soil chemistry—for instance, in trace element balances— might have small effects on wine flavours and aromas which are nevertheless dectectable by the sense of TASTE. To the extent that terroirs remain unique, and poorly understood, one can therefore hope that they will continue to help mould the infinite variety and individuality of the best wines, giving the special nuances of character that make wine such a fascinating study for wine-maker and consumer alike. *Vivent les différences*!

J.G. & R.E.S.

Dickenson, J., 'Viticultural geography: an introduction to the literature in English', *Journal of Wine Research*, 1 (1990), 5–24.
Dubos, J., 'Importance du terroir comme facteur de différenciation qualitative des vins', *Bulletin de l'O.I.V.*, 639 (1984), 861–73.
Halliday, J., and Johnson, H., *The Art and Science of Wine* (London, 1992).
Johnson, H., *The World Atlas of Wine* (Mitchell Beazley, London, 1971).
Laville, P., 'Le Terroir, un concept indispensable à l'élaboration et à la protection des appellations d'origine comme à la gestion des vignobles: le cas de la France', *Bulletin de l'O.I.V.*, 709–10 (1990), 217–41.
Seguin, G., ' "Terroirs" and pedology of wine growing', *Experientia*, 42 (1986), 861–73.

TÊTE DE CUVÉE, term occasionally used for selected top bottlings. Similar to CRÈME DE TÊTE.

TÊTES, French for the distillate known as HEADS.

TEXAS, south western state in the UNITED STATES and increasingly important as a producer of wines whose style is still emerging as a host of newcomers tackle varied terrain in a hot, dry climate. The youth of the Texas wine industry and its potential to be distinctive are neatly displayed in the surprising identities of two of its most memorable wines produced in the early years: a white French COLOMBARD 1990 (from Fall Creek) and a red CARNELIAN 1987.

Both grape varieties were more curiosities than trendsetters. CHENIN BLANC was Texas's most productive single grape variety at the beginning of the 1990s, followed in order by SAUVIGNON Blanc, CHARDONNAY, and CABERNET SAUVIGNON. Varieties present to a much more limited extent included CABERNET FRANC, MERLOT, RIESLING, TREBBIANO, and ZINFANDEL as well as Colombard and Carnelian. Total acreage then approached 3,000 (1,200 ha), with 26 wineries in commercial production. VARIETAL table wines accounted for nearly all wine made, although the state had two specialists in classic method sparkling wine (made like CHAMPAGNE).

More than two-thirds of the state's vineyards are on the high plains of west Texas. In Trans-Pecos most of the plantings are between Odessa and Fort Stockton. The other important western wine region, centred on Lubbock, is the Llano Estacado (Staked Plain), so called because the 18th century Spanish explorer Coronado marked his return route across the trackless semi-desert with stakes. Llano Estacado is also the name of the state's oldest (1976) and most reliable winery, located not far south of Lubbock. FROST can cause damage in some districts.

Recent rates of growth in plantings and number of wineries, however, suggest that Texas Hill Country, 200 miles/320 km east, may soon overtake the plains in spite of its later start. Three of Texas's four American Viticultural Areas (see AVA) are in Texas Hill Country: Bell Mountain AVA, Fredericksburg AVA, and Texas Hill Country AVA. (The fourth Texas AVA, Escondido Valley, is in Pecos County in Trans-Pecos region.)

The major force in Texas wine is the 1,000-acre Ste Genevieve Vineyard, in Trans-Pecos, developed jointly by the University of Texas and the large Bordeaux wine merchant CORDIER. Fall Creek Vineyards has been a leader in Texas Hill Country since its beginnings as a wine region.

English, S. J., *The Wines of Texas* (Austin, Tex., 1988).

TEXAS ROOT ROT, caused by the fungus *Phymatotrichum omnivorum* which lives in the soil. This vine FUNGAL DISEASE can prevent grape-growing in parts of the south western United States. A circular patch of vines can suddenly die in summer. The disease is avoided by planting disease-free material in non-infested soil. The vigorous ROOTSTOCK Dog Ridge can be planted where the fungus is suspected. R.E.S.

THAILAND, small country in south east Asia where some grape-bearing vines are grown successfully in a particularly warm, humid climate, by careful use of TRELLIS SYSTEMS and deliberate defoliation to simulate seasonal change.

THALIA, Portuguese name for the ubiquitous white grape variety known in France as UGNI BLANC and Italy as TREBBIANO.

THEOPHRASTUS (370–288 BC), philosopher and botanist from Lesbos who discusses viticulture in his 'plant researches'.

THERMOTHERAPY, a technique to eliminate VIRUS DISEASES from grapevines by growing infected plants at high temperatures (about 38 °C or 100 °F), and then propagating from shoot tips. These shoot tips can produce plants free of virus diseases, but diseases such as FANLEAF DEGENERATION virus are eliminated much more easily than others—LEAFROLL, for example. Each tip produced must be checked to see whether it is virus-free, and can become registered as a new CLONE. New techniques of TISSUE CULTURE have generally been found more effective at virus elimination. R.E.S.

THERMOVINIFICATION, process sometimes used in RED WINE-MAKING, particularly in cool climates or after particularly cool growing seasons, whereby heat, about 70 °C/158 °F, is applied to grape clusters or MUST before FERMENTATION to liberate ANTHOCYANS, or colour, from the skins (see TEMPERATURE effects). The heat treatment is immediately followed by PRESSING to liberate coloured juice, which is then fermented much as in traditional WHITE WINE-MAKING. Thermovinification is particularly valuable in making everyday wines from grape varieties low in anthocyans, or from better-coloured grape varieties affected by moulds such as BOTRYTIS rot, which destroys colour in dark-skinned grapes. In the latter case, the heat inactivates the colour-destroying enzymes secreted by the mould. Thermovinification is rarely used in making fine wines, however, which almost invariably rely on extended MACERATION to extract colour and flavour from the grape skins. A.D.W.

THIAMINE. See VITAMINS.

THINNING vines. See CROP THINNING and SHOOT THINNING.

THOMPSON SEEDLESS is the common CALIFORNIA name for the seedless white grape variety SULTANA. It acquired this name from an early grower of the variety, near Yuba City, one William Thompson. Thompson Seedless is California's most planted grape variety by far, its 263,000 acres/106,500 ha in 1991 dwarfing total plantings of California's second most planted white grape Chardonnay. Almost all of California's Thompson Seedless is planted in the hot, dry SAN JOAQUIN VALLEY, with nearly two-thirds in Fresno County, the powerhouse of California raisin production, alone. In the 1970s Thompson Seedless was particularly useful to the California wine industry in helping to bulk out inexpensive white JUG WINE blends at a time when demand far outstripped supply of premium white wine grape varieties, but today it is used chiefly for DRYING GRAPES.

THOUARSAIS, VINS DU, small southern Loire VDQS just west of Haut-POITOU. In 1990 only 17 ha/42 acres were officially producing this particularly light wine, mainly from Chenin Blanc with a little Chardonnay.

THRIPS, tiny (1–2 mm long), winged insects which readily feed on grapevine flowers and developing bunches, causing scarring and dwarfing of new shoots in early spring. Growers assess numbers present at this stage by sharply tapping the forming bunches on to a sheet of white paper. Thrips are also responsible for spot injury, which occurs when a female deposits an egg into a developing berry, producing a small dark scar surrounded by a lightened area. These spots may crack and allow decay organisms to enter, and the scarring is a defect in TABLE GRAPES. While thrips are sometimes thought to be the cause of poor FRUIT SET, there is little evidence to support this. Thrips are easily controlled by contact PESTICIDES if necessary. M.J.E.

TIBOUREN could almost be said to be *the* Provençal grape variety. It has a long history and the ability to produce such quintessentially Provençal wines as earthy rosés with a genuine scent of the *garrigue*. Although it is planted in strictly limited quantities, Tibouren is cultivated by a number of the more quality- and history-conscious producers of Provence and some of them bottle it as a varietal rosé. It is sensitive to COULURE and therefore yields irregularly. The deeply incised shape of its leaves reminds Galet of some Middle Eastern vine varieties, and certainly it could possibly have been imported by the Greeks via Marseilles, although its original sphere of influence was around St-Tropez, where it is thought by some to have been imported as recently as the end of the 18th century by a naval captain Antiboul, after whom it was named.

Galet, P., *Cépages et vignobles de France* (2nd edn., Montpellier, 1990).

TIERRA DE BARROS. Spanish wine zone. See EXTREMADURA.

TIGNANELLO, seminal central Italian wine first produced by the house of ANTINORI in the early 1970s. For more details, see VINO DA TAVOLA.

TIME and wine. See AGEING.

TINAJA, large, earthenware vessel, probably developed from the Roman AMPHORAE, used to ferment and store wine in central and southern SPAIN. *Tinajas* are still used in La MANCHA, VALDEPEÑAS, and MONTILLA-MORILES, although modern versions are mostly made from reinforced concrete. They are relatively cheap, but have the disadvantages that they are not very efficient in terms of space, are difficult to clean, and offer relatively poor TEMPERATURE CONTROL.

TINTA, the Spanish and Portuguese feminine adjective for red, is therefore the first word of many, unrelated Spanish and Portuguese names and synonyms for dark-skinned vine varieties. For Tinta Roriz see RORIZ, for example.

TINTA AMARELA, productive dark-skinned Portuguese grape variety once more extensively grown in the Douro and still grown in Portugal's Dão region. It can yield attractively scented wines but is not regarded as one of the finest port varieties and is particularly sensitive to rot. In southern Portugal it is known as Trincadeira.

TINTA BARROCA, relatively thick-skinned port grape variety which is best suited to higher or north-facing sites in Portugal's DOURO valley. Yields are variable and the vine can be depended upon to produce useful, dark-skinned grapes for a blend even in drought conditions. Perhaps because of this, Tinta Barroca has been the most popular port variety in South Africa's vineyards and unfortified VARIETAL Tinta Barroca dry red is a South African speciality.

TINTA CÃO, top-quality black grape variety for the production of PORT. Having almost disappeared from the vineyards of the DOURO valley in northern Portugal (despite its long history there), it is being planted with greater enthusiasm since it was identified as one of the five finest port varieties, although it is not one of the deepest coloured. It has also been planted experimentally at DAVIS in California.

TINTA FRANCISCA, lesser red grape variety used in the production of port in Portugal's DOURO valley where it is not regarded as one of the finest varieties. The wine produced can be notably sweet but is not particularly concentrated.

TINTA NEGRA MOLE, by far the most commonly planted vine variety on the island of MADEIRA. Although its

Tinajas used for maturing Montilla at Bodegas Alvear in southern Spain.

background is unknown, Negra Mole is a VINIFERA variety (unlike many of the vines that replaced the noble varieties SERCIAL, VERDELHO, BUAL, and MALVASIA after the ravages of DOWNY MILDEW and PHYLLOXERA in the 19th century). It yields relatively high quantities of very sweet, red wine which turns amber with the madeira production process and then yellow-green with age. A variety, which may be quite distinct, is also grown on the Portuguese mainland in the Algarve and, as Negramoll, in Spain.

TINTA PINHEIRA, ordinary Portuguese grape variety used for making red DÃO.

TINTO, Spanish and Portuguese for red, so that *vino* (*vinho* in Portuguese) *tinto* is red wine (as opposed to the lighter red CLARETE produced in Spain). The word is the derivation of the red wine once known in England as TENT.

Like TINTA, Tinto is also the first word of many Spanish and Portuguese names and synonyms for black grape varieties. TEMPRANILLO, for example, is known as Tinto Fino in Ribero del Duero, and as Tinto Madrid, Tinto de la Rioja, Tinto del Pais, and Tinto de Toro, to name but a few synonyms, in the rest of Spain.

TIPPING, the viticultural pratcice of cutting off shoot tips at flowering. Normally about 10 to 20 cm (8 in) of shoot tip are removed. For some varieties which commonly experience poor FRUIT SET this can help reduce the problem, known also as COULURE.

TIRAGE, French for that part of the SPARKLING WINE-MAKING process during which sugar and yeast are added to the blended base wines in order to provoke a second fermentation, thereby creating CARBON DIOXIDE gas. It is sometimes used to include the entire period during which the sparkling wine matures on the LEES of this second fermentation.

TISSUE CULTURE, the culturing of excised cells, tissues, and organs using artificial media of salts and nutrients, used particularly in genetic engineering. The techniques can be used to develop vines with particularly useful properties much faster than by conventional PROPAGATION. Usually

CALLUS develops first, then roots and buds develop within the callus leading to a new vine that can flower and set seed. The formation of roots or buds is achieved by subtle changes in the ingredients of the culture solution, especially in the relative amounts of the hormones AUXIN and CYTOKININ. Aseptic conditions are essential. The culture of the terminal 1 mm of vine shoot, especially after its fragmentation, has permitted the production of large numbers of plantlets in tubes that are free of some VIRUSES and CROWN GALL disease. Large numbers of vine plantlets can be 'micro-propagated' by these methods, which can rapidly build up populations of scarce VINE VARIETIES.

B.G.C.

TITRATABLE ACID. See TOTAL ACIDITY.

TOAST (*chauffe* in French), given to a barrel when forming it over a heat source, is one of the processes in BARREL MAKING that most obviously affect eventual wine flavour. The heat source also inevitably toasts the inside of the barrel to a degree that varies according to the heat of the fire and the

Steps involved in the **tissue culture** of grape vines

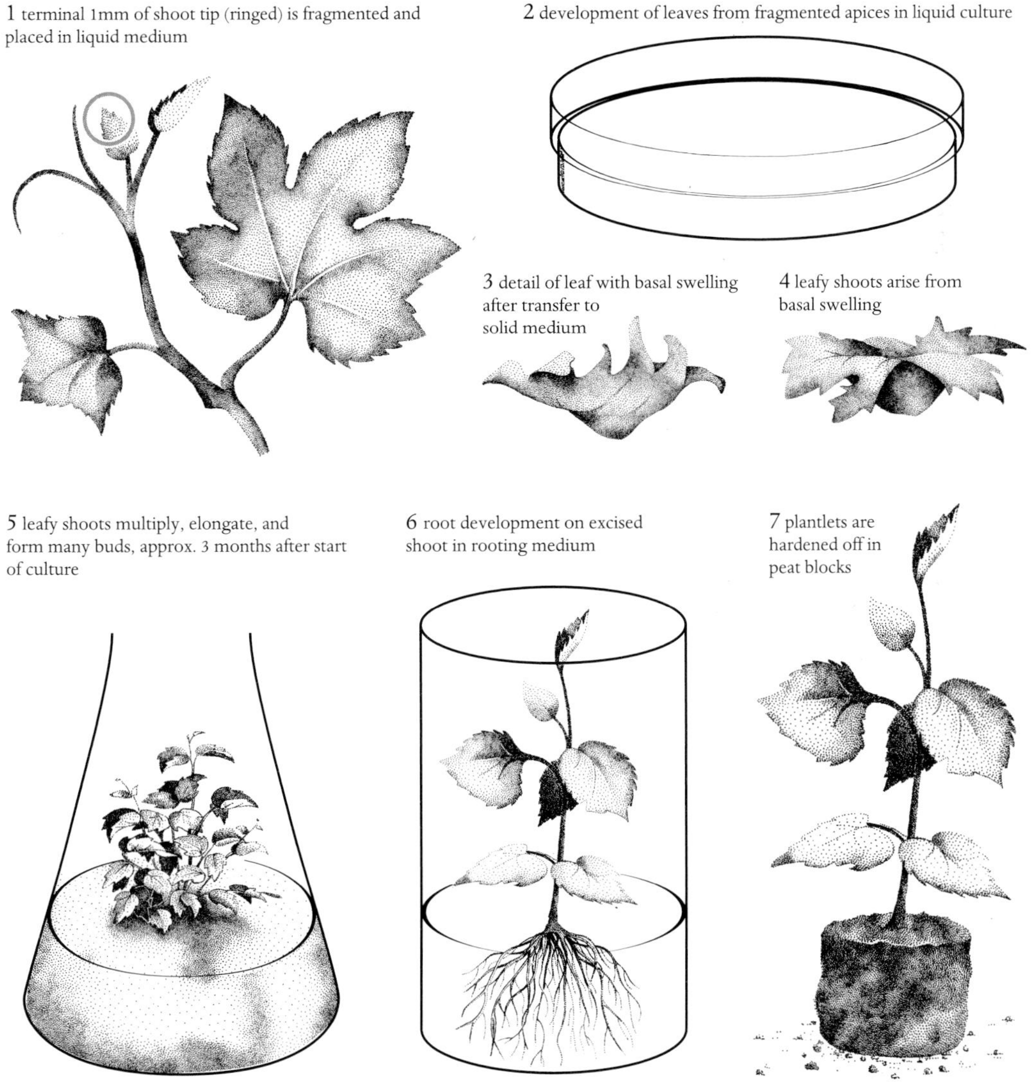
1 terminal 1mm of shoot tip (ringed) is fragmented and placed in liquid medium
2 development of leaves from fragmented apices in liquid culture
3 detail of leaf with basal swelling after transfer to solid medium
4 leafy shoots arise from basal swelling
5 leafy shoots multiply, elongate, and form many buds, approx. 3 months after start of culture
6 root development on excised shoot in rooting medium
7 plantlets are hardened off in peat blocks

length of time the barrel is held over it. This heating process dramatically alters the wood's physical and chemical composition. The toast provides a buffer between the ALCOHOL in wine and the TANNINS in wood. In general, the less a barrel is toasted, the more tannins and other wood characteristics will be leached into the wine by the alcohol. Wine matured in lightly toasted barrels therefore tend to taste 'oaky', 'woody', or even 'vegetal', while wine matured in heavily toasted barrels is more likely to taste 'toasty' or 'spicy'.

Burgundy barrels are in general more heavily toasted than Bordeaux barriques, perhaps partly because the STAVES are thicker, and partly because a heavy toast is better suited to the flavours of PINOT NOIR and CHARDONNAY grapes than to those of CABERNET SAUVIGNON, MERLOT, SAUVIGNON Blanc, and SÉMILLON. The following terms are used, although they are imprecise, and New World wine-makers are more likely to employ them than their European counterparts.

Light toast: there is little colour change in the wood. Wines aged in these barrels are usually quite fruity but can be somewhat tannic.

Medium toast: the wood is browner, probably having been toasted, over the fire for very approximately 15 minutes. The influence of the wood is more important on the wine. Wines aged in such barrels are said to have smells of vanilla and coffee. The greater toasting provides a buffer between the alcohol in the wine and the wood tannins. Therefore, wines aged in these barrels will normally be less tannic than those aged in light toast barrels.

Heavy toast: the wood is very dark. Wines aged in these barrels are usually marked by the heavy toast with aromas of roasted coffee beans, toasted bread, ginger, nutmeg, and smoked meats.

The above flavour descriptions apply to wine aged in French oak barrels. The word 'char' is usually associated with American whiskey barrels, which are made over steam or natural gas but then set on fire. Traditionally American oak wine barrels were simply un-charred bourbon barrels but American cooperages now toast to the customer's specifications.

M.K.

TOCAI, or **Tocai Friulano**, the most popular and widely planted white grape variety of the FRIULI region in north east Italy, has no connection at all with Tokay d'Alsace (an Alsace synonym for the PINOT GRIGIO which grows alongside Tocai in Friuli), and is probably completely unrelated to the TOKAY of Hungary (although see below). According to GALET, however, it is identical to SAUVIGNON Vert or Sauvignonasse, the variety planted in much of CHILE. In Italy in 1990 there were a total of nearly 7,000 ha / 17,290 acres planted with this variety.

In Friuli this productive, late budding vine variety produces the staple wine of the region's taverns and trattorie. Over 2,000 ha are currently in production in the major DOC zones (COLLI ORIENTALI, COLLIO, GRAVE DEL FRIULI, and ISONZO) accounting for nearly 20 per cent of the total vineyard area of these DOC zones, and over 30 per cent of the total area devoted to white varieties. Given its wide diffusion, it is not easy to single out particular areas of superior quality, but the Tocai of Buttrio, Manzano, and Rosazzo in the Colli Orientali, and that of the areas between Cormons and Brazzano, between Brazzano and Dolegna, and Capriva di Friuli in the Collio DOC, can be considered classic subzones for fine Tocai. The wine itself is light in colour and body, floral in aroma, and has pronounced almond notes on the palate and on the nose. It is designed to be drunk young.

Some Tocai, not identical to Tocai Friulano, is also grown in the VENETO.

Some Italian authorities, notably Gaetano Perusini, assert that the variety is closely related to the FURMINT grape of Tokay and was imported from Hungary by Count Ottelio di Ariis in 1863 at a time when Friuli was part of the Austro-Hungarian empire, while Friuli's historian Coronini claims that cuttings of Tocai were sent to King Bela IV of Hungary by Bertoldo di Andechs, patriach of Aquileia, in the first half of the 13th century. The dispute remains undecided, but, under pressure from Hungary, the Italians have agreed eventually to give up using the name Tocai.

A variety called Tocai Friulano is also cultivated to a limited extent in ARGENTINA, while a Sauvignon Vert is grown in UKRAINE.

D.T. & J.Ro.

Galet, P., *Cépages et vignobles de France*, ii: *l'Ampélographie française* (2nd edn., Montpellier, 1990).

TOKAY, simplified and commonly used version of the name of the great Hungarian wine **Tokaji**, from the wine region **Tokaj-Hegyalja** in the far north east of HUNGARY. (Tokay is also an extraordinary Australian fortified wine, described under LIQUEUR TOKAY. See also TOKAY D'ALSACE, a synonym for PINOT GRIS.)

According to Hungarian wine lore, the region's ability to produce unique sweet yet fragrant wines was discovered in 1650 when it was all owned by Zssuzsanna Lorántfly. The estate's priest, who was also in charge of wine production, ordered the harvest to be delayed because he feared an attack from the Turks. Some of the grapes were therefore attacked by NOBLE ROT and were picked and crushed separately before being poured into the must. The resulting wine, broached during Easter celebrations the following year, was much admired. Within the next 10 years the noble rot fungus is supposed to have been recognized (more than 100 years before it was in Germany at SCHLOSS JOHANNISBERG). By the 18th century this extraordinary wine had been introduced to the French court (see HUNGARY, history), and was subsequently introduced to the Russian imperial court by the Habsburgs. Only CONSTANTIA from the Cape of Good Hope, and to a lesser extent Moldavian COTNARI, rivalled Tokay as 'the wine of kings and king of wines' during this period of sweet wine worship, with Tokay Essencia or Essence regarded as an all-purpose restorative.

The Tokaj-Hegyalja region includes 28 villages, including Tokaj, which gives its name to the region and its wine. Among many hundreds of hectares of vines, the most famous vineyards are north of Tokaj in the villages of Tarcal, Mád,

Tokay cellars in north west Hungary, distinguished by their treasured thick black mould.

Tállya, and Tolcsva on the south eastern Zemplén Foothills of the Northern Massif. Geographically, the region extends over the border with Slovakia, although at one time CZECHOSLOVAKIA traded its right to use the term Tokay for a beer export deal with Hungary.

Vines are grown on two main soil types, either LOESS or soils of VOLCANIC origin, and the warming effect of the Carpathian mountains which shelter the region from the east, north, and west result in a MACROCLIMATE of humid nights and prolonged, warm autumns, which combination, together with the confluence of the Tisza and Bodrog rivers, favours the development of NOBLE ROT, here called *aszú*, the Hungarian equivalent of the Austrian term AUSBRUCH. Noble rot does not develop every year, but natural sugar levels of 20 g/l at picking qualify the grapes as Aszú.

Viticultural methods are similar to those elsewhere, except that particular attention should be paid to PRUNING in order not to dilute quality, and harvest is generally very late. The traditional start date of 28 October has been abandoned, but picking often continues late into November. Close and frequent inspection of vineyards is necessary in order to determine which of the varied sorts of Tokay can be made from each part. Tokay wines have for centuries been produced at different levels of sweetness and the purpose of modern wine law is merely to formalize tradition.

The principal grape variety grown here is the fiery FURMINT, enlivened and perfumed by up to half as much of the indigenous HÁRSLEVELŰ and occasionally softened by small quantities of the golden mutant of MUSCAT BLANC À PETITS GRAINS, here sometimes called Muscat Lunel, Yellow Muscat, or Muskotályos. All three of these ingredients (which play similar, respective parts to Sémillon, Sauvignon Blanc, and Muscadelle in SAUTERNES) are sometimes bottled as individual VARIETAL wines labelled, for example, Tokaji Furmint, but these dry to medium dry wines are called Tokay Ordinarium and are made from grapes unaffected by noble rot. These wines are bottled in regular 75-cl/27-fl oz bottles instead of the 50-cl flask that is characteristic of true Tokay.

Next up the scale of sweetness and, usually, quality, is Tokaji Szamorodni, or 'as it was grown'. These dry or sweet wines are made from a mixture of grapes both affected and unaffected by noble rot in which the proportion of Aszú grapes is less than 50 per cent. The sweetness of the resulting wine depends on this proportion. After crushing and destemming, the Szamorodni grapes are macerated for between 12 and 24 hours to encourage the formation of Aszú aromas, and are then pressed.

The third basic ingredient yielded by a typical Tokay vintage is the most precious. In those sections of the vineyard in which more than 50 per cent of the berries have been affected by noble rot, the affected shrivelled Aszú bunches, or even grapes, may be picked individually. They are then stored in tanks until the wine from unaffected grapes has been fermented, and are then kneaded to a sweet paste and added, in carefully controlled proportions, to lots of base wine specially selected for their superior levels of ALCOHOLIC STRENGTH, ACIDITY, and EXTRACT. Some remaining unfermented FRUCTOSE is also regarded as an advantage.

Base wine has traditionally been measured in the special small 136-l wooden casks made in nearby Gönc, while the Aszú paste was traditionally measured in *puttonyos*, special hods with a capacity of 20 to 25 kg (44–55 lbs). The higher the number of *puttonyos* added to a Gönc cask, the sweeter the wine. Today, Tokaji Aszú may be sold as 3, 4, 5, or 6 *puttonyos* according to certain minimum levels of RESIDUAL SUGAR and extract. A 6-*puttonyos* wine, for example, must contain 150 g/l residual sugar and 45 g/l sugar-free extract.

The paste is now made mechanically by gentle mashing of the Aszú berries and the base wine poured over the paste, stirred, and left to macerate and extract the special Aszú properties from the paste for between 24 and 36 hours. After gentle, usually pneumatic pressing, this new wine is racked into the special Gönc casks in which they are matured for between four and eight years, depending on style.

Another important ingredient in the unique style of Tokay is the curious low tunnels burrowed out of the hillsides, supposedly to protect the wines from marauding Turks, in which the wine is matured. The walls of these cool (10 °C/50 °F) cellars are lined with a fungus, *Racodium cellare*, which forms FILM-FORMING YEASTS very similar to, but colder and less active than, the FLOR of Jerez on the surface of the wine in the casks. TOPPING UP is deliberately discouraged, and thus Tokay is distinguished by a very high level of ALDEHYDES and ESTERS, as well as by the flavour of its particular grapes, high levels of acidity and extract, and varying levels of residual sugar.

The dry Tokaji Szamorodni exported through the Monimpex monopoly usually tastes like a rather flat SHERRY, although there is every reason to suppose that quality could improve substantially. A sweeter version was also made, but it lacks the natural vitality of true Tokaji Aszú, which tastes of botrytis and raisins in youth and takes on almond and bread flavours with age.

Two even sweeter forms of wine are made, in tiny quantities and only in the finest years, from *aszú* berries. Tokaji Essencia contains even more residual sugar than a 6-puttonyos Tokaji Aszú and a particularly powerful yeast is needed to achieve fermentation, after which the wine must be aged in cask for 10 years. Tokaji Essence is a lightly alcoholic syrup made from that small quantity of FREE-RUN juice that results from the storage of Aszú grapes before they are mashed to a paste. This is so high in sugar and non-fermentable components that it ferments extremely slowly, over many years, in cask and is intended for blending purposes only—although it is inevitably the object of much curiosity on the part of the increasing numbers of foreign visitors to the region.

See HUNGARY for more details of foreign investment in Tokay.

Katona, J., *A Guide to Hungarian Wine*, trans. by Z. Béres (Budapest, 1990).
Tokaj-Hegyaljai Album (1867).

TOKAY D'ALSACE, or simply **Tokay**, was for long the Alsace name for PINOT GRIS. The variety was probably taken to Hungary in the 14th century, where it was cultivated as Szürkebarat and, it is thought, brought back two centuries later by General Schwendi after his campaign against the Turks, to be planted in Kientzheim as 'Tokay', the name of Hungary's most famous wine even then (although the famously restorative wine TOKAY depends not on Pinot Gris but on FURMINT vines).

To avoid confusion with the famous Hungarian wine of the same name (although the wine-makers of Alsace would probably be horrified if anyone found the distinctive aromas of Hungarian Tokay in their Pinot Gris), Europe's vinous lawmakers proposed **Tokay Pinot Gris** as an alternative, an intermediate stage towards the eventual elimination of the word Tokay from Alsace.

Galet, P., *Cépages et vignobles de France* (2nd edn., Montpellier, 1990).

TONNEAU, traditional Bordeaux measure of wine volume, once a large wooden cask holding 900 l, or 252 imperial wine gallons, the equivalent of four BARRIQUES. A PARIS tonneau was 800 l, but, because of the prominence of GASCON merchants in London and English merchants in Bordeaux, the Bordeaux measure became the standard. By the end of the 18th century tonneaux had been replaced by the easier to transport smaller barrique, yet the tonneau, the exact equivalent of 100 CASES of wine, is still the measure in which the Bordeaux wine trade deals.

Such was the importance of wine to medieval trade in general (see BORDEAUX and DUTCH WINE TRADE), that a tonneau, or ton in English, evolved from being the space occupied by a tun of wine, to become the unit of measurement for the carrying capacity of any ship, whatever its load.

TONNERROIS, an up-and-coming wine area near CHABLIS around the town of Tonnerre.

TOPOCLIMATE, a local climate as determined by TOPOGRAPHY, for instance that of a particular hill, valley, or slope. It is commonly subsumed under the broader term MESOCLIMATE.

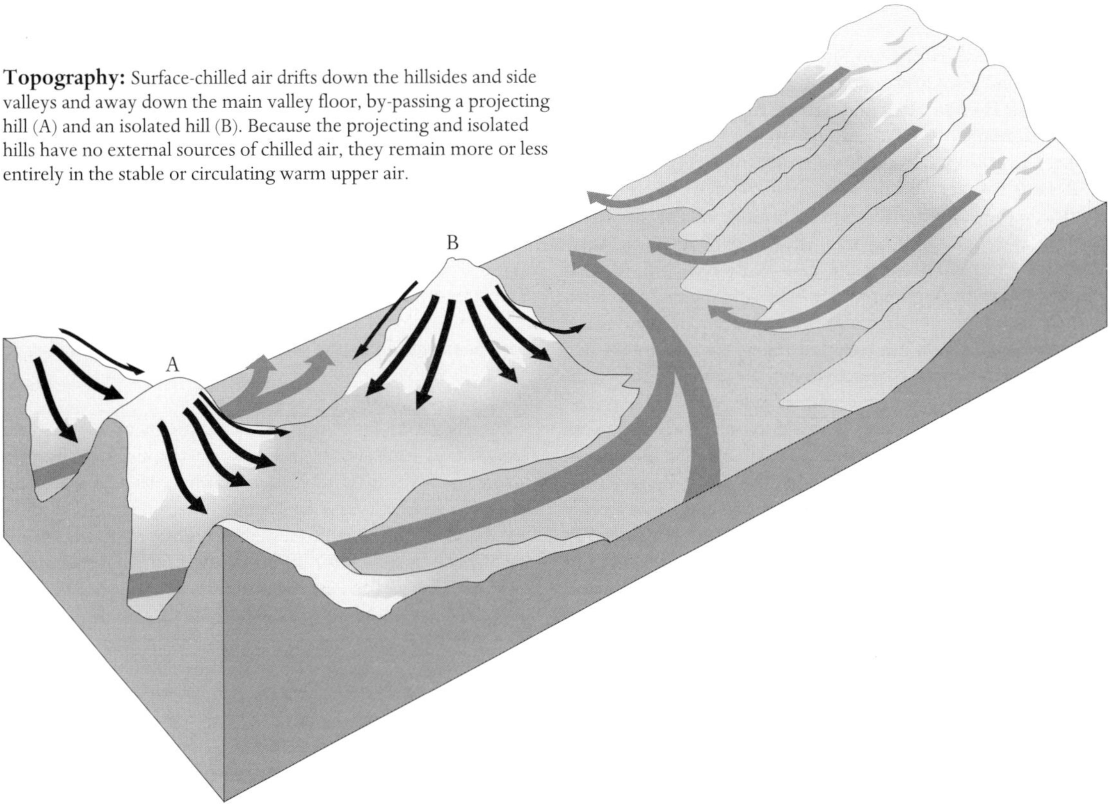

Topography: Surface-chilled air drifts down the hillsides and side valleys and away down the main valley floor, by-passing a projecting hill (A) and an isolated hill (B). Because the projecting and isolated hills have no external sources of chilled air, they remain more or less entirely in the stable or circulating warm upper air.

TOPOGRAPHY, a term describing the land surface features of any area, which can have considerable implications for local climate and therefore for viticulture. Geiger gives the most comprehensive general account of topographic effects on local climate. Some suggested detailed adjustments to temperature records, to allow for actual topographic features of vineyard sites, are listed under MESOCLIMATE. Topographic elements having the most influence on the climate are local ELEVATION or altitude; slope; the relative isolation of hills; aspect; and proximity to water masses such as oceans, lakes, and rivers.

1. *Local elevation or altitude* Other things being equal, temperature falls by about 0.6 °C/1.1 °F per 100 m/330 ft greater altitude.

2. *Slope* At night, air is chilled by direct contact with a land surface which is rapidly losing heat by radiation. The chilled air, being denser, flows down slopes to the flat land or valleys below, and is replaced by warmer air from above the land surface. The turbulent surface air over slopes at moderate elevations is therefore usually warmer at night, and in the early morning, than that settled over the adjacent flats and valley floors. This band on a hill slope is known as its 'thermal zone', and especially in cool climates is valued for viticulture because of its enhanced ripening potential and length of frost-free period. The steeper the slope, the more pronounced is its thermal zone. See also HILLSIDE VINEYARDS.

3. *Relative isolation of hills* Thermal zones are strongest on isolated and projecting hills or mountains, because these have little or no external source of surface-chilled air. Cooled air from their own surfaces that slips away can be replaced only by totally unchilled air from above. The implications of this are discussed under CLIMATE AND WINE QUALITY; see also TERROIR. Examples of viticulturally famous isolated hills include the hill of Corton at ALOXE-CORTON in Burgundy; the Kaiserstuhl in BADEN; and, on a larger scale, the Montagne de Reims in CHAMPAGNE.

4. *Aspect* Slopes which face the sun through much of the day (southerly aspects in the northern hemisphere, and northerly aspects in the southern hemisphere) are the warmest, and those facing away from the sun are the coolest. The most important consequences are felt at night. The differences in soil heating during times of sun exposure directly govern warming of the vines by reradiation at other times, when temperatures are lower and therefore more limiting. Differences in average soil temperature are themselves directly influential as well, through their effect on the vine roots. Warmth and activity of the roots are important not only for nutrition of the vine, but also for growth and fruiting

through export of the growth substance CYTOKININ to the vine tops.

The climatic contrasts among aspects are greatest at high latitudes, and also early and late in the vine-growing season, these being the situations and times when the sun is furthest from the vertical. Similarly, the steeper the slope, the more aspect will affect its climate.

Easterly aspects have the advantage that they are warmed earliest in the day, when soil and air temperatures are lowest, and therefore most limiting to vine growth or ripening. Also, east-facing slopes are the most sheltered from cold, stormy winds, which throughout the world come predominantly from the west; while to the extent that they are in the lee of major hill or mountain ranges, they generally enjoy the warmest and sunniest climates of their regions, which is a clear advantage in otherwise cool, wet regions. Notable examples of this are found in the CÔTE D'OR of Burgundy, and in the RHINE valley of Germany and Alsace. The combined result is that slopes facing east to south tend to be favoured for viticulture in the northern hemisphere, and those facing east to north tend to be favoured in the southern hemisphere, especially (but not exclusively) towards the cool limit of viticulture. West-facing slopes do, however, have some compensation in that they maintain their warmth longer into the night; while in west coastal regions, they can have better exposure to afternoon sea breezes (see below).

5. Proximity to oceans, lakes, and rivers Water absorbs and stores large quantities of heat, with relatively little change in temperature because of the depth to which the heat penetrates, together with the high specific heat of water compared with rocks or dry soil. Its resulting temperature inertia greatly modifies the temperature regimes of adjacent land, largely by the convectional circulation of air. Cool air from over the water is drawn to replace heated air rising over the land in the afternoons, while at night a reverse convection results from chilled air descending from the cold land surface and rising over the now relatively warm water. This daily alternating pattern of air circulation, when not prevailed over by stronger winds, makes the climate adjacent to water significantly more equable than it would otherwise be, in terms of both temperature and humidity. Both factors are important in CLIMATE AND WINE QUALITY. There is also a reduced incidence of spring FROSTS and WINTER FREEZE injury in regions liable to these. Examples include the Finger Lakes district of NEW YORK state and the vineyards of Ontario in CANADA.

The effects of rivers and lakes are normally confined to their immediate valleys, but maritime influences can extend considerable distances inland from coasts in the form of land and sea breezes. Notable examples of the latter occur in the BORDEAUX region of France; the NAPA Valley and SONOMA and other near-coastal regions of California; and the HUNTER VALLEY and SWAN VALLEY of Australia's east and west coasts respectively. J.G.

Geiger, R., *Das Klima der bodennahen Luftschicht* (4th edn., Brunswick, 1961), trans. as *The Climate near the Ground* (Cambridge, Mass., 1966).

TOPPING, the viticultural practice of cutting shoots to remove the younger growth. Normally 30 cm/12 in or so of shoot is cut off, which is significantly more than by the operation of TIPPING. See TRIMMING.

TOPPING UP, *ouillage* in French, the operation of refilling any sort of wooden container to replace wine lost through EVAPORATION. The container should be kept full or nearly full lest the ubiquitous ACETOBACTER use OXYGEN from the head space to start the process of transforming wine into VINEGAR. The well-run winery will have a strict regime of topping up all wooden containers on a regular basis.

A really good, tight BARREL closed with a sound, new, inert plastic BUNG loses liquid by diffusion through the barrel's staves. The HEAD SPACE created by this liquid loss is filled with water and alcohol vapours, together with traces of CARBON DIOXIDE. Since no oxygen can enter the head space, there is no danger of acetification and topping up is not necessary.

With older barrels, especially those in poor condition, in contrast, it is nearly impossible to achieve such a tight seal. Air inevitably seeps in around the bung or through poorly fitting joints between staves or tank heads. A regular topping-up regime is the only insurance against the development of vinegar in such containers.

Wine-makers differ in what they view as the ideal topping-up regime for various different wines, but modern practice is to top up at least monthly, using wine of the same provenance and, often, filling the barrel so that some wine is ejected when the BUNG is driven into the bunghole.

Depending on the amount of evaporation and the spare time available to the winery staff, topping up is done anywhere from twice a week to once every six weeks. In Bordeaux the bung is left at the top of the barrel so as to maximize AERATION of the young wine for the first six months, after which the barrel is rolled to one side so that the bung is in the so-called bung-over position. Thus the bung and bunghole region are kept moist and aeration is reduced. Many New World wineries have adopted this practice, even for Burgundian varieties, as it is much less labour intensive than constant topping up.

See also ULLAGE. A.D.W. & M.K.

TOP WORKING or **top grafting**, the viticultural operation of changing the fruiting VINE VARIETY of a mature vineyard by inserting a bud or graft of the selected variety in each vine to replace the former variety, but retaining the established root system. An array of approaches are available: CLEFT GRAFTING, NOTCH GRAFTING, CHIP BUDDING, or T-BUDDING, usually applied high on the original trunk just below the HEAD. If the operation is done well, only one season's crop is lost. The main risk is that of systemic disease spread from the

A bunch of **Sémillon** grapes at Ch d'**Yquem** in the progressive stages of **botrytis**, or **noble rot**, infection. Unaffected grapes are still hard and green before veraison (top left). Botrytis is just beginning to affect ripe grapes (top right). The lower picture shows the effects of partial (bottom left) and complete botrytis infection (bottom right) at which point the grapes are known as *grains rôtis*.

La Cité Mondiale Du Vin
Et Des Spiritueux
MARCHE PERMANENT
MART

original planting, especially VIRUS DISEASES to which different varieties and rootstocks have different tolerances. This operation was initially most common in the NEW WORLD as a response to market demand and FASHION, but is becoming increasingly prevalent in Old World regions. B.G.C.

TORBATO is a white-berried grape variety today most obviously associated with SARDINIA, where varietal dry whites are produced. Like GRENACHE Noir, known as Cannonau in Sardinia, its origins are disputed, thanks to the past extent of the kingdoms of Majorca and Aragon. Many believe it to be a Spanish variety which was imported many centuries ago. It is particularly successful around Alghero.

It was once quite widely cultivated in ROUSSILLON, where it is known as TOURBAT, or Malvoisie du Roussillon, but was abandoned before new and healthier plant material was imported from Sardinia in the 1980s.

TORGIANO, small hillside DOC zone between Perugia and Assisi in the central Italian region of UMBRIA. It has produced small quantities (less than 15,000 hl/396,000 gal in a normal year) of Umbria's finest red wine since the 1960s. The production of bottled wine is almost entirely in the hands of the LUNGAROTTI family, whose efforts have demonstrated that the SANGIOVESE vine can yield important results outside TUSCANY, results which have equalled those of CHIANTI CLASSICO, albeit in a completely different style. A significant amount of CANAIOLO grapes are used in the blend, but more important yet is the wine-making philosophy which emphasized a relatively brief period of CASK AGEING in large oval casks until the mid 1970s, and some BARREL MATURATION thereafter, followed by a lengthy period of BOTTLE AGEING—up to 10 years for the RISERVA. The house philosophy resulted in stellar wines in 1975 and 1979, although it is still too early to judge whether the same quality level has been maintained in the 1980s. D.T.

TORNA VIAGEM, literally means 'round trip' in Portuguese and is occasionally found on labels of ancient SETÚBAL which have been subjected to lengthy sea voyages for ageing purposes. This is the equivalent of the *vinho da roda* of MADEIRA.

TORO, Spanish red wine zone in CASTILE-LEÓN (see map on p. 907) whose reputation, like that of so many emerging wine regions in north and central Spain, now rests on one producer (although its wines were famous within Spain in medieval times). Bodegas Fariña (formerly Bodegas Porto) have, with their Colegiata label, almost single-handedly raised the profile of this wild and remote zone spanning the Duero valley east of Zamora since it was accorded DO status in 1987. At an ALTITUDE of between 600 and 750 m/2,000–2,800 ft, growing conditions are severe. The dry, stony soils can support cereals or vines. The region's principal grape variety, Tinto de Toro, is a variant of Rioja's TEMPRANILLO which has adapted to the climatic extremes of this part of Spain. The grapes need careful handling. Left to their own devices, they will easily ripen to a POTENTIAL ALCOHOL level of 16 per cent. Local regulations permit a maximum ALCOHOLIC STRENGTH of 15 per cent but the best wines usually have a strength of around 13.5 per cent. Although they are permitted under DO regulations, Toro produces few whites or rosés. So far the region has successfully staked its reputation on taming its powerful reds. R.J.M.

TORONTEL. The Chilean name for the aromatic white grape variety TORRONTÉS.

TORRES, MIGUEL SA, is Spain's largest family-owned producer of wine and Spanish BRANDY. The Torres family owns more than 900 ha/2,200 acres of vineyards in PENEDÈS in north east Spain, as well as properties in Chile and California.

The present company was founded in 1870 with the fruits of a chance investment by Jaime Torres in a Cuban oil company. A winery was established at Vilafranca del Penedès near Barcelona and its produce was shipped to Cuba in a fleet also belonging to Torres, whose heir was his nephew Juan. Juan expanded the business within Spain quite considerably and left a thriving family business to his son Miguel in 1932. After confiscation, disruption, and even winery destruction during the Spanish Civil War, Miguel rebuilt the business and as early as the 1950s decided to concentrate on selling wine in bottle rather than in bulk.

Perhaps the most significant development in the history of Torres came in 1959 when Miguel's son Miguel A. Torres went to study in DIJON. This rapidly resulted in experimental plantings of vine varieties imported from France and Germany such as Cabernet Sauvignon, Chardonnay, Riesling, Gewürztraminer, and Sauvignon Blanc. Torres also introduced vine TRELLIS SYSTEMS, a novelty then. A modern laboratory was established, temperature-controlled stainless steel fermentation vessels were installed, and red wines were bottled after just 18 months' BARREL MATURATION in cool cellars hewn out of the hillside. All of these techniques, and a host of other innovations, were then quite unknown elsewhere in Spain.

Vindication of Miguel A. Torres's achievements came in 1979, when, in some well-publicized 'wine olympics' organized by the French gastronomic magazine *Gault-Millau*, Torres Gran Coronas Black Label 1970 was voted winner of the top Cabernet class. In 1982/3 he spent a sabbatical year at MONTPELLIER, and has introduced higher VINE DENSITIES, increasingly ORGANIC methods, and MECHANICAL PRUNING. About a third of all Spanish wine produced by Torres is exported, notably to Sweden, Denmark, and the USA.

On the death of his father in 1991, Miguel A. Torres became president of the company with particular responsibilities for wine-making. He is also one of Spain's most prolific wine writers, and runs the 220-ha estate near Curico in CHILE which he established in 1978. His sister Marimar is a cookery writer

Bordeaux's Cîté Mondial du Vin, a commercial centre built in the late 1980s symbolizing the city's commitment to wine, and the decade.

The **Torres** family in the early 1990s (right to left): California-based Marimar, Miguel, and Juan-María, with their mother Doña Margarita.

based in San Francisco and manages a 56-ha vineyard in Sonoma.

TORRES VEDRAS, an IPR in western Portugal. See OESTE for more details.

TORRONTÉS, and **Torontés**, **Torontel**, white grape variety or varieties gaining increasing recognition in the Spanish-speaking world.

Torrontés is the name of a distinctively flavoured indigenous variety in GALICIA in north west Spain that is particularly common in the white wines of RIBEIRO. Within Spain the variety is occasionally found around Cordoba.

Much more important, however, are several white grape varieties known as Torrontés in ARGENTINA, where they were planted on a total of nearly 16,000 ha/39,500 acres in 1990. Although there was considerable emigration from Galicia to Argentina, no definite relationship between Spanish and Argentine Torrontés has been established. Some regard Torrontés as the Argentinian white wine variety with the greatest potential. Carefully vinified, Torrontés can produce wines that are light in body, high in acidity, and intriguingly aromatic in a way reminiscent of but not identical to MUSCAT, although much is also used for blending. The variety seems particularly well adapted to the arid growing conditions of Argentina, where its high natural acidity and assertive flavour distinguish it respectively from the PEDRO GIMÉNEZ and UGNI BLANC which still cover a greater area of vineyard.

Torrontés Riojano is the most common Argentine sub-variety and takes its name from the northern province of La Rioja, where it is by far the most planted single vine variety. **Torrontés Sanjuanino** is more commonly associated with the province of San Juan in Argentina and is rather less widely planted. It is less aromatic, and has bigger berries and more compact clusters. In Chile it is known as MOSCATEL DE AUSTRIA. Argentine vineyard statistics also distinguish the relatively rare **Torrontés Mendocino**, sometimes called **Torontés Mendozino**, which is actually most common in Río Negro province in the south and lacks Muscat aroma.

There are also several hundred hectares of a variety known as **Torontel** in CHILE.

TOSCANA, important central Italian region known in English as TUSCANY.

TOTAL ACIDITY, TA, or **titratable acidity**, measure of the total ACIDITY, both FIXED ACIDS and VOLATILE ACIDS, present in grape juice or wine. With ALCOHOLIC STRENGTH and RESIDUAL SUGAR, total acidity is one of the most common wine measurements involved in any wine ANALYSIS.

It is obtained by a laboratory process called titration, in which very small additions of an alkali of known strength are made to a measured quantity of the grape juice or wine until the amount of added alkali just equals the amount of acids in the sample. The value of these total acids can be calculated and expressed as grams of any number of different acids per litre of juice or wine. By tradition, different wine regions have chosen to express total acidity variously as TARTARIC ACID or sulphuric acid, or simply as the amount of acidic hydrogen ions (see PH which measures the concentration of active, rather than total, acidity) per litre.

In France and much of the rest of Europe, for example, it has become nearly standard to measure acids as if they were all sulphuric, even though the amount of this compound in grapes and wine is minuscule. In Germany, on the other hand, rather than choose a particular acid for reporting purposes, the measurement is often in milligram of hydrogen ion per litre. In the United States, Italy, South Africa, Australia, New Zealand, and United Kingdom meanwhile, total acidity is reported as if all acids were tartaric (and, as if the situation were not complicated enough already, sometimes titrated to an end point not of pH 7, but of pH 8.2). The total acidity of a young red bordeaux, for example, might be reported as 6.5 g/l of tartaric acid in Australia, 3.9 g/l of sulphuric acid in France, or 87 mg of hydrogen ions per l in Germany, even though the the wine in fact contains a complicated mixture of many different ACIDS.

The total acidity of wines expressed as tartaric acid normally varies between about 4.5 g/l (the minimum permitted within the EUROPEAN UNION although some hot climate wines may be less acid than this) and 8 g/l for wines made from underripe grapes or naturally high-acid grape varieties. The total acidity of ripe grape juice or must should ideally be in the general range of 7 to 10 g/l expressed as tartaric acid, although it may in practice be between 3 and 16 g/l. (Some acid is always lost during wine-making, as a result of MALOLACTIC FERMENTATION and cold STABILIZATION, so one must start with a higher acidity than the final one desired.)

A.D.W.

TOTAL DRY EXTRACT, or TDE. See EXTRACT.

TOUL, CÔTES DE, in the far north east of France, remains, with the even more northerly French wine region on the MOSELLE, as a reminder of what was once a flourishing Lorraine wine industry. It was subsequently marginalized by industrialization, injudicious replanting after PHYLLOXERA, the First World War, and the delimitation of the nearby CHAMPAGNE region which had once drawn wine from the region. Today Gamay is the most planted vine variety and is the usual ingredient in the local pale pink speciality VIN GRIS and such Pinot Noir as remains is reserved for Toul's relatively light reds. AUXERROIS is the most successful variety for dry whites.

George, R., *French Country Wines* (London, 1990).

TOURAINE, the most important Loire region centred on the town of Tours. This is 'the garden of France', and Loire châteaux country *par excellence*, a series of playgrounds for France's pre-revolutionary aristocrats, and now the Parisian weekender's rural paradise. The local TUFFEAU was quarried extensively to build these and more distant châteaux, leaving caves ideal for wine-making and wine maturation.

Touraine's most famous wines are the still red wines from the individual appellations of BOURGUEIL, CHINON, and St-Nicolas-de-Bourgueil and its still and sparkling, dry to sweet whites from VOUVRAY and MONTLOUIS.

Wines called simply Touraine come from a much larger zone, incorporating about 3,000 ha/7,400 acres of red grape vineyards and 2,500 ha of light-berried vines, that extends from SAUMUR in the west as far as the city of Blois in the east, encompassing very varied soils which may include clay, sand, tuffeau, and gravel. Viticulture is concentrated on the steep banks of the Loire and its tributary the Cher east of Tours. Cereals predominate on the cooler soils of the plateaux between river valleys. The climate of the region also shows considerable variation, with that of the most eastern vineyards being distinctly CONTINENTAL and affected by seriously cold winters, while vineyards at the western extreme are tempered by the influence of the Atlantic.

If soil and climate vary considerably throughout Touraine, there is an enormous range of grape varieties too. For all its proximity to Paris and the INAO headquarters, Touraine presents the APPELLATION CONTRÔLÉE authorities with their most severe test in their avowed aim to remove all VARIETAL names from labels of AC wines. White Touraine, for example, may be made from any combination of Chenin Blanc, Arbois, Sauvignon Blanc, and Chardonnay grapes, so long as Chardonnay constitutes no more than 20 per cent of the blend. A wine labelled Sauvignon de Touraine offers a very much clearer proposition to the potential buyer than one labelled simply Touraine.

Touraine Rouge, made in about the same quantity as Touraine Blanc, may be made from an even less specific blend, incorporating any or all of Cabernet Franc, Cabernet Sauvignon, Cot (Malbec), Pinot Noir, Meunier, Pinot Gris, Gamay, Pineau d'Aunis, and Grolleau.

In very general terms, Sauvignon and Gamay tend to be grown in the far east of the region, and are, respectively, the most common white and red varieties used for the Touraine appellation. From a conscientious producer, white Touraine can provide a less expensive alternative to the Loire's more famous Sauvignons produced in appellations such as SANCERRE and POUILLY-FUMÉ. Red Touraine is usually a distinctly leaner variant on the BEAUJOLAIS theme, however, although the relationship has been used to develop a Touraine PRIMEUR, and the adoption of SEMI-CARBONIC MACERATION has improved quality. Some producers label more substantial blended reds, made from Gamay, Cabernet, and Cot, Touraine Tradition, although the appellation Touraine-Villages has been proposed instead. Some white and red Touraine is, confusingly, made in quite a different style, however, most commonly but not necessarily from Chenin Blanc and Cabernet Franc grapes.

Such is Touraine's AMPELOGRAPHIC diversity that in the late 1980s, Arbois, for example, was still the third most planted variety in the Loir-et-Cher *département* which produces the bulk of generic Touraine, while there were also several hundred hectares of Cabernet Franc, Chenin Blanc, and Pineau d'Aunis.

An important commercial force in the region, with an admirable concern for quality, is the well-equipped Confrérie des Vignerons d'Oisly et Thésée, an association of some of the region's more ambitious vine-growers formed in 1961.

Small quantities of **Touraine Mousseux** (about a tenth as much as Saumur Mousseux, for example) and large quantities of **Touraine Primeur** (see PRIMEUR) are made but the region also has three subappellations in areas allowed to add their name to that of Touraine.

From its 200 ha/490 acres of vines on both banks of the Loire close to the famous château of Amboise, **Touraine-Amboise** produces mainly red wines from Gamay, Cabernet Franc, and Cot, the last of which can yield some wines with sufficient stuffing to be worth ageing. The appellation's white wines, dry to medium dry depending on the year, are made exclusively from the long lived Chenin Blanc.

Touraine-Azay-le-Rideau comprises fewer than 50 ha of vineyard on both banks of the Indre, south of the Loire between Tours and Chinon on soil that is clearly superior to that of the general Touraine appellation. It produces roughly equal quantities of either crisp whites from Chenin Blanc or light rosés mainly from Grolleau, which can be considerably more sprightly than the Rosé d'Anjou with which the variety is more readily associated.

Touraine-Mesland is the largest of these subappellations, with about 200 ha on a sand and gravel plateau immediately above the right bank of the Loire between Amboise and Blois. Gamay plus some Cabernet Franc and Cot is responsible for durable reds and rosés, and Chenin Blanc, together with some Chardonnay and Sauvignon, for dry whites. Touraine-Mesland's pale pink VIN GRIS enjoys a certain reputation.

See also LOIRE, and map on pp. 576–7.

TOURBAT is the ROUSSILLON name for Sardinia's white grape variety TORBATO. It is alternatively known as Malvoisie du Roussillon and is one of the many varieties allowed into the several VINS DOUX NATURELS of the region and Côtes du Roussillon whites.

TOURIGA is used as an Australian synonym for TOURIGA NACIONAL, but the Touriga of California is probably TOURIGA FRANCESA.

TOURIGA FRANCESA, robust and fine vine variety for red port that is widely grown in Portugal's DOURO valley and the TRÁS-OS-MONTES wine region. It is classified as one of the best port varieties, although the wine it produces is not as concentrated as that of TOURIGA NACIONAL. Its wines are notable for their perfume and persistent fruit. It should not be confused with the much less distinguished Portuguese variety TINTA FRANCISCA.

TOURIGA NACIONAL, the most revered vine variety for port, producing small quantities of very small berries in the DOURO valley and, increasingly, the Portuguese DÃO region which result in deep coloured, very tannic, concentrated wines. The vine is vigorous and robust but may produce just 300 g/10 oz of fruit per vine. Considerable work has been done on CLONAL SELECTION of the variety so that newer cuttings are slightly more productive and average sugar levels even higher. Touriga Nacional should constitute at least 20 per cent of all red Dão, although the wine's suitability as a vintage port ingredient is more obvious than as a red table wine. The variety is also planted to a limited extent in Australia, where it is used to add finesse to fortified wines.

TOURISM. Wine-related tourism has become increasingly important. For many centuries not even wine merchants travelled, but today many members of the general public deliberately make forays to explore a wine region or regions. This is partly a reflection of the increased interest in both wine and foreign travel generally, but also because most wine regions and many producers' premises are attractive places. VINEYARDS tend to be aesthetically pleasing in any case, and the sort of climate in which wine is generally produced is agreeable during most of the year. Getting to grips with this specialist form of agriculture combines urban dwellers' need to commune with nature with acquiring privileged, and generally admired, specialist knowledge. And then there is the possibility of TASTING, and buying wines direct from the source, which may involve keen prices and/or acquiring rarities.

Wine tourism is certainly not new to Germany. The RHINE has long welcomed tourists, who are encouraged to travel by steamer and stop at wine villages *en route*, and the MOSEL valley is surely one of the most photographed in the world. German tourists, on the other hand, have long plundered the Weinstuben of ALSACE and represent an important market for the region's wines.

In France, wine tourism was often accidental. Northern Europeans heading for the sun for decades travelled straight through BURGUNDY and the northern RHÔNE and could hardly fail to notice vineyards and the odd invitation 'Dégustation-Vente' (tasting-sale). (And it is true that a tasting almost invariably leads to a sale.) Wine producers in the LOIRE have long profited from their location in the midst of châteaux country, and within an easy Friday night's drive of Paris.

BORDEAUX has been one of the last important French wine regions to realize its potential for wine tourism. It was not until the late 1980s that the MÉDOC, the most famous cluster of top wine properties in the world, had a hotel and more than one restaurant suitable for international visitors. Alexis LICHINE was mocked for being virtually the only CLASSED GROWTH proprietor openly to welcome visitors.

Much of southern Europe is simply too hot, and too far from suitable resorts, to make wine tourism comfortable and feasible, but in various NEW WORLD wine regions, tourism has become an important aspect of business. Prominent examples here include NAPA and SONOMA, now almost part and parcel of the San Francisco tourist experience; SOUTH AFRICAN vineyards within easy reach of Cape Town; the HUNTER VALLEY for visitors to and residents of Sydney; and even the vineyards of ENGLAND.

Some tour operators and travel agents specialize in wine tourism, and the number of wine regions without their own special wine route or winery trail is decreasing rapidly.

TRACTOR, the most common vineyard machine. Tractor dimensions have had a significant impact on vineyard design. In many parts of Europe where tractors replaced horses, tractor designers obliged by creating either narrow or row-straddling, tractors (known in France as *tracteurs-enjambeurs*). The narrowest vineyard tractors are not much wider than their drivers, about 80 cm / 31 in. In the New World, however, vineyards were changed to accommodate the tractors, which included row spacings of 3 to 4 m to allow early tractor models between the rows.

The introduction of tractors and other forms of MECHANIZATION to viticulture has had profound economic and sociological effects. Less LABOUR was required and encouraged the population drift to the cities. R.E.S.

TRADE, WINE. Wine is better known for its sociability than its profitability. What is needed to make a small fortune in the wine business is said to be a large fortune. The wine trade is considerably more amusing, however, than many others. It routinely involves immersion in an often delicious product, travel to some of the more beautiful corners of the world (see TOURISM), and provides widely admired expertise.

One of the attractions of the wine trade is the people. It has for long attracted a wide range of individualists who, if they were not interesting and amusing before they or their visitors have tasted their wares, seem so afterwards. Producers and merchants alike tend to be generous, and to appreciate the fact that it is difficult to sell or buy wine without tasting and sharing it.

Apprenticeship is probably the easiest route into the wine trade, although some form of specialist EDUCATIONAL qualification can help too. The general areas in which full-time employment may be found include vineyard management, wine-making and quality control, sales and marketing, wholesaling, retailing, and, the job with potentially the most power and perks, buying.

See also wine MERCHANTS.

Tradition, as evinced by the old wooden ovals still treasured for white wine fermentation by producers such as Bürklin-Wolf in Germany's Pfalz.

TRADITION, an extremely important ingredient in viticulture and wine-making in many Old World regions, particularly those whose wines have, over the centuries, won devotees and esteem. A significant proportion of older small-scale producers in regions such as Burgundy and the Rhône, for example, do things in the vineyard and cellar precisely because their fathers did, even if their own children are likely to have been exposed to SCIENCE through some sort of formal training. These graduates of ACADEME may understand the reasons for some of these supposedly traditonal methods better than their parents, but they do not necessarily change them.

Some peasant wine-growers, for example, will perform operations such as RACKING or BOTTLING only when the moon is in a certain phase, or when the wind is, or is not, blowing from a certain direction. Superstition plays a very small part in making wine, and these traditions are likely to have evolved for a reason, often one that is eventually explained by science.

TRADITIONAL METHOD, alternative term for the champagne method of SPARKLING WINE-MAKING.

TRAINING in a wine context usually means VINE TRAINING. See also TRAINING SYSTEMS.

TRAINING SYSTEMS, methods of VINE TRAINING, which vary considerably around the world. Since the grapevine is a true VINE, and is not self-supporting like a tree, man has devised innumerable training systems for vines over the millennia of cultivation. The viticulturist's choice of training system will be affected by the cost of the system, the availability of any materials required, the availability of the skilled LABOUR required to install and manage it, vine VIGOUR, VINE VARIETY, MECHANIZATION requirements, and, in many instances, knowledge of alternative systems. In many places in the world, especially the OLD WORLD, little thought is given to using any but the region's traditional system.

A basic difference in training systems about which the casual observer may wonder is why some vineyards have trellis systems with wires, and others not. While self-supporting GOBELET vines are common in southern France, in many countries such vineyards are considered old-fashioned, and WIRES from which to suspend foliage are used instead. The control of vine VIGOUR and VINE DISEASES are the principal reasons for adopting more elaborate training systems. If vines were planted to the gobelet system in an area of summer rainfall such as northern France, the vines could be very prone to FUNGAL DISEASES because the leaves and fruit would be in a shaded, humid environment. It would also be difficult to gain access to the vineyard, as the shoots would cover the ground. Lifting the foliage up and containing it between wires allows TRIMMING of the ends and LEAF REMOVAL for better fruit exposure. Both tractor access to the vineyard and airflow within it are also improved.

Confusion between the terms training systems, TRELLIS SYSTEMS, and PRUNING is widespread. In fact they are three distinct, if closely related, entities. The vine is pruned in winter as a means of training the framework and buds into an appropriate position to be supported by the trellis system. In other words, the training system dictates to a certain extent which trellis system and method of pruning are used. Vines are trained to fit the physical trellis system, which is normally a man-made structure designed to support the vine's framework. Those training systems which involve trellises often incorporate the word trellis into their name.

A vine-training system should aim to maximize yield and quality, and to facilitate cultural operations such as spraying, cultivation, harvesting, and pruning. As the degree of mechanization increases, so does the need for the vineyard to be uniform and orderly. For example, mechanical leaf removal and harvesting are made easier by locating the bunches of grapes in a single zone. Similarly, mechanization of summer and winter pruning is made easier if the vine shoots and canes all point in the same direction, vertically upwards, for example. The vine framework should ideally be at a convenient height for any hand operations, neither too high nor too low. Some would argue that the fruit should be near the ground to absorb reflected heat, although this can involve back-breaking labour at HARVEST and pruning, and is extremely difficult to mechanize.

Until the 1980s it was extremely rare for any training system other than that traditional in a given region to be considered. Dr Jules GUYOT expressed similar sentiments in 1869 (see Huglin): 'Each province, each department, each canton and vineyard, are convinced that their traditional viticulture is the best, and it constitutes the last word in the art and the science of viticulture . . . The good results from one never benefit the others, and the training of the vines and the wines are abandoned to a thousand practices bizarre and narrow, resulting in complete anarchy, with logical progress impossible.' In many parts of the world, little has changed since this statement was made, although the recently developed vineyards of some NEW WORLD regions have evaluated the various systems and adopted those best suited to their requirements.

There is an almost infinite variety of vine-training systems, which is to be expected for a perennial plant like the grapevine which can be so easily trained according to the whims of every vine-grower. There are few plants whose cultivation can vary as much as between the densely planted (10,000 vines per ha / (4,000 per acre)), neatly trimmed vertical hedges of the vineyards of the Médoc and the vineyards of a few hundred vines per hectare trained up trees around agricultural fields in the Vinho Verde region of Portugal.

Vine-training systems can be classified in a number of ways. In France it is common to classify vines as low trained (*vignes basses*) or high trained (*vignes hautes*). For low vines the trunk is up to 50 cm/20 in high, but usually shorter. Such training systems are more economical, and are suited to lower-vigour vineyards. Grape RIPENING may benefit from their being closer to the ground, both HARVEST and PRUNING are much less comfortable manual operations, and vines may also be more disease prone. The many examples of low trained vines in France include the extensive southern areas of GOBELET, the CORDON DE ROYAT vines of Burgundy and Champagne, and the double GUYOT of Bordeaux.

High vines are less common in modern France but were certainly known by Roman authors (see AGRICULTURAL TREATISES). Interest in high vines was more recently rekindled by the 1950 publication of the Austrian LENZ MOSER. He recommended low-density vineyard with wide rows of trunks about 1.25 m high. Higher training does reduce FROST risk, but requires thicker and more expensive supports, although vineyard work is made easier. 'High culture' vines can be trained either cordon or Guyot. Vineyards of the New World have typically used high vine-training systems. Overhead trellises such as Italy's TENDONE are special examples of high vines.

There are other possible ways of classifying vine-training

systems, however. The cordons may be classed short, as in the 0.5 m in a closely spaced cordon de Royat, or many metres in length as for the Portuguese cruzeta (see below). An alternative classification takes account of whether the foliage is free, as for example in the gobelet vines of the Midi, or SHOOT POSITIONED or constrained into a plane, such as the vertical systems common in Alsace and Germany in which the foliage is held in place by WIRES and maintained by TRIMMING.

The vine canopies can also be classified by their plane: arbours or tendone trained vines have horizontal canopies about 2 m above the ground, while the Tatura trellis developed in Australia is inclined at 60 degrees to the ground, and most shoot positioned canopies are vertical. Some canopies have shoots all growing upwards, as in the lyre trellis, while the GENEVA DOUBLE CURTAIN (GDC) has shoots which grow downwards, and the SCOTT HENRY system has shoots trained both upwards and downwards. Vines may have a DIVIDED CANOPY in either the horizontal plane such as the GDC or LYRE trellis, or vertically as in the Scott Henry. Training systems can be simple, like the free-standing gobelet vines of the Rioja, or elaborate like the Ruakura twin two tier developed in New Zealand, which is both horizontally and vertically divided, and requires 20 wires per row to support fruit and foliage.

The following list gives brief details of some of the training systems in use around the world, including some new ones being used for deliberate CANOPY MANAGEMENT.

Alberate, an old form of vine-training system used in parts of Italy where the vines are trained on or between trees. There are local variations, such as those in Bologna, Tuscany, Veneto, and Romagna, with the common feature being that trees are used for support.

Alberello, see GOBELET.

Arbour, see TENDONE.

Arched cane, a variation on many different forms of training systems where canes are arched rather than being tied horizontally, see GUYOT. Alternative names include bow trained, *arcure* in French, Capovolto or Guyot *ad archetto* in Italy. This practice is claimed to lead to better BUDBREAK in the centre of the canes, where buds do not normally burst well. It can be considered a variation of GUYOT training.

Barra, used for monoculture in Vinho Verde whereby vines are trained in one direction along a single wire at shoulder height.

Basket training, often used for free-standing vines where canes are wound one around the other for mutual support. Common for some BUSH VINE systems which are pruned. Typically they are of low vigour.

Bush vines, see BUSH VINES and GOBELET.

Casarsa, or Casarsa Friuli, an Italian training system like the SYLVOZ, except the canes are not tied down after pruning.

Cassone padavano, a horizontally divided Italian system, pruned like the Sylvoz.

Cazenave, an Italian vine-training system which uses a modified form of Guyot pruning where short arms containing spurs and canes (five to six buds) are arranged along a horizontal CORDON. The canes are tied about vertically to a wire above. Because the pruner is able to leave so many buds per vine, this system is suited to fertile soils.

Château Thierry, a form of GUYOT training where the cane is tied in an arch to a stake beside the free-standing vine.

Cordon de Cazenave, an Italian and French system used for fertile soils, with one or more canes left on a CORDON DE ROYAT.

Cordon de Royat, see CORDON DE ROYAT.

Cordon vertical, a vertical cordon with alternating spurs to either side. Not used very commonly as growth tends to be mainly from the top buds.

Cruzeta, a system used in the VINHO VERDE area of Portugal where vines are trained to a wide cross arm about 2 m off the ground. More sophisticated than latada but less so than barra.

Duplex, a system developed in California in the 1960s with flexible cross arms to allow for machine harvesting. While the fruiting wires are horizontally divided by 1 m, the foliage was not shoot positioned to create two separate curtains as for the GENEVA DOUBLE CURTAIN. As a consequence, it is not nearly as beneficial in terms of yield, quality, and disease resistance.

Espalier, see ESPALIER.

Éventail, or fan, a French system with multiple arms, each giving rise to a spur or short cane. Originally the form used in Chablis, with the arms lying on the ground, this has been modified to the taille de Semur system, where each arm is tied to a lower wire in the one plane.

Factory roof system, commonly used for TABLE GRAPES, in South Africa and Israel, for example, where the CANOPY is trained up at an angle to meet in a gable near the row centre. This may also be called a closed, one-arm PERGOLA, and provides excellent access to the fruit for any hand work required.

Fan shaped, a training system distantly related to éventail that is used in central Europe, particularly Russia, where the vine trunks are spread out in the shape of a fan, which makes it easier to bury vines for WINTER PROTECTION. The Italian version is called ventagli.

Flachbogen, the German name for a training system like the Guyot whereby one cane is laid horizontally either side of the head, and shoots trained vertically between foliage wires. The shoots are trimmed at the top. See VERTICAL TRELLIS.

Geneva double curtain (GDC), see GENEVA DOUBLE CURTAIN.

Gobelet, see GOBELET.

Guyot, see GUYYOT.

Halbbogen, a German training system whereby the vine is pruned to one cane of about 15 buds' length, and is arched in the middle over a wire about 25 cm above the base and end of the cane. Shoots are trained each year vertically between foliage wires, and are trimmed at the top.

Hudson River umbrella, a system used in the eastern USA, where canes are arched downwards from a high head.

Isère, a training system much like Ch Thierry, where the cane is trained in a bow to a stake beside the vine.

Latada, traditional 3-m high trellis used in the Vinho Verde region for vines grown around fields of other crops.

Lenz Moser, see LENZ MOSER.

Lincoln canopy, a horizontal canopy developed at Lincoln College in New Zealand. It is like the arbour, but is at waist height and allows tractor access between rows.

Lyre, see LYRE.

MPCT, or minimal pruned cordon trained, which describes the system developed and extensively used in Australia, mainly for bulk wine production. Young vines are trained to a form of CORDON at about 1.5 m height and, apart from wrapping early cane growth on the wire, receive minimal hand work, including pruning. See MINIMAL PRUNING.

Palmette, an Italian training system, with one vine trained to four horizontal canes, one pair above the other.

Pendelbogen, the German name for the arched cane (see above) training system described above. There is a 50-cm height difference between the end of the cane and the highest point, which is considered to improve budbreak in the middle of the cane. Most of the shoots are trained vertically upright between foliage wires, and normally require trimming at the top. Pendelbogen means pendulum bow, and there are related training forms called not just Halbbogen (half bow), but also Rundbogen (round bow) and Doppelbogen (double bow). The name has also been applied to a mid height Sylvoz system in New Zealand.

Pergola, see PERGOLA.

Pyramid, an Italian training system where vine shoots are trained over a group of stakes tied together at the top, forming a pyramid.

Ramada, alternative name for latada above.

Raggi Bellussi, an Italian overhead training system suspended from above and with two vines planted together and trained in four directions. Pruned like the Sylvoz.

Raggiera or **raggi**, an Italian training system where vines are trained overhead on wires like the spokes of a wheel. Either one vine may be trained up a central stake or tree and divided into cordons, or several vines may be at the one position with each trained along a different radius.

Ruakura twin two tier trellis, a system developed at the Ruakura Research Centre in New Zealand with the canopy divided into four curtains, two above two. Well suited for high-vigour vineyards, but no mechanical harvester had been developed for it by the early 1990s.

Scott Henry, see SCOTT HENRY.

Slanting trellis. The canopy is trained along an inclined support. This trellis can be used for both table and wine grape production.

Smart-Dyson trellis, a modification of the SCOTT HENRY trellis, with curtains trained up and down from the one cordon, developed by John Dyson of California and Richard Smart of Australia.

Sylvoz, see SYLVOZ.

Tatura trellis. Developed at the Tatura Research Station in Australia and consisting of two inclined canopies at 60 degrees meeting in the middle of the row. Early studies indicated high productivity, but the system has not been used commercially for wine grapes, probably because of mechanization difficulties.

Te Kauwhata two tier. Developed at the Te Kauwhata Research Station in New Zealand this system is vertically divided, with shoots trained vertically upwards. Limited commercial use in California and New Zealand.

Tendone, see TENDONE.

Three wire trellis. Another California trellis system with a pair of fixed foliage wires above the cordon. Shoots are not positioned, and fall across these wires under their own weight.

Traverse trellis. European name for the T trellis.

T trellis. Common in Australia, where the vine is trained to two horizontal cordons about 0.5 m apart. It takes its name from the appearance of the vine trunk and cordons. Shoots are not positioned, and so the canopy is not divided. Can be machine prined and harvested, and is widely used in bulk wine-producing areas.

Tunnel, an alternative name for a form of overhead vine training where the vines are planted in two rows and trained overhead.

Two wire vertical trellis. Common terminology in California, where one wire is occupied by the cordon and the second is a fixed foliage wire. Shoots grow up and over this wire and fall under their own weight to form a bell-shaped canopy. When the vines are vigorous, the canopy is very shaded.

U, an alternative name for the LYRE trellis.

Umbrella kniffin. A system used in eastern America, where canes from a mid height head are trained over a top wire and tied below.

V, a vine-training system in the shape of the letter where shoots are trained upwards into two curtains. This form does not work as well as the lyre or U system, where the cordons are separated at the base.

Vase, another name for the GOBELET training system.

Vertical cordon, a rare training system as top buds tend to burst first, making it difficult to manage.

Vertical trellis, see VERTICAL TRELLIS.

VSP, or vertical shoot positioning, which describes a system used throughout the world where annual shoot growth is trained vertically and held in place by foliage wires. See VERTICAL TRELLIS.

Y, a vine-training system in the shape of the letter and equivalent to the V system except that the trunk of the vine forms the vertical part of the letter.

The above cannot pretend to be a comprehensive list of the multitude of training systems used world-wide, nor of all their local names, and how patterns of usage are changing, especially in the New World, but it does give some indication of the extraordinary variation in vine-training systems. The greatest complexity of training systems in the world is to be found in Italy, while those used in France tend to be slavishly regional. R.E.S.

Ambrosi, H., and Becker, H. (eds.), *Der deutsche Wein* (Munich, 1978).

Eynard, I., and Dalmasso, G., *Viticoltura moderna: manuale pratico* (Milan, 1990).
Galet, P., *Précis de viticulture* (4th edn., Montpellier, 1983).
Huglin, P., *Biologie et écologie de la vigne* (Lausanne, 1986).
Smart, R. E., and Robinson, M., *Sunlight into Wine: A Handbook for Winegrape Canopy Management* (Adelaide, 1991).
Champagnol, F., *Éléments de physiologie de la vigne et de viticulture générale* (St-Gely-du-Fesc, 1984).
Winkler, A. J., *et al.*, *General Viticulture* (2nd edn., Berkeley, Calif., 1974).

TRAJADURA, white grape variety used to add body and alcohol to Portugal's VINHO VERDE. It is known as TREIXADURA across the Spanish border in Galicia. It is often blended with LOUREIRO.

TRAMINER, the less aromatic, paler-skinned progenitor of the pink-skinned white wine grape variety GEWÜRZTRAMINER. It has been grown, for example, in Moravia in what was CZECHOSLOVAKIA, where it is also known as Prinç. The name derives from the town of Tramin, or Termeno, in the ALTO ADIGE. In countries as different as Germany, Italy, Austria, Romania, much of the CIS, and Australia, however, Traminer is also used as a synonym for Gewürztraminer, under which name more details can be found.

TRANSFER METHOD, SPARKLING WINE-MAKING process involving provoking a second fermentation in bottle and then transferring its contents into a tank where the wine is separated from the deposit.

TRANSLOCATION, plant physiological process whereby soluble materials such as dissolved salts, organic materials, and growth substances are moved around the vine in the PHLOEM. The phloem tissue is in the outer part of the trunk or stems, and so can be disrupted by CINCTURING. Sucrose is the principal form in which CARBOHYDRATES are moved, and the phloem sap also contains amino acids and organic acids, inorganic nutrients, plant hormones and alkaloids. Examples of translocation are the movement of inorganic nutrients absorbed from the soils by the root system to various organs of the plant where some may be incorporated into organic molecules; and finally the movement of products of PHOTOSYNTHESIS away from the leaves. From the wine point of view, the translocation of SUCROSE, MALIC ACID, TARTARIC ACID, elements, and compounds containing NITROGEN during RIPENING are crucial to the chemical composition of grapes, and thus to eventual wine quality.

The principal movement of the vine's foodstuffs is downward, yet for most of the season there is also some upward movement. Movement is invariably towards points of need such as growing shoot tips for the early part of the season, flowers, then developing berries, and also towards the permanent vine parts such as trunks and roots for the accumulation of reserves later in the season. HORMONES such as auxins, cytokinins, and gibberellins are shown to play an important role in regulating translocation. The vine is capable of translocating products over long distances, and so even though the shoot supporting a bunch may be shaded, the grapes will still ripen depending on materials imported from other parts of the vine. R.E.S.

TRANSPIRATION, physiological process whereby water taken up from a vine's roots is evaporated through the leaves, important in preventing the vine from overheating in sunny weather. Water and dissolved elements move in the so-called transpiration stream through the woody part of the vine called the XYLEM. The xylem fluid also contains relatively large amounts of amino acids, especially glutamine, organic acids, especially malic, and small amounts of sugars. Total water loss from a vineyard is called evapotranspiration, and this includes transpiration from the vines and also any weeds or cover crop present, plus EVAPORATION from the soil surface.

Transpiration is an energy-driven process, with the energy being provided by leaves absorbing sunlight. Water vapour passes from the leaf to the atmosphere via small pores on the underside called STOMATA. Energy is required to provide the latent heat of evaporation for the phase change from liquid to gas, which takes place in the cavity below the stomata. The cell walls of the substomatal cavity are wet from a long column of water extending to the roots. Provided the vine is well supplied with water, leaves facing the sun will be only 2–3 °C warmer than the air, while if water supply is limited then this figure can exceed 10 °C (18 °F) and the vine will suffer both HEAT STRESS and WATER STRESS.

Transpiration is controlled by both atmospheric and plant factors. High transpiration rates are due to weather patterns of low humidity, and high sunshine, temperature, and wind speed. Typically, during the day as temperature rises, humidity falls, and so transpiration is fastest in the early afternoon. As soils dry, the risk of water stress increases and so, by partially closing stomata, the vine is able to regulate its water status to some extent. However, as stomata close then PHOTOSYNTHESIS stops, as carbon dioxide entry into the leaf is inhibited.

Rates of transpiration vary with the weather and growth stage of the vineyard. Transpiration can be measured as an equivalent depth of water over the vineyard. For a vineyard in full leaf in the middle of the season, daily evapotranspiration rates may be as high as or 40,000 l/ha for a hot, dry, and sunny climate. For a vineyard planted with 2,000 vines per ha, this rate is equivalent to 20 l (4.4 gal) per vine per day. The amount of water transpired is very high relative to both the vine's growth overall and the fruit produced. For example, measurements cited by Smart and Coombe show 5,000 g and 80 g of water respectively for each gram of plant dry weight and gram of fruit produced. R.E.S.

Champagnol, F., *Éléments de physiologie de la vigne et de viticulture générale* (St-Gely-du-Fesc, 1984).
Smart, R. E., and Coombe, B. G., 'Water relations of vines', in T. T. Kozlowski (ed.), *Water Deficits and Plant Growth*, vii (New York, 1983).
Winkler, A. J., *et al.*, *General Viticulture* (2nd edn., Berkeley, Calif., 1974).

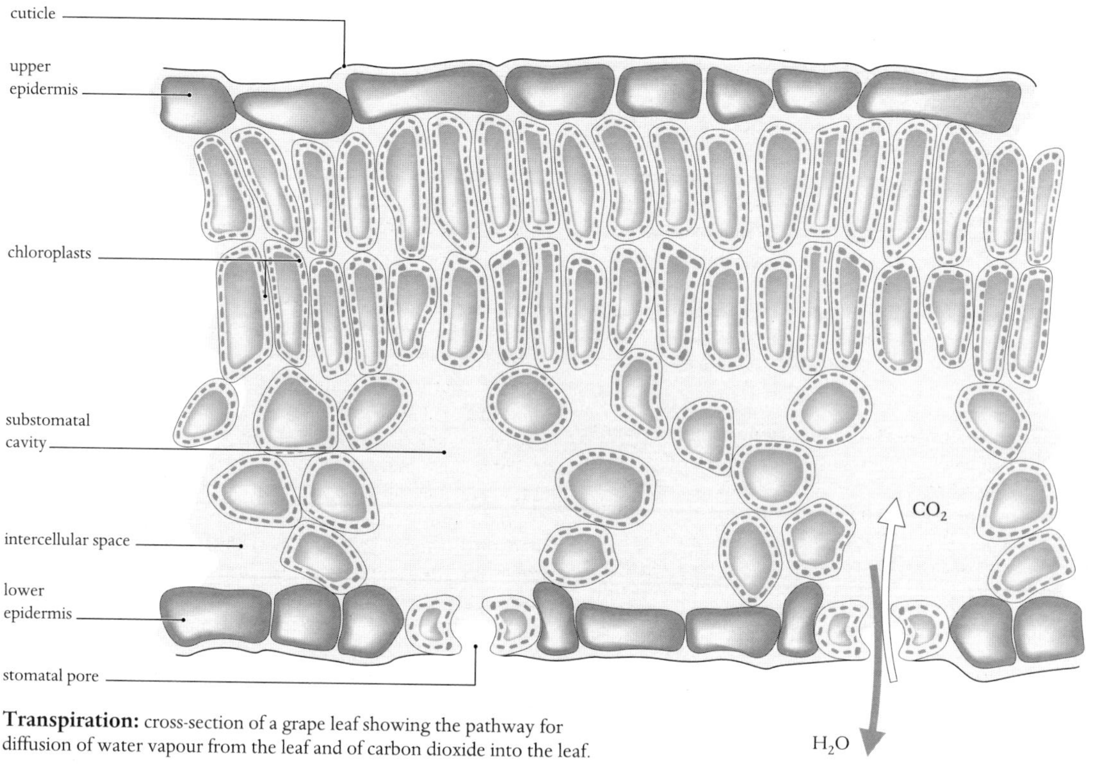

Transpiration: cross-section of a grape leaf showing the pathway for diffusion of water vapour from the leaf and of carbon dioxide into the leaf.

TRANSPORT OF WINE has changed considerably over the ages but a wide variety of different methods, from tanker to a bottle sent by mail, are still used.

Ancient history

Wine was transported in bulk in antiquity in a variety of ways. There are numerous representations throughout the classical period of huge wineskins loaded on the backs of two- or four-wheeled carts for movement overland. BARRELS also appear loaded on carts, but water-borne transport had a great advantage in antiquity because of the inefficency of the harnesses used on animals. For most of the Mediterranean area wine was carried in large AMPHORAE, which were loaded in the holds of ships. The pottery jars required considerable packing (heather, straw, etc.) to cushion them against breakages. They could be transferred to smaller vessels for transport up inland waterways. A recent discovery has been of wrecks carrying dolia (see DOLIUM), as a kind of tanker for the bulk transport of wine. Barrels were widely used in northern Europe (see CELTS) and later in the Mediterranean, although the amphora tradition died out completely only in the medieval period.

J.J.P.

Moulin, M. M., 'Le Transport du raisin ou du vin par la route à l'époque romaine en Gaule et dans les provinces voisines', in R. Chevallier, *et al.*, *Archéologie de la vigne et du vin* (Paris, 1990).

Peacock, D. P. S., and Williams, D. F., *Amphorae and the Roman Economy* (London, 1986).

Modern transport

In the Middle Ages RIVERS played an important role in transporting wine, and only those wine regions with access to good water transport (by sea and/or river) were likely to develop much trade. In the 19th and early 20th centuries, the advent of a RAILWAY system transformed wine regions as dissimilar as the LANGUEDOC-ROUSSILLON, Mendoza, RIOJA, and CHIANTI. Today wine is generally transported by road and sea (although, at the height of Beaujolais Nouveau's popularity in the early 1980s, planes, parachutes, and vintage cars were just some of the means used to race that particular wine to the consumer, and to the attention of newspaper editors).

For centuries the transport of wine meant BULK TRANSPORT, and the most common container used for transporting wine was the barrel. SHERRY, for example, was still shipped to British bottlers in its special casks, or BUTTS, until well into the 20th century (when the empty butts were used for Scotch whisky maturation). In the latter half of the 20th century, however, container shipment in bulk tankers became the norm, although, as an increasing proportion of wine is bottled not just in its country or region of origin but actually at the winery, the most common container for transport today is probably the BOTTLE. Barrels may be an awkward shape, but bottles are breakable, and pilferage of bottled wine is considerably easier than stealing BULK WINE. Wine transport across national frontiers or state lines can involve the additional problems associated with any product subject to TAXATION.

From the consumer's point of view, the most important aspect of the transport of wine is TEMPERATURE. If wine that has not been subject to considerable STABILIZATION, which includes most fine wine, is exposed to high temperatures, it may well deterioriate considerably. Conscientious producers try to avoid shipping wine in high summer, while scrupulous wholesalers insist that insulated containers are used for shipments in hot weather and/or through the TROPICS.

TRÁS-OS-MONTES, meaning 'behind the mountains', region of PORTUGAL in the far north east corner locked in by high mountains on one side and the Spanish frontier on the other (see map on p. 750). The inhabitants of Trás-os-Montes have always prided themselves on their independence but since the 1960s the economy has suffered as local people have been forced to leave this remote agricultural region to find profitable work in the coastal cities or abroad. The mountains which isolate Trás-os-Montes from the rest of Portugal cast a rain shadow over the region which becomes progressively more arid towards Spain. The climatic extremes and shallow granite-based soils make cultivation difficult, although farmers have been helped considerably by funds from the European Union and the World Bank. Wine is an important commodity in Trás-os-Montes, which includes the northern half of the PORT wine region. The high vineyards here, north of the DOURO valley, also supply wine for MATEUS Rosé and a number of imitative brands. Three Indicação de Proveniencia Regulamentada (IPR) regions have recently been designated in Trás-os-Montes: Chaves in the cooler west makes light red and white wines and includes the *vinhos dos mortos* (wines of the dead) of Boticas, so called because the bottles are buried in the ground for AGEING; Valpaços (probably the best of the three IPRs); and Planalto-Mirandes on the high plains above the Douro, which produces big alcoholic reds. R.J.M.

TREBBIANO, most common name for the undistinguished Ugni Blanc white grape variety in Italy, where it is by far the most planted white grape variety. The word Trebbiano in a wine name almost invariably signals something light, white, crisp, and uninspiring. This gold-, even amber-berried grape variety is so prolific, and so much planted in both France and Italy, the world's two major wine-producing countries, that it probably produces more wine than any other vine variety in the world—even though Spain's AIRÉN and Garnacha/GRENACHE cover a larger total vineyard area. Trebbiano in its many forms covers a greater area of vineyard even than SANGIOVESE. It is cited in more DOC regulations than any other single variety (about 80) and may well account for more than a third of Italy's entire DOC white wine production.

In France, where it found its way as a result of the Mediterranean trade that flourished between Italian and French ports during the 14th century, the variety is the country's most important white vine. See under its most common French name UGNI BLANC for details of Trebbiano in France.

Ugni Blanc's most common use, as base wine for brandy, provides a clue to the character of the wine produced by Trebbiano. It is, like most copiously produced wines, low in extract and character, relatively low in alcohol, but usefully high in acidity. This exceptionally vigorous vine buds late, thereby avoiding most spring frost damage, which underscores its high yields, which can easily reach 150 hl/ha (8.5 tons/acre). It has good resistance to POWDERY MILDEW and GREY ROT but can succumb to DOWNY MILDEW. Because it ripens relatively late, often as late as October in parts of Italy, there is a natural geographical limit on its cultivation but in areas such as Charentes it is simply picked before being fully ripe, as indeed it is in southern Italy to maximize acidity.

There are almost as many possible histories of Trebbiano as there are identified subvarieties in Italy. Trebbiano Toscano (Tuscan) and Trebbiano Giallo (yellow) ripen rather earlier than most other Trebbiano subvarieties. PLINY mentions a *vinum trebulanum* in CAMPANIA. There is no shortage of possible geographical references, with many towns and villages incorporating words like Trebbiano and the river Trebbia in EMILIA-ROMAGNA providing another possible source. The Bolognese agronomist PETRUS DE CRESCENTIIS certainly described the vine Trebbiano as early as 1303.

Today Trebbiano is planted all over Italy (with the exception of the cool far north), to the extent that it is likely that the great majority of basic *vino bianco* will contain at least some of the variety, if only to add acidity and volume. Its stronghold, however, is central Italy. **Trebbiano Toscano**, covering almost 60,000 ha/148,000 acres, was Italy's third most planted vine variety in 1990, while there were more than 20,000 ha of **Trebbiano Romagnolo**, nearly 12,000 ha of **Trebbiano d'Abruzzo**, nearly 5,000 ha of **Trebbiano Giallo**, and more than 2,000 ha of **Trebbiano di Soave**.

TREBBIANO DI ROMAGNA dominates white wine production in Emilia-Romagna, made chiefly from Trebbiano Romagnolo or the almost amber-berried Trebbiano della Fiamma. Some idea of Tebbiano's ubiquity is given by listing just some of the wines in which it is an ingredient: VERDICCHIO, ORVIETO, FRASCATI, together with in the north SOAVE from Trebbiano di Soave and LUGANA from Trebbiano di Lugana. The variety has after all had many centuries to adapt itself to local conditions. Between Tuscany and Rome, in UMBRIA, the variety is known as Procanico, which some agronomists believe is a superior, smaller-berried subvariety of Trebbiano. Only the fiercely varietal-conscious north eastern corner of Italy is virtually free of this bland ballast.

Trebbiano's malign influence was most noticeable in central TUSCANY in much of the 20th century, however, where Trebbiano was so well entrenched that CHIANTI and therefore VINO NOBILE DI MONTEPULCIANO laws sanctioned its inclusion in this red wine, thereby diluting its quality as well as its colour and damaging its reputation. Trebbiano is now very much an optional ingredient, however, which is increasingly spurned by the quality-conscious red wine producers of Tuscany.

The sea of Trebbiano still produced in Tuscany is being diverted into cool-vinified innocuous dry whites such as GALESTRO. Just as Viura (MACABEO) displaced the more interesting local white grape variety MALVASIA in Rioja, so the high-yielding Trebbiano has largely ousted Malvasia from Tuscany, although the latter makes a much more serious base for VIN SANTO.

Perhaps Italy's most exciting Trebbiano, Valentini's Trebbiano d'Abruzzo (see ABRUZZI), is not a Trebbiano at all but is made from BOMBINO BIANCO. Nevertheless, there was a dramatic increase in plantings of a variety known as Trebbiano d'Abruzzo in the 1980s.

Trebbiano has also managed to infiltrate Portugal's fiercely nationalistic vineyards, as Thalia, and is widely planted in BULGARIA and in parts of GREECE and RUSSIA. As well as being used for MEXICO's important brandy production, Trebbiano is well entrenched in the southern hemisphere, where its high yields and high acidity are valued. There were more than 4,000 ha of 'Ugni Blanc' in Argentina by the end of the 1980s as well as extensive plantings in Brazil and Uruguay.

South Africa also calls its relatively limited plantings Ugni Blanc but relies more on COLOMBARD for brandy production and cheap, tart blending material, as does California, whose few hundred acres of remaining 'St-Émilion' are exclusively in the Central Valley. Australia, however, has twice as much Trebbiano as Colombard, planted mainly in the irrigated areas, where it provides a usefully tart ingredient in basic blended whites and is also sometimes used by distillers.

The influence of Trebbiano / Ugni Blanc will surely decline as wine drinkers seek flavour with increasing determination.

See also UGNI BLANC.

TREBBIANO DI ROMAGNA, abundant VARIETAL central Italian dry white made from a grape variety which differs little either in AMPELOGRAPHY or wine personality from the TREBBIANO of Tuscany. The variety is cultivated across a wide swathe of ROMAGNA in the provinces of Bologna, Forlì, and Ravenna, with a total of approximately 3,000 ha / 7,400 acres producing about 95,000 hl / 2.5 million gal of DOC wine a year. Permitted yields of almost 100 hl / ha (5.7 tons / acre) do little to assist a grape not known for its striking personality, and most Trebbiano di Romagna is, at best, suitable for a picnic.

D.T.

TREIXADURA, white grape variety grown in GALICIA in north west Spain and known as TRAJADURA across the Portuguese border. In Galicia it is regarded as one of the more aromatic varieties.

TRELLIS SYSTEMS, support structures for the vine framework required for a given TRAINING SYSTEM. Normally these are man made, although vines are still occasionally trained to trees. The trellis system in its simplest form consists of a STAKE driven beside a vine to which the vine trunk or shoots are tied. Flexibility for vine training is increased by suspending WIRES along the line of stakes, thus forming rows of foliage. In many older vineyards, the wires are not tight and so provide little support for the vines and foliage. The development of high-tensile galvanized wire has allowed modern trellis systems which consist of end assemblies and line posts, interconnected by various configurations of very tightly strained wire which can support much heavier loads.

There are several designs of end assemblies but they are all firmly anchored in the ground so as to support the strain in the wire due to the weight of the crop, the vines, and any wind stresses. At intervals along the row are so-called intermediate posts which also help carry the vine weight. In a well-constructed trellis system, the wires should be strained so tight that the wire does not sag, and this in turn facilitates MECHANIZATION. Details of some common trellis systems and end assemblies are given by Smart and Robinson. Vineyard POSTS are made from wood, concrete, plastic, steel, stone, or even cane. If made from softwood, vineyard posts must be chemically treated to stop wood-rotting fungi.

The majority of the world's vineyards, however, have very simple trellis systems. For many, the vines are free standing (see GOBELET), or have loose wires running from vine to vine supported by occasional stakes. The major support for the weight of the vine and crop is from the vine trunk and CORDON or HEAD.

For more information on the wide range of trellis systems used in various regions, see TRAINING SYSTEMS. R.E.S.

Smart, R. E., and Robinson, M., *Sunlight into Wine: A Handbook for Winegrape Canopy Management* (Adelaide, 1991).

TRENTINO, the southern and principally Italian-speaking half of Italy's central alpine region of TRENTINO-ALTO ADIGE. Trento is the regional capital. Viticulture is centred on the valley of the Adige and the hills immediately to the east and west of the river, with an occasional excursion to side valleys such as the Valle dei Laghi and the Val di Cembra. The terrain further east and west into the Dolomites and the Gruppo di Brenta mountains is too rugged and mountainous for viticulture. Although the region is far to Italy's north, and Trento is on the 46th degree of LATITUDE, the climate is not necessarily cool, as heat rapidly builds up at lower altitudes during the summer months (see TOPOGRAPHY). Viticulture is therefore by no means confined to early ripening vine varieties. Annual average regional production is just over 1 million hl / 26.4 million gal per year. More than 70 per cent of the vineyards are registered for DOC wine production, a proportion second only to the ALTO ADIGE in Italy.

The DOC structure consists of one large regional DOC, supplemented by the various VARIETAL wines, together with five more or less geographically specific supplementary DOC zones. The Sorni DOC is minuscule. Teroldego Rotaliano suggests that the TEROLDEGO grape seems to have found its ideal soil in the GRAVELLY, pebbly terrain of the Rotaliano plain, although the DOC limits of 120 hl / ha (6.8 tons / acre) do not encourage quality. The DOC zone of Caldaro, on both sides of Lake Caldaro, is shared with the Alto Adige and

Late 15th century French painting illustrating **Petrus de Crescentiis**'s work showing medieval **trellis systems**.

SCHIAVA is the dominant grape. Valdadige, a long stretch of the Adige river, including a part of the Alto Adige and a north western chunk of the Veneto, is the DOC for predominantly a red blend of Schiava and LAMBRUSCO and a white blend of various INTERNATIONAL VARIETIES (PINOT BLANC, PINOT GRIS, MÜLLER-THURGAU, CHARDONNAY, and WELSCHRIESLING). Casteller is a DOC zone on both sides of the border with the province of Verona for a red blend of Schiava, MERLOT, and Lambrusco.

The Trentino's most important wines, however (with the exception of the 5 million bottles of Chardonnay-based SPUMANTE produced every year), are unquestionably the 17 VARIETAL wines of the Trentino DOC. Chardonnay is the most important white, followed by Müller-Thurgau, Pinot Gris, and Pinot Blanc; Cabernet, Merlot, MARZEMINO, LAGREIN, and Pinot Noir are the leading reds. Yields are too generous (from 14 to 15 tons per ha for the whites, from 13 to 15 tons per ha for the reds) to give wines of superior quality, but the Trentino's greatest handicap is the market-driven spirit of wine production, which has planted and vinified according to consumer tastes of the moment without much regard for specific characteristics of soil and MESOCLIMATE. The fact that 117 of the 222 townships of the Trentino are in one or another of the various DOCs is eloquent testimony of this productivist viewpoint, which has not served the area's viticulture well.

Significant historical traditions matching individual

varieties and individual subzones do exist none the less: Müller-Thurgau in Faedo and the Val di Cembra; Cabernet in the Vallagarina and between Pressano and Lavis; Lagrein in the Campo Rotaliano and in Roverè della Luna; NOSIOLA in Lavis, Faedo, and the Valle dei Laghi; Pinot Noir in Civezzano and in the hills to the north of Trento; Chardonnay in vineyards over 400 m / 1,300 ft in altitude. High-level Chardonnay, Müller-Thurgau, Cabernet and Merlot, and Pinot Noir, frequently treated to BARREL MATURATION, began to emerge from these specific subzones in the 1980s, indicating an important potential for high-quality wines which has yet to be tapped. CO-OPERATIVES market nearly three-quarters of the total production. The region's centre of ACADEME is SAN MICHELE ALL'ADIGE. D.T.

TRENTINO-ALTO ADIGE, northern Italian region through which flows the Adige river (called Etsch by the region's many German speakers). It is made up of ALTO ADIGE, or the South Tyrol, in the north and TRENTINO in the south (see map on p. 517).

TRESALLIER is a white grape variety grown in the Allier *département* notably for ST-POURÇAIN that is closely related to the SACY of the Yonne. It is certainly traditional there, but not unanimously acclaimed nowadays.

TRI, French for a sorting process, notably postal but, in a wine-making context, it means the selection of suitable grapes. This usually takes the form of a TRIAGE on reception of the grapes at the winery or cellar but in the production of BOTRYTIZED wines a *tri*, or several *tris*, is made in the vineyard whereby the pickers proceed along the rows selecting only those clusters, and occasionally only those berries, that have been successfully attacked by NOBLE ROT. In a difficult year such as 1972 as many as 11 *tris* might be made at Ch d'YQUEM, and in the end no SAUTERNES carrying that illustrious name was produced.

TRIAGE is the French and common wine-making term for the sorting of grapes according to quality prior to wine-making. Freshly picked bunches of grapes are typically spread on a sorting table or slowly moving belt so that substandard examples can be plucked off and thrown away. For most wines, clusters that are unevenly ripe, or underripe, or have suffered DISEASE or VINE PEST damage are rejected. In the production of BOTRYTIZED sweet white wines, however, all but the grapes uniformly infected with NOBLE ROT are rejected. Such sorting is a labour-intensive process that requires training and has so far resisted mechanization. Its expense can be justified only for relatively fine wines but its use increased considerably in the early 1990s, with the damp vintage of 1992 resulting in particularly widespread adoption in Bordeaux. A.D.W.

TRICASTIN, COTEAUX DU, extensive appellation on the eastern fringes of the southern RHÔNE for mainly red and rosé wines with a very small amount of white. Although the climate here is definitively MEDITERRANEAN, the generally higher altitudes and more exposed terrain produce rather lighter wines than those of Côtes-du-Rhône which they resemble. The best wine comes from sheltered, south-facing slopes, but acidity levels are usually noticeable beneath the superficial warmth of the southern vine variety perfume. The region was substantially redeveloped by *pieds noirs* returning from North Africa in the late 1960s. Large areas of scrub were cleared and planted with southern Rhône vine varieties. The appellation benefited from standard-bearers such as Domaine Tour d'Élyssas and Domaine du Vieux Micocoulier.

Grenache, Cinsaut, and Syrah are the principal vine varieties grown, although up to 20 per cent of Carignan, and of the permitted white varieties Grenache Blanc, Clairette, Picpoul, Bourboulenc, Ugni Blanc, Marsanne, Roussanne and Viognier may also be included. The basic maximum yield allowed is 52 hl / ha (3 tons / acre).

The wines are similar to those of Côtes du VENTOUX to the immediate south, which was also promoted to full APPELLATION CONTRÔLÉE status in 1973, but few of them are exported.

TRICHLORANISOLE, more properly **2,4,6-trichloroanisole**, or **TCA**, is the musty, unpleasant-smelling compound caused by the action of chlorine on cork bark or wood and associated with CORKED wine. Cork is by no means its only source, however. It has been found in BULK WINE and is also recognized in the food industry as a common cause of taint.

TRIMBACH, family-run wine producer based at Ribeauvillé in ALSACE. The company was established in 1626. Today it is particularly successful in the United States and its wines are characterized by very fine fruit and high acidity. Even its Sylvaner can stand many years' BOTTLE AGEING. Two of its most famous bottlings are Rieslings: the rare and long-lived Clos Ste-Hune (in fact from the Alsace Grand Cru Rosacker) and Cuvée Frédéric Émile, named after the 19th century Trimbach who expanded the business to become an important merchant house as well as vine-grower.

TRIMMING, the vineyard operation of removing unwanted shoot growth which can cause SHADING and can hinder SPRAYING. Although it is usually done with a trimming machine mounted on a tractor, it may also be carried out with a hand held machete or similar device. The shoots are normally trimmed to about 10–20 NODES, or 70–150 cm / 27–58 in long. Trimming is essential in vineyards with high VINE DENSITY to stop shoots from adjacent rows from growing together. Regrowth may be such as to demand up to six trimmings a year, particularly in vineyards well supplied with water (by rainfall or irrigation). If shoots are trimmed too short then there may be insufficient leaf area to ripen the crop properly (see LEAF TO FRUIT RATIO). Resulting wines will be lower in

Riesling grapes arriving at **Trimbach's** cellars in Ribeauvillé, Alsace

JOHN DEERE
6591
68

alcohol and of lighter body and colour. Sometimes vineyards are trimmed so neatly on the top and sides that vine rows can look like a recently trimmed hedge. R.E.S.

TROCKEN, German for dry, and an emotive term when applied to the wines of GERMANY. Wine drinkers within Germany fell for this style in the early 1980s, years ahead of foreigners, who are slowly being won over by the products of particularly ripe vintages in the late 1980s and early 1990s.

The term can be applied to a still wine with a maximum of 4 g/l RESIDUAL SUGAR, or up to 9 g/l if the TOTAL ACIDITY is less than the residual sugar by no more than 2 g/l (9 g/l residual sugar and total acidity not less than 7 g/l). The proportion of German still wine that is described as trocken varies considerably between regions (with a higher proportion in southern regions) but it averages about 16 per cent.

Because CARBON DIOXIDE reduces the impression of sweetness, a sparkling wine containing between 17 and 35 g/l residual sugar may be described as trocken (or, according to EUROPEAN UNION law, sec, secco, or dry, etc.). Many of the big-volume sparkling wines produced in Germany (see SEKT) are trocken, while top-quality versions are usually drier and labelled BRUT or extra brut.

In Austria trocken signified a maximum residual sugar level of under 4 g/l until 1994 when it was raised to 9 g/l.

See also HALBTROCKEN and SWEETNESS.

TROCKENBEERENAUSLESE, sometimes known as TBA, the ripest and rarest of the Prädikats in the QMP quality-wine category defined by the GERMAN WINE LAW. *Trockenbeeren* refers to grapes (*beeren*) shrivelled by NOBLE ROT. Many VINTAGES yield no Trockenbeerenauslese wine at all in Germany (although it is more frequent in Austria). Even riper grapes and higher MUST WEIGHTS are needed for this ultra-rich, usually deep golden-orange, usually heavily BOTRYTIZED wine than for BEERENAUSLESE. An even higher minimum POTENTIAL ALCOHOL is required than for SAUTERNES, generally produced in a much warmer climate. It is inevitable therefore that these rarities command exceptionally high prices which go some way to compensating the producer for the many passages through the vineyard, the risk of losing all the grapes to GREY ROT or rain, and the difficulty of vinifying such sticky juice. There has been a tendency to produce slightly less sweet Trockenbeerenauslesen than was the norm in the 1970s, while EISWEIN production has become more common.

See also AUSTRIA.

TROIS GLORIEUSES, annual weekend devoted to wine, and food, in and around Beaune. See HOSPICES DE BEAUNE and MEURSAULT for more details.

TROLLINGER is the most common German name for the distinctly ordinary black grape variety known as SCHIAVA in Italy, VERNATSCH in the Tyrol and Black Hamburg by many who grow and buy table grapes. It almost certainly originated in what is now the Italian Tyrol (see ALTO ADIGE) and its German name is a corruption of Tirolinger. In Germany it is grown almost exclusively in WÜRTTEMBERG, where its cultivation even as early as the 14th century is documented (see GERMAN HISTORY). Indeed only 10 of the 2,300 ha/5,680 acres of Trollinger counted in German vineyards in 1991 grew outside this distinctive region of smallholdings centred on Stuttgart whose speciality is red, or at least dark pink, wine. To suit local tastes (and most Trollinger is consumed within Württemberg and within the year), the wines are often relatively sweet and are rarely worth serious study. Growers coax absurdly high yields from this willing provider, the most productive clone of Vernatsch known as Schiava Grossa or Grossvernatsch. Although the variety remains popular with growers in Württemberg, where it constitutes one vine in every three, its extremely late ripening (later than Riesling) makes it unpopular elsewhere in Germany.

TRONÇAIS is a sort of French OAK named after a forest near NEVERS.

TROPICAL VITICULTURE. Although the grapevine is regarded by many to be a strictly temperate plant, it is now increasingly grown in the tropics, defined approximately as the region bordered by the tropics of Cancer and Capricorn. Countries in which some grapes are cultivated in tropical conditions includes AUSTRALIA, Colombia, BOLIVIA, BRAZIL, ECUADOR, INDIA, Indonesia, KENYA, Laos, MEXICO, Nigeria, the Philippines, Sri Lanka, THAILAND, and VENEZUELA.

Within the tropics there are many different climates, modified by differences in ALTITUDE and RAINFALL. Lowland tropical areas can be divided into those regions which are almost continuously wet, those with pronounced wet and dry seasons, and those which are virtually arid. In the lowland wet tropics, grapevines adopt an evergreen growth habit and can be manipulated into cropping more than once per year, mainly by PRUNING and by the application of chemicals which induce dormant buds to burst. Other chemicals are used which retard growth and induce flower buds to form. In areas within the tropics with pronounced wet and dry seasons, WATER STRESS can substitute for cold stress and induce a form of DORMANCY which causes vines to follow a seasonal cycle. In arid tropical areas, IRRIGATION is essential to permit vine growth. Here budburst is initiated by pruning and withholding irrigation water. Highland tropical areas with altitudes in excess of 1000 m/3,280 ft can have climates that are almost temperate with temperatures that are sufficiently low (less than 15 °C/59 °F) to induce normal dormancy and allow grapevines to follow a climate-controlled growth cycle.

The majority of tropical grapes are consumed as TABLE GRAPES. However, increasing amounts are used as DRYING GRAPES, especially in India, or fermented into wine. Grapevines can be very productive in the tropics, giving YIELDS of fresh fruit of 140 to 280 hl/ha, or 8 to 16 tons/acre. Depending on the climate, tropical grapes can be programmed to reach maturity at times of the year when other fresh fruit is not available, or when international prices are very high. J.V.P.

Communal singing and Burgundian joie de vivre at one of the **Trois Glorieuses**, at Clos de Vougeot.

TROPICS. For information on vine-growing within the tropics of Cancer and Capricorn, see TROPICAL VITICULTURE. Wine tasting in a tropical climate can be an arduous exercise, especially if humidity as well as the temperature is high. Most drinks need to be heavily chilled to offer any refreshment in a natural tropical environment, which means that sparkling wines and light reds such as Beaujolais can taste considerably more appealing than tannic reds and alcoholic white wines.

TROUSSEAU is the name of one of the two principal dark grape varieties indigenous to the JURA, and is more robust and deeply coloured than POULSARD although it is in serious decline as Pinot Noir, and Chardonnay, become ever more popular. It buds late and therefore avoids devastation by most spring frosts but is an irregular yielder. As long ago as the mid 19th century the early French AMPELOGRAPHER Comte A. Odart maintained that Trousseau is the same as Portugal's BASTARDO, and a variety for long called Cabernet Gros and occasionally, erroneously, Touriga in Australia. In both of these countries it is commonly used for sweet, dessert wines and flourishes in very different conditions from its native Jura. Galet also posits that the relatively rare variety known as Malvoisie Noire in the Lot may be Trousseau.

The lighter-berried mutation **Trousseau Gris** may well be the variety called Gray Riesling in CALIFORNIA, where there were still nearly 300 acres/120 ha planted in 1991, mainly in cooler sites. Just how this relatively obscure variety made its way around the world remains a mystery, although a number of other cuttings were taken from Portugal to Australia.

Galet, P., *Cépages et vignobles de France* (2nd edn., Montpellier, 1990).
—— 'La Culture de la vigne aux États-Unis et au Canada', *France viticole* (Sept.–Oct. 1980 and Jan.–Feb. 1981).

TRUNK, the main stem of a tree, from the ground to the first branches or, in the case of a grapevine, to the CORDONS. Newly formed vine trunks are pliable and need support (see VINE TRAINING). The height of the trunk of a grapevine is variable, from 10 cm/4 in (in BUSH VINES) to 10 m/30 ft (in vines growing up trees), and is determined by the specifications set for each TRAINING SYSTEM and TRELLIS. The trunk height determines the position of the CANOPY relative to the ground. Vine trunks are woody and form part of the bulk needed for

Oak trees in the **Tronçais** forest in the Allier *département*, the largest oak forest in Europe, whose wood is sought after by wine-makers all over the world. Closely planted trees result in tight grained wood.

storage reserves, especially of CARBOHYDRATES and NITROGEN compounds. In climates with freezing winters, multiple trunks are used to facilitate replacement after winter killing, and in extremely cold climates trunks are buried during the winter (see WINTER PROTECTION).

The trunk of any plant (including the OAK trees, used for COOPERAGE and CORKS) contains a sleeve of conducting tissue with the CAMBIUM in its centre, bark (with PHLOEM) on the outside, and wood (with XYLEM) on the inside. Through these tissues, xylem sap moves upward, carrying water, minerals, and compounds from the roots to the leaves, and phloem sap moves multi-directionally carrying sugars and elaborated molecules from the leaves to the rest of the vine. The downward passage of phloem sap in vines can be interrupted by trunk CINCTURING or girdling. B.G.C.

TRUNKED, a common form of VINE TRAINING where the vine has a trunk of variable height which ends in a HEAD or CORDONS. The term trunked is particularly used in eastern Europe and CIS countries, where such vines are considered high or low trunked, in contrast with trunkless vines, which are easier to bury for WINTER PROTECTION.

TUFA, a common mistranslation of the French term TUFFEAU.

TUFFEAU, a common rock type in the central LOIRE. *Tuffeau blanc* is CALCAREOUS but provides much better DRAINAGE than most LIMESTONES. This is the rock used to build many of the châteaux of the Loire and remaining hollows in the rock have been adapted for wine-making and storage.

The overlying *tuffeau jaune* is more sandy, and is particularly suitable for the Cabernet Franc vine, underlying some of the best vineyards in CHINON and SAUMUR-CHAMPIGNY. J.M.H.

TUNISIA, North African country which in some years produces more wine than MOROCCO and almost as much as ALGERIA. Viticulture was probably introduced when the Phoenicians established the city of CARTHAGE on the coast. Total vineyard area had fallen to about 29,000 ha/71,630 acres by the early 1990s, according to OIV figures, and just over half were dedicated to wine production as opposed to TABLE GRAPES. Tunisia exports about a third of her annual vintage of between 200,000 hl/5.3 million gal and 400,000 hl.

The more important wine regions are Nābul and Cap Bon, although small amounts of wine are produced in Aryānah, Bizerte, Bin 'Arūs, and Zaghwān.

Grape varieties planted include Carignan, Alicante Bouschet, Cinsaut, Cabernet Sauvignon, Mourvèdre, and most of the wines produced are either full bodied reds or light rosés, although some dry Muscat of Alexandria is also produced.

TURKEY, eastern Mediterranean country that is the world's fifth most important grower of grapes, fewer than three per cent of which are made into wine. Turkey is regularly the world's biggest producer of TABLE GRAPES and second only to California in its production of raisins and other DRYING GRAPES. And more than a third of all grapes grown in Turkey go into other non-fermented products such as GRAPE JUICE and GRAPE CONCENTRATE.

Modern Turkey includes Mount Ararat (see BIBLE) in ASIA MINOR, part of the region most closely identified with the ORIGINS OF VITICULTURE. Archaeological finds support the theory that wine was produced there at least 6,000 years ago. The region is therefore rich in indigenous VINIFERA vine varieties of which between 600 and 1,200 have been identified but fewer than 60 are grown commercially. Many serve as table grapes as well as wine grapes, which is how they survived many centuries of Ottoman rule and the ban on alcohol consumption under ISLAM. Kemal Atatürk himself, founder of modern Turkey, established the country's first winery for seven centuries in 1925 as part of his westernization programme.

The country's grape-growing regions include considerable climatic variation. The Thrace region in the hinterland of Istanbul is very much part of Europe and shares the warm coastal climate of its neighbours the far south west of BULGARIA and the extreme north east of GREECE. Responsible for 40 per cent of Turkish wine production, the region grows such European grape varieties as GAMAY, SÉMILLON, CLAIRETTE, PINOT NOIR, and RIESLING as well as such Turkish varieties as Yapincak and Papazkarasi. European varieties such as Sémillon, GRENACHE, and CARIGNAN are also grown on the Aegean coast, which accounts for about 20 per cent of Turkey's wine production, also from high-yield, low-altitude vineyards.

Anatolia, which produces the remainder of Turkish wine, has the most demanding climate, where vineyards, up to 1,250 m/4,000 ft above sea level, have to withstand very severe winters with temperatures sometimes down to −25 °C/−13 °F. Average summer temperatures are extremely high, however, and average sunshine up to 12 hours a day. Eastern Anatolia, where such grape varieties as Oküzgözü, Boğazkere for reds and Narince for whites are grown, borders GEORGIA and ARMENIA and has similar climatic conditions. Yields average less than 35 hl/ha (2 tons/acre).

Wine production is dominated by the state-owned Tekel together with two big private companies Kavaklidere and Doluca. In the early 1990s the head of the family-owned Anatolian company Diren could claim to be Turkey's only fully qualified OENOLOGIST. REFRIGERATION and STAINLESS STEEL tanks were still novelties.

Wine production is divided fairly equally between often-oxidized whites and relatively alcoholic reds with a few rosés. A quality wine scheme has been instituted but is used principally by the state-owned producer for its top bottlings. The state makes almost a quarter of each year's wine production into BRANDY and the aniseed-flavoured spirit *raki* (like ARAK) which, drunk with water, is the Turks' favoured alcoholic drink. Wine is for export and tourists.

TURKMENISTAN, central Asian republic of the CIS that sprawls between the Caspian Sea, UZBEKISTAN, AFGHANISTAN, and IRAN. A minor wine producer, it specializes in TABLE GRAPES and RAISINS. The vast Karakumy desert occupies a large part of this hot, dry country.

There are large daily and annual temperature fluctuations. the average January temperature is −4 °C/25 °F, that of July is 28 °C. The annual rainfall is 80 mm/3 in in the north east and 300 mm in the mountains, the largest amount of rainfall being recorded in spring and winter. Evidence of vine-growing in the country dates back to the 3rd century BC. Greek and Roman writers report that grapes were cultivated in Marghian (the Murgab valley) and in Aria (the Tejen valley). The Kopetdag ravines still have a great diversity of WILD VINES that have served as a basis for many indigenous varieties. Different wine vessels depicting grape bunches found during excavations of the village of Baghir near the capital Ashkhabad testify to the fact that Turkmenistan has a long history of wine-making.

For many years the nomadic way of life of Turkmenistan's population did not favour the development of agriculture, viticulture included, which had to wait until the country was annexed to RUSSIA at the end of the 19th century and the Ashkhabad railroad was built. In 1898, the total vineyard area was just 308 ha/760 acres. Thereafter it increased and reached 2,500 ha in 1928, 4,000 ha in 1940, and 11,000 ha in 1975. In 1990 its 27,000 ha of vineyard produced just 120,000 hl/3.2 million gal of wine.

Almost all vineyards need IRRIGATION, but only the north part of the Tashauz region needs WINTER PROTECTION. The Karakumy canal provided the chance to increase vineyard areas and their production. In the early 1990s, viticultural farms were changing over to large-scale technological grape cultivation. High-trunked vines on trellises were introduced into vineyards previously planted with low-trunked and high-trunked GOBELET vines.

The vineyards are in the Ashkhabad region (70 per cent of the total grape area), the Mary region (15 per cent), and the Chardzhou region.

Turkmenistan is a unique region suitable for early, mid, and late maturing table and raisin grapes. Provided assorted varieties are planted, grapes can be harvested from the middle of June until October. Only 21 grape varieties were cultivated on a commercial scale in the early 1990s, however, with eight wine varieties such as Terbash, Tara Uzüm Ashkhabadski, RIESLING, SAPERAVI, Kizil Sapak, and Bayan Shirey. In 1990 Turkmenistan produced about 120,000 hl of wine, typically strong and slightly OXIDIZED. V.R.

Kosheleva, R. V., Melkumova, Z. S., 'The Soviet Socialist Republic of Turkmenia' (Russian), in A. I. Timush (ed.), *Encyclopaedia of Viticulture* (Kishinëv, 1986).

Myznikova, S. L., and Kulakova-Alexeyeva, M. K., *Turkmenia's Enology and Wine* (Russian) (Ashkhabad, 1962).

Shapkin, Yu. D., *The Development of Viticulture in Turkmenistan* (Russian) (Ashkhabad, 1958).

TURSAN, small VDQS of about 300 ha/740 acres in the Landes in SOUTH WEST FRANCE producing wine made from mainly red, mainly TANNAT grapes, mostly from the CO-OPERATIVE and sold locally. The white version is of more interest and is virtually a one-producer wine, but what a producer: three-star chef Michel Guérard of Eugénie-lès-Bains, who lavishes such care as BARREL MATURATION on the local white grape variety, the BAROQUE, under which are more details.

TUSCANY, or **Toscana** in Italian, the most important region in central ITALY (see map on p. 517). Today Tuscany is at the centre neither of Italy's economic life nor of its political life, but it is the region which formed Italy's language, its literature, and its art, and has thus assumed a central place in the country's culture and self-image. The landscape, immortalized in the work of artists from Giotto to Michelangelo and part of every European's cultural baggage, has remained largely unchanged to this day: a succession of hills and valleys covered with cypresses, umbrella pines, vineyards, and olive groves.

Ancient history

In the ancient world, Tuscany, and at certain points of its history a much larger area, was known as Etruria. See ETRUSCANS for the ancient history of Tuscany.

Medieval history

If we know more about the wines of medieval Tuscany than we do about the wines of other regions of medieval Italy, it is not because they were better or there were more of them: the reason is Tuscany's economic and political importance. Florence was the banking capital of Europe, and Tuscany's bankers, notaries, and merchants kept records, many of which survive. The mass migration from the country to the towns that took place from the 11th to the 14th century created the great city states of northern and central Italy (see GENOA and VENICE): the population of Florence grew from a mere 6,000 to 90,000. Florence and Siena were the most powerful of the self-governing cities of Tuscany, and their fierce and bloody rivalry dominates the region's history in the Middle Ages, along with the wars between the Guelphs, who supported the pope, and the Ghibellines, who were on the side of the Hohenstaufen emperors.

Viticulture flourished despite the frequent civil wars, which were on too small a scale to devastate the Tuscan countryside. The region produced more or less equal amounts of oil and wine, but by far the largest crop, about two-thirds of the total, was wheat. Smallholders were rare in this part of Italy, since the land was mostly owned by monasteries, the local aristocracy, and, increasingly, by merchants in the cities. The system of agriculture was often that known as *mezzadria*, whereby the landowner would provide the working capital and the land in return for half (*mezzo*, hence the name) the crop. In 1132, for instance, the Badia (Abbey) di Passignano (whose wine is sold by the merchants ANTINORI) leased some of its land to a wealthy cobbler for half his crop of olive oil and wine. Of the other Vallombrosan monasteries that made wine, Badia a Coltibuono is still a well-known producer of CHIANTI.

The regional centre for market sales was the Mercato Vecchio in Florence. The earliest reference to wine retailers in the city dates from 1079, and in 1282 the wine sellers formed a guild, the Arte dei Vinattieri. Giovanni di Piero Antinori joined it in 1385, a member of the noble family that continues to make and sell wine in Tuscany today. In order to uphold the profession's reputation, the guild imposed a strict code of practice. The statutes insisted on cleanliness and exact measures; the shop was not to be situated within 100 yd of a church and it was not to serve children under 15. No cooked food could be sold, and shops were not to shelter ruffians, thieves, or prostitutes. The wine trade was vital to the Florentine economy. Tax records show that more than 300,000 hl/7.9 million gal of wine entered the city every year in the 14th century. The Florentine historian Villani, writing in 1338, estimated that weekly consumption of wine was a gallon a head. Given that Florence had approximately 90,000 inhabitants, this meant that well over 90 per cent was sold elsewhere, to the surrounding country or other Tuscan cities, some overseas via the port of Pisa, mainly to Flanders, PARIS, and Marseilles.

By no means all of this wine would have been Tuscan: a lot of it had come from Crete (Candia), Corsica, or NAPLES. Tuscany itself produced red wine, which was usually called simply *vino vermihlio*, but occasionally names appear. The reds of MONTEPULCIANO and Cortona were heavy, those of Casentino lighter. In the late 14th century we find Montalcino referred to as BRUNELLO. The most important of Tuscany's white wines were called 'Vernaccia' and 'Trebbiano', probably named after their respective grape varieties VERNACCIA and TREBBIANO, but neither was an exclusively Tuscan wine. Of the two, Vernaccia was the more highly reputed. In its sweet form it was associated primarily with LIGURIA, and particularly with Cinqueterre and Corniglia, although sweet Vernaccia was also made in Tuscany. The dry style of Vernaccia, made in San Gimignano (but also elsewhere), which is not found before the 14th century, was not exported overseas, because only the sweet version was capable of surviving the long sea voyage to France, Flanders, or England. Trebbiano, too, could be dry or sweet. The first recorded mention of CHIANTI is in the correspondence of the Tuscan merchant Francesco di Marco Datini in 1398, and it is a *white* wine. Datini was fond of it: in 1404 Amadeo Gherardini of Vignamaggio, which is still a well-known estate, wrote to Datini sending him half a barrel of his personal stock. Another of Datini's favourites was (red) CARMIGNANO.

Datini's letters, of which there are some 150,000 extant, give us an idea of what a rich merchant bought for his own consumption. He had MALMSEY sent to him from Venice and Genoa, and, more exotically, the equally strong, sweet wine of Tyre from Venice. These foreign wines were luxury items. Another expensive wine from outside Tuscany that Datini loved was Greco, which despite its name was an Italian wine, though probably from a Greek grape (GRECO or GRECHETTO perhaps?). It was grown in APULIA and so highly prized was it that in the 14th century the commune of San Gimignano

Farmhouse near Greve in Chianti Classico, typical **Tuscan** landscape, complete with vines and cypresses.

abandoned its tradition of giving distinguished visitors a few ounces of saffron and instead made them a present of the precious Greco.

Dante and Boccaccio both mention Vernaccia. It was a byword for luxury: Dante pictures Pope Martin IV fasting in purgatory to purge himself of the eels of Lake Bolzano which he used to eat stewed in Vernaccia (*Purgatorio* 24). In Boccaccio's *Decamerone* Vernaccia is a restorative for a rich and worn-out husband (2. 10).

No Tuscan author wrote exclusively about the wines of the region until Francesco Redi. His *Bacco in Toscana* ('Bacchus in Tuscany'), published in 1685, is subtitled *ditirambo*, the Greek dithyramb being a choral lyric in praise of DIONYSUS. Redi's poem, however, has little to do with the classical genre and is no more than an excuse for showing off his learning to fellow members of the Accademia della Crusca: he provides 228 pages of unhelpful and pretentious notes to deluge 980 lines of verse. Neither the poem nor the notes contains anything interesting or new about Tuscan wine and viticulture, and the notes Leigh Hunt wrote to his translation (1825) of *Bacco in Toscana* are a good deal more amusing (although of more use to the historian of language than to the historian of wine). The only wines Redi mentions, and praises, are VERNACCIA, CHIANTI, CARMIGNANO, and, finally, MONTEPULCIANO, which he regards as the king of all wines. H.M.W.

Flower, R., *Chianti: The Land, the People and the Wine* (London, 1979).

Melis, F., 'Produzione e commercio dei vini italiani nei secoli XIII–XVIII', *Annales cisalpines d'histoire sociale*, 1/3 (1972), 107–33.

Geography and vine varieties

The Tuscan countryside is famously undulating. A full 68 per cent of the region is officially classified as hilly (a mere eight per cent of the land is flat) and HILLSIDE VINEYARDS, at ALTITUDES of between 150 and 500 m supply the vast majority of the better-quality wines. The SANGIOVESE vine, the backbone of the regional production, seems to require the concentration of SUNLIGHT that slopes can provide to ripen well in these latitudes, and growers value the significant TEMPERATURE VARIATION between day and night as an important factor in developing its aromatic qualities.

Sangiovese has been, until recently, virtually synonymous with fine wine in Tuscany and, although the variety is widely planted throughout central Italy, the Tuscan climate (harsh in winter) and the calcium-rich MARLS in the best zones have thus far given incomparable results for this variety. The Arno river marks the northern border for cultivation of Sangiovese in Tuscany, with only the small DOC zone of CARMIGNANO, which virtually touches the river's bank, giving interesting wines at a more northerly latitude. Southwards through the CHIANTI CLASSICO area to the zones of VINO NOBILE DI MONTEPULCIANO and BRUNELLO DI MONTALCINO the wines become richer, fuller, more intense, and more alcoholic. Montalcino is, in fact, the only viticultural area of Tuscany where Sangiovese has always been fermented on its own; both CHIANTI and Vino Nobile were blended wines in the past, with CANAIOLO, MALVASIA, and TREBBIANO being used to soften Sangiovese's youthful asperity. This practice is gradually dying out except for wines deliberately shaped and marketed for early consumption. Chianti Classico, Vino Nobile di Montepulciano, and Brunello di Montalcino are all DOCG wines and have all shown a gradual but notable increase in overall quality level since the late 1970s—a fact which can only be attributed to a better understanding of Sangiovese and a more rigorous approach to cultivating and fermenting it. The finest wines of each area are regularly included in lists of the world's outstanding wines, but it cannot be ignored that this period of rising fortunes followed a similar period of declining quality and prestige.

Tuscan viticulture was dominated until recently by large estates owned by wealthy local families, the majority of them of noble origin, and tilled by a work-force of sharecroppers. The demise of this system in the 1950s and 1960s led to a hiatus in investment or even ordinary maintenance, deterioration of the vineyards and cellars, plummeting quality, and an eventual sales of the properties to new owners with the requisite capital and energy to carry on the viticultural traditions of the past. Tuscan ownership of Tuscan viticulture is now part of history, and the new wave of vintners from Milan, Rome, and Genoa—joined in the 1980s by a sizeable contingent of foreigners—has shown both a commendable commitment to quality and an equally commendable openness to new and more cosmopolitan ideas. See also ANTINORI, FRESCOBALDI, and RICASOLI, local noble families with considerable wine interests.

White wines

Trebbiano has been for white wine what Sangiovese has been for red wine, the basis of the regional production, and more than a dozen Trebbiano-based DOC wines currently exist in Tuscany. The grape has been cultivated principally for its high productivity and its acid-conserving qualities in hot areas, but the wines have little character and have gradually gone out of FASHION in the market-place; their future, if any, appears to be confined to a quaffing public in search of low prices. Scattered patches of VERMENTINO exist along the Tuscan coast up to the border with Liguria, but the variety has yet to establish a clear identification with Tuscany as a region. Interest in white wines is strong, however, and pioneering producers in Chianti have been experimenting with white INTERNATIONAL VARIETIES—principally CHARDONNAY and SAUVIGNON—in higher vineyards where Sangiovese ripens poorly. Results have been mixed thus far, but the problems seem more a question of lack of experience and technique than of the unsuitability of the TERROIR, and some striking successes have also been achieved, even if these products are likely to remain small in volume and somewhat marginal in the overall picture.

Supertuscans

Far less marginal are the new breed of Tuscan red wines, the so-called Supertuscans, often made with the assistance of French VINE VARIETIES and in an international style. Their development dates from the late 1960s and early 1970s, first as experiments or even for mere *divertissement*, but the startling results obtained in such all-CABERNET wines as Sassicaia and such Sangiovese/Cabernet blends as Tignanello from ANTINORI have established these products as a fundamental category in the overall Tuscan picture. Few estates in Chianti have not joined in the scramble to produce a wine of this prestigious type, and small BARREL MATURATION, now extended to Sangiovese, has yielded a new style of Tuscan wine greatly appreciated by consumers who once disdained Chianti. MERLOT is increasingly planted as an alternative to Cabernet, with impressive results, and significant amounts of SYRAH vines are expected to bear fruit in the 1990s.

Chianti still towers over these new wines, none the less. With close to 900,000 hl/23.7 million gal produced in an abundant year, it is Italy's largest single group of DOCs (although it should be remembered that Chianti's name has been extended to subzones near Florence, Pisa, Pistoia, Arezzo, and Siena which have nothing to do with the historic zone of Chianti Classico between Florence and Siena), supplying 80 per cent of the region's annual total of 1.1 million hl of DOC wine and 28 per cent of the total Tuscan wine production of 3.2 million hl in an average year.

For more details of specific Tuscan wines, see BOLGHERI, BRUNELLO DI MONTALCINO, CARMIGNANO, CHIANTI, CHIANTI CLASSICO, CHIANTI RUFINA, ELBA, GALESTRO, MONTECARLO, PREDICATO, VERNACCIA, VINO DA TAVOLA, VINO NOBILE DI MONTEPULCIANO, VIN SANTO. D.T.

Anderson, B., *The Wine Atlas of Italy* (London and New York, 1990).
George, R., *Chianti and the Wines of Tuscany* (London, 1990).
Gleave, D., *The Wines of Italy* (London and New York, 1989).

TXAKOLI, Basque wine. See CHACOLÍ DE GUETARIA.

TYPICITY, a wine tasting term adapted from the French *typicité* or Italian *tipicita* (the English word is **typicality**) for a wine's quality of being typical of its type, geographical provenance, and even its VINTAGE year— a wine characteristic much discussed by professionals. And it is perhaps because typicity is a subjective notion, rather than a physical attribute that can be measured by ANALYSIS, that it is so much discussed. Individual tasters are likely to differ as to what they consider typical of a particular wine description, just as they are likely to differ in their impressions of the wine under consideration.

Typicity need not and may not concern the average wine drinker, who is right to demand merely that the wine tastes good, but it becomes important in wine JUDGING if the wine has been entered into a particular class. It is also important to professional wine buyers, particularly when choosing wines to represent a GENERIC range.

Each wine type demands a different set of characteristics. For example, a deep white wine of modest ACIDITY and relatively high ALCOHOLIC STRENGTH, smelling strongly of ALDEHYDES, would be extremely atypical of Chablis, but would display the typicity of a FINO style of SHERRY. Similarly, a very young red wine smelling strongly of CARBONIC MACERATION would be accorded high marks for typicity if a young BEAUJOLAIS, but none as a young BORDEAUX.

It should be added, however, that, as wine-makers increasingly travel between wine regions, absorbing and applying different techniques, some distinctions between what were regarded as wine archetypes are being eroded, and there is more disagreement than ever as to what constitutes typicity.

TYROL. Hardly any wine is made in this western part of Austria, but considerable quantities are made in that part of the Tyrol ceded to Italy after the First World War, now known as the South Tyrol, Südtirol in German, or ALTO ADIGE in Italian.

U

UGNI BLANC (which is in fact Italy's ubiquitous Trebbiano) is France's most planted white grape variety by far, outnumbering Chardonnay's area five to one at the end of the 1980s, and yet is rarely seen on a wine label. Just as AIRÉN, Spain's most planted white variety, supplies that country's voracious brandy stills, so the copious, thin, acid wine of Ugni Blanc washes through the stills of the COGNAC and ARMAGNAÇ regions. Cognac is particularly reliant on Ugni Blanc, often calling it St-Émilion, which represents a good 95 per cent of all vines grown there (as opposed to only 40 per cent of vines in Gascony where armagnac is made, also from BACO BLANC and COLOMBARD).

These two brandy regions between them accounted for more than 80,000 ha/200,000 acres of France's giant total of Ugni Blanc plantings (still more than 100,000 at the end of the 1980s despite EUROPEAN UNION encouragement to pull up poorer-quality vineyards in the cognac-country). Ugni Blanc supplanted the FOLLE BLANCHE that was pre-PHYLLOXERA the main ingredient in French brandy production because of its good resistance to oidium POWDERY MILDEW and grey rot.

It is not, however, a French variety but was imported from Italy, probably during the 14th century when the papal court was established at Avignon. Other Italian varieties were presumably similarly transported but Trebbiano's extraordinarily high yields and high acidity may have helped establish it in southern France, where it is still grown widely today. Often called Clairette Ronde (although not related to CLAIRETTE) it was still among the five most planted varieties in the southern Rhône and Provence in most of whose appellations it is allowed to play a subsidiary role. There are still small plantings of it in Corsica and it was only in the late 1980s that Sauvignon Blanc overtook Ugni Blanc as Bordeaux's second most planted white grape variety. It is still widely planted in the north west of the Gironde where, like COLOMBARD, it is allowed into Bordeaux Blanc up to 30 per cent and is sometimes tellingly called Muscadet Aigre, or 'sour Muscadet'.

For more details of this variety, which probably produces more wine than any other, see TREBBIANO (although the variety is usually known throughout South America, where it is widely planted, as Ugni Blanc).

UHUDLER, strange wine speciality of Südburgenland in AUSTRIA made from vines that are AMERICAN HYBRIDS.

UKRAINE, independent republic in the south west of the CIS, its third most important wine producer (after RUSSIA and MOLDOVA). Its capital is Kiev. The CRIMEA, with a strong sense of independence from the Ukraine, is viticulturally its most important region.

History

Grapes were grown in what is now Ukraine as early as the 4th century BC. The south coast of the Ukraine, including Crimea, was a developed centre of grape culture in ancient times. Archaeological evidence has revealed stone fences, remnants of viticultural plots and wineries, and wine AMPHORAE in the Tauric settlement of Uch-Bash near Inkerman (as old as the 10th to 7th centuries BC) and in the ancient town of Mirmecium in the east portion of the Kerch peninsula. The tomb of a SCYTHIAN chief of 500 BC was unearthed arranged with an amphora of Chian wine at its head. In the northern parts of Ukraine wine production originated in monastic vineyards established there much later, in the 11th to 12th centuries.

Viticulture and wine production waxed and waned in the Ukraine since the land suffered numerous raids of nomadic tribes and witnessed long periods of war. The development of capitalism in Ukraine necessitated new profitable branches of agriculture, vine-growing and wine-making included. In 1913, the total vineyard area of Ukraine was 54,000 ha/133,000 acres and the gross yield of grapes was 79,000 tons. The grape and wine industry suffered heavily after the First World War, however, and as a result of PHYLLOXERA. By 1919, the total vineyard area had been reduced to 13,000 ha.

Thereafter the restoration of viticulture took place steadily, and by 1940 the total vineyard area was 103,000 ha. However, the Second World War also caused great damage to the industry. The total vineyard area decreased once more, to 68,000 ha. Vineyards were completely neglected, with the proportion of missing vines reaching 40 to 50 per cent. In the post-war period state farms specializing in viticulture were established and were subsequently amalgamated into specialized trusts and large companies. Nurseries were also established to meet the need for propagation material.

By 1990 vineyards occupied 175,000 ha, a significant decline since 1970. Viticulture in the southern parts of Ukraine accounts for up to 20 per cent of agricultural activity.

Climate and geography

Ukraine is mostly flat and sometimes hilly, with the Ukrainian Carpathian mountains in the south west and the Crimean mountains in the south.

The climate is mild, mostly continental. The difference between summer and winter temperatures increases in the south, when rainfall and humidity drop, the thickness of snow cover decreases, and snow holds for a shorter period of time. The average temperature in January ranges from −8 °C/10 °F in the north east to +2 °C/35 °F on the south coast of the Crimea, while the average temperature in July is 19° (66 °F) in the north west to 24° in the south east. The duration of the frost-free period is 230 days in the north and 290 days in the south. The active temperature summation is 2,900–3,700°. The annual rainfall amount is 350–400 mm (13–15 in) in the south east and 1,200–1,500 mm in the Carpathian Mountains.

Commercial viticulture is concentrated in the Crimea (62,500 ha), in the Odessa region (49,700 ha), the Kherson region (19,700 ha), the Nikolayev region (14,100 ha), the Transcarpathian region (6,800 ha), and in the Zaporozh'ye region (1,700 ha). These vineyards account for 88 per cent of the total vineyard area. Small vineyard areas are found in the south of the Vinnitsa region, the Dnepropetrovsk region, the Donetsk region, and the Kirovograd region. About 700 state and collective farms grow grapes, and the largest of them are located in the Crimea. State farms in the Ukraine may export to Russia, KAZAKHSTAN, MOLDOVA, and other CIS members.

Viticulture

Average YIELDS in Ukraine have been increasing significantly and by 1990 had reached more than 200 hl/ha (11 tons/acre).

A typical modern Ukraine vineyard allows large-scale cultivation of widely spaced vines that do not need WINTER PROTECTION (unlike RUSSIA) and which are trained high enough to permit MECHANIZATION of 60 per cent of all vineyards. New varieties with improved resistance to environmental factors are increasingly planted. Since most vineyards are located in drier zones, IRRIGATION has played a major part in doubling yields. The irrigated vineyard area accounts for more than 20,000 ha, or more than 10 per cent of the state's total.

Vine varieties

Vineyards are planted mostly to VINIFERA varieties grafted on phylloxera-resistant ROOTSTOCKS, although some MUSCADINES are also grown, according to the Institute MAGARATCH. Ukraine had 56 wine and 45 table vine varieties planted in 1992. The largest areas are planted to wine grapes such as RKATSITELI, ALIGOTÉ, CABERNET SAUVIGNON, SAPERAVI, RIESLING, SAUVIGNON Vert, GEWÜRZTRAMINER, PINOT GRIS, SERCIAL, BASTARDO, Fetiaska (see FETEASCA), Bastardo Magarachski, and white Sukhomlinski. Newly bred varieties also being introduced (see RUSSIA) include Golubok, Saperavi Severny, Pervenets Magaracha, Fioletovy Ranni, Podarok Magaracha, Karmraiut, Stepniak, Olimpiiski, Sorok let Oktiabria, and a range of TABLE GRAPES. Areas planted to indigenous grape varieties such as Kefessia, Soldaia, Sary Pandas, Kokus Bely, and Jevat Kara are being restored. Wine grapes account for 85 per cent of the total vineyard area but table grapes are gaining ground.

Since the production of various types of wine and brandy is determined by both natural conditions and economic reasons, about 60 viticultural regions have been specified for Ukraine. Each of these regions has an assortment of varieties and produces grapes of different uses.

Wines produced

The Crimea has the most favourable soil and climatic conditions for viticulture. Wines produced by the MASSANDRA winery are the pride of the republic.

The Crimea also produces high-quality white and red table wines and 'yellow' FORTIFIED wines such as Sercial Magarach, Massandra, and Oreanda. Wines made in the style of SHERRY are made using FLOR film yeasts and/or submerged culture yeasts, while MADEIRA-like wines are made in oak casks in direct sunlight for two to four years, or in specially simulated 'sun chambers' at which the temperature is held at 40 to 45 °C (104–13 °F) for six months.

Microzones in the foothills near Sevastopol' produce grapes to be made into dry white VARIETALS: Aligoté Zolotaia Balka, Rkatsiteli Inkermanskoie, Riesling Alcadar, and Riesling Krymski (Crimean Riesling). Dry red wines such as Cabernet Kachinskoie, Cabernet Kolchuginskoie, and Alushta (a blend of mainly Cabernet Sauvignon, Morrastel, and Saperavi) are produced in the western valleys of the Alma, Belbek, and Kacha in the Crimea, and in the vicinity of the town of Alushta.

The southern coastal steppes of Ukraine and the Dnepr right bank area have a moderately continental climate and increasingly warm temperatures towards the end of summer. This favours the production of full bodied, dry wines such as Perlyna Stepu, Nadneprianskoie, and Oksamit Ukrainy.

Dry white wines such as Beregovskoie, Promeniste, Serednianskoie, and Riesling Xakarpatski are made in the Transcarpathian region.

Industry organization

In 1990 Ukraine produced 2.7 million hl/71 million gal of wine, a steep decline from the 5.8m million hl average of the early 1980s before Gorbachev's anti-alcohol campaign.

Grapes are initially processed by 120 state farms and wineries in the wine regions, but finishing and bottling takes place at large plants near population centres, as is common throughout the CIS.

SOVIET SPARKLING WINE production is important in Ukraine and wineries producing 50 million bottles of this popular drink each year are in the capital Kiev and in Artemovsk, Odessa, Sevastopol', Sudak, and Kharkov. In 1882, the Russian wine-maker prince Leo Golitsyn established a winery in the village of Novy Svet in the Crimea which marked the beginning of the production of sparkling wines in Russia. Most common grape varieties used for base wines are Pinot Blanc, Aligoté, Riesling, and Fetiaska. More than 100,000 hl/2.6 million gal of Ukrainian brandies are also made each year.

Viticultural and oenological research in Ukraine is carried out by the most famous centre of wine academe in the CIS, the Institute for Vine and Wine MAGARATCH, founded in 1828 in Yalta in the Crimea. There is also the Tairov Institute for Viticulture and Oenology in Odessa, and the Institute for Design of Orchards and Vineyards in Simferopol'.

Of all CIS members, Ukraine has made most notable progress towards establishing its own Wine Law. V.R.

Dokuchayeva, E. N. (ed), *Grape Varieties* (Russian) (Kiev, 1986).
Johnson, H., *The Story of Wine* (London and New York, 1989).
Liannoi, A. D., 'The Soviet Socialist Republic of Ukraine' (Russian), in A. I. Timush (ed.), *Encyclopaedia of Viticulture* (Kishinëv, 1987).
Troshin, L. P., and Sviridenko, N. A., *Resistant grape varieties* (Russian) (Simferopol', 1988).
Valouiko, G. G., *Grape Wines* (Russian) (Moscow, 1978).

ULLAGE, which derives from the French OUILLAGE, has had a variety of meanings and uses in the English-speaking wine trade. It can mean the process of EVAPORATION of wine held in wooden containers such as a BARREL. The HEAD SPACE left in the container is also called the ullage, or 'ullage space', and the wine in that state is said to be 'on ullage'. The word ullage is also used for any space in a stoppered wine bottle not occupied by wine (see FILL LEVEL). And ullage is also used as a verb so that a bottle or barrel not entirely full is said to be 'ullaged'.

The ullage space in a barrel is not empty but contains water and alcohol vapours together with some CARBON DIOXIDE previously dissolved in the wine. If the container is not completely gas tight, some air will seep in around poorly fitting joints between staves, the tank head, or the bung. Only relatively new and well-made barrels approach the degree of tightness required to prevent the entry of air, and with it the risk of OXYGEN. When wine is matured in any other form of wooden container it is particularly important that the ullage space is minimized by regular TOPPING UP. A.D.W.

Even bottles from the same case can have quite different levels of **ullage**.

ULL DE LLEBRE, meaning 'hare's eye', is the CATALONIAN name for TEMPRANILLO.

UMBRIA, fourth smallest of ITALY's 20 regions in terms of both physical size and population, with its viticulture of only minor significance in the regional economy (see map p. 517). Only the Valle d'AOSTA, BASILICATA, LIGURIA, MOLISE, SARDINIA, and CALABRIA produce less than Umbria's 1 million hl/26 million gal per year, and only 17 per cent of this production is of DOC quality. Umbria produces only one-third the wine of neighbouring Tuscany (where DOC wine represents a third of the total volume), and, despite the geological and climatic similarities between these two central Italian regions, Umbria has never enjoyed either the significant urban civilization or the important country estates that have made Tuscan wines among Italy's most prestigious.

ORVIETO is the region's most signficant DOC wine, accounting for two-thirds of the total DOC production; other DOC white wines based on TREBBIANO grapes, simple products at best, are made in the zones of Colli del Trasimeno, Colli Perugini, TORGIANO, Colli Altotiberini, Colli Martani, and Colli Amerini. Trebbiano is often referred to as Procanico in Umbria, although some claim that Procanico is actually a superior CLONE of Trebbiano which gives smaller bunches and a finer wine. So far their efforts to transmute the dross of Trebbiano into the finely spun gold of Procanico have been more convincing at a verbal level than at the gustatory level. SANGIOVESE is the region's principal red grape variety, giving pleasant, if not memorable, wines in the Colli Altotiberini, Colli Amerini, Colli Martani, Colli Perugini, and Colli del Trasimeno DOCs; the wines produced near Lake Trasimeno are allowed up to 40 per cent of the GAMAY grape in the blend, and to the west of the lake some all-Gamay wines are produced, although they are more an oddity than a serious imitation of BEAUJOLAIS.

Sangiovese has reached its heights in Umbria in the wines produced by LUNGAROTTI in the Torgiano DOCG, and, as Rosso di Montefalco, also gives good results in the hillside vineyards of the small Montefalco DOC zone between Assisi and Terni, where it is blended with a small percentage of the local SAGRANTINO. This last variety, which in the past has given notably rustic wines high in TANNINS, demonstrated towards the end of the 1980s that it can respond well to more careful vinification and ageing techniques. There was a considerable improvement in general in Umbrian Sangiovese in the 1980s, rewarded with the promotion of Torgiano from DOC to DOCG. The elevation of Sagrantino di Montefalco to DOCG status, however, is perhaps more of a vote of confidence in the future than an accurate reflection of the prevailing quality level of all producers. D.T.

Anderson, B., *The Wine Atlas of Italy* (London and New York, 1990).
Gleave, D., *The Wines of Italy* (London and New York, 1989).

UNITED KINGDOM. See Great BRITAIN.

UNITED STATES of America, important producer of wine and DRYING GRAPES, and a significant consumer of fine wine.

History

European settlement in what is now the USA goes back to the late 16th century (see also VÍNLAND), but it was two centuries later that wine was first successfully produced there. The long delay was not for lack of trying. The abundant native AMERICAN VINE SPECIES immediately drew the attention of the first settlers; wine-making was an official aim of the Virginia and Carolina colonies, and it was encouraged and repeatedly tried in all of the American colonies.

The first trials quickly showed that wine acceptable to European palates could not be made from the unameliorated native grape varieties. The next step was to import cuttings of European VINIFERA vines, beginning in Virginia around 1619. The experiment was frequently repeated over the whole length of the Atlantic seaboard with vines from every great European wine region, but the result was uniform failure. The vines were destroyed by extremes of climate, by native PESTS, and by previously unknown VINE DISEASES. The facts were not clearly understood for more than two centuries, since the trials were isolated and uncoordinated, and no adequate knowledge of plant pathology existed. The cycle of hopeful experiment followed by complete failure went on in profitless repetition.

All Europe took part in the effort. French vignerons were imported along with French vines by the Virginia Company in 1619, and French expertise continued to be sought thereafter: Huguenot exiles were employed in Carolina in 1680, in Virginia in 1700, in Pennsylvania in 1683. Germans attempted wine-growing at Germantown in Pennsylvania; in Florida a colony of Greeks, Italians, Frenchmen, and Spaniards tried vine-growing in 1767. All of these, and innumerable other efforts, were based on *vinifera* varieties and were accordingly doomed to rapid and entire failure (see PHYLLOXERA and FUNGAL DISEASES).

A new direction was taken through the discovery of a chance hybrid—the combination of a native *Vitis labrusca* and an unknown *vinifera*—called the Alexander grape, in Pennsylvania, not far from where William Penn had planted *vinifera* in 1683. Its hybrid character was unrecognized for many years, but it in fact showed the way in which vine-growing in the eastern United States would be developed. The first successful commercial wine production in the USA, based on the Alexander, began in Indiana around 1806. Thereafter, many new AMERICAN HYBRIDS of American vine species either with each other or with a European *vinifera* variety, formed almost invariably by chance, were introduced and contributed to the possibilities of wine-making in the USA.

The most important were the CATAWBA, DELAWARE, ISABELLA, and Norton, all introduced in the first half of the 19th century. Most were better adapted to white wine production than to red, and most had more or less of the so-called FOXY aroma. Whatever their defects, they would at least survive under American conditions, and they made wine production possible.

Permanent and extensive wine production was first established around Cincinnati, Ohio, in the 1830s by Nicholas Longworth; when the Cincinnati *vignoble* was devastated by BLACK ROT, the Ohio wine industry moved north to the shores of Lake Erie. The other main wine-making centres were around Hermann, Missouri, a German colony on the Missouri river, and around the Finger Lakes of upstate New York (see NEW YORK for more historical detail of the state's wine industry).

In the south before the Civil War, some wine-making, based both on the native hybrids and on the native *rotundifolia* vines (see AMERICAN VINE SPECIES) of the American south, grew up in the Carolinas and Georgia. Scattered vineyards, all growing American native or hybrid vines, and small wineries could be found throughout the settled regions, and extended to the frontiers of TEXAS and Kansas. The federal government supported vine-growing through plant exploration, the distribution of plants, and experimental work in the analysis of grapes and wines. In the decade before the Civil War interest in vine-growing burgeoned and many new hybrid varieties were introduced, some of them now the outcome of controlled rather than accidental hybridizing.

The most important single result of this activity was the CONCORD, a vine with good resistance to pests and diseases, well adapted to the extreme growing conditions of the area that then constituted the United States, but whose extremely FOXY grapes were particularly unsuitable for wine (or at least wine as most wine drinkers know it). The ubiquity of the Concord has had a large part in establishing a taste for grape juice rather than for wine among Americans.

Meanwhile, although the fact was quite unknown in the USA, *vinifera* grapes were successfully grown and wine made in the Spanish settlements on the Rio Grande in New Mexico and Texas (beginning around 1626) and in the Franciscan missions of California (beginning around 1779). The Mexican War of 1846–7, followed by the Gold Rush of 1849, brought the *vinifera*-growing regions of the south west into the USA; since then, California has dominated American wine production. At the time of the American conquest, the vine was already grown on a small but commercial scale in Los Angeles. Plantings thereafter spread over the state and production grew rapidly, from a few hundred thousand gallons in 1860 to more than 30 million gal/1 million hl by the end of the century.

The first *vinifera* variety grown in New Mexico and California was the MISSION, probably a New World seedling of an unknown European parent; it is at best a mediocre grape for wine. Importations and trials of many superior *vinifera*

United States: This 1591 illustration of the arrival of the French in Florida shows just how common wild vines were.

varieties quickly began, and although the Mission grape long dominated California, plantings of other, better varieties increased steadily. Among the most interesting is the distinctively Californian ZINFANDEL, which is still widely grown.

The economic growth of the California industry was unstable: a cyclical pattern of boom and bust persisted until 1894 (see CALIFORNIA, history), when the California Wine Association, a union of the largest producers and dealers in the state, was formed. The CWA was not a monopoly, but it controlled so large a share of the wine production of the state that it could stabilize costs and prices, and did so down to the advent of Prohibition. The CWA distributed its wines throughout the USA (where wine drinking continued to be almost wholly confined to the cities) and developed export markets, particularly Great BRITAIN.

Outside California, vine-growing continued to develop slowly, in much the same way as previously. New Jersey, Virginia, and Arkansas were added to the states where viticulture was already established: New York (where the production of sparkling wine had become a speciality), Ohio, and Missouri. By 1919, the last year before national PROHIBITION was enforced, the USA produced 55 million gal of wine. During the Prohibition years, from 1920 to 1933, some commercial wine production was allowed, and HOME WINEMAKING became more popular than ever before or since, resulting in an increase in total vine acreage thanks to demand for GRAPE CONCENTRATE, but the industry was destroyed.

Upon Repeal (from 1934) the US industry had to reconstitute itself. Some of the old firms reappeared; many new firms mushroomed. But it took time to put things right: the market was ignorant, or perverted by the intemperate habits encouraged by Prohibition; the producers were uninstructed or, sometimes, unscrupulous. The country was in the lowest depths of economic depression, and wine was an unfamiliar luxury. High alcohol sweet wines became the mainstay of the trade, and remained so for the next generation. The federal government failed to re-establish its research programmes for wine, but important OENOLOGICAL and VITICULTURAL research was carried out by the state universities of California at DAVIS and New York. Promotional work was largely in the hands of the Wine Institute of California, founded in 1934.

The Second World War, by cutting off European supplies, brought new prosperity to US industry but brought new instability as well. Large distilling companies bought up established wineries in order to have a product to sell. A seller's market prevailed until, after the war, the artificially stimulated demand collapsed. The distillers departed from the wine trade, which fell into somnolence. Little effort was made to develop new markets; wineries typically sold their wines in bulk to wholesalers for bottling under their own brands; American wines, after the bad old example set in the 19th century, continued to use GENERIC names such as Burgundy, Chablis, Sherry, and Champagne, and most wineries produced an entire 'line' of such types from a severely limited range of grape varieties.

In the east, especially, the decline was marked; in Ohio, for example, the 149 wineries of 1940 had dwindled to 47 in 1960. One valuable new development was the introduction, by Philip WAGNER, of hybrid grape varieties developed in France (see FRENCH HYBRIDS) such as SEYVAL, SEIBEL, and BACO into the eastern vineyards; these gave larger yields and made more attractive and interesting wines than the old native hybrids could produce. Another innovation was the effective introduction of VARIETAL labelling by the American merchant Frank SCHOONMAKER, a practice that was to become standard.

Beginning around 1970, wine production in the USA suddenly took on a new energy and a new glamour, a development not yet explained but doubtless the result of many different, slowly gathering social forces. New wineries, large and small, were started in California (there were 240 wineries in 1970, 771 in 1989, 755 in 1992). New vineyards were planted, and wine-growers made unprecedented efforts to find the best matches between grape variety and location. They increasingly concentrated on relatively few grape varieties and wine types instead of producing the old comprehensive 'line' of wines, aspiring to new levels of quality and complexity. Innovation in technology was eagerly sought, at the same time as traditional European methods were introduced and adapted. Large-scale foreign investment from Japanese, British, French, Spanish, Swiss, and German companies was attracted to the American wine industry, notably a number of French CHAMPAGNE firms who invested in California sparkling wine production in the 1980s.

The explosion of new activity in the industry was matched by consumer developments: wine classes, wine societies, wine publications proliferated to exploit the interest and anxieties of a public long ignorant and indifferent but now eager to learn. Consumption of wine—now dominated by table wine—rose from 267 million gal in 1970 to 523 million gal in 1989. As wineries proliferated, they offered a variety of choices such as Americans had never before seen. One firm, GALLO of Modesto, California, has succeeded in becoming the largest winery in the world and in dominating the popular market for wine to an extent unknown even in the old days of the California Wine Association.

Outside California the boom in wine was, proportionately, even greater. The old regions—New York and Ohio especially—began to sprout new enterprises after a long quiescence. The vineyards were transformed by the introduction not only of hybrids developed in France such as Seyval and Seibel, but by *vinifera* varieties, now, thanks to modern understanding of plant pathology and the availability of PESTICIDES and FUNGICIDES, at last grown successfully in the eastern USA after more than three centuries of failure. States such as New Jersey, Pennsylvania, and Virginia which had once supported viticulture on only a modest scale now saw the growth of a renewed and expanded industry. Texas and New Mexico, sites of very old but very small-scale *vinifera* wine-making, now boasted large viticultural developments. The Yakima Valley in WASHINGTON, the Willamette Valley in OREGON, undertook large plantings of *vinifera* and began to develop a reputation for particular types of wine. Thanks to the prolific Concord grape, New York continues to produce more wine than any state other than California. Washington, South Carolina, and Georgia all produce more wine than Oregon. The number of commercial wineries in the entire country in 1993 was 1,528, distributed over 43 states. Wine production, over a five-year average, was more than 420 million gal, making the USA the world's fifth or sixth most important wine producer, rivalling Argentina.

The USA is still far from being a wine-drinking country, however; annual per capita consumption was about 2 gal (9 l) in the early 1990s. Many obstacles to the production and sale of wine still exist, some of them natural, such as climate, some of them man made, such as the different taxes and restrictions imposed by the different states. The spirit of Prohibition is still vigorous, whether it take the old form of moral disapproval or the newer forms of disapproval on grounds of diet and HEALTH. Since 1989 the federal government has required warning labels on all bottles of wine sold in the USA. But, on any view, the US wine industry in the latter half of the 20th century underwent a remarkable development from the ruins left after Prohibition, renewing old activities, spreading into new regions, expanding production, developing new methods in viticulture and wine-making, and reaching new levels of quality. T.P.

Adams, L., *The Wines of America* (4th edn., New York, 1990).
Pinney, T., *A History of Wine in America* (Berkeley, Calif., 1989).
Schoonmaker, F., and Marvel, T., *American Wines* (New York, 1941).

Modern wine production

Wine is made in virtually every state of the United States. Much is sold locally, but the wines of CALIFORNIA, NEW YORK, WASHINGTON, OREGON, IDAHO, and TEXAS have become important commercially and have international distribution. Historically, the first areas to be planted were around large bodies of water. More recently, inland valleys and mountains have also been planted with grapevines.

The catalyst was a series of Farm Winery Acts passed since the early 1970s which defined a farm winery as one which produces at least 51 per cent of its wines from grapes grown on land it owns or leases (as opposed to a commercial winery which can bottle wine from grapes grown anywhere) and eased some of the restrictions and financial burdens for new, small-scale, wine-growers and producers—as well as allowing them in many states to sell wine on Sundays. These new freedoms, together with advances in viticultural knowledge and an increased enthusiasm for both foreign travel and a particularly glamorous form of farming, have led both professionals and hobbyists across the USA to attempt wine production in their own states, sometimes even moving to other states if growing conditions appear better, especially if land values are superior.

In the following survey several wine-producing states are grouped, sometimes across political boundaries, into regions of similar climate and geography. Vine varieties grown tend to be either *Vitis* VINIFERA varieties, or AMERICAN HYBRIDS, or more usually FRENCH HYBRIDS, or MUSCADINES. A significant proportion of American wines are FRUIT WINES, however, made from fruits other than grapes. An AVA is an officially recognized American Viticultural Area.

New England

Is a north east US region that includes, from north to south, the states of Maine, New Hampshire, Vermont, Massachusetts, Connecticut, and Rhode Island. The two AVAs are Western Connecticut Highlands and Southeastern New England. Coastal wineries enjoy a climate moderated by Long Island Sound and the Atlantic Ocean. The climate for inland wineries is more severe. Grapes grown are *viniferas*, especially Chardonnay, and red and white hybrids. Fruit wines are made from raspberries, strawberries, blueberries, cranberries, cherries, rhubarb, plums, peaches, and pears. Mead and cider are also made. Being so far north, vines are under threat of WINTER FREEZE every year. A system of PRUNING late, after FLOWERING in June, instead of the traditional late winter pruning time, enables growers to determine their crop size after the threat of winter kill or spring frost has passed.

Lake Erie

Is one of the Great Lakes bordering CANADA to the north, and whose eastern and southern shores border western Pennsylvania, Ohio, and western New York. Lake Erie is an AVA, the first US tri-state appellation, established in 1983. Original Pennsylvania wineries gravitated to the shores of Lake Erie in the north western part of the state, because of the important GRAPE JUICE industry there. A significant number of *vinifera* vineyards there also supply grapes to wine-makers throughout the state. Wines are produced from *vinifera*, hybrids, native American grapes, and other fruits, planted in a wide range of MESOCLIMATES that vary with the proximity to the Lake.

Ohio, west of Pennsylvania, has about 20 wineries in the Lake Erie Region, in the most northerly part of the state. Markko Vineyards is distinguished for growing the first *vinifera* vines in Ohio at Conneaut in the late 1960s. Bass Island, in Lake Erie, has the longest growing season, and is also known for *vinifera* plantings. It is part of the Isle St George subappellation. There are about another 20 wineries in the Central Ohio Region in the heartland of Ohio, and the Ohio River Region, an AVA at the south west border of the state. Wines are made from *vinifera*, hybrids, native American grapes, and other fruits. A great deal of SPARKLING WINE is made, and Meier's Wine Cellars, established in 1856, is noted for its FORTIFIED wines. The Ohio River Region is also a multi-state appellation, and includes some wineries in southern Indiana and Kentucky. They also use *vinifera*, hybrid grapes, and other fruits.

Lake Michigan

Another of the Great Lakes, is bordered by Michigan, Indiana, Illinois, and Wisconsin. Each state is considered separately, and there are no multi-state appellations as with Lake Erie. The most favourable sites are those of Michigan's wineries on the eastern shore, with Fennville to the south, and Leelanau Peninsula to the north, being AVAs. Lake Michigan moderates the extreme climate. In winter, it provides moisture to the prevailing westerly winds that create a snow cover, protecting the vines from severe low temperatures.

Middle Atlantic States

Include New Jersey, south eastern Pennsylvania, Maryland, West Virginia, and Virginia. Most of New Jersey's small wine industry is around Egg Harbor, better known for boat-building than wine-making. The majority of Pennsylvania's approximately 50 wineries are now in the south eastern part of the state, around the city of Lancaster. Grapes, as well as other fruits, are grown on the high plateau around the Susquehanna river in a historic area known as York Highlands. Maryland is well known for Boordy Vineyard and Nursery, begun by Philip and Jocelyn WAGNER, who supplied a high proportion of the ROOTSTOCKS and French hybrids planted in the rest of the USA since the 1940s. *Vinifera* grapes have joined hybrids in present-day vineyards. West Virginia grows mostly hybrids.

Perhaps the greatest growth in eastern viticulture has been in Virginia. Grapes have been planted there since the early settlers came to Jamestown in 1607, making the first wine in the New World from indigenous grapes. It is to Thomas JEFFERSON, however, that credit is given for importing fine French wines to his estate at Monticello (now an AVA), and for the short-lived success of *vinifera* varieties that he grew and vinified. Today *viniferas* outnumber hybrids three to one, with a small amount of *labruscanas* also grown. Chardonnay and the red Bordeaux varieties do exceptionally well. The climate is warm, but growers have to guard against the FUNGAL DISEASES that come with high summer humidity by frequent SPRAYING and thinning CANOPIES. There are over 50 wineries in several viticultural areas in Central Virginia around Charlottesville: eastern Virginia, influenced by the Chesapeake Bay; northern Virginia, close to urban Washington, DC; Shenandoah Valley (an AVA, not to be confused with the AVA of the same name in Amador County, California) nestled in the Blue Ridge Mountains; and south west Virginia.

Midwestern states

Include Missouri, Arkansas, and Iowa. The first AVA in the USA was Augusta, Missouri, approved in 1980. These areas' viticulture has been influenced by predominantly German and Swiss immigrants travelling westward in the New World in the 1800s, as well as by the French MISSIONARIES who occupied these territories before they achieved statehood. Harsh winters, with temperature extremes causing thaws followed by hard freezes, limit most growers to hybrid and *labruscana* grape varieties. A few wineries, however, such as Mount Pleasant in Augusta, do grow *vinifera* varieties successfully. The most important areas are Augusta, Hermann, the Ozarks (which extend to Arkansas), and western Missouri. A final area, Saints of the East (named because so many of its cities are named for saints), contains Ste Genevieve, Missouri's oldest permanent settlement, along with a winery of the same name. This area and its wines shows a strong French influence from northern Louisiana. Arkansas wineries are in the western part of the state near Altus, in the valley of the Arkansas river. In addition to growing *vinifera*, hybrid, and *labruscana* grapes commercially, *rotundifolia* and *aestivalis* species of VITIS are also produced. Iowa's wineries are in the Amana area, 80 miles/130 km west of the Mississippi river. They enjoy a local following.

South western states

Include TEXAS, New Mexico, Arizona, and Colorado. New Mexico is the oldest wine growing region of the USA since Franciscan priests first produced sacramental wines there in the 16th century (see above) in the southern Mesilla Valley (a present-day AVA). Today it has 19 wineries, another AVA in the nearby Mimbres Valley, and has made some impact commercially, particularly with traditional method sparkling wines grown in high-altitude vineyards south of Albuquerque. The arid desert climate gets little rainfall, but the Rio Grande provides water for IRRIGATION. Elevations can range from 3,700 ft/1,130 m to 6,400 ft, creating contrasts in temperature, with 30 °F/17 °C drops at night not uncommon. Furthermore, the sun is very intense due to cloudless skies. There are few pests and diseases in these growing conditions. While the south west is one of the hottest regions of the USA in the summer, the winters can be bitterly cold. *Vinifera* varieties do best in the warmer, southern part of the state, while hybrids can withstand the cold of the northern, high desert plateaux.

Arizona, just west of New Mexico, has similar growing conditions, but there is a strong focus on growing *vinifera* grapes. The TERRA ROSSA, or red soil, in the south east appears promising for Pinot Noir and Cabernet Sauvignon vines. Colorado, north of New Mexico, also favours *vinifera* production. The main vineyard areas are west of the Continental Divide, and the plains east of Denver.

South eastern states

Include Georgia, North and South Carolina, Florida, Tennessee, Louisiana, and Mississippi. Georgia and North Carolina are growing increasing proportions of *vinifera* grapes (to a limited extent only in Tennessee and Mississippi), but due to great summer heat and humidity, along with danger of winter frosts, *Vitis rotundifolia* vines, known as Muscadines, survive better than other species. They grow along the Atlantic seaboard from Virginia to Florida. The most famous muscadine grape is the SCUPPERNONG. The wines are more neutral than *vinifera*, and are often slightly sweet. Besides the Muscadines, *labruscanas* and some hybrids are cultivated, although many wines are made from fruits other than grapes. Grape harvest in these warm, humid states usually takes place in late July or early August.

See also specific entries on CALIFORNIA, WASHINGTON, OREGON, TEXAS, IDAHO, HAWAII, and NEW YORK. H.L.

Adams, L., *The Wines of America* (4th edn., New York, 1990).
Gayot, A., *Guide to the Best Wineries of North America* (New York, 1993).

URSPRUNGSLAGE, German term for a 'site of origin' and the proposed replacement for the GROSSLAGE collective site. The word Ursprungslage should appear on labels of wines from them, and, unlike Grosslage, each Ursprungslage may produce wines only of a particular style, according to officially registered grape variety, acidity, alcoholic strength, and residual sugar. The consumer should therefore have some idea what sort of wine to expect from a bottle carrying the name of a particular Ursprungslage.

URUGUAY is South America's fourth most important wine-producing country with annual production rising from around 600,000 hl in the late 1970s to almost 1 million hl/26 million gal in the early 1990s. Such is the enthusiasm of Uruguayans for their wine (see CONSUMPTION) that few efforts to export it were made before the mid 1990s. Until then Uruguayan wine was, typically, an internationally unfashionable deep rosé, not unlike a Spanish CLARETE, made from an unusually sweet and stern blend of TANNAT and MUSCAT HAMBURG, possibly bulked up by some of the hybrid ISABELLA. HYBRIDS are being replaced by more internationally acceptable grape varieties, however, such as Pinot Blanc (which may actually be Chenin), Sauvignon Blanc, Chardonnay, Cabernet Sauvignon, Cabernet Franc, and Merlot, together with some Riesling and Gewürztraminer.

Uruguay's viticultural history is relatively short, commercial vine-growing having been introduced to the country only at the end of the 19th century, notably by Basques who promulgated the Tannat vine, commonly known in Uruguay as Harriague after an early vine-grower, with such enthusiasm that total Uruguayan plantings overtook France's total area of Tannat vineyard. A high proportion of Tannat vineyard has had to be replaced because of virus infection, however. Some Petit MANSENG can also be found, thanks to the same Basque influence.

Vine-growing is widely spread over the country, typically on its low hills, with the original vineyards concentrated in the south around Montevideo. The wine regions of Colonia and Carmelo are being developed in the far south west at the confluence of the Uruguay and Paraná rivers, while vines are also planted upstream in the warmer far north of the country around Salto and Bella Unión, which shares basalt soils with some of Argentina's and Chile's vineyards. Further east along Uruguay's northern border, on what is effectively a continuation of BRAZIL's promising new Frontera viticultural region, are Uruguay's northern Cerro Chapeu vineyards in Rivera province, where yields from the deep, well-drained, sandy soils are relatively low. Humidity is very high here and over half of production is from hybrids. Perhaps the country's most distinctive wine region, however, is the central vineyards of Carpinteria and El Carmen, where good day/night temperature variation and poor, shallow soils have been cited by visiting French experts as evidence of greatest potential.

Summers are warm and rainfall sufficient to obviate the need for irrigation although yields can easily be as high as 150 hl/ha (8.5 tons/acre). The LYRE system of vine trellising was successfully introduced to Uruguay by the Bordeaux viticulturalist Alain Carbonneau in the 1980s. Greater wine-making sophistication (stainless steel was still a novelty in the early 1990s) should increase Uruguayan presence in the international market-place. A national body dedicated to promoting Uruguayan wine quality, INAVI (Instituto Nacional de Vitivinicultura), was created as recently as 1988.

USA. See UNITED STATES of America.

USSR. See SOVIET UNION.

UTIEL-REQUENA, Spanish wine region producing sturdy reds in the hills inland from VALENCIA in south east Spain (see map on p. 907). Utiel-Requena is the coolest of the five wine regions of the LEVANTE and was once famous for its heavy DOBLE PASTA reds. Consequently the region is dominated by the sweet, dark BOBAL grape variety, although the TEMPRANILLO vine is rapidly gaining in importance. Utiel-Requena produces large amounts of GRAPE CONCENTRATE, as well as some good, fresh flavoured rosés from Bobal, thanks to recent improvements in wine-making equipment. R.J.M.

UVA DI TROIA, good-quality southern Italian red grape variety fast declining in popularity with growers. The vine's connection with Troy remains a mystery. Italy's total plantings fell from 5,000 ha/12,000 acres in 1982 to about 3,000 ha in 1990. For more details see APULIA.

UVA RARA, red wine grape variety too widely grown in OLTREPÒ PAVESE in Lombardy in northern Italy to justify its Italian name, whose literal translation is 'rare grape'. Often called, misleadingly, BONARDA Novarese, it is grown in the Novara hills and used to soften the SPANNA grapes grown here in a range of scented red wines.

UZBEKISTAN, independent central Asian republic that is part of the CIS. It is a major supplier of TABLE GRAPES but also produces about as much wine as KAZAKHSTAN to the north. Its capital is Tashkent.

History

The grapes and wines of Uzbekistan have long been famous beyond its own frontiers. Between the 6th and 2nd centuries BC people in the Fergana valley grew wheat, barley, and grapes using artificial IRRIGATION and Fergana grapes were prized in CHINA to the east.

It is thought that some central Asian VINE VARIETIES originated as the wild subspecies VITIS *silvestris* Gmel as a result of long-term selection. Some varieties were brought to Uzbekistan from IRAN between the 6th and 4th centuries BC and other varieties were brought by Greeks and Arabs in the 7th and 8th centuries AD. Archaeological excavation has revealed grape seeds dating back to the 5th century BC during excavations of Tali Barzu near Samarkand.

Viticulture and wine-making flourished in Uzbekistan until the end of the 7th century when, as a result of the Arab conquest of central Asia, wine grape varieties gave way to table, raisin, and seedless raisin varieties (see ISLAM).

After central Asia was annexed to RUSSIA in the second half of the 19th century, demand for table grape varieties with good shipping qualities developed rapidly. European wine varieties from MOLDOVA, the Crimea in UKRAINE, and other regions were also imported into Uzbekistan. In 1917 Uzbekistan had 37,000 ha/91,000 acres of vineyards, mainly owned by individual smallholders. The first specialized state farms were established in the 1920s.

Modern viticulture

Uzbekistan is in the very heart of central Asia, on the same latitude as Italy. The country's relief varies considerably, with the Tian-Shan and the Pamir and Alai spines in the east, and mountains accounting for about 30 per cent of the total area of the country. The climate of Uzbekistan is very continental. The average January temperature is 3 to −3 °C (37–22 °F) and that of July is 26 to 32 °C (79–89 °F). Late spring and early autumn FROSTS are commonplace. The active temperature summation is 4,000 to 4,500 °C. The annual rainfall is 100 mm (4 in) in the lowlands to 1,000 mm in the mountains.

Commercial grape culture is centred on the 10 zones of Uzbekistan with the most suitable soil and climate conditions. The leading viticultural zones are the Samarkand, Tashkent, and Bukhara regions. Wineries located in the Tashkent region include Ogenek, Kibrai, and Nizhni Chirchik; in the Samarkand region they include Bulungur and Pastdargom; and in the Bukhara region is Gala Assiya.

About 90 per cent of vines have to be covered with soil for WINTER PROTECTION. Only vineyards in the mountains, at an altitude of 800–1,500 m (2,600–5,000 ft), where the annual rainfall amount is not less than 450 mm, do not require IRRIGATION. Vines planted in rows and trained in a fan shape with numerous canes, together with semi-fan-shaped, trunkless forms on vertical four-storey trellises, account for about 90 per cent of the total vineyard area (see TRAINING SYSTEMS), although some varieties are left to grow in BUSH form.

The country's assortment of vines still has features typical of the viticulture of central Asia. Table grape varieties predominate and the grape conveyor system is employed whereby early, mid, and late maturing grapes are harvested continuously for about 120 days. In 1992, 36 varieties were officially allowed for commercial viticulture, of which 20 were table and dried fruit varieties. Wine grape varieties included ALEATICO, RIESLING, Kuljinkski, Hungarian Muscat, MUSCAT Rosé, Soiaki, Bayan Shirey, SAPERAVI, RKATSITELI, MORRASTEL, and Khindogny.

Uzbekistan produces dry, strong, and dessert wines (nearly 650,000 hl/17 million gal in 1990) as well as sparkling wines and brandies.

The Shreder Research Institute for Horticulture, Viticulture, and Oenology is Uzbekistan's centre of wine ACADEME and the AMPELOGRAPHER A. M. Negrul is one of several important academics based in Uzbekistan. V.R.

Akhramov, I. K., 'The history of viticulture and enology in the Fergana valley' (Russian), *Vinodelie i vinogradarstvo SSSR*, 7 (1966), 43.
Mirzayev, M. M., 'The Soviet Socialist Republic of Uzbekistan' (Russian), in A. I. Timush (ed.), *Encyclopaedia of Viticulture* (Kishinëv, 1986).
—— Kuznetsov, V. V., and Borozdin, R. G., *Viticulture and Oenology of Uzbekistan* (Russian) (Tashkent, 1962).

V

VACCARESE, unusual red grape variety permitted in CHÂTEAUNEUF-DU-PAPE producing wines similar to CINSAUT.

VACQUEYRAS, after GIGONDAS, the second one of the Côtes-du-Rhône villages to be awarded its own appellation, in 1990. Vacqueyras may be red, white, or rosé, although only a minuscule proportion of its nearly 700 ha/1,700 acres of vines are planted with white grape varieties. Most of the wine is like a super-concentrated Côtes-du-Rhône-Villages, made in the communes of Vacqueyras and Sarrians between Gigondas and BEAUMES-DE-VENISE (see map on p. 796). The appellation rules are very similar to those of Gigondas, and thus to those of Châteauneuf-du-Pape, although only half the grapes in a red Vacqueyras have to be Grenache. The rest are usually Syrah, Mourvèdre, and Cinsaut. Vacqueyras tends to be distinctly more rustic than good Gigondas.

VACUOLE, the central compartment of plant CELLS, separated from cytoplasm by a membrane. In grape berries, vacuoles within flesh cells contain the solution that forms grape juice. B.G.C.

VACUUM EVAPORATION. See CONCENTRATION.

VALDADIGE, or Etschtaler in German, basic appellation of the Adige (Etsch) valley used principally by producers in TRENTINO and also by some in eastern VENETO. Vineyards in ALTO ADIGE theoretically qualify but the Alto Adige appellation is usually used instead.

VALDEORRAS, easternmost wine zone in GALICIA in north west Spain (see map on p. 907). Steeply terraced vineyards are planted predominantly with poor but productive vine varieties such as the black Alicante (the local name for GARNACHA) and the white PALOMINO. The indigenous white GODELLO which had all but disappeared from Galicia in the wake of PHYLLOXERA is also showing potential. This moderately productive variety is susceptible to disease and Valdeorras, protected from the Atlantic by mountains immediately to the west, seems to be the only part of Galicia where Godello can be grown successfully. If carefully vinified, it can produce an aromatic wine with an ALCOHOLIC STRENGTH of 12 to 13 per cent. MENCÍA, a black grape which is closely related to the French CABERNET FRANC, is similarly respected by a new wave of producers in Valdeorras. It makes light, fruity reds for early drinking which are becoming as popular in Spain as those of neighbouring RIAS BAIXAS. R.J.M.

VALDEPEÑAS, wine region in CASTILE-LA MANCHA in south central Spain producing soft, ripe red wines. The sea of rolling vineyards that is Valdepeñas is really an extension of La MANCHA (see map on p. 907), but Valdepeñas has developed a reputation for quality over and above its larger neighbour and has consequently earned a separate denomination, or DO. Physical conditions in Valdepeñas are similar to those in La Mancha. The Sierra Morena dividing CASTILE from ANDALUCÍA immediately to the south is a barrier to the moderating influence of the Mediterranean. At an altitude of 700 m/2,300 ft above sea level, Valdepeñas shares the arid, CONTINENTAL conditions that prevail through much of central Spain.

As in La Mancha, the white AIRÉN is the dominant grape variety, although Valdepeñas is traditionally known for red wine rather than white. The red Cencibel, as the TEMPRANILLO of Rioja is known here, is planted on just over 4,000 ha/9,900 acres of vineyard compared to 30,000 ha of the more popular, DROUGHT-resistant Airén. Consequently much of the red wine made in the region is a blend of red and white grapes somewhat lacking in colour and BODY. The best red wines, however, are made exclusively from Cencibel, which has the capacity to age well in oak. Most of the wines exported from Valdepeñas are either RESERVAS or GRAN RESERVAS matured in American OAK casks. Some of the wines can taste unappetizingly baked from the heat, but the best have the soft, smooth, vanilla character (although not the price tag) of a well-aged RIOJA. R.J.M.

VALDIGUIÉ, sometimes called Gros Auxerrois, enjoyed its finest hour in the late 19th century when, as a dark-berried grape variety from the Lot, it was valued for its productivity and its resistance to oïdium (POWDERY MILDEW). In the early 20th century it was known as 'the ARAMON of the south west' for its emphasis on quantity at the expense of quality. It has now been all but eradicated from France where there remained only a few hundred hectares, mainly in the Tarn *département*, by the 1988 census.

Eight years earlier French ampelographer Galet had visited the USA and identified the variety then sold rather successfully as Napa Gamay as none other than this undistinguished vine from south west France, of which there were then 4,000 acres/1,600 ha planted in California. By the 1990s it had disappeared from official statistics.

Galet, P., 'La Culture de la vigne aux États-Unis et au Canada', *France viticole* (Sept.–Oct. 1980 and Jan.–Feb. 1981).

Marano in the **Valpolicella** Classico zone.

VALENÇAY, VDQS region on the south bank of the Cher tributary of the Loire in northern France at the far south eastern end of the TOURAINE district. Only about 200 ha/500 acres of clay soils with a certain amount of limestone and silt are planted with vines. Some of the most successful are Sauvignon Blanc (Valençay is only about 20 miles/30 km from the appellations QUINCY and REUILLY) but there is the full central Loire gamut of Cabernets, Cot (Malbec), Gamay, Pinot Noir, Chardonnay, Arbois for crisp wines of all three colours.

See also LOIRE and map on pp. 576–7.

VALENCIA, Spain's biggest port and third largest city, also lends its name to an autonomous region and one of five wine denominations (see DO) in the Levante (see map on p. 907). The vineyards are well away from the city, inland from the fertile market gardens and paddy fields bordering the Mediterranean. Production of white wine exceeds red. Neutral dry whites are made from the MERSEGUERA grape, although the local Moscatel Romano (MUSCAT OF ALEXANDRIA) produces some good, pungent dessert MISTELAS. MONASTRELL and the pink-fleshed GARNACHA Tintorera together produce rather coarse red wines, although the latter can produce some fresh, dry rosé. Five large producers dominate Valencia and the surrounding DOs. For more details, see LEVANTE. R.J.M.

VALGELLA, subzone of VALTELLINA in the far north of Italy.

VALLE D'AOSTA. See AOSTA.

VALLE ISARCO, or Eisacktaler in German, pure, dry white wines from the ALTO ADIGE.

VALPOLICELLA, red wine of extremely varied quality from the VENETO region in north east Italy. The Valpolicella, like a number of other historic areas of Italy, saw its production zone greatly enlarged when it achieved DOC status in 1968. It was extended eastward as far as the very boundaries of the SOAVE white wine zone. The original Valpolicella zone, whose wines alone may be labelled Valpolicella CLASSICO, now accounts for less than half the total production of about 340,000 hl/9 million gal. Valpolicella SUPERIORE, with an ALCOHOLIC STRENGTH of at least 12 per cent and an obligatory ageing period of one year, is a more ambitious product than the regular bottling which may have only 11 per cent alcohol but there is no ageing requirement. The subzone of the Valpantena, where the Bertani family has important vineyard holdings, is a legally permitted subdenomination on labels.

The DOC regulations, which imposed a maximum limit of 70 per cent of CORVINA grapes in the wine, have not been helpful to Valpolicella; Corvina is generally considered the grape with the most personality in the blend. The high acidity of the Molinara and the neutral character of the Rondinella contribute little to the overall quality level. Wines made exclusively from Corvina began to appear in the late 1980s, but they qualify only as a VINO DA TAVOLA. By 1990, Corvina plantings outnumbered those of Rondinella 3 : 2. The widespread use of the best grapes either for the production of such DRIED GRAPE WINES as local specialities RECIOTO and AMARONE, or for Valpolicella Superiore, has doubtlessly weakened the regular Valpolicella bottlings, which are in Italy frequently dubbed 'twice-skimmed milk'.

There is no question, however, that the Valpolicella's single greatest handicap has been the socio-economic structure of the zone's production: over 50 per cent of the grapes are handled by the CO-OPERATIVES and 20 per cent by large industrial wineries, many of which have no vineyard holdings; both have been dedicated to a policy of high-volume production at low prices. Grape prices hardly rose between 1978 and 1988, despite a decade of galloping inflation in Italy. The result was substantial overcropping and a gradual extension of the vineyard area from the poorer soils of the hills to include the more fertile, more productive, more easily mechanized vineyards of the plains.

Professor Giovanni Dalmasso, the doyen of Italy's oenologists in the first half of the 20th century, suggested a minimum altitude of 100 m/330 ft for the vineyards of the Valpolicella, but this was widely disregarded when the DOC regulations were drawn up. There have been some attempts to recover the HILLSIDE VINEYARDS, now largely abandoned, by making them into the sole area of a future Valpolicella DOCG, with the vineyards in the plains remaining at the DOC level. A request to increase maximum permitted YIELDS from 84 hl/ha (4.8 tons/acre) to 98 hl/ha (5.6 tons/acre) in 1988 (with an additional tolerance of 20 per cent) met considerable opposition and was refused, although the justification of the request—to regularize an already existing situation—is eloquent evidence of production realities in the Valpolicella.

RIPASSO is a common technique employed by better producers for reinforcing the standard Valpolicella wines, and converts them, thanks to the increased ALCOHOLIC STRENGTH into a Valpolicella SUPERIORE. This technique requires, ideally, unpressed skins used for Amarone, or at least some partially dried grape skins. The fact remains, however, that there are not enough dried grapes or Amarone skins for the vast bulk of Valpolicella production, and the wine, which once had the reputation of a fruity, eminently drinkable, medium-weight product has become, for the most part, rather thin and acidic. In the long run the future of the zone lies in a recovery of its viticulture: a lowering of yields, a return to the hillside vineyards, and an attempt to fit the various production categories to their proper zones. The township of Negrar, for example, has a long history of Valpolicella Superiore from the subzone of Torbe, of Amarone from the subzone of Jago, and of Recioto from the subzone of Moron, but much of this tradition has been subsumed in the rush to produce quantity at the expense of quality.

See also AMARONE and RECIOTO. D.T.

VALRÉAS, one of the Côtes-du-Rhône Villages. See RHÔNE.

VALTELLINA, the northernmost zone in Italy where the NEBBIOLO grape (here called Chiavennasca) is cultivated, is a narrow valley formed by the river Adda as it flows from east to west before emptying its waters into Lake Como. Despite its 46-degree latitude, the valley—protected to the north by the Rhaetian and Lepontine alps—has a relatively privileged climate (not unlike the warmer wine regions across the border in SWITZERLAND) with a high percentage of sunny days during the year. The longer days of the summer supply ample amounts of solar radiation for grape RIPENING, partially compensating for lower median temperatures compared with the classic areas for Nebbiolo in PIEDMONT to the south west. None the less, the wines themselves, while unmistakably Nebbiolo, do tend to have less body and roundness, and more perceptible TANNINS and ACIDITY, than the classic wines of the LANGHE or those made from SPANNA in the Novara-Vercelli hills, and can be sold only at considerably lower prices. Although Nebbiolo seems well adapted to the Valtellina, it has arrived fairly recently; the detailed works of Francesco Saverio Quadrio in the 17th century make no mention of the grape and the beginning of its cultivation in the Valtellina appears to date from the early 19th century.

The production zone is divided into nearly 500 ha of Valtellina SUPERIORE (including the legally recognized subzones of Grumello, Inferno, Sassella, and Valgella; Paradiso, another name which frequently appears on labels, is not a legally recognized subzone, although its wines can be among the valley's best) and the nearly 700 ha of regular Valtellina. The Superiore zone, the historical nucleus of the valley's viticulture, produces an average of 25,000 hl/660,000 gal per year with a minimum ALCOHOLIC STRENGTH of 12 per cent. The 20,000 hl yearly production of regular Valtellina is generally a simpler and less age-worthy wine which need reach only 11 per cent of alcohol.

Three thousand growers share the 1,176 ha/2,900 acres of DOC vineyards, a factor which—along with the high costs of maintaining the TERRACES which have been hewn into the steep hillsides—has led to the commercial domination of the NÉGOCIANT houses which market 88 per cent of the Valtellina's production. Another substantial portion, 10 per cent, is marketed by co-operative wineries, leaving the zone with a virtual absence of the small producers whose work has been so fundamental in improving the quality and image of the famous Langhe wines BAROLO and BARBARESCO.

The Valtellina also produces a wine called Sforzato (also seen with dialect names of Sfursat or Sfurzat) from raisined grapes; unlike a RECIOTO, the wine is dry and must have a minimum of 14.5 per cent of alcohol. See DRIED GRAPE WINES for more details. D.T.

Anderson, B., *The Wine Atlas of Italy* (London and New York, 1990).
Gleave, D., *The Wines of Italy* (London and New York, 1989).

VANDYKE PRICE, PAMELA (1923–). The first woman to write seriously about wine in Britain did more than most to popularize wines after the Second World War. Coming from a background in public relations, journalism, and cookery (in the magazine *House and Garden*), she has written almost 30 books on food and wine. These range from general works of reference (the Penguin *Book of Spirits and Liqueurs*, 1980) to the specialist (*Wines of the Graves*, 1988). They all reflect her true love of wine and (most) wine people. She is probably most distinguished as a performer, however, having trained initially as an actress.

Vandyke Price, P., *Woman of Taste* (London, 1990).

VARIETAL, descriptive term for a wine named after the dominant grape variety from which it is made. A varietal wine is distinct from a wine named after its own geographical provenance (as the great majority of European wines are), or a GENERIC wine, one named after a supposed style, often haphazardly borrowed from European geography, such as 'Chablis' and 'Burgundy'. Varietal wines are most closely associated with the New World where they constitute the great majority of wines produced. The concept was advocated with particular enthusiasm by Frank SCHOONMAKER in the 1950s and 1960s, and was embraced during the CALIFORNIA wine boom of the 1970s to distinguish the more ambitious wines, often made from Cabernet Sauvignon and, increasingly, Chardonnay, from the lack-lustre generics of old. Varietal labelling was also adopted, for a similar purpose, in AUSTRALIA, SOUTH AFRICA, NEW ZEALAND, and elsewhere.

Originally, when the United States' acreage of classic vine varieties was relatively limited, a varietal needed only 51 per cent of that variety in the blend to be so labelled. In 1973 this requirement was increased to 75 per cent (although some particularly strongly flavoured NEW YORK state vine varieties were exempted from this increased requirement; see FOXY). Despite the emergence of the MERITAGE category of superior blends, varietal wines continue to be California's premier statement of quality.

The French INAO authorities are hostile towards varietal labelling, understanding that they have nothing to gain and much to lose by entering into this commonwealth of nomenclature. Within France, varietal wines (typically VIN DE PAYS) are called *vins de cépage*, and have been widely regarded as of lower rank than APPELLATION CONTRÔLÉE wines. The INAO stated in the early 1990s that its eventual aim was to eradicate grape varieties from the names and labels of all appellation contrôlée wines, possibly even those of ALSACE and certainly such familiar combinations of grape and geography as Sauvignon de TOURAINE.

In their 1990s attempts to reformulate the DOC system and wine quality categories, the Italian authorities have been equally keen to emphasize their uniqueness, place, over grape variety. Such attitudes are understandable and, in the long term, will probably pay dividends, but there is little doubt that an important factor in the success of many New World wines has been the ease with which consumers can grasp the concept of varietal labelling. In the 1980s Chardonnay and Cabernet Sauvignon became the most recognizable BRAND names in the world of wine.

So popular has the term varietal become that many use it (incorrectly) as synonymous with variety. For more details, see VINE VARIETIES.

VARIETY of vine or grape. See VINE VARIETIES.

VAROIS, COTEAUX, enclave within the Côtes de PROVENCE appellation which takes its name from the Var *département*. The wine achieved AC status in 1993 (only eight years after it was made a VDQS) when 1,500 ha/3,700 acres of vines produced vast quantities of rosé, some potentially exciting reds, and a small quantity of extremely varied white wine. The wooded hills around Brignoles are based on LIMESTONE and are so buffered from warming maritime influence by the hills of Ste-Baume that vines will not ripen at all reliably at altitudes of more than about 350 m/1,100 ft.

Reds and rosés may incorporate an almost dazzling array of varieties: Grenache, Syrah, Cinsaut, Mourvèdre (which will ripen only in the warmest sites), Cabernet Sauvignon, Carignan (limited to half of any one parcel of vines), and the ancient Provençal variety Tibouren. This gives the better producers an exciting palette from which to work; some of them produce several different blends which vary in style by virtue of both varietal mix and ÉLEVAGE. For white wines, Grenache Blanc is added to those varieties permitted for Côtes de Provence Blanc (see PROVENCE), although Rolle is being increasingly appreciated.

VARRO, MARCUS TERENTIUS (116–27 BC) was a prolific Roman writer who wrote on subjects as diverse as grammar, geography, history, law, science, philosophy, and education; the rhetorician Quintilian called him 'the most learned man among the Romans' (*Institutio oratoria* 10. 1. 95). Yet the only one of his works to survive in its entirety is his manual of agriculture, *De re rustica*. Varro started it in his 80th year and addressed it to his wife, who had bought a farm. Varro was a man of letters, and, unlike CATO's treatise, from which he borrows occasionally, his own is a literary exercise, written in a highly wrought style. *De re rustica* is full of antiquarian learning as well as practical advice, and Varro often looks back to the time when the inhabitants of Italy were all hard-working honest farmers and there was none of the decadence that prevails among the city dwellers of his day. The treatise is divided into three books, each of which is a dialogue; most of the material on wine comes in the first book, which deals with agriculture proper (Books 2 and 3 are concerned mainly with livestock). He defines old wine as at least a year old; some wine goes off before that, but some, like FALERNIAN, becomes the more valuable the longer it is kept. Varro's work was used by later writers such as VIRGIL, PLINY, COLUMELLA, and PALLADIUS. Varro's own chief authority, by his own admission, is Mago of CARTHAGE, about whom nothing is known and of whose work nothing survives, either in the original or in the Greek translation that Varro claims existed. Among the many Greek authors he mentions as his sources are Aristotle, Xenophon, and Theophrastus.

H.M.W.

Skydsgaard, J. E., *Varro the Scholar* (Copenhagen, 1968).

VASE PAINTING. Vases in Ancient GREECE from 600 to 300 BC are an important source for information about the SYMPOSIUM, the VINTAGE, and VITICULTURE generally.

VAT, large CONTAINER for STORING wine and/or AGEING or maturation. A vat may also be used as a FERMENTATION VESSEL. In English-speaking countries they may also be known as tanks; in France they are called CUVES.

For many centuries WOOD has been the most common material but in the mid to late 20th century inert materials such as cement, enamel, epoxy resin, and STAINLESS STEEL have replaced wood except in particularly traditional or traditionalist areas.

For details of wine maturation in wooden vats see CASK AGEING.

VAT SIZE varies enormously. FERMENTATION VESSELS in large commercial wineries contain, typically, between 50 and 300 hl, although smaller enterprises may use much smaller wooden vats. The ratio of height to width has implications for red wine-making in determining the area of the CAP. Blending tanks may contain several thousand hl: 15,000 hl in the case of Lindemans' Karadoc winery in Australia. Peñaflor, Argentina's largest wine company, boasts the largest wine vat in the world, with a capacity of about 50,000 hl—large enough to hold a dinner party for several hundred inside.

VDN is sometimes used as an abbreviation for VIN DOUX NATUREL.

VDP, or the **Verband Deutscher Prädikats- und Qualitätsweingüter e V,** important association of more than 150 of the finest wine estates in GERMANY. In 1910 the mayor of Trier in the MOSEL-SAAR-RUWER region persuaded all the regional organizations dedicated to wine quality, such as his own GROSSER RING, to band together to form this national association.

Members must exceed the legal norms set for all German wines, maintain high standards of both viticulture and OENOLOGY, and at least 70 per cent of the estate's vineyard must be planted with traditional grape varieties (and not new GERMAN CROSSINGS). VDP members are concentrated in the Mosel-Saar-Ruwer, NAHE, RHEINGAU, RHEINHESSEN, and PFALZ regions where, perhaps not coincidentally, a particularly high proportion of the great RIESLING grape is grown.

In 1993 there were 164 members, many of them historic estates in, often aristocratic, family hands. The VDP association has continued to impose much stricter controls and targets on its members than the German government. In 1991, for example (when membership totalled 170), the VDP instituted stringent restrictions on YIELDS and adopted an overtly ecological viticultural policy.

VDQS stands for **Vin Délimité de Qualité Supérieure,** France's interim wine quality designation between VIN DE PAYS and APPELLATION CONTRÔLÉE. The VDQS category is very much a testing ground for smaller wine regions, many of which are eventually promoted to full AC status. Some VDQS date from the early 1950s; none were created between 1984 and 1993 when Côtes de MILLAU was created from Vin de Pays des Gorges et Côtes de Millau. Total annual production of VDQS wines is only about one per cent of the average total vintage. There is a relatively high concentration of VDQS designations on the fringes of the LOIRE, and of SOUTH WEST FRANCE. The VDQS system is overseen by the AC authorities, INAO, and the regulations governing the more recently granted VDQS wines are every bit as strict as AC rules.

VEGA SICILIA, concentrated and long-lived red wine that is Spain's undisputed equivalent of a FIRST GROWTH, made on a single property now incorporated into the RIBERA DEL DUERO denomination. The wine was being made long before the present DO region took shape in the 1980s. This 1,000-ha/2,500-acre farm either side of the main road east of Valladolid has been making wine in its present form since 1864 when Eloy Lacanda y Chaves planted vines from Bordeaux alongside Tinto Fino, also known as Tinta del País (a local strain of TEMPRANILLO). A succession of different owners have since managed to maintain the quality and reputation of Vega Sicilia as Spain's finest red wine.

The 130 ha of vineyard on CHALK soils overlooking the river Duero (DOURO in Portugal) are planted mainly with Tinto Fino but CABERNET SAUVIGNON, MERLOT, and MALBEC together make up about 35 per cent of the total production. A tiny quantity of the white ALBILLO is planted ostensibly to develop the bouquet.

Bodegas Vega Sicilia once produced three wines, all red. Two styles of Valbuena were released after maturing for three and five years respectively in French and American oak; only a five-year-old VINTAGE-dated version is now made. But it is the Vega Sicilia Unico that attracts the most attention. Restricted to the best VINTAGES, it is often released after spending about 10 years in a combination of wooden tanks; small, new BARRIQUES; large, old barrels; and bottles. Vega Sicilia can hardly be described as an exuberant wine and, perhaps because of its high price, the Unico occasionally attracts criticism. It is, however, an extraordinarily compact yet powerful, persistent wine with a restrained yet complex character that is uncommon in most of Spain. The best vintages of Vega Sicilia Unico and the rare multi-vintage Reserva Especial last for decades.

In 1992 Bodegas Vega Sicilia acquired the nearby Liceo winery and launched a less expensive range of wines in 1994.

R.J.M.

VEGETATIVE PROPAGATION, reproduction of a plant by asexual means. In nature it occurs by corms, bulbs, stolons, rhizomes, and layers. In viticulture, CUTTINGS and GRAFTING, or any part of a vine on which both roots and shoots will grow, are used. Micropropagation (see TISSUE CULTURE) is a modern application in which small amounts of a MOTHER VINE may be propagated in large numbers rapidly. Unlike

SEXUAL PROPAGATION, the progeny of vegetative propagation is genetically identical, unless MUTATION intervenes. B.G.C.

VEIN BANDING, vine disease. See FANLEAF DEGENERATION.

VELTLINER, common synonym for the Austrian white grape variety GRÜNER VELTLINER, also known in darker-skinned mutations as **Roter Veltliner**, which can produce characterful wines in ripe years, and occasionally **Brauner Veltliner**. Another important white grape variety, chiefly encountered in Austria, is FRÜHROTER VELTLINER, sometimes known as Veltliner in the far north east of Italy.

VENDANGE, French word for HARVEST. A *vendangeur* is a grape-picker, and a temporary lodging for grape-pickers may be called a *vendangeoir*.

VENDANGE TARDIVE, means literally 'late harvest' and is used most commonly, and most specifically, in ALSACE, where strict regulations cover its production, even if too many producers are meeting only the bare minima. Although all Vendange Tardive wines are made from ripe grapes, without the aid of CHAPTALIZATION, the wines themselves vary considerably in how sweet they are, with some of them tasting rich but almost bone dry. See also AUSLESE and BEERENAUSLESE, their counterparts in Germany.

VENDEMMIA, Italian for VINTAGE year or HARVEST. **Vendimia** is Spanish for harvest.

VENDÔMOIS, COTEAUX DU, a VDQS producing a wide range of wines between the Coteaux du LOIR and the city of Vendôme. The wines are necessarily light and crisp, this far from the equator, but a pale pink VIN GRIS from the PINEAU D'AUNIS grape can be an attractive local speciality. Slightly more solid reds may be made from Pinot Noir, Gamay, or Cabernet, and Chenin Blanc is the principal grape for some particularly tart white wines which represent about one bottle in six.

See also LOIRE and map on pp. 576–7.

VENETO, historically and currently important wine region in north east ITALY (see map on p. 517). It stretches westward to Lake Garda and northward to the alps and the Austrian border from the terra firma behind the lagoons and city of VENICE, an important power in the wine trade of the Middle Ages whose legacy has shaped some wines in the Veneto and elsewhere. The region usually produces more wine than any others in Italy apart from APULIA and SICILY, with an average annual production of more than 8 million hl/200 million gal. Its Verona and Treviso provinces are regularly among the five top producing provinces of the peninsula, along with Trapani, Foggia, and Taranto—all in the deep south.

In theory, a significant proportion of Veneto wine is of good quality, with percentages of DOC wine that approach a quarter of the total, but the reality is somewhat different: these percentages have been artificially inflated both by drastic enlargements of the DOC zones (to plains which were cereal-growing areas prior to the Second World War in the case of Valpolicella and Soave) and/or by sanctioning extremely generous YIELDS (in the case of Valpolicella, Soave, Bardolino, and Prosecco). The resulting wines, though nominally of DOC level, are too frequently characterless. Good bottles of Bardolino, Valpolicella, and Soave are not difficult to find, however, and there the CORVINA vine variety which forms the basis of Valpolicella, and GARGANEGA, the base of Soave, are capable of giving interesting products if grown in their proper area: the hills on the 45 degrees 30 minutes of LATITUDE which run eastward from Lake Garda, to the north of the fertile Adige river plain. Other hillside zones of real potential are scattered about the region and include the Colli Berici to the south and Breganze to the north of Vicenza, the Colli Euganei to the south west of Padua, the hillside part of the Piave DOC zone. Although native varieties, in particular Tocai, Garganega, and Verduzzo, are cultivated in these zones, the most interesting wines and the greatest potential are undoubtedly represented by light, fruity styled Merlot and Cabernet, though the relatively high yields and cool climate can often give a leafy, vegetal quality which detracts from the freshness. The Garganega-based Bianco di Custoza and Gambellara, two country cousins of Soave, the lightly sparkling Prosecco of Conegliano with a bitter finish, and the Moscato of the Colli Euganei (no rival to MOSCATO D'ASTI but with the true, musky varietal character) round out the regional picture, a picture characterized by large quantities of pleasant and easy drinking wines which seem to suffer from a lack of ambition and competitive spirit.

The Veneto's centre of ACADEME is the experimental viticultural institute at CONEGLIANO.

For details of notable specific wines, see AMARONE, BARDOLINO, BIANCO DI CUSTOZA, BREGANZE, GAMBELLARA, LISON-PRAMAGGIORE, PIAVE, PROSECCO, RABOSO, RECIOTO, SOAVE, and VALPOLICELLA. D.T.

VENEZUELA is a minor South American wine producer, and consumer, but TROPICAL VITICULTURE has been practised, mainly for TABLE GRAPES, since the arrival of European immigrants at the end of the 19th century (although there is evidence that Jesuit MISSIONARIES first planted vines at Cumana in the 16th century, and vine-growers emigrated here from Baden in 1783; see GERMAN HISTORY. In the late 20th century wine producers used GRAPE CONCENTRATE as their raw material for products that range from LAMBRUSCO-like blends to base wines for SANGRÍA. Average temperatures are about 27 °C, vine DORMANCY is impossible, and the two harvests per year are dictated by the rainy seasons. One of the most viticulturally suitable regions is Mérida in Lagunillas where at altitudes of about 1,100 m the climate is cooler than elsewhere and annual total rainfall (unevenly spread) is between 300 and 400 mm. Vines are also grown in Barquistimeto and in even drier areas to the north. Most of the vine varieties grown are table grapes, HYBRIDS such as Jacquez and ISABELLA, and a relative of CRIOLLA. A little GRILLO, BARBERA, and MALVASIA are also grown, however.

VENICE, north east Italian cultural and, once, commercial centre which was to exert considerable and sometimes lasting influence on the wines of the world. Medieval Venice had no agriculture or viticulture and obtained its wine and grain from LOMBARDY to the east; Venice's importance was in its trade. In 840 a treaty, known as the Pactum Lotharii, between CHARLEMAGNE's grandson Lothair and the doge of Venice, protected Venice's neutrality and guaranteed its security from the mainland. This treaty, which is the oldest surviving document of Venetian diplomacy, made Venice independent from the west and from Byzantium. Thus Venice became the most important of the Italo-Byzantine ports, and its position was strengthened when the Byzantines discovered that Venice's rivals Amalfi, NAPLES, and Gaeta had been collaborating with the Saracens. Initially Venice owed its wealth to its trade, acquiring possession of Crete, Modon, and Coron in the Aegean and being granted exemptions from the TAXATION in Constantinople that was to ruin the Byzantine economy (see GREECE, medieval history). The CRUSADES only strengthened Venice's position at the frontier between northern Europe and the eastern Mediterranean.

With its eastern expansion came the trade in sweet wines, so much more esteemed by northern Europeans than their own thinner ferments. Most of these were from Crete, known then as Candia. Many of them carried the name of the Greek port from which they were shipped, Monemvasia (hence MALVASIA di Candia, and MALMSEY). Some of these wines were sold in Constantinople, others were taken to Venice for redistribution, either overland to Florence (via Ferrara), or by sea to PARIS, ENGLAND, and Flanders. In addition to buying and selling Aegean wines, Venice also dealt in Italian wines, from Trevi, the northern Adriatic, and the MARCHES, and in the even richer wines of Tyre (in modern LEBANON), which was owned by the Venetians for most of the 13th century.

However, in trade with Syria and Palestine, Venice came second to GENOA, and the rivalry extended to the trade with northern Europe: Genoa led the way there, and Venice, which was less well placed, did not start shipping wine to northern Europe until the early 14th century. By that time Genoa had already won the battle: at the end of the 13th century Venice had ceased to be the richest and most important port in Italy, but not before having imported the Greek techniques of increasing sugar and alcohol content by deliberately making DRIED GRAPE WINES. Johnson suggests a direct link between such practices, employed on the islands along the Dalmatian coast, and those subsequently, indeed currently, used by some in the VENETO hinterland of Venice to make PASSITO versions of Valpolicella and Soave.

Venice was also to become the centre of GLASS production, and therefore played an important, if indirect, role in the history of wine.

See also ITALY. H.M.W.

Johnson, H., *The Story of Wine* (London, 1989).

Lopez, R. S. 'The trade of mediaeval Europe: the south', in *The Cambridge Economic History of Europe*, 7 vols., ii: *Trade and Industry in the Middle Ages* (Cambridge, 1987).

15th century engraving of a **Venice** which supplied huge quantities of Mediterranean wines to northern Europe.

Melis, Frederigo, 'Produzione e commercio dei vini italiani nei secoli XIII–XVIII', *Annales cisalpines d'histoire sociale*, 1/3 (1972), 107–33.
Nicol, Donald M., *Byzantium and Venice* (Cambridge, 1988).

VENTOUX, CÔTES DU, large appellation on the south eastern fringes of the southern RHÔNE between the Coteaux du TRICASTIN (also promoted to full AC status in 1973) and the Côtes du LUBÉRON. The 6,900-ha/17,000-acre appellation takes its name from Mont Ventoux, the 2,000-m/6,500-ft high peak which dominates the region. The communes entitled to the appellation are on the western and southern flanks of this land mass, which has a significant cooling effect on the southern Rhône's generally MEDITERRANEAN CLIMATE. Historically this has been an area for producing TABLE GRAPES (along with other tree fruits such as cherries).

The predominantly red and rosé wines are made mainly from a blend of Grenache, Syrah, Cinsaut, and Carignan—very similar to those of Tricastin, except that the proportion of Carignan can be 30 per cent in Ventoux whereas it is 20 per cent in Tricastin. Ventoux is even more dominated by the CO-OPERATIVES than Tricastin, and the wines generally taste even lighter than those of Tricastin. The red wines in particular can taste refreshing when drunk chilled in the region's high summer, but they too often lack substance and real interest. Fermentations are brief and deliberate EXTRACTION rare, although the highly successful BRAND La Vieille Ferme, which has been based on Ventoux wines, provides an honorable exception to this. Most other producers would do well to heed Livingstone-Learmonth's suggestion that more ambition and closer co-operation with possible markets could have dramatic and exciting consequences on the wine styles of this under-performing appellation.

Clairette and Bourboulenc are the principal varieties for the small quantities of white produced. The Bourboulenc in particular could produce some wine of real interest here.

Livingstone-Learmonth, J., *The Wines of the Rhône* (3rd edn., London, 1992).

VERAISON, word used by English speakers for that intermediate stage of grape berry development which marks the beginning of RIPENING, when the grapes change from the hard, green state to their softened and coloured form. It is derived from the French term *véraison*. At the beginning of veraison, the berries are hard and green, and about half their final size. During veraison, the berries change skin colour and soften, SUGARS and volume increase, and ACIDITY decreases. The colour of the grape before veraison is due to green chlorophyll, and at veraison berry skin changes colour to red-black (see ANTHOCYANS) or yellow-green (see CAROTENOIDS), depending on the variety.

For any one berry, the inception of veraison is rapid and dramatic. The berries soften and begin to accumulate GLUCOSE and FRUCTOSE, and begin to grow about six days later. However, not all berries on a vine, nor indeed in a bunch, show veraison simultaneously. The first berries to soften are those which are exposed and in warmer MICROCLIMATES (near a stake, post, or wall, for example, and benefiting from nocturnal back radiation); the last berries to undergo veraison are those in the CANOPY shade and on short shoots. It is difficult therefore to be precise about the single date of veraison; more commonly a date is recorded when, say, 50 per cent of the berries on a vine show veraison. A more exact alternative is to measure when the berries soften, or when the grapes' sugar concentration reaches a given value—7° BRIX, for example. At about the same time as veraison occurs, CANE RIPENING (known as *aoûtement* in French) begins.

The onset of veraison (and cane ripening) is controlled by both plant and environmental factors. Exposed grapes on vines which have a high LEAF TO FRUIT RATIO and which are experiencing mild WATER STRESS (and hence no active shoot growth) undergo veraison first. By contrast, veraison is delayed in vines with large crops, with many actively growing shoot tips and shaded fruit. Veraison is observably early in vineyards producing high-quality fruit, with both veraison and cane ripening developing quickly. Environmental factors associated with the early onset of veraison are warm, sunny, and dry weather. R.E.S. & B.G.C.

Champagnol, F., *Éléments de physiologie de la vigne et de viticulture générale* (St-Gely-du-Fesc, 1984).
Huglin, P., *Biologie et écologie de la vigne* (Paris, 1986).

VÉRARGUES, or **Coteaux de Vérargues**, one of the named CRUS within the Coteaux du LANGUEDOC appellation in southern France. The zone overlaps substantially with that of MUSCAT DE LUNEL east of Montpellier and is immediately south of ST-CHRISTOL.

VERDEJO, characterful white grape variety grown in and around the Spanish RUEDA region.

VERDELHO, Portuguese white grape variety most closely associated with the island of Madeira, where it became increasingly rare in the post-PHYLLOXERA era but the name was for long used to denote a style of wine somewhere between SERCIAL and BUAL levels of richness. The relatively few Verdelho vines on Madeira produce small, hard grapes and musts high in acidity. It is probably the same as the GOUVEIO of the Douro and possibly the same as the VERDELLO of Italy. The variety has had most notable success in vibrant, lemony, full bodied table wines in Australia, particularly in some of the hotter regions of WESTERN AUSTRALIA.

See also MADEIRA.

VERDELLO, white grape variety known both in UMBRIA and SICILY. A connection with VERDELHO seems likely but is unproven.

VERDICCHIO, one of central Italy's classic white wines, is produced from the Verdicchio grape in two DOC zones of its home territory (since at least the 14th century) of the MARCHES: Verdicchio dei Castelli di Jesi, to the west of Ancona and a mere 30 km/20 miles from the Adriatic Sea, and Verdicchio di Matelica, considerably further inland and at higher altitudes, close to the regional border with UMBRIA. The wines share common characteristics, although the Verdicchio di Matelica, with lower yields (13 tons/ha against the 15 tons permitted for Verdicchio dei Castelli di Jesi) and better exposed HILLSIDE VINEYARDS, can be a fuller, more characterful wine. Matelica's 225-odd ha (560 acres) are dwarfed, however, by the more than 2,300 ha of the Castelli di Jesi. This latter DOC is divided into a CLASSICO zone, with over 85 per cent of the total vineyard area, and a zone of regular Verdicchio dei Castelli di Jesi with a mere 300 ha. Close to 60 per cent of the production of the Castelli di Jesi DOC is controlled by CO-OPERATIVES, and NÉGOCIANT houses control three-quarters of the remaining 40 per cent; small producers are of marginal significance both in terms of volume and in their impact on the market.

The wine has gained its fame, in fact, largely due to the efforts of Fazi-Battaglia, a large négociant firm with extensive vineyard holdings, which pioneered the large-scale marketing of Verdicchio and still controls over 20 per cent of the total production. It was Fazi-Battaglia which introduced the amphora-shaped bottle and scroll-shaped label, initially a positive factor in gaining recognition for the wine but later responsible for the image of kitsch and frivolity with which Verdicchio has been saddled.

Like many central Italian white wines, Verdicchio was once fermented on its skins, giving it a certain fullness and authority albeit often at the expense of any delicacy. The GOVERNO technique, whereby a second fermentation is induced by the addition of the must from dried grapes after the conclusion of the initial fermentation, was also employed to add a contrasting sweetness and an enlivening dash of CARBON DIOXIDE to the wine. These practices have been largely abandoned and Verdicchio is now made in a modern style, without SKIN CONTACT and with temperature-controlled fermentations. It is now a more 'correct', if perhaps less distinctive, wine, although the lemony acidity and the bitter almonds of the after-taste are still identifiably present in the better bottles of the DOC.

Perhaps partly because of its high natural ACIDITY Verdicchio was one of the first Italian SPUMANTES, with a tradition which can be traced back to the middle of the 19th century, and pleasant bottles of bubbly Verdicchio remain an integral part of the DOC production. Total Verdicchio plantings were nearly 4,000 ha/9,900 acres in the early 1990s. D.T.

Anderson, B., *The Wine Atlas of Italy* (London and New York, 1990).
Gleave, D., *The Wines of Italy* (London and New York, 1989).

VERDOT. See PETIT VERDOT.

VERDUZZO, white grape variety with a long documented history in north east Italy. It is cultivated principally in FRIULI (with the significant exception of the PIAVE DOC in the bordering province of Treviso in the Veneto) in six different DOC zones: AQUILEIA, COLLI ORIENTALI, GRAVE, ISONZO, LATISANA, and LISON-PRAMAGGIORE. Only the Grave and the Colli Orientali produce significant quantities—respectively 10,000 (264,000) and 5,000 hl (132,000 gal) annually—and the Verduzzo of the Colli Orientali is qualitatively far superior, the grape showing a decided preference for HILLSIDE VINEYARDS. The wine exists both in a dry and a sweet version, although the latter, obtained either by late harvesting or by raisining the grapes (see DRIED GRAPE WINES), can frequently be more medium dry than lusciously sweet. Sweet Verduzzo, although less common than dry Verduzzo, is the more interesting wine, golden in colour and often with a delightful density and honeyed aromas, even if it lacks the complexity of an outstanding dessert wine. Dry Verduzzo is less characterful, and the grapes' TANNINS often impart an odd astringency which is more noticeable when it has been fermented dry.

Ramandolo, to the north of Udine, is considered the classic zone for fine sweet Verduzzo, but the Colli Orientali di Friuli DOC, when first established, permitted the use of the name Ramandolo for any sweet Verduzzo in the production zone, converting, as it were, a place name into a generic name. This anomaly was recently corrected with the establishment of a separate Ramandolo DOC. Occasional bottles of Verduzzo from the Collio production zone can also be found, superior to the Verduzzo of the Grave DOC if not as good as the Colli Orientali Verduzzo, but they qualify only as a VINO DA TAVOLA.

Italy's 1990 vineyard survey found 2,600 ha/6,400 acres of Verduzzo Trevigiano vines and 1,800 ha of Verduzzo Friulano. D.T.

VERMENTINO is the attractive, aromatic white grape variety widely grown in Sardinia, Liguria, to a limited extent in Corsica, and to an increasing extent in Languedoc-Roussillon, where it is a recently permitted variety in many appellations, including white Côtes du Roussillon. It is thought to be identical to the variety long grown in eastern Provence as ROLLE and in north western Italy is sometimes called Rollo. In CORSICA it is sometimes called Malvoisie de Corse, and some believe that the variety is related to the MALVASIA family. Vermentino is Corsica's most planted white grape variety and dominates the island's white APPELLATION CONTRÔLÉE wines. In Sardinia it is picked deliberately early to retain acid levels but still manages to produce lively wines of character.

Italy has nearly 4,000 ha/10,000 acres of Vermentino vines.

VERMOUTH, herb-flavoured FORTIFIED wine available in many different styles and qualities but usually a much more industrial product than wine. The Romans certainly made herb-flavoured wines, and the Greeks before them used a wide range of additives (see Ancient GREECE), often using wormwood or *artemesia absinthum*, which was thought to have curative powers for gastric ills. Such FLAVOURED WINES were strictly of local minority interest until the 16th century when a Piedmontese, d'Alessio, began to market a medicinal wine similar to those he had noted in Bavaria flavoured with wormwood, there called *Wermuth*. The medicine, which enjoyed a certain success in French royal circles, subsequently became known as *vermutwein* and, in Anglicized form, vermouth. The diarist Samuel Pepys noted 'a glass of wormwood wine' without the comment it would have elicited had it been anything other than commonplace in late 17th century London. Modern large-scale vermouth production dates from 18th century Piedmont, close to the alps which could supply the necessary herbs. Brands such as Cinzano, Martini, and the French Noilly Prat threw off any pretence at curative powers during the cocktail age and were particularly popular in the early and mid 20th century.

So many herbs and spices are now used to flavour fortified wines that the definition of vermouth is necessarily elastic. The more classic version is the almost dry, bitter drink with the strong aroma of wormwood and other bitter herbs. The Italian Punt e Mes is one of the better-known examples. But the more popular version by far is sweeter, about 17 per cent alcohol, and more vaguely herbal. Such vermouths are traditionally known as Italian if red and sweet and French if gold and drier, although these styles are made wherever vermouth is produced. France's most delicately alpine vermouth is Chambéry, while its vermouth arguably most closely linked to fine wine is Lillet of Bordeaux, for long owned by the Borie family of the ST-JULIEN property Ch Ducru-Beaucaillou.

The vermouth industry has never sought fine wine as its base and is a useful outlet for some of the European WINE LAKE, absorbing millions of litres of basic table wine from the south of Italy and France. The alcohol used for FORTIFICATION comes from much the same source. Traditionally vermouths were flavoured by infusion of 'botanicals', herbs, peels, and spices gathered from the wild. Modern vermouth is more likely to be flavoured by the addition of a concentrate designed for consistency to match an imagined ideal blend of botanicals. After sweetening, usually with MISTELLE, and fortification, most modern vermouth is chilled for tartrate STABILIZATION and subjected to PASTEURIZATION and FILTRATION. The worst is anticipated for products exported as widely as these.

VERNACCIA, name used for several, unrelated Italian grape varieties, mainly white but sometimes red, from the extreme north of the peninsula (VERNATSCH being merely a Germanic version of Vernaccia) to the fizzy red **Vernaccia di Serrapetrona** of the MARCHES and the **Vernaccia di Oristano** which is an almost SHERRY-like wine made on the island of SARDINIA. The most highly regarded form is VERNACCIA DI SAN GIMIGNANO, which has no relationship to the Sardinian **Vernaccia di Cagliari** vine, according to the studies of Professor Liuzzi of Cagliari in the early 1930s.

The name is so common because it comes from the same root as the word 'vernacular', or indigenous. Wines called Vernaccia, or sometimes **vernage**, are often cited in the records of London wine merchants in the Middle Ages, but the term could have been used for virtually any sort of wine, Latin being the common language then. Vernaccia was a particularly common product of LIGURIA in north west Italy and Tuscany. For more details of medieval trade in Vernaccia, see GENOA, ITALY, and TUSCANY.

VERNACCIA DI SAN GIMIGNANO, distinctive dry white wine made from the local VERNACCIA vine variety, probably unrelated to any other Vernaccia, cultivated in the sandstone-based soils around the famous towers of San Gimignano in the province of Siena in TUSCANY in central Italy. There are references to Vernaccia in the archives of San Gimignano as early as 1276.

DOC recognition was awarded in March of 1966, making Vernaccia di San Gimignano the first ever DOC, which saved the wine from what seemed a fatal decline: the Dalmasso Commission of 1932 had described the wine as a curiosity and the wine became even rarer after the Second World War when so much TREBBIANO and MALVASIA were planted in the zone. Since the late 1960s, the wine has enjoyed a measure of success, thanks to its unquestioned superiority over the standard bland Tuscan white blend of Trebbiano and Malvasia.

Vernaccia vine trained up a tree with the towers of San Gimignano in the background.

At its best the wine has a crisp, refreshing quality and an attractively bitter finish. Despite its renewed popularity and attempts to give it further complexity with small BARREL MATURATION, the wine has only attained modest quality and price levels. In the long run it may well have a lesser significance in its own place of origin, as leading producers in San Gimignano have begun to achieve striking success with serious red wines based on SANGIOVESE grapes (which have always been grown here), and with more international varieties such as CABERNET SAUVIGNON and CHARDONNAY. D.T.

VERNATSCH, German name for the undistinguished light red grape variety SCHIAVA.

VERONELLI, LUIGI (1926–), Italy's most influential food and wine critic since 1956, when he founded the magazine *Il Gastronomo* and began to collaborate with Italy's major daily newspapers, news weeklies, and RAI-TV, the national television network. Born into an affluent Milanese family with a broad European culture, Veronelli was an unabashed Francophile from his first writings and a frank admirer of the French APPELLATION CONTRÔLÉE system, in particular of its designated CRUS, a CLASSIFICATION which he has attempted to apply to Italian vineyards and their products in his many books on his country's wines. Polemical in character and a romantic anarchist in his political convictions, Veronelli has long championed the cause of the small peasant proprietor and has been a particularly bitter opponent of Italy's DOC systems, which he considers rigged in favour of the country's large commercial wineries. His campaigns against the DOC system earned him a period of banishment from Italian television in the 1970s and 1980s. A trip to California in the early 1980s converted him to an enthusiast of the BARRIQUE, then almost unknown in Italy, and his writings were extremely influential in spreading the use of small oak barrels in Italy.

For many years Veronelli represented the only possible means of obtaining commercial recognition and visibility for Italy's small producers and he can be credited with the discovery and identification of the large majority of the country's better producers, a role which has won him a group of devoted friends and an equally large group of sworn enemies. His endorsement has signified instant commercial success for a number of producers whose wines he first brought to public attention, a success which has induced in some of these producers an even greater commitment to quality, in others an avaricious pricing policy designed to capitalize on his endorsement. If the career has been a controversial one, it is safe to say that the current Italian wine scene would be virtually unrecognizable without his work, and the emergence of Italian VITICULTURE and OENOLOGY dedicated to quality would have been considerably slower and more uncertain. D.T.

Belfrage, N., *Life beyond Lambrusco* (London, 1984).

VERS DE LA GRAPPE, insect pests and an important cause of BOTRYTIS BUNCH ROT.

VERTICAL TRELLIS, a vine-TRAINING SYSTEM widely used throughout the world, in which the shoots are trained vertically upwards in summer. The shoots are held in place by foliage wires which, in turn, are attached to vineyard posts. In many vineyards there are two pairs of foliage wires, and commonly the vines are subjected to TRIMMING at the top and sides to maintain a neat, hedge-like appearance. Both SPUR PRUNING and CANE PRUNING are possible. This trellis system is widely used in Alsace, Germany, eastern Europe, and New Zealand, with high vines (trunks of about 1 m/3 ft) and relatively low-density plantings. The vineyards of Bordeaux, Burgundy, and Champagne are also vertically shoot positioned, although the vines are planted more closely together and the trunks are much shorter. R.E.S.

VERTICILLIUM WILT, FUNGAL DISEASE which causes apparently healthy vines to collapse suddenly. The fungus *Verticillium dahliae* lives in the soil, and attacks new vineyards. Young vines are usually affected, and often the vine recovers. There is no control apart from avoiding planting on sites where the fungus exists. R.E.S.

VESPAIOLA, white grape variety grown in the VENETO region of north east Italy, said to take its name from the wasps (*vespe*) attracted by the sugar levels of its ripe grapes. Its most famous product is the Torcolato sweet wine of BREGANZE, although in this Vespaiola is blended with Tocai and Garganega, and the DRIED GRAPE WINE-making technique may well be the most important ingredient.

VESPOLINA, low-yielding red grape variety known almost exclusively in, and therefore probably native to, the area around GATTINARA in the PIEDMONT region of north west Italy. Commonly blended with NEBBIOLO, occasionally in the company of BONARDA Piemontese, it is also grown in the OLTREPÒ PAVESE zone across the border in LOMBARDY, where it is known as Ughetta.

Anderson, B., *The Wine Atlas of Italy* (London and New York, 1990).

VEUVE CLICQUOT-PONSARDIN, Champagne house as famous for its eponymous founder, the first great champagne widow (*veuve* in French), as for its wines. Nicole Barbe Ponsardin (1777–1866) married François Clicquot, an owner of Champagne vineyards, in 1798. The wedding took place in a Champagne cellar as churches were not yet reconsecrated following the French Revolution. François Clicquot died in 1805, leaving Mme Clicquot in charge of the company, which she renamed Veuve Clicquot-Ponsardin. The widow steered the house carefully through the turbulent years of the First and Second Empires, defying Napoleon's blockades to ship the wine to Russia, and finding an export market in virtually every European court. 'La Grande Dame' is credited with inventing the riddling process called REMUAGE, and adapting a piece of her own furniture into the first riddling table for that purpose. She devised the famous yellow label, still used for the NON-VINTAGE wine. On her death, the company passed

Seppelts' sparkling wine cellars at Great Western in the Australian state of **Victoria**.

to her former chief partner, another shrewd businessman, Édouard Werlé, and the house remained in the hands of the Werlé family until in 1987 it became part of the Moët Hennessy-Louis Vuitton group (see LVMH). The house style is based on Pinot Noir grapes and, in particular, those grown at Bouzy, where the house has large holdings. La Grande Dame is Clicquot's PRESTIGE CUVÉE, named, of course, after the widow. In 1990, the Champagne house purchased a majority stake in the WESTERN AUSTRALIAN winery Cape Mentelle and its New Zealand subsidiary CLOUDY BAY. S.A.

Crestin-Billet, F., *Veuve Clicquot, la grande dame de la Champagne* (Grenoble, 1992).

VICTORIA, third most important wine state in AUSTRALIA.

Hubert de Castella came to Victoria in 1854 from his native Switzerland, and was a leading figure in the golden age of Victorian viticulture up to 1890 (when it produced half the wine made in Australia). He wrote several books, the most famous entitled *John Bull's Vineyard*, a eulogy suggesting Victoria could supply England with all the wine it might ever need. Instead, a combination of PHYLLOXERA, changing land use, changing consumption patterns, the removal of state duties, and the First World War saw the end of the hundreds of vineyards and wineries spread across the very cool southern half of the state.

North east Victoria, centred on **Rutherglen** and including **Milawa**, became the focus of wine-making, producing a range of FORTIFIED and red table wines, the latter almost indistinguishable from some of the former. Foremost among the fortified wines were, and are, the unctuous LIQUEUR MUSCAT and Liqueur Tokay, wines of unique style and extraordinary concentration of flavour deriving in part from the shrivelled grapes and in part from long BARREL MATURATION in tin sheds which unconsciously mimic the *estufas* of MADEIRA. These unique wine styles are also called simply Muscat and Tokay.

The two outposts to survive along with north eastern Victoria were **Great Western** (with Seppelt and Bests wineries), the central **Goulburn Valley** (Ch Tahbilk), and the north west **Riverland** (Mildara). From its nadir in the mid 1950s, when there were fewer than 30 wineries in operation, Victoria has recovered to the point where its viticultural map once again resembles that of the 19th century, populated by almost 200 wineries.

Melbourne is now ringed by the **Yarra Valley**, the **Mornington Peninsula**, **Geelong**, **South Gippsland**, and

Macedon. Over 70 wineries here enjoy a range of climatic conditions all cooler than those of Bordeaux, variously cooled by ALTITUDE or maritime influences. PINOT NOIR and CHARDONNAY are the dominant varieties, capable of producing wines of world class. CABERNET SAUVIGNON, CABERNET FRANC, and MERLOT also flourish, particularly in the Yarra Valley.

Central Victoria spreads east from **Drumborg** in the far west, to include Great Western, the **Pyrenees**, **Bendigo** (with Ballarat), and the Goulburn Valley. Excepting the ultra-cool Drumborg (where Seppelt's substantial vineyards are primarily devoted to sparkling wine production), these regions are all noted for their red wines, and in particular SHIRAZ. Intriguingly, this variety can produce wines redolent of pepper and spice (harking to France's Rhône valley) or eucalypt mint (challenging the famous Martha's Vineyard of California's NAPA Valley), but always with masses of dark berry fruit and ample TANNINS.

The Murray river meanders east for over 500 km / 305 miles as it marks the border between Victoria and NEW SOUTH WALES with major areas of Riverland viticulture around Echuca, Swan Hill, Robinvale, and, most significantly, Mildura. Karadoc, just to the east of Mildura, is home to Lindemans and Australia's largest winery, crushing up to 50,000 tonnes a year, rather more than any single French winery. Merbein is home to Mildara, while Sunnycliffe, Alambie, and BRL-HARDY's Burgonga wineries (the latter just across the Murray river in New South Wales) are major producers. Lindemans tells it all with its Bin 65 Chardonnay, blended in 15,000-hl / 396,000-gal tanks, and one of the largest Chardonnay BRANDS in the world. J.H.

VIDAL, white grape variety and a FRENCH HYBRID more properly known as **Vidal Blanc** or **Vidal 256**. It is a hybrid of UGNI BLANC and one of the SEIBEL parents of SEYVAL BLANC, developed by nurseryman J. L. Villard. It is grown to a limited extent in the eastern United States and is particularly valued for its winter hardiness and the late harvest sweet wines it produces in CANADA.

VIDIGEIRA, town in southern Portugal whose co-operative is establishing a certain reputation for its wines. See ALENTEJO for more details.

VIEILLES VIGNES is French for 'old vines'. The term is used widely on wine labels in the hope that potential buyers are aware that wine quality is often associated with senior VINE AGE, at least in the Old World. There are few effective controls on the use of the term, however, and little agreement about exactly how many years it is before a vine can be deemed old. BOLLINGER was one of the first producers to use the term, for the produce of vines which were never grafted post-PHYLLOXERA.

VIENNA, capital city of AUSTRIA and, unusually, a wine region in its own right.

VIGNA is Italian for VINEYARD, while a **vignaiolo** is a vine-grower.

VIGNE is French for a VINE. **Vigneron** is French for a vine-grower, some say derived from *vigne ronde*, implying that a vigneron actually prunes the vines himself whereas a VITICULTEUR merely grows them.

The term *vigneron* is now used widely outside France for a wide range of people engaged in wine production. A **vignoble** is French for a VINEYARD, although the term *vignoble* can be used more broadly as in 'the entire French *vignoble*'.

VIGOUR in a viticultural sense is the vine's vegetative growth, an important aspect of any vine. Vines of high vigour may be described as **vigorous**, and demonstrate a lack of BALANCE between shoot and fruit growth. Vigorous vineyards show rapid shoot growth in the spring, and shoots continue to grow late into the growing season, even past VERAISON, the beginning of fruit ripening. Shoots on vigorous vines have long INTERNODES, thick stems, large leaves, and many LATERAL SHOOTS. Vigorous vineyards are usually, but not necessarily, associated with high YIELDS. The rank, vegetative growth may produce so much SHADE that FRUITFULNESS declines, leading to even more vegetative growth.

Vigorous vineyards have high LEAF TO FRUIT RATIOS and may even show values of more than 50 sq cm/g. Other measurements listed by Smart and Robinson which are used to quantify vigour are the weight of annual prunings, the average weight of a cane at winter pruning, and the ratio of weight of grapes to pruning weight. Typical values of these measurements for high-vigour vineyards are more than 0.6 kg prunings per metre of row length, more than 60 g cane weight, and a yield to pruning weight ratio of less than 3. Low-vigour vineyards have corresponding figures of less than 0.3 kg/m, less than 10 g, and more than 12. Balanced vines have values of about 0.5 kg/m, 30 g, and 7 respectively.

The vigour of a vineyard is essentially dependent on two features, the size and health of the root system, and also the pruning level. First, what grows above ground is some sort of mirror of what grows below. A vine with a large and healthy root system will have the reserves of CARBOHYDRATES and balance of HORMONES to support vigorous shoot growth. On the other hand, a vine with a small and/or unhealthy root system, be it due to shallow soil, drought, root pests such as PHYLLOXERA, or diseases such as ARMILLARIA ROOT ROT, will support only low-vigour growth.

Vines should be pruned to bud numbers relative to the amount of early shoot growth they can support. This is the concept of BALANCED PRUNING, and one criterion used is to retain at winter PRUNING about 30 buds per kg of pruning weight. Use of this sort of rule means that the subsequent shoot growth will be in balance with the vine's carbohydrate reserves, ensuring balance between shoot and fruit growth, and moderate vigour.

High vigour is a common problem of modern vineyards, for many and varied reasons. The vines may be planted in a region with a benign climate on too deep a soil, which is well

High- (top) and low-**vigour** vineyards at the same point in the growing season.

supplied with water (from rainfall and/or irrigation) and nutrients (from natural fertility or fertilizers or added compost). Modern control methods can also keep vines free of stress associated with weeds, pests, and diseases. R.E.S.

Smart, R. E., and Robinson, M., *Sunlight into Wine: A Handbook for Winegrape Canopy Management* (Adelaide, 1991).

Winkler, A. J., *et al.*, *General Viticulture* (2nd edn., Berkeley, Calif., 1974).

VILANA, white grape variety that is native to and the most widely grown on the island of Crete (see GREECE). It is responsible for the most delicate examples of dry white Peza made there.

VILA NOVA DE GAIA, or Gaia New Town, cramped, cobbled suburb on the opposite side of the DOURO river estuary from the Portuguese city of OPORTO where PORT is traditionally aged. From the waterfront, long, single-storey buildings called LODGES rise in steps up the hillside. Under the clay-tiled roofs, shippers mature their stocks of port, as well as TASTING, BLENDING, BOTTLING, and selling it. Until 1986, the law required that all port destined for export had to be shipped from within the strictly defined (and easy to monitor) area of the Gaia entrepôt. Port may now be shipped from anywhere within the demarcated Douro region so that export markets are open to small firms, quintas, and co-operatives without premises in Vila Nova de Gaia. R.J.M.

VILLAGES, common suffix of an APPELLATION CONTRÔLÉE name for a French wine. Generally speaking, an X-Villages wine must be made from one or several of a selection of communes whose produce is known to be superior to that of the rest of the X zone. See, for example, BEAUJOLAIS, MÂCON, and Côtes-du-RHÔNE.

VILLAGE WINE is a term used particularly in Burgundy for a wine which qualifies for an APPELLATION that coincides with the name of the village or commune in which the wine is made. It contrasts with a lesser GENERIC wine which takes the name of a region, and wines from PREMIER CRU and GRAND CRU vineyards.

VILLARD is the common French name for a great French viticultural secret, their most commonly planted HYBRIDS. Most are members of the vast SEYVE VILLARD group.

In France Villard Blanc is Seyve Villard 12.375 while Villard Noir is Seyve Villard 18.315. Villard Noir was planted all over France, from the northern Rhône to Bordeaux, and was treasured for its resistance to downy mildew. Villard Blanc made slightly more palatable wine (though the must can be difficult to process). Both varieties yield prodigiously and for that attribute were so beloved by growers that in 1968 there were 30,000 ha/74,000 acres of Villard Noir and 21,000 ha of Villard Blanc in France (making them fifth and third most planted black and white grape varieties respectively).

To the great credit of the authorities, and thanks to not inconsiderable bribes for grubbing up, within 20 years these totals had been shaved to 2,500 ha and 4,600 ha and Villards of both hues will be almost completely eradicated by the turn of the century. Particularly attached to Villard are the growers of Tarn and Ardèche, to Villard Noir.

Other hybrids once widely planted in France are BACO, CHAMBOURCIN, COUDERC, PLANTET, and various other members of the Seibel and Seyve Villard families.

For more information see FRENCH HYBRIDS.

VIN, French for wine and therefore a much-used term (see below). **Vin blanc** is white wine, **vin rosé** is pink, **vin rouge** is red wine, **vin mousseux** is sparkling wine, and so on. For **vin ordinaire**, see VIN DE TABLE. For **vin biologique**, see ORGANIC WINE. For **vin blanc cassis**, see KIR.

VIÑA, Spanish word for VINEYARD.

VIN DÉLIMITÉ DE QUALITÉ SUPÉRIEURE, France's interim wine quality designation between APPELLATION CONTRÔLÉE and VIN DE PAYS. See VDQS for more details.

VIN DE LIQUEUR, strong, sweet drink made by adding GRAPE SPIRIT to grape juice for a golden vin de liqueur, or to whole, dark-skinned grapes for a red vin de liqueur. The alcohol is added before the juice begins to ferment so that the resulting liquids have an alcoholic strength of 16 to 17 per cent but no secondary products of fermentation such as GLYCEROL or SUCCINIC ACID. The term has also been adopted by EUROPEAN UNION authorities (although not by this book) to encompass all FORTIFIED wines.

The principal members of this special category of French specialities, sometimes known as mistelles, are the PINEAU DES CHARENTES of Cognac country and its Armagnac counterpart FLOC DE GASCOGNE. Another vin de liqueur more recently awarded its own APPELLATION CONTRÔLÉE is MACVIN of the Jura, made from local MARC added to grape juice and tasting strongly of the distinctive flavour of this POMACE BRANDY. Most vins de liqueur are pale gold, but soft, fruity rosé versions of both Pineau and Floc can be found in the regions of production. Vin de liqueur differs from VIN DOUX NATUREL in that the alcohol is added earlier and the resulting drinks therefore tend to be, and taste, more spirit dominated. Some Muscat de FRONTIGNAN may also qualify. Many wine regions have their own versions of this easy-to-make strong, sweet aperitif: Champagne has its Ratafia, the Rhône its Rinquinquin, while the Languedoc has Cartagène, although, where there are no regulations governing their production, they are sometimes made further along the scale towards vins doux naturels. Like vins doux naturels, these sweet wines can be enhanced by serving them cool, and the wine in an opened bottle should retain its appeal for well over a week.

VIN DE PAILLE is French for 'straw wine' (Strohwein in German), a small group of necessarily expensive but often quite delicious, long-lived, sweet white wines. These are essentially a subgroup of DRIED GRAPE WINES made from grapes dried on straw mats. Cyrus REDDING's catalogue of wines produced in the early 19th century makes it clear that vins de paille were then much more common and, although he was most enthusiastic about 'Ermitage-paille' (from HERMITAGE vines), he found vins de paille in JURA, ALSACE, and Corrèze. At about the same time some producers in Rust in AUSTRIA were also using the technique.

Today, production of this rarity is virtually confined to particularly ripe vintages and the most conscientious producers of Hermitage, ARBOIS, occasionally L'ÉTOILE, and Côtes du JURA. For much of the 20th century no vin de paille was made in Hermitage, but Gérard Chave revived the practice with healthy, not late-picked, Marsanne grapes in 1974, dried on straw in the attic, and has since been followed by CHAPOUTIER and others. (Chapoutier still have some ancient but not decrepit 1848 Hermitage vin de paille, according to Livingstone-Learmonth.) Average yields are minuscule once the grapes have been raisined, but the results are luscious in the extreme, and are invariably bottled in a half-bottle.

The Jura producers often suspend their SAVAGNIN, POULSARD, or Chardonnay grapes to raisin them rather than laying them out on straw. The minimum POTENTIAL ALCOHOL allowed is 18 per cent (as opposed to 14 per cent in Hermitage). The grapes are generally pressed at Christmas time, and 100 kg/220 lbs of grapes may yield fewer than 20 l/5 gal of juice. Jura producers also customarily age their vins de paille in cask for several years. The wines often have a natural alcoholic strength of about 15 per cent and are capable of long BOTTLE AGEING.

There is renewed, if limited, experimentation with making vin de paille in Alsace and, unlike BOTRYTIZED wine, this is one wine style with which any curious and dedicated wine-maker can experiment.

Livingstone-Learmonth, J., *The Wines of the Rhône* (3rd edn., London, 1992).

VIN DE PAYS, French expression meaning 'country wines' which was adopted for an intermediate category of wines created in FRANCE in 1973, and formalized in 1979, to recognize and encourage the production of wines that are distinctly superior to basic VIN DE TABLE, and which, in theory at least, offer some stamp of regional identity. Hence the creation of more than 140 different vins de pays, all of them carrying some geographical designation mirroring the principles of the APPELLATION CONTRÔLÉE (AC) system. To qualify as a vin de pays, a wine must not be blended, must be produced in limited quantities, must be made of certain specified grape varieties, must reach a certain minimum ALCOHOLIC STRENGTH, and must be submitted to a tasting panel, as well as coming from a specified area. By 1993, more than a fifth of all wine produced in France was sold as a vin de pays of some sort.

In many regions the vine-grower has a clear choice between making an appellation wine, or producing a vin de pays either because yields are too high to qualify for an AC, or because he or she grows (as is often the case with new or imported INTERNATIONAL VARIETIES) grape varieties permitted by the local Vin de Pays regulations but prohibited by those of the local AC. In general vins de pays may be produced from grapes which yield up to 90 hl/ha (5 tons/acre) while 50 hl/ha or so is a more likely maximum YIELD permitted by appellation regulations.

There are three levels of vin de pays:

Four are regional: Vin de Pays d'Oc from the LANGUEDOC; Vin de Pays du Jardin de la France from the LOIRE; Vin de Pays du Comté Tolosan, most of SOUTH WEST FRANCE; and Vin de Pays des Comtés Rhodaniens incorporating ARDÈCHE, BEAUJOLAIS, JURA, SAVOIE, and the northern RHÔNE.

About 40 are departmental. These are named after one of France's *départements*, or counties, such as Vin de Pays de l'Hérault, Vin de Pays de Loire-Atlantique, Vin de Pays de Tarn-et-Garonne, or Vin de Pays de l'Ardèche (these are, respectively, specific *départements* within each of the regions above).

About 100 more are locally specific. These may be named after some historical or geographical phenomenon such as Vin de Pays des Coteaux de Murviel, Vin de Pays des Marches de Bretagne, Vin de Pays des Coteaux du Quercy, or Vin de Pays des Coteaux de l'Ardèche (each a local denomination within the three departmental vins de pays specified above).

Some of these locally specific vins de pays names are virtually unused, some of the smaller ones have been developed as commercially useful exclusivities by individual merchants, and many of them are unknown outside their district of origin. Their names in many cases bear no relation to current geography—although historical nomenclature has clearly been a useful source for local officials charged with finding names which would present no confusion with the name of any existing AC or VDQS wine. (The French authorities have been keen to make a very clear distinction between vins de pays and wines which may be accorded the full sanction of AC status.) Some of the local names are simply too difficult for export markets, often unsure of the exact spelling of even vin de pays, to grasp. Vin de Pays des Coteaux du Grésivaudan, for example, will not be asked for by name by many outside Savoie, while the name of the south western Vin de Pays des Terrasses et Coteaux de Montauban seems unnecessarily pedantic.

Other exercises in nomenclature have represented strokes of genius. The image of Corsica is transformed in the name Vin de Pays de l'Île de Beauté, just as the Loire sounds even prettier as the Jardin de la France, while Roussillon's vins de pays quite rightly emphasize the region's ethnic origins in Vin de Pays Catalans and Vin de Pays des Côtes Catalans.

A certain amount of red, and some white, vin de pays PRIMEUR is produced each year, and may be released on the third Thursday of October (thereby beating Beaujolais NOUVEAU by a full month).

The vins de pays which have enjoyed enormous success outside France are those labelled as VARIETALS, a concept viewed with such distaste by the INAO, which oversees AC labelling, that vins de pays present the modern consumer with virtually the only means of acquiring a wine that is both French and labelled with a familiar grape variety such as Chardonnay, Sauvignon Blanc, Merlot, or Cabernet Sauvignon (or, increasingly, with a less familiar variety such as Marsanne, Terret, or Viognier). Some non-French customers could be much more attracted by a Chardonnay, Vin de Pays d'Oc, than, for example, a full AC counterpart carrying a less familiar name such as St-Romain or a Bugey, for example. Reverence for the words 'appellation contrôlée' is a French phenomenon. Vins de pays have been particularly successful in Germany and Great Britain.

The most important single vin de pays is Vin de Pays d'Oc, which is France's prime source of varietal wine. About 85 per cent of all vins de pays come from the Languedoc-Roussillon, Provence, or the southern Rhône. A further six per cent come from the Loire. Vin de pays has also provided a useful way of selling the surplus produce of vines grown in regions specializing in BRANDY production. Crisp, dry white Vin de Pays des Côtes de Gascogne was in the early 1980s a commercial saviour in ARMAGNAC country, while the COGNAC counterpart is Vin de Pays Charentais.

In every ten bottles of vin de pays, about seven are red, two are rosé, and one is white. In general in the 1980s they sold at lower prices than most AC wines, often quite rightly as these wines can be thin on flavour. Some producers, however, are becoming increasingly ambitious in their wine-making techniques and a number of vins de pays may be the products of low yields and expensive BARREL FERMENTATION or BARREL MATURATION, and may be offered, and sold, at

FRANCE: VINS DE PAYS

LOIRE
(VdP du Jardin de la France)

VdP de départment:
1. VdP du Cher
2. VdP des Deux-Sèvres
3. VdP de l'Indre-et-Loire
4. VdP du Loir-et-Cher
5. VdP de la Loire-Atlantique
6. VdP du Loiret
7. VdP du Maine-et-Loire
8. VdP de la Nièvre
9. VdP de la Sarthe
10. VdP de la Vendée
11. VdP de la Vienne

VdP de zone:
12. VdP du Bourbonnais
13. VdP des Coteaux Charitois
14. VdP des Coteaux du Cher et de l'Arnon
15. VdP des Marches de Bretagne
16. VdP de Retz

AQUITAINE - CHARENTES

VdP de départment:
17. VdP de la Dordogne
18. VdP de la Gironde
19. VdP des Landes
20. VdP du Lot-et-Garonne

VdP de zone:
21. VdP de l'Agenais
22. VdP Charentais
23. VdP des Terroirs Landais
24. VdP de Thézac-Perricard

MIDI-PYRÉNÉES
(VdP du Comté Tolosan)

VdP de départment:
25. VdP de l'Aveyron
26. VdP du Gers
27. VdP de la Haute-Garonne
28. VdP du Lot
29. VdP des Pyrénées-Atlantique
30. VdP du Tarn-et-Garonne

VdP de zone:
31. VdP de Bigorre
32. VdP des Coteaux de Glanes
33. VdP des Coteaux du Quercy
34. VdP des Coteaux Terrasses de Montauban
35. VdP des Côtes de Gascogne
36. VdP des Côtes de Montestruc
37. VdP des Côtes du Condomois
38. VdP des Côtes du Tarn
39. Millau (promoted to VDQS)
40. VdP de Saint-Sardos

LANGUEDOC-ROUSSILLON
(VdP d'Oc)

VdP de départment:
41. VdP de l'Aude
42. VdP du Gard
43. VdP de l'Hérault
44. VdP des Pyrénées-Orientales

CORSICA

VDP de zone:
45. VdP de l'Île de Beauté

PROVENCE-CÔTE D'AZUR

VdP de département:
46. VdP des Alpes-de-Haute-Provence
47. VdP des Alpes-Maritimes
48. VdP des Bouches-du-Rhône
49. VdP des Hautes-Alpes
50. VdP du Var
51. VdP du Vaucluse

VDP de zone:
52. VdP d'Argens
53. VdP des Maures
54. VdP du Mont-Caume
55. VdP de la Petite Crau
56. VdP de la Principauté d'Orange
57. VdP des Coteaux du Verdon
58. VdP d'Aigues

RHÔNE-ALPES
(VdP des Comtés Rhodaniens)

VdP de départment:
59. VdP de l'Ardeche
60. VdP de la Drôme
61. VdP du Puy-de-Dôme

VdP de zone:
62. VdP d'Allobrogie
63. VdP des Balmes Dauphinoises
64. VdP des Collines Rhodaniennes
65. VdP du Comté de Grignan
66. VdP des Coteaux de l'Ardèche
67. VdP des Coteaux des Baronnies
68. VdP des Coteaux du Grésivaudan
69. VdP d'Urfe

NORTH E

VdP de dépa
70. VdP de
71. VdP de
72. VdP du
73. VdP du
74. VdP de

VdP de zone
75. VdP des de Coiff
76. VdP de Comté

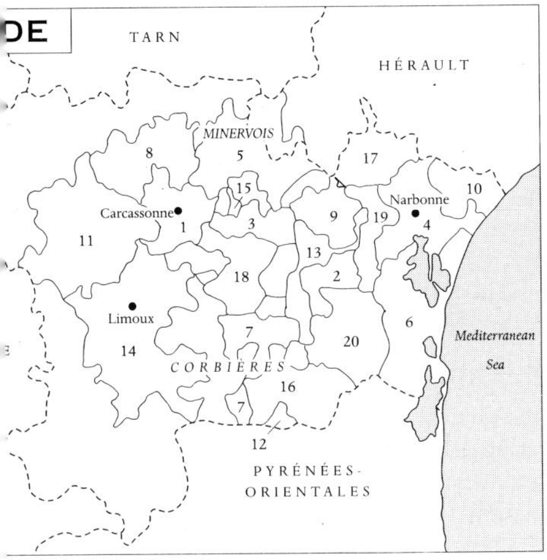

Cité de Carcassonne
:oteaux de la Cabrerisse
:oteaux de Miramont
:oteaux de Narbonne
:oteaux de Peyriac
:oteaux du Littoral Audois
:oteaux du Térmenes
:oteaux de Lastours
Côtes de Lézignan
Côtes de Pérignan

11. VdP des Côtes de Prouille
12. VdP de Cucugnan
13. VdP d'Hauterive en Pays d'Aude
14. VdP de la Haute-Vallée de l'Aude
15. VdP des Hauts-de-Badens
16. VdP du Torgan
17. VdP du Val de Cesse
18. VdP du Val de Dagne
19. VdP du Val d'Orbieu
20. VdP de la Vallée du Paradis

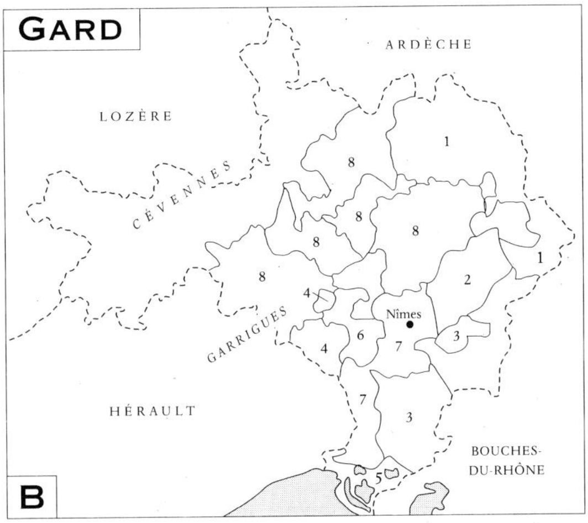

VdP de zone:
1. VdP des Coteaux de Cèze
2. VdP des Coteaux du Pont-du-Gard & VdP Duché d'Uzès
3. VdP des Coteaux Flaviens
4. VdP des Côtes du Vidourle
5. VdP des Sables-du-Golfe-du-Lion
6. VdP de la Vaunage
7. VdP de la Vistrenque
8. VdP des Cévennes

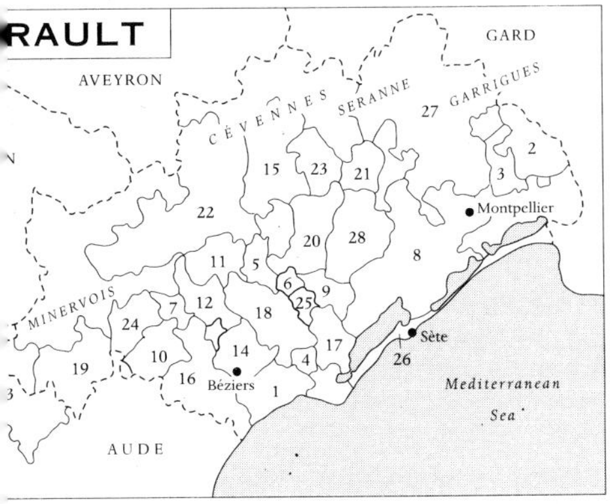

l'Ardhailhou
la Bénovie
Bérange
Bessan
Cassan
Caux
Cessenon
es Collines de la Moure
es Coteaux de Bessilles
es Coteaux de Fontcaude
es Coteaux de Laurens
es Coteaux de Murviel
es Coteaux de Peyriac
es Coteaux du Libron

15. VdP des Coteaux de Salagou
16. VdP des Coteaux de d'Enserune
17. VdP des Côtes de Thau
18. VdP des Côtes de Thongue
19. VdP des Côtes du Brian
20. VdP des Côtes du Céressou
21. VdP des Gorges de l'Hérault
22. VdP de la Haute-Vallée de l'Orb
23. VdP du Mont-Baudile
24. VdP des Monts de la Grage
25. VdP de Pézenas
26. VdP des Sables-du-Golfe-du-Lion
27. VdP du Val de Montferrand
28. VdP de la Vicomté d'Aumelas

VdP de zone:
1. VdP Catalan
2. VdP des Coteaux de Fenouillèdes
3. VdP des Côtes Catalanes
4. VdP de la Côte Vermeille
5. VdP des Vals d'Agly

relatively robust prices. The leader in this has been MAS de Daumas Gassac, an internationally famous wine which is sold merely as a departmental Vin de Pays de l'Hérault.

The vin de pays category is useful to the increasing number of producers trying to develop vineyards in isolated or new districts. The Swiss-backed Domaine de Ribonnet, for example, which produces ambitiously styled wines from vineyards south of Toulouse, sells its wines as Vin de Pays de la Haute-Garonne.

Atkin, T., *Vins de pays* (London, 1994).
Vins de pays of France (Paris, 1991).

VIN DE PRESSE. French for PRESS WINE.

VIN DE SAVOIE. See SAVOIE.

VIN DES GLACIERS, also known as **Vin du Glacier**, 'glacier wine' is a local speciality in the Val d'Anniviers near Sierre in the Valais of SWITZERLAND. The white wine, traditionally made of the now obscure Rèze variety, comes from communally cultivated vines and is stored at high altitudes in casks refilled just once a year on a SOLERA system. The resultant product is deliberately MADERIZED and valued for its rarity.

VIN DE TABLE, the French form of TABLE WINE and France's most basic level of wine which, in 1992, accounted for 23 per cent of the French harvest—not very much more than VIN DE PAYS, originally conceived as a sort of superior subcategory of vin de table, and considerably less than the amount of APPELLATION CONTRÔLÉE produced.

Vin de table was once known as *vin de consommation courante* (*VCC*) or, less formally, *vin ordinaire*. Today it is, typically, light red wine made in areas of the LANGUEDOC-ROUSSILLON not delimited as APPELLATION CONTRÔLÉE territory. There are no limits on YIELDS in table wine production and typical grape varieties are likely to be high-yielding CARIGNAN together with ARAMON and ALICANTE BOUSCHET (France's first, sixth, and 11th most planted red wine grape varieties according to the vineyard census of 1988). Some white vin de table is also made, and some vin de table is produced in virtually every part of France where vines are grown.

France's vin de table has been light and thin ever since the plains of the LANGUEDOC were planted at the end of the 19th century. Red vin de table has traditionally needed BLENDING with darker, more alcoholic wine which was originally imported from ALGERIA and subsequently from southern Italy and Sicily.

There is a serious SURPLUS of vin de table, and a significant proportion of it has been compulsorily DISTILLED as part of the EUROPEAN UNION's efforts to remedy this. The area of vineyard dedicated to vin de table production has also contracted markedly as the vin de pays designation has been developed, and as poorer-quality vineyard sites have been targeted by VINE PULL SCHEMES. The amount of vin de table produced each year is steadily declining, but not generally as fast as consumption of this sort of wine.

Much of it is sold locally, in bulk, for blending, with other table wines or to producers of VERMOUTHS or other FORTIFIED wines and wine-based products.

VIN DOUX NATUREL translates directly from French as a wine that is naturally sweet but is a term used to describe a French wine speciality that might well be considered *un*naturally sweet. Nature's sweetest wines contain so much grape sugar that the yeasts eventually give up the fermentation process of converting sugar into alcohol, leaving a residue of natural sugars in a stable wine of normal alcoholic strength (see SWEET WINE-MAKING). Vins doux naturels, on the other hand, are made by MUTAGE, by artificially arresting the conversion of grape sugar to alcohol by adding spirit half-way through, thereby incapacitating yeasts with alcohol and making a particularly strong, sweet half-wine in which grape flavours dominate wine flavours. They are normally made of the grape varieties MUSCAT and GRENACHE, and should have an alcoholic strength of at least 14 per cent.

The Greeks, happily ignorant of DISTILLATION, already knew how to make a sweet wine by adding concentrated must. Almost as soon as the techniques of distillation were introduced into western Europe, it was discovered that distilled wine, or alcoholic spirit, had the power to stop fermentation, thereby reliably retaining the sweetness so prized by our forebears. The Catalan alchemist ARNALDUS DE VILLANOVA (Arnaud de Villeneuve) of Montpellier University's then flourishing medical school perfected the process and in 1299 was granted a patent from the king of Majorca, then ruler of ROUSSILLON, which was to become the world's centre of vin doux naturel production.

This is essentially how PORT as we know it, created nearly 400 years later, is made strong and sweet, and the technique is also used in the production of MADEIRA and MÁLAGA. In each case spirit is added when the fermenting MUST has reached about six per cent alcohol, except that whereas the added spirit constitutes between five and 10 per cent of the final volume of a vin doux naturel, typically resulting in an alcoholic strength of just over 15 per cent, the added spirit usually represents 20 per cent of the final volume of port, whose alcoholic strength is closer to 20 per cent. The spirit added to vins doux naturels is considerably stronger than that added to port, however: about 95 per cent alcohol as opposed to the traditional 77 per cent used in port FORTIFICATION. Nowadays, however, the spirit may well come from exactly the same source, one of France's larger distilleries designed to reduce Europe's wine surplus (see WINE LAKE). Thus a vin doux naturel contains less alcohol, and less added water, than port.

A young vin doux naturel therefore, like port, tastes relatively simply of grapes, sugar, and alcohol (although, since some fermentation has usually taken place, it may contain a more interesting array of fermentation products than a VIN DE LIQUEUR). Naturally aromatic MUSCAT BLANC À PETITS GRAINS grapes are therefore particularly well suited to the production of vins doux naturels designed to be drunk young (and, usually, chilled to offset the sugar and alcohol). The best known of these golden sweet liquids that are made exclusively from this, the finest MUSCAT vine variety, was historically Muscat de FRONTIGNAN. The Languedoc has three other appellation contrôlée vins doux naturels, however: Muscats de LUNEL, MIREVAL, and, an exception far from the coast, ST-JEAN-DE-MINERVOIS, whose vineyards are even higher than most of those for the red, pink, and dry white wines of MINERVOIS. In the 1970s the similar, often even finer Muscat made in the Côtes-du-Rhône village of BEAUMES-DE-VENISE enjoyed renown on an international scale.

Muscat de Beaumes-de-Venise is probably easier for non-natives to appreciate than the southern Rhône's other vin doux naturel appellation of RASTEAU, whose Grenache-based heady red and tawny sweet wines, some of them deliberately made RANCIO, have more in common with the increasingly famous vins doux naturels of Roussillon. The best of these, like the best ports, owe their complex flavours necessarily to ageing, whether in cask, BONBONNE, or, occasionally, bottle. The greatest name is BANYULS, which has benefited from some impeccable wine-makers and, most important in this context, wine-éleveurs (see ÉLEVAGE). MAURY is a smaller appellation in the mountains with enormous and, occasionally, realized potential while the extensive coastal RIVESALTES and Muscat de Rivesaltes appellations are much more varied and sometimes traduced. Grand Roussillon is a largely theoretical vin doux naturel appellation designed as a lesser Rivesaltes.

Non-vintage-dated vins doux naturels are common, particularly among the Languedoc Muscats into which a little of the previous year's output may be blended so as to smooth out vintage differences. It is common in Roussillon, however, to find indications of age and vintage dates, although most vins doux naturels are ready to drink as soon as they are sold. Many, particularly the Muscats, benefit from being served chilled, but the alcohol preserves the freshness of wine in an opened bottle for at least a week.

George, R., *French Country Wines* (London, 1990).

VIN DU BUGEY. See BUGEY.

VINE, the plant, often known as the grapevine, whose fruit is transformed into WINE.

A vine in its broadest sense is any plant with a weak stem which supports itself by climbing on neighbouring plants, walls, or other supports. Of this group of plants the grapevine is the most famous, and the most commercially important. (In this work the word vine is used to mean the grapevine.) There are various forms of climbing vines which rely on different mechanisms for attachment. The so-called ramblers rest on each others' plants and some, as for roses, have spines to help adhesion. The grapevine is one of the so-called tendril climbers with TENDRILS on the stem; the garden pea has leaf tendrils.

Because the vine is unable to support itself, it is generally grown on TRELLIS SYSTEMS. Some TRAINING SYSTEMS still use trees for support, as for the *alberate* of Italy. However, most vineyards of the world are trained to some combination of wood posts and wire. Vines can be trained so that they are free standing but this requires special pruning and training to keep the trunk short, otherwise the vine will fall over. The GOBELET of the Mediterranean region is the most widespread of the free-standing forms.

Most of the world's wine is made from the VINIFERA species of the VITIS genus (see BOTANICAL CLASSIFICATION for a more detailed explanation of where the vine fits into the world of plants).

Grapevines are the world's most important fruit crop, with 8 million ha/20 million acres of vineyards producing about 60 million tonnes of fruit in the early 1990s. Grapes are used for wine-making in all of its forms, for BRANDY, for consumption as TABLE GRAPES and DRYING GRAPES, for fresh GRAPE JUICE, for GRAPE CONCENTRATE, RECTIFIED GRAPE MUST, and for limited industrial products. However, wine production is the major use and accounts for 80 per cent of all vineyard output.

The grapevine is grown on all continents except Antarctica, but most of the world's vineyards are in Europe. Three countries, Italy, Spain, and France, each have about 1 million ha of vineyards, and Italy and France each produce almost one-quarter of the world's wine. *Vitis vinifera* cannot tolerate extreme winter cold. Requiring warm summers for fruit maturation, the vine is grown approximately between the 10 and 20 °C isotherm in both hemispheres, or about between latitudes 30 degrees north and 50 degrees north, and 30 degrees south and 40 degrees south (see map of WORLD PRODUCTION). Principally in order to minimize the damage associated with FUNGAL DISEASES, the grapevine has traditionally been grown in MEDITERRANEAN CLIMATES with warm, dry summers and mild, wet winters. The ready availability of AGROCHEMICALS, and to a lesser extent disease-tolerant varieties, has allowed this range to be extended, especially since the Second World War. Winter DORMANCY is essential for vine longevity, and the hot and humid climates nearer the equator are not conducive to either grape production or wine quality (although see TROPICAL VITICULTURE).

Most of the world's vineyards are planted with traditional VINE VARIETIES, which have been perpetuated for centuries by vegetative propagation. Different CLONES of these varieties may also be distinguished.

Many viticultural practices are very traditional, especially in Europe, where in many cases they are prescribed by law. Cultural operations and the reasoning behind them are introduced under VITICULTURE, VINE PHYSIOLOGY, VINE DISEASES, and VINE PESTS. The effects of climate and soils are also discussed in, respectively, CLIMATE AND WINE QUALITY and SOIL AND WINE QUALITY.

See VINE MORPHOLOGY for discussion of the parts of the vine, and VINE PHYSIOLOGY for details of how the vine functions. See also VINE GROWTH CYCLE and, for a historical perspective, ORIGINS OF VITICULTURE. R.E.S.

Mullins, M. G., Bouquet, A., and Williams, L., *Biology of the Grapevine* (Cambridge, 1992).
Winkler, A. J., *et al.*, *General Viticulture* (2nd edn., Berkeley, Calif., 1974).

VINE AGE, easily observable by the width of the vine's trunk, is widely considered a factor affecting wine quality, with widespread consensus that, in general, older vines make better wine. Indeed this idea is enshrined in APPELLATION CONTRÔLÉE legislation which, in many cases, specifically excludes the produce of vines less than three or sometimes more years old. The limited amount of wine from young vines destined to produce AC wine is typically sold as VIN DE TABLE. Some French producers deliberately exclude wine from vines under a certain age from their top bottlings, and put it into SECOND WINES. The concept that older vines make better wine is much used in marketing wine in the Old World (see VIEILLES VIGNES) and has more recently been adopted in the New World, notably by some BAROSSA VALLEY producers. Conversely, some wine-makers observe that young vineyards produce their highest-quality wine in the first year or two of production.

Conventional VINE TRAINING takes two to three years to form the vine framework, and if any bunches are formed they are normally discarded before they ripen. Once a vine produces one to three or so normal crops and is about three to six years of age, it usually fills its allotted growing space above ground, and so the YIELD and annual shoot growth normally stabilize, and will change only with a major alteration to management or growing conditions. Vineyards which are protected from stresses, pests, and diseases, and from too much or too little water and mineral nutrients, can be long living. An outstanding example is the famous vine at Hampton Court Palace near London which is still producing large crops of grapes (under glass) despite being planted in 1769. Vineyards free from stresses are, however, rare. The vigour and yield of many commercial vineyards begin to decline after 20 years, and by 50 years many vineyards are yielding at such a low level as to be normally considered uneconomic.

Below ground, however, the picture can be different. Champagnol defines three stages of root growth. During the first stage the root system colonizes available space, and this takes until the seventh to tenth year, taking longer in poor soils and with low VINE DENSITY. In the so-called adult stage there is little change in the volume of soil exploited, but the final, senescent stage sees a reduction in root activity. This can be through the accumulation of cultivation wounds, or from the effects of drought, or from soil compaction by machinery, or lack of oxygen at depth. Root pests and diseases may also weaken the root system, and continued application of some fertilizers and spray materials can worsen SOIL ACIDITY and so reduce root health.

The parts of the vine above ground do seem to weaken with age, and senescence is more obvious. Despite perceptions to the contrary, winter PRUNING weakens the vine. Pruning wounds also allow the invasion of wood-rotting fungi, and continued summer TRIMMING is devigorating. In addition to this there are the continued effects of cultivation which can prune roots, and the exhaustion of the soil's mineral reserves.

The normal course of events, then, is for vines to show reduced VIGOUR as they age, and this is particularly evident for vines planted on sites with low SOIL potential. The conventional explanation for improved quality with vine age is

Vine age is reflected by the width of the plant's trunk. These vines in Gaillac may be 50 years old.

because of reduction in yield, and indeed for many celebrated vineyards the two go hand in hand. R.E.S.

Champagnol, F., *Éléments de physiologie de la vigne et de viticulture générale* (St-Gely-du-Fesc, 1984).
Smart, R. E., and Robinson, M., *Sunlight into Wine: A Handbook for Winegrape Canopy Management* (Adelaide, 1991).

VINE BREEDING, the crossing of one vine variety or species with another to produce a new variety. Grapevines are highly heterozygous outcrossers and do not breed true from seed, which is the reason for their universal vegetative PROPAGATION. If both parent varieties belong to the same species (in practice, usually the European VINIFERA) of the VITIS genus, then the result is commonly called a CROSS, while the results of crossing varieties from more than one species (typically, a *vinifera* variety and a member of an AMERICAN VINE SPECIES) are commonly called hybrids.

These NEW VARIETIES are traditionally created by dusting POLLEN from the male parent on to the receptive stigma of the female parent (see vine FLOWER), and then germinating the seed from the berry which subsequently grows (although see GENETIC ENGINEERING for more recent techniques). There is a very low probability that any one seedling will be a useful variety, and extensive testing, probably over more than 10 years, for viticultural and wine-making suitability is required before any new variety is released.

The convention is to express the female parent first, thus EMERALD RIESLING is a Muscadelle × Riesling cross, while BACO 22A is a Folle Blanche × Noah hybrid (Noah itself being an AMERICAN HYBRID).

Vine breeding was particularly important in the early 20th century, notably in France, Germany, and Romania, as a European response to the spread of the PHYLLOXERA pest (see HYBRIDS and FRENCH HYBRIDS). Breeding of new varieties which combined high yields with high MUST WEIGHTS, and subsequently those which combined high wine quality with good resistance to pests and diseases, has been an important activity in such German centres as GEILWEILERHOF and GEISENHEIM. See for example Professor Helmut BECKER.

The prospects for the breeding of new varieties are outlined by Einset and Pratt and Alleweldt and Possingham. They emphasize the availability of germplasm among *Vitis* species which contains resistance to the major pests, diseases, and environmental stresses of *vinifera*. *V amurensis* and *V riparia*, for example, contain genes for winter hardiness, and *V vinifera* and *V berlandieri* for lime soil tolerance (see CHLOROSIS). Among various *Vitis* species can be found genetic resistance to the fungal diseases DOWNY MILDEW, POWDERY MILDEW, BOTRYTIS BUNCH ROT; the bacterial diseases of CROWN GALL and PIERCE'S DISEASE; and the soil pests of PHYLLOXERA and NEMATODES. A desire to minimize the use of AGROCHEMICALS has encouraged vine breeding to combine these natural resistances, notably in Germany and the United States.

Because of increasing emphasis on a few familiar VINE VARIETIES, and also the lingering suspicion of hybrids caused by the poor wine performance of the early French hybrids, some consumers view the results of breeding programmes with suspicion. Yet such programmes can offer the opportunity of an improved range of flavours and styles produced from vineyards which do not require any other means of pest and disease protection.

See also NEW VARIETIES. R.E.S.

Alleweldt, G., and Possingham, J. V., 'Progress in grape breeding', *Theoretical and Applied Genetics*, 75 (1988), 669–73.
—— Spiegel-Roy, P., and Reisch, B., 'Grapes (*Vitis*)', in J. N. Moore and J. R. Ballington (eds.), *Genetic Resources of Temperate Fruit and Nut Crops: Acta horticulturae* 290 (1990), 289–327.
Einset, J., and Pratt, C., 'Grapes', in J. Janick and J. N. Moore (eds.), *Advances in Fruit Breeding* (West Lafayette, 1975).
Huglin, P., *Biologie et écologie de la vigne* (Paris, 1986).

VINE DENSITY is a measure of how closely spaced vines are in the vineyard, both within the row and between rows. Vine spacing is one of the most fundamental decisions in PLANTING a vineyard, and between, even within, the world's wine regions there is enormous variation in spacing. The traditional vineyards of France's Bordeaux, Burgundy, and Champagne regions have about 10,000 plants per ha (4,050 per acre) (and sometimes more), with vines spaced typically 1 m apart both within and between the rows. In many NEW WORLD vineyards, on the other hand, a spacing of 2.5 m/8 ft between vines along the row and 3.7 m/12 ft between rows, or 1,080 vines per ha, is quite common. Probably the most widely spaced vineyards of the world are those of the Vinho Verde region in Portugal, La Mancha in Spain, and some parts of Chile, Japan, and Italy (see TENDONE), with spacings as wide as 4 m by 4 m, or just 625 vines per ha.

It is widely held that high vine densities lead to improved wine quality. It is true that many of the world's most famous vineyards, especially in the Old World, have very narrow spacings, but it is difficult to argue that this is a prerequisite for quality production. Narrow spacings are indeed appropriate to vineyards of moderate VIGOUR, often a reflection of TERROIR effects and soil (see SOIL AND WINE QUALITY). Some New World vignerons have been encouraged to plant high-density vineyards on fertile vineyard soils in expectation of matching the quality of famous Old World vineyards. The theory is that such dense planting will cause root competition and substantial devigoration, but this has infrequently been demonstrated, and the result is often a vineyard of high vigour which is very difficult to manage. The quality of fruit is affected by excessive SHADE, and this potentially also reduces quantity. Research and commercial experience in Europe indicate that close row and vine spacings are suited only to vineyards of low SOIL FERTILITY, or more correctly of low soil potential. Some vine-growers have responded by removing only one vine in two down the row, and sometimes two in three. This has been found to restore vine BALANCE, and yield and quality have subsequently improved.

High-density vineyards are the traditional form of viticulture in many parts of the world, as spacing need only be sufficient to allow the workers unhindered access. Some vineyards are not even planted in rows but were haphazardly arranged, like a field of wheat. Before PHYLLOXERA invaded Europe, unhealthy plants could be replaced by LAYERING a cane from an adjacent vine. These considerations, and the fact that vines then were generally less vigorous, encouraged high-density vineyards and densities were as high as 40,000 plants per ha, or just a quarter of a square metre per plant. Once GRAFTING to ROOTSTOCKS developed as a response to phylloxera, however, then the additional cost of each plant encouraged lower vine densities. The introduction of first animals and then tractors led to the planting of vineyards in rows with a further reduction in vine density. The final factor leading to wider spacing between vines has been the need to provide sufficient space for modern, more vigorous vines. This follows from effective control of vine pests and diseases and weeds using AGROCHEMICALS, as well as the use of plants both VIRUS free and subject to CLONAL SELECTION.

OLD WORLD vineyards are generally planted more densely than those of the NEW WORLD. Many New World vineyards were planted after the introduction of TRACTORS, or even greater MECHANIZATION, necessitating row spacings of about 3 m. By contrast, most European vine-growers have chosen to persist with narrow rows and to develop either narrow tractors, or over-row tractors such as shown opposite p. 48, known in France as *tracteurs enjambeurs*.

Vineyard density is a major consideration affecting the vineyard's yield, quality, and therefore profitability. Planting costs are proportional to the number of plants used; costs for TRELLIS SYSTEMS and DRIP IRRIGATION are higher with narrower row spacings. The time taken to plough and spray is also greater when rows are closer together.

Under most circumstances, the YIELD of densely planted vineyards is higher, especially in the first years of the vineyard's life and with vines planted on low soil potential.

R.E.S.

Champagnol, F., *Éléments de physiologie de la vigne et de viticulture générale* (St-Gely-du-Fesc, 1984).
Galet, P., *Précis de viticulture* (4th edn., Montpellier, 1983).

VINE DISEASES. Diseases caused by microbes can limit the distribution of vines and affect both yield and quality. See BACTERIAL DISEASES, FUNGAL DISEASES, VIRUS DISEASES, MYCOPLASMA DISEASES, and the names of individual diseases.

VINE EXTRACTION. See RIPPING OUT for how it is done and VINE AGE and VINE PULL SCHEMES for some reasons why.

VINE FOLIAGE LIFTER, machine which lifts vine foliage in the growing season. Once the foliage is vertical it can be secured by WIRES and is then well placed for TRIMMING to maintain a constant CANOPY outline. See also SHOOT POSITIONING.

VINEGAR, sour liquid condiment that depends etymologically, and often materially, on wine. The French word for it, composed of *vin* (wine) and *aigre* (sour), is a direct descendant of its Latin equivalent. Not just wine but any solution containing a low concentration (less than 15 per cent) of ETHANOL will turn to vinegar if exposed to OXYGEN. The ethanol is oxidized first into an ALDEHYDE and then to ACETIC ACID by the oxygen in the atmosphere. Wine-makers over the centuries have learned to shelter wine from the action of atmospheric oxygen, and nowadays will do all they can to prevent their wines turning to vinegar, and 'vinegary' is a tasting term of great disapprobation (while 'winey' is quite a compliment when applied to a vinegar). Once the VOLATILE ACIDS in a wine have reached a certain point, however, it can have a potable future only as wine vinegar.

The OXIDATION of any dilute aqueous alcohol solution is greatly hastened by the action of a group of bacteria known as ACETOBACTER from the environment. These bacteria also hasten the reaction of some of the alcohol with some of the newly produced acetic acid to form the ESTER known as ETHYL ACETATE. This compound has a fruity flavour which, when added to the tart taste of acetic acid, gives the complex character to a good wine vinegar.

Vinegar can be made from many dilute aqueous alcohol solutions, based not just on grapes but on any fruits or vegetables containing fermentable sugar, or from compounds containing hydrolizable starch, or even from alcohol that is a petroleum or paper mill by-product (although colourless, synthetic vinegars are rarely used as table vinegars). The everyday vinegar of the market-place varies geographically. In southern Europe wine vinegar is the norm, for example, while in northern Europe malt, cider, and distilled vinegars predominate, and in the Far East rice vinegar is most usual.

Vinegar production must have started in ancient times as the natural result of exposure of wine and beer to the atmosphere when uses for soured wine would naturally have developed. The traditional technique for making vinegar is called the Orléans process and involves only partially filling barrels with wine and leaving it there, under the influence of desirable acetobacter, for several months. A trickling process, maximizing wine's exposure to air, was developed as both a batch and continuous process, at the beginning of the 20th century, but produces less complex vinegars in which the taste of ethyl acetate is much less pronounced than vinegars produced by the Orléans process. A development of the trickling process, the continuous acetator, or cavitator, was developed in the 1940s, borrowing techniques used for the large-scale production of penicillin at that time.

Today a wide range of vinegars are produced, many flavoured with herbs and fruits, some, such as Italian balsamic vinegar, given BARREL MATURATION according to rules as strict as those governing APPELLATION CONTRÔLÉE wine production. The most powerful vinegars are so strong in ethyl acetate that their flavour can overpower that of a subtle wine. In foods served with subtle wines, wine itself can be used as a condiment, contributing the same sort of ACIDITY as a vinegar would have done.

A domestic vinegar SOLERA is one solution for wine LEFT-OVERS.

A.D.W.

VINEGAR FLY. See FRUIT FLY.

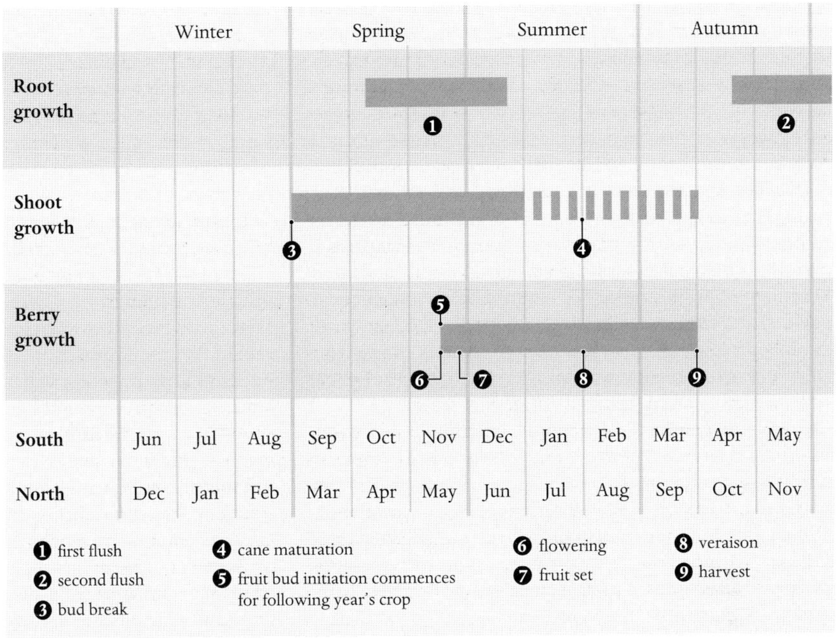

Vine growth cycle: patterns of root, shoot, and berry growth for the grapevine, for northern and southern hemispheres.

VINE GROWTH CYCLE, the annual march of the vine's development, which begins at budbreak in the spring, and concludes at leaf fall in the autumn. There are distinct developmental stages along the way (see PHENOLOGY), the principal ones being BUDBREAK, FLOWERING, FRUIT SET, VERAISON, HARVEST, when the grapes are mature, and LEAF FALL. The pace of development between these phenological stages varies greatly with vine variety. Very early varieties, such as MADELEINE ANGEVINE, go through the stages up to ripeness in a short time, and can therefore ripen in regions with a short growing season and relatively cool temperatures. In late varieties, such as MOURVÈDRE, CARIGNAN, and CLAIRETTE, all stages are prolonged and much more heat and time are needed to bring them to maturity. The length of the growth cycle also depends on climate, especially temperature. In hot regions, the period from budbreak to harvest may be as short as 130 days for early varieties, but in cooler regions this period can be over 200 days.

The vine often begins to grow later in the spring than most other deciduous plants, when the average air temperature is normally about 10 °C/50 °F in cool climates. The first sign is vines BLEEDING as the soil warms, then the buds swell, and eventually the first tinges of green are seen in the vineyards as the shoot tips burst from the buds. The young shoots grow very slowly at first, producing small leaves on each side of the shoot. This early shoot growth depends on the reserves of CARBOHYDRATES stored in the vine, but soon the leaves are old enough for PHOTOSYNTHESIS and produce the carbohydrates which become the tissue of further shoot growth.

After about four weeks in warm climates, the principal period of growth begins, and shoots grow much more rapidly. Shoots may grow more than 3 cm a day, and the observant can notice changes in shoot length from day to day. Shoot growth slackens at flowering or bloom, 40 to 80 days after budbreak, but can continue to the end of the season under conditions of mild temperatures and over-generous supplies of water and nitrogen. More commonly, WATER STRESS reduces shoot growth between flowering and veraison (or the beginning of grape RIPENING), and it may cease altogether later in the season. The shoot tips are sometimes trimmed, but will often grow again from lateral buds.

Small flower clusters are apparent on the young shoots as buttons, and in the few weeks before flowering they enlarge and the individual flowers are obvious. Flowering takes place when the average daily temperatures are about 15 to 20 °C, and is followed by the so-called fruit set process.

The next significant stage is that of veraison, when grapes change colour and begin to ripen. This takes place about 40 to 50 days after fruit set. Between set and veraison, the berries grow to about half their final size, but remain green and hard. They contain low concentrations of SUGARS, but are high in organic ACIDS. Veraison is an easily observable stage when the berries change colour to either red-black or yellow-green, depending on the variety. The berries also soften, and they begin rapidly to build up sugar. During this stage, the vines also rapidly accumulate carbohydrate reserves in the roots, trunk, and arms.

The most appropriate date of harvest depends on the

desired stage of maturity for WINE-MAKING. It is earliest for sparkling wines, intermediate for table wines, and delayed for dessert and fortified wines. Harvest date may also be influenced by weather conditions. Fruit ripening normally proceeds quickly in hot areas, with rapid increases in sugars and PH and a decline in ACIDITY, especially MALIC ACID. In cooler regions the rate of ripening is slower, and the fruit typically has lower sugars and higher acidity. Rainfall near harvest can cause problems due to berry splitting, BOTRYTIS, and other bunch rotting fungi (see ROT). After rain, there is normally a rush to harvest grapes while they are still sound.

Leaf fall marks the end of the season, and of all the developmental stages it is the least precisely marked. Some leaves may fall off during the growing season, especially if the vine comes under stress, for example by drought, disease, or shade. A significant proportion of the leaves may also be removed by MECHANICAL HARVESTING. With continued warm and sunny weather following harvest, the leaves remain healthy and are photosynthetically active in replacing carbohydrate reserves in the vine trunk and roots. Once these levels are built up, the vines often lose their green chlorophyll colour and turn yellow. The first frost of the season causes leaf fall, and the vines are then in a dormant state. After PRUNING in winter, the vines are ready for the growth cycle to begin again.

See also VINEYARD ANNUAL CYCLE. R.E.S.

Champagnol, F., *Éléments de physiologie de la vigne et de viticulture générale* (St-Gely-du-Fesc, 1984).
Coombe, B. G., 'Grape phenology', in B. G. Coombe and P. R. Dry (eds.), *Viticulture*, i: *Resources in Australia* (Adelaide, 1988).
Winkler, A. J., *et al.*, *General Viticulture* (2nd edn., Berkeley, Calif., 1974).

VINE IDENTIFICATION. See AMPELOGRAPHY and DNA 'FINGERPRINTING' for details of how to identify different VINE VARIETIES.

VINE IMPROVEMENT, a group of practices designed to improve vine planting material for the benefit of vineyard YIELD and the quality of the fruit and wine produced. This is currently focused on eliminating harmful VIRUS DISEASES and also on genetic improvement. CLONAL SELECTION is a technique which, by selecting high-performance vines, can achieve both ends. Other techniques of virus elimination include THERMOTHERAPY and TISSUE CULTURE. Genetic improvement can also be achieved through beneficial MUTATION and selection, by GENETIC ENGINEERING, and by VINE BREEDING.

Although virus diseases had affected European vines since the end of the 19th century, it took some time for preventive action to be taken on a national scale. The first attempt at controlling the quality of planting material in France was made in 1944, when the Section de Contrôle des Bois et Plantes de Vigne (now part of ONIVIT) was formed, charged with avoiding the spread of virus diseases, and also with ensuring that all rootstocks used had sufficient resistance to phylloxera. Previously, nurserymen had been free to propagate whichever vines they chose, with sometimes disastrous effects for their clients.

In Germany there has been a high regard for the health of buds and rootstock for grafting, and rigorous clonal selection programmes and registration of CLONES has ensured high-quality planting material. Similar schemes operate in other European countries.

In non-European countries there has also been an awareness of the importance of quality control of propagation material. After the Second World War, the California wine industry created a model system for improving the quality of planting material. Research at the University of California at DAVIS had demonstrated the importance of virus diseases, and had shown how they might be detected. A so-called 'clean rootstock program' was developed which aimed to distribute only virus-free cuttings to nurseries, using thermotherapy and INDEXING in particular to produce virus-free plants. This has subsequently become known as the Foundation Plant Material Service (FPMS), and has distributed high-health vines all around the world. In Australia and New Zealand, government officials worked with industry personnel to create at regional or state level a Vine Improvement Organization which became self-funding by the sales of improved planting material. R.E.S.

McCarthy, M. G., 'Grape planting material', in B. G. Coombe and P. R. Dry (eds.), *Viticulture*, i: *Resources in Australia* (Adelaide, 1988).

VINE MANAGEMENT, a term comprehending all management practices in the vineyard, including especially SOIL PREPARATION and DRAINAGE; PRUNING and CANOPY MANAGEMENT; use of FERTILIZERS, MULCHES, and COVER CROPS; CULTIVATION and WEED CONTROL; use of FUNGICIDES and PESTICIDES; IRRIGATION; vine TRIMMING and LEAF REMOVAL; CROP THINNING to control YIELD; and HARVEST methods.

VINE MORPHOLOGY is the study of the form and structure of the vine plant, as distinct from vine physiology which is the study of its function. See ANTHER, ARM, BEARER, BERRY, BRUSH, BUD, BUNCH, BUNCHSTEM, CAMBIUM, CANE, CALYPTRA, CELL, CORDON, FLOWERS, GRAPE, HEAD, INTERNODE, INFLORESCENCE, LATERAL SHOOT, LEAD, NODE, OVARY, PERICARP, PEDICEL, PETIOLE, PHLOEM, POLLEN, PULP, ROOT, SHOOT, SEEDS, SPUR, STAMEN, STEM, STOMA, TENDRIL, TRUNK, VINE, WATER SHOOT, and XYLEM. B.G.C.

VINE NUTRITION, the supply of inorganic nutrients (sometimes called mineral nutrients or nutrient elements) to the vine. Vines, like other plants, require three major nutrients, NITROGEN, PHOSPHORUS, and POTASSIUM, and the minor or trace elements MAGNESIUM, MANGANESE, IRON, ZINC, COPPER, and BORON.

Among horticultural plants, the vine is regarded as having low nutrition requirements. For example, a common recommendation for apple orchards is to apply an annual fer-

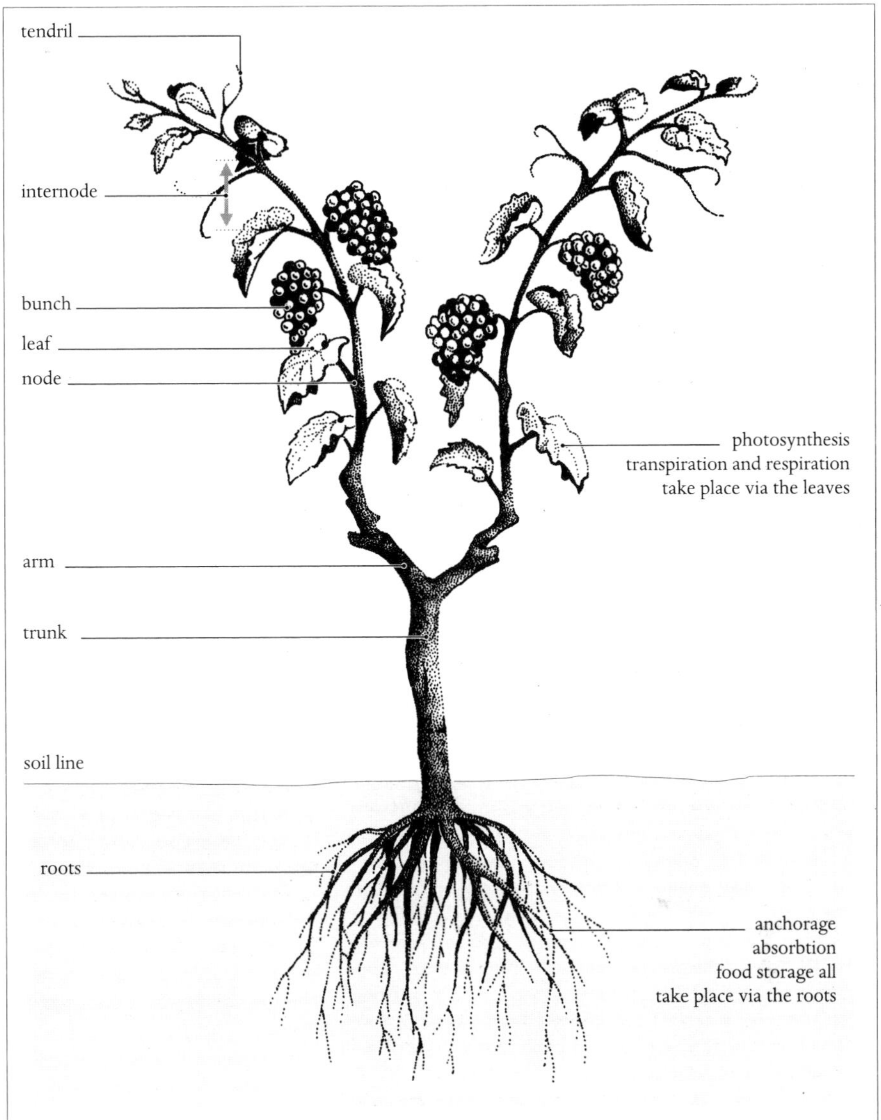

Vine morphology

tilizer dressing of 80 to 300 kg/ha (70–270 lb/acre) of nitrogen (N), 50 to 250 kg/ha of phosphorus (P), and 50 to 800 kg/ha of potassium (K). A similar suggestion for vineyards would be 0 to 100 kg/ha N, 0 to 50 kg/ha P, and 0 to 120 kg/ha K. These low requirements reflect the low levels of nutrients that are removed from the vineyard each year by the grape HARVEST.

Measurements have been made in many countries of the amounts of elements contained in the grapes picked, and also in the leaf litter and winter prunings. These values vary with region, variety, and yield, but are about 50 kg/ha of N, 15 kg/ha of P, and 45 kg/ha of K. A general recommendation therefore would be to apply this amount of FERTILIZER if there was any doubt that the vineyard soil would be able to supply it. In general, a soil test before PLANTING can indicate any likely deficiencies. In mature vineyards the standard procedure is to test either the leaves or the leaf stalks (PETIOLES) for their nutrient content, and apply fertilizers only as the need is indicated. For many crops, an annual addition of fertilizer will do little harm if it is not needed. For vines, however, such an addition is likely to be unnecessary and even wasteful since their needs are so low, and there is always the danger of over-fertilization, especially with nitrogen, which can directly and indirectly reduce wine quality. Similarly, high levels of potassium in soils can reduce wine quality because of increased wine PH.

Continued use of the same parcel of land for viticulture over extended periods of time reduces the levels of nutrients. Studies of old vineyard soils in Bordeaux have shown that fertility can be restored by heavy applications of ORGANIC MATTER, LIME, phosphorus, and potassium. Organic matter such as mulches and animal manures can be used to fertilize vineyards, but they are typically lower in nutrient content and more expensive. They often, however, improve soil structure by their organic matter content. Such forms of fertilizer are favoured for ORGANIC VITICULTURE.

Despite the common opinion to the contrary, there seems to be little connection between nutrition of the vine and wine character or quality other than through influences on vine VIGOUR. The lay perception is that soil directly affects wine quality through giving wines a special chemical signature which relates to their quality. This seems not to be the case, or at least has not been unequivocally demonstrated. See SOIL AND WINE QUALITY, and also TERROIR. R.E.S.

Winkler, A. J., *et al.*, *General Viticulture* (2nd edn., Berkeley, Calif., 1974).

VINE PESTS can make viticulture uneconomic and can have drastic effects on wine quality unless controlled. They include animals, insects, and nematodes (while VINE DISEASES include the microbes bacteria, fungi, mycoplasma, viroids, and virus).

The principal commercial wine grape VITIS VINIFERA is indigenous to Eurasia, whilst the majority of severe vine pests and diseases come principally from east and south east North America. Their accidental introduction to Europe from the 1850s onwards had dramatic consequences for local viticulture. The fungal disease POWDERY MILDEW was bad enough but fortunately a control was soon at hand. The insect pest PHYLLOXERA was not so easy to control, and for a period following its introduction in 1863 the entire French wine industry was threatened. Fortunately it was solved by grafting *vinifera* vines on to ROOTSTOCKS derived from AMERICAN VINE SPECIES which have natural resistance to phylloxera. This practice is now used world-wide.

In general, vine pests are easier to control than diseases, although the AGROCHEMICALS used to control insects (PESTICIDES) are among the most potent used in viticulture. The modern tendency is to depend less on PESTICIDES and to develop strategies such as INTEGRATED PEST MANAGEMENT. Phylloxera is a threat to only a small proportion of the world's vineyards as over 85 per cent are grafted to rootstocks considered resistant. However, the insect pest MARGARODES is at present confined to only a few vineyard regions of the southern hemisphere, and at present there is only limited chemical control.

Vine pests can have dramatic effects on wine quality. One end of the spectrum is the pest causing the vine severe stress, as for example with root damage due to NEMATODES or phylloxera. Indeed this effect is frequently transient as it is a prelude to death and/or vine removal (see RIPPING OUT).

The following are some examples of how some pests can affect vines and reduce wine quality. Leaf area removal by beetles, DEER, KANGAROOS, LOCUSTS, MOTHS, RABBITS, and SNAILS can jeopardize PHOTOSYNTHESIS and grape RIPENING. Leaves can also be damaged and photosynthesis reduced by LEAF HOPPERS and MITES. Vine growth and yield are reduced by attacks on roots from GOPHERS, phylloxera, margarodes, nematodes, and squirrels, and by destruction of the trunk and arms by BORERS and TERMITES. Damage to the grapes themselves by insects and birds can lead to BUNCH ROTS, which can be spread by fruit fly. Some pests can taint grapes, as for example the honeydew of MEALY BUGS and SCALE. Last but not least is the very important role of pests in carrying (vectoring) diseases. The dreaded and lethal bacterial PIERCE'S DISEASE is spread by LEAF HOPPERS, as is the mycoplasma disease FLAVESCENCE DORÉE. Important VIRUS DISEASES which can substantially reduce wine quality and yield are spread by nematodes and mealy bug.

For more detail see major entries under ANIMALS, BEETLES, BIRDS, FRUIT FLY, INSECT PESTS, MITES, NEMATODES, PHYLLOXERA; other entries are to be found under the pests' common name. R.E.S.

VINE PHYSIOLOGY, the science of the function of the VINE, including the growth and development of the vine shoot and root systems, its fruiting, and the major physiological processes such as PHOTOSYNTHESIS, TRANSLOCATION, and TRANSPIRATION. Physiology is also concerned with controls on plant growth and development, including both environmental and internal control by HORMONES. Both VINE NUTRITION and degree of WATER STRESS are important effects of the vineyard soil, and TEMPERATURE and SUNLIGHT are the most important climate effects.

The vine's physiology can be manipulated by vineyard management techniques to alter growth, yield, and quality. For example, decisions on TRAINING SYSTEMS and PRUNING levels will alter the light incident on leaves, thus affecting photosynthesis and sugar supply to the grapes during RIPENING. R.E.S.

Champagnol, F., *Éléments de physiologie de la vigne et de viticulture générale* (St-Gely-du-Fesc, 1984).
Mullins, M. G., Bouquet, A., and Williams, L., *Biology of the Vine.* (Cambridge, 1992).
Winkler, A. J., *et al.*, *General Viticulture* (2nd edn,, Berkeley, Calif., 1974).

VINE PRODUCTS, the range of products produced from the vine. The GRAPEVINE is the world's most important fruit crop, and WINE and its BRANDY distillates are by far the most important of its products. Other products include DRYING GRAPES, TABLE GRAPES, GRAPE JUICE, GRAPE CONCENTRATE, VINEGAR, grapeseed oil, and RECTIFIED GRAPE MUST. There are other minor products: grapevine cuttings (*sarments* in French) can be used for propagation or for barbecue firewood (although the latter is indeed a minor use); and vine leaves are used in Middle Eastern and Greek cuisine and for wrapping certain cheeses. R.E.S.

VINE PULL SCHEMES, schemes whereby growers receive some sort of incentive to pull out vines, a process known as *arrachage* in French. The most comprehensive of these schemes to combat various wine SURPLUSES is that embarked upon by the EUROPEAN UNION in 1988, which in the first five years encouraged growers, mainly in southern France and southern Italy, to pull out a total of 320,000 ha/790,400 acres, the equivalent of five times Australia's vineyard area. Many ageing vine-growers in these areas have come to expect this vine pull payment as they come to the end of their working life, regarding it as a retirement bonus. In few areas, however, have satisfactory alternative agricultural uses for the land been found.

An even more comprehensive vine pull scheme than the European Union's was enacted within a single country, the Soviet Union, as part of Gorbachev's attempts to curb alcohol consumption. Between 1985 and 1990, the total area under vine in the old USSR fell from more than 1.3 million ha to 880,000 ha.

Other national vine pull schemes may be directed at particular types of vine in an effort to reduce production of certain wine types—usually in recent history wine of the most basic sort. Such schemes were applied in both ARGENTINA and NEW ZEALAND in the late 1980s, for example.

For details of the mechanics of pulling out vines, see RIPPING OUT.

VINE REMOVAL. See RIPPING OUT.

VINE SPACING. See VINE DENSITY.

VINE TRAINING, the process of establishing a vine framework in the required shape. Training includes tying down and trimming growing shoots in summer, followed by suitable winter PRUNING. Normally vines are trained to a supporting structure which may be as simple as a stake in the ground, or may be a more complex trellis system made from wire and wood, metal, or concrete posts. Training is normally complete within the first two or three years of a vine's life and well established before grape production begins. It will, however, take longer where vines are planted at wide distances apart and with complex trellis systems such as the TENDONE. Training normally consists of forming the trunk, the cordons or head, and any arms required.

See under TRAINING SYSTEMS for more details of individual forms, and see also TRELLIS SYSTEMS for more details of their supports. R.E.S.

VINE-TRAINING SYSTEMS. See TRAINING SYSTEMS.

VINE VARIETIES, distinct types of vine within one species of the vine genus VITIS (see also BOTANICAL CLASSIFICATION). Different vine varieties produce different varieties of grape, so that the terms vine variety and grape variety are used almost interchangeably. Each variety of vine, or grape, may produce distinct and identifiable styles and flavours of wine.

The Doppelbogen, or double bow, **vine-training** system for Riesling vines in the Saar, fully exposed after winter pruning.

Vine variety is *cépage* in French, *cepa* in Spanish, *Rebsorte* in German, and *uva* in Italian.

Most of the vine varieties we know today (CABERNET SAUVIGNON and CHARDONNAY, for example) were selected by man from WILD VINES. Propagation by cuttings means that the new plants remain true to type (see PROPAGATION). These varieties have been supplemented by some which have developed naturally by MUTATION, and by HYBRIDS and CROSSES deliberately developed by man.

Most important vine varieties used to produce wine are of the European vine species *Vitis* VINIFERA. A number of varieties of AMERICAN VINE SPECIES and their AMERICAN HYBRIDS have also been used to make wine, however, and are also used as ROOTSTOCKS. Wine has also been made from a range of Asian vine varieties and from the FRENCH HYBRIDS.

It is clear that specific vine varieties were recognized in Ancient GREECE and ROME, since some are already described in CLASSICAL TEXTS such as those of Pliny and Columella (see ANCIENT VINE VARIETIES). The extent to which the vine varieties of Europe originate from wild vines or were introduced is not known. Also, with the fall of the Roman empire, cultivated vineyards were abandoned, and such varieties as were deliberately cultivated presumably interbred with local wild vines and native *Vitis vinifera*. The result of this intermixing over time is that many European regions have developed their own local varieties.

There are approximately 10,000 known varieties of *vinifera*. Ampelographers Pierre Viala and Victor Vermorel listed about 5,000 different varieties in their great seven-volume AMPELOGRAPHY published between 1902 and 1910 (see MONTPELLIER). Many of these were synonyms, and modern French authorities list fewer than 220 varieties of commercial significance in modern France. Italy and Portugal have a particularly rich heritage of vine varieties, however, and Galicia in north west Spain is reputed to boast as many as 1,000 indigenous vine varieties. Vine identification and the study of individual varieties' characteristics and aptitudes is a decidedly underdeveloped field of activity.

Vine varieties are often named for the colour of their berries, with many French varieties, for example, coming in *noir* (black), *rouge* (red), *violet*, *rose* (pink), *gris* (grey-pink), *jaune* (yellow), *vert* (green), and *blanc* (white) hues. This book uses the convention of adopting a capital letter for each word in a vine variety's name, although Pinot noir may be strictly more correct than Pinot Noir. Examples of mutants are Pinot Blanc and Pinot Gris, while Sauvignon Vert is a quite different variety from Sauvignon Blanc (itself completely unrelated to Cabernet Sauvignon). See individual variety names for more details.

Varieties were classified and grouped into families by Levadoux, but it has been difficult to establish the true origin for many varieties. Varieties can be broadly grouped into three major botanical categories called PROLES which are related to their geographical origins, and to some extent their end use. Varieties can also be classified in more detail by their country or region of origin, although as some varieties are becoming more international (see INTERNATIONAL VARIETIES) this distinction is becoming unclear.

Varieties may also be classified by their morphological features (see VINE MORPHOLOGY), of which a range is used to distinguish varieties and species in a scientific activity known as ampelography. Another classification is by end-product use, and so vine varieties may be described as being for wine, TABLE GRAPES, DRYING GRAPES, GRAPE JUICE, or for ROOTSTOCKS (although some varieties, such as SULTANA, are in practice used for several of these). Among wine vine varieties, some varieties are particularly well suited to different styles of wine: sparkling, fortified, still table wine, or brandy, for example. Within each group there are noble varieties and those suitable only for lower-value products.

Most widely planted varieties

Of all vine varieties, remarkably few have achieved an international reputation, and most of these are French. Obvious examples of these INTERNATIONAL VARIETIES include Cabernet Sauvignon, Pinot Noir, Syrah (Shiraz), Merlot, Chardonnay, Sauvignon Blanc, and Sémillon. There is little correlation between these most famous varieties and the vine varieties which cover the greatest total area of vineyard land: such varieties as AIRÉN, GRENACHE (GARNACHA), RKATSITELI, TREBBIANO (UGNI BLANC), and CARIGNAN are more widely planted even than Cabernet Sauvignon, some of these varieties being used substantially for BRANDY production and, in the case of the first two, being planted to Spain's relatively low VINE DENSITY.

Choice of variety

Vine-growers are rarely free to choose which vine variety to plant in a given vineyard. They may have acquired a planted vineyard in full production and cannot afford the crop loss involved in changing variety either by ripping out established vines or by FIELD GRAFTING a new variety on to the trunk and root system of the old one. Different varieties need different conditions of soil and climate. Cabernet Sauvignon simply will not ripen in many vineyards where the climate is too cool, for example.

In France, and much of the EUROPEAN UNION, the varieties permitted may be regulated. Some of these restrictions can be traced back to the Middle Ages (see PINOT NOIR), but formalization took place in 1935 with the APPELLATION CONTRÔLÉE (AC) laws which authorize only specified varieties for each appellation, distinguishing between principal and secondary varieties. Similarly, some varieties were completely banned (although it required more than 30 years for this law to have its effect). For the production of more basic VIN DE TABLE, l'Institut des Vins de Consommation Courante (IVCC, the precursor of ONIVIT) decreed in 1953 for each viticultural region three classifications of varieties: recommended, authorized, and tolerated until eventual removal. These laws have subsequently been overtaken by EU laws with the similar intent of allowing only specified varieties. For discussion of these restrictions, see VINE VARIETIES, EFFECT ON WINE.

In the New World, the choice of vine variety or varieties is often in practice determined by the style of wine that is eventually desired, many of them involving just one vine variety (often sold as a VARIETAL wine). Examples of monovarietal AC wines within France are Muscat de Frontignan, Muscadet, and Sancerre. Blends of two varieties often include those which are complementary, such as the productive and full bodied Marsanne mixed with the lighter, rarer Roussanne for the white Hermitage, or the lightly coloured Aramon with Alicante-Bouschet. Celebrated blends of three varieties include Sémillon, Sauvignon Blanc, and Muscadelle in Sauternes, and Pinot Noir, Chardonnay, and Meunier in champagne. Even more complex blends of varieties are common in red bordeaux and in Châteauneuf-du-Pape, both styles which are emulated in the New World. The mix of vine varieties that go into a single wine, or are planted on a single property, is called its *encépagement* in French and *uvaggio* in Italian.

Varieties themselves are often subdivided into various CLONES. While particular clones of many varieties have been selected through performance evaluation by CLONAL SELECTION, typically they cannot be separated by appearance.

NEW VARIETIES are being developed continually but may not be used for commercial wine-making for many years after they are bred. Most new varieties are bred for disease resistance. R.E.S. & J.Ro.

Galet, P., *Cépages et vignobles de France* (2nd edn., Montpellier, 1990).
—— *Précis de viticulture* (4th edn., Montpellier, 1983).
Mullins, M. G., Bouquet, A., and Williams, L., *Biology of the Grapevine* (Cambridge, 1992).
Robinson, J., *Vines, Grapes and Wines* (London, 1986).

VINE VARIETIES, EFFECT ON WINE. Of all the factors such as SOIL, CLIMATE, VITICULTURE, and detailed WINEMAKING techniques which have an effect on wine quality, vine variety is probably the easiest to detect in a BLIND TASTING. The colour of the grapes' skin determines what COLOUR of wine can be produced: red wine only from dark-skinned grapes. Only grape varieties which ripen readily and/or are prone to NOBLE ROT are likely to produce good SWEET WINES, while only those with high levels of natural acidity are likely to produce good BRANDY or SPARKLING WINES. But, even more important in identification, individual grape varieties tend to produce wines with identifiably different flavours. Indeed, in very general terms, it is a mark of quality in a vine variety that it is capable of producing wines with distinguished flavours, even if those flavours are heavily influenced by weather and TERROIR and vineyard practice. Lesser vine varieties tend to produce wines that are neutral and undistinguished, however promising the vineyard site.

When more than one vine variety is used to produce a single wine, it is important that the wines produced by those varieties are complementary. Cabernet Sauvignon tends to blend well with wines that have more obvious fruit such as Merlot or hot-climate Syrah/Shiraz, for example, while the weight of Sémillon is a good foil for the aroma and acidity of Sauvignon Blanc. Other French examples copied elsewhere include Grenache with Syrah and, possibly, Mourvèdre and Cabernet Sauvignon with Syrah.

Wine quality is maximized if the vine variety or vine varieties are well suited to the site, in terms of climate, soil structure, ROOTSTOCK, VINE DENSITY, TRAINING SYSTEM, PRUNING regime, and other viticultural methods. Matching vine variety to site is considered in its infancy in most of the NEW WORLD (although certain combinations such as Coonawarra for Cabernet Sauvignon vines, or Santa Barbara and Oregon for Pinot Noir, established themselves earlier than most). In parts of the Old World, on the other hand, the matching of vine variety to site, or even whole regions, is so entrenched (see VINE VARIETIES above) that some would argue it amounts to restriction. The varieties Cabernet Sauvignon and Merlot undoubtedly perform extremely well in Bordeaux, but it is perhaps an unnecessary constraint to forbid Bordeaux vine-growers from planting the Syrah grape of Hermitage (whose wines were regularly blended into those of Bordeaux to add weight when ADULTERATION AND FRAUD were rife).

The French APPELLATION CONTRÔLÉE system, which officially disapproves of citing vine varieties on the label, even as interpretation of a geographical appellation, is predicated on the belief that for every appellation there is an ideal vine variety or ENCÉPAGEMENT, or that the character of the appellation is stronger than that of any vine variety. While this is an attractive proposition (and it is certainly true that, for example, the appellation of a red bordeaux or a white Alsace wine is often more strongly identifiable than any single vine variety), it seems questionable for most wine regions, even within France. Regulations in other EUROPEAN UNION wine-producing countries tend to emulate those of France.

A contrary and quintessentially New World viewpoint has been summarized by Moran. The argument runs that appellation systems are essentially economic devices rather than environmental descriptions. A central plank to this argument is that in France the most famous wine regions' reputations are built on the best and best-known vine varieties, while lesser appellations are restricted to inferior varieties. Critics such as Moran see the more liberal New World approach as preferable, particularly in its commercial implications.

Galet, P., *Précis de viticulture* (4th edn., Montpellier, 1983).
Moran, W., 'The wine appellation: environmental description or economic device', *Auckland Cool Climate Symposium* (1988), 356–60.
Pouget, R., 'L'Encépagement des vignobles français d'appellation d'origine contrôlée: historique et possibilités d'évolution', *Bulletin de l'OIV*, 685–86 (1988), 183–95.

VINEYARD, name given to the field where grapevines are grown.

The contrast in connotations between the very words vineyard and field illustrates something of the special nature of vines as a crop. This may be partly connected with the symbolism of and pleasures associated with wine, but is also a function of the aesthetic appeal of vineyards in all seasons, whether the increasingly luxuriant green canopy of spring and summer, the flame-coloured leaves of autumn, or the rows of poignant black stumps in winter. The beauty of vineyards and vines plays an important part in wine TOURISM; it is difficult to imagine substantial numbers of people making a pilgrimage to a region famous for any other agricultural crop.

In most parts of the world the vineyard is a well-defined entity, generally well demarcated by the borders of the straight rows. *Vignoble* is a common French term for a vineyard at all quality levels. In Bordeaux, and elsewhere, CRU may be used synonymously with a top-quality vineyard, while in Burgundy the terms CLIMAT or, in the case of a walled vineyard, CLOS are more common. In Italy the terms cru, VIGNA, SORI, and RONCO are all used. Recognition of single vineyards is less developed in Spain although innovator Miguel TORRES uses the term *pago*.

Vineyards are typically monocultures with vines the only plants growing. Less frequently, however, vineyards are grown intermingled with other crops, the so-called *coltura promiscua* that was once the norm in much of central Italy. In the VINHO VERDE region of northern Portugal, vines are typically grown as borders around other fields which may contain field crops or orchards. Originally trained to wires attached to bordering trees, the vines of Vinho Verde are nowadays more commonly trained on wooden or metal supports, although they still surround fields in which other crops are grown.

Any one vineyard may be made up of smaller units, parcels, or fields, which may contain different vine varieties, clones, rootstocks, or vines of different ages. Sometimes fields are separated, as for example by headlands, hedges, or drainage ditches, and otherwise may be contiguous one with another.

Even relatively small vineyards are rarely homogeneous in terms of SOIL, TOPOGRAPHY, and MESOCLIMATE. Soils in particular may vary considerably within one single vineyard (see VOUGEOT or MONTRACHET, for example). Sometimes, when the soil, topography, and climate are uniform over an area much larger than a single vineyard, as in COONAWARRA in South Australia, then the region as a whole may earn a reputation for good quality rather than certain vineyards within it.

Vineyards vary in size, depending on many factors. Due to fragmentation of vineyards by inheritance, some vineyard owners in BURGUNDY may lay claim to only a few rows often indistinguishable to outsiders from the adjacent vines. At the other end of the scale in the New World there are often large corporate vineyards. One of the world's largest vineyards is the 2,800-ha/6,920-acre San Bernabe ranch in the Salinas Valley of MONTEREY in California.

Some vineyards are particularly famous for their wine because of their particular combination of VINE VARIETY, CLONE, ROOTSTOCK, and climate conditions, which can be distinguished at the various levels of MACROCLIMATE, MESOCLIMATE, and MICROCLIMATE. Of particular importance are the soil conditions, which, together with mesoclimate, constitute what the French (and others) call TERROIR. See under each of these entries for a discussion of their relative contribution. A feature, for example, of the famous Bordeaux PREMIERS CRUS is that as well as producing great wine in good years they are also able to do well in acknowledged low-quality years. This is a function not just of appropriate vineyard management, but also of the terroir which allows the vine to ripen the fruit adequately when other, less exalted vineyards, cannot.

See also HILLSIDE VINEYARDS, PLANTING, VINEYARD ANNUAL CYCLE, VINEYARD SITE SELECTION. R.E.S. & J.Ro.

VINEYARD ANNUAL CYCLE. The march of the seasons through the year dictates the work to be done in vineyards (see VINE GROWTH CYCLE). Spring is the time of budbreak, and early ploughing and spraying must be done. Early spring is also the common time for PLANTING vineyards. As the temperatures rise the vine shoots grow more rapidly, and FLOWERING takes place in early summer. This can be a busy period as often fungicide SPRAYS are to be applied, and the first SHOOT POSITIONING is carried out. Soon after FRUIT SET is the time for the second shoot positioning, and often the first TRIMMING. About this period the nurseryman is doing BENCH GRAFTING, and it is also the time for FIELD BUDDING AND GRAFTING. As the summer progresses the vine-grower is involved with further spraying of AGROCHEMICALS and often continued cultivation. Depending on the vine variety and region, the HARVEST may be in early, mid, or late summer, and sometimes in the autumn. Whenever it occurs it is one of the busiest periods in the vineyard, often involving SAMPLING to test grape ripeness before the HARVEST itself. Depending on the spread of varieties the harvest may be brief or protracted, but few other jobs are attended to in the vineyard at this time. The period immediately following harvest is busy in the wineries but not so in the vineyards, and vineyard workers and viticulturists often take their annual leave then. This is also the common time for soil RIPPING and maintenance of machinery and TRELLIS SYSTEMS. Once the leaves fall the serious business of PRUNING begins, and depending on the scale of operations this may continue right up until budbreak. This is also the time when CUTTINGS are taken for PROPAGATION. R.E.S.

VINEYARD SITE SELECTION is the single most important aspect of grape production in the NEW WORLD, and also in the Old World on the relatively rare occasions when it is practised. (Most Old World vineyards have been in existence for centuries, and when a new vineyard is created, or re-created, one important consideration may be whether or not it qualifies for a certain appellation.)

Vineyard site selection embraces more than just choosing the vineyard location, as the decision will affect the vineyard's YIELD, quality of the wine produced, and therefore the vineyard's long-term profitability. The site's regional CLIMATE, or MACROCLIMATE, for example, determines by virtue of temperature and sunshine hours which VINE VARIETIES should be grown, and the resulting likely wine style and quality. For example, lower temperatures produce more delicately flavoured wines, and hot climates produce wines relatively high in alcohol. Such effects are discussed under CLIMATE AND WINE QUALITY. Vineyards are often planted at higher ELEVATIONS to take advantage of lower temperatures. The site selection process might include evaluating climatic data from distinguished wine regions in an attempt to locate similar climates. With its enormous range of LATITUDE and ALTITUDE, Chile has a greater opportunity than most countries to match climates.

Similarly, rainfall and humidity affect the likelihood of many VINE DISEASES. For example, NEMATODES may be avoided by knowledge of indigenous types, or the previous crops grown on the site. It may even be possible to avoid introduction of PHYLLOXERA and other pests and diseases by creating a local QUARANTINE.

The site climate, or MESOCLIMATE, affects, for example, the extent to which cold air drains away, and the likelihood of spring and autumn FROST. A site's proximity to bodies of water such as lakes can be important in providing protection from injury due to particularly low temperatures, as in NEW YORK state and SWITZERLAND. These attributes depend on local TOPOGRAPHY.

The balance between rainfall and evaporation indicates the likelihood of DROUGHT, and for some regions at least whether IRRIGATION is desirable. In many parts of the world availability of high-quality water for irrigation is an essential factor in site selection. This may involve locating vineyards near streams or rivers, or with access to underground (artesian) water, or opportunities to build dams.

SOIL conditions present at the site will determine vineyard VIGOUR, with deep, fertile soils, for example, leading to vigorous growth and the possibility of high yields, but the concomitant need to manage problems this creates (see CANOPY MANAGEMENT). Premium-quality vineyards are typically found on soils with low water-holding capacity, and low SOIL FERTILITY. Site selection normally involves a process of soil mapping and physical and chemical analysis of soil samples. This allows potential problems such as poor DRAINAGE or SOIL ACIDITY to be treated appropriately before the vineyard is planted. Knowledge of soil depth indicates likely vine vigour.

Vegetation growing at the site, and the productivity and quality of other agricultural crops grown in the region, can be used as an indicator of the vineyard performance. The types of trees present give guidance as to the soil properties, and their size for their age indicates soil fertility and water supply.

Not all important features of potential vineyard sites are natural ones. Frontage to busy roads is essential if retail sales are expected from the vineyard site. Good communications with markets and proximity to a supply of LABOUR can also be significant. The performance and reputation of other vineyards in the area can also be commercially important.

R.E.S.

VIN GRIS is not, happily, a grey wine but a pink wine that is usually decidedly paler than most ROSÉ, made exactly as a white wine from dark-skinned grapes, and therefore without any MACERATION. No rules govern the term *vin gris*, but a wine labelled **gris de gris** must be made from lightly tinted grape varieties described as *gris* such as CINSAUT or GRENACHE GRIS.

In France, where it is a speciality of the Côtes de TOUL and certain parts of the Loire, it is usually made from pressing, but not macerating, dark-skinned grapes, often Gamay, which rarely ripen sufficiently to produce a deeply coloured red. It is also made in the Midi, notably beside the saltpans of the Camargue by Listel, where care is needed to tint rather than dye the resultant wine. The term is also occasionally encountered in the New World—although BLUSH wines are extremely similar to, if almost invariably sweeter than, *gris* wines. See also SCHILLERWEIN and other German light pinks.

VINHO, Portuguese for wine, and **vinho de mesa** is Portugal's basic TABLE WINE. A **vinho maduro** is one that has been matured, for at least a year. A **vinho verde**, on the other hand, is a 'green' or young wine, designed to be drunk early.

VINHO VERDE, light, acidic, often slightly sparkling, and highly distinctive wine produced in north west PORTUGAL whose name means 'green wine', a reference to the youthful state in which it is customarily sold. It is produced in verdant countryside inland from the coast north of the city of OPORTO which is known as the Costa Verde or Green Coast (see map on p. 750). The Vinho Verde DOC region is Portugal's largest demarcated wine region, extending from Vale da Cambra south of the river DOURO to the river Minho that forms the frontier with Spain over 130 km/80 miles to the north. Rain-bearing westerly winds from the Atlantic support intensive cultivation and the countryside north of Oporto is one of the most densely populated parts of rural Iberia. In order to make the best use of this cramped environment, vines have traditionally been grown high above the ground on arbours (see TENDONE), leaving space for other crops underneath. In the past, vines were often trained to grow up the trunks of tall poplar trees, but this form of viticulture has been largely replaced by an elaborate system of pergolas. Stout granite posts up to 4 metres high support a network of trellising covered by vines. Apart from making the best use of the limited available space, high trained vines help to reduce the risk of GREY ROT, which is endemic during the warm, damp, growing season. These practical advantages, however, are increasingly outweighed by such problems as the impossibility of MECHANIZATION. Many of the larger producers are therefore replanting vineyards on lower trellising systems.

The Vinho Verde DOC officially divides into six sub-regions, distinguished by climatic differences and the white grape varieties grown there. The area around the town of Monção on the Spanish border produces one of the best but least typical Vinhos Verdes from the ALVARINHO grape. Alcohol levels of up to 13 per cent set these wines apart, and thanks to a combination of consumer demand and low yields, they are relatively expensive. Further south around the towns of Braga, Barcelos, and Guimarães, the dominant grape varieties are LOUREIRO, TRAJADURA (both known, with slightly different spellings of their names, in GALICIA in Spain), and Pedernã (see ARINTO). These high-yielding vines produce wines that are light and acidic with an alcoholic strength typically between 8 and 10 per cent. Inland towards the river Douro around the town of Baião, AVESSO is the most important variety producing a slightly fuller style of wine in a warmer, drier climate.

However, half of all Vinho Verde produced is not the widely exported white wine but a fizzy, acidic, dry red made from grapes such as Azal, Vinhão, and Espadeiro and a large number of high-yielding HYBRIDS. With around 10 per cent of alcohol these deep coloured, rasping reds are something of an anathema to foreign palates and little red Vinho Verde leaves the north of Portugal.

The production of white Vinho Verde falls into two main camps. Until the 1950s nearly all Vinho Verde was made on a domestic scale. Following fermentation in open stone LAGARES, the wine would be run off into cask where the secondary MALOLACTIC FERMENTATION produced carbon dioxide. This was retained in the wine, giving it a slight sparkle. These rough and ready, usually cloudy, Vinhos Verdes are still drunk in rural bars and cafés. Since CO-OPERATIVE cellars were established in the 1950s and 1960s, more modern vinification methods have been used. Most vine-growers now deliver at least a portion of their crop either to the local co-operative or to one of the larger private wineries. Following mechanical pressing and fermentation in vat, the malolactic fermentation is suppressed and CARBON DIOXIDE is injected before bottling to give the wine its characteristic pétillance. In the 1980s a number of single estates or QUINTAS have also emerged, making high-quality VARIETAL wines from grapes such as Alvarinho, Loureiro, and Avesso. Although Vinho Verde is traditionally bone dry, most commercial BRANDS are sweetened to appeal to overseas markets. Unfortunately, few bottles carry a VINTAGE, but both red and white Vinho Verde should be drunk within a year after the harvest while the wine retains its characteristic fruit and freshness.

R.J.M.

VINIFERA, the European species of VITIS that is the vine most used for wine production, to which all the most familiar VINE VARIETIES belong. *Vinifera* is not a classical Latin word, but one made up by Linnaeus (see BOTANICAL CLASSIFICATION) to denote 'wine-grape bearing'.

The species is thought to originate in Transcaucasia (see ORIGINS OF VITICULTURE), and has been spread through the Mediterranean and Europe by the Phoenicians and Greeks and later by the Romans. *Vinifera* was spread through the New World, initially by Cortés in SOUTH AMERICA, and subsequently into western North America. The Dutch took *vinifera* grapevines to the Cape of Good Hope in 1616 (see SOUTH AFRICA), and the English to Australia, then New Zealand, beginning in 1788.

Vinifera is one of about 60 species of the *Vitis* genus, the majority of which originate in the Americas or Asia. *Vinifera* grapes are used principally for wine-making, table grapes, and drying grapes. See VINE for more details.

Vitis vinifera is distinguished from other *Vitis* species by a range of general botanical features, including vigorous shoots mostly free of hair, prominent NODES and BUDS, regularly intermittent TENDRILS, leaves generally orbicular, more or less deeply lobed, PETIOLAR sinus often in a U or lyre shape, and conspicuous dentation (so-called teeth) around the edge of the leaf. *Vinifera* flowers are typically hermaphroditic (both male and female), and there are differences in seeds too (see GRAPE). Because of man's selection of *vinifera* vines for their fruit characters, the seeds typically represent a small proportion of the berry weight, 10 per cent compared with 80 per cent for *Vitis berlandieri*.

Further details about *vinifera* can be found under the following entries which describe more fully aspects of the commercial culture of this species, emphasizing its use in wine-making. Especially important are the effects of CLIMATE and SOIL. See also VINE GROWTH CYCLE, VINE BREEDING, VINE DISEASES, VINE MORPHOLOGY, VINE PESTS, VINE PHYSIOLOGY, VINE PRODUCTS, VINE TRAINING, and VITICULTURE.

R.E.S.

VINIFICATION, the practical art of transforming grapes into wine. In its widest sense, it is synonymous with WINE-MAKING, but strictly encompasses only those processes which take place in the winery up to the point at which the ÉLEVAGE of the new wine begins. See also OENOLOGY.

VIN JAUNE, meaning literally 'yellow wine' in French, extraordinary style of wine made in France, mainly in the JURA region, using a technique similar to that used for making SHERRY.

In Jura, where the most famous *vin jaune* appellation is CH-CHALON, the wine must be made from the curious local white grape variety the SAVAGNIN or Naturé, grown ideally on MARL. The grapes are picked well ripened, often not until November, ideally at 13 to 15 per cent POTENTIAL ALCOHOL, and fermented as normal. The wine is then put into old 228-l/60-gal casks filled so that there is a good surface of wine on which the local benevolent FILM-FORMING YEAST, called here the *voile* or veil, can develop. It is similar to the FLOR which is responsible for FINO sherries but can develop at a lower alcoholic strength and, because temperatures are generally lower, is not as thick. The *voile* also has to survive the harsher temperatures of a Jura winter, and takes two or three years to develop fully. After full development it will wane in cooler weather. OXIDATION is an important element in making *vin jaune*. The wine is left in cask, untouched other than to allow regular sampling for a dangerous rise in VOLATILE ACIDS, for a full six years and three months. Considerable research is being undertaken to analyse precisely, and possibly replicate, the *voile*. (George observes that Chardonnay wine will develop *vin jaune* flavour under cultured yeasts designed to replicate the *voile* after about four years, but that it loses this nuttiness rapidly, unlike Savagnin.)

Jura producers claim that *vin jaune* will last for 50 or more years in its distinctive 62-cl *clavelin* bottle (the amount of wine left after keeping a litre in a cask for six years, supposedly). They advise opening the bottle half a day before serving, and that it should be drunk with all sorts of savoury dishes, particularly of course chicken cooked in the wine itself, a classic dish.

A similar wine, called *vin de voile*, is made by at least one producer in GAILLAC.

George, R., *French Country Wines* (London, 1990).

VÍNLAND. Driven westward by overpopulation in the second half of the 9th century, the Scandinavians colonized Iceland, then Greenland and finally, a century later, as some sources tell us, Vínland, 'Wine Land', which must have been on the east coast of America.

Two sagas, Grenlinga Saga, the 'Saga of the Greenlanders', composed in the late 12th century, and Eirik's Saga, dated mid 13th century, give accounts of the discovery of Vínland. Its colonization follows the same pattern as that of Iceland and Greenland: chance discovery, followed by further exploration, then settlement. A merchant on his way to Greenland in 985 or 986 is blown off course south west across the Atlantic and finds himself in unknown lands. Leif the Lucky, son of Eirik the Red, settler of Greenland, decides to explore the new country. He finds WILD VINES and wheat, rolling grasslands, timber, game, salmon, and a climate almost without winter frost. He names the country Vínland. After further voyages of exploration Leif's brother-in-law Thorfinn Karlsefni attempts to found a colony. He meets strong resistance from the natives, who resemble Native Americans but may also have been Eskimo, for they lived further south then than they do now. Thorfinn did not succeed in establishing a permanent Norse settlement in Vínland.

Scholars do not agree on the precise location of Vínland. The sagas do not give clues, and, although archaeologists have found what appear to be traces of Norse settlements on the east coast of America, the evidence is not conclusive. Besides, the climate was warmer around 1000 AD than now (hence the colonization of Greenland; see CLIMATE CHANGE) so that vines could survive further north.

Even though the stories told in the sagas differ in some respects, they are not fantasy. A foreign setting is a feature of the literary genre: the purpose of the sagas is to inform as well as to amuse, and the information they give about foreign countries is usually strikingly accurate. Moreover, an earlier and unrelated source supports the existence of Vínland. Around 1075 Adam of Bremen wrote a history of the archbishopric of Bremen and Hamburg, which until 1104 included the Scandinavian countries. Adam travelled to the royal court of Denmark, where his main informant was King Svein Ulfsson, nephew of King Canute. Svein Ulfsson tells him that Vínland has wild vines, which make excellent wine, and also wild wheat. Adam emphasizes that this is no mere fable, because it was told him for a fact by the Danes. So were the first wine-makers in America Norse colonists? But if they were, the wine must have been made not from the European *Vitis* VINIFERA, but from native AMERICAN VINE SPECIES, almost certainly VITIS *labrusca*, which grows wild on the eastern coast of the United States. H.M.W.

Jones, G., *The Norse Atlantic Saga Being the Norse Voyages of Discovery and Settlement to Iceland, Greenland, America* (Oxford, 1964).
Magnusson, M., and Pálsson, H., *The Vinland Sagas* (Harmondsworth, 1965).

VIN MUTÉ, wine that has undergone MUTAGE.

VINO, Italian for wine and, colloquially and unfairly, English for basic quaffing wine, or PLONK.

VINO DA MEDITAZIONE, unofficial but useful Italian category of wines too complex (and often too alcoholic and/or sweet) to drink with food. Such wines, many of them extra strong and/or sweet because they are DRIED GRAPE WINES, should be sipped meditatively after a meal.

Although they do not employ the same terminology, and produce wines much lighter in alcohol, many Germans effectively treat fine wine as a *vino da meditazione* to be drunk once the table has been cleared of food and, often, beer.

VINO DA TAVOLA, Italian for TABLE WINE, the official EUROPEAN UNION category denoting the lowest of the vinous low, but also much wider in scope in a country with such little regard for law as ITALY. While the great majority of each Italian wine harvest qualifies as basic vino da tavola, typically red from Apulia and white from Sicily, sold at rock bottom prices (or drained off into the European WINE LAKE), vino da tavola may also designate some of the finest, and most expensive, wines Italy produces, made outside the constraining rules of the official DOC and DOCG quality wine systems.

The birth of these new **vini da tavola** can be dated with some accuracy to the year 1974 and the appearance of Tignanello and Sassicaia, both marketed by the Florentine house of ANTINORI. Although the wines were produced in entirely different geographical zones (CHIANTI Classico for the first, BOLGHERI near the Tuscan coast for the second) and from entirely different grape varieties (CABERNET SAUVIGNON and CABERNET FRANC for the latter, a very high percentage of SANGIOVESE for the former), they shared four significant characteristics that were to mark the evolution of this category of wines. They both represented an attempt to give more body, intensity, and longevity to Tuscan red wines, which had become rather fruity and light-hearted in the preceding 15 years. Unlike the prevailing Tuscan red wine norm, these blends exclude white grapes (the first year of Tignanello in 1971 excluded TREBBIANO but retained three per cent of Malvasia; the second vintage, produced in 1975, eliminated white grapes altogether). Non-traditional, non-Italian varieties were used in both blends (the 1975 Tignanello substituted Cabernet Sauvignon for the native CANAIOLO). And, in a move that was to delight French COOPERS, small oak barrels, principally of French origin, were used for the BARREL MATURATION of both wines. This latter innovation was a radical break with the local practice of using large casks of Yugoslav oak, and marked a movement towards a more international style in the wines' flavour spectrum. The move was not welcomed by all in the domestic market and forced Antinori to seek a wider international public for the wines; it also forced them to seek more flavour intensity and concentration in the wines to avoid an overwhelming oakiness.

The blend of the 1975 Tignanello (80 per cent Sangiovese, 20 per cent Cabernet Sauvignon) rapidly became canonical and was to prove extremely influential over the following 15 years. Cabernet Sauvignon has remained principally a blending grape in Tuscany due both to a certain unfamiliarity with the variety on the part of growers and to the costs of transforming entire vineyards. A certain number of Cabernet Sauvignon-based wines began to appear, particularly after the middle of the 1980s. The native Sangiovese was hardly neglected, however, and a substantial number of BARRIQUE-aged, 100 per cent Sangiovese wines began to appear in the 1980s, the pioneering effort being Montevertine's Le Pergole Torte in 1977.

Experiments with earlier maturing varieties, MERLOT and SYRAH in particular, were less common, due at least partially to Tuscan producers' lack of familiarity with their characteristics, but the latter half of the 1980s saw various attempts to utilize them both for blending with Sangiovese and as wines on their own. Initial results left substantial grounds for optimism, especially for Merlot. The first PINOT NOIRS appeared at the same time, principally from vineyards at over 450 m/1,480 ft in altitude, where Sangiovese has traditionally had difficulties in ripening, although the suitability of this Burgundian variety to the Tuscan climate has yet to be demonstrated.

Although red wines represented the overwhelming majority of these new vini da tavola, the substantial availability of unfavourable exposures for red wine and/or higher vineyards where red varieties produced thin, acidic wines has also led to widespread plantings of non-traditional white varieties, with CHARDONNAY and SAUVIGNON Blanc being overwhelmingly favoured. The former is, in the majority of cases, aged in small oak barrels and often subjected to BARREL FERMENTATION beforehand.

Sassicaia was a pioneering wine, not only in its use of Cabernet but also in its revaluation of a zone never known for producing fine or even commercial wine. Its example has been followed by other peripheral areas of Tuscany. These cannot be DOC wines, just as non-traditional VARIETAL wines in an area like Chianti Classico cannot be given DOC status. The opposite phenomenon has occurred in certain DOCG areas outside Chianti Classico whose wines enjoy little prestige: the better producers have been progressively renouncing the use of the DOCG and labelling their best wines vino da tavola in order to obtain higher prices, thus reinforcing the Tuscan anomaly whereby the most prestigious and most remunerative wines are those that are the theoretically second-class citizen, the vino da tavola.

If high-priced vini da tavola were initially confined to Tuscany, the mid 1980s saw a significant expansion of the phenomenon. Ambitious producers saddled with poorly conceived DOCs and/or a poor image for the wines of their zone were quick to profit by the example of Tuscany. Superior Sangiovese from Romagna and superior versions of INTERNATIONAL VARIETIES from Friuli and the Trentino, frequently barrique aged, were the next to follow. This latter category of wines was a true reversal of formal values: the fruity and refreshing (if somewhat simple) Cabernet, Chardonnay, Sauvignon, and Pinot Noir of these two regions continued to be released as DOC wines while newer, more ambitious, more substantial versions of the same varieties, frequently from the same houses, were released as vini da tavola at substantially higher prices.

Piedmont, with a more consolidated viticultural tradition and with a certain number of prestigious DOCG wines, was slower to accept the idea that the term vino da tavola could be a viable alternative, but Barbera, the region's most widely planted variety, existed in a bewildering variety of styles. It was therefore almost inevitable that the first important small barrel-aged Barberas in Piedmont were vini da tavola and, as the number of these wines increased, many producers—not only in Asti or the Monferrato, but also in the LANGHE—began to release their basic Barbera as a DOC wine, their superior Barbera as a vino da tavola. As a region with a significant amount of experimentation with newly introduced international varieties, Piedmont has been forced to follow the example of Tuscany and classify the products of these grapes, many of them of very high quality, as vini da tavola. Younger producers' experiments with Nebbiolo/Barbera blends, or even more baroque blends such as Barbera/Cabernet Sauvignon, combinations obviously neither imagined nor covered by existing DOCs, had no alternative to vino da tavola status.

Italian wine thus does not follow the example of French or German viticultural classification, whose finest and most expensive products are almost inevitably the appellation wines and whose respective VIN DE TABLE and TAFELWEIN enjoy a generally low status. This is perhaps less of an anomaly than a reflection of the immaturity of Italy's fine wine tradition.

See also CAPITOLARE and SUPERTUSCAN. D.T.

VINO DE LA TIERRA, category of wines from specially designated zones in SPAIN which have not qualified for DO (Denominación de Origen) status. The category is the equivalent of the French VIN DE PAYS (although vinos de la tierra have been much slower to reach an exportable standard).

VINO DE MESA, Spanish term for TABLE WINE, the most basic category for wine coming from vineyards that do not qualify for either VINO DE LA TIERRA or DO (Denominación de Origen) status. If the wine is sold in bottle, its label may not normally display a grape variety, vintage, or geographic origin. Much of Spain's vino de mesa is sent for compulsory DISTILLATION under EUROPEAN UNION initiatives to diminish its wine SURPLUS.

VINO NOBILE DI MONTEPULCIANO, potentially majestic and certainly noble red wine made exclusively in the township of Montepulciano 120 km/75 miles south east of Florence in the hills of TUSCANY in central Italy. With BRUNELLO DI MONTALCINO, CHIANTI, and CARMIGNANO, it is one of Tuscany's four DOCG wines. Officially the wine is the classic Tuscan blend of SANGIOVESE, here called Prugnolo Gentile, with small amounts of CANAIOLO, TREBBIANO, and MALVASIA grapes. The DOCG regulations were modified in 1989, however, to permit the elimination of white grapes, and the better producers freely admit to making their wines entirely of Prugnolo Gentile even though the theoretical maximum is 80 per cent.

The soil of the zone has a higher percentage of sand than the production zones of Chianti Classico or Brunello; the slopes, which face mainly east to south east, are planted at altitudes of 250 m to 600 m/2,000 ft, although the best wines undoubtedly come from the lower vineyards.

Vino Nobile has an illustrious history, having been lauded as a 'perfect wine' by the cellarmaster of Pope Paul III in 1549, by Francesco Redi in his 'Bacchus in Tuscany' of 1685 (he called it 'the king of wines'), and by G. F. Neri in the late 18th century, who gave it the title 'noble'. The area planted rose rapidly after the introduction of the DOC in 1966. Between 1970 and 1989, the total vineyard rose from less than 150 ha/370 acres to 760 ha; production rose from 8,000 hl/211,000 gal to 30,700 hl; and the number of producers bottling their own wine increased from seven or eight to 40.

The wine itself is rather fuller in body and more alcoholic

than Chianti, reflecting its warmer production zone. It has so far not shown the aromatic finesse and elegance of the best Chianti or Brunello, possibly because of the lack of limestone in the soil, or because of Montepulciano's warmer evenings and nights. What is certain is that poor practices in both vineyard and cellar, with over-production and old casks being particular problems (accentuated by the obligatory two-year CASK AGEING period), led to a notable decline in the wine's quality between the late 1960s and the mid 1980s. Some progress has been made subsequently, but the wines have not been able to gain the prestige or fetch the prices in the marketplace of the better Chianti Classico Riservas and are undoubtedly the poor relation of Brunello di Montalcino and the more glamorous wines labelled VINO DA TAVOLA. Some experimentation with small oak barrels and with alternative vine varieties is taking place, though such developments remain marginal. Avignonesi is the most innovative producer, with a wide range of red and white vini di tavola.

Earlier maturing, lighter local wine is declassified as Rosso di Montepulciano, a DOC created in 1989. D.T.

Anderson, B., *The Wine Atlas of Italy* (London and New York, 1990).
Gleave, D., *The Wines of Italy* (London and New York, 1989).

VIN SANTO, 'holy wine', TUSCANY'S classic amber-coloured dessert wine, is produced throughout this central Italian region. It is made traditionally from the local white grapes TREBBIANO and MALVASIA (although the red SANGIOVESE was also used in the past) which have been dried on straw mats under the rafters, in the hottest and best-ventilated part of the peasant home (see DRIED GRAPE WINES). The grapes were normally crushed between the end of November and the end of March, depending on the desired RESIDUAL SUGAR level in the wine (the longer the drying process, the greater the evaporation and the sweeter the must), and then aged in small barrels holding between 50 l and 300 l/79 gal. These barrels, often bought second hand from the south of Italy, were frequently made of chestnut, but the 1980s saw a decisive turn towards OAK.

The wine comes in a bewildering range of styles from the ultra-sweet to a bone dry version which more closely resembles a dry FINO sherry than a dessert wine. The habit of keeping the barrels under the roof in a space called the *vinsantaia* encouraged refermentation each year when warm weather arrived and tended to exhaust the unfermented sugars that had remained in the wine. This stylistic variation was envisaged in the DOC rules, which define a dry, a semi-sweet, and a sweet Vin Santo with differing levels of alcohol and residual sugar.

Vin Santo currently has two DOCs, partially overlapping in terms of geography, although a high proportion of Vin Santo, which is made throughout Tuscany's wine zones, is non-DOC. The first, called Val d'Arbia, covers Radda, Monteriggioni, and a strip of territory south east of Siena to the boundaries of the Brunello di Montalcino zone. The second and more recent DOC, Colli dell'Etruria Centrale, is identical with the various DOC zones of the red wine CHIANTI. Both zones impose a substantial percentage of Trebbiano in the blend—75 per cent in the Val d'Arbia, 50 per cent for the Etruria Centrale DOC—despite the conviction of most of the better producers that it is the Malvasia grape that makes the better wine. The Etruria Centrale DOC authorities therefore caused a stir by imposing a five per cent ceiling on Malvasia and permitting the use of up to 45 per cent of such non-traditional, French grape varieties as PINOT BLANC, PINOT GRIS, CHARDONNAY, and SAUVIGNON Blanc.

The quality of the wine itself varies wildly not only as a result of variation in grape composition, residual sugar level, and wine-making competence, but because the land is divided between so many smallholders, all of whom seem to feel obliged to produce Vin Santo, the wine which was traditionally served to guests. Although some delicious Vin Santo is made, there is also a considerable proportion with serious wine FAULTS, particularly an excess of VOLATILITY, usually a direct consequence of lengthy BARREL MATURATION. DOC rules insist the wine is matured for at least three years, and the better producers rarely release their Vin Santo before five years. Cask maturation, without RACKING, lasts from four to more than 10 years for the most traditionally made Vin Santo. D.T.

Tachis, G., *Il Libro del Vin Santo* (Florence, 1988).

VINS DE MOSELLE. See MOSELLE.

VINTAGE can either mean the physical process of grape-picking and wine-making, for which see HARVEST, or it can mean the year or growing season which produced a particular wine, for which see VINTAGE YEAR. A vintage wine is one made from the produce of a single year.

VINTAGE ASSESSMENT is notoriously difficult because quality and character can vary so much between producers and properties. A vintage is often assessed at the most difficult stage in its life, its infancy, for reasons of commerce and curiosity. Wine merchants and wine writers habitually taste wines from the most recent vintage in a wine region important for INVESTMENT when they are just a few months old and are still in cask. Quite apart from the fact that the wines are at this stage still being made (see ÉLEVAGE), samples may give a misleading impression either because too long has elapsed since they were drawn from cask (OXIDATION is a common problem), or, if they are tasted directly from cask, because they are undergoing a distorting treatment such as FINING. Furthermore, this sort of vintage assessment is long before the ASSEMBLAGE process and can only provide a snapshot of embryonic wine from a small proportion of the total number of barrels produced.

This sort of comparative tasting can usually give some indication as to which are the most and least successful wines of a given vintage, but it can be extremely difficult to stand back from the individual samples, accurately remember exactly how the same wines from previous vintages tasted at

Year	Red Bordeaux	Sauternes	Red Burgundy	White Burgundy	Rhône	Loire (Moelleux)	Germany & Alsace (Late Harvest)	Champagne	Port
1945	7Δ	7Δ	7Δ	—	—	—	—	7Δ	—
1947	6Δ	6Δ	5Δ	—	—	7Δ	6Δ	—	—
1949	6Δ	7Δ	6Δ	—	—	5Δ	7Δ	7Δ	/
1953	6Δ	6Δ	4Δ	—	—	—	7Δ	6Δ	/
1959	6Δ	7†	7Δ	—	6†	—	6Δ	6Δ	/
1961	7†	5Δ	5Δ	—	7†	—	—	7Δ	/
1962	5Δ	6†	6Δ	—	5Δ	—	—	5Δ	/
1964	4Δ	—	6Δ	—	6†	6Δ	5Δ	6Δ	/
1966	6Δ	5Δ	6Δ	—	6†	—	—	6Δ	6†
1970	6Δ	5Δ	5Δ	—	6†	5Δ	—	6Δ	6†
1971	5Δ	6†	6Δ	6Δ	6†	6Δ	7Δ	6Δ	/
1975	5†	6†	—	—	4Δ	5Δ	6Δ	7Δ	4Δ
1976	4†	6Δ	5†	4Δ	5Δ	6†	6Δ	6†	/
1978	5†	3Δ	7†	6Δ	7†	5Δ	—	5†	/
1979	5†	4Δ	4Δ	6Δ	5Δ	5Δ	4Δ	6†	/
1981	5†	5†	3Δ	4Δ	4Δ	4Δ	4Δ	6†	/
1982	7†	4Δ	4†	5Δ	5†	5Δ	4Δ	7†	4Δ
1983	5†	6†	4Δ	4Δ	7*	5Δ	6Δ	5†	5*
1985	6†	4†	7*	6†	6*	6†	6†	5†	6*
1986	6*	6*	4†	6†	4†	6†	3†	5†	/
1988	5*	7*	7*	5Δ	6*	5*	5†	/	/
1989	6*	7*	6*	7*	6*	7*	7*	/	/
1990	6*	6*	7*	5*	6*	7*	6*	/	/
1991	3*	3*	5*	4*	4*	—	5*	/	5*
1992	3*	3*	5*	5*	5*	—	5*	/	/

*7 = the best 0 = no good * not yet ready † mature Δ drink soon*
— not readily available / no vintage generally (or yet) declared

Many excellent wines are produced in other countries, but district, climatic and grape variations make it difficult for the Society to give a balanced assessment of any one year. Good vintages not shown above: Port: 1948Δ, 1955Δ, 1960Δ, 1963†, 1977*, 1980*. Red Burgundy: 1969Δ, Sauternes: 1967† and Rhône: 1972Δ.

The International Wine & Food Society's **vintage chart** is one of the best known, and is fully revised annually by a committee of wine luminaries.

the same stage, and make any reliable assessment of the likely characteristics and potential of the young vintage as a whole. Vintages of which the collective assessment at this young stage was subsequently agreed to have been too enthusiastic include 1975 in Bordeaux and 1983 in Burgundy, but other examples abound. (Wine merchants have proved themselves much less likely to err on the side of caution.)

The assessment of a mature vintage is a much less hazardous process that is usually undertaken in the form of a horizontal TASTING, although of course SUBJECTIVITY plays its part as it does in all tasting.

VINTAGE CHARTS are both useful and notoriously fallible, partly because young VINTAGE ASSESSMENT is so fraught with difficulty. Most vintage charts take the form of a grid mapping ratings for each combination of wine region and year. The least sophisticated vintage charts content themselves with a NUMBER for each major wine region: Bordeaux 1990 '9' (out of 10), for instance. More sophisticated charts (that regularly updated in Robert PARKER's newsletter, for example) divide Bordeaux into its main districts, and add a letter indicating maturity: Margaux 1990 '90E' (90 out of 100, E for early maturing), for instance. The fact that this same vintage chart suggests that Graves 1990 is '90R' (R for ready to drink) already demonstrates how difficult it is to generalize about a district in which there may be hundreds of different producers, each with a different wine-making policy and style of wine.

The most useful vintage charts are the most detailed, but also those that are regularly updated on the basis of continuous and relevant tasting. The INTERNATIONAL WINE & FOOD SOCIETY was one of the first to issue a vintage chart, in 1935. The Society has since then issued an annual vintage chart, updated by a committee expressly charged with this task.

VINTAGE PORT, in France often called 'le vintage'. See PORT.

VINTAGE YEAR, the year in which a wine was produced and the characteristics of that year. Most, but not all, of its characteristics result from particular WEATHER conditions experienced. In the southern hemisphere, a **vintage-dated** wine invariably carries the year in which the grapes were picked, even though much of the VINE GROWTH CYCLE was actually in the previous year. In the northern hemisphere, vintage-dated wines carry the year in which both the vine growth occurred and the grapes were picked (with the exception of those rare examples of EISWEIN picked in early January, which are dated with the year whose vine growth produced the wine). The expression 'vintage year' is also sometimes used of a year producing particularly high quality wines.

In a literal sense, all young wine is vintage wine, being from a single year. Only at the BLENDING stage may wine of a recent year, or vintage, be mixed with older wines into an undated blend. Most everyday wines—such as the TABLE WINE category designated by the EUROPEAN UNION, the JUG WINES of the USA, and CASK WINE in Australia—are not vintage dated. Some top-quality CHAMPAGNE is NON-VINTAGE too. In most circumstances, however, a non-vintage wine is inferior to a vintage-dated one.

The vintage year printed on a wine label can help the consumer decide when to open a particular bottle, being particularly relevant to wine meant for AGEING (others, the great majority of wines, should simply be drunk as young as possible). Since the capacity of a wine to improve with age is one obvious test of its quality, a vintage's status is only fully established in retrospect (whatever those charged with selling it may say; see VINTAGE ASSESSMENT).

The concept of vintage year has a long history. OPIMIAN wine, made in the consular year of Lucius Opimius, 121 BC, was celebrated for decades afterwards as a particularly fine vintage. The wines must have been sweet and strong, made from very ripe or partially dried grapes and fermented to the extreme upper limit of natural fermentation (see DRIED GRAPE WINES) to have lasted as long as they did. Similar principles apply to the famous, long-lived vintages of the RHINE. The celebrated Steinwein of AD 1540, last drunk in 1961, was made in a freak year so hot and dry that the Rhine dried up, and could be walked across.

Vintage years did not become a normal commercial consideration until the end of the 17th century, when BOTTLES and CORKS replaced BARRELS for long-term wine storage. Vintages became particularly important towards the end of the 18th century, when the modern bottle shape evolved, allowing bottles to be stored on their sides. The better red wines of Bordeaux came to be 'laid down' for many years, and it was then that what is now regarded as the traditional Bordeaux style of WINE-MAKING for prolonged BOTTLE AGEING became established.

Penning-Rowsell gives details of some of the more famous Bordeaux vintages. The celebrated 1784 clarets, sought out and imported by America's wine-loving President Thomas JEFFERSON, were from one of the many fine vintages spanning the late 18th century and first years of the 19th century, culminating in the reputedly outstanding 'comet' year of 1811. Other runs of predominantly good Bordeaux vintages followed in the 1840s and again in the 1860s and the first half of the 1870s: a period long remembered as the crowning glory of the PRE-PHYLLOXERA era. The limited climatic records available suggest that these were predominantly warm periods (see CLIMATE CHANGE).

Vintage years in contemporary Bordeaux, and throughout central and western Europe, tend still to be those of ample sunshine (especially in spring, and again in late July and August), and average or higher TEMPERATURES leading to a normal or early HARVEST date. Bad vintage years have almost invariably been cool and/or wet, with below-average sunshine.

In hot and reliably sunny viticultural climates, on the other hand, the best years for table wines are usually average or cooler than average. This generalization does not apply to sweet FORTIFIED WINES, which need more or less unlimited warmth and sunshine. Nor does it necessarily apply to all table wines, or all hot areas. For instance wet, cloudy, and relatively cool summers in the very warm Hunter Valley of NEW SOUTH WALES are usually inferior for red table wines, although they may still produce good-quality white table wines.

The reactions of vines and grapes to seasonal conditions or weather events can also differ widely according to SOIL type within an area. As demonstrated by the extensive studies of Seguin in Bordeaux, vines on well-drained, deep soils may be little affected by variations in RAINFALL, whereas those on shallow and poorly drained soils will alternate between drought stress and waterlogging under the same rainfall. For this reason the best vineyards, with favourable TERROIR, are the least subject to vintage variation and can maintain consistently high quality.

In addition, VINE VARIETIES can react quite differently to the weather conditions depending on their individual timings of BUDBREAK, FLOWERING, and RIPENESS, and the relative sensitivities of their berries to rain, diseases, or damaging heat. PINOT NOIR, like most other early maturing red grape varieties, is very sensitive to heat or direct exposure of the berries to SUNLIGHT, readily suffering *coups de soleil*, or SUNBURN. ZINFANDEL, with its tightly packed bunches, is notoriously sensitive to any rain towards harvest time. The least rain and water uptake causes berry splitting and subsequent total BUNCH ROT. This is probably the main reason its extensive use is confined to California, where the ripening season is almost entirely free of rain. CHENIN BLANC is similarly susceptible, at least in climates such as those of California and South Africa where the preceding weather is mostly hot and dry. By contrast the CABERNET SAUVIGNON of Bordeaux is happily tolerant of both heat and rain, and is therefore generally less affected by vintage differences.

A final point is that critical weather events, particularly heavy rainfall and HAIL, are not necessarily uniform within a given district and year. Even if they were, management decisions can lead to quite different results—depending, for instance, on the extent to which SPRAYING has been practised, or whether grapes are picked before, during, or after rains at harvest time.

Nor is weather the only possible external influence on the characteristics of a particular vintage year. Market conditions may dictate how or whether certain viticultural practices such as PRUNING and CROP THINNING are carried out so as to influence crop quality or yield. Social history may also dictate some characteristics of a vintage year, as in some of the vintages ripened in European vineyards during the Second World War. There have also been instances of CONTAMINANTS from a new pesticide which have affected particular vintages of certain wines, sometimes on a less than localized scale, as in the use of Orthene in Germany in 1983.

For all these reasons, vintages are seldom uniformly good, medium, or bad, even within a small area (see VINTAGE ASSESSMENT). A generally recognized 'vintage' year can have its failures, often for reasons totally beyond the competence of vignerons and wine-makers. Equally, 'poor' vintages can usually still produce good wines from particular locations and grape varieties.

See AUCTIONS and INVESTING IN WINE for details of some individual vintages. See also LABELLING INFORMATION.

J.G. & R.E.S.

Penning-Rowsell, E., *The Wines of Bordeaux* (6th edn., London, 1989).

Seguin, G., '"Terroirs" and pedology of wine growing', *Experientia*, 42 (1986), 861–72.

VINTNER, late Middle English word for wine MERCHANT which superseded **vinter**. Mainly because of England's links with BORDEAUX, vintners were some of the most important people in the City of London in the 14th and early 15th centuries (four mayors of London were vintners in Edward II's reign). The **Vintners' Company** evolved from the 'Mistery of Vintners', a group of London and Gascon merchants who enjoyed a practical monopoly on London's important wine trade with Gascony from at least 1364. It was formally incorporated in 1437, and was recognized by Henry VIII as one of the '12 great' livery companies (along with the Mercers, Grocers, Drapers, Fishmongers, Goldsmiths, Skinners, Merchant Taylors, Haberdashers, Salters, Ironmongers, and Clothworkers). It is still based at **Vintners' Hall** by the Thames in London, in a section of the City known as **Vintry** ward, where for centuries wine would be unloaded for sale throughout southern England. Any member of the Vintners' Company is a freeman of the City of London and is still allowed to sell wine without applying for a licence. Today wine trade EDUCATION, regulation, and control are under its auspices, as is the Institute of MASTERS OF WINE.

Simon, A., *History of the Wine Trade in England*, ii (London, 1964).

VIN VINÉ is a traditional term for a wine made strong and sweet by the addition of alcohol to grape must at some point before fermentation is complete. A VIN DOUX NATUREL and a VIN DE LIQUEUR are both therefore *vins vinés*. See also MUTAGE.

VIOGNIER became one of the world's more fashionable white grape varieties in the early 1990s, mainly because its most famous wine CONDRIEU is both distinctive and, most importantly, scarce.

The vines can withstand drought well but are prone to POWDERY MILDEW. The grapes are a deep yellow and the resulting wine is high in colour, alcohol, and a very particular perfume redolent of apricots, peaches, and blossom. Condrieu is one of the few highly priced white wines that should probably be drunk young, while this perfume is at its most heady and before the wine's slightly low acidity fades.

The vine was at one time a common crop on the farmland south of Lyons and has been grown on the infertile terraces of the northern RHÔNE for centuries but its extremely low productivity saw it decline to an official total of just 14 ha/35 acres in the French agricultural census of 1968—mostly in the three north Rhône appellations in which it is allowed, Condrieu, CH GRILLET, and, to an even lesser extent, CÔTE-RÔTIE, in which it may be included as a perfuming agent up to 20 per cent of the Syrah-dominated total.

French nurserymen saw an increase in demand for Viognier cuttings from the mid 1980s, however (when the red wines of the Rhône enjoyed a renaissance of popularity), and by 1988 were selling half a million a year. By 1993 Viognier plantings in the Languedoc-Roussillon had reached 139 ha. In the early 1990s the consumer could choose from a range of recognizably perfumed, if slightly light, southern French varietal Viogniers, some of them produced at quite respectable levels, from cuttings field-grafted on to less fashionable varieties. The variety is also occasionally blended with other relative newcomers to the Languedoc-Roussillon such as MARSANNE and Rolle (VERMENTINO). As well as being grown in the Ardèche and throughout the Languedoc-Roussillon, Viognier became increasingly popular in California because of its modish associations with the Rhône. All but a third of the state's modest total acreage of Viognier in 1992 was too young to bear fruit. There are also limited plantings in Australia such as at Yalumba in South Australia. Galet also reports plantings of Viognier at Garibaldi in Brazil.

Galet, P., *Cépages et vignobles de France* (2nd edn., Montpellier, 1990).

VIRGIL (Publius Vergilius Maro) (70–19 BC), Latin poet and good, if unoriginal, source of information on viticulture in Ancient ROME. Like HORACE, Virgil benefited from the patronage of the Emperor Augustus, and much of his poetry was written in praise of Roman and Italian virtues. The rural virtues are expounded in the *Georgics*, a didactic poem about agriculture, written at the request of his patron Maecenas and published in 37 BC. The second of the four books is devoted mainly to vine-growing. Although it is of little use as a practical manual, it does give a lively and colourful picture of the life and problems of the vine-grower. Like HESIOD, Virgil's purpose was moral, and his main concern is to describe the farmer's virtues of austerity, integrity, and hard work, which made Rome great. Hence it is not surprising that his chief source should have been VARRO, as careful comparison shows, although he does not mention Varro by name. Although Virgil is the most interesting writer from a literary point of view, he is not an independent authority, and it is to his predecessors CATO and Varro, and to the later COLUMELLA and PLINY, that we must turn for first-hand information about Roman viticulture. Surprisingly, Virgil does not describe the HARVEST in detail, and he produces only a small selection of 15 ANCIENT VINE VARIETIES out of the 100 or so known from Latin authors, notably Columella. H.M.W. & H.H.A.

Griffin, J., *Latin Literature and Roman Life* (London, 1985).
Johnston, P. A., *Virgil's Agricultural Golden Age: A Study of the Georgics* (Leiden, 1980).

VIROIDS, particles smaller than VIRUSES which are thought capable of producing virus-like disease effects in the grapevine. Viroids can be found in nominally virus-free vines following THERMOTHERAPY, and are known to cause significant diseases for other crops such as hops and citrus fruits. Viroids are known to be transmitted by vegetative PROPAGATION as for viruses, but viroid-free grapevines can be produced by TISSUE CULTURE. R.E.S.

Mullins, M. G., Bouquet, A., and Williams, L., *Biology of the Grapevine* (Cambridge, 1992).

VIRUS DISEASES, group of VINE DISEASES caused by very small and simple organisms, consisting of ribonucleic acid wrapped in a protein sheath. Virus diseases began widely to affect European vines, and thus most of the vines used in wine production, from about 1890, when ROOTSTOCKS began to be used in France for the control of PHYLLOXERA. This is because GRAFTING doubles the risk of virus infection, as two different plants become merged; furthermore, rootstocks do not always show virus symptoms as do many fruiting varieties.

Virus diseases are mostly spread by man taking cuttings

Viticultural illustration to **Virgil's** *Georgics*.

from infected plants, although some are spread by NEMATODES and insects. They are mostly detected by inoculating sensitive plants, a process known as INDEXING, and more recently by serological techniques based on immunological reactions (see ELISA) and ribonucleic acid analysis. Often viruses do not kill the vine and they may frequently be overlooked, but each year they reduce both growth and yield. Sometimes virus diseases do not show symptoms, as, for example, with rootstocks infected with leafroll virus. This same virus can greatly reduce wine quality as it delays fruit ripening, and is probably the most important vine virus disease in many parts of the world. Considerable viticultural effort has been expended in VINE IMPROVEMENT in general, and in developing virus-free vines in particular.

Common virus diseases are CORKY BARK, FANLEAF DEGENERATION, LEAFROLL VIRUS, LEGNO RICCIO, NEPOVIRUSES.

Other groups of vine diseases include BACTERIAL DISEASES, FUNGAL DISEASES, MYCOPLASMA DISEASES. R.E.S.

Bovey, R., *et al.*, *Virus and Virus-Like Diseases of Vines: Colour Atlas of Symptoms* (Lausanne, 1980).

Pearson, R. C., and Goheen, A. C., *Compendium of Grape Diseases* (St Paul, Minn., 1988).

VISAN, one of the Côtes-du-Rhône Villages. See RHÔNE.

VISCOSITY, the quality of being **viscous**, the extent to which a solution resists flow or movement. Honey is more viscous than sugar syrup, for example, which is considerably more viscous than water. Viscosity, which approximates to what wine tasters call BODY, can be sensed by the human palate in the form of resistance as the solution is rinsed around the mouth.

A very sweet wine is more viscous than a dry one, even if they have the same ALCOHOLIC STRENGTH. Alcohol itself is more viscous than water, and higher-strength wines are therefore more viscous than lower-strength wines. An increase of one per cent in alcoholic strength increases viscosity relative to water by about 0.04 units, while an increase of 10 g/l in RESIDUAL SUGAR increases viscosity by about 0.03 units. The most viscous wines of all therefore are those that are both sweet and strong. The dissolved solids in wine, the wine's EXTRACT, also add marginally to its viscosity, so the less a wine has been subjected to FILTRATION and FINING, the more viscous it is.

It has been thought that the viscosity and the (quite unrelated) GLYCEROL content of a wine were the main factors in the formation of 'tears' on the inside of a wine glass. In fact, while they may be minor factors, the explanation is very different; see TEARS. A.D.W.

VITACEAE, the family in the plant kingdom which includes the genus VITIS containing the grapevine. There are 12 genera altogether with about 700 species, which are spread through tropical and temperate zones around the world. The plants in the family are characteristically climbers with leaves opposite tendrils. See BOTANICAL CLASSIFICATION. R.E.S.

VITAMINS, a group of organic compounds that are essential dietary components, deficiencies causing a variety of well-known disorders in humans. The levels of vitamins in grapes increase during ripening but the final values are relatively low compared with those of many other fruits. The most abundant is ASCORBIC ACID (vitamin C), the levels of which vary considerably—from 15 to 150 mg/l, which is only 10 per cent of that in oranges. Average values for the concentrations of other vitamins are about 1 to 10 ppm for niacin, pyridoxine, and pantothenic acid; 0.1 to 1 parts per million (ppm) for thiamine and riboflavin; and 0.001 to 0.01 ppm for biotin and folic acid. These levels in grapes are too low to be considered as a serious dietary source and are further reduced in wine by the use of SULPHUR DIOXIDE and YEAST growth (although AUTOLYSIS can add others). Wine also contains low concentrations of vitamin B_{12} (cobalamine).

The 'bioflavonoids', or vitamin P, a complex that includes D-catechin and many other flavonoids, occur in grape juice in large amounts, especially in dark-skinned berries. P is held to be a blood-capillary fragility factor and may play a part in warding off heart disease, although its credentials as a vitamin are contentious (see HEALTH). B.G.C. & A.D.W.

VITICULTEUR, French term for a vine-grower.

VITICULTURE, the science and practice of grape culture. Viticulture is practised consciously by VITICULTURISTS, often instinctively by grape-growers or vine-growers. Viticultural practices vary enormously around the world; some of these differences are highlighted under NEW WORLD, others under the relevant headings.

Grapes can be grown, over a wide range of LATITUDES, in climates ranging from very hot (southern California, central Australia) to very cool (England and Luxembourg). Viticulture is practised in very wet climates (parts of New Zealand) to very dry ones (Copiopo in Chile and the Central Valley in California). The TOPOGRAPHY can be very steep, as in the Mosel valley of Germany or the Douro of Portugal, or very flat plains, as in many regions of Australia. VINE DENSITY can vary enormously: from vineyards planted with large numbers of very small vines, as is common in Champagne and Bordeaux (10,000 vines per ha; 4,050 per acre), to few, large vines as in the Vinho Verde vineyards of Portugal (hardly more than 600 vines per ha). Some vineyards may be tended entirely by manual LABOUR, while others are mechanized so that most operations, including harvesting and pruning, are performed by machine. Vineyards may rely on IRRIGATION for their survival where they are grown in deserts, while in others, such as France, irrigation is forbidden.

The following entries follow the sequence of vineyard development from initial planning through to picking: VINEYARD SITE SELECTION; choice of ROOTSTOCK, VINE VARIETY, and CLONE; SOIL TESTING and SOIL PREPARATION; choice of VINE DENSITY and TRELLIS SYSTEM; vine PLANTING, TRAINING, and PRUNING; control of VINE PESTS, VINE DISEASES, and WEEDS; fruit SAMPLING and HARVEST. See also VINEYARD ANNUAL CYCLE.

Effects on wine quality

Quite apart from the decisions involved in vineyard site selection, there are obvious ways in which viticulture can influence wine quality, and some where the effects are more difficult to identify. The choice of vine variety has an obvious effect. Also important in affecting wine quality is the choice of clone and rootstock.

Usually premium-quality wines come from vineyards planted to soils with good DRAINAGE and of low SOIL FERTILITY. However, inappropriate vineyard management can destroy the potential for wine quality. For example, over-enthusiastic applications of nitrogen FERTILIZERS will result in excess vineyard VIGOUR which may delay RIPENING and encourage FUNGAL DISEASES. The SPRAYING regime adopted by the vine-grower can determine whether the grapes are affected by BUNCH ROT or not.

The choice of vine-TRAINING SYSTEM and associated trellis system can have fundamental effects on wine quality. Limits on YIELD are also imposed by appellation laws in some regions. Where vines are pruned lightly and carry too low a LEAF TO FRUIT RATIO then the fruit will not ripen properly and wine quality will be reduced.

Vineyards may require judicious IRRIGATION to prevent excessive WATER STRESS (although the practice is banned in many European regions), but excessive irrigation (like excessive rainfall) can cause delayed ripening and a loss of wine quality.

Vineyards should be subject to grape sampling programmes so that harvest takes place when the fruit is at optimum maturity.

See also VINE DISEASES, VINE PESTS, VINE PHYSIOLOGY, and VINE VARIETIES.

R.E.S.

Coombe, B. G., and Dry, P. R., *Viticulture, i: Resources in Australia* (Adelaide, 1988).
—— *Viticulture, ii: Practices* (Adelaide, 1992).
Galet, P., *Précis de viticulture* (4th edn., Montpellier, 1983).
Winkler, A. J., *et al.*, *General Viticulture* (2nd edn., Berkeley, Calif., 1974).

VITICULTURIST, someone who practises VITICULTURE. In many countries the grape-grower is termed simply 'grower' rather than 'viticulturist', which word is more often used for professional persons who typically have some formal tertiary training in viticulture. Grape-growers or vine-growers may also be termed wine-growers. R.E.S.

VITIS, the genus of the plant kingdom which includes the VINE (see BOTANICAL CLASSIFICATION). *Vitis* is one of 14 genera according to Galet in the family *Vitaceae* and contains in turn about 60 species. Most of the *Vitis* species can be found in the east and south east of North America, or in Asia, mainly in the temperate zones of the northern hemisphere, with a few in the tropics. The most important species for wine production is the single European species (strictly, Eurasian) *Vitis vinifera*, often written *V vinifera*, described in detail in VINIFERA.

As shown below, there are many different American species. AMERICAN VINE SPECIES became the subject of attention by early European settlers as *V vinifera* failed to cope with indigenous diseases in the early colonies on the east coast. However, they proved generally unsatisfactory for wine because of their strongly flavoured berries (see FOXY). These native American species have since been crossed with *V vinifera* to form new varieties (see AMERICAN HYBRIDS), and among themselves to produce the ROOTSTOCKS used in modern viticulture.

Asian species are little studied, and their exact number is still uncertain. One of them, however, *V amurensis*, is the world's most northerly vine species, and has been used to introduce cold hardiness into VINE BREEDING programmes (see AMURENSIS). Varieties of *V cognetiae* and *V thunbergii* are grown on a very limited scale in Japan.

Note: The systematic botanical classification of species within the *Vitis* genus has been a subject of confusion for more than a century. GALET clarified the taxonomy in 1967, but there is still some doubt about the taxonomy of Asian species. The French taxonomist Planchon proposed that *Vitis* species be divided into two so-called sections. The first, *Vitis* (but originally called *Euvitis*), contains the great majority of species including the 'European' wine grape species *vinifera*, and the second MUSCADINIA contains only three species indigeneous to the Americas. These two sections differ in chromosome number and many morphological features. The species of the section *Vitis* have proven to be closely enough related to interbreed easily when this has been attempted, but crossings between members of the two sections typically produces sterile hybrids. More recently it has been proposed that *Muscadinia* be considered a separate genus, which is adopted in some modern textbooks such as Mullins *et al.* but not others such as Galet and Antcliff. This volume follows Galet.

The following partial listing, of the most important species, is based on Mullins *et al.*, which in turn is from Galet's thesis. Only the more important species are listed. Other listings may be found in Winkler *et al.* and Galet.

Section *Vitis*	
European and Middle Eastern species	
Vitis vinifera	Europe, Middle East
American species	
Vitis aestivalis	North America (east)
Vitis berlandieri	North America (east)
Vitis californica	North America (west)
Vitis candicans	North America (east)
Vitis caribaea	North America (east)
Vitis champini[a]	North America (east)
Vitis cinerea	North America (east)
Vitis cordifolia	North America (east)
Vitis doaniana[b]	North America (east)
Vitis girdiana	North America (west)
Vitis labrusca[c]	North America (east)
Vitis linecumi	North America (east)
Vitis longii[d]	North America (east)
Vitis monticola	North America (east)
Vitis riparia[e]	North America (east)
Vitis rufomentosa	North America (east)
Vitis rupestris	North America (east)
Asian species	
Vitis amurensis	Asia
Vitis coignetiae	Asia
Vitis thunbergii	Asia
Section *Muscadinia*	
Vitis munsoniana	North America (east)
Vitis rotundifolia	North America (east)

[a] *Vitis champini* (sometimes spelt *champinii*) was originally described by the French ampelographer Planchon as a separate species, but it is now generally regarded as a group of natural *rupestris–candicans* hybrids.

[b] *Vitis doaniana*, a probable natural hybrid with *V candicans*.

[c] *Vitis labruscana* is sometimes used to describe natural hybrids of *V labrusca* with other species, including *V vinifera* as, for instance, the variety CONCORD.

[d] *Vitis longii* is sometimes given the name *V solonis* from a misreading on a bundle of cuttings sent to Europe. Some regard it as a natural hybrid between *V candicans* and other species, as for *V champini* and *V doaniana*.

[e] *Vitis riparia* is sometimes known as *V vulpina*.

See also VINE, VINIFERA, AMERICAN VINE SPECIES, VINE VARIETIES, PROLES, CLONE, HYBRIDS, CROSS. R.E.S.

Antcliff, A. J., 'Taxonomy: the grapevine as a member of the plant kingdom', in B. G. Coombe and P. R. Dry (eds.), *Viticulture, i: Resources in Australia* (Adelaide, 1988).

Galet, P., *Précis de viticulture* (4th edn., Montpellier, 1983).

Mullins, M. G., Bouquet, A., and Williams, L., *Biology of the Grapevine* (Cambridge, 1992).

Winkler, A. J., *et al., General Viticulture* (2nd edn., Berkeley, Calif., 1974).

VITIS VINIFERA, the species of vine from which most of the world's wine is made. The relationship of *vinifera* to other species of the Vitis genus is described above under VITIS, and details about the species and wine grapes in general are given under VINIFERA. The relationship of *Vitis vinifera* to other members of the plant kingdom is discussed under BOTANICAL CLASSIFICATION. The commercial culture of *Vitis vinifera* is introduced with the entry VITICULTURE.

VIURA is a common Spanish synonym for MACABEO and is therefore what Riojanos call their dominant white grape variety.

VIVARAIS, CÔTES DU, VDQS on the right bank of the RHÔNE immediately opposite Coteaux du TRICASTIN in the wild and beguiling Ardèche. Widely dispersed vineyards on mainly LIMESTONE soils in a much cooler and wetter climate than the rest of the southern Rhône total nearly 600 ha / 1,480 acres and produce mainly light reds and rosés from Grenache and Syrah grapes, with a little Carignan. A small amount of white is made from Clairette and Grenache Blanc. Production is dominated by CO-OPERATIVES whose more profitable business may be producing varietal VINS DE PAYS de l'Ardèche from non-appellation varieties.

VIZETELLY, HENRY (1820–94), prolific English wine writer whose detailed accounts of the history of port and champagne are particularly celebrated. Vizetelly came from a family of printers, and so it is particularly appropriate that today his influence is perhaps most marked in the continued, and increasingly imprecise, reproduction of the engravings which distinguished his many and various books about wine. He was introduced to wine in 1869 when he was sent to Paris to report on the French vintage for the *Pall Mall Gazette*, narrowly escaping execution during the Franco-Prussian War the next year. He spent much of the 1870s visiting the vineyards of France and Germany and in 1877 visited Portugal, Madeira, and the Canary islands. Whereas JULLIEN and REDDING provided global wine surveys for the specialist reader, Vizetelly managed both to delve more deeply into specific wine regions, and to produce books which appealed to a wider market. When based in France he was one of the first acknowledged wine 'experts' who was invited to serve as a judge of wines at the Vienna and Paris Exhibitions. On his eventual return to England, he became a publisher, often writing introductions to translations of foreign works. As Zola's English publisher, he was imprisoned and financially ruined.

Gabler, J. M., *Wine into Words: A History and Bibliography of Wine Books in the English Language* (Baltimore, 1985).

VOCABULARY, TASTING. See TASTING TERMS.

VOJVODINA, republic in the far north east of what was YUGOSLAVIA. The best of the vineyards enhance the lovely rolling countryside of Fruška Gora district north of Belgrade and south of the Hungarian border. They adjoin the vineyards of CROATIA to the west and sweep south beyond the town of Novi Sad nearly to Belgrade itself. Viticulturally they are an extension of the inland Croatian region with much the same mix of white grape varieties for the most part. There are also some good red wines made from CABERNET SAUVIGNON and MERLOT. The SMEDEREVKA vine, called after the town of Smederevo south of Belgrade, makes large amounts of very ordinary white wine usually drunk with mineral water as a SPRITZER and a Smederevka × TRAMINER crossing called Neoplanta which has a very perfumed aroma and oily texture not unlike a concentrated Pinot Gris. Some of the wines from this area are potentially the best-balanced whites in what was Yugoslavia.

Close to the Hungarian border lies a region which owes its roots much more to HUNGARY than to Yugoslavia. The sandy plains extend over the frontier; many of the people speak Hungarian more naturally than Serbian: and even the grapes reflect the Hungarian viticultural tradition. Laski Rizling (WELSCHRIESLING) still predominates but red wine grapes include KADARKA and Frankovka (BLAUFRÄNKISCH) while EZERJÓ and Kevedinka (the DINKA of Hungary) are among white wine grapes. Even MUSCAT OTTONEL tends to be more prevalent here and in Hungary than in the rest of Yugoslavia.

The sandy plain continues round into ROMANIA and a further, rather unexciting part of the Vojvodina vineyard sits on the northern bank of the Danube just where it crosses the Romanian border. More Smederevka and more Laski Rizling grow here. BANAT RIZLING grows here and in Romania and is reputed to have a better, more solid style than Laski Rizling.

In all, this region has about 14,000 ha / 34,600 acres of vineyards. A.H.M.

VOLATILE. All wines are volatile in that they contain volatile FLAVOUR COMPOUNDS and some level of VOLATILE ACIDS, but volatile is used as a pejorative tasting term for a wine in which the level of ACETIC ACID has risen unacceptably high.

VOLATILE ACIDITY of a wine is its total concentration of **volatile acids**, those naturally occurring organic ACIDS of wines that happen to be separable by DISTILLATION. Wine's most common volatile acid by far is ACETIC ACID. A few other acids such as formic, propionic, traces of SUCCINIC, and LACTIC, normally present in trace amounts in wines, are also volatile.

Acetic acid, in small amounts, is a by-product of the normal action of YEAST in grape juice. However, the major source is the action of a group of BACTERIA known as ACETOBACTER which require OXYGEN from the air for their growth and survival, and cause a reaction between the alcohol of the wine and the oxygen to produce acetic acid. Very low concentrations of acetic acid, below 0.2 g/l, do not affect the taste adversely. Increasing concentrations change the taste of the wine, however, from added complexity and fruitiness to a frankly vinegary flavour at levels much above 1.5 g/l. Most everyday wines are very low in acetic acid but some red wines may be excessively acetic. A few fine wines, usually mature reds in bottle, are rich enough in BODY, TANNINS, and ALCOHOL to bear concentrations of acetic acid that do not impair flavour but are sometimes said to 'lift' it.

It is not in fact the acetic acid itself that causes changes in the aroma but the ESTER known as ETHYL ACETATE, the reaction product of acetic acid and ETHANOL.

Exposure of wines to air in the presence of acetobacter starts the process of VINEGAR production, although if exposure to air is limited the wine will probably not be spoiled.

It was the research work of Louis PASTEUR, trying to find a reason for the spoilage of so much burgundy shipped to England, that resulted in the discovery of acetobacter. This work also resulted in the discovery that yeast is responsible for the conversion of grape sugars to wine. A.D.W.

VOLATILITY, property of having excessive VOLATILE ACIDS.

VOLCANIC, describes rocks which are the product of volcanic eruptions. These are variable in composition and therefore form a wide range of soils. Volcanic rocks seldom underlie major vineyard regions but there are several famous exceptions. In the Kaiserstuhl-Tuniberg region of BADEN in Germany, vines are grown in clays derived from volcanic rocks, while the PFALZ to the north is underlain by basalt. South Nahe has a feldspar-porphyry. The TOKAY of Hungary is said to be produced from grapes grown on volcanic rocks, mainly andesite.

The Finger Lakes region of NEW YORK state has stony but rich soil derived from volcanic rocks, where the vine roots can penetrate far below the winter frost level, and where SOIL WATER is available to the vines in dry summers. See entries prefixed SOIL. J.M.H.

VOLES can cause vine damage. See ANIMALS and VINE PESTS.

VOLNAY, attractive small village in the Côte de Beaune district of Burgundy's Côte d'Or producing elegant red wines from Pinot Noir. The wines of Volnay were celebrated under the *ancien régime* for their delicacy: Claude Arnoux, whose book on Burgundy (1728) begins with a Latin ode to the wines of Volnay, describes them as partridge-eye pink in colour, and the finest of all the wines of the Côte de Beaune, although they had to be drunk very young. Since then they have alternated in fame with those of neighbouring Pommard depending on whether FASHION dictated wines of breeding or of power.

More than half Volnay's vineyards are of PREMIER CRU status, stretching in a broad swathe from Pommard to Meursault, continuing into the latter village. Because Meursault is renowned for its white wines, its single really fine red wine vineyard of Les Santenots is sold as Volnay Santenots. The best part of this vineyard is Les Santenots-du-Milieu, although it is not as typical of Volnay as Le Cailleret, which it abuts, or Champans. These two vineyards express the astonishing, velvety finesse of Volnay. Clos des Chênes, just above Le Cailleret, is also very fine but a little lighter as the soil is even thinner.

Excellent vineyards close to the village include Taillepieds, the Clos de la Bousse d'Or, monopoly of Domaine de la Pousse d'Or which also owns an excellent enclave within Le Cailleret known as the Clos des 60 Ouvrées, and the Clos des Ducs of the Marquis d'Angerville, whose father pioneered DOMAINE BOTTLING in the 1930s.

See also CÔTE D'OR and its map. J.T.C.M.

Arnoux, C., *Dissertation sur la situation de Bourgogne* (Dijon, 1728).

VOSGES OAK comes from the mountains to the immediate west of ALSACE.

VÖSLAU, wine centre in lower AUSTRIA in what is now the Thermenregion district.

VOSNE-ROMANÉE, village in the Côte de Nuits district of Burgundy producing the finest red wines from Pinot Noir grapes. As well as excellent wines at VILLAGE and PREMIER CRU level there are six GRAND CRU vineyards three of which share the name Romanée, the suffix to which Vosne was hyphenated in 1866.

The grands crus are Romanée-Conti, La Romanée, La Tâche, Richebourg, Romanée-St-Vivant, and La Grande Rue. Between them they produce, with Musigny and Chambertin, the greatest wines of the Côte de Nuits. They have more finesse than any other but to this is allied as much power and stuffing as their nearest rivals.

A vineyard formerly known as Le Cloux was rechristened La Romanée in 1651, presumably on account of Roman remains being discovered nearby. In 1760 the property was bought by the Prince de Conti, subsequently becoming known as Romanée-Conti. Just above this sublime vineyard, whose wines can be the most expensive in the world, is La Romanée. Romanée-Conti has brown, CALCAREOUS soil about 60 cm/23 in deep with 45 to 49 per cent CLAY and liable to serious erosion in the upper, steeper part. La Romanée also has a notably steep slope with less clay and more RENDZINA in the make-up of the soil. The former is the monopoly of the DOMAINE DE LA ROMANÉE-CONTI, the latter of the Liger Belair family whose wine is distributed by BOUCHARD Père et Fils. About 300 cases are made each year from the tiny 0.84 ha/2 acres of La Romanée, double that from the 1.80 ha of Romanée-Conti.

Another monopoly of the Domaine de la Romanée-Conti, and regarded as nearly as fine as the vineyard from which it takes its name, is La Tâche, whose 6 ha (including the vineyard of Les Gaudichots which used to be separate but is regarded as being of the same quality) produce a wine which is explosively seductive even when young, whereas Romanée-Conti takes longer to show its astonishing completeness. La Tâche seems to thrive even in lesser years, being judged the only wine worthy of bottling by the Domaine de la Romanée-Conti in 1950 and 1951.

Next most sought-after Vosne-Romanée wine is Richebourg, whose 8 ha are shared between 10 growers, notably Domaine de la Romanée-Conti, Domaine LEROY, branches of the Gros family, and Domaine Méo-Camuzet. As the name suggests this is one of the most voluptuous wines of Burgundy and can equal La Tâche in some years.

Romanée-St-Vivant, taking its name from the monastery of St-Vivant founded at Vergy *c*.900 and subsequent owner of the vineyard, can also make very fine wine but it is usually lighter and less powerful than its neighbours, being further down the slope and having deeper soil. There are half a dozen owners of which the largest is Domaine de la Romanée-Conti (5.3 ha out of 9.43). Domaine Leroy and Louis LATOUR's Domaine de Corton Grancey are the next largest owners.

Between La Tâche to the south and La Romanée-Conti to the north lie the 1.4 ha of La Grande Rue, originally classified as PREMIER CRU but promoted, as its location suggests is only right, to grand cru. The vineyard is a monopoly of Domaine Lamarche, whose wines have not so far stood comparison with those of their illustrious neighbours.

Amongst the best of Vosne-Romanée's premier cru vineyards are Clos des Réas, Les Malconsorts, and Les Chaumes on the Nuits-St-Georges side, Cros Parantoux made famous by Henry Jayer, above the grands crus, and Les Beauxmonts and Les Suchots abutting Flagey-Échézeaux. Part of Les Beauxmonts is actually in the latter commune although it is sold as Vosne Romanée, as is the village wine of Flagey.

While the renown of the Domaine de la Romanée-Conti dominates Vosne-Romanée it should not overshadow other significant influences such as Henri Jayer, for his unparalleled wine-making skills; René Engel for his patriarchal influence and local historical research and publications during a long life; and now Lalou Bize-Leroy, who has bought and transformed the former Domaine Nöellat.

See also CÔTE D'OR and its map. J.T.C.M.

Olney, R., *Romanée-Conti* (Paris, 1991).

VOUGEOT, small village in the Côte de Nuits district of Burgundy producing red wines from the Pinot Noir grape. The name is derived from the diminutive of Vouge, a small stream flowing through the village. There are only 4.8 ha / 11.8 acres of vineyards producing VILLAGE WINE and 11.7 ha designated PREMIER CRU; the village's fame rests squarely with the 50.6 ha GRAND CRU, Clos de Vougeot.

The fame of Clos de Vougeot is historical since it was the flagship vineyard of the Cistercians, who planted and enclosed what is significantly the largest grand cru vineyard of the Côte d'Or. Geologically, this is not a homogeneous site: the top, abutting Bonnes Mares and Grands Échézeaux, has a light chalky and gravelly soil on oolitic limestone which drains beautifully and gives the wines of greatest distinction; the middle section is on softer limestone with clay and some gravel, with moderate drainage on a very gentle slope. The bottom section, almost flat, stretching down to the main RN74 road, consists of poorly drained alluvial clay.

When the wines could be blended by the monks to produce a complete wine from differing constituent parts, Clos de Vougeot doubtless deserved its reputation. Now that the vineyard is fragmented between 80 or more owners, far too many of the wines are below standard through the inadequacies of some of the raw material and many of the production techniques of the less conscientious producers.

Classic Clos de Vougeot is likely to be dense and ungiving when young, robust rather than elegant. However, after a decade it opens out into one of the most complete wines of the Côte d'Or with deep, rich flavours reminiscent of truffles and undergrowth.

Of the premier cru vineyards Le Clos Blanc, producing an unusual white wine from Chardonnay, is the monopoly of producers Héritier-Guyot, and Clos de la Perrière is in the sole possession of Domaine Bertagne. The other premiers crus are Les Cras, rarely seen, and Les Petits Vougeots.

See also CLOS DE VOUGEOT, and CÔTE D'OR and its map.

J.T.C.M.

VOUVRAY, the most important individual white wine appellation in the TOURAINE district of the Loire. The wines of Vouvray vary enormously in quality, thereby offering a true representation of the grape variety from which Vouvray is exclusively made. Vouvray is CHENIN BLANC and, to a certain extent, Chenin Blanc is Vouvray (although ARBOIS grapes are theoretically allowed into Vouvray too). No other wine made only from this long-lived middle Loire grape, often called Pineau de la Loire, is made in such quantity: about 60,000 hl / 1.6 million gal of still and 40,000 hl of sparkling wine produced from about 1,800 ha / 4,450 acres of vineyard. Only COTEAUX DU LAYON can rival Vouvray for the total area of Chenin Blanc planted, but this more westerly appellation has less than 1,200 ha.

Vouvray itself is a particularly pretty small town on the northern bank of the Loire just east of Tours, whose wines owe much to the MONKS AND MONASTERIES who refined local viticulture in the Middle Ages and subsequently. It was not until the creation of the Vouvray appellation in 1936 that Vouvray established an identity of its own; before then most of it was shipped out for blending by the energetic DUTCH WINE TRADE, and much of the wine sold as Vouvray came from anywhere in Touraine.

Houses, and wine cellars, have habitually been created out of the TUFFEAU on this right bank of the wide river, with vines planted in the clay and gravel topsoil over the tuffeau on the plateau above, dissected by small rivers and streams so that many vineyards have an ideal sheltered southerly aspect. The locals claim that this is where the Atlantic climate meets the CONTINENTAL climate.

Making top-quality Vouvray is as hazardous as making any top-quality sweet white wine which owes its sweetness to NOBLE ROT or extreme RIPENESS. The vine-grower is entirely

The Clos de **Vougeot**, Burgundy's largest enclosed vineyard and one of its most famous buildings, used today for wine-related jollity.

at the mercy of the weather, and the harvest in Vouvray is one of France's last, usually lasting until well into November, often involving a number of TRIS through the vineyard.

Wine-making here is distinguished by the need to bottle pure fruit and its naturally high acidity as early and as unadorned as possible. Thus, this is one of the few wine regions of the world of no commercial interest to the COOPERAGE business. Neutral fermentation vessels such as large old oak casks or stainless steel tanks are used, MALOLACTIC FERMENTATION is rigidly suppressed, and the AGEING process is expected to occur, extremely slowly, in bottle.

The style of wine made by the best producers such as Huet, Poniatowski, Champalou, and the large merchant house of Marc Brédif is determined completely by the weather. In the least generous VINTAGES only dry and possibly sparkling wines are made. The best years yield very sweet, golden nectars that are naturally MOELLEUX, or even LIQUOREUX, but are so high in acidity that most are almost unpleasant to drink in their middle age between about three years old and two to three decades. Some of the finest Vouvrays can still taste lively, and richly fruity, at nearly a century. A relatively high proportion of medium dry demi-sec is also produced in many years, and it too demands a considerable amount of BOTTLE AGEING before the acidity has muted and the wine can be served as a fine accompaniment to many savoury dishes, including those that are richly sauced.

Commercial Vouvray also exists, on the other hand, as simply a medium sweet, reasonably acid, white wine that has little capacity for development.

Vouvray Mousseux can often offer more interest than other Loire sparkling wines, to those who appreciate the honeyed aromas of Chenin Blanc, at least. The wines have weight and flavour, and are suitable for drinking with meals as well as before them.

See also LOIRE and map on pp. 576–7.

VQPRD, abbreviation for the EUROPEAN UNION term **Vin de Qualité Produit dans une Région Déterminée**, meaning QUALITY WINE. Although it is essentially a French expression, the initials are sometimes seen on labels of superior bottlings from any European country.

VRANAC, red grape variety that is a speciality of MONTENEGRO in what was YUGOSLAVIA. The wines produced are deep in colour and can be rich in EXTRACT, responding unusually well to oak AGEING. There is an element of refreshing bitterness on the finish of these wines that suggests some relationship to an Italian variety just across the Adriatic. Vranac is one of the few indigenous grape variety names to appear on the label of wines exported from what was Yugoslavia. It is also grown, less successfully, in MACEDONIA.

VSOP stands for 'very special old pale' and is used as a designation for superior COGNAC.

W

WÄDENSWIL, town on Lake Zurich and site of research station in German-speaking SWITZERLAND concerned with fruit growing, horticulture, and viticulture. It was founded in 1890 in response to the viticultural catastrophes of FUNGAL DISEASES and PHYLLOXERA, and because of the upheaval caused to the fruit and wine markets in Switzerland as a result of improved RAILWAY systems.

Wädenswil is concerned with research, development, testing, control, and advisory services. The station has developed a number of CLONES, notably of PINOT NOIR which have been planted as far away as Oregon, California, New Zealand, and South Africa. SUSTAINABLE VITICULTURE, in which pests and diseases are controlled by biological or biotechnological methods, is a particular concern here. A number of plant protection methods have been developed, such as the introduction of predators and pheromones for trapping and confusing INSECTS.

Wädenswil's counterpart in French-speaking Switzerland is at CHANGINS

WAGNER PHILIP, (1904–), Baltimore newspaper editor, VITICULTURIST, WINE-MAKER, and author of books on vines and wine. Beginning as a HOME WINE-MAKER during PROHIBITION, Wagner published *American Wines and How to Make Them* (1933). Interested in improving the basis of eastern American wine-making, Wagner began to import and test FRENCH HYBRID vines in 1939 and to distribute them from the nursery and vineyard he founded, Boordy Vineyard, in Maryland. His *A Wine-Grower's Guide* (1945) was the first work to publicize French hybrids in the USA; in the same year he opened a winery at Boordy Vineyard and produced the first French hybrid wine on record in the USA. Wagner's success with his wines, his activity in supplying French hybrids from his nursery, and the persuasiveness of his writing in favour of a better selection of VINE VARIETIES entitle him to be regarded as the man who changed the course of wine-making in the eastern USA. The clarity, grace, and authority of his books, which have passed through many editions and remain in print today, gave him an influence far beyond the sphere of Boordy Vineyard. T.P.

WAITER, WINE. See SOMMELIER.

WALES. Several small vineyards in sheltered corners of southern Wales produce Welsh wine. For more details, see ENGLAND.

WALKER BAY, coastal wine region in SOUTH AFRICA.

WAR, EFFECTS ON WINE. Wine is a way of life literally rooted in the soil. It is also capital and labour intensive and reliant on a complex distribution network, which make it highly vulnerable during time of war.

The most visible effect of war is the destruction of vineyards. Just as it was customary for warring ancient Greeks to cut down or burn the vines of their enemies, so the barbarian invaders of Roman Europe signalled victory in the same way.

Planting on newly captured territory likewise symbolized success. When the Christians drove the Moors from medieval SPAIN, they planted vines behind them, as did the Crusaders who briefly held parts of the Holy Land. A modern example might be the planting of vineyards on the Golan Heights in ISRAEL. It is difficult to imagine a clearer expression of a battle won and determination to stay than the planting of such a long-term crop as vines.

Certain regions have suffered ruin disproportionately because of their strategic geographical position. The location of the CHAMPAGNE region at the crossroads of northern Europe has ensured the destruction of its vineyards dozens of times, most famously when they were bisected by the trenches of the First World War.

The short-term effects of war have sometimes had permanent consequences. The Thirty Years War (1618–48) which ravaged 17th century Europe was so destructive that many northern German vineyard areas were never replanted (see GERMAN HISTORY). Recovery was hampered by the sheer scale of the devastation, by lack of manpower through depopulation, and by destruction of capital equipment.

Plundering of existing wine stocks is another common feature of European war with Champagne, once again, an obvious example. When Russian soldiers occupied the region in 1814 they were not slow to help themselves. In this case the Champagne houses did at least have the subsequent consolation that the Russians became their wines' most loyal peacetime consumers until 1917. In general, however, terrible hardship was the result of forced requisitioning and outright plunder. Civil conflicts, such as the French Wars of Religion in the 16th century, were at least as destructive.

The sale and distribution of wine is a complex operation which is inevitably dislocated by war. TRANSPORT becomes hazardous. During the HUNDRED YEARS WAR (1337–1453) ships carrying wine between Bordeaux and England were attacked so often that convoys were arranged for safety.

Wars also frequently had the consequence that trade with

ɔlumbia Crest winery in **Washington** state showing the original circular vineyards (and maize fields) designed for overhead irrigation.

ıemies was completely banned. When Britain and France ere at war in the early 18th century, French wine imports ıto Britain were prohibited. Smuggling was one answer to ıe problem, switching to wine produced by the ally Portugal as another. Thus war altered trading and consumption pat-ꞏrns, and PORT became the staple wine of Georgian England.

Wars do not bring uniform misfortune. The demand for ine to provision troops in some cases provided a stimulus ɔ wine regions not directly involved in the fighting. The oman army needed huge supplies to send it into battle. ecords show that, when Edward I embarked on his Scottish ımpaign in 1300, he first bought in vast quantities of wine om Bordeaux.

It is also probable that the influx of American forces into econd World War Europe and its aftermath was an import-ınt factor in building the wine market in the UNITED STATES.

Historically the effects of war on wine, as on so many other ɔmmercial activities, have been mixed and in some cases ıe grower's suffering made another's fortune. H.B.

Bonal, F., *Le Livre d'or de Champagne* (Lausanne, 1984).
Francis, A. D., *The Wine Trade* (London, 1972).
Johnson, H., *The Story of Wine* (London and New York, 1989).

WASHINGTON, state in the PACIFIC NORTHWEST of the United States which has, with little fuss or fanfare, crept into second position behind California as an American VINIFERA wine producer. Producing just five per cent of the national wine total (including New York state's 35,000 acres of mainly AMERICAN VINE SPECIES), Washington State's 11,000 acres/4,450 ha of vines made it a very distant second behind California's 300,000 or so in the early 1990s, but its reputation for quality is not so very far behind.

History

In the 1930s the Washington wine industry was based on the native American grape variety CONCORD which grows well in the Yakima Valley (see below). It is still abundantly planted there but is almost exclusively limited to the making of juice, jellies, and other non-wine confections. In 1969, when California's wine boom was well under way, there were just two wineries in Washington, each of them based on a single, small vineyard. By 1990 there were about 80 wineries in the state.

Wine styles

Almost all wines are VARIETAL. A Johannisberg Riesling 1972 from Ch Ste Michelle set Washington State wine on the path to national recognition when it bested all comers in a blind tasting conducted by the *Los Angeles Times*. Though a declining market hides the fact, Riesling remains a variety that the state grows particularly well, for both drier wines and sweeter late harvest ones, some of the latter being BOTRYTIZED. In cool vintages, especially, some producers mimic RHEINGAU Kabinett wines well enough to fool blind tasters.

By the early 1990s SEMILLON was delivering more exciting wines than Riesling, and with greater consistency. One after another of these wines has demonstrated the kind of structure and balance that promise well for longevity. In addition they have shown a subtlety perfectly adapted to Pacific Northwest regional seafoods. Most are made with little or no oak ageing to guard a maximim of fruit flavours. A few producers turned to BARREL FERMENTATION, LEES CONTACT, and other techniques intended to yield rivals to white burgundy.

The best performances of Riesling and Semillon notwithstanding, Chardonnay dominated vineyard and cellar alike in Washington state by the early 1990s, its acreage increasing by almost three-quarters between 1988 and 1991. While typical Chardonnays range from merely good to quite good, the variety's fortunes were sustained more by consumer demand than inherent superiority. Virtually all wineries use barrel fermentation, MALOLACTIC FERMENTATION and lees contact to broaden and deepen a modest varietal flavour.

Other white varieties with good track records from more limited plantings are SAUVIGNON Blanc and CHENIN BLANC. GEWÜRZTRAMINER has been steady, though workaday. MÜLLER-THURGAU has shown occasional brightness in a scattering of vineyards in the Puget Sound basin, an isolated patch of vines west of the Cascade Mountains (see below).

Not unreasonably, reds blossomed later than whites in Washington. The first great hope, CABERNET SAUVIGNON, remains important but was overtaken by Merlot in 1991. By nature Washington Cabernet Sauvignons lean towards raisiny ripe flavours and noticeable alcohol levels. The prevailing style has called for ample tannins and hearty oak flavours. The net effect has been wines dramatic in youth but without great staying power. MERLOT arrived in the vineyards several years behind Cabernet Sauvignon and quickly demonstrated richer flavours in wines of more restrained structure. Durability remains an unanswered question at the beginning of the 1990s, although several examples hint at the possibility of reasonably long life in bottle. Blends of these two BORDEAUX grape varieties are increasingly made and show promise. Among other red grape varieties, Washington has an American monopoly on the obscure Lemberger (see LIMBERGER and BLAUFRÄNKISCH) which several wineries produce as a quite rewarding fresh, fruit-rich wine meant to be drunk in its youth. One or two producers have even essayed large-scale, oak-aged wines with it, as in AUSTRIA.

Pinot Noir does not appear adapted to eastern Washington, but may have a restricted future directly across the Columbia river from Portland, OREGON, where climate conditions closely resemble those of Oregon's lower Willamette Valley. Two small vineyards there have yielded wines as similar to Oregonians as sun and soil promise. Howev[er] available land is limited.

Geography and climate

Pinot Noir is the perfect marker variety for the sharp diffe[r]ence between the climates of western and eastern Was[h]ington (see above). Western Washington is mild and dam[p] the year round because of the proximity of the Pacific Oce[an] and the inland sea called the Puget Sound, overlooked [by] Seattle. Eastern Washington, screened from marine air [by] the towering barrier of the Cascade Mountains, has h[ot] desert-dry summers and cold to arctically cold winters.

Population, limited space, and marginal growing co[n]ditions combine to limit plantings in **western Washingt[on]** to less than one per cent of the state's total.

Rigorous weather east of the Cascades has failed to halt t[he] march of the vine in **eastern Washington**, however. Vineya[rd] locations here are limited by the reach of IRRIGATION wat[er] and by air drainage. The first is vital in summer, the last ju[st] as vital in winter, where temperatures can plummet [to] −15 °F/−26 °C and stay there for a fortnight or more. Mo[st] vine plantings are on south and south west-facing slopes f[or] winter rather than summer warmth. Such freeze-susceptib[le] varieties as Merlot are limited to such slopes. Other varieti[es] more tender yet, such as Grenache, are disappearing after th[e] harsh winters of 1978/9 and 1990/1 killed high percentag[es] of the vines. The severity of these winters revived the Russia[n] technique of fan training which had been used for some ear[ly] plantings against winter cold (see vine TRAINING SYSTEMS).

Virtually all of the vineyards in eastern Washington fa[ll] within the 11 million-acre/4.4 million-ha embrace of the Co[l]umbia Valley AVA. Inside it, in turn, are the important Yakim[a] Valley appellation, which encompasses about 40 per cent [of] the state's vineyards, and the nascent Walla Walla Valley on[e]. Most vines are planted, ungrafted, widely spaced and traine[d] in bilateral CORDONS.

The producers

The dominant force in Washington wine is Stimson Lan[e] Company, a subsidiary of American Tobacco Company, an[d] the owner of a range of labels which includes Ch Ste Michell[e], Domaine Ste Michelle, Columbia Crest, Snoqualmie, Farro[n] Ridge, and Saddle Mountain. In the mid 1990s the firm owne[d] nearly a third of the state's vineyards. Other important labe[ls] by volume and reputation were Columbia Winery, als[o] Seattle based, and the Hogue Cellars, while Woodwar[d] Canyon was also achieving international recognition.

Clark, C., *American Wines of the Northwest* (New York, 1989).
Hill, C., *The Northwest Winery Guide* (Seattle, 1988).
Holden, R., and Holden, G., *Northwest Wine Country* (Seattle, 1990[)].
Meredith, T. J., *Northwest Wine* (4th edn., Kirkland, Wash., 1990)

WATER, is the most important constituent of wine (se[e] WINE COMPOSITION) and is as essential to those who produc[e] it as to those who consume it.

SOIL WATER, the product of RAINFALL and/or IRRIGATION, i[s] a prerequisite for vine growth and survival. PHOTOSYNTHESI[S] without which grapes would never ripen, depends on water being available (which is why RIPENING stops if WATER STRESS is too severe). Water in the form of well-timed rain can also be useful in dusting off grapes immediately prior to HARVEST.

Water is also vital in the winery: HYGIENE's best friend is the hosepipe, and many systems of TEMPERATURE CONTROL depend on copious supplies of water. In a small and decreasing number of wine regions, water may be added to wine to reduce ACIDITY.

And then there is water as a drink. For centuries wine was always diluted with water, indeed drinking undiluted wine was the mark of a barbarian in Ancient GREECE and Ancient ROME (but then their wines were strong relative to many of those drunk today). Wine was a safer drink than most available water until the 17th century in major cities, and much later than that elsewhere. In the late 1960s this writer was offered unlimited wine as part of her salary when working in a smart Italian hotel, but had to pay for bottled water, the only reliable drinking water.

The modern wine drinker rarely chooses to dilute his or her wine (other than to make the occasional SPRITZER) but for HEALTH reasons he or she is well advised to drink at least as much water alongside every glass of wine. Despite its frequent and incontravertible appeal, wine is a poor quencher of thirst.

WATER BERRY, an alternative name, current in California, for SHANKING, the physiological disorder of grape berry stems, drying and shrivelling grapes as they approach RIPENESS.

WATER SHOOT, a shoot that arises from the wood of the vine, not from buds left at pruning. In fact they mostly arise from base buds embedded in the wood and are generally not FRUITFUL. Suckers are a type of water shoot which arise at the base of the TRUNK at or below soil level. B.G.C.

WATER STRESS is the physiological state of plants, including vines, suffering from a shortage of water. Water stress during the later stages of the viticultural growing season is common, since a considerable proportion of the world's vines are grown in MEDITERRANEAN CLIMATES, where rain falls principally in the winter months. It is commonly held that some water stress is desirable for optimum wine quality, but there is little agreement about exactly how much.

Water stress depends on two components: the water content in the root zone of the vine, and the evaporative power of the atmosphere. The latter depends on factors affecting the rate of EVAPORATION, which is high on sunny, hot, windy days with low humidity. On days with extremely high evaporation, even well-watered vines can show temporary wilting. On the other hand, vines growing in dry soils but in overcast, cool, and humid climates do not show as much water stress. The combination of climate and soil which results in maximum vine stress is high evaporation and low soil water content; minimum stress results from low evaporation and wet soils. IRRIGATION can be used to overcome water stress, although it is outlawed in some countries.

Water stress is measured by vine physiologists as water potential in the plant, but is more easily understood in terms of the effect on the vine. One of the first signs of impending water stress is the drooping, or wilting, of tendrils near the shoot tip, followed by wilting of the young, then the mature leaves. With severe stress, the leaves exhibit CHLOROSIS, then NECROSIS, and eventually can fall off. As water stress develops in the vine, the plant responds by endeavouring to reduce water loss. A well-watered vine opens the pores called STOMATA on the underside of the leaf in response to the first light of dawn, and they remain open all day, allowing the free exchange of water vapour (the air humidity) and CARBON DIOXIDE between the leaf interior and the atmosphere. Water stress causes the vine leaf partially to close stomata during the day. Initially, this may be in the middle of the day, but subsequently, as the stress worsens, they are shut for most of the day. While this action is sufficient to reduce further water loss, PHOTOSYNTHESIS is reduced because of the lack of carbon dioxide.

Water stress also affects a range of other vine functions. Water stress of vineyards can substitute for winter cold in promoting dormancy in TROPICAL VITICULTURE. During the growing season, drought causes shoot growth to slow and then stop as the leaf tip loses activity. Leaves are smaller and paler in colour, and the growth of LATERAL SHOOTS is also inhibited. Severe stress early in the season can reduce FRUIT SET, and later stress reduces BERRY SIZE.

According to Champagnol, the effect of water stress on wine quality is not straightforward. There is no doubt that severe water stress interrupts grape RIPENING and reduces wine quality, as for example may be observed in Algeria. It is by no means clear whether water stress leads to higher SUGARS and better wine in dry viticultural areas such as the LANGUEDOC-ROUSSILLON in southern France. In humid maritime climates, such as that of BORDEAUX, however, there has been ample demonstration that mild water stress during ripening is favourable to wine quality. For example, the 1966 and 1967 growing seasons had similar weather, except that 1966 was a dry ripening season, and resulted in very much better-quality wines. R.E.S.

Champagnol, F., *Éléments de physiologie de la vigne et de viticulture générale* (St-Gely-du-Fesc, 1984).

WAUGH, HARRY (1904–), English wine merchant famous for his longevity, courtesy, and open mind. He did not enter the wine trade until he was 30, joining as a clerk in a long-established City of London business associated with the fashionable West End company of Block, Grey & Block, where he went to work and first displayed his ability in selecting and selling fine wines. At that time, few British wine merchants visited the sources of their wines, but relied on agents or their principals, who paid regular visits to Britain. In this way, Waugh met such well-known Bordeaux merchants as Christian CRUSE, Jean Calvet, and Ronald BARTON.

He also spent an annual holiday in the leading French wine areas with the late Allan SICHEL, wine importer and part-owner of Ch Palmer (see MARGAUX).

During the Second World War Waugh served in the Welsh Guards, and then at the beginning of 1946 joined the London office of HARVEYS of Bristol. With wine in very short supply after six years of war, there was great demand for red bordeaux, the favoured table wine among regular wine drinkers. Waugh took a further holiday in Bordeaux, where he was introduced by Édouard Cruse to the wines of POMEROL, then almost unknown in Britain. In 1950 he acquired and imported in cask the distinguished 1949 vintage of the then obscure Ch PÉTRUS; as by coincidence did that other Bristol wine merchant Ronald AVERY. He also visited for Harveys other French wine regions, including Beaujolais, then imported as a somewhat anonymous quaffing blend. He bought individual CRU Beaujolais and was invited to form a London chapter of the still flourishing Compagnons de Beaujolais CONFRÉRIE.

After the devastating FROSTS of February 1956 Waugh, by then a director of Harveys, went with a colleague to Bordeaux and, through broker Jean-Paul Gardère, bought large quantities of the fine 1955 vintage, thereby bypassing the négociants (see BORDEAUX WINE TRADE). He was a regular visitor for his firm to Oxford and Cambridge colleges, and in 1953 instituted an annual Oxbridge undergraduate wine-tasting competition, sponsored until 1990 by Harveys (and subsequently by POL ROGER champagne). During this period Harveys trained some of the leading lights of the British wine trade, including Michael BROADBENT.

Harry **Waugh**—still dining late in his own late 80s.

In 1962 the families who owned Ch LATOUR decided to sell and offered this famous Bordeaux first growth to Harveys. Although Waugh and his chairman were in favour, the majority of the board was against, so that Pearson, publishers of the *Financial Times*, acquired a 51 per cent stake, while Harveys were allotted only 25 per cent. Waugh became one of two Harvey representatives on the board, on which he remained during two changes of ownership. He introduced as joint managers Jean-Paul Gardère and his friend Henri Martin, proprietor of Ch Gloria (see ST-JULIEN). In 1966 Harveys was bought by Showerings, producers of Babycham, a popular perry, who later joined Allied Breweries (subsequently part of the multinational conglomerate Allied-DOMECQ). Waugh, then 62, retired. (Seven years later his first children, twins, were born.)

Then began Waugh's close association with wine amateurs in the United States. For many years he made regular lecture tours, and achieved a reputation in the USA unequalled by any other British wine professional. Several volumes of *Harry Waugh's Wine Diary* were published as a record of his punishing itineraries. He did much to publicize Ch Latour, as well as other Bordeaux châteaux's wines. He also introduced California wines to British (and east coast American) wine connoisseurs in the early 1970s when they were little known. For his services to French wines, he received the French Mérite Agricole in 1984 and in 1988 he was made a Chevalier de l'Ordre du Mérite National. In 1989 he was made an honorary member of the Institute of MASTERS OF WINE. He will always be remembered for his reply to someone who asked whether he had ever mistaken claret for burgundy: 'not since lunch.'

E.P.-R.

Waugh, H., *Harry Waugh's Wine Diaries* vols. i–ix (vols. i–v were individually entitled) (London, 1966–81).

WEATHER, probably the single most exasperatingly variable variable in the viticultural equation, as in most other farming activities. For details of overall weather patterns see CLIMATE, MACROCLIMATE, and CLIMATE CLASSIFICATION. For accounts of specific climatological phenomena with implications for wine production, see DEW, DROUGHT, FLOODING, FROST, HAIL, RAINFALL, SUNLIGHT, TEMPERATURE, and WIND. The weather in a specific growing season is the most important influence on the characteristics of a particular VINTAGE YEAR.

WEED CONTROL, a range of viticultural practices to avoid WEEDS competing for water and nutrients with vines, particularly young vines. The practices vary from region to region and with VINE AGE, with the common options being ploughing or HERBICIDES.

Mechanical control of weeds involves cultivating down the row alley using discs or tines. Cultivation directly under the row is more difficult, as the weeding device needs to avoid the trunks. A number of appropriate cultivators have been eveloped, with the swing back action achieved manually early models but now controlled automatically by touch nsing the trunk. Even so, such cultivation disturbs the ound under the vine row where the majority of roots are, nd many machines can cause some vine damage. Sauvignon anc trunks, for example, are particularly prone to a FUNGAL SEASE caused by injury due to mechanical undervine eeding. Hand hoeing of weeds is still found in some vine-rds, although often this is restricted to the control of par-cularly difficult weeds in young vineyards. The alternative to use herbicides, and spraying an undervine strip is ommon.

Mowing between the rows is common in summer rainfall eas, or where there is plentiful irrigation, otherwise the eeds growing there cause excessive WATER STRESS and some-mes NITROGEN deficiency, leading to incomplete fer-entations. Other methods of weed control include ulching, using cereal straw, for example, placed as a mat nder the rows. This has the added advantage of increasing ganic matter, earthworm populations, and water infil-ation. Weeds may also be controlled by placing a strip of astic sheet under the vines. This is especially common for oung vineyards, where weeds particularly hinder vine owth. R.E.S.

EEDER, implement used in vineyards for removing EEDS, typically from the vine row. These machines are ounted on a tractor, and a knife to cut under weeds is oved, either manually or automatically, in and out of the ne of trunks. Early versions of this machine were difficult to se and often removed the vine along with the weeds. The ontinued use of such machines has fallen from favour, due the death of some vines, and the introduction of some seases because of vine injury. In many parts of the world the se of undervine weeders has been replaced by herbicides. R.E.S.

EEDS. A weed is defined as a plant out of place, and any vine-growers regard a weedy vineyard as a sign of poor anagement. The presence of plants other than vines in the ineyard is a feature of so-called ORGANIC VITICULTURE, on the ther hand. Some vineyards are excessively cultivated to keep em free of weeds, to the detriment of SOIL STRUCTURE. More cently there has been a tendency to achieve the same result sing HERBICIDES, perhaps in combination with cultivation.

There is no doubt that weed growth inhibits the growth f vines, especially in young vines. When the vine root system small and shallow, weeds compete for water and nutrients, specially NITROGEN, but with older vines the competition an be less as the vine root system is larger and deeper. Some ant species seem to have a further effect in inhibiting others, phenomenon known as allelopathy. In very weedy vine-ards the weeds may also compete with the vines for light.

On the other hand, weeds can cause inconvenience and iscomfort to vineyard workers and can also harbour VINE ESTS and DISEASES, although they can also shelter predators f insect vine pests. In some vineyards, other plants may be deliberately encouraged to grow between the rows as a COVER CROP.

Weeds which occur in vineyards obviously vary from region to region, and are representative of the local flora. Those which occur depend on prior land use, soil prep-aration, seed reserves in the soil, and the extent to which seeds arrive in the vineyard, by wind or on implements, for example. Weeds which are difficult to control and can be found in many vineyards world-wide include field bindweed (*Convolvulus arvensis*), Johnson grass (*Holcus halepensis*), and Bermuda or couch grass (*Cynadon dactylon*). R.E.S.

Flaherty, D. L., *et al.* (eds.), *Grape Pest Management* (Oakland, Calif., 1992).

WEEVILS. See BEETLES.

WEIGHING of grapes is an important operation at any centre where grapes are received from a number of different growers who are paid by weight. This applies to most wine CO-OPERATIVES and many individual wineries, even if the more progressive take other factors such as grape quality and health into account before determining PRICE. This is normally done with large platform scales on which the lorry is weighed full and empty.

The amount of additives needed during the adjustment operations of ENRICHMENT, ACIDIFICATION, and DEACIDI-FICATION, as well as the BLENDING process, can be calculated more precisely on the basis of weight than volume. The weight of wine is calculated from the measured volume and the DENSITY. Blends calculated on a volume basis do not account for the contractions that occur when solutions of differing ALCOHOLIC STRENGTH are mixed. A.D.W.

WEIN, (pronouced 'vine') means 'wine' in GERMAN. It is therefore the first syllable of a host of important German wine names such as **Weinbau**, which means vine-growing, **Weinbrand**, which is German for basic BRANDY, and **Weingut**, meaning wine estate as distinct from a **Weinkellerei**, which buys in grapes, must, or wine but probably owns vineyards only if it describes itself as the all-purpose Weingut-Wein-kellerei. A **Weinprobe** is a wine tasting, **Weinsäure** is TAR-TARIC ACID, some of which may eventually be precipitated as crystal TARTRATES, or **Weinstein**.

WEISSER, meaning 'white' is a common prefix in German for pale-skinned grape varieties. Weisser Burgunder is PINOT BLANC, for example, while Blauer Burgunder is PINOT NOIR.

WEISSER RIESLING, common synonym for the great white RIESLING grape variety of Germany.

WEISSHERBST, special sort of pink wine made from a single grape variety in the AHR, RHEINGAU, RHEINHESSEN, PFALZ, WÜRTTEMBERG, and BADEN wine regions of GERMANY. It may be either a QBA or QMP wine and in Baden Weissherbst made from Spätburgunder (PINOT NOIR) has enjoyed local popularity. See also SCHILLERWEIN. The term is also used in German SWITZERLAND for very much the same style of wine.

WELSCHRIESLING, or **Wälschriesling**, white grape variety which, as Germans are keen to point out, is completely unrelated to the great RIESLING grape of Germany. Indeed it rankles with many Germans that the noble word is even allowed as a suffix in the name of this inferior variety; they would prefer that the word Rizling were used, as in **Welsch Rizling** or **Welschrizling**, which it is in many of its many synonyms.

Welschriesling may be the variety's most common name in AUSTRIA, but Welschrizling is obediently used in BULGARIA, its most common name in HUNGARY is OLASZ RIZLING, in SLOVENIA and VOJVODINA it is LASKI RIZLING, and in CZECHOSLOVAKIA it is the very similar Rizling Vlassky. Only in CROATIA does it acquire a name of any distinction, Graševina. The Italians call it RIESLING ITALICO (as opposed to Riesling Renano, which is the Riesling of Germany) and variants of this are used all over eastern Europe, notably in ROMANIA (although most of the 'Riesling' planted in the CIS is true German Riesling). The variety is one of the few common white wine grapes in ALBANIA, as it is in its close political ally CHINA.

The origins of this old variety are obscure. Although French origins have been posited, this seems unlikely as it is quite unknown in France (and Germany), it thrives best in dry climates and warmer soils, and has a tendency to produce excessively acid wines in cool climates.

Welsch simply means 'foreign' in Germanic languages, which provides few clues. But since Vlaska is the Slav name for Wallachia in Romania, and since the variety is particularly successful in that country, it is easy to develop a theory that it originated there, and that Laski is a corruption of Vlassy, or Wallachian.

Although Welschriesling has little in common with Riesling, it too is a late ripening vine whose grapes keep their acidity well and produce light bodied, relatively aromatic wines. Welschriesling can easily be persuaded to yield even more productively than Riesling, however, and indeed this and its useful acidity probably explain why it is so widely planted throughout eastern Europe and, partly, why so much of the wine it produces is undistinguished (although low technological standards in many wineries in what was YUGOSLAVIA, for example, have also played a part).

As a wine Welschriesling reaches its apogee in AUSTRIA, specifically in some particularly finely balanced, rich late harvest wines made on the shores of the Neusiedlersee in Burgenland where about two-thirds of Austria's total 5,000 ha / 12,350 acres of the variety are planted. In particularly favoured vintages, the NOBLE ROT forms to ripen grapes up to TROCKENBEERENAUSLESE level, while retaining the acidity that is Welschriesling's hallmark. Welschriesling may not have the aromatic character of Germany's Riesling, but since aroma plays only a small part in the appreciation of really sweet wines, this leaves Welschriesling at less of a disadvantage than Riesling addicts might imagine, although Austrian TBAs rarely have the longevity of their German counterparts. The bulk of Austria's Welschriesling, however, goes into light dryish wines for early drinking, notably in Burgenland and Styria. It has also been known as Riesler in Austria.

See also OLASZ RIZLING, LASKI RIZLING, and ITALIAN RIZLING.

WESTERN AUSTRALIA, or **WA**. AUSTRALIA's biggest state has the country's most isolated wine regions in its south west corner.

Nowhere have the winds of change blown harder since 1970 than in Western Australia. In that year more than 90 per cent of the state's wine was made from grapes grown in the Swan Valley; by 1980 the figure was 59 per cent; by 1990 it was 26 per cent and still falling. The other side of the coin has been the emergence of the Margaret River and Lower Great Southern regions spanning the far south western corner of the state.

In a manner reminiscent of the Barossa Valley in SOUTH AUSTRALIA, the hot Swan Valley remains the source of much of Western Australia's wine, largely through a single company, Houghton. As well as producing Houghton White Burgundy (as it has been called in Australia) from VERDELHO, CHENIN BLANC, and CHARDONNAY grown in the Swan Valley and at **Gingin** (just to the north), Houghton has large vineyards at Frankland in the Lower Great Southern, and is a major purchaser of grapes throughout that region and the Margaret River. The Swan Valley has the dubious distinction of being the hottest region in Australia, with vintage typically beginning in January.

The **Margaret River**, 240 km / 146 miles to the south, is still at a latitude of 34 degrees south, and therefore completely reliant upon the cooling influence of the Indian Ocean to provide its TEMPERATE climate. Here CABERNET SAUVIGNON produces a wine which consistently combines elegance with strength, redcurrant fruit with a seasoning of gravelly GOÛT *de terroir*. MERLOT is frequently blended with it. Pungently grassy and intense SEMILLON and SAUVIGNON Blanc also perform with distinction. These too are more often than not blended with each other (and sometimes with CHENIN BLANC as a third partner). CHARDONNAY is the other grape of importance, making wine which is often complex and sometimes long lived.

RIESLING has never succeeded in the Margaret River, but comes emphatically into its own in the far-flung, colder, and usually more CONTINENTAL sites of the Lower **Great Southern** area (including Mount Barker and Frankland). Here it produces crisp, tightly structured wines which evolve slowly but with grace, mirroring the slow development of the equally taut yet fragrant Cabernet Sauvignon. PINOT NOIR has proved its liking for Albany on the extreme southern coastline, and high hopes are held for it at Pemberton, to the north—this is a huge and diverse region. Chardonnay and SHIRAZ also do well, Sauvignon Blanc a little less so. If one had to nominate the most likely boom wine region for the 21st century the Lower Great Southern would be near the top of the list.

J.H.

ESTERN GRAPELEAF SKELETONIZER, a vine st and native insect of Mexico and the states of Arizona, w Mexico, and Texas, first found in California in 1941 in n Diego County. The young larvae feed on the soft leaf sue, leaving a skeleton framework. Chemical control is ective, but timing is critical. Left unchecked this insect will mpletely defoliate a vine. M.J.E.

HIP GRAFT, the form used in GRAFTING which simply volves an angled slice across the SCION stem and a similarly gled cut of the stock, with the two cuts then matched and e graft tied tightly with grafting tape. **Whip-and-tongue** is e same except that another cut is made to raise 'tongues' stem tissue that dovetail with each other and improve the ength of the graft. B.G.C.

HITE has a special meaning when applied both to grapes d wine. Any light-skinned grape may be called a white ape, even though the grape skin is not white but anything om pale green through gold to pink. In a similar fashion, nite wines are not white, but vary in colour from almost lourless to deep gold. See COLOUR.

HITE RIESLING, common synonym for the great nite RIESLING grape variety of Germany.

HITE ROT, FUNGAL DISEASE affecting vines that occurs in ose parts of Europe most prone to hailstorms, also known hail disease. Crop losses can be as high as 80 per cent. The uit is attacked after a hailstorm and, because the berry skin lifted from the flesh, the berries appear white, giving rise the name. High summer rainfall, high humidity, and high mperatures also favour the disease. The fungus responsible *Coniella diplodiella*, which is controlled by a range of chemi- sprays. R.E.S.

HITE WINE-MAKING, the production of wines with most imperceptible to golden COLOUR. If the juice is sep- ated from the grape skins gently and soon enough (as in e production of CHAMPAGNE), white wines can be made om black-skinned grapes, but the great majority of white ines are made from grapes with yellow or green skins. hite wines can be made from grapes of all hues, so long as ere is no SKIN CONTACT or MACERATION with dark-skinned apes. The only exception to this is the red-fleshed TEIN- RIERS. White grapes and wines are distinguished from their d counterparts by their absence of ANTHOCYANS.

As with any WINE-MAKING operation, the production of hite wines usually entails CRUSHING and DESTEMMING the ape clusters or bunches on arrival at the winery, although casionally white grapes may be crushed beforehand at a ld pressing station (and see also WHOLE BUNCH PRESSING). fter crushing and destemming, the sweet POMACE requires aining and PRESSING to separate the liquid from the solids. he timing of the separation of juice from solids constitutes e major difference between red and white wine-making: efore FERMENTATION for whites and afterwards for reds.

Prolonged contact between juice and grape skins (see SKIN CONTACT) encourages the transfer of soluble materials, most usefully FLAVOUR COMPOUNDS, from the skins to the juice. The extracted PHENOLICS, which provide a red wine with both colour and TANNIN, are generally undesirable, for they lead to astringent and bitter tastes and to the development of amber to brown colours deemed inappropriate for white wines.

Because of their light colour and delicate flavours, white wines show the unappetizing effects of OXIDATION much faster than red wines and so white wine-making is in general a more delicate operation than RED WINE-MAKING. Certain phenolics present in the pulp and extracted from the skins and seeds react rapidly with oxygen to generate amber to brown compounds. Small amounts of ACETALDEHYDE are produced by the reaction of oxygen with alcohol, and this compound can easily spoil the AROMA of a fresh, fruity young wine. There are two possible solutions to this inconvenience. Exposure to oxygen may be minimized or completely avoided throughout wine-making right up to and including bottling by techniques known collectively as PROTECTIVE.

Alternatively, a policy of unprotected handling is adopted whereby the MUST is deliberately, and sometimes in the case of everyday wines violently, aerated so that its susceptible phenolics oxidize, these brown compounds being removed by absorption into the dead yeast cells or LEES after fermentation. Most of the acetaldehyde produced by this sort of oxidation is reduced to alcohol during the subsequent fermentation. The disadvantage of this prefermentation oxidation is that it removes some of the compounds that would have contributed to BODY and AROMA as well as a bit of colour.

White wines are usually fermented and processed cooler than normal room TEMPERATURE, although the disadvantages of this are the cost of any REFRIGERATION used and the pressure on available FERMENTATION VESSELS since cool fermentations take longer.

Only a small, but much-vaunted, proportion of white wine comes into contact with WOOD but BARREL FERMENTATION followed by BARREL MATURATION is an increasingly common phenomenon, particularly for wines made from the CHARDONNAY grape. Among these barrel-fermented white wines, lees STIRRING is also increasingly popular, as is MALOLACTIC FERMENTATION, once associated predominantly with red wines. A.D.W.

WHITE WINES, made with much less SKIN CONTACT, are much lower in PHENOLICS than red wines. This does not necessarily mean, however, that they are inherently less interesting, or shorter lived (see AGEING). They vary enormously in colour from virtually colourless to deep gold and even, in extreme age, deep tawny (the same colour as some very old red wines). They are made in virtually all wine regions, although in hot regions ACIDIFICATION and some form of REFRIGERATION are usually needed to produce white wines suitable for modern tastes.

French for white is *blanc*, Italian is *bianco*, Spanish is *blanco*, Portuguese is *branco*, German is *weiss*, while in most eastern

White wine-making

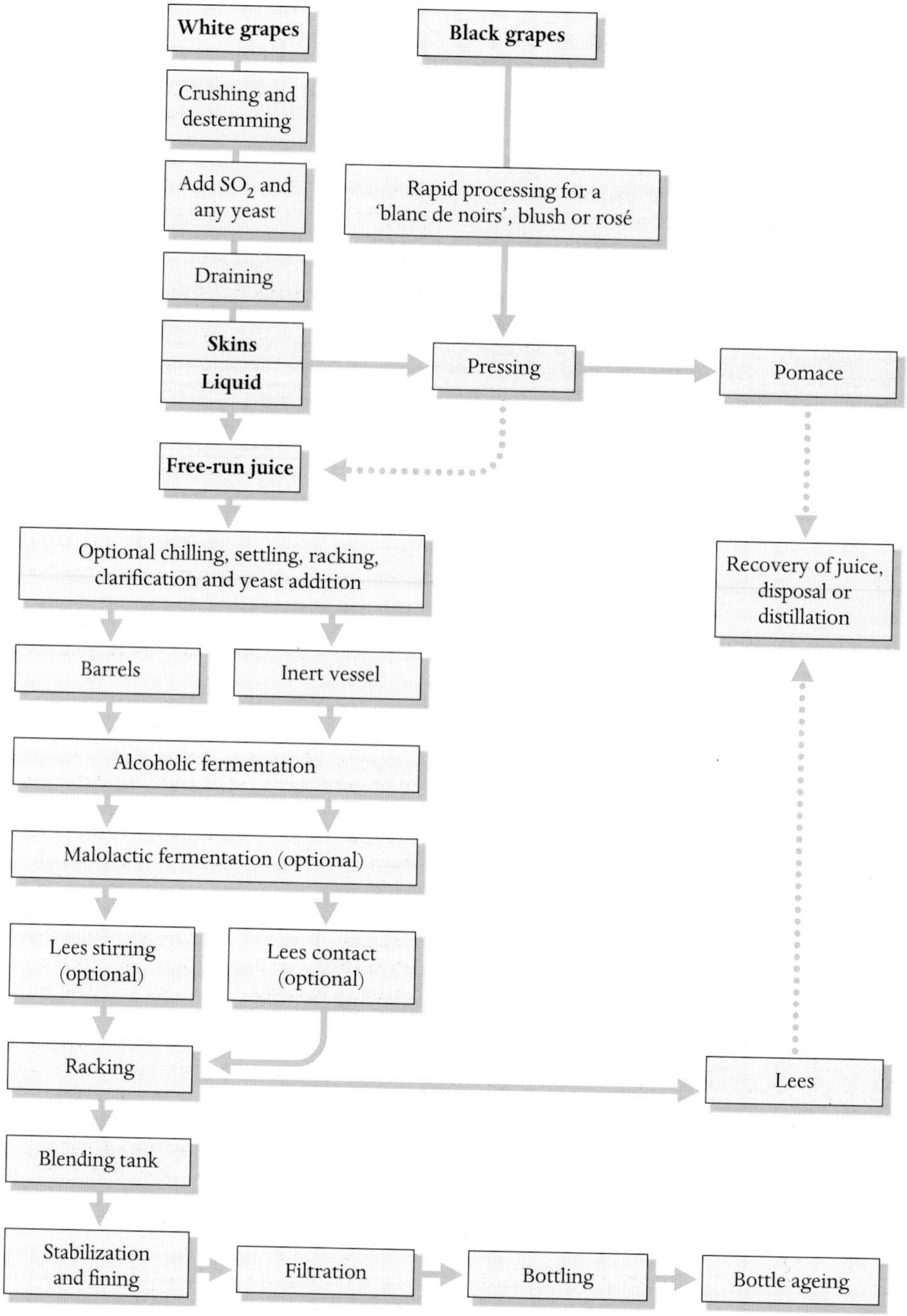

uropean languages, including Russian, the word for white s some variant of *byeli*.

WHITE ZINFANDEL, undeterred by the fact that it is either white nor crucially Zinfandel, was California's great ommercial success story of the 1980s. Although he was not he first to vinify California's ubiquitous ZINFANDEL grapes as white, and therefore BLUSH, wine, Bob Trinchero of Sutter Home launched 'White' Zinfandel down the commercial lipway in 1972 and was to see his own sales rocket from 5,000 cases in 1980 to 1.5 million cases six years later. The vine evolved as a way of making California's vast acreage f Zinfandel acceptable to the predominantly white winerinking American public. So successful was it that it stimuated an outbreak of new plantings of the variety expressly to eep pace with demand for this decidedly ersatz version. The vine is usually pale pink, decidedly sweet, often enlivened vith a touch of gas, and scented with more than a dash f other, more obviously aromatic, grape varieties such as Muscat or Riesling. So successful was the wine that it begat tyles such as **White Grenache**, designed to glamorize vineard Cinderellas.

WHOLE BUNCH FERMENTATION, ultra-traditional method of red wine FERMENTATION in which grape berries are ot subjected to DESTEMMING. The possible disadvantages are hat, unless the fruit is very ripe and MUST is handled very ently, the STEMS may impart harsh TANNINS to the wine. The echnique also involves a greater total capacity of FERMENTATION VESSELS which must be open topped to allow PUNCHNG DOWN of the CAP. The advantages are that the stems can ase the drainage of the juice through the cap, and encourage ealthy oxygenation by increasing the cap's interface with he atmosphere during MACERATION. This practice is most ommon in BURGUNDY.

WHOLE BUNCH PRESSING, special WHITE WINEMAKING technique whereby the grapes are not subjected to ESTEMMING and bunches of ripe grapes are pressed whole, vith the stems used as conduits for what can often be paricularly viscous juice. This works best for very ripe grapes nd would not be suitable if a period of SKIN CONTACT precedes RESSING since excess TANNINS could be leached into the wine rom the STEMS. This technique is almost universal in the roduction of top-quality SPARKLING WINES and most other vhite wines from dark-skinned grapes and in the direct pressng of BOTRYTIS-affected clusters of super-ripe grapes as in AUTERNES. It is also increasingly popular with some qualityonscious producers of white wines in some wine regions ince the juice that results tends to be low in PHENOLICS and igh in quality.

WHOLE GRAPE FERMENTATION. Alternative name or CARBONIC MACERATION.

WIEN. See VIENNA.

WILDBACHER, or **Blauer Wildbacher**, dark-skinned grape variety that is a speciality of western STYRIA in AUSTRIA, where almost all of the 230 ha/568 acres grown in the early 1990s were located. The variety has been increasingly popular with growers and almost all of it is made into the local pink speciality, Schilcher wine, enlivened by Wildbacher's high acidity and distinctive perfume.

WILD HORSE VALLEY, California wine region and AVA. See NAPA Valley.

WILD VINES, plants of the genus VITIS growing in their natural state without any cultivation by man. Such vines are often found climbing trees but may also grow as shrubs. They are widespread in the Americas, especially in the east and south east, in Asia, and up until the mid 1800s in Europe and western Asia. Generally the vines are indigenous, but sometimes they are feral, that is, they are derived from plants once cultivated rather than from indigenous plants. Examples of feral vines are the wild vines of the Pays BASQUE and, according to Mullins, the AMERICAN VINE SPECIES *Vitis riparia* and *Vitis rupestris* along the Rhône and Garonne rivers after importation as ROOTSTOCKS. Wild vines are typically spread by birds eating the berries and passing the seeds. Where wild vines of different species grow together it is common for natural HYBRIDS to develop, as for example in the east of America (see AMERICAN HYBRIDS.) Such hybrids can also develop from natural pollen interchange with cultivated grapes.

Perhaps the most famous of all wild vines are those described in the legend about Leif Ericsson, who sailed west from Greenland in AD 1001 and landed in unknown country (see VÍNLAND). The early settlers and explorers in the Americas and the Caribbean found profuse growth of wild vines in the woods. Such vines had tolerance to the harsh winter climate and indigenous pests such as PHYLLOXERA, and FUNGAL DISEASES such as DOWNY MILDEW and POWDERY MILDEW, and so could grow without check, while the *Vitis* VINIFERA vines imported from Europe perished in cultivation.

Wild vines of the wine-producing *vinifera* species were more widespread in Europe and western Asia, although they have disappeared from large areas of Europe since the introduction of the American pests and diseases noted above. Sometimes such wild vines are called *Vitis vinifera silvestris*, while cultivated vines are called *Vitis vinifera sativa*, although there are very few differences between the two forms. When they are both grown under the same conditions they appear similar; indeed there is more variation among different VINE VARIETIES of cultivated *vinifera* than there is among different types of wild *vinifera*. One fundamental difference, however, is that the wild vines are dioecious, that is that there are both male and female plants. The cultivated vine on the other hand has mostly perfect or hermaphrodite flowers (containing functional male and female parts), which results in better FRUIT SET, and would have been the basis of selection from the wild by man.

Wild vines are important to modern viticulture as they are the source of many of the present-day varieties. With the collapse of the Roman empire and the abandonment of vineyard cultivation, some ancient varieties became feral and interbred with native wild vines. So those of the modern varieties selected from the wild from that period onwards may have contained germplasm from both wild *Vitis vinifera* and Roman or Gallo-Roman varieties. R.E.S.

Mullins, M. G., Bouquet, A., and Williams, L., *Biology of the Grapevine* (Cambridge, 1992).

Pinney, T., *A History of Wine in America: From the Beginnings to Prohibition* (Berkeley, Calif., 1989).

WILLOW CREEK, California's northernmost wine region and AVA. A handful of tiny, unproven vineyards lie within this district in southern Humboldt County planted as recently as the late 1980s.

WIND, or strong air movement, is a problem on many coastal and otherwise exposed viticultural sites. Major valleys can also be windy, because they can act as funnels, and have their own distinctive systems of wind force and directions. The mistral of the southern Rhône is one of the more notorious examples of this. The detrimental effects of wind on vines are described under WIND STRESS; installing WINDBREAKS can provide a solution.

Hot, dry winds in summer are a particular hazard of viticultural regions bordering deserts. Most Australian vineyards are periodically affected. Coming out of the Australian central desert, such winds can last for up to several days. The sirocco of North Africa can similarly afflict the vineyards of southern Europe, occasionally reaching France.

The effects of wind are by no means all detrimental, however. The normally regular afternoon sea breezes of coastal regions with otherwise summer-dry climates, such as those of Portugal, California, and much of southern Australia, have a useful moderating effect on viticultural climate, and are thought to contribute significantly to the quality of their wines (see CLIMATE AND WINE QUALITY). In all environments some air movement is needed to prevent excessive humidity buildup within the vineyard, and to encourage drying of wet foliage and bunches, thereby reducing the risk of FUNGAL DISEASES. Night winds largely prevent radiation FROSTS (WIND MACHINES simulate this effect), while during sunlight hours the moderate movement of leaves encourages a more uniform spread of intermittent sunlight exposure among them, thus promoting a more efficient use of SUNLIGHT. Some degree of windiness is also often an unavoidable concomitant of the TOPOGRAPHIES that are viticulturally the best in other respects.

In summary, winds cannot be entirely avoided; nor are they wholly undesirable. The selection of sheltered sites, where possible, is important in windy regions. Beyond that, the answers to wind problems lie mainly in suitable vineyard strategies of TRELLISING and where necessary in the use of WINDBREAKS. J.G.

WINDBREAK, a barrier of vegetation or other materials to break the force of WINDS and avoid WIND STRESS. Large benefits have been shown in many environments, especially for exposed young vines and in early spring, when growth of the vines themselves is not enough to afford mutual protection.

The benefits of windbreaks go beyond reducing physical vine damage. A combination of reduced wind force and (in dry atmospheres) the maintenance of higher HUMIDITIES among the vines reduces closure of the leaf pores (STOMATA) and therefore enhances potential PHOTOSYNTHESIS. Quite substantial yield increases are commonly recorded in the lee of effective windbreaks, amply exceeding any losses that might be incurred through reduced vine area.

The best natural windbreaks are fast-growing trees or tall shrubs whose roots do not extend too far laterally. Poplars, elms, and eucalypts are common choices. Tall winter COVER CROPS such as cereal rye, planted between the vine rows, can also afford useful protection to young vineyards in early spring. This is only feasible where the spring FROST risk is small, and where summer rain or irrigation can ensure that the cover crop does not unduly compete with the vines for moisture. J.G. & R.E.S.

WIND MACHINE, a strong fan for stirring up and mixing cold, dense air settled on the land surface with warmer air from above, thereby preventing FROSTS on still spring nights when there is no WIND to do the job. Such machines, introducing an aeronautical look to vineyards, have been used on valley floors that are prone to radiation frosts, such as in the NAPA Valley of California. Helicopters can be used to the same effect. J.G.

WIND STRESS, can reduce vine YIELD and RIPENING in some exposed vineyards. Severe gusts of wind can have dramatic effects on vineyards, breaking shoots and removing leaves. However, even lower velocity wind can also cause vine problems which are apparent only to the trained eye. Wind cools plants by removing the warming effects of the sun's rays, as well as other more substantial effects on physiology. For some plants, including vines, wind can have a major effect on growth. Shoot length, leaf area, and fruit growth can all be substantially reduced. The problem is particularly acute for young vines, as in older vineyards the CANOPY can usually offer sufficient self-protection.

Some vines respond negatively to movement, probably a response involving plant HORMONES. A major effect of wind is that of closing STOMATA. Freeman and colleagues of the University of California showed that wind speeds of 3 m/10 ft per second in the Salinas Valley caused stomata to close partially, which has the effect of reducing both PHOTOSYNTHESIS and TRANSPIRATION. Vines ripening in windy places will show reduced ripening and higher PH.

Simon studied the effects of WINDBREAKS on vines in the San Rafael region of Argentina. Malbec vines adjacent to the 10-m/33-ft tall poplar windbreak showed earlier FLOWERING, FRUIT SET, and VERAISON and longer shoots with more grapes near the windbreak. The windbreak was also effective against occasional very strong winds in reducing mechanical damage. R.E.S.

Aerotechnology applied to **wind machines** in California's Napa Valley.

Freeman, B. M., Kliewer, W. M., and Stern, P., 'Influence of windbreaks and climatic region on diurnal fluctuation of leaf water potential, stomatal conductance, and leaf temperature of grapevines', *American Journal of Enology and Viticulture*, 33 (1982), 233–6.

Simon, J. C., 'Étude des influences agronomiques des brise-vents dans les périmètres irrigués du Centre-Ouest de l'Argentine. 1: Effets des brise-vents sur la croissance et le développement d'une culture type: la vigne,' *Annales agronomie*, 28 (1977), 75–93.

WINE, alcoholic drink made by fermenting the juice of fruits or berries (see FRUIT WINES). By extension, this most general definition can also include products of the FERMENTATION of sugar solutions flavoured with flowers or herbs, but it normally excludes those of hydrolysed barley starches involved in brewing, and the products of the fermentation of sugar-containing liquids destined for DISTILLATION. There are also certain drinks, such as mead, cider, and perry, which depend on sugar fermentations for their alcohol content but for historical reasons merit their own names.

The narrower definition, relevant to this book and accepted throughout Europe, is that wine is 'the alcoholic beverage obtained from the fermentation of the juice of freshly gathered grapes, the fermentation taking place in the district of origin according to local tradition and practice'. This is to distinguish 'proper' wine from alcoholic drinks made from imported grape concentrate, which are known in Europe as 'made wine'. These include BRITISH WINE and a significant proportion of the liquid produced by HOME WINEMAKING. New World definitions of wine are very similar except that the last phrase is omitted and wine may be made from a mixture of grapes grown many hundreds of miles apart.

Etymology

The modern English *wine* comes from Old English *wīn*, pronounced like modern 'wean': that indeed was how Chaucer pronounced his *wyn*, but Shakespeare's pronunciation was closer to our own. The Old English form was in turn descended from the Latin *vīnum*, or as the Romans wrote it VINVM, by way of a loan-word represented in all Germanic languages (e.g. German *Wein*, Icelandic *vín*); a similar loan into Celtic has yielded Welsh *gwin* and Irish *fíon*. The explanation is that the Germans and CELTS, whose native beverage was BEER, learnt to drink wine from the Romans (Caesar's statements that some German and Gaulish tribes forbade its import prove that it was already known); with it came the Latin word, borrowed while Latin *v* was still pronounced [w]. From Germanic territory drink and name passed in turn to the Slavs (e.g. Russian *vinó*) and Balts (Lithuanian *vŷnas*, Latvian *vīns*).

Within Latin itself, from *vīnum* comes the noun *vīnea* 'vineyard'; this word, reinterpreted of a single vine (classically *vītis*, whence 'viticulture'), yielded French *vigne*, which was naturally brought over to England by the Normans. However, once the native English began to learn their masters' language they adjusted it to suit their own speech-habits; since English then as now lacked the palatal sound of French *gn*, it was simplified to *n*, so that *vigne* became *vine*. This was adopted into English and subjected to the normal sound-changes of the late medieval and early modern period: the final *-e* ceased to be pronounced and the long *i* became a diphthong. The French word was also substituted in the term for the place where vines were grown, originally *wīngeard*, now 'vineyard', with the vowel shortened as often in compounds (e.g. 'shepherd' vs. 'sheep').

Whereas *vitis* can be related to an Indo-European verb-root meaning to 'wind' or 'twine', as in English *withy*, the ultimate origins of *vinum* and *vinea* are less clear: similar words are found in many Mediterranean languages, even those belonging to different language-families, but few interrelations can be established. For instance, although Latin ī often comes from *ei*, since the change did not take place till the late 2nd century BC it cannot have occurred in *vinum*, for which forms with *vin-* are found in the kindred languages of ancient Italy. This rules out a direct link with the term current in Ancient GREECE, according to dialect *woinos* (ϝοῖνος) or *oînos* (οἶνος), as in OENOLOGY, akin to the **woiniyo-* (* denotes a reconstructed form) underlying Armenian *gini* and sometimes associated with Sanskrit *veṇi* or *veṇī* 'braid'. The form *wiyana* and *wayana* are quoted from the ancient Anatolian languages (see ASIA MINOR) Hittite and Luvian: outside Indo-European, a Semitic noun **wayn*, 'grape, vine, wine', which yields Hebrew *yayin* and Ethiopic *wäyn* besides an Arabic *wayn* 'black grape' found in an ancient lexicon, has sometimes been considered the source of the Greek word and sometimes a derivative. Even Georgian *γvino* (see GEORGIA) has been proposed: no theory is convincing, except after a few glasses. L.A.H.-S.

Editorial note:

See WINE COMPOSITION, WINE-MAKING, WINE TYPES and the other entries which immediately follow. The word 'wine' appears only in their titles. Otherwise, for wine press see PRESS, for wine and religion see RELIGION AND WINE, for wine trade see TRADE, etc. For details of specific wines, see unde their names or their provenance.

WINE COMPOSITION differs quite considerably fror GRAPE COMPOSITION, partly because parts of the grape ar discarded during WINE-MAKING, and partly because the prc cesses involved effect a complicated series of transformation Alcoholic FERMENTATION, for example, transforms sugars int alcohol, while MALOLACTIC FERMENTATION reduces the level c malic acid in favour of lactic acid. The precise compositio of a wine varies with WINE TYPE, HARVEST conditions and date VINTAGE characteristics, and the age of the wine (see AGEIN for details of how wine composition may change with age Nevertheless, the following gives some guidance as to th likely range of concentrations of the essential constituents o the approximately 1,000 so far identified.

Component	Proportions per l	Comments
Dissolved gases		
CARBON DIOXIDE	0–50 cc	
SULPHUR DIOXIDE		
Total	80–200 mg	More in some sweet wine
Free	10–50 mg	Some in some unstable wines
Volatile substances		
WATER	700–900 mg	
ETHANOL (alcohol)	8.5–15 % by vol	More in fortified, less in low-alcohol wines
HIGHER ALCOHOLS	0.15–0.5 g	
ACETALDEHYDE	0.005–0.5 g	
ESTERS	0.5–1.5 g	
ACETIC ACID	0.3–0.5 g	Expressed as sulphuric acid
Fixed substances		
RESIDUAL SUGAR	0.8–180 g	According to type of wine more in botrytized wines
GLYCEROL	5–12 g	
PHENOLICS	0.4–4 g	
gums and PECTINS	1–3 g	Depending on the vintage
Organic acids		
TARTARIC ACID	5–10 g	Depending on grape origin
MALIC ACID	0–? g	According to extent of
LACTIC ACID	0–1 g	malolactic fermentation
SUCCINIC ACID	1–3 g	
CITRIC ACID	0–1 g	
Mineral salts		
Sulphates	0.1–0.4 g	Expressed as
Chlorides	0.25–0.85 g	potassium salts
Phosphates		
Mineral elements		
POTASSIUM	0.7–1.5 g	
CALCIUM	0.06–0.9 g	
COPPER	0.001–0.003 g	
IRON	0.002–0.005 g	

Navarre, C., *L'œnologie* (Paris, 1988).

WINE GRAPE, a term used to describe grapes used foi wine-making, as opposed to TABLE GRAPES for eating anc DRYING GRAPES for use by the dried fruit industry. For dis ussion about the plant which bears wine grapes see VINE, nd for more detail of the fruit itself, see GRAPE.

VINE LAKE, term coined for Europe's wine SURPLUS. With ne introduction of compulsory DISTILLATION in 1982, it was apidly transformed into an ALCOHOL lake. Of a typical annual vine surplus of just under 40 m hl, only about 15 m hl is kely to find a use as distilled alcohol. For more details, see UROPEAN UNION.

VINE-MAKER, one who makes WINE. In its broadest sense he term includes those who engage in HOME WINE-MAKING as hobby, although in a professional sense a wine-maker is omeone employed (sometimes by themselves) to produce vine. An increasing proportion of such people recognize that vine production includes every aspect of vineyard management, and there are wine producers all over the world whose production is so small that they personally conduct, r at least oversee, every stage from planting to marketing usually with markedly different degrees of success in each rea). A wine production unit of any size, however, will mploy both a VITICULTURALIST, or vineyard manager, and a vine-maker whose active responsibilities begin with receiving grapes from the vineyard and continue with their SAMPLING, CRUSHING, PRESSING, FERMENTATION, ÉLEVAGE, OTTLING, and storage—all those operations outlined in WINE-AKING. Larger wine producers may even employ a team of vine-makers, each with different responsibilities.

As one might expect in a field as international as wine, he term wine-maker has many synonyms: *maître-de-chai* in ordeaux; *Kellermeister* in Germany; *enologo* in Italy; *œnologue* n some French wineries. While most (though not all) nodern wine-makers have studied OENOLOGY, and will certainly consider themselves enologists, the term OENOLOGIST is more usually applied to an outside consultant rather than to a full-time employee in Europe.

Vine-makers can be more famous than winery owners, especially n the New World, as in the case of Philip Shaw of Rosemount in New South Wales.

Like the chef, the wine-maker enjoyed a brief period of near cult status during the early 1980s, when for a time certain men (and a few women) were treated as though capable of fashioning superior wine out of almost any quality of grapes, a FASHION that was most notable in the New World but by no means confined to it. VITICULTURISTS have been lobbying against this view, however, to become the wine gurus of the 1990s.

Most successful wine-makers understand that making fine wine depends not only on a respectful understanding of the complicated biochemistry involved but also, perhaps more importantly, on an appreciation of the greatest potential within each lot of grapes and then the skill and patience to reveal that potential in the finished wine.

Clarke, O., *New Classic Wines* (London, 1991).
Norman, R., *Burgundy* (London, 1992).

WINE-MAKING, the practical art of producing WINE. In its most general sense it encompasses all operations in both vineyard and cellar but for the purposes of this article wine-making excludes vine-growing, or VITICULTURE.

Wine-making, while a sophisticated practical art for several millennia, became an applied SCIENCE only towards the end of the 19th century after Louis PASTEUR's discovery of the existence and activities of BACTERIA and YEAST. Since then knowledge of the detailed chemical and biochemical reactions involved in their metabolic processes has steadily increased, as has the sophistication of the containers and equipment used in the professional cellar.

Wine-making in brief is a series of simple operations, the first of which is CRUSHING or smashing the fruit to liberate the SUGAR in the juice for FERMENTATION, which is the second step and occurs naturally when YEAST cells come into contact with sugar solutions. The new wine must then be subjected to various treatments to ensure CLARIFICATION and STABILIZATION and various other cellar operations which are collectively called élevage before the final step, BOTTLING.

Details in this sequence of operations vary considerably with WINE TYPE and its origin. General (as opposed to local) differences of technique dictated by different sorts of wine are outlined in WHITE WINE-MAKING, RED WINE-MAKING, ROSÉ WINE-MAKING, SWEET WINE-MAKING, SPARKLING WINE-MAKING, and under the names of various FORTIFIED WINES. One of the most obvious is the stage at which the juice is separated from the skins by PRESSING (before fermentation for white wines, after fermentation for red wines).

Before fermentation, some AMELIORATION of the grape juice may needed. Since more than half the sugar in grape juice is converted to end products other than ALCOHOL (mostly CARBON DIOXIDE), a sugar concentration of about 20 per cent by weight is needed in the crushed grapes (see MUST WEIGHT) to produce a sound wine of around 11 per cent (see ALCOHOLIC STRENGTH for the practical range of alcohol levels in wine). In many cooler wine regions fermentable sugars may be added to the basic fruit juice to increase the eventual alcoholic strength (see CHAPTALIZATION). In warmer regions on the other hand, ACIDIFICATION may be permitted at some point during wine-making. Some SULPHUR DIOXIDE is almost invariably added at this stage as a disinfectant.

The application of yeast is another crucial step in wine-making. Yeasts are single-celled plants which utilize sugar in building new yeast cells. In the presence of unlimited oxygen nearly all the sugar would be converted into cells, carbon dioxide, and water, but if the yeast's access to oxygen is restricted, as in a large container, after an initial multiplication phase, the yeast switches to a second metabolic process of which the end products are mainly ETHANOL, potable alcohol, and carbon dioxide. The alcohol produced dissolves additional substances such as plant ACIDS, TANNINS, colouring and flavouring materials from the grape pulp—and skins in the case of red wines. In a very real sense, wine is a by-product of the yeasts' metabolic activity operating under less than optimum conditions. Fortunately, yeasts make a number of other attractive flavour compounds during this second, less efficient metabolic process. Heat is another product generated by the yeasts' metabolism, and REFRIGERATION may well be needed in order to control TEMPERATURE below the level at which yeasts are fatally damaged.

The new wine is usually separated from its LEES once fermentation is complete (except in the case of some white wines deliberately matured with LEES CONTACT). The normal technique is to let all the debris settle on the bottom of the container for a few days before RACKING, drawing off the wine from the top. This wine, opaque with its load of suspended yeast cells and fine debris, is further clarified, usually by FILTRATION or CENTRIFUGATION. This clarification process is often encouraged by adding a FINING agent which attracts suspended particles towards it and then helps them fall to the bottom of the container.

A second, softening fermentation, MALOLACTIC FERMENTATION, may take place in wines high in MALIC ACID, naturally or encouraged, during or after the primary alcoholic fermentation.

Other optional steps include MACERATION of skins and pulp or wine which may take place before, during, and/or after fermentation, assisted in the case of red wines by REMONTAGE. Alternative methods of vinification include CARBONIC MACERATION, THERMOVINIFICATION, CONTINUOUS FERMENTATION.

It is important to minimize the new wine's exposure to OXYGEN, whatever its colour. In older wineries this was accomplished by keeping the wine in wooden containers and TOPPING UP at frequent intervals to replace losses by evaporation. Modern inert containers such as stainless steel tanks, once filled, lose no wine by evaporation. They have the additional advantage that, when there is insufficient wine to fill a tank completely, the empty HEAD SPACE can be filled with nitrogen or carbon dioxide, thus eliminating the problem of exposure of the wine to oxygen.

A common step immediately after red wine fermentation is to rack the wine off the skins into wooden BARRELS as this aids both clarification and the MATURATION process. For the highest-quality red wines, some time in new OAK barrels is common, the shape and size of barrel, duration of stay, and proportion of total production put into new oak varying according to wine type, vintage, and the producer's aspirations. New wine is capable of dissolving considerable flavour and tannins from a new barrel during the first year. Other red wines, or these wines after a year in new oak, may be aged in used oak or larger wooden casks, or red wines may proceed directly to inert storage tanks and omit a wood-ageing stage altogether. See ÉLEVAGE for more detail of the operations required during this post-fermentation stage.

Only a small proportion of white wines are aged in wood, STAINLESS STEEL being the preferred material for both fermentation and storage. An increasing proportion of top-quality white wines (especially those made from the Chardonnay grape), however, are fermented in small oak barrels (see BARREL FERMENTATION). They may then be allowed to rest on the lees from which certain flavour characteristics may be encouraged to develop by LEES STIRRING, or *bâtonnage*. Most white wine is clarified, stabilized, and bottled early to avoid exposure to oxygen and minimize any risk of OXIDATION.

The great majority of wines, whatever their colour, are bottled before the next vintage (so that storage capacity for only one year's production is needed). Wood-matured table wines will normally be bottled within two years of the vintage, however, while many fortified and some other wines treated to exceptionally long wood maturation (such as some Italian, Spanish, and Portuguese reds) may be matured in cask for much longer than this. (See ÉLEVAGE for a more detailed account of cellar work during this period.)

Before the wine can be bottled, it may be necessary to make a selection from different lots, and to assemble these ingredients into a final blend, although the BLENDING may well have been carried out at a much earlier point in the wine's evolution. (See also ASSEMBLAGE.)

The final step in the wine-making process before bottling is to subject the wine to ANALYSIS in order to check that it is stable and meets legal requirements.

Ideally wines should be given several months' BOTTLE AGEING before dispatch to ensure stability and to allow the wine to recover from the shock of bottling and, more specifically, possible BOTTLE SICKNESS. A.D.W.

Amerine, M., and Singleton, V., *Wine: An Introduction* (2nd edn., Berkeley, Calif., 1965).

Halliday, J., and Johnson, H., *The Art and Science of Wine* (London, 1992) or *The Vintner's Art* (New York, 1992).

Rankine, B., *Making Good Wine: A Manual of Winemaking Practice for Australia and New Zealand* (Melbourne, 1989).

WINE OF ORIGIN. Superior-quality designation scheme in SOUTH AFRICA.

WINE PRESS. See PRESS for details of the equipment used during PRESSING. For the interface between wine and the press, see WINE WRITERS.

One of the more spectacular modern **wineries**, the circular *cuverie* at Ch Pichon-Longueville (Baron) in Pauillac.

WINERY, modern, essentially NEW WORLD term for the premises on which wine is made; its first recorded use was in the United States in 1882. It may mean either the entire enterprise, or it may mean specifically the building or buildings used for wine-making. The nearest French equivalent is CAVE.

WINE SOCIETY, seminal British member-owned wine club-cum-wine merchant. The International Exhibition Co-operative Wine Society (IECWS), generally known as the Wine Society, was founded in 1874 by an architect, an eye surgeon, and a prominent Customs & Excise official following a food and wine exhibition in London's Albert Hall that year. The first chairman was the Scottish nobleman the Macleod of Macleod. The objects and rules included a membership holding of one share only, no dividends to be paid on these until extinction on the member's death, and the introduction of unfamiliar wines as well as those in general use—all to be bought 'for ready money only' at the lowest possible price. The Society remained small for many years, and attained its 5,000th member only in 1922, but grew substantially between the two World Wars. The number of shares now exceeds 160,000.

The Society has always had a considerable medical membership, and many DOCTORS have served on its Committee of Management, elected solely from the membership. Prospective members are sponsored by existing members and elected by the Committee. An annual dividend of five per cent is credited annually to each member shareholder, but is paid out only on the member's death, although, with the agreement of the Committee, many shares are inherited. Edmund PENNING-ROWSELL was the Society's longest-serving chairman, from 1964 until 1987.

The Society's cellars were under the London Palladium theatre and London Bridge railway station (where the London AUCTIONEERS subsequently stored their wine) until the Society moved out of London to purpose-built and regularly extended premises in Stevenage in 1965. In the early 1990s the Wine Society was the biggest independent retail wine merchant in Britain with a turnover exceeding £22 million. The policy of cash-with-order is retained. The Society is distinguished by its far-sighted, even-handed management, the efficiency of its bureaucracy, and the quality of wine STORAGE offered to members.

WINE TASTERS. The animate sort are humans, often of widely varying abilities, experiences, preferences, and prejudices, engaged in the pursuit of wine TASTING. The inanimate sort are shallow, usually silver, saucers for tasting young wines, known in French, and often in English, as TASTEVINS.

WINE TYPES may be classified in several ways, the most usual being by alcohol level. Those whose ALCOHOLIC STRENGTH is entirely due to FERMENTATION, and is usually in the range of nine to 15 per cent, are what we tend to call simply 'wine' or sometimes 'table wine' (although TABLE WINE has a specific meaning within the EUROPEAN UNION and elsewhere, as has QUALITY WINE). Such wines may be further classified by COLOUR into RED WINES, WHITE WINES, and ROSÉ WINES. Or they may be classified according to their concentration of dissolved carbon dioxide as SPARKLING WINES, still wines, and a host of terms in between such as PERLANT and FRIZZANTE. Such wine types may also be classified according to SWEETNESS.

Wines with higher concentrations of alcohol, between 15 and just over 20 per cent, are called FORTIFIED WINES in this book since (with the exception of some DRIED GRAPE WINES) they owe some of their alcoholic strength to the process of FORTIFICATION, or the addition of spirit. PORT and SHERRY are the best known of these wines, officially called 'vins de liqueur' in EU terminology. This higher-strength category also includes sweet alcoholic drinks made by adding grape spirit to fermenting grape juice at various points, for details of which see VIN DOUX NATUREL and VIN DE LIQUEUR as well as MISTELLE.

Wines which have been deliberately manipulated so that their alcohol levels are particularly low, say below 5.5 per cent, are sometimes called LOW ALCOHOL wines. (Some regular wines, such as MOSCATO D'ASTI and lighter SAAR wines, may have a natural alcoholic strength of between five and 9 per cent.)

Wine types may also be loosely, and somewhat subjectively, classified according to when they are drunk into APERITIF wines (sometimes called 'appetizer wines'), 'food wines' or 'dinner wines', and SWEET WINES or dessert wines.

Although geographical classifications are of wines not wine types, once-popular GENERIC wines represent an attempt at a geographical classification of wine types.

WINE WRITING, a parasitical activity enabled by vine-growing and wine-making but more usually associated with wine TASTING, and even wine drinking, than with either of the former. For an analysis of wine books through the ages, see LITERATURE OF WINE.

Since the 1970s, however, wine writing has escaped the restrictions of hard covers and can now be found in a wide variety of more ephemeral publications: from academic journals through specialist journals and newsletters and general interest magazines to newspapers of even the most populist sort. By the early 1980s, for probably the first time ever, it was possible, with luck and hard work, to make a living as a wine writer with no other source of income.

Even writers well known in other fields such as the English novelist Julian Barnes and columnist Auberon Waugh, and American investigative writer James Conaway, paid wine writers the compliment of dabbling in their chosen specialist subject.

By the 1990s, many women's magazines had replaced their wine columns with increased coverage of the health issues which so preoccupied them. An increasing proportion of the words written about wine resembled shopping lists rather than literature, and there were signs, from book publishers at least, that wine writing was likely to become an increasingly specialist activity.

WINKLER, ALBERT JULIUS, (1894–1989) scientist at the University of California at DAVIS whose name (and that of Maynard AMERINE) is commonly associated with a particular method of CLIMATE CLASSIFICATION involving heat summation whereby California was divided into five viticultural regions Regions I (the coolest) to V (the warmest). He edited *General Viticulture*, published in 1962 and revised in 1974, which was for long considered the most comprehensive book on viticulture in the English language.

WINTER FREEZE, a climatic stress which can be lethal to parts or all of the vine. In areas of high latitude and high altitude the risk of very cold winter weather is high, particularly in continental climates away from the moderating effects of oceans (although even in maritime climates winter freeze can kill thousands of vines in exceptionally cold winters such as that of 1956 in ST-ÉMILION and POMEROL). Such CONTINENTAL climates typically show colder temperatures, but also greater temperature range. Cold-hardy varieties, such as the American vine CONCORD, can be grown in the mid western United States in sites with annual minimum temperatures of −29 °C/−20 °F occurring once in three years. European VINIFERA varieties sensitive to cold require relatively warmer sites, however, where annual minimum temperatures of −20 °C (−4 °F) are recorded no more than once in a decade. CROWN GALL disease commonly develops on vines injured by winter freeze.

An essential first step towards avoiding winter freeze injury is wise SITE SELECTION. Sites which export cold air, such as those on free-standing hills, can avoid winter injury by being up to 5 °C/9 °F warmer than sites which import cold air, such as those on valley floors. Vineyard sites within a few kilometres of large bodies of water (such as the MÉDOC) are also preferred because of the moderating effects on temperature. Selecting varieties with noted winter hardiness is also important. Varieties such as CHARDONNAY and RIESLING are more winter hardy than PINOT NOIR, CHASSELAS, and CABERNET SAUVIGNON. In turn, *Vitis vinifera* is less hardy than some interspecific HYBRIDS such as SEYVAL, which in turn are less winter hardy than such American varieties as DELAWARE and CONCORD. Choice of ROOTSTOCKS which avoid stress is also critical for vine survival.

The vine's reserves of CARBOHYDRATES act like a biological antifreeze. The aim of vine management to avoid winter stress is to achieve maximum carbohydrate reserves at the end of the growing season. This entails choice of suitable TRAINING SYSTEM, appropriately severe PRUNING level, and THINNING so as to restrict YIELD, which, when excessive, can act to reduce levels of vine carbohydrates. Management of IRRIGATION and COVER CROPS or WEEDS to develop mild WATER STRESS to reduce late season shoot growth and hasten CANE RIPENING is desirable; late season shoot growth dramatically increases the likelihood of vine death as a result of low winter temperatures.

An alternative strategy to avoid winter kill is to bury the vines in autumn (see WINTER PROTECTION below). R.E.S.

Howell, S. A., 'Cultural manipulation of vine cold hardiness', in R. E. Smart, *et al.* (eds.), *Proceedings of the Second International Symposium for Cool Climate Viticulture and Oenology: 11–15 January 1988 Auckland, New Zealand* (Auckland, 1988).

WINTER PROTECTION, cumbersome viticultural technique aimed at protecting vines in cold, continental climates against the effects of WINTER FREEZE. Vines are buried in autumn to benefit from the fact that winter temperatures below the soil surface are never more than a few °C below freezing point, whereas the air temperature can be more than 20 °C/36 °F colder. Burying vines is, however, labour-intensive and expensive. This was traditionally practised in central Europe and North America, but is uncommon now because of the expense. Only in the vineyards of RUSSIA, parts of the UKRAINE, and central Asia is it still considered an acceptable price to pay for viticulture. The procedure has been modified so that just those few canes to be used for fruiting the following year are buried. Vines are also trained so that they have several trunks, so that those killed in winter can easily be replaced. See fan shaped TRAINING SYSTEMS. R.E.S.

WINZER, which is the German equivalent of the French vigneron, is a common prefix in Germany for a CO-OPERATIVE wine cellar, as in **Winzergenossenschaft**, **Winzerverein**, and **Winzervereinigung**.

WIRE, used to form vine trellis systems, along with POSTS. The widespread use of wire has revolutionized trellising of vines, since it is now possible to train vines to forms which maximize their production and MECHANIZATION. High-tensile wire can support very heavy loads without breaking, and wire can be galvanized to give it long life. Normally, thicker wire is used to support the weight of grapes in a trellis, and thinner wires to support foliage. The use of wire in fencing and for telegraph and wire rope in the 1840s lead to its more widespread availability, and galvanized wire has been used for farming since its introduction in England in 1851. See TRELLIS SYSTEMS and TRAINING SYSTEMS. R.E.S.

WOOD has been the most popular material for wine CONTAINERS both for transport and storage for centuries and even today trees are almost as important to some wines as vines. Merchants in Ancient ARMENIA shipped wine down the Tigris in palm-wood casks seven centuries BC, according to HERODOTUS. Wooden BARRELS eventually succeeded AMPHORAE as containers for both shipping and storage in the 3rd century AD.

It was not until the mid 20th century, however, that wood was irrevocably replaced by the bottle and tanker for shipment and widely replaced by inert materials such as cement and STAINLESS STEEL for storage and FERMENTATION. For fine wines, wood is still valued as the prime material for maturing (see BARREL MATURATION and CASK AGEING) and for fermenting certain types of white wine (see BARREL FERMENTATION).

The chemistry of wine's maturation in wood is still not fully understood but experience shows that wood (unlike amphorae and sealed tanks made of inert materials) inevitably exposes the wine to a certain amount of OXYGEN, and actively aids CLARIFICATION and STABILIZATION of the wine matured in it—quite apart from the wide range of flavours and characteristics which may be added and transformed as a result of exposure to that particular wood, either directly as WOOD FLAVOUR or indirectly as WOOD INFLUENCE.

See also WOOD TYPES.

Wood also plays a part in viticulture, not just because the vine's own wood is important (see CANE and TRUNK), but also because wood is a common material for POSTS and STAKES in the vineyard.

For more detail of wood structure, see CAMBIUM and XYLEM.

Guimberteau, G. (ed.), *Le Bois et la qualité des vins et eaux-de-vie* (Martillac, 1992).

WOOD ALCOHOL. Alternative name for harmful METHANOL.

WOOD FLAVOUR. The wood in which a wine is fermented and/or aged has a profound and often complex effect on its characteristics and flavour (see WOOD INFLUENCE). Certain substances present in wood may also be directly extracted and absorbed, without change, into the wine, however. Those extractable substances identified in OAK, the most commonly used wood, are listed below.

Lactones These compounds are responsible for what is generally called the aroma of oak, or 'oakiness', described as coconut-like. Toasting of the wood (see TOAST) may also increase this flavour. Open-air seasoning of the STAVES prior to BARREL MAKING generally decreases the lactones. These compounds can easily overpower a wine's inherent AROMA.

Phenolic aldehydes Vanillin is the best-known member of this group. Toasting increases the level of these, as does seasoning in the open air. BARREL FERMENTATION reduces their level.

Volatile phenols These impart a spice-like character reminiscent of cloves or carnations. These decrease with seasoning of the oak.

Terpenes These essential oils important in fruit, tea, and perfume are found in American oak and to a lesser degree in some French oak. It is likely but as yet unproven that they have flavour effects. This was a particularly active area of wine research in the early 1990s.

Carbohydrate degradation products This is a large and complex group that includes furfurals, which are produced from toasting wood sugars and have a bitter almond flavour. Maltol and cyclotene are also produced from the toasting process and not only have caramel-like flavours of their own, but also act as flavour potentiators. Like monosodium glutamate with food, these potentiators increase the perception of other flavours.

Tannins and other phenolics TANNINS and other PHENOLICS give colour and astringency but more importantly act as a reservoir to balance the oxidative/reductive reactions of the wine, protecting it from OXIDATION and lessening the chance of unpleasant REDUCTIVE aromas.

It is worth noting that wine in the barrel is biologically active. The YEASTS that affect the FERMENTATION of sugars to alcohol also transform some of these directly extracted oak compounds into other compounds with flavours different from the original. The furfurals, for instance, which have a bitter flavour when originally extracted, are transformed by the yeasts into compounds which have a range of flavours from smoked meat to leather. BACTERIA are also active in wine and, in the case of white wines, the barrel contributes compounds which bacteria can transform from relatively flavourless to highly aromatic ones reminscent of smoke, cloves, and coffee.

Those who cannot afford to extract their wood flavour from BARRELS may use OAK CHIPS or even OAK ESSENCE. L.B.

WOOD INFLUENCE. If a wine is fermented or matured in a wooden container, many different aspects of that container may shape its character and flavour, quite apart from those compounds that may be directly extracted from the oak and absorbed into the wine as WOOD FLAVOUR. The most obvious advantage of holding a wine in wood (see BARREL MATURATION and CASK AGEING) rather than an inert material is that wood encourages natural CLARIFICATION and STABILIZATION. The precise influence of a wooden container on any wine held in it is a function of the way that wine was made as well as of the following aspects.

Wood type

Barrels and tanks have been made from a variety of WOOD TYPES, although OAK is generally preferred. The exact choice of wood, or even oak, type can have a powerful effect on flavour and structure.

Manufacturing techniques

Several aspects of BARREL MAKING can have a marked impact on wine flavour. One particularly controversial issue is whether barrels made from hand-split staves are perceptibly superior to their counterparts made from sawn oak; carefully controlled research in this area is rare.

The method of drying the wood can also affect wine character. Wines, particularly wines naturally low in tannins themselves, can taste aggressively tannic after being matured in barrels made from kiln-dried, as opposed to air-dried, wood. It has been assumed that air drying extracts some wood TANNINS in a process illustrated by the black deposit left on the ground but Australian research by Sefton (see below) suggests that seasoning may be a much more complex process than was previously thought, with seasoning affecting not the actual level of tannins, but their sensory effect. Certainly the role played by wood tannins, which constitute as much as 10 per cent of the dry matter in oak, is not yet fully understood.

In an Australian study, lots of the same wood were dried in Australia and in France. The Australian lot, dried under hot and dry conditions, was analysed and compared to the lot aged in France under cool and moist conditions. As the rate of chemical reactions increases dramatically with temperature rise, differences were to be expected. It seems that the concentration of so-called 'whiskey' lactones (see WOOD FLAVOUR) was much higher in wood dried in Australia.

The degree to which the staves are heated while being bent, or barrel TOAST, has an obvious and profound effect on flavour. The more slowly this is done the better it is for both flavour and structure of a wine matured in that barrel. A deep medium toast produces the most desirable character for most woods, but there is variation in effect depending on geographic origin of the wood.

Size of container

The larger the container, the lower the ratio of surface area to volume will be. Barrels holding less than 190 l/50 gal can overwhelm wine with WOOD FLAVOURS. Containers holding more than 570 l/150 gal will provide little wood flavour, particularly after their first use. (See BARREL TYPES for detail of barrel sizes most commonly used.)

The use of large wooden VATS or tanks for wine has largely fallen out of favour since the advent of STAINLESS STEEL and other inert materials, because the latter are much easier to clean than wood and because TEMPERATURE is so difficult to control in large-volume wooden containers. A few top Bordeaux properties (Ch MARGAUX and MOUTON-ROTHSCHILD, for example) still use large oak vats for red wine FERMENTATION, as do some Burgundy and Rhône producers. Many of Italy's and some of Germany's and Alsace's most revered wines are the product of CASK AGEING in large, old wooden casks. Proponents of such wooden vats note that some of the greatest wines in the world are made in them and suggest that ageing in large wooden tanks provides a gentle oxygenation of the wine and, hence, a desirable form of pre-bottling maturation.

Age of container

Barrels may be valued simply because they are containers made from a material that clarifies and stabilizes the wine naturally, offers the wine some mild but useful useful oxygenation, or also because they can actually add WOOD FLAVOUR to the wine. The newer the barrel, the more wood flavour it is capable of imparting and in most wine regions new barrels command a premium, with one-year-old barrels selling for approximately 70 per cent, two-year-old barrels selling for less than 50 per cent, and five-year-old barrels selling for just 10 per cent of the cost of a new barrel.

New barrels may be the most expensive but they are not necessarily valued most highly by all wine-makers. Their strongly oaky flavour can overwhelm subtle wines and some wine-makers, especially in Burgundy, deliberately minimize this effect by using only a small proportion of new barrels or by 'breaking in' new barrels by using them on lesser wines.

Within a given type and style of wine, the richest wines will absorb the most oak with positive effects.

New barrels are used systematically for good vintages of classed growth red bordeaux and therefore for a high proportion of CABERNET SAUVIGNON (and CHARDONNAY) made by ambitious and well-funded wine-makers in newer wine regions. They are used with more moderation elsewhere.

Older barrels are important for wines where the wine-maker seeks slow oxygenation of the wine but no perceptible wood flavour, such as in making PORT, SHERRY, and, in many cases, RIOJA. Wine-makers here will often break in new barrels with lesser wines.

Time

Time remains the wine-maker's greatest tool. A wine's character is also influenced by how long it remains in wood, which, in the case of new oak, can vary from about two months for relatively light white wines to two years or even three in the case of a top-quality SAUTERNES. More traditionally minded producers in Spain, Italy, and Portugal may keep wines in old wooden cooperage for even longer. VEGA SICILIA, for example, may be matured for 10 years in barrel and some BRUNELLO DI MONTALCINO is given four years' CASK AGEING.

Vintage

The character of individual vintages also affects how they react to wood and therefore the influence of any wood on a wine's flavour. Wines, especially red wines, vary so much from vintage to vintage that it is impossible to specify the perfect barrel for a given wine. For this reason, many wine-makers order a range of different WOOD TYPES and with variation of TOAST in anticipation of each harvest. With white wines, which contain far fewer FLAVOUR COMPOUNDS than reds, the choices can be more specific.

Wine-making techniques

Up to this point our concerns have been with direct flavour effects from the oak, but equally important are the indirect or secondary flavour effects that are more the result of the wooden tank's or barrel's environment. For more details, see CASK AGEING and BARREL MATURATION respectively. White wines fermented in barrel may be changed enormously in character. For more details, see BARREL FERMENTATION.

Storage conditions

Exact temperature and humidity, even draughts, can affect the character of a wine held in a wooden container. For more details see BARREL MAINTENANCE. L.B. & M.K.

Naudin, R., *L'Élevage des vins de Bourgogne en fûts neufs* (Beaune, 1989).

Sefton, M. A., 'How does oak barrel maturation contribute to wine flavor?', *Australian and NZ Industry Journal* (Feb., 1991).

—— *et al.*, 'Influence of seasoning on the sensory characteristics and composition of oak extracts', in *International Oak Symposium* (San Francisco, 1993).

Singleton, V. L., 'Some aspects of the wooden container as a factor in wine maturation', in *Chemistry of Winemaking*, American Chemical Society (Washington, DC, 1974).

WOOD TYPES. Over the years many different kinds of wood have been used to make small BARRELS and larger VATS and casks. Acacia, cypress, chestnut, ash, redwood, pine, eucalyptus, and poplar are just a few of the woods that have been used.

Chestnut has long been popular for large oval casks in the Rhône, Beaujolais, and in parts of Italy and Portugal, but as this wood offers strong TANNINS and is also relatively porous, chestnut barrels and tanks are often coated with paraffin or silicone to neutralize the wood. Wines made in unlined new chestnut barrels can be so tannic as to be undrinkable.

In other countries pine, eucalyptus, and acacia have been used for casks, but these woods produce wines with flavours that strike many consumers as odd unless the wood is very well seasoned (see BARREL MAKING) or coated on the inside. In Chile the local evergreen beech, or *rauli*, wood is being replaced by more subtle, better-quality oak. Redwood was used for large upright tanks in America for many years, although very few have been built since the early 1970s. Redwood is rarely made into barrels because the wood is difficult to bend and the flavours are aggressive. Since the advent of neutral STAINLESS STEEL and enamel-lined tanks, wooden COOPERAGE must offer something extra to the wine to be worth the premium.

By far the most popular wood type in use in wine-making today is OAK, which has none of the disadvantages outlined above and whose particular aspects of WOOD INFLUENCE and WOOD FLAVOUR have come to be appreciated by both wine-makers and wine drinkers. M.K.

WORCESTER, hot inland wine region in SOUTH AFRICA.

WORLD PRODUCTION of wine is concentrated in two bands of generally TEMPERATE to MEDITERRANEAN CLIMATE in each hemisphere, as shown on the map pp. 1076–7. Although there are parts of the Far East which could still be developed for viticulture, total annual rainfall is generally too high. For more details see CLIMATE AND WINE QUALITY.

For details of the amounts of wine produced in various continents and countries of the world, see PRODUCTION. See also CONSUMPTION of wine.

WÜRTTEMBERG, relatively large wine region in southern GERMANY with 9,700 ha / 24,192 acres of vineyard which loosely follow the River Neckar and its tributaries (see map on p. 442). The main part of the region lies between Stuttgart and Heilbronn with the vineyards to the north mingling with those of BADEN. Steep and expensive-to-maintain terraced slopes look down on the Neckar. Besides being valued for the quality of their wine, these TERRACES add interest to the landscape and attract tourists. Where the gradient is greater than 30 per cent, IRRIGATION is allowed, which, by assisting PHOTOSYNTHESIS, can increase the POTENTIAL ALCOHOL content of the grape must by over one per cent. The regional climate varies from south to north, but is at its most CONTINENTAL in the BEREICH **Kocher-Jagst-Tauber**, where winters can be severe.

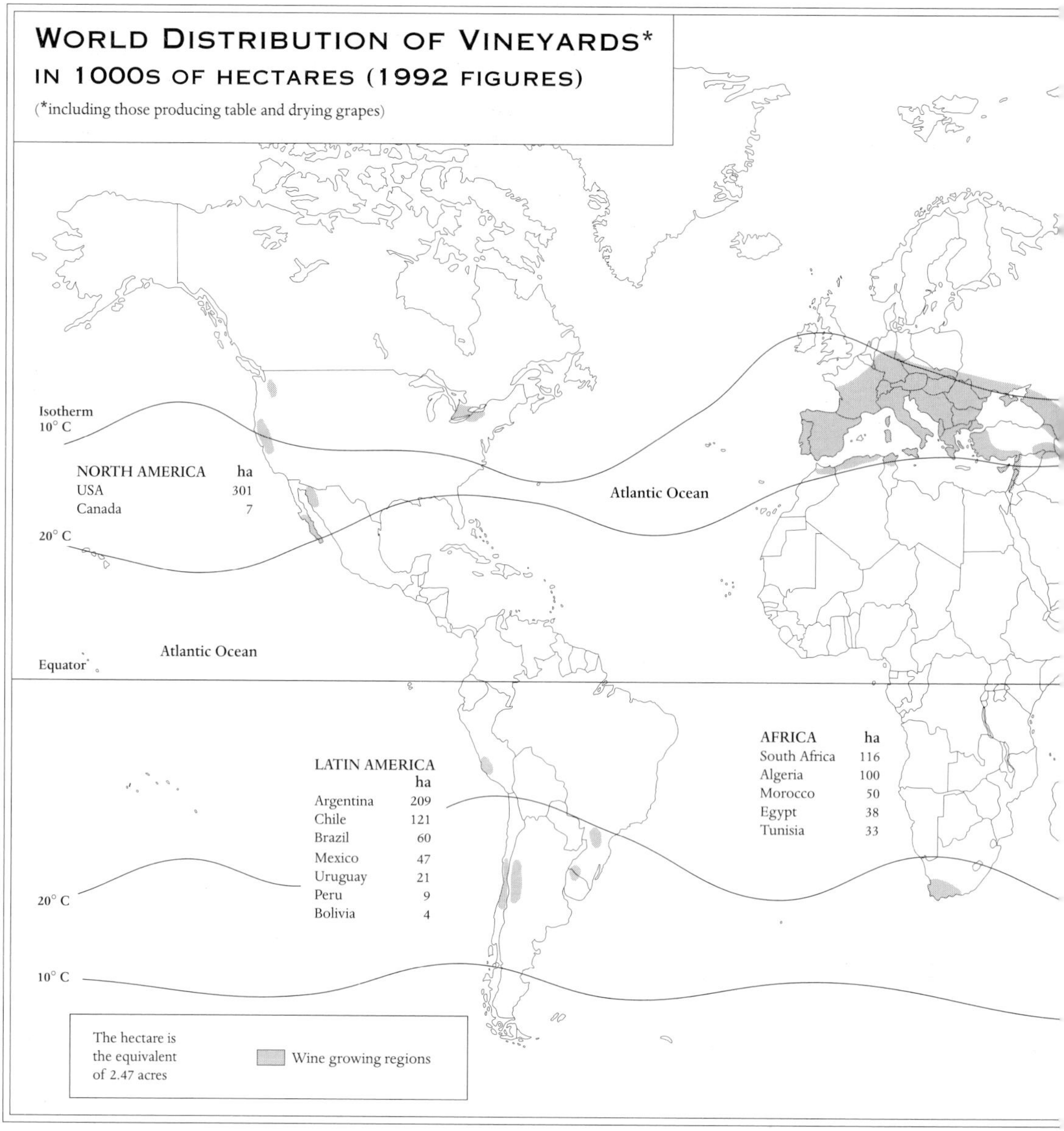

A quarter of the region is planted in RIESLING, with that produced at Flein, a few kilometres south of Heilbronn, enjoying much local esteem. Of the remaining white wine varieties, KERNER and MÜLLER-THURGAU both occupy about nine per cent of the area under vine. Of the red wine varieties, TROLLINGER is the most important followed by Müllerrebe (MEUNIER), known to the Württembergers as Schwarzriesling.

Most Württemberg red wine is a law unto itself. In the admittedly abundant 1989 vintage, the 1,526 ha of Trollinger in the Bereich **Württembergisch Unterland** produced an average yield of 222 hl/ha (12.6 tons/acre), and the figure for Spätburgunder (PINOT NOIR) was 149 hl/ha (nearly three times the yield allowed in BURGUNDY). With a crop of this magnitude red wine cannot be judged by normal international standards: most is extremely pale and has little backbone or perceptible TANNINS, but that is how the locals like it. Their per capita wine consumption is the highest in Germany, and although two-thirds of the wine drunk in the region is imported from elsewhere, there has yet to be a surplus of Württemberg red wine.

Of the 20,000 registered vine-growers, fewer than 3,000 own more than 1 ha/2.47 acres, so CO-OPERATIVE cellars are

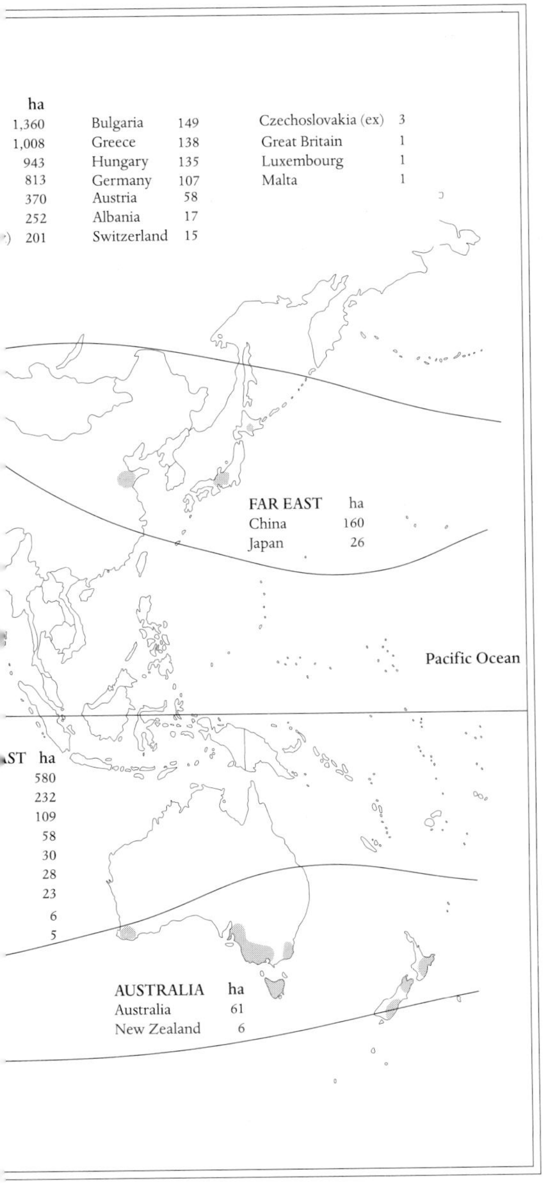

necessary. They handle over 80 per cent of the grape harvest: 64 operate as pressing stations for the central caller at Möglingen and 34 village co-operatives bottle their own wine. There is a small number of ancient and highly regarded state- and privately owned estates, of which 13 are members of the prestigious association the Verband Deutscher Prädikatsweingüter, or VDP. The best of their wines are serious and comparable in quality to those from good wine-makers in Baden. I.J.

WÜRZER is a Gewürztraminer × Müller-Thurgau crossing made at the German viticultural station of Alzey in 1932 and only planted in any significant quantity in the 1980s, at the end of which there were just over 100 ha / 247 acres, mainly in Rheinhessen. It is overpoweringly heady, yields well, but a little goes a very long way indeed.

X

XAREL-LO, white grape variety producing powerful still and sparkling wines in its native CATALONIA. It is particularly important in ALELLA, where it is known as Pansa Blanca. It is most commonly found in PENEDÈS, however, where, with Parellada and Macabeo, it makes up most CAVA blends. The vine is very vigorous and productive and buds early so is prone to spring frost damage. It needs careful pruning and the wine it produces can be very strongly flavoured.

XENOPHON, writer in Ancient GREECE in the late 5th century BC famous for his *Anabasis*. In the *Economics*, a dialogue between a farmer, Ischomachos, and the famous philosopher Socrates, the planting and care of vines is discussed: vines should be planted in well-dug earth, at an angle, and the earth should be trodden down around the vine. H.H.A.

XÉRÈS, French name for both JEREZ and SHERRY.

XERES, is the name of a variety available in California and exported to Australia thought to be the same as Rioja's GRACIANO.

XYLEM, the principal water-conducting tissue in vascular plants. In woody stem tissues, the secondary xylem forms the wood. The CAMBIUM differentiates xylem tissue on its inside. A single ring of xylem is produced each year with the first-formed vessels (in spring) being larger than those of late wood. This is how the annual rings which help to assess the age of a plant are formed (see OAK). In the grapevine, the vessels are large and porous so that its wood is very water conductive, a feature of vines generally. In autumn, however, vessels may become blocked by structures which plug the tubes, called tyloses, formed by the 'ballooning' of adjacent cell material into the vessel through pits in the walls; some vessels remain functional for up to seven years, but most become blocked by tyloses in their second or third year. The secondary xylem of QUERCUS forms the wood from which oak barrels are made. (See also PHLOEM.) B.G.C.

XYNISTERI, white grape variety commonly grown on the island of CYPRUS.

XYNOMAVRO, black grape variety grown all over northern GREECE as far south as the foothills of Mount Olympus, where Rapsani is produced. Its name means 'acid black' and the wines can indeed seem harsh in youth but they age well, as mature examples of Naoussa can demonstrate. One of the few Greek vine varieties which may not reach full ripeness in some years, it is blended with a small proportion of the local Negoska to produce Goumenissa and is also used as a base for sparkling wine on the exceptionally cool, high vineyards of Amindeo.

Y

YARRA VALLEY, cool and dynamic wine region just north east of Melbourne, the capital of Victoria in AUSTRALIA. For more detail see VICTORIA.

YEAST, single-celled agent vital to the FERMENTATION process which, starved of oxygen, transforms grape juice to wine. SUGARS are used as an energy source by yeast, with ALCOHOL and CARBON DIOXIDE as by-products of the reactions.

The word yeast (which may be singular or plural unless it encompasses yeasts from more than one species) is an old one whose meaning has changed significantly with the flowering of microbiological science. It originally derived from an ancient word meaning to boil, to seethe, or to be troubled. In 16th century English it referred to the froth on the top of a brewing tank and to the semi-solid material that could be collected both from that froth and from the bottom of the tank. From the mid 17th century, the meaning changed to that now current, by which yeast refers to a single-celled plant, a *thallophyte* and one of the lowest members of the vegetable kingdom along with algae, lichens, and fungi.

Nomenclature

The nomenclature of various yeasts is far from straightforward. Taxonomists, scientists who classify and name plants and animals, have traditionally had difficulty with the various micro-organisms because early microscopes revealed little detail, and because the appearance of an organism depended on the conditions of its growth, isolation, and preparation for observation. The result has been that names have changed over time as laboratory equipment improved and as new techniques were perfected.

Saccharomyces cerevisiae is the name now most frequently used for the yeast involved in making wine and beer and in leavening bread. *Saccharomyces*, the genus, means 'sugar fungus', and *cerevisiae* derives from the same root as 'cereals'. Older literature frequently called this yeast *Saccharomyces ellipsoideus* because the cells appeared more elliptical than circular. Within this yeast species are several hundred different strains or selections, each with real or fancied minor differences. Another species within the same genus, *Saccharomyces uvarum*, is often used in the distilling and brewing industries.

Cultured versus ambient yeast

Studies have shown that in long-established wine regions a number of other yeast genera are naturally present in significant populations and frequently participate in the wine-making process. Contrary to popular belief, such yeast are found not on grape skins but are airborne (Duncan could find yeast only in very small quantities on the brown speck at the base of ripe grapes, presumably as a result of water, containing yeast, draining off the berries). Spread around wineries and vineyards by insects, particularly FRUIT FLIES, these are collectively known as **wild yeast**, among which the most common genera are *Hansenula*, *Klöckera*, *Pichia*, and *Torulopsis*. More sensitive to SULPHUR DIOXIDE, and intolerant of an ALCOHOLIC STRENGTH much above five per cent, these wild yeast are generally active during the early stages of 'spontaneous fermentations', those occurring when no sulphur dioxide and no specially cultivated cultured yeast (see below) is added to the grape juice. Fortunately, there are usually enough *Saccharomyces cerevisiae* cells present with the wild yeast with the grapes as they come into the winery from the vineyard so that these latter yeast continue the fermentation above the unstable alcoholic strength of five per cent, depleting the supply of sugar and producing a stable wine. Once a winery begins to use wild yeast consistently, returning POMACE and LEES to vineyard soils to encourage the process, the wild yeast population tends to stabilize with a particular mixture of yeasts suitable for wine fermentation so that **ambient yeast** may be a more appropriate term. Such mixtures of yeast genera and species, often called **'natural yeast'**, have been much more commonly used in the traditional wine regions of Europe than cultured yeast.

The majority of New World wine-makers, however, and certainly all of those worried about minimizing risk, use **cultured yeast**, sometimes called **pure culture** or **inoculated yeast**. The advantage of cultured yeasts, of which only one strain is usually added, is that it has been specially selected (from ambient yeasts) so that its behaviour is predictable and the fermentation will proceed smoothly and, of most importance, to completion without the risk of a STUCK FERMENTATION. Individual wine-makers often favour certain strains of cultured yeast, often for practical WINE-MAKING reasons. The differences in the wines produced may often be too small to be detected by the average consumer.

The advantage of a well-adapted population of ambient or natural yeast is that there are many different strains and, because of their different abilities and aptitudes, they may be capable of producing a wine with a wider range of flavours and characteristics, a phenomenon that some wine-makers believe is even more marked when, as is increasingly the case, LEES CONTACT is encouraged. Such a view had not been confirmed by science in the mid 1990s, however, partly because of the difficulty of working with mixed culture fermentations and the difficulties of identification of the yeasts involved.

Cultured yeast characteristics
Yeast are cultured in large sterile tanks with vigorous aeration. They are then filtered, washed, dried, and packed in sterile containers for transfer to the winery (or brewery or bakery). Following use in wine-making, the yeast and grape debris are freed of as much wine as possible and most frequently discarded. A minor proportion may be processed to recover alcohol, TARTRATES, and occasionally grapeseed oil.

Among the many genera of yeast, there are astounding variations in terms of the production and tolerance of alcohol, aroma and flavour, rate of fermentation, temperature tolerance, flocculation characteristics, sulphur dioxide tolerance, reducing potential, and micro-nutrient requirements. Although some wild yeasts cannot tolerate alcohol concentrations above five per cent, some yeasts can tolerate concentrations of more than 20 per cent, for example (although a tolerance of up to 15 or 16 per cent is the norm for yeasts used in the production of table wine). Yeast with a high alcohol production and tolerance may be chosen for FORTIFICATION; yeast which flocculate particularly well, such as that called Épernay, may be used for SPARKLING WINE-MAKING; while a yeast with good tolerance of sulphur dioxide may be useful in certain examples of SWEET WINE-MAKING. Some cultured yeast strains are known internationally while others may be used merely locally.

How yeast works
Yeast, like most living organisms, need a carbon source, a good supply of NITROGEN, a few MINERALS, and a few trace substances or VITAMINS for growth and reproduction. Six-carbon SUGARS are the usual carbon source. AMINO ACIDS or ammonia most often supply the nitrogen. And most fruit juices, and certainly grape juice, can provide the MINERALS and VITAMINS necessary for growth. Wine yeast can also use SUCROSE. Nutrients such as diammonium phosphate based on nitrogen or vitamins may be specially added as growth factors to encourage yeast activity at the beginning of fermentation, especially in the case of ROT or underripe grapes.

In order to exist, to grow, and to produce more cells, the yeast cell needs energy which it can obtain from the GLUCOSE and FRUCTOSE of grape juice by a series of fairly complicated biochemical reactions known as **glycolosis**. This nearly universal process among living organisms is so complex and involves so many steps that it has taken scientists years of research for elucidation. Using its internal enzymes, the yeast cell splits the six-carbon sugar into one, PYRUVATE. From this glycolysis reaction series yeast obtain only a relatively small amount of energy.

If generous amounts of oygen are available, yeast will convert pyruvate nearly completely to carbon dioxide and water and harvest the maximum amount of the sugar's available energy. If limited amounts of oxygen are present, however, as in a large FERMENTATION VESSEL, the yeast have to use a considerably less efficient pathway (called FERMENTATION) which produces alcohol and CARBON DIOXIDE. (In small fermentation vessels, there is more oxygen per unit of sugar, resulting in poorer conversion of sugar to alcohol. This is why fermentation valves allowing carbon dioxide out but not oxygen in are used in HOME WINE-MAKING.) In this fermentative decomposition of pyruvate, the first step is removal of the terminal carbon dioxide from the pyruvate, leaving the two-carbon fragment ACETALDEHYDE. Acetaldehyde is then converted to ethyl alcohol and the carbon dioxide escapes as bubbles out of the fermentation vessel.

When the yeast have converted all of the sugar they die, flocculate, and fall to the bottom as gross LEES. In bottle-fermented sparkling wines, the interaction between this sediment and the wine in the bottle is an important element in SPARKLING WINE-MAKING (see AUTOLYSIS).

See also STUCK FERMENTATION, FILM-FORMING YEASTS, and FLOR.

A.D.W. & J.Ro.

Duncan, B., 'Grape epiflora at maturity with special reference to the stylar remnant', *Australian Grapegrower & Winemaker* (Apr. 1984).

Kunkee, R., 'The molds and yeasts of grapes and wines', in *Technology of Wine Making* (4th edn., Westport, Conn., 1979).

YECLA, wine zone in the LEVANTE, central south east Spain, producing mainly rather coarse red wines. Sandwiched between JUMILLA, ALICANTE, and ALMANSA (see map on p. 907), Yecla is dominated by La Purísima, the single largest co-OPERATIVE in Spain. The red MONASTRELL represents 80 per cent of all grapes grown in the region and, with a little help from GARNACHA, it has traditionally produced big, alcoholic wines for blending. A few smaller producers have turned their back on DOBLE PASTA production and are making fresher, lighter, wines using CARBONIC MACERATION.

R.J.M.

YELLOW MOSAIC, vine disease. See FANLEAF DEGENERATION.

YEMA BUD, alternative name for CHIP BUDDING.

YIELD, an important statistic in wine production, which measures how much a vineyard produces. It has been a subject of intense interest from at least the time of classical ROME.

Factors affecting yield
Vineyard yield depends on many factors, which will be briefly described here. For a more complete discussion see the individual factors listed.

Yield may be measured as either a weight of grapes or a volume of wine (see below), and is usually considered per unit area of vineyard, since this is what matters in farming economics. Those who believe that increasing VINE DENSITY is associated with improved wine quality argue that yield per vine is a more important consideration. Disciples of CANOPY MANAGEMENT, on the other hand, argue that the amount of sunlit leaf area per unit of land is more important than yield per vine.

Yield per vine depends on VINE AGE (very old vines often produce very little), the way the vines have been managed, and on the WEATHER over at least the last two years, together with other factors such as VINE PESTS and VINE DISEASES. Yield per vine depends on the number of bunches per vine, and the average bunch weight. The number of bunches per vine depends on the winter PRUNING policy, the BUDBREAK, and the number of bunches per shoot, or FRUITFULNESS. Bunch weight depends on the number of FLOWERS per bunch, and the success of FRUIT SET in forming berries, then on the weight of individual berries.

After pruning, the weather is one of the most important factors affecting vineyard yield. Cold winters, for example, promote a high degree of budbreak, but FROSTS in spring can kill young shoots and bunches. Warm, sunny weather promotes FLOWERING and POLLINATION, but cold, wet, and windy weather can cause poor FRUIT SET. Some varieties are more prone than others to poor set. Drought conditions can also reduce fruit set, but the more common DROUGHT effect is to reduce berry size, often to less than half that of vines well supplied with water. Rain will generally increase yield as it causes berries to swell, but too much rain near harvest causes BOTRYTIS BUNCH ROT and potentially a considerable, possibly total, loss in yield.

Strangely enough, the weather the preceding season can also have an effect on yield. It has been shown that warm, sunny weather during flowering encourages BUNCH INITIATION in the buds that are forming for next growing season. So this weather pattern can prepare the vine for a high potential yield the following year.

How yield is measured

Conventional units of yield are the weight of fresh grapes per unit land area, such as tonnes/ha, or tons/acre. (One ton/acre is about 2.5 tonnes/ha.) This is the standard measurement in most NEW WORLD wine regions. Although many Italians and Swiss measure yield in weight of grapes, in most European countries production is measured in volumes of wine per unit area, normally expressed as hectolitres per hectare, or hl/ha. In many cases, this measurement is an extremely important one, often limited to a maximum (depending on the VINTAGE) specified by local regulation (see APPELLATION CONTRÔLÉE, DOC, etc. and the note below).

The two measurements interrelate, although the volume of wine produced by a given weight of grapes can vary considerably according to vine variety, individual vintage conditions, winery equipment, wine-making policy, and, most importantly, wine type. To make 100 l (1 hl) of red wine, which is fermented in the presence of grape skins that can be pressed rather harder than white grape skins, about 130 kg (0.13 tonnes) of grapes are needed. To make 100 l of white wine, 150 kg are needed (more like 160 kg for top-quality SPARKLING wine-making). Assuming an average of 140 kg of grapes per 100 l of wine, one tonne/ha is about 7 hl/ha, while one ton/acre is about 17.5 hl/ha.

Interestingly, despite its importance in measuring yield, there is no uniform approach in determining the area of a vineyard. Excluding the essential and normally cultivated areas along the ends (called headlands) and at the sides, which are indubitably part of the productive unit, effectively reduces the size of many vineyards by 10 per cent or so, and the figure may be higher for small vineyards.

Wherever grapes are bought and sold in any quantity, there is normally a government-inspected WEIGHING scale.

Yields and wine quality

A necessary connection between low yields and high-quality wine has been assumed at least since Roman times when 'Bacchus amat colles' encapsulated the prevailing belief that low-yielding HILLSIDE VINEYARDS produced the best wine. Wine law in many European countries is predicated on the same belief and the much-imitated APPELLATION CONTRÔLÉE laws of France specify maximum permitted yields for each appellation (even if an additional allowance is often permitted; see PLC).

There is little doubt that heavily cropped vines with a low LEAF TO FRUIT RATIO ripen more slowly, so that in cooler climates the fruit may not reach full RIPENESS and wine quality suffers. It is less widely understood, however, that undercropping can also adversely affect wine quality. A high leaf to fruit ratio will certainly ripen grapes, but the shaded CANOPY MICROCLIMATE will produce grapes high in POTASSIUM and PH and low in PHENOLICS and flavour.

It should also be noted that, within a given wine region (Bordeaux is a notable example), there is no correlation between size of the crop and quality of the wine. Some of the finest red bordeaux VINTAGES of the 1980s, for example, were also those in which yields were relatively high; while the lowest crop levels of the decade were recorded in lesser vintages such as 1984 and 1980.

There are countless commercial examples of relatively high average annual vineyard yields associated with low quality, however. Very high yields are common to vineyards of high vigour, which in turn is typically due to planting on very fertile (or heavily fertilized) soil, well supplied with water. High-yielding vineyards are also often in hot climates, where the climate reduces the potential for wine quality anyway. Such vineyards are commonly planted with so-called 'bulk wine' varieties which also contribute to lower quality.

Very low yields may be the deliberate result of careful pruning, SHOOT THINNING, or even CROP THINNING, but they may also be associated with excessive vine stress. This can be due, for example, to weeds, pests, or disease, or to very shallow soils and WATER STRESS (as in much of Spain, for example), and a vine that is too severely stressed will not function properly and will not produce premium wine.

The yield which a vineyard can ripen properly will depend on the VINE VARIETY, the region, vine management practices (particularly pruning and vine-TRAINING SYSTEMS), and climate as well as weather. For example, a yield of 8 tonnes/ha, or 56 hl/ha, might be considered excessive in a very cool climate, but a yield five times this figure might be easily ripened to a similar or higher sugar level in a warmer climate. Some varieties seem more prone than others to crop level effects on wine quality. PINOT NOIR is an outstanding example, as the obvious inverse relationship between yield and quality in red burgundy demonstrates.

Some specific examples

Vineyard yields vary enormously around the world and, in some regions with less dependable climates, from year to year. Among the highest reported yields are about 100 tonnes/ha for TABLE GRAPES grown on complex trellises in Israel (if their juice were made into wine, this would convert into about 1,750 hl/ha!). The Argentine vine-breeder Angel Gargiulo was in the 1970s and 1980s encouraged to breed new wine grape varieties specifically designed for the Argentine environment which can yield up to 500 hl/ha (but were commercially planted only to a very limited extent). Commercial, well-managed vineyards in irrigated desert regions in California, Australia, and Argentina can routinely produce 15 tons/acre. At the other end of the spectrum, pests, disease, drought, or bunch rot can all reduce yields to less than 1 tonne/ha, or 7 hl/ha. See Ch d'YQUEM as well as Domaine LEROY and CHAPOUTIER for some examples of particularly low yields, encouraged for the sake of wine quality.

Some attempt at calculating national average yields may be attempted using OIV statistics, although these are more reliable for some countries than for others. According to those published in 1992, and discounting those vineyards dedicated to table or drying grapes, the United States has one of the highest national average yields, at 130 hl/ha/7.4 tons/acre. Germany's average yields are notoriously high, a remarkably even average of about 100 hl/ha in the 10 years to 1991. Countries with an average yield of around 70 hl/ha include France, Argentina, Chile, Australia, and Switzerland, while Italy's average yield is slightly lower (though the figure may be depressed by the extent of compulsory DISTILLATION in the south). Austria's average yield is just over 50 hl/ha, while countries such as Spain and Greece, with dry summers and virtually no irrigation, average yields of between 20 and 30 hl/ha, as does Portugal. Yields in eastern Europe's long-neglected vineyards are also low, averaging just 15 hl/ha in both Bulgaria and the ex-Soviet Union.

Certain wine types, most red wines, for example, are more sensitive to yield. Vineyards dedicated to sparkling wines, or base wines for brandy, are in general allowed to yield rather more than those dedicated to still wine production.

From a financial point of view, high yields are attractive to vine-growers, who have traditionally been paid on the simple basis of weight (although quality factors such as MUST WEIGHT are increasingly taken into account; see PRICE of grapes). Vine-growers whose aim is to produce good-quality wine may, however, deliberately restrict yields by such measures as pruning, crop thinning, and shoot thinning. One of the most important economic issues facing modern viticulture is whether high-vigour and high-yielding vineyards can produce high-quality wine using vineyard management techniques such as CANOPY MANAGEMENT.

The fact that yields are officially limited by regulation in the two most important wine-producing countries of France and Italy has undoubtedly encouraged world-wide respect for low yields, and perhaps some inertia in researching ways of increasing both quality and quantity. It should be noted, however, that the official maxima cited in wine regulations are now almost routinely increased in France by a device called the *plafond limite de classement*, or PLC, which allows a certain increase (often 20 per cent) on the base yield according to the conditions of the year. Average yields for the top appellations of the MÉDOC in 1989 and 1990, for example, were between 55 and 60 hl/ha when the theoretical maximum yield is 45 hl/ha.

See also PRUNING. R.E.S. & J.Ro.

Coombe, B. G., and Dry, P. R., *Viticulture: i: Resources in Australia* (Adelaide, 1988).
Gargiulo, A. A., 'Quality and quantity: Are they compatible?', *Journal of Wine Research*, 2/3 (1991), 161–81.

YORK MOUNTAIN, California wine region and AVA. See SAN LUIS OBISPO.

YQUEM, CHÂTEAU D', the greatest wine of SAUTERNES and, according to the famous 1855 CLASSIFICATION, of the entire BORDEAUX region. It is sweet, golden, and apparently almost immortal.

The origin of the name is obscure, although the Germanic *aig-helm* (meaning 'to have a helmet') is claimed. Probably the first vineyard-owning family were the de Sauvages, who, from being tenants, bought the estate in 1711. It was acquired by the Lur Saluces family, who still own the property, in 1785, when the last Sauvage d'Yquem married Comte Louis-Amadée de Lur Saluces. By then the wine was very well known, for in 1787 Thomas JEFFERSON wrote to 'M. d'Yquem', asking to buy some, stating, 'I know that yours is one of the best growths of Sauterne [sic]'. It is not known when Yquem was first made with BOTRYTIZED grapes, those affected by NOBLE ROT, but this painstaking technique probably originated early in the 19th century, although very sweet bottles dating from the latter part of the 18th century have been found. In the second half of the 19th century Yquem had a world-wide reputation, not least in tsarist RUSSIA. From before the First World War until 1968 the estate was run by the Marquis Bernard de Lur Saluces but since then it has been managed by Comte Alexandre, who also owns Ch de Farques in Sauternes.

The château, dating back to the 12th century and the Renaissance, stands on the crest of a small hill, with small towers at each corner and a large inner courtyard. The vineyard on all sides extends to 90 ha/220 acres in production out of a total of 102 ha. The vines planted are 80 per cent SÉMILLON and 20 per cent of the usually more productive SAUVIGNON Blanc. Production averages 5,500 cases, a fraction of the typical output of a top red wine property in the MÉDOC. The secret of Yquem's renown is its suceptibility to noble rot, and its ability to run risks and sacrifice quantity for painstakingly upheld quality. An average of six passages, or TRIS, are made through the vineyard each year so that only the BOTRYTIS-

orses are still used in the vineyards at Ch d'**Yquem**.

fected grapes are picked. The maximum yield is 9 hl/ha .5 tons/acre), compared with the normal 25 in Sauternes. he juice is pressed three times, and then treated to three ears' BARREL MATURATION in new OAK casks. Unlike nearly all ther Sauternes it is not sold until in bottle. The cost of the hole operation makes Yquem a very expensive wine. In 1987 acilities for CRYOEXTRACTION, or freeze concentration, were ontroversially installed for use in poor vintages.

Since 1959 a dry white wine, Y, or Ygrec, has been produced ut intermittently. Notably alcoholic, it has more than a hint f a Sauternes. E.P.-R.

Olney, R., *Yquem* (Paris, 1985, and London, 1986).

YUGOSLAVIA, eastern European union of peoples that xisted for barely 60 years before breaking up amid bloodhed, privation, and extreme ethnic tension at the beginning f the post-communist era in the early 1990s.

Viticulture in this war-torn collection of tribes and states s as rich and varied in potential as the people themselves. That potential was just beginning to be realized as civil war ntervened. For ease of reference, the name Yugoslavia is still ısed here, although no political implication is intended.

Yugoslavia runs from north west to south east parallel to, and on a latitude with, ITALY. The area of major white wine production runs inland along the north east border from eastern SLOVENIA through eastern CROATIA and into the northern half of SERBIA. Most of it is on hilly land, higher and steeper in the north and more gentle around the river Danube and its tributaries north and east of Belgrade.

The best of the reds come from the south eastern third of what was Yugoslavia along the coasts of MONTENEGRO and KOSOVO and on inland to MACEDONIA and eastern Serbia.

Considerable quantities of wine of both colours is produced along the rest of the coast and islands, the vast majority of which is consumed locally. In addition, Yugoslavia has substantial BRANDY and VERMOUTH industries.

Considering the geographical proximity and similarity to Italy, Yugoslavian wines are remarkably dissimilar to those produced across the Adriatic Sea, mainly because of the differences in vine variety mix between the two countries. PHYLLOXERA came relatively late to Yugoslavia, affecting the vineyards between 1890 and 1920. As in other countries, many vineyards were pulled out and remained permanently out of production, some were replanted with local grape varieties, but many (far more than in Italy) were converted to the better French, German, and Austrian varieties which were already well known and appreciated in other parts of eastern Europe.

Wine-making practices also frequently differ from Italy's. White wine-making especially is often either more rustic or more similar to Austrian or German traditions, accentuating aroma and, occasionally, sweetness. According to winemaker choice and market demand, reds are made either light and sweet with minimal EXTRACTION, as German red wines were traditionally, or strong and heavily coloured to a more eastern taste. Although wine-making techniques are relatively unsophisticated, the better wines often benefit by being offered for sale comparatively young rather than being subjected to years of wood ageing. Both white and red grape types can show very true, fully ripened VARIETAL characteristics which are more rarely seen in many of their Italian counterparts.

Yugoslavian wine production and consumption declined in the late 1980s, after a period of stable output and consumption well in excess of 6 million hl/158 million gal a year of wine from 250,000 ha/617,500 acres of vineyards. Some 20 per cent of this area was grubbed up between 1985 and 1991 following a similar decline in consumption on the home market.

Exports, once higher than a million hl a year, also fell sharply in the late 1980s and early 1990s. One-third of wine exports had been to other eastern bloc countries, which markets virtually disappeared as these newly independent post-communist states grappled with free market economies. One or two of the larger CO-OPERATIVES in eastern Yugoslavia which had specialized in making red wines for RUSSIA found themselves in 1992 with three unsold vintages on their hands. Two-thirds of Yugoslavia's wine exports had been to more developed countries, notably Germany and the UK. Despite repeated efforts in both these countries to widen the range of styles acceptable to their markets, the German market took huge amounts of light, sweetened red wine and the UK market took little other than huge amounts of medium dry whites based on Laski Rizling (WELSCHRIESLING) grapes. Both these styles came under tremendous price pressure in their respective markets which largely precluded the suppliers from making any effort to upgrade or update their vinification methods as their competitors were doing throughout the 1980s. By the mid 1990s these competitors included other former eastern bloc countries such as BULGARIA, CZECHOSLOVAKIA, HUNGARY, and MOLDOVA, which sold well in both markets and had far more success in attracting investment from the developed countries which should also have come Yugoslavia's way in the normal course of events.

The Japanese contributed to progress in Yugoslavia by setting an example of QUALITY CONTROL and investment aid to ensure their supply of attractive wines, but did little for Yugoslav morale by using the often very good wines produced under their surveillance for blends sold under Japanese brand names (see JAPAN).

Under the communist regime, Yugoslavia's cost of living was controlled, and there was full employment, but production standards were as low as the market would bear, and individual excellence was almost completely submerged, certainly in any wine offered for export. Wineries were also starved of investment, although the International Monetary Fund did invest in certain show-place wineries such as Vranje in Serbia. Vranje started to make excellent red wine but succumbed to a regime driven by quantity rather than quality after only a couple of years.

Unlike the more hard-line communist countries, however, Yugoslavia allowed considerable private land ownership. In 1990 180,000 ha, more than 70 per cent, of Yugoslavian vineyard were recorded as being in private hands. In spite of this, most of the wine is made by co-operative wineries or by the bottling and brand-owning companies which also own vineyards and were in turn owned or controlled indirectly by the state. Each of these companies had their own ties with specific co-operatives, giving the industry a level of protection on the home market, but leaving them in keen competition abroad. A 1988 publication promoted by the industry as a whole listed 36 such companies.

One or two private wine producers began to emerge from the more peaceful parts of Slovenia and Croatia in the early 1990s and it is to be hoped that their attempts to improve standards are heeded.

In 1993, erstwhile Yugoslavia seemed at least to be splitting up into components which corresponded reasonably well to the boundaries of the wine regions previously defined by state law. For more details, therefore, see (roughly from north to south) under SLOVENIA, CROATIA, VOJVODINA, SERBIA, KOSOVO, MONTENEGRO, BOSNIA HERCEGOVINA, and MACEDONIA.

Viticulture and climate

In most of the vineyards, with the exception of some of the coastal regions, the vines are trained along trellised rows. Although labour has been plentiful and cheap, vineyards are designed wherever possible to permit the passage of tractors for cultivation and treatment purposes. Pruning and harvesting remain almost entirely manual.

Training systems vary from double GUYOT through to LENZ MOSER and density of plantation follows suit. Distances between rows are usually fairly wide except on the more traditionally planted hillsides, where vines may even be trained up their own individual stake.

Under state control, little attention was paid to the quality of cultivation or ideal picking date. As a result, YIELDS a typically well under 50 hl/ha (2.8 tons/acre), less than h those of Germany, for example. Healthy red grapes are oft picked before they have reached full MATURITY and may th be subjected to trucking for very long distances to reach t winery to which they are contracted.

Of the vineyard areas, only Slovenia and Macedonia a particularly high compared with FRANCE or ITALY, there allowing a longer ripening season than latitude may sugge There is adequate rainfall and most of the countryside, w the exception of Macedonia, is pleasantly green and fert throughout the growing season, despite the fact that many the districts have a CONTINENTAL rather than MEDITERRANE climate and enjoy a high number of completely dry da Winters can be very cold, especially inland.

Wine-making

Such progress as Yugoslavia has made in vinification has be led by demand from export customers. The curious hyb of communism and capitalism by which the wine enterpris have been run developed heavy bureaucratic burdens anc lack of entrepreneurial spirit. Without the guarantee of lon term contracts, such enterprises have accordingly be unwilling or unable to make the investments necessary win new customers.

A further brake on progress was that those privileged ma agers who travelled to other wine regions of the world we often promoted beyond the point where they had any dire responsibility for handling wine. Perversely, the syste seemed almost designed to minimize the dissemination western expertise.

However, there was some investment in the 1980s. Ranks STAINLESS STEEL tanks crop up unexpectedly in some winerie Unfortunately, they are usually geared to large-scale pr duction and the storage of blended wines in bulk. It is ra to encounter both modern equipment such as good pipe pumps, presses, and heat exchangers and knowledge of hc to use it in the same place. And the energy necessary h been scarce and at a premium.

Even in the early 1990s, many of the co-operatives (su as one in the heart of Fruška Gora white wine country VOJVODINA) still had massive concrete cellars, three and fo stories of tanks high, with no means of TEMPERATU CONTROL. Often machinery which badly needs painting replacing to avoid metal CONTAMINATION in the wines cann be attended to in time for the harvest. Scant attention is pa to storage temperature, which particularly affects the hu surplus of reds which have so often been offered on the wor market as part of reciprocal deals by would-be importe Wines sweetened both for the home market and for expc more often than not have such BOUQUET as they possess fla tened by the use of very dull GRAPE CONCENTRATE.

It is possible to make wonderful wine from the grap grown here. Major exporters include Navip in Serbia, wh nursemaided the Japanese project referred to above in a we equipped winery near Belgrade, or Slovin and Vinag in Sl venia, who have for years supplied the UK market in gre

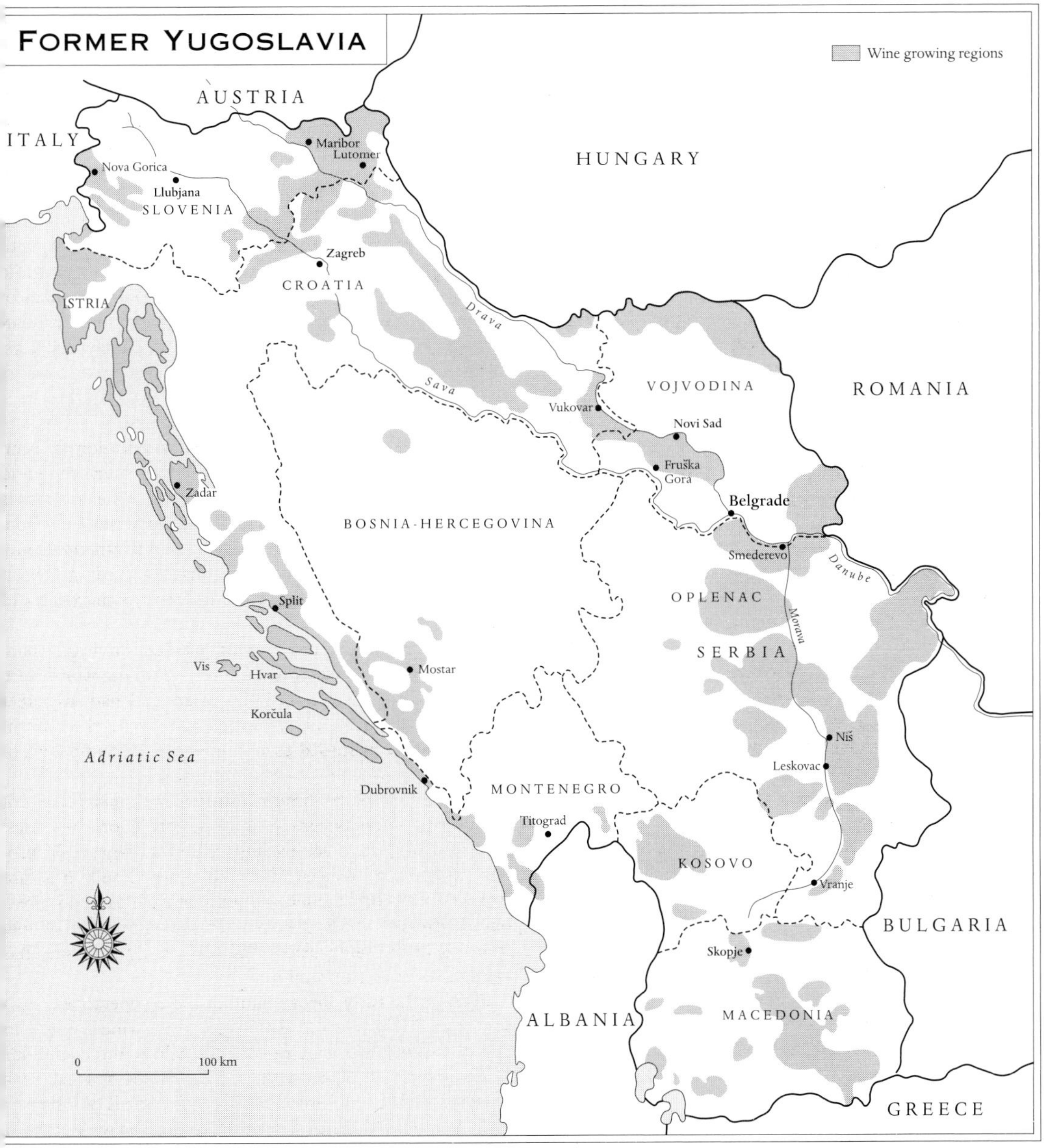

uantity. They are aware of the potential but have been unable ɔ market the quality they could produce because of the most evere price constraints. Perhaps some smaller enterprises ill finally capture the imagination of the outside world nd allow this part of the world to demonstrate just what it can do—if it is not already too late to halt the decline.

A.H.M.

Deretič, R., *Yugoslavia Wine Country* (Belgrade, 1988).

Gunn, A. W., 'Other vinelands of the world', in A. Simon, *Wines of the World*, ed. S. Sutcliffe (London, 1981).

Z

ZALEMA, Spanish white grape variety grown particularly in the southern CONDADO DE HUELVA zone, where its musts and wine can oxidize easily. It is being replaced by higher-quality varieties such as Palomino.

ZENTRALKELLEREI, a vast central co-operative wine cellar peculiar to GERMANY, where there are six, including the vast Badische Winzerkeller at Breisach in BADEN and Moselland in the MOSEL-SAAR-RUWER. These *Zentralkellereien* draw in wine from smaller CO-OPERATIVES, or *Winzergenossenschaften*. Other *Zentralkellereien* are at Kitzingen in FRANKEN, Bretzenheim in NAHE, Gau-Bickelheim in RHEINHESSEN, and Möglingen in WÜRTTEMBERG.

ZIBIBBO, Sicilian name for the MUSCAT OF ALEXANDRIA white grape variety, sometimes made into wine, notably Moscato di PANTELLERIA, although more usually sold as TABLE GRAPES. The 1990 Italian vineyard survey found scarcely 1,800 ha/4,450 acres of Zibibbo, as compared with 13,500 ha of Moscato Bianco (MUSCAT BLANC À PETITS GRAINS).

ZIERFANDLER, the more noble of the two white wine grape varieties traditionally associated with GUMPOLDSKIRCHEN, the dramatically full bodied, long-lived spicy white wine of the Thermenregion district of AUSTRIA. (The other is ROTGIPFLER.) At the end of the 1980s there were about 120 ha/296 acres of Zierfandler, which ripens very late, as its synonym Spätrot suggests, but keeps its acidity better than Rotgipfler. Unblended, Zierfandler has sufficient nerve to make late harvest wines with the ability to evolve over years in bottle, but most Zierfandler grapes are blended, and sometimes vinified, with Rotgipfler. The variety, as Cirfandli, is also known in Hungary.

ZILAVKA, relatively successful white grape variety planted in Hercegovina (see BOSNIA HERCEGOVINA) in what was YUGOSLAVIA. The variety manages to combine high alcohol with high acidity and a certain nuttiness of flavour. The Zilavka made around the inland town of Mostar is particularly prized. It is also increasingly planted in MACEDONIA, although it is not necessarily made exclusively from Zilavka grapes.

ZIMBABWE, southern African country with small-scale commercial wine industry. Launched in the 1950s, and nurtured in the sanctions period of the 1960s and 1970s, the industry showed a noticeable improvement in wine quality from the late 1980s. In this TROPICAL climate, temperature moderated by ALTITUDE in some of the better vineyard area Vines are sprayed with a calcium-based preparation to induc even budding in this warm, summer-rainfall country wher BOTRYTIS BUNCH ROT is an annual hazard. The most promisin vineyards are 40 km/25 miles east of the capital Harare a Marandera. Chenin Blanc, Colombard, and CAPE RIESLIN vines produce passable dry and off-dry whites with Sout African PINOTAGE making reds. There have also been BLUS wines, labelled 'Flirt' in Zimbabwe, which has no offici labelling or wine control regulations. The Monis Grou (whose best range is the Mukuyu Collection) and Africa Distillers are the biggest wineries, drawing from widely scat tered vineyards at Bulawayo and Mutare. Zimbabwe use South African, German, and occasionally Australian wine making expertise. Annual wine production was aroun 220,000 cases in the early 1990s. J.P. & J.Rc

ZINC, essential element for healthy vine growth. deficiency of zinc affects the plant's ability to synthesize th hormones AUXINS, which in turn results in a failure of th shoots to grow normally. The principal symptoms are CHLOR OSIS between the veins of young and old leaves, their sma size, and a widened leaf sinus where the PETIOLE attaches FRUIT SET can also be poor. Zinc deficiency commonly occur in vineyards on sandy soils, and is treated by daubing prunin wounds with pastes containing zinc, or spraying leaves i summer. R.E.S

Winkler, A. J., *et al.*, *General Viticulture* (2nd edn., Berkeley, Calif 1974).

ZINFANDEL is an exotic black grape variety of Europea origin cultivated predominantly in California that has tende to mirror the giddily changing fashions of the American win business.

For much of the 20th century the viticultural 'pioneer Agoston HARASZTHY was credited with introducing thi important variety to California from his native Hungary, bu a more worthy Zinfandel hero is the California historia Charles Sullivan who unearthed the truth, or at least part o it, about Zinfandel's route to California. It was he wh pointed out that there was no mention of Zinfandel in Har aszthy's copious promotional literature in the early 1860s and that, long before Haraszthy arrived in California in 1849 the variety was well known on the American East Coast

Called 'Zinfindal', it was exhibited at the Massachusetts Horticultural Society as early as 1834 and is frequently mentioned in the agricultural press of the 1840s and 1850s. In 1858 a Sacramento nurseryman exhibited a grape variety he called 'Zeinfindall' at the California state fair and by 1860 several California wines had been made from it. It seems highly likely that these cuttings came from the East Coast, although one San Jose nurseryman claimed, retrospectively and unverifiably, to have imported his Zinfandel directly from France to California in 1852 as 'Black St Peters'.

Because Zinfandel has no French connection, it has escaped the detailed scrutiny of the world's ampelographic centre in MONTPELLIER and its European origins rested on local hypothesis rather than internationally accredited fact until the application of DNA 'FINGERPRINTING' to vines in the early 1990s. Only then was it irrefutably demonstrated that Zinfandel is one and the same as the PRIMITIVO of southern Italy (which may have been imported from the United States). The relationship had already been sufficiently acknowledged by the Italians in the 1980s that some were exporting their Primitivo labelled, in direct appeal to the American market, Zinfandel. There may also be a link with the PLAVAC MALI of Dalmatia.

Zinfandel took firm hold on the California wine business in the 1880s, when its ability to produce in quantity was prized above all else. Many was the miner, and other beneficiary of California's GOLD RUSH, whose customary drink was Zinfandel. By the turn of the century Zinfandel was regarded as California's own claret and occupied some of the choicest North Coast vineyard. During Prohibition it was the choice of many a HOME WINE-MAKER but since then its viticultural popularity has become its undoing.

In 20th century California Zinfandel has occupied much the same place as Shiraz (Syrah) in Australia and has suffered the same lack of respect simply because it is the most planted black grape variety, often planted in unsuitably hot sites and expected to yield more than is good for it. Zinfandel may not be quite such a potentially noble grape variety as Syrah but it is certainly capable of producing fine wine if yields are restricted and the weather cool enough to allow a reasonably long growing season.

Zinfandel's viticultural disadvantages are that bunches can ripen unevenly, leaving harsh, green berries on the same bunch as those that have reached full maturity, and that once grapes reach full ripeness, in direct contrast to its great California rival Cabernet Sauvignon for example, they will soon turn to raisins if not picked quite rapidly. It therefore performs best in warm but not hot conditions and high-altitude vineyards can work particularly well.

Although Zinfandel has been required to transform itself into virtually every style and colour of wine that exists, it is probably best suited to dry, sturdy, unsubtle, but vigorous reds with an optimum lifespan of four to eight years. Such wines are rarely blends, although Ridge Vineyards are exponents of blending some PETITE SIRAH into Zinfandel. See CALIFORNIA for more details of Zinfandel the wine, both red and white. Dry Creek Valley in Sonoma has demonstrated a particular aptitude for this underestimated variety.

Thanks to the enormous popularity of WHITE ZINFANDEL, Zinfandel plantings, which had been declining, increased by up to 3,000 acres / 1,215 ha a year during the late 1980s, mostly in the Central Valley, so that they totalled 34,000 acres in 1992, just ahead of California's total acreage of its second most important black grape variety Cabernet Sauvignon.

It is also grown to a much more limited extent in warmer sites in other western states, and some South African growers have also taken advantage of their climate's suitability for Zinfandel.

Australia is another obvious location for this unusual variety and Cape Mentelle in Western Australia has been particularly successful with it.

Galet, P., 'La Culture de la vigne aux États-Unis et au Canada', *France viticole* (Sept.–Oct. 1980).

Sullivan, C. L., 'A viticultural mystery solved', *California History*, 57 (Summer 1978), 115–29.

ZWEIGELT, Zweigeltrebe, or **Blauer Zweigelt** is Austria's most popular dark-berried grape variety even though this crossing was bred only relatively recently, by a Dr Zweigelt at the KLOSTERNEUBURG research station in 1922. It is a BLAUFRÄNKISCH × ST-LAURENT crossing that at its best combines some of the bite of the first with the body of the second, although it is sometimes encouraged to produce too much dilute wine. It is popular with growers because it ripens earlier than Blaufränkisch but buds rather later than St Laurent, thereby tending to yield generously. It is widely grown throughout all Austrian wine regions and can occasionally make a serious, age-worthy wine, even though most examples are best drunk young. So successful has it been in Austria that the variety has also been planted on an experimental basis in Germany and England. The export fortunes of the variety may, oddly enough, be hampered by its originator's uncompromisingly Germanic surname. If only he had been called Dr Pinot Noir.

ILLUSTRATION SOURCES

The publishers wish to thank the following who have kindly given permission to reproduce illustrations on the pages indicated.

Black and White illustrations
Associazione Enologi Enotecnici Italiani 534
Averys of Bristol 82
Barnabys Picture Library 850
Bayer Staatsbibliothek Munich 277
Bibliothèque Nationale Paris 43
British Library 113, 989, 1049
British Museum 466, 564, 941
Robin Butler 260, 317, 416, 450
J. Allen Cash 692
Cephas/Jerry Alexander 656
Cephas/Nigel Blythe 204, 528, 981
Cephas/Andy Christodolo 52, 176
Cephas/Chris Davis 235
Cephas/Alan Proust 308, 389
Cephas/Mick Rock 12, 38, 79, 87, 102, 106, 126, 137, 168, 187, 206, 273, 331, 339, 344, 388, 456, 474, 536, 543, 609, 615, 629, 633, 660, 682, 693, 701, 732, 742, 757 bottom, 764, 769, 783, 797, 811, 814, 830, 839, 876, 924, 949, 965, 973, 991, 994, 1055, 1057, 1067
Cephas/Ted Stefan 512
Château Pichon-Longueville 221, 1071
Christies 840 top
CIVC 141, 327, 478, 481, 757, 767, 802
Jean-Loup Charmet 132, 346, 355
Reprinted from Pierre Galet: *A Practical Ampelography: Grapevine Identification*, translated and adapted by Lucie T. Morton. Copyright © 1979 by Cornell University. Used by permission of the publisher, Cornell University Press 31
Patrick Eagar endpapers, 63, 69, 103, 108, 114, 116, 122, 143, 160, 189, 193, 196, 201, 211, 215, 222, 227, 263, 274, 282, 307, 349, 375, 392, 412, 480, 488, 490, 533, 538, 549, 556, 568, 598, 600, 621, 645, 663, 673, 702, 731, 770, 826, 852, 862, 868, 897, 917, 920, 923, 963, 993, 997, 1002, 1011, 1019, 1021, 1030, 1069
E.T. Archive 371, 453, 762, 1004, 1016
John E. Fells and Sons Ltd 154, 320, 336, 500, 574, 744, 751, 774
Gaja 91, 419
German Wine Information Bureau 357, 541, 546, 792
Giraudon 202
Sonia Halliday Photographs 325, 946
Harveys Wine Museum 139, 261, 290, 484, 532, 865
International Wine and Food Society 1046
Kea/Francesco Venturi 120, 381, 596
Simon Loftus 503
Madeira Wine Company 370, 587
Mansell Collection 32, 35, 84, 244, 360, 363, 434, 518, 611, 630
Mary Evans Picture Library 325, 713
Merton College Oxford 840 bottom
Mouton Rothschild 60
Jean-Pierre Moueix 303, 778
Musée de l'École Carcassone 487
Peter Newark's Western Americana 531
Nucleus 396
Penfolds 711
Billett Potter 565, 712, 954, 1060
Janet Price 13, 405, 1037
Jan Read 228, 334, 393, 454, 777, 780, 806, 844, 892, 908, 970
Riedel 449
Saur/Visum 22
Scope/Jean-Luc Barda 55
Scope/Michel Guillard 662, 1083
Scope/Jacques Sierpinski 603
Scope/Jean-Daniel Sudres 788
Richard Smart 826, 1023
Sothebys 604
Swiss National Tourist Office 937
Tessiers 950
Torres 977
Professor L.E. Williams 394
Peter Woloszinski 378, 940

Colour illustrations all pictures except half-title and frontispiece facing page quoted
Bridgeman Art Library half-title
Michael Busselle 720
Cephas/Nigel Blythe 48
Cephas/Alain Proust 721
Cephas/Mick Rock frontispiece, 49, 177 bottom, 209, 304, 305, 336, 432, 464, 465, 592, 593, 816, 817, 944, 976
Cephas/Ted Stefanski 337
Patrick Eager 81, 177 top, 208, 433 bottom, 945
Foto Mas/Biblioteca Nacional Madrid 560
Sonia Halliday Photographs 561, 688, 689
Robert Harding Picture Library/Paolo Koch 433 top
Michael Holford 176
Images/Horizon/David Simmonds 849
Réunion des musées nationaux 80
from Jancis Robinson *Vines, Grapes & Wines*, 1986 Mitchell Beazley 848
Scope/Michel Guillard 977

Picture research by Anne-Marie Ehrlich.

Line diagrams on the pages indicated are drawn by Russell Birkett with reference to the following sources:
American Journal of Enology & Viticulture, Vol. 38, No 2., 1987. Copyright © Dr Ann C. Noble and *American Journal of Enology & Viticulture* 59, 459
B.G. Coombe and P.R. Dry (eds), *Viticulture, Volume 1: Resources in Australia, Volume 2: Practices* 186, 237, 250, 665, 920, 971
G. Dalmasso, *Viticoltura Moderna* 368
C. Fielden *Exploring Wines and Spirits* 754
J.S. Gladstone, *Viticulture and Environment* 255, 975
P. Huglin, *Biologie et écologie de la vigne* 28
J. Long, *Vignes et Vignobles* 477, 724, 875
R. Mayson, *Portugal's Wines & Wine Makers* 78
M.G. Mullins *et al*, *Biology of the Grapevine* 986
J. Renfrew, *Palaeoethnobotany* 703
L. Shanks, *Developing a Hillside Vineyard* 888
R. Smart and M. Robinson, *Sunlight into Wine* 88, 581, 860, 1033
R.J. Weaver, *Grape Growing* 455, 821, 1035
Winkler *et al*, *General Viticulture* 726

MEURSAULT 1991
MIS EN BOUTEILLE
CHATEAU LA ROSE POURRET
SAINT-EMILION GRAND CRU 1985
CHATEAU MEAUME
MARGAUX 1983
NOS CAVES
PAPES 1986
BORDEAUX
ESTATE BOTTLED
BORDEAUX SUPERIEUR
1987
MOUNTADAM VINEYARD
LA LAGUNE HAUT-MEDOC
SAINT-EMILION